BaseBall america

ALMANAC

A Comprehensive Review Of the 1995 Season, Featuring Statistics And Commentary

Baseball america's

1996
ALMANAC

PUBLISHED BY
Baseball America, Inc.

EDITOR
Allan Simpson

ASSISTANT EDITORS
James Bailey
Chris Wright

ASSOCIATE EDITORS
Jim Callis
Will Lingo
John Royster
Alan Schwarz

CONTRIBUTING WRITERS
Peter Barrouquere, Maureen Delany, Shannon Fears, Wayne Graczyk,
Sean Kernan, Andrew Linker, Javier Morales, Tim Pearrell, John Perratto, Curt Rallo,
Gene Sapakoff, Bob Sutton, George Schroeder, Larry Starks, Jeffrey Wilson

STATISTICAL PRODUCTION CONSULTANT
Howe Sportsdata International,
Boston, Mass.

Baseball america

| **EDITOR** | **PUBLISHER** | **GENERAL MANAGER** |
| Allan Simpson | Dave Chase | Joy C. Tempkins |

| **MANAGING EDITOR** | **ADVERTISING DIRECTOR** |
| Jim Callis | Kris Howard |

EDITOR'S NOTE
   Major league statistics are based on final, unofficial 1995 averages. Minor league statistics are official.
   The organization statistics, which begin on page 52, include all players who participated in at least one game during the 1995 season. Pitchers' batting statistics are not included, nor are the pitching statistics of field players who pitched on rare occasions. For players who played with more than one team in the same league, the player's cumulative statistics appear on the line immediately after the player's second-team statistics.
   Innings have been rounded off to the nearest full inning.

   *Lefthanded batter, pitcher   #Switch hitter

CONTENTS

Cover Photograph: Cal Ripken by Tom DiPace

MAJOR
LEAGUES

Damaging Labor Impasse Casts Black Cloud Over Baseball

By ALAN SCHWARZ

After all the magical moments, after Cal Ripken's 2,131st consecutive game, Hideo Nomo's explosion on the American landscape, Seattle's sudden infatuation for the game and Atlanta's first World Series conquest, a question still lingered on the minds of many baseball fans and observers:

Why?

Why did the regular season have to last just 144 games? Why did the players strike have to end with no meaningful resolution? Why did the 1995-96 offseason have to begin with as much uncertainty as the last?

Why couldn't the players and owners just get a deal done?

The 1995 season will be remembered for many wonderful accomplishments, but none matches the industry's lack of accomplishment during the previous year: The game's ruling bodies, for reasons inexcusable and almost incomprehensible to the average fan, couldn't reach accord on a new Basic Agreement and let their sniping distrust taint yet another season.

The strike, which began on Aug. 12, 1994 and canceled that season's playoffs and World Series, finally came to a close March 31 after a U.S. District court order forbade the owners from implementing new financial working conditions in the wake of a negotiations impasse. The court decided that conditions would revert to the old rules from the previous season—six-year free agency, arbitration, etc.—until the two sides came to an agreement through negotiation.

The players returned, ending the longest strike in sports history, as the owners licked their wounds. Soon the entire industry would be doing the same. While the owners and players fought over their pieces of the pie, each miscalculated how fast that pie would begin eroding.

Fan backlash during the season was greater than many expected. Attendance decreased across the majors some 17 percent, and in cities such as San Francisco, Minneapolis and Pittsburgh crowds were down almost 40 percent. Even National League Championship Series games in Cincinnati didn't sell out.

An answer did exist for the entire mess. The owners played harder ball than usual but lost their gamble to implement revenue sharing and a salary cap, and the players gambled that the damage to the industry would be less than it became.

Each side emerged from the fight with a better understanding of the damage they could inflict. That

might become the saving grace of the 1995 season.

"We're going to have to spend a little bit more time with the fans," Red Sox first baseman Dave Hollins said. "Guys can't be blowing them off like they do a lot."

Owners Don't Implement

Because the court order was obtained March 31, the players couldn't return quickly enough to avoid an adjustment in the season's schedule. Though replacement-player games were avoided, the season began April 25 and teams played just 144 games instead of 162.

KEY PLAYERS

Bud Selig

Don Fehr

Yet the disruption in the full season didn't seem to hurt the industry more than the overriding frustration over how the players and owners couldn't come to any agreement after such a long dispute. Very little was accomplished except, from the players' standpoint, the significant confirmation that the owners were barred from implementing their own terms and conditions upon the players.

After sparse bargaining sessions in the summer and fall of 1994, the owners declared an impasse in the negotiations Dec. 23 and set up a new financial labor system that temporarily turned the baseball world upside down:

■ Payrolls: Each team had to keep its payroll between 84 and 110 percent of half the average club revenue.

■ Free agency: Players with six years of service time had free agency as they were used to. Players with four and five years became restricted free agents if their old team made a qualifying offer, that being 110 percent of their previous year's salary. The old team could retain the rights to the player by matching any outside offer. Players with 4-5 years of service who did not receive qualifying offers would become unrestricted free agents.

■ Salary arbitration: eliminated.

These drastic changes, not bargained with the union, set up the March 31 showdown in federal court.

Red Sox CEO John Harrington called Implementation Day a "very frustrating and disappointing moment."

"I'm very disappointed," said David Cone, at the time the Royals' player representative. "I'm confused by why we're not still exchanging ideas. I thought the idea was to take a higher ground. I guess I was naive. It seems like legal posturing was more important to them. It seems that anything short of a total collapse by the Players Association wouldn't have gotten a deal."

The players quickly filed an unfair labor-practices complaint with the National Labor Relations Board. After the owners learned in early February that the NLRB was going to file such a complaint in federal court, they rescinded the cap and labor terms at least temporarily reverted to normal.

Even President Bill Clinton couldn't help reach a settlement in history's longest baseball argument. He had watched William J. Usery, widely regarded as the nation's top federal mediator, fail to get the two sides together for many weeks. So he entered the fray himself Feb. 7.

"The players and owners still remain far apart on their differences," Clinton said. "Clearly they are not capable of resolving this strike without an umpire."

Yet moving the dispute to the White House merely emphasized how tangled baseball's knot had become. Usery suggested the players and owners agree on a 50 percent tax on payrolls over $40 million and free agency for players with four years of service. The players refused, citing that such a tax would stagnate the free-agent market. Clinton asked both sides to accept binding arbitration. The owners refused that alternative.

In the end, Usery didn't even come close to getting the two sides together. The union, led by executive director Don Fehr, became critical of his lack of understanding of the issues involved.

Said Fehr: "When we ask an individual, 'Can you tell me why you made this recommendation, what is your rationale, how do you write the numbers, what are your assumptions, how much money do the players

Replacement fallout. Outspoken Dodgers outfielder Brett Butler, left, took exception to the presence in a Los Angeles uniform of replacement player Mike Busch.

lose or gain, how much money do the clubs lose or gain?' and the answer is, 'I don't know, Don,' it is not possible to take it seriously. And it is very regrettable that it happened.

"I think Bill Usery, in many respects, has done everything that he could. But, as I suggested to him the first day I met him, this would be far and away the hardest mediation he'd ever have to do. He agrees with that tonight."

Replacements Take Stage

With no end in sight, the owners went through with their plans for replacement baseball.

"We are committed to playing the 1995 season and will do so with the best players willing to play," said Brewers owner Bud Selig, the acting commissioner as chairman of the owners' Executive Council.

They never got to play during the regular season, but the use of replacement players in spring-training games caused predictable tension between them and the regular major leaguers. Other snags appeared as well.

Orioles owner Peter Angelos, a lawyer who had fought for union rights for decades, refused to field a replacement team during spring training and was outspoken in his disfavor for the plan. And local laws in Toronto forbade the use of strikebreakers, forcing the Blue Jays to make plans to play their regular-season games at their spring-training site in Dunedin, Fla.

But the most important hurdle the owners had to clear was the fans' lack of confidence that the replacement players were anything close to major league–

ATTENDANCE FALLOUT							
		1994			1995		
	Dates	Attendance	Average	Dates	Attendance	Average	Change (%)
Atlanta	54	2,539,240	47,022	72	2,561,831	35,581	-24
Baltimore	54	2,535,359	46,951	72	3,098,475	43,034	-8
Boston	61	1,775,826	29,111	72	2,164,378	30,061	+3
California	63	1,512,622	24,009	72	1,748,680	24,287	+1
Chicago NL	58	1,845,208	31,813	70	1,893,925	27,056	-15
Chicago AL	53	1,697,398	32,026	71	1,609,773	22,672	-29
Cincinnati	60	1,897,681	31,628	71	1,843,649	25,967	-18
Cleveland	51	1,995,174	39,121	71	2,842,725	40,038	+2
#Colorado	56	3,281,511	58,705	71	3,341,988	47,070	-20
Detroit	57	1,184,783	20,785	71	1,180,979	16,634	-20
Florida	59	1,937,467	32,838	69	1,670,255	24,206	-26
Houston	59	1,561,136	26,460	71	1,363,801	19,208	-27
Kansas City	57	1,400,494	24,570	70	1,232,969	17,614	-28
Los Angeles	55	2,279,421	41,444	72	2,766,251	38,420	-7
Milwaukee	56	1,268,397	22,650	71	1,087,560	15,318	-32
Minnesota	59	1,398,565	23,705	72	1,057,667	14,690	-38
Montreal	52	1,276,250	24,543	71	1,292,764	18,207	-26
New York NL	52	1,151,471	22,143	70	1,254,307	17,919	-19
New York AL	57	1,675,557	29,396	70	1,705,257	24,361	-17
Oakland	56	1,242,692	22,191	71	1,174,310	16,540	-25
Philadelphia	58	2,290,971	39,500	71	2,043,588	28,783	-27
Pittsburgh	60	1,222,517	20,375	70	905,517	12,936	-37
St. Louis	54	1,866,544	34,566	71	1,727,536	24,331	-30
San Diego	57	953,857	16,734	70	1,019,728	14,568	-13
San Francisco	59	1,704,614	28,892	72	1,241,497	17,243	-40
Seattle	44	1,103,798	25,086	73	1,640,992	22,479	-10
Texas	62	2,502,538	40,364	72	1,985,910	27,582	-32
Toronto	59	2,907,933	49,287	72	2,826,483	39,257	-20
Total	**1,582**	**50,009,023**	**31,611**	**1,919**	**50,282,795**	**26,202**	**-17**

#In 1995, the Rockies moved from spacious Mile High Stadium into cozy Coors Field, which held 50,200—nearly 30,000 fewer seats than Mile High.

caliber. Most of the players who agreed to play in spring training were either journeyman minor leaguers or minor leaguers who had been retired for years. Yankees DH Matt Stark weighed 275 pounds, and Mets right-hander Al Coghen, a 37-year-old refrigerator delivery man, had last pitched in A-ball in 1979.

Yet they all put on major league uniforms for six weeks, thrilled at the possibility of playing in the regular season and making big league money—a minimum of $115,000 per year. Many were enticed by the $5,000 bonus they received for signing just for spring training and the $25,000 they would receive if they were used in the regular season.

They never were. After the court order and the union's offer to come back to work on the eve of the sched-

Centerpiece. The Rockies were relatively unaffected by the strike because they played in brand-new Coors Field, one of the majors' best ballparks.

uled regular-season opener, the owners scrapped the replacement plan to minimize their losses. The replacement players were released, saving teams about $800,000 in the $25,000-per-player bonuses. The Marlins paid their players the $25,000 anyway, and other clubs gave them an extra $5,000 as a goodwill gesture, but the experience wasn't a financially rewarding one for most replacements.

"It kind of stinks it came down to the last day," Yankees pitcher Doug Cinella said. New York's scheduled Opening Day starter, Kent Wallace, had no regrets. "I got to do things I've never done before," he said. "I'd do it again."

The players who moved back home to their old jobs represented only a portion of the replacement players. Many were established minor leaguers who chose to play in major league spring-training games as a chance to advertise their skills for the future. When they returned to the minors and later earned promotions to the majors, the backlash from established big leaguers was hard to miss.

Nineteen former replacement players were promoted to the major leagues in 1995 and some were accepted more readily than others. The Brewers had few problems with Brian Givens, Jamie McAndrew and Ron Rightnowar, who comprised a significant portion of their pitching staff. But the Astros, for instance, resented righthander Craig McMurtry to the extent that he couldn't sit on the bullpen bench during a game. Giants players refused to welcome infielder Joel Chimelis, and he was sent back immediately to Triple-A Phoenix, avoiding clubhouse tension.

The most publicized shunning of a replacement player concerned Dodgers third baseman Mike Busch. With Brett Butler the resentment ringleader, Busch had to sit alone on the bench, in full view of national-television cameras, during his first

game.

"It was supposed to be the happiest moment of his life," said infielder Ron Maurer, a teammate of Busch both on the Dodgers' replacement team and at Triple-A Albuquerque. "I think we all expected him to get treated that way, but you'd think players would put that aside."

District Court Steps In

But back in March, no one was desperately concerned with how replacement players would mix with the normal major leaguers during the season. People still were worried that there would be no normal 1995 season at all.

With replacement baseball coming down the pike one week before Opening Day, the National Labor Relations Board authorized its general counsel to seek an injunction in United States District Court in Manhattan that would force the owners to reinstate certain elements of the old Basic Agreement. The players assured that winning the injunction hearing would assure their return if the owners didn't lock them out.

On March 31, judge Sonia Sotomayor, who grew up in a Bronx housing project just three miles from Yankee Stadium, ruled in favor of the players. In a swift and firm ruling, she prevented the owners from establishing new work rules in the absence of a collectively bargained agreement. She ordered them to reinstate competitive bidding for free agents and arbitration for eligible players.

"This strike has placed the entire concept of collective bargaining on trial," she said. "It is critical, therefore, that the board assure and that I protect its assurance that the spirit and the letter of Federal labor law be scrupulously followed."

Judge Sotomayor also said the owners had to come back to her before declaring an impasse in negoti-

REPLACEMENTS
A total of **19 players** who attended spring-training camps as replacement players were called to the major leagues in 1995. The list:
Scott Anderson, rhp, Royals
Doug Brady, 2b, White Sox
Mike Busch, 3b, Dodgers
Edgar Caceres, 2b, Royals
Joel Chimelis, 3b, Giants
Mike Christopher, rhp, Tigers
Brian Givens, lhp, Brewers
Jeff Grotewold, dh-c, Royals
Dave Hajek, 2b, Astros
Ron Mahay, of, Red Sox
Dan Masteller, 1b, Twins
Jamie McAndrew, rhp, Brewers
Craig McMurtry, rhp, Astros
Jose Mota, 2b, Royals
Dave Pavlas, rhp, Yankees
Rick Reed, rhp, Reds
Ron Rightnowar, rhp, Brewers
Joe Slusarski, rhp, Brewers
Scott Taylor, lhp, Rangers

1995 MAJOR LEAGUE ALL-STAR GAME

National League Makes Most Of Three Hits In 3-2 Victory

The American League pitching staff may have illustrated the truism that good pitching stops good hitting, but give the National League credit for making the most of its three hits in pulling out a pitching-dominated 3-2 victory July 11 at The Ballpark in Arlington, Texas.

No-hit through an All-Star Game record 5⅔ innings by the combined efforts of starter Randy Johnson, Kevin Appier and Dennis Martinez, the National League collected its first hit—and run—when Craig Biggio homered off Martinez in the sixth inning, trimming the AL's lead to 2-1. Frank Thomas, who won the home run derby the day before, had mashed a two-run missile in the fourth for the AL's only runs.

Mike Piazza tied the game in the seventh with a solo shot off crowd favorite Kenny Rogers and the NL won it an inning later when game MVP Jeff Conine crushed a home run in his first—and only—All-Star Game at-bat off loser Steve Ontiveros.

The loss spoiled a remarkable night for the AL pitchers, who combined for nine strikeouts, one walk, and allowed just one other baserunner besides the three home runs. The NL's three hits were the lowest winning total since 1952, when the National League also won 3-2 in a five-inning game shortened by rain.

TOP VOTE GETTERS

AMERICAN LEAGUE

CATCHER: 1. Ivan Rodriguez, Rangers (1,151,708); 2. Sandy Alomar, Indians (958,853); 3. Terry Steinbach, Athletics (467,853).

FIRST BASE: 1. Frank Thomas, White Sox (2,833,502); 2. Eddie Murray, Indians (729,027); 3. Will Clark, Rangers (505,103).

SECOND BASE: 1. Carlos Baerga, Indians (1,152,652); 2. Roberto Alomar, Blue Jays (1,003,550); 3. Chuck Knoblauch, Twins (583,195).

THIRD BASE: 1. Wade Boggs, Yankees (884,651); 2. Jim Thome, Indians (753,092); 3. Robin Ventura, White Sox (468,334).

SHORTSTOP: 1. Cal Ripken, Orioles (1,698,524); 2. Benji Gil, Rangers (675,963); 3. Omar Vizquel, Indians (666,506).

OUTFIELD: 1. Ken Griffey, Mariners (1,204,748); 2. Albert Belle, Indians (1,056,134); 3. Kirby Puckett, Twins (997,623); 4. Kenny Lofton, Indians (975,801); 5. Manny Ramirez, Indians (863,890); 6. Rickey Henderson, Athletics (702,257); 7. Joe Carter, Blue Jays (418,611); 8. Jose Canseco, Red Sox (404,758); 9. Paul Molitor, Blue Jays (387,060).

AMERICAN LEAGUE

CATCHER: 1. Mike Piazza, Dodgers (1,195,136); 2. Darren Daulton, Phillies (780,126); 3. Joe Girardi, Rockies (473,210).

FIRST BASE: 1. Fred McGriff, Braves (871,904); 2. Andres Galarraga, Rockies (802,672); 3. Jeff Bagwell, Astros (717,663).

SECOND BASE: 1. Craig Biggio, Astros (825,062); 2. Mickey Morandini, Phillies (737,270); 3. Delino DeShields, Dodgers (438,235).

THIRD BASE: 1. Matt Williams, Giants (1,029,519); 2. Scott Cooper, Cardinals (899,505); 3. Vinny Castilla, Rockies (604,823).

SHORTSTOP: 1. Ozzie Smith, Cardinals (1,367,518); 2. Barry Larkin, Reds (948,945); 3. Wil Cordero, Expos (634,885).

OUTFIELD: 1. Barry Bonds, Giants (1,392,180); 2. Lenny Dykstra, Phillies (903,952); 3. Tony Gwynn, Padres (898,951); 4. David Justice, Braves (851,644); 5. Dante Bichette, Rockies (706,249); 6. Larry Walker, Rockies (579,722); 7. Deion Sanders, Reds (564,231); 8. Ron Gant, Reds (532,814); 9. Raul Mondesi, Dodgers (446,119).

ROSTERS

NATIONAL LEAGUE

MANAGER: Felipe Alou, Expos.

PITCHERS: Tyler Green, Phillies; Tom Henke, Cardinals; Greg Maddux, Braves; Randy Myers, Cubs; Denny Neagle, Pirates; **Hideo Nomo, Dodgers**; Carlos Perez, Expos; Heathcliff Slocumb, Phillies; Todd Worrell, Dodgers.

CATCHERS: Mike Piazza, Dodgers; Darren Daulton, Phillies.

INFIELDERS: Craig Biggio (2b), Astros; Bobby Bonilla, Mets; **Vinny Castilla (3b), Rockies**; Mark Grace, Cubs; **Barry Larkin (ss), Reds**; **Fred McGriff (1b), Braves**; Mickey Morandini, Phillies; Jose Offerman, Dodgers; Ozzie Smith, Cardinals; Matt Williams, Giants.

OUFIELDERS: Dante Bichette, Rockies; **Barry Bonds (lf), Giants**; Jeff Conine, Marlins; **Lenny Dykstra (cf), Phillies**; **Ron Gant (dh), Reds**; **Tony Gwynn (rf), Padres**. Raul Mondesi, Dodgers; Reggie Sanders, Reds; Sammy Sosa, Cubs.

AMERICAN LEAGUE

MANAGER: Buck Showalter, Yankees.

PITCHERS: Kevin Appier, Royals; Chuck Finley, Angels; Erik Hanson, Red Sox; **Randy Johnson, Mariners**; Dennis Martinez, Indians; Jose Mesa, Indians; Steve Ontiveros, Athletics; Kenny Rogers, Rangers; Lee Smith, Angels; David Wells, Tigers.

CATCHERS: Ivan Rodriguez, Rangers; Mike Stanley, Yankees.

INFIELDERS: Roberto Alomar, Blue Jays; **Carlos Baerga (2b), Indians**; **Wade Boggs (3b), Yankees**; Gary DiSarcina, Angels; **Edgar Martinez (dh), Mariners**; Mark McGwire, Athletics; **Cal Ripken (ss), Orioles**; Kevin Seitzer, Brewers; Mo Vaughn, Red Sox; **Frank Thomas (1b), White Sox**.

OUFIELDERS: Albert Belle (lf), Indians; Jim Edmonds, Angels; Ken Griffey, Mariners; **Kenny Lofton (cf), Indians**; Paul O'Neill, Yankees; **Kirby Puckett (rf), Twins**; Manny Ramirez, Indians.

Starters in boldface type

BOX SCORE

July 11 in Arlington, Texas
National League 3, American League 2

National	ab	r	h	bi	bb	so	American	ab	r	h	bi	bb	so
Dykstra cf	2	0	0	0	1	0	Lofton cf	3	0	0	0	0	1
Sosa cf	1	0	0	0	0	0	Edmonds ph-cf	1	0	0	0	0	1
Gwynn rf	2	0	0	0	0	0	Baerga 2b	3	1	3	0	0	0
R.Sanders rf	1	0	0	0	0	1	Alomar ph-2b	1	0	0	0	0	0
Mondesi rf	1	0	0	0	0	0	E.Martinez dh	3	0	0	0	0	1
Bonds lf	3	0	0	0	0	1	T.Martinez ph	1	0	1	0	0	0
Bichette lf	1	0	0	0	0	0	Thomas 1b	2	1	1	2	0	0
Piazza c	3	1	1	1	0	0	Vaughn 1b	2	0	0	0	0	2
Daulton c	0	0	0	0	0	0	O'Neill lf	1	0	0	0	0	0
Belle lf	3	0	0	0	0	1	McGriff 1b	3	0	0	0	0	2
Grace 1b	0	0	0	0	0	0	Ripken ss	3	0	2	0	0	0
Gant dh	2	0	0	0	0	1	DiSarcina pr-ss	1	0	0	0	0	0
Conine ph	1	1	1	1	0	0	Boggs 3b	2	0	1	0	0	0
Larkin ss	3	0	0	0	0	0	Seitzer ph-3b	2	0	0	0	0	0
Offerman ss	0	0	0	0	0	0	Puckett rf	2	0	0	0	0	1
Castilla 3b	2	0	0	0	0	1	Ramirez ph-rf	0	0	0	0	2	0
Bonilla 3b	1	0	0	0	0	0	Rodriguez c	3	0	0	0	0	1
Biggio 2b	2	1	1	1	0	0	Stanley c	1	0	0	0	0	0
Morandini 2b	1	0	0	0	0	1							
Totals	**29**	**3**	**3**	**3**	**1**	**9**	**Totals**	**34**	**2**	**8**	**2**	**2**	**8**

National		000 001 110—3
American		000 200 000—2

LOB—National 0, American 7. 2B—Baerga. HR—Biggio, Piazza, Conine, Thomas. SB—Alomar. CS—Dykstra, Baerga.

National	ip	h	r	er	bb	so	American	ip	h	r	er	bb	so
Nomo	2	0	0	0	0	3	Johnson	2	0	0	0	1	3
Smiley	2	2	2	2	0	0	Appier	2	0	0	0	0	1
Green	1	2	0	0	0	1	D.Martinez	2	1	1	1	0	0
Neagle	1	0	0	0	0	1	Rogers	1	1	1	1	0	2
Perez	⅓	1	0	0	1	0	Ontiveros L	⅔	1	1	1	0	1
Slocumb W	1	1	0	0	0	2	Wells	⅓	0	0	0	0	1
Henke	⅔	0	0	0	0	1	Mesa	1	0	0	0	0	1
Myers S	1	0	0	0	1	0							

Umpires—HP—Durwood Merrill; 1B—Charlie Williams; 2B—Al Clark; 3B—Mike Winters. LF—Ted Hendry. RF—Ed Rapuano.
T—2:40. A—50,920.

ations in the future. Later, the United States Court of Appeals for the Second Circuit affirmed her ruling, denying the owners' request for a stay of the injunction, and chided the owners' lawyers for asserting that Sotomayor's ruling inhibited negotiations.

"When you're telling us that the injunction is stopping you from negotiating a collective bargaining agreement, you're telling us something that isn't so," Judge Jon Newman said. Other comments from the bench were similarly embarrassing to the owners' side.

Their stance weakened even before the appellate hearing, the owners decided not to lock out the players, fearing that would be ruled illegal, and allowed the players to return to spring training days after Judge Sotomayor's decision.

Teams scrambled to sign hundreds of unsigned players, and free agents scrambled to market themselves to interested teams. High salaries were harder to come by, with the owners' revenue significantly sapped by the previous year's canceled playoffs and their subsequent difficulty in selling season tickets. Many free agents advertised their skills at a special union-funded camp in Homestead, Fla.

But on April 25, when the Dodgers beat the Marlins 8-7 behind Raul Mondesi's two home runs, baseball had for the most part returned to normal. The game, and not the lawyers who controlled it for eight months, entered the spotlight again.

Ripken Resuscitates Baseball

No other event had a more positive effect on baseball's image in 1995 than when Cal Ripken stepped onto the field at Camden Yards on Sept. 6.

On that night in Baltimore, Ripken, the Orioles' steadfast shortstop, played in his 2,131st consecutive game, breaking Lou Gehrig's record that almost no one thought ever would be broken. Ripken's march

Defining moment. Baltimore's Cal Ripken provided baseball with its proudest moment in 1995.

toward the mark, set in 1939, reminded anyone who watched not only of baseball's charm, however sullied it might have become in the previous year, but also the positive effect the game can have on those who follow it.

"Tonight, I stand here overwhelmed as my name is connected with the great and courageous Lou Gehrig," Ripken said in a speech to Camden Yards' delirious fans. "I'm truly humbled to be mentioned in the same breath. Some may think our strongest connection is because we both played in many consecutive games. Yet, I believe in my heart, there truly is a common motivation: a love of the game, a passion for your team, and a desire to compete at the very highest level.

"I know that if Lou Gehrig is looking down on tonight's activities, he isn't concerned about someone playing one more consecutive game than he did. Instead, he's viewing tonight about what is good and right about the great American game."

Ripken's streak began on May 30, 1982, before he moved from third base to shortstop, where he became arguably the best player ever at that position. He played 18,984 of the Orioles' 19,146 innings during the 2,131 games and also appeared in 12 consecutive All-Star Games.

The record-breaking day became even more astounding than expected. He hit a home run in the fourth inning, his third in three nights.

Yet the tear-jerking moment came in the bottom of the fifth inning, when the game became official. The Baltimore crowd's ovation, which had been building for years as their hometown hero approached Gehrig's mark, let loose for 22 minutes. Ripken, a quiet and

Record hitter. Cleveland's Albert Belle became the first player in major league history to hit 50 doubles and 50 homers in a season.

1995 MAJOR LEAGUE FREE AGENTS

One hundred thirty-seven players with six or more seasons of major league service time filed for free agency following the 1995 season.

ATLANTA (6)

Player, Pos.	1995 Salary
Mike Devereaux, of	$800,000
Fred McGriff, 1b	4,250,000
Charlie O'Brien, c	550,000
Alejandro Pena, rhp	500,000
Luis Polonia, of	1,500,000
Dwight Smith, of	250,000

BALTIMORE (6)

Player, Pos.	1995 Salary
Harold Baines, of	$1,600,000
Kevin Bass, of	250,000
Kevin Brown, rhp	4,225,000
Mark Eichhorn, rhp	537,500
Doug Jones, rhp	1,000,000
Jamie Moyer, lhp	1,100,000

BOSTON (7)

Player, Pos.	1995 Salary
Rick Aguilera, rhp	$4,300,000
Jose Canseco, of	5,800,000
Erik Hanson, rhp	1,125,000
Mike Maddux, rhp	200,000
Mike Macfarlane, c	1,725,000
Willie McGee, of	200,000
Zane Smith, lhp	1,300,000

CALIFORNIA (13)

Player, Pos.	1995 Salary
Jim Abbott, lhp	$2,000,000
Mike Aldrete, 1b	430,000
Mike Bielecki, rhp	150,000
Chuck Finley, lhp	4,875,000
Dave Gallagher, of	250,000
Rene Gonzales, 3b	225,000
John Habyan, rhp	300,000
Greg Myers, c	800,000
Spike Owen, ss	3,500,000
Bob Patterson, lhp	225,000
Tony Phillips, of	4,366,667
Scott Sanderson, rhp	200,000
Dick Schofield, ss	350,000

CHICAGO/AL (2)

Player, Pos.	1995 Salary
Lance Johnson, of	$2,666,667
Dave Martinez, of	550,000
Dave Righetti, lhp	200,000

CHICAGO/NL (6)

Player, Pos.	1995 Salary
Shawon Dunston, ss	$3,775,000
Mark Grace, 1b	4,050,000
Howard Johnson, of	250,000
Randy Myers, lhp	3,833,334
Jaime Navarro, rhp	850,000
Mark Parent, c	300,000

CINCINNATI (6)

Player, Pos.	1995 Salary
Mariano Duncan, inf	$350,000
Ron Gant, of	3,500,000
Mike Jackson, rhp	750,000
Hal Morris, 1b	3,300,000
Benito Santiago, c	550,000
Frank Viola, lhp	400,000

CLEVELAND (7)

Player, Pos.	1995 Salary
Alvaro Espinoza, 3b	$450,000
John Farrell, rhp	250,000
Ken Hill, rhp	4,375,000
Eddie Murray, 1b	3,000,000
Tony Pena, c	450,000

California's Chuck Finley

Billy Ripken, ss	200,000
Dave Winfield, of	600,000

COLORADO (2)

Player, Pos.	1995 Salary
Mike Kingery, of	$600,000
Walt Weiss, ss	1,600,000

DETROIT (3)

Player, Pos.	1995 Salary
Scott Fletcher, 2b	$225,000
Franklin Stubbs, 1b	310,000
Lou Whitaker, 2b	3,783,334

FLORIDA (3)

Player, Pos.	1995 Salary
Jerry Browne, of	$650,000
Andre Dawson, of	500,000
Bryan Harvey, rhp	4,875,000

HOUSTON (6)

Player, Pos.	1995 Salary
Craig Biggio, 2b	$4,600,000
Pat Borders, c	310,000
John Cangelosi, of	175,000
Mike Henneman, rhp	4,833,334
Dave Magadan, 3b	275,000
Milt Thompson, of	525,000

KANSAS CITY (8)

Player, Pos.	1995 Salary
Tom Browning, lhp	$300,000
Gary Gaetti, 3b	700,000
Greg Gagne, ss	4,366,667
Tom Gordon, rhp	3,300,000
Mark Gubicza, rhp	650,000
Jeff Montgomery, rhp	4,166,667
Gregg Olson, rhp	400,000
Juan Samuel, of	325,000

LOS ANGELES (4)

Player, Pos.	1995 Salary
Tom Candiotti, rhp	$4,450,000
Roberto Kelly, of	3,733,334
Ramon Martinez, rhp	3,925,000
Tim Wallach, 3b	1,500,000

MILWAUKEE (6)

Player, Pos.	1995 Salary
Rob Dibble, rhp	$400,000
Darryl Hamilton, of	1,850,000
Joe Oliver, c	337,100
Kevin Seitzer, 3b	550,000
B.J. Surhoff, of	250,000
Bill Wegman, rhp	2,375,000

NEW YORK/AL (9)

Player, Pos.	1995 Salary
Wade Boggs, 3b	$4,624,316
David Cone, rhp	8,000,000
Rick Honeycutt, lhp	200,000
Steve Howe, lhp	2,300,000
Dion James, of	300,000
Don Mattingly, 1b	4,420,000
Jack McDowell, rhp	5,400,000
Mike Stanley, c	562,000
Randy Velarde, ss	350,000

NEW YORK/NL (2)

Player, Pos.	1995 Salary
Joe Orsulak, of	$850,000
Bill Spiers, inf	425,000

OAKLAND (5)

Player, Pos.	1995 Salary
Mike Gallego, ss	$300,000
Brian Harper, c	200,000
Ricky Henderson, of	3,800,000
Stan Javier, of	650,000
Steve Ontiveros, rhp	900,000

PHILADELPHIA (4)

Player, Pos.	1995 Salary
Jim Eisenreich, of	$1,200,000
Sid Fernandez, lhp	2,333,333
Charlie Hayes, 3b	1,000,000
Andy Van Slyke, of	550,000

PITTSBURGH (1)

Player, Pos.	1995 Salary
Don Slaught, c	$2,025,000

ST. LOUIS (4)

Player, Pos.	1995 Salary
Tom Henke, rhp	$1,500,000
Mike Morgan, rhp	3,375,000
Jose Oquendo, 2b	2,250,000
Jeff Parrett, rhp	300,000

SAN DIEGO (2)

Player, Pos.	1995 Salary
Jody Reed, 2b	$200,000
Fernandez Valenzuela, lhp	1,040,000

SAN FRANCISCO (3)

Player, Pos.	1995 Salary
Terry Mulholland, lhp	$1,250,000
Jeff Reed, c	700,000
Trevor Wilson, lhp	400,000

SEATTLE (4)

Player, Pos.	1995 Salary
Tim Belcher, rhp	$200,000
Andy Benes, rhp	3,400,000
Vince Coleman, of	250,000
Lee Guetterman, lhp	250,000

TEXAS (10)

Player, Pos.	1995 Salary
Danny Darwin, rhp	$300,000
Candy Maldonado, of	150,000
Roger McDowell, rhp	500,000
Otis Nixon, of	3,150,000
Mike Pagliarulo, 3b	300,000
Kenny Rogers, lhp	3,700,000
Jeff Russell, rhp	500,000
Mickey Tettleton, c-of	500,000
Bob Tewksbury, rhp	1,500,000
Bobby Witt, rhp	1,800,000

TORONTO (7)

Player, Pos.	1995 Salary
Roberto Alomar, 2b	5,500,000
Danny Cox, rhp	600,000
Al Leiter, lhp	795,000
Paul Molitor, dh	4,500,000
Lance Parrish, c	250,000
Duane Ward, rhp	4,750,000
Devon White, of	4,000,000

THE SPORTS GROUP

reserved man who had consistently dealt with the buildup of attention with dignity and class, took a victory lap around Camden Yards to slap hands with fans and reciprocate his appreciation.

"They should just rename shortstop the 'Ripken position,'" teammate Mike Mussina said. "You could play first, second, third or Ripken."

"Thirty years from now," former Baltimore manager Earl Weaver said, "there may be a kid going to bed and dreaming about playing 2,131 games like Cal Ripken did. I mean, talk about role models. This is one of a kind. This man stands alone."

Ripken didn't miss a game during the rest of the 1995 season. His streak continued into the offseason at 2,153. The professional baseball record stands at 2,215 games, the mark set by the Japanese leagues' Sachio Kinugasa from 1970-87.

Baseball Catches Nomomania

While Ripken provided the regular season's most memorable moment, some cited the international appeal of Japanese righthander Hideo Nomo as the most important ongoing story of 1995.

Nomo, 26, was signed by the Dodgers in February, became the first Japanese native to jump from that country's major leagues to the United States, and instantly took the big leagues by storm. His slow, whirling delivery tantalized hitters, and his astounding success captured the interest of even the most soured baseball fan. Everyone wanted to see just who this Nomo guy was.

"He's been awesome," Dodgers manager Tom Lasorda said in July. "He's been just overpowering. When we evaluated his ability in spring training, we thought he could win. But he's made a few adjustments and has become outstanding."

Nomo wound up being named Baseball America's 1995 Rookie of the Year. He finished the season 13-6 with a 2.56 ERA, second in the National League, and led the loop with 236 strikeouts. He started for the NL in the All-Star Game in Texas, and his win on the next-to-last day of the regular season clinched a playoff berth for Los Angeles.

The curiosity surrounding Nomo followed him throughout the season, most notably with an immense contingent of Japanese media following him wherever he went. He had been Japan's top pitcher from 1990-94 but retired after that last season in order to free himself from the Japanese leagues' free-agent rules. He signed with the Dodgers for a record $2 million bonus without any assurance that he could dominate in the United States as he had in Japan.

He quickly proved that he could. In June, he went 6-0 with a 0.89 ERA, winning NL pitcher-of-the-month honors. He became the biggest story in baseball, a reincarnation of the Fernandomania phenomenon from 14 years before, at a time when the industry desperately needed something to divert its attention from the labor woes.

"He's an attraction, because there is both talent there and an unusual story," Dodgers GM Fred Claire said. "But it all starts with the talent. It's like when Mark Fidrych was talking to the ball. If he didn't get anybody out, he would have been doing that at Toledo or someplace."

Indeed, Nomo was quite a pitcher, phenomenon or

Nomo-mania. Japanese sensation Hideo Nomo caused a big stir in 1995, winning Baseball America's Rookie-of-the-Year honors.

not. His fastball consistently was clocked in the low 90s, his control was superb, and because of his odd delivery hitters couldn't get a read on his devastating forkball. Many believed that after one time around the league, batters would get used to him. It didn't happen.

"He's our go-to guy," Dodgers catcher Mike Piazza said. "He's really something special."

New Wave Of Expansion

Despite all the uncertainty and acrimony on the labor front, two investment groups anted up $130 million to join the Major League Baseball fraternity. The Arizona Diamondbacks and Tampa Bay Devil Rays were the big winners in the expansion sweepstakes, being awarded franchises that will begin play in 1998.

It had not yet been announced in which leagues they would play. Because of scheduling reasons, both almost assuredly will join the same league unless interleague play is adopted.

Tampa Bay finally got its franchise after being teased for years with the prospect of getting one. The Florida Marlins won out for the 1993 wave of expansion, and the fertile Tampa Bay area had been used by other teams over the years as a threat for getting concessions from their cities. That happened with the Twins (in 1983), Athletics (1985), White Sox (1988), Rangers (1988), Mariners (1992) and Giants (1992).

"It's been a path of 10,000 steps, 10,000 phone calls, 10,000 frustrations," said Vince Naimoli, head of the Tampa Bay ownership group. "Now we're at the end of the path, but we start a new path. We start to focus on hiring a general manager, on the (Suncoast) Dome, on the development of the franchise, on the minor league system, on Opening Day 1998. We're

APRIL

26—Royals righthander Kevin Appier pitched 6⅔ no-hit innings against the Orioles before reaching his pitch limit and being removed from the game. The Royals held on for a 5-1 win.

29—In a 10-3 loss to the Yankees, Royals outfielder Jon Nunnally became the 70th major leaguer to homer in his first at-bat, taking Yankees righthander Melido Perez deep to lead off the game.

MAY

2—Red Sox shortstop John Valentin and first baseman Mo Vaughn hit grand slams in back-to-back innings, accounting for the only runs in Boston's 8-0 win over the Yankees. It was the 41st time in history that a team hit two grand slams in one game.

2—The Giants beat the Dodgers 4-3 in 13 innings after neither team scored through the first 12 innings.

3—Indians third baseman David Bell made his major league debut in a 14-7 victory over Detroit, making the Bells the second three-generation family in baseball (the Boones were the first). Bell's grandfather Gus died four days later.

Eddie Murray

6—The Rockies got pinch-hit home runs in back-to-back innings in a 17-11 loss to the Dodgers. John Vander Wal hit a three-run shot in the sixth and Mike Kingery hit a solo homer in the seventh. The two teams combined for a major league season-high 38 hits.

7—The Twins and Indians played the longest game in either team's history, a 17-inning affair that lasted six hours, 36 minutes. The Indians won 10-9. The teams also combined to leave on base a season-high 39 runners.

10—Angels DH Chili Davis had a career-high five hits in an 11-2 win over the Rangers. He had hits in his first three at-bats the next day to give him eight consecutive hits, tying a franchise record. Davis was one of 16 players to collect five hits in a game in 1995. Four players had six.

14—Indians DH Eddie Murray hit his 463rd career home run in a 3-1 victory against the Orioles, tying him for 18th place on the all-time list with teammate Dave Winfield. Murray finished the season with 479 career homers, good for 16th place all-time. Winfield finished at 465, in 19th place.

20—In a 10-6 loss to Seattle, Twins outfielder Marty Cordova homered in his fifth consecutive game, tying a major league rookie record.

23—Cubs righthander Kevin Foster and Rockies righthander Marvin Freeman homered off each other in a 7-6 Cubs win at Coors Field. They became just the 10th duo to accomplish the feat this century.

24—Mariners third baseman Mike Blowers tied a team record with eight RBIs in a 15-6 win over the Red Sox. He also set a team mark for extra-base hits in one game with two doubles, a triple and a home run. Blowers also had seven RBIs Aug. 18 against Boston.

28—San Diego tied a National League record by scoring nine runs in the 10th inning of a 13-5 win over Philadelphia. The Phillies scored once in the bottom of the 10th.

28—Detroit pounded a major league season-high seven home runs against Chicago—and still lost 14-12. The White Sox hit five, giving the two teams a combined one-game, major league record 12.

JUNE

1—Rangers lefthander Kenny Rogers ran his season-high, scoreless innings streak to 39 before surrendering a run to the Twins in a 6-3 Texas win. Orel Hershiser set the record of 59 straight in 1988.

2—Red Sox shortstop John Valentin homered three times

and had five hits in a 6-5 win over the Mariners. Valentin had an American League season-high 15 total bases in the game.

3—Expos righthander Pedro Martinez was perfect through nine innings, but lost his no-hitter when Padres left fielder Bip Roberts doubled to lead off the 10th. The Expos hung on to win 1-0.

6—Rockies coach Don Zimmer abruptly retired in the fifth inning of a 5-4 win over the Cardinals.

10—Orioles third baseman Jeff Manto became the 24th major leaguer to homer in four consecutive at-bats when he connected in the second inning of a 6-2 win over the Angels. Manto had hit two homers June 9 and homered in his last at-bat in the previous game. Altogether he homered five times in six at-bats in the three games.

11—Oakland first baseman Mark McGwire hit three solo home runs off Red Sox lefthander Zane Smith in an 8-1 Athletics win.

11—Expos outfielder Rondell White had six hits and five runs, and hit for the cycle in a 13-inning, 10-8 win over the Giants.

14—Giants third baseman Mike Benjamin went 6-for-7 in a 13-inning, 4-3 win over the Cubs, giving him a major league record 14 hits in three games. Benjamin was 14-for-18 in that stretch.

14—Los Angeles righthander Hideo Nomo struck out 16 Pirates batters in an 8-5 Dodgers win, the most in the National League in 1995.

16—Marlins outfielder Andre Dawson hit his 400th career National League home run, and his 429th overall, in a 2-1 win over Philadelphia. Dawson finished the season with 436 home runs, 22nd-best all-time.

18—Tigers manager Sparky Anderson moved into third place on the all-time wins list with his 2,158th, in a 10-8 victory over Baltimore. He passed Bucky Harris. Anderson finished with 2,194 victories, trailing only Connie Mack (3,731) and John McGraw (2,763).

25—Rockies first baseman Andres Galarraga became the fourth major leaguer to homer in three consecutive innings in an 11-3 win at San Diego. Galarraga, who had seven RBIs in the game, went deep in the sixth, seventh

Sparky Anderson

and eighth innings and was on deck when the last out was made in the ninth.

29—White Sox third baseman Robin Ventura had five hits in a 17-13 win over the Brewers. The teams combined for an American League season-high 36 hits in the game.

30—Angels outfielder Jim Edmonds failed to get a hit for the first time in 24 games in an 8-5 loss to Oakland. He and Dante Bichette (May 22-June 18) each enjoyed season-high 23-game hitting streaks.

30—Indians DH Eddie Murray collected his 3,000th career hit off righthander Mike Trombley in a 4-1 Cleveland win. Murray finished the year with 3,071 hits, 15th-best all-time.

JULY

3—Rockies first baseman Andres Galarraga went 6-for-6, including two home runs, in a 15-10 win over the Astros.

7—Oakland righthander Ariel Prieto made his major league debut, becoming the first 1995 draftee to reach the big leagues barely a month after the Cuban defector was drafted. Prieto pitched six innings, allowing seven hits and four earned runs in a 4-2 loss to Toronto.

14—Dodgers righthander Ramon Martinez threw a no-hitter against the Marlins, winning 7-0. Only a seventh-inning walk separated Martinez from a perfect game.

15—Mariners lefthander Randy Johnson recorded an American League season-high 16 strikeouts in a 3-0, three-hit shutout of Toronto.

18—Marlins first baseman Greg Colbrunn homered twice and had seven RBIs in a 14-inning, 12-10 win over the Giants.

29—Royals outfielder Vince Coleman had five hits as Kansas City set a club record with 21 singles in a 16-inning, 5-4 win over the Tigers. The Royals only extra-base hit was a home run by outfielder Jon Nunnally in the bottom of the 16th.

30—White Sox DH John Kruk retired with a .300 career batting average after getting a hit in his final major league at-bat in the top of the first inning of an 8-3 loss at Batimore.

30—The Angels scored eight times in an 8-3 win over the Brewers, giving them 201 runs in July—the most a team had scored in one month since the Yankees scored 202 in July 1958.

AUGUST

8—Pirates third baseman Jeff King hit two home runs in the second inning of Pittsburgh's 9-5 win over the Giants, becoming just the 16th National Leaguer to accomplish the feat.

10—Yankees catcher Mike Stanley hit three home runs and had seven RBIs in a 10-9 loss to the Indians.

10—Umpire Jim Quick halted a game in Los Angeles with one out in the bottom of the ninth after fans repeatedly threw baseballs on the field. The Dodgers were forced to forfeit the game, which the Cardinals had been leading 2-1.

15—Reds outfielder Reggie Sanders hit three home runs in an 11-3 win over the Rockies.

Ramon Martinez

18—Cardinals closer Tom Henke earned his 300th career save in a 4-3 win over the Braves.

18—Seattle third baseman Mike Blowers hit a grand slam and a three-run homer in his first two at-bats, giving him seven RBIs in a 9-3 win over the Red Sox.

18—The Cubs pounded out major league season-highs of 26 runs and 27 hits en route to a 26-7 win over the Rockies. The 33 runs the teams scored also were a season high.

23—Yankees third baseman Wade Boggs picked up his 2,500th career hit as a pinch-hitter in a 2-1 loss to Oakland.

25—Phillies first baseman Gregg Jefferies hit for the cycle in a 17-4 win over the Dodgers.

26—San Diego tied a National League record when outfielder Melvin Nieves hit the club's ninth grand slam of the season. Nieves' blast wasn't enough as the Padres lost to the Mets 7-6.

27—In a 2-1 win over Chicago, Blue Jays DH Paul Molitor went 4-for-4 for the second consecutive game, giving him eight consecutive hits, tying a club mark.

27—Dodgers catcher Mike Piazza doubled twice and homered twice, driving in seven runs in a 9-1 win over the Phillies. One of his home runs was a grand slam.

30—Tigers teammates Alan Trammell and Lou Whitaker played in their 1,914th game together, tying the American League record for teammates, in a 10-7 loss to Chicago.

31—Yankees outfielder Paul O'Neill hit three homers and drove in eight runs in an 11-6 win over the Angels. O'Neill had an AL-best 13 total bases in the game.

SEPTEMBER

1—Tigers manager Sparky Anderson managed his 4,000th major league game, a 14-4 loss to the Indians.

2—White Sox outfielder Tim Raines was caught stealing in a 10-4 win over the Blue Jays, snapping his string of 40 consecutive stolen bases, an American League record.

3—Yankees shortstop Tony Fernandez hit for the cycle in a 10-9 loss to Oakland.

4—White Sox third baseman Robin Ventura homered twice and drove in eight runs in a 14-3 win over the Rangers.

6—Orioles shortstop Cal Ripken played in his 2,131st consecutive game, breaking Lou Gehrig's record that had stood since 1939. Ripken homered in the bottom of the fourth inning and received a 22-minute ovation from the Camden Yards crowd in the middle of the fifth inning when he took a victory lap around the field. Baltimore beat California 4-2.

8—Cleveland ended a 41-year postseason drought by clinching the AL Central Division with a 3-2 win over Baltimore.

8—The Red Sox tied a major league record with four consecutive pinch hits in the eighth inning of an 8-4 loss to the Yankees.

9—Yankees first baseman Don Mattingly scored his 1,000th career run in a 9-1 win over the Red Sox.

12—In a 5-4 loss, the Reds turned their second triple play of the season.

15—Tigers first baseman Cecil Fielder hit his 250th career home run in a 3-2 win over the Rangers.

15—Cardinals shortstop Ozzie Smith turned his 1,554th double play in a 7-6 loss to the Dodgers, setting a major league record.

16—Braves righthander Greg Maddux set a major league record with his 17th consecutive road victory, a 6-1 win over the Reds.

17—In an 11-3 win over the Cubs, Padres third baseman Ken Caminiti hit home runs from each side of the plate for the second consecutive night.

18—Marlins outfielder Gary Sheffield went 3-for-3 with two homers and seven RBIs in a 13-10 loss to the Phillies, giving him eight consecutive hits over two games.

19—Rockies first baseman Andres Galarraga homered in a 15-4 loss to the Padres, giving the Rockies four players with 30 or more home runs—Dante Bichette, Vinny Castilla, Galarraga and Larry Walker. The 1977 Dodgers were the only other team ever to have four 30 home run hitters.

19—Indians outfielder Albert Belle homered in three straight at-bats in an 8-2 win over the White Sox.

19—Padres third baseman Ken Caminiti drove in eight runs while homering from both sides of the plate for the third time in four games—a major league record—in San Diego's 15-4 win over Colorado.

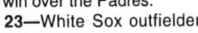

21—Rockies pinch-hitter John Vander Wal set a major league record with his 26th pinch hit of the season, a solo homer in a 5-3 loss to the Giants.

22—Orioles DH Harold Baines hit his 300th career home run in a 10-3 win over the Brewers.

22—Dodgers third baseman Tim Wallach picked up his 2,000th career hit in a 6-5 win over the Padres.

23—White Sox outfielder

Gary Sheffield

Lance Johnson went 6-for-6 with a season-best three triples and third baseman Robin Ventura went 5-for-6 with three doubles in a 14-4 win over the Twins. Johnson was the only AL player with six hits in a game in 1995.

30—Indians outfielder Albert Belle hit his 50th home run in a 3-2 win over the Royals, making him the first player ever to have 50 homers and 50 doubles in one season. He also became just the 12th player to hit 50 homers in one year.

OCTOBER

1—Righthander Mike Mussina pitched the Orioles fifth consecutive shutout, blanking the Tigers 4-0 on the last day of the season. The last time an AL staff threw five straight shutouts was 1974—also by the Orioles.

2—The Mariners defeated the Angels 9-1 in a one-game playoff for the AL West Division crown, advancing Seattle to postseason play for the first time in the team's 19-year history.

—Compiled by JAMES BAILEY

MAJOR LEAGUE DEBUTS, 1995

Player, Pos.	Club	Debut
Acevedo, Juan, rhp	Rockies	April 30
Adams, Terry, rhp	Cubs	Aug. 10
Ahearne, Pat, rhp	Tigers	June 14
Alberro, Jose, rhp	Rangers	April 27
Alfonzo, Edgar, 2b-3b	Mets	April 26
Alvarez, Tavo, rhp	Expos	Aug. 21
Andrews, Shane, 3b	Expos	April 26
Andujar, Luis, rhp	White Sox	Sept. 8
Aurilia, Rich, ss	Giants	Sept. 6
Bailey, Roger, rhp	Rockies	April 27
Baker, Scott, lhp	Athletics	July 17
Baldwin, James, rhp	White Sox	April 30
Barber, Brian, rhp	Cardinals	Aug. 12
Bark, Brian, lhp	Red Sox	July 6
Barry, Jeff, of	Mets	June 9
Bates, Jason, 2b	Rockies	April 26
Battle, Allen, of	Cardinals	April 26
Bell, David, 3b	Indians	May 3
Benard, Marvin, of	Giants	Sept. 5
Benes, Alan, rhp	Cardinals	Sept. 19
Benitez, Yamil, of	Expos	Sept. 16
Bennett, Erik, rhp	Angels	May 15
Bennett, Gary, c	Phillies	Sept. 24
Bertotti, Mike, lhp	White Sox	July 29
Berumen, Andres, rhp	Padres	April 27
Blomdahl, Ben, rhp	Tigers	April 28
Bochtler, Doug, rhp	Padres	May 5
Boehringer, Brian, rhp	Yankees	April 30
Borowski, Joe, rhp	Orioles	July 9
Bradshaw, Terry, of	Cardinals	May 4
Brady, Doug, 2b	White Sox	Sept. 5
Brandenburg, Mark, rhp	Rangers	July 20
Brewington, Jamie, rhp	Giants	July 24
Brito, Jorge, c	Rockies	May 6
Bunch, Melvin, rhp	Royals	May 6
Busch, Mike, 3b	Dodgers	Aug. 30
Byrd, Paul, rhp	Mets	July 28
Caceres, Edgar, 2b	Royals	June 8
Cameron, Mike, of	White Sox	Aug. 27
Carmona, Rafael, rhp	Mariners	May 18
Carrara, Giovanni, rhp	Blue Jays	July 29
Castillo, Alberto, c	Mets	May 29
Castro, Juan, ss	Dodgers	Sept. 2
Cedeno, Roger, of	Dodgers	June 20
Christiansen, Jason, lhp	Pirates	April 26
Clark, Tony, 1b	Tigers	Sept. 3
Clontz, Brad, rhp	Braves	April 26
Cookson, Brent, of	Royals	Aug. 12
Coomer, Ron, 3b	Twins	Aug. 1
Cordova, Marty, of	Twins	April 26
Cornelius, Reid, rhp	Expos	April 29
Counsell, Craig, ss	Rockies	Sept. 17
Courtright, John, lhp	Reds	May 6
Crabtree, Tim, rhp	Blue Jays	June 23
Creek, Doug, lhp	Cardinals	Sept. 17
Damon, Johnny, of	Royals	Aug. 12
Davison, Scott, rhp	Mariners	Sept. 4
Dedrick, Jim, rhp	Orioles	Aug. 12
Devarez, Cesar, c	Orioles	June 2
Dishman, Glenn, lhp	Padres	June 22
Dougherty, Jim, rhp	Astros	April 27
Dunbar, Matt, lhp	Marlins	April 26
Durham, Ray, 2b	White Sox	April 26
Eddy, Chris, lhp	Athletics	April 26
Edenfield, Ken, rhp	Angels	May 11
Encarnacion, Angelo, c	Pirates	May 2
Ericks, John, rhp	Pirates	June 24
Eshelman, Vaughn, lhp	Red Sox	May 2
Estes, Shawn, lhp	Giants	Sept. 16
Fermin, Ramon, rhp	Athletics	Aug. 6
Florence, Don, lhp	Mets	Aug. 8
Fonville, Chad, 2b-ss	Expos	April 28
Fordyce, Brook, c	Mets	April 26
Franco, Matt, 1b-3b	Cubs	Sept. 6
Garcia, Freddy, 3b	Pirates	May 3
Garcia, Karim, of	Dodgers	Sept. 2
Giambi, Jason, 3b	Athletics	May 8
Gibralter, Steve, of	Reds	June 1
Giles, Brian, of	Indians	Sept. 16
Giovanola, Ed, 3b	Braves	Sept. 10
Givens, Brian, lhp	Brewers	June 24
Goodwin, Curtis, of	Orioles	June 2
Grace, Mike, rhp	Phillies	Sept. 1
Grott, Matt, lhp	Reds	May 4
Grudzielanek, Mark, ss	Expos	April 28
Hajek, Dave, 2b	Astros	Sept. 15
Hancock, Lee, lhp	Pirates	Sept. 3
Hansell, Greg, rhp	Dodgers	April 28
Harikkala, Tim, rhp	Mariners	May 27
Hartgraves, Dean, lhp	Astros	May 3
Hatteberg, Scott, c	Red Sox	Sept. 8
Hawkins, LaTroy, rhp	Twins	April 29
Haynes, Jimmy, rhp	Orioles	Sept. 14
Heredia, Wilson, rhp	Rangers	April 27
Hermanson, Dustin, rhp	Padres	May 8
Herrera, Jose, of	Athletics	Aug. 12
Higginson, Bobby, of	Tigers	April 26
Hollandsworth, Todd, of	Dodgers	April 26
Hook, Chris, rhp	Giants	April 30
Hosey, Dwayne, of	Red Sox	Sept. 1
Hubbard, Mike, c	Cubs	July 13
Hudson, Joe, rhp	Red Sox	June 11
Huisman, Rich, rhp	Royals	Sept. 4
Hurtado, Edwin, rhp	Blue Jays	May 22
Isringhausen, Jason, rhp	Mets	July 17
James, Mike, rhp	Angels	April 19
Jeter, Derek, ss	Yankees	May 29
Johns, Doug, lhp	Athletics	July 8
Johnson, Mark, 1b	Pirates	April 26
Jordan, Kevin, 2b	Phillies	Aug. 8
Jordan, Ricardo, lhp	Blue Jays	June 23
Karchner, Matt, rhp	White Sox	July 18
Karl, Scott, lhp	Brewers	May 4
Karp, Ryan, lhp	Phillies	June 23
Keyser, Brian, rhp	White Sox	June 2
Konuszewski, Dennis, rhp	Pirates	Aug. 4
Kowitz, Brian, of	Braves	June 4
Krivda, Rick, lhp	Orioles	July 7
Kroon, Marc, rhp	Padres	July 7
Lawton, Matt, of	Twins	Sept. 5
Ledesma, Aaron, ss	Mets	July 2
Lira, Felipe, rhp	Tigers	April 27
Loaiza, Esteban, rhp	Pirates	April 29
Lomon, Kevin, rhp	Mets	April 27
Loretta, Mark, ss-2b	Brewers	Sept. 10
Mahay, Ron, of	Red Sox	May 21
Mantei, Matt, rhp	Marlins	June 18
Marquez, Isidro, rhp	White Sox	April 26
Martinez, Sandy, c	Blue Jays	June 24
Masteller, Dan, 1b	Twins	June 23
Mathews, T.J., rhp	Cardinals	July 28
Maxcy, Brian, rhp	Tigers	May 26
May, Darrell, lhp	Braves	Sept. 10
McAndrew, Jamie, rhp	Brewers	July 17
McCracken, Quinton, of	Rockies	Sept. 17
McCurry, Jeff, rhp	Pirates	May 6
Mecir, Jim, rhp	Mariners	Sept. 4
Menhart, Paul, rhp	Blue Jays	April 27
Mimbs, Mike, lhp	Phillies	May 6
Mintz, Steve, rhp	Giants	May 18
Morel, Ramon, rhp	Pirates	July 6
Mouton, Lyle, of	White Sox	June 7
Munoz, Noe, c	Dodgers	April 30
Munoz, Oscar, rhp	Twins	Aug. 6
Murray, Matt, rhp	Braves	Aug. 12
Myers, Mike, lhp	Marlins	April 27
Nevin, Phil, 3b	Astros	June 11
Nichting, Chris, rhp	Rangers	May 15
Nitkowski, C.J., lhp	Reds	June 3
Nomo, Hideo, rhp	Dodgers	May 2
Norman, Les, of	Royals	May 29
Nunnally, Jon, of	Royals	April 26
Ochoa, Alex, of	Mets	Sept. 11
Osuna, Antonio, rhp	Dodgers	April 26
Otero, Ricky, of	Mets	April 26
Owens, Eric, 2b	Reds	June 6
Palmeiro, Orlando, of	Angels	July 1
Parra, Jose, rhp	Dodgers	May 7
Parris, Steve, rhp	Pirates	June 21
Patterson, Jeff, rhp	Yankees	April 30
Pemberton, Rudy, of	Tigers	April 26
Penn, Shannon, 2b	Tigers	April 28
Percival, Troy, rhp	Angels	April 26
Perez, Carlos, lhp	Expos	April 27
Perez, Eddie, c	Braves	Sept. 10
Perez, Tomas, ss	Blue Jays	May 3
Person, Robert, rhp	Mets	Sept. 18
Pettitte, Andy, lhp	Yankees	April 29
Pierce, Jeff, rhp	Red Sox	April 26
Pittsley, Jim, rhp	Royals	May 23
Posada, Jorge, c	Yankees	Sept. 4
Powell, Jay, rhp	Marlins	Sept. 10
Pozo, Arquimedez, 2b	Mariners	Sept. 13
Prieto, Ariel, rhp	Athletics	July 2
Pulsipher, Bill, lhp	Mets	June 17
Raabe, Brian, 2b	Twins	Sept. 17
Radke, Brad, rhp	Twins	April 29
Randa, Joe, 3b	Royals	April 30
Rekar, Bryan, rhp	Rockies	July 19
Reyes, Alberto, rhp	Brewers	April 27
Ricci, Chuck, rhp	Phillies	Sept. 8
Rivera, Mariano, rhp	Yankees	May 23
Rivera, Roberto, lhp	Cubs	Sept. 3
Rivera, Ruben, of	Yankees	Sept. 3
Roa, Joe, rhp	Indians	Sept. 20
Roberson, Sid, lhp	Brewers	May 20
Robinson, Kenny, rhp	Blue Jays	July 20
Rodriguez, Felix, rhp	Dodgers	May 13
Rodriguez, Frank, rhp	Red Sox	April 26
Rodriguez, Steve, 2b	Red Sox	April 30
Rogers, Jimmy, rhp	Blue Jays	July 30
Rosselli, Joe, lhp	Giants	April 30
Santangelo, F.P., util	Expos	Aug. 2
Schall, Gene, 1b	Phillies	June 16
Schmidt, Curtis, rhp	Expos	April 28
Schmidt, Jason, rhp	Braves	April 28
Sefcik, Kevin, ss	Phillies	Sept. 8
Simas, Bill, rhp	White Sox	Aug. 15
Sirotka, Mike, lhp	White Sox	July 19
Snopek, Chris, 3b	White Sox	July 31
Sodowsky, Clint, rhp	Tigers	Sept. 4
Sparks, Steve, rhp	Brewers	April 28
Springer, Dennis, rhp	Phillies	Sept. 14
Steverson, Todd, of	Tigers	April 28
Stewart, Shannon, of	Blue Jays	Sept. 2
Sturtze, Tanyon, rhp	Cubs	May 3
Stynes, Chris, 2b	Royals	May 19
Sullivan, Scott, rhp	Reds	May 6
Suppan, Jeff, rhp	Red Sox	July 17
Swartzbaugh, Dave, rhp	Cubs	Sept. 3
Sweeney, Mark, 1b	Cardinals	Aug. 4
Sweeney, Mike, c	Royals	Sept. 18
Taylor, Scott, rhp	Rangers	July 28
Thobe, J.J., rhp	Expos	Sept. 18
Thobe, Tom, lhp	Braves	Sept. 12
Thomas, Larry, lhp	White Sox	Aug. 11
Thomas, Mike, lhp	Brewers	July 12
Timmons, Ozzie, of	Cubs	April 26
Torres, Dilson, rhp	Royals	April 29
Tremie, Chris, c	White Sox	July 1
Tucker, Michael, of	Royals	April 26
Unroe, Tim, 1b	Brewers	May 30
Urbina, Ugueth, rhp	Expos	May 9
Valdes, Marc, rhp	Marlins	Aug. 28
Valdez, Carlos, rhp	Giants	July 18
Veras, Quilvio, 2b	Marlins	April 26
Villone, Ron, lhp	Mariners	April 28
Vitiello, Joe, of-1b	Royals	April 29
Wade, Terrell, lhp	Braves	Sept. 12
Wagner, Billy, lhp	Astros	Sept. 14
Walker, Pete, rhp	Mets	June 7
Wall, Donne, rhp	Astros	Sept. 2
Ware, Jeff, rhp	Blue Jays	Sept. 2
Wasdin, John, rhp	Athletics	Aug. 24
Watkins, Scott, lhp	Twins	Aug. 2
Wengert, Don, rhp	Athletics	April 30
Whiteside, Sean, lhp	Tigers	Sept. 8
Widger, Chris, c	Mariners	June 23
Williams, George, c	Athletics	July 14
Williams, Todd, rhp	Dodgers	April 29
Wilson, Gary, rhp	Pirates	April 30
Wojciechowski, Steve, lhp	Athletics	July 18
Wolcott, Bob, rhp	Mariners	Aug. 18
Zaun, Gregg, c	Orioles	June 24

into the fun path."

Jerry Colangelo, owner of the National Basketball Association's Phoenix Suns, headed Arizona's group. He immediately hired Joe Garagiola Jr., the son of the former major leaguer and a former agent with no significant experience in a baseball front office, as his general manager. Garagiola hired Don Mitchell, a former assistant scouting director with the Braves, as his scouting director.

The Braves took an even larger hit when the Devil Rays tabbed Chuck LaMar as their general manager. LaMar had been an assistant GM in Atlanta and for five years had headed that club's immensely successful minor league and scouting departments.

LaMar chose Bill Livesey as his scouting director. Livesey had been the Yankees scouting director and an employee of that organization for 18 years before George Steinbrenner fired him in a shocking September purge of his team's minor league department.

Enshrined. New Hall of Famers, former Philadelphia stars Richie Ashburn, left, and Mike Schmidt.

JOHN KLEIN

Hall Inducts Schmidt, Others

Cooperstown invited five legends of the game to become enshrined in the Hall of Fame in 1995, among them a man considered to be the greatest third baseman of all time.

Mike Schmidt, who hit 548 home runs in his 18-year career, all with the Phillies, was elected during his first year on the ballot and was the only inductee in the writers' voting.

"If I had it to do all over again, I'd do it in Philadelphia," said Schmidt, who despite his excellence was embraced by Phillies fans only late in his career. "The only thing I would change would be me. I'd be less sensitive, I'd be more outgoing and I'd be more appreciative of what you expected of me.

"My relationship with the Philadelphia fans always has been misunderstood. Can we put that to rest here today? Sure, there were some tough nights and some tough games at Veterans Stadium, but what I remember most are the cheers of anticipation as I came up for a big at-bat and the curtain calls after home runs and the No. 20 hung on the outfield wall."

The Hall of Fame Veterans Committee inducted four other new members to Cooperstown:

■ Another former Phillie, Richie Ashburn, now the team's popular announcer. The outfielder had a lifetime .308 average during his 1948-62 career and had more hits than any player in the 1950s. He won batting titles in 1955 (.338) and 1958 (.350) and was considered one of the best defensive players of his time.

■ Former Negro League standout Leon Day, who died in Baltimore six days after being elected March 13. He pitched and played outfield and second base for the Newark Eagles in his 1934-50 career, and became the first Negro League star to be elected since Ray Dandridge in 1987.

"Leon had a vision of his induction right before his election," said Geraldine Day, Day's widow. "He said, 'Baby, I'm in.' I said, 'It's only 8 o'clock in the morning. They haven't even voted yet.'"

Mickey Mantle

"A few hours later, Leon's dream came true . . . Six days later, his weak heart gave out."

■ Righthander Vic Willis, who went 249-205 with a 2.63 ERA from 1898-1910 with the Boston, Pittsburgh and St. Louis National League clubs. He completed a whopping 388 games, 45 of them in 1902.

■ National League founder William Hulbert, who also served as NL president from 1877-82. He was most noted for his efforts to rid the game of gambling.

Bob Wolff, the longtime voice of the Washington Senators in his 57th year as a broadcaster, was inducted to the media wing of the Hall.

Baseball Mourns For Mantle

In a season of triumph and heartache, there was no sadder moment for many fans than when Mickey Mantle died Aug. 13 at the age of 63.

Arguably the best player of his era, Mantle left an indelible impression on baseball and those who watched him play. He was the definitive Yankee hero who could run as fast as he could hit a ball far. He played from 1951-69 and retired with 536 home runs, which today stands eighth all-time.

When he died in Dallas after a battle with liver cancer, during which he received a liver transplant and heightened awareness of the importance of organ donorship, the admitted alcoholic took his last chance to influence the millions who loved him.

"Don't be like me," he said. "God gave me a body and the ability to play baseball. He gave me everything. I just wasted it."

Major league ballparks across the nation held a moment of silence for the slugger the afternoon after he passed. Tributes to him were especially heartfelt in New York.

"I think the reason people loved him so much was that he portrayed the innocence of what we all want to be," said former Yankee and current team announcer Bobby Murcer, choking back tears. "I don't think that to this day that Mickey realized how people felt about him, how he touched their lives."

For the baseball community, it was the saddest day in an awfully sad year.

Ecstasy At Last For Team Of The '90s

By JOHN PERROTTO

Though they had won more games than any team in the 1990s, no one was ready to coronate the Atlanta Braves as The Team of the Decade.

Until the 1995 World Series.

The Braves finally put to rest the notion they didn't have what it takes to win it all as they defeated the Cleveland Indians in a tense six-game series, where  five games were decided by one run.

When Atlanta center fielder Marquis Grissom squeezed Carlos Baerga's fly ball for the final out of the series, clinching a 1-0 victory in Game Six, the Braves ended 30 years of frustration.

Gone were the nightmares of Series losses to Minnesota in 1991 and Toronto in 1992, along with the National League Championship Series defeat to Philadelphia in 1993 and the strike that dashed the Braves' postseason hopes in 1994.

After dispatching Colorado in four games in the new best-of-5 National League Division Series, then pulling off a stunning four-game sweep of Cincinnati in the National League Championship Series, the Braves had finally cleared their biggest hurdle.

"Now we'll be thought of as the team of the '90s," righthander John Smoltz said. "Toronto had two World Series championships (in 1992-93) but now we're right there with them."

"You always think about what it would finally be like to win the World Series," second baseman Mark Lemke said. "You think about how good the moment will feel when you finally get to that point, when it finally becomes a reality after you've tried so hard, but then you block it out. You realize that nothing has been given to you before, that everything always has been a battle in the World Series in the past, and that this will be a battle, too.

"Now that it's reality, though, it's the greatest feeling in the world."

"We've been through so much here, so I'm happy for everybody, especially the ones who were here during the bad times," lefthander Tom Glavine said.

Glavine Pitches Masterpiece

Glavine, who had been with the Braves longer than any other player, knew all too well about the bad times.

He broke in with Atlanta in 1987 as the Braves finished fifth in the six-team NL West. They wound up in last place each of the next three seasons before beginning their turnaround with a core of young players provided by Atlanta's first-rate minor league and scouting departments.

So, it was most fitting Glavine would be the World Series MVP and the star on a night Atlanta broke

World Series MVP. Braves lefthander Tom Glavine pitched one-hit ball for eight innings in Game Six to clinch the Series.

through and brought the South its first championship.

After getting the win in Game Two, allowing two runs on three hits in six innings, Glavine was masterful in the finale.

He pitched one-hit ball over eight innings in Game Six, allowing only a leadoff single to Tony Pena in the sixth. Mark Wohlers retired the side in order in the ninth for the save.

The victory was also sweet on another front for Glavine, booed earlier in the season by fans bitter that Glavine, the Braves' player representative, played such a visible role in baseball's labor woes.

"There has been so much talk about me being the perfect guy to pitch the clincher because I've been around here longer than anybody and through 100-loss seasons and what a great way to vindicate yourself from the strike," Glavine said. "I didn't think about that stuff. That wasn't the reason I was out there pitching. I was just trying to wrap up a championship for our club."

Justice Provides Spark

Glavine did it with help from another player looked at as controversial in the eyes of Braves' fans.

David Justice's leadoff solo homer off reliever Jim

Poole in the sixth inning accounted for the game's only run. The blast came one day after the right fielder blasted the home fans by telling the Atlanta Journal-Constitution, "If we don't win, they'll probably burn down our houses. You really have to do something great to get them out of their seats."

"The monkey was definitely there, sitting on my back," Justice said. "Heck, he was sitting on my door. I felt a lot of pressure coming to the stadium for this game, but several of the guys told me they were behind me.

"My brain was hurting. I felt the weight of the world on my shoulders. If we would have ended up losing this thing, it would have haunted me for a long time."

Justice's hit sent Braves fans, somewhat reserved after going through so many past postseason heartbreaks, out of their seats and into a frenzy.

But it was clearly pitching that won the World Series.

Atlanta had the major leagues' best ERA during the regular season, and Cleveland had scored the most runs. The time-honored truism "good pitching stops good hitting" was borne out, though. The Indians managed just 19 runs and a .179 batting average in the six games, flopping miserably in the franchise's first World Series appearance since 1954.

Many of Cleveland's big bats went silent as Eddie Murray hit .105, Baerga batted .192 and Manny Ramirez finished at .222. Kenny Lofton also faded, going 0-for-12 in the last three games after starting 5-for-12.

The frustration of the Cleveland hitters was obvious. Though Albert Belle hit two home runs later in the Series, he was clearly frustrated after going 1-for-6 in the first two games. For no apparent reason, he launched into an obscenity-laden tirade at NBC-TV reporter Hannah Storm before Game Three.

"We faced three aces," Cleveland righthander Orel Hershiser said. "The ace of aces is Greg Maddux, ace No. 2 is Tom Glavine and ace No. 3 is John Smoltz. Then they finish you off with Mark Wohlers. It is a deep staff that's well-managed. In a short series, a

Responds under pressure. Braves outfielder Dave Justice criticized Atlanta fans, then responded with a game-winning homer in Game Six.

pitching staff can get on a roll and set down a good lineup."

"This pitching staff is as good as it gets," Glavine said. "I'm not saying it's the best in baseball or one of the best ever. But we feel good about what we do."

"You have the pitching we've had the last five years and you have to think it's appropriate we shut down one of the best hitting teams in baseball," Atlanta manager Bobby Cox said.

Maddux Masterful

Atlanta's pitching showed early as Maddux tossed a two-hitter, allowing a pair of unearned runs, as the Braves took a 3-2 victory at home in Game One. The Braves pinned Hershiser with his first-ever postseason loss.

Glavine was credited with the 4-3 victory in Game Two. However, the big hero was catcher Javier Lopez. His two-run homer off Dennis Martinez in the sixth snapped a 2-2 tie and his pickoff of Ramirez at first base in the eighth thwarted a Cleveland rally in a one-run game.

The series shifted to Jacobs Field for Game Three and the Indians got their first win, 7-6 in 11 innings. Mur-

Braves mastermind. Atlanta manager Bobby Cox finally was rewarded for building the Braves into one of the game's marquee franchises.

WORLD SERIES
YEAR-BY-YEAR

Year	Winner	Manager	Loser	Manager	Result	MVP
1903	Boston (AL)	Jimmy Collins	Pittsburgh (NL)	Fred Clarke	5-3	None Selected
1904	NO SERIES					
1905	New York (NL)	John McGraw	Philadelphia (AL)	Connie Mack	4-1	None Selected
1906	Chicago (AL)	Fielder Jones	Chicago (NL)	Frank Chance	4-2	None Selected
1907	Chicago (NL)	Frank Chance	Detroit (AL)	Hugh Jennings	4-0	None Selected
1908	Chicago (NL)	Frank Chance	Detroit (AL)	Hugh Jennings	4-1	None Selected
1909	Pittsburgh (NL)	Fred Clarke	Detroit (AL)	Hugh Jennings	4-3	None Selected
1910	Philadelphia (AL)	Connie Mack	Chicago (NL)	Frank Chance	4-1	None Selected
1911	Philadelphia (AL)	Connie Mack	New York (NL)	John McGraw	4-2	None Selected
1912	Boston (AL)	Jake Stahl	New York (NL)	John McGraw	4-3-1	None Selected
1913	Philadelphia (AL)	Connie Mack	New York (NL)	John McGraw	4-1	None Selected
1914	Boston (NL)	George Stallings	Philadelphia (AL)	Connie Mack	4-0	None Selected
1915	Boston (AL)	Bill Carrigan	Philadelphia (NL)	Pat Moran	4-1	None Selected
1916	Boston (AL)	Bill Carrigan	Brooklyn (NL)	Wilbert Robinson	4-1	None Selected
1917	Chicago (AL)	Pants Rowland	New York (NL)	John McGraw	4-2	None Selected
1918	Boston (AL)	Ed Barrow	Chicago (NL)	Fred Mitchell	4-2	None Selected
1919	Cincinnati (NL)	Pat Moran	Chicago (AL)	Kid Gleason	5-3	None Selected
1920	Cleveland (AL)	Tris Speaker	Brooklyn (NL)	Wilbert Robinson	5-2	None Selected
1921	New York (NL)	John McGraw	New York (AL)	Miller Huggins	5-3	None Selected
1922	New York (NL)	John McGraw	New York (AL)	Miller Huggins	4-0	None Selected
1923	New York (AL)	Miller Huggins	New York (NL)	John McGraw	4-2	None Selected
1924	Washington (AL)	Bucky Harris	New York (NL)	John McGraw	4-3	None Selected
1925	Pittsburgh (NL)	Bill McKechnie	Washington (AL)	Bucky Harris	4-3	None Selected
1926	St. Louis (NL)	Rogers Hornsby	New York (AL)	Miller Huggins	4-3	None Selected
1927	New York (AL)	Miller Huggins	Pittsburgh (NL)	Donie Bush	4-0	None Selected
1928	New York (AL)	Miller Huggins	St. Louis (NL)	Bill McKechnie	4-0	None Selected
1929	Philadelphia (AL)	Connie Mack	Chicago (NL)	Joe McCarthy	4-1	None Selected
1930	Philadelphia (AL)	Connie Mack	St. Louis (NL)	Gabby Street	4-2	None Selected
1931	St. Louis (NL)	Gabby Street	Philadelphia (AL)	Connie Mack	4-3	None Selected
1932	New York (AL)	Joe McCarthy	Chicago (NL)	Charlie Grimm	4-0	None Selected
1933	New York (NL)	Bill Terry	Washington (AL)	Joe Cronin	4-1	None Selected
1934	St. Louis (NL)	Frankie Frisch	Detroit (AL)	Mickey Cochrane	4-3	None Selected
1935	Detroit (AL)	Mickey Cochrane	Chicago (NL)	Charlie Grimm	4-2	None Selected
1936	New York (AL)	Joe McCarthy	New York (NL)	Bill Terry	4-2	None Selected
1937	New York (AL)	Joe McCarthy	New York (NL)	Bill Terry	4-1	None Selected
1938	New York (AL)	Joe McCarthy	Chicago (NL)	Gabby Hartnett	4-0	None Selected
1939	New York (AL)	Joe McCarthy	Cincinnati (NL)	Bill McKechnie	4-0	None Selected
1940	Cincinnati (NL)	Bill McKechnie	Detroit (AL)	Del Baker	4-3	None Selected
1941	New York (AL)	Joe McCarthy	Brooklyn (NL)	Leo Durocher	4-1	None Selected
1942	St. Louis (NL)	Billy Southworth	New York (AL)	Joe McCarthy	4-1	None Selected
1943	New York (AL)	Joe McCarthy	St. Louis (NL)	Billy Southworth	4-1	None Selected
1944	St. Louis (NL)	Billy Southworth	St. Louis (AL)	Luke Sewell	4-2	None Selected
1945	Detroit (AL)	Steve O'Neill	Chicago (NL)	Charlie Grimm	4-3	None Selected
1946	St. Louis (NL)	Eddie Dyer	Boston (AL)	Joe Cronin	4-3	None Selected
1947	New York (AL)	Bucky Harris	Brooklyn (NL)	Burt Shotton	4-3	None Selected
1948	Cleveland (AL)	Lou Boudreau	Boston (NL)	Billy Southworth	4-2	None Selected
1949	New York (AL)	Casey Stengel	Brooklyn (NL)	Burt Shotton	4-1	None Selected
1950	New York (AL)	Casey Stengel	Philadelphia (NL)	Eddie Sawyer	4-0	None Selected
1951	New York (AL)	Casey Stengel	New York (NL)	Leo Durocher	4-2	None Selected
1952	New York (AL)	Casey Stengel	Brooklyn (NL)	Chuck Dressen	4-3	None Selected
1953	New York (AL)	Casey Stengel	Brooklyn (NL)	Chuck Dressen	4-2	None Selected
1954	New York (NL)	Leo Durocher	Cleveland (AL)	Al Lopez	4-0	None Selected
1955	Brooklyn (NL)	Walter Alston	New York (AL)	Casey Stengel	4-3	Johnny Podres, p, Brooklyn
1956	New York (AL)	Casey Stengel	Brooklyn (NL)	Walter Alston	4-3	Don Larsen, p, New York
1957	Milwaukee (NL)	Fred Haney	New York (AL)	Casey Stengel	4-3	Lew Burdette, p, Milwaukee
1958	New York (AL)	Casey Stengel	Milwaukee (NL)	Fred Haney	4-3	Bob Turley, p, New York
1959	Los Angeles (NL)	Walter Alston	Chicago (AL)	Al Lopez	4-2	Larry Sherry, p, Los Angeles
1960	Pittsburgh (NL)	Danny Murtaugh	New York (AL)	Casey Stengel	4-3	Bobby Richardson, 2b, New York
1961	New York (AL)	Ralph Houk	Cincinnati (NL)	Fred Hutchinson	4-1	Whitey Ford, p, New York
1962	New York (AL)	Ralph Houk	San Francisco (NL)	Alvin Dark	4-3	Ralph Terry, p, New York
1963	Los Angeles (NL)	Walter Alston	New York (AL)	Ralph Houk	4-0	Sandy Koufax, p, Los Angeles
1964	St. Louis (NL)	Johnny Keene	New York (AL)	Yogi Berra	4-3	Bob Gibson, p, St. Louis
1965	Los Angeles (NL)	Walter Alston	Minnesota (AL)	Sam Mele	4-3	Sandy Koufax, p, Los Angeles
1966	Baltimore (AL)	Hank Bauer	Los Angeles (NL)	Walter Alston	4-0	Frank Robinson, of, Baltimore
1967	St. Louis (NL)	Red Schoendienst	Boston (AL)	Dick Williams	4-3	Bob Gibson, p, St. Louis
1968	Detroit (AL)	Mayo Smith	St. Louis (NL)	Red Schoendienst	4-3	Mickey Lolich, p, Detroit
1969	New York (NL)	Gil Hodges	Baltimore (AL)	Earl Weaver	4-1	Donn Clendenon, 1b, New York
1970	Baltimore (AL)	Earl Weaver	Cincinnati (NL)	Sparky Anderson	4-1	Brooks Robinson, 3b, Baltimore
1971	Pittsburgh (NL)	Danny Murtaugh	Baltimore (AL)	Earl Weaver	4-3	Roberto Clemente, of, Pittsburgh
1972	Oakland (AL)	Dick Williams	Cincinnati (NL)	Sparky Anderson	4-3	Gene Tenace, c, Oakland
1973	Oakland (AL)	Dick Williams	New York (NL)	Yogi Berra	4-3	Reggie Jackson, of, Oakland
1974	Oakland (AL)	Alvin Dark	Los Angeles (NL)	Walter Alston	4-1	Rollie Fingers, p, Oakland
1975	Cincinnati (NL)	Sparky Anderson	Boston (AL)	Darrell Johnson	4-3	Pete Rose, 3b, Cincinnati
1976	Cincinnati (NL)	Sparky Anderson	New York (AL)	Billy Martin	4-0	Johnny Bench, c, Cincinnati
1977	New York (AL)	Billy Martin	Los Angeles (NL)	Tom Lasorda	4-2	Reggie Jackson, of, New York
1978	New York (AL)	Bob Lemon	Los Angeles (NL)	Tom Lasorda	4-2	Bucky Dent, ss, New York
1979	Pittsburgh (NL)	Chuck Tanner	Baltimore (AL)	Earl Weaver	4-3	Willie Stargell, 1b, Pittsburgh
1980	Philadelphia (NL)	Dallas Green	Kansas City (AL)	Jim Frey	4-2	Mike Schmidt, 3b, Philadelphia
1981	Los Angeles (NL)	Tom Lasorda	New York (AL)	Bob Lemon	4-2	Cey/Guerrero/Yeager, Los Angeles
1982	St. Louis (NL)	Whitey Herzog	Milwaukee (AL)	Harvey Kuenn	4-3	Darrell Porter, c, St. Louis
1983	Baltimore (AL)	Joe Altobelli	Philadelphia (NL)	Paul Owens	4-1	Rick Dempsey, c, Baltimore
1984	Detroit (AL)	Sparky Anderson	San Diego (NL)	Dick Williams	4-1	Alan Trammell, ss, Detroit
1985	Kansas City (AL)	Dick Howser	St. Louis (NL)	Whitey Herzog	4-3	Bret Saberhagen, p, Kansas City
1986	New York (NL)	Dave Johnson	Boston (AL)	John McNamara	4-3	Ray Knight, 3b, New York
1987	Minnesota (AL)	Tom Kelly	St. Louis (NL)	Whitey Herzog	4-3	Frank Viola, p, Minnesota
1988	Los Angeles (NL)	Tom Lasorda	Oakland (AL)	Tony La Russa	4-1	Orel Hershiser, p, Los Angeles
1989	Oakland (AL)	Tony La Russa	San Francisco (NL)	Roger Craig	4-0	Dave Stewart, p, Oakland
1990	Cincinnati (NL)	Lou Piniella	Oakland (AL)	Tony La Russa	4-0	Jose Rijo, p, Cincinnati
1991	Minnesota (AL)	Tom Kelly	Atlanta (NL)	Bobby Cox	4-3	Jack Morris, p, Minnesota
1992	Toronto (AL)	Cito Gaston	Atlanta (NL)	Bobby Cox	4-2	Pat Borders, c, Toronto
1993	Toronto (AL)	Cito Gaston	Philadelphia (NL)	Jim Fregosi	4-2	Paul Molitor, dh, Toronto
1994	NO SERIES					
1995	Atlanta (NL)	Bobby Cox	Cleveland (AL)	Mike Hargrove	4-2	Tom Glavine, p, Atlanta

ray drove home the game-winner with a single off Alejandro Pena after Baerga opened the inning with a double and Atlanta intentionally walked Belle to face Murray.

Cox made a controversial decision in Game Four, bypassing Maddux and the chance to pitch the four-time Cy Young Award winner three times in the Series.

Mike Hargrove

Instead, Steve Avery got the call. Avery struggled to a 7-13 record in the regular season, but was the winner as Atlanta moved in front 3-1 in the Series with a 5-2 victory.

Avery allowed one run on three hits in six innings. After Wohlers failed to retire the two batters he faced in the ninth, Pedro Borbon Jr., pitching for the first time in 19 days, nailed down the save.

At that point, the Series appeared over as Maddux took the mound for Game Five. However, Cleveland staved off elimination with a 5-4 win. Jim Thome's RBI single in the sixth put the Indians ahead for good at 3-2, and his solo homer in the eighth gave the Tribe a much-needed cushion at 5-2.

Whatever momentum Cleveland gained by beating Maddux ended in Game Six, though, as Glavine was close to perfection.

Bittersweet Season For Indians

It was a bitter end for the Indians, who had a 100-win season even though the regular season was shortened to 144 games. The Indians swept Boston in the American League Division Series and beat Seattle in six games in the ALCS.

"We had a great season in 1995," shortstop Omar Vizquel said. "Winning 100 games, winning 29 games in our last at-bat, clinching in Boston, coming back against Seattle and winning Game Five against Maddux. We just feel bad that we couldn't win tonight."

"We had fun," Lofton said. "That's the biggest thing I can say about this team. We never gave down on ourselves. We always fought back from little adversities. We had a great time winning and we tried to win it all. We just came up a little short."

"I don't care how many games you win in the regular season or what you do in the playoffs, the World Series is the biggest stage of all, the place where you really have to prove yourself," Cleveland manager Mike Hargrove said.

Ace closer. Braves righthander Mark Wohlers preserved Atlanta's 1-0 win in Game Six.

On losing side. Cleveland center fielder Kenny Lofton stole six bases in the 1995 World Series, but it wasn't enough to withstand the Braves.

"I think we made a good showing, showed the world the Cleveland Indians were for real. I think our lack of experience probably hurt us early in the Series. By the end of it, though, we proved we should be here."

With a roster filled with young stars, the Indians vowed they would return to the World Series and win it.

"Our time is coming," Thome said. "It'll happen and I think a lot of people on this team believe that. It's going to happen."

It finally happened for the Braves in 1995.

"From Day One, we were on a mission," Glavine said. "We were very businesslike and we knew the only thing that would make our season a success would be a World Series title."

If nothing else, it means the Braves are no longer the butt of jokes. The comparisons to the Buffalo Bills have ended.

"I've got to say I feel sorry for Buffalo, because they're standing alone now," Atlanta third baseman Chipper Jones said.

"I thought we handled it well, all the talk we would not be able to win a championship," Lemke said. "That was the most ridiculous thing I've heard in my life."

"It took us a while to get over the hump but we did it," Avery said. "People thought we were going to fall apart but we didn't. There was no way we'd fall apart. We knew right from the start this was going to be our year to win it all."

WORLD SERIES
BOX SCORES

Game One: October 21
Braves 3, Indians 2

CLEVE.	ab	r	h	bi	bb	so	ATLANTA	ab	r	h	bi	bb	so
Lofton cf	4	2	1	0	0	0	Grissom cf	4	0	1	0	0	1
Vizquel ss	4	0	0	0	0	1	Lemke 2b	3	0	1	0	1	1
Baerga 2b	4	0	0	1	0	1	Jones 3b	4	0	0	0	0	2
Belle lf	3	0	0	0	0	0	McGriff 1b	3	2	1	1	1	1
Murray 1b	3	0	0	0	0	0	Justice rf	1	1	0	0	2	0
Tavarez p	0	0	0	0	0	0	Klesko lf	2	0	0	0	0	2
Embree p	0	0	0	0	0	0	Devereaux ph-lf	0	0	0	0	1	0
Thome 3b	3	0	1	0	0	0	O'Brien c	2	0	0	0	0	1
Ramirez rf	3	0	0	0	0	2	Polonia ph	1	0	0	1	0	0
Alomar c	3	0	0	0	0	0	Lopez c	0	0	0	0	0	0
Hershiser p	2	0	0	0	0	0	Belliard ss	2	0	0	1	0	0
Assenmacher p	0	0	0	0	0	0	Maddux p	3	0	0	0	0	1
Sorrento 1b	1	0	0	0	0	0							
Totals	**30**	**2**	**2**	**1**	**0**	**4**	**Totals**	**25**	**3**	**3**	**3**	**5**	**9**

Cleveland	**100 000 001—2**
Atlanta	**010 000 20x—3**

E—Belliard (1), McGriff (1). **DP**—Cleveland 1. **LOB**—Cleveland 1, Atlanta 4. **HR**—McGriff (1). **SB**—Lofton 2 (2). **S**—Belliard.

Cleveland	ip	h	r	er	bb	so	Atlanta	ip	h	r	er	bb	so
Hershiser L	6	3	3	3	3	7	Maddux W	9	2	2	0	0	4
Assenmacher	0	0	0	0	1	0							
Tavarez	1⅓	0	0	0	1	0							
Embree	⅔	0	0	0	0	2							

Hershiser pitched to 2 batters in 7th. Assenmacher pitched to 1 batter in 7th.

Umpires: HP—Wendelstedt; **1B**—McKean; **2B**—Froemming; **3B**—Hirschbeck; **LF**—Pulli; **RF**—Brinkman.

T—2:37. **A**—51,876.

Game Two: October 22
Braves 4, Indians 3

CLEVE.	ab	r	h	bi	bb	so	ATLANTA	ab	r	h	bi	bb	so
Lofton cf	5	1	1	0	0	0	Grissom cf	3	1	1	0	0	0
Vizquel ss	4	0	1	0	1	0	Lemke 2b	3	1	1	0	1	0
Baerga 2b	4	0	0	0	1	0	Jones 3b	3	0	2	1	0	0
Belle lf	3	1	1	0	1	1	McGriff 1b	4	0	0	0	0	0
Murray 1b	3	1	1	2	1	0	Justice rf	3	1	2	1	1	0
Ramirez rf	4	0	2	0	0	1	Wohlers p	0	0	0	0	0	0
Thome 3b	3	0	0	0	1	1	Klesko lf	3	0	0	0	0	1
Pena c	3	0	0	0	0	0	Devereaux lf-rf	1	0	0	0	0	0
Sorrento ph	1	0	0	0	0	0	Lopez c	3	1	1	2	0	0
Alomar c	0	0	0	0	0	0	Belliard ss	4	0	0	0	0	1
Martinez p	2	0	0	0	0	0	Glavine p	1	0	0	0	1	1
Embree p	0	0	0	0	0	0	Smith ph	1	0	1	0	0	0
Kirby ph	1	0	0	0	0	1	McMichael p	0	0	0	0	0	0
Poole ph	0	0	0	0	0	0	Pena p	0	0	0	0	0	0
Tavarez p	0	0	0	0	0	0	Polonia lf	0	0	0	0	0	0
Amaro ph	1	0	0	0	0	1							
Totals	**34**	**3**	**6**	**2**	**5**	**5**	**Totals**	**29**	**4**	**8**	**4**	**3**	**3**

Cleveland	**020 000 100—3**
Atlanta	**002 002 00x—4**

E—Jones (1), Devereaux (1), Martinez (1), Belle (1). **DP**—Cleveland 2. **LOB**—Cleveland 9, Atlanta 7. **2B**—Jones (1). **HR**—Murray (1), Lopez (1). **SB**—Lofton 2 (4), Vizquel (1). **SF**—Jones.

Cleveland	ip	h	r	er	bb	so	Atlanta	ip	h	r	er	bb	so
Martinez L	5⅔	8	4	4	3	3	Glavine W	6	3	2	2	3	3
Embree	⅓	0	0	0	0	0	McMichael	⅔	1	1	0	1	1
Poole	1	0	0	0	0	0	Pena	1	1	0	0	1	0
Tavarez	1	0	0	0	0	0	Wohlers S	1⅓	1	0	0	0	1

WP—Glavine, McMichael. **HBP**—Grissom (by Martinez); Lopez (by Tavarez).

Umpires: HP—McKean; **1B**—Froemming; **2B**—Hirschbeck; **3B**—Pulli; **LF**—Brinkman; **RF**—Wendelstedt.

T—3:17. **A**—51,877.

Game Three: October 24
Indians 7, Braves 6

ATLANTA	ab	r	h	bi	bb	so	CLEVE.	ab	r	h	bi	bb	so
Grissom cf	6	1	2	0	0	2	Lofton cf	3	3	3	0	3	0
Polonia lf	4	1	1	1	1	1	Vizquel ss	6	2	2	1	0	1
Jones 3b	3	2	1	0	2	0	Baerga 2b	6	0	3	3	0	0
McGriff 1b	5	1	3	2	0	1	Espinoza pr	0	1	0	0	0	0
Justice rf	5	0	0	1	0	0	Belle lf	4	0	1	1	2	0
Klesko lf	3	1	2	1	0	0	Murray dh	6	0	1	1	0	3
Devereaux ph	2	0	1	1	0	1	Thome 3b	4	0	0	0	1	1
Lopez c	5	0	0	0	0	0	Ramirez rf	2	1	0	0	3	0
Lemke 2b	5	0	2	0	0	0	Sorrento 1b	4	0	1	0	0	3
Belliard ss	2	0	0	0	0	1	Kirby pr	0	0	0	0	0	0
Smith ph	1	0	0	0	0	0	Perry 1b	1	0	0	0	0	1
Mordecai ss	1	0	0	0	0	1	Alomar c	5	0	1	1	0	1
Totals	**42**	**6**	**12**	**6**	**3**	**7**	**Totals**	**41**	**7**	**12**	**7**	**9**	**10**

Atlanta	**100 001 130 00—6**
Cleveland	**202 000 110 01—7**

E—Belliard (2), Sorrento (1), Baerga (1). **DP**—Atlanta 1, Cleveland 2. **LOB**—Atlanta 7, Cleveland 12. **2B**—Jones (2), Grissom (1), Lofton (1), Alomar (1), Baerga (1). **3B**—Vizquel (1). **HR**—McGriff (2), Klesko (1). **SB**—Polonia (1), McGriff (1), Lofton (5), Ramirez (1). **CS**—Grissom (1), Lofton (1). **S**—Mordecai.

Atlanta	ip	h	r	er	bb	so	Cleveland	ip	h	r	er	bb	so
Smoltz	2⅓	6	4	4	2	4	Nagy	7	8	5	5	1	4
Clontz	2⅓	1	0	0	0	1	Assenmacher	⅓	0	1	1	1	0
Mercker	2	1	1	1	2	2	Tavarez	⅔	1	0	0	0	0
McMichael	⅔	1	1	1	1	1	Mesa W	3	3	0	0	1	3
Wohlers	2⅔	1	0	0	3	2							
Pena L	0	2	1	1	1	0							

Nagy pitched to 2 batters in 8th. Pena pitched to 3 batters in 11th.

Umpires: HP—Froemming; **1B**—Hirschbeck; **2B**—Pulli; **3B**—Brinkman; **LF**—Wendelstedt; **RF**—McKean.

T—4:09. **A**—43,584.

Game Four: October 25
Braves 5, Indians 2

ATLANTA	ab	r	h	bi	bb	so	CLEVE.	ab	r	h	bi	bb	so
Grissom cf	4	1	3	0	1	0	Lofton cf	5	0	0	0	0	1
Polonia lf	4	1	2	1	0	0	Vizquel ss	3	0	0	0	1	0
Devereaux lf	0	0	0	0	1	0	Baerga 2b	4	0	1	0	0	0
Jones 3b	4	1	0	0	1	0	Belle lf	3	1	1	1	1	1
McGriff 1b	3	1	1	0	2	1	Murray dh	2	0	0	0	2	0
Justice rf	5	0	1	2	0	0	Ramirez rf	3	1	1	1	1	0
Klesko dh	3	1	1	1	1	1	Perry 1b	3	0	0	0	0	1
Mordecai ph	1	0	0	0	0	0	Sorrento ph	1	0	1	0	0	0
Lopez c	5	0	2	1	0	1	Espinoza 3b	2	0	1	0	0	0
Lemke 2b	5	0	1	0	0	0	Thome ph-3b	2	0	1	0	0	1
Belliard ss	3	0	0	0	0	1	Alomar c	4	0	0	0	0	1
Totals	**37**	**5**	**11**	**5**	**6**	**4**	**Totals**	**32**	**2**	**6**	**2**	**5**	**5**

Atlanta	**000 001 301—5**
Cleveland	**000 001 001—2**

E—Lemke (1). **DP**—Atlanta 1. **LOB**—Atlanta 12, Cleveland 8. **2B**—Lopez 2 (2), Polonia (1), McGriff (1), Thome (1), Sorrento (1). **HR**—Klesko (2), Belle (1), Ramirez (1). **SB**—Grissom 2 (2). **CS**—Espinoza (1). **S**—Belliard.

Atlanta	ip	h	r	er	bb	so	Cleveland	ip	h	r	er	bb	so
Avery W	6	3	1	1	5	3	Hill L	6⅓	6	3	3	4	1
McMichael	2	1	0	0	0	0	Assenmacher	⅔	1	1	0	1	2
Wohlers	0	2	1	1	0	0	Tavarez	⅔	2	0	0	1	1
Borbon S	1	0	0	0	0	2	Embree	1⅓	2	1	1	0	0

Wohlers pitched to 2 batters in 9th.

PB—Alomar. **Balk**—Avery.

Umpires: HP—Hirschbeck; **1B**—Pulli; **2B**—Brinkman; **3B**—Wendelstedt; **LF**—McKean; **RF**—Froemming.

T—3:14. **A**—43,578.

Game Five: October 26
Indians 5, Braves 4

ATLANTA	ab	r	h	bi	bb	so	CLEVE.	ab	r	h	bi	bb	so
Grissom cf	4	0	1	1	0	0	Lofton cf	4	0	0	0	0	0
Polonia lf	4	1	1	1	0	1	Vizquel ss	3	1	1	0	1	1
Jones 3b	4	0	1	0	0	1	Baerga 2b	4	1	1	0	0	0
McGriff 1b	4	1	1	0	0	2	Belle lf	3	2	1	2	1	2
Justice rf	4	0	0	0	0	1	Murray dh	3	0	0	0	1	0
Klesko dh	4	2	2	2	0	0	Thome 3b	4	1	2	2	0	0
Lemke 2b	4	0	0	0	0	1	Ramirez rf	3	0	1	1	0	1
O'Brien c	1	0	0	0	0	0	Perry 1b	1	0	0	0	0	0
Lopez ph-c	1	0	0	0	0	0	Sorrento 1b	3	0	0	0	0	1
Belliard ss	1	0	0	0	0	1	Kirby rf	0	0	0	0	0	0
Smith ph	0	0	0	0	1	0	Alomar c	3	0	2	0	0	0
Mordecai ss	1	0	1	0	0	0							
Totals	**32**	**4**	**7**	**4**	**1**	**7**	**Totals**	**31**	**5**	**8**	**5**	**3**	**5**

Atlanta	**000 110 002—4**
Cleveland	**200 002 01x—5**

E—Hershiser (1). **DP**—Cleveland 2. **LOB**—Atlanta 3, Cleveland 5. **2B**—Jones (3), McGriff (2), Alomar (2), Baerga (2). **HR**—Polonia (1), Klesko (3), Belle (2), Thome (1). **CS**—Murray (1).

Atlanta	ip	h	r	er	bb	so	Cleveland	ip	h	r	er	bb	so
Maddux L	7	7	4	4	3	4	Hershiser W	8	5	2	1	1	6
Clontz	1	1	1	1	0	1	Mesa S	1	2	2	2	0	1

Umpires: HP—Pulli; **1B**—Brinkman; **2B**—Wendelstedt; **3B**—McKean; **LF**—Froemming; **RF**—Hirschbeck.

T—2:33. **A**—43,595.

Top hitter. Atlanta outfielder Marquis Grissom topped all World Series performers with a .360 average.

COMPOSITE BOX

CLEVELAND

Player, Pos.	AVG	G	AB	R	H	2B	3B	HR	RBI	BB	SO	SB
Alvaro Espinoza, 3b..	.500	2	2	1	1	0	0	0	0	0	0	0
Albert Belle, lf............	.235	6	17	4	4	0	0	2	4	7	5	0
Manny Ramirez, rf	.222	6	18	2	4	0	0	1	2	4	5	1
Jim Thome, ph-3b....	.211	6	19	1	4	1	0	1	2	2	5	0
Kenny Lofton, cf........	.200	6	25	6	5	1	0	0	0	3	1	6
Sandy Alomar, c	.200	5	15	0	3	2	0	0	1	0	2	0
Carlos Baerga, 2b......	.192	6	26	1	5	2	0	0	4	1	1	0
Paul Sorrento, ph-1b..	.182	5	11	0	2	1	0	0	0	0	4	0
Omar Vizquel, ss	.174	6	23	3	4	0	1	0	1	3	5	1
Tony Pena, c............	.167	2	6	0	1	0	0	0	0	0	0	0
Eddie Murray, 1b-dh..	.105	6	19	1	2	0	0	1	3	5	4	0
Herbert Perry, 1b	.000	3	5	0	0	0	0	0	0	0	2	0
Dennis Martinez, p.....	.000	2	3	0	0	0	0	0	0	0	1	0
Ruben Amaro, ph-rf ..	.000	2	2	0	0	0	0	0	0	0	1	0
Orel Hershiser, p.......	.000	2	2	0	0	0	0	0	0	0	0	0
Wayne Kirby, ph-rf	.000	3	1	0	0	0	0	0	0	0	1	0
Jim Poole, p	.000	2	1	0	0	0	0	0	0	0	0	0
Totals	**.179**	**6**	**195**	**19**	**35**	**7**	**1**	**5**	**17**	**25**	**37**	**8**

Pitcher	W	L	ERA	G	GS	SV	IP	H	R	ER	BB	SO
Julian Tavarez	0	0	0.00	5	0	0	4	3	0	0	2	1
Orel Hershiser	1	1	2.57	2	2	0	14	8	5	4	4	13
Alan Embree	0	0	2.70	4	0	0	3	2	1	1	2	2
Dennis Martinez	0	1	3.48	2	2	0	10	12	4	4	8	5
Jim Poole	0	1	3.86	2	0	0	2	1	1	1	0	1
Ken Hill	0	1	4.26	2	1	0	6	7	3	3	4	1
Jose Mesa	1	0	4.50	2	0	1	4	5	2	2	1	4
Charles Nagy	0	0	6.43	1	1	0	7	8	5	5	1	4
Paul Assenmacher....	0	0	6.75	4	0	0	1	1	2	1	3	3
Totals	**2**	**4**	**3.57**	**6**			**53**	**47**	**23**	**21**	**25**	**34**

ATLANTA

Player, Pos.	AVG	G	AB	R	H	2B	3B	HR	RBI	BB	SO	SB
Dwight Smith, ph.......	.500	3	2	0	1	0	0	0	0	1	0	0
Marquis Grissom, cf..	.360	6	25	3	9	1	0	0	1	1	3	3
Mike Mordecai, ph-ss	.333	3	3	0	1	0	0	0	0	0	1	0
Ryan Klesko, lf..........	.313	6	16	4	5	0	0	3	4	3	4	0
Chipper Jones, 3b.....	.286	6	21	3	6	3	0	0	1	4	5	0
Luis Polonia, ph-lf ...	.286	6	14	3	4	1	0	1	4	1	3	1
Mark Lemke, 2b.........	.273	6	22	1	6	0	0	0	2	3	2	0
Fred McGriff, 1b........	.261	6	23	5	6	2	0	2	3	5	5	1
David Justice, rf	.250	6	20	3	5	1	0	1	5	5	1	0
Mike Devereaux, rf-lf..	.250	5	4	0	1	0	0	0	1	2	1	0
Javy Lopez, c............	.176	6	17	1	3	2	0	1	3	1	1	0
Rafael Belliard, ss.....	.000	6	16	0	0	0	0	0	1	0	4	0
Tom Glavine, p	.000	2	4	0	0	0	0	0	0	1	2	0
Charlie O'Brien, c......	.000	2	3	0	0	0	0	0	0	0	1	0
Greg Maddux, p	.000	2	3	0	0	0	0	0	0	0	1	0
Totals	**.244**	**6**	**193**	**23**	**47**	**10**	**0**	**8**	**23**	**25**	**34**	**5**

Pitcher	W	L	ERA	G	GS	SV	IP	H	R	ER	BB	SO
Pedro Borbon............	0	0	0.00	1	0	1	1	0	0	0	0	2
Tom Glavine	2	0	1.29	2	2	0	14	4	2	2	6	11
Steve Avery	1	0	1.50	1	1	0	6	3	1	1	5	3
Mark Wohlers	0	0	1.80	4	0	2	5	4	1	1	3	3
Greg Maddux	1	1	2.25	2	2	0	16	9	6	4	3	8
Brad Clontz	0	0	2.70	2	0	0	3	2	1	1	0	2
Greg McMichael	0	0	2.70	3	0	0	3	3	2	1	2	2
Kent Mercker	0	0	4.50	1	0	0	2	1	1	1	2	2
Alejandro Pena	0	0	9.00	2	0	0	1	3	1	1	2	0
John Smoltz	0	1	15.43	1	1	0	2	6	4	4	2	4
Totals	**4**	**2**	**2.67**	**6**			**54**	**35**	**19**	**16**	**25**	**37**

Cleveland	522 003 222	01—19
Atlanta	112 115 633	00—23

DP—Atlanta 2, Cleveland 8. LOB—Cleveland 39, Atlanta 44.
E—Belliard 2, McGriff, Jones, Devereaux, Martinez, Belle, Sorrento, Baerga, Lemke, Hershiser, Thome. CS—Grissom, Lofton, Espinoza, Lemke, Belle. S—Belliard 2, Mordecai, O'Brien, Lemke. SF—Jones.
HBP—Grissom (by Martinez), Lopez (by Tavarez). PB—Alomar. Balk—Avery.
Umpires—Joe Brinkman, Bruce Froemming, John Hirschbeck, Jim McKean, Frank Pulli, Harry Wendelstedt.

Game Six: October 28
Braves 1, Indians 0

CLEVE.	ab	r	h	bi	bb	so	ATLANTA	ab	r	h	bi	bb	so
Lofton cf	4	0	0	0	0	0	Grissom cf	4	0	1	0	0	0
Vizquel ss	3	0	0	0	0	2	Lemke 2b	2	0	1	0	1	0
Sorrento ph	1	0	0	0	0	0	Jones 3b	3	0	2	0	1	0
Baerga 2b	4	0	0	0	0	0	McGriff 1b	4	0	0	0	0	2
Belle lf	1	0	0	0	2	1	Justice rf	2	1	2	1	2	0
Murray 1b	2	0	0	1	1	1	Klesko lf	1	0	0	0	2	0
Ramirez rf	3	0	0	0	0	1	Devereaux lf	1	0	0	0	0	0
Embree p	0	0	0	0	0	0	Lopez c	3	0	0	0	1	0
Tavarez p	0	0	0	0	0	0	Belliard ss	4	0	0	0	0	0
Assenmacher p	0	0	0	0	0	0	Glavine p	3	0	0	0	0	1
Thome 3b	3	0	0	0	0	2	Polonia ph	1	0	0	0	0	1
Pena c	3	0	1	0	0	0	Wohlers p	0	0	0	0	0	0
Martinez p	1	0	0	0	0	1							
Poole p	1	0	0	0	0	0							
Hill p	0	0	0	0	0	0							
Amaro rf	1	0	0	0	0	0							
Totals	**27**	**0**	**1**	**0**	**3**	**8**	**Totals**	**28**	**1**	**6**	**1**	**7**	**4**

Cleveland	000	000	000—0
Atlanta	000	001	00x—1

E—Thome (1). DP—Cleveland 1. LOB—Cleveland 3, Atlanta 11. 2B—Justice (1). HR—Justice (1). SB—Lofton (6), Grissom (3). CS—Belle (1), Lemke (1). S—Lemke.

Cleveland	ip	h	r	er	bb	so	Atlanta	ip	h	r	er	bb	so
Martinez	4⅔	4	0	0	5	2	Glavine W	8	1	0	0	3	8
Poole L	1⅓	1	1	1	0	1	Wohlers S	1	0	0	0	0	0
Hill	0	1	0	0	0	0							
Embree	1	0	0	0	2	0							
Tavarez	⅔	0	0	0	0	0							
Assenmacher	⅓	0	0	0	0	1							

Hill pitched to 1 batter in 7th.
Umpires: HP—Brinkman; 1B—Wendelstedt; 2B—McKean; 3B—Froemming; LF—Hirschbeck; RF—Pulli.
T—3:02. A—51,875.

Star-Crossed Indians End Long Dry Spell

By JOHN ROYSTER

Cleveland's dream wasn't lost after all. It turns out it was just deferred.

After 40 years of off-field calamity, front-office incompetence and just plain bad baseball, the Indians finally fielded a contender in 1994. But the most star-crossed franchise in the game was stopped by disaster again, this time in the form of the players' strike.

It was the kind of thing fatalistic Cleveland fans had come to expect. A team that goes 66-47 and is in line for at least a wild-card playoff berth isn't a contender if it has "Indians" across the front of its shirts. *Something* will happen.

But general manager John Hart, manager Mike Hargrove and the players clung to the belief that good baseball would overcome any jinxes. And then they went out and played their way into the 1995 World Series.

"I have to think that if we do things right," Hart said in 1994, "there will be magic here again."

Hart was more right than he knew, for in '95 the Indians seemed to specialize in late-inning, come-from-behind wins. Their success on the field made the Indians one of the few teams immune from fan backlash over the strike. Their attendance was more than 2.8 million during the strike-shortened regular season, second in the American League only to the Orioles, who drew more than 3 million.

"I'd like to think that our marketing was the main factor in all this," said Indians vice president of marketing Jeff Overton. "But it's the talent on the club that pulled us through this. We've got a great product, and we were really helped by the surge of energy we got from the players. Right out of the blocks this season, the team performed the way it did last year, and that got the ball rolling."

The Indians steadfastly refused to fold in the AL Championship Series against the Seattle Mariners, even after falling behind 2-1 in the best-of-7 series.

John Hart

They won three straight, putting themselves in the World Series for the first time since 1954. The crowning touch came in Game Six, when they beat the Mariners' seemingly invincible pitching ace, Randy Johnson, with three runs in the eighth inning. Kenny Lofton scored from second base on a passed ball, and Carlos Baerga hit a home run before Johnson departed.

The series had begun in surprising fashion, as Seattle's Bob Wolcott, a rookie who started the season in Double-A, beat the Indians 3-2. To borrow a football term, Wolcott bent but didn't break. He allowed eight

Supreme Effort. Veteran Orel Hershiser pitched Cleveland into the World Series, winning ALCS MVP honors.

hits and five walks in seven innings but left with a lead that relievers Jeff Nelson and Norm Charlton preserved. Cleveland left 12 runners on base.

But otherwise, Seattle couldn't win unless Johnson started. He kept the Mariners in Game Three for eight innings, and they won 5-2 with three runs in the 11th inning.

The other three games were dominated by Cleveland pitching—two strong starts by Orel Hershiser and a combined shutout by four pitchers, including starter Ken Hill.

Hershiser won Games Two and Five, allowing just two earned runs in 14 innings. In the Division Series he shut out the Red Sox for 7⅓ innings, and he had two fine outings in the World Series. It was his best work since he had career-threatening shoulder surgery in 1990, for a team that welcomed him with open arms after the Dodgers failed to renew his contract over the winter.

"I think I'll bring a lot to this team," Hershiser had said early in the season. "They wouldn't bring me here if they didn't think I'd contribute. They want somebody to give them a chance to win, bona fide, solid starters. At this stage of my career I won't blow hitters away, but I'll give them good, solid starts."

Page	EAST	W	L	PCT	GB	Manager	General Manager	Attend./Dates	Last Pennant
67	Boston Red Sox	86	58	.597	—	Kevin Kennedy	Dan Duquette	2,164,378 (72)	1986
164	New York Yankees*	79	65	.549	7	Buck Showalter	Gene Michael	1,705,257 (70)	1981
60	Baltimore Orioles	71	73	.493	15	Phil Regan	Roland Hemond	3,098,475 (72)	1983
112	Detroit Tigers	60	84	.417	26	Sparky Anderson	Joe Klein	1,180,979 (71)	1984
229	Toronto Blue Jays	56	88	.389	30	Cito Gaston	Gord Ash	2,826,483 (72)	1993
Page	CENTRAL	W	L	PCT	GB	Manager(s)	General Manager	Attend./Dates	Last Pennant
100	Cleveland Indians	100	44	.694	—	Mike Hargrove	John Hart	2,842,725 (71)	1995
131	Kansas City Royals	70	74	.486	30	Bob Boone	Herk Robinson	1,232,969 (70)	1985
81	Chicago White Sox	68	76	.472	32	Lamont/Bevington	Ron Schueler	1,609,773 (71)	1959
145	Milwaukee Brewers	65	79	.451	35	Phil Garner	Sal Bando	1,087,560 (71)	1982
152	Minnesota Twins	56	88	.389	44	Tom Kelly	Terry Ryan	1,057,667 (72)	1991
Page	WEST	W	L	PCT	GB	Manager	General Manager	Attend./Dates	Last Pennant
217	Seattle Mariners#	79	66	.545	—	Lou Piniella	Woody Woodward	1,640,992 (73)	None
74	California Angels	78	67	.538	1	Marcel Lachemann	Bill Bavasi	1,748,680 (72)	None
223	Texas Rangers	74	70	.514	5½	Johnny Oates	Doug Melvin	1,985,910 (72)	None
178	Oakland Athletics	67	77	.465	11½	Tony La Russa	Sandy Alderson	1,174,310 (71)	1990

*Won wild-card playoff berth #Won one-game divisional playoff
NOTE: Team's individual batting, pitching and fielding statistics can be found on page indicated in lefthand column.

When it counted most, Hershiser did better than that.

The Playoff Unit

Johnson and the Mariners provided more excitement than the Indians in the new AL Division Series. The Indians swept the Red Sox in three games, but the Mariners made things much more interesting against the Yankees.

They spotted New York a 2-0 lead in games, but that was before Johnson got into the act. He didn't appear until Game Three because he had pitched the one-game playoff against the Angels that gave the M's the AL West championship.

Working on three days' rest, Johnson threw 116 pitches in seven-plus innings, allowing two runs. The bullpen allowed two more runs, but Johnson was credited with the victory as the Mariners won 7-4.

After his team eked out another win in Game Four, Johnson found himself on the mound again in Game Five. This time, he came out of the bullpen with the score tied 4-4, two on and none out in the ninth.

He struck out Wade Boggs on three pitches, retired Bernie Williams on a popup and induced Paul O'Neill to foul out. The next inning, Johnson struck out the side.

Johnson finally surrendered a run in the 11th, but the Mariners rallied to win in the bottom of the inning on Edgar Martinez' two-run double.

All told, Johnson appeared in four games in two weeks in do-or-die situations. He extended his team's season three of the four times, until that fateful eighth inning against Cleveland.

"If you really think about who was the most valuable

Franchise Pitcher. AL Cy Young Award winner Randy Johnson led Seattle to its first playoff berth.

MICHAEL PONZINI

player to any team, it may have been Randy Johnson," said his manager, Lou Piniella.

The series also marked the long-awaited postseason debut of Yankees first baseman Don Mattingly, who had toiled for 13 seasons without reaching the playoffs. Mattingly acquitted himself well, batting .417 with six RBIs in 24 at-bats.

"It's been a tremendous relief for me to finally make it, to get rid of that asterisk next to my name," Mattingly said. "I've always kind of resented it."

The first game of the Cleveland-Boston series was a classic, a five-hour marathon which the Indians won 5-4 in 13 innings. Catcher Tony Pena won it with a home run. Each team had scored a run in the 11th, Cleveland on a home run by Albert Belle which provided the series' greatest moment of intrigue.

After the homer, the Red Sox had the umpires confiscate Belle's bat to check for cork. Belle had been suspended during the '94 regular season for using a corked bat. But when league officials sawed this bat open, all they found was wood.

The rest of the series was anticlimactic, characterized by Hershiser's pitching in Game Two and the Indians offense shelling Boston pitching sensation Tim Wakefield in Game Three.

Fallen Angels

If the 1995 season will be remembered for the revitalization of the Indians and Mariners, it also will be remembered for a folding act by the Angels.

California blew an 11-game lead in the AL West in the last two months of the season, placing the Angels

AMERICAN LEAGUE CHAMPIONS, 1901-95

NOTE: Most Valuable Player award formally recognized in 1931.
GA—Games ahead of second-place team

	Pennant	Pct.	GA
1901	Chicago	.610	4
1902	Philadelphia	.610	5
1903	Boston	.659	14½
1904	Boston	.617	1½
1905	Philadelphia	.622	2
1906	Chicago	.616	3
1907	Detroit	.613	1½
1908	Detroit	.588	½
1909	Detroit	.645	3½
1910	Philadelphia	.680	14½
1911	Philadelphia	.669	13½
1912	Boston	.691	14
1913	Philadelphia	.627	6½
1914	Philadelphia	.651	8½
1915	Boston	.669	2½
1916	Boston	.591	2
1917	Chicago	.649	9
1918	Boston	.595	2½
1919	Chicago	.629	3½
1920	Cleveland	.636	2
1921	New York	.641	4½
1922	New York	.610	1
1923	New York	.645	16
1924	Washington	.597	2
1925	Washington	.636	8½
1926	New York	.591	3
1927	New York	.714	19
1928	New York	.656	2½
1929	Philadelphia	.693	18
1930	Philadelphia	.662	8

	Pennant	Pct.	GA	MVP
1931	Philadelphia	.704	13½	Lefty Grove, lhp, Philadelphia
1932	New York	.695	13	Jimmie Foxx, 1b, Philadelphia
1933	Washington	.651	7	Jimmie Foxx, 1b, Philadelphia
1934	Detroit	.656	7	Mickey Cochrane, c, Detroit
1935	Detroit	.616	3	Hank Greenberg, 1b, Detroit
1936	New York	.667	19½	Lou Gehrig, 1b, New York
1937	New York	.662	13	Charlie Gehringer, 2b, Detroit
1938	New York	.651	9½	Jimmie Foxx, 1b, Boston
1939	New York	.702	17	Joe DiMaggio, of, New York
1940	Detroit	.584	1	Hank Greenberg, 1b, Detroit
1941	New York	.656	17	Joe DiMaggio, of, New York
1942	New York	.669	9	Joe Gordon, 2b, New York
1943	New York	.636	13½	Spud Chandler, rhp, New York
1944	St. Louis	.578	1	Hal Newhouser, lhp, Detroit
1945	Detroit	.575	1½	Hal Newhouser, lhp, Detroit
1946	Boston	.675	12	Ted Williams, of, Boston
1947	New York	.630	12	Joe DiMaggio, of, New York
1948	Cleveland	.626	1	Lou Boudreau, ss, Cleveland
1949	New York	.630	1	Ted Williams, of, Boston
1950	New York	.636	3	Phil Rizzuto, ss, New York
1951	New York	.636	5	Yogi Berra, c, New York
1952	New York	.617	2	Bobby Shantz, lhp, Philadelphia
1953	New York	.656	8½	Al Rosen, 3b, Cleveland
1954	Cleveland	.721	8	Yogi Berra, c, New York
1955	New York	.623	3	Yogi Berra, c, New York
1956	New York	.630	9	Mickey Mantle, of, New York
1957	New York	.636	8	Mickey Mantle, of, New York
1958	New York	.597	10	Jackie Jensen, of, Boston
1959	Chicago	.610	5	Nellie Fox, 2b, Chicago
1960	New York	.630	8	Roger Maris, of, New York
1961	New York	.673	8	Roger Maris, of, New York
1962	New York	.593	5	Mickey Mantle, of, New York
1963	New York	.646	10½	Elston Howard, c, New York
1964	New York	.611	1	Brooks Robinson, 3b, Baltimore
1965	Minnesota	.630	7	Zoilo Versalles, ss, Minnesota
1966	Baltimore	.606	9	Frank Robinson, of, Baltimore
1967	Boston	.568	1	Carl Yastrzemski, of, Boston
1968	Detroit	.636	12	Denny McLain, rhp, Detroit

	East. Div.	PCT	GA	West. Div.	PCT	GA	Pennant		MVP
1969	Baltimore	.673	19	Minnesota	.599	9	Baltimore	3-0	Harmon Killebrew, 1b-3b, Minnesota
1970	Baltimore	.667	15	Minnesota	.605	9	Baltimore	3-0	Boog Powell, 1b, Baltimore
1971	Baltimore	.639	12	Oakland	.627	16	Baltimore	3-0	Vida Blue, lhp, Oakland
1972	Detroit	.551	½	Oakland	.600	5½	Oakland	3-2	Dick Allen, 1b, Chicago
1973	Baltimore	.599	8	Oakland	.580	6	Oakland	3-2	Reggie Jackson, of, Oakland
1974	Baltimore	.562	2	Oakland	.556	5	Oakland	3-1	Jeff Burroughs, of, Texas
1975	Boston	.594	4½	Oakland	.605	7	Boston	3-0	Fred Lynn, of, Boston
1976	New York	.610	10½	Kansas City	.556	2½	New York	3-2	Thurman Munson, c, New York
1977	New York	.617	2½	Kansas City	.630	8	New York	3-2	Rod Carew, 1b, Minnesota
1978	New York	.613	1	Kansas City	.568	5	New York	3-1	Jim Rice, of, Boston
1979	Baltimore	.642	8	California	.543	3	Baltimore	3-1	Don Baylor, dh, California
1980	New York	.636	3	Kansas City	.599	14	Kansas City	3-0	George Brett, 3b, Kansas City
1981	New York*	.607	2	Oakland**	.587	—	New York	3-0	Rollie Fingers, rhp, Milwaukee
	Milwaukee	.585	1½	Kansas City	.566	1			
1982	Milwaukee	.586	1	California	.574	3	Milwaukee	3-2	Robin Yount, ss, Milwaukee
1983	Baltimore	.605	6	Chicago	.611	20	Baltimore	3-1	Cal Ripken Jr., ss, Baltimore
1984	Detroit	.642	15	Kansas City	.519	3	Detroit	3-0	Willie Hernandez, lhp, Detroit
1985	Toronto	.615	2	Kansas City	.562	1	Kansas City	4-3	Don Mattingly, 1b, New York
1986	Boston	.590	5½	California	.568	5	Boston	4-3	Roger Clemens, rhp, Boston
1987	Detroit	.605	2	Minnesota	.525	2	Minnesota	4-1	George Bell, of, Toronto
1988	Boston	.549	1	Oakland	.642	13	Oakland	4-0	Jose Canseco, of, Oakland
1989	Toronto	.549	2	Oakland	.611	7	Oakland	4-1	Robin Yount, of, Milwaukee
1990	Boston	.543	2	Oakland	.636	9	Oakland	4-0	Rickey Henderson, of, Oakland
1991	Toronto	.562	7	Minnesota	.586	8	Minnesota	4-1	Cal Ripken Jr., ss, Baltimore
1992	Toronto	.593	4	Oakland	.593	6	Toronto	4-2	Dennis Eckersley, rhp, Oakland
1993	Toronto	.586	7	Chicago	.580	8	Toronto	4-2	Frank Thomas, 1b, Chicago

	East Div.	PCT	GA	Central Div.	PCT	GA	West Div.	PCT	GA	MVP
1994	New York	.619	6½	Chicago	.593	1	Texas	.456	1	Frank Thomas, 1b, Chicago
1995	Boston	.597	7	Cleveland#	.694	30	Seattle	.545	1	Mo Vaughn, 1b, Boston

*Won first half; defeated Milwaukee 3-2 in best-of-5 playoff. #Won AL pennant, defeating Seattle 4-2.
**Won first half, defeated Kansas City 3-0 in best-of-5 playoff.

alongside the '51 Dodgers, the '64 Phillies, the '78 Red Sox and the '94 Democrats among the greatest collapses of all time.

Two nine-game losing streaks between late August and late September, and a streak in which the Mariners won 11 of 12, did the Angels in.

Seattle took first place on Sept. 22 and led by three games with five to play. Miraculously, the Angels won all five to force the one-game playoff, but then they ran into Johnson and lost 9-1.

No division title. No wild-card berth. No nothing. Except a dubious place in baseball history.

"We gave it away," said a downcast Angels center fielder Jim Edmonds. "It's not like we got beat. It's not like they beat us out of first place. We just gave it away."

Still, the Angels' future appeared better than their past, thanks to an expected infusion of marketing savvy from new owners, the Walt Disney Co. Disney bought 25 percent of the team from Gene and Jackie Autry for a reported $30 million and assumed control of day-to-day operations. Disney also has an option to buy the rest of the team upon Gene Autry's death.

"You've got one of the finest businesses in the United States backing you," Angels assistant general manager Tim Mead said of Disney, which also owns the NHL's Anaheim Mighty Ducks. "That's exciting. Everything that happens associated with Disney is positive."

Other Clubs Change Hands

Elsewhere, however, the league was hemorrhaging good owners.

Early in the year, the Haas family sold the Athletics to Bay Area businessmen Steve Schott and Ken Hofmann after 14 years of sensible stewardship. Under managing general partner Walter Haas Jr. the A's went to two World Series, winning the title in 1989 over their cross-bay rivals, the Giants.

Haas, who also owned the Levi Strauss company, died just a week before ownership officially changed hands at the end of the season.

Mighty Hitter. DH Edgar Martinez led the American League in hitting, then powered Seattle to a victory over New York in the Division Series.

In Toronto, the Labatt brewery announced plans to divest itself of its shares in the Blue Jays. The brewery had quietly helped make the Jays a rock of stability since their creation in 1977.

And in Minnesota, owner Carl Pohlad announced that the Twins were for sale, though no buyer had yet been found.

Mariners Seek New Dome

Seattle-area voters defeated a referendum to finance a new stadium for the Mariners, even as the team was catching the Angels and drawing its largest, most boisterous crowds ever.

It's tempting to speculate what the fate of the Sept. 19 referendum might have been had it been held just two weeks later, but its failure placed Seattle's baseball future in jeopardy. Ownership said it would be

AMERICAN LEAGUE ALL-STARS

Selected by Baseball America

Pos.	Player, Team	B-T	Ht.	Wt.	Age	'95 Salary	AVG	AB	R	H	2B	3B	HR	RBI	SB
C	Ivan Rodriguez, Texas	R-R	5-9	205	23	$2,575,000	.303	492	56	149	32	2	12	67	0
1B	Mo Vaughn, Boston	L-R	6-1	245	27	2,675,000	.300	550	98	165	28	3	39	126	11
2B	Chuck Knoblauch, Minn.	R-R	5-9	170	27	2,987,500	.333	538	107	179	34	8	11	63	46
3B	Jim Thome, Cleveland	L-R	6-4	220	25	825,000	.314	452	92	142	29	3	25	73	4
SS	John Valentin, Boston	R-R	6-0	185	28	612,500	.298	520	108	155	37	2	27	102	20
OF	Albert Belle, Cleveland	R-R	6-2	210	29	4,300,000	.317	546	121	173	52	1	50	126	5
	Jay Buhner, Seattle	R-R	6-3	210	31	4,066,666	.262	470	86	123	23	0	40	121	0
	Tim Salmon, California	R-R	6-3	220	27	900,000	.330	537	111	177	34	3	34	105	5
DH	Edgar Martinez, Seattle	R-R	5-11	190	32	3,566,367	.356	511	121	182	52	0	29	113	4

Pos.	Player, Team	B-T	Ht.	Wt.	Age	'95 Salary	W	L	ERA	G	SV	IP	H	BB	SO
P	David Cone, Toronto-NY	L-R	6-1	190	32	8,000,000	18	8	3.57	30	0	229	195	88	191
	Randy Johnson, Seattle	R-L	6-10	225	32	4,425,000	18	2	2.48	30	0	214	159	65	294
	Mike Mussina, Baltimore	R-R	6-2	185	26	2,925,000	19	9	3.29	32	0	222	187	50	158
	Tim Wakefield, Boston	R-R	6-2	204	29	170,000	16	8	2.95	27	0	195	163	68	119
RP	Jose Mesa, Cleveland	R-R	6-3	225	29	900,000	3	0	1.13	62	46	64	49	17	58

Player of the Year: Albert Belle, of, Cleveland. **Pitcher of the Year:** Randy Johnson, lhp, Seattle. **Rookie of the Year:** Garret Anderson, of, California.
Manager of the Year: Lou Piniella, Seattle. **Executive of the Year:** John Hart, Cleveland.

AMERICAN LEAGUE
YEAR-BY-YEAR LEADERS: BATTING

Year	Batting Average	Home Runs	RBIs
1901	Nap Lajoie, Philadelphia .422	Nap Lajoie, Philadelphia 14	Nap Lajoie, Philadelphia 125
1902	Ed Delahanty, Wash. .376	Socks Seybold, Philadelphia 16	Buck Freeman, Boston 121
1903	Nap Lajoie, Cleveland .355	Buck Freeman, Boston 13	Buck Freeman, Boston 104
1904	Nap Lajoie, Cleveland .381	Harry Davis, Philadelphia 10	Nap Lajoie, Cleveland 102
1905	Elmer Flick, Cleveland .306	Harry Davis, Philadelphia 8	Harry Davis, Philadelphia 83
1906	George Stone, St. Louis .358	Harry Davis, Philadelphia 12	Harry Davis, Philadelphia 96
1907	Ty Cobb, Detroit .350	Harry Davis, Philadelphia 8	Ty Cobb, Detroit 116
1908	Ty Cobb, Detroit .324	Sam Crawford, Detroit 7	Ty Cobb, Detroit 101
1909	Ty Cobb, Detroit .377	Ty Cobb, Detroit 9	Ty Cobb, Detroit 115
1910	Ty Cobb, Detroit .385	Jake Stahl, Boston 10	Sam Crawford, Detroit 115
1911	TyCobb, Detroit .420	Frank Baker, Philadelphia 11	Ty Cobb, Detroit 144
1912	Ty Cobb, Detroit .410	2 tied at 10	Frank Baker, Philadelphia 133
1913	Ty Cobb, Detroit .390	Frank Baker, Philadelphia 12	Frank Baker, Philadelphia 126
1914	Ty Cobb, Detroit .368	Frank Baker, Philadelphia 9	Sam Crawford, Detroit 112
1915	Ty Cobb, Detroit .370	Braggo Roth, Cleveland 7	Sam Crawford, Detroit 116
1916	Tris Speaker, Cleveland .386	Wally Pipp, New York 12	Wally Pipp, New York 99
1917	Ty Cobb, Detroit .383	Wally Pipp, New York 9	Bob Veach, Detroit 115
1918	Ty Cobb, Detroit .382	2 tied at 11	2 tied at 74
1919	Ty Cobb, Detroit .384	Babe Ruth, Boston 29	Babe Ruth, Boston 112
1920	George Sisler, St. Louis .407	Babe Ruth, New York 54	Babe Ruth, New York 137
1921	Harry Heilmann, Detroit .394	Babe Ruth, New York 59	Babe Ruth, New York 171
1922	George Sisler, St. Louis .420	Kenny Williams, St. Louis 39	Kenny Williams, St. Louis 155
1923	Harry Heilmann, Detroit .403	Babe Ruth, New York 41	Babe Ruth, New York 131
1924	Babe Ruth, New York .378	Babe Ruth, New York 46	Goose Goslin, Wash. 129
1925	Harry Heilmann, Detroit .393	Bob Meusel, New York 33	Bob Meusel, New York 138
1926	Heinie Manush, Detroit .377	Babe Ruth, New York 47	Babe Ruth, New York 145
1927	Harry Heilmann, Detroit .398	Babe Ruth, New York 60	Lou Gehrig, New York 175
1928	Goose Goslin, Wash. .379	Babe Ruth, New York 54	2 tied at 142
1929	Lew Fonseca, Cleveland .369	Al Simmons, Philadelphia 46	Al Simmons, Philadelphia 157
1930	Al Simmons, Philadelphia .381	Babe Ruth, New York 49	Lou Gehrig, New York 174
1931	Al Simmons, Philadelphia .390	Lou Gehrig, New York 46	Lou Gehrig, New York 184
1932	Dale Alexander, Det.-Bos. .367	Jimmie Foxx, Philadelphia 58	Jimmie Foxx, Philadelphia 169
1933	Jimmie Foxx, Philadelphia .356	Jimmie Foxx, Philadelphia 48	Jimmie Foxx, Philadelphia 163
1934	Lou Gehrig, New York .363	Lou Gehrig, New York 49	Lou Gehrig, New York 165
1935	Buddy Myer, Washington .349	2 tied at 36	Hank Greenberg, Detroit 170
1936	Luke Appling, Chicago .388	Lou Gehrig, New York 49	Hal Trosky, Cleveland 162
1937	Charlie Gehringer, Detroit .371	Joe DiMaggio, New York 46	Hank Greenberg, Detroit 183
1938	Jimmie Foxx, Boston .349	Hank Greenberg, Detroit 58	Jimmie Foxx, Boston 175
1939	Joe DiMaggio, New York .381	Jimmie Foxx, Boston 35	Ted Williams, Boston 145
1940	Joe DiMaggio, New York .352	Hank Greenberg, Detroit 41	Hank Greenberg, Detroit 150
1941	Ted Williams, Boston .406	Ted Williams, Boston 37	Joe DiMaggio, New York 125
1942	Ted Williams, Boston .356	Ted Williams, Boston 36	Ted Williams, Boston 137
1943	Luke Appling, Chicago .328	Rudy York, Detroit 34	Rudy York, Detroit 118
1944	Lou Boudreau, Cleve. .327	Nick Etten, New York 22	Vern Stephens, St. Louis 109
1945	Snuffy Stirnweiss, New York .309	Vern Stephens, St. Louis 24	Nick Etten, New York 111
1946	Mickey Vernon, Wash. .353	Hank Greenberg, Detroit 44	Hank Greenberg, Detroit 127
1947	Ted Williams, Boston .343	Ted Williams, Boston 32	Ted Williams, Boston 114
1948	Ted Williams, Boston .369	Joe DiMaggio, New York 39	Joe DiMaggio, New York 155
1949	George Kell, Detroit .343	Ted Williams, Boston 43	2 tied at 159
1950	Billy Goodman, Boston .354	Al Rosen, Cleveland 37	2 tied at 144
1951	Ferris Fain, Philadelphia .344	Gus Zernial, Chi.-Phil. 33	Gus Zernial, Chi.-Phil. 129
1952	Ferris Fain, Philadelphia .327	Larry Doby, Cleveland 32	Al Rosen, Cleveland 105
1953	Mickey Vernon, Washington .337	Al Rosen, Cleveland 43	Al Rosen, Cleveland 145
1954	Bobby Avila, Cleveland .341	Larry Doby, Cleveland 32	Larry Doby, Cleveland 126
1955	Al Kaline, Detroit .340	Mickey Mantle, New York 37	2 tied at 116
1956	Mickey Mantle, New York .353	Mickey Mantle, New York 52	Mickey Mantle, New York 130
1957	Ted Williams, Boston .388	Roy Sievers, Washington 42	Roy Sievers, Washington 114
1958	Ted Williams, Boston .328	Mickey Mantle, New York 42	Jackie Jensen, Boston 122
1959	Harvey Kuenn, Detroit .353	2 tied at 42	Jackie Jensen, Boston 112
1960	Pete Runnels, Boston .320	Mickey Mantle, New York 40	Roger Maris, New York 112
1961	Norm Cash, Detroit .361	Roger Maris, New York 61	Roger Maris, New York 142
1962	Pete Runnels, Boston .326	Harmon Killebrew, Minn. 48	Harmon Killebrew, Minn. 126
1963	Carl Yastrzemski, Boston .321	Harmon Killebrew, Minn. 45	Dick Stuart, Boston 118
1964	Tony Oliva, Minnesota .323	Harmon Killebrew, Minn. 49	Brooks Robinson, Baltimore 118
1965	Tony Oliva, Minnesota .321	Tony Conigliaro, Boston 32	Rocky Colavito, Cleveland 108
1966	Frank Robinson, Baltimore .316	Frank Robinson, Baltimore 49	Frank Robinson, Baltimore 122
1967	Carl Yastrzemski, Boston .326	2 tied at 44	Carl Yastrzemski, Boston 121
1968	Carl Yastrzemski, Boston .301	Frank Howard, Washington 44	Ken Harrelson, Boston 109
1969	Rod Carew, Minnesota .332	Harmon Killebrew, Minn. 49	Harmon Killebrew, Minn. 140
1970	Alex Johnson, California .329	Frank Howard, Washington 44	Frank Howard, Washington 126
1971	Tony Oliva, Minnesota .337	Bill Melton, Chicago 33	Harmon Killebrew, Minn. 119
1972	Rod Carew, Minnesota .318	Dick Allen, Chicago 37	Dick Allen, Chicago 113
1973	Rod Carew, Minnesota .350	Reggie Jackson, Oakland 32	Reggie Jackson, Oakland 117
1974	Rod Carew, Minnesota .364	Dick Allen, Chicago 32	Jeff Burroughs, Texas 118
1975	Rod Carew, Minnesota .359	Reggie Jackson, Oakland 36	George Scott, Milwaukee 109
1976	George Brett, Kansas City .333	Graig Nettles, New York 32	Lee May, Baltimore 109
1977	Rod Carew, Minnesota .388	Jim Rice, Boston 39	Larry Hisle, Minnesota 119
1978	Rod Carew, Minnesota .333	Jim Rice, Boston 46	Jim Rice, Boston 139
1979	Fred Lynn, Boston .333	Gorman Thomas, Mil. 45	Don Baylor, California 139
1980	George Brett, Kansas City .390	2 tied at 41	Cecil Cooper, Milwaukee 122
1981	Carney Lansford, Boston .336	4 tied at 22	Eddie Murray, Baltimore 78
1982	Willie Wilson, Kansas City .332	2 tied at 39	Hal McRae, Kansas City 133
1983	Wade Boggs, Boston .361	Jim Rice, Boston 39	Cecil Cooper, Milwaukee 126
1984	Don Mattingly, New York .343	Tony Armas, Boston 43	Tony Armas, Boston 123
1985	Wade Boggs, Boston .368	Darrell Evans, Detroit 40	Don Mattingly, New York 145
1986	Wade Boggs, Boston .357	Jesse Barfield, Toronto 40	Joe Carter, Cleveland 121
1987	Wade Boggs, Boston .363	Mark McGwire, Oakland 49	George Bell, Toronto 134
1988	Wade Boggs, Boston .366	Jose Canseco, Oakland 42	Jose Canseco, Oakland 124
1989	Kirby Puckett, Minn. .339	Fred McGriff, Toronto 36	Ruben Sierra, Texas 119
1990	George Brett, Kansas City .329	Cecil Fielder, Detroit 51	Cecil Fielder, Detroit 132
1991	Julio Franco, Texas .341	Cecil Fielder, Detroit 44	Cecil Fielder, Detroit 133
1992	Edgar Martinez, Seattle .343	Juan Gonzalez, Texas 43	Cecil Fielder, Detroit 124
1993	John Olerud, Toronto .363	Juan Gonzalez, Texas 46	Albert Belle, Cleveland 129
1994	Paul O'Neill, New York .359	Ken Griffey, Seattle 40	Kirby Puckett, Minnesota 112
1995	Edgar Martinez, Seattle .356	Albert Belle, Cleveland 50	2 tied at 126

AMERICAN LEAGUE
YEAR-BY-YEAR LEADERS: PITCHING

Year	Wins		ERA		Strikeouts	
1901	Cy Young, Boston	33	Cy Young, Boston	1.63	Cy Young, Boston	158
1902	Cy Young, Boston	32	Ed Siever, Detroit	1.91	Rube Waddell, Philadelphia	210
1903	Cy Young, Boston	28	Earl Moore, Cleveland	1.77	Rube Waddell, Philadelphia	302
1904	Jack Chesbro, New York	41	Addie Joss, Cleveland	1.59	Rube Waddell, Philadelphia	349
1905	Rube Waddell, Philadelphia	26	Rue Waddell, Philadelphia	1.48	Rube Waddell, Philadelphia	287
1906	Al Orth, New York	27	Doc White, Chicago	1.52	Rube Waddell, Philadelphia	196
1907	2 tied at	27	Ed Walsh, Chicago	1.60	Rube Waddell, Philadelphia	232
1908	Ed Walsh, Chicago	40	Addie Joss, Cleveland	1.16	Ed Walsh, Chicago	269
1909	George Mullin, Detroit	29	Harry Krause, Philadelphia	1.39	Frank Smith, Chicago	177
1910	Jack Coombs, Philadelphia	31	Ed Walsh, Chicago	1.27	Walter Johnson, Washington	313
1911	Jack Coombs, Philadelphia	28	Vean Gregg, Cleveland	1.81	Ed Walsh, Chicago	255
1912	Joe Wood, Boston	34	Walter Johnson, Wash	1.39	Walter Johnson, Washington	303
1913	Walter Johnson, Wash	36	Walter Johnson, Wash	1.14	Walter Johnson, Washington	243
1914	Walter Johnson, Wash	28	Dutch Leonard, Bos	1.00	Walter Johnson, Washington	225
1915	Walter Johnson, Wash	27	Joe Wood, Boston	1.49	Walter Johnson, Washington	203
1916	Walter Johnson, Wash	25	Babe Ruth, Boston	1.75	Walter Johnson, Washington	228
1917	Ed Cicotte, Chicago	28	Ed Cicotte, Chicago	1.53	Walter Johnson, Washington	188
1918	Walter Johnson, Wash	23	Walter Johnson, Wash	1.27	Walter Johnson, Washington	162
1919	Ed Cicotte, Chicago	29	Walter Johnson, Wash	1.49	Walter Johnson, Washington	147
1920	Jim Bagby, Cleveland	31	Bob Shawkey, New York	2.45	Stan Coveleski, Cleveland	133
1921	2 tied at	27	Red Faber, Chicago	2.48	Walter Johnson, Washington	143
1922	Eddie Rommel, Phil	27	Red Faber, Chicago	2.80	Urban Shocker, St. Louis	149
1923	George Uhle, Cleveland	26	Stan Coveleski, Cleveland	2.76	Walter Johnson, Washington	130
1924	Walter Johnson, Wash	23	Walter Johnson, Wash	2.72	Walter Johnson, Washington	158
1925	2 tied at	21	Stan Coveleski, Wash	2.84	Lefty Grove, Philadelphia	116
1926	George Uhle, Cleveland	27	Lefty Grove, Philadelphia	2.51	Lefty Grove, Philadelphia	194
1927	2 tied at	22	Wilcy Moore, New York	2.28	Lefty Grove, Philadelphia	174
1928	2 tied at	24	Garland Braxton, Wash	2.52	Lefty Grove, Philadelphia	183
1929	George Earnshaw, Phil	24	Lefty Grove, Philadelphia	2.82	Lefty Grove, Philadelphia	170
1930	Lefty Grove, Philadelphia	28	Lefty Grove, Philadelphia	2.54	Lefty Grove, Philadelphia	209
1931	Lefty Grove, Philadelphia	31	Lefty Grove, Philadelphia	2.05	Lefty Grove, Philadelphia	175
1932	General Crowder, Wash	26	Red Ruffing, New York	2.84	Red Ruffing, New York	190
1933	2 tied at	24	Monte Pearson, Cleveland	2.33	Lefty Gomez, New York	163
1934	Lefty Gomez, New York	26	Lefty Gomez, New York	2.33	Lefty Gomez, New York	158
1935	Wes Ferrell, Boston	25	Lefty Grove, Boston	2.70	Tommy Bridges, Detroit	163
1936	Tommy Bridges, Detroit	23	Lefty Grove, Boston	2.81	Tommy Bridges, Detroit	175
1937	Lefty Gomez, New York	21	Lefty Gomez, New York	2.33	Lefty Gomez, New York	194
1938	Red Ruffing, New York	21	Lefty Grove, Philadelphia	3.07	Bob Feller, Cleveland	240
1939	Bob Feller, Cleveland	24	Lefty Grove, Philadelphia	2.54	Bob Feller, Cleveland	246
1940	Bob Feller, Cleveland	27	Bob Feller, Cleveland	2.62	Bob Feller, Cleveland	261
1941	Bob Feller, Cleveland	25	Thornton Lee, Chicago	2.37	Bob Feller, Cleveland	260
1942	Tex Hughson, Boston	22	Ted Lyons, Chicago	2.10	2 tied at	113
1943	2 tied at	20	Spud Chandler, New York	1.64	Allie Reynolds, Cleveland	151
1944	Hal Newhouser, Detroit	29	Dizzy Trout, Detroit	2.12	Hal Newhouser, Detroit	187
1945	Hal Newhouser, Detroit	25	Hal Newhouser, Detroit	1.81	Hal Newhouser, Detroit	212
1946	2 tied at	26	Hal Newhouser, Detroit	1.94	Bob Feller, Cleveland	348
1947	Bob Feller, Cleveland	20	Spud Chandler, New York	2.46	Bob Feller, Cleveland	196
1948	Hal Newhouser, Detroit	21	Gene Bearden, Cleveland	2.43	Bob Feller, Cleveland	164
1949	Mel Parnell, Boston	25	Mel Parnell, Boston	2.78	Virgil Trucks, Detroit	153
1950	Bob Lemon, Cleveland	23	Early Wynn, Cleveland	3.20	Bob Lemon, Cleveland	170
1951	Bob Feller, Cleveland	22	Saul Rogovin, Det.-Chi.	2.78	Vic Raschi, New York	164
1952	Bobby Shantz, Philadelphia	24	Allie Reynolds, New York	2.07	Allie Reynolds, New York	160
1953	Bob Porterfield, Wash	22	Eddie Lopat, New York	2.43	Billy Pierce, Chicago	186
1954	3 tied at	23	Mike Garcia, Cleveland	2.64	Bob Turley, Baltimore	185
1955	3 tied at	18	Billy Pierce, Chicago	1.97	Herb Score, Cleveland	245
1956	Frank Lary, Detroit	21	Whitey Ford, New York	2.47	Herb Score, Cleveland	263
1957	2 tied at	20	Bobby Shantz, New York	2.45	Early Wynn, Cleveland	184
1958	2 tied at	21	Whitey Ford, New York	2.01	Early Wynn, Chicago	179
1959	Early Wynn, Chicago	22	Hoyt Wilhelm, Balt.	2.19	Jim Bunning, Detroit	201
1960	2 tied at	18	Frank Baumann, Chicago	2.68	Jim Bunning, Detroit	201
1961	Whitey Ford, New York	25	Dick Donovan, Washington	2.40	Camilo Pascual, Minnesota	221
1962	Ralph Terry, New York	23	Hank Aguirre, Detroit	2.21	Camilo Pascual, Minnesota	206
1963	Whitey Ford, New York	24	Gary Peters, Chicago	2.33	Camilo Pascual, Minnesota	202
1964	2 tied at	20	Dean Chance, L.A.	1.65	Al Downing, New York	217
1965	Mudcat Grant, Minnesota	21	Sam McDowell, Cleveland	2.18	Sam McDowell, Cleveland	325
1966	Jim Kaat, Minnesota	25	Gary Peters, Chicago	1.98	Sam McDowell, Cleveland	225
1967	2 tied at	22	Joel Horlen, Chicago	2.06	Jim Lonborg, Boston	246
1968	Denny McLain, Detroit	31	Luis Tiant, Cleveland	1.60	Sam McDowell, Cleveland	283
1969	Denny McLain, Detroit	24	Dick Bosman, Washington	2.19	Sam McDowell, Cleveland	279
1970	3 tied at	24	Diego Segui, Oakland	2.56	Sam McDowell, Cleveland	304
1971	Mickey Lolich, Detroit	25	Vida Blue, Oakland	1.82	Mickey Lolich, Detroit	308
1972	2 tied at	24	Luis Tiant, Boston	1.91	Nolan Ryan, California	329
1973	Wilbur Wood, Chicago	24	Jim Palmer, Baltimore	2.40	Nolan Ryan, California	383
1974	2 tied at	25	Catfish Hunter, Oakland	2.49	Nolan Ryan, California	367
1975	2 tied at	23	Jim Palmer, Baltimore	2.09	Frank Tanana, California	269
1976	Jim Palmer, Baltimore	22	Mark Fidrych, Detroit	2.34	Nolan Ryan, California	327
1977	3 tied at	20	Frank Tanana, California	2.54	Nolan Ryan, California	341
1978	Ron Guidry, New York	25	Ron Guidry, New York	1.74	Nolan Ryan, California	260
1979	Mike Flanagan, Baltimore	23	Ron Guidry, New York	2.78	Nolan Ryan, California	223
1980	Steve Stone, Baltimore	25	Rudy May, New York	2.47	Len Barker, Cleveland	187
1981	Steve McCatty, Oak.	14	Steve McCatty, Oak.	2.32	Len Barker, Cleveland	127
1982	LaMarr Hoyt, Chicago	19	Rick Sutcliffe, Cleveland	2.96	Floyd Bannister, Seattle	209
1983	LaMarr Hoyt, Chicago	24	Rick Honeycutt, Texas	2.42	Jack Morris, Detroit	232
1984	Mike Boddicker, Balt.	20	Mike Boddicker, Balt.	2.79	Mark Langston, Seattle	204
1985	Ron Guidry, New York	22	Dave Stieb, Toronto	2.48	Bert Blyleven, Cleveland-Minn.	206
1986	Roger Clemens, Boston	24	Roger Clemens, Boston	2.48	Mark Langston, Seattle	245
1987	2 tied at	20	Jimmy Key, Toronto	2.76	Mark Langston, Seattle	262
1988	Frank Viola, Minnesota	24	Allan Anderson, Minnesota	2.45	Roger Clemens, Boston	291
1989	Bret Saberhagen, K.C.	23	Bret Saberhagen, K.C.	2.16	Nolan Ryan, Texas	301
1990	Bob Welch, Oakland	27	Roger Clemens, Boston	1.93	Nolan Ryan, Texas	232
1991	2 tied at	20	Roger Clemens, Boston	2.62	Roger Clemens, Boston	241
1992	2 tied at	21	Roger Clemens, Boston	2.41	Randy Johnson, Seattle	241
1993	Jack McDowell, Chicago	22	Kevin Appier, Kansas City	2.56	Randy Johnson, Seattle	308
1994	Jimmy Key, New York	17	Steve Ontiveros, Oakland	2.65	Randy Johnson, Seattle	204
1995	Mike Mussina, Baltimore	19	Randy Johnson, Seattle	2.48	Randy Johnson, Seattle	294

AMERICAN LEAGUE
DEPARTMENT LEADERS

BATTING

AT-BATS
Lance Johnson, Chicago	607
Otis Nixon, Texas	589
Chad Curtis, Detroit	586
Travis Fryman, Detroit	567
Bernie Williams, New York	563

RUNS
Albert Belle, Cleveland	121
Edgar Martinez, Seattle	121
Jim Edmonds, California	120
Tony Phillips, California	119
Tim Salmon, California	111

HITS
Lance Johnson, Chicago	186
Edgar Martinez, Seattle	182
Chuck Knoblauch, Minnesota	179
Tim Salmon, California	177
Carlos Baerga, Cleveland	175

TOTAL BASES
Albert Belle, Cleveland	377
Rafael Palmeiro, Baltimore	323
Edgar Martinez, Seattle	321
Tim Salmon, California	319
Mo Vaughn, Boston	316

DOUBLES
Albert Belle, Cleveland	52
Edgar Martinez, Seattle	52
Kirby Puckett, Minnesota	39
John Valentin, Boston	37
Tino Martinez, Seattle	35

TRIPLES
Kenny Lofton, Cleveland	13
Lance Johnson, Chicago	12
Brady Anderson, Baltimore	10
Bernie Williams, New York	9
Chuck Knoblauch, Minnesota	8

HOME RUNS
Albert Belle, Cleveland	50
Frank Thomas, Chicago	40
Jay Buhner, Seattle	40
Mo Vaughn, Boston	39
Rafael Palmeiro, Baltimore	39
Mark McGwire, Oakland	39

HOME RUN RATIO
(At-Bats Per HR)
Albert Belle, Cleveland	10.9
Jay Buhner, Seattle	11.8
Frank Thomas, Chicago	12.3
Mickey Tettleton, Texas	13.4
Mo Vaughn, Boston	14.1

RUNS BATTED IN
Mo Vaughn, Boston	126
Albert Belle, Cleveland	126
Jay Buhner, Seattle	121
Edgar Martinez, Seattle	113
Tino Martinez, Seattle	111
Frank Thomas, Chicago	111

SACRIFICE BUNTS
Tom Goodwin, Kansas City	14
Luis Alicea, Boston	13
Joey Cora, Seattle	13
Brent Mayne, Kansas City	11
Four tied at	10

SACRIFICE FLIES
Frank Thomas, Chicago	12
Will Clark, Texas	11
Paul O'Neill, New York	11
Brent Gates, Oakland	11
Omar Vizquel, Cleveland	10

HIT BY PITCH
Ed Sprague, Toronto	15

Heavenly Slugger. Angels outfielder Tim Salmon finished among AL leaders in runs (111), hits (177), total bases (319) and slugging percentage (.594).

Mo Vaughn, Boston	14
Mike Macfarlane, Boston	14
Mark McGwire, Oakland	11
Pat Meares, Minnesota	11

WALKS
Frank Thomas, Chicago	136
Edgar Martinez, Seattle	116
Tony Phillips, California	113
Mickey Tettleton, Texas	107
Jim Thome, Cleveland	97

INTENTIONAL WALKS
Frank Thomas, Chicago	29
Edgar Martinez, Seattle	19
Kirby Puckett, Minnesota	18
Mo Vaughn, Boston	17
Tino Martinez, Seattle	15

STRIKEOUTS
Mo Vaughn, Boston	150
Benji Gil, Texas	147
Tony Phillips, California	135
Jim Edmonds, California	130
Mike Blowers, Seattle	128

TOUGHEST TO STRIKE OUT
(Plate Appearances Per SO)
Lance Johnson, Chicago	20.8
Carlos Baerga, Cleveland	19.4
Joey Cora, Seattle	15.7
Mike Greenwell, Boston	15.0
Don Mattingly, New York	14.5

STOLEN BASES
Kenny Lofton, Cleveland	54
Tom Goodwin, Kansas City	50
Otis Nixon, Texas	50
Chuck Knoblauch, Minnesota	46
Vince Coleman, KC-Seattle	42

CAUGHT STEALING
Otis Nixon, Texas	21
Tom Goodwin, Kansas City	18
Chuck Knoblauch, Minnesota	18
Vince Coleman, KC-Seattle	16
Chad Curtis, Detroit	15
Kenny Lofton, Cleveland	15

GIDP
Paul O'Neill, New York	25
Albert Belle, Cleveland	24
Ed Sprague, Toronto	19
Travis Fryman, Detroit	18
Mike Blowers, Seattle	18
Mike Greenwell, Boston	18

HITTING STREAKS
Jim Edmonds, California	23
Bobby Bonilla, Baltimore	20
Roberto Alomar, Toronto	19
Chad Curtis, Detroit	18
Mark McGwire, Oakland	18

MULTIPLE-HIT GAMES
Chuck Knoblauch, Minnesota	56
Tim Salmon, California	55
Edgar Martinez, Seattle	54
Lance Johnson, Chicago	54
Carlos Baerga, Cleveland	52

SLUGGING PERCENTAGE
Albert Belle, Cleveland	.690
Edgar Martinez, Seattle	.628
Frank Thomas, Chicago	.606
Tim Salmon, California	.594
Rafael Palmeiro, Baltimore	.583

ON-BASE PERCENTAGE
Edgar Martinez, Seattle	.479
Frank Thomas, Chicago	.454
Jim Thome, Cleveland	.438
Tim Salmon, California	.429
Chili Davis, California	.429

PITCHING

WINS
Mike Mussina, Baltimore	19
Randy Johnson, Seattle	18
David Cone, Toronto-New York	18
Kenny Rogers, Texas	17
Tim Wakefield, Boston	16
Charles Nagy, Cleveland	16
Orel Hershiser, Cleveland	16

LOSSES

Kevin Gross, Texas 15
Mike Moore, Detroit 15
Jason Bere, Chicago 15
Pat Hentgen, Toronto 14
Juan Guzman, Toronto 14
Mark Gubicza, Kansas City 14
Brad Radke, Minnesota 14

WINNING PERCENTAGE

Randy Johnson, Seattle .... .900
David Wells, Detroit .... .769
Eric Hanson, Boston .... .750
Charles Nagy, Cleveland .... .727
Orel Hershiser, Cleveland .... .727

GAMES

Jesse Orosco, Baltimore 65
Roger McDowell, Texas 64
Bob Wickman, New York 63
Bobby Ayala, Seattle 63
Stan Belinda, Boston 63

GAMES STARTED

Mark Gubicza, Kansas City 33
Mike Mussina, Baltimore 32
Chuck Finley, California 32
Nine players at 31

COMPLETE GAMES

Jack McDowell, New York 8
Mike Mussina, Baltimore 7
Scott Erickson, Minn.-Balt. 7
Tim Wakefield, Boston 6
Randy Johnson, Seattle 6
David Cone, Toronto-New York 6

SHUTOUTS

Mike Mussina, Baltimore 4
Randy Johnson, Seattle 3
Six tied at 2

GAMES FINISHED

Roberto Hernandez, Chicago 57
Jose Mesa, Cleveland 57
John Wetteland, New York 56
Rick Aguilera, Boston 51
Lee Smith, California 51

SAVES

Jose Mesa, Cleveland 46
Lee Smith, California 37
Roberto Hernandez, Chicago 32
Rick Aguilera, Boston 32

Mo Vaughn
126 RBIs

John Wetteland, New York 31
Jeff Montgomery, Kansas City 31

INNINGS PITCHED

David Cone, Toronto-New York 229
Mike Mussina, Baltimore 222
Jack McDowell, New York 218
Randy Johnson, Seattle 214
Mark Gubicza, Kansas City 213

HITS ALLOWED

Pat Hentgen, Toronto 236
Todd Stottlemyre, Oakland 228
Mark Gubicza, Kansas City 222
Ricky Bones, Milwaukee 218
Scott Erickson, Baltimore 213

RUNS ALLOWED

Pat Hentgen, Toronto 129
Kevin Gross, Texas 124
Jason Bere, Chicago 120
Mike Moore, Detroit 118
Todd Stottlemyre, Oakland 117

HOME RUNS ALLOWED

Brad Radke, Minnesota 32
Kevin Gross, Texas 27
Ricky Bones, Milwaukee 26
Todd Stottlemyre, Oakland 26
Kenny Rogers, Texas 26

WALKS

Al Leiter, Toronto 108
Jason Bere, Chicago 106
Wilson Alvarez, Chicago 93
Chuck Finley, California 93
Roger Pavlik, Texas 90
Pat Hentgen, Toronto 90

HIT BATSMEN

Roger Clemens, Boston 14
Dennis Martinez, Cleveland 12
Tim Wakefield, Boston 9
Kevin Brown, Baltimore 9
Four tied at 8

STRIKEOUTS

Randy Johnson, Seattle 294
Todd Stottlemyre, Oakland 205
Chuck Finley, California 195
David Cone, New York 191
Kevin Appier, Kansas City 185

STRIKEOUTS PER 9 INNINGS

Randy Johnson, Seattle 12.3
Todd Stottlemyre, Oakland 8.8
Chuck Finley, California 8.6
Kevin Appier, Kansas City 8.3
Al Leiter, Toronto 7.5

WILD PITCHES

Al Leiter, Toronto 14
Chuck Finley, California 13
Sean Bergman, Detroit 13
Tim Wakefield, Boston 11
Todd Stottlemyre, Oakland 11
David Cone, Toronto-New York 11
Edwin Hurtado, Toronto 11

BALKS

Brian Anderson, California 3
Tim Fortugno, Chicago 3
Fourteen tied at 2

OPPONENTS BATTING AVERAGE

Randy Johnson, Seattle .... .201
Kevin Appier, Kansas City .... .221
Mike Mussina, Baltimore .... .226
Tim Wakefield, Boston .... .227
David Cone, Toronto-New York .... .238
Al Leiter, Toronto .... .238

FIELDING

PITCHER

PCT Mark Gubicza, K.C. 1.000
PO Kevin Brown, Baltimore 40
A Dennis Martinez, Cleve. 36
E Two tied at 4
TC Kevin Brown, Baltimore 84

Jose Mesa.
46 saves

DP Ricky Bones, Milwaukee 8

CATCHER

PCT Chris Hoiles, Baltimore .... .996
PO Ivan Rodriguez, Texas 707
A Ivan Rodriguez, Texas 67
E John Flaherty, Detroit 11
TC Ivan Rodriguez, Texas 782
DP Brent Mayne, Kansas City 11
PB Mike Macfarlane, Boston 26

FIRST BASE

PCT Wally Joyner, Kansas City ...... .998
PO Mo Vaughn, Boston 1262
A Rafael Palmeiro, Baltimore 119
E Mark McGwire, Oakland 12
TC Mo Vaughn, Boston 1,368
DP Mo Vaughn, Boston 128

SECOND BASE

PCT Roberto Alomar, Toronto .... .994
PO Roberto Alomar, Toronto 272
A Carlos Baerga, Cleveland 444
E Joey Cora, Seattle 22
TC Luis Alicea, Boston 699
DP Luis Alicea, Boston 103

THIRD BASE

PCT Wade Boggs, New York .... .981
PO Ed Sprague, Toronto 133
A Travis Fryman, Detroit 337
E Tony Phillips, California 19
TC Travis Fryman, Detroit 458
DP Travis Fryman, Detroit 38

SHORTSTOP

PCT Cal Ripken, Baltimore .... .989
PO Mike Bordick, Oakland 245
A Jose Valentin, Boston 414
E Three tied at 18
TC John Valentin, Boston 659
DP Cal Ripken, Baltimore 100

OUTFIELD

PCT Stan Javier, Oakland 1.000
PO Bernie Williams, New York 432
A Bobby Higginson, Detroit 13
E Two tied at 8
TC Bernie Williams, New York 441
DP Rich Becker, Minnesota 5

AMERICAN LEAGUE
1995 BATTING, PITCHING STATISTICS

CLUB BATTING

	AVG	G	AB	R	H	2B	3B	HR	BB	SO	SB
Cleveland	.291	144	5028	840	1461	279	23	207	542	766	132
Chicago	.280	145	5060	755	1417	252	37	146	576	767	110
Boston	.280	144	4997	791	1399	286	31	175	560	923	99
Minnesota	.279	144	5005	703	1398	270	34	120	471	916	105
California	.277	145	5019	801	1390	252	25	186	564	889	58
New York	.276	145	4947	749	1365	280	34	122	625	851	50
Seattle	.276	145	4996	796	1377	276	20	182	549	871	110
Milwaukee	.266	144	5000	740	1329	249	42	128	502	800	105
Texas	.265	144	4913	691	1304	247	24	138	526	877	90
Oakland	.264	144	4916	730	1296	228	18	169	565	911	112
Baltimore	.262	144	4837	704	1267	229	27	173	574	803	92
Kansas City	.260	144	4903	629	1275	240	35	119	475	849	120
Toronto	.260	144	5036	642	1309	275	27	140	492	906	75
Detroit	.247	144	4865	654	1204	228	29	159	551	987	73

CLUB PITCHING

	ERA	G	CG	SHO	SV	IP	H	R	ER	BB	SO
Cleveland	3.83	144	10	10	50	1301	1261	607	554	445	926
Baltimore	4.31	144	19	10	29	1267	1165	640	607	523	930
Boston	4.41	144	7	9	39	1293	1338	698	634	476	888
Kansas City	4.48	144	11	10	37	1288	1323	691	642	503	763
Seattle	4.52	145	9	8	39	1289	1343	708	647	591	1068
California	4.53	145	8	9	42	1284	1310	697	646	486	901
New York	4.56	145	18	5	35	1285	1286	688	651	535	908
Texas	4.66	144	14	4	34	1285	1385	720	666	514	838
Milwaukee	4.82	144	7	4	31	1286	1391	747	689	603	699
Chicago	4.85	145	12	4	36	1283	1374	758	693	617	892
Toronto	4.88	144	16	8	22	1293	1336	777	701	654	894
Oakland	4.97	144	8	4	34	1273	1320	761	703	556	890
Detroit	5.50	144	5	3	38	1275	1509	844	779	536	729
Minnesota	5.77	144	7	2	27	1273	1450	889	816	533	790

CLUB FIELDING

	PCT	PO	A	E	DP		PCT	PO	A	E	DP
Baltimore	.986	3801	1441	72	141	Minnesota	.981	3818	1487	100	141
New York	.986	3854	1416	74	121	Milwaukee	.981	3858	1669	105	186
Kansas City	.984	3854	1660	90	168	Oakland	.981	3819	1486	102	151
Texas	.982	3855	1589	98	156	Detroit	.981	3825	1594	106	143
California	.982	3853	1416	95	120	Seattle	.980	3868	1357	104	108
Cleveland	.982	3903	1598	101	142	Chicago	.980	3854	1415	108	131
Toronto	.982	3878	1399	97	131	Boston	.978	3878	1581	120	151

INDIVIDUAL BATTING LEADERS
(Minimum 446 Plate Appearances)

	AVG	G	AB	R	H	2B	3B	HR	RBI	BB	SO	SB
Martinez, Edgar, Seattle	.356	145	511	121	182	52	0	29	113	116	87	4
Knoblauch, Chuck, Minn.	.333	136	538	107	179	34	8	11	63	78	95	46
Salmon, Tim, California	.330	143	537	111	177	34	3	34	105	91	111	5
Boggs, Wade, New York	.324	126	460	76	149	22	4	5	63	74	50	1
Murray, Eddie, Cleveland	.323	113	436	68	141	21	0	21	82	39	65	5
Surhoff, B.J., Milwaukee	.320	117	415	72	133	26	3	13	73	37	43	7
Davis, Chili, California	.318	119	424	81	135	23	0	20	86	89	79	3
Belle, Albert, Cleveland	.317	143	546	121	173	52	1	50	126	73	80	5
Baerga, Carlos, Cleveland	.314	135	557	87	175	28	2	15	90	35	31	11
Thome, Jim, Cleveland	.314	137	452	92	142	29	3	25	73	97	113	4

INDIVIDUAL PITCHING LEADERS
(Minimum 144 Innings)

	W	L	ERA	G	GS	CG	SV	IP	H	R	ER	BB	SO
Johnson, Randy, Seattle	18	2	2.48	30	30	6	0	214	159	65	59	65	294
Wakefield, Tim, Boston	16	8	2.95	27	27	6	0	195	163	76	64	68	119
Martinez, Dennis, Cleveland	12	5	3.08	28	28	3	0	187	174	71	64	46	99
Mussina, Mike, Baltimore	19	9	3.29	32	32	7	0	222	187	86	81	50	158
Rogers, Kenny, Texas	17	7	3.38	31	31	3	0	208	192	87	78	76	140
Cone, David, Tor.-NY	18	8	3.57	30	30	6	0	229	195	95	91	88	191
Brown, Kevin, Baltimore	10	9	3.60	26	26	3	0	172	155	73	69	48	117
Leiter, Al, Toronto	11	11	3.64	28	28	2	0	183	162	80	74	108	153
Abbott, Jim, Chi.-Calif.	11	8	3.70	30	30	4	0	197	209	93	81	64	86
Gubicza, Mark, KC	12	14	3.75	33	33	3	0	213	222	97	89	62	81

AWARD WINNERS

Selected by Baseball Writers Association of America

MVP

Player, Team	1st	2nd	3rd	Total
Mo Vaughn, Boston	12	12	4	308
Albert Belle, Cleveland	11	10	7	300
Edgar Martinez, Seattle	4	5	12	244
Jose Mesa, Cleveland	1	0	1	130
Jay Buhner, Seattle	0	0	1	120
Randy Johnson, Seattle	0	1	2	111
Tim Salmon, Calif.	0	0	0	110
Frank Thomas, Chicago	0	0	1	86
John Valentin, Boston	0	0	0	57
Gary Gaetti, K.C.	0	0	0	45
Rafael Palmeiro, Balt.	0	0	0	34
Manny Ramirez, Cleve.	0	0	0	30
Tim Wakefield, Boston	0	0	0	20
Jim Edmonds, Calif.	0	0	0	18
Paul O'Neill, N.Y.	0	0	0	14
Mark McGwire, Oak.	0	0	0	7
Chuck Knoblauch, Minn.	0	0	0	5
Wade Boggs, N.Y.	0	0	0	5
Gary DiSarcina, Calif.	0	0	0	3
Cal Ripken, Baltimore	0	0	0	3
Kirby Puckett, Minn.	0	0	0	2

Cy Young Award

Player, Team	1st	2nd	3rd	Total
Randy Johnson, Seattle	26	2	0	136
Jose Mesa, Cleveland	2	13	5	54
Tim Wakefield, Boston	0	6	11	29
David Cone, Tor.-N.Y.	0	5	3	18
Mike Mussina, Balt.	0	2	8	14
Charles Nagy, Cleve.	0	0	1	1

Rookie of the Year

Player, Team	1st	2nd	3rd	Total
Marty Cordova, Minn.	13	13	1	105
Garret Anderson, Calif.	13	10	4	99
Andy Pettitte, N.Y.	1	1	8	16
Troy Percival, Calif.	1	2	2	13
Shawn Green, Tor.	0	2	2	8
Ray Durham, Chicago	0	0	3	3
Julian Tavarez, Cleve.	0	0	3	3
Jon Nunnally, K.C.	0	0	2	2
Tom Goodwin, K.C.	0	0	1	1
Brad Radke, Minn.	0	0	1	1
Steve Sparks, Mil.	0	0	1	1

Manager of the Year

Manager, Team	1st	2nd	3rd	Total
Lou Piniella, Seattle	9	12	5	86
Kevin Kennedy, Bos.	11	5	4	74
Mike Hargrove, Cle.	8	8	7	71
Buck Showalter, N.Y.	0	1	5	8
Marcel Lachemann, Cal.	0	1	2	5
Phil Garner, Mil.	0	1	1	4
Bob Boone, K.C.	0	0	3	3
Johnny Oates, Texas	0	0	1	1

NOTE: MVP balloting based on 14 points for first-place vote, nine for second, eight for third, etc.; Cy Young Award, Rookie of the Year and Manager of the Year balloting based on five points for first-place vote, three for second and one for third.

compelled to move the team if arrangements for a new ballpark couldn't be made.

Still, the team's play and the fans' enthusiasm might have saved baseball for Seattle. Shortly after the Mariners were eliminated from the playoffs, both the state and local governments approved money for a stadium. What it will look like and when it will be finished remained unclear.

The Brewers also won their battle for a new stadium when, on Oct. 12, Wisconsin Gov. Tommy Thompson signed legislation which provided tax money for financing.

Plans call for a $250 million stadium with a retractable roof to be ready in time for the 1999 season.

He Wouldn't Knuckle Under

Wakefield offered a lesson in perseverance as he went 16-8 with a 2.95 for the Red Sox.

He first burst onto the scene in 1992, when he was called up at midseason by the Pirates, went 8-1 with a 2.15 ERA and beat the Atlanta Braves twice in the National League Championship Series.

But for two years after '92 his lowest ERA, in the majors or minors, was 5.61. He was released by the Pirates in the spring of 1995, picked up by the Red Sox and assigned to Triple-A Pawtucket.

Whereupon he made his second rise from the ashes. Wakefield made just four starts for Pawtucket, going 2-1, 2.52, before the Red Sox called him up.

TOM DiPACE

Tim Wakefield

He was even better in the majors. By late August, he was 14-1, 1.65 and had won 10 straight starts. He even ranked among the league's top 10 in fewest walks per nine innings, a rarity for a knuckleballer. And he was on at least equal footing with Johnson in the AL Cy Young Award race.

Wakefield faded after that and got embarrassed in his only playoff start against the Indians. But his bad streaks seem to be only temporary.

"I'm just glad to be back in the big leagues again," Wakefield said. "I never had any doubt I'd be back. I didn't know with whom. When the Pirates released me in spring training, Jim Leyland told me that I would get back up soon, that a change of scenery would do me well."

Wakefield's team may have been vanquished quickly in the playoffs, but it did a remarkable job just to get there. New general manager Dan Duquette was charged with cutting the player payroll from $42 million to $28 million, and he was working with a new manager, Kevin Kennedy, and a new coaching staff.

The Red Sox used 53 players, changed pitching coaches twice during the season and overcame injuries to outfielder Jose Canseco and righthanders Roger Clemens and Aaron Sele.

"It's been very satisfying," Duquette said, "but I'm

from here, so you never get total satisfaction until you win it all."

Straw Still Stirs

Leave it to the Yankees to create a sensation with a player who gets only 87 at-bats. Or one who doesn't play at all.

Publicity-seeking Yankees owner George Steinbrenner signed former Mets stars Darryl Strawberry and Dwight Gooden, each with a history of drug and injury problems.

The June signing of Strawberry reportedly came over the objection of general manager Gene Michael, and many observers said the team needed pitching much more than another bat. The Yankees were slow to bring Strawberry to the major league team, extending his tuneup in the minors for weeks.

Once he did arrive, Strawberry played well but not very often. He batted .276 in 87 at-bats. In the Division Series, he went 0-for-2 in two pinch-hitting

AL: BEST TOOLS

A Baseball America survey of American League managers, conducted at midseason 1995, ranked AL players with the best tools:

BEST HITTER	BEST PICKOFF MOVE
1. Edgar Martinez, Mariners	1. Mark Langston, Angels
2. Frank Thomas, White Sox	2. Ed Vosberg, Rangers
3. Ken Griffey, Mariners	3. Jack McDowell, Yankees
BEST POWER HITTER	**BEST RELIEVER**
1. Mark McGwire, Athletics	1. Jose Mesa, Indians
2. Frank Thomas, White Sox	2. Lee Smith, Angels
3. Cecil Fielder, Tigers	3. Dennis Eckersley, Athletics
BEST BUNTER	**BEST DEFENSIVE C**
1. Kenny Lofton, Indians	1. Ron Karkovice, White Sox
2. Roberto Alomar, Blue Jays	2. Ivan Rodriguez, Rangers
3. Otis Nixon, Rangers	3. Terry Steinbach, Athletics
BEST HIT-AND-RUN ARTIST	**BEST DEFENSIVE 1B**
1. Kevin Seitzer, Brewers	1. Don Mattingly, Yankees
2. Chuck Knoblauch, Twins	2. J.T. Snow, Angels
3. Mike Bordick, Athletics	3. Rafael Palmeiro, Orioles
BEST BASERUNNER	**BEST DEFENSIVE 2B**
1. Kenny Lofton, Indians	1. Roberto Alomar, Blue Jays
2. Paul Molitor, Blue Jays	2. Chuck Knoblauch, Twins
3. Roberto Alomar, Blue Jays	3. Ray Durham, White Sox
FASTEST BASERUNNER	**BEST DEFENSIVE 3B**
1. Kenny Lofton, Indians	1. Wade Boggs, Yankees
2. Tom Goodwin, Royals	2. Robin Ventura, White Sox
3. Vince Coleman, Royals	3. Gary Gaetti, Royals
BEST PITCHER	**BEST DEFENSIVE SS**
1. Kevin Appier, Royals	1. Omar Vizquel, Indians
2. Randy Johnson, Mariners	2. Greg Gagne, Royals
3. Dennis Martinez, Indians	3. Mike Bordick, Athletics
BEST FASTBALL	**BEST INFIELD ARM**
1. Randy Johnson, Mariners	1. Mike Blowers, Mariners
2. Jose Mesa, Indians	2. Travis Fryman, Tigers
3. Troy Percival, Angels	3. John Valentin, Red Sox
BEST CURVEBALL	**BEST DEFENSIVE OF**
1. Tom Gordon, Royals	1. Kenny Lofton, Indians
2. Erik Hanson, Red Sox	2. Ken Griffey, Mariners
3. Dennis Martinez, Indians	3. Devon White, Blue Jays
BEST SLIDER	**BEST OUTFIELD ARM**
1. Randy Johnson, Mariners	1. Jay Buhner, Mariners
2. David Cone, Blue Jays	2. Mark Whiten, Red Sox
3. Kevin Appier, Royals	3. Tim Salmon, Angels
BEST CHANGEUP	**MOST EXCITING PLAYER**
1. Erik Hanson, Red Sox	1. Ken Griffey, Mariners
2. Mike Mussina, Orioles	2. Kenny Lofton, Indians
3. Kenny Rogers, Rangers	3. Roberto Alomar, Blue Jays
BEST CONTROL	**BEST MANAGER**
1. Bob Tewksbury, Rangers	1. Tony La Russa, Athletics
2. Dennis Martinez, Indians	2. Buck Showalter, Yankees
3. Kevin Appier, Royals	3. Mike Hargrove, Indians

appearances.

After their playoff defeat the Yankees signed Gooden, who had been suspended for the season for violating his drug aftercare program. Both players were dispatched to Puerto Rico for winter ball.

Murray Reaches 3,000 Hits

Eddie Murray, a quietly consistent player for 19 seasons, became the 19th player to record 3,000 career hits.

No. 3,000 came on June 30, a nondescript single to right field off Twins righthander Mike Trombley in Minneapolis. The first teammate to greet Murray after the hit was Dave Winfield, who in 1993 became the 18th player to reach 3,000.

Murray, never enthusiastic about speaking with media, held a press conference after the game.

"I hope things get back to normal," he said. "It'll be a lot better once I'm done playing. I never set 3,000 as a goal. I know there were people out there happier than I was. It's not what I was focused on."

Big Names Quit

The usual postseason game of musical chairs among general managers and field managers had a new twist in 1995—many of those who left their jobs did so voluntarily.

Five managers and two GMs, some of them marquee names, left their posts. A third GM, the Tigers' Joe Klein, was let go when his contract expired at the end of the year. Former Padres GM Randy Smith was named to succeed Klein.

Sparky Anderson, who led teams in Cincinnati and Detroit to World Series titles, stepped down as Tigers manager after the season. The much-beloved Anderson knew the club was about to embark on a youth movement and decided he wasn't the man for the job.

Buck Showalter

Only one manager, the White Sox' Gene Lamont, left during the season. He was fired after the team, which had won the most recent AL West title in 1993, got off to a disappointing start. His replacement was third-base coach Terry Bevington.

Two teams, the Orioles and Yankees, lost both their GM and manager. Maverick Orioles owner Peter Angelos began talking to candidates for both jobs while GM Roland Hemond and manager Phil Regan still were in place. Both eventually were fired, with Regan later replaced by Davey Johnson from the Reds.

In New York, both GM Gene Michael and manager Buck Showalter were offered extensions, but both said no thanks. Rather than accept a pay cut from $600,000 to $400,000 as GM, Michael took a $150,000 scouting job with the Yankees. Bob Watson was unexpectedly hired away from the Astros to replace him.

Both Michael and Showalter had been in their jobs longer than anyone under Steinbrenner.

Another big-name manager, Oakland's Tony La Russa, quit of his own accord to make his first foray into the National League with the Cardinals.

AMERICAN LEAGUE

DIVISION SERIES

SEATTLE vs. NEW YORK

BOX SCORES

Game One: October 3
Yankees 9, Mariners 6

SEATTLE	ab	r	h	bi	bb	so	NEW YORK	ab	r	h	bi	bb	so
Coleman lf	4	1	0	0	1	1	Boggs 3b	5	2	3	2	0	0
Cora 2b	4	1	0	0	1	0	Kelly pr-2b	0	1	0	0	0	0
Griffey cf	5	3	3	3	0	0	B. Williams cf	5	2	3	2	0	0
E.Martinez dh	4	1	3	1	1	0	O'Neill rf	3	0	1	1	1	0
T.Martinez 1b	3	0	1	1	2	1	Sierra dh	5	1	1	2	0	1
Buhner rf	5	0	1	0	0	0	James lf	4	1	2	1	0	0
Blowers 3b	4	0	0	0	1	3	G. Williams pr-lf	1	0	0	0	0	1
Wilson c	3	0	0	1	1	1	Stanley c	4	0	1	1	0	0
Sojo ss	4	0	1	0	0	0	Fernandez ss	3	0	0	0	1	0
							Velarde 2b-3b	3	2	1	0	0	0
Totals	36	6	9	6	7	6	Totals	36	9	13	9	2	2

Seattle		000	101	202—6
New York		002	002	41x—9

LOB—Seattle 10, New York 7. **2B**—B. Williams (1), Mattingly (1), Boggs (1). **HR**—Griffey 2 (2), Boggs (1), Sierra (1). **SF**—O'Neill.

Seattle	ip	h	r	er	bb	so	New York	ip	h	r	er	bb	so
Bosio	5⅔	6	4	4	1	1	Cone W	8	6	4	4	6	5
Nelson L	⅓	1	1	1	0	0	Wetteland	1	3	2	2	1	1
Ayala	⅓	4	3	3	0	0							
Risley	⅔	0	0	0	0	1							
Wells	1	2	1	1	0	1							

Nelson pitched to one batter in 7th.

HBP—Velarde (by Nelson).

Umpires: **HP**—Reilly; **1B**—Scott; **2B**—McKean; **3B**—McCoy; **LF**—Garcia; **RF**—Joyce.

T—3:38. **A**—57,178.

Game Two: October 4
Yankees 7, Mariners 5

SEATTLE	ab	r	h	bi	bb	so	NEW YORK	ab	r	h	bi	bb	so
Coleman lf	5	2	2	1	0	1	Boggs 3b	4	1	0	0	2	1
Widger c	2	0	0	0	0	2	Posada c	0	1	0	0	0	0
Sojo ss	7	0	1	1	0	2	Davis 3b	1	0	1	0	0	0
Griffey cf	6	1	2	2	0	0	B. Williams cf	6	0	1	1	1	1
E.Martinez dh	6	1	3	0	1	1	O'Neill rf	6	1	2	1	1	2
Buhner rf	6	0	3	0	1	1	Sierra dh	7	1	2	2	0	2
Blowers 3b	3	0	0	0	1	0	Mattingly 1b	6	1	3	1	1	1
Strange ph-3b	3	0	0	0	0	1	James lf	3	0	0	0	0	1
T.Martinez 1b	7	0	2	1	0	1	G. Williams lf	1	0	0	0	0	0
Wilson c	3	0	0	0	0	0	Strawberry ph	1	0	0	0	0	1
Diaz ph-lf	3	0	1	0	0	1	Kelly 2b	0	1	0	0	1	0
Cora 2b	4	1	2	0	0	0	Leyritz c	6	1	1	2	0	0
Fermin 2b	1	0	0	0	0	1	Fernandez ss	5	0	1	0	1	1
							Velarde 2b-lf	5	0	0	0	0	0
Totals	56	5	16	5	3	11	Totals	51	7	11	7	8	11

Seattle		001	001	200	001	000—5
New York		000	012	100	001	002—7

E—Sojo (1), Cora (1). **DP**—Seattle 2, New York 1. **LOB**—Seattle 11, New York 11. **2B**—B. Williams (2), Sierra (1), E. Martinez (1), Cora (1), Buhner (1). **HR**—Griffey (3), Coleman (1), Sierra (2), Mattingly (1), O'Neill (1), Leyritz (1). **CS**—Buhner (1), T. Martinez (1). **S**—Cora, Kelly. **SF**—Griffey.

Seattle	ip	h	er	r	bb	so	New York	ip	h	er	r	bb	so
Benes	5	6	3	3	3	3	Pettitte	7	9	4	4	3	0
Risley	1	0	0	0	0	2	Wickman	1⅓	2	0	0	0	2
Charlton	4	1	1	1	0	5	Wetteland	3⅓	3	1	1	0	4
Nelson	1⅓	0	1	1	1	3	Rivera W	3⅓	2	0	0	0	5
Belcher L	3	4	2	2	4	0							

Benes pitched to two batters in 6th.

HBP—Leyritz (by Risley).

Umpires: **HP**—Scott; **1B**—McKean; **2B**—McCoy; **3B**—Garcia; **LF**—Joyce; **RF**—Reilly.

T—5:13. **A**—57,126.

MICHAEL YELMAN

Playoff Star. Despite missing most of the regular season, Seattle's Ken Griffey slugged five home runs in the AL Division Series.

Game Three: October 6
Mariners 7, Yankees 4

NEW YORK	ab	r	h	bi	bb	so	SEATTLE	ab	r	h	bi	bb	so
Velarde lf	3	0	0	0	1	1	Coleman lf	4	2	2	0	0	1
B. Williams cf	3	2	3	2	1	0	Cora 2b	2	1	0	0	1	0
Stanley c	4	1	2	1	0	0	Griffey cf	3	0	0	0	1	1
Sierra dh	3	0	0	0	1	0	E.Martinez dh	1	2	0	0	3	0
Mattingly 1b	4	0	0	0	0	3	T.Martinez 1b	4	2	3	3	0	0
G.Williams rf	2	1	0	0	1	1	Buhner rf	4	0	1	1	0	1
O'Neill ph-rf	1	0	0	0	0	1	Blowers 3b	2	0	1	1	1	1
Davis 3b	4	0	0	0	0	2	Sojo ss	3	0	0	1	0	0
Fernandez ss	4	0	1	0	0	1	Wilson c	4	0	0	0	0	3
Kelly 2b	3	0	0	1	0	3							
Totals	**31**	**4**	**6**	**4**	**4**	**12**	**Totals**	**27**	**7**	**7**	**6**	**6**	**7**

New York	**000 100 120—4**
Seattle	**000 024 10x—7**

E—Velarde (1), Stanley (1). **DP**—New York 2. **LOB**—New York 5, Seattle 5. **3B**—Coleman (1). **HR**—T.Martinez (1), B.Williams 2 (2), Stanley (1). **SB**—B.Williams (1), Coleman (1), Cora (1), Griffey (1). **S**—Cora. **SF**—Kelly, Sojo.

New York	ip	h	er	r	bb	so	Seattle	ip	h	er	r	bb	so
McDowell L	5⅓	3	5	5	4	4	Johnson W	7	4	2	2	4	10
Howe	0	1	1	1	0	0	Risley	⅔	2	2	2	0	0
Wickman	⅔	2	0	0	0	1	Charlton S	1⅓	0	0	0	0	2
Hitchcock	⅔	1	1	0	2	0							
Rivera	1⅓	0	0	0	0	2							

Howe pitched to 1 batter in 6th.

HBP—Blowers (by McDowell). **WP**—McDowell.

Umpires: HP—Brinkman; **1B**—Roe; **2B**—Evans; **3B**—Morrison; **LF**—Welke; **RF**—Hirschbeck.

T—3:04. **A**—57,944.

Game Four: October 7
Mariners 11, Yankees 8

NEW YORK	ab	r	h	bi	bb	so	SEATTLE	ab	r	h	bi	bb	so
Boggs 3b	5	1	2	1	1	1	Coleman lf	4	1	0	0	1	1
Kelly pr	0	0	0	0	0	0	Cora 2b	4	2	2	0	1	0
B. Williams cf	5	2	2	0	1	1	Griffey cf	4	3	2	1	0	2
O'Neill rf	3	2	2	2	2	1	E.Martinez dh	4	2	3	7	1	0
Sierra dh	4	0	1	1	0	2	T.Martinez 1b	5	1	1	0	0	1
Mattingly 1b	5	1	4	2	0	0	Buhner rf	4	2	3	1	1	0
James lf	4	0	0	0	0	0	Blowers 3b	4	0	1	0	0	1
G.Williams lf	0	0	0	0	0	0	Sojo ss	4	0	3	1	0	0
Strawberry ph	1	0	0	0	0	0	Fermin ss	0	0	0	0	0	0
Stanley c	4	1	1	1	1	1	Wilson c	4	0	1	0	1	0
Fernandez ss	5	0	1	0	0	0							
Velarde 2b	2	1	1	0	3	0							
Totals	**38**	**8**	**14**	**7**	**8**	**6**	**Totals**	**37**	**11**	**16**	**10**	**5**	**5**

New York	**302 000 012— 8**
Seattle	**004 011 05x—11**

E—Mattingly (1). **DP**—New York 1, Seattle 2. **LOB**—New York 12, Seattle 10. **2B**—Boggs (2), Sierra (2), Mattingly 2 (3). **HR**—Griffey (4), E. Martinez 2 (2), Buhner (1), O'Neill (2). **CS**—Velarde (1). **S**—Blowers. **SF**—Sierra, Sojo.

New York	ip	h	er	r	bb	so	Seattle	ip	h	er	r	bb	so
Kamieniecki	5	9	5	4	4	4	Bosio	2	4	5	5	3	1
Hitchcock	1	1	1	1	0	1	Nelson	4	6	0	0	2	4
Wickman	1	1	0	0	0	0	Belcher	1⅓	0	1	1	1	0
Wetteland L	0	2	4	4	1	0	Charlton W	⅔	2	1	1	1	1
Howe	1	3	1	1	0	0	Ayala	⅓	2	1	1	1	0
							Risley S	⅔	0	0	0	0	0

Bosio pitched to 2 batters in 3rd. Nelson pitched to 1 batter in 7th. Wetteland pitched to 4 batters in 8th. Charlton pitched to 1 batter in 9th.

HBP—Griffey (by Wetteland). **WP**—Charlton.

Umpires: HP—Roe; 1B—Evans; **2B**—Morrison; **3B**—Welke; **LF**—Hirschbeck; **RF**—Brinkman.

T—4:08. **A**—57,180.

Game Five: October 8
Mariners 6, Yankees 5

NEW YORK	ab	r	h	bi	bb	so	SEATTLE	ab	r	h	bi	bb	so
Boggs 3b	5	0	0	0	0	3	Coleman lf	6	0	1	0	0	0
Leyritz ph-c	1	0	0	0	0	1	Cora 2b	5	2	2	1	0	0
B. Williams cf	2	2	0	0	4	1	Griffey cf	5	2	2	1	1	1
O'Neill rf	5	2	1	2	1	1	E. Martinez dh	6	0	3	2	0	1
Sierra dh	4	0	0	0	1	2	T. Martinez 1b	3	1	2	0	1	1
Mattingly 1b	5	0	1	2	0	1	Rodriguez pr-ss	1	1	0	0	0	0
James lf	2	0	0	0	1	0	Buhner rf	5	0	3	1	0	2
G. Williams pr-lf	1	0	0	0	1	1	Sojo ss	2	0	0	0	0	1
Stanley c	4	0	1	0	1	0	Newson ph	1	0	0	0	0	1
Kelly pr-2b	0	1	0	0	0	0	Fermin ss	0	0	0	0	0	0
Fernandez ss	4	0	2	0	0	0	Diaz ph	0	0	0	0	1	0
Velarde 2b-3b	4	0	1	1	1	2	Widger c	1	0	0	0	0	1
							Wilson c	3	0	1	0	0	2
							Strange ph-3b	1	0	0	1	1	0
							Blowers 3b-1b	5	0	1	0	0	2
Totals	**37**	**5**	**6**	**5**	**10**	**12**	**Totals**	**44**	**6**	**15**	**6**	**4**	**12**

New York	**000 202 000 01—5**
Seattle	**001 100 020 02—6**

DP—Seattle 1. **LOB**—New York 10, Seattle 13. **2B**—Fernandez 2 (2), Mattingly (4), T.Martinez (1), E.Martinez 2 (3). **HR**—Griffey (5), O'Neill (3), Cora (1). **S**—Fernandez, Cora.

New York	ip	h	er	r	bb	so	Seattle	ip	h	er	r	bb	so
Cone	7⅔	9	4	4	3	9	Benes	6⅔	4	4	4	6	5
Rivera	⅔	1	0	0	1	1	Charlton	1⅓	1	0	0	2	1
McDowell L	1⅔	5	2	2	0	2	Johnson W	3	1	1	1	2	6

Charlton pitched to 2 batters in 9th. McDowell pitched to 3 batters in 11th.

WP—Cone 2.

Umpires: HP—Evans; **1B**—Morrison; **2B**—Welke; **3B**—Hirschbeck; **LF**—Brinkman; **RF**—Roe.

T—4:18. **A**—57,411.

COMPOSITE BOX

SEATTLE

Player, Pos.	AVG	G	AB	R	H	2B	3B	HR	RBI	BB	SO	SB
Edgar Martinez, dh	.571	5	21	6	12	3	0	2	10	6	2	0
Jay Buhner, rf	.458	5	24	2	11	1	0	1	3	2	4	0
Tino Martinez, 1b	.409	5	22	4	9	1	0	1	5	3	4	0
Ken Griffey, cf	.391	5	23	9	9	0	0	5	7	2	3	1
Alex Diaz, ph-lf	.333	2	3	0	1	0	0	0	0	1	1	0
Joey Cora, 2b	.316	5	19	7	6	1	0	1	1	3	1	1
Luis Sojo, ss	.250	5	20	0	5	0	0	0	3	0	3	0
Vince Coleman, lf	.217	5	23	6	5	0	1	1	1	2	4	1
Mike Blowers, 3b	.167	5	18	0	3	0	0	0	1	3	7	0
Dan Wilson, c	.118	5	17	0	2	0	0	0	1	2	6	0
Doug Strange, ph-3b	.000	2	4	0	0	0	0	0	1	1	1	0
Chris Widger, c	.000	2	3	0	0	0	0	0	0	0	3	0
Felix Fermin, 2b	.000	3	1	0	0	0	0	0	0	0	1	0
Alex Rodriguez, ph-ss	.000	1	1	1	0	0	0	0	0	0	0	0
Warren Newson, ph	.000	1	1	0	0	0	0	0	0	0	1	0
Totals	**.315**	**5**	**200**	**35**	**63**	**6**	**1**	**11**	**33**	**25**	**41**	**3**

Pitcher	W	L	ERA	G	GS	SV	IP	H	R	ER	BB	SO
Norm Charlton	1	0	2.45	4	0	1	7	4	2	2	3	9
Randy Johnson	2	0	2.70	2	1	0	10	5	3	3	6	16
Jeff Nelson	0	1	3.18	3	0	0	6	7	2	2	3	7
Andy Benes	0	0	5.40	2	2	0	12	10	7	7	9	8
Bill Risley	0	0	6.00	4	0	1	3	2	2	2	0	1
Tim Belcher	0	1	6.23	2	0	0	4	4	3	3	5	0
Bob Wells	0	0	9.00	1	0	0	1	2	1	1	1	0
Chris Bosio	0	0	0.57	2	2	0	8	10	9	9	4	2

Bobby Ayala.............. 0 0 54.00 2 0 0 1 6 4 4 1 0
Totals 3 2 5.79 5 5 2 51 50 33 33 32 43

NEW YORK

Player, Pos.	AVG	G	AB	R	H	2B	3B	HR	RBI	BB	SO	SB
Bernie Williams, cf	.429	5	21	8	9	2	0	2	5	7	3	1
Don Mattingly, 1b	.417	5	24	3	10	4	0	1	6	1	5	0
Paul O'Neill, rf	.333	5	18	5	6	0	0	3	6	5	5	0
Bob Stanley, c	.313	5	16	2	5	0	0	1	3	2	1	0
Wade Boggs, 3b	.263	4	19	4	5	2	0	1	3	3	5	0
Tony Fernandez, ss	.238	5	21	0	5	2	0	0	0	2	2	0
Russ Davis, 3b	.200	2	5	0	1	0	0	0	0	0	2	0
Randy Velarde, 2b-3b-lf	.176	5	17	3	3	0	0	0	1	6	4	0
Ruben Sierra, dh	.174	5	23	2	4	2	0	2	5	2	7	0
Jim Leyritz, c	.143	2	7	1	1	0	0	1	2	0	1	0
Dion James, lf	.083	4	12	0	1	0	0	0	0	1	1	0
Gerald Williams, pr-lf-rf	.000	5	5	1	0	0	0	0	0	2	3	0
Pat Kelly, pr-2b	.000	4	3	3	0	0	0	1	1	3	0	
Darryl Strawberry, ph	.000	2	2	0	0	0	0	0	0	0	1	0
Jorge Posada, pr	.000	1	0	1	0	0	0	0	0	0	0	0
Totals	.259	5	193	33	50	12	0	11	32	32	43	1

Pitcher	W	L	ERA	G	GS	SV	IP	H	R	ER	BB	SO
Mariano Rivera	1	0	0.00	3	0	0	5	3	0	0	1	8
Bob Wickman	0	0	0.00	3	0	0	3	5	0	0	0	3
David Cone	1	0	4.60	2	2	0	16	15	8	8	9	14
Andy Pettitte	0	0	5.14	1	1	0	7	9	4	4	3	0
Jimmy Hitchcock	0	0	5.40	2	0	0	2	2	2	1	2	1
Scott Kamieniecki	0	0	7.20	1	1	0	5	9	5	4	4	4
Jack McDowell	0	2	9.00	2	1	0	7	8	7	7	4	6
John Wetteland	0	1	14.55	3	0	0	4	8	7	7	2	5
Steve Howe	0	0	18.00	2	0	0	1	4	2	2	0	0
Totals	2	3	5.94	5	5	0	50	63	35	33	25	41
Seattle							006	237	572	021	000	—35
New York							304	316	642	011	002	—33

DP—Seattle 5, New York 4. **LOB**—Seattle 49, New York 45.
E—Sojo, Cora, Stanley, Velarde, Mattingly. **CS**—Buhner, T. Martinez, Velarde. **S**—Cora 3, Kelly, Blowers, Fernandez. **SF**—Sojo 2, O'Neill, Griffey, Kelly, Sierra.
HBP—Velarde (by J. Nelson), Leyritz (by Risley), Blowers (by McDowell), Griffey (by Wetteland). **WP**—Cone 2, McDowell, Charlton.

Umpires—Joe Brinkman, Jim Evans, Rich Garcia, John Hirschbeck, Tim Joyce, Larry McCoy, Jim McKean, Dan Morrison, Mike Reilly, Rocky Roe, Dale Scott, Tim Welke.

CLEVELAND vs. BOSTON

BOX SCORES

Game One: October 3
Indians 5, Red Sox 4

BOSTON	ab	r	h	bi	bb	so	CLEVE.	ab	r	h	bi	bb	so
Hosey rf	5	1	0	1	0	1	Lofton cf	5	0	1	0	0	2
Valentin ss	4	1	2	2	2	0	Vizquel ss	3	1	0	0	2	1
Vaughn 1b	6	0	0	0	0	3	Baerga 2b	5	1	2	0	0	1
Canseco dh	6	0	0	0	1	Belle lf	5	2	2	3	1	1
Greenwell lf	6	0	3	0	0	1	Murray dh	6	0	1	1	0	0
Naehring 3b	5	1	2	1	0	1	Thome 3b	6	0	1	0	0	3
Tinsley cf	5	0	0	1	2	Ramirez rf	6	0	0	0	0	1
Macfarlane c	3	0	0	0	0	1	Sorrento 1b	5	0	1	0	0	2
Stairs ph	1	0	0	0	0	1	Perry ph	1	0	0	0	0	0
Haselman c	0	0	0	0	0	0	Alomar c	4	0	1	0	0	0
Alicea 2b	5	1	4	1	0	0	Kirby pr	0	0	0	0	0	0
							Pena c	2	1	1	1	0	0
Totals	48	4	11	4	4	10	Totals	48	5	10	5	3	11
Boston							002	000	010	010	0—4	
Cleveland							000	003	000	010	1—5	

E—Macfarlane (1), Alicea (1), Sorrento (1), Lofton (1). **DP**—Cleveland 1. **LOB**—Boston 10, Cleveland 11. **2B**—Alicea (1), Belle (1). **HR**—Valentin (1), Alicea (1), Naehring (1), Belle (1), Pena (1). **SB**—Vizquel (1), Alicea (1). **CS**—Valentin (1). **S**—Naehring, Vizquel.

Boston	ip	h	er	r	bb	so	Cleveland	ip	h	er	r	bb	so
Clemens	7	5	3	3	1	5	Martinez	6	5	2	2	0	2
Cormier	⅓	0	0	0	1	1	Tavarez	1⅓	2	1	1	0	2
Belinda	⅓	0	0	0	0	1	Assenmacher	⅓	0	0	0	0	1
Stanton	2⅓	1	0	0	0	4	Plunk	1⅓	1	0	0	1	1
Aguilera	⅔	3	1	1	0	1	Mesa	1	0	0	0	1	0
Maddux	⅔	0	0	0	0	0	Poole	1⅔	2	1	1	1	2
Smith L	1⅓	1	1	1	0	0	Hill W	1⅓	1	0	0	0	2

HBP—Baerga (by Cormier); Lofton (by Maddux).
Umpires: HP—Welke; 1B—Hirschbeck; 2B—Brinkman; 3B—Roe; LF—Denkinger; RF—Morrison.
T—5:01. **A**—44,218.

Game Two: October 4
Indians 4, Red Sox 0

BOSTON	ab	r	h	bi	bb	so	CLEVE.	ab	r	h	bi	bb	so
Hosey cf	4	0	0	0	0	0	Lofton cf	3	1	0	0	1	0
Valentin ss	4	0	0	0	0	1	Vizquel ss	4	0	1	2	0	0
Vaughn 1b	4	0	0	0	0	2	Baerga 2b	4	0	0	0	0	0
Canseco dh	4	0	0	0	0	1	Belle lf	2	1	1	0	2	0
Greenwell lf	4	0	0	0	0	0	Murray dh	4	1	2	2	0	1
Naehring 3b	4	0	0	0	0	0	Thome 3b	4	0	0	0	0	3
McGee rf	3	0	1	0	0	2	Ramirez rf	4	0	0	0	0	1
Macfarlane c	3	0	2	0	0	1	Kirby rf	0	0	0	0	0	0
Alicea 2b	1	0	0	0	2	1	Sorrento 1b	1	1	0	1	0	0
							Alomar c	2	0	0	0	0	0
Totals	31	0	3	0	2	8	Totals	28	4	4	4	5	
Boston							000	000	000	—0		
Cleveland							000	020	02x	—4		

E—Valentin (1), Belle (1), Sorrento (2). **LOB**—Boston 6, Cleveland 6. **2B**—Vizquel (1). **3B**—Murray (1). **HR**—Murray (1). **SB**—Hosey (1). **S**—Alomar.

Boston	ip	h	r	er	bb	so	Cleveland	ip	h	r	er	bb	so
Hanson L	8	4	4	4	4	5	Hershiser W	7⅓	3	0	0	2	7
							Tavarez	⅓	0	0	0	0	0
							Assenmacher	⅓	0	0	0	0	1
							Mesa	1	0	0	0	0	0

HBP—Sorrento (by Hanson). **WP**—Hershiser. **PB**—Macfarlane.
Umpires: HP—Hirschbeck; 1B—Brinkman; 2B—Roe; 3B—Denkinger; LF—Morrison; RF—Welke.
T—2:33. **A**—44,264.

Game Three: October 6
Indians 8, Red Sox 2

CLEVE.	ab	r	h	bi	bb	so	BOSTON	ab	r	h	bi	bb	so
Lofton cf	5	0	1	0	0	1	Hosey cf	3	0	0	0	1	2
Vizquel ss	5	1	1	2	0	0	McGee ph-cf	1	0	0	1	0	0
Baerga 2b	5	1	2	1	0	0	Valentin ss	4	0	1	0	1	0
Belle lf	4	0	0	1	2	0	Vaughn 1b	4	0	0	1	1	2
Murray dh	3	2	2	0	2	0	Canseco rf	3	0	0	0	2	0
Thome 3b	3	1	1	3	1	0	Greenwell lf	5	0	0	0	0	1
Espinoza 3b	1	0	0	0	0	0	Jefferson dh	4	1	1	0	0	1
Ramirez rf	2	1	0	1	0	0	Naehring 3b	4	1	2	0	0	0
Kirby rf	1	0	1	0	0	0	Alicea 2b	4	0	2	0	0	1
Sorrento 1b	4	2	1	1	1	1	Macfarlane c	3	0	1	1	0	1
Alomar c	5	1	1	1	0	1							
Pena c	0	0	0	0	0	0							
Totals	38	8	11	8	6	6	Totals	35	2	7	2	5	8
Cleveland							021	005	000	—8		
Boston							000	100	010	—2		

E—Lofton (2), Baerga (1), Macfarlane (2). **LOB**—Cleveland 10, Boston 12. **2B**—Baerga (1), Alomar (1), Valentin (1). **HR**—Thome (1). **SF**—Macfarlane.

Cleveland	ip	h	r	er	bb	so	Boston	ip	h	r	er	bb	so
Nagy W	7	4	1	1	5	6	Wakefield L	5⅓	5	7	7	5	4
Tavarez	1	3	1	1	0	1	Cormier	½	2	1	1	0	1
Assenmacher	1	0	0	0	0	1	Maddux	2⅓	2	0	0	0	1
							Hudson	1	2	0	0	1	0

HBP—Ramirez (by Wakefield). **WP**—Hudson. **PB**—Macfarlane.
Umpires: HP—McKean; 1B—McCoy; 2B—Garcia; 3B—Joyce; LF—Reilly; RF—Scott.
T—3:18. **A**—34,211.

COMPOSITE BOX

CLEVELAND

Player Pos.	AVG	G	AB	R	H	2B	3B	HR	RBI	BB	SO	SB
Wayne Kirby, pr-rf	1.000	2	1	0	1	0	0	0	0	0	0	0
Tony Pena, c	.500	2	2	1	1	0	0	1	1	0	0	0
Eddie Murray, dh	.385	3	13	3	5	0	1	1	3	2	1	0
Paul Sorrento, 1b	.300	3	10	2	3	0	0	0	1	2	3	0
Carlos Baerga, 2b	.286	3	14	2	4	1	0	0	1	0	1	0
Albert Belle, lf	.273	3	11	3	3	1	0	1	4	3	3	0
Sandy Alomar, c	.182	3	11	1	2	1	0	0	1	0	1	0
Omar Vizquel, ss	.167	3	12	2	2	1	0	0	4	2	1	1
Kenny Lofton, cf	.154	3	13	1	2	0	0	0	0	1	3	0
Jim Thome, 3b	.154	3	13	1	2	0	0	1	3	1	6	0
Herbert Perry, 1b	.000	1	1	0	0	0	0	0	0	0	0	0
Manny Ramirez, rf	.000	3	12	1	0	0	0	0	1	2	0	
Alvaro Espinoza, 3b	.000	1	1	0	0	0	0	0	0	0	0	0
Totals	.219	3	114	17	25	4	1	4	17	13	22	1

Pitcher	W	L	ERA	G	GS	SV	IP	H	R	ER	BB	SO
Paul Assenmacher	0	0	0.00	3	0	0	2	0	0	0	0	3
Orel Hershiser	1	0	0.00	1	1	0	7	3	0	0	2	7
Ken Hill	1	0	0.00	1	0	1	1	1	0	0	0	2
Jose Mesa	0	0	0.00	2	0	1	2	0	0	0	2	0

Pitcher	W	L	ERA	G	GS	SV	IP	H	R	ER	BB	SO
Eric Plunk	0	0	0.00	1	0	0	1	1	0	0	1	1
Charles Nagy	1	0	0.78	1	1	0	7	4	1	1	5	6
Dennis Martinez	0	0	3.00	1	1	0	6	5	2	2	0	2
Jim Poole	0	0	5.40	1	0	0	2	2	1	1	1	2
Julian Tavarez	0	0	6.75	3	0	0	3	5	2	2	0	3
Totals	**3**	**0**	**1.74**	**3**	**3**	**1**	**31**	**21**	**6**	**6**	**11**	**26**

BOSTON

Player Pos.	AVG	G	AB	R	H	2B	3B	HR	RBI	BB	SO	SB
Luis Alicea, 2b	.600	3	10	1	6	1	0	1	1	3	2	1
Mike Macfarlane, c	.333	3	9	0	3	0	0	0	1	0	3	0
Willie McGee, rf-ph	.333	2	3	0	1	0	0	0	1	0	2	0
Tim Naehring, 3b	.308	3	13	2	4	0	0	1	1	0	1	0
John Valentin, ss	.250	3	12	1	3	1	0	1	2	3	1	0
Reggie Jefferson, dh	.250	1	4	1	1	0	0	0	0	0	1	0
Mike Greenwell, lf	.200	3	15	0	3	0	0	0	0	0	1	0
Jose Canseco, dh	.000	3	13	0	0	0	0	0	0	2	2	0
Dwayne Hosey, rf	.000	3	12	1	0	0	0	0	0	2	3	1
Bill Haselman, c	.000	1	2	0	0	0	0	0	0	0	0	0
Matt Stairs, ph	.000	1	1	0	0	0	0	0	0	0	1	0
Lee Tinsley, cf	.000	1	5	0	0	0	0	0	0	1	2	0
Mo Vaughn, 1b	.000	3	14	0	0	0	0	0	0	1	7	0
Totals	**.184**	**3**	**114**	**6**	**21**	**2**	**0**	**3**	**6**	**11**	**26**	**2**

Pitcher	W	L	ERA	G	GS	SV	IP	H	R	ER	BB	SO
Stan Belinda	0	0	0.00	1	0	0	1	0	0	0	0	0
Mike Maddux	0	0	0.00	2	0	0	3	2	0	0	1	1
Joe Hudson	0	0	0.00	1	0	0	1	2	0	0	1	0
Mike Stanton	0	0	0.00	1	0	0	2	1	0	0	0	4
Roger Clemens	0	0	3.86	1	1	0	7	5	3	3	1	5
Erik Hanson	0	1	4.50	1	1	0	8	4	4	4	4	5
Zane Smith	0	1	6.75	1	0	0	1	1	1	1	0	0
Tim Wakefield	0	1	11.81	1	1	0	5	5	7	7	5	4
Rheal Cormier	0	0	13.50	2	0	0	1	2	1	1	1	2
Rick Aguilera	0	0	13.50	1	0	0	1	3	1	1	0	1
Totals	**0**	**3**	**5.16**	**3**	**3**	**0**	**30**	**25**	**17**	**17**	**13**	**22**

Cleveland	**021 028 020 010 1—17**
Boston	**002 100 020 010 0— 6**

DP—Boston 0, Cleveland 1. **LOB**—Boston 28, Cleveland 27.

E—Lofton 2, Baerga, Macfarlane 2. **CS**—Valentin. **S**—Alomar, Naehring, Vizquel. **SF**—Macfarlane.

HBP—Lofton (by Maddux), Baerga (by Cormier), Sorrento (by Hanson), M. Ramirez (by Wakefield). **WP**—Hershiser, Hudson. **PB**—Macfarlane 2.

Umpires—Joe Brinkman, Don Denkinger, Rich Garcia, John Hirschbeck, Tim Joyce, Larry McCoy, Jim McKean, Dan Morrison, Mike Reilly, Rocky Roe, Dale Scott, Tim Welke.

CHAMPIONSHIP SERIES

SEATTLE vs. CLEVELAND

BOX SCORES

Game One: October 10
Mariners 3, Indians 2

CLEVE.	ab	r	h	bi	bb	so	SEATTLE	ab	r	h	bi	bb	so
Lofton cf	3	0	3	0	2	0	Coleman lf	4	0	0	0	0	2
Vizquel ss	4	0	0	0	1	0	Cora 2b	4	0	2	0	0	0
Baerga 2b	4	1	1	0	1	1	Griffey cf	3	0	2	0	1	1
Belle lf	4	1	1	1	1	2	E.Martinez dh	3	0	0	0	1	0
Murray dh	5	0	0	0	0	1	T.Martinez 1b	3	0	0	0	1	0
Thome 3b	4	0	2	1	0	0	Buhner rf	3	2	1	0	1	2
Ramirez rf	4	0	1	0	0	0	Blowers 3b	4	1	1	2	0	0
Sorrento 1b	4	0	1	0	0	1	Sojo ss	3	0	1	1	0	0
Alomar c	4	0	1	0	0	0	Wilson c	3	0	0	0	0	1
Amaro pr	0	0	0	0	0	0							
Pena c	0	0	0	0	0	0							
Totals	**36**	**2**	**10**	**2**	**5**	**5**	**Totals**	**30**	**3**	**7**	**3**	**4**	**6**

Cleveland	**001 000 100—2**
Seattle	**020 000 10x—3**

E—Thome (1). **DP**—Cleveland 1, Seattle 1. **LOB**—Cleveland 12, Seattle 7. **2B**—Sorrento (1), Cora (2), Buhner (2), Sojo (1), Griffey (1). **3B**—Lofton (1). **HR**—Belle (2), Blowers (1). **CS**—Griffey.

Cleve.	ip	h	r	er	bb	so	Seattle	ip	h	r	er	bb	so
D.Martinez L	6⅓	6	3	3	2	4	Wolcott W	7	8	2	2	5	2
Tavarez	1	1	0	0	1	1	Nelson	⅔	1	0	0	0	1
Assenmacher	0	0	0	0	1	0	Charlton S	1⅓	1	0	0	0	2
Plunk	⅔	0	0	0	0	1							

Assenmacher pitched to 1 batter in 8th.

Umpires: HP—Phillips; **1B**—Cousins; **2B**—Reed; **3B**—Ford; **LF**—McClelland; **RF**—Coble.

T—3:07. **A**—57,065.

Game Two: October 11
Indians 5, Mariners 2

CLEVE.	ab	r	h	bi	bb	so	SEATTLE	ab	r	h	bi	bb	so
Lofton cf	4	1	1	0	1	1	Coleman lf	4	0	1	0	0	3
Vizquel ss	3	0	0	0	2	0	Cora 2b	3	0	0	0	0	0
Baerga 2b	5	0	2	2	0	0	Griffey cf	4	1	2	1	0	0
Belle lf	3	0	1	0	2	0	E. Martinez dh	3	0	0	0	1	0
Murray dh	5	0	2	0	0	0	T. Martinez 1b	4	0	0	0	0	2
Thome 3b	4	0	0	0	0	1	Buhner rf	4	1	1	1	0	1
Espinoza 3b	1	0	0	0	0	0	Blowers 3b	4	0	1	0	0	1
Ramirez rf	4	2	4	2	0	0	Sojo ss	3	0	0	0	0	0
Kirby rf	0	0	0	0	0	0	A. Diaz dh	1	0	1	0	0	0
Sorrento 1b	4	2	1	0	0	0	Wilson c	3	0	0	0	0	0
Alomar c	4	0	1	1	0	1	Strange ph	1	0	0	0	0	0
Totals	**37**	**5**	**12**	**5**	**5**	**3**	**Totals**	**34**	**2**	**6**	**2**	**1**	**7**

Cleveland	**000 022 010—5**
Seattle	**000 001 001—2**

E—Sojo (2). **DP**—Seattle 2. **LOB**—Cleveland 10, Seattle 7. **3B**— Alomar (1). **HR**—Ramirez 2 (2), Griffey (6), Buhner (2). **SB**—Coleman (2), Vizquel (2).

Cleveland	ip	h	r	er	bb	so	Seattle	ip	h	r	er	bb	so
Hershiser W	8	4	1	1	1	7	Belcher L	5⅔	9	4	4	2	1
Mesa	1	2	1	1	0	0	Ayala	2⅔	2	1	1	3	2
							Risley	⅔	1	0	0	0	0

HBP—Cora (by Hershiser). **WP**—Hershiser.

Umpires: HP—Cousins; **1B**—Reed; **2B**—Ford; **3B**—McClelland; **LF**—Coble; **RF**—Phillips.

T—3:14. **A**—58,144.

Game Three: October 13
Mariners 5, Indians 2

SEATTLE	ab	r	h	bi	bb	so	CLEVE.	ab	r	h	bi	bb	so
Coleman lf	5	0	0	0	0	0	Lofton cf	5	1	2	1	0	2
Widger c	0	0	0	0	0	0	Vizquel ss	4	0	0	1	0	0
Cora 2b	4	1	1	0	0	0	Baerga 2b	5	0	1	0	0	1
Fermin 2b	0	0	0	0	0	0	Belle lf	4	0	0	0	0	0
Griffey cf	5	1	2	0	0	1	Murray dh	4	0	0	0	0	1
E.Martinez dh	5	0	0	0	0	1	Amaro pr-dh	1	0	0	0	0	0
T.Martinez 1b	4	1	1	0	1	1	Ramirez rf	3	0	0	0	1	2
Buhner rf	5	2	2	4	0	1	Perry 1b	3	0	0	0	1	1
Blowers 3b	3	0	1	0	0	0	Alomar c	3	0	0	0	1	0
Diaz ph-lf	2	0	0	0	0	1	Espinoza 3b	3	0	1	0	0	1
Sojo ss	4	0	2	0	0	0	Kirby pr	0	1	0	0	0	0
Wilson c	3	0	0	0	0	2	Thome 3b	1	0	0	0	0	0
Strange ph-3b	1	0	0	0	0	0							
Totals	**41**	**5**	**9**	**4**	**1**	**7**	**Totals**	**36**	**2**	**4**	**2**	**3**	**8**

Seattle	**011 000 000 03—5**
Cleveland	**000 100 010 00—2**

E—Alomar, Buhner, Espinoza. **DP**—Cleveland 1. **LOB**—Seattle 5, Cleveland 6. **3B**—Lofton (2). **HR**—Buhner 2 (4). **SB**—Griffey (2), Cora (2), Lofton (1). **CS**—Perry, E. Martinez. **SF**—Vizquel.

Seattle	ip	h	r	er	bb	so	Cleveland	ip	h	r	er	bb	so
Johnson	8	4	2	1	2	6	Nagy	8	5	2	1	0	6
Charlton W	3	0	0	0	1	2	Mesa	1	1	0	0	0	0
							Tavarez L	1	2	1	1	0	0
							Assenmacher	⅓	0	0	0	0	0
							Plunk	⅔	1	2	2	1	1

Tavarez pitched to 1 batter in 11th.

HBP—Cora (by Nagy), Belle (by Charlton).

Umpires: HP—Reed; **1B**—Ford; **2B**—McClelland; **3B**—Coble; **LF**—Phillips; **RF**—Cousins.

T—3:18. **A**—43,643.

Game Four: October 14
Indians 7, Mariners 0

SEATTLE	ab	r	h	bi	bb	so	CLEVE.	ab	r	h	bi	bb	so
Coleman lf	3	0	0	0	1	0	Lofton cf	3	1	1	1	1	0
Cora 2b	4	0	0	0	0	0	Vizquel ss	4	1	1	1	1	2
Griffey cf	3	0	0	0	1	1	Baerga 2b	4	1	2	1	0	0
E.Martinez dh	4	0	1	0	0	1	Murray dh	3	1	1	2	1	1
T.Martinez 1b	4	0	1	0	0	2	Thome 3b	3	1	1	2	1	1
Buhner rf	3	0	3	0	1	0	Ramirez rf	3	0	1	0	1	1
Blowers 3b	4	0	0	0	0	3	Sorrento 1b	3	0	0	0	1	1
Sojo ss	3	0	1	0	0	1	Pena c	3	1	1	0	1	0
Amaral ph	1	0	0	0	0	1	Kirby lf	4	1	1	0	0	0
Wilson c	2	0	0	0	0	0							
Widger c	1	0	0	0	0	1							
Strange ph	0	0	0	0	0	0							
Rodriguez ph	1	0	0	0	0	1							
Totals	**33**	**0**	**6**	**0**	**3**	**11**	**Totals**	**30**	**7**	**9**	**7**	**7**	**6**

Seattle	**000 000 000—0**
Cleveland	**312 001 00x—7**

E—Wilson (1). **DP**—Seattle 2. **LOB**—Seattle 9, Cleveland 7. **2B**—Buhner (3), Vizquel (2). **HR**—Murray (2), Thome (2). **SB**—Griffey (3), Coleman (3), Lofton (2), Kirby (1). **SF**—Lofton.

Seattle	ip	h	r	er	bb	so	Cleveland	ip	h	r	er	bb	so
Benes L	2⅓	6	6	6	2	3	Hill W	7	5	0	0	3	6
Wells	3	2	1	1	2	2	Poole	1	0	0	0	0	0
Ayala	1	1	0	0	0	1	Ogea	⅔	1	0	0	0	2
Nelson	1⅓	0	0	0	2	0	Embree	⅓	0	0	0	0	1
Risley	⅓	0	0	0	1	0							

WP—Ogea.

Umpires: **HP**—Ford; **1B**—McClelland; **2B**—Coble; **3B**—Phillips; **LF**—Cousins; **RF**—Reed.

T—3:30. **A**—43,686.

Game Five: October 15
Indians 3, Mariners 2

SEATTLE	ab	r	h	bi	bb	so	CLEVE.	ab	r	h	bi	bb	so
Cora 2b	4	2	1	0	1	0	Lofton cf	5	0	2	0	0	1
E.Martinez dh	5	0	0	0	0	2	Vizquel ss	4	1	1	0	1	0
Griffey cf	3	0	1	1	1	1	Baerga 2b	3	0	1	0	1	0
Buhner rf	4	0	0	0	0	3	Belle lf	3	0	0	0	0	2
T.Martinez 1b	4	0	1	0	0	1	Kirby lf	0	0	0	0	0	0
Strange 3b	2	0	0	0	0	2	Murray dh	3	1	3	1	1	0
Coleman ph	0	0	0	0	1	0	Thome 3b	3	1	1	2	1	1
Blowers 3b	0	0	0	0	0	0	Espinoza 3b	0	0	0	0	0	0
Diaz lf	3	0	2	0	1	0	Ramirez rf	4	0	0	0	1	0
Sojo ss	4	0	0	0	0	0	Sorrento 1b	2	0	0	1	1	1
Wilson c	3	0	0	0	0	1	Perry 1b	1	0	0	0	0	1
Amaral ph	1	0	0	0	0	0	Alomar c	4	0	2	0	0	0
							Pena c	0	0	0	0	0	0
Totals	**33**	**2**	**5**	**1**	**4**	**10**	**Totals**	**32**	**3**	**10**	**3**	**5**	**7**

```
Seattle        001 000 000—2
Cleveland      100 002 00x—3
```

E—T. Martinez (1), Griffey (1), Belle 2 (3), Sorrento 2 (4). **DP**—Seattle 2, Cleveland 1. **LOB**—Seattle 9, Cleveland 11. **2B**—Diaz (1), Griffey (3), Alomar (2), Murray (1). **HR**—Thome (2). **SB**—Cora (3), Coleman (4), Vizquel 2 (4), Lofton 2 (4). **S**—Strange, Kirby.

Seattle	ip	h	r	er	bb	so	Cleveland	ip	h	r	er	bb	so
Bosio L	5⅓	7	3	2	2	3	Hershiser W	6	5	2	1	2	8
Nelson	1	2	0	0	3	2	Tavarez	⅓	0	0	0	0	0
Risley	1⅔	1	0	0	0	2	Assenmacher	1	0	0	0	0	2
							Plunk	⅔	0	0	0	2	0
							Mesa S	1	0	0	0	0	0

Umpires: **HP**—McClelland; **1B**—Coble; **2B**—Cousins; **3B**—Reed; **LF**—Ford; **RF**—Phillips.

T—3:37. **A**—43,607.

Game Six: October 17
Indians 4, Mariners 0

CLEVE.	ab	r	h	bi	bb	so	SEATTLE	ab	r	h	bi	bb	so
Lofton cf	4	1	2	1	0	2	Coleman lf	4	0	1	0	0	1
Vizquel ss	4	0	0	0	0	0	Widger c	0	0	0	0	0	0
Baerga 2b	4	1	3	1	0	1	Cora 2b	4	0	0	0	0	0
Belle lf	4	0	2	0	0	1	Griffey cf	3	0	0	1	0	0
Murray dh	4	0	0	0	0	1	E.Martinez dh	3	0	1	0	1	1
Ramirez rf	3	0	0	0	0	1	T.Martinez 1b	3	0	0	0	1	1
Kirby rf	1	0	0	0	0	0	Buhner rf	4	0	0	0	0	1
Perry 1b	4	0	0	0	0	1	Blowers 3b	3	0	1	0	0	1
Espinoza 3b	4	1	0	0	0	2	Sojo ss	3	0	1	0	0	1
Pena c	3	0	1	0	0	0	Fermin ss	0	0	0	0	0	0
Amaro pr	0	1	0	0	0	0	Wilson c	2	0	0	0	0	0
Alomar c	0	0	0	0	0	0	Diaz ph-lf	1	0	0	0	0	0
Totals	**35**	**4**	**8**	**2**	**0**	**8**	**Totals**	**30**	**0**	**4**	**0**	**2**	**5**

```
Cleveland      000 010 030—4
Seattle        000 000 000—0
```

E—Cora (2). **DP**—Cleveland 1. **LOB**—Cleveland 4, Seattle 6. **2B**—Belle (2), Pena (1), Sojo (2). **HR**—Baerga (1). **SB**—Coleman (5), Lofton (5), E.Martinez (1).

Cleveland	ip	h	r	er	bb	so	Seattle	ip	h	r	er	bb	so
D. Martinez W	7	4	0	0	1	3	Johnson L	7⅓	8	4	3	0	7
Tavarez	1	0	0	0	1	0	Charlton	1⅔	0	0	0	0	1
Mesa	1	0	0	0	1	1							

HBP—E. Martinez (by D.Martinez). **PB**—Wilson.

Umpires: **HP**—Coble; **1B**—Kaiser; **2B**—Cousins; **3B**—Reed; **LF**—Ford; **RF**—McClelland.

T—2:54. **A**—58,489.

COMPOSITE BOX

CLEVELAND

Player, Pos.	AVG	G	AB	R	H	2B	3B	HR	RBI	BB	SO	SB
Kenny Lofton, cf	.458	6	24	4	11	0	2	0	3	6	4	5
Carlos Baerga, 2b	.400	6	25	3	10	0	0	1	4	3	2	0
Tony Pena, c	.333	4	6	1	2	1	0	0	0	0	1	0
Manny Ramirez, rf	.286	6	21	2	6	0	0	2	2	5	2	0
Sandy Alomar, c	.267	5	15	0	4	1	0	0	1	1	1	0
Jim Thome, 3b	.267	5	15	2	4	0	0	2	5	3	2	0
Eddie Murray, dh	.250	6	24	2	6	1	0	1	3	3	2	0
Albert Belle, lf	.222	5	18	1	4	1	0	1	1	5	3	0
Wayne Kirby, pr-rf	.200	5	5	2	1	0	0	0	0	0	0	1
Paul Sorrento, 1b	.154	4	13	2	2	1	0	0	3	3	2	0
Alvaro Espinoza, 3b	.125	4	8	1	1	0	0	0	0	3	0	0
Omar Vizquel, ss	.087	6	23	2	2	1	0	0	2	2	5	3
Herbert Perry, 1b	.000	3	8	0	0	0	0	0	0	3	1	0
Ruben Amaro, pr	.000	3	1	1	0	0	0	0	0	0	0	0
Totals	**.257**	**6**	**206**	**23**	**53**	**6**	**3**	**7**	**21**	**37**	**25**	**9**

Pitcher	W	L	ERA	G	GS	SV	IP	H	R	ER	BB	SO
Ken Hill	1	0	0.00	1	1	0	7	5	0	0	3	6
Paul Assenmacher	0	0	0.00	3	0	0	1	0	0	0	0	3
Jim Poole	0	0	0.00	1	0	0	1	0	0	0	0	2
Chad Ogea	0	0	0.00	1	0	0	1	1	0	0	0	2
Alan Embree	0	0	0.00	1	0	0	1	0	0	0	0	1
Charles Nagy	0	0	1.12	1	1	0	8	5	2	1	0	6
Orel Hershiser	2	0	1.29	2	2	0	14	9	3	2	3	15
Dennis Martinez	1	1	2.03	2	2	0	13	10	3	3	3	7
Jose Mesa	0	0	2.25	4	0	1	4	3	1	1	1	1
Julian Tavarez	0	1	2.70	4	0	0	3	3	1	1	1	2
Eric Plunk	0	0	9.00	3	0	0	2	1	2	2	3	2
Totals	**4**	**2**	**1.64**	**6**		**1**	**55**	**37**	**12**	**10**	**15**	**46**

SEATTLE

Player, Pos.	AVG	G	AB	R	H	2B	3B	HR	RBI	BB	SO	SB
Alex Diaz, ph-lf	.429	4	7	0	3	1	0	0	0	1	1	0
Ken Griffey, cf	.333	6	21	2	7	2	0	1	2	4	4	1
Jay Buhner, rf	.304	6	23	5	7	2	0	3	5	2	8	0
Luis Sojo, ss	.250	6	20	2	5	2	0	0	1	0	2	0
Mike Blowers, 3b	.222	6	18	1	4	0	0	1	2	0	4	0
Joey Cora, 2b	.174	6	23	2	4	1	0	0	0	1	0	1
Tino Martinez, 1b	.136	6	22	0	3	0	0	0	3	7	0	0
Vince Coleman, lf	.100	6	20	2	2	0	0	0	0	2	6	1
Edgar Martinez, dh	.087	6	23	0	2	0	0	0	1	2	5	0
Dan Wilson, c	.000	6	16	0	0	0	0	0	0	0	4	0
Doug Strange, ph-3b	.000	4	4	0	0	0	0	0	0	0	2	0
Rich Amaral ph	.000	2	2	0	0	0	0	0	0	0	1	0
Alex Rodriguez, ph	.000	1	1	0	0	0	0	0	0	0	1	0
Chris Widger, c	.000	3	1	0	0	0	0	0	0	0	1	0
Felix Fermin, 2b-ss	.000	1	0	0	0	0	0	0	0	0	0	0
Totals	**.184**	**6**	**201**	**12**	**37**	**8**	**0**	**5**	**10**	**15**	**46**	**3**

Pitcher	W	L	ERA	G	GS	SV	IP	H	R	ER	BB	SO
Norm Charlton	1	0	0.00	3	0	1	6	1	0	0	1	5
Jeff Nelson	0	0	0.00	3	0	0	3	3	0	0	5	3
Bill Risley	0	0	0.00	3	0	0	3	2	0	0	1	2
Randy Johnson	0	1	2.35	2	2	0	15	12	6	4	2	13
Bobby Ayala	0	0	2.45	2	0	0	4	3	1	1	3	3
Bob Wolcott	1	0	2.57	1	1	0	7	8	2	2	5	2
Bob Wells	0	0	3.00	1	0	0	3	2	1	1	2	2
Chris Bosio	0	1	3.38	1	1	0	5	7	3	2	2	3
Tim Belcher	0	1	6.35	1	1	0	6	9	4	4	2	1
Andy Benes	0	1	23.14	1	1	0	2	6	6	6	2	3
Totals	**2**	**4**	**3.33**	**6**		**1**	**54**	**53**	**23**	**20**	**25**	**37**

```
Cleveland      413 135 150 00—23
Seattle        032 011 101 03—12
```

DP—Cleveland 4, Seattle 7. **LOB**—Cleveland 44, Seattle 49.

E—Thome, Sojo (2), Buhner, Alomar, Espinoza, Wilson, T. Martinez, Perry. **CS**—Griffey, E. Martinez, Perry. **S**—Strange, Kirby. **SF**—Vizquel, Lofton.

HBP—Cora 2 (by Hershiser, Nagy), Belle (by Charlton), E. Martinez (by D. Martinez). **WP**—Hershiser, Ogea. **PB**—Wilson.

Umpires—Drew Coble, Derryl Cousins, Dale Ford, Tim McClelland, Dave Phillips, Rick Reed.

Braves Make Quick Work Of Cincinnati

By WILL LINGO

It was supposed to be a classic. It was the matchup that most fans looked forward to from the beginning of the 1995 season. It was great pitching against great hitting.

It was a rout.

The Atlanta Braves jumped on the Cincinnati Reds from the beginning of the National League Championship Series, with Braves pitchers Tom Glavine and John Smoltz holding the Reds to three runs in two games in Cincinnati.

Coming home to Atlanta, leading the series two games to none, the Braves ran out Greg Maddux and Steve Avery to stomp out the little life that was left in the Reds' bats. Finally coming into his own, hard-throwing reliever Mark Wohlers closed out three of the four games.

All told in the Braves' series sweep, the Reds batted .209 in the four games and scored five runs, easily a new record for a four-game series (the previous low was Pittsburgh's 10 runs in 1974).

Rookie third baseman Chipper Jones and first baseman Fred McGriff provided the bulk of the offense for the Braves, with seven hits each.

But the series MVP was Mike Devereaux, who found new life with the Braves as a late-season acquisition from the White Sox. After toiling in relative obscurity for seven major league seasons, Devereaux became the man of the hour with his timely hitting.

It started in Game One, when Devereaux came in as a defensive replacement after the Braves scored a run in the top of the ninth to tie the game at 1-1. He stayed in the game as it moved to the 11th inning and hit the game-winning single.

In Game Two, Devereaux started and had an RBI in a 6-2 Braves win. He started again in Game Three and scored a run in a 5-2 win.

The topper came in Game Four, when he started only because David Justice was out with a sore right knee, injured when a line drive hit it during batting practice. Devereaux came through in a big way, hitting a three-run homer in the seventh inning that broke the game open and broke the Reds' back. The Braves went on to win 6-0, and Devereaux finished the series batting .308 (4-

Cy Young winner. Righthander Greg Maddux won 19 games and pitched the Braves to the NL pennant.

GEORGE GOJKOVICH

Mike Devereaux

MORRIS FOSTOFF

for-13) with a team-leading five RBIs.

"To be where I am right now is unbelievable," Devereaux said. "I never even dreamed about it."

Probably not when he was in Chicago anyway, with the White Sox sinking like a stone in the American League Central. When told of the trade to Atlanta for minor league outfielder Andre King, Devereaux thought it was a joke.

He was glad to find out otherwise. And though Devereaux, 32, had to adjust from playing every day to taking a part-time job, he made the most of it.

"I think I can still play every day," he said. "But remember, they got me to help them win the World Series. For them to feel that way, I've got to feel good. This is like a second life for me."

It was like a slow death for the Reds, who not only saw their offensive heroes disappear but also played in front of thousands of empty seats at Riverfront Stadium.

After such a successful regular season, the series left a bad taste in the Reds' mouths. Reggie Sanders was 2-for-16 (part of a general postseason collapse) with a staggering 10 strikeouts. Ron Gant was 3-for-16, and Hal Morris was 2-for-12.

The fans in Cincinnati apparently didn't care anyway. The Reds drew 36,762 fans for Game One and 43,257 for Game Two, not even close to Riverfront's capacity of 52,952.

All that coupled with Reds manager Davey Johnson's slow procession to the exit ended a bittersweet year for the Reds. Johnson's contract dictated that he step aside after the 1995 season to make way for Ray Knight. He was to become a consultant in the Reds' front office but instead he took over as manager of the Orioles.

No Early Upsets

On top of being the best teams during the 1995 regular season, the performance of the Reds and the Braves in the first-ever National League divisional playoffs indicated a classic matchup for the pennant.

The Reds swept the Los Angeles Dodgers, and the Braves dispatched the Colorado Rockies in four games.

The Dodgers won the NL West but didn't put up much of a fight against the Reds after slugging it out with the Rockies for division supremacy for much of the season.

The Reds outpitched and outhit the Dodgers, outscoring them 22-7. When Game Three rolled around, the Reds had champagne on ice, and the Dodgers already had their bags packed.

It started in the first inning of the first game, with the Reds scoring four runs and never looking back. Benito Santiago hit a two-run homer, and Morris went 3-for-4 with two runs and two RBIs in a 7-2 win.

Dodgers rookie Ismael Valdes kept Game Two close, staking the Dodgers to a 2-2 tie going into the eighth inning. But the bullpen gave up three runs, and a Dodgers rally in the bottom of the ninth fell a run short, with the Reds winning 5-4.

The Reds came home to Riverfront, with Dodgers sensation Hideo Nomo starting as the Dodgers last line of defense. But Nomo was erratic, and the Reds hung five runs on him in five innings and cruised to a 10-1 victory.

The Rockies played with more spirit in their first postseason appearance, but the Braves' superior talent won out in a three games to one series win.

The Braves won the first two games in delirious Coors Field with ninth-inning rallies. Game One was tied 4-4 going into the ninth when Jones came through with a two-out, solo home run. Wohlers picked up the save with a scoreless ninth, striking out Rockies left-hander Lance Painter with the bases loaded to end the game after manager Don Baylor ran out of position players.

The Rockies led Game Two going into the ninth, 4-3, but the roof fell in on the Colorado bullpen. Rookie utilityman Mike Mordecai hit a two-out single to drive in the winning run, and the Braves put up two more runs for good measure in a 7-4 win.

Most people expected a sweep as the series went back to Atlanta, but the resilient Rockies survived yet another Braves rally to win 7-5 in 10 innings.

That forced the Braves to bring back Maddux, who pitched seven innings and got no decision in Game One. He gave up four runs in seven innings this time, but the Braves bats came alive, with Fred McGriff exploding for five RBIs in a 10-4 Atlanta win.

The division series did not name MVPs, but Atlanta center fielder Marquis Grissom was the standout. Playing in the postseason for the first time, Grissom went

MORRIS FOSTOFF

Steady shortstop. Barry Larkin hit .319 and stole 51 bases to lead Cincinnati to the NL Central title.

11-for 21 (.524) with three home runs, four RBIs and five runs.

Though the Rockies lost, outfielder Dante Bichette said it was a valuable experience for the team.

"These were the four most fun games I have ever played in my life," he said. "What the team learned was how to win and what it takes to win. We didn't have what it takes, but we learned what it takes."

Rockies Buy A Contender

The Rockies were disappointed by their playoff loss, but it was anything but a disappointing season for the sweethearts of the Rocky Mountains.

With fans packing Coors Field in its debut season, Colorado became the first expansion team to make it to the playoffs before its eighth season. The Rockies were playing their third.

The Rockies also were the first team to have four players hit at least 30 home runs since the 1977 Dodgers. Bichette, Vinny Castilla, Andres Galarraga and Larry Walker did it for Colorado.

It all became possible when Denver embraced its team in a way beyond anyone's dreams, and when Jerry McMorris acquired the team from its original ownership group.

The Rockies were set to build slowly by developing players through their minor league system, but McMorris told general manager Bob Gebhard that the team had enough money to think big.

So the Rockies gave up draft picks to sign Ellis Burks, Howard Johnson and Walt Weiss for the 1994 season. The thin air of Colorado had already rejuvenated the careers of Galarraga and Bichette.

Page	EAST	W	L	PCT	GB	Manager	General Manager	Attend./Dates	Last Pennant
53	Atlanta Braves	90	54	.625	—	Bobby Cox	John Schuerholz	2,561,831 (72)	1995
171	New York Mets	69	75	.479	21	Dallas Green	Joe McIlvaine	1,254,307 (70)	1986
184	Philadelphia Phillies	69	75	.479	21	Jim Fregosi	Lee Thomas	2,043,588 (71)	1993
119	Florida Marlins	67	76	.468	22½	Rene Lachemann	Dave Dombrowski	1,670,255 (69)	None
158	Montreal Expos	66	78	.458	24	Felipe Alou	Kevin Malone	1,292,764 (71)	None
Page	CENTRAL	W	L	PCT	GB	Manager(s)	General Manager	Attend./Dates	Last Pennant
94	Cincinnati Reds	85	59	.590	—	Davey Johnson	Jim Bowden	1,843,649 (71)	1990
125	Houston Astros	76	68	.527	9	Terry Collins	Bob Watson	1,363,801 (71)	None
88	Chicago Cubs	73	71	.507	12	Jim Riggleman	Ed Lynch	1,893,925 (70)	1945
197	St. Louis Cardinals	62	81	.434	22½	Torre/Jorgensen	Walt Jocketty	1,727,536 (71)	1987
190	Pittsburgh Pirates	58	86	.403	27	Jim Leyland	Cam Bonifay	905,517 (70)	1979
Page	WEST	W	L	PCT	GB	Manager	General Manager	Attend./Dates	Last Pennant
138	Los Angeles Dodgers	78	66	.542	—	Tommy Lasorda	Fred Claire	2,766,251 (72)	1988
106	Colorado Rockies*	77	67	.535	1	Don Baylor	Bob Gebhard	3,341,998 (71)	None
204	San Diego Padres	70	74	.486	8	Bruce Bochy	Randy Smith	1,019,728 (70)	1984
211	San Francisco Giants	67	77	.465	11	Dusty Baker	Bob Quinn	1,241,497 (72)	1989

*Won wild-card playoff berth
NOTE: Team's individual batting, pitching and fielding statistics can be found on page indicated in lefthand column.

So when the Rockies went out to get righthander Bill Swift and Walker, fans had a right to be optimistic.

"The Rockies made the best offer, but I wanted to come here anyway," Walker said. "My agent even asked where I'd prefer to come and I said Colorado. You get 50,000 fans a game, and I can see this team winning in the future. In Montreal, 50,000 people is a week's work."

Indeed, the Rockies' rapid rise would not have been possible without their fan support. The team drew 7.7 million in its two seasons at Mile High Stadium, and at beautiful Coors Field in downtown Denver, the Rockies drew 3.3 million.

The new ballpark is much smaller than Mile High, but it brings in more money because of its higher average ticket prices and a lease that gives the Rockies all the concession money and 80 percent of the parking profits.

The Rockies were even able to pull off the classic, late-season deal to fortify their lineup for the playoffs. Colorado beat out all the other contenders to get Bret Saberhagen from the Mets for pitching prospect Juan Acevedo.

Alas, Saberhagen was a bit of a disappointment, and pitching proved to be the Rockies' undoing in the playoffs. But Walker and the Rockies were already looking forward to 1996.

"We have no reason to hang our heads," he said. "Whoever said we don't belong here was wrong. We went up against the best team in the league and played them tough. We gave them a fight."

Many Mediocre Markets

The news was not as happy in other markets, where teams were having to slash their payrolls and rebuild their rosters, or look for better markets in which to

All-star catcher. Mike Piazza led the NL West champion Dodgers with a .346 average.

play, or both.

The luckless Montreal Expos, who took years to build the best team in baseball from the ground up, not only saw their best season ruined by the strike but also saw their team ripped apart before the 1995 season began.

The Expos went 74-40 in 1994, but it amounted to nothing after the strike. That team was led by home-grown standouts Moises Alou, Grissom and Walker in the field and Ken Hill, Mel Rojas and John Wetteland on the mound.

By the time the 1995 season rolled around, only Alou and Rojas were still in Montreal, and it was clear that neither could shoulder the load that had been dropped on them. Up-and-comers Wil Cordero and Rondell White showed their talent, but fellow youngster Cliff Floyd suffered a devastating broken wrist that at one time was thought to threaten his career.

By the end of the season, the team was talking about trading Cordero, general manager Kevin Malone resigned in frustration over the tight payroll, and owner Claude Brochu was denying persistent reports of the Expos being sold.

But the Expos rumors were pushed aside when the Astros became the main target of the northern Virginia group led by telecommunications executive William Collins.

Collins, whose group lost out in the expansion race to Arizona and Tampa Bay, started looking for teams to move soon after that. Many teams were discussed, but he and Astros owner Drayton McLane got into serious negotiations.

McLane, who only a few years ago was seen as the savior of baseball in Houston, said he could not afford to continue to lose millions of dollars in Houston.

Collins had already arranged for whatever team he

NATIONAL LEAGUE CHAMPIONS, 1901-95

NOTE: Most Valuable Player award formally recognized in 1931
GA—Games ahead of second-place team

Pennant		Pct.	GA
1901	Pittsburgh	.647	1½
1902	Pittsburgh	.741	27½
1903	Pittsburgh	.650	6½
1904	New York	.693	13
1905	New York	.686	9
1906	Chicago	.763	20
1907	Chicago	.704	17
1908	Chicago	.643	1
1909	Pittsburgh	.724	6½
1910	Chicago	.675	13
1911	New York	.647	7½
1912	New York	.682	10
1913	New York	.664	12½
1914	Boston	.614	10½
1915	Philadelphia	.592	7
1916	Brooklyn	.610	2½
1917	New York	.636	10
1918	Chicago	.651	10½
1919	Cincinnati	.686	9
1920	Brooklyn	.604	7
1921	New York	.614	4
1922	New York	.604	7
1923	New York	.621	4½
1924	New York	.608	1½
1925	Pittsburgh	.621	8½
1926	St. Louis	.578	2
1927	Pittsburgh	.610	1½
1928	St. Louis	.617	2
1929	Chicago	.645	10½
1930	St. Louis	.597	2

Pennant		Pct.	GA	MVP
1931	St. Louis	.656	13	Frankie Frisch, 2b, St. Louis
1932	Chicago	.584	4	Chuck Klein, of, Philadelphia
1933	New York	.599	5	Carl Hubbell, lhp, New York
1934	St. Louis	.621	2	Dizzy Dean, rhp, St. Louis
1935	Chicago	.649	4	Gabby Hartnett, c, Chicago
1936	New York	.597	5	Carl Hubbell, lhp, New York
1937	New York	.625	3	Joe Medwick, of, St. Louis
1938	Chicago	.586	2	Ernie Lombardi, c, Cincinnati
1939	Cincinnati	.630	4½	Bucky Walters, rhp, Cincinnati
1940	Cincinnati	.654	12	Frank McCormick, 1b, Cincinnati
1941	Brooklyn	.649	2½	Dolf Camilli, 1b, Brooklyn
1942	St. Louis	.688	2	Mort Cooper, rhp, St. Louis
1943	St. Louis	.682	18	Stan Musial, of, St. Louis
1944	St. Louis	.682	14½	Marty Marion, ss, St. Louis
1945	Chicago	.636	3	Phil Cavarretta, 1b, Chicago
1946	St. Louis	.628	2	Stan Musial, 1b, St. Louis
1947	Brooklyn	.610	5	Bob Elliott, 3b, Boston
1948	Boston	.595	6½	Stan Musial, of, St. Louis
1949	Brooklyn	.630	1	Jackie Robinson, 2b, Brooklyn
1950	Philadelphia	.591	2	Jim Konstanty, rhp, Philadelphia
1951	New York	.624	1	Roy Campanella, c, Brooklyn
1952	Brooklyn	.627	4½	Hank Sauer, of, Chicago
1953	Brooklyn	.682	13	Roy Campanella, c, Brooklyn
1954	New York	.630	5	Willie Mays, of, New York
1955	Brooklyn	.641	13½	Roy Campanella, c, Brooklyn
1956	Brooklyn	.604	1	Don Newcombe, rhp, Brooklyn
1957	Milwaukee	.617	8	Hank Aaron, of, Milwaukee
1958	Milwaukee	.597	8	Ernie Banks, ss, Chicago
1959	Los Angeles	.564	2	Ernie Banks, ss, Chicago
1960	Pittsburgh	.617	7	Dick Groat, ss, Pittsburgh
1961	Cincinnati	.604	4	Frank Robinson, of, Cincinnati
1962	San Francisco	.624	1	Maury Wills, ss, Los Angeles
1963	Los Angeles	.611	6	Sandy Koufax, lhp, Los Angeles
1964	St. Louis	.574	1	Ken Boyer, 3b, St. Louis
1965	Los Angeles	.599	2	Willie Mays, of, San Francisco
1966	Los Angeles	.586	1½	Roberto Clemente, of, Pittsburgh
1967	St. Louis	.627	10½	Orlando Cepeda, 1b, St. Louis
1968	St. Louis	.599	9	Bob Gibson, rhp, St. Louis

	East. Div.	PCT	GA	West. Div.	PCT	GA	Pennant		MVP
1969	New York	.617	8	Atlanta	.574	3	New York	3-0	Willie McCovey, 1b, San Francisco
1970	Pittsburgh	.549	5	Cincinnati	.630	14½	Cincinnati	3-0	Johnny Bench, c, Cincinnati
1971	Pittsburgh	.599	7	San Francisco	.556	1	Pittsburgh	3-1	Joe Torre, 3b, St. Louis
1972	Pittsburgh	.619	11	Cincinnati	.617	10½	Cincinnati	3-2	Johnny Bench, c, Cincinnati
1973	New York	.509	1½	Cincinnati	.611	3½	New York	3-2	Pete Rose, of, Cincinnati
1974	Pittsburgh	.543	1½	Los Angeles	.630	4	Los Angeles	3-1	Steve Garvey, 1b, Los Angeles
1975	Pittsburgh	.571	6½	Cincinnati	.667	20	Cincinnati	3-0	Joe Morgan, 2b, Cincinnati
1976	Philadelphia	.623	9	Cincinnati	.630	10	Cincinnati	3-0	Joe Morgan, 2b, Cincinnati
1977	Philadelphia	.623	5	Los Angeles	.605	10	Los Angeles	3-1	George Foster, of, Cincinnati
1978	Philadelphia	.556	1½	Los Angeles	.586	2½	Los Angeles	3-1	Dave Parker, of, Pittsburgh
1979	Pittsburgh	.605	2	Cincinnati	.559	1½	Pittsburgh	3-0	Hernandez, St. Louis; Stargell, Pittsburgh
1980	Philadelphia	.562	1	Houston	.571	1	Philadelphia	3-2	Mike Schmidt, 3b, Philadelphia
1981	Montreal*	.566	½	Los Angeles**	.632	½	Los Angeles	3-2	Mike Schmidt, 3b, Philadelphia
	Philadelphia	.618	1½	Houston	.623	1			
1982	St. Louis	.568	3	Atlanta	.549	1	St. Louis	3-0	Dale Murphy, of, Atlanta
1983	Philadelphia	.556	6	Los Angeles	.562	3	Philadelphia	3-1	Dale Murphy, of, Atlanta
1984	Chicago	.596	6½	San Diego	.568	12	San Diego	3-2	Ryne Sandberg, 2b, Chicago
1985	St. Louis	.623	3	Los Angeles	.586	5½	St. Louis	4-2	Willie McGee, of, St. Louis
1986	New York	.667	21½	Houston	.593	10	New York	4-2	Mike Schmidt, 3b, Philadelphia
1987	St. Louis	.586	3	San Francisco	.556	6	St. Louis	4-3	Andre Dawson, of, Chicago
1988	New York	.625	15	Los Angeles	.584	7	Los Angeles	4-3	Kirk Gibson, of, Los Angeles
1989	Chicago	.571	6	San Francisco	.568	3	San Francisco	4-1	Kevin Mitchell, of, San Francisco
1990	Pittsburgh	.586	4	Cincinnati	.562	5	Cincinnati	4-2	Barry Bonds, of, Pittsburgh
1991	Pittsburgh	.605	14	Atlanta	.580	1	Atlanta	4-3	Terry Pendleton, 3b, Atlanta
1992	Pittsburgh	.593	9	Atlanta	.605	8	Atlanta	4-3	Barry Bonds, of, Pittsburgh
1993	Philadelphia	.599	3	Atlanta	.642	1	Philadelphia	4-2	Barry Bonds, of, San Francisco

	East Div.	PCT	GA	Central Div.	PCT	GA	West Div.		PCT	GA	MVP
1994	Montreal	.649	6	Cincinnati	.593	½	Los Angeles		.509	3½	Jeff Bagwell, 1b, Houston
1995	Atlanta#	.625	21	Cincinnati	.590	9	Los Angeles		.542	1	Barry Larkin, ss, Cincinnati

*Won second half; defeated Philadelphia 3-2 in best-of-5 playoff.   #Won NL pennant, defeating Cincinnati 4-2.
**Won first half; defeated Houston 3-2 in best-of-5 playoff.

brought in to play two or three seasons in RFK Stadium in Washington, D.C., before moving to a ballpark to be built in northern Virginia.

The other team most likely to move seemed to be the Pittsburgh Pirates, who went through all kinds of struggles to find a buyer. The team had been on the block for more than a year, but no one came through until newspaper heir Kevin McClatchy emerged with a bid to buy the team.

The city of Pittsburgh sought buyers who would keep the team, which was said to be at least $60 million in debt, in Pittsburgh, and McClatchy seemed to be the last hope to do that. Collins was ready to pounce on the team if McClatchy couldn't get his deal put together, but he did and it appears for now that the Pirates will stay.

St. Louis, long one of the National League's most stable franchises, was put up for sale following the 1995 season by the Anheuser-Busch Corporation, which had owned the team since 1953.

The San Diego Padres got some needed stability when a group led by Larry Lucchino and John Moores bought the team in December 1994. They moved quickly to show things would be different in San Diego by engineering a blockbuster 12-player trade with the Astros (see below).

But the honeymoon was over by the end of the season, with GM Randy Smith resigning over his difficulties in working with Lucchino. De facto team spokesman Tony Gwynn said, "I think Larry and Randy are having their problems because Randy can't do his job. He's a GM. GMs should make decisions about signing people or trades. Larry wants to be involved in that too. I think they're kind of not meshing."

Blockbuster Aids Both Teams

The Padres and Astros actually made the biggest trade of the year on Dec. 28, 1994. It involved 12 players and was the biggest trade in baseball since 1957.

The Padres sent outfielder Derek Bell, righthander Doug Brocail, shortstop Ricky Gutierrez, lefthander Pedro A. Martinez, outfielder Phil Plantier and third baseman Craig Shipley to the Astros for third baseman

Repeat winner. San Diego outfielder Tony Gwynn won his sixth batting title in 1995, hitting .368.

Ken Caminiti, shortstop Andujar Cedeno, outfielder Steve Finley, first baseman Roberto Petagine, righthander Brian Williams and a player to be named (who turned out to be lefthander Sean Fesh).

Part of the deal turned out to be short-lived: the Astros returned Plantier to the Padres in July after he struggled with injuries that limited him to just 22 games with the Astros. The Astros acquired minor league pitchers Jeff Tabaka and Rich Loiselle in the return deal.

Caminiti and Finley posted career-high numbers with the Padres, enabling them to stay in the NL West

NATIONAL LEAGUE ALL-STARS

Selected by Baseball America

Pos.	Player, Team	B-T	Ht.	Wt.	Age	'95 Salary	AVG	AB	R	H	2B	3B	HR	RBI	SB
C	Mike Piazza, Los Angeles...	R-R	6-3	220	27	$900,000	.346	434	82	150	17	0	32	93	1
1B	Mark Grace, Chicago	L-L	6-2	190	31	4,050,000	.326	552	97	180	51	3	16	92	6
2B	Craig Biggio, Houston........	R-R	5-11	180	29	4,600,000	.302	553	123	167	30	2	22	77	33
3B	Ken Caminiti, San Diego.....	B-R	6-0	200	32	4,550,000	.302	526	74	159	33	0	26	94	12
SS	Barry Larkin, Cincinnati......	R-R	6-0	195	31	5,700,000	.319	496	98	158	29	6	15	66	51
OF	Dante Bichette, Colorado....	R-R	6-3	235	31	3,100,000	.340	579	102	197	38	2	40	128	1
	Tony Gwynn, San Diego......	L-L	5-11	210	35	4,583,334	.368	535	82	197	33	1	9	90	17
	Reggie Sanders, Cincinnati	R-R	6-1	185	27	1,975,000	.306	484	91	148	36	6	28	99	36

Pos.	Player, Team	B-T	Ht.	Wt.	Age	'95 Salary	W	L	ERA	G	SV	IP	H	BB	SO
P	Tom Glavine, Atlanta	L-L	6-1	185	29	4,750,000	16	7	3.08	29	0	199	182	66	127
	Greg Maddux, Atlanta.........	R-R	6-0	175	29	5,500,000	19	2	1.63	28	0	210	147	23	181
	Hideo Nomo, Los Angeles..	R-R	6-2	210	27	109,000	13	6	2.54	28	0	191	124	78	236
	Pete Schourek, Cincinnati...	L-L	6-5	205	26	725,000	18	7	3.22	29	0	190	158	45	160
RP	Mark Wohlers, Atlanta	R-R	6-4	207	25	202,500	7	3	2.09	65	25	65	51	24	90

Player of the Year: Dante Bichette, of, Colorado. **Pitcher of the Year:** Greg Maddux, rhp, Atlanta. **Rookie of the Year:** Hideo Nomo, rhp, Los Angeles. **Manager of the Year:** Davey Johnson, Cincinnati. **Executive of the Year:** Jim Bowden, Cincinnati.

Year	Batting Average	Home Runs	RBIs
1901	Jesse Burkett, St. Louis .382	Sam Crawford, Cincinnati 16	Honus Wagner, Pittsburgh 126
1902	Ginger Beaumont, Pitt. .357	Tom Leach, Pittsburgh 6	Honus Wagner, Pittsburgh 91
1903	Honus Wagner, Pitt. .355	Jim Sheckard, Brooklyn 9	Sam Mertes, New York 104
1904	Honus Wagner, Pitt. .349	Harry Lumley, Brooklyn 9	Bill Dahlen, New York 80
1905	Cy Seymour, Cincinnati .377	Fred Odwell, Cincinnati 9	Cy Seymour, Cincinnati 121
1906	Honus Wagner, Pitt. .339	2 tied at 12	2 tied at 83
1907	Honus Wagner, Pitt. .350	Dave Brain, Boston 10	Sherry Magee, Philadelphia 85
1908	Honus Wagner, Pitt. .354	Tim Jordan, Brooklyn 12	Honus Wagner, Pittsburgh 109
1909	Honus Wagner, Pitt. .339	Red Murray, New York 7	Honus Wagner, Pittsburgh 100
1910	Sherry Magee, Phil. .331	2 tied at 10	Sherry Magee, Philadelphia 123
1911	Honus Wagner, Pitt. .334	Wildfire Schulte, Chicago 21	Wildfire Schulte, Chicago 121
1912	Heinie Zimmerman, Chi. .372	Heinie Zimmerman, Chicago 14	Heinie Zimmerman, Chi. 103
1913	Jake Daubert, Brooklyn .350	Gavvy Cravath, Philadelphia 19	Gavvy Cravath, Philadelphia 128
1914	Jake Daubert, Brooklyn .329	Gavvy Cravath, Philadelphia 19	Sherry Magee, Phil. 103
1915	Larry Doyle, New York .320	Gavvy Cravath, Philadelphia 24	Gavvy Cravath, Philadelphia 115
1916	Hal Chase, Cincinnati .339	2 tied at 12	Heinie Zimmerman, Chi.-N.Y. 83
1917	Edd Roush, Cincinnati .341	Gavvy Cravath, Philadelphia 12	Heinie Zimmerman, N.Y. 102
1918	Zack Wheat, Brooklyn .335	Gavvy Cravath, Philadelphia 8	Sherry Magee, Cincinnati 76
1919	Edd Roush, Cincinnati .321	Gavvy Cravath, Philadelphia 12	Hy Myers, Brooklyn 73
1920	Rogers Hornsby, St.L .370	Cy Williams, Philadelphia 15	2 tied at 94
1921	Rogers Hornsby, St.L .397	George Kelly, New York 23	Rogers Hornsby, St. Louis 126
1922	Rogers Hornsby, St.L .401	Rogers Hornsby, St. Louis 42	Rogers Hornsby, St. Louis 152
1923	Rogers Hornsby, St.L .384	Cy Williams, Philadelphia 41	Emil Meusel, New York 125
1924	Rogers Hornsby, St.L .424	Jack Fournier, Brooklyn 27	George Kelly, New York 136
1925	Rogers Hornsby, St.L .403	Rogers Hornsby, St. Louis 39	Rogers Hornsby, St. Louis 143
1926	Bubbles Hargrave, Cinc. .353	Hack Wilson, Chicago 21	Jim Bottomley, St. Louis 131
1927	Paul Waner, Pittsburgh .380	2 tied at 30	Paul Waner, Pittsburgh 131
1928	Rogers Hornsby, St.L. .387	2 tied at 31	Jim Bottomley, St. Louis 136
1929	Lefty O'Doul, Philadelphia .398	Chuck Klein, Philadelphia 43	Hack Wilson, Chicago 159
1930	Bill Terry, New York .401	Hack Wilson, Chicago 56	Hack Wilson, Chicago 190
1931	Chick Hafey, St. Louis .349	Chuck Klein, Philadelphia 31	Chuck Klein, Philadelphia 121
1932	Lefty O'Doul, Brooklyn .368	2 tied at 38	Frank Hurst, Philadelphia 143
1933	Chuck Klein, Philadelphia .368	Chuck Klein, Philadelphia 28	Chuck Klein, Philadelphia 120
1934	Paul Waner, Pittsburgh .362	2 tied at 35	Mel Ott, New York 135
1935	Arky Vaughan, Pittsburgh .385	Wally Berger, Boston 34	Wally Berger, Boston 130
1936	Paul Waner, Pittsburgh .373	Mel Ott, New York 33	Joe Medwick, St. Louis 138
1937	Joe Medwick, St. Louis .374	Mel Ott, New York 31	Joe Medwick, St. Louis 154
1938	Ernie Lombardi, Cincinnati .342	Mel Ott, New York 36	Joe Medwick, St. Louis 122
1939	Johnny Mize, St. Louis .349	Johnny Mize, St. Louis 28	Frank McCormick, Cinc. 128
1940	Debs Garms, Pittsburgh .355	Johnny Mize, St. Louis 43	Johnny Mize, St. Louis 137
1941	Pete Reiser, Brooklyn .343	Dolf Camilli, Brooklyn 34	Dolf Camilli, Brooklyn 120
1942	Ernie Lombardi, Boston .330	Mel Ott, New York 30	Johnny Mize, New York 110
1943	Stan Musial, St. Louis .357	Bill Nicholson, Chicago 29	Bill Nicholson, Chicago 128
1944	Dixie Walker, Brooklyn .357	Bill Nicholson, Chicago 33	Bill Nicholson, Chicago 122
1945	Phil Cavarretta, Chicago .355	Tommy Holmes, Boston 28	Dixie Walker, Brooklyn 124
1946	Stan Musial, St. Louis .365	Ralph Kiner, Pittsburgh 23	Enos Slaughter, St. Louis 130
1947	Harry Walker, St.L-Phil. .363	2 tied at 51	Johnny Mize, New York 138
1948	Stan Musial, St. Louis .376	2 tied at 40	Stan Musial, St. Louis 131
1949	Jackie Robinson, Brook. .342	Ralph Kiner, Pittsburgh 54	Ralph Kiner, Pittsburgh 127
1950	Stan Musial, St. Louis .346	Ralph Kiner, Pittsburgh 47	Del Ennis, Philadelphia 126
1951	Stan Musial, St. Louis .355	Ralph Kiner, Pittsburgh 42	Monte Irvin, New York 121
1952	Stan Musial, St. Louis .336	2 tied at 37	Hank Sauer, Chicago 121
1953	Carl Furillo, Brooklyn .344	Eddie Mathews, Milwaukee 47	Roy Campanella, Brooklyn 142
1954	Willie Mays, New York .345	Ted Kluszewski, Cincinnati 49	Ted Kluszewski, Cincinnati 141
1955	Richie Ashburn, Phil. .338	Willie Mays, New York 51	Duke Snider, Brooklyn 136
1956	Hank Aaron, Milwaukee .328	Duke Snider, Brooklyn 43	Stan Musial, St. Louis 109
1957	Stan Musial, St. Louis .351	Hank Aaron, Milwaukee 44	Hank Aaron, Milwaukee 132
1958	Richie Ashburn, Phil. .350	Ernie Banks, Chicago 47	Ernie Banks, Chicago 129
1959	Hank Aaron, Milwaukee .355	Eddie Mathews, Milwaukee 46	Ernie Banks, Chicago 143
1960	Dick Groat, Pittsburgh .325	Ernie Banks, Chicago 41	Hank Aaron, Milwaukee 126
1961	Roberto Clemente, Pitt. .351	Orlando Cepeda, San Fran. 46	Orlando Cepeda, San Fran. 142
1962	Tommy Davis, L.A. .346	Willie Mays, San Francisco 49	Tommy Davis, Los Angeles 153
1963	Tommy Davis, L.A. .326	Hank Aaron, Milwaukee 44	Hank Aaron, Milwaukee 130
1964	Roberto Clemente, Pitt. .339	Willie Mays, San Francisco 47	Ken Boyer, St. Louis 119
1965	Roberto Clemente, Pitt. .329	Willie Mays, San Francisco 52	Deron Johnson, Cincinnati 130
1966	Matty Alou, Pittsburgh .342	Hank Aaron, Atlanta 44	Hank Aaron, Atlanta 127
1967	Roberto Clemente, Pitt. .357	Hank Aaron, Atlanta 39	Orlando Cepeda, San Fran. 111
1968	Pete Rose, Cincinnati .335	Willie McCovey, San Fran. 36	Willie McCovey, San Fran. 105
1969	Pete Rose, Cincinnati .348	Willie McCovey, San Fran. 45	Willie McCovey, San Fran. 126
1970	Rico Carty, Atlanta .366	Johnny Bench, Cincinnati 45	Johnny Bench, Cincinnati 148
1971	Joe Torre, St. Louis .363	Willie Stargell, Pittsburgh 48	Joe Torre, St. Louis 137
1972	Billy Williams, Chicago .333	Johnny Bench, Cincinnati 40	Johnny Bench, Cincinnati 125
1973	Pete Rose, Cincinnati .338	Willie Stargell, Pittsburgh 44	Willie Stargell, Pittsburgh 119
1974	Ralph Garr, Atlanta .353	Mike Schmidt, Philadelphia 36	Johnny Bench, Cincinnati 129
1975	Bill Madlock, Chicago .354	Mike Schmidt, Philadelphia 38	Greg Luzinski, Philadelphia 120
1976	Bill Madlock, Chicago .339	Mike Schmidt, Philadelphia 38	George Foster, Cincinnati 121
1977	Dave Parker, Pittsburgh .338	George Foster, Cincinnati 52	George Foster, Cincinnati 149
1978	Dave Parker, Pittsburgh .334	George Foster, Cincinnati 40	George Foster, Cincinnati 120
1979	Keith Hernandez, St.L. .344	Dave Kingman, Chicago 48	Dave Winfield, San Diego 118
1980	Bill Buckner, Chicago .324	Mike Schmidt, Philadelphia 48	Mike Schmidt, Philadelphia 121
1981	Bill Madlock, Pittsburgh .341	Mike Schmidt, Philadelphia 31	Mike Schmidt, Philadelphia 91
1982	Al Oliver, Montreal .331	Dave Kingman, New York 37	Dale Murphy, Atlanta 109
1983	Bill Madlock, Pittsburgh .323	Mike Schmidt, Philadelphia 40	Dale Murphy, Atlanta 121
1984	Tony Gwynn, San Diego .351	2 tied at 36	2 tied at 106
1985	Willie McGee, St. Louis .353	Dale Murphy, Atlanta 37	Dave Parker, Cincinnati 125
1986	Tim Raines, Montreal .334	Mike Schmidt, Philadelphia 37	Mike Schmidt, Philadelphia 119
1987	Tony Gwynn, San Diego .370	Andre Dawson, Chicago 49	Andre Dawson, Chicago 137
1988	Tony Gwynn, San Diego .313	Darryl Strawberry, New York 39	Will Clark, San Francisco 109
1989	Tony Gwynn, San Diego .336	Kevin Mitchell, S.F. 47	Kevin Mitchell, S.F. 125
1990	Willie McGee, Chicago .335	Ryne Sandberg, Chicago 40	Matt Williams, S.F. 122
1991	Terry Pendleton, Atlanta .319	Howard Johnson, New York 38	Howard Johnson, N.Y. 117
1992	Gary Sheffield, S.D. .330	Fred McGriff, San Diego 35	Darren Daulton, Phil. 109
1993	Andres Galarraga, Colo. .370	Barry Bonds, San Francisco 46	Barry Bonds, S.F. 123
1994	Tony Gwynn, San Diego .394	Matt Williams, S.F. 43	Jeff Bagwell, Houston 116
1995	Tony Gwynn, San Diego .368	Dante Bichette, Colorado 40	Dante Bichette, Colorado 128

NATIONAL LEAGUE
YEAR-BY-YEAR LEADERS: PITCHING

Year	Wins	ERA	Strikeouts
1901	Bill Donovan, Brooklyn... 25	Jesse Tannehill, Pittsburgh. 2.18	Noodles Hahn, Cin. ... 233
1902	Jack Chesbro, Pittsburgh. 28	Jack Taylor, Chicago... 1.33	Vic Willis, Boston... 226
1903	Joe McGinnity, New York. 31	Sam Leever, Pittsburgh.. 2.06	Christy Mathewson, N.Y. 267
1904	Joe McGinnity, New York. 35	Joe McGinnity, New York.. 1.61	Christy Mathewson, N.Y. 212
1905	Christy Mathewson, N.Y.. 32	Christy Mathewson, N.Y... 1.27	Christy Mathewson, N.Y. 206
1906	Joe McGinnity, New York. 27	Mordecai Brown, Chicago.. 1.04	Fred Beebe, Chi.-StL.... 171
1907	Christy Mathewson, New York. 24	Jack Pfiester, Chicago.... 1.15	Christy Mathewson, N.Y. 178
1908	Christy Mathewson, N.Y. 37	Christy Mathewson, N.Y. 1.43	Christy Mathewson, N.Y. 259
1909	Mordecai Brown, Chicago. 27	Orval Overall, Chicago... 1.14	Orval Overall, Chicago.. 205
1910	Christy Mathewson, N.Y.. 27	George McQuillan, Phil. 1.60	Christy Mathewson, N.Y. 190
1911	Grover Alexander, Phil. 28	Christy Mathewson, N.Y. 1.99	Rube Marquard, New York 237
1912	2 tied at... 26	Jeff Tesreau, New York. 1.96	Grover Alexander, Phil. 195
1913	Tom Seaton, Philadelphia 27	Christy Mathewson, N.Y. 2.06	Tom Seaton, Philadelphia 168
1914	Grover Alexander, Phil. 27	Bill Doak, St. Louis. 1.72	Grover Alexander, Phil. 214
1915	Grover Alexander, Phil. 31	Grover Alexander, Phil. 1.22	Grover Alexander, Phil. 241
1916	Grover Alexander, Phil. 33	Grover Alexander, Phil. 1.55	Grover Alexander, Phil. 167
1917	Grover Alexander, Phil. 30	Grover Alexander, Phil. 1.85	Grover Alexander, Phil. 200
1918	Hippo Vaughn, Chicago. 22	Hippo Vaughn, Chicago. 1.74	Hippo Vaughn, Chicago. 148
1919	Jesse Barnes, New York. 25	Grover Alexander, Chicago 1.72	Hippo Vaughn, Chicago. 141
1920	Grover Alexander, Chicago 27	Grover Alexander, Chicago 1.91	Grover Alexander, Chicago 173
1921	2 tied at... 22	Bill Doak, St. Louis. 2.58	Burleigh Grimes, Brooklyn. 136
1922	Eppa Rixey, Cincinnati. 25	Rosy Ryan, New York. 3.00	Dazzy Vance, Brooklyn. 134
1923	Dolf Luque, Cincinnati. 27	Dolf Luque, Cincinnati. 1.93	Dazzy Vance, Brooklyn. 197
1924	Dazzy Vance, Brooklyn. 28	Dazzy Vance, Brooklyn. 2.16	Dazzy Vance, Brooklyn. 262
1925	Dazzy Vance, Brooklyn. 22	Dolf Luque, Cincinnati. 2.63	Dazzy Vance, Brooklyn. 221
1926	4 tied at... 20	Ray Kremer, Pittsburgh. 2.61	Dazzy Vance, Brooklyn. 140
1927	Charlie Root, Chicago. 26	Ray Kremer, Pittsburgh. 2.47	Dazzy Vance, Brooklyn. 184
1928	2 tied at... 25	Dazzy Vance, Brooklyn. 2.09	Dazzy Vance, Brooklyn. 200
1929	Pat Malone, Chicago. 22	Bill Walker, New York. 3.08	Pat Malone, Chicago. 166
1930	2 tied at... 20	Dazzy Vance, Brooklyn. 2.61	Bill Hallahan, St. Louis. 177
1931	3 tied at... 19	Bill Walker, New York. 2.26	Bill Hallahan, St. Louis. 159
1932	Lon Warneke, Chicago. 22	Lon Warneke, Chicago. 2.37	Dizzy Dean, St. Louis. 191
1933	Carl Hubbell, New York. 23	Carl Hubbell, New York. 1.66	Dizzy Dean, St. Louis. 199
1934	Dizzy Dean, St. Louis. 30	Carl Hubbell, New York. 2.30	Dizzy Dean, St. Louis. 195
1935	Dizzy Dean, St. Louis. 28	Cy Blanton, Pittsburgh. 2.59	Dizzy Dean, St. Louis. 182
1936	Carl Hubbell, New York. 26	Carl Hubbell, New York. 2.31	Van Lingle Mungo, Brooklyn. 238
1937	Carl Hubbell, New York. 22	Jim Turner, Boston. 2.38	Carl Hubbell, New York. 159
1938	Bill Lee, Chicago. 22	Bill Lee, Chicago. 2.66	Clay Bryant, Chicago. 135
1939	Bucky Walters, Cincinnati. 27	Bucky Walters, Cincinnati. 2.29	Bucky Walters, Cincinnati. 137
1940	Bucky Walters, Cincinnati. 22	Bucky Walters, Cincinnati. 2.48	Kirby Higbe, Philadelphia. 137
1941	2 tied at... 22	Elmer Riddle, Cincinnati. 2.24	Johnny Vander Meer, Cin. 202
1942	Mort Cooper, St. Louis. 22	Mort Cooper, St. Louis. 1.77	Johnny Vander Meer, Cin. 186
1943	3 tied at... 21	Howie Pollet, St. Louis. 1.75	Johnny Vander Meer, Cin. 174
1944	Bucky Walters, Cincinnati. 23	Ed Heusser, Cincinnati. 2.38	Bill Voiselle, New York. 161
1945	Red Barrett, Bos.-St.L. 23	Hank Borowy, Chicago. 2.14	Preacher Roe, Pittsburgh. 148
1946	Howie Pollet, St. Louis. 21	Howie Pollet, St. Louis. 2.10	John Schmitz, Chicago. 135
1947	Ewell Blackwell, Cincinnati 22	Warren Spahn, Boston. 2.33	Ewell Blackwell, Cincinnati. 193
1948	Johnny Sain, Boston. 24	Harry Brecheen, St. Louis. 2.24	Harry Brecheen, St. Louis. 149
1949	Warren Spahn, Boston. 21	Dave Koslo, New York. 2.50	Warren Spahn, Boston. 151
1950	Warren Spahn, Boston. 21	Jim Hearn, St.L-New York. 2.49	Warren Spahn, Boston. 191
1951	2 tied at... 23	Chet Nichols, Boston. 2.88	2 tied at... 164
1952	Robin Roberts, Philadelphia 28	Hoyt Wilhelm, New York. 2.43	Warren Spahn, Boston. 183
1953	Warren Spahn, Milwaukee. 23	Warren Spahn, Milwaukee. 2.10	Robin Roberts, Philadelphia 198
1954	Robin Roberts, Philadelphia 23	John Antonelli, New York. 2.29	Robin Roberts, Philadelphia 185
1955	Robin Roberts, Philadelphia 23	Bob Friend, Pittsburgh. 2.84	Sam Jones, Chicago. 198
1956	Don Newcombe, Brooklyn 27	Lew Burdette, Milwaukee. 2.71	Sam Jones, Chicago. 176
1957	Warren Spahn, Milwaukee 21	Johnny Podres, Brooklyn. 2.66	Jack Sanford, Philadelphia. 188
1958	2 tied at... 22	Stu Miller, San Francisco. 2.47	Sam Jones, St. Louis. 225
1959	3 tied at... 21	Sam Jones, San Francisco. 2.82	Don Drysdale, Los Angeles 242
1960	2 tied at... 21	Mike McCormick, San Fran. 2.70	Don Drysdale, Los Angeles 246
1961	Warren Spahn, Milwaukee. 21	Warren Spahn, Milwaukee. 3.01	Sandy Koufax, Los Angeles 269
1962	Don Drysdale, Los Angeles 25	Sandy Koufax, Los Angeles 2.54	Don Drysdale, Los Angeles 232
1963	Sandy Koufax, Los Angeles 25	Sandy Koufax, Los Angeles 1.88	Sandy Koufax, Los Angeles 306
1964	Larry Jackson, Chicago. 24	Sandy Koufax, Los Angeles 1.74	Bob Veale, Pittsburgh. 250
1965	Sandy Koufax, Los Angeles 26	Sandy Koufax, Los Angeles 2.04	Sandy Koufax, Los Angeles 382
1966	Sandy Koufax, Los Angeles 27	Sandy Koufax, Los Angeles 1.73	Sandy Koufax, Los Angeles 317
1967	Mike McCormick, San Fran. 22	Phil Niekro, Atlanta. 1.87	Jim Bunning, Philadelphia. 253
1968	Juan Marichal, San Fran. 26	Bob Gibson, St. Louis. 1.12	Bob Gibson, St. Louis. 268
1969	Tom Seaver, New York. 25	Juan Marichal, San Fran. 2.10	Ferguson Jenkins, Chicago 273
1970	2 tied at... 23	Tom Seaver, New York. 2.81	Tom Seaver, New York. 283
1971	Ferguson Jenkins, Chicago 24	Tom Seaver, New York. 1.76	Tom Seaver, New York. 289
1972	Steve Carlton, Philadelphia 27	Steve Carlton, Philadelphia 1.98	Steve Carlton, Philadelphia. 310
1973	Ron Bryant, San Francisco 24	Tom Seaver, New York. 2.08	Tom Seaver, New York. 251
1974	Buzz Capra, Atlanta. 20	Buzz Capra, Atlanta. 2.28	Steve Carlton, Philadelphia. 240
1975	Tom Seaver, New York. 22	Randy Jones, San Diego. 2.24	Tom Seaver, New York. 243
1976	Randy Jones, San Diego. 22	John Denny, St. Louis. 2.52	Tom Seaver, New York. 235
1977	Steve Carlton, Philadelphia 23	John Candelaria, Pittsburgh 2.34	Phil Niekro, Atlanta. 252
1978	Gaylord Perry, San Diego. 21	Craig Swan, New York. 2.43	J.R. Richard, Houston. 303
1979	2 tied at... 21	J.R. Richard, Houston. 2.71	J.R. Richard, Houston. 313
1980	Steve Carlton, Philadelphia 24	Don Sutton, Los Angeles. 2.21	Steve Carlton, Philadelphia. 286
1981	Tom Seaver, Cincinnati. 14	Nolan Ryan, Houston. 1.69	Fernando Valenzuela, L.A. 180
1982	Steve Carlton, Philadelphia 23	Steve Rogers, Montreal. 2.40	Steve Carlton, Philadelphia. 286
1983	John Denny, Philadelphia. 19	Atlee Hammaker, San Fran. 2.25	Steve Carlton, Philadelphia. 275
1984	Joaquin Andujar, St. Louis 20	Alejandro Pena, Los Angeles 2.48	Dwight Gooden, New York. 276
1985	Dwight Gooden, New York. 24	Dwight Gooden, New York. 1.53	Dwight Gooden, New York. 268
1986	Fernando Valenzuela, L.A. 21	Mike Scott, Houston. 2.22	Mike Scott, Houston. 306
1987	Rick Sutcliffe, Chicago. 18	Nolan Ryan, Houston. 2.76	Nolan Ryan, Houston. 270
1988	Joe Magrane, St. Louis. 23	Joe Magrane, St. Louis. 2.18	Nolan Ryan, Houston. 228
1989	Mike Scott, Houston. 20	Scott Garrelts, San Fran. 2.28	Jose DeLeon, St. Louis. 201
1990	Doug Drabek, Pittsburgh. 22	Danny Darwin, Houston. 2.21	David Cone, New York. 233
1991	2 tied at... 20	Dennis Martinez, Mon. 2.39	David Cone, New York. 241
1992	2 tied at... 20	Bill Swift, San Francisco. 2.08	John Smoltz, Atlanta. 215
1993	2 tied at... 22	Jose Rijo, Cincinnati. 2.36	Jose Rijo, Cincinnati. 227
1994	Greg Maddux, Atlanta. 16	Greg Maddux, Atlanta. 1.56	Andy Benes, San Diego. 189
1995	Greg Maddux, Atlanta. 19	Greg Maddux, Atlanta. 1.63	Hideo Nomo, Los Angeles 236

NATIONAL LEAGUE
DEPARTMENT LEADERS

BATTING

AT-BATS
Brian McRae, Chicago 580
Dante Bichette, Colorado 579
Sammy Sosa, Chicago 564
Steve Finley, San Diego................... 562
Andres Galarraga, Colorado 554

RUNS
Craig Biggio, Houston 123
Barry Bonds, San Francisco............. 109
Steve Finley, San Diego................... 104
Dante Bichette, Colorado 102
Barry Larkin, Cincinnati 98

HITS
Dante Bichette, Colorado 197
Tony Gwynn, San Diego 197
Mark Grace, Chicago 180
Brian McRae, Chicago 167
Steve Finley, San Diego................... 167
Craig Biggio, Houston 167

TOTAL BASES
Dante Bichette, Colorado 359
Larry Walker, Colorado 300
Vinny Castilla, Colorado 297
Eric Karros, Los Angeles 295
Barry Bonds, San Francisco............. 292

DOUBLES
Mark Grace, Chicago 51
Brian McRae, Chicago 38
Dante Bichette, Colorado 38
Reggie Sanders, Cincinnati................ 36
Will Cordero, Montreal........................ 35
Ray Lankford, St. Louis 35

TRIPLES
Eric Young, Colorado 9
Brett Butler, N.Y.-L.A............................ 9
Luis Gonzalez, Houston-Chicago 8
Deion Sanders, Cinc.-S.F..................... 8
Steve Finley, San Diego 8

HOME RUNS
Dante Bichette, Colorado 40
Sammy Sosa, Chicago 36
Larry Walker, Colorado...................... 36
Barry Bonds, San Francisco.............. 33
Mike Piazza, Los Angeles 32
Eric Karros, Los Angeles 32
Vinny Castilla, Colorado 32

HOME RUN RATIO
(At-Bats per Home Runs)
Mike Piazza, Los Angeles 13.6
Larry Walker, Colorado.................... 13.7
Ron Gant, Cincinnati 14.1
Dante Bichette, Colorado 14.5
Barry Bonds, San Francisco............. 15.3

RUNS BATTED IN
Dante Bichette, Colorado 128
Sammy Sosa, Chicago 119
Andres Galarraga, Colorado............ 106
Eric Karros, Los Angeles 105
Jeff Conine, Florida 105

SACRIFICE BUNTS
Bobby Jones, New York 18
Andy Ashby, San Diego 17
Jose Vizcaino, New York.................... 13
Ramon Martinez, Los Angeles 13
Darren Lewis, S.F.-Cinc..................... 12
Pete Schourek, Cincinnati 12
Joe Girardi, Colorado 12
Dave Mlicki, New York........................ 12

SACRIFICE FLIES
Jeff Conine, Florida 12
Jeff King, Pittsburgh 8
Raul Mondesi, Los Angeles................. 7

Mile high masher. Colorado slugger Dante Bichette led the National League with 40 home runs and 359 total bases.

MORRIS FOSTOFF

Craig Biggio, Houston............................ 7
Mark Grace, Chicago............................. 7
Roberto Kelly, Los Angeles 7
Dante Bichette, Colorado 7

HIT BY PITCH
Craig Biggio, Houston.......................... 22
Larry Walker, Colorado........................ 14
Andres Galarraga, Colorado............... 13
John Patterson, San Francisco 12
Jeff Blauser, Atlanta 12

INTENTIONAL WALKS
Barry Bonds, San Francisco................ 22
Jeff Branson, Cincinnati...................... 14
Larry Walker, Colorado........................ 13
Jeff Bagwell, Houston.......................... 12
Tony Tarasco, Montreal........................ 12

STRIKEOUTS
Andres Galarraga, Colorado............. 146
Sammy Sosa, Chicago 134
Reggie Sanders, Cincinnati 122
Eric Karros, Los Angeles 115
Rico Brogna, New York 111

TOUGHEST TO STRIKE OUT
(Plate Appearances per SO)
Tony Gwynn, San Diego.................... 38.5
Gregg Jefferies, Philadelphia 20.0
Mark Grace, Chicago........................ 13.6
Jody Reed, San Diego....................... 13.6
Brett Butler, N.Y.-L.A......................... 11.7

STOLEN BASES
Quilvio Veras, Florida 56
Barry Larkin, Cincinnati 51
Delino DeShields, Los Angeles 39
Reggie Sanders, Cincinnati................ 36
Steve Finley, San Diego 36

CAUGHT STEALING
Quilvio Veras, Florida 21

Darren Lewis, S.F.-Cinc. 18
Delino DeShields, Los Angeles 14
Eric Young, Colorado 12
Reggie Sanders, Cincinnati 12
Steve Finley, San Diego 12
Jacob Brumfield, Pittsburgh................ 12

GIDP
Charlie Hayes, Philadelphia 22
Eddie Williams, San Diego 21
Tony Gwynn, San Diego...................... 20
Fred McGriff, Atlanta 20
Bernard Gilkey, St. Louis.................... 17
Mark Lemke, Atlanta........................... 17

HITTING STREAKS
Dante Bichette, Colorado 23
Carlos Garcia, Pittsburgh 21
Eric Young, Colorado 19
Dante Bichette, Colorado 19
David Segui, Montreal 18

MULTIPLE-HIT GAMES
Tony Gwynn, San Diego...................... 65
Dante Bichette, Colorado 58
Craig Biggio, Houston......................... 53
Mark Grace, Chicago.......................... 53
Brian McRae, Chicago........................ 52

SLUGGING PERCENTAGE
Dante Bichette, Colorado 620
Larry Walker, Colorado.....................607
Mike Piazza, Los Angeles 606
Reggie Sanders, Cincinnati 579
Barry Bonds, San Francisco.............577

ON-BASE PERCENTAGE
Barry Bonds, San Francisco.............431
Craig Biggio, Houston.......................406
Tony Gwynn, San Diego....................404
Walt Weiss, Colorado........................403
Mike Piazza, Los Angeles 400

PITCHING

WINS
Greg Maddux, Atlanta 19
Pete Schourek, Cincinnati 18
Ramon Martinez, Los Angeles 17
Tom Glavine, Atlanta........................... 16
Four tied at 14

LOSSES
Paul Wagner, Pittsburgh 16
John Burkett, Florida 14
Jeff Fassero, Montreal......................... 14
Tom Candiotti, Los Angeles 14
Steve Avery, Atlanta............................ 13
Terry Mulholland, San Francisco......... 13
Steve Trachsel, Chicago 13

WINNING PERCENTAGE
Greg Maddux, Atlanta .... .905
Pete Schourek, Cincinnati .... .720
Dave Burba, S.F.-Cincinnati............. .714
Ramon Martinez, Los Angeles .... .708
John Smiley, Cincinnati .... .706

GAMES
Curtis Leskanic, Colorado 76
Dave Veres, Houston 72
Steve Reed, Colorado 71
Yorkis Perez, Florida 69
Todd Jones, Houston 68
Darren Holmes, Colorado.................... 68
Mike Perez, Chicago 68

GAMES STARTED
Danny Neagle, Pittsburgh 31
Andy Ashby, San Diego 31
Doug Drabek, Houston 31
Mark Portugal, S.F.-Cinc. 31
Esteban Loaiza, Pittsburgh................. 31

COMPLETE GAMES
Greg Maddux, Atlanta 10
Mark Leiter, San Francisco 7
Ismael Valdes, Los Angeles 6
Denny Neagle, Pittsburgh 5
Four tied with 4

SHUTOUTS
Hideo Nomo, Los Angeles 3
Greg Maddux, Atlanta 3
Ten tied with 2

GAMES FINISHED
Heathcliff Slocumb, Philadelphia........ 54
Robb Nen, Florida 54
Todd Worrell, Los Angeles 53
Rod Beck, San Francisco..................... 53
Trevor Hoffman, San Diego................. 51
Danny Miceli, Pittsburgh...................... 51

Craig Biggio
123 runs

R&R SPORTS GROUP

Barry Bonds
.431 OBA

DAN ARNOLD

SAVES
Randy Myers, Chicago 36
Tom Henke, St. Louis 36
Rod Beck, San Francisco 33
Heathcliff Slocumb, Philadelphia......... 32
Todd Worrell, Los Angeles 32

INNINGS PITCHED
Greg Maddux, Atlanta......................... 210
Denny Neagle, Pittsburgh.................. 210
Ramon Martinez, Los Angeles 206
Joey Hamilton, San Diego 204
Jaime Navarro, Chicago 200

HITS ALLOWED
Denny Neagle, Pittsburgh.................. 221
Paul Quantrill, Philadelphia............... 212
Bobby Jones, New York 209
John Burkett, Florida 208
Jeff Fassero, Montreal........................ 207

RUNS ALLOWED
Esteban Loaiza, Pittsburgh................ 115
Terry Mulholland, San Francisco....... 112
Bobby Jones, New York 107
Doug Drabek, Houston 104
Steve Trachsel, Chicago 104

HOME RUNS ALLOWED
Kevin Foster, Chicago 32
Terry Mulholland, San Francisco......... 25
Steve Trachsel, Chicago 25
Juan Bautista, San Francisco.............. 24
Dave Mlicki, New York......................... 23

WALKS
Ramon Martinez, Los Angeles 81
Hideo Nomo, Los Angeles................... 78
Pat Rapp, Florida................................. 76
Steve Trachsel, Chicago 76
Mike Mimbs, Philadelphia................... 75

HIT BATSMEN
Mark Leiter, San Francisco................. 17
Darryl Kile, Houston............................ 12
Pedro Martinez, Montreal 11
Andy Ashby, San Diego....................... 11
Joey Hamilton, San Diego 11

STRIKEOUTS
Hideo Nomo, Los Angeles................. 236
John Smoltz, Atlanta.......................... 193
Greg Maddux, Atlanta........................ 181
Shane Reynolds, Houston 175
Pedro Martinez, Montreal 174

STRIKEOUTS PER 9 INNINGS
Hideo Nomo, Los Angeles............... 11.1
John Smoltz, Atlanta........................... 9.0
Shane Reynolds, Houston.................. 8.3
Pedro Martinez, Montreal 8.0
Kevin Foster, Chicago 7.8

WILD PITCHES
Hideo Nomo, Los Angeles................... 19
Hector Carrasco, Cincinnati................ 15
John Smoltz, Atlanta........................... 13
Toby Borland, Philadelphia................. 12
John Ericks, Pittsburgh....................... 11
Darryl Kile, Houston............................ 11

BALKS
Hideo Nomo, Los Angeles.................... 5
William VanLandingham, S.F. 4
Carlos Perez, Montreal......................... 4
Ismael Valdes, Los Angeles 3
Paul Quantrill, Philadelphia 3
Mark Leiter, San Francisco 3
John Habyan, St. Louis 3

OPPONENTS BATTING AVERAGE
Hideo Nomo, Los Angeles............... .182
Greg Maddux, Atlanta...................... .197
Pedro Martinez, Montreal .... .227
Ismael Valdes, Los Angeles .... .228
Pete Schourek, Cincinnati .... .228

FIELDING

PITCHER
PCT Greg Maddux, Atlanta.......... 1.000
PO   Doug Drabek, Houston 24
A   Greg Maddux, Atlanta.............. 53
E   Two tied with............................. 6
TC   Greg Maddux, Atlanta.............. 71
DP   Tom Glavine, Atlanta 6

CATCHER
PCT Benito Santiago, Cincinnati ... .996
PO   Mike Piazza, Los Angeles 805
A   Two tied with 63
E   Scott Servais, Hous.-Chi. 12
TC   Mike Piazza, Los Angeles 866
DP   Brad Ausmus, San Diego 14

FIRST BASE
PCT Rico Brogna, New York .... .998
PO   Andres Galarraga, Colorado 1,299
A   Jeff Bagwell, Houston 129
E   Andres Galarraga, Colorado.... 13
TC   Andres Galarraga, Colorado 1,432
DP   Andres Galarraga, Colorado... 129

SECOND BASE
PCT Bret Boone, Cincinnati .... .994
PO   Bret Boone, Cincinnati............ 311
A   Craig Biggio, Houston............. 419
E   Two tied with 11
TC   Craig Biggio, Houston............. 728
DP   Bret Boone, Cincinnati 106

THIRD BASE
PCT Tim Wallach, Los Angeles ..... .976
PO   Two tied with 104
A   Ken Caminiti, San Diego 295
E   Ken Caminiti, San Diego 27
TC   Ken Caminiti, San Diego 424
DP   Ken Caminiti, San Diego 28

SHORTSTOP
PCT Jose Vizcaino, New York....... .984
PO   Will Cordero, Montreal............ 223
A   Two tied with 411
E   Jose Offerman, Los Angeles ... 35
TC   Royce Clayton, San Francisco. 654
DP   Walt Weiss, Colorado 99

OUTFIELD
PCT Jim Eisenreich, Philadelphia . 1.000
PO   Brian McRae, Chicago............ 345
A   Raul Mondesi, Los Angeles...... 16
E   Sammy Sosa, Chicago............. 13
TC   Brian McRae, Chicago............ 352
DP   Two tied with............................. 4

race for most of the season. Caminiti batted .302 with 26 home runs and 94 RBIs, all career highs. Finley's .297 average and 104 runs were also career highs. Shortstop Andujar Cedeno was the biggest disappointment for the Padres, batting just .210 while also struggling on defense.

The Astros, who missed the playoffs by just a game, benefited most from Bell, who was in the thick of the NL batting race until he missed the final six weeks of the season with a thigh injury. He finished up the season hitting .334 with 86 RBIs. No one else from the deal had a dramatic impact with Houston.

Magnificent Martinezes

The Martinez brothers were nearly perfect in 1995—at least on a given night.

Ramon Martinez pitched the only major league no-hitter against the Florida Marlins on July 14. It was the first no-hitter since Kenny Rogers did it on July 28, 1994, when Texas played California.

Martinez actually was only one walk away from pitching a perfect game in his 7-0 win. When Quilvio Veras flied out to left fielder Roberto Kelly to end the game, Martinez jumped into Mike Piazza's arms.

Martinez, 27, had struggled coming into the game, but he was dominant in throwing the fifth no-hitter since the Dodgers moved to Los Angeles. The game seemed to propel him through the rest of the season.

"I have pride and I wanted to let people know that I can still pitch," said Martinez, who finished the season at 17-7 with a 3.66 ERA. "You know something, I think people had forgotten about me."

When Martinez got home that night, he had a long message from his younger brother Pedro waiting for him. It was only a month earlier that Pedro had flirted with history.

Pedro pitched nine perfect innings but had to settle for a one-hit victory over the Padres on June 3.

Martinez, who lost a no-hitter in the ninth inning against the Reds in 1994, struck out nine in his bid for the 14th perfect game in major league history.

All-star lefty. Cincinnati's Pete Schourek had his best major league season, winning 18 games.

But the Expos couldn't score until the 10th, and Martinez gave up a double to Bip Roberts in the Padres' half of the inning. Mel Rojas then came in to pick up the save.

"I know I'm still young, but I've been around long enough now that I think I've shown people what I can do," said Martinez, 23. He had only two days earlier received notification from the NL office that he would be fined $500 for hitting Luis Gonzalez with a pitch.

NL: BEST TOOLS

A Baseball America survey of National League managers, conducted at midseason 1995, ranked NL players with the best tools:

BEST HITTER
1. Tony Gwynn, Padres
2. Barry Bonds, Giants
3. Mike Piazza, Dodgers

BEST POWER HITTER
1. Matt Williams, Giants
2. Mike Piazza, Dodgers
3. Barry Bonds, Giants

BEST BUNTER
1. Brett Butler, Mets
2. Jay Bell, Pirates
3. Robby Thompson, Giants

BEST HIT-AND-RUN ARTIST
1. Tony Gwynn, Padres
2. Craig Biggio, Astros
3. Jay Bell, Pirates

BEST BASERUNNER
1. Barry Larkin, Reds
2. Marquis Grissom, Braves
3. Jeff Bagwell, Astros

FASTEST BASERUNNER
1. Deion Sanders, Reds
2. Marquis Grissom, Braves
3. Chuck Carr, Marlins

BEST PITCHER
1. Greg Maddux, Braves
2. Hideo Nomo, Dodgers
3. Pedro Martinez, Expos

BEST FASTBALL
1. Mark Wohlers, Braves
2. Pedro Martinez, Expos
3. Bret Saberhagen, Mets

BEST CURVEBALL
1. Darryl Kile, Astros
2. Doug Drabek, Astros
3. John Smoltz, Braves

BEST SLIDER
1. John Smoltz, Braves
2. Jose Rijo, Reds
3. Greg Maddux, Braves

BEST CHANGEUP
1. Tom Glavine, Braves
2. Greg Maddux, Braves
3. Ramon Martinez, Dodgers

BEST CONTROL
1. Greg Maddux, Braves
2. Bret Saberhagen, Mets
3. John Burkett, Marlins

BEST PICKOFF MOVE
1. Jose Rijo, Reds
2. Terry Mulholland, Giants
3. Armando Reynoso, Rockies

BEST RELIEVER
1. Heathcliff Slocumb, Phillies
2. Randy Myers, Cubs
3. Rod Beck, Giants

BEST DEFENSIVE C
1. Tom Pagnozzi, Cardinals
2. Kirt Manwaring, Giants
3. Charles Johnson, Marlins

BEST DEFENSIVE 1B
1. Mark Grace, Cubs
2. Jeff Bagwell, Astros
3. Andres Galarraga, Rockies

BEST DEFENSIVE 2B
1. Mark Lemke, Braves
2. Craig Biggio, Astros
3. Rey Sanchez, Cubs

BEST DEFENSIVE 3B
1. Matt Williams, Giants
2. Ken Caminiti, Padres
3. Charlie Hayes, Phillies

BEST DEFENSIVE SS
1. Barry Larkin, Reds
2. Jay Bell, Pirates
3. Ozzie Smith, Cardinals

BEST INFIELD ARM
1. Shawon Dunston, Cubs
2. Ken Caminiti, Padres
3. Matt Williams, Giants

BEST DEFENSIVE OF
1. Marquis Grissom, Braves
2. Barry Bonds, Giants
3. Raul Mondesi, Dodgers

BEST OUTFIELD ARM
1. Raul Mondesi, Dodgers
2. Larry Walker, Rockies
3. Sammy Sosa, Cubs

MOST EXCITING PLAYER
1. Barry Bonds, Giants
2. Deion Sanders, Reds
3. Raul Mondesi, Dodgers

BEST MANAGER
1. Jim Leyland, Pirates
2. Felipe Alou, Expos
3. Jim Fregosi, Phillies

NATIONAL LEAGUE
1995 BATTING, PITCHING STATISTICS

CLUB BATTING

	AVG	G	AB	R	H	2B	3B	HR	BB	SO	SB
Colorado	.282	144	4994	785	1406	259	43	200	484	943	125
Houston	.275	144	5097	747	1403	260	22	109	566	992	176
San Diego	.272	144	4950	668	1345	231	20	116	447	872	124
Cincinnati	.270	144	4903	747	1326	277	35	161	519	946	190
New York	.267	144	4958	657	1323	218	34	125	446	994	58
Chicago	.265	144	4963	693	1315	267	39	158	440	953	105
Los Angeles	.264	144	4942	634	1303	191	31	140	468	1023	127
Philadelphia	.262	144	4950	615	1296	263	30	94	497	884	72
Florida	.262	143	4886	673	1278	214	29	144	517	916	131
Pittsburgh	.259	144	4937	629	1281	245	27	125	456	972	84
Montreal	.259	144	4905	621	1268	265	24	118	400	901	120
San Francisco	.253	145	4971	652	1256	229	33	152	472	1060	138
Atlanta	.250	144	4814	645	1202	210	27	168	520	933	73
St. Louis	.247	144	4779	563	1182	238	24	107	436	920	79

CLUB PITCHING

	ERA	G	CG	SHO	SV	IP	H	R	ER	BB	SO
Atlanta	3.44	144	18	11	34	1293	1184	540	494	436	1087
Los Angeles	3.67	144	16	11	37	1295	1188	609	528	462	1060
New York	3.87	144	9	9	36	1291	1296	618	556	401	901
Cincinnati	4.03	144	8	10	38	1289	1270	623	578	424	903
Houston	4.06	144	6	8	32	1320	1357	674	596	460	1056
St. Louis	4.10	144	4	6	38	1266	1290	658	576	445	842
Montreal	4.11	144	7	9	42	1284	1286	638	586	416	950
Chicago	4.13	144	6	12	45	1301	1313	671	597	518	926
San Diego	4.15	144	6	10	35	1285	1242	672	592	512	1047
Philadelphia	4.20	144	8	8	41	1290	1241	658	603	538	980
Florida	4.27	143	12	7	29	1286	1299	673	611	562	994
Pittsburgh	4.71	144	11	7	29	1275	1407	736	667	477	871
San Francisco	4.86	145	12	5	34	1294	1368	776	699	505	801
Colorado	4.97	144	1	1	43	1288	1443	783	711	512	891

CLUB FIELDING

	PCT	PO	A	E	DP		PCT	PO	A	E	DP
Cincinnati	.986	3868	1507	79	140	St. Louis	.980	3797	1622	113	156
Philadelphia	.982	3871	1520	97	139	New York	.979	3873	1603	115	125
Atlanta	.982	3875	1569	100	113	Chicago	.979	3903	1563	115	115
Colorado	.981	3865	1665	107	146	Florida	.979	3858	1467	115	143
San Francisco	.980	3881	1548	108	142	Houston	.979	3961	1639	121	120
San Diego	.980	3854	1538	108	130	Pittsburgh	.978	3826	1589	122	138
Montreal	.980	3851	1557	109	119	Los Angeles	.976	3885	1491	130	120

INDIVIDUAL BATTING LEADERS
(Minimum 446 Plate Appearances)

	AVG	G	AB	R	H	2B	3B	HR	RBI	BB	SO	SB
Gwynn, Tony, San Diego	.368	135	535	82	197	33	1	9	90	35	15	17
Piazza, Mike, LA	.346	112	434	82	150	17	0	32	93	39	80	1
Bichette, Dante, Colorado	.340	139	579	102	197	38	2	40	128	22	96	13
Bell, Derek, Houston	.334	112	452	63	151	21	2	8	86	33	71	27
Grace, Mark, Chicago	.326	143	552	97	180	51	3	16	92	65	46	6
Larkin, Barry, Cincinnati	.319	131	496	98	158	29	6	15	66	61	49	51
Castilla, Vinny, Colorado	.309	139	527	82	163	34	2	32	90	30	87	2
Segui, David, NY-Mtl	.309	130	456	68	141	25	4	12	68	40	47	2
Jefferies, Gregg, Phil	.306	114	480	69	147	31	2	11	56	35	26	9
Sanders, Reggie, Cinc.	.306	133	484	91	148	36	6	28	99	69	122	36

INDIVIDUAL PITCHING LEADERS
(Minimum 144 Innings)

	W	L	ERA	G	GS	CG	SV	IP	H	R	ER	BB	SO
Maddux, Greg, Atlanta	19	2	1.63	28	28	10	0	210	147	39	38	23	181
Nomo, Hideo, Los Angeles	13	6	2.54	28	28	4	0	191	124	63	54	78	236
Ashby, Andy, San Diego	12	10	2.94	31	31	2	0	193	180	79	63	62	150
Valdes, Ismael, LA	13	11	3.05	33	27	6	1	198	168	76	67	51	150
Glavine, Tom, Atlanta	16	7	3.08	29	29	3	0	199	182	76	68	66	127
Hamilton, Joey, San Diego	6	9	3.08	31	30	2	0	204	189	89	70	56	123
Smoltz, John, Atlanta	12	7	3.18	29	29	2	0	193	166	76	68	72	193
Castillo, Frank, Chicago	11	10	3.21	29	29	2	0	188	179	75	67	52	135
Schourek, Pete, Cinc.	18	7	3.22	29	29	2	0	190	158	72	68	45	160
Navarro, Jaime, Chicago	14	6	3.28	29	29	1	0	200	194	79	73	56	128

AWARD WINNERS

Selected by Baseball Writers Association of America

MVP

Player, Team	1st	2nd	3rd	Total
Barry Larkin, Cinc.	11	5	7	281
Dante Bichette, Colo	6	6	6	251
Greg Maddux, Atlanta	7	8	5	249
Mike Piazza, L.A.	3	7	6	214
Eric Karros, L.A.	0	2	3	135
Reggie Sanders, Cinc.	0	0	0	120
Larry Walker, Colo.	0	0	1	88
Sammy Sosa, Chicago	0	0	0	81
Tony Gwynn, San Diego	0	0	0	72
Craig Biggio, Houston	0	0	0	58
Ron Gant, Cincinnati	1	0	0	31
Barry Bonds, S.F.	0	0	0	21
Mark Grace, Chicago	0	0	0	14
Derek Bell, Houston	0	0	0	12
Jeff Bagwell, Houston	0	0	0	5
Charlie Hayes, Phil.	0	0	0	4
Andres Galarraga, Colo.	0	0	0	4
Chipper Jones, Atlanta	0	0	0	3
Vinny Castilla, Colo.	0	0	0	2
Fred McGriff, Atlanta	0	0	0	2
Pete Schourek, Cinc.	0	0	0	2
Jeff Conine, Florida	0	0	0	1
Tom Henke, St. Louis	0	0	0	1

Cy Young Award

Player, Team	1st	2nd	3rd	Total
Greg Maddux, Atlanta	28	0	0	140
Pete Schourek, Cinc.	0	16	7	55
Tom Glavine, Atlanta	0	6	12	30
Hideo Nomo, L.A.	0	5	4	19
Ramon Martinez, L.A.	0	1	5	8

Rookie of the Year

Player, Team	1st	2nd	3rd	Total
Hideo Nomo, L.A.	18	9	1	118
Chipper Jones, Atlanta	10	18	0	104
Quilvio Veras, Florida	0	1	11	14
Jason Isringhausen, N.Y.	0	0	4	4
John Mabry, St. Louis	0	0	4	4
Carlos Perez, Montreal	0	0	4	4
Chad Fonville, L.A.	0	0	1	1
Brian Hunter, Houston	0	0	1	1
Charles Johnson, Fla.	0	0	1	1
Ismael Valdes, L.A.	0	0	1	1

Manager of the Year

Manager, Team	1st	2nd	3rd	Total
Don Baylor, Colorado	19	9	0	122
Davey Johnson, Cin.	8	15	4	89
Bobby Cox, Atlanta	1	1	12	20
Terry Collins, Houston	0	2	5	11
Jim Riggleman, Chicago	0	1	3	6
Dallas Green, New York	0	0	3	3
Bruce Bochy, San Diego	0	0	1	1

NOTE: MVP balloting based on 14 points for first-place vote, nine for second, eight for third, etc. Cy Young Award, Rookie of the Year and Manager of the Year balloting based on five points for first-place vote, three for second and one for third.

NATIONAL LEAGUE
DIVISION SERIES
ATLANTA vs. COLORADO
BOX SCORES

Game One: October 3
Braves 5, Rockies 4

ATLANTA	ab	r	h	bi	bb	so	COLORADO	ab	r	h	bi	bb	so
Grissom cf	5	1	2	1	0	0	Young 2b	4	0	2	0	1	0
Lemke 2b	5	0	1	0	0	1	Girardi c	3	0	1	0	0	0
Jones 3b	5	2	2	2	0	0	Vander Wal ph	1	0	0	0	0	0
McGriff 1b	5	0	1	0	0	1	Munoz p	0	0	0	0	0	0
Justice rf	2	1	1	0	2	0	Holmes p	0	0	0	0	0	0
Klesko lf	4	1	3	0	0	1	Kingery cf	1	0	1	0	0	0
McMichael p	0	0	0	0	0	0	Bichette lf	4	1	2	0	1	0
Pena p	0	0	0	0	0	0	Walker rf	3	1	1	0	2	0
Wohlers p	0	0	0	0	0	0	Galarraga 1b	5	1	2	0	0	1
O'Brien c	2	0	0	0	0	1	Burks cf	3	0	2	2	0	0
Polonia ph	1	0	0	1	0	0	Leskanic p	0	0	0	0	0	0
Lopez c	1	0	1	0	0	0	Painter ph	1	0	0	0	0	1
Blauser ss	2	0	0	0	1	1	Castilla 3b	3	1	2	2	0	0
Smith ph	1	0	1	1	0	0	Hubbard pr	0	0	0	0	0	0
Belliard ss	0	0	0	0	0	0	Owens c	1	0	0	0	0	1
Maddux p	3	0	0	0	0	1	Weiss ss	2	0	0	0	1	0
Devereaux ph-lf	1	0	0	0	0	0	Ritz p	2	0	0	0	0	0
							Reed p	0	0	0	0	0	0
							Ruffin p	0	0	0	0	0	0
							Bates ph-3b	1	0	0	0	0	0
Totals	37	5	12	5	3	7	**Totals**	34	4	13	4	5	3

Atlanta	001 002 011—5
Colorado	000 300 010—4

E—Justice (1), Ritz (1), Castilla (1), Burks (1), Girardi (1). **DP**—Atlanta 4, Colorado 2. **LOB**—Atlanta 8, Colorado 11. **2B**—Grissom (1), Young (1), Castilla (1), Burks (1). **HR**—Grissom (1), Jones 2 (2), Castilla (1). **SB**—Polonia (1). **S**—Bates. **SF**—Burks.

Atlanta	ip	h	r	er	bb	so	Colorado	ip	h	r	er	bb	so
Maddux	7	9	3	3	2	0	Ritz	5⅓	7	3	2	2	4
McMichael	⅓	1	1	1	1	0	Reed	1	1	0	0	1	1
Pena W	⅔	1	0	0	1	1	Ruffin	⅔	0	0	0	0	0
Wohlers S	1	2	0	0	1	2	Munoz	⅔	1	1	1	0	1
							Holmes	⅓	2	0	0	0	0
							Leskanic L	1	1	1	1	0	1

HBP—Weiss (by Maddux).
Umpires: HP—McSherry; **1B**—Layne; **2B**—West; **3B**—Tata; **LF**—Wendelstedt; **RF**—Reliford.
T—3:19. **A**—50,040.

Game Two: October 4
Braves 7, Rockies 4

ATLANTA	ab	r	h	bi	bb	so	COLORADO	ab	r	h	bi	bb	so
Grissom cf	6	2	2	2	0	2	Young 2b	5	0	1	0	0	1
Lemke 2b	4	1	1	0	1	0	Burks cf	3	1	0	0	0	1
Jones 3b	5	1	3	0	0	0	Kingery cf	2	0	0	0	0	0
McGriff 1b	4	1	1	1	1	2	Bichette lf	4	2	3	0	0	0
Justice rf	4	0	1	0	1	0	Walker rf	4	1	1	3	0	1
Lopez c	4	0	1	1	0	2	Galarraga 1b	4	0	1	1	0	1
Klesko lf	3	0	0	0	0	1	Castilla 3b	3	0	0	0	0	0
Devereaux ph-lf	2	1	1	0	0	0	Girardi c	4	0	0	0	0	0
Blauser ss	2	0	0	0	0	1	Weiss ss	3	0	1	0	1	1
Polonia ph	1	0	0	0	0	1	Painter p	1	0	0	0	0	0
Avery p	0	0	0	0	0	0	Hubbard ph	1	0	0	0	0	0
Pena p	0	0	0	0	0	0	Reed p	0	0	0	0	0	0
Mordecai ph	1	1	1	1	0	0	Ruffin p	0	0	0	0	0	0
Wohlers p	0	0	0	0	0	0	Bates ph	1	0	1	0	0	0
Glavine p	3	0	1	0	0	1	Leskanic p	0	0	0	0	0	0
Smith ph	1	0	1	0	0	0	Munoz p	0	0	0	0	0	0
Belliard ss	1	0	0	0	0	0	Holmes p	0	0	0	0	0	0
							Vander Wal ph	1	0	0	0	0	1
Totals	41	7	13	5	3	10	**Totals**	36	4	8	4	1	6

Atlanta	101 100 004—7
Colorado	000 003 010—4

E—Blauser (1), Young 2 (2). **LOB**—Atlanta 12, Colorado 7. **2B**—Smith (1), Jones (1), Bichette 2 (2), Galarraga (1). **HR**—Grissom 2 (3), Walker (1). **SF**—Lopez.

Atlanta	ip	h	r	er	bb	so	Colorado	ip	h	r	er	bb	so
Glavine	7	5	3	2	1	3	Painter	5	5	3	3	2	4
Avery	⅔	1	1	1	0	1	Reed	1⅓	1	0	0	0	1
Pena W	⅓	1	0	0	0	0	Ruffin	⅔	2	0	0	1	1
Wohlers S	1	1	0	0	0	2	Leskanic	1	2	1	1	0	2
							Munoz L	⅓	1	1	1	0	0
							Holmes	⅔	2	2	0	0	2

Leskanic pitched to 1 batter in 9th.
HBP—Blauser (by Reed), Castilla (by Pena).
Umpires: HP—Layne; **1B**—West; **2B**—Tata; **3B**—Wendelstedt; **LF**—Reliford; **RF**—McSherry.
T—3:08. **A**—50,063.

Game Three: October 6
Rockies 7, Braves 5

COLORADO	ab	r	h	bi	bb	so	ATLANTA	ab	r	h	bi	bb	so
Young 2b	3	2	1	2	1	0	Grissom cf	5	0	2	0	0	1
Reed p	0	0	0	0	0	0	Lemke 2b	5	0	0	0	0	1
Munoz p	0	0	0	0	0	0	Jones 3b	5	0	1	0	0	1
Leskanic p	0	0	0	0	0	0	McGriff 1b	4	1	1	0	1	0
Ruffin p	0	0	0	0	0	0	Justice rf	3	1	0	0	1	0
Holmes p	0	0	0	0	0	0	Klesko lf	4	3	3	1	0	1
Vander Wal ph	1	0	0	0	0	0	Lopez c	4	0	2	2	0	1
Thompson p	0	0	0	0	0	0	Blauser ss	2	0	0	0	0	1
Kingery cf	4	0	0	0	0	1	Belliard ss	0	0	0	0	0	0
Bichette lf	5	2	3	0	0	2	Smith ph	0	0	0	0	0	0
Walker rf	3	1	1	0	1	1	Mordecai ph-ss	2	0	1	1	0	0
Galarraga 1b	5	0	1	1	0	3	Smoltz p	2	0	0	0	0	0
Castilla 3b	5	1	2	3	0	1	Clontz p	0	0	0	0	0	0
Girardi c	5	0	0	0	0	1	Devereaux ph	1	0	0	0	0	0
Weiss ss	3	1	1	0	1	1	Borbon p	0	0	0	0	0	0
Swift p	3	0	0	0	0	2	McMichael p	0	0	0	0	0	0
Bates 2b	1	0	0	0	0	0	Polonia ph	1	0	1	1	0	0
							Wohlers p	0	0	0	0	0	0
							Mercker p	0	0	0	0	0	0
Totals	38	7	9	6	3	12	**Totals**	38	5	11	5	2	6

Colorado	102 002 000 2—7
Atlanta	000 300 101 0—5

DP—Colorado 3. **LOB**—Colorado 6, Atlanta 5. **2B**—Bichette (3), Klesko (1), Mordecai (1). **HR**—Young (1), Castilla (2). **SB**—Walker (1), Weiss (1), Grissom (1). **CS**—Grissom (1), Lopez (1). **S**—Kingery.

Colorado	ip	h	r	er	bb	so	Atlanta	ip	h	r	er	bb	so
Swift	6	7	4	4	2	3	Smoltz	5⅔	5	5	5	1	6
Reed	⅓	0	0	0	0	1	Clontz	1⅓	0	0	0	0	2
Munoz	0	1	0	0	0	0	Borbon	1	1	0	0	0	3
Leskanic	1	0	0	0	0	1	McMichael	1	0	0	0	1	1
Ruffin	1	1	1	1	0	1	Wohlers L	⅔	3	2	2	1	0
Holmes W	⅔	2	0	0	0	0	Mercker	⅓	0	0	0	0	0
Thompson S	1	0	0	0	0	0							

Swift pitched to 1 batter in 7th. Munoz pitched to 1 batter in 7th.
HBP—Walker (by Smoltz). **WP**—Smoltz.
Umpires: HP—Gregg; **1B**—Pulli; **2B**—Froemming; **3B**—Darling; **LF**—Montague; **RF**—Davidson.
T—3:16. **A**—51,300.

Game Four: October 7
Braves 10, Rockies 4

COLORADO	ab	r	h	bi	bb	so	ATLANTA	ab	r	h	bi	bb	so
Young 2b	4	1	3	0	0	1	Grissom cf	5	2	5	1	0	0
Kingery cf	3	1	1	0	0	0	Lemke 2b	5	2	2	1	0	1
Bichette lf	4	1	2	3	0	1	Jones 3b	3	1	1	2	2	1
Walker rf	4	0	0	0	0	2	McGriff 1b	5	2	3	5	0	0
Galarraga 1b	4	0	1	0	0	1	Justice rf	4	0	1	0	1	1
Castilla 3b	4	1	3	1	0	0	Klesko lf	4	1	1	0	0	0
Girardi c	4	0	1	0	0	1	Devereaux lf	1	0	0	0	0	0
Weiss ss	4	0	0	0	0	1	O'Brien c	3	0	1	0	1	0
Saberhagen p	1	0	0	0	0	0	Belliard ss	4	1	0	0	0	1
Hubbard ph	1	0	0	0	0	0	Maddux p	3	1	1	0	0	0
Ritz p	0	0	0	0	0	0	Smith ph	1	0	0	0	0	0
Munoz p	0	0	0	0	0	0	Pena p	0	0	0	0	0	0
Bates ph	1	0	0	0	0	0							
Reynoso p	0	0	0	0	0	0							
Ruffin p	0	0	0	0	0	0							
Vander Wal ph	1	0	0	0	0	1							
Totals	35	4	11	4	0	8	**Totals**	38	10	15	9	4	4

Colorado	003 001 000—4
Atlanta	004 213 00x—10

E—Young (3). **DP**—Colorado 1, Atlanta 1. **LOB**—Colorado 5, Atlanta 8. **2B**—Grissom (2), Lemke (1), Jones (2). **HR**—McGriff 2 (2), Bichette (1), Castilla (3). **SB**—Young (1), Grissom (2). **S**—Kingery.

Colorado	ip	h	r	er	bb	so	Atlanta	ip	h	r	er	bb	so
Saberhagen L	4	7	6	5	1	3	Maddux W	7	10	4	4	0	7
Ritz	1⅔	5	4	4	1	1	Pena	2	1	0	0	0	1
Munoz	⅓	1	0	0	1	0							
Reynoso	1	2	0	0	0	0							
Ruffin	1	0	0	0	1	0							

Umpires: HP—Pulli; **1B**—Froemming; **2B**—Darling; **3B**—Montague; **LF**—Davidson; **RF**—Gregg.
T—2:38. **A**—50,027.

COMPOSITE BOX

ATLANTA

Player Pos.	AVG	G	AB	R	H	2B	3B	HR	RBI	BB	SO	SB
Dwight Smith, ph	.667	4	3	0	2	1	0	0	1	0	0	0
Mike Mordecai, ph	.667	2	3	1	2	1	0	0	2	0	0	0
Marquis Grissom, cf	.524	4	21	5	11	2	0	3	4	0	3	2
Ryan Klesko, lf	.467	4	15	5	7	1	0	0	1	0	3	0
Javier Lopez, c	.444	3	9	0	4	0	0	0	3	0	3	0
Chipper Jones, 3b	.389	4	18	4	7	2	0	2	4	2	2	0
Fred McGriff, 1b	.333	4	18	4	6	0	0	2	6	2	3	0
Tom Glavine, p	.333	1	3	0	1	0	0	0	0	0	1	0
Luis Polonia, ph	.333	3	3	0	1	0	0	0	2	0	1	1
David Justice, rf	.231	4	13	2	3	0	0	0	5	2	0	
Mark Lemke, 2b	.211	4	19	3	4	1	0	0	1	1	3	0
Mike Devereaux, ph-lf	.200	4	5	1	1	0	0	0	0	0	0	0
Charlie O'Brien, c	.200	2	5	0	1	0	0	0	0	1	1	0
Greg Maddux, p	.167	2	6	1	1	0	0	0	0	0	1	0
Jeff Blauser, ss	.000	3	6	0	0	0	0	0	0	1	3	0
Rafael Belliard, ss	.000	4	5	1	0	0	0	0	0	0	1	0
John Smoltz, p	.000	1	2	0	0	0	0	0	0	0	0	0
Totals	**.331**	**4**	**154**	**27**	**51**	**8**	**0**	**7**	**24**	**12**	**27**	**3**

Pitcher	W	L	ERA	G	GS	SV	IP	H	R	ER	BB	SO
Brad Clontz	0	0	0.00	1	0	0	1	0	0	0	0	2
Alejandro Pena	2	0	0.00	3	0	0	3	3	0	0	1	2
Pedro Borbon	0	0	0.00	1	0	0	1	1	0	0	0	3
Kent Mercker	0	0	0.00	1	0	0	0	0	0	0	0	0
Tom Glavine	0	0	2.57	1	1	0	7	5	3	2	1	3
Greg Maddux	1	0	4.50	2	2	0	14	19	7	7	2	7
Mark Wohlers	0	1	6.75	3	0	2	3	6	2	2	2	4
Greg McMichael	0	0	6.75	3	0	0	1	1	1	1	2	1
John Smoltz	0	0	7.94	1	1	0	6	5	5	5	1	6
Steve Avery	0	0	13.50	1	0	0	1	1	1	1	0	1
Totals	**3**	**1**	**4.38**	**4**	**4**	**2**	**37**	**41**	**19**	**18**	**9**	**29**

COLORADO

Player Pos.	AVG	G	AB	R	H	2B	3B	HR	RBI	BB	SO	SB
Dante Bichette, lf	.588	4	17	6	10	3	0	1	3	1	3	0
Vinny Castilla, 3b	.467	4	15	3	7	1	0	3	6	0	1	0
Eric Young, 2b	.438	4	16	3	7	1	0	1	2	2	2	1
Ellis Burks, cf	.333	2	6	1	2	1	0	0	2	0	1	0
Andres Galarraga, 1b	.278	4	18	1	5	1	0	0	2	0	6	0
Jason Bates, ph-3b	.250	4	4	0	1	0	0	0	0	0	0	0
Larry Walker, rf	.214	4	14	3	3	0	0	1	3	3	4	1
Mike Kingery, cf	.200	4	10	1	2	0	0	0	0	0	1	0
Walt Weiss, ss	.167	4	12	1	2	0	0	0	0	3	2	1
Joe Girardi, c	.125	4	16	0	2	0	0	0	0	2	0	0
John Vander Wal, ph	.000	4	4	0	0	0	0	0	0	0	2	0
Bill Swift, p	.000	1	3	0	0	0	0	0	0	0	1	0
Lance Painter, p-ph	.000	2	2	0	0	0	0	0	0	0	1	0
Kevin Ritz, p	.000	2	2	0	0	0	0	0	0	0	0	0
Trent Hubbard, pr-ph	.000	3	2	0	0	0	0	0	0	0	0	0
Jayhawk Owens, ss	.000	1	1	0	0	0	0	0	0	0	1	0
Bret Saberhagen, p	.000	1	1	0	0	0	0	0	0	0	1	0
Totals	**.287**	**4**	**143**	**19**	**41**	**7**	**0**	**6**	**18**	**9**	**29**	**3**

Pitcher	W	L	ERA	G	GS	SV	IP	H	R	ER	BB	SO
Steve Reed	0	0	0.00	3	0	0	3	2	0	0	1	3
Darren Holmes	1	0	0.00	3	0	0	2	6	2	0	0	2
Mark Thompson	0	0	0.00	1	0	1	1	0	0	0	0	0
Armando Reynoso	0	0	0.00	1	0	0	1	2	0	0	0	0
Bruce Ruffin	0	0	2.70	4	0	0	3	3	1	1	2	2
Lance Painter	0	0	5.40	1	0	0	5	5	3	3	2	4
Bill Swift	0	0	6.00	1	1	0	6	7	4	4	2	3
Curtis Leskanic	0	1	6.00	3	0	0	3	3	2	2	0	4
Kevin Ritz	0	0	7.71	2	1	0	7	12	7	6	3	5
Bret Saberhagen	0	1	11.25	1	1	0	4	7	6	5	1	3
Mike Munoz	0	1	13.50	4	0	0	1	4	2	1	1	1
Totals	**1**	**3**	**5.75**	**4**	**4**	**1**	**36**	**51**	**27**	**23**	**12**	**27**

DP—Atlanta 5, Colorado 6. LOB—Atlanta 33, Colorado 29.
E—Justice, Ritz, Castilla, Burks, Girardi, Blauser, E. Young 3.
CS—Grissom, Lopez. S—Kingery 2, Bates. SF—Burks, Lopez.
HBP—Weiss (by Maddux), Castilla (by Pena), Blauser (by Reed), Walker (by Smoltz). Umpires—Gary Darling, Bob Davidson, Bruce Froemming, Eric Gregg, Jerry Layne, John McSherry, Ed Montague, Frank Pulli, Charlie Reliford, Terry Tata, Harry Wendelstedt, Joe West.

CINCINNATI vs. LOS ANGELES
BOX SCORES

Game One: October 3
Reds 7, Dodgers 2

CINCINNATI	ab	r	h	bi	bb	so	L.A.	ab	r	h	bi	bb	so
Howard cf	3	0	1	0	0	1	Butler cf	5	0	1	1	0	1
Walton ph-cf-lf	2	0	0	0	0	1	Fonville ss	4	0	1	0	0	1
Larkin ss	4	1	2	0	1	1	Piazza c	4	1	2	1	0	0
Gant lf	5	1	1	0	0	1	Karros 1b	4	0	1	0	0	0
D. Lewis cf	0	0	0	0	0	0	Wallach 3b	3	0	0	1	1	1
Sanders rf	5	1	1	0	0	2	Mondesi rf	4	0	0	0	0	2
Morris 1b	4	2	3	2	1	0	DeShields 2b	3	1	2	0	1	0
Santiago c	3	1	3	1	1	1	Kelly lf	4	0	1	0	0	0
Boone 2b	4	1	1	0	0	2	Martinez p	1	0	0	0	0	0
Branson 3b	3	0	2	2	1	0	Cummings p	0	0	0	0	0	0
Schourek p	2	0	0	0	0	1	Ashley ph	0	0	0	1	0	0
Duncan ph	1	0	0	0	0	0	Astacio p	0	0	0	0	0	0
Jackson p	0	0	0	0	0	0	Webster ph	1	0	0	0	0	0
Brantley p	0	0	0	0	0	0	Guthrie p	0	0	0	0	0	0
							Osuna p	0	0	0	0	0	0
							Hansen ph	1	0	0	0	0	0
Totals	**36**	**7**	**12**	**7**	**4**	**10**	**Totals**	**34**	**2**	**8**	**2**	**3**	**5**

Cincinnati	400	030	000—7
Los Angeles	000	011	000—2

DP—Cincinnati 1, Los Angeles 1. LOB—Cincinnati 8, Los Angeles 8. 2B—Morris (1), Howard (1), Sanders (1), Boone (1), Branson (1). HR—Santiago (1), Piazza (1). SB—Larkin 2 (2). S—Schourek. SF—Santiago.

Cincinnati	ip	h	r	er	bb	so	Los Angeles	ip	h	r	er	bb	so
Schourek W	7	5	2	2	3	5	Martinez L	4⅓	10	7	7	2	3
Jackson	1	2	0	0	0	0	Cummings	⅔	1	0	0	0	1
Brantley	1	1	0	0	0	0	Astacio	2	0	0	0	0	4
							Guthrie	1	0	0	0	1	1
							Osuna	1	1	0	0	1	1

Umpires: HP—Montague; 1B—Davidson; 2B—Gregg; 3B—Pulli; LF—Froemming; RF—Darling.
T—3:15. A—44,199.

Game Two: October 4
Reds 5, Dodgers 4

CINCINNATI	ab	r	h	bi	bb	so	L.A.	ab	r	h	bi	bb	so
Howard cf	4	0	0	0	0	0	Butler cf	5	1	3	0	0	0
D. Lewis cf	1	0	0	0	0	0	Fonville ss	4	1	4	0	0	0
Larkin ss	4	0	1	1	0	1	Piazza c	5	0	0	0	0	1
Gant lf	4	1	0	0	0	1	Karros 1b	4	2	3	4	1	0
Jackson p	0	0	0	0	0	0	Wallach 3b	5	0	1	0	0	1
Brantley p	0	0	0	0	0	0	DeShields 2b	5	0	0	0	0	0
Sanders rf	3	2	1	2	1	2	Mondesi rf	3	0	1	0	0	0
Morris 1b	3	1	1	1	0	0	Hollandsworth rf	1	0	0	0	0	0
Santiago c	3	0	1	1	1	1	Kelly lf	4	0	1	0	0	0
Boone 2b	3	0	0	0	0	1	Valdes p	3	0	0	0	0	0
Burba p	0	0	0	0	0	0	Osuna p	0	0	0	0	0	0
Walton lf	0	0	0	1	1	0	Hansen ph	1	0	1	0	0	0
Branson 3b	3	0	0	0	0	1	Offerman pr	0	0	0	0	0	0
M. Lewis ph-3b	1	0	1	0	0	0	Tapani p	0	0	0	0	0	0
Smiley p	2	0	0	0	0	1	Guthrie p	0	0	0	0	0	0
Duncan 2b	2	1	2	0	0	0	Astacio p	0	0	0	0	0	0
Totals	**33**	**5**	**6**	**5**	**4**	**7**	**Totals**	**40**	**4**	**14**	**4**	**1**	**2**

Cincinnati	000	200	012—5
Los Angeles	100	100	002—4

E—Fonville (1), Osuna (1). DP—Los Angeles 1. LOB—Cincinnati 5, Los Angeles 11. 2B—Karros (1). HR—Sanders (1), Karros 2 (2). SB—Duncan (1), Sanders 2 (2), Morris (1). S—Fonville.

Cincinnati	ip	h	r	er	bb	so	Los Angeles	ip	h	r	er	bb	so
Smiley	6	9	2	2	0	1	Valdes	7	3	2	0	1	6
Burba W	1	2	0	0	1	0	Osuna L	1	2	1	1	0	0
Jackson	1	1	0	0	0	0	Tapani	⅓	0	2	2	3	1
Brantley S	1	2	2	2	0	1	Guthrie	⅓	0	0	0	0	0
							Astacio	⅓	1	0	0	0	0

Umpires: HP—Davidson; 1B—Gregg; 2B—Pulli; 3B—Froemming; LF—Darling; RF—Montague.
T—3:21. A—46,051.

Game Three: October 6
Reds 10, Dodgers 1

L.A.	ab	r	h	bi	bb	so	CINCINNATI	ab	r	h	bi	bb	so
Butler cf	5	0	0	0	0	2	Howard cf	3	0	0	0	0	1
Fonville ss	4	0	1	0	0	0	D. Lewis ph-cf	2	0	0	0	0	1
Gwynn ph	1	0	0	0	0	1	Larkin ss	5	1	2	0	0	0
Piazza c	5	0	1	0	0	1	Gant lf	4	1	2	2	0	1
Karros 1b	4	1	2	0	0	0	Walton lf	1	0	0	0	0	0
Wallach 3b	4	0	0	0	0	1	Sanders rf	5	0	0	0	0	5

	ab	r	h	bi	bb	so			ab	r	h	bi	bb	so
DeShields 2b	4	0	1	0	0	3	Morris 1b		3	2	1	0	1	1
Mondesi rf	2	0	1	1	0	0	Santiago c		3	1	1	0	1	1
Holl'worth ph-rf	1	0	0	0	0	0	Boone 2b		3	3	2	1	1	0
Kelly lf	3	0	2	0	1	0	Branson 3b		1	0	0	0	1	0
Nomo p	2	0	0	0	0	2	M. Lewis ph-3b		1	2	1	4	1	0
Tapani p	0	0	0	0	0	0	Wells p		3	0	1	0	0	1
Guthrie p	0	0	0	0	0	0	Jackson p		1	0	1	3	0	0
Astacio p	0	0	0	0	0	0	Brantley p		0	0	0	0	0	0
Webster ph	1	0	0	0	0	0								
Cummings p	0	0	0	0	0	0								
Osuna p	0	0	0	0	0	0								
Hansen ph	1	0	1	0	0	0								
Totals	37	1	9	1	1	10	Totals		35	10	11	10	5	11

Los Angeles		000	100	000—		1
Cincinnati		002	104	30x—		10

E—Kelly (1), Sanders (1), M. Lewis (1). LOB—Los Angeles 11, Cincinnati 6. 2B—Piazza (1), Jackson (1). HR—Gant (1), Boone (1), M. Lewis (1). SB—Larkin 2 (4), Boone (1).

L.A.	ip	h	r	er	bb	so	Cincinnati	ip	h	r	er	bb	so
Nomo L	5	7	5	5	2	6	Wells W	6⅓	6	1	0	1	8
Tapani	0	0	1	1	1	0	Jackson	1⅔	1	0	0	0	1
Guthrie	0	2	1	1	0	0	Brantley	1	2	0	0	0	1
Astacio	1	0	0	0	0	1							
Cummings	⅔	2	3	3	2	2							
Osuna	1⅓	0	0	0	0	0							

Nomo pitched to 2 batters in 6th, Tapani pitched to 1 batter in 6th, Guthrie pitched to 2 batters in 6th.
HBP—Mondesi (by Wells). WP—Nomo.
Umpires—HP—West; 1B—Tata; 2B—Wendelstedt; 3B—Reliford; LF—McSherry; RF—Layne.
T—3:27. A—53,276.

COMPOSITE BOX

CINCINNATI

Player Pos.	AVG	G	AB	R	H	2B	3B	HR	RBI	BB	SO	SB
Mike Jackson, p	1.000	3	1	0	1	1	0	0	3	0	0	0
Mariano Duncan, ph-2b	.667	2	3	1	2	0	0	0	1	0	0	1
Hal Morris, 1b	.500	3	10	5	5	1	0	0	2	3	1	1
Marc Lewis, ph-3b	.500	2	2	2	1	0	0	1	5	1	0	0
Barry Larkin, ss	.385	3	13	2	5	0	0	1	1	2	4	
Benito Santiago, c	.333	3	9	2	3	0	0	1	3	2	3	0
David Wells, p	.333	3	3	0	1	0	0	0	0	0	1	0
Bret Boone, 2b	.300	3	10	4	3	1	0	1	1	1	3	1
Jeff Branson, 3b	.286	3	7	0	2	1	0	0	2	2	0	0
Ron Gant, lf	.231	3	13	3	3	0	0	1	2	0	3	0
Reggie Sanders, rf	.154	3	13	3	2	1	0	1	2	2	9	2
Thomas Howard, cf	.100	3	10	0	1	1	0	0	0	2	0	
Darren Lewis, ph-cf	.000	3	3	0	0	0	0	0	0	1	0	
Jerome Walton, ph-cf-lf	.000	3	3	0	0	0	0	0	0	1	1	0
Pete Schourek, p	.000	1	2	0	0	0	0	0	0	0	1	0
John Smiley, p	.000	1	2	0	0	0	0	0	0	1	0	
Totals	.279	3	104	22	29	6	0	5	22	13	28	9

Pitcher	W	L	ERA	G	GS	SV	IP	H	R	ER	BB	SO
David Wells	1	0	0.00	1	1	0	6	6	1	0	1	8
Mike Jackson	0	0	0.00	3	0	0	4	4	0	0	0	1
Dave Burba	1	0	0.00	1	0	0	1	2	0	0	1	0
Pete Schourek	1	0	2.57	1	1	0	7	5	2	2	3	5
John Smiley	0	0	3.00	1	1	0	6	9	2	2	0	1
John Brantley	0	0	6.00	3	0	1	3	5	2	2	0	2
Totals	3	0	2.00	3	3	1	27	31	7	6	5	17

LOS ANGELES

Player Pos.	AVG	G	AB	R	H	2B	3B	HR	RBI	BB	SO	SB
Dave Hansen ph	.667	3	3	0	2	0	0	0	0	0	0	0
Chad Fonville ss	.500	3	12	1	6	0	0	0	0	0	0	0
Eric Karros 1b	.500	3	12	3	6	1	0	2	4	1	0	0
Roberto Kelly lf	.364	3	11	0	4	0	0	0	0	1	0	0
Brett Butler cf	.267	3	15	1	4	0	0	1	0	3	0	
Delino DeShields 2b	.250	3	12	1	3	0	0	0	0	3	0	
Mike Piazza c	.214	3	14	1	3	1	0	1	1	2	0	
Raul Mondesi rf	.222	3	9	2	2	0	0	1	2	0		
Tim Wallach 3b	.083	3	12	0	1	0	0	0	0	1	3	0
Ismael Valdes p	.000	1	3	0	0	0	0	0	0	0	0	
Todd Hollandsworth rf	.000	2	2	0	0	0	0	0	0	0	0	
Lenny Webster ph	.000	2	2	0	0	0	0	0	0	1	0	
Hideo Nomo p	.000	1	2	0	0	0	0	0	0	2	0	
Ramon Martinez p	.000	1	1	0	0	0	0	0	0	0	0	
Chris Gwynn p	.000	1	1	0	0	0	0	0	0	1	0	
Billy Ashley, ph	.000	1	0	0	0	0	0	0	0	1	0	0
Totals	.279	3	111	7	31	2	0	3	7	5	17	0

Pitcher	W	L	ERA	G	GS	SV	IP	H	R	ER	BB	SO
Ismael Valdes	0	0	0.00	1	1	0	7	3	2	0	1	6
Pedro Astacio	0	0	0.00	3	0	0	3	1	0	0	5	
Antonio Osuna	0	1	2.70	3	0	0	3	3	1	1	1	3
Mark Guthrie	0	0	6.75	3	0	0	1	2	1	1	1	1
Hideo Nomo	0	1	9.00	1	1	0	5	7	5	2	2	6
Ramon Martinez	0	1	14.54	1	1	0	4	10	7	7	2	3
John Cummings	0	0	20.25	2	0	0	1	3	3	3	2	3
Kevin Tapani	0	0	81.00	2	0	0	0	3	3	4	1	
Totals	0	3	6.92	3	3	0	26	29	22	20	13	28

DP—Cincinnati 1, Los Angeles 2. LOB—Cincinnati 19, Los Angeles 30.
E—Kelly, Sanders, M. Lewis. S—Schourek, Fonville. SF—Santiago.
HBP—Mondesi (by Wells).
Umpires—Gary Darling, Bob Davidson, Bruce Froemming, Eric Gregg, Jerry Layne, John McSherry, Ed Montague, Frank Pulli, Charlie Reliford, Terry Tata, Harry Wendelstedt, Joe West.

CHAMPIONSHIP SERIES

ATLANTA vs. CINCINNATI

BOX SCORES

Game One: October 10
Braves 2, Reds 1

ATLANTA	ab	r	h	bi	bb	so	CINCINNATI	ab	r	h	bi	bb	so
Grissom cf	5	0	1	0	0	3	Walton cf-lf	4	0	0	0	0	0
Lemke 2b	5	0	0	0	0	0	Howard ph	1	0	1	0	0	0
Jones 3b	5	1	2	0	0	0	Larkin ss	5	1	2	0	0	0
McGriff 1b	4	1	1	0	1	0	Gant lf	4	0	2	1	0	2
Justice rf	4	0	1	1	0	1	D. Lewis cf	0	0	0	0	0	0
Polonia pr-lf	0	0	0	0	0	0	Harris ph	0	0	0	0	0	0
Lopez c	5	0	1	0	0	0	Duncan ph	0	0	0	1	0	0
Klesko lf	2	0	0	0	2	2	Sanders rf	4	0	0	0	1	1
Devereaux rf	1	0	1	1	0	0	Santiago c	3	0	1	0	1	0
Blauser ss	4	0	0	0	1	2	Morris 1b	3	0	1	0	0	0
Clontz p	0	0	0	0	0	0	Boone 2b	4	0	0	0	0	1
Avery p	0	0	0	0	0	0	M. Lewis 3b	3	0	1	0	0	1
McMichael p	0	0	0	0	0	0	Branson ph-3b	1	0	0	0	0	1
Glavine p	1	0	0	1	0	0	Schourek p	3	0	0	0	0	3
Mordecai ph	1	0	0	0	0	1	Brantley p	0	0	0	0	0	0
Pena p	0	0	0	0	0	0	Anthony ph	1	0	0	0	0	1
Smith ph	1	0	0	0	0	0	Jackson p	0	0	0	0	0	0
Wohlers p	0	0	0	0	0	0							
Belliard ss	0	0	0	0	0	0							
Totals	38	2	7	2	5	9	Totals	36	1	8	1	3	10

Atlanta	000	000	001	01—2
Cincinnati	000	100	000	00—1

E—None. DP—Atlanta 5, Cincinnati 1. LOB—Atlanta 9, Cincinnati 6. 2B—Larkin (1), Morris (2), Howard (2). 3B—Larkin (1). CS—Klesko (1). S—Polonia.

Atlanta	ip	h	r	er	bb	so	Cinc.	ip	h	r	er	bb	so
Glavine	7	7	1	1	2	5	Schourek	8⅓	6	1	1	2	8
Pena	1	0	0	0	0	1	Brantley	1⅔	0	0	0	2	1
Wohlers W	2	0	0	0	0	4	Jackson L	1	1	1	1	1	0
Clontz	⅓	1	0	0	0	0							
Avery	0	0	0	0	1	0							
McMichael S	⅔	0	0	0	0	0							

Avery pitched to 1 batter in 11th.
HBP—Morris (by Glavine). WP—Schourek.
Umpires: HP—Runge; 1B—Quick; 2B—DeMuth; 3B—Davis; LF—Marsh; RF—Crawford.
T—3:18. A—40,382.

Game Two: October 11
Braves 6, Reds 2

ATLANTA	ab	r	h	bi	bb	so	CINCINNATI	ab	r	h	bi	bb	so
Grissom cf	4	1	1	0	1	0	Howard cf	3	0	1	0	1	0
Lemke 2b	4	1	1	0	1	0	Jackson p	0	0	0	0	0	0
Jones 3b	5	0	1	1	0	0	Brantley p	0	0	0	0	0	0
McGriff 1b	4	2	3	0	1	0	Duncan ph	1	0	0	0	0	0
Justice rf	4	1	1	0	1	0	Portugal p	0	0	0	0	0	0
Devereaux lf	4	0	1	1	0	0	Larkin ss	5	0	3	0	0	0
Klesko ph-lf	1	0	0	0	0	0	Gant lf	4	0	0	0	0	1
Lopez c	5	1	3	1	0	1	Sanders rf	5	1	0	0	0	4
Belliard ss	3	0	0	0	1	0	Morris 1b	4	0	0	1	1	0
Polonia lf	1	0	0	0	0	0	Santiago c	4	0	1	0	1	0
Mordecai ss	1	0	0	0	0	0	Boone 2b	3	1	2	0	0	0
Smoltz p	3	0	1	0	0	0	Branson 3b	3	1	0	0	0	0
Pena p	0	0	0	0	0	0	Smiley p	0	0	0	0	0	0
Smith ph	1	0	0	0	0	0	Harris ph	1	0	1	1	0	0
McMichael p	0	0	0	0	0	0	Burba p	0	0	0	0	0	0
Wohlers p	0	0	0	0	0	0	Anthony ph	0	0	0	1	0	0
							Lewis pr-cf	1	0	0	0	0	0
Totals	40	6	11	5	4	2	Totals	36	2	9	1	4	6

Atlanta	100	100	000	4—6
Cincinnati	000	020	000	0—2

E—Sanders (2), Smoltz (1). DP—Cincinnati 1. LOB—Atlanta 8, Cincinnati 9. 2B—McGriff 3 (3), Devereaux (1), Larkin (2). HR—Lopez (1). SB—Smoltz (1), Harris (1), Branson (1), Larkin (5), Morris (2). CS—Howard (1), Sanders (1). S—Branson.

Atlanta	ip	h	r	er	bb	so	Cincinnati	ip	h	r	er	bb	so
Smoltz	7	7	2	2	2	2	Smiley	5	5	2	2	0	1
Pena	1	1	0	0	1	2	Burba	2	2	0	0	3	0
McMichael W	1	0	0	0	1	0	Jackson	1	1	0	0	0	1
Wohlers	1	1	0	0	0	2	Brantley	1	0	0	0	0	0
							Portugal L	1	3	4	4	1	0

WP—Burba, Portugal. Balk—Jackson.

Umpires: HP—Quick; 1B—DeMuth; 2B—Davis; 3B—Marsh; LF—Crawford; RF—Runge.

T—3:26. A—44,624.

Game Three: October 14
Braves 5, Reds 2

CINCINNATI	ab	r	h	bi	bb	so	ATLANTA	ab	r	h	bi	bb	so
Howard cf	3	0	0	1	1	0	Grissom cf	5	0	1	0	0	1
Larkin ss	5	0	1	0	0	0	Lemke 2b	4	1	1	0	0	0
Gant lf	3	1	1	0	0	0	Jones 3b	4	1	3	2	0	0
Sanders rf	4	0	1	0	0	3	McGriff 1b	4	1	2	0	0	0
Morris 1b	4	0	1	1	0	0	Justice rf	3	0	1	0	1	0
Santiago c	3	0	0	0	1	0	Devereaux lf	3	1	1	0	1	1
Boone 2b	4	0	1	0	0	1	O'Brien c	4	1	2	3	0	0
Branson 3b	4	1	1	0	0	0	Belliard ss	4	0	1	0	0	1
Wells	2	0	1	0	0	0	Maddux p	3	0	0	0	0	1
Harris ph	1	0	1	0	0	0	Klesko ph	1	0	0	0	0	1
Hernandez p	0	0	0	0	0	0	Wohlers p	0	0	0	0	0	0
Carrasco p	0	0	0	0	0	0							
Taubensee ph	1	0	0	0	0	0							
Totals	34	2	8	2	2	4	**Totals**	35	5	12	5	2	6

Cincinnati   000 000 011—2
Atlanta   000 003 20x—5

E—Grissom (1). DP—Cincinnati 1. LOB—Cincinnati 9, Atlanta 8. 2B—Branson (2), McGriff (4). HR—O'Brien (1), Jones (3). SB—Jones (1). CS—Larkin (1). SF—Howard.

Cincinnati	ip	h	r	er	bb	so	Atlanta	ip	h	r	er	bb	so
Wells L	6	8	3	3	2	3	Maddux W	8	7	1	1	2	4
Hernandez	⅔	3	2	2	0	0	Wohlers	1	1	1	1	0	0
Carrasco	1⅓	1	0	0	0	3							

HBP—Gant (by Maddux). WP—Maddux.

Umpires: HP—DeMuth; 1B—Davis; 2B—Marsh; 3B—Crawford; LF—Runge; RF—Quick.

T—2:42. A—51,424.

Game Four: October 15
Braves 6, Reds 0

CINCINNATI	ab	r	h	bi	bb	so	ATLANTA	ab	r	h	bi	bb	so
Walton cf	3	0	0	0	0	2	Grissom cf	5	1	2	0	0	0
Howard ph-cf	1	0	0	0	0	0	Lemke 2b	5	0	1	1	0	0
Larkin ss	3	0	1	0	1	1	Jones 3b	2	1	1	0	3	1
Gant lf	4	0	0	0	0	1	McGriff 1b	4	1	1	0	1	0
Sanders rf	3	0	0	0	1	2	Devereaux rf	5	1	1	3	0	1
Duncan 1b	2	0	0	0	0	1	Lopez c	4	1	3	0	0	0
Morris ph-1b	1	0	0	0	0	0	Klesko lf	3	0	0	0	1	1
Santiago c	3	0	1	0	0	2	Belliard ss	4	1	1	0	0	2
Jackson p	0	0	0	0	0	0	Avery p	2	0	1	0	0	0
Burba p	0	0	0	0	0	0	O'Brien ph	1	0	0	0	0	0
Boone 2b	3	0	0	0	0	0	McMichael p	0	0	0	0	0	0
M. Lewis 3b	3	0	0	1	0	0	Polonia ph	1	0	1	1	0	0
Branson ph-3b	1	0	0	0	0	1	Pena p	0	0	0	0	0	0
Schourek p	2	0	0	0	0	1	Wohlers p	0	0	0	0	0	0
Taubensee	1	0	1	0	0	0							
Totals	28	0	3	0	3	11	**Totals**	36	6	12	5	5	5

Cincinnati   000 000 000—0
Atlanta   001 000 50x—6

E—Belliard (1), Larkin (1). DP—Cincinnati 1, Atlanta 1. LOB—Cincinnati 4, Atlanta 11. 2B—Lopez (1). 3B—Grissom (1). HR—Devereaux (1).

Cincinnati	ip	h	r	er	bb	so	Atlanta	ip	h	r	er	bb	so
Schourek L	6	8	1	1	1	5	Avery W	6	2	0	0	3	6
Jackson	⅓	3	5	5	3	0	McMichael	1	0	0	0	0	2
Burba	1⅔	1	0	1	0	0	Pena	1	1	0	0	0	1
							Wohlers	1	0	0	0	0	2

PB—Taubensee.

Umpires: HP—Davis; 1B—Marsh; 2B—Crawford; 3B—Runge; LF—Quick; RF—DeMuth.

T—2:54. A—52,067.

COMPOSITE BOX

ATLANTA

Player, Pos.	AVG	G	AB	R	H	2B	3B	HR	RBI	BB	SO	SB
Luis Polonia, pr-lf	.500	3	2	0	1	0	0	0	1	0	0	0
Steve Avery, p	.500	2	2	0	1	0	0	0	0	0	0	0
Chipper Jones, 3b	.438	4	16	3	7	0	0	1	3	3	1	1
Fred McGriff, 1b	.438	4	16	5	7	4	0	0	3	0	0	0
Charlie O'Brien, c	.400	2	5	1	2	0	0	1	3	0	1	0
Javier Lopez, c	.357	3	14	2	5	1	0	1	3	0	1	0
John Smoltz, p	.333	1	3	0	1	0	0	0	0	0	1	1
Mike Devereaux, rf-lf	.308	4	13	2	4	1	0	1	5	1	2	0
Rafael Belliard, ss	.273	4	11	1	3	0	0	0	0	0	3	0
David Justice, rf	.273	3	11	1	3	0	0	0	1	2	1	0
Marquis Grissom, cf	.263	4	19	2	5	0	1	0	1	4	0	
Mark Lemke, 2b	.167	4	18	2	3	0	0	0	1	1	0	0
Ryan Klesko, lf	.000	4	7	0	0	0	0	0	3	4	0	
Jeff Blauser, ss	.000	1	4	0	0	0	0	0	1	2	0	
Greg Maddux, p	.000	2	3	0	0	0	0	0	0	1	0	
Mike Mordecai, ph-ss	.000	2	2	0	0	0	0	0	0	1	0	
Dwight Smith, ph	.000	2	2	0	0	0	0	0	0	0	0	
Tom Glavine, p	.000	1	1	0	0	0	0	0	0	1	0	
Totals	.282	4	149	19	42	6	1	4	17	16	22	2

Pitcher	W	L	ERA	G	GS	SV	IP	H	R	ER	BB	SO
Steve Avery	1	0	0.00	2	1	0	6	2	0	0	4	6
Alejandro Pena	0	0	0.00	3	0	0	3	2	0	0	1	4
Greg McMichael	1	0	0.00	3	0	1	3	0	0	0	1	2
Brad Clontz	0	0	0.00	1	0	0	1	0	0	0	0	0
Greg Maddux	1	0	1.12	1	1	0	8	7	1	1	2	4
Tom Glavine	0	0	1.29	1	1	0	7	7	1	1	2	5
Mark Wohlers	1	0	1.80	4	0	5	2	1	1	0	8	
John Smoltz	0	0	2.57	1	1	0	7	7	2	2	2	2
Totals	4	0	1.15	4	4	1	39	28	5	5	12	31

CINCINNATI

Player, Pos.	AVG	G	AB	R	H	2B	3B	HR	RBI	BB	SO	SB
Lenny Harris, ph	1.000	3	2	0	2	0	0	0	0	1	0	0
Eddie Taubensee, c	.500	2	2	0	1	0	0	0	0	0	0	0
David Wells, p	.500	1	2	0	1	0	0	0	0	0	0	0
Barry Larkin, ss	.389	4	18	1	7	2	1	0	0	1	1	1
Thomas Howard, cf-ph	.250	4	8	0	2	1	0	0	1	2	0	0
Mark Lewis, 3b	.250	2	4	0	1	0	0	0	0	1	1	0
Benito Santiago, c	.231	4	13	0	3	0	0	0	0	2	3	0
Bret Boone, 2b	.214	4	14	1	3	0	0	0	0	1	2	0
Ron Gant, lf	.188	4	16	1	3	0	0	1	0	3	0	
Hal Morris, 1b	.167	4	12	0	2	1	0	0	1	1	1	1
Reggie Sanders, rf	.125	4	16	0	2	0	0	0	0	2	10	0
Jeff Branson, ph-3b	.111	4	9	2	1	1	0	0	0	0	2	1
Jerome Walton, cf-lf	.000	2	7	0	0	0	0	0	0	0	2	0
Pete Schourek, p	.000	2	5	0	0	0	0	0	0	0	1	0
Mariano Duncan, ph	.000	3	3	0	0	0	0	0	0	1	1	0
Eric Anthony, ph	.000	2	1	0	0	0	0	0	0	1	1	0
Darren Lewis, cf	.000	2	1	0	0	0	0	0	0	0	0	0
John Smiley, p	.000	1	0	0	0	0	0	0	0	0	0	0
Totals	.209	4	134	5	28	5	1	0	4	12	31	4

Pitcher	W	L	ERA	G	GS	SV	IP	H	R	ER	BB	SO
Jeff Brantley	0	0	0.00	2	0	0	3	0	0	0	2	1
Dave Burba	0	0	0.00	4	0	0	4	3	0	0	4	0
Hector Carrasco	0	0	0.00	1	0	0	1	1	0	0	0	3
Pete Schourek	0	1	1.26	2	2	0	14	14	2	2	3	13
John Smiley	0	0	3.60	1	1	0	5	5	2	2	0	1
David Wells	0	1	4.50	1	1	0	6	8	3	3	2	3
Mike Jackson	0	1	23.14	3	0	0	2	5	6	6	4	1
Xavier Hernandez	0	0	27.00	1	0	0	1	3	2	2	0	0
Mark Portugal	0	1	36.00	1	0	0	1	3	4	4	1	0
Totals	0	4	4.62	4	4	0	37	42	19	19	16	22

Atlanta   101 103 701 41—19
Cincinnati   000 120 011 00— 5

DP—Atlanta 8, Cincinnati 4. LOB—Atlanta 36, Cincinnati 28.

E—Smoltz, Grissom, Belliard. CS—Klesko, Howard, Sanders, Larkin. S—Polonia, Branson. SF—Howard.

HBP—Morris (by Glavine), Gant (by Maddux). WP—Schourek, Burba, Portugal, Maddux. PB—Taubensee. Bk—Jackson.

Umpires—Gerry Crawford, Jerry Davis, Randy Marsh, Dana DeMuth, Jim Quick, Paul Runge.

ORGANIZATION STATISTICS

ATLANTA BRAVES

Manager: Bobby Cox.   **1995 Record:** 90-54, .625 (1st, NL East).

BATTING	AVG	G	AB	R	H	2B	3B	HR	RBI	BB	SO	SB	CS	B	T	HT	WT	DOB	1st Yr	Resides
Belliard, Rafael	.222	75	180	12	40	2	1	0	7	6	28	2	2	R	R	5-6	160	10-24-61	1980	Boca Raton, Fla.
Blauser, Jeff	.211	115	431	60	91	16	2	12	31	57	107	8	5	R	R	6-1	180	11-8-65	1984	Alpharetta, Ga.
Devereaux, Mike	.255	29	55	7	14	3	0	1	8	2	11	2	0	R	R	6-0	195	4-10-63	1985	Tampa, Fla.
Giovanola, Ed	.071	13	14	2	1	0	0	0	0	3	5	0	0	L	R	5-10	170	3-4-69	1990	San Jose, Calif.
Grissom, Marquis	.258	139	551	80	142	23	3	12	42	47	61	29	9	R	R	5-11	192	4-17-67	1988	Red Oak, Ga.
Jones, Chipper	.265	140	524	87	139	22	3	23	86	73	99	8	4	S	R	6-3	195	4-24-72	1990	New Smyrna Beach, Fla.
Justice, Dave	.253	120	411	73	104	17	2	24	78	73	68	4	2	L	L	6-3	200	4-14-66	1985	Atlanta, Ga.
Kelly, Mike	.190	97	137	26	26	6	1	3	17	11	49	7	3	R	R	6-4	195	6-2-70	1991	Los Alamitos, Calif.
Klesko, Ryan	.310	107	329	48	102	25	2	23	70	47	72	5	4	L	L	6-3	220	6-12-71	1989	Boynton Beach, Fla.
Kowitz, Brian	.167	10	24	3	4	1	0	0	3	2	5	0	1	L	L	5-10	175	8-7-69	1990	Owings Mills, Md.
Lemke, Mark	.253	116	399	42	101	16	5	5	38	44	40	2	2	S	R	5-9	167	8-13-65	1983	Atlanta, Ga.
Lopez, Javy	.315	100	333	37	105	11	4	14	51	14	57	0	1	R	R	6-3	185	11-5-70	1988	Ponce, P.R.
McGriff, Fred	.280	144	528	85	148	27	1	27	93	65	99	3	6	L	L	6-3	215	10-31-63	1981	Tampa, Fla.
Mordecai, Mike	.280	69	75	10	21	6	0	3	11	9	16	0	0	R	R	5-11	175	12-13-67	1989	Pinson, Ala.
O'Brien, Charlie	.227	67	198	18	45	7	0	9	23	29	40	0	1	R	R	6-2	205	5-1-61	1982	Tulsa, Okla.
Oliva, Jose	.156	48	109	7	17	4	0	5	12	7	22	0	0	R	R	6-1	215	3-3-71	1988	San Pedro de Macoris, D.R.
Perez, Eddie	.308	7	13	1	4	1	0	1	4	0	2	0	0	R	R	6-1	175	5-4-68	1987	Maracaibo, Venez.
Polonia, Luis	.264	28	53	6	14	7	0	0	2	3	9	3	0	L	L	5-8	150	10-27-64	1984	Santiago City, D.R.
Sharperson, Mike	.143	7	7	1	1	0	0	0	2	0	2	0	0	R	R	6-3	190	10-4-61	1982	Stone Mountain, Ga.
Smith, Dwight	.252	103	131	16	33	8	2	3	21	13	35	0	3	L	R	5-11	177	11-8-63	1984	Atlanta, Ga.

PITCHING	W	L	ERA	G	GS	CG	SV	IP	H	R	ER	BB	SO	B	T	HT	WT	DOB	1st Yr	Resides
Avery, Steve	7	13	4.67	29	29	3	0	173	165	92	90	52	141	L	L	6-4	205	4-14-70	1988	Taylor, Mich.
Bedrosian, Steve	1	2	6.11	29	0	0	0	28	40	21	19	12	22	R	R	6-3	205	12-6-57	1978	Senoia, Ga.
Borbon, Pedro	2	2	3.09	41	0	0	2	32	29	12	11	17	33	L	L	6-1	205	11-15-67	1988	Houston, Texas
Clark, Terry	0	0	4.91	3	0	0	0	4	3	2	2	3	2	R	R	6-2	196	10-10-60	1979	La Puente, Calif.
Clontz, Brad	8	1	3.65	59	0	0	4	69	71	29	28	22	55	R	R	6-1	180	4-25-71	1992	Patrick Spring, Va.
Glavine, Tom	16	7	3.08	29	29	3	0	199	182	76	68	66	127	L	L	6-1	185	3-25-66	1984	Alpharetta, Ga.
Maddux, Greg	19	2	1.63	28	28	10	0	210	147	39	38	23	181	R	R	6-0	175	4-14-66	1984	Las Vegas, Nev.
May, Darrell	0	0	11.25	2	0	0	0	4	10	5	5	0	1	L	L	6-2	170	6-13-72	1992	Rogue River, Ore.
McMichael, Greg	7	2	2.79	67	0	0	2	81	64	27	25	32	74	R	R	6-3	215	12-1-66	1988	Alpharetta, Ga.
Mercker, Kent	7	8	4.15	29	26	0	0	143	140	73	66	61	102	L	L	6-2	195	2-1-68	1986	Dublin, Ohio
Murray, Matt	0	2	6.75	4	1	0	0	11	10	8	8	5	3	L	R	6-6	235	9-26-70	1988	Swampscott, Mass.
Nichols, Rod	0	0	5.40	5	0	0	0	7	14	11	4	5	3	R	R	6-2	190	12-29-64	1985	Columbus, Ga.
Pena, Alejandro	0	0	4.15	14	0	0	0	13	11	6	6	4	18	R	R	6-1	200	6-25-59	1979	Roswell, Ga.
2-team (13 Florida)	2	0	2.61	27	0	0	0	31	22	9	9	7	39							
Schmidt, Jason	2	2	5.76	9	2	0	0	25	27	17	16	18	19	R	R	6-5	185	1-29-73	1991	Kelso, Wash.
Smoltz, John	12	7	3.18	29	29	2	0	193	166	76	68	72	193	R	R	6-3	185	5-15-67	1986	Duluth, Ga.
Stanton, Mike	1	1	5.59	26	0	0	1	19	31	14	12	6	13	L	L	6-1	190	6-2-67	1987	Houston, Texas
Thobe, Tom	0	0	10.80	3	0	0	0	3	7	4	4	0	2	L	L	6-5	195	9-3-69	1988	Huntington Beach, Calif.
Wade, Terrell	0	1	4.50	3	0	0	0	4	3	2	2	4	3	L	L	6-3	204	1-25-73	1991	Rembert, S.C.
Wohlers, Mark	7	3	2.09	65	0	0	25	65	51	16	15	24	90	R	R	6-4	207	1-23-70	1988	Atlanta, Ga.
Woodall, Brad	1	1	6.10	9	0	0	0	10	13	10	7	8	5	S	L	6-0	175	6-25-69	1991	Blythewood, S.C.

FIELDING

Catcher	PCT	G	PO	A	E	DP	PB
Lopez	.988	93	625	50	8	5	8
O'Brien	.992	64	446	23	4	4	0
Perez	1.000	5	31	2	0	2	0

First Base	PCT	G	PO	A	E	DP
Klesko	.957	4	20	2	1	0
McGriff	.996	144	1285	96	5	103
Mordecai	1.000	9	24	2	0	3
Oliva	.000	1	0	0	0	0
Perez	1.000	1	3	0	0	1

Second Base	PCT	G	PO	A	E	DP
Belliard	1.000	32	41	91	0	11
Giovanola	1.000	7	9	5	0	1
Lemke	.990	115	205	305	5	61
Mordecai	1.000	21	14	19	0	8

Third Base	PCT	G	PO	A	E	DP
Giovanola	.000	3	0	0	0	0
Jones	.931	123	81	254	25	19
Mordecai	1.000	6	0	5	0	0

	PCT	G	PO	A	E	DP
Oliva	.902	25	14	41	6	3
Sharperson	.000	1	0	0	0	0

Shortstop	PCT	G	PO	A	E	DP
Belliard	.992	40	33	90	1	11
Blauser	.970	115	151	337	15	62
Giovanola	1.000	1	0	2	0	0
Mordecai	1.000	6	1	5	0	1

Outfield	PCT	G	PO	A	E	DP
Devereaux	1.000	27	41	0	0	0
Grissom	.994	136	309	9	2	1
Jones	1.000	20	22	1	0	0
Justice	.984	120	233	8	4	0
Kelly	.940	83	63	0	4	0
Klesko	.942	102	111	2	7	0
Kowitz	1.000	8	6	0	0	0
Mordecai	.000	1	0	0	0	0
Polonia	1.000	15	9	0	0	0
Smith	.923	25	24	0	2	0

LEE R. SCHMID

Fred McGriff

BRAVES

Lefthander Tom Glavine won 16 games for Atlanta

MICHAEL YELMAN

Braves minor league Player of the Year Andruw Jones

MORRIS FOSTOFF

FARM SYSTEM

Assistant General Manager/Player Personnel: Chuck LaMar.

Class	Farm Team	League	W	L	Pct.	Finish*	Manager	First Yr
AAA	Richmond (Va.) Braves	International	75	66	.532	2nd (10)	Grady Little	1966
AA	Greenville (S.C.) Braves	Southern	59	83	.415	10th (10)	Bruce Benedict	1984
#A	Durham (N.C.) Bulls	Carolina	63	76	.453	7th (8)	Matt West	1980
A	Macon (Ga.) Braves	South Atlantic	71	70	.504	9th (14)	Nelson Norman	1991
A	Eugene (Ore.) Emeralds	Northwest	37	39	.487	T-4th (8)	Paul Runge	1995
#R	Danville (Va.) Braves	Appalachian	27	40	.403	9th (10)	Max Venable	1993
R	West Palm Beach (Fla.) Braves	Gulf Coast	14	43	.246	16th (16)	Jim Saul	1976

*Finish in overall standings (No. of teams in league)   #Advanced level

ORGANIZATION LEADERS

MAJOR LEAGUERS

BATTING
*AVG	Javy Lopez	.315
R	Chipper Jones	87
H	Fred McGriff	148
TB	Fred McGriff	258
2B	Fred McGriff	27
3B	Mark Lemke	5
HR	Fred McGriff	27
RBI	Fred McGriff	93
BB	Two tied at	73
SO	Jeff Blauser	107
SB	Marquis Grissom	29

PITCHING
W	Greg Maddux	19
L	Steve Avery	13
#ERA	Greg Maddux	1.63
G	Greg McMichael	67
CG	Greg Maddux	10
SV	Mark Wohlers	25
IP	Greg Maddux	210
BB	John Smoltz	72
SO	John Smoltz	193

LEE R. SCHMID

Mark Wohlers. 25 saves

MINOR LEAGUERS

BATTING
*AVG	Aldo Pecorilli, Greenville/Richmond	.344
R	Andruw Jones, Macon	104
H	Jose Munoz, Richmond	151
TB	Andruw Jones, Macon	275
2B	Andruw Jones, Macon	41
3B	Brett Brewer, Macon	8
HR	Ron Wright, Macon	32
RBI	Ron Wright, Macon	104
BB	Gus Kennedy, Macon	95
SO	Gus Kennedy, Macon	151
SB	Andruw Jones, Macon	56

PITCHING
W	Two tied at	14
L	Jamie Arnold, Durham/Greenville	13
#ERA	Tom Thobe, Richmond	1.84
G	Matt Byrd, Durham	60
CG	Jerry Koller, Greenville	3
SV	Matt Byrd, Durham	27
IP	Derrin Ebert, Macon	182
BB	Jacob Shumate, Danville/Macon	119
SO	Damian Moss, Macon	177

*Minimum 250 At-Bats   #Minimum 75 Innings

TOP 10 PROSPECTS

How the Braves Top 10 prospects, as judged by Baseball America prior to the 1995 season, fared in 1995:

Chipper Jones

Player, Pos.	Club (Class—League)	AVG	AB	R	H	2B	3B	HR	RBI	SB
1. Chipper Jones, ss-3b	Atlanta	.265	524	87	139	22	3	23	86	8
2. Andruw Jones, of	Macon (A—South Atlantic)	.277	537	104	149	41	5	25	100	56
5. Glenn Williams, ss	Eugene (A—Northwest)	.224	268	39	60	11	4	7	36	7
	Macon (A—South Atlantic)	.175	120	13	21	4	0	0	14	2
6. Jermaine Dye, of	Greenville (AA—Southern)	.285	403	50	115	26	4	15	71	4
7. Damon Hollins, of	Greenville (AA—Southern)	.247	466	64	115	26	2	18	77	6
8. Fernando Lunar, c	Eugene (A—Northwest)	.238	130	13	31	6	0	2	16	0
	Macon (A—South Atlantic)	.179	134	13	24	2	0	0	9	1
10. Jose Oliva, 3b	Atlanta	.156	107	7	17	4	0	5	12	0
	St. Louis	.122	74	8	9	1	0	2	8	0

		W	L	ERA	G	SV	IP	H	BB	SO
3. Jason Schmidt, rhp	Richmond (AAA—International)	8	6	2.25	19	0	116	97	48	95
	Atlanta	2	2	5.76	9	0	25	27	18	19
4. Terrell Wade, lhp	Richmond (AAA—International)	10	9	4.56	24	0	142	137	63	124
	Atlanta	0	1	4.50	3	0	4	3	4	3
9. Damian Moss, lhp	Macon (A—South Atlantic)	9	10	3.56	27	0	149	134	70	177

INTERNATIONAL LEAGUE

BATTING	AVG	G	AB	R	H	2B	3B	HR	RBI	BB	SO	SB	CS	B	T	HT	WT	DOB	1st Yr	Resides
Cabrera, Francisco	.231	36	104	7	24	5	0	1	14	5	22	0	1	R	R	6-4	195	10-10-66	1986	Santo Domingo, D.R.
Giovanola, Ed	.321	99	321	45	103	18	2	4	36	55	37	8	7	L	R	5-10	170	3-4-69	1990	San Jose, Calif.
Graffanino, Tony	.190	50	179	20	34	6	0	4	17	15	49	2	2	R	R	6-1	200	6-6-72	1990	Seneca, S.C.
Grijak, Kevin	.298	106	309	35	92	16	5	12	56	25	47	1	3	L	R	6-2	195	8-6-70	1991	Sterling Heights, Mich.
Houston, Tyler	.255	103	349	41	89	10	3	12	42	18	62	3	5	L	R	6-2	210	1-17-71	1989	Las Vegas, Nev.
Kelly, Mike	.289	15	45	5	13	1	0	2	8	5	17	0	1	R	R	6-4	195	6-2-70	1991	Los Alamitos, Calif.
Kelly, Pat	.182	11	22	2	4	1	0	0	2	0	5	0	1	R	R	5-11	175	1-22-67	1989	Waukegan, Ill.
Kowitz, Brian	.280	100	353	53	99	14	5	2	34	41	43	11	8	L	L	5-10	175	8-7-69	1990	Owings Mills, Md.
Martinez, Pablo	.229	14	48	5	11	0	2	0	4	2	7	1	1	S	R	5-10	155	6-29-69	1989	San Juan Baron, D.R.
Moore, Bobby	.258	108	329	45	85	18	2	3	27	27	27	9	7	R	R	5-11	165	10-27-65	1987	Cincinnati, Ohio
Munoz, Jose	.290	135	520	65	151	18	5	3	45	53	65	7	10	S	R	5-11	165	11-11-67	1987	Yabucoa, P.R.
O'Connor, Kevin	.222	94	203	33	45	2	3	4	14	27	42	14	4	L	R	6-0	180	6-8-69	1990	Huntington Beach, Calif.
Olmeda, Jose	.253	80	241	22	61	11	3	1	24	16	41	2	1	S	R	5-9	155	6-20-68	1989	Gurabo, P.R.
Orton, John	.180	17	50	6	9	3	0	1	6	3	22	2	2	R	R	6-1	192	12-8-65	1987	Atascadero, Calif.
Pecorilli, Aldo	.260	49	127	16	33	3	0	6	17	19	20	0	0	R	R	5-11	185	9-12-70	1992	Sterling Heights, Mich.
Perez, Eddie	.265	92	324	31	86	19	0	5	40	12	58	1	2	R	R	6-1	175	5-4-68	1987	Maracaibo, Venez.
Reed, Darren	.265	57	136	11	36	7	0	5	22	11	28	0	0	R	R	6-1	205	10-16-65	1984	Ventura, Calif.
Roa, Hector	.258	40	120	15	31	5	0	2	7	3	23	0	1	S	R	5-11	170	6-11-69	1988	San Pedro de Macoris, D.R.
Scott, Gary	.151	27	86	7	13	1	0	0	2	10	13	0	1	R	R	6-0	175	8-22-68	1989	Pelham, N.Y.
Sharperson, Mike	.319	87	298	42	95	16	1	3	47	35	34	7	2	R	R	6-3	190	10-4-61	1982	Stone Mountain, Ga.
Swann, Pedro	.211	15	38	2	8	1	0	0	3	1	2	0	2	L	R	6-0	195	10-27-70	1991	Townsend, Del.
Toth, David	.231	7	13	1	3	0	0	0	1	1	2	0	1	R	R	6-1	195	12-8-69	1990	West Keansburg, N.J.
Tucker, Scooter	.167	22	66	5	11	3	1	0	6	8	16	0	0	R	R	6-2	205	11-18-66	1988	Cantonment, Fla.
Twardoski, Mike	.138	19	58	7	8	1	0	0	5	10	8	1	1	L	L	5-11	185	7-13-64	1986	Lockport, N.Y.
Villanueva, Hector	.211	10	19	1	4	1	0	1	3	1	3	0	0	R	R	6-1	220	10-2-64	1985	Rio Piedras, P.R.
Warner, Mike	.206	28	97	10	20	4	1	2	8	10	21	0	3	L	L	5-10	170	5-9-71	1992	Palm Beach Gardens, Fla.
Williams, Juan	.264	45	129	18	34	5	0	5	11	17	38	1	3	L	R	6-0	180	10-9-72	1990	Riverside, Calif.

PITCHING	W	L	ERA	G	GS	CG	SV	IP	H	R	ER	BB	SO	B	T	HT	WT	DOB	1st Yr	Resides
Alvarez, Jose	1	3	3.62	5	5	0	0	27	26	15	11	7	16	R	R	5-11	175	4-12-56	1978	Piedmont, S.C.
Bark, Brian	2	2	3.54	13	5	0	0	41	42	16	16	17	22	L	L	5-9	170	8-26-68	1990	Baltimore, Md.
Blair, Dirk	1	1	6.48	8	0	0	0	8	12	8	6	4	2	R	R	6-3	215	5-19-69	1991	Durant, Okla.
Brock, Chris	2	8	5.40	22	9	0	0	60	68	37	36	27	43	R	R	6-0	175	2-5-70	1992	Altamonte Springs, Fla.
Brown, Jeff	1	2	3.22	12	0	0	1	22	23	10	8	5	12	L	L	6-0	165	9-8-70	1990	Grand Prairie, Texas
Coffman, Kevin	1	0	3.00	2	1	0	0	6	4	2	2	4	7	R	R	6-3	205	1-19-65	1983	Victoria, Texas
Harrison, Tom	2	1	3.21	9	6	0	1	42	34	17	15	20	16	R	R	6-2	185	9-30-71	1993	Miamisburg, Ohio
King, Richard	1	1	2.57	14	0	0	0	14	13	8	4	6	3	R	R	6-2	205	12-30-69	1992	Stone Mountain, Ga.
Lomon, Kevin	1	2	3.00	32	3	0	1	60	62	23	20	32	52	R	R	6-1	195	11-20-71	1991	Cameron, Okla.
Martin, Tom	0	0	9.00	7	0	0	0	9	10	9	9	3	3	L	L	6-1	185	5-21-70	1989	Panama City, Fla.
May, Darrell	4	2	3.71	9	9	0	0	51	53	21	21	16	42	L	L	6-2	170	6-13-72	1992	Rogue River, Ore.
Minutelli, Gino	0	0	4.41	5	3	0	0	16	20	8	8	3	8	L	L	6-0	190	5-23-64	1985	Nashville, Tenn.
Murray, Matt	10	3	2.78	19	19	0	0	123	108	41	38	34	78	L	R	6-6	235	9-26-70	1988	Swampscott, Mass.
Nichols, Rod	1	2	2.53	41	3	0	25	57	54	16	16	6	57	R	R	6-2	190	12-29-64	1985	Columbus, Ga.
Polley, Dale	3	2	1.56	47	0	0	7	63	51	15	11	20	60	R	L	6-0	165	8-9-65	1987	Frankfort, Ky.
Potts, Mike	5	5	3.79	38	1	0	1	74	79	35	31	37	52	L	L	5-9	170	9-5-70	1990	Lithonia, Ga.
Schmidt, Jason	8	6	2.25	19	19	0	0	116	97	40	29	48	95	R	R	6-5	185	1-29-73	1991	Kelso, Wash.
Seelbach, Chris	4	6	4.66	14	14	1	0	73	64	39	38	39	65	R	R	6-4	180	12-18-72	1991	Lufkin, Texas
Thobe, Tom	7	0	1.84	48	2	1	5	88	65	27	18	26	57	L	L	6-5	195	9-3-69	1988	Huntington Beach, Calif.
Thomas, Royal	7	7	3.48	39	8	1	0	88	103	43	34	24	39	R	R	6-2	187	9-3-69	1987	Beaumont, Texas
Wade, Terrell	10	9	4.56	24	23	1	0	142	137	76	72	63	124	L	L	6-3	204	1-25-73	1991	Rembert, S.C.
Woodall, Brad	4	4	5.10	13	11	0	0	65	70	39	37	17	44	S	L	6-0	175	6-25-69	1991	Blythewood, S.C.

FIELDING

Catcher	PCT	G	PO	A	E	DP	PB
Cabrera	1.000	3	7	2	0	1	2
Houston	.986	21	124	13	2	2	1
Orton	1.000	17	83	10	0	1	0
Pecorilli	1.000	2	1	2	0	0	0
Perez	.989	83	539	69	7	7	2
Reed	.978	7	41	3	1	0	1
Toth	.947	5	15	3	1	0	0
Tucker	.984	20	107	16	2	1	4
Villanueva	1.000	2	5	1	0	0	0

First Base	PCT	G	PO	A	E	DP
Cabrera	1.000	10	79	3	0	5
Grijak	.992	51	355	25	3	26
Houston	.987	61	421	33	6	44
O'Connor	1.000	1	2	0	0	0
Pecorilli	1.000	27	170	11	0	16
Perez	1.000	2	1	0	0	0
Sharperson	1.000	6	43	7	0	5
Twardoski	1.000	19	165	15	0	8
Villanueva	1.000	4	26	1	0	2

Second Base	PCT	G	PO	A	E	DP
Graffanino	.983	50	102	127	4	30
P. Kelly	.833	1	3	2	1	1
Martinez	.875	2	5	2	1	1
Munoz	.988	51	111	146	3	36
O'Connor	1.000	1	4	3	0	1
Olmeda	.968	3	40	50	3	10
Roa	.969	13	23	40	2	5
Scott	1.000	4	10	5	0	1
Sharperson	1.000	3	3	6	0	3

Third Base	PCT	G	PO	A	E	DP
Giovanola	1.000	2	0	2	0	0
Houston	.939	13	9	22	2	5
P. Kelly	1.000	4	1	9	0	1
Munoz	.930	36	24	56	6	5
Pecorilli	1.000	6	0	1	0	0
Roa	1.000	15	4	23	0	0
Scott	.909	23	14	46	6	4
Sharperson	.969	69	32	125	5	9

Shortstop	PCT	G	PO	A	E	DP
Giovanola	.965	90	125	284	15	52

	PCT	G	PO	A	E	DP
Martinez	.982	12	16	38	1	5
Munoz	.916	36	44	119	15	9
Olmeda	.824	3	6	8	3	4
Roa	.957	9	10	34	2	5

Outfield	PCT	G	PO	A	E	DP
Grijak	1.000	4	4	0	0	0
Houston	.963	15	25	1	1	0
M. Kelly	1.000	12	24	0	0	0
P. Kelly	1.000	7	11	1	0	0
Kowitz	.969	97	217	2	7	0
Moore	1.000	100	179	9	0	3
Munoz	.957	25	20	2	1	1
O'Connor	.976	79	118	4	3	0
Olmeda	.946	48	84	4	5	1
Pecorilli	1.000	11	18	0	0	0
Reed	1.000	30	52	1	0	0
Swann	1.000	9	9	1	0	0
Twardoski	.000	1	0	0	0	0
Warner	.950	27	57	0	3	0
Williams	.961	40	69	5	3	1

SOUTHERN LEAGUE

BATTING	AVG	G	AB	R	H	2B	3B	HR	RBI	BB	SO	SB	CS	B	T	HT	WT	DOB	1st Yr	Resides
Ayrault, Joe	.245	89	302	27	74	20	0	7	42	13	70	2	4	R	R	6-3	190	10-8-71	1990	Sarasota, Fla.
Dye, Jermaine	.285	104	403	60	115	26	4	15	71	27	74	4	8	R	R	6-0	195	1-28-74	1993	Vacaville, Calif.
Grijak, Kevin	.432	21	74	14	32	5	0	2	11	7	9	0	1	L	R	6-2	195	8-6-70	1991	Sterling Heights, Mich.
Hollins, Damon	.247	129	466	64	115	26	2	18	77	44	120	6	6	R	L	5-11	180	6-12-74	1992	Vallejo, Calif.
Hughes, Troy	.255	73	200	24	51	7	1	6	25	17	52	3	6	R	R	6-4	212	1-3-71	1989	Mt. Vernon, Ill.
Klesko, Ryan	.231	4	13	1	3	0	0	1	4	2	1	0	0	L	L	6-3	220	6-12-71	1989	Boynton Beach, Fla.
Malloy, Marty	.278	124	461	73	128	20	3	10	59	39	58	11	12	L	R	5-10	160	7-6-72	1992	Trenton, Fla.
Martinez, Pablo	.255	120	462	70	118	22	4	5	29	37	89	12	12	S	R	5-10	155	6-29-69	1989	San Juan Baron, D.R.
Nunez, Ramon	.261	81	241	34	63	15	2	9	34	15	63	1	1	R	R	6-0	150	9-22-72	1990	Manzanillo, D.R.
Olmeda, Jose	.250	31	108	16	27	5	1	4	10	7	18	1	0	S	R	5-9	155	6-20-68	1989	Gurabo, P.R.
Pecorilli, Aldo	.385	70	265	51	102	17	2	7	42	22	39	2	8	R	R	5-11	185	9-12-70	1992	Sterling Heights, Mich.
Rippelmeyer, Brad	.182	53	165	8	30	8	0	2	16	11	54	1	0	R	R	6-2	190	2-6-70	1991	Valmeyer, Ill.
Robinson, Don	.214	13	28	2	6	1	1	0	3	4	4	1	0	L	R	6-0	185	1-16-72	1990	Haynesville, La.
Smith, Robert	.261	127	444	75	116	27	3	14	58	40	109	12	6	R	R	6-3	190	4-10-74	1992	Oakland, Calif.
Sparks, Greg	.214	65	145	15	31	6	0	5	21	17	41	0	0	L	L	6-0	185	3-31-64	1984	Phoenix, Ariz.
Swann, Pedro	.324	102	339	57	110	24	2	11	64	45	63	14	11	L	R	6-0	195	10-27-70	1991	Townsend, Del.
Warner, Mike	.237	53	173	31	41	12	0	0	7	47	36	12	4	L	L	5-10	170	5-9-71	1992	Palm Beach Gardens, Fla.
Williams, Juan	.313	62	192	40	60	14	2	15	39	19	44	4	3	L	R	6-0	180	10-9-72	1990	Riverside, Calif.
Wollenburg, Doug	.191	66	162	22	31	5	0	1	12	13	31	4	3	R	R	6-2	185	10-11-70	1992	Newark, Ohio

PITCHING	W	L	ERA	G	GS	CG	SV	IP	H	R	ER	BB	SO	B	T	HT	WT	DOB	1st Yr	Resides
Arnold, Jamie	1	5	6.35	10	10	0	0	57	76	42	40	25	19	R	R	6-2	188	3-24-74	1992	Kissimmee, Fla.
Blair, Dirk	2	2	4.21	40	0	0	2	62	69	29	29	11	38	R	R	6-3	215	5-19-69	1991	Durant, Okla.
Burgess, Kurt	1	1	7.20	8	0	0	0	10	16	8	8	2	3	L	L	6-0	175	6-10-69	1991	Tulsa, Okla.
D'Andrea, Mike	3	6	4.88	40	0	2	100	110	65	54	53	61	R	R	5-10	195	12-23-69	1992	Old Town, Maine
Etheridge, Roger	2	10	5.67	32	16	1	0	102	120	73	64	52	47	L	L	6-5	215	5-31-72	1992	Linden, Ala.
Harrison, Tom	6	4	4.38	14	14	1	0	88	87	50	43	27	57	R	R	6-2	185	9-30-71	1993	Miamisburg, Ohio
Hollinger, Adrian	1	4	4.63	7	6	1	0	45	43	26	23	20	28	L	R	6-0	180	9-23-70	1991	Mira Loma, Calif.
Hostetler, Marcus	5	2	4.12	33	0	0	2	44	47	30	20	21	24	R	R	6-3	210	7-4-69	1993	Kalona, Iowa
Hostetler, Mike	10	10	5.26	28	28	0	0	163	182	102	95	46	93	R	R	6-2	195	6-5-70	1991	Marietta, Ga.
Koller, Jerry	9	12	4.94	25	25	3	0	148	163	86	81	37	84	R	R	6-3	190	6-30-72	1990	Martinsville, Ind.
May, Darrell	2	8	3.55	15	15	0	0	91	81	44	36	20	79	L	L	6-2	170	6-13-72	1992	Rogue River, Ore.
Murray, Matt	4	0	1.53	5	5	0	0	29	20	5	5	8	25	L	R	6-6	235	9-26-70	1988	Swampscott, Mass.
Paige, Carey	1	4	5.01	7	7	0	0	41	45	30	23	11	26	R	R	6-3	175	3-2-74	1992	Abilene, Texas
Schutz, Carl	3	7	4.94	51	0	0	26	58	53	36	32	36	56	L	L	5-11	200	8-22-71	1993	Paulina, La.
Seelbach, Chris	6	0	1.64	9	9	1	0	60	38	15	11	30	65	R	R	6-4	180	12-18-72	1991	Lufkin, Texas
Shafer, Bill	2	2	5.01	42	0	0	1	59	69	37	33	38	44	R	R	6-4	215	10-6-72	1991	Arlington, Texas
Simmons, John	1	5	4.62	48	0	0	1	60	67	35	31	22	54	L	L	6-6	220	10-12-70	1992	Tinley Park, Ill.
Turnier, Aaron	0	1	5.19	8	0	0	0	17	17	13	10	18	16	L	L	6-3	190	9-30-70	1992	Las Vegas, Nev.

FIELDING

Catcher	PCT	G	PO	A	E	DP	PB
Ayrault	.986	88	516	64	8	4	3
Pecorilli	.913	6	39	3	4	0	0
Rippelmeyer	.972	53	287	28	9	3	4

First Base	PCT	G	PO	A	E	DP
Grijak	.986	20	202	7	3	16
Nunez	.985	45	305	25	5	29
Olmeda	1.000	5	1	0	0	0
Pecorilli	.996	34	245	24	1	15
Sparks	.983	55	340	12	6	29
Swann	.954	7	59	3	3	6
Wollenburg	.977	5	41	2	1	3

Second Base	PCT	G	PO	A	E	DP
Malloy	.973	124	246	321	16	69
Nunez	.978	10	26	19	1	5
Olmeda	1.000	3	10	13	0	2
Wollenburg	.956	16	31	34	3	8

Third Base	PCT	G	PO	A	E	DP
Nunez	.667	1	0	2	1	0
Olmeda	1.000	1	0	5	0	0
Pecorilli	.867	3	2	11	2	0
Smith	.937	126	120	265	26	25
Wollenburg	.852	21	11	35	8	1

Shortstop	PCT	G	PO	A	E	DP
Martinez	.966	118	167	340	18	55

	PCT	G	PO	A	E	DP
Olmeda	.959	22	36	58	4	12
Wollenburg	.909	6	8	12	2	6

Outfield	PCT	G	PO	A	E	DP
Dye	.981	103	234	22	5	2
Hollins	.978	129	330	18	8	3
Hughes	.968	53	83	7	3	1
Klesko	1.000	2	2	0	0	0
Pecorilli	.923	6	12	0	1	0
Robinson	1.000	6	5	1	0	1
Swann	.966	48	83	3	3	0
Warner	.953	48	100	1	5	0
Williams	.991	51	104	2	1	0
Wollenburg	1.000	1	1	0	0	0

CAROLINA LEAGUE

BATTING	AVG	G	AB	R	H	2B	3B	HR	RBI	BB	SO	SB	CS	B	T	HT	WT	DOB	1st Yr	Resides
Benbow, Lou	.220	82	245	20	54	7	0	4	17	11	53	2	3	R	R	6-0	167	1-12-71	1991	Laguna Hills, Calif.
Correa, Miguel	.236	118	398	43	94	19	1	19	70	19	95	9	13	S	R	6-2	165	9-10-71	1990	Arroyo, P.R.
French, Anton	.269	7	26	3	7	1	0	0	2	3	2	4	1	S	R	5-10	175	7-25-75	1993	St. Louis, Mo.
Garcia, Adrian	.250	5	12	2	3	1	0	0	4	4	1	0	0	R	R	5-11	190	9-12-72	1990	Elizabeth, N.J.
Hicks, Jamie	.219	41	105	9	23	6	0	0	14	5	18	0	2	R	R	6-2	200	11-15-71	1994	Hermitage, Tenn.
Jimenez, Manny	.245	121	375	40	92	16	2	2	23	17	71	8	6	R	R	5-11	160	7-4-71	1990	Pueblo Nuevo Mao, D.R.
King, Andre	.252	111	421	59	106	22	3	9	33	39	126	15	13	R	R	6-1	190	11-26-73	1993	Ft. Lauderdale, Fla.
Knott, John	.267	112	344	55	92	14	3	11	46	63	100	11	13	R	R	5-11	185	12-7-70	1993	St. Louis, Mo.
Magee, Danny	.256	76	266	38	68	11	1	4	29	11	46	7	5	R	R	6-2	175	11-25-74	1993	Denham Springs, La.
McBride, Gator	.236	102	360	60	85	15	1	13	56	54	109	11	4	R	R	5-10	170	8-12-73	1993	Hurricane, W.Va.
Monds, Wonderful	.279	81	297	44	83	17	0	6	33	17	63	28	7	R	R	6-3	190	1-11-73	1993	Fort Pierce, Fla.
Newell, Brett	.215	33	79	10	17	1	0	0	3	4	20	0	1	R	R	6-0	180	10-25-72	1993	El Segundo, Calif.
Nunez, Ramon	.370	17	54	13	20	4	0	5	15	8	9	0	0	R	R	6-0	155	9-22-72	1990	Manzanillo, D.R.
Pagano, Scott	.266	110	354	47	94	12	1	1	26	38	75	41	21	S	R'	5-11	175	4-26-71	1992	Dania, Fla.
Simon, Randall	.264	122	420	56	111	18	1	18	79	36	63	6	5	L	L	6-0	180	5-26-75	1993	Willemstad, Curacao
Smith, Sean	.280	32	93	10	26	8	0	3	13	9	22	1	0	L	R	5-10	185	2-15-74	1992	Oconomowoc, Wisc.
Toth, Dave	.245	85	257	20	63	6	0	6	26	25	42	3	3	R	R	6-1	195	12-8-69	1990	West Keansburg, N.J.
Warner, Ken	.226	51	137	12	31	11	1	2	13	12	32	1	2	R	R	5-10	175	7-1-74	1992	Amite, La.
Weaver, Colby	.278	8	18	2	5	2	0	0	2	4	6	0	0	R	R	6-0	185	4-17-73	1994	Warwick, N.Y.
Webb, Kevin	.182	43	121	17	22	4	0	5	11	18	39	2	0	R	R	6-4	215	12-27-69	1991	Yorba Linda, Calif.
Wieser, Mike	.210	28	62	5	13	2	0	1	3	2	12	0	1	R	R	6-4	200	3-24-73	1991	Fargo, N.D.

GAMES BY POSITION: C—Garcia 5, Hicks 39, Smith 27, Toth 82, Weaver 5, Webb 1. **1B**—Knott 20, Nunez 7, Simon 113, Webb 7, Wieser 2. **2B**—Benbow 7, Jimenez 95, Knott 1, Newell 3, Warner 47, Wieser 1. **3B**—Benbow 18, Jimenez 21, Knott 55, Newell 26, Smith 1, Webb 32, Wieser 16. **SS**—Benbow 57, Jimenez 9, Magee 73, Newell 4, Wieser 9. **OF**—Correa 91, French 7, King 97, Knott 32, McBride 78, Monds 51, Pagano 84, Toth 1.

PITCHING	W	L	ERA	G	GS	CG	SV	IP	H	R	ER	BB	SO	B	T	HT	WT	DOB	1st Yr	Resides
Arnold, Jamie	4	8	3.94	15	14	1	0	80	86	42	35	21	44	R	R	6-2	188	3-24-74	1992	Kissimmee, Fla.
Binkley, Brett	2	2	5.97	24	0	0	0	29	34	20	19	21	20	L	L	5-10	175	9-28-71	1993	Lilburn, Ga.
Bock, Jeff	5	1	3.36	32	4	0	2	67	58	31	25	31	45	R	R	6-5	200	4-26-71	1993	Cary, N.C.
Bowie, Micah	4	11	3.59	23	23	1	0	130	119	65	52	61	91	L	L	6-4	185	11-10-74	1993	Humble, Texas
Burgess, Kurt	2	4	7.83	34	0	0	0	44	48	44	38	34	25	L	L	6-0	175	6-10-69	1991	Tulsa, Okla.
Byrd, Matt	5	4	2.97	60	0	0	27	70	52	24	23	32	79	S	R	6-2	200	5-17-71	1993	Brighton, Mich.
Christmas, Maurice	2	7	4.83	31	18	0	0	114	135	68	61	19	68	R	R	6-4	190	2-26-74	1992	Winchester, Mass.
Daniels, Lee	1	4	4.24	21	0	0	4	23	26	13	11	14	24	R	R	6-4	180	3-31-71	1990	Rochelle, Ga.
Green, Jason	2	4	5.58	39	1	0	3	50	31	31	31	79	59	R	R	6-2	195	11-15-73	1993	Hercules, Calif.
Harrison, Tom	3	1	0.96	7	6	0	0	38	22	5	4	13	25	R	R	6-2	185	9-30-71	1993	Miamisburg, Ohio
Hostetler, Marcus	1	1	6.61	12	0	0	0	16	23	13	12	7	6	R	R	6-3	210	7-4-69	1993	Kalona, Iowa
Jacobs, Ryan	11	6	3.51	29	25	1	0	149	145	72	58	57	99	R	L	6-5	175	2-3-74	1992	Winston-Salem, N.C.
Lavenia, Mark	0	1	5.56	6	0	0	0	11	14	8	7	5	9	R	L	6-1	175	8-30-72	1993	Latham, N.Y.
Leroy, John	6	9	5.44	24	22	1	0	126	128	82	76	57	77	R	R	6-3	175	4-19-75	1993	Bellevue, Wash.
Mathews, Del	7	8	3.54	33	16	1	1	112	117	53	44	38	77	L	L	6-3	200	10-31-74	1993	Fernandina Beach, Fla.
Nelson, Earl	0	1	4.95	15	0	0	2	20	27	17	11	17	17	R	L	6-1	185	5-2-72	1991	San Antonio, Texas
Paige, Carey	5	3	3.38	10	10	1	0	64	53	24	24	15	37	R	R	6-3	175	3-2-74	1992	Abilene, Texas
Place, Mike	2	1	10.57	7	0	0	0	8	11	11	9	6	2	R	R	6-4	190	8-13-70	1990	Seminole, Fla.
Raines, Ken	1	0	4.94	19	0	0	0	24	38	19	13	12	15	R	L	6-2	175	10-14-72	1994	Freeland, Mich.
Wells, David	0	0	4.73	7	0	0	0	13	21	8	7	2	6	R	R	6-5	200	6-20-72	1993	Logansport, Ind.

MACON   A
SOUTH ATLANTIC LEAGUE

BATTING	AVG	G	AB	R	H	2B	3B	HR	RBI	BB	SO	SB	CS	B	T	HT	WT	DOB	1st Yr	Resides
Brewer, Brett	.241	128	452	78	109	25	8	8	60	60	113	15	5	R	R	6-2	180	10-16-74	1993	Snowflake, Ariz.
Dawson, Charles	.246	42	122	19	30	6	0	3	13	18	27	1	0	R	R	5-11	200	1-27-72	1994	Waldo, Ark.
Delgado, Jose	.237	45	169	19	40	5	3	3	16	11	28	3	4	S	R	5-11	155	3-20-75	1993	Carolina, P.R.
Eaglin, Mike	.266	129	530	82	141	15	4	2	30	64	94	41	13	R	R	5-10	170	4-25-73	1992	San Pablo, Calif.
Helms, Wes	.276	136	539	89	149	32	1	11	85	50	107	2	2	R	R	6-4	210	5-12-76	1994	Gastonia, N.C.
Jones, Andruw	.277	139	537	104	149	41	5	25	100	70	122	56	11	R	R	6-1	170	4-23-77	1994	Willemstad, Curacao
Kennedy, Gus	.253	128	439	83	111	29	5	24	76	95	151	20	6	R	R	5-10	195	12-26-73	1994	Seligman, Ariz.
Landry, Dan	.226	13	53	4	12	1	0	0	6	6	12	0	0	R	R	5-10	180	1-20-73	1995	Plaquemine, La.
Lombard, George	.206	49	180	32	37	6	1	3	16	27	44	16	4	L	R	6-0	208	9-14-75	1994	Atlanta, Ga.
Lunar, Fernando	.179	39	134	13	24	2	0	0	9	10	38	1	0	R	R	6-2	185	5-25-77	1994	Anaco, Venez.
Matos, Pasqual	.185	72	238	23	44	11	1	5	26	11	86	2	2	R	R	6-2	160	12-23-74	1992	Barahona, D.R.
Newell, Brett	.256	76	285	39	73	9	1	0	29	24	72	5	1	R	R	6-0	180	10-25-72	1994	El Segundo, Calif.
Saturnino, Sherton	.188	42	117	6	22	2	0	2	13	3	36	1	2	R	R	5-9	185	10-16-71	1993	Willemstad, Curacao
Utting, Ben	.218	21	55	5	12	2	0	0	6	7	13	1	1	L	R	6-1	160	12-22-75	1993	Melbourne, Australia
Vaske, Terry	.169	53	148	14	25	7	0	5	18	18	58	0	1	L	R	6-5	190	3-1-71	1992	Dyersville, Iowa
Waldrop, Tom	.237	60	194	19	46	11	1	3	24	14	52	1	5	L	L	6-3	195	1-10-70	1992	Decatur, Ill.
Weaver, Colby	.243	14	37	4	9	0	0	1	6	5	8	1	0	R	R	6-0	195	4-17-73	1994	Warwick, N.Y.
Williams, Glenn	.175	38	120	13	21	4	0	0	14	16	42	2	1	S	R	6-1	185	7-18-77	1994	Ingleburn, Australia
Wright, Ron	.293	14	58	7	17	3	1	2	10	4	13	0	0	R	R	6-1	205	1-21-76	1994	Kennewick, Wash.

GAMES BY POSITION: C—Dawson 38, Lunar 32, Matos 72, Vaske 1, Weaver 14. **1B**—Vaske 21, Wright 120. **2B**—Delgado 4, Eaglin 128, Landry 2, Newell 9, Utting 1. **3B**—Helms 133, Landry 2, Newell 8, Vaske 3. **SS**—Delgado 41, Landry 8, Newell 47, Utting 20, Williams 32. **OF**—Brewer 112, Jones 130, Kennedy 109, Lombard 35, Saturnino 25, Vaske 1, Waldrop 24.

PITCHING	W	L	ERA	G	GS	CG	SV	IP	H	R	ER	BB	SO	B	T	HT	WT	DOB	1st Yr	Resides
Blythe, Billy	0	2	10.34	7	2	0	1	16	15	20	18	14	15	R	R	6-2	190	1-25-76	1994	Lexington, Ky.
Bowie, Micah	4	1	2.28	5	5	0	0	28	9	8	7	11	36	L	L	6-4	185	11-10-74	1993	Humble, Texas
Briggs, Anthony	8	5	2.99	29	24	1	0	147	145	76	49	56	114	R	R	6-2	162	9-14-73	1994	Manning, S.C.
Brown, Darold	3	1	3.29	31	0	0	5	55	39	22	20	32	55	L	L	6-0	175	8-16-73	1993	Atlanta, Ga.
Cain, Travis	1	2	7.52	14	2	0	0	26	25	23	22	31	32	L	R	6-3	185	8-10-75	1993	Anderson, S.C.
Collins, Zach	0	0	5.40	4	0	0	0	3	7	4	2	2	3	S	L	6-0	175	1-7-73	1994	Bowie, Md.
Culp, Wes	4	6	3.53	39	5	0	3	105	100	56	41	44	56	R	R	6-2	175	12-23-74	1994	Austin, Texas
Ebert, Derrin	14	5	3.31	28	28	0	0	182	184	87	67	46	124	L	L	6-3	175	8-21-76	1994	Hesperia, Calif.
Evangelista, Alberto	4	3	4.50	24	2	1	0	54	42	29	21	16	51	R	R	6-1	160	10-10-73	1993	Cotui, D.R.
Giard, Kenneth	1	0	0.68	5	0	0	0	13	7	1	1	5	19	R	R	6-3	210	4-2-73	1991	Warwick, R.I.
Graham, Steve	1	1	9.35	5	0	0	0	9	17	12	9	5	7	R	R	6-4	190	7-20-71	1994	West Warwick, R.I.
Lavenia, Mark	4	3	2.14	24	3	0	4	46	38	17	11	14	45	R	L	6-1	175	8-30-72	1993	Latham, N.Y.
Millwood, Kevin	5	6	4.63	29	12	0	0	103	86	65	53	57	89	R	R	6-4	205	12-24-74	1993	Bessemer City, N.C.
Moss, Damian	9	10	3.56	27	27	0	0	149	134	73	59	70	177	R	L	6-0	187	11-24-76	1994	Sadler, Australia
Olszewski, Eric	2	5	3.76	35	1	0	5	81	54	37	34	50	103	L	R	6-3	205	11-4-74	1993	Spring, Texas
Raines, Ken	1	1	1.93	14	0	0	8	19	11	4	4	5	22	R	L	6-2	175	10-14-72	1994	Freeland, Mich.
Rocker, John	4	4	4.50	16	16	0	0	86	86	50	43	52	61	R	L	6-4	205	10-17-74	1993	Macon, Ga.
Shumate, Jacob	0	8	7.23	17	14	0	0	56	38	56	45	87	49	R	R	6-2	180	1-22-76	1994	Hartsville, S.C.
Thompson, Mark	3	2	4.71	13	0	0	2	21	13	12	11	4	15	R	R	6-2	200	9-22-70	1994	Ladd, Ill.
Tyner, Mark	2	2	3.28	29	0	0	3	47	48	31	17	17	38	R	R	6-2	195	4-11-72	1993	Richmond, Calif.
Zedalis, Craig	1	1	4.76	12	0	0	0	23	25	12	12	8	17	R	R	6-5	210	8-27-72	1994	Bartlett, Ill.

EUGENE   A
NORTHWEST LEAGUE

BATTING	AVG	G	AB	R	H	2B	3B	HR	RBI	BB	SO	SB	CS	B	T	HT	WT	DOB	1st Yr	Resides
Brown, Roosevelt	.309	57	165	28	51	12	4	7	32	13	30	6	3	L	R	5-10	190	8-3-75	1993	Vicksburg, Miss.
Daugherty, Keith	.125	2	8	1	1	0	0	0	0	0	2	0	0	R	R	6-4	230	7-11-73	1995	Opelika, Ala.
DeLeon, Reymundo	.189	50	127	14	24	2	1	1	11	13	48	2	3	R	R	6-0	175	11-20-74	1994	San Pedro de Macoris, D.R.
Ellison, Skeeter	.133	19	15	5	2	0	0	0	1	5	7	4	2	S	R	5-10	177	9-15-75	1995	Provo, Utah
Foote, Derek	.000	1	0	0	0	0	0	0	0	1	0	0	0	L	R	6-4	235	11-18-74	1993	Smithfield, N.C.

58 · 1996 ALMANAC

BATTING

BATTING	AVG	G	AB	R	H	2B	3B	HR	RBI	BB	SO	SB	CS	B	T	HT	WT	DOB	1st Yr	Resides
Hacker, Steve	.211	16	57	4	12	3	0	2	9	1	13	0	0	R	R	6-5	230	9-6-74	1995	St. Louis, Mo.
Hines, Pooh	.242	44	124	26	30	7	3	2	13	20	27	13	2	R	R	5-11	165	9-13-74	1995	Decatur, Ga.
Hodges, Randy	.291	61	206	29	60	7	5	2	28	12	35	10	6	L	R	6-0	185	1-20-73	1995	Ocala, Fla.
Lombard, George	.252	68	262	38	66	5	3	5	19	23	91	35	13	L	R	6-0	208	9-14-75	1994	Atlanta, Ga.
Lunar, Fernando	.244	38	131	13	32	6	0	2	16	9	28	0	1	R	R	6-2	205	5-25-77	1994	Anaco, Venez.
Mahoney, Mike	.241	43	112	14	27	6	0	1	15	15	17	6	2	R	R	6-3	175	12-5-72	1995	Des Moines, Iowa
Person, Wilton	.264	62	197	25	52	8	1	0	23	20	21	7	6	R	R	6-3	175	8-16-73	1994	Starkville, Miss.
Rust, Brian	.204	53	157	18	32	7	1	4	19	7	43	2	1	R	R	6-3	205	8-1-74	1995	Portland, Ore.
Sasser, Rob	.269	57	216	40	58	9	1	9	32	23	51	14	4	R	R	6-4	190	3-6-75	1993	Oakland, Calif.
Saturnino, Sherton	.238	8	21	4	5	0	0	1	1	1	7	2	0	R	R	5-9	185	10-16-71	1991	Willemstad, Curacao
Shy, Jason	.241	20	54	6	13	2	0	2	6	1	12	0	0	R	R	5-11	200	11-17-73	1995	Chico, Calif.
Spiegel, Rich	.143	7	14	0	2	0	0	0	2	3	0	0	0	R	R	6-0	185	12-6-73	1994	Pasadena, Md.
Taylor, Matthew	.000	10	24	1	0	0	0	0	0	5	8	0	1	L	R	6-0	175	3-7-74	1995	Richmond, Calif.
Tocco, Todd	.197	59	117	12	23	3	0	1	8	17	32	0	1	L	R	6-3	202	6-20-72	1995	Chuluota, Fla.
Trippy, Joe	.309	75	259	48	80	16	0	2	38	24	31	29	13	L	L	5-10	185	7-31-73	1995	Seattle, Wash.
Williams, Glenn	.224	71	268	39	60	11	4	7	36	21	71	7	4	S	R	6-1	185	7-18-77	1994	Ingleburn, Australia

GAMES BY POSITION: C—Foote 1, Lombard 2, Lunar 37, Mahoney 41, Shy 9, Spiegel 4. **1B**—Daugherty 2, Ellison 1, Hacker 12, Person 50, Spiegel 1, Tocco 29. **2B**—Brown 1, Ellison 4, Hines 29, Hodges 46, Taylor 6. **3B**—Hines 1, Hodges 10, Person 1, Rust 51, Sasser 4, Tocco 28. **SS**—Hines 12, Person 1, Rust 2, Sasser 54, Taylor 4, Williams 9. **OF**—Brown 44, DeLeon 46, Ellison 7, Hodges 5, Lombard 65, Person 10, Saturnino 6, Shy 12, Trippy 74.

PITCHING

PITCHING	W	L	ERA	G	GS	CG	SV	IP	H	R	ER	BB	SO	B	T	HT	WT	DOB	1st Yr	Resides
Blythe, Billy	1	6	9.80	14	10	0	1	38	45	55	41	49	24	R	R	6-2	190	1-25-76	1994	Lexington, Ky.
Brooks, Antone	2	0	0.53	15	0	0	0	17	9	5	1	8	26	L	L	6-0	176	12-20-73	1995	Florence, S.C.
Brown, Darold	0	3	4.24	3	3	0	0	17	18	16	8	6	13	L	L	6-0	175	8-16-73	1993	Atlanta, Ga.
Butler, Adam	4	1	2.49	23	0	0	8	25	15	9	7	12	50	L	L	6-2	225	8-17-73	1995	Burke, Va.
Chrismon, Thad	2	2	2.61	32	0	0	3	38	31	15	11	21	28	R	R	6-0	195	1-30-73	1995	Apex, N.C.
Cruz, Charlie	2	7	2.55	15	15	0	0	81	68	34	23	36	90	L	L	5-11	175	10-22-73	1995	Miami, Fla.
Garcia, Jose	3	3	3.86	14	14	0	0	70	64	43	30	35	62	R	R	6-1	165	2-26-75	1994	Santo Domingo, D.R.
Gerland, Greg	4	2	2.16	19	2	0	1	42	39	18	10	15	33	L	L	6-2	175	11-20-72	1995	Euclid, Ohio
Giard, Ken	1	2	3.28	25	0	0	2	34	31	9	9	5	44	R	R	6-3	210	4-2-73	1991	Warwick, R.I.
Koehler, P.K.	0	2	22.50	2	2	0	0	4	4	10	10	12	5	L	L	6-4	215	8-10-73	1994	Medford, Ore.
Mayhew, Keith	0	1	4.54	24	1	0	1	40	46	29	20	17	35	R	R	5-11	180	10-21-71	1995	Spout Spring, Va.
Mazzone, Tony	3	1	3.89	25	0	0	2	44	50	24	19	12	38	R	R	6-1	170	9-24-72	1994	Rawlings, Md.
McKnight, Chris	5	2	2.92	13	13	0	0	65	63	31	21	21	30	L	L	6-3	195	7-3-73	1995	Fayetteville, Ga.
McMullen, Jerry	1	1	1.47	22	0	0	1	31	28	7	5	8	31	L	L	6-2	190	10-13-73	1995	Redmond, Ore.
McWilliams, Matt	2	3	2.01	24	4	0	0	49	34	21	11	16	42	R	R	6-4	225	1-27-73	1995	Charlotte, N.C.
Rocker, John	1	5	5.16	12	12	0	0	59	45	40	34	36	74	R	L	6-4	205	10-17-74	1994	Macon, Ga.
Zedalis, Craig	0	0	2.70	8	0	0	0	13	16	6	4	4	10	R	R	6-5	210	8-27-72	1994	Bartlett, Ill.

DANVILLE · R

APPALACHIAN LEAGUE

BATTING

BATTING	AVG	G	AB	R	H	2B	3B	HR	RBI	BB	SO	SB	CS	B	T	HT	WT	DOB	1st Yr	Resides
Anglen, Toby	.253	63	221	32	56	11	0	3	35	24	33	14	4	L	R	5-10	175	9-11-73	1994	Sperry, Okla.
Bass, Jayson	.224	64	268	38	60	17	4	0	17	28	61	24	8	S	R	6-0	175	6-19-74	1995	Fayette, Ala.
Cross, Adam	.304	50	181	25	55	15	0	1	16	11	16	15	11	R	R	6-1	180	8-22-73	1995	Bluff City, Tenn.
Dougherty, Keith	.294	25	85	14	25	5	1	5	14	3	14	1	1	R	R	6-4	230	7-11-73	1995	Opelika, Ala.
Duncan, Angel	.232	49	142	23	33	3	1	0	8	29	45	5	3	L	L	5-10	170	9-21-75	1994	Killeen, Texas
Espada, Angel	.301	33	113	17	34	0	1	1	8	12	16	16	4	R	R	5-9	150	8-15-74	1994	Salinas, P.R.
Foote, Derek	.362	17	58	10	21	4	0	3	9	3	21	0	0	L	R	6-4	235	11-18-74	1994	Smithfield, N.C.
Franklin, James	.243	51	148	30	36	5	2	0	17	28	51	9	5	R	R	6-2	210	9-14-74	1993	Hodgenville, Ky.
Hodges, Randy	.250	2	8	1	2	0	0	1	1	0	2	0	1	L	R	6-0	185	1-20-73	1995	Ocala, Fla.
Langford, Derrick	.341	27	85	7	29	3	0	1	16	9	18	1	2	R	R	6-1	212	11-21-74	1995	Richmond, Calif.
Martin, Ryan	.214	5	14	2	3	1	0	0	2	3	5	0	1	R	R	6-5	225	10-21-75	1994	Pierron, Ill.
McWhite, Ray	.260	64	231	37	60	16	1	12	53	16	76	8	4	S	R	6-0	190	9-8-73	1994	Jacksonville, Fla.
Mullen, Adam	.137	17	51	2	7	0	1	0	3	4	17	1	1	R	R	6-4	195	2-27-76	1994	Beaufort, S.C.
Pickett, Cory	.220	61	218	20	48	5	5	0	26	19	67	9	4	L	R	6-2	180	10-16-75	1994	San Jose, Calif.
Pointer, Corey	.278	46	158	33	44	5	3	8	27	19	60	8	4	R	R	6-2	205	9-2-75	1994	Waxahachie, Texas
Sasser, Rob	.319	12	47	8	15	2	1	0	7	4	7	5	1	R	R	6-4	190	3-6-75	1993	Oakland, Calif.
Shy, Jason	.231	8	13	1	3	0	0	0	2	3	0	0	0	R	R	5-11	200	11-17-73	1995	Chico, Calif.
Utting, Ben	.238	55	189	30	45	8	1	0	15	27	34	12	4	L	R	6-1	160	12-22-75	1993	Melbourne, Australia

GAMES BY POSITION: C—Foote 14, Martin 3, Mullen 16, Pointer 35, Shy 8. **1B**—Anglen 1, Daugherty 19, Foote 1, McWhite 51. **2B**—Anglen 11, Cross 27, Espada 31, Hodges 2. **3B**—Anglen 45, Cross 4, Daugherty 2, McWhite 9, Sasser 11. **SS**—Anglen 6, Cross 10, Utting 55. **OF**—Bass 62, Duncan 43, Franklin 9, Langford 9, Pickett 57.

PITCHING

PITCHING	W	L	ERA	G	GS	CG	SV	IP	H	R	ER	BB	SO	B	T	HT	WT	DOB	1st Yr	Resides
Abreu, Winston	6	3	2.31	13	13	1	0	74	54	29	19	13	90	R	R	6-2	155	4-5-77	1994	Cotui, D.R.
Chen, Bruce	4	4	3.97	14	13	1	0	70	78	42	31	19	56	L	L	6-1	150	6-19-77	1994	Panama City, Panama
Cochrane, Andrew	1	4	4.63	6	0	0	0	12	14	11	6	9	5	L	L	6-2	205	10-8-74	1995	Richmond, B.C.
Collins, Ken	1	0	4.18	18	1	0	0	32	36	31	15	15	29	R	R	6-7	235	4-23-74	1995	Dunn, N.C.
Cooper, Ken	1	0	1.65	17	0	0	4	27	20	9	5	5	23	R	R	5-11	190	11-14-73	1995	Highgate Falls, Vt.
Giuliano, Joe	2	5	7.25	11	11	0	0	50	71	45	40	19	48	R	R	6-2	170	1-1-76	1994	Hamilton, Ohio
Gobert, Chris	0	0	0.00	3	0	0	0	6	1	0	0	3	3	L	L	6-4	185	3-20-73	1994	Lafayette, La.
Knowland, Sam	4	2	2.86	20	0	0	1	35	37	23	11	10	21	R	R	6-2	195	6-30-73	1995	The Dalles, Ore.
Koehler, P.K.	0	2	3.54	11	6	0	1	41	39	21	16	16	46	L	L	6-4	215	8-10-73	1994	Medford, Ore.
Loewe, Kevin	1	3	3.79	20	0	0	5	38	24	20	16	10	43	L	L	5-11	175	7-20-73	1994	Baltimore, Md.
McKnight, Chris	0	1	3.00	1	1	0	0	3	2	1	1	6	L	L	6-3	195	7-3-73	1995	Fayetteville, Ga.
Osting, Jimmy	1	0	7.15	11	10	0	0	39	46	34	31	25	43	R	L	6-5	185	4-7-77	1995	Louisville, Ky.
Raines, Ken	0	0	0.71	11	0	0	6	13	8	4	1	0	14	R	R	6-2	175	10-14-72	1994	Freeland, Mich.
Reynolds, Walker	1	3	3.99	20	0	0	1	38	26	19	17	19	30	R	R	6-1	185	10-18-73	1995	Demopolis, Ala.
Schnur, Curt	1	4	5.74	18	0	0	0	31	34	24	20	22	31	R	R	6-3	210	11-2-72	1995	Butler, Pa.
Shumate, Jacob	1	2	10.80	7	2	0	0	13	6	21	16	32	16	R	R	6-2	180	1-22-76	1994	Hartsville, S.C.
Wise, James	0	1	15.43	2	0	0	0	2	3	4	4	1	3	L	L	6-4	200	3-20-76	1995	Meldrim, Ga.
Wise, William	0	3	5.63	10	10	0	0	46	42	33	29	23	24	R	R	6-4	203	9-10-75	1994	Plains, Ga.

GULF COAST LEAGUE

BATTING	AVG	G	AB	R	H	2B	3B	HR	RBI	BB	SO	SB	CS	B	T	HT	WT	DOB	1st Yr	Resides
Carubelli, Gustavo	.196	49	148	13	29	8	0	2	6	24	31	3	3	R	R	6-0	195	7-28-74	1995	Santa Fe, Argentina
Colon, Ariel	.202	30	84	6	17	2	0	0	7	9	25	1	0	R	R	6-1	185	9-17-77	1995	Carolina, P.R.
Corzo, Beau	.207	27	87	7	18	3	0	3	7	5	22	0	0	R	R	6-2	190	9-9-77	1995	Maracaibo, Venez.
Ellison, Skeeter	.226	20	62	4	14	4	1	0	4	6	27	1	4	S	R	5-10	177	9-15-75	1995	Provo, Utah
Landry, Dan	.238	38	122	16	29	5	0	2	7	11	25	4	1	R	R	5-10	180	1-20-73	1995	Plaquemine, La.
Lopez, Edgar	.214	38	117	14	25	4	0	0	5	20	13	5	5	R	R	6-0	155	10-6-74	1995	Rivas, Nicaragua
Monds, Wonderful	.133	4	15	1	2	0	0	0	1	1	8	2	1	R	R	6-3	190	1-11-73	1993	Fort Pierce, Fla.
Otero, Oscar	.128	29	86	3	11	0	0	0	2	3	16	1	2	R	R	6-1	165	5-28-77	1995	Cayey, P.R.
Pendergrass, Tyrone	.181	52	188	19	34	4	0	1	7	15	51	8	4	S	R	6-1	174	7-31-76	1995	Hartsville, S.C.
Scharrer, Jim	.180	48	172	10	31	4	0	2	22	13	43	1	3	R	R	6-4	220	11-5-76	1995	Erie, Pa.
Selivanov, Andrei	.154	23	52	4	8	3	0	0	4	7	7	0	0	L	R	5-10	170	2-6-77	1995	Moscow, Russia
Smith, Phillip	.123	38	114	5	14	1	0	0	5	4	37	0	1	R	R	6-1	208	12-18-76	1995	Phillipsburg, N.J.
Spencer, Jeffrey	.234	48	171	17	40	8	1	4	21	12	42	7	2	R	R	6-2	170	6-25-77	1995	Melbourne, Australia
Taylor, Matthew	.161	35	112	9	18	2	0	0	6	10	11	1	4	L	R	6-0	175	3-7-74	1995	Richmond, Calif.
Torrealba, Steve	.207	30	92	3	19	4	0	0	10	11	20	0	0	R	R	6-0	175	2-24-78	1995	Barquisimeto, Venez.
Vecchioni, Gerald	.172	33	99	10	17	1	0	0	2	10	23	2	3	R	R	6-0	172	3-18-77	1995	Baltimore, Md.

GAMES BY POSITION: C—Corzo 25, Selivanov 10, Torrealba 30. **1B**—Colon 23, Landry 1, Scharrer 36. **2B**—Landry 3, Lopez 36, Otero 4, Taylor 20. **3B**—Landry 8, Otero 6, Spencer 42, Taylor 2. **SS**—Landry 14, Lopez 1, Otero 2, Taylor 13, Vecchioni 30. **OF**—Carubelli 49, Ellison 18, Landry 9, Monds 4, Otero 4, Pendergrass 52, Selivanov 4, Smith 37.

PITCHING	W	L	ERA	G	GS	CG	SV	IP	H	R	ER	BB	SO	B	T	HT	WT	DOB	1st Yr	Resides
Bauldree, Joe	0	0	7.09	12	0	0	0	27	26	21	21	26	19	R	R	6-5	175	3-23-77	1995	Wake Forest, N.C.
Bell, Robbie	1	6	6.88	10	8	0	0	34	38	29	26	14	33	R	R	6-5	225	1-17-77	1995	Marlboro, N.Y.
Birrell, Simon	2	3	5.97	13	3	0	1	38	47	37	25	23	18	R	R	6-6	185	10-7-77	1995	Ephrata, Wash.
Collins, Zach	0	0	2.57	3	0	0	1	7	6	2	2	1	2	S	L	6-0	175	1-7-73	1994	Bowie, Md.
Cooper, Keith	1	0	3.00	2	0	0	0	3	2	1	1	1	3	R	R	5-11	190	11-14-72	1995	Highgate Falls, Vt.
Corba, Lisandro	0	2	1.06	6	3	0	0	17	9	5	2	1	18	R	R	6-3	200	9-2-75	1995	Santa Fe, Argentina
Fowler, Ben	1	2	1.09	12	0	0	1	25	17	13	3	13	23	S	R	6-4	185	1-21-77	1995	Alpharetta, Ga.
Gerland, Greg	1	0	0.00	2	0	0	0	4	1	0	0	1	3	L	L	6-2	175	11-20-72	1995	Euclid, Ohio
Johnson, Joaquin	0	0	5.00	11	2	0	0	27	25	17	15	16	15	L	L	6-4	195	10-15-76	1994	Emeryville, Calif.
Jolliffee, Brian	0	2	6.65	11	0	0	1	23	36	24	17	9	15	R	L	6-2	205	9-15-74	1995	Cumberland, Maine
Pacheco, Delvis	1	8	2.55	13	13	0	0	60	47	26	17	38	52	L	L	6-0	150	6-7-78	1994	Las Matas de Farfan, D.R.
Perez, Odaliz	3	5	2.22	12	12	1	0	65	48	22	16	18	62	L	L	6-0	150	6-7-78	1994	Las Matas de Farfan, D.R.
Shiell, Jason	1	3	4.43	12	0	0	2	22	23	16	11	10	13	R	R	6-0	180	10-19-76	1995	Savannah, Ga.
Shurman, Ryan	1	6	6.75	10	7	0	0	35	37	31	26	21	26	R	R	6-4	180	8-28-76	1995	Tualatin, Ore.
White, Eric	1	1	6.75	13	1	0	0	32	39	37	24	22	10	R	R	6-4	235	8-23-77	1995	Enfield, Conn.
Wise, William	0	2	6.75	4	0	0	0	7	11	8	5	3	6	L	L	6-4	200	3-20-76	1995	Meldrim, Ga.
Wyatt, Ben	1	3	2.98	12	8	1	1	42	36	25	14	27	24	L	L	6-4	170	11-14-76	1995	Little Rock, Ark.

BALTIMORE ORIOLES

Manager: Phil Regan. **1995 Record:** 71-73, .493 (3rd, AL East)

BATTING	AVG	G	AB	R	H	2B	3B	HR	RBI	BB	SO	SB	CS	B	T	HT	WT	DOB	1st Yr	Resides
Alexander, Manny	.236	94	242	35	57	9	1	3	23	20	30	11	4	R	R	5-10	165	3-20-71	1988	San Pedro de Macoris, D.R.
Anderson, Brady	.262	143	554	108	145	33	10	16	64	87	111	26	7	L	L	6-1	195	1-18-64	1985	Newport Beach, Calif.
Baines, Harold	.299	126	385	60	115	19	1	24	63	70	45	0	2	L	L	6-2	195	3-15-59	1977	St. Michaels, Md.
Barberie, Bret	.241	90	237	32	57	14	0	2	25	36	50	3	3	S	R	5-11	180	8-16-67	1989	Cerritos, Calif.
Bass, Kevin	.244	111	295	32	72	12	0	5	32	24	47	8	8	S	R	6-0	190	5-12-59	1977	Sugar Land, Texas
Bonilla, Bobby	.333	61	237	47	79	12	4	10	46	23	31	0	2	S	R	6-3	240	2-23-63	1981	Bradenton, Fla.
Brown, Jarvis	.148	18	27	2	4	1	0	0	1	7	9	1	1	R	R	5-7	170	3-26-67	1986	Mt. Zion, Ill.
Buford, Damon	.063	24	32	6	2	0	0	0	2	6	7	3	1	R	R	5-10	170	6-12-70	1990	Sherman Oaks, Calif.
Devarez, Cesar	.000	6	4	0	0	0	0	0	0	0	0	0	0	R	R	5-10	175	9-22-69	1988	San Pedro de Macoris, D.R.
Gomez, Leo	.236	53	127	16	30	5	0	4	12	18	23	0	1	R	R	6-0	208	3-2-67	1986	Canovanas, P.R.
Goodwin, Curtis	.263	87	289	40	76	11	3	1	24	15	53	22	4	L	L	5-11	180	9-30-72	1991	San Leandro, Calif.
Hammonds, Jeffrey	.242	57	178	18	43	9	1	4	23	9	30	4	2	R	R	6-0	180	3-5-71	1992	Scotch Plains, N.J.
Hoiles, Chris	.250	114	352	53	88	15	1	19	58	67	80	1	0	R	R	6-0	213	3-20-65	1986	Cockeysville, Md.
Huson, Jeff	.248	66	161	24	40	4	2	1	19	15	20	5	4	L	R	6-3	180	8-15-64	1986	Bedford, Texas
Manto, Jeff	.256	89	254	31	65	9	0	17	38	24	69	0	3	R	R	6-3	210	8-23-64	1985	Bristol, Pa.
Nokes, Matt	.122	26	49	4	6	1	0	2	6	4	11	0	0	L	R	6-1	195	10-31-63	1981	San Diego, Calif.
Obando, Sherman	.263	16	38	0	10	1	0	0	3	2	12	1	0	R	R	6-4	215	1-23-70	1988	Changuinola, Panama
Palmeiro, Rafael	.310	143	554	89	172	30	2	39	104	62	65	3	1	L	L	6-0	188	9-24-64	1985	Arlington, Texas
Ripken, Cal	.262	144	550	71	144	33	2	17	88	52	59	0	1	R	R	6-4	220	8-24-60	1978	Reisterstown, Md.
Smith, Mark	.231	37	104	11	24	5	0	3	15	12	22	3	0	R	R	6-3	205	5-7-70	1991	Arcadia, Calif.
Van Slyke, Andy	.159	17	63	6	10	1	0	3	8	5	15	0	0	L	R	6-2	195	12-21-60	1980	Chesterfield, Mo.
Voigt, Jack	1.000	3	1	1	1	0	0	0	0	0	0	0	0	R	R	6-1	175	5-17-66	1987	Venice, Fla.
Zaun, Greg	.260	40	104	18	27	5	0	3	14	16	14	1	1	S	R	5-10	170	4-14-71	1989	Glendale, Calif.

PITCHING	W	L	ERA	G	GS	CG	SV	IP	H	R	ER	BB	SO	B	T	HT	WT	DOB	1st Yr	Resides
Benitez, Armando	1	5	5.66	44	0	0	2	48	37	33	30	37	56	R	R	6-4	220	11-3-72	1990	San Pedro de Macoris, D.R.
Borowski, Joe	0	0	1.23	6	0	0	0	7	5	1	1	4	3	R	R	6-2	225	5-4-71	1989	Bayonne, N.J.
Brown, Kevin	10	9	3.60	26	26	3	0	172	155	73	69	48	117	R	R	6-4	215	2-14-72	1991	Brampton, Ontario
Clark, Terry	2	5	3.46	38	0	0	1	39	40	15	15	18	18	R	R	6-2	196	10-10-60	1979	La Puente, Calif.
Dedrick, Jim	0	0	2.35	6	0	0	0	8	8	2	2	6	3	S	R	6-0	185	4-4-68	1990	Everett, Wash.
DeSilva, John	1	0	7.27	2	2	0	0	9	8	7	7	7	1	R	R	6-0	193	9-30-67	1989	Fort Bragg, Calif.
Erickson, Scott	9	4	3.89	17	16	7	0	109	111	47	47	35	61	R	R	6-4	225	2-2-68	1989	Sunnyvale, Calif.
2-team (15 Minn.)	13	10	4.81	32	31	7	0	196	213	108	105	67	106							
Fernandez, Sid	0	4	7.39	8	7	0	0	28	36	26	23	17	31	L	L	6-1	220	10-12-62	1981	Kailua, Hawaii
Harris, Gene	0	0	4.50	3	0	0	0	4	4	2	2	1	4	R	R	5-11	190	12-5-64	1986	Okeechobee, Fla.
Hartley, Mike	1	0	1.29	3	0	0	0	7	5	1	1	1	4	R	R	6-1	197	8-31-61	1982	El Cajon, Calif.
2-team (5 Boston)	1	0	5.14	8	0	0	0	14	13	8	8	3	6							
Haynes, Jimmy	2	1	2.25	4	3	0	0	24	11	6	6	12	22	R	R	6-4	185	9-5-72	1991	LaGrange, Ga.
Jones, Doug	0	4	5.01	52	0	0	22	47	55	30	26	16	42	R	R	6-2	195	6-24-57	1978	Tucson, Ariz.
Klingenbeck, Scott	2	2	4.88	6	5	0	0	31	32	17	17	18	15	R	R	6-2	205	2-3-71	1992	Cincinnati, Ohio
Krivda, Rick	2	7	4.54	13	13	1	0	75	76	40	38	25	53	R	L	6-1	180	1-19-70	1991	McKeesport, Pa.
Lee, Mark	2	0	4.86	39	0	0	1	33	31	18	18	18	27	L	L	6-3	195	7-20-64	1985	Colorado Springs, Colo.
McDonald, Ben	3	6	4.16	14	13	1	0	80	67	40	37	38	62	R	R	6-7	210	11-24-67	1989	Denham Springs, La.
Mills, Alan	3	0	7.43	21	0	0	0	23	30	20	19	18	16	R	R	6-1	192	10-18-66	1986	Lakeland, Fla.
Moyer, Jamie	8	6	5.21	27	18	0	0	116	117	70	67	30	65	L	L	6-0	170	11-18-62	1984	Granger, Ill.
Mussina, Mike	19	9	3.29	32	32	7	0	222	187	86	81	50	158	R	R	6-2	185	12-8-68	1990	Montoursville, Pa.
Oquist, Mike	2	1	4.17	27	0	0	0	54	51	27	25	41	27	R	R	6-2	170	5-30-68	1989	La Junta, Colo.
Orosco, Jesse	2	4	3.26	65	0	0	3	50	28	19	18	27	58	R	L	6-2	205	4-21-57	1978	Poway, Calif.
Pennington, Brad	0	1	8.10	8	0	0	0	7	3	7	6	11	10	L	L	6-6	215	4-14-69	1989	Salem, Ind.
Rhodes, Arthur	2	5	6.21	19	9	0	0	75	68	53	52	48	77	L	L	6-2	204	10-24-69	1988	Sarasota, Fla.

FIELDING

Catcher	PCT	G	PO	A	E	DP	PB
Devarez	1.000	6	14	0	0	0	0
Hoiles	.996	107	659	33	3	6	4
Nokes	.989	16	83	5	1	0	1
Zaun	.987	39	216	13	3	4	3

First Base	PCT	G	PO	A	E	DP
Gomez	1.000	3	5	0	0	0
Manto	1.000	4	28	2	0	5
Palmeiro	.997	142	1181	119	4	120
Voigt	1.000	1	1	1	0	0

Second Base	PCT	G	PO	A	E	DP
Alexander	.971	81	136	165	9	48
Barberie	.977	74	114	187	7	45
Huson	1.000	21	38	44	0	14

Third Base	PCT	G	PO	A	E	DP
Alexander	.500	2	1	0	1	0
Barberie	1.000	3	0	1	0	0
Bonilla	.952	24	14	46	3	5
Gomez	.978	44	23	68	2	3

	PCT	G	PO	A	E	DP
Huson	1.000	33	21	44	0	5
Manto	.959	69	40	101	6	11

Shortstop	PCT	G	PO	A	E	DP
Alexander	1.000	7	2	5	0	1
Huson	.500	1	0	1	1	0
Ripken	.989	144	206	409	7	100

Outfield	PCT	G	PO	A	E	DP
Anderson	.989	142	268	1	3	0
Bass	.984	77	123	3	2	1
Bonilla	.971	39	66	2	2	0
Brown	1.000	17	16	0	0	0
Buford	1.000	24	40	0	0	0
Goodwin	.990	84	202	1	2	1
Hammonds	.989	46	88	1	1	0
Obando	.923	7	12	0	1	0
Smith	1.000	32	60	2	0	0
Van Slyke	.978	17	42	2	1	1

Rafael Palmeiro

MICHAEL PONZINI

ORIOLES

RON VESELY

Righthander Mike Mussina led the Orioles with 19 wins

Orioles minor league Player of the Year Rocky Coppinger

MEL BAILEY

FARM SYSTEM

Director of Player Development: Syd Thrift.

Class	Farm Team	League	W	L	Pct.	Finish*	Manager	First Yr
AAA	Rochester (N.Y.) Red Wings	International	73	69	.514	3rd (10)	Marv Foley	1961
AA	Bowie (Md.) Baysox	Eastern	68	74	.479	6th (10)	Bob Miscik	1993
#A	Frederick (Md.) Keys	Carolina	58	79	.449	8th (8)	Mike O'Berry	1989
#A	High Desert (Calif.) Mavericks	California	46	94	.329	10th (10)	Tim Blackwell	1995
#R	Bluefield (W.Va.) Orioles	Appalachian	49	16	.754	1st (10)	Andy Etchebarren	1958
R	Sarasota (Fla.) Orioles	Gulf Coast	34	25	.576	7th (16)	Julio Garcia	1991

*Finish in overall standings (No. of teams in league)   #Advanced level

ORGANIZATION LEADERS

MAJOR LEAGUERS

BATTING
*AVG	Rafael Palmeiro	.310
R	Brady Anderson	108
H	Rafael Palmeiro	172
TB	Rafael Palmeiro	323
2B	Two tied at	33
3B	Brady Anderson	10
HR	Rafael Palmeiro	39
RBI	Rafael Palmeiro	104
BB	Brady Anderson	87
SO	Brady Anderson	111
SB	Brady Anderson	26

PITCHING
W	Mike Mussina	19
L	Two tied at	9
#ERA	Mike Mussina	3.29
G	Jesse Orosco	65
CG	Mike Mussina	7
SV	Doug Jones	22
IP	Mike Mussina	222
BB	Mike Mussina	50
SO	Mike Mussina	158

Tommy Davis. 232 total bases

MINOR LEAGUERS

BATTING
*AVG	Matt Howard, Bowie	.303
R	Jarvis Brown, Bowie/Rochester	91
H	Tommy Davis, Frederick/Bowie	143
TB	Tommy Davis, Frederick/Bowie	232
2B	Jose Millares, Bowie	30
3B	Tom D'Aquila, High Desert	11
HR	Two tied at	21
RBI	Billy Owens, Bowie/Rochester	92
BB	Brad Tyler, Rochester	71
SO	Tommy Davis, Frederick/Bowie	114
SB	Miguel Mejia, Bluefield/High Desert	52

PITCHING
W	Rocky Coppinger, Fred./Bowie/Roch.	16
L	Ryan Griffin, High Desert	15
#ERA	Rocky Coppinger, Fred./Bowie/Roch.	1.97
G	Chris Lemp, Frederick/Bowie/Roch.	62
CG	Rocky Coppinger, Fred./Bowie/Roch.	4
SV	Chris Lemp, Frederick/Bowie/Roch.	23
IP	Rocky Coppinger, Fred./Bowie/Roch.	187
BB	Rocky Coppinger, Fred./Bowie/Roch.	84
SO	Rocky Coppinger, Fred./Bowie/Roch.	172

*Minimum 250 At-Bats   #Minimum 75 Innings

TOP 10 PROSPECTS

How the Orioles Top 10 prospects, as judged by Baseball America prior to the 1995 season, fared in 1995:

Armando Benitez

Player, Pos.	Club (Class—League)	AVG	AB	R	H	2B	3B	HR	RBI	SB
2. *Alex Ochoa, of	Rochester (AAA—International)	.274	336	41	92	18	2	8	46	17
	Norfolk (AAA—International)	.309	123	17	38	6	2	2	15	7
	New York Mets	.297	37	7	11	1	0	0	0	1
4. Curtis Goodwin, of	Rochester (AAA—International)	.264	140	24	37	3	3	0	7	17
	Baltimore	.263	289	40	76	11	3	1	24	22
6. Manny Alexander, 2b	Baltimore	.236	242	35	57	9	1	3	23	11
7. Tommy Davis, 3b	Frederick (A—Carolina)	.268	496	62	133	26	3	15	57	7
	Bowie (AA—Eastern)	.313	32	5	10	3	0	3	10	0

		W	L	ERA	G	SV	IP	H	BB	SO
1. Armando Benitez, rhp	Rochester (AAA—International)	2	2	1.25	17	8	22	10	7	37
	Baltimore	1	5	5.66	44	2	47	37	37	56
3. Jimmy Haynes, rhp	Rochester (AAA—International)	12	8	3.29	26	0	167	162	49	140
	Baltimore	2	1	2.25	4	0	24	11	12	22
5. Rocky Coppinger, rhp	Frederick (A—Carolina)	7	1	1.57	11	0	69	46	24	91
	Bowie (AA—Eastern)	6	2	2.69	13	0	84	58	43	62
	Rochester (AAA—International)	3	0	1.04	5	0	35	23	17	19
8. Brian Sackinsky, rhp	Rochester (AAA—International)	3	3	4.60	14	0	63	70	10	42
9. Calvin Maduro, rhp	Frederick (A—Carolina)	8	5	2.94	20	0	122	109	34	120
	Bowie (AA—Eastern)	0	6	5.09	7	0	35	39	27	26
10. William Percibal, rhp	High Desert (A—California)	7	6	3.23	21	0	128	123	55	105
	Bowie (AA—Eastern)	1	0	0.00	2	0	14	7	7	7

*Traded to New York Mets

ROCHESTER — AAA

INTERNATIONAL LEAGUE

BATTING	AVG	G	AB	R	H	2B	3B	HR	RBI	BB	SO	SB	CS	B	T	HT	WT	DOB	1st Yr	Resides
Alfonzo, Edgar	.185	18	54	5	10	3	0	1	6	2	10	0	0	R	R	6-0	167	6-10-67	1985	Santa Teresa Del Tuy, Venez.
Bartee, Kimera	.154	15	52	5	8	2	1	0	3	0	16	0	0	S	R	6-0	180	7-21-72	1993	Omaha, Neb.
Batiste, Kim	.281	66	260	31	73	13	1	3	29	8	27	4	8	R	R	6-0	193	3-15-68	1987	Prairieville, La.
2-team (32 Scranton)	.264	98	382	41	101	17	2	7	47	10	41	5	8							
Brown, Jarvis	.314	17	70	12	22	4	2	0	4	10	20	1	1	R	R	5-7	170	3-26-67	1986	Mt. Zion, Ill.
2-team (45 Norfolk)	.294	62	218	41	64	16	5	0	21	28	49	7	4							
Buford, Damon	.309	46	188	40	58	12	3	4	18	17	26	17	4	R	R	5-10	170	6-12-70	1990	Sherman Oaks, Calif.
Carey, Paul	.236	89	284	39	67	13	0	9	50	40	68	1	2	L	R	6-4	215	1-8-68	1990	Weymouth, Mass.
Crowley, Jim	.173	34	98	7	17	3	0	1	6	7	21	0	1	R	R	6-0	190	10-16-69	1991	Cockeysville, Md.
DeJardin, Bobby	.314	9	35	6	11	2	0	0	3	3	3	1	0	S	R	5-11	180	1-8-67	1988	Huntington Beach, Calif.
Devarez, Cesar	.250	67	240	32	60	12	1	1	21	7	25	2	2	R	R	5-10	175	9-22-69	1988	San Pedro de Macoris, D.R.
Friedman, Jason	.377	25	61	9	23	4	0	4	9	6	8	0	0	L	L	6-1	200	8-8-69	1989	Cypress, Calif.
2-team (14 Paw.)	.339	39	112	15	38	7	0	6	18	8	11	0	0							
Goodwin, Curtis	.264	36	140	24	37	3	3	0	7	12	15	17	3	L	L	5-11	180	9-30-72	1991	San Leandro, Calif.
Gresham, Kris	.250	21	64	5	16	2	1	0	4	4	15	0	0	R	R	6-2	206	8-30-70	1991	Mt. Pleasant, N.C.
Huson, Jeff	.251	60	223	28	56	9	0	3	21	26	29	16	5	L	R	6-3	180	8-15-64	1986	Bedford, Texas
Knapp, Mike	.183	40	126	10	23	1	1	1	12	12	26	1	1	R	R	6-0	195	10-6-64	1986	Sacramento, Calif.
Lewis, T.R.	.295	22	78	12	23	7	0	4	19	7	14	1	1	R	R	6-0	180	4-17-71	1989	Jacksonville, Fla.
McClain, Scott	.251	61	199	32	50	9	1	8	22	23	34	0	1	R	R	6-3	209	5-19-72	1990	Glendale, Ariz.
McGinnis, Russ	.182	20	55	8	10	2	0	3	11	17	19	0	0	R	R	6-3	225	6-18-63	1985	Phoenix, Ariz.
Noboa, Junior	.100	6	20	1	2	0	0	0	2	0	0	0	0	R	R	5-10	165	11-10-64	1981	Santo Domingo, D.R.
Obando, Sherman	.296	85	324	42	96	26	6	9	53	29	57	1	1	R	R	6-4	215	1-23-70	1988	Changuinola, Panama
Ochoa, Alex	.274	91	336	41	92	18	2	8	46	26	50	17	7	R	R	6-0	185	3-29-72	1991	Miami Lakes, Fla.
Owens, Billy	.143	9	28	2	4	0	0	0	1	1	6	0	0	S	R	6-1	210	4-12-71	1992	Fresno, Calif.
Robertson, Rod	.278	101	338	54	94	21	2	15	58	22	63	8	7	S	R	5-9	175	1-16-68	1986	Orange, Texas
Smith, Greg	.229	52	210	32	48	6	1	4	21	21	24	14	3	S	R	6-0	180	4-5-67	1985	Palm Springs, Calif.
Smith, Mark	.277	96	364	55	101	25	3	12	66	24	69	7	3	R	R	6-3	205	5-7-70	1991	Arcadia, Calif.
Tyler, Brad	.258	114	361	60	93	17	3	17	52	71	63	10	5	L	R	6-2	175	3-3-69	1990	Aurora, Ind.
Wawruck, Jim	.302	39	149	21	45	12	3	1	23	13	23	5	4	L	L	5-11	185	4-23-70	1991	Glastonbury, Conn.
Woods, Tyrone	.261	70	238	30	62	17	1	8	31	24	68	2	3	R	R	6-1	190	8-19-69	1988	Brooksville, Fla.
Zaun, Greg	.293	42	140	26	41	13	1	6	18	14	21	0	3	S	R	5-10	170	4-14-71	1989	Glendale, Calif.

PITCHING	W	L	ERA	G	GS	CG	SV	IP	H	R	ER	BB	SO	B	T	HT	WT	DOB	1st Yr	Resides
Benitez, Armando	2	2	1.25	17	0	0	8	22	10	4	3	7	37	R	R	6-4	220	11-3-72	1990	San Pedro de Macoris, D.R.
Borowski, Joe	1	3	4.04	28	0	0	6	36	32	16	16	18	32	R	R	6-2	225	5-4-71	1989	Bayonne, N.J.
Chavez, Carlos	0	0	10.80	1	0	0	0	2	3	2	2	3	1	R	R	6-1	200	8-25-72	1992	El Paso, Texas
Chitren, Steve	0	0	2.45	2	0	0	0	4	6	3	1	3	0	R	R	6-0	180	6-8-67	1989	Las Vegas, Nev.
Clark, Terry	1	2	2.70	9	0	0	5	10	5	3	3	2	10	R	R	6-2	196	10-10-60	1979	La Puente, Calif.
Coppinger, Rocky	3	0	1.04	5	5	0	0	35	23	5	4	17	19	R	R	6-5	245	3-19-74	1994	El Paso, Texas
Dedrick, Jim	4	0	1.77	24	2	0	1	46	45	9	9	14	31	S	R	6-0	185	4-4-68	1990	Everett, Wash.
Dettmer, John	4	7	4.68	21	11	1	1	83	98	52	43	16	46	R	R	6-0	185	3-4-70	1992	Glencoe, Mo.
DeSilva, John	11	9	4.18	26	25	2	0	151	156	78	70	51	82	R	R	6-0	193	9-30-67	1989	Fort Bragg, Calif.
Forney, Rick	0	0	3.94	3	3	0	0	16	19	9	7	6	12	R	R	6-4	210	10-24-71	1991	Arnold, Md.
Hartley, Mike	0	1	0.82	8	0	0	0	11	4	1	1	2	12	R	R	6-1	197	8-31-61	1982	El Cajon, Calif.
2-team (26 Paw.)	1	2	3.43	34	1	0	1	58	51	22	22	14	51							
Haynes, Jimmy	12	8	3.29	26	25	3	0	167	162	77	61	49	140	R	R	6-4	185	9-5-72	1991	LaGrange, Ga.
Holman, Brad	0	1	0.00	1	1	0	0	2	5	4	0	2	0	R	R	6-5	200	2-9-68	1990	Wichita, Kan.
Hurst, James	1	1	3.79	10	0	0	0	19	17	8	8	4	17	L	L	6-0	165	6-1-67	1990	Sebring, Fla.
Klingenbeck, Scott	3	1	2.72	8	7	0	0	43	46	14	13	10	29	R	R	6-2	205	2-3-71	1992	Cincinnati, Ohio
Krivda, Rick	6	5	3.19	16	16	1	0	102	96	44	36	32	74	R	L	6-1	180	1-19-70	1991	McKeesport, Pa.
Lane, Aaron	0	0	6.30	9	0	0	0	10	11	11	7	5	9	L	L	6-1	180	6-2-71	1992	Taylorville, Ill.
Lee, Mark	4	2	1.57	25	0	0	3	29	18	6	5	5	35	L	L	6-3	195	7-20-64	1985	Colorado Springs, Colo.
Lemp, Chris	0	1	11.25	3	0	0	0	4	7	5	5	3	4	R	R	6-0	175	7-23-71	1991	Sacramento, Calif.
Magee, Bo	0	0	13.50	2	0	0	0	2	4	3	3	1	1	R	L	6-4	180	4-9-68	1991	Jackson, Miss.
McDonald, Ben	0	0	2.45	1	1	0	0	4	1	2	1	4	1	R	R	6-7	210	11-24-67	1989	Denham Springs, La.
McGehee, Kevin	11	9	5.83	27	20	0	0	127	150	89	82	33	84	R	R	6-0	190	1-18-69	1990	Pineville, La.
Mills, Alan	0	1	0.00	1	1	0	0	3	2	6	0	5	2	S	R	6-1	192	10-18-66	1986	Lakeland, Fla.
Myers, Jimmy	0	4	3.06	55	0	0	6	65	72	28	22	29	31	R	R	6-1	185	4-28-69	1987	Crowder, Okla.
Oquist, Mike	0	0	5.25	7	0	0	2	12	17	8	7	5	11	R	R	6-2	170	5-30-68	1989	La Junta, Colo.
Rhodes, Arthur	2	1	2.70	4	4	1	0	30	27	12	9	8	33	L	L	6-2	204	10-24-69	1988	Sarasota, Fla.
Ryan, Kevin	0	3	9.35	6	2	0	0	17	27	20	18	4	7	R	R	6-1	187	9-23-70	1991	Oklahoma City, Okla.
Sackinsky, Brian	3	3	4.60	14	11	0	0	63	70	33	32	10	42	R	R	6-4	220	6-22-71	1992	Library, Pa.
Seminara, Frank	1	0	3.28	29	0	0	0	36	31	13	13	14	20	R	R	6-2	195	5-16-67	1988	Brooklyn, N.Y.
Shea, John	0	1	2.95	38	0	0	4	40	38	16	13	17	37	R	L	6-6	210	6-23-66	1986	Dunedin, Fla.
Wegmann, Tom	3	2	3.44	9	5	1	0	34	30	15	13	9	23	R	R	6-0	190	8-29-68	1990	Dyersville, Iowa
Williams, Jimmy	1	2	7.11	5	3	0	0	13	21	13	10	9	12	L	L	6-7	232	5-18-65	1984	Butler, Ala.
2-team (27 Norfolk)	12	6	3.48	32	16	0	2	119	110	55	46	65	100							

FIELDING

Catcher	PCT	G	PO	A	E	DP	PB
Devarez	.995	52	331	40	2	4	5
Gresham	.965	21	127	12	5	3	0
Knapp	.996	36	203	23	1	1	3
McGinnis	1.000	2	12	1	0	0	1
Robertson	1.000	2	7	2	0	0	1
Zaun	.989	34	243	18	3	1	1

First Base	PCT	G	PO	A	E	DP
Carey	.991	76	633	47	6	61
Crowley	1.000	2	21	0	0	1
Friedman	1.000	11	82	10	0	8
McGinnis	1.000	4	29	1	0	2
Obando	.962	16	137	14	6	15
Owens	.985	9	60	4	1	3
Robertson	.944	4	17	0	1	1
Woods	.988	30	227	18	3	22
Alfonzo	1.000	1	1	3	0	0

Second Base	PCT	G	PO	A	E	DP
Crowley	.982	24	49	61	2	19
DeJardin	.974	8	15	23	1	5
Huson	1.000	8	25	28	0	9
Noboa	.909	6	9	11	2	0
Robertson	.907	12	22	27	5	11
Tyler	.970	94	171	252	13	46

Third Base	PCT	G	PO	A	E	DP
Alfonzo	.750	3	0	3	1	0
Batiste	.934	63	51	104	11	9
Crowley	1.000	8	3	10	0	3
DeJardin	1.000	2	1	1	0	0
Knapp	.000	1	0	0	0	0
McClain	.940	61	41	130	11	9
Robertson	.935	10	5	24	2	3

Shortstop	PCT	G	PO	A	E	DP
Alfonzo	.971	9	13	21	1	5
Batiste	1.000	3	3	3	0	0
Huson	.974	54	85	175	7	43

Shortstop	PCT	G	PO	A	E	DP
Robertson	.926	33	40	86	10	16
G. Smith	.963	52	83	149	9	26

Outfield	PCT	G	PO	A	E	DP
Bartee	1.000	15	37	2	0	0
Brown	.949	17	55	1	3	1

	PCT	G	PO	A	E	DP
Buford	.983	46	115	2	2	0
Friedman	1.000	4	5	0	0	0
Goodwin	.965	36	81	1	3	0
Lewis	.905	10	19	0	2	0
Obando	.960	29	47	1	2	0
Ochoa	.975	91	183	9	5	1

	PCT	G	PO	A	E	DP
Robertson	.909	39	57	3	6	0
M. Smith	.961	95	167	4	7	1
Tyler	.964	15	26	1	1	0
Wawruck	1.000	30	75	6	0	1
Woods	.938	14	14	1	1	0

BOWIE   AA

EASTERN LEAGUE

BATTING	AVG	G	AB	R	H	2B	3B	HR	RBI	BB	SO	SB	CS	B	T	HT	WT	DOB	1st Yr	Resides
Alfonzo, Edgar	.304	28	112	14	34	6	0	1	19	10	16	1	2	R	R	6-0	167	6-10-67	1985	Santa Teresa, Venez.
Arnold, Ken	.000	10	22	3	0	0	0	0	0	6	8	0	0	R	R	6-1	180	5-10-69	1991	Atco, N.J.
Avila, Rolando	.233	16	43	8	10	2	0	0	4	6	8	2	2	R	R	5-8	170	8-10-73	1994	Paramount, Calif.
Bartee, Kimera	.284	53	218	45	62	9	1	3	19	23	45	22	7	S	R	6-0	180	7-21-72	1993	Omaha, Neb.
Batiste, Kim	.358	24	95	16	34	5	0	4	27	6	14	2	0	R	R	6-0	193	3-15-68	1987	Prairieville, La.
Bautista, Juan	.105	13	38	3	4	2	0	0	0	3	5	1	0	R	R	6-1	185	6-24-75	1992	San Pedro de Macoris, D.R.
Berrios, Harry	.245	56	208	32	51	13	0	5	21	26	44	12	2	R	R	5-11	205	12-2-71	1993	Grand Rapids, Mich.
Brown, Jarvis	.279	58	219	50	61	12	1	6	23	33	49	12	3	R	R	5-7	170	3-26-67	1986	Mt. Zion, Ill.
Byrne, Clayton	.218	14	55	5	12	2	1	1	6	4	8	2	1	R	R	6-2	215	2-12-72	1991	Perth, Australia
Castaldo, Gregg	.234	104	265	37	62	12	3	2	26	39	61	5	3	R	R	6-0	180	3-14-71	1992	Grover, Mo.
Castaneda, Hector	.154	34	65	3	10	2	0	0	6	10	10	0	0	L	R	6-2	190	11-1-71	1992	Mexico City, Mexico
Chavez, Eric	.196	14	51	5	10	2	0	2	4	4	17	0	0	R	R	5-11	212	9-7-70	1992	Carlsbad, N.M.
Crowley, Jim	.214	29	98	11	21	5	0	2	13	23	23	1	1	R	R	6-0	190	10-16-69	1991	Cockeysville, Md.
Davis, Tommy	.313	9	32	5	10	3	0	3	10	1	9	0	0	R	R	6-1	195	5-21-73	1994	Semmes, Ala.
Friedman, Jason	.232	63	228	22	53	11	0	3	27	16	23	1	1	L	L	6-1	200	8-8-69	1989	Cypress, Calif.
Fully, Ed	.218	34	119	15	26	5	0	2	6	6	23	2	3	R	R	5-11	191	7-14-71	1989	St. Lucie, Fla.
2-team (18 Bing.)	.213	52	155	19	33	6	0	3	9	6	28	2	5							
Gresham, Kris	.077	5	13	1	1	0	0	0	0	3	5	1	0	R	R	6-2	206	8-30-70	1991	Mt. Pleasant, N.C.
Hammonds, Jeffrey	.387	9	31	7	12	3	1	1	11	10	7	3	0	R	R	6-0	180	3-5-71	1992	Scotch Plains, N.J.
Hodge, Roy	.172	29	99	11	17	1	1	0	9	18	15	2	0	R	R	6-2	191	6-22-71	1990	St. Thomas, V.I.
Howard, Matt	.303	70	251	42	76	8	2	1	15	29	27	22	4	R	R	5-10	170	9-22-67	1989	San Diego, Calif.
Hugo, Sean	.222	43	117	15	26	3	0	0	10	20	29	1	1	L	L	6-1	185	9-7-72	1994	Oklahoma City, Okla.
Lamb, David	.250	1	4	0	1	0	0	0	1	0	1	0	0	S	R	6-2	165	6-6-75	1993	Newbury Park, Calif.
Lewis, T.R.	.294	86	309	57	91	19	1	5	44	40	43	12	3	R	R	6-0	180	4-17-71	1989	Jacksonville, Fla.
Manto, Jeff	.250	1	4	1	1	0	0	0	0	0	2	0	0	R	R	6-3	210	8-23-64	1985	Bristol, Pa.
McClain, Scott	.278	70	259	41	72	14	1	13	61	25	44	2	1	R	R	6-3	209	5-19-72	1990	Glendale, Ariz.
Mercedes, Feliciano	.150	28	80	10	12	1	0	0	7	6	14	2	3	S	R	5-10	145	7-9-73	1990	Villa Magdalena, D.R.
Michael, Jeff	.167	4	12	2	2	0	0	0	0	4	4	0	0	R	R	6-0	174	8-8-71	1993	Hamilton, Ohio
Millares, Jose	.248	120	411	50	102	30	3	4	50	20	62	7	6	R	R	5-11	190	3-24-68	1990	Palmdale, Calif.
Owens, Billy	.269	122	453	57	122	27	0	17	91	43	87	2	1	S	R	6-1	210	4-12-71	1992	Fresno, Calif.
Rodriguez, Nerio	.000	3	4	0	0	0	0	0	0	0	2	0	0	R	R	6-1	195	3-22-73	1991	San Pedro de Macoris, D.R.
Valdez, Trovin	.000	2	0	0	0	0	0	0	0	0	0	0	0	S	R	5-10	163	11-18-73	1993	New York, N.Y.
Van Slyke, Andy	.500	2	6	2	3	0	0	0	2	3	0	0	0	L	R	6-2	195	12-21-60	1980	Chesterfield, Mo.
Virgilio, George	.234	41	107	11	25	3	0	1	13	13	11	0	0	S	R	5-9	170	2-15-71	1989	Elizabeth, N.J.
2-team (27 Harr.)	.202	68	163	20	33	3	0	2	18	33	22	1	1							
Waszgis, B.J.	.253	130	438	53	111	22	0	10	50	70	91	2	4	R	R	6-2	210	8-24-70	1991	Omaha, Neb.
Wawruck, Jim	.278	56	212	29	59	7	1	6	30	20	31	7	3	L	L	5-11	185	4-23-70	1991	Glastonbury, Conn.

PITCHING	W	L	ERA	G	GS	CG	SV	IP	H	R	ER	BB	SO	B	T	HT	WT	DOB	1st Yr	Resides
Borowski, Joe	2	2	3.92	16	0	0	7	21	16	9	9	7	32	R	R	6-2	225	5-4-71	1989	Bayonne, N.J.
Chavez, Carlos	0	0	0.00	1	0	0	0	2	2	0	0	1	2	R	R	6-1	200	8-25-72	1991	El Paso, Texas
Conner, Scott	5	1	4.17	44	0	0	0	82	57	43	38	74	82	R	R	6-2	192	3-22-72	1991	Irvine, Calif.
Coppinger, Rocky	6	2	2.69	13	13	2	0	84	58	33	25	43	62	R	R	6-5	245	3-19-74	1994	El Paso, Texas
Dedrick, Jim	4	2	2.98	10	10	0	0	60	59	24	20	25	48	S	R	6-0	185	4-4-68	1990	Everett, Wash.
Devereux, Charles	0	1	5.21	12	0	0	0	19	24	13	11	17	27	R	R	6-2	185	7-22-70	1992	Derwood, Md.
Emerson, Scott	0	2	5.06	4	4	0	0	16	19	18	9	14	13	R	R	6-3	185	4-22-69	1992	Phoenix, Ariz.
Faino, Jeff	0	2	2.72	31	0	0	0	43	34	18	13	15	17	R	L	6-0	185	11-22-72	1992	Danvers, Mass.
2-team (5 Trenton)	1	3	2.66	36	0	0	0	51	43	21	15	16	22							
Fernandez, Sid	1	0	0.75	2	2	1	0	12	4	2	1	3	10	L	L	6-1	220	10-12-62	1981	Kailua, Hawaii
Forney, Rick	7	7	5.75	23	19	1	0	97	110	69	62	42	73	R	R	6-4	210	10-24-71	1991	Arnold, Md.
Harris, Doug	3	5	4.01	11	11	2	0	61	66	30	27	15	32	R	R	6-4	205	9-27-69	1990	Carlisle, Pa.
Hurst, James	0	0	0.00	1	0	0	0	1	2	3	0	1	1	L	L	6-0	165	6-1-67	1990	Sebring, Fla.
Jarvis, Matt	9	8	5.11	26	21	0	0	118	154	71	67	42	60	R	L	6-4	185	2-22-72	1991	Albuquerque, N.M.
Knowles, Greg	5	2	4.14	37	1	0	0	74	83	44	34	26	37	R	R	6-3	196	1-9-69	1991	Plantation, Fla.
Lane, Aaron	5	3	4.17	40	0	0	2	45	45	23	21	31	31	L	L	6-1	180	6-21-72	1992	Taylorville, Ill.
Lehman, Toby	1	3	7.94	4	4	0	0	17	20	15	15	11	14	R	R	6-0	200	8-12-71	1992	San Marcos, Calif.
Lemp, Chris	2	4	5.40	18	0	0	4	20	28	13	12	7	14	R	R	6-0	175	7-23-71	1991	Sacramento, Calif.
Maduro, Calvin	0	6	5.09	7	7	0	0	35	39	28	20	27	26	R	R	6-0	175	9-5-74	1992	Santa Cruz, Aruba
Magee, Bo	1	1	5.40	5	1	0	0	8	10	8	5	6	7	R	L	6-4	180	4-9-68	1991	Jackson, Miss.
2-team (21 Canton)	1	3	6.63	26	1	0	1	38	43	34	28	34	32							
Newlin, Jim	3	5	3.68	40	1	0	11	64	69	35	26	22	51	R	R	6-2	205	9-11-66	1989	Leawood, Kan.
Nieto, Tony	0	0	15.00	1	1	0	0	3	6	5	5	3	3	S	R	6-1	170	4-19-73	1994	Monterey Park, Calif.
Percibal, William	1	0	0.00	2	2	0	0	14	7	0	0	7	7	R	R	6-1	170	2-2-74	1992	San Pedro de Macoris, D.R.
Pierce, Ed	2	6	6.43	7	4	0	1	21	32	16	15	9	16	L	L	6-1	190	6-26-68	1989	San Dimas, Calif.
Ryan, Kevin	4	3	3.43	39	0	0	5	63	67	31	24	15	31	R	R	6-1	187	9-23-70	1991	Oklahoma City, Okla.
Shenk, Larry	0	0	6.52	6	0	0	0	10	6	8	7	8	8	R	R	6-0	185	6-13-69	1992	Federal Way, Wash.
Stephenson, Garrett	7	10	3.64	29	29	1	0	175	154	87	71	47	139	R	R	6-4	185	1-2-72	1992	Kimberly, Md.
Wegmann, Tom	2	3	4.18	14	11	0	0	65	56	35	30	22	49	R	R	6-0	190	8-29-68	1990	Dyersville, Iowa

Catcher	PCT	G	PO	A	E	DP	PB
Castaneda	.984	32	113	12	2	2	3
Gresham	.971	5	33	1	1	0	0
Rodriguez	1.000	3	13	1	0	0	0
Waszgis	.982	125	782	89	16	6	23

First Base	PCT	G	PO	A	E	DP
Arnold	1.000	2	1	0	0	0
E. Chavez	.981	12	99	7	2	8
Davis	1.000	3	28	2	0	4
Friedman	.987	44	359	35	5	31
Millares	.966	3	24	4	1	3
Owens	.988	82	665	60	9	62
Waszgis	1.000	1	1	0	0	0

Second Base	PCT	G	PO	A	E	DP
Alfonzo	1.000	19	36	38	0	10
Castaldo	.971	48	86	116	6	28
Crowley	.976	8	19	21	1	6
Mercedes	.982	26	44	67	2	11

	PCT	G	PO	A	E	DP
Millares	.938	30	54	51	7	15
Virgilio	.947	26	46	62	6	12

Third Base	PCT	G	PO	A	E	DP
Alfonzo	1.000	1	0	1	0	0
Batiste	.881	23	14	38	7	1
Castaldo	1.000	2	2	0	0	0
Chavez	.875	2	1	6	1	1
Crowley	.964	20	15	38	2	6
McClain	.933	70	57	165	16	15
Millares	.874	25	20	56	11	3
Virgilio	1.000	1	1	4	0	0

Shortstop	PCT	G	PO	A	E	DP
Alfonzo	.889	12	13	27	5	6
Arnold	.964	7	6	21	1	5
Batiste	.833	1	1	4	1	0
Bautista	.907	12	21	28	5	8
Castaldo	.948	46	64	120	10	16
Howard	.972	67	86	196	8	38

	PCT	G	PO	A	E	DP
Lamb	.800	1	1	3	1	2
Michael	.750	4	8	7	5	2

Outfield	PCT	G	PO	A	E	DP
Avila	.935	13	28	1	2	0
Bartee	.964	53	155	4	6	1
Berrios	.979	54	94	1	2	0
Brown	.972	58	135	4	4	1
Byrne	1.000	14	27	2	0	1
Friedman	1.000	2	2	0	0	0
Fully	.932	33	80	2	6	1
Hammonds	.923	7	12	0	1	0
Hodge	.968	27	54	6	2	0
Hugo	1.000	34	64	2	0	0
Lewis	.942	76	128	1	8	0
Millares	1.000	20	23	2	0	0
Valdez	.000	1	0	0	0	0
VanSlyke	1.000	2	4	0	0	0
Wawruck	.986	51	68	3	1	0

HIGH DESERT · A

CALIFORNIA LEAGUE

BATTING	AVG	G	AB	R	H	2B	3B	HR	RBI	BB	SO	SB	CS	B	T	HT	WT	DOB	1st Yr	Resides
Avila, Rolando	.239	52	180	26	43	10	1	2	10	29	26	19	8	R	R	5-8	170	8-10-73	1994	Paramount, Calif.
Bautista, Juan	.262	99	374	54	98	13	4	11	51	18	74	22	9	R	R	6-1	185	6-24-75	1992	San Pedro de Macoris, D.R.
Bishop, Steve	.116	12	43	5	5	1	1	0	3	4	12	1	0	R	R	6-4	205	9-14-70	1993	Atlanta, Ga.
Bogle, Bryan	.172	19	64	7	11	2	1	0	4	8	18	3	1	R	R	6-1	205	5-18-73	1994	Merritt Island, Fla.
Byrne, Clayton	.236	54	199	24	47	10	2	1	19	7	36	7	5	R	R	6-2	215	2-12-72	1991	Perth, Australia
Cabrera, Jairo	.205	14	39	2	8	0	0	0	3	3	7	1	0	R	R	5-11	180	6-13-72	1991	Colon, Panama
Chavez, Eric	.232	74	254	38	59	15	0	14	37	27	74	4	2	R	R	5-11	212	9-7-70	1992	Carlsbad, N.M.
Clark, Howie	.258	100	329	50	85	20	2	5	40	32	51	12	6	L	R	5-10	171	2-13-74	1992	Huntington Beach, Calif.
Clyburn, Danny	.281	45	160	20	45	3	1	12	37	17	41	2	1	R	R	6-3	217	4-6-74	1992	Lancaster, S.C.
Curtis, Kevin	.293	112	399	70	117	26	1	21	70	54	83	8	6	R	R	6-2	210	8-19-72	1993	Upland, Calif.
D'Aquila, Tom	.264	110	386	48	102	10	11	11	63	45	111	8	7	R	R	6-1	190	4-15-73	1994	Middletown, Conn.
Eaddy, Keith	.244	99	336	58	82	17	4	12	42	43	107	20	9	R	R	5-9	180	11-23-70	1992	Newark, N.J.
Fully, Ed	.369	38	149	28	55	11	0	6	34	7	22	9	6	R	R	5-11	191	7-14-71	1989	St. Lucie, Fla.
Gargiulo, Mike	.206	14	34	2	7	1	0	0	4	1	9	0	1	L	R	6-1	175	1-22-75	1993	Harrisburg, Pa.
Gresham, Kris	.257	47	140	25	36	8	0	5	15	12	31	1	3	R	R	6-2	206	8-30-70	1991	Mt. Pleasant, N.C.
Harmer, Frank	.250	6	12	3	3	1	0	1	1	5	5	0	0	S	R	6-3	210	5-21-75	1994	Altamonte Springs, Fla.
Hodge, Roy	.300	42	140	31	42	8	1	3	15	36	24	8	7	R	R	6-2	191	6-22-71	1990	St. Thomas, V.I.
Hugo, Sean	.240	28	75	8	18	3	1	1	13	12	21	1	1	L	L	6-1	185	9-7-72	1994	Oklahoma City, Okla.
Knapp, Mike	.267	5	15	1	4	1	0	0	1	2	6	0	1	R	R	6-0	195	10-6-64	1986	Sacramento, Calif.
Martin, Lincoln	.240	54	150	27	36	7	2	1	12	28	37	7	4	S	R	5-10	170	10-20-71	1993	Douglasville, Ga.
Mejia, Miguel	.269	37	119	14	32	6	1	0	12	14	17	16	7	R	R	6-1	155	3-25-75	1992	San Pedro de Macoris, D.R.
Mercedes, Feliciano	.234	31	107	10	25	4	1	0	10	5	24	5	0	S	R	5-10	145	7-9-73	1990	Villa Magdalena, D.R.
Nadeau, Mike	.246	22	57	5	14	0	0	0	4	6	12	3	2	R	R	5-9	180	8-31-73	1994	Portland, Ore.
Pagan, Angel	.157	35	115	12	18	3	1	1	10	4	29	3	2	S	R	6-1	175	4-23-74	1992	Arecibo, P.R.
Rodriguez, Nerio	.236	58	144	20	34	7	0	4	12	18	50	5	3	R	R	6-1	195	3-22-73	1991	San Pedro de Macoris, D.R.
Serra, Jose	.261	76	234	30	61	6	1	0	22	18	30	11	5	R	R	5-11	160	3-28-73	1991	San Pedro de Macoris, D.R.
Short, Rick	.418	29	98	14	41	3	0	4	12	10	5	1	2	R	R	6-0	190	12-6-72	1994	South Elgin, Ill.
Williamson, Joel	.167	24	66	5	11	2	0	1	3	18	1	0	0	R	R	6-0	175	10-18-69	1993	Winnetka, Ill.
Wolff, Mike	.271	94	292	32	79	17	3	5	44	16	53	3	5	L	L	6-3	205	2-17-73	1994	Granger, Ind.

GAMES BY POSITION: C—Cabrera 14, Chavez 12, Clark 1, Gargiulo 14, Gresham 47, Harmer 5, Knapp 5, Rodriguez 50, Williamson 24. **1B**—Chavez 4, Clark 1, Curtis 70, Wolff 79. **2B**—Clark 9, Martin 36, Mercedes 24, Nadeau 20, Pagan 11, Serra 40, Short 25. **3B**—Bogle 16, Chavez 37, Clark 82, Nadeau 2, Pagan 10, Serra 2, Short 5. **SS**—Bautista 96, Clark 1, Mercedes 8, Pagan 14, Serra 35, Short 2. **OF**—Avila 49, Bishop 9, Bogle 1, Byrne 51, Chavez 8, Clark 4, Clyburn 42, Curtis 1, D'Aquila 73, Eaddy 84, Fully 34, Hodge 36, Hugo 24, Martin 4, Mejia 34.

PITCHING	W	L	ERA	G	GS	CG	SV	IP	H	R	ER	BB	SO	B	T	HT	WT	DOB	1st Yr	Resides
Brewer, Brian	1	9	5.47	17	15	1	0	81	96	66	49	42	65	L	L	5-11	210	12-10-71	1993	Fairfield, Calif.
Brown, Cory	2	7	5.36	30	10	0	3	94	104	66	56	32	80	R	R	6-3	166	6-29-73	1992	St. Petersburg, Fla.
Cafaro, Rocco	4	5	4.46	44	1	0	8	67	69	42	33	25	52	R	R	6-0	175	12-2-72	1993	Brandon, Fla.
Crills, Brad	1	2	5.51	5	3	0	0	16	19	15	10	8	10	R	R	6-0	195	10-16-71	1994	Ephrata, Pa.
Daigle, Tim	0	1	4.95	19	0	0	4	44	46	33	24	20	36	L	L	5-11	170	2-4-72	1994	Marrero, La.
Dyess, Todd	6	9	5.10	23	22	0	0	125	145	94	71	58	118	R	R	6-3	192	3-20-73	1994	Florence, Miss.
Dykhoff, Radhames	1	5	5.02	34	2	0	3	81	95	68	45	44	88	L	L	6-0	205	9-27-74	1993	Oranjestad, Aruba
Gambs, Chris	0	0	12.00	3	0	0	0	3	4	4	4	4	1	R	R	6-2	210	10-26-73	1991	Richmond, Calif.
Griffin, Ryan	6	15	6.80	31	25	0	3	143	182	129	108	80	90	R	R	6-5	195	10-15-73	1993	Dunedin, Fla.
Hackett, Jason	3	1	5.18	18	2	0	1	40	43	30	23	31	29	L	L	6-1	176	3-10-75	1994	Worton, Md.
Hill, Chris	0	2	9.00	5	1	0	0	13	20	13	13	7	10	L	L	6-1	175	4-13-69	1988	Duncanville, Texas
Karns, Tim	1	0	0.59	7	0	0	0	15	10	6	1	9	9	R	R	6-4	195	9-21-72	1993	Lakewood, Colo.
LaRocca, Todd	0	7	7.41	15	7	0	1	51	68	53	42	29	31	R	R	6-1	185	9-21-72	1994	Atlanta, Ga.
Pena, Alex	3	4	6.66	34	6	0	3	77	97	68	57	28	44	R	R	6-0	175	9-9-72	1993	El Paso, Texas
Percibal, William	7	6	3.23	21	20	2	0	128	123	63	46	55	105	R	R	6-1	170	2-2-74	1992	San Pedro de Macoris, D.R.
Rodriguez, Nerio	0	0	1.80	7	0	0	0	10	8	2	2	7	10	R	R	6-1	195	3-22-73	1991	San Pedro de Macoris, D.R.
Rogers, Jason	1	3	7.83	5	5	0	0	23	32	26	20	18	10	L	L	6-6	215	4-5-73	1994	Reno, Nev.
Saneaux, Francisco	8	10	5.93	23	11	0	1	53	56	77	62	72	64	R	R	6-1	180	3-3-74	1991	Santo Domingo, D.R.
Sauritch, Chris	1	0	6.14	7	0	0	0	15	20	10	10	8	10	S	R	5-10	175	3-24-72	1994	Lake Forest, Calif.
Shenk, Larry	0	0	16.88	2	0	0	0	3	6	5	5	3	2	R	R	6-0	185	6-13-69	1992	Federal Way, Wash.
Smith, Hut	3	4	9.13	11	9	0	0	46	58	54	47	15	38	R	R	6-3	195	6-8-73	1992	Kannapolis, N.C.
Trimarco, Mike	6	6	5.27	40	1	0	2	101	109	70	59	36	52	R	R	6-0	170	12-22-71	1993	Aurora, Ill.

CAROLINA LEAGUE

BATTING	AVG	G	AB	R	H	2B	3B	HR	RBI	BB	SO	SB	CS	B	T	HT	WT	DOB	1st Yr	Resides
Avila, Rolando	.263	52	175	26	46	8	1	1	13	14	27	15	5	R	R	5-8	170	8-10-73	1994	Paramount, Calif.
Berrios, Harry	.208	71	240	33	50	5	2	10	28	32	66	10	6	R	R	5-11	205	12-2-71	1993	Grand Rapids, Mich.
Bridgers, Brandon	.161	10	31	3	5	3	0	0	5	11	5	1	1	R	R	5-11	170	8-31-72	1993	Fayetteville, N.C.
Brown, Todd	.237	32	59	6	14	4	0	0	2	5	21	6	2	S	R	5-10	155	4-14-72	1994	Venice, Fla.
Byrne, Clayton	.228	35	136	16	31	7	0	3	13	5	29	3	4	R	R	6-2	215	2-12-72	1991	Perth, Australia
Cabrera, Jairo	.183	25	60	7	11	1	0	0	1	7	13	0	1	R	R	5-11	180	6-13-72	1991	Colon, Panama
Castaneda, Hector	.213	17	47	6	10	1	1	0	4	6	9	0	0	L	R	6-2	190	11-1-71	1992	Mexico City, Mexico
Clyburn, Danny	.200	15	45	4	9	4	0	0	4	4	18	1	1	R	R	6-3	217	4-6-74	1992	Lancaster, S.C.
2-team (59 W-S)	.250	74	272	31	68	14	2	11	45	17	77	3	5							
Davis, Tommy	.268	130	496	62	133	26	3	15	57	41	105	7	1	R	R	6-1	195	5-21-73	1994	Semmes, Ala.
Dellucci, David	.281	28	96	16	27	3	0	1	10	12	10	1	2	L	L	5-10	180	10-31-73	1995	Baton Rouge, La.
Foster, Jim	.261	128	429	44	112	27	3	6	56	51	63	2	3	R	R	6-4	220	8-18-71	1993	Warwick, R.I.
Garcia, Jesse	.225	124	365	52	82	11	3	3	27	49	75	5	10	R	R	5-10	155	9-24-73	1993	Robstown, Texas
Gargiulo, Mike	.273	6	11	1	3	0	0	0	0	0	4	0	0	L	R	6-1	175	1-22-75	1993	Harrisburg, Pa.
Hawkins, Wes	.211	78	199	13	42	10	2	0	16	11	49	4	1	R	R	6-0	195	12-10-71	1993	Mansfield, La.
Hendricks, Ryan	.133	5	15	1	2	1	0	1	3	2	6	0	0	L	R	6-3	205	8-3-72	1994	Randallstown, Md.
Hodge, Roy	.256	48	172	19	44	12	1	1	17	16	31	4	3	R	R	6-2	191	6-22-71	1990	St. Thomas, V.I.
Hugo, Sean	.281	29	89	13	25	4	0	4	13	21	24	0	0	L	L	6-1	185	9-7-72	1994	Oklahoma City, Okla.
Hunter, Lanier	.143	7	14	1	2	1	0	0	1	7	0	0	0	S	R	5-11	168	2-13-73	1992	Hopewell, Va.
Kirgan, Chris	.201	124	378	25	76	18	2	11	47	25	107	3	2	L	L	6-4	225	6-29-73	1994	Littleton, Colo.
Lamb, David	.222	124	436	39	97	14	2	2	34	38	81	6	7	S	R	6-2	165	6-6-75	1993	Newbury Park, Calif.
LeCronier, Jason	.282	40	131	17	37	8	1	6	19	12	40	1	0	L	R	6-0	180	3-30-73	1995	Bay City, Mich.
Manto, Jeff	.375	2	8	1	3	0	0	1	3	0	1	0	0	R	R	6-3	210	8-23-64	1985	Bristol, Pa.
Michael, Jeff	.246	66	203	19	50	12	0	0	17	24	46	3	4	R	R	6-0	174	8-8-71	1993	Hamilton, Ohio
Pagan, Angel	.194	31	72	8	14	3	1	1	6	5	19	0	1	S	R	5-11	175	4-23-74	1992	Arecibo, P.R.
Quillin, Ty	.122	16	41	4	5	0	0	0	3	4	15	0	1	L	R	6-4	221	1-23-72	1990	Buhler, Kan.
Riemer, Matt	.182	27	77	6	14	2	0	1	10	4	22	0	1	R	R	6-3	173	9-1-72	1992	Baltimore, Md.
Sauritch, Chris	.067	9	15	2	1	0	0	0	1	5	6	2	1	S	R	5-10	175	3-24-72	1994	Lake Forest, Calif.
Short, Rick	.077	5	13	1	1	0	0	0	2	1	2	1	0	R	R	6-0	190	12-6-72	1994	South Elgin, Ill.
Valdez, Trovin	.245	112	375	51	92	12	4	0	13	18	77	34	21	S	R	5-10	163	11-18-73	1993	New York, N.Y.
Van Slyke, Andy	.000	1	2	1	0	0	0	0	0	2	1	0	0	L	R	6-2	195	12-21-60	1980	Chesterfield, Mo.

GAMES BY POSITION: C—Cabrera 25, Castaneda 10, Foster 112, Gargiulo 3, Pagan 1. **1B**—Davis 1, Hendricks 2, Hugo 4, Kirgan 115, Michael 28, Riemer 12. **2B**—Garcia 123, Lamb 1, Michael 12, Pagan 13, Quillin 1, Riemer 1, Sauritch 1. **3B**—Davis 120, Foster 1, Manto 1, Michael 15, Pagan 9, Riemer 1, Sauritch 1, Short 1. **SS**—Lamb 120, Michael 15, Pagan 5, Sauritch 1. **OF**—Avila 51, Berrios 46, Bridgers 10, Brown 27, Byrne 34, Clyburn 10, Davis 1, Dellucci 23, Hawkins 41, Hodge 47, Hugo 19, Hunter 3, LeCronier 27, Quillin 8, Riemer 7, Valdez 106, Van Slyke 1.

PITCHING	W	L	ERA	G	GS	CG	SV	IP	H	R	ER	BB	SO	B	T	HT	WT	DOB	1st Yr	Resides
Brewer, Brian	2	4	2.53	14	8	0	1	68	49	22	19	19	48	L	L	5-11	210	12-10-71	1993	Fairfield, Calif.
Chavez, Carlos	5	5	2.55	43	1	0	6	81	62	38	23	40	107	R	R	6-1	200	8-25-72	1992	El Paso, Texas
Coppinger, Rocky	7	1	1.57	11	11	2	0	69	46	16	12	24	91	R	R	6-5	245	3-19-74	1994	El Paso, Texas
Crills, Brad	2	5	3.06	9	9	3	0	62	63	26	21	12	33	R	R	6-0	195	10-16-71	1994	Ephrata, Pa.
Daigle, Tim	0	2	8.53	6	0	0	0	6	9	12	6	5	9	L	L	5-11	170	2-4-72	1994	Marrero, La.
Dawley, Joey	1	2	6.34	24	0	0	1	33	41	28	23	22	29	R	R	6-4	205	9-19-71	1993	Moreno Valley, Calif.
Dyess, Todd	0	2	6.59	3	3	0	0	14	17	10	10	5	8	R	R	6-3	192	3-20-73	1994	Florence, Miss.
Faino, Jeff	0	0	4.76	4	0	0	0	6	7	5	3	2	8	R	L	6-0	185	11-22-72	1992	Danvers, Mass.
Hale, Shane	0	2	10.93	6	2	0	0	14	21	18	17	6	6	R	L	6-1	180	12-30-68	1990	Mobile, Ala.
Hernandez, Francisco	0	1	6.00	3	0	0	1	3	3	2	2	3	3	R	R	6-0	160	12-17-76	1994	San Pedro de Macoris, D.R.
Huber, Jeff	2	0	5.21	21	0	0	0	19	29	16	11	5	11	R	L	6-4	220	12-17-70	1990	Scottsdale, Ariz.
Kitchen, Ron	2	2	7.23	30	0	0	0	37	55	35	30	10	10	R	R	6-1	218	7-4-71	1993	Belle Vernon, Pa.
LaRocca, Todd	3	1	1.76	5	5	0	0	31	22	7	6	16	24	R	R	6-1	185	9-21-72	1994	Atlanta, Ga.
Lehman, Toby	0	5	4.25	19	10	1	0	55	44	30	26	27	48	R	R	6-0	200	8-12-71	1992	San Marcos, Calif.
Lemp, Chris	2	3	2.38	41	0	0	19	45	44	16	12	17	50	R	R	6-0	175	7-23-71	1991	Sacramento, Calif.
Lombardi, John	0	4	7.16	6	3	0	0	16	22	13	13	6	13	R	R	6-3	210	4-24-73	1993	Warwick, R.I.
Maduro, Calvin	8	5	2.94	20	20	2	0	122	109	43	40	34	120	R	R	6-0	175	9-5-74	1992	Santa Cruz, Aruba
Magee, Bo	2	1	4.05	5	5	0	0	27	28	15	12	5	28	R	L	6-4	180	4-9-68	1991	Jackson, Miss.
Maine, Dalton	1	1	3.68	19	0	0	0	22	20	10	9	11	21	R	R	6-3	185	3-22-72	1995	Framingham, Mass.
Mansur, Jeff	0	0	4.70	12	0	0	0	15	20	8	8	5	12	L	L	5-11	185	8-2-70	1991	Hood River, Ore.
Marenghi, Matt	4	13	5.08	30	16	0	2	113	108	73	64	41	85	R	R	6-2	185	1-22-73	1994	Las Vegas, Nev.
Mayse, Robert	1	0	3.72	6	0	0	0	10	9	5	4	8	7	R	R	6-2	200	12-21-73	1994	Conowingo, Md.
Nieto, Tony	1	4	3.92	21	0	0	0	39	38	19	17	9	14	S	R	5-11	170	4-19-73	1994	Monterey Park, Calif.
Rhodes, Joe	0	1	4.50	2	1	0	0	6	8	3	3	2	2	R	R	6-4	190	1-8-75	1994	Hendersonville, N.C.
Rogers, Jason	1	3	4.32	15	14	1	0	67	64	38	32	45	52	L	L	6-6	215	4-5-73	1994	Reno, Nev.
Smith, Hut	3	2	6.47	20	2	0	2	32	39	23	23	31	28	R	R	6-3	195	6-8-73	1992	Kannapolis, N.C.
Stewart, Rachaad	8	8	3.64	26	26	1	0	151	126	71	61	66	140	L	L	6-4	212	10-8-74	1994	Elgin, Ill.
Walker, Jimmy	2	2	3.48	9	0	0	0	21	15	12	8	9	19	R	R	6-0	180	2-26-71	1993	Nickerson, Kan.
White, Gary	1	0	3.00	1	1	0	0	6	3	2	2	2	4	L	L	6-2	200	8-14-72	1995	Sarasota, Fla.

APPALACHIAN LEAGUE

BATTING	AVG	G	AB	R	H	2B	3B	HR	RBI	BB	SO	SB	CS	B	T	HT	WT	DOB	1st Yr	Resides
Almonte, Wady	.307	51	189	37	58	12	1	6	30	9	49	6	5	R	R	6-0	180	4-20-75	1993	Higuey, D.R.
Bogle, Bryan	.452	10	31	11	14	2	0	1	4	4	2	1	0	R	R	6-1	205	5-18-73	1994	Merritt Island, Fla.
Bryant, Chris	.287	58	195	39	56	10	1	5	37	25	30	6	4	R	R	6-2	195	12-15-72	1993	Middlesex, N.C.
Daedelow, Craig	.000	5	13	1	0	0	0	0	1	4	3	0	1	R	R	5-11	175	4-3-76	1994	Huntington Beach, Calif.
Dellucci, David	.333	20	69	11	23	5	1	2	12	6	7	3	1	L	L	5-10	180	10-31-73	1995	Baton Rouge, La.
Gabriel, Denio	.289	53	180	39	52	4	0	1	24	25	36	31	8	S	R	6-0	150	10-25-75	1993	La Romana, D.R.
Gargiulo, Mike	.289	48	180	24	52	7	4	3	21	10	35	1	2	L	R	6-1	175	1-22-75	1993	Harrisburg, Pa.
Harmer, Frank	.190	18	58	5	11	3	0	0	10	9	14	1	0	S	R	6-3	210	5-21-75	1994	Altamonte, Springs, Fla.
Higman, Joel	.208	11	24	2	5	0	0	0	3	3	8	2	0	R	R	6-1	185	3-30-74	1995	Villas, N.J.

BATTING	AVG	G	AB	R	H	2B	3B	HR	RBI	BB	SO	SB	CS	B	T	HT	WT	DOB	1st Yr	Resides
Isom, Johnny	.344	59	212	47	73	14	4	6	56	25	27	9	2	R	R	5-11	210	8-9-73	1995	Forth Worth, Texas
Kerr, Brian	.167	3	6	0	1	1	0	0	1	0	2	0	0	R	R	6-0	180	12-26-75	1994	Farmington, N.M.
Kingsale, Eugene	.316	47	171	45	54	11	2	0	16	27	31	20	8	S	R	6-3	170	8-20-76	1994	Aruba, Aruba
LeCronier, Jason	.246	21	69	11	17	4	1	2	10	11	17	1	1	L	R	6-0	180	3-30-75	1995	Bay City, Mich.
Martinez, Eddy	.308	57	185	42	57	11	3	1	35	23	42	5	5	R	R	6-2	150	10-23-77	1995	San Pedro de Macoris, D.R.
Mejia, Miguel	.298	51	181	50	54	6	3	3	30	18	30	36	5	R	R	6-1	155	3-25-75	1992	San Pedro de Macoris, D.R.
Ramos, Noel	.196	31	107	18	21	5	1	5	18	10	43	1	0	R	R	6-1	230	10-25-76	1994	Isabela, P.R.
Russin, Tom	.312	57	215	42	67	21	1	5	41	18	27	1	1	R	R	6-2	200	9-9-73	1995	Sarasota, Fla.
Short, Rick	.282	11	39	9	11	2	0	2	12	2	1	2	1	R	R	6-0	190	12-6-72	1994	South Elgin, Ill.
Winn, Wess	.224	24	49	4	11	2	0	0	9	12	12	2	2	S	R	5-10	175	5-5-72	1995	Waxahachie, Texas

GAMES BY POSITION: C—Gargiulo 48, Harmer 18. **1B**—Ramos 27, Russin 40. **2B**—Daedelow 2, Gabriel 50, Short 7, Winn 15. **3B**—Bogle 6, Bryant 58, Daedelow 1, Russin 1, Short 4. **SS**—Daedelow 2, Gabriel 3, Martinez 56, Winn 8. **OF**—Almonte 47, Dellucci 12, Higman 8, Isom 48, Kerr 1, Kingsale 44, LeCronier 5, Mejia 45.

PITCHING	W	L	ERA	G	GS	CG	SV	IP	H	R	ER	BB	SO	B	T	HT	WT	DOB	1st Yr	Resides
Bates, Shawn	2	0	2.45	14	2	0	3	26	22	13	7	16	31	L	L	6-3	169	2-27-75	1994	Wichita Falls, Texas
Crills, Brad	3	0	0.90	4	4	0	0	20	15	3	2	5	15	R	R	6-0	195	10-16-71	1994	Ephrata, Pa.
Dean, Greg	6	2	3.89	10	6	0	1	37	34	22	16	17	33	R	R	6-1	220	4-16-74	1995	Ada, Okla.
Eibey, Scott	3	1	5.56	14	6	0	2	44	51	32	27	24	26	L	L	6-4	210	1-19-74	1995	Waterloo, Iowa
Fussell, Chris	9	1	2.19	12	12	1	0	66	37	18	16	32	98	R	R	6-2	185	5-19-76	1994	Oregon, Ohio
Hackett, Jason	3	1	3.02	13	6	0	1	51	45	28	17	28	54	L	L	6-1	176	3-10-75	1994	Worton, Md.
LaRocca, Todd	4	1	3.05	8	6	1	0	44	38	17	15	14	38	R	R	6-1	185	9-21-72	1994	Atlanta, Ga.
Maine, Dalton	0	1	11.25	1	0	0	0	4	7	5	5	0	2	R	R	6-3	185	3-22-72	1995	Framingham, Mass.
Mercedes, Carlos	0	0	9.00	1	0	0	0	1	2	1	1	1	0	R	R	6-0	175	3-29-76	1994	El Seibo, D.R.
Moreno, Julio	4	3	4.20	9	8	0	0	49	61	31	23	12	36	R	R	6-1	145	10-23-75	1994	Los Lanos, D.R.
Morseman, Robert	1	0	2.02	18	1	0	6	36	22	9	8	14	38	L	L	6-4	190	6-10-74	1995	Westfield, Pa.
Olszewski, Tim	3	2	3.06	16	0	0	3	35	34	19	12	19	29	R	R	6-2	200	2-24-74	1995	Germantown, Wisc.
Ponson, Sidney	6	3	4.17	13	13	0	0	78	79	44	36	16	56	R	R	6-1	200	11-2-76	1994	Aruba, Aruba
Reed, Dan	1	0	2.57	6	1	0	1	14	10	5	4	5	11	R	L	6-3	195	10-20-74	1995	McLean, Va.
Santos, Juan	0	0	0.00	1	0	0	0	3	1	0	0	0	2	R	R	6-2	160	2-23-76	1993	Ramon Santana, D.R.
Sauritch, Chris	4	1	3.72	13	0	0	3	19	18	13	8	11	16	S	R	5-10	175	3-24-72	1994	Lake Forest, Calif.
Snyder, Matt	0	0	1.04	17	0	0	8	35	35	9	4	13	46	R	R	5-11	190	7-7-74	1995	Newtown, Pa.

SARASOTA R

GULF COAST LEAGUE

BATTING	AVG	G	AB	R	H	2B	3B	HR	RBI	BB	SO	SB	CS	B	T	HT	WT	DOB	1st Yr	Resides
Akins, Carlos	.283	42	138	35	39	9	1	3	20	22	28	9	3	R	R	6-0	180	7-12-74	1995	Oklahoma City, Okla.
Alfonzo, Edgar	.167	6	18	1	3	0	0	0	1	0	0	0	0	R	R	6-0	167	6-10-67	1985	Santa Teresa, Venez.
Alley, Charles	.300	12	30	10	9	4	0	0	3	11	4	0	0	S	R	6-3	190	12-20-76	1995	West Palm Beach, Fla.
Bartee, Kimera	.238	5	21	5	5	0	0	1	3	3	2	1	1	R	R	6-0	180	7-21-72	1993	Omaha, Neb.
Brown, Derek	.233	49	146	15	34	5	0	0	11	23	32	3	3	R	R	6-0	170	7-23-76	1994	Hagerstown, Md.
Casimiro, Carlos	.252	32	107	14	27	4	2	2	11	10	22	1	3	R	R	6-0	155	11-8-76	1994	San Pedro de Macoris, D.R.
Charles, Curtis	.159	25	63	6	10	2	0	0	3	9	29	1	1	R	R	6-1	179	3-15-76	1995	Caracas, Venez.
Daedelow, Craig	.259	49	170	35	44	9	0	1	11	24	19	7	2	R	R	5-11	175	4-3-76	1994	Huntington Beach, Calif.
Dent, Darrell	.280	36	125	24	35	7	3	0	6	21	22	6	2	L	L	6-2	172	5-26-77	1995	Panorama City, Calif.
DiSalle, Javier	.333	4	12	0	4	0	0	0	1	0	1	1	1	R	R	6-0	170	7-12-75	1994	Caracas, Venez.
Higman, Joel	.143	6	21	2	3	0	0	0	1	2	7	1	0	R	R	6-1	185	3-30-74	1995	Villas, N.J.
Kerr, Brian	.184	10	38	4	7	2	1	1	7	2	10	1	0	R	R	6-0	180	12-26-75	1994	Farmington, N.M.
King, Brian	.277	17	47	4	13	2	0	0	4	2	12	1	0	R	R	6-0	200	9-1-76	1995	Oviedo, Fla.
Ortiz, James	.217	14	46	1	10	2	0	0	3	3	13	1	0	R	R	6-0	175	10-29-76	1994	Levittown, P.R.
Paxton, Chris	.226	11	31	1	7	1	1	0	6	1	4	0	0	L	R	6-2	210	12-11-76	1995	Palmdale, Calif.
Pickering, Calvin	.500	15	60	8	30	10	0	1	22	2	6	0	0	L	L	6-3	283	9-29-76	1995	Temple Terrace, Fla.
Porter, Kedric	.218	47	147	20	32	4	1	1	12	21	17	11	3	R	R	5-10	175	11-7-74	1994	Tampa, Fla.
Ramos, Noel	.200	4	15	1	3	1	0	0	5	2	6	0	1	R	R	6-1	230	10-25-76	1994	Isabela, P.R.
Ribaudo, Mike	.244	16	41	3	10	1	0	0	4	3	10	0	0	R	R	6-2	175	6-21-75	1995	Sarasota, Fla.
Rivera, Roberto	.293	42	150	21	44	7	3	3	26	10	38	6	3	R	R	6-2	160	11-25-76	1994	La Romana, D.R.
Robertson, Dean	.156	28	90	18	14	4	0	0	6	14	18	4	4	R	R	6-1	166	2-19-76	1994	Geelong, Australia
Serra, Joaquin	.141	29	85	7	12	0	0	0	3	6	12	2	2	R	R	5-9	164	9-5-75	1995	Beverly Hills, Calif.
Stephens, Joel	.232	23	82	8	19	3	1	0	10	5	25	2	1	R	R	6-1	207	3-15-76	1995	Tioga, Pa.
Sullivan, Davey	.232	38	125	13	29	6	0	1	12	10	23	1	1	R	R	6-0	210	1-3-76	1995	Waynesboro, Pa.
Taylor, Avery	.033	13	30	2	1	0	0	0	2	3	12	0	0	R	R	6-0	202	11-30-75	1995	Long Beach, Miss.
Winn, Wess	.222	13	36	4	8	2	4	0	5	3	9	0	0	S	R	5-10	175	5-5-72	1995	Waxahachie, Texas

GAMES BY POSITION: C—Alley 12, DiSalle 4, Paxton 11, Sullivan 38. **1B**—Brown 16, Pickering 11, Ramos 4, Ribaudo 4, Robertson 28, Serra 1. **2B**—Alfonzo 2, Brown 2, Casimiro 22, Daedelow 1, Kerr 9, Serra 24, Taylor 7, Winn 2. **3B**—Alfonzo 1, Brown 33, King 17, Ribaudo 9, Serra 2, Taylor 1, Winn 4. **SS**—Alfonzo 1, Casimiro 13, Daedelow 49, Serra 2. **OF**—Akins 39, Bartee 5, Charles 8, Dent 31, Higman 4, Kerr 1, Ortiz 5, Porter 42, Rivera 32, Stephens 16.

PITCHING	W	L	ERA	G	GS	CG	SV	IP	H	R	ER	BB	SO	B	T	HT	WT	DOB	1st Yr	Resides
Bray, Chris	3	2	3.68	12	2	0	0	29	27	20	12	16	22	R	R	6-4	190	10-28-74	1995	Currituck, N.C.
Fisher, Louis	4	3	1.85	9	7	2	0	39	27	23	8	24	29	R	R	6-1	189	10-14-76	1995	Oakland, Calif.
Hacen, Abraham	2	3	2.54	13	8	0	2	46	34	21	13	32	37	R	R	6-2	175	6-22-71	1993	La Romana, D.R.
Hale, Shane	0	0	1.29	2	2	0	0	7	6	2	1	4	6	R	L	6-1	180	12-30-68	1990	Mobile, Ala.
Harris, Doug	1	0	0.00	1	0	0	1	2	2	0	0	0	0	R	R	6-4	205	9-27-69	1990	Carlisle, Pa.
Hernandez, Francisco	2	2	1.32	24	0	0	11	27	18	4	4	6	23	R	R	6-0	160	12-17-76	1994	San Pedro de Macoris, D.R.
Huntsman, Brandon	6	3	3.86	13	12	1	0	65	53	38	28	33	64	R	R	6-8	195	11-19-75	1994	Pleasant Grove, Utah
Maine, Dalton	1	0	2.08	18	0	0	2	30	24	7	7	9	32	R	R	6-3	185	3-22-72	1995	Framingham, Mass.
Mansur, Jeff	0	0	3.38	3	0	0	0	5	11	5	2	0	2	L	L	5-11	185	8-2-70	1995	Hood River, Ore.
Mercedes, Carlos	2	1	2.55	10	1	0	0	25	22	8	7	2	10	R	R	6-0	175	3-29-76	1994	El Seibo, D.R.
Mills, Alan	0	0	0.00	1	1	0	0	2	3	0	0	2	1	S	R	6-1	192	10-18-66	1986	Lakeland, Fla.
Moreno, Julio	3	2	1.59	5	5	1	0	34	17	9	6	7	29	R	R	6-1	145	10-23-75	1994	Los Lanos, D.R.
Perez, Leonardo	1	1	4.41	8	0	0	0	16	14	13	8	7	7	R	R	6-1	165	7-31-74	1991	Sabana Palenque, D.R.
Rhodes, Joe	4	2	3.04	13	11	0	0	71	72	36	24	28	43	R	R	6-4	190	1-8-75	1994	Hendersonville, N.C.
Santos, Juan	0	2	3.20	21	0	0	2	25	25	11	9	4	16	R	R	6-2	160	2-23-76	1993	Ramon Santana, D.R.
White, Gary	5	4	2.17	12	10	2	0	66	52	26	16	16	56	L	L	6-2	200	8-14-72	1995	Sarasota, Fla.

BOSTON RED SOX

Manager: Kevin Kennedy. **1995 Record:** 86-58, .597 (1st, AL East).

BATTING	AVG	G	AB	R	H	2B	3B	HR	RBI	BB	SO	SB	CS	B	T	HT	WT	DOB	1st Yr	Resides
Alicea, Luis	.270	132	419	64	113	20	3	6	44	63	61	13	10	S	R	5-9	177	7-29-65	1986	Loxahatchie, Fla.
Bell, Juan	.154	17	26	7	4	2	0	1	2	2	10	0	0	S	R	5-11	175	3-29-68	1985	San Pedro de Macoris, D.R.
Canseco, Jose	.306	102	396	64	121	25	1	24	81	42	93	4	0	R	R	6-3	185	7-2-64	1982	Miami, Fla.
Chamberlain, Wes	.119	19	42	4	5	1	0	1	1	3	11	1	0	R	R	6-2	219	4-13-66	1987	Chicago, Ill.
Donnels, Chris	.253	40	91	13	23	2	2	2	11	9	18	0	0	L	R	6-0	185	4-21-66	1987	Aliso Viejo, Calif.
Greenwell, Mike	.297	120	481	67	143	25	4	15	76	38	35	9	5	L	R	6-0	205	7-18-63	1982	Cape Coral, Fla.
Haselman, Bill	.243	64	152	22	37	6	1	5	23	17	30	0	2	R	R	6-3	215	5-25-66	1987	Saratoga, Calif.
Hatteberg, Scott	.500	2	2	1	1	0	0	0	0	0	0	0	0	L	R	6-1	185	12-14-69	1991	Yakima, Wash.
Hollins, Dave	.154	5	13	2	2	0	0	0	1	4	7	0	0	S	R	6-1	207	5-25-66	1987	Orchard Park, N.Y.
Hosey, Dwayne	.338	24	68	20	23	8	1	3	7	8	16	6	0	S	R	5-10	170	3-11-67	1987	Altadena, Calif.
James, Reggie	.167	16	24	2	4	1	0	0	1	1	4	0	0	R	R	6-1	202	10-4-62	1982	Alto, Texas
2-team (26 KC)	.268	42	82	8	22	4	0	2	8	7	14	1	0							
Jefferson, Reggie	.289	46	121	21	35	8	0	5	26	9	24	0	0	L	L	6-4	215	9-25-68	1986	Tallahassee, Fla.
Macfarlane, Mike	.225	115	364	45	82	18	1	15	51	38	78	2	1	R	R	6-1	205	4-12-64	1985	Overland Park, Kan.
Mahay, Ron	.200	5	20	3	4	2	0	1	3	1	6	0	0	L	L	6-2	185	6-28-71	1991	Crestwood, Ill.
McGee, Willie	.285	67	200	32	57	11	3	2	15	9	41	5	2	S	R	6-1	185	11-2-58	1977	Hercules, Calif.
Naehring, Tim	.307	126	433	61	133	27	2	10	57	77	66	0	2	R	R	6-2	200	2-1-67	1988	Cincinnati, Ohio
O'Leary, Troy	.308	112	399	60	123	31	6	10	49	29	64	5	3	L	L	6-0	190	8-4-69	1987	Rialto, Calif.
Rhodes, Karl	.080	10	25	2	2	1	0	0	1	3	4	0	0	L	L	5-11	170	8-21-68	1986	Cincinnati, Ohio
Rodriguez, Carlos	.333	13	30	5	10	2	0	0	5	2	2	0	0	S	R	5-9	160	11-1-67	1987	Columbus, Ohio
Rodriguez, Steve	.125	6	8	1	1	0	0	0	0	1	1	1	0	R	R	5-9	170	11-29-70	1992	Las Vegas, Nev.
Rowland, Rich	.172	14	29	1	5	1	0	0	1	0	11	0	0	R	R	6-1	215	2-25-67	1988	Lakeland, Fla.
Shumpert, Terry	.234	21	47	6	11	3	0	0	3	4	13	3	1	R	R	5-11	185	8-16-66	1987	Paducah, Ky.
Stairs, Matt	.261	39	88	8	23	7	1	1	17	4	14	0	1	L	R	5-9	175	2-27-69	1989	Stanley, N.B.
Tinsley, Lee	.284	100	341	61	97	17	1	7	41	39	74	18	8	S	R	5-10	180	3-4-69	1987	Shelbyville, Ky.
Valentin, John	.298	135	520	108	155	37	2	27	102	81	67	20	5	R	R	6-0	185	2-18-67	1988	Braintree, Mass.
Vaughn, Mo	.300	140	550	98	165	28	3	39	126	68	150	11	4	L	R	6-1	230	12-15-67	1989	Braintree, Mass.
Whiten, Mark	.185	32	108	13	20	3	0	1	10	8	23	1	0	S	R	6-3	215	11-25-66	1986	Pensacola, Fla.

PITCHING	W	L	ERA	G	GS	CG	SV	IP	H	R	ER	BB	SO	B	T	HT	WT	DOB	1st Yr	Resides
Aguilera, Rick	2	2	2.67	30	0	0	20	30	26	9	9	7	23	R	R	6-5	203	12-31-61	1983	Chanhassen, Minn.
2-team (22 Minn.)	3	3	2.60	52	0	0	32	55	46	16	16	13	52							
Bark, Brian	0	0	0.00	3	0	0	0	2	2	0	0	1	0	L	L	5-9	170	8-26-68	1990	Baltimore, Md.
Belinda, Stan	8	1	3.10	63	0	0	10	70	51	25	24	28	57	R	R	6-3	215	8-6-66	1985	Alexandria, Pa.
Clemens, Roger	10	5	4.18	23	23	0	0	140	141	70	65	60	132	R	R	6-4	220	8-4-62	1983	Houston, Texas
Cormier, Rheal	7	5	4.07	48	12	0	0	115	131	60	52	31	69	L	L	5-10	185	4-23-67	1989	Moncton, N.B.
Eshelman, Vaughn	6	3	4.85	23	14	0	0	82	86	47	44	36	41	L	L	6-3	205	5-22-69	1991	Houston, Texas
Gunderson, Eric	2	1	5.11	19	0	0	0	12	13	7	7	9	9	R	L	6-0	195	3-29-66	1987	Portland, Ore.
Hanson, Erik	15	5	4.24	29	29	1	0	187	187	94	88	59	139	R	R	6-6	215	5-18-65	1986	Kirkland, Wash.
Hartley, Mike	0	0	9.00	5	0	0	0	7	8	7	7	2	2	R	R	6-1	197	8-31-61	1982	El Cajon, Calif.
Hudson, Joe	0	1	4.11	39	0	0	1	46	53	21	21	23	29	R	R	6-1	180	9-29-70	1992	Medford, N.J.
Johnston, Joel	0	0	11.25	4	0	0	0	4	2	5	5	3	4	R	R	6-4	234	3-8-67	1988	West Chester, Pa.
Lilliquist, Derek	2	1	6.26	28	0	0	0	23	27	17	16	9	9	L	L	5-10	195	2-20-66	1987	Vero Beach, Fla.
Looney, Brian	0	1	17.36	3	1	0	0	5	12	9	9	4	2	L	L	5-10	180	9-26-69	1991	Cheshire, Conn.
Maddux, Mike	4	1	3.61	36	4	0	1	90	86	40	36	15	65	L	R	6-2	188	8-27-61	1982	Las Vegas, Nev.
Murray, Matt	0	1	18.90	2	1	0	0	3	11	10	7	3	1	R	R	6-6	235	9-26-70	1988	Swampscott, Mass.
Pena, Alejandro	1	1	7.40	17	0	0	0	24	33	23	20	12	25	R	R	6-1	200	6-25-59	1979	Roswell, Ga.
Pierce, Jeff	0	3	6.60	12	0	0	0	15	16	12	11	14	12	R	R	6-1	200	6-7-69	1991	Staatsburg, N.Y.
Rodriguez, Frank	0	2	10.57	9	2	0	0	15	21	19	18	10	14	R	R	6-0	175	12-11-72	1991	Oviedo, Fla.
Ryan, Ken	0	4	4.96	28	0	0	7	33	34	20	18	24	34	R	R	6-3	215	10-24-68	1986	Attleboro, Mass.
Sele, Aaron	3	1	3.06	6	6	0	0	32	32	14	11	14	21	R	R	6-5	218	6-25-70	1991	Poulsbo, Wash.
Shepherd, Keith	0	0	36.00	2	0	0	0	1	4	4	4	2	0	R	R	6-1	197	1-21-68	1986	Wabash, Ind.
Smith, Zane	8	8	5.61	24	21	0	0	111	144	78	69	23	47	L	L	6-1	207	12-28-60	1982	Stone Mountain, Ga.
Stanton, Mike	1	0	3.00	22	0	0	1	21	17	9	7	8	10	L	L	6-1	190	6-2-67	1987	Houston, Texas
Suppan, Jeff	1	2	5.96	8	3	0	0	23	29	15	15	5	19	R	R	6-1	200	1-2-75	1993	West Hills, Calif.
Vanegmond, Tim	0	1	9.45	4	1	0	0	7	9	7	7	6	5	R	R	6-2	185	5-31-69	1991	Senoia, Ga.
Wakefield, Tim	16	8	2.95	27	27	6	0	195	163	76	64	68	119	R	R	6-2	204	8-2-66	1988	Melbourne, Fla.

FIELDING

Catcher	PCT	G	PO	A	E	DP	PB
Haselman	.989	48	257	16	3	0	3
Hatteberg	1.000	2	4	0	0	0	0
Macfarlane	.993	111	618	49	5	8	26
Rowland	.977	11	39	3	1	2	0

First Base	PCT	G	PO	A	E	DP
Donnels	1.000	8	36	6	0	8
Haselman	1.000	1	2	0	0	0
Jefferson	1.000	7	26	4	0	4
Vaughn	.992	138	1262	95	11	128

Second Base	PCT	G	PO	A	E	DP
Alicea	.977	132	254	429	16	103
Bell	1.000	5	9	11	0	4
Donnels	1.000	3	1	1	0	1
C. Rodriguez	.960	7	9	15	1	3

	PCT	G	PO	A	E	DP
S. Rodriguez	1.000	1	1	2	0	0
Shumpert	1.000	8	12	15	0	4

Third Base	PCT	G	PO	A	E	DP
Bell	1.000	1	0	1	0	0
Donnels	.927	27	17	34	4	2
Haselman	.000	1	0	0	0	0
Naehring	.954	124	85	244	16	23
C. Rodriguez	1.000	1	0	1	0	0
Shumpert	1.000	5	2	7	0	0

Shortstop	PCT	G	PO	A	E	DP
Bell	.857	6	6	12	3	1
C. Rodriguez	1.000	6	7	11	0	3
S. Rodriguez	.667	4	0	2	1	0
Shumpert	.909	3	7	13	2	3
Valentin	.973	135	227	414	18	95

Outfield	PCT	G	PO	A	E	DP
Canseco	1.000	1	1	0	0	0
Chamberlain	.955	12	20	1	1	0
Greenwell	.972	118	201	11	6	1
Hollins	1.000	2	3	0	0	0
Hosey	1.000	21	46	1	0	0
James	1.000	8	14	0	0	0
Jefferson	1.000	2	2	0	0	0
Mahay	1.000	5	9	0	0	0
McGee	.973	64	101	7	3	1
O'Leary	.976	105	196	6	5	1
Rhodes	.947	9	18	0	1	0
Stairs	.913	23	19	2	2	0
Tinsley	.979	97	228	4	5	1
Whiten	1.000	31	52	4	0	1

Shortstop John Valentin led the Red Sox with 37 doubles

Red Sox minor league Player of the Year Rafael Orellano

MORRIS FOSTOFF

RED SOX

FARM SYSTEM

Director of Player Development and Administration: Ed Kenney.

Class	Farm Team	League	W	L	Pct.	Finish*	Manager	First Yr
AAA	Pawtucket (R.I.) Red Sox	International	70	71	.496	7th (10)	Buddy Bailey	1973
AA	Trenton (N.J.) Thunder	Eastern	73	69	.514	T-3rd (10)	Ken Macha	1995
#A	Sarasota (Fla.) Red Sox	Florida State	65	68	.489	T-7th (14)	Tom Barrett	1994
A	Michigan Battle Cats	Midwest	75	62	.547	4th (14)	DeMarlo Hale	1995
A	Utica (N.Y.) Blue Sox	New York-Penn	33	40	.452	11th (14)	Bob Geren	1993
R	Fort Myers (Fla.) Red Sox	Gulf Coast	21	36	.368	13th (16)	Felix Maldonado	1993

*Finish in overall standings (No. of teams in league)   #Advanced level

ORGANIZATION LEADERS

MAJOR LEAGUERS

BATTING

*AVG	Troy O'Leary	.308
R	John Valentin	108
H	Mo Vaughn	165
TB	Mo Vaughn	316
2B	John Valentin	37
3B	Troy O'Leary	6
HR	Mo Vaughn	39
RBI	Mo Vaughn	126
BB	John Valentin	81
SO	Mo Vaughn	150
SB	John Valentin	20

PITCHING

W	Tim Wakefield	16
L	Two tied at	8
#ERA	Tim Wakefield	2.95
G	Stan Belinda	63
CG	Tim Wakefield	6
SV	Rick Aguilera	20
IP	Tim Wakefield	195
BB	Tim Wakefield	68
SO	Erik Hanson	139

Troy O'Leary. .308 average

MORRIS FOSTOFF

MINOR LEAGUERS

BATTING

*AVG	Ryan McGuire, Trenton	.333
R	Donnie Sadler, Michigan	103
H	Ryan McGuire, Trenton	138
TB	Clyde Pough, Trenton/Pawtucket	245
2B	David Gibralter, Michigan	34
3B	Two tied at	8
HR	Clyde Pough, Trenton/Pawtucket	26
RBI	Clyde Pough, Trenton/Pawtucket	92
BB	Donnie Sadler, Michigan	79
SO	Clyde Pough, Trenton/Pawtucket	128
SB	Donnie Sadler, Michigan	41

PITCHING

W	Three tied at	11
L	Wes Brooks, Trenton	11
#ERA	Darrell Tillmon, GCL Sox/Michigan	2.13
G	Shayne Bennett, Sarasota/Trenton	62
CG	Two tied at	5
SV	Shayne Bennett, Sarasota/Trenton	27
IP	Rafael Orellano, Trenton	187
BB	Two tied at	78
SO	Rafael Orellano, Trenton	160

*Minimum 250 At-Bats   #Minimum 75 Innings

TOP 10 PROSPECTS

How the Red Sox Top 10 prospects, as judged by Baseball America prior to the 1995 season, fared in 1995:

Nomar Garciaparra

MORRIS FOSTOFF

Player, Pos.	Club (Class—League)	AVG	AB	R	H	2B	3B	HR	RBI	SB
1. Nomar Garciaparra, ss	Trenton (AA—Eastern)	.267	513	77	137	20	8	8	47	35
3. Trot Nixon, of	Sarasota (A—Florida State)	.303	264	43	80	11	4	5	39	7
	Trenton (AA—Eastern)	.160	94	9	15	3	1	2	8	2
5. Jose Malave, of	Pawtucket (AAA—International)	.270	318	55	86	12	1	23	57	0
7. #Steve Rodriguez, 2b	Pawtucket (AAA—International)	.241	324	39	78	16	3	1	24	12
	Boston	.125	8	1	1	0	0	0	0	1
	Detroit	.194	31	4	6	1	0	0	0	1
8. Donnie Sadler, ss	Michigan (A—Midwest)	.283	438	103	124	25	8	9	55	41
9. Glenn Murray, of	Pawtucket (AAA—International)	.244	336	66	82	15	0	25	66	5
10. %Marc Lewis, of	Utica (A—New York-Penn)	.301	272	47	82	15	5	5	39	24
	Michigan (A—Midwest)	.152	92	14	14	2	1	1	5	10

Player, Pos.	Club (Class—League)	W	L	ERA	G	SV	IP	H	BB	SO
2. *Frank Rodriguez, rhp	Pawtucket (AAA—International)	1	1	4.00	13	2	27	19	8	18
	Boston	0	2	10.57	9	0	15	21	10	14
	Minnesota	5	6	5.38	16	0	91	93	47	45
4. Jeff Suppan, rhp	Trenton (AA—Eastern)	6	2	2.36	15	0	99	86	26	88
	Pawtucket (AAA—International)	2	3	5.32	7	0	46	50	9	32
	Boston	1	2	5.96	8	0	23	29	5	19
6. Rafael Orellano, lhp	Trenton (AA—Eastern)	11	7	2.99	27	0	187	146	72	160

*Traded to Minnesota #Claimed on waivers by Detroit %Traded to Atlanta

INTERNATIONAL LEAGUE

BATTING	AVG	G	AB	R	H	2B	3B	HR	RBI	BB	SO	SB	CS	B	T	HT	WT	DOB	1st Yr	Resides
Barbara, Don	.217	40	129	19	28	8	0	2	10	12	18	2	0	L	L	6-2	220	10-27-68	1990	Huntington Beach, Calif.
Bell, Juan	.263	68	262	42	69	18	1	6	23	21	46	4	5	S	R	5-11	175	3-29-68	1985	San Pedro de Macoris, D.R.
Blosser, Greg	.200	17	50	5	10	0	0	1	4	5	13	0	0	L	L	6-3	205	6-26-71	1989	Sarasota, Fla.
Brown, Randy	.250	74	212	27	53	6	1	2	12	10	53	5	1	R	R	5-11	160	5-1-70	1989	Houston, Texas
Canseco, Jose	.167	2	6	1	1	0	0	0	1	1	5	0	0	R	R	6-3	185	7-2-64	1982	Miami, Fla.
Chamberlain, Wes	.350	48	183	28	64	17	1	12	40	3	45	5	3	R	R	6-2	219	4-13-66	1987	Chicago, Ill.
Delgado, Alex	.252	44	107	14	27	3	0	5	12	6	12	0	0	R	R	6-0	160	1-11-71	1988	Palmerejo, Venez.
Donnels, Chris	.400	4	15	1	6	0	0	1	4	1	3	0	0	L	R	6-0	185	4-21-66	1987	Aliso Vista, Calif.
Friedman, Jason	.294	14	51	6	15	3	0	2	9	2	3	0	0	L	L	6-1	200	8-8-69	1989	Cypress, Calif.
Fulton, Ed	.294	9	17	0	5	2	0	0	2	3	6	0	0	L	R	6-0	195	1-7-66	1987	Danville, Va.
Greenwell, Mike	.500	1	4	0	2	2	0	0	0	1	0	1	0	L	R	6-0	205	7-18-63	1982	Cape Coral, Fla.
Hardge, Mike	.253	29	91	9	23	3	0	1	5	8	16	1	3	R	R	5-11	183	1-27-72	1990	Killeen, Texas
Hatteberg, Scott	.271	85	251	36	68	15	1	7	27	40	39	2	0	L	R	6-1	185	12-14-69	1991	Yakima, Wash.
Howard, Tim	.311	38	90	13	28	5	1	0	11	7	11	7	3	L	R	5-10	155	6-2-69	1988	Brawley, Calif.
Lennon, Pat	.273	40	128	20	35	6	2	3	20	16	42	6	4	R	R	6-2	200	4-27-68	1986	Whiteville, N.C.
LeVangie, Dana	.235	6	17	1	4	0	0	0	2	3	0	0	0	R	R	5-10	185	8-11-69	1991	Whitman, Mass.
Mahay, Ron	.318	11	44	5	14	4	0	0	3	4	9	1	0	L	L	6-2	185	6-28-71	1991	Crestwood, Ill.
Malave, Jose	.270	91	318	55	86	12	1	23	57	30	67	0	1	R	R	6-2	195	5-31-71	1990	Cumana, Venez.
Malzone, John	.111	6	18	0	2	0	0	0	2	0	4	0	0	R	R	6-0	170	10-29-67	1989	Needham, Mass.
McGee, Willie	.476	5	21	9	10	0	0	0	2	0	4	2	0	S	R	6-1	185	11-2-58	1977	Hercules, Calif.
Murray, Glenn	.244	104	336	66	82	15	0	25	66	34	109	5	6	R	R	6-2	200	11-23-70	1989	Manning, S.C.
Pough, Clyde	.232	30	99	12	23	8	1	5	23	7	27	0	0	R	R	6-0	173	12-25-69	1988	Avon Park, Fla.
Rhodes, Karl	.285	69	246	40	70	13	3	10	43	34	46	8	6	L	L	5-11	170	8-21-68	1986	Cincinnati, Ohio
Rodriguez, Carlos	.293	40	133	19	39	7	0	0	13	20	8	1	0	S	R	5-9	160	11-1-67	1987	Columbus, Ohio
Rodriguez, Steve	.241	82	324	39	78	16	3	1	24	25	34	12	10	R	R	5-9	170	11-29-70	1992	Las Vegas, Nev.
Rodriguez, Tony	.268	96	317	37	85	15	2	0	21	15	39	11	5	R	R	5-11	165	8-15-70	1991	Cidra, P.R.
Rodriguez, Victor	.276	31	116	10	32	5	0	0	8	2	13	1	1	R	R	5-11	173	7-14-61	1977	Villa Carolina, P.R.
Rowland, Rich	.258	34	124	20	32	7	0	8	24	7	24	0	1	R	R	6-1	215	2-25-67	1988	Lakeland, Fla.
Shumpert, Terry	.271	37	133	17	36	7	0	2	11	14	27	10	4	R	R	5-11	185	8-16-66	1987	Paducah, Ky.
Snyder, Cory	.227	20	66	9	15	4	0	3	8	5	25	0	0	R	R	6-3	205	11-11-62	1985	Laguna Hills, Calif.
Stairs, Matt	.284	75	271	40	77	17	0	13	56	29	41	3	3	L	R	5-9	175	2-27-69	1989	Stanley, N.B.
Wade, Scott	.148	7	27	2	4	1	0	0	0	0	11	0	0	R	R	6-2	200	4-26-63	1984	Seabrook, Md.
Waggoner, Aubrey	.188	16	48	3	9	1	0	0	8	10	22	2	2	L	R	5-11	185	12-6-66	1985	San Bernardino, Calif.
Wedge, Eric	.234	108	376	52	88	17	1	20	68	63	96	1	3	R	R	6-3	215	1-27-68	1989	Fort Wayne, Ind.
Whiten, Mark	.284	28	102	19	29	3	1	4	13	19	30	4	2	S	R	6-3	215	11-25-66	1986	Pensacola, Fla.

PITCHING	W	L	ERA	G	GS	CG	SV	IP	H	R	ER	BB	SO	B	T	HT	WT	DOB	1st Yr	Resides
Bakkum, Scott	1	0	1.71	15	0	0	2	26	21	13	5	7	15	R	R	6-4	205	11-20-69	1992	La Crosse, Wisc.
Bark, Brian	3	1	2.27	30	0	0	7	32	21	8	8	14	21	L	L	5-9	170	8-26-68	1990	Baltimore, Md.
2-team (13 Rich)	5	3	2.99	43	5	0	7	72	63	24	24	31	43							
Barnes, Brian	7	5	4.23	21	18	2	0	106	107	62	50	30	90	L	L	5-9	170	3-25-67	1989	Smyrna, Ga.
Bennett, Joel	2	4	5.84	20	13	0	0	77	91	57	50	45	50	R	R	6-1	161	1-31-70	1991	Kirkwood, N.Y.
Cain, Tim	4	0	2.28	14	0	0	4	28	24	7	7	8	19	S	R	6-1	180	10-9-69	1990	Piscataway, N.J.
Ciccarella, Joe	0	1	3.86	11	5	0	0	26	22	15	11	10	13	L	L	6-3	190	12-29-69	1991	Huntington Beach, Calif.
Clemens, Roger	0	0	0.00	1	1	0	0	5	1	0	0	3	5	R	R	6-4	220	8-4-62	1983	Houston, Texas
Culberson, Calvain	0	0	6.39	6	0	0	0	13	18	12	9	11	4	R	R	5-10	195	11-14-66	1988	Rome, Ga.
Finnvold, Gar	0	0	0.00	1	1	0	0	4	1	1	0	1	3	R	R	6-5	195	3-11-68	1990	Boca Raton, Fla.
Gakeler, Dan	0	2	6.10	4	4	0	0	21	24	14	14	9	13	R	R	6-6	215	5-1-64	1984	Greensboro, N.C.
Hansen, Brent	7	5	4.29	14	14	2	0	92	90	48	44	23	50	R	R	6-2	195	8-4-70	1992	Carlsbad, Calif.
Hartley, Mike	1	1	4.05	26	1	0	1	47	47	21	21	12	39	R	R	6-1	197	8-31-61	1982	El Cajon, Calif.
Hill, Chris	2	3	6.10	10	6	0	0	31	31	24	21	25	20	L	L	6-1	175	4-13-69	1988	Duncanville, Texas
Hoeme, Steve	0	2	4.62	15	2	0	1	39	40	21	20	15	21	R	R	6-6	230	11-2-67	1987	Preston, Kan.
Howard, Chris	3	1	3.92	17	0	0	0	21	25	11	9	4	19	R	L	6-0	185	11-18-65	1986	Nahant, Mass.
Johnston, Joel	1	2	6.75	30	0	0	6	41	54	31	31	19	39	R	R	6-4	234	3-8-67	1988	West Chester, Pa.
Jones, Calvin	5	2	4.03	33	0	0	8	38	37	23	17	15	36	R	R	6-3	185	9-26-63	1984	Perris, Calif.
Langbehn, Gregg	0	0	0.00	7	0	0	0	2	0	0	0	6	1	R	L	5-11	182	11-14-69	1988	Schofield, Wisc.
Lewis, Scott	0	0	3.86	3	0	0	0	5	7	2	2	0	1	R	R	6-3	178	12-5-65	1988	Tustin, Calif.
Looney, Brian	4	7	3.49	18	18	1	0	101	106	44	39	33	78	L	L	5-10	180	9-26-69	1991	Cheshire, Conn.
Pierce, Jeff	4	2	4.14	23	3	0	0	41	34	21	19	16	43	R	R	6-1	200	6-7-69	1991	Staatsburg, N.Y.
Plummer, Dale	9	9	5.19	34	10	1	0	101	140	73	58	18	47	R	R	6-4	190	1-26-65	1988	Bath, Maine
Rodriguez, Frank	1	1	4.00	13	2	0	2	27	19	12	12	8	18	R	R	6-0	175	12-11-72	1991	Oviedo, Fla.
Ryan, Ken	0	1	6.30	9	0	0	0	10	12	7	7	4	6	R	R	6-3	215	10-24-68	1986	Attleboro, Mass.
Satre, Jason	1	5	6.16	9	5	0	0	31	38	23	21	16	14	R	R	6-1	180	8-24-70	1988	Arlington, Texas
Sele, Aaron	0	0	9.00	2	2	0	0	5	9	5	5	2	1	R	R	6-5	218	6-25-70	1991	Poulsbo, Wash.
Senior, Shawn	0	1	6.00	1	1	0	0	6	9	4	4	2	1	L	L	6-1	195	3-17-72	1993	Cherry Hill, N.J.
Smith, Zane	0	0	0.00	1	1	0	0	7	5	0	0	0	5	L	L	6-1	207	12-28-60	1982	Stone Mountain, Ga.
Suppan, Jeff	2	3	5.32	7	7	0	0	46	50	29	27	9	32	R	R	6-1	200	1-2-75	1993	West Hills, Calif.
Vanegmond, Tim	5	3	3.92	12	12	0	0	67	66	32	29	21	47	R	R	6-2	185	5-31-69	1991	Sharpsburg, Ga.
Wakefield, Tim	2	1	2.52	4	4	0	0	25	23	10	7	9	14	R	R	6-2	204	8-2-66	1988	Melbourne, Fla.
Wengert, Bill	0	1	5.40	7	0	0	0	12	17	7	7	4	10	R	R	6-5	210	1-4-68	1988	Sioux City, Iowa
Wertz, Bill	4	5	5.80	29	6	0	2	64	74	47	41	31	55	R	R	6-6	220	1-15-67	1988	Cleveland, Ohio
Whitehurst, Wally	1	3	6.51	6	6	0	0	28	36	21	20	5	13	R	R	6-3	185	4-11-64	1985	Madisonville, La.
Wiggs, Johnny	1	0	5.79	14	0	0	0	9	11	6	6	3	6	L	L	5-11	165	3-13-67	1989	Lakeland, Fla.

FIELDING

Catcher	PCT	G	PO	A	E	DP	PB
Delgado	.974	33	157	32	5	1	7
Fulton	.971	7	31	2	1	1	2
Hatteberg	.984	77	446	45	8	5	7
LeVangie	1.000	6	32	4	0	0	0
Rowland	.984	27	177	8	3	0	3

	PCT	G	PO	A	E	DP	PB
Wedge	1.000	9	42	6	0	0	2

First Base	PCT	G	PO	A	E	DP
Barbara	.985	29	235	20	4	15
Chamberlain	1.000	1	1	0	0	0
Delgado	1.000	5	16	2	0	1

	PCT	G	PO	A	E	DP
Friedman	1.000	10	79	3	0	7
Pough	.994	20	144	20	1	11
T. Rodriguez	1.000	1	2	0	0	0
V. Rodriguez	.985	10	62	4	1	10
Rowland	1.000	3	28	1	0	1

	PCT	G	PO	A	E	DP
Snyder	1.000	3	23	4	0	4
Wedge	.995	74	554	40	3	49
Bell	.981	23	49	55	2	11
Second Base	**PCT**	**G**	**PO**	**A**	**E**	**DP**
Brown	1.000	2	3	6	0	0
Hardge	.959	16	32	39	3	7
S. Rodriguez	.975	80	167	191	9	37
T. Rodriguez	.986	33	65	80	2	13
Shumpert	1.000	3	2	1	0	0
Third Base	**PCT**	**G**	**PO**	**A**	**E**	**DP**
Bell	.833	2	3	2	1	0
Delgado	1.000	4	1	5	0	1
Donnels	.833	3	2	3	1	0
Hardge	.906	13	8	21	3	0

	PCT	G	PO	A	E	DP
Malzone	.833	5	2	8	2	1
Pough	.778	1	1	6	2	1
T. Rodriguez	.938	59	44	122	11	10
V. Rodriguez	1.000	24	14	45	0	2
Rowland	1.000	1	0	1	0	0
Shumpert	.896	30	27	68	11	12
Snyder	.907	14	15	24	4	4
Shortstop	**PCT**	**G**	**PO**	**A**	**E**	**DP**
Bell	.929	43	56	87	11	11
Brown	.949	67	102	161	14	33
C. Rodriguez	.962	38	51	99	6	13
T. Rodriguez	.963	12	10	16	1	1
Outfield	**PCT**	**G**	**PO**	**A**	**E**	**DP**
Blosser	.886	16	30	1	4	0

	PCT	G	PO	A	E	DP
Brown	1.000	4	3	0	0	0
Chamberlain	.945	33	66	3	4	0
T. Howard	.965	31	55	0	2	0
Lennon	.951	35	54	4	3	1
Mahay	1.000	11	30	2	0	0
Malave	.966	65	113	2	4	0
McGee	.875	3	7	0	1	0
Murray	.975	95	227	5	6	0
Rhodes	.967	65	172	6	6	3
Shumpert	1.000	1	0	0	0	0
Snyder	1.000	2	2	0	0	0
Stairs	1.000	51	79	13	0	2
Wade	1.000	7	15	1	0	0
Waggoner	.939	13	31	0	2	0
Whiten	.940	20	43	4	3	0

TRENTON   AA
EASTERN LEAGUE

BATTING	AVG	G	AB	R	H	2B	3B	HR	RBI	BB	SO	SB	CS	B	T	HT	WT	DOB	1st Yr	Resides
Abad, Andy	.240	89	287	29	69	14	3	4	32	36	58	5	7	L	L	6-1	185	8-25-72	1993	Jupiter, Fla.
Blosser, Greg	.246	49	179	25	44	13	0	11	34	13	42	3	2	L	L	6-3	205	6-26-71	1989	Sarasota, Fla.
Brown, Matt	.182	4	11	1	2	0	0	0	0	1	2	0	0	R	R	6-0	195	4-4-69	1990	Foster City, Calif.
Carey, Todd	.272	76	228	30	62	11	1	8	36	28	44	3	4	L	R	6-1	180	8-14-71	1992	Cumberland, R.I.
Delgado, Alex	.333	23	72	13	24	1	0	3	14	9	8	0	0	R	R	6-0	165	1-11-71	1988	Palmerejo, Venez.
Fuller, Aaron	.196	58	204	27	40	7	4	0	10	15	45	16	4	S	R	5-10	170	9-7-71	1993	Sacramento, Calif.
Garciaparra, Nomar	.267	125	513	77	137	20	8	8	47	50	42	35	12	R	R	6-1	175	7-23-73	1994	Whittier, Calif.
Graham, Tim	.160	8	25	2	4	1	0	0	0	1	5	0	1	L	R	6-0	185	9-4-71	1989	Lancaster, Ohio
Hardge, Mike	.244	40	127	18	31	4	1	0	12	11	26	3	4	R	R	5-11	183	1-27-72	1990	Killeen, Texas
Hecker, Doug	.204	61	221	20	45	16	0	5	32	18	43	2	0	R	R	6-4	210	1-21-71	1992	Wantagh, N.Y.
Johnson, J.J.	.500	2	6	1	3	0	0	0	1	0	0	0	0	R	R	6-0	195	8-31-73	1991	Pine Plains, N.Y.
Juday, Rob	.100	3	10	0	1	0	0	0	0	2	4	0	0	S	R	6-0	180	12-29-70	1992	Midland, Mich.
Lennon, Pat	.398	27	98	19	39	7	0	1	8	14	22	7	2	R	R	6-2	200	4-27-68	1986	Whiteville, N.C.
LeVangie, Dana	.178	42	129	10	23	3	1	0	7	11	30	1	3	R	R	5-10	185	8-11-69	1991	Whitman, Mass.
Mahay, Ron	.235	93	310	37	73	12	3	5	28	44	90	5	6	L	L	6-2	185	6-28-71	1991	Crestwood, Ill.
Martin, Jeff	.217	78	254	25	55	10	1	4	30	16	83	3	3	R	R	6-4	220	7-14-70	1992	Goodlettsville, Tenn.
McGuire, Ryan	.333	109	414	59	138	29	1	7	59	58	51	11	8	L	L	6-1	195	11-23-71	1993	Woodland Hills, Calif.
McKeel, Walt	.238	29	84	11	20	3	1	2	11	8	15	2	1	R	R	6-2	200	1-17-72	1990	Stantonsburg, N.C.
Merloni, Lou	.277	93	318	42	88	16	1	1	30	39	50	7	7	R	R	5-10	188	4-6-71	1993	Framingham, Mass.
Murphy, Pat	.228	35	114	17	26	4	0	0	11	6	21	10	6	L	R	5-10	160	3-24-72	1993	Mobile, Ala.
Nava, Lipso	.216	20	51	7	11	3	0	1	7	1	5	1	0	R	R	6-2	175	11-28-68	1990	Maracaibo, Venez.
Nixon, Trot	.160	25	94	9	15	3	1	2	8	7	20	2	1	L	L	6-1	195	4-11-74	1993	Wilmington, N.C.
Pough, Clyde	.278	97	363	68	101	23	5	21	69	50	101	11	5	R	R	6-0	173	12-25-69	1988	Avon Park, Fla.
Selby, Bill	.286	117	451	64	129	29	2	13	68	46	52	4	6	L	R	5-9	190	6-11-70	1992	Walls, Miss.
Shelton, Ben	.186	35	118	23	22	2	0	4	13	27	31	1	1	R	L	6-3	210	9-21-69	1987	Oak Park, Ill.
2-team (56 N.B.)	.218	91	294	60	64	7	0	17	43	67	89	5	1							
Tinsley, Lee	.389	4	18	3	7	1	0	0	3	1	5	1	0	S	R	5-10	180	3-4-69	1987	Shelbyville, Ky.
Zambrano, Eddie	.147	19	68	5	10	1	0	1	7	6	25	0	0	R	R	6-2	175	2-1-66	1985	Maracaibo, Venez.
Zambrano, Jose	.242	22	62	7	15	6	0	2	7	11	15	2	1	R	R	6-3	195	3-18-71	1988	Maracaibo, Venez.

PITCHING	W	L	ERA	G	GS	CG	SV	IP	H	R	ER	BB	SO	B	T	HT	WT	DOB	1st Yr	Resides
Amos, Chad	0	0	12.60	6	0	0	0	5	10	8	7	3	1	R	R	6-6	230	10-8-71	1992	New Matamoras, Ohio
Bakkum, Scott	6	4	1.34	28	0	0	0	47	31	12	7	9	24	R	R	6-4	205	11-20-69	1992	La Crosse, Wisc.
Bennett, Shayne	0	1	5.06	10	0	0	3	11	16	6	6	3	6	R	R	6-5	226	4-10-72	1993	Modbury, Australia
Blais, Mike	2	0	2.52	13	0	0	0	25	19	8	7	7	20	R	R	6-0	195	10-2-71	1993	East Lyme, Conn.
Bogott, Kurt	0	1	2.70	2	0	0	0	3	3	1	1	1	2	L	L	6-4	195	9-30-72	1993	Sterling, Ill.
Brooks, Wes	5	11	4.12	29	23	5	0	162	149	87	74	43	85	R	R	6-3	200	1-11-72	1992	Lebanon, Ill.
Cain, Tim	4	3	3.73	29	1	0	4	51	46	25	21	17	45	S	R	6-1	180	10-9-69	1990	Piscataway, N.J.
Carter, Glenn	1	1	3.07	14	0	0	8	15	15	8	5	4	10	R	R	6-0	175	11-29-67	1988	Melrose Park, Ill.
Caruso, Joe	1	1	11.37	11	0	0	0	13	21	16	16	8	8	R	R	6-3	195	9-16-70	1991	Petaluma, Calif.
Cederblad, Brett	3	2	3.63	8	5	2	0	45	43	19	18	11	36	S	R	6-5	195	3-6-73	1995	Sydney, Australia
Ciccarella, Joe	2	1	2.73	22	2	0	0	33	31	13	10	12	33	L	L	6-3	190	12-29-69	1991	Huntington Beach, Calif.
Emerson, Scott	0	0	4.76	4	0	0	0	6	9	3	3	2	5	S	L	6-5	175	12-22-71	1992	Phoenix, Ariz.
2-team (4 Bowie)	0	2	4.98	8	4	0	0	22	28	21	12	16	18							
Eshelman, Vaughn	0	1	0.00	2	2	0	0	7	3	1	0	0	7	L	L	6-3	205	5-22-69	1991	Houston, Texas
Faino, Jeff	1	1	2.35	5	0	0	0	8	9	3	2	1	5	R	L	6-0	185	11-22-72	1992	Danvers, Mass.
Fernandez, Jared	5	4	3.90	11	10	1	0	67	64	32	29	28	40	R	R	6-2	225	2-2-72	1994	West Valley, Utah
Hansen, Brent	4	5	3.26	11	11	3	0	77	70	32	28	17	52	R	R	6-2	195	8-4-70	1992	Carlsbad, Calif.
Hill, Chris	0	0	9.00	1	0	0	0	6	7	6	6	6	10	L	L	6-1	175	4-13-69	1988	Duncanville, Texas
Hoeme, Steve	2	0	3.33	20	0	0	6	24	23	9	9	8	17	R	R	6-6	230	11-2-67	1987	Preston, Kan.
Hudson, Joe	0	1	1.71	22	0	0	8	32	20	8	6	17	24	R	R	6-1	180	9-29-70	1992	Medford, N.J.
Ingram, Todd	1	1	5.84	18	0	0	0	25	27	19	16 , 21	16	R	R	6-4	200	4-1-68	1991	Bellevue, Wash.
Johnson, Dom	1	2	9.42	5	2	0	0	14	19	16	15	12	11	R	R	6-5	230	8-9-68	1987	Poway, Calif.
Langbehn, Gregg	0	1	5.40	14	0	0	1	13	9	9	8	9	11	R	L	5-11	182	11-14-69	1988	Schofield, Wisc.
Malloy, Chuck	0	0	4.76	1	1	0	0	6	9	5	3	1	1	R	R	6-4	225	3-1-72	1994	Philadelphia, Pa.
Orellano, Rafael	11	7	3.09	27	27	2	0	187	146	68	64	72	160	L	L	6-2	160	4-28-73	1993	Humacao, P.R.
Peterson, Dean	4	8	5.38	20	14	1	0	89	96	57	53	27	47	R	R	6-3	200	8-3-72	1993	Cortland, Ohio
Riley, Ed	0	0	2.76	16	0	0	1	16	14	6	5	9	10	L	L	6-2	195	2-10-70	1988	Worcester, Mass.
Ryan, Ken	0	2	5.82	11	0	0	2	17	23	13	11	5	16	R	R	6-3	215	10-24-68	1986	Attleboro, Mass.
Sele, Aaron	0	1	3.38	2	2	0	0	8	8	3	3	2	9	R	R	6-5	218	6-25-70	1991	Poulsbo, Wash.
Senior, Shawn	11	7	4.52	27	27	0	0	151	154	91	76	68	90	L	L	6-3	195	3-17-72	1993	Cherry Hill, N.J.
Sullivan, Mike	3	1	1.37	15	0	0	2	20	17	5	3	3	16	R	R	6-3	195	1-27-68	1989	Dallas, Texas
Suppan, Jeff	6	2	2.36	15	15	1	0	99	86	35	26	22	88	R	R	6-1	200	1-2-75	1993	West Hills, Calif.

FIELDING

Catcher

Catcher	PCT	G	PO	A	E	DP	PB
Brown	1.000	4	19	1	0	0	0
Delgado	.978	19	114	19	3	1	1
LeVangie	.996	42	248	26	1	3	5
Martin	.989	75	484	43	6	4	13
McKeel	.979	17	84	11	2	1	4

First Base	PCT	G	PO	A	E	DP
Carey	1.000	8	49	4	0	3
Hardge	1.000	1	0	1	0	0
Hecker	.994	30	283	26	2	16
McGuire	.989	70	642	48	8	51
McKeel	1.000	3	4	0	0	0
Pough	.980	32	262	31	6	17
Shelton	.983	6	59	0	1	3

Second Base	PCT	G	PO	A	E	DP
Carey	.973	21	46	63	3	15
Hardge	.951	13	17	41	3	7
Juday	1.000	3	2	3	0	0

	PCT	G	PO	A	E	DP
Merloni	.952	72	149	168	16	25
Murphy	.951	7	17	22	2	7
Selby	.966	35	70	70	5	14

Third Base	PCT	G	PO	A	E	DP
Carey	.925	27	16	46	5	3
Delgado	.000	1	0	0	0	0
Hardge	.920	9	7	16	2	2
Merloni	.945	20	16	53	4	5
Murphy	.900	10	9	18	3	1
Nava	1.000	4	4	10	0	0
Pough	.969	8	9	22	1	0
Selby	.885	74	49	136	24	11

Shortstop	PCT	G	PO	A	E	DP
Carey	.985	14	20	45	1	7
Garciaparra	.963	125	205	396	23	61
Hardge	.786	3	3	8	3	0
Merloni	1.000	1	1	1	0	0

	PCT	G	PO	A	E	DP
Nava	1.000	3	6	5	0	1

Outfield	PCT	G	PO	A	E	DP
Abad	.987	86	143	9	2	1
Blosser	1.000	35	59	5	0	1
Fuller	.972	56	135	6	4	2
Graham	1.000	8	14	0	0	0
Hardge	.955	14	18	3	1	0
Hecker	.929	18	24	2	2	0
J.J.Johnson	1.000	2	1	0	0	0
Lennon	.919	22	32	2	3	0
Mahay	.970	91	187	9	6	2
McGuire	.973	37	66	7	2	1
Murphy	.944	14	17	0	1	0
Nava	1.000	11	18	0	0	0
Nixon	1.000	25	66	2	0	0
Tinsley	1.000	3	4	0	0	0
E. Zambrano	1.000	16	38	2	0	1
J. Zambrano	.975	21	38	1	1	0

SARASOTA   A

FLORIDA STATE LEAGUE

BATTING

	AVG	G	AB	R	H	2B	3B	HR	RBI	BB	SO	SB	CS	B	T	HT	WT	DOB	1st Yr	Resides
Abad, Andy	.288	18	59	5	17	3	0	0	10	6	13	4	3	L	L	6-1	185	8-25-72	1993	Jupiter, Fla.
Borrero, Rikchy	.204	34	98	9	20	5	0	0	4	5	22	0	1	R	R	6-1	195	1-5-73	1990	Hormigueros, P.R.
Braddy, Junior	.264	114	413	41	109	12	5	2	36	31	99	13	12	R	R	6-3	205	10-4-71	1994	Lexington, Ky.
Carey, Todd	.306	25	85	15	26	6	0	4	19	9	17	2	1	L	R	6-1	180	8-14-71	1992	Cumberland, R.I.
Clark, Kevin	.225	84	293	23	66	11	0	4	31	21	63	2	5	R	R	6-1	200	4-30-73	1993	Henderson, Nev.
Collier, Dan	.256	67	242	30	62	12	1	12	44	20	83	5	9	R	R	6-3	205	8-13-70	1991	Ozark, Ala.
Davenport, Jeff	.000	10	22	1	0	0	0	0	3	1	8	0	0	R	R	6-3	205	12-21-70	1994	Greenville, Ohio
Henry, Antoine	.226	16	62	14	14	0	1	2	8	8	7	5	2	R	R	6-0	180	5-29-73	1991	San Diego, Calif.
Jackson, Gavin	.266	100	342	61	91	19	1	0	36	40	43	11	12	R	R	5-10	170	7-19-73	1993	Sylvester, Ga.
Johnson, J.J.	.276	107	391	49	108	16	4	10	43	74	7	8		R	R	6-0	195	8-31-73	1991	Pine Plains, N.Y.
Lombardi, Mark	.263	7	19	2	5	2	0	0	1	0	4	0	0	R	R	5-10	190	12-25-69	1991	Worcester, Mass.
McKeel, Walt	.333	62	198	26	66	14	0	8	35	25	28	6	3	R	R	6-2	200	1-17-72	1990	Stantonsburg, N.C.
Murphy, Pat	.201	54	189	18	38	4	0	2	15	8	26	12	5	L	R	5-10	160	3-24-72	1993	Mobile, Ala.
Nava, Lipso	.258	20	62	11	16	4	0	2	10	7	7	1	0	R	R	5-10	175	11-28-68	1990	Maracaibo, Venez.
Nixon, Trot	.303	73	264	43	80	11	4	5	39	45	46	7	5	L	L	6-1	195	4-11-74	1993	Wilmington, N.C.
Ortiz, Nick	.247	91	304	38	75	20	1	5	38	27	68	6	4	R	R	6-0	165	7-9-73	1991	Cidra, P.R.
Patton, Greg	.217	8	23	1	5	0	0	0	2	8	0	0		R	R	6-4	190	3-8-72	1993	Springfield, Va.
Raifstanger, John	.270	102	326	52	88	19	1	2	24	34	63	6	1	R	R	6-0	190	6-2-73	1994	Great Barrington, Mass.
Ramirez, Hiram	.186	40	140	13	26	2	0	2	12	3	29	3	2	R	R	6-2	200	9-10-72	1991	Ensenada, P.R.
Sheffield, Tony	.238	103	315	45	75	17	3	1	25	28	109	9	11	L	L	6-1	195	2-17-74	1992	Tullahoma, Tenn.
Smith, Dave	.299	23	67	12	20	5	1	0	6	9	10	1	5	R	R	5-10	160	2-18-72	1993	Cheektowaga, N.Y.
Tebbs, Nathan	.291	118	440	58	128	15	4	2	52	39	80	25	15	S	R	5-11	175	12-14-72	1993	Riverton, Utah
Varriano, Mark	.000	8	16	0	0	0	0	0	0	1	9	0	0	R	R	6-1	195	10-5-72	1995	Grand Forks, N.D.
Zambrano, Jose	.367	10	30	4	11	1	0	2	8	12	11	1	1	R	R	6-0	165	3-18-71	1988	Maracaibo, Venez.

GAMES BY POSITION: C—Borrero 30, Clark 30, Davenport 9, Lombardi 7, McKeel 56, Ramirez 14, Varriano 7. 1B—Abad 12, Braddy 1, Carey 12, Clark 46, McKeel 2, Patton 2, Raifstanger 49, Ramirez 18. 2B—Murphy 22, Ortiz 1, Raifstanger 33, Smith 19, Tebbs 71. 3B—Carey 6, Jackson 1, Murphy 21, Nava 4, Ortiz 76, Patton 1, Raifstanger 8, Tebbs 16. SS—Carey 3, Jackson 94, Murphy 1, Nava 6, Ortiz 13, Patton 4, Smith 2, Tebbs 23. OF—Abad 8, Braddy 99, Collier 24, Henry 12, Johnson 97, Murphy 6, Nixon 69, Raifstanger 10, Sheffield 2, Tebbs 2, Zambrano 6.

PITCHING

	W	L	ERA	G	GS	CG	SV	IP	H	R	ER	BB	SO	B	T	HT	WT	DOB	1st Yr	Resides
Antoszek, Chris	1	2	4.15	3	3	0	0	17	21	10	8	4	9	R	R	6-2	205	4-30-71	1994	Palatine, Ill.
Barkley, Brian	8	10	3.25	24	24	2	0	147	147	66	53	37	70	L	L	6-2	170	12-8-75	1994	Waco, Texas
Belinda, Stan	0	0	4.50	1	1	0	0	2	2	1	1	0	2	R	R	6-3	215	8-6-66	1985	Alexandria, Pa.
Bennett, Shayne	2	5	2.56	52	0	0	24	60	50	23	17	21	69	R	R	6-5	200	4-10-72	1993	Modbury, Australia
Bogott, Kurt	6	4	3.05	41	9	0	0	89	89	44	30	41	62	L	L	6-4	195	9-30-72	1993	Sterling, Ill.
Cederblad, Brett	7	6	4.09	24	12	0	0	92	98	50	42	21	71	S	R	6-5	195	3-6-73	1995	Sydney, Australia
Clemens, Roger	0	0	0.00	1	1	0	0	4	0	0	0	2	7	R	R	6-4	220	8-4-62	1983	Houston, Texas
Emerson, Scott	2	5	4.77	16	11	1	0	60	66	38	32	29	47	S	L	6-5	175	12-21-71	1992	Phoenix, Ariz.
Ferran, Alex	0	0	0.00	1	0	0	0	1	4	4	2	0	1	R	R	6-0	165	6-11-69	1988	Miami, Fla.
Hartgrove, Lyle	3	1	3.98	47	1	0	2	75	73	36	33	21	52	R	R	6-1	160	2-2-72	1994	Asheboro, N.C.
Hecker, Doug	1	2	3.43	10	1	0	1	21	24	9	8	7	16	R	R	6-4	210	1-21-71	1992	Wantagh, N.Y.
Howard, Chris	0	2	5.23	6	5	0	0	10	10	6	6	4	7	R	L	6-0	185	11-18-65	1986	Nahant, Mass.
Huffman, Jeff	4	4	4.58	15	11	0	0	77	72	43	39	36	55	R	L	6-2	190	11-17-71	1994	Raeford, N.C.
Kramer, Dan	2	0	6.14	21	0	0	0	15	18	12	10	7	13	R	L	6-0	190	10-31-74	1994	Downey, Calif.
Malloy, Charles	6	4	3.54	16	12	2	0	86	72	38	34	39	51	R	R	6-4	225	3-1-72	1994	Philadelphia, Pa.
Marquez, Ihosvany	1	1	3.00	12	0	0	1	15	10	6	5	13	18	R	R	6-0	195	9-8-71	1990	Hialeah, Fla.
Martinez, Cesar	6	6	3.75	34	10	0	0	110	108	62	46	40	61	L	L	6-2	200	4-29-73	1991	San Diego, Calif.
McLaughlin, Denis	3	2	3.26	54	0	0	6	66	57	31	24	66	79	R	R	6-5	215	11-19-72	1994	Warwick, N.Y.
Merrill, Ethan	11	7	3.78	27	25	1	0	150	155	86	63	67	78	L	L	6-3	210	4-21-72	1994	Burlington, Vt.
Pena, Juan	1	1	4.91	2	2	0	0	7	8	4	4	3	5	R	R	6-5	210	6-27-77	1995	Hialeah, Fla.
Peterson, Dean	1	3	6.75	4	4	0	0	17	25	17	13	10	15	R	R	6-3	200	8-3-72	1993	Cortland, Ohio
Sele, Aaron	0	0	0.00	2	2	0	0	7	6	0	0	1	8	R	R	6-5	218	6-25-70	1991	Poulsbo, Wash.
Telgheder, Jim	0	3	6.48	22	0	0	0	25	30	20	18	15	24	R	R	6-3	210	3-22-71	1993	Slate Hill, N.Y.

MIDWEST LEAGUE

BATTING	AVG	G	AB	R	H	2B	3B	HR	RBI	BB	SO	SB	CS	B	T	HT	WT	DOB	1st Yr	Resides
Allison, Chris	.315	87	298	46	94	8	4	0	22	52	39	36	4	R	R	5-10	165	10-22-71	1994	Rock Island, Ill.
Bazzani, Matt	.116	29	69	8	8	5	0	0	6	11	28	1	0	R	R	6-1	205	9-17-73	1994	Foster City, Calif.
Borrero, Rikchy	.229	23	70	8	16	4	1	2	6	6	17	0	1	R	R	6-1	195	1-5-73	1990	Hormigueros, P.R.
Bowles, John	.241	106	352	48	85	18	0	4	46	46	70	5	8	L	R	5-11	188	9-6-74	1992	Rockville, Md.
Chevalier, Virgil	.667	2	6	2	4	1	0	0	0	1	0	1	0	R	R	6-2	230	10-31-73	1995	Burnt Hills, N.Y.
Coleman, Michael	.268	112	422	70	113	16	2	11	61	40	93	29	5	R	R	5-11	210	8-16-75	1994	Nashville, Tenn.
DePastino, Joe	.277	98	325	47	90	20	4	10	53	30	70	3	3	R	R	6-2	210	9-4-73	1992	Sarasota, Fla.
DeRosso, Tony	.233	106	382	57	89	20	1	13	50	38	93	9	1	R	R	6-3	215	11-7-75	1994	Moultrie, Ga.
Faggett, Ethan	.243	115	399	56	97	11	7	8	47	37	112	23	7	L	L	6-0	190	8-21-74	1992	Burleson, Texas
Gibralter, David	.252	121	456	48	115	34	1	16	82	20	79	3	4	R	R	6-3	215	6-19-75	1993	Duncanville, Texas
Hamilton, Joe	.217	119	405	65	88	15	2	16	59	73	124	8	7	L	R	6-0	185	7-12-74	1992	Rehoboth, Mass.
Kurek, Chris	.193	52	145	14	28	8	2	0	18	13	47	0	0	R	R	6-0	195	1-25-72	1994	Buffalo, N.Y.
Lewis, Marc	.152	36	92	14	14	2	1	1	5	9	16	10	3	R	R	6-2	175	5-20-75	1994	Decatur, Ala.
Patton, George	.248	69	226	34	56	13	0	9	27	31	58	4	3	R	R	6-4	190	3-8-72	1993	Springfield, Va.
Sadler, Donnie	.283	118	438	103	124	25	8	9	55	79	85	41	13	R	R	5-7	160	6-17-75	1994	Valley Mills, Texas
Smith, Dave	.219	61	187	18	41	11	0	1	23	20	46	1	1	R	R	5-10	160	2-18-72	1993	Cheektowaga, N.Y.
Stasio, Tony	.305	87	315	44	96	22	1	7	47	25	70	1	1	R	R	6-2	200	6-21-71	1993	Davie, Fla.
Wojtkowski, Steve	.000	6	14	2	0	0	0	0	0	3	3	0	0	L	R	6-2	185	4-10-73	1994	Middletown, N.Y.

GAMES BY POSITION: C—Bazzani 23, Borrero 16, Chevalier 1, DePastino 68, Kurek 49. **1B**—Bazzani 1, Bowles 3, Chevalier 1, DePastino 9, Gibralter 92, Patton 2, Stasio 40. **2B**—Allsion 83, Bowles 28, Patton 7, Smith 36, Wojtkowski 2. **3B**—Bowles 19, DeRosso 80, Gibralter 16, Patton 24, Smith 2, Wojtkowski 2. **SS**—Allsion 1, Patton 19, Sadler 112, Smith 12. **OF**—Bowles 38, Coleman 111, Faggett 107, Hamilton 115, Lewis 31, Stasio 33.

PITCHING	W	L	ERA	G	GS	CG	SV	IP	H	R	ER	BB	SO	B	T	HT	WT	DOB	1st Yr	Resides
Barksdale, Joe	9	8	4.53	24	24	1	0	141	139	91	71	78	93	R	R	6-3	200	9-6-73	1993	Augusta, Ga.
Betti, Rich	0	0	0.00	1	0	0	0	2	0	0	0	1	1	R	L	5-11	170	9-16-73	1993	Milford, Mass.
Blais, Mike	2	1	1.96	32	0	0	10	46	34	12	10	11	35	R	R	6-5	226	10-2-71	1993	East Lyme, Conn.
Bonilla, Welnis	1	1	6.17	12	0	0	1	12	12	12	8	10	11	R	R	6-3	190	10-18-75	1993	Valverde Mao, D.R.
Bush, Craig	7	3	3.82	34	2	0	6	75	68	37	32	30	78	R	R	6-3	195	8-13-73	1991	Lancaster, Ohio
Cook, Jake	5	3	4.83	21	11	1	0	76	68	48	41	39	50	R	R	6-6	220	8-31-74	1993	Greenville, Ohio
Domenico, Brian	0	2	2.89	6	1	0	0	9	11	12	3	11	5	R	R	6-2	190	2-10-73	1992	Lincoln, R.I.
Dutch, John	4	7	7.94	32	0	0	1	51	80	50	45	20	23	R	R	6-1	200	9-24-72	1994	Laurinburg, N.C.
Farrell, Jim	3	2	3.65	13	13	1	0	69	62	34	28	23	70	R	R	6-1	180	11-1-73	1995	Hartville, Ohio
Hale, Tim	6	3	2.48	42	0	0	2	69	68	27	19	13	49	R	L	6-6	245	8-3-71	1994	Thornville, Ohio
Jones, Scott	2	0	5.68	5	0	0	0	6	3	5	4	8	13	R	R	6-0	200	3-1-73	1995	Union, Ohio
Mamott, Joe	3	6	5.96	14	13	1	0	77	76	56	51	50	66	R	R	6-4	235	9-13-73	1994	Lancaster, N.Y.
Marquez, Ihosvany	1	0	7.71	3	0	0	0	5	3	4	4	2	7	R	R	6-0	195	9-8-71	1990	Hialeah, Fla.
Mitchell, Alvin	6	8	5.31	30	17	0	1	115	120	75	68	64	74	R	R	6-3	220	7-7-71	1994	Rowlett, Texas
Padilla, Roy	0	1	6.48	4	1	0	0	8	10	9	6	7	7	L	L	6-7	230	8-4-75	1993	Panama City, Panama
Pavano, Carl	6	6	3.44	22	22	1	0	141	118	63	54	52	138	R	R	6-5	225	1-8-76	1994	Southington, Conn.
Renfroe, Chad	1	3	3.13	12	3	0	2	32	28	16	11	15	25	L	R	6-2	195	10-31-73	1993	Pedro, Ohio
Rose, Brian	8	5	3.44	21	20	2	0	136	127	63	52	31	105	R	R	6-2	190	2-13-76	1995	Dartmouth, Mass.
Telgheder, Jim	5	1	1.80	22	1	0	4	35	29	8	7	8	39	R	R	6-3	210	3-22-71	1993	Slate Hill, N.Y.
Tillmon, Darrell	6	3	2.24	13	10	0	0	76	56	25	19	12	53	L	L	6-2	170	3-30-73	1995	Wadesboro, N.C.
Tyrell, Jim	2	3	3.60	16	0	0	4	25	17	17	10	15	37	R	L	5-11	170	10-14-72	1992	Poughkeepsie, N.Y.

NEW YORK-PENN LEAGUE

BATTING	AVG	G	AB	R	H	2B	3B	HR	RBI	BB	SO	SB	CS	B	T	HT	WT	DOB	1st Yr	Resides
Austin, Kevie	.242	34	91	10	22	3	0	1	6	8	38	5	2	R	R	6-0	185	7-12-73	1995	Marietta, Ga.
Bazzani, Matt	.243	29	74	15	18	4	3	3	17	4	17	1	0	R	R	6-1	205	9-17-73	1994	Foster City, Calif.
Brannon, Tony	.216	42	125	11	27	5	1	1	18	9	20	5	2	R	R	5-9	170	1-15-75	1995	Johnstown, Ohio
Chamblee, James	.255	62	200	36	51	9	1	2	16	23	45	9	7	R	R	6-4	175	5-6-75	1995	Denton, Texas
Chevalier, Virgil	.308	64	250	34	77	12	2	7	46	11	35	15	6	R	R	6-2	230	10-31-73	1995	Burnt Hills, N.Y.
Goodwin, Keith	.260	39	146	26	38	4	1	2	16	14	22	10	1	R	R	6-2	188	2-5-75	1994	Sulphur, La.
Lebron, Ruben	.287	52	150	30	43	6	3	1	15	11	28	16	7	S	R	5-10	140	8-10-75	1992	San Pedro de Macoris, D.R.
Lewis, Marc	.301	69	272	47	82	15	5	5	39	17	32	24	9	R	R	6-2	175	5-20-75	1994	Decatur, Ala.
Norman, Ty	.252	49	159	23	40	5	0	3	15	8	28	8	4	R	R	5-11	165	6-29-74	1992	Haddock, Ga.
Prodanov, Peter	.244	55	172	26	42	10	0	3	22	16	31	12	2	R	R	6-1	200	9-4-73	1995	Princeton, N.J.
Rathmell, Lance	.285	66	228	34	65	10	1	1	30	28	25	4	5	R	R	6-1	185	8-1-73	1995	Williamsport, Pa.
Rivera, Wilfredo	.210	44	138	14	29	2	3	1	15	5	35	3	1	R	R	6-2	200	5-12-74	1993	Vega Alta, P.R.
Sagers, Kory	.182	25	66	11	12	1	1	0	7	5	18	1	1	S	R	6-3	180	8-22-73	1995	Las Vegas, Nev.
Sapp, Damien	.198	37	111	19	22	5	1	1	14	14	34	0	2	R	R	6-3	225	5-20-76	1994	Pleasant Grove, Utah
Tippin, Greg	.228	68	232	20	53	7	1	2	27	16	68	12	6	L	L	6-0	190	3-4-73	1995	Anaheim, Calif.
Variano, Mark	.091	4	11	2	1	0	0	0	1	2	3	0	0	R	R	6-1	195	10-5-72	1995	Grand Forks, N.D.

GAMES BY POSITION: C—Bazzani 23, Chevalier 21, Sapp 35, Variano 4. **1B**—Chevalier 19, Lewis 1, Prodanov 4, Rathmell 2, Sapp 1, Tippin 56. **2B**—Lebron 48, Prodanov 1, Rathmell 20, Sagers 15. **3B**—Brannon 41, Prodanov 11, Rathmell 22. **SS**—Chamblee 62, Lebron 1, Prodanov 11, Rathmell 11, Sagers 7. **OF**—Austin 29, Bazzani 1, Chevalier 1, Goodwin 36, Lewis 66, Norman 47, Prodanov 14, Rivera 43, Tippin 6.

PITCHING	W	L	ERA	G	GS	CG	SV	IP	H	R	ER	BB	SO	B	T	HT	WT	DOB	1st Yr	Resides
Betti, Rich	2	1	1.02	12	0	0	2	18	9	2	2	2	25	R	L	5-11	170	9-16-73	1993	Milford, Mass.
Cannon, Kevan	3	4	3.39	9	9	1	0	61	59	33	23	23	51	L	L	6-3	215	8-24-74	1995	Columbus, Ohio
Fernandes, Jamie	0	1	4.66	3	1	0	1	10	9	5	5	3	7	R	R	6-5	225	8-4-71	1993	Plymouth, Mass.
Fernandez, Jared	3	2	1.89	5	5	1	0	38	30	11	8	9	23	R	R	6-2	225	2-2-72	1994	West Valley, Utah
Jacobs, Mike	8	3	2.71	13	13	2	0	86	83	35	26	37	51	R	R	6-6	235	5-3-73	1994	Stockbridge, Ga.
Jones, Scott	0	1	1.35	20	0	0	13	20	11	3	3	9	26	R	R	6-0	200	3-1-73	1995	Union, Ohio
Mamott, Joe	4	6	6.68	9	6	0	0	32	40	35	24	28	36	R	R	6-4	235	9-13-73	1994	Lancaster, N.Y.
Marquez, Ihosvany	0	0	2.70	12	0	0	0	20	13	6	6	13	23	R	R	6-0	195	9-8-71	1990	Hialeah, Fla.
Mejia, Carlos	1	1	4.73	10	0	0	1	13	15	8	7	5	14	L	L	6-2	194	11-14-73	1992	La Vega, D.R.

PITCHING	W	L	ERA	G	GS	CG	SV	IP	H	R	ER	BB	SO	B	T	HT	WT	DOB	1st Yr	Resides
Munro, Peter	5	4	2.60	14	14	0	0	90	79	38	26	33	74	R	R	6-2	185	6-14-75	1994	Little Neck, N.Y.
Noffke, Andy	0	2	7.71	23	0	0	0	26	34	30	22	24	24	R	R	6-6	220	6-19-73	1995	Springfield, Ohio
Perez, Hilario	2	2	4.81	20	3	0	1	43	50	38	23	22	22	R	R	6-2	175	10-11-72	1991	Elias Pina, D.R.
Pinango, Simon	2	4	6.91	20	0	0	0	29	30	27	22	16	27	L	L	6-0	190	12-9-73	1991	Sucre, Venezuela
Romboli, Curtis	2	3	4.56	14	6	2	0	51	60	32	26	16	34	L	L	6-0	190	2-7-73	1995	Randolph, Mass.
Santiago, Antonio	0	3	5.30	4	4	0	0	19	24	17	11	13	11	L	L	6-1	185	8-30-76	1994	Carolina, P.R.
Sauve, Jeff	1	1	4.70	11	0	0	1	15	19	12	8	8	16	R	R	6-4	200	6-27-73	1995	Camp Hill, Pa.
Welch, Robb	4	4	5.68	12	12	1	0	65	76	45	41	39	35	R	R	6-4	190	12-30-75	1994	Twin Falls, Idaho

FORT MYERS   R

GULF COAST LEAGUE

BATTING	AVG	G	AB	R	H	2B	3B	HR	RBI	BB	SO	SB	CS	B	T	HT	WT	DOB	1st Yr	Resides
Alayon, Elvis	.200	25	85	7	17	3	0	0	5	3	10	4	1	L	R	5-11	170	12-14-74	1995	New York, N.Y.
Betancourt, Rafael	.256	51	168	18	43	5	0	0	19	13	31	8	5	R	R	6-1	187	4-29-74	1994	Cumana, Venez.
Cardona, Luis	.213	42	136	14	29	6	0	1	15	8	35	0	1	R	R	6-1	198	9-14-77	1995	San Sebastian, P.R.
Davenport, Jeff	.077	5	13	0	1	0	0	0	0	0	3	0	0	R	R	6-3	205	12-21-70	1990	Greenville, Ohio
Ferguson, Dwight	.194	22	62	10	12	3	0	0	6	17	24	4	3	L	L	6-1	170	12-9-76	1995	Carol City, Fla.
Flores, Oswaldo	.273	14	33	8	9	0	0	1	6	3	11	1	1	R	R	6-3	180	4-24-78	1995	Caracas, Venez.
Goodwin, Rawlin	.429	18	63	15	27	2	0	0	11	3	8	10	1	R	R	6-2	188	2-5-75	1994	Sulphur, La.
Gruber, Nick	.111	13	27	1	3	0	0	0	1	2	5	0	0	R	R	6-0	185	10-14-76	1995	Westmont, N.J.
Jenkins, Corey	.145	35	124	12	18	1	0	1	6	11	43	5	2	R	R	6-2	195	8-25-76	1995	Columbia, S.C.
Johnson, Rontrez	.254	52	193	37	49	4	2	0	11	30	30	25	5	R	R	5-10	160	12-12-76	1995	Marshall, Texas
Liniak, Cole	.266	23	79	9	21	7	0	1	8	4	8	2	0	R	R	6-1	181	8-23-76	1995	Encinitas, Calif.
Lomasney, Steve	.163	29	92	10	15	6	0	0	7	8	16	2	1	R	R	6-0	185	8-9-77	1995	Peabody, Mass.
Nova, Geraldo	.077	16	26	1	2	0	0	0	3	4	7	0	0	S	R	6-0	168	3-1-78	1995	Santo Domingo, D.R.
Olmeda, Jose	.217	42	129	15	28	4	1	4	14	11	42	3	3	S	R	6-0	165	7-7-77	1995	Fajardo, P.R.
Rodriguez, Carlos	.214	13	42	12	9	3	0	0	9	3	0	1	1	S	R	5-9	160	11-1-67	1987	Columbus, Ohio
Rojas, Moises	.207	42	140	22	29	5	0	1	16	20	34	5	3	R	R	5-11	180	11-25-76	1995	Hialeah, Fla.
Roman, Felipe	.227	50	176	14	40	8	2	1	17	7	38	1	0	R	R	6-3	199	12-17-76	1995	Rio Piedras, P.R.
Tardiff, Jeremy	.130	10	23	2	3	0	1	1	4	1	2	0	0	R	R	6-1	195	11-21-77	1995	Mechanic Falls, Maine
Variano, Mark	.163	18	49	4	8	1	0	0	6	6	10	0	0	R	R	6-1	195	10-5-72	1995	Grand Forks, N.D.
Veras, Wilton	.264	31	91	7	24	1	0	0	5	7	9	1	2	R	R	6-1	180	1-19-78	1995	Santo Domingo, D.R.
Zambrano, Eddie	.000	1	1	0	0	0	0	0	0	0	0	0	0	R	R	6-2	175	2-1-66	1985	Maracaibo, Venez.
Zambrano, Jose	.286	10	28	5	8	0	0	2	9	8	10	2	0	R	R	6-0	165	3-18-71	1988	Maracaibo, Venez.

GAMES BY POSITION: C—Cardona 20, Davenport 5, **1B**—Cardona 3, Nova 1, Roman 47, Veras 9. **2B**—Alayon 20, Betancourt 22, Nova 12, Rodriguez 8. **3B**—Betancourt 19, Liniak 21, Rodriguez 8. **SS**—Betancourt 13, Olmeda 42, Rodriguez 3. **OF**—Ferguson 20, Flores 13, Goodwin 15, Jenkins 32, Johnson 48, Rojas 37, Roman 1, Tardiff 9, J.Zambrano 8.

PITCHING	W	L	ERA	G	GS	CG	SV	IP	H	R	ER	BB	SO	B	T	HT	WT	DOB	1st Yr	Resides
Asher, Ray	0	3	6.92	10	3	0	0	26	32	29	20	26	21	R	R	6-4	190	10-2-74	1993	Vallejo, Calif.
Betti, Rich	1	0	2.45	3	1	0	1	7	7	3	2	3	4	R	L	5-11	170	9-16-73	1993	Milford, Mass.
Black, Jayson	4	5	4.43	12	9	3	0	65	83	42	32	14	50	R	R	6-2	195	1-12-76	1994	Convoy, Ohio
Butler, Robert	1	4	5.01	14	8	0	0	47	48	36	26	32	58	R	L	6-0	185	9-30-74	1994	Henderson, Ky.
Cannon, Kevan	2	1	0.68	5	3	1	0	27	14	6	2	9	38	L	L	6-3	215	8-24-74	1995	Columbus, Ohio
Crawford, Paxton	2	4	2.74	12	7	1	2	46	38	17	14	12	44	R	R	6-3	190	8-4-77	1995	Carlsbad, N.M.
Farrell, Jim	1	0	1.50	1	1	0	0	6	2	1	1	1	3	R	R	6-1	180	11-1-73	1995	Hartville, Ohio
Hecker, Doug	0	0	5.40	2	0	0	0	2	4	2	1	0	4	R	R	6-4	210	1-21-71	1992	Wantagh, N.Y.
Kinney, Matt	1	3	2.93	8	2	0	2	28	29	13	9	10	11	R	R	6-4	190	12-16-76	1995	Bangor, Maine
Martinez, Humberto	0	3	3.62	14	0	0	1	27	25	14	11	17	19	R	R	6-2	175	12-26-74	1993	San Pedro de Macoris, D.R.
Pena, Juan	3	2	1.95	13	4	2	1	55	41	17	12	6	47	R	R	6-5	210	6-27-77	1995	Hialeah, Fla.
Rauch, Robert	0	1	4.76	7	0	0	2	6	8	4	3	2	6	R	R	6-1	195	6-28-73	1995	Beaumont, Texas
Santana, Pedro	2	4	6.41	12	6	0	0	39	51	40	28	20	14	R	R	6-3	186	11-22-77	1995	San Pedro de Macoris, D.R.
Santiago, Antonio	2	2	4.32	6	3	0	0	25	30	17	12	3	24	L	L	6-1	185	8-30-76	1994	Carolina, P.R.
Stallings, Ben	0	1	7.82	8	0	0	0	13	14	11	11	11	7	R	R	6-1	200	9-30-76	1995	Owensboro, Ky.
Tillmon, Darrell	1	0	1.13	3	1	0	0	8	4	2	1	0	5	L	L	6-2	170	3-30-73	1995	Wadesboro, N.C.
Valencia, Enrique	1	2	4.76	14	4	0	0	34	51	25	18	9	19	L	L	6-4	165	5-10-77	1995	Merida, Venez.
Yount, Andy	0	1	2.76	5	5	0	0	16	13	8	5	6	17	R	R	6-2	185	2-14-77	1995	Kingwood, Texas

CALIFORNIA ANGELS

Manager: Marcel Lachemann. **1995 Record:** 78-67, .538 (2nd, AL West).

BATTING	AVG	G	AB	R	H	2B	3B	HR	RBI	BB	SO	SB	CS	B	T	HT	WT	DOB	1st Yr	Resides
Aldrete, Mike	.250	18	24	1	6	0	0	0	3	0	8	0	0	L	L	5-11	180	1-29-61	1983	Monterey, Calif.
2-team (60 Oakland)	.268	78	149	19	40	8	0	4	24	19	31	0	0							
Allanson, Andy	.171	35	82	5	14	3	0	3	10	7	12	0	1	R	R	6-5	225	12-22-61	1983	Cleveland, Ohio
Anderson, Garret.........	.321	106	374	50	120	19	1	16	69	19	65	6	2	L	L	6-3	190	6-30-72	1990	Granada Hills, Calif.
Correia, Rod	.238	14	21	3	5	1	1	0	3	0	5	0	0	R	R	5-11	185	9-13-67	1988	Rehoboth, Mass.
Dalesandro, Mark.........	.100	11	10	1	1	1	0	0	0	0	2	0	0	R	R	6-0	185	5-14-68	1990	Chicago, Ill.
Davis, Chili	.318	119	424	81	135	23	0	20	86	89	79	3	3	S	R	6-3	217	1-17-60	1978	Scottsdale, Ariz.
DiSarcina, Gary...........	.307	99	362	61	111	28	6	5	41	20	25	7	4	R	R	6-1	178	11-19-67	1988	East Grandwich, Mass.
Easley, Damion	.216	114	357	35	77	14	2	4	35	32	47	5	2	R	R	5-11	155	11-11-69	1989	Glendale, Ariz.
Edmonds, Jim	.290	141	558	120	162	30	4	33	107	51	130	1	4	L	L	6-1	190	6-27-70	1988	Diamond Bar, Calif.
Fabregas, Jorge	.247	73	227	24	56	10	0	1	22	17	28	0	2	L	R	6-3	205	3-13-70	1991	Miami, Fla.
Flora, Kevin	.000	2	1	1	0	0	0	0	0	0	1	0	0	R	R	6-0	185	6-10-69	1987	Chandler, Ariz.
Gallagher, Dave	.188	11	16	1	3	1	0	0	0	2	1	0	0	R	R	6-0	185	9-20-60	1980	Trenton, N.J.
Gonzales, Rene	.333	30	18	1	6	1	0	1	3	0	4	0	0	R	R	6-3	215	9-3-61	1982	Newport Beach, Calif.
Hudler, Rex	.265	84	223	30	59	16	0	6	27	10	48	13	0	R	R	6-2	180	9-2-60	1978	Fresno, Calif.
Lind, Jose	.163	15	43	5	7	2	0	0	1	3	4	0	0	R	R	5-11	180	5-1-64	1983	Dorado, P.R.
2-team (29 KC)	.236	44	140	9	33	5	0	0	7	6	12	0	1							
Martinez, Carlos	.180	26	61	7	11	1	0	1	9	6	7	0	0	R	R	6-5	215	8-11-65	1984	La Guaira, Venezuela
Myers, Greg	.260	85	273	35	71	12	2	9	38	17	49	0	1	L	R	6-2	215	4-14-66	1984	Riverside, Calif.
Owen, Spike	.229	82	218	17	50	9	3	1	28	18	22	3	2	S	R	5-9	165	4-19-61	1982	Austin, Texas
Palmeiro, Orlando	.350	15	20	3	7	0	0	0	1	1	1	0	0	L	R	5-11	155	1-19-69	1991	Miami, Fla.
Perez, Eduardo	.169	29	71	9	12	4	1	1	7	12	9	0	2	R	R	6-4	215	9-11-69	1991	Santurce, P.R.
Phillips, Tony	.261	139	525	119	137	21	1	27	61	113	135	13	10	S	R	5-10	175	4-25-59	1978	Scottsdale, Ariz.
Salmon, Tim	.330	143	537	111	177	34	3	34	105	91	111	5	5	R	R	6-3	220	8-24-68	1989	Phoenix, Ariz.
Schofield, Dick	.250	12	20	1	5	0	0	0	2	4	2	0	0	R	R	5-10	178	11-21-62	1981	Laguna Hills, Calif.
Snow, J.T.	.289	143	544	80	157	22	1	24	102	52	91	2	1	S	L	6-2	202	2-26-68	1989	Corona Del Mar, Calif.
Turner, Chris	.100	5	10	0	1	0	0	0	1	0	3	0	0	R	R	6-1	190	3-23-69	1991	Bowling Green, Ky.

PITCHING	W	L	ERA	G	GS	CG	SV	IP	H	R	ER	BB	SO	B	T	HT	WT	DOB	1st Yr	Resides
Abbott, Jim...................	5	4	4.15	13	13	1	0	85	93	43	39	29	41	L	L	6-3	210	9-19-67	1989	Newport Beach, Calif.
2-team (17 Chicago)	11	8	3.70	30	30	4	0	197	209	93	81	64	86							
Anderson, Brian...........	6	8	5.87	18	17	1	0	100	110	66	65	30	45	S	L	6-1	180	4-26-72	1993	Geneva, Ohio
Bennett, Erik	0	0	0.00	1	0	0	0	0	0	0	0	0	0	R	R	6-2	205	9-13-68	1989	Yreka, Calif.
Bielecki, Mike	4	6	5.97	22	11	0	0	75	80	56	50	31	45	R	R	6-3	195	7-31-59	1979	Crownsville, Md.
Boskie, Shawn	7	7	5.64	20	20	1	0	112	127	73	70	25	51	R	R	6-3	205	3-28-67	1986	Reno, Nev.
Butcher, Mike	6	1	4.73	40	0	0	0	51	49	28	27	31	29	R	R	6-1	200	5-10-65	1986	Phoenix, Ariz.
Edenfield, Ken	0	0	4.26	7	0	0	0	13	15	7	6	5	6	R	R	6-1	165	3-18-67	1990	Knoxville, Tenn.
Finley, Chuck	15	12	4.21	32	32	2	0	203	192	106	95	93	195	L	L	6-6	214	11-26-62	1985	Newport Beach, Calif.
Habyan, John	1	2	4.13	28	0	0	0	33	36	16	15	12	25	R	R	6-2	195	1-29-64	1982	Bel Air, Md.
Harkey, Mike	3	4	4.55	12	8	1	0	61	80	32	31	16	28	R	R	6-5	235	10-25-66	1987	Chino Hills, Calif.
2-team (14 Oakland) .8		9	5.44	26	20	1	0	127	155	78	77	47	56							
Holzemer, Mark	0	1	5.40	12	0	0	0	8	11	6	5	7	5	L	L	6-0	165	8-20-69	1988	Littleton, Colo.
James, Mike	3	0	3.88	46	0	0	1	56	49	27	24	26	36	R	R	6-3	180	8-15-67	1988	Mary Esther, Fla.
Langston, Mark	15	7	4.63	31	31	2	0	200	212	109	103	64	142	R	L	6-2	184	8-20-60	1981	Anaheim Hills, Calif.
Monteleone, Rich	1	0	2.00	9	0	0	0	9	8	2	2	3	5	R	R	6-2	217	3-22-63	1982	Tampa, Fla.
Patterson, Bob	5	2	3.04	62	0	0	0	53	48	18	18	13	41	R	L	6-2	185	5-16-59	1982	Hickory, N.C.
Percival, Troy	3	2	1.95	62	0	0	3	74	37	19	16	26	94	R	R	6-3	200	8-9-69	1990	Moreno Valley, Calif.
Sanderson, Scott..........	1	3	4.12	7	7	0	0	39	48	23	18	4	23	R	R	6-5	192	7-22-56	1977	Northbrook, Ill.
Smith, Lee	0	5	3.47	52	0	0	37	49	42	19	19	25	43	R	R	6-6	269	12-4-57	1975	Castor, La.
Springer, Russ..............	2	6	6.10	19	6	0	1	52	60	37	35	25	38	R	R	6-4	195	11-7-68	1989	Pollack, La.
Williams, Mitch	1	2	6.75	20	0	0	0	11	13	10	8	21	9	L	L	6-4	200	11-17-64	1982	Hico, Texas

FIELDING

Catcher	PCT	G	PO	A	E	DP	PB
Allanson	.994	35	164	15	1	1	3
Dalesandro....	1.000	8	10	0	0	0	0
Fabregas........	.986	73	391	36	6	4	8
Myers	.989	61	341	21	4	4	1
Turner............	1.000	4	17	2	0	0	1

First Base	PCT	G	PO	A	E	DP
Aldrete...........	1.000	1	1	0	0	0
Hudler............	1.000	2	8	0	0	1
Martinez	1.000	4	20	0	0	2
Snow	.997	143	1161	57	4	105

Second Base	PCT	G	PO	A	E	DP
Correia	1.000	3	0	3	0	0
Easley	.981	88	145	209	7	41

	PCT	G	PO	A	E	DP
Gonzales........	1.000	6	4	6	0	0
Hudler............	.986	52	93	115	3	32
Lind	1.000	15	24	40	0	10
Owen..............	1.000	16	27	21	0	7

Third Base	PCT	G	PO	A	E	DP
Correia	.750	2	0	6	2	1
Gonzales........	1.000	18	2	6	0	0
Martinez	.968	16	5	25	1	7
Owen..............	.945	29	16	36	3	3
Perez	.883	23	16	37	7	3
Phillips	.924	88	53	178	19	17

Shortstop	PCT	G	PO	A	E	DP
Correia	.850	7	6	11	3	4
DiSarcina	.986	98	146	275	6	49

	PCT	G	PO	A	E	DP
Easley	.973	25	41	67	3	18
Gonzales.........	.000	1	0	0	0	0
Owen..............	.952	25	22	38	3	7
Schofield	1.000	12	8	23	0	2

Outfield	PCT	G	PO	A	E	DP
Aldrete...........	1.000	2	7	0	0	0
Anderson........	.978	100	213	7	5	0
Dalesandro.....	1.000	1	1	0	0	0
Edmonds........	.998	139	401	8	1	2
Gallagher	1.000	6	9	1	0	1
Hudler............	.955	22	21	0	1	0
Palmeiro	1.000	7	7	0	0	0
Phillips	.991	48	113	1	1	0
Salmon...........	.988	142	320	7	4	0

Jim Edmonds led the Angels with 120 runs and 107 RBIs

Angels minor league
Player of the Year
Todd Greene

THE SPORTS GROUP

FRANK RAGSDALE

ANGELS

FARM SYSTEM

Director of Player Development: Ken Forsch.

Class	Farm Team	League	W	L	Pct.	Finish*	Manager	First Yr
AAA	Vancouver (B.C.) Canadians	Pacific Coast	81	60	.574	2nd (10)	Don Long	1993
AA	Midland (Texas) Angels	Texas	66	70	.485	5th (8)	Mario Mendoza	1985
#A	Lake Elsinore (Calif.) Storm	California	81	57	.587	2nd (10)	Mitch Seoane	1994
A	Cedar Rapids (Iowa) Kernels	Midwest	76	62	.551	3rd (14)	Tom Lawless	1993
A	Boise (Idaho) Hawks	Northwest	48	27	.640	1st+ (8)	Tom Kotchman	1990
R	Mesa (Ariz.) Angels	Arizona	35	21	.625	2nd (6)	Bruce Hines	1989

*Finish in overall standings (No. of teams in league)   #Advanced level   +Won league championship

ORGANIZATION LEADERS

MAJOR LEAGUERS

BATTING

*AVG	Tim Salmon	.330
R	Jim Edmonds	120
H	Tim Salmon	177
TB	Tim Salmon	319
2B	Tim Salmon	34
3B	Gary DiSarcina	6
HR	Tim Salmon	34
RBI	Jim Edmonds	107
BB	Tony Phillips	113
SO	Tony Phillips	135
SB	Tony Phillips	13

PITCHING

W	Two tied at	15
L	Chuck Finley	12
#ERA	Jim Abbott	
G	Two tied at	62
CG	Two tied at	2
SV	Lee Smith	37
IP	Chuck Finley	203
BB	Chuck Finley	93
SO	Chuck Finley	195

Tim Salmon. .330-34-105

FRANK RAGSDALE

MINOR LEAGUERS

BATTING

*AVG	Demond Smith, Cedar Rapids/Lake Els.	.344
R	Demond Smith, Cedar Rapids/Lake Els.	96
H	Jovino Carvajal, Midland/Vancouver	162
TB	Todd Greene, Midland/Vancouver	292
2B	Demond Smith, Cedar Rapids/Lake Els.	33
3B	Leon Glenn, Midland	11
HR	Todd Greene, Midland/Vancouver	40
RBI	George Arias, Midland	104
BB	Aaron Guiel, Lake Elsinore	69
SO	Leon Glenn, Midland	126
SB	Demond Smith, Cedar Rapids/Lake Els.	51

PITCHING

W	Matt Beaumont, Lake Elsinore	16
L	Geoff Edsell, Lake Elsinore/Midland	15
#ERA	Mike Holtz, Lake Elsinore	2.29
G	Mike Holtz, Lake Elsinore	56
CG	Jason Dickson, Cedar Rapids	9
SV	Carlos Castillo, Lake Elsinore	32
IP	Ryan Hancock, Midland	176
BB	Geoff Edsell, Lake Elsinore/Midland	83
SO	Geoff Edsell, Lake Elsinore/Midland	153

*Minimum 250 At-Bats   #Minimum 75 Innings

TOP 10 PROSPECTS

How the Angels Top 10 prospects, as judged by Baseball America prior to the 1995 season, fared in 1995:

Garret Anderson

BARBARA JEAN GERMANO

Player, Pos.	Club (Class—League)	AVG	AB	R	H	2B	3B	HR	RBI	SB
2. Garret Anderson, of	Vancouver (AAA—Pacific Coast)	.311	61	9	19	7	0	0	12	0
	California	.321	374	50	120	19	1	16	69	6
4. *McKay Christensen, of	Did not play—On Mormon mission									
5. Todd Greene, c	Midland (AA—Texas)	.327	318	59	104	19	1	26	57	3
	Vancouver (AAA—Pacific Coast)	.250	168	28	42	3	1	14	35	1
6. Marquis Riley, of	Vancouver (AAA—Pacific Coast)	.262	477	70	125	6	6	0	43	29
10. #Kevin Flora, 2b-of	Vancouver (AAA—Pacific Coast)	.298	124	22	37	7	0	3	14	7
	California	.000	1	0	0	0	0	0	0	0
	Philadelphia	.213	75	12	16	3	0	2	7	1

Player, Pos.	Club (Class—League)	W	L	ERA	G	SV	IP	H	BB	SO
1. *Andrew Lorraine, lhp	Vancouver (AAA—Pacific Coast)	6	6	3.96	18	0	98	105	30	51
	Nashville (AAA—American Assoc.)	4	1	6.00	7	0	39	54	12	26
	Chicago White Sox	0	0	3.38	5	0	8	3	2	5
3. Troy Percival, rhp	California	3	2	1.95	62	3	74	37	26	94
7. Ryan Hancock, rhp	Midland (AA—Texas)	12	9	4.56	28	0	176	222	45	79
8. *Bill Simas, rhp	Vancouver (AAA—Pacific Coast)	6	3	3.55	30	6	38	44	14	44
	Nashville (AAA—American Assoc.)	1	1	3.86	7	0	12	12	3	12
	Chicago White Sox	1	1	2.57	14	0	14	15	10	16
9. Jeff Schmidt, rhp	Midland (AA—Texas)	4	12	5.83	20	0	100	127	48	46

*Traded to Chicago White Sox   #Traded to Philadelphia

PACIFIC COAST LEAGUE

BATTING	AVG	G	AB	R	H	2B	3B	HR	RBI	BB	SO	SB	CS	B	T	HT	WT	DOB	1st Yr	Resides
Anderson, Garret	.311	14	61	9	19	7	0	0	12	5	14	0	0	L	L	6-3	190	6-30-72	1990	Granada Hills, Calif.
Carvajal, Jovino	.325	41	163	25	53	3	3	1	10	3	18	10	7	S	R	6-1	160	9-2-68	1987	La Romana, D.R.
Cohick, Emmitt	.333	10	24	3	8	2	0	0	5	5	8	0	1	L	L	6-2	175	8-8-68	1991	Yorba Linda, Calif.
Correia, Rod	.303	73	264	42	80	6	5	1	39	26	33	8	4	R	R	5-11	185	9-13-67	1988	Rehoboth, Mass.
Dalesandro, Mark	.333	34	123	16	41	13	1	1	18	6	12	2	0	R	R	6-0	185	5-14-68	1990	Chicago, Ill.
Deer, Rob	.288	25	80	16	23	5	1	4	20	16	32	0	0	R	R	6-3	225	9-29-60	1978	Scottsdale, Ariz.
Durham, Leon	.273	18	55	7	15	1	0	2	10	5	11	0	0	L	L	6-2	215	7-31-57	1976	Cincinnati, Ohio
Fabregas, Jorge	.247	21	73	9	18	3	0	4	10	9	12	0	0	L	R	6-3	205	3-13-70	1991	Miami, Fla.
Flora, Kevin	.298	38	124	22	37	7	0	3	14	16	33	7	4	R	R	6-0	185	6-10-69	1987	Chandler, Ariz.
Forbes, P.J.	.274	109	369	47	101	22	3	1	52	21	46	4	6	R	R	5-10	160	9-22-67	1990	Pittsburg, Kan.
Gonzales, Rene	.273	50	165	27	45	12	0	4	18	24	25	0	0	R	R	6-3	215	9-3-61	1982	Newport Beach, Calif.
Grebeck, Brian	.245	81	241	41	59	11	2	5	30	38	38	4	0	R	R	5-7	160	8-31-67	1990	Cerritos, Calif.
Greene, Todd	.250	43	168	28	42	3	1	14	35	11	36	1	0	R	R	5-10	195	5-8-71	1993	Martinez, Ga.
Hosey, Steve	.271	16	59	10	16	3	0	2	6	7	16	2	0	R	R	6-3	225	4-2-69	1989	Inglewood, Calif.
Jackson, John	.301	35	113	20	34	7	1	1	11	22	15	8	3	L	L	6-0	185	1-2-67	1990	Diamond Bar, Calif.
Jordan, Ricky	.222	19	63	5	14	2	0	2	9	3	7	0	0	R	R	6-3	205	5-26-65	1983	Gold River, Calif.
Lind, Jose	.222	10	36	2	8	2	0	0	5	1	4	1	0	R	R	5-11	180	5-1-64	1983	Dorado, P.R.
Martinez, Carlos	.247	25	97	17	24	3	0	1	6	7	17	1	2	R	R	6-5	215	8-11-65	1984	La Guaira, Venezuela
Molina, Ben	.000	1	2	0	0	0	0	0	0	0	1	0	0	R	R	5-11	190	7-20-74	1993	Vega Alta, P.R.
Monzon, Jose	.217	13	23	5	5	1	0	1	5	3	2	0	0	R	R	6-1	178	11-8-68	1987	Municipio Vargas, Venez.
Munoz, Orlando	.100	4	10	0	1	0	0	0	0	0	3	0	1	S	R	5-11	175	5-4-71	1989	Miranda, Venez.
Palmeiro, Orlando	.307	107	398	66	122	21	4	0	47	41	34	16	7	L	R	5-11	155	1-19-69	1991	Miami, Fla.
Peguero, Jose	.254	17	59	6	15	6	0	0	3	0	8	1	0	R	R	6-0	195	2-8-65	1985	Jersey City, N.J.
Perez, Eduardo	.325	69	246	39	80	12	7	6	37	25	34	6	2	R	R	6-4	215	9-11-69	1991	Santurce, P.R.
Pritchett, Chris	.276	123	434	66	120	27	4	8	53	56	79	2	3	L	R	6-4	185	1-31-70	1991	Modesto, Calif.
Ramirez, J.D.	.000	1	4	0	0	0	0	0	0	0	1	0	0	R	R	5-9	160	11-19-66	1989	Douglas, Ariz.
Raven, Luis	.244	37	135	18	33	11	1	5	26	11	35	3	1	R	R	6-4	230	11-19-68	1989	La Guaira, Venez.
Riley, Marquis	.262	120	477	70	125	6	6	0	43	49	69	29	10	R	R	5-10	170	12-27-70	1992	Ashdown, Ark.
Schofield, Dick	.189	16	53	5	10	4	0	0	9	3	3	0	0	R	R	5-10	178	11-21-62	1981	Laguna Hills, Calif.
Sweeney, Mark	.345	69	226	48	78	14	2	7	59	43	33	3	1	L	L	6-1	195	10-26-69	1991	Holliston, Mass.
Tejero, Fausto	.260	37	96	10	25	3	0	0	8	10	22	2	0	R	R	6-2	205	10-26-68	1990	Hialeah, Fla.
Turner, Chris	.266	80	282	44	75	20	2	3	48	34	54	3	0	R	R	6-1	190	3-23-69	1991	Bowling Green, Ky.
Vaughn, Derek	.667	1	3	0	2	0	0	0	0	0	0	1	0	R	R	6-1	190	1-11-70	1991	Lancaster, Calif.

PITCHING	W	L	ERA	G	GS	CG	SV	IP	H	R	ER	BB	SO	B	T	HT	WT	DOB	1st Yr	Resides
Akerfelds, Darrel	3	3	4.50	9	9	0	0	48	60	24	24	19	27	R	R	6-2	210	6-12-61	1983	Denver, Colo.
Bennett, Erik	6	0	4.26	28	0	0	2	51	44	24	24	18	39	R	R	6-2	205	9-13-68	1989	Yreka, Calif.
Bielecki, Mike	1	0	0.00	3	1	0	0	5	2	3	0	2	4	R	R	6-3	195	7-31-59	1979	Crownsville, Md.
Boskie, Shawn	1	0	3.00	1	1	0	0	6	4	2	2	4	1	R	R	6-3	205	3-28-67	1986	Reno, Nev.
Butler, Mike	0	0	4.50	3	0	0	0	6	4	3	3	2	3	L	L	6-1	195	12-14-70	1991	Denton, Md.
Chavez, Tony	2	0	1.50	8	0	0	1	12	7	4	2	4	8	R	R	5-11	180	10-22-70	1992	Merced, Calif.
Edenfield, Ken	7	2	3.45	33	0	0	0	60	56	24	23	25	44	R	R	6-1	165	3-18-67	1990	Knoxville, Tenn.
Fortugno, Tim	1	1	1.54	10	0	0	1	12	8	2	2	4	7	L	L	6-0	185	4-11-62	1986	Huntington Beach, Calif.
Heredia, Julian	5	3	3.63	51	0	0	10	74	69	34	30	23	65	R	R	6-1	160	9-22-69	1989	La Romana, D.R.
Holdridge, David	0	2	4.61	11	0	0	1	14	18	10	7	7	13	R	R	6-3	195	2-5-69	1988	Huntington Beach, Calif.
Holzemer, Mark	3	2	2.47	28	4	0	2	55	45	18	15	24	35	L	L	6-0	165	8-20-69	1988	Littleton, Colo.
Janicki, Pete	1	4	7.03	9	9	0	0	49	64	38	38	23	34	R	R	6-4	190	1-26-71	1992	Mesa, Ariz.
Keling, Korey	0	2	4.08	3	0	0	0	18	18	9	8	6	16	R	R	6-5	210	11-24-68	1991	Shawnee, Kan.
Leftwich, Phil	2	0	3.19	6	5	1	0	37	28	13	13	9	25	R	R	6-5	205	5-19-69	1990	Mesa, Ariz.
Lorraine, Andrew	6	6	3.96	18	18	4	0	98	105	49	43	30	51	L	L	6-3	195	8-11-72	1993	Valencia, Calif.
Mack, Tony	0	1	4.50	4	3	0	0	20	19	10	10	6	15	R	R	5-10	177	4-30-61	1994	Lexington, Ky.
Monteleone, Rich	1	0	3.24	7	1	0	1	17	19	7	6	3	7	R	R	6-2	217	3-22-63	1982	Tampa, Fla.
Morrison, Keith	14	9	4.93	28	26	4	0	161	178	97	88	40	84	R	R	6-4	190	11-22-69	1990	Suwannee, Ga.
Patterson, Ken	0	0	0.82	8	0	0	1	11	12	1	1	4	4	L	L	6-4	222	7-8-64	1985	McGregor, Texas
Ratekin, Mark	2	5	5.33	19	3	0	0	51	62	35	30	18	14	R	R	6-4	215	11-14-70	1991	Tehachapi, Calif.
Renko, Steve	2	5	4.21	10	9	0	0	51	53	29	24	18	22	R	R	6-3	205	8-1-67	1990	Overland Park, Kan.
Simas, Bill	6	3	3.55	30	0	0	6	38	44	19	15	14	44	L	R	6-3	220	11-28-71	1992	Fresno, Calif.
Springer, Russ	3	0	3.44	6	6	0	0	34	24	16	13	23	23	R	R	6-4	195	11-7-68	1989	Pollack, La.
Valera, Julio	2	5	5.70	13	13	2	0	71	85	54	45	21	43	R	R	6-2	215	10-13-68	1986	San Sebastian, P.R.
VanRyn, Ben	2	0	3.07	11	5	0	0	29	29	10	10	9	20	L	L	6-5	195	8-9-71	1990	Kendallville, Ind.
Watson, Ron	0	1	4.76	5	0	0	0	6	3	3	3	6	3	L	R	6-5	240	9-12-68	1990	Gilford, N.H.
Williams, Shad	9	7	3.37	25	25	3	0	150	142	65	56	48	114	R	R	6-0	185	3-10-71	1991	Fresno, Calif.
Willis, Carl	2	2	4.11	20	0	0	1	35	40	17	16	11	17	L	R	6-4	210	12-28-60	1983	Durham, N.C.

FIELDING

Catcher	PCT	G	PO	A	E	DP	PB
Dalesandro	1.000	4	10	0	0	0	0
Fabregas	.969	21	112	12	4	2	0
Greene	.995	30	175	17	1	1	5
Molina	1.000	1	4	0	0	0	0
Monzon	1.000	5	41	5	0	0	2
Tejero	.995	37	186	29	1	3	2
Turner	.990	51	282	23	3	2	5

First Base	PCT	G	PO	A	E	DP
Dalesandro	1.000	1	9	0	0	0
Deer	.977	5	40	2	1	4
Durham	1.000	2	5	0	0	0
Gonzales	1.000	1	8	2	0	2
Jordan	1.000	1	6	0	0	0
Munoz	1.000	1	1	0	0	0

	PCT	G	PO	A	E	DP
Perez	.986	8	67	4	1	3
Pritchett	.989	117	995	92	12	99
Raven	.971	3	32	1	1	6
Sweeney	.958	3	22	1	1	2
Turner	1.000	6	45	3	0	7

Second Base	PCT	G	PO	A	E	DP
Correia	.944	8	15	19	2	5
Forbes	.986	103	180	257	6	63
Gonzales	.903	7	10	18	3	5
Grebeck	.973	16	37	34	2	11
Lind	1.000	10	23	21	0	8
Munoz	1.000	3	3	5	0	1
Ramirez	1.000	1	1	5	0	0

Third Base	PCT	G	PO	A	E	DP
Correia	.875	6	4	10	2	1

	PCT	G	PO	A	E	DP
Dalesandro	.846	7	4	7	2	0
Gonzales	.966	11	10	18	1	2
Grebeck	.957	11	6	16	1	3
Martinez	.970	24	17	48	2	3
Munoz	1.000	1	2	1	0	1
Peguero	.929	17	6	33	3	2
Perez	.958	42	27	86	5	11
Raven	.873	21	9	46	8	6
Turner	.909	14	7	23	3	2

Shortstop	PCT	G	PO	A	E	DP
Correia	.961	60	106	193	12	35
Forbes	1.000	6	10	14	0	1
Gonzales	.947	26	25	82	6	18
Grebeck	.959	38	53	109	7	19
Schofield	.932	16	24	44	5	9

Outfield	PCT	G	PO	A	E	DP
Anderson	.957	11	22	0	1	0
Carvajal	.980	38	92	5	2	0
Cohick	.905	7	19	0	2	0
Dalesandro	1.000	18	33	1	0	0
Deer	.917	9	11	0	1	0

	PCT	G	PO	A	E	DP
Flora	.986	35	65	4	1	1
Grebeck	1.000	12	11	0	0	0
Hosey	.962	15	22	3	1	0
Jackson	1.000	10	31	56	3	0
Palmeiro	.995	103	192	4	1	2

	PCT	G	PO	A	E	DP
Pritchett	1.000	1	4	0	0	0
Riley	.994	119	326	2	2	0
Sweeney	.988	38	80	1	1	0
Turner	1.000	3	11	0	0	0
Vaughn	1.000	1	3	0	0	0

MIDLAND — AA

TEXAS LEAGUE

BATTING

	AVG	G	AB	R	H	2B	3B	HR	RBI	BB	SO	SB	CS	B	T	HT	WT	DOB	1st Yr	Resides
Arias, George	.279	134	520	91	145	19	10	30	104	63	119	3	1	R	R	5-11	190	3-12-72	1993	Tucson, Ariz.
Boykin, Tyrone	.271	62	210	34	57	11	3	7	25	21	36	2	1	R	R	6-0	195	4-25-68	1991	Columbia, S.C.
Carpenter, Jerry	.000	2	2	1	0	0	0	0	0	0	1	0	0	R	R	6-0	180	3-27-72	1994	Lakeland, Fla.
Carvajal, Jovino	.313	79	348	58	109	13	5	2	23	18	42	39	21	S	R	6-1	160	9-2-68	1987	La Romana, D.R.
Cohick, Emmitt	.229	56	153	25	35	13	2	2	23	33	45	3	2	L	L	6-2	175	8-8-68	1991	Yorba Linda, Calif.
Daniels, Moe	.202	25	84	9	17	5	0	1	4	14	22	2	4	R	R	6-2	190	1-14-71	1992	Tallahassee, Fla.
Diaz, Alfredo	.240	8	25	3	6	3	0	0	4	0	12	0	0	S	R	5-11	175	9-10-72	1992	El Monte, Calif.
Glenn, Leon	.254	120	433	68	110	19	11	17	65	34	126	16	11	L	R	6-2	200	9-16-69	1988	Louisville, Miss.
Gonzales, Rene	.176	5	17	1	3	0	0	0	2	4	1	0	1	R	R	6-3	215	9-3-61	1982	Newport Beach, Calif.
Greene, Todd	.327	82	318	59	104	19	1	26	57	17	55	3	5	R	R	5-10	195	5-8-71	1993	Martinez, Ga.
Guerrero, Pedro	.302	66	252	40	76	13	0	7	40	28	34	0	2	R	R	6-0	195	6-29-56	1973	Los Angeles, Calif.
Harkrider, Tim	.291	124	460	66	134	22	4	2	39	48	36	3	5	S	R	6-0	180	9-5-71	1993	Carthage, Texas
Hosey, Steve	.239	30	88	16	21	4	0	2	16	12	31	5	4	R	R	6-3	225	4-2-69	1989	Inglewood, Calif.
Monzon, Jose	.289	57	180	29	52	11	1	1	19	22	36	0	0	R	R	6-1	178	11-8-68	1987	Municipio Vargas, Venez.
Munoz, Orlando	.314	87	309	39	97	19	4	1	44	33	33	9	5	S	R	5-11	175	5-4-71	1989	Miranda, Venez.
Ortiz, Bo	.275	96	360	48	99	10	3	8	56	17	40	12	11	R	R	5-11	170	4-4-70	1991	Hartford, Conn.
Ramirez, J.D.	.271	80	251	34	68	16	1	10	36	22	49	1	1	R	R	5-9	160	11-19-66	1989	Douglas, Ariz.
Raven, Luis	.267	21	86	9	23	2	1	5	15	4	30	1	1	R	R	6-4	230	11-19-68	1989	La Guaira, Venez.
Redington, Tom	.250	9	32	5	8	2	0	0	3	6	5	0	0	R	R	6-1	200	2-13-69	1987	Anaheim, Calif.
Takayoshi, Todd	.278	7	18	2	5	0	1	0	0	1	4	1	0	L	R	6-1	190	10-4-70	1993	Cleveland, Ohio
Tejero, Fausto	.226	16	53	7	12	3	0	1	11	1	13	0	1	R	R	6-2	205	10-26-68	1990	Hialeah, Fla.
Urso, Joe	.324	12	37	6	12	3	0	0	4	5	3	0	0	R	R	5-7	160	7-28-70	1992	Tampa, Fla.
Wolff, Mike	.303	127	445	76	135	28	3	14	70	65	83	10	9	R	R	6-1	195	12-19-70	1992	Wilmington, N.C.

PITCHING

	W	L	ERA	G	GS	CG	SV	IP	H	R	ER	BB	SO	B	T	HT	WT	DOB	1st Yr	Resides
Akerfelds, Darrel	3	1	3.44	29	1	0	0	55	46	21	21	26	16	R	R	6-2	210	6-12-61	1983	Denver, Colo.
Blyleven, Todd	3	1	5.02	8	0	0	0	14	13	8	8	3	8	S	R	6-5	230	9-27-72	1993	Villa Park, Calif.
Bonanno, Rob	1	1	9.45	3	3	0	0	13	24	16	14	6	6	R	R	6-0	195	1-5-71	1994	Tampa, Fla.
Brown, Willard	9	10	5.18	27	27	2	0	148	188	92	85	47	80	R	R	6-4	215	4-14-72	1993	Marblehead, Mass.
Butler, Mike	1	1	4.50	19	0	0	0	24	24	12	12	9	14	L	L	6-1	195	12-14-70	1991	Denton, Md.
Chavez, Tony	0	1	8.00	7	0	0	2	9	13	9	8	1	4	R	R	5-11	180	10-22-70	1992	Merced, Calif.
Edsell, Geoff	2	3	5.91	5	5	1	0	32	39	26	21	16	19	R	R	6-2	195	12-10-71	1993	Muncy, Pa.
Hancock, Ryan	12	9	4.56	28	28	5	0	176	222	107	89	45	79	R	R	6-2	220	11-11-71	1993	Cupertino, Calif.
Harris, Bryan	6	5	4.94	39	4	0	0	78	105	50	43	32	60	L	L	6-2	205	9-11-71	1993	Peachtree City, Ga.
Holdridge, David	1	0	1.78	14	0	0	1	25	20	8	5	8	23	R	R	6-3	195	2-5-69	1988	Huntington Beach, Calif.
Keling, Korey	8	5	3.46	29	12	1	1	122	113	53	47	52	101	R	R	6-5	210	11-24-68	1991	Shawnee, Kan.
Mack, Tony	0	0	0.00	3	0	0	0	6	3	0	0	1	5	R	R	5-10	177	4-30-61	1994	Lexington, Ky.
Nieves, Ernesto	0	1	4.05	6	1	0	0	13	15	7	6	10	3	R	R	5-11	183	8-26-70	1990	Brooklyn, N.Y.
Pricher, John	0	0	4.50	8	0	0	1	10	16	7	5	6	7	S	R	5-10	200	11-13-70	1992	Orlando, Fla.
Ratekin, Mark	0	0	5.94	11	0	0	0	17	19	12	11	5	11	R	R	6-4	215	11-14-70	1991	Tehachapi, Calif.
Renko, Steve	3	5	4.81	22	9	0	1	77	100	51	41	28	44	R	R	6-3	205	8-1-67	1990	Overland Park, Kan.
Schmidt, Jeff	4	12	5.83	20	20	0	0	100	127	75	65	48	46	R	R	6-5	210	2-21-71	1992	La Crosse, Wisc.
Schooler, Mike	3	3	1.79	54	0	0	20	65	49	16	13	19	55	R	R	6-3	210	8-10-62	1985	Renton, Wash.
Sebach, Kyle	1	2	10.31	5	5	0	0	18	31	24	21	12	7	R	R	6-4	195	9-6-71	1993	Santee, Calif.
Snyder, John	8	9	5.74	21	21	4	0	133	158	93	85	48	81	R	R	6-3	185	8-16-74	1992	Thousand Oaks, Calif.
Thibert, John	0	0	4.18	12	0	0	2	24	19	12	11	17	15	R	R	6-1	190	1-9-70	1990	Okeechobee, Fla.
VanRyn, Ben	1	1	2.78	19	0	0	1	32	33	10	10	12	24	L	L	6-5	195	8-9-71	1990	Kendallville, Ind.
Watson, Ron	0	0	4.91	3	0	0	0	4	2	2	2	6	3	L	R	6-5	240	9-12-68	1990	Gilford, N.H.

FIELDING

Catcher	PCT	G	PO	A	E	DP	PB
Carpenter	1.000	1	1	0	0	0	0
Glenn	1.000	1	6	1	0	0	0
Greene	.992	65	311	44	3	3	9
Monzon	.976	57	312	61	9	9	6
Takayoshi	1.000	6	28	2	0	0	0
Tejero	.990	16	90	13	1	0	5

First Base	PCT	G	PO	A	E	DP
Boykin	.980	19	131	17	3	14
Glenn	.988	110	1009	60	13	112
Greene	1.000	2	3	0	0	0
Guerrero	.895	2	16	1	2	1
Munoz	1.000	3	23	3	0	4
Raven	1.000	6	45	5	0	10
Redington	1.000	7	62	6	0	8
Urso	.000	1	0	0	0	0

Second Base	PCT	G	PO	A	E	DP
Diaz	1.000	3	5	4	0	2
Gonzales	.964	5	11	16	1	6
Munoz	.994	69	131	185	2	50
Ortiz	1.000	1	0	3	0	0
Ramirez	.974	62	143	200	9	42
Redington	.000	1	0	0	0	0
Urso	.956	9	17	26	2	11

Third Base	PCT	G	PO	A	E	DP
Arias	.936	129	127	300	29	40
Diaz	1.000	1	1	4	0	0
Glenn	.889	3	3	5	1	0
Munoz	.778	3	1	6	2	1
Raven	.929	4	4	9	1	1

Shortstop	PCT	G	PO	A	E	DP
Arias	1.000	1	1	0	0	0

Shortstop	PCT	G	PO	A	E	DP
Diaz	1.000	4	5	6	0	2
Harkrider	.948	124	177	402	32	95
Munoz	.949	13	16	40	3	6

Outfield	PCT	G	PO	A	E	DP
Boykin	.970	34	61	3	2	0
Carvajal	.983	79	161	10	3	2
Cohick	.945	36	49	3	3	1
Daniels	.962	24	46	4	2	2
Glenn	1.000	5	9	1	0	0
Hosey	1.000	22	35	1	0	0
Munoz	.000	2	0	0	0	0
Ortiz	.974	92	165	20	5	5
Ramirez	.000	1	0	0	0	0
Raven	.909	8	8	2	1	2
Wolff	.973	127	309	18	9	3

LAKE ELSINORE — A

CALIFORNIA LEAGUE

BATTING

	AVG	G	AB	R	H	2B	3B	HR	RBI	BB	SO	SB	CS	B	T	HT	WT	DOB	1st Yr	Resides
Allanson, Andy	.317	22	82	22	26	9	0	4	22	16	8	2	2	R	R	6-5	225	12-22-61	1983	Cleveland, Ohio
Brakebill, Mark	.143	2	7	0	1	0	0	0	0	1	2	0	0	R	R	6-1	200	8-15-69	1989	Phoenix, Ariz.
Burke, Jamie	.274	106	365	47	100	15	6	2	56	32	53	6	4	R	R	6-0	195	9-24-71	1993	Roseburg, Ore.

BATTING	AVG	G	AB	R	H	2B	3B	HR	RBI	BB	SO	SB	CS	B	T	HT	WT	DOB	1st Yr	Resides
Carpenter, Jerry	.000	1	2	0	0	0	0	0	0	1	0	0	0	R	R	6-0	180	3-27-72	1994	Lakeland, Fla.
Cunningham, Earl	.239	78	284	50	68	13	2	15	55	15	97	8	3	R	R	6-2	250	6-3-70	1989	Lancaster, S.C.
Daniels, Moe	.305	39	151	26	46	8	2	0	11	18	35	6	4	R	R	6-2	190	1-14-71	1993	Tallahassee, Fla.
Davis, Doug	.333	1	3	0	1	0	0	0	0	1	1	0	0	R	R	6-0	195	9-24-62	1984	Bloomsburg, Pa.
Diaz, Alfredo	.235	49	149	25	35	12	2	1	25	11	54	1	1	S	R	5-11	175	9-10-72	1992	El Monte, Calif.
Doty, Derrin	.247	94	324	46	80	12	0	8	35	37	54	16	6	R	R	6-2	220	6-3-70	1993	Oak Harbor, Wash.
Erstad, Darin	.363	25	113	24	41	7	3	5	24	6	22	3	0	L	L	6-2	195	6-4-74	1995	Jamestown, N.D.
Guiel, Aaron	.269	113	409	73	110	25	7	7	58	69	96	7	6	L	R	5-10	190	10-5-72	1993	Langley, B.C.
Hemphill, Bret	.199	45	146	12	29	7	0	1	17	18	36	2	1	S	R	6-3	210	12-17-71	1994	Santa Clara, Calif.
Luuloa, Keith	.263	102	380	50	100	22	7	5	53	24	47	1	5	R	R	6-1	175	12-24-74	1993	Kaunakakai, Hawaii
Moeder, Tony	.238	68	252	39	60	18	1	6	26	27	61	2	3	R	R	6-2	205	7-14-71	1994	San Diego, Calif.
Molina, Ben	.385	27	96	21	37	7	2	2	12	8	7	0	0	R	R	5-11	190	7-20-74	1993	Vega Alta, P.R.
Owen, Spike	.200	3	10	1	2	1	0	0	0	2	2	0	0	S	R	5-9	165	4-19-61	1982	Austin, Texas
Powell, Chris	.200	13	40	7	8	2	1	1	2	13	10	0	2	L	L	6-0	180	9-1-68	1993	Huntington Beach, Calif.
Raven, Luis	.417	6	24	5	10	2	1	2	6	5	7	1	0	R	R	6-4	230	11-19-68	1989	La Guaira, Venez.
Redington, Tom	.328	76	271	50	89	26	1	6	54	51	43	2	1	R	R	6-1	200	2-13-69	1987	Anaheim, Calif.
Shockey, Greg	.327	114	441	85	144	32	3	20	88	42	88	2	2	L	L	6-1	190	4-11-70	1992	Huntington Beach, Calif.
Simmons, Mark	.202	81	238	35	48	7	1	1	25	32	61	10	8	S	R	6-1	195	9-23-72	1990	Chicago, Ill.
Smith, Demond	.351	34	148	32	52	8	2	7	26	11	36	14	3	S	R	5-11	170	11-6-72	1990	Rialto, Calif.
Smith, Joel	.205	30	88	12	18	4	0	3	19	11	15	0	0	R	R	5-9	195	12-12-68	1992	Tallahassee, Fla.
2-team (67 Visalia)	.266	97	350	44	93	16	3	12	62	26	80	0	1							
Takayoshi, Todd	.242	60	157	19	38	6	1	3	30	42	30	1	1	L	R	6-1	190	10-4-70	1993	Cleveland, Ohio
Tejero, Fausto	.238	8	21	5	5	1	0	0	3	5	6	1	0	R	R	6-2	205	10-26-68	1990	Hialeah, Fla.
Urso, Joe	.316	65	244	48	77	16	2	3	34	34	41	7	5	R	R	5-7	160	7-28-70	1992	Tampa, Fla.
Vaughn, Derek	.265	94	328	66	87	15	7	6	50	43	61	22	5	R	R	6-1	190	1-11-70	1991	Lancaster, Calif.

GAMES BY POSITION: C—Allanson 22, Carpenter 1, Hemphill 45, Molina 27, J. Smith 17, Takayoshi 35, Tejero 9. **1B**—Brakebill 1, Burke 21, Diaz 1, Moeder 61, Redington 56, Shockey 1, J. Smith 3, Takayoshi 6. **2B**—Diaz 2, Guiel 108, Owen 1, Simmons 16, Urso 22. **3B**—Brakebill 1, Burke 89, Diaz 30, Owen 1, Raven 1, Redington 1, Simmons 23, Urso 1. **SS**—Diaz 12, Luuloa 101, Simmons 8, Urso 24. **OF**—Cunningham 8, Daniels 38, Doty 91, Erstad 25, Powell 13, Shockey 107, Simmons 34, D. Smith 34, Vaughn 92.

PITCHING	W	L	ERA	G	GS	CG	SV	IP	H	R	ER	BB	SO	B	T	HT	WT	DOB	1st Yr	Resides
Aguirre, Jose	0	1	3.83	29	0	0	0	47	48	26	20	20	35	R	L	5-11	165	11-25-73	1992	Anaheim, Calif.
Anderson, Brian	1	1	1.93	3	3	0	0	14	10	3	3	1	13	S	L	6-1	180	4-26-72	1993	Geneva, Ohio
Beaumont, Matt	16	9	3.29	27	26	0	0	175	162	80	64	57	149	L	L	6-3	210	4-22-73	1994	Rittman, Ohio
Bielecki, Mike	0	0	4.91	3	2	0	0	4	2	2	2	2	2	R	R	6-3	195	7-31-59	1979	Crownsville, Md.
Blyleven, Todd	0	1	4.32	6	0	0	0	8	12	9	4	5	8	S	R	6-5	230	9-27-72	1993	Villa Park, Calif.
Bonanno, Rob	8	4	3.05	17	17	4	0	112	112	49	38	16	72	R	R	6-0	195	1-5-71	1994	Tampa, Fla.
Boskie, Shawn	0	0	4.09	3	3	0	0	11	15	7	5	4	8	R	R	6-3	205	3-28-67	1986	Reno, Nev.
Castillo, Carlos	2	1	2.41	52	0	0	32	52	55	18	14	15	40	R	R	6-2	225	5-9-71	1991	Anaheim, Calif.
Castro, Tony	0	0	5.56	8	0	0	0	11	15	9	7	8	9	R	R	6-2	175	7-9-71	1989	Phoenix, Ariz.
Chavez, Tony	4	2	4.23	33	0	0	9	45	51	28	21	19	48	R	R	5-11	180	10-22-70	1992	Merced, Calif.
Dafun, George	0	2	5.54	3	3	0	0	13	8	8	8	11	13	R	R	6-1	205	11-14-74	1993	Kihei, Hawaii
DeClue, Jon	5	1	3.57	9	4	0	0	40	50	16	16	5	22	R	L	6-2	198	9-17-70	1994	Apopka, Fla.
2-team (21 Visalia)	11	6	3.52	30	18	0	0	143	145	64	56	32	112							
Drysdale, Brooks	1	0	2.00	8	0	0	0	9	8	3	2	4	8	R	R	5-10	175	6-15-71	1993	Petaluma, Calif.
Edsell, Geoff	8	12	3.67	23	22	1	0	140	127	81	57	67	134	R	R	6-2	195	12-10-71	1993	Muncy, Pa.
Gomez, Marcial	1	0	5.84	7	0	0	0	12	11	10	8	10	10	R	R	6-4	200	3-1-72	1991	Hialeah, Fla.
Hinson, Dean	0	0	5.40	5	0	0	0	7	8	9	4	6	4	R	R	6-3	215	7-15-71	1993	Bloomfield, N.M.
2-team (23 Visalia)	1	1	4.17	28	0	0	3	41	38	27	19	22	39							
Holdridge, David	3	0	0.98	12	0	0	0	18	13	3	2	5	18	R	R	6-3		2-5-69	1988	Huntington Beach, Calif.
Holtz, Mike	4	4	2.29	56	0	0	3	83	70	26	21	23	101	L	L	5-9	172	10-10-72	1994	Ebensburg, Ark.
James, Mike	0	0	9.53	5	1	0	0	6	9	6	6	3	8	R	R	6-3	180	8-15-67	1988	Mary Esther, Fla.
Janicki, Pete	9	4	3.06	20	20	0	0	123	130	66	42	28	106	R	R	6-4	190	1-26-71	1992	Mesa, Ariz.
Patterson, Ken	0	0	0.00	6	0	0	1	10	7	0	0	1	5	L	L	6-4	222	7-8-64	1985	McGregor, Texas
Perisho, Matt	8	9	6.32	24	22	0	0	115	137	91	81	60	68	L	L	6-0	190	6-8-75	1993	Chandler, Ariz.
Pricher, John	1	0	3.38	5	0	0	0	8	9	4	3	4	3	S	R	5-10	200	11-13-70	1992	Orlando, Fla.
Sebach, Kyle	7	2	4.60	14	13	0	0	76	91	40	39	29	60	R	R	6-4	195	9-6-71	1991	Santee, Calif.
Slade, Shawn	1	0	5.14	15	0	0	0	14	15	11	8	5	15	R	R	6-2	200	10-26-70	1993	Seekonk, Mass.
Watson, Ron	1	0	4.76	10	0	0	0	11	6	6	6	6	8	L	R	6-5	240	9-12-68	1990	Gilford, N.H.
Williard, Brian	2	4	4.26	29	3	0	0	61	64	32	29	13	44	R	R	6-2	220	5-1-73	1991	St. Petersburg, Fla.

CEDAR RAPIDS   A

MIDWEST LEAGUE

BATTING	AVG	G	AB	R	H	2B	3B	HR	RBI	BB	SO	SB	CS	B	T	HT	WT	DOB	1st Yr	Resides
Alvarez, Luis	.195	42	123	14	24	7	1	2	13	12	15	2	2	L	L	6-4	210	10-25-69	1994	Canoga Park, Calif.
Betten, Randy	.233	36	60	8	14	2	0	0	4	13	8	6	2	R	R	5-11	170	7-28-71	1995	Highland, Calif.
Carpenter, Jerry	.100	11	30	2	3	0	0	2	4	9	0	0	R	R	6-0	180	3-27-72	1994	Lakeland, Fla.
Choi, Kyung	.228	36	123	14	28	4	2	1	6	9	12	4	1	L	L	6-1	180	5-12-72	1995	Seoul, Korea
Davalillo, David	.270	44	141	17	38	7	1	0	16	7	32	1	0	R	R	5-8	170	8-17-74	1993	Santa Teresa, Venez.
Donati, John	.286	116	381	63	109	24	2	16	75	57	92	5	3	R	R	6-1	200	5-4-73	1991	Concord, Calif.
Encarnacion, Anito	.209	42	86	4	18	3	0	0	6	2	12	0	0	R	R	6-2	185	8-26-72	1991	Sabana Perdida, D.R.
Espiritu, Michael	.167	9	24	1	4	0	0	0	2	7	3	1	1	R	R	5-9	195	2-1-72	1994	Seaside, Calif.
Failla, Paul	.253	129	459	77	116	23	4	2	48	66	102	30	19	S	R	6-2	195	12-8-71	1994	Sewickley, Pa.
Hemphill, Bret	.252	72	234	36	59	11	1	8	28	21	54	0	2	S	R	6-3	210	12-17-71	1994	Santa Clara, Calif.
Henderson, Juan	.229	123	402	61	92	12	1	2	28	36	79	47	12	R	R	5-10	160	4-17-74	1993	Santo Domingo, D.R.
Herrick, Jason	.285	104	358	54	102	21	4	11	57	38	84	19	3	L	L	6-0	175	7-29-73	1991	Franklin, Wisc.
Iatarola, Aaron	.260	115	388	62	101	20	1	16	69	44	92	7	4	L	L	5-11	189	9-28-71	1993	Longwood, Fla.
Moeder, Tony	.268	48	168	32	45	11	1	15	47	19	36	2	2	R	R	6-2	205	7-14-71	1994	San Diego, Calif.
Molina, Ben	.293	39	133	19	39	9	4	17	15	11	1	1	R	R	5-11	190	7-20-74	1993	Vega Alta, P.R.
Morris, Greg	.287	103	355	65	102	18	0	14	57	61	59	8	2	R	R	6-2	190	1-29-72	1994	Carmichael, Calif.
Olmstead, Nate	.232	59	155	20	36	8	0	1	15	20	37	1	0	S	R	6-4	200	3-24-72	1994	Davis, Calif.
Powell, Chris	.159	25	63	11	10	3	1	0	4	11	17	6	0	L	L	6-0	180	9-1-68	1993	Huntington Beach, Calif.
Robbins, Lance	.235	38	81	18	19	4	0	0	9	16	11	1	3	R	R	6-2	185	4-2-71	1993	Sioux City, Iowa

BATTING

BATTING	AVG	G	AB	R	H	2B	3B	HR	RBI	BB	SO	SB	CS	B	T	HT	WT	DOB	1st Yr	Resides
Ryder, Derek	.095	17	21	1	2	0	0	0	2	5	7	0	1	R	R	6-1	190	3-30-73	1995	Wallingford, Pa.
Smith, Demond	.341	79	317	64	108	25	7	7	41	32	61	37	12	S	R	5-11	170	11-6-72	1990	Rialto, Calif.
Young, Kevin	.291	119	395	58	115	22	2	2	46	37	42	17	12	R	R	6-0	195	1-22-72	1994	Northville, Mich.

GAMES BY POSITION: C—Carpenter 11, Encarnacion 14, Espiritu 9, Hemphill 68, Molina 39, Ryder 16. **1B**—Donati 72, Moeder 40, Olmstead 33, Robbins 1. **2B**—Betten 20, Davalillo 8, Henderson 114, Robbins 12. **3B**—Betten 2, Davalillo 30, Donati 2, Morris 102, Robbins 15. **SS**—Betten 2, Davalillo 4, Failla 129, Henderson 7, Robbins 2. **OF**—Alvarez 3, Choi 33, Donati 1, Herrick 100, Iatarola 72, Moeder 7, Olmstead 6, Powell 23, Smith 79, Young 116.

PITCHING	W	L	ERA	G	GS	CG	SV	IP	H	R	ER	BB	SO	B	T	HT	WT	DOB	1st Yr	Resides
Aguirre, Jose	0	0	3.86	6	2	0	0	14	12	6	6	10	12	R	L	5-11	165	11-25-73	1992	Anaheim, Calif.
Bushart, John	2	2	7.36	19	3	0	0	37	47	34	30	17	24	L	L	6-5	200	2-10-71	1993	Thousand Oaks, Calif.
Cintron, Jose	5	3	3.84	13	9	1	0	68	65	36	29	9	38	R	R	6-2	185	9-12-75	1993	Yabucoa, P.R.
Crossley, Chad	0	0	7.71	12	0	0	1	16	18	16	14	15	9	R	R	6-4	215	1-22-72	1993	Brandon, Fla.
Dafun, George	0	1	3.27	5	1	0	0	11	15	5	4	10	13	R	R	6-1	205	11-14-74	1992	Kihei, Hawaii
Deakman, Josh	4	2	3.59	13	13	0	0	73	67	33	29	24	53	R	R	6-5	185	2-25-74	1995	Beaverton, Ore.
Dickson, Jason	14	6	2.86	25	25	9	0	173	151	71	55	45	134	L	R	6-0	190	3-30-73	1994	Chatham, N.B.
Freehill, Michael	4	5	2.62	54	0	0	28	55	54	25	16	23	60	R	R	6-3	177	6-2-71	1994	Phoenix, Ariz.
Grenert, Geoff	3	4	4.13	27	4	0	1	72	76	43	33	23	55	R	R	6-3	181	2-18-71	1993	Scottsdale, Ariz.
Hill, Jason	2	1	4.55	48	0	0	2	59	59	38	30	41	49	R	L	5-11	175	4-14-72	1994	Redding, Calif.
Knox, Jeff	7	6	4.92	25	17	0	0	108	125	69	59	24	56	R	R	6-3	205	8-1-72	1991	Deltona, Fla.
Petroff, Dan	9	10	4.62	27	27	2	0	146	153	86	75	47	98	R	R	6-4	220	4-5-74	1994	Punxsutawney, Pa.
Sick, David	6	5	3.67	50	0	0	3	74	72	41	30	27	64	R	R	6-2	195	10-31-71	1994	Wilmington, N.C.
Skuse, Nick	13	7	4.04	26	25	3	0	147	155	84	66	61	116	R	R	6-7	240	1-9-72	1994	Los Gatos, Calif.
Slade, Shawn	3	1	4.25	30	0	0	3	42	42	24	20	19	35	R	R	6-2	200	10-26-70	1993	Seekonk, Mass.
Thurmond, Travis	2	5	5.31	14	2	0	2	39	36	25	23	20	55	R	R	6-3	200	12-8-73	1992	Hillsboro, Ore.
Warren, Deshawn	2	3	3.26	7	7	1	0	30	20	12	11	13	26	L	L	6-0	172	5-5-74	1992	Butler, Ala.
Washburn, Jarrod	0	1	3.44	3	3	0	0	18	17	7	7	7	20	L	L	6-1	185	8-13-74	1995	Webster, Wisc.

BOISE · A

NORTHWEST LEAGUE

BATTING	AVG	G	AB	R	H	2B	3B	HR	RBI	BB	SO	SB	CS	B	T	HT	WT	DOB	1st Yr	Resides
Alzualde, Daniel	.284	24	67	3	19	3	0	1	8	5	19	0	0	R	R	6-3	227	3-28-72	1992	Caracas, Venez.
Baughman, Justin	.233	58	215	26	50	4	3	1	20	18	38	19	4	R	R	5-11	175	8-1-74	1995	Reno, Nev.
Betten, Randy	.375	2	8	2	3	0	0	0	2	1	2	0	0	R	R	5-11	170	7-28-71	1995	Highland, Calif.
Bilderback, Ty	.322	61	177	35	57	11	2	3	25	29	29	10	5	L	L	6-2	180	10-29-73	1995	El Centro, Calif.
Bryan, Leonardo	.200	42	80	8	16	3	1	0	6	16	18	3	2	R	R	6-1	180	3-24-73	1991	Santo Domingo, D.R.
Buxbaum, Danny	.329	68	231	46	76	15	0	8	51	49	31	1	0	R	R	6-4	217	1-17-75	1995	Alachua, Fla.
Choi, Kyung	.299	21	67	14	20	2	0	0	5	9	5	3	1	L	L	6-1	180	5-12-72	1995	Seoul, Korea
Dalton, Jed	.262	48	126	10	33	8	1	0	10	8	20	1	1	R	R	6-1	190	4-3-73	1995	Omaha, Neb.
Davalillo, David	.223	36	112	17	25	9	1	1	12	6	21	1	0	R	R	5-8	170	8-17-74	1993	Santa Teresa, Venez.
Durrington, Trent	.171	50	140	23	24	4	1	3	19	17	35	20	0	R	R	5-10	185	8-27-75	1994	Broadbeach Waters, Aust.
Graves, Bryan	.208	32	53	9	11	2	0	1	5	17	12	0	0	R	R	6-0	200	10-8-74	1995	Bogalusa, La.
Ham, Kevin	.315	69	238	39	75	7	3	7	43	40	57	2	2	R	R	6-1	195	9-14-74	1993	El Paso, Texas
Hutchins, Norm	.250	45	176	34	44	6	2	2	11	15	44	10	6	S	L	6-2	185	11-20-75	1994	Greenburgh, N.Y.
Kane, Ryan	.276	74	283	39	78	14	2	14	59	25	57	0	0	R	R	6-4	210	1-25-74	1995	Acton, Mass.
McAninch, John	.250	42	112	16	28	9	0	2	12	11	24	0	0	R	R	6-0	205	8-1-73	1995	Oak Harbor, Wash.
Mota, Alfonso	.288	51	104	25	30	5	0	2	16	21	11	4	0	L	R	5-7	165	2-25-74	1992	San Pedro de Macoris, D.R.
Vallone, Gar	.242	37	99	21	24	6	0	0	16	20	33	4	2	S	R	6-00	175	5-9-73	1995	Placentia, Calif.
Vander Griend, Jon	.287	56	157	30	45	8	0	3	24	26	32	7	3	L	R	6-5	220	4-25-72	1995	Lynden, Wash.
Wagner, Kyle	.141	36	78	14	11	1	0	1	14	17	18	1	0	R	R	6-0	195	4-18-73	1995	New Cumberland, Pa.

GAMES BY POSITION: C—Alzualde 21, Bryan 1, Graves 26, McAninch 20, Vander Griend 1, Wagner 36. **1B**—Buxbaum 56, Dalton 1, McAninch 11, Vander Griend 16. **2B**—Betten 2, Davalillo 24, Durrington 37, Mota 9, Vallone 21. **3B**—Dalton 2, Davalillo 10, Kane 69, Mota 1, Vallone 2. **SS**—Baughman 57, Durrington 12, Mota 1, Vallone 14. **OF**—Bilderback 58, Bryan 36, Choi 20, Dalton 33, Davalillo 1, Ham 59, Hutchins 45, Vander Griend 19.

PITCHING	W	L	ERA	G	GS	CG	SV	IP	H	R	ER	BB	SO	B	T	HT	WT	DOB	1st Yr	Resides
Agosto, Stevenson	6	2	2.92	13	11	0	0	52	39	20	17	30	34	L	L	5-10	175	9-2-75	1994	Rio Grande, P.R.
Alvarez, Juan	0	0	0.77	9	0	0	0	12	12	1	1	2	11	L	L	6-1	180	8-9-73	1995	Miami, Fla.
Avila, Edwin	1	1	10.35	14	1	0	0	20	27	27	23	14	17	R	R	6-2	175	6-15-74	1992	Santo Domingo, D.R.
Coe, Keith	2	5	4.69	13	12	0	0	56	49	35	29	38	42	R	R	6-4	195	8-28-73	1994	Jamesburg, N.J.
Cooper, Brian	3	2	3.92	13	11	0	1	62	60	31	27	22	66	R	R	6-1	175	8-19-74	1995	Glendora, Calif.
Crossley, Chad	0	0	20.25	2	0	0	0	1	3	4	3	1	0	R	R	6-4	215	1-22-72	1993	Brandon, Fla.
Dafun, George	4	4	5.31	16	12	0	1	59	57	40	35	33	61	R	R	6-1	205	11-14-74	1992	Kihei, Hawaii
Deakman, Josh	1	1	1.54	3	3	0	0	12	11	8	2	4	8	R	R	6-5	185	2-25-74	1995	Beaverton, Ore.
De la Cruz, Fernando	0	0	13.50	1	0	0	0	1	3	6	2	2	4	R	R	6-0	165	1-25-71	1993	La Romana, D.R.
Farfan, David	1	0	2.53	14	0	0	0	21	19	9	6	12	17	R	R	5-7	185	5-30-74	1995	Livermore, Calif.
Mayer, Aaron	3	1	5.40	20	1	0	0	35	38	29	21	22	32	R	R	6-6	200	8-13-74	1993	San Ramon, Calif.
O'Quinn, James	0	0	4.84	23	0	0	0	22	22	12	12	18	26	L	L	6-0	190	8-27-73	1995	Jacksonville, Fla.
Petri, Tom	1	0	4.18	10	1	0	0	24	27	12	11	13	9	R	R	6-2	205	5-16-73	1995	Green Bay, Wisc.
Renko, Todd	0	0	7.36	5	0	0	0	4	6	3	3	2	4	R	R	6-2	210	6-16-73	1995	Leawood, Kan.
Scutero, Brian	1	2	4.91	22	0	0	12	22	17	13	12	16	17	R	R	6-1	190	8-15-73	1995	Winter Park, Fla.
Sumter, Kevin	0	1	2.27	21	0	0	0	32	15	8	8	31	38	R	R	6-0	185	9-4-72	1995	Oakdale, Calif.
Thurmond, Travis	9	3	3.11	16	15	4	0	101	75	36	35	31	93	R	R	6-3	200	12-8-73	1992	Hillsboro, Ore.
Valdez, Ken	1	0	4.63	5	0	0	0	12	11	8	6	7	9	R	R	6-0	195	10-4-74	1992	Tampa, Fla.
Vermillion, Grant	12	3	1.96	30	0	0	6	60	49	19	13	16	50	R	R	5-11	195	10-7-71	1995	Sun City, Calif.
Washburn, Jarrod	3	2	3.33	8	8	0	0	46	35	17	17	14	54	L	L	6-1	185	8-13-74	1995	Webster, Wisc.

MESA · R

ARIZONA LEAGUE

BATTING	AVG	G	AB	R	H	2B	3B	HR	RBI	BB	SO	SB	CS	B	T	HT	WT	DOB	1st Yr	Resides
Balcazar, Carlos	.301	35	93	11	28	5	1	1	11	12	20	2	0	L	R	6-2	197	2-12-74	1993	Barranquilla, Colombia
Barnes, Larry	.310	56	197	42	61	8	3	3	37	27	40	12	5	L	L	6-1	195	7-23-74	1995	Bakersfield, Calif.
Barrios, Esteban	.211	28	71	11	15	1	1	0	2	17	9	3	1	L	L	5-9	175	11-22-75	1995	Miami, Fla.

BATTING

BATTING	AVG	G	AB	R	H	2B	3B	HR	RBI	BB	SO	SB	CS	B	T	HT	WT	DOB	1st Yr	Resides
Castro, Nelson	.195	55	190	34	37	1	2	0	22	27	50	15	7	S	R	5-11	182	6-4-76	1994	Villa Vasquez, D.R.
Cowsill, Brendon	.257	34	113	18	29	5	3	0	13	18	28	7	0	R	R	6-3	190	1-7-75	1994	La Crescenta, Calif.
De la Cruz, Jesus........	.241	31	79	6	19	4	1	0	10	3	17	1	2	R	R	5-11	159	12-15-73	1992	San Pedro de Macoris, D.R.
Delgado, Ariel..............	.206	53	189	26	39	5	3	0	19	15	36	5	3	L	L	6-2	193	9-11-76	1994	Carolina, P.R.
Erstad, Darin	.556	4	18	2	10	1	0	0	1	1	1	1	0	L	L	6-2	195	6-4-74	1995	Jamestown, N.D.
Hutchins, Norm	.271	14	59	9	16	1	1	0	7	4	10	8	4	S	L	6-2	185	11-20-75	1994	Greenburgh, N.Y.
Lawrence, Mike	.162	18	37	5	6	1	0	0	5	7	11	1	0	S	R	6-4	200	2-18-76	1995	Chico, Calif.
Llanos, Alexis	.283	26	53	6	15	1	2	0	3	3	11	0	0	S	R	6-1	160	9-20-76	1995	Carolina, P.R.
Rodriguez, Juan	.298	54	215	27	64	8	8	1	31	7	49	4	7	S	R	5-10	185	12-16-74	1994	Arecibo, P.R.
Saucedo, Robert	.280	30	75	13	21	1	1	1	9	12	11	3	1	R	R	6-0	205	9-26-75	1994	Monterrey, Mexico
Stuart, Rich.................	.299	56	204	42	61	10	6	2	33	25	42	20	8	R	R	5-11	175	7-31-76	1994	Arecibo, P.R.
Veras, Illuminado	.253	32	87	9	22	4	1	1	9	5	13	2	2	R	R	6-0	190	5-13-75	1993	Santo Domingo, D.R.
Wardrop, Adam	.253	49	146	26	37	4	2	0	10	30	36	8	7	S	R	6-0	170	4-28-75	1994	Mermaid Waters, Australia

GAMES BY POSITION: C—Balcazar 20, Saucedo 20, Veras 30. **1B**—Balcazar 4, Barnes 54, Barrios 1, Rodriguez 2. **2B**—De la Cruz 21, Llanos 10, Wardrop 37. **3B**—Cowsill 33, De la Cruz 5, Lawrence 17, Wardrop 10. **SS**—Castro 55, Llanos 4, Wardrop 3. **OF**—Barnes 2, Barrios 13, Delgado 51, Erstad 3, Hutchins 14, Rodriguez 40, Stuart 51.

PITCHING

PITCHING	W	L	ERA	G	GS	CG	SV	IP	H	R	ER	BB	SO	B	T	HT	WT	DOB	1st Yr	Resides
Agosto, Stevenson........	0	1	5.40	1	1	0	0	5	3	5	3	2	2	L	L	5-10	175	9-2-75	1994	Rio Grande, P.R.
Ashley, Antonio	0	0	2.25	5	0	0	0	8	6	3	2	1	4	R	R	6-4	242	11-15-76	1995	Vallejo, Calif.
Blevins, Jeremy	5	1	2.45	11	9	0	0	51	39	20	14	32	48	R	R	6-3	195	10-5-77	1995	Bristol, Tenn.
Darrell, Thomas............	4	3	1.71	18	5	0	2	63	51	18	12	14	49	R	R	6-6	210	7-21-76	1995	Dunbar, Pa.
Drysdale, Brooks	0	0	8.10	4	0	0	1	3	4	4	3	1	7	R	R	5-10	175	6-15-71	1993	Petaluma, Calif.
Gomez, Alex	4	3	5.58	13	3	0	0	31	30	21	19	23	31	R	R	6-0	170	7-1-74	1994	Barranquilla, Colombia
Hamada, Nori	0	0	13.50	1	0	0	0	1	1	1	1	1	0	R	R	6-3	180	8-22-73	1994	Tottori, Japan
Leftwich, Phil	1	1	0.45	4	4	0	0	20	13	4	1	2	32	R	R	6-5	205	5-19-69	1990	Mesa, Ariz.
Lopez, Jose	2	2	2.40	11	7	0	0	41	45	18	11	13	36	R	R	6-1	170	9-30-76	1994	Navojoa, Mexico
McGuire, Brandon	1	0	3.38	2	0	0	0	5	3	3	2	3	6	S	R	6-3	210	8-10-77	1995	Big Spring, Texas
Patterson, Ken.............	0	0	0.00	1	1	0	0	3	0	0	0	1	3	L	L	6-4	222	7-8-64	1985	McGregor, Texas
Quinteros, Steve...........	0	1	4.38	7	1	0	0	12	19	10	6	3	13	R	R	6-3	196	6-2-76	1995	San Diego, Calif.
Richmond, Terrance......	0	0	9.00	1	0	0	0	1	1	1	1	1	0	R	R	6-2	190	5-14-77	1995	Oakland, Calif.
Riley, Brian	0	1	3.00	17	0	0	9	15	11	5	5	10	16	R	R	6-1	185	7-29-75	1995	Miami, Fla.
Rodriguez, Hector	2	2	2.92	9	2	1	0	25	21	9	8	9	21	R	R	6-3	210	3-21-75	1994	Caguas, P.R.
Rojas, Miguel................	1	0	4.66	9	0	0	0	10	10	6	5	5	7	R	R	5-11	195	11-17-75	1995	Arecibo, P.R.
Romero, John................	7	3	2.41	18	6	2	1	71	57	29	19	18	64	R	R	6-2	175	9-1-75	1995	Sylmar, Calif.
Soriano, Jacobo	0	1	3.09	11	0	0	4	12	9	6	4	7	10	R	R	5-11	175	11-28-74	1992	San Pedro de Macoris, D.R.
Stockstill, Jason............	3	1	5.08	12	7	2	0	44	38	29	25	22	31	L	L	6-4	185	11-13-76	1995	Anaheim, Calif.
Volkman, Keith	5	2	2.53	13	10	0	0	68	61	30	19	25	49	L	L	6-2	215	1-13-76	1994	Pasadena, Md.

CHIGAGO
WHITE SOX

Managers: Gene Lamont, Terry Bevington. **1995 Record:** 68-76, .472 (3rd, AL Central).

BATTING	AVG	G	AB	R	H	2B	3B	HR	RBI	BB	SO	SB	CS	B	T	HT	WT	DOB	1st Yr	Resides
Brady, Doug	.190	12	21	4	4	1	0	0	3	2	4	0	1	S	R	5-11	165	11-23-69	1991	Las Vegas, Nev.
Cameron, Mike	.184	28	38	4	7	2	0	1	2	3	15	0	0	R	R	6-1	170	1-8-73	1991	LaGrange, Ga.
Devereaux, Mike	.306	92	333	48	102	21	1	10	55	25	51	6	6	R	R	6-0	195	4-10-63	1985	Tampa, Fla.
Durham, Ray	.257	125	471	68	121	27	6	7	51	31	83	18	5	S	R	5-8	170	11-30-71	1990	Charlotte, N.C.
Grebeck, Craig	.260	53	154	19	40	12	0	1	18	21	23	0	0	R	R	5-7	148	12-29-64	1987	Cerritos, Calif.
Guillen, Ozzie	.248	122	415	50	103	20	3	1	41	13	25	6	7	L	R	5-11	164	1-20-64	1981	Guarenas, Venez.
Johnson, Lance	.306	142	607	98	186	18	12	10	57	32	31	40	6	L	L	5-11	160	7-6-63	1984	Mobile, Ala.
Karkovice, Ron	.217	113	323	44	70	14	1	13	51	39	84	2	3	R	R	6-1	215	8-8-63	1982	Orlando, Fla.
Kruk, John	.308	45	159	13	49	7	0	2	23	26	33	0	1	L	L	5-10	214	2-9-61	1981	Burlington, W.Va.
LaValliere, Mike	.245	46	98	7	24	6	0	1	19	9	15	0	0	L	R	5-10	210	8-18-60	1981	Bradenton, Fla.
Lyons, Barry	.266	27	64	8	17	2	0	5	16	4	14	0	0	R	R	6-1	200	6-3-60	1982	Biloxi, Miss.
Martin, Norberto	.269	72	160	17	43	7	4	2	17	3	25	5	0	S	R	5-10	164	12-10-66	1984	Hato Rey, P.R.
Martinez, Dave	.307	119	303	49	93	16	4	5	37	32	41	8	2	L	L	5-10	175	9-26-64	1983	Safety Harbor, Fla.
Mouton, Lyle	.302	58	179	23	54	16	0	5	27	19	46	1	0	R	R	6-4	240	5-13-69	1991	Lafayette, La.
Newson, Warren	.235	51	85	19	20	0	2	3	9	23	27	1	1	L	L	5-7	202	7-3-64	1986	Newnan, Ga.
Raines, Tim	.285	133	502	81	143	25	4	12	67	70	52	13	2	S	R	5-8	185	9-16-59	1977	Heathrow, Fla.
Sabo, Chris	.254	20	71	10	18	5	0	1	8	3	12	2	0	R	R	6-0	185	1-19-62	1983	Sarasota, Fla.
Snopek, Chris	.324	22	68	12	22	4	0	1	7	9	12	1	0	R	R	6-1	185	9-20-70	1992	Cynthiana, Ky.
Thomas, Frank	.308	145	493	102	152	27	0	40	111	136	74	3	2	R	R	6-5	257	5-27-68	1989	Burr Ridge, Ill.
Tremie, Chris	.167	10	24	0	4	0	0	0	1	2	3	0	0	R	R	6-0	200	10-17-69	1992	Houston, Texas
Ventura, Robin	.295	135	492	79	145	22	0	26	93	75	98	4	3	L	R	6-1	185	7-14-67	1989	Santa Maria, Calif.

PITCHING	W	L	ERA	G	GS	CG	SV	IP	H	R	ER	BB	SO	B	T	HT	WT	DOB	1st Yr	Resides
Abbott, Jim	6	4	3.36	17	17	3	0	112	116	50	42	35	45	L	L	6-3	210	9-19-67	1989	Newport Beach, Calif.
Alvarez, Wilson	8	11	4.32	29	29	3	0	175	171	96	84	93	118	L	L	6-1	235	3-24-70	1987	Maracaibo, Venez.
Andujar, Luis	2	1	3.26	5	5	0	0	30	26	12	11	14	9	R	R	6-2	175	11-22-72	1991	Bani, D.R.
Baldwin, James	0	1	12.89	6	4	0	0	15	32	22	21	9	10	R	R	6-4	210	7-15-71	1990	Southern Pines, N.C.
Bere, Jason	8	15	7.19	27	27	1	0	138	151	120	110	106	110	R	R	6-3	185	5-26-71	1990	Wilmington, Mass.
Bertotti, Mike	1	1	12.56	4	4	0	0	14	23	20	20	11	15	L	L	6-1	185	1-18-70	1991	Highland Mills, N.Y.
Bolton, Rod	0	2	8.18	8	3	0	0	22	33	23	20	14	10	R	R	6-2	190	9-23-68	1990	Chattanooga, Tenn.
DeLeon, Jose	5	3	5.19	38	0	0	0	68	60	41	39	28	53	R	R	6-3	215	12-20-60	1979	Boca Raton, Fla.
Dibble, Rob	0	1	6.28	16	0	0	1	14	7	10	10	27	16	L	R	6-4	230	1-24-64	1983	Cincinnati, Ohio
Fernandez, Alex	12	8	3.80	30	30	5	0	204	200	98	86	65	159	R	R	6-0	195	8-13-69	1990	Hialeah, Fla.
Fortugno, Tim	1	3	5.59	37	0	0	0	39	30	24	24	19	24	L	L	6-0	185	4-11-62	1986	Huntington Beach, Calif.
Hammaker, Atlee	0	0	12.79	13	0	0	0	6	11	9	9	8	3	S	L	6-2	204	1-24-58	1979	Knoxville, Tenn.
Hernandez, Roberto	3	7	3.92	60	0	0	32	60	63	30	26	28	84	R	R	6-4	235	11-11-64	1986	Cobo Rojo, P.R.
Karchner, Matt	4	2	1.69	31	0	0	0	32	33	8	6	12	24	R	R	6-4	245	6-28-67	1989	Berwick, Pa.
Keyser, Brian	5	6	4.97	23	10	0	0	92	114	53	51	27	48	R	R	6-1	180	10-31-66	1989	Walnut Creek, Calif.
Lorraine, Andrew	0	0	3.38	5	0	0	0	8	3	3	3	2	5	L	L	6-3	195	8-11-72	1993	Valencia, Calif.
Marquez, Isidro	0	1	6.75	7	0	0	0	7	9	5	5	2	8	R	R	6-3	190	5-15-65	1985	Navojoa, Mexico
McCaskill, Kirk	6	4	4.89	55	1	0	2	81	97	50	44	33	50	R	R	6-1	205	4-9-61	1982	Corona Del Mar, Calif.
Radinsky, Scott	2	1	5.45	46	0	0	1	38	46	23	23	17	14	L	L	6-3	204	3-3-68	1986	Simi Valley, Calif.
Righetti, Dave	3	2	4.20	10	9	0	0	49	65	24	23	18	29	L	L	6-4	219	11-28-58	1977	Los Altos, Calif.
Ruffcorn, Scott	0	0	7.88	4	0	0	0	8	10	7	7	13	5	R	R	6-4	215	12-29-69	1991	Austin, Texas
Shaw, Jeff	0	0	6.52	9	0	0	0	10	12	7	7	1	6	R	R	6-2	185	7-7-66	1986	Wash. Courthouse, Ohio
Simas, Bill	1	1	2.57	14	0	0	0	14	15	5	4	10	16	L	R	6-3	220	11-28-71	1992	Fresno, Calif.
Sirotka, Mike	1	2	4.19	6	6	0	0	34	39	16	16	17	19	L	L	6-1	190	5-13-71	1993	Houston, Texas
Thomas, Larry	0	0	1.32	17	0	0	0	14	8	2	2	6	12	R	L	6-1	190	10-25-69	1991	Mobile, Ala.

FIELDING

Catcher	PCT	G	PO	A	E	DP	PB
Karkovice	.991	113	629	42	6	2	7
LaValliere	.996	46	202	20	1	1	1
Lyons	.987	16	64	10	1	2	4
Tremie	.976	9	39	2	1	0	0

First Base	PCT	G	PO	A	E	DP
Kruk	.909	1	10	0	1	1
Lyons	.974	4	33	4	1	4
Martinez	.997	47	311	23	1	38
Sabo	.909	1	10	0	1	1
Thomas	.991	90	738	34	7	67
Ventura	.981	18	95	10	2	12

Second Base	PCT	G	PO	A	E	DP
Brady	1.000	6	14	21	0	4
Durham	.973	122	245	298	15	67
Grebeck	1.000	8	11	14	0	2
Martin	.950	17	35	41	4	12

Third Base	PCT	G	PO	A	E	DP
Grebeck	.970	18	14	18	1	3

	PCT	G	PO	A	E	DP
Martin	.818	9	2	7	2	2
Sabo	1.000	1	0	1	0	0
Snopek	1.000	17	11	13	0	0
Ventura	.948	121	106	206	17	15

Shortstop	PCT	G	PO	A	E	DP
Grebeck	.961	31	51	95	6	20
Guillen	.976	120	167	319	12	58
Martin	.962	7	8	17	1	2
Snopek	.941	6	14	18	2	5

Outfield	PCT	G	PO	A	E	DP
Cameron	1.000	28	33	1	0	0
Devereaux	.985	90	187	4	3	1
Johnson	.991	140	338	8	3	2
Martin	1.000	12	7	2	0	0
Martinez	.976	59	81	2	2	1
Mouton	.990	53	93	5	1	1
Newson	.978	24	44	1	1	0
Raines	.980	108	193	7	4	1

BERNARD TRONCALE

Frank Thomas

Alex Fernandez led the White Sox with 12 wins and 159 strikeouts

White Sox minor league Player of the Year Luis Andujar

WHITE SOX

R&R SPORTS GROUP

FARM SYSTEM

Director of Minor League Operations: Steve Noworyta.

Class	Farm Team	League	W	L	Pct.	Finish*	Manager	First Yr
AAA	Nashville (Tenn.) Sounds	American Assoc.	68	76	.472	6th (8)	Rick Renick	1993
AA	Birmingham (Ala.) Barons	Southern	80	64	.556	3rd (10)	Terry Francona	1986
#A	Prince William (Va.) Cannons	Carolina	64	76	.457	6th (8)	Dave Huppert	1994
A	South Bend (Ill.) Silver Hawks	Midwest	66	69	.489	9th (14)	Fred Kendall	1988
A	Hickory (N.C.) Crawdads	South Atlantic	49	89	.355	14th (14)	Mike Rojas	1993
#R	Bristol (Va.) White Sox	Appalachian	28	39	.418	7th (10)	Chris Cron	1995
R	Sarasota (Fla.) White Sox	Gulf Coast	36	22	.621	4th (16)	Mike Gellinger	1964

*Finish in overall standings (No. of teams in league)   #Advanced level

ORGANIZATION LEADERS

MAJOR LEAGUERS

BATTING
*AVG	Frank Thomas	.308
R	Frank Thomas	102
H	Lance Johnson	186
TB	Frank Thomas	299
2B	Two tied at	27
3B	Lance Johnson	12
HR	Frank Thomas	40
RBI	Frank Thomas	111
BB	Frank Thomas	136
SO	Robin Ventura	98
SB	Lance Johnson	40

PITCHING
W	Alex Fernandez	12
L	Jason Bere	15
#ERA	Alex Fernandez	3.80
G	Roberto Hernandez	60
CG	Alex Fernandez	5
SV	Roberto Hernandez	32
IP	Alex Fernandez	204
BB	Jason Bere	106
SO	Alex Fernandez	159

Lance Johnson. 186 hits, 40 steals

MORRIS FOSTOFF

MINOR LEAGUERS

BATTING
*AVG	Kevin Coughlin, Birmingham/Nash.	.372
R	Essex Burton, Birmingham	95
H	Jeff Abbott, Prince William/Birm.	155
TB	Nilson Robledo, South Bend	243
2B	Frank Menechino, Prince William	31
3B	Three tied at	6
HR	Juan Thomas, Prince William	26
RBI	Nilson Robledo, South Bend	108
BB	Frank Menechino, Prince William	96
SO	Juan Thomas, Prince William	156
SB	Essex Burton, Birmingham	60

PITCHING
W	Tom Fordham, Prince William/Birm.	15
L	Brian Woods, Prince William	15
#ERA	Barry Johnson, Birmingham	1.85
G	David Welch, Hickory	60
CG	David Lundquist, South Bend	5
SV	Two tied at	20
IP	Jack Ford, Hickory	174
BB	Two tied at	73
SO	Russell Herbert, South Bend/Hickory	163

*Minimum 250 At-Bats   #Minimum 75 Innings

TOP 10 PROSPECTS

How the White Sox Top 10 prospects, as judged by Baseball America prior to the 1995 season, fared in 1995:

Scott Ruffcorn

Player, Pos.	Club (Class—League)	AVG	AB	R	H	2B	3B	HR	RBI	SB
3. Ray Durham, 2b	Chicago	.257	471	68	121	27	6	7	51	18
4. Jimmy Hurst, of	Birmingham (AA—Southern)	.189	301	47	57	11	0	12	34	12
5. Chris Snopek, 3b-ss	Nashville (AAA—American Assoc.)	.323	393	56	127	23	4	12	55	2
	Chicago	.324	68	12	22	4	0	1	7	1
6. Jeff Abbott, of	Prince William (A—Carolina)	.348	264	41	92	16	0	4	47	7
	Birmingham (AA—Southern)	.320	197	25	63	11	1	3	28	1
8. Eddie Pearson, 1b	GCL White Sox (R—Gulf Coast)	.300	20	7	6	2	0	1	6	0
	Birmingham (AA—Southern)	.224	201	20	45	13	0	2	25	1
10. Greg Norton, 3b	Birmingham (AA—Southern)	.249	469	65	117	23	2	6	60	19

		W	L	ERA	G	SV	IP	H	BB	SO
1. Scott Ruffcorn, rhp	GCL White Sox (R—Gulf Coast)	0	0	0.90	3	0	10	7	5	7
	Birmingham (AA—Southern)	0	2	5.63	3	0	16	17	10	13
	Nashville (AAA—American Assoc.)	0	0	108.00	2	0	0	3	3	0
	Chicago	0	0	7.88	4	0	8	10	13	5
2. James Baldwin, rhp	Nashville (AAA—American Assoc.)	5	9	5.85	18	0	95	120	44	89
	Chicago	0	1	12.89	6	0	15	32	9	10
7. Scott Christman, lhp	Prince William (A—Carolina)	4	4	3.59	13	0	85	83	19	56
	Birmingham (AA—Southern)	2	5	6.39	12	0	62	76	24	37
9. Carlos Castillo, rhp	Hickory (A—South Atlantic)	5	6	3.73	14	1	80	85	18	67

AMERICAN ASSOCIATION

BATTING	AVG	G	AB	R	H	2B	3B	HR	RBI	BB	SO	SB	CS	B	T	HT	WT	DOB	1st Yr	Resides
Brady, Doug	.298	125	450	71	134	15	6	5	27	31	76	32	6	S	R	5-11	165	11-23-69	1991	Las Vegas, Nev.
Cappuccio, Carmine ...	.273	66	216	30	59	14	0	5	24	29	26	0	2	L	R	6-3	185	2-1-70	1992	Malden, Mass.
Cotto, Henry	.131	17	61	4	8	1	0	1	4	1	20	0	1	R	R	6-2	180	1-5-61	1980	Renton, Wash.
Coughlin, Kevin	.182	10	22	0	4	1	0	0	0	4	3	0	1	L	L	6-0	175	9-7-70	1989	Clarksburg, Md.
Cron, Chris	.217	21	69	3	15	2	0	2	10	8	20	0	0	R	R	6-2	207	3-31-64	1984	Placentia, Calif.
Fraraccio, Dan.............	.250	10	28	2	7	0	0	0	3	1	6	2	0	R	R	5-11	175	9-18-70	1992	Bradenton, Fla.
Howard, Tim................	.233	37	103	8	24	3	1	2	13	13	12	4	3	L	R	5-10	155	6-2-69	1988	Brawley, Calif.
Howitt, Dann...............	.226	45	133	16	30	6	1	3	15	16	32	0	3	L	R	6-5	205	2-13-64	1986	Medford, Ore.
Lyons, Barry	.257	71	265	37	68	16	1	8	38	20	56	0	0	R	R	6-1	200	6-3-60	1982	Biloxi, Miss.
Machado, Robert	.143	16	49	7	7	3	0	1	5	7	12	0	1	R	R	6-1	150	6-3-73	1991	Carabobo, Venez.
Milstien, Dave..............	.235	11	34	1	8	1	0	0	2	3	4	0	0	R	R	6-0	170	9-11-68	1986	Simi Valley, Calif.
Mouton, Lyle	.296	71	267	40	79	17	0	8	41	23	58	10	4	R	R	6-4	240	5-13-69	1991	Lafayette, La.
Noriega, Rey	.164	20	55	6	9	4	0	1	3	3	20	0	0	S	R	6-0	175	3-15-68	1989	Miami, Fla.
Ortiz, Javier	.167	7	24	3	4	0	0	1	1	1	5	0	0	R	R	6-4	210	1-22-63	1983	Hialeah, Fla.
Ortiz, Junior	.186	64	172	13	32	9	0	1	16	12	27	0	0	R	R	5-11	185	10-24-59	1977	Humacao, P.R.
Ramsey, Fernando	.310	98	406	61	126	19	3	5	45	13	47	26	8	R	R	6-2	175	12-20-65	1987	Arcoiris, Panama
Robertson, Mike	.248	139	499	55	124	17	4	19	52	50	72	2	4	L	L	6-0	180	10-9-70	1991	Placentia, Calif.
Saenz, Olmedo	.304	111	415	60	126	26	1	13	74	45	60	0	2	R	R	6-2	185	10-8-70	1990	Chitre Herrera, Panama
Snopek, Chris..............	.323	113	393	56	127	23	4	12	55	50	72	2	5	R	R	6-1	185	9-20-70	1992	Cynthiana, Ky.
Tremie, Chris	.200	67	190	13	38	4	0	2	16	13	37	0	0	R	R	6-0	200	10-17-69	1992	Houston, Texas
Valrie, Kerry	.250	138	544	75	136	30	3	7	55	40	107	22	15	R	R	5-10	195	10-31-68	1990	Loxley, Ala.
Wilson, Brandon..........	.294	27	85	8	25	5	0	1	10	4	11	3	1	R	R	6-1	175	2-26-69	1990	Owensboro, Ky.
Wolak, Jerry	.229	108	385	43	88	21	1	14	63	20	83	5	3	R	R	5-10	170	7-27-70	1988	West Covina, Calif.
Zupcic, Bob	.244	13	41	9	10	2	0	2	5	13	6	1	0	R	R	6-4	220	8-18-66	1987	Charlotte, N.C.

PITCHING	W	L	ERA	G	GS	CG	SV	IP	H	R	ER	BB	SO	B	T	HT	WT	DOB	1st Yr	Resides
Baldwin, James	5	9	5.85	18	18	0	0	95	120	76	62	44	89	R	R	6-4	210	7-15-71	1990	Southern Pines, N.C.
Bere, Jason	1	0	3.38	1	1	0	0	5	6	2	2	2	7	R	R	6-3	185	5-26-71	1990	Wilmington, Mass.
Bertotti, Mike...............	2	3	8.72	7	6	0	0	32	41	34	31	17	35	L	L	6-1	185	1-18-70	1991	Highland Mills, N.Y.
Bolton, Rod..................	14	3	2.88	20	20	3	0	131	127	44	42	23	76	R	R	6-2	190	9-23-68	1990	Chattanooga, Tenn.
Bolton, Tom	5	7	4.43	19	17	1	0	102	106	52	50	31	82	L	L	6-3	185	5-6-62	1980	Smyrna, Tenn.
Costello, Fred	0	2	5.11	7	0	0	0	12	17	9	7	7	6	R	R	6-4	190	10-1-66	1986	San Bruno, Calif.
Davis, John..................	1	1	0.00	4	0	0	1	3	3	2	0	3	0	R	R	6-6	205	1-5-63	1981	Northridge, Calif.
Ellis, Robert	1	1	2.18	4	4	0	0	21	16	7	5	10	9	R	R	6-5	220	12-15-70	1990	Baton Rouge, La.
Gajkowski, Steve	0	1	2.55	15	0	0	0	25	26	15	7	8	12	R	R	6-2	200	12-30-69	1990	Bellevue, Wash.
Hammaker, Atlee	1	2	1.27	15	0	0	1	28	27	4	4	7	20	S	L	6-2	204	1-24-58	1979	Knoxville, Tenn.
Johnson, Dane	4	4	2.41	46	0	0	15	56	48	24	15	28	51	R	R	6-5	205	2-10-63	1993	Miami, Fla.
Jones, Calvin	0	0	6.75	5	0	0	0	7	13	8	5	3	5	R	R	6-3	185	9-26-63	1984	Perris, Calif.
Karchner, Matt..............	3	3	1.45	28	0	0	9	37	39	7	6	10	29	R	R	6-4	245	6-28-67	1989	Berwick, Pa.
Keyser, Brian	2	4	2.36	10	10	2	0	72	49	23	19	9	40	R	R	6-1	180	10-31-66	1989	Walnut Creek, Calif.
Levine, Alan.................	0	2	5.14	3	3	0	0	14	20	10	8	7	14	L	R	6-3	180	5-22-68	1991	Hanover Park, Ill.
Lorraine, Andrew	4	1	6.00	7	7	0	0	39	51	29	26	12	26	L	L	6-3	195	8-11-72	1993	Valencia, Calif.
Marquez, Isidro	7	4	4.75	46	0	0	4	72	80	41	38	27	57	R	R	6-3	190	5-15-65	1985	Navojoa, Mex
Mongiello, Mike	3	3	5.14	31	8	1	1	91	104	59	52	37	72	R	R	6-2	215	1-19-68	1989	Secaucus, N.J.
Novoa, Rafael	0	1	10.80	3	3	0	0	10	17	13	12	9	3	L	L	6-1	180	10-26-67	1989	Phoenix, Ariz.
Olsen, Steve	1	7	4.79	14	14	0	0	77	85	44	41	16	45	R	R	6-4	225	11-2-69	1991	La Grange, Ky.
Pall, Donn	4	3	3.98	44	0	0	3	86	89	40	38	20	79	R	R	6-1	180	1-11-62	1985	Bloomingdale, Ill.
Righetti, Dave	4	5	3.23	16	15	1	0	84	81	40	30	20	44	L	L	6-4	219	11-28-58	1977	Los Altos, Calif.
Ruffcorn, Scott..............	0	0	108.00	2	2	0	0	0	3	4	4	3	0	R	R	6-4	185	12-29-69	1991	Austin, Texas
Simas, Bill	1	1	3.86	7	0	0	0	12	12	5	5	3	12	L	R	6-3	220	11-28-71	1992	Fresno, Calif.
Sirotka, Mike	1	5	2.83	8	8	0	0	54	51	21	17	13	34	L	L	6-1	190	5-13-71	1993	Houston, Texas
Vierra, Joey	2	2	4.17	56	1	0	4	58	47	28	27	19	57	L	L	5-7	170	1-31-66	1987	Honolulu, Hawaii
Wilson, Steve	2	2	4.56	20	7	0	1	51	60	32	26	17	26	L	L	6-3	190	12-13-64	1985	Tempe, Ariz.

FIELDING

Catcher	PCT	G	PO	A	E	DP	PB
Lyons	1.000	31	172	15	0	3	1
Machado	.972	15	87	17	3	1	2
Jun. Ortiz	.985	56	301	31	5	4	8
Tremie	.998	67	394	30	1	5	5

First Base	PCT	G	PO	A	E	DP
Coughlin	1.000	2	14	0	0	1
Cron	1.000	2	9	0	0	2
Lyons	.993	17	128	7	1	10
Robertson	.992	137	1172	75	10	111

Second Base	PCT	G	PO	A	E	DP
Brady	.975	116	238	304	14	88
Howard	.984	12	32	28	1	8
Milstien	1.000	2	5	5	0	2
B. Wilson	.950	20	32	63	5	8

Third Base	PCT	G	PO	A	E	DP
Cron	.833	10	8	17	5	1
Fraraccio	.000	1	0	0	0	0
Howard	.930	19	10	43	4	5
Milstien	1.000	4	4	7	0	1
Saenz	.939	111	82	289	24	24
Snopek	.714	3	0	5	2	0

	PCT	G	PO	A	E	DP
Wolak	.667	1	0	2	1	0

Shortstop	PCT	G	PO	A	E	DP
Brady..............	.800	1	1	3	1	0
Fraraccio	.933	8	17	39	4	8
Howard............	.000	2	0	0	0	0
Milstien	.947	5	4	14	1	1
Noriega...........	.871	17	23	31	8	5
Snopek...........	.942	110	133	353	30	71
B. Wilson.........	.933	7	6	22	2	6

Outfield	PCT	G	PO	A	E	DP
Cappuccio	.978	51	86	3	2	2
Cotto..............	.833	5	5	0	1	0
Coughlin	1.000	6	12	0	0	0
Howard............	.000	1	0	0	0	0
Howitt	1.000	14	14	2	0	0
Mouton	.978	62	123	8	3	1
Ramsey...........	.973	87	211	4	6	1
Robertson	.889	5	8	0	1	0
Valrie..............	.972	124	265	11	8	6
B. Wilson	.000	1	0	0	0	0
Wolak	.970	83	155	8	5	0
Zupcic.............	.923	9	9	3	1	0

Chris Snopek

SOUTHERN LEAGUE

BATTING	AVG	G	AB	R	H	2B	3B	HR	RBI	BB	SO	SB	CS	B	T	HT	WT	DOB	1st Yr	Resides
Abbott, Jeff	.320	55	197	25	63	11	1	3	28	19	20	1	3	R	L	6-2	190	8-17-72	1994	Atlanta, Ga.
Burton, Essex	.255	142	554	95	141	15	2	1	43	80	79	60	22	R	R	5-9	155	5-16-69	1991	San Diego, Calif.
Cameron, Mike	.249	107	350	64	87	20	5	11	60	54	104	21	12	R	R	6-1	170	1-8-73	1991	LaGrange, Ga.
Cappuccio, Carmine	.278	65	248	34	69	13	3	4	38	22	21	2	2	L	R	6-3	185	2-1-70	1992	Malden, Mass.
Coughlin, Kevin	.385	96	327	56	126	29	2	3	49	34	43	5	2	L	L	6-0	175	9-7-70	1989	Clarksburg, Md.
DiSarcina, Glenn	.269	9	26	4	7	1	0	0	2	2	3	0	0	L	R	6-1	180	4-29-70	1991	Billerica, Mass.
Fryman, Troy	.222	112	356	48	79	13	3	8	41	49	97	9	1	L	R	6-4	195	10-2-71	1991	Pensacola, Fla.
Gonzalez, Paul	.269	8	26	4	7	1	0	2	4	2	7	0	1	L	R	6-0	185	4-22-69	1990	Fort Worth, Texas
Hurst, Jimmy	.189	91	301	47	57	11	0	12	34	33	95	12	5	R	R	6-6	225	3-1-72	1991	Tuscaloosa, Ala.
Manning, Henry	.300	11	30	3	9	1	0	2	11	1	1	0	0	R	R	5-11	185	7-3-68	1991	Rutherford, N.J.
Noriega, Rey	.190	42	100	9	19	5	0	0	5	11	27	1	2	S	R	6-0	175	3-15-68	1989	Miami, Fla.
Norton, Greg	.249	133	469	65	117	23	2	6	60	64	90	19	12	S	R	6-1	182	7-6-72	1993	Walnut Creek, Calif.
Pearson, Eddie	.224	50	201	20	45	13	0	2	25	7	36	1	0	L	R	6-3	225	1-31-74	1992	Mobile, Ala.
Poe, Charles	.283	120	427	75	121	28	2	13	60	51	79	19	4	R	R	6-0	185	11-9-71	1990	West Covina, Calif.
Rose, Pete	.385	5	13	1	5	1	0	0	2	3	3	0	0	L	R	6-1	180	11-16-69	1989	Cincinnati, Ohio
Vinas, Julio	.269	102	372	47	100	16	2	6	61	37	80	3	3	R	R	6-0	200	2-14-73	1991	Hialeah, Fla.
Vollmer, Scott	.236	81	258	35	61	5	0	6	39	42	39	0	1	R	R	6-1	175	2-9-71	1993	Thousand Oaks, Calif.
Wilson, Craig	.289	132	471	56	136	19	1	4	46	43	44	2	2	R	R	6-1	190	9-3-70	1992	Phoenix, Ariz.

PITCHING	W	L	ERA	G	GS	CG	SV	IP	H	R	ER	BB	SO	B	T	HT	WT	DOB	1st Yr	Resides
Anduiar, Luis	14	8	2.85	27	27	2	0	167	147	64	53	44	146	R	R	6-2	175	11-22-72	1991	Bani, D.R.
Bertotti, Mike	2	7	5.00	12	12	1	0	63	60	38	35	36	53	L	L	6-1	185	1-18-70	1991	Highland Mills, N.Y.
Christman, Scott	2	5	6.39	12	12	0	0	62	76	49	44	24	37	L	L	6-3	190	12-3-71	1993	Vancouver, Wash.
Dibble, Rob	0	1	7.36	8	0	0	1	7	4	6	6	5	15	L	R	6-4	230	1-24-64	1983	Cincinnati, Ohio
Fordham, Tom	3	3	3.38	14	14	2	0	83	79	35	31	28	61	L	L	6-2	210	2-20-74	1993	El Cajon, Calif.
Gajkowski, Steve	4	4	4.18	35	0	0	2	52	64	27	24	16	29	R	R	6-2	200	12-30-69	1990	Bellevue, Wash.
Johnson, Barry	7	4	1.85	47	0	0	0	78	64	21	16	15	53	R	R	6-4	200	8-21-69	1991	Joliet, Ill.
Johnston, Sean	5	2	4.21	34	13	0	0	98	120	53	46	36	44	L	L	6-0	185	12-10-70	1990	Berlin, Conn.
Levine, Alan	4	3	2.34	43	1	0	7	73	61	22	19	25	68	L	R	6-3	180	5-22-68	1991	Hanover Park, Ill.
McCarthy, Greg	3	3	5.04	38	0	0	3	45	37	28	25	29	48	L	L	6-2	193	10-30-68	1987	Shelton, Conn.
Mongiello, Mike	3	1	1.99	7	5	0	0	32	23	8	7	6	23	R	R	6-2	215	1-19-68	1989	Secaucus, N.J.
Moore, Tim	7	5	3.68	29	19	0	0	120	118	58	49	40	78	R	R	6-4	190	9-4-70	1992	Irving, Texas
Olsen, Steve	8	3	3.48	14	14	2	0	85	84	44	33	21	56	R	R	6-4	225	11-2-69	1991	La Grange, Ky.
Pierson, Jason	0	2	8.10	4	4	0	0	23	29	22	21	6	15	R	L	6-0	190	1-6-71	1992	Berwyn, Pa.
Ruffcorn, Scott	0	2	5.63	3	3	0	0	16	17	11	10	10	13	R	R	6-4	215	12-29-69	1991	Austin, Texas
Sirotka, Mike	7	6	3.20	16	16	1	0	101	95	42	36	22	79	L	L	6-1	190	5-13-71	1993	Houston, Texas
Snyder, John	1	0	6.64	5	4	0	0	20	24	16	15	6	13	R	R	6-3	185	8-16-74	1992	Thousand Oaks, Calif.
Thomas, Larry	4	1	1.34	35	0	0	2	40	24	9	6	15	47	R	L	6-1	190	10-25-69	1991	Mobile, Ala.
Watkins, Jason	0	0	3.95	10	0	0	0	14	18	7	6	3	10	R	R	6-0	195	3-26-70	1992	Longview, Texas
Woodfin, Chris	3	3	4.50	48	0	0	20	64	59	34	32	24	72	R	R	6-1	190	2-23-68	1991	Statesville, N.C.
Worrell, Steve	0	1	8.31	4	0	0	0	4	5	5	4	2	2	L	L	6-2	190	11-25-69	1992	Cape May, N.J.

FIELDING

Catcher	PCT	G	PO	A	E	DP	PB
Manning	.985	11	57	10	1	2	1
Vinas	.976	57	356	50	10	4	5
Vollmer	.992	79	554	70	5	8	10

First Base	PCT	G	PO	A	E	DP
Coughlin	.989	26	160	13	2	15
Fryman	.985	86	655	53	11	67
Gonzalez	1.000	2	21	0	0	1
Pearson	.987	33	286	25	4	25
Vinas	1.000	8	69	3	0	7

Second Base	PCT	G	PO	A	E	DP
Burton	.957	140	311	337	29	94
Noriega	1.000	8	14	10	0	1

Third Base	PCT	G	PO	A	E	DP
Gonzalez	1.000	5	3	11	0	0
Noriega	.941	6	5	11	1	0
Norton	.938	131	102	277	25	23
Rose	1.000	4	4	8	0	0

Shortstop	PCT	G	PO	A	E	DP
DiSarcina	1.000	3	5	4	0	2
Noriega	.909	14	15	25	4	7

	PCT	G	PO	A	E	DP
Wilson	.945	132	193	389	34	80

Outfield	PCT	G	PO	A	E	DP
Abbott	.966	42	55	1	2	0
Cameron	.985	107	250	7	4	1
Cappuccio	.985	65	119	9	2	0
Coughlin	.971	73	128	7	4	3
Fryman	1.000	11	15	0	0	0
Hurst	.931	66	131	3	10	0
Noriega	1.000	12	13	0	0	0
Poe	.968	78	143	7	5	1

CAROLINA LEAGUE

BATTING	AVG	G	AB	R	H	2B	3B	HR	RBI	BB	SO	SB	CS	B	T	HT	WT	DOB	1st Yr	Resides
Abbott, Jeff	.348	70	264	41	92	16	0	4	47	26	25	7	1	R	L	6-2	190	8-17-72	1994	Atlanta, Ga.
Buchanan, Shawn	.000	4	1	2	0	0	0	0	0	0	0	0	0	R	R	6-0	190	2-1-69	1991	Gary, Ind.
Durso, Joe	.213	58	178	16	38	3	2	4	22	16	31	0	0	R	R	6-2	210	1-3-71	1992	Glendale, N.Y.
Fraraccio, Dan	.230	24	74	11	17	5	0	2	6	8	12	0	0	R	R	5-11	175	9-18-70	1992	Bradenton, Fla.
Goligoski, Jason	.217	95	300	42	65	7	2	0	24	52	47	16	5	L	R	6-1	180	10-2-71	1993	Hamilton, Mon.
Gonzalez, Paul	.207	92	290	25	60	10	0	7	34	31	85	1	1	L	R	6-0	185	4-22-69	1990	Fort Worth, Texas
Izquierdo, Sergio	.188	10	32	6	6	2	0	0	2	2	3	0	0	R	R	5-9	182	8-11-72	1994	Hialeah, Fla.
King, Andre	.156	9	32	4	5	1	1	0	3	6	9	1	0	R	R	6-1	190	11-26-73	1993	Ft. Lauderdale, Fla.
2-team (111 Durham)	.245	120	453	63	111	23	4	9	36	45	135	16	13							
Machado, Robert	.254	83	272	37	69	14	3	1	40	47	0	0	0	R	R	6-1	150	6-3-73	1991	Carabobo, Venez.
McKinnon, Sandy	.253	125	494	64	125	19	5	2	23	39	93	35	17	R	R	5-8	175	9-20-73	1993	Nicholls, Ga.
Menechino, Frank	.261	137	476	65	124	31	3	6	58	96	75	6	2	R	R	5-9	175	1-7-71	1993	Staten Island, N.Y.
Newhouse, Andre	.213	78	268	29	57	13	0	1	22	16	59	7	2	R	R	6-0	190	6-30-72	1990	Houston, Texas
Ordonez, Magglio	.238	131	487	61	116	24	2	12	65	41	71	11	5	R	R	5-11	185	1-28-74	1991	Caracas, Venez.
Polidor, Wil	.249	95	346	34	86	14	4	0	24	9	33	2	6	S	R	6-1	158	9-23-73	1991	Caracas, Venez.
Richardson, Eric	.167	9	12	2	2	0	0	0	1	1	3	0	1	R	R	6-0	179	5-7-71	1993	Brenham, Texas
Spinello, Joe	.133	10	30	1	4	1	0	0	2	0	9	0	0	R	R	5-10	220	6-5-72	1995	Kansas City, Mo.
Thomas, Juan	.235	132	464	64	109	20	4	26	69	40	156	4	5	R	R	6-5	240	4-17-72	1991	Ashland, Ky.
Walker, Joe	.333	1	3	1	1	0	1	0	2	1	1	0	0	S	R	6-3	210	11-15-71	1993	Saginaw, Mich.
Watson, Marty	.259	23	85	12	22	3	2	5	14	5	21	2	1	R	R	6-1	205	12-3-70	1993	Chandler, Ind.
Williams, Harold	.282	129	472	56	133	30	1	14	72	48	98	4	2	L	L	6-4	200	2-14-71	1993	Garyville, La.

GAMES BY POSITION: C—Durso 50, Izquierdo 10, Machado 76, Spinello 9, Walker 1. **1B—**Thomas 68, Williams 72. **2B—**Menechino 137, Polidor 5. **3B—**Fraraccio 24, Goligoski 38, Gonzalez 84, Newhouse 1, Polidor 1. **SS—**Fraraccio 2, Goligoski 56, Polidor 89. **OF—**Abbott 62, Gonzalez 1, King 9, McKinnon 123, Newhouse 72, Ordonez 130, Richardson 6, Watson 22.

PITCHING	W	L	ERA	G	GS	CG	SV	IP	H	R	ER	BB	SO	B	T	HT	WT	DOB	1st Yr	Resides
Call, Mike	4	7	5.42	28	9	3	1	105	114	66	63	37	62	R	R	6-0	180	11-6-68	1991	Seattle, Wash.
Callistro, Rob	1	1	4.00	8	0	0	0	18	19	8	8	7	18	R	R	6-2	178	9-25-69	1989	Concord, Calif.
Christman, Scott	4	4	3.59	13	13	1	0	85	83	38	34	19	56	L	L	6-3	190	12-3-71	1993	Vancouver, Wash.
Clemons, Chris	7	12	4.73	27	27	1	0	137	136	78	72	64	92	R	R	6-4	220	10-31-72	1994	McGregor, Texas
Cruz, Nelson	2	1	0.47	9	0	0	1	19	12	1	1	6	18	R	R	6-1	160	9-13-72	1990	Miami, Fla.
Fordham, Tom	9	0	2.04	13	13	1	0	84	66	20	19	35	78	L	L	6-2	210	2-20-74	1993	El Cajon, Calif.
Heathcott, Mike	4	9	4.67	27	14	1	3	89	96	56	46	36	68	R	R	6-3	180	5-16-69	1991	Chicago, Ill.
Lindemann, Wayne	2	0	5.86	19	0	0	1	43	54	30	28	20	32	L	L	6-1	205	12-19-69	1992	Longview, Wash.
Pierson, Jason	5	4	4.42	21	12	0	0	92	91	48	45	22	69	R	L	6-0	190	1-6-71	1992	Berwyn, Pa.
Pratt, Rich	5	11	3.14	25	25	2	0	152	139	66	53	42	120	L	L	6-3	201	5-7-71	1993	Hartford, Conn.
Rizzo, Todd	3	5	2.78	36	0	0	1	68	68	30	21	39	59	R	L	6-3	220	5-24-71	1992	Aston, Pa.
Tagle, Hank	3	2	3.09	33	0	0	2	70	58	28	24	15	66	L	L	6-0	175	4-24-68	1991	Sierra Vista, Ariz.
Vazquez, Archie	3	4	3.59	47	0	0	20	58	53	26	23	30	70	R	R	6-4	233	4-11-72	1991	Hialeah, Fla.
Woods, Brian	9	15	5.17	27	27	3	0	139	155	89	80	53	102	L	R	6-6	212	6-7-71	1993	West Caldwell, N.J.
Worrell, Steve	3	1	1.52	29	0	0	3	47	32	10	8	7	52	L	L	6-2	190	11-25-69	1992	Cape May, N.J.

SOUTH BEND   A

MIDWEST LEAGUE

BATTING	AVG	G	AB	R	H	2B	3B	HR	RBI	BB	SO	SB	CS	B	T	HT	WT	DOB	1st Yr	Resides
Boulware, Ben	.258	129	476	68	123	19	5	2	60	32	78	24	13	R	R	5-11	185	2-25-72	1993	Los Gatos, Calif.
Buchanan, Shawn	.269	103	350	45	94	16	4	2	35	46	72	10	8	R	R	6-0	190	2-1-69	1991	Gary, Ind.
Carone, Rick	.254	111	347	56	88	16	1	9	51	84	91	0	3	R	R	6-0	195	1-17-71	1993	Cary, Ill.
Evans, Jason	.280	101	336	70	94	17	4	6	36	79	74	11	4	S	R	5-11	187	2-11-71	1992	Chatsworth, Calif.
LaValliere, Mike	.600	2	5	1	3	1	0	0	1	1	0	0	0	L	R	5-10	210	8-18-60	1981	Bradenton, Fla.
Levias, Andres	.234	25	77	13	18	1	0	0	12	6	14	7	3	S	R	6-1	175	10-1-73	1992	Lakewood, Calif.
Mathews, Byron	.199	97	332	40	66	11	4	1	34	32	70	16	11	S	R	6-2	175	11-30-70	1992	Ballwin, Mo.
Moore, Brandon	.257	132	510	75	131	9	3	0	37	48	49	34	8	R	R	5-11	175	8-23-72	1994	Springville, Ala.
Richardson, Eric	.231	63	199	32	46	11	1	0	19	19	39	23	6	R	R	6-0	179	9-6-72	1991	Brenham, Texas
Rincones, Wuarnner	.214	20	56	4	12	1	0	0	7	6	13	0	1	R	R	6-2	175	9-3-73	1991	Guayama, Venez.
Robledo, Nilson	.285	135	537	71	153	24	3	20	108	30	100	0	2	R	R	6-1	165	11-3-68	1989	Entrega General, Panama
Rosario, Melvin	.273	118	450	58	123	30	6	15	57	30	109	1	8	S	R	6-0	191	5-25-73	1992	Miami, Fla.
Rose, Pete	.277	116	423	56	117	24	6	4	65	54	45	2	0	L	R	6-1	180	11-16-69	1989	Cincinnati, Ohio
Spinello, Joe	.214	7	14	2	3	0	0	1	2	3	0	0	R	R	5-10	220	6-5-72	1995	Kansas City, Mo.
Topham, Ryan	.250	14	48	4	12	3	0	0	2	4	12	0	0	L	L	6-3	200	12-17-73	1995	Portage, Mich.
Walker, Joe	.000	6	6	0	0	0	0	0	0	4	4	0	0	S	R	6-3	210	11-15-71	1995	Saginaw, Mich.
Wambach, James	.214	9	28	1	6	0	0	0	2	2	6	0	0	L	L	6-4	220	10-24-69	1994	Barrington, Ill.
Whittaker, Jay	.220	67	227	29	50	14	3	5	31	26	58	14	5	R	R	6-2	190	11-17-73	1994	Long Beach, Calif.
Zerpa, Mauro	.221	41	86	5	19	1	0	0	5	6	20	1	0	R	R	6-0	165	5-11-75	1992	Carabobo, Venez.

GAMES BY POSITION: C— Carone 83, LaValliere 2, Rosario 49, Spinello 4, Walker 6. **1B—**Robledo 135, Rose 1. **2B—**Boulware 129, Zerpa 8. **3B—**Buchanan 1, Rincones 20, Rose 113, Zerpa 15. **SS—**Moore 132, Zerpa 12. **OF—**Boulware 1, Buchanan 94, Evans 87, Levias 23, Mathews 89, Richardson 49, Topham 1, Whittaker 61.

PITCHING	W	L	ERA	G	GS	CG	SV	IP	H	R	ER	BB	SO	B	T	HT	WT	DOB	1st Yr	Resides
Ambrose, John	1	1	5.40	3	3	1	0	17	18	13	10	10	15	R	R	6-5	171	11-1-74	1994	St. Petersburg, Fla.
Bigham, Dave	8	7	3.29	25	23	1	0	153	176	62	56	39	62	L	L	5-11	190	9-20-70	1989	Mankato, Minn.
Broome, Curtis	5	8	4.48	29	4	1	1	90	101	53	45	39	62	R	R	6-2	195	4-30-72	1993	Gary, Ind.
Dixon, Jim	1	2	4.86	10	1	0	0	17	25	16	9	4	11	R	R	6-3	195	10-7-72	1993	Raton, N.M.
Droll, Jeff	0	1	3.21	8	0	0	1	14	25	11	5	4	9	R	R	6-2	195	2-2-71	1992	Bigler, Pa.
Duncan, Sean	0	0	0.79	12	0	0	0	11	8	2	1	3	8	L	L	6-2	195	6-9-73	1994	Arlington, Texas
Fletcher, Paul	4	4	2.98	36	0	0	5	57	55	21	19	24	49	L	L	5-10	195	12-9-69	1992	Alpharetta, Ga.
Garcia, Ariel	4	2	3.14	10	10	0	0	57	54	23	20	19	46	R	R	6-0	158	10-3-75	1993	Panama City, Panama
Gomez, Gus	7	6	4.13	25	25	1	0	144	120	85	66	68	99	R	R	5-10	170	10-28-73	1991	Caracas, Venez.
Herbert, Russell	2	4	3.52	9	9	0	0	54	46	25	21	27	48	R	R	6-4	200	4-21-72	1994	Mentor, Ohio
Leiber, Zane	0	0	6.91	14	0	0	1	29	35	26	22	9	21	R	R	6-2	190	9-15-73	1993	Tucson, Ariz.
Lindemann, Wayne	1	0	7.36	7	6	0	0	22	32	21	18	16	15	L	L	6-1	205	12-19-69	1992	Longview, Wash.
Lundquist, David	8	4	3.58	18	18	5	0	118	107	54	47	38	60	R	R	6-2	200	6-4-73	1993	Carson City, Nev.
McCormack, Andy	1	2	4.63	6	4	0	0	23	26	14	12	10	16	R	L	6-1	205	2-4-74	1993	Raynham, Mass.
Place, Mike	4	5	3.95	28	2	0	3	55	56	30	24	19	34	R	R	6-4	190	8-13-70	1990	Seminole, Fla.
Portillo, Alex	0	1	4.91	2	0	0	0	4	5	2	2	0	4	L	L	6-1	175	12-27-74	1992	Anzoategui, Venez.
Quirk, John	3	2	3.96	22	1	0	0	52	52	32	23	36	30	L	L	6-4	210	11-20-70	1993	Bronx, N.Y.
Radinsky, Scott	0	0	0.00	6	0	0	2	10	5	0	0	0	11	L	L	6-3	204	3-3-68	1986	Simi Valley, Calif.
Salmon, Fabian	4	1	3.80	15	0	0	3	24	18	15	10	11	15	S	R	6-1	180	10-4-71	1992	Hollywood, Fla.
Smith, Charles	10	10	2.69	26	25	4	0	167	128	70	50	61	145	R	R	6-1	175	10-21-69	1991	Cleveland, Ohio
Surratt, Jamie	3	3	3.12	26	0	0	11	40	32	15	14	12	34	R	R	5-10	175	12-17-69	1993	Midland, Texas
Theodile, Robert	1	2	7.62	7	4	0	0	26	45	30	22	13	16	R	R	6-3	190	9-16-72	1992	Jeanerette, La.

HICKORY   A

SOUTH ATLANTIC LEAGUE

BATTING	AVG	G	AB	R	H	2B	3B	HR	RBI	BB	SO	SB	CS	B	T	HT	WT	DOB	1st Yr	Resides
Albert, Rashad	.213	88	328	34	70	16	2	5	20	19	108	22	12	R	R	6-1	165	9-18-75	1994	Fernandina Beach, Fla.
Antczak, Chuck	.200	6	5	0	1	0	0	0	1	0	2	0	0	R	R	6-0	185	10-8-73	1995	Sarasota, Fla.
Bearden, Doug	.156	44	141	9	22	5	1	2	12	5	44	1	1	R	R	6-2	170	9-11-75	1994	Inman, S.C.
Cancel, David	.288	76	240	24	69	3	2	2	13	11	37	11	10	S	R	5-11	168	3-3-74	1994	San Sebastian, D.R.
Drent, Brian	.188	24	69	8	13	5	1	1	5	6	28	0	4	R	R	6-3	205	7-27-73	1994	Worthington, Minn.
Friedrich, Steve	.252	136	532	56	134	24	6	6	50	16	107	19	16	R	L	6-0	175	5-29-73	1993	Yorba Linda, Calif.
Gomez, Ramon	.229	76	231	26	53	6	0	0	9	18	64	17	9	R	R	6-2	175	10-6-75	1994	San Pedro de Macoris, D.R.
Hayes, Darren	.245	58	196	18	48	12	2	3	19	16	53	7	2	R	R	6-1	195	11-12-72	1995	Lenoir, N.C.
Izquierdo, Sergio	.146	45	123	6	18	2	0	0	4	8	20	0	0	R	R	5-9	182	8-11-74	1994	Hialeah, Fla.

BATTING	AVG	G	AB	R	H	2B	3B	HR	RBI	BB	SO	SB	CS	B	T	HT	WT	DOB	1st Yr	Resides
Johnson, Jeff	.229	53	170	15	39	9	0	2	14	13	40	2	2	R	R	5-10	175	6-8-73	1995	Clinton, Miss.
Johnson, Mark	.182	107	319	31	58	9	0	2	17	59	52	3	5	L	R	6-0	185	9-12-75	1994	Warner Robins, Ga.
Koerick, Thomas	.185	73	200	15	37	10	1	2	20	15	85	2	2	R	R	6-3	205	11-16-72	1994	Radnor, Pa.
Lee, Carlos	.248	63	218	18	54	9	1	4	30	8	34	1	5	R	R	6-2	205	6-20-76	1994	Panama City, Panama
McClure, Craig	.169	49	154	13	26	3	1	2	8	17	56	6	2	R	R	6-1	175	8-4-75	1993	Littleton, Colo.
Mendoza, Jesus	.251	116	434	49	109	24	2	8	49	36	53	2	7	R	R	5-10	160	11-10-74	1992	Bolivar, Venez.
Navas, Jesus	.228	79	202	23	46	7	0	1	16	28	36	3	6	S	R	6-0	170	1-11-75	1994	Palo Negro, Venez.
Simmons, Brian	.190	41	163	13	31	6	1	2	11	19	44	4	4	S	R	6-2	191	9-4-73	1995	McMurray, Pa.
Tidick, Michael	.212	56	132	17	28	9	2	2	9	21	41	5	4	R	R	6-2	185	3-7-71	1994	Endicott, N.Y.
Valdez, Mario	.272	130	441	65	120	30	5	11	56	67	107	9	7	L	R	6-2	190	11-19-74	1994	Hialeah, Fla.
Wilhelm, Brent	.225	67	240	19	54	9	2	2	24	15	36	4	3	R	R	6-0	185	1-22-73	1995	Independence, Mo.

GAMES BY POSITION: C—Antczak 1, Izquierdo 44, M. Johnson 100, Koerick 12. **1B**—Friedrich 1, Gomez 1, Izquierdo 1, Koerick 26, Valdez 120. **2B**—Friedrich 89, Mendoza 46, Navas 18. **3B**—Friedrich 30, Koerick 13, Lee 44, Wilhelm 67. **SS**—Bearden 44, J. Johnson 50, Lee 1, Navas 56, Wilhelm 1. **OF**—Albert 85, Cancel 66, Drent 23, Friedrich 3, Gomez 72, Hayes 56, McClure 46, Simmons 41, Tidick 47.

PITCHING	W	L	ERA	G	GS	CG	SV	IP	H	R	ER	BB	SO	B	T	HT	WT	DOB	1st Yr	Resides
Ambrose, John	4	8	3.95	14	14	0	0	73	65	41	32	35	49	R	R	6-5	171	11-1-74	1994	St. Petersburg, Fla.
Anez, Maycoll	0	0	2.25	2	0	0	0	4	3	2	1	4	4	R	R	6-3	185	7-21-76	1994	Caracas, Venez.
Beirne, Kevin	0	0	4.50	3	0	0	0	4	7	2	2	0	4	L	R	6-4	210	1-1-74	1995	The Woodlands, Texas
Broome, John	0	1	9.64	4	0	0	0	5	8	5	5	4	3	R	R	6-0	185	6-26-73	1993	Maple Shade, N.J.
Buteaux, Shane	2	7	7.29	13	13	0	0	67	90	63	54	32	30	R	R	6-3	202	12-28-71	1994	New Iberia, La.
Carlson, Garret	0	0	32.40	3	0	0	0	2	6	6	6	4	2	R	R	6-3	195	10-15-73	1995	Spokane, Wash.
Castillo, Carlos	5	6	3.73	14	12	2	1	80	85	42	33	18	67	R	R	6-2	230	4-21-75	1994	Miami, Fla.
Crine, Dennis	3	6	6.12	15	11	0	1	60	74	52	41	20	20	R	R	6-5	230	8-28-74	1994	Henderson, Nev.
Cruz, Nelson	2	7	2.70	44	0	0	9	67	65	31	20	15	68	R	R	6-1	160	9-13-72	1990	Miami, Fla.
Dixon, Jim	4	1	1.93	35	0	0	5	51	43	23	11	16	56	R	R	6-3	195	10-7-72	1993	Raton, N.M.
Fereira, Marcos	0	2	16.88	4	0	0	0	3	6	6	5	4	1	R	R	6-3	150	12-13-74	1991	Valencia, Venez.
Forbes, Adam	0	0	9.82	4	0	0	0	4	8	5	4	5	3	L	L	6-3	175	1-27-75	1993	Cambridge, Australia
Ford, Jack	8	14	3.89	27	27	3	0	174	174	86	75	66	157	L	L	6-0	170	11-30-71	1992	Paris, Texas
Halley, Allen	2	1	2.55	13	9	0	1	60	46	21	17	12	58	S	R	6-1	195	9-7-71	1995	St. Maarten, Neth. Antilles
Herbert, Russell	3	8	2.67	18	18	1	0	115	83	48	34	46	115	R	R	6-4	200	4-21-72	1994	Mentor, Ohio
Leiber, Zane	1	0	5.60	14	0	0	0	18	19	13	11	5	13	R	R	6-2	190	9-15-73	1993	Tucson, Ariz.
Mejias, Fernando	2	9	4.59	30	16	0	0	112	128	78	57	38	76	R	R	6-3	215	3-15-72	1991	Maracay, Venez.
Moore, David	1	0	6.18	20	0	0	0	28	41	20	19	7	15	R	R	6-3	185	10-9-74	1993	Windemere, Fla.
Portillo, Alex	0	3	2.25	33	0	0	2	56	57	24	14	10	36	L	L	6-1	175	12-27-74	1992	Anzoategui, Venez.
Ruiz, Rafael	1	0	15.75	5	0	0	0	4	7	8	7	5	5	L	L	6-0	170	2-17-75	1992	Caracas, Venez.
Surratt, Jamie	1	1	1.76	12	0	0	3	15	13	8	3	8	19	R	R	5-10	175	12-17-69	1993	Midland, Texas
Theodile, Robert	6	9	3.79	20	17	1	0	107	103	61	45	53	77	R	R	6-3	190	9-16-72	1992	Jeanerette, La.
Welch, David	4	5	2.67	60	0	0	5	78	68	39	23	21	82	L	L	6-3	210	4-30-70	1992	Violet, La.
Wells, David	1	1	5.17	17	1	0	0	38	44	28	22	13	30	R	R	6-5	200	6-20-72	1993	Logansport, Ind.

BRISTOL

R

APPALACHIAN LEAGUE

BATTING	AVG	G	AB	R	H	2B	3B	HR	RBI	BB	SO	SB	CS	B	T	HT	WT	DOB	1st Yr	Resides
Albert, Chernan	.270	38	152	27	41	5	3	5	14	9	37	12	8	R	R	6-1	165	9-18-75	1994	Fernandina Beach, Fla.
Anderson, Frank	.222	46	153	10	34	7	1	2	16	7	52	2	3	R	R	6-1	200	9-1-75	1995	Stockbridge, Ga.
Antczak, Chuck	.305	24	59	11	18	4	0	1	10	6	16	2	0	R	R	6-0	185	10-8-73	1995	Sarasota, Fla.
Bagley, Sean	.203	35	64	8	13	1	1	0	5	8	25	9	3	R	R	6-3	195	6-20-76	1994	Gig Harbor, Wash.
Bearden, Doug	.234	46	167	26	39	10	1	3	22	6	40	5	0	R	R	6-2	170	9-11-75	1994	Lexington, S.C.
Bowness, Brian	.223	54	202	20	45	4	0	1	23	12	37	0	1	R	R	6-3	205	5-23-74	1995	East Hanover, N.J.
Drent, Brian	.242	49	161	31	39	13	0	5	26	39	58	16	2	R	R	6-3	205	7-27-73	1994	Worthington, Mn
Helms, Ryan	.164	48	146	16	24	2	1	0	9	11	33	3	1	S	R	6-0	165	12-2-75	1994	Cincinnati, Ohio
Hollins, Darontaye	.248	62	222	24	55	7	2	0	14	20	75	14	5	R	R	6-0	200	9-6-74	1995	Roseville, Calif.
Lee, Carlos	.346	67	269	43	93	17	1	7	45	8	34	17	7	R	R	6-2	205	6-20-76	1994	Panama City, Panama
McClure, Craig	.233	64	223	26	52	4	2	2	26	22	65	7	8	R	R	6-1	175	8-4-75	1993	Littleton, Colo.
Rincones, Wuarnner	.317	61	189	25	60	10	4	1	25	32	29	2	0	R	R	6-2	175	9-3-73	1991	Guayama, Venez.
Spry, Shane	.233	15	43	5	10	2	0	0	6	10	7	0	0	L	L	5-11	185	9-4-75	1993	Spearwood, Australia
Strasser, John	.226	46	159	24	36	3	2	0	10	24	37	2	0	R	R	6-0	165	11-28-74	1995	Glendale, Ariz.

GAMES BY POSITION: C—Anderson 46, Antczak 23, Bagley 12. **1B**—Bowness 54, Lee 5, Rincones 13. **2B**—Helms 47, Rincones 5, Strasser 20. **3B**—Bearden 3, Lee 58, Rincones 11. **SS**—Bearden 43, Strasser 29. **OF**—Albert 35, Bagley 11, Drent 44, Hollins 56, McClure 59, Spry 2.

PITCHING	W	L	ERA	G	GS	CG	SV	IP	H	R	ER	BB	SO	B	T	HT	WT	DOB	1st Yr	Resides
Anez, Maycoll	0	2	5.74	7	2	0	1	16	24	14	10	8	11	R	R	6-3	185	7-21-76	1994	Caracas, Venez.
Beirne, Kevin	1	0	0.00	9	0	0	2	9	4	0	0	4	12	L	R	6-4	210	1-1-74	1995	The Woodlands, Texas
Buteaux, Shane	7	6	4.26	13	13	1	0	74	72	45	35	41	49	R	R	6-3	202	12-28-71	1994	New Iberia, La.
Cruz, Nelson	0	0	9.00	1	0	0	0	1	2	1	1	0	2	R	R	6-1	160	9-13-72	1990	Miami, Fla.
Desrosiers, Erik	0	2	3.09	22	0	0	2	32	22	13	11	7	47	R	R	6-4	210	9-21-74	1995	Fountain Hills, Ariz.
Garber, Joel	5	1	1.20	19	6	0	0	60	37	13	8	12	66	L	L	6-4	200	10-14-73	1994	Manhattan Beach, Calif.
Halley, Allen	1	0	12.00	2	0	0	0	3	8	4	4	1	4	S	R	6-1	195	9-7-71	1995	St. Maarten, Neth. Antilles
Hasselhoff, Derek	7	3	3.66	12	11	0	0	66	66	32	27	14	46	R	R	6-2	185	10-19-75	1995	Pasadena, Md.
Hunt, Jon	2	4	4.47	13	13	0	0	58	52	39	29	34	54	L	L	6-2	190	5-17-74	1995	Ironton, Ohio
Kraus, Tim	1	2	2.35	5	0	0	1	'8	3	3	2	7	9	L	R	6-1	190	12-26-72	1995	Cincinnati, Ohio
Kruse, Kelly	0	1	12.32	15	0	0	0	19	29	32	26	16	21	R	R	6-3	210	5-1-72	1995	Russellville, Mo.
Moore, David	1	0	5.16	15	0	0	0	30	34	22	17	11	37	R	R	6-3	185	10-9-74	1993	Windemere, Fla.
Ruiz, Rafael	1	2	2.15	22	0	0	1	38	26	14	9	15	49	L	L	6-0	170	2-17-75	1992	Caracas, Venez.
Secoda, Jason	2	8	5.35	13	12	0	0	66	78	57	39	33	63	R	R	6-1	195	9-2-74	1995	Fullerton, Calif.
Virchis, Adam	0	7	5.30	10	10	1	0	56	65	39	33	7	33	R	R	6-3	180	10-15-73	1995	Chula Vista, Calif.
Vota, Michael	1	2	4.60	22	0	0	3	31	33	19	16	14	24	R	R	6-4	175	12-29-72	1995	DuBois, Pa.

GULF COAST LEAGUE

BATTING	AVG	G	AB	R	H	2B	3B	HR	RBI	BB	SO	SB	CS	B	T	HT	WT	DOB	1st Yr	Resides
Amaya, Edilberto	.192	26	78	9	15	3	0	1	9	3	20	0	1	R	R	6-3	172	5-24-76	1994	Panama City, Panama
DiSarcina, Glenn	.194	9	36	6	7	3	1	0	3	0	4	1	0	L	R	6-1	180	4-29-70	1991	Billerica, Mass.
Downs, Brian	.285	37	130	22	37	8	0	2	18	7	27	0	1	R	R	6-2	210	4-10-75	1995	Chino, Calif.
Encarnacion, Pedro	.333	10	24	1	8	0	0	0	1	1	4	2	1	R	R	6-1	165	4-29-75	1993	San Pedro de Macoris, D.R.
Fauske, Joshua	.257	33	105	18	27	7	0	4	18	11	22	1	0	R	R	6-4	230	3-16-74	1995	Mercer Island, Wash.
Garcia, Luis	.230	45	161	33	37	5	2	0	12	20	29	9	3	R	R	6-3	200	9-22-75	1995	Hermosillo, Mexico
Gomez, Ramon	.262	30	103	16	27	3	0	1	6	12	22	12	4	R	R	6-2	175	10-6-75	1994	San Pedro de Macoris, D.R.
Hayes, Darren	.300	6	20	2	6	0	0	0	2	2	1	0	0	R	R	6-1	195	11-12-72	1995	Lenoir, N.C.
Horn, Marvin	.240	38	129	13	31	7	2	1	14	11	38	0	1	L	L	6-4	195	8-2-74	1995	Hawthorne, Calif.
Klee, Chuck	.213	44	155	24	33	8	0	0	19	19	41	3	2	R	R	6-3	175	5-15-77	1995	Lighthouse Point, Fla.
Lutz, Manny	.281	46	160	23	45	10	3	3	31	19	42	0	0	L	R	6-2	230	6-14-76	1995	Spring Valley, Calif.
Nova, Fernando	.208	36	125	17	26	6	0	0	7	16	46	1	3	R	R	6-0	168	2-9-76	1995	San Pedro de Macoris, D.R.
Pearson, Eddie	.300	6	20	7	6	2	0	1	6	3	2	0	0	L	R	6-3	225	1-31-74	1992	Mobile, Ala.
Rengifo, Daliene	.208	27	72	7	15	2	0	0	5	10	21	5	2	R	R	6-0	165	6-16-77	1994	Miranda, Venez.
Rodriguez, Liubiemithz	.227	36	119	18	27	6	1	1	11	23	19	4	2	S	R	5-9	170	11-5-76	1995	Caracas, Venez.
Shelton, Barry	.282	33	103	10	29	5	0	2	13	10	16	0	1	R	R	5-11	210	8-4-73	1995	Roanoke, Va.
Simmons, Brian	.176	5	17	5	3	1	0	1	5	6	1	0	0	S	R	6-2	191	9-4-73	1995	McMurray, Pa.
Solano, Angel	.232	44	151	20	35	5	1	1	13	9	23	7	3	R	R	5-11	160	5-9-76	1995	Villa Magdella, D.R.
Stevens, Clayton	.224	42	143	19	32	1	4	5	21	20	40	3	2	R	R	6-3	210	7-28-75	1995	Bay Minette, Ala.
Weisner, Randy	.286	5	7	1	2	1	0	0	4	1	0	0	0	L	R	6-2	210	4-25-72	1995	Pompano Beach, Fla.

GAMES BY POSITION: C—Downs 37, Fauske 25, Shelton 1, Weisner 5. **1B**—Amaya 25, Horn 36, Pearson 2, Shelton 1. **2B**—Rodriguez 36, Solano 25. **3B**—Garcia 1, Lutz 34, Shelton 26, Solano 1. **SS**—DiSarcina 2, Klee 42, Solano 16. **OF**—DiSarcina 1, Encarnacion 10, Garcia 41, Gomez 26, Hayes 5, Nova 30, Rengifo 24, Simmons 5, Stevens 36.

PITCHING	W	L	ERA	G	GS	CG	SV	IP	H	R	ER	BB	SO	B	T	HT	WT	DOB	1st Yr	Resides
Anez, Maycoll	4	1	0.93	7	1	0	1	29	19	6	3	4	21	R	R	6-3	185	7-21-76	1994	Caracas, Venez.
Bales, Joe	3	1	3.97	11	9	1	0	45	44	27	20	31	44	R	R	6-5	175	9-13-74	1993	Reno, Nev.
Beirne, Kevin	0	0	2.45	2	0	0	2	4	2	2	1	1	3	L	R	6-4	210	1-1-74	1995	The Woodlands, Texas
Brown, Tighe	0	0	1.17	3	0	0	0	8	3	1	1	2	12	R	R	6-4	195	9-10-76	1995	Louisville, Ky.
Buckman, Tom	1	2	3.08	18	0	0	7	26	26	15	9	6	18	R	R	6-6	200	6-28-74	1995	Pembroke Pines, Fla.
Carlson, Garret	2	0	0.00	2	0	0	0	5	2	0	0	0	3	R	R	6-3	195	10-15-73	1995	Spokane, Wash.
Chantres, Carlos	2	3	3.21	11	11	2	0	62	65	32	22	14	47	R	R	6-3	175	4-1-76	1994	Miami, Fla.
De la Rosa, Raul	4	1	1.67	11	2	0	0	27	22	9	5	16	22	R	R	6-2	168	6-3-76	1993	San Pedro de Macoris, D.R.
Demorejon, Pedro	3	4	3.60	12	0	0	1	30	28	14	12	5	34	R	R	6-1	180	10-16-74	1995	Miami, Fla.
Duncan, Sean	0	0	0.00	3	0	0	1	6	5	3	0	1	6	L	L	6-2	195	6-9-73	1994	Arlington, Texas
Eyre, Scott	0	2	2.30	9	9	0	0	27	16	7	7	12	40	L	L	6-1	160	5-30-72	1991	Magna, Utah
Fereira, Marcos	0	1	14.73	7	0	0	0	7	11	14	12	8	4	R	R	6-3	150	12-13-74	1991	Valencia, Venez.
Gray, Jason	4	2	2.02	14	4	0	1	36	35	10	8	9	37	R	R	6-2	185	4-28-77	1995	North Lauderdale, Fla.
Hundley, Chanin	0	0	6.23	3	0	0	0	4	7	5	3	2	2	R	R	6-1	185	1-19-74	1995	Hialeah, Fla.
Kruse, Kelly	1	0	4.50	3	0	0	0	4	4	2	2	1	2	R	R	6-3	210	5-1-72	1995	Russellville, Mo.
Lakman, Jason	3	0	3.27	9	5	0	0	41	44	17	15	12	23	R	R	6-4	220	10-17-76	1995	Woodinville, Wash.
McCaskey, Tom	1	1	3.00	6	1	0	0	18	17	6	6	7	16	R	R	6-3	200	10-8-75	1995	San Marcos, Calif.
McCormack, Andy	1	0	1.50	1	1	0	0	6	4	1	1	0	4	R	L	6-1	205	2-4-74	1993	Raynham, Mass.
Mendoza, Geronimo	0	1	4.30	10	0	0	0	15	8	9	7	7	11	R	R	6-4	160	1-23-78	1995	Santo Domingo, D.R.
Nichols, James	7	2	2.89	11	10	0	0	65	64	31	21	12	38	R	R	6-4	215	1-22-76	1995	Bear, Del.
Ruffcorn, Scott	0	0	0.90	3	3	0	0	10	7	4	1	5	7	R	R	6-4	215	12-29-69	1991	Austin, Texas
Schrenk, Steve	0	1	0.00	2	2	0	0	7	5	2	0	0	6	R	R	6-3	185	11-20-68	1987	Aurora, Ore.

CHICAGO CUBS

Manager: Jim Riggleman.　　**1995 Record:** 73-71, .507 (3rd, NL Central).

BATTING	AVG	G	AB	R	H	2B	3B	HR	RBI	BB	SO	SB	CS	B	T	HT	WT	DOB	1st Yr	Resides
Buechele, Steve	.189	32	106	10	20	2	0	1	9	11	19	0	0	R	R	6-2	200	9-26-61	1982	Arlington, Texas
Bullett, Scott	.273	104	150	19	41	5	7	3	22	12	30	8	3	L	L	6-2	190	12-25-68	1988	Martinsburg, W.Va.
Dunston, Shawon	.296	127	477	58	141	30	6	14	69	10	75	10	5	R	R	6-1	175	3-21-63	1982	Fremont, Calif.
Franco, Matt	.294	16	17	3	5	1	0	0	1	0	4	0	0	L	R	6-3	195	8-19-69	1987	Thousand Oaks, Calif.
Gonzalez, Luis	.290	77	262	34	76	19	4	7	34	39	33	5	5	L	R	6-2	180	9-3-67	1988	Houston, Texas
2-team (56 Houston)	.276	133	471	69	130	29	8	13	69	57	63	6	8							
Grace, Mark	.326	143	552	97	180	51	3	16	92	65	46	6	2	L	L	6-2	190	6-28-64	1986	Pacific Palisades, Calif.
Haney, Todd	.411	25	73	11	30	8	0	2	6	7	11	0	0	R	R	5-9	165	7-30-65	1987	Waco, Texas
Hernandez, Jose	.245	93	245	37	60	11	4	13	40	13	69	1	0	R	R	6-0	180	7-14-69	1987	Vega Alta, P.R.
Hubbard, Mike	.174	15	23	2	4	0	0	0	1	2	2	0	0	R	R	6-1	180	2-16-71	1992	Madison Heights, Va.
Johnson, Howard	.195	87	169	26	33	4	1	7	22	34	46	1	1	S	R	5-10	195	11-29-60	1979	Poway, Calif.
Kmak, Joe	.245	19	53	7	13	3	0	1	6	6	12	0	0	R	R	6-0	185	5-3-63	1985	Foster City, Calif.
McRae, Brian	.288	137	580	92	167	38	7	12	48	47	92	27	8	S	R	6-0	185	8-27-67	1985	Leawood, Kan.
Parent, Mark	.250	12	32	5	8	2	0	3	5	3	7	0	0	R	R	6-5	225	9-16-61	1979	San Diego, Calif.
2-team (69 Pitt.)	.234	81	265	30	62	11	0	18	38	26	69	0	0							
Pratt, Todd	.133	25	60	3	8	2	0	0	4	6	21	0	0	R	R	6-3	195	2-9-67	1985	Boca Raton, Fla.
Rhodes, Karl	.125	13	16	2	2	0	0	0	2	0	4	0	0	L	L	5-11	170	8-21-68	1986	Cincinnati, Ohio
Roberson, Kevin	.184	32	38	5	7	1	0	4	6	6	14	0	1	S	R	6-4	210	1-29-68	1988	Decatur, Ill.
Sanchez, Rey	.278	114	428	57	119	22	2	3	27	14	48	6	4	R	R	5-10	180	10-5-67	1986	Rio Piedras, P.R.
Servais, Scott	.286	52	175	31	50	12	0	12	35	23	37	2	1	R	R	6-2	195	6-4-67	1989	Coon Valley, Wisc.
2-team (28 Houston)	.265	80	264	38	70	22	0	13	47	32	52	2	2							
Sosa, Sammy	.268	144	564	89	151	17	3	36	119	58	134	34	7	R	R	6-0	165	11-12-68	1986	San Pedro de Macoris,D.R.
Timmons, Ozzie	.263	77	171	30	45	10	1	8	28	13	32	3	0	R	R	6-2	205	9-18-70	1991	Tampa, Fla.
Wilkins, Rick	.191	50	162	24	31	2	0	6	14	36	51	0	0	L	R	6-2	210	6-4-67	1987	Jacksonville, Fla.
Zeile, Todd	.227	79	299	34	68	16	0	9	30	16	53	0	0	R	R	6-1	185	9-9-65	1986	Valencia, Calif.
2-team (34 St.L)	.246	113	426	50	105	22	0	14	52	34	76	1	0							

PITCHING	W	L	ERA	G	GS	CG	SV	IP	H	R	ER	BB	SO	B	T	HT	WT	DOB	1st Yr	Resides
Adams, Terry	1	1	6.50	18	0	0	1	18	22	15	13	10	15	R	R	6-3	180	3-6-73	1991	Semmes, Ala.
Banks, Willie	0	1	15.43	10	0	0	0	12	27	23	20	12	9	R	R	6-1	202	2-27-69	1987	Jersey City, N.J.
Bullinger, Jim	12	8	4.14	24	24	1	0	150	152	80	69	65	93	R	R	6-2	180	8-21-65	1986	Sarasota, Fla.
Casian, Larry	1	0	1.93	42	0	0	0	23	23	6	5	15	11	R	L	6-0	173	10-28-65	1987	Salem, Ore.
Castillo, Frank	11	10	3.21	29	29	2	0	188	179	75	67	52	135	R	R	6-1	185	4-1-69	1987	El Paso, Texas
Edens, Tom	1	0	6.00	5	0	0	0	3	6	3	2	3	2	L	R	6-2	185	6-9-61	1983	Clarkston, Wash.
Foster, Kevin	12	11	4.51	30	28	0	0	168	149	90	84	65	146	R	R	6-1	160	1-13-69	1988	Evanston, Ill.
Garces, Rich	0	0	3.27	7	0	0	0	11	11	6	4	3	6	R	R	6-0	230	5-18-71	1988	Maracay, Venez.
Hickerson, Bryan	2	3	6.82	38	0	0	1	32	36	28	24	15	28	L	L	6-2	203	10-13-63	1986	Scottsdale, Ariz.
Morgan, Mike	2	1	2.19	4	4	0	0	25	19	8	6	9	15	R	R	6-2	222	10-8-59	1978	Ogden, Utah
Myers, Randy	1	2	3.88	57	0	0	38	56	49	25	24	28	59	L	L	6-1	210	9-19-62	1982	Vancouver, Wash.
Nabholz, Chris	0	1	5.40	34	0	0	0	23	22	15	14	14	21	L	L	6-5	210	1-5-67	1989	Pottsville, Pa.
Navarro, Jaime	14	6	3.28	29	29	1	0	200	194	79	73	56	128	R	R	6-4	225	3-27-67	1987	Orlando, Fla.
Perez, Mike	2	6	3.66	68	0	0	2	71	72	30	29	27	49	R	R	6-0	187	10-19-64	1986	Yauco, P.R.
Rivera, Roberto	0	0	5.40	7	0	0	0	5	8	3	3	2	2	L	L	6-0	175	1-1-69	1988	Bayamon, P.R.
Sturtze, Tanyon	0	0	9.00	2	0	0	0	2	2	2	2	1	0	R	R	6-5	190	10-12-70	1990	Worcester, Mass.
Swartzbaugh, Dave	0	0	0.00	1	0	0	0	7	5	2	0	3	5	R	R	6-2	195	2-11-68	1989	Middletown, Ohio
Trachsel, Steve	7	13	5.15	30	29	2	0	161	174	104	92	76	117	R	R	6-3	185	10-31-70	1991	Yorba Linda, Calif.
Walker, Mike	1	3	3.22	42	0	0	1	45	45	22	16	24	20	R	R	6-1	195	10-4-66	1986	Brooksville, Fla.
Wendell, Turk	3	1	4.92	43	0	0	0	60	71	35	33	24	50	S	R	6-2	175	5-19-67	1988	Dalton, Mass.
Young, Anthony	3	4	3.70	32	1	0	2	41	47	20	17	14	15	R	R	6-2	200	1-19-66	1987	Houston, Texas

FIELDING

Catcher	PCT	G	PO	A	E	DP	PB
Hubbard	.971	9	33	0	1	0	0
Kmak	1.000	18	93	1	0	0	1
Parent	1.000	10	66	5	0	0	2
Pratt	.981	25	149	9	3	1	1
Servais	.981	52	328	33	7	3	9
Wilkins	.988	49	288	29	4	7	6

First Base	PCT	G	PO	A	E	DP
Franco	1.000	1	2	0	0	0
Grace	.995	143	1211	114	7	93
Johnson	1.000	3	15	1	0	3
Wilkins	1.000	2	6	2	0	1
Zeile	1.000	1	17	0	0	3

Second Base	PCT	G	PO	A	E	DP
Franco	1.000	3	0	2	0	0
Haney	.978	17	31	57	2	12
Hernandez	.971	29	56	76	4	18
Johnson	.889	8	7	9	2	2
Sanchez	.987	111	194	342	7	58

Third Base	PCT	G	PO	A	E	DP
Buechele	.942	32	26	55	5	3
Franco	.000	1	0	0	0	0

	PCT	G	PO	A	E	DP
Haney	1.000	4	3	4	0	0
Hernandez	1.000	20	12	36	0	1
Johnson	.926	34	10	53	5	4
Kmak	1.000	1	0	1	0	0
Zeile	.939	75	35	134	11	13

Shortstop	PCT	G	PO	A	E	DP
Dunston	.969	125	187	336	17	51
Hernandez	.961	43	45	77	5	18
Johnson	1.000	1	1	2	0	1
Sanchez	1.000	4	1	9	0	2

Outfield	PCT	G	PO	A	E	DP
Bullett	.968	64	59	1	2	0
Gonzalez	.978	76	172	5	4	1
Johnson	1.000	13	12	0	0	0
McRae	.991	137	345	4	3	0
Rhodes	.889	11	8	0	1	0
Roberson	1.000	11	8	0	0	0
Sosa	.962	143	320	13	13	4
Timmons	.970	55	63	1	2	1
Zeile	.000	2	0	0	1	0

Randy Myers

Mark Grace led the Cubs with a .326 average and 51 doubles

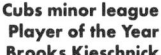

Cubs minor league Player of the Year Brooks Kieschnick

FARM SYSTEM

Director of Player Development: Jim Hendry.

Class	Farm Team	League	W	L	Pct.	Finish*	Manager	First Yr
AAA	Iowa Cubs	American Assoc.	69	74	.483	5th (8)	Ron Clark	1981
AA	Orlando (Fla.) Cubs	Southern	76	67	.531	4th (10)	Bruce Kimm	1993
#A	Daytona (Fla.) Cubs	Florida State	87	48	.644	1st+ (14)	Dave Trembley	1993
A	Rockford (Ill.) Cubbies	Midwest	75	65	.536	T-5th (14)	Steve Roadcap	1995
A	Williamsport (Pa.) Cubs	New York-Penn	37	39	.487	7th (14)	Oneri Fleita	1994
R	Fort Myers (Fla.) Cubs	Gulf Coast	35	22	.614	5th (16)	Sandy Alomar Sr.	1993

*Finish in overall standings (No. of teams in league)   #Advanced level   +Won league championship

ORGANIZATION LEADERS

MAJOR LEAGUERS

Sammy Sosa. 36 homers, 119 RBIs

BATTING
*AVG	Mark Grace	.326
R	Mark Grace	97
H	Mark Grace	180
TB	Mark Grace	285
2B	Mark Grace	51
3B	Two tied at	7
HR	Sammy Sosa	36
RBI	Sammy Sosa	119
BB	Mark Grace	65
SO	Sammy Sosa	134
SB	Sammy Sosa	34

PITCHING
W	Jaime Navarro	14
L	Steve Trachsel	13
#ERA	Frank Castillo	3.21
G	Mike Perez	68
CG	Two tied at	2
SV	Randy Myers	38
IP	Jaime Navarro	200
BB	Steve Trachsel	76
SO	Kevin Foster	146

MINOR LEAGUERS

BATTING
*AVG	Michael Carter, Iowa	.325
R	Scott Samuels, Daytona/Orlando	95
H	Brooks Kieschnick, Iowa	149
TB	Brooks Kieschnick, Iowa	250
2B	Two tied at	33
3B	Scott Samuels, Daytona/Orlando	12
HR	Brooks Kieschnick, Iowa	23
RBI	Robin Jennings, Orlando	79
BB	Ken Coleman, Orlando	76
SO	Two tied at	104
SB	Two tied at	40

PITCHING
W	Alfredo Garcia, Rockford	14
L	Kennie Steenstra, Iowa	12
#ERA	Greg Twiggs, Daytona	1.41
G	Rob Taylor, Iowa	54
CG	Kennie Steenstra, Iowa	6
SV	Jason Hart, Daytona/Orlando	27
IP	Alfredo Garcia, Rockford	177
BB	Mike Anderson, Iowa	69
SO	Amaury Telemaco, Orlando	151

*Minimum 250 At-Bats   #Minimum 75 Innings

TOP 10 PROSPECTS

How the Cubs Top 10 prospects, as judged by Baseball America prior to the 1995 season, fared in 1995:

Amaury Telemaco

Player, Pos.	Club (Class—League)	AVG	AB	R	H	2B	3B	HR	RBI	SB
1. Brooks Kieschnick, of	Iowa (AAA—American Assoc.)	.295	505	61	149	30	1	23	73	2
3. Kevin Orie, 3b	Daytona (A—Florida State)	.244	409	54	100	17	4	9	51	5
6. Mike Hubbard, c	Iowa (AAA—American Assoc.)	.260	254	28	66	6	3	5	23	6
	Chicago	.174	23	2	4	0	0	0	1	0
9. Doug Glanville, of	Iowa (AAA—American Assoc.)	.270	419	48	113	16	2	4	37	13

Player, Pos.	Club (Class—League)	W	L	ERA	G	SV	IP	H	BB	SO
2. Amaury Telemaco, rhp	Orlando (AA—Southern)	8	8	3.29	22	0	148	112	42	151
4. *Derek Wallace, rhp	Wichita (AA—Texas)	4	3	4.40	26	6	43	51	13	24
	Binghamton (AA—Eastern)	0	1	5.28	15	2	15	11	9	8
5. Jayson Peterson, rhp	Williamsport (A—New York-Penn)	2	0	3.71	3	0	17	15	5	14
	Rockford (A—Midwest)	4	7	6.47	13	0	65	67	47	45
7. Javier Martinez, rhp	Rockford (A—Midwest)	6	6	3.96	18	0	105	100	39	53
8. Jason Ryan, rhp	Daytona (A—Florida State)	11	5	3.48	26	0	135	128	54	98
10. Brian Stephenson, rhp	Daytona (A—Florida State)	10	9	3.96	26	0	150	145	58	109

*Traded to Royals, then to New York Mets

IOWA — AAA

AMERICAN ASSOCIATION

BATTING	AVG	G	AB	R	H	2B	3B	HR	RBI	BB	SO	SB	CS	B	T	HT	WT	DOB	1st Yr	Resides
Benavides, Freddie	.241	106	315	30	76	14	4	4	26	25	47	2	3	R	R	6-2	180	4-7-66	1987	Laredo, Texas
Bream, Scott	.159	29	82	10	13	1	0	2	9	11	20	1	0	R	R	6-1	170	11-4-70	1989	Omaha, Neb.
Carter, Michael	.325	107	421	57	137	16	3	8	40	14	46	12	12	R	R	5-9	170	5-5-69	1990	Vicksburg, Miss.
Colon, Cris	.260	106	366	35	95	18	1	4	36	17	51	1	0	S	R	6-2	180	1-3-69	1987	La Guaira, Venez.
Cox, Darron	.234	33	94	7	22	6	0	1	14	8	21	0	0	R	R	6-1	205	11-21-67	1989	Norman, Okla.
Fanning, Steve	.000	4	5	0	0	0	0	0	0	1	4	0	0	R	R	6-3	180	5-16-67	1988	Conyers, Ga.
Fariss, Monty	.182	10	33	5	6	0	0	1	2	9	7	0	0	R	R	6-4	205	10-13-67	1988	Cashion, Okla.
Franco, Matt	.281	121	455	51	128	28	5	6	58	37	44	1	1	L	R	6-3	195	8-19-69	1987	Thousand Oaks, Calif.
Gardner, Jeff	.323	65	235	35	76	11	0	3	24	23	27	1	2	L	R	5-11	165	2-4-64	1985	Costa Mesa, Calif.
Glanville, Doug	.270	112	419	48	113	16	2	4	37	16	64	13	9	R	R	6-2	170	8-25-70	1991	Teaneck, N.J.
Gousha, Sean	.000	2	5	0	0	0	0	0	0	0	3	0	0	R	R	6-4	200	9-19-70	1992	Escondido, Calif.
Haney, Todd	.313	90	326	38	102	20	2	4	30	28	21	2	2	R	R	5-9	165	7-30-65	1987	Waco, Texas
Hubbard, Mike	.260	75	254	28	66	6	3	5	23	26	60	6	1	R	R	6-1	180	2-16-71	1992	Madison Heights, Va.
Jose, Felix	.135	10	37	2	5	3	0	0	1	1	6	0	0	S	R	6-1	220	5-8-65	1984	Boca Raton, Fla.
Kessinger, Keith	.229	68	210	21	48	11	0	2	20	25	23	1	1	S	R	6-2	185	2-19-67	1989	Oxford, Miss.
Kieschnick, Brooks	.295	138	505	61	149	30	1	23	73	58	91	2	3	L	R	6-4	228	6-6-72	1993	Caldwell, Texas
Kmak, Joe	.173	34	98	6	17	3	0	2	7	6	24	0	0	R	R	6-0	185	5-3-63	1985	Foster City, Calif.
Kosco, Bryn	.251	119	363	50	91	24	3	15	52	30	85	2	2	L	R	6-1	185	3-9-67	1988	Poland, Ohio
Martinez, Manny	.290	122	397	63	115	17	8	8	49	20	64	11	8	R	R	6-2	169	10-3-70	1988	San Pedro de Macoris, D.R.
O'Halloran, Greg	.158	7	19	1	3	1	0	0	1	0	7	0	0	L	R	6-2	200	5-21-68	1989	Mississauga, Ontario
Pledger, Kinnis	.083	9	24	1	2	0	0	0	2	12	0	0	1	L	R	6-4	215	7-17-68	1987	Benton, Ark.
Pratt, Todd	.328	23	58	3	19	1	0	0	5	4	17	0	0	R	R	6-3	195	2-9-67	1985	Boca Raton, Fla.

PITCHING	W	L	ERA	G	GS	CG	SV	IP	H	R	ER	BB	SO	B	T	HT	WT	DOB	1st Yr	Resides
Abbott, Paul	7	7	3.67	46	11	0	0	115	104	50	47	64	127	R	R	6-3	195	9-15-67	1985	Fullerton, Calif.
Adams, Terry	0	0	0.00	7	0	0	5	6	3	0	0	2	10	R	R	6-3	180	3-6-73	1991	Semmes, Ala.
Anderson, Mike	7	9	3.46	27	27	3	0	172	156	71	66	69	123	R	R	6-3	205	7-30-66	1988	Georgetown, Texas
Campbell, Mike	9	3	2.45	21	15	0	0	103	93	31	28	29	88	R	R	6-3	210	2-17-64	1985	Kirkland, Wash.
Casian, Larry	0	0	2.13	13	0	0	1	13	9	3	3	2	9	R	L	6-0	173	10-28-65	1987	Salem, Ore.
Dabney, Fred	4	6	5.95	33	1	0	0	56	68	42	37	29	33	R	L	6-3	190	11-20-67	1988	Sarasota, Fla.
DeLeon, Luis	0	1	13.50	2	0	0	0	2	6	3	3	0	3	R	R	6-1	159	8-19-58	1977	Ponce, P.R.
Dixon, Steve	6	3	2.85	53	0	0	0	41	34	16	13	19	38	L	L	6-0	195	8-3-69	1989	Louisville, Ky.
Edens, Tom	2	0	3.46	20	3	0	1	42	36	17	16	17	28	R	R	6-2	185	6-9-61	1983	Clarkston, Wash.
Garces, Rich	0	2	2.86	23	0	0	7	28	25	10	9	8	36	R	R	6-0	230	5-18-71	1988	Maracay, Venez.
Gozzo, Mauro	0	3	4.15	6	6	0	0	30	37	22	14	11	11	R	R	6-3	226	3-7-66	1984	Kensington, Conn.
Grant, Mark	5	2	3.13	11	11	2	0	69	58	28	24	10	39	R	R	6-2	215	10-24-63	1981	Alpine, Calif.
Meier, Kevin	1	2	8.44	3	2	0	0	11	18	10	10	3	7	R	R	6-4	200	2-20-66	1987	Southington, Conn.
Morton, Kevin	1	7	4.79	28	12	1	0	92	97	52	49	42	49	R	L	6-2	185	3-8-68	1989	Winter Park, Fla.
Nabholz, Chris	0	2	6.41	6	5	0	0	20	27	17	14	12	16	L	L	6-5	210	1-5-67	1989	Pottsville, Pa.
Shifflett, Steve	5	1	5.33	26	0	0	0	27	30	18	16	6	10	R	R	6-3	200	1-5-66	1989	Pleasant Hill, Mo.
Smith, Ottis	1	3	10.45	5	5	0	0	21	34	25	24	13	12	R	L	6-1	160	1-28-71	1990	Fond du Lac, Wisc.
Steenstra, Kennie	9	12	3.89	29	26	6	0	171	174	85	74	48	96	R	R	6-5	220	10-13-70	1992	Lynchburg, Mo.
Sturtze, Tanyon	4	7	6.80	23	17	1	0	86	108	66	65	42	48	R	R	6-5	190	10-12-70	1990	Worcester, Mass.
Swartzbaugh, Dave	3	0	1.53	30	0	0	0	47	33	10	8	18	38	R	R	6-2	195	2-11-68	1988	Middletown, Ohio
Taylor, Rob	4	2	2.81	54	0	0	18	58	42	20	18	28	48	R	R	6-3	225	3-25-66	1984	College Park, Md.
Walker, Mike	1	1	4.10	16	1	0	0	26	22	13	12	19	13	R	R	6-1	195	10-4-66	1986	Brooksville, Fla.
Young, Anthony	0	1	11.25	1	1	0	0	4	9	5	5	4	6	R	R	6-2	200	1-19-66	1987	Houston, Texas

FIELDING

Catcher	PCT	G	PO	A	E	DP	PB
Cox	.986	28	187	18	3	4	1
Franco	.000	1	0	0	0	0	0
Gousha	1.000	2	7	0	0	0	0
Hubbard	.982	71	446	33	9	3	8
Kmak	.992	33	209	26	2	3	1
O'Halloran	.935	5	28	1	2	0	1
Pratt	.985	8	59	5	1	0	0

First Base	PCT	G	PO	A	E	DP
Colon	.984	52	357	24	6	31
Fariss	1.000	7	62	3	0	5
Franco	.996	36	222	18	1	26
Kieschnick	1.000	7	13	3	0	2
Kosco	.993	70	548	43	4	57
Pratt	.963	6	23	3	1	0

Second Base	PCT	G	PO	A	E	DP
Benavides	1.000	1	2	5	0	2
Bream	.980	25	43	57	2	17
Colon	.990	23	39	61	1	16
Gardner	.988	49	103	153	3	39
Haney	.975	33	64	95	4	16
Kessinger	1.000	23	44	70	0	16

Third Base	PCT	G	PO	A	E	DP
Benavides	.903	17	7	21	3	3
Bream	1.000	1	0	2	0	0
Colon	.945	21	8	44	3	5
Franco	.925	95	61	161	18	11
Gardner	.857	7	4	8	2	2
Haney	.938	16	12	33	3	4
Kosco	.833	8	5	5	2	0

Shortstop	PCT	G	PO	A	E	DP
Benavides	.968	85	113	220	11	49
Bream	.857	2	3	3	1	0
Fanning	1.000	1	0	2	0	0
Haney	.975	22	26	53	2	13
Kessinger	.931	41	47	115	12	28

Outfield	PCT	G	PO	A	E	DP
Carter	.980	97	189	7	4	1
Glanville	.982	101	209	9	4	3
Haney	.957	13	21	1	1	0
Jose	1.000	8	12	0	0	0
Kieschnick	.989	117	166	12	2	1
Martinez	.983	108	281	16	5	2
O'Halloran	.000	1	0	0	0	0
Pledger	1.000	5	7	0	0	0

ORLANDO — AA

SOUTHERN LEAGUE

BATTING	AVG	G	AB	R	H	2B	3B	HR	RBI	BB	SO	SB	CS	B	T	HT	WT	DOB	1st Yr	Resides
Brown, Brant	.271	121	446	67	121	27	4	6	53	39	77	8	5	L	L	6-3	220	6-22-71	1992	Porterville, Calif.
Burton, Darren	.306	62	222	40	68	16	2	4	21	27	42	7	4	S	R	6-1	185	9-16-72	1990	Somerset, Ky.
Coleman, Ken	.277	127	394	82	109	19	3	4	37	76	55	25	7	S	R	5-10	175	2-6-67	1988	Jersey City, N.J.
Cox, Darron	.284	33	102	8	29	5	0	4	15	8	16	3	3	R	R	6-1	205	11-21-67	1989	Norman, Okla.
Dowler, Dee	.226	9	31	6	7	2	0	0	1	2	5	1	0	R	R	5-9	175	7-23-71	1993	Indianapolis, Ind.
Duross, Gabe	.262	68	244	23	64	10	1	3	40	10	20	3	2	L	L	6-1	195	4-6-72	1992	Kingston, N.Y.
Erdman, Brad	.111	14	36	4	4	0	0	0	1	6	0	0	0	R	R	6-3	190	2-23-70	1989	Casper, Wyom.
Gomez, Rudy	.192	93	214	18	41	11	1	1	16	15	45	0	0	R	R	5-10	165	8-8-69	1991	Tempe, Ariz.
Jennings, Robin	.296	132	490	71	145	27	7	17	79	44	61	7	14	L	L	6-2	200	4-11-72	1992	Miami, Fla.
Johnson, Jack	.221	25	68	3	15	0	0	0	4	7	11	1	3	R	R	6-3	205	3-24-70	1991	Chicago, Ill.
Kessinger, Keith	.258	18	62	8	16	5	0	0	5	3	6	0	0	S	R	6-2	185	2-19-67	1989	Oxford, Miss.
Kingston, Mark	.266	66	199	17	53	13	0	5	24	22	41	0	1	S	R	6-4	210	5-16-70	1991	Midland, Ga.

BATTING

BATTING	AVG	G	AB	R	H	2B	3B	HR	RBI	BB	SO	SB	CS	B	T	HT	WT	DOB	1st Yr	Resides
Larregui, Ed	.300	122	423	55	127	18	1	11	60	32	39	3	10	R	R	6-0	185	12-1-72	1990	Carolina, P.R.
Madsen, Dan	.192	15	26	6	5	0	1	0	6	6	2	0	1	S	L	6-0	185	2-10-71	1992	Carson City, Nev.
Manahan, Austin	.212	94	260	34	55	12	0	3	19	16	57	13	6	S	R	6-1	185	4-12-70	1988	Scottsdale, Ariz.
Morales, Francisco	.167	2	6	0	1	0	0	0	0	1	2	0	0	R	R	6-3	180	1-31-73	1991	San Pedro de Macoris, D.R.
Ortiz, Hector	.234	96	299	13	70	12	0	0	18	20	39	0	5	R	R	6-0	178	10-14-69	1988	Canovanas, P.R.
Petersen, Chris	.212	125	382	48	81	10	3	4	36	45	97	7	3	R	R	5-10	160	11-6-70	1992	Southington, Conn.
Samuels, Scott	.286	5	21	3	6	1	0	1	4	3	4	2	0	L	R	5-11	190	5-19-71	1992	San Jose, Calif.
Snyder, Jared	.500	1	4	2	2	0	0	0	0	0	0	0	0	R	R	6-2	215	3-8-70	1993	Saugus, Calif.
Torres, Paul	.298	63	228	38	68	14	1	10	45	29	40	0	3	R	R	6-3	210	10-19-70	1989	San Lorenzo, Calif.
Valdes, Pedro	.300	114	426	57	128	28	3	7	68	37	77	3	6	L	L	6-1	160	6-29-73	1991	Loiza, P.R.
Viera, Jose	.121	12	33	2	4	0	0	1	2	2	8	0	0	R	R	6-1	190	2-23-71	1990	Arecibo, P.R.

PITCHING

PITCHING	W	L	ERA	G	GS	CG	SV	IP	H	R	ER	BB	SO	B	T	HT	WT	DOB	1st Yr	Resides
Adams, Terry	2	3	1.43	37	0	0	19	38	23	9	6	16	26	R	R	6-3	180	3-6-73	1991	Semmes, Ala.
Bradford, Troy	1	1	4.91	4	4	0	0	22	22	13	12	9	6	R	R	6-2	200	2-25-69	1990	St. David, Ariz.
Bullinger, Jim	0	0	0.00	1	1	0	0	4	3	0	0	1	2	R	R	6-2	180	8-21-65	1986	Sarasota, Fla.
Burlingame, Ben	9	2	3.53	37	10	0	1	97	93	39	38	38	73	R	R	6-5	210	1-31-70	1991	Newton, Mass.
Connolly, Matt	3	4	4.08	21	4	0	2	40	34	18	18	11	43	R	R	6-8	230	10-1-68	1991	Richmond Hill, N.Y.
Dabney, Fred	2	1	2.08	13	0	0	1	17	13	9	4	10	9	R	L	6-3	190	11-20-67	1988	Sarasota, Fla.
DeLeon, Luis	0	1	2.00	4	0	0	0	9	7	2	2	2	3	R	R	6-1	159	8-19-58	1977	Ponce, P.R.
Dreyer, Darren	1	3	4.18	14	0	0	0	24	24	11	11	3	10	R	R	6-0	208	5-21-71	1992	Taft, Texas
Haas, David	0	3	4.97	3	3	0	0	13	18	10	7	10	4	R	R	6-1	200	10-19-65	1988	Wichita, Kan.
Harrah, Doug	5	2	1.94	44	0	0	5	70	58	21	15	34	49	R	R	6-0	175	4-23-69	1991	Newton Falls, Ohio
Hart, Jason	0	1	2.12	14	0	0	3	17	14	5	4	4	20	R	R	6-0	195	11-14-71	1994	Round Rock, Texas
Hutcheson, David	8	10	4.01	28	27	1	0	168	178	84	75	45	103	R	R	6-2	185	8-29-71	1993	Tampa, Fla.
Johnson, Chris	5	4	3.45	46	0	0	5	70	68	34	27	24	49	R	R	6-8	215	12-7-68	1987	Hixson, Tenn.
Meier, Kevin	4	1	2.64	11	11	0	0	65	55	24	19	13	52	R	R	6-4	200	2-20-66	1987	Southington, Conn.
Morgan, Mike	0	2	7.59	2	2	0	0	11	13	9	9	7	5	R	R	6-2	222	10-8-59	1978	Ogden, Utah
Petersen, Matt	3	9	5.87	24	15	1	0	89	107	66	58	39	59	R	R	6-4	190	5-21-70	1992	Omaha, Neb.
Ratliff, Jon	10	5	3.47	26	25	1	0	140	143	67	54	42	94	R	R	6-5	200	12-22-71	1993	Clay, N.Y.
Rivera, Roberto	6	2	2.38	49	0	0	6	68	50	18	18	11	34	L	L	6-0	175	1-1-69	1988	Bayamon, P.R.
Smith, Ottis	4	5	3.07	17	17	0	0	108	109	50	37	38	51	R	L	6-1	160	4-15-70	1990	Fond du Lac, Wisc.
Swartzbaugh, Dave	4	0	2.48	16	0	0	0	29	18	10	8	7	37	R	R	6-2	195	2-11-68	1989	Middletown, Ohio
Telemaco, Amaury	8	8	3.29	22	22	3	0	148	112	60	54	42	151	R	R	6-3	180	1-19-74	1991	La Romana, D.R.
Wendell, Turk	1	0	3.86	5	0	0	1	7	6	3	3	4	7	S	R	6-2	175	5-19-67	1988	Dalton, Mass.
Young, Anthony	0	0	0.00	2	2	0	0	5	6	1	0	3	5	R	R	6-2	200	1-19-66	1987	Houston, Texas

FIELDING

Catcher	PCT	G	PO	A	E	DP	PB
Cox	.973	31	157	24	5	1	2
Erdman	.986	14	70	3	1	0	0
J. Johnson	.977	21	111	14	3	2	2
Kingston	1.000	4	3	1	0	0	1
Morales	1.000	2	6	1	0	0	2
Ortiz	.991	94	567	72	6	5	3
Snyder	1.000	1	6	1	0	0	0

First Base	PCT	G	PO	A	E	DP
Brown	.990	107	917	92	10	75
Duross	.992	38	328	24	3	31
Kingston	1.000	4	10	0	0	1
Torres	1.000	2	15	0	0	0

Second Base	PCT	G	PO	A	E	DP
Coleman	.974	79	121	180	8	33

	PCT	G	PO	A	E	DP
Gomez	.972	77	106	136	7	31
Kessinger	.970	13	31	33	2	9
Manahan	.898	21	42	46	10	9

Third Base	PCT	G	PO	A	E	DP
Coleman	.942	77	23	91	7	8
Gomez	.000	1	0	0	0	0
Kessinger	1.000	1	0	1	0	0
Kingston	.946	58	38	85	7	6
Manahan	.808	19	8	13	5	0
Torres	.913	38	19	65	8	4
Viera	.913	9	7	14	2	1

Shortstop	PCT	G	PO	A	E	DP
Coleman	.917	4	7	4	1	2
Gomez	.958	26	28	64	4	17

	PCT	G	PO	A	E	DP
Kessinger	.913	5	8	13	2	2
Petersen	.964	125	212	357	21	66

Outfield	PCT	G	PO	A	E	DP
Brown	1.000	8	14	0	0	0
Burton	.981	49	101	4	2	1
Dowler	1.000	9	16	3	0	0
Duross	1.000	1	1	0	0	0
Jennings	.963	126	242	15	10	2
Larregui	.976	92	156	6	4	2
Madsen	1.000	9	16	1	0	0
Manahan	.963	32	52	0	2	0
Samuels	1.000	5	11	0	0	0
Torres	1.000	37	59	3	0	1
Valdes	.979	106	172	11	4	4

DAYTONA · A

FLORIDA STATE LEAGUE

BATTING	AVG	G	AB	R	H	2B	3B	HR	RBI	BB	SO	SB	CS	B	T	HT	WT	DOB	1st Yr	Resides
Cabrera, Alex	.294	54	214	26	63	14	0	2	35	9	36	2	4	R	R	6-2	217	12-24-71	1991	El Tigre, Venez.
Dowler, Dee	.251	112	415	70	104	12	2	3	59	45	51	26	15	R	R	5-9	175	7-23-71	1993	Indianapolis, Ind.
Duross, Gabe	.241	60	224	20	54	9	0	3	34	11	12	4	4	L	L	6-1	195	4-6-72	1992	Kingston, N.Y.
Ellis, Kevin	.270	120	430	57	116	17	6	6	66	26	73	6	3	R	R	6-0	210	11-21-71	1993	Waco, Texas
Erdman, Brad	.154	8	26	4	4	1	0	0	3	4	6	0	0	R	R	6-3	190	2-23-70	1989	Casper, Wyom.
Forkerway, Trey	.202	75	188	22	38	4	0	1	11	20	29	10	1	R	R	5-11	175	5-17-71	1993	Abilene, Texas
Gousha, Sean	.250	5	8	1	2	2	0	0	0	1	0	0	0	R	R	6-4	200	9-19-70	1992	Escondido, Calif.
Johnson, Andre	.071	5	14	2	1	0	0	0	2	0	4	0	0	R	R	6-0	205	11-7-69	1991	Baltimore, Md.
Johnson, Jack	.375	4	8	1	3	0	0	1	2	1	4	0	0	R	R	6-3	205	3-24-70	1991	Chicago, Ill.
Kingston, Mark	.235	49	170	23	40	8	0	2	23	14	33	1	1	S	R	6-4	200	5-16-70	1992	Midland, Tex.
Madsen, Dan	.194	13	36	7	7	1	0	1	3	3	11	4	2	S	L	6-0	185	2-10-71	1992	Carson City, Nev.
Maxwell, Jason	.263	117	388	66	102	13	3	10	58	63	68	12	7	R	R	6-0	175	3-21-72	1993	Lewisburg, Tenn.
Micucci, Mike	.195	23	41	4	8	2	0	0	3	4	9	0	0	L	R	5-11	185	12-15-72	1994	Emerson, N.J.
Molina, Jose	.236	82	233	27	55	9	1	1	19	29	53	1	0	R	R	6-1	180	6-3-75	1993	Vega Alta, P.R.
Morales, Francisco	.257	36	101	17	26	4	0	6	23	16	28	1	1	R	R	6-3	180	1-31-73	1991	San Pedro de Macoris, D.R.
Morris, Bobby	.308	95	344	44	106	18	2	3	51	48	46	22	8	L	R	6-0	180	11-22-72	1993	Munster, Ind.
Orie, Kevin	.244	119	409	54	100	17	4	9	51	42	71	5	4	R	R	6-4	215	9-1-72	1993	Pittsburgh, Pa.
Perez, Richard	.220	85	255	31	56	8	0	0	26	28	41	4	2	R	R	6-2	175	1-30-73	1991	Lara, Venez.
Pico, Brandon	.245	16	49	4	12	2	0	0	4	7	8	1	1	L	L	6-1	185	1-2-74	1992	Newport, R.I.
Porter, Bo	.217	113	336	54	73	12	2	3	19	32	104	22	10	R	R	6-1	188	7-5-72	1994	Newark, N.J.
Samuels, Scott	.327	112	388	92	127	29	12	2	42	69	63	38	14	L	R	5-11	190	5-19-71	1992	San Jose, Calif.
Snyder, Jared	.167	18	36	2	6	0	0	0	6	2	4	3	0	R	R	6-2	215	3-8-70	1993	Saugus, Calif.
Whatley, Gabe	.262	15	42	8	11	3	0	1	5	7	5	2	0	L	R	6-0	180	12-29-71	1993	Stone Mountain, Ga.

GAMES BY POSITION: C—Erdman 5, Gousha 5, J. Johnson 2, Kingston 1, Micucci 22, Molina 82, Morales 29, Snyder 18. **1B**—Cabrera 39, Duross 60, Ellis 5, J. Johnson 2, Kingston 37, Whatley 1. **2B**—Forkerway 40, Morris 64, Perez 47. **3B**—Orie 106, Perez 37, Whatley 1. **SS**—Forkerway 30, Maxwell 116, Perez 1. **OF**—Dowler 109, Ellis 69, Forkerway 1, A. Johnson 1, Madsen 13, Pico 11, Porter 110, Samuels 106, Whatley 10.

PITCHING	W	L	ERA	G	GS	CG	SV	IP	H	R	ER	BB	SO	B	T	HT	WT	DOB	1st Yr	Resides
Box, Shawn	8	6	3.05	25	23	0	0	124	114	50	42	35	90	R	R	5-11	180	3-13-73	1994	Mereta, Texas
Connolly, Matt	7	1	0.98	18	2	0	2	55	37	14	6	9	77	R	R	6-8	230	10-1-68	1991	Richmond Hill, N.Y.
Culberson, Don	1	1	4.56	12	0	0	0	24	27	15	12	15	15	R	R	6-2	195	12-31-70	1990	Philadelphia, Miss.
Devries, Andrew	1	0	3.57	21	1	0	0	45	45	21	18	22	21	L	L	6-3	205	3-19-73	1993	Venice, Fla.
Dreyer, Darren	3	5	1.94	29	0	0	7	56	42	18	12	9	45	R	R	6-0	208	5-21-71	1992	Taft, Texas
Gonzalez, Geremis	5	1	1.22	19	2	0	4	44	34	15	6	13	30	R	R	6-1	180	1-8-75	1992	Maracaibo, Venez.
Hart, Jason	0	3	2.21	37	0	0	24	41	29	15	10	18	50	R	R	6-0	195	11-14-71	1994	Round Rock, Texas
Hill, Shawn	5	3	3.68	37	0	0	3	59	48	31	24	17	71	R	R	5-11	190	5-4-70	1993	Nashua, N.H.
Khoury, Tony	2	0	4.05	7	0	0	0	7	10	3	3	2	4	R	R	6-1	185	6-16-71	1993	Toledo, Ohio
Lopez, Orlando	7	2	2.68	44	0	0	8	81	75	30	24	32	76	L	L	6-0	185	3-28-73	1992	Isabela, P.R.
Petersen, Matt	2	1	4.15	3	3	0	0	17	13	8	8	3	13	R	R	6-4	190	5-21-70	1992	Omaha, Neb.
Rodriguez, Chris	1	0	5.91	5	0	0	0	11	14	7	7	2	6	R	R	6-1	195	10-8-71	1991	Caguas, P.R.
Ryan, Jason	5	3	3.48	26	26	0	0	135	128	61	52	54	98	S	R	6-2	180	1-23-76	1994	Bound Brook, N.J.
Stephenson, Brian	10	9	3.96	26	26	0	0	150	145	79	66	58	109	R	R	6-3	205	7-17-73	1994	Fullerton, Calif.
Stevenson, Jason	2	0	2.95	8	0	0	1	18	11	6	6	6	15	R	R	6-3	180	8-11-74	1994	Phenix City, Ala.
Twiggs, Greg	3	1	3.41	18	13	1	0	89	64	30	14	28	80	R	L	5-10	155	10-15-71	1993	Winter Springs, Fla.
Walker, Wade	8	6	2.53	25	24	2	0	135	113	50	38	36	117	R	R	6-1	190	9-18-71	1993	Gonzales, La.
Wendell, Turk	0	0	1.17	4	2	0	0	8	5	2	1	1	8	S	R	6-2	175	5-19-67	1988	Dalton, Mass.
Winslett, Dax	4	4	2.28	12	12	0	0	67	61	24	17	18	52	R	R	6-1	200	1-1-72	1993	Houston, Texas
2-team (14 Vero Beach)	12	6	2.78	26	25	0	0	152	148	59	47	39	111							
Young, Anthony	0	0	5.63	6	1	0	0	8	5	5	5	4	3	R	R	6-2	200	1-19-66	1987	Houston, Texas

ROCKFORD A

MIDWEST LEAGUE

BATTING	AVG	G	AB	R	H	2B	3B	HR	RBI	BB	SO	SB	CS	B	T	HT	WT	DOB	1st Yr	Resides
Avalos, Gilbert	.237	104	350	57	83	15	1	2	34	39	74	18	4	R	R	5-11	175	3-26-73	1993	Houston, Texas
Barnes, Kelvin	.167	5	12	1	2	0	0	0	1	3	0	0	R	R	6-2	183	9-4-74	1994	Battleboro, N.C.
Barton, Scott	.231	14	26	2	6	3	0	2	3	6	0	1	L	R	6-0	180	1-26-74	1992	Jasper, Tenn.
Bogle, Bryan	.206	36	97	13	20	3	0	2	11	8	20	4	1	R	R	6-1	205	5-18-73	1994	Merritt Island, Fla.
Bustos, Saul	.253	95	289	46	73	12	2	10	47	22	66	5	2	R	R	5-11	170	9-30-72	1994	Odessa, Texas
Cline, Pat	.272	112	390	65	106	27	0	13	77	58	93	6	1	R	R	6-3	220	10-9-74	1993	Bradenton, Fla.
Dennis, Brian	.206	51	102	10	21	3	0	2	16	13	28	1	1	R	R	6-1	210	3-4-72	1994	Culver City, Calif.
Freeman, Richard	.273	131	466	89	127	33	5	11	67	61	57	8	3	R	R	6-4	205	2-3-72	1994	Houston, Texas
Fric, Sean	.235	7	17	3	4	1	0	0	2	4	2	0	0	R	R	6-1	190	6-7-73	1993	Port Lavaca, Texas
Gazarek, Marty	.261	107	399	57	104	24	1	3	53	27	58	7	5	R	R	6-2	190	6-1-73	1994	North Baltimore, Ohio
Hightower, Vee	.265	64	238	51	63	11	1	7	36	39	52	23	6	S	R	6-5	205	4-26-72	1993	Mt. Lebanon, Pa.
Johnson, Jack	.214	24	70	5	15	2	0	1	14	8	17	0	0	R	R	6-3	205	3-24-70	1991	Chicago, Ill.
Kimbler, Doug	.286	102	353	69	101	33	2	12	67	39	61	7	3	R	R	5-10	185	8-27-68	1990	West Chazy, N.Y.
Livsey, Shane	.283	57	226	39	64	10	1	2	27	22	30	21	7	S	R	5-11	180	7-21-73	1991	Chicago, Ill.
Madsen, Dan	.261	29	88	18	23	6	2	0	11	14	15	14	4	S	L	6-0	185	2-10-71	1992	Carson City, Nev.
Medina, Alger	.194	26	62	8	12	1	0	1	8	7	15	6	1	R	R	6-0	176	6-30-74	1992	Santo Domingo, D.R.
Olinde, Chad	.238	54	164	21	39	11	0	1	26	23	42	3	2	L	R	5-10	170	5-26-72	1994	Oscar, La.
Perez, Mike	.245	39	106	12	26	3	1	0	11	13	24	3	3	R	R	5-10	165	6-2-72	1995	San Antonio, Texas
Pico, Brandon	.300	96	383	59	115	27	4	4	47	34	53	7	7	L	L	6-1	185	1-2-74	1992	Newport, R.I.
Salzano, Jerry	.286	6	21	0	6	1	0	2	1	1	0	1	R	R	6-0	175	10-27-74	1992	Trenton, N.J.
Snyder, Jared	.185	24	65	7	12	2	0	1	6	6	15	0	0	R	R	6-2	215	3-8-70	1993	Saugus, Calif.
Walker, Steve	.289	103	415	78	120	24	7	3	44	37	104	40	16	S	R	6-1	180	2-11-72	1991	Leesburg, Ga.
Whatley, Gabe	.257	95	339	54	87	23	2	7	54	44	99	4	3	R	R	6-1	180	12-29-71	1993	Stone Mountain, Ga.

GAMES BY POSITION: C—Barton 5, Cline 91, Dennis 17, Johnson 19, Snyder 24. **1B**—Dennis 9, Freeman 131, Johnson 4, Kimbler 1, Salzano 3, Whatley 7. **2B**—Avalos 32, Kimbler 5, Livsey 52, Olinde 39, Perez 37. **3B**—Avalos 72, Barnes 4, Bustos 1, Kimbler 49, Olinde 17, Salzano 3, Whatley 10. **SS**—Bustos 94, Kimbler 54. **OF**—Avalos 1, Bogle 33, Fric 5, Gazarek 70, Hightower 17, Madsen 29, Medina 20, Pico 94, Salzano 1, Walker 99, Whatley 74.

PITCHING	W	L	ERA	G	GS	CG	SV	IP	H	R	ER	BB	SO	B	T	HT	WT	DOB	1st Yr	Resides
Bair, Dennis	4	2	1.51	9	7	0	0	54	41	10	9	6	40	L	R	6-5	215	11-17-74	1995	Monhall, Pa.
Barker, Richard	2	0	3.71	32	0	0	1	44	45	20	18	20	23	R	R	6-2	195	10-29-72	1994	Malden, Mass.
Bogle, Sean	1	0	1.21	13	0	0	0	22	17	3	3	9	15	R	R	6-2	195	10-3-73	1994	Indianapolis, Ind.
Bryant, Chris	2	2	6.43	21	0	0	0	35	32	26	25	17	29	L	L	6-1	180	8-13-75	1993	Tampa, Fla.
Byrne, Earl	4	3	4.65	13	11	0	0	60	54	36	31	38	51	L	L	6-1	165	7-2-74	1994	Melbourne, Australia
Casey, Ryan	2	6	6.05	16	0	0	1	19	19	15	13	11	12	R	R	6-1	195	8-29-72	1994	Killeen, Texas
Dennis, Brian	0	0	3.60	3	0	0	1	5	6	2	2	1	4	R	R	6-1	210	3-4-72	1994	Culver City, Calif.
Faulkner, Neal	2	3	3.90	40	0	0	1	67	61	36	29	29	47	R	R	6-9	230	4-16-75	1994	Montgomery, Ala.
Fennell, Barry	2	1	2.35	4	4	0	0	23	19	8	6	13	8	R	L	6-4	200	9-30-76	1994	Pennsauken, N.J.
Garcia, Alfredo	14	9	3.76	27	27	1	0	177	176	94	74	43	120	S	R	6-2	175	6-11-74	1993	Buena Park, Calif.
Gonzalez, Geremis	4	4	5.10	12	12	1	0	65	63	43	37	28	36	R	R	6-1	180	1-8-75	1992	Maracaibo, Venez.
Khoury, Tony	4	2	4.60	28	1	0	0	45	49	37	23	26	38	R	R	6-1	185	6-16-71	1993	Toledo, Ohio
Krause, Kevin	6	7	3.81	30	13	0	0	99	96	53	42	41	58	R	R	6-0	165	8-27-73	1992	Syracuse, N.Y.
Martinez, Javier	6	6	3.96	18	18	1	0	105	100	56	46	39	53	R	R	6-2	195	2-5-77	1994	Bayamon, P.R.
May, Scott	3	0	1.71	8	3	0	0	26	20	7	5	9	24	R	R	6-5	185	11-11-61	1994	Waupaca, Wisc.
Montelongo, Joseph	10	7	4.26	20	20	1	0	118	109	62	56	49	82	R	R	6-0	190	9-12-73	1994	Cleveland, Ohio
Ormonde, Troy	0	3	8.14	7	5	0	0	24	29	29	22	28	13	R	R	6-3	205	1-7-75	1994	Colville, Wash.
Peterson, Jayson	4	6	6.47	13	13	0	0	65	67	56	47	47	45	S	R	6-4	185	11-2-75	1994	Commerce City, Colo.
Putrich, Josh	0	2	7.45	6	1	0	0	10	10	8	8	5	6	R	R	6-1	175	2-25-74	1994	Farmington, Ill.
Rain, Steve	5	2	1.21	53	0	0	23	59	38	12	8	23	66	R	R	6-6	225	6-2-75	1993	Walnut, Calif.
Stevenson, Jason	4	3	5.59	33	5	0	2	77	85	50	48	31	54	R	R	6-3	180	8-11-74	1994	Phenix City, Ala.

WILLIAMSPORT A

NEW YORK-PENN LEAGUE

BATTING	AVG	G	AB	R	H	2B	3B	HR	RBI	BB	SO	SB	CS	B	T	HT	WT	DOB	1st Yr	Resides
Barton, Scott	.222	16	45	3	10	5	2	0	13	4	13	0	1	L	R	6-0	180	1-26-74	1992	Jasper, Tenn.
Bentley, Kevin	.217	50	115	14	25	4	3	2	13	14	48	1	3	R	R	6-2	210	9-21-72	1995	Bedford, Texas
Conley, Brian	.251	69	259	42	65	18	1	1	23	24	49	7	3	R	R	5-11	180	12-5-74	1995	Cincinnati, Ohio

BATTING	AVG	G	AB	R	H	2B	3B	HR	RBI	BB	SO	SB	CS	B	T	HT	WT	DOB	1st Yr	Resides
Ellison, Tony	.222	5	18	5	4	0	0	1	2	2	5	0	0	R	R	6-0	195	7-12-74	1995	Grifton, N.C.
Jasco, Elinton	.320	6	25	2	8	2	0	0	4	0	5	2	0	R	R	5-10	150	5-11-75	1993	San Pedro de Macoris, D.R.
Joseph, Terry	.292	70	260	49	76	8	10	1	34	30	33	18	6	R	R	5-9	185	11-20-73	1995	Harvey, La.
Lauterhahn, Mike	.143	5	14	5	2	1	0	0	0	5	5	1	1	R	R	6-0	170	1-1-73	1995	Wanaque, N.J.
Maleski, Tom	.232	40	112	13	26	8	1	0	14	19	25	1	1	R	R	6-0	200	12-23-77	1995	Richardson, Texas
McDonald, Ashanti	.249	59	193	26	48	4	1	1	20	13	46	4	5	L	R	6-0	185	4-25-73	1995	Chicago, Ill.
Nieves, Jose	.214	69	276	46	59	13	1	4	44	21	39	11	10	R	R	6-0	153	6-16-75	1992	Guacara, Venez.
Nova, Jose	.221	52	172	25	38	7	1	0	13	21	48	2	1	R	R	6-0	190	5-23-75	1995	Tempe, Ariz.
Perez, Mike	.294	7	17	2	5	0	1	0	3	3	3	0	0	R	R	5-10	165	6-2-72	1995	San Antonio, Texas
Putko, James	.270	47	141	18	38	12	0	3	23	16	34	0	1	L	R	6-3	205	6-26-74	1995	Hubbard, Ohio
Salzano, Jerry	.298	62	218	28	65	13	2	0	23	22	28	4	3	R	R	6-0	175	10-27-74	1992	Trenton, N.J.
Seidel, Ryan	.296	64	203	27	60	8	5	0	20	17	37	13	2	R	R	6-0	180	5-21-73	1995	Westlake Village, Calif.
Speed, Dorian	.216	60	204	30	44	8	3	2	23	28	56	18	5	R	R	6-3	190	3-1-74	1995	Tempe, Ariz.
Vieira, Scott	.318	61	214	35	68	8	2	6	46	25	37	3	1	R	R	5-11	185	8-17-73	1995	San Ramon, Calif.
Zuleta, Julio	.173	30	75	9	13	3	1	0	6	11	12	0	1	R	R	6-6	230	3-28-75	1993	Juan Diaz, Panama

GAMES BY POSITION: C—Bartori 14, Maleski 28, Vieira 27, Zuleta 25. **1B**—Maleski 3, Putko 36, Salzano 53, Seidel 2, Vieira 1. **2B**—Conley 50, Jasco 6, McDonald 8, Nieves 9, Perez 7. **3B**—Maleski 3, McDonald 25, Nova 52, Salzano 1, Vieira 2. **SS**—Conley 3, McDonald 24, Nieves 54. **OF**—Bentley 43, Ellison 3, Joseph 66, Lauterhahn 4, Salzano 17, Seidel 59, Speed 58, Vieira 5.

PITCHING	W	L	ERA	G	GS	CG	SV	IP	H	R	ER	BB	SO	B	T	HT	WT	DOB	1st Yr	Resides
Bair, Dennis	2	3	1.60	7	7	0	0	39	33	13	7	2	31	L	R	6-5	215	11-17-74	1995	Monhall, Pa.
Bogle, Sean	1	0	2.05	12	0	0	1	22	22	12	5	8	15	R	R	6-2	195	10-3-73	1994	Indianapolis, Ind.
Diaz, Jairo	1	7	2.98	30	0	0	0	45	39	21	15	10	55	R	R	6-2	198	8-21-75	1994	Maracay, Venez.
Greene, Brian	3	2	3.33	18	5	0	0	46	52	28	17	16	25	R	R	6-2	200	11-30-73	1995	Ft. Thomas, Ky.
Hammack, Brandon	1	5	4.18	27	0	0	6	32	32	20	15	14	40	R	R	6-5	240	3-5-73	1995	San Antonio, Texas
Kelley, Jason	1	1	1.62	3	3	0	0	17	14	3	3	7	6	R	R	6-1	225	11-14-75	1994	Live Oak, Fla.
Kendrick, Scott	2	1	3.33	5	5	0	0	27	26	14	10	8	15	L	R	6-3	185	11-21-75	1995	Monroe, N.Y.
McNeese, John	5	3	1.86	13	12	0	0	73	73	24	15	10	47	R	L	6-0	180	11-25-71	1995	Columbia, Miss.
McNichol, Brian	3	1	3.08	9	9	0	0	50	57	28	17	8	35	L	L	6-6	210	5-20-74	1995	Woodbridge, Va.
Mosley, Tim	2	0	4.28	23	0	0	1	34	40	23	16	16	26	R	R	6-0	180	10-16-74	1995	New Castle, Pa.
Ormonde, Troy	2	4	4.29	14	14	0	0	71	61	50	34	39	41	R	R	6-3	205	1-7-75	1994	Colville, Wash.
Peterson, Jayson	2	0	3.71	3	3	0	0	17	15	7	7	5	14	S	R	6-4	185	11-25-75	1994	Commerce City, Colo.
Ricketts, Chad	4	5	4.19	12	12	0	0	69	89	46	32	16	37	R	R	6-5	195	2-12-75	1995	St. Petersburg, Fla.
Speier, Justin	2	1	1.49	30	0	0	12	36	27	6	6	4	39	R	R	6-4	195	11-6-73	1995	Scottsdale, Ariz.
Weber, David	2	3	7.94	22	2	0	0	34	51	38	30	15	28	R	R	5-11	175	11-19-74	1993	Jersey City, N.J.
Wood, Kerry	0	0	10.38	2	2	0	0	4	5	8	5	5	5	R	R	6-5	190	6-16-77	1995	Grand Prairie, Texas
Wyatt, Cortez	4	3	2.63	22	2	0	0	48	38	16	14	8	35	R	R	6-1	195	8-29-72	1994	Atlanta, Ga.

FORT MYERS   R

GULF COAST LEAGUE

BATTING	AVG	G	AB	R	H	2B	3B	HR	RBI	BB	SO	SB	CS	B	T	HT	WT	DOB	1st Yr	Resides
Abreu, Nelson	.214	57	173	21	37	3	2	2	24	19	37	12	8	R	R	6-0	170	8-16-76	1994	Maracay, Venez.
Barnes, Kelvin	.286	49	168	28	48	6	6	6	37	24	37	11	4	R	R	6-2	183	9-4-74	1994	Battleboro, N.C.
Borges, Victor	.213	35	94	20	20	0	1	0	6	17	18	8	2	L	L	6-1	180	5-1-76	1994	Miranda, Venez.
Campos, Miguel	.209	36	115	21	24	6	0	3	13	8	37	5	1	R	R	6-1	185	3-28-76	1994	Carabobo, Venez.
Colon, Jose	.227	40	119	14	27	4	0	2	11	10	30	8	5	R	R	6-2	190	1-25-76	1995	Melbourne, Fla.
Connell, Jerry	.211	22	76	6	16	5	0	1	6	6	12	1	1	R	R	6-2	197	7-17-77	1995	Avenel, N.J.
Crutchfield, David	.231	31	104	19	24	5	4	0	8	11	33	13	1	L	R	6-0	195	6-5-75	1994	Rockville, Md.
Gil, Daniel	.167	9	6	0	1	0	0	0	1	0	0	0	0	R	R	6-3	190	7-3-74	1993	San Diego, Calif.
Gordon, Buck	.100	4	10	0	1	0	0	0	2	2	2	0	0	R	R	6-1	220	9-29-74	1995	Shenandoah, Va.
Green, Ronald	.319	34	119	28	38	7	4	2	12	18	33	13	7	R	R	5-10	170	9-12-72	1995	Tupelo, Miss.
Jasco, Elinton	.379	34	124	28	47	6	3	1	17	16	18	29	9	R	R	5-10	150	5-11-73	1993	San Pedro de Macoris, D.R.
Kinnie, Donald	.250	35	120	20	30	6	4	0	14	12	36	12	1	R	R	6-2	185	10-4-73	1995	Tuscaloosa, Ala.
Macero, Victor	.234	41	128	17	30	5	0	2	11	14	25	4	2	R	R	6-2	205	6-8-77	1994	Caracas, Venez.
Medina, Alger	.224	23	76	10	17	5	1	0	11	10	4	7	4	R	R	6-0	176	6-30-74	1992	Santo Domingo, D.R.
Payano, Alexi	.297	29	91	20	27	4	1	2	14	11	16	1	0	S	R	6-2	185	4-8-77	1994	Bani, D.R.
Pressley, Kasey	.236	39	140	12	33	4	1	0	16	11	47	1	1	L	R	6-4	220	9-5-76	1995	Orlando, Fla.
Salazar, Juan	.285	36	130	12	37	7	1	2	24	9	12	3	1	R	R	6-1	180	1-14-75	1994	Valencia, Venez.

GAMES BY POSITION: C—Campos 20, Gordon 2, Payano 19, Salazar 20. **1B**—Macero 28, Pressley 23, Salazar 7. **2B**—Campos 9, Jasco 34, Medina 17. **3B**—Barnes 46, Campos 7, Medina 5. **SS**—Abreu 57, Campos 2. **OF**—Barnes 2, Borges 27, Campos 1, Colon 38, Connell 20, Crutchfield 28, Green 33, Kinnie 30, Macero 1, Medina 3.

PITCHING	W	L	ERA	G	GS	CG	SV	IP	H	R	ER	BB	SO	B	T	HT	WT	DOB	1st Yr	Resides
Birsner, Roark	3	2	2.70	12	12	0	0	50	40	18	15	22	42	R	R	6-4	180	12-2-75	1994	Berlin, N.J.
Booker, Chris	3	2	2.76	13	7	0	1	42	36	22	13	16	43	R	R	6-3	205	11-9-75	1995	Monroeville, Ala.
Bryant, Chris	0	0	4.91	6	0	0	0	11	11	6	6	5	13	L	L	6-1	180	8-13-75	1993	Tampa, Fla.
Corrales, Rafael	1	1	2.42	12	0	0	2	22	23	8	6	8	10	R	R	6-5	190	5-29-75	1995	Miami, Fla.
Dickson, Lance	1	0	0.00	2	1	0	0	3	2	0	0	3	3	R	L	6-1	185	10-19-69	1990	La Mesa, Calif.
Farnsworth, Kyle	3	2	0.87	16	0	0	1	31	22	8	3	11	18	R	R	6-4	190	4-14-76	1994	Roswell, Ga.
Feliz, Jose	3	2	1.75	13	5	0	1	36	29	20	7	10	27	R	R	6-1	175	8-31-76	1994	Santo Domingo, D.R.
Gil, Daniel	1	1	3.46	7	0	0	2	13	9	7	5	8	9	R	R	6-3	190	7-3-74	1993	San Diego, Calif.
Guzman, Jose	0	1	1.50	2	0	0	0	6	5	1	1	0	3	R	R	6-3	195	4-9-63	1981	Arlington, Texas
Hammons, Matt	3	1	2.35	10	8	0	0	46	35	14	12	16	32	R	R	6-3	195	4-9-77	1995	San Diego, Calif.
Holobinko, Mike	3	2	1.74	8	1	0	0	21	16	8	4	8	11	L	L	6-2	210	12-24-75	1995	Rahway, N.J.
Kelley, Jason	1	1	0.70	7	5	0	0	26	10	11	2	19	20	R	R	6-1	225	11-14-75	1994	Live Oak, Fla.
Licciardi, Ron	4	3	2.43	17	1	0	0	33	24	13	9	16	22	L	L	6-2	190	3-26-76	1995	Oakdale, Conn.
Macero, Victor	0	1	5.40	1	0	0	0	5	3	3	3	1	3	R	R	6-2	205	6-8-77	1994	Caracas, Venez.
Markey, Barret	0	1	1.76	17	1	0	4	41	43	11	8	7	24	R	R	6-5	195	7-20-76	1995	St. Petersburg, Fla.
Martino, Jason	0	0	0.00	8	0	0	2	11	4	2	0	5	4	R	R	6-2	180	6-11-77	1995	Pittstown, N.J.
Peraza, Jose	0	0	0.00	3	0	0	0	2	0	0	0	1	2	L	L	6-3	200	2-7-75	1995	Norwalk, Calif.
Ricketts, Chad	1	0	0.00	2	0	0	0	9	1	1	0	1	5	R	R	6-5	195	2-12-75	1995	St. Petersburg, Fla.
Stading, Kris	0	0	0.66	11	0	0	0	14	8	4	1	14	12	L	L	6-7	235	12-24-76	1995	Phoenix, Ariz.
Villegas, Ismael	3	2	2.40	11	10	0	0	61	43	17	11	11	26	R	R	6-0	177	8-12-76	1994	Caguas, P.R.
Vizcaino, Edward	1	1	2.70	14	0	0	1	17	15	10	5	6	11	R	R	6-0	160	4-17-77	1994	Bani, D.R.
Wood, Kerry	0	0	0.00	1	1	0	0	3	0	0	0	1	2	R	R	6-5	190	6-16-77	1995	Grand Prairie, Texas

CINCINNATI REDS

Manager: Davey Johnson.   **1995 Record:** 85-59, .590 (1st, NL Central).

BATTING	AVG	G	AB	R	H	2B	3B	HR	RBI	BB	SO	SB	CS	B	T	HT	WT	DOB	1st Yr	Resides
Anthony, Eric	.269	47	134	19	36	6	0	5	23	13	30	2	1	L	L	6-2	195	11-8-67	1986	Houston, Texas
Berryhill, Damon	.183	34	82	6	15	3	0	2	11	10	19	0	0	S	R	6-0	205	12-3-63	1984	Laguna Niguel, Calif.
Boone, Bret	.267	138	513	63	137	34	2	15	68	41	84	5	1	R	R	5-10	180	4-6-69	1990	Villa Park, Calif.
Branson, Jeff	.260	122	331	43	86	18	2	12	45	44	69	2	1	L	R	6-0	180	1-26-67	1989	Silas, Ala.
Duncan, Mariano	.290	29	69	16	20	2	1	3	13	5	19	0	1	R	R	6-0	185	3-13-63	1982	Cherry Hill, N.J.
2-team (52 Phil.)	.287	81	265	36	76	14	2	6	36	5	62	1	3							
Gant, Ron	.276	119	410	79	113	19	4	29	88	74	108	23	8	R	R	6-0	200	3-2-65	1983	Smyrna, Ga.
Gibralter, Steve	.333	4	3	0	1	0	0	0	0	0	0	0	0	R	R	6-0	170	10-9-72	1990	Duncanville, Texas
Greene, Willie	.105	8	19	1	2	0	0	0	3	7	0	0	0	L	R	5-11	184	9-23-71	1989	Haddock, Ga.
Harris, Lenny	.208	101	197	32	41	8	3	2	16	14	20	10	1	L	R	5-10	205	10-28-64	1983	Miami, Fla.
Howard, Tom	.302	113	281	42	85	15	2	3	26	20	37	17	8	S	R	6-2	205	12-11-64	1986	Elk Grove, Calif.
Hunter, Brian	.215	40	79	9	17	6	0	1	9	11	21	2	1	R	L	6-0	195	3-4-68	1987	Anaheim, Calif.
Larkin, Barry	.319	131	496	98	158	29	6	15	66	61	49	51	5	R	R	6-0	190	4-28-64	1985	Cincinnati, Ohio
Lewis, Darren	.245	58	163	19	40	1	0	8	17	20	11	11	R	R	6-0	180	8-28-67	1988	San Mateo, Calif.
2-team (74 SF)	.250	132	472	66	118	13	3	1	24	34	57	32	18							
Lewis, Mark	.339	81	171	25	58	13	1	3	30	21	33	0	3	R	R	6-1	190	11-30-69	1988	Hamilton, Ohio
Morris, Hal	.279	101	359	53	100	25	2	11	51	29	58	1	1	L	L	6-4	215	4-9-65	1986	Union, Ky.
Owens, Eric	1.000	2	2	0	2	0	0	0	1	0	0	0	0	R	R	6-1	184	2-3-71	1992	Danville, Va.
Sanders, Deion	.240	33	129	19	31	2	3	1	10	9	18	16	3	L	L	6-1	195	8-9-67	1988	Alpharetta, Ga.
Sanders, Reggie	.306	133	484	91	148	36	6	28	99	69	122	36	12	R	R	6-1	180	12-1-67	1988	Cincinnati, Ohio
Santiago, Benito	.286	81	266	40	76	20	0	11	44	24	48	2	2	R	R	6-1	182	3-9-65	1983	La Jolla, Calif.
Taubensee, Eddie	.284	80	218	32	62	14	2	9	44	22	52	2	2	L	R	6-4	205	10-31-68	1986	Houston, Texas
Walton, Jerome	.290	102	162	32	47	12	1	8	22	17	25	10	7	R	R	6-1	175	7-8-65	1986	Fairburn, Ga.
Wilson, Nigel	.000	5	7	0	0	0	0	0	0	0	4	0	0	L	L	6-1	170	1-12-70	1988	Ajax, Ontario
Worthington, Craig	.278	10	18	1	5	1	0	1	2	2	1	0	0	R	R	6-0	200	4-17-65	1985	Anaheim, Calif.

PITCHING	W	L	ERA	G	GS	CG	SV	IP	H	R	ER	BB	SO	B	T	HT	WT	DOB	1st Yr	Resides
Brantley, Jeff	3	2	2.82	56	0	0	28	70	53	22	22	20	62	R	R	5-10	189	9-5-63	1985	Clinton, Miss.
Burba, Dave	6	2	3.27	15	9	1	0	63	52	24	23	26	50	R	R	6-4	240	7-7-66	1987	Springfield, Ohio
2-team (37 SF)	10	4	3.97	52	9	1	0	107	90	50	47	51	96							
Carrasco, Hector	2	7	4.12	64	0	0	5	87	86	45	40	46	64	R	R	6-2	175	10-22-69	1988	San Pedro de Macorís, D.R.
Courtright, John	0	0	9.00	1	0	0	0	1	2	1	1	0	0	L	L	6-2	185	5-30-70	1991	Columbus, Ohio
Grott, Matt	0	0	21.60	2	0	0	0	2	6	4	4	0	2	L	L	6-1	205	12-5-67	1989	Glendale, Ariz.
Hernandez, Xavier	7	2	4.60	59	0	0	3	90	95	47	46	31	84	R	R	6-2	185	8-16-65	1986	Missouri City, Texas
Jackson, Mike	6	1	2.39	40	0	0	2	49	38	13	13	19	41	R	R	6-2	223	12-22-64	1984	Spring, Texas
Jarvis, Kevin	3	4	5.70	19	11	1	0	79	91	56	50	32	33	L	R	6-2	200	8-1-69	1991	Lexington, Ky.
McElroy, Chuck	3	4	6.02	44	0	0	0	40	46	29	27	15	27	L	L	6-0	195	10-1-67	1986	Friendswood, Texas
Nitkowski, C.J.	1	3	6.12	9	7	0	0	32	41	25	22	15	18	L	L	6-2	185	3-9-73	1994	Milford, Pa.
Pennington, Brad	0	0	5.59	6	0	0	0	10	9	8	6	11	7	L	L	6-6	215	4-14-69	1989	Salem, Ind.
Portugal, Mark	6	5	3.82	14	14	0	0	78	79	35	33	22	33	R	R	6-0	190	10-30-62	1981	Missouri City, Texas
2-team (17 SF)	11	10	4.01	31	31	1	0	182	185	91	81	56	96							
Pugh, Tim	6	5	3.84	28	12	0	0	98	100	46	42	32	38	R	R	6-6	225	1-26-67	1989	Florence, Ky.
Reed, Rick	0	0	5.82	4	3	0	0	17	18	12	11	3	10	R	R	6-0	200	8-16-64	1986	Huntington, W.Va.
Remlinger, Mike	0	0	9.00	2	0	0	0	1	2	1	1	3	1	L	L	6-0	195	3-23-66	1987	Plymouth, Mass.
2-team (5 NY)	0	1	6.43	7	0	0	0	7	9	6	5	5	7							
Rijo, Jose	5	4	4.17	14	14	0	0	69	76	33	32	22	62	R	R	6-3	210	5-13-65	1981	San Cristobal, D.R.
Roper, John	0	0	10.29	2	2	0	0	7	13	9	8	4	6	R	R	6-0	175	11-21-71	1990	Raeford, N.C.
Ruffin, Johnny	0	1	1.35	10	0	0	0	13	4	3	2	11	11	R	R	6-3	170	7-29-71	1988	Butler, Ala.
Schourek, Pete	18	7	3.22	29	29	2	0	190	158	72	68	45	160	L	L	6-5	195	5-10-69	1987	Falls Church, Va.
Smiley, John	12	5	3.46	28	27	1	0	177	173	72	68	39	124	L	L	6-4	215	3-17-65	1983	Warrendale, Pa.
Smith, Pete	1	2	6.66	11	2	0	0	24	30	19	18	7	14	R	R	6-2	200	2-27-66	1984	Smyrna, Ga.
Sullivan, Scott	0	0	4.91	3	0	0	0	4	4	2	2	2	2	R	R	6-3	210	3-13-71	1993	Carrollton, Ala.
Viola, Frank	0	1	6.28	3	3	0	0	14	20	11	10	3	4	L	L	6-4	209	4-19-60	1981	Longwood, Fla.
Wells, David	6	5	3.59	11	11	3	0	73	74	34	29	16	50	L	L	6-4	225	5-20-63	1982	Palm Harbor, Fla.

FIELDING

Catcher	PCT	G	PO	A	E	DP	PB
Berryhill	.988	29	152	12	2	1	1
Santiago	.996	75	461	33	2	4	6
Taubensee	.983	65	326	21	6	0	4

First Base	PCT	G	PO	A	E	DP
Anthony	.966	17	102	10	4	11
Berryhill	1.000	1	1	0	0	0
Branson	.000	1	0	0	0	0
Duncan	1.000	6	32	0	0	1
Harris	1.000	23	127	13	0	10
Hunter	.983	23	164	12	3	20
Morris	.994	99	757	73	5	78
Santiago	1.000	8	19	2	0	2
Taubensee	1.000	3	12	1	0	2
Walton	1.000	3	3	0	0	0
Worthington	1.000	4	24	2	0	3

Second Base	PCT	G	PO	A	E	DP
Boone	.994	138	311	362	4	106
Branson	1.000	8	1	1	0	0
Duncan	.963	7	13	13	1	3
Harris	1.000	1	2	0	0	0
M. Lewis	1.000	0	0	3	0	0

Third Base	PCT	G	PO	A	E	DP
Branson	.971	98	52	179	7	23
Greene	1.000	7	1	13	0	1
Harris	.939	24	9	53	4	3
M. Lewis	.968	72	19	103	4	4
Owens	.000	2	0	0	0	0
Worthington	1.000	2	2	2	0	0

Shortstop	PCT	G	PO	A	E	DP
Branson	.980	32	31	65	2	15
Duncan	1.000	6	8	13	0	2

	PCT	G	PO	A	E	DP
Larkin	.980	130	192	341	11	72
M. Lewis	1.000	2	0	1	0	0

Outfield	PCT	G	PO	A	E	DP
Anthony	1.000	24	39	2	0	0
Duncan	1.000	3	6	0	0	0
Gant	.985	117	191	7	3	0
Gibralter	1.000	2	1	0	0	0
Harris	1.000	8	9	2	0	0
Howard	.985	82	127	2	2	1
Hunter	1.000	4	7	1	0	0
D. Lewis	.992	73	121	3	1	0
D. Sanders	.968	33	88	2	3	1
R. Sanders	.982	130	268	12	5	2
Walton	.982	89	107	2	2	0
Wilson	1.000	2	2	0	0	0

DAN ARNOLD

Pete Schourek led the Reds with 18 wins and a 3.22 ERA

Reds minor league Player of the Year Eric Owens

STAN DENNY

REDS

FARM SYSTEM

Director of Player Development: Chief Bender.

Class	Farm Team	League	W	L	Pct.	Finish*	Manager	First Yr
AAA	Indianapolis (Ind.) Indians	American Assoc.	88	56	.611	1st (8)	Marc Bombard	1993
AA	Chattanooga (Tenn.) Lookouts	Southern	83	60	.580	2nd (10)	Dave Miley	1988
#A	Winston-Salem (N.C.) Warthogs	Carolina	69	68	.504	3rd (8)	Mark Berry	1993
A	Charleston (W.Va.) Wheelers	South Atlantic	77	65	.542	6th (14)	Razor Shines	1990
#R	Billings (Mont.) Mustangs	Pioneer	49	20	.710	1st (8)	Donnie Scott	1974
#R	Princeton (W.Va.) Reds	Appalachian	31	32	.492	5th (10)	Brad Kelley	1991

*Finish in overall standings (No. of teams in league)   #Advanced level

ORGANIZATION LEADERS

MAJOR LEAGUERS

BATTING
*AVG	Barry Larkin	.319
R	Barry Larkin	98
H	Barry Larkin	158
TB	Reggie Sanders	280
2B	Reggie Sanders	36
3B	Two tied at	6
HR	Ron Gant	29
RBI	Reggie Sanders	99
BB	Ron Gant	74
SO	Reggie Sanders	122
SB	Barry Larkin	51

PITCHING
W	Pete Schourek	18
L	Two tied at	7
#ERA	Pete Schourek	3.22
G	Hector Carrasco	64
CG	David Wells	3
SV	Jeff Brantley	28
IP	Pete Schourek	190
BB	Hector Carrasco	46
SO	Pete Schourek	160

MORRIS FOSTOFF

Reggie Sanders. 99 RBIs

MINOR LEAGUERS

BATTING
*AVG	Thomas Scott, Billings	.352
R	Ruben Santana, Chattanooga	89
H	Ruben Santana, Chattanooga	163
TB	Ruben Santana, Chattanooga	239
2B	Dan Rohrmeier, Chattanooga/Ind.	34
3B	Two tied at	10
HR	Two tied at	20
RBI	Two tied at	79
BB	Nick Morrow, Charleston	77
SO	Nick Morrow, Charleston	123
SB	Terry Wright, Charleston	46

PITCHING
W	Two tied at	13
L	Clint Koppe, Charleston	13
#ERA	Chris Murphy, Princeton/W-S	1.83
G	Rusty Kilgo, Chattanooga/Indianapolis	56
CG	Cedric Allen, Charleston	5
SV	Rusty Kilgo, Chattanooga/Indianapolis	29
IP	Mike Ferry, Chattanooga/Indianapolis	172
BB	Chris Reed, Winston-Salem	68
SO	Tommy Kramer, Chattanooga	126

*Minimum 250 At-Bats   #Minimum 75 Innings

TOP 10 PROSPECTS

How the Reds Top 10 prospects, as judged by Baseball America prior to the 1995 season, fared in 1995:

LARRY KINKER

Pokey Reese

Player, Pos.	Club (Class—League)	AVG	AB	R	H	2B	3B	HR	RBI	SB
1. Pokey Reese, ss	Indianapolis (AAA—Amer. Assoc.)	.239	343	51	82	21	1	10	46	8
2. Pat Watkins, of	Winston-Salem (A—Carolina)	.206	107	14	22	3	1	4	13	1
	Chattanooga (AA—Southern)	.291	358	57	104	26	2	12	57	5
6. Chad Mottola, of	Chattanooga (AA—Southern)	.293	181	32	53	13	1	10	39	1
	Indianapolis (AAA—Amer. Assoc.)	.259	239	40	62	11	1	8	37	8
7. Aaron Boone, 3b	Winston-Salem (A—Carolina)	.261	395	61	103	19	1	14	50	11
	Chattanooga (AA—Southern)	.227	66	6	15	3	0	0	3	2
8. Decomba Conner, of	Princeton (R—Appalachian)	.125	16	2	2	2	0	0	5	2
	Charleston (A—South Atlantic)	.263	308	55	81	10	7	5	40	22
9. Tim Belk, 1b	Indianapolis (AAA—Amer. Assoc.)	.301	193	30	58	11	0	4	18	2
10. Steve Gibralter, of	Indianapolis (AAA—Amer. Assoc.)	.316	263	49	83	19	3	18	63	0

Player, Pos.	Club (Class—League)	W	L	ERA	G	SV	IP	H	BB	SO
3. *C.J. Nitkowski, lhp	Chattanooga (AA—Southern)	4	2	2.50	8	0	50	39	20	52
	Indianapolis (AAA—Amer. Assoc.)	0	2	5.20	6	0	28	28	10	21
	Cincinnati	1	3	6.12	9	0	32	41	15	18
	Detroit	1	4	7.09	11	0	39	53	20	13
4. Kevin Jarvis, rhp	Indianapolis (AAA—Amer. Assoc.)	4	2	4.45	10	0	61	62	18	37
	Cincinnati	3	4	5.70	19	0	79	91	32	33
5. Scott Sullivan, rhp	Indianapolis (AAA—Amer. Assoc.)	4	3	3.53	44	1	59	51	24	54
	Cincinnati	0	0	4.91	3	0	4	4	2	2

*Traded to Detroit

AMERICAN ASSOCIATION

BATTING	AVG	G	AB	R	H	2B	3B	HR	RBI	BB	SO	SB	CS	B	T	HT	WT	DOB	1st Yr	Resides
Anthony, Eric	.292	7	24	7	7	0	0	4	8	6	4	2	0	L	L	6-2	195	11-8-67	1986	Houston, Texas
Arias, Amador	.400	5	15	2	6	0	0	0	1	2	1	1	0	S	R	5-10	160	5-28-72	1990	Maracay, Venez.
Belk, Tim	.301	57	193	30	58	11	0	4	18	16	30	2	5	R	R	6-3	200	4-6-70	1992	Houston, Texas
Bess, Johnny	.000	2	5	0	0	0	0	0	0	0	2	0	0	S	R	6-1	190	4-6-70	1992	Grand Junction, Colo.
Briley, Greg	.233	46	146	17	34	8	0	3	17	22	34	9	2	L	R	5-8	180	5-24-65	1986	Greenville, N.C.
Brooks, Jerry	.283	90	325	41	92	19	2	14	52	22	38	3	1	R	R	6-0	195	3-23-67	1988	Syracuse, N.Y.
Brown, Chris	.000	3	7	0	0	0	0	0	0	1	0	0	0	R	R	6-2	218	8-15-61	1979	Los Angeles, Calif.
Denson, Drew	.277	107	357	59	99	21	0	18	69	34	68	1	0	R	R	6-5	220	11-16-65	1984	Cincinnati, Ohio
Dismuke, Jamie	.250	13	36	6	9	1	0	0	2	3	3	0	0	L	R	6-1	210	10-17-69	1989	Syracuse, N.Y.
Dorsett, Brian	.262	91	313	40	82	25	1	16	58	25	47	1	1	R	R	6-4	222	4-9-61	1983	Terre Haute, Ind.
Gibralter, Steve	.316	79	263	49	83	19	3	18	63	25	70	0	2	R	R	6-0	170	10-9-72	1990	Duncanville, Texas
Gordon, Keith	.264	89	265	36	70	14	1	6	38	15	94	3	4	R	R	6-1	205	1-22-69	1990	Olney, Md.
Greene, Willie	.243	91	325	57	79	12	2	19	45	38	67	3	3	L	R	5-11	184	9-23-71	1988	Haddock, Ga.
Hunter, Brian	.361	9	36	7	13	5	0	4	11	6	11	0	1	R	L	6-0	195	3-4-68	1987	Anaheim, Calif.
Knapp, Mike	.256	14	39	8	10	2	0	1	6	3	7	1	0	R	R	6-0	195	10-6-64	1986	Sacramento, Calif.
Kremblas, Frank	.160	27	75	7	12	2	0	0	3	12	25	4	2	R	R	5-11	180	10-25-66	1989	Carroll, Ohio
Magdaleno, Ricky	.125	4	8	1	1	0	0	1	1	0	3	0	0	R	R	6-1	170	7-6-74	1993	Baldwin Park, Calif.
McCarty, David	.336	37	140	31	47	10	1	8	32	15	30	0	0	R	L	6-5	207	11-23-69	1991	Houston, Texas
Mitchell, Keith	.244	70	213	40	52	11	2	11	36	40	40	4	4	R	R	5-10	180	8-6-69	1987	San Diego, Calif.
Morris, Hal	.400	2	5	2	2	0	0	0	1	1	0	0	0	L	L	6-4	215	4-9-65	1986	Union, Ky.
Mottola, Chad	.259	69	239	40	62	11	1	8	37	20	50	8	1	R	R	6-3	215	10-15-71	1992	Pembroke Pines, Fla.
Owens, Eric	.314	108	427	86	134	24	8	12	63	52	61	33	12	R	R	6-1	184	2-3-71	1992	Danville, Va.
Reese, Pokey	.239	89	343	51	82	21	1	10	46	36	81	8	5	R	R	6-0	160	6-10-73	1991	Columbia, S.C.
Rohrmeier, Dan	.176	10	34	5	6	3	1	0	3	0	4	0	0	R	R	6-0	185	9-27-65	1987	Woodridge, Ill.
Sellers, Rick	.263	5	19	3	5	1	0	3	7	1	3	0	0	R	R	6-0	210	2-22-67	1989	Remus, Mich.
Smith, Greg	.214	4	14	1	3	0	0	0	2	3	0	0	0	S	R	6-0	180	4-5-67	1985	Palm Springs, Calif.
2-team (59 N.O.)	.212	63	184	19	39	3	1	0	9	19	25	11	7							
Stillwell, Kurt	.264	100	341	50	90	14	3	7	30	45	51	4	3	S	R	5-11	185	6-4-65	1983	Poway, Calif.
Trafton, Todd	.000	5	5	0	0	0	0	0	0	0	2	0	0	R	R	6-2	210	3-16-64	1986	Elk Grove, Calif.
Wilson, Brandon	.167	4	12	3	2	0	0	0	2	1	0	0	0	R	R	6-1	175	2-26-69	1990	Owensboro, Ky.
2-team (27 Nashville)	.278	31	97	11	27	5	1	0	10	6	12	3	1							
Wilson, Nigel	.313	82	304	53	95	27	3	17	51	13	95	5	3	L	L	6-1	170	1-12-70	1988	Ajax, Ontario
Worthington, Craig	.318	81	277	48	88	19	0	9	41	31	51	1	1	R	R	6-0	200	4-17-65	1985	Anaheim, Calif.

PITCHING	W	L	ERA	G	GS	CG	SV	IP	H	R	ER	BB	SO	B	T	HT	WT	DOB	1st Yr	Resides
Beatty, Blaine	7	1	3.61	20	8	0	0	67	80	33	27	16	37	L	L	6-2	190	4-25-64	1986	Victoria, Texas
Belcher, Tim	0	0	1.80	2	2	0	0	10	6	2	2	1	8	R	R	6-3	220	10-19-61	1984	Mt. Gilead, Ohio
Buckley, Travis	10	9	4.70	23	18	3	0	132	141	80	69	33	85	R	R	6-4	208	6-15-70	1989	Overland Park, Kan.
Courtright, John	2	1	4.28	13	2	0	0	34	29	18	16	15	13	L	L	6-2	185	5-30-70	1991	Columbus, Ohio
Davis, Storm	0	0	3.38	4	0	0	0	5	4	2	2	3	4	R	R	6-4	225	12-26-61	1979	Cockeysville, Md.
Donnelly, Brendan	1	1	23.63	3	0	0	0	3	7	8	7	2	1	R	R	6-3	200	7-4-71	1992	Albuquerque, N.M.
Drahman, Brian	0	0	0.00	2	0	0	0	3	3	0	0	1	3	R	R	6-3	231	11-7-66	1986	Ft. Lauderdale, Fla.
2-team (22 Okla. City)	2	2	2.83	24	0	0	4	35	39	11	11	15	22							
Ferry, Mike	1	2	5.19	3	3	0	0	17	21	15	10	3	3	R	R	6-3	195	7-26-69	1990	Auburn, Ala.
Grott, Matt	7	3	4.24	25	18	2	2	115	99	61	54	24	74	L	L	6-1	205	12-5-67	1989	Glendale, Ariz.
Hurst, James	0	0	5.40	3	0	0	1	3	2	2	2	1	1	L	L	6-0	165	6-1-67	1990	Sebring, Fla.
2-team (28 Okla. City)	1	5	7.20	31	7	0	5	50	73	42	40	26	43							
Jackson, Mike	0	0	0.00	2	1	0	0	2	0	0	0	0	1	R	R	6-2	223	12-22-64	1984	Spring, Texas
Jarvis, Kevin	4	2	4.45	10	10	2	0	61	62	33	30	18	37	L	R	6-2	200	8-1-69	1991	Lexington, Ky.
Jean, Domingo	1	0	0.00	2	0	0	0	2	1	0	0	1	0	R	R	6-2	175	1-9-69	1990	San Pedro de Macoris, D.R.
Kilgo, Rusty	0	0	4.50	2	0	0	0	2	4	2	1	1	1	L	L	6-0	175	8-9-66	1989	Houston, Texas
Mathile, Mike	0	2	2.51	14	3	0	0	29	22	10	8	6	16	R	R	6-4	220	11-24-68	1990	Brookville, Ohio
Moore, Marcus	1	0	4.97	7	1	0	1	13	13	8	7	14	6	S	R	6-5	204	11-2-70	1989	Oakland, Calif.
Nitkowski, C.J.	0	2	5.20	6	6	0	0	28	28	16	16	10	21	L	L	6-2	185	3-9-73	1994	Milford, Pa.
Pennington, Brad	0	0	10.29	11	2	0	0	14	17	19	16	21	15	L	L	6-6	215	4-14-69	1989	Salem, Ind.
Pugh, Tim	2	4	4.68	6	6	1	0	42	42	24	22	14	20	R	R	6-6	225	1-26-67	1989	Florence, Ky.
Reed, Rick	11	4	3.33	22	21	3	0	135	127	60	50	10	91	R	R	6-0	200	8-16-64	1986	Huntington, W.Va.
Remlinger, Mike	5	3	4.05	41	1	0	0	47	40	24	21	32	58	L	L	6-0	195	3-23-66	1987	Plymouth, Mass.
Roper, John	2	5	4.97	8	8	0	0	42	47	26	23	16	23	R	R	6-0	175	11-21-71	1990	Raeford, N.C.
Ruffin, Johnny	3	1	2.90	36	1	0	0	50	27	19	16	37	58	R	R	6-3	190	7-29-71	1988	Butler, Ala.
Salkeld, Roger	12	4	4.22	20	20	1	0	119	96	60	56	57	86	R	R	6-5	215	3-6-71	1989	Saugus, Calif.
Sauveur, Rich	5	2	2.05	52	0	0	15	57	43	17	13	18	47	L	L	6-4	170	11-23-63	1983	Falls Church, Va.
Scudder, Scott	1	4	5.17	7	7	0	0	38	43	24	22	9	13	R	R	6-2	190	2-14-68	1986	Austin, Texas
Service, Scott	4	1	2.18	36	0	0	18	41	33	13	10	15	48	R	R	6-6	226	2-26-67	1986	Cincinnati, Ohio
Sullivan, Scott	4	3	3.53	44	0	0	1	59	51	31	23	24	54	R	R	6-3	210	3-13-71	1993	Carrollton, Ala.
Vasquez, Marcos	0	0	.00	2	0	0	1	4	1	0	0	0	1	R	R	5-10	170	11-5-68	1987	Rio Piedras, P.R.
Viola, Frank	3	3	4.09	6	6	0	0	33	33	17	15	6	25	L	L	6-4	209	4-19-60	1981	Longwood, Fla.
Warren, Brian	2	1	1.61	41	0	0	2	56	56	18	10	9	35	R	R	6-1	165	4-26-67	1990	Bridgewater, Mass.

FIELDING

Catcher	PCT	G	PO	A	E	DP	PB
Brooks	.986	52	323	22	5	1	12
Dorsett	.982	87	506	34	10	4	5
Knapp	1.000	13	60	3	0	0	1
Sellers	1.000	5	19	4	0	0	2

First Base	PCT	G	PO	A	E	DP
Anthony	.909	2	9	1	1	1
Belk	.989	50	428	20	5	24
Brooks	1.000	7	64	5	0	5
Denson	.983	15	108	9	2	19
Dismuke	.981	11	91	10	2	9
Hunter	1.000	4	35	1	0	0
McCarty	.994	37	335	14	2	27
Morris	1.000	2	13	2	0	0
Worthington	.996	30	217	26	1	15

Second Base	PCT	G	PO	A	E	DP
Arias	.938	5	10	20	2	7
Kremblas	.966	7	13	15	1	3
Owens	.967	105	219	274	17	63
Smith	.950	4	10	9	1	3
Stillwell	.980	28	39	61	2	7
B. Wilson	1.000	1	1	1	0	0

Third Base	PCT	G	PO	A	E	DP
Brooks	1.000	2	1	7	0	1
Brown	1.000	2	1	2	0	0
Greene	.952	62	41	118	8	6
Kremblas	.900	12	3	24	3	4
Magdaleno	.000	1	0	0	0	0
Stillwell	.904	24	17	49	7	6
Worthington	.947	52	28	114	8	11

Shortstop	PCT	G	PO	A	E	DP
Greene	.933	14	14	42	4	5
Magdaleno	.833	3	1	4	1	.0
Reese	.935	88	131	258	27	37
Stillwell	.960	44	56	113	7	27
B. Wilson	.818	3	3	6	2	0

Outfield	PCT	G	PO	A	E	DP
Anthony	1.000	2	5	0	0	0
Belk	1.000	7	12	1	0	0
Bess	1.000	1	0	0	0	0
Briley	.972	44	69	1	2	0
Brooks	.932	32	39	2	3	0
Gibralter	.977	78	207	2	5	0
Gordon	.988	80	155	3	2	2
Greene	1.000	3	5	0	0	0

	PCT	G	PO	A	E	DP		PCT	G	PO	A	E	DP		PCT	G	PO	A	E	DP
Hunter	.889	7	7	1	1	0	Mitchell	.979	65	136	4	3	1	Rohrmeier	1.000	8	10	0	0	0
Kremblas	1.000	2	6	0	0	0	Mottola	.976	69	151	11	4	2	N. Wilson	.958	69	111	4	5	1

CHATTANOOGA   AA

SOUTHERN LEAGUE

BATTING	AVG	G	AB	R	H	2B	3B	HR	RBI	BB	SO	SB	CS	B	T	HT	WT	DOB	1st Yr	Resides
Arias, Amador	.222	71	108	17	24	3	1	0	4	6	15	3	2	S	R	5-10	160	5-28-72	1990	Maracay, Venez.
Boone, Aaron	.227	23	66	6	15	3	0	0	3	5	12	2	0	R	R	6-2	190	3-9-73	1994	Villa Park, Calif.
Brown, Adam	.266	77	233	24	62	14	2	5	32	24	36	0	1	L	R	6-0	203	8-10-66	1986	Monroe, Ga.
Buckley, Troy	.241	10	29	1	7	0	0	0	0	6	6	0	0	R	R	6-4	215	3-3-68	1990	Campbell, Calif.
Dismuke, Jamie	.285	99	347	56	99	11	0	20	69	44	45	0	0	L	R	6-1	210	10-17-69	1989	Syracuse, N.Y.
Hyzdu, Adam	.263	102	312	55	82	14	1	13	48	45	56	3	2	R	R	6-2	210	12-6-71	1990	Mesa, Ariz.
Jenkins, Dee	.059	8	17	1	1	1	0	0	1	3	7	1	1	R	R	5-9	175	6-28-73	1991	Columbia, S.C.
Koelling, Brian	.296	107	432	71	128	21	7	3	44	40	63	30	12	R	R	6-1	185	6-11-69	1991	Cleveland, Ohio
Kopriva, Dan	.281	51	121	14	34	8	0	1	11	11	14	1	1	R	R	5-11	190	11-6-69	1992	Traer, Iowa
Kremblas, Cleveland	.149	19	67	8	10	2	0	1	6	7	10	1	1	R	R	5-11	180	10-25-66	1989	Carroll, Ohio
Ladell, Cleveland	.292	135	517	76	151	28	7	5	43	39	88	28	15	R	R	5-11	170	9-19-70	1992	Dallas, Texas
Magdaleno, Ricky	.175	11	40	2	7	2	0	1	2	4	13	0	0	R	R	6-1	170	7-6-74	1993	Baldwin Park, Calif.
Merchant, Mark	.208	25	53	4	11	0	0	1	6	7	15	0	0	S	R	6-2	185	1-23-69	1987	Chuluota, Fla.
Mota, Domingo	.000	5	6	0	0	0	0	0	0	0	1	0	0	R	R	5-8	180	8-4-69	1990	La Crescenta, Calif.
Mottola, Chad	.293	51	181	32	53	13	1	10	39	13	32	1	2	R	R	6-3	215	10-15-71	1992	Pembroke Pines, Fla.
Rohrmeier, Dan	.326	118	426	77	139	31	0	17	76	41	63	0	1	R	R	6-0	185	9-27-65	1987	Woodridge, Ill.
Rumfield, Toby	.264	92	273	32	72	12	1	8	53	26	47	0	3	R	R	6-3	190	9-4-72	1991	Belton, Texas
Sanders, Deion	.571	2	7	1	4	0	0	1	2	0	1	1	0	L	L	6-1	195	8-9-67	1988	Alpharetta, Ga.
Santana, Ruben	.293	142	556	89	163	23	10	11	79	50	77	2	5	R	R	6-2	175	3-7-70	1990	Santo Domingo, D.R.
Sellers, Rick	.238	89	281	40	67	13	3	8	41	45	66	2	1	R	R	6-0	210	2-22-67	1989	Remus, Mich.
Vasquez, Chris	.400	7	15	3	6	1	0	1	1	2	3	0	0	L	R	5-11	170	10-23-71	1990	Saugus, Calif.
Watkins, Pat	.291	105	358	57	104	26	2	12	57	33	53	5	5	R	R	6-2	185	9-2-72	1993	Garner, N.C.
Wilson, Brandon	.328	75	308	56	101	29	1	9	50	28	52	12	6	R	R	6-1	175	2-26-69	1990	Owensboro, Ky.

PITCHING	W	L	ERA	G	GS	CG	SV	IP	H	R	ER	BB	SO	B	T	HT	WT	DOB	1st Yr	Resides
Beatty, Blaine	3	2	3.46	8	8	1	0	52	60	22	20	17	34	L	L	6-2	190	4-25-64	1986	Victoria, Texas
Bene, Bill	0	0	13.50	4	0	0	0	7	6	6	9	4		R	R	6-4	205	11-21-67	1988	Montebello, Calif.
Brumley, Duff	5	1	1.68	25	0	0	1	48	31	11	9	16	60	R	R	6-4	195	8-25-70	1990	Cleveland, Tenn.
Buckley, Travis	1	2	7.53	3	3	0	0	14	21	12	12	5	10	R	R	6-4	208	6-15-70	1989	Overland Park, Kan.
Burgos, John	3	5	2.78	44	3	0	0	100	95	42	31	19	82	L	L	5-11	170	8-2-67	1986	Humacao, P.R.
Connors, Chad	0	1	2.79	10	0	0	0	10	9	3	3	9	15	R	R	6-0	200	10-18-71	1993	Dayton, Ohio
Cullop, Nick	0	0	7.90	8	0	0	0	14	15	13	12	7	8	R	R	6-7	180	10-4-71	1992	Kingsport, Tenn.
Farmer, Howard	0	1	6.75	1	1	0	0	4	5	6	3	1	2	R	R	6-2	184	1-18-66	1987	Gary, Ind.
Ferry, Mike	9	5	3.77	24	24	1	0	155	191	75	65	23	74	R	R	6-3	195	7-26-69	1990	Auburn, Ala.
Fox, Chad	4	5	5.06	20	17	0	0	80	76	49	45	52	56	R	R	6-2	180	9-3-70	1992	Houston, Texas
Jackson, Mike	0	0	0.00	3	2	0	0	3	2	0	0	0	2	R	R	6-2	223	12-22-64	1984	Spring, Texas
Kilgo, Rusty	8	2	2.32	54	0	0	29	66	67	21	17	13	61	L	L	6-0	175	8-9-66	1989	Houston, Texas
Kramer, Tommy	12	1	3.33	21	18	2	0	127	117	54	47	28	126	S	R	6-0	205	1-9-68	1987	St. Bernard, Ohio
Luebbers, Larry	10	6	4.65	28	21	0	0	118	112	71	61	59	87	R	R	6-6	190	10-11-69	1990	Florence, Ky.
Moore, Marcus	6	1	4.98	36	0	0	2	43	31	24	24	34	57	S	R	6-5	204	11-2-70	1989	Oakland, Calif.
Nitkowski, C.J.	4	2	2.50	8	8	0	0	50	39	20	14	20	52	L	L	6-2	185	3-9-73	1994	Milford, Pa.
Nix, James	3	5	3.20	40	5	0	2	84	84	43	30		71	R	R	5-11	175	9-6-70	1992	Burton, Texas
Pickett, Ricky	4	5	3.28	40	0	0	9	47	22	20	17	44	69	L	L	6-0	185	1-19-70	1992	Fort Worth, Texas
Roper, John	0	0	1.00	3	3	0	0	9	5	1	1	1	6	R	R	6-0	175	11-21-71	1990	Raeford, N.C.
Smith, Mike	0	2	17.47	3	2	0	0	6	11	13	11	5	5	R	R	6-3	180	10-31-63	1984	San Antonio, Texas
Tranbarger, Mark	3	1	1.95	48	0	0	0	55	50	15	12	20	46	L	L	6-2	205	9-17-69	1991	Cincinnati, Ohio
Tuttle, Dave	1	6	7.01	8	7	0	0	35	40	29	27	21	20	R	R	6-3	190	9-29-69	1992	Los Gatos, Calif.
VanRyn, Ben	0	1	9.24	5	3	0	0	13	22	18	13	6	6	L	L	6-5	195	8-9-71	1990	Kendallville, Ind.
Vasquez, Marcos	7	6	3.68	26	18	0	1	120	125	63	49	46	80	R	R	5-10	170	11-5-68	1987	Rio Piedras, P.R.

FIELDING

Catcher	PCT	G	PO	A	E	DP	PB
Brown	.992	65	440	35	4	7	7
Buckley	1.000	8	61	3	0	0	1
Rumfield	1.000	2	2	0	0	0	0
Sellers	.987	88	567	55	8	7	11

First Base	PCT	G	PO	A	E	DP
Brown	.000	1	0	0	0	0
Dismuke	.989	95	647	69	8	64
Kopriva	1.000	3	4	0	0	0
Merchant	1.000	1	1	0	0	0
Rohrmeier	.969	7	29	2	1	4
Rumfield	.983	55	353	53	7	38
Santana	1.000	1	8	4	0	0

Second Base	PCT	G	PO	A	E	DP
Arias	.966	40	40	45	3	10

	PCT	G	PO	A	E	DP
Jenkins	.917	7	11	11	2	3
Koelling	.980	56	132	117	5	23
Kremblas	.956	19	44	42	4	12
Mota	.000	1	0	0	0	0
Santana	.945	50	76	114	11	21

Third Base	PCT	G	PO	A	E	DP
Boone	.875	22	14	28	6	4
Kopriva	.848	33	19	48	12	2
Rohrmeier	.889	12	14	10	3	2
Santana	.929	98	64	160	17	14

Shortstop	PCT	G	PO	A	E	DP
Arias	.871	9	8	19	4	3
Koelling	.932	51	87	117	15	28
Magdaleno	.839	11	20	32	10	6

	PCT	G	PO	A	E	DP
Wilson	.951	75	97	195	15	37

Outfield	PCT	G	PO	A	E	DP
Hyzdu	.995	99	182	4	1	0
Ladell	.985	135	312	6	5	2
Merchant	1.000	4	1	0	0	0
Mota	.000	1	0	0	0	0
Mottola	.974	50	106	6	3	2
Rohrmeier	1.000	56	103	7	0	2
Rumfield	1.000	12	12	0	0	0
Sanders	1.000	1	3	1	0	1
Santana	1.000	1	2	0	0	0
C. Vasquez	1.000	3	5	0	0	0
Watkins	.960	104	185	8	8	1

WINSTON-SALEM   A

CAROLINA LEAGUE

BATTING	AVG	G	AB	R	H	2B	3B	HR	RBI	BB	SO	SB	CS	B	T	HT	WT	DOB	1st Yr	Resides
Akers, Chad	.260	103	361	41	94	14	1	2	29	27	49	25	8	R	R	5-8	160	5-30-72	1993	Lake, W.Va.
Bako, Paul	.285	82	249	29	71	11	2	7	27	42	66	3	1	L	R	6-2	205	6-20-72	1993	Lafayette, La.
Bess, Johnny	.187	88	246	35	46	10	2	4	21	30	83	12	4	S	R	6-1	190	4-6-70	1992	Grand Junction, Colo.
Boone, Aaron	.261	108	395	61	103	19	1	14	50	43	77	11	7	R	R	6-2	190	3-9-73	1994	Villa Park, Calif.
Broach, Donald	.261	117	460	74	120	23	4	8	34	50	73	16	14	R	R	6-0	185	7-18-71	1993	Cincinnati, Ohio
Brown, Ray	.265	122	445	63	118	26	0	19	77	52	85	3	2	L	R	6-2	205	7-30-72	1994	Redding, Calif.
Clyburn, Danny	.260	59	227	27	59	10	2	11	41	13	59	2	4	R	R	6-3	217	4-6-74	1992	Lancaster, S.C.

BATTING	AVG	G	AB	R	H	2B	3B	HR	RBI	BB	SO	SB	CS	B	T	HT	WT	DOB	1st Yr	Resides
Cradle, Cobi	.183	23	71	14	13	2	0	0	2	21	8	9	2	L	L	5-11	165	7-7-71	1993	Cerritos, Calif.
Frye, Dan	.182	7	11	3	2	1	0	1	2	5	4	0	0	R	R	6-0	180	2-22-70	1992	Logansport, Ind.
Gann, Steve	.244	15	41	5	10	2	0	0	5	2	5	0	1	R	R	6-1	180	6-19-70	1993	Houston, Texas
Garcia, Guillermo	.237	78	245	26	58	10	2	3	29	28	32	2	2	R	R	6-3	190	4-4-72	1990	Santo Domingo, D.R.
Jenkins, Dee	.289	50	149	25	43	7	1	4	14	18	25	0	6	L	R	5-9	175	6-28-73	1991	Columbia, S.C.
Kopriva, Dan	.345	17	58	4	20	4	1	0	5	4	6	1	0	R	R	5-11	190	11-6-69	1992	Traer, Iowa
Larkin, Stephen	.220	13	50	2	11	1	0	0	4	3	12	2	2	L	L	6-0	190	7-24-73	1994	Cincinnati, Ohio
Lofton, James	.220	38	123	15	27	5	1	0	14	8	22	1	4	S	R	5-9	170	3-6-74	1993	Los Angeles, Calif.
Magdaleno, Ricky	.223	91	309	30	69	13	1	7	40	15	69	3	1	R	R	6-1	170	7-6-74	1993	Baldwin Park, Calif.
Meggers, Mike	.246	76	272	45	67	18	1	20	54	32	69	7	3	R	R	6-2	200	7-6-70	1992	Sacramento, Calif.
Oyas, Danny	.214	50	173	19	37	6	0	8	31	10	45	1	1	R	R	6-0	180	3-19-73	1992	San Bernardino, Calif.
Robertson, Robbie	.216	91	278	34	60	11	0	8	32	22	77	2	4	L	L	6-4	190	9-11-71	1993	Mobile, Ala.
Sexton, Chris	.400	4	15	3	6	0	0	1	5	4	0	0	0	R	R	5-11	180	8-3-71	1993	Cincinnati, Ohio
Thomas, Rod	.222	20	54	7	12	2	0	2	7	8	22	2	3	R	R	6-1	195	8-22-73	1991	Reddick, Fla.
Watkins, Pat	.206	27	107	14	22	3	1	4	13	10	24	1	0	R	R	6-2	185	9-2-72	1993	Garner, N.C.
White, Jimmy	.261	31	111	15	29	5	1	7	18	4	33	1	1	R	R	6-1	170	12-1-72	1990	Tampa, Fla.
Wilson, Brian	.224	20	58	10	13	1	0	2	8	7	16	1	2	R	R	6-1	185	7-14-72	1994	Albany, Texas

GAMES BY POSITION: C—Bako 78, Bess 20, Garcia 54. **1B**—Bess 19, Brown 100, Garcia 10, Larkin 3, Robertson 12. **2B**—Akers 75, Gann 1, Jenkins 31, Lofton 36. **3B**—Boone 108, Frye 5, Gann 7, Garcia 6, Kopriva 16. **SS**—Akers 24, Bess 1, Frye 1, Gann 3, Garcia 1, Magdaleno 91, Sexton 4, Wilson 20. **OF**—Bess 21, Broach 116, Clyburn 49, Cradle 21, Larkin 10, Meggers 67, Oyas 42, Robertson 54, Thomas 18, Watkins 26.

PITCHING	W	L	ERA	G	GS	CG	SV	IP	H	R	ER	BB	SO	B	T	HT	WT	DOB	1st Yr	Resides
Connors, Chad	2	2	6.86	16	0	0	2	20	28	16	15	11	13	R	R	6-0	200	10-18-71	1993	Dayton, Ohio
Cullop, Glen	0	1	0.90	6	0	0	0	10	7	1	1	5	4	R	R	6-0	180	10-4-71	1992	Kingsport, Tenn.
Donnelly, Brendan	1	2	1.02	23	0	0	2	35	20	6	4	14	32	R	R	6-3	200	7-4-71	1992	Albuquerque, N.M.
Doyle, Tom	3	1	3.45	21	3	0	1	31	32	18	12	12	22	L	L	6-3	205	1-20-70	1988	Redondo Beach, Calif.
Etler, Todd	6	12	3.69	24	23	3	0	154	148	71	63	49	78	R	R	6-0	205	4-18-74	1992	Villa Hills, Ky.
Giron, Emiliano	2	0	2.30	17	0	0	0	27	23	15	7	10	29	R	R	6-2	165	1-5-72	1990	Santo Domingo, D.R.
Hagan, Danny	1	0	1.80	1	1	0	0	5	5	1	1	4	2	R	L	6-2	205	6-14-72	1993	Louisville, Ky.
Harvell, Pete	0	1	12.60	4	0	0	0	5	9	7	7	4	1	L	L	6-2	190	10-14-71	1993	San Jose, Calif.
Jesperson, Bob	2	1	4.26	5	0	0	0	6	5	3	3	4	1	R	R	6-1	195	5-25-69	1991	White Lake, Wisc.
Kummerfeldt, Jason	4	6	3.48	37	3	0	3	78	78	37	30	19	51	R	R	6-4	220	12-17-69	1992	Billings, Mon.
Lyons, Curt	9	9	2.98	26	26	0	0	160	139	66	53	67	122	R	R	6-5	228	10-17-74	1992	Richmond, Ky.
Maberry, Louis	1	0	4.34	20	0	0	0	37	40	20	18	7	19	R	R	5-11	180	12-6-70	1992	Abilene, Texas
Magre, Pete	1	1	3.09	17	0	0	2	32	39	14	11	15	27	R	R	6-1	180	10-31-70	1993	Cameron, Texas
McKenzie, Scott	3	4	2.75	49	0	0	20	72	42	27	22	30	55	R	R	6-0	185	9-30-70	1993	Arlington, Texas
Murphy, Chris	2	1	2.70	4	3	0	0	20	13	7	6	5	22	L	L	6-8	235	2-16-72	1995	Cincinnati, Ohio
Priest, Eddie	5	5	3.63	12	12	1	0	67	60	32	27	22	60	R	L	6-1	200	4-8-74	1994	Horton, Ala.
Reed, Chris	10	7	3.32	24	24	3	0	149	116	63	55	68	104	R	R	6-3	206	8-25-73	1991	Anaheim, Calif.
Robbins, Jason	9	6	3.06	23	23	3	0	141	113	62	48	42	106	R	R	6-3	195	12-20-72	1993	South Bend, Ind.
Ruyak, Todd	5	6	3.99	34	9	0	0	86	99	44	38	20	48	L	L	6-3	215	9-18-70	1992	Hamilton Square, N.J.
Tuttle, Dave	3	3	3.18	10	10	2	0	62	49	28	22	19	54	R	R	6-3	190	9-29-69	1992	Los Gatos, Calif.

CHARLESTON, W.Va.   A

SOUTH ATLANTIC LEAGUE

BATTING	AVG	G	AB	R	H	2B	3B	HR	RBI	BB	SO	SB	CS	B	T	HT	WT	DOB	1st Yr	Resides
Allen, Marlon	.270	117	396	47	107	26	0	9	76	42	108	2	2	R	R	6-6	228	3-28-73	1994	Columbus, Ga.
Bragga, Matt	.248	88	258	35	64	11	5	0	26	28	62	6	5	L	R	6-1	190	7-20-72	1994	Jefferson, Ohio
Brown, Ray	.118	6	17	3	2	1	0	0	0	4	3	0	0	L	R	6-2	205	7-30-72	1994	Redding, Calif.
Carvajal, Jhonny	.263	135	486	78	128	18	5	0	42	58	77	44	19	R	R	5-10	165	7-24-74	1993	Barcelona, Venez.
Conner, Decomba	.263	91	308	55	81	10	7	5	40	39	77	22	5	R	R	5-10	184	7-17-73	1994	Mooresville, N.C.
Eddie, Steve	.275	115	331	45	91	16	3	6	47	24	46	10	3	R	R	6-1	185	1-6-71	1993	Storm Lake, Iowa
Fussell, Denny	.250	20	44	4	11	2	0	0	7	4	10	1	0	L	L	6-1	190	5-11-71	1992	San Antonio, Texas
Gann, Steve	.208	15	48	3	10	1	0	0	4	6	7	1	1	R	R	6-1	180	6-19-70	1993	Houston, Texas
Hampton, Mike	.245	96	302	46	74	16	3	1	32	53	70	17	4	R	R	6-2	195	1-17-72	1994	Colorado Springs, Colo.
Herider, Jeremy	.133	8	15	2	2	0	0	0	2	6	0	0	0	S	R	5-10	180	4-9-72	1995	Lancaster, Calif.
Jenkins, Dee	.244	31	86	14	21	1	1	0	5	15	19	5	0	L	R	5-9	175	6-28-73	1991	Columbia, S.C.
Lofton, James	.208	65	192	20	40	10	1	0	14	18	43	8	5	S	R	5-9	170	3-6-74	1993	Los Angeles, Calif.
Morrow, Nick	.251	139	467	67	117	28	9	4	54	77	123	41	17	R	R	5-11	180	4-17-72	1994	Lexington, N.C.
Ordaz, Luis	.231	112	359	43	83	14	7	2	42	13	47	12	5	R	R	5-11	170	8-12-75	1993	Maracaibo, Venez.
Preston, Doyle	.125	7	16	1	2	1	0	0	2	4	5	0	2	L	R	6-3	195	2-9-73	1994	Saltillo, Texas
Sanders, Rod	.204	81	152	22	31	7	2	1	11	12	45	4	8	R	R	5-9	175	9-27-73	1992	Florence, S.C.
Sharp, Scott	.211	55	161	7	34	2	2	0	16	7	63	1	2	R	R	6-2	200	10-16-72	1993	Sykesville, Md.
Thomas, Rod	.146	29	82	8	12	3	0	1	6	7	25	3	0	R	R	6-1	195	8-22-73	1991	Reddick, Fla.
Towle, Justin	.268	107	343	54	92	22	2	8	60	44	95	3	6	R	R	6-3	210	2-21-74	1992	Seattle, Wash.
White, Jimmy	.169	20	65	7	11	3	1	1	8	6	27	1	1	L	R	6-1	170	12-1-72	1990	Tampa, Fla.
Wilson, Brian	.308	5	13	3	4	1	0	0	1	3	0	0	0	R	R	6-1	185	7-14-72	1994	Albany, Texas
Wright, Terry	.283	125	410	68	116	13	10	2	56	50	43	46	16	L	L	5-11	175	11-1-70	1994	Ellenboro, N.C.

GAMES BY POSITION: C—Eddie 2, Sharp 53, Towle 100. **1B**—Allen 64, Bragga 26, Brown 2, Eddie 76, Fussell 1, Towle 1. **2B**—Carvajal 106, Eddie 4, Herider 1, Jenkins 24, Lofton 22. **3B**—Eddie 31, Gann 14, Hampton 94, Lofton 9, Preston 7. **SS**—Carvajal 35, Eddie 2, Herider 5, Ordaz 111, Wilson 5. **OF**—Bragga 24, Carvajal 1, Conner 90, Eddie 10, Lofton 20, Morrow 138, Sanders 62, Thomas 18, Wright 115.

PITCHING	W	L	ERA	G	GS	CG	SV	IP	H	R	ER	BB	SO	B	T	HT	WT	DOB	1st Yr	Resides
Allen, Cedric	13	7	2.85	27	27	5	0	170	143	64	54	46	108	L	L	5-10	183	1-13-72	1994	Belton, Texas
Callahan, Damon	2	1	6.12	6	6	0	0	25	33	22	17	14	17	R	R	6-4	190	12-10-75	1994	Cleveland, Tenn.
Caruthers, Clayton	11	7	3.70	27	27	0	0	139	149	67	57	50	105	S	R	6-2	200	11-20-72	1994	N. Richland Hills, Texas
Donnelly, Brendan	1	1	1.19	24	0	0	12	30	14	4	4	7	33	R	R	6-3	200	7-4-71	1992	Albuquerque, N.M.
Doyle, Tom	6	4	4.35	14	12	1	0	62	57	34	30	30	66	L	L	6-3	205	1-20-70	1988	Redondo Beach, Calif.
Franklin, Joel	3	3	4.97	24	1	0	2	51	49	28	28	22	58	S	R	6-3	200	4-18-73	1993	Coronado, Calif.
Giron, Emiliano	0	0	0.94	30	0	0	20	29	12	3	3	8	39	R	R	6-2	165	1-5-72	1990	Santo Domingo, D.R.
Harvell, Pete	0	0	2.93	27	0	0	0	28	25	11	9	10	17	L	L	6-2	190	10-14-71	1993	San Jose, Calif.
Koppe, Clint	7	13	3.37	30	22	0	0	158	144	66	59	47	119	R	R	6-4	220	8-14-73	1993	Lake Jackson, Texas
Lott, Brian	8	7	3.46	28	20	0	1	138	155	56	53	33	96	R	R	6-0	200	5-15-72	1994	Cleveland, Ohio
Maberry, Louis	0	1	0.00	4	0	0	0	5	2	1	0	3	5	R	R	5-11	180	12-6-70	1992	Abilene, Texas
Magre, Pete	2	1	5.08	21	0	0	0	28	34	16	16	8	19	R	R	6-1	180	10-31-70	1993	Cameron, Texas

PITCHING	W	L	ERA	G	GS	CG	SV	IP	H	R	ER	BB	SO	B	T	HT	WT	DOB	1st Yr	Resides
Nieto, Tony	3	4	3.44	13	8	2	0	55	55	37	21	21	35	S	R	6-1	170	4-19-73	1994	Monterey Park, Calif.
Runyan, Paul	6	2	4.13	15	5	0	0	52	56	29	24	17	28	R	R	6-2	200	8-5-71	1994	San Antonio, Texas
Smith, Justin	4	5	3.61	44	0	0	1	62	66	28	25	24	43	R	R	6-0	195	2-7-72	1994	Eustis, Fla.
Solomon, David	1	2	3.40	43	0	0	6	40	38	19	15	23	29	R	L	5-10	185	9-30-71	1994	Saginaw, Mich.
Tomko, Brett	4	2	1.84	9	7	0	0	49	41	12	10	9	46	R	R	6-4	205	4-7-73	1995	Tampa, Fla.
Tweedlie, Brad	2	4	6.16	19	7	0	0	50	46	36	34	34	40	R	R	6-2	215	12-9-71	1993	Enfield, Conn.
Vejil, Aaron	2	0	0.00	6	0	0	0	3	2	0	0	3	5	R	L	6-0	178	2-11-75	1994	Sante Fe, N.M.
Weiss, Marc	1	0	5.52	11	0	0	0	15	23	10	9	13	12	R	R	6-4	205	8-3-73	1994	Los Angeles, Calif.
Wilkerson, Steven	1	1	5.49	16	0	0	0	20	21	13	12	18	15	R	R	6-2	200	11-8-72	1993	Farmington, N.M.

PRINCETON   R

APPALACHIAN LEAGUE

BATTING	AVG	G	AB	R	H	2B	3B	HR	RBI	BB	SO	SB	CS	B	T	HT	WT	DOB	1st Yr	Resides
Boyette, Tony	.293	61	222	41	65	15	1	10	49	21	41	2	0	R	R	6-0	200	12-7-75	1994	Alachua, Fla.
Bracho, Darwin	.207	31	82	5	17	5	0	0	7	4	16	0	2	S	R	5-10	175	4-10-75	1995	Maracaibo, Venez.
Concepcion, David	.236	60	203	44	48	10	2	6	24	42	44	10	0	S	R	5-10	175	4-28-75	1995	Miami, Fla.
Conner, Decomba	.125	6	16	2	2	2	0	0	5	3	3	2	0	R	R	5-10	184	7-17-73	1994	Mooresville, N.C.
Davis, James	.276	58	225	40	62	10	4	3	29	14	33	8	0	R	R	6-4	205	4-14-73	1995	Franklin, Ky.
Ennis, Wayne	.048	10	21	4	1	0	0	0	2	0	8	0	0	R	R	6-6	190	9-7-76	1994	Raleigh, N.C.
Guthrie, David	.204	55	181	28	37	11	0	0	13	18	41	7	1	S	R	6-2	185	5-21-74	1995	Birmingham, Ala.
Hall, Darran	.120	9	25	3	3	0	0	0	1	5	10	1	2	L	L	5-10	160	9-8-75	1993	San Diego, Calif.
Herrera, Jesus	.242	46	149	18	36	8	0	1	9	7	38	6	5	S	R	6-2	160	8-25-76	1995	Maracaibo, Venez.
Ingram, Darron	.275	60	233	37	64	6	3	14	53	11	78	3	1	R	R	6-3	210	6-7-76	1994	Lexington, Ky.
Mapp, Eric	.224	61	210	32	47	11	0	5	23	18	58	10	1	R	R	6-2	185	11-10-77	1995	Douglas, Ariz.
Mason, Lamont	.167	26	78	11	13	3	1	0	3	16	21	6	4	R	R	5-9	169	7-10-72	1995	Lexington, Ky.
Mepri, Sal	.200	6	5	0	1	0	0	0	0	0	3	0	0	R	R	6-1	185	9-18-76	1994	Santo Domingo, D.R.
Patellis, Anthony	.253	46	166	21	42	7	1	11	32	11	58	4	2	R	R	5-10	190	3-1-74	1995	Campbell, Ohio
Pennyfeather, William	.000	1	3	0	0	0	0	0	0	0	1	0	0	R	R	6-2	215	5-25-68	1988	Perth Amboy, N.J.
Salano, Manuel	.216	30	74	12	16	4	0	1	14	7	20	2	2	R	R	5-11	172	5-17-78	1995	Villa Mella, D.R.
Smalley, Jevon	.258	39	97	17	25	5	1	2	14	16	31	3	2	L	R	6-2	230	3-14-73	1995	Upper Sandusky, Ohio
Terry, Tony	.170	47	106	15	18	3	0	0	8	17	40	7	4	S	R	6-1	185	8-2-75	1994	Abbeville, S.C.

GAMES BY POSITION: C—Boyette 12, Bracho 18, Davis 40, Mepri 5. **1B**—Boyette 39, Davis 4, Ennis 8, Smalley 20. **2B**—Bracho 6, Concepcion 36, Guthrie 4, Mason 25. **3B**—Concepcion 20, Guthrie 8, Patellis 41. **SS**—Guthrie 48, Herrera 1, Salano 27. **OF**—Bracho 3, Conner 6, Hall 9, Herrera 37, Ingram 57, Mapp 61, Pennyfeather 1, Terry 36.

PITCHING	W	L	ERA	G	GS	CG	SV	IP	H	R	ER	BB	SO	B	T	HT	WT	DOB	1st Yr	Resides
Angerhofer, Chad	2	4	7.22	13	7	0	0	39	52	37	31	17	38	L	L	6-1	180	10-5-75	1995	Gainesville, Fla.
Cloud, Tony	4	5	4.20	12	12	0	0	56	47	34	26	26	46	R	R	6-0	185	8-12-75	1995	Lancaster, S.C.
Corey, Mark	1	1	3.68	4	3	0	0	15	12	7	6	6	8	R	R	6-3	210	11-16-74	1995	Austin, Pa.
Cushman, Dwayne	2	3	3.09	26	0	0	8	35	33	21	12	15	40	R	R	6-0	175	11-27-71	1995	Port Salerno, Fla.
Davis, Lance	3	7	3.88	15	9	0	0	58	77	39	25	25	43	R	L	6-0	165	9-1-76	1995	Polk City, Fla.
Fonceca, Chad	0	0	7.25	11	1	0	0	22	27	19	18	10	21	L	R	6-2	185	1-2-76	1995	Victorville, Calif.
Giron, Roberto	1	1	5.50	24	0	0	4	36	33	23	22	14	41	R	R	6-2	175	3-24-76	1994	Villa Mella, D.R.
Mattox, Gene	0	0	11.32	11	0	0	0	10	13	13	13	12	10	R	R	6-2	205	3-24-75	1995	Jacksonville, Fla.
Montgomery, Joe	3	0	2.38	13	3	0	0	45	45	19	12	14	27	R	R	6-0	155	10-15-72	1995	Richmond, Ky.
Murphy, Chris	7	1	3.16	10	10	1	0	64	51	23	11	19	52	L	L	6-8	235	2-16-72	1995	Cincinnati, Ohio
Roberts, Randolph	4	5	3.16	15	9	0	0	63	51	35	22	33	74	R	R	6-3	180	1-19-74	1992	San Cristobal, D.R.
Schleuss, Will	0	3	4.50	23	0	0	1	32	29	20	16	22	34	L	L	6-2	190	3-5-74	1995	Martinsburg, W Va.
Sparks, Jeff	2	0	3.23	16	2	0	2	39	32	19	14	27	49	R	R	6-3	210	4-4-72	1995	Houston, Texas
Vicentino, Andy	2	2	7.50	10	7	0	0	30	36	30	25	27	23	L	L	6-1	184	1-10-76	1992	Maracaibo, Venez.

BILLINGS   R

PIONEER LEAGUE

BATTING	AVG	G	AB	R	H	2B	3B	HR	RBI	BB	SO	SB	CS	B	T	HT	WT	DOB	1st Yr	Resides
Burress, Andrew	.262	35	103	17	27	9	2	2	18	6	16	0	2	R	R	6-0	180	7-18-77	1995	McRae, Ga.
Claybrook, Stephen	.287	63	188	45	54	9	0	1	14	45	52	21	6	L	R	6-0	170	12-30-72	1995	Robstown, Texas
Fehrenbach, Todd	.094	15	32	2	3	0	0	0	5	13	1	0	L	R	6-0	203	5-5-76	1995	Inverness, Fla.
Goodhart, Steven	.340	65	250	48	85	12	4	0	45	28	34	9	4	R	R	6-0	170	2-14-73	1995	Heath, Ohio
Goodman, Herbert	.203	37	79	10	16	3	0	0	4	9	24	3	1	R	R	6-0	190	3-25-75	1995	Florence, S.C.
Hall, Darran	.148	15	27	11	4	0	1	0	2	8	3	1	1	L	L	5-10	160	9-8-75	1993	San Diego, Calif.
LaRue, Michael	.273	58	183	35	50	8	1	5	31	16	28	3	5	R	R	5-11	195	3-19-74	1995	Spring Branch, Texas
Montgomery, Andre	.254	44	122	18	31	2	1	1	9	8	20	4	4	R	R	5-10	160	6-27-77	1995	Louisville, Ky.
Parsons, Jason	.315	60	222	47	70	20	1	6	48	32	41	3	1	R	R	6-3	220	9-2-72	1995	Newport Beach, Calif.
Preston, Doyle	.285	65	242	40	69	12	1	6	43	42	60	1	2	L	R	6-3	195	2-9-73	1994	Saltillo, Texas
Rojas, Christian	.263	68	270	48	71	15	5	11	56	35	57	6	6	R	R	6-1	170	6-3-75	1994	Santo Domingo, D.R.
Scott, Thomas	.353	67	252	68	89	24	4	7	43	44	65	17	9	R	R	6-0	185	3-29-73	1995	Canby, Ore.
Sorg, Jay	.296	67	247	42	73	14	1	7	40	26	52	4	3	L	R	6-3	195	5-10-73	1994	Louisville, Ky.
Wilson, Brian	.287	62	209	32	60	14	1	9	35	36	49	7	7	R	R	6-1	185	7-14-72	1994	Albany, Texas

GAMES BY POSITION: C—Burress 23, Fehrenbach 8, LaRue 54. **1B**—Parsons 9, Sorg 62. **2B**—Goodhart 65, Wilson 8. **3B**—Preston 64, Wilson 11. **SS**—Montgomery 33, Preston 1, Wilson 52. **OF**—Claybrook 63, Goodman 32, Hall 12, Montgomery 1, Rojas 68, Scott 66.

PITCHING	W	L	ERA	G	GS	CG	SV	IP	H	R	ER	BB	SO	B	T	HT	WT	DOB	1st Yr	Resides
Atchley, Justin	10	4	3.51	13	13	0	0	77	91	33	30	20	65	L	L	6-2	205	9-5-73	1995	Sedro Woolley, Wash.
Bailey, Ben	6	4	2.96	13	13	0	0	79	74	32	26	29	68	R	R	6-2	220	8-31-74	1995	Howe, Ind.
Bryant, Adam	4	2	3.13	29	0	0	11	37	39	13	13	5	30	R	R	6-6	225	12-27-71	1994	Levittown, Pa.
Callahan, Damon	9	2	2.91	14	14	0	0	80	62	36	26	26	68	R	R	6-4	190	12-10-75	1994	Cleveland, Tenn.
Garcia, Eddy	3	2	2.63	15	5	0	1	48	38	20	14	12	45	R	R	6-0	205	5-31-74	1995	San Cristobal, D.R.
King, Raymond	3	0	1.67	28	0	0	5	43	31	11	8	15	43	L	L	6-1	221	1-15-74	1995	Ripley, Tenn.
Lapka, Rick	8	4	3.76	14	14	0	0	79	66	33	33	43	66	R	R	6-4	195	11-18-71	1994	Cicero, Ill.
Lawrence, Rich	0	1	3.24	13	2	0	1	25	25	18	9	11	27	R	R	6-0	185	9-22-74	1995	Naples, Fla.
MacRae, Scott	0	1	5.67	18	0	0	1	27	32	24	17	20	9	R	R	6-3	205	8-13-74	1995	Marietta, Ga.
Marine, Justin	1	1	1.75	18	0	0	2	26	21	9	5	11	20	R	R	6-3	220	11-14-74	1995	Calabasas, Calif.
Riedling, John	2	2	7.04	13	7	0	1	38	51	38	30	21	28	R	R	5-11	190	8-29-75	1994	Pompano Beach, Fla.
Weiss, Marc	1	2	7.62	18	1	0	1	26	36	26	22	15	14	R	R	6-4	205	8-3-73	1994	Los Angeles, Calif.
Wright, Scott	2	0	3.62	17	0	0	0	27	28	15	11	7	29	R	R	6-2	205	10-15-72	1995	Medford, Ore.

CLEVELAND INDIANS

Manager: Mike Hargrove.   **1995 Record:** 100-44, .694 (1st, AL Central).

BATTING	AVG	G	AB	R	H	2B	3B	HR	RBI	BB	SO	SB	CS	B	T	HT	WT	DOB	1st Yr	Resides
Alomar, Sandy	.300	66	203	32	61	6	0	10	35	7	26	3	1	R	R	6-5	215	6-18-66	1984	Westlake, Ohio
Amaro, Ruben	.200	28	60	5	12	3	0	1	7	4	6	1	3	S	R	5-10	175	2-12-65	1987	Philadelphia, Pa.
Baerga, Carlos	.314	135	557	87	175	28	2	15	90	35	31	11	2	S	R	5-11	200	11-4-68	1986	Westlake, Ohio
Bell, David	.000	2	2	0	0	0	0	0	0	0	0	0	0	R	R	5-10	170	9-14-72	1990	Cincinnati, Ohio
Belle, Albert	.317	143	546	121	173	52	1	50	126	73	80	5	2	R	R	6-2	210	8-25-66	1987	Euclid, Ohio
Burnitz, Jeromy	.571	9	7	4	4	1	0	0	0	0	0	0	0	L	R	6-0	190	4-14-69	1990	Key Largo, Fla.
Espinoza, Alvaro	.252	66	143	15	36	4	0	2	17	2	16	0	2	R	R	6-0	190	2-19-62	1979	Bergenfield, N.J.
Giles, Brian	.556	6	9	6	5	0	0	1	3	0	1	0	0	L	L	5-11	195	1-20-71	1989	El Cajon, Calif.
Kirby, Wayne	.207	101	188	29	39	10	2	1	14	13	32	10	3	L	R	5-10	185	1-22-64	1983	Yorktown, Va.
Levis, Jesse	.333	12	18	1	6	2	0	0	3	1	0	0	0	L	R	5-9	180	4-14-68	1989	Philadelphia, Pa.
Lofton, Kenny	.310	118	481	93	149	22	13	7	53	40	49	54	15	L	L	6-0	180	5-31-67	1988	Tucson, Ariz.
Murray, Eddie	.323	113	436	68	141	21	0	21	82	39	65	5	1	S	R	6-2	220	2-24-56	1973	Canyon Country, Calif.
Pena, Tony	.262	91	263	25	69	15	0	5	28	14	44	1	0	R	R	6-0	184	6-4-57	1976	Santiago, D.R.
Perry, Herbert	.315	52	162	23	51	13	1	3	23	13	28	1	3	R	R	6-2	210	9-15-69	1991	Mayo, Fla.
Ramirez, Manny	.308	137	484	85	149	26	1	31	107	75	112	6	6	R	R	6-0	190	5-30-72	1991	Brooklyn, N.Y.
Ripken, Billy	.412	8	17	4	7	0	0	2	3	0	3	0	0	R	R	6-1	188	12-16-64	1982	Cockeysville, Md.
Sorrento, Paul	.235	104	323	50	76	14	0	25	79	51	71	1	1	L	R	6-2	220	11-17-65	1986	Peabody, Mass.
Thome, Jim	.314	137	452	92	142	29	3	25	73	97	113	4	3	L	R	6-4	220	8-27-70	1989	Peoria, Ill.
Tucker, Scooter	.000	17	20	2	0	0	0	0	5	4	0	0	0	R	R	6-2	205	11-18-66	1988	Cantonment, Fla.
Vizquel, Omar	.266	136	542	87	144	28	0	6	56	59	59	29	11	S	R	5-9	165	4-24-67	1984	Caracas, Venez.
Winfield, Dave	.191	46	115	11	22	5	0	2	4	14	26	1	0	R	R	6-6	246	10-3-51	1973	Fort Myers, Fla.

PITCHING	W	L	ERA	G	GS	CG	SV	IP	H	R	ER	BB	SO	B	T	HT	WT	DOB	1st Yr	Resides
Assenmacher, Paul	6	2	2.82	47	0	0	0	38	32	13	12	12	40	L	L	6-3	195	12-10-60	1983	Stone Mountain, Ga.
Black, Bud	4	2	6.85	11	10	0	0	47	63	42	36	16	34	L	L	6-2	185	6-30-57	1979	San Diego, Calif.
Clark, Mark	9	7	5.27	22	21	2	0	125	143	77	73	42	68	R	R	6-5	225	5-12-68	1988	Bath, Ill.
Cook, Dennis	0	0	6.39	11	0	0	0	13	16	9	9	10	13	L	L	6-3	190	10-4-62	1985	Austin, Texas
Embree, Alan	3	2	5.11	23	0	0	1	25	23	16	14	16	23	L	L	6-2	190	1-23-70	1990	Brush Prairie, Wash.
Farrell, John	0	0	3.86	1	0	0	0	5	7	4	2	0	4	R	R	6-4	210	8-4-62	1984	Westlake, Ohio
Grimsley, Jason	0	0	6.09	15	2	0	1	34	37	24	23	32	25	R	R	6-3	180	8-7-67	1985	Cleveland, Texas
Hershiser, Orel	16	6	3.87	26	26	1	0	167	151	76	72	51	111	R	R	6-3	193	9-16-58	1979	Pasadena, Calif.
Hill, Ken	4	1	3.98	12	11	1	0	75	77	36	33	32	48	R	R	6-2	175	12-14-65	1985	Lynn, Mass.
Lopez, Albie	0	0	3.13	6	2	0	0	23	17	8	8	7	22	R	R	6-2	205	8-18-71	1991	Mesa, Ariz.
Martinez, Dennis	12	5	3.08	28	28	3	0	187	174	71	64	46	99	R	R	6-1	183	5-14-55	1974	Miami, Fla.
Mesa, Jose	3	0	1.13	62	0	0	46	64	49	9	8	17	58	R	R	6-3	225	5-22-66	1982	Westlake, Ohio
Nagy, Charles	16	6	4.55	29	29	2	0	178	194	95	90	61	139	L	R	6-3	200	5-5-67	1989	Westlake, Ohio
Ogea, Chad	8	3	3.05	20	14	1	0	106	95	38	36	29	57	R	R	6-2	200	11-9-70	1991	Lake Charles, La.
Olson, Gregg	0	0	13.50	3	0	0	0	3	5	4	4	2	0	R	R	6-4	212	10-11-66	1988	Reisterstown, Md.
Plunk, Eric	6	2	2.67	56	0	0	2	64	48	19	19	27	71	R	R	6-5	220	9-3-63	1981	Riverside, Calif.
Poole, Jim	3	3	3.75	42	0	0	0	50	40	22	21	17	41	L	L	6-2	203	4-28-66	1988	Ellicott City, Md.
Roa, Joe	0	1	6.00	1	1	0	0	6	9	4	4	2	0	R	R	6-1	194	10-11-71	1989	Hazel Park, Mich.
Shuey, Paul	0	2	4.26	7	0	0	0	6	5	4	3	5	5	R	R	6-3	215	9-16-70	1992	Raleigh, N.C.
Tavarez, Julian	10	2	2.44	57	0	0	0	85	76	36	23	21	68	R	R	6-2	165	5-22-73	1990	Santiago, D.R.

FIELDING

Catcher	PCT	G	PO	A	E	DP	PB
Alomar	.995	61	364	22	2	3	4
Levis	1.000	12	33	5	0	1	0
Pena	.987	91	508	36	7	6	6
Tucker	.982	17	53	3	1	0	1

First Base	PCT	G	PO	A	E	DP
Espinoza	1.000	2	9	0	0	1
Murray	.984	18	160	22	3	12
Perry	1.000	45	388	30	0	30
Sorrento	.992	91	816	58	7	88

Second Base	PCT	G	PO	A	E	DP
Baerga	.973	134	231	444	19	99
Espinoza	.966	32	18	39	2	7
Ripken	1.000	7	7	6	0	1

Third Base	PCT	G	PO	A	E	DP
Bell	1.000	2	0	2	0	0

	PCT	G	PO	A	E	DP
Espinoza	.974	22	10	27	1	1
Perry	1.000	1	3	0	0	0
Ripken	.000	1	0	0	0	0
Thome	.948	134	75	214	16	22

Shortstop	PCT	G	PO	A	E	DP
Espinoza	.960	19	13	35	2	8
Vizquel	.986	136	210	405	9	84

Outfield	PCT	G	PO	A	E	DP
Amaro	1.000	22	35	0	0	0
Belle	.981	142	304	7	6	1
Burnitz	1.000	6	10	0	0	0
Giles	1.000	3	2	0	0	0
Kirby	.990	68	94	2	1	1
Lofton	.970	114	248	11	8	3
Ramirez	.978	131	220	3	5	2

Jose Mesa

Manny Ramirez hit .308 with 31 homers and 107 RBIs for the Indians

Indians minor league Player of the Year Bartolo Colon

MEL BAILEY

RODGER WOOD

INDIANS

FARM SYSTEM

Director of Minor League Operations: Mark Shapiro.

Class	Farm Team	League	W	L	Pct.	Finish*	Manager	First Yr
AAA	Buffalo (N.Y.) Bisons	American Assoc.	82	62	.569	2nd (10)	Brian Graham	1995
AA	Canton-Akron (Ohio) Indians	Eastern	67	75	.472	T-7th (10)	Ted Kubiak	1989
#A	Kinston (N.C.) Indians	Carolina	81	56	.591	2nd+ (8)	Gordy MacKenzie	1987
A	Columbus (Ga.) RedStixx	South Atlantic	80	62	.563	3rd (14)	Jeff Datz	1991
A	Watertown (N.Y.) Indians	New York-Penn	46	27	.630	3rd+ (14)	Joel Skinner	1989
#R	Burlington (N.C.) Indians	Appalachian	26	38	.406	8th (10)	Harry Spilman	1986

*Finish in overall standings (No. of teams in league)   #Advanced level   +Won league championship

ORGANIZATION LEADERS

MAJOR LEAGUERS

BATTING

*AVG	Eddie Murray	.323
R	Albert Belle	121
H	Carlos Baerga	175
TB	Albert Belle	377
2B	Albert Belle	52
3B	Kenny Lofton	13
HR	Albert Belle	50
RBI	Albert Belle	126
BB	Jim Thome	97
SO	Jim Thome	113
SB	Kenny Lofton	54

PITCHING

W	Two tied at	16
L	Mark Clark	7
#ERA	Julian Tavarez	2.44
G	Jose Mesa	62
CG	Dennis Martinez	3
SV	Jose Mesa	46
IP	Dennis Martinez	187
BB	Charles Nagy	61
SO	Charles Nagy	139

Kenny Lofton. 13 triples, 54 steals

MEL BAILEY

MINOR LEAGUERS

BATTING

*AVG	Tim Jorgensen, Watertown	.325
R	Torey Lovullo, Buffalo	84
H	Alex Ramirez, Bakersfield/Canton	164
TB	Rod McCall, Bakersfield/Canton	253
2B	Two tied at	34
3B	Tim Jorgensen, Watertown	9
HR	Rod McCall, Bakersfield/Canton	29
RBI	Rod McCall, Bakersfield/Canton	88
BB	Todd Betts, Kinston	88
SO	James Betzsold, Kinston	137
SB	Ricky Gutierrez, Kinston	43

PITCHING

W	Joe Roa, Buffalo	17
L	Jay Vaught, Kinston	12
#ERA	Bartolo Colon, Kinston	1.96
G	Dan Graves, Kinston/Canton/Buffalo	58
CG	Two tied at	4
SV	Two tied at	31
IP	John Farrell, Buffalo	184
BB	Teddy Warrecker, Columbus	80
SO	Bartolo Colon, Kinston	152

*Minimum 250 At-Bats   #Minimum 75 Innings

TOP 10 PROSPECTS

How the Indians Top 10 prospects, as judged by Baseball America prior to the 1995 season, fared in 1995:

Jaret Wright

MEL BAILEY

Player, Pos.	Club (Class—League)	AVG	AB	R	H	2B	3B	HR	RBI	SB
5. Herbert Perry, 1b	Buffalo (AAA—American Assoc.)	.317	180	27	57	14	1	2	17	1
	Cleveland	.315	162	23	51	13	1	3	23	1
6. *David Bell, 3b-2b	Buffalo (AAA—American Assoc.)	.272	254	34	69	11	1	8	34	0
	Cleveland	.000	2	0	0	0	0	0	0	0
	Louisville (AAA—American Assoc.)	.276	76	9	21	3	1	1	9	4
	St. Louis	.250	144	13	36	7	2	2	19	1
7. Enrique Wilson, ss	Kinston (A—Carolina)	.267	464	55	124	24	7	6	52	18
8. Damian Jackson, ss	Canton-Akron (AA—Eastern)	.248	484	67	120	20	2	3	34	40

Player, Pos.	Club (Class—League)	W	L	ERA	G	SV	IP	H	BB	SO
1. Jaret Wright, rhp	Columbus (A—South Atlantic)	5	6	3.00	24	0	129	93	79	113
2. Paul Shuey, rhp	Buffalo (AAA—American Assoc.)	1	2	2.63	25	11	27	21	7	27
	Cleveland	0	2	4.26	7	0	6	5	5	5
3. Daron Kirkreit, rhp	Kinston (A—Carolina)	0	1	5.93	3	0	14	14	6	14
	Canton-Akron (AA—Eastern)	2	9	5.69	14	0	81	74	46	67
4. Julian Tavarez, rhp	Cleveland	10	2	2.44	57	0	85	76	21	68
9. Alan Embree, lhp	Buffalo (AAA—American Assoc.)	3	4	0.89	30	5	41	31	19	56
	Cleveland	3	2	5.11	23	1	25	23	16	23
10. John Carter, rhp	Canton-Akron (AA—Eastern)	1	2	3.95	5	0	27	27	13	14

*Traded to St. Louis

AMERICAN ASSOCIATION

BATTING

BATTING	AVG	G	AB	R	H	2B	3B	HR	RBI	BB	SO	SB	CS	B	T	HT	WT	DOB	1st Yr	Resides
Amaro, Ruben	.305	54	213	42	65	15	3	6	22	18	29	6	1	S	R	5-10	175	2-12-65	1987	Philadelphia, Pa.
Bell, David	.272	70	254	34	69	11	1	8	34	22	37	0	3	R	R	5-10	170	9-14-72	1990	Cincinnati, Ohio
Bolick, Frank	.246	20	65	11	16	6	0	3	10	3	13	0	1	S	R	5-10	177	6-28-66	1987	Mt. Carmel, Pa.
Burnitz, Jeromy	.284	128	443	72	126	26	7	19	85	50	83	13	5	L	R	6-0	190	4-14-69	1990	Key Largo, Fla.
Candaele, Casey	.247	97	364	50	90	10	7	4	38	22	42	9	2	S	R	5-9	165	1-12-61	1983	San Luis Obispo, Calif.
Costo, Tim	.247	105	324	41	80	11	2	11	60	27	65	2	0	R	R	6-5	230	2-16-69	1990	Glen Ellyn, Ill.
Flores, Miguel	.283	31	113	13	32	8	1	0	12	5	13	5	0	R	R	5-11	185	8-16-70	1990	Monterrey, Mexico
Fordyce, Brook	.250	58	176	18	44	13	0	0	9	14	20	1	0	R	R	6-1	185	5-7-70	1989	Old Lyme, Conn.
Giles, Brian	.310	123	413	67	128	18	8	15	67	54	40	7	3	L	L	5-11	195	1-20-71	1989	El Cajon, Calif.
Howitt, Dann	.303	41	119	19	36	8	3	4	18	14	30	0	0	L	R	6-5	205	2-13-64	1986	Medford, Ore.
2-team (45 Nash.)	.262	86	252	35	66	14	4	7	33	30	62	0	3							
Humphreys, Mike	.246	34	126	17	31	4	0	1	5	8	22	5	1	R	R	6-0	185	4-10-67	1988	De Soto, Texas
Levis, Jesse	.311	66	196	26	61	16	0	4	20	32	11	0	3	L	R	5-9	180	4-14-68	1989	Philadelphia, Pa.
Lopez, Luis	.262	123	455	62	119	21	1	17	66	29	47	1	1	R	R	6-1	190	9-1-64	1983	Brooklyn, N.Y.
Lovullo, Torey	.255	132	474	84	121	20	5	16	61	70	62	3	1	S	R	6-0	185	7-25-65	1987	Northridge, Calif.
Marini, Marc	.271	32	85	12	23	5	0	3	15	7	14	0	0	L	L	6-1	185	3-17-70	1991	Tunkhannock, Pa.
Martindale, Ryan	.161	11	31	4	5	1	0	0	0	9	1	0	0	R	R	6-3	215	12-2-68	1991	Omaha, Neb.
Martinez, Carmelo	.278	11	36	8	10	1	0	2	9	7	10	0	0	R	R	6-2	220	7-28-60	1979	Dorado, P.R.
Massarelli, John	.000	3	1	0	0	0	0	0	0	1	0	0	0	R	R	6-2	200	1-23-66	1987	Canton, Ohio
McClendon, Lloyd	.278	37	108	19	30	6	0	5	19	20	20	0	0	R	R	6-0	208	1-11-59	1980	Merrillville, Ind.
Perry, Herbert	.317	49	180	27	57	14	1	2	17	15	18	1	0	R	R	6-2	210	9-15-69	1991	Mayo, Fla.
Riles, Ernest	.278	6	18	5	5	0	0	1	7	3	1	0	0	L	R	6-1	180	10-2-60	1981	Tallahassee, Fla.
Ripken, Billy	.292	130	448	51	131	34	1	4	56	28	38	6	4	R	R	6-1	188	12-16-64	1982	Cockeysville, Md.
Smith, Ed	.323	13	31	4	10	0	1	3	9	3	5	0	1	R	R	6-4	220	6-5-69	1987	Browns Mills, N.J.
Wrona, Rick	.226	31	93	9	21	6	0	0	10	3	19	0	1	R	R	6-0	180	12-10-63	1985	Tulsa, Okla.
Yelding, Eric	.346	29	81	13	28	7	0	1	9	6	12	3	1	R	R	5-11	165	2-22-65	1984	Daphne, Ala.

PITCHING

PITCHING	W	L	ERA	G	GS	CG	SV	IP	H	R	ER	BB	SO	B	T	HT	WT	DOB	1st Yr	Resides
Austin, Jim	1	1	12.00	2	1	0	0	3	7	6	4	2	1	R	R	6-2	200	12-7-63	1986	Richmond, Va.
Bell, Eric	13	9	3.90	28	24	3	0	161	177	76	70	47	86	L	L	6-0	165	10-27-63	1982	Modesto, Calif.
Chapin, Darrin	0	1	8.31	6	0	0	0	9	12	10	8	2	4	R	R	6-0	170	2-1-66	1986	Courtland, Ohio
Clark, Mark	4	0	3.57	5	5	0	0	35	39	14	14	10	17	R	R	6-5	225	5-12-68	1988	Bath, Ill.
Crawford, Carlos	0	1	5.64	13	3	0	1	30	36	22	19	12	15	R	R	6-1	185	10-4-71	1990	Charlotte, N.C.
Embree, Alan	3	4	0.89	30	0	0	5	41	31	10	4	19	56	L	L	6-2	190	1-23-70	1990	Brush Prairie, Wash.
Farrell, Jim	11	9	4.54	29	28	2	0	184	198	97	93	61	92	R	R	6-4	210	8-4-62	1984	Westlake, Ohio
Frohwirth, Todd	1	1	3.34	26	0	0	3	32	31	13	12	12	16	R	R	6-4	204	9-28-62	1984	Milwaukee, Wisc.
Graves, Danny	0	0	3.00	3	0	0	0	3	5	4	1	1	2	R	R	5-11	200	8-7-73	1995	Valrico, Fla.
Grimsley, Jason	5	3	2.91	10	10	2	0	68	61	26	22	19	40	R	R	6-3	180	8-7-67	1985	Cleveland, Texas
Harris, Pep	2	1	2.48	14	0	0	0	33	32	11	9	15	18	R	R	6-2	185	9-23-72	1991	Lancaster, S.C.
Klink, Joe	2	1	3.00	45	0	0	8	39	31	13	13	15	32	L	L	5-11	170	2-3-62	1983	Pembroke Pines, Fla.
Lancaster, Les	5	4	4.31	45	3	1	0	88	90	45	42	19	68	R	R	6-2	205	4-21-62	1985	Irving, Texas
Lewis, James	6	4	3.64	18	16	1	0	94	101	42	38	25	50	R	R	6-4	195	1-31-70	1991	Jacksonville, Fla.
Lopez, Albie	5	10	4.44	18	18	1	0	101	101	57	50	51	82	R	R	6-2	205	8-18-71	1991	Mesa, Ariz.
Lynch, David	1	2	4.30	14	0	0	0	15	16	8	7	7	14	R	L	6-3	205	10-7-65	1987	Redondo Beach, Calif.
Ogea, Chad	0	1	4.58	4	4	0	0	18	16	12	9	8	11	R	R	6-2	190	11-9-70	1991	Lake Charles, La.
Olson, Gregg	1	0	2.49	18	0	0	13	22	16	6	6	9	25	R	R	6-4	212	10-11-66	1988	Reisterstown, Md.
Perschke, Greg	1	1	5.74	3	3	0	0	16	13	10	10	6	11	R	R	6-3	180	8-3-67	1989	La Porte, Ind.
Poole, Jim	0	0	27.00	1	1	0	0	3	7	8	8	2	0	L	L	6-2	203	4-28-66	1988	Ellicott City, Md.
Roa, Joe	17	3	3.50	25	24	3	0	165	168	71	64	28	93	R	R	6-1	194	10-11-71	1989	Hazel Park, Mich.
Shuey, Paul	1	2	2.63	25	0	0	11	27	21	9	8	7	27	R	R	6-3	215	9-16-70	1992	Raleigh, N.C.
Slusarski, Joe	1	1	6.32	4	2	0	0	16	18	12	11	4	9	R	R	6-4	195	12-19-66	1989	Springfield, Ill.
Telford, Anthony	4	1	3.46	16	2	0	0	39	35	15	15	10	24	R	R	6-0	175	3-6-66	1987	Pinellas Park, Fla.
Turner, Matt	0	1	5.23	10	0	0	3	10	16	7	6	5	10	R	R	6-5	215	2-18-67	1986	Lexington, Ky.

FIELDING

Catcher	PCT	G	PO	A	E	DP	PB
Fordyce	.991	51	306	18	3	2	2
Levis	.994	60	338	20	2	5	3
Lopez	1.000	4	12	1	0	1	0
Martindale	.978	11	41	4	1	0	1
Wrona	.995	31	167	16	1	3	4

First Base	PCT	G	PO	A	E	DP
Bolick	1.000	1	9	0	0	1
Costo	.991	66	584	47	6	56
Howitt	.000	1	0	0	0	0
Lopez	.989	27	252	17	3	23
Lovullo	.974	11	70	6	2	6
Martinez	.500	1	0	1	1	0
Perry	.994	48	419	44	3	42
Smith	1.000	1	1	0	0	0

Second Base	PCT	G	PO	A	E	DP
Bell	1.000	3	4	8	0	4
Candaele	.985	52	103	165	4	27

	PCT	G	PO	A	E	DP
Flores	.980	29	53	92	3	22
Lovullo	.984	69	132	175	5	47
Ripken	1.000	4	13	12	0	2

Third Base	PCT	G	PO	A	E	DP
Bell	.954	66	37	151	9	9
Bolick	.943	17	8	25	2	1
Candaele	1.000	1	0	4	0	0
Costo	.750	3	1	2	1	0
Lopez	.958	11	3	20	1	2
Lovullo	.930	58	30	116	11	13
McClendon	1.000	2	0	1	0	0
Smith	1.000	2	3	1	0	0

Shortstop	PCT	G	PO	A	E	DP
Bell	.900	5	5	13	2	4
Bolick	.000	1	0	0	0	0
Candaele	.881	19	20	32	7	8
Lovullo	1.000	2	3	6	0	2

	PCT	G	PO	A	E	DP
Ripken	.978	126	150	389	12	80

Outfield	PCT	G	PO	A	E	DP
Amaro	.990	49	102	2	1	0
Burnitz	.981	127	241	12	5	0
Candaele	.962	30	49	1	2	0
Costo	.909	12	10	0	1	0
Fordyce	.000	3	0	0	0	0
Giles	.981	118	248	4	5	0
Howitt	.965	31	53	2	2	0
Humphreys	1.000	33	80	4	0	1
Lopez	1.000	7	5	1	0	0
Marini	1.000	18	17	1	0	0
Martinez	1.000	2	2	0	0	0
McClendon	.941	24	32	0	2	0
Smith	.750	9	9	0	3	0
Yelding	.979	19	45	2	1	0

EASTERN LEAGUE

BATTING

BATTING	AVG	G	AB	R	H	2B	3B	HR	RBI	BB	SO	SB	CS	B	T	HT	WT	DOB	1st Yr	Resides
Alomar, Sandy	.400	6	15	3	6	1	0	0	1	1	1	0	0	R	R	6-5	215	6-18-66	1984	Westlake, Ohio
Biasucci, Joe	.244	41	135	19	33	8	0	2	16	20	35	0	0	R	R	5-11	180	4-28-70	1990	Hollywood, Fla.
Bryant, Pat	.259	127	421	60	109	22	3	17	59	52	116	16	8	R	R	5-11	182	10-27-72	1990	Sherman Oaks, Calif.
Cameron, Stanton	.256	35	82	11	21	8	0	1	12	10	18	1	0	R	R	6-5	195	7-5-69	1987	Powell, Tenn.

BATTING

BATTING	AVG	G	AB	R	H	2B	3B	HR	RBI	BB	SO	SB	CS	B	T	HT	WT	DOB	1st Yr	Resides
Campbell, Darrin	.000	2	7	1	0	0	0	0	0	0	1	0	0	R	R	5-9	180	7-1-67	1988	Cleveland, Ohio
Castillo, Ben	.224	32	116	15	26	7	2	2	15	11	23	1	2	R	R	6-1	192	7-15-66	1988	Cooper City, Fla.
Crosby, Mike	.165	75	224	18	37	5	1	5	20	10	60	1	1	L	R	6-1	200	2-24-69	1992	Warwick, R.I.
Davenport, Adell	.276	9	29	2	8	1	0	0	5	3	5	0	0	R	R	5-11	195	7-16-67	1988	Greenville, Miss.
Hagy, Gary	.294	6	17	2	5	2	0	0	3	1	2	0	0	R	R	6-3	195	4-7-69	1991	Ephrata, Wash.
Harvey, Ray	.259	122	444	52	115	20	1	3	32	43	75	1	4	L	L	6-1	185	1-1-69	1991	Brentwood, Tenn.
Hood, Dennis	.217	8	23	6	5	1	0	0	2	2	7	1	0	R	R	6-2	180	7-3-66	1984	Reston, Va.
Jackson, Damian	.248	131	484	67	120	20	2	3	34	65	103	40	22	R	R	5-10	160	8-16-73	1992	Concord, Calif.
Lantigua, Eduardo	.196	13	46	5	9	2	0	1	4	1	14	0	0	R	R	6-0	198	9-4-73	1991	Moca, D.R.
Marini, Marc	.306	83	310	41	95	28	1	3	56	30	51	3	3	L	L	6-1	185	3-17-70	1991	Tunkhannock, Pa.
Martindale, Ryan	.375	2	8	2	3	0	0	0	1	1	0	0	1	R	R	6-3	215	12-2-68	1991	Omaha, Neb.
Massarelli, John	.281	55	178	17	50	10	2	2	22	16	28	17	6	R	R	6-2	200	1-23-66	1987	Canton, Ohio
Maxwell, Pat	.247	84	267	19	66	7	0	4	25	15	26	1	1	L	R	6-0	170	3-28-70	1991	Wichita Falls, Texas
McCall, Rod	.274	26	95	16	26	5	0	9	18	12	21	1	1	L	R	6-7	235	11-4-71	1990	Stanton, Calif.
McNabb, Buck	.167	19	48	3	8	0	0	0	1	6	14	0	1	R	R	6-0	180	1-17-73	1991	Fort Walton Beach, Fla.
Murphy, Mike	.043	10	23	1	0	0	0	0	4	3	0	1	1	R	R	6-2	185	1-23-72	1990	Canton, Ohio
Neal, Mike	.267	134	419	64	112	24	2	5	46	71	79	5	6	R	R	6-1	180	11-5-71	1993	Hammond, La.
Ramirez, Alex	.248	33	133	15	33	3	4	1	11	5	24	3	5	R	R	5-11	176	10-3-74	1991	Miranda, Venez.
Ramirez, Omar	.324	10	34	6	11	0	0	0	3	3	3	0	0	R	R	5-9	170	11-2-70	1990	Santiago, D.R.
Smith, Ed	.241	103	365	41	88	18	2	11	52	36	93	0	2	R	R	6-4	220	6-5-69	1987	Browns Mills, N.J.
Soliz, Steve	.173	32	81	9	14	3	0	2	7	13	16	0	0	R	R	5-10	180	1-27-71	1993	Oxnard, Calif.
Taylor, Jamie	.000	4	11	0	0	0	0	0	0	0	4	0	0	L	R	6-2	220	10-10-70	1992	Bloomingdale, Ohio
Townsend, Chad	.262	116	404	39	106	22	1	9	50	31	90	3	2	L	L	6-5	222	7-4-71	1992	Palm Desert, Calif.
Wakamatsu, Don	.266	51	143	16	38	10	0	4	23	17	21	0	0	R	R	6-2	200	2-22-63	1985	Hayward, Calif.
Yelding, Eric	.351	10	37	5	13	1	0	0	7	1	6	3	0	R	R	5-11	165	2-22-65	1984	Daphne, Ala.

PITCHING

PITCHING	W	L	ERA	G	GS	CG	SV	IP	H	R	ER	BB	SO	B	T	HT	WT	DOB	1st Yr	Resides
Brown, Dickie	8	5	4.67	37	9	0	3	98	88	56	51	67	51	R	R	5-9	170	8-13-70	1990	North Little Rock, Ark.
Cabrera, Jose	5	3	3.28	24	11	1	0	85	83	32	31	21	61	R	R	6-0	160	3-24-72	1991	Santiago, D.R.
Carter, John	1	2	3.95	5	0	0	0	27	27	13	12	13	14	R	R	6-1	195	2-16-72	1991	Chicago, Ill.
Chapin, Darrin	0	1	4.50	4	0	0	0	8	12	7	4	2	6	R	R	6-0	170	2-1-66	1986	Courtland, Ohio
Crawford, Carlos	2	2	2.61	8	2	0	0	52	47	19	15	15	36	R	R	6-1	185	10-4-71	1990	Charlotte, N.C.
De la Maza, Roland	2	1	4.10	7	7	0	0	37	35	19	17	18	27	R	R	6-2	195	11-11-71	1993	Arleta, Calif.
De la Rosa, Maximo	0	0	54.00	1	0	0	0	1	2	2	1	0	2	R	R	5-11	170	7-12-71	1990	Villa Mella, D.R.
Driskill, Travis	3	4	4.66	33	0	0	4	46	46	24	24	19	39	R	R	6-0	185	8-1-71	1993	Austin, Texas
Fronio, Jason	1	3	7.22	8	5	1	0	29	32	25	23	16	23	R	R	6-2	205	12-26-69	1991	Riverside, Conn.
Graves, Danny	1	0	0.00	11	0	0	10	23	10	1	0	2	11	R	R	5-11	200	8-7-73	1995	Valrico, Fla.
Harris, Pep	6	3	2.39	32	7	0	10	83	78	34	22	23	40	R	R	6-2	185	9-23-72	1991	Lancaster, S.C.
Hrusovsky, John	1	7	7.11	35	4	0	1	70	77	64	55	35	59	R	R	6-1	195	9-12-70	1991	Vero Beach, Fla.
Kirkreit, Daron	2	9	5.69	14	14	1	0	81	74	54	51	46	49	R	R	6-6	225	8-7-72	1993	Norco, Calif.
Kline, Steve	2	3	2.42	14	14	0	0	89	86	34	24	30	45	S	L	6-2	200	8-22-72	1993	Winfield, Pa.
Koller, Rod	0	0	7.23	9	1	0	1	19	26	17	15	4	3	R	R	6-4	195	7-13-70	1991	Texarkana, Texas
Magee, Bo	0	2	6.98	21	0	0	1	30	33	26	23	26	25	R	L	6-4	180	4-28-66	1991	Jackson, Miss.
Matthews, Mike	5	8	5.93	15	15	1	0	74	82	62	49	43	37	L	L	6-2	175	10-24-73	1992	Woodbridge, Va.
Perschke, Greg	1	0	3.38	3	0	0	0	5	4	2	2	2	4	R	R	6-3	180	8-3-67	1989	La Porte, Ind.
Popplewell, Tom	2	0	9.74	15	0	0	0	20	33	22	22	16	14	R	R	6-3	225	8-3-67	1987	Hamilton, Ohio
Steph, Rod	8	10	3.81	32	20	1	0	137	150	74	58	33	82	R	R	5-11	185	8-27-69	1991	Plano, Texas
Taylor, Tommy	1	1	3.72	5	0	0	0	10	9	4	4	6	3	R	R	6-1	180	7-16-70	1989	Louisa, Va.
Telford, Anthony	2	0	0.82	2	2	0	0	11	6	2	1	4	4	R	R	6-0	175	3-6-66	1987	Pinellas Park, Fla.
Trlicek, Rick	5	3	3.05	24	0	0	3	38	33	16	13	16	27	R	R	6-3	200	4-26-69	1987	Houston, Texas
Whitten, Casey	9	8	3.31	20	20	2	0	114	100	49	42	38	91	L	L	6-0	175	5-23-72	1993	Terre Haute, Ind.
Williams, Greg	0	0	4.23	24	0	0	0	28	15	14	13	21	17	L	L	6-1	195	4-30-72	1993	Portland, Ore.

FIELDING

Catcher	PCT	G	PO	A	E	DP	PB
Alomar	.958	5	23	1	1	0	0
Campbell	.923	2	11	1	1	0	0
Crosby	.984	73	389	53	7	7	5
Martindale	1.000	2	13	0	0	0	0
Soliz	.979	32	161	24	4	1	3
Wakamatsu	.992	47	219	22	2	2	5

First Base	PCT	G	PO	A	E	DP
Cameron	1.000	1	2	0	0	0
Davenport	1.000	6	45	2	0	3
Harvey	.987	10	71	7	1	8
McCall	.992	12	111	7	1	6
Smith	.987	12	70	4	1	6
Townsend	.985	111	904	73	15	92

Second Base	PCT	G	PO	A	E	DP
Biasucci	1.000	4	11	11	0	1
Maxwell	.960	20	40	57	4	10

	PCT	G	PO	A	E	DP
Neal	.959	121	238	340	25	78
Smith	1.000	1	0	1	0	1
Third Base	**PCT**	**G**	**PO**	**A**	**E**	**DP**
Biasucci	.941	7	4	12	1	3
Cameron	.000	1	0	0	0	0
Hagy	.000	1	0	0	0	0
Lantigua	.811	13	8	22	7	1
Maxwell	.944	42	20	82	6	6
Neal	.947	6	6	12	1	1
Smith	.938	81	38	160	13	15
J. Taylor	1.000	3	2	6	0	1
Shortstop	**PCT**	**G**	**PO**	**A**	**E**	**DP**
Hagy	.963	5	8	18	1	3
Jackson	.939	122	220	337	36	80
Maxwell	.907	15	29	49	8	7
Neal	.793	6	11	12	6	2

Outfield	PCT	G	PO	A	E	DP
Biasucci	.000	1	0	0	0	0
Bryant	.975	120	302	8	8	1
Cameron	.955	23	38	4	2	2
Castillo	.941	31	59	5	4	0
Harvey	.977	51	85	0	2	0
Hood	1.000	8	10	1	0	1
Marini	.994	83	150	3	1	0
Massarelli	.983	52	114	2	2	1
McNabb	1.000	18	31	0	0	0
Murphy	1.000	9	18	1	0	1
A. Ramirez	.975	32	72	5	2	2
O. Ramirez	1.000	3	2	0	0	0
Smith	.923	14	23	1	2	0
Yelding	1.000	9	20	1	0	0

KINSTON A

CAROLINA LEAGUE

BATTING	AVG	G	AB	R	H	2B	3B	HR	RBI	BB	SO	SB	CS	B	T	HT	WT	DOB	1st Yr	Resides
Anderson, Milt	.000	4	5	1	0	0	0	0	0	0	0	0	0	S	R	5-10	175	9-7-72	1995	Fitzgerald, Ga.
Aven, Bruce	.261	130	479	70	125	23	5	23	69	41	109	15	9	R	R	5-9	180	3-4-72	1994	Orange, Texas
Betts, Todd	.272	109	331	52	90	15	3	9	44	88	56	2	3	L	R	6-0	190	6-24-73	1993	Scarborough, Ontario
Betzsold, James	.268	126	455	77	122	22	2	25	71	55	137	3	5	R	R	6-3	210	8-7-72	1994	Orange, Calif.
Cawhorn, Gerad	.210	85	262	23	55	12	0	1	22	29	60	4	1	R	R	6-1	185	8-27-71	1993	Brea, Calif.
Claudio, Patricio	.265	89	298	37	79	7	4	5	27	26	73	27	11	R	R	6-0	173	4-12-72	1991	Santiago, D.R.
Diaz, Einar	.263	104	373	46	98	21	0	6	43	12	29	3	6	R	R	5-10	165	12-28-72	1991	Chiriqui, Panama
Gutierrez, Ricky	.262	117	439	63	115	21	7	4	46	67	62	43	16	R	R	6-0	170	3-23-70	1994	Long Beach, Calif.
Hagy, Gary	.134	52	142	12	19	3	0	3	9	12	34	3	2	R	R	6-3	195	4-7-69	1991	Ephrata, Wash.
Harriss, Robin	.245	15	49	8	12	3	1	2	6	3	8	0	0	R	R	6-1	205	8-7-71	1994	San Angelo, Texas

BATTING

BATTING	AVG	G	AB	R	H	2B	3B	HR	RBI	BB	SO	SB	CS	B	T	HT	WT	DOB	1st Yr	Resides
Johnson, Todd	.232	21	56	4	13	2	1	0	9	0	13	0	0	R	R	5-11	205	12-18-70	1993	Fresno, Calif.
Lemons, Rich	.250	5	12	1	3	1	0	0	2	4	1	0	0	L	R	6-4	215	9-9-71	1993	Tucson, Ariz.
Mader, Chris	.074	11	27	1	2	0	0	0	2	1	5	0	0	R	R	6-0	195	10-6-70	1992	Tewksbury, Mass.
Melusky, Mitch	.241	8	29	5	7	5	0	0	2	2	9	0	0	R	R	6-0	185	9-18-73	1992	Yakima, Wash.
Murphy, Mike	.232	67	177	26	41	6	0	1	15	15	30	13	4	R	R	6-2	185	1-23-72	1990	Canton, Ohio
Prieto, Rich	.193	26	88	12	17	2	1	1	10	13	20	3	1	S	R	5-10	175	8-24-72	1993	Carmel, Calif.
Sexson, Richie	.306	131	494	80	151	34	0	22	85	43	115	4	6	R	R	6-6	206	12-29-74	1993	Brush Prairie, Wash.
Thomas, Greg	.219	102	329	32	72	21	0	11	43	25	98	0	2	L	L	6-3	200	7-19-72	1993	Orlando, Fla.
Wilson, Enrique	.267	117	464	55	124	24	7	6	52	25	38	18	19	S	R	5-11	160	7-27-75	1992	Santo Domingo, D.R.

GAMES BY POSITION: C—Diaz 103, Harriss 15, Johnson 21, Mader 1, Meluskey 7. **1B**—Cawhorn 4, Hagy 1, Sexson 125, Thomas 12. **2B**—Cawhorn 13, Gutierrez 116, Hagy 14, Prieto 1, Wilson 1. **3B**—Betts 92, Cawhorn 50, Diaz 2, Hagy 6. **SS**—Gutierrez 1, Hagy 24, Wilson 114. **OF**—Anderson 1, Aven 110, Betzsold 123, Claudio 89, Lemons 2, Murphy 57, Prieto 25, Thomas 20.

PITCHING

PITCHING	W	L	ERA	G	GS	CG	SV	IP	H	R	ER	BB	SO	B	T	HT	WT	DOB	1st Yr	Resides
Brabant, Dan	7	4	4.23	47	0	0	1	94	81	47	44	49	89	R	R	6-1	211	4-16-73	1993	Longueuil, Quebec.
Colon, Bartolo	13	3	1.96	21	21	0	0	129	91	31	28	39	152	R	R	6-0	185	5-24-75	1994	Puerto Plata, D.R.
De la Maza, Roland	6	0	2.37	26	12	0	1	110	99	31	29	28	100	R	R	6-2	195	11-11-71	1993	Arleta, Calif.
De la Rosa, Maximo	5	2	2.19	43	0	0	8	62	46	23	15	37	61	R	R	5-11	170	7-12-71	1990	Villa Mella, D.R.
Driskill, Travis	0	2	2.74	15	0	0	0	23	17	7	7	5	24	R	R	6-0	185	8-1-71	1993	Austin, Texas
Graves, Danny	3	1	0.82	38	0	0	21	44	30	11	4	12	46	R	R	5-11	200	8-7-73	1995	Valrico, Fla.
Hanson, Kris	5	6	5.04	20	18	1	0	96	102	56	54	24	53	R	R	6-5	240	1-5-71	1993	Stevens Point, Wisc.
Heiserman, Rick	9	9	3.74	19	19	1	0	113	97	55	47	42	86	R	R	6-7	220	2-22-73	1994	Omaha, Neb.
Kirkreit, Daron	0	1	5.93	3	3	0	0	14	14	9	9	6	14	R	R	6-6	225	8-7-72	1993	Norco, Calif.
Martinez, Johnny	0	0	1.64	6	0	0	2	11	9	2	2	4	13	R	R	6-3	168	11-25-72	1991	Guayabin, D.R.
Mesa, Rafael	4	3	2.94	35	1	0	1	52	34	19	17	20	29	R	R	6-4	175	10-9-73	1991	Azua, D.R.
Montoya, Wilmer	1	0	5.40	1	0	0	0	3	4	2	2	1	2	R	R	5-10	165	3-15-74	1993	Carabobo, Venez.
Najera, Noe	0	1	2.25	8	3	0	0	20	10	6	5	9	14	L	L	6-2	190	12-9-70	1992	Norwalk, Calif.
Oropeza, Igor	2	3	4.50	20	2	0	1	38	24	19	19	29	31	R	R	6-3	160	7-11-72	1992	La Guaira, Venez.
Ramos, Cesar	2	2	3.65	8	0	0	0	12	16	6	5	3	4	R	R	6-0	178	12-2-73	1992	Monte Cristi, D.R.
Runion, Tony	7	11	4.09	28	24	0	0	143	131	70	65	57	84	R	R	6-3	220	12-6-71	1993	Florence, Ky.
Sexton, Jeff	5	1	2.53	8	8	2	0	57	52	17	16	7	41	R	R	6-2	190	10-4-71	1993	Indianola, Okla.
Vaught, Jay	8	12	3.37	27	26	4	0	171	184	80	64	28	82	L	R	6-1	185	12-21-71	1994	Deer Park, Texas
Williams, Greg	2	1	2.45	30	0	0	3	22	15	9	6	8	18	L	L	6-1	190	4-30-72	1993	Portland, Ore.

COLUMBUS — A

SOUTH ATLANTIC LEAGUE

BATTING	AVG	G	AB	R	H	2B	3B	HR	RBI	BB	SO	SB	CS	B	T	HT	WT	DOB	1st Yr	Resides
Afenir, Tom	.077	5	13	1	1	0	0	0	0	0	5	0	0	R	R	6-0	180	8-9-71	1995	San Diego, Calif.
Branyan, Russell	.256	76	277	46	71	8	6	19	55	27	120	1	1	S	R	6-3	195	12-19-75	1994	Warner Robins, Ga.
Cardenas, Epi	.290	125	513	69	149	28	4	7	56	30	64	11	7	R	R	5-10	160	1-28-72	1992	Bandera, Texas
Carpenter, Matt	.286	2	7	2	2	1	0	1	3	0	2	0	0	R	R	6-0	195	9-28-72	1994	Euclid, Ohio
2-team (9 Asheville)	.143	11	28	2	4	2	0	1	6	1	4	0	0							
Chambers, Mack	.000	2	4	0	0	0	0	0	0	1	1	0	1	R	R	5-10	155	2-8-73	1993	Spiro, Okla.
Chapman, Eric	.241	54	199	27	48	9	3	0	8	19	42	23	6	R	R	6-1	178	9-9-71	1993	Charlottesville, Va.
Colombino, Carlo	.000	1	2	0	0	0	0	0	0	1	0	0	0	R	R	5-10	180	9-28-64	1985	Point Pleasant, N.J.
Glass, Chip	.289	115	402	70	116	17	5	5	45	37	47	37	8	L	L	5-11	180	6-24-71	1994	Ukiah, Calif.
Harriss, Robin	.223	51	179	18	40	6	0	2	18	11	30	0	3	R	R	6-1	205	8-7-71	1994	San Angelo, Texas
Lantigua, Eduardo	.241	23	87	13	21	5	0	1	10	4	20	2	1	R	R	6-0	198	9-4-73	1991	Moca, D.R.
Lewis, Andreaus	.261	76	245	35	64	8	5	2	23	36	86	18	7	S	R	6-2	215	1-24-73	1993	Decatur, Ga.
Lewis, Rob	.152	20	66	6	10	1	0	2	8	9	18	0	1	R	R	5-11	190	12-15-70	1993	El Segundo, Calif.
Matos, Julius	.245	52	155	16	38	7	3	0	13	11	21	2	2	R	R	5-11	170	12-12-74	1994	Racine, Wisc.
Mercedes, Guillermo	.191	55	183	23	35	5	1	2	8	18	19	6	3	S	R	5-11	155	1-17-74	1991	La Romana, D.R.
Moyle, Mike	.203	73	227	19	46	7	0	6	31	35	46	2	3	R	R	6-2	200	9-8-71	1992	Perth, Australia
Oram, Jon	.217	64	198	20	43	6	3	2	19	13	40	2	5	R	R	6-1	180	10-29-73	1993	Olympia, Wash.
Perry, Chan	.285	114	411	64	117	30	4	9	50	53	49	7	2	R	R	6-2	200	9-13-72	1994	Mayo, Fla.
Prieto, Rich	.222	4	18	1	4	0	0	1	2	0	4	0	0	S	R	5-10	175	8-24-72	1993	Carmel, Calif.
Stumberger, Darren	.270	127	448	62	121	27	0	11	57	56	72	3	3	R	R	6-3	205	4-11-73	1994	Boca Raton, Fla.
Thompson, Leroy	.214	82	248	34	53	15	3	7	35	40	78	1	2	L	L	6-0	180	10-25-74	1992	Fernandina Beach, Fla.
Valera, Willy	.163	31	104	8	17	3	1	2	6	4	35	0	1	R	R	6-0	155	7-23-75	1993	San Cristobal, D.R.
Warner, Bryan	.239	119	393	47	94	14	4	8	58	25	73	8	2	L	L	5-9	185	8-7-74	1994	Monrovia, Calif.
White, Eric	.317	113	404	73	128	13	2	46	51	40	73	3	2	R	R	6-1	180	10-13-72	1992	Diamond Bar, Calif.

GAMES BY POSITION: C—Afenir 5, Carpenter 2, Harriss 51, Lewis 20, Moyle 67. **1B**—Lantigua 4, Moyle 2, Oram 1, Perry 64, Stumberger 76. **2B**—Cardenas 124, Chambers 1, Matos 6, Oram 9, White 4. **3B**—Branyan 62, Colombino 1, Lantigua 9, Matos 1, Oram 15, White 68. **SS**—Chambers 1, Matos 30, Mercedes 54, Oram 33, Valera 31. **OF**—Chapman 51, Glass 111, Lantigua 7, Lewis 75, Matos 14, Oram 4, Perry 17, Prieto 4, Thompson 37, Warner 110, White 38.

PITCHING

PITCHING	W	L	ERA	G	GS	CG	SV	IP	H	R	ER	BB	SO	B	T	HT	WT	DOB	1st Yr	Resides
Caldwell, David	11	10	4.40	27	27	0	0	151	162	87	74	58	104	L	L	6-3	190	11-14-74	1994	Brooklyn, N.Y.
Dinnen, Kevin	2	7	4.14	49	0	0	1	59	47	34	27	34	43	R	R	6-1	185	12-1-71	1993	Pembroke Pines, Fla.
Done, J.J.	0	3	9.00	4	3	0	0	12	21	15	12	9	8	R	R	6-1	165	10-23-75	1993	Miami, Fla.
Donovan, Scot	0	6	4.81	40	0	0	10	49	53	38	26	36	38	R	R	6-3	195	7-3-72	1994	Dunwoody, Ga.
Dougherty, Tony	4	4	4.72	27	10	0	0	88	85	61	46	50	78	R	R	6-2	205	4-12-73	1994	Slippery Rock, Pa.
Granata, Chris	11	5	2.47	33	12	0	0	113	94	43	31	53	93	R	R	6-0	205	2-26-72	1994	Columbus, Ohio
Kramer, Scott	2	2	2.08	19	1	0	2	52	45	19	12	14	53	R	R	5-11	180	10-6-73	1994	Wyomissing, Pa.
Martinez, Johnny	6	1	1.83	16	2	0	0	54	37	15	11	14	43	R	R	6-3	168	11-25-72	1991	Guayabin, D.R.
Montoya, Wilmer	3	3	3.12	51	0	0	31	81	65	33	28	36	91	R	R	5-10	165	3-15-74	1993	Carabobo, Venez.
Najera, Noe	3	1	3.38	43	0	0	1	43	34	20	16	24	53	L	L	6-2	190	12-9-70	1992	Norwalk, Calif.
Oropeza, Igor	4	1	1.48	9	8	0	0	49	39	13	8	13	46	R	R	6-3	160	7-11-72	1992	La Guaira, Venez.
Perez, Julio	8	5	4.02	22	17	0	1	110	109	53	49	39	100	R	R	6-1	163	5-18-74	1993	San Cristobal, D.R.
Sanders, Frankie	1	1	3.00	2	0	0	0	9	9	3	3	4	9	R	R	5-11	165	8-27-75	1995	Sarasota, Fla.
Sexton, Jeff	4	2	2.19	14	13	2	0	82	66	27	20	16	71	R	R	6-2	190	10-4-71	1993	Indianola, Okla.
Warrecker, Teddy	10	5	4.13	24	24	1	0	131	104	76	60	80	125	L	R	6-6	215	10-1-72	1994	Santa Barbara, Calif.
Weber, Lenny	4	0	1.84	17	0	0	2	29	19	6	6	10	32	R	R	6-1	180	8-6-72	1994	Jeanerette, La.
Wright, Jaret	5	6	3.00	24	24	0	0	129	93	55	43	79	113	R	R	6-2	220	12-29-75	1994	Anaheim, Calif.
Zubiri, John	0	0	0.00	1	1	0	0	3	3	0	0	0	3	R	R	6-2	170	11-15-74	1992	Hanford, Calif.

WATERTOWN
NEW YORK-PENN LEAGUE

BATTING	AVG	G	AB	R	H	2B	3B	HR	RBI	BB	SO	SB	CS	B	T	HT	WT	DOB	1st Yr	Resides
Afenir, Tom	.200	6	15	2	3	2	0	0	3	0	3	0	0	R	R	6-0	180	8-9-71	1995	San Diego, Calif.
Budzinski, Mark	.253	70	253	50	64	12	8	3	25	52	49	15	5	L	L	6-2	175	8-26-73	1995	Severna Park, Md.
Carpenter, Matt	.323	12	31	4	10	3	0	0	4	4	7	0	0	R	R	6-0	195	9-28-72	1994	Euclid, Ohio
Casey, Sean	.329	55	207	26	68	18	0	2	37	18	21	3	0	L	R	6-4	215	7-2-74	1995	Pittsburgh, Pa.
Choate, Jon	.219	59	196	28	43	10	2	2	24	24	36	2	3	L	R	5-11	185	9-14-73	1994	Houston, Texas
Coats, Nathan	.276	12	29	2	8	2	1	0	3	4	11	0	0	R	R	5-11	185	5-1-74	1995	Sparks, Nev.
Culp, Matt	.129	33	85	7	11	3	0	1	8	14	26	1	0	L	R	6-3	205	5-8-73	1994	Overland Park, Kan.
Deshenes, Marc	.208	42	144	18	30	4	1	1	14	18	45	6	2	R	R	6-0	175	1-6-73	1995	Dracut, Mass.
Gonzalez, Rich	.266	55	184	24	49	4	1	1	17	17	19	1	0	R	R	6-0	185	11-13-74	1995	Miami, Fla.
Hayes, Heath	.212	15	52	4	11	3	0	0	6	7	14	1	1	R	R	6-3	195	2-29-72	1994	Citrus Heights, Calif.
Jorgensen, Tim	.325	73	295	44	96	19	9	8	52	32	63	4	1	L	R	6-3	200	11-30-72	1995	Luxemburg, Wisc.
Minici, Jason	.208	66	231	28	48	5	0	6	27	25	65	4	3	R	R	6-0	190	10-29-73	1995	Irvine, Calif.
Morgan, Scott	.262	66	244	42	64	18	0	2	33	26	63	6	5	R	R	6-7	230	7-19-73	1995	Spokane, Wash.
Owens, Walter	.273	23	44	9	12	1	0	0	3	6	10	2	1	R	R	5-11	175	4-9-73	1994	Mascoutah, Ill.
Stadler, Mike	.238	6	21	2	5	1	0	0	2	0	6	0	0	R	R	6-2	190	7-5-74	1992	El Cajon, Calif.
Taylor, Jerry	.286	5	21	3	6	1	0	0	3	1	3	0	0	R	R	5-10	210	12-19-72	1995	Goliad, Texas
Thornhill, Chad	.250	55	164	34	41	8	1	0	16	37	31	0	0	L	R	6-3	180	8-22-72	1995	Fresno, Calif.
Valera, Willy	.254	65	240	33	61	13	3	3	29	14	57	4	2	R	R	6-0	155	7-23-75	1993	San Cristobal, D.R.

GAMES BY POSITION: C—Afenir 6, Carpenter 4, Coats 12, Gonzalez 55, Stadler 5. **1B**—Casey 52, Culp 9, Hayes 13, Thornhill 6. **2B**—Deshenes 35, Thornhill 48. **3B**—Jorgensen 73. **SS**—Deshenes 12, Thornhill 1, Valera 65. **OF**—Budzinski 70, Choate 40, Culp 4, Minici 63, Morgan 40, Owens 18.

PITCHING	W	L	ERA	G	GS	CG	SV	IP	H	R	ER	BB	SO	B	T	HT	WT	DOB	1st Yr	Resides
Adge, Jason	5	1	1.58	19	0	0	1	46	40	10	8	9	26	L	R	6-0	195	10-18-71	1995	Sacramento, Calif.
Arellano, Carlos	0	0	3.60	2	2	0	0	5	3	2	2	4	4	R	R	6-2	180	4-9-75	1994	Mexicali, Mexico
Atkins, Dannon	5	2	3.26	13	10	0	1	61	52	28	22	26	46	R	R	6-3	195	8-7-73	1995	Miami, Fla.
Bennett, Jason	3	3	3.76	16	12	0	0	79	86	36	33	20	53	R	R	6-0	200	7-15-74	1995	Montoursville, Pa.
Crowell, Jim	5	2	2.86	12	9	0	0	57	50	22	18	27	48	L	L	6-4	220	5-14-74	1995	Indianapolis, Ind.
Grife, Richard	1	2	2.53	5	0	0	0	11	10	5	3	5	8	R	R	6-6	235	2-3-72	1995	Des Moines, Iowa
Harvey, Terry	6	2	1.82	8	8	0	0	54	36	13	11	6	33	R	R	6-1	180	1-29-73	1995	Dacula, Ga.
Horn, Keith	3	2	2.86	8	8	0	0	44	39	18	14	12	36	R	R	5-11	185	5-17-74	1995	Jonesboro, Ark.
Hritz, Derrick	0	1	2.10	18	0	0	1	30	28	9	7	16	23	L	L	6-0	200	9-21-72	1993	Gahanna, Ohio
Mathis, Sammie	4	1	4.36	18	0	0	0	33	39	22	16	15	21	R	R	6-1	195	12-16-72	1995	El Dorado, Ark.
Merrick, Brett	2	1	1.93	22	0	0	4	37	15	10	8	18	44	L	L	6-0	180	5-30-74	1995	Lynnwood, Wash.
Negrette, Richard	3	3	5.52	18	5	0	3	46	42	30	28	23	35	S	R	6-2	175	3-6-76	1994	Maracaibo, Venez.
Rakers, Jason	4	3	3.00	14	14	1	0	75	72	27	25	24	93	R	R	6-2	197	6-29-73	1995	Pittsburgh, Pa.
Schultz, Scott	1	3	4.70	9	5	0	2	31	39	24	16	11	20	R	R	5-10	185	7-16-72	1995	Sterling, Va.
Weber, Lenny	1	0	2.00	5	0	0	0	9	5	2	2	6	11	R	R	6-1	180	8-6-72	1994	Jeanerette, La.
Winchester, Scott	3	1	2.83	23	0	0	11	29	24	10	9	6	27	R	R	6-2	210	4-20-73	1995	Midland, Mich.

BURLINGTON
APPALACHIAN LEAGUE

BATTING	AVG	G	AB	R	H	2B	3B	HR	RBI	BB	SO	SB	CS	B	T	HT	WT	DOB	1st Yr	Resides
Anderson, Milton	.257	58	210	45	54	7	3	3	19	41	44	38	6	S	R	5-10	175	9-7-72	1995	Fitzgerald, Ga.
Coats, Nathan	.313	20	64	8	20	5	0	1	5	4	15	1	0	R	R	5-11	185	5-1-74	1995	Sparks, Nev.
Edwards, Donald	.169	43	130	20	22	2	0	0	5	17	35	5	2	R	R	6-1	185	11-24-76	1995	Mechanicsburg, Pa.
Glavine, Mike	.245	46	155	28	38	10	0	11	28	22	37	1	0	L	L	6-3	210	1-24-73	1995	Billerica, Mass.
Hardy, Brian	.200	29	80	15	16	4	0	5	12	10	40	1	0	L	R	6-4	240	3-26-77	1995	Arlington, Texas
Jensen, Blair	.191	21	47	3	9	1	0	0	2	6	21	2	0	R	R	6-1	185	8-4-75	1994	Kingsbury, Calif.
Lugo, Ursino	.245	32	94	13	23	0	0	0	5	3	20	9	4	S	R	6-0	158	11-9-74	1993	Bani, D.R.
McNeal, Pepe	.281	27	89	4	25	2	0	2	15	4	20	2	0	R	R	6-3	205	8-11-75	1994	Thonotosassa, Fla.
Messner, Jake	.222	46	144	17	32	2	4	0	9	14	40	8	5	L	L	6-0	192	5-18-77	1995	Sacramento, Calif.
Mota, Christian	.282	59	234	37	66	17	3	2	36	6	55	7	3	S	R	5-11	165	3-31-76	1994	San Pedro de Macoris, D.R.
Murphy, Quinn	.175	40	126	12	22	5	0	2	9	14	56	2	5	L	R	6-1	195	9-28-75	1994	Moline, Ill.
Pena, Jose	.200	23	70	7	14	2	0	2	6	0	21	0	1	R	R	6-2	175	6-29-74	1993	Monte Cristi, D.R.
Ramirez, Alonso	.167	10	18	3	3	0	0	1	3	6	0	0	0	R	R	6-2	210	9-6-73	1995	Berwyn, Ill.
Santiago, Arnold	.285	35	123	15	35	5	1	0	11	4	22	3	1	R	R	6-3	220	10-29-74	1994	Carolina, P.R.
Taylor, Jerry	.296	10	27	7	8	1	1	2	8	8	6	1	0	R	R	5-10	210	12-19-72	1995	Goliad, Texas
Tiller, Brad	.236	55	195	24	46	10	1	1	23	11	49	11	5	R	R	5-10	165	11-21-75	1994	Inez, Ky.
Whitaker, Chad	.238	47	181	20	43	13	1	5	27	14	59	2	3	L	R	6-2	190	9-16-76	1995	Ft. Lauderdale, Fla.
Williams, Jewell	.219	46	146	20	32	6	1	4	15	13	52	11	4	R	R	6-2	185	6-25-77	1995	Las Vegas, Nev.

GAMES BY POSITION: C—Coats 19, McNeal 27, Pena 21, Ramirez 9, Santiago 30. **1B**—Glavine 38, Hardy 2, Jensen 1, Santiago 30. **2B**—Murphy 35, Tiller 32. **3B**—Jensen 10, Mota 59, Murphy 3, Santiago 1. **SS**—Edwards 41, Mota 1, Tiller 24. **OF**—Anderson 58, Lugo 22, Messner 43, Mota 1, Whitaker 39, Williams 42.

PITCHING	W	L	ERA	G	GS	CG	SV	IP	H	R	ER	BB	SO	B	T	HT	WT	DOB	1st Yr	Resides
Anderson, Gary	1	2	6.35	14	0	0	3	17	18	12	12	8	22	R	R	5-10	180	12-31-73	1995	Brenham, Texas
Edwards, Jon	3	2	5.30	19	1	0	1	37	44	28	22	16	31	R	R	6-0	175	6-15-73	1995	Walla Walla, Wash.
Feingold, Leon	0	0	216.00	1	0	0	0	0	8	8	8	1	0	S	R	6-5	230	5-1-73	1994	Oceanside, N.Y.
Feliz, Bienvenido	4	2	2.71	12	12	1	0	73	55	29	22	20	78	R	R	6-0	175	6-4-77	1994	Santo Domingo, D.R.
Fleetwood, Tony	2	4	4.71	18	0	0	0	29	25	18	15	14	34	L	L	6-3	200	12-31-71	1995	Marlow, Okla.
Grife, Richard	2	0	2.32	16	0	0	1	31	20	12	8	10	31	R	R	6-6	235	2-3-72	1995	Des Moines, Iowa
Harrison, Scott	0	1	9.00	5	0	0	0	16	22	19	16	13	13	R	R	5-9	195	7-3-77	1995	Pinole, Calif.
Loudermilk, Darren	2	2	5.05	21	1	0	0	41	40	27	23	23	38	R	R	6-3	220	10-11-74	1995	Oklahoma City, Okla.
Lowry, Elliott	0	0	5.85	10	0	0	0	20	26	15	13	10	13	R	L	6-1	170	9-10-74	1994	Wilmington, N.C.
Martinez, Dennis	1	1	7.90	15	2	0	0	27	35	31	24	18	22	S	R	6-3	170	11-16-73	1995	Miami, Fla.
Martinez, Willie	0	7	9.45	11	11	0	0	40	64	50	42	25	36	R	R	6-2	165	1-4-78	1995	Barquisimeto, Venez.
Oldham, Bob	3	6	5.50	18	8	0	0	52	55	43	32	32	55	R	R	6-5	200	4-4-74	1994	Connellsville, Pa.
Ortiz, Steve	1	3	4.55	22	0	0	7	28	30	16	14	20	46	L	L	5-11	190	1-30-73	1994	Killeen, Texas
Sanders, Frankie	3	3	2.96	12	12	3	0	70	48	31	23	32	80	R	R	5-11	165	8-27-75	1995	Sarasota, Fla.
Wagner, Ken	5	5	3.16	13	12	0	0	68	54	34	24	23	80	R	R	6-4	218	8-3-74	1995	West Palm Beach, Fla.

COLORADO
ROCKIES

Manager: Don Baylor.   **1995 Record:** 77-67, .535 (2nd, NL West).

BATTING

	AVG	G	AB	R	H	2B	3B	HR	RBI	BB	SO	SB	CS	B	T	HT	WT	DOB	1st Yr	Resides
Bates, Jason	.267	116	322	42	86	17	4	8	46	42	70	3	6	S	R	5-11	170	1-5-71	1992	Norwalk, Calif.
Bichette, Dante	.340	139	579	102	197	38	2	40	128	22	96	13	9	R	R	6-3	235	11-18-63	1984	Palm Beach Gardens, Fla.
Brito, Jorge	.216	18	51	5	11	3	0	0	7	2	17	1	0	R	R	6-1	188	6-22-66	1986	Athens, Ala.
Burks, Ellis	.266	103	278	41	74	10	6	14	49	39	72	7	3	R	R	6-2	205	9-11-64	1983	Denver, Colo.
Castellano, Pedro	.000	4	5	0	0	0	0	0	0	2	3	0	0	R	R	6-1	195	3-11-70	1988	Lara, Venez.
Castilla, Vinny	.309	139	527	82	163	34	2	32	90	30	87	2	8	R	R	6-1	185	7-4-67	1990	Oaxaca, Mex
Counsell, Craig	.000	3	1	0	0	0	0	0	0	1	0	0	0	L	R	6-0	177	8-21-70	1992	Whitefish Bay, Wisc.
Galarraga, Andres	.280	143	554	89	155	29	3	31	106	32	146	12	2	R	R	6-3	245	6-18-61	1979	Caracas, Venez.
Girardi, Joe	.262	125	462	63	121	17	2	8	55	29	76	3	3	R	R	5-11	195	10-14-64	1986	Lake Forest, Ill.
Hubbard, Trenidad	.310	24	58	13	18	4	0	3	9	8	6	2	1	R	R	5-8	180	5-11-66	1986	Houston, Texas
Kingery, Mike	.269	119	350	66	94	18	4	8	37	45	40	13	5	L	L	6-0	185	3-29-61	1980	Atwater, Minn.
McCracken, Quinton	.000	3	1	0	0	0	0	0	0	0	1	0	0	S	R	5-8	170	3-16-70	1992	Southport, N.C.
Mejia, Roberto	.154	23	52	5	8	1	0	1	4	0	17	0	1	R	R	5-11	160	4-14-72	1989	Hato Mayor, D.R.
Nokes, Matt	.182	10	11	1	2	1	0	0	1	4	0	0	0	L	R	6-1	195	10-31-63	1981	San Diego, Calif.
Owens, Jayhawk	.244	18	45	7	11	2	0	4	12	2	15	0	0	R	R	6-0	200	2-10-69	1990	Sardinia, Ohio
Pulliam, Harvey	.400	5	5	1	2	1	0	1	3	0	2	0	0	R	R	6-0	205	10-20-67	1986	San Francisco, Calif.
Tatum, Jimmy	.235	34	34	4	8	1	0	4	1	7	0	0	0	R	R	6-2	200	10-9-67	1985	Lakeside, Calif.
Vander Wal, John	.347	105	101	15	35	8	1	5	21	16	23	1	1	L	L	6-1	190	4-29-66	1987	Hudsonville, Mich.
Walker, Larry	.306	131	494	96	151	31	5	36	101	49	72	16	3	L	R	6-2	185	12-1-66	1985	Maple Ridge, B.C.
Weiss, Walt	.260	137	427	65	111	17	3	1	25	98	57	15	3	S	R	6-0	178	11-28-63	1985	Danville, Calif.
Young, Eric	.317	120	366	68	116	21	9	6	36	49	29	35	12	R	R	5-9	017	5-18-67	1989	New Brunswick, N.J.

PITCHING

	W	L	ERA	G	GS	CG	SV	IP	H	R	ER	BB	SO	B	T	HT	WT	DOB	1st Yr	Resides
Acevedo, Juan	4	6	6.44	17	11	0	0	66	82	53	47	20	40	R	R	6-2	195	5-5-70	1992	Carpentersville, Ill.
Bailey, Roger	7	6	4.98	39	6	0	0	81	88	49	45	39	33	R	R	6-1	180	10-3-70	1992	Tallahassee, Fla.
Freeman, Marvin	3	7	5.89	22	18	0	0	95	122	64	62	41	61	R	R	6-7	222	4-10-63	1984	Country Club Hills, Ill.
Grahe, Joe	4	3	5.08	17	9	0	0	57	69	42	32	27	27	R	R	6-0	200	8-14-67	1989	Palm Beach Gardens, Fla.
Hickerson, Bryan	1	0	11.88	18	0	0	0	17	33	24	22	13	12	L	L	6-2	203	10-13-63	1986	Scottsdale, Ariz.
2-team (38 Chicago)	3	3	8.57	56	0	0	1	48	69	52	46	28	40							
Holmes, Darren	6	1	3.24	68	0	0	14	67	59	26	24	28	61	R	R	6-0	199	4-25-66	1984	Fletcher, N.C.
Leskanic, Curt	6	3	3.40	76	0	0	10	98	83	38	37	33	107	R	R	6-0	180	4-2-68	1990	Pineville, La.
Munoz, Mike	2	4	7.42	64	0	0	2	44	54	38	36	27	37	L	L	6-2	190	7-12-65	1986	West Covina, Calif.
Nied, Dave	0	0	20.77	2	0	0	0	4	11	10	10	3	3	R	R	6-2	185	12-22-68	1988	Denver, Colo.
Olivares, Omar	1	3	7.39	11	6	0	0	32	44	28	26	21	15	R	R	6-1	183	7-6-67	1987	San German, P.R.
Painter, Lance	3	0	4.37	33	1	0	1	45	55	23	22	10	36	L	L	6-1	195	7-21-67	1990	Milwaukee, Wisc.
Reed, Steve	5	2	2.14	71	0	0	3	84	61	24	20	21	79	R	R	6-2	195	3-11-66	1988	Lewiston, Idaho
Rekar, Bryan	4	6	4.98	15	14	1	0	85	95	51	47	24	60	R	R	6-3	205	6-3-72	1993	Orland Park, Ill.
Reynoso, Armando	7	7	5.32	20	18	0	0	93	116	61	55	36	40	R	R	6-0	196	5-1-66	1989	Lagos de Moreno, Mexico
Ritz, Kevin	11	11	4.21	31	28	0	2	173	171	91	81	65	120	R	R	6-4	220	6-8-65	1986	Cambridge, Ohio
Ruffin, Bruce	0	1	2.12	37	0	0	11	34	26	8	8	19	23	S	L	6-2	213	10-4-63	1985	Austin, Texas
Saberhagen, Bret	2	1	6.28	9	9	0	0	43	60	33	30	13	29	R	R	6-1	200	4-11-64	1983	Babylon, N.Y.
2-team (16 NY)	7	6	4.18	25	25	3	0	153	165	78	71	33	100							
Sager, A.J.	0	0	7.36	10	0	0	0	15	19	16	12	7	10	R	R	6-4	220	3-3-65	1988	Kirkersville, Ohio
Swift, Bill	9	3	4.94	19	19	0	0	106	122	62	58	43	68	R	R	6-0	191	10-27-61	1985	South Portland, Maine
Thompson, Mark	2	3	6.53	21	5	0	0	51	73	42	37	22	30	R	R	6-2	205	4-7-71	1992	Russellville, Ky.

FIELDING

Catcher	PCT	G	PO	A	E	DP	PB
Brito	.991	18	109	6	1	0	4
Girardi	.988	122	730	60	10	7	5
Nokes	.909	3	10	0	1	0	0
Owens	.988	16	79	6	1	2	1
Tatum	1.000	1	3	0	0	0	0

First Base	PCT	G	PO	A	E	DP
Galarraga	.991	142	1299	120	13	129
Kingery	.963	5	25	1	1	0
Vander Wal	.957	10	42	3	2	3

Second Base	PCT	G	PO	A	E	DP
Bates	.991	82	136	188	3	50
Mejia	.971	16	36	30	2	4
Young	.973	77	165	228	11	55

Third Base	PCT	G	PO	A	E	DP
Bates	.973	15	10	26	1	1
Castellano	1.000	3	1	0	0	0

	PCT	G	PO	A	E	DP
Castilla	.958	137	84	256	15	21

Shortstop	PCT	G	PO	A	E	DP
Bates	.985	20	24	41	1	5
Castilla	1.000	5	2	1	0	1
Counsell	1.000	3	1	1	0	1
Weiss	.974	136	201	406	16	99

Outfield	PCT	G	PO	A	E	DP
Bichette	.986	136	208	9	3	0
Burks	.970	80	158	3	5	0
Hubbard	1.000	16	16	1	0	0
Kingery	.979	108	180	4	4	0
McCracken	.000	1	0	0	0	0
Pulliam	.000	1	0	0	0	0
Tatum	1.000	2	1	0	0	0
Vander Wal	1.000	10	9	1	0	0
Walker	.988	129	225	13	3	1
Young	1.000	19	15	3	0	0

Larry Walker

Third baseman Vinny Castilla was one of four Colorado players to hit 30 homers in 1995

GEORGE GOJKOVICH

Rockies minor league Player of the Year Derrick Gibson

FRANK RAGSDALE

ROCKIES

FARM SYSTEM

Vice President, Player Personnel: Dick Balderson.

Class	Farm Team	League	W	L	Pct.	Finish*	Manager	First Yr
AAA	Colo. Springs (Colo.) Sky Sox	Pacific Coast	77	66	.538	4th+ (10)	Brad Mills	1993
AA	New Haven (Conn.) Ravens	Eastern	79	63	.556	2nd (10)	Paul Zuvella	1994
#A	Salem (Va.) Avalanche	Carolina	68	72	.486	T-4th (8)	Bill Hayes	1995
A	Asheville (N.C.) Tourists	South Atlantic	76	63	.547	5th (14)	Bill McGuire	1994
A	Portland (Ore.) Rockies	Northwest	41	34	.547	3rd (8)	P.J. Carey	1995
R	Chandler (Ariz.) Rockies	Arizona	13	42	.236	6th (6)	Jim Eppard	1992

*Finish in overall standings (No. of teams in league)   #Advanced level   +Won league championship

ORGANIZATION LEADERS

MAJOR LEAGUERS

BATTING
*AVG	Dante Bichette	.340
R	Dante Bichette	102
H	Dante Bichette	197
TB	Dante Bichette	359
2B	Dante Bichette	38
3B	Eric Young	9
HR	Dante Bichette	40
RBI	Dante Bichette	128
BB	Walt Weiss	98
SO	Andres Galarraga	146
SB	Eric Young	35

PITCHING
W	Kevin Ritz	11
L	Kevin Ritz	11
#ERA	Steve Reed	84
G	Curt Leskanic	76
CG	Bryan Rekar	1
SV	Darren Holmes	14
IP	Kevin Ritz	173
BB	Kevin Ritz	65
SO	Kevin Ritz	120

Quinton McCracken. .359 average

R&R SPORTS GROUP

MINOR LEAGUERS

BATTING
*AVG	Quinton McCracken, N.H./Colo. Spgs.	.359
R	Trenidad Hubbard, Colorado Springs	102
H	Quinton McCracken, N.H./Colo. Spgs.	167
TB	Derrick Gibson, Asheville	280
2B	Pete Carranza, Asheville/Salem	34
3B	Two tied at	10
HR	Derrick Gibson, Asheville	32
RBI	Derrick Gibson, Asheville	115
BB	Chris Sexton, Salem/New Haven	93
SO	Derrick Gibson, Asheville	136
SB	Two tied at	51

PITCHING
W	Brent Crowther, Asheville/Salem	15
L	Luther Hackman, Asheville	11
#ERA	Mike Vavrek, Portland/Asheville	1.69
G	Jim Czajkowski, Colorado Springs	60
CG	Brent Crowther, Asheville/Salem	6
SV	Luis Colmenares, Asheville	21
IP	Brent Crowther, Asheville/Salem	183
BB	Doug Million, Salem	79
SO	Brent Crowther, Asheville/Salem	133

*Minimum 250 At-Bats   #Minimum 75 Innings

TOP 10 PROSPECTS

How the Rockies Top 10 prospects, as judged by Baseball America prior to the 1995 season, fared in 1995:

Doug Million

Player, Pos.	Club (Class—League)	AVG	AB	R	H	2B	3B	HR	RBI	SB
4. Derrick Gibson, of	Asheville (A—South Atlantic)	.292	506	91	148	16	10	32	115	31
6. Neifi Perez, ss	New Haven (AA—Eastern)	.253	427	59	108	28	3	5	43	5

Player, Pos.	Club (Class—League)	W	L	ERA	G	SV	IP	H	BB	SO
1. Doug Million, lhp	Salem (A—Carolina)	5	7	4.62	24	0	111	111	79	85
2. *Juan Acevedo, rhp	Colo. Springs (AAA—Pacific Coast)	1	1	6.14	3	0	15	18	7	7
	Norfolk (AAA—International)	0	0	0.00	2	0	3	0	1	2
	Colorado	4	6	6.44	17	0	66	82	20	40
3. Mark Thompson, rhp	Colo. Springs (AAA—Pacific Coast)	5	3	6.10	11	0	62	73	25	38
	Colorado	2	3	6.53	21	0	51	73	22	30
5. John Burke, rhp	Colo. Springs (AAA—Pacific Coast)	7	1	4.55	19	1	87	79	48	65
7. John Thomson, rhp	New Haven (AA—Eastern)	7	8	4.18	26	0	131	132	56	82
8. Jamey Wright, rhp	Salem (A—Carolina)	10	8	2.47	26	0	171	160	72	95
9. Bryan Rekar, rhp	New Haven (AA—Eastern)	6	3	2.13	12	0	80	65	16	80
	Colo. Springs (AAA—Pacific Coast)	4	2	1.49	7	0	48	29	13	39
	Colorado	4	6	4.98	15	0	85	95	24	60
10. Ivan Arteaga, rhp	New Haven (AA—Eastern)	2	4	5.56	14	0	34	36	21	18

*Traded to New York Mets

PACIFIC COAST LEAGUE

BATTING	AVG	G	AB	R	H	2B	3B	HR	RBI	BB	SO	SB	CS	B	T	HT	WT	DOB	1st Yr	Resides
Bolick, Frank	.235	23	68	8	16	3	1	2	7	8	14	0	0	S	R	5-10	177	6-28-66	1987	Mt. Carmel, Pa.
Brito, Jorge	.229	32	96	9	22	4	1	2	15	2	20	0	0	R	R	6-1	188	6-22-66	1986	Athens, Ala.
Burks, Ellis	.310	8	29	9	9	2	1	2	6	4	8	0	0	R	R	6-2	205	9-11-64	1983	Denver, Colo.
Case, Mike	.286	7	14	2	4	1	0	0	0	4	1	1		R	R	6-2	185	12-26-68	1992	Yorba Linda, Calif.
Castellano, Pete	.266	99	334	40	89	23	2	9	47	24	56	2	0	R	R	6-1	195	3-11-70	1988	Lara, Venez.
Cockrell, Alan	.313	106	355	58	111	22	1	12	58	30	65	0	3	R	R	6-2	210	12-5-62	1984	Galena, Kan.
Cole, Stu	.274	76	208	28	57	15	2	2	24	17	19	1	2	R	R	6-2	190	2-7-66	1987	Charlotte, N.C.
Counsell, Craig	.281	118	399	60	112	22	6	5	53	34	47	10	2	L	R	6-0	177	8-21-70	1992	Whitefish Bay, Wisc.
Gainer, Jay	.291	112	358	57	104	19	1	23	86	42	64	2	3	L	L	6-0	188	10-8-66	1990	Ellsburg, Va.
Garrison, Webster	.293	126	460	83	135	32	6	12	77	46	74	12	4	R	R	5-11	170	8-24-65	1984	Marrero, La.
Hubbard, Trenidad	.340	123	480	102	163	29	7	12	66	61	59	37	14	R	R	5-8	180	5-11-66	1986	Houston, Texas
Landrum, Ced	.259	82	166	31	43	5	2	2	19	11	29	12	5	L	R	5-8	170	9-3-63	1986	Sweetwater, Ala.
Martinez, Chito	.155	42	110	18	17	8	0	4	6	12	32	0	2	L	L	5-10	185	12-19-65	1984	Metairie, La.
McCracken, Quinton	.361	61	244	55	88	14	6	3	28	23	30	17	6	S	R	5-8	170	3-16-70	1992	Southport, N.C.
Mejia, Roberto	.294	38	143	18	42	10	2	2	14	7	29	0	2	R	R	5-11	160	4-14-72	1989	Hato Mayor, D.R.
Nokes, Matt	.216	12	37	7	8	2	0	4	10	2	4	0	0	L	R	6-1	195	10-31-63	1981	San Diego, Calif.
Owens, Jayhawk	.294	70	221	47	65	13	5	12	48	20	61	2	1	R	R	6-0	200	2-10-69	1990	Sardinia, Ohio
Perez, Neifi	.278	11	36	4	10	4	0	0	2	0	5	1	1	S	R	6-0	175	6-2-75	1993	Villa Mella, D.R.
Pulliam, Harvey	.327	115	407	90	133	30	6	25	91	49	59	6	2	R	R	6-0	205	10-20-67	1986	San Francisco, Calif.
Strittmatter, Mark	.294	5	17	1	5	2	0	0	3	0	3	0	0	R	R	6-1	200	4-4-69	1992	Ridgewood, N.J.
Tatum, Jim	.323	27	93	17	30	7	0	6	18	6	21	0	1	R	R	6-2	200	10-9-67	1985	Lakeside, Calif.
Van Burkleo, Ty	.286	76	231	43	66	14	2	14	57	29	57	2	1	L	L	6-4	210	10-7-63	1982	Mesa, Ariz.
Walters, Dan	.284	52	155	15	44	9	2	3	23	7	20	0	0	R	R	6-2	190	8-15-66	1985	Santee, Calif.

PITCHING	W	L	ERA	G	GS	CG	SV	IP	H	R	ER	BB	SO	B	T	HT	WT	DOB	1st Yr	Resides
Acevedo, Juan	1	1	6.14	3	3	0	0	15	18	11	10	7	7	R	R	6-2	195	5-5-70	1992	Carpentersville, Ill.
Bailey, Roger	0	0	2.70	3	3	0	0	17	15	9	5	8	13	R	R	6-1	180	10-3-70	1992	Tallahassee, Fla.
Bullard, Jason	0	0	7.27	4	0	0	0	9	18	13	7	5	5	R	R	6-2	185	10-23-68	1991	Sweeny, Texas
Burke, John	7	1	4.55	19	17	0	1	87	79	46	44	48	65	S	R	6-4	220	2-9-70	1992	Highlands Ranch, Colo.
Bustillos, Albert	8	4	4.61	34	19	0	3	133	151	82	68	33	77	R	R	6-1	230	4-8-68	1988	San Jose, Calif.
Conroy, Brian	0	2	6.11	5	5	0	0	28	36	19	19	11	9	S	R	6-2	185	8-29-68	1989	Needham, Mass.
Crowther, Brent	0	1	7.50	1	1	0	0	6	11	6	5	2	1	R	R	6-4	220	5-15-72	1994	North Vancouver, B.C.
Czajkowski, Jim	3	10	5.06	60	0	0	17	84	90	54	47	52	56	S	R	6-4	215	12-18-63	1986	Cary, N.C.
Fredrickson, Scott	11	3	3.45	58	1	0	4	76	70	40	29	47	70	R	R	6-3	215	8-19-67	1990	San Antonio, Texas
Grahe, Joe	1	1	3.27	2	2	1	0	11	7	4	4	3	4	R	R	6-0	200	8-14-67	1989	Palm Beach Gardens, Fla.
Grundt, Ken	0	0	4.76	9	0	0	0	6	9	5	3	4	5	L	L	6-4	195	8-26-69	1991	Chicago, Ill.
Hawblitzel, Ryan	5	3	4.55	21	14	0	0	83	88	47	42	17	40	R	R	6-2	170	4-30-71	1990	Lake Worth, Fla.
Hunter, Jim	2	2	6.96	10	4	0	0	32	43	27	25	17	13	R	R	6-3	205	6-22-64	1985	Middletown, N.J.
Johnston, Joel	2	2	5.96	18	0	0	0	23	26	16	15	12	14	R	R	6-4	234	3-8-67	1988	West Chester, Pa.
Jones, Bobby	1	2	7.30	11	8	0	0	41	50	38	33	33	48	R	L	6-0	175	4-11-72	1992	Rutherford, N.J.
Kotarski, Mike	2	2	10.80	22	0	0	0	30	48	37	36	20	21	L	L	6-1	195	9-18-70	1993	Peabody, Mass.
Logsdon, Kevin	0	0	24.00	2	0	0	0	3	8	8	8	5	2	S	L	5-11	215	12-23-70	1991	Baker City, Ore.
Nied, David	1	1	4.99	7	7	0	0	31	31	18	17	25	21	R	R	6-2	185	12-22-68	1988	Denver, Colo.
Olivares, Omar	0	1	5.40	3	2	0	0	12	14	7	7	2	6	R	R	6-1	183	7-6-67	1987	San German, P.R.
Painter, Lance	0	3	5.96	11	4	0	0	26	32	20	17	11	12	L	L	6-1	195	7-21-67	1990	Milwaukee, Wisc.
Peever, Lloyd	3	2	5.36	8	8	0	0	42	45	26	25	16	25	R	R	5-11	185	9-15-71	1992	Stonewall, Okla.
Rekar, Bryan	4	2	1.49	7	7	2	0	48	29	10	8	13	39	R	R	6-3	205	6-3-72	1993	Orland Park, Ill.
Reynoso, Armando	2	1	1.57	5	5	0	0	23	14	4	4	6	17	R	R	6-0	190	5-1-66	1989	Lagos de Moreno, Mexico
Romanoli, Paul	3	1	4.50	31	0	0	3	20	27	13	10	10	23	L	L	6-2	182	9-22-69	1991	Germantown, Tenn.
Sager, A.J.	8	5	3.50	23	22	1	0	134	153	61	52	23	80	R	R	6-4	220	3-3-65	1988	Kirkersville, Ohio
Scott, Darryl	4	10	4.70	59	1	0	4	96	113	63	50	41	77	R	R	6-1	185	8-6-68	1990	Prior Lake, Mn
Shifflett, Steve	4	3	6.87	23	0	0	0	38	61	33	29	13	21	R	R	6-1	200	1-5-66	1989	Pleasant Hill, Mo.
Thompson, Mark	5	3	6.10	11	10	0	0	62	73	43	42	25	38	R	R	6-2	205	4-7-71	1992	Russellville, Ky.

FIELDING

Catcher	PCT	G	PO	A	E	DP	PB
Brito	.983	31	163	13	3	2	2
Nokes	.979	8	43	3	1	1	0
Owens	.989	68	390	46	5	8	4
Strittmatter	.973	5	32	4	1	0	0
Tatum	.667	1	2	0	1	0	0
Walters	.984	48	222	17	4	2	3

First Base	PCT	G	PO	A	E	DP
Bolick	1.000	1	8	1	0	1
Castellano	.995	26	186	9	1	24
Gainer	.986	63	508	48	8	57
Martinez	.941	3	16	0	1	3
Van Burkleo	.982	65	521	29	10	53

Second Base	PCT	G	PO	A	E	DP
Cole	.987	14	34	41	1	15
Garrison	.971	100	193	307	15	66
Mejia	.973	35	80	97	5	28

Third Base	PCT	G	PO	A	E	DP
Bolick	.927	17	12	26	3	1
Case	.625	3	1	4	3	0
Castellano	.973	73	36	110	4	15
Cole	.912	18	8	23	3	3
Garrison	.914	22	12	41	5	4
Tatum	.945	23	13	39	3	6

Shortstop	PCT	G	PO	A	E	DP
Cole	.964	23	24	57	3	14

	PCT	G	PO	A	E	DP
Counsell	.950	115	182	386	30	86
Perez	.936	11	16	28	3	5

Outfield	PCT	G	PO	A	E	DP
Burks	1.000	7	16	0	0	0
Cockrell	.981	87	153	5	3	1
Hubbard	.980	120	285	11	6	0
Landrum	.961	46	70	3	3	0
Martinez	.981	27	50	1	1	0
McCracken	.991	57	104	5	1	1
Pulliam	.985	112	186	8	3	6

EASTERN LEAGUE

BATTING	AVG	G	AB	R	H	2B	3B	HR	RBI	BB	SO	SB	CS	B	T	HT	WT	DOB	1st Yr	Resides
Case, Mike	.245	102	310	55	76	16	2	10	46	43	72	6	2	R	R	6-2	185	12-26-68	1992	Yorba Linda, Calif.
Dixon, Colin	.191	14	47	3	9	2	2	0	7	2	7	0	1	R	R	6-5	215	8-27-68	1989	West Vancouver, B.C.
Echevarria, Angel	.300	124	453	78	136	30	1	21	100	56	93	8	3	R	R	6-4	215	5-25-71	1992	Bridgeport, Conn.
Gonzalez, Mauricio	.268	73	164	20	44	5	3	0	12	7	29	0	1	S	R	5-11	170	2-13-72	1990	Santo Domingo, D.R.
Hartung, Andy	.097	12	31	4	3	2	0	0	0	2	7	1	0	R	R	6-1	205	2-12-69	1990	Stoneham, Mass.
Higgins, Mike	.245	17	49	4	12	0	0	0	6	3	10	0	0	R	R	6-0	205	6-3-71	1993	Nutley, N.J.
Jones, Terry	.269	124	472	78	127	12	1	1	26	39	104	51	19	S	R	5-10	160	2-15-71	1993	Pinson, Ala.
Kennedy, David	.306	128	484	75	148	22	2	22	96	48	131	4	1	R	R	6-4	215	9-3-72	1992	Glen Ridge, N.J.

BATTING

	AVG	G	AB	R	H	2B	3B	HR	RBI	BB	SO	SB	CS	B	T	HT	WT	DOB	1st Yr	Resides
List, Lou	.278	82	212	26	59	10	4	6	44	20	43	2	2	R	R	6-3	200	11-17-65	1987	No. Hollywood, Calif.
McCracken, Quinton	.357	55	221	33	79	11	4	1	26	21	32	26	8	S	R	5-8	170	3-16-70	1992	Southport, N.C.
Myrow, John	.246	96	353	52	87	18	1	3	50	25	67	16	5	R	R	6-0	177	2-11-72	1993	Pacific Palisades, Calif.
Perez, Neifi	.253	116	427	59	108	28	3	5	43	24	52	5	2	S	R	6-0	175	6-2-75	1993	Villa Mella, D.R.
Rogers, Lamarr	.283	109	371	68	105	15	0	0	31	64	50	21	7	R	R	5-8	165	6-24-71	1992	Altadena, Calif.
Scalzitti, Will	.187	39	123	9	23	6	0	1	14	10	17	0	0	R	R	6-0	190	8-29-72	1992	Hollywood, Fla.
Schmidt, Tom	.217	115	423	55	92	25	3	6	49	24	99	2	1	R	R	6-3	200	2-12-73	1992	Perry Hall, Md.
Sexton, Chris	.000	1	3	0	0	0	0	0	0	0	0	0	0	R	R	5-11	180	8-3-71	1993	Cincinnati, Ohio
Snyder, Randy	.235	5	17	2	4	1	0	0	2	0	3	0	2	R	R	6-2	210	3-28-67	1988	Kent, Wash.
Strittmatter, Mark	.243	90	288	44	70	12	1	7	42	47	51	1	0	R	R	6-1	200	4-4-69	1992	Ridgewood, N.J.
Wells, Forry	.214	4	14	3	3	0	0	0	1	1	2	0	0	L	R	6-4	205	3-21-71	1994	Belleville, Ill.
White, Billy	.232	58	181	25	42	9	1	3	34	27	44	2	2	R	R	6-0	185	7-3-68	1989	Louisville, Ky.

PITCHING

	W	L	ERA	G	GS	CG	SV	IP	H	R	ER	BB	SO	B	T	HT	WT	DOB	1st Yr	Resides
Alston, Garvin	4	4	2.84	47	0	0	6	67	47	24	21	26	73	R	R	6-2	188	12-8-71	1992	Mt. Vernon, N.Y.
Aminoff, Matt	0	2	1.54	6	0	0	0	12	9	7	2	6	10	R	R	6-1	185	12-29-71	1993	Santa Monica, Calif.
Arteaga, Ivan	2	4	5.56	14	11	0	0	34	36	26	21	21	18	L	R	6-2	220	7-20-72	1989	Puerto Cabello, Venez.
Brownson, Mark	0	0	1.50	1	1	0	0	6	4	2	1	1	4	R	R	6-2	175	6-17-75	1994	Wellington, Fla.
Farmer, Mike	10	5	4.89	40	12	0	0	110	117	63	60	35	77	S	L	6-1	200	7-3-68	1990	Gary, Ind.
Grundt, Ken	2	2	2.13	28	0	0	3	38	26	14	9	10	27	L	L	6-4	195	8-26-69	1991	Chicago, Ill.
Henderson, Chris	0	0	0.00	3	0	0	0	4	1	0	0	2	2	R	R	6-3	205	12-15-71	1992	Boca Raton, Fla.
Holman, Brad	0	0	3.38	7	1	0	0	16	8	6	6	5	9	R	R	6-5	200	2-9-68	1990	Wichita, Kan.
Hutchins, Jason	0	0	3.86	12	1	0	1	14	13	6	6	14	14	R	R	6-1	185	3-20-70	1992	Irvine, Calif.
Johnson, Jason	6	3	5.32	19	12	0	0	68	77	43	40	29	37	R	R	6-6	225	1-7-71	1993	Williamsport, Pa.
Jones, Bobby	5	2	2.58	27	8	0	3	73	61	27	21	36	70	R	L	6-4	205	4-11-72	1992	Rutherford, N.J.
Kotarski, Mike	2	3	3.24	31	0	0	2	50	43	25	18	36	54	L	L	6-1	195	9-18-70	1992	Peabody, Mass.
Moore, Joel	14	6	3.20	27	26	1	0	157	156	69	56	67	102	L	R	6-2	200	8-13-72	1993	Elgin, Ill.
Neier, Chris	10	4	4.16	38	18	1	0	123	164	62	57	47	74	R	R	6-2	185	12-22-68	1988	Denver, Colo.
Nied, David	0	0	8.10	1	1	0	0	3	4	3	3	0	0	R	R	6-3	205	6-3-73	1993	Orland Park, Ill.
Rekar, Bryan	6	3	2.13	12	12	1	0	80	65	28	19	16	80	R	R	6-3	205	6-3-72	1993	Austin, Texas
Ruffin, Bruce	0	0	0.00	2	2	0	0	2	1	0	0	0	2	S	L	6-2	213	10-4-63	1985	Austin, Texas
Salamon, John	1	0	6.10	6	0	0	0	10	9	7	7	16	9	R	R	6-1	220	3-30-72	1991	McKees Rocks, Pa.
Schneider, Phil	0	1	7.71	2	2	0	0	7	8	8	6	8	9	R	R	6-1	215	4-26-71	1993	Westbury, N.Y.
Tellers, Dave	2	5	2.87	33	3	0	1	69	60	29	22	14	63	R	R	5-10	175	3-13-68	1990	Buena Park, Calif.
Thomson, John	7	8	4.18	26	24	0	0	131	132	69	61	56	82	R	R	6-3	175	10-1-73	1993	Sulphur, La.
Viano, Jacob	3	6	3.38	57	0	0	19	72	51	31	27	38	85	R	R	5-11	180	9-4-73	1993	Long Beach, Calif.
Voisard, Mark	2	0	3.23	27	0	0	2	31	31	12	11	14	22	R	R	6-5	210	11-4-69	1992	Sidney, Ohio
Wright, Jamey	0	1	9.00	1	1	0	0	3	6	3	3	3	0	R	R	6-6	205	12-24-74	1993	Richardson, Texas
Zolecki, Mike	3	4	3.25	9	7	0	0	55	56	25	20	20	32	R	R	6-2	195	12-6-71	1993	South Milwaukee, Wisc.

FIELDING

Catcher	PCT	G	PO	A	E	DP	PB
Higgins	.980	17	92	7	2	0	4
Scalzitti	.996	39	220	28	1	0	4
Snyder	.941	5	30	2	2	0	1
Strittmatter	.990	90	664	48	7	3	4

First Base	PCT	G	PO	A	E	DP
Case	.984	39	222	18	4	22
Hartung	.966	3	26	2	1	1
Kennedy	.984	117	938	70	16	105

Second Base	PCT	G	PO	A	E	DP
Gonzalez	.986	17	31	40	1	7
Rogers	.984	104	203	290	8	61

	PCT	G	PO	A	E	DP
White	.963	31	57	101	6	27

Third Base	PCT	G	PO	A	E	DP
Case	1.000	12	8	8	0	1
Dixon	.815	12	9	13	5	0
Gonzalez	1.000	5	1	3	0	0
Hartung	.923	5	6	6	1	1
Schmidt	.897	113	79	181	30	21
White	1.000	8	6	12	0	3

Shortstop	PCT	G	PO	A	E	DP
Gonzalez	.933	22	22	61	6	13
Perez	.967	114	175	358	18	80

	PCT	G	PO	A	E	DP
Sexton	1.000	1	0	3	0	0
White	.917	10	10	23	3	6

Outfield	PCT	G	PO	A	E	DP
Case	.979	52	86	8	2	1
Echevarria	.978	105	202	20	5	0
T. Jones	.966	121	264	18	10	0
List	.920	18	22	1	2	0
McCracken	.971	53	92	10	3	0
Myrow	.977	94	161	11	4	0
Wells	1.000	4	5	0	0	0

SALEM

CAROLINA LEAGUE

A

BATTING	AVG	G	AB	R	H	2B	3B	HR	RBI	BB	SO	SB	CS	B	T	HT	WT	DOB	1st Yr	Resides
Bernhardt, Steven	.217	59	180	18	39	3	2	4	16	8	38	2	3	R	R	6-0	180	10-9-70	1993	Timonium, Md.
Carpenter, Matt	.000	1	0	0	0	0	0	0	0	0	0	0	0	R	R	6-0	195	9-28-72	1994	Euclid, Ohio
Carranza, Pete	.216	18	51	9	11	2	0	4	8	9	8	2	0	R	R	5-9	185	9-29-71	1993	El Centro, Calif.
Culp, Brian	.279	128	459	69	128	33	1	8	63	71	80	8	3	R	R	6-0	195	7-5-70	1993	Overland Park, Kan.
Dixon, Colin	.291	57	220	25	64	13	1	5	30	13	30	0	0	R	R	6-5	215	8-27-68	1989	West Vancouver, B.C.
Garcia, Vicente	.243	119	457	62	111	26	1	10	41	53	73	5	0	R	R	6-0	170	2-14-75	1993	Maracaibo, Venez.
Giudice, John	.258	99	356	49	92	21	4	7	48	24	81	7	4	R	R	6-1	205	6-19-71	1993	New Britain, Conn.
Grunewald, Keith	.265	118	412	48	109	22	1	6	45	46	84	8	4	S	R	6-1	185	10-15-71	1993	Marietta, Ga.
Higgins, Mike	.241	53	158	9	38	9	0	0	18	17	30	1	3	R	R	6-0	205	6-3-71	1993	Nutley, N.J.
Holdren, Nate	.245	119	420	48	103	16	2	15	69	34	126	6	3	R	R	6-4	240	12-8-71	1993	Richland, Wash.
Jones, Pookie	.208	16	53	9	11	3	0	1	3	3	16	1	1	R	R	6-1	190	7-13-71	1994	Killen, Ala.
Lezeau, James	.000	4	5	0	0	0	0	0	0	1	3	0	0	L	R	6-3	190	7-11-72	1994	Prescott Valley, Ariz.
Pozo, Yohel	.170	43	135	7	23	4	0	0	3	2	21	0	1	R	R	6-2	188	10-17-73	1992	Maracaibo, Venez.
Scalzitti, Will	.200	11	5	4	1	0	0	0	0	4	5	0	1	R	R	6-0	190	8-29-72	1992	Hollywood, Fla.
Sexton, Chris	.267	123	461	81	123	16	6	4	32	93	55	14	11	R	R	5-11	180	8-3-71	1993	Cincinnati, Ohio
2-team (4 W-S)	.271	127	476	84	129	16	6	5	37	97	55	14	11							
Smith, Jason	.093	30	86	4	8	1	1	1	5	11	38	0	0	R	R	6-4	225	9-12-70	1993	Arlington, Texas
Snyder, Randy	.289	23	76	19	22	5	0	3	14	18	13	2	1	R	R	6-2	210	3-28-67	1988	Kent, Wash.
Velazquez, Edgard	.300	131	497	74	149	25	6	13	69	40	102	7	10	R	R	6-0	170	12-15-75	1993	Guaynabo, P.R.
Wells, Forry	.254	119	402	60	102	23	4	18	67	56	105	6	3	L	R	6-4	205	3-21-71	1994	Belleville, Ill.
Wells, Mark	.195	66	236	24	46	8	0	10	31	13	83	0	3	L	R	6-0	195	4-4-72	1994	Mission Viejo, Calif.

GAMES BY POSITION: C—Dixon 2, Higgins 51, Pozo 42, Scalzitti 11, Smith 24, Snyder 23. **1B**—Bernhardt 2, Dixon 38, Grunewald 1, Holdren 90, Smith 1, F. Wells 19. **2B**—Bernhardt 25, Garcia 114, Grunewald 2, Sexton 3. **3B**—Bernhardt 21, Carranza 13, Dixon 1, Grunewald 87, Holdren 1, F. Wells 1. **SS**—Grunewald 26, Sexton 116. **OF**—Bernhardt 3, Carranza 1, Culp 106, Giudice 98, Lezeau 3, Sexton 3, Velasquez 131, F. Wells 39, M. Wells 56.

PITCHING	W	L	ERA	G	GS	CG	SV	IP	H	R	ER	BB	SO	B	T	HT	WT	DOB	1st Yr	Resides
Aminoff, Matt	4	6	3.21	39	0	0	16	53	53	28	19	22	31	R	R	6-1	185	12-29-71	1993	Santa Monica, Calif.
Barnes, Keith	4	5	5.35	15	15	1	0	79	90	52	47	24	43	L	L	6-3	189	8-9-74	1992	Hixson, Tenn.
Bliss, Bill	3	2	4.23	34	0	0	4	45	38	24	21	25	23	R	R	6-6	205	10-10-69	1991	Stoneboro, Pa.
Brownson, Mark	2	1	4.02	9	1	0	1	16	16	8	7	10	9	R	R	6-2	175	6-17-75	1994	Wellington, Fla.
Conley, Curt	4	1	3.61	39	0	0	3	47	42	22	19	27	35	L	L	6-2	210	2-19-71	1993	Clayton, Ohio
Crowther, Brent	3	6	2.76	12	12	3	0	78	70	31	24	25	60	R	R	6-4	220	5-15-72	1994	North Vancouver, B.C.
Dietrich, Jason	1	0	8.59	6	0	0	0	7	9	7	7	8	9	R	R	5-11	190	11-15-72	1994	Garden Grove, Calif.
Garrett, Neil	1	0	12.27	5	0	0	0	4	5	8	5	5	3	R	R	6-1	170	7-4-74	1992	Joliet, Ill.
Goldman, Barry	0	3	5.79	8	0	0	0	9	8	7	6	7	6	R	R	6-0	185	8-24-68	1993	Tempe, Ariz.
Johnson, Jason	1	2	2.05	5	4	0	0	22	23	6	5	5	9	R	R	6-6	225	1-7-71	1993	Williamsport, Pa.
Kusiewicz, Mike	0	0	1.50	1	1	0	0	6	7	1	1	0	7	R	L	6-2	185	11-1-76	1995	Nepean, Ontario
Larock, Scott	5	4	3.90	52	1	0	4	102	96	52	44	27	92	R	R	6-1	195	9-17-72	1994	Cheshire, Conn.
Locklear, Jeff	0	0	12.79	6	0	0	0	6	10	9	9	4	3	L	L	6-4	210	2-6-70	1991	Glen Burnie, Md.
Million, Doug	5	7	4.62	24	23	0	0	111	111	71	57	89	95	L	L	6-4	175	10-13-75	1994	Sarasota, Fla.
Pool, Matt	9	9	4.80	28	28	2	0	165	191	90	88	50	95	S	R	6-6	190	7-8-73	1994	Fresno, Calif.
Saipe, Mike	5	3	3.48	21	9	0	3	85	68	35	33	32	90	R	R	6-1	190	9-10-73	1994	San Diego, Calif.
Salamon, John	1	0	6.14	8	0	0	1	15	13	10	10	5	9	R	R	6-1	220	3-30-72	1991	McKees Rocks, Pa.
Sobkoviak, Jeff	5	3	4.80	40	5	0	2	86	96	52	46	37	44	R	R	6-7	225	8-22-71	1992	Iroquois, Ill.
Stewart, Chris	0	2	8.53	10	0	0	0	13	18	15	12	11	10	R	R	6-2	190	7-20-71	1993	Memphis, Tenn.
Voisard, Mark	0	0	7.36	6	0	0	0	7	8	6	6	4	5	R	R	6-5	210	11-4-69	1992	Sidney, Ohio
Waldron, Joe	1	2	2.51	9	0	0	0	14	23	5	4	1	17	L	L	6-0	180	7-4-69	1990	McAlester, Okla.
Walls, Doug	5	5	3.84	15	15	0	0	80	61	39	34	49	79	L	R	6-3	200	3-21-74	1993	Union, Ohio
Wright, Jamey	10	8	2.47	26	26	2	0	171	160	74	47	72	95	R	R	6-6	205	12-24-74	1993	Richardson, Texas
Zolecki, Mike	0	1	7.20	9	0	0	0	15	22	15	12	7	12	R	R	6-2	195	12-6-71	1993	South Milwaukee, Wisc.

ASHEVILLE   A
SOUTH ATLANTIC LEAGUE

BATTING	AVG	G	AB	R	H	2B	3B	HR	RBI	BB	SO	SB	CS	B	T	HT	WT	DOB	1st Yr	Resides
Arias, Rogelio	.160	67	213	9	34	4	0	0	4	7	25	0	3	R	R	6-0	165	6-9-76	1993	Santo Domingo, D.R.
Carpenter, Matt	.095	9	21	0	2	1	0	0	3	1	2	0	0	R	R	6-0	195	9-28-72	1994	Euclid, Ohio
Carranza, Pete	.254	111	433	67	110	32	2	5	29	45	49	10	9	R	R	5-9	185	9-29-71	1993	El Centro, Calif.
Elam, Brett	.000	1	2	0	0	0	0	0	0	0	1	0	0	R	R	6-0	170	8-1-72	1995	Council Bluffs, Iowa
Fantauzzi, John	.213	107	329	38	70	20	4	8	44	51	79	1	1	L	L	6-6	220	11-26-71	1992	Lakeland, Fla.
Figueroa, Danny	.233	80	227	34	53	22	1	3	22	24	73	3	7	R	R	5-11	182	3-6-74	1992	Rio Piedras, P.R.
Gambill, Chad	.256	106	367	34	94	25	1	8	57	16	92	6	4	R	R	6-2	190	11-27-74	1993	Clearwater, Fla.
Gibson, Derrick	.292	135	506	91	148	16	10	32	115	29	136	31	13	R	R	6-2	238	2-5-75	1993	Winter Haven, Fla.
Hall, Ronnie	.299	130	448	64	134	20	4	4	46	44	78	26	13	R	R	6-4	195	10-14-75	1993	Tustin, Calif.
Helton, Todd	.254	54	201	24	51	11	1	1	15	25	32	1	1	L	L	6-2	195	8-20-73	1995	Powell, Tenn.
Houser, Kyle	.211	112	361	43	76	11	0	2	32	34	43	5	4	R	R	6-0	150	1-21-75	1993	Dallas, Texas
Jarrett, Link	.235	116	404	46	95	11	0	0	20	62	60	12	10	S	R	5-10	165	1-26-72	1994	Tallahassee, Fla.
Jones, Pookie	.349	16	63	16	22	6	2	0	8	2	14	3	0	R	R	6-1	190	7-13-71	1994	Killen, Ala.
Light, Tal	.270	23	63	13	17	4	0	4	13	18	17	0	0	R	R	6-3	205	11-28-73	1995	Lumberton, Texas
Mayber, Chan	.193	34	88	11	17	4	0	3	7	9	19	7	0	R	R	5-11	160	10-7-72	1994	Pueblo, Colo.
Meskauskas, John	.278	30	79	11	22	4	0	3	13	4	16	0	1	R	R	5-11	205	1-16-73	1994	Palm City, Fla.
Myers, Aaron	.138	20	65	1	9	3	0	0	6	3	27	0	0	R	R	6-1	200	5-14-76	1994	Santa Maria, Calif.
Oakland, Mike	.208	18	48	4	10	1	0	0	2	10	6	0	0	R	R	6-4	215	7-18-70	1992	San Leandro, Calif.
Ocasio, Fred	.308	14	39	3	12	0	0	2	3	7	0	2	0	R	R	5-11	190	12-28-70	1994	Stillwater, Okla.
Ortman, Ben	.158	14	38	7	6	1	0	1	4	4	9	1	1	R	R	5-10	175	2-13-71	1993	Corvallis, Ore.
Pena, Elvis	.228	48	145	27	33	2	0	0	4	28	32	23	6	S	R	5-11	155	9-15-76	1994	Santo Domingo, D.R.
Pozo, Yohel	.216	40	139	7	30	3	0	1	15	4	32	0	3	R	R	6-2	188	10-17-73	1992	Maracaibo, Venez.
Resetar, Gary	.000	2	2	0	0	0	0	0	0	0	1	0	0	L	R	6-3	205	12-20-66	1988	Bayonne, N.J.
Smith, Jason	.100	24	80	7	8	3	0	1	8	8	40	0	1	R	R	6-2	225	9-12-70	1993	Arlington, Texas
Wells, Mark	.287	40	115	21	33	6	3	8	23	9	38	1	3	L	R	6-0	195	4-4-72	1994	Mission Viejo, Calif.

GAMES BY POSITION: C—Arias 67, Carpenter 9, Meskauskas 29, Pozo 40, Smith 8. **1B**—Carranza 2, Fantauzzi 85, Figueroa 1, Helton 44, Oakland 7, Smith 5. **2B**—Carranza 1, Jarrett 80, Mayber 7, Ocasio 10, Pena 48. **3B**—Carranza 102, Elam 1, Mayber 22, Meskauskas 1, Myers 20, Ocasio 3. **SS**—Carranza 1, Jarrett 32, Mayber 2. **OF**—Carranza 3, Figueroa 49, Gambill 9, Gibson 125, Hall 130, Ortman 10, Wells 28.

PITCHING	W	L	ERA	G	GS	CG	SV	IP	H	R	ER	BB	SO	B	T	HT	WT	DOB	1st Yr	Resides
Barnes, Keith	2	0	1.98	10	1	0	1	36	25	10	8	15	21	L	L	6-3	189	8-9-74	1992	Hixson, Tenn.
Bost, Heath	4	1	1.52	9	2	0	0	24	20	6	4	3	17	R	R	6-4	200	10-13-74	1995	Taylorsville, N.C.
Brownson, Mark	6	7	4.01	23	12	0	1	99	106	52	44	29	94	R	R	6-2	175	6-17-75	1994	Wellington, Fla.
Burdick, Morgan	0	1	4.39	17	0	0	0	27	26	13	13	10	19	R	R	6-2	175	5-15-75	1993	Dunlap, Calif.
Colmenares, Luis	2	2	2.29	45	0	0	21	55	37	15	14	29	74	R	R	5-11	189	11-25-76	1994	Valencia, Venez.
Crowther, Brent	12	3	3.28	15	15	3	0	99	79	31	25	25	72	R	R	6-4	220	5-15-72	1994	North Vancouver, B.C.
Eden, Bill	5	3	2.14	33	0	0	9	67	55	22	16	14	80	L	L	6-2	205	4-4-73	1994	Franklin, Tenn.
Gonzalez, Jhonny	4	3	2.48	21	0	0	3	33	23	13	9	15	31	L	L	6-0	190	9-27-76	1994	Maracaibo, Venez.
Gooch, Arnold	5	8	2.94	21	21	1	0	129	111	51	42	57	117	R	R	6-2	195	11-12-76	1994	Levittown, Pa.
Grundt, Ken	0	0	0.30	20	0	0	1	30	18	1	1	7	38	L	L	6-4	195	8-26-69	1991	Chicago, Ill.
Hackman, Luther	11	11	4.64	28	28	2	0	165	162	95	85	65	108	R	R	6-3	205	10-10-74	1994	Columbus, Miss.
Henderson, Chris	1	1	1.63	17	0	0	1	28	20	6	5	18	28	R	R	6-3	205	12-15-71	1992	Boca Raton, Fla.
Kusiewicz, Mike	8	4	2.06	21	21	0	0	122	92	40	28	34	103	R	L	6-2	185	11-1-76	1995	Nepean, Ontario
Lasbury, Robert	0	2	8.64	6	0	0	0	8	10	11	8	6	5	R	R	6-2	195	8-5-72	1993	Waterbury, Conn.
Martin, Chandler	4	3	3.83	8	8	0	0	49	48	23	21	27	32	R	R	6-1	180	10-23-73	1995	Salem, Ore.
McAdams, Denny	0	0	3.86	5	0	0	0	7	7	4	3	2	7	R	R	6-0	175	11-20-73	1994	San Marcos, Calif.
McClinton, Patrick	1	2	3.51	18	0	0	2	33	27	16	13	9	12	L	L	6-5	210	8-9-71	1993	Louisville, Ky.
Rose, Brian	1	0	4.91	10	1	0	0	15	14	8	8	2	15	R	R	6-1	195	10-7-74	1994	Potsdam, N.Y.
Slamka, John	1	1	4.09	6	1	0	0	11	9	5	5	4	7	R	L	6-3	190	4-2-74	1994	Phoenix, Ariz.
Swanson, David	1	4	4.97	8	0	0	1	13	14	7	7	7	7	L	L	6-0	184	10-19-72	1991	Berlin, Conn.
2-team (27 Columbia)	8	5	2.02	37	4	0	4	80	62	21	18	38	67							
Vavrek, Mike	5	4	2.00	12	12	1	0	77	64	24	17	25	54	L	L	6-2	185	4-23-74	1995	Glendale Heights, Ill.
Waldrep, Art	0	3	5.68	15	3	0	1	32	48	23	20	10	21	R	R	6-2	180	6-4-72	1994	Cherokee, Ala.
Wehn, Kevin	2	2	6.30	5	0	0	1	10	9	7	7	4	9	R	R	6-2	205	8-23-72	1993	Cooper City, Fla.
Zolecki, Mike	0	2	3.80	5	0	0	1	43	34	20	18	29	33	R	R	6-2	195	12-6-71	1993	South Milwaukee, Wisc.

PORTLAND

NORTHWEST LEAGUE

BATTING	AVG	G	AB	R	H	2B	3B	HR	RBI	BB	SO	SB	CS	B	T	HT	WT	DOB	1st Yr	Resides
Arias, Rogelio	.279	13	43	4	12	1	0	0	3	1	3	3	1	R	R	6-0	165	6-9-76	1993	Santo Domingo, D.R.
Barthol, Blake	.236	56	191	20	45	10	2	1	25	22	32	5	2	R	R	6-0	200	4-7-73	1995	Emmaus, Pa.
Brzozoski, Marc	.233	66	240	22	56	6	2	2	25	25	71	6	4	R	R	6-1	195	7-27-73	1995	Calhoun, Ga.
Drizos, Justin	.205	71	224	37	46	15	1	3	24	54	55	7	1	L	L	6-2	200	12-8-73	1995	Irvine, Calif.
Elam, Brett	.143	33	84	11	12	0	0	0	8	17	17	3	2	R	R	6-0	170	8-1-72	1995	Council Bluffs, Iowa
Feuerstein, David	.268	70	269	40	72	10	3	5	44	23	41	20	8	R	R	6-2	200	7-19-73	1995	Scarsdale, N.Y.
Groseclose, Harold	.333	5	12	2	4	1	0	0	2	2	2	0	1	R	R	5-11	165	10-4-72	1995	Covington, Va.
Hallead, John	.168	45	143	17	24	5	2	1	16	15	49	9	5	L	L	5-10	180	2-4-76	1994	Ellensburg, Wash.
Jimenez, Elvis	.179	37	123	8	22	0	2	1	9	8	36	7	4	R	R	5-11	170	3-12-76	1994	Santo Domingo, D.R.
Mayber, Chan	.205	27	78	13	16	2	1	0	8	13	22	6	3	R	R	5-11	160	10-7-72	1994	Pueblo, Colo.
Meskauskas, John	.345	9	29	4	10	3	0	1	9	8	7	2	2	R	R	5-11	205	1-16-73	1994	Palm City, Fla.
Myers, Aaron	.201	57	184	25	37	5	0	6	24	23	44	1	3	R	R	6-1	200	5-14-76	1994	Santa Maria, Calif.
Neubart, Garrett	.266	39	128	23	34	8	0	0	8	21	24	12	3	R	R	5-10	160	11-7-73	1995	Livingston, N.J.
Pena, Elvis	.251	58	215	29	54	6	3	0	18	26	45	28	7	S	R	5-11	155	9-15-76	1994	Santo Domingo, D.R.
Reynolds, Paul	.207	45	135	15	28	7	1	1	6	5	43	9	3	R	R	6-2	205	11-27-72	1994	Snowflake, Ariz.
Twist, Jeff	.139	27	79	6	11	3	0	0	6	9	18	0	2	S	R	6-3	220	6-17-73	1994	Bakersfield, Calif.
Whitley, Bill	.230	64	230	40	53	10	2	0	20	35	33	8	3	R	R	6-0	170	3-29-72	1995	Dunwoody, Ga.

GAMES BY POSITION: C—Arias 13, Barthol 47, Meskauskas 7, Twist 14. 1B—Drizos 71, Twist 8. 2B—Elam 4, Groseclose 4, Mayber 17, Myers 1, Pena 5. 3B—Elam 14, Mayber 9, Myers 51, Reynolds 16. SS—Elam 15, Groseclose 1, Mayber 1, Whitley 58. OF—Brzozoski 52, Feuerstein 64, Hallead 38, Jimenez 27, Neubart 3, Reynolds 25.

PITCHING	W	L	ERA	G	GS	CG	SV	IP	H	R	ER	BB	SO	B	T	HT	WT	DOB	1st Yr	Resides
Bevel, Bobby	2	3	3.54	25	0	0	1	28	24	13	11	18	25	L	L	6-3	180	10-10-73	1995	West Plains, Md.
Bost, Heath	1	0	3.38	10	0	0	0	16	15	6	6	0	25	R	R	6-4	200	10-13-74	1995	Taylorsville, N.C.
D'Alessandro, Marc	9	3	2.96	16	15	2	0	97	85	41	32	28	64	L	L	6-2	195	7-23-75	1994	Ocean, N.J.
Dietrich, Jason	0	0	0.00	10	1	0	4	13	5	0	0	5	24	R	R	5-11	190	11-15-72	1994	Garden Grove, Calif.
Emiliano, Jamie	4	1	3.49	28	0	0	11	39	31	18	15	16	41	R	R	5-10	210	8-2-74	1995	Andrews, Texas
Gonzalez, Laril	3	4	4.06	15	11	0	2	58	44	31	26	43	48	R	R	6-4	180	5-25-76	1994	San Cristobal, D.R.
Kammerer, James	2	1	1.53	11	5	0	0	35	24	8	6	11	17	L	L	6-3	205	7-21-73	1995	Winona, Mn
Keehn, Drew	2	4	3.80	20	0	0	0	43	38	22	18	17	30	R	R	6-2	185	9-19-74	1995	Chandler, Ariz.
Macca, Chris	3	2	3.28	24	0	0	5	36	25	15	13	17	41	R	R	6-2	185	11-14-74	1995	Plant City, Fla.
Martin, Chandler	4	1	1.66	7	7	0	0	38	20	10	7	21	34	R	R	6-1	180	10-23-75	1995	Salem, Ore.
Murphy, Sean	2	0	1.59	21	0	0	0	40	21	11	7	16	39	R	R	6-1	180	12-7-72	1995	Hays, Kan.
Nied, David	0	0	0.00	1	1	0	0	3	1	0	0	1	5	R	R	6-2	185	12-22-68	1988	Denver, Colo.
Randall, Scott	7	3	1.99	15	15	1	0	95	76	35	21	28	78	R	R	6-3	178	10-29-75	1995	Goleta, Calif.
Reitzenstein, Brad	1	1	10.13	7	0	0	0	8	12	10	9	6	10	R	R	5-11	195	4-5-73	1995	Vancouver, Wash.
Romine, Jason	0	1	6.39	4	3	0	0	13	14	9	9	7	5	R	R	6-5	215	4-11-75	1995	Omak, Wash.
Rose, Brian	1	1	5.19	5	0	0	0	9	10	5	5	6	11	R	R	6-1	195	10-7-72	1994	Potsdam, N.Y.
Vavrek, Mike	0	0	0.00	3	0	0	0	14	8	0	0	3	14	L	L	6-2	185	4-23-74	1995	Glendale Heights, Ill.
Wuestenhoefer, Brady	1	9	4.64	14	14	1	0	78	88	50	40	23	50	R	R	6-3	215	3-7-75	1995	Greenville, Miss.

CHANDLER

ARIZONA LEAGUE

BATTING	AVG	G	AB	R	H	2B	3B	HR	RBI	BB	SO	SB	CS	B	T	HT	WT	DOB	1st Yr	Resides
Acevedo, Juan	.211	29	90	10	19	2	1	0	8	9	25	2	4	R	R	5-11	168	11-29-76	1994	Santo Domingo, D.R.
Alamo, Efrain	.252	39	147	14	37	4	4	0	14	7	36	4	2	R	R	6-2	190	10-5-76	1994	Canovanas, P.R.
Cespedes, Angel	.211	19	57	11	12	1	1	0	11	7	12	1	4	S	R	5-11	168	10-25-77	1995	Azua, D.R.
Clark, John	.203	52	192	22	39	5	1	0	12	14	52	6	1	R	R	6-3	185	10-17-76	1995	Cibolo, Texas
Duverge, Salvador	.287	46	164	22	47	9	3	1	18	20	36	11	4	R	R	6-0	165	5-14-76	1994	San Cristobal, D.R.
Gordon, Gary	.252	36	135	20	34	2	1	0	8	22	37	20	7	R	R	5-10	190	12-13-76	1995	Willingboro, N.J.
Groseclose, Harold	.252	31	119	19	30	4	1	0	8	15	26	4	0	R	R	5-11	165	10-4-72	1995	Covington, Va.
Kirkpatrick, Brian	.139	38	122	11	17	1	0	1	7	11	54	4	1	R	R	6-3	170	9-7-76	1995	King City, Calif.
Lindsey, John	.235	48	179	23	42	10	0	2	22	11	48	0	2	R	R	6-3	230	1-30-77	1995	Hattiesburg, Miss.
McNally, Jason	.213	41	141	18	30	2	0	0	18	18	39	2	1	R	R	6-1	200	3-2-72	1995	Prescott, Ariz.
Niles, David	.198	40	116	21	23	3	0	0	9	22	50	3	0	L	L	6-2	195	9-6-76	1994	Summerland Key, Fla.
Rushdan, Rasheed	.000	6	18	1	0	0	0	0	3	2	5	0	0	R	R	6-2	200	4-14-76	1994	Cheraw, S.C.
Selga, Andres	.179	21	67	7	12	2	0	0	5	5	29	1	1	R	R	6-2	173	7-29-77	1995	Valencia, Venez.
Silverio, Richard	.272	35	136	19	37	4	4	1	19	8	34	2	3	L	L	6-2	159	11-7-76	1994	Santo Domingo, D.R.
Vidal, Carlos	.287	49	136	19	39	11	1	0	20	23	20			R	R	6-2	190	4-21-75	1995	Rio Piedras, P.R.

GAMES BY POSITION: C—McNally 23, Vidal 34. 1B—Lindsey 26, McNally 1, Niles 34. 2B—Cespedes 15, Clark 17, Groseclose 23, Kirkpatrick 3. 3B—Acevedo 15, Clark 3, Kirkpatrick 23, McNally 17. SS—Cespedes 4, Clark 32, Groseclose 8, Kirkpatrick 12. OF—Acevedo 12, Alamo 36, Duverge 39, Gordon 32, Niles 1, Rushdan 5, Selga 13, Silverio 31.

PITCHING	W	L	ERA	G	GS	CG	SV	IP	H	R	ER	BB	SO	B	T	HT	WT	DOB	1st Yr	Resides
Contreras, Orlando	2	2	6.04	16	0	0	1	28	40	27	19	17	18	R	R	6-0	162	9-17-76	1995	Maracaibo, Venez.
Douglas, Reggie	0	1	9.33	15	0	0	1	27	37	29	28	19	17	R	R	6-5	216	2-2-77	1995	Los Angeles, Calif.
Druckrey, Chris	0	8	5.04	14	13	0	0	70	75	54	39	38	65	R	R	6-5	220	8-18-74	1995	St. Anne, Ill.
Florentino, Osmil	0	2	6.85	19	0	0	2	43	55	42	33	17	27	R	R	6-5	180	12-6-77	1994	Bonao, D.R.
Kammerer, James	1	0	0.96	6	0	0	0	9	11	5	1	3	14	L	L	6-3	205	7-21-73	1995	Winona, Mn
Mahlberg, John	2	3	4.38	10	7	0	0	39	44	27	19	21	52	R	R	6-2	197	10-21-76	1995	Coquille, Ore.
Martino, Wil	3	1	5.32	16	3	0	0	44	48	27	26	23	44	L	L	6-4	188	12-6-77	1995	Santo Domingo, D.R.
Nivar, Amaury	0	0	11.12	6	0	0	0	11	14	18	14	14	10	R	R	6-0	190	2-17-78	1995	Santo Domingo, D.R.
Podjan, James	2	7	9.00	17	5	0	0	45	71	58	45	27	30	R	R	6-2	180	3-4-75	1995	St. Joseph, Mich.
Rosa, Cristy	0	0	5.37	12	12	0	0	59	77	56	35	16	42	R	R	6-1	155	10-5-77	1995	Guanica, P.R.
Segura, Juan	0	1	5.22	20	0	0	1	29	32	19	17	19	20	L	L	6-2	185	7-8-75	1994	San Pedro de Macoris, D.R.
Stahl, Anders	3	5	3.46	12	12	0	0	52	42	31	20	19	44	R	R	6-0	175	7-20-75	1994	Anderson, Calif.
Williams, Patrick	0	2	5.65	5	3	0	0	14	21	16	9	10	6	R	R	6-0	180	4-2-76	1995	Kent, Wash.

DETROIT TIGERS

Manager: Sparky Anderson. **1995 Record:** 60-84, .417 (4th, AL East).

BATTING	AVG	G	AB	R	H	2B	3B	HR	RBI	BB	SO	SB	CS	B	T	HT	WT	DOB	1st Yr	Resides
Bautista, Danny	.203	89	271	28	55	9	0	7	27	12	68	4	1	R	R	5-11	170	5-24-72	1989	Santo Domingo, D.R.
Clark, Tony	.238	27	101	10	24	5	1	3	11	8	30	0	0	S	R	6-8	240	6-15-72	1990	El Cajon, Calif.
Curtis, Chad	.268	144	586	96	157	29	3	21	67	70	93	27	15	R	R	5-10	175	11-6-68	1989	Middleville, Mich.
Cuyler, Milt	.205	41	88	15	18	1	4	0	5	8	16	2	1	S	R	5-10	185	10-7-68	1986	Lakeland, Fla.
Fielder, Cecil	.243	136	494	70	120	18	1	31	82	75	116	0	1	R	R	6-3	250	9-21-63	1982	Grosse Point Farms, Mich.
Flaherty, John	.243	112	354	39	86	22	1	11	40	18	47	0	0	R	R	6-1	202	10-21-67	1988	West Nyack, N.Y.
Fletcher, Scott	.231	67	182	19	42	10	1	1	17	19	27	1	0	R	R	5-11	173	7-30-58	1979	Fayetteville, Ga.
Fryman, Travis	.275	144	567	79	156	21	5	15	81	63	100	4	2	R	R	6-1	194	3-25-69	1987	Cantonment, Fla.
Gibson, Kirk	.260	70	227	37	59	12	2	9	35	33	61	9	2	L	L	6-3	225	5-28-57	1978	Grosse Pointe, Mich.
Gomez, Chris	.223	123	431	49	96	20	2	11	50	41	96	4	1	R	R	6-1	183	6-16-71	1992	Lakewood, Calif.
Hall, Joe	.133	7	15	2	2	0	0	0	2	2	3	0	0	R	R	6-0	180	3-6-66	1988	Paducah, Ky.
Higginson, Bob	.224	131	410	61	92	17	5	14	43	62	107	6	4	L	R	5-11	180	8-18-70	1992	Philadelphia, Pa.
Nevin, Phil	.219	29	96	9	21	3	1	2	12	11	27	0	0	R	R	6-2	185	1-19-71	1992	Placentia, Calif.
Pemberton, Rudy	.300	12	30	3	9	3	1	0	3	1	5	0	0	R	R	6-1	185	12-17-69	1987	San Pedro de Macoris, D.R.
Penn, Shannon	.333	3	9	0	3	0	0	0	0	1	2	0	0	S	R	5-10	163	9-11-69	1989	Cincinnati, Ohio
Rodriguez, Steve	.194	12	31	4	6	1	0	0	0	5	9	1	2	R	R	5-9	170	11-29-70	1992	Las Vegas, Nev.
2-team (6 Boston)	.179	18	39	5	7	1	0	0	0	6	10	2	2							
Samuel, Juan	.281	76	171	28	48	10	1	10	34	24	38	5	4	R	R	5-11	180	12-9-60	1980	Santo Domingo, D.R.
Steverson, Todd	.262	30	42	11	11	0	0	2	6	6	10	2	0	R	R	6-2	185	11-15-71	1992	Inglewood, Calif.
Stubbs, Franklin	.250	62	116	13	29	11	0	2	19	19	27	0	1	L	L	6-2	208	10-21-60	1982	Chino Hills, Calif.
Tingley, Ron	.226	54	124	14	28	8	1	4	18	15	38	0	1	R	R	6-2	194	5-27-59	1977	Riverside, Calif.
Trammell, Alan	.269	74	223	28	60	12	0	2	23	27	19	3	1	R	R	6-0	185	2-21-58	1976	Bloomfield Hills, Mich.
Whitaker, Lou	.293	84	249	36	73	14	0	14	44	31	41	4	0	L	R	5-11	180	5-12-57	1975	Lakeland, Fla.
White, Derrick	.188	39	48	3	9	2	0	0	2	0	7	1	0	R	R	6-1	215	10-12-69	1991	San Rafael, Calif.

PITCHING	W	L	ERA	G	GS	CG	SV	IP	H	R	ER	BB	SO	B	T	HT	WT	DOB	1st Yr	Resides
Ahearne, Pat	0	2	11.70	4	3	0	0	10	20	13	13	5	4	R	R	6-3	195	12-10-69	1992	Atascadero, Calif.
Bergman, Sean	7	10	5.12	28	28	1	0	135	169	95	77	67	86	R	R	6-4	205	4-11-70	1991	Joliet, Ill.
Blomdahl, Ben	0	0	7.77	14	0	0	1	24	36	21	21	13	15	R	R	6-2	185	12-30-70	1991	Riverside, Calif.
Boever, Joe	5	7	6.39	60	0	0	3	99	128	74	70	44	71	R	R	6-1	200	10-4-60	1982	Palm Harbor, Fla.
Bohanon, Brian	1	1	5.54	52	10	0	1	106	121	68	65	41	63	L	L	6-3	220	8-1-68	1987	Houston, Texas
Christopher, Mike	4	0	3.82	36	0	0	1	61	71	28	26	14	34	R	R	6-5	205	11-3-63	1985	Petersburg, Va.
Doherty, John	5	9	5.10	48	2	0	6	113	130	66	64	37	46	R	R	6-4	210	6-11-67	1989	Tuckahoe, N.Y.
Gardiner, Mike	0	0	14.59	9	0	0	0	12	27	20	20	2	7	S	R	6-0	190	10-19-65	1987	Canton, Mass.
Gohr, Greg	1	0	0.87	10	0	0	0	10	9	1	1	3	12	R	R	6-3	205	10-29-67	1989	Campbell, Calif.
Groom, Buddy	1	3	7.52	23	4	0	1	41	55	35	34	26	23	L	L	6-2	200	7-10-65	1987	Red Oak, Texas
Henneman, Mike	0	1	1.53	29	0	0	18	29	24	5	5	9	24	R	R	6-4	205	12-11-61	1984	Colleyville, Texas
Henry, Dwayne	1	0	6.23	10	0	0	5	9	11	6	6	10	9	R	R	6-3	205	2-16-62	1980	Glen Allen, Va.
Lima, Jose	3	9	6.11	15	15	0	0	74	85	52	50	18	37	R	R	6-2	170	9-30-72	1989	Santiago, D.R.
Lira, Felipe	9	13	4.31	37	22	0	1	146	151	74	70	56	89	R	R	6-0	170	4-26-72	1990	Miranda, Venez.
Maxcy, Brian	4	5	6.88	41	0	0	0	52	61	48	40	31	20	R	R	6-1	170	5-4-71	1992	Amory, Miss.
Moore, Mike	5	15	7.53	25	25	1	0	133	179	118	111	68	64	R	R	6-4	205	11-26-59	1981	Tempe, Ariz.
Myers, Mike	1	0	9.95	11	0	0	0	6	10	7	7	4	4	L	L	6-3	197	6-26-69	1990	Wheeling, Ill.
Nitkowski, C.J.	1	4	7.09	11	11	0	0	39	53	32	31	20	13	L	L	6-2	185	3-9-73	1994	Milford, Pa.
Sodowsky, Clint	1	3	5.01	6	6	0	0	23	24	15	13	18	14	L	R	6-3	180	7-13-72	1991	Ponca City, Okla.
Wells, David	10	3	3.04	18	18	3	0	130	120	54	44	37	83	L	L	6-4	225	5-20-63	1982	Palm Harbor, Fla.
Whiteside, Sean	0	0	14.73	2	0	0	0	4	7	6	6	4	2	L	L	6-4	190	4-19-71	1992	Cordele, Ga.
Wickander, Kevin	0	0	2.60	21	0	0	1	17	18	6	5	9	9	L	L	6-3	200	1-4-65	1986	Glendale, Ariz.

FIELDING

Catcher	PCT	G	PO	A	E	DP	PB
Flaherty	.982	112	569	33	11	5	0
Tingley	.991	53	198	19	2	2	3

First Base	PCT	G	PO	A	E	DP
Clark	.985	27	252	18	4	25
Fielder	.993	77	631	73	5	66
Fletcher	1.000	1	2	0	0	0
Samuel	.983	37	271	23	5	26
Stubbs	.972	20	134	5	4	13
Tingley	1.000	1	0	0	0	0
White	.981	16	47	5	1	4

Second Base	PCT	G	PO	A	E	DP
Fletcher	1.000	63	109	161	0	49
Gomez	.979	31	54	82	3	20
Penn	.864	3	10	9	3	4
Rodriguez	.982	12	21	34	1	6
Samuel	.955	6	9	12	1	3
Whitaker	.985	63	107	163	4	32

Third Base	PCT	G	PO	A	E	DP
Fryman	.969	144	107	337	14	38

Shortstop	PCT	G	PO	A	E	DP
Fletcher	1.000	3	0	1	0	0
Gomez	.973	97	155	279	12	61
Rodriguez	.000	1	0	0	0	0
Trammell	.980	60	86	158	5	34

Outfield	PCT	G	PO	A	E	DP
Bautista	.988	86	164	3	2	0
Curtis	.992	144	362	5	3	1
Cuyler	.929	36	50	2	4	0
Gibson	.000	1	0	0	0	0
Hall	1.000	5	11	1	0	0
Higginson	.985	123	247	13	4	3
Nevin	.963	27	50	2	2	0
Pemberton	1.000	8	15	0	0	0
Samuel	.750	9	9	0	3	0
Steverson	1.000	27	22	1	0	0
Stubbs	.955	20	21	0	1	0
White	.889	9	8	0	1	0

Cecil Fielder

Chad Curtis led the Tigers with 96 runs, 255 total bases and 27 steals

Tigers minor league Player of the Year Brandon Reed

MORRIS FOSTOFF

JOHN SPEAR

TIGERS

FARM SYSTEM

Director of Scouting and Player Development: Jeff Scott.

Class	Farm Team	League	W	L	Pct.	Finish*	Manager(s)	First Yr
AAA	Toledo (Ohio) Mud Hens	International	71	71	.500	6th (10)	Tom Runnells	1987
AA	Jacksonville (Fla.) Suns	Southern	75	69	.521	5th (10)	Bill Plummer	1995
#A	Lakeland (Fla.) Tigers	Florida State	64	69	.481	9th (14)	Dave Anderson	1960
A	Fayetteville (N.C.) Generals	South Atlantic	86	55	.610	1st (14)	Dwight Lowry	1987
A	Jamestown (N.Y.) Jammers	New York-Penn	32	44	.421	13th (14)	Bruce Fields	1994
R	Lakeland (Fla.) Tigers	Gulf Coast	33	24	.579	6th (16)	Kevin Bradshaw	1995

*Finish in overall standings (No. of teams in league)   #Advanced level

ORGANIZATION LEADERS

MAJOR LEAGUERS

BATTING
*AVG	Travis Fryman	.275
R	Chad Curtis	96
H	Chad Curtis	157
TB	Chad Curtis	255
2B	Chad Curtis	29
3B	Two tied at	5
HR	Cecil Fielder	31
RBI	Cecil Fielder	82
BB	Cecil Fielder	75
SO	Cecil Fielder	116
SB	Chad Curtis	27

PITCHING
W	David Wells	10
L	Mike Moore	15
#ERA	David Wells	3.04
G	Joe Boever	60
CG	David Wells	3
SV	Mike Henneman	18
IP	Felipe Lira	146
BB	Mike Moore	68
SO	Felipe Lira	89

RON VESELY

Travis Fryman. *.275* average

MINOR LEAGUERS

BATTING
*AVG	Joe Hall, Toledo	.320
R	Richard Almanzar, Fayetteville/Lake.	76
H	Daryle Ward, Fayetteville	149
TB	Ivan Cruz, Jacksonville/Toledo	233
2B	Two tied at	32
3B	Three tied at	7
HR	Ivan Cruz, Jacksonville/Toledo	31
RBI	Daryle Ward, Fayetteville	106
BB	Ivan Cruz, Jacksonville/Toledo	66
SO	Glen Barker, Jacksonville	143
SB	Richard Almanzar, Fayetteville/Lake.	50

PITCHING
W	Cam Smith, Fayetteville	13
L	Greg Granger, Lakeland	12
#ERA	Scott Gardner, Fayetteville/Lakeland	2.15
G	John Kelly, Jacksonville	66
CG	Clint Sodowsky, Jacksonville/Toledo	6
SV	Brandon Reed, Fayetteville	41
IP	Clint Sodowsky, Jacksonville/Toledo	184
BB	Cam Smith, Fayetteville	87
SO	Cam Smith, Fayetteville	166

*Minimum 250 At-Bats   #Minimum 75 Innings

TOP 10 PROSPECTS

TY SPORT GROUP

Tony Clark

How the Tigers Top 10 prospects, as judged by Baseball America prior to the 1995 season, fared in 1995:

Player, Pos.	Club (Class—League)	AVG	AB	R	H	2B	3B	HR	RBI	SB
1. Tony Clark, 1b	Toledo (AAA—International)	.242	405	50	98	17	2	14	63	0
	Detroit	.238	101	10	24	5	1	3	11	0
2. Matt Brunson, ss	Fayetteville (A—South Atlantic)	.222	144	18	32	3	3	1	8	16
	Lakeland (A—Florida State)	.129	132	10	17	2	1	0	7	9
4. Bob Higginson, of	Detroit	.224	410	61	92	17	5	14	43	6
6. Keith Smith, ss	Did not play—Retired									
9. Jayson Bass, of	Fayetteville (A—South Atlantic)	.215	368	47	79	15	6	10	48	14

		W	L	ERA	G	SV	IP	H	BB	SO
3. Cade Gaspar, rhp	Lakeland (A—Florida State)	7	6	3.90	23	0	99	95	44	97
5. Jose Lima, rhp	Toledo (AAA—International)	5	3	3.01	11	0	75	69	14	40
	Detroit	3	9	6.11	15	0	74	85	18	37
7. Cam Smith, rhp	Fayetteville (A—South Atlantic)	13	8	3.81	29	0	149	110	87	166
8. Justin Thompson, lhp	Lakeland (A—Florida State)	2	1	4.88	6	0	24	30	8	20
	Jacksonville (AA—Southern)	6	7	3.73	18	0	123	110	38	98
10. Sean Whiteside, lhp	Jacksonville (AA—Southern)	2	0	3.78	27	0	33	34	20	17

INTERNATIONAL LEAGUE

BATTING	AVG	G	AB	R	H	2B	3B	HR	RBI	BB	SO	SB	CS	B	T	HT	WT	DOB	1st Yr	Resides
Baez, Kevin	.231	116	376	30	87	13	2	4	37	22	57	1	6	R	R	6-0	170	1-10-67	1988	Brooklyn, N.Y.
Bautista, Danny	.241	18	58	6	14	3	0	0	4	1	10	1	2	R	R	5-11	170	5-24-72	1989	Santo Domingo, D.R.
Briley, Greg	.238	31	84	8	20	4	1	1	7	6	25	0	2	L	R	5-8	180	5-24-65	1986	Greenville, N.C.
Brock, Tarrik	.194	9	31	4	6	1	0	0	2	17	2	2	1	L	L	6-3	170	12-25-73	1991	Hawthorne, Calif.
Clark, Tony	.242	110	405	50	98	17	2	14	63	52	129	0	2	S	R	6-8	240	6-15-72	1990	El Cajon, Calif.
Cruz, Ivan	.194	11	36	5	7	2	0	0	3	6	9	0	0	L	L	6-3	210	5-3-68	1989	Fajardo, P.R.
Cuyler, Milt	.305	54	203	33	62	10	4	6	28	20	40	6	7	S	R	5-10	185	10-7-68	1986	Lakeland, Fla.
Delli Carri, Joe	.250	4	12	4	3	0	0	1	1	1	2	1	0	R	R	6-1	178	1-16-67	1989	River Vale, N.J.
Givens, Jim	.237	79	219	23	52	5	1	0	14	26	40	7	5	S	R	6-1	173	11-11-67	1991	Findlay, Ohio
Gonzalez, Pete	.211	6	19	0	4	1	0	0	2	3	6	0	0	R	R	6-0	190	11-24-69	1989	Hialeah, Fla.
Hall, Joe	.320	91	319	52	102	19	2	11	47	36	50	4	1	R	R	6-0	180	3-6-66	1988	Paducah, Ky.
Hecht, Steve	.236	25	72	14	17	5	1	0	6	7	6	5	0	L	R	5-9	165	11-12-65	1988	Broken Arrow, Okla.
Leiper, Tim	.212	18	66	3	14	1	0	0	6	4	8	0	0	L	R	5-11	175	7-19-66	1985	Cary, N.C.
Lukachyk, Rob	.254	104	346	43	88	24	7	7	26	33	75	8	5	L	R	6-0	185	7-24-68	1987	Sarasota, Fla.
Mashore, Justin	.220	72	223	32	49	4	3	4	21	14	62	12	9	R	R	5-9	190	2-14-72	1991	Concord, Calif.
McGriff, Terry	.271	58	188	14	51	8	0	4	23	20	29	0	0	R	R	6-2	180	9-23-63	1981	Fort Pierce, Fla.
Mendenhall, Kirk	.200	11	30	2	6	1	0	1	4	5	1	2	0	R	R	5-9	160	9-17-67	1990	Rochester, Ill.
Milne, Darren	.150	7	20	0	3	1	0	0	4	1	4	0	0	R	R	6-1	190	3-24-71	1992	Sandy, Utah
Nevin, Phil	.304	7	23	3	7	2	0	1	3	1	5	0	0	R	R	6-2	185	1-19-71	1992	Placentia, Calif.
Pemberton, Rudy	.344	67	224	31	77	15	3	7	23	15	36	8	4	R	R	6-1	185	12-17-69	1987	San Pedro de Macoris, D.R.
Penn, Shannon	.248	63	218	41	54	4	1	1	15	17	40	15	9	S	R	5-10	163	9-11-69	1989	Cincinnati, Ohio
Rice, Lance	.268	15	41	2	11	1	0	1	6	4	6	0	3	S	R	6-1	195	10-19-66	1988	Salem, Ore.
Springer, Steve	.265	25	102	14	27	7	1	2	10	4	18	1	1	R	R	6-0	190	2-11-61	1982	Huntington Beach, Calif.
Steverson, Todd	.107	9	28	6	3	0	0	1	1	5	13	0	2	R	R	6-2	185	11-15-71	1992	Inglewood, Calif.
Tackett, Jeff	.269	96	301	32	81	15	0	6	30	35	46	2	1	R	R	6-2	206	12-1-65	1984	Cockeysville, Md.
White, Derrick	.265	87	309	50	82	15	3	14	49	29	65	6	6	R	R	6-1	215	10-12-69	1991	San Rafael, Calif.
Wilson, Craig	.263	121	468	56	123	31	0	9	65	37	61	8	2	R	R	5-11	210	11-28-64	1984	Annapolis, Md.
Zinter, Alan	.222	101	334	42	74	15	4	13	48	36	102	4	4	S	R	6-2	190	5-19-68	1989	El Paso, Texas

PITCHING	W	L	ERA	G	GS	CG	SV	IP	H	R	ER	BB	SO	B	T	HT	WT	DOB	1st Yr	Resides
Ahearne, Pat	7	9	4.70	25	23	1	0	140	165	83	73	37	54	R	R	6-3	195	12-10-69	1992	Atascadero, Calif.
Bauer, Matt	2	1	3.46	13	0	0	0	13	17	7	5	4	10	L	L	6-1	195	3-25-70	1991	Saginaw, Mich.
Bergman, Sean	0	1	6.00	1	1	0	0	3	4	2	2	0	4	R	R	6-4	205	4-11-70	1991	Joliet, Ill.
Blomdahl, Ben	5	4	3.54	41	0	0	3	56	55	24	22	13	39	R	R	6-2	185	12-30-70	1991	Riverside, Calif.
Bottenfield, Kent	5	11	4.54	27	19	2	1	137	148	80	69	55	68	R	R	6-2	225	11-14-68	1986	Royal Palm Beach, Fla.
Buckels, Gary	2	2	2.15	31	0	0	0	46	37	14	11	20	38	R	R	6-0	185	7-22-65	1987	Huntington Beach, Calif.
Carlyle, Ken	8	8	4.33	32	20	0	0	125	139	65	60	44	63	R	R	6-1	185	9-16-69	1992	Cordova, Tenn.
Christopher, Mike	2	4	2.23	36	0	0	21	36	38	14	9	8	32	R	R	6-5	205	11-3-63	1985	Petersburg, Va.
Gardiner, Mike	0	1	4.41	11	1	0	0	16	19	8	8	13	10	S	R	6-0	200	10-19-65	1987	Canton, Mass.
Gohr, Greg	0	2	2.87	6	4	0	0	16	16	9	5	8	15	R	R	6-3	205	10-29-67	1989	Campbell, Calif.
Gonzales, Frank	3	2	3.31	49	0	0	0	52	43	23	19	17	54	R	L	6-0	185	3-12-68	1989	La Junta, Colo.
Groom, Buddy	2	3	1.91	6	5	1	0	33	31	14	7	4	24	L	L	6-2	200	7-10-65	1987	Red Oak, Texas
Henry, Dwayne	1	1	3.35	41	0	0	11	48	43	21	18	24	52	R	R	6-3	205	2-16-62	1980	Glen Allen, Va.
Kiely, John	0	0	1.46	14	0	0	0	12	13	4	2	6	8	R	R	6-3	215	10-4-64	1988	Brockton, Mass.
Kramer, Tommy	3	1	4.61	6	5	0	0	27	23	15	14	16	15	S	R	6-2	205	1-9-68	1987	St. Bernard, Ohio
Lima, Jose	5	3	3.01	11	11	1	0	75	69	26	25	14	40	R	R	6-2	170	9-30-72	1989	Santiago, D.R.
Marshall, Randy	7	3	2.30	20	17	2	0	109	99	38	28	29	67	L	L	6-3	170	10-12-66	1989	Ypsilanti, Mich.
Martel, Ed	0	1	1.59	4	0	0	0	6	4	1	1	5	3	R	R	6-1	190	3-2-69	1987	New Baltimore, Mich.
Maxcy, Brian	1	3	5.26	20	0	0	2	26	32	20	15	11	11	R	R	6-1	170	5-4-71	1992	Amory, Miss.
Myers, Mike	0	0	4.32	6	0	0	0	8	6	4	4	3	8	L	L	6-3	197	6-26-69	1990	Wheeling, Ill.
2-team (37 Charlotte)	0	5	5.40	43	0	0	0	45	47	29	27	18	32							
Santos, Henry	0	1	6.75	1	0	0	0	3	3	2	2	2	4	L	L	6-1	175	1-17-73	1990	Santiago, D.R.
Sodowsky, Clint	5	1	2.85	9	9	1	0	60	47	21	19	30	32	L	R	6-3	180	7-13-72	1991	Ponca City, Okla.
Tunnell, Lee	0	1	3.14	7	0	0	0	14	9	5	5	2	7	R	R	6-1	178	10-30-60	1981	Austin, Texas
Weston, Mickey	11	7	2.90	28	27	2	0	180	170	68	58	41	69	R	R	6-1	180	3-26-61	1982	Fenton, Mich.
Wickander, Kevin	2	1	2.13	16	0	0	1	13	11	3	3	5	8	L	L	6-3	200	1-4-65	1986	Glendale, Ariz.

FIELDING

Catcher	PCT	G	PO	A	E	DP	PB
Gonzalez	.957	6	40	5	2	0	0
McGriff	1.000	40	167	18	0	1	2
Rice	1.000	15	70	9	0	1	0
Tackett	.987	93	485	58	7	5	6
Zinter	1.000	3	5	1	0	0	0

First Base	PCT	G	PO	A	E	DP
Clark	.981	62	615	51	13	73
Cruz	.969	9	89	6	3	9
Lukachyk	.929	2	13	0	1	1
White	.985	26	241	16	4	22
Zinter	.992	48	476	32	4	48

Second Base	PCT	G	PO	A	E	DP
Briley	.957	13	31	2	6	
Delli Carri	.970	4	14	18	1	6
Givens	.972	39	56	116	5	29
Hall	1.000	1	0	1	0	0
Hecht	.989	15	43	51	1	16

	PCT	G	PO	A	E	DP
Leiper	.933	6	17	11	2	2
Penn	.962	58	106	173	11	37
Springer	.976	22	46	75	3	19
Wilson	.966	7	8	20	1	4

Third Base	PCT	G	PO	A	E	DP
Givens	.839	12	8	18	5	3
Hall	.885	12	3	20	3	1
Leiper	1.000	2	3	6	0	0
McGriff	.786	3	4	7	3	3
Springer	.944	6	3	14	1	3
Tackett	1.000	1	2	2	0	0
Wilson	.921	113	72	256	28	18

Shortstop	PCT	G	PO	A	E	DP
Baez	.975	116	205	414	16	92
Givens	.952	28	37	83	6	17
Mendenhall	.955	9	14	28	2	10
Springer	.000	1	0	0	0	0

Outfield	PCT	G	PO	A	E	DP
Bautista	.943	18	32	1	2	0
Briley	.973	16	36	0	1	0
Brock	.929	9	12	1	1	0
Cuyler	.960	51	95	1	4	0
Hall	.993	73	145	5	1	1
Hecht	1.000	7	13	0	0	0
Leiper	1.000	4	11	0	0	0
Lukachyk	.988	96	157	2	2	1
Mashore	.986	68	140	6	2	1
Milne	1.000	6	3	1	0	0
Nevin	1.000	4	2	0	0	0
Pemberton	.953	43	59	2	3	2
Steverson	.818	7	8	1	2	0
White	.947	48	86	4	5	0
Zinter	.955	15	21	0	1	0

MICHAEL YELMAN

LARRY KINKER

Twin Killers. Detroit shortstop Alan Trammell, left, and second baseman Lou Whitaker set a major league record for most games played by a double play combination.

JACKSONVILLE AA
SOUTHERN LEAGUE

BATTING	AVG	G	AB	R	H	2B	3B	HR	RBI	BB	SO	SB	CS	B	T	HT	WT	DOB	1st Yr	Resides
Barker, Glen	.239	133	507	74	121	26	4	10	49	33	143	39	16	R	R	5-10	180	5-10-71	1993	Albany, N.Y.
Briley, Greg	.087	8	23	2	2	0	0	1	4	2	6	0	1	L	R	5-8	180	5-24-65	1986	Greenville, N.C.
Brock, Tarrik	.115	9	26	4	3	0	0	0	2	3	14	2	0	L	L	6-3	170	12-25-73	1991	Hawthorne, Calif.
Catalanotto, Frank	.226	134	491	66	111	19	5	8	48	49	56	13	8	L	R	6-0	170	4-27-74	1992	Smithtown, N.Y.
Colon, Felix	.259	31	81	5	21	7	0	2	8	13	13	0	0	R	R	6-0	176	9-15-70	1989	Levittown, P.R.
Cooper, Gary	.276	99	337	66	93	22	1	18	66	59	83	8	4	R	R	6-1	200	8-13-64	1986	Orem, Utah
Cruz, Ivan	.282	108	397	65	112	17	1	31	93	60	94	0	0	L	L	6-3	210	5-3-68	1989	Fajardo, P.R.
Danapilis, Eric	.258	129	415	47	107	24	1	10	63	61	100	3	3	R	R	6-2	220	6-11-71	1993	St. Joseph, Mich.
Delanuez, Rex	.263	111	331	47	87	22	1	9	41	49	74	10	6	R	R	5-10	175	1-7-68	1989	Burbank, Calif.
Fermin, Carlos	.173	59	127	10	22	4	0	1	9	5	16	0	2	R	R	5-9	140	7-12-73	1990	Mao Valverde, D.R.
Fernandez, Daniel	.165	94	230	18	38	5	0	4	16	29	60	1	3	R	R	5-11	180	6-6-66	1988	San Lorenzo, Calif.
Garcia, Luis	.277	17	47	6	13	0	0	0	5	1	8	2	1	R	R	6-0	174	5-20-75	1993	San Fran. de Macoris, D.R.
Hansen, Terrel	.223	55	179	22	40	8	0	9	22	10	40	0	1	R	R	6-3	210	9-25-66	1987	Bremerton, Wash.
Kimsey, Keith	.161	34	118	8	19	4	1	1	10	7	39	1	1	R	R	6-7	200	8-15-72	1991	Lakeland, Fla.
Leiper, Tim	.259	110	375	60	97	19	1	8	46	48	30	3	3	L	R	5-11	175	7-19-66	1985	Cary, N.C.
Lidle, Kevin	.163	36	80	12	13	7	0	1	5	1	31	1	0	R	R	5-11	170	3-22-72	1992	West Covina, Calif.
Mashore, Justin	.243	40	148	26	36	8	2	4	15	6	41	5	1	R	R	5-9	190	2-14-72	1991	Concord, Calif.
Perona, Joe	.147	13	34	2	5	3	0	0	3	2	5	0	0	R	R	6-0	195	2-8-70	1991	Spring Valley, Ill.
Pevey, Marty	.259	20	58	2	15	2	0	1	7	4	17	0	2	L	R	6-1	190	9-18-61	1982	Savannah, Ga.
Pratte, Evan	.250	18	52	2	13	2	0	0	1	7	9	0	3	S	R	5-10	175	12-18-68	1991	Ballwin, Mo.
Rendina, Mike	.224	31	98	12	22	5	0	3	16	7	20	0	1	L	L	6-4	215	9-28-70	1988	El Cajon, Calif.
Rice, Lance	.123	65	154	8	19	1	1	3	11	11	23	0	0	S	R	6-1	195	10-19-66	1988	Salem, Ore.
Sanchez, Yuri	.213	121	342	52	73	8	7	6	26	38	116	15	6	L	R	6-1	165	11-11-73	1992	Lynn, Mass.
Wooten, Shawn	.129	20	70	4	9	1	0	2	7	1	17	0	0	R	R	5-11	205	7-24-72	1993	LaVerne, Calif.

PITCHING	W	L	ERA	G	GS	CG	SV	IP	H	R	ER	BB	SO	B	T	HT	WT	DOB	1st Yr	Resides
Aldred, Scott	1	0	0.00	2	2	0	0	12	9	0	0	1	11	L	L	6-4	195	6-12-68	1987	Lakeland, Fla.
Bauer, Matt	1	1	4.12	27	0	0	0	44	43	22	20	22	30	L	L	6-1	195	3-25-70	1991	Saginaw, Mich.
Berlin, Mike	0	0	2.45	3	0	0	0	4	3	1	1	0	1	R	R	6-1	185	2-14-71	1992	Moundsville, W.Va.
Cedeno, Blas	3	2	3.46	48	5	0	0	81	71	34	31	36	53	R	R	6-0	165	11-15-72	1991	Carabobo, Venez.
Drumright, Mike	0	1	3.69	5	5	0	0	32	30	13	13	15	34	L	R	6-4	210	4-19-74	1995	Valley Center, Kan.
Gaillard, Eddie	0	1	5.63	8	0	0	0	8	11	5	5	5	4	R	R	6-1	180	8-13-70	1993	West Palm Beach, Fla.
Goldsmith, Gary	4	7	4.61	15	15	0	0	82	78	52	42	31	42	R	R	6-2	205	7-4-71	1993	Alamogordo, N.M.
Greene, Rick	6	2	3.49	32	0	0	0	39	45	19	15	15	29	R	R	6-5	200	1-2-71	1992	Miami, Fla.
Grimm, John	2	1	8.62	13	0	0	0	16	23	17	15	10	9	R	R	5-11	170	9-13-70	1992	Reynoldsburg, Ohio
Guilfoyle, Michael	5	1	2.88	56	0	0	3	59	55	23	19	31	50	L	L	5-11	187	4-29-68	1990	Bayonne, N.J.
Gutierrez, Jim	8	4	2.76	45	1	0	4	59	60	22	18	25	36	R	R	6-2	190	11-28-70	1989	Burlington, Wash.
Kelley, Rich	1	0	4.50	7	0	0	0	6	9	3	3	0	2	L	L	6-3	200	5-27-70	1991	Scituate, Mass.
Kelly, John	7	7	2.09	66	0	0	29	77	76	24	18	21	47	R	R	6-4	185	7-3-67	1990	Buford, Ga.

PITCHING

PITCHING	W	L	ERA	G	GS	CG	SV	IP	H	R	ER	BB	SO	B	T	HT	WT	DOB	1st Yr	Resides
Miller, Trever	8	2	2.72	31	16	3	0	122	122	46	37	34	77	R	L	6-3	175	5-29-73	1991	Louisville, Ky.
Moehler, Brian	8	10	4.82	28	27	0	0	162	176	94	87	52	89	R	R	6-3	195	12-31-71	1993	Rockingham, N.C.
Norman, Scott	1	3	2.48	4	4	2	0	29	31	12	8	6	9	R	R	6-0	195	9-1-72	1993	Sarasota, Fla.
Rosengren, John	2	7	4.52	14	13	0	0	68	73	39	34	40	59	L	L	6-4	190	8-10-72	1992	Rye, N.Y.
Sodowsky, Clint	5	5	2.55	19	19	5	0	124	102	46	35	50	77	L	R	6-3	180	7-13-72	1991	Ponca City, Okla.
Thompson, Justin	6	7	3.73	18	18	3	0	123	110	55	51	38	98	L	L	6-3	175	3-8-73	1991	Spring, Texas
Whiteside, Sean	2	0	3.78	27	1	0	0	33	34	17	14	20	17	L	L	6-4	190	4-19-71	1992	Cordele, Ga.
Withem, Shannon	5	8	5.75	19	18	0	0	108	142	77	69	24	80	R	R	6-3	185	9-21-72	1990	Ypsilanti, Mich.

FIELDING

Catcher	PCT	G	PO	A	E	DP	PB
Fernandez	.991	93	464	61	5	7	5
Lidle	.990	20	90	10	1	1	0
Perona	.909	6	17	3	2	0	0
Pevey	.952	5	19	1	1	0	0
Rice	.994	63	284	43	2	9	5

First Base	PCT	G	PO	A	E	DP
Colon	1.000	15	137	13	0	13
Cooper	1.000	5	38	3	0	3
Cruz	.992	81	795	60	7	86
Leiper	.986	26	250	23	4	23
Perona	1.000	1	1	0	0	0
Pevey	1.000	4	27	2	0	2
Rendina	1.000	23	219	10	0	20

Second Base	PCT	G	PO	A	E	DP
Catalanotto	.974	133	252	411	18	98
Fermin	1.000	7	4	12	0	2

	PCT	G	PO	A	E	DP
Leiper	1.000	10	13	32	0	7
Mashore	.000	1	0	0	0	0
Pratte	1.000	4	14	15	0	7
Sanchez	1.000	2	4	3	0	0

Third Base	PCT	G	PO	A	E	DP
Cooper	.957	75	38	162	9	11
Fermin	.889	18	6	26	4	2
Garcia	.000	1	0	0	0	0
Leiper	.944	33	21	80	6	12
Lidle	.786	6	2	9	3	2
Perona	.900	7	2	7	1	1
Pratte	.933	9	5	23	2	1
Wooten	.921	20	8	50	5	3

Shortstop	PCT	G	PO	A	E	DP
Cooper	.000	1	0	0	0	0
Fermin	.939	32	53	85	9	25

	PCT	G	PO	A	E	DP
Garcia	.929	15	19	46	5	8
Pratte	.857	4	3	3	1	0
Sanchez	.957	116	170	366	24	70

Outfield	PCT	G	PO	A	E	DP
Barker	.973	120	284	9	8	3
Briley	1.000	7	11	0	0	0
Brock	.929	9	12	1	1	0
Danapilis	.981	78	100	4	2	1
Delanuez	.992	82	117	9	1	1
Hansen	.986	44	69	3	1	1
Kimsey	.984	30	57	5	1	1
Leiper	.988	57	75	7	1	1
Lidle	.500	1	1	0	1	0
Mashore	1.000	40	88	2	0	1
Pevey	1.000	6	8	0	0	0

LAKELAND   A

FLORIDA STATE LEAGUE

BATTING

BATTING	AVG	G	AB	R	H	2B	3B	HR	RBI	BB	SO	SB	CS	B	T	HT	WT	DOB	1st Yr	Resides
Almanzar, Richard	.307	42	140	29	43	9	0	1	14	18	20	11	9	R	R	5-10	155	4-3-76	1993	San Fran. de Macoris, D.R.
Arano, Eloy	.283	102	353	35	100	9	1	0	33	9	55	5	6	S	R	5-11	170	3-5-74	1993	Veracruz, Mexico
Aybar, Ramon	.125	3	8	1	1	0	0	0	0	1	5	0	0	L	R	5-9	150	5-10-76	1994	Bani, D.R.
Borel, Jamie	.122	16	41	8	5	1	0	0	1	6	6	2	1	R	R	5-11	170	9-20-71	1994	Raleigh, N.C.
Brock, Tarrik	.209	28	91	12	19	3	0	0	5	12	32	5	3	L	L	6-3	170	12-25-73	1991	Hawthorne, Calif.
Brown, Shawn	.167	10	24	2	4	1	0	0	0	4	5	0	0	R	R	6-1	176	4-16-71	1993	Tabernacle, N.J.
Brunson, Matt	.129	45	132	10	17	2	1	0	7	26	41	9	2	S	R	5-11	165	9-2-74	1993	Englewood, Colo.
Christmon, Drew	.220	79	273	34	60	8	6	9	39	14	96	7	2	L	R	5-10	200	6-8-72	1993	Midwest City, Okla.
De la Cruz, Carlos	.000	2	3	0	0	0	0	0	0	0	2	0	0	R	R	6-2	175	7-24-75	1994	Santo Domingo, D.R.
DeJesus, Malvin	.301	73	239	39	72	7	5	3	23	27	51	7	6	R	R	5-9	160	9-16-71	1992	Carolina, P.R.
Driskell, Jeff	.262	23	61	8	16	4	0	2	8	5	17	0	0	R	R	6-2	212	1-20-72	1994	Vero Beach, Fla.
Facione, Chris	.293	110	400	44	117	17	6	5	56	35	76	20	10	R	R	6-3	190	9-21-70	1993	Millbrae, Calif.
Freeman, Sean	.290	114	414	42	120	21	2	6	65	49	98	3	4	L	L	6-3	205	9-10-71	1994	Andover, Ohio
Garcia, Luis	.280	102	361	39	101	10	4	2	35	8	42	9	10	R	R	6-0	174	5-20-75	1993	San Fran. de Macoris, D.R.
Hare, Rich	.150	9	20	3	3	0	0	0	2	1	4	0	0	R	R	6-2	175	10-28-71	1994	Dallas, Texas
Kimsey, Keith	.217	54	175	30	38	8	2	6	16	22	58	1	1	R	R	6-7	200	8-15-72	1991	Lakeland, Fla.
Landry, Lonny	.161	19	56	2	9	1	0	0	4	2	16	0	0	R	R	5-10	185	11-2-72	1993	Broussard, La.
Marine, Del	.241	77	257	27	62	14	0	4	25	13	63	5	1	R	R	6-0	195	10-18-71	1992	Woodland Hills, Calif.
Martin, Mike	.176	6	17	1	3	0	0	0	1	3	1	0	0	R	R	5-9	170	1-12-72	1994	Swansea, Mass.
Martinez, Dalvis	.189	38	111	12	21	5	0	0	5	12	26	0	1	R	R	5-10	185	12-5-73	1993	Santo Domingo, D.R.
Roberts, David	.303	92	357	67	108	10	5	3	30	39	43	30	8	L	L	5-10	172	5-31-72	1993	Oceanside, Calif.
Rodriguez, Adam	.250	30	88	8	22	4	0	1	10	8	17	1	0	R	R	5-10	195	3-16-71	1993	Tucson, Ariz.
Rojas, Roberto	.250	4	12	1	3	0	0	0	2	1	4	1	0	L	L	6-0	185	11-23-70	1991	Santo Domingo, D.R.
Thompson, Billy	.242	73	223	26	54	13	1	5	28	15	45	4	0	R	R	5-11	185	11-5-70	1994	Wayne, W. Va.
Trammell, Bubba	.284	122	454	61	129	32	3	16	72	48	80	13	3	R	R	6-2	205	11-6-71	1994	Knoxville, Tenn.
Williams, Ed	.267	4	15	1	4	1	1	0	1	0	4	0	0	S	R	6-3	220	1-22-72	1991	Miami, Fla.
Wooten, Shawn	.230	38	135	11	31	10	1	2	11	10	28	0	1	R	R	5-11	205	7-24-72	1993	LaVerne, Calif.

GAMES BY POSITION: C—Driskell 13, Marine 58, Rodriguez 15, B.Thompson 66, Williams 1. **1B**—Freeman 118, Marine 15, Rodriguez 13. **2B**—Almanzar 36, Arano 17, Aybar 3, Brunson 30, DeJesus 45, Garcia 9, Martin 6. **3B**—Almanzar 4, Arano 55, Brown 9, Martinez 38, Rodriguez 1, Wooten 38. **SS**—Arano 27, Borel 1, Brock 28, Christmon 54, De la Cruz 2, Facione 105, Hare 7, Kimsey 49, Landry 19, Roberts 31, Rojas 4, Trammell 113. **OF**—Arano 27, Brunson 4, DeJesus 4, Garcia 92.

PITCHING

PITCHING	W	L	ERA	G	GS	CG	SV	IP	H	R	ER	BB	SO	B	T	HT	WT	DOB	1st Yr	Resides
Aldred, Scott	4	2	3.19	13	7	0	2	68	57	25	24	19	64	L	L	6-4	195	6-12-68	1987	Lakeland, Fla.
Berlin, Mike	2	1	3.06	16	0	0	1	32	25	13	11	21	23	R	R	6-1	185	2-14-71	1992	Moundsville, W. Va.
Borkowski, David	1	0	0.00	1	1	0	0	5	2	0	0	1	3	R	R	6-1	200	2-7-77	1995	Sterling Heights, Mich.
Brown, Alvin	2	3	4.24	9	0	0	0	47	35	23	22	33	35	R	R	6-1	200	9-2-70	1989	Los Angeles, Calif.
Drumright, Mike	1	1	4.29	5	5	0	0	21	19	11	10	9	19	L	R	6-4	210	4-19-74	1995	Valley Center, Kan.
Gaillard, Eddy	2	4	1.31	43	0	0	25	55	48	13	8	18	51	R	R	6-1	180	8-13-70	1993	West Palm Beach, Fla.
Gardner, Scott	0	0	2.77	5	0	0	0	13	10	6	4	7	14	S	R	6-5	210	9-30-71	1990	El Centro, Calif.
Gaspar, Cade	7	6	3.90	23	23	0	0	99	95	48	43	44	97	R	R	6-3	175	8-21-73	1994	Mission Viejo, Calif.
Gonzalez, Generoso	0	0	0.00	1	0	0	0	3	1	0	0	1	1	R	R	6-4	170	2-19-76	1993	Santo Domingo, D.R.
Granger, Greg	9	12	5.01	27	25	1	0	142	176	93	79	46	91	R	R	6-3	200	3-7-73	1993	Ellettsville, Ind.
Housely, Adam	0	1	6.00	19	1	0	1	30	39	23	20	11	23	S	R	6-3	198	8-13-71	1994	Napa, Calif.
Jordan, Jason	1	3	5.95	4	4	0	0	20	32	20	13	7	8	R	R	6-3	220	10-2-72	1994	Wichita, Kan.
Kostich, Bill	1	0	0.00	1	0	0	0	6	2	0	0	2	2	L	L	6-0	190	2-1-71	1989	Taylor, Mich.
Lima, Jose	3	1	2.57	4	4	0	0	21	23	11	6	0	20	R	R	6-2	170	9-30-72	1989	Santiago, D.R.
Marrero, Kenny	1	4	3.72	37	0	0	5	56	54	28	23	28	46	R	R	6-3	208	5-13-70	1991	Dorado, P.R.
McLain, Mike	1	1	3.58	21	0	0	2	38	33	13	11	7	27	L	R	6-2	205	3-18-70	1992	Elk Grove, Calif.
Mysel, David	1	1	5.83	20	0	0	2	29	36	22	19	14	32	R	R	6-5	215	4-13-71	1992	Hummelstown, Pa.
Norman, Scott	7	7	4.07	22	21	3	0	128	141	86	58	38	63	R	R	6-0	195	9-1-72	1993	Sarasota, Fla.
Rosengren, John	3	3	3.99	13	8	0	0	56	46	33	25	36	35	L	L	6-4	190	8-10-72	1992	Rye, N.Y.

PITCHING	W	L	ERA	G	GS	CG	SV	IP	H	R	ER	BB	SO	B	T	HT	WT	DOB	1st Yr	Resides
Salazar, Mike	7	3	3.19	42	3	0	5	87	86	37	31	21	52	L	L	6-4	200	4-16-71	1993	Clovis, Calif.
Santos, Henry	5	6	4.24	35	10	0	0	98	111	59	46	40	80	L	L	6-1	175	1-17-73	1990	Santiago, D.R.
Serna, Joe	0	1	2.00	5	0	0	1	9	10	4	2	5	3	S	R	6-1	230	12-18-73	1993	Valinda, Calif.
Siler, Jeff	2	2	2.28	27	0	0	1	28	21	9	7	7	26	L	L	6-0	180	10-1-70	1994	Merrill, Mich.
Stentz, Brent	0	0	0.00	2	0	0	0	2	0	0	0	0	4	R	R	6-5	225	7-24-75	1995	Brooksville, Fla.
Thompson, Justin	2	1	4.88	6	6	0	0	24	30	13	13	8	20	L	L	6-3	175	3-8-73	1991	Spring, Texas
Tuttle, Dave	1	4	2.90	6	4	1	0	31	31	11	10	12	28	R	R	6-3	190	9-29-69	1992	Los Gatos, Calif.
Whiteman, Greg	1	2	6.05	4	4	0	0	19	18	16	13	15	20	L	L	6-2	185	6-12-73	1994	Wileyford, W. Va.

FAYETTEVILLE   A
SOUTH ATLANTIC LEAGUE

BATTING	AVG	G	AB	R	H	2B	3B	HR	RBI	BB	SO	SB	CS	B	T	HT	WT	DOB	1st Yr	Resides
Almanzar, Richard	.247	80	308	47	76	12	1	0	16	29	32	39	15	R	R	5-10	155	4-3-76	1993	San Fran. de Macoris, D.R.
Balfe, Ryan	.261	113	398	53	104	20	2	10	49	48	85	1	1	S	R	6-1	180	11-11-75	1994	Cornwall, N.Y.
Balint, Rob	.242	13	33	4	8	2	0	1	4	1	15	0	0	R	R	6-1	189	6-1-74	1994	Winter Garden, Fla.
Bass, Jayson	.215	108	368	47	79	15	6	10	48	37	111	14	3	L	L	6-3	212	6-22-74	1993	Seattle, Wash.
Borel, Jamie	.244	86	279	60	68	9	3	0	20	41	43	36	14	R	R	5-11	170	9-20-71	1994	Raleigh, N.C.
Brunson, Matt	.222	43	144	18	32	3	3	1	8	22	34	16	6	S	R	5-11	165	9-2-74	1993	Englewood, Colo.
Cardona, Javier	.206	51	165	18	34	8	0	3	19	13	30	1	0	R	R	6-0	185	9-15-75	1994	Dorado, P.R.
Darr, Mike	.289	112	395	58	114	21	2	5	66	58	88	5	2	L	R	6-3	205	3-21-76	1994	Corona, Calif.
Encarnacion, Juan	.282	124	457	62	129	31	7	16	72	30	113	5	6	R	R	6-2	160	3-8-76	1993	Las Matas de Farfan, D.R.
Garcia, Neil	.231	88	251	46	58	12	1	7	33	59	49	3	6	S	R	6-0	185	4-6-73	1994	Tustin, Calif.
Lidle, Kevin	.142	36	113	15	16	4	1	4	13	16	44	0	1	R	R	5-11	170	3-22-72	1992	West Covina, Calif.
Martinez, Davis	.255	30	102	17	26	7	0	3	15	16	35	1	0	R	R	5-10	185	12-5-73	1993	Santo Domingo, D.R.
Monroe, Darryl	.259	104	382	55	99	21	2	3	28	23	76	23	12	R	R	6-1	175	3-2-72	1993	Lawrence, Kan.
Perez, Santiago	.238	130	425	54	101	15	1	4	44	30	98	10	9	S	R	6-2	150	12-30-75	1993	Santo Domingo, D.R.
Rives, Sherron	.227	56	150	15	34	8	0	0	19	11	36	3	1	R	R	6-2	195	10-29-71	1994	St. Louis, Mo.
Rodriguez, Adam	.302	39	139	16	42	14	1	4	25	9	25	0	1	R	R	5-10	195	3-16-71	1993	Tucson, Ariz.
Ward, Daryle	.284	137	524	75	149	32	0	14	106	46	111	1	2	L	L	6-2	230	6-27-75	1994	Riverside, Calif.

GAMES BY POSITION: C—Balint 2, Cardona 48, Garcia 52, Lidle 23, Rodriguez 24. 1B—Balint 5, Garcia 6, Lidle 1, Rives 3, Rodriguez 13, Ward 121. 2B—Almanzar 79, Brunson 33, Garcia 2, Rives 36. 3B—Balfe 104, Balint 2, Garcia 3, Lidle 9, Martinez 26, Rives 10. SS—Brunson 10, Martinez 1, Perez 129, Rives 8. OF—Bass 95, Borel 70, Cardona 1, Darr 97, Encarnacion 102, Lidle 1, Martinez 1, Monroe 70, Rives 1, Rodriguez 1.

PITCHING	W	L	ERA	G	GS	CG	SV	IP	H	R	ER	BB	SO	B	T	HT	WT	DOB	1st Yr	Resides
Bajda, Mike	0	0	3.00	4	0	0	0	9	8	5	3	10	4	R	R	6-4	215	8-7-73	1994	Shelton, Conn.
Clark, Doug	0	1	11.57	4	0	0	0	5	10	11	6	3	3	R	R	6-2	195	6-1-71	1995	Jacksonville Beach, Fla.
Cordero, Francisco	0	3	6.30	4	4	0	0	20	26	16	14	12	19	R	R	6-2	170	8-11-77	1994	Santo Domingo, D.R.
Dinyar, Eric	4	3	2.49	42	0	0	5	87	77	34	24	25	71	R	R	6-6	210	8-13-73	1994	Johnstown, Pa.
Gardner, Scott	6	3	2.06	49	1	0	4	87	62	26	20	24	112	S	R	6-5	210	9-30-71	1990	El Centro, Calif.
Housley, Adam	3	1	2.37	19	0	0	1	38	26	14	10	11	43	S	R	6-3	198	8-13-71	1994	Napa, Calif.
Jacobson, Kelton	5	7	5.82	25	12	0	0	68	72	52	44	44	64	R	R	6-3	205	2-17-71	1994	Seattle, Wash.
Jordan, Jason	10	4	2.28	24	24	0	0	138	128	48	35	43	103	R	R	6-3	220	10-2-72	1994	Wichita, Kan.
Martinez, Osvaldo	0	0	4.15	6	0	0	0	13	11	6	6	1	15	R	R	6-0	175	5-9-75	1992	Villa Gonzalez, D.R.
Newton, Chris	0	0	5.79	2	0	0	0	5	6	3	3	1	3	R	L	6-1	185	7-25-72	1994	Winnetka, Ill.
Powell, Brian	4	0	1.61	5	5	0	0	28	15	5	5	11	37	R	R	6-2	205	10-10-73	1995	Bainbridge, Ga.
Reed, Brandon	3	0	0.97	55	0	0	41	65	40	11	7	18	70	R	R	6-4	185	12-18-74	1994	Lapeer, Mich.
Roberts, Willis	6	3	2.70	17	15	0	0	80	72	33	24	40	52	R	R	6-3	175	6-19-75	1992	San Cristobal, D.R.
Serna, Joe	4	0	2.36	12	0	0	0	27	14	13	7	10	21	S	R	6-1	230	12-18-73	1993	Valinda, Calif.
Siler, Jeff	1	1	0.40	21	0	0	1	23	16	2	1	11	25	L	L	6-0	180	10-1-70	1994	Merrill, Mich.
Skrmetta, Matt	9	4	2.71	44	2	0	2	90	66	36	27	35	105	R	R	6-3	220	11-6-72	1993	Satellite Beach, Fla.
Smith, Cam	13	8	3.81	29	29	2	0	149	110	75	63	87	166	R	R	6-3	190	9-20-73	1993	Selkirk, N.Y.
Sobik, Trad	8	5	4.16	18	18	0	0	102	100	68	47	24	60	R	R	6-2	175	1-29-76	1994	Palm Harbor, Fla.
Whiteman, Greg	6	8	4.23	23	23	1	0	126	108	68	59	58	145	L	L	6-2	185	6-12-73	1994	Wileyford, W Va.
Whiteman, Tony	0	1	3.96	28	0	0	0	25	25	16	11	18	23	L	L	6-1	185	12-30-70	1994	Wileyford, W Va.
Wilson, Mike	4	3	4.38	17	8	0	0	49	43	29	24	19	36	R	R	6-5	220	4-4-73	1993	Dallas, Texas

JAMESTOWN   A
NEW YORK-PENN LEAGUE

BATTING	AVG	G	AB	R	H	2B	3B	HR	RBI	BB	SO	SB	CS	B	T	HT	WT	DOB	1st Yr	Resides
Caballero, Manuel	.197	52	142	23	28	4	1	5	20	32	42	3	2	L	R	6-3	205	10-18-73	1995	Gilbert, Ariz.
De la Rosa, Elvis	.238	14	42	3	10	2	0	0	5	1	15	1	1	R	R	5-11	195	5-5-75	1993	Elias Pina, D.R.
Engleka, Doug	.283	44	166	32	47	8	2	2	20	20	28	11	5	R	R	5-10	170	10-6-72	1995	Dayton, Ohio
Fuller, Brian	.270	40	137	28	37	9	1	6	24	19	26	4	2	R	R	6-2	205	11-5-72	1995	Plover, Wisc.
Garcia, Apostol	.235	60	200	25	47	8	3	0	21	10	36	10	6	S	R	6-0	155	8-3-76	1994	Las Matas de Farfan, D.R.
Gray, Ricky	.152	32	79	15	12	3	1	2	8	17	30	4	0	L	L	5-9	185	5-9-72	1995	Orland, Maine
Hare, Rich	.193	27	57	6	11	4	0	4	3	13	4	1	R	R	6-2	175	10-28-71	1994	Dallas, Texas
Kapler, Gabriel	.288	63	236	38	68	19	4	4	34	23	37	1	2	R	R	6-1	190	7-31-75	1995	Reseda, Calif.
Koonce, Graham	.280	73	289	37	81	16	1	3	34	35	63	8	3	L	L	6-3	195	5-15-75	1994	Julian, Calif.
Lemonis, Chris	.236	57	191	19	45	7	2	0	21	18	32	5	1	R	R	5-11	185	9-7-71	1995	New York, N.Y.
Miller, Mike	.228	64	197	39	45	9	1	3	27	60	66	10	7	R	R	6-1	200	12-22-72	1995	Smithtown, N.Y.
Milord, Clausel	.207	34	87	13	18	3	1	1	12	20	21	6	4	R	R	5-10	170	12-27-73	1995	Brooklyn, N.Y.
Mitchell, Rivers	.282	60	234	28	66	8	6	0	17	13	35	15	7	R	R	6-0	195	6-24-72	1995	Seattle, Wash.
Rojas, Ron	.213	17	47	8	10	1	0	1	8	8	9	4	0	S	R	5-11	185	3-27-73	1995	Burbank, Ill.
Waggoner, Jay	.245	63	204	21	50	5	4	3	24	22	40	2	3	L	R	5-11	195	10-2-72	1995	Birmingham, Ala.
Weaver, Scott	.301	65	236	33	71	11	2	5	34	38	33	16	5	L	L	5-11	190	9-21-73	1995	Sault Ste. Marie, Mich.

GAMES BY POSITION: C—Caballero 37, De la Rosa 14, Fuller 31. 1B—Koonce 72, Waggoner 5. 2B—Engleka 21, Garcia 1, Lemonis 51, Rojas 10. 3B—Engleka 6, Lemonis 4, Miller 64, Rojas 6, Waggoner 3. SS—Engleka 22, Garcia 60, Rojas 1. OF—Gray 27, Hare 15, Kapler 61, Milord 28, Mitchell 52, Weaver 62.

PITCHING	W	L	ERA	G	GS	CG	SV	IP	H	R	ER	BB	SO	B	T	HT	WT	DOB	1st Yr	Resides
Bajda, Mike	2	2	7.99	13	3	0	0	24	35	26	21	17	14	R	R	6-4	215	8-7-73	1994	Shelton, Conn.
Barker, Jeff	2	2	3.94	14	0	0	0	16	15	10	7	8	14	R	R	6-4	185	2-19-74	1994	Rancho Cucamonga, Calif.
Bettencourt, Justin	2	8	4.84	14	14	0	0	74	73	53	40	41	63	L	L	6-2	198	12-19-73	1994	Capitola, Calif.
Brown, Shawn	1	2	6.05	18	0	0	0	19	27	16	13	6	10	R	R	6-1	176	4-16-71	1993	Tabernacle, N.J.
Cordero, Francisco	4	7	5.22	15	14	0	0	88	96	62	51	37	54	R	R	6-2	170	8-11-77	1994	Santo Domingo, D.R.
Corey, Bryan	2	2	3.86	29	0	0	10	28	21	14	12	12	41	R	R	6-1	170	10-21-73	1993	Newbury Park, Calif.
Cummins, Brian	2	1	3.38	18	0	0	1	35	37	22	13	8	24	L	L	6-0	210	5-2-73	1995	Orland Park, Ill.
Durkovic, Peter	0	0	5.92	14	1	0	1	24	28	17	16	10	10	L	L	6-4	215	7-9-73	1995	Flushing, N.Y.
Eby, Michael	2	1	1.52	23	0	0	2	30	20	7	5	5	33	L	L	6-1	190	2-25-72	1995	Westlake, Calif.
Foran, John	1	2	5.82	14	0	0	1	17	17	15	11	6	18	R	R	6-1	185	10-22-73	1995	Alford, Fla.
Groves, Brian	0	1	4.44	16	0	0	0	24	21	17	12	17	15	L	L	6-2	215	12-14-72	1995	Athens, Ga.
Martinez, Osvaldo	4	4	3.77	15	15	1	0	91	85	46	38	30	56	R	R	6-4	175	5-9-75	1992	Villa Gonzalez, D.R.
Neese, Josh	3	1	3.72	20	2	0	0	36	29	15	15	14	38	R	R	6-1	185	4-22-72	1993	Freedom, Okla.
Oakley, Matt	0	0	18.00	1	0	0	0	1	3	2	2	1	0	R	R	6-2	225	7-12-73	1995	Raleigh, N.C.
Powell, Brian	2	1	3.08	5	5	0	0	26	19	12	9	8	15	R	R	6-2	205	10-10-73	1995	Bainbridge, Ga.
Reinfelder, David	2	5	4.60	16	14	0	0	78	85	48	40	17	55	R	L	6-1	180	4-24-74	1995	Vassar, Mich.
Weber, Eric	2	2	5.23	15	3	0	0	33	35	25	19	11	22	R	R	6-3	185	10-3-74	1993	Saginaw, Mich.
Wilson, Mike	1	3	6.55	5	5	0	0	22	27	20	16	6	12	R	R	6-5	220	4-4-73	1993	Dallas, Texas

LAKELAND   R

GULF COAST LEAGUE

BATTING	AVG	G	AB	R	H	2B	3B	HR	RBI	BB	SO	SB	CS	B	T	HT	WT	DOB	1st Yr	Resides
Aybar, Ramon	.241	38	112	22	27	2	1	0	10	18	38	16	5	L	R	5-9	150	5-10-76	1994	Bani, D.R.
Balint, Rob	.200	1	5	1	1	0	0	1	1	0	2	0	0	R	R	6-1	189	6-1-74	1994	Winter Garden, Fla.
Capallen, Rene	.317	33	101	17	32	3	1	0	13	13	14	6	4	R	R	5-11	160	4-24-78	1995	Santo Domingo, D.R.
Cedeno, Jesus	.255	40	110	20	28	2	2	3	14	16	26	2	2	R	R	5-11	160	6-24-76	1994	Santo Domingo, D.R.
Cordero, Edward	.214	49	126	17	27	2	2	0	11	12	23	11	5	R	R	6-0	155	6-6-75	1992	Santo Domingo, D.R.
De la Cruz, Carlos	.329	47	155	24	51	7	1	2	17	20	45	28	4	R	R	6-2	175	7-24-75	1994	Santo Domingo, D.R.
Domingo, Tyrone	.206	35	107	18	22	1	2	0	1	5	25	20	4	R	R	5-8	169	10-22-74	1991	Los Angeles, Calif.
Hagge, Kirk	.177	43	96	8	17	0	0	0	3	16	32	3	2	S	R	6-4	200	10-31-75	1994	La Crescenta, Calif.
Jones, Bryan	.247	33	93	13	23	2	0	0	7	11	34	7	1	R	R	6-0	185	1-21-75	1995	Plantation, Fla.
Katayama, Daiki	.180	28	50	5	9	1	0	2	4	3	13	0	0	R	R	6-0	175	2-24-75	1995	Nishinomiya City, Japan
Kopacz, Derek	.285	53	165	24	47	12	3	2	30	25	40	11	3	R	R	5-10	185	4-2-75	1995	Orland Park, Ill.
Lignitz, Jeremiah	.232	30	82	9	19	1	1	1	7	9	27	1	3	L	R	6-2	210	5-18-77	1995	Davidson, Mich.
Peniche, Fray	.157	28	83	8	13	1	0	1	4	2	31	2	0	R	R	6-2	185	11-2-76	1995	Santiago, D.R.
Ramirez, Francisco	.217	41	143	15	31	4	5	2	22	7	38	6	4	R	R	6-2	195	1-21-76	1995	Santo Domingo, D.R.
Ruiz, Cesar	.288	45	132	17	38	6	5	1	19	11	35	4	2	S	R	6-1	150	9-14-74	1992	Haina, D.R.
Shipman, Thomas	.183	30	60	8	11	2	0	1	10	10	21	4	0	S	R	6-0	190	2-22-77	1995	New Port Richey, Fla.
Stevenson, Chad	.158	32	95	11	15	4	1	3	12	11	23	1	0	R	R	6-4	215	2-3-76	1994	Henderson, Nev.

GAMES BY POSITION: C—Katayama 24, Lignitz 22, Stevenson 28. **1B**—Balint 1, Hagge 42, Katayama 4, Ruiz 26. **2B**—Aybar 33, Jones 25, Kopacz 3, Ruiz 2. **3B**—Capallen 3, Kopacz 47, Ruiz 16. **SS**—Capallen 21, Cordero 47. **OF**—Capallen 13, Cedeno 33, De la Cruz 33, Domingo 29, Peniche 28, Ramirez 26, Shipman 26.

PITCHING	W	L	ERA	G	GS	CG	SV	IP	H	R	ER	BB	SO	B	T	HT	WT	DOB	1st Yr	Resides
Alicea, Patrick	5	2	1.93	12	8	2	1	51	45	21	11	14	43	R	R	6-3	180	6-29-76	1995	New York, N.Y.
Borkowski, David	3	2	2.96	10	10	1	0	52	45	24	17	8	36	R	R	6-1	200	2-7-77	1995	Sterling Heights, Mich.
Bruner, Clayton	0	1	3.94	5	4	0	0	16	15	12	7	10	15	R	R	6-3	190	10-16-76	1995	Weatherford, Okla.
Dessellier, Chris	0	0	0.00	1	0	0	1	1	0	0	0	1	3	R	R	6-5	210	6-29-74	1992	Ypsilanti, Mich.
Fuduric, Tony	5	2	2.97	16	0	0	0	30	25	13	10	21	21	R	R	6-3	185	9-6-74	1993	Huntsburg, Ohio
Gonzalez, Generoso	3	3	3.89	16	4	0	1	39	29	19	17	16	45	R	R	6-4	170	2-19-76	1993	Santo Domingo, D.R.
Kauflin, David	2	1	4.86	5	3	0	0	17	11	11	9	7	13	R	R	6-4	230	5-20-76	1994	Clinton Township, Mich.
Lawrie, Jason	0	1	4.50	4	4	0	0	12	10	8	6	12	12	R	R	6-2	175	10-31-76	1995	San Jose, Calif.
Manser, Chris	2	2	2.45	6	5	0	0	29	24	10	8	5	26	R	R	6-2	215	6-8-76	1995	Lutz, Fla.
Martinez, Romulo	0	0	7.50	16	0	0	1	24	27	22	20	13	14	R	R	6-1	170	12-5-76	1994	Santiago, D.R.
McFarlane, Joseph	0	0	0.00	1	0	0	0	1	1	0	0	0	1	R	R	6-3	185	2-20-77	1995	Anacortes, Wash.
Persails, Mark	1	4	4.41	11	10	0	0	51	50	37	25	25	30	R	R	6-3	185	10-25-75	1995	Vassar, Mich.
Rodriguez, Tomas	0	0	2.53	14	0	0	1	21	14	13	6	8	21	R	R	6-5	220	6-11-75	1993	Santo Domingo, D.R.
Romo, Greg	3	1	2.63	5	5	0	0	27	25	9	8	5	25	L	R	6-3	175	5-14-75	1995	Wasco, Calif.
Santamaria, Juan	0	0	5.40	12	0	0	1	20	26	17	12	11	17	R	R	6-1	165	5-6-77	1995	Barrio, D.R.
Stentz, Brent	2	1	2.36	24	0	0	16	27	21	7	7	12	28	R	R	6-5	225	7-24-75	1995	Brooksville, Fla.
Yonemura, Kazuki	2	4	2.32	14	4	0	1	43	38	20	11	9	49	R	R	6-0	175	4-10-74	1995	Nishinomiya City, Japan

FLORIDA MARLINS

Manager: Rene Lachemann. **1995 Record:** 67-76, .469 (4th, NL East).

BATTING	AVG	G	AB	R	H	2B	3B	HR	RBI	BB	SO	SB	CS	B	T	HT	WT	DOB	1st Yr	Resides
Abbott, Kurt	.255	120	420	60	107	18	7	17	60	36	110	4	3	R	R	6-0	170	6-2-69	1989	St. Petersburg, Fla.
Arias, Alex	.269	94	216	22	58	9	2	3	26	22	20	1	0	R	R	6-3	185	11-20-67	1987	New York, N.Y.
Browne, Jerry	.255	77	184	21	47	4	0	1	17	25	20	1	1	S	R	5-10	170	2-13-66	1983	Arlington, Texas
Carr, Chuck	.227	105	308	54	70	20	0	2	20	46	49	25	11	S	R	5-10	165	8-10-68	1986	Tucson, Ariz.
Colbrunn, Greg	.277	138	528	70	146	22	1	23	89	22	69	11	3	R	R	6-0	200	7-26-69	1988	Fontana, Calif.
Conine, Jeff	.302	133	483	72	146	26	2	25	105	66	94	2	0	R	R	6-1	220	6-27-66	1988	Rialto, Calif.
Dawson, Andre	.257	79	226	30	58	10	3	8	37	9	45	0	0	R	R	6-3	195	7-10-54	1975	Miami, Fla.
Decker, Steve	.226	51	133	12	30	2	1	3	13	19	22	1	0	R	R	6-3	205	10-25-65	1988	Keizer, Ore.
Diaz, Mario	.230	49	87	5	20	3	0	1	6	1	12	0	0	R	R	5-10	160	1-10-62	1979	Yabucoa, P.R.
Gregg, Tommy	.237	72	156	20	37	5	0	6	20	16	33	3	1	L	L	6-1	190	7-29-63	1985	Smyrna, Ga.
Johnson, Charles	.251	97	315	40	79	15	1	11	39	46	71	0	2	R	R	6-2	215	7-20-71	1992	Ft. Pierce, Fla.
Morman, Russ	.278	34	72	9	20	2	1	3	7	3	12	0	0	R	R	6-4	215	4-28-62	1983	Blue Springs, Mo.
Natal, Bob	.233	16	43	2	10	2	1	2	6	1	9	0	0	R	R	5-11	190	11-13-65	1987	Chula Vista, Calif.
Pendleton, Terry	.290	133	513	70	149	32	1	14	78	38	84	1	2	S	R	5-9	195	7-16-60	1982	Duluth, Ga.
Sheffield, Gary	.324	63	213	46	69	8	0	16	46	55	45	19	4	R	R	5-11	190	11-18-68	1986	St. Petersburg, Fla.
Tavarez, Jesus	.289	63	190	31	55	6	2	2	13	16	27	7	5	S	R	6-0	170	3-26-71	1990	Santo Domingo, D.R.
Veras, Quilvio	.261	124	440	86	115	20	7	5	32	80	68	56	21	S	R	5-8	168	4-3-71	1990	Santo Domingo, D.R.
Whitmore, Darrell	.190	27	58	6	11	2	0	1	2	5	15	0	0	L	R	6-1	210	11-18-68	1990	Front Royal, Va.
Zosky, Eddie	.200	6	5	0	1	0	0	0	0	0	0	0	0	R	R	6-0	175	2-10-68	1989	Whittier, Calif.

PITCHING	W	L	ERA	G	GS	CG	SV	IP	H	R	ER	BB	SO	B	T	HT	WT	DOB	1st Yr	Resides
Banks, Willie	2	3	4.32	9	9	0	0	50	43	27	24	30	30	R	R	6-1	202	2-27-69	1987	Jersey City, N.J.
3-team (10 Chi.-6 LA)	2	6	5.66	25	15	0	0	91	106	71	57	58	62							
Bowen, Ryan	2	0	3.78	4	3	0	0	17	23	11	7	12	15	R	R	6-0	185	2-10-68	1987	Houston, Texas
Burkett, John	14	14	4.30	30	30	4	0	188	208	95	90	57	126	R	R	6-3	205	11-28-64	1983	Scottsdale, Ariz.
Dunbar, Matt	0	1	11.57	8	0	0	0	7	12	9	9	11	5	L	L	6-0	160	10-15-68	1990	Tallahassee, Fla.
Garces, Rich	0	2	5.40	11	0	0	0	13	14	9	8	8	16	R	R	6-0	230	5-18-71	1988	Maracay, Venez.
2-team (7 Chicago)	0	2	4.44	18	0	0	0	24	25	15	12	11	22							
Gardner, Mark	5	5	4.49	39	11	1	1	102	109	60	51	43	87	R	R	6-1	190	3-1-62	1985	Fresno, Calif.
Groom, Buddy	1	2	7.20	14	0	0	0	15	26	12	12	6	12	L	L	6-2	200	7-10-65	1987	Red Oak, Texas
Hammond, Chris	9	6	3.80	25	24	3	0	161	157	73	68	47	126	L	L	6-1	195	1-21-66	1986	Birmingham, Ala.
Harvey, Bryan	0	0	0.00	1	0	0	0	0	2	3	3	1	0	R	R	6-2	212	6-2-63	1985	Catawba, N.C.
Hernandez, Jeremy	0	0	11.57	7	0	0	0	7	12	9	9	3	5	R	R	6-6	195	7-6-66	1987	Yuma, Ariz.
Johnstone, John	0	0	3.86	4	0	0	0	5	7	2	2	3	3	R	R	6-3	195	11-25-68	1987	Liverpool, N.Y.
Lewis, Richie	0	1	3.75	21	1	0	0	36	30	15	15	15	32	R	R	5-10	175	1-25-66	1987	Losantville, Ind.
Mantei, Matt	0	1	4.73	12	0	0	0	13	12	8	7	13	15	R	R	6-1	181	7-7-73	1991	Sawyer, Mich.
Mathews, Terry	4	4	3.38	57	0	0	3	83	70	32	31	27	72	L	R	6-2	225	10-5-64	1987	Boyce, La.
Murphy, Rob	1	1	9.82	8	0	0	0	7	8	9	8	5	5	L	L	6-2	215	5-26-60	1981	Miami, Fla.
2-team (6 LA)	1	2	11.25	14	0	0	0	12	14	16	15	8	7							
Myers, Mike	0	0	0.00	2	0	0	0	2	1	0	0	3	0	L	L	6-3	197	6-26-69	1990	Wheeling, Ill.
Nen, Robb	0	7	3.29	62	0	0	23	66	62	26	24	23	68	R	R	6-4	190	11-28-69	1987	Seal Beach, Calif.
Pena, Alejandro	2	0	1.50	13	0	0	0	18	11	3	3	3	21	R	R	6-1	200	6-25-59	1979	Roswell, Ga.
Perez, Yorkis	2	6	5.21	69	0	0	1	47	35	29	27	28	47	L	L	6-0	160	9-30-67	1983	Haina, D.R.
Powell, Jay	0	0	1.08	9	0	0	0	8	7	2	1	6	4	R	R	6-4	220	1-9-72	1993	Collinsville, Tenn.
Rapp, Pat	14	7	3.44	28	28	3	0	167	158	72	64	76	102	R	R	6-3	210	7-13-67	1989	Sulphur, La.
Scheid, Rich	0	0	6.10	6	0	0	0	10	14	7	7	7	10	L	L	6-3	185	2-3-65	1986	Summit, N.J.
Small, Aaron	1	0	1.42	7	0	0	0	6	7	2	1	6	5	R	R	6-5	200	11-23-71	1989	Victorville, Calif.
Valdes, Marc	0	0	14.14	3	3	0	0	7	17	13	11	9	2	R	R	6-0	170	12-20-71	1993	Tampa, Fla.
Veres, Randy	4	4	3.88	47	0	0	1	49	46	25	21	32	31	R	R	6-3	187	11-25-65	1985	Rancho Cordova, Calif.
Weathers, Dave	4	5	5.98	28	15	0	0	90	104	68	60	52	60	R	R	6-3	205	9-25-69	1988	Leoma, Tenn.
Witt, Bobby	2	7	3.90	19	19	1	0	111	104	52	48	47	95	R	R	6-2	205	5-11-64	1985	Colleyville, Texas

FIELDING

Catcher	PCT	G	PO	A	E	DP	PB
Decker	.985	46	296	24	5	3	3
Johnson	.992	97	641	63	6	9	5
Natal	.988	13	80	3	1	1	0

First Base	PCT	G	PO	A	E	DP
Colbrunn	.996	134	1066	90	5	108
Conine	.991	14	97	11	1	10
Decker	1.000	2	3	0	0	0
Gregg	1.000	2	17	1	0	2
Morman	1.000	3	10	2	0	1

Second Base	PCT	G	PO	A	E	DP
Arias	1.000	6	9	19	0	3
Browne	.992	27	62	66	1	13
Diaz	.944	9	15	19	2	8
Veras	.986	122	297	315	9	85
Zosky	1.000	1	0	1	0	1

Third Base	PCT	G	PO	A	E	DP
Arias	.939	21	8	23	2	3
Browne	1.000	7	1	10	0	0

	PCT	G	PO	A	E	DP
Diaz	1.000	3	1	0	0	0
Pendleton	.952	129	104	250	18	24

Shortstop	PCT	G	PO	A	E	DP
Abbott	.959	115	149	290	19	66
Arias	.947	36	40	85	7	15
Diaz	1.000	5	6	11	0	4
Zosky	.667	4	1	1	1	0

Outfield	PCT	G	PO	A	E	DP
Browne	.959	29	45	2	2	2
Carr	.987	103	217	8	3	1
Conine	.976	118	195	7	5	2
Dawson	.908	59	76	3	8	2
Gregg	.984	38	63	0	1	0
Morman	.955	18	21	0	1	0
Sheffield	.942	61	109	5	7	1
Tavarez	1.000	61	118	1	0	1
Veras	1.000	2	2	0	0	0
Whitmore	.960	16	24	0	1	0

Jeff Conine

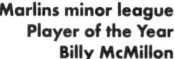

First baseman Greg Colbrunn hit .277 with 23 homers and 89 RBIs

Marlins minor league Player of the Year Billy McMillon

MORRIS FOSTOFF

MARLINS

FARM SYSTEM

Director of Player Development: John Boles.

Class	Farm Team	League	W	L	Pct.	Finish*	Manager	First Yr
AAA	Charlotte (N.C.) Knights	International	59	81	.421	9th (10)	Sal Rende	1995
AA	Portland (Maine) Sea Dogs	Eastern	86	56	.606	1st (10)	Carlos Tosca	1994
#A	Brevard County (Fla.) Manatees	Florida State	61	74	.452	12th (14)	Fredi Gonzalez	1994
A	Kane County (Ill.) Cougars	Midwest	69	69	.500	7th (14)	Lynn Jones	1993
A	Elmira (N.Y.) Pioneers	New York-Penn	25	51	.329	14th (14)	Paul Kirsch	1993
R	Melbourne (Fla.) Marlins	Gulf Coast	40	16	.714	1st (16)	Juan Bustabad	1992

*Finish in overall standings (No. of teams in league)   #Advanced level

ORGANIZATION LEADERS

MAJOR LEAGUERS

BATTING
*AVG	Jeff Conine.............	.302
R	Quilvio Veras............	86
H	Terry Pendleton......	149
TB	Jeff Conine.............	251
2B	Terry Pendleton........	32
3B	Two tied at	7
HR	Jeff Conine.............	25
RBI	Jeff Conine.............	105
BB	Quilvio Veras	80
SO	Kurt Abbott.............	110
SB	Quilvio Veras	56

PITCHING
W	Two tied at	14
L	John Burkett.............	14
#ERA	Terry Mathews	3.38
G	Yorkis Perez	69
CG	John Burkett.............	4
SV	Robb Nen.................	23
IP	John Burkett.............	188
BB	Pat Rapp..................	76
SO	Two tied at	126

Quilvio Veras. NL-best 56 steals

AL SOLOMON

MINOR LEAGUERS

BATTING
*AVG	Luis Castillo, Kane County	.326
R	Ralph Milliard, Portland	104
H	Billy McMillon, Portland	162
TB	Billy McMillon, Portland	239
2B	Ryan Jackson, Kane County	39
3B	Todd Dunwoody, Kane County	8
HR	Two tied at..	14
RBI	Billy McMillon, Portland	93
BB	Billy McMillon, Portland	96
SO	Josh Booty, Elmira/Kane County..........	130
SB	Amaury Garcia, Elmira/Kane County	46

PITCHING
W	Two tied at..	12
L	Marc Valdes, Charlotte	13
#ERA	Clemente Nunez, Brevard County........	2.48
G	Dan Chergey, Portland.........................	55
CG	Clemente Nunez, Brevard County.............	4
SV	Jay Powell, Portland............................	24
IP	Marc Valdes, Charlotte.........................	170
BB	Walter Miranda, Kane County	88
SO	Bryan Ward, Brevard County/Portland ..	136

*Minimum 250 At-Bats   #Minimum 75 Innings

TOP 10 PROSPECTS

How the Marlins Top 10 prospects, as judged by Baseball America prior to the 1995 season, fared in 1995:

Charles Johnson

Player, Pos.	Club (Class—League)	AVG	AB	R	H	2B	3B	HR	RBI	SB
1. Charles Johnson, c	Florida	.251	315	40	79	15	1	11	39	0
2. Josh Booty, 3b	Elmira (A—New York-Penn)	.220	287	33	63	18	1	6	37	4
	Kane County (A—Midwest)	.101	109	6	11	2	0	1	6	1
5. Edgar Renteria, ss	Portland (AA—Eastern)	.289	508	70	147	15	7	7	68	30
7. Quilvio Veras, 2b	Florida	.261	440	86	115	20	7	5	32	56
8. Luis Castillo, 2b	Kane County (A—Midwest)	.326	340	71	111	4	4	0	23	41
10. Victor Rodriguez, ss	Kane County (A—Midwest)	.235	472	65	111	9	1	0	43	18

Player, Pos.	Club (Class—League)	W	L	ERA	G	SV	IP	H	BB	SO
3. Andy Larkin, rhp	Portland (AA—Eastern)	1	2	3.38	9	0	40	29	11	23
4. Marc Valdes, rhp	Charlotte (AAA—International)	9	13	4.86	27	0	170	189	59	104
	Florida	0	0	14.14	3	0	7	17	9	2
6. Brian Meadows, rhp	Kane County (A—Midwest)	9	9	4.22	26	0	147	163	41	103
9. Will Cunnane, rhp	Portland (AA—Eastern)	9	2	3.67	21	0	118	120	34	83

INTERNATIONAL LEAGUE

BATTING	AVG	G	AB	R	H	2B	3B	HR	RBI	BB	SO	SB	CS	B	T	HT	WT	DOB	1st Yr	Resides
Abbott, Kurt	.278	5	18	3	5	0	0	1	3	1	3	1	0	R	R	6-0	170	6-2-69	1989	St. Petersburg, Fla.
Boston, Daryl	.188	18	64	7	12	5	0	1	2	6	12	0	0	L	L	6-3	210	1-4-63	1981	Cincinnati, Ohio
Brewer, Rod	.322	69	236	31	76	15	1	9	55	33	45	0	0	L	L	6-3	208	2-24-66	1987	Zellwood, Fla.
Capra, Nick	.256	119	406	60	104	17	1	9	51	54	45	22	12	R	R	5-8	165	3-8-58	1979	Oklahoma City, Okla.
Carr, Chuck	.217	7	23	5	5	0	1	1	2	2	1	2	0	S	R	5-10	165	8-10-68	1986	Tucson, Ariz.
Carter, Jeff	.269	124	428	78	115	20	3	0	22	62	86	22	10	S	R	5-10	160	10-20-63	1985	Evanston, Ill.
Carter, Steve	.250	24	72	9	18	0	0	3	15	7	6	0	0	L	R	6-4	205	12-12-64	1987	Charlottesville, Va.
Castaldo, Vince	.200	7	10	2	2	0	0	0	1	3	3	0	0	L	R	6-0	190	7-19-67	1990	Ballwin, Mo.
Dascenzo, Doug	.260	75	265	51	69	9	0	4	26	25	30	14	9	S	L	5-8	160	6-30-64	1985	La Belle, Pa.
Ford, Curt	.305	57	167	18	51	10	0	3	17	9	29	2	4	L	R	5-10	150	10-11-60	1981	Creve Coeur, Mo.
Gregg, Tommy	.387	34	124	30	48	10	1	9	32	21	13	7	0	L	L	6-1	190	7-29-63	1985	Smyrna, Ga.
Hernandez, Kiki	.240	60	150	13	36	6	0	7	28	16	26	0	0	R	R	5-11	195	4-16-69	1988	Florida, P.R.
Jorgensen, Terry	.264	99	356	38	94	14	0	7	52	39	40	3	3	R	R	6-4	210	9-2-66	1987	Green Bay, Wisc.
Massarelli, John	.244	65	254	37	62	7	2	2	8	26	55	14	10	R	R	6-2	200	1-23-66	1987	Canton, Ohio
Millette, Joe	.187	74	193	22	36	6	1	0	20	10	36	1	1	R	R	6-1	175	8-12-66	1989	Lafayette, Calif.
Morman, Russ	.314	44	169	28	53	7	1	6	36	14	22	2	2	R	R	6-4	215	4-28-62	1983	Blue Springs, Mo.
Natal, Rob	.314	53	191	23	60	14	0	3	24	11	23	0	0	R	R	5-11	190	11-13-65	1987	Chula Vista, Calif.
Pappas, Erik	.221	122	389	48	86	28	3	10	52	61	78	10	7	R	R	6-0	195	4-25-66	1984	Chicago, Ill.
Rudolph, Mason	.250	2	4	1	1	0	0	0	0	0	1	0	0	R	R	6-1	204	1-28-70	1988	Mesa, Ariz.
Schunk, Jerry	.224	101	343	36	77	13	0	6	33	19	31	8	0	R	R	5-11	186	10-5-65	1986	Cincinnati, Ohio
Tavarez, Jesus	.300	39	140	15	42	6	2	1	8	9	19	7	7	S	R	6-0	171	3-26-71	1990	Santo Domingo, D.R.
Zosky, Eddie	.247	92	312	27	77	15	2	3	42	7	48	2	3	R	R	6-0	175	2-10-68	1989	Whittier, Calif.
Zupcic, Bob	.295	72	254	34	75	12	0	11	47	24	35	2	2	R	R	6-4	220	8-18-66	1987	Charlotte, N.C.

PITCHING	W	L	ERA	G	GS	CG	SV	IP	H	R	ER	BB	SO	B	T	HT	WT	DOB	1st Yr	Resides
Adamson, Joel	8	4	3.29	19	18	2	0	115	113	51	42	20	80	L	L	6-4	180	7-2-71	1990	Lakewood, Calif.
Batista, Miguel	6	12	4.80	34	18	0	0	116	118	79	62	60	58	R	R	6-0	160	2-19-71	1988	San Pedro de Macoris, D.R.
Bowen, Ryan	0	1	9.64	1	1	0	0	5	5	5	5	4	3	R	R	6-0	185	2-10-68	1987	Houston, Texas
Brown, Keith	0	1	2.45	4	0	0	0	7	6	3	2	2	3	S	R	6-4	215	2-14-64	1986	Antioch, Tenn.
Clary, Marty	2	2	4.74	9	2	0	0	19	26	16	10	1	8	R	R	6-4	190	4-3-62	1983	Clawson, Mich.
Davis, Mark	0	0	5.00	9	0	0	0	9	13	8	5	1	5	L	L	6-4	210	10-19-60	1979	Marietta, Ga.
Drahman, Brian	2	1	6.30	21	0	0	4	20	28	14	14	11	17	R	R	6-3	231	11-7-66	1986	Ft. Lauderdale, Fla.
Hammond, Chris	0	0	0.00	1	1	0	0	4	3	1	0	2	3	L	L	6-1	195	1-21-66	1986	Birmingham, Ala.
Hancock, Chris	0	1	13.50	3	0	0	0	3	6	6	5	4	2	L	L	6-3	205	9-12-69	1988	Riverside, Calif.
Hernandez, Jeremy	0	2	5.58	15	3	0	0	31	37	20	19	15	24	R	R	6-6	195	7-6-66	1987	Yuma, Ariz.
Lemon, Don	0	0	5.40	6	0	0	0	12	11	7	7	3	8	R	R	6-4	195	6-2-67	1989	Locust Grove, Ga.
Lewis, Richie	5	2	3.20	17	8	1	0	59	50	22	21	20	45	R	R	5-10	175	1-25-66	1987	Losantville, Ind.
Long, Steve	5	4	5.96	33	6	0	4	74	71	57	49	46	46	R	R	6-4	220	7-17-69	1990	Worth, Ill.
Mantei, Matt	0	1	2.57	6	0	0	0	7	1	3	2	5	10	R	R	6-1	181	7-7-73	1991	Sawyer, Mich.
Mathews, Terry	0	0	4.91	2	0	0	0	4	5	2	2	0	5	L	R	6-2	225	10-5-64	1987	Boyce, La.
Miller, Kurt	8	11	4.62	22	22	0	0	127	143	76	65	55	83	R	R	6-5	200	8-24-72	1990	Bakersfield, Calif.
Murphy, Rob	0	0	0.00	3	0	0	2	3	2	0	0	0	1	L	L	6-2	215	5-26-60	1981	Miami, Fla.
Mutis, Jeff	0	1	3.72	27	0	0	2	36	31	18	15	14	21	L	L	6-2	185	12-20-66	1988	Allentown, Pa.
Myers, Mike	0	5	5.65	37	0	0	0	37	41	25	23	15	24	L	L	6-3	197	6-26-69	1990	Wheeling, Ill.
Newlin, Jim	0	0	4.26	5	0	0	0	6	6	3	3	1	0	R	R	6-1	200	6-25-59	1979	Roswell, Ga.
Pena, Alejandro	0	0	0.96	9	0	0	5	9	2	1	1	1	7	R	R	6-1	200	6-25-59	1979	Roswell, Ga.
Perigny, Don	1	1	5.14	6	0	0	0	7	8	6	4	1	10	R	R	5-11	175	1-9-68	1990	Lowell, Mass.
Rapp, Pat	0	1	6.00	1	1	0	0	6	6	4	4	1	5	R	R	6-3	210	7-13-67	1989	Sulphur, La.
Rojas, Euclides	0	0	3.00	2	0	0	0	3	2	1	1	2	2	R	R	6-0	180	8-25-67	1995	Miami, Fla.
Scheid, Rich	1	4	5.93	19	8	0	0	55	74	40	36	15	37	L	L	6-3	185	2-3-65	1986	Summit, N.J.
Shepherd, Keith	1	1	21.21	4	0	0	0	5	11	11	11	3	2	R	R	6-2	197	1-21-68	1986	Wabash, Ind.
Small, Aaron	2	1	2.88	33	0	0	10	41	36	15	13	10	31	R	R	6-5	200	11-23-71	1989	Victorville, Calif.
2-team (1 Syracuse)	2	1	2.98	34	0	0	10	42	39	16	14	11	33							
Smith, Pete	3	1	3.86	10	8	0	0	49	51	21	21	17	20	R	R	6-2	200	2-27-66	1984	Smyrna, Ga.
Spencer, Stan	1	4	7.84	9	9	0	0	41	61	37	36	24	19	R	R	6-3	195	8-2-68	1991	Battle Ground, Wash.
Spradlin, Jerry	3	3	3.03	41	0	0	1	59	59	26	20	15	38	S	R	6-7	240	6-14-67	1988	Anaheim, Calif.
Valdes, Marc	9	13	4.86	27	27	3	0	170	189	98	92	59	104	R	R	6-0	190	12-20-71	1993	Tampa, Fla.
Veres, Randy	1	0	2.70	6	0	0	1	7	3	2	2	5	5	R	R	6-3	187	11-25-65	1985	Rancho Cordova, Calif.
Wainhouse, David	0	0	4.00	4	0	0	0	4	6	4	4	2	4	L	R	6-2	185	11-7-67	1989	Mercer Island, Wash.
2-team (26 Syracuse)	3	2	4.50	30	0	0	5	28	35	19	14	15	20							
Weathers, David	0	1	9.00	1	1	0	0	5	10	5	5	5	0	R	R	6-3	205	9-25-69	1988	Leoma, Tenn.
Zimmerman, Mike	2	2	5.30	31	7	0	0	70	84	46	41	41	30	R	R	6-0	180	2-6-69	1990	Brooklyn, N.Y.

FIELDING

Catcher	PCT	G	PO	A	E	DP	PB
Hernandez	.964	30	119	16	5	0	1
Massarelli	1.000	2	11	0	0	0	1
Natal	.997	43	259	41	1	3	4
Pappas	.982	75	398	37	8	4	5
Rudolph	1.000	2	6	0	0	0	0

First Base	PCT	G	PO	A	E	DP
Brewer	.990	65	541	50	6	57
Capra	1.000	1	7	0	0	0
Gregg	.993	13	123	12	1	14
Jorgensen	1.000	4	13	1	0	1
Morman	.998	40	407	23	1	42
Natal	1.000	1	8	2	0	1

	PCT	G	PO	A	E	DP
Pappas	.995	23	187	17	1	22
Zupcic	1.000	4	21	1	0	1
Second Base	PCT	G	PO	A	E	DP
Capra	1.000	3	2	1	0	0
J. Carter	.951	68	148	199	18	40
Millette	.951	47	75	139	11	32
Schunk	.978	32	50	82	3	27
Zosky	.970	13	20	44	2	14
Third Base	PCT	G	PO	A	E	DP
Capra	.892	23	22	36	7	5
Castaldo	1.000	2	1	1	0	0

	PCT	G	PO	A	E	DP
Jorgensen	.962	97	73	208	11	21
Millette	.857	1	1	5	1	1
Natal	.909	4	4	6	1	0
Schunk	.914	15	9	23	3	0
Zosky	.975	13	16	23	1	8
Zupcic	.000	1	0	0	0	0
Shortstop	PCT	G	PO	A	E	DP
Abbott	.909	5	5	15	2	3
Capra	1.000	1	1	0	0	0
Millette	.934	19	25	46	5	10
Schunk	.966	60	104	177	10	44
Zosky	.966	66	125	212	12	52

Outfield	PCT	G	PO	A	E	DP		PCT	G	PO	A	E	DP		PCT	G	PO	A	E	DP
Boston	1.000	8	12	1	0	0	Dascenzo	1.000	70	157	3	0	0	Morman	.900	3	9	0	1	0
Capra	.972	85	133	7	4	0	Ford	.987	45	69	5	1	1	Pappas	.956	21	38	5	2	0
Carr	1.000	7	9	0	0	0	Gregg	1.000	13	17	1	0	0	Tavarez	.979	38	92	2	2	0
J. Carter	1.000	43	73	5	0	2	Massarelli	.983	64	110	8	2	0	Zupcic	.977	54	81	4	2	0
S. Carter	.900	12	15	3	2	0														

PORTLAND AA
EASTERN LEAGUE

BATTING	AVG	G	AB	R	H	2B	3B	HR	RBI	BB	SO	SB	CS	B	T	HT	WT	DOB	1st Yr	Resides
Clapinski, Chris	.236	87	208	32	49	9	3	4	30	28	44	5	2	S	R	6-0	165	8-20-71	1992	Rancho Mirage, Calif.
Clark, Tim	.271	134	499	62	135	34	2	8	88	59	86	0	5	L	L	6-3	210	2-10-69	1990	Philadelphia, Pa.
Johnson, Charles	.000	2	7	0	0	0	0	0	1	3	0	0	0	R	R	6-2	215	7-20-71	1992	Fort Pierce, Fla.
Katzaroff, Rob	.304	116	441	87	134	16	4	10	49	49	33	18	10	R	R	5-8	170	7-29-68	1990	Phoenix, Ariz.
Kremers, Jimmy	.223	85	264	32	59	11	5	7	37	27	70	1	0	L	R	6-3	205	10-8-65	1988	Broken Arrow, Okla.
Lucca, Lou	.276	112	388	57	107	28	1	9	64	59	77	4	4	R	R	5-11	210	10-13-70	1992	S. San Francisco, Calif.
McMillon, Billy	.313	141	518	92	162	29	3	14	93	96	90	15	9	L	L	5-11	172	11-17-71	1993	Sumter, S.C.
Milliard, Ralph	.267	128	464	104	124	22	3	11	40	85	83	22	10	R	R	5-10	160	12-30-73	1993	Soest, Neth. Antilles
Redmond, Mike	.255	105	333	37	85	11	1	3	39	22	27	2	2	R	R	6-0	190	5-5-71	1993	Spokane, Wash.
Renteria, Edgar	.289	135	508	70	147	15	7	7	68	32	85	30	11	R	R	6-1	172	8-7-75	1992	Barranquilla, Columbia
Rudolph, Mason	.197	41	76	9	15	4	1	4	16	1	29	0	1	R	R	6-1	204	1-28-70	1988	Mesa, Ariz.
Sheff, Chris	.276	131	471	85	130	25	7	12	91	72	84	23	6	R	R	6-3	210	2-4-71	1992	Laguna Hills, Calif.
Torres, Tony	.296	58	81	15	24	3	2	0	4	11	23	9	0	R	R	5-9	165	6-1-70	1994	San Pablo, Calif.
Waller, Casey	.222	14	36	4	8	2	1	0	5	6	4	1	0	S	R	5-11	180	12-15-67	1989	South Boston, Va.
Wilson, Pookie	.273	107	348	51	95	13	5	3	44	18	51	9	4	L	L	5-10	180	10-24-70	1992	Sylacauga, Ala.

PITCHING	W	L	ERA	G	GS	CG	SV	IP	H	R	ER	BB	SO	B	T	HT	WT	DOB	1st Yr	Resides
Alfonseca, Antonio	9	3	3.64	19	17	1	0	96	81	43	39	42	75	R	R	6-4	160	4-16-72	1990	La Romana, D.R.
Chergey, Dan	6	7	3.47	55	0	0	5	80	62	35	31	26	75	R	R	6-2	195	1-29-71	1993	Thousand Oaks, Calif.
Cunnane, Will	9	2	3.67	21	21	1	0	118	120	48	48	34	83	R	R	6-2	195	4-24-74	1993	Congers, N.Y.
Hancock, Chris	0	0	0.00	1	0	0	0	2	1	1	0	0	1	L	L	6-3	205	9-12-69	1988	Riverside, Calif.
Heredia, Wilson	4	0	2.00	4	4	0	0	27	22	7	6	14	19	R	R	6-0	165	3-30-72	1990	San Pedro de Macoris, D.R.
Juelsgaard, Jarod	3	1	3.89	48	0	0	2	72	65	35	31	44	44	R	R	6-3	190	6-27-68	1991	Elk Horn, Iowa
Larkin, Andy	1	2	3.38	9	9	0	0	40	29	16	15	11	23	R	R	6-4	181	6-27-74	1992	Medford, Ore.
Leahy, Pat	1	1	4.50	13	6	0	0	42	32	24	21	20	37	R	R	6-6	245	10-31-70	1992	Yakima, Wash.
Lemon, Don	1	6	3.61	30	3	0	1	62	60	30	25	19	47	R	R	6-4	195	6-2-67	1989	Locust Grove, Ga.
Mantei, Matt	1	0	2.38	8	0	0	1	11	10	3	3	5	15	R	R	6-1	181	7-7-73	1991	Sawyer, Mich.
McGraw, Tom	5	0	1.81	55	0	0	2	75	69	21	15	31	60	L	L	6-2	195	12-8-67	1990	Yacolt, Wash.
Mendoza, Reynol	9	10	3.43	27	27	1	0	168	163	73	64	69	120	R	R	6-0	215	10-27-70	1992	San Antonio, Texas
Mix, Greg	6	4	4.68	24	13	0	0	92	98	51	48	25	56	R	R	6-4	210	8-21-71	1993	Albuquerque, N.M.
Pettit, Doug	3	1	3.69	21	0	0	2	32	30	13	13	6	24	L	R	6-1	220	4-10-70	1992	Deer Park, Texas
Powell, Jay	5	4	1.87	50	0	0	24	53	42	12	11	15	53	R	R	6-4	220	1-9-72	1993	Collinsville, Tenn.
Rojas, Euclides	1	1	7.77	14	1	0	1	22	27	20	19	13	22	R	R	6-0	190	8-25-67	1995	Miami, Fla.
Spencer, Stan	1	4	7.38	8	8	0	0	39	57	39	32	19	32	R	R	6-3	195	8-2-68	1991	Battle Ground, Wash.
Wainhouse, David	2	1	7.20	17	0	0	0	25	39	22	20	8	16	L	R	6-2	195	11-7-67	1989	Mercer Island, Wash.
Ward, Bryan	7	3	4.50	20	11	1	2	72	70	42	36	31	71	L	L	6-2	210	1-28-72	1993	Mt. Holly, N.J.
Whisenant, Matt	10	6	3.50	23	22	2	0	129	106	57	50	65	107	S	L	6-3	215	6-8-71	1990	La Canada, Calif.

FIELDING

Catcher	PCT	G	PO	A	E	DP	PB		PCT	G	PO	A	E	DP		PCT	G	PO	A	E	DP
Johnson	.958	2	21	2	1	0	0	Milliard	.975	128	299	357	17	71	Renteria	.944	134	179	379	33	55
Kremers	.980	45	263	32	6	3	5	Torres	.970	10	14	18	1	4	Torres	.935	9	8	21	2	6
Redmond	.992	104	656	95	6	6	9	**Third Base**	**PCT**	**G**	**PO**	**A**	**E**	**DP**	**Outfield**	**PCT**	**G**	**PO**	**A**	**E**	**DP**
Rudolph	1.000	16	44	2	0	0	1	Clapinski	.978	30	24	64	2	4	Clapinski	1.000	5	6	0	0	0
First Base	**PCT**	**G**	**PO**	**A**	**E**	**DP**		Lucca	.952	111	56	261	16	23	Clark	.000	3	0	0	0	0
Clapinski	.900	1	9	0	1			Redmond	1.000	1	1	0	0	0	Katzaroff	.985	99	193	1	3	0
Clark	.991	129	1158	98	11	93		Torres	1.000	12	2	18	0	3	McMillon	.982	131	207	14	4	3
Kremers	.987	18	142	6	2	4		Waller	1.000	1	0	6	0	1	Sheff	.985	113	191	4	3	0
Second Base	**PCT**	**G**	**PO**	**A**	**E**	**DP**		**Shortstop**	**PCT**	**G**	**PO**	**A**	**E**	**DP**	Wilson	.988	88	159	3	2	1
Clapinski	1.000	15	32	28	0	9		Clapinski	.971	10	9	25	1	2							

BREVARD COUNTY A
FLORIDA STATE LEAGUE

BATTING	AVG	G	AB	R	H	2B	3B	HR	RBI	BB	SO	SB	CS	B	T	HT	WT	DOB	1st Yr	Resides
Babin, Brady	.248	32	105	15	26	3	2	2	19	9	20	0	1	R	R	6-0	170	9-17-75	1993	Gonzales, La.
Baugh, Gavin	.188	81	250	24	47	11	2	1	21	26	70	10	3	S	R	6-3	197	7-26-73	1992	San Mateo, Calif.
Berg, David	.298	114	382	71	114	18	1	3	39	68	61	9	4	R	R	5-11	185	9-3-70	1993	Roseville, Calif.
Brown, Ron	.260	121	404	48	105	22	3	3	59	31	79	6	12	R	R	6-3	185	1-17-70	1993	Tampa, Fla.
Brown, Willie	.222	63	189	26	42	6	1	6	23	25	74	4	3	L	R	6-2	197	8-31-70	1992	Edison, Ga.
Browne, Jerry	.286	3	7	2	2	0	0	0	2	1	1	0	0	S	R	5-10	170	2-13-66	1983	Arlington, Texas
Dawson, Andre	.100	3	10	0	1	0	0	0	0	0	2	0	0	R	R	6-3	195	7-10-54	1975	Miami, Fla.
Gonzalez, Alex	.203	17	59	6	12	2	1	0	8	1	14	1	1	R	R	6-0	150	2-15-77	1994	Turmero, Venez.
Hastings, Lionel	.273	120	469	60	128	20	0	7	45	44	64	3	3	R	R	5-9	175	1-26-73	1994	Orange, Calif.
Kingman, Brendan	.253	95	348	37	88	19	4	8	47	31	45	1	0	R	R	6-1	195	5-22-73	1992	Sydney, Australia
Long, Justin	.118	9	17	3	2	0	0	0	1	1	10	0	0	R	R	6-0	180	12-1-71	1994	Fontana, Calif.
Martinez, Ramon	.263	99	372	47	98	7	2	2	24	29	84	21	4	S	R	6-0	170	9-8-69	1990	Villa Gonzalez, D.R.
Millar, Kevin	.288	129	459	53	132	32	2	13	68	70	66	4	4	R	R	6-1	195	9-24-71	1993	Encino, Calif.
Prater, Andrew	.150	73	173	18	26	5	0	2	16	18	49	0	2	R	R	6-1	195	7-4-72	1990	Austin, Texas
Reeves, Glen	.270	117	415	68	112	22	2	1	33	78	78	6	7	R	R	6-0	175	1-19-74	1993	Glen Waverly, Australia
Robinson, Dan	.237	105	354	38	84	17	3	7	52	35	81	10	6	L	R	6-1	195	8-19-70	1992	Shreveport, La.
Sims, Michael	.185	89	260	24	48	6	0	1	20	15	52	4	2	R	R	5-11	185	2-23-71	1993	Lancaster, Calif.
Southard, Scott	.210	68	219	18	46	7	1	2	21	20	40	4	3	R	R	5-10	165	10-14-71	1993	Pensacola, Fla.

GAMES BY POSITION: C—Kingman 1, Prater 73, Sims 89. **1B**—Baugh 1, Kingman 3, Millar 125, Robinson 13. **2B**—Baugh 3, Berg 7, Hastings 118, Southard 15. **3B**—Baugh 72, Berg 52, Browne 1, Southard 15. **SS**—Babin 32, Berg 56, Gonzalez 17, Southard 39. **OF**—R. Brown 121, W. Brown 49, Browne 1, Long 6, Martinez 93, Reeves 111, Robinson 51.

PITCHING	W	L	ERA	G	GS	CG	SV	IP	H	R	ER	BB	SO	B	T	HT	WT	DOB	1st Yr	Resides
Andersen, Mark	0	1	3.96	20	0	0	0	36	42	25	16	17	21	R	R	6-2	210	9-27-71	1994	Eugene, Ore.
Bowen, Mitchel	0	2	2.56	41	3	0	3	88	87	36	25	32	51	R	R	6-5	225	10-24-72	1993	La Crescenta, Calif.
Bowen, Ryan	0	2	2.45	3	3	0	0	11	6	3	3	6	10	R	R	6-0	185	2-10-68	1987	Houston, Texas
Carl, Todd	3	4	3.96	15	7	0	1	52	44	26	23	27	19	R	R	6-5	220	1-3-73	1993	Stitzer, Wisc.
Davis, Mark	0	0	0.00	3	0	0	0	5	2	0	0	4	4	L	L	6-4	210	10-19-60	1979	Marietta, Ga.
Delgado, Ernie	1	6	7.07	18	10	0	0	62	74	51	49	59	36	R	R	6-2	190	7-21-75	1993	Tucson, Ariz.
Delahoya, Javier	1	0	1.74	5	0	0	0	10	6	2	2	2	8	R	R	6-2	160	2-21-70	1989	North Hollywood, Calif.
Ehler, Daniel	5	6	3.57	16	15	0	0	88	88	46	35	26	66	R	R	6-3	180	2-17-75	1993	Covina, Calif.
Hammond, Chris	0	0	0.00	1	1	0	0	4	3	1	0	0	4	L	L	6-1	195	1-21-66	1986	Birmingham, Ala.
Heredia, Felix	6	4	3.57	34	8	0	1	96	101	52	38	36	76	L	L	6-0	160	6-18-76	1993	Barahona, D.R.
Hernandez, Jeremy	0	0	2.35	4	2	0	0	8	5	2	2	2	5	R	R	6-6	195	7-6-66	1987	Yuma, Ariz.
Hollinger, Adrian	0	2	5.40	11	4	0	2	25	26	17	15	18	18	L	R	6-0	180	9-23-70	1991	Mira Loma, Calif.
Hurst, William	1	4	3.02	39	4	0	12	51	33	20	17	41	35	R	R	6-7	220	4-28-70	1990	Miami, Fla.
Leahy, Pat	4	4	3.88	11	11	0	0	46	41	29	20	22	43	R	R	6-6	245	10-31-70	1992	Yakima, Wash.
Lewis, Michael	4	5	2.32	43	0	0	1	62	48	22	16	22	44	L	L	6-2	195	10-4-68	1991	Bakersfield, Calif.
Militello, Sam	0	1	7.84	4	4	0	0	10	7	10	9	20	18	R	R	6-3	200	11-26-69	1990	Tampa, Fla.
Mix, Greg	1	3	3.94	5	4	1	0	30	27	13	13	10	17	R	R	6-4	210	8-21-71	1993	Albuquerque, N.M.
Nunez, Clemente	12	6	2.48	19	19	4	0	123	99	48	34	22	79	R	R	5-11	181	2-10-75	1992	Bonao, D.R.
Pettit, Doug	2	5	2.83	27	0	0	4	35	37	18	11	13	22	L	R	6-1	220	4-10-70	1992	Deer Park, Texas
Saunders, Tony	6	5	3.04	13	13	0	0	71	60	29	24	15	54	L	L	6-1	189	4-29-74	1992	Ellicott City, Md.
Stanifer, Robert	3	6	4.14	18	13	0	0	83	97	47	38	15	45	R	R	6-2	195	3-10-72	1994	Easley, S.C.
Thornton, Paul	4	5	3.27	42	1	0	4	72	66	34	26	27	56	R	R	6-2	210	6-21-70	1993	Callahan, Fla.
Tidwell, Jason	0	0	0.00	4	1	0	0	7	5	3	0	3	3	R	R	6-3	190	8-2-71	1992	Cartersville, Ga.
Ward, Bryan	5	1	2.88	11	11	0	0	72	68	27	23	17	65	L	L	6-2	210	1-28-72	1993	Mt. Holly, N.J.
Weathers, Dave	0	0	0.00	1	1	0	0	4	4	0	0	1	3	R	R	6-3	205	9-25-69	1988	Leoma, Tenn.
Whitten, Michael	1	4	3.96	22	0	0	1	39	47	21	17	9	25	L	L	6-4	200	12-27-68	1992	Raleigh, N.C.

KANE COUNTY — A

MIDWEST LEAGUE

BATTING	AVG	G	AB	R	H	2B	3B	HR	RBI	BB	SO	SB	CS	B	T	HT	WT	DOB	1st Yr	Resides
Booty, Josh	.101	31	109	6	11	2	0	1	6	11	45	1	0	R	R	6-3	210	4-29-75	1994	Shreveport, La.
Cady, Todd	.251	115	387	47	97	23	1	11	66	47	104	1	0	S	R	6-4	222	11-25-72	1994	La Mesa, Calif.
Castillo, Luis	.326	89	340	71	111	4	4	0	23	55	50	41	18	R	R	5-11	146	9-12-75	1993	San Pedro de Macoris, D.R.
Castro, Dennis	.246	46	138	12	34	9	0	5	21	15	33	1	0	L	R	6-2	195	11-25-72	1994	Gilroy, Calif.
Cole, Abdul	.123	56	122	10	15	3	0	1	7	17	48	3	1	R	R	6-1	185	8-4-75	1994	San Francisco, Calif.
Cook, Hayward	.280	78	261	50	73	5	1	8	23	12	61	23	4	R	R	5-10	195	6-24-72	1994	San Jose, Calif.
Darden, Tony	.287	86	286	42	82	15	5	3	31	40	40	5	5	R	R	6-0	170	5-29-74	1994	Gilmer, Texas
Dunwoody, Todd	.283	132	494	89	140	20	8	14	89	52	105	39	11	L	L	6-2	185	4-11-75	1993	West Lafayette, Ind.
Garcia, Amaury	.241	26	58	19	14	4	1	1	5	18	12	5	2	R	R	5-10	160	5-20-75	1993	Santo Domingo, D.R.
Goodell, Steve	.286	2	7	0	2	0	0	0	1	2	2	0	0	R	R	6-3	196	4-23-75	1995	Dublin, Calif.
Gugino, Mark	.244	58	164	29	40	13	2	3	20	35	29	5	3	R	R	6-0	195	10-28-72	1994	Columbia, S.C.
Harvey, Aaron	.292	100	336	58	98	25	3	7	54	25	70	11	7	L	R	5-10	180	6-11-73	1994	Donvale, Australia
Jackson, Ryan	.293	132	471	78	138	39	6	10	82	67	74	13	8	L	L	6-2	195	11-15-71	1994	Sarasota, Fla.
Kuilan, Hector	.000	2	7	0	0	0	0	0	0	0	1	0	0	R	R	5-11	190	4-3-76	1994	Vega Alta, P.R.
Reyes, Michael	.189	14	37	8	7	3	0	0	4	7	11	0	2	R	R	6-1	190	4-21-72	1994	La Coste, Texas
Rodriguez, Maximo	.191	72	236	18	45	7	1	5	30	18	65	0	1	R	R	6-0	170	11-18-73	1993	La Romana, D.R.
Rodriguez, Victor	.235	127	472	65	111	9	1	0	43	40	47	18	6	R	R	5-7	175	10-25-76	1994	Guayama, P.R.
Roskos, John	.297	114	418	74	124	36	3	12	88	42	86	2	0	R	R	5-11	198	11-19-74	1993	Rio Rancho, N.M.
White, Walter	.285	63	207	30	59	18	2	1	23	32	52	3	2	R	R	6-1	190	12-12-71	1994	Rohnert Park, Calif.

GAMES BY POSITION: C—Cady 7, Kuilan 2, M. Rodriguez 65, Roskos 71. **1B**—Cady 88, Castro 1, Jackson 52. **2B**—Castillo 89, Darden 10, Garcia 4, White 44. **3B**—Booty 31, Castro 42, Darden 47, Garcia 20, Gugino 1, White 8. **SS**—Darden 1, Goodell 2, V. Rodriguez 127, White 13. **OF**—Cole 50, Cook 65, Darden 26, Dunwoody 129, Gugino 36, Harvey 57, Jackson 59, Reyes 13.

PITCHING	W	L	ERA	G	GS	CG	SV	IP	H	R	ER	BB	SO	B	T	HT	WT	DOB	1st Yr	Resides
Alejo, Nigel	4	1	2.39	48	0	0	7	53	48	17	14	25	47	R	R	6-0	171	1-12-75	1993	Palo Negro, Venez.
Andersen, Mark	1	2	3.46	15	0	0	1	26	29	13	10	13	15	R	R	6-2	210	9-27-71	1994	Eugene, Ore.
Bussa, Todd	0	1	0.86	36	0	0	14	42	20	4	4	15	38	R	R	5-11	170	12-13-72	1991	Palm Beach Gardens, Fla.
Carl, Todd	0	5	8.54	12	7	0	0	39	69	37	37	11	22	R	R	6-5	220	1-3-73	1993	Stitzer, Wisc.
DeWitt, Scott	0	0	0.00	1	1	0	0	3	0	0	0	1	2	R	L	6-4	200	10-6-74	1995	Springfield, Ore.
Farmer, Jon	1	4	6.98	29	11	0	0	79	97	65	61	32	60	L	L	6-3	215	9-12-73	1994	Porterville, Calif.
Filbeck, Ryan	1	4	3.67	25	0	0	1	42	40	19	17	17	28	R	R	6-2	200	12-23-72	1993	El Toro, Calif.
Gonzalez, Gabe	4	4	2.28	32	0	0	1	43	32	18	11	14	41	S	L	6-1	160	5-24-72	1995	Long Beach, Calif.
Hebbert, Allan	0	1	12.38	5	2	0	0	8	9	12	11	15	3	R	R	6-3	180	10-8-74	1994	Rancho Cucamonga, Calif.
Mays, Marcus	1	2	6.17	8	0	0	0	12	15	8	8	7	6	L	L	6-4	175	5-4-74	1993	DeKalb, Ill.
Meadows, Brian	9	9	4.22	26	26	1	0	147	163	90	69	41	103	R	R	6-4	210	11-21-75	1994	Troy, Ala.
Micknich, Steve	1	0	2.31	9	0	0	0	12	13	3	3	6	10	R	R	6-1	190	12-17-71	1994	Elmira, N.Y.
Miles, Chad	1	1	7.24	19	0	0	0	27	35	33	22	23	14	L	L	6-3	195	2-26-73	1994	Renton, Wash.
Miranda, Walter	8	7	4.08	25	25	1	0	128	102	68	58	88	106	R	R	6-4	190	1-6-75	1992	Cartagena, Colombia
Parisi, Mike	11	8	3.29	26	26	2	0	164	152	73	60	42	113	R	R	6-3	195	6-18-73	1994	Arcadia, Calif.
Pineda, Leonel	2	2	3.51	5	5	1	0	33	44	14	13	6	10	R	R	6-2	175	8-20-76	1993	Valverde Mao, D.R.
Press, Greg	10	3	3.60	29	21	0	0	132	127	72	53	37	82	R	R	6-3	200	9-21-71	1994	Santa Cruz, Calif.
Stark, Zachary	1	1	15.51	5	4	0	0	16	27	30	27	17	5	R	L	6-6	205	8-7-74	1994	Leawood, Kan.
Tidwell, Jason	1	4	8.62	6	4	0	0	16	19	17	15	14	13	R	R	6-3	190	8-2-71	1992	Cartersville, Ga.
Vardijan, Dan	0	0	6.00	1	1	0	0	3	5	3	2	2	2	R	R	6-5	193	12-1-76	1995	Glenview, Ill.
Ybarra, Jamie	5	5	3.00	50	2	0	2	96	62	37	32	40	104	R	R	6-0	164	6-17-71	1994	San Jose, Calif.
Zanolla, Dan	4	4	3.58	28	3	0	0	60	58	34	24	28	54	R	R	6-0	185	9-18-70	1993	Hobart, Ind.

ELMIRA — A

NEW YORK-PENN LEAGUE

BATTING	AVG	G	AB	R	H	2B	3B	HR	RBI	BB	SO	SB	CS	B	T	HT	WT	DOB	1st Yr	Resides
Babin, Brady	.350	6	20	4	7	1	1	0	2	3	1	0	0	R	R	6-0	170	9-17-75	1993	Gonzales, La.
Booty, Josh	.220	74	287	33	63	18	1	6	37	19	85	4	4	R	R	6-3	210	4-29-75	1994	Shreveport, La.

BATTING	AVG	G	AB	R	H	2B	3B	HR	RBI	BB	SO	SB	CS	B	T	HT	WT	DOB	1st Yr	Resides
Erwin, Mat	.262	68	260	22	68	12	2	4	39	22	36	2	1	R	R	6-0	195	2-28-73	1995	Fair Oaks, Calif.
Funaro, Joe	.265	56	189	24	50	10	3	2	16	17	21	5	2	R	R	5-9	170	3-20-73	1995	Hamden, Conn.
Garcia, Amaury	.273	62	231	40	63	7	3	0	17	34	50	41	12	R	R	5-10	160	5-20-75	1993	Santo Domingo, D.R.
Garrett, Jason	.221	41	131	15	29	4	1	1	11	11	31	2	1	R	R	6-2	180	6-10-75	1995	Manchaca, Texas
Goodell, Steve	.253	69	253	42	64	14	4	7	30	36	50	4	5	R	R	6-3	196	4-23-75	1995	Dublin, Calif.
Hernandez, Rob	.040	8	25	0	1	0	0	0	0	5	7	1	0	S	R	5-10	190	8-29-72	1995	San Jose, Calif.
Jefferson, Dave	.077	5	13	1	1	0	0	0	0	1	3	2	0	R	R	6-2	190	6-18-75	1993	Palo Alto, Calif.
Jones, Jaime	.284	31	116	21	33	6	2	4	11	9	30	5	4	L	L	6-3	190	8-2-76	1995	Poway, Calif.
Long, Justin	.210	56	186	25	39	6	1	5	17	17	54	13	3	R	R	6-0	180	12-1-71	1994	Fontana, Calif.
McCartney, Sommer	.179	33	112	11	20	4	0	1	5	6	29	1	3	R	R	6-0	200	8-2-72	1994	San Jose, Calif.
Miller, Kumandac	.201	47	154	9	31	4	3	0	15	8	40	2	4	R	R	6-1	210	10-9-73	1992	Sacramento, Calif.
Rascon, Rene	.219	34	114	12	25	4	1	0	11	20	34	3	3	L	L	6-3	210	9-27-73	1995	Watsonville, Calif.
Shanahan, Jason	.239	64	230	19	55	9	4	4	28	30	50	7	3	S	R	6-2	210	8-27-73	1995	Missoula, Mon.
Winn, Randy	.315	51	213	38	67	7	4	6	22	15	31	19	7	S	R	6-2	175	6-9-74	1995	Danville, Calif.

GAMES BY POSITION: C—Erwin 57, Hernandez 6, McCartney 15. 1B—Garrett 19, McCartney 1, Shanahan 57. 2B—Funaro 17, Garcia 60. 3B—Booty 72, Funaro 1, Goodell 1, Shanahan 2. SS—Babin 5, Booty 1, Funaro 3, Goodell 65, Shanahan 2. OF—Funaro 33, Jefferson 5, Jones 30, Long 52, Miller 42, Rascon 26, Winn 51.

PITCHING	W	L	ERA	G	GS	CG	SV	IP	H	R	ER	BB	SO	B	T	HT	WT	DOB	1st Yr	Resides
Beagle, Chad	1	3	5.73	5	5	0	0	22	25	16	14	13	21	L	L	6-5	195	3-31-71	1995	Roanoke, Va.
Burgus, Travis	7	5	3.48	15	15	0	0	88	84	45	34	29	68	L	L	6-2	185	11-6-72	1995	Mission Viejo, Calif.
Enard, Tony	0	5	7.63	15	5	0	0	31	33	36	26	22	27	R	R	6-4	220	8-16-74	1995	Sparks, Nev.
Farr, Mark	0	5	6.08	9	9	0	0	40	45	34	27	31	24	R	R	6-4	180	7-14-73	1994	Grafton, Ohio
Garcia, Rick	1	7	5.97	15	15	0	0	75	80	56	50	46	53	R	R	6-4	210	8-25-73	1995	El Paso, Texas
Howard, Tom	0	0	7.43	10	0	0	0	13	9	13	11	7	21	R	L	6-4	180	7-29-75	1993	Cocoa Beach, Fla.
Johnson, Scott	0	0	4.32	4	0	0	0	8	10	4	4	1	4	R	R	6-4	218	7-28-74	1992	Greeley, Colo.
Micknich, Steve	0	0	0.00	4	0	0	2	5	1	0	0	2	6	R	R	6-1	190	12-17-71	1994	Elmira, N.Y.
Miles, Chad	1	1	6.65	14	0	0	0	22	29	18	16	10	10	L	L	6-3	195	2-26-73	1994	Renton, Wash.
Miller, David	1	1	4.32	9	0	0	1	17	17	8	8	7	11	R	R	6-7	220	8-31-73	1995	Sanford, N.C.
Moore, Sam	1	2	1.84	15	0	0	3	29	23	8	6	4	22	R	R	6-3	190	10-29-71	1995	Charleston, S.C.
Pailthorpe, Bob	2	7	4.88	13	12	0	1	52	69	41	28	17	38	R	R	6-1	210	12-6-72	1995	Fremont, Calif.
Reichstein, Derek	1	4	5.23	22	2	0	1	52	52	37	30	27	37	R	R	6-5	230	11-22-72	1994	Los Gatos, Calif.
Ross, Jeremy	1	0	3.00	20	0	0	2	42	38	17	14	20	40	R	R	6-4	185	5-23-74	1994	Murray, Utah
Santoro, Gary	1	4	3.75	24	0	0	6	36	45	21	15	10	34	R	R	6-3	205	12-15-72	1995	Watertown, Conn.
Stephens, Shannon	8	5	2.58	17	12	0	0	91	72	38	26	17	74	R	R	6-2	205	8-28-73	1995	Grover Beach, Calif.
Treend, Pat	0	2	6.29	17	1	0	0	34	43	32	24	16	29	R	R	6-4	220	11-1-71	1995	Westhills, Calif.

MELBOURNE   R
GULF COAST LEAGUE

BATTING	AVG	G	AB	R	H	2B	3B	HR	RBI	BB	SO	SB	CS	B	T	HT	WT	DOB	1st Yr	Resides
Agnoly, Earl	.272	55	213	39	58	5	1	0	20	16	18	19	5	R	R	6-0	170	11-18-75	1993	Cativa, Panama
Bautista, Jorge	.206	42	126	16	26	6	1	0	4	12	23	0	0	R	R	5-9	165	7-12-76	1995	San Cristobal, D.R.
Camilo, Jose	.335	48	155	37	52	5	5	4	22	41	28	19	6	L	L	5-11	175	9-28-76	1994	Trujillo Alto, P.R.
Chastain, Dan	.200	4	10	0	2	0	0	0	0	0	1	1	0	R	R	5-11	205	12-27-72	1995	Fort Collins, Colo.
Fagley, Daniel	.182	16	33	4	6	0	0	0	4	4	8	0	0	R	R	5-10	185	12-18-74	1994	Riverton, N.J.
Franco, Raul	.277	49	184	30	51	12	0	0	22	16	14	9	3	R	R	5-11	150	1-14-76	1994	San Pedro de Macoris, D.R.
Gonzalez, Alex	.294	53	187	30	55	7	4	2	30	19	27	11	2	R	R	6-2	205	2-15-77	1994	Turmero, Venez.
Green, Raymond	.000	3	5	0	0	0	0	0	0	0	0	0	0	R	R	6-2	205	5-3-74	1995	Greenfield, Calif.
Jones, Jaime	.222	5	18	2	4	0	0	0	3	5	4	0	0	L	L	6-3	190	8-2-76	1995	Poway, Calif.
Kuilan, Hector	.248	48	153	14	38	8	0	0	27	17	20	4	1	R	R	5-11	190	4-3-76	1994	Vega Alta, P.R.
Owen, Tom	.227	28	66	13	15	3	0	0	10	12	6	0	2	R	R	6-0	180	2-13-73	1995	Elkhart, Iowa
Ramirez, Julio	.284	48	204	35	58	9	4	2	13	13	42	17	6	R	R	5-11	160	8-10-77	1994	Santo Domingo, D.R.
Reynoso, Ismael	.221	25	68	12	15	0	0	0	8	12	18	1	0	R	R	5-10	165	6-17-78	1994	La Romana, D.R.
Rolison, Nate	.276	37	134	22	37	10	2	1	19	15	34	0	1	L	R	6-5	225	3-27-77	1995	Petal, Miss.
Rosario, Juan	.000	5	7	1	0	0	0	0	0	4	2	1	0	R	R	6-4	195	11-3-75	1993	Perth Amboy, N.J.
Sime, Rafael	.240	55	204	26	49	7	6	2	22	20	48	7	1	L	L	6-1	155	9-30-76	1994	Valverde Mao, D.R.
Truitt, Theron	.179	24	67	8	12	0	0	0	0	22	15	31	19	R	R	6-2	175	8-3-75	1995	LaGrange, Calif.

GAMES BY POSITION: C—Chastain 2, Fagley 15, Green 2, Kuilan 47. 1B—Agnoly 26, Chastain 1, Rolison 30. 2B—Bautista 11, Franco 49, Reynoso 4. 3B—Bautista 31, Owen 20, Reynoso 14. SS—Gonzalez 52, Reynoso 8. OF—Agnoly 20, Camilo 34, Jones 4, Ramirez 46, Rosario 1, Sime 52, Truitt 15.

PITCHING	W	L	ERA	G	GS	CG	SV	IP	H	R	ER	BB	SO	B	T	HT	WT	DOB	1st Yr	Resides
Austin, Swan	0	2	3.10	15	0	0	4	20	22	9	7	12	15	R	R	6-2	210	10-31-76	1995	Douglasville, Ga.
Bair, Wayne	2	2	2.96	6	6	0	0	24	21	10	8	7	22	L	L	6-5	255	1-27-77	1995	Manchester, Md.
DeWitt, Scott	5	3	1.98	11	10	1	0	64	48	15	14	9	70	R	L	6-4	200	10-6-74	1995	Springfield, Ore.
Duvall, Michael	5	0	2.22	16	1	0	1	28	15	8	7	12	34	R	L	6-0	185	10-11-74	1995	Centerville, Va.
Getz, Rod	1	1	3.38	6	6	0	0	29	25	12	11	4	30	R	R	5-9	180	2-17-76	1995	Lawrenceberg, Ind.
Hurtado, Victor	3	1	0.81	7	7	1	0	33	14	5	3	16	28	R	R	6-1	155	6-14-77	1994	Santo Domingo, D.R.
Izquierdo, Hansel	0	0	0.00	1	0	0	0	2	3	3	0	2	0	R	R	6-2	200	1-2-77	1995	Miami, Fla.
Lara, Nelson	1	1	3.74	11	0	0	1	22	21	13	9	11	9	R	R	6-0	165	7-15-78	1995	Santo Domingo, D.R.
Marriott, Michael	0	0	1.13	2	2	0	0	8	2	2	1	7	6	R	R	6-3	195	3-12-77	1995	Spring, Texas
Richardson, David	0	2	2.30	9	0	0	1	16	8	5	4	5	8	R	R	6-3	187	12-4-73	1994	San Pedro de Macoris, D.R.
Rojas, Euclides	2	0	0.90	2	2	0	0	10	6	1	1	1	7	R	R	6-0	190	8-25-67	1995	Miami, Fla.
Ross, Jeremy	2	0	0.00	2	0	0	0	8	8	1	0	1	11	R	R	6-4	185	5-23-74	1994	Murray, Utah
Santiago, Derek	5	1	2.48	11	10	0	0	58	55	20	16	17	59	R	R	6-1	155	10-10-75	1995	Aurora, Ill.
Stark, Zac	3	1	1.73	11	1	0	2	26	18	7	5	3	16	R	L	6-6	205	8-7-74	1994	Leawood, Kan.
Tejera, Michael	3	1	2.65	11	3	0	2	34	28	13	10	16	28	L	L	5-9	175	10-18-76	1995	Miami, Fla.
Vardijan, Dan	5	0	1.64	9	8	0	0	44	21	11	8	10	34	R	R	6-5	193	12-1-76	1995	Glenview, Ill.
West, Kenyon	2	1	2.45	13	0	0	3	29	32	17	8	6	9	R	R	6-2	195	1-26-76	1996	Miami, Fla.
Widerski, Jonathan	1	0	3.33	14	0	0	1	24	16	13	9	18	12	R	R	6-4	190	5-17-77	1995	Minneapolis, Minn.

HOUSTON
ASTROS

Manager: Terry Collins.　　**1995 Record:** 76-68, .528 (2nd, NL Central).

BATTING	AVG	G	AB	R	H	2B	3B	HR	RBI	BB	SO	SB	CS	B	T	HT	WT	DOB	1st Yr	Resides
Bagwell, Jeff	.290	114	448	88	130	29	0	21	87	79	102	12	5	R	R	6-0	195	5-27-68	1989	Houston, Texas
Bell, Derek	.334	112	452	63	151	21	2	8	86	33	71	27	9	R	R	6-2	200	12-11-68	1987	Tampa, Fla.
Biggio, Craig	.302	141	553	123	167	30	2	22	77	80	85	33	8	R	R	5-11	180	12-14-65	1987	Houston, Texas
Borders, Pat	.114	11	35	1	4	0	0	0	2	7	0	0	0	R	R	6-2	195	5-14-63	1982	Lake Wales, Fla.
Brumley, Mike	.056	18	18	1	1	0	0	1	0	0	6	1	0	S	R	5-10	175	4-9-63	1983	Tulsa, Okla.
Cangelosi, John	.318	90	201	46	64	5	2	2	18	48	42	21	5	S	L	5-8	160	3-10-63	1982	Chicago, Ill.
Donnels, Chris	.300	19	30	4	9	0	0	0	2	3	6	0	0	L	R	6-0	185	4-21-66	1987	Aliso Vista, Calif.
Eusebio, Tony	.299	113	368	46	110	21	1	6	58	31	59	0	2	R	R	6-2	185	4-27-67	1985	Kissimmee, Fla.
Goff, Jerry	.154	12	26	2	4	2	0	1	3	4	13	0	0	L	R	6-3	207	4-12-64	1986	San Rafael, Calif.
Gonzalez, Luis	.258	56	209	35	54	10	4	6	35	18	30	1	3	L	R	6-2	180	9-3-67	1988	Houston, Texas
Gutierrez, Ricky	.276	52	156	22	43	6	0	0	12	10	33	5	0	R	R	6-1	175	5-23-70	1988	Miami, Fla.
Hajek, Dave	.000	5	2	0	0	0	0	0	0	1	1	1	0	R	R	5-10	165	10-14-67	1990	Colorado Springs, Colo.
Hunter, Brian L.	.302	78	321	52	97	14	5	2	28	21	52	24	7	R	R	6-4	180	3-5-71	1989	Vancouver, Wash.
Magadan, Dave	.313	127	348	44	109	24	0	2	51	71	56	2	1	L	R	6-3	200	9-30-62	1983	Tampa, Fla.
May, Derrick	.301	78	206	29	62	15	1	8	41	19	24	5	0	L	R	6-4	200	7-14-68	1986	Newark, Del.
Miller, Orlando	.262	92	324	36	85	20	1	5	36	22	71	3	4	R	R	6-1	180	1-13-69	1988	El Dorado, Panama
Mouton, James	.262	104	298	42	78	18	2	4	27	25	59	25	8	R	R	5-9	175	12-29-68	1991	Sacramento, Calif.
Nevin, Phil	.117	18	60	4	7	1	0	0	1	7	13	1	0	R	R	6-2	185	1-19-71	1992	Placentia, Calif.
Plantier, Phil	.250	22	68	12	17	2	0	4	15	11	19	0	0	L	R	5-11	195	1-27-69	1987	San Diego, Calif.
Servais, Scott	.225	28	89	7	20	10	0	1	12	9	15	0	1	R	R	6-2	195	6-4-67	1989	Coon Valley, Wisc.
Shipley, Craig	.263	92	232	23	61	8	1	3	24	8	28	6	1	R	R	6-0	168	1-7-63	1984	Jupiter, Fla.
Simms, Mike	.256	50	121	14	31	4	0	9	24	13	28	1	2	R	R	6-4	185	1-12-67	1985	Houston, Texas
Stankiewicz, Andy	.115	43	52	6	6	1	0	0	7	12	19	4	2	R	R	5-9	165	8-10-64	1986	La Habra, Calif.
Thompson, Milt	.220	92	132	14	29	9	0	2	19	14	37	4	2	L	R	5-11	170	1-5-59	1979	Ballwin, Mo.
Tucker, Scooter	.286	5	7	1	2	0	0	1	1	0	0	0	0	R	R	6-2	205	11-18-66	1988	Cantonment, Fla.
Wilkins, Rick	.250	15	40	6	10	1	0	1	5	10	10	0	0	L	R	6-2	210	6-4-67	1987	Jacksonville, Fla.
2-team (50 Chicago)	.203	65	202	30	41	3	0	7	19	46	61	0	0							

PITCHING	W	L	ERA	G	GS	CG	SV	IP	H	R	ER	BB	SO	B	T	HT	WT	DOB	1st Yr	Resides
Brocail, Doug	6	4	4.19	36	7	0	1	77	87	40	36	22	39	L	R	6-5	190	5-16-67	1986	Lamar, Colo.
Dougherty, Jim	8	4	4.92	56	0	0	0	68	76	37	37	25	49	R	R	6-0	210	3-8-68	1991	Kitty Hawk, N.C.
Drabek, Doug	10	9	4.77	31	31	2	0	185	205	104	98	54	143	R	R	6-1	185	7-25-62	1983	The Woodlands, Texas
Hampton, Mike	9	8	3.35	24	24	0	0	151	141	73	56	49	115	R	L	5-10	180	9-9-72	1990	Homosassa, Fla.
Hartgraves, Dean	2	0	3.22	40	0	0	0	36	30	14	13	16	24	R	L	6-0	185	8-12-66	1987	Central Point, Ore.
Henneman, Mike	0	1	3.00	21	0	0	8	21	21	7	7	4	19	R	R	6-4	205	12-11-61	1984	Colleyville, Texas
Hudek, John	2	2	5.40	19	0	0	7	20	19	12	12	5	29	S	R	6-1	200	8-8-66	1988	Tampa, Fla.
Jones, Todd	6	5	3.07	68	0	0	15	100	89	38	34	52	96	L	R	6-3	200	4-24-68	1989	Pell City, Ala.
Kile, Darryl	4	12	4.96	25	21	0	0	127	114	81	70	73	113	R	R	6-5	185	12-2-68	1988	Corona, Calif.
Martinez, Pedro A.	0	0	7.40	25	0	0	0	21	29	18	17	16	17	L	L	5-11	155	11-29-68	1987	Villa Mella, D.R.
McMurtry, Craig	0	1	7.84	11	0	0	0	10	15	11	9	9	4	R	R	6-5	192	11-5-59	1980	Troy, Texas
Powell, Ross	0	0	11.00	15	0	0	0	9	16	12	11	11	8	L	L	6-0	180	1-24-68	1989	Antioch, Tenn.
Reynolds, Shane	10	11	3.47	30	30	3	0	189	196	87	73	37	175	R	R	6-3	210	3-26-68	1989	Houston, Texas
Swindell, Greg	10	9	4.47	33	26	1	0	153	180	86	76	39	96	R	L	6-3	225	1-2-65	1986	Houston, Texas
Tabaka, Jeff	1	0	2.22	24	0	0	0	24	17	6	6	12	19	R	L	6-2	195	1-17-64	1986	Clinton, Ohio
2-team (5 SD)	1	0	3.23	34	0	0	0	31	27	11	11	17	25							
Veres, Dave	5	1	2.26	72	0	0	1	103	89	29	26	30	94	R	R	6-2	195	10-19-66	1986	Gresham, Ore.
Wagner, Billy	0	0	0.00	1	0	0	0	0	0	0	0	0	0	L	L	5-10	180	7-25-71	1993	Tannersville, Va.
Wall, Donne	3	1	5.55	6	5	0	0	24	33	19	15	5	16	R	R	6-1	180	7-11-67	1989	Festus, Mo.

FIELDING

Catcher	PCT	G	PO	A	E	DP	PB
Borders	.987	11	70	5	1	2	2
Eusebio	.993	103	645	49	5	9	11
Goff	1.000	11	80	6	0	1	1
Servais	.977	28	198	17	5	3	0
Tucker	1.000	3	7	1	0	0	0
Wilkins	1.000	13	87	4	0	0	0

First Base	PCT	G	PO	A	E	DP
Bagwell	.994	114	1004	129	7	81
Brumley	1.000	1	1	1	0	0
Magadan	1.000	11	66	4	0	5
May	.000	1	0	0	0	0
Shipley	1.000	1	1	0	0	0
Simms	.995	25	204	17	1	17

Second Base	PCT	G	PO	A	E	DP
Biggio	.986	141	299	419	10	78

	PCT	G	PO	A	E	DP
Donnels	1.000	1	0	1	0	0
Shipley	1.000	5	5	10	0	1
Stankiewicz	1.000	6	3	7	0	0

Third Base	PCT	G	PO	A	E	DP
Brumley	.000	1	0	1	0	0
Donnels	.818	9	3	6	2	2
Gutierrez	.000	2	0	0	0	0
Magadan	.922	100	55	159	18	9
Nevin	.933	16	10	32	3	4
Shipley	.982	65	27	82	2	5
Stankiewicz	1.000	3	2	1	0	0

Shortstop	PCT	G	PO	A	E	DP
Brumley	1.000	3	0	1	0	0
Gutierrez	.956	44	64	108	8	17

	PCT	G	PO	A	E	DP
Miller	.964	89	131	270	15	52
Shipley	.971	11	10	24	1	2
Stankiewicz	.985	14	15	51	1	6

Outfield	PCT	G	PO	A	E	DP
Bell	.963	110	201	10	8	2
Brumley	1.000	3	2	0	0	0
Cangelosi	.950	59	92	3	5	0
Gonzalez	.980	55	94	2	2	0
Hunter	.955	74	182	8	9	2
May	.974	55	74	0	2	0
Mouton	1.000	94	136	4	0	0
Plantier	.962	20	25	0	1	0
Simms	1.000	12	17	0	0	0
Thompson	.979	34	45	2	1	1

ASTROS

TY SPORTS GROUP

Jeff Bagwell led the Astros with 87 RBIs

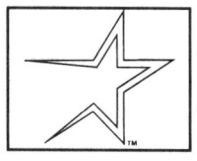

Astros minor league Player of the Year Donne Wall

FARM SYSTEM

Director of Player Development: Fred Nelson.

Class	Farm Team	League	W	L	Pct.	Finish*	Manager	First Yr
AAA	Tucson (Ariz.) Toros	Pacific Coast	87	56	.608	1st (10)	Rick Sweet	1980
AA	Jackson (Miss.) Generals	Texas	62	73	.459	7th (8)	Tim Tolman	1991
#A	Kissimmee (Fla.) Cobras	Florida State	55	81	.404	13th (14)	Dave Engle	1985
A	Quad City (Iowa) River Bandits	Midwest	76	61	.555	2nd (14)	Jim Pankovits	1993
A	Auburn (N.Y.) Astros	New York-Penn	40	34	.541	5th (14)	Manny Acta	1982
R	Kissimmee (Fla.) Astros	Gulf Coast	32	26	.552	T-8th (16)	Bobby Ramos	1977

*Finish in overall standings (No. of teams in league)   #Advanced level

ORGANIZATION LEADERS

MAJOR LEAGUERS

BATTING
*AVG	Derek Bell	.334
R	Craig Biggio	123
H	Craig Biggio	167
TB	Craig Biggio	267
2B	Craig Biggio	30
3B	Brian Hunter	5
HR	Craig Biggio	22
RBI	Jeff Bagwell	87
BB	Craig Biggio	80
SO	Jeff Bagwell	102
SB	Craig Biggio	33

PITCHING
W	Three tied at	10
L	Darryl Kile	12
#ERA	Dave Veres	2.26
G	Dave Veres	72
CG	Shane Reynolds	3
SV	Todd Jones	15
IP	Shane Reynolds	189
BB	Darryl Kile	73
SO	Shane Reynolds	175

MORRIS FOSTOFF

Craig Biggio. 22 homers

MINOR LEAGUERS

BATTING
*AVG	Donovan Mitchell, Quad City	.329
R	Dave Hajek, Tucson	99
H	Dave Hajek, Tucson	164
TB	Dave Hajek, Tucson	221
2B	Dave Hajek, Tucson	37
3B	Bob Abreu, Tucson	17
HR	Ray Montgomery, Jackson/Tucson	21
RBI	Ray Montgomery, Jackson/Tucson	92
BB	Tim Forkner, Kissimmee/Jackson	79
SO	Trevor Froschauer, Kissimmee	121
SB	Carlos Hernandez, Quad City	58

PITCHING
W	Donne Wall, Tucson	17
L	Dan Lock, Quad City	15
#ERA	Tony Mounce, Quad City	2.43
G	Two tied at	55
CG	Tony Mounce, Quad City	3
SV	Manuel Barrios, Quad City	23
IP	Donne Wall, Tucson	177
BB	Scott Elarton, Quad City	71
SO	Billy Wagner, Jackson/Tucson	157

*Minimum 250 At-Bats   #Minimum 75 Innings

TOP 10 PROSPECTS

How the Astros Top 10 prospects, as judged by Baseball America prior to the 1995 season, fared in 1995:

Brian Hunter

Player, Pos.	Club (Class—League)	AVG	AB	R	H	2B	3B	HR	RBI	SB
1. Brian Hunter, of	Tucson (AAA—Pacific Coast)	.329	155	28	51	5	1	1	16	11
	Houston	.302	321	52	97	14	5	2	28	24
3. Richard Hidalgo, of	Jackson (AA—Texas)	.266	489	59	130	28	6	14	59	8
4. Orlando Miller, ss	Houston	.262	324	36	85	20	1	5	36	3
5. Bob Abreu, of	Tucson (AAA—Pacific Coast)	.304	415	72	126	24	17	10	75	16
6. *Phil Nevin, 3b-of	Tucson (AAA—Pacific Coast)	.291	223	31	65	16	0	7	41	2
	Houston	.117	60	4	7	1	0	0	1	1
	Toledo (AAA—International)	.304	23	3	7	2	0	1	3	0
	Detroit	.219	96	9	21	3	1	2	12	0
10. Ramon Castro, c	Auburn (A—New York-Penn)	.299	224	40	67	17	0	9	49	0
	Kissimmee (A—Florida State)	.208	120	6	25	5	0	0	8	0

		W	L	ERA	G	SV	IP	H	BB	SO
2. Billy Wagner, lhp	Jackson (AA—Texas)	2	2	2.57	12	0	70	49	36	77
	Tucson (AAA—Pacific Coast)	5	3	3.18	13	0	76	70	32	80
7. Scott Elarton, rhp	Quad City (A—Midwest)	13	7	4.45	26	0	150	149	71	112
8. Kevin Gallaher, rhp	Kissimmee (A—Florida State)	1	1	5.71	7	0	17	8	24	21
	Jackson (AA—Texas)	2	2	3.40	6	0	42	31	23	28
	Tucson (AAA—Pacific Coast)	1	1	6.43	3	0	14	19	9	11
9. #Rich Huisman, rhp	Tucson (AAA—Pacific Coast)	6	1	4.45	42	6	55	58	28	47
	Omaha (AAA—American Assoc.)	0	0	1.80	5	1	5	3	1	13
	Kansas City	0	0	7.45	7	0	10	14	1	12

*Traded to Detroit #Traded to Kansas City

PACIFIC COAST LEAGUE

BATTING

BATTING	AVG	G	AB	R	H	2B	3B	HR	RBI	BB	SO	SB	CS	B	T	HT	WT	DOB	1st Yr	Resides
Abreu, Bob	.304	114	415	72	126	24	17	10	75	67	120	16	14	L	R	6-0	160	3-11-74	1991	Turmero, Venez.
Ball, Jeff	.293	110	362	58	106	25	2	4	56	25	66	11	5	R	R	5-10	185	4-17-69	1990	Merced, Calif.
Brumley, Mike	.261	94	330	56	86	20	10	4	33	41	67	17	6	S	R	5-10	175	4-9-63	1983	Tulsa, Okla.
Cangelosi, John	.368	30	106	18	39	4	1	0	9	19	11	11	3	S	L	5-8	160	3-10-63	1982	Chicago, Ill.
Chavez, Raul	.262	32	103	14	27	5	0	0	10	8	13	0	1	R	R	5-11	175	3-18-73	1990	Valencia, Venez.
Goff, Jerry	.222	68	207	23	46	11	1	6	34	29	56	0	0	L	R	6-3	207	4-12-64	1986	San Rafael, Calif.
Guerrero, Juan	.294	72	194	21	57	10	1	2	21	14	42	1	1	R	R	5-11	160	2-1-67	1987	Haina, D.R.
Gutierrez, Ricky	.301	64	236	46	71	12	4	1	26	28	28	9	7	R	R	6-1	175	5-23-70	1988	Miami, Fla.
Hajek, Dave	.327	131	502	99	164	37	4	4	79	39	27	12	7	R	R	5-10	165	10-14-67	1990	Colorado Springs, Colo.
Hatcher, Chris	.286	94	290	59	83	19	2	14	50	42	107	7	3	R	R	6-3	220	1-7-69	1990	Carter Lake, Iowa
Hunter, Brian	.329	38	155	28	51	5	1	1	16	17	13	11	3	R	R	6-4	180	3-5-71	1989	Vancouver, Wash.
Kellner, Frank	.180	28	89	11	16	3	1	0	7	15	12	1	0	S	R	5-11	175	1-5-67	1990	Tucson, Ariz.
Makarewicz, Scott	.266	62	192	21	51	9	0	5	31	10	23	1	0	R	R	6-0	200	3-1-67	1989	Grand Rapids, Mich.
Montgomery, Ray	.302	88	291	48	88	19	0	11	68	24	58	5	3	R	R	6-3	195	8-8-69	1990	Bronxville, N.Y.
Mora, Melvin	.600	2	5	3	3	0	1	0	1	2	0	1	0	R	R	5-10	160	2-2-72	1991	Naquanqua, Venez.
Mouton, James	.455	3	11	1	5	0	0	1	1	0	2	0	1	R	R	5-9	175	12-29-68	1991	Sacramento, Calif.
Nevin, Phil	.291	62	223	31	65	16	0	7	41	27	39	2	3	R	R	6-2	185	1-19-71	1992	Placentia, Calif.
Plantier, Phil	.250	10	24	6	6	2	0	1	4	5	4	0	0	L	R	5-11	195	1-27-69	1987	San Diego, Calif.
Ramos, Ken	.315	112	327	57	103	24	8	3	47	51	27	14	5	L	L	6-1	185	6-8-67	1989	Pueblo, Colo.
Rohde, Dave	.276	73	170	27	47	8	2	0	20	32	17	2	2	S	R	6-2	182	5-8-64	1986	Newport Beach, Calif.
Simms, Mike	.295	85	319	56	94	26	8	13	66	35	65	1	0	R	R	6-4	185	1-12-67	1985	Houston, Texas
Stankiewicz, Andy	.276	25	87	16	24	4	0	1	15	14	8	3	1	R	R	5-9	165	8-10-64	1986	La Habra, Calif.
Wilkins, Rick	.333	4	12	0	4	0	0	0	4	2	0	0	0	L	R	6-2	210	6-4-67	1987	Jacksonville, Fla.

PITCHING

PITCHING	W	L	ERA	G	GS	CG	SV	IP	H	R	ER	BB	SO	B	T	HT	WT	DOB	1st Yr	Resides
Bennett, Erik	3	1	4.76	14	1	0	1	23	27	17	12	14	24	R	R	6-2	205	9-13-68	1989	Yreka, Calif.
2-team (28 Van.)	9	1	4.42	42	1	0	3	73	71	41	36	32	63							
Brocail, Doug	1	0	3.86	3	3	0	0	16	18	9	7	4	16	L	R	6-5	190	5-16-67	1986	Lamar, Colo.
Castillo, Juan	0	4	10.93	11	10	0	0	40	66	51	49	27	21	R	R	6-4	216	6-23-70	1988	Caracas, Venez.
Daspit, Jim	5	1	3.57	36	0	0	1	63	63	30	25	22	49	R	R	6-7	210	8-10-69	1990	Sacramento, Calif.
Dougherty, Jim	1	0	3.27	8	0	0	1	11	11	4	4	5	12	R	R	6-0	210	3-8-68	1991	Kitty Hawk, N.C.
Evans, Dave	0	0	0.00	2	0	0	0	3	2	0	0	1	4	R	R	6-3	185	1-1-68	1990	Houston, Texas
Fesh, Sean	1	0	1.35	10	0	0	0	13	11	2	2	3	7	L	L	6-2	165	11-3-72	1991	Bethel, Conn.
Gallaher, Kevin	1	1	6.43	3	3	0	0	14	19	11	10	9	11	R	R	6-3	190	8-1-68	1991	Vienna, Va.
Gardner, Chris	1	4	8.54	16	2	0	0	26	43	26	25	19	6	R	R	6-0	175	3-30-69	1988	Paso Robles, Calif.
Hartgraves, Dean	3	2	2.11	14	0	0	5	21	21	6	5	5	15	R	L	6-0	185	8-12-66	1987	Central Point, Ore.
Holt, Chris	5	8	4.10	20	19	0	0	119	155	65	54	32	69	R	R	6-4	205	9-18-71	1992	Dallas, Texas
Huisman, Rick	6	1	4.45	42	0	0	6	55	58	33	27	28	47	R	R	6-3	200	5-17-69	1990	Bensenville, Ill.
Jean, Domingo	2	1	6.59	3	3	0	0	14	15	10	10	7	14	R	R	6-2	175	1-9-69	1990	San Pedro de Macoris, D.R.
Ketchen, Doug	3	6	6.28	19	12	0	1	72	101	55	50	26	30	R	R	6-1	190	7-9-68	1990	Calgary, Alberta
Kile, Darryl	2	1	8.51	4	4	0	0	24	29	23	23	12	15	R	R	6-5	185	12-2-68	1988	Corona, Calif.
Loiselle, Rich	0	0	2.61	2	1	0	0	10	8	4	3	4	4	R	R	6-5	225	1-12-72	1991	Oshkosh, Wisc.
2-team (8 Las Vegas)	2	2	5.97	10	8	1	0	38	44	31	25	13	20							
Martinez, Pedro	1	1	6.62	20	3	0	2	34	44	28	25	13	21	L	L	6-2	155	11-29-68	1987	Villa Mella, D.R.
McMurtry, Craig	6	1	1.29	13	13	1	0	70	54	11	10	19	41	R	R	6-5	192	11-5-59	1980	Troy, Texas
Mlicki, Doug	1	2	5.56	6	6	0	0	34	44	27	21	6	22	R	R	6-3	175	4-23-71	1992	Dublin, Ohio
Morman, Alvin	5	1	3.91	45	0	0	3	48	50	26	21	20	36	L	L	6-3	210	1-6-69	1991	Rockingham, N.C.
Patrick, Bronswell	5	1	4.19	43	4	0	1	82	91	42	38	21	62	R	R	6-1	205	9-16-70	1988	Greenville, N.C.
Powell, Ross	3	3	3.08	13	4	0	0	38	37	16	13	15	34	L	L	6-0	180	1-24-68	1989	Antioch, Tenn.
Sepeda, Jamie	3	2	4.91	8	8	0	0	40	52	22	22	12	19	R	R	6-2	200	12-8-70	1992	Sinton, Texas
Small, Mark	3	3	4.09	51	0	0	19	66	74	32	30	19	51	R	R	6-3	205	11-12-67	1989	Seattle, Wash.
Wagner, Billy	5	3	3.18	13	13	0	0	76	70	28	27	32	80	L	L	5-10	180	7-25-71	1993	Tannersville, Va.
Waldron, Joe	1	0	4.32	4	0	0	0	8	6	4	4	2	11	L	L	6-0	180	7-4-69	1990	McAlester, Okla.
Wall, Donne	17	6	3.30	28	28	0	0	177	190	72	65	32	119	R	R	6-1	180	7-11-67	1989	Festus, Mo.
Waring, Jim	2	2	8.46	5	5	0	0	22	30	24	21	8	5	L	R	6-2	180	9-19-69	1991	DeLand, Fla.
Westbrook, Destry	0	0	7.30	5	0	0	0	12	20	10	10	7	8	R	R	6-1	195	12-13-70	1992	Montrose, Colo.
White, Chris	1	1	8.71	5	1	0	0	10	16	10	10	2	6	R	R	6-0	180	9-15-69	1991	Greenville, Pa.

FIELDING

Catcher	PCT	G	PO	A	E	DP	PB
Chavez	.980	32	203	39	5	3	4
Goff	.989	62	336	39	4	5	12
Makarewicz	.981	61	338	28	7	8	2
Wilkins	1.000	4	27	4	0	0	1

First Base	PCT	G	PO	A	E	DP
Ball	.990	35	272	16	3	25
Brumley	1.000	2	3	0	0	0
Goff	.938	3	15	0	1	0
Hatcher	.977	73	590	40	15	62
Simms	.985	48	376	24	6	43

Second Base	PCT	G	PO	A	E	DP
Abreu	1.000	1	3	0	0	1
Ball	.000	2	0	0	0	0
Brumley	.929	4	3	10	1	1
Guerrero	.947	5	10	8	1	0
Hajek	.982	124	269	398	12	100
Kellner	1.000	1	1	2	0	0

	PCT	G	PO	A	E	DP
Rohde	.982	16	28	26	1	5
Stankiewicz	.947	4	7	11	1	3

Third Base	PCT	G	PO	A	E	DP
Ball	.957	46	19	93	5	11
Brumley	.938	17	5	25	2	0
Goff	.000	1	0	0	0	0
Guerrero	.900	28	16	38	6	5
Nevin	.923	57	39	128	14	17
Rohde	.893	15	6	19	3	1
Stankiewicz	1.000	2	2	8	0	1

Shortstop	PCT	G	PO	A	E	DP
Brumley	.961	24	22	52	3	9
Guerrero	1.000	2	0	1	0	1
Gutierrez	.977	61	91	167	6	34
Kellner	.974	25	39	72	3	22
Rohde	.948	32	30	62	5	11
Stankiewicz	.978	20	27	62	2	9

Outfield	PCT	G	PO	A	E	DP
Abreu	.969	111	204	18	7	5
Ball	1.000	15	19	0	0	0
Brumley	.948	42	68	5	4	2
Cangelosi	.986	29	67	2	1	0
Guerrero	1.000	4	10	0	0	0
Hajek	1.000	1	2	0	0	0
Hatcher	1.000	6	9	0	0	0
Hunter	1.000	37	91	1	0	0
Montgomery	.965	87	182	10	7	3
Mora	1.000	2	2	0	0	0
Mouton	.500	3	1	0	1	0
Plantier	1.000	9	9	0	0	0
Ramos	.988	100	165	5	2	1
Rohde	.000	1	0	0	0	0
Simms	.964	34	48	6	2	1

TEXAS LEAGUE

BATTING	AVG	G	AB	R	H	2B	3B	HR	RBI	BB	SO	SB	CS	B	T	HT	WT	DOB	1st Yr	Resides
Bagwell, Jeff	.167	4	12	0	2	0	0	0	0	3	2	0	0	R	R	6-0	195	5-27-68	1989	Houston, Texas
Bridges, Kary	.301	118	418	56	126	22	4	3	43	49	17	10	12	L	R	5-10	165	10-27-71	1993	Hattiesburg, Miss.
Centeno, Henri	.256	92	172	24	44	3	1	2	12	24	31	6	4	S	R	5-11	159	1-1-70	1990	Casanay, Venez.
Chavez, Raul	.287	58	188	16	54	8	0	4	25	8	17	0	4	R	R	5-11	175	3-18-73	1990	Valencia, Venez.
Colon, Dennis	.224	106	379	33	85	10	0	5	31	24	38	3	6	L	R	5-10	165	8-4-73	1991	Manati, P.R.
Donnels, Chris	.167	4	12	1	2	1	0	0	1	4	4	0	0	L	R	6-0	185	4-21-66	1987	Aliso Vista, Calif.
Forkner, Tim	.269	35	119	19	32	11	0	3	23	19	14	1	3	L	R	5-11	180	3-28-73	1993	Greeley, Colo.
Gilmore, Tony	.212	53	146	10	31	3	0	1	15	10	27	0	0	R	R	6-2	195	10-15-68	1990	Tulsa, Okla.
Groppuso, Mike	.215	24	79	5	17	3	1	1	5	16	17	2	1	R	R	6-3	195	3-9-70	1991	Lake Kattrine, N.Y.
Hatcher, Chris	.308	11	39	5	12	1	0	1	3	4	6	0	2	R	R	6-3	220	1-7-69	1990	Carter Lake, Iowa
Hidalgo, Richard	.266	133	489	59	130	28	6	14	59	32	76	8	9	R	R	6-2	175	7-2-75	1991	Guarenas, Venez.
Hunter, Brian	.500	2	6	1	3	0	0	0	1	0	0	0	0	R	R	6-4	180	3-5-71	1989	Vancouver, Wash.
Johnson, Russ	.249	132	475	65	118	16	2	9	53	50	60	10	5	R	R	5-10	185	2-22-73	1994	Baton Rouge, La.
Kellner, Frank	.316	75	269	31	85	15	1	0	29	35	52	1	7	S	R	5-11	175	1-5-67	1990	Tucson, Ariz.
Luce, Roger	.212	18	52	4	11	2	1	1	4	3	12	0	0	R	R	6-4	215	5-7-69	1991	Houston, Texas
McNabb, Buck	.260	15	50	4	13	1	0	0	3	5	11	1	0	L	R	6-0	180	1-17-73	1991	Fort Walton Beach, Fla.
Mitchell, Tony	.266	96	331	45	88	17	2	19	61	35	83	1	2	S	R	6-4	225	10-14-70	1989	Detroit, Mich.
Montgomery, Ray	.299	35	127	24	38	8	1	10	24	13	13	6	3	R	R	6-3	195	8-8-69	1990	Bronxville, N.Y.
Mora, Melvin	.298	123	467	63	139	32	0	3	45	32	57	22	11	R	R	5-10	160	2-2-72	1991	Naquanqua, Venez.
Nevers, Tom	.242	83	298	36	72	7	3	8	35	24	58	5	2	R	R	6-1	175	9-13-71	1990	Edina, Minn.
Probst, Alan	.236	28	89	11	21	5	0	1	8	7	25	0	0	R	R	6-4	205	10-24-70	1992	Avis, Pa.
Verduzco, Steve	.241	18	29	4	7	3	0	1	1	0	8	0	1	R	R	6-1	185	9-10-72	1993	Cupertino, Calif.
Wesson, Barry	.667	4	3	2	2	0	1	0	1	0	0	0	0	R	R	6-2	195	4-6-77	1995	Glen Allan, Miss.
White, Chad	.273	32	77	11	21	4	0	0	3	8	9	2	1	S	R	6-2	180	5-26-71	1993	Brewer, Maine
White, Jimmy	.000	2	1	1	0	0	0	0	0	1	0	0	0	L	R	6-1	170	12-1-72	1990	Tampa, Fla.
Wilkins, Rick	.000	4	11	0	0	0	0	0	0	3	2	0	0	L	R	6-2	210	6-4-67	1987	Jacksonville, Fla.

PITCHING	W	L	ERA	G	GS	CG	SV	IP	H	R	ER	BB	SO	B	T	HT	WT	DOB	1st Yr	Resides
Allen, Ron	2	0	5.91	4	0	0	0	11	13	7	7	5	3	R	R	5-11	185	5-10-70	1991	Kirkland, Wash.
Castillo, Juan	4	4	4.01	12	12	0	0	67	68	39	30	27	38	R	R	6-4	216	6-23-70	1988	Caracas, Venez.
Creek, Ryan	9	7	3.63	26	24	1	0	144	137	74	58	64	120	R	R	6-1	180	9-24-72	1993	Martinsburg, W.Va.
Duey, Kyle	0	2	5.40	7	0	0	2	7	11	4	4	2	4	R	R	6-2	215	11-8-67	1990	Vancouver, Wash.
Evans, Dave	2	9	3.33	49	0	0	18	68	50	29	25	28	54	R	R	6-3	185	1-1-68	1990	Houston, Texas
Gallaher, Kevin	2	2	3.40	6	6	1	0	42	31	18	16	23	28	R	R	6-3	190	8-1-68	1991	Vienna, Va.
Grzanich, Mike	5	3	2.74	50	0	0	8	66	55	22	20	38	44	R	R	6-1	180	8-24-72	1992	Champaign, Ill.
Hingle, Larry	0	2	11.12	9	0	0	0	11	11	15	14	15	5	L	L	6-3	200	12-12-70	1992	Ormond Beach, Fla.
Holt, Chris	2	1	1.67	5	5	1	0	32	27	8	6	5	24	R	R	6-4	205	9-18-71	1992	Dallas, Texas
Humphrey, Rich	1	1	1.69	9	0	0	0	16	11	5	3	9	9	R	R	6-1	185	6-24-71	1993	Lakeland, Fla.
Ketchen, Doug	3	3	3.59	15	5	0	1	53	55	23	21	15	45	R	R	6-1	190	7-9-68	1990	Calgary, Alberta
Lister, Martin	4	3	4.00	15	13	1	0	70	80	35	31	24	27	L	L	6-2	210	6-12-72	1992	Pensacola, Fla.
Mercado, Hector	1	4	7.80	8	7	0	0	30	36	33	26	32	20	L	L	6-3	205	4-29-74	1992	Dorado, P.R.
Mlicki, Doug	8	3	2.79	16	16	2	0	97	73	41	30	33	72	R	R	6-3	175	4-23-71	1992	Dublin, Ohio
Narcisse, Tyrone	5	14	3.24	27	27	2	0	164	140	76	59	60	93	R	R	6-5	205	2-4-72	1990	Port Arthur, Texas
Sepeda, Jaime	0	1	9.00	1	1	0	0	4	7	4	4	2	1	R	R	6-2	200	12-8-70	1992	Sinton, Texas
Wagner, Billy	2	2	2.57	12	12	0	0	70	49	25	20	36	77	L	L	5-10	180	7-25-71	1993	Tannersville, Va.
Waldron, Joe	1	2	3.71	28	0	0	2	51	57	22	21	11	39	L	L	6-0	180	7-4-69	1990	McAlester, Okla.
Walker, Jamie	4	2	4.50	50	0	0	2	58	59	29	29	24	48	L	L	6-2	190	7-1-71	1992	Clarksville, Tenn.
Waring, Jim	1	4	8.01	17	5	0	2	52	77	49	46	15	27	L	L	6-2	180	9-19-69	1991	DeLand, Fla.
White, Chris	6	3	5.09	38	2	0	0	71	71	45	40	24	45	R	R	6-0	180	9-15-69	1991	Greenville, Pa.

FIELDING

Catcher	PCT	G	PO	A	E	DP	PB
Chavez	.987	55	316	52	5	8	7
Gilmore	.991	50	284	29	3	2	12
Luce	.949	16	71	4	4	1	2
Probst	.994	25	137	19	1	3	4
Wilkins	1.000	4	23	1	0	0	0

First Base	PCT	G	PO	A	E	DP
Bagwell	1.000	3	24	6	0	3
Colon	.985	101	893	79	15	89
Groppuso	1.000	8	56	4	0	4
Hatcher	1.000	3	28	4	0	1
Kellner	1.000	23	200	17	0	20
Luce	1.000	1	9	1	0	0
Montgomery	.980	5	43	5	1	2

Second Base	PCT	G	PO	A	E	DP
Bridges	.975	68	118	198	8	42
Centeno	.966	58	82	116	7	41

	PCT	G	PO	A	E	DP
Kellner	1.000	20	30	59	0	18
Mora	.000	1	0	0	0	0
Nevers	.938	13	27	33	4	8

Third Base	PCT	G	PO	A	E	DP
Centeno	1.000	2	0	1	0	0
Chavez	.000	1	0	0	0	0
Donnels	.929	4	6	7	1	0
Forkner	.900	34	27	63	10	8
Groppuso	.965	15	14	41	2	3
Kellner	.919	21	12	22	3	2
Mora	.667	1	0	2	1	0
Nevers	.907	68	57	158	22	13

Shortstop	PCT	G	PO	A	E	DP
Centeno	1.000	1	0	1	0	0
Johnson	.978	128	182	383	13	78

	PCT	G	PO	A	E	DP
Kellner	.933	7	12	16	2	4
Nevers	1.000	5	5	8	0	1

Outfield	PCT	G	PO	A	E	DP
Bridges	.955	28	39	3	2	0
Hatcher	.875	6	13	1	2	1
Hidalgo	.981	129	238	14	5	3
Hunter	1.000	2	5	0	0	0
McNabb	1.000	13	23	0	0	0
Mitchell	.933	73	118	7	9	2
Montgomery	1.000	25	59	5	0	0
Verduzco	.981	119	244	14	5	6
Wesson	1.000	2	3	0	0	0
Chad White	.981	30	51	1	1	0

FLORIDA STATE LEAGUE

BATTING	AVG	G	AB	R	H	2B	3B	HR	RBI	BB	SO	SB	CS	B	T	HT	WT	DOB	1st Yr	Resides
Basey, Marsalis	.230	91	317	37	73	6	0	0	16	18	35	12	5	R	R	5-8	175	12-10-71	1990	Martinsburg, W.Va.
Beyna, Terry	.167	15	42	4	7	1	0	0	2	2	12	0	0	R	R	6-1	195	8-1-72	1993	Mt. Prospect, Ill.
Castro, Ramon	.208	36	120	6	25	5	0	0	8	6	21	0	0	R	R	6-3	195	3-1-76	1994	Vega Baja, P.R.
Forkner, Tim	.284	89	296	42	84	20	4	1	34	60	40	4	2	L	R	5-11	180	3-28-73	1993	Greeley, Colo.
Froschauer, Trevor	.197	102	325	32	64	8	1	12	40	49	121	2	0	R	R	6-6	230	9-21-72	1993	Springfield, Ill.
Halemanu, Joshua	.133	6	15	1	2	0	0	0	1	7	0	0	1	L	L	6-3	195	8-27-73	1994	Honolulu, Hawaii
Landaker, Dave	.206	96	287	30	59	7	2	0	18	42	47	8	10	R	R	6-0	185	2-20-74	1992	Simi Valley, Calif.
Mangham, Rodney	.209	42	134	19	28	7	1	0	12	22	31	5	3	S	L	5-11	165	10-19-71	1994	College Park, Ga.
Marsh, Roy	.216	114	393	51	85	18	3	4	23	38	95	22	11	R	R	5-8	180	11-22-73	1994	Baltimore, Md.

BATTING	AVG	G	AB	R	H	2B	3B	HR	RBI	BB	SO	SB	CS	B	T	HT	WT	DOB	1st Yr	Resides
Meluskey, Mitch	.215	78	261	23	56	18	1	3	31	27	33	3	0	S	R	6-0	185	9-18-73	1992	Yakima, Wash.
Nelson, Bryant	.327	105	395	47	129	34	5	3	52	20	37	14	10	S	R	5-10	170	1-27-74	1994	Crossett, Ark.
Perez, Jhonny	.271	65	214	24	58	12	0	4	31	22	37	23	7	R	R	5-10	150	10-23-76	1994	Santo Domingo, D.R.
Peterson, Nate	.280	76	257	34	72	17	0	4	22	21	42	3	1	L	R	6-2	185	7-12-71	1993	Melbourne, Australia
Ramos, Eddie	.114	30	105	5	12	3	1	0	8	4	27	0	0	R	R	6-2	195	12-20-72	1991	Miami, Fla.
Roche, Marlon	.227	26	97	10	22	7	0	0	7	3	24	3	2	R	R	6-1	172	4-11-75	1992	Caracas, Venez.
Sanchez, Victor	.268	78	272	34	73	11	0	7	38	23	69	6	3	R	R	5-11	175	12-20-71	1994	Stockton, Calif.
Saylor, Jamie	.228	89	289	38	66	4	1	2	19	22	58	13	6	L	R	5-11	185	9-11-74	1993	Garland, Texas
Scolaro, Donnie	.302	23	63	9	19	3	0	0	3	7	12	1	0	R	R	5-10	170	2-7-72	1994	Brandon, Fla.
Stewart, Tom	.251	52	167	9	42	4	1	1	15	17	48	0	2	S	R	5-9	170	10-18-72	1995	Daingerfield, Texas
Verduzco, Steve	.250	98	348	47	87	17	0	7	50	37	50	18	4	R	R	6-1	185	9-10-72	1993	Cupertino, Calif.
White, Jimmy	.182	16	55	6	10	3	1	0	3	9	9	4	0	L	R	6-1	170	12-1-72	1990	Tampa, Fla.

GAMES BY POSITION: C—Castro 34, Froschauer 33, Meluskey 75, Sanchez 9. **1B**—Beyna 4, Froschauer 64, Halemanu 1, Landaker 10, Ramos 29, Sanchez 37. **2B**—Basey 73, Landaker 1, Nelson 6, Saylor 57, Scolaro 8. **3B**—Basey 1, Beyna 3, Forkner 89, Landaker 36, Nelson 6, Perez 1, Scolaro 3, Stewart 7, Verduzco 2. **SS**—Landaker 4, Nelson 59, Perez 33, Saylor 22, Scolaro 9, Stewart 19. **OF**—Basey 18, Beyna 3, Halemanu 2, Landaker 44, Mangham 42, Marsh 112, Nelson 20, Peterson 46, Roche 26, Scolaro 2, Stewart 29, Verduzco 94, White 5.

PITCHING	W	L	ERA	G	GS	CG	SV	IP	H	R	ER	BB	SO	B	T	HT	WT	DOB	1st Yr	Resides
Albaladejo, Randy	0	0	11.42	7	0	0	0	9	13	13	11	10	5	R	R	6-3	190	4-10-73	1991	Vega Alta, P.R.
Breitenstein, Keith	0	1	3.00	4	0	0	0	6	7	2	2	3	4	R	L	6-1	185	1-12-72	1994	Kettering, Ohio
Brown, Brett	0	0	0.00	1	0	0	0	1	1	0	0	0	0	L	L	6-3	210	4-26-74	1995	Lewes, Del.
Dace, Derek	0	1	16.88	1	1	0	0	3	4	5	5	5	1	L	L	6-7	200	4-9-75	1994	Sullivan, Mo.
Dault, Donnie	4	7	3.08	41	5	0	6	108	95	52	37	36	95	R	R	6-6	185	4-15-72	1991	Austin, Texas
Gallaher, Kevin	1	1	5.71	7	7	0	0	17	8	11	11	24	21	R	R	6-3	190	8-1-68	1991	Vienna, Va.
Gandolph, Dave	0	2	5.28	12	4	0	0	15	15	11	9	20	8	L	L	6-4	220	3-20-70	1991	Greenwood, Ind.
Gunderson, Mike	0	0	0.00	1	0	0	0	2	1	0	0	0	0	R	R	6-4	235	3-24-73	1994	Detroit Lakes, Mn
Hartnett, Bill	1	1	4.01	32	2	0	2	74	87	52	33	32	61	R	R	6-4	200	3-2-71	1993	Brookline, Mass.
Henriquez, Oscar	3	4	5.04	20	0	0	1	45	40	29	25	30	36	R	R	6-4	175	1-28-74	1991	La Guaira, Venez.
Hingle, Larry	0	0	18.78	10	0	0	0	8	15	18	16	11	2	L	L	6-3	200	12-12-70	1992	Ormond Beach, Fla.
Humphrey, Rich	3	1	1.96	46	0	0	14	55	45	16	12	20	33	R	R	6-1	185	6-24-71	1993	Lakeland, Fla.
Loiz, Niuman	0	8	5.56	13	13	0	0	57	71	48	35	30	33	R	R	6-4	170	12-12-73	1991	Caracas, Venez.
Lopez, Johann	5	5	2.61	18	12	0	1	69	55	30	20	25	67	R	R	6-2	170	4-4-75	1992	Agua Negra, Venez.
Mercado, Hector	6	8	3.46	19	17	2	0	104	96	50	40	37	75	L	L	6-3	205	4-29-74	1992	Dorado, P.R.
O'Malley, Paul	8	10	3.61	27	27	0	0	147	148	86	59	62	80	R	R	6-3	180	12-20-72	1994	Skokie, Ill.
Ramos, Edgar	4	0	0.41	4	4	0	0	22	11	4	1	1	16	R	R	6-4	170	3-6-75	1992	Cumana, Venez.
Root, Derek	0	0	4.50	5	0	0	0	6	10	3	3	2	3	L	L	6-5	190	5-26-75	1993	Lakewood, Ohio
Sacharko, Mark	0	1	6.59	6	1	0	0	14	16	10	10	11	6	R	R	6-1	200	4-18-76	1994	Lancaster, Texas
Shrum, Dennis	7	6	3.24	38	0	0	5	92	96	44	33	28	69	R	R	6-1	180	8-29-71	1992	Madera, Calif.
Steinke, Brock	0	3	6.61	8	5	0	0	33	48	28	24	16	15	R	R	6-2	180	6-27-75	1993	Cedar Rapids, Iowa
Tucker, Julien	2	11	5.00	19	15	0	0	68	86	61	38	27	28	L	R	6-7	200	4-19-73	1993	Chataeauguay, Quebec
Walter, Michael	4	3	5.55	41	0	0	0	71	78	58	44	42	42	R	R	6-1	190	10-23-74	1993	San Diego, Calif.
Waring, Jim	2	1	1.78	5	5	1	0	30	23	10	6	11	16	L	R	6-2	180	9-19-69	1991	DeLand, Fla.
Westbrook, Destry	0	1	10.07	10	0	0	1	20	34	24	22	13	22	R	R	6-1	195	12-13-70	1992	Montrose, Colo.
Williams, Matt	4	6	4.63	19	18	2	0	101	115	60	52	44	71	S	L	6-0	185	4-12-71	1992	Virginia Beach, Va.
Wright, Howard	1	0	3.60	2	0	0	0	5	1	3	2	4	3	L	R	5-11	185	11-14-70	1994	Las Vegas, N.M.

QUAD CITY — A

MIDWEST LEAGUE

BATTING	AVG	G	AB	R	H	2B	3B	HR	RBI	BB	SO	SB	CS	B	T	HT	WT	DOB	1st Yr	Resides
Alexander, Chad	.286	2	7	2	2	0	0	0	1	0	0	0	0	R	R	6-0	190	5-22-74	1995	Lufkin, Texas
Amezcua, Adan	.246	46	142	13	35	8	2	4	12	5	28	2	3	R	R	6-1	180	3-9-74	1993	Mazatlan, Mexico
Bowers, R.J.	.242	110	372	52	90	19	1	12	58	35	119	10	9	R	R	6-1	210	2-10-74	1992	West Middlesex, Pa.
Coe, Ryan	.261	38	92	16	24	7	0	5	18	13	20	1	2	R	R	5-10	200	1-16-73	1995	East Ridge, Tenn.
Freire, Alejandro	.305	125	417	71	127	23	1	15	65	50	83	9	5	R	R	6-1	170	8-23-74	1992	Caracas, Venez.
Gonzalez, Jimmy	.244	35	78	4	19	3	1	1	14	8	13	1	2	R	R	6-3	210	3-8-73	1991	Hartford, Conn.
Hernandez, Carlos	.260	126	470	74	122	19	6	4	40	39	68	58	21	R	R	5-9	160	12-12-75	1993	Caracas, Venez.
Mitchell, Donovan	.329	111	383	72	126	23	1	4	42	29	38	21	15	L	R	5-9	175	11-27-69	1992	White Plains, N.Y.
Nelson, Bryant	.038	6	26	1	1	1	0	0	2	0	3	0	0	S	R	5-10	170	1-27-74	1994	Crossett, Ark.
Pratt, Wes	.227	14	44	5	10	1	1	2	10	7	11	2	0	R	R	6-3	180	3-5-73	1994	Northeast, Md.
Probst, Alan	.258	52	151	23	39	12	1	7	27	13	28	2	0	R	R	6-4	205	10-24-70	1992	Avis, Pa.
Rennhack, Mike	.271	100	299	46	81	14	1	1	47	39	37	15	4	S	L	6-2	175	8-25-74	1992	Encinitas, Calif.
Rodriguez, Noel	.311	109	386	48	120	26	5	8	71	28	49	4	5	R	R	6-3	180	12-5-73	1991	Yabucoa, P.R.
Ross, Tony	.257	107	339	46	87	11	4	3	41	31	57	21	5	R	R	5-11	175	5-11-75	1992	Kansas City, Mo.
Sanchez, Victor	.235	13	34	3	8	0	0	0	1	6	10	1	0	R	R	5-11	175	12-20-71	1994	Stockton, Calif.
Santana, Jose	.227	88	229	36	52	10	2	1	21	24	40	6	4	S	R	6-0	160	4-30-72	1990	San Pedro de Macoris, D.R.
Trammell, Gary	.298	103	336	44	100	12	3	2	33	33	62	14	8	L	R	6-0	180	10-16-72	1993	Garland, Texas
Truby, Chris	.233	118	400	68	93	23	4	9	64	41	66	27	8	R	R	6-2	185	12-9-73	1993	Mukilteo, Wash.
White, Chad	.244	75	242	36	59	14	0	0	18	37	35	12	4	S	R	6-2	180	5-26-71	1993	Brewer, Maine

GAMES BY POSITION: C—Amezcua 46, Coe 30, Gonzalez 30, Probst 52, Sanchez 6. **1B**—Coe 2, Freire 101, Rodriguez 46, Sanchez 2. **2B**—Hernandez 98, Mitchell 50. **3B**—Mitchell 4, Nelson 1, Trammell 21, Truby 118. **SS**—Hernandez 30, Mitchell 42, Nelson 1, Santana 80. **OF**—Alexander 2, Bowers 107, Freire 3, Nelson 5, Pratt 14, Rennhack 93, Ross 96, Trammell 37, Truby 1, White 73.

PITCHING	W	L	ERA	G	GS	CG	SV	IP	H	R	ER	BB	SO	B	T	HT	WT	DOB	1st Yr	Resides
Barrios, Manuel	1	5	2.25	50	0	0	23	52	44	16	13	17	55	R	R	6-0	145	9-21-74	1993	Cabecera, Panama
Blanco, Alberto	3	3	3.13	11	11	1	0	55	47	22	19	19	58	L	L	6-1	170	6-27-76	1993	Miranda, Venez.
Diorio, Mike	6	4	3.24	33	11	0	1	92	82	39	33	36	81	R	R	6-1	170	3-1-73	1993	Pueblo, Colo.
Elarton, Scott	13	7	4.45	26	26	0	0	150	149	86	74	71	112	R	R	6-8	225	2-23-76	1994	Lamar, Colo.
Gunderson, Mike	3	2	2.74	44	0	0	1	66	46	25	20	27	48	R	R	6-4	235	3-24-73	1994	Detroit Lakes, Minn.
Halama, John	1	2	2.02	55	0	0	2	62	48	16	14	22	56	L	L	6-5	195	2-22-72	1994	Brooklyn, N.Y.
Hall, Billy	4	2	2.15	36	0	0	7	50	29	18	12	18	36	R	R	6-0	200	9-4-73	1994	Jennings, Okla.
Kester, Tim	12	5	2.97	28	23	2	0	161	158	80	53	20	111	R	R	6-4	185	12-1-71	1993	Coral Springs, Fla.
Lock, Dan	8	15	4.15	27	27	1	0	143	152	94	66	58	90	R	L	6-5	210	3-27-73	1994	Brighton, Mich.
Mounce, Tony	16	8	2.43	25	25	3	0	159	118	55	43	57	143	L	L	6-2	185	2-8-75	1994	Kennewick, Wash.
Ramos, Edgar	0	1	15.43	2	2	0	0	5	5	9	8	7	5	R	R	6-4	170	3-6-75	1992	Cumana, Venez.

PITCHING	W	L	ERA	G	GS	CG	SV	IP	H	R	ER	BB	SO	B	T	HT	WT	DOB	1st Yr	Resides
Runyan, Sean	4	6	3.66	22	11	0	0	76	67	37	31	29	65	L	L	6-3	200	6-21-74	1992	Urbandale, Iowa
Shaver, Tony	2	0	1.61	35	0	0	1	56	35	15	10	19	40	R	R	5-11	185	2-15-72	1994	Orlando, Fla.
Sikorski, Brian	1	0	0.00	2	0	0	0	3	1	1	0	0	4	R	R	6-1	190	7-27-74	1995	Roseville, Mich.
Steinke, Brock	2	1	4.34	21	1	0	0	37	30	20	18	27	18	R	R	6-2	180	6-27-75	1993	Cedar Rapids, Iowa

AUBURN   A

NEW YORK-PENN LEAGUE

BATTING	AVG	G	AB	R	H	2B	3B	HR	RBI	BB	SO	SB	CS	B	T	HT	WT	DOB	1st Yr	Resides
Adams, Jason	.215	51	181	28	39	6	0	0	18	27	19	3	1	L	L	6-1	180	6-22-73	1995	Rose Hill, Kan.
Alexander, Chad	.291	71	278	45	81	15	5	5	43	25	37	7	1	R	R	6-0	190	5-22-74	1995	Lufkin, Texas
Bovender, Jason	.313	71	243	42	76	15	4	5	41	30	70	1	2	R	R	6-3	180	4-10-73	1995	Charlotte, N.C.
Brunner, Michael	.193	26	83	7	16	6	0	2	11	5	25	2	1	R	R	6-3	195	12-30-71	1995	Schenectady, N.Y.
Castro, Ramon	.299	63	224	40	67	17	0	9	49	24	27	0	1	R	R	6-3	195	3-1-76	1994	Vega Baja, P.R.
Halemanu, Joshua	.197	52	157	25	31	6	0	7	25	29	60	2	2	L	L	6-3	195	8-27-73	1994	Honolulu, Hawaii
Lugo, Julio	.291	59	230	36	67	6	3	1	16	26	31	17	7	R	R	5-11	155	11-16-75	1995	Brooklyn, N.Y.
Pratt, Wes	.266	66	256	42	68	11	0	2	44	20	43	6	3	R	R	6-3	180	3-5-73	1994	Northeast, Md.
Robinson, Hassan	.265	65	245	32	65	8	1	0	18	9	25	12	2	R	R	6-3	180	9-22-72	1994	Queens Village, N.Y.
Robles, Oscar	.287	58	216	49	62	9	1	0	19	39	15	8	2	L	R	5-11	155	4-9-76	1994	San Diego, Calif.
Scolaro, Donald	.239	49	159	14	38	6	0	0	25	11	27	1	3	R	R	5-10	170	2-7-72	1994	Brandon, Fla.
Tribolet, Scott	.250	50	172	23	43	7	4	1	22	13	31	2	2	R	R	6-1	200	3-2-72	1995	Huntington, Ind.

GAMES BY POSITION: C—Brunner 24, Castro 54. **1B**—Adams 1, Halemanu 52, Scolaro 4. **2B**—Adams 47, Lugo 20, Scolaro 8. **3B**—Adams 1, Bovender 58, Scolaro 16. **SS**—Lugo 19, Robles 55. **OF**—Alexander 67, Lugo 3, Pratt 54, Robinson 59, Tribolet 40.

PITCHING	W	L	ERA	G	GS	CG	SV	IP	H	R	ER	BB	SO	B	T	HT	WT	DOB	1st Yr	Resides
Albaladejo, Randy	0	0	5.23	9	0	0	2	10	12	6	6	5	7	R	R	6-3	190	4-10-73	1991	Vega Alta, P.R.
Corominas, Mike	2	1	6.94	13	0	0	0	23	22	20	18	24	14	L	L	6-2	190	10-31-74	1995	Glendora, Calif.
Fuller, Stephen	6	5	4.86	14	14	0	0	67	67	51	36	51	29	R	R	6-5	195	7-8-74	1995	St. Charles, Ill.
Green, Jason	8	2	3.81	14	14	2	0	83	82	48	35	29	48	R	R	6-4	190	6-5-75	1994	Port Hope, Ontario
Loiz, Niuman	1	1	2.63	3	3	1	0	14	7	5	4	8	11	R	R	6-4	170	12-12-73	1991	Caracas, Venez.
Phillips, Jon	2	0	0.00	2	0	0	0	5	6	0	0	1	5	L	L	6-0	190	6-29-72	1993	Collins, N.Y.
Root, Derek	2	0	3.29	17	3	0	1	38	28	14	14	24	37	L	L	6-5	190	5-26-75	1993	Lakewood, Ohio
Rosenbohm, Jim	2	4	3.66	22	1	0	1	52	48	23	21	32	50	R	R	6-1	170	9-19-73	1992	Omaha, Neb.
Schulte, Troy	1	2	4.88	23	0	0	6	31	30	20	17	9	22	R	R	6-2	200	7-15-71	1993	Westphalia, Iowa
Sikorski, Brian	1	2	2.10	23	0	0	12	34	22	8	8	14	35	R	R	6-1	190	7-27-74	1995	Roseville, Mich.
Smith, Eric	3	6	3.93	14	14	0	0	71	70	37	31	30	56	R	R	6-0	185	5-17-74	1995	Garden City, Kan.
Smyth, Gregg	6	6	4.56	14	14	1	0	75	87	48	38	25	48	L	L	6-1	180	6-22-73	1995	Stamford, Conn.
Stachler, Eric	1	2	8.42	18	0	0	2	36	47	35	34	27	32	R	R	6-3	215	4-18-73	1995	Coldwater, Ohio
Steinke, Brock	1	0	2.08	6	0	0	0	9	11	2	2	3	6	R	R	6-2	180	6-27-75	1993	Cedar Rapids, Iowa
Tickell, Brian	5	3	5.57	13	11	2	0	73	79	47	45	18	31	R	R	6-2	185	11-9-74	1995	Grand Prairie, Texas

KISSIMMEE   R

GULF COAST LEAGUE

BATTING	AVG	G	AB	R	H	2B	3B	HR	RBI	BB	SO	SB	CS	B	T	HT	WT	DOB	1st Yr	Resides
Alleyne, Roberto	.218	35	110	12	24	2	0	1	11	8	27	5	5	R	R	6-4	195	5-15-77	1994	Panama City, Panama
Barksdale, Shane	.258	47	159	19	41	9	1	3	25	20	61	7	11	L	R	6-4	195	9-6-76	1994	Gallant, Ala.
Burns, Kevin	.250	42	136	17	34	4	1	3	23	12	24	8	3	L	L	6-5	210	9-9-75	1995	El Dorado, Ark.
Chapman, Scott	.286	14	28	3	8	1	0	0	1	4	4	1	1	R	R	6-3	205	1-30-78	1995	Albany, Ohio
Cole, Eric	.270	39	122	17	33	3	1	0	12	7	21	7	5	R	R	6-1	180	11-15-75	1995	Lancaster, Calif.
DeShazer, Jeremy	.245	38	106	13	26	6	1	0	11	8	19	6	1	S	R	5-10	175	8-18-76	1995	Kirkland, Wash.
Griffin, Juan	.172	26	64	11	11	1	1	0	10	6	22	5	1	R	R	6-2	165	7-20-75	1993	San Pedro de Macoris, D.R.
Guillen, Carlos	.295	30	105	17	31	4	2	2	15	9	17	17	1	R	R	6-0	150	9-30-75	1993	Maracay, Venez.
Mejia, Marlon	.235	34	98	19	23	1	0	0	5	8	21	2	3	R	R	6-1	175	11-17-74	1995	Jersey City, N.J.
Miles, Aaron	.257	47	171	32	44	9	3	0	18	14	14	9	6	L	R	5-9	160	12-15-76	1995	Antioch, Calif.
Roche, Marlon	.326	29	92	20	30	5	0	0	11	10	19	8	9	R	R	6-1	172	4-11-75	1992	Caracas, Venez.
Rose, Mike	.258	35	89	13	23	2	1	1	9	11	18	2	1	R	R	6-1	190	8-25-76	1995	Elk Grove, Calif.
Samboy, Nelson	.313	55	192	39	60	12	2	1	22	26	19	21	8	R	R	5-10	155	9-4-76	1994	Pedernales, D.R.
Smith, Jermaine	.149	23	67	9	10	3	2	1	5	3	23	2	2	R	R	6-2	220	10-21-76	1994	Auburn, N.Y.
Ubaldo, Nelson	.243	34	103	12	25	4	2	1	9	8	32	9	2	R	R	6-2	200	6-27-74	1995	Cambridge, Mass.
Wesson, Barry	.188	45	138	14	26	2	2	2	18	19	40	4	0	R	R	6-2	195	4-6-77	1995	Glen Allan, Miss.
White, Mickey	.000	1	4	1	0	0	0	0	0	0	0	0	0	R	R	6-2	235	2-20-76	1995	Wenatchee, Wash.

GAMES BY POSITION: C—Chapman 13, Griffin 26, Rose 33. **1B**—Alleyne 22, Burns 39, Rose 1, Smith 1. **2B**—Miles 21, Samboy 39. **3B**—Cole 32, Samboy 14, Smith 17. **SS**—Cole 4, Mejia 33, Miles 25. **OF**—Alleyne 13, Barksdale 46, DeShazer 27, Roche 27, Ubaldo 30, Wesson 44, White 1.

PITCHING	W	L	ERA	G	GS	CG	SV	IP	H	R	ER	BB	SO	B	T	HT	WT	DOB	1st Yr	Resides
Anderson, John	0	2	3.00	2	0	0	0	3	3	3	1	1	5	R	R	6-2	180	8-11-73	1994	Upland, Calif.
Beckerman, Andy	0	0	0.00	2	0	0	0	3	1	0	0	0	3	L	R	6-1	185	12-21-69	1992	Plano, Texas
Brown, Brett	0	0	3.18	12	0	0	1	11	12	7	4	6	12	L	L	6-3	210	4-26-74	1995	Lewes, Del.
Crawford, Chris	1	0	3.62	10	5	0	0	32	29	15	13	25	22	R	R	6-8	225	5-13-75	1995	Kalamazoo, Mich.
Dace, Derek	3	4	1.95	11	10	2	0	69	60	20	15	6	77	L	L	6-7	200	4-9-75	1994	Sullivan, Mo.
Garcia, Freddy	6	3	4.47	11	11	0	0	58	60	32	29	14	58	R	R	6-3	180	10-6-76	1994	Miranda, Venez.
Gosch, Grant	0	0	0.00	1	0	0	0	1	0	0	0	1	1	L	L	6-2	180	6-3-75	1993	Belmont, Calif.
Hook, Jeff	1	0	0.00	2	0	0	0	6	4	0	0	2	4	L	R	6-4	175	8-26-74	1994	Newbury Park, Calif.
Lynch, James	2	1	1.56	17	1	0	4	35	14	12	6	26	49	R	R	6-4	195	12-12-75	1994	Evansville, Ind.
McCarter, Jason	0	1	2.86	16	0	0	2	22	16	8	7	16	21	R	R	6-3	196	9-26-76	1995	Watsonville, Calif.
McFerrin, Chris	4	4	2.86	20	0	0	5	35	28	20	11	17	39	L	R	6-5	175	6-30-76	1995	Fresno, Calif.
McKnight, Tony	1	1	3.86	3	3	0	0	12	14	5	5	2	8	R	R	6-5	205	6-29-77	1995	Texarkana, Ark.
Medina, Tomas	1	1	8.46	11	1	0	0	22	37	26	21	14	23	R	R	6-2	165	4-12-75	1994	Barquisimeto, Venez.
Prestash, J.D.	4	3	2.63	11	11	0	0	51	48	18	15	24	56	L	L	6-2	190	8-14-75	1995	Phillipsburg, Pa.
Ramos, Edgar	0	1	1.84	5	5	0	0	15	14	6	3	5	16	R	R	6-4	170	3-6-75	1992	Cumana, Venez.
Sacharko, Mark	1	2	3.75	12	0	0	0	24	23	14	10	12	22	R	R	6-1	200	4-18-76	1994	Lancaster, Texas
Turley, Jason	5	0	5.63	11	0	0	0	16	14	13	10	13	14	R	R	6-2	190	2-13-75	1994	Evanston, Wyom.
Yanez, Luis	2	5	2.95	11	11	0	0	61	52	29	20	15	63	R	R	6-2	187	12-1-77	1995	Anzoategui, Venez.

KANSAS CITY
ROYALS

Manager: Bob Boone. **1995 Record:** 70-74, .486 (2nd, AL Central).

BATTING	AVG	G	AB	R	H	2B	3B	HR	RBI	BB	SO	SB	CS	B	T	HT	WT	DOB	1st Yr	Resides
Borders, Pat	.231	52	143	14	33	8	1	4	13	7	22	0	0	R	R	6-2	195	5-14-63	1982	Lake Wales, Fla.
Caceres, Edgar	.239	55	117	13	28	6	2	1	17	8	15	2	2	S	R	6-1	170	6-6-64	1984	Barquisimeto, Venez.
Coleman, Vince	.287	75	293	39	84	13	4	4	20	27	48	26	9	S	R	6-1	185	9-22-61	1982	St. Louis, Mo.
Cookson, Brent	.143	22	35	2	5	1	0	0	5	2	7	1	0	R	R	5-11	200	9-7-69	1991	Santa Paula, Calif.
Damon, Johnny	.282	47	188	32	53	11	5	3	23	12	22	7	0	L	L	6-0	175	11-5-73	1992	Orlando, Fla.
Gaetti, Gary	.261	137	514	76	134	27	0	35	96	47	91	3	3	R	R	6-0	200	8-19-58	1979	Raleigh, N.C.
Gagne, Greg	.256	120	430	58	110	25	4	6	49	38	60	3	5	R	R	5-11	180	11-12-61	1979	Rehoboth, Mass.
Goodwin, Tom	.288	133	480	72	138	16	3	4	28	38	72	50	18	L	R	6-1	165	7-27-68	1989	Fresno, Calif.
Grotewold, Jeff	.278	15	36	4	10	1	0	1	6	9	7	0	0	L	R	6-0	215	12-8-65	1987	Lake Arrowhead, Calif.
Hamelin, Bob	.168	72	208	20	35	7	1	7	25	26	56	0	1	L	L	6-0	235	11-29-67	1988	Charlotte, N.C.
Hiatt, Phil	.204	52	113	11	23	6	0	4	12	9	37	1	0	R	R	6-3	200	5-1-69	1990	Pensacola, Fla.
Howard, Dave	.243	95	255	23	62	13	4	0	19	24	41	6	1	S	R	6-0	175	2-26-67	1987	Sarasota, Fla.
James, Chris	.310	26	58	6	18	3	0	2	7	6	10	1	0	R	R	6-1	202	10-4-62	1982	Alto, Texas
Jose, Felix	.133	9	30	2	4	1	0	0	1	2	9	0	0	S	R	6-1	220	5-8-65	1984	Boca Raton, Fla.
Joyner, Wally	.310	131	465	69	144	28	0	12	83	69	65	3	2	L	L	6-2	200	6-16-62	1983	Lee's Summitt, Mo.
Lind, Jose	.268	29	97	4	26	3	0	0	6	3	8	0	1	R	R	5-11	180	5-1-64	1983	Dorado, P.R.
Lockhart, Keith	.321	94	274	41	88	19	3	6	33	14	21	8	1	L	R	5-10	170	11-10-64	1986	Largo, Fla.
Mayne, Brent	.251	110	307	23	77	18	1	1	27	25	41	0	1	L	R	6-1	190	4-19-68	1989	Costa Mesa, Calif.
McGinnis, Russ	.000	3	5	1	0	0	0	0	0	1	1	0	0	R	R	6-3	225	6-18-63	1985	Phoenix, Ariz.
Mercedes, Henry	.256	23	43	7	11	2	0	0	9	8	13	0	0	R	R	5-11	185	7-23-69	1988	Santo Domingo, D.R.
Miller, Keith	.333	9	15	2	5	0	0	1	3	2	4	0	0	R	R	5-11	185	6-12-63	1985	Leawood, Kan.
Mota, Jose	.000	2	2	0	0	0	0	0	0	0	0	0	0	S	R	5-9	155	3-16-65	1985	Glendale, Calif.
Norman, Les	.225	24	40	6	9	0	1	0	4	6	6	0	1	R	R	6-1	185	2-25-69	1991	Greenfield, Ill.
Nunnally, Jon	.244	119	303	51	74	15	6	14	42	51	86	6	4	L	R	5-10	188	11-9-71	1992	Pelham, N.C.
Randa, Joe	.171	34	70	6	12	2	0	1	5	6	17	0	1	R	R	5-11	190	12-18-69	1991	Delafield, Wisc.
Samuel, Juan	.176	15	34	3	6	0	0	2	5	5	11	1	0	R	R	5-11	180	12-9-60	1980	Santo Domingo, D.R.
2-team (76 Detroit)	.263	91	205	31	54	10	1	12	39	29	49	6	4							
Stynes, Chris	.171	22	35	7	6	1	0	0	2	4	3	0	0	R	R	5-9	170	1-19-73	1991	Boca Raton, Fla.
Sweeney, Mike	.250	4	4	1	1	0	0	0	0	0	0	0	0	R	R	6-1	195	7-22-73	1991	Ontario, Calif.
Tucker, Michael	.260	62	177	23	46	10	4	4	17	18	51	2	3	L	R	6-2	185	6-25-71	1992	Chase City, Va.
Vitiello, Joe	.254	53	130	13	33	4	0	7	21	8	25	0	0	R	R	6-2	215	4-11-70	1991	Stoneham, Mass.

PITCHING	W	L	ERA	G	GS	CG	SV	IP	H	R	ER	BB	SO	B	T	HT	WT	DOB	1st Yr	Resides
Anderson, Scott	1	0	5.33	6	4	0	0	25	29	15	15	8	8	R	R	6-5	195	5-1-62	1984	Vancouver, Wash.
Appier, Kevin	15	10	3.89	31	31	4	0	201	163	90	87	80	185	R	R	6-2	195	12-6-67	1987	Overland Park, Kan.
Brewer, Billy	2	4	5.56	48	0	0	0	45	54	28	28	20	31	L	L	6-1	175	4-15-68	1990	Waco, Texas
Browning, Tom	0	2	8.10	2	2	0	0	10	13	9	9	5	3	L	L	6-1	190	4-28-60	1982	Edgewood, Ky.
Bunch, Mel	1	3	5.63	13	5	0	0	40	42	25	25	14	19	R	R	6-1	165	11-4-71	1992	Texarkana, Texas
Converse, Jim	1	0	5.84	9	0	0	0	12	12	8	8	8	5	L	R	5-9	180	8-17-71	1990	Citrus Heights, Calif.
2-team (6 Seattle)	1	3	6.56	15	1	0	1	23	28	17	17	16	14							
Fleming, Dave	0	1	3.66	9	5	0	0	32	27	17	13	19	14	L	L	6-3	200	11-7-69	1990	Mahopac, N.Y.
2-team (16 Seattle)	1	6	5.96	25	12	1	0	80	84	61	53	53	40							
Gordon, Tom	12	12	4.43	31	31	2	0	189	204	110	93	89	119	R	R	5-9	180	11-18-67	1986	Avon Park, Fla.
Gubicza, Mark	12	14	3.75	33	33	3	0	213	222	97	89	62	81	R	R	6-5	230	8-14-62	1981	Northridge, Calif.
Haney, Chris	3	4	3.65	16	13	1	0	81	78	35	33	33	31	L	L	6-3	195	11-16-68	1990	Barboursvile, Va.
Huisman, Rich	0	0	7.45	7	0	0	0	10	14	8	8	1	12	R	R	6-3	200	5-17-69	1990	Bensenville, Ill.
Jacome, Jason	4	6	5.36	15	14	1	0	84	101	52	50	21	39	L	L	6-0	180	11-24-70	1991	Tucson, Ariz.
Linton, Doug	0	1	7.25	7	2	0	0	22	22	21	18	10	13	R	R	6-1	190	9-22-67	1987	Kingsport, Tenn.
Magnante, Mike	1	1	4.23	28	0	0	0	45	45	23	21	16	28	L	L	6-1	190	6-17-65	1988	Burbank, Calif.
Meacham, Rusty	4	3	4.98	49	0	0	2	60	72	36	33	19	30	R	R	6-2	175	1-27-68	1988	Palm City, Fla.
Montgomery, Jeff	2	3	3.43	54	0	0	31	66	60	27	25	25	49	R	R	5-11	180	1-7-62	1983	Leawood, Kan.
Olson, Gregg	3	3	3.26	20	0	0	3	30	23	11	11	17	21	R	R	6-4	212	10-11-66	1988	Reisterstown, Md.
2-team (3 Cleve.)	3	3	4.09	23	0	0	3	33	28	15	15	19	21							
Pichardo, Hipolito	8	4	4.36	44	0	0	1	64	66	34	31	30	43	R	R	6-1	185	8-22-69	1988	Esperanza, D.R.
Pittsley, Jim	0	0	13.50	1	1	0	0	3	7	5	5	1	0	R	R	6-7	215	4-3-74	1992	DuBois, Pa.
Rasmussen, Dennis	1	1	9.00	5	1	0	0	10	13	10	10	6	4	L	L	6-7	240	4-18-59	1980	Omaha, Neb.
Torres, Dilson	1	2	6.09	24	2	0	0	44	56	30	30	17	28	R	R	6-1	215	5-31-70	1991	Suredo, Venez.

FIELDING

Catcher	PCT	G	PO	A	E	DP	PB
Borders	1.000	45	182	18	0	3	5
Hamelin	.000	1	0	0	0	0	0
Mayne	.995	103	540	40	3	11	4
Mercedes	.986	22	62	8	1	1	2
Sweeney	.875	4	7	0	1	0	0

First Base	PCT	G	PO	A	E	DP
Caceres	1.000	6	11	0	0	2
Gaetti	.990	11	92	10	1	10
Grotewold	.750	1	3	0	1	1
Hamelin	1.000	8	66	9	0	11
Howard	1.000	1	3	0	0	1
Joyner	.998	126	1111	118	3	121
McGinnis	1.000	1	8	0	0	0
Samuel	1.000	1	8	0	0	0
Vitiello	.982	8	51	3	1	3

Second Base	PCT	G	PO	A	E	DP
Caceres	.992	36	49	71	1	10
Howard	.994	41	68	99	1	21
James	.000	1	0	0	0	0
Lind	.992	29	56	75	1	17
Lockhart	.974	61	106	160	7	43
Mota	1.000	2	1	3	0	0
Randa	.957	9	7	15	1	3
Stynes	.982	17	21	35	1	14

Third Base	PCT	G	PO	A	E	DP
Caceres	1.000	3	2	3	0	2
Gaetti	.954	123	90	218	15	21
Lockhart	.958	17	5	18	1	1
McGinnis	1.000	1	1	0	0	0
Randa	.949	22	8	29	2	1

Shortstop	PCT	G	PO	A	E	DP
Caceres	1.000	8	10	18	0	6

	PCT	G	PO	A	E	DP
Gagne	.969	118	174	389	18	88
Howard	.986	33	47	93	2	25

Outfield	PCT	G	PO	A	E	DP
Coleman	.975	69	109	7	3	2
Cookson	1.000	12	14	0	0	0
Damon	.991	47	110	0	1	0
Goodwin	.990	130	292	6	3	2
Hiatt	.957	47	63	4	3	1
Howard	.945	30	49	3	3	0
James	1.000	5	9	0	0	0
Jose	1.000	7	15	2	0	0
McGinnis	.000	1	0	0	0	0
Miller	1.000	4	5	1	0	0
Norman	.958	17	22	1	1	0
Nunnally	.971	107	197	5	6	1
Samuel	1.000	5	3	0	0	0
Tucker	.986	36	67	3	1	0

Righthander Jeff Montgomery led the Royals with 31 saves

Royals minor league Player of the Year Johnny Damon

MORRIS FOSTOFF

STAN DENNY

ROYALS

FARM SYSTEM

Director of Minor League Operations: Bob Hegman.

Class	Farm Team	League	W	L	Pct.	Finish*	Manager	First Yr
AAA	Omaha (Neb.) Royals	American Assoc.	76	68	.528	3rd (8)	Mike Jirschele	1969
AA	Wichita (Kan.) Wranglers	Texas	72	64	.603	2nd (8)	Ron Johnson	1995
#A	Wilmington (Del.) Blue Rocks	Carolina	83	55	.601	1st (8)	John Mizerock	1993
A	Springfield (Ill.) Sultans	Midwest	65	74	.468	10th (14)	Brian Poldberg	1995
A	Spokane (Wash.) Indians	Northwest	36	39	.480	6th (8)	Al Pedrique	1995
R	Fort Myers (Fla.) Royals	Gulf Coast	47	12	.797	1st+(16)	Bob Herold	1993

*Finish in overall standings (No. of teams in league)   #Advanced level   +Won league championship

ORGANIZATION LEADERS

MAJOR LEAGUERS

BATTING
*AVG	Keith Lockhart	.321
R	Gary Gaetti	76
H	Wally Joyner	144
TB	Gary Gaetti	266
2B	Wally Joyner	28
3B	Jon Nunnally	6
HR	Gary Gaetti	35
RBI	Gary Gaetti	96
BB	Wally Joyner	69
SO	Gary Gaetti	91
SB	Tom Goodwin	50

PITCHING
W	Kevin Appier	15
L	Mark Gubicza	14
#ERA	Chris Haney	3.65
G	Jeff Montgomery	54
CG	Kevin Appier	4
SV	Jeff Montgomery	31
IP	Mark Gubicza	213
BB	Tom Gordon	89
SO	Kevin Appier	185

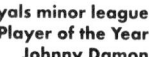

Jaime Bluma. 26 saves

JOHN SPEAR

MINOR LEAGUERS

BATTING
*AVG	Johnny Damon, Wichita	.343
R	Jeremy Carr, Bakersfield/Wilmington	94
H	Rod Myers, Wichita	153
TB	Mandy Romero, Wichita	230
2B	Mandy Romero, Wichita	32
3B	Rodolfo Mendez, Springfield	11
HR	Sal Fasano, Wilmington/Wichita	22
RBI	Mandy Romero, Wichita	82
BB	Jeff Grotewold, Omaha	82
SO	Rodolfo Mendez, Springfield	121
SB	Jeremy Carr, Bakersfield/Wilmington	52

PITCHING
W	Glendon Rusch, Wilmington	14
L	Three tied at	10
#ERA	Glendon Rusch, Wilmington	1.74
G	Jaime Bluma, Wichita/Omaha	60
CG	Dennis Rasmussen, Omaha	3
SV	Jaime Bluma, Wichita/Omaha	26
IP	Tim Byrdak, Wilmington	166
BB	Bart Evans, Wilmington/Wichita	89
SO	Glendon Rusch, Wilmington	147

*Minimum 250 At-Bats   #Minimum 75 Innings

TOP 10 PROSPECTS

How the Royals Top 10 prospects, as judged by Baseball America prior to the 1995 season, fared in 1995:

Michael Tucker

Player, Pos.	Club (Class—League)	AVG	AB	R	H	2B	3B	HR	RBI	SB
1. Johnny Damon, of	Wichita (AA—Texas)	.343	423	83	145	15	9	16	54	26
	Kansas City	.282	188	32	53	11	5	3	23	7
2. Michael Tucker, of	Omaha (AAA—American Assoc.)	.305	275	37	84	18	4	4	28	11
	Kansas City	.260	177	23	46	10	0	4	17	2
4. Sergio Nunez, 2b	Wilmington (A—Carolina)	.237	460	63	109	10	2	4	25	33
6. Joe Vitiello, 1b-of	Omaha (AAA—American Assoc.)	.279	229	33	64	14	2	12	42	0
	Kansas City	.254	130	13	33	4	0	7	21	0
7. Felix Martinez, ss	Wichita (AA—Texas)	.263	426	53	112	15	3	3	30	44
9. Matt Smith, 1b	Springfield (A—Midwest)	.226	412	49	93	18	1	6	46	8
10. Joe Randa, 3b	Omaha (AAA—American Assoc.)	.275	233	33	64	10	2	8	33	2
	Kansas City	.171	70	6	12	2	0	1	5	0

Player, Pos.	Club (Class—League)	W	L	ERA	G	SV	IP	H	BB	SO
3. Jim Pittsley, rhp	Omaha (AAA—American Assoc.)	4	1	3.21	8	0	48	38	16	39
	Kansas City	0	0	13.50	1	0	3	7	1	0
5. Jeff Granger, lhp	Wichita (AA—Texas)	4	7	5.93	18	0	96	122	40	81
8. Ken Ray, rhp	Wilmington (A—Carolina)	6	4	2.69	13	0	77	74	22	63
	Wichita (AA—Texas)	4	5	5.97	14	0	75	83	46	53

MORRIS FOSTOFF

TY SPORTS GROUP

Royalty. Kansas City got 35 home runs from slugging third baseman Gary Gaetti, left, and 15 wins from ace righthander Kevin Appier.

OMAHA   AAA
AMERICAN ASSOCIATION

BATTING	AVG	G	AB	R	H	2B	3B	HR	RBI	BB	SO	SB	CS	B	T	HT	WT	DOB	1st Yr	Resides
Bruett, J.T.	.279	44	129	20	36	6	1	2	14	17	19	6	4	L	L	5-11	180	10-8-67	1988	Plymouth, Minn.
Burton, Darren	.000	2	5	0	0	0	0	0	0	0	1	0	0	S	R	6-1	185	9-16-72	1990	Somerset, Ky.
Caceres, Edgar	.206	37	107	13	22	3	1	0	12	8	10	3	1	S	R	6-1	170	6-6-64	1984	Barquisimeto, Venez.
Chamberlain, Wes	.219	16	64	2	14	3	0	1	6	2	15	0	0	R	R	6-2	219	4-13-66	1987	Chicago, Ill.
Coleman, Vince	.395	9	38	7	15	2	0	1	5	2	6	3	0	S	R	6-1	185	9-22-61	1982	St. Louis, Mo.
Cookson, Brent	.401	40	137	28	55	13	0	4	20	17	24	0	0	R	R	5-11	200	9-7-69	1991	Santa Paula, Calif.
Elster, Kevin	.238	11	42	5	10	4	0	0	6	5	8	0	0	R	R	6-2	200	8-3-64	1984	Huntington Beach, Calif.
Garber, Jeff	.143	6	14	1	2	0	0	0	0	0	5	0	0	R	R	5-11	180	9-27-66	1988	Valdosta, Ga.
Green, Gary	.169	26	71	5	12	2	0	0	3	3	14	0	0	R	R	6-3	180	1-14-62	1985	Arlington, Texas
Grotewold, Jeff	.294	105	350	70	103	19	0	17	60	82	88	0	2	L	R	6-0	215	12-8-65	1987	Lake Arrowhead, Calif.
Halter, Shane	.230	124	392	42	90	19	3	8	39	40	97	2	3	R	R	5-10	160	11-8-69	1991	Papillion, Neb.
Hamelin, Bob	.294	36	119	25	35	12	0	10	32	31	34	2	3	L	L	6-0	235	11-29-67	1988	Charlotte, N.C.
Hatcher, Billy	.276	26	105	14	29	5	1	1	12	9	6	4	2	R	R	5-10	190	10-4-60	1981	Cincinnati, Ohio
Hiatt, Phil	.158	20	76	7	12	5	0	2	8	2	25	0	0	R	R	6-3	200	5-1-69	1990	Pensacola, Fla.
Hosey, Dwayne	.295	75	271	59	80	21	4	12	50	29	45	15	6	S	R	5-10	170	3-11-67	1987	Altadena, Calif.
Hughes, Keith	.289	103	342	51	99	22	2	11	46	30	41	4	2	L	L	6-3	210	9-12-63	1982	Berwyn, Pa.
James, Chris	.167	3	12	3	2	1	0	1	3	1	2	0	0	R	R	6-1	202	10-4-62	1982	Alto, Texas
Lockhart, Keith	.378	44	148	24	56	7	1	5	19	16	10	1	3	L	R	5-10	170	11-10-64	1986	Largo, Fla.
Long, Kevin	.250	22	64	7	16	3	0	0	5	8	1	2	1	L	L	5-9	165	12-30-66	1989	Phoenix, Ariz.
Lyden, Mitch	.253	71	237	26	60	8	1	12	44	11	66	0	0	R	R	6-3	225	12-14-64	1983	Ft. Lauderdale, Fla.
Mercedes, Henry	.215	86	275	37	59	12	0	11	37	22	90	2	0	R	R	5-11	185	7-23-69	1988	Santo Domingo, D.R.
Miller, Keith	.250	7	20	3	5	2	0	0	2	4	2	1	0	R	R	5-11	185	6-12-63	1985	Leawood, Kan.
Mota, Jose	.322	27	87	6	28	4	0	0	10	6	9	1	2	S	R	5-9	155	3-16-65	1985	Glendale, Calif.
Norman, Les	.284	83	313	46	89	19	3	9	33	18	48	5	3	R	R	6-1	185	2-25-69	1991	Greenfield, Ill.
Randa, Joe	.275	64	233	33	64	10	2	8	33	22	33	2	2	R	R	5-11	190	12-18-69	1991	Delafield, Wisc.
Reynolds, Harold	.202	38	109	12	22	6	1	1	11	13	10	2	3	S	R	5-11	185	11-26-60	1981	Baltimore, Md.
Sisco, Steve	.208	7	24	4	5	1	0	0	0	2	8	0	0	R	R	5-9	180	12-2-69	1992	Thousand Oaks, Calif.
Stewart, Andy	.301	44	156	24	47	11	0	3	21	12	18	0	1	R	R	5-11	205	12-5-70	1990	Oshawa, Ontario
Strickland, Chad	.273	8	22	3	6	2	0	0	5	1	4	0	0	R	R	6-1	180	3-16-72	1990	Midwest City, Okla.
Stynes, Chris	.275	83	306	51	84	12	5	9	42	27	24	4	5	R	R	5-9	170	1-19-73	1991	Boca Raton, Fla.
Tucker, Michael	.305	71	275	37	84	18	4	4	28	24	39	11	4	L	R	6-2	185	6-25-71	1992	Chase City, Va.
Vitiello, Joe	.279	59	229	33	64	14	2	12	42	12	50	0	1	R	R	6-2	215	4-11-70	1991	Stoneham, Mass.

PITCHING	W	L	ERA	G	GS	CG	SV	IP	H	R	ER	BB	SO	B	T	HT	WT	DOB	1st Yr	Resides
Anderson, Scott	5	3	4.17	15	11	1	0	73	63	37	34	16	47	R	R	6-5	195	5-1-62	1984	Vancouver, Wash.
Bevil, Brian	1	3	9.41	6	6	0	0	22	40	31	23	14	10	R	R	6-3	190	9-5-71	1991	Houston, Texas
Bluma, Jaime	0	0	3.04	18	0	0	4	24	21	13	8	14	12	R	R	5-11	195	5-18-72	1994	Owasso, Okla.
Brewer, Billy	0	0	0.00	6	0	0	0	7	1	0	0	7	5	L	L	6-1	175	4-15-68	1990	Waco, Texas

PITCHING	W	L	ERA	G	GS	CG	SV	IP	H	R	ER	BB	SO	B	T	HT	WT	DOB	1st Yr	Resides
Brown, Kevin	0	0	7.62	7	1	0	0	13	20	13	11	12	5	L	L	6-1	185	3-5-66	1986	Broderick, Calif.
Browning, Tom	0	1	3.43	5	5	0	0	21	13	8	8	5	5	L	L	6-1	190	4-28-60	1982	Edgewood, Ky.
Bunch, Melvin	1	7	4.57	12	11	1	0	65	63	37	33	20	50	R	R	6-1	165	11-4-71	1992	Texarkana, Texas
Converse, Jim	1	0	0.00	4	0	0	0	5	1	0	0	1	9	L	R	5-9	180	8-17-71	1990	Citrus Heights, Calif.
DeJesus, Jose	3	6	6.13	36	6	0	10	62	56	45	42	52	49	R	R	6-5	225	1-6-65	1983	Cidra, P.R.
Dorlarque, Aaron	2	2	4.24	24	1	0	4	40	38	19	19	15	24	R	R	6-3	180	2-16-70	1992	Vancouver, Wash.
Eddy, Chris	1	1	7.27	14	0	0	0	17	20	15	14	12	12	L	L	6-3	200	11-27-69	1992	Duncanville, Texas
Fleming, Dave	1	0	3.38	3	3	0	0	16	17	6	6	7	8	L	L	6-3	200	11-7-69	1990	Mahopac, N.Y.
Fyhrie, Mike	3	4	4.45	14	11	0	0	61	71	34	30	14	39	R	R	6-2	190	12-9-69	1991	Westminster, Calif.
Garretts, Scott	1	2	5.30	9	1	0	1	19	17	12	11	13	15	R	R	6-4	205	10-30-61	1979	Shreveport, La.
Harris, Reggie	0	1	18.00	2	0	0	0	2	5	4	4	1	2	R	R	6-1	190	8-12-68	1987	Waynesboro, Va.
Harrison, Brian	4	2	6.13	16	8	1	0	54	76	39	37	10	12	R	R	6-1	175	12-18-68	1992	Bryan, Texas
Huisman, Rich	0	1	1.80	5	0	0	1	5	3	1	1	1	3	R	R	6-3	200	5-17-69	1990	Bensenville, Ill.
Kutzler, Jerry	8	5	4.02	37	5	0	4	103	128	48	46	27	45	L	R	6-1	175	3-25-65	1987	Zion, Ill.
Linton, Doug	7	7	4.40	18	18	2	0	108	129	60	53	24	85	R	R	6-1	190	9-22-67	1987	Kingsport, Tenn.
Magnante, Mike	5	1	2.84	15	8	0	0	57	55	23	18	13	38	L	L	6-1	190	6-17-65	1988	Burbank, Calif.
Mallicoat, Rob	0	1	3.00	3	0	0	0	3	1	1	1	3	1	L	L	6-3	215	11-16-64	1984	Houston, Texas
Melendez, Jose	3	4	4.89	21	1	0	0	35	44	21	19	14	30	R	R	6-2	190	9-2-65	1984	Naguabo, P.R.
Milacki, Bob	8	3	3.33	15	15	2	0	105	90	42	39	31	63	R	R	6-4	230	7-28-64	1984	Lake Havasu, Ariz.
Munoz, J.J.	2	3	3.38	57	0	0	6	56	48	23	21	19	51	L	L	5-9	170	11-1-67	1990	Mesquite, Texas
Myers, Rod	4	5	4.10	38	0	0	2	48	52	26	22	19	38	R	R	6-1	190	6-26-69	1990	Rockford, Ill.
Olson, Gregg	0	0	0.00	1	0	0	0	1	0	0	0	1	1	R	R	6-4	212	10-11-66	1988	Reisterstown, Md.
2-team (18 Buffalo)	1	0	2.38	19	0	0	13	23	16	6	6	10	26							
Perry, Pat	0	0	5.79	5	0	0	3	5	5	3	3	2	4	L	L	6-1	190	2-4-59	1978	St. Louis, Mo.
Pierce, Ed	0	0	7.36	3	0	0	0	4	9	4	3	1	1	L	L	6-1	190	10-6-68	1989	San Dimas, Calif.
Pittsley, Jim	4	1	3.21	8	8	0	0	48	38	20	17	16	39	R	R	6-7	215	4-3-74	1992	DuBois, Pa.
Rasmussen, Dennis	6	3	2.89	10	10	3	0	65	63	22	21	17	51	L	L	6-7	240	4-18-59	1980	Omaha, Neb.
Strange, Don	0	0	7.47	9	0	0	1	16	24	13	13	6	11	R	R	6-0	195	5-26-67	1989	Springfield, Mass.
Torres, Dilson	3	1	2.63	5	5	1	0	27	28	11	8	7	12	R	R	6-1	215	5-31-70	1991	Suredo, Venez.
Toth, Robert	1	2	3.61	8	8	1	0	47	53	25	19	8	31	R	R	6-2	180	7-30-72	1990	Cypress, Calif.

FIELDING

Catcher	PCT	G	PO	A	E	DP	PB
Lyden	.993	44	269	28	2	5	5
Mercedes	.987	78	418	55	6	9	12
Stewart	.981	25	140	16	3	2	3
Strickland	1.000	8	32	3	0	0	1

First Base	PCT	G	PO	A	E	DP
Caceres	1.000	2	23	0	0	1
Grotewold	.981	75	645	49	15	84
Hamelin	.967	19	157	19	6	21
Lyden	1.000	6	18	3	0	2
Norman	1.000	1	0	1	0	0
Stewart	1.000	11	72	13	0	5
Vitiello	.984	28	221	21	4	26

Second Base	PCT	G	PO	A	E	DP
Caceres	.977	8	18	25	1	7
Halter	.921	21	42	51	8	15
Mota	1.000	9	13	23	0	6
Reynolds	.966	33	63	80	5	22
Sisco	.956	7	16	27	2	8

	PCT	G	PO	A	E	DP
Stynes	.966	69	136	176	11	51

Third Base	PCT	G	PO	A	E	DP
Caceres	1.000	15	8	32	0	0
Garber	1.000	3	0	2	0	0
Green	.846	5	3	8	2	0
Grotewold	1.000	3	5	3	0	1
Lockhart	.928	37	31	72	8	10
Mercedes	.895	7	1	16	2	2
Randa	.958	64	42	96	6	8
Reynolds	1.000	2	1	7	0	0
Stewart	.000	1	0	0	2	0
Stynes	.947	13	8	28	2	5

Shortstop	PCT	G	PO	A	E	DP
Caceres	.913	5	9	12	2	6
Elster	1.000	11	22	30	0	12
Green	1.000	19	20	52	0	8
Halter	.978	103	183	304	11	75
Mota	.918	13	17	28	4	5

Outfield	PCT	G	PO	A	E	DP
Bruett	.977	39	84	0	2	0
Burton	1.000	2	6	0	0	0
Caceres	1.000	2	1	0	0	0
Chamberlain	1.000	14	24	2	0	1
Coleman	.950	9	19	0	1	0
Cookson	1.000	26	56	3	0	1
Hatcher	.981	26	52	0	1	0
Hiatt	.974	19	37	1	1	0
Hosey	.971	62	125	10	4	2
Hughes	.965	74	130	9	5	2
Long	1.000	18	32	0	0	0
Miller	1.000	1	2	0	0	0
Mota	1.000	3	4	1	0	0
Norman	.979	81	180	8	4	1
Stewart	.000	1	0	0	0	0
Tucker	.986	70	133	11	2	1
Vitiello	1.000	2	4	0	0	0

WICHITA   AA
TEXAS LEAGUE

BATTING	AVG	G	AB	R	H	2B	3B	HR	RBI	BB	SO	SB	CS	B	T	HT	WT	DOB	1st Yr	Resides
Burton, Darren	.239	41	163	13	39	1		1	20	12	27	6	6	S	R	6-1	185	9-16-72	1992	Somerset, Ky.
Damon, Johnny	.343	111	423	83	145	15	9	16	54	67	35	26	15	L	L	6-0	175	11-5-73	1992	Orlando, Fla.
Diaz, Lino	.350	62	226	40	79	15	3	6	43	14	21	0	3	R	R	5-11	182	7-22-70	1993	Altoona, Pa.
Fasano, Sal	.290	87	317	60	92	19	2	20	66	27	61	3	6	R	R	6-2	220	8-10-71	1993	Hanover Park, Ill.
Gonzalez, Raul	.291	22	79	14	23	3	2	1	11	8	13	4	0	R	R	5-8	175	12-27-73	1991	Villa Carolina, P.R.
Jennings, Lance	.182	13	44	2	8	0	0	0	3	1	8	0	0	R	R	6-0	195	10-3-71	1989	Modesto, Calif.
Long, Kevin	.292	67	250	38	73	14	1	1	26	41	29	9	6	L	L	5-9	165	12-30-66	1989	Phoenix, Ariz.
Long, Ryan	.231	102	342	36	79	26	0	5	34	10	48	4	4	R	R	6-0	175	2-3-73	1991	Houston, Texas
Marshall, Jason	.226	60	146	14	33	1	1	0	9	4	23	0	0	R	R	6-0	175	6-27-72	1992	Abilene, Texas
Martinez, Felix	.263	127	426	53	112	15	3	3	30	31	71	44	20	S	R	6-0	168	5-18-74	1993	Nagua, D.R.
Martinez, Ramon	.275	103	393	58	108	20	2	3	51	42	50	11	8	R	R	6-1	170	10-10-72	1993	Toa Alta, P.R.
Medrano, Anthony	.000	1	5	0	0	0	0	0	0	0	0	0	0	R	R	5-11	155	12-8-74	1993	Long Beach, Calif.
Murphy, Steve	.333	18	39	9	13	2	0	0	4	4	5	0	1	L	R	5-8	165	4-13-71	1992	Germantown, Tenn.
Myers, Rod	.307	131	499	71	153	22	6	7	62	34	77	29	16	L	L	6-0	190	1-14-73	1991	Conroe, Texas
Romero, Mandy	.302	121	440	73	133	32	1	21	82	69	60	1	3	S	R	5-11	196	10-19-67	1988	Miami, Fla.
Sisco, Steve	.301	54	209	29	63	12	1	3	23	15	31	3	1	R	R	5-9	180	12-2-69	1992	Thousand Oaks, Calif.
Smiley, Rueben	.240	41	104	16	25	3	1	2	13	8	20	1	3	L	L	6-4	185	8-27-68	1988	Los Angeles, Calif.
Sparks, Rodney	.000	5	0	0	0	0	0	0	0	0	0	0	0	R	R	6-0	165	11-7-71	1993	Phoenix, Ariz.
Stewart, Andy	.259	60	216	28	56	18	0	3	32	11	31	1	2	R	R	6-1	205	12-5-70	1990	Oshawa, Ontario
Strickland, Chad	.224	51	183	16	41	7	0	1	21	5	22	0	0	R	R	6-1	185	3-16-72	1990	Midwest City, Okla.
Sutton, Larry	.269	53	197	31	53	11	1	5	32	26	33	1	1	L	L	5-11	175	5-14-70	1992	Temecula, Calif.
Williams, Ted	.000	0	0	0	0	0	0	0	0	0	0	0	0	S	R	6-1	160	1-25-71	1993	Columbus, Miss.

PITCHING	W	L	ERA	G	GS	CG	SV	IP	H	R	ER	BB	SO	B	T	HT	WT	DOB	1st Yr	Resides
Atkinson, Neil	3	0	4.80	40	0	0	1	51	52	29	27	21	32	L	L	6-0	190	1-14-71	1993	San Antonio, Texas
Bevil, Brian	5	7	5.84	15	15	0	0	74	85	51	48	35	57	R	R	6-3	190	9-5-71	1991	Houston, Texas
Bluma, Jaime	3	3	3.09	42	0	0	22	55	38	19	19	9	31	R	R	5-11	195	5-18-72	1994	Owasso, Okla.
Bovee, Mike	8	6	4.18	20	20	1	0	114	118	60	53	43	72	R	R	5-10	200	8-21-73	1991	Mira Mesa, Calif.

PITCHING	W	L	ERA	G	GS	CG	SV	IP	H	R	ER	BB	SO	B	T	HT	WT	DOB	1st Yr	Resides
Brewer, Nevin	3	2	3.96	19	4	1	0	50	54	31	22	21	21	R	R	6-4	195	8-1-71	1993	Wilmington, N.C.
Browning, Tom	1	0	7.50	1	1	0	0	6	10	5	5	1	5	L	L	6-1	190	4-28-60	1982	Edgewood, Ky.
Connolly, Chris	1	0	5.68	13	0	0	0	13	18	11	8	11	2	L	L	6-2	192	12-4-70	1991	Lynchburg, Va.
Dorlarque, Aaron	1	1	1.15	20	1	0	0	47	37	8	6	10	32	R	R	6-3	180	2-16-70	1992	Vancouver, Wash.
Eddy, Chris	1	0	4.00	9	0	0	1	9	8	4	4	3	10	L	L	6-3	200	11-27-69	1992	Duncanville, Texas
Evans, Bart	0	4	10.48	7	7	0	0	22	22	28	26	45	13	R	R	6-1	190	12-30-70	1992	Ozark, Mo.
Fyhrie, Mike	3	2	3.04	17	9	0	1	74	76	31	25	23	41	R	R	6-2	190	12-9-69	1991	Westminster, Calif.
Granger, Jeff	4	7	5.93	18	18	0	0	96	122	76	63	40	81	R	L	6-4	200	12-16-71	1993	Orange, Texas
Grundy, Phil	1	1	8.31	6	2	0	0	17	16	17	16	7	11	R	R	6-2	195	9-8-72	1993	Somerset, Ky.
Harrison, Brian	1	1	4.73	15	0	0	2	27	35	18	14	7	11	R	R	6-1	175	12-18-68	1992	Bryan, Texas
McDill, Allen	1	0	2.11	12	1	0	1	21	16	7	5	5	20	L	L	6-1	160	8-23-71	1992	Hot Springs, Ark.
Morones, Geno	3	6	4.10	17	16	0	0	79	85	49	36	39	32	R	R	5-11	197	3-26-71	1991	San Leandro, Calif.
Paskievitch, Tom	1	1	5.06	5	0	0	0	5	6	3	3	2	3	R	R	6-3	210	7-19-68	1991	Erie, Pa.
Ralston, Kris	9	4	3.56	18	16	0	0	94	85	40	37	28	84	R	R	6-2	205	8-8-71	1993	Carthage, Mo.
Rawitzer, Kevin	6	4	5.25	28	3	0	1	48	48	30	28	19	42	L	L	5-10	185	2-28-71	1993	Danville, Calif.
Ray, Ken	4	5	5.97	14	14	0	0	75	83	55	50	46	53	R	R	6-2	160	11-27-74	1993	Roswell, Ga.
Sheehan, Chris	0	2	5.51	31	0	0	2	51	51	35	31	16	31	R	R	6-4	205	1-5-69	1992	Kirkland, Wash.
Strange, Don	0	1	1.50	24	0	0	8	36	28	7	6	7	36	R	R	6-0	195	5-26-67	1989	Springfield, Mass.
Toth, Robert	8	4	2.17	21	9	1	0	104	95	30	25	27	77	R	R	6-2	180	7-30-72	1990	Cypress, Calif.
Wallace, Derek	4	3	4.40	26	0	0	6	43	51	23	21	13	24	R	R	6-3	200	9-1-71	1992	Oxnard, Calif.

FIELDING

Catcher	PCT	G	PO	A	E	DP	PB
Fasano	.976	44	286	34	8	5	3
Jennings	1.000	13	61	10	0	0	1
Romero	.982	26	146	17	3	1	1
Stewart	.964	17	74	6	3	1	1
Strickland	.977	50	285	50	8	2	5

First Base	PCT	G	PO	A	E	DP
Fasano	.982	35	303	30	6	36
K. Long	.970	4	31	1	1	1
Marshall	.989	11	82	4	1	5
Myers	.857	2	6	0	1	0
Romero	.933	2	13	1	1	3
Stewart	.994	41	328	28	2	33
Sutton	.986	52	452	25	7	39

Second Base	PCT	G	PO	A	E	DP
Diaz	.833	2	1	4	1	1
Marshall	1.000	16	19	28	0	3
R. Martinez	.984	100	182	299	8	67
Medrano	.909	1	3	7	1	0
Sisco	.993	29	59	80	1	15

Third Base	PCT	G	PO	A	E	DP
Diaz	.965	61	40	124	6	13
R. Long	.912	69	43	134	17	6
Marshall	.929	9	2	11	1	1
Sisco	1.000	6	1	15	0	1
Stewart	1.000	2	0	2	0	0

Shortstop	PCT	G	PO	A	E	DP
Marshall	.970	21	26	38	2	8
F. Martinez	.922	125	222	371	50	76

	PCT	G	PO	A	E	DP
R. Martinez	.941	2	4	12	1	1

Outfield	PCT	G	PO	A	E	DP
Burton	.963	41	73	4	3	1
Damon	.984	108	296	11	5	2
Gonzalez	.957	21	38	6	2	0
K. Long	.986	60	129	8	2	0
R. Long	1.000	22	40	1	0	0
Marshall	1.000	3	3	0	0	0
Murphy	.960	14	24	0	1	0
Myers	.967	129	256	8	9	2
Sisco	1.000	2	2	0	0	0
Smiley	.938	24	28	2	2	1
Stewart	1.000	2	1	1	0	0
Strickland	1.000	1	1	0	0	0

WILMINGTON
CAROLINA LEAGUE

BATTING	AVG	G	AB	R	H	2B	3B	HR	RBI	BB	SO	SB	CS	B	T	HT	WT	DOB	1st Yr	Resides
Brooks, Ramy	.218	94	326	41	71	16	0	8	30	25	82	2	1	R	R	6-2	180	4-12-70	1990	Blanchard, Okla.
Byington, Jimmie	.223	92	273	24	61	6	1	0	23	13	33	12	6	R	R	6-0	170	8-22-73	1993	Tulsa, Okla.
Carr, Jeremy	.231	5	13	1	3	1	0	0	0	1	3	0	0	R	R	5-10	170	3-30-71	1993	Boise, Idaho
Delaney, Donovan	.250	114	360	22	90	13	7	3	39	25	82	6	9	R	R	5-11	200	3-24-74	1994	Haughton, La.
Diaz, Lino	.301	51	173	20	52	6	2	2	23	11	9	0	5	R	R	5-11	182	7-22-70	1993	Altoona, Pa.
Evans, Michael	.218	96	317	26	69	15	1	8	36	27	79	0	2	L	R	6-0	190	8-7-72	1993	Houston, Texas
Fasano, Sal	.227	23	88	12	20	2	1	2	7	5	16	0	0	R	R	6-2	220	8-10-71	1993	Hanover Park, Ill.
Gonzalez, Raul	.292	86	308	36	90	19	3	11	49	14	54	8	4	R	R	5-8	175	12-27-73	1991	Villa Carolina, P.R.
Jimenez, Oscar	.251	121	374	42	94	18	4	1	31	53	92	11	8	R	R	6-0	190	12-18-74	1991	Panama City, Panama
Knowles, Brian	.000	9	25	1	0	0	0	0	1	0	5	0	0	R	R	6-1	190	10-22-71	1994	Melbourne, Fla.
Lopez, Mendy	.271	130	428	41	116	29	3	2	36	28	73	18	10	R	R	6-2	165	10-15-74	1992	Santo Domingo, D.R.
Medrano, Anthony	.285	123	460	69	131	26	6	3	43	34	42	11	6	R	R	5-11	155	12-8-74	1993	Long Beach, Calif.
Mendez, Carlos	.273	107	396	46	108	19	2	7	61	18	36	0	4	R	R	6-1	195	6-18-74	1991	Caracas, Venez.
Montilla, Julio	.222	8	27	0	6	0	0	0	1	4	6	0	0	S	R	5-10	170	6-9-73	1992	Caracas, Venez.
Nunez, Sergio	.237	124	460	63	109	10	2	4	25	51	66	33	19	R	R	5-11	155	1-3-75	1992	Santo Domingo, D.R.
Oglesby, Luke	.200	53	60	18	12	0	0	0	1	4	21	19	6	L	R	5-7	155	6-27-73	1993	Fort Collins, Colo.
Paul, Kortney	.111	8	9	1	1	0	0	0	0	1	5	0	0	R	R	6-1	190	1-7-72	1994	Fort Worth, Texas
Sweeney, Mike	.310	99	332	61	103	23	1	18	53	60	39	6	1	R	R	6-1	195	7-22-73	1991	Ontario, Calif.
Teeters, Brian	.228	64	162	25	37	7	0	6	26	19	51	11	5	L	L	5-10	175	11-12-72	1992	Bakersfield, Calif.

GAMES BY POSITION: C—Brooks 53, Evans 1, Fasano 17, Mendez 1, Paul 7, Sweeney 72. **1B**—Byington 8, Evans 43, Fasano 2, Mendez 95. **2B**—Byington 9, Carr 1, Medrano 12, Montilla 5, Nunez 124. **3B**—Byington 12, Diaz 32, Lopez 108, Montilla 1, Sweeney 1. **SS**—Byington 13, Lopez 22, Medrano 113, Montilla 3. **OF**—Byington 48, Carr 1, Delaney 110, Evans 15, Gonzalez 76, Jimenez 119, Knowles 7, Oglesby 39, Teeters 51.

PITCHING	W	L	ERA	G	GS	CG	SV	IP	H	R	ER	BB	SO	B	T	HT	WT	DOB	1st Yr	Resides
Anderson, Eric	3	1	2.93	16	0	0	2	28	28	9	9	4	19	R	R	6-1	190	10-20-74	1993	Blue Springs, Mo.
Atkinson, Neil	1	1	2.86	8	0	0	3	22	21	7	7	6	20	L	L	6-0	190	1-14-71	1993	San Antonio, Texas
Brewer, Nevin	1	1	0.93	17	0	0	8	29	19	4	3	15	20	R	R	6-4	195	8-1-71	1993	Wilmington, N.C.
Byrdak, Tim	11	5	2.16	27	26	0	0	166	118	46	40	48	127	L	L	5-11	170	10-31-73	1994	Oak Forest, Ill.
Connolly, Chris	5	2	3.48	27	0	0	1	44	38	23	17	23	29	L	L	6-2	192	12-4-70	1991	Lynchburg, Va.
Dickens, John	3	1	1.77	48	0	0	9	76	57	17	15	17	59	L	L	6-3	195	6-25-71	1992	Fort Worth, Texas
Downs, John	1	0	5.40	8	0	0	0	12	19	7	7	2	7	R	R	6-2	185	9-15-70	1991	Englewood, Ohio
Evans, Bart	4	1	2.89	16	6	0	2	47	30	21	15	44	47	R	R	6-1	190	12-30-70	1992	Ozark, Mo.
Flury, Pat	2	1	2.45	15	0	0	1	22	18	6	6	7	13	R	R	6-2	205	3-14-73	1993	Sparks, Nev.
Gamboa, Javier	3	4	4.04	8	8	0	0	49	42	23	22	13	33	R	R	6-1	185	3-17-74	1994	Paso Robles, Calif.
Grundy, Phil	6	6	3.31	20	16	0	1	106	106	46	39	32	90	R	R	6-2	195	9-8-72	1993	Somerset, Ky.
Hodges, Kevin	2	3	4.53	12	10	0	0	54	53	31	27	25	27	R	R	6-2	190	6-24-73	1991	Spring, Texas
Rawitzer, Kevin	2	0	2.33	15	1	0	3	27	21	8	7	8	22	L	L	5-10	185	2-28-71	1993	Danville, Calif.
Ray, Ken	6	4	2.69	13	13	1	0	77	74	32	23	22	63	R	R	6-2	160	11-27-74	1993	Roswell, Ga.
Roberts, Ray	1	2	3.32	13	0	0	4	19	18	7	7	2	16	L	L	6-0	190	6-29-73	1994	American Canyon, Calif.
Rosado, Jose	10	7	3.13	25	25	0	0	138	128	53	48	30	117	L	L	6-0	175	11-9-74	1994	Dorado, P.R.
Rusch, Glendon	14	6	1.74	26	26	1	0	166	110	41	32	34	147	L	L	6-2	170	11-7-74	1993	Seattle, Wash.

PITCHING	W	L	ERA	G	GS	CG	SV	IP	H	R	ER	BB	SO	B	T	HT	WT	DOB	1st Yr	Resides
Sheehan, Chris............	2	1	1.86	13	0	0	3	19	7	5	4	2	27	R	R	6-4	205	1-5-69	1992	Kirkland, Wash.
Sinnes, David	0	2	3.04	18	0	0	3	24	15	12	8	24	34	R	R	5-11	185	5-12-71	1993	Miami, Fla.
Smith, Toby	5	7	3.08	30	7	0	4	79	67	32	27	20	65	R	R	6-6	225	11-16-71	1993	Guthrie, Okla.
Towns, Ryan	1	0	5.63	12	0	0	1	16	12	11	10	18	8	R	R	6-2	210	6-26-72	1991	Gonzales, Texas
Winkle, Ken	1	1	10.54	11	0	0	1	14	16	18	16	10	14	R	R	6-2	235	1-8-72	1994	Seminole, Fla.

SPRINGFIELD   A
MIDWEST LEAGUE

BATTING	AVG	G	AB	R	H	2B	3B	HR	RBI	BB	SO	SB	CS	B	T	HT	WT	DOB	1st Yr	Resides
Brandon, Jelani	.243	74	230	32	56	12	1	3	37	35	37	6	2	R	R	6-1	190	3-21-74	1992	Florence, Ky.
Burgos, Carlos	.181	27	72	8	13	2	0	0	8	7	11	0	0	R	R	6-2	225	6-13-72	1991	Luquillo, P.R.
Cedeno, Eduardo........	.224	81	210	30	47	7	2	7	27	14	67	7	3	R	R	6-0	150	8-2-72	1990	La Romana, D.R.
Delaney, Sean............	.298	62	188	24	56	8	2	5	22	19	27	5	1	R	R	5-11	190	5-22-70	1992	Berwyn, Ill.
Hansen, Jed	.258	122	414	86	107	27	7	9	50	78	73	44	10	R	R	6-1	195	8-19-72	1994	Olympia, Wash.
McNally, Sean	.271	132	479	60	130	28	8	12	79	35	119	6	3	R	R	6-4	205	12-14-72	1994	Rye, N.Y.
Mendez, Rodolfo	.276	129	449	70	124	28	11	10	72	34	121	40	10	R	R	5-11	180	8-22-74	1994	Santo Domingo, D.R.
Mendoza, Francisco.....	.253	96	308	38	78	18	1	11	49	24	65	4	1	R	R	6-0	190	10-4-72	1992	Santo Domingo, D.R.
Oglesby, Luke	.197	50	122	27	24	0	0	2	6	19	26	24	5	L	R	5-7	155	6-27-71	1993	Fort Collins, Colo.
Price, Chris................	.264	52	159	22	42	7	1	3	14	23	32	6	2	R	R	6-1	192	8-28-72	1995	Lebanon, Tenn.
Prieto, Alejandro..........	.251	124	431	61	108	9	3	2	44	40	69	11	7	S	R	5-11	150	6-19-76	1993	Caracas, Venez.
Ramos, Jeff	.219	39	96	14	21	8	0	4	20	9	25	0	0	L	R	6-2	190	4-14-75	1994	Toronto, Ontario
Rocha, Juan	.233	94	292	53	68	21	1	10	41	16	65	5	2	R	R	5-11	175	9-8-73	1994	Santa Fe, Calif.
Smith, Matt	.226	117	412	49	93	18	1	6	46	24	96	8	5	L	L	6-4	215	6-2-76	1994	Grants Pass, Ore.
Sparks, Rodney	.219	43	96	11	21	4	0	1	7	8	14	0	0	R	R	6-0	165	11-7-71	1993	Phoenix, Ariz.
Treanor, Matt	.185	75	211	17	39	6	2	3	19	21	59	1	1	R	R	6-1	188	3-3-76	1994	Anaheim, Calif.
Walls, Eric	.227	101	299	53	68	14	1	2	21	17	65	20	7	L	L	6-0	155	9-13-72	1992	Centralia, Ill.
Welch, Coby	.171	19	35	3	6	0	0	0	1	3	9	0	0	R	R	6-2	195	9-6-73	1994	Tallahassee, Fla.

GAMES BY POSITION: C—Burgos 12, Delaney 45, Ramos 12, Treanor 74, Welch 18. 1B—Burgos 8, McNally 1, Mendoza 20, Smith 116. 2B—Cedeno 7, Hansen 120, Sparks 23. 3B—Cedeno 6, McNally 128, Mendoza 12, Sparks 4. SS—Cedeno 26, Prieto 123, Sparks 6. OF—Brandon 57, Cedeno 29, Mendez 124, Oglesby 42, Price 48, Rocha 75, Walls 83.

PITCHING	W	L	ERA	G	GS	CG	SV	IP	H	R	ER	BB	SO	B	T	HT	WT	DOB	1st Yr	Resides
Anderson, Eric	9	5	3.40	21	14	1	1	93	89	39	35	34	52	R	R	6-1	190	10-20-74	1993	Blue Springs, Mo.
Bernal, Manuel	1	5	7.38	8	8	0	0	43	55	37	35	9	17	R	R	6-2	163	4-29-74	1994	Los Mochis, Mexico
Brewer, Billy................	0	0	0.00	1	0	0	1	2	2	1	0	1	2	L	L	6-1	175	4-15-68	1990	Waco, Texas
Brixey, Dustin	4	5	3.79	36	8	0	2	102	101	51	43	40	44	R	R	6-4	190	10-16-73	1993	Jay, Okla.
Carter, Lance	9	5	3.99	27	24	1	0	138	151	77	61	22	118	R	R	6-1	170	12-18-74	1994	Bradenton, Fla.
Fitzpatrick, Ken	2	2	3.92	12	7	0	0	44	36	26	19	17	29	R	R	6-6	230	8-25-74	1992	Bell Gardens, Calif.
Flury, Pat	2	6	4.31	34	0	0	1	54	65	32	26	24	35	R	R	6-2	205	3-14-73	1993	Sparks, Nev.
Gamboa, Javier	6	6	3.15	19	19	1	0	106	83	45	37	32	66	R	R	6-1	185	3-17-74	1994	Paso Robles, Calif.
MacDonald, Mike	6	5	3.30	55	0	0	12	63	49	24	23	27	49	R	R	6-0	165	8-12-72	1994	Miami, Fla.
Mull, Blaine	4	10	4.88	25	25	0	0	125	142	79	68	50	71	R	R	6-4	186	8-14-76	1994	Morganton, N.C.
Nelson, Rodney	6	10	5.46	25	21	1	0	115	131	82	70	73	58	R	R	6-6	230	8-28-74	1994	Wharton, Texas
Phillips, Marc	2	3	3.05	38	2	0	3	86	88	47	29	38	41	L	L	6-2	195	5-30-72	1994	Waynesboro, Va.
Ritter, Jason	1	0	12.34	7	0	0	0	12	19	20	16	6	12	R	R	6-2	185	7-16-74	1994	Tulsa, Okla.
Robbins, Michael........	2	3	4.50	8	8	0	0	40	47	22	20	10	26	L	L	6-1	190	2-7-74	1995	Oakland, Calif.
Roberts, Ray	2	5	4.52	38	0	0	1	66	86	38	33	17	43	L	L	6-2	195	6-29-73	1994	American Canyon, Calif.
Steed, Sam................	2	0	2.45	8	0	0	0	15	14	4	4	6	14	L	L	5-10	170	2-28-69	1994	Malden, Mass.
Towns, Ryan	0	1	5.58	18	1	0	0	31	33	24	19	17	31	R	R	6-2	210	6-26-72	1991	Gonzales, Texas
Upchurch, Wayne........	2	3	4.25	18	2	0	1	30	40	19	14	4	13	R	R	6-7	195	3-15-72	1994	Carrollton, Texas
Winkle, Ken	1	1	9.49	9	0	0	0	12	16	13	13	2	8	R	R	6-2	235	1-8-72	1994	Seminole, Fla.

SPOKANE   A
NORTHWEST LEAGUE

BATTING	AVG	G	AB	R	H	2B	3B	HR	RBI	BB	SO	SB	CS	B	T	HT	WT	DOB	1st Yr	Resides
Escandon, Emiliano	.318	13	44	7	14	1	1	1	12	6	11	1	0	S	R	5-10	170	11-6-74	1995	Ontario, Calif.
Finnieston, Adam	.237	10	38	4	9	0	0	0	4	1	9	0	1	R	R	6-0	190	10-11-72	1995	Miami, Fla.
Frazier, Tyrone............	.170	51	147	15	25	3	0	0	9	11	46	8	4	R	R	6-0	183	10-26-74	1993	Shreveport, La.
Hallmark, Patrick	.304	56	227	36	69	11	0	4	25	13	37	5	3	R	R	6-0	170	12-31-73	1995	Houston, Texas
Kortmeyer, Scott	.141	21	64	6	9	2	0	0	2	5	26	0	0	R	R	6-2	200	11-6-73	1995	Glendale, Ariz.
Lewis, Dwayne	.208	46	149	24	31	2	1	1	8	30	55	8	8	L	R	5-9	160	5-18-73	1995	Brooklyn, N.Y.
Melito, Mark	.250	61	200	24	50	7	1	3	20	27	30	2	2	R	R	6-1	175	2-4-72	1995	Glen Ridge, N.J.
Miranda, Tony	.271	71	266	53	72	17	0	2	22	28	36	15	10	R	R	5-10	175	5-23-73	1995	Lynwood, Calif.
Moreno, Victor	.167	7	24	3	4	1	0	0	0	2	10	0	0	R	R	6-2	185	9-7-75	1994	Corona, N.Y.
Nations, Joel	.214	40	140	15	30	6	1	0	16	20	26	1	1	R	R	5-10	175	7-27-72	1995	Seattle, Wash.
Paulin, Randy	.204	54	191	14	39	6	0	3	22	14	49	0	1	R	R	6-3	215	9-1-71	1995	Miamisburg, Ohio
Pinoni, Scott	.184	11	38	4	7	2	0	0	4	5	9	0	0	R	R	6-1	250	3-28-73	1994	Columbus, Ohio
Quinn, Mark	.284	44	162	28	46	12	2	6	37	15	28	0	1	R	R	6-1	185	5-21-74	1995	San Dimas, Calif.
Robles, Juan	.000	4	9	0	0	0	0	0	0	1	5	0	0	R	R	5-9	178	3-17-72	1995	Hermosillo, Mexico
Roland, William	.218	70	262	26	57	16	1	4	30	26	53	1	1	R	R	5-10	190	10-23-73	1994	Corpus Christi, Texas
Schafer, Brett	.195	62	205	23	40	7	0	1	19	39	42	11	1	R	R	5-11	175	7-3-73	1995	Malibu, Calif.
Vida, James	.323	74	291	38	94	13	1	4	39	19	32	0	0	L	L	6-0	195	9-13-70	1995	St. Petersburg, Fla.
Weathersby, Leon........	.229	37	118	13	27	4	3	1	12	9	42	2	3	R	R	6-0	180	5-13-75	1993	Los Angeles, Calif.

GAMES BY POSITION: C—Hallmark 51, Paulin 24, Robles 4, Vida 1. 1B—Hallmark 2, Moreno 3, Paulin 14, Pinoni 4, Vida 57. 2B—Lewis 13, Nations 37, Schafer 28. 3B—Escandon 2, Quinn 13, Roland 58, Schafer 6. SS—Escandon 10, Lewis 9, Melito 61. OF—Finnieston 9, Frazier 50, Kortmeyer 21, Lewis 22, Miranda 60, Moreno 5, Quinn 19, Schafer 29, Weathersby 34.

PITCHING	W	L	ERA	G	GS	CG	SV	IP	H	R	ER	BB	SO	B	T	HT	WT	DOB	1st Yr	Resides
Adam, Justin	3	4	5.29	15	8	0	1	49	45	34	29	31	35	R	R	6-4	218	8-22-74	1994	Windsor, Ontario
Albrecht, Jon	2	2	3.38	17	0	0	6	21	14	8	8	12	15	L	L	6-1	200	10-31-71	1995	Liberal, Kan.
Charles, Israel	1	0	4.50	4	0	0	0	6	6	3	3	3	5	R	R	6-3	176	6-20-73	1991	El Seybo, D.R.
Hodge, Hal	3	1	4.26	16	15	0	0	70	81	39	33	20	45	L	L	6-3	220	9-11-72	1995	Millbrook, Ala.

PITCHING	W	L	ERA	G	GS	CG	SV	IP	H	R	ER	BB	SO	B	T	HT	WT	DOB	1st Yr	Resides
Judice, Bryan	0	1	7.91	14	0	0	1	19	29	18	17	10	14	R	R	6-2	185	10-30-72	1995	Riverside, Calif.
Kaysner, Brent	0	2	1.56	19	0	0	4	35	15	7	6	24	37	R	R	6-6	235	4-23-74	1994	Bothell, Wash.
Liz, Jesus	0	0	7.11	9	0	0	0	13	19	15	10	12	11	L	L	6-3	200	4-12-75	1995	Hialeah, Fla.
Prihoda, Stephen	1	6	3.25	14	13	1	0	69	65	36	25	18	63	R	L	6-6	220	12-7-72	1995	Weimer, Texas
Ritter, Jason	3	1	3.21	10	4	0	0	34	25	12	12	15	29	R	R	6-2	185	7-16-74	1994	Tulsa, Okla.
Robbins, Mike	1	3	2.33	5	5	0	0	27	23	9	7	6	16	L	L	6-1	190	2-7-74	1995	Oakland, Calif.
Saier, Matthew	1	2	3.31	16	0	0	4	35	24	14	13	12	41	R	R	6-2	192	1-29-73	1995	Gulf Breeze, Fla.
Sanders, Allen	4	5	4.47	14	10	0	0	56	67	43	28	18	36	R	R	6-3	195	4-15-75	1995	Deer Park, Texas
Sanders, Craig	3	1	1.94	22	0	0	3	46	32	11	10	24	32	S	R	6-4	225	7-31-72	1995	Lincoln, Neb.
Santiago, Jose	2	4	3.14	22	0	0	1	49	60	26	17	20	32	R	R	6-3	200	11-5-74	1994	Loiza, P.R.
Soto, Daniel	0	3	5.06	3	2	0	0	11	11	6	6	4	10	R	R	6-0	200	1-21-74	1994	Mexico City, Mexico
Upchurch, Wayne	1	1	6.39	7	0	0	0	13	22	12	9	5	7	R	R	6-7	195	3-15-72	1994	Carrollton, Texas
Villarreal, Modesto	8	2	2.90	16	11	0	0	81	73	30	26	23	57	R	R	6-0	195	10-29-75	1993	Panama City, Panama
Williamson, Jeremy	3	1	1.43	11	7	0	0	44	32	12	7	9	35	L	L	6-3	190	8-19-74	1995	Sumrall, Miss.
Winders, Brian	0	1	30.00	2	1	0	0	3	10	10	10	3	2	R	R	6-4	205	9-21-72	1995	Baton Rouge, La.

FORT MYERS   R

GULF COAST LEAGUE

BATTING	AVG	G	AB	R	H	2B	3B	HR	RBI	BB	SO	SB	CS	B	T	HT	WT	DOB	1st Yr	Resides
Bales, Taylor	.000	8	14	2	0	0	0	0	0	4	6	0	0	R	R	6-0	195	9-25-73	1995	Pasadena, Texas
Beltran, Carlos	.278	52	180	29	50	9	0	0	23	13	30	5	3	S	R	6-1	175	4-24-77	1995	Manati, P.R.
Blosser, Doug	.255	50	161	18	41	10	1	7	33	32	39	0	0	L	R	6-3	215	10-1-76	1995	Sarasota, Fla.
Cepeda, Jose	.348	54	187	32	65	6	4	0	21	15	5	2	2	R	R	6-0	185	8-1-74	1995	Fajardo, P.R.
Coffee, Gary	.328	52	189	30	62	9	3	11	45	28	38	2	0	R	R	6-3	195	3-13-75	1994	Atlanta, Ga.
Dasher, Melvin	.200	16	35	3	7	2	0	1	5	1	15	0	0	R	R	6-2	195	9-9-76	1995	Palatka, Fla.
Febles, Carlos	.282	54	188	40	53	13	5	3	20	26	30	16	8	R	R	5-11	165	5-24-76	1994	La Romana, D.R.
Lebron, Juan	.177	47	147	17	26	5	2	2	13	10	38	0	3	R	R	6-4	195	6-7-77	1995	Arroyo, P.R.
Longueira, Tony	.242	41	95	12	23	5	0	1	13	9	11	3	0	R	R	6-0	170	9-24-74	1995	Pembroke Pines, Fla.
Montas, Ricardo	.071	22	28	2	2	0	0	1	3	3	6	0	0	R	R	6-1	160	3-9-77	1994	Santo Domingo, D.R.
Montilla, Julio	.239	17	46	6	11	3	0	0	3	1	8	0	0	S	R	5-10	170	6-9-73	1992	Caracas, Venez.
Pitts, Shedrick	.253	34	79	25	20	1	0	2	6	13	23	11	1	S	R	6-1	180	3-13-76	1994	Seattle, Wash.
Radcliff, Victor	.260	38	123	25	32	8	2	4	15	12	24	3	6	R	R	5-10	180	9-23-76	1995	Beech Island, S.C.
Ramos, Jeff	.227	28	75	10	17	4	0	3	7	7	16	0	1	L	R	6-2	190	4-14-75	1994	Toronto, Ontario
Robles, Juan	.162	29	74	9	12	3	0	0	7	9	9	0	0	R	R	5-9	178	3-17-72	1994	Hermosillo, Mexico
Stafford, Kimani	.164	39	67	13	11	1	1	0	4	12	30	0	0	R	R	5-11	170	6-17-76	1995	Richmond, Calif.
Tillero, Adrian	.252	36	103	14	26	7	1	1	11	8	33	1	1	R	R	6-0	165	4-26-78	1995	Tampa, Fla.
Welch, Coby	.279	16	43	7	12	2	0	0	9	3	8	0	0	R	R	6-0	195	9-6-73	1994	Tallahassee, Fla.

GAMES BY POSITION: C—Bales 8, Ramos 25, Robles 28, Welch 14. **1B**—Blosser 20, Coffee 34, Montilla 10, Ramos 3, Welch 1. **2B**—Cepeda 4, Febles 54, Longueira 3, Montas 5, Montilla 2, Stafford 1. **3B**—Cepeda 52, Longueira 3, Montas 9, Montilla 1, Radcliff 8. **SS**—Cepeda 4, Longueira 37, Montas 6, Montilla 5, Radcliff 26. **OF**—Beltran 51, Coffee 2, Dasher 12, Lebron 46, Pitts 32, Radcliff 1, Stafford 33, Tillero 36.

PITCHING	W	L	ERA	G	GS	CG	SV	IP	H	R	ER	BB	SO	B	T	HT	WT	DOB	1st Yr	Resides
Aguilar, Alonzo	0	1	3.76	15	1	0	1	26	26	14	11	10	24	R	R	6-0	185	12-15-74	1995	Los Angeles, Calif.
Bernal, Manuel	3	0	1.36	6	6	0	0	33	29	9	5	4	25	R	R	6-2	163	4-29-74	1994	Los Mochis, Mexico
Burton, Jamie	0	0	8.25	6	1	0	0	12	13	11	11	10	14	R	L	6-5	198	5-28-75	1995	Central Point, Ore.
Carmano, Kevin	6	1	2.12	15	0	0	2	34	25	18	8	9	16	R	R	6-1	185		1995	Panama City, Panama
Fleming, Dave	0	0	0.00	1	1	0	0	3	2	1	0	0	1	L	L	6-3	200	11-7-69	1990	Mahopac, N.Y.
Key, Francis	1	2	2.57	16	0	0	2	28	17	13	8	12	34	R	R	5-10	162	10-4-76	1995	Cantonment, Fla.
Martin, Jeffrey	3	1	1.47	11	10	1	0	55	35	12	9	11	53	R	R	6-4	195	1-25-74	1995	Las Vegas, Nev.
Meady, Todd	3	3	2.63	12	6	0	2	38	33	21	11	6	26	R	R	6-4	216	9-13-76	1995	Middlebury, Conn.
Moore, David	2	2	4.18	14	1	0	2	28	28	17	13	12	12	R	R	6-2	205	2-13-76	1995	Ft. Lauderdale, Fla.
Moreno, Orber	1	1	2.45	8	3	0	0	22	15	9	6	7	21	R	R	6-4	140	4-27-77	1994	Los Autos, Venez.
Mullis, Steven	2	1	2.92	8	1	0	1	12	7	6	4	7	13	L	L	6-4	189	2-19-75	1995	Gastonia, N.C.
Paredes, Carlos	4	2	3.53	10	10	0	0	51	56	28	20	17	37	R	R	6-0	170	5-10-76	1995	Sabana de la Mar, D.R.
Penny, Tony	2	0	5.06	10	0	0	0	16	17	9	9	4	7	R	R	6-4	185	3-23-76	1995	Newberry, S.C.
Ritter, Jason	0	0	0.00	2	0	0	1	4	3	1	0	1	2	R	R	6-2	185	7-16-74	1994	Tulsa, Okla.
Sanders, Allen	0	0	0.00	1	0	0	1	2	1	0	0	0	3	R	R	6-3	195	4-15-75	1995	Deer Park, Texas
Shannon, Bobby	1	1	3.25	16	0	0	2	28	28	11	10	3	26	R	L	5-11	185	9-21-77	1995	Shippensburg, Pa.
Thorn, Todd	4	2	3.23	11	10	0	0	47	43	23	17	14	58	L	L	6-1	175	11-4-76	1995	Stratford, Ontario
Wallace, Jeff	5	3	1.23	12	7	0	1	44	28	20	6	15	51	L	L	6-2	237	4-12-76	1995	Paris, Ohio

LOS ANGELES DODGERS

Manager: Tommy Lasorda. **1995 Record:** 78-66, .542 (1st, NL West).

BATTING	AVG	G	AB	R	H	2B	3B	HR	RBI	BB	SO	SB	CS	B	T	HT	WT	DOB	1st Yr	Resides
Ashley, Billy	.237	81	215	17	51	5	0	8	27	25	88	0	0	R	R	6-7	230	7-11-70	1988	Belleville, Mich.
Busch, Mike	.235	13	17	3	4	0	0	3	6	0	7	0	0	R	R	6-5	241	7-7-68	1990	Farmington, Iowa
Butler, Brett	.274	39	146	24	40	5	2	0	13	24	9	11	1	L	L	5-10	160	6-15-57	1979	Atlanta, Ga.
2-team (90 NY)	.300	129	513	78	154	18	9	1	38	67	51	32	8							
Castro, Juan	.250	11	4	0	1	0	0	0	0	1	1	0	0	R	R	5-10	163	6-20-72	1991	Los Mochis, Mexico
Cedeno, Roger	.238	40	42	4	10	2	0	0	3	3	10	1	0	S	R	6-1	165	8-16-74	1992	Carabobo, Venez.
DeShields, Delino	.256	127	425	66	109	18	3	8	37	63	83	39	14	L	R	6-1	170	1-15-69	1987	West Palm Beach, Fla.
Fonville, Chad	.276	88	308	41	85	6	1	0	16	23	39	20	5	S	R	5-7	155	3-5-71	1992	Midway Park, N.C.
2-team (14 Mtl.)	.278	102	320	43	89	6	1	0	16	23	42	20	7							
Garcia, Karim	.200	13	20	1	4	0	0	0	0	0	4	0	0	L	L	6-0	200	10-29-75	1993	Ciudad Obregon, Mexico
Gwynn, Chris	.214	67	84	8	18	3	2	1	10	6	23	0	0	L	L	6-0	220	10-13-64	1985	Alta Loma, Calif.
Hansen, Dave	.287	100	181	19	52	10	0	1	14	28	28	0	0	L	R	6-0	195	11-24-68	1986	Long Beach, Calif.
Hernandez, Carlos	.149	45	94	3	14	1	0	2	8	7	25	0	0	R	R	5-11	185	5-24-67	1985	Caracas, Venez.
Hollandsworth, Todd	.233	41	103	16	24	2	0	5	13	10	29	2	1	L	L	6-2	193	4-20-73	1991	San Ramon, Calif.
Ingram, Garey	.200	44	55	5	11	2	0	0	3	9	8	3	0	R	R	5-11	178	7-25-70	1990	Columbus, Ga.
Karros, Eric	.298	143	551	83	164	29	3	32	105	61	115	4	4	R	R	6-4	205	11-4-67	1988	Manhattan Beach, Calif.
Kelly, Roberto	.279	112	409	47	114	19	2	6	48	15	65	15	7	R	R	6-2	192	10-1-64	1982	Panama City, Panama
2-team (24 Mtl.)	.278	136	504	58	140	23	2	7	52	22	79	19	10							
Mondesi, Raul	.285	139	536	91	153	23	6	26	88	33	96	27	4	R	R	5-11	210	3-12-71	1988	New York, N.Y.
Munoz, Noe	.000	2	1	0	0	0	0	0	0	0	0	0	0	R	R	6-0	195	11-11-67	1994	Los Mochis, Mexico
Offerman, Jose	.287	119	429	69	123	14	6	4	33	69	67	2	7	S	R	6-0	160	11-8-68	1988	San Pedro de Macoris, D.R.
Parker, Rick	.276	27	29	3	8	0	0	0	4	2	4	1	1	R	R	6-0	185	3-20-63	1985	Independence, Mo.
Piazza, Mike	.346	112	434	82	150	17	0	32	93	39	80	1	0	R	R	6-3	200	9-4-68	1989	Valley Forge, Pa.
Prince, Tom	.200	18	40	3	8	2	1	1	4	4	10	0	0	R	R	5-11	185	8-13-64	1984	Bradenton, Fla.
Pye, Eddie	.000	7	8	0	0	0	0	0	0	0	4	0	0	R	R	5-10	170	2-13-67	1988	Columbia, Tenn.
Rodriguez, Henry	.263	21	80	6	21	4	1	1	10	5	17	0	1	L	L	6-1	210	11-8-67	1986	New York, N.Y.
Schofield, Dick	.100	9	10	0	1	0	0	0	1	3	0	0	0	R	R	5-10	178	11-21-62	1981	Laguna Hills, Calif.
Treadway, Jeff	.118	17	17	2	2	0	1	0	3	0	2	0	0	L	R	5-11	175	1-22-63	1984	Griffin, Ga.
Wallach, Tim	.266	97	327	24	87	22	2	9	38	27	69	0	0	R	R	6-3	200	9-14-57	1979	Tustin, Calif.
Webster, Mitch	.179	54	56	6	10	1	1	1	3	4	14	0	0	S	L	6-1	191	5-16-59	1977	Great Bend, Kan.
Williams, Reggie	.091	15	11	2	1	0	0	0	1	2	3	0	0	S	R	6-1	180	5-5-66	1988	Laurens, S.C.

PITCHING	W	L	ERA	G	GS	CG	SV	IP	H	R	ER	BB	SO	B	T	HT	WT	DOB	1st Yr	Resides
Astacio, Pedro	7	8	4.24	48	11	1	0	104	103	53	49	29	80	R	R	6-2	195	11-28-69	1988	Miami, Fla.
Banks, Willie	0	2	4.03	6	6	0	0	29	36	21	13	16	23	R	R	6-1	202	2-27-69	1987	Jersey City, N.J.
Bruske, Jim	0	0	4.50	9	0	0	1	10	12	7	5	4	5	R	R	6-1	185	10-7-64	1986	Palmdale, Calif.
Candiotti, Tom	7	14	3.50	30	30	1	0	190	187	93	74	58	141	R	R	6-2	220	8-31-57	1979	Danville, Calif.
Cummings, John	3	1	3.00	35	0	0	0	39	38	16	13	10	21	L	L	6-3	200	5-10-69	1990	Laguna Niguel, Calif.
Daal, Omar	4	0	7.20	28	0	0	0	20	29	16	16	15	11	L	L	6-3	185	3-1-72	1990	Valencia, Venez.
Eischen, Joey	0	0	3.10	17	0	0	0	20	19	9	7	11	15	L	L	6-1	190	5-25-70	1989	West Covina, Calif.
Guthrie, Mark	0	2	3.66	24	0	0	0	20	19	11	8	9	19	S	L	6-4	205	9-22-65	1987	Bradenton, Fla.
Hansell, Greg	0	1	7.45	20	0	0	0	19	29	17	16	6	13	R	R	6-5	215	3-12-71	1989	La Palma, Calif.
Martinez, Ramon	17	7	3.66	30	30	4	0	206	176	95	84	81	138	L	R	6-4	173	3-22-68	1985	Santo Domingo, D.R.
Murphy, Rob	0	1	12.60	6	0	0	0	5	6	7	7	3	2	L	L	6-2	215	5-26-60	1981	Miami, Fla.
Nomo, Hideo	13	6	2.54	28	28	4	0	191	124	63	54	78	236	R	R	6-2	226	8-31-68	1995	Osaka, Japan
Osuna, Antonio	2	4	4.43	39	0	0	0	45	39	22	22	20	46	R	R	5-11	160	4-12-73	1991	Sinaloa, Mexico
Park, Chan Ho	0	0	4.50	2	1	0	0	4	2	2	2	2	7	R	R	6-2	185	6-30-73	1994	Glendale, Calif.
Parra, Jose	0	0	4.35	8	0	0	0	10	10	8	5	6	7	R	R	5-11	160	11-28-72	1990	Santiago, D.R.
Rodriguez, Felix	1	1	2.53	11	0	0	0	11	11	3	3	5	8	R	R	6-1	190	12-5-72	1990	Monte Cristi, D.R.
Seanez, Rudy	1	3	6.75	37	0	0	3	35	39	27	26	18	29	R	R	5-11	185	10-20-68	1985	El Centro, Calif.
Tapani, Kevin	4	2	5.05	13	11	0	0	57	72	37	32	14	43	R	R	6-0	175	2-18-64	1986	Eden Prairie, Minn.
Valdes, Ismael	13	11	3.05	33	27	6	1	198	168	76	67	51	150	R	R	6-3	183	8-21-73	1991	Tamaulipas, Mexico
Williams, Todd	0	0	5.12	16	0	0	0	19	19	11	11	11	5	R	R	6-3	185	2-13-71	1991	East Syracuse, N.Y.
Worrell, Todd	4	1	2.02	59	0	0	32	62	50	15	14	19	61	R	R	6-5	200	9-28-59	1982	Temple City, Calif.

FIELDING

Catcher	PCT	G	PO	A	E	DP	PB
Hernandez	.983	41	210	25	4	4	5
Munoz	1.000	2	6	0	0	0	0
Piazza	.990	112	805	52	9	8	12
Prince	.988	17	71	8	1	2	2

First Base	PCT	G	PO	A	E	DP
Busch	1.000	2	8	1	0	2
Gwynn	1.000	2	5	1	0	2
Karros	.995	143	1234	109	7	101
Rodriguez	1.000	1	1	0	0	0
Wallach	1.000	1	11	0	0	0

Second Base	PCT	G	PO	A	E	DP
DeShields	.980	113	204	330	11	55
Fonville	.966	36	71	98	6	14
Ingram	1.000	7	7	11	0	3
Treadway	1.000	1	1	1	0	1

Third Base	PCT	G	PO	A	E	DP
Busch	.875	10	2	5	1	0
Castro	1.000	7	2	3	0	0
Hansen	.933	58	27	70	7	6
Ingram	.750	12	9	15	8	0
Parker	.000	2	0	0	0	0
Pye	.000	2	0	0	0	0
Schofield	.000	1	0	0	0	0
Treadway	.000	2	0	0	0	0
Wallach	.976	96	50	156	5	10

Shortstop	PCT	G	PO	A	E	DP
Castro	1.000	4	1	4	0	2
Fonville	.971	38	38	95	4	13
Offerman	.932	115	165	312	35	61
Parker	.000	2	0	0	0	0
Schofield	1.000	3	3	9	0	3

Outfield	PCT	G	PO	A	E	DP
Ashley	.972	69	102	2	3	0
Butler	.987	39	75	0	1	0
Cedeno	.977	36	43	0	1	0
Fonville	.947	11	16	2	1	1
Garcia	1.000	5	5	0	0	0
Gwynn	1.000	17	21	0	0	0
Hollandsworth	.938	37	60	1	4	0
Ingram	1.000	4	1	0	0	0
Kelly	.969	110	183	2	6	1
Mondesi	.980	138	282	16	6	3
Parker	1.000	21	20	1	0	1
Rodriguez	1.000	20	36	0	0	0
Webster	1.000	25	12	0	0	0
Williams	1.000	14	6	0	0	0

DODGERS

GEORGE GOJKOVICH

Dodgers outfielder Raul
Mondesi hit .285 with
26 homers

**Dodgers minor league
Player of the Year
Adam Riggs**

LARRY GOREN

FARM SYSTEM

Director of Minor League Operations: Charlie Blaney.

Class	Farm Team	League	W	L	Pct.	Finish*	Manager	First Yr
AAA	Albuquerque (N.M.) Dukes	Pacific Coast	75	69	.521	5th (10)	Rick Dempsey	1963
AA	San Antonio (Texas) Missions	Texas	64	72	.471	6th (8)	John Shelby	1977
#A	San Bernardino (Calif.) Spirit	California	84	54	.609	1st+ (10)	Ron Roenicke	1995
#A	Vero Beach (Fla.) Dodgers	Florida State	74	59	.556	4th (14)	Jon Debus	1980
A	Yakima (Wash.) Bears	Northwest	27	48	.360	8th (8)	Joe Vavra	1988
#R	Great Falls (Mont.) Dodgers	Pioneer	31	38	.449	6th (8)	John Shoemaker	1984

*Finish in overall standings (No. of teams in league)   #Advanced level   +Won league championship

ORGANIZATION LEADERS

MAJOR LEAGUERS

BATTING
*AVG	Mike Piazza	.346
R	Raul Mondesi	91
H	Eric Karros	164
TB	Eric Karros	295
2B	Eric Karros	29
3B	Two tied at	6
HR	Two tied at	32
RBI	Eric Karros	105
BB	Jose Offerman	69
SO	Eric Karros	115
SB	Delino DeShields	39

PITCHING
W	Ramon Martinez	17
L	Tom Candiotti	14
#ERA	Hideo Nomo	2.54
G	Todd Worrell	59
CG	Ismael Valdes	6
SV	Todd Worrell	32
IP	Ramon Martinez	206
BB	Ramon Martinez	81
SO	Hideo Nomo	236

TOM DiPACE

Ramon Martinez. 17 wins

MINOR LEAGUERS

BATTING
*AVG	Adam Riggs, San Bernardino	.362
R	Adam Riggs, San Bernardino	111
H	Adam Riggs, San Bernardino	196
TB	Adam Riggs, San Bernardino	317
2B	Adam Riggs, San Bernardino	39
3B	Two tied at	10
HR	Adam Riggs, San Bernardino	24
RBI	Adam Riggs, San Bernardino	106
BB	Chris Latham, Vero Beach/S.A./Alb.	90
SO	Brian Richardson, San Bernardino	122
SB	Mike Metcalfe, Vero Beach/S.A.	61

PITCHING
W	Gary Rath, San Antonio/Albuquerque	16
L	Mike Iglesias, San Bern./Bakersfield	12
#ERA	Kevin Pincavitch, San Bern./Vero Beach	1.74
G	Rich Linares, Bakersfield	55
CG	Gary Rath, San Antonio/Albuquerque	3
SV	Joe Jacobsen, San Bern./Vero Beach	34
IP	Dave Pyc, San Antonio/Albuquerque	164
BB	Joe Lagarde, San Bern./Bakersfield	81
SO	Joe Lagarde, San Bern./Bakersfield	127

*Minimum 250 At-Bats   #Minimum 75 Innings

TOP 10 PROSPECTS

How the Dodgers Top 10 prospects, as judged by Baseball America prior to the 1995 season, fared in 1995:

MORRIS FOSTOFF

Todd Hollandsworth

Player, Pos.	Club (Class—League)	AVG	AB	R	H	2B	3B	HR	RBI	SB
1. Todd Hollandsworth, of	San Bernardino (A—California)	.500	2	0	1	0	0	0	0	0
	Albuquerque (AAA—Pacific Coast)	.237	38	9	9	2	0	2	4	1
	Los Angeles	.233	103	16	24	2	0	5	13	2
3. Roger Cedeno, of	Albuquerque (AAA—Pacific Coast)	.305	367	67	112	19	9	2	44	23
	Los Angeles	.238	42	4	10	2	0	0	3	1
4. Paul Konerko, c	San Bernardino (A—California)	.277	448	77	124	21	1	19	77	3
6. Karim Garcia, of	Albuquerque (AAA—Pacific Coast)	.319	474	88	151	26	10	20	91	12
	Los Angeles	.200	20	1	4	0	0	0	0	0

		W	L	ERA	G	SV	IP	H	BB	SO
2. Antonio Osuna, rhp	San Bernadino (A—California)	0	0	1.29	5	0	7	3	5	11
	Albuquerque (AAA—Pacific Coast)	0	1	4.42	19	11	18	15	9	19
	Los Angeles	2	4	4.43	39	0	45	39	20	46
5. Chan Ho Park, rhp	Albuquerque (AAA—Pacific Coast)	6	7	4.91	23	0	110	93	76	101
	Los Angeles	0	0	4.50	2	0	4	2	2	7
7. Rick Gorecki, rhp	Vero Beach (A—Florida State)	1	2	0.67	6	0	27	19	9	24
8. *Greg Hansell, rhp	Albuquerque (AAA—Pacific Coast)	1	1	8.44	8	1	16	25	6	15
	Los Angeles	0	1	7.45	20	0	19	29	6	13
	Salt Lake (AAA—Pacific Coast)	3	1	5.01	7	0	32	39	4	17
9. Felix Rodriguez, rhp	Albuquerque (AAA—Pacific Coast)	3	2	4.24	14	0	51	52	26	46
	Los Angeles	1	1	2.53	11	0	11	11	5	5
10. Kym Ashworth, lhp	Vero Beach (A—Florida State)	7	4	3.53	24	0	120	111	64	97

*Traded to Minnesota

PACIFIC COAST LEAGUE

BATTING

	AVG	G	AB	R	H	2B	3B	HR	RBI	BB	SO	SB	CS	B	T	HT	WT	DOB	1st Yr	Resides
Blanco, Henry	.227	29	97	11	22	4	1	2	13	10	23	0	0	R	R	5-11	168	8-29-71	1990	Guarenas, Venez.
Bournigal, Rafael	.129	15	31	2	4	1	0	0	1	1	2	0	0	R	R	5-11	165	5-12-66	1987	Santo Domingo, D.R.
Busch, Mike	.269	121	443	68	119	32	1	18	62	42	103	2	2	R	R	6-5	241	7-7-68	1990	Farmington, Iowa
Candaele, Casey	.259	12	27	2	7	0	0	0	2	4	4	0	1	S	R	5-9	165	1-12-61	1983	San Luis Obispo, Calif.
Castro, Juan	.267	104	341	51	91	18	4	3	43	20	42	4	4	R	R	5-10	163	6-20-72	1991	Los Mochis, Mexico
Cedeno, Roger	.305	99	367	67	112	19	9	2	44	53	56	23	18	S	R	6-1	165	8-16-74	1992	Carabobo, Venez.
Coomer, Ron	.322	85	323	54	104	23	2	16	76	18	28	5	2	R	R	5-11	195	11-18-66	1987	Crest Hill, Ill.
Demetral, Chris	.278	87	187	34	52	7	1	3	19	24	28	1	6	L	R	5-11	175	12-8-69	1991	Sterling Heights, Mich.
Garcia, Karim	.319	124	474	88	151	26	10	20	91	38	102	12	6	L	L	6-0	200	10-29-75	1993	Ciudad Obregon, Mexico
Guerrero, Wilton	.327	14	49	10	16	1	1	0	2	1	7	2	3	R	R	5-11	145	10-24-74	1992	Santo Domingo, D.R.
Hollandsworth, Todd	.237	10	38	9	9	2	0	2	4	6	8	1	0	L	L	6-2	193	4-20-73	1991	San Ramon, Calif.
Huckaby, Ken	.324	89	278	30	90	16	2	1	40	12	26	3	1	R	R	6-1	205	1-27-71	1991	Manteca, Calif.
Ingram, Garey	.246	63	232	28	57	11	4	1	30	21	40	10	4	R	R	5-11	178	7-25-70	1990	Columbus, Ga.
Kirkpatrick, Jay	.250	13	40	4	10	1	1	1	6	2	6	0	0	L	R	6-4	220	7-10-69	1991	Tallahassee, Fla.
Latham, Chris	.167	5	18	2	3	0	1	0	3	1	4	1	0	S	R	6-0	188	5-26-73	1991	Las Vegas, Nev.
Lott, Billy	.315	41	146	23	46	7	2	5	26	13	48	1	2	R	R	6-4	210	8-16-70	1989	Petal, Miss.
Marrero, Oreste	.348	7	23	5	8	2	0	2	6	1	5	0	0	L	L	6-0	205	10-31-69	1987	Bayamon, P.R.
Martin, James	.253	25	75	8	19	3	1	1	7	8	20	3	3	L	R	6-1	210	12-10-70	1992	Eufaula, Okla.
Maurer, Ron	.259	84	185	29	48	14	2	5	25	19	34	1	2	R	R	6-1	185	6-10-68	1990	Beachwood, N.J.
Munoz, Noe	.224	23	58	1	13	1	0	0	3	2	8	0	0	R	R	6-0	195	11-11-67	1994	Los Mochis, Mexico
Parker, Rick	.280	58	175	33	49	7	2	1	14	27	17	1	6	R	R	6-0	185	3-20-63	1985	Independence, Mo.
Pose, Scott	.188	7	16	5	3	1	0	0	1	2	0	2	0	L	R	5-11	165	2-11-67	1989	West Des Moines, Iowa
Prince, Tom	.318	61	192	30	61	15	0	7	36	27	41	0	0	R	R	5-11	185	8-13-64	1984	Bradenton, Fla.
Pye, Eddie	.295	84	302	49	89	20	1	3	32	30	36	11	2	R	R	5-10	170	2-13-67	1988	Columbia, Tenn.
Spearman, Vernon	.172	22	29	7	5	0	1	0	2	11	4	2	2	L	L	5-10	160	12-17-69	1991	Union City, Calif.
Traxler, Brian	.283	110	353	46	100	24	1	11	50	24	27	1	3	L	L	5-10	200	9-26-67	1988	San Antonio, Texas
Wallach, Tim	.333	1	3	1	1	0	0	0	1	0	2	0	0	R	R	6-3	200	9-14-57	1979	Tustin, Calif.
Williams, Reggie	.312	66	234	44	73	15	5	6	29	30	46	6	4	S	R	6-1	180	5-5-66	1988	Laurens, S.C.

PITCHING

	W	L	ERA	G	GS	CG	SV	IP	H	R	ER	BB	SO	B	T	HT	WT	DOB	1st Yr	Resides
Alicea, Miguel	1	1	4.05	7	0	0	3	7	6	5	3	4	0	R	R	6-2	192	11-10-59	1978	Santa Isabel, P.R.
Brosnan, Jason	2	0	4.35	23	1	0	2	31	30	16	15	9	18	L	L	6-1	190	1-26-68	1989	San Leandro, Calif.
Bruske, Jim	7	5	4.11	43	6	0	4	114	128	54	52	41	99	R	R	6-1	185	10-7-64	1986	Palmdale, Calif.
Castro, Nelson	0	0	0.00	2	0	0	1	2	0	0	0	0	2	R	R	6-1	185	12-10-71	1990	Los Angeles, Calif.
Correa, Ramser	0	0	0.00	2	0	0	0	4	5	0	0	1	3	R	R	6-5	225	11-13-70	1987	Carolina, P.R.
Daal, Omar	2	3	3.88	17	9	0	1	53	56	28	23	26	46	L	L	6-3	185	3-1-72	1990	Valencia, Venez.
Edwards, Wayne	1	2	5.06	14	0	0	1	16	17	16	9	17	12	L	L	6-5	185	5-7-64	1985	Sepulveda, Calif.
Eischen, Joey	3	0	0.00	13	0	0	2	16	8	0	0	3	14	L	L	6-1	190	5-25-70	1989	West Covina, Calif.
Garcia, Jose	1	3	6.32	11	0	0	0	16	19	11	11	7	10	R	R	6-3	146	6-12-72	1991	Monte Cristi, D.R.
Hansell, Greg	1	1	8.44	8	1	0	1	16	25	15	15	6	15	R	R	6-5	215	3-12-71	1989	La Palma, Calif.
Holman, Shawn	5	6	5.13	49	1	0	5	79	107	58	45	39	60	R	R	6-1	200	11-10-64	1982	Sewickley, Pa.
Lilliquist, Derek	0	0	2.70	13	0	0	5	13	18	4	4	3	9	L	L	5-10	195	2-20-66	1987	Vero Beach, Fla.
Martinez, Jesus	1	1	4.50	2	0	0	0	4	4	2	2	4	5	L	L	6-2	145	3-13-74	1991	Santo Domingo, D.R.
McCarthy, Tom	3	3	6.00	13	8	0	0	48	61	41	32	22	28	R	R	6-0	185	6-18-61	1979	Lexington, N.C.
Milchin, Mike	8	4	4.32	18	17	2	0	83	94	43	40	30	50	L	L	6-3	190	2-28-68	1989	Richmond, Va.
Mimbs, Mark	6	5	2.97	23	16	1	0	106	105	40	35	22	96	L	L	6-2	180	2-13-69	1990	Macon, Ga.
Montalvo, Rafael	3	5	2.65	49	0	0	4	98	105	44	29	34	65	R	R	6-0	190	3-31-64	1980	Puerto Nuevo, P.R.
O'Donoghue, John	5	6	3.82	25	18	1	0	92	97	58	39	25	59	L	L	6-6	210	5-26-69	1990	Elkton, Md.
Osuna, Antonio	0	1	4.42	19	0	0	11	18	15	9	9	9	19	R	R	5-11	160	4-12-73	1991	Sinaloa, Mexico
Park, Chan Ho	6	7	4.91	23	22	0	0	110	93	64	60	76	101	R	R	6-2	185	6-30-73	1994	Glendale, Calif.
Parra, Jose	3	2	5.13	12	10	1	1	53	62	33	30	17	33	R	R	5-11	160	11-28-72	1990	Santiago, D.R.
Pyc, Dave	0	1	3.86	1	1	0	0	7	7	5	3	2	3	L	L	6-3	235	2-11-71	1992	Depew, N.Y.
Rath, Gary	3	5	5.08	8	8	0	0	39	46	31	22	20	23	L	L	6-2	185	1-10-73	1994	Long Beach, Miss.
Rodriguez, Felix	3	2	4.24	14	11	0	0	51	52	29	24	26	46	R	R	6-1	190	12-5-72	1990	Monte Cristi, D.R.
Treadwell, Jody	3	5	3.96	30	15	1	1	125	121	61	55	32	79	R	R	6-0	190	12-14-68	1990	Jacksonville, Fla.
Williams, Todd	4	1	3.38	25	0	0	0	45	59	21	17	15	23	R	R	6-3	185	2-13-71	1991	East Syracuse, N.Y.

FIELDING

Catcher

	PCT	G	PO	A	E	DP	PB
Huckaby	.973	80	515	61	16	5	9
Maurer	1.000	5	18	3	0	0	0
Munoz	.991	19	89	16	1	1	3
Prince	.989	55	310	34	4	7	3

First Base

	PCT	G	PO	A	E	DP
Blanco	1.000	11	97	6	0	3
Busch	.994	40	303	21	2	30
Coomer	.979	35	314	17	7	33
Huckaby	1.000	1	3	0	0	0
Kirkpatrick	1.000	6	51	4	0	1
Marrero	1.000	1	6	0	0	2
Maurer	1.000	1	1	0	0	0
Traxler	.992	66	569	23	5	61

Second Base

	PCT	G	PO	A	E	DP
Candaele	.958	6	23	23	2	8
J. Castro	1.000	10	4	17	0	2
Demetral	.978	40	59	115	4	23
Ingram	.975	48	90	144	6	38
Maurer	.977	25	38	46	2	12
Parker	1.000	3	4	2	0	0
Pye	.971	41	83	116	6	26

Third Base

	PCT	G	PO	A	E	DP
Blanco	.967	19	17	41	2	6
Busch	.941	75	31	143	11	14
Candaele	1.000	1	0	1	0	0
Coomer	.980	44	21	76	2	5
Maurer	.967	17	5	24	1	1
Parker	1.000	3	1	4	0	0
Pye	1.000	3	1	2	0	0
Wallach	1.000	1	0	1	0	0

Shortstop

	PCT	G	PO	A	E	DP
Bournigal	.951	12	7	32	2	4
J. Castro	.971	92	148	327	14	67
Guerrero	.852	14	13	39	9	6
Maurer	1.000	13	12	33	0	3
Parker	.000	1	0	0	0	0

Outfield

	PCT	G	PO	A	E	DP
Pye	.947	29	48	78	7	17
Blanco	1.000	1	1	0	0	0
Busch	.800	6	4	0	1	0
Cedeno	.985	94	189	3	3	0
Demetral	.952	16	18	2	1	1
Garcia	.932	122	185	7	14	0
Guerrero	1.000	1	0	0	0	0
Hollandsworth	1.000	10	19	3	0	0
Ingram	1.000	19	25	0	0	0
Latham	1.000	5	7	0	0	0
Lott	.988	40	76	4	1	3
Marrero	1.000	5	8	0	0	0
Martin	.971	24	34	0	1	0
Maurer	1.000	8	12	0	0	0
Parker	.975	44	78	1	2	0
Pose	1.000	4	2	0	0	0
Spearman	1.000	8	11	0	0	0
R. Williams	1.000	61	141	10	0	4

Dynamic Duo. The Dodgers won the National League West title in 1995 on the strength of catcher Mike Piazza (.346-32-93) and first baseman Eric Karros (.298-32-105).

SAN ANTONIO
TEXAS LEAGUE

AA

BATTING	AVG	G	AB	R	H	2B	3B	HR	RBI	BB	SO	SB	CS	B	T	HT	WT	DOB	1st Yr	Resides
Blanco, Henry	.255	88	302	37	77	18	4	12	48	29	52	1	1	R	R	5-11	168	8-29-71	1990	Guarenas, Venez.
Butterfield, Chris	.000	2	6	0	0	0	0	0	0	2	3	0	0	S	R	6-1	193	8-27-67	1989	Modesto, Calif.
Cairo, Miguel	.278	107	435	53	121	20	1	1	41	26	32	33	16	R	R	6-1	160	5-4-74	1991	Anaco, Venez.
Dandridge, Brad	.417	3	12	1	5	0	0	0	1	0	1	0	1	R	R	6-0	190	11-29-71	1993	Santa Maria, Calif.
Guerrero, Wilton	.348	95	382	53	133	13	6	0	26	26	63	21	22	R	R	5-11	145	10-24-74	1992	Santo Domingo, D.R.
Jaime, Angel	.364	9	22	5	8	0	0	1	2	2	3	2	1	R	R	6-0	160	3-6-73	1992	Santo Domingo, D.R.
Landrum, Tito	.238	87	260	42	62	13	1	8	25	26	64	5	6	R	R	6-4	210	8-26-70	1991	Sweetwater, Ala.
Latham, Chris	.299	58	214	38	64	14	5	9	37	33	59	11	11	S	R	6-0	188	5-26-73	1991	Las Vegas, Nev.
LoDuca, Paul	.246	61	199	27	49	8	0	1	8	26	25	5	5	R	R	5-10	193	4-12-72	1993	Phoenix, Ariz.
Luzinski, Ryan	.229	44	144	18	33	5	0	1	9	13	32	1	1	R	R	6-0	215	8-22-73	1992	Medford, N.J.
Maness, Dwight	.223	57	179	29	40	2	3	5	24	20	44	4	6	R	R	6-0	205	10-31-69	1987	Bayamon, P.R.
Marrero, Oreste	.258	125	445	60	115	25	3	21	86	64	98	5	2	L	L	6-0	205	10-31-69	1987	Bayamon, P.R.
Martin, James	.235	95	327	43	77	20	3	4	36	36	83	18	10	L	R	6-1	210	12-10-70	1992	Eufaula, Okla.
Melendez, Dan	.261	128	464	46	121	28	1	7	59	51	66	0	3	L	L	6-4	195	1-4-71	1992	Los Angeles, Calif.
Metcalfe, Mike	.244	10	41	10	10	1	0	0	2	7	2	1	2	S	R	5-10	175	1-2-73	1994	Orlando, Fla.
Otanez, Willis	.240	27	100	8	24	4	1	1	7	6	25	0	1	R	R	5-11	150	4-19-73	1990	Las Matas De Cotui, D.R.
Puchales, Javier	.228	31	57	4	13	1	0	0	1	3	6	0	2	L	L	6-0	170	3-29-72	1989	Caguas, P.R.
Rios, Eddie	.285	98	365	43	104	22	4	5	53	20	47	2	4	R	R	5-10	160	10-13-72	1991	Charallave, Venez.
Romero, Willie	.266	105	376	46	100	20	1	7	44	40	69	10	12	R	R	5-11	158	8-5-74	1991	Candelaria, Venez.
Steed, Dave	.252	40	123	13	31	10	1	3	16	11	32	0	1	R	R	6-1	205	2-25-73	1993	Starkville, Miss.
Yard, Bruce	.359	16	39	7	14	3	0	0	4	5	6	0	1	L	R	6-0	175	10-17-71	1993	McIntyre, Pa.

PITCHING	W	L	ERA	G	GS	CG	SV	IP	H	R	ER	BB	SO	B	T	HT	WT	DOB	1st Yr	Resides
Brosnan, Jason	1	0	3.57	19	0	0	2	23	24	9	9	4	21	L	L	6-1	190	1-26-68	1989	San Leandro, Calif.
Brunson, William	4	5	4.95	14	14	0	0	80	105	46	44	22	44	L	L	6-4	185	3-20-70	1992	DeSoto, Texas
Camacho, Dan	1	1	1.59	11	0	0	2	11	9	2	2	8	8	R	R	5-11	190	11-11-73	1992	San Diego, Calif.
Castro, Nelson	5	7	5.20	48	1	0	3	81	98	51	47	30	51	R	R	6-1	185	12-10-71	1992	Los Angeles, Calif.
Correa, Ramser	1	4	4.53	42	0	0	17	50	54	29	25	21	34	R	R	6-5	225	11-13-70	1987	Carolina, P.R.
Cummings, John	0	2	3.95	6	5	0	0	27	28	13	12	7	13	L	L	6-3	200	5-10-69	1990	Laguna Niguel, Calif.
Garcia, Jose	2	6	4.03	38	0	0	2	58	50	32	26	24	36	R	R	6-3	146	6-12-72	1991	Monte Cristi, D.R.
Herges, Matt	0	3	4.88	19	0	0	8	28	34	16	15	16	18	R	R	6-0	200	4-1-70	1992	Champaign, Ill.
Hubbs, Dan	2	1	3.54	31	0	0	0	61	58	25	24	16	52	R	R	6-2	200	1-23-71	1993	Renton, Wash.
Martinez, Jesus	6	9	3.54	24	24	1	0	140	129	64	55	71	83	L	L	6-2	145	3-13-74	1991	Santo Domingo, D.R.
Oropesa, Eddie	1	1	3.12	16	0	0	1	17	22	8	6	12	16	L	L	6-2	200	11-23-71	1993	Miami, Fla.
Prado, Jose	7	11	3.48	28	22	0	1	145	126	70	56	64	93	R	R	6-2	195	5-9-72	1993	Miami, Fla.
Pyc, Dave	12	6	3.38	26	26	1	0	157	170	72	59	49	78	L	L	6-3	235	2-11-71	1992	Depew, N.Y.
Rath, Gary	13	3	2.77	18	18	3	0	117	96	42	36	48	81	L	L	6-2	185	1-10-73	1994	Long Beach, Miss.
Troutman, Keith	1	2	3.15	38	0	0	2	66	64	24	23	18	50	R	R	6-1	200	5-29-73	1992	Candler, N.C.
Weaver, Eric	8	11	4.07	27	26	1	0	142	147	83	64	72	105	R	R	6-5	230	8-4-73	1991	Illiopolis, Ill.

FIELDING

Catcher	PCT	G	PO	A	E	DP	PB
Blanco	1.000	1	2	0	0	0	0
Dandridge	1.000	2	9	0	0	0	1
LoDuca	.975	56	346	38	10	7	8
Luzinski	.986	43	246	33	4	6	5
Steed	.981	40	227	27	5	2	3
Yard	1.000	2	3	0	0	0	0

First Base	PCT	G	PO	A	E	DP
LoDuca	1.000	2	7	0	0	1
Marrero	.994	19	154	13	1	17
Melendez	.997	120	1068	98	3	103

Second Base	PCT	G	PO	A	E	DP
Cairo	.963	80	159	227	15	50

Second Base	PCT	G	PO	A	E	DP
Rios	.974	62	107	156	7	34
Yard	1.000	1	2	3	0	1

Third Base	PCT	G	PO	A	E	DP
Blanco	.963	88	79	210	11	21
LoDuca	.833	2	0	5	1	0
Otanez	.957	27	18	48	3	4
Rios	1.000	56	15	65	0	8
Yard	.000	1	0	0	0	0

Shortstop	PCT	G	PO	A	E	DP
Cairo	.946	30	51	89	8	22
Guerrero	.953	88	121	263	19	46
Jaime	.944	4	4	13	1	1

Shortstop	PCT	G	PO	A	E	DP
Metcalfe	.957	10	14	31	2	7
Yard	.950	9	19	19	2	6

Outfield	PCT	G	PO	A	E	DP
Jaime	1.000	4	3	0	0	0
Landrum	.955	82	144	5	7	2
Latham	.972	58	135	2	4	0
Maness	.952	55	156	1	8	0
Marrero	.984	34	60	0	1	0
Martin	.916	81	125	6	12	1
Puchales	.963	18	22	4	1	0
Romero	.966	103	215	14	8	6

SAN BERNARDINO   A
CALIFORNIA LEAGUE

BATTING	AVG	G	AB	R	H	2B	3B	HR	RBI	BB	SO	SB	CS	B	T	HT	WT	DOB	1st Yr	Resides
Asencio, Alex	.257	29	105	15	27	1	4	2	18	6	31	2	0	L	L	6-0	177	5-30-74	1991	San Cristobal, D.R.
Dandridge, Brad	.320	82	322	56	103	14	2	11	61	14	34	16	5	R	R	6-0	190	11-29-71	1993	Santa Maria, Calif.
Durkin, Chris	.268	57	164	24	44	10	1	8	31	28	48	9	6	L	L	6-6	247	8-12-70	1991	Youngstown, Ohio
Faircloth, Kevin	.185	56	146	23	27	3	0	0	6	14	40	7	3	R	R	6-2	170	6-6-73	1994	Winston-Salem, N.C.
Gibbs, Kevin	.231	5	13	1	3	1	0	0	0	0	2	1	0	S	R	6-2	182	4-3-74	1995	Davidsonville, Md.
Hilo, Johnny	.247	38	93	14	23	2	1	1	9	15	23	3	2	L	R	6-2	185	10-23-73	1994	Baldwin Park, Calif.
Hollandsworth, Todd	.500	1	2	0	1	0	0	0	0	0	1	0	1	L	L	6-2	193	4-20-73	1991	San Ramon, Calif.
Hunter, Scott	.285	113	379	68	108	19	3	11	59	36	83	27	8	R	R	6-1	195	12-17-75	1994	Philadelphia, Pa.
Johnson, Keith	.242	111	417	64	101	26	1	17	68	17	83	20	12	R	R	5-11	190	4-17-71	1992	Stockton, Calif.
Kirkpatrick, Jay	.270	71	267	38	72	19	0	15	50	40	75	3	0	L	R	6-4	220	7-10-69	1991	Tallahassee, Fla.
Konerko, Paul	.277	118	448	77	124	21	1	19	77	59	88	3	1	R	R	6-3	210	3-5-76	1994	Paradise Valley, Ariz.
Nelson, Charlie	.250	1	4	0	1	0	0	0	0	0	0	0	0	L	L	5-10	180	8-11-71	1994	Perham, Minn.
Newstrom, Doug	.291	97	316	53	92	22	1	6	58	40	58	19	9	L	R	6-1	195	9-18-71	1993	Goodyear, Ariz.
Richardson, Brian	.284	127	462	68	131	18	1	12	58	35	122	17	16	R	R	6-2	190	8-31-75	1992	Diamond Bar, Calif.
Riggs, Brian	.362	134	542	111	196	39	5	24	106	59	93	31	10	R	R	6-0	190	10-4-72	1994	Andover, N.J.
Roberge, J.P.	.287	116	450	92	129	22	1	17	59	34	62	31	8	R	R	6-0	180	9-12-72	1994	Arcadia, Calif.
Schaaf, Bob	.252	52	151	18	38	7	0	5	21	12	32	4	4	R	R	5-10	170	10-15-72	1994	Frankfort, Ill.
Smith, Frank	.205	58	122	19	25	7	1	3	15	30	54	9	3	R	R	6-2	205	8-11-72	1990	Riverside, Calif.
Spearman, Vernon	.288	93	365	78	105	15	7	3	36	56	50	43	12	L	L	5-10	160	12-17-69	1991	Union City, Calif.
Stuckenschneider, Eric	.250	8	20	2	5	1	0	0	2	7	6	1	0	R	R	6-0	180	8-24-71	1994	Freeburg, Mo.
Wallach, Tim	.467	4	15	2	7	3	0	0	4	1	3	0	0	R	R	6-3	200	9-14-57	1979	Tustin, Calif.

GAMES BY POSITION: C—Dandridge 43, Konerko 95, Newstrom 14. 1B—Kirkpatrick 95, Newstrom 51, Richardson 6, Roberge 35, Smith 1. 2B—Faircloth 12, Riggs 121, Roberge 5, Schaaf 9. 3B—Johnson 5, Richardson 122, Roberge 1, Schaaf 18, Wallach 4. SS—Faircloth 42, Johnson 105, Schaaf 4. OF—Asencio 29, Dandridge 23, Durkin 53, Gibbs 5, Hilo 34, Hollandsworth 1, Hunter 111, Nelson 1, Newstrom 10, Roberge 46, Schaaf 5, Smith 51, Spearman 93, Stuckenschneider 2.

PITCHING	W	L	ERA	G	GS	CG	SV	IP	H	R	ER	BB	SO	B	T	HT	WT	DOB	1st Yr	Resides
Aquino, Julio	2	2	7.84	25	3	0	0	60	96	59	52	23	42	R	R	6-1	173	12-12-72	1991	Guerra, D.R.
Brunson, William	10	0	2.05	13	13	0	0	83	68	24	19	21	70	L	L	6-4	185	3-20-70	1992	DeSoto, Texas
Camacho, Dan	6	2	3.95	43	1	0	9	68	66	32	30	30	79	R	R	5-11	190	11-11-73	1992	San Diego, Calif.
Colon, Julio	6	3	4.33	49	0	0	12	79	68	47	38	37	75	R	R	6-2	202	10-30-72	1993	Los Angeles, Calif.
Davis, Eddie	0	0	3.77	5	1	0	1	14	17	10	6	6	6	R	R	6-0	195	12-22-72	1993	New Orleans, La.
Herges, Matt	5	2	3.66	22	2	0	1	52	58	29	21	15	35	R	R	6-0	200	4-1-70	1992	Champaign, Ill.
Iglesias, Mike	1	2	6.60	4	3	0	0	15	26	14	11	2	12	R	R	6-5	215	11-9-72	1991	Castro Valley, Calif.
2-team (24 Bak.)	8	12	3.57	28	26	2	0	159	150	79	63	40	120							
Jacobsen, Joe	0	0	0.00	4	0	0	2	4	4	2	0	2	5	R	R	6-3	215	12-26-71	1992	Clovis, Calif.
Lagarde, Joe	5	10	4.60	24	24	0	0	123	135	83	63	68	102	R	R	5-9	180	1-17-75	1993	Washington, D.C.
Oropesa, Eddie	0	0	0.00	1	0	0	1	0	0	0	0	0	0	L	L	6-2	200	11-23-71	1993	Miami, Fla.
Osuna, Antonio	0	0	1.29	5	0	0	0	7	3	1	1	5	11	R	R	5-11	160	4-12-73	1991	Sinaloa, Mexico
Paluk, Jeff	6	3	5.71	41	0	0	1	52	65	34	33	30	52	R	R	6-4	215	9-28-72	1994	Plymouth, Mich.
Parra, Julio	5	5	5.19	14	13	0	0	69	76	45	40	29	65	R	R	6-1	245	9-2-74	1994	Los Mochis, Mexico
Pearsall, J.J.	0	1	8.44	6	0	0	0	11	15	10	10	7	5	L	L	6-2	202	9-9-73	1995	Burnt Hills, N.Y.
Pincavitch, Kevin	2	0	2.70	3	0	0	0	10	8	5	3	6	10	R	R	5-11	180	7-5-70	1992	Greensboro, Pa.
Pivaral, Hugo	6	4	4.63	24	24	0	0	103	106	61	53	43	89	R	R	6-5	220	1-2-77	1994	Guatemala City, Guatemala
Price, Tom	10	5	5.20	42	13	2	3	152	145	99	88	47	82	L	L	6-0	190	3-19-72	1994	Edwardsville, Ill.
Ricabal, Dan	4	1	3.88	43	0	0	2	72	63	35	31	33	62	R	R	6-1	185	7-8-72	1994	Rosemead, Calif.
Roach, Petie	1	2	3.00	30	0	0	8	33	28	16	11	14	38	L	L	6-2	180	9-19-70	1992	Redding, Calif.
Rolocut, Brian	1	0	5.68	11	3	0	0	13	15	10	8	16	10	R	R	6-1	195	4-8-74	1993	Gambrills, Md.
Seanez, Rudy	2	0	.00	4	0	0	1	6	2	0	0	3	5	R	R	5-10	185	10-20-68	1986	El Centro, Calif.
Stone, Ricky	3	5	6.52	12	12	0	0	58	79	50	42	25	31	R	R	6-2	173	2-28-75	1994	Hamilton, Ohio
Zerbe, Chad	11	7	4.57	28	27	1	0	163	168	103	83	64	94	L	L	6-0	190	4-27-72	1991	Tampa, Fla.

VERO BEACH   A
FLORIDA STATE LEAGUE

BATTING	AVG	G	AB	R	H	2B	3B	HR	RBI	BB	SO	SB	CS	B	T	HT	WT	DOB	1st Yr	Resides
Anderson, Cliff	.271	113	365	48	99	20	2	6	44	10	58	1	4	L	R	5-8	165	7-4-70	1994	Kodiak, Alaska
Asencio, Alex	.266	58	184	24	49	8	3	2	21	6	22	4	3	L	L	6-0	177	5-30-74	1991	San Cristobal, D.R.
Biltimier, Mike	.225	127	422	62	95	14	0	14	50	48	109	0	1	L	L	6-1	215	10-30-70	1993	Aurora, Colo.
Boyd, Quincy	.152	31	66	4	10	2	0	0	1	9	20	0	0	R	R	6-0	180	2-24-71	1994	Prosperity, S.C.
Cooney, Kyle	.278	105	356	44	99	11	2	6	54	17	50	4	3	R	R	6-2	200	3-31-73	1994	Meriden, Conn.
Gibbs, Kevin	.250	7	20	1	5	1	0	0	2	0	1	0	1	S	R	6-2	182	4-3-74	1995	Davidsonville, Md.
Gross, Rafael	.252	35	115	18	29	4	1	0	8	13	15	5	4	R	R	5-11	185	8-15-74	1993	Santo Domingo, D.R.
Hernaiz, Juan	.212	50	156	17	33	1	1	2	9	3	39	5	1	R	R	5-11	185	2-15-75	1992	Carolina, P.R.
Latham, Chris	.286	71	259	53	74	13	4	6	39	56	54	42	11	S	R	6-0	188	5-26-73	1991	Las Vegas, Nev.

BATTING

BATTING	AVG	G	AB	R	H	2B	3B	HR	RBI	BB	SO	SB	CS	B	T	HT	WT	DOB	1st Yr	Resides
Lewis, Tyrone	.000	1	1	0	0	0	0	0	0	0	1	0	0	R	R	5-10	185	1-22-74	1992	Waco, Texas
Luzinski, Ryan	.336	38	134	15	45	12	0	5	23	9	21	1	0	R	R	6-0	215	8-22-73	1992	Medford, N.J.
Majeski, Brian	.224	69	147	22	33	3	1	2	11	26	34	9	8	R	R	6-0	180	1-10-72	1991	Plantsville, Conn.
Maness, Dwight	.231	43	143	16	33	3	0	3	23	11	29	13	5	R	R	6-3	180	4-3-74	1992	New Castle, Del.
Metcalfe, Mike	.301	120	435	86	131	13	3	3	35	60	37	60	27	S	R	5-10	175	1-2-73	1994	Orlando, Fla.
Moore, Michael	.273	7	22	3	6	1	0	1	6	8	0	1	R	R	6-4	200	3-7-71	1992	Beverly Hills, Calif.
Nelson, Charlie	.271	80	277	37	75	13	2	0	30	46	50	33	13	L	L	5-10	180	8-11-71	1994	Perham, Minn.
Otanez, Willis	.260	92	354	39	92	24	0	10	53	28	59	1	1	R	R	5-11	150	4-19-73	1990	Las Matas De Cotui, D.R.
Post, David	.237	52	114	16	27	2	1	0	11	23	11	3	0	R	R	5-11	170	9-3-73	1992	Kingston, N.Y.
Roberge, J.P.	.000	3	9	1	0	0	0	0	0	0	2	0	0	R	R	6-0	180	9-12-72	1994	Arcadia, Calif.
Schaaf, Rob	.217	21	60	7	13	1	0	1	5	1	13	0	0	R	R	5-10	170	10-15-72	1994	Frankfort, Ill.
Sell, Donald	.270	80	222	21	60	6	1	1	23	18	33	1	3	L	R	6-2	195	6-19-71	1994	Woodburn, Ore.
Sosa, Juan	.222	8	27	2	6	1	1	1	6	0	4	0	2	R	R	6-1	175	8-19-75	1993	San Fran. de Macoris, D.R.
Sowards, Ryan	.286	75	196	36	56	13	0	3	34	47	32	1	0	L	R	6-0	180	8-11-73	1994	Bothell, Wash.
Steed, David	.251	59	195	11	49	16	0	0	24	18	53	0	0	R	R	6-1	205	2-25-73	1993	Starkville, Miss.

GAMES BY POSITION: C—Boyd 13, Cooney 59, Luzinski 23, Steed 52. **1B**—Biltimier 127, Boyd 5, Roberge 1, Schaaf 2, Sell 3, Sowards 4. **2B**—Anderson 97, Post 39, Schaaf 11, Sosa 5, Sowards 1. **3B**—Anderson 1, Gross 35, Otanez 89, Sowards 12. **SS**—Anderson 17, Metcalfe 120, Sosa 2. **OF**—Asencio 58, Cooney 1, Gibbs 7, Hernaiz 46, Latham 59, Majeski 58, Maness 43, Nelson 76, Post 4, Roberge 1, Schaaf 6, Sell 67, Sowards 17.

PITCHING

PITCHING	W	L	ERA	G	GS	CG	SV	IP	H	R	ER	BB	SO	B	T	HT	WT	DOB	1st Yr	Resides
Aquino, Julio	0	0	0.00	3	0	0	1	3	1	0	0	3	0	R	R	6-1	173	12-12-72	1991	Guerra, D.R.
Ashworth, Kym	7	4	3.53	24	24	1	0	120	111	56	47	64	97	L	L	6-3	185	7-31-76	1993	Para Hills West, Australia
Challinor, John	2	6	3.86	37	1	0	1	75	62	36	32	35	59	R	R	6-3	190	1-31-75	1994	Morphett Vale, Australia
Duran, Roberto	7	4	3.38	23	22	0	0	101	82	42	38	70	114	L	L	6-0	190	3-6-73	1990	Moca, D.R.
Gorecki, Rick	1	2	0.67	6	5	0	0	27	19	6	2	9	24	R	R	6-3	180	8-27-73	1991	Oak Forest, Ill.
Groot, Franz	0	0	5.83	14	1	0	1	29	28	21	19	18	15	R	R	6-6	187	11-3-70	1991	Nederland, Netherlands
Henderson, Ryan	11	5	3.88	39	6	0	2	104	98	53	45	58	86	R	R	6-1	190	9-30-69	1992	Dana Point, Calif.
Hollis, Ron	2	5	2.47	43	0	0	0	73	55	22	20	38	56	L	R	6-3	205	8-13-73	1994	Brighton, Mich.
Jacobsen, Joe	3	1	3.67	47	0	0	32	49	42	20	20	15	51	R	R	6-3	215	12-26-71	1992	Clovis, Calif.
Liquet, Wilton	0	0	4.05	4	1	0	0	7	5	3	3	5	3	R	R	5-11	160	6-16-73	1991	Monte Cristi, D.R.
Oropesa, Eddie	3	1	3.81	19	1	0	1	28	25	12	12	10	23	L	L	6-2	200	11-23-71	1993	Miami, Fla.
Paluk, Jeff	1	0	6.75	2	0	0	0	4	5	3	3	2	4	R	R	6-4	215	9-28-72	1994	Plymouth, Mich.
Parra, Julio	7	3	2.85	22	1	0	0	41	39	21	13	20	36	R	R	5-11	180	7-5-70	1992	Los Mochis, Mexico
Pincavitch, Kevin	10	7	1.66	32	13	2	2	125	83	37	23	48	103	R	R	5-11	180	6-8-73	1994	Greensboro, Pa.
Reed, Jason	0	0	3.42	21	0	0	0	24	18	9	9	11	17	L	L	6-3	215	6-8-73	1994	Lakeside, Calif.
Reyes, Dennis	1	0	1.80	3	2	0	0	10	8	2	2	6	9	R	L	6-3	220	4-19-77	1994	Higuera de Zaragoza, Mex.
Sikes, Ken	3	4	5.06	14	12	0	0	64	64	44	36	36	50	R	R	6-5	230	1-25-73	1993	Warner Robins, Ga.
Urbina, Dan	5	7	4.32	18	16	0	0	92	90	56	44	52	48	R	R	6-0	160	11-13-74	1992	Miranda, Venez.
Watts, Brandon	5	3	4.04	13	8	0	0	49	46	29	22	22	42	L	L	6-3	190	9-13-72	1991	Ruston, La.
Winslett, Dax	6	4	3.18	14	13	0	0	85	87	35	30	21	59	R	R	6-1	200	1-1-72	1993	Houston, Texas
Yocum, David	2	1	2.96	8	7	0	0	27	12	9	12	20	L	L	6-0	175	6-10-74	1995	Miami, Fla.

YAKIMA
NORTHWEST LEAGUE

BATTING	AVG	G	AB	R	H	2B	3B	HR	RBI	BB	SO	SB	CS	B	T	HT	WT	DOB	1st Yr	Resides
Backowski, Lance	.193	34	114	8	22	1	1	0	8	8	16	4	1	R	R	6-0	180	6-8-75	1995	Fresno, Calif.
Carpentier, Mike	.255	53	188	20	48	8	4	4	28	13	23	4	5	R	R	5-11	180	8-1-74	1995	Redlands, Calif.
Cuevas, Trent	.203	38	123	13	25	7	0	1	8	14	22	3	4	R	R	5-11	175	12-25-76	1995	Placentia, Calif.
Gibbs, Kevin	.313	52	182	36	57	6	4	1	18	36	46	38	5	S	R	6-2	182	4-3-74	1995	Davidsonville, Md.
Granzow, Judd	.224	50	156	12	35	5	2	4	13	15	53	3	1	L	R	6-4	200	8-8-76	1995	Granada Hills, Calif.
Gross, Rafael	.254	40	142	17	36	4	1	3	15	13	17	12	2	R	R	5-11	185	8-15-74	1993	Santo Domingo, D.R.
Harmon, Brian	.254	22	59	4	15	3	0	0	8	12	9	0	0	R	R	6-2	195	3-21-76	1994	Palos Heights, Ill.
Hernaiz, Juan	.278	50	158	23	44	9	2	0	16	6	30	9	3	R	R	5-11	185	2-15-75	1992	Carolina, P.R.
Hilo, Johnny	.250	50	168	18	42	10	0	3	22	23	33	5	2	L	R	6-2	185	10-23-73	1994	Baldwin Park, Calif.
Malave, Joshua	.270	44	137	12	37	13	2	1	15	6	41	1	1	R	R	6-0	196	3-22-75	1995	Ft. Lauderdale, Fla.
Markert, Jason	.272	34	81	10	22	4	1	0	10	14	17	1	1	R	R	5-10	190	9-28-73	1995	Dupo, Ill.
McClain, Terrance	.204	33	54	12	11	2	0	0	2	12	23	7	3	R	R	6-0	168	3-28-72	1995	College Park, Ga.
Meyer, Travis	.205	36	83	9	17	7	0	0	5	11	22	0	0	R	R	6-0	205	9-18-73	1995	Westerville, Ohio
Morimoto, Ken	.270	55	178	27	48	4	2	0	14	19	40	19	4	R	R	6-1	163	9-22-74	1995	Eleele, Hawaii
Owen, Andy	.242	56	165	16	40	12	1	0	17	9	35	6	1	L	L	5-10	180	7-12-73	1995	Escondido, Calif.
Rasmussen, Nate	.234	44	128	12	30	3	1	0	5	4	43	1	1	L	L	6-6	240	10-19-74	1994	Lakeville, Minn.
Sosa, Juan	.235	61	217	26	51	10	4	3	16	15	39	8	1	R	R	6-1	175	8-19-75	1993	San Fran. de Macoris, D.R.
Tucker, Jon	.165	41	115	6	19	3	0	1	5	13	35	0	0	L	L	6-5	200	12-17-76	1995	Northridge, Calif.
Walkanoff, A.J.	.232	38	112	7	25	5	0	0	8	5	23	0	0	R	R	6-4	220	3-4-74	1995	Zion, Ill.

GAMES BY POSITION: C—Malave 3, Markert 30, Meyer 32, Owen 1, Rasmussen 1, Walkanoff 36. **1B**—Harmon 4, Malave 14, Rasmussen 40, Tucker 38. **2B**—Backowski 16, Carpentier 11, Sosa 51. **3B**—Backowski 16, Gross 40, Malave 23, Sosa 7. **SS**—Carpentier 41, Cuevas 35, Morimoto 1, Sosa 3. **OF**—Backowski 1, Gibbs 36, Granzow 36, Gross 1, Hernaiz 39, Hilo 9, McClain 1, Meyer 1, Morimoto 48, Owen 34.

PITCHING	W	L	ERA	G	GS	CG	SV	IP	H	R	ER	BB	SO	B	T	HT	WT	DOB	1st Yr	Resides
Babineaux, Darrin	1	6	3.64	12	10	0	0	59	53	33	24	18	36	R	R	6-4	210	7-10-74	1995	Rayne, La.
Cervantes, Peter	3	5	4.65	13	10	0	0	50	55	32	26	16	35	L	R	6-2	185	10-13-74	1995	Los Angeles, Calif.
Chambers, Scott	1	2	5.34	20	1	0	1	29	31	20	17	13	37	L	L	5-11	175	7-10-75	1995	Benton, Ky.
Coyle, Bryan	2	0	1.40	6	1	0	0	19	14	3	3	8	17	R	R	6-1	183	8-4-75	1994	Vancouver, Wash.
Davis, Eddie	2	3	4.89	20	4	0	1	53	61	33	29	32	36	R	R	6-0	195	12-22-72	1993	New Orleans, La.
Foster, Kris	2	3	2.89	15	10	0	3	56	38	27	18	25	59	R	R	6-1	200	8-30-74	1993	Lehigh Acres, Fla.
Keppen, Jeff	2	2	5.66	20	3	0	0	41	46	35	26	32	32	R	R	6-2	190	1-31-75	1995	Lawrenceville, Ga.
Masaoka, Onan	2	4	3.65	15	7	0	3	49	28	25	20	47	75	R	L	6-0	188	10-27-77	1995	Hilo, Hawaii
McNeely, Mitch	3	4	4.25	24	3	0	1	53	53	30	25	15	31	L	L	6-6	190	2-14-74	1995	New Albany, Miss.
Pearsall, J.J.	2	3	3.26	20	1	0	1	39	39	18	14	14	26	L	L	6-2	202	9-9-73	1995	Burnt Hills, N.Y.
Sanchez, Mike	1	2	0.95	18	1	0	5	28	16	4	3	20	27	R	R	6-3	175	11-23-75	1995	Riverside, Calif.
Soto, Seferino	2	4	7.75	15	6	0	0	36	30	37	31	54	34	R	R	6-1	185	8-26-75	1995	Escondido, Calif.
South, Carl	3	6	6.14	13	10	0	0	56	72	47	38	19	30	R	R	6-5	210	4-14-75	1994	Roswell, Ga.
Stone, Ricky	4	4	5.25	16	6	0	2	48	54	31	28	20	28	R	R	6-2	173	2-28-75	1994	Hamilton, Ohio

PITCHING	W	L	ERA	G	GS	CG	SV	IP	H	R	ER	BB	SO	B	T	HT	WT	DOB	1st Yr	Resides
Tapia, Elias.................	0	1	5.40	13	1	0	0	23	23	20	14	13	15	R	R	6-2	205	5-31-76	1994	South Gate, Calif.
Thomas, Robbie............	0	1	3.60	7	2	0	0	20	15	11	8	11	17	L	L	6-4	200	4-5-72	1994	Roswell, Ga.
Vukson, John................	0	0	16.71	11	0	0	0	7	9	20	13	26	6	R	R	6-3	195	10-27-75	1993	Clovis, Calif.

GREAT FALLS
PIONEER LEAGUE
R

BATTING	AVG	G	AB	R	H	2B	3B	HR	RBI	BB	SO	SB	CS	B	T	HT	WT	DOB	1st Yr	Resides
Baker, Jason	.260	55	104	17	27	3	0	4	22	11	23	2	1	R	L	6-0	185	12-31-73	1995	Rome, N.Y.
Barlock, Todd	.274	59	190	43	52	12	5	1	31	29	45	10	3	R	R	6-4	220	8-8-71	1995	Bristol, Conn.
Bethea, Larry...............	.172	21	29	2	5	0	0	0	3	1	7	0	0	R	R	6-4	230	10-9-76	1995	Red Springs, N.C.
Bramlett, Jeff	.145	32	55	5	8	2	1	0	5	12	23	1	2	R	R	6-0	200	4-27-76	1995	Cleveland, Tenn.
Brown, Eric.................	.255	54	145	26	37	10	5	3	36	22	56	6	3	R	R	6-1	205	2-28-77	1995	La Place, La.
Carpentier, Mike..........	.263	6	19	4	5	2	0	0	2	1	3	0	0	R	R	5-11	180	8-1-74	1995	Redlands, Calif.
Flores, Eric	.229	40	83	12	19	5	1	0	9	16	28	3	1	R	R	6-3	190	7-7-76	1995	Oxnard, Calif.
Garcia, Miguel	.222	59	171	32	38	7	2	1	20	18	47	22	4	S	R	6-2	175	2-15-75	1992	Santiago, D.R.
Gonzalez, Manuel	.360	59	197	35	71	9	3	4	30	9	27	16	7	S	R	6-2	173	5-30-76	1994	Santo Domingo, D.R.
Illig, Brett	.167	23	42	4	7	1	0	0	1	3	14	0	0	R	R	6-3	185	9-4-77	1995	Phoenixville, Pa.
Manfredi, Joel	.219	33	73	6	16	2	0	1	10	6	14	0	0	R	R	6-2	205	2-24-76	1995	Stockton, Calif.
Martinez, Rafael	.273	58	183	30	50	13	3	4	30	23	36	6	3	L	L	6-3	185	8-24-75	1992	Santo Domingo, D.R.
Mateo, Jose.................	.245	40	110	20	27	2	0	0	3	13	30	4	3	S	R	6-0	160	12-28-76	1994	Santo Domingo, D.R.
Mauch, Dennis	.253	28	79	10	20	2	0	0	9	10	19	4	2	R	R	6-3	190	11-12-73	1995	Sacramento, Calif.
McCarty, Matt	.227	16	22	3	5	0	0	0	1	1	4	0	1	R	R	6-0	172	2-2-76	1995	Nashville, Tenn.
Meyer, Bobby	.150	25	40	4	6	0	1	0	4	3	14	0	0	R	R	5-11	170	9-17-74	1995	Dubuque, Iowa
Morrison, Greg	.323	54	164	29	53	8	2	2	30	12	15	1	3	L	L	6-1	185	2-23-76	1995	Medicine Hat, Alberta
Ozuna, Rafael	.327	62	245	45	80	15	5	3	34	17	36	5	6	S	R	5-11	176	7-11-74	1993	San Cristobal, D.R.
Pena, Angel.................	.290	49	138	24	40	11	1	4	15	21	32	2	1	R	R	6-0	220	2-16-75	1993	San Pedro de Macoris, D.R.
Prokopec, Luke	.244	43	119	16	29	6	2	2	24	8	37	5	2	L	R	6-0	180	2-23-78	1995	Renmark, Australia
Stuckenschneider, Eric	.314	40	118	32	37	8	2	4	16	32	26	10	7	R	R	6-0	190	8-24-71	1994	Freeburg, Mo.

GAMES BY POSITION: C—Manfredi 12, Mauch 28, Pena 45, Prokopec 2. **1B**—Bethea 8, Bramlett 27, Martinez 58. **2B**—Bramlett 1, Carpentier 1, Flores 4, Illig 1, Mateo 4, McCarty 1, Meyer 15, Ozuna 62. **3B**—Barlock 56, Illig 11, Manfredi 19. **SS**—Carpentier 6, Flores 36, Garcia 1, Illig 10, Mateo 36, McCarty 12, Ozuna 1. **OF**—Baker 52, Barlock 1, Bramlett 2, Brown 36, Garcia 55, Gonzalez 48, Meyer 2, Morrison 44, Prokopec 34, Stuckenschneider 3.

PITCHING	W	L	ERA	G	GS	CG	SV	IP	H	R	ER	BB	SO	B	T	HT	WT	DOB	1st Yr	Resides
Bourbakis, Michael........	1	2	5.14	11	1	0	0	14	16	10	8	8	13	R	R	6-2	195	11-19-76	1995	Brooklyn, N.Y.
Chapa, Javier	2	2	5.69	13	9	0	0	49	54	36	31	17	37	R	R	6-3	182	5-27-74	1995	Nuevo Laredo, Mexico
Charbonneau, Marc ...	4	1	3.61	14	7	0	0	42	37	28	17	27	30	R	L	6-3	185	9-29-75	1995	Ottawa, Ontario
Davis, John	2	2	2.81	11	1	0	0	32	24	20	10	19	26	R	R	6-4	218	8-31-73	1995	Swainsboro, Ga.
Feliciano, Pedro	0	0	13.50	6	0	0	0	7	12	12	10	7	9	L	L	5-11	165	8-25-76	1995	Dorado, P.R.
Fernandez, Omar	3	1	4.84	19	2	0	0	35	39	28	19	21	27	R	R	6-2	200	9-4-73	1995	Miami, Fla.
Flores, Ignacio	6	4	4.72	16	12	0	0	69	66	42	36	38	76	R	R	6-2	188	5-8-75	1995	La Paz, Mexico
Nakashima, Toni	2	4	5.60	20	3	0	0	35	39	25	22	20	32	L	L	5-9	160	3-17-78	1995	Sao Paulo, Brazil
Neal, Billy...................	0	1	5.84	6	1	0	0	12	19	12	8	4	8	R	R	6-0	201	9-20-71	1995	Scottsdale, Ariz.
Ochsenfeld, Chris	1	4	6.86	14	7	0	1	42	50	45	32	33	32	L	L	6-2	210	8-21-76	1994	Hampton, Va.
Reed, Jason	2	5	4.09	15	12	0	1	73	79	42	33	28	45	L	L	6-3	215	6-8-73	1994	Lakeside, Calif.
Rivera, Oscar	2	1	4.13	18	1	0	1	28	28	19	13	17	30	L	R	6-2	185	11-18-75	1995	La Paz, Mexico
Sangeado, Juan	1	3	4.30	16	3	0	1	46	47	28	22	25	46	R	R	5-11	179	4-29-75	1995	Pichucalco, Mexico
Sweezey, Gary	2	1	3.21	17	0	0	2	28	34	22	10	6	18	R	R	6-3	200	5-22-76	1995	Southington, Conn.
Taczy, Craig	0	4	3.52	18	2	0	0	31	25	20	12	28	24	L	L	6-6	215	4-15-77	1995	Crestwood, Ill.
Torres, Jackson	3	3	4.59	14	8	0	1	51	66	37	26	11	32	R	R	6-2	198	8-19-74	1992	Azua, D.R.

MILWAUKEE BREWERS

Manager: Phil Garner.   **1995 Record:** 65-79, .451 (4th, AL Central).

BATTING	AVG	G	AB	R	H	2B	3B	HR	RBI	BB	SO	SB	CS	B	T	HT	WT	DOB	1st Yr	Resides
Cirillo, Jeff	.277	125	328	57	91	19	4	9	39	47	42	7	2	R	R	6-2	180	9-23-69	1991	Van Nuys, Calif.
Hamilton, Darryl	.271	112	398	54	108	20	6	5	44	47	35	11	1	L	R	6-1	180	12-3-64	1986	Sugar Land, Texas
Hulse, David	.251	119	339	46	85	11	6	3	47	18	60	15	3	L	L	5-11	170	2-25-68	1990	San Angelo, Texas
Jaha, John	.313	88	316	59	99	20	2	20	65	36	66	2	1	R	R	6-1	205	5-27-66	1985	Portland, Ore.
Listach, Pat	.219	101	334	35	73	8	2	0	25	25	61	13	3	S	R	5-9	170	9-12-67	1988	Woodway, Texas
Loretta, Mark	.260	19	50	13	13	3	0	1	3	4	7	1	1	R	R	6-0	175	8-14-71	1993	Laguna Niguel, Calif.
Matheny, Mike	.247	80	166	13	41	9	1	0	21	12	28	2	1	R	R	6-3	205	9-22-70	1991	Reynoldsburg, Ohio
May, Derrick	.248	32	113	15	28	3	1	1	9	5	18	0	1	L	R	6-4	200	7-14-68	1986	Newark, Del.
Mieske, Matt	.251	117	267	42	67	13	1	12	48	27	45	2	4	R	R	6-0	185	2-13-68	1990	Livonia, Mich.
Nilsson, Dave	.278	81	263	41	73	12	1	12	53	24	41	2	0	L	R	6-3	215	12-14-69	1987	Everton Hills, Australia
Oliver, Joe	.273	97	337	43	92	20	0	12	51	27	66	2	4	R	R	6-3	220	7-24-65	1983	Orlando, Fla.
Seitzer, Kevin	.311	132	492	56	153	33	3	5	69	64	57	2	0	R	R	5-11	190	3-26-62	1983	Overland Park, Kan.
Singleton, Duane	.065	13	31	0	2	0	0	0	0	1	10	1	0	L	R	6-1	170	8-6-72	1990	Staten Island, N.Y.
Surhoff, B.J.	.320	117	415	72	133	26	3	13	73	37	43	7	3	L	R	6-1	200	8-4-64	1985	Franklin, Wisc.
Unroe, Tim	.250	2	4	0	1	0	0	0	0	0	0	0	0	R	R	6-3	200	10-7-70	1992	Round Lake Beach, Ill.
Valentin, Jose	.219	112	338	62	74	23	3	11	49	37	83	16	8	S	R	5-10	175	10-12-69	1987	Manati, P.R.
Vaughn, Greg	.224	108	392	67	88	19	1	17	59	55	89	10	4	R	R	6-0	205	7-3-65	1986	Elk Grove, Calif.
Vina, Fernando	.257	113	288	46	74	7	7	3	29	22	28	6	3	L	R	5-9	170	4-16-69	1993	Sacramento, Calif.
Ward, Turner	.264	44	129	19	34	3	1	4	16	14	21	6	1	S	R	6-2	182	4-11-65	1986	Saraland, Ala.

PITCHING	W	L	ERA	G	GS	CG	SV	IP	H	R	ER	BB	SO	B	T	HT	WT	DOB	1st Yr	Resides
Bones, Ricky	10	12	4.63	32	31	3	0	200	218	108	103	83	77	R	R	6-0	190	4-7-69	1986	Guayama, P.R.
Bronkey, Jeff	0	0	3.65	8	0	0	0	12	15	6	5	6	5	R	R	6-3	215	9-18-65	1986	Klamath Falls, Ore.
Dibble, Rob	1	1	8.25	15	0	0	0	12	9	11	11	19	10	L	R	6-4	230	1-24-64	1983	Cincinnati, Ohio
2-team (16 Chicago)	1	2	7.18	31	0	0	1	26	16	21	21	46	26							
Eldred, Cal	1	1	3.42	4	4	0	0	24	24	10	9	10	18	R	R	6-4	235	11-24-67	1989	Center Point, Iowa
Fetters, Mike	0	3	3.38	40	0	0	22	35	40	16	13	20	33	R	R	6-4	215	12-19-64	1986	Gilbert, Ariz.
Givens, Brian	5	7	4.95	19	19	0	0	107	116	71	59	54	73	R	L	6-6	220	11-6-65	1984	Aurora, Colo.
Ignasiak, Mike	4	1	5.90	25	0	0	0	40	51	27	26	23	26	S	R	5-11	190	3-12-66	1988	Casco, Mich.
Karl, Scott	6	7	4.14	25	18	1	0	124	141	65	57	50	59	L	L	6-2	195	8-9-71	1992	Carlsbad, Calif.
Kiefer, Mark	4	1	3.44	24	0	0	0	50	37	20	19	27	41	R	R	6-4	184	11-13-68	1988	Kingsland, Texas
Lloyd, Graeme	0	5	4.50	33	0	0	4	32	28	16	16	8	13	L	L	6-7	230	4-9-67	1988	Gnarwarre, Australia
McAndrew, Jamie	2	3	4.71	10	4	0	0	36	37	21	19	12	19	R	R	6-2	190	9-2-67	1989	Fort Myers, Fla.
Mercedes, Jose	0	1	9.82	5	0	0	0	7	12	9	8	8	6	R	R	6-1	180	3-5-71	1990	Las Palmillas, D.R.
Miranda, Angel	4	5	5.23	30	10	0	1	74	83	47	43	49	45	L	L	6-1	195	11-9-69	1987	Arecibo, P.R.
Reyes, Al	1	1	2.43	27	0	0	1	33	19	9	9	18	29	R	R	6-0	165	4-10-71	1988	Santo Domingo, D.R.
Rightnowar, Ron	2	1	5.40	34	0	0	1	37	35	23	22	18	22	R	R	6-3	190	9-5-64	1987	Toledo, Ohio
Roberson, Sid	6	4	5.76	26	13	0	0	84	102	55	54	30	40	L	L	5-9	170	9-7-71	1992	Orange Park, Fla.
Scanlan, Bob	4	7	6.59	17	14	0	0	83	101	66	61	44	29	R	R	6-8	215	8-9-66	1984	Beverly Hills, Calif.
Slusarski, Joe	1	1	5.40	12	0	0	0	15	21	11	9	6	6	R	R	6-4	195	12-19-66	1989	Springfield, Ill.
Sparks, Steve	9	11	4.63	33	27	3	0	202	210	111	104	86	96	R	R	6-0	180	7-2-65	1987	Tulsa, Okla.
Thomas, Mike	0	0	0.00	1	0	0	0	1	2	0	0	1	0	L	L	6-1	175	9-2-69	1989	Cabot, Ark.
Wegman, Bill	5	7	5.35	37	4	0	2	71	89	45	42	21	50	R	R	6-5	235	12-19-62	1981	Cincinnati, Ohio
Wickander, Kevin	0	0	0.00	8	0	0	1	6	1	0	0	3	2	L	L	6-3	200	1-4-65	1986	Glendale, Ariz.
2-team (21 Detroit)	0	0	1.93	29	0	0	1	23	19	6	5	12	11							

FIELDING

Catcher	PCT	G	PO	A	E	DP	PB
Matheny	.986	80	261	18	4	2	10
Nilsson	1.000	2	2	0	0	0	1
Oliver	.982	91	408	40	8	4	16
Surhoff	.984	18	57	6	1	0	8

First Base	PCT	G	PO	A	E	DP
Cirillo	1.000	3	16	1	0	1
Jaha	.997	81	649	60	2	86
Nilsson	1.000	7	16	2	0	1
Oliver	1.000	2	6	0	0	1
Seitzer	.990	36	288	21	3	38
Surhoff	.992	55	348	29	3	45
Unroe	1.000	2	11	0	0	3

Second Base	PCT	G	PO	A	E	DP
Cirillo	.984	25	52	75	2	16
Listach	1.000	59	104	169	0	44
Loretta	1.000	4	5	9	0	2
Vina	.983	99	183	225	7	71

Third Base	PCT	G	PO	A	E	DP
Cirillo	.938	108	45	153	13	22
Listach	1.000	2	1	0	0	0

	PCT	G	PO	A	E	DP
Seitzer	.968	88	52	160	7	18
Valentin	1.000	1	0	2	0	1
Vina	.000	2	0	0	0	0

Shortstop	PCT	G	PO	A	E	DP
Cirillo	1.000	2	0	1	0	0
Listach	.963	56	54	103	6	31
Loretta	.979	13	13	33	1	5
Valentin	.971	104	164	333	15	85
Vina	.969	6	11	20	1	4

Outfield	PCT	G	PO	A	E	DP
Hamilton	.989	109	262	4	3	1
Hulse	.984	115	180	2	3	1
Listach	1.000	11	10	1	0	0
May	.971	32	65	1	2	1
Mieske	.979	108	177	7	4	2
Nilsson	.981	58	99	5	2	0
Singleton	1.000	11	22	1	0	0
Surhoff	.993	60	125	9	1	1
Ward	.989	40	81	5	1	1
Wegman	.000	1	0	0	0	0

B.J. Surhoff

Third baseman Kevin Seitzer led the Brewers with 153 hits and 33 doubles

THE SPORTS GROUP

Brewers minor league Player of the Year Jeff D'Amico

LARRY KINKER

FARM SYSTEM

Director of Player Development: Fred Stanley.

Class	Farm Team	League	W	L	Pct.	Finish*	Manager	First Yr
AAA	New Orleans (La.) Zephyrs	American Assoc.	63	79	.444	7th (8)	Chris Bando	1993
AA	El Paso (Texas) Diablos	Texas	68	68	.500	4th (8)	Tim Ireland	1981
#A	Stockton (Calif.) Ports	California	74	65	.532	5th (10)	Bob Mariano	1979
A	Beloit (Wis.) Snappers	Midwest	88	51	.633	1st+ (14)	Dub Kilgo	1982
#R	Helena (Mont.) Brewers	Pioneer	44	28	.611	2nd+ (8)	Alex Morales	1985
R	Chandler (Ariz.) Brewers	Arizona	34	22	.607	3rd (6)	Ralph Dickenson	1988

*Finish in overall standings (No. of teams in league)   #Advanced level   +Won league championship

ORGANIZATION LEADERS

MAJOR LEAGUERS

BATTING
*AVG	B.J. Surhoff	.320
R	B.J. Surhoff	72
H	Kevin Seitzer	153
TB	Kevin Seitzer	207
2B	Kevin Seitzer	33
3B	Fernando Vina	7
HR	John Jaha	20
RBI	B.J. Surhoff	73
BB	Kevin Seitzer	64
SO	Greg Vaughn	89
SB	Jose Valentin	16

PITCHING
W	Ricky Bones	10
L	Ricky Bones	12
#ERA	Scott Karl	4.14
G	Mike Fetters	40
CG	Two tied at	3
SV	Mike Fetters	22
IP	Steve Sparks	202
BB	Steve Sparks	86
SO	Steve Sparks	96

THE SPORTS GROUP

Mike Fetters. 22 saves

MINOR LEAGUERS

BATTING
*AVG	Mike Kinkade, Helena	.353
R	Dave Milstien, Beloit/Stockton	84
H	Hector Ortega, Stockton	162
TB	Derek Hacopian, Beloit	244
2B	Brian Banks, El Paso	39
3B	Two tied at	10
HR	Derek Hacopian, Beloit	23
RBI	Derek Hacopian, Beloit	92
BB	Two tied at	81
SO	Scott Krause, Beloit	126
SB	Greg Martinez, Stockton	55

PITCHING
W	Two tied at	13
L	Kelly Wunsch, Beloit/Stockton	13
#ERA	Josh Bishop, AZL Brewers	2.16
G	Luis Salazar, Stockton	52
CG	Kelly Wunsch, Beloit/Stockton	4
SV	Doug Webb, Stockton/El Paso	30
IP	Kelly Wunsch, Beloit/Stockton	160
BB	Frankie Rodriguez, El Paso	80
SO	Josh Bishop, AZL Brewers	134

*Minimum 250 At-Bats   #Minimum 75 Innings

TOP 10 PROSPECTS

How the Brewers Top 10 prospects, as judged by Baseball America prior to the 1995 season, fared in 1995:

JOHN SPEAR

Antone Williamson

Player, Pos.	Club (Class—League)	AVG	AB	R	H	2B	3B	HR	RBI	SB
1. Antone Williamson, 3b	El Paso (AA—Texas)	.309	392	62	121	30	6	7	90	3
2. Duane Singleton, of	New Orleans (AAA—Amer. Assoc.)	.268	355	48	95	10	4	4	29	31
	Milwaukee	.065	31	0	2	0	0	0	0	1
3. Danny Klassen, ss	Beloit (A—Midwest)	.275	218	27	60	15	2	2	25	12
4. Mark Loretta, ss	New Orleans (AAA—Amer. Assoc.)	.286	479	48	137	22	5	7	79	8
	Milwaukee	.260	50	13	13	3	0	1	3	1
6. Tim Unroe, 1b	New Orleans (AAA—Amer. Assoc.)	.261	371	43	97	21	2	6	45	4
	Milwaukee	.250	4	0	1	0	0	0	0	0
8. Derek Wachter, of	New Orleans (AAA—Amer. Assoc.)	.257	382	44	98	23	1	8	45	2
9. Todd Dunn, of	Stockton (A—California)	.293	249	44	73	20	2	7	40	14

		W	L	ERA	G	SV	IP	H	BB	SO
5. Jeff D'Amico, rhp	Beloit (A—Midwest)	13	3	2.39	21	0	132	102	31	119
7. Marshall Boze, rhp	New Orleans (AAA—Amer. Assoc.)	3	9	4.27	23	1	112	134	45	47
10. Sid Roberson, lhp	New Orleans (AAA—Amer. Assoc.)	0	2	7.62	4	0	13	20	10	8
	Milwaukee	6	4	5.76	26	0	84	102	37	40

AMERICAN ASSOCIATION

BATTING	AVG	G	AB	R	H	2B	3B	HR	RBI	BB	SO	SB	CS	B	T	HT	WT	DOB	1st Yr	Resides
Barker, Tim	.258	80	264	44	68	9	5	1	24	29	39	10	8	R	R	6-0	175	6-30-68	1989	Salisbury, Md.
Basse, Mike	.247	121	381	49	94	14	2	0	35	58	62	15	9	L	L	6-0	185	3-7-70	1991	San Juan Capistrano, Calif.
Byington, John	.255	13	47	5	12	1	0	1	3	2	4	1	0	R	R	5-8	165	11-4-67	1989	Baytown, Texas
Dodson, Bo	.281	62	203	29	57	5	1	9	34	36	27	0	0	L	L	6-2	195	12-7-70	1989	West Sacramento, Calif.
Finn, Mike	.325	35	117	20	38	4	1	3	19	13	7	9	2	R	R	5-8	168	10-18-67	1989	Oakland, Calif.
Gonzalez, Javier	.248	43	113	20	28	11	0	5	15	7	24	0	0	R	R	6-0	193	10-3-68	1986	Carolina, P.R.
Harris, Mike	.232	21	56	3	13	3	0	0	5	4	9	1	1	L	L	5-11	195	4-30-70	1991	Lexington, Ky.
Jaha, John	.400	3	10	2	4	1	0	1	3	2	1	0	0	R	R	6-1	205	5-27-66	1985	Portland, Ore.
Koslofski, Kevin	.212	105	321	41	68	18	4	7	35	34	100	4	2	L	R	5-8	175	9-24-66	1984	Maroa, Ill.
Lofton, Rodney	.217	102	240	30	52	7	0	1	18	15	48	9	3	R	R	5-11	185	10-7-67	1988	East St. Louis, Ill.
Lopez, Pedro	.000	3	8	0	0	0	0	0	0	0	3	0	0	R	R	6-0	160	3-29-69	1988	Vega Baja, P.R.
Loretta, Mark	.286	127	479	48	137	22	5	7	79	34	47	8	9	R	R	6-0	175	8-14-71	1993	Laguna Niguel, Calif.
Matheny, Mike	.353	6	17	3	6	2	0	3	4	0	5	0	0	R	R	6-3	205	9-22-70	1991	Reynoldsburg, Ohio
Nilsson, Dave	.444	3	9	1	4	0	0	1	4	2	0	0	0	L	R	6-3	215	12-14-69	1987	Everton Hills, Australia
Oliver, Joe	.077	4	13	0	1	1	0	0	0	0	3	0	0	R	R	6-3	220	7-24-65	1983	Orlando, Fla.
Perez, Danny	.294	12	34	5	10	1	0	0	0	5	9	0	0	R	R	5-10	188	2-26-71	1992	El Paso, Texas
Singleton, Duane	.268	106	355	48	95	10	4	4	29	39	63	31	15	L	R	6-1	170	8-6-72	1990	Staten Island, N.Y.
Smith, Greg	.212	59	170	18	36	3	1	0	9	17	22	11	7	S	R	6-0	180	4-5-67	1985	Palm Springs, Calif.
Staton, Dave	.252	108	325	42	82	11	1	19	46	46	96	0	3	R	R	6-5	215	4-12-68	1989	Auburn, Calif.
Stefanski, Mike	.246	78	228	30	56	10	2	2	24	14	28	2	0	R	R	6-2	190	9-12-69	1991	Redford, Mich.
Sutko, Glenn	.208	42	101	7	21	8	0	3	14	7	35	0	0	R	R	6-3	225	5-9-69	1988	Alpharetta, Ga.
Talanoa, Scott	.143	31	98	9	14	4	0	1	3	6	26	0	0	R	R	6-5	240	11-12-69	1991	Lawndale, Calif.
Unroe, Tim	.261	102	371	43	97	21	2	6	45	18	94	4	3	R	R	6-3	200	10-7-70	1992	Round Lake Beach, Ill.
Wachter, Derek	.257	112	382	44	98	23	1	8	45	39	67	2	2	R	R	6-2	195	8-28-70	1991	Miller Place, N.Y.
Ward, Turner	.242	11	33	3	8	1	1	1	3	4	10	0	0	S	R	6-2	182	4-11-65	1986	Saraland, Ala.
Weger, Wes	.286	64	234	28	67	16	0	2	24	10	31	0	2	R	R	6-0	170	10-3-70	1992	Longwood, Fla.

PITCHING	W	L	ERA	G	GS	CG	SV	IP	H	R	ER	BB	SO	B	T	HT	WT	DOB	1st Yr	Resides
Archer, Kurt	2	6	3.25	38	0	0	2	61	57	23	22	17	41	R	R	6-4	230	4-27-69	1990	Burlington, Wash.
Boze, Marshall	3	9	4.27	23	19	1	1	112	134	65	53	45	47	R	R	6-1	212	5-23-71	1990	Springfield, Ill.
Bronkey, Jeff	0	1	2.25	2	1	0	0	8	8	2	2	1	2	R	R	6-3	215	9-18-65	1986	Klamath Falls, Ore.
Combs, Pat	1	1	5.40	12	2	0	0	15	19	11	9	13	10	L	L	6-4	213	10-29-66	1989	Houston, Texas
Dibble, Rob	0	1	0.00	4	0	0	0	4	1	2	0	2	6	L	R	6-4	230	1-24-64	1983	Cincinnati, Ohio
Duncan, Chip	1	4	6.29	14	5	0	0	34	44	26	24	18	23	R	R	5-11	185	6-25-67	1987	Fort Myers, Fla.
2-team (3 Okla. City)	1	4	5.90	17	5	0	0	40	50	28	26	19	26							
Farrell, Mike	8	10	4.57	25	24	0	0	142	173	84	72	38	74	R	R	6-2	184	1-28-69	1991	Logansport, Ind.
Fritz, John	6	3	3.97	41	6	0	1	82	70	38	36	42	56	R	R	6-1	170	3-6-69	1988	Koppel, Pa.
Ganote, Joe	7	4	3.42	14	13	2	0	82	88	35	31	21	56	R	R	6-5	185	1-22-68	1990	Lake Wylie, S.C.
Givens, Brian	7	4	2.55	16	11	2	0	78	67	28	22	33	75	R	L	6-6	220	11-6-65	1984	Aurora, Colo.
Ignasiak, Mike	1	1	2.50	4	2	0	0	18	9	5	5	8	19	S	R	5-11	190	3-12-66	1988	Casco, Mich.
Jones, Stacy	3	2	3.02	34	0	0	6	48	51	16	16	12	39	R	R	6-6	225	5-26-67	1988	Attalla, Ala.
Karl, Scott	3	4	3.30	8	6	1	0	46	47	18	17	12	29	L	L	6-2	195	8-9-71	1992	Carlsbad, Calif.
Kiefer, Mark	8	2	2.82	12	12	1	0	70	60	22	22	19	52	R	R	6-4	184	11-13-68	1988	Kingsland, Texas
McAndrew, Jamie	7	5	3.97	17	17	3	0	104	102	48	46	44	62	R	R	6-2	190	9-2-67	1989	Fort Myers, Fla.
McClellan, Paul	0	3	6.06	3	3	1	0	16	19	11	11	8	8	R	R	6-2	190	2-3-66	1986	Redwood City, Calif.
Parker, Clay	0	0	6.75	2	0	0	0	1	3	2	1	2	2	R	R	6-1	175	12-19-62	1985	Hixson, Tenn.
Popplewell, Tom	0	2	6.75	10	0	0	0	13	13	11	10	11	16	R	R	6-3	225	8-3-67	1987	Hamilton, Ohio
Rambo, Dan	0	4	5.20	7	6	0	0	36	39	23	21	9	22	R	R	6-0	190	10-7-66	1989	Sault St. Marie, Mich.
Rightnowar, Ron	1	1	2.67	25	0	0	10	30	37	16	9	9	22	R	R	6-3	190	9-5-64	1987	Toledo, Ohio
Roberson, Sid	0	2	7.62	4	3	0	0	13	20	11	11	10	8	L	L	5-9	170	9-7-71	1992	Orange Park, Fla.
Scanlan, Bob	0	1	5.40	3	3	0	0	12	17	7	7	3	5	R	R	6-8	215	8-9-66	1984	Beverly Hills, Calif.
Seminara, Frank	2	3	7.96	11	7	0	0	37	54	35	33	14	19	R	R	6-2	195	5-16-67	1988	Brooklyn, N.Y.
Shinall, Zak	0	0	7.62	9	0	0	0	13	15	11	11	7	5	R	R	6-3	215	10-14-68	1987	Vero Beach, Fla.
Slusarski, Joe	1	1	1.12	33	0	0	11	48	37	10	6	11	30	R	R	6-4	195	12-19-66	1989	Springfield, Ill.
2-team (4 Buffalo)	2	2	2.39	37	2	0	11	64	55	22	17	15	39							
Swingle, Paul	1	4	4.57	35	0	0	0	43	42	25	22	16	47	R	R	6-0	185	12-21-66	1989	Mesa, Ariz.
Taylor, Scott	1	0	2.38	2	2	0	0	11	10	3	3	3	9	R	R	6-3	200	10-3-66	1989	Wichita, Kan.
Thomas, Mike	0	1	4.05	35	0	0	1	33	37	18	15	18	28	L	L	6-1	175	9-2-69	1989	Cabot, Ark.

FIELDING

Catcher	PCT	G	PO	A	E	DP	PB
Gonzalez	.996	43	239	27	1	5	4
Lofton	.000	1	0	0	0	0	0
Lopez	1.000	2	14	1	0	0	0
Matheny	1.000	6	30	4	0	0	0
Oliver	1.000	3	14	7	0	1	0
Stefanski	.995	70	355	35	2	5	7
Sutko	.991	39	192	20	2	2	6

First Base	PCT	G	PO	A	E	DP
Barker	1.000	10	62	4	0	7
Dodson	.995	47	400	32	2	40
Harris	.000	1	0	0	0	0
Jaha	1.000	1	9	2	0	3
Singleton	1.000	1	3	0	0	0
Staton	.993	54	419	33	3	45
Stefanski	1.000	1	8	0	0	3
Talanoa	1.000	5	30	3	0	3
Unroe	1.000	47	321	23	0	46
Wachter	1.000	1	1	0	0	0

Second Base	PCT	G	PO	A	E	DP
Barker	1.000	23	48	55	0	19

	PCT	G	PO	A	E	DP
Finn	.961	14	17	32	2	5
Lofton	.983	57	98	134	4	35
Loretta	1.000	1	1	1	0	1
Smith	.973	19	31	40	2	8
Weger	.974	53	115	145	7	48

Third Base	PCT	G	PO	A	E	DP
Barker	.902	18	6	31	4	3
Byington	.885	11	3	20	3	1
Dodson	1.000	1	0	1	0	0
Finn	.667	1	1	1	1	0
Lofton	.963	31	20	57	3	8
Loretta	1.000	4	3	9	0	0
Singleton	1.000	1	0	1	0	0
Staton	1.000	2	0	1	0	0
Stefanski	1.000	3	1	2	0	0
Sutko	.750	2	1	5	2	1
Unroe	.940	67	51	137	12	16
Weger	.941	5	6	10	1	1

Shortstop	PCT	G	PO	A	E	DP
Barker	1.000	2	4	9	0	2
Lofton	1.000	5	6	13	0	4
Loretta	.958	123	200	366	25	79
Smith	.974	15	21	53	2	13
Weger	.909	2	3	7	1	2

Outfield	PCT	G	PO	A	E	DP
Barker	1.000	34	41	2	0	0
Basse	.988	91	150	8	2	0
Dodson	1.000	7	10	1	0	0
Finn	.972	23	33	2	1	0
Harris	1.000	4	5	1	0	0
Koslofski	.996	101	231	19	1	2
Nilsson	1.000	1	2	0	0	0
Singleton	.978	85	165	12	4	2
Staton	1.000	2	1	0	0	0
Stefanski	.000	1	0	0	0	0
Unroe	1.000	1	1	0	0	0
Wachter	.983	106	154	17	3	3
Ward	.900	9	9	0	1	0

Mark Loretta
.286-7-79 for New Orleans

Brian Banks
.308-12-78 for El Paso

Todd Landry
.292-16-79 for El Paso

EL PASO

TEXAS LEAGUE

AA

BATTING	AVG	G	AB	R	H	2B	3B	HR	RBI	BB	SO	SB	CS	B	T	HT	WT	DOB	1st Yr	Resides
Banks, Brian	.308	128	441	81	136	39	10	12	78	81	113	9	9	S	R	6-3	200	9-28-70	1993	Mesa, Ariz.
Dodson, Bo	.359	63	223	46	80	20	4	7	43	37	42	1	1	L	L	6-2	195	12-7-70	1989	West Sacramento, Calif.
Dumas, Mike	.217	12	23	5	5	0	1	0	4	3	0	2	1	R	R	5-9	163	5-28-71	1992	Hattiesburg, Miss.
Felder, Kenny	.272	114	367	51	100	24	4	12	55	48	94	2	6	R	R	6-3	235	2-9-71	1992	Niceville, Fla.
Felix, Lauro	.277	81	220	51	61	13	1	3	25	45	44	6	1	R	R	5-9	160	6-24-70	1992	El Paso, Texas
Guerrero, Mike	.310	23	71	14	22	1	0	1	7	7	5	0	0	S	R	5-11	155	1-8-68	1987	Santo Domingo, D.R.
Harris, Mike	.333	8	24	4	8	2	0	1	5	2	3	0	0	L	L	5-11	195	4-30-70	1991	Lexington, Ky.
Hughes, Bobby	.266	51	173	11	46	12	0	7	27	12	30	0	2	R	R	6-4	220	3-10-71	1992	North Hollywood, Calif.
Jenkins, Geoff	.278	21	79	12	22	4	2	1	13	8	23	3	1	L	L	6-1	195	7-21-74	1995	Rancho Cordova, Calif.
Kappesser, Bob	.191	61	115	17	22	5	2	1	17	12	19	2	2	R	R	5-9	180	2-14-67	1989	Auburn, N.Y.
Landry, Todd	.292	132	511	76	149	33	4	16	79	33	99	9	7	R	L	6-4	215	8-21-72	1993	Donaldsonville, La.
Lopez, Pedro	.312	84	218	32	68	15	2	4	28	18	45	0	3	R	R	6-0	160	3-29-69	1988	Vega Baja, P.R.
Lopez, Roberto	.312	114	417	80	130	22	8	1	44	77	63	9	4	S	R	5-9	150	11-15-71	1994	Bayamon, P.R.
Martinez, Gabby	.278	44	133	13	37	3	2	0	11	2	22	5	1	S	R	6-2	170	1-7-74	1992	Santurce, P.R.
Millan, Bernie	.242	13	33	2	8	1	0	1	3	0	3	0	0	S	R	6-1	202	12-27-70	1990	Rio Piedras, P.R.
Nevers, Tom	.254	35	118	19	30	5	1	1	12	11	21	2	1	R	R	6-1	175	9-13-71	1990	Edina, Minn.
2-team (83 Jackson)	.245	118	416	55	102	12	4	9	47	35	79	7	3							
Nicholas, Darrell	.205	15	39	4	8	0	1	0	2	0	11	4	0	R	R	6-0	180	5-26-72	1994	Garyville, La.
Nilsson, Dave	.467	5	15	1	7	1	0	1	4	0	1	1	0	L	R	6-3	215	12-14-69	1987	Everton Hills, Australia
Odor, Rouglas	.294	6	17	2	5	0	0	0	2	2	2	0	0	R	R	5-11	165	1-26-68	1988	New Orleans, La.
Perez, Danny	.276	22	76	16	21	1	1	0	7	4	14	1	0	R	R	5-10	188	2-26-71	1992	El Paso, Texas
Richardson, Scott	.254	82	256	29	65	9	6	1	29	16	42	8	6	R	R	6-1	175	2-19-71	1992	Rialto, Calif.
Rodriques, Cecil	.266	72	244	36	65	9	7	2	24	15	51	5	2	R	R	6-0	175	9-3-71	1991	Fort Pierce, Fla.
Samples, Todd	.000	2	4	1	0	0	0	0	0	1	1	0	0	R	R	6-2	185	8-1-69	1990	Springfield, Mo.
Shabazz, Basil	.216	47	102	19	22	2	3	0	7	14	23	9	5	R	R	6-0	185	1-31-72	1991	Pine Bluff, Ark.
Stefanski, Mike	.407	6	27	5	11	3	0	1	6	0	3	1	0	R	R	6-2	190	9-12-69	1991	Redford, Mich.
Sutko, Glenn	.277	44	119	18	33	9	1	4	20	20	34	1	0	R	R	6-3	225	5-9-69	1988	Alpharetta, Ga.
Talanoa, Scott	.222	2	9	0	2	2	0	0	1	1	0	0	0	R	R	6-5	240	11-12-69	1991	Lawndale, Calif.
Thompson, Fletcher	.192	11	26	3	5	0	0	0	3	1	9	0	0	L	R	5-11	180	9-14-68	1990	Jackson, Miss.
Weger, Wes	.256	45	160	22	41	9	2	0	19	10	14	1	1	R	R	6-0	170	10-3-70	1992	Longwood, Fla.
Williamson, Antone	.309	104	392	62	121	30	6	7	90	47	57	3	1	L	R	6-1	195	7-18-73	1994	Torrance, Calif.

PITCHING	W	L	ERA	G	GS	CG	SV	IP	H	R	ER	BB	SO	B	T	HT	WT	DOB	1st Yr	Resides
Archer, Kurt	0	0	3.00	4	0	0	1	6	4	2	2	1	5	R	R	6-4	230	4-27-69	1990	Burlington, Wash.
Browne, Byron	10	4	3.43	25	20	2	0	126	106	55	48	78	110	R	R	6-7	200	8-8-70	1991	Phoenix, Ariz.
Caruso, Gene	2	1	6.08	46	1	0	2	71	87	55	48	36	53	L	L	6-0	185	7-20-69	1992	Las Vegas, Nev.
Cimorelli, Frank	0	0	4.50	2	0	0	0	2	1	1	1	2	0	R	R	6-0	175	8-2-68	1989	Hyde Park, N.Y.
Cole, Jim	1	4	8.75	6	6	0	0	24	42	28	23	11	14	R	R	6-2	200	2-19-71	1993	Augusta, Ga.
Duda, Steve	1	3	4.87	24	4	0	1	44	58	33	24	16	29	R	R	5-11	170	6-27-71	1993	Thousand Oaks, Calif.
Gamez, Francisco	2	1	5.29	27	8	0	2	68	79	46	40	39	33	R	R	6-2	185	4-2-70	1990	Tucson, Ariz.
Ganote, Joe	5	1	1.61	12	7	0	1	50	40	18	9	16	39	R	R	6-1	185	1-22-68	1990	Lake Wylie, S.C.
Gerstein, Ron	8	12	4.55	28	22	1	0	127	155	90	64	58	69	L	L	6-1	200	1-1-69	1990	Santa Cruz, Calif.
Jones, Stacy	1	1	2.03	8	0	0	3	13	12	7	3	4	14	R	R	6-6	225	5-26-67	1988	Attalla, Ala.
Kappesser, Bob	0	0	9.28	8	0	0	0	11	18	11	11	5	2	R	R	5-9	180	2-14-67	1989	Auburn, N.Y.
Kloek, Kevin	7	11	4.93	28	27	3	0	157	196	103	86	48	121	R	R	6-3	175	8-15-70	1992	Santa Barbara, Calif.
Kosenski, John	3	1	5.72	16	0	0	0	28	41	19	18	17	25	R	R	6-5	195	1-28-69	1991	Boulder, Colo.
Langben, Gregg	2	1	5.24	16	0	0	0	22	19	16	13	12	20	R	L	5-11	182	11-14-69	1988	Schofield, Wisc.
Lidle, Cory	5	4	3.36	45	9	0	2	110	126	52	41	36	78	R	R	6-0	175	3-22-72	1991	West Covina, Calif.
Linares, Yfrain	1	1	9.45	8	0	0	0	13	21	15	14	12	9	R	R	6-2	180	12-7-69	1988	Maracay, Venez.
Maloney, Sean	7	5	4.18	43	0	0	15	65	69	41	30	28	54	R	R	6-7	200	5-25-71	1993	North Kingstown, R.I.
Montoya, Norm	2	5	3.42	51	0	0	2	76	88	36	29	18	43	L	L	6-1	190	9-24-70	1990	Newark, Calif.
Popplewell, Tom	0	0	15.00	4	0	0	0	3	7	5	5	6	1	R	R	6-3	225	8-3-67	1987	Hamilton, Ohio
Rodriguez, Frankie	9	8	4.98	28	27	1	0	143	157	90	79	80	129	R	R	5-9	170	1-6-73	1992	Brea, Calif.
Wagner, Joe	0	4	9.95	5	5	0	0	19	32	31	21	22	8	R	R	6-1	195	12-8-71	1993	Janesville, Wisc.
Webb, Doug	2	1	4.42	18	0	0	8	18	11	9	9	13	11	R	R	6-3	205	8-25-73	1994	Draper, Utah

FIELDING

Catcher

Catcher	PCT	G	PO	A	E	DP	PB
Banks	.947	3	17	1	1	0	2
Hughes	.976	51	299	29	8	2	6
Kappesser	.975	35	157	37	5	0	7
Lopez	.985	48	231	37	4	5	5
Sutko	.975	34	198	34	6	2	3

First Base

First Base	PCT	G	PO	A	E	DP
Banks	.975	5	37	2	1	1
Dodson	1.000	11	100	7	0	12
Guerrero	1.000	1	1	0	0	0
Landry	.989	121	1015	123	13	101
Lopez	.875	5	6	1	1	1
Millan	1.000	3	2	0	0	0
Montoya	1.000	1	1	0	0	0
Nevers	1.000	3	10	0	0	3
Richardson	.750	1	3	0	1	0
Sutko	1.000	2	3	1	0	0
Williamson	1.000	6	32	1	0	8

Second Base

Second Base	PCT	G	PO	A	E	DP
Dumas	.960	5	12	12	1	1
Felix	.957	20	44	49	4	18
Guerrero	1.000	1	2	2	0	0
Kappesser	1.000	8	2	6	0	2
Lopez	.972	110	228	295	15	69

	PCT	G	PO	A	E	DP
Millan	1.000	5	3	10	0	2
Nevers	1.000	1	1	0	0	0
Odor	.833	1	1	4	1	1
Richardson	.000	2	0	0	1	0
Thompson	1.000	6	13	26	0	3

Third Base

Third Base	PCT	G	PO	A	E	DP
Banks	1.000	2	1	1	0	0
Dumas	.833	3	3	7	2	0
Felix	.950	15	5	33	2	4
Guerrero	.333	2	0	1	2	0
Kappesser	.882	11	4	11	2	0
Millan	.833	2	2	3	1	0
Nevers	.805	32	20	46	16	3
Richardson	.000	2	0	0	0	0
Stefanski	.842	6	2	14	3	2
Thompson	.714	3	2	3	2	1
Weger	1.000	1	0	3	0	0
Williamson	.866	76	47	134	28	6

Shortstop

Shortstop	PCT	G	PO	A	E	DP
Dumas	.818	2	5	4	2	1
Felix	.939	47	71	99	11	24
Guerrero	.938	18	35	40	5	7
Lopez	.909	6	4	6	1	0

	PCT	G	PO	A	E	DP
Martinez	.949	43	65	103	9	27
Nevers	.833	2	2	3	1	2
Odor	.962	5	11	14	1	6
Weger	.931	37	62	100	12	16

Outfield

Outfield	PCT	G	PO	A	E	DP
Banks	.960	117	206	8	9	1
Caruso	.000	1	0	0	0	0
Dodson	1.000	1	1	0	0	0
Felder	.966	108	156	14	6	0
Gamez	.000	1	0	0	0	0
Jenkins	.857	20	41	1	7	0
Kappesser	.000	4	0	0	0	0
Landry	.875	17	13	1	2	0
Langbehn	.000	1	0	0	0	0
Lopez	.000	1	0	0	0	0
Nicholas	.903	14	28	0	3	0
Nilsson	1.000	5	4	0	0	0
Richardson	.958	75	109	5	5	3
Rodriques	.976	65	118	2	3	0
Samples	1.000	1	3	0	0	0
Shabazz	.938	40	53	8	4	1
Sutko	.000	1	0	0	0	0

STOCKTON

A

CALIFORNIA LEAGUE

BATTING

BATTING	AVG	G	AB	R	H	2B	3B	HR	RBI	BB	SO	SB	CS	B	T	HT	WT	DOB	1st Yr	Resides
Campillo, Rob	.302	35	106	10	32	3	0	0	17	7	13	0	0	R	R	6-0	195	11-2-71	1992	Tucson, Ariz.
Carrasquel, Domingo	.269	67	160	19	43	10	0	0	20	18	21	2	5	S	R	5-11	168	8-18-71	1991	Barquisimeto, Venez.
Dobrolsky, Bill	.270	88	252	28	68	14	3	2	30	25	37	3	4	R	R	6-2	205	3-16-70	1991	Orwigsburg, Pa.
Dumas, Mike	.235	74	243	41	57	7	3	1	17	27	26	21	12	R	R	6-0	195	5-28-71	1992	Hattiesburg, Miss.
Dunn, Todd	.293	67	249	44	73	20	2	7	40	19	67	14	3	R	R	6-5	220	7-29-70	1993	Jacksonville, Fla.
Fitzpatrick, Will	.207	13	29	5	6	1	0	1	4	8	16	0	0	L	R	6-6	230	11-17-70	1993	San Mateo, Calif.
Hamlin, Jonas	.332	99	388	65	129	32	5	16	69	17	86	5	4	R	R	6-4	210	4-18-70	1990	West Valley City, Utah
Hostetler, Brian	.000	3	7	0	0	0	0	0	0	0	3	0	0	L	R	6-1	205	3-21-70	1992	Edwardsburg, Mich.
Hughes, Bobby	.235	52	179	22	42	9	2	8	31	17	41	2	2	R	R	6-4	220	3-10-71	1992	North Hollywood, Calif.
Jenkins, Geoff	.255	13	47	13	12	2	0	3	12	10	12	2	0	L	L	6-1	195	7-21-74	1995	Rancho Cordova, Calif.
Martinez, Gabby	.258	64	213	25	55	13	3	1	20	10	25	13	6	S	R	6-2	170	1-7-74	1992	Santurce, P.R.
Martinez, Greg	.276	114	410	80	113	8	2	0	43	69	64	55	9	S	R	5-10	168	1-27-72	1993	Las Vegas, Nev.
McGonigle, Bill	.262	78	210	33	55	8	1	0	21	23	35	3	4	R	R	6-1	175	11-13-71	1994	Glendale, Ariz.
Milstien, Dave	.276	58	214	36	59	14	1	4	37	25	16	0	3	R	R	6-0	170	9-11-68	1986	Simi Valley, Calif.
Morreale, John	.239	30	88	13	21	2	1	0	8	8	16	0	3	R	R	6-1	195	8-29-71	1994	New Orleans, La.
Nevers, Tom	.286	4	14	2	4	0	0	0	6	1	6	1	0	R	R	6-0	180	9-13-71	1990	Edina, Minn.
Nicholas, Darrell	.320	87	350	54	112	16	3	5	39	23	75	26	8	R	R	6-3	183	8-31-72	1989	Garyville, La.
Ortega, Hector	.301	137	539	81	162	27	4	8	76	39	109	26	13	R	R	6-1	202	9-27-70	1989	Puerto Cabello, Venez.
Powell, Gordon	.254	111	389	58	99	19	5	12	48	21	85	22	6	R	R	6-1	175	2-19-71	1992	Rialto, Calif.
Richardson, Scott	.225	24	80	12	18	4	1	2	14	6	16	8	3	R	R	6-2	205	5-14-75	1993	El Seibo, D.R.
Rodriguez, Miguel	.300	12	10	2	3	1	1	0	1	1	4	0	0	R	R	6-0	175	9-3-71	1991	Fort Pierce, Fla.
Rodriques, Cecil	.266	65	173	21	46	6	3	4	20	13	48	8	8	R	R	6-2	195	2-2-70	1991	Lincoln, Ill.
Seitzer, Brad	.308	127	428	66	132	28	3	6	56	72	68	7	4	R	R	6-2	195	2-2-70	1991	Lincoln, Ill.

GAMES BY POSITION: C—Campillo 35, Dobrolsky 79, Hughes 45, Rodriguez 11. **1B**—Hamlin 98, Hughes 1, Ortega 2, Powell 4, Seitzer 47. **2B**—Carrasquel 31, Dumas 34, Morreale 11, Nevers 2, Powell 73, Richardson 1. **3B**—Carrasquel 1, Milstien 1, Morreale 8, Nevers 1, Ortega 72, Seitzer 67. **SS**—Carrasquel 30, Dumas 1, Ga. Martinez 64, Milstien 56, Nevers 1. **OF**—Dumas 34, Dunn 63, Jenkins 13, Gr. Martinez 109, McGonigle 53, Ortega 46, Richardson 20, Rodriques 45.

PITCHING

PITCHING	W	L	ERA	G	GS	CG	SV	IP	H	R	ER	BB	SO	B	T	HT	WT	DOB	1st Yr	Resides
Brown, Keith	1	0	1.62	12	0	0	0	17	11	4	3	6	8	R	L	5-10	195	7-7-71	1995	East Williston, N.Y.
Cole, Jim	7	4	3.48	14	0	0	0	85	88	43	33	20	52	R	R	6-2	200	2-19-71	1993	Augusta, Ga.
Duda, Steve	3	6	4.33	12	12	2	0	79	87	48	38	20	59	R	L	5-11	170	6-27-71	1993	Thousand Oaks, Calif.
Felix, Ruben	0	2	12.79	6	0	0	0	6	9	9	9	5	3	R	L	5-10	160	6-24-70	1995	El Paso, Texas
Gamez, Francisco	2	1	2.78	4	3	0	0	23	20	8	7	11	7	R	R	6-2	185	4-2-70	1990	Tucson, Ariz.
Hartmann, Pete	2	0	4.50	12	0	0	0	14	9	7	7	11	9	L	R	6-2	200	5-13-71	1993	Arvada, Colo.
Kramer, Jeff	12	7	4.47	32	24	0	1	149	174	87	74	58	108	R	R	6-4	180	10-6-73	1994	Rincon, Ga.
Kyslinger, Dan	4	1	3.59	37	0	0	1	53	58	24	21	37	44	R	R	6-4	236	7-17-71	1992	Winston-Salem, N.C.
Linares, Yfrain	2	0	1.17	7	3	0	0	23	20	7	3	16	17	R	R	6-2	180	12-7-69	1988	Maracay, Venez.
McGonigle, Bill	0	0	6.75	4	0	0	0	4	5	3	3	3	3	R	R	6-1	175	11-13-71	1994	Glendale, Ariz.
Murphy, Matt	2	1	5.91	5	4	0	0	21	25	14	14	13	9	L	L	6-2	200	7-28-70	1993	Woodstock, Vt.
Paul, Andy	7	5	4.06	38	13	0	1	106	116	59	48	42	87	R	R	6-4	205	9-4-71	1992	Whitehouse Station, N.J.
Rosenkranz, Terry	1	2	6.20	35	1	0	0	49	44	34	34	49	43	L	L	6-4	205	11-5-70	1992	Greenville, Ky.
Sadler, Alan	4	9	4.42	14	14	1	2	114	113	62	56	59	82	R	R	6-6	185	2-10-72	1992	Conyers, Ga.
Salazar, Luis	6	2	2.32	52	0	0	10	89	66	28	23	18	71	R	R	5-11	170	7-7-70	1988	Maracay, Venez.
Schenbeck, T.J.	1	5	7.05	31	1	0	2	45	66	41	35	16	32	R	R	6-1	200	6-21-72	1992	Aurora, Colo.
Wagner, Jim	7	6	4.35	20	0	0	0	108	124	62	52	53	76	R	R	6-1	195	12-8-71	1993	Janesville, Wisc.
Webb, Doug	0	0	1.70	32	0	0	22	37	17	7	7	8	34	R	R	6-3	205	8-25-73	1994	Draper, Utah
Wilstead, Judd	8	9	5.09	31	21	0	0	140	165	94	79	71	72	L	R	6-4	205	3-14-73	1991	Washington, Utah
Wunsch, Kelly	5	6	5.33	14	13	1	0	74	89	51	44	39	62	L	L	6-5	192	7-12-72	1993	Houston, Texas

MIDWEST LEAGUE

BATTING	AVG	G	AB	R	H	2B	3B	HR	RBI	BB	SO	SB	CS	B	T	HT	WT	DOB	1st Yr	Resides
Andreopoulos, Alex....	.301	60	163	32	49	9	0	1	20	35	16	5	3	L	R	5-10	190	8-19-72	1995	Toronto, Ontario
Belliard, Ron...............	.297	130	461	76	137	28	5	13	76	36	67	16	12	R	R	5-9	176	4-7-75	1994	Miami, Fla.
Betances, Junior	.293	122	427	66	125	21	8	1	52	61	67	21	9	R	R	5-10	170	5-26-73	1991	La Vega, D.R.
Burckel, Brad...............	.147	13	34	4	5	1	0	0	3	3	11	0	3	R	R	5-11	173	10-10-71	1994	Metairie, La.
Campillo, Rob..............	.211	47	123	17	26	4	0	0	13	7	20	0	0	R	R	6-0	195	11-2-71	1994	Tucson, Ariz.
Cephas, Ruben	.170	76	94	17	16	0	0	0	1	7	25	13	3	L	R	5-11	155	6-11-73	1992	Seaford, Del.
Dumas, Mike...............	.254	20	71	11	18	1	2	0	4	11	11	9	6	R	R	5-9	163	5-28-71	1992	Hattiesburg, Miss.
Fitzpatrick, Will	.200	55	115	18	23	5	1	2	14	38	35	5	3	L	R	6-6	230	11-17-70	1993	San Mateo, Calif.
Garcia, Franklin	.230	26	61	7	14	2	0	0	6	5	14	5	2	R	R	5-11	150	5-4-75	1993	San Jose de Ochoa, D.R.
Hacopian, Derek	.324	123	442	75	143	30	1	23	92	56	35	4	5	R	R	6-0	200	1-1-70	1992	Potomac, Md.
Harris, Mike	.341	12	41	8	14	1	1	0	5	4	5	7	1	L	L	5-11	195	4-30-70	1991	Lexington, Ky.
Jaha, John..................	.000	1	4	0	0	0	0	0	0	0	1	0	0	R	R	6-1	205	5-27-66	1985	Portland, Ore.
Klassen, Danny	.275	59	218	27	60	15	2	2	25	16	43	12	4	R	R	6-0	175	9-22-75	1993	Port St. Lucie, Fla.
Kominek, Toby	.278	55	187	38	52	14	2	7	30	18	56	12	2	R	R	6-2	205	6-13-73	1995	Erie, Mich.
Krause, Scott..............	.247	134	481	83	119	30	4	13	76	50	126	24	10	R	R	6-1	187	8-16-73	1994	Willowick, Ohio
Mealing, John..............	.220	19	41	4	9	2	0	0	2	3	17	2	1	L	R	6-2	195	12-30-73	1993	Edgefield, S.C.
Mendez, Emilio............	.059	7	17	1	1	0	0	0	0	1	9	0	0	R	R	6-0	160	5-17-73	1992	Miami Beach, Fla.
Milstien, Dave	.327	53	196	47	64	12	1	2	21	23	15	8	4	R	R	6-0	170	9-11-68	1986	Simi Valley, Calif.
Montiel, David	.160	74	100	20	16	1	0	0	11	11	19	19	10	S	R	5-9	170	9-21-72	1994	Ft. Lauderdale, Fla.
Nilsson, Dave	.545	3	11	2	6	3	0	1	7	2	0	0	0	L	R	6-3	215	12-14-69	1987	Everton Hills, Australia
Smith, John	.211	76	261	38	55	16	4	10	44	20	88	8	2	R	R	5-9	175	7-7-69	1994	Indianapolis, Ind.
Snook, Robert..............	.000	3	6	0	0	0	0	0	0	2	3	0	0	R	R	6-0	185	11-18-73	1994	Ottawa, Ill.
Tyler, Josh	.237	77	186	24	44	5	0	2	27	36	40	3	6	R	R	6-1	185	9-6-73	1994	Green Lane, Pa.
Ward, Turner	.000	2	5	0	0	0	0	0	0	3	1	0	0	S	R	6-2	182	4-11-65	1986	Saraland, Ala.
Williams, Drew	.267	135	427	66	114	21	2	14	66	81	76	8	8	L	R	5-11	200	3-27-72	1994	Jacksonville, Fla.
Wilson, Chris	.190	28	63	12	12	1	1	0	6	3	14	5	1	R	R	5-9	160	1-7-71	1994	Tampa, Fla.
Zwisler, Josh	.234	98	252	29	59	12	1	1	18	28	46	8	4	R	R	5-10	185	9-30-74	1993	Cuyahoga Falls, Ohio

GAMES BY POSITION: C—Andreopoulos 55, Campillo 45, Snook 3, Tyler 2, Williams 2, Zwisler 67. **1B**—Burckel 1, Fitzpatrick 13, Hacopian 27, Krause 1, Milstien 1, Tyler 6, Williams 124, Zwisler 2. **2B**—Belliard 119, Betances 7, Dumas 1, Garcia 20, Krause 1, Milstien 2, Tyler 1. **3B**—Belliard 15, Betances 102, Burckel 1, Dumas 3, Klassen 2, Kominek 3, Tyler 40, Williams 1. **SS**—Betances 23, Burckel 9, Dumas 9, Garcia 2, Klassen 56, Mendez 7, Milstien 49. **OF**—Betances 1, Cephas 63, Dumas 7, Hacopian 74, Kominek 51, Krause 131, Linares 1, Mealing 14, Milstien 1, Montiel 55, Smith 73, Tyler 4, Ward 2, Williams 5, Wilson 20, Zwisler 19.

PITCHING	W	L	ERA	G	GS	CG	SV	IP	H	R	ER	BB	SO	B	T	HT	WT	DOB	1st Yr	Resides
Beck, Greg	5	2	4.72	35	5	0	2	74	73	46	39	35	91	R	R	6-4	215	10-21-72	1994	Fort Myers, Fla.
Bronkey, Jeff	0	1	3.68	3	3	0	0	7	5	5	3	3	8	R	R	6-3	215	9-18-65	1986	Klamath Falls, Ore.
Burt, Chris.................	1	3	3.80	36	0	0	27	43	34	19	18	17	42	R	R	6-3	200	1-11-73	1994	Beloit, Wisc.
D'Amico, Jeff	13	3	2.39	21	20	3	0	132	102	40	35	31	119	R	R	6-7	250	12-27-75	1993	Pinellas Park, Fla.
Dalton, Brian	4	3	2.74	34	4	0	4	82	70	31	25	44	75	R	R	6-1	190	6-24-72	1994	Brooksville, Fla.
Felix, Ruben	4	5	5.40	45	0	0	0	48	49	33	29	36	60	R	L	5-10	160	6-24-70	1991	El Paso, Texas
Fitzpatrick, Will	0	0	2.45	3	0	0	0	4	3	1	1	2	2	L	R	6-6	230	11-17-70	1993	San Mateo, Calif.
Gonzalez, Juan	11	5	4.16	42	6	0	6	89	86	50	41	37	53	R	R	6-1	188	1-28-75	1992	Bani, D.R.
Gooda, David	0	0	3.77	3	0	0	0	14	13	8	6	8	9	L	L	6-3	196	8-17-76	1993	Brisbane, Australia
Huntsman, Scott..........	4	3	2.72	43	0	0	1	50	42	17	15	34	49	R	R	6-2	230	10-28-72	1994	Zanesville, Ohio
Ignasiak, Mike	0	0	0.00	1	1	0	0	3	0	0	0	2	4	S	R	5-11	190	3-12-66	1988	Casco, Mich.
Linares, Yfrain	3	3	4.29	19	12	0	0	71	75	42	34	43	63	R	R	6-2	190	12-7-69	1988	Maracay, Venez.
Mercado, Gabby	11	6	5.36	24	23	0	0	129	138	89	77	50	89	R	R	5-11	175	11-26-72	1993	Luquillo, P.R.
Mullins, Greg	3	1	3.96	15	4	0	2	36	26	16	16	14	48	L	L	6-0	160	12-13-71	1995	Palatka, Fla.
Nate, Scott.................	1	0	2.77	20	0	0	2	26	26	12	8	13	12	R	L	6-8	205	9-2-73	1994	Dowagiac, Mich.
Rantz, Ron	0	1	16.20	10	0	0	0	8	12	15	15	12	12	R	L	6-5	250	5-23-73	1994	Phoenix, Ariz.
Rosenkranz, Terry.......	0	0	0.00	4	0	0	0	8	2	2	0	2	4	L	L	6-4	205	11-5-70	1992	Greenville, Ky.
Schenbeck, T.J............	4	2	3.62	18	1	0	5	37	35	18	15	23	37	R	R	6-0	200	6-21-72	1992	Aurora, Colo.
Tollberg, Brian	13	4	3.41	22	22	1	0	132	119	59	50	27	110	R	R	6-3	195	9-16-72	1994	Bradenton, Fla.
Woodard, Steve...........	7	4	4.54	21	21	1	0	115	113	68	58	31	94	L	R	6-4	225	5-15-75	1994	Hartselle, Ala.
Wunsch, Kelly	4	7	4.20	14	14	3	0	86	90	47	40	37	66	L	L	6-5	192	7-12-72	1993	Houston, Texas

PIONEER LEAGUE

BATTING	AVG	G	AB	R	H	2B	3B	HR	RBI	BB	SO	SB	CS	B	T	HT	WT	DOB	1st Yr	Resides
Andreopoulos, Alex......	.556	3	9	3	5	0	0	2	7	4	0	0	0	L	R	5-10	190	8-19-72	1995	Toronto, Ontario
Arevalos, Ryan............	.241	47	137	40	33	11	0	3	18	39	38	5	4	R	R	6-0	180	3-12-73	1995	San Antonio, Texas
Cancel, Robinson........	.240	46	154	18	37	9	0	0	24	9	20	8	3	R	R	5-11	195	5-4-76	1994	Lajas, P.R.
Elliott, Dave	.262	54	172	35	45	11	1	7	37	33	29	3	5	R	R	6-2	192	8-10-73	1995	Gladstone, Mich.
Guerrero, Sergio	.302	41	129	26	39	10	1	4	17	13	12	5	1	R	R	5-9	180	12-22-74	1995	McAllen, Texas
Iapoce, Anthony	.301	39	146	43	44	7	0	0	13	28	24	19	3	R	L	5-10	178	8-23-73	1994	Ridgewood, N.Y.
Jenkins, Geoff	.321	7	28	2	9	0	1	0	9	3	11	0	2	L	L	6-1	195	7-21-74	1995	Rancho Cordova, Calif.
Johnson, Brian	.247	32	85	24	21	2	0	2	10	9	17	3	4	R	R	6-1	190	9-24-72	1995	Arlington, Texas
Johnson, Ledowick	.253	35	95	18	24	3	0	1	18	20	25	5	6	L	R	5-11	170	10-21-72	1995	Greenville, N.C.
Judge, Mike................	.348	30	112	28	39	13	1	0	25	11	12	1	2	R	R	6-2	190	4-26-72	1994	Stafford, Texas
Kinkade, Mike	.353	69	266	76	94	19	1	4	39	43	38	26	9	R	R	6-1	210	5-6-73	1995	Tigard, Ore.
Knight, Brook	.235	16	34	4	8	1	0	0	4	8	2	1	0	R	R	5-10	185	11-20-72	1995	Corvallis, Ore.
Kominek, Toby	.333	13	48	7	16	1	1	3	18	3	9	2	1	R	R	6-2	205	6-13-73	1995	Erie, Mich.
Lopez, Mickey	.324	57	225	66	73	19	2	1	41	38	20	12	8	S	R	5-9	165	11-17-73	1995	Miami, Fla.
Mealing, John..............	.349	55	169	35	59	11	4	4	31	23	43	17	7	L	R	6-2	195	12-30-73	1993	Edgefield, S.C.
O'Neal, Troy	.357	4	14	5	5	1	0	0	1	1	0	0	0	R	R	5-11	190	4-24-72	1995	Greenville, Del.
2-team (43 Leth.)...	.242	47	149	22	36	3	1	0	16	22	21	3	3							
Parent, Gerald	.355	57	200	50	72	16	0	7	63	50	30	1	7	L	R	6-3	220	12-7-73	1995	Assonet, Mass.
Ritter, Ryan	.281	47	167	32	47	7	1	9	38	14	50	10	2	R	R	6-0	195	11-26-73	1995	Marietta, Ga.
Roche, Michael	.118	4	17	4	2	0	0	0	1	2	4	1	0	R	R	5-10	165	11-17-75	1995	North Lauderdale, Fla.
Smith, Rick	.307	61	218	42	67	19	1	8	44	36	40	0	4	L	R	6-2	205	1-5-72	1995	Big Rapids, Mich.

GAMES BY POSITION: C—Andreopoulos 3, Cancel 45, Kinkade 18, Knight 14, O'Neal 4. **1B**—Judge 16, Kinkade 21, Parent 13, Smith 27. **2B**—Arevalos 12, Guerrero 7, Lopez 26, Ritter 27, Roche 4. **3B**—Guerrero 23, Judge 1, Kinkade 25, Kominek 6, Parent 20. **SS**—Arevalos 35, Elliott 1, Guerrero 10, Lopez 31, Ritter 1, Smith 1. **OF**—Elliott 48, Iapoce 39, Jenkins 6, B. Johnson 31, L. Johnson 29, Kominek 6, Mealing 48, Parent 17, Ritter 17, Smith 1.

PITCHING	W	L	ERA	G	GS	CG	SV	IP	H	R	ER	BB	SO	B	T	HT	WT	DOB	1st Yr	Resides
Barnes, Larry	2	0	2.25	3	2	0	0	12	5	5	3	6	15	S	R	6-5	230	8-11-76	1994	Jacksonville, Fla.
Benny, Peter	5	0	3.88	11	7	0	0	46	48	25	20	24	47	R	R	6-3	196	11-9-75	1993	Tempe, Ariz.
Berninger, Darren	3	1	7.71	21	0	0	0	28	45	28	24	34	11	R	R	6-3	225	1-4-73	1995	Baton Rouge, La.
Bowles, Matt	1	0	15.19	6	3	0	0	11	17	18	18	18	10	R	R	6-1	195	5-4-75	1995	Huntington, W.Va.
Camp, Jared	1	4	8.65	8	8	0	0	34	44	39	33	20	26	R	R	6-3	225	8-26-76	1994	Union, N.J.
Collins, Ed	5	3	5.86	14	13	0	0	55	50	44	36	63	33	R	R	6-3	225	8-26-76	1994	Union, N.J.
Dawsey, Jason	3	0	2.74	9	8	0	0	43	40	15	13	23	47	L	L	5-8	165	5-27-74	1995	Lexington, S.C.
Estrada, Horacio	1	2	5.40	13	0	0	0	30	27	21	18	24	30	L	L	6-0	160	10-19-75	1992	San Joaquin, Venez.
Gaskill, Derek	5	2	3.70	31	0	0	3	56	50	30	23	23	59	R	R	6-6	190	5-6-74	1992	Portsmouth, Va.
Gooda, David	4	4	4.17	10	10	0	0	58	54	32	27	33	33	L	L	6-3	196	8-17-76	1995	Brisbane, Australia
Hommel, Brian	2	0	0.45	15	0	0	2	20	7	3	1	14	32	L	L	5-10	170	10-26-72	1995	Indianapolis, Ind.
Lenhardt, Bruce	0	1	1.93	9	0	0	0	9	7	6	2	11	10	R	R	6-9	210	1-31-74	1995	Barnhart, Mo.
Miller, Shawn	2	0	4.82	16	0	0	0	28	37	18	15	16	33	R	R	6-4	221	5-7-74	1995	Bensenville, Ill.
Mullins, Greg	4	0	2.74	4	4	0	0	23	22	7	7	6	14	L	L	6-0	160	12-13-71	1995	Palatka, Fla.
Nate, Scott	0	2	9.00	3	0	0	1	2	4	3	2	0	2	R	L	6-8	205	9-2-73	1994	Dowagiac, Mich.
Pasqualicchio, Mike	0	3	3.16	8	7	0	0	31	30	14	11	20	21	R	L	6-1	205	8-17-74	1995	Astoria, N.Y.
Pavlovich, Tony	0	0	0.93	9	0	0	4	10	4	1	1	3	14	R	R	5-11	185	8-23-74	1994	Pavo, Ga.
Preston, George	1	0	8.10	3	2	0	0	7	11	9	6	2	9	R	R	5-11	175	9-22-73	1993	Brenham, Texas
Richardson, Jesse	3	1	4.62	25	0	0	2	39	44	23	20	27	34	R	L	6-1	195	9-30-72	1995	Oxford, N.C.
Sheldon, Shane	0	0	13.50	17	0	0	0	15	18	28	23	25	15	R	R	6-3	205	10-22-72	1993	Portage, Mich.
Smith, Travis	4	2	2.41	20	7	0	5	56	41	16	15	19	63	R	R	5-10	170	11-7-72	1995	Bend, Ore.

CHANDLER   R

ARIZONA LEAGUE

BATTING	AVG	G	AB	R	H	2B	3B	HR	RBI	BB	SO	SB	CS	B	T	HT	WT	DOB	1st Yr	Resides
Allen, Tony	.221	46	113	19	25	0	5	0	14	14	35	7	2	R	R	6-1	175	6-19-76	1995	Kearneysville, W.Va.
Campusano, Carlos	.249	54	173	25	43	4	1	1	15	14	27	7	3	R	R	5-11	155	9-2-75	1994	Palave, D.R.
Harris, Mike	.304	6	23	5	7	2	1	0	4	2	7	0	1	L	L	5-11	195	4-30-70	1991	Lexington, Ky.
Harris, Rico	.279	48	172	40	48	6	3	0	22	37	22	26	10	S	R	5-7	146	1-7-75	1995	Jacksonville, Fla.
Iapoce, Anthony	.333	3	3	2	1	0	0	0	0	1	1	1	0	R	L	5-10	178	8-23-73	1994	Ridgewood, N.Y.
Judge, Mike	.293	16	41	8	12	2	1	0	6	8	9	2	1	R	R	6-2	190	4-26-72	1994	Stafford, Texas
Moore, Donald	.239	38	71	10	17	0	0	1	6	8	27	3	1	R	R	6-2	184	6-12-76	1995	York, Pa.
Peters, Tony	.244	51	172	25	42	8	2	2	24	29	55	9	3	R	R	6-2	210	10-28-74	1995	Garrettsville, Ohio
Rendon, Miguel	.259	48	162	23	42	5	2	0	25	9	18	4	2	R	R	6-0	181	3-5-75	1993	Cumana, Venez.
Ritter, Ryan	.200	4	15	1	3	3	0	0	2	0	0	0	0	R	R	6-0	190	11-26-73	1995	Marietta, Ga.
Roche, Michael	.255	47	161	33	41	11	2	0	31	18	42	9	3	R	R	5-10	165	11-17-75	1995	North Lauderdale, Fla.
Rodriguez, Miguel	.313	48	163	24	51	12	1	1	18	11	34	9	2	R	R	6-2	205	5-14-75	1993	El Seibo, D.R.
Rogue, Francisco	.226	19	62	10	14	3	1	0	10	1	9	0	0	R	R	6-1	170	11-22-75	1993	Santo Domingo, D.R.
Schaub, Greg	.274	33	95	12	26	4	3	0	11	5	20	5	4	R	R	6-1	185	3-30-77	1995	Oxford, Pa.
Singleton, Sam	.245	47	139	28	34	4	3	0	19	20	33	2	3	L	R	5-9	150	2-10-76	1995	Rand, W Va.
Walther, Chris	.259	50	174	28	45	3	2	0	19	10	9	4	3	R	R	6-2	200	8-28-76	1995	Odessa, Fla.
Wilkerson, Adrian	.331	54	187	22	51	9	1	1	20	18	26	18	7	R	R	6-0	185	4-6-75	1995	Douglas, Ga.

GAMES BY POSITION: C—Rodriguez 45, Rogue 16. **1B**—Judge 5, Peters 24, Rendon 4, Rogue 4, Walther 26. **2B**—Campusano 4, Harris 40, Roche 20. **3B**—Campusano 36, Roche 18, Schaub 11. **SS**—Campusano 19, Ritter 3, Singleton 46. **OF**—Allen 43, R. Harris 1, Iapoce 2, Moore 35, Peters 26, Rendon 18, Schaub 20, Walther 23, Wilkerson 53.

PITCHING	W	L	ERA	G	GS	CG	SV	IP	H	R	ER	BB	SO	B	T	HT	WT	DOB	1ST-YR	RESIDES
Barnes, Larry	0	1	1.77	6	5	0	0	20	16	4	4	14	31	S	R	6-5	230	8-11-74	1994	Jacksonville, Fla.
Bishop, Josh	8	2	2.16	14	13	3	0	96	64	34	23	29	134	R	R	6-4	180	7-16-74	1995	Sedalia, Mo.
Bowles, Matt	0	1	6.60	7	0	0	0	15	20	12	11	3	4	R	R	6-7	220	2-21-73	1995	Glasgow, Ky.
De los Santos, Valerio	4	6	2.20	14	12	0	0	82	81	34	20	12	57	L	L	6-4	185	10-6-75	1993	San Joaquin, D.R.
Estrada, Horacio	0	1	3.71	8	1	0	2	17	13	9	7	8	21	L	L	6-0	160	10-19-75	1992	San Joaquin, Venez.
Glick, Dave	2	0	4.26	18	0	0	0	25	24	13	12	14	29	L	L	6-1	190	4-2-76	1995	Palmdale, Calif.
Gutierrez, Alfredo	0	0	6.48	7	0	0	0	8	10	9	6	8	7	R	R	6-0	170	3-22-76	1994	Riverside, Calif.
Guzman, Jonathan	0	0	10.38	11	0	0	0	13	18	16	15	8	4	L	L	6-2	205	8-26-77	1995	Levittown, P.R.
Hill, Tyrone	0	0	3.18	4	4	0	0	11	8	4	4	9	11	L	L	6-5	195	3-7-72	1991	Yucaipa, Calif.
Ishee, Gabe	9	2	3.63	15	12	2	0	79	78	41	32	41	90	S	R	6-2	175	8-14-74	1995	Biloxi, Miss.
Lenhardt, Bruce	1	0	3.86	2	0	0	0	5	8	2	2	1	3	R	R	6-9	210	1-31-74	1995	Barnhart, Mo.
Norris, MacKenzie	1	0	0.61	2	0	0	0	15	7	4	1	6	14	R	R	6-7	205	3-19-76	1995	Mesa, Ariz.
Pavlovich, Tony	0	2	4.00	19	0	0	10	18	20	10	8	3	20	R	R	5-11	185	8-23-74	1994	Pavo, Ga.
Perez, Jesse	2	2	2.70	16	0	0	4	20	16	6	6	4	20	R	R	5-11	185	8-15-75	1995	Cantel, Calif.
Prempas, Lyle	6	5	4.09	13	6	0	0	51	49	33	23	28	67	L	L	6-7	205	12-3-74	1993	West Chester, Ill.
Preston, George	1	0	0.00	2	0	0	0	8	5	1	0	3	15	R	R	5-11	175	9-22-73	1993	Brenham, Texas
Tijerina, Tano	0	0	4.50	1	1	0	0	2	3	1	1	2	1	R	R	6-4	225	6-23-74	1993	Waco, Texas
Torres, Derek	1	0	1.69	6	0	0	0	5	2	1	1	2	7	R	R	5-11	180	9-28-76	1995	Rio Grande, P.R.
Updike, Jon	0	0	12.00	4	0	0	0	3	2	4	4	8	3	S	R	6-5	210	1-26-73	1993	Deltona, Fla.

MINNESOTA TWINS

Manager: Tom Kelly. **1995 Record:** 56-88, .389 (5th, AL Central).

BATTING	AVG	G	AB	R	H	2B	3B	HR	RBI	BB	SO	SB	CS	B	T	HT	WT	DOB	1st Yr	Resides
Becker, Rich	.237	106	392	45	93	15	1	2	33	34	95	8	9	S	L	5-10	180	2-1-72	1990	Aurora, Ill.
Brito, Bernardo	.200	5	5	1	1	0	0	1	1	0	3	0	0	R	R	6-1	210	12-4-63	1981	San Cristobal, D.R.
Clark, Jerald	.339	36	109	17	37	8	3	3	15	2	11	3	0	R	R	6-4	202	8-10-63	1985	Crockett, Texas
Cole, Alex	.342	28	79	10	27	3	2	1	14	8	15	1	3	L	L	6-2	183	8-17-65	1985	St. Petersburg, Fla.
Coomer, Ron	.257	37	101	15	26	3	1	5	19	9	11	0	1	R	R	5-11	195	11-18-66	1987	Crest Hill, Ill.
Cordova, Marty	.277	137	512	81	142	27	4	24	84	52	111	20	7	R	R	6-0	190	7-10-69	1989	Las Vegas, Nev.
Dunn, Steve	.000	5	6	0	0	0	0	0	0	1	3	0	0	L	L	6-4	220	4-18-70	1988	Fairfax, Va.
Hale, Chip	.262	69	103	10	27	4	0	2	18	11	20	0	0	L	R	5-10	175	12-2-64	1987	Hermosa Beach, Calif.
Hocking, Denny	.200	9	25	4	5	0	2	0	3	2	2	1	0	S	R	5-10	180	4-2-70	1990	Torrance, Calif.
Ingram, Riccardo	.125	4	8	0	1	0	0	0	1	2	1	0	0	R	R	6-0	198	9-10-66	1988	Douglas, Ga.
Knoblauch, Chuck	.333	136	538	107	179	34	8	11	63	78	95	46	18	R	R	5-9	181	7-7-68	1989	Houston, Texas
Lawton, Matt	.317	21	60	11	19	4	1	1	12	7	11	1	1	L	R	5-9	180	11-3-71	1991	Saucier, Miss.
Leius, Scott	.247	117	372	51	92	16	5	4	45	49	54	2	1	R	R	6-3	208	9-24-65	1986	Minnetonka, Minn.
Maas, Kevin	.193	22	57	5	11	4	0	1	5	7	11	0	0	L	L	6-3	205	1-20-65	1986	Berkeley, Calif.
Masteller, Dan	.237	71	198	21	47	12	0	3	21	18	19	1	2	L	L	6-0	185	3-17-68	1989	Lyndhurst, Ohio
McCarty, Dave	.218	25	55	10	12	3	1	0	4	4	18	0	1	R	L	6-5	207	11-23-69	1991	Houston, Texas
Meares, Pat	.269	116	390	57	105	19	4	12	49	15	68	10	4	R	R	5-11	180	9-6-68	1990	Salina, Kan.
Merullo, Matt	.282	76	195	19	55	14	1	1	27	14	27	0	1	L	R	6-2	200	8-4-65	1986	Ridgefield, Conn.
Munoz, Pedro	.301	104	376	45	113	17	0	18	58	19	86	0	3	R	R	5-11	203	9-19-68	1985	Ponce, P.R.
Puckett, Kirby	.314	137	538	83	169	39	0	23	99	56	89	3	2	R	R	5-9	215	3-14-61	1982	Chicago, Ill.
Raabe, Brian	.214	6	14	4	3	0	0	0	1	1	0	0	0	R	R	5-9	170	11-5-67	1990	North Branch, Minn.
Reboulet, Jeff	.292	87	216	39	63	11	0	4	23	27	34	1	2	R	R	6-0	168	4-30-64	1986	Kettering, Ohio
Stahoviak, Scott	.266	94	263	28	70	19	0	3	23	30	61	5	1	L	R	6-5	208	3-6-70	1991	Wheeling, Ill.
Walbeck, Matt	.257	115	393	40	101	18	1	1	44	25	71	3	1	S	R	5-11	195	10-2-69	1987	Sacramento, Calif.

PITCHING	W	L	ERA	G	GS	CG	SV	IP	H	R	ER	BB	SO	B	T	HT	WT	DOB	1st Yr	Resides
Aguilera, Rick	1	1	2.52	22	0	0	12	25	20	7	7	6	29	R	R	6-5	203	12-31-61	1983	Chanhassen, Minn.
Campbell, Kevin	0	0	4.66	6	0	0	0	10	8	5	5	5	5	R	R	6-2	225	12-6-64	1986	Des Arc, Ark.
Erickson, Scott	4	6	5.95	15	15	0	0	88	102	61	58	32	45	R	R	6-4	225	2-2-68	1989	Sunnyvale, Calif.
Guardado, Eddie	4	9	5.12	51	5	0	2	91	99	54	52	45	71	R	L	6-0	187	10-2-70	1991	Stockton, Calif.
Guthrie, Mark	5	3	4.46	36	0	0	0	42	47	22	21	16	48	S	L	6-4	205	9-22-65	1987	Bradenton, Fla.
Harris, Greg W.	0	5	8.82	7	6	0	0	33	50	35	32	16	21	R	R	6-2	195	12-1-63	1985	Las Vegas, Nev.
Hawkins, LaTroy	2	3	8.67	6	6	1	0	27	39	29	26	12	9	R	R	6-5	195	12-21-72	1991	Gary, Ind.
Horsman, Vince	0	0	7.00	6	0	0	0	9	12	8	7	4	4	R	L	6-2	175	3-9-67	1985	Dartmouth, N.S.
Klingenbeck, Scott	0	2	8.57	18	4	0	0	48	69	48	46	24	27	R	R	6-2	205	2-3-71	1992	Cincinnati, Ohio
2-team (6 Baltimore)	2	4	7.12	24	9	0	0	80	101	65	63	42	42							
Mahomes, Pat	4	10	6.37	47	7	0	3	95	100	74	67	47	67	R	R	6-4	210	8-9-70	1988	Lindale, Texas
Munoz, Oscar	2	1	5.60	10	3	0	0	35	40	28	22	17	25	R	R	6-2	205	9-25-69	1990	Hialeah, Fla.
Parra, Jose	1	5	7.59	12	12	0	0	62	83	59	52	22	29	R	R	5-11	160	11-28-72	1990	Santiago, D.R.
Radke, Brad	11	14	5.32	29	28	2	0	181	195	112	107	47	75	R	R	6-2	180	10-27-72	1991	Tampa, Fla.
Robertson, Rich	2	0	3.83	25	4	1	0	52	48	22	22	31	38	L	L	6-4	175	9-15-68	1990	Waller, Texas
Rodriguez, Frank	5	6	5.38	16	16	0	0	90	93	64	54	47	45	R	R	6-0	175	12-11-72	1991	Oviedo, Fla.
2-team (9 Boston)	5	8	6.13	25	18	0	0	106	114	83	72	57	59							
Sanford, Mo	0	0	5.30	11	0	0	0	19	16	11	11	16	17	R	R	6-6	225	12-24-66	1988	Starkville, Miss.
Schullstrom, Erik	0	0	6.89	37	0	0	0	47	66	36	36	22	21	R	R	6-5	220	3-25-69	1990	San Leandro, Calif.
Stevens, Dave	5	4	5.07	56	0	0	10	66	74	40	37	32	47	R	R	6-3	210	3-4-70	1990	La Habra, Calif.
Tapani, Kevin	6	11	4.92	20	20	3	0	134	155	79	73	34	88	R	R	6-0	175	2-18-64	1986	Eden Prarie, Minn.
Trombley, Mike	4	8	5.62	20	18	0	0	98	107	68	61	42	68	R	R	6-2	200	4-14-67	1989	Naples, Fla.
Watkins, Scott	0	0	5.40	27	0	0	0	22	22	14	13	11	11	L	L	6-3	180	5-15-70	1992	Sand Springs, Okla.
Willis, Carl	0	0	94.50	3	0	0	0	1	5	7	7	5	2	R	R	6-4	210	12-28-60	1983	Durham, N.C.

FIELDING

Catcher	PCT	G	PO	A	E	DP	PB
Merullo	.987	46	210	11	3	2	3
Reboulet	.000	1	0	0	0	0	0
Walbeck	.991	113	604	35	6	3	8

First Base	PCT	G	PO	A	E	DP
Clark	1.000	11	33	3	0	4
Coomer	.993	22	131	13	1	13
Dunn	1.000	3	5	0	0	2
Hale	1.000	3	13	0	0	0
Maas	.936	8	43	1	3	4
McCarty	.993	18	128	10	1	13
Merullo	1.000	5	2	0	0	0
Munoz	.727	3	7	1	3	1
Reboulet	1.000	17	80	13	0	7
Stahoviak	.998	69	494	61	1	48

Second Base	PCT	G	PO	A	E	DP
Hale	1.000	7	2	5	0	1

	PCT	G	PO	A	E	DP
Knoblauch	.985	136	253	400	10	88
Puckett	1.000	1	0	1	0	0
Raabe	1.000	4	5	8	0	3
Reboulet	.979	15	17	29	1	5

Third Base	PCT	G	PO	A	E	DP
Coomer	.962	13	6	19	1	1
Hale	1.000	5	1	1	0	1
Leius	.945	112	60	182	14	27
Puckett	.000	1	0	0	0	0
Raabe	.000	2	0	0	0	0
Reboulet	.960	22	14	34	2	2
Stahoviak	.907	22	9	30	4	3

Shortstop	PCT	G	PO	A	E	DP
Hocking	.971	6	13	20	1	5
Knoblauch	1.000	2	1	0	0	0
Leius	1.000	7	0	5	0	0
Meares	.965	114	186	317	18	69

	PCT	G	PO	A	E	DP
Puckett	.000	1	0	0	0	0
Reboulet	.993	39	53	84	1	22

Outfield	PCT	G	PO	A	E	DP
Becker	.986	105	275	12	4	5
Clark	1.000	23	47	1	0	0
Cole	.938	23	44	1	3	0
Coomer	1.000	1	1	0	0	0
Cordova	.986	137	345	12	5	3
Lawton	.972	19	34	1	1	0
Masteller	1.000	22	32	0	0	0
McCarty	1.000	5	2	0	0	0
Meares	1.000	3	1	0	0	0
Munoz	.926	25	22	3	2	0
Puckett	.981	109	195	9	4	1

Outfielder Marty Cordova hit .277 and led the Twins with 24 home runs

LARRY KINKER

MORRIS FOSTOFF

Twins minor league Player of the Year Todd Walker

FARM SYSTEM

Director of Minor Leagues: Jim Rantz.

Class	Farm Team	League	W	L	Pct.	Finish*	Manager	First Yr
AAA	Salt Lake (Utah) Buzz	Pacific Coast	79	65	.549	3rd (10)	Phil Roof	1994
AA	Hardware City (Conn.) Rock Cats	Eastern	65	77	.458	9th (10)	Sal Butera	1995
#A	Fort Myers (Fla.) Miracle	Florida State	75	55	.577	2nd (14)	Al Newman	1993
A	Fort Wayne (Ind.) Wizards	Midwest	75	65	.536	T-5th (14)	Dan Rohn	1993
#R	Elizabethton (Tenn.) Twins	Appalachian	33	31	.516	3rd (10)	John Russell	1974
R	Fort Myers (Fla.) Twins	Gulf Coast	20	35	.364	14th (16)	Mike Boulanger	1989

*Finish in overall standings (No. of teams in league) #Advanced level

ORGANIZATION LEADERS

MAJOR LEAGUERS

BATTING
*AVG	Chuck Knoblauch...	.333
R	Chuck Knoblauch....	107
H	Chuck Knoblauch....	179
TB	Kirby Puckett...........	277
2B	Kirby Puckett.............	39
3B	Chuck Knoblauch	8
HR	Marty Cordova	24
RBI	Kirby Puckett.............	99
BB	Chuck Knoblauch......	78
SO	Marty Cordova	111
SB	Chuck Knoblauch......	46

PITCHING
W	Brad Radke..............	11
L	Brad Radke..............	14
#ERA	Kevin Tapani..........	4.92
G	Dave Stevens	56
CG	Kevin Tapani............	3
SV	Rick Aguilera.............	12
IP	Brad Radke..............	181
BB	Two tied at	47
SO	Kevin Tapani............	88

BERNARD TRONCALE

Kirby Puckett. 99 RBIs

MINOR LEAGUERS

BATTING
*AVG	Riccardo Ingram, Salt Lake..................	.348
R	Brian Raabe, Salt Lake	88
H	Riccardo Ingram, Salt Lake	166
TB	Riccardo Ingram, Salt Lake	249
2B	Riccardo Ingram, Salt Lake	43
3B	Anthony Byrd, Hardware City	8
HR	Todd Walker, Hardware City	21
RBI	Tom Quinlan, Salt Lake..........................	88
BB	Ben Shelton, Hardware City/Salt Lake	73
SO	Tom Quinlan, Salt Lake.........................	124
SB	Carlos Garcia, Elizabethton/Ft. Wayne ...	38

PITCHING
W	Two tied at..	13
L	Marc Barcelo, Salt Lake	13
#ERA	Keith Linebarger, Fort Myers................	2.10
G	Sean Gavaghan, Hardware City/SL	56
CG	Brett Roberts, Hardware City	5
SV	Scott Watkins, Salt Lake	20
IP	Brett Roberts, Hardware City	174
BB	Dan Serafini, Hardware City/Salt Lake....	73
SO	Travis Miller, Hardware City	151

*Minimum 250 At-Bats   #Minimum 75 Innings

TOP 10 PROSPECTS

How the Twins Top 10 prospects, as judged by Baseball America prior to the 1995 season, fared in 1995:

LaTroy Hawkins

Player, Pos.	Club (Class—League)	AVG	AB	R	H	2B	3B	HR	RBI	SB
2. Todd Walker, 2b	Hardware City (AA—Eastern)	.290	513	83	149	27	3	21	85	23
4. Marty Cordova, of	Minnesota	.277	512	81	142	27	4	24	84	20
5. Rich Becker, of	Salt Lake (AAA—Pacific Coast)	.309	123	26	38	7	0	6	28	6
	Minnesota	.237	392	45	93	15	1	2	33	8
6. Torii Hunter, of	Fort Myers (A—Florida State)	.246	391	64	96	15	2	7	36	7
9. Scott Stahoviak, 3b-1b	Salt Lake (AAA—Pacific Coast)	.303	33	6	10	1	0	0	5	2
	Minnesota	.266	263	28	70	19	0	3	23	5

Player, Pos.	Club (Class—League)	W	L	ERA	G	SV	IP	H	BB	SO
1. LaTroy Hawkins, rhp	Salt Lake (AAA—Pacific Coast)	9	7	3.55	22	0	144	150	40	74
	Minnesota	2	3	8.67	6	0	27	39	12	9
3. Marc Barcelo, rhp	Salt Lake (AAA—Pacific Coast)	8	13	7.05	28	0	143	214	59	63
7. Dan Serafini, lhp	Hardware City (AA—Eastern)	12	9	3.38	27	0	163	155	72	123
	Salt Lake (AAA—Pacific Coast)	0	0	6.75	1	1	4	4	1	4
8. Travis Miller, lhp	Hardware City (AA—Eastern)	7	9	4.37	28	0	163	172	65	151
10. Gus Gandarillas, rhp	Hardware City (AA—Eastern)	2	4	6.12	25	7	32	38	16	25
	Salt Lake (AAA—Pacific Coast)	2	3	6.44	22	2	29	34	19	17

PACIFIC COAST LEAGUE

BATTING	AVG	G	AB	R	H	2B	3B	HR	RBI	BB	SO	SB	CS	B	T	HT	WT	DOB	1st Yr	Resides
Becker, Rich	.309	36	123	26	38	7	0	6	28	26	24	6	1	S	L	5-10	180	2-1-72	1990	Aurora, Ill.
Brito, Bernardo	.306	51	186	31	57	10	1	15	49	17	58	1	0	R	R	6-1	210	12-4-63	1981	San Cristobal, D.R.
Corbin, Ted	.200	4	10	0	2	0	0	0	1	0	1	0	0	S	R	5-9	150	4-27-71	1992	Naples, Fla.
De la Rosa, Juan	.224	31	49	7	11	2	0	0	5	1	6	0	0	R	R	6-1	190	12-1-68	1986	La Romana, D.R.
Duncan, Andres	.278	12	36	2	10	2	1	0	6	4	5	2	0	S	R	5-11	155	11-30-71	1989	San Pedro de Macoris, D.R.
Dunn, Steve	.316	109	402	57	127	31	1	12	83	30	63	3	2	L	L	6-4	220	4-18-70	1988	Fairfax, Va.
Durant, Mike	.251	85	295	40	74	15	3	2	23	20	31	11	7	R	R	6-2	198	9-14-69	1991	Columbus, Ohio
Hale, Chip	.286	16	49	5	14	4	0	0	2	7	5	0	1	L	R	5-10	175	12-2-64	1987	Hermosa Beach, Calif.
Hazlett, Steve	.300	127	427	71	128	25	6	4	49	41	65	8	10	R	R	5-11	170	3-30-70	1991	Longmont, Colo.
Hocking, Denny	.282	117	397	51	112	24	2	8	75	25	41	12	8	S	R	5-10	180	4-2-70	1990	Torrance, Calif.
Horn, Jeff	.500	3	10	0	5	1	0	0	2	0	1	0	0	R	R	6-1	190	8-23-70	1992	Riverside, Calif.
Ingram, Riccardo	.348	122	477	80	166	43	2	12	85	41	60	4	5	R	R	6-0	198	9-10-66	1988	Douglas, Ga.
Jackson, John	.278	55	194	39	54	14	3	4	21	22	20	8	2	L	L	6-0	185	1-2-67	1990	Diamond Bar, Calif.
2-team (35 Van.)	.287	90	307	59	88	21	4	5	32	44	35	16	5							
Lennon, Pat	.400	34	115	26	46	15	0	6	29	12	29	2	1	R	R	6-2	200	4-27-68	1986	Whiteville, N.C.
Masteller, Dan	.303	48	152	25	46	10	7	4	18	15	17	4	1	L	L	6-0	185	3-17-68	1989	Lyndhurst, Ohio
Miller, Damian	.285	83	295	39	84	23	1	3	41	15	39	2	4	R	R	6-2	190	10-13-69	1990	West Salem, Wisc.
Pose, Scott	.310	70	203	41	63	9	1	0	19	29	28	13	4	L	R	5-11	165	2-11-67	1989	West Des Moines, Iowa
2-team (7 Alb.)	.301	77	219	46	66	10	1	0	20	31	28	15	4							
Quinlan, Tom	.279	130	466	78	130	22	6	17	88	39	124	6	3	R	R	6-3	210	3-27-68	1987	Maplewood, Minn.
Raabe, Brian	.305	112	440	88	134	32	6	3	60	45	14	15	0	R	R	5-9	170	11-5-67	1990	North Branch, Minn.
Shelton, Ben	.242	9	33	7	8	1	1	1	6	6	16	0	0	R	L	6-3	210	9-21-69	1987	Oak Park, Ill.
Simons, Mitch	.325	130	480	87	156	34	4	3	46	47	45	32	16	R	R	5-9	170	12-13-68	1991	Midwest City, Okla.
Snider, Van	.357	32	115	25	41	7	0	7	28	7	17	1	0	L	R	6-3	200	8-11-63	1982	Birmingham, Ala.
Stahoviak, Scott	.303	9	33	6	10	1	0	0	5	6	3	2	0	L	R	6-5	208	3-6-70	1991	Wheeling, Ill.

PITCHING	W	L	ERA	G	GS	CG	SV	IP	H	R	ER	BB	SO	B	T	HT	WT	DOB	1st Yr	Resides
Barcelo, Marc	8	13	7.05	28	28	2	0	143	214	131	112	59	63	R	R	6-3	210	1-10-72	1993	Tucson, Ariz.
Bryant, Shawn	4	1	4.88	31	0	0	0	48	62	31	26	16	27	R	L	6-3	205	6-10-69	1990	Oklahoma City, Okla.
Courtright, John	3	7	6.80	18	17	1	0	85	108	70	64	36	42	L	L	6-2	185	5-30-70	1991	Columbus, Ohio
Gandarillas, Gus	2	3	6.44	22	0	0	2	29	34	23	21	19	17	R	R	6-0	180	7-19-71	1992	Hialeah, Fla.
Gavaghan, Sean	1	4	5.51	35	0	0	5	47	53	32	29	31	28	R	R	6-1	185	12-19-69	1992	Ft. Washington, Pa.
Hansell, Greg	3	1	5.01	7	5	0	0	32	39	20	18	4	17	R	R	6-5	215	3-12-71	1989	La Palma, Calif.
2-team (8 Alb.)	4	2	6.14	15	6	0	1	48	64	35	33	10	32							
Hawkins, LaTroy	9	7	3.55	22	22	4	0	144	150	63	57	40	74	R	R	6-5	195	12-21-72	1991	Gary, Ind.
Henry, Jon	1	0	6.75	3	2	0	0	12	15	9	9	2	3	R	R	6-5	215	8-1-68	1990	Jamestown, N.Y.
Horsman, Vince	1	0	10.38	16	0	0	0	13	23	15	15	4	10	L	L	6-2	175	3-9-67	1985	Dartmouth, N.S.
Johnson, Judd	1	1	3.43	17	0	0	1	21	27	11	8	12	11	R	L	6-0	185	5-4-66	1988	Peebles, Ohio
Misuraca, Mike	9	6	5.34	31	19	1	0	143	174	93	85	36	67	R	R	6-0	188	8-21-68	1989	Covina, Calif.
Munoz, Oscar	8	6	4.95	19	19	1	0	113	121	67	62	35	74	R	R	6-2	205	9-25-69	1990	Hialeah, Fla.
Naulty, Dan	2	6	5.18	42	8	0	4	90	92	55	52	47	76	R	R	6-6	202	1-6-70	1992	Huntington Beach, Calif.
Pulido, Carlos	8	1	4.67	43	3	0	3	71	87	42	37	20	38	L	L	6-0	182	8-5-71	1989	Caracas, Venez.
Robertson, Rich	5	0	2.44	7	7	1	0	44	31	13	12	12	40	L	L	6-4	175	9-15-68	1990	Waller, Texas
Sanford, Mo	0	1	6.35	4	0	0	0	6	6	4	4	4	8	R	R	6-6	225	12-24-66	1988	Starkville, Miss.
Schullstrom, Erik	2	0	4.66	10	0	0	2	10	12	5	5	4	8	R	R	6-5	220	3-25-69	1990	San Leandro, Calif.
Serafini, Dan	0	0	6.75	1	0	0	1	4	4	3	3	1	4	S	L	6-1	185	1-25-74	1992	San Bruno, Calif.
Stevens, Matt	0	0	3.52	7	0	0	1	8	9	4	3	2	5	R	R	6-1	200	1-20-67	1989	Glens Falls, N.Y.
Trombley, Mike	5	3	3.62	12	12	0	0	70	71	32	28	26	59	R	R	6-2	200	4-14-67	1989	Naples, Fla.
Watkins, Scott	4	2	2.80	45	0	0	20	55	45	18	17	13	57	L	L	6-3	180	5-15-70	1992	Sand Springs, Okla.
Wissler, Bill	3	3	4.62	37	2	0	1	60	69	32	31	24	56	R	R	6-3	205	8-27-70	1991	Harrisburg, Pa.

FIELDING

Catcher	PCT	G	PO	A	E	DP	PB
Durant	.990	70	354	30	4	3	2
Horn	1.000	3	18	1	0	0	2
Miller	.998	76	394	52	1	5	7

First Base	PCT	G	PO	A	E	DP
Dunn	.991	102	916	59	9	75
Durant	.917	1	11	0	1	0
Hale	1.000	3	25	2	0	5
Ingram	1.000	1	1	0	0	0
Masteller	.990	10	84	12	1	4
Quinlan	1.000	21	149	7	0	18
Shelton	.970	7	59	5	2	10
Snider	.986	7	66	3	1	6
Stahoviak	1.000	5	32	1	0	2

Second Base	PCT	G	PO	A	E	DP
Corbin	.875	2	3	4	1	1

	PCT	G	PO	A	E	DP
Duncan	1.000	1	4	0	0	1
Hale	1.000	5	3	13	0	2
Hocking	1.000	1	2	3	0	0
Raabe	.989	56	98	169	3	37
Simons	.984	90	195	244	7	63

Third Base	PCT	G	PO	A	E	DP
Hale	1.000	9	5	11	0	2
Quinlan	.940	110	66	231	19	18
Raabe	.975	31	16	63	2	1
Stahoviak	1.000	7	4	15	0	2

Shortstop	PCT	G	PO	A	E	DP
Corbin	1.000	2	3	5	0	3
Duncan	.966	11	25	32	2	6
Hocking	.966	114	171	390	20	72
Raabe	.958	9	6	17	1	4

	PCT	G	PO	A	E	DP
Simons	.949	15	24	50	4	5

Outfield	PCT	G	PO	A	E	DP
Becker	.991	36	108	5	1	0
Brito	1.000	4	15	0	0	0
De la Rosa	1.000	23	42	1	0	0
Durant	1.000	3	5	0	0	0
Hazlett	.986	124	273	13	4	0
Ingram	.990	112	197	10	2	0
Jackson	.971	52	99	1	3	0
Lennon	1.000	6	10	0	0	0
Masteller	1.000	31	53	2	0	0
Miller	1.000	1	1	0	0	0
Pose	.980	62	90	8	2	0
Shelton	1.000	2	3	0	0	0
Simons	1.000	12	12	0	0	0
Snider	1.000	22	33	2	0	0

HARDWARE CITY   AA
EASTERN LEAGUE

BATTING	AVG	G	AB	R	H	2B	3B	HR	RBI	BB	SO	SB	CS	B	T	HT	WT	DOB	1st Yr	Resides
Brede, Brent	.274	134	449	71	123	28	2	3	39	69	82	14	6	L	L	6-4	175	9-13-71	1990	New Baden, Ill.
Byrd, Anthony	.247	123	442	54	109	20	8	3	51	28	85	21	10	R	R	5-11	180	11-13-70	1992	La Grange, Ga.
Duncan, Andres	.226	83	230	28	52	5	2	0	14	10	51	10	5	S	R	5-11	155	11-30-71	1989	San Pedro de Macoris, D.R.
Garrow, David	.143	6	14	0	2	0	0	0	1	2	2	0	0	R	R	6-3	190	9-26-70	1991	Mesa, Ariz.
Gerald, Ed	.111	6	18	1	2	1	0	0	3	2	9	0	0	S	R	6-3	205	7-18-70	1989	St. Paul's, N.C.
Grifol, Pedro	.177	77	226	23	40	9	0	3	21	23	33	1	0	R	R	6-1	205	11-28-69	1991	Miami, Fla.
Hunter, Greg	.077	6	13	1	1	0	0	0	0	1	1	1	0	L	R	6-2	180	1-17-68	1970	Wenatchee, Wash.

BATTING

BATTING	AVG	G	AB	R	H	2B	3B	HR	RBI	BB	SO	SB	CS	B	T	HT	WT	DOB	1st Yr	Resides
Jackson, John	.298	16	57	8	17	2	1	3	8	11	7	3	4	L	L	6-0	185	1-2-67	1990	Diamond Bar, Calif.
Kontorinis, Andrew	.289	36	114	12	33	4	0	2	17	14	18	1	1	L	R	6-0	198	11-18-69	1992	Astoria, N.Y.
Lawton, Matt	.269	114	412	75	111	19	5	13	54	56	70	26	9	L	R	5-9	180	11-3-71	1991	Saucier, Miss.
Legree, Keith	.200	43	110	10	22	2	0	0	6	21	33	3	1	L	R	6-2	195	12-26-71	1991	Statesboro, Ga.
Lopez, Rene	.246	82	264	22	65	8	0	3	26	27	48	0	0	R	R	5-11	195	12-10-71	1992	Downey, Calif.
Moore, Tim	.241	90	311	39	75	19	1	9	45	24	86	4	2	S	L	5-9	215	8-27-71	1989	Greenville, N.C.
Norman, Kenny	.290	12	31	4	9	1	0	1	5	9	9	1	5	R	R	5-10	180	7-13-71	1989	Sweetwater, Texas
Ogden, Jamie	.284	117	384	54	109	22	1	13	61	48	90	6	5	L	L	6-5	215	1-19-72	1990	White Bear Lake, Minn.
Roper, Chad	.226	120	443	41	100	22	3	11	61	27	86	2	3	R	R	6-1	212	3-29-74	1992	Belton, S.C.
Shelton, Ben	.239	56	176	37	42	5	0	13	30	40	58	4	0	R	L	6-3	210	9-21-69	1987	Oak Park, Ill.
Smith, Bubba	.243	42	148	20	36	11	0	6	21	6	41	0	0	R	R	6-2	225	12-18-69	1991	Riverside, Calif.
Tirpack, Ken	.250	7	16	4	4	2	0	2	3	5	3	1	0	L	R	6-0	186	10-3-69	1992	Campbell, Ohio
Valette, Ramon	.214	111	346	40	74	11	2	4	32	21	52	19	2	R	R	6-1	160	1-20-72	1990	Palenque, D.R.
Walker, Todd	.290	137	513	83	149	27	3	21	85	63	101	23	9	L	R	6-0	180	5-25-73	1994	Bossier City, La.

PITCHING

PITCHING	W	L	ERA	G	GS	CG	SV	IP	H	R	ER	BB	SO	B	T	HT	WT	DOB	1st Yr	Resides
DeJesus, Javy	0	0	1.59	4	0	0	0	6	8	2	1	1	3	L	L	5-11	198	8-3-71	1992	Beaumont, Texas
Fultz, Aaron	0	2	6.60	3	3	0	0	15	11	12	11	9	12	L	L	5-11	183	9-4-73	1992	Munford, Tenn.
Gandarilla, Gus	2	4	6.12	25	0	0	7	32	38	26	22	16	25	R	R	6-0	180	7-19-71	1992	Hialeah, Fla.
Gavaghan, Sean	2	1	2.20	21	0	0	5	29	18	10	7	10	30	R	R	6-1	185	12-19-69	1992	Ft. Washington, Pa.
Konieczki, Dom	0	1	1.95	39	0	0	1	32	28	10	7	19	35	R	L	6-1	170	6-16-69	1991	Erie, Pa.
Legault, Kevin	6	1	3.21	47	1	0	3	87	79	31	31	28	52	R	R	6-1	200	3-5-71	1992	Watervliet, N.Y.
Maldonado, Jay	0	0	11.81	5	0	0	0	5	7	8	7	3	4	R	R	6-0	195	3-24-73	1992	San Antonio, Texas
Mansur, Jeff	0	0	1.42	5	0	0	1	6	5	1	1	2	3	L	L	5-11	185	8-2-70	1991	Hood River, Ore.
Miller, Travis	7	9	4.37	28	27	1	0	163	172	93	79	65	151	R	L	6-3	205	11-2-72	1994	West Manchester, Ohio
Moten, Scott	8	5	3.94	40	1	0	3	75	65	40	33	36	43	R	R	6-1	198	4-12-72	1992	Bellflower, Calif.
Norris, Joe	5	6	3.59	46	0	0	5	83	79	42	33	36	47	R	R	6-4	215	11-29-70	1989	Inyokern, Calif.
Ohme, Kevin	3	4	3.46	35	11	0	0	101	89	51	39	45	52	L	L	6-1	175	4-13-71	1993	West Palm Beach, Fla.
Ritchie, Todd	4	9	5.73	24	21	0	0	113	135	78	72	54	60	R	R	6-3	185	11-7-71	1990	Duncanville, Texas
Roberts, Brett	11	9	3.41	28	28	5	0	174	162	72	66	50	135	R	R	6-7	225	3-24-70	1991	South Webster, Ohio
Saccavino, Craig	1	6	5.66	27	1	0	1	41	48	36	26	32	34	R	R	6-4	195	10-1-69	1992	Stuart, Fla.
Serafini, Dan	12	9	3.38	27	27	1	0	163	155	74	61	72	123	S	L	6-1	185	1-25-74	1992	San Bruno, Calif.
Trinidad, Hector	4	11	4.61	23	22	0	0	121	137	67	62	22	92	R	R	6-2	190	9-8-73	1991	Whittier, Calif.

FIELDING

Catcher	PCT	G	PO	A	E	DP	PB
Grifol	.980	74	442	42	10	2	12
Lopez	.983	79	498	69	10	4	5

First Base	PCT	G	PO	A	E	DP
Brede	1.000	10	69	7	0	5
Kontorinis	.991	14	107	8	1	5
Ogden	.987	66	582	41	8	49
Shelton	.988	49	446	36	6	40
Smith	1.000	7	48	3	0	6
Tirpack	.953	5	38	3	2	3

Second Base	PCT	G	PO	A	E	DP
Duncan	1.000	6	8	7	0	1
Hunter	1.000	2	1	1	0	0
Valette	.963	26	38	91	5	26

Third Base	PCT	G	PO	A	E	DP
Garrow	1.000	3	2	5	0	1
Hunter	.667	1	0	2	1	0
Kontorinis	.750	3	1	2	1	0
Lopez	1.000	2	3	5	0	0
Roper	.938	117	69	248	21	21
Walker	.865	21	5	27	5	1

Shortstop	PCT	G	PO	A	E	DP
Duncan	.941	68	119	184	19	43
Garrow	1.000	3	3	5	0	0
Hunter	.800	3	2	2	1	0
Roper	1.000	2	3	10	0	1

Outfield	PCT	G	PO	A	E	DP
Walker	.961	117	210	328	22	65
Valette	.927	84	90	215	24	34
Brede	.962	120	238	12	10	3
Byrd	.977	119	247	7	6	1
Duncan	1.000	1	1	0	0	0
Gerald	.750	2	2	1	1	0
Jackson	.880	13	21	1	3	1
Lawton	.991	110	221	12	2	2
Legree	.957	28	44	0	2	0
Moore	.882	15	15	0	2	0
Norman	1.000	5	6	1	0	0
Ogden	.988	40	78	3	1	0

FORT MYERS — A
FLORIDA STATE LEAGUE

BATTING	AVG	G	AB	R	H	2B	3B	HR	RBI	BB	SO	SB	CS	B	T	HT	WT	DOB	1st Yr	Resides
Baker, Jason	.239	91	276	35	66	9	0	0	26	30	38	8	8	L	L	5-10	176	7-31-72	1992	Shelbyville, Tenn.
Brown, Armann	.190	23	63	6	12	2	3	0	9	3	15	1	0	R	R	6-1	163	9-10-72	1992	Austin, Texas
Caraballo, Gary	.307	85	309	51	95	24	2	5	55	34	44	5	6	R	R	5-11	205	7-11-71	1989	Yauco, P.R.
Champion, Jim	.227	99	308	38	70	14	4	3	33	26	88	3	1	L	L	6-3	195	8-9-73	1994	Corvallis, Ore.
Hilt, Scott	.167	19	42	3	7	0	0	1	3	3	12	0	0	R	R	6-2	215	12-9-72	1994	Westfield, Mass.
Horn, Jeff	.266	66	199	25	53	5	1	0	20	38	30	2	3	R	R	6-1	190	8-23-70	1992	Riverside, Calif.
Hunter, Torii	.246	113	391	64	96	15	2	7	36	38	77	7	4	R	R	6-2	205	7-18-75	1993	Pine Bluff, Ark.
Jones, Ben	.239	109	335	60	80	10	2	0	31	41	53	19	6	R	R	5-10	175	9-15-73	1992	Alexandria, La.
Knauss, Tom	.237	99	316	37	75	19	1	1	26	28	72	2	8	R	R	6-2	205	6-16-74	1992	Arlington Heights, Ill.
McCalmont, Jim	.228	92	285	30	65	13	2	4	21	23	54	2	7	R	R	6-0	185	10-6-71	1994	Scottsdale, Ariz.
Mientkiewicz, Doug	.245	38	110	9	27	6	1	1	15	18	19	2	2	L	R	6-2	190	6-19-74	1995	Miami, Fla.
Motte, James	.235	119	392	47	92	17	2	4	37	31	78	8	10	R	R	6-2	170	5-4-72	1993	Pueblo, Colo.
Nava, Marlon	.242	112	376	47	91	18	0	1	37	22	45	5	9	R	R	5-10	165	6-18-73	1991	Ciudid Ojeda, Venez.
Nihart, Tom	.200	4	10	1	2	2	0	0	2	1	3	0	0	R	R	6-2	200	7-5-72	1994	Easley, S.C.
Radmanovich, Ryan	.317	12	41	3	13	2	0	0	5	2	8	0	0	L	R	6-2	185	8-9-71	1993	Calgary, Alberta
Rupp, Chad	.266	107	376	44	100	23	1	12	52	38	77	14	3	R	R	6-3	215	9-30-71	1993	Tampa, Fla.
Smith, Bubba	.330	60	176	27	58	15	0	13	51	16	38	1	2	R	R	6-2	225	12-18-69	1991	Riverside, Calif.
Stricklin, Scott	.187	65	166	20	31	1	0	0	8	41	25	4	4	L	R	5-11	180	2-17-72	1993	The Plains, Ohio
Venezia, Danny	.245	16	49	5	12	1	1	0	4	7	8	1	0	R	R	6-1	180	11-4-71	1993	Brooklyn, N.Y.

GAMES BY POSITION: C—Hilt 13, Horn 65, Nihart 4, Stricklin 65. **1B**—Caraballo 1, Champion 57, Mientkiewicz 24, Rupp 55, Smith 8. **2B**—McCalmont 71, Nava 61, Venezia 15. **3B**—Caraballo 83, McCalmont 13, Nava 35, Radmanovich 11, Smith 6. **SS**—Motte 116, Nava 22. **OF**—Baker 84, Brown 19, Champion 31, Hunter 103, Jones 103, Knauss 88, Nava 1.

PITCHING	W	L	ERA	G	GS	CG	SV	IP	H	R	ER	BB	SO	B	T	HT	WT	DOB	1st Yr	Resides
Biehl, Rod	2	0	4.05	12	0	0	0	20	15	9	9	8	20	L	L	5-11	190	6-11-69	1991	North Lake, Ill.
Bowers, Shane	13	5	2.16	23	23	1	0	146	119	43	35	32	103	R	R	6-6	215	7-27-71	1993	Covina, Calif.
Caridad, Ron	2	3	2.40	17	0	0	3	41	27	15	11	18	38	R	R	5-10	180	3-22-72	1990	Miami, Fla.
Carrasco, Troy	12	4	3.13	25	25	2	0	138	131	62	48	63	99	S	L	5-11	172	1-27-75	1993	Tampa, Fla.
DeBrino, Rob	11	3	3.14	41	0	0	4	49	38	24	17	25	30	R	R	6-2	205	9-25-73	1992	Northvale, N.J.
Fultz, Aaron	3	6	3.25	21	21	2	0	122	115	52	44	41	127	L	L	5-11	183	9-4-73	1992	Munford, Tenn.

PITCHING	W	L	ERA	G	GS	CG	SV	IP	H	R	ER	BB	SO	B	T	HT	WT	DOB	1st Yr	Resides
Harris, Greg	1	0	0.95	3	3	1	0	19	12	3	2	4	11	R	R	6-2	195	12-1-63	1985	Las Vegas, Nev.
Lehoisky, Russ	0	5	3.29	26	0	0	0	52	45	25	19	38	29	R	R	6-5	205	1-30-71	1993	Comstock, N.Y.
Linebarger, Keith	7	4	2.10	29	10	1	4	103	74	30	24	35	73	R	R	6-6	220	5-11-71	1992	Ringgold, Ga.
Maldonado, Jay	0	1	6.23	5	0	0	0	4	6	4	3	4	4	R	R	6-0	195	3-24-73	1992	San Antonio, Texas
Miller, Shawn	4	1	1.90	30	0	0	4	71	68	16	15	13	35	R	R	6-3	195	4-27-73	1991	Modesto, Calif.
Morse, Paul	3	1	3.82	35	0	0	15	61	57	30	26	12	56	R	R	6-2	185	2-27-73	1995	Danville, Ky.
O'Brien, Brian	0	3	2.88	24	0	0	0	34	31	20	11	15	20	L	L	6-3	195	7-4-71	1993	Bellevue, Neb.
Redman, Mark	2	1	2.76	8	5	0	0	33	28	13	10	13	26	L	L	6-5	215	1-5-74	1995	Del Mar, Calif.
Sampson, Benj	11	9	3.49	28	27	3	0	160	148	71	62	52	95	L	L	6-0	185	4-27-75	1993	Bondurant, Iowa
Tatar, Jason	4	5	2.61	21	15	0	1	83	64	33	24	36	60	R	R	6-0	185	8-15-74	1992	Rantoul, Ill.

FORT WAYNE
MIDWEST LEAGUE

BATTING	AVG	G	AB	R	H	2B	3B	HR	RBI	BB	SO	SB	CS	B	T	HT	WT	DOB	1st Yr	Resides
Alvarez, Rafael	.283	99	374	62	106	17	5	5	36	34	53	15	11	L	L	5-11	160	1-22-77	1994	Valencia, Venez.
Brown, Armann	.233	78	253	35	59	9	2	1	25	30	72	6	5	R	R	6-1	163	9-10-72	1992	Austin, Texas
Fortin, Troy	.258	112	407	49	105	21	1	7	48	38	69	4	5	R	R	5-11	200	2-24-75	1993	Lundar, Manitoba
Fraser, Joe	.200	5	15	0	3	0	0	0	2	0	5	1	0	R	R	6-1	200	8-23-74	1995	Westminster, Calif.
Garcia, Carlos	.189	34	95	13	18	5	0	0	10	7	13	11	0	R	R	5-11	165	5-21-76	1993	Coraballeda, Venez.
Gordon, Adrian	.240	75	217	34	52	10	1	2	18	26	63	16	7	R	R	6-3	217	3-8-74	1992	Alexandria, La.
Gunderson, Shane	.253	26	87	17	22	7	0	2	12	10	17	2	1	R	R	6-0	205	10-16-73	1995	Faribault, Minn.
Hilt, Scott	.185	30	92	13	17	5	1	1	15	11	28	0	0	L	R	6-2	215	12-9-72	1994	Westfield, Mass.
Koskie, Corey	.310	123	462	64	143	37	5	16	78	38	79	2	4	L	R	6-3	215	6-28-73	1994	Dugold, Manitoba
Lane, Ryan	.266	115	432	69	115	37	1	6	56	65	92	17	9	R	R	6-1	175	7-6-74	1993	Bellefontaine, Ohio
McCalmont, Jim	.333	7	33	5	11	3	0	3	7	3	3	2	0	R	R	6-0	185	10-6-71	1994	Scottsdale, Ariz.
Moriarty, Mike	.227	62	203	26	46	6	3	4	26	27	44	8	0	R	R	5-10	166	3-8-74	1995	Clayton, N.J.
Mucker, Kelcey	.230	109	405	48	93	16	1	7	47	27	59	12	4	R	R	6-4	220	2-17-75	1993	Lawrenceburg, Ind.
Paez, Israel	.260	113	388	41	101	12	2	2	45	35	55	12	11	R	R	5-10	168	12-23-76	1994	Carabobo, Venez.
Patterson, Jake	.264	116	435	56	115	23	5	14	68	35	118	0	2	L	L	6-0	230	8-1-73	1994	Golden, Colo.
Pearson, Kevin	.141	29	78	10	11	1	1	1	7	6	30	1	0	R	R	6-5	195	2-20-73	1992	Fergus Falls, Minn.
Pierzynski, A.J.	.310	22	84	10	26	5	1	2	14	2	10	0	0	L	R	6-3	210	12-30-76	1995	Orlando, Fla.
Valentin, Jose	.321	112	383	59	123	26	5	19	65	47	75	0	5	S	R	5-10	185	9-19-75	1993	Manati, P.R.
Vizcaino, Romulo	.248	103	343	44	85	13	4	1	22	35	56	6	6	S	R	6-2	160	1-20-74	1991	Santo Domingo, D.R.

GAMES BY POSITION: C—Fortin 4, Hilt 30, Pierzynski 20, Valentin 101. **1B**—Fortin 80, Gunderson 4, Patterson 56, Pearson 8. **2B**—Fraser 4, Garcia 9, Lane 42, McCalmont 6, Paez 91. **3B**—Fraser 1, Garcia 14, Koskie 109, McCalmont 2, Paez 19, Valentin 9. **SS**—Lane 75, Moriarty 62, Paez 8. **OF**—Alvarez 96, Brown 76, Garcia 7, Gordon 41, Gunderson 21, Mucker 105, Pearson 14, Vizcaino 98.

PITCHING	W	L	ERA	G	GS	CG	SV	IP	H	R	ER	BB	SO	B	T	HT	WT	DOB	1st Yr	Resides
Alvarado, Luis	1	1	2.92	16	1	0	2	37	41	18	12	14	24	R	R	6-0	163	8-28-74	1992	Cayey, P.R.
Bedinger, Doug	6	6	4.61	46	0	0	9	66	74	37	34	28	62	R	R	6-1	190	8-22-74	1994	Channalton, Ill.
Bell, Jason	3	1	1.31	9	6	0	0	34	26	11	5	6	40	R	R	6-3	205	9-30-74	1995	Orlando, Fla.
Chapman, Walker	2	6	6.24	14	11	0	1	53	59	41	37	36	31	R	R	6-3	210	2-25-76	1994	Frostburg, Md.
Cobb, Trevor	4	4	3.88	11	10	0	0	53	51	26	23	18	46	L	L	6-2	185	7-13-73	1992	Marysville, Wash.
Dowhower, Deron	3	0	3.27	35	0	0	3	77	53	32	28	49	97	R	R	6-2	195	2-14-72	1993	Ashburn, Va.
Fidge, Darren	6	5	3.68	39	17	1	13	134	126	62	55	37	106	R	R	6-2	175	11-12-74	1992	Adelaide, Australia
Gourdin, Tom	6	6	4.42	41	0	0	6	90	90	49	44	32	74	R	R	6-3	190	5-24-73	1992	Murray, Utah
Meyhoff, Jason	2	1	6.59	17	10	0	0	55	70	52	40	30	35	L	L	6-0	185	3-13-73	1994	Center, N.D.
Mott, Tom	13	4	4.03	25	25	1	0	130	123	67	58	48	64	R	R	6-3	215	10-9-73	1994	San Luis Obispo, Calif.
Nartker, Mike	5	5	3.10	17	16	1	0	96	87	36	33	20	79	R	R	6-2	205	11-26-71	1995	Hillsboro, Ohio
Pavicich, Paul	4	3	3.01	39	0	0	5	87	75	39	29	28	100	L	L	6-2	190	1-10-73	1994	Los Gatos, Calif.
Perkins, Dan	7	12	5.49	29	22	0	0	121	133	86	74	69	89	R	R	6-2	175	3-15-75	1993	Miami, Fla.
Peters, Brannon	1	1	4.38	11	1	0	0	25	29	17	12	16	24	R	L	6-3	215	2-16-72	1994	Homer, La.
Radlosky, Robert	11	8	4.03	30	18	1	0	121	111	64	54	55	102	R	R	6-2	170	1-7-74	1994	Lantana, Fla.
Ruch, Rob	0	1	2.73	9	3	0	1	26	17	8	8	16	27	R	R	6-3	210	7-5-72	1994	Westville, Ill.
Rushing, Will	1	1	1.78	13	0	0	1	25	15	11	5	10	25	L	L	6-3	190	11-8-72	1995	Statesboro, Ga.
Williams, Juan	0	0	4.50	3	0	0	0	6	7	4	3	3	4	R	L	6-0	175	12-24-73	1993	Irvington, N.J.

ELIZABETHTON
APPALACHIAN LEAGUE

BATTING	AVG	G	AB	R	H	2B	3B	HR	RBI	BB	SO	SB	CS	B	T	HT	WT	DOB	1st Yr	Resides
Brown, Jerome	.183	17	71	10	13	2	0	0	1	5	25	5	0	S	R	5-10	168	1-19-76	1994	Smithville, Okla.
Colburn, Brian	.175	11	40	3	7	0	0	0	4	3	8	2	0	L	L	5-7	170	5-15-76	1994	La Crosse, Wisc.
Davidson, Cleatus	.296	39	152	27	45	6	2	3	27	11	31	10	4	S	R	5-10	160	11-1-76	1994	Lake Wales, Fla.
Fraser, Joe	.261	46	184	29	48	4	0	4	21	20	22	5	4	R	R	6-1	200	8-23-74	1995	Westminster, Calif.
Garcia, Carlos	.306	62	235	42	72	15	1	5	34	16	41	27	8	R	R	5-11	165	5-21-76	1993	Coraballeda, Venez.
Gunderson, Shane	.309	37	139	32	43	11	2	7	30	20	24	4	0	R	R	6-0	205	10-16-73	1995	Faribault, Minn.
Herdman, Eli	.212	62	217	36	46	10	0	10	36	34	60	1	2	L	R	6-0	190	3-24-76	1994	Bremerton, Wash.
Johnson, Heath	.209	59	201	31	42	10	0	1	16	41	51	4	5	L	R	6-3	210	8-25-76	1994	Lakefield, Minn.
Johnson, Travis	.341	14	44	6	15	5	1	2	4	5	10	2	1	L	R	6-0	210	11-23-73	1995	Monticello, Minn.
Jones, Ivory	.199	47	136	21	27	4	1	2	11	22	43	6	5	L	L	5-10	160	2-28-73	1995	Vallejo, Calif.
Juarez, Raul	.283	40	120	25	34	7	0	3	16	23	50	10	3	R	R	5-8	185	10-28-75	1994	Carabobo, Venez.
Lakovic, Greg	.244	14	41	7	10	2	0	0	8	3	8	0	1	L	R	6-2	185	1-31-75	1994	Coquitlam, B.C.
Pena, Francisco	.190	10	21	4	4	2	0	0	2	2	10	0	0	R	R	6-1	205	8-22-76	1994	Santo Domingo, D.R.
Pierzynski, A.J.	.332	56	205	29	68	13	1	7	45	14	23	0	2	L	R	6-3	210	12-30-76	1995	Orlando, Fla.
Reyes, Freddy	.277	40	130	17	36	10	1	5	21	6	28	0	0	R	R	6-1	214	4-8-76	1995	Levittown, P.R.
Schroeder, John	.263	62	236	44	62	7	2	6	30	16	39	1	1	L	R	6-4	220	10-9-75	1994	Coeur D'Alene, Idaho

GAMES BY POSITION: C—Gunderson 10, Lakovic 4, Pena 7, Pierzynski 49. **1B**—Gunderson 1, Lakovic 1, Pierzynski 1, Reyes 18, Schroeder 47. **2B**—Brown 2, Fraser 45, Garcia 20. **3B**—Garcia 5, Herdman 58, Reyes 2. **SS**—Brown 6, Davidson 38, Garcia 24. **OF**—Brown 8, Colburn 10, Garcia 17, Gunderson 25, H. Johnson 56, T. Johnson 13, Jones 41, Juarez 35, Schroeder 1.

PITCHING	W	L	ERA	G	GS	CG	SV	IP	H	R	ER	BB	SO	B	T	HT	WT	DOB	1st Yr	Resides
Anderson, Eric	3	2	2.95	21	2	0	0	40	48	21	13	19	31	L	L	6-0	180	2-25-73	1993	Downers Grove, Ill.
Bartels, Todd	6	2	4.11	13	9	2	0	57	66	27	26	3	45	R	R	6-4	215	11-16-73	1995	Omaha, Neb.

PITCHING	W	L	ERA	G	GS	CG	SV	IP	H	R	ER	BB	SO	B	T	HT	WT	DOB	1st Yr	Resides
Blank, John..............	3	0	4.54	15	5	0	0	36	40	21	18	16	32	L	L	6-4	205	10-22-73	1995	Jennings, La.
Boggs, Harold.............	3	5	5.82	12	12	0	0	60	77	53	39	20	55	R	R	6-4	225	8-30-74	1995	Lizemore, W.Va.
Chapman, Walker	0	1	5.63	4	1	0	0	8	9	6	5	1	7	R	R	6-3	210	2-25-76	1994	Frostburg, Md.
Harris, Jeffrey	1	3	3.82	21	0	0	0	33	42	15	14	13	27	R	R	6-1	190	7-4-74	1995	San Pablo, Calif.
Mahaffey, Alan	5	6	3.47	13	12	1	0	70	66	42	27	21	73	L	L	6-3	200	2-2-74	1995	Springfield, Mo.
Niedermaier, Brad	2	0	2.21	7	7	0	0	41	33	14	10	17	47	R	R	6-3	205	2-9-73	1995	Niles, Ill.
Peters, Tim	2	3	1.65	27	0	0	0	33	27	16	6	5	36	L	L	6-0	190	12-1-72	1995	Houston, Texas
Rath, Fred..................	1	1	1.35	27	0	0	12	33	20	8	5	11	50	R	R	6-3	205	1-5-73	1995	Tampa, Fla.
Richardson, Kasey	1	0	2.33	3	3	0	0	19	12	8	5	13	11	L	L	6-4	180	8-27-76	1994	Huntingtown, Md.
Sellner, Aaron	1	2	2.14	19	1	0	0	34	30	15	8	10	32	L	R	6-2	195	9-6-73	1994	West Haven, Conn.
Splittorff, Jamie............	5	4	3.24	13	12	1	0	72	64	40	26	29	72	L	R	6-3	185	10-12-73	1995	Blue Springs, Mo.
Tanksley, Scott.............	0	2	4.11	11	0	0	1	15	16	13	7	5	17	S	R	5-11	185	11-1-73	1995	Kemp, Texas

FORT MYERS   R

GULF COAST LEAGUE

BATTING	AVG	G	AB	R	H	2B	3B	HR	RBI	BB	SO	SB	CS	B	T	HT	WT	DOB	1st Yr	Resides
Astacio, Onofre	.224	47	165	21	37	3	1	0	8	17	42	26	6	S	R	6-0	165	4-10-76	1993	Bayaguana, D.R.
Ayuso, Julio	.169	25	71	5	12	0	0	0	3	7	20	0	1	R	R	6-2	180	6-23-77	1995	Carolina, P.R.
Bunkley, Antuan	.298	49	181	24	54	9	0	6	23	15	35	11	4	R	R	6-0	205	9-20-75	1994	West Palm Beach, Fla.
Cruz, Andres	.241	32	112	10	27	5	1	0	9	7	19	1	0	R	R	5-11	174	6-11-77	1995	Salinas, P.R.
Davidson, Cleatus	.200	21	75	11	15	2	1	0	5	10	17	8	3	S	R	5-10	160	11-1-76	1994	Lake Wales, Fla.
Harrison, Jamal	.143	5	14	0	2	1	0	0	2	2	1	0	0	R	R	6-4	207	7-15-77	1995	Palo Alto, Calif.
Johnson, Carlisle.........	.180	19	50	2	9	1	0	0	4	11	13	1	1	R	R	6-3	220	9-14-76	1995	Pierson, Fla.
Johnson, Travis	.316	24	76	14	24	5	0	1	10	11	9	5	4	L	R	6-0	210	11-23-73	1995	Monticello, Mn
Juarez, Raul	.346	7	26	3	9	1	1	1	6	0	5	0	0	R	R	6-3	185	10-28-75	1994	Carabobo, Venez.
Lorenzo, Juan	.217	14	46	3	10	0	0	0	2	4	6	0	0	S	R	6-0	155	6-10-78	1995	Cambito Garabitos, D.R.
McHenry, Joe	.219	34	114	9	25	8	0	0	7	9	38	2	3	R	R	6-1	175	5-24-76	1995	Murfreesboro, Tenn.
Millwood, Terry	.217	47	161	15	35	5	3	0	11	17	29	5	2	R	R	6-1	209	7-6-75	1994	Brisbane, Australia
Nelson, Kevin	.145	45	138	7	20	8	0	1	11	11	36	1	1	R	R	6-3	210	2-9-77	1995	Alexander, Ark.
Orndorff, Dave	.209	23	67	12	14	0	0	1	3	13	11	5	0	R	R	5-10	175	8-10-77	1995	Shippensburg, Pa.
Pena, Frank	.188	21	69	7	13	6	0	0	5	5	18	0	0	R	R	6-1	205	8-22-76	1995	Santo Domingo, D.R.
Prada, Nelson	.269	24	78	5	21	4	1	0	13	3	12	0	0	R	R	6-2	200	2-2-76	1995	Barquisimeto, Venez.
Quezado, Dalmiro	.155	32	103	5	16	6	0	0	6	1	17	1	1	R	R	5-11	150	10-18-76	1995	Santo Domingo, D.R.
Reyes, Freddy	.238	6	21	2	5	1	0	1	4	1	6	0	0	R	R	6-1	214	4-8-76	1995	Levittown, P.R.
Vilchez, Jose	.225	45	142	14	32	6	0	0	6	1	29	7	5	S	R	5-11	180	4-20-76	1994	Maracaibo, Venez.

GAMES BY POSITION: C—Orndorff 20, Pena 14, Prada 24. **1B**—Bunkley 29, Cruz 21, Harrison 4, Reyes 5. **2B**—Astacio 17, Davidson 7, Millwood 1, Quezado 30. **3B**—Bunkley 24, Nelson 36, Quezado 30. **SS**—Astacio 30, Davidson 14, Lorenzo 14. **OF**—Ayuso 15, C. Johnson 12, T. Johnson 22, McHenry 33, Millwood 44, Vilchez 44.

PITCHING	W	L	ERA	G	GS	CG	SV	IP	H	R	ER	BB	SO	B	T	HT	WT	DOB	1st Yr	Resides
Cobb, Trevor	2	0	0.95	3	3	0	0	19	11	5	2	7	15	L	L	6-2	185	7-13-73	1992	Marysville, Wash.
Ellison, Austin..............	0	0	3.78	11	0	0	2	17	17	10	7	15	11	R	R	6-1	200	9-17-75	1995	Austin, Texas
Espina, Randy	0	1	0.90	4	2	0	0	10	11	10	1	6	3	L	L	6-0	180	5-11-78	1995	Cabimas, Venez.
Forster, Peter	2	5	3.71	10	7	2	0	44	37	21	18	27	36	L	L	6-4	185	6-4-75	1994	Gladstone, Mo.
Garff, Jeffery	4	2	1.77	15	6	0	1	46	34	12	9	5	30	R	R	6-4	195	12-3-75	1995	Bountiful, Utah
Malko, Bryan	1	2	2.73	10	4	0	1	33	23	14	10	23	29	R	R	6-3	185	1-23-77	1995	Piscataway, N.J.
Marquez, Ralph	0	4	4.09	11	0	0	1	22	19	13	10	18	19	R	R	6-2	185	7-16-76	1995	Hialeah, Fla.
Marshall, Lee	0	1	4.91	6	1	0	0	11	16	10	6	8	7	R	R	6-1	205	9-25-76	1995	Ariton, Ala.
McBride, Rodney..........	3	7	3.08	12	11	1	1	61	63	38	21	34	36	R	R	6-1	190	11-15-74	1994	Memphis, Tenn.
Meyhoff, Jason	0	0	4.50	2	0	0	0	2	3	3	1	0	3	L	L	6-3	185	3-13-73	1994	Center, N.D.
Ocando, Stewart	0	1	5.96	14	0	0	0	23	26	25	15	22	20	R	R	5-11	183	11-12-77	1995	Aragua, Venez.
Puffer, Brandon	0	3	2.88	14	5	0	1	41	29	21	13	21	35	R	R	6-3	172	10-5-75	1994	Mission Viejo, Calif.
Reilly, Sean	1	0	5.27	6	0	0	0	14	19	12	8	6	11	R	L	6-2	180	6-10-77	1995	Burlington, Ontario
Richardson, Kasey	5	2	1.15	7	7	2	0	47	38	10	6	11	35	L	L	6-4	180	8-27-76	1994	Huntingtown, Md.
Ruch, Rob	1	3	3.86	7	2	0	2	23	16	13	10	16	30	R	R	6-3	210	7-5-72	1994	Westville, Ill.
Stewart, Scott	0	0	6.35	3	1	0	0	6	7	4	4	4	9	R	L	6-2	200	8-14-75	1994	Stanley, N.C.
Vanderbush, Matt.........	2	3	4.00	8	6	0	0	36	37	23	16	9	28	L	L	6-5	230	6-3-74	1995	Glenwood, N.J.

MONTREAL
EXPOS

Manager: Felipe Alou. **1995 Record:** 66-78, .458 (5th, NL East).

BATTING	AVG	G	AB	R	H	2B	3B	HR	RBI	BB	SO	SB	CS	B	T	HT	WT	DOB	1st Yr	Resides
Alou, Moises	.273	93	344	48	94	22	0	14	58	29	56	4	3	R	R	6-3	195	7-3-66	1986	Redwood City, Calif.
Andrews, Shane	.214	84	220	27	47	10	1	8	31	17	68	1	1	R	R	6-1	205	8-28-71	1990	Carlsbad, N.M.
Benitez, Yamil	.385	14	39	8	15	2	1	2	7	1	7	0	2	R	R	6-2	180	10-5-72	1990	San Juan, P.R.
Berry, Sean	.318	103	314	38	100	22	1	14	55	25	53	3	8	R	R	5-11	210	3-22-66	1986	Rolling Hills Estates, Calif.
Cordero, Wil	.286	131	514	64	147	35	2	10	49	36	88	9	5	R	R	6-2	185	10-3-71	1988	Mayaguez, P.R.
Fletcher, Darrin	.286	110	350	42	100	21	1	11	45	32	23	0	1	L	R	6-2	195	10-3-66	1987	Oakwood, Ill.
Floyd, Cliff	.130	29	69	6	9	1	0	1	8	7	22	3	0	L	R	6-4	220	12-5-72	1991	Markham, Ill.
Foley, Tom	.208	11	24	2	5	2	0	0	2	2	4	1	0	L	R	6-1	175	9-9-59	1977	Miami, Fla.
Fonville, Chad	.333	14	12	2	4	0	0	0	0	0	3	0	2	S	R	5-7	155	3-5-71	1992	Midway Park, N.C.
Frazier, Lou	.190	35	63	6	12	2	0	0	3	8	12	4	0	S	R	6-2	175	1-26-65	1986	St. Louis, Mo.
Grudzielanek, Mark	.245	78	269	27	66	12	2	1	20	14	47	8	3	R	R	6-1	170	6-30-70	1991	El Paso, Texas
Kelly, Roberto	.274	24	95	11	26	4	0	1	9	7	14	4	3	R	R	6-2	192	10-1-64	1982	Panama City, Panama
Laker, Tim	.234	64	141	17	33	8	1	3	20	14	38	0	1	R	R	6-2	175	11-27-69	1988	Simi Valley, Calif.
Lansing, Mike	.255	127	467	47	119	30	2	10	62	28	65	27	4	R	R	6-0	175	4-3-68	1990	Casper, Wyom.
Pride, Curtis	.175	48	63	10	11	1	0	0	2	5	16	3	2	L	R	5-11	195	12-17-68	1986	Silver Spring, Md.
Rodriguez, Henry	.207	24	58	7	12	0	0	1	5	6	11	0	0	L	L	6-1	210	11-8-67	1986	New York, N.Y.
2-team (21 LA)	.239	45	138	13	33	4	1	2	15	11	28	0	1							
Santangelo, F.P.	.296	35	98	11	29	5	1	1	9	12	9	1	1	S	R	5-10	165	10-24-67	1989	El Dorado Hills, Calif.
Segui, David	.305	97	383	59	117	22	3	10	57	28	38	1	4	S	L	6-1	202	7-19-66	1988	Kansas City, Kan.
2-team (33 NY)	.309	130	456	68	141	25	4	12	68	40	47	2	7							
Siddall, Joe	.300	7	10	4	3	0	0	1	3	3	0	0	0	L	R	6-1	197	10-25-67	1988	Windsor, Ontario
Silvestri, Dave	.264	39	72	12	19	6	0	2	7	9	27	2	0	R	R	6-0	180	9-29-67	1989	St. Louis, Mo.
Spehr, Tim	.257	41	35	4	9	5	0	1	3	6	7	0	0	R	R	6-2	205	7-2-66	1988	Waco, Texas
Tarasco, Tony	.249	126	438	64	109	18	4	14	40	51	78	24	3	L	R	6-1	205	12-9-70	1988	Santa Monica, Calif.
Treadway, Jeff	.240	41	50	4	12	2	0	0	10	5	2	0	1	L	R	5-11	175	1-22-63	1984	Griffin, Ga.
2-team (17 LA)	.209	58	67	6	14	2	1	0	13	5	4	0	1							
White, Rondell	.295	130	474	87	140	33	4	13	57	41	87	25	5	R	R	6-1	193	2-23-72	1990	Gray, Ga.

PITCHING	W	L	ERA	G	GS	CG	SV	IP	H	R	ER	BB	SO	B	T	HT	WT	DOB	1st Yr	Resides
Alvarez, Tavo	1	5	6.75	8	8	0	0	37	46	30	28	14	17	R	R	6-3	183	11-25-71	1990	Tucson, Ariz.
Aquino, Luis	0	2	3.86	29	0	0	2	37	47	24	16	11	22	R	R	6-1	190	5-19-65	1982	Caguas, P.R.
Cornelius, Reid	0	0	8.00	8	0	0	0	9	11	8	8	5	4	R	R	6-0	190	6-2-70	1989	Thomasville, Ala.
DeLeon, Jose	0	1	7.56	7	0	0	0	8	7	7	7	7	12	R	R	6-3	215	12-20-60	1979	Boca Raton, Fla.
Eversgerd, Bryan	0	0	5.14	25	0	0	0	21	22	13	12	9	8	R	L	6-1	185	2-11-69	1989	Centralia, Ill.
Fassero, Jeff	13	14	4.33	30	30	1	0	189	207	102	91	74	164	L	L	6-1	180	1-5-63	1988	Springfield, Ill.
Fraser, Willie	2	1	5.61	22	0	0	2	26	25	17	16	9	12	R	R	6-1	206	5-26-64	1985	Newburgh, N.Y.
Harris, Greg	2	3	2.61	45	0	0	0	48	45	18	14	16	47	S	R	6-0	175	11-2-55	1977	Orleans, Mass.
Henry, Butch	7	9	2.84	21	21	1	0	127	133	47	40	28	60	L	L	6-1	195	10-7-68	1987	El Paso, Texas
Heredia, Gil	5	6	4.31	40	18	0	1	119	137	60	57	21	74	R	R	6-1	190	10-26-65	1987	Tucson, Ariz.
Leiper, Dave	0	2	2.86	26	0	0	2	22	16	8	7	6	12	L	L	6-1	160	6-18-62	1982	Plano, Texas
Martinez, Pedro	14	10	3.51	30	30	2	0	195	158	79	76	66	174	R	R	5-11	150	7-25-71	1988	Santo Domingo, D.R.
Perez, Carlos	10	8	3.69	28	23	2	0	141	142	61	58	28	106	L	L	6-3	200	4-14-71	1990	San Cristobal, D.R.
Rojas, Mel	1	4	4.12	59	0	0	30	68	69	32	31	29	61	R	R	5-11	165	12-10-66	1986	Santo Domingo, D.R.
Rueter, Kirk	5	3	3.23	9	9	1	0	47	38	17	17	9	28	L	L	6-3	190	12-1-70	1991	Hoyleton, Ill.
Schmidt, Curt	0	0	6.97	11	0	0	0	10	15	8	8	9	7	R	R	6-6	223	3-16-70	1992	Miles City, Mon.
Scott, Tim	2	0	3.98	62	0	0	2	63	52	30	28	23	57	R	R	6-2	205	11-16-66	1984	Hanford, Calif.
Shaw, Jeff	1	6	4.62	50	0	0	3	62	58	35	32	26	45	R	R	6-2	185	7-7-66	1986	Wash. Courthouse, Ohio
Thobe, J.J.	0	0	9.00	4	0	0	0	4	6	4	4	3	0	R	R	6-6	200	11-19-70	1992	Huntington Beach, Calif.
Urbina, Ugueth	2	2	6.17	7	4	0	0	23	26	17	16	14	15	R	R	6-2	170	2-15-74	1991	Caracas, Venez.
White, Gabe	1	2	7.01	19	1	0	0	26	26	21	20	9	25	L	L	6-2	200	11-20-71	1990	Sebring, Fla.

FIELDING

Catcher	PCT	G	PO	A	E	DP	PB
Fletcher	.994	98	613	44	4	8	0
Laker	.977	61	265	27	7	1	4
Siddall	.882	7	14	1	2	0	2
Spehr	.990	38	92	12	1	3	0

First Base	PCT	G	PO	A	E	DP
Andrews	.977	29	160	11	4	11
Berry	1.000	3	22	4	0	0
Floyd	.987	18	143	12	2	13
Foley	1.000	4	21	2	0	1
Rodriguez	1.000	10	82	7	0	8
Segui	.997	97	840	70	3	68
Silvestri	1.000	4	21	1	0	4

Second Base	PCT	G	PO	A	E	DP
Foley	1.000	3	2	5	0	2
Fonville	.000	2	0	0	0	0

Second Base	PCT	G	PO	A	E	DP
Frazier	1.000	·	1	0	1	0	0
Grudzielanek	.963	13	26	26	2	5
Lansing	.991	127	306	373	6	77
Santangelo	1.000	5	1	0	0	0
Silvestri	1.000	3	3	2	0	0
Treadway	1.000	11	11	15	0	2

Third Base	PCT	G	PO	A	E	DP
Andrews	.973	51	22	86	3	2
Berry	.947	83	54	161	12	19
Grudzielanek	.935	31	18	68	6	2
Silvestri	.938	8	2	13	1	0
Treadway	1.000	1	0	1	0	0

Shortstop	PCT	G	PO	A	E	DP
Cordero	.960	105	124	280	17	47
Grudzielanek	.987	34	50	104	2	17

Shortstop	PCT	G	PO	A	E	DP
Lansing	1.000	2	0	1	0	0
Silvestri	1.000	9	8	20	0	1

Outfield	PCT	G	PO	A	E	DP
Alou	.981	92	147	5	3	2
Benitez	.950	14	18	1	1	0
Cordero	.900	26	44	1	5	0
Floyd	.750	4	3	0	1	0
Frazier	.973	25	36	0	1	0
Kelly	1.000	24	42	1	0	0
Pride	.920	24	23	0	2	0
Rodriguez	.857	8	6	0	1	0
Santangelo	.979	25	46	0	1	0
Segui	.000	2	0	0	0	0
Silvestri	.000	3	0	0	0	0
Tarasco	.979	117	230	7	5	3
White	.986	119	270	5	4	2

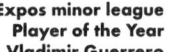

Rondell White led Montreal with 87 runs while hitting .295

BILL SETLIFF

MORRIS FOSTOFF

Expos minor league Player of the Year Vladimir Guerrero

EXPOS

FARM SYSTEM

Director of Player Development: Bill Geivett.

Class	Farm Team	League	W	L	Pct.	Finish*	Manager	First Yr
AAA	Ottawa (Ont.) Lynx	International	72	70	.507	5th+ (10)	Pete Mackanin	1993
AA	Harrisburg (Pa.) Senators	Eastern	61	80	.433	10th (10)	Pat Kelly	1991
#A	West Palm Beach (Fla.) Expos	Florida State	54	81	.400	12th (14)	Gomer Hodge	1969
A	Albany (Ga.) Polecats	South Atlantic	62	78	.443	11th (14)	Doug Sisson	1995
A	Vermont Expos	New York-Penn	49	27	.645	1st (14)	Jim Gabella	1994
R	West Palm Beach (Fla.) Expos	Gulf Coast	21	35	.375	12th (16)	Luis Dorante	1986

*Finish in overall standings (No. of teams in league)   #Advanced level   +Won league championship

ORGANIZATION LEADERS

MAJOR LEAGUERS

BATTING
*AVG	Sean Berry	.318
R	Rondell White	87
H	Wil Cordero	147
TB	Rondell White	220
2B	Wil Cordero	35
3B	Three tied at	4
HR	Three tied at	14
RBI	Mike Lansing	62
BB	Tony Tarasco	51
SO	Wil Cordero	88
SB	Mike Lansing	27

PITCHING
W	Pedro Martinez	14
L	Jeff Fassero	14
#ERA	Butch Henry	2.84
G	Tim Scott	62
CG	Two tied at	2
SV	Mel Rojas	30
IP	Pedro Martinez	195
BB	Jeff Fassero	74
SO	Pedro Martinez	174

MORRIS FOSTOFF

Pedro Martinez. 14 wins

MINOR LEAGUERS

BATTING
*AVG	Vladimir Guerrero, Albany	.333
R	Mike Berry, Visalia/West Palm	85
H	Brad Fullmer, Albany	151
TB	Vladimir Guerrero, Albany	229
2B	Brad Fullmer, Albany	38
3B	Two tied at	10
HR	Julian Yan, Ottawa	22
RBI	Julian Yan, Ottawa	78
BB	Bob Henley, Albany	83
SO	Chris Schwab, Albany	173
SB	Hiram Bocachica, Albany	47

PITCHING
W	Chris Weidert, Vermont/Albany	12
L	Three tied at	12
#ERA	Chris Weidert, Vermont/Albany	2.38
G	Kirk Bullinger, Harrisburg	56
CG	Steve Falteisek, Harrisburg/Ottawa	6
SV	Jake Benz, West Palm Beach	22
IP	Steve Falteisek, Harrisburg/Ottawa	191
BB	Neil Weber, Harrisburg	90
SO	Everett Stull, Harrisburg	132

*Minimum 250 At-Bats   #Minimum 75 Innings

TOP 10 PROSPECTS

How the Expos Top 10 prospects, as judged by Baseball America prior to the 1995 season, fared in 1995:

Ugueth Urbina

Player, Pos.	Club (Class—League)	AVG	AB	R	H	2B	3B	HR	RBI	SB
3. Hiram Bocachica, ss	Albany (A—South Atlantic)	.284	380	65	108	20	10	2	30	47
4. Vladimir Guerrero, of	Albany (A—South Atlantic)	.333	421	77	140	21	10	16	63	12
5. Brad Fullmer, 3b	Albany (A—South Atlantic)	.323	468	69	151	38	4	8	67	10
6. Shane Andrews, 3b	Montreal	.214	220	27	47	10	1	8	31	1
9. Mark Grudzielanek, ss	Ottawa (AAA—International)	.298	181	26	54	9	1	1	22	12
	Montreal	.245	269	27	66	12	2	1	20	8

Player, Pos.	Club (Class—League)	W	L	ERA	G	SV	IP	H	BB	SO
1. Ugueth Urbina, rhp	West Palm Beach (A—Florida State)	1	0	0.00	2	0	9	4	1	11
	Ottawa (AAA—International)	6	2	3.04	13	0	68	46	26	55
	Montreal	2	2	6.17	7	0	23	26	14	15
2. Everett Stull, rhp	Harrisburg (AA—Eastern)	3	12	5.54	24	0	127	114	79	132
7. Rod Henderson, rhp	Harrisburg (AA—Eastern)	3	6	4.31	12	0	56	51	18	53
8. Carlos Perez, lhp	Montreal	10	8	3.69	28	0	141	142	28	106
10. Scott Gentile, rhp	Harrisburg (AA—Eastern)	2	2	3.44	37	11	50	36	15	48

INTERNATIONAL LEAGUE

BATTING	AVG	G	AB	R	H	2B	3B	HR	RBI	BB	SO	SB	CS	B	T	HT	WT	DOB	1st Yr	Resides
Alvarez, Clemente	.231	50	143	15	33	7	0	4	20	10	34	0	0	R	R	5-11	180	5-18-68	1987	Anzoategui, Venezuela
Barron, Tony	.245	50	147	20	36	10	0	10	22	14	22	0	2	R	R	6-0	185	8-17-66	1987	Tacoma, Wash.
Benitez, Yamil	.259	127	474	66	123	24	6	18	69	44	128	14	6	R	R	6-2	180	10-5-72	1990	San Juan, P.R.
Bournigal, Rafael	.204	19	54	2	11	4	0	0	6	2	4	0	0	R	R	5-11	165	5-12-66	1987	Santo Domingo, D.R.
Buccheri, Jim	.268	133	470	64	126	16	4	0	30	49	58	44	11	R	R	6-1	165	11-12-68	1988	Fountain Valley, Calif.
Cairo, Sergio	.333	2	6	1	2	1	0	0	0	0	1	0	0	R	R	6-1	165	10-22-70	1988	San Pedro de Macoris, D.R.
Castleberry, Kevin	.294	118	428	65	126	18	4	7	56	52	59	9	7	L	R	5-10	170	4-22-68	1989	Midwest City, Okla.
Delima, Rafael	.259	10	27	4	7	0	0	0	3	5	3	2	0	L	L	5-11	175	12-21-67	1986	Valencia, Venez.
Felix, Junior	.225	51	160	22	36	7	3	3	24	15	48	1	2	S	R	5-11	165	10-3-67	1986	Surfside Beach, S.C.
Foley, Tom	.306	23	62	13	19	5	0	0	7	8	7	1	0	L	R	6-1	175	9-9-59	1977	Miami, Fla.
Frazier, Lou	.218	31	110	11	24	3	0	1	10	13	20	10	1	S	R	6-2	175	1-26-65	1986	St. Louis, Mo.
Grudzielanek, Mark	.298	49	181	26	54	9	1	1	22	10	17	12	1	R	R	6-1	170	6-30-70	1991	El Paso, Texas
Heffernan, Ray	.216	36	102	13	22	5	0	1	12	7	13	1	0	L	R	5-10	185	3-3-65	1988	Stony Brook, N.Y.
Jacobs, Frank	.250	11	32	9	8	2	2	0	4	11	3	0	1	L	L	6-4	250	5-22-68	1991	Highland Heights, Ky.
2-team (8 Norfolk)	.246	19	57	11	14	3	2	1	10	11	7	0	1							
Martin, Chris	.257	126	412	55	106	19	1	3	40	46	59	30	5	R	R	6-1	170	1-25-68	1990	Los Angeles, Calif.
Martinez, Ray	.250	39	108	17	27	6	0	0	9	6	17	3	0	R	R	6-0	165	10-1-68	1987	Highland Park, Calif.
Pride, Curtis	.279	42	154	25	43	8	3	4	24	12	35	8	4	L	R	5-11	195	12-17-68	1986	Silver Spring, Md.
Rodriguez, Henry	.200	4	15	0	3	1	0	0	2	1	4	0	0	L	L	6-1	210	11-8-67	1986	New York, N.Y.
Rundels, Matt	.250	14	36	7	9	1	1	0	4	7	8	1	1	R	R	5-11	180	4-26-70	1992	Pataskala, Ohio
Santangelo, F.P.	.255	95	267	37	68	15	3	2	25	32	22	7	4	S	R	5-10	165	10-24-67	1989	El Dorado Hills, Calif.
Siddall, Joe	.214	83	248	26	53	14	2	1	23	23	42	3	3	L	R	6-1	197	10-25-67	1988	Windsor, Ontario
Tovar, Raul	.304	20	56	8	17	2	0	0	7	8	5	0	0	R	R	6-1	183	11-14-58	1977	Caracas, Venez.
Velasquez, Guillermo	.250	45	112	11	28	5	0	1	9	8	14	1	2	L	R	6-0	170	4-23-68	1986	Calexico, Mexico
Wilstead, Randy	.292	9	24	6	7	2	1	0	3	6	3	0	0	L	L	6-4	200	4-5-68	1990	Provo, Utah
Wood, Ted	.267	98	326	35	87	16	1	8	49	37	63	9	2	L	L	6-2	187	1-4-67	1989	New Orleans, La.
Yan, Julian	.280	114	372	49	104	22	3	22	79	15	90	5	1	R	R	6-3	190	7-24-65	1985	El Seibo, D.R.

PITCHING	W	L	ERA	G	GS	CG	SV	IP	H	R	ER	BB	SO	B	T	HT	WT	DOB	1st Yr	Resides
Alvarez, Tavo	2	1	2.49	3	3	0	0	22	17	6	6	5	11	R	R	6-3	183	11-25-71	1990	Tucson, Ariz.
Baxter, Bob	5	5	3.92	39	13	0	0	101	125	51	44	25	39	L	L	6-1	180	2-17-69	1990	Norwood, Mass.
Boucher, Denis	5	5	5.69	14	11	0	0	55	65	39	35	31	22	R	L	6-1	195	3-7-68	1988	Lachine, Quebec
Cornelius, Reid	1	1	6.75	4	3	0	0	11	16	12	8	5	7	R	R	6-0	190	6-2-70	1989	Thomasville, Ala.
Diaz, Rafael	0	3	6.56	32	2	0	0	48	51	38	35	25	31	R	R	6-1	175	12-12-69	1988	Maywood, Calif.
Eischen, Joey	2	1	1.72	11	0	0	0	16	9	4	3	8	13	L	L	6-1	190	5-25-70	1989	West Covina, Calif.
Eversgerd, Bryan	6	2	2.38	38	0	0	2	53	49	21	14	26	45	R	L	6-1	185	2-11-69	1989	Centralia, Ill.
Fajardo, Hector	0	0	4.11	11	0	0	0	15	18	7	7	6	9	R	R	6-4	200	11-6-70	1989	Michoacan, Mexico
Falteisek, Steve	2	0	1.17	3	3	1	0	23	17	4	3	5	18	R	R	6-2	200	1-28-72	1992	Floral Park, N.Y.
Fraser, Willie	7	6	3.19	19	19	1	0	107	94	44	38	18	84	R	R	6-1	206	5-26-64	1985	Newburgh, N.Y.
Garcia, Miguel	0	0	1.35	5	0	0	0	7	6	1	1	3	4	L	L	6-1	170	4-19-66	1988	Caracas, Venez.
Harris, Greg	3	0	1.06	11	0	0	1	17	7	3	2	3	17	S	R	6-0	175	11-2-55	1977	Orleans, Mass.
Kerley, Collin	2	0	2.16	5	0	0	0	8	11	3	2	3	3	R	R	6-3	200	3-26-70	1992	Houston, Texas
Layana, Tim	1	1	8.50	26	0	0	4	36	56	35	34	20	27	R	R	6-2	190	3-2-64	1986	Florence, Ky.
Leiper, Dave	0	0	0.00	2	0	0	0	3	1	0	0	1	2	L	L	6-1	160	6-18-62	1982	Plano, Texas
Magrane, Joe	3	6	4.84	12	12	0	0	67	69	43	36	31	37	R	L	6-6	230	7-2-64	1985	Chesterfield, Mo.
Manuel, Barry	5	12	4.59	35	22	1	1	127	125	71	65	50	85	R	R	5-11	185	8-12-65	1987	Mamou, La.
Mitchell, John	0	1	4.32	6	0	0	0	8	8	4	4	3	5	R	R	6-2	165	8-11-65	1983	Nashville, Tenn.
Pacheco, Alex	1	0	6.23	4	0	0	0	9	8	6	6	5	4	R	R	6-3	170	7-19-73	1990	Caracas, Venez.
Pena, Jim	0	0	3.68	7	0	0	0	7	4	3	3	8	7	L	L	6-1	185	9-17-64	1986	Phoenix, Ariz.
Rueter, Kirk	9	7	3.06	20	20	3	0	121	120	50	41	25	67	L	L	6-3	190	12-1-70	1991	Hoyleton, Ill.
Schmidt, Curt	5	0	2.22	43	0	0	15	53	40	14	13	18	38	R	R	6-6	223	3-16-70	1992	Miles City, Mon.
Thobe, J.J.	5	8	3.27	55	0	0	5	88	79	37	32	16	36	R	R	6-6	200	11-19-70	1992	Huntington Beach, Calif.
Torres, Ricky	3	8	5.01	32	11	1	0	92	90	58	51	26	58	R	R	6-2	210	12-31-63	1984	Rio Piedras, P.R.
Urbina, Ugueth	6	2	3.04	13	11	2	0	68	46	26	23	26	55	R	R	6-2	170	2-15-74	1991	Caracas, Venez.
White, Gabe	2	3	3.90	12	12	0	0	62	58	31	27	17	37	L	L	6-2	200	11-20-71	1990	Sebring, Fla.

FIELDING

Catcher	PCT	G	PO	A	E	DP	PB
Alvarez	.988	48	292	26	4	3	3
Heffernan	.987	28	140	15	2	3	3
Santangelo	1.000	1	5	0	0	0	0
Siddall	.990	78	346	56	4	6	8

First Base	PCT	G	PO	A	E	DP
Jacobs	1.000	1	9	0	0	2
Velasquez	.996	29	216	16	1	14
Wilstead	1.000	3	35	2	0	3
Wood	.986	33	260	20	4	21
Yan	.997	105	876	57	3	88

Second Base	PCT	G	PO	A	E	DP
Bournigal	1.000	1	0	2	0	0
Buccheri	.973	12	14	22	1	7
Castleberry	.977	96	205	257	11	58
Foley	.984	10	27	34	1	11
Martin	1.000	7	19	18	0	4

	PCT	G	PO	A	E	DP
Rundels	.967	10	13	45	2	5
Santangelo	1.000	20	32	54	0	9

Third Base	PCT	G	PO	A	E	DP
Castleberry	.873	23	16	46	9	5
Foley	1.000	5	5	9	0	0
Martin	.921	46	36	115	13	12
Martinez	.944	31	16	68	5	3
Rundels	1.000	2	2	4	0	0
Santangelo	.946	53	27	113	8	4
Siddall	.750	1	2	1	1	0

Shortstop	PCT	G	PO	A	E	DP
Bournigal	.984	15	15	48	1	10
Foley	1.000	6	13	19	0	4
Grudzielanek	.939	49	58	156	14	29
Martin	.952	70	101	195	15	45
Martinez	.875	5	2	5	1	1

	PCT	G	PO	A	E	DP
Santangelo	.958	5	7	16	1	5

Outfield	PCT	G	PO	A	E	DP
Barron	1.000	31	59	2	0	0
Benitez	.964	116	177	10	7	2
Buccheri	.984	116	235	7	4	0
Cairo	1.000	2	3	0	0	0
Delima	1.000	8	6	2	0	0
Felix	1.000	33	60	0	0	0
Frazier	.974	30	73	3	2	0
Heffernan	.800	1	4	0	1	0
Pride	.974	37	69	5	2	1
Rundels	1.000	1	1	0	0	0
Santangelo	.952	12	18	2	1	1
Tovar	.963	14	26	0	1	0
Wood	.987	50	73	4	1	0
Yan	.600	3	3	0	2	0

EASTERN LEAGUE

BATTING	AVG	G	AB	R	H	2B	3B	HR	RBI	BB	SO	SB	CS	B	T	HT	WT	DOB	1st Yr	Resides
Alcantara, Israel	.211	71	237	25	50	12	2	10	29	21	81	1	1	R	R	6-2	165	5-6-73	1991	Santo Domingo, D.R.
Allen, Matt	.143	5	14	2	2	0	0	0	1	2	2	0	0	R	R	6-2	190	12-25-69	1991	Tampa, Fla.
Barron, Tony	.291	29	103	20	30	5	0	10	23	10	21	0	0	R	R	6-0	185	8-17-66	1987	Tacoma, Wash.
Bournigal, Rafael	.221	29	95	12	21	3	1	0	7	11	8	1	0	R	R	5-11	165	5-12-66	1987	Santo Domingo, D.R.

BATTING

BATTING	AVG	G	AB	R	H	2B	3B	HR	RBI	BB	SO	SB	CS	B	T	HT	WT	DOB	1st Yr	Resides
Buckley, Troy	.291	48	158	16	46	10	0	2	15	9	19	0	1	R	R	6-4	215	3-3-68	1990	Campbell, Calif.
Cabrera, Jolbert	.286	9	35	4	10	2	0	0	1	1	3	3	1	R	R	6-0	177	12-8-72	1991	Cartagena, Colombia
Cairo, Sergio	.000	4	13	0	0	0	0	0	0	1	2	0	0	R	R	6-1	165	10-22-70	1988	San Pedro de Macoris, D.R.
Charbonnet, Mark	.251	120	407	34	102	14	4	8	57	19	104	3	6	L	L	6-1	185	4-5-71	1989	Norwalk, Calif.
Chick, Bruce	.268	12	41	4	11	2	1	0	6	0	9	0	0	R	R	6-4	210	3-7-69	1990	St. Petersburg, Fla.
Dauphin, Phil	.244	111	398	53	97	20	2	5	38	43	61	17	7	L	L	6-1	180	5-11-69	1990	Worthington, Ohio
Everson, Darin	.214	5	14	0	3	1	0	0	1	0	2	0	0	L	R	6-3	224	4-22-71	1994	Ada, Minn.
Fitzpatrick, Rob	.167	15	42	3	7	1	0	1	3	6	11	0	0	R	R	6-0	190	9-14-68	1990	Midland Park, N.J.
Grissom, Antonio	.257	82	237	32	61	10	0	4	23	33	48	13	8	R	R	6-1	195	1-11-70	1990	Red Oak, Ga.
Hinton, Steve	.222	10	18	4	4	0	0	0	0	7	5	0	0	L	L	6-2	200	9-5-69	1991	Elgin, Ill.
Horne, Tyrone	.296	87	294	59	87	17	4	14	47	58	65	14	8	L	R	5-10	185	11-2-70	1989	Troy, N.C.
Hymel, Gary	.189	95	302	35	57	10	2	11	36	22	97	3	2	R	R	6-2	195	5-21-68	1991	Cypress, Texas
Jacobs, Frank	.316	78	269	44	85	19	0	9	51	48	41	1	3	L	L	6-4	250	5-22-68	1991	Highland Heights, Ky.
2-team (23 Bing.)	.312	101	337	56	105	22	0	13	60	58	56	1	3							
Kounas, Tony	.235	66	196	15	46	5	0	1	22	19	27	1	1	R	R	6-2	180	12-5-69	1992	Laguna Beach, Calif.
Lane, Dan	.123	39	81	5	10	1	0	0	1	3	21	0	1	R	R	6-2	180	4-25-73	1989	Montreal, Quebec
Marabella, Tony	.225	30	89	10	20	1	0	1	11	7	11	0	1	L	R	5-11	179	4-25-73	1989	Montreal, Quebec
Martinez, Ray	.237	48	152	18	36	6	0	1	13	20	24	3	2	R	R	6-0	165	10-1-68	1987	Highland Park, Calif.
Northrup, Kevin	.309	40	152	23	47	14	0	1	27	10	16	0	1	R	R	6-1	190	1-27-70	1992	Sanford, N.C.
Rundels, Matt	.247	120	462	72	114	30	4	11	55	47	112	19	11	R	R	5-11	180	4-26-70	1992	Pataskala, Ohio
Saffer, Jon	.237	20	76	9	18	4	0	0	4	6	14	2	1	L	R	6-2	200	7-6-73	1992	Tucson, Ariz.
Tovar, Edgar	.202	81	247	28	50	7	2	3	21	16	24	1	3	R	R	6-1	170	11-28-73	1992	Turmero, Venez.
Ventress, Leroy	.220	11	41	4	9	0	0	0	0	5	19	3	0	S	R	6-0	173	8-14-68	1986	Maringouin, La.
Vidro, Jose	.260	64	246	33	64	16	2	4	38	20	37	3	7	S	R	5-11	175	8-27-74	1992	Sabana Grande, P.R.
Virgilio, George	.143	27	56	9	8	0	0	1	5	20	11	1	1	S	R	5-9	170	2-15-71	1989	Elizabeth, N.J.

PITCHING

PITCHING	W	L	ERA	G	GS	CG	SV	IP	H	R	ER	BB	SO	B	T	HT	WT	DOB	1st Yr	Resides
Alvarez, Tavo	2	1	2.25	3	3	0	0	16	17	8	4	5	14	R	R	6-3	183	11-25-71	1990	Tucson, Ariz.
Aucoin, Derek	2	4	4.96	29	0	0	1	53	52	34	29	28	48	R	R	6-7	226	3-27-70	1989	Montreal, Quebec
Botkin, Alan	0	0	8.31	3	0	0	1	4	5	4	4	2	4	L	L	6-3	204	10-6-67	1989	West Palm Beach, Fla.
Bullinger, Kirk	5	3	2.42	56	0	0	7	67	61	22	18	25	42	R	R	6-2	170	10-28-69	1992	Hammond, La.
DeHart, Rick	6	7	4.84	35	12	0	0	93	94	62	50	39	64	L	L	6-1	180	3-21-70	1992	Topeka, Kan.
Diaz, Rafael	2	2	5.59	11	1	0	0	19	17	13	12	9	16	R	R	6-1	175	12-12-69	1988	Maywood, Calif.
Falteisek, Steve	9	6	2.95	25	25	5	0	168	152	74	55	64	112	R	R	6-2	200	1-28-72	1992	Floral Park, N.Y.
Gentile, Scott	2	2	3.44	37	0	0	11	50	36	19	19	15	48	R	R	5-11	210	12-21-70	1992	Berlin, Conn.
Henderson, Rod	3	6	4.31	12	12	0	0	56	51	28	27	18	53	R	R	6-4	195	3-11-71	1992	Glasgow, Ky.
Kendrena, Ken	3	2	2.51	30	0	0	1	65	58	27	18	25	46	R	R	5-11	170	10-29-70	1992	Rancho Cucamonga, Calif.
Kerley, Collin	0	0	0.00	2	0	0	0	7	5	0	0	1	3	R	R	6-3	200	3-26-70	1992	Houston, Texas
Mikkelsen, Linc	1	2	5.37	21	5	0	0	54	57	33	32	24	39	R	R	6-0	186	7-27-67	1990	Montague, Mich.
Pacheco, Alex	9	7	4.27	45	0	0	4	86	76	45	41	31	88	R	R	6-3	170	7-19-73	1990	Caracas, Venez.
Paniagua, Jose	7	12	5.34	25	25	2	0	126	140	84	75	62	89	R	R	6-1	160	8-20-73	1991	Santo Domingo, D.R.
Paxton, Darrin	0	1	1.29	7	0	0	0	7	5	2	1	3	7	L	L	6-4	220	4-17-70	1991	Wichita, Kan.
Pollard, Damon	0	0	8.64	6	0	0	0	8	11	11	8	4	10	S	R	5-8	165	9-29-67	1990	Hattiesburg, Miss.
Pote, Lou	0	1	5.40	9	4	0	0	28	32	17	17	7	24	R	R	6-3	195	8-27-71	1991	Chicago, Ill.
Puig, Benny	0	0	0.00	1	0	0	0	2	3	2	0	1	0	L	L	5-10	183	10-16-65	1985	Arecibo, P.R.
Shaw, Cedric	0	1	4.66	5	2	0	0	19	25	10	10	6	13	L	L	5-11	175	5-28-67	1988	Brusly, La.
Stull, Everett	3	12	5.54	24	24	0	0	127	114	88	78	99	132	R	R	6-3	195	8-24-71	1992	Stone Mountain, Ga.
Tirado, Aris	1	0	0.77	8	0	0	1	12	8	1	1	5	10	R	R	5-8	160	3-31-63	1985	Vega Baja, P.R.
Weber, Neil	6	11	5.01	28	28	0	0	153	157	98	85	90	119	L	L	6-5	205	12-6-72	1993	Irvine, Calif.

FIELDING

Catcher	PCT	G	PO	A	E	DP	PB
Allen	.943	5	31	2	2	0	0
Buckley	.997	43	313	36	1	6	5
Everson	1.000	2	12	1	0	0	0
Fitzpatrick	.991	14	98	9	1	3	3
Hymel	.986	49	324	30	5	0	16
Kounas	.975	38	234	34	7	4	4

First Base	PCT	G	PO	A	E	DP
Charbonnet	.983	6	50	8	1	5
Everson	1.000	3	19	0	0	1
Hinton	.978	8	45	0	1	1
Hymel	.985	25	186	17	3	19
Jacobs	.978	74	601	57	15	53
Kounas	.977	18	121	7	3	7
Lane	1.000	1	2	0	0	0
Marabella	1.000	7	42	4	0	5
Martinez	.986	8	58	10	1	5
Virgilio	1.000	2	11	0	0	2

Second Base	PCT	G	PO	A	E	DP
Lane	1.000	10	21	16	0	1
Marabella	1.000	1	0	1	0	0
Martinez	1.000	17	29	39	0	7
Rundels	.954	93	196	241	21	64
Vidro	.964	27	61	73	5	12

Third Base	PCT	G	PO	A	E	DP
Alcantara	.892	68	48	118	20	9
Lane	1.000	2	0	1	0	0
Marabella	.904	17	16	31	5	1
Martinez	.932	16	10	31	3	8
Rundels	.750	1	1	2	1	0
Tovar	.958	12	6	17	1	2
Vidro	.963	19	8	44	2	4
Virgilio	.921	16	9	26	3	2

Shortstop	PCT	G	PO	A	E	DP
Bournigal	.968	29	27	64	3	14
Cabrera	.935	9	11	18	2	5
Lane	.935	20	11	32	3	4
Martinez	1.000	3	3	11	0	1
Rundels	.875	9	11	24	5	4
Tovar	.949	63	92	171	14	35
Vidro	.973	20	28	45	2	9
Virgilio	.750	3	2	7	3	1

Outfield	PCT	G	PO	A	E	DP
Barron	.975	22	37	2	1	0
Cairo	1.000	3	4	0	0	0
Charbonnet	.995	91	182	3	1	1
Chick	.875	10	13	1	2	0
Dauphin	.977	104	207	4	5	0
Grissom	.956	59	106	3	5	0
Horne	.971	70	130	5	4	0
Marabella	1.000	1	2	0	0	0
Northrup	.959	32	46	1	2	0
Rundels	.978	20	44	1	1	0
Saffer	.972	17	35	0	1	0
Tovar	1.000	1	1	0	0	0
Ventress	1.000	9	18	2	0	2
Virgilio	.000	1	0	0	0	0

WEST PALM BEACH

FLORIDA STATE LEAGUE

BATTING	AVG	G	AB	R	H	2B	3B	HR	RBI	BB	SO	SB	CS	B	T	HT	WT	DOB	1st Yr	Resides
Adolfo, Carlos	.185	28	81	6	15	1	0	1	7	5	22	1	0	R	R	5-11	160	4-20-76	1994	Santo Domingo, D.R.
Alcantara, Israel	.276	39	134	16	37	7	2	3	22	9	35	3	0	R	R	6-2	165	5-6-73	1991	Santo Domingo, D.R.
Alvarado, Basilio	.222	6	18	0	4	0	0	0	0	1	5	0	0	R	R	5-11	199	7-20-74	1992	Santo Domingo, D.R.
Berry, Michael	.165	24	79	16	13	3	1	1	2	13	16	0	1	R	R	5-10	185	8-12-70	1993	Rolling Hills, Calif.
Blum, Geoff	.263	125	457	54	120	20	2	1	62	34	61	6	5	S	R	6-3	193	4-26-73	1994	Chino, Calif.
Cabrera, Jolbert	.286	103	357	62	102	23	2	1	25	38	61	19	12	R	R	6-0	177	12-8-72	1991	Cartagena, Colombia
Cabrera, Orlando	.200	3	5	0	1	0	0	0	0	0	1	0	0	R	R	5-11	165	3-2-74	1994	Cartagena, Colombia
Campos, Jesus	.221	107	326	32	72	6	2	0	21	25	40	18	7	R	R	5-9	145	10-12-73	1991	San Pedro de Macoris, D.R.

BATTING

BATTING	AVG	G	AB	R	H	2B	3B	HR	RBI	BB	SO	SB	CS	B	T	HT	WT	DOB	1st Yr	Resides
Chick, Bruce	.100	3	10	0	1	0	0	0	1	1	3	0	0	R	R	6-4	210	3-7-69	1990	St. Petersburg, Fla.
Everson, Darin	.219	38	105	7	23	2	0	1	13	12	22	0	0	L	R	6-3	224	4-22-71	1994	Ada, Minn.
Fitzpatrick, Rob	.209	17	43	3	9	1	0	1	5	9	12	3	3	R	R	6-0	190	9-14-68	1990	Midland Park, N.J.
Foster, Jeff	.207	65	179	22	37	7	3	4	26	10	42	10	3	L	R	6-2	175	2-25-72	1993	Knoxville, Tenn.
Grissom, Antonio	.200	8	20	3	4	1	0	0	1	4	6	2	1	R	R	6-1	195	1-11-70	1990	Red Oak, Ga.
Koeyers, Ramsey	.189	77	244	19	46	6	1	0	18	9	64	2	1	R	R	6-1	187	8-7-74	1991	Brievengst, Curacao
Marabella, Tony	.259	60	201	22	52	6	1	0	21	13	23	1	1	L	R	5-11	179	4-25-73	1989	Montreal, Quebec
Niethammer, Marc	.187	96	315	34	59	11	3	10	31	31	105	4	6	L	R	6-5	230	9-28-73	1992	Lake Wales, Fla.
Ottaviano, Paul	.235	112	395	35	93	20	2	1	37	34	44	13	6	L	L	6-1	190	4-22-73	1994	Flanders, N.J.
Pachot, John	.251	67	227	17	57	10	0	0	23	12	38	1	2	R	R	6-2	168	11-11-74	1993	Ponce, P.R.
Raleigh, Matt	.207	66	179	29	37	11	0	2	18	54	64	4	2	R	R	5-11	205	7-18-70	1992	Swanton, Vt.
Saffer, Jon	.318	92	324	60	103	10	6	4	35	53	49	18	5	L	R	6-2	200	7-6-73	1992	Tucson, Ariz.
Stovall, Darond	.232	121	461	52	107	22	2	4	51	44	117	18	12	S	L	6-1	185	1-3-73	1993	East St. Louis, Ill.
Vidro, Jose	.325	44	163	20	53	15	2	3	24	8	21	0	1	S	R	5-11	175	8-27-74	1992	Sabana Grande, P.R.

GAMES BY POSITION: C—Alvarado 6, Everson 5, Fitzpatrick 63, Koeyers 65, Pachot 60, Raleigh 1. **1B**—Everson 21, Koeyers 1, Marabella 19, Niethammer 73, Ottaviano 11, Raleigh 20. **2B**—Berry 10, Blum 60, J. Cabrera 14, Foster 19, Marabella 2, Raleigh 3, Vidro 35. **3B**—Alcantara 29, Berry 11, Blum 13, J. Cabrera 10, Foster 15, Marabella 31, Raleigh 29, Vidro 3. **SS**—Berry 1, Blum 38, J. Cabrera 80, O. Cabrera 2, Foster 19, Raleigh 1, Vidro 6. **OF**—Adolfo 22, Alcantara 3, Berry 1, Campos 9, Grissom 4, Ottaviano 100, Saffer 77, Stovall 114.

PITCHING

PITCHING	W	L	ERA	G	GS	CG	SV	IP	H	R	ER	BB	SO	B	T	HT	WT	DOB	1st Yr	Resides
Benz, Jake	0	2	1.17	44	0	0	22	54	44	13	7	18	48	L	L	5-9	162	2-27-72	1994	Pleasant Hill, Calif.
Clelland, Rick	2	4	2.69	35	5	0	0	70	59	30	21	46	66	R	R	6-4	205	10-1-71	1990	Brilliant, Ohio
DaSilva, Fernando	7	10	3.70	27	20	2	0	124	136	61	51	31	54	R	R	6-2	194	9-6-71	1991	Brossard, Quebec
Forster, Scott	6	11	4.05	26	26	1	0	147	129	78	66	80	92	R	L	6-1	194	10-27-71	1991	Flourtown, Pa.
Hmielewski, Chris	1	3	3.59	36	2	0	0	58	57	31	23	28	41	L	L	6-4	210	7-18-70	1991	Franklin Park, Ill.
Kendrena, Ken	3	3	3.04	16	0	0	2	24	23	9	8	11	19	R	R	6-1	170	10-29-70	1992	Rancho Cucamonga, Calif.
Kerley, Collin	1	3	3.95	19	0	0	0	27	28	16	12	11	17	R	R	6-3	200	3-26-70	1992	Houston, Texas
Knieper, Aaron	2	4	3.95	32	6	0	0	71	67	38	31	46	48	R	R	6-5	205	6-15-72	1993	Saginaw, Mich.
Markham, Andy	7	11	3.94	24	23	1	0	121	129	62	53	44	58	R	R	6-3	200	11-12-72	1993	Phoenix, Ariz.
McCommon, Jason	7	11	3.75	26	26	3	0	156	153	75	65	38	94	R	R	6-0	190	8-9-71	1994	Memphis, Tenn.
Moraga, David	1	1	3.94	3	3	0	0	16	20	7	7	10	10	L	L	6-0	184	7-8-75	1994	Suisun, Calif.
Phelps, Tommy	0	2	16.20	2	2	0	0	5	10	10	9	11	5	L	L	6-3	192	3-4-74	1993	Tampa, Fla.
Pisciotta, Scott	5	4	2.52	53	0	0	2	61	55	26	17	36	38	R	R	6-7	225	6-8-73	1991	Marietta, Ga.
Pollard, Damon	4	3	3.35	28	0	0	1	51	38	21	19	26	43	S	R	5-8	165	9-29-67	1990	Hattiesburg, Miss.
Rushworth, Jim	1	0	3.65	10	0	0	1	12	11	5	5	6	9	R	R	6-0	180	7-3-71	1992	West Monroe, La.
Schneider, Tom	0	1	10.80	4	0	0	0	3	8	5	4	2	3	R	L	6-4	205	9-27-72	1993	Shreveport, La.
Urbina, Ugueth	1	0	0.00	2	2	0	0	9	4	0	0	1	11	R	R	6-2	170	2-15-74	1991	Caracas, Venez.
Yan, Esteban	6	8	3.07	24	21	1	1	138	139	63	47	33	89	R	R	6-4	180	6-22-74	1991	La Higuera, D.R.

ALBANY   A

SOUTH ATLANTIC LEAGUE

BATTING	AVG	G	AB	R	H	2B	3B	HR	RBI	BB	SO	SB	CS	B	T	HT	WT	DOB	1st Yr	Resides
Acosta, Ed	.152	51	105	9	16	1	0	0	9	8	30	1	3	R	R	6-1	160	12-5-71	1993	Rock Falls, Ill.
Adolfo, Carlos	.243	57	214	31	52	13	5	4	33	17	65	5	6	R	R	5-11	160	4-20-76	1994	Santo Domingo, D.R.
Alderman, Kurt	.248	55	161	21	40	8	1	2	17	11	40	2	1	L	R	6-3	200	3-11-71	1994	Davis, Calif.
Bocachica, Hiram	.284	96	380	65	108	20	10	2	30	52	78	47	17	R	R	5-11	165	3-4-76	1994	Bayamon, P.R.
Brinkley, Josh	.174	22	69	8	12	3	0	1	5	3	11	2	2	R	R	5-10	175	8-5-73	1993	Raleigh, N.C.
Brown, Nate	.254	117	397	34	101	23	3	4	49	32	112	4	8	L	L	6-5	225	2-3-71	1993	Berkeley, Calif.
Camilli, Jason	.188	53	181	28	34	5	0	3	16	38	50	13	10	R	R	6-0	178	10-18-75	1994	Phoenix, Ariz.
Coquillette, Trace	.269	128	458	67	123	27	4	3	57	64	91	17	16	R	R	5-11	165	6-4-74	1993	Orangevale, Calif.
Estrada, Josue	.213	70	235	27	50	11	1	2	17	24	70	2	3	R	R	6-0	185	1-21-75	1993	Rio Piedras, P.R.
Fullmer, Brad	.323	123	468	69	151	38	4	8	67	36	33	10	10	L	R	6-1	185	1-17-75	1994	Chatsworth, Calif.
Guerrero, Vladimir	.333	110	421	77	140	21	10	16	63	30	45	12	7	R	R	6-2	158	2-9-76	1993	Bani, D.R.
Haas, Matt	.235	52	166	18	39	7	0	0	15	18	30	1	5	L	R	6-1	175	2-1-72	1994	Paducah, Ky.
Henley, Bob	.281	102	335	45	94	20	1	3	46	83	57	1	2	R	R	6-2	190	1-30-73	1993	Grand Bay, Ala.
Pond, Simon	.213	23	80	4	17	5	0	0	7	4	25	1	0	L	R	6-1	175	10-27-76	1994	North Vancouver, B.C.
Rosado, Juan	.182	5	11	0	2	1	0	0	3	0	4	1	0	L	L	5-11	180	8-6-74	1994	Camuy, P.R.
Schwab, Chris	.227	122	484	60	110	22	3	5	43	48	173	4	6	R	L	6-3	215	7-25-74	1993	Eagan, Minn.
Seguignol, Fernando	.208	121	457	59	95	22	2	12	66	28	141	12	8	S	R	6-5	179	1-19-75	1993	Panama City, Panama
Van Oeveren, Ryan	.163	49	135	11	22	4	0	1	7	14	44	1	1	S	R	6-0	175	11-20-72	1995	Grandvile, Mich.

GAMES BY POSITION: C—Alderman 23, Haas 31, Henley 94. **1B**—Brown 102, Fullmer 32, Haas 12. **2B**—Acosta 13, Bocachica 2, Brinkley 1, Camilli 18, Coquillette 110, Van Oeveren 8. **3B**—Acosta 26, Adolfo 1, Brinkley 20, Coquillette 18, Fullmer 41, Haas 2, Pond 22, Van Oeveren 31. **SS**—Acosta 6, Bocachica 94, Brinkley 1, Camilli 37, Van Oeveren 12. **OF**—Acosta 7, Adolfo 50, Brown 11, Coquillette 5, Estrada 61, Guerrero 94, Haas 1, Rosado 5, Schwab 106, Seguignol 110.

PITCHING	W	L	ERA	G	GS	CG	SV	IP	H	R	ER	BB	SO	B	T	HT	WT	DOB	1st Yr	Resides
Bell, Mike	3	3	2.61	12	0	0	0	21	13	8	6	8	14	L	R	6-2	195	10-14-72	1995	Sarasota, Fla.
Civit, Xavier	3	7	7.62	12	1	0	0	26	34	30	22	18	29	R	R	6-2	175	5-17-73	1993	Barcelona, Spain
Cole, Jason	3	3	4.37	32	4	0	1	58	67	33	28	22	51	R	R	6-3	198	9-8-72	1994	Coventry, R.I.
Durocher, Jayson	3	7	3.91	24	22	1	0	122	105	67	53	56	88	R	R	6-3	195	8-18-74	1993	Scottsdale, Ariz.
Handy, Russell	2	7	4.27	30	5	0	2	72	78	50	34	37	57	R	R	6-4	200	8-4-74	1993	Bakersfield, Calif.
LaPoint, Jason	5	2	3.52	33	0	0	0	61	72	34	24	15	52	L	L	6-4	180	8-1-70	1993	La Porte, Texas
Mattes, Troy	0	2	5.03	4	4	0	0	20	21	12	11	12	15	R	R	6-7	185	8-26-75	1994	Sarasota, Fla.
Mikkelsen, Linc	0	1	1.93	12	0	0	5	23	24	14	5	8	17	S	R	6-0	186	7-27-67	1990	Montague, Mich.
Moraga, David	8	8	2.68	25	24	1	0	148	136	63	44	46	109	L	L	6-0	184	7-8-75	1994	Suisun, Calif.
Nygaard, Chris	6	4	2.86	41	0	0	1	57	60	25	18	8	43	R	R	6-4	230	4-29-72	1994	Coral Springs, Fla.
Phelps, Tommy	10	9	3.33	24	24	1	0	135	142	76	50	45	119	L	L	6-3	192	3-4-74	1993	Tampa, Fla.
Powell, Jeremy	1	0	1.59	1	1	0	0	6	4	1	1	1	6	R	R	6-5	230	6-18-76	1994	Sacramento, Calif.
Rhodriguez, Rory	3	4	3.50	37	0	2	0	90	84	44	35	34	83	R	R	5-10	175	2-26-71	1991	Carol City, Fla.
Rushworth, Jim	1	2	8.31	6	0	0	1	9	10	9	8	6	5	R	R	6-0	180	7-3-71	1992	West Monroe, La.
Stephens, Bill	1	3	5.75	13	1	0	0	20	25	16	13	9	16	S	R	6-5	215	10-31-72	1991	Ringgold, Ga.
Stubbs, Jerry	3	2	3.22	47	1	0	3	101	106	51	36	30	80	R	R	6-2	180	4-72	1993	Hutchinson, Pa.
Thurman, Mike	3	8	5.47	22	22	2	0	110	133	79	67	32	77	R	R	6-5	190	7-22-73	1994	Philomath, Ore.
Vazquez, Javier	6	6	5.08	21	21	1	0	103	109	67	58	47	87	R	R	6-2	175	6-25-76	1994	Ponce, P.R.
Weidert, Chris	1	2	7.84	3	3	0	0	10	16	14	9	5	17	R	R	6-3	210	4-3-74	1993	Emporia, Kan.
Woodring, Jason	1	1	2.66	48	0	0	16	51	46	19	15	20	50	R	R	6-3	190	4-2-74	1993	Trinidad, Colo.

VERMONT

NEW YORK-PENN LEAGUE

BATTING	AVG	G	AB	R	H	2B	3B	HR	RBI	BB	SO	SB	CS	B	T	HT	WT	DOB	1st Yr	Resides
Bady, Ed	.329	72	295	51	97	15	3	2	25	24	52	34	19	S	R	5-11	170	2-5-73	1994	Queens, N.Y.
Barrett, Michael	.100	3	10	0	1	0	0	0	1	1	1	0	0	R	R	6-3	185	10-22-76	1995	Alpharetta, Ga.
Blakeney, Mo	.265	39	132	17	35	8	1	2	17	8	23	12	2	R	R	5-10	185	1-17-73	1995	Kannapolis, N.C.
Brinkley, Josh	.221	38	122	14	27	2	0	0	11	14	26	6	1	R	R	5-10	175	8-5-73	1993	Raleigh, N.C.
Cabrera, Orlando	.282	65	248	37	70	12	5	3	33	16	28	15	8	R	R	5-11	165	3-2-74	1994	Cartagena, Colombia
Camilli, Jason	.243	63	243	37	59	10	2	1	21	30	52	17	10	R	R	6-0	178	10-18-75	1994	Phoenix, Ariz.
Culp, Randy	.000	1	3	0	0	0	0	0	0	0	0	0	0	R	R	6-1	195	8-18-74	1993	Killeen, Texas
Denning, Wes	.196	56	168	30	33	0	2	0	17	23	45	16	5	L	R	5-11	180	12-30-72	1995	St. Paul, Minn.
Fernandez, Jose	.274	66	270	38	74	6	7	4	41	13	51	29	4	R	R	6-2	210	11-2-74	1993	Santiago, D.R.
Garcia, Jaime	.242	50	149	22	36	7	2	2	16	27	30	1	1	R	R	5-8	180	5-8-72	1995	Tolleson, Ariz.
Macias, Jose	.239	53	176	24	42	4	2	0	9	19	19	11	7	R	R	5-10	173	1-25-74	1992	Panama City, Panama
Olsen, D.C.	.256	70	270	33	69	16	1	7	44	20	52	3	4	R	R	6-0	220	5-3-72	1995	Oakhurst, Calif.
Rosado, Juan	.245	48	155	20	38	4	2	1	24	18	16	4	5	L	L	5-11	180	8-6-74	1994	Camuy, P.R.
Steinkemper, Jake	.164	21	61	4	10	3	0	0	5	10	15	1	3	R	R	6-3	205	2-27-74	1995	Phoenix, Ariz.
Wolger, Mike	.256	60	203	27	52	7	1	2	23	34	47	3	3	L	L	6-2	195	9-12-72	1995	Redwood City, Calif.

GAMES BY POSITION: C—Brinkley 16, Garcia 50, Steinkemper 15, **1B**—Olsen 48, Wolger 28. **2B**—Brinkley 2, Cabrera 53, Macias 21. **3B**—Brinkley 7, Fernandez 63, Macias 9. **SS**—Barrett 1, Brinkley 1, Cabrera 12, Camilli 62. **OF**—Bady 71, Blakeney 38, Denning 55, Macias 23, Rosado 48.

PITCHING	W	L	ERA	G	GS	CG	SV	IP	H	R	ER	BB	SO	B	T	HT	WT	DOB	1st Yr	Resides
Baker, Jason	6	5	4.13	14	14	0	0	72	59	40	33	47	57	R	R	6-4	195	11-21-74	1993	Midland, Texas
Bell, Mike	0	0	0.54	7	0	0	1	17	7	5	1	5	12	L	L	6-2	195	10-14-72	1995	Sarasota, Fla.
Centeno, Jose	0	0	0.90	6	0	0	1	10	8	2	1	0	6	L	L	6-3	168	11-9-72	1993	Anzoategui, Venez.
Civit, Xavier	3	3	2.85	19	0	0	1	54	44	21	17	21	44	R	R	6-2	175	5-17-73	1993	Barcelona, Spain
Dixon, Tim	7	2	1.83	18	9	0	1	69	58	20	14	16	58	L	L	6-2	215	2-26-72	1995	San Jose, Calif.
Ferguson, Tim	0	0	7.71	3	0	0	0	5	2	4	4	2	2	L	L	6-0	195	5-1-72	1995	Lake Worth, Fla.
Herr, David	6	3	3.76	18	7	0	1	55	53	26	23	18	35	R	R	6-5	210	7-7-73	1995	West Chester, Pa.
Marquez, Robert	1	1	0.84	29	0	0	21	32	15	5	3	11	32	R	R	6-0	180	4-21-73	1995	Houston, Texas
Mattes, Troy	3	4	3.72	10	10	0	0	46	51	34	19	25	23	R	R	6-7	185	8-26-75	1994	Sarasota, Fla.
Mitchell, Scott	3	1	2.23	18	1	0	1	40	35	18	10	15	30	R	R	5-11	170	3-19-73	1995	Citrus Heights, Calif.
Morris, Chad	1	0	2.40	9	0	0	0	15	11	4	4	9	19	R	R	6-3	193	7-6-72	1995	Florence, S.C.
Powell, Jeremy	5	5	4.34	15	15	0	0	87	88	48	42	34	47	R	R	6-5	230	6-18-76	1994	Sacramento, Calif.
Smart, J.D.	0	1	2.28	5	5	0	0	28	29	9	7	7	21	L	R	6-2	185	11-12-73	1995	Austin, Texas
Stephens, Bill	3	1	1.65	13	0	0	3	27	17	5	5	7	30	S	R	6-5	215	10-31-72	1991	Ringgold, Ga.
Stern, Marty	0	0	3.38	8	0	0	0	13	12	5	5	6	10	R	R	6-5	210	1-3-74	1995	Pompano Beach, Fla.
Weidert, Chris	11	1	1.79	15	15	1	0	95	67	31	19	21	52	R	R	6-3	210	4-3-74	1994	Emporia, Kan.

WEST PALM BEACH

GULF COAST LEAGUE

BATTING	AVG	G	AB	R	H	2B	3B	HR	RBI	BB	SO	SB	CS	B	T	HT	WT	DOB	1st Yr	Resides
Alvarado, Basilio	.297	28	74	8	22	6	1	1	12	4	11	1	1	R	R	5-11	199	7-20-74	1992	Santo Domingo, D.R.
Barrett, Michael	.311	50	183	22	57	13	4	0	19	15	19	7	6	R	R	6-3	185	10-22-76	1995	Alpharetta, Ga.
Chick, Bruce	.235	15	51	4	12	5	0	1	9	5	8	1	2	R	R	6-4	210	3-7-69	1990	St. Petersburg, Fla.
Colson, Jeremiah	.063	23	48	4	3	0	1	0	4	2	24	1	2	L	L	5-11	170	6-20-76	1995	St. Paul's, N.C.
Culp, Randy	.152	10	33	2	5	2	0	0	1	1	9	0	1	R	R	6-1	195	8-18-74	1993	Killeen, Texas
Daniels, Ronny	.162	20	74	6	12	4	2	0	3	4	27	3	1	R	L	6-3	210	9-17-76	1995	Lake Wales, Fla.
Davis, Torrance	.273	45	139	19	38	1	1	0	5	12	25	13	7	R	R	6-1	180	12-25-75	1995	Texarkana, Texas
Fitzpatrick, Rob	.200	9	25	5	5	3	0	0	4	7	4	0	0	R	R	6-0	190	9-14-68	1990	Midland Park, N.J.
James, Kenny	.212	43	156	20	33	1	0	0	3	20	43	11	8	S	R	6-0	198	10-9-76	1995	Sebring, Fla.
King, Kevin	.263	14	38	6	10	3	0	0	2	2	19	3	0	R	R	6-1	175	4-7-74	1993	St. Croix, Virgin Islands
LaForest, Pierre	.000	2	6	1	0	0	0	0	0	2	4	0	0	L	R	6-1	190	1-27-78	1995	Gatineau, Quebec
Llanos, Francisco	.149	37	114	15	17	9	0	0	5	10	40	3	2	R	R	6-2	218	10-20-76	1995	Carolina, P.R.
Mateo, Henry	.148	38	122	11	18	0	0	0	6	14	47	2	7	S	R	5-11	170	10-14-76	1995	Santurce, P.R.
Miyauchi, Hector	.233	16	43	9	10	2	0	1	2	7	8	3	1	R	R	6-0	185	6-19-67	1995	Hontomon, Japan
Oropeza, William	.231	45	143	14	33	8	1	3	27	9	28	2	5	R	R	6-1	175	10-16-75	1994	LaGuaira, Venez.
Ovalles, Homy	.234	30	64	7	15	3	1	0	2	4	18	1	1	R	R	5-10	160	7-6-76	1994	Miranda, Venez.
Pond, Simon	.150	45	133	13	20	6	1	0	12	22	34	2	3	L	L	6-0	210	10-27-76	1994	North Vancouver, B.C.
Santos, Edgardo	.221	23	68	4	15	2	1	0	4	3	6	2	2	L	L	6-0	210	1-22-74	1994	Ponce, P.R.
Schneider, Brian	.227	30	97	7	22	3	0	0	4	14	23	2	4	L	R	6-1	180	11-26-76	1995	Cherryville, Pa.
Ware, Jeremy	.241	38	116	18	28	9	4	2	15	18	28	5	4	L	L	6-1	190	10-23-75	1995	Guelph, Ontario

GAMES BY POSITION: C—Alvarado 28, Fitzpatrick 2, Oropeza 6, Schneider 27. **1B**—Culp 5, Llanos 32, Oropeza 5, Santos 22. **2B**—Mateo 37, Ovalles 17, Pond 12. **3B**—Barrett 1, Culp 1, LaForest 1, Oropeza 30, Ovalles 1, Pond 31. **SS**—Barrett 48, Mateo 2, Ovalles 11. **OF**—Chick 11, Colson 18, Davis 41, James 41, King 14, Llanos 1, Miyauchi 16, Pond 3, Ware 37.

PITCHING	W	L	ERA	G	GS	CG	SV	IP	H	R	ER	BB	SO	B	T	HT	WT	DOB	1st Yr	Resides
Boike, Todd	2	4	3.94	23	1	0	2	48	54	32	21	13	35	R	R	6-0	185	11-22-75	1995	Taylor, Mich.
Boyd, Bradley	1	1	5.01	17	0	0	1	23	27	17	13	13	10	R	R	6-8	235	12-21-75	1995	Merrylands, Australia
Centeno, Jose	1	0	2.45	15	0	0	1	26	18	7	7	6	17	L	L	6-3	168	11-9-72	1993	Anzoategui, Venez.
Figueroa, Julio	2	3	3.08	10	10	0	0	50	44	27	17	20	37	R	R	6-1	179	6-29-74	1992	La Romana, D.R.
Fortune, Peter	3	5	4.69	11	11	1	0	48	46	33	25	18	27	L	L	6-2	190	3-4-75	1995	Valley Cottage, N.Y.
Garsky, Brian	2	3	3.12	14	6	0	1	43	48	25	15	19	43	R	R	6-1	172	10-14-75	1995	Clinton Township, Mich.
Lacey, James	1	1	8.34	12	1	0	0	23	35	29	21	14	10	R	R	6-2	210	3-30-76	1995	North Lauderdale, Fla.
Lara, Yovanny	1	2	5.10	11	4	0	0	30	35	21	17	19	16	R	R	6-2	163	9-20-75	1993	San Cristobal, D.R.
Lebron, John	0	0	0.00	2	0	0	0	2	0	0	0	3	0	R	R	6-0	190	11-7-70	1988	Patillas, P.R.
Martin, Trey	2	5	4.85	17	4	0	2	43	43	26	23	22	26	R	R	6-1	175	10-2-76	1995	Phoenix, Ariz.
Mattes, Troy	2	0	0.00	2	2	0	0	12	7	0	0	3	8	R	R	6-7	185	8-26-75	1994	Sarasota, Fla.
Quezada, Edward	0	7	4.99	12	10	0	0	52	52	36	29	10	36	R	R	6-2	150	1-15-75	1993	Santana Nizao, D.R.
Sanchez, Bienvenido	1	1	1.46	16	1	0	5	37	27	7	6	12	29	R	R	6-1	185	10-14-75	1995	Arecibo, P.R.
Smart, J.D.	2	0	1.69	2	2	0	0	11	10	2	2	1	6	L	R	6-2	185	11-12-73	1995	Austin, Texas
Sorzano, Ronnie	1	2	5.21	4	4	0	0	19	24	13	11	6	10	R	R	6-3	180	3-7-76	1994	Caracas, Venez.

NEW YORK YANKEES

Manager: Buck Showalter. **1995 Record:** 79-65, .549 (2nd, AL East).

BATTING

BATTING	AVG	G	AB	R	H	2B	3B	HR	RBI	BB	SO	SB	CS	B	T	HT	WT	DOB	1st Yr	Resides
Boggs, Wade	.324	126	460	76	149	22	4	5	63	74	50	1	1	L	R	6-2	197	6-15-58	1976	Tampa, Fla.
Davis, Russ	.276	40	98	14	27	5	2	2	12	10	26	0	0	R	R	6-0	170	9-13-69	1988	Hueytown, Ala.
Eenhoorn, Robert	.143	5	14	1	2	1	0	0	2	1	3	0	0	R	R	6-3	175	2-9-68	1990	Rotterdam, Netherlands
Elster, Kevin	.118	10	17	1	2	1	0	0	0	1	5	0	0	R	R	6-2	200	8-3-64	1984	Huntington Beach, Calif.
Fernandez, Tony	.245	108	384	57	94	20	2	5	45	42	40	6	6	S	R	6-2	175	6-30-62	1980	Santo Domingo, D.R.
James, Dion	.287	85	209	22	60	6	1	2	26	20	16	4	1	L	L	6-1	175	11-9-62	1980	Sacramento, Calif.
Jeter, Derek	.250	15	48	5	12	4	1	0	7	3	11	0	0	R	R	6-3	175	6-26-74	1992	Kalamazoo, Mich.
Kelly, Pat	.237	89	270	32	64	12	1	4	29	23	65	8	3	R	R	6-0	180	10-14-67	1988	Bangor, Pa.
Leyritz, Jim	.269	77	264	37	71	12	0	7	37	37	73	1	1	R	R	6-0	190	12-27-63	1986	Plantation, Fla.
Mattingly, Don	.288	128	458	59	132	32	2	7	49	40	35	0	2	L	L	6-0	175	4-20-61	1979	Evansville, Ind.
O'Neill, Paul	.300	127	460	82	138	30	4	22	96	71	76	1	2	L	L	6-4	215	2-25-63	1981	Cincinnati, Ohio
Polonia, Luis	.261	67	238	37	62	9	3	2	15	25	29	10	4	L	L	5-8	150	10-27-64	1984	Santiago City, D.R.
Posada, Jorge	.000	1	0	0	0	0	0	0	0	0	0	0	0	S	R	6-0	167	8-17-71	1991	Rio Piedras, P.R.
Rivera, Ruben	.000	5	1	0	0	0	0	0	0	0	1	0	0	R	R	6-3	190	11-14-73	1992	Chorrera, Panama
Sierra, Ruben	.260	56	215	33	56	15	0	7	44	22	34	1	0	S	R	6-1	200	10-6-65	1983	Carolina, P.R.
2-team (70 Oakland)	.263	126	479	73	126	32	0	19	86	46	76	5	4							
Silvestri, Dave	.095	17	21	4	2	0	0	1	4	4	9	0	0	R	R	6-0	180	9-29-67	1989	St. Louis, Mo.
Stanley, Mike	.268	118	399	63	107	29	1	18	83	57	106	1	1	R	R	6-0	190	6-25-63	1985	Oviedo, Fla.
Strawberry, Darryl	.276	32	87	15	24	4	1	3	13	10	22	0	0	L	L	6-6	215	3-12-62	1980	Glendale, Calif.
Tartabull, Danny	.224	59	192	25	43	12	0	6	28	33	54	0	0	R	R	6-1	210	10-30-62	1980	Malibu, Calif.
Velarde, Randy	.278	111	367	60	102	19	1	7	46	55	64	5	1	R	R	6-0	185	11-24-62	1985	Midland, Texas
Williams, Bernie	.307	144	563	93	173	29	9	18	82	75	98	8	6	S	R	6-2	196	9-13-68	1986	Vega Alta, P.R.
Williams, Gerald	.247	100	182	33	45	18	2	6	28	22	34	4	2	R	R	6-2	185	8-10-66	1987	LaPlace, La.

PITCHING

PITCHING	W	L	ERA	G	GS	CG	SV	IP	H	R	ER	BB	SO	B	T	HT	WT	DOB	1st Yr	Resides
Ausanio, Joe	2	0	5.73	28	0	0	1	38	42	24	24	23	36	R	R	6-1	205	12-9-65	1988	Kingston, N.Y.
Bankhead, Scott	1	1	6.00	20	1	0	0	39	44	26	26	16	20	R	R	5-10	185	7-31-63	1985	Asheboro, N.C.
Boehringer, Brian	0	3	13.75	7	3	0	0	18	24	27	27	22	10	S	R	6-2	180	1-8-69	1991	Fenton, Mo.
Cone, David	9	2	3.82	13	13	1	0	99	82	42	42	47	89	R	R	6-1	190	1-2-63	1981	Leawood, Kan.
2-team (17 Toronto)	18	8	3.57	30	30	6	0	229	195	95	91	88	191							
Eiland, Dave	1	1	6.30	4	1	0	0	10	16	10	7	3	6	R	R	6-3	205	7-5-66	1987	Dade City, Fla.
Hitchcock, Sterling	11	10	4.70	27	27	4	0	168	155	91	88	68	121	L	L	6-1	195	4-29-71	1989	Seffner, Fla.
Honeycutt, Rick	0	0	27.00	3	0	0	0	1	2	3	3	1	0	L	L	6-1	192	6-29-54	1976	La Habra Heights, Calif.
Howe, Steve	6	3	4.96	56	0	0	2	49	66	29	27	17	28	L	L	5-11	195	3-10-58	1979	Whitefish, Mont.
Kamieniecki, Scott	7	6	4.01	17	16	1	0	90	83	43	40	49	43	R	R	6-0	190	4-19-64	1987	Flint, Mich.
Key, Jimmy	1	2	5.64	5	5	0	0	30	40	20	19	6	14	R	L	6-1	185	4-22-61	1982	Tarpon Springs, Fla.
MacDonald, Bob	1	1	4.86	33	0	0	0	46	50	25	25	22	41	L	L	6-2	208	4-27-65	1987	Toms River, N.J.
Manzanillo, Josias	0	0	2.08	11	0	0	0	17	19	4	4	9	11	R	R	6-0	190	10-16-67	1983	Hyde Park, Mass.
McDowell, Jack	15	10	3.93	30	30	8	0	218	211	106	95	78	157	R	R	6-5	185	1-16-66	1987	Chicago, Ill.
Patterson, Jeff	0	0	2.70	3	0	0	0	3	3	1	1	3	3	R	R	6-2	200	10-1-68	1989	Anaheim, Calif.
Pavlas, Dave	0	0	3.18	4	0	0	0	6	8	2	2	0	3	R	R	6-7	195	8-12-62	1985	Phoenix, Ariz.
Perez, Melido	5	5	5.58	13	12	1	0	69	70	46	43	31	44	R	R	6-4	180	2-15-66	1984	San Cristobal, D.R.
Pettitte, Andy	12	9	4.17	31	26	3	0	175	183	86	81	63	114	L	L	6-5	220	6-15-72	1991	Deer Park, Texas
Rivera, Mariano	5	3	5.51	19	10	0	0	67	71	43	41	30	51	R	R	6-4	168	11-29-69	1990	Puerto Caimito, Panama
Wetteland, John	1	5	2.93	60	0	0	31	61	40	22	20	14	66	R	R	6-2	195	8-21-66	1985	Monroe, La.
Wickman, Bob	2	4	4.05	63	1	0	1	80	77	38	36	33	51	R	R	6-1	220	2-6-69	1990	Abrams, Wisc.

FIELDING

Catcher	PCT	G	PO	A	E	DP	PB
Leyritz	.993	46	286	18	2	2	5
Posada	1.000	1	1	0	0	0	0
Stanley	.993	107	651	35	5	10	15

First Base	PCT	G	PO	A	E	DP
Boggs	1.000	9	45	5	0	4
Davis	1.000	2	1	0	0	0
James	1.000	6	31	4	0	1
Leyritz	.993	18	131	6	1	11
Mattingly	.994	125	997	80	7	90
Silvestri	1.000	4	26	2	0	2

Second Base	PCT	G	PO	A	E	DP
Eenhoorn	1.000	3	10	6	0	2
Elster	.000	1	0	0	0	0
Fernandez	1.000	4	7	9	0	2
Kelly	.983	87	161	256	7	54
Silvestri	1.000	1	0	0	0	0
Velarde	.976	62	102	140	6	25

Third Base	PCT	G	PO	A	E	DP
Boggs	.981	117	69	193	5	11

	PCT	G	PO	A	E	DP
Davis	.968	34	15	45	2	1
Velarde	1.000	19	6	30	0	2

Shortstop	PCT	G	PO	A	E	DP
Eenhoorn	.750	2	1	2	1	0
Elster	1.000	10	10	14	0	2
Fernandez	.976	103	141	274	10	63
Jeter	.962	15	17	34	2	7
Silvestri	.000	1	0	0	0	0
Velarde	.976	28	37	87	3	21

Outfield	PCT	G	PO	A	E	DP
James	.968	29	30	0	1	0
O'Neill	.987	121	220	3	3	0
Polonia	1.000	64	132	5	0	1
Sierra	.950	10	18	1	1	0
Strawberry	.909	11	18	2	2	1
Tartabull	1.000	18	27	1	0	1
Velarde	.960	20	23	1	1	0
B. Williams	.982	144	432	1	8	0
G. Williams	.993	92	138	6	1	2

Wade Boggs

Outfielder Bernie Williams led the Yankees with 173 hits and 274 total bases

R&R SPORTS GROUP

YANKEES

MORRIS FOSTOFF

Yankees minor league Player of the Year Ruben Rivera

FARM SYSTEM

Vice President, Player Development and Scouting: Bill Livesey.

Class	Farm Team	League	W	L	Pct.	Finish*	Manager	First Yr
AAA	Columbus (Ohio) Clippers	International	71	68	.511	4th (10)	Bill Evers	1979
AA	Norwich (Conn.) Navigators	Eastern	70	71	.496	5th (10)	Jimmy Johnson	1995
#A	Tampa (Fla.) Yankees	Florida State	72	64	.529	5th (14)	Jake Gibbs	1994
A	Greensboro (N.C.) Bats	South Atlantic	70	70	.500	10th (14)	Trey Hillman	1990
A	Oneonta (N.Y.) Yankees	New York-Penn	34	41	.453	T-9th (14)	Rob Thomson	1967
R	Tampa (Fla.) Yankees	Gulf Coast	32	26	.552	T-8th (16)	Hector Lopez	1980

*Finish in overall standings (No. of teams in league)   #Advanced level

ORGANIZATION LEADERS

MAJOR LEAGUERS

MORRIS FOSTOFF

Jack McDowell. 15 wins

BATTING
- *AVG Wade Boggs .... .324
- R Bernie Williams 93
- H Bernie Williams ... 173
- TB Bernie Williams 274
- 2B Don Mattingly 32
- 3B Bernie Williams 9
- HR Paul O'Neill 22
- RBI Paul O'Neill 96
- BB Bernie Williams 75
- SO Mike Stanley 106
- SB Luis Polonia 10

PITCHING
- W Jack McDowell 15
- L Two tied at 10
- #ERA David Cone 3.82
- G Bob Wickman 63
- CG Jack McDowell 8
- SV John Wetteland 31
- IP Jack McDowell 218
- BB Jack McDowell 78
- SO Jack McDowell 157

MINOR LEAGUERS

BATTING
- *AVG Derek Jeter, Columbus .... .317
- R Derek Jeter, Columbus 96
- H Don Sparks, Columbus 170
- TB Ruben Rivera, Norwich/Columbus 238
- 2B Jorge Posada, Columbus 32
- 3B Andy Fox, Norwich/Columbus 11
- HR Ruben Rivera, Norwich/Columbus 24
- RBI Don Sparks, Columbus 90
- BB R.D. Long, Tampa/Norwich 79
- SO Ruben Rivera, Norwich/Columbus 139
- SB Rod Smith, Oneonta/Greensboro 41

PITCHING
- W Matt Drews, Tampa 15
- L Mike Buddie, Norwich 12
- #ERA Chris Corn, Greensboro/Tampa 1.85
- G Mike DeJean, Norwich 59
- CG Two tied at 3
- SV Two tied at 24
- IP Ray Ricken, Gboro/Tampa/Norwich 193
- BB Mike Buddie, Norwich 81
- SO Ray Ricken, Gboro/Tampa/Norwich 178

*Minimum 250 At-Bats   #Minimum 75 Innings

TOP 10 PROSPECTS

How the Yankees Top 10 prospects, as judged by Baseball America prior to the 1995 season, fared in 1995:

STAN DENNY

Derek Jeter

Player, Pos.	Club (Class—League)	AVG	AB	R	H	2B	3B	HR	RBI	SB
1. Ruben Rivera, of	Norwich (AA—Eastern)	.293	256	49	75	16	8	9	39	16
	Columbus (AAA—International)	.270	174	37	47	8	2	15	35	8
	New York	.000	1	0	0	0	0	0	0	0
2. Derek Jeter, ss	Columbus (AAA—International)	.317	486	96	154	27	9	2	45	20
	New York	.250	48	5	12	4	1	0	7	0
4. Russ Davis, 3b	Columbus (AAA—International)	.250	76	12	19	4	1	2	15	0
	New York	.276	98	14	27	5	2	2	12	0
7. Jorge Posada, c	Columbus (AAA—International)	.255	368	60	94	32	5	8	51	4
	New York	.000	0	0	0	0	0	0	0	0
8. Tate Seefried, 1b	Norwich (AA—Eastern)	.226	274	34	62	18	1	5	33	0
	Columbus (AAA—International)	.164	110	7	18	6	0	1	12	0
10. Brian Buchanan, of	Greensboro (A—South Atlantic)	.302	96	19	29	3	0	3	12	7

		W	L	ERA	G	SV	IP	H	BB	SO
3. Andy Pettitte, lhp	Columbus (AAA—International)	0	0	0.00	2	0	12	7	0	8
	New York	12	9	4.17	31	0	175	183	63	114
5. Matt Drews, rhp	Tampa (A—Florida State)	15	7	2.27	28	0	182	142	58	140
6. Brien Taylor, lhp	GCL Yankees (R—Gulf Coast)	2	5	6.08	11	0	40	29	54	38
9. Mariano Rivera, rhp	Columbus (AAA—International)	2	2	2.10	7	0	30	25	3	30
	New York	5	3	5.51	19	0	67	71	30	51

THE SPORTS GROUP

TOM DiPACE

Lefthanded Power. The Yankees earned an American League wild-card berth in 1995 as Paul O'Neill, left, hit .300 with 22 homers and Don Mattingly hit .288.

COLUMBUS AAA

INTERNATIONAL LEAGUE

BATTING	AVG	G	AB	R	H	2B	3B	HR	RBI	BB	SO	SB	CS	B	T	HT	WT	DOB	1st Yr	Resides
Barnwell, Rich	.231	46	130	22	30	4	2	1	17	13	32	7	3	R	R	6-0	190	2-29-68	1989	Hawthorne, Calif.
Benzinger, Todd	.280	12	50	4	14	3	0	1	4	2	10	0	0	S	R	6-1	195	2-11-63	1981	Cincinnati, Ohio
Carpenter, Bubba	.246	116	374	57	92	12	3	11	49	40	70	13	6	L	L	6-1	185	7-23-68	1991	Winslow, Ariz.
Davis, Russ	.250	20	76	12	19	4	1	2	15	17	23	0	0	R	R	6-0	170	9-13-69	1988	Hueytown, Ala.
DeBerry, Joe	.292	10	24	3	7	2	2	0	4	1	6	0	0	L	L	6-2	195	6-30-70	1991	Colorado Springs, Colo.
Eenhoorn, Robert	.252	92	318	36	80	11	3	5	32	20	54	2	4	R	R	6-3	175	2-9-68	1990	Rotterdam, Netherlands
Epps, Scott	.143	4	7	0	1	0	0	0	0	0	1	0	0	R	R	5-11	180	12-8-69	1992	Jenks, Okla.
Figga, Mike	.280	8	25	2	7	1	0	1	3	3	5	0	0	R	R	6-0	200	7-31-70	1990	Tampa, Fla.
Fleming, Carlton	.221	32	86	9	19	6	0	0	5	8	6	0	2	S	R	5-11	175	8-25-71	1992	Freeport, N.Y.
Fox, Andy	.348	82	302	61	105	16	6	9	37	43	41	22	4	L	R	6-4	185	1-12-71	1989	Sacramento, Calif.
Hill, Lew	.271	54	144	15	39	5	0	4	20	5	36	6	5	S	R	5-10	190	4-16-69	1987	Cleveland, Ohio
Jeter, Derek	.317	123	486	96	154	27	9	2	45	61	56	20	12	R	R	6-3	175	6-26-74	1992	Kalamazoo, Mich.
Leach, Jalal	.243	88	272	37	66	12	5	6	31	22	60	11	4	L	L	6-2	200	3-14-69	1990	Novato, Calif.
Livesey, Jeff	.264	42	91	8	24	3	0	0	7	7	18	0	0	R	R	6-0	185	5-24-66	1988	Spring Hill, Fla.
Luke, Matt	.299	23	77	11	23	4	1	3	12	2	12	1	1	L	L	6-5	225	2-26-71	1992	Brea, Calif.
Maas, Kevin	.280	44	161	28	45	7	2	9	33	23	40	0	0	L	L	6-3	205	1-20-65	1986	Berkeley, Calif.
Masse, Billy	.224	49	165	19	37	6	2	4	24	24	31	3	3	R	R	6-1	190	7-6-66	1989	Wethersfield, Conn.
McDowell, Oddibe	.217	14	46	5	10	0	1	1	2	6	9	0	1	L	L	5-9	160	8-25-62	1985	Arlington, Texas
Melvin, Bob	.288	19	66	7	19	5	0	1	4	3	12	0	0	R	R	6-4	205	10-28-61	1981	Scottsdale, Ariz.
Perezchica, Tony	.257	101	358	43	92	12	4	7	44	18	74	3	3	R	R	5-11	165	4-30-66	1986	Mesa, Ariz.
Posada, Jorge	.255	108	368	60	94	32	5	8	51	54	101	4	4	S	R	6-0	167	8-17-71	1991	Rio Piedras, P.R.
Rivera, Ruben	.270	48	174	37	47	8	2	15	35	26	62	8	4	R	R	6-3	190	11-14-73	1992	Chorrera, Panama
Seefried, Tate	.164	29	110	7	18	6	0	1	12	1	34	0	0	L	R	6-4	180	4-22-72	1990	El Segundo, Calif.
Sparks, Don	.312	137	545	67	170	26	10	7	90	29	75	2	0	R	R	6-2	185	6-19-66	1988	Long Beach, Calif.
Strawberry, Darryl	.301	22	83	20	25	3	1	7	29	15	17	1	1	L	L	6-6	215	3-12-62	1980	Glendale, Calif.
Thoutsis, Paul	.215	52	130	10	28	4	1	0	15	· 4	16	1	0	L	R	6-1	185	10-23-65	1983	Worcester, Mass.
Wilson, Tom	.258	22	62	11	16	3	1	0	9	9	10	0	0	R	R	6-3	185	12-19-70	1991	Yorba Linda, Calif.

PITCHING	W	L	ERA	G	GS	CG	SV	IP	H	R	ER	BB	SO	B	T	HT	WT	DOB	1st Yr	Resides
Ausanio, Joe	1	0	7.50	11	0	0	3	12	12	10	10	5	20	R	R	6-1	205	12-9-65	1988	Kingston, N.Y.
Boehringer, Brian	8	6	2.77	17	17	3	0	104	101	39	32	31	58	S	R	6-2	180	1-8-69	1991	Fenton, Mo.
Carper, Mark	8	9	4.82	33	14	0	1	106	114	61	57	55	61	R	R	6-2	200	9-29-68	1991	Highland, Md.
Cook, Andy	2	3	3.36	37	2	0	2	56	53	24	21	19	28	R	R	6-5	215	8-30-67	1988	Memphis, Tenn.
Croghan, Andy	1	1	3.60	20	0	0	4	25	21	10	10	22	22	R	R	6-5	205	10-26-69	1991	Yorba Linda, Calif.
Dunbar, Matt	2	3	4.06	36	0	0	0	44	50	22	20	19	33	L	L	6-0	160	10-15-68	1990	Tallahassee, Fla.
Eiland, Dave	8	7	3.14	19	18	1	0	109	109	44	38	22	62	R	R	6-3	205	7-5-66	1987	Dade City, Fla.
Frazier, Ron	2	2	4.50	24	5	0	0	54	54	33	27	23	31	R	R	6-5	185	6-13-69	1990	Otis, Mass.
Hernandez, Willie	2	1	7.67	22	0	0	0	27	43	24	23	12	16	L	L	6-3	170	11-14-54	1974	Rio Piedras, P.R.
Hutton, Mark	2	6	8.43	11	11	0	0	52	64	51	49	24	23	R	R	6-6	225	2-6-70	1989	West Lakes, Australia
Kamieniecki, Scott	1	1	0.00	1	1	0	0	7	2	0	0	1	10	R	R	6-0	190	4-19-64	1987	Flint, Mich.
MacDonald, Bob	2	1	2.33	13	0	0	0	19	22	7	5	5	13	L	L	6-2	208	4-27-65	1987	Toms River, N.J.
Mendoza, Ramiro	1	0	2.57	2	2	0	0	14	10	4	4	2	13	R	R	6-2	154	6-15-72	1992	Los Santos, Panama

PITCHING	W	L	ERA	G	GS	CG	SV	IP	H	R	ER	BB	SO	B	T	HT	WT	DOB	1st Yr	Resides
Musset, Jose	0	0	6.23	5	0	0	0	4	4	4	3	2	4	R	R	6-3	186	9-18-68	1987	Monte Plata, D.R.
Ojala, Kirt	8	7	3.95	32	20	0	1	146	138	74	64	54	107	L	L	6-2	200	12-24-68	1990	Portage, Mich.
Patterson, Jeff	5	3	3.61	33	0	0	0	62	56	30	25	30	36	R	R	6-2	200	10-1-68	1989	Anaheim, Calif.
Pavlas, Dave	3	3	2.61	48	0	0	18	59	43	19	17	20	51	R	R	6-7	195	8-12-62	1985	Phoenix, Ariz.
Pettitte, Andy	0	0	0.00	2	2	0	0	12	7	0	0	0	8	L	L	6-5	220	6-15-72	1991	Deer Park, Texas
Quirico, Rafael	0	0	4.70	20	0	0	0	23	15	14	12	14	21	L	L	6-3	170	9-7-69	1987	Santo Domingo, D.R.
Rivera, Mariano	2	2	2.10	7	7	1	0	30	25	10	7	3	30	R	R	6-4	168	11-29-69	1990	Puerto Caimito, Panama
Rumer, Tim	10	8	5.22	28	25	0	0	141	156	98	82	76	110	L	L	6-3	205	8-8-69	1990	Princeton, N.J.
Segura, Jose	0	2	8.71	11	0	0	4	10	18	12	10	8	8	R	R	5-11	180	1-26-63	1981	Fundacion, D.R.
Smith, Daryl	0	3	4.03	13	7	0	0	51	54	31	23	20	23	R	R	6-4	220	7-29-60	1980	Baltimore, Md.
Sutherland, John	0	0	9.00	3	0	0	0	3	5	3	3	0	2	R	R	6-2	185	10-11-68	1991	Walnut Creek, Calif.
Wallace, Kent	4	1	3.02	9	9	0	0	51	44	19	17	11	31	L	R	6-3	192	8-22-70	1992	Paducah, Ky.

FIELDING

Catcher	PCT	G	PO	A	E	DP	PB
Epps	.941	4	15	1	1	0	0
Figga	1.000	5	29	4	0	0	1
Livesey	.984	26	113	7	2	0	0
Melvin	.971	12	66	2	2	0	0
Posada	.993	93	500	58	4	7	14
Wilson	.962	22	109	16	5	2	0

First Base	PCT	G	PO	A	E	DP
Benzinger	.986	12	131	8	2	12
Carpenter	1.000	3	20	1	0	3
Davis	1.000	2	8	1	0	1
DeBerry	.974	5	36	2	1	1
Livesey	.000	1	0	0	0	0
Maas	1.000	11	89	8	0	13
Melvin	1.000	1	11	1	0	1
Seefried	.993	28	271	25	2	27
Sparks	.994	80	762	55	5	76
Thoutsis	1.000	5	28	3	0	4

Second Base	PCT	G	PO	A	E	DP
Eenhoorn	.979	82	162	219	8	63
Fleming	.934	20	37	62	7	12
Fox	1.000	4	2	5	0	2
Perezchica	.981	48	75	128	4	28

Third Base	PCT	G	PO	A	E	DP
Davis	.848	19	9	30	7	1
Eenhoorn	1.000	5	3	6	0	0
Epps	1.000	1	1	0	0	0
Fox	.968	69	59	184	8	22
Perezchica	.923	19	15	33	4	3
Sparks	.975	39	25	92	3	15

Shortstop	PCT	G	PO	A	E	DP
Eenhoorn	1.000	5	3	6	0	2
Fox	.970	10	10	22	1	3
Jeter	.953	123	189	394	29	74
Perezchica	.956	11	24	41	3	7

Outfield	PCT	G	PO	A	E	DP
Barnwell	.986	44	66	2	1	1
Carpenter	.982	104	211	4	4	2
Fox	1.000	8	13	0	0	0
Hill	.984	37	62	0	1	0
Leach	.943	64	97	2	6	0
Luke	.949	23	36	1	2	0
Maas	1.000	22	26	0	0	0
Masse	.961	44	72	1	3	0
McDowell	1.000	14	26	0	0	0
Perezchica	.957	20	21	1	1	0
Rivera	.975	48	113	6	3	2
Sparks	1.000	2	1	0	0	0
Strawberry	1.000	9	9	0	0	0
Thoutsis	.953	31	41	0	2	0

NORWICH

AA

EASTERN LEAGUE

BATTING	AVG	G	AB	R	H	2B	3B	HR	RBI	BB	SO	SB	CS	B	T	HT	WT	DOB	1st Yr	Resides
Burnett, Roger	.222	104	356	32	79	14	0	3	29	28	64	3	3	R	R	6-1	185	11-14-69	1991	Broken Arrow, Okla.
Cabreja, Alexis	.091	6	11	1	1	0	0	0	1	3	0	1	0	R	R	6-1	205	3-22-69	1993	Woodland Hills, Calif.
Delvecchio, Nick	.260	125	430	66	112	23	4	19	74	72	133	2	1	L	R	6-5	203	1-23-70	1992	Natick, Mass.
DeBerry, Joe	.000	2	4	0	0	0	0	0	0	0	2	0	0	L	L	6-2	195	6-30-70	1991	Colorado Springs, Colo.
Epps, Scott	.247	33	73	6	18	6	0	0	7	9	21	0	0	R	R	5-11	180	12-8-69	1992	Jenks, Okla.
Figga, Mike	.271	109	399	59	108	22	4	13	61	43	90	1	0	R	R	6-0	200	7-31-70	1990	Tampa, Fla.
Fleming, Carlton	.304	40	125	15	38	3	1	0	16	12	10	5	3	S	R	5-11	175	8-25-71	1992	Freeport, N.Y.
Fox, Andy	.206	44	175	23	36	3	5	5	17	19	36	8	1	L	R	6-4	185	1-12-71	1989	Sacramento, Calif.
Hawkins, Kraig	.222	12	45	5	10	0	0	0	3	7	11	7	2	S	R	6-2	170	12-4-71	1992	Lake Charles, La.
Hinds, Robert	.252	132	445	71	112	8	1	1	37	50	102	27	10	R	R	6-1	180	4-26-71	1992	Cerritos, Calif.
Horne, Tyrone	.283	46	166	23	47	16	1	2	22	26	36	4	2	L	R	5-10	185	11-2-70	1989	Troy, N.C.
2-team (87 Harr.)	.291	133	460	82	134	33	5	16	69	84	101	18	10							
Hughes, Troy	.327	15	55	7	18	2	1	1	8	4	11	0	2	R	R	6-4	212	1-3-71	1989	Mt. Vernon, Ill.
Long, R.D.	.212	9	33	4	7	3	0	0	5	7	11	2	1	S	R	6-1	183	4-2-71	1992	Penfield, N.Y.
Luke, Matt	.260	93	365	48	95	17	5	8	53	20	68	5	4	L	L	6-5	225	2-26-71	1992	Brea, Calif.
Phillips, Steve	.258	11	31	2	8	1	0	2	7	6	8	0	0	L	L	6-2	205	1-12-68	1991	Fairfield, Ohio
Renteria, Dave	.105	15	38	4	4	0	0	0	3	13	1	0	0	R	R	6-0	175	12-1-72	1992	Belen, N.M.
Riggs, Kevin	.330	57	179	38	59	16	1	4	36	51	28	5	5	L	R	5-11	190	2-3-69	1990	East Hartford, Conn.
Rivera, Ruben	.293	71	256	49	75	16	8	9	39	37	77	16	8	R	R	6-3	190	11-14-73	1992	Chorrera, Panama
Robertson, Jason	.276	117	456	60	126	29	10	6	54	41	106	19	12	L	L	6-2	200	3-24-71	1989	Country Club Hills, Ill.
Romano, Scott	.246	100	353	43	87	15	1	7	51	48	57	7	2	R	R	6-1	185	8-3-71	1989	Tampa, Fla.
Salcedo, Edwin	.000	3	2	0	0	0	0	0	0	0	2	0	0	R	R	6-0	214	7-8-70	1990	Lakeridge, Va.
Seefried, Tate	.226	77	274	34	62	18	1	5	33	31	86	0	1	L	R	6-4	180	4-22-72	1990	El Segundo, Calif.
Turner, Brian	.296	86	311	39	92	21	3	4	43	25	72	3	2	L	L	6-2	210	6-9-71	1989	Orwell, Ohio
Wilson, Tom	.143	28	84	6	12	4	0	0	4	17	22	0	0	R	R	6-3	185	12-19-70	1991	Yorba Linda, Calif.

PITCHING	W	L	ERA	G	GS	CG	SV	IP	H	R	ER	BB	SO	B	T	HT	WT	DOB	1st Yr	Resides
Antolick, Jeff	1	1	6.75	2	2	0	0	9	17	9	7	2	5	R	R	6-6	205	3-3-71	1992	Drums, Pa.
Buddie, Mike	10	12	4.81	29	27	2	1	150	155	102	80	81	106	R	R	6-3	210	12-7-70	1992	Berea, Ohio
Carper, Mark	0	0	10.80	1	1	0	0	5	9	6	6	1	3	R	R	6-2	200	9-29-68	1991	Highland, Md.
Carter, Tom	3	7	5.57	28	15	0	0	97	128	69	60	47	65	L	L	6-8	215	4-30-70	1991	Anniston, Ala.
Coleman, Billy	6	4	4.05	46	0	0	2	73	56	52	33	57	64	R	R	6-2	185	1-18-69	1991	Roanoke, Texas
DeJean, Mike	5	5	2.99	59	0	0	20	78	58	29	26	34	57	R	R	6-3	205	9-28-70	1992	Denham Springs, La.
Hines, Rich	3	5	3.63	54	0	0	7	62	58	38	25	56	53	L	L	6-1	185	5-20-69	1990	Milton, Fla.
Hubbard, Mark	4	4	4.21	13	12	0	1	73	81	38	34	25	39	L	L	6-2	190	2-2-70	1991	Dover, Fla.
Janzen, Marty	1	2	4.95	3	3	0	0	20	17	11	11	7	16	R	R	6-3	197	5-31-73	1991	Gainesville, Fla.
Kozelewski, Blaise	1	0	4.91	29	0	0	0	55	53	35	30	27	33	R	R	6-3	185	11-2-69	1992	Somerdale, N.J.
Long, Joe	4	2	4.85	43	1	0	2	82	103	54	44	48	34	R	R	6-4	200	6-23-71	1991	Glendora, Calif.
Mendoza, Ramiro	5	6	3.21	19	19	2	0	90	87	39	32	33	68	R	R	6-2	154	6-15-72	1992	Los Santos, Panama
Musselwhite, Jim	5	9	4.58	24	24	1	0	132	136	75	67	34	96	R	R	6-1	190	10-25-71	1993	Apopka, Fla.
Musset, Jose	4	1	3.33	34	0	0	4	49	43	21	18	24	42	R	R	6-3	186	9-18-68	1987	Monte Plata, D.R.
Pantoja, Johnny	1	2	6.48	11	2	0	0	25	29	23	18	14	19	R	R	6-0	190	2-24-78	1994	Cartagena, Colombia
Perez, Melido	1	0	0.00	2	2	0	0	9	7	0	0	3	9	R	R	6-4	180	2-15-66	1984	San Cristobal, D.R.
Ricken, Ray	4	2	2.72	8	8	1	0	53	44	21	16	24	43	R	R	6-5	225	8-11-73	1994	Warren, Mich.
Standish, Scott	4	3	5.67	17	9	0	0	60	73	43	38	30	47	R	R	6-5	225	10-5-72	1993	Omaha, Neb.
Sullivan, Grant	0	0	54.00	1	0	0	0	1	4	4	4	0	0	L	L	6-5	210	3-19-70	1991	Signal Mountain, Tenn.
Sutherland, John	1	0	2.77	13	0	0	2	13	12	5	4	3	12	R	R	6-2	185	10-11-68	1991	Walnut Creek, Calif.
Wallace, Kent	4	2	3.52	18	16	0	0	95	93	41	37	24	72	L	R	6-3	192	8-22-70	1992	Paducah, Ky.

FIELDING

Catcher	PCT	G	PO	A	E	DP	PB
Epps	.971	27	120	15	4	0	2
Figga	.985	105	640	92	11	4	15
Salcedo	1.000	3	8	0	0	0	0
Wilson	.993	19	129	12	1	0	3

First Base	PCT	G	PO	A	E	DP
Delvecchio	.985	58	498	43	8	38
Epps	1.000	1	7	0	0	0
Riggs	.966	3	27	1	1	1
Seefried	.989	58	497	39	6	52
Turner	.990	26	197	11	2	20

Second Base	PCT	G	PO	A	E	DP
Fleming	.950	32	57	75	7	14
Hinds	.960	111	248	322	24	73
Long	1.000	2	1	4	0	0

	PCT	G	PO	A	E	DP
Renteria	1.000	3	5	1	0	1

Third Base	PCT	G	PO	A	E	DP
Burnett	.915	21	7	47	5	3
Epps	.500	3	0	1	1	0
Hinds	.769	13	6	14	6	1
Long	.750	1	1	2	1	1
Renteria	1.000	6	5	10	0	0
Romano	.913	99	70	236	29	19
Wilson	.800	7	6	14	5	0

Shortstop	PCT	G	PO	A	E	DP
Burnett	.931	75	116	194	23	39
Fox	.958	44	77	127	9	23
Hinds	.926	13	22	28	4	9
Long	.800	6	6	14	5	3

	PCT	G	PO	A	E	DP
Renteria	.800	5	7	9	4	3

Outfield	PCT	G	PO	A	E	DP
Cabreja	.800	5	4	0	1	0
Delvecchio	.957	42	62	4	3	0
Epps	1.000	2	1	0	0	0
Fleming	1.000	3	3	0	0	0
Hawkins	1.000	12	28	0	0	0
Horne	.900	20	34	2	4	0
Hughes	.875	12	21	0	3	0
Luke	.979	93	178	12	4	1
Phillips	1.000	11	21	0	0	0
Rivera	.984	71	176	7	3	1
Robertson	.979	116	227	4	5	0
Romano	.000	2	0	0	0	0
Turner	.990	50	98	2	1	1

TAMPA   A
FLORIDA STATE LEAGUE

BATTING

	AVG	G	AB	R	H	2B	3B	HR	RBI	BB	SO	SB	CS	B	T	HT	WT	DOB	1st Yr	Resides
Bierek, Kurt	.248	126	447	60	111	16	2	4	53	61	73	3	4	L	R	6-4	200	9-13-72	1993	Hillsboro, Ore.
Cooper, Tim	.176	63	170	16	30	3	1	3	13	24	44	1	1	R	R	6-3	190	3-10-71	1989	Sacramento, Calif.
Delafield, Wil	.269	7	26	4	7	1	0	1	6	2	11	1	0	R	R	6-2	185	2-15-72	1992	Baton Rouge, La.
DeBerry, Joe	.224	58	196	16	44	9	3	1	18	19	45	1	0	L	L	6-2	195	6-30-70	1991	Colorado Springs, Colo.
Donato, Dan	.250	3	8	1	2	0	0	1	1	0	2	0	0	L	R	6-1	205	11-15-72	1995	Dedham, Mass.
Fithian, Grant	.250	3	4	0	1	0	0	0	1	0	2	0	0	R	R	6-0	192	11-20-71	1994	Rockwall, Texas
Hansen, Elston	.193	61	187	28	36	12	1	2	19	23	45	0	1	R	R	6-1	185	11-16-71	1990	Curacao, Neth. Antilles
Hawkins, Kraig	.243	111	432	56	105	9	3	1	19	66	95	28	14	S	R	6-2	170	12-4-71	1992	Lake Charles, La.
Kelly, Pat	.235	3	17	0	4	1	0	0	2	0	1	0	0	R	R	6-0	180	10-14-67	1988	Bangor, Pa.
Knowles, Eric	.271	115	391	45	106	24	4	1	33	45	58	7	3	R	R	6-0	190	10-21-73	1991	Miami, Fla.
Long, R.D.	.250	110	384	70	96	15	10	4	36	72	100	28	13	S	R	6-1	183	4-2-71	1992	Penfield, N.Y.
Mitchell, Mike	.266	102	368	40	98	16	1	8	61	29	52	1	0	L	R	6-3	205	4-5-73	1994	Camarillo, Calif.
Motuzas, Jeff	.159	28	69	6	11	0	0	1	8	4	24	1	0	R	R	6-2	205	10-1-71	1990	Nashua, N.H.
Renteria, David	.217	33	69	6	15	3	1	1	4	4	16	1	1	R	R	6-0	175	12-1-72		Belen, N.M.
Schmitz, Mike	.231	4	13	2	3	1	0	0	0	0	1	0	0	R	R	6-3	215	4-22-71	1993	Coconut Creek, Fla.
Smith, Sloan	.260	124	412	61	107	23	1	13	64	74	136	6	8	S	R	6-4	215	11-29-72	1993	Evanston, Ill.
Spencer, Shane	.300	134	500	87	150	31	3	16	88	61	60	14	8	R	R	5-11	192	2-22-72	1990	El Cajon, Calif.
Strawberry, Darryl	.222	2	9	1	2	1	0	0	1	2	1	2	0	L	L	6-6	215	3-12-62	1980	Glendale, Calif.
Suplee, Ray	.233	98	317	33	74	9	1	7	37	33	94	4	2	R	R	6-3	200	12-15-70	1992	Sarasota, Fla.
Torborg, Dale	.000	2	1	0	0	0	0	0	0	0	1	0	0	R	R	6-5	205	10-24-71	1994	Mountainside, N.J.
2-team (5 St. Lucie)	.100	7	10	0	1	0	0	0	1	0	5	0	0							
Torres, Jaime	.239	107	364	45	87	17	0	8	45	28	29	1	1	R	R	6-0	176	3-12-73	1992	Aragua, Venez.
Troilo, Jason	.000	1	2	0	0	0	0	0	0	0	2	0	0	R	R	6-1	195	9-7-72	1994	Avondale, Pa.
Twitty, Sean	.250	1	4	0	1	0	0	0	0	0	1	0	0	R	R	6-3	190	10-23-70	1989	Astoria, N.Y.
Wilson, Tom	.167	17	48	3	8	0	0	0	2	11	13	1	0	R	R	6-3	185	12-19-70	1991	Yorba Linda, Calif.

GAMES BY POSITION: C—Fithian 3, Motuzas 28, Torres 105, Troilo 1, Wilson 13. **1B**—Cooper 32, DeBerry 49, Long 1, Mitchell 57, Schmitz 1, Torborg 1. **2B**—Hansen 42, Kelly 3, Long 94, Renteria 8. **3B**—Bierek 122, Cooper 16, Donato 1, Hansen 1, Renteria 1. **SS**—Knowles 115, Long 7, Renteria 20. **OF**—Cooper 2, Delafield 3, Donato 1, Hawkins 111, Smith 124, Spencer 109, Suplee 66.

PITCHING

	W	L	ERA	G	GS	CG	SV	IP	H	R	ER	BB	SO	B	T	HT	WT	DOB	1st Yr	Resides
Berry, Jason	2	0	0.92	7	0	0	0	20	14	3	2	10	14	R	R	6-4	220	4-2-74	1993	Brockton, Mass.
Cindrich, Jeff	1	4	4.35	24	0	0	0	39	50	28	19	17	32	R	R	6-6	230	2-22-71	1991	Cape Coral, Fla.
Corn, Chris	0	1	3.18	4	0	0	0	6	3	2	2	3	9	R	R	6-2	170	10-4-71	1994	Louisville, Ky.
Cumberland, Chris	1	2	1.82	5	5	0	0	25	28	10	5	5	16	R	L	6-1	185	1-15-73	1993	Safety Harbor, Fla.
Drews, Matt	15	7	2.27	28	28	3	0	182	142	73	46	58	140	R	R	6-8	205	8-29-74	1994	Sarasota, Fla.
Drumheller, Al	3	3	1.34	32	0	0	2	40	24	11	6	14	45	R	L	6-0	185	7-31-71	1993	Shenandoah, Pa.
Gordon, Mike	4	6	3.04	21	21	1	0	124	111	54	42	49	96	L	R	6-2	195	11-30-72	1992	Quincy, Fla.
Hubbard, Mark	4	4	1.84	13	11	1	0	68	52	22	14	21	40	L	L	6-2	190	2-2-70	1971	Dover, Fla.
Janzen, Marty	10	3	2.61	18	18	1	0	114	102	38	33	30	104	R	R	6-3	197	5-31-73	1991	Gainesville, Fla.
Jerzembeck, Mike	0	1	9.00	2	0	0	0	3	5	4	3	2	1	R	R	6-1	185	5-18-72	1993	Queens Village, N.Y.
Kamieniecki, Scott	1	0	1.80	1	1	0	0	5	6	2	1	1	2	R	R	6-0	190	4-19-64	1987	Flint, Mich.
Kozeniewski, Blaise	3	1	0.95	11	0	0	0	19	11	3	2	3	17	R	R	6-3	185	11-2-69	1992	Somerdale, N.J.
Lankford, Frank	4	6	2.59	15	0	0	15	54	64	29	21	22	58	R	R	6-2	190	3-26-71	1993	Atlanta, Ga.
Leshnock, Donnie	10	6	3.08	28	10	0	2	88	78	41	30	45	67	L	R	6-4	220	4-20-71	1992	Columbus, Ohio
Medina, Rafael	2	2	2.37	6	6	0	0	30	29	12	8	12	25	R	R	6-3	194	2-15-75	1993	Panama City, Panama
Meyer, David	3	4	6.52	12	11	0	0	58	84	49	42	29	29	L	L	6-5	215	12-15-71	1994	Grapevine, Texas
Rathbun, Jason	1	0	4.05	10	5	0	0	27	27	17	12	10	14	R	R	6-2	200	8-29-72	1993	Houston, Texas
Resz, Greg	0	1	3.38	12	0	0	1	13	10	9	5	9	16	L	R	6-5	215	12-25-71	1993	Springfield, Mo.
Ricken, Ray	4	2	2.15	11	11	1	0	75	47	25	18	27	58	R	R	6-5	215	8-11-73	1994	Warren, Mich.
Rios, Dan	0	4	2.00	57	0	0	24	67	67	24	15	20	72	R	R	6-2	208	11-11-72	1993	Hialeah, Fla.
Rodriguez, Salvador	0	1	11.05	6	0	0	0	7	13	10	9	4	7	R	R	6-2	200	12-29-74	1994	Santiago, Mexico
Rojano, Jason	0	2	6.23	4	0	0	0	4	4	3	3	2	4	R	R	6-3	164	1-14-71	1995	Cartegena, Colombia
Santiago, Sandi	3	3	3.90	34	3	0	0	58	54	28	25	29	55	R	R	6-1	175	3-16-70	1989	Bani, D.R.
Schlomann, Brett	2	0	1.64	2	2	0	0	11	10	6	2	0	5	R	R	6-1	185	7-31-74	1994	Collinsville, Okla.
Shoemaker, Steve	0	1	1.08	3	2	0	0	17	9	5	2	13	12	L	R	6-1	195	2-3-73	1994	Phoenixville, Pa.
Standish, Scott	0	0	2.57	4	2	0	0	14	10	5	4	4	10	R	R	6-5	225	10-5-72	1993	Omaha, Neb.

GREENSBORO A
SOUTH ATLANTIC LEAGUE

BATTING	AVG	G	AB	R	H	2B	3B	HR	RBI	BB	SO	SB	CS	B	T	HT	WT	DOB	1st Yr	Resides
Ashby, Chris	.274	88	288	45	79	23	1	9	45	61	68	3	3	R	R	6-3	185	12-15-74	1993	Boca Raton, Fla.
Beeney, Ryan	.278	57	227	32	63	6	0	0	21	29	48	9	8	R	R	6-3	200	8-22-72	1994	Newark, Ohio
Brown, Vick	.227	118	432	66	98	10	1	2	36	44	93	24	9	R	R	6-1	165	11-14-72	1993	Cypress, Fla.
Buchanan, Brian	.302	23	96	19	29	3	0	3	12	9	17	7	1	R	R	6-4	220	7-21-73	1994	Clifton, Va.
Delafield, Wil	.208	107	384	37	80	14	0	4	29	16	107	3	7	R	R	6-2	185	2-15-72	1992	Baton Rouge, La.
DeBerry, Joe	.400	12	45	14	18	3	0	5	11	9	6	0	0	L	L	6-2	195	6-30-70	1991	Colorado Springs, Colo.
Donato, Dan	.318	108	387	55	123	30	1	7	69	37	46	7	6	L	R	6-1	205	11-15-72	1995	Dedham, Mass.
Dukart, Derek	.256	86	305	35	78	21	2	6	40	28	59	2	3	L	R	6-4	205	8-17-71	1994	Lincoln, Neb.
Fithian, Grant	.225	51	151	16	34	8	1	2	12	19	45	5	4	R	R	6-0	192	11-20-71	1994	Rockwall, Texas
Giardi, Mike	.168	46	101	10	17	4	0	1	5	15	17	3	4	R	R	6-2	205	7-14-72	1994	Salem, Mass.
Gipner, Marcus	.150	7	20	0	3	1	0	0	2	1	6	0	0	S	R	6-3	190	9-1-73	1991	Safety Harbor, Fla.
Ledee, Ricky	.269	89	335	65	90	16	6	14	49	51	66	10	4	L	L	6-2	160	11-22-73	1990	Salinas, P.R.
Lobaton, Jose	.243	60	185	26	45	6	5	0	23	22	58	11	6	R	R	5-11	154	3-29-74	1992	Acarigua, Venez.
McLamb, Brian	.226	81	252	34	57	11	0	6	32	25	61	11	4	S	R	6-3	185	12-13-72	1993	Jacksonville, Fla.
Shumpert, Derek	.216	56	153	21	33	3	1	0	14	18	41	4	2	S	R	6-2	185	9-30-75	1993	St. Louis, Mo.
Smith, Rod	.243	62	235	31	57	5	6	0	9	34	41	17	12	S	R	6-0	185	9-2-75	1994	Lexington, Ky.
Torborg, Dale	.198	33	81	10	16	4	0	1	11	7	28	1	0	R	R	6-5	205	10-24-71	1994	Mountainside, N.J.
Trimble, Rob	.133	33	83	5	11	2	0	0	5	4	22	0	1	R	R	6-1	200	6-2-72	1993	Carthage, Texas
Troilo, Jason	.288	19	59	6	17	4	0	3	9	3	19	0	1	R	R	6-1	195	9-7-72	1994	Avondale, Pa.
Twitty, Sean	.283	80	293	49	83	25	1	10	58	29	83	6	2	R	R	6-3	190	10-23-70	1989	Astoria, N.Y.
Wuerch, Carlos	.188	31	85	4	16	2	0	0	8	11	20	2	2	L	R	6-2	200	7-14-71	1991	Leamington, Ontario
Yedo, Carlos	.246	117	435	65	107	22	1	13	57	53	126	2	1	L	L	6-4	210	2-24-74	1994	Miami, Fla.

GAMES BY POSITION: C—Ashby 62, Donato 1, Fithian 51, Trimble 24, Troilo 16. **1B**—DeBerry 12, Donato 6, Giardi 1, Gipner 1, Torborg 14, Wuerch 5, Yedo 111. **2B**—Brown 117, Giardi 12, McLamb 21, Smith 1. **3B**—Donato 54, Dukart 73, Giardi 5, McLamb 13, Wuerch 3. **SS**—Beeney 56, Brown 1, Dukart 1, Giardi 2, Lobaton 58, McLamb 27. **OF**—Buchanan 23, Delafield 105, Donato 8, Giardi 11, Ledee 87, McLamb 8, Shumpert 51, Smith 62, Twitty 66, Wuerch 14.

PITCHING	W	L	ERA	G	GS	CG	SV	IP	H	R	ER	BB	SO	B	T	HT	WT	DOB	1st Yr	Resides
Alazaus, Shawn	3	1	5.54	33	0	0	1	39	43	25	24	18	40	L	L	6-4	195	3-20-72	1993	Carrollton, Ohio
Benson, Jeremy	0	0	0.00	3	0	0	0	4	1	0	0	2	4	L	L	6-3	210	9-11-72	1994	Baltimore, Md.
Beverlin, Jason	2	4	2.65	7	7	1	0	51	49	15	15	6	31	L	R	6-5	230	11-27-73	1994	Royal Oak, Mich.
Binversie, Brian	0	4	4.96	31	0	0	0	45	53	30	25	18	32	R	R	6-3	201	11-11-72	1994	Howards Grove, Wis.
Brown, Charlie	4	4	4.42	45	2	0	4	57	57	31	28	23	69	R	R	6-3	178	9-13-73	1992	Fort Pierce, Fla.
Corn, Chris	8	7	1.76	49	0	0	24	82	54	20	16	22	101	R	R	6-2	170	10-4-71	1994	Louisville, Ky.
Cubillan, Darwin	5	5	3.62	22	14	1	0	97	86	50	39	38	78	R	R	6-1	190	11-16-74	1994	Maracay, Venez.
Ford, Ben	0	0	5.14	7	0	0	0	7	4	4	4	5	8	R	R	6-7	200	8-15-75	1994	Cedar Rapids, Iowa
Jarvis, Jason	8	7	3.01	22	16	0	0	111	103	47	37	38	82	R	R	6-1	170	10-27-73	1994	West Bountiful, Utah
Judd, Mike	0	0	0.00	1	0	0	0	3	2	0	0	1	4	R	R	6-2	200	6-30-75	1995	La Mesa, Calif.
Medina, Rafael	4	4	4.01	19	19	1	0	99	86	48	44	38	108	R	R	6-3	194	2-15-75	1993	Panama City, Panama
Meyer, David	8	4	4.86	14	14	1	0	87	104	52	47	28	54	L	L	6-5	215	12-15-71	1994	Grapevine, Texas
Mittauer, Casey	3	6	1.94	49	0	0	8	74	60	26	16	14	59	R	R	6-5	225	9-1-72	1993	Cooper City, Fla.
Parotte, Frisco	3	1	2.80	22	0	0	0	35	40	20	11	16	35	R	R	6-3	180	9-10-75	1994	Levittown, P.R.
Ricken, Ray	3	2	2.23	10	10	0	0	65	42	20	16	16	77	R	R	6-5	225	8-11-73	1994	Warren, Mich.
Robinson, Martin	1	0	7.56	2	1	0	0	8	8	7	7	12	5	L	L	6-1	180	9-13-76	1994	Cape Coral, Fla.
Rojano, Rafael	0	0	6.58	19	1	0	1	26	35	24	19	13	38	R	R	6-3	164	1-14-71	1995	Cartegena, Colombia
Schaffner, Eric	0	1	5.06	1	1	0	0	5	5	8	3	5	0	R	R	6-4	190	10-19-74	1994	Keizer, Ore.
Schlomann, Brett	10	7	3.90	25	25	1	0	148	144	76	64	54	140	R	R	6-1	185	7-31-74	1994	Collinsville, Okla.
Shelby, Anthony	3	8	4.01	27	13	0	0	90	87	54	40	28	81	L	L	6-3	200	12-11-73	1993	Sarasota, Fla.
Shoemaker, Steve	4	4	3.11	17	17	0	0	81	62	33	28	52	82	L	R	6-1	195	2-3-73	1994	Phoenixville, Pa.

ONEONTA A
NEW YORK-PENN LEAGUE

BATTING	AVG	G	AB	R	H	2B	3B	HR	RBI	BB	SO	SB	CS	B	T	HT	WT	DOB	1st Yr	Resides
Antrim, Patrick	.192	26	78	6	15	1	0	0	5	1	23	3	1	S	R	6-2	170	8-18-73	1995	Mission Viejo, Calif.
Camfield, Eric	.270	73	296	46	80	11	3	1	42	22	41	17	7	L	L	6-2	185	1-7-73	1995	Fairborn, Ohio
Dennis, Les	.264	48	148	24	39	6	1	1	13	14	40	5	2	R	R	6-0	175	6-3-73	1995	West Linn, Ore.
Emmons, Scott	.198	67	242	25	48	15	3	2	32	25	62	1	1	R	R	6-4	205	12-25-73	1995	Norco, Calif.
Gipner, Marcus	.099	25	81	6	8	1	0	0	0	15	20	1	1	S	R	6-3	190	9-1-73	1991	Safety Harbor, Fla.
Imrisek, Jason	.077	6	13	1	1	0	0	0	1	1	2	0	0	R	R	5-11	185	6-10-74	1995	Orland Park, Ill.
Lobaton, Jose	.221	41	145	23	32	11	3	1	11	13	30	4	1	R	R	5-11	154	3-29-74	1992	Acarigua, Venez.
Lowell, Mike	.260	72	281	36	73	18	0	1	27	23	34	3	1	R	R	6-4	195	2-24-74	1995	Coral Gables, Fla.
McCormick, Cody	.276	74	268	33	74	16	2	6	32	30	60	4	2	R	R	6-3	200	7-30-74	1995	Berkeley, Calif.
Morenz, Shea	.276	33	116	11	32	5	3	1	20	15	27	1	4	L	R	6-2	205	1-22-74	1995	San Angelo, Texas
Nelson, Trey	.146	16	48	5	7	3	0	0	8	4	21	0	0	R	R	6-3	210	10-15-74	1992	Covina, Calif.
Palmer, Jim	.070	15	43	4	3	0	0	0	4	7	16	0	0	R	R	6-3	195	9-11-74	1993	Coral Springs, Fla.
Samuel, Cody	.274	37	124	15	34	7	1	4	17	10	42	2	0	R	R	6-1	210	4-10-74	1992	Redondo Beach, Calif.
Shumpert, Derek	.209	62	196	25	41	7	3	0	11	29	58	13	3	S	R	6-2	185	9-30-75	1993	St. Louis, Mo.
Smith, Rod	.235	49	187	34	44	8	3	0	10	30	49	24	7	S	R	6-0	185	9-2-75	1994	Lexington, Ky.
Wilcox, Luke	.327	59	223	25	73	16	7	1	28	20	28	9	3	L	R	6-4	190	11-15-73	1995	St. Johns, Mich.

GAMES BY POSITION: C—Emmons 37, Imrisek 1, McCormick 38. **1B**—Emmons 13, Gipner 23, Palmer 7, Samuel 37. **2B**—Antrim 1, Dennis 31, Smith 49. **3B**—Lowell 72, Palmer 3. **SS**—Antrim 23, Dennis 17, Lobaton 41. **OF**—Camfield 67, Morenz 31, Nelson 13, Shumpert 60, Wilcox 59.

PITCHING	W	L	ERA	G	GS	CG	SV	IP	H	R	ER	BB	SO	B	T	HT	WT	DOB	1st Yr	Resides
Barnes, Monte	0	0	3.86	3	0	0	0	5	5	2	2	3	4	L	L	6-6	255	5-14-74	1994	Wilton Manors, Fla.
Becker, Tom	6	6	5.33	15	15	0	0	78	83	55	46	40	65	R	R	6-3	205	1-13-75	1994	Adelaide, Australia
Berry, Jason	2	0	0.00	8	0	0	0	13	9	1	0	4	19	R	R	6-4	220	4-2-74	1993	Brockton, Mass.
Boardman, Eric	3	4	3.82	11	6	0	0	33	30	24	14	21	23	R	R	6-3	215	10-14-75	1995	Norwalk, Calif.
Brandt, Dale	1	2	3.73	23	0	0	0	31	36	21	13	15	24	L	L	6-1	190	1-11-74	1994	Vero Beach, Fla.
Einertson, Darrel	0	4	1.88	25	0	0	0	38	32	20	8	15	35	R	R	6-2	190	9-4-72	1995	Urbandale, Iowa

PITCHING	W	L	ERA	G	GS	CG	SV	IP	H	R	ER	BB	SO	B	T	HT	WT	DOB	1st Yr	Resides
Ford, Ben	5	0	0.87	29	0	0	0	52	39	23	5	16	50	R	R	6-7	200	8-15-75	1994	Cedar Rapids, Iowa
Horton, Aaron	0	2	3.22	6	3	0	0	22	19	13	8	4	12	L	L	6-5	196	10-10-74	1995	Cardington, Ohio
Lail, Jerry	5	6	3.97	13	13	0	0	68	66	38	30	31	59	R	R	6-0	185	9-10-74	1995	Taylorsville, N.C.
Olivier, Rich	3	3	3.88	12	12	0	0	60	63	36	26	21	50	R	R	6-0	155	11-22-74	1992	Santo Domingo, D.R.
Randolph, Steve	0	3	7.48	6	6	0	0	22	19	22	18	23	31	L	L	6-3	185	5-1-74	1995	Austin, Texas
Robbins, Jake	0	0	0.00	1	0	0	0	1	0	0	0	0	1	R	R	6-5	195	5-23-76	1994	Charlotte, N.C.
St. Pierre, Bob	5	3	2.83	15	15	0	0	89	83	39	28	24	91	R	R	6-1	190	4-11-74	1995	Huntington, Md.
Tessmer, Jay	2	0	0.95	34	0	0	20	38	27	8	4	12	52	R	R	6-3	190	12-26-72	1995	Cochranton, Pa.
Whitworth, Clint	0	2	5.93	12	1	0	0	27	31	23	18	15	15	R	R	6-7	210	9-11-71	1993	Frederick, Okla.
Wilkinson, Arrow	0	2	4.13	14	0	0	0	28	28	19	13	23	24	R	R	6-4	220	9-27-72	1995	Ardmore, Okla.
Wilson, Mike	2	4	4.20	14	4	0	0	41	41	24	19	19	41	R	R	6-3	220	3-10-73	1995	Houston, Texas

TAMPA   R
GULF COAST LEAGUE

BATTING	AVG	G	AB	R	H	2B	3B	HR	RBI	BB	SO	SB	CS	B	T	HT	WT	DOB	1st Yr	Resides
Antrim, Patrick	.250	16	52	9	13	2	1	0	4	4	13	3	0	S	R	6-2	170	8-18-73	1995	Mission Viejo, Calif.
Beaumont, Hamil	.104	18	48	6	5	0	0	1	3	5	22	1	0	R	R	6-3	200	1-3-75	1993	Panama City, Panama
Butler, Garrett	.232	48	185	40	43	4	4	0	16	16	45	11	0	S	R	6-2	165	5-20-76	1994	Miami, Fla.
De la Cruz, Wilfredo	.195	43	118	17	23	1	0	0	7	15	36	6	2	R	R	6-0	160	2-2-74	1994	Santo Domingo, D.R.
Garcia, Julio	.154	4	13	1	2	0	0	0	3	1	3	2	0	R	R	6-2	160	2-2-73	1990	Boca Chica, D.R.
Imrisek, Jason	.283	15	53	5	15	3	0	1	8	2	12	2	2	R	R	5-11	185	6-10-74	1995	Orland Park, Ill.
Jimenez, D'Angelo	.280	57	214	41	60	14	8	2	28	23	31	6	3	S	R	6-0	160	12-21-77	1995	Santo Domingo, D.R.
Keech, Erik	.225	37	120	6	27	7	0	1	19	12	18	0	1	L	R	6-2	195	9-7-74	1995	Sarasota, Fla.
Kelly, Pat	.000	1	2	2	0	0	0	0	1	1	0	0	0	R	R	6-0	180	10-14-67	1988	Bangor, Pa.
Kerr, James	.241	26	83	12	20	2	0	0	6	5	24	0	0	R	R	6-1	180	4-28-75	1994	Coral Springs, Fla.
Kofler, Eric	.246	19	69	11	17	3	2	3	13	3	8	1	1	L	L	6-1	170	2-11-76	1995	Palm Harbor, Fla.
Leon, Donny	.171	16	41	3	7	1	0	0	5	3	14	0	1	S	R	6-2	180	5-7-76	1995	Ponce, P.R.
Maas, Kevin	.444	2	9	1	4	0	0	1	3	0	0	0	0	L	L	6-3	205	1-20-65	1986	Berkeley, Calif.
McDonald, Donzell	.236	28	110	23	26	5	1	0	9	16	24	11	2	S	R	6-0	165	2-20-75	1995	Glendale, Colo.
Pinto, Rene	.184	15	49	2	9	0	1	0	4	7	11	0	0	R	R	6-0	195	7-17-77	1994	Palo Negra, Venez.
Rosado, Luis	.256	52	168	25	43	7	0	2	16	22	31	2	1	R	R	6-2	183	10-4-75	1994	San Pedro de Macoris, D.R.
Saffer, Jeffrey	.293	50	184	30	54	10	1	4	33	17	55	0	2	R	R	6-4	220	6-30-75	1995	Tucson, Ariz.
Strawberry, Darryl	.250	7	20	3	5	2	0	0	4	9	5	2	0	L	L	6-6	215	3-12-62	1980	Glendale, Calif.
Valencia, Victor	.241	25	58	5	14	1	0	1	8	6	22	0	0	R	R	6-2	185	5-30-77	1995	Maracay, Venez.
Velazquez, Jose	.287	58	209	33	60	9	2	3	34	30	20	3	4	L	R	6-3	205	8-24-75	1994	Guayama, P.R.
Zambrano, Victor	.205	27	78	10	16	3	1	0	5	5	15	2	3	S	R	6-1	170	8-6-74	1994	Losteques, Venez.

GAMES BY POSITION: C—Imrisek 14, Keech 18, Leon 3, Pinto 10, Valencia 25. **1B**—Velazquez 58. **2B**—Antrim 13, Garcia 4, Kelly 1, Kerr 20, Zambrano 23. **3B**—Leon 10, Rosado 51. **SS**—Antrim 1, Jimenez 56, Zambrano 3. **OF**—Beaumont 10, Butler 48, De la Cruz 34, Kofler 18, Maas 2, McDonald 28, Saffer 40, Strawberry 4.

PITCHING	W	L	ERA	G	GS	CG	SV	IP	H	R	ER	BB	SO	B	T	HT	WT	DOB	1st Yr	Resides
Aguilar, Carlo	6	0	2.08	18	0	0	1	39	36	11	9	13	34	R	R	6-1	165	11-7-75	1993	Carabobo, Venez.
Armas, Antonio	0	1	0.64	5	4	0	0	14	12	9	1	6	13	R	R	6-4	175	4-29-78	1994	Puerto Piritu, Venez.
Brand, Scott	0	0	0.90	4	0	0	0	10	5	1	1	3	8	R	R	6-3	200	1-1-76	1995	Lubbock, Texas
Cumberland, Chris	0	1	1.29	4	4	0	0	7	3	1	1	1	7	R	L	6-1	185	1-15-73	1993	Safety Harbor, Fla.
De los Santos, Luis	0	0	0.00	2	0	0	0	5	5	2	0	2	6	R	R	6-2	187	11-1-77	1995	San Pedro de Macoris, D.R.
Horton, Aaron	2	1	1.57	8	6	0	0	23	17	7	4	6	21	L	L	6-5	196	10-10-74	1995	Cardington, Ohio
Judd, Mike	1	1	1.11	21	0	0	8	32	18	5	4	6	30	R	R	6-2	200	6-30-75	1995	La Mesa, Calif.
Mejia, Felix	2	0	3.45	9	0	0	0	16	11	6	6	13	21	R	R	6-1	210	3-12-76	1994	Hialeah, Fla.
Mota, Daniel	2	3	2.20	14	0	0	0	33	27	9	8	4	35	R	R	6-0	170	10-9-75	1994	Santo Domingo, D.R.
Parotte, Frisco	0	0	2.79	9	0	0	1	10	9	3	3	6	8	R	R	6-3	180	9-10-75	1994	Levittown, P.R.
Randolph, Steve	4	0	2.22	8	3	0	0	24	11	7	6	16	34	L	L	6-3	185	5-1-74	1995	Austin, Texas
Rangel, Julio	1	3	4.40	14	0	0	2	29	20	18	14	16	30	R	R	6-3	190	9-28-75	1994	Panama City, Panama
Robbins, Jake	2	5	5.54	14	0	0	0	37	32	26	23	18	17	R	R	6-5	195	5-23-76	1994	Charlotte, N.C.
Robinson, Martin	6	1	2.48	11	8	2	0	62	54	20	17	13	56	L	L	6-1	180	9-13-76	1994	Cape Coral, Fla.
Schaffner, Eric	2	2	1.65	11	7	0	0	44	31	17	8	16	48	R	R	6-4	190	10-19-74	1994	Keizer, Ore.
Taylor, Brien	2	5	6.08	11	11	0	0	40	29	37	27	54	38	L	L	6-4	215	12-26-71	1991	Beaufort, N.C.
Trimble, Rob	0	0	0.57	11	0	0	1	16	12	2	1	4	14	L	R	6-1	200	6-2-72	1993	Carthage, Texas
Verdin, Cesar	2	2	3.46	11	5	0	0	26	26	15	10	10	35	L	L	6-3	210	11-11-76	1995	San Diego, Calif.
Williams, Brad	0	3	5.32	11	7	0	0	24	14	19	14	34	28	L	L	6-5	205	11-26-76	1995	Tucson, Ariz.

NEW YORK METS

Manager: Dallas Green. **1995 Record:** 69-75, .479 (T-2nd, NL East).

BATTING	AVG	G	AB	R	H	2B	3B	HR	RBI	BB	SO	SB	CS	B	T	HT	WT	DOB	1st Yr	Resides
Alfonzo, Edgardo.........	.278	101	335	26	93	13	5	4	41	12	37	1	1	R	R	5-11	185	8-11-73	1991	Caracas, Venez.
Barry, Jeff...................	.133	15	15	2	2	1	0	0	0	1	8	0	0	S	R	6-0	200	9-22-68	1990	San Diego, Calif.
Bogar, Tim..................	.290	78	145	17	42	7	0	1	21	9	25	1	0	R	R	6-2	198	10-28-66	1987	Kankakee, Ill.
Bonilla, Bobby.............	.325	80	317	49	103	25	4	18	53	31	48	0	3	S	R	6-3	240	2-23-63	1981	Bradenton, Fla.
Brogna, Rico...............	.289	134	495	72	143	27	2	22	76	39	111	0	0	L	L	6-2	200	4-18-70	1988	Watertown, Conn.
Buford, Damon.............	.235	44	136	24	32	5	0	4	12	19	28	7	7	R	R	5-10	170	6-12-70	1990	Sherman Oaks, Calif.
Butler, Brett...............	.311	90	367	54	114	13	7	1	25	43	42	21	7	L	L	5-10	160	6-15-57	1979	Atlanta, Ga.
Castillo, Alberto..........	.103	13	29	2	3	0	0	0	0	3	9	1	0	R	R	6-0	184	2-10-70	1987	Las Matas de Farfan, D.R.
Everett, Carl...............	.260	79	289	48	75	13	1	12	54	39	67	2	5	S	R	6-0	190	6-3-71	1990	Tampa, Fla.
Fordyce, Brook............	.500	4	2	1	1	1	0	0	0	1	0	0	0	R	R	6-1	185	5-7-70	1989	Old Lyme, Conn.
Hundley, Todd.............	.280	90	275	39	77	11	0	15	51	42	64	1	0	S	R	5-11	185	5-27-69	1987	Port St. Lucie, Fla.
Huskey, Butch.............	.189	28	90	8	17	1	0	3	11	10	16	1	0	R	R	6-3	240	11-10-71	1989	Lawton, Okla.
Jones, Chris...............	.280	79	182	33	51	6	2	8	31	13	45	2	1	R	R	6-2	205	11-16-65	1984	Cedar Rapids, Iowa
Kent, Jeff..................	.278	125	472	65	131	22	3	20	65	29	89	3	3	R	R	6-1	185	3-7-68	1989	Huntington Beach, Calif.
Ledesma, Aaron...........	.242	21	33	4	8	0	0	0	3	6	7	0	0	R	R	6-2	200	6-3-71	1990	Union City, Calif.
Ochoa, Alex................	.297	11	37	7	11	1	0	0	2	0	10	1	0	R	R	6-0	185	3-29-72	1991	Miami Lakes, Fla.
Orsulak, Joe...............	.283	108	290	41	82	19	2	1	37	19	35	1	3	L	L	6-1	203	5-31-62	1981	Cockeysville, Md.
Otero, Ricky...............	.137	35	51	5	7	2	0	0	1	3	10	2	1	S	R	5-7	150	4-15-72	1991	Vega Baja, P.R.
Segui, David...............	.329	33	73	9	24	3	1	2	11	12	9	1	3	S	L	6-1	202	7-19-66	1988	Kansas City, Kan.
Spiers, Bill................	.208	63	72	5	15	2	1	0	11	12	15	0	1	L	R	6-2	190	6-5-66	1987	Elloree, S.C.
Stinnett, Kelly............	.219	77	196	23	43	8	1	4	18	29	65	2	0	R	R	5-11	195	2-14-70	1990	Lawton, Okla.
Thompson, Ryan...........	.251	75	267	39	67	13	0	7	31	19	77	3	1	R	R	6-3	200	11-4-67	1987	Edesville, Md.
Vizcaino, Jose.............	.287	135	509	66	146	21	5	3	56	35	76	8	3	S	R	6-1	180	3-26-68	1987	El Cajon, Calif.

PITCHING	W	L	ERA	G	GS	CG	SV	IP	H	R	ER	BB	SO	B	T	HT	WT	DOB	1st Yr	Resides
Birkbeck, Mike.............	0	1	1.63	4	4	0	0	28	22	5	5	2	14	R	R	6-2	185	3-10-61	1983	Canton, Ohio
Byrd, Paul..................	2	0	2.05	17	0	0	0	22	18	6	5	7	26	R	R	6-1	185	12-3-70	1991	Louisville, Ky.
Cornelius, Reid............	3	7	5.15	10	10	0	0	58	64	36	33	25	35	R	R	6-0	190	6-2-70	1989	Thomasville, Ala.
2-team (8 Montreal)...	3	7	5.54	18	10	0	0	67	75	44	41	30	39							
DiPoto, Jerry..............	4	6	3.78	58	0	0	2	79	77	41	33	29	49	R	R	6-2	200	5-24-68	1989	North Olmstead, Ohio
Florence, Don.............	3	0	1.50	14	0	0	0	12	17	3	2	6	5	R	L	6-0	195	3-16-67	1988	New Boston, N.H.
Franco, John...............	5	3	2.44	48	0	0	29	52	48	17	14	17	41	L	L	5-10	185	9-17-60	1981	Brooklyn, N.Y.
Gunderson, Eric...........	1	1	3.70	30	0	0	0	24	25	10	10	8	19	R	L	6-0	195	3-29-66	1987	Portland, Ore.
Harnisch, Pete............	2	8	3.68	18	18	0	0	110	111	55	45	24	82	R	R	6-4	205	12-10-63	1986	Hartland, Wisc.
Henry, Doug...............	3	6	2.96	51	0	0	4	67	48	23	22	25	62	R	R	6-4	205	12-10-63	1986	Hartland, Wisc.
Isringhausen, Jason......	9	2	2.81	14	14	1	0	93	88	29	29	31	55	R	R	6-3	196	9-7-72	1992	Brighton, Ill.
Jacome, Jason.............	0	4	10.29	5	5	0	0	21	33	24	24	15	11	L	L	6-0	180	11-24-70	1991	Tucson, Ariz.
Jones, Bobby..............	10	10	4.19	30	30	3	0	196	209	107	91	53	127	R	R	6-4	205	2-10-70	1991	Kerman, Calif.
Lomon, Kevin...............	0	1	6.75	6	0	0	0	9	17	8	7	5	6	R	R	6-1	185	11-20-71	1991	Cameron, Okla.
Manzanillo, Josias........	1	2	7.88	12	0	0	0	16	18	15	14	6	14	R	R	6-0	190	10-16-67	1983	Hyde Park, Mass.
Minor, Blas................	4	2	3.66	35	0	0	1	47	44	21	19	13	43	R	R	6-3	200	3-20-66	1988	Gilbert, Ariz.
Mlicki, Dave...............	9	7	4.26	29	25	0	0	161	160	82	76	54	123	R	R	6-4	190	6-8-68	1990	Galloway, Ohio
Person, Robert............	1	0	0.75	3	1	0	0	12	5	1	1	2	10	R	R	5-11	180	1-8-69	1989	St. Louis, Mo.
Pulsipher, Bill.............	5	7	3.98	17	17	2	0	127	122	58	56	45	81	L	L	6-3	200	10-9-73	1991	Clifton, Va.
Remlinger, Mike...........	0	1	6.35	5	0	0	0	6	7	5	4	2	6	L	L	6-0	195	3-23-66	1987	Plymouth, Mass.
Saberhagen, Bret.........	5	5	3.35	16	16	3	0	110	105	45	41	20	71	R	R	6-1	200	4-11-64	1983	Babylon, N.Y.
Telgheder, Dave..........	1	2	5.61	7	4	0	0	26	34	18	16	7	16	R	R	6-3	212	11-11-66	1989	Slate Hill, N.Y.
Walker, Pete...............	1	0	4.58	13	0	0	0	18	24	9	9	5	5	R	R	6-2	184	4-8-69	1990	East Lyme, Conn.

FIELDING

Catcher	PCT	G	PO	A	E	DP	PB
Castillo	.974	12	66	9	2	0	2
Hundley	.987	89	488	29	7	8	6
Stinnett	.983	67	380	22	7	1	6

First Base	PCT	G	PO	A	E	DP
Bogar............	1.000	10	47	5	0	6
Bonilla...........	1.000	10	85	3	0	5
Brogna...........	.998	131	1112	93	3	95
Jones............	1.000	5	43	3	0	3
Ledesma........	1.000	2	3	0	0	0
Orsulak.........	1.000	1	3	1	0	0
Segui............	1.000	7	41	3	0	4

Second Base	PCT	G	PO	A	E	DP
Alfonzo..........	.989	29	36	51	1	7
Bogar............	.929	7	6	20	2	6
Kent..............	.984	122	245	353	10	69
Spiers...........	1.000	6	4	12	0	1
Vizcaino.........	1.000	1	0	1	0	0

Third Base	PCT	G	PO	A	E	DP
Alfonzo..........	.962	58	40	111	6	9
Bogar............	.950	25	9	29	2	4
Bonilla..........	.882	46	24	73	13	8

	PCT	G	PO	A	E	DP
Huskey	.925	27	14	60	6	2
Ledesma	.875	10	2	12	2	0
Spiers	.794	11	9	18	7	2

Shortstop	PCT	G	PO	A	E	DP
Alfonzo	1.000	6	5	9	0	3
Bogar............	.971	27	20	46	2	5
Ledesma........	.000	2	0	0	0	0
Vizcaino.........	.984	134	189	411	10	80

Outfield	PCT	G	PO	A	E	DP
Barry..............	1.000	2	2	0	0	0
Bogar.............	.000	1	0	0	0	0
Bonilla...........	.983	31	55	4	1	0
Buford...........	.972	39	67	2	2	0
Butler............	.995	90	207	6	1	1
Everett..........	.981	77	147	9	3	3
Huskey	1.000	1	2	0	0	0
Jones............	.976	52	79	3	2	1
Ochoa............	1.000	10	20	1	0	0
Orsulak..........	.965	86	108	3	4	0
Otero	1.000	23	31	1	0	0
Segui............	1.000	18	15	2	0	0
Thompson........	.985	74	193	4	3	2

John Franco

First baseman Rico Brogna led the Mets with 22 homers and 76 RBIs.

MORRIS FOSTOFF

Mets minor league Player of the Year Jason Isringhausen

TOM DiPACE

FARM SYSTEM

Director of Minor League Operations: Steve Phillips.

Class	Farm Team	League	W	L	Pct.	Finish*	Manager	First Yr
AAA	Norfolk (Va.) Tides	International	86	56	.606	1st (10)	Toby Harrah	1969
AA	Binghamton (N.Y.) Mets	Eastern	67	75	.472	T-7th (10)	John Tamargo	1992
#A	St. Lucie (Fla.) Mets	Florida State	61	73	.455	11th (14)	Rafael Landestoy	1988
A	Columbia (S.C.) Bombers	South Atlantic	72	68	.514	8th (14)	Howie Freiling	1983
A	Pittsfield (Mass.) Mets	New York-Penn	34	42	.447	12th (14)	Ron Gideon	1989
#R	Kingsport (Tenn.) Mets	Appalachian	48	18	.727	2nd+ (10)	John Gibbons	1980
R	St. Lucie (Fla.) Mets	Gulf Coast	38	19	.667	2nd (16)	John Stephenson	1988

*Finish in overall standings (No. of teams in league)   #Advanced level   +Won league championship

ORGANIZATION LEADERS

MAJOR LEAGUERS

BATTING

*AVG	Bobby Bonilla	.325
R	Rico Brogna	72
H	Jose Vizcaino	146
TB	Rico Brogna	240
2B	Rico Brogna	27
3B	Two tied at	5
HR	Rico Brogna	22
RBI	Rico Brogna	76
BB	Todd Hundley	42
SO	Rico Brogna	111
SB	Brett Butler	21

PITCHING

W	Bobby Jones	10
L	Bobby Jones	10
#ERA	Jason Isringhausen	2.81
G	Jerry DiPoto	58
CG	Bobby Jones	3
SV	John Franco	29
IP	Bobby Jones	196
BB	Dave Mlicki	54
SO	Bobby Jones	127

THE SPORTS GROUP

Bobby Jones. 10 wins

MINOR LEAGUERS

BATTING

*AVG	Omar Garcia, Binghamton/Norfolk	.318
R	Jay Payton, Binghamton/Norfolk	92
H	Jay Payton, Binghamton/Norfolk	170
TB	Jay Payton, Binghamton/Norfolk	269
2B	Jason Hardtke, Binghamton/Norfolk	43
3B	Jeramie Simpson, Kingsport	10
HR	Butch Huskey, Norfolk	28
RBI	Butch Huskey, Norfolk	87
BB	Jason Hardtke, Binghamton/Norfolk	68
SO	Bryon Gainey, Columbia	157
SB	Julio Zorilla, Columbia	42

PITCHING

W	Eric Ludwick, Binghamton/Norfolk	13
L	Two tied at	13
#ERA	Jason Isringhausen, Bing./Norfolk	1.97
G	Jim McCready, Binghamton/Norfolk	60
CG	Paul Wilson, Binghamton/Norfolk	8
SV	Mike Welch, St. Lucie/Binghamton	15
IP	Mark Guerra, St. Lucie/Binghamton	193
BB	Eric Hiljus, St. Lucie/Binghamton	82
SO	Paul Wilson, Binghamton/Norfolk	194

*Minimum 250 At-Bats   #Minimum 75 Innings

TOP 10 PROSPECTS

How the Mets Top 10 prospects, as judged by Baseball America prior to the 1995 season, fared in 1995:

Player, Pos.	Club (Class—League)	AVG	AB	R	H	2B	3B	HR	RBI	SB
3. Rey Ordonez, ss	Norfolk (AAA—International)	.214	439	49	94	21	4	2	50	11
4. Edgardo Alfonzo, 3b-2b	New York	.278	335	26	93	13	5	4	41	1
6. Carl Everett, of	Norfolk (AAA—International)	.300	260	52	78	16	4	6	35	12
	New York	.260	289	48	75	13	1	12	54	2
7. Jay Payton, of	Binghamton (AA—Eastern)	.345	357	59	123	20	3	14	54	16
	Norfolk (AAA—International)	.240	196	33	47	11	4	4	30	11
8. Terrance Long, of	Pittsfield (A—New York-Penn)	.257	187	24	48	9	4	4	31	11
	Columbia (A—South Atlantic)	.197	178	27	35	1	2	2	13	8
10. Preston Wilson, 3b	Columbia (A—South Atlantic)	.269	442	70	119	26	5	20	61	20

Player, Pos.	Club (Class—League)	W	L	ERA	G	SV	IP	H	BB	SO
1. Bill Pulsipher, lhp	Norfolk (AAA—International)	6	4	3.14	13	0	92	84	33	63
	New York	5	7	3.98	17	0	127	122	45	81
2. Paul Wilson, rhp	Binghamton (AA—Eastern)	6	3	2.17	16	0	120	89	24	127
	Norfolk (AAA—International)	5	3	2.85	10	0	66	59	20	67
5. Jason Isringhausen, rhp	Binghamton (AA—Eastern)	2	1	2.85	6	0	41	26	12	59
	Norfolk (AAA—International)	9	1	1.55	12	0	87	64	24	75
	New York	9	2	2.81	14	0	93	88	31	55
9. Kirk Presley, rhp	Columbia (A—South Atlantic)	1	2	5.14	4	0	21	30	13	8

BILL SETLIFF

Bill Pulsipher

INTERNATIONAL LEAGUE

BATTING	AVG	G	AB	R	H	2B	3B	HR	RBI	BB	SO	SB	CS	B	T	HT	WT	DOB	1st Yr	Resides
Abner, Shawn	.258	11	31	3	8	0	0	0	1	1	7	0	0	R	R	6-1	194	6-17-66	1984	San Diego, Calif.
Alicea, Ed	.245	122	436	63	107	17	4	3	39	45	78	21	13	S	R	5-10	175	3-9-67	1988	Guaynabo, P.R.
Azuaje, Jesus	.429	5	14	1	6	1	0	0	0	2	2	1	1	R	R	5-10	170	1-16-73	1992	Bolivar, Venezuela
Barry, Jeff	.220	12	41	3	9	2	0	0	6	3	6	0	0	S	R	6-0	200	9-22-68	1990	San Diego, Calif.
Boka, Ben	.143	19	21	0	3	0	0	0	1	0	8	0	0	R	R	6-4	215	1-9-73	1991	Downington, Pa.
Brown, Jarvis	.284	45	148	29	42	12	3	0	17	18	29	6	3	R	R	5-7	170	3-26-67	1986	Mt. Zion, Ill.
Castillo, Alberto	.267	69	217	23	58	13	1	4	31	26	32	2	3	R	R	6-0	184	2-10-70	1987	Las Matas de Farfan, D.R.
Daubach, Brian	.000	2	7	0	0	0	0	0	0	2	0	0	0	L	R	6-1	201	2-11-72	1990	Belleville, Ill.
Davis, Jay	.192	10	26	1	5	1	1	0	3	0	2	0	1	L	L	5-11	172	10-3-70	1989	Chicago, Ill.
Diaz, Cesar	.182	3	11	2	2	0	0	0	0	0	2	0	0	R	R	6-3	185	7-12-74	1990	Maracay, Venez.
Everett, Carl	.300	67	260	52	78	16	4	6	35	20	47	12	6	S	R	6-0	190	6-3-71	1990	Tampa, Fla.
Garcia, Omar	.309	115	430	55	133	21	7	3	64	21	58	3	4	R	R	6-0	192	11-16-71	1989	Carolina, P.R.
Graham, Greg	.197	47	122	14	24	5	0	0	9	15	23	1	2	S	R	6-0	181	1-30-69	1990	Bowling Green, Ky.
Greene, Charlie	.193	27	88	6	17	3	0	0	4	3	28	0	1	R	R	6-1	177	1-23-71	1991	Miami, Fla.
Hardtke, Jason	.286	4	7	1	2	1	0	0	0	2	0	1	1	S	R	5-10	175	9-15-71	1990	San Jose, Calif.
Huskey, Butch	.284	109	394	66	112	18	1	28	87	39	88	8	6	R	R	6-3	240	11-10-71	1989	Lawton, Okla.
Jacobs, Frank	.240	8	25	2	6	1	0	1	6	0	4	0	0	L	L	6-4	250	5-22-68	1991	Highland Heights, Ky.
Jones, Chris	.333	33	114	20	38	12	1	3	19	11	20	5	2	R	R	6-2	205	11-16-65	1984	Cedar Rapids, Iowa
Ledesma, Aaron	.299	56	201	26	60	12	1	0	28	10	22	6	3	R	R	6-2	200	6-3-71	1990	Union City, Calif.
Lee, Derek	.254	112	351	56	89	17	0	18	60	48	62	11	6	L	R	6-1	200	7-28-66	1988	Reston, Va.
McCoy, Trey	.209	25	67	6	14	5	0	3	7	5	11	0	0	R	R	6-3	215	10-12-66	1988	Virginia Beach, Va.
Morgan, Kevin	.323	19	62	10	20	1	0	0	8	4	8	1	3	R	R	6-1	170	3-3-70	1991	Duson, La.
Ochoa, Alex	.309	34	123	17	38	6	2	2	15	14	12	7	3	R	R	6-0	185	3-29-72	1991	Miami Lakes, Fla.
2-team (91 Roch.)	.283	125	459	58	130	24	4	10	61	40	62	24	10							
Ordonez, Rey	.214	125	439	49	94	21	4	2	50	27	50	11	13	R	R	5-9	159	1-11-72	1993	Miami, Fla.
Orton, John	.288	56	170	20	49	8	0	3	20	14	45	1	3	R	R	6-1	192	12-8-65	1987	Atascadero, Calif.
2-team (17 Rich.)	.264	73	220	26	58	11	0	4	26	17	67	3	5							
Otero, Ricky	.268	72	295	37	79	8	6	1	23	27	33	16	13	S	R	5-7	150	4-15-72	1991	Vega Baja, P.R.
Payton, Jay	.240	50	196	33	47	11	4	4	30	11	22	11	3	R	R	5-10	190	11-22-72	1994	Zanesville, Ohio
Sanders, Tracy	.227	64	110	21	25	6	0	4	14	34	34	3	1	L	R	6-0	206	7-26-69	1990	Dallas, N.C.
Saunders, Chris	.232	16	56	9	13	3	1	3	7	9	15	1	1	R	R	6-1	203	7-19-70	1992	Clovis, Calif.
Spiers, Bill	.220	12	41	4	9	2	0	0	4	8	6	0	1	L	R	6-2	190	6-5-66	1987	Elloree, S.C.
Thompson, Ryan	.340	15	53	7	18	3	0	2	11	4	15	4	1	R	R	6-3	200	11-4-67	1987	Edesville, Md.
Tijerina, Tony	.000	1	0	0	0	0	0	0	0	0	0	0	0	S	R	5-11	190	12-19-69	1991	Georgetown, Texas

PITCHING	W	L	ERA	G	GS	CG	SV	IP	H	R	ER	BB	SO	B	T	HT	WT	DOB	1st Yr	Resides
Acevedo, Juan	0	0	0.00	2	0	0	0	3	0	0	0	1	2	R	R	6-2	195	5-5-70	1992	Carpentersville, Ill.
Birkbeck, Mike	5	3	2.36	9	9	0	0	53	52	20	14	13	39	R	R	6-2	185	3-10-61	1983	Canton, Ohio
Byrd, Paul	3	5	2.79	22	10	1	6	87	71	29	27	21	61	R	R	6-1	185	12-3-70	1991	Louisville, Ky.
Cornelius, Reid	7	0	0.90	10	10	1	0	70	57	10	7	19	43	R	R	6-0	190	6-2-70	1989	Thomasville, Ala.
2-team (4 Ottawa)	8	1	1.67	14	13	1	0	81	73	22	15	24	50							
Crawford, Joe	1	1	1.93	8	0	0	0	19	9	5	4	4	13	L	L	6-3	225	5-2-70	1991	Hillsboro, Ohio
Engle, Tom	0	1	12.00	1	1	0	0	3	5	4	4	3	5	R	R	6-3	215	2-14-71	1989	Lancaster, Ohio
Florence, Don	0	1	0.96	41	0	0	4	47	37	6	5	17	29	R	L	6-0	195	3-16-67	1988	New Boston, N.H.
Fuller, Mark	0	0	2.08	4	0	0	1	4	7	2	1	0	2	L	R	6-6	216	8-5-70	1992	Melbourne, Fla.
Isringhausen, Jason	9	1	1.55	12	12	3	0	87	64	17	15	24	75	R	R	6-3	196	9-7-72	1992	Brighton, Ill.
Jacome, Jason	2	4	3.92	8	8	0	0	44	40	21	19	13	31	L	L	6-0	180	11-24-70	1991	Tucson, Ariz.
Ludwick, Eric	1	1	5.85	4	3	0	0	20	22	15	13	7	9	R	R	6-5	210	12-14-71	1993	Las Vegas, Nev.
McCready, Jim	0	1	2.01	28	0	0	0	40	41	14	9	20	21	R	R	6-1	187	11-25-69	1991	Norwood, Mass.
Osuna, Al	3	1	3.00	14	4	0	0	42	39	14	14	12	31	R	L	6-3	200	8-10-65	1987	Houston, Texas
Paxton, Darrin	0	0	9.00	1	0	0	0	2	3	2	2	2	0	L	L	6-4	220	4-17-70	1991	Wichita, Kan.
Person, Robert	2	1	4.50	5	4	0	0	32	30	17	16	13	33	R	R	5-11	180	1-8-69	1989	St. Louis, Mo.
Pulsipher, Bill	6	4	3.14	13	13	4	0	92	84	36	32	33	63	L	L	6-3	200	10-9-73	1991	Clifton, Va.
Roberts, Chris	7	13	5.52	25	25	2	0	150	197	99	92	58	88	R	L	5-10	185	6-25-71	1992	Middleburg, Fla.
Rogers, Bryan	8	3	2.21	56	0	0	10	77	58	22	19	22	50	R	R	5-11	170	10-30-67	1988	Hollister, Calif.
Stidham, Phil	6	2	3.21	34	6	0	1	70	56	33	25	36	56	R	R	6-0	180	11-18-68	1991	Tulsa, Okla.
Stoddard, Bob	0	1	6.75	3	0	0	0	3	5	2	2	1	1	R	R	6-1	190	3-8-58	1978	Bellevue, Wash.
Telgheder, Dave	5	4	2.24	29	11	0	3	92	77	34	23	8	75	R	R	6-3	212	11-11-66	1989	Slate Hill, N.Y.
Walker, Pete	5	2	3.91	34	1	0	8	48	51	24	21	16	39	R	R	6-2	184	4-8-69	1990	East Lyme, Conn.
Williams, Jimmy	11	4	3.05	27	13	0	2	106	89	42	36	56	88	L	L	6-7	232	5-18-65	1984	Butler, Ala.
Wilson, Paul	5	3	2.85	10	10	4	0	66	59	25	21	20	67	R	R	6-5	235	3-28-73	1994	Orlando, Fla.

FIELDING

Catcher	PCT	G	PO	A	E	DP	PB
Boka	.970	14	28	4	1	1	4
Castillo	.987	67	469	44	7	4	1
Diaz	.938	3	13	2	1	1	0
Greene	1.000	27	157	25	0	1	0
Orton	.994	46	290	38	2	5	3
Tijerina	1.000	1	1	0	0	0	0

First Base	PCT	G	PO	A	E	DP
Barry	.984	12	117	9	2	10
Daubach	1.000	2	21	3	0	3
Garcia	.988	107	963	67	12	89
Huskey	.988	18	155	6	2	21
Jacobs	1.000	2	12	0	0	0
Ledesma	1.000	3	33	0	0	4
McCoy	.952	3	16	4	1	1
Sanders	1.000	3	14	1	0	3

Second Base	PCT	G	PO	A	E	DP
Alicea	.965	114	224	325	20	75

	PCT	G	PO	A	E	DP
Azuaje	1.000	3	10	6	0	2
Graham	.963	7	7	19	1	5
Hardtke	1.000	2	5	2	0	0
Morgan	1.000	10	25	26	0	8
Spiers	.936	8	19	25	3	7

Third Base	PCT	G	PO	A	E	DP
Alicea	.929	3	4	9	1	0
Azuaje	1.000	2	1	6	0	0
Graham	.926	23	9	41	4	7
Huskey	.943	56	28	122	9	9
Ledesma	.929	48	39	91	10	8
Saunders	.923	16	8	28	3	1
Spiers	.889	4	4	4	1	0

Shortstop	PCT	G	PO	A	E	DP
Graham	.918	12	14	31	4	5
Ledesma	1.000	1	1	3	0	0

	PCT	G	PO	A	E	DP
Morgan	.976	7	12	29	1	2
Ordonez	.967	124	188	436	21	88

Outfield	PCT	G	PO	A	E	DP
Abner	1.000	3	2	0	0	0
Brown	.960	43	71	1	3	0
Davis	1.000	8	11	0	0	0
Everett	1.000	64	133	7	0	0
Huskey	.972	41	65	4	2	0
Jones	.985	30	62	4	1	2
Lee	.959	65	86	8	4	1
McCoy	1.000	2	4	0	0	0
Ochoa	.971	33	66	1	2	0
Otero	.970	72	147	12	5	5
Payton	.982	49	106	3	2	0
Sanders	.980	27	47	1	1	0
Thompson	1.000	13	15	2	0	0

EASTERN LEAGUE

BATTING

BATTING	AVG	G	AB	R	H	2B	3B	HR	RBI	BB	SO	SB	CS	B	T	HT	WT	DOB	1st Yr	Resides
Agbayani, Benny	.275	88	295	38	81	11	2	1	26	39	51	12	3	R	R	5-11	175	12-28-71	1993	Aiea, Hawaii
Azuaje, Jesus	.198	24	86	10	17	5	0	0	8	11	25	1	1	R	R	5-10	170	1-16-73	1992	Bolivar, Venez.
Barry, Jeff	.269	80	290	49	78	17	6	11	53	31	61	4	1	S	R	6-0	200	9-22-68	1990	San Diego, Calif.
Bates, Fletcher	.000	2	8	1	0	0	0	0	0	1	6	0	0	S	R	6-1	193	3-24-74	1994	Wilmington, N.C.
Benbow, Lou	1.000	3	1	0	1	0	0	0	0	1	0	0	0	R	R	6-0	167	1-12-71	1991	Laguna Hills, Calif.
Cradle, Cobi	.000	2	2	0	0	0	0	0	0	0	0	0	0	L	L	5-11	165	7-7-71	1993	Cerritos, Calif.
Daly, Bob	.000	1	4	1	0	0	0	0	0	1	1	0	0	R	R	6-1	205	10-8-72	1992	Downers Grove, Ill.
Daubach, Brian	.245	135	469	61	115	25	2	10	72	51	104	6	2	L	R	6-1	201	2-11-72	1990	Belleville, Ill.
Davis, Jay	.255	116	443	64	113	17	6	3	50	26	68	11	5	L	L	5-11	172	10-3-70	1989	Chicago, Ill.
Diaz, Cesar	.170	13	47	5	8	2	0	0	5	6	20	0	1	R	R	6-3	185	7-12-74	1990	Maracay, Venezuela
Epperson, Chad	.059	7	17	0	1	0	1	0	0	1	8	1	0	S	R	6-3	221	3-26-72	1992	Fort Myers, Fla.
Fully, Ed	.194	18	36	4	7	1	0	1	3	0	5	0	2	R	R	5-11	191	7-14-71	1989	Port St. Lucie, Fla.
Garcia, Omar	.526	5	19	4	10	1	1	0	1	4	0	0	0	R	R	6-0	192	11-16-71	1989	Carolina, P.R.
Greene, Charlie	.237	100	346	26	82	13	0	2	34	15	47	2	1	R	R	6-1	177	1-23-71	1991	Miami, Fla.
Hardtke, Jason	.286	121	455	65	130	42	4	4	52	66	58	6	8	S	R	5-10	175	9-15-71	1990	San Jose, Calif.
Jacobs, Frank	.294	23	68	12	20	3	0	4	9	10	15	0	0	L	L	6-4	250	5-22-68	1991	Highland Heights, Ky.
Keister, Tripp	.219	66	146	23	32	7	1	1	10	29	26	3	4	L	L	5-9	172	9-27-70	1992	Newark, Del.
Mahalik, John	.225	67	187	19	42	6	1	5	19	19	34	1	1	R	R	6-2	190	7-28-71	1993	Irving, Texas
Miller, Ryan	.053	9	19	3	1	0	0	0	0	2	4	1	0	R	R	6-0	175	10-22-72	1994	Tulare, Calif.
Morgan, Kevin	.277	114	430	63	119	21	1	4	51	44	52	9	9	R	R	6-1	170	3-3-70	1991	Duson, La.
Payton, Jay	.345	85	357	59	123	20	3	14	54	29	32	16	7	R	R	5-10	190	11-22-72	1994	Zanesville, Ohio
Sanders, Tracy	.281	10	32	6	9	3	0	2	8	5	11	1	0	L	R	6-0	206	7-26-69	1990	Dallas, N.C.
Saunders, Chris	.259	122	441	58	114	22	5	8	66	45	98	3	6	R	R	6-1	203	7-19-70	1992	Clovis, Calif.
Smith, Brandon	.000	2	2	0	0	0	0	0	0	0	1	0	0	R	R	6-2	200	3-9-73	1991	Roswell, Ga.
Smith, John	.083	9	12	2	1	1	0	0	1	2	6	0	0	R	R	5-9	175	7-7-69	1992	Indianapolis, Ind.
Thompson, Ryan	.500	2	8	2	4	0	0	1	4	1	2	0	0	R	R	6-3	200	11-4-67	1987	Edesville, Md.
Tijerina, Tony	.178	32	118	3	21	5	0	0	9	1	22	0	0	S	R	5-11	190	12-19-69	1991	Georgetown, Texas
White, Don	.236	94	314	48	74	17	2	3	20	40	56	25	6	R	R	5-10	180	3-13-72	1991	Rock Island, Ill.
Wipf, Mark	.091	4	11	1	1	0	0	0	1	1	8	1	0	S	R	6-4	195	1-11-73	1991	Santa Barbara, Calif.
Zuniga, David	.000	3	1	1	0	0	0	0	0	0	0	0	0	R	R	5-8	140	4-19-71	1993	Los Banos, Calif.

PITCHING

PITCHING	W	L	ERA	G	GS	CG	SV	IP	H	R	ER	BB	SO	B	T	HT	WT	DOB	1st Yr	Resides
Arffa, Steve	0	0	4.50	1	1	0	0	6	7	3	3	1	1	R	L	6-2	195	1-26-73	1994	Glendora, Calif.
Bullock, Craig	0	3	6.89	11	0	0	0	16	20	12	12	7	12	R	R	6-3	222	2-11-72	1990	Houston, Texas
Cosman, Jeff	4	7	7.08	10	10	0	0	48	57	40	38	18	23	R	R	6-4	193	2-8-71	1993	Memphis, Tenn.
Crawford, Joe	7	2	2.23	42	1	0	0	61	48	17	15	17	43	L	L	6-3	225	5-2-70	1991	Hillsboro, Ohio
Edmondson, Brian	7	11	4.76	23	22	2	0	134	150	82	71	59	69	R	R	6-2	165	1-29-73	1991	Riverside, Calif.
Engle, Tom	1	5	5.40	13	2	0	0	28	28	19	17	7	15	R	R	6-2	215	2-14-71	1989	Lancaster, Ohio
Fiegel, Todd	0	1	15.00	4	0	0	0	3	4	5	5	3	4	L	L	6-2	195	10-16-69	1991	Springfield, Va.
Fuller, Mark	4	3	2.95	47	1	0	1	79	83	33	26	22	34	L	R	6-6	216	8-5-70	1992	Melbourne, Fla.
Guerra, Mark	1	1	5.79	6	5	1	0	33	35	24	21	9	24	R	R	6-2	185	11-4-71	1994	Grand Ridge, Fla.
Hiljus, Erik	2	4	5.86	10	10	0	0	55	60	38	36	32	40	R	R	6-5	230	12-25-72	1991	Santa Clarita, Calif.
Isringhausen, Jason	2	1	2.85	6	6	1	0	41	26	15	13	12	59	R	R	6-3	196	9-7-72	1992	Brighton, Ill.
Kindell, Scott	0	0	0.00	1	0	0	0	1	2	0	0	0	1	L	L	6-2	204	11-18-72	1990	Fort Pierce, Fla.
Knackert, Brent	7	7	2.30	48	0	0	11	82	53	23	21	26	69	R	R	6-3	195	8-1-69	1987	Huntington Beach, Calif.
Ludwick, Eric	12	5	2.95	23	22	3	0	143	108	52	47	68	131	R	R	6-5	210	12-14-71	1993	Las Vegas, Nev.
McCready, Jim	1	1	3.23	32	0	0	4	39	42	21	14	14	17	R	R	6-1	187	11-25-69	1991	Norwood, Mass.
McDill, Allen	3	5	4.56	12	12	1	0	73	69	42	37	38	44	L	L	6-1	160	8-23-71	1992	Hot Springs, Ark.
Novoa, Rafael	0	1	2.25	4	0	0	0	8	6	2	2	5	6	L	L	6-1	180	10-26-67	1989	Phoenix, Ariz.
Paxton, Darrin	1	1	3.89	21	3	0	0	37	41	20	16	10	20	L	L	6-4	220	4-17-70	1991	Wichita, Kan.
2-team (7 Harr.)	1	2	3.48	28	3	0	0	44	46	22	17	13	27							
Person, Robert	5	4	3.11	26	7	1	7	67	46	27	23	25	65	R	R	5-11	180	1-8-69	1989	St. Louis, Mo.
Ramirez, Hector	4	12	4.60	20	20	2	0	123	127	69	63	48	63	R	R	6-3	218	12-15-71	1988	El Seibo, D.R.
Schorr, Brad	0	2	9.18	4	4	0	0	17	21	21	17	20	6	R	R	6-2	201	1-21-72	1990	Columbus, Ga.
Stidham, Phil	0	0	4.66	7	0	0	0	10	9	6	5	9	7	R	R	6-0	180	11-18-68	1991	Tulsa, Okla.
Tam, Jeff	0	2	4.50	14	0	0	3	18	20	11	9	4	9	R	R	6-1	185	8-19-70	1993	Tallahassee, Fla.
Wallace, Derek	0	1	5.28	15	0	0	2	15	11	9	9	9	8	R	R	6-3	200	9-1-71	1992	Oxnard, Calif.
Welch, Mike	0	0	0.00	1	0	0	0	1	0	0	0	0	2	L	R	6-2	207	8-25-72	1993	Nashua, N.H.
Wilson, Paul	6	3	2.17	16	16	4	0	120	89	34	29	24	127	R	R	6-5	235	3-28-73	1994	Orlando, Fla.

FIELDING

Catcher	PCT	G	PO	A	E	DP	PB
Diaz	.987	13	72	2	1	0	5
Epperson	1.000	5	12	2	0	0	
Greene	.995	100	670	54	4	3	9
Smith	1.000	2	3	1	0	1	0
Tijerina	.991	32	199	14	2	1	10

First Base	PCT	G	PO	A	E	DP
Barry	1.000	4	13	1	0	1
Daly	1.000	1	8	2	0	1
Daubach	.992	131	1137	98	10	111
Fully	1.000	1	1	0	0	1
Garcia	.978	4	43	2	1	3
Jacobs	.962	9	69	6	3	4
Saunders	1.000	1	7	2	0	1

Second Base	PCT	G	PO	A	E	DP
Azuaje	.989	20	31	63	1	16
Hardtke	.970	115	197	346	17	68
Mahalik	.976	10	16	25	1	5
Miller	1.000	2	1	4	0	0
Zuniga	1.000	1	0	1	0	1

Third Base	PCT	G	PO	A	E	DP
Azuaje	.833	3	3	2	1	0
Daubach	.000	1	0	0	0	0
Hardtke	.875	5	4	10	2	0
Mahalik	.938	25	12	48	4	6
Saunders	.951	118	47	223	14	17

Shortstop	PCT	G	PO	A	E	DP
Mahalik	.944	27	30	72	6	11
Miller	1.000	3	9	8	0	6

	PCT	G	PO	A	E	DP
Morgan	.962	114	192	340	21	73

Outfield	PCT	G	PO	A	E	DP
Agbayani	.972	60	100	3	3	0
Barry	1.000	74	116	5	0	0
Bates	1.000	2	7	0	0	0
Davis	.965	112	210	9	8	1
Fully	1.000	9	16	3	0	3
Keister	.952	18	16	4	1	0
Payton	.988	83	230	7	3	1
Sanders	.909	7	10	0	1	0
Smith	1.000	3	3	0	0	0
Thompson	1.000	2	2	0	0	0
White	.984	78	180	7	3	0
Wipf	.750	4	6	0	2	0

FLORIDA STATE LEAGUE

BATTING	AVG	G	AB	R	H	2B	3B	HR	RBI	BB	SO	SB	CS	B	T	HT	WT	DOB	1st Yr	Resides
Agbayani, Benny	.310	44	155	24	48	9	3	2	29	26	27	8	3	R	R	5-11	175	12-28-71	1993	Aiea, Hawaii
Azuaje, Jesus	.239	91	306	35	73	5	1	2	20	36	55	14	9	R	R	5-10	170	1-16-73	1992	Bolivar, Venez.
Benbow, Lou	.364	12	33	4	12	2	0	0	2	1	7	0	1	R	R	6-0	167	1-12-71	1991	Laguna Hills, Calif.
Cradle, Cobi	.233	78	257	34	60	5	1	1	12	37	45	19	3	L	L	5-11	165	7-7-71	1993	Cerritos, Calif.
Diaz, Cesar	.233	102	361	33	84	17	2	6	40	19	91	0	5	R	R	6-3	185	7-12-74	1990	Maracay, Venezuela
Epperson, Chad	.190	42	121	7	23	7	1	1	14	17	32	1	0	S	R	6-3	221	3-26-72	1992	Fort Myers, Fla.
Ferrier, Ross	.201	68	234	27	47	6	2	7	23	18	69	2	5	R	R	6-5	228	8-10-71	1993	Waterloo, Ontario
Hammell, Al	.157	34	70	7	11	1	0	1	3	16	19	2	1	R	R	5-11	195	7-23-71	1992	Pleasant Valley, N.Y.
Keister, Tripp	.330	28	94	15	31	5	2	0	14	14	11	5	4	L	L	5-9	172	9-27-70	1992	Newark, Del.
Lopez, Jose	1.000	1	2	0	2	0	0	0	1	2	0	0	0	R	R	6-1	175	8-4-75	1994	Santiago, D.R.
Madonna, Chris	.000	3	5	0	0	0	0	0	0	0	1	0	0	L	R	5-11	190	3-13-73	1994	Smithtown, N.Y.
Maness, Dwight	.205	14	44	4	9	4	0	0	5	7	6	1	2	R	R	6-3	180	4-3-74	1992	New Castle, Del.
2-team (43 V.B.)	.225	57	187	20	42	7	0	3	28	18	35	14	7							
Miller, Ryan	.244	89	279	32	68	10	3	2	23	13	42	5	3	R	R	6-0	175	10-22-72	1994	Tulare, Calif.
Motes, Jeff	.200	12	35	7	7	0	0	0	4	1	7	0	0	R	R	6-0	185	6-11-71	1995	Port Sulphur, La.
Northrup, Kevin	.297	17	64	7	19	1	1	0	12	4	6	2	1	R	R	6-1	190	1-27-70	1992	Sanford, N.C.
Petrulis, Paul	.227	104	291	33	66	10	0	1	16	45	51	3	11	R	R	5-10	160	1-25-72	1993	River Forest, Ill.
Pichardo, Sandy	.274	125	478	55	131	10	6	0	27	28	64	29	17	S	R	5-11	173	11-26-74	1991	Santiago, D.R.
Shirley, Al	.186	59	183	27	34	6	3	5	18	23	94	8	4	R	R	6-1	209	10-18-73	1991	Danville, Va.
Terrell, Matt	.197	86	193	24	38	6	2	0	9	18	53	11	2	R	R	6-2	195	6-2-72	1993	Sturgis, Mich.
Torborg, Dale	.111	5	9	0	1	0	0	0	1	0	4	0	0	R	R	6-5	205	10-24-71	1994	Mountainside, N.J.
Warner, Randy	.260	122	446	43	116	23	6	10	70	27	86	6	7	R	R	6-2	200	8-5-73	1991	Seattle, Wash.
Whitehurst, Todd	.222	58	189	13	42	7	1	0	18	21	37	2	3	S	R	6-5	220	4-28-72	1990	San Jose, Calif.
Wipf, Mark	.246	123	435	52	107	20	6	4	53	39	95	15	7	S	R	6-4	195	1-11-73	1991	Santa Barbara, Calif.
Zuniga, David	.172	10	29	1	5	0	0	0	1	6	0	1	0	R	R	5-8	140	4-19-71	1993	Los Banos, Calif.

GAMES BY POSITION: C—Diaz 96, Epperson 17, Hammell 34, Madonna 2. **1B**—Epperson 15, Torborg 5, Warner 104, Whitehurst 20. **2B**—Azuaje 50, Miller 6, Pichardo 79, Zuniga 6. **3B**—Azuaje 26, Benbow 2, Epperson 1, Lopez 1, Motes 9, Petrulis 69, Whitehurst 39. **SS**—Azuaje 16, Benbow 10, Miller 82, Motes 3, Petrulis 33, Zuniga 4. **OF**—Agbayani 19, Cradle 57, Ferrier 44, Keister 16, Maness 9, Northrup 14, Pichardo 22, Shirley 56, Terrell 70, Warner 4, Wipf 114.

PITCHING	W	L	ERA	G	GS	CG	SV	IP	H	R	ER	BB	SO	B	T	HT	WT	DOB	1st Yr	Resides
Arffa, Steve	5	5	4.30	32	10	1	2	88	99	46	42	22	46	R	L	6-2	195	1-26-73	1994	Glendora, Calif.
Bullock, Craig	4	5	2.52	40	0	0	5	50	47	15	14	13	27	R	R	6-3	222	2-11-72	1990	Houston, Texas
Cosman, Jeff	4	9	3.12	15	15	6	0	101	96	43	35	27	72	R	R	6-4	193	2-8-71	1993	Memphis, Tenn.
Dotel, Octavio	1	0	5.63	3	0	0	0	8	10	5	5	4	9	R	R	6-5	160	11-25-73	1993	Santo Domingo, D.R.
Engle, Tom	3	3	1.80	9	9	1	0	50	34	16	10	15	41	R	R	6-3	215	2-14-71	1989	Lancaster, Ohio
Grennan, Steve	0	0	2.16	9	0	0	0	8	8	3	2	4	10	L	L	5-10	153	7-3-70	1991	Salina, Kan.
Guerra, Mark	9	9	2.64	23	23	4	0	160	148	55	47	33	110	R	R	6-2	185	11-4-71	1994	Grand Ridge, Fla.
Hiljus, Erik	8	4	2.99	17	17	0	0	111	85	46	37	50	98	R	R	6-5	230	12-25-72	1991	Santa Clarita, Calif.
Kenny, Sean	4	9	2.70	46	0	0	2	57	51	22	17	15	26	R	R	6-2	205	8-3-72	1993	Ann Arbor, Mich.
Larson, Toby	6	7	2.52	19	18	3	0	122	122	44	34	30	82	R	R	6-3	195	2-22-73	1994	Olympia, Wash.
McDill, Allen	4	2	1.64	7	7	1	0	49	36	11	9	13	28	L	L	6-1	160	8-23-71	1992	Hot Springs, Ark.
Newell, Brandon	2	2	2.96	39	0	0	3	49	42	18	16	29	39	R	R	6-0	205	1-1-72	1993	Blaine, Wash.
Pack, Steve	0	0	4.82	5	0	0	0	9	15	6	5	1	5	R	R	6-3	185	8-6-73	1993	Fallbrook, Calif.
Petcka, Joe	1	1	5.98	30	1	0	0	47	39	35	31	35	28	R	R	6-3	195	10-20-70	1992	Clintonville, Wis.
Roque, Rafael	6	9	3.56	24	24	2	0	137	114	65	54	72	81	L	L	6-4	186	1-1-72	1991	Santo Domingo, D.R.
Sauerbeck, Scott	0	1	2.03	20	1	0	0	27	26	10	6	14	25	R	L	6-3	190	11-9-71	1994	Cincinnati, Ohio
Turrentine, Rich	0	3	6.05	4	4	0	0	19	17	14	13	17	14	R	R	6-0	175	5-21-71	1989	Texarkana, Ark.
Welch, Mike	4	4	5.40	44	6	0	15	70	96	50	42	18	51	L	R	6-2	207	8-25-73	1993	Nashua, N.H.

SOUTH ATLANTIC LEAGUE

BATTING	AVG	G	AB	R	H	2B	3B	HR	RBI	BB	SO	SB	CS	B	T	HT	WT	DOB	1st Yr	Resides
Arvelo, Tom	.125	8	16	4	2	0	0	0	0	3	7	2	0	S	R	6-2	170	12-11-73	1991	Santo Domingo, D.R.
Boka, Ben	.083	8	12	1	1	0	0	0	1	4	0	0	0	R	R	6-4	215	1-9-73	1991	Downington, Pa.
Collum, Gary	.250	9	24	2	6	0	1	0	7	2	7	2	0	R	L	5-11	180	7-14-71	1993	Pitman, N.J.
Ferrier, Ross	.186	23	70	6	13	1	0	2	5	8	20	5	0	R	R	6-5	228	8-10-71	1993	Waterloo, Ontario
Gainey, Bryon	.243	124	448	49	109	20	5	14	64	30	157	1	3	L	R	6-5	209	1-23-76	1994	Mobile, Ala.
Gomez, Paul	.204	68	181	19	37	10	1	4	20	33	65	0	3	R	R	5-11	190	3-8-73	1992	Miami, Fla.
Guerrero, Rafael	.277	116	415	47	115	18	3	7	56	25	63	13	8	R	R	6-2	191	12-3-74	1991	Santo Domingo, D.R.
Hammell, Al	.000	3	6	0	0	0	0	0	0	2	4	0	0	R	R	5-11	195	7-23-71	1992	Pleasant Valley, N.Y.
Hunter, Scott	.250	12	40	2	10	0	0	0	1	2	13	2	1	R	R	6-1	195	12-17-75	1994	Philadelphia, Pa.
Lackey, Steve	.191	67	178	21	34	8	0	1	21	11	42	9	2	R	R	5-11	159	9-25-74	1992	Riverside, Calif.
Long, Terrence	.197	55	178	27	35	1	2	2	13	28	43	8	5	L	L	6-1	179	2-29-76	1994	Millbrook, Ala.
Lopez, Jose	.232	82	280	37	65	17	4	5	38	35	76	7	2	R	R	6-1	175	8-4-75	1994	Santiago, D.R.
Morales, Eric	.275	38	109	12	30	4	0	0	11	12	18	2	1	R	R	5-11	191	9-26-73	1992	Moca, D.R.
Mota, Guillermo	.243	123	400	45	97	24	3	4	45	32	127	8	3	R	R	6-5	185	7-25-73	1991	San Pedro de Macoris, D.R.
Ozario, Yudith	.217	123	456	59	99	12	2	2	33	34	113	40	15	R	R	5-11	155	1-1-75	1991	La Romana, D.R.
Sanderson, David	.237	121	363	53	86	11	5	5	36	38	81	20	10	L	L	6-3	185	10-2-72	1994	Fulton, Mo.
Turner, Rocky	.176	12	17	2	3	0	0	0	0	2	5	0	0	R	R	6-0	170	2-12-72	1994	Arlington, Texas
Whitehurst, Todd	.164	21	61	10	10	3	0	1	1	11	19	2	1	S	R	6-5	220	4-28-72	1990	San Jose, Calif.
Wilson, Preston	.269	111	442	70	119	26	5	20	61	19	114	20	6	R	R	6-2	193	7-19-74	1992	Eastover, S.C.
Wilson, Vance	.250	91	324	34	81	11	0	6	32	19	45	4	3	R	R	5-11	180	3-17-73	1994	Mesa, Ariz.
Winterlee, Scott	.429	4	7	0	3	0	0	0	0	2	0	0	0	R	R	6-0	205	12-22-70	1993	Mt. Morris, Mich.
Zorrilla, Julio	.276	133	518	65	143	15	3	0	31	31	75	42	18	S	R	5-11	156	2-20-75	1993	San Pedro de Macoris, D.R.
Zuniga, David	.178	36	73	6	13	2	0	0	4	7	19	0	2	R	R	5-8	140	4-19-71	1993	Los Banos, Calif.

GAMES BY POSITION: C—Boka 7, Gomez 26, Hammell 3, Morales 35, V. Wilson 85, Winterlee 1. **1B**—Boka 1, Gainey 118, Gomez 6, Guerrero 26, Lackey 1, Mota 1, Whitehurst 2. **2B**—Arvelo 4, Lackey 4, Zorrilla 128, Zuniga 8. **3B**—Gomez 1, Lackey 38, Lopez 79, Whitehurst 20, Zuniga 20. **SS**—Arvelo 2, Lackey 25, Mota 122, Zuniga 1. **OF**—Collum 5, Ferrier 13, Guerrero 59, Hunter 12, Long 49, Ozario 115, Sanderson 74, Turner 8, P. Wilson 104.

PITCHING	W	L	ERA	G	GS	CG	SV	IP	H	R	ER	BB	SO	B	T	HT	WT	DOB	1st Yr	Resides
Adair, Scott	0	1	10.38	3	0	0	0	4	10	8	5	0	4	R	R	6-0	190	11-10-75	1993	Riverside, Calif.
Atwater, Joe	9	6	2.69	27	18	3	1	147	106	52	44	28	127	L	L	6-3	160	2-12-75	1993	Graham, N.C.
Baker, Derek	2	8	3.30	36	0	0	6	63	52	25	23	35	44	R	R	6-3	207	6-19-73	1992	San Luis Obispo, Calif.
Gooch, Arnold	2	3	4.46	6	6	0	0	38	39	25	19	15	34	R	R	6-2	195	11-12-76	1994	Levittown, Pa.
2-team (21 Asheville)	5	8	2.94	21	21	1	0	129	111	51	42	57	117							
Johnston, Sean	11	6	3.03	23	22	2	0	148	132	60	50	63	105	L	L	6-4	187	6-28-76	1994	Highland Park, Ill.
Kelly, John	8	8	3.88	28	28	3	0	167	148	80	72	65	124	R	R	6-0	180	12-13-72	1994	Leominster, Mass.
Kindell, Scott	0	0	0.00	1	0	0	0	0	0	0	0	0	0	L	L	6-2	204	11-18-72	1990	Fort Pierce, Fla.
Larson, Toby	3	3	2.63	8	8	0	0	51	43	24	15	19	53	R	R	6-3	210	2-22-73	1994	Olympia, Wash.
McEntire, Ethan	3	2	3.34	6	6	1	0	32	26	14	12	23	31	L	L	6-1	195	7-19-75	1993	Clarkesville, Ga.
Pack, Steve	2	7	3.70	36	0	0	12	56	63	33	23	20	35	R	R	6-3	195	8-6-73	1993	Fallbrook, Calif.
Presley, Kirk	1	2	5.14	4	4	0	0	21	30	17	12	13	8	R	R	6-3	195	4-17-75	1994	Tupelo, Miss.
Sanchez, Jesus	9	7	3.13	27	27	4	0	170	154	76	59	58	177	L	L	5-10	153	10-11-74	1992	Bani, D.R.
Sauerbeck, Scott	5	4	3.27	19	0	0	2	33	28	14	12	14	33	R	L	6-3	190	11-9-71	1994	Cincinnati, Ohio
Short, Barry	4	3	1.97	40	1	0	4	78	63	22	17	22	56	R	R	6-3	182	12-15-73	1994	Mansfield, Mo.
Swanson, David	7	1	1.46	29	4	0	3	68	48	14	11	31	60	L	L	6-0	184	10-19-72	1991	Berlin, Conn.
Tatis, Ramon	2	3	5.63	18	2	0	0	32	34	27	20	14	27	L	L	6-2	180	1-5-73	1991	Guayubin, D.R.
Turrentine, Rich	4	4	2.51	26	14	0	2	104	70	38	29	60	111	R	R	6-0	175	5-21-71	1989	Texarkana, Ark.
Wolff, Tom	0	0	4.37	15	0	0	0	23	21	13	11	8	16	R	R	6-2	185	7-29-73	1993	Hillsdale, Mich.

PITTSFIELD
NEW YORK-PENN LEAGUE
A

BATTING	AVG	G	AB	R	H	2B	3B	HR	RBI	BB	SO	SB	CS	B	T	HT	WT	DOB	1st Yr	Resides
Arvelo, Tom	.305	79	279	41	85	8	7	0	17	16	63	24	6	S	R	6-1	170	12-11-73	1991	Santo Domingo, D.R.
Bates, Fletcher	.326	75	276	52	90	14	9	6	37	41	72	17	9	S	R	6-1	193	3-24-74	1994	Wilmington, N.C.
Daly, Rob	.294	76	303	43	89	22	3	3	60	22	28	4	1	R	R	6-1	205	10-8-72	1992	Downers Grove, Ill.
Dieguez, Mike	.215	59	181	31	39	7	1	0	17	31	29	0	5	R	R	6-3	200	7-12-72	1994	New Hyde Park, N.Y.
Jaroncyk, Ryan	.231	4	13	5	3	0	0	0	3	5	5	0	0	R	R	6-0	160	3-26-77	1995	Escondido, Calif.
Lackey, Steve	.240	21	75	7	18	5	0	0	6	2	16	1	0	R	R	5-11	159	9-25-74	1992	Riverside, Calif.
LeClair, Paul	.180	31	100	10	18	3	0	0	6	7	35	0	1	R	R	5-11	185	8-9-72	1994	Huntsville, Ala.
Long, Terrence	.257	51	187	24	48	9	4	4	31	18	36	11	4	L	L	6-1	179	2-29-76	1994	Millbrook, Ala.
Martinez, Roger	.101	23	69	1	7	3	0	0	3	5	20	1	0	R	R	5-10	175	12-6-72	1995	Corpus Christi, Texas
Morales, Eric	.241	66	237	18	57	6	1	1	28	20	36	2	2	R	R	5-11	171	9-26-73	1992	Moca, P.R.
Mota, Gleydel	.162	14	37	4	6	0	0	2	4	11	2	2	1	L	L	5-8	161	3-30-75	1992	San Pedro de Macoris, D.R.
Motes, Jeff	.231	52	169	14	39	7	3	0	15	21	33	1	1	R	R	6-0	185	6-11-71	1995	Port Sulphur, La.
Parker, Michael	.500	3	2	0	1	0	0	0	0	0	1	0	0	R	R	5-10	190	8-5-72	1995	South Bend, Ind.
Parsons, Jeff	.227	49	172	31	39	4	0	0	10	37	33	25	7	R	R	6-0	190	11-16-73	1995	Shawnee, Okla.
Pelis, Andy	.053	8	19	3	1	0	0	0	4	7	0	0	0	R	R	6-0	200	8-27-72	1995	Northampton, Mass.
Pileski, Mark	.161	8	31	2	5	1	0	0	4	1	2	1	0	R	R	6-1	175	4-13-74	1995	Brockton, Mass.
Soriano, Carlos	.176	5	17	1	3	2	0	0	1	1	2	1	0	R	R	6-0	165	10-24-74	1992	San Pedro de Macoris, D.R.
Turner, Rocky	.259	33	116	9	30	4	0	0	10	7	17	8	7	R	R	6-0	170	2-12-72	1994	Arlington, Texas
Viruet, Willie	.188	11	32	4	6	0	0	0	5	4	7	0	0	R	R	5-11	165	1-4-74	1995	Hialeah, Fla.
Yoder, Paul	.213	55	183	25	39	6	4	0	18	30	34	0	5	R	R	6-2	185	8-25-74	1995	Bethlehem, Pa.

GAMES BY POSITION: C—Martinez 17, Morales 57, Parker 3, Pelis 8. **1B**—Daly 76, Morales 1. **2B**—Arvelo 67, Parsons 1, Soriano 2, Turner 1, Viruet 9. **3B**—Dieguez 52, Motes 24, Soriano 3, Viruet 1. **SS**—Arvelo 1, Jaroncyk 4, Lackey 21, Motes 9, Parsons 40, Pileski 3. **OF**—Bates 70, LeClair 29, Long 51, Mota 11, Turner 27, Yoder 46.

PITCHING	W	L	ERA	G	GS	CG	SV	IP	H	R	ER	BB	SO	B	T	HT	WT	DOB	1st Yr	Resides
Atwater, Joe	1	0	2.25	1	1	0	0	8	8	2	2	3	6	L	L	6-3	160	2-12-75	1993	Graham, N.C.
Ballew, Preston	1	0	0.00	1	1	0	0	5	2	0	0	3	4	L	L	5-10	175	5-13-77	1995	Carlsbad, N.M.
Bowman, Paul	0	1	9.64	2	0	0	0	5	7	6	5	5	3	R	R	6-2	188	3-27-73	1993	Steubenville, Ohio
Coronado, Osvaldo	4	5	3.87	15	15	0	0	91	91	52	39	26	57	R	R	6-2	185	12-30-73	1992	Puerto Plata, D.R.
Ferullo, Matt	1	0	0.00	2	0	0	0	5	3	0	0	1	6	R	R	6-5	225	5-16-73	1995	Revere, Mass.
Gulin, Lindsey	0	0	3.86	1	1	0	0	7	4	4	3	3	8	L	L	6-3	160	11-22-76	1995	Issaquah, Wash.
Howatt, Jeff	1	2	4.15	17	0	0	1	39	37	22	18	15	26	R	R	6-6	225	1-30-74	1995	Fillmore, Calif.
Kindell, Scott	4	1	2.36	20	0	0	0	27	25	11	7	6	14	L	L	6-2	204	11-18-72	1990	Fort Pierce, Fla.
Koenig, Matthew	4	5	4.27	15	12	0	0	78	81	47	37	23	43	R	R	6-2	189	7-19-72	1994	Brielle, N.J.
Lisio, Joseph	2	2	1.62	28	0	0	12	33	27	8	6	14	24	R	R	6-2	205	8-5-73	1994	West Hempstead, N.Y.
McEntire, Ethan	4	2	5.06	13	13	0	0	69	81	43	39	46	41	L	L	6-1	195	7-19-75	1993	Clarkesville, Ga.
Murray, Dan	0	6	1.97	22	0	0	0	32	24	17	7	16	34	R	R	6-1	185	11-21-73	1995	Garden Grove, Calif.
Patterson, Casey	0	4	9.53	12	4	0	0	34	47	43	36	28	18	R	R	6-0	165	6-18-73	1995	Clovis, Calif.
Pyrtle, Joe	0	1	3.48	17	0	0	2	31	32	18	12	12	17	R	R	6-1	200	11-21-73	1995	Wilmington, N.C.
Short, Barry	0	0	4.50	2	0	0	1	2	4	1	1	1	2	R	R	6-3	182	12-15-73	1994	Mansfield, Mo.
Tatis, Ramon	4	5	3.63	13	13	1	0	79	88	40	32	27	69	L	L	6-2	180	1-5-73	1991	Guayubin, D.R.
Trumpour, Andy	7	6	2.57	15	2	0	0	105	95	44	30	32	75	R	R	6-4	185	10-22-73	1992	Anaheim, Calif.
Wolff, Tom	0	2	8.00	4	1	0	0	9	15	11	8	5	8	R	R	6-2	185	7-29-73	1993	Hillsdale, Mich.

KINGSPORT
APPALACHIAN LEAGUE
R

BATTING	AVG	G	AB	R	H	2B	3B	HR	RBI	BB	SO	SB	CS	B	T	HT	WT	DOB	1st Yr	Resides
Black, Brandon	.292	31	106	17	31	5	0	3	20	8	23	7	1	L	R	6-0	185	12-16-74	1995	Florence, Ky.
Cox, Robert	.197	57	188	29	37	9	0	3	25	30	59	1	3	R	R	6-1	176	11-11-75	1994	Culver City, Calif.
Edmondson, Tracy	.265	44	155	36	41	11	0	3	25	27	34	8	1	R	R	6-0	165	6-10-75	1995	Riverside, Calif.
Erickson, Corey	.333	2	9	1	3	0	0	1	4	0	3	0	0	R	R	5-11	185	1-10-77	1995	Springfield, Ill.
Frost, Robert	.333	11	30	3	10	2	0	0	7	1	5	1	0	R	R	6-3	215	1-14-73	1995	Florissant, Mo.
Gill, Sean	.000	8	18	2	0	0	0	0	0	1	10	0	0	R	R	6-2	195	11-19-71	1995	Cincinnati, Ohio
Hoover, Will	.190	11	21	1	4	1	0	0	3	2	10	0	0	R	R	6-2	177	12-10-74	1995	Camp Hill, Pa.
Lantigua, Miguel	.125	6	16	0	2	0	0	0	1	1	6	0	0	S	R	6-2	185	7-23-73	1994	Santo Domingo, D.R.
McCarthy, Kevin	.132	26	91	11	12	2	1	0	4	17	18	1	2	L	L	6-4	198	7-5-76	1994	Pittsburgh, Pa.
Mendoza, Carlos	.328	51	192	56	63	9	0	0	24	27	24	28	6	L	L	5-11	160	11-4-74	1994	Bolivar, Venez.
Mifflin, Brian	.250	1	4	1	1	0	0	0	1	0	0	0	0	R	R	6-2	234	7-2-73	1994	Lewes, Del.
Mota, Gleydel	.000	1	3	1	0	0	0	0	0	1	2	0	0	L	L	5-8	161	3-30-75	1992	San Pedro de Macoris, D.R.

BATTING	AVG	G	AB	R	H	2B	3B	HR	RBI	BB	SO	SB	CS	B	T	HT	WT	DOB	1st Yr	Resides
Naples, Brandon	.275	32	109	22	30	1	1	1	23	11	11	2	0	R	L	6-0	190	11-5-72	1995	Reading, Pa.
Patterson, Jarrod	.279	64	240	45	67	17	3	13	57	28	50	3	1	L	R	6-0	190	9-7-73	1993	Clanton, Ala.
Polanco, Enohel	.229	62	205	28	47	5	2	2	21	18	60	7	6	R	R	5-11	140	8-11-75	1992	Puerto Plata, D.R.
Ramirez, Daniel	.248	62	226	30	56	6	2	2	32	15	44	21	10	R	R	6-0	175	2-22-74	1994	San Pedro de Macoris, D.R.
Simpson, Jeramie	.323	59	229	50	74	11	10	0	28	20	37	25	5	L	R	5-10	160	11-28-74	1994	Edmond, Okla.
Soriano, Juan	.262	40	107	29	28	5	1	0	12	20	21	7	2	R	R	5-11	155	10-24-74	1994	San Pedro de Macoris, D.R.
Torbett, Hanes	.261	19	46	10	12	1	2	0	5	9	8	0	0	R	R	5-11	180	9-12-72	1995	Johnson City, Tenn.
Valera, Yojanny	.294	56	204	30	60	13	0	3	36	11	33	2	1	R	R	6-1	170	8-17-76	1993	San Cristobal, D.R.

GAMES BY POSITION: C—Frost 8, Hoover 8, Lantigua 3, Valera 53. **1B**—Lantigua 1, Naples 15, Patterson 54, Torbett 1. **2B**—Edmondson 41, Erickson 1, Simpson 4, Soriano 21, Torbett 6. **3B**—Cox 57, Soriano 14, Torbett 3. **SS**—Polanco 61, Soriano 7. **OF**—Black 26, Gill 2, McCarthy 25, Mendoza 33, Mifflin 1, Mota 1, Naples 11, Ramirez 62, Simpson 46, Torbett 2.

PITCHING	W	L	ERA	G	GS	CG	SV	IP	H	R	ER	BB	SO	B	T	HT	WT	DOB	1st Yr	Resides
Beebe, Joey	5	1	3.25	9	7	0	0	44	43	16	16	12	34	L	L	6-4	175	4-30-75	1994	Berlin, N.J.
Blang, Michael	0	2	3.18	23	0	0	7	28	19	10	10	7	18	R	R	6-4	230	1-22-73	1995	Monona, Wis.
Cooper, Chadwick	0	0	3.03	22	1	0	6	30	21	12	10	12	38	R	R	6-2	205	5-15-75	1995	Petersburg, W.Va.
Cope, Craig	0	0	8.44	12	0	0	0	11	9	12	10	12	10	L	L	6-1	174	3-21-76	1994	Windsor, Ontario
DeWitt, Chris	1	0	3.86	23	0	0	5	28	31	18	12	7	16	R	R	6-5	215	3-24-74	1995	Ozark, Mo.
Figueroa, Nelson	7	3	3.07	12	12	2	0	76	57	31	26	22	79	S	R	6-1	165	5-18-74	1995	Brooklyn, N.Y.
Herbison, Brett	1	0	7.20	1	1	0	0	5	6	4	4	2	4	R	R	6-5	175	6-13-77	1995	Elgin, Ill.
Kessel, Kyle	4	0	1.80	5	5	0	0	30	33	11	6	10	23	L	L	6-0	160	6-2-76	1994	Mundelein, Ill.
Ojeda, Erick	6	2	2.40	14	5	0	0	60	47	18	16	12	60	L	L	5-10	177	10-15-75	1993	Carabobo, Venez.
Olson, Phil	6	2	2.42	12	10	2	1	67	47	24	18	23	45	R	R	6-3	225	10-24-73	1995	Sarasota, Fla.
Poupart, Melvin	1	1	5.06	18	0	0	1	27	27	17	15	10	13	R	R	6-0	193	7-1-75	1994	Humacao, P.R.
Pumphrey, Kenny	7	3	3.86	12	12	0	0	65	50	32	28	42	76	R	R	6-6	195	9-10-76	1994	Glen Burnie, Md.
Santamaria, Bill	5	3	4.18	13	13	1	0	71	62	37	33	29	55	R	R	6-2	223	1-6-76	1994	Lakewood, N.J.
Villafuerte, Brandon	5	1	5.63	20	0	0	0	32	28	21	20	26	42	R	R	5-11	165	12-17-75	1995	Morgan Hill, Calif.

PORT ST. LUCIE — R
GULF COAST LEAGUE

BATTING	AVG	G	AB	R	H	2B	3B	HR	RBI	BB	SO	SB	CS	B	T	HT	WT	DOB	1st Yr	Resides
Bishop, Tim	.237	47	156	31	37	6	5	2	15	13	38	4	2	R	R	6-0	168	5-25-74	1994	Valparaiso, Ind.
Black, Brandon	.352	30	105	16	37	12	3	1	25	10	11	1	1	L	R	6-0	185	12-16-74	1995	Florence, Ky.
Bowers, Kevin	.220	36	123	20	27	4	1	2	19	21	38	1	0	R	R	6-2	225	2-3-77	1995	St. George, Utah
Engle, Beau	.179	10	28	3	5	2	1	0	1	2	3	0	0	R	R	6-1	180	11-9-74	1994	Altus, Okla.
Erickson, Corey	.281	53	178	38	50	6	1	7	35	37	40	10	3	R	R	5-11	185	1-10-77	1995	Springfield, Ill.
Jaroncyk, Ryan	.276	44	174	31	48	5	3	0	14	13	28	7	2	R	R	6-0	160	3-26-77	1995	Escondido, Calif.
Jelsovsky, Craig	.233	18	43	6	10	2	0	0	6	3	4	0	2	R	R	6-1	165	6-2-76	1994	El Cajon, Calif.
Lantigua, Miguel	.262	27	84	11	22	6	0	0	7	4	16	4	2	S	R	6-2	167	7-23-73	1994	Santo Domingo, D.R.
McCarthy, Kevin	.133	22	75	5	10	1	0	1	5	2	13	0	0	L	L	6-4	198	7-5-76	1994	Pittsburgh, Pa.
Mifflin, Brian	.306	51	193	29	59	13	1	5	40	5	43	1	1	R	R	6-2	234	7-2-73	1994	Lewes, Del.
Morrison, Ryan	.255	38	110	20	28	7	0	1	11	17	21	3	0	R	R	6-2	188	3-29-75	1995	Liverpool, N.Y.
Mota, Gleydel	.320	34	122	32	39	6	2	0	18	19	27	21	5	L	L	5-8	161	3-30-75	1992	San Pedro de Macoris, D.R.
Rodriguez, Sammy	.278	6	18	1	5	0	0	0	1	2	4	0	1	R	R	5-10	180	8-20-75	1995	New York, N.Y.
Shirley, Al	.333	4	15	4	5	2	0	0	0	3	4	3	1	R	R	6-2	209	10-18-73	1991	Danville, Va.
Soriano, Carlos	.263	47	167	25	44	11	3	5	24	15	24	1	2	R	R	6-0	165	10-24-74	1992	San Pedro de Macoris, D.R.
Soriano, Juan	.219	10	32	5	7	2	0	1	3	4	9	3	0	R	R	5-11	155	10-24-74	1994	San Pedro de Macoris, D.R.
Tessmar, Tim	.209	56	196	20	41	5	4	0	28	30	27	4	1	L	L	6-3	185	1-22-74	1995	Rochester Hills, Mich.
Zamora, Junior	.232	20	56	9	13	2	2	0	4	5	10	0	0	R	R	6-2	168	5-3-76	1994	San Pedro de Macoris, D.R.

GAMES BY POSITION: C—Bowers 21, Engle 10, Lantigua 26, Rodriguez 6. **1B**—Erickson 1, Jelsovsky 2, Lantigua 1, Mifflin 3, C. Soriano 1, Tessmar 56. **2B**—Erickson 45, Jelsovsky 4, C. Soriano 6, J. Soriano 9. **3B**—Erickson 1, Jelsovsky 4, Morrison 1, C. Soriano 38, Zamora 20. **SS**—Erickson 6, Jaroncyk 31, Jelsovsky 12, J. Soriano 1. **OF**—Bishop 47, Black 30, McCarthy 22, Mifflin 16, Morrison 33, Mota 33, Shirley 4.

PITCHING	W	L	ERA	G	GS	CG	SV	IP	H	R	ER	BB	SO	B	T	HT	WT	DOB	1st Yr	Resides
Ballew, Preston	3	0	1.75	14	2	0	4	36	27	8	7	6	42	L	L	5-10	175	5-13-77	1995	Carlsbad, N.M.
Borkowski, Bob	0	0	2.25	5	0	0	1	8	6	2	2	3	1	R	R	6-2	190	11-10-76	1994	Wilmington, Del.
Brito, Juan	3	2	3.89	13	4	0	2	37	42	20	16	10	33	L	L	5-10	152	2-10-76	1994	San Pedro de Macoris, D.R.
Burke, Ethan	1	2	4.34	13	0	0	5	19	19	9	9	5	14	R	R	6-4	205	9-6-75	1994	Baker, Ore.
Burnett, Allan	2	3	4.28	9	8	1	0	34	27	16	16	23	26	R	R	6-5	204	1-3-77	1995	North Little Rock, Ark.
Dotel, Octavio	7	4	2.18	13	12	2	0	74	48	23	18	17	86	R	R	6-5	160	11-25-73	1993	Santo Domingo, D.R.
Enloe, Mark	2	1	3.12	11	2	0	0	26	24	14	9	16	25	L	L	6-3	200	2-5-77	1995	Cleveland, Texas
Gulin, Lindsey	6	0	1.71	10	4	0	0	47	36	11	9	13	48	L	L	6-3	160	11-22-76	1995	Issaquah, Wash.
Herbison, Brett	3	0	2.20	9	9	0	0	41	31	13	10	16	31	R	R	6-5	175	6-13-77	1995	Elgin, Ill.
Kessel, Kyle	3	0	1.80	7	7	0	0	40	29	12	8	11	47	L	L	6-0	160	6-2-76	1994	Mundelein, Ill.
Manley, Kevin	0	0	6.75	2	0	0	0	1	1	1	1	3	0	R	R	6-4	195	10-29-75	1994	Frostproof, Fla.
Newell, Brandon	0	0	0.00	1	0	0	0	1	1	2	0	2	2	R	R	6-0	205	1-1-72	1993	Blaine, Wash.
Olson, Phil	0	0	4.50	1	0	0	0	2	1	1	1	3	3	R	R	6-3	225	10-24-73	1995	Sarasota, Fla.
Petcka, Joe	0	0	0.00	1	0	0	0	2	1	0	0	0	4	R	R	6-3	195	10-20-70	1992	Clintonville, Wis.
Roberts, Grant	2	1	2.15	11	3	0	0	29	19	13	7	14	24	R	R	6-3	187	9-13-77	1995	El Cajon, Calif.
Samboy, Javier	5	3	2.98	12	4	0	1	48	40	17	16	17	31	L	L	6-2	160	2-13-75	1992	Pedernales, D.R.
Tam, Jeff	0	0	3.00	2	1	0	0	3	2	1	1	1	2	R	R	6-1	185	8-19-70	1993	Tallahassee, Fla.
Torres, Eric	0	2	0.44	11	0	0	3	21	11	5	1	6	8	R	R	6-2	198	6-11-77	1995	Mayaguez, P.R.
Wicks, Ross	0	1	3.38	12	1	0	0	19	15	7	7	6	15	R	R	6-2	180	7-13-76	1994	Eugene, Ore.

OAKLAND ATHLETICS

Manager: Tony La Russa.   **1995 Record:** 67-77, .465 (4th, AL West).

BATTING	AVG	G	AB	R	H	2B	3B	HR	RBI	BB	SO	SB	CS	B	T	HT	WT	DOB	1st Yr	Resides
Aldrete, Mike	.272	60	125	18	34	8	0	4	21	19	23	0	0	L	L	5-11	180	1-29-61	1983	Monterey, Calif.
Berroa, Geronimo	.278	141	546	87	152	22	3	22	88	63	98	7	4	R	R	6-0	165	3-18-65	1984	Santo Domingo, D.R.
Bordick, Mike...............	.264	126	428	46	113	13	0	8	44	35	48	11	3	R	R	5-11	170	7-21-65	1986	Winterport, Maine
Brosius, Scott	.262	123	389	69	102	19	2	17	46	41	67	4	2	R	R	6-1	190	8-15-66	1987	McMinnville, Ore.
Cruz, Fausto.................	.217	8	23	0	5	0	0	0	5	3	5	1	1	R	R	5-11	165	1-5-72	1990	Villa Vasquez, D.R.
Gallego, Mike	.233	43	120	11	28	0	0	0	8	9	24	0	1	R	R	5-8	160	10-31-60	1981	Yorba Linda, Calif.
Gates, Brent	.254	136	524	60	133	24	4	5	56	46	84	3	3	S	R	6-1	180	3-14-70	1991	Grandville, Mich.
Giambi, Jason	.256	54	176	27	45	7	0	6	25	28	31	2	1	L	R	6-2	200	1-8-71	1992	Covina, Calif.
Harper, Brian...............	.000	2	7	0	0	0	0	0	0	0	1	0	0	R	R	6-2	206	10-16-59	1977	Scottsdale, Ariz.
Helfand, Eric...............	.163	38	86	9	14	2	1	0	7	11	25	0	0	L	R	6-0	210	3-25-69	1990	San Diego, Calif.
Henderson, Rickey.......	.300	112	407	67	122	31	1	9	54	72	66	32	10	R	L	5-10	195	12-25-58	1976	Oakland, Calif.
Herrera, Jose	.243	33	70	9	17	1	2	0	2	6	11	1	3	L	L	6-0	164	8-30-72	1991	Santo Domingo, D.R.
Javier, Stan	.278	130	442	81	123	20	2	8	56	49	63	36	5	S	R	6-0	185	1-9-64	1981	Santo Domingo, D.R.
McGwire, Mark	.274	104	317	75	87	13	0	39	90	88	77	1	1	R	R	6-5	225	10-1-63	1984	Claremont, Calif.
Paquette, Craig	.226	105	283	42	64	13	1	13	49	12	88	5	2	R	R	6-0	190	3-28-69	1989	Garden Grove, Calif.
Sierra, Ruben	.265	70	264	40	70	17	0	12	42	24	42	4	4	S	R	6-1	200	10-6-65	1983	Carolina, P.R.
Steinbach, Terry..........	.278	114	406	43	113	26	1	15	65	25	74	1	3	R	R	6-1	175	3-2-62	1983	Plymouth, Minn.
Tartabull, Danny..........	.261	24	88	9	23	4	0	2	7	10	28	0	2	R	R	6-1	210	10-30-62	1980	Malibu, Calif.
2-team (59 N.Y.)	.236	83	280	34	66	16	0	8	35	43	82	0	2							
Tomberlin, Andy	.212	46	85	15	18	0	0	4	10	5	22	4	1	L	L	5-11	160	11-7-66	1986	Monroe, N.C.
Williams, George..........	.291	29	79	13	23	5	1	3	14	11	21	0	0	S	R	5-10	190	4-22-69	1991	La Crosse, Wisc.
Young, Ernie	.200	26	50	9	10	3	0	2	5	8	12	0	0	R	R	6-1	190	7-8-69	1990	Chicago, Ill.

PITCHING	W	L	ERA	G	GS	CG	SV	IP	H	R	ER	BB	SO	B	T	HT	WT	DOB	1st Yr	Resides
Acre, Mark	1	2	5.71	43	0	0	0	52	52	35	33	28	47	R	R	6-8	235	9-16-68	1991	Corning, Calif.
Baker, Scott.................	0	0	9.82	1	0	0	0	4	5	4	4	5	3	L	L	6-2	175	5-18-70	1990	Henderson, Nev.
Briscoe, John...............	0	1	8.35	16	0	0	0	18	25	17	17	21	19	R	R	6-3	195	9-22-67	1988	Richardson, Texas
Corsi, Jim....................	2	4	2.20	38	0	0	2	45	31	14	11	26	26	R	R	6-1	220	9-9-61	1982	Natick, Mass.
Darling, Ron	4	7	6.23	21	21	1	0	104	124	79	72	46	69	R	R	6-3	195	8-19-60	1981	New York, N.Y.
Eckersley, Dennis	4	6	4.83	52	0	0	29	50	53	29	27	11	40	R	R	6-2	195	10-3-54	1972	Sudbury, Mass.
Eddy, Chris	0	0	7.36	6	0	0	0	4	7	3	3	2	2	L	L	6-3	200	11-27-69	1992	Duncanville, Texas
Fermin, Ramon	0	0	13.50	1	0	0	0	1	4	2	2	1	0	R	R	6-3	180	11-25-72	1990	San Fran. de Macoris, D.R.
Harkey, Mike	4	6	6.27	14	12	0	0	66	75	46	46	31	28	R	R	6-5	220	10-25-66	1987	Chino Hills, Calif.
Honeycutt, Rick	5	1	2.42	49	0	0	2	45	37	13	12	9	21	L	L	6-1	192	6-29-54	1976	La Habra Heights, Calif.
Johns, Doug	5	3	4.61	11	9	1	0	55	44	32	28	26	25	R	L	6-2	185	12-19-67	1990	Plantation, Fla.
Leiper, Dave	1	1	3.57	24	0	0	0	23	23	10	9	13	10	L	L	6-1	190	6-18-62	1982	Plano, Texas
Mohler, Mike...............	1	1	3.04	28	0	0	1	24	16	8	8	18	15	R	L	6-2	195	7-26-68	1990	Gonzales, La.
Ontiveros, Steve	9	6	4.37	22	22	2	0	130	144	75	63	38	77	R	R	6-0	180	3-5-61	1982	Stafford, Texas
Phoenix, Steve	0	0	32.40	1	0	0	0	2	3	6	6	3	3	R	R	6-3	195	1-31-68	1990	El Cajon, Calif.
Prieto, Ariel	2	6	4.97	14	9	1	0	58	57	35	32	32	37	R	R	6-3	225	10-22-66	1995	Beverly Hills, Calif.
Reyes, Carlos	4	6	5.09	40	1	0	0	69	71	43	39	28	48	S	R	6-1	190	4-19-69	1991	Macon, Ga.
Stewart, Dave	3	7	6.89	16	16	0	0	81	101	65	62	39	58	R	R	6-2	200	2-19-57	1975	Emeryville, Calif.
Stottlemyre, Todd	14	7	4.55	31	31	2	0	210	228	117	106	80	205	L	R	6-3	195	5-20-65	1986	Yakima, Wash.
Van Poppel, Todd	4	8	4.88	36	14	1	0	138	125	77	75	56	122	R	R	6-5	210	12-9-71	1990	Arlington, Texas
Wasdin, John...............	1	5	4.67	5	2	0	0	17	14	9	9	3	6	R	R	6-2	195	8-5-72	1993	Tallahassee, Fla.
Wengert, Don	1	1	3.34	19	0	0	0	30	30	14	11	12	16	R	R	6-3	205	11-6-69	1992	Sioux City, Iowa
Wojciechowski, Steve ..	2	3	5.18	14	7	0	0	49	51	28	28	28	13	L	L	6-2	185	7-29-70	1991	Calumet City, Ill.

FIELDING

Catcher	PCT	G	PO	A	E	DP	PB
Harper	1.000	2	6	0	0	0	0
Helfand...........	.994	36	167	13	1	4	0
Steinbach........	.993	111	681	57	5	8	3
Williams...........	.956	13	58	7	3	0	1

First Base	PCT	G	PO	A	E	DP
Aldrete............	.989	35	175	10	2	16
Brosius............	.984	18	110	17	2	26
Gates............	1.000	1	8	4	0	1
Giambi............	.994	26	167	10	1	20
McGwire...........	.986	91	775	64	12	65
Paquette........	1.000	3	10	1	0	1
Steinbach........	.833	2	5	0	1	3

Second Base	PCT	G	PO	A	E	DP
Brosius...........	1.000	3	3	4	0	1
Gallego...........	.960	18	25	47	3	9
Gates............	.982	132	233	424	12	81

Third Base	PCT	G	PO	A	E	DP
Brosius	.918	60	27	96	11	8
Gallego...........	.882	12	5	10	2	1
Giambi............	.960	30	27	45	3	4

	PCT	G	PO	A	E	DP
Javier...............	.000	1	0	0	0	0
Paquette........	.935	75	38	78	8	11

Shortstop	PCT	G	PO	A	E	DP
Bordick...........	.983	126	245	338	10	93
Brosius	1.000	3	2	2	0	1
Cruz................	.971	8	9	24	1	2
Gallego...........	1.000	14	16	32	0	6
Paquette.......	1.000	8	5	12	0	6

Outfield	PCT	G	PO	A	E	DP
Aldrete...........	.941	16	16	0	1	0
Berroa	.971	71	129	5	4	2
Brosius	.971	49	66	2	2	0
Henderson	.988	90	162	5	2	1
Herrera..........	.956	25	41	2	2	1
Javier.............	1.000	124	332	3	0	1
Paquette.........	1.000	20	19	1	0	0
Sierra.............	.957	62	89	1	4	0
Tartabull..........	1.000	1	1	0	0	0
Tomberlin	.979	42	45	1	1	0
Young..............	.946	24	35	0	2	0

Mark McGwire

MIKE PONZINI

Outfielder Rickey Henderson led Oakland with a .300 average and 31 doubles

A's minor league Player of the Year Steve Cox

R&R SPORTS GROUP

MEL BAILEY

ATHLETICS

FARM SYSTEM

Director of Player Development: Keith Lieppman.

Class	Farm Team	League	W	L	Pct.	Finish*	Manager	First Yr
AAA	Edmonton (Alta.) Trappers	Pacific Coast	68	76	.472	6th (10)	Gary Jones	1995
AA	Huntsville (Ala.) Stars	Southern	70	74	.486	6th (10)	Dick Scott	1985
#A	Modesto (Calif.) A's	California	78	62	.557	3rd (10)	Glenn Ezell	1975
A	West Michigan Whitecaps	Midwest	67	69	.493	8th (14)	Jim Colborn	1994
A	Southern Oregon A's	Northwest	33	43	.434	7th (8)	Tony DeFrancesco	1979
R	Scottsdale (Ariz.) Athletics	Arizona	37	19	.661	1st+ (6)	Juan Navarette	1988

*Finish in overall standings (No. of teams in league)   #Advanced level   +Won league championship

ORGANIZATION LEADERS

MAJOR LEAGUERS

BATTING
*AVG	Rickey Henderson	.300
R	Geronimo Berroa	87
H	Geronimo Berroa	152
TB	Geronimo Berroa	246
2B	Rickey Henderson	31
3B	Brent Gates	4
HR	Mark McGwire	39
RBI	Mark McGwire	90
BB	Mark McGwire	88
SO	Geronimo Berroa	98
SB	Stan Javier	36

PITCHING
W	Todd Stottlemyre	14
L	Todd Van Poppel	8
#ERA	Steve Ontiveros	4.37
G	Dennis Eckersley	52
CG	Two tied at	2
SV	Dennis Eckersley	29
IP	Todd Stottlemyre	210
BB	Todd Stottlemyre	80
SO	Todd Stottlemyre	205

Dennis Eckersley. 29 saves

MIKE PONZINI

MINOR LEAGUERS

BATTING
*AVG	George Williams, Edmonton	.310
R	Jason McDonald, Modesto	109
H	Scott Spiezio, Huntsville	149
TB	Steve Cox, Modesto	269
2B	Two tied at	33
3B	Scott Spiezio, Huntsville	8
HR	Two tied at	30
RBI	Steve Cox, Modesto	110
BB	Jason McDonald, Modesto	110
SO	Gary Hust, Modesto	169
SB	Jason McDonald, Modesto	70

PITCHING
W	Bobby Chouinard, Huntsville	14
L	Stacy Hollins, Huntsville/Edmonton	15
#ERA	Derek Manning, Modesto/Huntsville	2.85
G	Mike Maurer, Modesto/Huntsville	56
CG	Two tied at	2
SV	Mike Maurer, Modesto/Huntsville	24
IP	John Wasdin, Edmonton	174
BB	Curtis Shaw, Edmonton	88
SO	Brad Rigby, Modesto	145

*Minimum 250 At-Bats   #Minimum 75 Innings

TOP 10 PROSPECTS

How the Athletics Top 10 prospects, as judged by Baseball America prior to the 1995 season, fared in 1995:

Ben Grieve

FRANK RAGSDALE

Player, Pos.	Club (Class—League)	AVG	AB	R	H	2B	3B	HR	RBI	SB
1. Ben Grieve, of	West Michigan (A—Midwest)	.261	371	53	97	16	1	4	62	11
	Modesto (A—California)	.262	107	17	28	5	0	2	14	2
3. Jose Herrera, of	Huntsville (AA—Southern)	.282	358	37	101	11	4	6	45	9
	Oakland	.243	70	9	17	1	2	0	2	1
4. Jason Giambi, 3b	Edmonton (AAA—Pacific Coast)	.342	190	34	65	26	1	3	41	0
	Oakland	.256	176	27	45	7	0	6	25	2
6. Ernie Young, of	Edmonton (AAA—Pacific Coast)	.277	347	70	96	21	4	15	72	2
	Oakland	.200	50	9	10	3	0	2	5	0

Player, Pos.	Club (Class—League)	W	L	ERA	G	SV	IP	H	BB	SO
2. John Wasdin, rhp	Edmonton (AAA—Pacific Coast)	12	8	5.52	29	0	174	193	38	111
	Oakland	1	1	4.67	5	0	17	14	3	6
5. Stacy Hollins, rhp	Huntsville (AA—Southern)	3	8	5.33	11	0	83	80	42	62
	Edmonton (AAA—Pacific Coast)	0	7	10.31	7	0	30	47	21	25
7. Steve Wojciechowski, lhp	Edmonton (AAA—Pacific Coast)	6	3	3.69	14	0	78	75	21	39
	Oakland	2	3	5.18	14	0	49	51	28	13
8. Willie Adams, rhp	Huntsville (AA—Southern)	6	5	3.01	13	0	81	75	17	72
	Edmonton (AAA—Pacific Coast)	2	5	4.37	11	0	68	73	15	40
9. Don Wengert, rhp	Edmonton (AAA—Pacific Coast)	1	1	7.38	16	1	39	55	16	20
	Oakland	1	1	3.34	19	0	30	30	12	16
10. Heath Haynes, rhp	Edmonton (AAA—Pacific Coast)	2	0	6.27	12	0	19	21	11	13

BATTING

	AVG	G	AB	R	H	2B	3B	HR	RBI	BB	SO	SB	CS	B	T	HT	WT	DOB	1st Yr	Resides
Beard, Garrett	.230	22	61	5	14	2	0	0	10	3	7	0	0	R	R	6-1	190	2-1-69	1989	Irwin, Pa.
Beauchamp, Kash	.200	1	5	0	1	0	0	0	1	0	0	0	0	R	R	6-3	165	1-8-63	1982	Fortston, Ga.
Bowie, Jim	.267	141	531	69	142	26	2	3	70	54	51	4	1	L	L	6-0	200	2-17-65	1986	Suisun City, Calif.
Bryant, Scott	.288	119	406	58	117	33	3	10	69	49	87	1	3	R	R	6-2	215	10-31-67	1989	San Antonio, Texas
Cruz, Fausto	.281	114	448	72	126	23	2	11	67	34	67	7	5	R	R	5-11	165	1-5-72	1990	Villa Vasquez, D.R.
Faries, Paul	.300	117	424	67	127	15	2	0	46	34	47	14	8	R	R	5-10	170	2-20-65	1987	San Diego, Calif.
Gallego, Mike	.278	6	18	1	5	1	0	0	1	0	4	0	0	R	R	5-8	160	10-31-60	1981	Yorba Linda, Calif.
Giambi, Jason	.342	55	190	34	65	26	1	3	41	34	26	0	0	L	R	6-2	200	1-8-71	1992	Covina, Calif.
Helfand, Eric	.214	19	56	5	12	4	2	1	12	9	10	0	1	L	R	6-0	210	3-25-69	1990	San Diego, Calif.
Jones, Tim	.500	2	6	1	3	1	0	0	1	0	0	0	0	L	R	5-10	172	12-1-62	1985	Sumter, S.C.
Lydy, Scott	.290	104	400	78	116	29	7	16	65	33	66	15	4	R	R	6-5	205	10-26-68	1989	Mesa, Ariz.
Maksudian, Mike	.265	100	324	54	86	24	4	3	34	46	55	5	1	L	R	5-11	220	5-28-66	1987	Libertyville, Ill.
Mashore, Damon	.300	117	337	50	101	19	5	1	37	42	77	17	5	S	R	5-11	195	10-31-69	1991	Concord, Calif.
Molina, Izzy	.167	2	6	0	1	0	0	0	0	0	2	0	0	R	R	6-0	200	6-3-71	1990	Miami, Fla.
Moore, Kevin	.279	72	265	53	74	14	4	2	26	47	67	10	3	S	R	6-1	190	10-29-70	1988	Detroit, Mich.
Northrup, Kevin	.182	17	44	4	8	2	0	0	1	5	8	0	0	R	R	6-1	190	1-27-70	1992	Sanford, N.C.
Saunders, Doug	.188	5	16	2	3	2	1	0	4	0	2	0	0	R	R	6-0	172	12-13-69	1988	Port St. Lucie, Fla.
Sheldon, Scott	.258	45	128	21	33	7	1	4	12	15	15	4	2	R	R	6-3	185	11-28-68	1991	Houston, Texas
Tomberlin, Andy	.250	14	52	9	13	3	0	2	7	5	15	0	0	L	L	5-11	160	11-7-66	1986	Monroe, N.C.
Williams, George	.310	81	290	53	90	20	0	13	55	50	52	0	4	S	R	5-10	190	4-22-69	1991	La Crosse, Wis.
Wolfe, Joel	.205	11	39	4	8	3	0	0	4	2	7	0	2	R	R	6-3	205	6-18-70	1991	Northridge, Calif.
Wood, Jason	.235	127	421	49	99	20	5	2	50	29	72	1	4	R	R	6-1	170	12-16-69	1991	Fresno, Calif.
Young, Ernie	.277	95	347	70	96	21	4	15	72	49	73	2	2	R	R	6-1	190	7-8-69	1990	Chicago, Ill.

PITCHING

	W	L	ERA	G	GS	CG	SV	IP	H	R	ER	BB	SO	B	T	HT	WT	DOB	1st Yr	Resides
Adams, Willie	2	5	4.37	11	10	1	0	68	73	35	33	15	40	R	R	6-7	215	10-8-72	1993	La Mirada, Calif.
Baker, Scott	4	7	5.28	22	20	1	0	107	123	69	63	46	56	L	L	6-2	175	5-18-70	1990	Henderson, Nev.
Bankhead, Scott	1	3	7.85	12	0	0	1	18	28	18	16	7	15	R	R	5-10	185	7-31-63	1985	Asheboro, N.C.
Bittiger, Jeff	2	0	5.28	6	1	0	0	15	17	10	9	7	15	R	R	5-10	175	4-13-62	1980	Colonia, N.J.
Brink, Brad	0	1	4.88	9	3	0	0	24	24	20	13	16	15	R	R	6-2	203	1-20-65	1986	Modesto, Calif.
2-team (11 Phoenix)	2	6	6.29	20	12	0	0	69	79	55	48	46	48							
Briscoe, John	0	0	3.00	3	0	0	0	6	5	2	2	5	3	R	R	6-3	195	9-22-67	1988	Richardson, Texas
Brock, Russ	1	8	6.87	18	8	0	1	55	75	44	42	31	44	R	R	6-5	210	10-13-69	1991	Lockland, Ohio
Corsi, Jim	0	0	0.00	3	0	0	3	3	0	0	0	1	3	R	R	6-1	220	9-9-61	1982	Natick, Mass.
Daspit, Jim	0	1	10.80	2	0	0	0	5	6	6	6	2	5	R	R	6-7	210	8-10-69	1990	Sacramento, Calif.
2-team (36 Tucson)	5	2	4.10	38	0	0	1	68	69	36	31	24	54							
Haynes, Heath	2	0	6.27	12	0	0	0	19	21	14	13	11	13	R	R	6-0	175	11-30-68	1991	Wheeling, W.Va.
Hollins, Stacy	0	7	10.31	7	7	0	0	30	47	43	34	21	25	R	R	6-3	195	7-31-72	1992	Willis, Texas
Hostetler, Tom	0	0	12.60	4	0	0	0	5	9	7	7	8	7	R	R	5-10	165	10-10-64	1987	Villa Park, Ill.
Jimenez, Miguel	0	0	12.27	6	3	0	0	7	12	10	10	10	4	R	R	6-2	205	8-19-69	1991	New York, N.Y.
Johns, Doug	9	5	3.41	23	21	0	0	132	148	55	50	43	70	R	L	6-2	185	12-19-67	1990	Plantation, Fla.
Kubinski, Tim	1	2	4.78	6	5	0	0	32	34	18	17	10	12	L	L	6-4	205	1-20-72	1993	San Luis Obispo, Calif.
Leiper, Dave	1	0	13.50	2	0	0	0	1	4	2	2	2	1	L	L	6-1	160	6-18-62	1982	Plano, Texas
Mohler, Mike	2	1	2.60	29	0	0	5	45	40	16	13	20	28	R	L	6-2	195	7-26-68	1990	Gonzales, La.
Murphy, Dan	0	1	5.40	1	0	0	0	2	1	1	1	3	2	R	R	6-2	195	9-18-64	1983	Hesperia, Calif.
Peek, Tim	0	0	4.57	12	0	0	0	22	20	11	11	7	6	R	R	6-2	210	1-23-68	1987	Elkhart, Ind.
Phoenix, Steve	4	3	4.50	40	0	0	5	64	66	36	32	28	28	R	R	6-3	183	1-31-68	1990	El Cajon, Calif.
Revenig, Todd	4	5	4.31	45	0	0	10	54	53	32	26	15	28	R	R	6-1	185	6-28-69	1990	Baxter, Minn.
Rose, Scott	0	2	6.30	5	1	0	0	10	13	7	7	7	0	R	R	6-3	200	5-12-70	1990	Tampa, Fla.
Sanchez, Alex	0	0	5.19	8	0	0	0	17	18	12	10	10	8	R	R	6-2	200	4-8-66	1987	Antioch, Calif.
Shaw, Curtis	6	5	4.67	42	3	0	2	98	91	60	51	88	52	L	L	6-2	190	8-16-69	1990	Bartlesville, Okla.
Smith, Tim	3	2	6.03	9	7	0	0	37	44	27	25	22	22	R	R	6-2	185	10-24-69	1991	Westerville, Ohio
Stanhope, Chuck	1	1	4.50	6	0	0	0	6	8	3	3	1	2	R	R	6-4	185	3-23-64	1985	Pensacola, Fla.
Swan, Russ	3	3	4.34	17	0	0	4	19	23	9	9	11	10	L	L	6-4	210	1-3-64	1986	Kent, Wash.
Telford, Anthony	3	2	7.18	8	0	0	0	36	47	32	29	16	17	R	R	6-0	175	3-6-66	1987	Pinellas Park, Fla.
Wasdin, John	12	8	5.52	29	28	2	0	174	193	117	107	38	111	R	R	6-2	195	8-5-72	1993	Tallahassee, Fla.
Wengert, Don	1	1	7.38	16	6	0	1	39	55	32	32	16	20	R	R	6-3	205	11-6-69	1992	Sioux City, Iowa
Wojciechowski, Steve	6	3	3.69	14	12	0	0	78	75	37	32	21	39	L	L	6-2	185	7-29-70	1991	Calumet City, Ill.

FIELDING

Catcher	PCT	G	PO	A	E	DP	PB
Beard	.977	17	75	10	2	1	0
Helfand	.968	16	79	11	3	2	1
Maksudian	.989	54	241	33	3	2	8
Molina	1.000	2	9	1	0	0	0
Williams	.981	64	310	44	7	6	4

First Base	PCT	G	PO	A	E	DP
Beard	.000	1	0	0	0	0
Bowie	.996	138	1215	126	6	127
Bryant	.980	10	45	4	1	5
Giambi	1.000	3	7	0	0	1
Maksudian	1.000	4	16	1	0	0
Sheldon	1.000	3	21	2	0	2

Second Base	PCT	G	PO	A	E	DP
Faries	.984	105	230	261	8	75
Gallego	1.000	3	2	2	0	0

	PCT	G	PO	A	E	DP
Jones	1.000	1	0	1	0	0
Saunders	1.000	4	16	17	0	5
Sheldon	1.000	1	0	2	0	0
Wood	.968	39	84	98	6	17

Third Base	PCT	G	PO	A	E	DP
Bryant	.700	2	4	3	3	1
Faries	.857	3	3	3	1	0
Gallego	1.000	1	0	2	0	1
Giambi	.935	48	31	98	9	10
Jones	1.000	1	1	4	0	0
Maksudian	1.000	11	7	23	0	3
Sheldon	.959	32	20	74	4	8
Wood	.939	59	48	136	12	15

Shortstop	PCT	G	PO	A	E	DP
Cruz	.958	113	196	355	24	72
Faries	1.000	3	2	15	0	2

	PCT	G	PO	A	E	DP
Gallego	1.000	1	0	4	0	0
Sheldon	.933	3	3	11	1	2
Wood	.945	30	41	97	8	20

Outfield	PCT	G	PO	A	E	DP
Beauchamp	1.000	1	3	0	0	0
Bryant	.942	53	93	5	6	0
Lydy	.968	92	202	12	7	1
Maksudian	1.000	19	23	1	0	0
Mashore	.981	114	197	12	4	1
Moore	.974	63	147	5	4	2
Northrup	.933	10	12	2	1	0
Tomberlin	.929	12	25	1	2	0
Williams	.000	1	0	0	0	0
Wolfe	.923	11	12	0	1	0
Young	.971	90	194	7	6	0

SOUTHERN LEAGUE

BATTING

	AVG	G	AB	R	H	2B	3B	HR	RBI	BB	SO	SB	CS	B	T	HT	WT	DOB	1st Yr	Resides
Batista, Tony	.255	120	419	55	107	23	1	16	61	29	98	7	8	R	R	6-0	180	12-9-73	1992	Mao Valverde, D.R.
Beard, Garrett	.190	43	126	18	24	2	0	1	8	15	21	2	3	R	R	6-1	190	2-1-69	1989	Irwin, Pa.
Felix, Lauro	.111	10	27	3	3	0	0	1	1	2	8	0	0	R	R	5-9	160	6-24-70	1992	El Paso, Texas
Francisco, David	.279	129	477	75	133	17	1	5	48	38	92	30	8	R	R	6-0	165	2-27-72	1991	Santiago, D.R.
Gubanich, Creighton	.219	94	274	37	60	7	1	13	43	48	82	1	0	R	R	6-4	220	3-27-72	1991	Phoenixville, Pa.
Hart, Chris	.262	36	103	11	27	3	2	2	20	10	30	1	3	R	R	6-0	190	5-2-69	1990	Harrisonburg, Va.
Herrera, Jose	.282	92	358	37	101	11	4	6	45	27	58	9	8	L	L	6-0	164	8-30-72	1991	Santo Domingo, D.R.
Lesher, Brian	.261	127	471	78	123	23	2	19	71	64	110	7	8	R	L	6-5	205	3-5-71	1992	Newark, Del.
Molina, Izzy	.259	83	301	38	78	16	1	8	26	26	62	3	4	R	R	6-0	200	6-3-71	1990	Miami, Fla.
Neill, Mike	.299	33	107	11	32	6	1	2	16	12	29	1	0	L	L	6-2	189	4-27-70	1991	Langhorne, Pa.
Sheldon, Scott	.217	66	235	25	51	10	2	4	15	23	60	5	0	R	R	6-3	185	11-28-68	1991	Houston, Texas
Sobolewski, Mark	.205	83	307	35	63	14	1	7	34	22	62	2	1	R	R	5-11	185	2-10-70	1992	Southington, Conn.
Spiezio, Scott	.282	141	528	78	149	33	8	13	86	67	78	10	3	S	R	6-2	205	9-21-72	1993	Morris, Ill.
Waggoner, Jim	.200	51	110	18	22	5	1	0	15	34	29	1	2	L	R	5-11	185	4-17-67	1989	Hermitage, Tenn.
Walker, Dane	.232	110	370	46	86	13	2	2	35	57	84	9	7	L	R	5-10	180	11-16-69	1991	Lake Oswego, Ore.
White, Jason	.234	48	167	20	39	4	1	8	27	24	49	2	1	R	L	6-3	215	2-26-70	1992	Mulvane, Kan.
Wolfe, Joel	.256	108	399	58	102	15	2	12	41	54	75	23	12	R	R	6-3	205	6-18-70	1991	Northridge, Calif.

PITCHING

	W	L	ERA	G	GS	CG	SV	IP	H	R	ER	BB	SO	B	T	HT	WT	DOB	1st Yr	Resides
Abbott, Todd	0	0	4.05	4	0	0	0	7	6	3	3	3	4	R	R	6-4	200	9-13-73	1995	North Little Rock, Ark.
Adams, Willie	6	5	3.01	13	13	0	0	81	75	33	27	17	72	R	R	6-7	215	10-8-72	1993	La Mirada, Calif.
Banks, Jim	3	2	4.73	44	1	0	2	67	72	39	35	40	52	R	R	6-0	200	1-3-70	1992	Olive Branch, Miss.
Bennett, Bob	10	7	4.22	23	21	0	0	117	119	62	55	38	96	R	R	6-4	205	12-30-70	1992	Rapid City, S.D.
Chouinard, Bobby	14	8	3.62	29	29	1	0	167	155	81	67	50	106	R	R	6-1	188	5-1-72	1990	Forest Grove, Ore.
Dressendorfer, Kirk	0	1	3.15	9	4	0	0	20	13	7	7	5	18	R	R	5-11	180	4-8-69	1990	Pearland, Texas
Fermin, Ramon	6	7	3.86	32	13	0	7	100	105	53	43	45	58	R	R	6-3	180	11-25-72	1990	San Fran. de Macoris, D.R.
Grigsby, Benji	3	5	4.01	30	6	0	3	76	66	40	34	20	55	R	R	6-1	200	12-2-70	1992	Lafayette, La.
Haught, Gary	1	1	4.30	9	3	0	0	23	23	14	11	8	20	S	R	6-1	195	9-29-70	1992	Choctaw, Okla.
Hollins, Stacy	3	8	5.33	15	15	0	0	83	80	52	49	42	62	R	R	6-3	195	7-31-72	1992	Willis, Texas
Jimenez, Miguel	3	2	3.60	6	6	0	0	30	25	12	12	11	28	R	R	6-2	205	8-19-69	1991	New York, N.Y.
Lemke, Steve	4	9	4.38	25	19	0	0	125	144	72	61	29	65	R	R	6-1	185	1-4-70	1992	Lincolnshire, Ill.
Manning, Derek	1	2	4.50	5	5	0	0	28	26	14	14	7	22	L	L	6-4	220	7-21-70	1993	Wilmington, N.C.
Maurer, Mike	0	2	6.53	17	0	0	6	21	34	18	15	5	19	R	R	6-2	195	7-4-72	1994	Burnsville, Minn.
Michalak, Chris	1	1	11.12	7	0	0	1	6	10	7	7	5	4	L	L	6-2	195	1-4-71	1993	Lemont, Ill.
Pierce, Rob	1	1	9.87	15	0	0	0	17	26	21	19	14	16	R	R	6-2	200	12-17-70	1991	Mapleton, Utah
Plaster, Allen	1	0	3.18	43	0	0	2	68	63	26	24	26	47	R	R	6-3	210	8-13-70	1991	Kernersville, N.C.
Rose, Scott	4	6	2.59	38	5	0	13	80	70	24	23	23	35	R	R	6-3	200	5-12-70	1990	Tampa, Fla.
Shoemaker, Steve	4	4	3.43	43	0	0	5	76	62	33	29	31	63	R	R	6-3	195	2-24-70	1991	Columbus, Ohio
Taylor, Aaron	1	1	2.13	5	4	0	0	25	26	7	6	8	24	R	R	6-4	185	2-13-71	1989	Reno, Nev.
Thomas, Carlos	2	2	4.97	7	0	0	0	13	13	8	7	5	12	R	R	6-4	215	8-6-68	1991	Memphis, Tenn.
Zongor, Steve	2	0	7.62	9	0	0	0	13	13	11	11	9	11	R	L	6-0	190	6-30-70	1993	Franklin, Tenn.

FIELDING

Catcher	PCT	G	PO	A	E	DP	PB
Beard	.978	29	162	17	4	1	3
Gubanich	.997	43	253	47	1	4	8
Molina	.980	78	455	74	11	11	14

First Base	PCT	G	PO	A	E	DP
Beard	1.000	2	5	0	0	0
Gubanich	.990	21	179	22	2	20
Lesher	.941	3	14	2	1	2
Molina	.889	1	7	1	1	0
Sheldon	.991	10	103	5	1	9
Spiezio	1.000	2	17	0	0	3
White	.986	48	445	32	7	45
Wolfe	.992	62	592	48	5	60

Second Base	PCT	G	PO	A	E	DP
Batista	.970	18	35	61	3	14

	PCT	G	PO	A	E	DP
Sheldon	.974	27	57	90	4	19
Sobolewski	.964	83	160	238	15	58
Spiezio	1.000	1	1	4	0	1
Waggoner	.979	21	39	55	2	12

Third Base	PCT	G	PO	A	E	DP
Beard	1.000	1	0	1	0	0
Gubanich	.765	5	3	10	4	1
Sheldon	1.000	2	3	5	0	2
Spiezio	.932	134	104	291	29	34
Waggoner	1.000	6	5	6	0	1

Shortstop	PCT	G	PO	A	E	DP
Batista	.945	102	133	310	26	59
Felix	.964	9	7	20	1	6

	PCT	G	PO	A	E	DP
Sheldon	.948	25	40	88	7	23
Waggoner	.986	17	22	50	1	9

Outfield	PCT	G	PO	A	E	DP
Felix	.000	1	0	0	0	0
Francisco	.979	128	267	15	6	4
Gubanich	.000	1	0	0	0	0
Hart	.980	28	48	2	1	1
Herrera	.958	90	176	6	8	0
Lesher	.974	114	184	5	5	2
Neill	1.000	13	24	0	0	0
Walker	.944	50	65	2	4	0
Wolfe	1.000	24	44	2	0	0

CALIFORNIA LEAGUE

BATTING

	AVG	G	AB	R	H	2B	3B	HR	RBI	BB	SO	SB	CS	B	T	HT	WT	DOB	1st Yr	Resides
Banks, Tony	.198	28	81	10	16	3	0	1	10	13	17	3	0	L	L	5-11	190	9-21-71	1993	Oakland, Calif.
Bellhorn, Mark	.258	56	229	35	59	12	0	6	31	27	52	5	2	S	R	6-1	195	8-23-74	1995	Oviedo, Fla.
Bengoechea, Brandy	.261	134	467	60	122	19	4	5	44	47	96	7	10	R	R	5-11	170	8-2-71	1993	Lewiston, Idaho
Bordick, Mike	.000	2	2	0	0	0	0	0	0	0	0	0	1	R	R	5-11	170	7-21-65	1986	Winterport, Maine
Cox, Steve	.298	132	483	95	144	29	3	30	110	84	88	5	4	L	L	6-4	225	10-31-74	1992	Strathmore, Calif.
Cromer, D.T.	.259	108	378	59	98	18	5	14	52	36	66	5	7	L	L	6-2	205	3-19-71	1992	Murrells Inlet, S.C.
Grieve, Ben	.262	28	107	17	28	5	0	2	14	15	22	2	0	L	R	6-4	200	5-4-76	1994	Arlington, Texas
Guillen, Jose	.257	41	113	16	29	2	1	1	11	11	24	9	3	R	R	5-11	160	6-1-73	1991	Santo Domingo, D.R.
Hust, Gary	.238	128	467	85	111	20	2	27	87	61	169	10	4	R	R	6-4	215	3-15-72	1992	Petal, Miss.
Keel, David	.200	9	25	4	5	0	0	1	3	3	7	0	0	L	R	6-3	205	7-23-72	1992	Toney, Ala.
Martins, Eric	.290	106	407	71	118	17	5	1	54	62	74	7	8	R	R	5-10	175	11-19-72	1994	Rowland Heights, Calif.
McDonald, Jason	.262	133	493	109	129	25	7	6	50	110	84	70	20	S	R	5-8	175	3-20-72	1993	Elk Grove, Calif.
Moore, Kerwin	.245	15	53	8	13	3	1	1	6	11	16	3	3	S	R	6-1	190	10-29-70	1988	Detroit, Mich.
Moore, Mark	.261	77	261	40	68	16	0	10	48	42	76	3	2	R	R	6-2	215	7-22-70	1992	Prairie Village, Kan.
Morales, Willie	.277	109	419	49	116	32	0	4	60	28	75	1	4	R	R	5-10	182	9-7-72	1993	Tucson, Ariz.
Moschetti, Mike	.351	23	77	5	27	6	0	0	9	6	16	0	2	R	R	6-0	175	3-14-75	1993	La Mirada, Calif.
Neill, Mike	.276	71	257	39	71	17	1	6	36	34	65	4	4	L	L	6-2	189	4-27-70	1991	Langhorne, Pa.

BATTING	AVG	G	AB	R	H	2B	3B	HR	RBI	BB	SO	SB	CS	B	T	HT	WT	DOB	1st Yr	Resides
Ortega, Randy	.174	10	23	2	4	1	0	0	1	6	7	0	0	R	R	6-1	205	7-5-72	1993	Stockton, Calif.
Paulino, Arturo	.111	5	9	2	1	0	0	0	0	4	4	1	0	R	R	5-11	170	7-18-74	1993	San Cristobal, D.R.
Reese, Mat	.200	15	50	4	10	4	0	1	6	4	23	0	2	L	L	6-3	205	5-3-71	1993	Maricopa, Ariz.
White, Jason	.307	76	267	63	82	16	1	22	71	54	71	1	2	R	L	6-3	215	2-26-70	1992	Mulvane, Kan.

GAMES BY POSITION: C—M. Moore 37, Morales 101, Ortega 7. 1B—Bengoechea 4, Cox 114, Cromer 4, Morales 3, Ortega 1, White 16. 2B—Bengoechea 4, Guillen 12, Martins 98, McDonald 14, Moschetti 20. 3B—Bengoechea 129, Guillen 7, Martins 11, Morales 1, Ortega 2, Paulino 1. SS—Bellhorn 55, Bengoechea 1, Bordick 1, Guillen 5, McDonald 78, Paulino 4. OF—Banks 25, Cromer 95, Grieve 27, Guillen 2, Hust 128, Keel 9, McDonald 43, K. Moore 15, Neill 59, Reese 6, White 26.

PITCHING	W	L	ERA	G	GS	CG	SV	IP	H	R	ER	BB	SO	B	T	HT	WT	DOB	1st Yr	Resides
Baldwin, Scott	0	1	6.08	5	3	0	0	13	16	11	9	19	10	L	L	6-2	205	3-27-70	1993	Lewiston, Idaho
Baxter, Herb	4	7	6.60	29	14	0	0	91	104	75	67	64	73	L	L	6-2	165	8-25-71	1992	Pinewood, S.C.
Briscoe, John	0	0	1.59	4	4	0	0	6	5	1	1	2	5	R	R	6-3	195	9-22-67	1988	Richardson, Texas
Dressendorfer, Kirk	0	6	4.62	27	16	0	0	37	39	24	19	18	50	R	R	5-11	180	4-8-69	1990	Pearland, Texas
Haught, Gary	9	5	2.60	34	4	0	4	87	76	29	25	24	81	R	R	6-1	190	9-29-70	1992	Choctaw, Okla.
Huber, Aaron	0	0	0.00	4	0	0	0	5	7	3	0	3	5	R	R	6-2	190	8-24-72	1993	Humble, Texas
Jimenez, Miguel	1	2	6.00	4	4	0	0	18	14	13	12	14	11	R	R	6-2	205	8-19-69	1991	New York, N.Y.
Kubinski, Tim	6	10	4.95	25	17	0	2	109	126	73	60	24	83	L	L	6-4	205	1-20-72	1993	San Luis Obispo, Calif.
Manning, Derek	10	1	2.43	25	12	0	3	111	112	43	30	25	102	L	L	6-4	220	7-24-70	1993	Wilmington, N.C.
Maurer, Mike	2	1	1.79	39	0	0	18	40	27	9	8	9	44	R	R	6-2	195	7-4-72	1994	Burnsville, Minn.
Michalak, Chris	3	2	2.62	44	0	0	2	65	56	26	19	27	49	L	L	6-2	195	1-4-71	1993	Lemont, Ill.
Nelson, Chris	0	2	0.90	2	2	0	0	10	4	1	1	4	5	S	R	6-3	185	1-26-73	1995	San Diego, Calif.
Rigby, Brad	11	4	3.84	31	23	0	2	155	135	70	66	48	145	R	R	6-6	203	5-14-73	1994	Longwood, Fla.
Rossiter, Mike	7	2	4.19	18	7	0	0	69	68	33	32	19	70	R	R	6-6	230	6-20-73	1991	Burbank, Calif.
Sawyer, Zach	7	1	5.40	15	0	0	3	70	68	45	42	28	72	R	R	6-4	215	3-19-73	1993	Clinton, Mass.
Urbina, William	2	0	5.27	30	0	0	1	41	51	28	24	16	18	R	R	6-4	210	2-9-74	1992	Tucson, Ariz.
Walsh, Matt	2	7	4.65	44	9	0	5	101	98	64	52	45	108	R	R	6-2	197	12-12-72	1993	Melrose, Mass.
Whitaker, Ryan	5	10	4.41	32	25	0	0	151	177	90	74	54	88	R	R	6-0	175	2-3-72	1993	Broken Arrow, Okla.
Zongor, Steve	2	4	4.07	37	0	0	1	55	57	29	25	21	55	R	L	6-0	190	6-30-70	1993	Franklin, Tenn.

WEST MICHIGAN   A
MIDWEST LEAGUE

BATTING	AVG	G	AB	R	H	2B	3B	HR	RBI	BB	SO	SB	CS	B	T	HT	WT	DOB	1st Yr	Resides
Brown, Emil	.251	124	459	63	115	17	3	3	67	52	77	35	19	R	R	6-2	200	12-29-74	1994	Chicago, Ill.
Castro, Jose	.240	113	409	76	98	20	2	2	40	76	94	51	20	S	R	5-10	165	10-15-74	1994	Villa Vasquez, D.R.
D'Amico, Jeff	.226	125	434	56	98	24	1	7	55	56	94	8	5	R	R	6-3	190	11-9-74	1993	Redmond, Wash.
DaSilva, Manny	.316	7	19	5	6	2	1	0	3	4	4	0	0	R	R	6-1	195	8-17-72	1994	Mebane, N.C.
DeBoer, Rob	.242	104	339	57	82	25	2	6	50	58	110	11	6	R	R	5-10	205	2-4-71	1994	Omaha, Neb.
Francisco, Vicente	.245	85	277	41	68	8	2	1	25	30	48	4	8	S	R	6-2	150	7-5-72	1990	Mao Valverde, D.R.
Grieve, Ben	.261	102	371	53	97	16	1	4	62	60	75	11	3	L	R	6-4	200	5-4-76	1994	Arlington, Texas
Hamburg, Leon	.183	85	268	40	49	16	2	2	32	42	78	12	3	R	R	6-0	195	1-4-75	1993	Granite Bay, Calif.
Harris, Eric	.168	70	202	29	34	9	2	7	29	26	73	5	0	R	R	6-2	220	2-9-73	1993	Columbia, Tenn.
Miranda, Alex	.232	124	393	53	91	21	2	8	60	75	78	6	8	L	L	6-2	195	5-14-72	1994	Miami, Fla.
Moschetti, Mike	.318	8	22	6	7	2	0	0	3	3	8	1	0	R	R	6-0	175	3-14-75	1993	La Mirada, Calif.
Newhan, David	.219	25	96	9	21	5	0	3	8	13	26	3	2	L	R	5-10	180	9-7-73	1995	Yorba Linda, Calif.
Ortega, Randy	.216	48	162	8	35	4	0	0	13	13	27	0	2	R	R	6-1	205	7-5-72	1993	Stockton, Calif.
Rondon, Alex	.216	25	74	11	16	3	0	2	5	7	13	1	0	R	R	6-0	175	7-4-74	1994	Guatire, Venez.
Sanders, Pat	.208	11	24	4	5	0	0	0	3	4	6	0	0	L	L	6-0	205	8-28-71	1993	Huntsville, Ala.
Smith, Demond	.313	8	32	6	10	1	1	2	3	2	8	3	2	S	R	5-11	170	11-6-72	1990	Rialto, Calif.
2-team (79 Cedar Rap.)	.338	87	349	70	118	26	8	9	44	34	69	40	14							
Soriano, Fred	.262	107	305	68	80	7	3	3	32	51	72	40	6	S	R	5-9	160	8-5-74	1993	Bani, D.R.
Soriano, Jose	.213	123	413	64	88	12	2	6	43	30	103	35	12	R	R	6-1	180	4-4-74	1992	Bani, D.R.

GAMES BY POSITION: C—DaSilva 5, DeBoer 83, Hamburg 2, Ortega 42, Rondon 21. 1B—Francisco 3, Harris 24, Miranda 118, Sanders 6. 2B—Castro 99, Francisco 41, Hamburg 4, Moschetti 6. 3B—D'Amico 108, Francisco 36, Ortega 2. SS—Castro 14, D'Amico 21, Francisco 11, F. Soriano 106. OF—Brown 109, Castro 2, Grieve 92, Hamburg 61, Harris 6, Newhan 23, Smith 7, J. Soriano 121.

PITCHING	W	L	ERA	G	GS	CG	SV	IP	H	R	ER	BB	SO	B	T	HT	WT	DOB	1st Yr	Resides
Beverlin, Jason	3	9	4.04	22	14	0	0	89	76	51	40	40	84	L	R	6-5	230	11-27-73	1994	Royal Oak, Mich.
Cochrane, Chris	6	4	3.07	41	4	0	9	85	79	37	29	28	48	R	R	6-3	205	12-21-72	1994	South Plainfield, N.J.
Delvalle, Henry	1	1	3.38	3	0	0	0	5	4	2	2	4	8	L	L	6-0	190	9-19-72	1995	Chicago, Ill.
Epstein, Ian	5	0	5.89	18	0	0	0	18	24	14	12	10	16	L	L	6-3	215	3-29-71	1994	Piedmont, Calif.
Gunther, Kevin	1	3	3.71	9	0	0	2	27	28	16	11	3	17	R	R	6-0	200	2-6-73	1995	Olympia, Wash.
Hause, Brendan	8	7	3.87	31	18	0	0	137	136	75	59	57	106	L	L	6-1	185	10-21-74	1994	San Diego, Calif.
King, Bill	9	7	3.34	30	18	0	2	148	152	75	55	41	95	R	R	6-5	225	2-18-73	1994	Mobile, Ala.
Leibee, Skye	0	1	11.74	9	0	0	8	9	13	10	13	5	5	L	L	5-10	180	10-29-73	1993	Taft, Calif.
Lowe, Jason	0	0	11.00	7	0	0	0	9	17	14	11	6	7	R	R	5-11	185	12-27-72	1993	Pensacola, Fla.
Morrison, Chris	4	1	4.98	13	0	0	0	22	28	13	12	4	13	R	R	6-0	195	4-3-72	1995	Lithonia, Ga.
Newman, Damon	3	4	3.74	21	9	0	1	67	57	32	28	50	52	R	R	6-3	210	7-17-73	1993	Greensboro, N.C.
Perez, Juan	11	8	3.64	30	19	1	1	141	129	73	57	55	117	L	L	6-0	168	3-28-73	1992	La Romana, D.R.
Rajotte, Jason	2	2	3.12	44	0	0	13	52	51	27	18	38	52	L	L	6-0	175	12-15-72	1993	West Warwick, R.I.
Rivette, Scott	1	0	2.93	8	0	0	2	15	12	5	5	5	15	S	R	6-2	200	1-8-74	1995	Upland, Calif.
Silva, Luis	1	0	6.75	10	1	0	0	21	31	16	16	7	21	R	R	6-4	200	4-18-75	1994	Guatire, Venez.
Smith, Andy	4	10	3.89	30	22	0	2	123	117	71	53	72	68	R	R	6-5	220	1-29-75	1993	Kannapolis, N.C.
Smith, John	1	0	4.05	25	0	0	1	33	32	21	15	18	33	L	L	6-1	200	2-7-72	1994	Steelton, Pa.
Sosa, Helpis	3	5	4.70	21	6	0	2	54	59	47	28	26	37	R	R	6-4	198	6-26-74	1993	Santo Domingo, D.R.
Weinberg, Todd	4	5	4.76	36	9	0	1	87	86	52	46	56	54	R	L	6-3	225	6-13-72	1993	Somerset, Mass.
Zancanaro, Dave	0	2	2.20	16	16	0	0	33	19	8	8	15	42	L	L	6-1	170	1-8-69	1990	Sacramento, Calif.

SOUTHERN OREGON   A
NORTHWEST LEAGUE

BATTING	AVG	G	AB	R	H	2B	3B	HR	RBI	BB	SO	SB	CS	B	T	HT	WT	DOB	1st Yr	Resides
Ardoin, Danny	.234	58	175	28	41	9	1	2	23	31	50	2	1	R	R	6-0	195	7-8-74	1995	Ville Platte, La.

BATTING	AVG	G	AB	R	H	2B	3B	HR	RBI	BB	SO	SB	CS	B	T	HT	WT	DOB	1st Yr	Resides
Christenson, Ryan	.190	49	158	14	30	4	1	1	16	22	33	5	5	R	R	5-11	175	3-28-74	1995	Apple Valley, Calif.
DaVanon, Jeff	.251	57	167	29	42	6	2	1	17	34	49	6	5	S	R	6-0	185	12-8-73	1995	Del Mar, Calif.
DaSilva, Manny	.246	55	195	31	48	14	4	3	33	26	25	3	1	R	R	6-1	195	8-17-72	1994	Mebane, N.C.
Filchner, Duane	.275	62	189	34	52	4	0	6	34	35	28	12	8	L	L	6-1	185	2-28-73	1995	Northampton, Pa.
Harris, Robert	.252	63	230	31	58	14	1	1	16	32	32	9	5	R	R	5-8	175	2-1-72	1995	Sugar Land, Texas
Klostermeyer, Mike	.237	64	186	31	44	7	0	3	19	31	36	4	2	L	L	6-2	195	4-26-74	1995	Papillion, Neb.
Knight, Bill	.206	48	136	21	28	7	1	2	19	21	43	5	4	R	R	6-0	195	8-27-72	1995	Holliston, Mass.
Moschetti, Mike	.241	39	141	21	34	4	1	0	15	20	27	13	1	R	R	6-0	175	3-14-75	1993	La Mirada, Calif.
Newhan, David	.269	42	145	25	39	8	1	6	21	29	30	10	5	L	R	5-10	180	9-7-73	1995	Yorba Linda, Calif.
Rondon, Alex...............	.359	14	39	7	14	4	0	0	7	4	12	0	1	R	R	6-0	175	7-4-74	1994	Guatire, Venez.
Slemmer, David	.224	66	246	36	55	5	3	1	20	36	42	16	4	R	R	6-0	187	3-29-73	1995	Edwardsville, Ill.
Tejada, Miguel	.245	74	269	45	66	15	5	8	44	41	54	19	2	R	R	5-10	180	5-25-76	1994	Bani, D.R.
Valenti, Jon.................	.209	35	110	13	23	5	0	2	16	8	18	2	0	R	R	6-1	195	11-26-73	1994	Bakersfield, Calif.
Welch, Brandon...........	.147	39	102	6	15	3	0	0	11	15	30	1	0	L	R	6-1	190	2-7-73	1995	Arkansas City, Kan.

GAMES BY POSITION: C—Ardoin 57, DaSilva 16, Rondon 10. **1B**—DaSilva 12, Filchner 3, Klostermeyer 57, Rondon 2, Slemmer 2, Valenti 16. **2B**—Harris 39, Moschetti 29, Slemmer 13. **3B**—DaSilva 4, Harris 15, Slemmer 51, Valenti 16. **SS**—Harris 4, Slemmer 4, Tejada 72. **OF**—Christenson 48, DaVanon 40, Filchner 56, Klostermeyer 1, Knight 45, Newhan 3, Welch 26.

PITCHING	W	L	ERA	G	GS	CG	SV	IP	H	R	ER	BB	SO	B	T	HT	WT	DOB	1st Yr	Resides
Abbott, Todd	2	3	2.96	17	5	0	1	49	39	22	16	18	41	R	R	6-4	200	9-13-73	1995	North Little Rock, Ark.
Batchelder, Bill	1	4	5.52	18	5	0	0	44	56	30	27	13	20	R	R	6-3	190	10-19-72	1995	North Andover, Mass.
Connelly, Steven	2	4	3.81	17	0	0	2	28	29	17	12	14	19	R	R	6-3	210	4-27-71	1995	Long Beach, Calif.
Costello, T.J.	0	0	6.23	3	0	0	0	4	8	4	3	2	5	L	L	6-2	195	12-29-73	1995	North Long Branch, N.J.
Epstein, Ian.................	2	2	2.90	23	0	0	1	40	32	17	13	9	36	L	L	6-3	215	3-29-71	1994	Piedmont, Calif.
French, Jon	1	2	6.41	20	0	0	0	27	34	21	19	17	18	R	R	6-4	175	10-9-72	1995	Kennett, Mo.
Gunther, Kevin	1	1	1.42	5	5	0	0	19	14	6	3	2	11	R	R	6-0	200	2-6-73	1995	Olympia, Wash.
Hilton, Willy	1	4	4.40	16	1	0	1	31	37	22	15	12	31	R	R	6-2	190	12-26-72	1995	Forrest City, Ark.
Holden, Jason	2	6	4.72	19	8	0	0	61	64	42	32	23	30	R	R	6-2	190	8-5-73	1994	Southaven, Miss.
Kjos, Ryan	2	0	2.45	9	0	0	2	11	9	4	3	5	16	R	R	6-5	220	3-4-73	1995	Hopkins, Minn.
Leibee, Skye................	0	0	3.86	2	0	0	0	2	1	1	1	1	3	L	L	5-10	180	10-29-73	1993	Taft, Calif.
McDonald, Matt	3	2	3.14	13	9	0	0	52	42	22	18	18	47	L	L	6-4	200	6-10-74	1994	Princeton, Ill.
Mimnaugh, Scott	2	3	3.24	3	3	0	0	8	10	8	3	4	8	R	R	6-5	230	4-9-71	1994	Ashland, Ore.
Mlodik, Kevin	2	2	3.15	20	10	0	0	60	62	35	21	20	43	R	R	6-1	205	8-21-74	1995	Rosholt, Wis.
Morrison, Chris	2	1	2.40	6	0	0	0	15	14	4	4	1	8	R	R	6-0	195	4-3-72	1995	Lithonia, Ga.
Nelson, Chris	2	3	3.48	16	6	0	1	54	43	25	21	13	52	S	R	6-3	185	1-26-73	1995	San Diego, Calif.
Newman, Damon	3	3	3.61	14	7	0	1	47	51	32	19	24	35	R	R	6-3	210	7-17-73	1993	Greensboro, N.C.
Rivette, Scott	2	0	0.95	9	1	0	2	19	16	5	2	11	22	S	R	6-2	200	4-28-74	1995	Upland, Calif.
Rolish, Chad	1	0	3.00	4	0	0	1	6	6	3	2	4	1	L	L	5-10	180	10-31-72	1995	Yorba Linda, Calif.
Silva, Luis	4	3	3.81	19	14	0	1	78	79	43	33	20	76	R	R	6-4	200	4-18-75	1994	Guatire, Venez.
Sosa, Helpis	0	1	6.75	6	2	0	0	13	21	11	10	6	17	R	R	6-4	198	6-26-73	1992	Santo Domingo, D.R.

SCOTTSDALE   R

ARIZONA LEAGUE

BATTING	AVG	G	AB	R	H	2B	3B	HR	RBI	BB	SO	SB	CS	B	T	HT	WT	DOB	1st Yr	Resides
Cesar, Dionys	.322	48	171	41	55	11	4	2	21	23	35	29	7	S	R	5-10	155	9-27-76	1994	Santo Domingo, D.R.
Chambers, Victor	.309	34	110	11	34	2	3	0	16	14	17	12	4	L	R	5-9	172	4-2-76	1995	Vallejo, Calif.
Ducasse, Luis...............	.063	6	16	1	1	0	0	1	5	8	0	0	R	R	6-0	190	12-21-76	1995	New York, N.Y.
Freeman, Terrance	.242	34	95	14	23	0	1	0	5	10	25	3	3	R	R	5-9	165	1-24-75	1995	Brandon, Fla.
Guerrero, Diogene	.228	41	136	27	31	4	5	1	13	29	48	11	7	R	R	5-9	175	6-1-75	1994	La Romana, D.R.
Hernandez, Ramon	.364	48	143	37	52	9	6	4	37	39	16	6	2	R	R	6-0	170	5-20-76	1994	Caracas, Venez.
Hernandez, Victor	.152	21	46	5	7	0	0	3	5	21	0	2	R	R	6-0	167	2-28-77	1995	Ciales, P.R.
Johnson, Jace	.132	17	38	4	5	1	0	1	4	4	16	1	1	R	R	6-0	175	7-24-74	1995	Phoenix, Ariz.
Jones, Timothy.............	.198	32	96	7	19	2	2	0	10	6	36	5	3	L	R	6-0	208	9-13-77	1995	Buena Park, Calif.
Lara, Edward	.288	47	184	42	53	6	6	1	26	22	19	23	9	R	R	5-10	160	10-30-75	1993	Bani, D.R.
Law, Khris	.165	36	103	17	17	1	0	2	11	15	37	5	3	S	R	6-0	172	1-31-75	1994	Danville, Va.
Martinez, Hipolito	.221	46	149	23	33	4	4	2	27	16	47	8	4	R	R	6-1	185	1-30-77	1994	Bani, D.R.
Paulino, Arturo	.256	31	117	18	30	2	4	0	13	14	36	14	1	R	R	5-11	170	7-18-74	1993	San Cristobal, D.R.
Polanco, Juan	.296	48	179	41	53	11	5	2	23	17	35	18	8	R	R	6-0	190	1-6-75	1993	Bani, D.R.
Rauer, Troy	.160	30	100	13	16	2	1	1	12	12	43	3	3	R	R	6-4	225	11-18-72	1995	St. Joseph, Mo.
Scheker, Luis	.250	16	60	9	15	3	1	1	11	11	16	1	1	R	R	6-3	200	4-18-74	1994	Santo Domingo, D.R.
Ventura, Wilfredo	.279	34	104	19	29	3	1	3	20	20	32	7	3	R	R	5-11	212	10-11-76	1993	Santo Domingo, D.R.

GAMES BY POSITION: C—R. Hernandez 30, V. Hernandez 1, Ventura 29. **1B**—R. Hernandez 13, Johnson 1, Jones 1, Paulino 4, Polanco 11, Rauer 10, Scheker 16, Ventura 5. **2B**—Cesar 34, Ducasse 1, Freeman 25, Guerrero 1, Lara 1, Paulino 2, Polanco 3. **3B**—Cesar 4, Guerrero 2, Hernandez 6, Lara 2, Paulino 5, Polanco 34. **SS**—Cesar 8, Lara 45, Paulino 7, Polanco 1. **OF**—Chambers 29, Ducasse 6, Guerrero 38, V. Hernandez 13, Jones 22, Law 32, Martinez 40, Rauer 8.

PITCHING	W	L	ERA	G	GS	CG	SV	IP	H	R	ER	BB	SO	B	T	HT	WT	DOB	1st Yr	Resides
Abreu, Oscar	1	2	7.96	20	1	0	0	26	33	30	23	35	29	R	R	6-1	155	12-7-73	1994	Santo Domingo, D.R.
Baez, Benito	5	1	3.34	14	11	1	0	70	64	35	26	28	83	R	R	6-0	180	5-6-77	1994	Bonao, D.R.
Bennett, Tom...............	1	1	2.72	11	6	0	0	36	20	16	11	16	46	R	R	6-4	180	5-13-76	1995	Alameda, Calif.
Costello, Terrance	2	3	3.74	12	6	0	1	43	46	22	18	9	41	L	L	6-2	195	12-29-75	1995	North Long Branch, N.J.
Foster, Cliff	0	0	27.00	1	0	0	0	1	4	4	3	0	0	R	R	6-0	182	12-24-71	1992	Texarkana, Texas
Kazmirski, Robert	4	0	2.13	28	0	0	10	38	36	13	9	6	32	R	R	6-3	200	6-24-72	1995	Agoura Hills, Calif.
Kjos, Ryan	0	0	19.64	3	0	0	0	4	9	10	8	1	5	R	R	6-5	220	3-4-73	1995	Hopkins, Minn.
Knickerbocker, Tom	4	3	3.92	17	7	0	1	44	39	27	19	25	40	L	L	6-4	200	7-15-75	1995	Prairie du Chien, Wis.
McDonald, Matt	0	0	2.20	5	1	0	0	16	11	7	4	9	23	L	L	6-4	200	6-10-74	1994	Princeton, Ill.
Moreno, Juan	6	2	1.21	20	0	0	0	45	36	10	6	20	49	L	L	6-1	200	2-28-75	1994	Caracas, Venez.
Nix, Wayne	0	1	5.79	6	3	0	0	14	15	10	9	4	14	R	R	6-5	210	9-16-76	1995	North Hills, Calif.
Osteen, Gavin	0	0	0.00	1	1	0	0	2	1	0	0	0	1	R	L	6-0	195	11-27-69	1989	Bethany Beach, Del.
Paulino, Jose	9	2	3.19	15	13	0	0	87	74	35	31	17	51	R	R	5-11	170	1-2-77	1994	San Cristobal, D.R.
Plant, David	4	2	1.76	14	6	0	2	51	34	11	10	12	51	R	R	6-1	190	2-1-76	1995	Modesto, Calif.
Suazo, Rigoberto..........	1	0	1.69	2	0	0	1	5	4	1	1	2	5	R	R	6-2	175	1-10-77	1994	Villa Sombrero, D.R.

PHILADELPHIA PHILLIES

Manager: Jim Fregosi. **1995 Record:** 69-75, .479 (T-2nd, NL East).

BATTING	AVG	G	AB	R	H	2B	3B	HR	RBI	BB	SO	SB	CS	B	T	HT	WT	DOB	1st Yr	Resides
Bennett, Gary	.000	1	1	0	0	0	0	0	0	0	1	0	0	R	R	6-0	190	4-17-72	1990	Waukegan, Ill.
Daulton, Darren	.249	98	342	44	85	19	3	9	55	55	52	3	0	L	R	6-2	201	1-3-62	1980	Safety Harbor, Fla.
Duncan, Mariano	.286	52	196	20	56	12	1	3	23	0	43	1	2	R	R	6-0	185	3-13-63	1982	Cherry Hill, N.J.
Dykstra, Lenny	.264	62	254	37	67	15	1	2	18	33	28	10	5	L	L	5-10	160	2-10-63	1981	Philadelphia, Pa.
Eisenreich, Jim	.316	129	377	46	119	22	2	10	55	38	44	10	0	L	L	5-11	200	4-18-59	1980	Blue Springs, Mo.
Elster, Kevin	.208	26	53	10	11	4	1	1	9	7	14	0	0	R	R	6-2	200	8-3-64	1984	Huntington Beach, Calif.
Flora, Kevin	.213	24	75	12	16	3	0	2	7	4	22	1	0	R	R	6-0	185	6-10-69	1987	Chandler, Ariz.
Gallagher, Dave	.318	62	157	12	50	12	0	1	12	16	20	0	0	R	R	6-0	185	9-20-60	1980	Trenton, N.J.
Hayes, Charlie	.276	141	529	58	146	30	3	11	85	50	88	5	1	R	R	6-0	224	5-29-65	1983	Hattiesburg, Miss.
Hollins, Dave	.229	65	205	46	47	12	2	7	25	53	38	1	1	S	R	6-1	207	5-25-66	1987	Orchard Park, N.Y.
Jefferies, Gregg	.306	114	480	69	147	31	2	11	56	35	26	9	5	S	R	5-10	185	8-1-67	1985	Millbrae, Calif.
Jordan, Kevin	.185	24	54	6	10	1	0	2	6	2	9	0	0	R	R	6-1	185	10-9-69	1990	San Francisco, Calif.
Lieberthal, Mike	.255	16	47	1	12	2	0	0	4	5	5	0	0	R	R	6-0	170	1-18-72	1990	Westlake Village, Calif.
Longmire, Tony	.356	59	104	21	37	7	0	3	19	11	19	1	1	L	R	6-1	180	8-12-68	1986	Vallejo, Calif.
Marsh, Tom	.294	43	109	13	32	3	1	3	15	4	25	0	1	R	R	6-2	190	12-27-65	1988	Toledo, Ohio
Morandini, Mickey	.283	127	494	65	140	34	7	6	49	42	80	9	6	L	R	5-11	171	4-22-66	1989	Valparaiso, Ind.
Ready, Randy	.138	23	29	3	4	0	0	0	0	3	6	0	1	R	R	5-11	180	1-8-60	1980	Cardiff, Calif.
Schall, Gene	.231	24	65	2	15	2	0	0	5	6	16	0	0	R	R	6-3	190	6-5-70	1991	Willow Grove, Pa.
Sefcik, Kevin	.000	5	4	1	0	0	0	0	0	0	2	0	0	R	R	5-1	175	2-10-71	1993	Tinley Park, Ill.
Stocker, Kevin	.218	125	412	42	90	14	3	1	32	43	75	6	1	S	R	6-1	175	2-13-70	1991	Spokane, Wash.
Van Slyke, Andy	.243	63	214	26	52	10	2	3	16	28	41	7	0	L	R	6-2	195	12-21-60	1980	Chesterfield, Mo.
Varsho, Gary	.252	72	103	7	26	1	1	0	11	7	17	2	0	L	R	5-10	180	6-20-61	1982	Marshfield, Wisc.
Webster, Lenny	.267	49	150	18	40	9	0	4	14	16	27	0	0	R	R	5-9	195	2-10-65	1986	Charlotte, N.C.
Whiten, Mark	.269	60	212	38	57	10	1	11	37	31	63	7	0	S	R	6-3	215	11-25-66	1986	Pensacola, Fla.

PITCHING	W	L	ERA	G	GS	CG	SV	IP	H	R	ER	BB	SO	B	T	HT	WT	DOB	1st Yr	Resides
Abbott, Kyle	2	0	3.81	18	0	0	0	28	28	12	12	16	21	L	L	6-4	195	2-18-68	1989	Cherry Hill, N.J.
Borland, Toby	1	3	3.77	50	0	0	6	74	81	37	31	37	59	R	R	6-7	175	5-29-69	1989	Quitman, La.
Bottalico, Ricky	5	3	2.46	62	0	0	1	88	50	25	24	42	87	L	R	6-1	190	8-26-69	1991	Newington, Conn.
Carter, Andy	0	0	6.14	4	0	0	0	7	4	5	5	2	6	L	L	6-5	190	11-9-68	1987	Erdenheim, Pa.
Charlton, Norm	2	5	7.36	25	0	0	0	22	23	19	18	15	12	S	L	6-3	205	1-6-63	1984	Jamaica Beach, Texas
Deshaies, Jim	0	1	20.25	2	2	0	0	5	15	12	12	1	6	L	L	6-4	225	6-23-60	1982	Massena, N.Y.
Fernandez, Sid	6	1	3.34	11	11	0	0	65	48	25	24	21	79	L	L	6-1	220	10-12-62	1981	Kailua, Hawaii
Fletcher, Paul	1	0	5.40	10	0	0	2	13	15	8	8	9	10	R	R	6-1	185	1-14-67	1988	Ravenswood, W. Va.
Frey, Steve	0	0	0.84	9	0	0	1	11	3	1	1	2	2	R	L	5-9	170	7-29-63	1983	Newtown, Pa.
Grace, Mike	1	1	3.18	2	2	0	0	11	10	4	4	4	7	R	R	6-4	210	6-20-70	1991	Joliet, Ill.
Green, Tyler	8	9	5.31	26	25	4	0	141	157	86	83	66	85	R	R	6-5	185	2-18-70	1991	Englewood, Colo.
Greene, Tommy	0	5	8.29	11	6	0	0	34	45	32	31	20	24	R	R	6-5	225	4-6-67	1985	Richmond, Va.
Harris, Gene	2	2	4.26	21	0	0	0	19	19	9	9	8	9	R	R	5-11	190	12-5-64	1986	Okeechobee, Fla.
Juden, Jeff	2	4	4.02	13	10	1	0	63	53	31	28	31	47	R	R	6-7	245	1-19-71	1989	Salem, Mass.
Karp, Ryan	0	0	4.50	1	0	0	0	2	1	1	1	3	2	L	L	6-4	205	4-5-70	1992	Coral Gables, Fla.
Mimbs, Mike	9	7	4.15	35	19	2	1	137	127	70	63	75	93	L	L	6-2	182	2-13-69	1990	Macon, Ga.
Munoz, Bobby	0	2	5.74	3	3	0	0	16	15	13	10	9	6	R	R	6-7	237	3-3-68	1989	Hialeah, Fla.
Olivares, Omar	0	1	5.40	5	0	0	0	10	11	6	6	2	7	R	R	6-1	183	7-6-67	1987	San German, P.R.
2-team (11 Colo.)	1	4	7.29	16	6	0	0	42	55	34	32	23	22							
Quantrill, Paul	11	12	4.67	33	29	0	0	179	212	102	93	44	103	L	R	6-1	185	11-3-68	1989	Cobourg, Ontario
Ricci, David	1	0	1.80	7	0	0	0	10	9	2	2	3	9	R	R	6-2	180	11-20-68	1987	Laurel, Md.
Schilling, Curt	7	5	3.57	17	17	1	0	116	96	52	46	26	114	R	R	6-4	215	11-14-66	1986	Marlton, N.J.
Slocumb, Heath	5	6	2.89	61	0	0	32	65	64	26	21	35	63	R	R	6-3	180	6-7-66	1984	Jamaica, N.Y.
Springer, Dennis	0	3	4.84	4	4	0	0	22	21	15	12	9	15	R	R	5-10	185	2-12-65	1987	Fresno, Calif.
Springer, Russ	3	0	3.71	14	0	0	0	27	22	11	11	10	32	R	R	6-4	195	11-7-68	1989	Pollack, La.
West, David	3	2	3.79	8	8	0	0	38	34	17	16	19	25	L	L	6-6	225	9-1-64	1983	Stuart, Fla.
Williams, Mike	3	3	3.29	33	8	0	0	88	78	37	32	29	57	R	R	6-2	190	7-29-69	1990	Newport, Va.

FIELDING

Catcher	PCT	G	PO	A	E	DP	PB
Daulton	.994	95	631	45	4	5	9
Lieberthal	.991	14	95	10	1	1	7
Webster	.990	43	274	18	3	1	3

First Base	PCT	G	PO	A	E	DP
Duncan	.980	12	90	6	2	10
Elster	1.000	4	17	0	0	1
Hollins	.988	61	532	30	7	53
Jefferies	.994	59	492	33	3	53
Ready	.967	3	28	1	1	4
Schall	.984	14	112	10	2	9

Second Base	PCT	G	PO	A	E	DP
Duncan	.957	24	50	60	5	17

	PCT	G	PO	A	E	DP
Jordan	.984	9	28	33	1	8
Morandini	.989	122	269	337	7	74
Ready	1.000	1	1	1	0	0

Third Base	PCT	G	PO	A	E	DP
Duncan	1.000	1	2	2	0	0
Elster	1.000	2	2	2	0	0
Hayes	.963	141	104	264	14	27
Jordan	1.000	1	1	2	0	0
Sefcik	1.000	2	0	1	0	1

Shortstop	PCT	G	PO	A	E	DP
Duncan	.956	14	14	51	3	9
Elster	.982	19	18	36	1	11

	PCT	G	PO	A	E	DP
Stocker	.969	125	147	383	17	72

Outfield	PCT	G	PO	A	E	DP
Dykstra	.987	61	153	2	2	1
Eisenreich	1.000	111	205	2	0	1
Flora	1.000	20	33	1	0	1
Gallagher	1.000	55	89	1	0	0
Jefferies	1.000	55	87	3	0	1
Longmire	1.000	23	33	2	0	0
Marsh	.939	29	44	2	3	0
Schall	1.000	4	3	0	0	0
Van Slyke	.984	56	117	5	2	1
Varsho	.939	25	31	0	2	0
Whiten	.965	55	105	4	4	0

MORRIS FOSTOFF

Gregg Jefferies led Philadelphia with 69 runs and 147 hits

Phillies minor league Player of the Year Rich Hunter

PHILLIES

FARM SYSTEM

Director of Player Development: Del Unser.

Class	Farm Team	League	W	L	Pct.	Finish*	Manager	First Yr
AAA	Scranton/W-B (Pa.) Red Barons	International	70	72	.493	8th (10)	Mike Quade	1989
AA	Reading (Pa.) Phillies	Eastern	73	69	.514	T-3rd+ (10)	Bill Dancy	1967
#A	Clearwater (Fla.) Phillies	Florida State	79	59	.572	3rd (14)	Don McCormack	1985
A	Piedmont (N.C.) Phillies	South Atlantic	82	58	.586	2nd (14)	Roy Majtyka	1995
A	Batavia (N.Y.) Clippers	New York-Penn	41	34	.547	4th (14)	Al LeBoeuf	1988
#R	Martinsville (Va.) Phillies	Appalachian	30	37	.448	6th (10)	Ramon Henderson	1988

*Finish in overall standings (No. of teams in league)   #Advanced level   +Won league championship

ORGANIZATION LEADERS

MAJOR LEAGUERS

BATTING

*AVG	Jim Eisenreich	.316
R	Gregg Jefferies	69
H	Gregg Jefferies	147
TB	Two tied at	215
2B	Mickey Morandini	34
3B	Mickey Morandini	7
HR	Three tied at	11
RBI	Charlie Hayes	85
BB	Darren Daulton	55
SO	Charlie Hayes	88
SB	Two tied at	10

PITCHING

W	Paul Quantrill	11
L	Paul Quantrill	12
#ERA	Ricky Bottalico	2.46
G	Ricky Bottalico	62
CG	Tyler Green	4
SV	Heathcliff Slocumb	32
IP	Paul Quantrill	179
BB	Mike Mimbs	75
SO	Curt Schilling	114

Jim Eisenreich. .316 average

THE SPORTS GROUP

MINOR LEAGUERS

BATTING

*AVG	Wendell Magee, Clearwater/Reading	.338
R	Larry Huff, Piedmont	86
H	Wendell Magee, Clearwater/Reading	177
TB	David Doster, Reading	254
2B	David Doster, Reading	39
3B	Matt Guiliano, Piedmont	12
HR	Fred McNair, Reading/Scranton	23
RBI	Dan Held, Clearwater/Reading	85
BB	Two tied at	74
SO	Dan Held, Clearwater/Reading	128
SB	Scott Shores, Clearwater	30

PITCHING

W	Rich Hunter, Piedmont/Clear./Read.	19
L	Two tied at	11
#ERA	Gary Yeager, Batavia	2.56
G	Chuck Ricci, Scranton	68
CG	Ryan Nye, Clearwater	5
SV	Brian Stumpf, Piedmont	28
IP	Blaise Ilsley, Scranton	185
BB	Larry Mitchell, Reading	72
SO	Matt Beech, Clearwater/Reading	155

*Minimum 250 At-Bats   #Minimum 75 Innings

TOP 10 PROSPECTS

How the Phillies Top 10 prospects, as judged by Baseball America prior to the 1995 season, fared in 1995:

THE SPORTS GROUP

Scott Rolen

Player, Pos.	Club (Class—League)	AVG	AB	R	H	2B	3B	HR	RBI	SB
1. Scott Rolen, 3b	Clearwater (A—Florida State)	.290	238	45	69	13	2	10	39	4
	Reading (AA—Eastern)	.289	76	16	22	3	0	3	15	1
5. Rick Holifield, of	Reading (AA—Eastern)	.247	93	18	23	3	1	1	5	5
	Scranton (AAA—International)	.206	223	32	46	6	3	3	24	21
6. Kevin Jordan, 2b	Scranton (AAA—International)	.310	410	61	127	29	4	5	60	3
	Philadelphia	.185	54	6	10	1	0	2	6	0
7. Mike Lieberthal, c	Scranton (AAA—International)	.281	278	44	78	20	2	6	42	1
	Philadelphia	.255	47	1	12	2	0	0	4	0
10. Jon McMullen, 1b	Clearwater (A—Florida State)	.237	118	17	28	7	0	1	14	0

Player, Pos.	Club (Class—League)	W	L	ERA	G	SV	IP	H	BB	SO
2. Wayne Gomes, rhp	Reading (AA—Eastern)	7	4	3.96	22	0	105	89	70	102
3. Ricky Bottalico, rhp	Philadelphia	5	3	2.46	62	1	88	50	42	87
4. Carlton Loewer, rhp	Clearwater (A—Florida State)	7	5	3.30	20	0	115	124	36	83
	Reading (AA—Eastern)	4	1	2.16	8	0	50	42	31	55
8. Tyler Green, rhp	Philadelphia	8	9	5.31	26	0	141	157	66	85
9. Ryan Nye, rhp	Clearwater (A—Florida State)	12	7	3.40	27	0	167	164	33	116

INTERNATIONAL LEAGUE

BATTING

BATTING	AVG	G	AB	R	H	2B	3B	HR	RBI	BB	SO	SB	CS	B	T	HT	WT	DOB	1st Yr	Resides
Batiste, Kim	.230	32	122	10	28	4	1	4	18	2	14	1	0	R	R	6-0	193	3-15-68	1987	Prairieville, La.
Bennett, Gary	.150	7	20	1	3	0	0	0	1	2	2	0	0	R	R	6-0	190	4-17-72	1990	Waukegan, Ill.
Bieser, Steve	.269	95	245	37	66	12	6	1	33	22	56	14	5	S	R	5-10	170	8-4-67	1989	St. Genevieve, Mo.
Brophy, E.J.	.200	34	65	7	13	2	0	1	6	8	15	0	0	R	R	6-3	210	4-17-70	1992	Montgomery, Ala.
Butler, Rob	.300	92	327	46	98	16	4	3	35	24	39	5	8	L	L	5-11	185	4-10-70	1991	Toronto, Ontario
Elster, Kevin	.294	5	17	2	5	3	0	0	2	2	3	0	0	R	R	6-2	200	8-3-64	1984	Huntington Beach, Calif.
Geisler, Phil	.186	20	43	2	8	5	0	1	7	2	13	0	0	L	L	6-3	200	10-23-69	1991	Springfield, Ore.
Gilbert, Shawn	.263	136	536	84	141	26	2	2	42	64	102	16	11	R	R	5-9	170	3-12-65	1987	Glendale, Ariz.
Grable, Rob	.229	26	83	7	19	4	0	3	11	7	34	3	0	R	R	6-2	200	1-20-70	1991	Bohemia, N.Y.
Hayden, Dave	.293	20	41	6	12	1	0	2	3	6	13	0	2	R	R	5-11	170	12-1-69	1991	Okahumpka, Fla.
Holifield, Rick	.206	76	223	32	46	6	3	3	24	24	52	21	5	L	L	6-2	165	3-25-70	1988	Montclair, Calif.
Jordan, Kevin	.310	106	410	61	127	29	4	5	60	28	36	3	0	R	R	6-1	185	10-9-69	1990	San Francisco, Calif.
Koelling, Brian	.264	16	53	5	14	1	0	0	3	1	14	3	1	R	R	6-1	185	6-11-69	1991	Cleveland, Ohio
Liebertbal, Mike	.281	85	278	44	78	20	2	6	42	44	36	1	1	R	R	6-0	170	1-18-72	1990	Westlake Village, Calif.
Manahan, Anthony	.288	90	299	36	86	11	1	3	32	28	39	6	1	R	R	6-0	190	12-15-68	1990	Scottsdale, Ariz.
Marsh, Tom	.307	78	296	46	91	22	5	10	47	13	39	9	3	R	R	6-2	180	12-27-65	1988	Toledo, Ohio
McNair, Fred	.240	9	25	1	6	1	0	0	2	3	6	0	0	R	R	6-4	215	1-31-70	1989	Mesa, Ariz.
Montoyo, Charlie	.243	92	288	32	70	13	1	3	34	50	45	2	3	R	R	5-10	170	10-17-65	1987	Florida, P.R.
Schall, Gene	.313	92	320	52	100	25	4	12	63	49	54	3	3	R	R	6-3	190	6-5-70	1991	Willow Grove, Pa.
Sefcik, Kevin	.346	7	26	5	9	6	1	0	6	3	1	0	0	R	R	5-1	175	2-10-71	1993	Tinley Park, Ill.
Taylor, Sam	.143	3	7	3	1	0	0	1	1	1	2	0	0	L	L	5-11	185	8-6-68	1989	Murray, Ky.
Tokheim, David	.271	127	450	64	122	18	8	11	66	18	55	6	7	L	L	6-1	185	5-25-69	1991	Menlo Park, Calif.
Vatcher, Jim	.375	9	24	4	9	1	0	0	2	1	4	1	0	R	R	5-9	172	5-27-65	1987	Pacific Palisades, Calif.
Zuber, Jon	.287	119	418	53	120	19	5	3	50	49	68	1	2	L	L	6-1	175	12-10-69	1992	Moraga, Calif.

PITCHING

PITCHING	W	L	ERA	G	GS	CG	SV	IP	H	R	ER	BB	SO	B	T	HT	WT	DOB	1st Yr	Resides
Borland, Toby	0	0	0.00	8	0	0	1	11	5	0	0	6	15	R	R	6-7	175	5-29-69	1989	Quitman, La.
Carter, Andy	1	2	4.35	14	1	0	0	21	17	10	10	13	18	L	L	6-5	190	11-9-68	1987	Erdenheim, Pa.
Combs, Pat	4	4	5.43	22	6	0	0	56	71	37	34	25	36	L	L	6-4	213	10-29-66	1989	Houston, Texas
Deshaies, Jim	7	8	3.45	19	19	2	0	117	105	51	45	26	79	L	L	6-4	225	6-23-60	1982	Massena, N.Y.
DuBois, Brian	1	5	4.56	49	0	0	1	51	58	31	26	25	48	L	L	5-8	180	4-18-67	1985	Sarasota, Fla.
Fletcher, Paul	4	1	3.10	52	0	0	2	61	45	33	21	28	48	R	R	6-1	185	1-14-67	1988	Ravenswood, W.Va.
Frey, Steve	0	0	1.80	4	0	0	0	5	3	1	1	2	3	L	L	5-9	170	7-29-63	1983	Newtown, Pa.
Gaddy, Bob	5	7	6.28	17	17	0	0	86	100	72	60	56	42	R	L	6-1	202	1-11-67	1989	Pensacola, Fla.
Grace, Mike	2	0	1.59	2	2	1	0	17	17	3	3	2	13	R	R	6-4	210	6-20-70	1991	Joliet, Ill.
Greene, Tommy	3	0	2.22	4	4	0	0	28	18	8	7	6	19	R	R	6-5	225	4-6-67	1985	Richmond, Va.
Hill, Eric	4	3	4.30	21	0	0	2	23	24	13	11	9	16	R	R	6-2	190	11-19-67	1990	Corryton, Tenn.
Ilsley, Blaise	8	10	3.88	29	29	2	0	185	210	96	80	34	102	L	L	6-1	185	4-9-64	1985	Alpena, Mich.
Innis, Jeff	0	2	4.30	15	0	0	6	15	13	8	7	8	14	R	R	6-1	180	7-5-62	1983	Jupiter, Fla.
Juden, Jeff	6	4	4.10	14	13	0	0	83	73	43	38	33	65	R	R	6-7	245	1-19-71	1989	Salem, Mass.
Juhl, Mike	0	0	0.00	1	0	0	0	0	0	0	0	1	0	L	L	5-9	180	8-10-69	1991	Lake Katrine, N.Y.
Karp, Ryan	7	1	4.20	13	13	0	0	81	81	43	38	31	73	L	L	6-4	205	4-5-70	1992	Coral Gables, Fla.
Melendez, Jose	0	0	6.00	2	0	0	0	3	6	4	2	2	1	R	R	6-2	190	9-2-65	1984	Naguabo, P.R.
Munoz, Bobby	1	0	0.56	2	2	1	0	16	8	2	1	3	10	R	R	6-7	237	3-3-68	1989	Hialeah, Fla.
Olivares, Omar	0	3	4.87	7	7	0	0	44	49	25	24	20	28	R	R	6-1	183	7-6-67	1987	San German, P.R.
Ricci, Chuck	4	3	2.49	68	0	0	25	65	48	22	18	24	66	R	R	6-2	180	11-20-68	1987	Laurel, Md.
Springer, Dennis	10	11	4.68	30	23	4	0	171	163	101	89	47	115	R	R	5-10	185	2-12-65	1987	Fresno, Calif.
Tranberg, Mark	1	4	7.23	11	2	0	0	24	32	19	19	6	15	R	R	6-4	210	2-28-69	1992	Buena Park, Calif.
West, David	1	0	0.00	1	1	1	0	7	2	0	0	0	6	L	L	6-6	225	9-1-64	1983	Stuart, Fla.
Wiegandt, Scott	1	3	2.98	47	0	0	2	54	55	19	18	27	41	L	L	5-11	180	12-9-67	1989	Louisville, Ky.
Williams, Mike	0	1	4.66	3	3	1	0	10	8	5	5	2	8	R	R	6-2	190	7-29-69	1990	Newport, Fla.

FIELDING

Catcher	PCT	G	PO	A	E	DP	PB
Bennett	1.000	7	38	4	0	0	1
Bieser	.973	39	230	25	7	3	7
Brophy	.980	30	132	16	3	2	3
Lieberthal	.993	83	503	45	4	2	8

First Base	PCT	G	PO	A	E	DP
McNair	1.000	3	25	2	0	3
Montoyo	1.000	2	3	0	0	0
Schall	.992	43	355	20	3	34
Zuber	.996	104	825	63	4	86

Second Base	PCT	G	PO	A	E	DP
Jordan	.976	102	217	279	12	70
Koelling	.935	16	39	33	5	9
Manahan	.976	24	64	58	3	10
Montoyo	1.000	2	3	1	0	0

	PCT	G	PO	A	E	DP
Sefcik	1.000	7	13	16	0	4
Third Base	**PCT**	**G**	**PO**	**A**	**E**	**DP**
Batiste	.952	28	24	56	4	7
Bieser	.714	2	2	3	2	0
Gilbert	.929	3	2	11	1	2
Grable	.846	4	4	7	2	2
Hayden	.917	13	7	15	2	2
Lieberthal	.500	1	0	1	1	0
Manahan	.901	37	28	63	10	6
Montoyo	.952	71	46	114	8	9
Schall	.000	2	0	0	0	0

Shortstop	PCT	G	PO	A	E	DP
Elster	.947	5	6	12	1	4
Gilbert	.953	107	156	347	25	71

	PCT	G	PO	A	E	DP
Hayden	1.000	1	0	3	0	0
Manahan	.925	17	31	43	6	12
Montoyo	.947	16	23	31	3	3
Outfield	**PCT**	**G**	**PO**	**A**	**E**	**DP**
Bieser	.988	39	82	1	1	0
Butler	.974	85	147	4	4	1
Geisler	1.000	12	19	1	0	0
Gilbert	.967	23	55	3	2	0
Grable	1.000	14	25	0	0	0
Holifield	.964	72	131	4	5	0
Marsh	.994	75	156	4	1	2
Schall	.988	45	76	5	1	0
Taylor	1.000	1	2	0	0	0
Tokheim	.982	92	158	8	3	2
Vatcher	1.000	4	8	0	0	0

EASTERN LEAGUE

BATTING

BATTING	AVG	G	AB	R	H	2B	3B	HR	RBI	BB	SO	SB	CS	B	T	HT	WT	DOB	1st Yr	Resides
Bennett, Gary	.236	86	271	27	64	11	0	4	40	22	36	0	0	R	R	6-0	190	4-17-72	1990	Waukegan, Ill.
Bigler, Jeff	.091	13	44	4	4	1	0	0	2	6	10	0	0	R	R	6-0	190	9-13-69	1991	Mequon, Wis.
Blasingame, Kent	.205	86	195	38	40	4	2	1	17	29	43	9	7	L	L	6-0	175	2-4-69	1993	Scottsdale, Ariz.
Brito, Luis	.333	2	3	1	1	0	0	0	1	0	1	0	1	S	R	6-0	155	4-12-71	1989	San Pedro de Macoris, D.R.
Brophy, E.J.	.500	2	4	0	2	1	0	0	0	0	1	0	0	R	R	6-3	210	4-17-70	1992	Montgomery, Ala.
Burke, Alan	.200	11	20	5	4	2	0	1	3	1	6	0	0	R	R	6-0	190	11-28-70	1992	Anaheim, Calif.
Doster, David	.265	139	551	84	146	39	3	21	79	51	61	11	7	R	R	5-10	185	10-8-70	1993	New Haven, Ind.
Eason, Tommy	.255	96	333	43	85	18	3	14	50	18	61	2	2	R	R	6-0	200	7-8-70	1991	La Grange, N.C.
Estalella, Bobby	.235	10	34	5	8	2	0	2	9	4	7	0	0	R	R	6-1	200	8-23-74	1993	Pembroke Pines, Fla.

BATTING

BATTING	AVG	G	AB	R	H	2B	3B	HR	RBI	BB	SO	SB	CS	B	T	HT	WT	DOB	1st Yr	Resides
Fisher, David	.230	79	204	18	47	18	1	1	20	14	29	4	4	R	R	6-0	160	2-26-70	1992	Joplin, Mo.
Geisler, Phil	.232	76	272	27	63	10	3	2	35	21	65	4	2	L	L	6-3	200	10-23-69	1991	Springfield, Ore.
Grable, Rob	.300	103	353	71	106	24	1	16	67	67	85	15	11	R	R	6-2	200	1-20-70	1991	Bohemia, N.Y.
Hayden, Dave	.234	68	192	22	45	6	0	3	11	26	39	0	3	R	R	5-11	170	12-1-69	1991	Okahumpka, Fla.
Held, Dan	.500	2	4	2	2	1	0	1	3	2	1	1	0	R	R	6-0	200	10-7-70	1993	Neosho, Wis.
Holifield, Rick	.247	30	93	18	23	3	1	1	5	22	18	5	2	L	L	6-2	165	3-25-70	1988	Montclair, Calif.
Magee, Wendell	.294	39	136	17	40	9	1	3	21	21	17	3	4	R	R	6-0	225	8-3-72	1994	Hattiesburg, Miss.
McConnell, Chad	.276	94	319	46	88	12	1	11	52	27	59	8	3	R	R	6-1	180	10-13-70	1992	Sioux Falls, S.D.
McNair, Fred	.271	108	395	64	107	24	1	23	68	38	86	3	2	R	R	6-4	215	1-31-70	1989	Mesa, Ariz.
Millan, Adam	.350	10	20	3	7	3	0	1	7	4	3	0	0	R	R	6-0	195	3-26-72	1994	Montebello, Calif.
Moler, Jason	.265	22	83	17	22	3	0	2	14	12	13	2	2	R	R	6-1	195	10-29-69	1992	Yorba Linda, Calif.
Mota, Gary	.227	33	110	13	25	4	2	1	9	8	23	0	2	R	R	6-0	195	10-6-70	1990	La Cresenta, Calif.
Rolen, Scott	.289	20	76	16	22	3	0	3	15	7	14	1	0	R	R	6-4	210	4-4-75	1993	Jasper, Ind.
Sefcik, Kevin	.272	128	508	68	138	18	4	4	46	38	48	14	11	R	R	5-1	175	2-10-71	1993	Tinley Park, Ill.
Solomon, Steve	.228	119	356	50	81	19	6	3	42	48	82	17	4	L	L	6-0	180	4-9-70	1992	Los Angeles, Calif.
Waco, David	.300	5	10	1	3	0	0	1	0	2	0	2	0	R	R	6-0	185	12-8-69	1993	Northridge, Calif.

PITCHING

PITCHING	W	L	ERA	G	GS	CG	SV	IP	H	R	ER	BB	SO	B	T	HT	WT	DOB	1st Yr	Resides
Andersen, Larry	0	0	6.23	5	0	0	0	4	6	3	3	1	7	R	R	6-3	205	5-6-53	1971	Bellevue, Wash.
Beech, Matt	2	4	2.96	14	13	0	0	79	67	33	26	33	70	L	L	6-2	190	1-20-72	1994	San Antonio, Texas
Blazier, Ron	4	5	3.29	56	3	0	1	107	93	44	39	31	102	R	R	6-6	215	7-30-71	1990	Bellwood, Pa.
Brown, Dan	1	0	7.71	2	0	0	0	2	4	4	2	0	2	R	R	6-5	210	12-26-68	1991	Vinita, Okla.
Dodd, Robert	0	0	0.00	1	0	0	0	1	0	0	0	2	0	L	L	6-3	195	3-14-73	1994	Plano, Texas
Doolan, Blake	11	5	2.22	60	0	0	16	73	63	22	18	27	50	R	R	6-0	178	2-11-69	1992	Pasadena, Texas
Foster, Mark	1	1	5.66	25	0	0	1	21	25	15	13	17	15	L	L	6-1	200	12-24-71	1993	Severn, Md.
Gilmore, Joel	2	0	6.25	18	3	0	0	36	45	27	25	18	27	R	R	6-6	230	12-16-69	1991	Conroe, Texas
Gomes, Wayne	7	4	3.96	22	22	1	0	105	89	54	46	70	102	R	R	6-0	215	1-15-73	1993	Hampton, Va.
Grace, Mike	13	6	3.54	24	24	2	0	147	137	65	58	35	118	R	R	6-4	210	6-20-70	1991	Joliet, Ill.
Hanselman, Carl	4	3	6.37	24	1	0	2	41	45	29	29	17	35	L	L	6-5	190	5-23-70	1988	Shreveport, La.
Heflin, Bronson	0	0	0.00	1	0	0	0	1	0	0	0	1	2	R	R	6-3	195	8-29-71	1994	Clarksville, Tenn.
Hill, Eric	4	3	2.90	38	0	0	4	59	55	23	19	27	52	R	R	6-2	190	11-19-67	1990	Corryton, Tenn.
Holman, Craig	1	1	3.49	32	1	0	1	57	55	27	22	16	40	R	R	6-3	200	3-13-69	1991	Attalla, Ala.
Hunter, Rich	3	0	2.05	3	3	0	0	22	14	6	5	6	17	R	R	6-1	180	9-25-74	1993	Temecula, Calif.
Juhl, Mike	1	8	4.27	49	0	0	0	46	43	32	22	28	39	L	L	5-9	180	8-10-69	1991	Lake Katrine, N.Y.
Karp, Ryan	1	2	3.06	7	7	0	0	47	44	18	16	15	37	L	L	6-4	205	4-5-70	1992	Coral Gables, Fla.
Loewer, Carlton	4	1	2.16	8	8	0	0	50	42	17	12	31	35	S	R	6-6	220	9-24-73	1995	Eunice, La.
Mitchell, Larry	6	11	5.54	25	24	1	0	128	136	85	79	72	107	R	R	6-1	200	10-16-71	1992	Charlottesville, Va.
Munoz, Bobby	0	4	10.80	4	4	0	0	15	28	19	18	3	8	R	R	6-7	237	3-3-68	1989	Hialeah, Fla.
Smith, Eric	1	0	20.25	4	0	0	0	4	11	9	9	4	5	R	R	6-3	200	12-9-69	1992	Salem, Utah
Tranberg, Mark	6	6	3.73	18	18	3	0	111	110	50	46	30	62	R	R	6-4	210	2-28-69	1992	Buena Park, Calif.
Trisler, John	2	4	5.16	30	10	0	0	82	96	51	47	26	50	R	R	6-4	235	3-19-70	1991	Indianapolis, Ind.
West, David	0	0	1.50	1	1	0	0	6	2	1	1	3	8	L	L	6-6	225	9-1-64	1983	Stuart, Fla.

FIELDING

Catcher

Catcher	PCT	G	PO	A	E	DP	PB
Bennett	.994	82	551	65	4	13	6
Brophy	1.000	2	3	0	0	0	0
Eason	.990	58	368	32	4	7	10
Estalella	.986	10	60	9	1	1	3
Millan	1.000	5	30	0	0	0	0

First Base

First Base	PCT	G	PO	A	E	DP
Bigler	.992	13	125	6	1	8
Eason	.987	26	209	18	3	17
Fisher	1.000	1	6	0	0	0
Geisler	.987	18	137	11	2	10
Held	1.000	1	6	0	0	2
McNair	.987	88	765	46	11	73
Millan	1.000	1	8	0	0	1
Moler	1.000	1	9	1	0	0

Second Base

Second Base	PCT	G	PO	A	E	DP
Doster	.983	137	261	420	12	91
Fisher	1.000	5	18	0	2	

Third Base

Third Base	PCT	G	PO	A	E	DP
Grable	.956	34	25	40	3	6
Hayden	.924	58	33	89	10	7
Moler	.967	21	15	43	2	4
Rolen	.934	20	10	47	4	3
Sefcik	1.000	21	9	33	0	5

Shortstop

Shortstop	PCT	G	PO	A	E	DP
Brito	1.000	2	2	4	0	1
Fisher	.935	40	50	80	9	17
Hayden	.000	2	0	0	0	0
Sefcik	.963	112	157	316	18	63

Outfield

Outfield	PCT	G	PO	A	E	DP
Blasingame	.904	46	64	2	7	0
Burke	.875	6	7	0	1	0
Doster	.000	1	0	0	0	0
Geisler	.984	58	121	6	2	2
Grable	.980	72	94	2	2	0
Hayden	1.000	2	3	0	0	0
Held	1.000	1	2	0	0	0
Holifield	.989	30	84	3	1	1
Magee	.932	39	65	4	5	0
McConnell	.975	85	149	7	4	2
Mota	.946	24	33	2	2	1
Solomon	.990	97	197	8	2	0

CLEARWATER   A

FLORIDA STATE LEAGUE

BATTING	AVG	G	AB	R	H	2B	3B	HR	RBI	BB	SO	SB	CS	B	T	HT	WT	DOB	1st Yr	Resides
Amador, Manuel	.279	96	330	45	92	19	4	6	47	22	38	5	2	S	R	6-0	165	11-21-75	1993	Santo Domingo, D.R.
Angeli, Doug	.191	16	47	4	9	3	0	0	3	3	13	0	1	R	R	5-11	183	1-7-71	1993	Springfield, Ill.
Brito, Domingo	.000	1	1	0	0	0	0	0	0	0	1	0	0	R	R	6-0	160	7-6-75	1994	Santo Domingo, D.R.
Brito, Luis	.274	109	383	42	105	14	3	3	41	17	35	12	5	S	R	6-0	155	4-12-71	1989	San Pedro de Macorís, D.R.
Burke, Alan	.222	3	9	2	2	0	0	1	2	0	2	0	0	R	R	6-0	190	11-28-70	1992	Anaheim, Calif.
Costello, Brian	.249	112	406	52	101	19	2	9	56	37	88	14	9	R	R	6-1	195	10-4-74	1993	Orlando, Fla.
Diaz, Linardo	.212	11	33	1	7	1	0	0	1	3	7	0	0	R	R	6-1	165	12-30-74	1993	Berabona, D.R.
Estalella, Bobby	.260	117	404	61	105	24	1	15	58	56	76	0	3	R	R	6-0	200	8-23-74	1993	Pembroke Pines, Fla.
Evans, Stan	.248	89	286	34	71	5	3	0	32	29	33	10	5	L	R	5-11	175	12-17-70	1992	Oak Hill, Fla.
Flores, Jose	.222	49	185	25	41	4	3	1	19	15	27	12	5	R	R	5-11	160	4-26-73	1994	New York, N.Y.
Gallone, Santy	.244	90	283	45	69	15	1	6	40	47	39	5	3	R	R	5-11	190	8-9-71	1993	Bellmore, N.Y.
Gyselman, Jeff	.172	26	64	8	11	0	0	0	3	6	14	0	0	R	R	6-3	193	7-10-70	1993	Bothell, Wash.
Haws, Scott	.000	2	1	0	0	0	0	0	0	1	0	0	0	R	R	6-0	190	1-11-72	1992	Fairless Hills, Pa.
Held, Dan	.272	134	489	82	133	35	1	21	82	56	127	2	1	R	R	6-0	200	10-7-70	1993	Neosho, Wis.
Kendall, Jeremey	.215	36	135	18	29	1	2	3	10	14	40	15	5	R	R	5-9	170	9-3-71	1992	East Troy, Wis.
Magee, Wendell	.353	96	388	67	137	24	5	6	46	33	40	7	10	R	R	6-0	225	8-3-72	1994	Hattiesburg, Miss.
McMullen, Jon	.237	30	118	17	28	7	0	1	14	20	19	0	0	L	R	6-0	240	11-30-73	1992	Ventura, Calif.
Northeimer, Jamie	.316	6	19	1	6	1	0	0	5	3	4	0	0	R	R	5-10	174	7-5-72	1994	Sacramento, Calif.
Nuneviller, Tom	.233	12	43	2	10	2	0	0	6	4	6	0	0	R	R	6-3	210	5-15-69	1990	Ottsville, Pa.
O'Brien, Joe	.140	13	50	6	7	1	0	1	7	3	13	1	0	R	R	6-0	200	7-21-72	1994	Philadelphia, Pa.
Rolen, Scott	.290	66	238	45	69	13	2	10	39	37	46	4	0	R	R	6-4	210	4-4-75	1993	Jasper, Ind.

BATTING	AVG	G	AB	R	H	2B	3B	HR	RBI	BB	SO	SB	CS	B	T	HT	WT	DOB	1st Yr	Resides
Shores, Scott	.254	133	460	74	117	23	5	7	52	55	127	30	16	R	R	6-1	190	2-4-72	1994	Phoenix, Ariz.
Waco, David	.223	59	193	22	43	8	1	0	13	23	27	2	2	R	R	6-0	185	12-8-69	1993	Northridge, Calif.

GAMES BY POSITION: C—Estalella 114, Gyselman 26, Northeimer 6. **1B**—Held 132, Waco 8. **2B**—Amador 47, D. Brito 1, L. Brito 3, Flores 9, Gallone 42, Waco 47. **3B**—Amador 6, L. Brito 11, Flores 30, Gallone 15, O'Brien 12, Rolen 65, Waco 4. **SS**—Amador 23, Angeli 16, L. Brito 96, Flores 10. **OF**—Burke 1, Costello 99, Diaz 11, Evans 72, Gallone 4, Kendall 36, Magee 93, Nuneviller 8, Shores 103, Waco 1.

PITCHING	W	L	ERA	G	GS	CG	SV	IP	H	R	ER	BB	SO	B	T	HT	WT	DOB	1st Yr	Resides
Agostinelli, Peter	4	4	4.34	57	0	0	6	46	54	26	22	22	32	L	L	6-3	195	11-7-68	1992	Spencerport, N.Y.
Beech, Matt	9	4	4.19	15	15	0	0	86	87	45	40	30	85	L	L	6-2	190	1-20-72	1994	San Antonio, Texas
Costa, Tony	9	10	3.85	25	25	2	0	145	155	75	62	39	71	R	R	6-4	210	12-19-70	1992	Lemoore, Calif.
Dodd, Robert	8	7	3.16	26	26	0	0	151	144	64	53	58	110	L	L	6-3	195	3-14-73	1994	Plano, Texas
Fiore, Tony	6	2	3.71	24	10	0	0	70	70	41	29	44	45	R	R	6-0	200	10-12-71	1992	Chicago, Ill.
Foster, Mark	0	1	5.40	24	0	0	1	23	30	17	14	10	13	L	L	6-1	200	12-24-71	1993	Severn, Md.
Franek, Tom	0	0	3.55	9	0	0	0	13	12	6	5	3	9	R	R	6-3	200	11-16-70	1993	Fort Collins, Colo.
Greene, Tommy	0	3	3.15	3	3	0	0	20	12	7	7	7	20	R	R	6-5	225	4-6-67	1985	Richmond, Va.
Heflin, Bronson	2	3	2.95	57	0	0	21	61	52	25	20	21	84	R	R	6-3	195	8-29-71	1994	Clarksville, Tenn.
Herrmann, Gary	7	2	3.60	42	3	0	3	70	64	31	28	28	56	R	L	6-4	205	10-15-69	1992	Houston, Texas
Hunter, Rich	6	0	2.93	9	9	0	0	58	62	23	19	7	46	R	R	6-1	180	9-25-74	1993	Temecula, Calif.
Loewer, Carlton	7	5	3.30	20	20	1	0	115	124	59	42	36	83	S	R	6-6	220	9-24-73	1995	Eunice, La.
Metheney, Nelson	5	5	3.00	59	0	0	1	72	65	32	24	25	38	R	R	6-3	205	6-14-71	1993	Salem, Va.
Nye, Ryan	12	9	3.40	27	27	5	0	167	164	71	63	33	116	R	R	6-2	195	6-24-73	1994	Cameron, Okla.
Perkins, Ron	1	1	2.84	6	0	0	0	6	6	3	2	5	3	R	R	6-3	210	3-27-68	1990	Hamden, Conn.
Rama, Shelby	0	0	4.32	4	0	0	0	8	12	4	4	1	2	R	R	6-6	210	1-22-72	1993	Phoenix, Ariz.
Smith, Eric	0	0	0.00	8	0	0	4	8	3	0	0	1	7	R	R	6-3	200	12-9-69	1992	Salem, Utah
Swan, Tyrone	2	3	3.40	37	0	0	0	48	50	25	18	19	46	R	R	6-7	195	5-7-69	1993	Sparks, Nev.
Valley, Jason	0	0	12.46	4	0	0	0	4	9	6	6	4	4	R	R	6-1	190	9-30-72	1994	Belfair, Wash.
Vandemark, John	1	2	5.67	24	0	0	0	27	24	21	17	21	18	L	L	6-1	205	9-28-71	1990	Lockport, N.Y.

PIEDMONT   A

SOUTH ATLANTIC LEAGUE

BATTING	AVG	G	AB	R	H	2B	3B	HR	RBI	BB	SO	SB	CS	B	T	HT	WT	DOB	1st Yr	Resides
Amador, Manny	.000	1	4	0	0	0	0	0	0	0	0	0	1	S	R	6-0	165	11-21-75	1993	Santo Domingo, D.R.
Diaz, Linardo	.083	9	12	0	1	1	0	0	0	0	2	0	0	R	R	6-1	165	12-30-74	1993	Berabona, D.R.
Flores, Jose	.263	61	186	22	49	7	0	0	19	24	29	11	8	R	R	5-11	160	6-26-73	1994	New York, N.Y.
Guiliano, Matt	.226	129	451	67	102	22	12	4	59	51	114	6	8	R	R	5-7	175	6-7-72	1994	Ronkonkoma, N.Y.
Hooker, Kevin	.174	16	46	4	8	2	0	0	6	9	13	1	0	R	R	5-11	165	7-25-72	1995	Corvallis, Ore.
Huff, Larry	.272	130	481	86	131	26	4	1	51	74	64	26	8	R	R	6-0	175	1-24-72	1994	Las Vegas, Nev.
Key, Jeff	.258	111	384	55	99	18	6	10	54	26	100	5	7	L	R	6-1	200	11-22-74	1993	Covington, Ga.
Millan, Adam	.294	107	394	69	116	25	2	10	64	44	45	1	4	R	R	6-0	195	3-26-72	1994	Montebello, Calif.
Mobilia, Bill	.240	55	150	17	36	5	2	0	17	13	39	1	0	R	R	6-1	190	11-29-70	1994	Ely, Minn.
Nitschke, Bear	.000	2	4	0	0	0	0	0	0	0	3	0	0	L	R	6-3	205	4-20-71	1994	Fresno, Calif.
Northeimer, Jamie	.291	115	392	56	114	24	4	1	54	53	72	9	4	R	R	5-10	174	7-5-72	1994	Sacramento, Calif.
O'Brien, Joe	.217	60	189	27	41	4	1	1	31	19	38	2	5	R	R	6-0	200	7-21-72	1994	Philadelphia, Pa.
Petillo, Bruce	.111	2	9	0	1	0	0	0	2	0	3	0	0	R	R	6-1	200	11-21-70	1993	Yorba Linda, Calif.
Pullen, Shane	.251	118	435	65	109	26	4	7	57	34	70	4	2	L	R	5-11	160	6-16-73	1994	Kosciusko, Miss.
Reyes, Winston	.176	6	17	1	3	0	1	0	5	1	8	0	1	R	R	6-0	175	4-12-74	1992	Mocaibao, D.R.
Royster, Aaron	.264	126	489	73	129	23	3	8	58	39	106	22	9	R	R	6-1	220	11-30-72	1994	Chicago, Ill.
Schreimann, Eric	.174	7	23	1	4	1	0	0	1	1	4	0	0	R	R	6-1	205	4-22-75	1994	Jefferson City, Mo.
Stingley, Derek	.179	39	84	20	15	2	0	1	5	6	24	13	2	R	R	6-0	185	4-9-71	1993	Chicago, Ill.
Torok, John	.188	91	202	26	38	4	5	1	22	45	39	11	7	L	R	6-1	172	7-5-72	1994	Riverview, Mich.
Wampler, Sam	.000	1	3	0	0	0	0	0	0	0	2	0	0	S	R	6-1	190	9-22-74	1994	Idaho Falls, Idaho
Watts, Josh	.234	111	355	50	83	13	0	5	43	45	96	8	5	L	R	6-1	205	3-24-75	1993	Glendale, Ariz.
Williamson, Matt	.235	88	285	44	67	10	2	1	25	35	67	3	4	R	R	6-3	195	7-4-72	1994	Plano, Texas

GAMES BY POSITION: C—Millan 31, Nitschke 2, Northeimer 108, Petillo 1, Schreimann 5. **1B**—Key 1, Millan 75, Mobilia 15, O'Brien 1, Pullen 59, Reyes 3. **2B**—Amador 1, Flores 9, Hooker 2, Huff 127, Mobilia 1, Williamson 7. **3B**—Flores 44, Hooker 10, Huff 1, Mobilia 18, O'Brien 14, Reyes 2, Williamson 68. **SS**—Flores 8, Guiliano 129, Mobilia 1, Williamson 4. **OF**—Diaz 9, Key 61, O'Brien 31, Pullen 19, Royster 123, Schreimann 2, Stingley 30, Torok 89, Watts 106.

PITCHING	W	L	ERA	G	GS	CG	SV	IP	H	R	ER	BB	SO	B	T	HT	WT	DOB	1st Yr	Resides
Antonini, Adrian	2	0	3.80	6	5	0	0	21	19	10	9	2	26	R	R	6-3	225	7-27-72	1994	Miami, Fla.
Barbao, Joe	8	4	3.38	43	0	0	1	67	70	34	25	12	24	R	R	6-1	190	4-18-72	1994	Crown Point, Ind.
Boyd, Jason	6	8	3.58	26	24	1	0	151	151	77	60	44	129	R	R	6-2	165	2-23-73	1994	Edwardsville, Ill.
Censale, Silvio	10	6	3.15	22	21	0	0	120	96	54	42	54	123	L	L	6-2	195	11-21-71	1993	Lodi, N.J.
Estavil, Mauricio	3	5	3.68	42	0	0	1	44	33	20	18	37	58	L	L	6-0	185	6-27-72	1994	Calabasas, Calif.
Gambs, Chris	0	0	6.86	9	0	0	0	20	24	17	15	14	15	R	R	6-2	210	10-26-73	1991	Richmond, Calif.
Genke, Todd	3	2	3.91	31	1	0	1	53	50	30	23	18	37	R	R	6-1	190	4-8-71	1993	Greenfield, Wis.
Hamilton, Paul	1	0	4.71	15	1	0	0	21	24	11	11	7	10	R	R	6-4	185	10-31-71	1993	Cleveland, Texas
Humphry, Trevor	5	7	3.62	28	20	2	0	119	122	67	48	63	102	R	R	6-2	210	10-31-71	1992	Delight, Ark.
Hunter, Rich	10	2	2.77	15	15	3	0	104	79	37	32	19	80	R	R	6-1	180	9-25-74	1993	Temecula, Calif.
Karvala, Kyle	5	1	3.44	20	0	0	2	18	13	9	7	7	17	L	L	6-3	220	2-11-71	1994	New Berlin, Wis.
Kosek, Kory	1	2	0.00	15	0	0	3	20	13	8	0	5	24	R	R	6-1	185	4-8-73	1995	Glencoe, Minn.
Legrow, Brett	0	1	5.14	8	2	0	1	14	16	10	8	5	8	L	L	6-2	200	3-2-71	1994	Russellville, Ark.
Manning, Len	10	10	2.64	27	26	1	0	160	130	68	47	58	154	L	L	6-2	195	12-30-71	1994	New Brighton, Minn.
Mitchell, Courtney	0	1	10.38	5	0	0	0	4	7	5	5	5	3	S	L	5-9	178	11-20-72	1994	Garyville, La.
Nyari, Pete	5	1	4.52	35	1	0	1	62	58	40	31	39	49	R	R	5-11	200	9-4-71	1994	Erie, Pa.
Phipps, Chris	0	2	1.96	11	0	0	0	23	24	9	5	8	10	R	R	6-3	220	2-27-74	1992	Bristol, Tenn.
Stumpf, Brian	3	3	2.34	55	0	0	28	62	59	20	16	19	66	L	R	6-3	200	5-22-72	1994	Springfield, Pa.
Wimberly, Larry	10	3	2.67	24	24	0	0	135	99	48	40	44	139	L	L	6-2	185	8-22-75	1994	Winter Garden, Fla.

BATAVIA   A

NEW YORK-PENN LEAGUE

BATTING	AVG	G	AB	R	H	2B	3B	HR	RBI	BB	SO	SB	CS	B	T	HT	WT	DOB	1st Yr	Resides
Anderson, Marlon	.295	74	312	52	92	13	4	3	40	15	20	22	8	L	R	5-10	190	1-3-74	1995	Prattville, Ala.
Brito, Domingo	.125	11	32	1	4	0	0	0	2	9	9	0	0	R	R	6-0	160	7-6-75	1994	Santo Domingo, D.R.
Carver, Steve	.304	56	217	35	66	13	2	7	41	17	29	2	1	L	R	6-3	215	9-27-72	1995	Jacksonville, Fla.

BATTING	AVG	G	AB	R	H	2B	3B	HR	RBI	BB	SO	SB	CS	B	T	HT	WT	DOB	1st Yr	Resides
Cornelius, Jonathon	.262	68	263	29	69	11	4	3	41	22	59	4	2	R	R	6-1	195	11-30-73	1995	Covina, Calif.
Cox, Charles	.218	38	124	13	27	4	2	0	11	11	41	2	0	R	R	6-2	190	1-28-73	1995	Pasadena, Texas
Crane, Todd	.246	27	69	15	17	3	0	0	8	13	25	2	0	R	R	6-1	185	7-2-73	1995	Roswell, Ga.
Dawkins, Walter	.315	58	203	46	64	11	4	1	31	27	36	15	6	R	R	5-10	190	8-6-72	1995	Garden Grove, Calif.
Diaz, Linardo	.240	22	75	13	18	4	1	1	7	3	17	4	1	R	R	6-1	165	12-30-74	1993	Berabona, D.R.
Fana, Alberto	.262	20	61	5	16	1	0	0	4	2	11	0	0	R	R	6-0	180	2-27-74	1994	Santo Domingo, D.R.
Kimm, Tyson	.270	14	37	8	10	2	0	0	6	6	6	0	0	S	R	6-1	175	11-30-72	1995	Amana, Iowa
Leaman, Jeff	.264	62	220	30	58	10	1	4	22	20	55	2	4	R	R	6-0	190	12-30-72	1995	Litchfield, Calif.
Pettiford, Torrey	.311	41	151	21	47	5	2	0	17	5	18	12	2	R	R	5-9	163	5-30-73	1994	Cedar Grove, N.C.
Pierce, Kirk	.218	30	101	18	22	5	1	0	7	10	23	0	0	R	R	6-0	200	5-26-73	1995	Murrieta, Calif.
Raynor, Mark	.262	66	267	49	70	10	6	3	37	38	42	13	4	R	R	6-0	180	4-1-73	1995	Williamston, N.C.
Robinson, David	.219	56	201	27	44	9	3	2	26	20	45	9	3	L	L	5-11	195	11-29-72	1995	Dayton, Ohio
Russell, Jason	.191	40	141	9	27	3	1	2	18	11	25	0	2	R	R	5-11	190	3-2-74	1995	Salina, Okla.
Schreimann, Eric	.269	15	52	9	14	1	0	4	13	1	7	0	1	R	R	6-1	205	4-22-75	1994	Jefferson City, Mo.
Snusz, Chris	.227	21	66	9	15	1	1	1	5	5	12	1	1	R	R	6-0	195	11-8-72	1995	Buffalo, N.Y.

GAMES BY POSITION: C—Cox 34, Pierce 27, Schreimann 1, Snusz 18. **1B**—Carver 40, Fana 13, Leaman 19, Pierce 1. **2B**—Anderson 73, Brito 3, Pettiford 3. **3B**—Cox 1, Leaman 38, Russell 40. **SS**—Brito 9, Kimm 1, Leaman 2, Raynor 66. **OF**—Cornelius 63, Cox 2, Crane 21, Dawkins 51, Diaz 21, Leaman 4, Robinson 54, Schreimann 14.

PITCHING	W	L	ERA	G	GS	CG	SV	IP	H	R	ER	BB	SO	B	T	HT	WT	DOB	1st Yr	Resides
Antonini, Adrian	0	1	9.53	3	3	0	0	6	12	6	6	1	8	R	R	6-3	225	7-27-72	1995	Miami, Fla.
Barnett, Marty	1	6	6.20	10	10	0	0	49	67	45	34	10	32	R	R	6-3	210	3-10-74	1995	Harlan, Iowa
Choi, Chang Yang	1	3	4.96	7	7	0	0	33	35	20	18	14	32	R	R	6-2	190	6-3-73	1995	Seoul, Korea
Ford, Brian	3	1	1.18	29	0	0	10	38	24	8	5	5	44	R	L	6-3	210	1-7-73	1995	Hope Mills, N.C.
Gaiko, Rob	1	1	8.18	20	0	0	0	33	50	34	30	11	25	R	R	6-3	225	4-14-73	1995	Stillwater, Okla.
Gambs, Chris	3	2	5.50	7	7	0	0	34	31	21	21	22	21	R	R	6-2	210	10-26-73	1991	Richmond, Calif.
Hamilton, Bo	7	2	2.58	14	13	1	0	84	73	30	24	23	62	R	R	6-4	185	10-31-71	1993	Cleveland, Texas
Kawabata, Kyle	2	0	3.58	18	0	0	0	33	34	16	13	5	30	R	R	6-0	195	1-2-74	1995	Kailua, Hawaii
McClurg, Clint	2	2	4.30	10	5	1	0	38	41	26	18	21	14	R	R	6-5	195	11-29-73	1993	Arvada, Colo.
Mendes, Jaime	1	1	3.92	30	0	0	3	41	50	23	18	6	35	R	R	5-10	185	4-6-73	1995	Las Cruces, N.M.
Mensink, Brian	4	1	2.98	11	8	0	0	48	56	23	16	10	37	R	R	6-4	215	11-1-73	1995	Rochester, Minn.
Mitchell, Courtney	0	5	4.89	28	0	0	1	42	46	28	23	23	40	S	L	5-9	178	11-20-72	1994	Garyville, La.
Noone, Bill	1	0	14.29	6	0	0	0	6	14	11	9	3	2	R	R	6-2	190	5-5-73	1995	Pittston, Pa.
Shumaker, Anthony	2	1	1.62	9	4	1	0	39	38	10	7	4	31	L	L	6-5	223	5-14-73	1995	Kokomo, Ind.
Smith, Justin	4	3	4.26	15	10	0	0	61	71	35	29	20	37	R	R	6-3	205	1-19-72	1994	Pittsford, N.Y.
Yeager, Gary	9	4	2.56	19	8	1	0	81	74	33	23	16	57	R	R	6-1	190	11-6-73	1995	Elizabethtown, Pa.

MARTINSVILLE   R

APPALACHIAN LEAGUE

BATTING	AVG	G	AB	R	H	2B	3B	HR	RBI	BB	SO	SB	CS	B	T	HT	WT	DOB	1st Yr	Resides
Andino, Luis	.192	27	73	13	14	5	1	1	11	4	27	1	2	R	R	6-4	176	1-27-75	1994	Carolina, P.R.
Brito, Domingo	.148	29	81	8	12	0	0	0	3	11	32	1	0	R	R	6-0	160	7-6-75	1994	Santo Domingo, D.R.
Buckles, Matt	.190	22	58	6	11	2	0	0	4	2	17	2	0	L	R	5-11	195	12-29-76	1995	East Palatka, Fla.
Elliott, Zach	.358	45	151	46	54	10	4	2	19	32	30	13	5	R	R	6-0	180	9-1-73	1995	Tustin, Calif.
Hooker, Kevin	.335	49	179	38	60	16	1	9	46	21	34	2	3	R	R	5-11	185	7-25-72	1995	Corvallis, Ore.
Janke, Jared	.242	46	149	24	36	11	0	3	27	26	25	5	1	R	R	6-5	225	5-17-74	1995	Coeur D'Alene, Idaho
Kearney, Chad	.225	29	80	9	18	1	0	1	5	10	32	1	2	R	R	5-11	190	5-24-74	1994	Central Islip, N.Y.
Kennedy, Justin	.199	43	146	11	29	7	1	0	15	7	36	11	0	L	L	6-1	188	8-16-77	1995	Bastrop, La.
Livingston, Clyde	.212	33	104	15	22	5	2	2	25	8	22	1	0	L	R	5-10	190	2-28-73	1995	Prosperity, S.C.
Mata, Manuel	.400	2	5	1	2	0	0	0	2	0	0	0	0	L	L	6-1	186	7-15-76	1995	Caracas, Venez.
O'Connor, Richard	.224	53	174	27	39	4	1	0	11	26	52	13	8	R	R	6-1	185	9-23-73	1995	Walkerton, Ind.
Oliveros, Leonardo	.284	48	155	17	44	9	0	2	18	14	18	0	0	R	R	5-10	185	12-1-75	1994	Maturin, Venez.
Raio, Domenick	.214	6	14	1	3	0	0	0	1	1	4	0	0	R	R	6-1	200	10-8-73	1995	Atco, N.J.
Schreimann, Eric	.299	38	127	12	38	8	0	2	18	10	20	2	1	R	R	6-1	205	4-22-75	1994	Jefferson City, Mo.
Serafin, Ricardo	.189	22	53	8	10	1	0	1	4	1	20	4	0	R	R	6-0	160	2-20-77	1994	San Pedro de Macoris, D.R.
Serbio, Carmen	.229	28	83	15	19	6	1	2	12	20	23	0	1	R	R	5-10	170	9-9-72	1995	Fayetteville, N.C.
Stone, Matthew	.252	40	111	15	28	8	0	0	13	29	37	3	0	L	L	6-4	220	2-7-75	1993	Vista, Calif.
Taylor, Reggie	.222	64	239	36	53	4	6	2	32	23	58	18	7	L	R	6-1	180	1-12-77	1995	Newberry, S.C.
Townsend, Terric	.286	5	14	4	4	0	0	0	1	3	2	1	0	R	R	6-3	170	1-16-74	1995	Wichita, Kan.
Wampler, Sam	.136	11	22	0	3	0	0	0	1	3	10	0	0	S	R	6-1	190	9-22-74	1994	Idaho Falls, Idaho
Williams, Errick	.239	36	113	19	27	1	0	0	11	6	32	13	2	R	R	6-0	215	5-21-77	1995	San Diego, Calif.

GAMES BY POSITION: C—Livingston 9, Oliveros 40, Raio 3, Schreimann 14, Wampler 9. **1B**—Janke 36, Mata 3, Stone 35. **2B**—Brito 2, Hooker 43, O'Connor 23, Serbio 1. **3B**—Andino 1, Brito 17, Elliott 1, Hooker 6, O'Connor 25, Serbio 19, Townsend 2. **SS**—Brito 10, Elliott 43, O'Connor 7, Serbio 8, Townsend 3. **OF**—Andino 20, Buckles 15, Kearney 23, Kennedy 41, Raio 1, Schreimann 3, Serafin 19, Taylor 63, Williams 33.

PITCHING	W	L	ERA	G	GS	CG	SV	IP	H	R	ER	BB	SO	B	T	HT	WT	DOB	1st Yr	Resides
Aguiar, Douglas	2	2	5.56	15	7	0	0	45	46	28	28	21	42	R	R	6-0	160	2-20-77	1995	Zulia, Venez.
Bowser, Robert	2	2	3.90	17	0	0	1	32	30	15	14	9	35	R	R	6-5	220	11-26-73	1995	Indianapolis, Ind.
Burger, Rob	2	4	4.65	9	9	0	0	41	47	25	21	23	54	R	R	6-1	190	3-25-76	1994	Willow Street, Pa.
Coggin, David	5	3	3.00	11	11	0	0	48	45	25	16	31	43	R	R	6-4	195	10-30-76	1995	Upland, Calif.
Dunne, Brian	3	4	4.28	16	6	0	1	48	67	39	23	10	33	S	L	6-2	215	10-2-73	1995	Brooklyn, N.Y.
Frace, Ryan	3	2	2.17	14	0	0	1	29	20	14	7	9	31	R	R	6-2	205	2-23-72	1995	Fullerton, Calif.
Kershner, Jason	4	2	5.14	13	13	0	0	63	67	42	36	19	53	L	L	6-2	160	12-19-76	1995	Scottsdale, Ariz.
Knoll, Randy	0	3	8.83	6	0	0	0	17	21	18	17	9	22	R	R	6-4	190	3-21-77	1995	Corona, Calif.
Kosek, Kory	1	0	2.37	9	0	0	2	19	10	5	5	4	17	R	R	6-1	185	4-8-73	1995	Glencoe, Minn.
Miller, Brian	6	4	5.16	23	0	0	3	45	46	28	26	15	35	R	R	6-0	200	1-26-73	1995	Two Rivers, Wis.
Mosquea, Alberto	0	4	4.58	9	3	0	0	20	13	10	10	25	15	R	R	6-1	151	9-4-75	1994	Santo Domingo, D.R.
Noone, Bill	0	0	2.08	1	1	0	0	4	3	1	1	1	5	R	R	6-2	190	5-5-73	1995	Pittston, Pa.
Pizarro, Melvin	0	0	6.23	10	0	0	0	17	20	13	12	5	17	L	L	6-1	185	12-30-78	1995	Carolina, P.R.
Reed, Kenny	0	1	7.43	13	0	0	0	23	29	22	19	21	15	R	R	6-6	175	5-22-75	1995	Rolla, Mo.
Shumaker, Anthony	1	3	4.50	6	4	0	0	28	31	16	14	8	26	L	L	6-5	223	5-14-73	1995	Kokomo, Ind.
Sikes, Jason	0	3	5.94	4	3	0	0	17	23	13	11	9	13	R	R	6-5	225	6-17-76	1994	Perry, Ga.
Tebbetts, Scott	1	3	2.25	22	0	0	9	32	31	15	8	7	30	R	R	6-0	200	10-8-72	1995	San Diego, Calif.
Yoder, Jason	1	2	5.40	8	4	0	0	28	33	20	17	11	23	R	R	6-10	230	5-1-75	1995	Palmyra, N.J.

PITTSBURGH PIRATES

Manager: Jim Leyland.   **1995 Record:** 58-86, .403 (5th, NL Central).

BATTING	AVG	G	AB	R	H	2B	3B	HR	RBI	BB	SO	SB	CS	B	T	HT	WT	DOB	1st Yr	Resides
Aude, Rich	.248	42	109	10	27	8	0	2	19	6	20	1	2	R	R	6-5	220	7-13-71	1989	Chatsworth, Calif.
Bell, Jay	.262	138	530	79	139	28	4	13	55	55	110	2	5	R	R	6-1	175	12-11-65	1984	Valrico, Fla.
Brumfield, Jacob	.271	116	402	64	109	23	2	4	26	37	71	22	12	R	R	6-0	180	5-27-65	1983	Atlanta, Ga.
Clark, Dave	.281	77	196	30	55	6	0	4	24	24	38	3	3	L	R	6-2	210	9-3-62	1983	Tupelo, Miss.
Cummings, Midre	.243	59	152	13	37	7	1	2	15	13	30	1	0	L	R	6-0	196	10-14-71	1990	St. Croix, Virgin Islands
Encarnacion, Angelo	.226	58	159	18	36	7	2	2	10	13	28	1	1	R	R	5-8	180	4-18-73	1990	Santo Domingo, D.R.
Garcia, Carlos	.294	104	367	41	108	24	2	6	50	25	55	8	4	R	R	6-1	193	10-15-67	1987	Lancaster, N.Y.
Garcia, Freddy	.140	42	57	5	8	1	1	0	1	8	17	0	1	R	R	6-2	186	8-1-72	1991	La Romana, D.R.
Johnson, Mark	.208	79	221	32	46	6	1	13	28	37	66	5	2	L	L	6-4	220	10-17-67	1990	Worcester, Mass.
King, Jeff	.265	122	445	61	118	27	2	18	87	55	63	7	4	R	R	6-1	180	12-26-64	1986	Wexford, Pa.
Liriano, Nelson	.286	107	259	29	74	12	1	5	38	24	34	2	2	S	R	6-1	175	6-3-64	1983	Puerta Plata, D.R.
Martin, Al	.282	124	439	70	124	25	3	13	41	44	92	20	11	L	L	6-2	210	11-24-67	1985	Scottsdale, Ariz.
Merced, Orlando	.300	132	487	75	146	29	4	15	83	52	74	7	2	L	R	5-11	170	11-2-66	1985	Ocala, Fla.
Parent, Mark	.232	69	233	25	54	9	0	15	33	23	62	0	0	R	R	6-5	225	9-16-61	1979	San Diego, Calif.
Pegues, Steve	.246	82	171	17	42	8	0	6	16	4	36	1	2	R	R	6-2	190	5-21-68	1987	Pontotoc, Miss.
Sasser, Mackey	.154	14	26	1	4	1	0	0	0	0	0	0	0	L	R	6-1	210	8-3-62	1984	Lynn Haven, Fla.
Slaught, Don	.304	35	112	13	34	6	0	0	13	9	8	0	0	R	R	6-1	190	9-11-58	1980	Arlington, Texas
Wehner, John	.308	52	107	13	33	0	3	0	5	10	17	3	1	R	R	6-3	205	6-29-67	1988	Pittsburgh, Pa.
Young, Kevin	.232	56	181	13	42	9	0	6	22	8	53	1	3	R	R	6-2	219	6-16-69	1990	Kansas City, Kan.

PITCHING	W	L	ERA	G	GS	CG	SV	IP	H	R	ER	BB	SO	B	T	HT	WT	DOB	1st Yr	Resides
Christiansen, Jason	1	3	4.15	63	0	0	0	56	49	28	26	34	53	R	L	6-5	235	9-21-69	1991	Elkhorn, Neb.
Dyer, Mike	4	5	4.34	55	0	0	0	75	81	40	36	30	53	R	R	6-3	200	9-8-66	1986	Fullerton, Calif.
Ericks, John	3	9	4.58	19	18	1	0	106	108	59	54	50	80	R	R	6-7	220	9-16-67	1988	Tinley Park, Ill.
Gott, Jim	2	4	6.03	25	0	0	3	31	38	26	21	12	19	R	R	6-4	230	8-3-59	1977	Altadena, Calif.
Hancock, Lee	0	0	1.93	11	0	0	0	14	10	3	3	2	6	L	L	6-4	215	6-27-67	1988	Saratoga, Calif.
Hope, John	0	0	30.86	3	0	0	0	2	8	8	8	4	2	R	R	6-3	206	12-21-70	1989	Ft. Lauderdale, Fla.
Konuszewski, Dennis	0	0	54.00	1	0	0	0	3	2	2	1	0	0	R	R	6-3	210	2-4-71	1992	Bridgeport, Mich.
Lieber, Jon	4	7	6.32	21	12	0	0	73	103	56	51	14	45	L	R	6-3	205	4-2-70	1992	Council Bluffs, Iowa
Loaiza, Esteban	8	9	5.16	32	31	1	0	173	205	115	99	55	85	R	R	6-2	172	12-31-71	1991	Imperial Beach, Calif.
Maddux, Mike	1	0	9.00	8	0	0	0	9	14	9	9	3	4	L	R	6-2	188	8-27-61	1982	Las Vegas, Nev.
Manzanillo, Ravelo	0	0	4.91	5	0	0	0	4	3	3	2	2	1	L	L	5-10	190	10-17-63	1981	San Pedro de Macoris,D.R.
McCurry, Jeff	1	4	5.02	55	0	0	1	61	82	38	34	30	27	R	R	6-7	210	1-21-70	1991	Houston, Texas
Miceli, Danny	4	4	4.66	58	0	0	21	58	61	30	30	28	56	R	R	5-11	205	9-9-70	1990	Orlando, Fla.
Morel, Ramon	0	1	2.84	5	0	0	0	6	6	2	2	2	3	R	R	6-2	170	8-15-74	1991	Villa Gonzalez, D.R.
Neagle, Denny	13	8	3.43	31	31	5	0	210	221	91	80	45	150	L	L	6-2	215	9-13-68	1989	Gambrills, Md.
Parris, Steve	6	6	5.38	15	15	1	0	82	89	49	49	33	61	R	R	6-0	190	12-17-67	1989	Joliet, Ill.
Plesac, Dan	4	4	3.58	58	0	0	3	60	53	26	24	27	57	L	L	6-5	215	2-4-62	1983	Hales Corners, Wisc.
Powell, Ross	0	2	5.23	12	3	0	0	21	20	14	12	10	12	L	L	6-0	180	1-24-68	1989	Antioch, Tenn.
2-team (15 Houston)	0	2	6.98	27	3	0	0	30	36	26	23	21	20							
Wagner, Paul	5	16	4.80	33	25	3	1	165	174	96	88	72	120	R	R	6-1	202	11-14-67	1989	Germantown, Wisc.
White, Rick	2	3	4.75	15	9	0	0	55	66	33	29	18	29	R	R	6-4	215	12-23-68	1990	Springfield, Ohio
Wilson, Gary	0	1	5.02	10	0	0	0	14	13	8	8	5	8	R	R	6-3	180	1-1-70	1992	Arcata, Calif.

FIELDING

Catcher	PCT	G	PO	A	E	DP	PB
Encarnacion	.979	55	278	43	7	2	4
Parent	.990	67	364	39	4	1	7
Sasser	1.000	11	35	3	0	0	0
Slaught	.996	33	220	9	1	2	1
Wehner	1.000	1	2	0	0	0	0

First Base	PCT	G	PO	A	E	DP
Aude	.996	32	223	11	1	28
Johnson	.986	70	527	36	8	53
King	.994	35	296	27	2	22
Merced	.995	35	175	15	1	22
Young	1.000	6	30	2	0	2

Second Base	PCT	G	PO	A	E	DP
C. Garcia	.982	92	217	265	9	70
King	1.000	8	8	14	0	4
Liriano	.981	67	130	132	5	31

Third Base	PCT	G	PO	A	E	DP
Bell	1.000	3	1	6	0	1
F. Garcia	.955	8	6	15	1	4

	PCT	G	PO	A	E	DP
King	.942	84	48	164	13	14
Liriano	1.000	5	0	5	0	0
Wehner	1.000	19	11	26	0	1
Young	.919	48	28	108	12	7

Shortstop	PCT	G	PO	A	E	DP
Bell	.978	136	205	409	14	88
C. Garcia	.895	15	17	34	6	6
King	.333	2	0	1	2	0
Liriano	.000	1	0	0	0	0
Wehner	1.000	1	0	2	0	0

Outfield	PCT	G	PO	A	E	DP
Brumfield	.969	104	241	8	8	1
Clark	.961	61	98	4	4	0
Cummings	.988	41	79	2	1	0
Martin	.977	121	206	8	5	2
Merced	.976	107	199	8	5	2
Pegues	.954	53	81	2	4	1
Wehner	1.000	23	22	1	0	1

Denny Neagle

Third baseman Jeff King led Pittsburgh with 18 homers and 87 RBIs

GEORGE GOJKOVICH

PIRATES

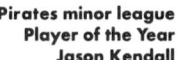

Pirates minor league Player of the Year Jason Kendall

BILL SETLIFF

FARM SYSTEM

Director of Minor Leagues: Chet Montgomery.

Class	Farm Team	League	W	L	Pct.	Finish*	Manager	First Yr
AAA	Calgary (Alta.) Cannons	Pacific Coast	58	83	.411	10th (10)	Bobby Meacham	1995
AA	Carolina (N.C.) Mudcats	Southern	89	55	.618	1st+ (10)	Trent Jewett	1991
#A	Lynchburg (Va.) Hillcats	Carolina	67	71	.486	T-4th (8)	Marc Hill	1995
A	Augusta (Ga.) GreenJackets	South Atlantic	76	62	.551	4th+ (14)	Jeff Banister	1988
A	Erie (Pa.) SeaWolves	New York-Penn	34	41	.453	T-9th (14)	Scott Little	1995
R	Bradenton (Fla.) Pirates	Gulf Coast	23	36	.390	11th (16)	Woody Huyke	1967

*Finish in overall standings (No. of teams in league)   #Advanced level   +Won league championship

ORGANIZATION LEADERS

MAJOR LEAGUERS

BATTING
*AVG	Orlando Merced	.300
R	Jay Bell	79
H	Orlando Merced	146
TB	Orlando Merced	228
2B	Orlando Merced	29
3B	Two tied at	4
HR	Jeff King	18
RBI	Jeff King	87
BB	Two tied at	55
SO	Jay Bell	110
SB	Jacob Brumfield	22

PITCHING
W	Denny Neagle	13
L	Paul Wagner	16
#ERA	Denny Neagle	3.43
G	Jason Christiansen	63
CG	Denny Neagle	5
SV	Dan Miceli	21
IP	Denny Neagle	210
BB	Paul Wagner	72
SO	Denny Neagle	150

Orlando Merced. .300 average

MINOR LEAGUERS

BATTING
*AVG	Keith Osik, Calgary	.336
R	Adrian Brown, Augusta/Lynchburg	94
H	Trey Beamon, Calgary	151
TB	George Canale, Carolina	245
2B	Erik Johnson, Calgary	35
3B	Three tied at	6
HR	Two tied at	21
RBI	George Canale, Carolina	102
BB	Rob Leary, Lynchburg/Carolina	84
SO	Shon Walker, Augusta	127
SB	Derek Swafford, Augusta	52

PITCHING
W	Elmer Dessens, Carolina	15
L	Jeff Kelly, Augusta	11
#ERA	Chris Peters, Lynchburg/Carolina	2.33
G	Marc Pisciotta, Carolina	56
CG	Matt Ruebel, Carolina	4
SV	Matt Ryan, Carolina/Calgary	27
IP	Matt Ruebel, Carolina	169
BB	John Dillinger, Lynchburg	67
SO	Chris Peters, Lynchburg/Carolina	139

*Minimum 250 At-Bats   #Minimum 75 Innings

TOP 10 PROSPECTS

How the Pirates Top 10 prospects, as judged by Baseball America prior to the 1995 season, fared in 1995:

TYLER TRAVIS-BOLDEN

Trey Beamon

Player, Pos.	Club (Class—League)	AVG	AB	R	H	2B	3B	HR	RBI	SB
1. Trey Beamon, of	Calgary (AAA—Pacific Coast)	.334	452	74	151	29	5	5	62	18
2. Lou Collier, ss	Lynchburg (A—Carolina)	.276	399	68	110	19	3	4	38	31
3. Mark Farris, ss	Injured—Did not play									
4. Freddy Garcia, 3b	Pittsburgh	.140	57	5	8	1	1	0	1	0
5. Charles Peterson, of	Lynchburg (A—Carolina)	.274	391	61	107	9	4	7	51	31
	Carolina (AA—Southern)	.329	70	13	23	3	1	0	7	2
7. Jason Kendall, c	Carolina (AA—Southern)	.326	429	87	140	26	1	8	71	10
9. Micah Franklin, of	Calgary (AAA—Pacific Coast)	.293	358	64	105	28	0	21	71	3
10. Rich Aude, 1b	Calgary (AAA—Pacific Coast)	.333	195	34	65	14	2	9	42	3
	Pittsburgh	.248	109	10	27	8	0	2	19	1

		W	L	ERA	G	SV	IP	H	BB	SO
6. Esteban Loaiza, rhp	Pittsburgh	8	9	5.16	32	0	173	205	55	85
8. Ramon Morel, rhp	Lynchburg (A—Carolina)	3	7	3.47	12	0	73	80	13	44
	Carolina (AA—Southern)	3	3	3.52	10	0	69	71	10	34
	Pittsburgh	0	1	2.84	5	0	6	6	2	3

Not Their Fault. The Pirates finished last in the National League Central in 1995, despite the efforts of shortstop Jay Bell (.262-13-55), left, and outfielder Al Martin (.282-13-41).

CALGARY   AAA

PACIFIC COAST LEAGUE

BATTING	AVG	G	AB	R	H	2B	3B	HR	RBI	BB	SO	SB	CS	B	T	HT	WT	DOB	1st Yr	Resides
Allensworth, Jermaine..	.316	51	190	46	60	13	4	3	11	13	30	13	4	R	R	5-11	180	1-11-72	1993	Anderson, Ind.
Aude, Rich....................	.333	50	195	34	65	14	2	9	42	12	30	3	2	R	R	6-5	220	7-13-71	1989	Chatsworth, Calif.*
Beamon, Trey................	.334	118	452	74	151	29	5	5	62	39	55	18	8	L	R	6-3	195	2-11-74	1992	Dallas, Texas
Cameron, Stanton........	.208	7	24	8	5	4	0	0	4	4	4	0	0	R	R	6-5	195	7-5-69	1987	Powell, Tenn.
Cummings, Midre.........	.277	45	159	19	44	9	1	1	16	6	27	1	1	L	R	6-0	196	10-14-71	1990	St. Croix, Virgin Islands
Encarnacion, Angelo.....	.250	21	80	8	20	3	0	1	6	1	12	1	0	R	R	5-8	180	4-18-73	1990	Santo Domingo, D.R.
Franklin, Micah............	.293	110	358	64	105	28	0	21	71	47	95	3	3	S	R	6-0	195	4-25-72	1990	San Francisco, Calif.
Hanel, Marcus..............	.125	2	8	1	1	0	0	0	0	0	1	0	0	R	R	6-4	205	10-19-71	1989	Racine, Wisc.
Horn, Sam....................	.333	36	99	21	33	8	2	8	22	14	21	0	0	L	L	6-5	250	11-2-63	1982	Bessemer, Ala.
Johnson, Erik	.297	123	455	64	135	35	6	3	58	39	40	5	4	R	R	5-11	175	10-11-65	1987	San Ramon, Calif.
Johnson, Mark..............	.304	9	23	7	7	4	0	2	8	6	4	1	0	L	L	6-4	220	10-17-67	1990	Worcester, Mass.
Knabenshue, Chris	.000	4	10	2	0	0	0	0	1	4	3	0	0	L	R	6-1	175	10-30-63	1985	Aurora, Colo.
Marx, Tim	.297	61	185	27	55	11	1	1	12	19	16	2	3	R	R	6-2	190	11-27-68	1991	Evansville, Ind.
Matos, Francisco..........	.323	100	341	36	110	11	6	3	40	5	25	9	2	R	R	6-1	160	4-8-70	1988	Azua, D.R.
Mercedes, Luis.............	.262	25	84	18	22	1	0	1	8	11	10	1	2	R	R	6-3	183	2-20-68	1987	San Pedro de Macoris, D.R.
Osik, Keith..................	.336	90	301	40	101	25	1	10	59	21	42	2	2	R	R	6-0	195	10-22-68	1990	Rocky Point, N.Y.
Polcovich, Kevin...........	.282	62	213	31	60	8	1	3	27	11	32	5	6	R	R	5-9	165	6-28-70	1992	Auburn, N.Y.
Ratliff, Daryl................	.343	95	286	41	98	11	1	0	37	18	30	9	6	R	R	6-1	180	10-15-69	1989	Santa Cruz, Calif.
Richardson, Jeff	.333	7	18	4	6	0	0	0	3	2	1	0	0	R	R	6-1	172	8-26-65	1986	Lincoln, Neb.
Rodriguez, Boi.............	.256	11	39	10	10	2	0	2	10	3	5	1	0	L	R	6-0	180	4-14-66	1987	Dorado Beach, P.R.
Simmons, Nelson..........	.281	107	299	44	84	17	0	9	58	30	45	1	1	S	R	6-1	215	6-27-63	1981	Spring Valley, Calif.
Sveum, Dale................	.284	118	408	71	116	34	1	12	70	48	78	2	2	S	R	6-3	185	11-23-63	1982	Glendale, Ariz.
Wehner, John...............	.329	40	158	30	52	12	2	4	24	12	16	8	4	R	R	6-3	205	6-29-67	1988	Pittsburgh, Pa.
Womack, Tony..............	.280	30	107	12	30	3	1	0	6	12	11	7	5	L	R	5-9	153	9-25-69	1991	Chatham, Va.
Young, Kevin................	.356	45	163	24	58	23	1	8	34	15	21	6	3	R	R	6-2	219	6-16-69	1990	Kansas City, Kan.

PITCHING	W	L	ERA	G	GS	CG	SV	IP	H	R	ER	BB	SO	B	T	HT	WT	DOB	1st Yr	Resides
August, Don.................	0	2	4.50	2	2	0	0	8	10	7	4	4	4	R	R	6-3	190	7-3-63	1985	New Berlin, Wisc.
Ayrault, Bob.................	0	0	4.91	6	0	0	0	7	7	4	4	3	4	R	R	6-4	235	4-27-66	1989	Reno, Nev.
Backlund, Brett............	2	3	5.22	12	8	0	0	50	59	29	29	9	29	R	R	6-0	195	12-16-69	1992	Salem, Ore.
Bennett, Chris..............	0	0	5.14	4	0	0	0	7	11	7	4	1	7	R	R	6-6	205	9-8-65	1986	Yreka, Calif.
Corbin, Archie..............	1	5	8.56	47	1	0	1	61	76	63	58	55	54	R	R	6-4	187	12-30-67	1986	Beaumont, Texas
De los Santos, Mariano.	3	6	6.15	14	14	0	0	72	85	57	49	22	36	R	R	5-10	200	7-13-70	1989	Santo Domingo, D.R.
Ericks, John................	2	1	2.48	5	5	0	0	29	20	8	8	13	25	R	R	6-7	220	9-16-67	1988	Tinley Park, Ill.
Flynt, Will...................	1	0	5.40	12	1	0	0	22	27	15	13	12	12	L	L	6-5	215	11-23-67	1991	San Diego, Calif.
Gibson, Paul................	0	2	3.72	19	0	0	1	19	21	11	8	9	17	R	L	6-0	185	1-4-60	1978	Center Moriches, N.Y.
Hancock, Lee...............	6	10	5.07	34	17	1	0	114	146	78	64	27	49	L	L	6-4	215	6-27-67	1988	Saratoga, Calif.
Hill, Milt....................	1	3	4.90	24	5	0	0	61	69	38	33	14	31	R	R	6-0	180	8-22-65	1987	Cumming, Ga.
Hope, John	7	1	2.79	13	13	3	0	81	76	29	25	11	41	R	R	6-3	206	12-21-70	1989	Ft. Lauderdale, Fla.
Lieber, Jon..................	1	5	7.01	14	14	0	0	77	122	69	60	19	34	L	R	6-3	205	4-2-70	1992	Council Bluffs, Iowa

PITCHING

PITCHING	W	L	ERA	G	GS	CG	SV	IP	H	R	ER	BB	SO	B	T	HT	WT	DOB	1st Yr	Resides
Manzanillo, Ravelo	0	2	12.75	8	1	0	0	12	23	18	17	10	2	L	L	5-10	190	10-17-63	1981	San Pedro de Macoris,D.R.
Maysey, Matt	8	7	5.50	44	12	0	1	103	122	67	63	44	71	R	R	6-4	225	1-8-67	1985	Yuma, Ariz.
McCurry, Jeff	0	0	1.80	3	0	0	0	5	3	1	1	2	2	R	R	6-7	210	1-21-70	1991	Houston, Texas
Ralph, Curtis	1	4	8.44	28	0	0	1	32	43	35	30	23	27	R	R	6-0	205	8-6-68	1988	Sacramento, Calif.
Ryan, Matt	0	0	1.93	5	0	0	1	5	5	1	1	1	2	R	R	6-5	190	3-20-72	1993	Memphis, Tenn.
Rychel, Kevin	0	1	10.38	10	0	0	0	9	14	11	10	6	4	L	L	5-9	176	9-24-71	1989	Midland, Texas
Shouse, Brian	4	4	6.18	8	8	1	0	39	62	35	27	7	17	L	L	5-11	180	9-26-68	1990	Effingham, Ill.
St. Claire, Randy	3	5	5.00	54	0	0	19	54	72	31	30	21	43	R	R	6-3	190	8-23-60	1979	Whitehall, N.Y.
Taylor, Scott	5	8	4.11	27	25	1	0	140	144	73	64	35	83	L	L	6-1	190	8-2-67	1988	Fort Myers, Fla.
White, Rick	6	4	4.20	14	11	1	0	79	97	40	37	10	56	R	R	6-4	215	12-23-68	1990	Springfield, Ohio
Willis, Travis	2	2	7.15	22	0	0	0	39	57	35	31	15	13	R	R	6-2	185	11-28-68	1989	Somis, Calif.
Wilson, Gary	1	2	5.51	6	4	0	0	16	19	16	10	9	12	R	R	6-3	180	1-1-70	1992	Arcata, Calif.
Winston, Darrin	4	6	4.80	53	0	0	2	51	59	33	27	17	40	R	L	6-0	195	7-6-66	1988	Fords, N.J.

FIELDING

Catcher

Catcher	PCT	G	PO	A	E	DP	PB
Encarnacion	.984	21	113	14	2	1	3
Hanel	.923	2	12	0	1	0	1
Marx	.977	54	268	27	7	5	5
Osik	.990	74	372	24	4	3	6

First Base

First Base	PCT	G	PO	A	E	DP
Aude	.988	49	447	31	6	58
Horn	.976	16	157	5	4	15
M. Johnson	.972	8	65	5	2	4
Osik	1.000	11	83	9	0	3
Rodriguez	.975	7	73	4	2	5
Simmons	.956	9	62	3	3	7
Sveum	.986	36	313	39	5	32
Young	.978	12	124	11	3	11

Second Base

Second Base	PCT	G	PO	A	E	DP
E. Johnson	.974	81	159	218	10	66

	PCT	G	PO	A	E	DP
Matos	.967	48	84	123	7	29
Richardson	.963	5	11	15	1	7
Wehner	.931	5	15	12	2	4
Womack	.967	15	15	44	2	4

Third Base

Third Base	PCT	G	PO	A	E	DP
E. Johnson	1.000	11	7	25	0	0
Osik	1.000	1	2	2	0	0
Rodriguez	.625	2	0	5	3	1
Sveum	.963	70	40	196	9	20
Wehner	.909	31	14	86	10	7
Young	.913	31	20	74	9	4

Shortstop

Shortstop	PCT	G	PO	A	E	DP
E. Johnson	.920	26	32	71	9	9
Matos	.944	45	56	145	12	32
Polcovich	.959	61	90	215	13	49

	PCT	G	PO	A	E	DP
Sveum	.778	1	3	4	2	3
Womack	.960	15	22	50	3	5

Outfield

Outfield	PCT	G	PO	A	E	DP
Allensworth	.989	46	90	2	1	0
Beamon	.960	110	201	14	9	0
Cameron	1.000	7	10	0	0	0
Cummings	.943	41	96	4	6	1
Franklin	.965	100	162	3	6	0
Knabenshue..	1.000	2	1	0	0	0
Mercedes	.940	25	43	4	3	2
Osik	1.000	3	1	0	0	0
Ratliff	.978	79	177	4	4	0
Simmons	.965	35	51	4	2	2
Wehner	1.000	5	7	0	0	0

CAROLINA · AA

SOUTHERN LEAGUE

BATTING	AVG	G	AB	R	H	2B	3B	HR	RBI	BB	SO	SB	CS	B	T	HT	WT	DOB	1st Yr	Resides
Allensworth, Jermaine..	.269	56	219	37	59	14	2	1	14	25	34	13	8	R	R	5-11	180	1-11-72	1993	Anderson, Ind.
Austin, Jake	.236	102	352	29	83	19	2	4	40	17	51	5	3	R	R	6-0	205	4-30-70	1992	Atlanta, Ga.
Beasley, Tony	.281	105	335	59	94	16	4	2	34	31	44	20	4	R	R	5-8	165	12-5-66	1989	Bowling Green, Va.
Brown, Michael	.238	60	223	29	53	13	1	8	33	28	62	0	3	L	L	6-7	245	11-4-71	1989	Vacaville, Calif.
Brumfield, Jacob	.417	3	12	2	5	0	0	2	2	1	2	0	2	R	R	6-0	180	5-27-65	1983	Atlanta, Ga.
Canale, George	.287	130	487	71	140	30	6	21	102	46	83	1	3	L	R	6-1	195	8-11-65	1986	Roanoke, Va.
Conger, Jeff	.289	39	128	15	37	6	1	1	17	18	31	8	2	L	L	6-0	185	8-6-71	1990	Charlotte, N.C.
Cranford, Jay	.229	93	288	30	66	12	1	5	42	52	67	3	4	R	R	6-3	175	4-7-71	1992	Macon, Ga.
Edge, Tim	.214	45	126	15	27	5	0	4	19	10	33	0	0	R	R	6-0	210	10-26-68	1990	Snellville, Ga.
Espinosa, Ramon	.286	134	489	69	140	28	2	3	48	17	64	14	6	R	R	6-0	175	2-7-72	1990	San Pedro de Macoris, D.R.
Farrell, Joe	.220	94	314	34	69	13	0	10	47	15	82	3	4	R	R	6-2	185	7-30-71	1991	Jacksonville, Fla.
Hanel, Marcus	.183	21	60	1	11	1	0	0	3	4	18	0	1	R	R	6-4	205	10-19-71	1989	Racine, Wisc.
Kendall, Jason	.326	117	429	87	140	16	1	8	71	56	22	10	7	R	R	6-0	170	6-26-74	1992	Torrance, Calif.
Krevokuch, Jim	.282	70	174	20	49	13	0	1	11	12	20	1	1	R	R	5-11	175	5-13-69	1991	West Newton, Pa.
Leary, Rob	.305	67	243	38	74	14	3	6	42	40	38	3	3	L	L	6-3	195	7-9-71	1991	Bayside, N.Y.
Munoz, Omer	.265	67	234	29	62	10	1	2	25	5	23	2	0	R	R	5-9	156	3-3-66	1985	Oshkosh, Wisc.
Peterson, Charles	.329	20	70	13	23	3	1	0	7	9	15	2	1	R	R	6-3	200	5-8-74	1993	Laurens, S.C.
Polcovich, Kevin	.317	64	221	27	70	8	0	3	18	14	29	10	5	R	R	5-9	165	6-28-70	1992	Auburn, N.Y.
Ratliff, Daryl	.286	16	63	10	18	4	0	1	5	8	10	2	1	R	R	6-1	180	10-15-69	1989	Santa Cruz, Calif.
Rodarte, Raul	.370	16	54	8	20	5	1	0	11	10	14	2	2	R	R	5-11	190	4-9-70	1991	Diamond Bar, Calif.
Sanford, Chance	.278	16	36	6	10	3	1	3	10	5	7	3	1	L	R	5-10	165	6-2-72	1992	Houston, Texas
Slaught, Don	.250	3	12	1	3	1	0	0	1	0	3	0	0	R	R	6-1	190	9-11-58	1980	Arlington, Texas
Womack, Tony	.256	82	332	52	85	9	4	1	19	19	36	27	10	L	R	5-9	153	9-25-69	1991	Chatham, Va.

PITCHING	W	L	ERA	G	GS	CG	SV	IP	H	R	ER	BB	SO	B	T	HT	WT	DOB	1st Yr	Resides
Backlund, Brett	5	6	3.58	22	14	0	0	93	81	46	37	35	80	R	R	6-0	195	12-16-69	1992	Salem, Ore.
Bennett, Chris	0	1	6.67	18	0	0	1	27	42	22	20	9	13	R	R	6-6	205	9-8-65	1986	Yreka, Calif.
Cooke, Steve	0	0	7.20	1	1	0	0	5	5	4	4	5	4	R	L	6-6	220	1-14-70	1990	Tigard, Ore.
De los Santos, Mariano	1	0	3.62	21	0	0	0	27	28	16	11	14	20	R	R	5-10	200	7-13-70	1989	Santo Domingo, D.R.
Dessens, Elmer	15	8	2.49	27	27	1	0	152	170	62	42	21	68	R	R	6-0	190	1-13-72	1993	Hermosillo, Mexico
Evans, Sean	5	2	5.33	29	2	0	0	49	47	35	29	25	44	R	R	6-1	185	11-6-70	1991	Buffalo, N.Y.
Figueroa, Fernando	0	0	3.38	6	0	0	0	8	12	5	3	2	4	L	L	6-1	170	8-19-64	1986	Caguas, P.R.
Flynt, Will	0	0	0.00	4	0	0	0	4	3	0	0	2	6	L	L	6-5	215	11-23-67	1991	San Diego, Calif.
Hill, Milt	2	2	4.02	10	10	0	0	56	53	27	25	4	46	R	R	6-0	180	8-22-65	1987	Cumming, Ga.
Konuszewski, Dennis....	7	7	3.65	48	0	0	2	62	63	33	25	26	48	R	R	6-3	210	2-4-71	1992	Bridgeport, Mich.
Lawrence, Sean	0	2	5.48	12	3	0	0	21	27	13	13	8	19	L	L	6-4	215	9-2-70	1992	Ephraim, Ill.
Morel, Ramon	3	3	3.52	10	10	0	0	69	71	31	27	10	34	R	R	6-2	170	8-15-74	1991	Villa Gonzalez, D.R.
Nezelek, Andy	1	0	5.14	6	0	0	1	14	16	9	8	3	14	L	R	6-6	218	10-24-65	1986	Richmond, Va.
Parris, Steve	9	1	2.51	14	14	2	0	90	61	25	25	16	86	R	R	6-0	190	12-17-67	1989	Joliet, Ill.
Peters, Chris	2	0	1.29	2	2	0	0	14	9	2	2	2	7	L	L	6-1	170	1-28-72	1993	McMurray, Pa.
Pisciotta, Marc	6	4	4.15	56	0	0	9	69	60	37	32	45	57	R	R	6-5	240	8-7-70	1991	Charlotte, N.C.
Ralph, Curtis	1	1	2.42	18	1	0	1	26	23	8	7	10	17	R	R	6-0	205	8-6-68	1988	Sacramento, Calif.
Rivera, Lino	0	0	6.00	4	0	0	0	6	10	6	4	3	4	R	R	5-11	173	12-2-66	1985	Venus Garden, P.R.
Ruebel, Matt	13	5	2.76	27	27	4	0	169	150	68	52	45	136	L	L	6-2	180	10-16-69	1991	Ames, Iowa
Ryan, Matt	2	1	1.57	44	0	0	26	46	33	10	8	15	41	R	R	6-5	190	3-20-72	1993	Memphis, Tenn.
Rychel, Kevin	3	2	3.33	40	0	0	1	51	35	21	19	24	60	L	L	5-9	176	9-24-71	1989	Midland, Texas
Shouse, Brian	7	6	4.47	21	20	0	0	115	126	64	57	19	76	L	L	5-11	180	9-26-68	1990	Effingham, Ill.
Tolar, Kevin	1	0	3.65	12	0	0	0	12	16	5	5	7	9	R	L	6-3	225	1-28-71	1989	Panama City, Fla.

PITCHING	W	L	ERA	G	GS	CG	SV	IP	H	R	ER	BB	SO	B	T	HT	WT	DOB	1st Yr	Resides
Tsamis, George	0	0	4.09	12	0	0	0	11	12	5	5	5	7	R	L	6-2	175	6-14-67	1989	Clearwater, Fla.
Wilkins, Marc	5	3	3.99	37	12	0	0	99	91	47	44	44	80	R	R	5-11	215	10-21-70	1992	Mansfield, Ohio
Willis, Travis	1	1	2.91	16	0	0	3	22	23	10	7	10	12	R	R	6-2	185	11-28-68	1989	Somis, Calif.
Wilson, Gary	0	0	0.00	1	1	0	0	5	0	0	0	3	5	R	R	6-3	180	1-1-70	1992	Arcata, Calif.

FIELDING

Catcher	PCT	G	PO	A	E	DP	PB
Edge	.983	34	198	31	4	3	2
Hanel	1.000	18	103	13	0	4	6
Kendall	.989	98	692	54	8	7	11
Slaught	1.000	3	24	1	0	0	0

First Base	PCT	G	PO	A	E	DP
Brown	.991	56	503	36	5	33
Canale	.994	38	294	22	2	34
Farrell	1.000	1	2	0	0	0
Hanel	1.000	1	2	0	0	1
Leary	.985	59	557	36	9	51
Munoz	1.000	1	1	0	0	0

Second Base	PCT	G	PO	A	E	DP
Beasley	.968	80	146	217	12	44
Krevokuch	.987	24	31	47	1	8

	PCT	G	PO	A	E	DP
Munoz	.987	48	103	130	3	28
Rodarte	.800	3	3	5	2	2
Womack	.956	11	16	27	2	5

Third Base	PCT	G	PO	A	E	DP
Beasley	1.000	2	0	2	0	0
Canale	.942	26	18	31	3	2
Cranford	.914	86	69	177	23	14
Krevokuch	.918	38	22	68	8	5
Munoz	.000	1	0	0	0	0
Rodarte	.871	9	6	21	4	2

Shortstop	PCT	G	PO	A	E	DP
Beasley	.960	23	36	60	4	11
Cranford	.800	3	1	1	1	0
Krevokuch	1.000	1	1	0	0	0

	PCT	G	PO	A	E	DP
Polcovich	.943	63	88	208	18	36
Womack	.953	68	110	214	16	49

Outfield	PCT	G	PO	A	E	DP
Allensworth	.985	54	131	3	2	1
Austin	.974	93	136	12	4	2
Beasley	1.000	1	1	0	0	0
Brumfield	1.000	3	9	0	0	0
Canale	.962	30	45	5	2	0
Conger	.969	39	90	3	3	3
Espinosa	.956	125	232	9	11	2
Farrell	.957	79	147	10	7	2
Krevokuch	1.000	1	2	0	0	0
Leary	1.000	2	5	0	0	0
Peterson	.977	20	40	2	1	0
Ratliff	.967	15	29	0	1	0

LYNCHBURG

A

CAROLINA LEAGUE

BATTING	AVG	G	AB	R	H	2B	3B	HR	RBI	BB	SO	SB	CS	B	T	HT	WT	DOB	1st Yr	Resides
Austin, Jake	.270	18	74	7	20	6	0	1	11	3	8	0	3	L	R	6-0	205	4-30-70	1992	Atlanta, Ga.
Bonifay, Ken	.245	116	375	57	92	22	2	10	54	63	88	3	5	L	R	6-1	185	9-1-70	1991	Kingsport, Tenn.
Brooks, Eddie	.118	27	68	6	8	1	0	0	2	8	21	0	1	R	R	6-1	175	11-23-72	1994	Lexington, Ky.
Brown, Adrian	.242	54	215	30	52	5	2	1	14	12	20	11	6	S	R	6-0	185	2-7-74	1992	Summit, Miss.
Canetto, John	.250	13	28	5	7	2	0	0	2	3	13	0	0	S	R	5-11	185	9-19-72	1995	Hillsdale, N.Y.
Collier, Lou	.276	114	399	68	110	19	3	4	38	51	60	31	11	R	R	5-10	170	8-21-73	1993	Chicago, Ill.
Conger, Jeff	.264	90	318	44	84	13	5	3	23	35	74	26	16	L	L	6-0	185	8-6-71	1990	Charlotte, N.C.
Cornelius, Brian	.154	12	39	2	6	3	0	0	4	4	11	0	1	L	R	6-0	170	2-16-67	1989	Homestead, Fla.
Daniel, Mike	.284	50	169	31	48	11	1	10	35	29	36	0	2	R	R	6-1	195	9-21-69	1991	Weatherford, Okla.
Hanel, Marcus	.185	40	135	14	25	4	1	3	8	4	33	0	1	R	R	6-4	205	10-19-71	1989	Racine, Wisc.
House, Mitch	.180	16	50	7	9	3	0	1	6	9	13	0	1	R	R	6-2	205	5-28-72	1990	Dante, Va.
Knoblauh, Jay	.277	87	264	40	73	16	2	8	47	16	62	3	2	R	R	6-0	185	11-3-65	1988	Houston, Texas
Leary, Rob	.260	63	208	42	54	9	0	8	31	44	43	9	4	L	L	6-3	195	7-9-71	1991	Bayside, N.Y.
Mendez, Sergio	.246	65	236	30	58	13	0	8	35	9	49	9	4	R	R	6-2	180	10-12-73	1992	Santo Domingo, D.R.
Peterson, Charles	.274	107	391	61	107	9	4	7	51	43	73	31	17	R	R	6-3	200	5-8-74	1993	Laurens, S.C.
Reynolds, Chance	.200	5	15	0	3	0	0		2	3	2	0	1	S	R	5-10	185	9-16-71	1993	Byromville, Ga.
Robertson, Tommy	.273	61	161	16	44	7	0	1	23	20	41	3	7	L	R	6-1	195	12-27-71	1990	Ridgeway, S.C.
Rodarte, Raul	.286	104	346	57	99	18	2	12	48	35	49	19	13	R	R	5-11	180	4-9-70	1991	Diamond Bar, Calif.
Rodriguez, Roman	.254	44	130	11	33	4	0	0	9	7	25	1	0	R	R	6-1	180	3-30-69	1988	San Mateo, Venez.
Sanford, Chance	.333	16	66	8	22	4	0	3	14	7	13	1	0	L	R	5-10	165	6-2-72	1992	Houston, Texas
Secrist, Reed	.282	112	380	60	107	18	3	19	75	54	88	3	4	L	R	6-1	200	5-7-70	1992	Farmington, Utah
Zapata, Ramon	.298	119	416	59	124	27	2	8	45	42	58	6	8	R	R	5-8	155	1-14-71	1990	Santo Domingo, D.R.

GAMES BY POSITION: C—Canetto 11, Daniel 19, Hanel 40, Mendez 60, Reynolds 5, Rodarte 2, Secrist 14. 1B—Bonifay 57, Daniel 8, Hanel 1, Knoblauh 4, Leary 23, Rodarte 2, Sanford 16, Zapata 98. 2B—Brooks 18, House, Knoblauh 4, Leary 23, Rodarte 2, Secrist 38. 3B—Bonifay 24, Brooks 5, Rodarte 95, Rodriguez 11, Secrist 18. SS—Brooks 8, Collier 112, Rodriguez 2, Zapata 13. OF—Austin 18, Bonifay 17, Brown 54, Conger 85, Cornelius 12, Daniel 2, Knoblauh 54, Leary 34, Peterson 104, Robertson 42, Secrist 25.

PITCHING	W	L	ERA	G	GS	CG	SV	IP	H	R	ER	BB	SO	B	T	HT	WT	DOB	1st Yr	Resides
Abramavicius, Jason	1	0	7.30	9	0	0	0	12	22	13	10	5	11	L	L	6-4	190	12-14-69	1993	Marengo, Ill.
Anderson, Jimmy	1	5	4.13	10	9	0	0	52	56	29	24	21	32	L	L	6-1	180	1-22-76	1994	Chesapeake, Va.
Caruso, Joe	4	0	2.95	29	0	0	4	40	36	13	13	16	27	R	R	6-3	195	9-16-70	1991	Petaluma, Calif.
Chaves, Rafael	1	3	2.66	42	0	0	22	47	35	17	14	13	45	R	R	6-0	195	11-1-68	1986	Isabela, P.R.
DeLeon, Ercilio	2	0	4.24	13	0	0	0	17	12	9	8	11	9	R	R	6-1	170	4-12-70	1992	La Romana, D.R.
Dillinger, John	6	6	4.02	27	22	0	0	123	111	62	55	67	97	R	R	6-6	230	8-28-73	1992	Connellsville, Pa.
Doornweerd, Dave	0	1	6.75	5	0	0	0	8	8	6	6	5	9	R	R	6-1	185	9-29-72	1991	New Port Richey, Fla.
Farson, Bryan	1	3	5.82	27	6	0	0	51	54	41	33	19	35	L	L	6-2	198	7-22-72	1992	Massillon, Ohio
Hartzog, Cullen	6	4	3.34	43	1	0	0	59	49	23	22	30	45	R	R	6-1	190	11-11-69	1988	Panama City, Fla.
Johnson, Jason	1	4	4.91	10	10	0	0	55	58	37	30	20	41	R	R	6-6	220	10-27-73	1992	Burlington, Ky.
Lawrence, Sean	5	8	4.22	20	19	0	0	111	115	56	52	25	82	L	L	6-4	215	9-9-70	1991	Ephraim, Ill.
LaPlante, Michel	1	1	8.22	5	2	0	0	15	21	14	14	3	13	R	R	6-2	180	12-9-69	1992	East Montreal, Quebec
Mattson, Craig	2	0	3.09	11	0	0	0	12	11	5	4	0	5	R	R	6-4	205	11-25-73	1993	Belvidere, Ill.
Mesewicz, Mark	0	1	23.14	6	0	0	0	5	13	12	12	2	3	L	L	6-3	195	10-13-69	1992	Newark, Ohio
Morel, Ramon	3	7	3.47	12	12	1	0	73	80	35	28	13	44	R	R	6-3	170	8-15-74	1991	Villa Gonzalez, D.R.
Perkins, Paul	0	3	3.94	25	0	0	1	30	34	15	13	10	28	R	R	6-4	210	8-4-70	1990	Fairfield, Calif.
Peters, Chris	11	5	2.43	24	24	3	0	145	126	57	39	35	132	L	L	6-1	170	1-28-72	1992	McMurray, Pa.
Pfaff, Jason	5	6	3.23	35	10	0	0	114	115	56	41	31	95	R	R	6-2	215	10-19-69	1991	Cincinnati, Ohio
Pickford, Kevin	0	3	4.94	4	4	0	0	27	31	15	15	0	15	L	L	6-3	200	3-12-75	1993	Fresno, Calif.
Pontbriant, Matt	7	7	5.05	27	17	1	0	109	137	67	61	28	60	L	L	6-4	200	9-2-72	1990	Norwich, Conn.
Sosa, Jose	0	0	6.88	10	0	0	0	17	27	14	13	6	12	R	R	6-2	185	9-2-72	1990	Santo Domingo, D.R.
Tolar, Kevin	2	0	2.79	18	0	0	0	19	13	7	6	6	19	R	L	6-3	225	1-28-71	1989	Panama City, Fla.
Young, Danny	2	4	7.40	24	2	0	0	41	52	37	34	27	34	L	L	6-5	180	11-3-71	1991	Woodbury, Tenn.

SOUTH ATLANTIC LEAGUE

BATTING	AVG	G	AB	R	H	2B	3B	HR	RBI	BB	SO	SB	CS	B	T	HT	WT	DOB	1st Yr	Resides
Asche, Mike	.266	106	376	62	100	17	6	6	59	35	60	21	5	R	R	6-2	190	2-13-72	1994	Kearney, Neb.
Brooks, Eddie	.273	67	238	40	65	13	5	2	37	28	61	3	5	R	R	6-1	175	11-23-72	1994	Lexington, Ky.
Brown, Adrian	.300	76	287	64	86	15	4	4	31	33	23	25	14	S	R	6-0	185	2-7-74	1992	Summit, Miss.
Edwards, Aaron	.263	47	160	29	42	4	2	0	9	11	39	10	4	R	R	6-2	180	8-5-73	1994	Ontario, Calif.
Gonzalez, Wikleman	.241	84	278	41	67	17	0	3	36	26	32	5	4	R	R	5-11	175	5-17-74	1992	Palo Negro, Venez.
Guillen, Jose	.235	10	34	6	8	1	1	2	6	2	9	0	0	R	R	5-11	165	5-17-76	1993	San Cristobal, D.R.
Harris, G.G.	.245	100	368	38	90	23	0	2	46	17	50	2	6	R	R	6-2	215	5-14-73	1992	Lancaster, S.C.
Kelley, Erskine	.218	105	349	47	76	13	5	4	32	22	86	24	7	R	R	6-5	210	2-27-71	1992	Freeport, N.Y.
Pollock, Elton	.234	26	94	8	22	5	1	0	10	7	23	8	3	R	R	5-11	185	4-17-73	1995	Clinton, S.C.
Reynolds, Chance	.215	24	65	8	14	2	0	1	6	12	11	0	2	S	R	5-10	185	9-16-71	1993	Byromville, Ga.
Rice, Andy	.222	14	54	8	12	3	0	1	8	2	14	0	0	S	R	6-2	220	8-31-75	1993	Birmingham, Ala.
Robinson, Tony	.229	96	297	34	68	9	0	2	37	38	60	21	11	R	R	6-0	185	6-11-76	1994	Diamond Bar, Calif.
Segura, Juan	.225	25	80	3	18	2	0	0	4	1	21	0	2	R	R	6-1	160	1-27-74	1992	Valverde Mao, D.R.
Staton, T.J.	.292	112	391	43	114	21	5	5	53	27	97	27	13	L	L	6-3	200	2-17-75	1993	Elyria, Ohio
Subero, Carlos	.186	31	97	8	18	2	0	0	6	2	24	1	0	S	R	6-0	155	6-15-72	1991	Caracas, Venez.
Swafford, Derek	.253	119	447	69	113	15	5	3	48	33	101	52	16	L	R	5-10	175	1-21-75	1993	Ventura, Calif.
Sweet, Jonathan	.285	87	267	28	76	9	1	1	22	18	31	5	4	L	R	6-0	183	11-10-71	1994	Columbus, Ohio
Thobe, Steve	.299	84	291	43	87	12	2	6	38	29	71	1	3	R	R	6-7	230	5-26-72	1994	Huntington Beach, Calif.
Walker, Shon	.229	110	358	49	82	20	0	6	54	68	127	10	9	L	L	6-1	182	6-9-74	1992	Cynthiana, Ky.

GAMES BY POSITION: C—Gonzalez 49, Reynolds 22, Sweet 77. **1B**—Harris 70, Rice 10, Thobe 61. **2B**—Brooks 24, Segura 5, Subero 1, Swafford 115. **3B**—Asche 97, Brooks 27, Segura 3, Thobe 15. **SS**—Brooks 5, Robinson 93, Segura 18, Subero 29. **OF**—Brooks 1, Brown 68, Edwards 43, Guillen 6, Kelley 96, Pollock 26, Staton 100, Walker 96.

PITCHING	W	L	ERA	G	GS	CG	SV	IP	H	R	ER	BB	SO	B	T	HT	WT	DOB	1st Yr	Resides
Anderson, Jimmy	4	2	1.53	14	14	0	0	77	51	15	13	31	75	L	L	6-1	180	1-22-76	1994	Chesapeake, Va.
Chaves, Rafael	1	0	2.08	7	0	0	2	9	3	2	6	9	R	R	6-0	195	11-1-68	1986	Isabela, P.R.
Cooke, Steve	1	0	0.00	1	1	0	0	5	2	0	0	1	6	R	L	6-6	220	1-14-70	1990	Tigard, Ore.
Davis, Kane	12	6	3.75	26	25	1	0	139	136	73	58	43	78	R	R	6-3	180	6-25-75	1993	Reedy, W.Va.
France, Aaron	6	6	2.47	18	15	0	0	95	80	29	26	26	77	L	R	6-2	175	4-17-74	1994	Anaheim, Calif.
Garcia-Luna, Francisco	2	1	2.86	14	10	1	0	63	57	31	20	17	48	R	R	6-3	190	4-6-73	1991	Mexico City, Mexico
Grebe, Brett	2	2	3.62	32	0	0	2	37	42	19	15	16	36	R	R	6-2	185	11-24-70	1989	Westminster, Calif.
Hampton, Mark	5	5	4.13	39	0	0	0	57	46	32	26	38	45	R	R	6-3	196	9-20-69	1989	Hammond, La.
Johnson, Jason	3	5	4.36	11	11	1	0	54	57	32	26	17	42	R	R	6-6	220	10-27-73	1992	Burlington, Ky.
Kelly, Jeff	6	11	3.47	26	26	0	0	143	134	68	55	51	114	L	L	6-6	215	1-11-75	1994	Staten Island, N.Y.
Maskivish, Joe	2	1	2.12	26	0	0	20	30	23	9	7	9	33	R	R	6-4	180	8-14-71	1994	Shadyside, Ohio
Nuttle, Jamison	0	0	1.17	6	0	0	0	8	5	3	1	8	10	R	R	6-5	205	2-2-72	1992	Spencerville, Ind.
Paugh, Rick	6	2	2.59	52	0	0	2	59	60	23	17	17	61	L	L	6-6	190	2-6-72	1994	Bridgeport, W.Va.
Pelka, Brian	1	3	5.98	26	0	0	0	41	46	31	27	20	29	R	R	6-6	185	3-14-72	1992	Philipsburg, Pa.
Phillips, Jason	4	3	3.60	30	6	0	0	80	76	46	32	53	65	R	R	6-6	215	3-22-74	1992	Muncy, Pa.
Pickford, Kevin	7	3	2.00	16	16	0	0	86	85	28	19	16	59	L	L	6-3	200	3-12-75	1993	Fresno, Calif.
Reid, Rayon	2	5	4.38	12	11	1	0	62	52	36	30	28	47	R	R	6-0	185	7-25-73	1993	North Miami Beach, Fla.
Spade, Matt	6	5	2.92	51	1	0	5	71	50	23	23	19	71	R	R	6-0	180	12-4-72	1994	Boyertown, Pa.
Temple, Jason	5	2	2.26	51	0	0	5	72	45	26	18	28	84	R	R	6-1	185	11-8-74	1993	Woodhaven, Mich.
Young, Danny	1	0	2.51	6	2	0	0	14	9	6	4	16	11	L	L	6-5	180	11-3-71	1991	Woodbury, Tenn.

NEW YORK-PENN LEAGUE

BATTING	AVG	G	AB	R	H	2B	3B	HR	RBI	BB	SO	SB	CS	B	T	HT	WT	DOB	1st Yr	Resides
Adamson, Jason	.286	2	7	0	2	0	0	0	2	0	1	0	0	R	R	6-3	192	5-5-76	1995	Moorpark, Calif.
Borges, Mariano	.111	17	45	4	5	0	0	0	2	3	11	1	1	R	R	6-0	170	12-7-72	1993	Arecibo, P.R.
Boryczewski, Marty	.094	10	32	0	3	0	0	0	1	6	0	0	0	R	R	6-2	190	8-17-72	1994	Parsippany, N.J.
Canetto, John	.160	11	25	5	4	0	0	1	7	7	0	0	S	R	5-11	185	9-19-72	1995	Hillsdale, N.Y.
Davis, Albert	.230	44	152	31	35	12	0	2	12	19	26	8	2	R	R	5-9	175	10-5-76	1994	Alcoa, Tenn.
Edwards, Aaron	.264	15	53	10	14	0	0	0	3	6	10	7	2	R	R	6-2	180	8-5-73	1994	Ontario, Calif.
Flanigan, Steven	.271	25	85	8	23	4	1	1	10	1	23	1	0	R	R	6-1	210	10-23-71	1995	Kittanning, Pa.
Guillen, Jose	.314	66	258	41	81	17	1	12	46	10	44	1	5	R	R	5-11	165	5-17-76	1993	San Cristobal, D.R.
Hermansen, Chad	.273	44	165	30	45	8	3	6	25	18	39	4	2	R	R	6-2	185	9-10-77	1995	Henderson, Nev.
Long, Garrett	.278	29	108	17	30	4	0	2	16	15	25	2	2	R	R	6-3	195	10-5-76	1995	Houston, Texas
Mackert, Jamie	.218	35	101	18	22	4	4	2	17	22	46	0	4	R	R	6-1	190	5-2-74	1992	West Chicago, Ill.
May, Freddie	.267	27	90	10	24	3	1	1	12	5	23	5	5	L	L	6-2	190	1-24-76	1995	Seattle, Wash.
Maynor, Tonka	.129	11	31	2	4	1	0	1	3	4	2	0	0	L	R	6-2	220	1-3-72	1994	Pembroke, N.C.
Miyake, Chris	.308	61	227	34	70	6	5	2	25	12	31	14	6	R	R	6-2	185	5-18-74	1995	San Gabriel, Calif.
Pollock, Elton	.299	43	174	29	52	7	1	2	21	12	30	12	5	R	R	5-11	185	4-17-73	1995	Clinton, S.C.
Reynolds, Paul	.242	37	120	17	29	2	0	0	18	14	18	0	2	S	R	5-10	185	9-16-71	1993	Byromville, Ga.
Rice, Andy	.316	70	269	44	85	15	2	8	33	19	59	7	5	S	R	6-2	220	8-31-75	1993	Birmingham, Ala.
Schreiber, Stan	.286	3	7	1	2	0	0	2	1	2	0	0	R	R	5-10	175	9-8-75	1994	Appleton, Wisc.
Segura, Juan	.257	26	105	10	27	2	3	2	9	3	24	1	1	R	R	6-1	160	1-27-74	1992	Valverde Mao, D.R.
Smith, Akili	.125	14	40	6	5	0	0	1	4	13	1	0	R	R	6-3	210	8-21-75	1993	San Diego, Calif.
Springfield, Bo	.263	25	76	11	20	1	2	1	6	13	20	8	4	L	R	5-10	173	1-25-76	1994	Denison, Texas
Venezia, Richard	.204	38	108	11	22	2	0	1	10	13	24	5	1	R	R	5-9	155	9-24-73	1994	Pittsburgh, Pa.
Whipple, Boomer	.253	67	225	29	57	4	0	3	33	30	18	4	3	R	R	6-1	185	2-9-73	1995	Lincolnshire, Ill.

GAMES BY POSITION: C—Boryczewski 10, Canetto 10, Flanigan 22, Reynolds 36. **1B**—Long 17, Mackert 22, Maynor 8, Rice 31, Smith 2. **2B**—Miyake 38, Pollock 3, Schreiber 2, Segura 12, Venezia 22, Whipple 2. **3B**—Mackert 12, Segura 2, Venezia 3, Whipple 64. **SS**—Hermansen 39, Miyake 18, Segura 12, Venezia 8. **OF**—Adamson 2, Borges 16, Davis 44, Edwards 13, Guillen 64, Long 9, May 25, Pollock 41, Smith 7, Springfield 17.

PITCHING	W	L	ERA	G	GS	CG	SV	IP	H	R	ER	BB	SO	B	T	HT	WT	DOB	1st Yr	Resides
Beach, Scott	1	0	7.50	14	0	0	0	18	24	21	15	17	8	R	R	6-4	175	10-18-73	1995	Prairie Village, Kan.
Bigler, Cory	0	6	4.66	10	4	0	0	29	34	21	15	13	13	R	R	6-2	210	1-20-73	1995	Mequon, Wisc.
Bullock, Derek	4	4	2.35	11	11	1	0	65	65	21	17	15	27	R	R	6-2	186	2-24-73	1995	Sioux City, Iowa
Chew, Greg	2	3	3.23	24	0	0	3	31	37	18	11	15	23	R	R	6-4	197	1-16-74	1994	Erma, N.J.

PITCHING	W	L	ERA	G	GS	CG	SV	IP	H	R	ER	BB	SO	B	T	HT	WT	DOB	1st Yr	Resides
Collie, Tim	3	6	2.00	29	0	0	11	36	32	18	8	9	27	R	R	5-11	185	7-5-73	1995	Charlotte, N.C.
Duffy, Ryan	1	2	4.76	19	8	0	0	51	59	33	27	14	31	R	L	6-3	185	6-1-73	1994	Sombra, Ontario
Farrow, Jason	3	1	2.23	20	4	0	0	48	44	18	12	20	50	R	R	6-2	195	7-30-73	1995	Palestine, Texas
Goedde, Roger	1	3	7.97	5	5	0	0	20	31	23	18	17	8	R	R	6-4	180	5-19-76	1994	Evansville, Ind.
Hernandez, Elvin	6	1	2.89	14	14	2	0	90	82	40	29	22	54	R	R	6-1	165	8-20-77	1994	Laguna Salada Monte, D.R.
Nuttle, Jamison	0	1	3.07	13	0	0	1	15	8	8	5	7	13	R	R	6-5	205	2-2-72	1992	Spencerville, Ind.
Pena, Jesus	0	3	12.66	3	3	0	0	11	18	16	15	7	5	L	L	6-0	170	3-8-75	1993	Santo Domingo, D.R.
Perez, Gil	2	2	2.79	18	1	0	0	39	39	19	12	15	27	R	R	6-1	160	9-1-72	1990	San Cristobal, D.R.
Reid, Rayon	3	3	2.45	8	7	0	0	48	37	16	13	11	47	R	R	6-0	185	7-25-73	1993	North Miami Beach, Fla.
Reyes, Jose	2	3	3.39	19	7	1	0	58	53	25	22	29	44	R	R	6-1	188	5-1-73	1993	Villa Vazquez, D.R.
Santos, Rafael	0	0	0.00	2	0	0	0	1	0	0	0	2	1	R	R	6-2	185	10-24-75	1993	Haina, D.R.
Thomas, Rob	1	1	4.60	15	0	0	0	16	9	10	8	17	9	L	L	6-0	200	5-28-74	1995	Sinton, Texas
Viegas, Randy	0	0	6.30	8	1	0	0	10	14	9	7	9	9	L	L	6-2	175	8-22-75	1994	Roseville, Calif.
Young, Ryan	5	2	2.79	16	10	1	1	68	62	34	21	17	38	R	R	6-0	175	6-16-73	1995	Brentwood, Tenn.

BRADENTON   R

GULF COAST LEAGUE

BATTING	AVG	G	AB	R	H	2B	3B	HR	RBI	BB	SO	SB	CS	B	T	HT	WT	DOB	1st Yr	Resides
Adamson, Jason	.255	42	145	20	37	9	0	1	16	17	21	1	1	R	R	6-3	192	5-5-76	1995	Moorpark, Calif.
Antigua, Nilson	.242	27	99	6	24	3	1	0	9	2	19	0	1	R	R	6-2	175	12-14-75	1993	Monte Plata, D.R.
Davis, Albert	.302	10	43	8	13	3	0	3	9	1	6	1	0	R	R	5-9	175	10-5-76	1994	Alcoa, Tenn.
Delgado, Daniel	.179	33	106	15	19	2	0	0	7	15	16	6	0	R	R	5-9	165	12-29-76	1995	Miami, Fla.
Elliott, Dawan	.220	34	109	8	24	1	2	0	9	6	30	2	0	L	L	6-3	200	7-30-76	1995	Long Branch, N.J.
Feliz, Edgar	.236	17	55	4	13	4	0	0	8	2	14	0	2	S	R	6-2	143	12-14-77	1994	Jimani, D.R.
Frias, Ovidio	.283	29	99	16	28	5	2	0	7	7	10	1	0	R	R	5-11	165	3-19-77	1995	Santo Domingo, D.R.
Hermansen, Chad	.304	24	92	14	28	10	1	3	17	9	19	0	0	R	R	6-2	185	9-10-77	1995	Henderson, Nev.
Hernandez, Alex	.269	49	186	24	50	5	3	1	17	17	33	4	4	L	L	6-4	190	5-28-77	1995	Levittown, P.R.
Knabenshue, Chris	.176	4	17	1	3	0	0	1	2	0	1	0	0	L	R	6-1	185	10-30-63	1985	Aurora, Colo.
Long, Garrett	.349	20	63	13	22	2	1	1	8	17	10	0	1	R	R	6-3	195	10-5-76	1995	Houston, Texas
May, Freddie	.333	29	96	18	32	5	2	2	13	18	16	2	4	L	L	6-2	190	1-24-76	1995	Seattle, Wash.
McSparin, Paul	.292	23	72	14	21	5	0	3	13	4	19	1	1	R	R	6-2	210	4-16-74	1994	Harrisburg, Ill.
Pascual, Edison	.228	41	136	19	31	3	2	3	18	10	26	3	0	L	L	6-3	170	9-10-76	1994	Santo Domingo, D.R.
Pena, Adelis	.282	54	202	27	57	7	2	0	23	3	26	6	1	R	R	6-1	175	4-19-77	1994	Cumana, Venez.
Pena, Alex	.238	48	172	15	41	7	3	1	20	6	26	3	3	R	R	6-2	175	9-9-77	1995	Ensanche Luperon, D.R.
Sanford, Chance	.211	6	19	2	4	0	0	1	1	2	2	0	0	L	R	5-10	165	6-2-72	1992	Houston, Texas
Schreiber, Stan	.258	38	128	16	33	1	2	0	10	21	23	8	1	R	R	5-10	175	9-8-75	1994	Appleton, Wisc.
Shipp, Skip	.130	18	54	4	7	0	0	0	4	5	13	0	0	R	R	6-2	205	1-12-76	1995	Kennesaw, Ga.
Springfield, Bo	.000	3	6	1	0	0	0	0	0	1	1	1	0	L	R	5-10	173	1-25-76	1994	Denison, Texas

GAMES BY POSITION: C—Antigua 25, McSparin 19, Shipp 18. **1B**—Antigua 1, Hernandez 9, Long 14, Pascual 37. **2B**—Delgado 9, Frias 14, Sanford 4, Schreiber 35. **3B**—Feliz 1, Frias 4, Long 1, Ad. Pena 54, Al. Pena 1. **SS**—Delgado 22, Feliz 16, Hermansen 16, Ad. Pena 1. **OF**—Adamson 28, Davis 9, Elliott 30, Hernandez 36, Knabenshue 3, May 25, Pascual 3, Al. Pena 45, Springfield 2.

PITCHING	W	L	ERA	G	GS	CG	SV	IP	H	R	ER	BB	SO	B	T	HT	WT	DOB	1st Yr	Resides
Alvarado, Carlos	0	0	6.00	2	0	0	0	3	1	2	2	5	2	R	R	6-4	195	1-24-78	1995	Arecibo, P.R.
Alvarado, David	1	0	4.80	9	2	0	1	15	15	8	8	4	15	R	R	6-3	180	4-29-78	1995	Falcon, Venez.
Arroyo, Bronson	5	4	4.26	13	9	0	1	61	72	39	29	9	48	R	R	6-5	165	2-24-77	1995	Brooksville, Fla.
Batista, Mario	0	1	5.40	1	1	0	0	5	7	4	3	3	2	R	R	6-0	160	10-17-74	1992	Santo Domingo, D.R.
Bonilla, Miguel	0	0	1.93	2	0	0	0	5	5	1	1	1	2	R	R	6-2	195	8-23-73	1995	Santo Domingo, D.R.
Cook, O.J.	0	4	3.63	12	7	0	2	35	33	24	14	22	25	R	R	6-3	195	12-13-76	1995	Bethlehem, Pa.
Deutsch, Curry	2	4	2.83	14	0	0	1	35	40	17	11	11	19	L	L	6-0	175	9-11-72	1994	Lee Center, Mn
Dunn, Cordell	1	1	5.40	5	0	0	0	10	13	9	6	4	5	R	R	6-2	185	11-3-75	1994	Tunica, Miss.
Fisher, Ryan	0	0	0.00	1	0	0	0	1	1	0	0	0	1	L	L	6-2	190	4-26-74	1995	Milltown, Wisc.
Gaerte, Travis	0	0	6.00	6	0	0	0	12	14	9	8	2	5	R	R	6-3	180	10-21-76	1995	Fremont, Ind.
Gillispie, Ryan	0	1	2.45	4	0	0	0	7	8	4	2	6	4	R	R	6-6	200	3-29-77	1995	San Diego, Calif.
Goedde, Roger	1	1	2.61	6	6	1	0	31	31	12	9	7	25	R	R	6-4	180	5-19-76	1994	Evansville, Ind.
LaPlante, Michel	0	0	0.00	2	0	0	1	3	1	0	0	0	4	R	R	6-2	180	12-9-69	1992	East Montreal, Quebec
Mason, Roger	1	0	0.00	1	0	0	0	1	2	0	0	0	1	R	R	6-6	220	9-18-58	1981	Bellaire, Mich.
Mesewicz, Mark	0	0	3.86	3	0	0	0	5	5	2	2	1	6	L	L	6-3	195	10-13-69	1992	Newark, Ohio
Nezelek, Andy	0	0	7.71	4	0	0	1	7	12	7	6	2	6	L	R	6-0	175	10-24-65	1986	Richmond, Va.
O'Conner, Brian	2	2	1.88	14	5	0	1	43	33	22	9	13	43	L	L	6-2	175	1-4-77	1995	Cincinnati, Ohio
Pena, Jesus	0	0	2.57	7	6	0	0	35	20	11	10	19	36	L	L	6-0	170	3-8-75	1993	Santo Domingo, D.R.
Santos, Rafael	2	5	6.31	11	10	1	0	51	63	49	36	27	26	R	R	6-2	185	10-24-75	1993	Haina, D.R.
Scofield, Josh	0	0	9.00	2	0	0	0	2	3	2	2	4	4	R	L	6-2	185	11-5-76	1995	East Hampton, Conn.
Settle, Brian	0	2	8.27	11	0	0	0	21	25	22	19	20	11	R	R	6-5	190	7-17-77	1995	Portsmouth, Va.
Symmonds, Mike	1	1	4.70	6	0	0	0	8	3	5	4	9	9	L	L	5-9	180	3-13-73	1995	Norfolk, Va.
Viegas, Randy	3	2	2.54	6	4	0	0	28	28	13	8	5	24	L	L	6-2	175	8-22-75	1994	Roseville, Calif.
Villar, Maximo	1	1	7.20	6	3	0	1	20	29	21	16	9	13	R	R	6-3	175	10-11-76	1994	Bani, D.R.
Ward, Kerry	2	6	4.87	11	6	0	0	44	59	33	24	13	27	R	R	6-3	190	10-2-74	1993	Bradenton, Fla.

ST. LOUIS CARDINALS

Managers: Joe Torre, Mike Jorgensen. **1995 Record:** 62-81, .434 (4th, NL Central).

BATTING	AVG	G	AB	R	H	2B	3B	HR	RBI	BB	SO	SB	CS	B	T	HT	WT	DOB	1st Yr	Resides
Battle, Allen	.271	61	118	13	32	5	0	0	2	15	26	3	3	R	R	6-0	170	11-29-68	1991	Mt. Olive, N.C.
Bell, David	.250	39	144	13	36	7	2	2	19	4	25	1	2	R	R	5-10	170	9-14-72	1990	Cincinnati, Ohio
Bradshaw, Terry	.227	19	44	6	10	1	1	0	2	2	10	1	2	L	R	6-0	180	2-3-69	1990	Zuni, Va.
Caraballo, Ramon	.202	34	99	10	20	4	1	2	3	6	33	3	2	S	R	5-7	150	5-23-69	1989	Santo Domingo, D.R.
Coles, Darnell	.225	63	138	13	31	7	0	3	16	16	20	0	0	R	R	6-1	185	6-2-62	1991	Safety Harbor, Fla.
Cooper, Scott	.230	118	374	29	86	18	2	3	40	49	85	0	3	L	R	6-3	205	10-13-67	1986	St. Charles, Mo.
Cromer, Tripp	.226	105	345	36	78	19	0	5	18	14	66	0	0	R	R	6-2	160	11-21-67	1989	Lexington, S.C.
Giannelli, Ray	.091	9	11	0	1	0	0	0	3	4	0	0	0	L	R	6-0	195	2-5-66	1988	Lindenhurst, N.Y.
Gilkey, Bernard	.298	121	480	73	143	33	4	17	69	42	70	12	6	R	R	6-0	170	9-24-66	1985	St. Louis, Mo.
Hemond, Scott	.144	57	118	11	17	1	0	3	9	12	31	0	0	R	R	6-0	215	11-18-65	1986	Dunedin, Fla.
Hulett, Tim	.182	4	11	0	2	0	0	0	0	0	3	0	0	R	R	6-0	199	1-12-60	1980	Springfield, Ill.
Jordan, Brian	.296	131	490	83	145	20	4	22	81	22	79	24	9	R	R	6-1	205	3-29-67	1988	Baltimore, Md.
Lankford, Ray	.277	132	483	81	134	35	2	25	82	63	110	24	8	L	L	5-11	180	6-5-67	1987	Modesto, Calif.
Lee, Manuel	1.000	1	1	1	1	0	0	0	0	0	0	0	0	S	R	5-9	161	6-17-65	1982	San Pedro de Macoris, D.R.
Mabry, John	.307	129	388	35	119	21	1	5	41	24	45	0	3	L	R	6-4	195	10-17-70	1991	Warwick, Md.
Oliva, Jose	.122	22	74	8	9	1	0	2	8	5	24	0	0	R	R	6-1	215	3-3-71	1988	San Pedro de Macoris, D.R.
2-team (48 Atlanta)	.142	70	183	15	26	5	0	7	20	12	46	0	0							
Oquendo, Jose	.209	88	220	31	46	8	3	2	17	35	21	1	1	S	R	5-10	156	7-4-63	1979	Rio Piedras, P.R.
Pagnozzi, Tom	.215	62	219	17	47	14	1	2	15	11	31	0	1	R	R	6-1	190	7-30-62	1983	Tucson, Ariz.
Pena, Geronimo	.267	32	101	20	27	6	1	1	8	16	30	3	2	S	R	6-1	170	3-29-67	1985	Los Alcarrizos, D.R.
Perry, Gerald	.165	65	79	4	13	4	0	0	5	6	12	0	0	L	R	5-11	180	10-30-60	1978	Smyrna, Ga.
Sabo, Chris	.154	5	13	0	2	1	0	0	3	1	2	1	0	R	R	6-0	185	1-19-62	1983	Sarasota, Fla.
Sheaffer, Danny	.231	76	208	24	48	10	1	5	30	23	38	0	0	R	R	6-0	190	8-21-61	1981	Winston-Salem, N.C.
Smith, Ozzie	.199	44	156	16	31	5	1	0	11	17	12	4	3	S	R	5-10	150	12-26-54	1977	Ladue, Mo.
Sweeney, Mark	.273	37	77	5	21	2	0	2	13	10	15	1	1	L	L	6-1	195	10-26-69	1991	Holliston, Mass.
Zeile, Todd	.291	34	127	16	37	6	0	5	22	18	23	1	0	R	R	6-1	185	9-9-65	1986	Valencia, Calif.

PITCHING	W	L	ERA	G	GS	CG	SV	IP	H	R	ER	BB	SO	B	T	HT	WT	DOB	1st Yr	Resides
Arocha, Rene	3	5	3.99	41	0	0	0	50	55	24	22	18	25	R	R	6-0	180	2-24-66	1992	Miami, Fla.
Bailey, Cory	0	0	7.36	3	0	0	0	4	2	3	3	2	5	R	R	6-1	210	1-24-71	1991	Marion, Ill.
Barber, Brian	2	1	5.22	9	4	0	0	29	31	17	17	16	27	R	R	6-1	172	3-4-73	1991	Orlando, Fla.
Benes, Alan	1	2	8.44	3	3	0	0	16	24	15	15	4	20	R	R	6-5	215	1-21-72	1993	Lake Forest, Ill.
Creek, Doug	0	0	0.00	6	0	0	0	7	2	0	0	3	10	L	L	5-10	205	3-1-69	1991	Martinsburg, W Va.
DeLucia, Rich	8	7	3.39	56	1	0	0	82	63	38	31	36	76	R	R	6-0	185	10-7-64	1986	Columbia, S.C.
Fossas, Tony	3	0	1.47	58	0	0	0	37	28	6	6	10	40	L	L	6-0	187	9-23-57	1979	Ft. Lauderdale, Fla.
Frascatore, John	1	1	4.41	14	4	0	0	33	39	19	16	16	21	R	R	6-1	200	2-4-70	1991	Oceanside, N.Y.
Habyan, John	3	2	2.88	31	0	0	0	41	32	18	13	15	35	R	R	6-2	195	1-29-64	1982	Bel Air, Md.
Henke, Tom	1	1	1.82	52	0	0	36	54	42	11	11	18	48	R	R	6-5	225	12-21-57	1980	Jefferson City, Mo.
Hill, Ken	6	7	5.06	18	18	0	0	110	125	71	62	45	50	R	R	6-2	175	12-14-65	1985	Lynn, Mass.
Jackson, Danny	2	12	5.90	19	19	2	0	101	120	82	66	48	52	R	L	6-0	205	1-5-62	1982	Overland Park, Kan.
Mathews, T.J.	1	1	1.52	23	0	0	2	30	21	7	5	11	28	R	R	6-2	200	1-19-70	1992	Columbia, Ill.
Morgan, Mike	5	6	3.88	17	17	1	0	107	114	48	46	25	46	R	R	6-2	222	10-8-59	1978	Ogden, Utah
2-team (4 Chicago)	7	7	3.56	21	21	1	0	131	133	56	52	34	61							
Osborne, Donovan	4	6	3.81	19	19	0	0	113	112	58	48	34	82	L	L	6-2	195	6-21-69	1990	Carson City, Nev.
Palacios, Vicente	2	3	5.80	20	5	0	0	40	48	29	26	19	34	R	R	6-2	180	7-19-63	1983	Veracruz, Mexico
Parrett, Jeff	4	7	3.64	59	0	0	0	77	71	33	31	28	71	R	R	6-3	185	8-26-61	1983	Lexington, Ky.
Petkovsek, Mark	6	6	4.00	26	21	1	0	137	136	71	61	35	71	R	R	6-0	185	11-18-65	1987	Beaumont, Texas
Rodriguez, Rich	0	0	0.00	1	0	0	0	2	0	0	0	0	0	L	L	5-11	200	3-1-63	1984	Knoxville, Tenn.
Urbani, Tom	3	5	3.70	24	13	0	0	83	99	40	34	21	52	L	L	6-1	190	1-21-68	1990	Santa Cruz, Calif.
Watson, Allen	7	9	4.96	21	19	0	0	114	126	68	63	41	49	L	L	6-3	195	11-18-70	1991	Middle Village, N.Y.

FIELDING

Catcher	PCT	G	PO	A	E	DP	PB
Hemond	.985	38	185	15	3	1	7
Pagnozzi	.995	61	336	38	2	4	1
Sheaffer	.993	67	360	37	3	9	1

First Base	PCT	G	PO	A	E	DP
Coles	.992	18	122	7	1	7
Giannelli	1.000	2	8	0	0	1
Mabry	.994	73	595	53	4	63
Oliva	1.000	2	16	1	0	2
Perry	1.000	11	69	3	0	4
Sabo	.929	2	11	2	1	1
Sheaffer	1.000	3	31	4	0	1
Sweeney	.994	19	153	11	1	20
Zeile	.980	34	310	30	7	31

Second Base	PCT	G	PO	A	E	DP
Bell	.967	37	75	103	6	27

	PCT	G	PO	A	E	DP
Caraballo	.956	24	56	73	6	20
Cromer	.969	11	15	16	1	4
Hemond	1.000	6	4	7	0	0
Hulett	.941	2	5	11	1	3
Lee	.800	1	2	2	1	0
Oquendo	.981	62	114	148	5	37
Pena	.976	25	50	73	3	18

Third Base	PCT	G	PO	A	E	DP
Bell	.875	3	2	5	1	0
Coles	.951	22	13	26	2	1
Cooper	.945	110	65	243	18	24
Oliva	.977	18	11	31	1	4
Oquendo	.000	2	0	0	0	0
Sabo	1.000	1	0	1	0	0
Sheaffer	1.000	1	0	2	0	1

Shortstop	PCT	G	PO	A	E	DP
Cromer	.960	95	111	276	16	57
Hulett	.750	1	1	2	1	0
Oquendo	.988	24	20	61	1	14
Smith	.964	41	60	129	7	28

Outfield	PCT	G	PO	A	E	DP
Battle	.984	32	61	0	1	0
Bradshaw	.952	10	19	1	1	0
Coles	1.000	1	0	0	0	0
Giannelli	1.000	2	2	0	0	0
Gilkey	.986	118	206	10	3	4
Jordan	.996	126	267	4	1	2
Lankford	.990	129	300	7	3	2
Mabry	1.000	39	57	5	0	2
Oquendo	.000	1	0	0	0	0
Sweeney	.000	1	0	0	1	0

Outfielder Brian Jordan led St. Louis with 83 runs and 145 hits

GEORGE GOJKOVICH

Cardinals minor league Player of the Year Steve Montgomery

JOHN SPEAR

CARDINALS

FARM SYSTEM

Director of Player Development: Mike Jorgensen.

Class	Farm Team	League	W	L	Pct.	Finish*	Manager	First Yr
AAA	Louisville (Ky.) Redbirds	American Assoc.	74	70	.514	4th+ (8)	Joe Pettini	1982
AA	Arkansas Travelers	Texas	70	65	.519	3rd (8)	Mike Ramsey	1966
#A	St. Petersburg (Fla.) Cardinals	Florida State	64	67	.489	T-7th (14)	Chris Maloney	1966
A	Peoria (Ill.) Chiefs	Midwest	62	72	.463	11th (14)	Roy Silver	1995
A	Savannah (Ga.) Cardinals	South Atlantic	56	83	.403	12th (14)	Scott Melvin	1984
A	New Jersey Cardinals	New York-Penn	35	41	.461	8th (14)	Luis Melendez	1994
#R	Johnson City (Tenn.) Cardinals	Appalachian	35	33	.515	4th (10)	Steve Turco	1975

*Finish in overall standings (No. of teams in league)   #Advanced level   +Won league championship

ORGANIZATION LEADERS

MAJOR LEAGUERS

BATTING
*AVG	John Mabry	.307
R	Brian Jordan	83
H	Brian Jordan	145
TB	Ray Lankford	248
2B	Ray Lankford	35
3B	Two tied at	4
HR	Ray Lankford	25
RBI	Ray Lankford	82
BB	Ray Lankford	63
SO	Ray Lankford	110
SB	Two tied at	24

PITCHING
W	Rich DeLucia	8
L	Danny Jackson	12
#ERA	Rich DeLucia	3.39
G	Jeff Parrett	59
CG	Danny Jackson	2
SV	Tom Henke	36
IP	Mark Petkovsek	137
BB	Danny Jackson	48
SO	Donovan Osborne	82

MORRIS FOSTOFF

Ray Lankford. 25 homers, 82 RBIs

MINOR LEAGUERS

BATTING
*AVG	Jeff Berblinger, Arkansas	.319
R	Anton French, Peoria	71
H	Miguel Rivera, Savannah	130
TB	Mike Gulan, Arkansas/Louisville	213
2B	Tracy Woodson, Louisville	35
3B	Three tied at	8
HR	Anthony Lewis, Arkansas	24
RBI	Anthony Lewis, Arkansas	85
BB	Dave Madsen, St. Petersburg	70
SO	Nate Dishington, Savannah	154
SB	Anton French, Peoria	57

PITCHING
W	Two tied at	11
L	Rafael Ramirez, Savannah	15
#ERA	Brian Reed, Peoria	1.79
G	Matthew Golden, Savannah	64
CG	Mike Badorek, Arkansas	4
SV	Steve Montgomery, Arkansas	36
IP	Mike Busby, Arkansas/Louisville	172
BB	Sean Lowe, Arkansas	64
SO	Kris Detmers, St. Petersburg	150

*Minimum 250 At-Bats   #Minimum 75 Innings

TOP 10 PROSPECTS

How the Cardinals Top 10 prospects, as judged by Baseball America prior to the 1995 season, fared in 1995:

STAN DENNY

Alan Benes

Player, Pos.	Club (Class—League)	AVG	AB	R	H	2B	3B	HR	RBI	SB
4. Terry Bradshaw, of	Louisville (AAA—Amer. Assoc.)	.283	389	65	110	24	8	8	42	20
	St. Louis	.227	44	6	10	1	1	0	2	1
5. John Mabry, of-1b	Louisville (AAA—Amer. Assoc.)	.083	12	0	1	0	0	0	0	0
	St. Louis	.307	388	35	119	21	1	5	41	0
7. Allen Battle, of	Louisville (AAA—Amer. Assoc.)	.280	164	28	46	12	1	3	18	7
	St. Louis	.271	118	13	32	5	0	0	2	3
9. Aaron Holbert, ss	Louisville (AAA—Amer. Assoc.)	.257	401	57	103	16	4	9	40	14
10. Dmitri Young, of	Arkansas (AA—Texas)	.292	367	54	107	18	6	10	62	2

Player, Pos.	Club (Class—League)	W	L	ERA	G	SV	IP	H	BB	SO
1. Alan Benes, rhp	Louisville (AAA—Amer. Assoc.)	4	2	2.41	11	0	56	37	14	54
	St. Louis	1	2	8.44	3	0	16	24	4	20
2. Brian Barber, rhp	Louisville (AAA—Amer. Assoc.)	6	5	4.70	20	0	107	105	40	94
	St. Louis	2	1	5.22	9	0	29	31	16	27
3. Bret Wagner, lhp	St. Petersburg (A—Florida State)	5	4	2.12	17	0	93	77	28	59
	Arkansas (AA—Texas)	1	2	3.19	6	0	37	34	18	31
6. Corey Avrard, rhp	Savannah (A—South Atlantic)	1	6	3.98	13	0	54	38	33	51
8. Jay Witasick, rhp	St. Petersburg (A—Florida State)	7	7	2.74	18	0	105	80	36	109
	Arkansas (AA—Texas)	2	4	6.88	7	0	34	46	16	26

John Mabry
.307-5-41 for St. Louis

Tom Henke
36 saves for St. Louis

Tracy Woodson
.262-18-76 for Louisville

MORRIS FOSTOFF · MEL BAILEY · DAN ARNOLD

LOUISVILLE AAA
AMERICAN ASSOCIATION

BATTING	AVG	G	AB	R	H	2B	3B	HR	RBI	BB	SO	SB	CS	B	T	HT	WT	DOB	1st Yr	Resides
Anderson, Charlie	.000	1	0	0	0	0	0	0	0	0	0	0	0	R	R	6-1	190	3-18-70	1992	Jacksonville, Fla.
Aversa, Joe	.220	85	141	23	31	6	0	0	9	26	29	7	3	S	R	5-10	155	5-20-68	1990	Huntington Beach, Calif.
Battle, Allen	.280	47	164	28	46	12	1	3	18	28	32	7	1	R	R	6-0	170	11-29-68	1991	Mt. Olive, N.C.
Bell, David	.276	18	76	9	21	3	1	1	9	2	10	4	0	R	R	5-10	170	9-14-72	1990	Cincinnati, Ohio
2-team (70 Buffalo)	.273	88	330	43	90	14	2	9	43	24	47	4	3							
Bradshaw, Terry	.283	111	389	65	110	24	8	8	42	53	60	20	7	L	R	6-0	180	2-3-69	1990	Zuni, Va.
Caraballo, Ramon	.318	69	245	38	78	10	1	8	25	19	42	14	4	S	R	5-7	150	5-23-69	1989	Santo Domingo, D.R.
Cholowsky, Dan	.218	76	238	27	52	9	1	7	25	36	64	10	4	R	R	6-0	195	10-30-70	1991	San Jose, Calif.
Deak, Brian	.228	54	162	19	37	5	0	6	31	26	47	2	0	R	R	6-0	185	10-25-67	1986	Scottsdale, Ariz.
Deak, Darrel	.241	106	336	42	81	21	2	7	34	53	90	2	2	S	R	6-0	180	7-5-69	1991	Scottsdale, Ariz.
Difelice, Mike	.270	21	63	8	17	4	0	0	3	5	11	1	0	R	R	6-2	205	5-28-69	1991	Knoxville, Tenn.
Diggs, Tony	.250	23	36	4	9	3	0	0	0	5	4	2	1	S	R	6-0	175	4-20-67	1989	Starke, Fla.
Giannelli, Ray	.295	119	390	56	115	19	1	16	70	44	85	3	7	L	R	6-0	195	2-5-66	1988	Lindenhurst, N.Y.
Gilkey, Bernard	.333	2	6	3	2	1	0	1	1	1	0	0	0	R	R	6-0	170	9-24-66	1985	St. Louis, Mo.
Gulan, Mike	.236	58	195	21	46	10	4	5	27	10	53	2	2	R	R	6-1	190	12-18-70	1992	Steubenville, Ohio
Hemond, Scott	.000	1	3	1	0	0	0	0	0	0	0	0	0	R	R	6-0	215	11-18-65	1986	Dunedin, Fla.
Holbert, Aaron	.257	112	401	57	103	16	4	9	40	20	60	14	6	R	R	6-0	160	1-9-73	1990	Long Beach, Calif.
Hulett, Tim	.300	3	10	1	3	1	0	0	3	2	0	0	1	R	R	6-0	199	1-12-60	1980	Springfield, Ill.
Johns, Keith	.000	5	10	0	0	0	0	0	0	2	0	0	0	R	R	6-1	175	7-19-71	1992	Jacksonville, Fla.
Lee, Manuel	.273	6	22	2	6	0	0	0	0	0	2	1	0	S	R	5-9	161	6-17-65	1982	San Pedro de Macoris,D.R.
Mabry, John	.083	4	12	0	1	0	0	0	0	0	0	0	0	L	R	6-4	195	10-17-70	1991	Warwick, Md.
Martinez, Domingo	.261	64	222	26	58	15	0	9	31	15	49	0	0	R	R	6-2	185	8-4-67	1985	Santo Domingo, D.R.
McNeely, Jeff	.236	109	271	31	64	6	1	0	19	23	53	5	8	R	R	6-2	200	10-18-69	1989	Monroe, N.C.
Pagnozzi, Tom	.500	5	16	4	8	2	0	1	3	1	0	0	0	R	R	6-1	190	7-30-62	1983	Tucson, Ariz.
Pena, Geronimo	.381	6	21	5	8	1	0	2	6	3	1	0	0	S	R	6-1	170	3-29-67	1985	Los Alcarrizos, D.R.
Prager, Howard	.255	54	102	9	26	5	0	6	15	19	25	1	1	L	L	6-2	200	4-6-66	1989	Dallas, Texas
Ronan, Marc	.213	78	225	15	48	8	0	0	8	14	42	4	3	L	R	6-2	190	9-19-69	1990	Tallahassee, Fla.
Sabo, Chris	.393	9	28	5	11	0	0	1	4	1	4	0	0	R	R	6-0	185	1-19-62	1983	Sarasota, Fla.
Sweeney, Mark	.368	22	76	15	28	8	0	2	22	14	8	2	0	L	L	6-1	195	10-26-69	1991	Holliston, Mass.
Thomas, Skeets	.249	84	273	29	68	15	1	9	34	18	76	0	0	L	R	5-11	195	9-9-68	1990	Hamlet, N.C.
Woodson, Tracy	.262	118	431	62	113	30	0	18	76	27	43	12	4	R	R	6-3	215	10-5-62	1984	Raleigh, N.C.
Wrona, Rick	.226	16	31	1	7	1	1	1	2	2	6	0	0	R	R	6-0	180	12-10-63	1985	Tulsa, Okla.
2-team (31 Buffalo)	.226	47	124	10	28	7	1	1	12	5	25	0	1							
Young, Dmitri	.286	2	7	3	2	0	0	0	0	1	1	0	0	S	R	6-2	215	10-11-73	1991	Camarillo, Calif.
Zeile, Todd	.125	2	8	0	1	0	0	0	0	0	2	0	0	R	R	6-1	185	9-9-65	1986	Valencia, Calif.

PITCHING	W	L	ERA	G	GS	CG	SV	IP	H	R	ER	BB	SO	B	T	HT	WT	DOB	1st Yr	Resides
Bailey, Cory	5	3	4.55	55	0	0	25	59	51	30	30	30	49	R	R	6-1	210	1-24-71	1991	Marion, Ill.
Barber, Brian	6	5	4.70	23	19	0	0	107	105	67	56	40	94	R	R	6-1	172	3-4-73	1991	Orlando, Fla.
Batchelor, Richard	5	4	3.28	50	6	0	0	85	85	39	31	16	61	R	R	6-1	195	4-8-67	1990	Hartsville, S.C.
Beltran, Rigo	8	9	5.21	24	24	0	0	130	156	81	75	34	92	L	L	5-11	185	11-13-69	1991	San Diego, Calif.
Benes, Alan	4	2	2.41	11	11	2	0	56	37	16	15	14	54	R	R	6-5	215	1-21-72	1993	Lake Forest, Ill.
Buckels, Gary	1	2	5.51	13	0	0	5	16	18	11	10	13	8	R	R	6-0	185	7-22-65	1987	Huntington Beach, Calif.
Busby, Mike	2	3	3.29	6	6	1	0	38	28	18	14	11	26	R	R	6-4	215	12-27-72	1991	Wilmington, Calif.
Cadaret, Greg	1	0	3.09	12	0	0	0	12	14	4	4	1	7	L	L	6-3	215	2-27-62	1983	Mesa, Ariz.
Carpenter, Cris	2	5	2.43	49	0	0	5	67	59	18	18	20	41	R	R	6-1	185	4-5-65	1988	Gainesville, Ga.
Cimorelli, Frank	1	1	9.00	6	0	0	0	5	12	7	5	0	3	R	R	6-0	175	8-2-68	1989	Hyde Park, N.Y.
Creek, Doug	3	2	3.23	26	0	0	0	31	20	12	11	21	29	L	L	5-10	205	3-1-69	1991	Martinsburg, W.Va.
Davis, Clint	0	0	12.27	4	0	0	0	4	6	5	5	2	4	R	R	6-3	205	9-26-69	1991	Irving, Texas
De la Rosa, Francisco	2	5	4.06	28	19	1	0	115	104	56	52	38	66	S	R	5-11	185	3-3-66	1985	La Romana, D.R.
Frascatore, John	2	8	3.95	28	10	1	5	82	89	54	36	34	55	R	R	6-1	200	2-4-70	1991	Oceanside, N.Y.
Jackson, Danny	1	0	1.29	1	1	1	0	7	8	1	1	2	2	R	L	6-0	205	1-5-62	1982	Overland Park, Kan.
Martinez, Frankie	2	1	3.61	38	0	0	0	52	60	25	21	21	23	R	R	6-2	180	4-24-68	1987	Santo Domingo, D.R.

PITCHING	W	L	ERA	G	GS	CG	SV	IP	H	R	ER	BB	SO	B	T	HT	WT	DOB	1st Yr	Resides
Mathews, T.J.	9	4	2.70	32	7	0	1	67	60	35	20	27	50	R	R	6-2	200	1-19-70	1992	Columbia, Ill.
Minchey, Nate	8	7	3.73	26	24	1	0	147	153	77	61	42	67	R	R	6-7	225	8-31-69	1987	San Antonio, Texas
Osborne, Donovan	0	1	3.86	1	1	0	0	7	8	3	3	0	3	L	L	6-2	195	6-21-69	1990	Carson City, Nev.
Petkovsek, Mark	4	1	2.32	8	8	2	0	54	38	16	14	8	30	R	R	6-0	185	11-18-65	1987	Beaumont, Texas
Raczka, Mike	5	3	3.86	55	0	0	1	49	49	23	21	20	43	L	L	6-2	180	11-16-62	1984	Southington, Conn.
Simmons, Scott	0	2	8.00	2	2	0	0	9	11	9	8	1	2	R	L	6-2	200	8-15-69	1991	St. Charles, Mo.
Urbani, Tom	1	1	2.93	2	2	0	0	15	16	6	5	5	11	L	L	6-1	190	1-21-68	1990	Santa Cruz, Calif.
Watson, Allen	2	2	2.63	4	4	1	0	24	20	10	7	6	19	L	L	6-3	195	11-18-70	1991	Middle Village, N.Y.

FIELDING

Catcher	PCT	G	PO	A	E	DP	PB
B. Deak	.993	51	247	18	2	0	4
Difelice	.984	21	111	10	2	2	2
Hemond	1.000	1	6	0	0	0	1
Pagnozzi	1.000	5	19	0	0	0	0
Ronan	.993	76	417	35	3	1	8
Wrona	.984	13	57	4	1	1	0

First Base	PCT	G	PO	A	E	DP
Aversa	1.000	1	1	0	0	0
Cholowsky	.961	6	48	1	2	3
D. Deak	.983	45	333	16	6	28
Giannelli	.988	17	71	9	1	10
Martinez	.988	35	299	30	4	24
Prager	.980	33	188	13	4	13
Sabo	1.000	7	32	4	0	2
Sweeney	.990	22	176	19	2	14
Woodson	.965	12	102	9	4	4
Zeile	.923	2	11	1	1	0

Second Base	PCT	G	PO	A	E	DP
Aversa	.951	32	28	49	4	5

	PCT	G	PO	A	E	DP
Bell	.989	18	39	54	1	7
Caraballo	.981	58	126	178	6	39
Cholowsky	.950	6	7	12	1	0
D. Deak	.959	45	71	92	7	16
Giannelli	1.000	1	2	1	0	1
Hulett	1.000	3	6	5	0	0
Johns	1.000	3	7	4	0	1
Pena	.926	5	9	16	2	3

Third Base	PCT	G	PO	A	E	DP
Anderson	1.000	1	1	0	0	0
Aversa	.957	16	3	19	1	2
Cholowsky	1.000	1	1	0	0	0
D. Deak	.929	9	5	8	1	0
Giannelli	.900	5	3	6	1	1
Gulan	.948	54	38	90	7	2
Johns	.000	1	0	0	0	0
Woodson	.960	75	58	160	9	16

Shortstop	PCT	G	PO	A	E	DP
Aversa	.985	35	43	87	2	14

	PCT	G	PO	A	E	DP
Caraballo	.969	8	8	23	1	5
Diggs	.000	1	0	0	0	0
Holbert	.936	109	153	302	31	53
Johns	1.000	1	0	5	0	0
Lee	1.000	6	4	3	0	2

Outfield	PCT	G	PO	A	E	DP
Aversa	.000	1	0	0	0	0
Battle	.982	47	106	1	2	0
Bradshaw	.969	107	248	1	8	0
Cholowsky	.973	61	104	4	3	0
Diggs	1.000	18	21	1	0	0
Giannelli	.983	95	164	9	3	2
Gilkey	1.000	2	2	0	0	0
Mabry	.889	4	8	0	1	0
McNeely	.993	98	144	1	1	0
Thomas	.969	57	87	7	3	1
Young	.750	2	3	0	1	0

ARKANSAS   AA

TEXAS LEAGUE

BATTING	AVG	G	AB	R	H	2B	3B	HR	RBI	BB	SO	SB	CS	B	T	HT	WT	DOB	1st Yr	Resides
Anderson, Charlie	.283	77	240	31	68	15	2	4	29	21	55	1	2	R	R	6-1	190	3-18-70	1992	Jacksonville, Fla.
Berblinger, Jeff	.319	87	332	66	106	15	4	5	29	48	40	16	16	R	R	6-0	190	11-19-70	1993	Goddard, Kan.
Bethea, Scott	.176	11	34	6	6	1	0	0	4	2	5	1	0	L	R	5-11	175	6-17-69	1990	Jonesboro, Ark.
Cholowsky, Dan	.311	54	190	41	59	12	0	7	35	24	41	7	6	R	R	6-0	195	10-30-70	1991	San Jose, Calif.
Christopher, Chris	.274	23	62	7	17	1	0	1	3	1	6	4	1	R	R	5-11	175	11-16-71	1993	Greenville, N.C.
Difelice, Mike	.267	62	176	14	47	10	1	1	24	23	29	0	2	R	R	6-2	205	5-28-69	1991	Knoxville, Tenn.
Diggs, Tony	.268	78	235	33	63	9	8	2	21	35	41	7	6	S	R	6-0	175	4-20-67	1989	Starke, Fla.
Ellis, Paul	.227	78	229	17	52	6	0	2	25	49	18	0	1	L	R	6-1	205	11-28-68	1990	San Ramon, Calif.
Griffin, Ty	.274	94	263	38	72	16	1	9	44	36	59	17	2	S	R	5-11	185	9-5-67	1988	Tampa, Fla.
Gulan, Mike	.314	64	242	47	76	16	3	12	48	11	52	4	2	R	R	6-1	190	12-18-70	1992	Steubenville, Ohio
Johns, Keith	.280	111	396	69	111	13	2	2	28	55	53	14	7	R	R	6-1	175	7-19-71	1992	Jacksonville, Fla.
Jones, Chris	.226	50	84	11	19	2	0	0	4	9	12	3	3	L	L	5-10	160	1-28-71	1991	Paducah, Ky.
Lewis, Anthony	.251	115	407	55	102	21	3	24	85	44	117	0	2	L	L	5-11	185	2-2-71	1989	North Las Vegas, Nev.
McEwing, Joe	.248	42	121	16	30	4	0	2	12	9	13	3	2	R	R	5-10	170	10-19-72	1992	Bristol, Pa.
Norton, Chris	.240	10	25	6	6	2	0	0	6	11	5	0	0	R	R	6-2	215	9-21-70	1992	Maitland, Fla.
Pimentel, Wander	.000	2	2	0	0	0	0	0	0	0	0	0	0	R	R	5-11	185	9-18-72	1990	Bani, D.R.
Radziewicz, Doug	.233	34	116	15	27	5	0	1	13	18	14	0	0	L	L	6-1	195	4-24-69	1991	Somerville, N.J.
Rupp, Brian	.325	23	77	10	25	3	0	0	6	6	12	0	1	R	R	6-5	185	9-20-71	1992	Florissant, Mo.
Silvia, Brian	.241	12	29	4	7	1	0	0	3	4	9	0	0	R	R	6-0	195	9-13-71	1992	Columbia, Miss.
Torres, Paul	.225	66	231	24	52	11	0	10	33	21	56	2	1	R	R	6-3	210	10-19-70	1989	San Lorenzo, Calif.
Velez, Jose	.296	107	287	37	85	13	1	7	41	13	36	5	4	S	L	6-1	160	3-6-73	1990	Mayaguez, P.R.
Warner, Ron	.245	47	98	9	24	3	0	0	8	16	15	0	0	R	R	6-3	185	12-2-68	1991	Redlands, Calif.
Young, Dmitri	.292	97	367	54	107	18	6	10	62	30	46	2	4	S	R	6-2	215	10-11-73	1991	Camarillo, Calif.

PITCHING	W	L	ERA	G	GS	CG	SV	IP	H	R	ER	BB	SO	B	T	HT	WT	DOB	1st Yr	Resides
Alkire, Jeff	0	0	3.00	2	0	0	0	3	4	1	1	0	2	R	L	6-1	200	11-15-69	1992	San Jose, Calif.
Anderson, Paul	0	0	3.26	38	1	0	0	58	60	27	21	11	31	R	R	6-4	215	12-19-68	1990	San Diego, Calif.
Arrandale, Matt	3	5	3.28	47	3	0	2	69	72	28	25	22	28	R	R	6-0	165	12-14-70	1993	St. Louis, Mo.
Badorek, Mike	7	5	4.35	18	17	4	1	101	119	61	49	30	50	R	R	6-5	230	5-15-69	1991	Mt. Zion, Ill.
Busby, Mike	7	6	3.29	20	20	1	0	134	125	63	49	30	95	R	R	6-4	215	12-27-72	1991	Wilmington, Calif.
Carpenter, Brian	2	1	4.96	17	4	0	0	53	57	32	29	21	35	R	R	6-0	225	3-3-71	1992	Marble Falls, Texas
Corona, John	1	1	7.20	5	0	0	0	5	7	5	4	6	3	L	L	6-0	185	5-28-69	1989	Santa Fe Springs, Calif.
Creek, Doug	4	2	2.88	26	0	0	1	34	24	12	11	16	50	L	L	5-10	205	3-1-69	1991	Martinsburg, W.Va.
Davis, Ray	7	6	4.50	21	18	0	0	110	112	67	55	30	70	R	R	6-1	225	2-6-73	1991	Palatka, Fla.
Long, Tony	4	4	3.74	32	0	0	0	55	58	28	23	14	35	L	L	6-4	200	11-20-69	1990	Silver Spring, Md.
Lowe, Sean	9	8	4.88	24	24	0	0	129	143	84	70	64	77	R	R	6-2	205	3-29-71	1992	Mesquite, Texas
Martinez, Francisco	1	1	1.29	11	0	0	1	21	10	3	3	7	13	R	R	6-2	180	4-24-68	1987	Santo Domingo, D.R.
Matranga, Jeff	0	0	0.00	7	0	0	0	8	1	0	0	3	4	R	R	6-2	170	12-14-70	1992	Lakeside, Calif.
Mesewicz, Mark	0	1	6.75	5	0	0	0	13	9	7	7	1	7	L	L	6-3	195	10-13-69	1992	Newark, Ohio
Montgomery, Steve	5	2	3.25	55	0	0	36	61	52	22	22	22	56	R	R	6-4	200	12-25-70	1992	Corona Del Mar, Calif.
Oehrlein, Dave	4	7	4.87	23	10	1	0	78	80	48	42	28	52	L	L	6-0	185	9-1-69	1992	Rockville, Minn.
Osborne, Donovan	0	0	2.45	2	2	0	0	11	12	4	3	2	6	L	L	6-2	195	6-21-69	1990	Carson City, Nev.
Simmons, Scott	11	9	3.43	22	22	1	0	139	145	66	53	28	73	R	L	6-2	200	8-15-69	1991	St. Charles, Mo.
Wagner, Bret	1	2	3.19	6	6	0	0	37	34	14	13	18	31	L	L	6-0	190	4-17-73	1994	New Cumberland, Pa.
Watson, Allen	1	0	0.00	1	1	0	0	5	4	1	0	0	7	L	L	6-3	195	11-18-70	1991	Middle Village, N.Y.
Witasick, Jay	2	4	6.88	7	7	0	0	34	46	29	26	16	26	R	R	6-4	205	8-28-72	1993	Bel Air, Md.

ST. PETERSBURG   A

FLORIDA STATE LEAGUE

BATTING	AVG	G	AB	R	H	2B	3B	HR	RBI	BB	SO	SB	CS	B	T	HT	WT	DOB	1st Yr	Resides
Bellum, Donnie	.195	64	118	16	23	3	0	0	9	12	23	0	2	R	R	6-1	185	5-25-70	1992	Grants Pass, Ore.
Dalton, Dee	.205	118	385	36	79	16	1	2	30	45	81	10	4	R	R	5-11	170	6-17-72	1993	Roanoke, Va.
Deares, Greg	.235	20	51	3	12	1	0	0	6	2	8	0	0	L	R	6-2	180	4-22-71	1993	Baltimore, Md.
Fick, Chris	.293	113	348	56	102	25	3	13	52	38	79	1	2	L	R	6-2	190	10-4-69	1994	Thousand Oaks, Calif.
Garcia, Osmel	.175	105	315	37	55	4	0	0	13	28	66	24	11	R	R	6-1	180	10-14-73	1993	Hialeah, Fla.
Lee, Manuel	.353	6	17	2	6	1	0	0	3	2	3	0	0	S	R	5-9	161	6-17-65	1982	San Pedro de Macoris,D.R.
Madsen, Dave	.281	121	388	48	109	20	3	4	64	70	62	1	0	R	R	6-2	195	6-14-72	1993	Murray, Utah
Marrero, Elieser	.211	107	383	43	81	16	1	10	55	23	55	9	4	R	R	6-0	180	10-17-71	1993	Miami, Fla.
Matvey, Mike	.273	87	304	32	83	15	4	0	20	40	67	1	5	R	R	6-0	180	10-17-71	1993	Charlotte, N.C.
McEwing, Joe	.228	75	281	33	64	13	0	1	23	25	49	2	3	R	R	5-10	170	10-19-72	1992	Bristol, Pa.
McKinnon, Tom	.267	53	172	15	46	16	0	2	10	5	39	1	1	L	R	6-5	185	5-16-73	1991	Lakewood, Calif.
Morales, Francisco	.195	28	87	10	17	5	0	2	10	11	29	1	1	R	R	6-3	180	1-31-73	1991	San Pedro de Macoris, D.R.
2-team (36 Daytona)	.229	64	188	27	43	11	0	8	33	27	57	2	1							
Mota, Santo	.156	64	173	27	27	8	0	1	11	15	40	6	0	S	R	5-9	150	4-4-73	1991	San Pedro de Macoris, D.R.
Murphy, Jeff	.180	50	122	9	22	3	1	2	14	19	36	0	0	S	R	6-2	210	12-27-70	1992	Las Vegas, Nev.
Rupp, Brian	.277	90	325	30	90	12	2	0	23	27	43	0	0	R	R	6-5	185	9-20-71	1992	Florissant, Mo.
Sabo, Chris	.231	14	39	10	9	0	0	2	7	10	6	1	0	R	R	6-0	185	1-19-62	1983	Sarasota, Fla.
Santucci, Steven	.236	106	292	25	69	5	3	4	25	27	60	9	3	R	R	6-1	190	12-16-71	1993	Leominster, Mass.
Taylor, Mike	.239	70	159	13	38	3	1	2	15	28	24	0	2	L	L	6-0	185	9-17-70	1993	Girard, Ohio
Ugueto, Jesus	.130	37	77	3	10	1	0	0	3	3	18	0	1	R	R	6-0	145	12-29-72	1990	Catia La Mar, Venez.
Wyrick, Chris	.237	55	139	20	33	6	1	1	15	10	25	3	5	R	R	6-0	185	7-12-71	1993	Jefferson City, Mo.

GAMES BY POSITION: **C**—Marrero 81, Morales 22, Murphy 40. **1B**—Madsen 55, Rupp 59, Sabo 10, Taylor 20. **2B**—Dalton 22, Lee 1, McEwing 72, Mota 43, Ugueto 4, Wyrick 1. **3B**—Dalton 99, Madsen 11, Mota 1, Rupp 13, Sabo 2, Ugueto 10, Wyrick 13. **SS**—Dalton 1, Lee 5, Matvey 87, Mota 10, Ugueto 20, Wyrick 30. **OF**—Bellum 59, Deares 17, Fick 105, Garcia 102, McEwing 2, McKinnon 52, Mota 3, Rupp 19, Sabo 1, Santucci 96, Taylor 1.

PITCHING	W	L	ERA	G	GS	CG	SV	IP	H	R	ER	BB	SO	B	T	HT	WT	DOB	1st Yr	Resides
Aybar, Manuel	2	5	3.35	9	9	0	0	48	42	27	18	16	43	R	R	6-1	165	10-5-74	1991	Bani, D.R.
Blake, Todd	2	2	2.59	42	0	0	0	56	58	25	16	17	35	L	L	6-2	205	9-22-70	1992	Durham, N.C.
Cain, Chance	1	0	3.27	7	0	0	0	11	18	6	4	2	4	R	R	6-3	195	2-4-71	1993	Canton, Ga.
Carpenter, Brian	5	3	2.14	16	7	0	0	59	40	17	14	11	51	R	R	6-0	225	3-3-71	1992	Marble Falls, Texas
Croushore, Rick	6	4	3.51	12	11	0	0	59	44	25	23	32	57	R	R	6-4	210	8-7-70	1993	Houston, Texas
Detmers, Kris	10	9	3.25	25	25	1	0	147	120	64	53	57	150	S	L	6-5	215	6-22-74	1994	Nokomis, Ill.
Garcia, Frank	0	1	10.26	16	0	0	1	17	27	22	19	18	8	R	R	5-11	170	3-5-74	1994	Azua, D.R.
Grasser, Craig	4	2	1.36	26	0	0	0	33	26	5	5	12	27	R	R	6-3	190	4-24-70	1992	Baltimore, Md.
Hartmann, Rich	0	0	1.65	13	0	0	0	16	13	5	3	3	12	R	R	6-3	220	8-27-72	1994	Sayville, N.Y.
Heiserman, Rick	2	3	5.46	6	5	0	0	28	28	18	17	11	18	R	R	6-5	205	2-22-73	1994	Omaha, Neb.
King, Curtis	7	8	2.58	28	21	3	0	136	117	49	39	49	65	R	R	6-5	205	10-25-70	1994	Conshohocken, Pa.
Lovinger, Kevin	1	0	1.66	22	0	0	0	22	9	4	4	10	14	L	L	6-1	190	8-29-71	1994	Mission Viejo, Calif.
Marquardt, Scott	3	4	3.78	9	9	0	0	52	55	24	22	15	39	R	R	6-2	195	8-25-72	1993	Baytown, Texas
Matranga, Jeff	3	4	2.74	53	0	0	3	66	49	27	20	21	39	R	R	6-2	190	12-14-72	1992	Lakeside, Calif.
Matulevich, Jeff	1	5	2.76	51	0	0	30	59	50	20	18	30	61	R	R	6-3	200	4-15-70	1992	Haddam, Conn.
Morris, Matt	3	2	2.38	6	6	1	0	34	22	16	9	11	31	R	R	6-4	210	8-9-74	1995	Montgomery, N.Y.
Raggio, Brady	2	3	3.80	20	3	0	0	47	43	24	20	13	35	R	R	6-2	190	7-17-72	1992	Danville, Calif.
Stewart, Chris	0	1	5.35	30	0	0	0	34	29	22	20	25	36	R	R	6-2	190	7-20-71	1993	Memphis, Tenn.
Wagner, Bret	5	4	2.12	17	17	1	0	93	77	36	22	28	59	L	L	6-0	190	4-17-73	1994	New Cumberland, Pa.
Witasick, Jay	7	7	2.74	18	18	1	0	105	80	39	32	36	109	R	R	6-4	205	8-28-72	1993	Bel Air, Md.

PEORIA   A

MIDWEST LEAGUE

BATTING	AVG	G	AB	R	H	2B	3B	HR	RBI	BB	SO	SB	CS	B	T	HT	WT	DOB	1st Yr	Resides
Ballara, Juan	.255	86	243	33	62	12	6	8	27	17	53	5	3	R	R	6-2	150	3-30-72	1990	Santo Domingo, D.R.
Bautista, Juan	.222	84	189	31	42	4	1	2	22	4	43	18	8	R	R	6-1	165	6-12-73	1991	Boca Chica, D.R.
Biermann, Steve	.238	59	122	10	29	3	0	0	10	15	16	4	3	S	R	6-0	175	9-30-71	1993	St. Louis, Mo.
Contreras, Efrain	.258	98	271	35	70	9	2	10	48	27	45	1	3	L	R	5-11	190	12-22-74	1994	Rio Piedras, P.R.
Dean, Mark	.205	75	190	19	39	2	2	0	12	14	42	4	0	S	R	6-0	160	5-4-71	1993	Wadsworth, Ohio
French, Anton	.273	116	417	71	114	19	5	10	37	37	98	57	16	S	R	5-10	175	7-25-75	1993	St. Louis, Mo.
Gerteisen, Aaron	.216	73	218	24	47	6	1	2	17	25	29	7	5	L	R	6-0	165	10-26-72	1993	Tallahassee, Fla.
Grandizio, Steve	.280	117	379	65	106	18	4	1	33	42	63	21	8	R	R	6-3	190	9-13-71	1994	Media, Pa.
Hall, Ryan	.271	108	317	38	86	24	0	4	44	49	70	1	2	L	R	6-0	205	2-25-72	1994	Springville, Utah
Jumonville, Joe	.228	113	378	37	86	18	4	4	45	9	47	2	1	R	R	6-1	205	8-18-70	1993	New Iberia, La.

BATTING

BATTING	AVG	G	AB	R	H	2B	3B	HR	RBI	BB	SO	SB	CS	B	T	HT	WT	DOB	1st Yr	Resides
Llanos, Victor	.277	21	47	7	13	2	0	0	3	3	7	0	1	R	R	6-2	190	6-26-73	1991	Carolina, P.R.
Lugo, Jesus	.265	65	219	26	58	11	2	2	29	12	31	1	1	R	R	6-3	180	5-8-75	1993	Puerto La Cruz, Venez.
McDonald, Keith	.268	65	179	22	48	6	0	1	20	22	38	0	1	R	R	6-2	215	2-8-73	1994	Yorba Linda, Calif.
Nunez, Isaias	.217	120	378	37	82	19	6	2	43	25	66	1	6	L	L	6-2	150	4-10-74	1992	Haina, D.R.
Polanco, Placido	.266	103	361	43	96	7	4	2	41	18	30	7	6	R	R	5-10	168	10-10-75	1994	Miami, Fla.
Robinson, Darek	.240	113	363	36	87	15	0	2	23	37	60	2	5	S	R	5-11	180	2-14-73	1993	Pleasant Grove, Utah

GAMES BY POSITION: C—Ballara 52, Dean 1, Hall 39, McDonald 62. **1B**—Ballara 2, Bautista 1, Grandizio 1, Hall 18, Llanos 9, Nunez 119. **2B**—Biermann 9, Dean 25, Polanco 1, Robinson 111. **3B**—Biermann 3, Dean 34, Jumonville 112, Llanos 1. **SS**—Biermann 40, Contreras 1, Dean 11, Polanco 101. **OF**—Bautista 63, Contreras 78, Dean 2, French 113, Gerteisen 66, Grandizio 93, Lugo 36.

PITCHING

PITCHING	W	L	ERA	G	GS	CG	SV	IP	H	R	ER	BB	SO	B	T	HT	WT	DOB	1st Yr	Resides
Carroll, David	2	2	4.38	24	6	0	0	51	53	33	25	24	41	S	L	6-3	205	7-23-72	1993	Fairfax, Va.
Corrigan, Cory	4	7	2.32	47	10	0	0	113	90	36	29	23	84	R	R	6-0	170	9-14-71	1993	Athens, Ohio
Crump, Jody	1	1	6.19	25	0	0	0	36	40	25	25	26	16	L	L	6-6	210	10-5-72	1994	Sadieville, Ky.
Curran, Tighe	3	0	2.90	24	0	0	0	40	35	18	13	21	21	L	L	6-0	180	12-28-73	1993	Newbury Park, Calif.
Dale, Carl	9	9	2.94	24	24	2	0	144	124	66	47	62	104	R	R	6-2	215	12-7-72	1994	Cookeville, Tenn.
Foderaro, Kevin	3	8	6.20	15	14	0	0	70	80	58	48	24	36	R	R	6-3	215	10-3-72	1994	Valencia, Calif.
Gautreau, Mike	4	3	4.55	45	0	0	0	63	62	42	32	29	55	R	R	5-11	195	9-28-71	1994	Lafayette, La.
Hall, Yates	2	5	4.53	9	8	0	0	46	45	25	23	24	47	R	R	6-2	190	3-29-73	1994	Front Royal, Va.
Johnson, Ron	5	7	3.17	22	19	0	0	102	105	56	36	36	61	R	L	6-0	198	4-20-72	1994	Parker, Texas
Pontes, Dan	2	5	1.60	34	6	0	1	68	47	19	12	15	88	R	R	6-3	200	4-27-71	1993	Geneva, N.Y.
Raggio, Brady	3	0	1.85	8	8	3	0	49	42	13	10	2	34	R	R	6-4	210	9-17-72	1992	Danville, Calif.
Reed, Brian	11	3	1.79	63	0	0	4	90	55	29	18	25	119	R	R	6-2	185	9-1-71	1994	Lexington, Ky.
Roettgen, Mark	0	4	10.29	4	4	0	0	14	24	20	16	15	14	R	R	6-5	213	8-15-76	1994	Jefferson City, Mo.
Scott, Ron	0	2	8.47	21	1	0	0	34	37	36	32	30	21	L	L	5-9	170	7-24-71	1993	Sarasota, Fla.
Slininger, Dennis	0	3	10.97	3	3	0	0	11	16	13	13	7	12	R	R	6-2	190	6-29-72	1991	Largo, Fla.
Stein, Blake	10	6	3.80	27	27	1	0	140	122	69	59	61	133	R	R	6-7	210	8-3-73	1994	Folsom, La.
Welch, Travis	3	4	4.50	46	0	0	31	46	40	26	23	18	45	R	R	6-0	202	1-30-74	1993	Loomis, Calif.
West, Adam	0	3	12.08	4	4	0	0	13	22	21	17	24	5	L	L	6-1	185	10-10-73	1994	Thousand Oaks, Calif.

SAVANNAH · A

SOUTH ATLANTIC LEAGUE

BATTING

BATTING	AVG	G	AB	R	H	2B	3B	HR	RBI	BB	SO	SB	CS	B	T	HT	WT	DOB	1st Yr	Resides
Abell, Tony	.122	17	49	1	6	1	0	0	2	4	18	1	1	R	R	5-10	175	1-13-75	1994	Ekron, Ky.
Almond, Greg	.161	18	56	2	9	2	0	0	3	8	16	0	1	R	R	6-0	195	4-14-71	1993	Panama City, Fla.
Ambrosina, Pete	.239	129	464	55	111	10	2	1	36	69	100	20	12	S	R	5-10	175	11-5-73	1994	Harrogate, Tenn.
Bowen, Glenn	.231	16	52	1	12	3	0	0	2	0	17	0	1	R	R	6-2	175	11-18-73	1992	Mayo, S.C.
Coach, Calvin	.197	65	218	15	43	2	1	0	10	20	58	8	4	L	L	6-0	175	11-10-72	1994	Clearwater, S.C.
Cooper, Steve	.250	48	156	13	39	7	0	0	12	22	51	2	0	R	R	6-1	195	5-26-70	1995	Orem, Utah
Dishington, Nate	.214	124	444	56	95	17	5	11	44	62	154	13	7	L	R	6-3	210	1-8-75	1993	Glendale, Calif.
Ealy, Tracey	.243	101	370	38	90	18	1	7	35	41	103	8	5	S	R	6-0	210	7-8-71	1988	Las Vegas, Nev.
Falciglia, Tony	.169	23	71	4	12	2	0	0	5	9	17	1	1	R	R	5-11	185	9-29-72	1995	Bronx, N.Y.
Green, Bert	.228	132	429	48	98	7	6	1	25	55	101	26	9	R	R	5-10	170	6-9-74	1993	Ballwin, Mo.
Harper, Rantie	.208	91	318	34	66	12	2	3	31	34	114	13	3	R	R	6-1	180	5-20-75	1993	San Diego, Calif.
Leon, Geraldo	.165	41	133	15	22	4	1	0	11	10	46	0	1	R	R	6-0	160	12-8-76	1994	Cayey, P.R.
McDougal, Mike	.080	15	50	2	4	0	0	0	4	2	17	1	1	R	R	6-4	210	3-22-75	1994	Las Vegas, Nev.
McMillan, Tom	.214	85	262	21	56	8	1	7	21	35	91	5	4	R	R	6-0	190	9-6-75	1993	Guaynabo, P.R.
McNally, Shawn	.219	49	169	21	37	8	2	1	14	24	48	8	2	R	R	6-2	215	1-29-73	1995	Winder, Ga.
Morales, Francisco	.147	19	75	3	11	3	0	2	4	4	23	0	2	R	R	6-3	180	1-31-73	1991	San Pedro de Macoris, D.R.
Rivera, Miguel	.253	128	514	44	130	14	3	4	41	21	76	10	6	R	R	5-10	175	4-14-74	1993	Racine, Wisc.
Robles, Rafael	.197	56	142	15	28	2	1	0	7	39	43	2	4	S	R	6-1	175	5-8-73	1991	Villa Mella, D.R.
Silvia, Brian	.247	59	198	25	49	14	2	8	33	31	39	4	2	R	R	6-0	195	9-13-71	1992	Columbia, Miss.
Taylor, Byron	.103	14	29	2	3	0	0	0	0	1	10	0	0	L	R	5-8	190	2-28-73	1994	Centerville, Ill.
Williams, Curtis	.187	51	134	14	25	2	1	1	9	20	44	2	5	L	L	6-1	175	9-27-72	1993	Lewisville, Ark.
Williams, Mark	.154	64	201	19	31	2	0	4	13	33	57	0	0	R	R	6-0	180	11-17-72	1992	Coral Springs, Fla.

GAMES BY POSITION: C—Almond 11, Bowen 16, Falciglia 18, Morales 18, Silvia 24, M. Williams 62. **1B**—Cooper 36, Dishington 85, McDougal 112, McMillan 1, Robles 2, Silvia 8. **2B**—Ambrosina 121, Rivera 1, Robles 18. **3B**—Ambrosina 1, Harper 1, Leon 20, Rivera 117, Robles 6. **SS**—Green 132, Robles 10. **OF**—Abell 17, Coach 63, Ealy 97, Harper 85, Leon 1, McMillan 67, McNally 49, Robles 5, Silvia 2, Taylor 4, C. Williams 47, M. Williams 1.

PITCHING

PITCHING	W	L	ERA	G	GS	CG	SV	IP	H	R	ER	BB	SO	B	T	HT	WT	DOB	1st Yr	Resides
Almanza, Armando	3	9	3.92	20	20	0	0	108	108	62	47	40	72	L	L	6-3	205	10-26-72	1993	El Paso, Texas
Avrard, Corey	1	6	3.98	13	0	0	0	54	38	25	24	33	51	R	R	6-3	185	12-6-76	1994	Metairie, La.
Aybar, Manuel	3	8	3.04	18	18	2	0	113	82	46	38	36	99	R	R	6-1	165	10-5-74	1991	Bani, D.R.
Bledsoe, Randy	2	1	6.42	28	0	0	0	34	41	25	24	22	28	R	R	6-3	195	1-25-72	1992	Huntington, Texas
Conway, Keith	7	2	1.46	60	0	0	10	74	49	14	12	26	87	R	L	6-2	200	5-8-73	1993	Philadelphia, Pa.
Cruise, Mark	0	0	3.68	6	0	0	0	7	8	5	3	1	5	R	R	6-5	225	10-1-72	1993	San Pablo, Calif.
Garcia, Frank	0	3	3.16	34	0	0	24	37	26	17	13	15	41	R	R	5-11	170	3-5-74	1994	Azua, D.R.
Glauber, Keith	2	1	3.73	40	0	0	0	63	50	29	26	36	62	R	R	6-2	190	1-18-72	1994	Morganville, N.J.
Golden, Matthew	7	3	2.00	64	0	0	1	90	71	22	20	21	94	R	R	6-3	190	1-23-72	1994	Woodbridge, N.J.
Hartmann, Rich	1	2	5.05	31	0	0	0	41	35	26	23	20	52	R	R	6-3	220	8-27-72	1994	Sayville, N.Y.
Helvey, Rob	1	1	7.97	18	0	0	0	20	28	22	18	16	25	R	R	6-0	185	5-22-72	1994	St. Louis, Mo.
Logan, Marcus	3	6	3.32	34	7	0	0	87	73	42	32	38	83	R	R	6-0	170	5-8-72	1994	Evanston, Ill.
Lovinger, Kevin	6	3	1.34	38	0	0	1	47	35	14	7	21	54	L	L	6-1	190	8-29-71	1994	Mission Viejo, Calif.
McNeill, Kevin	3	4	4.96	29	21	0	0	111	131	74	61	47	87	R	R	6-4	210	12-22-70	1994	Waller, Texas
Minor, Tom	1	1	4.91	8	0	0	0	7	10	7	4	2	9	R	R	6-3	195	2-12-72	1994	Walnut Creek, Calif.
Ramirez, Rafael	6	15	3.91	26	25	0	0	147	160	81	64	42	91	R	R	6-2	175	10-20-74	1992	San Pedro de Macoris, D.R.
Reames, Britt	3	5	3.46	10	10	1	0	55	41	23	21	15	63	R	R	5-11	170	8-19-73	1995	Seneca, S.C.
Windham, Mike	6	9	4.07	26	25	0	0	133	133	73	60	60	115	R	R	6-1	185	3-8-72	1993	West Palm Beach, Fla.

NEW YORK-PENN LEAGUE

BATTING	AVG	G	AB	R	H	2B	3B	HR	RBI	BB	SO	SB	CS	B	T	HT	WT	DOB	1st Yr	Resides
Betts, Darrell	.152	54	151	22	23	4	0	0	11	32	38	3	6	S	R	5-10	160	2-3-73	1995	Cincinnati, Ohio
Cameron, Ken	.239	39	138	18	33	9	1	0	10	12	20	5	0	L	L	6-0	185	3-1-73	1995	Pullman, Wash.
Cardona, Ruben	.251	49	195	36	49	5	4	0	24	21	24	7	2	L	R	5-9	170	11-15-71	1995	Brooklyn, N.Y.
Deluca, Nic	.250	3	8	1	2	0	0	0	0	0	2	0	0	R	R	6-0	175	12-22-71	1995	Salt Lake City, Utah
Deman, Lou	.220	52	186	22	41	8	0	2	24	12	60	2	3	R	R	6-2	225	7-1-73	1995	Egg Harbor, N.J.
Doezie, Troy	.190	23	84	15	16	5	2	1	12	10	18	0	1	R	R	6-2	210	9-6-73	1992	Sandy, Utah
Freitas, Joe	.191	14	47	8	9	6	0	0	9	5	18	2	0	R	R	6-3	195	8-2-73	1995	Hanford, Calif.
Garman, Sean	.195	50	133	20	26	5	0	0	8	21	25	1	0	S	R	6-0	175	3-12-74	1994	Caldwell, Idaho
Hall, Andy	.310	64	252	30	78	10	5	1	34	19	44	19	6	S	R	6-0	175	4-29-74	1995	Camarillo, Calif.
Insunza, Miguel	.242	55	207	30	50	6	0	0	21	24	18	11	8	R	R	5-10	170	7-16-72	1995	Biddeford, Maine
Lariviere, Jason	.280	33	100	13	28	3	1	0	9	14	10	8	2	R	R	5-10	180	9-30-73	1995	Cottonwood, Ariz.
McClendon, Travis	.286	50	161	25	46	9	1	1	18	10	25	6	3	R	R	5-11	185	10-22-72	1995	Cottonwood, Ariz.
McHugh, Ryan	.194	26	98	7	19	4	0	1	14	8	39	2	0	R	R	6-6	215	7-29-73	1995	Stamford, Conn.
McNally, Shawn	.256	24	90	11	23	5	0	1	10	8	18	5	1	R	R	6-2	215	1-29-73	1995	Winder, Ga.
Mueller, Bret	.262	70	267	39	70	5	8	2	39	20	61	7	3	R	R	6-1	195	3-26-73	1995	Oakhurst, Calif.
Richard, Chris	.282	75	284	36	80	14	3	3	43	47	31	6	6	L	L	6-2	185	6-7-74	1995	San Diego, Calif.
Ugueto, Hector	.287	54	202	37	58	7	2	1	28	17	36	9	2	R	R	6-0	147	12-16-73	1991	Catia La Mar, Venez.

GAMES BY POSITION: C—Deman 22, Doezie 14, McClendon 46. **1B**—Garman 5, Richard 75. **2B**—Cardona 48, Deluca 1, Hall 4, Insunza 25. **3B**—Deluca 2, Garman 44, Hall 37, Insunza 3. **SS**—Betts 51, Insunza 28. **OF**—Cameron 28, Freitas 14, Lariviere 33, McHugh 24, McNally 24, Mueller 66, Ugueto 53.

PITCHING	W	L	ERA	G	GS	CG	SV	IP	H	R	ER	BB	SO	B	T	HT	WT	DOB	1st Yr	Resides
Benes, Adam	5	3	3.36	19	10	0	0	75	71	30	28	23	47	L	R	6-2	195	3-12-73	1995	Lake Forest, Ill.
Bennett, Matt	3	0	3.42	23	0	0	0	47	49	30	18	13	34	R	R	6-3	215	9-13-73	1991	Modesto, Calif.
Donnelly, Robert	1	3	3.54	36	0	0	0	48	37	21	19	30	63	R	R	6-0	180	9-27-73	1995	Fresno, Calif.
Frascatore, Steve	4	6	4.68	16	15	0	0	83	86	56	43	30	43	R	R	6-2	190	2-28-72	1994	Oceanside, N.Y.
Hall, Yates	3	0	1.37	5	5	0	0	26	19	7	4	11	22	R	R	6-2	190	3-29-73	1994	Front Royal, Va.
Helvey, Rob	2	1	0.73	11	0	0	2	12	7	1	1	5	15	R	L	6-0	185	5-27-72	1994	St. Louis, Mo.
Kast, Nick	5	1	1.38	29	0	0	0	46	29	11	7	21	64	R	L	5-11	165	8-17-72	1995	Wichita Falls, Texas
Miedreich, Kevin	2	6	4.70	15	15	0	0	75	84	47	39	33	39	R	R	6-3	210	3-19-73	1995	Eldred, N.Y.
Morris, Matt	2	0	1.64	2	2	0	0	11	12	3	2	3	13	R	R	6-5	210	8-9-74	1995	Montgomery, N.Y.
Reames, Britt	2	1	1.52	5	5	0	0	30	19	7	5	12	42	R	R	5-11	170	8-19-73	1995	Seneca, S.C.
Severino, Jose	3	3	5.29	17	10	0	0	66	65	48	39	37	68	R	R	6-3	178	11-24-73	1991	Santo Domingo, D.R.
Spaulding, Scott	1	0	2.59	35	0	0	2	49	36	17	14	14	40	R	R	6-3	215	8-8-73	1995	Claremont, N.H.
Swenson, Mike	2	4	4.82	19	6	0	0	52	53	35	28	32	54	L	L	6-2	195	11-16-72	1995	Tampa, Fla.
Villafana, Jose	0	6	4.91	27	0	0	13	29	35	17	16	21	28	R	R	6-3	195	4-22-74	1995	Sylmar, Calif.
Ward, Jon	0	7	8.07	9	8	0	0	32	47	42	29	18	35	R	R	6-6	220	11-13-74	1995	Huntington Beach, Calif.

APPALACHIAN LEAGUE

BATTING	AVG	G	AB	R	H	2B	3B	HR	RBI	BB	SO	SB	CS	B	T	HT	WT	DOB	1st Yr	Resides
Abell, Antonio	.258	55	190	27	49	10	2	0	16	22	76	8	8	R	R	5-10	175	1-13-75	1994	Ekron, Ky.
Cardona, Alex	.217	22	46	9	10	3	0	0	7	11	4	0	1	R	R	5-11	190	10-19-74	1993	Kissmmee, Fla.
Current, Jeremy	.254	23	63	5	16	3	0	0	6	8	23	0	0	R	R	6-1	175	9-15-75	1993	Mt. Zion, Ill.
Deck, Billy	.259	59	205	27	53	12	0	1	30	30	52	4	6	L	L	6-0	180	9-16-76	1995	South Venice, Fla.
Diaz, Ivan	.214	6	14	0	3	0	0	0	2	0	3	0	0	R	R	5-11	185	1-21-75	1994	Santo Domingo, D.R.
Falciglia, Tony	.314	33	118	18	37	14	0	4	26	12	34	0	1	R	R	5-11	185	9-29-72	1995	Bronx, N.Y.
Haas, Chris	.269	67	242	43	65	15	3	7	50	52	93	1	3	L	R	6-2	210	10-15-76	1995	Paducah, Ky.
Harris, Rodger	.182	45	121	26	22	5	1	0	7	19	44	5	2	S	R	5-9	165	8-30-75	1995	Hanford, Calif.
Jimenez, Ruben	.164	41	116	13	19	0	4	0	20	16	27	5	6	S	R	5-11	155	8-18-75	1993	San Pedro de Macoris, D.R.
Lee, Jason	.105	28	76	10	8	1	0	0	4	8	38	2	4	L	R	6-1	185	4-22-77	1995	Burlington, Iowa
Martinez, Tony	.234	24	77	18	18	0	1	2	8	26	14	3	2	R	R	5-10	170	1-23-73	1995	Tinton Falls, N.J.
McDougal, Mike	.175	32	97	8	17	3	1	3	12	6	27	0	2	R	R	6-4	210	3-22-75	1994	Las Vegas, Nev.
McNeal, Pepe	.175	27	97	9	17	6	0	0	12	15	22	2	0	R	R	6-3	205	8-11-75	1994	Thonotosassa, Fla.
2-team (27 Burl.)	.226	54	186	13	42	8	0	2	27	19	48	4	0							
Milledge, Tony	.276	31	87	14	24	7	1	3	12	7	15	1	0	R	R	5-11	195	12-30-75	1994	Palmetto, Fla.
Munoz, Juan	.347	57	190	43	66	12	1	7	31	27	17	13	2	L	L	5-9	170	3-27-74	1995	Miami, Fla.
Robinson, Kerry	.296	60	250	44	74	12	8	1	26	16	30	14	10	L	L	6-0	175	10-3-73	1995	Spanish Lake, Mo.
Schofield, Andy	.227	40	119	22	27	8	0	0	11	19	30	6	1	R	R	5-11	185	11-11-73	1995	Danville, Ill.
Sturges, Brian	.143	17	42	5	6	1	0	0	6	2	7	0	0	R	R	6-0	185	12-21-72	1995	Thousand Oaks, Calif.
Woolf, Jason	.279	31	111	16	31	7	1	0	14	8	21	6	3	S	R	6-1	170	6-6-77	1995	Miami, Fla.

GAMES BY POSITION: C—Cardona 19, Falciglia 20, McNeal 26, Sturges 13. **1B**—Cardona 2, Deck 58, McDougal 11. **2B**—Diaz 4, Harris 42, Jimenez 22, Milledge 9, Sturges 8. **3B**—Haas 64, Jimenez 1, Milledge 8. **SS**—Jimenez 19, Martinez 23, Milledge 2, Woolf 28. **OF**—Abell 52, Current 20, Lee 19, McDougal 1, Munoz 55, Robinson 25.

PITCHING	W	L	ERA	G	GS	CG	SV	IP	H	R	ER	BB	SO	B	T	HT	WT	DOB	1st Yr	Resides
Barfield, Rodney	2	7	9.82	10	10	0	0	37	52	50	40	30	18	R	R	6-1	190	8-26-74	1995	Albany, Ga.
DeWitt, Matt	2	6	7.04	13	12	0	0	63	84	56	49	32	45	R	R	6-4	220	9-4-77	1995	Las Vegas, Nev.
Jimenez, Jose	5	7	3.49	14	14	1	0	90	81	48	35	25	85	R	R	6-3	170	7-7-73	1992	San Pedro de Macoris, D.R.
King, Matt	0	0	67.50	1	0	0	0	1	2	5	5	4	2	R	R	6-3	192	4-11-76	1995	Toledo, Ohio
Kown, John	4	2	2.65	16	4	1	0	51	44	31	15	18	42	L	R	6-5	215	12-15-72	1995	Marietta, Ohio
McCaffrey, Dennis	2	0	4.78	24	0	0	0	32	36	24	17	17	24	R	R	6-2	180	10-11-75	1994	Browns Mills, N.J.
Mear, Rich	7	3	3.35	14	14	0	0	78	68	37	29	40	75	L	L	6-3	218	6-30-76	1994	Rowland Heights, Calif.
Mendez, Manuel	0	3	3.08	30	0	0	19	38	33	13	13	12	61	L	L	6-0	190	5-27-74	1994	Fresno, Calif.
Reed, Steve	2	2	4.43	31	0	0	1	43	48	24	21	15	41	R	R	6-2	205	9-24-75	1994	Juno Beach, Fla.
Roettgen, Mark	4	5	5.59	13	13	0	0	66	63	48	41	40	60	R	R	6-5	213	8-15-76	1994	Jefferson City, Mo.
Rogan, Sean	1	0	5.59	13	0	0	0	29	30	22	18	17	22	L	L	5-11	185	11-20-73	1995	Glencoe, Mo.
Roque, Jorge	2	0	5.12	14	0	0	0	19	15	11	11	9	22	R	R	6-0	195	10-15-74	1995	Santurce, P.R.
West, Adam	1	1	2.85	18	1	0	0	41	41	26	13	19	41	L	L	6-1	185	10-10-73	1994	Thousand Oaks, Calif.

SAN DIEGO PADRES

Manager: Bruce Bochy. **1995 Record:** 70-74, .486 (3rd, NL West).

BATTING	AVG	G	AB	R	H	2B	3B	HR	RBI	BB	SO	SB	CS	B	T	HT	WT	DOB	1st Yr	Resides
Ausmus, Brad	.293	103	328	44	96	16	4	5	34	31	56	16	5	R	R	5-11	185	4-14-69	1988	Cheshire, Conn.
Bean, Billy	.000	4	7	1	0	0	0	0	0	1	4	0	0	L	L	6-1	185	5-11-64	1986	Hollywood, Calif.
Caminiti, Ken	.302	143	526	74	159	33	0	26	94	69	94	12	5	S	R	6-0	200	4-21-63	1985	Richmond, Texas
Cedeno, Andujar	.210	120	390	42	82	16	2	6	31	28	92	5	3	R	R	6-1	168	8-21-69	1987	La Romana, D.R.
Cianfrocco, Archi	.263	51	118	22	31	7	0	5	31	11	28	0	2	R	R	6-5	200	10-6-66	1987	Rome, N.Y.
Clark, Phil	.216	75	97	12	21	3	0	2	7	8	18	0	2	R	R	6-0	180	5-6-68	1986	Toledo, Ohio
Finley, Steve	.297	139	562	104	167	23	8	10	44	59	62	36	12	L	L	6-2	180	3-12-65	1987	Houston, Texas
Gwynn, Tony	.368	135	535	82	197	33	1	9	90	35	15	17	5	L	L	5-11	210	5-9-60	1981	Poway, Calif.
Holbert, Ray	.178	63	73	11	13	2	1	2	5	8	20	4	0	R	R	6-0	165	9-25-70	1988	Moreno Valley, Calif.
Hyers, Tim	.000	6	6	0	0	0	0	0	0	0	1	0	0	L	L	6-1	180	10-3-71	1990	Covington, Ga.
Johnson, Brian	.251	68	207	20	52	9	0	3	29	11	39	0	0	R	R	6-2	210	1-8-68	1989	Oakland, Calif.
Livingstone, Scott	.337	99	196	26	66	15	0	5	32	15	22	2	1	L	R	6-0	198	7-15-65	1988	Southlake, Texas
McDavid, Ray	.176	11	17	2	3	0	0	0	2	6	11	1	1	L	R	6-3	195	7-20-71	1989	San Diego, Calif.
Newfield, Marc	.309	21	55	6	17	5	1	1	7	2	8	0	0	R	R	6-4	205	10-19-72	1990	Huntington Beach, Calif.
Nieves, Melvin	.205	98	234	32	48	6	1	14	38	19	88	2	3	S	R	6-2	186	12-28-71	1988	Bayamon, P.R.
Petagine, Roberto	.234	89	124	15	29	8	0	3	17	26	41	0	0	L	L	6-1	172	6-7-71	1990	Nueva Esparta, Venez.
Plantier, Phil	.257	54	148	21	38	4	0	5	19	17	29	1	1	L	R	5-11	195	1-27-69	1987	San Diego, Calif.
2-team (22 Houston)	.255	76	216	33	55	6	0	9	34	28	48	1	1							
Reed, Jody	.256	131	445	58	114	18	1	4	40	59	38	6	4	R	R	5-9	165	7-26-62	1984	Tampa, Fla.
Roberts, Bip	.304	73	296	40	90	14	0	2	25	17	36	20	2	S	R	5-7	160	10-27-63	1982	San Diego, Calif.
Williams, Eddie	.260	97	296	35	77	11	1	12	47	23	47	0	0	R	R	6-0	175	11-1-64	1983	La Mesa, Calif.

PITCHING	W	L	ERA	G	GS	CG	SV	IP	H	R	ER	BB	SO	B	T	HT	WT	DOB	1st Yr	Resides
Ashby, Andy	12	10	2.94	31	31	2	0	193	180	79	63	62	150	R	R	6-5	180	7-11-67	1986	Kansas City, Mo.
Benes, Andy	4	7	4.17	19	19	1	0	119	121	65	55	45	126	R	R	6-6	238	8-20-67	1989	Poway, Calif.
Berumen, Andres	2	3	5.68	37	0	0	1	44	37	29	28	36	42	R	R	6-1	205	4-5-71	1989	Banning, Calif.
Blair, Willie	7	5	4.34	40	12	0	0	114	112	60	55	45	83	R	R	6-1	185	12-18-65	1986	Lexington, Ky.
Bochtler, Doug	4	4	3.57	34	0	0	1	45	38	18	18	19	45	R	R	6-3	200	7-5-70	1989	West Palm Beach, Fla.
Dishman, Glenn	4	8	5.01	19	16	0	0	97	104	60	54	34	43	L	L	6-1	195	11-5-70	1993	Fremont, Calif.
Elliott, Donnie	0	0	0.00	1	0	0	0	2	0	0	0	1	3	R	R	6-4	190	9-20-68	1988	Deer Park, Texas
Florie, Bryce	2	2	3.01	47	0	0	1	69	49	30	23	38	68	R	R	6-0	170	5-21-70	1988	Hanahan, S.C.
Hamilton, Joey	6	9	3.08	31	30	2	0	204	189	89	70	56	123	R	R	6-4	220	9-9-70	1991	Statesboro, Ga.
Hermanson, Dustin	3	1	6.82	26	0	0	0	32	35	26	24	22	19	R	R	6-3	195	12-21-72	1994	Springfield, Ohio
Hoffman, Trevor	7	4	3.88	55	0	0	31	53	48	25	23	14	52	R	R	6-0	195	10-13-67	1989	Williamsville, N.Y.
Kroon, Marc	0	1	10.80	2	0	0	0	2	1	2	2	2	2	S	R	6-2	175	4-2-73	1991	Phoenix, Ariz.
Krueger, Bill	0	0	7.04	6	0	0	0	8	13	6	6	4	6	L	L	6-5	205	4-24-58	1980	Seattle, Wash.
Mauser, Tim	0	1	9.53	5	0	0	0	6	4	6	6	9	9	R	R	6-0	185	10-4-66	1988	Fort Worth, Texas
Sanders, Scott	5	5	4.30	17	15	1	0	90	79	46	43	31	88	R	R	6-4	220	3-25-69	1990	Thibodaux, La.
Tabaka, Jeff	0	0	7.11	10	0	0	0	6	10	5	5	6	6	R	L	6-2	195	1-17-64	1986	Clinton, Ohio
Valenzuela, Fernando	8	3	4.98	29	15	0	0	90	101	53	50	34	57	L	L	5-11	202	11-1-60	1978	Los Angeles, Calif.
Villone, Ron	2	1	4.21	19	0	0	1	26	24	12	12	11	37	L	L	6-3	235	1-16-70	1992	Bergenfield, N.J.
Williams, Brian	3	10	6.00	44	6	0	0	72	79	54	48	38	75	R	R	6-2	195	2-15-69	1990	Cayce, S.C.
Worrell, Tim	1	0	4.73	9	0	0	0	13	16	7	7	6	13	R	R	6-4	215	7-5-67	1990	Arcadia, Calif.

FIELDING

Catcher	PCT	G	PO	A	E	DP	PB
Ausmus	.992	100	656	63	6	14	3
Johnson	.993	55	394	32	3	2	5

First Base	PCT	G	PO	A	E	DP
Ausmus	.000	1	0	0	0	0
Cianfrocco	1.000	30	76	7	0	7
Clark	1.000	2	7	0	0	1
Hyers	1.000	1	1	1	0	0
Johnson	.900	2	9	0	1	0
Livingstone	.991	43	297	17	3	25
Nieves	.917	2	11	0	1	1
Petagine	.996	51	262	22	1	21
Williams	.989	81	571	49	7	53

Second Base	PCT	G	PO	A	E	DP
Cianfrocco	1.000	3	7	6	0	1
Holbert	1.000	7	3	3	0	1
Livingstone	1.000	4	2	3	0	1
Reed	.994	130	364	362	4	79
Roberts	.981	25	37	68	2	11

Third Base	PCT	G	PO	A	E	DP
Caminiti	.936	143	102	295	27	28
Cedeno	.500	1	0	1	1	0

	PCT	G	PO	A	E	DP
Cianfrocco	.000	3	0	0	0	0
Livingstone	1.000	13	1	13	0	0

Shortstop	PCT	G	PO	A	E	DP
Cedeno	.965	116	139	304	16	58
Cianfrocco	.945	15	11	33	3	7
Holbert	.940	30	24	55	5	12
Reed	1.000	5	1	3	0	1
Roberts	.960	7	6	18	1	4

Outfield	PCT	G	PO	A	E	DP
Bean	.750	4	3	0	1	0
Cianfrocco	1.000	7	11	2	0	0
Clark	1.000	34	25	0	0	0
Finley	.977	138	291	8	7	0
Gwynn	.992	133	245	8	2	1
Holbert	.000	1	0	0	0	0
McDavid	1.000	7	5	0	0	0
Newfield	1.000	19	24	1	0	0
Nieves	.990	79	95	5	1	1
Petagine	1.000	2	1	0	0	0
Plantier	.958	39	64	5	3	1
Roberts	.989	50	92	2	1	0

Ken Caminiti

Outfielder Steve Finley led San Diego with 104 runs and 36 stolen bases

MORRIS FOSTOFF

Padres minor league Player of the Year Derrek Lee

MEL BAILEY

PADRES

FARM SYSTEM

Director of Minor League Operations: Priscilla Oppenheimer.

Class	Farm Team	League	W	L	Pct.	Finish*	Manager	First Yr
AAA	Las Vegas (Nev.) Stars	Pacific Coast	61	83	.424	9th (10)	Tim Flannery	1983
AA	Memphis (Tenn.) Chicks	Southern	68	74	.479	7th (10)	Jerry Royster	1995
#A	Rancho Cuca. (Calif.) Quakes	California	68	70	.493	7th (10)	Marty Barrett	1993
A	Clinton (Iowa) Lumber Kings	Midwest	51	86	.372	14th (14)	Ed Romero	1995
#R	Idaho Falls (Idaho) Braves	Pioneer	42	29	.592	3rd (8)	Mike Basso	1995
R	Peoria (Ariz.) Padres	Arizona	24	31	.436	4th (6)	Dan Norman	1988

*Finish in overall standings (No. of teams in league)   #Advanced level

ORGANIZATION LEADERS

MAJOR LEAGUERS

BATTING
*AVG	Tony Gwynn	.368
R	Steve Finley	104
H	Tony Gwynn	197
TB	Ken Caminiti	270
2B	Two tied at	33
3B	Steve Finley	8
HR	Ken Caminiti	26
RBI	Ken Caminiti	94
BB	Ken Caminiti	69
SO	Ken Caminiti	94
SB	Steve Finley	36

PITCHING
W	Andy Ashby	12
L	Two tied at	10
#ERA	Andy Ashby	2.94
G	Trevor Hoffman	55
CG	Two tied at	2
SV	Trevor Hoffman	31
IP	Joey Hamilton	204
BB	Andy Ashby	62
SO	Andy Ashby	150

GEORGE GOJKOVICH

Tony Gwynn. .368 average

MINOR LEAGUERS

BATTING
*AVG	Larry See, Rancho Cuca./Las Vegas	.330
R	Derrek Lee, Rancho Cuca./Memphis	82
H	Derrek Lee, Rancho Cuca./Memphis	152
TB	Derrek Lee, Rancho Cuca./Memphis	250
2B	Greg LaRocca, Rancho Cuca./Memphis	36
3B	Two tied at	8
HR	Derrek Lee, Rancho Cuca./Memphis	23
RBI	Derrek Lee, Rancho Cuca./Memphis	96
BB	Gordon Amerson, Idaho Falls/Clinton	74
SO	Stoney Briggs, Memphis	133
SB	Keith Thomas, Memphis	43

PITCHING
W	Heath Murray, Rancho Cuca./Memphis	14
L	Greg Keagle, Rancho Cuca./Mem./L.V.	15
#ERA	James Sak, Idaho Falls/Clinton	1.85
G	Two tied at	58
CG	Rob Mattson, Memphis	11
SV	Todd Schmitt, Memphis/Las Vegas	20
IP	Rob Mattson, Memphis	202
BB	Matt Clement, Idaho Falls/Rancho Cuca.	91
SO	Shane Dennis, Clinton/Rancho Cuca.	157

*Minimum 250 At-Bats   #Minimum 75 Innings

TOP 10 PROSPECTS

How the Padres Top 10 prospects, as judged by Baseball America prior to the 1995 season, fared in 1995:

MEL BAILEY

Dustin Hermanson

Player, Pos.	Club (Class—League)	AVG	AB	R	H	2B	3B	HR	RBI	SB
2. Raul Casanova, c	Memphis (AA—Southern)	.271	306	42	83	18	0	12	44	4
4. Derrek Lee, 1b	Rancho Cuca. (A—California)	.301	502	82	151	25	2	23	95	14
	Memphis (AA—Southern)	.111	9	0	1	0	0	0	1	0
5. Melvin Nieves, of	San Diego	.205	234	32	48	6	1	14	38	2
6. Homer Bush, 2b	Memphis (AA—Southern)	.280	432	53	121	12	5	5	37	34
7. Ray McDavid, of	AZL Padres (R—Arizona)	.464	28	13	13	2	1	1	6	3
	Las Vegas (AAA—Pacific Coast)	.271	166	28	45	8	1	5	27	7
	San Diego	.176	17	2	3	0	0	0	0	1
10. Julio Bruno, 3b	Memphis (AA—Southern)	.270	196	16	53	6	3	2	25	3
	Las Vegas (AAA—Pacific Coast)	.245	139	13	34	6	1	0	6	1

		W	L	ERA	G	SV	IP	H	BB	SO
1. Dustin Hermanson, rhp	Las Vegas (AAA—Pacific Coast)	0	1	3.50	31	11	36	35	29	42
	San Diego	3	1	6.82	26	0	32	35	22	19
3. Marc Kroon, rhp	Memphis (AA—Southern)	7	5	3.51	22	2	115	90	61	123
8. Bryce Florie, rhp	San Diego	2	2	3.01	47	1	69	49	38	68
9. Glenn Dishman, lhp	Las Vegas (AAA—Pacific Coast)	6	3	2.55	14	0	106	91	20	64
	San Diego	4	8	5.01	19	0	97	104	34	43

PACIFIC COAST LEAGUE

BATTING	AVG	G	AB	R	H	2B	3B	HR	RBI	BB	SO	SB	CS	B	T	HT	WT	DOB	1st-Yr	RESIDES
Bean, Billy	.290	119	445	67	129	34	2	15	77	46	55	2	2	L	L	6-1	185	5-11-64	1986	Hollywood, Calif.
Bream, Scott	.241	87	303	33	73	7	1	0	15	35	59	7	5	S	R	6-1	170	11-4-70	1989	Omaha, Neb.
Bruno, Julio	.245	38	139	13	34	6	1	0	6	8	24	1	3	R	R	5-11	190	10-15-72	1990	Puerta Plata, D.R.
Bullock, Eric	.263	84	190	32	50	4	1	4	25	12	22	6	0	L	L	5-11	185	2-16-60	1981	Carson, Calif.
Cianfrocco, Archi	.311	89	322	51	100	20	2	10	58	16	61	5	0	R	R	6-5	200	10-6-66	1987	Rome, N.Y.
Colbert, Craig	.249	74	241	30	60	8	1	1	24	21	44	1	0	R	R	6-0	214	2-13-65	1986	Pearland, Texas
Deer, Rob	.291	64	223	38	65	18	3	14	45	31	57	2	2	R	R	6-3	225	9-29-60	1978	Scottsdale, Ariz.
2-team (25 Van.)	.290	89	303	54	88	23	4	18	65	47	89	2	2							
Hall, Billy	.225	86	249	42	56	3	1	1	22	20	47	22	5	S	R	5-9	180	6-17-69	1991	Wichita, Kan.
Holbert, Ray	.115	9	26	3	3	1	0	0	3	5	10	1	1	R	R	6-0	165	9-25-70	1988	Moreno Valley, Calif.
Hyers, Tim	.290	82	259	46	75	12	1	1	23	24	33	0	3	L	L	6-1	180	10-3-71	1990	Covington, Ga.
McDavid, Ray	.271	52	166	28	45	8	1	5	27	30	35	7	1	L	R	6-3	195	7-20-71	1989	San Diego, Calif.
Mulligan, Sean	.274	101	339	34	93	20	1	7	43	27	61	0	0	R	R	6-2	205	4-25-70	1991	Diamond Bar, Calif.
Newfield, Marc	.343	20	70	10	24	5	1	3	12	3	11	2	0	R	R	6-4	205	10-19-72	1990	Huntington Beach, Calif.
2-team (53 Tacoma)	.295	73	268	40	79	16	1	8	42	12	41	3	0							
Petagine, Roberto	.214	19	56	8	12	2	1	1	5	13	17	1	0	L	L	6-1	172	6-7-71	1990	Nueva Esparta, Venez.
Roberts, Bip	.333	3	12	1	4	0	0	0	2	0	3	1	0	S	R	5-7	160	10-27-63	1982	San Diego, Calif.
Rossy, Rico	.301	98	316	44	95	11	2	1	45	55	36	3	7	R	R	5-10	175	2-16-64	1985	Bayamon, P.R.
Russo, Paul	.297	44	148	17	44	10	0	4	19	9	31	0	1	R	R	5-11	215	8-26-69	1990	Tampa, Fla.
See, Larry	.307	38	114	11	35	8	1	2	20	5	12	0	0	R	R	6-1	195	6-20-60	1980	Norwalk, Calif.
Smiley, Reuben	.219	34	96	10	21	4	1	3	17	8	19	6	3	L	L	6-4	185	8-27-68	1988	Los Angeles, Calif.
Smith, Ira	.325	59	209	39	68	19	5	3	22	13	25	5	4	R	R	5-11	185	8-4-67	1990	Chestertown, Md.
Snyder, Cory	.265	8	34	4	9	1	0	0	5	1	10	0	0	R	R	6-3	205	11-11-62	1985	Laguna Hills, Calif.
Springer, Steve	.218	35	87	7	19	3	0	1	10	2	17	1	1	R	R	6-0	190	2-11-61	1982	Huntington Beach, Calif.
Thurston, Jerrey	.200	5	20	2	4	1	0	0	0	0	5	0	0	R	R	6-4	200	4-17-72	1990	Longwood, Fla.
Vatcher, Jim	.292	101	356	56	104	31	3	7	43	33	46	3	4	R	R	5-9	172	5-27-65	1987	Pacific Palisades, Calif.
Velandia, Jorge	.242	66	206	25	54	12	3	0	25	13	37	0	0	R	R	5-9	160	1-12-75	1992	Caracas, Venez.

PITCHING	W	L	ERA	G	GS	CG	SV	IP	H	R	ER	BB	SO	B	T	HT	WT	DOB	1st Yr	Resides
Arvesen, Scott	0	0	15.00	2	0	0	0	3	4	5	5	2	0	R	R	6-6	210	7-15-68	1989	Orland Park, Ill.
Berumen, Andres	0	0	5.40	4	0	0	0	3	4	2	2	2	3	R	R	6-1	205	4-5-71	1989	Banning, Calif.
Bochtler, Doug	2	3	4.25	18	2	0	1	36	31	18	17	26	32	R	R	6-3	200	7-5-70	1990	West Palm Beach, Fla.
Cadaret, Greg	3	5	5.88	28	4	0	0	52	56	40	34	22	52	L	L	6-3	215	2-27-62	1983	Mesa, Ariz.
Cole, Victor	0	2	6.41	4	0	0	0	20	19	17	14	10	12	S	R	5-10	160	1-23-68	1988	Monterey, Calif.
Cromwell, Nate	0	0	13.50	9	3	0	0	15	35	27	23	14	11	L	L	6-1	185	8-23-68	1987	Las Vegas, Nev.
Dishman, Glenn	6	3	2.55	14	14	3	0	106	91	37	30	20	64	L	R	6-1	195	11-5-70	1993	Fremont, Calif.
Elliott, Donnie	1	0	4.50	7	0	0	1	8	8	4	4	4	2	R	R	6-4	190	9-20-68	1988	Deer Park, Texas
Ettles, Mark	0	0	7.82	10	0	0	0	13	21	11	11	3	10	R	R	6-0	178	10-30-66	1989	South Perth, Australia
Fesh, Sean	2	1	3.32	30	0	0	1	38	53	21	14	16	18	L	L	6-2	165	11-3-72	1991	Bethel, Conn.
2-team (10 Tucson)	3	1	2.81	40	0	0	1	51	64	23	16	19	25							
Harriger, Denny	9	9	4.07	29	28	7	0	177	187	94	80	60	97	R	R	5-11	185	7-21-69	1987	Ford City, Pa.
Hathaway, Hilly	4	6	6.22	14	14	1	0	64	76	49	44	27	37	L	L	6-4	195	9-12-69	1990	Jacksonville, Fla.
Hermanson, Dustin	0	1	3.50	31	0	0	11	36	35	23	14	29	42	R	R	6-3	195	12-21-72	1994	Springfield, Ohio
Hernandez, Fernando	1	6	7.65	8	8	0	0	38	43	32	32	31	40	R	R	6-2	185	6-16-71	1990	Santiago, D.R.
Keagle, Greg	7	6	4.28	14	13	0	0	76	76	47	36	42	49	R	R	6-2	185	6-28-71	1993	Horseheads, N.Y.
Loiselle, Rich	2	2	7.24	8	7	1	0	27	36	27	22	9	16	R	R	6-5	225	1-12-72	1991	Oshkosh, Wisc.
Long, Joey	1	3	4.60	25	0	0	0	31	38	22	16	16	13	R	L	6-2	215	7-15-70	1991	Rosewood, Ohio
Martinez, Jose	6	10	4.75	27	25	2	0	152	156	86	80	44	64	R	R	6-2	155	4-1-71	1989	Santiago, D.R.
Mauser, Tim	3	4	4.80	35	0	0	0	51	63	39	27	20	32	R	R	6-0	185	10-4-66	1988	Fort Worth, Texas
McFarlin, Terric	7	6	3.96	58	2	0	7	123	120	67	54	59	85	S	R	6-0	160	4-6-69	1991	Brooklyn, N.Y.
Merriman, Brett	2	2	8.25	11	0	0	0	12	14	12	11	12	7	R	R	6-2	180	7-15-66	1988	Chandler, Ariz.
Plantenberg, Erik	0	0	81.00	2	0	0	0	0	3	3	3	0	1	S	L	6-1	180	10-30-68	1990	Bellevue, Wash.
Sanders, Scott	0	0	0.00	1	1	0	0	3	3	0	0	1	2	R	R	6-4	220	3-25-69	1990	Thibodaux, La.
Schmitt, Todd	0	2	7.82	12	0	0	2	13	16	11	11	9	6	R	R	6-2	170	2-12-70	1992	Clinton Township, Mich.
Tabaka, Jeff	0	1	1.99	19	0	0	6	23	16	6	5	14	27	R	L	6-2	195	1-17-64	1986	Clinton, Ohio
Taylor, Kerry	2	2	4.38	8	8	0	0	37	44	21	18	21	21	R	R	6-3	200	1-25-71	1989	Roseau, Minn.
Weber, Weston	3	4	4.81	9	8	1	0	49	59	37	26	9	32	R	R	6-0	175	1-5-64	1986	Dodge Center, Minn.
2-team (20 Tacoma)	6	11	4.67	29	21	2	0	150	170	92	78	50	86							
Worrell, Tim	0	2	6.00	10	3	0	0	24	27	21	16	17	18	R	R	6-4	215	7-5-67	1990	Arcadia, Calif.

FIELDING

Catcher	PCT	G	PO	A	E	DP	PB
Cianfrocco	1.000	1	1	0	0	0	0
Colbert	.985	69	343	42	6	4	8
Mulligan	.987	82	439	33	6	5	11
Thurston	.976	5	36	4	1	0	1

First Base	PCT	G	PO	A	E	DP
Bean	1.000	9	77	3	0	8
Bullock	.667	1	2	0	1	0
Cianfrocco	.985	42	371	35	6	33
Colbert	.857	2	6	0	1	0
Deer	.976	12	73	9	2	6
Hyers	.998	54	450	24	1	40
Newfield	1.000	1	10	1	0	1
Petagine	.975	14	110	7	3	13
See	.995	24	195	15	1	18
Springer	1.000	3	32	3	0	2

Second Base	PCT	G	PO	A	E	DP
Bream	.975	65	134	177	8	42

	PCT	G	PO	A	E	DP
Hall	.928	69	108	149	20	32
Holbert	.972	9	9	26	1	5
Roberts	1.000	1	0	2	0	0
Rossy	.973	14	30	43	2	12

Third Base	PCT	G	PO	A	E	DP
Bruno	.925	38	25	99	10	10
Cianfrocco	.880	31	17	64	11	3
Colbert	.000	1	0	0	0	0
Rossy	.894	27	20	56	9	3
Russo	.960	43	30	91	5	10
Smith	.000	1	0	0	0	0
Snyder	.600	2	1	2	2	0
Springer	.957	9	6	16	1	1

Shortstop	PCT	G	PO	A	E	DP
Bream	.967	24	26	63	3	11
Roberts	.938	3	2	13	1	1
Rossy	.951	58	88	205	15	34

	PCT	G	PO	A	E	DP
Springer	.920	4	4	19	2	3
Velandia	.903	66	97	190	31	39

Outfield	PCT	G	PO	A	E	DP
Bean	.983	110	219	6	4	2
Bream	.000	1	0	0	0	0
Bullock	.959	35	46	1	2	0
Cianfrocco	1.000	14	23	1	0	0
Colbert	1.000	2	3	1	0	0
Deer	.971	40	66	0	2	0
Hall	.000	1	0	0	0	0
Hyers	.953	23	40	1	2	0
McDavid	1.000	49	134	0	0	0
Newfield	.978	19	44	1	1	0
Smiley	.933	26	41	1	3	0
Smith	.957	54	87	3	4	1
Snyder	1.000	6	8	1	0	0
Springer	.800	3	4	0	1	0
Vatcher	.994	95	164	8	1	3

SOUTHERN LEAGUE

BATTING	AVG	G	AB	R	H	2B	3B	HR	RBI	BB	SO	SB	CS	B	T	HT	WT	DOB	1st Yr	Resides
Alvarez, Gabe	.556	2	9	0	5	1	0	0	4	1	1	0	0	R	R	6-1	185	3-6-74	1995	El Monte, Calif.
Briggs, Stoney	.247	118	385	60	95	14	7	8	46	40	133	17	8	R	R	6-3	215	12-26-71	1991	Seaford, Del.
Bruno, Julio	.270	59	196	16	53	6	3	2	25	8	35	3	2	R	R	5-11	190	10-15-72	1990	Puerta Plata, D.R.
Bush, Homer	.280	108	432	53	121	12	5	5	37	15	83	34	12	R	R	5-11	180	11-11-72	1991	East St. Louis, Ill.
Casanova, Raul	.271	89	306	42	83	18	0	12	44	25	51	4	1	R	R	6-0	192	8-24-72	1990	Ponce, P.R.
Cotton, John	.253	121	407	60	103	19	8	12	47	38	101	15	6	L	R	6-0	170	10-30-70	1989	Huntsville, Texas
Davis, Josh	.500	1	2	0	1	0	0	0	0	1	1	0	0	R	R	6-0	180	6-13-76	1994	Locust Grove, Okla.
DeLeon, Roberto	.267	73	236	24	63	10	0	7	34	12	32	2	2	R	R	5-10	188	3-29-71	1992	Missouri City, Texas
Dotel, Mariano	.280	8	25	7	7	2	0	0	5	2	10	0	1	S	R	6-2	160	4-3-71	1989	San Pedro de Macoris, D.R.
Drinkwater, Sean	.240	102	287	29	69	12	1	6	26	26	49	3	4	R	R	6-3	195	6-22-71	1992	El Toro, Calif.
Gennaro, Brad	.267	104	397	46	106	19	1	5	60	21	62	11	8	L	L	6-1	175	8-2-71	1992	La Mesa, Calif.
Harley, Quentin	.245	50	159	21	39	5	3	3	14	13	34	7	1	S	R	5-11	165	11-11-71	1990	Eugene, Ore.
Johnson, Earl	.200	2	10	0	2	0	0	0	0	1	0	0	1	S	R	5-9	163	10-3-71	1991	Detroit, Mich.
Killeen, Tim	.235	77	230	27	54	14	0	9	40	27	71	2	0	L	R	6-0	195	7-26-70	1992	Phoenix, Ariz.
LaRocca, Greg	.143	2	7	0	1	0	0	0	0	0	1	0	1	R	R	5-11	185	11-10-72	1994	Bedford, N.H.
Lee, Derrek	.111	2	9	0	1	0	0	0	1	0	2	0	0	R	R	6-5	220	9-6-75	1993	Folsom, Calif.
Mack, Quinn	.238	20	63	6	15	1	0	2	6	8	8	2	1	L	L	5-10	180	9-11-65	1987	Cerritos, Calif.
Russo, Paul	.311	45	122	19	38	9	1	6	18	22	33	1	0	R	R	5-11	215	8-26-69	1990	Tampa, Fla.
Schwenke, Matt	.242	23	62	7	15	3	0	0	4	3	16	0	0	R	R	6-2	210	8-12-72	1993	Poway, Calif.
Smith, Ira	.303	64	238	40	72	13	3	5	36	23	32	11	4	R	R	5-11	185	8-4-67	1990	Chestertown, Md.
Thomas, Keith	.253	109	356	60	90	13	4	10	33	20	85	43	11	S	R	6-1	180	9-12-68	1986	Chicago, Ill.
Thompson, Jason	.272	137	475	62	129	20	1	20	64	62	131	7	3	L	L	6-4	200	6-13-71	1993	Laguna Hills, Calif.
Tredaway, Chad	.267	10	30	5	8	1	0	0	4	3	5	1	0	S	R	6-0	180	6-18-72	1992	Edinburg, Texas
Triessl, Mike	.167	4	6	0	1	0	0	0	0	0	0	0	0	R	R	6-1	215	2-27-71	1993	Malverne, N.Y.
Velandia, Jorge	.204	63	186	23	38	10	2	4	17	14	37	0	2	R	R	5-9	160	1-12-75	1992	Caracas, Venez.

PITCHING	W	L	ERA	G	GS	CG	SV	IP	H	R	ER	BB	SO	B	T	HT	WT	DOB	1st Yr	Resides
Baker, Jared	1	0	14.73	4	0	0	0	7	10	12	12	8	6	L	R	6-5	220	3-25-71	1992	Goose Creek, S.C.
Barnes, Jon	0	1	3.24	2	1	0	0	8	9	3	3	2	4	R	R	6-1	197	4-11-73	1991	Lancaster, S.C.
Beckett, Robbie	3	4	4.80	36	8	2	0	86	65	57	46	73	98	R	L	6-1	235	7-16-72	1990	Austin, Texas
Clark, Dera	2	2	2.39	23	0	0	5	26	18	7	7	14	29	R	R	6-1	204	4-14-65	1987	Lindsay, Texas
Cole, Victor	1	0	1.35	8	2	0	0	20	15	5	3	8	17	S	R	5-10	160	1-23-68	1988	Monterey, Calif.
Freitas, Mike	0	6	3.66	54	0	0	2	59	55	26	24	26	36	R	R	6-1	160	9-22-69	1989	Sacramento, Calif.
Hanson, Craig	0	3	6.43	25	3	0	1	49	64	36	35	39	33	R	R	6-3	190	9-30-70	1991	Roseville, Minn.
Harrison, Brian	2	1	3.25	38	0	0	0	36	32	21	13	33	29	L	L	6-1	190	11-26-66	1986	Oxnard, Calif.
Hernandez, Fernando	4	6	5.16	12	12	0	0	66	72	46	38	42	74	R	R	6-2	185	6-16-71	1990	Santiago, D.R.
Huber, Jeff	0	0	11.57	5	0	0	0	5	7	6	6	0	6	R	L	6-4	220	12-17-70	1990	Scottsdale, Ariz.
Kaufman, Brad	11	10	5.76	27	27	0	0	148	142	112	95	90	119	R	R	6-2	210	4-26-72	1993	Traer, Iowa
Keagle, Greg	4	9	5.11	15	15	1	0	81	82	52	46	41	82	R	R	6-2	185	6-28-71	1993	Horseheads, N.Y.
Kroon, Marc	7	5	3.51	22	19	0	2	115	90	49	45	61	123	S	R	6-2	175	4-2-73	1991	Phoenix, Ariz.
Loiselle, Rich	6	3	3.55	13	13	1	0	79	82	46	31	33	48	R	R	6-5	225	1-12-72	1991	Oshkosh, Wisc.
Long, Joey	0	2	3.32	25	0	0	0	22	28	15	8	10	18	R	L	6-2	215	7-15-70	1991	Rosewood, Ohio
Mattson, Rob	12	13	4.11	30	28	11	0	202	199	109	92	73	139	L	R	6-1	190	11-18-66	1991	Palm Beach Gardens, Fla.
Murray, Heath	5	4	3.38	14	14	0	0	77	83	36	29	42	71	L	L	6-4	205	4-19-73	1994	Troy, Ohio
Plantenberg, Erik	2	0	1.66	20	0	0	2	22	19	4	4	2	16	S	L	6-1	180	10-30-68	1990	Bellevue, Wash.
Schmitt, Todd	0	0	1.30	26	0	0	18	28	18	4	4	11	27	R	R	6-2	170	2-12-70	1992	Clinton Township, Mich.
Thomas, Carlos	1	1	10.13	11	0	0	0	13	15	16	15	14	10	R	R	6-4	215	8-6-68	1991	Memphis, Tenn.
2-team (7 Huntsville)	3	3	7.62	18	0	0	0	26	28	24	22	19	24							
Veras, Dario	7	3	3.81	58	0	0	1	83	81	38	35	27	70	R	R	6-2	165	3-13-73	1991	Villa Vasquez, D.R.

FIELDING

Catcher	PCT	G	PO	A	E	DP	PB
Casanova	.980	75	531	55	12	6	12
Davis	1.000	1	6	0	0	0	0
Killeen	.985	59	408	55	7	5	11
Schwenke	.972	20	130	8	4	1	4
Triessl	.889	3	8	0	1	0	0

First Base	PCT	G	PO	A	E	DP
Cotton	1.000	1	2	0	0	1
DeLeon	1.000	1	1	0	0	1
Drinkwater	.982	10	50	4	1	2
Killeen	1.000	1	1	0	0	0
Lee	1.000	2	16	3	0	1
Russo	1.000	1	12	2	0	0
Thompson	.994	135	1044	88	7	102

Second Base	PCT	G	PO	A	E	DP
Alvarez	.833	2	0	5	1	1
Bush	.969	106	235	268	16	69
Cotton	.800	2	3	1	1	1

	PCT	G	PO	A	E	DP
DeLeon	1.000	3	2	3	0	1
Drinkwater	.974	6	13	24	1	4
Harley	.970	26	41	55	3	9
Tredaway	.929	7	10	16	2	4

Third Base	PCT	G	PO	A	E	DP
Briggs	.000	1	0	0	0	0
Bruno	.934	52	32	109	10	15
Cotton	1.000	1	0	0	0	0
DeLeon	.875	7	1	6	1	0
Drinkwater	.963	62	44	113	6	17
Harley	.737	7	4	10	5	2
Russo	.961	35	20	53	3	3
Thomas	.000	1	0	0	0	0
Tredaway	1.000	2	0	1	0	0

Shortstop	PCT	G	PO	A	E	DP
Alvarez	1.000	1	0	1	0	0
Cotton	.941	24	30	34	4	7

	PCT	G	PO	A	E	DP
DeLeon	.941	54	73	134	13	19
Dotel	1.000	8	9	19	0	4
Drinkwater	.935	14	18	25	3	4
Harley	1.000	1	0	2	0	0
LaRocca	.889	2	6	2	1	1
Velandia	.952	60	88	152	12	29

Outfield	PCT	G	PO	A	E	DP
Briggs	.959	89	136	6	6	1
Cotton	.969	90	178	10	6	1
Drinkwater	1.000	2	2	0	0	0
Gennaro	.984	102	172	10	3	1
Harley	1.000	5	7	0	0	0
Johnson	.800	2	4	0	1	0
Kaufman	.000	1	0	0	0	0
Mack	1.000	16	33	0	0	0
Smith	.972	59	98	5	3	1
Thomas	.982	88	160	7	3	1

CALIFORNIA LEAGUE

BATTING	AVG	G	AB	R	H	2B	3B	HR	RBI	BB	SO	SB	CS	B	T	HT	WT	DOB	1st Yr	Resides
Alvarez, Gabe	.344	59	212	41	73	17	2	6	36	29	30	1	0	R	R	6-1	185	3-6-74	1995	El Monte, Calif.
Conway, Jeff	.254	28	67	9	17	1	0	0	5	4	10	1	1	L	L	6-1	188	12-20-72	1994	Carrollton, Texas
Corps, Erick	.191	73	183	21	35	6	0	1	13	22	54	1	1	S	R	6-0	180	9-6-74	1992	Carolina, P.R.
Cuevas, Eduardo	.243	43	140	14	34	5	2	1	24	7	16	5	1	R	R	5-10	155	12-1-73	1992	Santo Domingo, D.R.
Derotal, Francisco	.196	29	56	9	11	2	0	2	5	3	20	1	0	R	R	5-11	180	4-15-74	1993	Puerto Cabello, Venez.
Grass, Darren	.241	23	58	6	14	6	0	1	9	2	15	0	0	R	R	6-2	220	9-6-71	1994	St. Paul, Minn.

MORRIS FOSTOFF

DAN ARNOLD

Padres Pitchers. San Diego posted a 70-74 record in the National League West as Andy Ashby, left, led starters with 12 wins, and Trevor Hoffman had a team-high 31 saves.

BATTING	AVG	G	AB	R	H	2B	3B	HR	RBI	BB	SO	SB	CS	B	T	HT	WT	DOB	1st Yr	Resides
Johnson, Earl	.293	81	341	51	100	11	3	0	25	25	51	34	12	S	R	5-9	163	10-3-71	1991	Detroit, Mich.
Koscielniak, Dwain	.222	7	9	1	2	0	0	1	2	3	2	0	0	R	R	5-10	205	5-16-73	1994	Gaylord, Mich.
LaRocca, Greg	.322	125	466	77	150	36	5	8	74	44	77	15	4	R	R	5-11	185	11-10-72	1994	Bedford, N.H.
Lee, Derrek	.301	128	502	82	151	25	2	23	95	49	130	14	7	R	R	6-5	220	9-6-75	1993	Folsom, Calif.
Marnell, Anthony	.043	16	23	3	1	0	0	0	1	1	13	0	0	R	R	6-1	200	1-2-74	1995	Las Vegas, Nev.
McKinnis, Leroy	.245	15	49	9	12	1	0	1	6	10	10	1	0	R	R	6-1	185	11-14-72	1993	Madison, Ala.
Moore, Vince	.227	84	299	50	68	11	1	15	57	35	102	10	5	L	L	6-1	190	9-22-71	1991	Houston, Texas
Mowry, Dave	.239	50	142	19	34	10	0	3	23	21	38	0	0	L	L	6-3	225	10-22-71	1990	Long Beach, Calif.
Prieto, Chris	.273	114	366	80	100	12	6	2	35	64	55	39	14	L	L	5-10	170	8-24-72	1993	Carmel, Calif.
Rivera, Santiago	.215	61	130	11	28	5	1	0	10	13	36	2	0	S	R	5-11	180	12-15-72	1993	Rio Piedras, P.R.
Roberts, Bip	.000	1	3	1	0	0	0	0	0	1	1	1	0	S	R	5-7	160	10-27-63	1982	San Diego, Calif.
Roberts, John	.278	98	327	59	91	16	3	6	51	44	86	27	8	R	R	5-9	185	9-30-73	1991	Pine Bluff, Ark.
Schwenke, Matt	.179	22	56	7	10	2	0	0	7	2	20	0	0	R	R	6-2	210	8-12-72	1993	Poway, Calif.
See, Larry	.345	49	171	34	59	10	0	14	50	14	31	0	2	R	R	6-1	195	6-20-60	1980	Norwalk, Calif.
Tena, Dario	.172	11	29	1	5	1	0	0	0	3	4	2	1	S	R	5-10	160	12-19-72	1990	San Cristobal, D.R.
Thurston, Jerrey	.220	76	200	24	44	9	0	1	13	21	64	1	0	R	R	6-4	200	4-17-72	1990	Longwood, Fla.
Tredaway, Chad	.277	109	408	53	113	17	2	6	57	29	43	4	2	S	R	6-0	180	6-18-72	1992	Edinburg, Texas
Triessl, Mike	.254	49	138	13	35	8	0	0	20	5	32	1	0	R	R	6-1	215	2-27-71	1993	Malverne, N.Y.
2-team (22 River.)	.292	71	212	28	62	10	0	3	34	17	47	1	0							
Woodridge, Dickie	.282	116	358	67	101	9	3	3	58	71	40	9	4	L	R	5-9	180	1-24-71	1993	Jordan, N.Y.

GAMES BY POSITION: C—Grass 21, Marnell 16, McKinnis 10, Schwenke 22, See 1, Thurston 75, Triessl 29. **1B**—Lee 121, Mowry 8, Rivera 1, See 11, Triessl 4. **2B**—Corps 15, Cuevas 14, LaRocca 24, Rivera 1, Tredaway 4, Woodridge 97. **3B**—Alvarez 9, Corps 9, Koscielniak 4, LaRocca 11, Rivera 24, Thurston 1, Tredaway 97. **SS**—Alvarez 43, Corps 6, LaRocca 87, Rivera 15. **OF**—Conway 25, Corps 34, Cuevas 2, Derotal 27, Johnson 81, Moore 84, Mowry 1, Prieto 89, Rivera 9, J. Roberts 95, Tena 11, Woodridge 4.

PITCHING	W	L	ERA	G	GS	CG	SV	IP	H	R	ER	BB	SO	B	T	HT	WT	DOB	1st Yr	Resides
Arroyo, Luis	7	10	5.25	26	24	0	0	129	158	97	75	62	102	L	L	6-0	175	9-29-73	1992	Arecibo, P.R.
Baker, Jared	7	2	4.44	31	15	1	1	101	98	57	50	49	98	L	R	6-5	220	3-25-71	1992	Goose Creek, S.C.
Barnes, Jon	0	0	1.69	5	1	0	0	11	6	3	2	2	10	R	R	6-1	197	4-11-73	1991	Lancaster, S.C.
Baron, Jimmy	0	0	16.88	3	0	0	0	3	7	8	5	6	3	L	L	6-3	230	2-22-74	1992	Humble, Texas
Barrett, Mark	1	0	3.58	32	0	0	1	33	39	18	13	11	29	L	L	6-1	215	9-24-71	1994	Bowie, Md.
Berumen, Andres	0	0	2.45	4	0	0	1	7	6	2	2	1	11	R	R	6-1	205	4-5-71	1989	Banning, Calif.
Clement, Matt	3	4	4.24	12	12	0	0	57	61	37	27	49	33	R	R	6-3	190	8-12-74	1994	Butler, Pa.
Cromwell, Nate	0	1	3.52	4	4	0	0	15	15	7	6	6	14	L	L	6-1	185	8-23-68	1987	Las Vegas, Nev.
Dennis, Shane	8	2	2.51	11	11	2	0	79	63	27	22	22	77	R	L	6-3	200	7-3-71	1994	Uniontown, Kan.
Dixon, Bubba	10	7	3.24	47	12	2	5	142	118	61	51	46	133	L	L	5-10	165	1-7-72	1994	Lucedale, Miss.
Drewien, Dan	1	2	6.35	17	0	0	1	28	30	20	20	11	26	R	R	6-1	185	8-29-72	1993	San Diego, Calif.
Erdos, Todd	0	0	13.50	1	0	0	0	3	5	4	4	0	4	R	R	6-1	185	11-21-73	1992	Meadville, Pa.
Ettles, Mark	0	0	6.35	3	0	0	0	6	7	5	4	1	7	R	R	6-0	178	10-30-66	1989	South Perth, Australia
Garrett, Hal	0	4	2.79	23	1	0	0	42	40	21	13	25	43	R	R	6-1	160	4-27-75	1993	Mt. Juliet, Tenn.
Gates, Sean	0	0	0.00	1	0	0	0	3	1	0	0	2	0	R	R	5-10	185	4-6-72	1994	Hammond, La.
Hanson, Craig	3	4	6.14	9	9	0	0	37	43	29	25	19	31	R	R	6-3	190	9-30-70	1991	Roseville, Minn.
Hathaway, Hilly	0	1	3.46	3	3	0	0	13	11	6	5	4	10	L	L	6-4	195	9-12-69	1990	Jacksonville, Fla.
Hermanson, Mike	4	6	5.67	42	0	0	0	75	69	52	47	49	74	R	R	6-3	195	11-26-71	1992	Chicago, Ill.

PITCHING	W	L	ERA	G	GS	CG	SV	IP	H	R	ER	BB	SO	B	T	HT	WT	DOB	1st Yr	Resides
Isom, Jeff	1	0	9.00	4	0	0	0	4	6	4	4	0	2	L	L	6-0	185	9-22-72	1993	West Lafayette, Ind.
Keagle, Greg	0	0	4.50	2	2	0	0	14	14	9	7	2	11	R	R	6-2	185	6-28-71	1993	Horseheads, N.Y.
LaChappa, Matt	11	7	5.56	28	28	1	0	154	163	103	95	88	106	L	L	6-2	175	6-29-75	1993	Lakeside, Calif.
Murray, Heath	9	4	3.12	14	14	4	0	92	80	37	32	38	81	L	L	6-4	205	4-19-73	1994	Troy, Ohio
Schlutt, Jason	0	1	4.91	11	0	0	2	15	16	9	8	4	11	R	L	6-0	190	1-21-72	1993	Baroda, Mich.
White, Darell	0	5	6.22	42	0	0	0	59	69	49	41	43	49	R	R	6-2	200	4-16-72	1992	Alexandria, La.
Whitman, Ryan	1	2	4.96	14	0	0	0	16	23	13	9	7	13	R	R	6-3	210	1-7-72	1990	Lake Park, Fla.
Wolff, Bryan	2	7	3.32	54	0	0	18	57	39	23	21	54	77	R	R	6-1	195	3-16-72	1993	St. Louis, Mo.
Worrell, Tim	0	2	5.16	9	3	0	1	23	25	17	13	6	17	R	R	6-4	215	7-5-67	1990	Arcadia, Calif.

CLINTON   A

MIDWEST LEAGUE

BATTING	AVG	G	AB	R	H	2B	3B	HR	RBI	BB	SO	SB	CS	B	T	HT	WT	DOB	1st Yr	Resides
Allen, Dusty	.266	36	139	25	37	12	1	5	31	12	29	1	0	R	R	6-4	215	8-9-72	1995	Oklahoma City, Okla.
Amerson, Gordon	.157	48	134	15	21	2	0	1	8	35	41	5	5	L	L	6-1	185	10-10-76	1994	San Bernardino, Calif.
Carmona, Cesarin	.178	42	129	13	23	2	1	0	5	15	35	10	7	S	R	5-11	180	12-20-76	1994	Palla Bani, D.R.
Cuevas, Eduardo	.259	69	263	39	68	11	1	2	31	9	31	17	3	R	R	5-10	155	12-1-73	1992	Santo Domingo, D.R.
Davis, Josh	.200	8	15	2	3	0	0	0	2	1	5	1	0	R	R	6-0	180	6-13-76	1994	Locust Grove, Okla.
DeLeon, Raymond	.267	9	30	3	8	1	0	0	4	2	3	0	1	L	L	6-4	235	3-19-70	1994	Missouri City, Texas
Ebbert, Chad	.000	2	5	0	0	0	0	0	0	0	1	0	0	R	R	6-4	225	10-1-73	1994	Lake Mary, Fla.
Espinal, Juan	.208	116	336	28	70	11	0	7	46	47	79	3	3	R	R	6-0	185	4-15-75	1992	La Vega, D.R.
Johnson, Jay	.118	8	17	0	2	0	0	0	0	1	3	0	1	R	R	5-11	160	6-25-73	1994	Highland, Calif.
Jones, Ken	.184	31	76	8	14	2	0	0	7	6	20	1	0	R	R	5-11	185	10-26-71	1995	Auburn, Ind.
Keefe, Jamie	.240	67	175	28	42	3	1	1	10	23	42	12	3	R	R	5-11	180	8-2-73	1992	Rochester, N.H.
Lowry, Curt	.214	57	182	33	39	1	2	0	16	26	51	7	6	R	R	6-0	170	9-22-72	1995	Paris, Texas
Martin, Mike	.189	51	127	10	24	3	0	0	14	24	24	2	0	L	R	6-1	175	2-19-73	1995	Tallahassee, Fla.
Martinez, Erik	.102	29	59	4	6	0	0	0	2	3	10	2	0	R	R	5-9	162	12-11-71	1994	North Hollywood, Calif.
Matthews, Gary	.238	128	421	57	100	18	4	2	40	68	109	28	8	S	R	6-3	185	8-25-74	1994	Canoga Park, Calif.
Melo, Juan	.282	134	479	65	135	32	1	5	46	33	88	12	10	S	R	6-3	185	11-5-76	1994	Bani, D.R.
Root, Mitch	.275	89	309	37	85	20	1	3	42	37	52	3	1	R	R	6-3	185	10-26-73	1991	Chatsworth, Calif.
Sanchez, Marcos	.111	6	18	0	2	1	0	0	0	1	6	0	0	S	R	6-0	190	9-25-74	1992	Santo Domingo, D.R.
Schwenke, Matt	.190	36	100	3	19	5	1	1	8	2	34	0	0	R	R	6-2	210	8-12-72	1993	Poway, Calif.
Tena, Dario	.183	99	295	30	54	6	0	0	19	25	41	33	10	S	R	5-10	160	12-19-72	1990	San Cristobal, D.R.
Totman, Jason	.288	61	229	32	66	19	3	0	32	26	27	6	1	R	R	5-9	175	11-3-72	1995	McPherson, Kan.
Tyrus, Jason	.226	65	159	15	36	5	1	2	17	10	53	4	5	R	R	6-2	200	6-6-72	1994	Milpitas, Calif.
Ullan, Dave	.208	43	96	8	20	1	0	1	11	20	16	0	2	R	R	6-1	195	8-7-72	1994	La Grande, Ore.
Winget, Jeremy	.269	120	375	49	101	30	2	5	44	67	75	4	4	L	L	6-1	212	6-5-73	1991	Murray, Utah
Wulfert, Mark	.245	48	147	17	36	10	1	1	16	17	34	9	2	R	R	5-11	175	8-20-72	1995	Farmington, N.M.

GAMES BY POSITION: C—Davis 8, Ebbert 2, Jones 31, Martin 50, Sanchez 6, Schwenke 31, Ullan 37, Winget 1. **1B**—Allen 23, DeLeon 3, Martin 1, Root 56, Schwenke 6, Winget 60. **2B**—Carmona 36, Cuevas 6, Keefe 40, Martinez 8, Root 1, Totman 57. **3B**—Cuevas 30, Espinal 107, Keefe 4, Martinez 2, Root 2. **SS**—Keefe 9, Martinez 7, Melo 132. **OF**—Allen 18, Amerson 47, Johnson 7, Keefe 2, Lowry 56, Martinez 7, Matthews 127, Tena 90, Tyrus 53, Wulfert 46.

PITCHING	W	L	ERA	G	GS	CG	SV	IP	H	R	ER	BB	SO	B	T	HT	WT	DOB	1st Yr	Resides
Baron, Jimmy	0	8	6.22	11	9	1	0	51	65	42	35	16	31	L	L	6-3	230	2-22-74	1992	Humble, Texas
Davis, Keith	2	5	5.22	36	8	0	2	71	64	41	41	45	54	R	R	6-1	195	11-1-72	1994	Vacherie, La.
Dennis, Shane	3	9	3.87	14	14	3	0	86	68	51	37	35	80	R	L	6-3	200	7-3-71	1994	Uniontown, Kan.
Erdos, Todd	0	0	5.40	5	1	0	0	5	4	3	3	1	6	R	R	6-1	185	11-21-73	1992	Meadville, Pa.
Garrett, Hal	3	8	5.59	11	11	1	0	58	58	43	36	34	41	R	R	6-1	160	4-27-75	1993	Mt. Juliet, Tenn.
Gates, Sean	0	2	4.99	29	0	0	1	40	39	23	22	19	27	R	R	5-10	185	4-6-72	1994	Hammond, La.
Hammerschmidt, Andy	5	5	3.87	14	14	1	0	86	89	40	37	18	51	L	L	6-1	220	6-21-72	1995	New Ulm, Minn.
Isom, Jeff	8	8	3.40	35	15	2	2	116	123	56	44	42	94	L	L	6-0	185	9-22-72	1993	West Lafayette, Ind.
Jenkins, A.J.	1	12	6.60	33	13	2	0	91	109	80	67	55	54	R	R	6-2	195	12-13-71	1994	Palestine, Texas
Leach, Jarman	1	3	3.71	19	0	0	0	27	30	17	11	7	12	L	L	6-1	195	11-7-72	1994	Novato, Calif.
Logan, Chris	4	6	2.18	53	0	0	17	62	62	29	15	27	61	R	R	6-1	185	11-10-70	1994	Hattiesburg, Miss.
Martinez, Uriel	0	0	5.19	11	0	0	0	17	27	15	10	3	8	R	R	6-1	180	10-22-74	1995	Mexico City, Mexico
Mix, Derek	1	0	5.14	35	0	0	1	49	34	42	28	54	48	R	R	6-4	220	5-11-74	1993	Moreno Valley, Calif.
Newman, Eric	1	7	7.65	11	10	1	0	42	52	41	36	38	31	R	R	6-4	220	8-27-72	1995	Fremont, Calif.
Perez, Jayson	0	1	6.53	13	1	0	0	21	31	28	15	15	17	R	R	6-2	152	6-27-74	1992	Mayaguez, P.R.
Sak, James	6	1	1.98	7	7	3	0	50	42	12	11	13	44	R	R	6-1	195	8-18-73	1995	Chicago, Ill.
Thomas, Carlos	2	0	2.45	13	0	0	1	18	19	9	5	10	14	R	R	6-4	215	8-6-68	1991	Memphis, Tenn.
Torres, Luis	0	0	13.50	3	0	0	0	2	5	3	3	5	1	R	R	6-2	228	1-13-76	1994	Manati, P.R.
Van De Weg, Ryan	6	4	4.15	15	15	1	0	91	92	56	42	32	89	R	R	6-0	180	2-24-74	1995	West Olive, Mich.
Walters, Brett	8	7	2.71	32	19	4	1	146	133	58	44	27	122	R	R	6-0	185	9-30-74	1994	Bateman, Australia

IDAHO FALLS   R

PIONEER LEAGUE

BATTING	AVG	G	AB	R	H	2B	3B	HR	RBI	BB	SO	SB	CS	B	T	HT	WT	DOB	1st Yr	Resides
Abernathy, George	.293	63	256	52	75	12	5	9	45	26	64	6	4	L	R	5-11	200	10-13-73	1995	Jackson, Tenn.
Allen, Dusty	.327	29	104	21	34	7	0	4	24	21	19	1	2	R	R	6-4	215	8-9-72	1995	Oklahoma City, Okla.
Amerson, Gordon	.305	46	167	40	51	16	5	1	22	39	33	8	7	L	L	6-1	185	10-10-76	1995	San Bernardino, Calif.
Bucci, Carmen	.186	50	113	22	21	2	0	0	7	14	32	7	2	R	R	5-11	180	3-29-73	1995	Oak Forest, Ill.
Davis, Ben	.279	52	197	36	55	8	3	5	46	17	36	0	0	S	R	6-4	195	3-10-77	1995	Aston, Pa.
Davis, Josh	.222	4	18	3	4	1	0	0	1	1	2	0	0	R	R	6-0	180	6-13-76	1994	Locust Grove, Okla.
Ebbert, Chad	.333	1	3	0	1	0	0	0	0	0	1	0	0	R	R	6-4	225	10-1-73	1994	Lake Mary, Fla.
Gama, Rick	.320	70	266	71	85	16	2	8	58	55	29	17	4	R	R	5-10	170	4-27-73	1995	Mexico City, Mexico
Hills, Rich	.308	61	224	49	69	14	1	7	48	31	27	4	1	R	R	6-0	195	7-28-73	1995	Springdale, Ark.
Hunt, Kenya	.219	32	73	13	16	2	0	2	15	16	32	1	0	R	R	6-4	190	9-2-72	1994	Oceanside, Calif.
Langdon, Trajan	.174	11	23	4	4	0	0	1	3	3	9	0	1	R	R	6-4	190	5-13-76	1994	Anchorage, Alaska
Lindsey, Rodney	.265	35	155	30	41	4	4	0	14	13	37	21	7	R	R	5-8	175	1-28-76	1994	Opelika, Ala.
Marnell, Anthony	.125	3	8	0	1	1	0	0	1	2	1	0	1	R	R	6-5	200	1-2-74	1995	Las Vegas, Nev.
Martinez, Obed	.275	53	193	31	53	7	1	1	31	15	33	3	3	R	R	6-1	190	7-19-75	1994	Rio Piedras, P.R.

BATTING	AVG	G	AB	R	H	2B	3B	HR	RBI	BB	SO	SB	CS	B	T	HT	WT	DOB	1st Yr	Resides
Merila, Mark	.284	56	197	42	56	7	0	0	39	43	21	5	3	S	R	5-9	180	11-9-71	1994	Plymouth, Minn.
Moore, James	.255	15	47	10	12	5	1	0	6	7	9	1	0	R	R	6-0	200	8-19-74	1995	Sweetwater, Texas
Rosario, Eliezer	.246	20	69	9	17	3	1	0	7	3	9	4	2	R	R	6-0	165	11-11-75	1994	Cayey, P.R.
Sanchez, Marcos	.327	42	165	35	54	8	2	4	33	11	36	5	0	S	R	6-0	190	9-25-74	1992	Santo Domingo, D.R.
Watkins, Sean	.372	67	247	51	92	20	1	13	67	43	55	0	1	L	L	6-4	210	10-6-74	1995	Peoria Heights, Ill.

GAMES BY POSITION: C—B. Davis 48, J. Davis 4, Ebbert 1, Marnell 3, Sanchez 19. **1B**—Allen 3, Hunt 9, Sanchez 3, Watkins 65. **2B**—Bucci 4, Gama 69, Merila 2. **3B**—Bucci 12, Hills 32, Langdon 9, Merila 36. **SS**—Bucci 31, Hills 30, Rosario 20. **OF**—Abernathy 61, Allen 12, Amerson 45, Hunt 8, Lindsey 36, Martinez 14, Moore 14, Sanchez 2.

PITCHING	W	L	ERA	G	GS	CG	SV	IP	H	R	ER	BB	SO	B	T	HT	WT	DOB	1st Yr	Resides
Bales, Daniel	0	1	10.67	10	1	0	1	14	26	24	17	13	8	R	R	6-3	200	10-27-73	1995	Summit, Miss.
Baron, Jimmy	2	3	5.65	27	1	0	0	43	51	31	27	19	43	L	L	6-3	230	2-22-74	1992	Humble, Texas
Campbell, Tim	1	1	5.20	18	0	0	1	36	37	21	21	17	38	R	R	6-0	190	12-22-72	1995	Seattle, Wash.
Clark, Chris	0	0	4.50	1	1	0	0	6	3	3	3	4	9	R	R	6-1	180	10-29-74	1994	Aurora, Colo.
Clement, Matt	6	3	4.33	14	14	0	0	81	61	53	39	42	65	R	R	6-3	190	8-12-74	1994	Butler, Pa.
Erdos, Todd	5	3	3.48	32	0	0	1	41	34	19	16	30	48	R	R	6-1	185	11-21-73	1994	Meadville, Pa.
Graves, Jon	0	0	13.50	4	0	0	0	4	5	7	6	12	0	R	R	6-1	165	8-5-71	1992	San Diego, Calif.
Guzman, Domingo	2	2	6.66	27	0	0	11	26	25	22	19	25	33	R	R	6-3	198	4-5-75	1994	San Cristobal, D.R.
Henderson, James	3	0	2.25	4	4	0	0	20	19	6	5	9	16	R	R	6-5	195	2-14-73	1995	Ringgold, Ga.
Irvine, Michael	2	1	5.85	28	0	0	2	52	59	40	34	28	52	R	R	6-3	190	8-18-73	1995	Waterloo, Iowa
Kolb, Brandon	2	3	7.04	9	8	0	0	38	42	33	30	29	21	R	R	6-1	190	11-20-73	1995	Danville, Calif.
Newman, Eric	8	4	4.41	15	14	0	0	82	91	49	40	35	65	R	R	6-4	220	8-27-72	1995	Fremont, Calif.
Perez, Jayson	0	0	0.00	1	0	0	0	1	1	0	0	2	1	R	R	6-2	152	6-27-74	1992	Mayaguez, P.R.
Remington, Jake	5	5	5.15	15	15	1	0	87	106	62	50	29	54	R	R	6-4	175	8-26-75	1994	Broken Arrow, Okla.
Sak, James	3	1	1.65	13	0	0	1	33	15	9	6	12	55	R	R	6-1	195	8-18-73	1995	Chicago, Ill.
Spear, Russell	3	2	6.21	14	13	0	0	67	83	65	46	36	53	R	R	6-3	190	8-30-77	1995	Albanvale, Australia
Torres, Luis	0	1	27.00	1	0	0	0	1	3	3	3	2	2	R	R	6-2	228	1-13-76	1994	Manati, P.R.

PEORIA   R

ARIZONA LEAGUE

BATTING	AVG	G	AB	R	H	2B	3B	HR	RBI	BB	SO	SB	CS	B	T	HT	WT	DOB	1st Yr	Resides
Carmona, Cesarin	.255	15	51	7	13	2	2	1	4	5	10	3	3	S	R	5-11	180	12-20-76	1994	Palla Bani, D.R.
Chavez, Steven	.259	55	197	30	51	7	5	0	24	24	48	5	6	L	R	5-11	190	7-30-75	1995	Carlsbad, N.M.
Cruz, Francisco	.000	1	2	0	0	0	0	0	0	1	0	0	0	R	R	6-3	183	12-9-74	1993	Bani, D.R.
Davis, Josh	.203	37	128	20	26	4	1	0	7	14	35	3	3	R	R	6-0	180	6-13-76	1994	Locust Grove, Okla.
Ebbert, Chad	.315	35	127	18	40	5	3	2	21	9	29	2	2	R	R	6-4	225	10-1-73	1994	Lake Mary, Fla.
Hunter, Andy	.208	35	106	14	22	2	2	0	11	17	39	2	1	R	R	6-2	175	12-28-76	1995	Arlington, Texas
Jackson, Rod	.253	45	150	16	38	6	0	0	6	9	39	11	3	R	R	5-11	155	2-24-75	1994	Camden, Ark.
Jacobo, Roberto	.241	46	166	18	40	2	3	0	15	12	49	10	7	S	L	6-4	174	6-7-76	1994	Haina, D.R.
Jacobus, Brian	.194	44	144	12	28	7	0	0	11	8	32	0	1	L	L	6-0	175	6-8-76	1995	Puyallup, Wash.
Jones, Ken	.500	1	4	0	2	1	0	0	1	0	1	0	0	R	R	5-11	185	10-26-71	1995	Auburn, Ind.
Marnell, Anthony	.400	1	5	1	2	1	0	0	3	0	2	0	0	R	R	6-1	200	1-2-74	1995	Las Vegas, Nev.
McDavid, Ray	.464	9	28	13	13	2	1	1	6	8	7	3	1	L	R	6-3	195	7-20-71	1988	San Diego, Calif.
Moore, James	.320	15	50	7	16	4	1	0	9	4	17	1	2	R	R	6-0	200	8-19-74	1995	Sweetwater, Texas
Paciorek, Pete	.257	54	183	32	47	11	3	5	24	33	58	6	4	S	L	6-3	195	5-19-76	1994	San Gabriel, Calif.
Pernell, Brandon	.247	48	174	22	43	11	1	2	29	16	54	8	2	R	R	6-2	180	4-11-77	1995	Torrance, Calif.
Rodriguez, John	.202	31	94	12	19	1	1	1	11	2	27	0	3	R	R	6-0	180	11-25-75	1995	Corpus Christi, Texas
Rosario, Eliezer	.259	7	27	3	7	3	0	0	3	5	6	1	0	R	R	6-0	165	11-11-75	1994	Cayey, P.R.
Rutherford, Daryl	.333	47	186	29	62	12	4	5	27	11	28	13	7	R	R	6-0	175	10-30-75	1994	Union, S.C.

GAMES BY POSITION: C—Davis 24, Ebbert 29, Jones 1, Marnell 1. **1B**—Jacobo 4, Paciorek 53. **2B**—Davis 3, Jackson 44, Rodriguez 7, Rosario 2, Rutherford 3. **3B**—Chavez 51, Rodriguez 4, Rutherford 2. **SS**—Carmona 14, Rodriguez 18, Rosario 5, Rutherford 25. **OF**—Cruz 1, Hunter 32, Jacobo 41, Jacobus 41, McDavid 1, Moore 13, Pernell 44.

PITCHING	W	L	ERA	G	GS	CG	SV	IP	H	R	ER	BB	SO	B	T	HT	WT	DOB	1st Yr	Resides
Clark, Chris	5	5	2.10	13	12	1	0	73	52	30	17	38	82	R	R	6-1	180	10-29-74	1994	Aurora, Colo.
Desabrias, Mark	2	3	3.11	19	2	0	0	55	52	28	19	20	28	S	R	6-2	180	7-10-75	1995	Casselberry, Fla.
Drewien, Dan	0	0	0.00	1	0	0	0	3	2	1	0	0	2	R	R	6-1	185	8-29-72	1993	San Diego, Calif.
Duncan, DeVohn	4	5	3.12	11	10	0	0	52	47	39	18	22	40	R	R	6-4	212	4-1-75	1993	Jersey City, N.J.
Ettles, Mark	0	0	5.79	3	0	0	0	5	6	6	3	4	2	R	R	6-0	178	10-30-66	1989	South Perth, Australia
Henderson, James	0	0	8.22	3	1	0	0	8	12	8	7	6	12	R	R	6-5	195	2-14-73	1995	Ringgold, Ga.
Kolb, Brandon	1	1	1.17	4	4	1	0	23	13	10	3	13	21	R	R	6-1	190	11-20-73	1995	Danville, Calif.
Lopez, Rodrigo	1	1	5.45	11	7	0	1	35	41	29	21	14	33	R	R	5-11	170	12-14-75	1995	Thalnepantla, Mexico
Matlack, Dan	0	2	3.58	16	0	0	0	28	20	15	11	14	16	R	R	6-2	200	7-25-75	1995	Sugar Grove, Ohio
Nash, Damond	1	3	7.31	15	3	1	0	44	55	42	36	27	32	L	R	6-2	200	3-7-76	1995	Texarkana, Ark.
Neiman, Joshua	1	1	4.24	10	0	0	1	17	20	9	8	3	18	R	R	6-4	210	10-19-74	1994	Durango, Colo.
Perez, Jayson	0	0	9.00	2	0	0	0	2	3	2	2	2	1	R	R	6-2	152	6-27-74	1992	Mayaguez, P.R.
Schroeder, Scott	0	1	7.36	2	2	0	0	7	12	7	6	2	8	R	R	6-6	235	9-8-74	1994	Portland, Ore.
Smith, Josh	1	2	1.69	8	0	0	1	11	12	8	2	8	8	L	L	5-11	175	8-26-77	1995	Houston, Texas
Torres, Luis	4	3	4.75	22	0	0	8	36	36	24	19	20	34	R	R	6-2	228	1-13-76	1994	Manati, P.R.
Walker, Kevin	5	5	3.01	13	12	0	0	72	74	34	24	12	69	L	L	6-4	190	9-20-76	1995	Grand Prairie, Texas

SAN FRANCISCO GIANTS

Manager: Dusty Baker.   **1995 Record:** 67-77, .465 (4th, NL West).

BATTING	AVG	G	AB	R	H	2B	3B	HR	RBI	BB	SO	SB	CS	B	T	HT	WT	DOB	1st Yr	Resides
Aurilia, Rich	.474	9	19	4	9	3	0	2	4	1	2	1	0	R	R	6-0	170	9-2-71	1992	Brooklyn, N.Y.
Benard, Marvin	.382	13	34	5	13	2	0	1	4	1	7	1	0	L	L	5-10	180	1-20-71	1992	Cudahy, Calif.
Benjamin, Mike	.220	68	186	19	41	6	0	3	12	8	51	11	1	R	R	6-0	169	11-22-65	1987	Chandler, Ariz.
Benzinger, Todd	.200	9	10	2	2	0	0	1	2	2	3	0	0	S	R	6-1	195	2-11-63	1981	Cincinnati, Ohio
Bonds, Barry	.294	144	506	109	149	30	7	33	104	120	83	31	10	L	L	6-1	185	7-24-64	1985	Murrieta, Calif.
Carreon, Mark	.301	117	396	53	119	24	0	17	65	23	37	0	1	R	L	6-0	195	7-9-63	1981	Tucson, Ariz.
Clayton, Royce	.244	138	509	56	124	29	3	5	58	38	109	24	9	R	R	6-0	183	1-2-70	1988	Inglewood, Calif.
Faneyte, Rikkert	.198	46	86	7	17	4	1	0	4	11	27	1	0	R	R	6-1	170	5-31-69	1991	Amsterdam, Netherlands
Hill, Glenallen	.264	132	497	71	131	29	4	24	86	39	98	25	5	R	R	6-2	210	3-22-65	1983	Boca Raton, Fla.
Lampkin, Tom	.276	65	76	8	21	2	0	1	9	9	8	2	0	L	R	5-11	183	3-4-64	1986	Boring, Ore.
Leonard, Mark	.190	14	21	4	4	1	0	1	4	5	2	0	0	L	R	6-0	212	8-14-64	1986	San Jose, Calif.
Lewis, Darren	.252	74	309	47	78	10	3	1	16	17	37	21	7	R	R	6-0	200	8-28-67	1988	San Mateo, Calif.
Manwaring, Kirt	.251	118	379	21	95	15	2	4	36	27	72	1	0	R	R	5-11	203	7-15-65	1986	Scottsdale, Ariz.
McCarty, David	.250	12	20	1	5	1	0	0	2	2	4	1	0	R	L	6-5	207	11-23-69	1991	Houston, Texas
Patterson, John	.205	95	205	27	42	5	3	1	14	14	41	4	2	S	R	5-9	168	2-11-67	1988	Phoenix, Ariz.
Phillips, J.R.	.195	92	231	27	45	9	0	9	28	19	69	1	1	L	L	6-1	185	4-29-70	1988	Moreno Valley, Calif.
Reed, Jeff	.265	66	113	12	30	2	0	0	9	20	17	0	0	L	R	6-2	190	11-12-62	1980	Elizabethton, Tenn.
Sanders, Deion	.285	52	214	29	61	9	5	5	18	18	42	8	6	L	L	6-1	195	8-9-67	1988	Alpharetta, Ga.
2-team (33 Cinc.)	.268	85	343	48	92	11	8	6	28	27	60	24	9							
Scarsone, Steve	.266	80	233	33	62	10	3	11	29	18	82	3	2	R	R	6-2	170	4-11-66	1986	Anaheim, Calif.
Thompson, Robby	.223	95	336	51	75	15	0	8	23	42	76	1	2	R	R	5-11	173	5-10-62	1983	Tequesta, Fla.
Williams, Matt	.336	76	283	53	95	17	1	23	65	30	58	2	0	R	R	6-2	205	11-28-65	1986	Scottsdale, Ariz.

PITCHING	W	L	ERA	G	GS	CG	SV	IP	H	R	ER	BB	SO	B	T	HT	WT	DOB	1st Yr	Resides
Aquino, Luis	0	1	14.40	5	0	0	0	5	10	10	8	2	4	R	R	6-1	190	5-19-65	1982	Caguas, P.R.
2-team (29 Montreal)	0	3	5.10	34	0	0	2	42	57	34	24	13	26							
Barton, Shawn	4	1	4.26	52	0	0	1	44	37	22	21	19	22	R	L	6-3	195	5-14-63	1984	Reading, Pa.
Bautista, Jose	3	8	6.44	52	6	0	0	101	120	77	72	26	45	R	R	6-2	207	7-25-64	1981	Cooper City, Fla.
Beck, Rod	5	6	4.45	60	0	0	33	59	60	31	29	21	42	R	R	6-1	236	8-3-68	1986	Scottsdale, Ariz.
Brewington, Jamie	6	4	4.54	13	13	0	0	75	68	38	38	45	45	R	R	6-4	180	9-28-71	1992	Greenville, N.C.
Burba, Dave	4	2	4.98	37	0	0	0	43	38	26	24	25	46	R	R	6-4	240	7-7-66	1987	Springfield, Ohio
Burgos, Enrique	0	0	8.64	5	0	0	0	8	14	8	8	6	12	L	L	6-4	230	10-7-65	1983	Panama City, Panama
Dewey, Mark	1	0	3.13	27	0	0	0	32	30	12	11	17	32	R	R	6-0	216	1-3-65	1987	Jenison, Mich.
Estes, Shawn	0	3	6.75	3	3	0	0	17	16	14	13	5	14	L	R	6-2	200	2-28-73	1991	Gardnerville, Nev.
Frey, Steve	0	1	4.26	9	0	0	0	6	7	6	3	2	5	L	L	5-9	170	7-29-63	1983	Newtown, Pa.
Gomez, Pat	0	0	5.14	18	0	0	0	14	16	8	8	12	15	L	L	5-11	185	3-17-68	1986	Citrus Heights, Calif.
Greer, Kenny	0	2	5.25	8	0	0	0	12	15	12	7	5	7	R	R	6-2	215	5-12-67	1988	Hull, Mass.
Hook, Chris	5	1	5.50	45	0	0	0	52	55	33	32	29	40	S	R	6-5	195	8-4-68	1989	Florence, Ky.
Leiter, Mark	10	12	3.82	30	29	7	0	196	185	91	83	55	129	R	R	6-3	210	4-13-63	1983	West Caldwell, N.J.
Mintz, Steve	1	2	7.45	14	0	0	0	19	26	16	16	12	7	L	R	5-11	190	11-24-68	1990	Leland, N.C.
Mulholland, Terry	5	13	5.80	29	24	2	0	149	190	112	96	38	65	L	R	6-3	200	3-9-63	1984	Scottsdale, Ariz.
Portugal, Mark	5	5	4.15	17	17	1	0	104	106	56	48	34	63	R	R	6-0	190	10-30-62	1981	Missouri City, Texas
Roper, John	0	0	27.00	1	0	0	0	1	2	3	3	2	0	R	R	6-0	175	11-21-71	1990	Raeford, N.C.
Rosselli, Joe	2	1	8.70	9	5	0	0	30	39	29	29	20	7	R	L	6-1	170	5-28-72	1990	Woodland Hills, Calif.
Service, Scott	3	1	3.19	28	0	0	0	31	18	11	11	20	30	R	R	6-6	226	2-26-67	1986	Cincinnati, Ohio
Torres, Salomon	0	1	9.00	4	1	0	0	8	13	8	8	7	2	R	R	5-11	150	3-11-72	1990	San Pedro de Macoris, D.R.
Valdez, Carlos	0	1	6.14	11	0	0	0	15	19	10	10	8	7	R	R	5-11	165	12-26-71	1990	Nizao, D.R.
Valdez, Sergio	4	5	4.75	13	11	1	0	66	78	43	35	17	29	R	R	6-1	190	9-7-65	1983	Santo Domingo, D.R.
VanLandingham, William	6	3	3.67	18	18	1	0	123	124	58	50	40	95	R	R	6-2	210	7-16-70	1991	Franklin, Tenn.
Wilson, Trevor	3	4	3.92	17	17	0	0	83	82	42	36	38	38	L	L	6-0	204	6-7-66	1985	Scottsdale, Ariz.

FIELDING

Catcher	PCT	G	PO	A	E	DP	PB
Lampkin	1.000	17	59	5	0	1	1
Manwaring	.990	118	607	55	7	10	5
Reed	.995	42	175	21	1	2	1

First Base	PCT	G	PO	A	E	DP
Benzinger	1.000	5	15	0	0	3
Carreon	.993	81	703	44	5	65
McCarty	1.000	2	14	0	0	0
Phillips	.993	79	535	37	4	47
Scarsone	1.000	11	79	6	0	12

Second Base	PCT	G	PO	A	E	DP
Benjamin	1.000	8	7	14	0	0
Patterson	.983	53	114	112	4	34
Scarsone	.954	13	26	36	3	12
Thompson	.993	91	181	238	3	51

Third Base	PCT	G	PO	A	E	DP
Benjamin	.964	43	29	77	4	3
Scarsone	.927	50	30	71	8	8
Williams	.958	74	49	178	10	10

Shortstop	PCT	G	PO	A	E	DP
Aurilia	1.000	6	8	16	0	4
Benjamin	1.000	16	15	30	0	6
Clayton	.969	136	223	411	20	93

Outfield	PCT	G	PO	A	E	DP
Benard	1.000	7	19	0	0	0
Bonds	.980	143	279	12	6	2
Carreon	.938	22	29	1	2	0
Faneyte	.981	34	49	3	1	0
Hill	.959	125	226	10	10	1
Lampkin	1.000	6	3	0	0	0
Leonard	1.000	6	9	0	0	0
Lewis	.995	57	200	2	1	1
McCarty	.833	4	5	0	1	0
Phillips	1.000	1	1	0	0	0
Sanders	.984	52	127	0	2	0

Barry Bonds

GEORGE GOJKOVICH

GEORGE GOJKOVICH

Matt Williams played only 76 games, but led the Giants with a .336 average

Giants minor league Player of the Year Jesse Ibarra

LARRY GOREN

GIANTS

FARM SYSTEM

Director of Player Development: Jack Hiatt

Class	Farm Team	League	W	L	Pct.	Finish*	Manager(s)	First Yr
AAA	Phoenix (Ariz.) Firebirds	Pacific Coast	62	82	.431	8th (10)	Keith Bodie/Jim Davenport	1966
AA	Shreveport (La.) Captains	Texas	88	47	.652	1st+ (8)	Ron Wotus	1979
#A	San Jose (Calif.) Giants	California	77	63	.550	4th (10)	Carlos Lezcano	1988
A	Burlington (Iowa) Bees	Midwest	54	81	.400	13th (14)	Mike Hart	1995
A	Bellingham (Wash.) Giants	Northwest	43	33	.566	2nd (8)	Glenn Tufts	1995

*Finish in overall standings (No. of teams in league)   #Advanced level   +Won league championship

ORGANIZATION LEADERS

MAJOR LEAGUERS

BATTING
*AVG	Matt Williams	.336
R	Barry Bonds	109
H	Barry Bonds	149
TB	Barry Bonds	292
2B	Barry Bonds	30
3B	Barry Bonds	7
HR	Barry Bonds	33
RBI	Barry Bonds	104
BB	Barry Bonds	120
SO	Royce Clayton	109
SB	Barry Bonds	31

PITCHING
W	Mark Leiter	10
L	Terry Mulholland	13
#ERA	Wm. VanLandingham	3.67
G	Rod Beck	60
CG	Mark Leiter	7
SV	Rod Beck	33
IP	Mark Leiter	196
BB	Mark Leiter	55
SO	Mark Leiter	129

TOM DiPACE

Rod Beck. 33 saves

MINOR LEAGUERS

BATTING
*AVG	Jason McFarlin, Shreveport	.337
R	Jacob Cruz, Shreveport	88
H	Bill Mueller, Shreveport/Phoenix	153
TB	Jesse Ibarra, Burlington/San Jose	283
2B	Armando Rios, San Jose	34
3B	Benji Simonton, San Jose/Shreveport	9
HR	Jesse Ibarra, Burlington/San Jose	34
RBI	Jesse Ibarra, Burlington/San Jose	100
BB	Mark Leonard, Phoenix	81
SO	Don Denbow, Burlington	143
SB	Armando Rios, San Jose	51

PITCHING
W	Three tied at	13
L	Randy Phillips, Phoenix	13
#ERA	Carlos Valdez, Shreveport	1.74
G	Shawn Purdy, Shreveport	52
CG	Eight tied at	2
SV	Jeffrey Keith, Burlington	23
IP	Steve Bourgeois, Shreveport/Phoenix	180
BB	Brook Smith, Burlington	72
SO	Keith Foulke, San Jose	168

*Minimum 250 At-Bats   #Minimum 75 Innings

TOP 10 PROSPECTS

How the Giants Top 10 prospects, as judged by Baseball America prior to the 1995 season, fared in 1995:

BILL SETLIFF

J.R. Phillips

Player, Pos.	Club (Class—League)	AVG	AB	R	H	2B	3B	HR	RBI	SB
1. J.R. Phillips, 1b	San Francisco	.195	231	27	45	9	0	9	28	1
2. Dante Powell, of	San Jose (A—California)	.248	505	74	125	23	8	10	70	43
7. Jay Canizaro, ss	Shreveport (AA—Texas)	.293	440	83	129	25	7	12	60	16
8. Marcus Jensen, c	Shreveport (AA—Texas)	.283	321	55	91	22	8	4	45	0
9. Keith Williams, of	Shreveport (AA—Texas)	.305	275	39	84	20	1	9	55	5
	Phoenix (AAA—Pacific Coast)	.301	83	7	25	4	1	2	14	0
10. Chris Wimmer, 2b	Phoenix (AAA—Pacific Coast)	.263	449	55	118	23	4	2	44	13

Player, Pos.	Club (Class—League)	W	L	ERA	G	SV	IP	H	BB	SO
3. Steve Soderstrom, rhp	Shreveport (AA—Texas)	9	5	3.41	22	0	116	106	51	91
4. Joe Rosselli, lhp	Phoenix (AAA—Pacific Coast)	4	3	4.99	13	0	79	94	12	34
	San Francisco	2	1	8.70	9	0	30	39	20	7
5. Fausto Macey, rhp	San Jose (A—California)	8	9	3.89	28	0	171	167	50	94
6. Andy Taulbee, rhp	San Jose (A—California)	3	2	3.02	10	0	63	50	22	33
	Shreveport (AA—Texas)	4	5	3.95	14	0	87	107	27	38

PACIFIC COAST LEAGUE

BATTING	AVG	G	AB	R	H	2B	3B	HR	RBI	BB	SO	SB	CS	B	T	HT	WT	DOB	1st Yr	Resides
Aurilia, Rich	.279	71	258	42	72	12	0	5	34	35	29	2	2	R	R	6-0	170	9-2-71	1992	Hazlet, N.J.
Bellinger, Clay	.274	97	277	34	76	16	1	2	32	27	52	3	2	R	R	6-3	195	11-18-68	1989	Oneonta, N.Y.
Benard, Marvin	.304	111	378	70	115	14	6	6	32	50	66	10	13	L	L	5-10	180	1-20-71	1992	Cudahy, Calif.
Brewer, Rod	.244	15	45	8	11	4	0	1	8	3	10	1	1	L	L	6-3	208	2-24-66	1987	Zellwood, Fla.
Chimelis, Joel	.259	118	398	48	103	32	1	7	66	28	53	1	2	R	R	6-0	165	7-27-67	1988	Brooklyn, N.Y.
Christopherson, Eric	.220	94	282	21	62	9	1	1	25	35	54	1	1	R	R	6-1	190	4-25-69	1990	Westminster, Calif.
Cookson, Brent	.300	68	210	38	63	9	3	15	46	25	36	3	3	R	R	5-11	200	9-7-69	1991	Santa Paula, Calif.
Daugherty, Jack	.152	10	33	4	5	1	0	0	3	2	4	0	0	S	L	6-0	190	7-3-60	1983	San Diego, Calif.
Ehmann, Kurt	.269	67	216	21	58	5	2	0	7	24	41	8	3	R	R	6-1	185	8-18-70	1992	Ukiah, Calif.
Faneyte, Rikkert	.274	38	135	22	37	8	1	1	17	15	22	2	5	R	R	6-0	170	5-31-69	1991	Amsterdam, Netherlands
Jones, Dax	.267	112	404	47	108	21	3	2	45	31	52	11	10	R	R	6-0	170	8-4-70	1991	Waukegan, Ill.
Leonard, Mark	.296	112	392	73	116	25	3	14	79	81	63	3	2	L	R	6-0	210	8-14-64	1986	San Jose, Calif.
McCarty, David	.351	37	151	31	53	19	2	4	19	17	27	1	1	R	L	6-5	207	11-23-69	1991	Houston, Texas
Miller, Barry	.224	71	156	18	35	8	1	2	21	23	35	0	2	L	L	6-5	210	7-10-68	1990	Hampton, Va.
Miller, Roger	.212	43	137	14	29	4	1	1	10	9	15	0	0	R	R	6-0	190	4-4-67	1989	Sarasota, Fla.
Mirabelli, Doug	.167	23	66	3	11	0	1	0	7	12	10	1	0	R	R	6-1	205	10-18-70	1992	Las Vegas, Nev.
Mueller, Bill	.297	41	172	23	51	13	6	2	19	19	31	0	0	S	R	5-11	173	3-17-71	1993	Maryland Heights, Mo.
Murray, Calvin	.180	13	50	8	9	1	0	4	10	4	6	2	2	R	R	5-11	185	7-30-71	1992	Dallas, Texas
Ortiz, Ray	.242	66	190	22	46	10	2	4	29	13	36	1	0	L	L	6-2	215	4-27-68	1989	San Francisco, Calif.
Scott, Gary	.265	68	219	33	58	16	2	5	26	26	39	2	2	R	R	6-0	175	8-22-68	1989	Pelham, N.Y.
Williams, Keith	.301	24	83	7	25	4	1	2	14	5	11	0	0	R	R	6-0	190	4-21-72	1993	Bedford, Pa.
Wimmer, Chris	.263	132	449	55	118	23	4	2	44	31	49	13	7	R	R	5-11	170	9-25-70	1992	Wichita, Kan.

PITCHING	W	L	ERA	G	GS	CG	SV	IP	H	R	ER	BB	SO	B	T	HT	WT	DOB	1st Yr	Resides
Barton, Shawn	2	0	1.80	15	0	0	0	25	20	5	5	5	25	R	L	6-3	195	5-14-63	1984	Reading, Pa.
Bourgeois, Steve	1	1	3.38	6	5	0	0	35	38	13	13	23	R	R	6-1	220	8-4-72	1993	Paulina, La.
Brink, Brad	2	5	7.05	11	9	0	0	45	55	35	35	30	33	R	R	6-2	203	1-20-65	1986	Modesto, Calif.
Burcham, Tim	1	0	5.06	5	0	0	0	11	18	7	6	2	6	R	R	6-4	175	10-7-63	1985	Hampton, Va.
Burgos, Enrique	2	6	6.14	41	2	0	2	59	63	44	40	40	77	L	L	6-4	230	10-7-65	1983	Panama City, Panama
Carlson, Dan	9	5	4.27	23	22	2	0	133	138	67	63	66	93	R	R	6-1	185	1-26-70	1990	Portland, Ore.
Clayton, Royal	0	2	5.87	5	5	0	0	23	35	18	15	6	13	R	R	6-2	210	11-25-65	1987	Inglewood, Calif.
Gamez, Bob	3	5	5.59	36	9	0	2	66	76	46	41	27	41	L	L	6-5	185	11-18-68	1988	Newark, Calif.
Gardella, Mike	0	0	13.50	3	0	0	0	4	9	6	6	1	3	L	L	5-10	195	1-18-67	1989	Sapulpa, Okla.
Gomez, Pat	0	0	27.00	2	0	0	0	1	5	5	4	3	1	L	L	5-11	185	3-17-68	1986	Citrus Heights, Calif.
Greer, Ken	5	2	3.98	38	0	0	1	63	65	29	28	19	41	R	R	6-2	215	5-12-67	1988	Hull, Mass.
Hook, Chris	0	0	1.50	4	0	0	0	6	2	1	1	3	5	S	R	6-5	195	8-4-68	1989	Florence, Ky.
Jones, Stacy	0	1	8.53	4	0	0	0	6	9	6	6	4	4	R	R	6-6	225	5-26-67	1988	Attalla, Ala.
Knudsen, Kurt	0	1	5.03	11	1	0	1	20	18	13	11	11	20	R	R	6-3	200	2-20-67	1988	Folsom, Calif.
Menendez, Tony	5	6	3.92	50	0	0	13	64	67	34	28	32	61	R	R	6-2	195	2-20-65	1984	Carol City, Fla.
Mintz, Steve	5	2	2.39	31	0	0	7	49	42	16	13	21	36	L	R	5-11	190	11-24-68	1990	Leland, N.C.
Mulholland, Terry	0	0	2.25	1	1	0	0	4	4	3	1	1	4	R	L	6-3	200	3-9-63	1984	Scottsdale, Ariz.
Phillips, Randy	4	13	5.11	25	24	2	0	132	155	83	75	40	66	R	R	6-3	210	3-18-71	1992	Pine Bluff, Ark.
Piatt, Doug	0	1	5.87	6	0	0	0	8	7	5	5	5	3	L	R	6-1	190	9-26-65	1988	Beaver, Pa.
Robinson, Scott	5	7	4.66	31	15	0	0	124	134	68	64	37	61	R	R	6-2	200	11-15-68	1990	Cordova, Ala.
Rogers, Kevin	0	0	4.15	3	1	0	0	4	9	2	2	2	1	S	L	6-1	198	8-20-68	1988	Parchman, Miss.
Roper, John	0	1	9.00	1	1	0	0	3	5	3	3	0	2	R	R	6-0	175	11-21-71	1990	Raeford, N.C.
Rosselli, Joe	4	3	4.99	13	13	1	0	79	94	47	44	12	34	R	L	6-1	170	5-28-72	1990	Woodland Hills, Calif.
Torres, Salomon	0	0	0.00	1	0	0	0	2	2	0	0	0	5	R	R	5-11	150	3-11-72	1990	San Pedro de Macoris, D.R.
Trlicek, Rick	5	4	5.29	38	0	0	0	63	72	44	37	21	43	R	R	6-3	200	4-26-69	1987	Houston, Texas
Valdez, Carlos	1	0	2.76	18	0	0	2	29	29	10	9	13	30	R	R	5-11	165	12-26-71	1990	Bani, D.R.
Valdez, Sergio	6	7	4.45	18	18	2	0	109	117	58	54	25	64	R	R	6-1	190	9-7-65	1983	Santo Domingo, D.R.
Vanderweele, Doug	2	4	6.10	11	4	1	0	38	57	29	26	11	20	R	R	6-3	200	3-18-70	1991	Las Vegas, Nev.
Whitaker, Steve	0	5	7.00	16	10	0	0	54	72	47	42	36	30	L	L	6-6	225	4-15-70	1991	Atwater, Calif.
Whitehurst, Wally	0	1	7.16	4	0	0	0	16	20	13	13	8	7	R	R	6-3	185	4-11-64	1985	Madisonville, La.

FIELDING

Catcher	PCT	G	PO	A	E	DP	PB
Bellinger	1.000	1	2	0	0	0	0
Christopherson	.993	91	543	44	4	6	5
Ehmann	.750	1	3	0	1	0	2
R. Miller	.972	41	221	23	7	5	2
Mirabelli	.985	23	115	17	2	4	2

First Base	PCT	G	PO	A	E	DP
Bellinger	1.000	3	10	1	0	2
Brewer	1.000	13	134	14	0	12
Chimelis	.998	51	395	25	1	41
Leonard	.989	13	89	1	1	11
McCarty	.994	35	327	31	2	39
B. Miller	.994	38	290	17	2	31
Ortiz	.990	13	91	6	1	15

Second Base	PCT	G	PO	A	E	DP
Bellinger	.956	16	15	28	2	3
Chimelis	.958	20	34	34	3	15
Ehmann	1.000	2	5	5	0	3
Mueller	1.000	1	3	3	0	1
Wimmer	.983	127	224	371	10	96

Third Base	PCT	G	PO	A	E	DP
Bellinger	.981	27	15	37	1	5
Chimelis	.938	24	15	45	4	4
Ehmann	.913	13	7	14	2	2
Mueller	.938	40	23	82	7	8
Scott	.921	60	33	107	12	8

Shortstop	PCT	G	PO	A	E	DP
Aurilia	.975	71	104	246	9	56
Bellinger	.960	29	42	79	5	19

	PCT	G	PO	A	E	DP
Chimelis	.911	8	16	25	4	2
Ehmann	.949	51	79	165	13	45

Outfield	PCT	G	PO	A	E	DP
Bellinger	1.000	23	32	0	0	0
Benard	.959	97	183	5	8	2
Cookson	.967	56	86	2	3	1
Daugherty	.909	7	10	0	1	0
Faneyte	.944	36	83	2	5	1
Jones	.980	105	284	9	6	0
Leonard	.976	89	154	9	4	3
McCarty	1.000	3	3	1	0	0
Murray	1.000	13	19	2	0	0
Ortiz	1.000	26	29	2	0	0
Williams	1.000	19	38	1	0	0

TEXAS LEAGUE

BATTING	AVG	G	AB	R	H	2B	3B	HR	RBI	BB	SO	SB	CS	B	T	HT	WT	DOB	1st Yr	Resides
Alguacil, Jose	.250	1	4	1	1	0	0	0	1	0	1	1	0	L	R	6-2	175	8-9-72	1993	Caracas, Venez.
Aurilia, Rich	.327	64	226	29	74	17	1	4	42	27	26	10	3	R	R	6-0	170	9-2-71	1992	Hazlet, N.J.
Canizaro, Jay	.293	126	440	83	129	25	7	12	60	58	98	16	9	R	R	5-10	175	7-4-73	1993	Orange, Texas
Cruz, Jacob	.297	127	458	88	136	33	1	13	77	57	72	9	8	L	L	6-0	175	1-28-73	1994	Oxnard, Calif.

BATTING

BATTING	AVG	G	AB	R	H	2B	3B	HR	RBI	BB	SO	SB	CS	B	T	HT	WT	DOB	1st Yr	Resides
Ehmann, Kurt	.231	38	130	24	30	5	0	1	17	22	15	1	2	R	R	6-1	185	8-18-70	1992	Ukiah, Calif.
Florez, Tim	.268	100	295	37	79	11	2	9	46	26	49	4	3	R	R	5-10	170	7-23-69	1991	Goleta, Calif.
Jenkins, Bernie	.167	5	12	1	2	0	0	1	1	2	5	0	0	R	R	6-4	195	9-12-67	1988	Brooklyn, N.Y.
Jensen, Marcus	.283	95	321	55	91	22	8	4	45	41	68	0	0	S	R	6-4	195	12-14-72	1990	Oakland, Calif.
Mayes, Craig	.222	9	18	0	2	1	0	0	3	0	2	0	0	L	R	5-10	195	5-8-70	1992	Washington, Mich.
McFarlin, Jason	.337	93	252	39	85	13	2	6	37	25	26	8	7	L	L	6-0	175	6-28-70	1989	Pensacola, Fla.
Miller, Roger	.274	19	62	11	17	6	0	2	10	6	1	0	0	R	R	6-0	190	4-4-67	1989	Sarasota, Fla.
Mirabelli, Doug	.302	40	126	14	38	13	0	0	16	20	14	1	0	R	R	6-1	205	10-18-70	1992	Las Vegas, Nev.
Morrow, Chris	.246	83	240	31	59	17	0	7	35	31	44	1	1	L	L	6-1	190	11-8-69	1988	Pacifica, Calif.
Mueller, Bill	.309	88	330	56	102	16	2	1	39	53	36	6	5	S	R	5-11	173	3-17-71	1993	Maryland Heights, Mo.
Murray, Calvin	.236	110	441	77	104	17	3	2	29	59	70	26	10	R	R	5-11	185	7-30-71	1992	Dallas, Texas
Reid, Derek	.143	8	14	2	2	0	1	0	1	0	4	0	0	R	R	6-3	195	2-4-70	1990	Cincinnati, Ohio
Simonton, Benji	.306	38	108	18	33	9	3	4	30	11	32	3	1	R	R	6-1	225	5-12-72	1992	Tempe, Ariz.
Williams, Keith	.305	75	275	39	84	20	1	9	55	23	39	5	3	R	R	6-0	190	4-21-72	1993	Bedford, Pa.
Wilson, Desi	.286	122	482	77	138	27	3	5	72	40	68	11	9	L	L	6-7	230	5-9-68	1991	Glen Cove, N.Y.
Witkowski, Matt	.289	17	38	7	11	1	0	0	5	8	7	0	0	R	R	6-0	175	2-5-70	1988	Glendale, Ariz.
Woods, Kenny	.254	89	209	30	53	11	0	3	23	23	29	4	5	R	R	5-10	173	8-2-70	1992	Los Angeles, Calif.

PITCHING

PITCHING	W	L	ERA	G	GS	CG	SV	IP	H	R	ER	BB	SO	B	T	HT	WT	DOB	1st Yr	Resides
Bourgeois, Steve	12	3	2.85	22	22	2	0	145	140	50	46	53	91	R	R	6-1	220	8-4-72	1993	Paulina, La.
Brannon, Cliff	0	0	5.40	3	1	0	0	10	13	7	6	4	7	R	R	6-6	190	7-28-67	1989	Kennesaw, Ga.
Brewington, Jamie	8	3	3.06	16	16	1	0	88	72	39	30	55	74	R	R	6-4	180	9-28-71	1992	Greenville, N.C.
Castillo, Mariano	3	1	3.13	22	0	0	0	37	38	17	13	13	31	R	R	6-0	168	3-17-71	1990	Boca Chica, D.R.
Corps, Edwin	13	6	3.86	27	27	2	0	166	195	80	71	41	53	R	R	5-11	180	11-3-72	1994	Carolina, P.R.
Estes, Shawn	2	0	2.01	4	4	0	0	22	14	5	5	10	18	R	L	6-2	200	2-28-73	1991	Gardnerville, Nev.
Frontera, Chad	3	5	4.17	20	13	0	1	82	88	45	38	39	52	R	R	6-2	195	11-22-72	1994	Brooklyn, N.Y.
Hyde, Rich	5	1	3.89	33	0	0	7	44	48	21	19	10	24	R	R	6-0	185	12-24-68	1991	Mahomet, Ill.
McLain, Mike	2	1	3.12	11	0	0	1	17	13	7	6	3	11	L	R	6-2	205	3-18-70	1992	Elk Grove, Calif.
Peterson, Mark	4	3	1.27	37	0	0	2	64	51	15	9	6	38	L	L	5-11	195	11-27-70	1992	Kirkland, Wash.
Pickett, Ricky	2	0	1.71	14	0	0	3	21	9	5	4	9	23	L	L	6-0	185	1-19-70	1992	Fort Worth, Texas
Pote, Lou	2	2	5.33	28	0	0	3	51	53	41	30	26	30	R	R	6-3	190	8-27-71	1991	Chicago, Ill.
Purdy, Shawn	6	3	3.75	52	1	0	21	62	61	31	26	18	33	R	R	6-0	205	7-30-68	1991	St. Cloud, Fla.
Richey, Jeff	1	2	2.45	8	0	0	1	22	20	7	6	8	11	R	R	6-0	185	9-30-69	1992	Monroe, La.
Soderstrom, Steve	9	5	3.41	22	22	0	0	116	106	53	44	51	91	R	R	6-3	215	4-3-72	1994	Turlock, Calif.
Taulbee, Andy	4	5	3.95	14	14	1	0	87	107	47	38	27	38	R	R	6-4	210	10-5-72	1994	Tucker, Ga.
Valdez, Carlos	3	2	1.27	22	3	0	5	64	40	11	9	14	51	R	R	5-11	165	12-26-71	1990	Nizao, D.R.
Vanderweele, Doug	5	2	2.52	13	9	0	0	64	61	18	18	13	22	R	R	6-3	200	3-18-70	1991	Las Vegas, Nev.
Wanke, Chuck	2	3	4.35	43	0	0	0	41	35	23	20	22	40	R	L	6-5	200	2-2-71	1990	Beaverton, Ore.
Whitaker, Steve	2	0	3.86	4	3	0	0	16	17	8	7	10	10	L	L	6-6	225	4-15-70	1991	Atwater, Calif.

FIELDING

Catcher

Catcher	PCT	G	PO	A	E	DP	PB
Ehmann	.000	1	0	0	1	0	0
Jensen	.991	89	471	70	5	5	11
Mayes	1.000	1	4	0	0	0	0
Miller	.984	19	116	11	2	3	4
Mirabelli	.984	35	166	21	3	1	2

First Base

First Base	PCT	G	PO	A	E	DP
Florez	.875	1	7	0	1	1
Mirabelli	1.000	3	27	0	0	2
Morrow	1.000	2	19	2	0	0
Simonton	1.000	9	81	5	0	11
Wilson	.992	118	1113	72	9	112
Witkowski	.960	8	45	3	2	8
Woods	1.000	3	21	0	0	5

Second Base

Second Base	PCT	G	PO	A	E	DP
Canizaro	.965	105	228	295	19	84
Florez	.977	42	65	102	4	23
Mueller	1.000	2	5	1	0	0
Witkowski	.966	4	12	16	1	5
Woods	.857	1	3	3	1	1

Third Base

Third Base	PCT	G	PO	A	E	DP
Florez	.920	48	22	81	9	12
Mueller	.977	85	47	168	5	13
Witkowski	.833	2	1	4	1	0
Woods	.895	21	14	37	6	2

Shortstop

Shortstop	PCT	G	PO	A	E	DP
Alguacil	.750	1	2	1	1	1
Aurilia	.962	63	122	237	14	52

	PCT	G	PO	A	E	DP
Canizaro	.941	19	26	38	4	10
Ehmann	.973	38	53	126	5	23
Florez	.941	6	6	10	1	3
Woods	.906	21	32	55	9	12

Outfield

Outfield	PCT	G	PO	A	E	DP
Cruz	.996	114	235	16	1	2
Jenkins	.833	4	5	0	1	0
McFarlin	.956	64	84	3	4	1
Morrow	1.000	56	90	4	0	1
Murray	.993	109	286	9	2	1
Reid	1.000	5	3	0	0	0
Simonton	.938	18	29	1	2	1
Williams	.966	63	109	4	4	0
Woods	.974	38	34	3	1	2

SAN JOSE — A

CALIFORNIA LEAGUE

BATTING	AVG	G	AB	R	H	2B	3B	HR	RBI	BB	SO	SB	CS	B	T	HT	WT	DOB	1st Yr	Resides
Alguacil, Jose	.236	58	225	30	53	10	3	0	17	14	44	11	6	L	R	6-2	175	8-9-72	1993	Caracas, Venez.
Alimena, Charles	.205	54	171	17	35	3	2	1	18	11	44	1	0	L	L	6-3	210	1-21-72	1990	Sacramento, Calif.
Cavanagh, Mike	.125	6	16	2	2	0	1	0	3	2	8	0	0	R	R	6-0	205	6-20-70	1992	Holyoke, Mass.
Delgado, Wilson	.000	1	0	0	0	0	0	0	0	0	0	0	0	S	R	5-11	165	7-15-75	1993	Santo Domingo, D.R.
Ealy, Tracey	.156	12	32	7	5	0	0	0	2	2	12	0	0	S	R	6-0	210	7-8-71	1989	Las Vegas, Nev.
Galarza, Joel	.292	58	209	28	61	13	1	7	44	11	35	6	2	R	R	5-11	214	10-14-73	1993	Yabucoa, P.R.
Gulseth, Mark	.234	22	64	8	15	4	1	0	6	10	16	1	0	L	R	6-4	200	11-12-71	1993	Callaway, Minn.
Ibarra, Jesse	.333	3	9	1	3	2	0	0	4	1	1	0	0	S	R	6-3	195	7-12-72	1994	El Monte, Calif.
Keene, Andre	.254	103	323	62	82	15	1	15	62	76	101	7	6	L	L	6-5	265	3-11-71	1991	Lanham, Md.
Keifer, Greg	.212	28	66	9	14	2	0	2	12	9	31	2	0	R	R	6-3	200	1-21-73	1994	Westerville, Ohio
King, Brett	.274	107	394	61	108	29	4	3	41	41	86	28	8	R	R	6-1	195	7-20-72	1993	Apopka, Fla.
Marval, Raul	.278	10	36	1	10	0	0	0	3	1	5	1	1	R	R	6-0	170	12-13-75	1993	Cabodare, Venez.
Mayes, Craig	.252	90	318	34	80	17	4	0	39	27	50	3	1	L	R	5-10	195	5-8-70	1992	Washington, Mich.
Phillips, Gary	.264	106	363	51	96	17	8	1	32	26	68	3	1	R	R	5-11	170	9-25-71	1992	Tullahoma, Tenn.
Powell, Dante	.248	135	505	74	125	23	8	10	70	46	131	43	12	R	R	6-2	185	8-25-73	1994	Long Beach, Calif.
Rios, Armando	.293	128	488	76	143	34	3	8	75	74	75	51	10	L	L	5-9	178	9-13-71	1994	Carolina, P.R.
Sbrocco, Jon	.301	120	425	66	128	14	5	2	46	55	43	12	10	L	R	5-10	165	1-5-71	1993	Willoughby Hills, Ohio
Schneider, Dan	.167	13	36	3	6	1	0	0	2	1	7	0	0	R	R	6-2	195	4-18-72	1994	Greensboro, N.C.
Shepherd, Brian	.156	13	32	1	5	0	0	0	1	1	6	0	2	R	R	6-0	210	11-6-72	1994	Salinas, Calif.
Simonton, Benji	.289	61	225	38	65	9	6	8	37	40	78	7	0	R	R	6-1	225	5-12-72	1992	Tempe, Ariz.
Singleton, Chris	.277	94	405	55	112	13	5	2	31	17	49	33	13	L	L	6-2	195	8-15-72	1993	Hercules, Calif.
Thielen, D.J.	.213	91	282	38	60	13	1	8	34	38	81	4	5	R	R	6-2	185	8-5-71	1991	Portland, Ore.
Wallace, Brian	.222	25	81	15	18	1	0	2	8	9	18	3	0	R	R	6-2	200	9-10-71	1992	Newark, Del.

BATTING	AVG	G	AB	R	H	2B	3B	HR	RBI	BB	SO	SB	CS	B	T	HT	WT	DOB	1st Yr	Resides
Williams, Matt	.182	4	11	2	2	0	0	1	2	0	3	0	0	R	R	6-2	205	11-28-65	1986	Scottsdale, Ariz.
Wilson, Todd	.239	37	117	14	28	7	1	0	13	6	19	1	0	R	R	6-0	210	11-20-69	1994	San Diego, Calif.

GAMES BY POSITION: C—Cavanagh 6, Galarza 37, Mayes 84, Schneider 12, Shepherd 13. **1B**—Alguacil 1, Alimena 35, Galarza 5, Gulseth 16, Keene 50, Simonton 35, Wallace 1, Wilson 6. **2B**—Alguacil 25, Marval 4, Phillips 1, Sbrocco 114, Wallace 3. **3B**—Alguacil 14, Phillips 103, Thielen 2, Wallace 5, Williams 4, Wilson 25. **SS**—Alguacil 19, Delgado 1, King 107, Marval 7, Phillips 1, Wallace 16. **OF**—Alguacil 4, Alimena 3, Ealy 3, King 3, Keifer 22, Powell 130, Rios 118, Singleton 91, Thielen 79.

PITCHING	W	L	ERA	G	GS	CG	SV	IP	H	R	ER	BB	SO	B	T	HT	WT	DOB	1st Yr	Resides
Andrakin, Rob	2	1	2.36	29	0	0	7	46	38	14	12	19	49	R	R	6-1	180	2-11-69	1993	San Jose, Calif.
Aquino, Luis	0	0	0.00	4	4	0	0	10	9	1	0	1	13	R	R	6-1	190	5-19-65	1982	Caguas, P.R.
Brohawn, Troy	7	3	1.65	11	10	0	0	65	45	14	12	20	57	L	L	6-1	190	1-14-73	1994	Woolford, Md.
Castillo, Mariano	4	4	1.59	21	0	0	3	57	49	14	10	13	51	R	R	6-0	168	3-17-71	1990	Boca Chica, D.R.
Estes, Shawn	5	2	2.17	9	8	0	0	50	32	13	12	17	61	R	L	6-2	200	2-28-73	1991	Gardnerville, Nev.
Foulke, Keith	13	6	3.50	28	26	2	0	177	166	85	69	32	168	R	R	6-0	195	10-19-72	1994	Huffman, Texas
Gomez, Dennys	2	0	2.08	13	0	0	0	30	27	13	7	15	23	S	R	6-0	195	6-21-71	1994	Miami, Fla.
Gomez, Pat	0	0	1.42	3	2	0	0	6	5	2	1	5	5	L	L	5-11	185	3-17-68	1986	Citrus Heights, Calif.
Hartvigson, Chad	4	4	3.54	32	7	0	4	84	85	38	33	24	63	R	L	6-3	195	12-15-70	1994	Kirkland, Wash.
Henrikson, Dan	0	1	7.71	7	0	0	0	7	8	6	6	4	6	L	L	6-0	180	9-12-68	1989	Everett, Wash.
Howry, Bobby	12	10	3.54	27	25	1	0	165	171	79	65	54	107	L	R	6-5	215	8-4-73	1994	Glendale, Ariz.
Hyde, Rich	0	2	2.00	16	0	0	7	18	19	6	4	5	13	R	R	6-0	185	12-24-68	1991	Mahomet, Ill.
Macey, Fausto	8	9	3.89	28	25	1	0	171	167	84	74	50	94	R	R	6-4	185	10-9-75	1994	Santo Domingo, D.R.
Martin, Jeff	5	6	3.30	36	0	0	5	71	60	34	26	25	63	R	R	6-2	195	3-28-73	1991	Phoenix, Ariz.
McLain, Mike	0	1	2.29	9	0	0	2	20	16	5	5	6	21	L	R	6-2	205	3-18-70	1992	Elk Grove, Calif.
Ortiz, Russell	0	1	1.50	5	0	0	0	6	4	1	1	2	7	R	R	6-1	190	6-5-74	1995	Burbank, Calif.
Peters, Don	3	3	4.24	20	13	0	2	68	68	33	32	24	38	R	R	6-0	190	10-7-69	1990	Crestwood, Ill.
Prater, Pete	2	0	3.18	5	4	0	0	23	18	8	8	7	14	R	R	6-4	190	7-20-72	1994	Corning, Ark.
Rogers, Kevin	0	2	1.80	4	4	0	0	10	2	2	1	5	5	S	L	6-1	198	8-20-68	1988	Parchman, Miss.
Schramm, Carl	6	4	2.54	37	0	0	3	71	57	23	20	16	68	R	R	6-4	200	6-10-70	1991	Crete, Ill.
Taulbee, Andy	3	2	3.02	10	9	1	0	63	50	27	21	22	33	R	R	6-4	210	10-5-72	1994	Tucker, Ga.
VanLandingham, Wm.	1	0	0.00	1	1	0	0	7	4	0	0	2	5	R	R	6-2	210	7-16-70	1991	Franklin, Tenn.
Villano, Mike	0	1	1.65	21	0	0	1	33	27	7	6	11	42	R	R	6-1	200	8-10-71	1994	Bay City, Mich.
Whitaker, Steve	0	0	4.50	2	0	0	1	6	7	3	3	2	1	L	L	6-6	225	4-15-70	1991	Atwater, Calif.
Wilson, Trevor	0	1	1.35	2	2	0	0	7	5	4	1	3	5	L	L	6-0	204	6-7-66	1985	Scottsdale, Ariz.

BURLINGTON   A

MIDWEST LEAGUE

BATTING	AVG	G	AB	R	H	2B	3B	HR	RBI	BB	SO	SB	CS	B	T	HT	WT	DOB	1st Yr	Resides
Alguacil, Jose	.221	38	136	15	30	2	0	0	5	7	27	13	1	L	R	6-2	175	8-9-72	1993	Caracas, Venez.
Altman, Heath	.125	20	24	4	3	0	0	1	2	4	15	1	0	S	R	6-5	200	6-2-71	1993	Hamlet, N.C.
Bray, Notorris	.200	15	45	8	9	0	1	0	6	8	12	3	0	R	R	6-0	183	7-27-73	1994	La Grange, Ga.
Castillo, Alberto	.165	34	103	7	17	4	0	4	13	7	43	2	0	L	L	6-3	205	7-5-75	1994	Miami Lakes, Fla.
Cordero, Pablo	.242	59	190	21	46	9	2	2	21	14	38	2	1	R	R	6-0	189	6-24-73	1991	El Seibo, D.R.
Corujo, Rey	.133	14	45	2	6	1	0	0	2	8	1	1	0	R	R	5-11	165	10-19-71	1995	Bayamon, P.R.
Cruz, Deivi	.138	16	58	2	8	1	0	1	9	4	7	1	1	R	R	6-0	175	6-11-75	1993	Nizao, D.R.
Dantzler, Eric	.167	30	84	6	14	1	0	1	7	12	24	2	0	R	R	6-3	205	5-5-73	1994	Joliet, Ill.
Delgado, Wilson	.310	93	365	52	113	20	3	5	37	32	57	9	9	S	R	5-11	165	7-15-75	1993	Santo Domingo, D.R.
2-team (19 Wis.)	.299	112	435	65	130	23	3	5	44	35	72	12	9							
Denbow, Don	.178	105	326	42	58	7	1	12	33	42	143	14	2	R	R	6-4	215	4-30-73	1993	Corsicana, Texas
Glenn, Darrin	.214	62	182	35	39	4	1	9	27	23	59	4	3	R	R	6-0	195	1-4-71	1993	El Paso, Texas
Gulseth, Mark	.277	41	137	15	38	7	0	4	19	18	30	3	3	L	R	6-4	200	11-12-71	1993	Callaway, Minn.
Ibarra, Jesse	.330	129	437	72	144	30	1	34	96	77	94	1	2	S	R	6-3	195	7-12-72	1994	El Monte, Calif.
Keifer, Greg	.143	6	14	3	2	1	0	0	2	2	4	1	0	R	R	6-3	200	1-21-73	1994	Westerville, Ohio
Marval, Raul	.267	88	296	42	79	8	2	1	19	10	32	4	6	R	R	6-0	170	12-13-75	1993	Cabodare, Venez.
Poor, Jeff	.242	101	322	33	78	23	1	4	38	27	68	1	0	R	R	6-1	200	5-23-74	1994	El Segundo, Calif.
Reid, Derek	.285	95	354	74	101	16	4	13	55	31	55	22	4	R	R	6-2	195	2-4-70	1990	Cincinnati, Ohio
Schneider, Dan	.213	51	141	13	30	4	0	2	12	10	27	1	1	R	R	6-2	195	4-18-72	1994	Greensboro, N.C.
Swift, Scott	.191	68	209	29	40	3	1	0	17	37	33	9	5	S	R	6-1	180	10-18-70	1994	Ballwin, Mo.
Wallace, Brian	.213	97	338	48	72	12	0	9	38	34	65	7	5	R	R	6-2	200	9-10-71	1992	Newark, Del.
Watson, Kevin	.186	80	247	29	46	5	1	7	25	18	88	1	2	R	R	6-3	200	9-8-72	1994	Portland, Ore.
Wilson, Todd	.257	30	105	8	27	5	0	2	11	6	12	1	0	R	R	6-0	210	11-20-69	1994	San Diego, Calif.
Zaletel, Brian	.227	27	97	9	22	4	0	2	5	4	19	0	0	R	R	6-1	185	1-9-71	1993	Largo, Fla.

GAMES BY POSITION: C—Glenn 4, Ibarra 22, Poor 74, Schneider 51. **1B**—Altman 1, Castillo 33, Dantzler 12, Glenn 5, Gulseth 40, Ibarra 56. **2B**—Cruz 14, Marval 79, Swift 53. **3B**—Cruz 2, Glenn 11, Wallace 97, Wilson 29. **SS**—Alguacil 36, Castillo 1, Cruz 1, Delgado 93, Marval 11. **OF**—Altman 13, Bray 15, Cordero 57, Corujo 13, Dantzler 9, Denbow 105, Glenn 1, Keifer 1, Reid 95, Swift 2, Watson 21, Zaletel 21.

PITCHING	W	L	ERA	G	GS	CG	SV	IP	H	R	ER	BB	SO	B	T	HT	WT	DOB	1st Yr	Resides
Abreu, Jose	1	0	3.46	8	0	0	0	13	9	8	5	12	14	R	R	6-2	184	5-4-75	1993	Puerto Plata, D.R.
Abreu, Juan	0	0	0.00	2	0	0	0	2	1	3	0	4	0	L	L	6-0	207	10-26-75	1993	Quibor, Venez.
Ali, Sam	0	0	2.25	3	0	0	0	4	4	1	1	0	2	R	R	6-3	200	1-12-71	1995	Everett, Mass.
Altman, Heath	0	0	2.45	3	0	0	0	4	3	2	1	6	5	S	R	6-5	200	6-2-71	1993	Hamlet, N.C.
Alvarez, Ivan	1	2	4.85	4	2	0	0	13	17	12	7	5	12	L	L	6-3	220	5-19-70	1993	Canoga Park, Calif.
Cardona, Isbell	0	4	7.00	6	4	0	0	18	19	21	14	20	12	R	R	6-4	185	9-6-71	1990	La Guaira, Venez.
Charlton, Aaron	0	1	4.13	16	0	0	0	24	18	13	11	13	16	R	R	6-0	185	8-4-72	1994	Brea, Calif.
Estes, Shawn	0	0	4.11	4	4	0	0	15	13	8	7	12	22	R	L	6-2	200	2-28-73	1991	Gardnerville, Nev.
2-team (2 Wisc.)	0	0	2.84	6	6	0	0	25	18	9	8	17	33							
Gomez, Dennys	1	1	3.74	14	0	0	0	22	25	11	9	11	26	S	R	6-0	195	6-21-71	1994	Miami, Fla.
Grote, Jason	0	1	9.35	6	0	0	1	9	10	9	9	5	8	R	R	6-0	180	4-13-75	1994	Gresham, Ore.
Hernandez, Santos	5	8	2.66	44	0	0	9	64	54	27	19	20	85	R	R	6-1	172	11-3-72	1994	Chiriqui, Panama
Hutzler, Jeff	3	5	3.48	9	9	0	0	52	51	34	20	17	44	R	R	6-6	220	12-5-72	1995	San Antonio, Texas
Keith, Jeffrey	1	3	2.98	47	0	0	23	66	35	26	22	42	74	L	L	6-1	205	6-1-72	1994	Troy, N.Y.
Lake, Kevin	10	7	4.45	28	21	0	0	119	136	75	59	61	85	L	L	6-0	190	6-28-73	1994	Lompoc, Calif.
Lintern, Cory	1	0	6.00	9	0	0	0	15	19	10	10	5	8	S	R	6-0	190	12-13-71	1994	Colton, Calif.
McMillan, Leonard	1	0	5.27	8	0	0	0	14	15	8	8	10	4	L	R	6-0	170	4-22-74	1994	Catoosa, Okla.
McMullen, Mike	4	10	5.49	29	11	2	0	84	98	76	51	54	53	R	R	6-6	210	10-13-73	1993	Granada Hills, Calif.

PITCHING	W	L	ERA	G	GS	CG	SV	IP	H	R	ER	BB	SO	B	T	HT	WT	DOB	1st Yr	Resides
Mosman, Marc	0	0	0.00	8	0	0	0	9	5	0	0	4	6	R	R	6-2	210	8-16-73	1995	Lake Forest, Calif.
Myers, Jason	2	9	5.02	16	16	1	0	95	109	64	53	26	85	L	L	6-4	210	9-19-73	1993	Fontana, Calif.
Prater, Pete	7	5	3.69	21	20	2	0	115	112	58	47	56	80	R	R	6-4	190	7-20-72	1994	Corning, Ark.
Ratliff, Chris	2	6	6.34	15	14	1	0	61	74	49	43	32	33	R	R	6-3	195	6-26-73	1994	El Sobrante, Calif.
Rector, Bobby	9	11	4.11	27	24	0	0	136	135	78	62	59	102	R	R	6-1	170	9-24-74	1994	Carpinteria, Calif.
Rosenbohm, Jim	0	0	19.80	3	0	0	0	5	9	11	11	11	3	R	R	6-1	170	9-19-73	1992	Omaha, Neb.
Schiefelbein, Mike	0	0	0.00	1	0	0	0	0	0	0	0	1	0	R	R	6-1	190	8-8-72	1994	Littleton, Colo.
Smith, Brook	3	2	5.01	39	4	0	1	88	85	67	49	72	70	L	L	6-0	180	11-4-71	1993	Waukesha, Wisc.
Smith, Mason	0	4	6.94	8	4	0	0	23	26	18	18	12	19	R	R	6-4	190	9-30-72	1994	Portland, Ore.
Smith, Shad	0	1	6.23	2	2	0	0	9	10	8	6	6	4	R	R	6-4	220	5-21-67	1990	League City, Texas
Villano, Mike	3	1	2.84	16	0	0	1	25	20	12	8	21	29	R	R	6-1	200	8-10-71	1994	Bay City, Mich.

BELLINGHAM A

NORTHWEST LEAGUE

BATTING	AVG	G	AB	R	H	2B	3B	HR	RBI	BB	SO	SB	CS	B	T	HT	WT	DOB	1st Yr	Resides
Benner, Brian	.125	2	8	0	1	1	0	0	1	1	4	0	0	R	R	6-1	205	8-22-75	1993	Mission Viejo, Calif.
Bray, Notorris	.500	2	4	3	2	0	0	0	3	1	0	1	0	R	R	6-0	183	7-27-73	1994	La Grange, Ga.
Calderon, Ricardo	.227	67	216	23	49	9	0	6	35	22	73	1	2	L	L	6-2	195	12-22-75	1994	Carolina, P.R.
Castillo, Alberto	.213	74	263	19	56	11	0	5	23	35	99	0	1	L	L	6-3	205	7-5-75	1994	Miami Lakes, Fla.
Corujo, Rey	.221	60	208	23	46	15	1	6	34	23	27	6	4	R	R	5-11	185	10-19-71	1995	Bayamon, P.R.
Cruz, Deivi	.296	62	223	32	66	17	0	3	28	19	21	6	3	R	R	6-0	175	6-11-75	1993	Nizao, D.R.
Dantzler, Eric	.118	6	17	2	2	1	0	1	1	0	5	0	0	R	R	6-3	205	5-5-73	1994	Joliet, Ill.
Felix, Pedro	.274	43	113	14	31	2	1	0	16	7	33	1	1	R	R	6-1	180	4-27-77	1994	Azua, D.R.
Keifer, Greg	.278	10	36	6	10	1	2	1	3	4	14	0	1	R	R	6-3	200	1-21-73	1994	Westerville, Ohio
Morales, Julio	.254	66	248	43	63	18	3	6	25	34	60	26	9	R	R	6-0	190	2-15-74	1995	Palm Beach Gardens, Fla.
Nathan, Joe	.232	56	177	23	41	7	2	3	20	22	48	3	2	R	R	6-4	195	11-22-74	1995	Circleville, N.Y.
Norton, Andy	.218	25	55	3	12	1	0	0	5	8	15	0	0	R	R	6-0	200	2-9-73	1995	Woodinville, Wash.
Prospero, Teodoro	.138	41	109	7	15	2	0	1	6	6	45	0	1	R	R	5-11	160	2-12-77	1995	San Pedro de Macoris, D.R.
Rand, Ian	.128	23	47	4	6	0	0	0	1	4	25	0	0	R	R	6-4	190	1-30-77	1995	La Mesa, Calif.
Thompson, Bruce	.232	66	241	49	56	7	2	2	13	43	75	18	6	L	R	5-11	180	10-30-72	1995	Brandon, Fla.
Topping, Dan	.267	57	180	15	48	5	0	5	31	14	24	0	0	R	R	6-0	210	1-18-76	1994	St. Petersburg, Fla.
Torrealba, Yolvit	.155	26	71	2	11	3	0	0	8	2	14	0	1	R	R	5-11	180	7-19-78	1995	Guarenas, Venez.
Watson, Jon	.299	65	231	42	69	9	0	2	27	20	41	16	9	R	R	6-0	185	12-18-73	1995	Wallington, N.J.
Weaver, Terry	.250	37	116	24	29	2	0	3	13	9	30	2	1	R	R	6-1	175	10-8-72	1995	Dalton, Ohio

GAMES BY POSITION: C—Norton 24, Topping 47, Torrealba 26. **1B**—Calderon 1, Castillo 74, Dantzler 3, Felix 4. **2B**—Cruz 6, Prospero 36, Watson 44. **3B**—Cruz 54, Felix 25, Watson 7. **SS**—Nathan 54, Weaver 24. **OF**—Bray 1, Calderon 52, Corujo 35, Keifer 6, Morales 64, Rand 22, Thompson 64.

PITCHING	W	L	ERA	G	GS	CG	SV	IP	H	R	ER	BB	SO	B	T	HT	WT	DOB	1st Yr	Resides
Abreu, Jose	1	2	4.63	13	0	0	1	23	17	12	12	12	29	R	R	6-2	184	5-4-75	1993	Puerto Plata, D.R.
Ali, Sam	0	2	7.88	5	0	0	0	8	10	7	7	4	3	R	R	6-3	200	1-12-71	1995	Everett, Mass.
Bailey, Philip	6	1	1.36	19	4	0	0	60	51	15	9	15	39	L	L	6-1	185	10-4-73	1995	Benton, Ark.
Barcelo, Lorenzo	3	2	3.45	12	11	0	0	47	43	23	18	19	34	R	R	6-4	200	9-10-77	1994	San Pedro de Macoris, D.R.
Bermudez, Manuel	1	2	3.81	13	13	0	0	57	51	28	24	25	39	R	R	6-1	180	12-15-76	1995	Antioch, Calif.
Blasingim, Joseph	1	1	4.26	13	1	0	0	25	31	14	12	14	22	R	R	6-4	190	2-16-73	1995	Moro, Ill.
Blood, Darin	6	3	2.54	14	13	0	0	74	63	26	21	32	78	L	R	6-2	205	8-31-74	1995	Post Falls, Idaho
Brester, Jason	1	0	4.13	8	6	0	0	24	23	11	11	12	17	L	L	6-3	190	12-7-76	1995	Burlington, Wash.
Fontenot, Joe	0	3	1.93	6	6	0	0	19	14	5	4	10	14	R	R	6-2	185	3-20-77	1995	Scott, La.
Gomez, Dennys	0	1	7.50	4	0	0	1	6	8	6	5	3	6	S	R	6-0	195	6-21-71	1994	Miami, Fla.
Herrera, Ivan	0	0	0.00	1	0	0	0	2	0	0	0	1	1	R	R	6-6	215	12-16-76	1995	Acarigua, Venez.
Hutzler, Jeff	2	2	1.72	7	7	0	0	31	35	9	6	8	19	R	R	6-6	220	12-5-72	1995	San Antonio, Texas
Knoll, Brian	5	2	2.05	22	2	0	0	57	44	22	13	17	35	R	R	6-3	200	8-4-73	1995	Corona, Calif.
Lintern, Cory	2	0	0.87	3	0	0	1	10	6	2	1	2	6	S	R	6-0	190	12-13-71	1994	Colton, Calif.
Medero, Gadiel	0	0	6.35	4	0	0	0	6	10	7	4	4	4	R	R	6-6	210	11-25-75	1995	Trujillo Alto, P.R.
Mosman, Marc	0	0	5.81	12	3	0	0	26	38	21	17	8	21	R	R	6-2	210	8-16-73	1995	Lake Forest, Calif.
Ortiz, Russell	2	0	0.52	25	0	0	11	34	19	4	2	13	55	R	R	6-1	190	6-5-74	1995	Burbank, Calif.
Rodriguez, Luis	0	0	6.00	4	0	0	0	6	6	5	4	8	8	L	L	6-3	195	3-3-76	1994	Carolina, P.R.
Schiefelbein, Mike	0	0	0.00	3	0	0	0	1	1	0	0	3	1	R	R	6-1	190	8-8-72	1994	Littleton, Colo.
Stoops, Jim	6	5	3.43	24	0	0	4	42	32	23	16	17	58	R	R	6-2	180	6-30-72	1995	Somerset, N.J.
Takahashi, Kurt	1	2	5.61	17	0	0	0	26	28	18	16	14	20	R	R	6-4	215	2-22-74	1995	Porterville, Calif.
Tucker, Ben	2	1	1.91	12	10	0	0	57	53	21	12	19	48	R	R	6-4	210	11-6-73	1995	Fresno, Calif.
Woodrow, Jim	4	4	3.65	27	0	0	3	44	35	18	18	25	34	R	R	6-6	240	5-4-73	1995	Bradenton, Fla.

SEATTLE MARINERS

Manager: Lou Piniella.   **1995 Record:** 79-66, .545 (1st, AL West).

BATTING	AVG	G	AB	R	H	2B	3B	HR	RBI	BB	SO	SB	CS	B	T	HT	WT	DOB	1st Yr	Resides
Amaral, Rich	.282	90	238	45	67	14	2	2	19	21	33	21	2	R	R	6-0	175	4-1-62	1983	Seattle, Wash.
Blowers, Mike	.257	134	439	59	113	24	1	23	96	53	128	2	1	R	R	6-2	210	4-24-65	1986	Tacoma, Wash.
Bragg, Darren	.234	52	145	20	34	5	1	3	12	18	37	9	0	L	R	5-9	180	9-7-69	1991	Wolcott, Conn.
Buhner, Jay	.262	126	470	86	123	23	0	40	121	60	120	0	1	R	R	6-3	210	8-13-64	1984	League City, Texas
Coleman, Vince	.290	40	162	27	47	10	2	1	9	10	32	16	7	S	R	6-1	185	9-22-61	1982	St. Louis, Mo.
2-team (75 K.C.)	.288	115	455	66	131	23	6	5	29	37	80	42	16							
Cora, Joey	.297	120	427	64	127	19	2	3	39	37	31	18	7	S	R	5-8	155	5-14-65	1985	Caguas, P.R.
Diaz, Alex	.248	103	270	44	67	14	0	3	27	13	27	18	8	S	R	5-11	180	10-5-68	1987	San Sebastian, P.R.
Fermin, Felix	.195	73	200	21	39	6	0	0	15	6	6	2	0	R	R	5-11	170	10-9-63	1983	Santiago, D.R.
Griffey, Ken Jr.	.258	72	260	52	67	7	0	17	42	52	53	4	2	L	L	6-3	205	11-21-69	1987	Renton, Wash.
Kreuter, Chad	.227	26	75	12	17	5	0	1	8	5	22	0	0	S	R	6-2	190	8-26-64	1985	Arlington, Texas
Martinez, Edgar	.356	145	511	121	182	52	0	29	113	116	87	4	3	R	R	5-11	190	1-2-63	1983	Kirkland, Wash.
Martinez, Tino	.293	141	519	92	152	35	3	31	111	62	91	0	0	L	R	6-2	210	12-7-67	1989	Tampa, Fla.
Newfield, Marc	.188	24	85	7	16	3	0	3	14	3	16	0	0	R	R	6-4	205	10-19-72	1990	Huntington Beach, Calif.
Newson, Warren	.292	33	72	15	21	2	0	2	6	16	18	1	0	L	L	5-7	202	7-3-64	1986	Newnan, Ga.
2-team (51 Chicago)	.261	84	157	34	41	2	2	5	15	39	45	2	1							
Pirkl, Greg	.235	10	17	2	4	0	0	0	0	1	7	0	0	R	R	6-5	225	8-7-70	1988	Phoenix, Ariz.
Pozo, Arquimedez	.000	1	1	0	0	0	0	0	0	0	0	0	0	R	R	5-10	160	8-24-73	1991	Santo Domingo, D.R.
Rodriguez, Alex	.232	48	142	15	33	6	2	5	19	6	42	4	2	R	R	6-2	190	7-27-75	1994	Miami, Fla.
Sojo, Luis	.289	102	339	50	98	18	2	7	39	23	19	4	2	R	R	5-11	174	1-3-66	1987	Barquisimeto, Venez.
Strange, Doug	.271	74	155	19	42	9	2	2	21	10	25	0	3	S	R	6-2	170	4-13-64	1985	Scottsdale, Ariz.
Thurman, Gary	.320	13	25	3	8	2	0	0	3	1	3	5	2	R	R	5-10	180	11-12-64	1983	Indianapolis, Ind.
Widger, Chris	.200	23	45	2	9	0	0	1	2	3	11	0	0	R	R	6-3	195	5-21-71	1992	Pennsville, N.J.
Wilson, Dan	.278	119	399	40	111	22	3	9	51	33	63	2	1	R	R	6-3	190	3-25-69	1990	St. Louis Park, Ill.

PITCHING	W	L	ERA	G	GS	CG	SV	IP	H	R	ER	BB	SO	B	T	HT	WT	DOB	1st Yr	Resides
Ayala, Bobby	6	5	4.44	63	0	0	19	71	73	42	35	30	77	R	R	6-3	200	7-8-69	1988	Oxnard, Calif.
Belcher, Tim	10	12	4.52	28	28	1	0	179	188	101	90	88	96	R	R	6-3	220	10-19-61	1984	Mt. Gilead, Ohio
Benes, Andy	7	2	5.86	12	12	0	0	63	72	42	41	33	45	R	R	6-6	238	8-20-67	1989	Poway, Calif.
Bosio, Chris	10	8	4.92	31	31	0	0	170	211	98	93	69	85	R	R	6-3	225	4-3-63	1982	Shingle Springs, Calif.
Carmona, Rafael	2	4	5.66	15	3	0	1	48	55	31	30	34	28	L	R	6-2	185	10-2-72	1993	Comerio, P.R.
Charlton, Norm	2	1	1.51	30	0	0	14	48	23	12	8	16	58	S	L	6-3	205	1-6-63	1984	Jamaica Beach, Texas
Converse, Jim	0	3	7.36	6	1	0	1	11	16	9	9	8	9	L	R	5-9	180	8-17-71	1990	Citrus Heights, Calif.
Cummings, John	0	0	11.81	4	0	0	0	5	8	7	7	4	4	L	L	6-3	200	5-10-69	1990	Laguna Niguel, Calif.
Davis, Tim	2	1	6.38	5	5	0	0	24	30	21	17	18	19	L	L	5-11	165	7-14-70	1992	Bristol, Fla.
Davison, Scott	0	0	6.23	3	0	0	0	4	7	3	3	1	3	R	R	6-0	190	10-16-70	1988	Redondo Beach, Calif.
Fleming, Dave	1	5	7.50	16	7	1	0	48	57	44	40	34	26	L	L	6-3	200	11-7-69	1990	Mahopac, N.Y.
Frey, Steve	0	3	4.76	13	0	0	0	11	16	7	6	6	7	R	L	5-9	170	7-29-63	1983	Newtown, Pa.
Guetterman, Lee	0	0	6.88	23	0	0	1	17	21	13	13	11	11	L	L	6-8	225	11-22-58	1981	Lenoir City, Tenn.
Harikkala, Tim	0	0	16.20	1	0	0	0	3	7	6	6	1	1	R	R	6-2	185	7-15-71	1992	Lake Worth, Fla.
Johnson, Randy	18	2	2.48	30	30	6	0	214	159	65	59	65	294	R	L	6-10	225	9-10-63	1985	Bellevue, Wash.
King, Kevin	0	0	12.27	2	0	0	0	4	7	5	5	1	3	L	L	6-4	200	2-11-69	1990	Tulsa, Okla.
Krueger, Bill	2	1	5.85	6	5	0	0	20	37	17	13	4	10	L	L	6-5	205	4-24-58	1980	Seattle, Wash.
Mecir, Jim	0	0	0.00	2	0	0	0	5	5	1	0	2	3	S	R	6-1	195	5-16-70	1991	St. James, N.Y.
Nelson, Jeff	7	3	2.17	62	0	0	2	79	58	21	19	27	96	R	R	6-8	225	11-17-66	1984	Baltimore, Md.
Risley, Bill	2	1	3.13	45	0	0	1	60	55	21	21	18	65	R	R	6-2	210	5-29-67	1987	Farmington, N.M.
Torres, Salomon	3	8	6.00	16	13	1	0	72	87	53	48	42	45	R	R	5-11	150	3-11-72	1990	San Pedro de Macoris, D.R.
Villone, Ron	0	2	7.91	19	0	0	0	19	20	19	17	23	26	L	L	6-3	235	1-16-70	1992	Bergenfield, N.J.
Wells, Bob	4	3	5.75	30	4	0	0	77	88	51	49	39	38	R	R	6-0	180	11-1-66	1989	Yakima, Wash.
Wolcott, Bob	3	2	4.42	7	6	0	0	37	43	18	18	14	19	R	R	6-0	190	9-8-73	1992	Medford, Ore.

FIELDING

Catcher	PCT	G	PO	A	E	DP	PB
Kreuter	.976	23	151	12	4	3	3
Widger	1.000	19	61	1	0	0	2
Wilson	.995	119	895	52	5	5	8

First Base	PCT	G	PO	A	E	DP
Blowers	.974	7	32	5	1	7
E. Martinez	.968	3	29	1	1	0
T. Martinez	.993	139	1048	101	8	88
Pirkl	1.000	6	32	3	0	1

Second Base	PCT	G	PO	A	E	DP
Cora	.955	112	205	262	22	53
Fermin	.991	29	32	75	1	12
Pozo	1.000	1	0	1	0	0
Sojo	.957	19	23	44	3	5
Strange	1.000	5	3	5	0	1

Third Base	PCT	G	PO	A	E	DP
Blowers	.947	126	80	169	14	9
E. Martinez	.800	4	1	3	1	0
Strange	.948	41	28	64	5	2

Shortstop	PCT	G	PO	A	E	DP
Cora	.000	1	0	0	1	0
Fermin	.971	46	75	93	5	31
Rodriguez	.953	46	56	106	8	14
Sojo	.983	80	110	176	5	35

Outfield	PCT	G	PO	A	E	DP
Amaral	.992	73	121	6	1	0
Blowers	.800	5	4	0	1	0
Bragg	.989	47	83	7	1	2
Buhner	.989	120	180	5	2	0
Coleman	.988	38	82	2	1	0
Diaz	.987	88	145	4	2	2
Griffey	.990	70	190	5	2	1
Newfield	1.000	24	44	0	0	0
Newson	.971	23	33	1	1	0
Sojo	.900	6	8	1	1	0
Strange	1.000	4	8	0	0	0
Thurman	1.000	9	15	0	0	0
Widger	1.000	3	3	0	0	0

Tino Martinez

RON VESELY

MARINERS

FARM SYSTEM

Director of Player Development: Jim Beattie.

Class	Farm Team	League	W	L	Pct.	Finish*	Manager	First Yr
AAA	Tacoma (Wash.) Rainiers	Pacific Coast	68	76	.472	6th (10)	Steve Smith	1995
AA	Port City (N.C.) Roosters	Southern	62	80	.437	8th (10)	Dave Myers	1995
#A	Riverside (Calif.) Pilots	California	72	67	.518	6th (10)	Dave Brundage	1993
A	Wisconsin Timber Rattlers	Midwest	63	75	.457	12th (14)	Mike Goff	1993
A	Everett (Wash.) Aquasox	Northwest	37	39	.487	T-4th (8)	Orlando Gomez	1995
R	Peoria (Ariz.) Mariners	Arizona	24	32	.429	5th (6)	Tom LeVasseur	1988

*Finish in overall standings (No. of teams in league)   #Advanced level

ORGANIZATION LEADERS

MAJOR LEAGUERS

BATTING

*AVG	Edgar Martinez	.356
R	Edgar Martinez	121
H	Edgar Martinez	182
TB	Edgar Martinez	321
2B	Edgar Martinez	52
3B	Two tied at	3
HR	Jay Buhner	40
RBI	Jay Buhner	121
BB	Edgar Martinez	116
SO	Mike Blowers	128
SB	Rich Amaral	21

PITCHING

W	Randy Johnson	18
L	Tim Belcher	12
#ERA	Jeff Nelson	2.17
G	Bobby Ayala	63
CG	Randy Johnson	6
SV	Bobby Ayala	19
IP	Randy Johnson	214
BB	Tim Belcher	88
SO	Randy Johnson	294

Mariners minor league Player of the Year Raul Ibanez

THE SPORTS GROUP

MINOR LEAGUERS

BATTING

*AVG	Raul Ibanez, Riverside	.332
R	Randy Jorgensen, Riverside	78
H	Randy Jorgensen, Riverside	148
TB	James Bonnici, Port City	246
2B	James Bonnici, Port City	36
3B	Gary Thurman, Tacoma	12
HR	Two tied at	20
RBI	Raul Ibanez, Riverside	108
BB	James Bonnici, Port City	76
SO	Jason Varitek, Port City	126
SB	Kyle Towner, Wisconsin	34

PITCHING

W	Trey Moore, Riverside	14
L	Roy Smith, Wisconsin	14
#ERA	Todd Niemeier, Everett	2.81
G	Dan Sullivan, Riverside	53
CG	Three tied at	4
SV	Dean Crow, Riverside	22
IP	Derek Bieniasz, Wisconsin	175
BB	Matt Apana, Port City/Tacoma	85
SO	Marino Santana, Wisconsin/Riverside	167

*Minimum 250 At-Bats   #Minimum 75 Innings

TOP 10 PROSPECTS

How the Mariners Top 10 prospects, as judged by Baseball America prior to the 1995 season, fared in 1995:

Alex Rodriguez

FRANK RAGSDALE

Player, Pos.	Club (Class—League)	AVG	AB	R	H	2B	3B	HR	RBI	SB
1. Alex Rodriguez, ss	Tacoma (AAA—Pacific Coast)	.360	214	37	77	12	3	15	45	2
	Seattle	.232	142	15	33	6	2	5	19	4
2. *Marc Newfield, of	Tacoma (AAA—Pacific Coast)	.278	198	30	55	11	0	5	30	1
	Seattle	.188	85	7	16	3	0	3	14	0
	Las Vegas (AAA—Pacific Coast)	.343	70	10	24	5	1	3	12	2
	San Diego	.309	55	6	17	5	1	1	7	0
4. Desi Relaford, ss-2b	Port City (AA—Southern)	.287	352	51	101	11	2	7	27	25
	Tacoma (AAA—Pacific Coast)	.239	113	20	27	5	1	2	7	6
6. Chris Widger, c	Tacoma (AAA—Pacific Coast)	.276	174	29	48	11	1	9	21	0
	Seattle	.200	45	2	9	0	0	1	2	0
10. Greg Pirkl, 1b	Tacoma (AAA—Pacific Coast)	.293	174	29	51	8	2	15	44	1
	Seattle	.235	17	2	4	0	0	0	0	0

Player, Pos.	Club (Class—League)	W	L	ERA	G	SV	IP	H	BB	SO
3. *Ron Villone, lhp	Tacoma (AAA—Pacific Coast)	1	0	0.61	22	13	30	9	19	43
	Seattle	0	2	7.91	19	0	19	20	23	26
	San Diego	2	1	4.21	19	1	26	24	11	37
5. Makoto Suzuki, rhp	AZL Mariners (R—Arizona)	1	0	6.75	4	0	4	5	0	3
	Riverside (A—California)	0	1	4.70	6	0	8	10	6	6
7. Matt Wagner, rhp	Port City (AA—Southern)	5	8	2.82	23	0	137	121	33	111
	Tacoma (AAA—Pacific Coast)	1	5	6.27	6	0	33	43	17	33
8. Bob Wolcott, rhp	Port City (AA—Southern)	7	3	2.20	12	0	86	60	13	53
	Tacoma (AAA—Pacific Coast)	6	3	4.08	13	0	79	94	16	43
	Seattle	3	2	4.42	7	0	37	43	14	19
9. #Shawn Estes, lhp	Wisconsin (A—Midwest)	0	0	0.90	2	0	10	5	5	11
	Burlington (A—Midwest)	0	0	4.11	4	0	15	13	12	22
	San Jose (A—California)	5	2	2.17	9	0	50	32	17	61
	Shreveport (AA—Texas)	2	0	2.01	4	0	22	14	10	18
	San Francisco	0	3	6.75	3	0	17	16	5	14

*Traded to San Diego   #Traded to San Francisco

PACIFIC COAST LEAGUE

BATTING	AVG	G	AB	R	H	2B	3B	HR	RBI	BB	SO	SB	CS	B	T	HT	WT	DOB	1st Yr	Resides
Barron, Tony	.200	9	25	4	5	0	0	0	2	2	3	0	0	R	R	6-0	185	8-17-66	1987	Tacoma, Wash.
Bragg, Darren	.307	53	212	24	65	13	3	4	31	23	39	10	3	L	R	5-9	180	9-7-69	1991	Wolcott, Conn.
Diaz, Alex	.250	10	40	3	10	1	0	0	4	2	5	1	2	S	R	5-11	180	10-5-68	1987	San Sebastian, P.R.
Diaz, Eddy	.333	11	36	5	12	2	0	0	5	4	2	0	0	R	R	5-10	160	9-29-71	1990	Barquisimeto, Venez.
Fermin, Felix	.333	1	3	0	1	0	0	0	0	0	0	0	0	R	R	5-11	170	10-9-63	1983	Santiago, D.R.
Griffey, Ken	.000	1	3	0	0	0	0	0	0	0	1	0	0	L	L	6-3	205	11-21-69	1987	Renton, Wash.
Hansen, Terrel	.220	20	50	5	11	1	0	3	10	2	12	0	0	R	R	6-3	210	9-25-66	1987	Bremerton, Wash.
Howard, Chris	.243	83	268	33	65	14	0	4	31	18	70	0	1	R	R	6-2	200	2-27-66	1988	Houston, Texas
Humphreys, Mike	.200	18	35	3	7	2	0	0	1	3	11	0	0	R	R	6-0	185	4-10-67	1988	DeSoto, Texas
Kreuter, Chad	.292	15	48	6	14	5	0	1	11	8	11	0	0	S	R	6-2	190	8-26-64	1985	Arlington, Texas
Litton, Greg	.309	117	388	58	120	25	1	9	56	43	69	2	2	R	R	6-0	185	7-13-64	1984	Pensacola, Fla.
Mack, Quinn	.265	70	204	30	54	11	0	1	17	24	21	9	2	L	L	5-10	180	9-11-65	1987	Cerritos, Calif.
Maynard, Scott	.000	1	1	0	0	0	0	0	0	0	0	0	0	R	R	6-2	215	8-28-77	1995	Laguna Niguel, Calif.
Newfield, Marc	.278	53	198	30	55	11	0	5	30	19	30	1	0	R	R	6-4	205	10-19-72	1990	Huntington Beach, Calif.
Noland, J.D.	.275	76	251	27	69	10	3	5	28	13	37	14	6	L	R	5-9	173	12-5-68	1989	Lexington, Ky.
Peguero, Julio	.200	11	25	2	5	0	1	0	1	1	7	0	0	S	R	5-11	160	9-7-68	1987	Santo Domingo, D.R.
Pevey, Marty	.105	7	19	2	2	0	0	0	0	1	5	0	0	L	R	6-1	190	9-18-61	1982	Savannah, Ga.
Pirkl, Greg	.293	47	174	29	51	8	2	15	44	14	28	1	1	R	R	6-5	225	8-7-70	1988	Phoenix, Ariz.
Pozo, Arquimedez	.300	122	450	57	135	19	6	10	62	26	31	3	3	R	R	5-10	160	8-24-73	1991	Santo Domingo, D.R.
Relaford, Desi	.239	30	113	20	27	5	1	2	7	13	24	6	0	S	R	5-8	155	9-16-73	1991	Jacksonville, Fla.
Roberson, Kevin	.236	42	157	17	37	6	1	6	17	19	51	1	1	S	R	6-4	210	1-29-68	1988	Decatur, Ill.
Rodriguez, Alex	.360	54	214	37	77	12	3	15	45	18	44	2	4	R	R	6-2	190	7-27-75	1994	Miami, Fla.
Saunders, Doug	.281	50	135	19	38	5	2	5	24	7	30	0	0	R	R	6-0	172	12-13-69	1988	Port St. Lucie, Fla.
2-team (5 Edmonton)	.272	55	151	21	41	7	3	5	28	7	32	0	0							
Sealy, Scot	.300	4	10	1	3	0	0	0	0	0	0	0	0	R	R	6-4	225	2-10-71	1992	Satsuma, Ala.
Sheets, Andy	.293	132	437	57	128	29	9	2	47	32	83	8	3	R	R	6-2	180	11-19-71	1992	St. Amant, La.
Sherman, Darrell	.257	119	350	59	90	9	3	2	31	54	49	19	6	L	L	5-9	160	12-4-67	1989	Lynwood, Calif.
Sojo, Luis	.176	4	17	1	3	0	0	1	1	0	2	0	0	R	R	5-11	174	1-3-66	1987	Barquisimeto, Venez.
Thurman, Gary	.300	93	363	65	109	10	12	5	46	20	62	22	8	R	R	5-10	180	11-12-64	1983	Indianapolis, Ind.
Turang, Brian	.240	59	196	22	47	4	1	1	18	13	35	7	4	R	R	5-10	170	6-14-67	1989	Long Beach, Calif.
Wakamatsu, Don	.156	9	32	3	5	1	0	0	6	2	8	0	0	R	R	6-2	200	2-22-63	1985	Hayward, Calif.
Widger, Chris	.276	50	174	29	48	11	1	9	21	9	29	0	0	R	R	6-3	195	5-21-71	1992	Pennsville, N.J.
Wilkerson, Curtis	.222	5	18	1	4	0	0	0	3	1	3	0	0	S	R	5-9	175	4-26-61	1980	Arlington, Texas
Willard, Jerry	.268	85	228	33	61	16	0	9	47	45	43	0	0	L	R	6-2	195	3-14-60	1980	Port Hueneme, Calif.

PITCHING	W	L	ERA	G	GS	CG	SV	IP	H	R	ER	BB	SO	B	T	HT	WT	DOB	1st Yr	Resides
Apana, Matt	8	8	4.95	21	20	0	0	104	121	72	57	61	58	R	R	6-0	195	1-16-71	1993	Honolulu, Hawaii
Campbell, Kevin	3	2	3.67	31	0	0	1	49	50	28	20	14	34	R	R	6-2	225	12-6-64	1986	Des Arc, Ark.
Carmona, Rafael	4	3	5.06	8	8	1	0	48	52	29	27	19	37	L	R	6-2	185	10-2-72	1993	Comerio, P.R.
Converse, Jim	4	7	5.99	17	12	0	0	74	96	57	49	36	43	L	R	5-9	180	8-17-71	1990	Citrus Heights, Calif.
Cummings, John	0	1	7.71	1	1	0	0	2	6	4	2	3	3	L	L	6-3	200	5-10-69	1990	Laguna Niguel, Calif.
Darwin, Jeff	7	2	2.70	46	0	0	12	63	51	21	19	21	51	R	R	6-3	180	7-6-69	1989	Gainesville, Texas
Davis, Tim	0	1	5.40	2	2	0	0	13	15	8	8	4	13	L	L	5-11	165	7-14-70	1992	Bristol, Fla.
Davison, Scott	1	1	5.32	8	3	0	0	22	21	14	13	4	12	R	R	6-0	190	10-16-70	1988	Redondo Beach, Calif.
Glinatsis, George	1	2	7.34	8	8	0	0	31	39	25	25	13	13	R	R	6-4	195	6-29-69	1991	Youngstown, Ohio
Gould, Clint	0	0	0.00	1	0	0	0	0	0	0	0	0	0	R	R	6-1	230	8-18-71	1994	Kent, Wash.
Graybill, Dave	0	0	6.75	6	0	0	0	9	12	8	7	6	1	R	R	6-2	210	10-9-62	1984	Tempe, Ariz.
Green, Otis	4	1	5.76	18	0	0	0	25	26	19	16	12	17	L	L	6-2	192	3-11-64	1983	Miami, Fla.
Guetterman, Lee	1	2	2.95	33	1	0	4	37	33	12	12	9	21	L	L	6-8	225	11-22-58	1981	Lenoir City, Tenn.
Harikkala, Tim	5	12	4.24	25	24	4	0	146	151	78	69	55	73	R	R	6-2	185	7-15-71	1992	Lake Worth, Fla.
Holman, Brad	1	0	8.10	5	0	0	0	7	9	6	6	3	1	R	R	6-5	200	2-9-68	1990	Wichita, Kan.
King, Kevin	0	0	7.56	16	0	0	0	17	33	14	14	7	10	L	L	6-4	200	2-11-69	1990	Tulsa, Okla.
Krueger, Bill	5	3	4.26	10	8	0	0	51	52	30	24	9	39	L	L	6-5	205	4-24-58	1980	Seattle, Wash.
Lewis, Jeff	1	1	9.64	3	2	0	0	9	13	10	10	4	11	R	R	6-3	178	12-5-65	1988	Tustin, Calif.
Mecir, Jim	1	4	3.10	40	0	0	8	70	63	29	24	28	46	S	R	6-1	195	5-16-70	1991	St. James, N.Y.
Milacki, Bob	6	4	5.27	12	12	1	0	72	94	50	42	23	31	R	R	6-4	230	7-28-64	1984	Lake Havasu, Ariz.
Phillips, Tony	3	2	4.12	47	1	0	1	87	98	44	40	14	44	R	R	6-4	195	6-9-69	1991	Hattiesburg, Miss.
Risley, Bill	0	0	0.00	1	0	0	0	1	0	0	0	1	2	R	R	6-2	210	5-29-67	1987	Farmington, N.M.
Salkeld, Roger	1	0	1.80	4	3	0	1	15	8	4	3	7	11	R	R	6-5	215	3-6-71	1989	Saugus, Calif.
Thompson, John	0	1	0.00	1	0	0	0	3	2	0	0	0	4	R	R	6-2	200	1-18-73	1992	Spokane, Wash.
Torres, Salomon	1	1	3.21	5	4	0	0	28	20	10	10	13	19	R	R	5-11	150	3-11-72	1990	San Pedro de Macoris, D.R.
2-team (1 Phoenix)	1	1	3.00	6	4	0	0	30	22	10	10	13	24							
Villone, Ron	1	0	0.61	22	0	0	13	30	9	6	2	19	42	L	L	6-3	235	1-16-70	1992	Bergenfield, N.J.
Wagner, Matt	1	5	6.27	6	6	1	0	33	43	29	23	17	33	R	R	6-5	215	4-4-72	1994	Cedar Falls, Iowa
Weber, Weston	3	7	4.60	20	13	0	0	102	111	55	52	41	54	R	R	6-0	175	1-5-64	1986	Dodge Center, Minn.
Williams, Jeff	0	3	8.22	8	3	0	0	23	31	21	21	12	8	R	R	6-4	230	4-16-69	1990	Arlington, Texas
Wolcott, Bob	6	3	4.08	13	13	2	0	79	94	49	36	16	43	R	R	6-0	190	9-8-73	1992	Medford, Ore.

FIELDING

Catcher	PCT	G	PO	A	E	DP	PB
Howard	.987	77	405	47	6	3	8
Kreuter	.988	14	70	10	1	3	1
Litton	1.000	2	2	0	0	0	0
Maynard	1.000	1	6	0	0	0	0
Pevey	1.000	7	36	1	0	0	1
Sealy	.933	4	14	0	1	0	1
Wakamatsu	.952	9	53	6	3	1	0
Widger	.980	37	176	21	4	3	4
Willard	1.000	12	38	0	0	0	1

First Base	PCT	G	PO	A	E	DP
Barron	1.000	1	1	0	0	0
Hansen	1.000	9	71	6	0	5
Litton	.990	79	575	48	6	53
Pirkl	.983	33	276	19	5	31
Saunders	1.000	4	35	3	0	2
Turang	1.000	1	6	0	0	0
Willard	.976	46	324	35	9	26

Second Base	PCT	G	PO	A	E	DP
E. Diaz	.966	7	10	18	1	4
Pozo	.971	81	162	245	12	49

	PCT	G	PO	A	E	DP
Relaford	.958	29	50	88	6	18
Saunders	.974	7	17	20	1	6
Sheets	1.000	8	9	31	0	5
Sojo	1.000	2	3	6	0	0
Turang	.947	52	25	29	3	5
Wilkerson	1.000	5	8	19	0	4

Third Base	PCT	G	PO	A	E	DP
E. Diaz	1.000	4	2	5	0	1
Litton	.948	39	33	59	5	7
Pozo	.946	33	29	59	5	2

	PCT	G	PO	A	E	DP
Saunders	.947	34	18	54	4	9
Sheets	.913	33	11	83	9	2
Turang	.917	14	9	24	3	3

Shortstop	PCT	G	PO	A	E	DP
Fermin	.000	1	0	0	0	0
Litton	1.000	2	0	4	0	0
Relaford	1.000	2	2	5	0	0
Rodriguez	.961	51	90	157	10	28
Saunders	.000	1	0	0	0	0

	PCT	G	PO	A	E	DP
Sheets	.957	93	137	268	18	59
Sojo	1.000	1	1	3	0	1

Outfield	PCT	G	PO	A	E	DP
Barron	1.000	5	11	0	0	0
Bragg	.968	47	115	7	4	2
A. Diaz	1.000	9	15	1	0	0
Hansen	1.000	5	3	0	0	0
Humphreys	.955	15	21	0	1	0
Litton	1.000	3	2	1	0	0

	PCT	G	PO	A	E	DP
Mack	.960	56	94	3	4	3
Newfield	.966	30	55	1	2	0
Noland	.947	42	68	4	4	1
Peguero	1.000	7	9	1	0	0
Roberson	.981	29	51	2	1	0
Sherman	.974	112	252	12	7	1
Thurman	.965	86	180	13	7	2
Turang	.982	30	56	0	1	0
Widger	1.000	6	13	1	0	0

PORT CITY   AA

SOUTHERN LEAGUE

BATTING	AVG	G	AB	R	H	2B	3B	HR	RBI	BB	SO	SB	CS	B	T	HT	WT	DOB	1st Yr	Resides
Adams, Tommy	.220	30	118	10	26	7	0	3	16	6	27	5	3	R	R	6-1	205	11-26-69	1991	Mission Viejo, Calif.
Bonnici, James	.283	138	508	75	144	36	3	20	91	76	97	2	2	R	R	6-4	230	1-21-72	1991	Ortonville, Mich.
Cardenas, John	.226	57	195	17	44	9	0	0	17	9	45	1	3	R	R	6-3	210	7-23-70	1993	Fort Worth, Texas
Cora, Manny	.226	80	261	17	59	8	3	0	15	8	38	1	6	S	R	6-0	183	12-20-73	1991	Levittown, P.R.
Delgado, Wilson	.195	13	41	3	8	4	0	0	1	6	8	0	0	S	R	5-11	165	7-15-75	1993	Santo Domingo, D.R.
Diaz, Eddy	.261	110	421	66	110	22	0	16	47	40	39	9	7	R	R	5-10	160	9-29-71	1990	Barquisimeto, Venez.
Gipson, Charles	.223	112	391	36	87	11	2	0	29	30	66	10	12	R	R	6-0	188	12-16-72	1992	Orange, Calif.
Gomez, Fabio	.237	29	93	7	22	4	0	1	11	12	20	1	3	R	R	6-0	185	5-12-68	1987	Tucson, Ariz.
Griffey, Craig	.177	96	299	43	53	11	1	0	24	46	77	13	3	R	R	5-11	175	6-3-71	1991	West Chester, Ohio
Hickey, Mike	.262	120	447	59	117	24	1	6	59	60	83	6	3	S	R	6-2	180	6-22-70	1992	Honolulu, Hawaii
Koehler, Jim	.000	2	2	0	0	0	0	0	0	0	1	0	0	L	L	6-3	215	11-5-70	1991	Pleasanton, Calif.
Peguero, Julio	.316	71	256	42	81	15	1	3	18	16	34	12	8	S	R	5-11	160	9-7-68	1987	Santo Domingo, D.R.
Rackley, Keifer	.256	114	430	55	110	17	2	6	40	39	96	8	4	L	R	6-1	200	2-27-71	1993	Birmingham, Ala.
Ramirez, Roberto	.278	129	490	67	136	24	6	17	82	35	98	11	10	R	R	6-2	180	3-18-70	1989	Phoenix, Ariz.
Relaford, Desi	.287	90	352	51	101	11	2	7	27	41	58	25	9	S	R	5-8	155	9-16-73	1991	Jacksonville, Fla.
Saunders, Doug	.263	28	114	13	30	9	1	4	16	10	28	2	0	R	R	6-0	172	12-13-69	1988	Port St. Lucie, Fla.
Sutherland, Alex	.205	13	44	1	9	3	0	0	3	5	7	1	0	R	R	5-11	170	9-13-71	1991	Maracaibo, Venez.
Varitek, Jason	.224	104	352	42	79	14	2	10	44	61	126	0	1	S	R	6-2	210	4-11-72	1995	Longwood, Fla.

PITCHING	W	L	ERA	G	GS	CG	SV	IP	H	R	ER	BB	SO	B	T	HT	WT	DOB	1st Yr	Resides
Adam, Dave	6	10	4.34	31	13	0	0	112	107	58	54	48	85	R	R	6-3	202	2-14-69	1990	Shelton, Conn.
Apana, Matt	1	3	4.32	6	6	0	0	33	34	24	16	24	28	R	R	6-0	195	1-16-71	1993	Honolulu, Hawaii
Carmona, Rafael	1	1	1.80	15	0	0	4	15	11	5	3	3	17	L	R	6-2	185	10-2-72	1993	Comerio, P.R.
Davison, Scott	2	0	0.89	34	0	0	10	41	22	4	4	16	50	R	R	6-0	190	10-16-70	1988	Redondo Beach, Calif.
Fernandez, Osvaldo	12	7	3.57	27	26	0	0	156	139	78	62	60	160	L	L	6-2	193	4-15-70	1994	San Fernando, Calif.
Fitzer, Doug	0	0	5.40	4	0	0	0	5	3	4	3	1	4	L	L	6-5	210	7-2-69	1990	Farmington Hills, Mich.
Franklin, Ryan	6	10	4.32	31	20	1	0	146	153	84	70	43	102	R	R	6-3	160	3-5-73	1993	Spiro, Okla.
Glinatsis, George	6	7	5.30	18	18	1	0	93	104	63	55	44	68	R	R	6-4	195	6-29-69	1991	Youngstown, Ohio
King, Kevin	1	1	3.77	20	0	0	0	31	35	15	13	11	19	L	L	6-4	200	2-11-69	1990	Tulsa, Okla.
Lowe, Derek	1	6	6.08	10	10	1	0	53	70	41	36	22	30	R	R	6-6	170	6-1-73	1991	Dearborn, Mich.
Nickell, Jackie	5	8	3.73	27	9	0	0	89	74	40	37	30	81	R	R	5-10	175	4-20-70	1992	Tiburon, Calif.
Resendez, Oscar	0	2	4.24	11	0	0	0	17	16	8	8	8	15	R	R	6-1	175	9-1-71	1991	Alice, Texas
Russell, Lagrande	4	3	3.24	39	0	0	1	72	68	32	26	43	54	R	R	6-2	175	8-20-70	1990	Hallsboro, N.C.
Tsamis, George	0	0	2.61	7	0	0	0	10	11	4	3	11	3	R	L	6-2	175	6-14-67	1989	Clearwater, Fla.
2-team (12 Carolina)	0	0	3.38	19	0	0	0	21	23	9	8	16	10							
Urso, Sal	2	0	2.17	51	0	0	1	46	41	13	11	21	44	R	L	5-11	195	1-19-72	1990	Tampa, Fla.
Wagner, Matt	5	8	2.82	23	23	0	0	137	121	57	43	33	111	R	R	6-5	215	4-4-72	1994	Cedar Falls, Iowa
Witte, Trey	3	2	1.73	48	0	0	11	62	48	17	12	14	39	R	R	6-1	190	1-15-70	1991	Houston, Texas
Wolcott, Bob	7	3	2.20	12	12	0	2	86	60	26	21	13	53	R	R	6-0	190	9-8-73	1992	Medford, Ore.
Worley, Robert	1	7	4.58	22	5	0	0	57	60	42	29	30	26	R	R	6-3	185	2-15-71	1992	Westerville, Ohio

FIELDING

Catcher	PCT	G	PO	A	E	DP	PB
Cardenas	.989	48	328	34	4	5	10
Sutherland	.990	13	91	10	1	0	0
Varitek	.988	89	589	59	8	7	21

First Base	PCT	G	PO	A	E	DP
Bonnici	.995	137	1274	87	7	136
Cardenas	1.000	5	25	0	0	2
Hickey	1.000	7	44	0	0	7
Koehler	1.000	1	1	0	0	0

Second Base	PCT	G	PO	A	E	DP
Cora	.968	67	155	213	12	50
Diaz	.978	36	65	112	4	26

	PCT	G	PO	A	E	DP
Gipson	.900	2	2	7	1	2
Hickey	.945	34	74	99	10	23
Relaford	.941	5	5	11	1	2

Third Base	PCT	G	PO	A	E	DP
Diaz	.932	29	25	44	5	6
Gomez	.914	17	13	40	5	6
Hickey	.927	73	35	142	14	10
Saunders	.963	28	14	63	3	7

Shortstop	PCT	G	PO	A	E	DP
Cora	.944	6	5	12	1	3
Delgado	.917	13	10	45	5	7

	PCT	G	PO	A	E	DP
Diaz	.940	46	75	129	13	30
Relaford	.929	84	129	265	30	62

Outfield	PCT	G	PO	A	E	DP
Adams	1.000	19	27	3	0	1
Gipson	.980	110	233	12	5	4
Griffey	.982	92	152	8	3	1
Peguero	.961	36	72	2	3	1
Rackley	.960	78	116	4	5	0
Ramirez	.961	102	165	8	7	3

RIVERSIDE   A

CALIFORNIA LEAGUE

BATTING	AVG	G	AB	R	H	2B	3B	HR	RBI	BB	SO	SB	CS	B	T	HT	WT	DOB	1st Yr	Resides
Adams, Tommy	.287	69	251	46	72	17	4	8	40	28	40	12	4	R	R	6-1	205	11-26-69	1991	Mission Viejo, Calif.
Barger, Mike	.317	82	344	77	109	10	1	2	41	38	45	33	14	R	R	6-0	165	4-6-71	1993	Fenton, Mo.
Cook, Jason	.190	6	21	9	4	1	0	0	3	5	4	0	0	R	R	6-0	180	12-9-71	1993	Fairfax Station, Va.
Cruz, Jose Jr.	.257	35	144	34	37	7	1	7	29	24	50	3	1	S	R	6-0	190	4-19-74	1995	Houston, Texas
Cuellar, Jose	.111	19	45	7	5	0	0	2	12	9	0	0	0	R	R	6-1	200	6-5-70	1994	Hialeah, Fla.
Dean, Chris	.251	116	407	56	102	16	8	6	45	49	98	13	10	S	R	5-10	178	1-3-74	1993	Hayward, Calif.
Guevara, Giomar	.243	83	292	53	71	12	3	2	34	30	71	7	4	S	R	5-9	158	10-23-72	1991	Guarenas, Venez.
Ibanez, Raul	.332	95	361	59	120	23	9	20	108	41	49	4	3	L	R	6-2	210	6-2-72	1992	Miami, Fla.
Jorgensen, Randy	.299	133	495	78	148	32	2	12	97	46	74	4	2	L	L	6-2	200	4-3-72	1993	Snohomish, Wash.
Ladjevich, Rick	.309	122	470	74	145	26	0	7	71	26	65	3	2	R	R	6-3	220	2-17-72	1994	West Middlesex, Pa.

BATTING	AVG	G	AB	R	H	2B	3B	HR	RBI	BB	SO	SB	CS	B	T	HT	WT	DOB	1st Yr	Resides
Marquez, Jesus	.237	84	312	42	74	9	2	2	26	18	62	4	5	L	L	6-1	160	3-12-73	1990	Caracas, Venez.
Miller, Roy	.183	65	175	21	32	4	0	1	18	12	49	3	4	R	R	5-10	190	12-22-71	1993	Newberg, Ore.
Patel, Manny	.285	83	274	45	78	8	6	0	32	33	30	9	4	L	R	5-10	165	4-22-72	1993	Tampa, Fla.
Sealy, Scot	.243	58	206	23	50	5	0	2	30	16	36	2	2	R	R	6-4	205	2-10-71	1992	Satsuma, Ala.
Smith, Scott	.235	56	179	28	42	6	0	2	20	21	60	2	1	R	R	6-3	215	10-14-71	1994	Coppell, Texas
Sturdivant, Marcus	.274	99	347	60	95	13	5	1	34	39	41	31	13	L	L	5-10	150	10-29-73	1992	Oakboro, N.C.
Tejcek, John	.260	105	416	72	108	22	3	10	54	32	116	23	3	R	R	5-10	185	7-16-71	1993	San Diego, Calif.
Triessl, Mike	.365	22	74	15	27	2	0	3	14	12	15	0	0	R	R	6-1	215	2-27-71	1993	Malverne, N.Y.

GAMES BY POSITION: C—Cuellar 19, Ibanez 63, Ladjevich 4, Sealy 54, Triessl 11. 1B—Jorgensen 131, Ladjevich 6, Sealy 1, Smith 2, Sturdivant 1. 2B—Dean 115, Miller 21, Patel 27. 3B—Ladjevich 94, Patel 34, Smith 4. SS—Guevara 83, Miller 38, Patel 21. OF—Adams 48, Barger 78, Cruz 33, Marquez 68, Miller 1, Smith 32, Sturdivant 78, Tejcek 92.

PITCHING	W	L	ERA	G	GS	CG	SV	IP	H	R	ER	BB	SO	B	T	HT	WT	DOB	1st Yr	Resides
Clayton, Craig	9	8	5.00	28	28	0	0	160	171	102	89	83	156	R	R	6-0	185	11-29-70	1991	Anaheim, Calif.
Cope, Robin	2	4	7.39	11	5	0	0	32	50	31	26	18	13	L	R	6-5	230	4-26-73	1991	Okeechobee, Fla.
Crow, Dean	3	4	2.63	51	0	0	22	62	54	21	18	13	46	L	R	6-5	212	8-21-72	1993	Houston, Texas
Fitzer, Doug	0	0	4.61	25	0	0	0	27	26	15	14	15	13	L	L	6-5	210	7-2-69	1990	Farmington Hills, Mich.
Hinchliffe, Brett	8	6	6.61	15	15	0	0	78	110	69	57	35	68	S	R	6-4	205	7-21-74	1992	Detroit, Mich.
Ippolito, Rob	1	3	4.20	35	0	0	1	60	59	41	28	31	43	R	R	6-2	195	7-28-72	1994	La Mesa, Calif.
Montane, Ivan	5	5	5.63	24	16	0	0	93	101	67	58	71	79	R	R	6-2	195	6-3-73	1992	Miami, Fla.
Moore, Trey	14	6	3.09	24	24	0	0	148	122	65	51	58	134	L	L	6-1	200	10-2-72	1994	South Lake, Texas
Newton, Geronimo	4	4	3.15	46	0	0	2	71	74	35	25	24	42	L	L	6-0	165	12-31-73	1992	Christiansted, V.I.
Santana, Marino	3	5	6.19	9	9	0	0	44	44	47	33	25	57	R	R	6-1	188	5-10-72	1990	Boca Chica, D.R.
Smith, Ryan	10	7	3.11	23	23	2	0	142	142	68	49	50	108	R	R	6-3	215	11-11-71	1991	Toledo, Ohio
Sullivan, Dan	4	4	4.13	53	0	0	8	85	98	49	39	38	59	R	R	6-4	205	2-5-70	1991	Pittsburgh, Pa.
Suzuki, Makoto	0	1	4.70	6	0	0	0	8	10	4	4	6	6	R	R	6-4	195	5-31-75	1992	Kobe, Japan
Theron, Greg	4	2	5.03	40	0	0	1	68	72	44	38	23	45	R	R	6-6	215	9-20-73	1992	Mesa, Ariz.
Vanhof, John	1	1	10.59	4	4	0	0	17	26	25	20	12	12	L	L	6-3	180	12-4-73	1992	Southgate, Mich.
Winchester, Marty	3	1	4.57	35	4	0	0	67	67	40	34	45	56	L	L	6-6	225	7-25-72	1992	Long Beach, Calif.
Worley, Robert	6	4	5.31	11	11	0	0	61	64	44	36	30	44	R	R	6-3	185	2-15-71	1992	Westerville, Ohio

WISCONSIN   A
MIDWEST LEAGUE

BATTING	AVG	G	AB	R	H	2B	3B	HR	RBI	BB	SO	SB	CS	B	T	HT	WT	DOB	1st Yr	Resides
Augustine, Andy	.171	56	129	17	22	0	0	1	6	19	43	3	1	R	R	5-10	190	1-13-72	1993	Rothschild, Wisc.
Buhner, Shawn	.240	87	292	24	70	14	3	2	36	16	65	0	2	R	R	6-2	190	8-29-72	1993	League City, Texas
Carroll, Doug	.225	90	276	29	62	18	0	5	40	18	60	0	1	L	R	6-2	195	8-31-73	1994	Holliston, Mass.
Clifford, James	.244	101	307	46	75	26	3	10	44	40	87	8	4	L	L	6-2	225	3-23-70	1992	Seattle, Wash.
Cook, Jason	.269	117	405	61	109	24	3	5	64	44	44	12	5	R	R	6-0	180	12-9-71	1993	Fairfax Station, Va.
Darcuiel, Faruq	.259	83	282	29	73	10	3	1	20	22	50	27	6	L	L	5-11	180	11-28-72	1994	Fresno, Calif.
DeLeon, Santo	.105	9	19	0	2	0	0	0	0	3	5	1	0	S	R	5-11	170	10-28-73	1992	San Luis, D.R.
Delgado, Wilson	.243	19	70	13	17	3	0	0	7	3	15	3	0	S	R	5-11	165	7-15-75	1993	Santo Domingo, D.R.
Heath, Jason	.268	70	235	29	63	20	2	4	32	19	60	3	3	R	R	6-2	195	2-5-71	1993	Shawnee, Okla.
Hinds, Collin	.071	5	14	0	1	0	0	0	1	2	8	1	0	R	R	6-1	190	3-1-74	1994	Los Angeles, Calif.
Lanza, Mike	.204	101	333	28	68	13	1	2	29	22	67	10	5	R	R	6-1	190	10-22-73	1994	Port Chester, N.Y.
Mathis, Joe	.266	117	376	59	100	17	3	6	43	43	91	26	6	L	R	5-10	180	8-10-74	1993	Johnston, S.C.
Molina, Luis	.255	109	337	45	86	18	1	3	42	42	72	7	9	R	R	5-11	170	3-22-74	1993	Panama City, Panama
Monahan, Shane	.283	59	233	34	66	9	6	1	32	11	40	9	2	L	R	6-0	200	8-12-74	1995	Marietta, Ga.
Ramirez, Joel	.083	7	24	1	2	1	0	0	1	0	4	1	0	R	R	5-10	155	8-17-73	1994	Miami, Fla.
Smith, Scott	.327	34	107	13	35	12	1	3	17	11	21	0	1	R	R	6-3	215	10-14-71	1994	Coppell, Texas
Sutherland, Alex	.224	90	303	36	68	17	2	1	35	19	56	2	0	R	R	5-11	170	9-13-71	1991	Maracaibo, Venez.
Towner, Kyle	.226	104	301	64	68	12	0	1	24	63	59	34	11	S	R	5-6	170	11-11-72	1994	Saraland, Ala.
Villalobos, Carlos	.260	110	389	64	101	16	4	9	53	35	76	16	4	R	R	6-0	170	4-5-74	1993	Cartagena, Colombia
Wathan, Dusty	.091	5	11	1	1	0	0	1	3	0	3	0	0	S	R	6-5	215	8-22-73	1994	Blue Springs, Mo.

GAMES BY POSITION: C—Augustine 55, Heath 13, Sutherland 85, Wathan 5. 1B—Buhner 62, Clifford 81, Heath 1. 2B—Cook 59, Lanza 39, Molina 43, Ramirez 5. 3B—Cook 35, Lanza 1, Molina 5, Villalobos 104. SS—Cook 1, Delgado 19, Lanza 58, Molina 63, Ramirez 2. OF—Carroll 47, Cook 20, Darcuiel 76, DeLeon 6, Hinds 4, Mathis 112, Monahan 59, Smith 28, Towner 98.

PITCHING	W	L	ERA	G	GS	CG	SV	IP	H	R	ER	BB	SO	B	T	HT	WT	DOB	1st Yr	Resides
Beck, Chris	12	8	3.88	28	19	2	2	130	113	62	56	61	119	R	R	6-3	205	6-11-72	1994	Garden Grove, Calif.
Bieniasz, Derek	11	10	3.13	27	27	4	0	175	145	76	61	54	99	R	R	6-4	190	4-19-74	1993	Toronto, Ontario
Cloude, Ken	9	8	3.24	25	25	4	0	161	137	64	58	43	140	R	R	6-1	185	1-9-75	1994	Baltimore, Md.
Daniels, John	4	5	2.66	39	0	0	7	74	63	28	22	22	60	S	R	6-3	185	2-7-74	1993	Valinda, Calif.
Doughty, Brian	5	7	3.95	32	3	0	4	84	83	50	37	26	54	R	R	6-5	210	9-21-74	1992	Bothell, Wash.
Estes, Shawn	0	0	0.90	2	2	0	0	10	5	1	1	5	11	R	L	6-2	185	2-28-73	1991	Gardnerville, Nev.
Gould, Clint	0	0	5.77	25	0	0	0	34	34	24	22	28	20	R	R	6-1	230	8-18-71	1994	Kent, Wash.
Green, Chris	1	5	3.67	35	0	0	2	56	55	31	23	21	43	L	R	6-0	180	8-13-74	1993	La Mesa, Calif.
Krueger, Robert	0	0	4.50	19	0	0	0	22	21	12	11	12	8	L	L	6-2	185	10-19-71	1993	Oak Forest, Ill.
Morgan, Eric	0	0	1.35	7	0	0	1	13	5	6	2	7	7	R	R	6-0	190	10-24-72	1994	Cocoa, Fla.
Pearce, Jeff	0	1	7.03	27	0	0	0	24	21	21	19	25	19	L	L	6-2	205	11-24-69	1990	Sebastopol, Calif.
Santana, Marino	8	3	1.77	15	15	2	0	97	57	26	19	25	110	R	R	6-1	188	5-10-72	1990	Boca Chica, D.R.
Scheffer, Aaron	0	1	6.59	9	0	0	0	14	17	14	10	5	8	L	R	6-1	190	8-15-75	1994	Westland, Mich.
Smith, Roy	7	14	5.38	27	27	1	0	149	179	100	89	54	109	R	R	6-7	210	5-18-76	1994	Pinellas Park, Fla.
Thompson, John	3	8	4.13	38	7	0	19	70	65	41	32	43	69	R	R	6-2	200	1-18-73	1992	Spokane, Wash.
Vanhof, Dave	4	5	4.16	15	13	1	0	63	52	42	29	50	27	L	L	6-3	180	12-4-73	1992	Southgate, Mich.
Wiesner, Chad	0	0	3.00	1	0	0	0	3	3	1	1	1	2	R	R	6-1	180	10-5-71	1994	Rochester, Minn.

EVERETT   A
NORTHWEST LEAGUE

BATTING	AVG	G	AB	R	H	2B	3B	HR	RBI	BB	SO	SB	CS	B	T	HT	WT	DOB	1st Yr	Resides
Amado, Jose	.265	57	215	33	57	15	1	8	33	24	19	15	5	R	R		194	1-1-75	1994	San Cristobal, Venez.
Burrows, Mike	.206	67	223	28	46	5	3	7	33	42	72	13	8	L	L	6-4	180	1-19-76	1994	American Fork, Utah
Cruz, Jose Jr.	.455	3	11	6	5	0	0	0	2	3	1	0		S	R	6-0	190	4-19-74	1995	Houston, Texas

BATTING

BATTING	AVG	G	AB	R	H	2B	3B	HR	RBI	BB	SO	SB	CS	B	T	HT	WT	DOB	1st Yr	Resides
Griffin, Chad	.183	36	82	11	15	2	0	1	5	16	36	1	0	L	R	5-10	160	4-28-74	1993	Charlotte, N.C.
Heams, Shane	.197	27	61	5	12	4	0	1	4	3	28	2	0	R	R	6-1	175	9-29-75	1995	Lambertville, Mich.
Medrano, Teodoro	.333	1	3	0	1	0	0	0	0	1	0	0	0	R	R	5-11	190	9-17-75	1993	Santo Domingo, D.R.
Pomierski, Joe	.221	59	217	31	48	15	3	11	38	26	58	4	2	L	R	6-2	192	4-15-74	1992	Biloxi, Miss.
Ramirez, Joel	.251	70	243	31	61	12	0	1	31	37	39	9	6	R	R	5-10	155	8-17-73	1994	Miami, Fla.
Rodriguez, Javier	.133	20	60	2	8	1	0	0	1	7	13	0	0	R	R	6-2	195	8-21-74	1994	Miami, Fla.
Sachse, Matt	.230	59	191	34	44	6	0	1	14	29	76	5	4	L	L	6-0	205	6-29-76	1995	Spokane, Wash.
Sheffer, Chad	.280	56	193	31	54	9	1	0	18	27	38	28	8	S	R	6-0	180	12-17-73	1995	Dover, Fla.
Simonton, Cy Leon	.206	48	155	17	32	2	1	0	15	14	36	8	4	L	L	6-0	180	8-23-76	1994	Pittsburg, Calif.
Thomasson, Shane	.210	40	100	10	21	0	1	0	3	2	23	7	2	R	R	6-2	190	4-3-73	1994	Whitwell, Tenn.
Thompson, Karl	.246	54	187	29	46	13	1	5	26	16	39	4	0	R	R	6-0	180	12-30-73	1995	Diamond Bar, Calif.
Tinoco, Luis	.286	62	203	34	58	10	2	9	31	35	41	9	3	R	R	6-2	200	7-24-74	1992	Maracaibo, Venez.
Vickers, Randy	.256	68	266	35	68	13	2	12	37	20	102	5	2	R	R	6-3	200	7-21-75	1994	West Covina, Calif.
Wathan, Dusty	.271	53	181	32	49	9	1	6	25	17	26	2	1	S	R	6-5	215	8-22-73	1994	Blue Springs, Mo.

GAMES BY POSITION: C—Medrano 1, Simonton 1, Thompson 37, Wathan 41. **1B**—Amado 3, Pomierski 58, Tinoco 13, Wathan 7. **2B**—Amado 4, Griffin 20, Ramirez 66, Thomasson 1, Vickers 3. **3B**—Amado 44, Griffin 4, Heams 1, Pomierski 1, Ramirez 1, Sheffer 1, Thomasson 28. **SS**—Griffin 3, Ramirez 9, Sheffer 53, Thomasson 28. **OF**—Burrows 67, Cruz 3, Heams 22, Sachse 50, Simonton 45, Thomasson 1, Tinoco 58, Vickers 10.

PITCHING

PITCHING	W	L	ERA	G	GS	CG	SV	IP	H	R	ER	BB	SO	B	T	HT	WT	DOB	1st Yr	Resides
Brizek, Seth	0	2	6.97	8	0	0	1	10	13	10	8	8	16	R	R	6-3	190	12-19-73	1995	Blandon, Pa.
Clifford, Eric	3	2	2.40	28	0	0	4	45	39	17	12	11	39	R	R	6-1	210	9-18-74	1994	Chandler, Ariz.
Collett, Andy	0	0	0.00	1	0	0	0	0	1	0	0	2	0	L	R	6-3	215	10-28-73	1995	Arroyo Grande, Calif.
Conway, Robert	1	0	4.00	6	0	0	0	9	6	4	11	3	8	R	R	6-3	200	2-14-72	1995	New Iberia, La.
Cooper, David	1	2	7.36	17	2	0	0	33	36	31	27	31	20	R	R	6-4	195	5-16-75	1994	Hesperia, Calif.
Gryboski, Kevin	1	5	3.50	25	0	0	2	36	27	18	14	18	25	R	R	6-5	220	11-15-73	1995	Plains, Pa.
Iddon, Brent	3	5	4.36	14	14	1	0	74	86	49	36	25	67	R	R	6-2	180	2-4-76	1995	Sydney, Australia
Kurtz, Danny	5	2	3.12	14	12	1	0	69	60	27	24	32	43	R	R	6-1	190	5-23-74	1995	Highland, N.Y.
Marte, Damaso	2	2	2.21	11	5	0	0	37	25	11	9	10	39	L	L	6-2	194	2-14-74	1993	Santo Domingo, D.R.
Mitchell, Kelvin	3	2	4.62	25	0	0	1	37	41	26	19	23	24	R	L	6-2	195	10-17-74	1993	Butler, Ala.
Niemeier, Todd	4	3	2.81	15	15	0	0	80	74	33	25	26	80	L	L	6-1	165	1-28-73	1995	Evansville, Ind.
Ruskey, Jason	0	0	6.08	3	3	0	0	13	15	13	9	9	7	L	L	6-2	220	3-30-73	1994	Springfield, Ill.
Scheer, Greg	0	1	4.15	18	0	0	1	22	16	12	10	19	23	R	L	6-5	205	2-23-72	1995	Louisville, Ky.
Scheffer, Aaron	2	5	3.74	24	0	0	1	43	44	23	18	16	38	L	R	6-1	190	8-15-75	1994	Westland, Mich.
Soden, Chad	4	3	3.38	13	12	0	0	61	55	30	23	17	52	L	L	6-1	195	9-7-75	1995	Tuckerman, Ark.
Szimanski, Tom	2	0	1.69	16	0	0	5	21	13	4	4	6	19	R	R	6-2	205	9-9-72	1994	Baltimore, Md.
Trawick, Tim	6	2	3.14	16	13	0	0	86	66	34	30	30	63	R	R	6-4	208	3-7-72	1995	Columbus, Ga.

PEORIA   R

ARIZONA LEAGUE

BATTING

BATTING	AVG	G	AB	R	H	2B	3B	HR	RBI	BB	SO	SB	CS	B	T	HT	WT	DOB	1st Yr	Resides
Arias, David	.332	48	184	30	61	18	4	4	37	23	52	2	0	L	L	6-4	230	11-18-75	1993	Haina, D.R.
Cruz, Cirilo	.308	39	146	22	45	8	0	0	20	16	37	0	2	R	R	6-0	185	5-29-75	1995	Arroyo, P.R.
Figueroa, Luis	.292	32	120	14	35	2	0	0	11	12	9	1	2	R	R	5-11	177	3-2-77	1995	Carolina, P.R.
Fowler, Marvin	.258	26	97	13	25	4	3	0	8	7	29	4	4	L	R	6-2	210	6-23-75	1995	Palatka, Fla.
Harrison, Adonis	.290	45	155	31	45	7	5	1	14	37	37	7	9	L	R	5-9	165	9-28-76	1995	Pasadena, Calif.
Isom, Daleon	.258	28	89	17	23	4	1	1	8	18	19	11	8	R	R	6-3	190	7-3-75	1994	Benton Harbor, Mich.
Johnson, Duan	.351	43	174	33	61	9	3	0	28	8	14	3	2	R	R	6-1	190	2-23-76	1995	St. Paul's, N.C.
Maynard, Scott	.236	21	72	6	17	2	0	1	12	9	21	0	0	R	R	6-2	215	8-28-77	1995	Laguna Niguel, Calif.
McDougall, Matt	.238	27	101	17	24	3	0	0	9	12	21	9	4	R	R	5-11	192	7-29-76	1995	Henley Beach, Australia
Medrano, Teodoro	.000	1	3	0	0	0	0	0	0	0	0	0	0	R	R	5-11	190	9-17-75	1993	Santo Domingo, D.R.
Needham, Scott	.177	21	62	12	11	5	1	0	10	14	22	0	1	R	R	6-1	190	1-15-75	1995	Bentonville, Ark.
Randolph, Ed	.281	41	135	22	38	11	4	3	25	12	30	5	5	S	R	6-2	205	10-17-74	1993	Dallas, Texas
Rodriguez, Frank	.298	16	57	14	17	0	1	0	1	8	18	3	0	R	R	5-9	165	10-18-75	1994	Gualey, D.R.
Rose, Carlos	.152	27	92	10	14	1	0	1	6	3	33	4	1	R	R	6-2	208	8-21-75	1995	Cleveland, Miss.
Rowson, James	.189	30	106	9	20	6	1	0	9	6	38	9	2	L	R	5-11	190	9-12-76	1995	Mount Vernon, N.Y.
Stewart, Keith	.196	15	46	12	9	0	1	1	6	11	23	3	0	L	R	6-0	170	9-26-73	1995	Clay City, Ky.
Tolbert, Ernest	.176	26	91	16	16	3	2	1	7	9	24	2	2	R	R	6-1	200	1-29-76	1995	San Diego, Calif.
Vazquez, Ramon	.206	39	141	20	29	3	1	0	11	19	27	4	3	L	R	5-11	170	8-21-76	1995	Cayey, P.R.
Williams, Marcus	.227	22	88	6	20	7	1	0	6	0	23	4	2	R	R	6-5	185	1-24-77	1995	Detroit, Mich.

GAMES BY POSITION: C—Maynard 21, McDougall 3, Medrano 1, Randolph 40. **1B**—Arias 46, Cruz 1, Johnson 1, Williams 11. **2B**—Cruz 1, Figueroa 2, Harrison 43, Rodriguez 14, Vazquez 1. **3B**—Cruz 22, Figueroa 24, Johnson 8, Rodriguez 2, Vazquez 3. **SS**—Figueroa 1, Harrison 1, Johnson 20, Vazquez 35. **OF**—Cruz 9, Fowler 26, Isom 26, McDougall 25, Randolph 1, Rose 25, Rowson 28, Stewart 11, Tolbert 24, Williams 10.

PITCHING

PITCHING	W	L	ERA	G	GS	CG	SV	IP	H	R	ER	BB	SO	B	T	HT	WT	DOB	1st Yr	Resides
Blanco, Roger	1	6	5.50	12	12	0	0	54	60	43	33	24	27	R	R	6-6	220	8-29-76	1993	La Sabana, Venez.
Bonilla, Denis	1	1	3.06	21	0	0	2	35	39	21	12	9	39	L	L	6-1	204	3-15-74	1992	Santo Domingo, D.R.
Burton, Isaac	0	0	3.00	2	0	0	0	3	1	2	1	4	2	R	R	6-4	196	1-3-73	1995	Los Angeles, Calif.
Craig, Casey	1	0	6.00	2	0	0	0	3	5	2	2	0	0	R	R	6-2	185	10-8-75	1993	Jackson, Mich.
Derenches, Albert	1	2	3.31	19	0	0	0	35	36	15	13	21	40	S	L	6-3	190	8-17-76	1995	Tampa, Fla.
Gonzalez, Jose	4	4	5.30	12	10	0	0	56	56	40	33	31	66	R	R	6-1	190	3-4-77	1994	Maracaibo, Venez.
Gutierrez, Javier	1	4	5.88	14	4	1	0	34	43	31	22	19	38	R	R	6-2	175	8-26-74	1994	Guanta, Venez.
Jacob, Russell	6	2	2.88	12	11	0	0	56	47	29	18	31	54	R	R	6-6	225	1-2-75	1994	Winter Haven, Fla.
Jimenez, Jhonny	1	2	4.45	19	0	0	0	32	39	23	16	14	28	R	R	6-1	185	4-26-76	1994	Los Lanos, D.R.
Johnson, Shelby	1	1	5.29	9	0	0	0	17	24	16	10	9	14	R	R	6-1	185	4-3-74	1995	Jackson, Miss.
Kaye, Justin	0	1	10.71	12	0	0	0	19	33	28	23	19	13	S	R	6-4	185	6-9-76	1995	Las Vegas, Nev.
Lowe, Derek	1	0	0.93	2	2	0	0	10	5	1	1	2	11	R	R	6-6	170	6-1-73	1991	Dearborn, Mich.
Mays, Joe	2	3	3.25	10	10	0	0	44	41	24	16	18	44	S	R	6-1	160	12-10-75	1995	Bradenton, Fla.
Nogowski, Brandon	0	2	2.70	20	0	0	7	27	30	10	8	13	27	L	L	6-0	185	5-13-76	1995	Hood River, Ore.
Palki, Jeromy	0	0	7.94	4	0	0	0	6	7	7	5	2	7	R	R	6-1	195	4-14-76	1995	Oakland, Ore.
Suzuki, Makoto	1	0	6.75	4	3	0	0	4	5	4	3	0	3	R	R	6-4	195	5-31-75	1992	Kobe, Japan
Szimanski, Tom	1	0	4.15	4	0	0	0	4	2	2	2	3	4	R	R	6-2	205	9-9-72	1994	Baltimore, Md.
Tisdale, Warren	1	1	1.64	13	0	0	1	22	17	5	4	10	19	R	R	6-4	198	9-7-76	1995	Jacksonville, Fla.
Weymouth, Martin	2	3	3.98	9	4	0	0	32	37	23	14	10	26	R	R	6-2	180	8-6-77	1995	Romeo, Mich.

TEXAS
RANGERS

Manager: Johnny Oates.   **1995 Record:** 74-70, .514 (3rd, AL West).

BATTING	AVG	G	AB	R	H	2B	3B	HR	RBI	BB	SO	SB	CS	B	T	HT	WT	DOB	1st Yr	Resides
Beltre, Esteban............	.217	54	92	7	20	8	0	0	7	4	15	0	0	R	R	5-10	172	12-26-67	1984	San Pedro de Macoris,D.R.
Buechele, Steve..........	.125	9	24	0	3	0	0	0	0	4	3	0	0	R	R	6-2	200	9-26-61	1982	Arlington, Texas
Clark, Will	.302	123	454	85	137	27	3	16	92	68	50	0	1	L	L	6-1	196	3-13-64	1985	New Orleans, La.
Fox, Eric	.000	10	15	2	0	0	0	0	0	3	4	0	0	S	L	5-10	180	8-15-63	1986	Paso Robles, Calif.
Frazier, Lou	.212	49	99	19	21	2	0	0	8	7	20	9	1	S	R	6-2	175	1-26-65	1986	St. Louis, Mo.
Frye, Jeff	.278	90	313	38	87	15	2	4	29	24	45	3	3	R	R	5-9	180	8-31-66	1988	Las Vegas, Nev.
Gil, Benji	.219	130	415	36	91	20	3	9	46	26	147	2	4	R	R	6-2	180	10-6-72	1991	San Diego, Calif.
Gonzalez, Juan	.295	90	352	57	104	20	2	27	82	17	66	0	0	R	R	6-3	210	10-16-69	1986	Vega Baja, P.R.
Greer, Rusty	.271	131	417	58	113	21	2	13	61	55	66	3	1	L	L	6-0	190	1-21-69	1990	Albertville, Ala.
Hare, Shawn	.250	18	24	2	6	1	0	0	2	4	6	0	0	L	L	6-1	200	3-26-67	1989	Lakeland, Fla.
Hatcher, Billy	.083	6	12	2	1	1	0	0	0	1	1	0	0	R	R	5-10	190	10-4-60	1981	Cincinnati, Ohio
Horn, Sam	.111	11	9	0	1	0	0	0	1	6	0	0	0	L	L	6-5	250	11-2-63	1982	Bessemer, Ala.
Maldonado, Candy	.233	13	30	6	7	3	0	2	5	7	5	0	1	R	R	6-0	205	9-5-60	1978	Arecibo, P.R.
2-team (61 Tor.)	.263	74	190	28	50	16	0	9	30	32	50	1	2							
Marzano, John	.333	2	6	1	2	0	0	0	0	0	0	0	0	R	R	5-11	195	2-14-63	1985	Philadelphia, Pa.
McLemore, Mark	.261	129	467	73	122	20	5	5	41	59	71	21	11	S	R	5-11	207	10-4-64	1982	Gilbert, Ariz.
Nixon, Otis	.295	139	589	87	174	21	2	0	45	58	85	50	21	S	R	6-2	180	1-9-59	1979	Alpharetta, Ga.
Ortiz, Luis	.231	41	108	10	25	5	2	1	18	6	18	0	1	R	R	6-0	195	5-25-70	1991	Santo Domingo, D.R.
Pagliarulo, Mike.........	.232	86	241	27	56	16	0	4	27	15	49	0	0	L	R	6-2	195	3-15-60	1981	Melrose, Mass.
Palmer, Dean	.336	36	119	30	40	6	0	9	24	21	21	1	1	R	R	6-2	195	12-27-68	1986	Tallahassee, Fla.
Rodriguez, Ivan	.303	130	492	56	149	32	2	12	67	16	48	0	2	R	R	5-9	205	11-30-71	1989	Vega Baja, P.R.
Tettleton, Mickey	.238	134	429	76	102	19	1	32	78	107	110	0	0	S	R	6-2	212	9-16-60	1981	Farmington, Hills, Mich.
Valle, Dave	.240	36	75	7	18	3	0	0	5	6	18	1	0	R	R	6-2	220	10-30-60	1978	Renton, Wash.
Voigt, Jack	.161	33	62	8	10	3	0	2	8	10	14	0	0	R	R	6-1	175	5-17-66	1987	Venice, Fla.
2-team (3 Baltimore).	.175	36	63	9	11	3	0	2	8	10	14	0	0							
Worthington, Craig	.221	26	68	4	15	4	0	2	6	7	8	0	0	R	R	6-0	200	4-17-65	1985	Anaheim, Calif.

PITCHING	W	L	ERA	G	GS	CG	SV	IP	H	R	ER	BB	SO	B	T	HT	WT	DOB	1st Yr	Resides
Alberro, Jose	0	0	7.40	12	0	0	0	21	26	18	17	12	10	R	R	6-2	190	6-29-69	1991	San Juan, P.R.
Brandenburg, Mark	0	1	5.93	11	0	0	0	27	36	18	18	7	21	R	R	6-0	170	7-14-70	1992	Humble, Texas
Burrows, Terry	2	2	6.45	28	3	0	1	45	60	37	32	19	22	L	L	6-1	185	11-28-68	1990	Lake Charles, La.
Cook, Dennis	0	2	4.00	35	1	0	2	45	47	23	20	16	40	L	L	6-3	190	10-4-62	1985	Austin, Texas
2-team (11 Cleve.).....	0	2	4.53	46	1	0	2	58	63	32	29	26	53							
Darwin, Danny	2	2	7.15	7	4	0	0	34	40	27	27	7	22	R	R	6-3	202	10-25-55	1976	Valley View, Texas
2-year (13 Toronto)...	3	10	7.45	20	15	1	0	99	131	87	82	31	58							
Dettmer, John..............	0	0	27.00	1	0	0	0	0	2	1	1	0	0	R	R	6-0	185	3-4-70	1992	Glencoe, Mo.
Fajardo, Hector............	0	0	7.80	5	0	0	0	15	19	13	13	5	9	R	R	6-4	200	11-26-70	1989	Michoacan, Mexico
Gross, Kevin	9	15	5.54	31	30	4	0	184	200	124	113	89	106	R	R	6-5	215	6-8-61	1981	Claremont, Calif.
Helling, Rick...............	0	2	6.57	3	3	0	0	12	17	11	9	8	5	R	R	6-3	215	12-15-70	1992	West Fargo, N.D.
Heredia, Wilson	0	1	3.75	6	0	0	0	12	9	5	5	15	6	R	R	6-0	165	3-30-72	1990	San Pedro de Macoris, D.R.
Howard, Chris	0	0	0.00	4	0	0	0	4	3	0	0	1	2	R	L	6-0	185	11-18-65	1996	Nahant, Mass.
McDowell, Roger..........	7	4	4.02	64	0	0	4	85	86	39	38	34	49	R	R	6-1	195	12-21-60	1982	Stuart, Fla.
Nichting, Chris	0	0	7.03	13	0	0	0	24	36	19	19	13	6	R	R	6-1	205	5-13-66	1988	Cincinnati, Ohio
Oliver, Darren	4	2	4.22	17	7	0	0	49	47	25	23	32	39	R	L	6-0	170	10-6-70	1988	Rio Linda, Calif.
Pavlik, Roger	10	10	4.37	31	31	2	0	192	174	96	93	90	149	R	R	6-2	220	10-4-67	1987	Houston, Texas
Rogers, Kenny	17	7	3.38	31	31	3	0	208	192	87	78	76	140	L	L	6-1	205	11-10-64	1982	Arlington, Texas
Russell, Jeff	1	0	3.03	37	0	0	20	33	36	12	11	9	21	R	R	6-3	205	9-2-61	1980	Colleyville, Texas
Taylor, Scott M.	1	2	9.39	3	3	0	0	15	25	16	16	5	10	R	R	6-3	200	10-3-66	1989	Wichita, Kan.
Tewksbury, Bob...........	8	7	4.58	21	21	4	0	130	169	75	66	20	53	R	R	6-4	200	11-30-60	1981	Penacook, N.H.
Vosberg, Ed...............	5	5	3.00	44	0	0	4	36	32	15	12	16	36	L	L	6-1	190	9-28-61	1983	Tucson, Ariz.
Whiteside, Matt............	5	4	4.08	40	0	0	3	53	48	24	24	19	46	R	R	6-0	185	8-8-67	1990	Charleston, Mo.
Witt, Bobby	3	4	4.55	10	10	1	0	61	81	35	31	21	46	R	R	6-2	205	5-11-64	1985	Colleyville, Texas

FIELDING

Catchers	PCT	G	PO	A	E	DP	PB
Marzano	1.000	2	7	1	0	0	0
Rodriguez.......	.990	127	707	67	8	8	8
Tettleton	1.000	3	5	1	0	0	0
Valle	.993	29	137	12	1	0	2

First Base	PCT	G	PO	A	E	DP
Clark..............	.994	122	1076	88	7	125
Greer..............	.935	3	29	0	2	4
Hare	1.000	1	1	0	0	0
Pagliarulo.......	.987	11	69	8	1	5
Tettleton	1.000	9	80	6	0	7
Valle	1.000	7	20	1	0	2
Voigt..............	.952	5	19	1	1	3

Second Base	PCT	G	PO	A	E	DP
Beltre..............	.953	15	13	28	2	6
Frye	.975	83	173	248	11	55
McLemore.......	.993	66	108	184	2	42

Third Base	PCT	G	PO	A	E	DP
Beltre..............	.000	1	0	0	0	0
Buechele	1.000	7	10	0	2	
Ortiz...............	.867	35	9	43	8	2
Pagliarulo	.963	68	42	113	6	12
Palmer............	.948	36	19	72	5	9
Worthington.....	.980	26	13	36	1	3

Shortstop	PCT	G	PO	A	E	DP
Beltre..............	.969	36	40	53	3	13

	PCT	G	PO	A	E	DP
Gil...................	.974	130	226	409	17	95

Outfield	PCT	G	PO	A	E	DP
Fox	1.000	8	13	0	0	0
Frazier	.973	47	69	2	2	0
Gonzalez	1.000	5	6	1	0	0
Greer..............	.982	125	211	9	4	0
Hare	1.000	9	9	1	0	0
Hatcher	1.000	5	9	1	0	0
Maldonado	1.000	11	20	1	0	0
McLemore........	.986	73	140	0	2	0
Nixon..............	.989	138	357	4	4	1
Tettleton	.972	63	100	3	3	1
Voigt..............	1.000	25	36	1	0	0

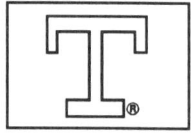

Lefthander Kenny Rogers led Texas pitchers with 17 wins and a 3.30 ERA

MORRIS FOSTOFF

Rangers minor league Player of the Year Fernando Tatis

JIM McLEAN

FARM SYSTEM

Director of Player Development: Reid Nichols

Class	Farm Team	League	W	L	Pct.	Finish*	Manager	First Yr
AAA	Oklahoma City 89ers	American Assoc.	54	89	.378	8th (8)	Greg Biagini	1983
AA	Tulsa (Okla.) Drillers	Texas	52	83	.385	8th (8)	Bobby Jones	1977
#A	Charlotte (Fla.) Rangers	Florida State	65	67	.492	6th (14)	Butch Wynegar	1987
A	Charleston (S.C.) RiverDogs	South Atlantic	50	89	.360	13th (14)	Mike Berger	1993
A	Hudson Valley (N.Y.) Renegades	New York-Penn	47	27	.635	2nd (14)	Bump Wills	1994
R	Port Charlotte (Fla.) Rangers	Gulf Coast	24	34	.414	10th (16)	Chino Cadahia	1973

*Finish in overall standings (No. of teams in league)   #Advanced level

ORGANIZATION LEADERS

MAJOR LEAGUERS

BATTING
*AVG	Ivan Rodriguez	.303
R	Otis Nixon	87
H	Otis Nixon	174
TB	Ivan Rodriguez	221
2B	Ivan Rodriguez	32
3B	Mark McLemore	5
HR	Mickey Tettleton	32
RBI	Will Clark	92
BB	Mickey Tettleton	107
SO	Benji Gil	147
SB	Otis Nixon	50

PITCHING
W	Kenny Rogers	17
L	Kevin Gross	15
#ERA	Kenny Rogers	3.38
G	Roger McDowell	64
CG	Two tied at	4
SV	Jeff Russell	20
IP	Kenny Rogers	208
BB	Roger Pavlik	90
SO	Roger Pavlik	149

Will Clark. 92 RBIs

MORRIS FOSTOFF

MINOR LEAGUERS

BATTING
*AVG	Cliff Brumbaugh, Hudson Valley	.358
R	Mark Little, Charlotte	75
H	Fernando Tatis, Charleston	151
TB	Fernando Tatis, Charleston	247
2B	Fernando Tatis, Charleston	43
3B	Brian Thomas, Tulsa	9
HR	Mike Smith, Tulsa	16
RBI	Fernando Tatis, Charleston	84
BB	Johnny Monell, Tulsa	67
SO	Mark Little, Charlotte	108
SB	Dom Gatti, Charleston	39

PITCHING
W	Jeff Davis, Charlotte/Tulsa	13
L	David Perez, Tulsa/Oklahoma City	14
#ERA	Scott Mudd, Hudson Valley	2.24
G	Rodney Cook, Charleston	60
CG	Dave Geeve, Tulsa/Oklahoma City	5
SV	Brian Martineau, Hudson Valley	18
IP	Jim Brower, Charlotte	174
BB	Julio Santana, Charlotte./Tulsa/Okla. City	75
SO	Nelson Perpetuo, Charleston/Charlotte	132

*Minimum 250 At-Bats   #Minimum 75 Innings

TOP 10 PROSPECTS

How the Rangers Top 10 prospects, as judged by Baseball America prior to the 1995 season, fared in 1995:

Julio Santana

MEL BAILEY

Player, Pos.	Club (Class—League)	AVG	AB	R	H	2B	3B	HR	RBI	SB
2. Benji Gil, ss	Texas	.219	415	36	91	20	3	9	46	2
3. Terrell Lowery, of	GCL Rangers (R—Gulf Coast)	.265	34	10	9	3	1	3	7	1
	Charlotte (A—Florida State)	.257	35	4	9	2	2	0	4	1
4. Edwin Diaz, 2b	Charlotte (A—Florida State)	.284	450	48	128	26	5	8	56	8
5. Mike Bell, 3b	Charlotte (A—Florida State)	.260	470	49	122	20	1	5	52	9
6. Andrew Vessel, of	Charlotte (A—Florida State)	.265	498	67	132	26	2	9	78	3
7. Kevin Brown, c	Charlotte (A—Florida State)	.265	355	48	94	25	1	11	57	2
	Okla. City (AAA—Amer. Assoc.)	.400	10	1	3	1	0	0	0	0

Player, Pos.	Club (Class—League)	W	L	ERA	G	SV	IP	H	BB	SO
1. Julio Santana, rhp	Charlotte (A—Florida State)	0	3	3.73	5	0	31	32	16	27
	Tulsa (AA—Texas)	6	4	3.23	15	0	103	91	52	71
	Okla. City (AAA—Amer. Assoc.)	0	2	39.00	2	0	3	9	7	6
8. Jim Brower, rhp	Charlotte (A—Florida State)	7	10	3.89	27	0	174	170	62	110
9. Jerry Martin, rhp	Tulsa (AA—Texas)	3	7	5.18	22	0	89	100	51	46
10. Ritchie Moody, lhp	GCL Rangers (R—Gulf Coast)	0	0	2.70	2	0	10	10	6	10
	Charlotte (A—Florida State)	0	1	6.23	1	0	4	3	8	0
	Tulsa (AA—Texas)	0	1	6.97	11	0	21	24	18	9

RANGERS

AMERICAN ASSOCIATION

BATTING	AVG	G	AB	R	H	2B	3B	HR	RBI	BB	SO	SB	CS	B	T	HT	WT	DOB	1st Yr	Resides
Borrelli, Dean	.200	54	185	17	37	9	1	2	17	18	50	0	1	R	R	6-2	210	10-20-66	1988	Salisbury, Mass.
Brown, Kevin	.400	3	10	1	4	1	0	0	0	2	4	0	0	R	R	6-2	200	4-21-73	1994	Winslow, Ind.
Brown, Marty	.168	30	101	12	17	5	0	3	12	8	25	0	0	R	R	6-1	195	1-23-63	1985	Rolla, Mo.
Buechele, Steve	.308	3	13	1	4	0	0	1	3	1	1	0	0	R	R	6-2	200	9-26-61	1982	Arlington, Texas
Byington, John	.259	109	390	44	101	15	2	2	29	19	37	6	2	R	R	5-8	165	11-4-67	1989	Baytown, Texas
2-team (13 N.O.)	.261	122	437	49	113	16	2	3	32	22	41	6	2							
Cameron, Stanton	.167	5	12	2	2	1	0	0	4	3	0	0	0	R	R	6-5	195	7-5-69	1987	Powell, Tenn.
Chance, Tony	.214	63	196	19	42	12	0	2	20	15	55	1	1	R	R	6-1	191	10-26-64	1983	Charleston, W.Va.
Clinton, Jim	.000	8	13	0	0	0	0	0	0	1	6	0	0	R	R	6-2	185	6-17-67	1986	Lewistown, Mon.
Dostal, Bruce	.212	88	293	35	62	14	6	4	31	30	49	11	3	L	L	6-0	195	3-10-65	1987	Towaco, N.J.
Figueroa, Bien	.100	9	20	1	2	0	0	0	2	0	2	1	0	R	R	5-10	167	2-7-64	1986	Tallahassee, Fla.
Fox, Eric	.278	92	349	52	97	22	5	6	50	30	68	5	5	S	L	5-10	180	8-15-63	1986	Paso Robles, Calif.
Goldberg, Lonnie	.233	10	30	2	7	3	0	1	5	2	4	1	0	R	R	5-10	170	8-1-70	1993	Falls Church, Va.
Hare, Shawn	.265	68	238	27	63	13	3	4	30	23	47	3	1	L	L	6-1	200	3-26-67	1989	Lakeland, Fla.
Harris, Donald	.200	12	40	4	8	1	1	0	7	3	7	0	2	R	R	6-1	185	11-12-67	1989	Waco, Texas
Hecht, Steve	.261	67	238	26	62	6	3	3	14	16	45	9	5	L	R	5-9	165	11-12-65	1988	Broken Arrow, Okla.
Hinzo, Tommy	.252	82	254	33	64	10	1	0	20	13	38	8	3	S	R	5-11	175	6-18-64	1986	Chula Vista, Calif.
Horn, Sam	.308	46	156	26	48	8	1	9	12	42	25	49	0	2	L	L	6-5	250	11-2-63	1982	Bessemer, Ala.
Hulett, Tim	.213	39	141	14	30	6	1	1	7	7	33	0	0	R	R	6-0	199	1-12-60	1980	Springfield, Ill.
2-team (3 Louis.)	.219	42	151	15	33	7	1	1	10	9	33	0	1							
Kennedy, Darryl	.182	3	11	1	2	0	0	1	3	0	2	0	0	R	R	5-10	170	1-23-69	1991	Davenport, Fla.
Lindeman, Jim	.252	83	294	52	74	16	3	12	36	33	54	0	1	R	R	6-1	200	1-10-62	1983	Des Plaines, Ill.
Luce, Roger	.000	1	3	0	0	0	0	0	0	0	2	0	0	R	R	6-4	215	5-7-69	1991	Houston, Texas
Marzano, John	.309	120	427	55	132	41	3	9	56	33	54	3	4	R	R	5-11	195	2-14-63	1985	Philadelphia, Pa.
McCoy, Trey	.310	9	29	4	9	1	0	0	2	7	7	0	0	R	R	6-3	215	10-12-66	1988	Virginia Beach, Va.
Ortiz, Luis	.306	47	170	19	52	10	5	2	20	8	20	1	1	R	R	6-0	195	5-25-70	1991	Santo Domingo, D.R.
Parra, Franklin	.167	6	18	0	3	1	0	0	1	2	4	1	0	S	R	6-0	165	7-8-71	1989	Puerto Plata, D.R.
Ritchie, Gregg	.179	9	28	5	5	0	0	1	4	6	4	1	0	L	L	6-0	180	1-25-64	1986	Stafford, Va.
Rivera, Luis	.138	19	58	3	8	4	0	1	3	1	6	0	0	R	R	5-10	172	1-3-64	1982	Cidra, P.R.
Rolls, David	.000	2	5	0	0	0	0	0	1	1	4	0	0	R	R	6-0	195	10-1-66	1988	Tucson, Ariz.
Sagmoen, Marc	.223	56	188	20	42	11	3	3	25	16	31	5	2	L	L	5-11	180	4-6-71	1993	Seattle, Wash.
Schu, Rick	.271	110	398	49	108	19	3	12	57	40	63	5	3	R	R	6-0	185	1-26-62	1981	Carmichael, Calif.
Shave, Jon	.205	32	83	10	17	1	0	0	5	7	28	1	0	R	R	6-0	180	11-4-67	1990	Fernandina Beach, Fla.
Vargas, Hector	.275	98	305	38	84	10	2	0	27	30	54	6	1	R	R	5-11	155	6-3-66	1986	Arecibo, P.R.

PITCHING	W	L	ERA	G	GS	CG	SV	IP	H	R	ER	BB	SO	B	T	HT	WT	DOB	1st Yr	Resides
Alberro, Jose	4	2	3.36	20	10	0	0	78	73	34	29	27	55	R	R	6-2	190	6-29-69	1991	San Juan, P.R.
Barfield, John	0	0	0.00	4	0	0	1	7	4	2	0	1	2	L	L	6-1	195	10-15-64	1986	Pine Bluff, Ark.
Brandenburg, Mark	0	5	2.02	35	0	0	2	58	52	16	13	15	51	R	R	6-0	170	7-14-70	1992	Humble, Texas
Brumley, Duff	1	1	5.40	3	0	0	1	5	6	4	3	2	3	R	R	6-4	195	8-25-70	1990	Cleveland, Tenn.
Burrows, Terry	0	0	10.13	5	0	0	0	3	5	4	3	2	4	L	L	6-1	185	11-28-68	1990	Lake Charles, La.
Bushing, Chris	0	0	13.50	3	0	0	0	1	5	2	2	0	2	R	R	6-0	190	11-4-67	1986	Plantation, Fla.
Curtis, Chris	3	5	5.00	51	0	0	5	77	81	53	43	39	40	R	R	6-2	185	5-8-71	1991	Duncanville, Texas
Darwin, Danny	0	0	0.00	1	1	0	0	3	1	0	0	0	4	R	R	6-3	202	10-25-55	1976	Valley View, Texas
Dettmer, John	0	0	2.08	5	0	0	0	9	10	3	2	4	10	R	R	6-0	185	3-4-70	1992	Glencoe, Mo.
Drahman, Brian	2	2	3.09	22	0	0	4	32	36	11	11	14	19	R	R	6-3	231	11-7-66	1986	Ft. Lauderdale, Fla.
Duncan, Chip	0	0	3.38	3	0	0	0	5	6	2	2	1	3	R	R	5-11	185	6-27-65	1987	Fort Myers, Fla.
Geeve, Dave	2	5	5.66	10	10	2	0	56	72	36	35	13	30	R	R	6-3	190	10-19-69	1991	Niles, Ill.
Goetz, Barry	4	6	5.72	40	6	0	1	90	97	60	57	49	46	R	R	6-2	195	8-28-68	1990	Arlington, Texas
Helling, Rick	8	2	5.33	20	20	3	0	110	132	73	65	41	80	R	R	6-3	215	12-15-70	1992	West Fargo, N.D.
Heredia, Wilson	1	4	6.82	8	7	0	0	32	40	26	24	25	21	R	R	6-0	165	3-30-72	1990	San Pedro de Macoris, D.R.
Hurst, James	1	5	7.33	28	7	0	4	47	71	40	38	25	42	L	L	6-0	165	6-1-67	1990	Sebring, Fla.
Jean, Domingo	3	8	6.14	24	13	1	0	88	102	70	60	61	72	R	R	6-2	175	1-9-69	1990	San Pedro de Macoris, D.R.
Lacy, Kerry	0	0	0.00	1	0	0	1	2	0	0	0	0	1	R	R	6-2	195	8-7-72	1991	Higdon, Ala.
Nichting, Chris	5	5	2.13	23	7	3	1	68	58	19	16	19	72	R	R	6-1	205	5-13-66	1988	Cincinnati, Ohio
Patterson, Danny	1	0	1.65	14	0	0	2	27	23	8	5	9	9	R	R	6-0	168	2-17-71	1990	Rosemead, Calif.
Perez, David	5	12	5.57	20	20	1	0	103	120	71	64	34	74	R	R	5-11	170	5-23-68	1989	San Antonio, Texas
Santana, Julio	0	2	39.00	2	2	0	0	3	9	14	13	7	6	R	R	6-0	175	10-20-73	1990	San Pedro de Macoris, D.R.
Schuermann, Lance	1	4	4.67	33	13	0	0	89	101	51	46	40	44	L	L	6-2	200	2-7-70	1991	St. Louis, Mo.
Taylor, Scott	7	8	3.66	22	19	1	0	118	122	59	48	38	65	R	R	6-3	200	10-3-66	1989	Wichita, Kan.
2-team (2 N.O.)	8	8	3.55	24	21	1	0	129	132	62	51	41	74							
Vosberg, Ed	0	0	0.00	1	0	0	0	2	1	0	0	1	2	L	L	6-1	190	9-28-61	1983	Tucson, Ariz.
Wishnevski, Rob	6	3	3.47	41	8	0	3	109	101	51	42	53	78	R	R	6-1	215	1-2-67	1987	Valparaiso, Ind.

FIELDING

Catcher	PCT	G	PO	A	E	DP	PB
Borrelli	.997	49	282	24	1	4	14
K. Brown	.750	2	6	0	2	0	0
Kennedy	.931	3	24	3	2	0	0
Luce	1.000	1	6	0	0	0	0
Marzano	.992	93	551	64	5	12	4
Rolls	1.000	2	15	1	0	0	1

First Base	PCT	G	PO	A	E	DP
Borrelli	.972	3	33	2	1	4
M. Brown	1.000	2	22	0	0	2
Byington	.994	22	151	9	1	13
Clinton	1.000	3	20	3	0	1
Horn	1.000	2	11	0	0	0
Lindeman	.989	74	640	48	8	67
McCoy	1.000	7	64	3	0	11

	PCT	G	PO	A	E	DP
Ortiz	1.000	1	6	0	0	2
Schu	1.000	18	130	11	0	17
Vargas	1.000	22	154	10	0	18

Second Base	PCT	G	PO	A	E	DP
M. Brown	.955	6	8	13	1	1
Byington	.941	15	26	38	4	8
Clinton	1.000	1	1	1	0	0
Hecht	.965	32	65	99	6	28
Hinzo	.955	56	112	122	11	41
Hulett	1.000	4	5	7	0	2
Schu	1.000	3	6	7	0	1
Shave	.964	28	43	64	4	16
Vargas	.958	17	33	35	3	8

Third Base	PCT	G	PO	A	E	DP
M. Brown	.938	20	12	48	4	6
Buechele	.818	3	3	6	2	0
Byington	.945	66	63	143	12	24
Goldberg	.000	1	0	0	0	0
Hulett	1.000	4	4	9	0	2
Ortiz	.931	38	29	93	9	7
Schu	.889	21	9	31	5	4
Vargas	1.000	2	0	3	0	0

Shortstop	PCT	G	PO	A	E	DP
M. Brown	.778	1	1	6	2	1
Clinton	1.000	3	3	0	0	0
Figueroa	.974	9	11	26	1	4
Goldberg	.975	8	7	32	1	4
Hinzo	.957	26	27	63	4	14

	PCT	G	PO	A	E	DP
Hulett	.921	27	45	72	10	19
Parra	.800	4	3	9	3	1
Rivera	.962	19	24	51	3	11
Schu	.961	63	85	162	10	34

Outfield	PCT	G	PO	A	E	DP
M. Brown	1.000	1	1	0	0	0

	PCT	G	PO	A	E	DP
Cameron	1.000	5	8	2	0	1
Chance	.990	58	90	6	1	1
Dostal	.986	81	204	7	3	1
Fox	.982	87	157	4	3	0
Hare	.966	63	110	4	4	2
Harris	1.000	10	23	1	0	0
Hecht	.985	30	64	3	1	0

	PCT	G	PO	A	E	DP
Lindeman	1.000	1	1	0	0	0
Parra	.000	1	0	0	0	0
Ritchie	1.000	6	11	0	0	0
Sagmoen	.980	54	97	3	2	0
Schu	.917	7	11	0	1	0
Vargas	.971	47	62	6	2	2

TULSA   AA

TEXAS LEAGUE

BATTING

	AVG	G	AB	R	H	2B	3B	HR	RBI	BB	SO	SB	CS	B	T	HT	WT	DOB	1st Yr	Resides
Charles, Frank	.253	126	479	51	121	24	3	13	72	22	92	1	0	R	R	6-4	210	2-23-69	1991	Anaheim, Calif.
Clinton, Jim	.193	28	57	6	11	2	0	1	7	7	16	2	0	R	R	6-2	185	6-17-67	1989	Lewistown, Mon.
Edwards, Mike	.216	38	111	11	24	3	1	3	13	15	13	0	0	R	R	6-1	205	3-9-70	1991	Placentia, Calif.
Estrada, Osmani	.266	120	410	44	109	23	3	3	43	35	49	0	2	R	R	5-8	180	1-23-69	1993	Woodland Hills, Calif.
Frias, Hanley	.281	93	360	44	101	18	4	0	27	45	53	14	12	S	R	6-0	160	12-5-73	1991	Villa Altagracia, D.R.
Kennedy, Darryl	.251	61	195	26	49	9	1	3	26	17	22	0	0	R	R	5-10	170	1-23-69	1991	Davenport, Fla.
Mercedes, Guillermo	.119	15	42	4	5	1	0	0	1	4	6	0	0	S	R	5-11	155	1-17-74	1991	La Romana, D.R.
Monell, Johnny	.306	121	434	55	133	18	1	12	64	67	53	0	1	S	R	5-10	180	10-31-65	1985	Bronx, N.Y.
Nunez, Rogelio	.224	82	263	27	59	4	0	2	17	10	43	0	7	S	R	6-0	180	5-6-70	1988	Santiago, D.R.
Parra, Franklin	.245	71	261	27	64	9	2	2	26	12	51	7	9	S	R	6-0	165	7-8-71	1989	Puerto Plata, D.R.
Sagmoen, Marc	.231	63	242	36	56	8	5	6	22	23	23	5	4	L	L	5-11	180	4-6-71	1993	Seattle, Wash.
Sims, Wesley	.233	12	43	4	10	1	1	0	5	6	3	0	0	S	R	6-0	175	11-7-71	1993	Charlotte, Tenn.
Smith, Mike	.257	132	499	65	128	22	3	16	64	60	72	11	6	R	R	6-0	180	12-1-69	1992	Piqua, Ohio
Texidor, Jose	.269	129	494	55	133	33	1	5	64	31	61	1	1	R	R	6-0	150	12-14-71	1989	Juana Diaz, P.R.
Thomas, Brian	.269	131	458	61	123	24	9	4	35	50	87	8	4	L	R	6-0	185	5-6-71	1993	Portland, Ore.
Turco, Frank	.208	53	149	23	31	3	1	1	12	18	34	4	3	R	R	5-11	165	7-3-68	1990	Cooper City, Fla.
Voigt, Jack	.188	4	16	1	3	0	0	1	3	2	5	1	0	R	R	6-1	175	5-17-66	1987	Venice, Fla.

PITCHING

	W	L	ERA	G	GS	CG	SV	IP	H	R	ER	BB	SO	B	T	HT	WT	DOB	1st Yr	Resides
Castillo, Felipe	2	2	3.82	14	0	0	0	33	42	19	14	11	16	R	R	6-3	161	8-23-66	1986	La Romana, D.R.
Cather, Mike	0	2	3.32	18	0	0	0	22	20	11	8	7	15	R	R	6-2	180	12-17-70	1993	Folsom, Calif.
Davidson, Jackie	0	2	21.86	2	2	0	0	7	21	18	17	1	5	S	R	6-0	175	9-20-64	1984	Everman, Texas
Davis, Jeff	1	0	0.00	1	1	0	0	7	2	0	0	1	4	R	R	6-0	170	9-20-72	1993	Somerset, Mass.
Dreyer, Steve	2	4	2.89	10	10	1	0	62	56	22	20	19	48	R	R	6-3	180	11-19-69	1990	Cedar Falls, Iowa
Duncan, Chip	2	1	3.00	17	1	0	1	36	34	12	12	17	31	R	R	5-11	185	6-27-65	1987	Fort Myers, Fla.
Escamilla, Jaime	0	0	1.80	4	0	0	0	5	6	4	1	2	5	R	L	5-9	165	5-25-72	1994	San Diego, Calif.
Geeve, Dave	3	8	5.17	15	14	3	0	94	108	61	54	20	38	R	R	6-3	190	10-19-69	1991	Niles, Ill.
Heredia, Wilson	4	2	3.18	8	7	1	1	45	42	19	16	21	34	R	R	6-0	165	3-30-72	1990	San Pedro de Macoris, D.R.
Keusch, Joseph	0	0	0.00	1	0	0	0	3	1	0	0	0	1	L	R	6-1	175	1-20-72	1994	Huntingburg, Ind.
Kimel, Jack	2	2	7.32	17	2	0	0	36	52	33	29	23	10	L	L	6-1	175	12-24-69	1992	Clemmons, N.C.
Knox, Kerry	2	2	3.41	5	4	0	0	29	28	12	11	9	14	L	L	6-0	188	4-10-67	1989	Fort Worth, Texas
Lacy, Kerry	2	7	4.28	28	7	0	9	82	94	47	39	39	49	R	R	6-2	195	8-7-72	1991	Higdon, Ala.
Martin, Jerry	3	7	5.18	22	17	0	0	89	100	55	51	51	46	R	R	6-3	175	3-15-72	1992	McMinnville, Tenn.
Martinez, Ramiro	0	5	5.17	13	5	0	0	47	53	29	27	31	34	L	L	6-2	185	1-28-72	1992	Los Angeles, Calif.
Moody, Ritchie	0	1	6.97	11	0	0	0	21	24	18	16	18	9	R	L	6-1	185	2-22-71	1992	Brookville, Ohio
Morvay, Joe	5	8	5.21	37	0	0	8	66	82	45	38	28	30	L	R	6-4	210	2-8-71	1993	Boardman, Ohio
Patterson, Danny	2	2	6.19	26	0	0	5	36	45	27	25	13	24	R	R	6-0	168	2-17-71	1990	Rosemead, Calif.
Perez, David	3	2	5.24	8	7	0	0	46	49	30	27	18	25	R	R	5-11	170	5-23-68	1989	San Antonio, Texas
Powell, John	1	4	3.89	7	7	0	0	39	45	21	17	16	27	R	R	5-10	180	4-7-71	1994	Snellville, Ga.
Santana, Julio	6	4	3.15	15	15	3	0	103	91	40	36	52	71	R	R	6-0	175	1-20-73	1990	San Pedro de Macoris, D.R.
Smith, Scotty	5	8	6.00	29	13	1	0	102	144	83	68	31	38	R	R	6-3	200	3-8-71	1993	Chattanooga, Tenn.
Wheeler, Earl	1	1	5.40	5	0	0	0	8	14	8	5	2	6	R	R	6-2	205	12-3-69	1993	Stillwater, Okla.
Wiley, Chad	6	9	3.89	26	23	0	0	160	165	78	69	52	69	R	R	5-11	175	11-20-71	1992	Lenexa, Kan.

FIELDING

Catcher	PCT	G	PO	A	E	DP	PB
Charles	.000	1	0	0	0	0	0
Kennedy	.979	59	281	43	7	6	5
Nunez	.967	82	420	72	17	5	7

First Base	PCT	G	PO	A	E	DP
Charles	.984	123	1107	73	19	116
Clinton	.972	7	64	5	2	7
Kennedy	1.000	1	2	0	0	1
Turco	.932	8	35	6	3	5
Voigt	1.000	1	8	1	0	0

Second Base	PCT	G	PO	A	E	DP
Estrada	1.000	5	11	16	0	6

	PCT	G	PO	A	E	DP
Sims	1.000	1	3	2	0	1
Smith	.982	131	310	411	13	93

Third Base	PCT	G	PO	A	E	DP
Edwards	.911	25	28	44	7	6
Estrada	.926	92	73	164	19	17
Parra	.944	22	18	33	3	4

Shortstop	PCT	G	PO	A	E	DP
Clinton	1.000	2	2	4	0	1
Estrada	.966	18	30	56	3	13
Frias	.948	93	137	301	24	64
Mercedes	.938	15	23	52	5	10

	PCT	G	PO	A	E	DP
Parra	1.000	1	0	2	0	1
Sims	.939	10	15	31	3	10

Outfield	PCT	G	PO	A	E	DP
Clinton	1.000	14	13	1	0	1
Parra	.902	45	81	2	9	0
Sagmoen	.993	62	135	7	1	3
Texidor	.993	128	264	9	2	2
Thomas	.992	131	340	16	3	2
Turco	.987	36	66	8	1	2
Voigt	.000	2	0	0	0	0

CHARLOTTE   A

FLORIDA STATE LEAGUE

BATTING

	AVG	G	AB	R	H	2B	3B	HR	RBI	BB	SO	SB	CS	B	T	HT	WT	DOB	1st Yr	Resides
Bell, Mike	.260	129	470	49	122	20	1	5	52	48	72	9	8	R	R	6-2	185	12-7-74	1993	Cincinnati, Ohio
Blair, Brian	.223	69	264	34	59	5	3	0	9	34	42	14	6	L	L	5-9	180	4-9-72	1993	Belton, Texas
Bokemeier, Matt	.236	105	385	42	91	16	1	8	34	26	76	7	7	S	R	6-2	190	8-7-72	1994	Fresno, Calif.
Brown, Kevin	.265	107	355	48	94	25	1	11	57	50	96	2	3	R	R	6-2	200	4-21-73	1994	Winslow, Ind.
Cossins, Tim	.059	7	17	1	1	0	0	0	0	4	5	0	1	R	R	6-1	192	3-31-70	1993	Windsor, Calif.
Crespo, Mike	.162	28	74	6	12	2	0	0	3	6	23	0	0	S	R	5-10	175	11-18-70	1990	Vega Alta, P.R.
Diaz, Edwin	.284	115	450	48	128	26	5	8	56	33	94	8	13	R	R	5-11	170	1-15-75	1993	Vega Alta, P.R.
Frias, Hanley	.333	13	120	13	40	6	3	0	14	15	11	8	6	S	R	6-0	160	12-5-73	1991	Villa Altagracia, D.R.
Little, Mark	.256	115	438	75	112	31	8	9	50	51	108	20	14	R	R	6-0	200	7-11-72	1994	Edwardsville, Ill.
Lowery, Terrell	.257	11	35	4	9	2	2	0	4	6	6	1	0	R	R	6-3	175	10-25-70	1991	Oakland, Calif.
Macon, Leland	.259	119	405	52	105	15	3	2	38	41	85	14	12	R	R	6-2	205	5-4-73	1993	Kirkwood, Mo.
Malone, Scott	.236	100	314	33	74	14	1	2	40	45	41	5	2	L	R	6-3	215	4-16-71	1992	Aledo, Texas

BATTING	AVG	G	AB	R	H	2B	3B	HR	RBI	BB	SO	SB	CS	B	T	HT	WT	DOB	1st Yr	Resides
Mercedes, Guillermo	.218	33	110	10	24	2	0	0	5	7	12	1	2	S	R	5-11	155	1-17-74	1991	La Romana, D.R.
Perez, Joe	.257	24	74	8	19	4	0	1	9	9	12	1	1	L	L	5-11	195	5-26-70	1989	Bronx, N.Y.
Rijo, Rafael	.304	16	46	3	14	2	0	0	5	5	11	2	0	R	R	6-2	170	9-19-69	1988	La Romana, D.R.
Sauve, Erik	.143	31	70	9	10	3	0	0	4	9	13	0	2	R	R	5-9	165	3-20-72	1994	Mechanicsburg, Pa.
Shugars, Shawn	.348	10	23	4	8	1	1	0	3	3	4	0	0	L	L	5-11	185	11-7-71	1994	Charlotte Hall, Md.
Sims, Wes	.273	5	11	2	3	1	0	0	1	2	5	0	0	S	R	6-0	175	11-7-71	1993	Charlotte, Tenn.
Subero, Carlos	.136	17	44	3	6	1	0	0	4	0	10	0	0	R	R	6-0	155	6-15-72	1991	Caracas, Venez.
Unrat, Chris	.250	66	172	22	43	8	1	1	17	23	38	1	2	L	R	6-1	205	3-28-71	1993	Kirkland, Quebec
Vessel, Andrew	.265	129	498	67	132	26	2	9	78	32	75	3	17	R	R	6-3	205	3-11-75	1993	Richmond, Calif.

GAMES BY POSITION: C—Brown 96, Cossins 3, Crespo 19, Unrat 33. 1B—Blair 8, Bokemeier 13, Brown 1, Malone 99, Sauve 13, Unrat 12. 2B—Bokemeier 10, Diaz 110, Sauve 12, Sims 2, Subero 9. 3B—Bell 126, Bokemeier 6, Sauve 2, Sims 1. SS—Bokemeier 62, Diaz 1, Frias 33, Mercedes 33, Sims 1, Subero 6, Unrat 1. OF—Blair 49, Little 96, Lowery 11, Macon 107, Malone 1, Perez 15, Rijo 10, Shugars 6, Vessel 110.

PITCHING	W	L	ERA	G	GS	CG	SV	IP	H	R	ER	BB	SO	B	T	HT	WT	DOB	1st Yr	Resides
Baine, David	1	3	4.10	21	3	0	1	48	47	23	22	24	29	L	6-5	200	12-24-69	1992	Novato, Calif.	
Briscoe, Janos	0	0	0.00	1	0	0	0	2	3	0	0	0	2	R	R	6-3	175	3-31-73	1994	Franklin, Ky.
Brower, Jim	7	10	3.89	27	27	2	0	174	170	93	75	62	110	R	R	6-2	205	12-29-72	1994	Minnetonka, Minn.
Buckles, Bucky	2	9	3.13	48	0	0	16	69	70	29	24	21	43	R	R	6-1	190	6-19-73	1994	Victorville, Calif.
Davis, Jeff	12	7	2.89	26	26	0	0	165	159	74	53	37	105	R	R	6-0	170	9-20-72	1993	Somerset, Mass.
Hartmann, Pete	2	4	7.32	15	2	0	2	36	46	34	29	26	30	L	L	6-2	200	5-13-71	1993	Arvada, Colo.
Johnson, Jonathan	1	5	2.70	8	7	1	0	43	34	14	13	16	25	R	R	6-0	180	7-16-74	1995	Ocala, Fla.
Kell, Rob	1	0	3.05	11	0	0	1	21	16	9	7	15	21	R	L	6-1	200	9-21-70	1993	Hatfield, Pa.
Keusch, Joseph	9	4	1.82	40	0	0	8	64	56	19	13	14	36	L	R	6-1	175	1-20-72	1994	Huntingdon, Ind.
Manning, David	9	5	3.50	26	20	0	0	129	127	56	50	46	66	R	R	6-3	205	8-14-71	1992	Lantana, Fla.
Martinez, Ramiro	2	2	4.08	14	6	0	2	46	45	21	21	15	30	L	L	6-2	185	1-28-72	1992	Los Angeles, Calif.
Moody, Eric	5	5	2.75	13	13	2	0	88	84	30	27	13	57	R	R	6-6	185	1-6-71	1993	Williamston, S.C.
Moody, Ritchie	0	1	6.23	1	1	0	0	4	3	3	3	8	0	R	L	6-1	185	2-22-71	1992	Brookville, Ohio
Perpetuo, Nelson	0	0	7.71	5	0	0	0	7	5	7	6	5	7	R	L	5-11	165	7-6-70	1991	Monroe, Conn.
Powell, John	4	1	3.00	19	2	0	2	48	44	18	16	13	47	R	R	5-10	180	4-7-71	1994	Snellville, Ga.
Reyes, Jose	1	3	4.40	30	2	0	3	61	67	38	30	22	41	R	R	5-10	170	8-22-69	1988	Santo Domingo, D.R.
Roman, Dan	2	2	7.71	7	5	0	0	26	30	22	22	19	21	L	L	6-5	220	3-22-71	1992	Staten Island, N.Y.
Santana, Julio	0	3	3.73	5	5	1	0	31	32	16	13	16	27	R	R	6-0	175	1-20-73	1990	San Pedro de Macoris, D.R.
Seip, Rod	1	2	2.00	6	4	0	0	27	26	9	6	6	23	R	R	6-2	190	3-12-74	1992	Thebes, Ill.
Smith, Dan	5	1	2.95	9	9	1	0	58	53	23	19	16	34	R	R	6-2	175	9-15-75	1993	Girard, Kan.
Tewksbury, Bob	1	0	0.00	1	1	0	0	6	3	0	0	0	4	R	R	6-4	200	11-30-60	1981	Penacook, N.H.

CHARLESTON, S.C.   A
SOUTH ATLANTIC LEAGUE

BATTING	AVG	G	AB	R	H	2B	3B	HR	RBI	BB	SO	SB	CS	B	T	HT	WT	DOB	1st Yr	Resides
Aguila, Hector	.152	13	33	4	5	1	0	0	3	5	13	0	1	R	R	5-11	185	9-8-74	1995	Arecibo, P.R.
Barkett, Andy	.218	21	78	7	17	6	0	0	12	10	27	0	3	L	L	6-1	205	9-5-74	1995	Raleigh, N.C.
Comeaux, Eddie	.210	90	243	38	51	7	1	0	19	39	58	10	7	R	R	6-3	185	7-16-73	1994	Pomona, Calif.
Cooney, James	.087	18	46	2	4	0	0	1	2	3	14	1	0	R	R	6-3	225	3-5-72	1995	Grayslake, Ill.
Cossins, Tim	.203	22	59	8	12	5	0	1	8	9	13	2	0	R	R	6-1	192	3-31-70	1993	Windsor, Calif.
Gatti, Dom	.230	96	335	50	77	8	4	0	32	53	38	39	15	R	R	5-10	175	11-2-71	1993	New Hyde Park, N.Y.
Goldberg, Lonnie	.218	100	340	29	74	12	1	2	31	26	54	17	11	R	R	5-10	170	8-1-70	1993	Falls Church, Va.
Gonzalez, Mario	.207	11	29	3	6	1	0	0	1	3	4	2	1	S	R	5-11	155	2-21-74	1992	La Guaira, Venez.
Heller, Brad	.224	76	214	27	48	13	0	4	15	21	37	3	1	R	R	5-11	190	12-8-71	1995	Tucson, Ariz.
Larkin, Stephen	.255	113	369	50	94	19	1	5	45	54	80	18	10	L	L	6-0	190	7-24-73	1994	Cincinnati, Ohio
Lopez, Victor	.289	12	38	4	11	3	0	0	2	4	3	3	0	R	R	5-10	185	4-26-73	1994	Los Mochis, Mexico
Luciano, Virgilio	.218	104	285	30	62	14	1	2	31	26	76	18	9	L	L	5-11	165	6-25-76	1994	Santiago, D.R.
Millican, Kevin	.215	88	270	27	58	17	0	5	28	31	81	2	4	R	R	5-10	200	5-31-72	1994	Jennings, La.
Pearson, Cory	.208	61	183	21	38	8	0	1	13	18	53	13	6	R	R	6-0	170	7-30-74	1992	Logan, W.Va.
Perez, Joe	.272	67	243	24	66	14	2	3	29	18	55	10	3	L	L	5-11	195	5-26-70	1989	Bronx, N.Y.
Rutz, Ryan	.220	133	491	60	108	20	1	1	22	55	88	36	26	L	L	5-5	155	7-22-72	1994	Kennewick, Wash.
Santa, Roberto	.261	99	295	35	77	11	1	5	46	55	37	0	6	L	L	6-3	205	6-17-72	1994	Arecibo, P.R.
Shugars, Shawn	.227	8	22	2	5	1	0	0	3	1	3	0	2	L	L	5-11	185	11-7-71	1994	Charlotte Hall, Md.
Tatis, Fernando	.303	131	499	74	151	43	4	15	84	45	94	22	19	S	R	6-1	175	1-1-75	1993	San Pedro de Macoris, D.R.
Vasquez, Danilo	.214	44	131	12	28	6	2	1	7	6	42	6	3	R	R	5-11	175	1-26-74	1994	Bronx, N.Y.
Veras, Juan	.203	102	305	39	62	11	2	0	17	32	69	16	8	R	R	5-11	165	8-13-74	1994	West Palm Beach, Fla.

GAMES BY POSITION: C—Cooney 4, Cossins 19, Heller 65, Lopez 12, Millican 62. 1B—Barkett 16, Cooney 7, Goldberg 4, Heller 1, Larkin 55, Millican 8, Santa 64. 2B—Aguila 1, Goldberg 13, Rutz 131, Veras 2. 3B—Aguila 7, Goldberg 15, Tatis 124. SS—Aguila 2, Goldberg 46, Gonzalez 7, Rutz 1, Veras 94. OF—Aguila 1, Barkett 5, Comeaux 80, Gatti 96, Goldberg 16, Larkin 28, Luciano 81, Millican 3, Pearson 50, Perez 5, Shugars 2, Vasquez 42.

PITCHING	W	L	ERA	G	GS	CG	SV	IP	H	R	ER	BB	SO	B	T	HT	WT	DOB	1st Yr	Resides
Chavarria, David	3	5	3.92	52	0	0	6	62	55	33	27	38	68	L	R	6-7	195	5-19-73	1991	Burnaby, B.C.
Cook, Rodney	3	8	2.53	60	0	0	11	96	83	32	27	39	88	R	R	6-3	170	6-7-71	1994	Atlanta, Texas
Escamilla, Jaime	3	4	4.42	32	0	0	2	71	59	38	35	18	76	R	L	5-9	165	5-25-72	1994	San Diego, Calif.
Gogolewski, Chris	5	13	4.23	30	19	2	0	140	169	93	66	38	84	L	L	6-5	182	8-4-73	1994	Oshkosh, Wisc.
Hausmann, Isaac	0	0	9.45	5	0	0	0	7	10	10	7	1	6	R	R	6-4	170	6-27-76	1994	Covina, Calif.
Hower, Dan	4	7	7.29	22	17	0	1	83	96	88	67	59	55	L	L	6-1	190	2-19-73	1994	Omaha, Neb.
Kell, Rob	1	4	3.48	7	7	0	0	44	38	20	17	9	47	R	L	6-1	200	9-21-70	1993	Hatfield, Pa.
Knight, Brandon	4	2	3.13	9	9	0	0	55	37	22	19	21	52	L	R	6-0	170	10-15-75	1995	Oxnard, Calif.
Knighton, Toure	1	9	4.88	22	19	1	0	107	121	64	58	46	100	R	R	6-3	180	7-4-75	1994	Tucson, Ariz.
Morillo, Donald	1	4	2.10	18	0	0	1	26	22	7	6	17	28	R	R	6-0	185	9-1-73	1995	Charleston, S.C.
Mortimer, Mick	0	0	0.00	5	0	0	0	13	10	2	0	6	11	R	R	5-11	180	5-4-73	1994	Tillamook, Ore.
O'Flynn, Gardner	9	10	2.96	30	24	2	0	167	156	70	55	61	110	S	L	6-2	205	7-5-71	1993	Ipswich, Mass.
Pauls, Matthew	3	3	4.22	16	0	2	1	21	22	20	10	10	19	R	R	6-1	190	7-26-74	1994	Monahans, Texas
Perpetuo, Nelson	6	4	3.21	32	10	1	0	104	80	47	37	51	125	R	L	5-11	165	7-6-70	1991	Monroe, Conn.
Reyes, Jose	0	0	18.00	4	0	0	0	4	10	8	8	3	5	R	R	5-10	170	8-22-69	1988	Santo Domingo, D.R.
Runion, Jeff	1	1	3.18	2	2	0	0	11	12	8	4	6	4	R	R	6-5	185	8-29-74	1992	Riverdale, Ga.
Ryan, Reid	4	9	9.38	22	5	0	0	47	64	57	49	40	39	R	R	6-2	190	4-21-71	1994	Alvin, Texas
Silva, Ted	5	4	3.38	11	11	0	0	67	59	26	25	12	66	R	R	6-0	175	8-4-74	1995	Redondo Beach, Calif.
Stewart, Scott	1	7	3.69	11	11	1	0	76	76	38	31	14	47	R	L	6-2	200	8-14-75	1994	Stanley, N.C.

HUDSON VALLEY   A
NEW YORK-PENN LEAGUE

BATTING	AVG	G	AB	R	H	2B	3B	HR	RBI	BB	SO	SB	CS	B	T	HT	WT	DOB	1st Yr	Resides
Briones, Chris	.221	48	163	18	36	12	1	5	26	4	53	0	0	R	R	5-11	205	6-5-73	1995	Brea, Calif.
Brumbaugh, Clif	.358	74	282	44	101	19	4	2	45	39	51	15	3	R	R	6-2	205	4-21-74	1995	New Castle, Del.
Echols, Mandell	.284	58	215	31	61	8	3	1	21	14	48	15	13	R	R	6-2	190	11-16-73	1995	Barfield, Miss.
Evans, Kyle	.238	57	189	31	45	11	1	4	25	27	39	4	1	L	L	5-10	180	12-17-73	1995	Anaheim, Calif.
Gallagher, Shawn	.150	5	20	1	3	2	0	0	4	1	4	0	0	R	R	6-0	187	11-8-76	1995	Wilmington, N.C.
Goodwin, Joe	.282	57	181	29	51	6	0	1	27	20	20	2	1	R	R	5-10	170	4-19-74	1995	New Windsor, Md.
Gorecki, Ryan	.296	59	189	24	56	4	0	0	20	17	10	8	6	L	R	5-9	160	7-18-73	1995	East Rockaway, N.Y.
Johnson, Jason	.240	46	150	27	36	7	3	5	16	12	38	10	6	R	R	6-2	190	2-1-76	1994	Vallejo, Calif.
Martinez, Dave	.250	44	124	19	31	6	0	0	17	13	25	1	1	L	L	6-5	230	1-28-74	1995	Cerritos, Calif.
McAulay, John	.212	24	52	7	11	0	0	0	4	8	9	1	1	R	R	6-0	180	6-10-73	1995	Lumberton, Miss.
McLendon, Craig	.000	4	6	0	0	0	0	0	0	0	3	0	0	R	R	6-3	185	11-26-75	1994	Jonesboro, Ga.
Podsednik, Scott	.266	65	252	42	67	3	0	0	20	35	31	20	6	L	L	6-0	170	3-18-76	1994	West, Texas
Reed, Billy	.216	45	134	16	29	4	1	1	11	17	24	3	2	R	R	5-10	160	5-9-73	1995	Birmingham, Ala.
Stratton, Kelly	.207	30	58	10	12	2	0	1	8	7	6	1	1	L	L	6-3	190	6-23-72	1995	Aptos, Calif.
Vasquez, Danny	.267	69	240	38	64	9	4	4	31	15	58	16	5	R	R	5-11	175	1-26-74	1994	Bronx, N.Y.
Vopata, Nathan	.281	68	231	37	65	12	8	0	30	23	36	10	5	L	R	5-10	175	2-6-73	1995	Visalia, Calif.
Walker, Rodney	.077	13	26	2	2	0	0	0	1	0	10	1	0	R	R	6-1	167	2-8-76	1993	Chicago, Ill.

GAMES BY POSITION: C—Briones 5, Goodwin 57, McAulay 24, McLendon 4. **1B**—Brumbaugh 2, Evans 53, Gallagher 5, Johnson 1, Martinez 24, Walker 2. **2B**—Gorecki 53, Vopata 27, Walker 1. **3B**—Brumbaugh 73, Gorecki 1, Vopata 5, Walker 1. **SS**—Reed 42, Vopata 37, Walker 7. **OF**—Echols 56, Johnson 36, Podsednik 65, Stratton 18, Vazquez 67.

PITCHING	W	L	ERA	G	GS	CG	SV	IP	H	R	ER	BB	SO	B	T	HT	WT	DOB	1st Yr	Resides
Bauer, Charles	4	3	3.17	15	15	0	0	82	81	42	29	32	62	R	R	6-0	185	11-10-72	1995	Rensselaer, N.Y.
Codd, Tim	3	0	3.08	25	0	0	0	38	36	15	13	21	38	R	R	6-3	195	10-4-73	1995	North Tonawanda, N.Y.
Dempster, Ryan	1	0	3.18	1	1	0	0	6	7	2	2	1	6	R	R	6-2	195	5-3-77	1995	Gibsons, B.C.
Draeger, Mark	3	4	5.40	21	2	0	0	40	40	33	24	26	33	R	R	6-3	180	11-19-72	1995	Lockport, Ill.
Glynn, Ryan	3	3	4.70	9	8	0	0	44	56	27	23	16	21	R	R	6-3	200	11-1-74	1995	Portsmouth, Va.
Kahlon, Bobby	5	5	2.32	30	0	0	3	54	35	16	14	21	76	R	R	6-0	175	9-15-72	1995	El Sobrante, Calif.
Link, Bryan	5	3	3.49	15	15	1	0	90	79	39	35	25	88	R	L	6-1	170	4-6-73	1995	Wylie, Texas
Martineau, Brian	5	2	1.30	30	0	0	18	42	30	10	6	10	39	R	R	6-2	205	12-16-74	1995	Riverside, Calif.
McHugh, Michael	0	0	8.40	10	0	0	0	15	26	17	14	14	9	L	L	5-11	180	4-9-73	1995	Pittsburgh, Pa.
Moore, Robert	2	3	5.43	13	13	0	0	63	77	45	38	13	45	R	R	6-5	217	3-27-73	1995	Kalispell, Mon.
Mudd, Scott	7	1	2.24	15	15	3	0	101	91	37	25	18	62	R	R	6-0	195	10-12-72	1995	Louisville, Ky.
Sagedal, Brent	0	2	7.08	14	5	0	1	34	42	29	27	18	25	R	R	6-2	200	8-6-73	1995	Woodville, Wisc.
Venafro, Michael	9	2	2.13	32	0	0	2	51	37	13	12	21	32	L	L	5-10	170	8-2-73	1995	Chantilly, Va.

PORT CHARLOTTE   R
GULF COAST LEAGUE

BATTING	AVG	G	AB	R	H	2B	3B	HR	RBI	BB	SO	SB	CS	B	T	HT	WT	DOB	1st Yr	Resides
Aguila, Hector	.192	53	182	20	35	7	5	0	17	12	27	6	2	R	R	5-11	185	9-8-74	1995	Arecibo, P.R.
Cossins, Tim	.000	2	4	0	0	0	0	0	0	0	1	0	0	R	R	6-1	192	3-31-70	1993	Windsor, Calif.
Gallagher, Shawn	.338	58	210	34	71	13	3	7	40	19	44	17	4	R	R	6-0	187	11-8-76	1995	Wilmington, N.C.
Lima, Estivinson	.180	31	89	10	16	5	0	1	7	8	19	0	1	R	R	6-1	186	10-19-76	1994	Santo Domingo, D.R.
Llibre, Brian	.269	24	67	4	18	2	0	0	8	2	21	1	0	R	R	6-4	201	9-16-77	1995	West Covina, Calif.
Lowery, Terrell	.265	10	34	10	9	3	1	3	7	6	7	1	0	R	R	6-3	175	10-25-70	1991	Oakland, Calif.
McLendon, Craig	.242	25	66	7	16	2	0	0	4	5	10	1	0	R	R	6-3	185	11-26-75	1994	Jonesboro, Ga.
Mercado, Julio	.167	55	156	13	26	5	0	0	12	10	49	9	2	R	R	6-0	180	5-11-77	1995	Stafford, Va.
Monroe, Craig	.249	54	193	22	48	6	2	0	33	18	25	13	2	R	R	6-2	195	2-27-77	1995	Texarkana, Texas
Nunez, Juan	.241	43	137	16	33	2	1	1	7	15	46	26	9	S	R	5-10	165	1-11-77	1994	Esperanza, D.R.
Ortiz, Asbel	.305	43	128	18	39	10	1	3	23	8	26	4	2	S	R	5-10	155	6-20-76	1994	Cidra, P.R.
Parra, Jose	.156	45	135	16	21	4	2	0	7	24	41	12	6	S	R	6-0	155	4-23-77	1994	Santiago, D.R.
Pena, Jose	.242	50	153	26	37	4	4	0	10	12	29	22	5	R	R	6-2	175	10-13-76	1994	Santiago, D.R.
Rivera, Juan	.186	28	70	8	13	2	0	0	6	13	29	5	1	R	R	6-2	184	4-30-77	1995	Rio Grande, P.R.
Rose, Damian	.097	13	31	5	3	0	0	0	2	4	16	3	1	R	R	5-10	173	10-11-76	1995	San Jose, Calif.
Suero, Rey	.216	39	111	19	24	3	1	0	5	14	23	12	5	R	R	5-10	170	9-5-77	1994	Santo Domingo, D.R.
Terry, Reggie	.294	5	17	3	5	0	0	0	0	4	2	0	0	R	R	6-0	180	9-19-73	1995	Hampton, Va.

GAMES BY POSITION: C—Cossins 2, Lima 3, Llibre 11, McLendon 25, Rivera 28. **1B**—Gallagher 57, Lima 1. **2B**—Nunez 31, Ortiz 2, Suero 27. **3B**—Aguila 52, Llibre 1, Ortiz 10. **SS**—Ortiz 17, Parra 43. **OF**—Aguila 1, Lima 10, Lowery 3, Mercado 55, Monroe 53, Ortiz 4, Pena 47, Rose 12, Suero 2, Terry 4.

PITCHING	W	L	ERA	G	GS	CG	SV	IP	H	R	ER	BB	SO	B	T	HT	WT	DOB	1st Yr	Resides
Battaglia, Chuck	4	3	4.97	10	8	0	0	42	46	31	23	13	35	R	R	6-3	235	4-19-75	1994	Massapequa Park, N.Y.
Bryant, Scooter	0	0	0.00	1	0	0	0	1	0	0	0	1	1	L	L	6-2	170	1-1-77	1995	Sulphur, La.
Dempster, Ryan	3	1	2.36	8	6	1	0	34	34	21	9	17	37	R	R	6-2	195	5-3-77	1995	Gibsons, B.C.
Dreyer, Steve	0	1	1.00	2	2	0	0	9	6	1	1	2	7	R	R	6-3	180	11-19-69	1990	Cedar Falls, Iowa
Gaston, Ryan	0	0	1.99	10	1	0	2	23	19	9	5	6	23	R	R	5-10	175	5-24-77	1995	Longview, Texas
Hausmann, Isaac	1	2	2.67	18	0	0	6	30	24	11	9	9	23	R	R	6-4	170	6-27-76	1994	Covina, Calif.
Knight, Brandon	2	1	5.25	3	2	0	0	12	12	7	7	6	11	L	R	6-0	170	10-1-75	1995	Oxnard, Calif.
Kolb, Dan	1	7	2.21	12	11	0	0	53	38	22	13	28	46	R	R	6-0	190	3-29-75	1995	Sterling, Ill.
Martinez, Juan	1	2	5.40	12	6	0	0	38	43	28	23	11	27	R	R	6-0	152	5-20-75	1992	Santo Domingo, D.R.
Moody, Ritchie	0	0	2.70	2	2	0	0	10	10	3	3	6	10	R	L	6-1	185	2-22-71	1992	Brookville, Ohio
Moreno, Ricardo	1	0	1.80	4	1	1	1	15	13	3	3	1	8	R	R	6-2	180	3-3-76	1995	Guadalajara, Mexico
Ovalle, Bonelly	4	2	3.72	17	5	1	1	58	51	29	24	20	58	R	R	5-11	164	7-30-78	1995	Santiago, D.R.
Reynolds, Mark	0	2	5.40	7	1	0	0	10	8	10	6	11	10	L	R	5-11	190	3-22-73	1995	Des Moines, Iowa
Roberts, Franklin	0	0	27.00	1	0	0	0	1	1	2	2	4	0	R	R	6-3	170	1-23-75	1994	Seaford, Del.
Ryan, Michael-Sean	2	5	2.35	17	0	0	2	38	36	15	10	8	22	R	R	6-8	210	5-22-76	1994	Annapolis, Md.
Simmons, Carlos	4	3	3.28	14	9	0	0	58	57	33	21	22	44	R	R	6-1	200	1-22-74	1994	Clinton, Md.
Smith, Dan	0	3	4.26	4	3	0	0	19	19	9	9	5	12	R	R	6-3	175	9-15-75	1993	Girard, Kan.
Smith, Tom	0	0	27.00	5	0	0	0	3	6	14	9	17	4	R	R	6-3	210	7-27-76	1995	Petaluma, Calif.
Styles, Bobby	0	0	6.55	12	1	0	0	22	31	24	16	9	21	R	R	6-8	270	1-10-77	1995	Hendersonville, N.C.

TORONTO BLUE JAYS

Manager: Cito Gaston.   **1995 Record:** 56-88, .389 (5th, AL East).

BATTING	AVG	G	AB	R	H	2B	3B	HR	RBI	BB	SO	SB	CS	B	T	HT	WT	DOB	1st Yr	Resides
Alomar, Roberto	.300	130	517	71	155	24	7	13	66	47	45	30	3	S	R	6-0	175	2-5-68	1985	Salinas, P.R.
Battle, Howard	.200	9	15	3	3	0	0	0	0	4	8	1	0	R	R	6-0	197	3-25-72	1990	Ocean Springs, Miss.
Carter, Joe	.253	139	558	70	141	23	0	25	76	37	87	12	1	R	R	6-3	215	3-7-60	1981	Leawood, Kan.
Cedeno, Domingo	.236	51	161	18	38	6	1	4	14	10	35	0	1	S	R	6-1	170	11-4-68	1988	La Romana, D.R.
Delgado, Carlos	.165	37	91	7	15	3	0	3	11	6	26	0	0	L	R	6-3	206	6-25-72	1989	Aguadilla, P.R.
Gonzalez, Alex	.243	111	367	51	89	19	4	10	42	44	114	4	4	R	R	6-0	182	4-8-73	1991	Miami, Fla.
Green, Shawn	.288	121	379	52	109	31	4	15	54	20	68	1	2	L	L	6-4	180	11-10-72	1992	Santa Ana, Calif.
Huff, Mike	.232	61	138	14	32	9	1	1	9	22	21	1	1	R	R	6-1	190	8-11-63	1985	Chicago, Ill.
Knorr, Randy	.212	45	132	18	28	8	0	3	16	11	28	0	0	R	R	6-2	212	11-12-68	1986	Covina, Calif.
Maldonado, Candy	.269	61	160	22	43	13	0	7	25	25	45	1	1	R	R	6-0	205	9-5-60	1978	Arecibo, P.R.
Martinez, Sandy	.241	62	191	12	46	12	0	2	25	7	45	0	0	L	R	6-2	200	10-3-72	1990	Villa Mella, D.R.
Molitor, Paul	.270	130	525	63	142	31	2	15	60	61	57	12	0	R	R	6-0	185	8-22-56	1977	Mequon, Wisc.
Olerud, John	.291	135	492	72	143	32	0	8	54	84	54	0	0	L	L	6-5	218	8-5-68	1989	Bellevue, Wash.
Parrish, Lance	.202	70	178	15	36	9	0	4	22	15	52	0	0	R	R	6-3	220	6-15-56	1974	Yorba Linda, Calif.
Perez, Robert	.188	17	48	2	9	2	0	1	3	0	5	0	0	R	R	6-0	195	4-8-73	1991	Bolivar, Venez.
Perez, Tomas	.245	41	98	12	24	3	1	1	8	7	18	0	1	R	R	5-11	165	12-29-73	1991	Santo Domingo, D.R.
Sprague, Ed	.244	144	521	77	127	27	2	18	74	58	96	0	0	R	R	6-2	215	7-25-67	1989	Lodi, Calif.
Stewart, Shannon	.211	12	38	2	8	0	0	0	1	5	5	2	0	R	R	6-1	185	2-25-74	1992	Miami, Fla.
White, Devon	.283	101	427	61	121	23	5	10	53	29	97	11	2	S	R	6-2	178	12-29-62	1981	Mesa, Ariz.

PITCHING	W	L	ERA	G	GS	CG	SV	IP	H	R	ER	BB	SO	B	T	HT	WT	DOB	1st Yr	Resides
Carrara, Giovanni	2	4	7.21	12	7	1	0	49	64	46	39	25	27	R	R	6-2	210	3-4-68	1990	Anzoategui, Venezuela
Castillo, Tony	1	5	3.22	55	0	0	13	73	64	27	26	24	38	L	L	5-10	190	3-1-63	1983	Barquisimeto, Venez.
Cone, David	9	6	3.38	17	17	5	0	130	113	53	49	41	102	L	R	6-1	190	1-2-63	1981	Leawood, Kan.
Cornett, Brad	0	0	9.00	5	0	0	0	5	6	5	5	3	4	R	R	6-3	190	2-4-69	1992	Odessa, Texas
Cox, Danny	1	3	7.40	24	0	0	0	45	57	40	37	33	38	R	R	6-4	225	9-21-59	1981	Freeburg, Ill.
Crabtree, Tim	0	2	3.09	31	0	0	0	32	30	16	11	13	21	R	R	6-4	205	10-13-69	1992	Jackson, Mich.
Darwin, Danny	1	8	7.62	13	11	1	0	65	91	60	55	24	36	R	R	6-3	202	10-25-55	1976	Valley View, Texas
Guzman, Juan	4	14	6.32	24	24	3	0	135	151	101	95	73	94	R	R	5-11	190	10-28-66	1985	Manoguayabo, D.R.
Hall, Darren	0	2	4.41	17	0	0	3	16	21	9	8	9	11	R	R	6-3	205	7-14-64	1986	Irving, Texas
Hentgen, Pat	10	14	5.11	30	30	2	0	201	236	129	114	90	135	R	R	6-2	200	11-13-68	1986	Fraser, Mich.
Hurtado, Edwin	5	2	5.45	14	10	1	0	78	81	50	47	40	33	R	R	6-2	215	2-1-70	1991	Naguaonagua, Venez.
Jordan, Ricardo	1	0	6.60	15	0	0	1	15	18	11	11	13	10	L	L	5-11	165	6-27-70	1990	Delray Beach, Fla.
Leiter, Al	11	11	3.64	28	28	2	0	183	162	80	74	108	153	L	L	6-1	190	10-23-65	1984	Plantation, Fla.
Menhart, Paul	1	4	4.92	21	9	1	0	79	72	49	43	47	50	R	R	6-2	190	3-25-69	1990	Conyers, Ga.
Robinson, Ken	1	2	3.69	21	0	0	0	39	25	21	16	22	31	R	R	5-9	175	11-3-69	1991	Akron, Ohio
Rogers, Jimmy	2	4	5.70	19	0	0	0	24	21	15	15	18	13	R	R	6-0	190	1-3-67	1987	Tulsa, Okla.
Timlin, Mike	4	3	2.14	31	0	0	5	42	38	13	10	17	36	R	R	6-4	210	3-10-66	1987	Olsmar, Fla.
Ward, Duane	0	1	27.00	4	0	0	0	3	11	10	8	5	3	R	R	6-4	210	5-28-64	1982	Las Vegas, Nev.
Ware, Jeff	2	1	5.47	5	5	0	0	26	28	18	16	21	18	R	R	6-3	190	11-11-70	1991	Virginia Beach, Va.
Williams, Woody	1	2	3.69	23	3	0	0	54	44	23	22	28	41	R	R	6-0	190	8-19-66	1988	Houston, Texas

FIELDING

Catcher	PCT	G	PO	A	E	DP	PB
Knorr	.971	45	243	22	8	2	8
Martinez	.986	61	329	28	5	6	14
Parrish	1.000	67	346	41	0	7	9

First Base	PCT	G	PO	A	E	DP
Carter	1.000	7	47	3	0	2
Delgado	1.000	4	20	1	0	3
Olerud	.997	133	1099	89	4	103
Sprague	.971	7	34	0	1	3

Second Base	PCT	G	PO	A	E	DP
Alomar	.994	128	272	367	4	84
Cedeno	1.000	20	30	42	0	8
T. Perez	1.000	7	10	12	0	3

Third Base	PCT	G	PO	A	E	DP
Battle	1.000	6	1	6	0	0
Cedeno	.000	1	0	0	0	0

	PCT	G	PO	A	E	DP
Gonzalez	.895	9	6	11	2	1
T. Perez	.000	1	0	0	0	0
Sprague	.958	139	133	234	16	20

Shortstop	PCT	G	PO	A	E	DP
Cedeno	.980	30	55	90	3	18
Gonzalez	.957	97	158	216	17	46
T. Perez	.954	31	38	65	5	14

Outfield	PCT	G	PO	A	E	DP
Carter	.975	128	269	9	7	1
Delgado	1.000	17	34	1	0	0
Green	.973	109	207	9	6	3
Huff	.980	55	95	3	2	0
Maldonádo	.988	58	78	2	1	0
R. Perez	1.000	15	30	0	0	0
Stewart	.955	12	20	1	1	0
White	.989	100	261	7	3	0

MORRIS FOSTOFF

Roberto Alomar

BLUE JAYS

Outfielder Joe Carter led the Blue Jays with 25 homers and 76 RBIs

THE PICTURE DESK

Blue Jays minor league Player of the Year Robert Perez

MORRIS FOSTOFF

FARM SYSTEM

Director of Player Development: Mel Queen.

Class	Farm Team	League	W	L	Pct.	Finish*	Manager(s)	First Yr
AAA	Syracuse (N.Y.) Chiefs	International	59	82	.418	10th (10)	Bob Didier/Rich Hebner	1978
AA	Knoxville (Tenn.) Smokies	Southern	54	90	.375	10th (10)	Garth Iorg	1980
#A	Dunedin (Fla.) Blue Jays	Florida State	63	74	.460	10th (14)	Jim Nettles	1987
A	Hagerstown (Md.) Suns	South Atlantic	73	68	.518	7th (14)	Omar Malave	1993
A	St. Catharines (Ont.) Stompers	New York-Penn	38	37	.507	6th (14)	J.J. Cannon	1986
#R	Medicine Hat (Alta.) Blue Jays	Pioneer	35	37	.486	4th (8)	Darren Balsley	1978
R	Dunedin (Fla.) Blue Jays	Gulf Coast	19	40	.322	15th (16)	Rocket Wheeler	1993

*Finish in overall standings (No. of teams in league)   #Advanced level

ORGANIZATION LEADERS

MAJOR LEAGUERS

BATTING
*AVG	Roberto Alomar	.300
R	Ed Sprague	77
H	Roberto Alomar	155
TB	Joe Carter	239
2B	John Olerud	32
3B	Roberto Alomar	7
HR	Joe Carter	25
RBI	Joe Carter	76
BB	John Olerud	84
SO	Alex Gonzalez	114
SB	Roberto Alomar	30

PITCHING
W	Al Leiter	11
L	Two tied at	14
#ERA	Al Leiter	3.64
G	Tony Castillo	55
CG	Juan Guzman	3
SV	Tony Castillo	13
IP	Pat Hentgen	201
BB	Al Leiter	108
SO	Al Leiter	153

TY SPORT PHOTOS

Al Leiter. 153 strikeouts

MINOR LEAGUERS

BATTING
*AVG	Robert Perez, Syracuse	.343
R	Shannon Stewart, Knoxville	89
H	Robert Perez, Syracuse	172
TB	Robert Perez, Syracuse	249
2B	Robert Perez, Syracuse	38
3B	Lorenzo de la Cruz, Knoxville	12
HR	Carlos Delgado, Syracuse	22
RBI	Ryan Jones, Dunedin	78
BB	Shannon Stewart, Knoxville	89
SO	Kevin Witt, Hagerstown	148
SB	Lonell Roberts, Knoxville	57

PITCHING
W	Mark Sievert, Hagerstown	12
L	Two tied at	12
#ERA	Brian Smith, Hagerstown	0.87
G	Rick Steed, Knoxville/Syracuse	58
CG	Three tied at	3
SV	Brian Smith, Hagerstown	21
IP	Chris Carpenter, Dunedin/Knoxville	164
BB	Chris Carpenter, Dunedin/Knoxville	81
SO	Mark Sievert, Hagerstown	140

*Minimum 250 At-Bats   #Minimum 75 Innings

TOP 10 PROSPECTS

How the Blue Jays Top 10 prospects, as judged by Baseball America prior to the 1995 season, fared in 1995:

Shawn Green

Player, Pos.	Club (Class—League)	AVG	AB	R	H	2B	3B	HR	RBI	SB
1. Shawn Green, of	Toronto	.288	379	52	109	31	4	15	54	1
2. Alex Gonzalez, ss	Toronto	.243	367	51	89	19	4	10	42	4
4. Shannon Stewart, of	Knoxville (AA—Southern)	.287	498	89	143	24	6	5	55	42
	Toronto	.211	38	2	8	0	0	0	1	2
5. Sandy Martinez, c	Knoxville (AA—Southern)	.229	144	14	33	8	1	2	22	0
	Toronto	.241	191	12	46	12	0	2	25	0
9. *Chris Stynes, 2b	Omaha (AAA—American Assoc.)	.275	306	51	84	15	5	9	42	4
	Kansas City	.171	35	7	6	1	0	0	2	0
10. Howard Battle, 3b	Syracuse (AAA—International)	.251	443	43	111	17	4	8	48	10
	Toronto	.200	15	3	3	0	0	0	0	1

Player, Pos.	Club (Class—League)	W	L	ERA	G	SV	IP	H	BB	SO
3. Jose Silva, rhp	Knoxville (AA—Southern)	0	0	9.00	3	0	2	3	6	2
6. Chris Carpenter, rhp	Dunedin (A—Florida State)	3	5	2.17	15	0	99	83	50	56
	Knoxville (AA—Southern)	3	7	5.18	12	0	64	71	31	53
7. Jose Pett, rhp	Knoxville (AA—Southern)	8	9	4.26	26	0	142	132	48	89
8. Edwin Hurtado, rhp	Knoxville (AA—Southern)	2	4	4.45	11	0	55	54	25	38
	Toronto	5	2	5.45	14	0	78	81	40	33

*Traded to Kansas City

INTERNATIONAL LEAGUE

BATTING	AVG	G	AB	R	H	2B	3B	HR	RBI	BB	SO	SB	CS	B	T	HT	WT	DOB	1st Yr	Resides
Battle, Howard	.251	118	443	43	111	17	4	8	48	39	73	10	11	R	R	6-0	197	3-25-72	1990	Ocean Springs, Miss.
Bowers, Brent	.252	111	305	38	77	16	5	5	26	10	57	5	1	L	R	6-3	200	5-2-71	1989	Bridgeview, Ill.
Brito, Tilson	.242	90	327	49	79	16	3	7	32	29	69	17	8	R	R	6-0	170	5-28-72	1990	Los Trinitarios, D.R.
Brooks, Eric	.192	47	120	12	23	3	1	0	5	12	27	0	2	R	R	6-2	195	5-18-69	1988	La Mirada, Calif.
Butler, Rich	.161	69	199	20	32	4	2	2	14	9	45	2	3	L	R	6-1	180	5-1-73	1991	Toronto, Ontario
Canate, Willie	.238	114	345	48	82	17	2	3	30	23	62	8	5	R	R	6-0	170	12-11-71	1989	Maracaibo, Venez.
Crespo, Felipe	.294	88	347	56	102	20	5	13	41	41	56	12	7	S	R	5-11	190	3-5-73	1991	Caguas, P.R.
Delgado, Carlos	.318	91	333	59	106	23	4	22	74	45	78	0	4	L	R	6-3	206	6-25-72	1989	Aguadilla, P.R.
Diaz, Edgar	.302	15	43	5	13	0	1	0	2	7	6	0	0	R	R	6-1	175	2-8-64	1982	San Juan, P.R.
Johnson, Matt	.500	5	6	1	3	2	0	0	0	0	1	0	0	R	R	5-10	175	5-15-70	1992	Arvada, Colo.
Kelly, Pat	.132	30	68	6	9	1	0	2	8	6	15	0	0	R	R	5-11	175	1-22-67	1978	Waukegan, Ill.
2-team (11 Rich.)	.144	41	90	8	13	2	0	2	10	6	20	0	1							
Knorr, Randy	.269	18	67	6	18	5	1	1	6	5	14	0	0	R	R	6-2	212	11-12-68	1986	Covina, Calif.
Lis, Joe	.262	130	485	68	127	33	4	17	56	46	54	6	2	R	R	5-10	170	11-3-68	1991	Newburgh, Ind.
Lutz, Brent	.163	35	86	5	14	0	0	1	5	4	23	1	2	R	R	6-1	185	5-7-70	1991	Issaquah, Wash.
Montalvo, Robert	.038	11	26	0	1	0	0	0	1	2	8	0	0	R	R	6-1	165	3-25-70	1988	West New York, N.J.
Perez, Robert	.343	122	502	70	172	38	6	9	67	13	60	7	5	R	R	6-3	195	6-4-69	1990	Bolivar, Venez.
Ramos, John	.252	116	413	59	104	24	1	20	75	38	83	2	2	R	R	6-0	190	8-6-65	1986	Tampa, Fla.
Sawkiw, Warren	.190	11	42	3	8	1	0	0	0	5	8	2	0	S	R	5-11	180	1-19-68	1990	Lakeland, Fla.
Townley, Jason	.261	96	264	25	69	11	0	8	30	38	71	0	3	R	R	6-2	220	6-18-69	1987	Pensacola, Fla.
Weinke, Chris	.226	113	341	42	77	12	2	10	41	44	74	4	3	L	R	6-3	205	7-31-72	1991	St. Paul, Minn.

PITCHING	W	L	ERA	G	GS	CG	SV	IP	H	R	ER	BB	SO	B	T	HT	WT	DOB	1st Yr	Resides
Baptist, Travis	3	4	4.33	15	13	0	0	79	83	56	38	32	52	S	L	6-0	190	12-30-71	1990	Aloha, Ore.
Brow, Scott	1	5	9.00	11	5	0	0	31	52	39	31	18	14	R	R	6-3	200	3-17-69	1990	Hillsboro, Ore.
Brown, Chad	1	1	3.27	11	0	0	0	22	21	11	8	20	14	L	L	6-0	185	12-9-71	1992	Gastonia, N.C.
Brown, Tim	3	8	6.27	19	12	0	0	75	95	69	52	28	54	R	R	6-3	185	9-16-68	1988	Brandon, Fla.
Carrara, Giovanni	7	7	3.96	21	21	0	0	132	116	72	58	56	81	R	R	6-2	210	3-4-68	1990	Anzoategui, Venez.
Cornett, Brad	0	1	4.91	3	3	0	0	11	13	6	6	4	3	R	R	6-3	190	2-4-69	1992	Odessa, Texas
Cox, Danny	0	0	0.00	4	0	0	0	7	2	0	0	5	9	R	R	6-4	225	9-21-59	1981	Freeburg, Ill.
Crabtree, Tim	0	2	5.40	26	0	0	5	32	38	25	19	12	22	R	R	6-4	205	10-13-69	1992	Jackson, Mich.
Flener, Huck	6	11	3.94	30	23	1	0	135	131	70	59	41	83	S	L	5-11	180	2-25-69	1990	Fairfield, Calif.
Ganote, Joe	0	2	10.13	3	3	0	0	11	16	15	12	4	3	R	R	6-1	185	1-22-68	1990	Lake Wylie, S.C.
Gibson, Paul	0	1	4.81	26	0	0	3	24	24	16	13	6	28	R	L	6-0	185	1-4-60	1978	Center Moriches, N.Y.
Gray, Dennis	2	2	4.44	15	0	0	0	24	27	16	12	10	15	L	L	6-6	225	12-24-69	1991	Banning, Calif.
Guzman, Juan	0	0	0.00	1	1	0	0	5	1	0	0	3	5	R	R	5-11	190	10-28-66	1985	Manoguayabo, D.R.
Heble, Kurt	0	0	5.79	4	0	0	0	5	6	4	3	2	5	R	R	6-3	205	2-9-69	1991	West Columbia, Texas
Jordan, Ricardo	0	0	6.57	13	0	0	0	12	15	9	9	7	17	L	L	5-11	165	6-27-70	1990	Delray Beach, Fla.
Menhart, Paul	2	4	6.31	10	10	0	0	51	62	42	36	25	30	R	R	6-2	190	3-25-69	1990	Conyers, Ga.
Montoya, Al	0	0	0.00	7	0	0	0	4	3	1	0	3	2	L	L	6-2	168	6-10-69	1991	Roswell, N.M.
Robinson, Ken	5	3	3.22	38	0	0	2	50	37	18	18	12	61	R	R	5-9	175	11-3-69	1991	Akron, Ohio
Rogers, Jimmy	3	4	3.05	38	0	0	1	74	65	26	25	31	82	R	R	6-2	190	1-3-67	1987	Tulsa, Okla.
Small, Aaron	0	0	5.40	1	0	0	0	2	3	1	1	1	2	R	R	6-5	200	11-23-71	1989	Victorville, Calif.
Spoljaric, Paul	2	10	4.93	43	9	0	10	88	69	51	48	54	108	R	L	6-3	205	9-24-70	1990	Kelowna, B.C.
Steed, Rick	4	3	3.72	31	0	0	1	56	51	29	23	23	34	R	R	6-2	185	9-8-70	1989	West Covina, Calif.
Tilmon, Pat	0	0	1.50	4	0	0	0	6	8	3	1	4	2	R	R	6-0	177	5-4-66	1987	Hopewell, Va.
Timlin, Mike	1	1	1.04	8	0	0	0	17	13	6	2	4	13	R	R	6-4	210	3-10-66	1987	Olsmar, Fla.
Wainhouse, Dave	3	2	3.70	26	0	0	5	24	29	13	10	11	18	L	R	6-2	185	11-7-67	1989	Mercer Island, Wash.
Ward, Duane	1	1	15.00	6	0	0	0	6	14	10	10	2	4	R	R	6-4	210	5-28-64	1982	Las Vegas, Nev.
Ware, Jeff	7	0	3.00	16	16	0	0	75	62	29	25	46	76	R	R	6-3	190	11-11-70	1991	Virginia Beach, Va.
Weber, Ben	4	5	5.40	25	15	0	1	92	111	62	55	27	38	R	R	6-4	180	11-17-69	1991	Groves, Texas
Whitehurst, Wally	3	1	3.86	6	4	0	0	28	32	16	12	7	21	R	R	6-3	185	4-11-64	1985	Madisonville, La.
2-team (6 Paw.)	1	3	6.51	6	6	0	0	28	36	21	20	5	13							
Williams, Woody	0	0	3.52	5	1	0	1	8	5	3	3	5	13	R	R	6-0	190	8-19-66	1988	Houston, Texas
York, Mike	1	4	7.00	20	5	0	0	45	55	50	35	27	37	R	R	6-1	180	9-6-64	1983	Justice, Ill.

FIELDING

Catcher	PCT	G	PO	A	E	DP	PB
Brooks	.988	46	235	15	3	0	5
Knorr	.979	17	129	14	3	3	0
Lutz	.975	19	71	8	2	0	2
Ramos	.959	10	68	2	3	0	0
Townley	.990	74	473	32	5	5	6

First Base	PCT	G	PO	A	E	DP
Delgado	.995	79	696	47	4	63
Lis	1.000	2	16	0	0	1
Lutz	1.000	1	2	0	0	1
Ramos	.983	14	108	8	2	9
Townley	.935	6	22	7	2	3
Weinke	.991	50	379	46	4	28

Second Base	PCT	G	PO	A	E	DP
Brito	1.000	4	3	5	0	0
Crespo	.938	86	160	220	25	38
Diaz	.667	2	0	2	1	0
Kelly	.975	11	15	24	1	3

	PCT	G	PO	A	E	DP
Lis	.994	42	64	111	1	22
Montalvo	.917	7	14	19	3	5
Third Base	PCT	G	PO	A	E	DP
Battle	.913	90	40	192	22	11
Diaz	.000	1	0	0	0	0
Johnson	1.000	1	0	1	0	0
Kelly	.000	2	0	0	0	0
Lis	.914	35	35	82	11	4
Lutz	.714	3	1	4	2	0
Montalvo	1.000	2	1	2	0	1
Sawkiw	.813	7	4	9	3	0
Weinke	.875	18	9	19	4	1
Shortstop	PCT	G	PO	A	E	DP
Battle	.923	34	42	89	11	11
Brito	.952	88	120	235	18	48
Diaz	.950	12	28	29	3	7
Johnson	1.000	5	2	7	0	1

	PCT	G	PO	A	E	DP
Kelly	.950	15	19	38	3	9
Lis	1.000	2	0	3	0	0
Montalvo	1.000	1	2	5	0	1
Outfield	PCT	G	PO	A	E	DP
Bowers	.945	94	150	5	9	0
Brooks	.000	1	0	0	0	0
Butler	.965	64	101	9	4	2
Canate	.963	112	223	14	9	4
Delgado	1.000	14	28	2	0	0
Kelly	1.000	1	1	0	0	0
Lis	.980	31	48	2	1	1
Lutz	.923	13	12	0	1	0
Montalvo	.000	2	0	0	0	0
Perez	.964	119	208	7	8	0
Ramos	.917	7	11	0	1	0
Sawkiw	.933	7	13	1	1	0
Weinke	.915	28	43	0	4	0

SOUTHERN LEAGUE

BATTING	AVG	G	AB	R	H	2B	3B	HR	RBI	BB	SO	SB	CS	B	T	HT	WT	DOB	1st Yr	Resides
Adriana, Sharnol	.284	75	261	33	74	17	1	3	33	32	64	12	13	R	R	6-1	185	11-13-70	1991	Willemstad, Curacao
Boston, D.J.	.244	132	479	51	117	27	1	11	71	47	100	12	8	L	L	6-7	230	9-6-71	1991	Cincinnati, Ohio

BATTING	AVG	G	AB	R	H	2B	3B	HR	RBI	BB	SO	SB	CS	B	T	HT	WT	DOB	1st Yr	Resides
Brooks, Eric	.283	21	53	6	15	3	0	4	12	12	9	0	1	R	R	6-2	195	5-18-69	1988	La Mirada, Calif.
Butler, Rich	.267	58	217	27	58	12	3	4	33	25	41	11	3	L	R	6-1	180	5-1-73	1991	Toronto, Ontario
Coolbaugh, Mike	.240	142	500	71	120	32	2	9	56	37	110	7	11	R	R	6-1	190	6-5-72	1990	San Antonio, Texas
Cradle, Rickey	.179	41	117	17	21	5	1	4	13	17	29	3	3	R	R	6-2	180	6-20-73	1991	Cerritos, Calif.
De la Cruz, Lorenzo	.274	140	508	63	139	20	12	8	61	36	129	11	11	R	R	6-1	199	9-5-71	1991	Santo Domingo, D.R.
Harmes, Kris	.228	86	259	28	59	14	2	4	29	36	47	0	1	L	R	6-2	190	6-13-71	1990	Mount Joy, Pa.
Henry, Santiago	.220	138	454	47	100	25	4	2	30	10	91	16	6	R	R	5-11	156	7-27-72	1991	San Pedro de Macoris, D.R.
Johnson, Matt	.181	57	144	8	26	4	0	0	11	17	32	1	1	R	R	5-10	175	5-15-70	1992	Arvada, Colo.
Kelly, Pat	.242	47	161	22	39	6	1	2	14	13	30	1	1	R	R	5-11	175	1-22-67	1989	Waukegan, Ill.
Ladd, Jeff	.292	9	24	1	7	1	1	0	2	5	8	0	0	R	R	6-3	200	7-10-70	1992	Oregon, Ohio
Lutz, Brent	.132	52	144	14	19	6	0	2	12	15	59	4	1	R	R	6-1	185	5-7-70	1991	Issaquah, Wash.
Martinez, Sandy	.229	41	144	14	33	8	1	2	22	6	34	0	1	L	R	6-2	200	10-3-72	1990	Villa Mella, D.R.
Morland, Mike	.179	11	28	6	5	1	0	0	1	1	4	0	0	R	R	6-0	190	8-17-69	1991	Cascade Locks, Ore.
Moultrie, Pat	.255	13	51	3	13	0	0	0	7	4	6	2	1	L	L	5-11	160	4-27-73	1992	Fresno, Calif.
Roberts, Lonell	.236	116	454	66	107	12	3	1	29	27	97	57	18	S	R	6-0	172	6-7-71	1989	Bloomington, Calif.
Sawkiw, Warren	.248	44	121	11	30	4	1	1	11	13	36	2	2	S	R	5-11	180	1-19-68	1990	Lakeland, Fla.
Stewart, Shannon	.287	138	498	89	143	24	6	5	55	89	61	42	16	R	R	6-1	185	2-25-74	1992	Miami, Fla.

PITCHING	W	L	ERA	G	GS	CG	SV	IP	H	R	ER	BB	SO	B	T	HT	WT	DOB	1st Yr	Resides
Almanzar, Carlos	3	12	3.99	35	19	0	2	126	144	77	56	32	93	R	R	6-2	166	11-6-73	1991	Santo Domingo, D.R.
Beltran, Alonso	3	6	5.69	28	6	0	1	87	111	60	55	32	54	R	R	6-3	180	3-4-72	1991	El Paso, Texas
Brandow, Derek	5	6	4.29	25	21	1	1	107	95	60	51	50	106	R	R	6-1	190	1-25-70	1992	London, Ontario
Brown, Chad	1	3	4.57	40	0	0	1	41	38	23	21	22	35	L	L	6-0	185	12-9-71	1992	Gastonia, N.C.
Carpenter, Chris	3	7	5.18	12	12	0	0	64	71	47	37	31	53	R	R	6-6	220	4-27-75	1994	Raymond, N.H.
Doman, Roger	0	3	5.87	14	0	0	0	31	42	25	20	11	16	R	R	6-5	185	1-26-73	1991	Cassville, Mo.
Freeman, Chris	2	3	5.42	39	5	0	8	81	78	53	49	38	80	R	R	6-4	205	8-27-72	1994	Knoxville, Tenn.
Gray, Dennis	0	3	6.34	24	0	0	0	33	29	25	23	20	22	L	L	6-6	225	12-24-69	1991	Banning, Calif.
Heble, Kurt	3	7	6.02	47	0	0	6	52	52	36	35	24	44	R	R	6-3	205	2-9-69	1991	West Columbia, Texas
Hurtado, Edwin	2	4	4.45	11	11	0	0	55	54	34	27	25	38	R	R	6-2	215	2-1-70	1991	Carabobo, Venez.
Ingram, Todd	1	1	3.71	20	0	0	3	34	26	17	14	16	19	R	R	6-4	200	4-1-68	1991	Bellevue, Wash.
Janzen, Marty	5	1	2.63	7	7	2	0	48	35	14	14	14	44	R	R	6-3	197	5-31-73	1991	Gainesville, Fla.
Jersild, Aaron	2	2	5.98	14	5	0	0	41	47	28	27	21	29	L	L	6-0	180	6-28-69	1992	Columbia, S.C.
Kotes, Chris	3	9	4.91	36	11	1	1	106	109	66	58	45	74	R	R	6-3	195	5-11-69	1991	Hopewell Junction, N.Y.
Meinershagen, Adam	1	1	10.80	3	3	0	0	12	17	14	14	2	4	R	R	6-4	190	7-25-73	1991	St. Louis, Mo.
Pace, Scott	6	8	4.57	18	18	1	0	102	117	66	52	48	71	L	L	6-4	210	9-16-71	1994	Cieba, P.R.
Pett, Jose	8	9	4.26	26	25	1	0	142	132	87	67	48	89	R	R	6-6	190	1-8-76	1992	Sao Paulo, Brazil
Silva, Jose	0	0	9.00	3	0	0	0	2	3	2	2	6	2	R	R	6-5	210	12-19-73	1991	San Diego, Calif.
Steed, Rick	2	4	3.69	27	0	0	9	32	23	15	13	16	29	R	R	6-2	185	9-8-70	1989	West Covina, Calif.
Weber, Ben	4	1	3.91	12	1	0	0	25	26	12	11	6	16	R	R	6-4	180	11-17-69	1991	Groves, Texas

FIELDING

Catcher	PCT	G	PO	A	E	DP	PB
Brooks	.986	19	122	16	2	1	3
Harmes	.974	43	275	34	8	3	2
Ladd	.977	7	38	4	1	0	0
Lutz	.971	39	217	19	7	1	9
Martinez	.980	38	219	30	5	0	4
Morland	.985	9	60	5	1	0	1

First Base	PCT	G	PO	A	E	DP
Boston	.986	132	1129	91	17	117
Coolbaugh	1.000	7	65	5	0	0
Harmes	1.000	3	28	0	0	0
Lutz	1.000	1	6	1	0	0
Sawkiw	.947	3	16	2	1	1

Second Base	PCT	G	PO	A	E	DP
Coolbaugh	1.000	6	8	12	0	2

	PCT	G	PO	A	E	DP
Henry	.972	106	209	269	14	69
Johnson	.988	28	27	58	1	13
Kelly	1.000	1	1	4	0	0
Sawkiw	.974	11	15	23	1	5

Third Base	PCT	G	PO	A	E	DP
Adriana	1.000	3	1	3	0	0
Coolbaugh	.935	126	83	279	25	30
Harmes	.667	3	2	2	2	0
Johnson	1.000	5	1	7	0	0
Kelly	1.000	9	5	25	0	1
Sawkiw	.833	5	1	14	3	1

Shortstop	PCT	G	PO	A	E	DP
Adriana	.928	71	88	209	23	36
Henry	.918	32	51	94	13	14

	PCT	G	PO	A	E	DP
Johnson	.833	8	3	12	3	1
Kelly	.939	37	45	94	9	24

Outfield	PCT	G	PO	A	E	DP
Butler	.974	48	106	5	3	1
Coolbaugh	1.000	2	3	0	0	0
Cradle	.980	31	45	3	1	0
De la Cruz	.964	119	224	14	9	1
Johnson	.750	2	3	0	1	0
Lutz	.923	8	11	1	1	0
Moultrie	1.000	13	22	0	0	0
Roberts	.947	81	159	3	9	0
Sawkiw	1.000	5	6	0	0	0
Stewart	.980	132	283	6	6	1

DUNEDIN   A
FLORIDA STATE LEAGUE

BATTING	AVG	G	AB	R	H	2B	3B	HR	RBI	BB	SO	SB	CS	B	T	HT	WT	DOB	1st Yr	Resides
Candelaria, Ben	.259	125	471	66	122	21	5	5	49	53	98	11	4	L	R	5-11	167	1-29-75	1992	Hatillo, P.R.
Cradle, Rickey	.275	50	178	33	49	10	3	7	27	28	49	6	2	R	R	6-2	180	6-20-73	1991	Cerritos, Calif.
Cromer, Brandon	.237	106	329	40	78	11	3	6	43	43	84	0	5	L	R	6-2	175	1-25-74	1992	Lexington, S.C.
Davila, Vic	.257	109	331	48	85	14	5	6	45	24	66	1	3	L	R	6-0	185	10-27-72	1993	New York, N.Y.
Evans, Tom	.279	130	444	63	124	29	3	9	66	51	80	7	2	R	R	6-1	180	7-9-74	1992	Kirkland, Wash.
Jones, Ryan	.249	127	478	65	119	28	0	18	78	41	92	1	1	R	R	6-3	220	11-5-74	1993	Irvine, Calif.
Loeb, Marc	.223	64	193	17	43	12	0	1	22	24	46	1	1	R	R	6-3	210	11-14-69	1989	Rialto, Calif.
Melhuse, Adam	.215	123	428	43	92	20	0	4	41	61	87	6	1	S	R	6-2	185	3-27-72	1993	Stockton, Calif.
Moultrie, Pat	.246	92	349	40	86	8	4	1	29	27	65	15	4	L	L	5-11	160	4-27-73	1992	Fresno, Calif.
Patzke, Jeff	.264	129	470	68	124	32	6	11	75	85	81	5	3	S	R	6-0	170	11-19-73	1992	Klamath Falls, Ore.
Querecuto, Juan	.179	53	140	16	25	4	1	1	10	8	31	0	0	R	R	6-4	175	12-3-69	1989	Anzoategui, Venez.
Ramirez, Angel	.275	131	541	78	149	19	5	8	52	21	99	17	12	R	R	5-10	166	1-24-73	1991	Azua, D.R.
Sanchez, Omar	.250	39	120	25	30	5	0	0	8	21	20	3	2	R	R	6-0	170	7-24-70	1992	Guarico, Venez.
Solano, Fausto	.208	41	144	19	30	5	2	1	10	17	30	3	2	R	R	5-9	145	6-19-74	1992	Santo Domingo, D.R.

GAMES BY POSITION: C—Loeb 40, Melhuse 94, Querecuto 14. **1B**—Davila 1, Jones 119, Loeb 1, Melhuse 3, Querecuto 21. **2B**—Davila 24, Patzke 117. **3B**—Davila 12, Evans 108, Moultrie 1, Querecuto 2. **SS**—Cromer 94, Patzke 13, Solano 38. **OF**—Candelaria 121, Cradle 48, Davila 12, Evans 1, Melhuse 1, Moultrie 76, Querecuto 3, Ramirez 130, Sanchez 34.

PITCHING	W	L	ERA	G	GS	CG	SV	IP	H	R	ER	BB	SO	B	T	HT	WT	DOB	1st Yr	Resides
Adkins, Tim	7	4	3.75	45	0	0	17	48	36	29	20	33	49	L	L	6-0	195	5-12-74	1992	Huntington, W.Va.
Carpenter, Chris	5	2	2.17	15	15	0	0	99	83	29	24	25	89	R	R	6-6	220	4-27-75	1994	Raymond, N.H.
Gordon, Mike	1	2	5.89	7	6	0	0	37	44	32	24	24	36	L	R	6-2	195	11-30-72	1992	Quincy, Fla.
Halperin, Mike	3	5	3.62	14	12	0	0	70	70	36	28	29	63	L	L	5-10	170	9-8-73	1994	Naples, Fla.

PITCHING	W	L	ERA	G	GS	CG	SV	IP	H	R	ER	BB	SO	B	T	HT	WT	DOB	1st Yr	Resides
Harris, D.J.	3	3	3.22	42	0	0	2	67	54	29	24	41	56	R	R	5-10	190	4-11-71	1993	Las Vegas, Nev.
Jersild, Aaron	2	6	4.81	22	3	0	1	49	54	30	26	17	39	L	L	6-0	180	6-28-69	1992	Columbia, S.C.
Largusa, Levon	4	4	4.10	16	7	1	0	59	68	32	27	28	37	L	L	5-11	180	5-21-71	1992	San Leandro, Calif.
Lukasiewicz, Mark	3	6	5.60	31	13	0	1	88	80	62	55	42	71	L	L	6-5	230	3-8-73	1994	Secaucus, N.J.
Mallory, Trevor	0	5	5.01	37	3	0	0	70	80	53	39	41	46	R	R	6-4	180	5-31-72	1991	St. Petersburg, Fla.
Meinershagen, Adam	5	9	3.75	21	13	1	0	98	115	59	41	23	53	R	R	6-4	190	7-25-73	1991	St. Louis, Mo.
Romano, Mike	11	7	4.13	28	26	1	0	150	141	79	69	75	102	S	R	6-2	195	3-3-72	1993	Chalmette, La.
Sinacori, Chris	0	1	6.75	12	0	0	2	12	13	9	9	4	11	R	R	6-4	200	8-19-70	1991	Wantagh, N.Y.
Sinclair, Steve	5	3	2.59	46	0	0	2	73	69	26	21	17	52	L	L	6-2	172	8-2-71	1991	Victoria, B.C.
Smith, Keilan	11	6	4.11	26	24	1	0	149	164	83	68	53	85	R	R	6-4	175	12-20-73	1992	Memphis, Tenn.
Spring, Josh	1	0	1.05	18	0	0	2	26	16	6	3	17	23	R	R	6-1	210	11-26-72	1991	Lebanon, Ohio
Steinert, Rob	3	4	4.70	17	11	0	0	75	82	48	39	29	41	R	R	6-2	195	9-29-71	1993	Greenlawn, N.Y.
Toney, Mike	1	2	8.03	12	0	0	3	12	19	14	11	13	6	R	R	6-3	205	7-31-73	1993	Sierra Vista, Ariz.
Viola, Frank	0	1	3.97	3	3	0	0	11	12	9	5	3	8	L	L	6-4	209	4-19-60	1981	Longwood, Fla.
Ward, Duane	0	1	6.23	3	2	0	0	4	4	3	3	1	4	R	R	6-4	210	5-28-64	1982	Las Vegas, Nev.

HAGERSTOWN — A
SOUTH ATLANTIC LEAGUE

BATTING	AVG	G	AB	R	H	2B	3B	HR	RBI	BB	SO	SB	CS	B	T	HT	WT	DOB	1st Yr	Resides
Holley, Battle	.203	23	79	6	16	4	0	0	7	3	18	0	2	R	R	6-0	188	3-5-77	1994	Tabor City, N.C.
Ladd, Jeff	.305	94	311	54	95	17	3	19	58	78	94	6	3	R	R	6-3	200	7-10-70	1992	Oregon, Ohio
Llanos, Aurelio	.251	106	378	54	95	25	1	17	63	29	115	9	7	R	R	6-4	215	10-14-70	1988	Carolina, P.R.
Morgan, Dave,	.265	67	249	26	66	14	1	4	26	18	53	1	0	R	R	6-4	215	11-19-71	1993	Needham, Mass.
Mosquera, Julio	.291	108	406	64	118	22	5	3	46	29	53	5	5	R	R	5-10	165	1-29-72	1991	Panama City, Panama
Mummau, Rob	.257	107	366	63	94	17	3	5	42	42	74	6	1	R	R	5-11	180	8-21-71	1993	Manheim, Pa.
Prensi, Dagoberto	.208	104	361	40	75	18	5	4	33	18	106	10	6	R	R	6-3	170	12-16-72	1991	La Romana, D.R.
Reilly, John	.000	1	2	1	0	0	0	0	0	0	0	0	0	R	R	5-10	190	10-14-72	1994	Glendale, N.Y.
Rivers, Jonathon	.294	123	429	54	126	16	6	6	48	40	104	18	5	R	R	6-2	200	8-17-74	1992	Tallassee, Ala.
Sanders, Anthony	.232	133	512	72	119	28	1	8	48	52	103	26	14	R	R	6-2	180	3-2-74	1993	Tucson, Ariz.
Stone, Craig	.276	96	355	47	98	20	4	8	52	34	104	3	2	R	R	6-2	190	7-12-75	1993	Quaker Hill, Australia
Strange, Mike	.234	96	290	51	68	9	2	1	27	61	92	13	3	R	R	6-0	172	4-21-74	1994	Melbourne, Fla.
Thompson, Andy	.239	124	461	48	110	19	2	6	57	29	108	2	3	R	R	6-3	210	10-8-75	1995	Sun Prairie, Wisc.
Witt, Kevin	.232	119	479	58	111	35	1	14	50	28	148	1	5	L	R	6-4	185	1-5-76	1993	Jacksonville, Fla.

GAMES BY POSITION: C—Ladd 26, Morgan 23, Mosquera 98. **1B**—Ladd 15, Llanos 17, Morgan 19, Mosquera 1, Mummau 1, Stone 95. **2B**—Holley 1, Mummau 54, Strange 93. **3B**—Holley 12, Mummau 12, Thompson 119. **SS**—Mummau 26, Witt 117. **OF**—Holley 2, Llanos 70, Prensi 103, Rivers 122, Sanders 133.

PITCHING	W	L	ERA	G	GS	CG	SV	IP	H	R	ER	BB	SO	B	T	HT	WT	DOB	1st Yr	Resides
Arias, Alfredo	4	6	4.16	35	1	0	1	71	67	37	33	35	59	R	R	6-2	160	11-5-72	1991	San Pedro de Macoris, D.R.
Crowther, John	1	3	5.45	11	11	0	0	38	52	36	23	27	21	R	R	6-5	231	9-23-73	1994	Savannah, Ga.
Davenport, Joe	0	1	6.11	13	0	0	0	18	22	19	12	13	13	R	R	6-5	225	3-24-76	1994	Santee, Calif.
Davey, Tom	4	1	3.38	8	8	0	0	37	29	23	14	31	25	R	R	6-7	215	9-11-73	1994	Canton, Mich.
Doman, Roger	2	2	4.41	14	6	0	1	51	65	32	25	13	24	R	R	6-5	185	1-26-73	1991	Cassville, Mo.
Hartshorn, Tyson	3	4	5.36	12	7	0	0	49	59	37	29	20	28	R	R	6-5	190	8-3-74	1993	Lamar, Colo.
Hibbard, Billy	2	1	3.89	16	0	0	0	35	42	16	15	6	20	R	R	6-3	198	6-24-76	1994	Orlando, Fla.
Jarvis, Jason	4	3	3.60	8	8	0	0	50	49	27	20	13	42	R	R	6-1	170	10-27-73	1994	West Bountiful, Utah
Lee, Jeremy	7	11	4.20	26	26	1	0	148	160	82	69	29	118	R	R	6-8	235	10-20-74	1993	Galesburg, Ill.
McBride, Chris	5	10	4.29	19	19	2	0	107	121	61	51	27	52	L	R	6-5	210	10-13-73	1994	Leland, N.C.
Meiners, Doug	8	4	2.99	18	18	3	0	117	121	52	39	14	73	R	R	6-8	190	5-16-74	1992	Staten Island, N.Y.
Nunez, Maximo	1	1	5.54	22	0	0	0	37	40	29	23	20	21	R	R	6-5	165	1-15-73	1991	Villa Mella, D.R.
Pace, Scott	4	2	1.09	11	6	2	1	58	32	8	7	12	57	L	L	6-4	210	9-16-71	1994	Cieba, P.R.
Peterman, Ernie	1	1	12.60	2	0	0	0	5	9	7	7	1	4	R	R	6-2	205	2-27-72	1995	Nanty Glo, Pa.
Rhine, Kendall	3	3	2.60	42	0	0	13	55	41	20	16	28	49	R	R	6-6	205	11-27-70	1992	Lilburn, Ga.
Schneider, Jeff	0	1	27.00	2	0	0	0	1	1	2	2	4	0	R	R	6-6	205	6-23-73	1994	Euless, Texas
Sievert, Mark	12	6	2.91	27	27	3	0	161	126	79	52	46	140	L	R	6-4	180	2-16-73	1991	Janesville, Wisc.
Smith, Brian	9	1	0.87	47	0	0	21	104	77	18	10	16	101	R	R	5-11	185	7-19-72	1994	Salisbury, N.C.
Spring, Josh	1	4	4.17	19	4	0	0	45	44	23	21	19	33	R	R	6-1	210	11-26-72	1991	Lebanon, Ohio
Toney, Mike	3	3	2.48	20	0	0	4	29	21	11	8	17	26	R	R	6-3	205	7-31-73	1993	Sierra Vista, Ariz.

ST. CATHARINES — A
NEW YORK-PENN LEAGUE

BATTING	AVG	G	AB	R	H	2B	3B	HR	RBI	BB	SO	SB	CS	B	T	HT	WT	DOB	1st Yr	Resides
Bourne, Charles	.199	55	176	24	35	11	0	1	17	18	50	12	3	R	R	6-2	180	5-21-75	1993	Altadena, Calif.
Freel, Ryan	.280	65	243	30	68	10	5	3	29	22	49	12	7	R	R	5-10	175	3-8-76	1995	Jacksonville, Fla.
Hayes, Chris	.306	70	271	39	83	17	3	2	36	24	50	8	7	R	R	6-2	190	12-23-73	1995	Jacksonville, Fla.
Holley, Battle	.240	65	246	33	59	2	1	3	26	22	47	3	3	R	R	6-0	188	3-5-77	1994	Tabor City, N.C.
Johnson, Damon	.216	63	232	26	50	9	5	1	25	8	73	9	2	R	R	6-1	195	8-22-75	1993	Crossett, Ark.
Landers, Mark	.232	74	271	43	63	11	0	10	52	45	86	1	2	L	L	6-0	200	10-2-71	1994	Charleston, W Va.
Reilly, John	.260	32	77	8	20	2	2	1	10	6	20	0	0	R	R	5-10	190	10-14-72	1994	Glendale, N.Y.
Rodriguez, Luis	.276	66	257	22	71	16	2	1	20	10	49	2	4	R	R	5-9	160	1-3-74	1991	Charallave, Venez.
Rosario, Felix	.226	64	217	24	49	6	0	1	21	18	44	9	3	R	R	6-3	165	12-30-71	1991	Villa Mella, D.R.
Sanchez, Omar	.301	74	292	62	88	16	6	3	23	19	50	26	10	R	R	5-9	160	7-24-70	1992	Guarico, Venez.
Solano, Fausto	.285	57	207	28	59	17	1	2	24	30	28	14	4	R	R	5-9	144	6-19-74	1992	Santo Domingo, D.R.
Williams, Brian	.194	24	67	5	13	2	0	0	6	6	22	0	3	R	R	6-1	195	2-9-75	1995	Dickinson, Texas

GAMES BY POSITION: C—Reilly 4, Rodriguez 62, Williams 16. **1B**—Hayes 2, Landers 74. **2B**—Freel 65, Holley 8, Sanchez 7. **3B**—Hayes 28, Holley 46, Rodriguez 2. **SS**—Hayes 14, Holley 5, Solano 57. **OF**—Bourne 53, Hayes 3, Johnson 60, Reilly 3, Rosario 55, Sanchez 60.

PITCHING	W	L	ERA	G	GS	CG	SV	IP	H	R	ER	BB	SO	B	T	HT	WT	DOB	1st Yr	Resides
Crowther, John	3	6	5.40	15	14	0	0	68	87	43	41	34	44	R	R	6-5	231	9-23-73	1994	Savannah, Ga.
Davey, Tom	3	3	3.32	7	7	0	0	38	27	19	14	23	29	R	R	6-7	215	9-11-73	1994	Canton, Mich.
De la Cruz, Narciso	1	1	7.20	21	0	0	0	35	39	31	28	22	19	L	L	6-0	160	7-15-73	1995	El Seybo, D.R.
Fitterer, Scott	0	0	1.14	22	0	0	9	24	18	7	3	13	22	R	R	6-2	200	11-4-73	1995	Kent, Wash.
Hartshorn, Tyson	3	4	4.26	13	13	1	0	70	83	45	33	25	25	R	R	6-5	190	8-3-74	1993	Lamar, Colo.
Horton, Eric	6	2	2.84	21	7	0	3	70	50	26	22	26	51	R	R	6-2	180	8-9-70	1994	Cedar Bluff, Ala.

PITCHING	W	L	ERA	G	GS	CG	SV	IP	H	R	ER	BB	SO	B	T	HT	WT	DOB	1st Yr	Resides
Hoy, Wayne	5	3	2.21	24	1	0	3	57	39	20	14	23	34	R	R	6-4	210	4-16-71	1994	Bayville, N.Y.
Lowe, Ben	4	5	4.35	15	15	0	0	79	89	43	38	40	61	S	L	5-10	185	6-13-74	1994	Key West, Fla.
Nunez, Maximo	1	0	9.39	7	0	0	0	8	11	10	8	7	6	R	R	6-5	165	1-15-73	1991	Villa Mella, D.R.
Peguero, Jose	2	1	4.50	17	0	0	0	34	31	19	17	19	19	R	R	6-2	170	12-20-75	1994	San Cristobal, D.R.
Peterman, Ernie	1	1	5.94	4	3	0	0	17	18	11	11	2	8	R	R	6-2	205	2-27-72	1995	Nanty Glo, Pa.
Smith, Randy	0	2	3.27	18	0	0	2	33	34	14	12	9	26	R	R	6-0	190	7-11-72	1995	Duncan, Okla.
Volkert, Oreste	2	3	2.67	22	0	0	2	54	53	20	16	14	44	R	R	6-6	187	1-16-75	1993	La Habra, Calif.
Young, Joe	6	5	2.04	15	15	0	0	84	72	29	19	35	73	R	R	6-4	205	4-28-75	1993	Fort McMurray, Alberta

MEDICINE HAT   R
PIONEER LEAGUE

BATTING	AVG	G	AB	R	H	2B	3B	HR	RBI	BB	SO	SB	CS	B	T	HT	WT	DOB	1st Yr	Resides
Curl, John	.319	69	270	47	86	26	1	7	63	31	61	5	1	L	R	6-3	205	11-10-72	1995	College Station, Texas
Farner, Matt	.275	45	142	28	39	3	3	2	24	26	48	9	5	L	L	6-4	185	10-15-74	1993	Enola, Pa.
Gordon, Herman	.232	51	181	26	42	2	1	5	20	10	57	2	1	S	R	6-2	190	11-5-74	1994	Oceanside, Calif.
Hampton, Robbie	.235	55	187	28	44	14	1	7	27	11	73	2	3	R	R	6-3	200	2-21-76	1994	Mount Pleasant, Texas
McCormick, Andrew	.295	69	258	64	76	18	2	5	37	64	67	15	5	R	R	5-11	190	6-21-73	1995	Tempe, Ariz.
Peeples, Michael	.312	72	285	55	89	14	4	3	50	35	46	27	5	R	R	5-11	160	9-3-76	1994	Green Cove Springs, Fla.
Shatley, Andy	.226	70	261	32	59	12	2	2	30	29	66	1	3	R	R	6-3	185	1-23-76	1994	Jonesboro, Ark.
Snelling, Allen	.226	35	115	9	26	2	0	1	11	7	31	1	2	R	R	6-1	180	6-13-73	1995	Newport, Ore.
Stewart, Paxton	.248	50	161	30	40	13	2	0	17	23	34	4	2	L	R	6-3	185	5-4-74	1995	New York, N.Y.
Timmons, Shayne	.167	24	42	5	7	1	0	0	3	6	11	0	1	R	R	5-11	185	1-23-72	1994	New Castle, Del.
Valdespino, Jose	.190	35	105	14	20	3	2	3	13	18	34	1	1	R	R	6-1	186	6-15-74	1991	Panama City, Panama
Wilson, Craig	.283	49	184	33	52	14	1	7	35	24	41	8	2	R	R	6-2	195	11-30-76	1995	Huntington Beach, Calif.
Woodward, Chris	.232	72	241	44	56	8	0	3	21	33	41	9	4	R	R	6-0	160	6-27-76	1995	Covina, Calif.

GAMES BY POSITION: C—Timmons 13, Valdespino 31, Wilson 35. 1B—Curl 63, Stewart 8, Timmons 5, Valdespino 1. 2B—Peeples 45, Snelling 30. 3B—Peeples 1, Shatley 70, Snelling 1, Stewart 1, Timmons 4. SS—Snelling 2, Woodward 72. OF—Farner 42, Gordon 45, Hampton 53, McCormick 67, Peeples 8, Stewart 12.

PITCHING	W	L	ERA	G	GS	CG	SV	IP	H	R	ER	BB	SO	B	T	HT	WT	DOB	1st Yr	Resides
Brabec, William	0	1	7.03	19	0	0	0	24	31	33	19	20	25	R	R	6-4	210	9-30-73	1995	Lombard, Ill.
Castillo, Vic	0	0	0.00	2	0	0	0	2	5	5	0	1	2	R	R	6-1	175	5-14-74	1994	Villa Mella, D.R.
Corral, Ruben	4	8	4.81	14	14	2	0	86	92	65	46	34	50	L	R	6-6	200	5-1-76	1993	El Monte, Calif.
Done, J.J.	5	5	4.59	22	1	0	1	33	35	25	17	15	29	R	R	5-11	165	11-25-75	1993	Santo Domingo, D.R.
Escobar, Kelvin	3	3	5.71	14	14	1	0	69	66	47	44	33	75	R	R	6-1	195	4-11-76	1992	La Guaira, Venez.
Gomez, Miguel	2	5	5.10	14	14	1	0	72	79	55	41	32	46	R	R	6-3	170	5-31-74	1992	Panama City, Panama
Hibbard, Billy	1	1	3.57	4	3	0	0	18	14	8	7	4	15	R	R	6-3	198	6-24-76	1994	Orlando, Fla.
James, Jhon	0	0	18.00	2	0	0	0	1	2	2	2	3	1	R	R	6-3	170	5-11-75	1993	La Sabana, Venez.
Johnson, Mike	4	1	3.86	19	0	0	3	49	46	26	21	25	32	L	R	6-2	175	10-3-75	1993	Edmonton, Alberta
Mann, James	5	4	4.29	14	14	1	0	78	78	47	37	37	66	R	R	6-3	225	11-17-74	1994	Holbrook, Mass.
Mitchell, John	2	2	2.50	25	0	0	11	36	20	15	10	17	50	R	R	6-4	200	8-25-74	1995	Camarillo, Calif.
Rodriguez, Victor	4	1	3.88	17	2	0	0	58	42	31	25	40	45	R	R	6-2	190	8-31-73	1994	Pensacola, Fla.
Rosario, Nelson	0	1	7.82	10	0	0	0	13	21	13	11	6	5	L	L	5-11	155	8-1-75	1993	El Seybo, D.R.
Smith, Ramon	1	4	3.63	19	0	0	2	22	15	16	9	24	26	S	L	5-11	175	7-5-73	1994	Alameda, Calif.
Veniard, Jay	4	1	2.71	11	10	0	0	63	67	34	19	21	43	L	L	6-4	215	8-16-74	1995	Jacksonville, Fla.

DUNEDIN   R
GULF COAST LEAGUE

BATTING	AVG	G	AB	R	H	2B	3B	HR	RBI	BB	SO	SB	CS	B	T	HT	WT	DOB	1st Yr	Resides
Bejarano, Brian	.254	52	173	20	44	6	4	3	25	11	53	1	1	R	R	6-3	200	1-29-75	1995	Laveen, Ariz.
Charles, Steve	.214	48	145	17	31	4	2	0	15	24	47	7	1	L	R	6-2	190	8-20-74	1994	London, Ontario
Cisar, Ryan	.153	35	72	10	11	1	0	0	5	20	24	0	0	R	R	6-1	175	1-5-77	1995	New Martinsville, W.Va.
Douglas, John	.235	55	179	21	42	6	0	2	26	24	35	6	4	R	R	6-3	185	7-20-73	1995	Vienna, Va.
Fortin, Blaine	.205	42	112	13	23	4	1	1	14	5	16	0	2	R	R	6-3	205	8-1-77	1995	Lundar, Manitoba
Kehoe, John	.274	57	201	32	55	17	5	2	32	35	52	8	0	R	R	6-0	185	1-9-73	1995	South Bend, Ind.
Maloney, Jeff	.163	39	92	9	15	5	0	0	12	6	24	2	1	R	R	6-4	190	11-27-76	1995	Basking Ridge, N.J.
Maysonet, Jose	.145	29	69	14	10	2	0	0	1	14	11	1	2	R	R	6-1	155	5-12-76	1994	Arecibo, P.R.
Medina, Robert	.177	30	62	5	11	1	1	2	8	4	23	1	1	R	R	6-2	193	4-25-76	1995	Caguas, P.R.
Nobles, Ivan	.143	36	105	14	15	3	1	0	12	13	40	2	1	R	R	6-1	170	5-14-75	1993	Brandon, Fla.
Peck, Thomas	.270	59	215	42	58	12	2	2	22	40	39	10	6	L	R	6-1	160	7-2-74	1995	Coral Gables, Fla.
Phillips, Darren	.136	20	44	3	6	0	0	0	3	4	21	0	1	S	R	6-2	187	11-14-75	1994	Condell Park, Australia
Solano, Fausto	.295	11	44	12	13	5	0	2	7	3	6	2	1	R	R	5-9	144	6-19-74	1992	Santo Domingo, D.R.
Villa, Willie	.181	40	138	20	25	6	2	0	11	14	28	2	1	R	R	6-2	220	3-24-76	1994	Nanakuli, Hawaii
Whitlock, Brian	.256	54	168	27	43	10	3	3	22	41	48	5	0	L	R	6-3	200	12-14-76	1995	Oakland, Calif.

GAMES BY POSITION: C—Cisar 20, Fortin 31, Medina 26, Phillips 15. 1B—Bejarano 15, Phillips 2, Whitlock 45. 2B—Douglas 2, Kehoe 49, Maysonet 12. 3B—Bejarano 12, Douglas 42, Kehoe 9, Phillips 4. SS—Bejarano 1, Douglas 8, Maloney 27, Maysonet 15, Solano 11. OF—Bejarano 8, Charles 47, Cisar 1, Nobles 32, Peck 58, Villa 36.

PITCHING	W	L	ERA	G	GS	CG	SV	IP	H	R	ER	BB	SO	B	T	HT	WT	DOB	1st Yr	Resides
Bowles, Brian	0	1	2.40	8	0	0	0	15	18	12	4	3	11	R	R	6-5	205	8-18-76	1995	Manhattan Beach, Calif.
Burchart, Kyle	1	3	7.64	13	2	0	0	35	55	45	30	20	27	R	R	6-5	190	8-18-76	1995	Tulsa, Okla.
Coe, Michael	0	1	3.38	2	0	0	0	8	8	4	3	6	1	R	L	6-4	187	10-22-74	1993	Indianapolis, Ind.
Davenport, Joe	2	3	5.66	15	10	1	1	56	67	47	35	30	29	R	R	6-5	225	3-24-76	1994	Santee, Calif.
Geraldo, Antonio	0	0	1.50	2	2	0	0	6	6	1	1	1	6	R	R	6-2	170	1-13-75	1992	Azua, D.R.
Glover, Mike	3	7	4.91	10	10	2	0	62	62	48	34	26	46	R	R	6-5	180	12-3-76	1994	DeLand, Fla.
Halladay, Roy	3	5	3.40	10	8	0	0	50	35	25	19	16	48	R	R	6-6	200	5-14-77	1995	Arvada, Colo.
Johnson, Mike	0	2	7.20	3	3	0	0	5	20	15	12	8	13	L	R	6-2	175	10-3-75	1993	Edmonton, Alberta
Lawrence, Clint	1	5	4.57	12	9	0	0	45	40	33	23	26	40	L	L	6-4	200	10-19-76	1995	Oakville, Ontario
Mendoza, David	2	5	4.99	12	10	0	0	49	58	37	27	14	39	R	R	6-7	205	2-29-76	1994	Oceanside, Calif.
Schneider, Jeff	0	2	15.43	3	2	0	0	5	9	10	8	7	2	R	R	6-6	205	6-23-73	1994	Euless, Texas
Seabury, Jaron	3	0	3.18	15	0	0	1	40	35	16	14	17	18	R	R	6-4	215	1-31-76	1995	Mt. Vernon, Wash.
Severino, Edy	1	3	5.63	24	0	0	0	24	31	25	15	13	13	R	R	6-4	170	6-8-76	1994	Yamasa, D.R.
Vaninetti, Gene	0	2	4.98	20	0	0	2	22	25	14	12	6	7	R	R	6-3	210	2-20-75	1992	Morphett Vale, Australia
Wells, David	2	0	0.82	3	1	0	0	11	4	2	1	2	18	L	L	6-4	215	8-16-74	1995	Jacksonville, Fla.
Zavershnik, Mike	1	1	5.45	19	0	0	2	36	44	29	22	11	26	R	L	6-8	185	2-21-76	1994	Mississauga, Ontario

INDEPENDENT/CO-OP
TEAMS

BAKERSFIELD A
CALIFORNIA LEAGUE

BATTING	AVG	G	AB	R	H	2B	3B	HR	RBI	BB	SO	SB	CS	B	T	HT	WT	DOB	1st Yr	Resides
3 Breuer, Jim	.048	10	21	0	1	0	0	0	3	2	13	0	0	R	R	6-4	200	8-15-73	1993	Bismarck, N.D.
2 Carr, Jeremy	.257	128	499	92	128	22	2	1	38	79	73	52	21	R	R	5-10	170	3-30-71	1993	Boise, Idaho
1 Claudio, Patricio	.281	32	128	19	36	9	3	1	9	13	26	5	7	R	R	6-0	173	4-12-72	1991	Santiago, D.R.
1 Hence, Sam	.125	4	8	1	1	0	0	0	0	0	1	0	0	R	R	5-11	205	1-3-71	1990	Wiggins, Miss.
1 Johnson, Todd	.360	9	25	2	9	2	1	0	2	3	4	0	1	R	R	5-11	205	12-18-70	1993	Fresno, Calif.
1 Lemons, Rich	.282	36	124	18	35	5	0	4	16	13	42	4	2	L	R	6-4	215	9-9-71	1993	Tucson, Ariz.
1 McCall, Rod	.330	96	345	61	114	19	1	20	70	40	90	2	5	L	R	6-7	235	11-4-71	1990	Stanton, Calif.
1 McNabb, Buck	.300	63	237	34	71	8	1	0	27	38	38	11	1	L	R	6-0	180	1-17-73	1991	Fort Walton Beach, Fla.
3 Meilan, Tony	.211	12	38	3	8	1	0	0	2	2	4	1	1	R	R	5-10	170	10-21-71	1994	Miami, Fla.
2 Morillo, Cesar	.305	108	371	41	113	25	1	1	37	31	71	4	12	S	R	5-11	180	7-21-73	1990	Eugene, Ore.
1 Prieto, Rich	.222	74	248	34	55	12	2	2	22	29	46	15	2	S	R	5-10	175	8-24-72	1993	Carmel, Calif.
1 Ramirez, Alex	.323	98	406	56	131	25	2	10	52	18	76	13	9	R	R	5-11	176	10-3-74	1991	Miranda, Venez.
3 Rasmussen, Nate	.197	23	71	12	14	4	0	0	6	12	23	0	0	L	L	6-6	240	10-19-74	1994	Lakeville, Minn.
3 Soliz, Steve	.245	44	159	9	39	5	0	1	11	15	34	2	1	R	R	5-10	180	1-27-71	1993	Oxnard, Calif.
3 Stare, Lonny	.272	104	372	54	101	21	2	9	59	33	65	14	10	R	R	5-11	185	5-20-71	1994	San Diego, Calif.
4 Tyrus, Jason, of	.173	25	81	12	14	0	0	4	10	7	28	4	2	R	R	6-2	200	6-6-72	1994	Milpitas, Calif.
3 Wingate, Ervan	.234	121	445	51	104	23	1	8	59	42	86	5	8	R	R	6-0	185	2-4-74	1992	Redlands, Calif.
3 Wittig, Paul	.278	93	331	44	92	17	1	7	53	20	66	6	3	R	R	6-1	190	7-31-73	1992	Bremerton, Wash.
3 Yard, Bruce	.230	59	191	19	44	8	1	1	27	27	22	2	5	L	R	6-0	175	10-17-71	1993	McIntyre, Pa.
3 Zahner, Kevin	.233	82	257	25	60	7	2	2	31	12	37	4	1	R	R	6-1	187	9-13-72	1991	Ellington, Conn.
3 Zellers, Kevin	.241	96	332	39	80	16	1	5	27	39	106	5	6	R	R	6-1	180	11-21-72	1994	Seven Hills, Ohio

GAMES BY POSITION: C—Johnson 7, Soliz 44, Wittig 61, Zahner 47. **1B**—Breuer 2, McCall 52, Rasmussen 19, Wingate 56, Wittig 2, Zahner 15. **2B**—Carr 121, Morillo 10, Wingate 9. **3B**—Morillo 18, Wingate 33, Zellers 94. **SS**—Meilan 12, Morillo 73, Prieto 2, Stare 1, Wingate 2, Yard 53. **OF**—Breuer 7, Carr 1, Claudio 32, Hence 2, Lemons 35, McNabb 63, Prieto 68, Ramirez 84, Stare 99, Tyrus 24, Wingate 18, Zahner 1.

PITCHING	W	L	ERA	G	GS	CG	SV	IP	H	R	ER	BB	SO	B	T	HT	WT	DOB	1st Yr	Resides
3 Bland, Nathan	4	9	5.22	27	23	0	0	122	155	89	71	55	46	L	L	6-5	205	12-27-74	1993	Birmingham, Ala.
3 Eaddy, Brad	4	5	2.95	42	1	0	5	79	66	29	26	36	68	L	L	6-5	200	6-6-70	1994	Florence, S.C.
3 Edwards, Wayne	9	8	3.36	21	21	1	0	129	125	63	48	56	83	L	L	6-5	185	5-7-64	1985	Sepulveda, Calif.
3 Iglesias, Mike	7	10	3.26	24	23	2	0	144	124	65	52	38	108	R	R	6-5	215	11-9-72	1991	Castro Valley, Calif.
3 Jaye, Jamie	1	2	4.39	5	5	0	0	27	30	16	13	10	22	L	L	6-7	235	3-27-73	1994	Bay Minette, Ala.
4 Kenady, Jake	4	10	6.72	23	16	0	0	87	107	76	65	68	69	L	L	6-4	190	9-21-73	1991	Apple Valley, Minn.
3 Lagarde, Joe	1	1	2.91	4	4	0	0	22	19	8	7	13	25	R	R	5-9	180	1-17-75	1993	Washington, D.C.
2-team (24 San Bem.)	4	10	6.72	23	16	0	0	87	107	76	65	68	69							
3 Linares, Rich	4	4	2.27	55	0	0	20	67	64	18	17	17	57	R	R	6-0	200	8-31-72	1992	Long Beach, Calif.
1 Meade, Paul	2	2	7.55	24	0	0	0	54	70	47	45	25	32	S	R	6-0	175	2-14-69	1991	Urbandale, Iowa
3 Mitchell, Kendrick	1	2	5.34	36	0	0	0	57	61	46	34	38	36	R	L	6-4	210	12-6-73	1992	Portland, Ore.
3 Nomo, Hideo	0	1	3.38	1	1	0	0	5	6	2	2	1	6	R	R	6-2	226	8-31-68	1995	Osaka, Japan
1 Ramos, Cesar	6	3	3.56	24	4	0	2	61	63	28	24	17	35	R	R	6-0	178	12-2-73	1992	Monte Cristi, D.R.
3 Scafa, Bob	5	8	4.23	42	5	0	4	79	92	56	37	26	61	L	L	5-10	205	9-13-72	1994	Park Ridge, Ill.
3 Scheffler, Craig	3	8	6.02	32	19	0	0	106	118	85	66	65	51	S	L	6-2	195	9-13-71	1993	Wausau, Wisc.
3 Tapia, Elias	0	1	3.90	17	0	0	1	32	35	22	14	14	14	R	R	6-2	205	5-31-76	1994	South Gate, Calif.
3 Thomas, Robbie	1	6	7.48	26	6	0	0	49	55	51	41	36	39	L	L	6-4	200	4-5-72	1994	Roswell, Ga.
1 Williams, Matt	2	0	2.36	7	7	0	0	34	34	9	9	14	30	S	L	6-0	185	4-12-71	1992	Virginia Beach, Va.
1 York, Charles	4	2	5.82	31	5	0	1	68	75	47	44	24	69	L	L	6-4	240	12-5-70	1992	Orange Park, Fla.

Property of Cleveland (1), Kansas City (2), Los Angeles (3), San Diego (4).

VISALIA A
CALIFORNIA LEAGUE

BATTING	AVG	G	AB	R	H	2B	3B	HR	RBI	BB	SO	SB	CS	B	T	HT	WT	DOB	1st Yr	Resides
6 Berry, Michael	.307	98	368	69	113	28	4	9	61	57	70	12	6	R	R	5-10	185	8-12-70	1993	Rolling Hills, Calif.
Bethea, Scott	.241	105	370	51	89	17	3	0	27	47	35	14	9	R	R	6-2	195	12-20-71	1990	Waverly, Ohio
4 Bonds, Bobby	.223	109	373	56	83	12	6	11	30	42	114	26	12	R	R	6-4	180	3-7-70	1992	Tampa, Fla.
3 Brock, Tarrik	.225	45	138	21	31	5	2	1	15	17	52	11	1	L	L	6-3	170	12-25-73	1991	Hawthorne, Calif.
8 Fernandez, Antonio	.227	90	309	25	70	10	1	2	32	14	48	1	0	R	R	6-0	195	5-24-73	1994	Tucson, Ariz.
1 Fuller, Aaron	.253	49	186	27	47	7	3	1	19	19	32	11	10	S	R	5-10	170	9-7-71	1993	Sacramento, Calif.
3 Garcia, Manuel	.100	12	40	3	4	2	1	0	4	1	18	3	0	R	R	6-0	180	11-9-68	1987	San Pedro de Macoris, D.R.
1 Graham, John	.248	98	306	45	76	8	1	1	30	36	77	12	6	L	R	5-10	170	5-7-71	1993	Abington, Mass.
Hayashi, Hiroyasu	.268	40	138	19	37	6	0	0	15	26	27	2	3	L	L	5-7	168	6-15-71	1995	Tokyo, Japan
1 Hecker, Doug	.071	8	14	2	1	0	0	0	0	3	5	0	1	R	R	6-4	210	1-21-71	1992	Wantagh, N.Y.
4 Jennings, Lance	.301	85	316	31	95	15	1	6	41	36	56	0	2	R	R	6-0	195	10-3-71	1989	Modesto, Calif.
3 Kruger, Andy	.253	100	356	46	90	9	7	4	32	28	65	10	15	L	L	5-11	180	11-7-72	1993	Dowagiac, Mich.
Ohmura, Iwao	.261	45	153	15	40	9	0	1	18	9	32	1	1	R	R	6-1	185	5-31-69	1995	Wakanai, Japan
3 Pagee, Shawn	.114	22	44	1	5	0	0	0	4	2	17	0	1	S	R	6-0	185	3-18-71	1994	Menlo Park, Calif.
2 Parker, Alan	.230	121	395	40	91	18	2	0	36	27	81	6	7	R	R	5-11	165	5-27-72	1994	Tampa, Fla.
4 Pinoni, Scott	.320	73	259	44	83	19	0	14	45	33	50	1	1	R	R	6-1	250	3-28-73	1994	Columbus, Ohio
5 Priest, Chris	.232	55	185	18	43	8	0	1	15	19	34	3	3	R	R	5-11	185	12-30-71	1995	Joliet, Ill.
2 Smith, Joel	.286	67	262	32	75	12	3	9	43	15	65	0	1	R	R	5-9	195	12-12-68	1992	Tallahassee, Fla.

BATTING	AVG	G	AB	R	H	2B	3B	HR	RBI	BB	SO	SB	CS	B	T	HT	WT	DOB	1st Yr	Resides
Tachikawa, Takashi ..	.176	47	119	10	21	2	1	1	14	8	28	1	1	R	R	6-0	180	10-7-75	1995	Tokyo, Japan
Tohyama, Shoji	.297	51	155	15	46	9	2	2	24	8	38	1	1	L	L	5-11	185	7-21-67	1995	Tokyo, Japan
3 Wyngarden, Brett	.263	76	270	21	71	14	0	3	24	12	81	1	2	R	R	6-2	200	10-8-70	1992	St Joseph, Mich.

GAMES BY POSITION: C—Jennings 76, Pagee 17, Smith 28, Wyngarden 36. **1B**—Fernandez 13, Hecker 6, Pagee 1, Pinoni 68, Smith 12, Tohyama 46, Wyngarden 7. **2B**—Berry 46, Bethea 74, Fernandez 13, Fuller 1, Gracia 11, Priest 1. **3B**—Berry 48, Fernandez 60, Fuller 2, Parker 2, Priest 35. **SS**—Bethea 27, Parker 118. **OF**—Bonds 103, Brock 39, Fuller 47, Graham 65, Hayashi 26, Kruger 71, Ohmura 42, Priest 15, Tachikawa 36.

PITCHING	W	L	ERA	G	GS	CG	SV	IP	H	R	ER	BB	SO	B	T	HT	WT	DOB	1st Yr	Resides
2 DeClue, Jon.	6	5	3.50	21	14	0	0	103	95	48	40	27	90	R	L	6-2	198	9-17-70	1994	Apopka, Fla.
Endo, Masataka	9	9	3.76	28	27	6	0	187	162	87	78	62	178	R	R	6-1	194	9-8-72	1995	Fukushima, Japan
Enoki, Yasuhiro	4	7	5.45	13	13	2	0	74	104	52	45	11	51	R	R	6-0	176	5-22-72	1995	Tokyo, Japan
2 Fetchel, Tony...........	0	1	6.66	18	1	0	0	24	22	20	18	32	11	R	R	6-2	186	8-12-71	1994	South Gate, Calif.
1 Hecker, Doug	0	0	0.00	2	0	0	0	2	1	1	0	1	2	R	R	6-4	210	1-21-71	1992	Wantagh, N.Y.
2 Hinson, Dean............	1	1	3.93	23	0	0	3	34	30	18	15	16	35	R	R	6-3	215	7-15-71	1989	Bloomfield, N.M.
Idemoto, Kenichiro	5	6	4.10	31	8	2	2	101	104	54	46	27	83	L	L	5-10	154	10-2-73	1995	Mie, Japan
7 Jenkins, Jon	1	1	5.55	33	1	0	0	47	43	34	29	38	38	R	R	6-8	210	6-3-68	1990	Culpeper, Va.
2 Locklear, Dean	3	3	3.93	9	9	0	0	53	50	29	23	21	27	R	L	6-1	190	10-12-69	1990	Granite, Okla.
7 Magnelli, Anthony......	2	5	4.24	29	0	0	11	40	40	20	19	6	30	R	R	5-11	185	9-8-70	1993	Suffern, N.Y.
Meadows, Jimmy	7	6	4.37	27	21	1	0	126	136	71	61	51	94	R	R	6-3	200	12-28-64	1984	Wingate, N.C.
Muto, Junichiro	1	2	3.52	17	0	0	5	38	33	16	15	5	35	R	R	6-0	172	3-15-69	1995	Tokyo, Japan
7 Myers, Tom	3	8	6.43	30	13	0	0	85	108	81	61	45	34	L	L	5-11	175	8-12-69	1991	San Jose, Calif.
1 Rowland, Thad	0	1	4.91	7	0	0	0	11	18	8	6	4	5	L	L	6-0	180	11-25-70	1994	Charleston, S.C.
9 Ryan, Reid...............	0	6	9.38	12	5	0	0	32	51	43	33	26	14	R	R	6-2	190	4-21-71	1994	Alvin, Texas
Seki, Kiyokazu	5	6	4.94	35	3	0	3	86	79	53	47	29	84	R	R	6-0	176	9-26-64	1995	Tokyo, Japan
7 Spiller, Derron	5	8	6.03	32	11	0	0	88	114	64	59	16	52	R	L	6-4	225	12-20-69	1989	Camarillo, Calif.
Wada, Takashi	1	4	4.62	17	1	0	0	37	44	23	19	18	43	R	R	5-11	165	10-7-70	1995	Tokyo, Japan
Yoshida, Atsushi........	5	7	3.60	13	13	0	0	75	88	37	30	12	68	R	R	5-11	170	9-29-70	1995	Tokyo, Japan

Property of Boston (1), California (2), Detroit (3), Kansas City (4), Minnesota (5), New York Mets (6), St. Louis (7), San Diego (8), Texas (9).

BUTTE   R

PIONEER LEAGUE

BATTING	AVG	G	AB	R	H	2B	3B	HR	RBI	BB	SO	SB	CS	B	T	HT	WT	DOB	1st Yr	Resides
Arrollado, Courtney	.269	62	216	34	58	11	0	0	21	19	38	9	2	R	R	6-1	190	9-5-74	1993	San Diego, Calif.
Barkett, Andy...............	.333	45	162	33	54	11	5	5	51	33	39	1	0	L	L	6-1	205	9-5-74	1995	Raleigh, N.C.
Benner, Brian	.302	67	245	42	74	15	5	2	40	44	83	5	2	R	R	6-1	205	8-22-75	1993	Mission Viejo, Calif.
Bogle, Bryan...............	.333	2	9	0	3	1	0	0	2	1	4	0	0	R	R	6-1	205	5-18-73	1994	Merritt Island, Fla.
Bray, Notorris	.255	60	188	50	48	9	1	1	14	46	35	27	10	R	R	6-0	183	7-27-73	1994	La Grange, Ga.
DeSensi, Craig	.208	29	72	10	15	2	1	0	5	6	14	2	0	R	R	5-11	195	10-27-72	1995	Louisville, Ky.
Giallella, Brian	.240	33	100	12	24	3	0	2	20	11	14	0	1	S	R	5-10	165	2-13-73	1995	Trenton, N.J.
Kernan, Phil................	.275	59	200	24	55	9	7	4	39	26	57	0	2	L	R	6-3	180	12-20-72	1995	Pleasanton, Calif.
Levias, Andres	.294	57	228	47	67	7	6	1	26	30	35	33	12	S	R	6-1	175	10-1-73	1992	Lakewood, Calif.
Messick, J.T.	.200	40	130	16	26	5	1	0	14	21	23	0	0	R	R	6-0	190	12-17-72	1995	Coweta, Okla.
Perez, Nelson..............	.223	61	215	24	48	5	5	2	20	9	44	2	2	R	R	6-1	175	1-11-74	1993	San Pedro de Macoris, D.R.
Rodriguez, Sammy	.246	17	57	7	14	1	0	1	6	4	13	2	1	R	R	5-10	180	8-20-75	1995	New York, N.Y.
Shanks, Cliff	.279	42	147	19	41	8	1	2	22	5	37	0	1	R	R	6-2	195	8-30-71	1995	Clinton, Miss.
Shapiro, Tony..............	.289	40	121	13	35	9	1	3	15	9	34	2	0	R	R	6-2	210	5-26-73	1995	Novato, Calif.
Underwood, Devin	.237	55	190	22	45	12	0	0	17	30	31	0	4	S	R	6-1	180	4-22-74	1994	Anaheim, Calif.
Zumwalt, Rusty	.274	41	113	19	31	5	2	0	10	15	20	5	1	L	L	6-0	175	9-12-73	1995	Bixby, Okla.

GAMES BY POSITION: C—Messick 8, Rodriguez 14, Shanks 2, Shapiro 1, Underwood 54. **1B**—Barkett 45, Kernan 11, Messick 1, Shanks 15. **2B**—Arrollado 58, Giallella 17. **3B**—Arrollado 4, Barkett 1, DeSensi 26, Messick 29, Shanks 21. **SS**—DeSensi 1, Giallella 13, Messick 2, Perez 61. **OF**—Benner 59, Bogle 2, Bray 60, Levias 56, Shapiro 18, Zumwalt 36.

PITCHING	W	L	ERA	G	GS	CG	SV	IP	H	R	ER	BB	SO	B	T	HT	WT	DOB	1st Yr	Resides
Abreu, Juan	1	4	8.74	8	5	0	0	23	27	31	22	28	21	L	L	6-0	207	10-26-75	1993	Quibor, Venez.
Bonilla, Welnis.............	2	2	4.38	27	2	0	5	39	46	34	19	33	30	R	R	6-3	190	10-18-75	1993	Valverde Mao, D.R.
Cardona, Isbell	0	2	7.04	3	3	0	0	15	26	13	12	7	9	R	R	6-1	186	9-6-71	1990	La Guaira, Venez.
Dillon, Chad	0	5	10.23	15	7	0	0	41	60	58	47	39	26	R	R	6-5	220	12-21-75	1994	Cincinnati, Ohio
Fernandes, Jamie	4	6	4.02	12	12	0	0	64	75	52	43	32	44	R	R	6-5	225	8-4-71	1993	Plymouth, Mass.
Grote, Jason	2	5	7.04	22	7	0	4	47	67	46	37	23	35	R	R	6-0	180	4-13-75	1994	Gresham, Ore.
Holding, Brook	4	3	5.14	27	0	0	3	42	36	26	24	33	49	R	R	6-3	210	11-17-72	1995	Blanchard, Okla.
Johnson, Scott.............	0	2	6.58	20	0	0	0	40	59	31	29	11	31	R	R	6-4	218	7-28-74	1992	Greeley, Colo.
Jones, Matthew	0	1	7.97	21	0	0	0	35	54	40	31	17	30	R	R	6-3	225	5-2-72	1995	Etters, Pa.
Justiniano, Rene...........	0	8	7.50	12	12	0	0	60	86	58	50	26	40	R	R	6-1	188	5-13-74	1994	Chicago, Ill.
McMillan, Len	0	1	9.88	10	0	0	0	14	18	17	15	18	15	L	R	6-0	170	4-22-74	1994	Catoosa, Okla.
Medero, Gadiel	0	0	15.30	8	1	0	0	10	22	19	17	7	4	R	R	6-0	210	11-25-75	1995	Trujillo Alto, P.R.
Mejia, Carlos	2	1	3.76	10	7	0	0	38	37	16	16	17	28	L	L	6-2	194	11-14-73	1992	La Vega, D.R.
Padilla, Roy	2	7	5.91	15	14	0	0	70	80	60	46	54	49	L	L	6-7	230	8-4-75	1993	Panama City, Panama
Rodriguez, Luis	0	1	9.49	7	0	0	0	12	12	14	13	12	10	L	L	6-3	195	3-3-76	1994	Carolina, P.R.
Waites, Steve	2	5	4.78	28	0	0	0	43	60	33	23	22	26	R	R	6-5	205	1-12-73	1995	Spring, Texas

LETHBRIDGE   R

PIONEER LEAGUE

BATTING	AVG	G	AB	R	H	2B	3B	HR	RBI	BB	SO	SB	CS	B	T	HT	WT	DOB	1st Yr	Resides
Aviles, Ronnel	.078	43	77	6	6	2	0	0	0	9	22	0	1	S	R	6-1	186	5-6-77	1995	Ponce, P.R.
Burks, Donny...............	.155	62	181	19	28	3	2	0	6	34	40	4	2	R	R	6-3	185	1-10-73	1995	Baltimore, Md.
Cook, John	.264	58	220	26	58	10	2	1	29	18	32	4	3	R	R	6-0	210	1-2-73	1995	Elmira, N.Y.
Cropper, Roger	.284	65	243	38	69	11	7	1	24	24	53	16	5	S	R	6-2	185	12-1-72	1994	Frederiksted, V.I.
Dillingham, Dan............	.174	51	161	21	28	7	0	3	16	15	49	4	2	R	R	6-3	205	3-8-74	1994	Bradenton, Fla.
Hinds, Collin	.186	69	220	26	41	7	0	4	27	21	87	5	5	R	R	6-1	190	3-1-74	1995	Los Angeles, Calif.
Hutchison, Tom	.276	62	217	43	60	7	3	1	17	32	21	33	6	R	R	5-11	175	9-15-72	1994	Levittown, N.Y.
Johnson, Anthony	.297	61	229	30	68	10	3	2	41	18	33	6	8	R	R	6-2	210	2-17-73	1995	Neptune, N.J.

BATTING	AVG	G	AB	R	H	2B	3B	HR	RBI	BB	SO	SB	CS	B	T	HT	WT	DOB	1st Yr	Resides
Lewis, Dwayne	.255	16	47	8	12	3	2	0	8	15	9	0	1	L	R	5-9	160	5-18-73	1995	Brooklyn, N.Y.
McCarty, Matt	.305	38	141	27	43	3	4	1	14	12	31	6	2	R	R	6-0	172	2-2-76	1995	Nashville, Tenn.
2-team (16 G.F.)	.294	54	163	30	48	3	4	1	15	13	35	6	3							
Messick, J.T.	.316	6	19	2	6	2	0	0	6	2	4	0	0	R	R	6-0	190	12-17-72	1995	Coweta, Okla.
2-team (40 Butte)	.215	46	149	18	32	7	1	0	20	23	27	0	0							
Moreno, Victor	.280	46	157	25	44	10	3	4	24	18	43	7	2	R	R	6-2	185	9-7-75	1994	Corona, N.Y.
O'Neal, Troy	.230	43	135	17	31	2	1	0	15	21	21	3	3	R	R	5-11	190	4-24-72	1995	Greenville, Del.
Paul, Kortney	.239	58	201	28	48	11	0	3	24	25	48	3	2	R	R	6-1	190	1-7-72	1994	Fort Worth, Texas
Walker, Rodney	.264	39	125	21	33	4	1	0	8	20	31	7	4	R	R	5-11	205	4-28-72	1995	Cleveland, Okla.
Ward, Jason	.125	11	24	3	3	0	0	0	2	6	6	0	0	L	R	5-11	167	2-8-76	1993	Chicago, Ill.

GAMES BY POSITION: C—Cook 2, O'Neal 38, Paul 38. **1B**—Cook 46, Dillingham 1, Johnson 28, Messick 3. **2B**—Burks 11, Hutchison 53, Lewis 9, Walker 8. **3B**—Burks 1, Hutchison 8, McCarty 27, Messick 2, Moreno 24, Walker 10, Ward 11. **SS**—Burks 49, Hutchison 1, Lewis 6, McCarty 2, Walker 22. **OF**—Aviles 37, Cropper 64, Dillingham 25, Hinds 69, Johnson 34, Lewis 1, Moreno 20, Walker 1.

PITCHING	W	L	ERA	G	GS	CG	SV	IP	H	R	ER	BB	SO	B	T	HT	WT	DOB	1st Yr	Resides
Battaglia, Chuck	0	3	3.98	4	3	0	0	20	24	11	9	6	9	R	R	6-3	235	4-19-75	1994	Massapequa Park, N.Y.
Burge, Jason	2	4	3.44	23	0	0	5	34	27	17	13	13	49	L	L	6-0	160	3-29-73	1995	Fort Worth, Texas
Falls, Curtis	2	2	3.71	24	4	1	1	53	56	27	22	19	49	R	R	6-2	215	12-10-73	1994	Yarmouth, N.S.
Friedman, Matt	0	8	6.60	20	6	0	4	44	55	40	32	26	36	R	R	6-2	185	9-27-72	1995	Fort Worth, Texas
Gullard, Jack	0	2	6.60	26	2	0	1	30	38	27	22	13	34	L	L	5-11	165	12-26-70	1995	Billings, Mon.
Harper, Terry	2	2	6.53	15	0	0	0	21	21	15	15	14	28	R	R	6-1	175	8-1-74	1995	Benton, Ark.
2-team (8 Ogden)	1	4	8.33	23	1	0	0	31	35	36	29	25	39							
Hokanson, Don	0	0	7.98	8	0	0	0	15	32	21	13	7	7	R	R	6-3	205	7-17-72	1995	Lockport, Ill.
Jenkins, Scott	1	3	6.51	15	6	0	0	47	56	49	34	40	43	S	R	6-2	190	2-5-73	1995	Abilene, Texas
Judice, Bryan	1	1	3.00	7	0	0	3	6	5	4	2	3	8	R	R	6-4	190	11-4-72	1995	Riverside, Calif.
Kirkman, Casey	5	6	4.55	15	15	1	0	95	94	56	48	39	91	R	R	6-2	185	10-30-72	1995	Exeter, Calif.
LaRue, Shaun	2	2	2.97	26	0	0	0	36	30	13	12	24	42	L	R	6-2	225	10-30-71	1995	Spring Branch, Texas
Neal, Billy	3	2	3.23	10	8	1	0	53	53	30	19	20	47	R	R	6-0	201	9-20-71	1995	Scottsdale, Ariz.
2-team (6 G.F.)	3	3	3.72	16	9	1	0	65	74	42	27	24	55							
Richardson, Darrell	5	4	5.00	15	15	1	0	85	106	63	47	38	85	R	R	5-10	190	9-22-71	1995	Dallas, Texas
Robins, Doug	2	2	5.13	15	4	0	0	40	43	29	23	16	28	R	R	6-1	190	7-19-73	1995	Levittown, N.Y.
Upchurch, Wayne	2	6	5.60	9	9	1	0	53	68	44	33	19	39	R	R	6-7	195	3-15-72	1994	Carrollton, Texas

OGDEN   R

PIONEER LEAGUE

BATTING	AVG	G	AB	R	H	2B	3B	HR	RBI	BB	SO	SB	CS	B	T	HT	WT	DOB	1st Yr	Resides
Bledsoe, Jim	.359	38	131	17	47	14	0	3	22	19	27	3	1	R	R	6-0	195	9-22-71	1995	Valley, Ala.
Coca, Mark	.296	70	277	61	82	11	1	0	36	54	43	11	13	R	R	5-10	180	7-25-74	1995	San Jose, Calif.
Cornish, Tim	.119	13	42	3	5	1	0	0	2	4	19	1	0	R	R	6-1	175	10-16-72	1992	Somis, Calif.
Demetral, Scott	.273	60	231	37	63	11	1	1	27	22	42	3	4	L	R	5-10	175	5-31-73	1995	Sterling Heights, Mich.
Gavello, Tim	.269	8	26	3	7	3	0	0	4	8	5	0	0	L	L	5-11	190	12-29-71	1994	Castro Valley, Calif.
Gronowski, Craig	.333	10	36	11	12	1	0	0	3	12	5	4	2	L	L	5-10	165	8-1-72	1994	South Holland, Ill.
Jones, Shane	.323	70	297	46	96	21	2	8	69	17	55	3	3	R	R	6-0	210	12-10-71	1994	West Jordan, Utah
Keighley, Chris	.188	47	133	21	25	5	0	2	21	36	31	1	1	R	R	5-10	187	11-27-72	1995	Cooper City, Fla.
King, Brian	.257	9	35	4	9	3	1	0	5	4	10	0	0	L	L	6-1	188	5-19-73	1995	El Dorado Hills, Calif.
Lopez, Louis	.357	46	182	36	65	15	0	7	39	16	20	1	1	R	R	6-3	190	10-5-72	1995	Brooklyn, N.Y.
Lopiccolo, Jamie	.388	70	260	74	101	13	3	12	55	55	40	15	7	R	R	5-9	162	12-11-71	1994	North Hollywood, Calif.
Martinez, Erik	.259	34	116	21	30	9	0	1	13	11	26	1	0	R	R	5-9	185	1-25-71	1993	Elverta, Calif.
Martinez, Matt	.200	4	10	3	2	0	0	0	0	1	2	0	0	R	R	5-10	185	8-14-64	1995	Pacifica, Calif.
Morales, Rich	.000	1	0	0	0	0	0	0	0	0	0	0	0	R	R	5-10	185			
Phair, Kelly	.250	62	188	35	47	7	2	0	25	26	28	8	5	R	R	6-2	185	6-2-73	1995	Cincinnati, Ohio
Sanchez, Ismael	.283	20	60	16	17	2	0	0	8	16	13	2	1	R	R	5-11	190	2-8-73	1995	El Centro, Calif.
Scheffer, Lawrence	.283	61	233	34	66	11	0	7	41	10	43	1	3	R	R	6-2	210	3-27-73	1995	Westland, Mich.
Schock, Jared	.091	7	11	1	1	0	0	0	0	1	3	0	0	R	R	6-1	200	7-25-74	1995	San Jose, Calif.
Srebroski, Andrew	.067	10	30	3	2	0	0	0	0	7	12	0	1	R	R	6-2	195	4-28-72	1994	Pasadena, Md.
Vallero, Rich	.228	46	127	17	29	6	0	0	9	16	35	1	2	L	R	6-0	205	5-8-73	1995	Pacifica, Calif.

GAMES BY POSITION: C—Keighley 44, Vallero 36. **1B**—Jones 70, Vallero 1. **2B**—Coca 2, Demetral 38, E. Martinez 29, M. Martinez 2, Phair 5, Schock 2. **3B**—Bledsoe 5, Demetral 13, King 1, Lopez 44, Lopiccolo 11, E. Martinez 1, Schock 1. **SS**—Demetral 7, E. Martinez 1, M. Martinez 1, Phair 57, Schock 1, Srebroski 10. **OF**—Bledsoe 2, Coca 69, Cornish 12, Gronowski 10, Keighley 1, King 8, Lopiccolo 58, E. Martinez 1, Sanchez 19, Scheffer 41.

PITCHING	W	L	ERA	G	GS	CG	SV	IP	H	R	ER	BB	SO	B	T	HT	WT	DOB	1st Yr	Resides
Alexander, Don	2	4	6.40	19	1	0	0	32	43	32	23	26	30	R	R	5-10	140	1-2-72	1995	Englewood, Colo.
Besser, Mike	1	1	5.14	4	0	0	0	7	10	4	4	2	1	L	L	5-11	185	7-4-72	1995	Las Vegas, Nev.
Caravelli, Mike	1	2	3.93	5	3	0	0	18	27	11	8	3	13	R	L	6-2	200	7-27-72	1995	Santa Monica, Calif.
Cooke, Alan	0	5	5.13	16	5	0	0	40	52	26	23	32	23	S	R	6-0	190	3-27-75	1995	Sarasota, Fla.
Fox, Ryan	0	0	7.71	2	0	0	0	2	7	6	2	0	2	R	R	6-3	205	6-12-74	1995	Troy, Ohio
Gamez, Rene	4	2	6.29	10	10	0	0	54	53	41	38	30	42	R	R	5-11	185	3-3-73	1995	Tucson, Ariz.
Harper, Terry	1	2	11.81	8	1	0	0	11	14	21	14	11	11	R	R	6-1	175	8-1-74	1995	Benton, Ark.
Hindy, Mark	2	3	4.73	24	6	0	1	70	89	52	37	24	44	L	L	6-3	215	7-20-73	1995	Brooklyn, N.Y.
Jamie, Jorge	0	0	4.32	10	0	0	1	17	22	8	8	4	8	S	L	5-4	180	7-8-70	1995	Phoenix, Ariz.
Kazama, Yuhito	0	1	14.04	6	1	0	0	8	16	17	13	8	4	R	R	6-4	210	6-4-75	1995	Nagano, Japan
Kline, Jason	3	4	5.43	25	6	0	2	58	80	45	35	25	37	L	L	6-4	210	5-17-73	1995	Goreville, Ill.
Lee, Calvin	1	2	7.52	5	5	0	0	21	23	17	21	15	15	R	R	6-0	170	8-5-73	1992	Garyville, La.
Martin, Jeremy	1	1	7.64	9	2	0	0	18	23	16	15	11	11	L	L	6-0	180	12-8-71	1995	Lawrenceburg, Ind.
Novak, Troy	5	1	3.88	15	15	2	0	97	101	50	42	19	77	R	R	6-1	185	1-21-72	1995	Muskegon, Mich.
O'Hearn, Paul	1	4	8.91	11	7	0	0	32	41	45	32	26	27	S	R	6-4	210	9-23-70	1994	Santa Ana, Calif.
Porzio, Mike	4	3	6.38	8	8	2	0	48	66	39	34	15	26	L	L	6-3	190	8-20-72	1993	Norwalk, Conn.
Schultea, Matt	4	2	4.67	34	0	0	0	54	59	37	28	18	43	R	R	6-0	180	7-17-74	1995	Houston, Texas
Whitson, Eric	2	1	8.59	22	0	0	4	29	35	33	28	16	31	S	R	6-0	180	8-15-72	1995	Weaverville, N.C.

APPALACHIAN LEAGUE

BATTING	AVG	G	AB	R	H	2B	3B	HR	RBI	BB	SO	SB	CS	B	T	HT	WT	DOB	1st Yr	Resides
4 Andrews, Jeff	.107	34	112	10	12	0	0	1	12	6	31	1	1	R	R	6-0	185	10-22-71	1994	Union Grove, Ala.
8 Coburn, Todd	.281	62	228	37	64	12	3	4	39	22	47	7	1	R	R	6-2	205	2-26-72	1994	Carson City, Nev.
9 Fernandez, Randy ...	.308	15	39	2	12	0	0	0	3	5	16	2	4	L	L	6-0	174	3-17-74	1992	Villa Mella, D.R.
2 Hendricks, Ryan.......	.258	58	178	38	46	12	0	11	36	46	50	8	1	L	R	6-3	205	8-3-72	1994	Randallstown, Md.
2 Higman, Joel	.267	13	45	4	12	1	0	0	4	3	18	1	0	R	R	6-1	185	3-30-74	1995	Villas, N.J.
2-team (11 Blue.)..	.246	24	69	6	17	1	0	0	7	6	26	3	0							
5 Hobbie, Matt.............	.227	60	211	25	48	12	5	2	24	23	49	17	5	L	L	5-10	185	12-12-74	1993	Sarasota, Fla.
2 Hunter, Lanier	.250	62	216	36	54	12	2	4	18	32	64	15	10	S	R	5-11	168	2-13-73	1992	Hopewell, Va.
3 Malin, Edgar.............	.175	21	63	12	11	1	0	1	8	10	27	3	2	R	R	6-2	179	10-25-74	1994	West New York, N.J.
5 Mastrullo, Mike	.179	46	134	20	24	5	2	0	14	25	43	5	4	R	R	5-11	180	5-1-75	1994	Billerica, Mass.
4 McCroskey, Jackie...	.288	49	156	26	45	12	5	2	27	26	31	12	3	L	L	5-10	177	8-23-73	1993	Louisville, Ky.
7 Nolte, Bruce	.220	61	209	30	46	6	2	3	21	21	46	16	5	R	R	6-0	160	4-4-74	1993	Pennsauken, N.J.
6 Raymondi, Mike	.220	28	82	8	18	3	0	1	8	5	27	1	0	R	R	5-11	196	9-28-75	1994	Watertown, S.D.
8 Reyes, Winston........	.265	20	68	5	18	4	0	0	8	3	17	3	2	R	R	6-0	175	4-12-74	1992	Mocaibao, D.R.
1 Roberson, Gerald.....	.213	52	188	28	40	11	1	3	14	13	31	12	4	R	R	5-10	177	8-22-74	1993	Pontotoc, Miss.
1 Wood, Tony.............	.268	56	205	26	55	5	2	0	19	15	55	5	2	R	R	5-9	170	7-6-72	1994	Tacoma, Wash.

GAMES BY POSITION: C—Andrews 34, Coburn 27, Raymondi 11. **1B**—Coburn 14, Hendricks 52, Mastrullo 1, Raymondi 2. **2B**—Mastrullo 24, Roberson 39, Wood 6. **3B**—Mastrullo 13, Reyes 18, Wood 40. **SS**—Nolte 60, Roberson 2, Wood 9. **OF**—Coburn 1, Fernandez 11, Higman 13, Hobbie 58, Hunter 59, Malin 17, Mastrullo 1, McCroskey 41, Roberson 9.

PITCHING	W	L	ERA	G	GS	CG	SV	IP	H	R	ER	BB	SO	B	T	HT	WT	DOB	1st Yr	Resides
7 Adair, Scott...............	2	9	4.70	13	13	1	0	75	96	47	39	13	28	R	R	6-0	190	11-10-75	1993	Riverside, Calif.
9 Alexis, Julio	1	6	4.74	14	13	0	0	82	89	55	43	21	65	R	R	6-3	175	7-12-73	1991	San Pedro de Macoris, D.R.
6 Alvarado, Luis...........	3	4	3.68	11	5	1	0	44	43	28	18	12	43	R	R	6-0	163	8-28-74	1992	Cayey, P.R.
3 Fereira, Marcos	0	1	15.63	5	1	0	0	6	9	16	11	14	3	R	R	6-3	150	12-13-74	1991	Valencia, Venez.
1 Hoalton, Brandon	1	3	5.34	6	6	0	0	29	31	23	17	11	26	S	R	6-3	190	12-25-73	1994	Garden Grove, Calif.
9 Manon, Julio	3	4	3.65	16	8	2	1	74	75	34	30	30	77	R	R	6-1	183	7-10-73	1992	Boca Chica, D.R.
2 Pierce, Drew	2	4	6.21	22	0	0	2	33	46	29	23	10	42	R	R	6-4	195	8-1-74	1994	Twin Falls, Idaho
3 Prejean, Alex	3	2	9.38	14	3	0	0	32	37	36	33	31	23	R	R	6-1	180	11-2-74	1994	Seabrook, Texas
8 Quintana, Urbano......	1	2	5.71	19	1	0	3	35	43	26	22	12	35	R	R	6-0	160	2-9-75	1993	Esperanza Mao, D.R.
2 Spang, R.J.................	2	4	4.60	18	0	0	3	31	31	21	16	9	31	R	R	6-0	188	10-19-74	1992	Racine, Wis.
6 Starling, Marcus	0	2	15.19	13	3	0	0	21	36	39	36	25	22	L	L	6-1	190	1-31-73	1994	MacClenny, Fla.
4 Vejil, Aaron	1	0	5.95	14	0	0	2	20	19	15	13	10	21	R	L	6-0	178	2-11-75	1994	Sante Fe, N.M.
2 Young, Ty..................	4	6	4.67	14	14	2	0	79	75	56	41	36	49	L	R	6-4	190	6-11-73	1991	Kountz, Texas

Property of Atlanta (1), Baltimore (2), Chicago Cubs (3), Cincinnati (4), Cleveland (5), Minnesota (6), New York Mets (7), Philadelphia (8), St. Louis (9)

MINOR LEAGUES

Skyrocketing Franchise Values
A Sign Of Prosperity In Minors

By WILL LINGO

As the minor leagues continue to ride a wave of popular and financial success, franchises become more like businesses. They are more coveted and fought over than ever.

The illustrations of that were everywhere in 1995, with a city buying its franchise to keep it, owners arranging an unprecedented franchise swap, cities fighting to get franchises and other cities losing franchises after only a few years.

The best morality play was in the Eastern League, where the mayor of Harrisburg, Pa., had the last pitch and saved his city's team by throwing nearly everyone a curve.

Old Kent Park. The West Michigan Whitecaps shattered their own Class A attendance record in 1995, drawing 506,989 to Old Kent Park.

After months of speculation that Harrisburg had little chance to keep the Senators from moving, the city council agreed to buy the franchise for $6.7 million rather than lose it to Springfield, Mass., after the 1996 season.

That came two weeks after the National Association told the Senators' owners it wouldn't act on their request to move the franchise until they reopened negotiations with Harrisburg mayor Stephen Reed.

Reed, who had offered to buy the team before league owners voted to allow it to move, agreed to pay $2.6 million more than the Senators' new owners paid in January 1995 for the team.

"There is nominal risk in my view," Reed said. "The far greater risk would have been had we lost the present franchise."

Jerome Mileur bought the team in 1981 for $85,000 and sold it 14 years later for $4.1 million to a group from Philadelphia. The group attempted to move the Senators 90 miles east to the Allentown-Easton area. When that failed, they agreed in May to move the team to Springfield.

Officials in Springfield threatened litigation when Harrisburg nixed their deal. "We're going berserk. We're ballistic," said Paul Stelzer, co-chairman of Springfield's Bring Baseball Back Committee.

But the cities eventually settled their dispute when Harrisburg paid Springfield $115,000, Springfield's expenses in pursuit of the franchise.

Franchise Swap In Works

The Nashville Sounds had almost as turbulent a 1995 season, starting off hoping to have Michael Jordan in uniform and finishing with plans to downgrade to Double-A.

The Sounds picked themselves up and got on with the season when Jordan decided early in spring training to go back to basketball.

"We've made it for 17 years without him, and we hope to have 17 more," said Mike Schmittou, the son of Sounds president Larry Schmittou and the team's director of merchandising. "We knew things would change, and sure enough they did."

That was the least of their changes, in fact. Larry Schmittou tentatively agreed to swap

ORGANIZATION STANDINGS

TEAM	—1995— W	L	Pct.	1994 Pct.	1993 Pct.	1992 Pct.
Cincinnati (6)	397	301	.569	.539	.511	.570
California (6)	388	297	.566	.507	.479	.540
Milwaukee (6)	376	308	.550	.544	.541	.567
Chicago-NL (6)	379	315	.546	.446	.483	.456
Cleveland (6)	382	320	.544	.521	.579	.543
New York-NL (7)	406	351	.536	.509	.516	.509
Kansas City (6)	369	321	.535	.589	.513	.519
Philadelphia (6)	375	329	.533	.475	.456	.507
Detroit (6)	361	332	.521	.454	.494	.496
Houston (6)	352	331	.515	.501	.473	.466
San Francisco (5)	324	306	.514	.497	.532	.506
Minnesota (6)	347	328	.514	.502	.503	.530
Los Angeles (6)	357	340	.512	.514	.424	.467
Colorado (6)	354	340	.510	.477	.451	.462
Oakland (6)	353	343	.507	.556	.526	.501
New York-AL (6)	349	340	.507	.512	.527	.509
Pittsburgh (6)	347	348	.499	.430	.457	.459
Florida (6)	340	347	.495	.496	.536	.533
Boston (6)	337	347	.493	.485	.426	.444
Baltimore (6)	328	357	.479	.515	.536	.478
St. Louis (7)	396	431	.479	.542	.548	.511
Chicago-AL (7)	391	435	.473	.524	.527	.552
Seattle (6)	326	369	.469	.518	.479	.478
Montreal (6)	319	371	.462	.529	.522	.534
San Diego (6)	314	374	.456	.458	.446	.462
Atlanta (7)	346	417	.453	.485	.528	.490
Toronto (7)	341	428	.453	.498	.497	.463
Texas (6)	292	389	.429	.450	.499	.512
Independents (6)	214	345	.383	.383	.429	.382

Number of farm teams in parentheses

PLAYER OF YEAR

Curacao Product Earns Top Prize

Curacao, an island in the Netherlands Antilles, just north of Venezuela, has a population of just 150,000. It has produced only a handful of professional baseball players, including a special one who spent the summer of 1995 at Class A Macon: Andruw Jones.

Jones hit 25 home runs, drove in 100 runs and stole 56 bases. A season like that hadn't happened in the minors since 1961, when Jose Cardenal achieved a similar trifecta in the old Class D Sophomore League. Jones also hit .277 with 104 runs, 41 doubles and 275 total bases.

Andruw Jones

MORRIS FOSTOFF

But numbers don't tell the whole story. They're not what makes Jones special.

"It makes me happy because people from Curacao will be happy with me," says Jones, 18. "But I don't really worry too much because I just play the game, just get more experience, because with experience you learn more and you get better."

In 1995, he was the best in the minor leagues, Baseball America's Minor League Player of the Year.

"He just has so much natural ability," said Nelson Norman, his manager at Macon. "There is something there that you don't see at his age. You look at him and you can see something there that other players don't have. He can do so many things so well."

No doubt the Braves

saw something special when they found Jones. Though he was only 15 and couldn't sign a contract until he was 16, the Braves knew what they had and snapped him up.

Most observers think he has it all.

Paul Snyder, the Braves' director of scouting, talks about none of Jones' specific skills. But Snyder, one of those who helped sign Jones, mentions Grissom, Griffey, Aaron.

And then his favorite story when he's asked about his first impression of Jones.

"It was his first time at bat, and he hit a ball to right-center. He came around first at full speed, saw the outfielder come up with the ball and just hit the brakes. He skidded standing up," Snyder said. "The only other time in my life I had seen something like that was in 1960 in Philadelphia at Shibe Park."

The player? Roberto Clemente.

"It just gave me a special feeling," Snyder says. "I knew then he was something special.

"I am not smart enough to tell you where it's going to stop. It doesn't matter whether he has a bat or glove in his hands. He stands out. We just want to keep challenging him and keep him reaching."

Jones knows he needs some time, but he doesn't think he'll need much.

"I just want to get to the big leagues right now, but you got to have more experience to get to the big leagues," he says. "This is the first full season I got. And maybe two more full seasons, or maybe one more full season, I will be ready to hit against major league pitchers."

PREVIOUS WINNERS

1981—Mike Marshall, 1b, Albuquerque (Dodgers)
1982—Ron Kittle, of, Edmonton (White Sox)
1983—Dwight Gooden, rhp, Lynchburg (Mets)
1984—Mike Bielecki, rhp, Hawaii (Pirates)
1985—Jose Canseco, of, Huntsville/Tacoma (Athletics)
1986—Gregg Jefferies, ss, Columbia/Lynchburg (Mets)
1987—Gregg Jefferies, ss, Jackson (Mets)
1988—Tom Gordon, rhp, Appleton/Memphis/Omaha (Royals)
1989—Sandy Alomar Jr., c, Las Vegas (Padres)
1990—Frank Thomas, 1b, Birmingham (White Sox)
1991—Derek Bell, of, Syracuse (Blue Jays)
1992—Tim Salmon, of, Edmonton (Angels)
1993—Manny Ramirez, of, Canton/Charlotte (Indians)
1994—Derek Jeter, ss, Tampa/Albany/Columbus (Yankees)

---

franchises with David Hersh, owner of the Memphis Chicks, moving from the American Association to the Southern League.

It would be an unprecedented move. Under the terms of the deal, the franchises would trade places and Hersh would pay Schmittou about $3.5 million. But the deal still had to be approved by the leagues and the National Association.

Schmittou said Herschel Greer Stadium could no longer accommodate a Triple-A team adequately. That might sound like another negotiating tack in Schmittou's continual effort to get a new stadium from the city, but the city's new arena and pursuit of professional football, hockey and basketball franchises appeared to be its chief interests.

It was unclear if a Triple-A team would begin play in Memphis in 1996 or in 1997. In addition to the minor league organizations, the teams' major league affiliates, particularly the Chicago White Sox, also

had concerns about the plan. Chicago is Nashville's parent club.

The city of Austin, Texas, one of the nation's largest untapped minor league markets, looked like it would end up with nothing after being in line to get two franchises. But it still could be a factor in the moves of several franchises.

First, the Shreveport Captains were tentatively sold to an Austin group. But when the Phoenix Firebirds were displaced by the expansion Arizona Diamondbacks, they swooped in and claimed the Austin territory on the grounds that Triple-A has priority over Double-A when a virgin market is at stake.

That put the Captains back in Shreveport, at least for the time being.

"This clears the way for Phoenix to come to Austin," Firebirds general manager Craig Pletenik said. "The only thing remaining is to sell the seat options and build a stadium."

CLASSIFICATION ALL-STARS
Selected by Baseball America

TRIPLE-A

Pos. Player, Club	B-T	Ht.	Wt.	Age	AVG	AB	R	H	2B	3B	HR	RBI	SB
C John Marzano, Okla. City (American Assoc.)	R-R	5-11	195	32	.309	427	55	132	41	3	9	56	3
1B Carlos Delgado, Syracuse (International)	L-R	6-3	220	23	.318	333	59	106	23	4	22	74	0
2B Eric Owens, Indianapolis (American Assoc.)	R-R	6-1	185	24	.314	427	86	134	24	8	12	63	33
3B Butch Huskey, Norfolk (International)	R-R	6-3	244	23	.284	394	66	112	18	1	28	87	8
SS Alex Rodriguez, Tacoma (Pacific Coast)	R-R	6-3	190	20	.360	214	37	77	12	3	15	45	2
OF Karim Garcia, Albuquerque (Pacific Coast)	L-L	6-0	172	19	.319	474	88	151	26	10	20	90	12
OF Steve Gibralter, Indianapolis (Amer. Assoc.)	R-R	6-0	190	22	.316	263	49	83	19	3	18	63	0
OF Riccardo Ingram, Salt Lake (Pacific Coast)	R-R	6-0	205	28	.348	477	80	166	43	2	12	85	4
DH Brooks Kieschnick, Iowa (American Assoc.)	L-R	6-4	228	23	.295	505	61	149	30	1	23	73	2

Pos. Player, Club	B-T	Ht.	Wt.	Age	W	L	ERA	G	SV	IP	H	BB	SO
P Rod Bolton, Nashville (American Assoc.)	R-R	6-2	190	26	14	3	2.88	20	0	131	125	23	76
P Jason Isringhausen, Norfolk (International)	R-R	6-3	196	22	9	1	1.55	12	0	87	64	24	75
P Matt Murray, Richmond (International)	L-R	6-6	235	24	10	3	2.78	19	0	123	108	34	78
P Joe Roa, Buffalo (American Assoc.)	R-R	6-1	194	23	17	3	3.50	25	0	165	168	28	93
P Donne Wall, Tucson (Pacific Coast)	R-R	6-1	180	28	17	6	3.30	28	0	177	190	32	119

Player of the Year: Jason Isringhausen, rhp, Norfolk.   **Manager of the Year:** Marc Bombard, Indianapolis (American Assoc.).

DOUBLE-A

Pos. Player, Club	B-T	Ht.	Wt.	Age	AVG	AB	R	H	2B	3B	HR	RBI	SB
C Jason Kendall, Carolina (Southern)	R-R	6-0	180	21	.326	429	87	140	26	1	8	71	10
1B David Kennedy, New Haven (Eastern)	R-R	6-4	215	24	.306	484	75	148	22	2	22	96	4
2B Todd Walker, Hardware City (Eastern)	L-R	6-0	170	22	.290	513	83	149	27	3	21	85	23
3B George Arias, Midland (Texas)	R-R	5-11	190	23	.279	520	91	145	19	10	30	104	3
SS Nomar Garciaparra, Trenton (Eastern)	R-R	6-0	165	22	.267	513	77	137	20	8	8	47	35
OF Johnny Damon, Wichita (Texas)	L-L	6-0	175	21	.343	423	83	145	15	9	16	54	26
OF Billy McMillon, Portland (Eastern)	L-L	5-11	172	23	.313	518	92	162	29	3	14	93	15
OF Jay Payton, Binghamton (Eastern)	R-R	5-10	185	22	.345	357	59	123	20	3	14	54	16
DH Todd Greene, Midland (Texas)	R-R	5-9	195	24	.327	318	59	104	19	1	26	57	3

Pos. Player, Club	B-T	Ht.	Wt.	Age	W	L	ERA	G	SV	IP	H	BB	SO
P Luis Andujar, Birmingham (Southern)	R-R	6-2	175	22	14	8	2.85	27	0	167	147	44	146
P Steve Bourgeois, Shreveport (Texas)	R-R	6-1	220	23	12	3	2.85	22	0	145	140	53	91
P Elmer Dessens, Carolina (Southern)	R-R	6-0	190	23	15	8	2.49	27	0	152	170	21	68
P Gary Rath, San Antonio (Texas)	L-L	6-2	185	22	13	3	2.77	18	0	117	96	48	81
P Paul Wilson, Binghamton (Eastern)	R-R	6-5	235	22	6	3	2.17	16	0	120	89	24	127

Player of the Year: Johnny Damon, of, Wichita.   **Manager of the Year:** Dave Miley, Chattanooga (Southern).

CLASS A

Pos. Player, Club	B-T	Ht.	Wt.	Age	AVG	AB	R	H	2B	3B	HR	RBI	SB
C Raul Ibanez, Riverside (California)	L-R	6-2	200	23	.332	361	59	120	23	3	20	108	4
1B Richie Sexson, Kinston (Carolina)	R-R	6-6	200	20	.306	494	80	151	34	0	22	85	4
2B Adam Riggs, San Bernardino (California)	R-R	5-11	180	22	.362	542	111	196	39	5	24	106	31
3B Fernando Tatis, Charleston, S.C. (So. Atlantic)	B-R	6-1	175	20	.303	499	74	151	43	4	15	84	22
SS Donnie Sadler, Michigan (Midwest)	R-R	5-6	165	20	.283	438	103	124	25	8	9	55	41
OF Derrick Gibson, Asheville (South Atlantic)	R-R	6-2	228	20	.292	506	91	148	16	10	32	115	31
OF Andruw Jones, Macon (South Atlantic)	R-R	6-1	170	18	.277	537	104	149	41	5	25	100	56
OF Demond Smith, C.R./W. Mich. (MWL)/L.E. (Cal)	B-R	5-11	170	22	.342	497	102	170	34	10	16	70	54
DH Jesse Ibarra, Burlington(MWL)/San Jose (Cal)	B-R	6-3	195	23	.330	446	73	147	32	1	34	100	1

Pos. Player, Club	B-T	Ht.	Wt.	Age	W	L	ERA	G	SV	IP	H	BB	SO
P Bartolo Colon, Kinston (Carolina)	R-R	6-0	185	20	13	3	1.96	21	0	129	91	39	152
P Jeff D'Amico, Beloit (Midwest)	R-R	6-7	250	19	13	3	2.39	21	0	132	102	31	119
P Matt Drews, Tampa (Florida State)	R-R	6-8	230	21	15	7	2.27	28	0	182	142	58	140
P Brandon Reed, Fayetteville (South Atlantic)	R-R	6-3	165	20	3	0	0.97	55	41	65	40	18	78
P Glendon Rusch, Wilmington (Carolina)	L-L	6-2	170	20	14	6	1.74	26	0	166	110	34	147

Player of the Year: Andruw Jones, of, Macon.   **Manager of the Year:** Dave Trembley, Daytona (Florida State).

SHORT-SEASON

Pos. Player, Club	B-T	Ht.	Wt.	Age	AVG	AB	R	H	2B	3B	HR	RBI	SB
C Ramon Castro, Auburn (New York-Penn)	R-R	6-3	195	19	.299	224	40	67	17	0	9	49	0
1B Sean Watkins, Idaho Falls (Pioneer)	L-L	6-4	210	20	.372	247	51	92	20	1	13	67	0
2B Rick Gama, Idaho Falls (Pioneer)	R-R	5-10	170	22	.320	266	71	85	16	2	8	58	17
3B Cliff Brumbaugh, Hudson Valley (NY-Penn)	R-R	6-2	205	21	.358	282	44	101	19	4	2	45	15
SS Chad Hermansen, Pirates (GCL)/Erie (NY-P)	R-R	6-2	185	17	.284	257	44	73	18	4	9	42	4
OF Fletcher Bates, Pittsfield (New York-Penn)	B-R	6-1	193	21	.326	276	52	90	14	9	6	37	17
OF Jose Guillen, Erie (New York-Penn)	R-R	5-11	165	19	.314	258	41	81	17	1	12	46	1
OF Jamie Lopiccolo, Ogden (Pioneer)	R-R	6-3	195	22	.388	260	74	101	11	3	12	55	15
DH Danny Buxbaum, Boise (Northwest)	R-R	6-4	215	22	.329	231	46	76	15	0	8	51	1

Pos. Player, Club	B-T	Ht.	Wt.	Age	W	L	ERA	G	SV	IP	H	BB	SO
P Josh Bishop, Brewers (Arizona)	R-R	6-4	180	21	8	2	2.16	14	0	96	64	29	134
P Chris Fussell, Bluefield (Appalachian)	R-R	6-2	185	19	9	1	2.19	12	0	66	37	32	98
P Russell Ortiz, Bellingham (Northwest)	R-R	6-1	190	21	2	0	0.52	25	12	34	19	15	55
P Jay Tessmer, Oneonta (New York-Penn)	R-R	6-3	182	22	2	0	0.95	34	20	38	27	12	52
P Chris Weidert, Vermont (New York-Penn)	R-R	6-3	210	21	11	1	1.79	15	0	95	67	21	52

Player of the Year: Chad Hermansen, ss, GCL Pirates/Erie.   **Manager of the Year:** Tom Kotchman, Boise (Northwest).

MINOR LEAGUE ALL-STARS

Selected by Baseball America

Pos.	Player, Club	B-T	Ht.	Wt.	Age	AVG	AB	R	H	2B	3B	HR	RBI	SB
C	Todd Greene, Midland/Vancouver	R-R	5-9	195	24	.300	486	87	146	22	2	40	92	4
1B	Richie Sexson, Kinston	R-R	6-6	200	20	.306	494	80	151	34	0	22	85	4
2B	Adam Riggs, San Bernardino	R-R	5-11	180	22	.362	542	111	196	39	5	24	106	31
3B	Butch Huskey, Norfolk	R-R	6-3	244	23	.284	394	66	112	18	1	28	87	8
SS	Alex Rodriguez, Tacoma	R-R	6-3	190	20	.360	214	37	77	12	3	15	45	2
OF	Johnny Damon, Wichita	L-L	6-0	175	21	.343	423	83	145	15	9	16	54	26
OF	Karim Garcia, Albuquerque	L-L	6-0	172	19	.319	474	88	151	26	10	20	90	12
OF	Andruw Jones, Macon	R-R	6-1	170	18	.277	537	104	149	41	5	25	100	56
DH	Jesse Ibarra, Burlington/San Jose	B-R	6-3	195	23	.330	446	73	147	32	1	34	100	1

Pos.	Player, Club	B-T	Ht.	Wt.	Age	W	L	ERA	G	SV	IP	H	BB	SO
P	Bartolo Colon, Kinston	R-R	6-0	185	20	13	3	1.96	21	0	129	91	39	152
P	Rocky Coppinger, Frederick/Bowie/Roch.	R-R	6-5	245	21	16	3	1.97	29	0	188	127	84	172
P	Jason Isringhausen, Binghamton/Norfolk	R-R	6-3	196	22	11	2	1.97	18	0	128	90	36	134
P	Donne Wall, Tucson	R-R	6-1	180	28	17	6	3.30	28	0	177	190	32	119
P	Paul Wilson, Binghamton/Norfolk	R-R	6-5	235	22	11	6	2.42	26	0	186	148	44	194

Player of the Year: Andruw Jones, Macon.   **Manager of the Year:** Marc Bombard, Indianapolis.

That proved to be a big hurdle. The seat-option proposal was modeled after a trend in professional sports in which fans pay for the rights to buy tickets for the best seats in the park.

Austin's city council approved the stadium financing plan, which called for the city to pay $10 million and the franchise to pay $10 million (through its seat options) to build a 12,000-seat stadium.

But citizens balked at the council ramrodding the plan through with little public debate. Seat-options sales proved to be sluggish and the outcry prompted the council to hold a referendum on the financing plan.

The plan was soundly voted down, the Firebirds were back in Phoenix for 1996, and both they and Austin were forced to start from scratch.

Polecats Leave Smell In Albany

The season-long rumors that Richard Holtzman would sell the Albany Polecats or try to move the South Atlantic League team proved true when he sold the team to a group that will move it to Salisbury, Md.

Then he ripped Albany, which built Polecat Park for the team when it moved from Sumter, S.C., for the 1992 season.

"Those who believe there is no such thing as a bad baseball town need only to examine Albany, Ga., closely," Holtzman said in a statement. "Those who truly know how to run a minor league baseball franchise can never dispute our efforts."

Albany finished last in the league in attendance, but local officials blamed economic fallout from devastating floods that struck the city the year before.

Mayor-elect Tommy Coleman defended Albany. "I really don't think that shows a lot of class," he said. "I don't know why you'd want to kick anybody when you leave."

Holtzman sold the franchise to Maryland Baseball Limited Partnership, the group headed by Peter Kirk that already owns Maryland's Bowie Baysox (Eastern) and Frederick Keys (Carolina).

The new club is called the Delmarva Shorebirds and will play on Maryland's Eastern Shore.

Albany wasn't alone in losing its team, though. The Sultans of Springfield (Midwest) will become the Lansing Lugnuts in 1996 and the Riverside Pilots (California) will become the Lancaster Jethawks after lackluster support in those cities.

The Pilots are the second team to leave Riverside in

Paul Wilson. The top pick in the 1994 draft went 11-6 and led the minor leagues with 194 strikeouts.

five years. The Red Wave moved to Adelanto, Calif., in 1990 and became the High Desert Mavericks, one of the more successful franchises in the minors until a downturn in 1994-95.

The Pilots moved to Riverside in 1993 and were at the bottom of the Cal League in attendance each season. In Lancaster, the team will play in a new, 4,500-seat stadium.

"A league is only as good as its weakest club, and Riverside has been a real sore spot," Lake Elsinore general manager Kevin Haghian said. "For the league as a whole, the move is fantastic."

Orphans Still Wandering

With more major league expansion on the horizon, the minors had better brace for more upheaval. The fallout from the last round of expansion still is being felt.

The Southern League's traveling road show, which played in Wilmington, N.C., as the Port City Roosters in 1995, now targets Ozark, Mo., as its permanent home, though it has had many permanent homes before.

DEPARTMENT LEADERS
MINOR LEAGUES

*Full-Season Teams Only

TEAM

WINS
Carolina (Southern) 89
Beloit (Midwest) 88
Indianapolis (American Assoc.) 88
Shreveport (Texas) 88
Daytona (Florida State) 87
Tucson (Pacific Coast) 87

LONGEST WINNING STREAK
Bluefield (Appalachian) 16
Helena (Pioneer) 15
Colorado Springs (Pacific Coast) 15
Tampa (Florida State) 14
Fort Myers (Florida State) 12

LOSSES
High Desert (California) 94
Knoxville (Southern) 90
Charleston, S.C. (South Atlantic) 89
Hickory (South Atlantic) 89
Oklahoma City (American Assoc.) 89

LONGEST LOSING STREAK
New Jersey (New York-Penn) 14
Durham (Carolina) 13
Phoenix (Pacific Coast) 13
Rockies (Arizona) 13

BATTING AVERAGE*
Salt Lake (Pacific Coast) .... .304
Calgary (Pacific Coast) .... .302
Colorado Springs (Pacific Coast) .... .291
Tucson (Pacific Coast) .... .289
El Paso (Texas) .... .286

HOME RUNS
Indianapolis (American Assoc.) 193
Colorado Springs (Pacific Coast) 157
Pawtucket (International) 156
San Bernardino (California) 154
Omaha (American Association) 144

STOLEN BASES
San Bernardino (California) 246
Charleston, W.Va. (South Atlantic) 230
West Michigan (Midwest) 226
Stockton (California) 220
Charleston, S.C. (South Atlantic) 218

EARNED RUN AVERAGE*
Tampa (Florida State) 2.80
Daytona (Florida State) 2.82
Wilmington (Carolina) 2.84

Kevin Coughlin
Minors' best .372 average

Todd Greene
Led minors with 40 homers

Fort Myers (Florida State) 2.85
Norfolk (International) 3.01

STRIKEOUTS
Fayetteville (South Atlantic) 1183
Macon (South Atlantic) 1136
Greensboro (South Atlantic) 1130
Savannah (South Atlantic) 1118
Columbus (South Atlantic) 1103

FIELDING AVERAGE*
Salt Lake (Pacific Coast) .... .981
New Orleans (American Association) .980
Buffalo (American Association) .... .979
Binghamton (Eastern) .... .978
Iowa (American Association) .... .978
Kinston (Carolina) .... .978
Vancouver (Pacific Coast) .... .978

INDIVIDUAL BATTING

BATTING AVERAGE*
(Minimum 350 At-Bats)
Kevin Coughlin, Birm./Nashville .... .372
Adam Riggs, San Bernardino .... .362
Quinton McCracken, N.H./Colo. Spr. .. .359
Pat Lennon, Paw./Trenton/Salt Lake . .352
Riccardo Ingram, Salt Lake .... .348
Wilton Guerrero, San Antonio/Albuq. .346
Aldo Pecorilli, Greenville/Richmond... .344
Johnny Damon, Wichita .... .343
Robert Perez, Syracuse .... .343
Demond Smith, L.E./C.Rap./W. Mich. .342

RUNS
Adam Riggs, San Bernardino 111
Jason McDonald, Modesto 109
Andruw Jones, Macon 104
Ralph Milliard, Portland 104
Donnie Sadler, Michigan 103

HITS
Adam Riggs, San Bernardino 196
Wendell Magee, Clearwater/Reading . 177
Robert Perez, Syracuse 172
Don Sparks, Columbus 170
Demond Smith, L.E./C. Rap./W. Mich. 170
Jay Payton, Binghamton/Norfolk 170

TOP HITTING STREAKS
Doug Brady, Nashville 30
Trenidad Hubbard, Colorado Springs ... 29
Jay Payton, Binghamton 25
Preston Wilson, Columbia 24

MOST HITS, ONE GAME
George Canale, Port City 6
Rick Ladjevich, Riverside 6
Daryl Monroe, Fayetteville 6

TOTAL BASES
Adam Riggs, San Bernardino 317
Todd Greene, Midland/Vancouver 292
Jesse Ibarra, Burlington/San Jose 283
Derrick Gibson, Asheville 280
Andruw Jones, Macon 275

EXTRA-BASE HITS
Andruw Jones, Macon 71
Adam Riggs, San Bernardino 68
Jesse Ibarra, Burlington/San Jose 67
Todd Greene, Midland/Vancouver 64
Clyde Pough, Trenton/Pawtucket 63
David Doster, Reading 63

DOUBLES
Jason Hardtke, Binghamton/Norfolk 43
Riccardo Ingram, Salt Lake 43
Fernando Tatis, Charleston, S.C. 43
Andruw Jones, Macon 41
John Marzano, Oklahoma City 41

TRIPLES
Bob Abreu, Tucson 17
Lorenzo De la Cruz, Knoxville 12
Matt Guiliano, Piedmont 12
Scott Samuels, Daytona/Orlando 12
Gary Thurman, Tacoma........................ 12

HOME RUNS
Todd Greene, Midland/Vancouver 40
Jesse Ibarra, Burlington/San Jose 34
Derrick Gibson, Asheville 32
Ron Wright, Macon 32
Ivan Cruz, Jacksonville/Toledo 31

RUNS BATTED IN
Derrick Gibson, Asheville 115
Steve Cox, Modesto 110
Nilson Robledo, South Bend 108
Raul Ibanez, Riverside 108
Adam Riggs, San Bernardino 106
Daryle Ward, Fayetteville 106

MOST RBIs, ONE GAME
Steve Verduzco, Kissimmee 10
Chad Alexander, Auburn 8

Asheville's Derrick Gibson
Topped minors with 115 RBIs

FRANK RAGSDALE

Tucson's Bob Abreu
17 triples

Steve Cox, Modesto 8
Andruw Jones, Macon 8
Harvey Pulliam, Colorado Springs.......... 8
Ryan Ritter, Helena 8
Richie Sexson, Kinston 8

STOLEN BASES
Jason McDonald, Modesto 70
Mike Metcalfe, Vero Beach/San Ant..... 61
Anton French, Peoria/Durham 61
Essex Burton, Birmingham 60
Carlos Hernandez, Quad City.............. 58

BASE ON BALLS
Jason McDonald, Modesto 110
Chris Sexton, W-S/Salem/New Haven . 97
Frank Menechino, Prince William 96
Billy McMillon, Port City 96
Gus Kennedy, Macon 95

STRIKEOUTS
Chris Schwab, Albany 173
Gary Hust, Modesto............................ 169
Bryon Gainey, Columbia..................... 157
Juan Thomas, Prince William 156
Nate Dishington, Savannah................ 154

SLUGGING PERCENTAGE*
Jesse Ibarra, Burlington/San Jose..... .635
Harvey Pulliam, Colorado Springs....... .614
Raul Ibanez, Riverside .... .612
Carlos Delgado, Syracuse.................. .610
Todd Greene, Midland/Vancouver..... .601

ON-BASE PERCENTAGE*
Jeff Ladd, Hagerstown/Knoxville .... .452
Kevin Coughlin, Birm./Nashville .... .439
Bob Henley, Albany .... .436
Johnny Damon, Wichita..................... .434
Jeff Grotewold, Omaha...................... .434

BATTING AVERAGE*
By Position
(Minimum 350 At-Bats)
CATCHER
Raul Ibanez, Riverside .... .332
Jason Kendall, Carolina...................... .326
Jose Valentin, Fort Wayne .... .324
Mike Sweeney, Wilmington .... .310
John Marzano, Oklahoma City .... .309

FIRST BASEMEN
Aldo Pecorilli, Greenville/Richmond .. .344
Ryan McGuire, Trenton .... .333
Jonas Hamlin, Stockton...................... .332
Kevin Grijak, Greenville/Richmond..... .324
Bo Dodson, El Paso/New Orleans..... .322

SECOND BASEMEN
Adam Riggs, San Bernardino .... .362
Donovan Mitchell, Quad City .... .329
Dave Hajek, Tucson .... .327
Luis Castillo, Kane County .... .326

Mitch Simons, Salt Lake .... .325
THIRD BASEMEN
Lino Diaz, Wilmington/Wichita .... .328
Eric White, Columbus .... .317
Dan Donato, Greensboro/Tampa .... .316
Corey Koskie, Fort Wayne .... .310
Antone Williamson, El Paso............... .309
Rick Ladjevich, Riverside................... .309

SHORTSTOPS
Wilson Guerrero, San Antonio/Albuq. .346
Chris Snopek, Nashville...................... .323
Ed Giovanola, Richmond .... .321
Greg LaRocca, R.C./Memphis........... .319
Derek Jeter, Columbus .... .317

OUTFIELDERS
Kevin Coughlin, Birm./Nashville......... .372
Quinton McCracken, N.H./Colo. Spr. . .359
Riccardo Ingram, Salt Lake .... .348
Johnny Damon, Wichita...................... .343
Robert Perez, Syracuse...................... .343

INDIVIDUAL PITCHING

EARNED RUN AVERAGE*
(Minimum 112 Innings)
Glendon Rucsh, Wilmington 1.74
Kevin Pincavitch, V.B./San Bern........ 1.74
Bryan Rekar, N.H./Colo. Springs 1.89
Bartolo Colon, Kinston 1.96
Rocky Coppinger, Fred./Bowie/Roch. 1.97
Jason Isringhausen, Bing./Norfolk..... 1.97
Mike Kusiewicz, Asheville/Salem........ 2.03
Tim Byrdak, Wilmington 2.16
Shane Bowers, Fort Myers 2.16
Tom Price, San Bernardino 2.20

WINS
Rich Hunter, Piedmont/Reading 19
Joe Roa, Buffalo 17
Donne Wall, Tucson 17
Matt Beaumont, Lake Elsinore............. 16
Rocky Coppinger, Fred./Bowie/Roch.... 16
Marty Janzen, Tampa/Norwich/Knox.... 16
Tony Mounce, Quad City 16
Gary Rath, San Antonio/Albuquerque .. 16

LOSSES
Geoff Edsell, Lake Elsinore/Midland..... 15
Ryan Griffin, High Desert..................... 15
Stacy Hollins, Huntsville/Edmonton 15
Greg Keagle, R.C./Mempis/L.V. 15
Dan Lock, Quad City 15
Rafael Ramirez, Savannah................... 15
Brian Woods, Prince William 15

GAMES
Chuck Ricci, Scranton/Wilkes-Barre..... 68
John Kelly, Jacksonville 66
Matthew Golden, Savannah 64
Brian Reed, Peoria 63
Shayne Bennett, Sarasota/Trenton 62

MEL BAILEY

Modesto's Jason McDonald
70 steals led minors

Chris Lemp, Frederick/Bowie............... 62
Rick Trlicek, Phoenix/Canton-Akron 62
COMPLETE GAMES
Rob Mattson, Memphis 11
Jason Dickson, Cedar Rapids 9
Paul Wilson, Binghamton/Norfolk 8
Denny Harriger, Las Vegas 7
Jeff Cosman, St. Lucie/Binghamton 6
Brent Crowther, Ashe./Salem/Colo. Spr. 6
Masataka Endo, Visalia 6
Steve Falteisek, Harrisburg/Ottawa 6
Clint Sodowsky, Jacksonville/Toledo 6
Kennie Steenstra, Iowa.......................... 6

SAVES
Brandon Reed, Fayetteville 41
Steve Montgomery, Arkansas............... 36
Joe Jacobsen, Vero Beach/San Bern... 34
Carlos Castillo, Lake Elsinore.............. 32
Danny Graves, Kinston/Canton/Buffalo 31
Wilmer Montoya, Columbus/Kinston..... 31
Travis Welch, Peoria............................. 31

INNINGS PITCHED
Rob Mattson, Memphis 202
Ray Ricken, Gboro/Tampa/Norwich ... 193
Mark Guerra, St. Lucie/Binghamton ... 193
Steve Falteisek, Harrisburg/Ottawa 191
Rocky Coppinger, Fred./Bowie/Roch.. 187

BASE ON BALLS
Jacob Shumate, Macon/Danville 119
Matt Clement, Rancho Cuca./Idaho Falls.. 91
Brad Kaufman, Memphis 90
Neil Weber, Harrisburg 90
Bart Evans, Wichita/Wilmington............ 89

STRIKEOUTS
Paul Wilson, Binghamton/Norfolk 194
Ray Ricken, Gboro/Tampa/Norwich 178
Masataka Endo, Visalia 178
Damian Moss, Macon 177
Jesus Sanchez, Columbia 177

STRIKEOUTS/9 INNINGS*
(Starters)
Damian Moss, Macon 10.67
Marino Santana, Wisc./Riverside..... 10.39
Greg Whiteman, Lake./Fayetteville.. 10.24
Roberto Duran, Vero Beach 10.13
Cam Smith, Fayetteville 10.03

STRIKEOUTS/9 INNINGS*
(Relievers)
Bronson Heflin, Clear./Reading 12.48
Ricky Pickett, Chatt./Shreveport 12.24
Bryan Wolff, Rancho Cucamonga 12.16
Brian Reed, Peoria 11.86
Scott Gardner, Lake./Fayetteville 11.30

BATTING AVERAGE AGAINST*
(Starters)
Glendon Rusch, Wilmington .... .188
Rocky Coppinger, Fred./Bowie/Roch. .191
Marino Santana, Wisc./Riverside...... .195
Ray Ricken, Gboro/Tampa/Norwich ... .196
Tim Byrdak, Wilmington.................... .198

BATTING AVERAGE AGAINST*
(Relievers)
Ricky Pickett, Chatt./Shreveport .... .135
Doug Webb, Stockton/El Paso .... .145
Brian Reed, Peoria .... .172
Brandon Reed, Fayetteville .... .173
Jason Temple, Augusta .... .173

MOST STRIKEOUTS IN ONE GAME
Josh Bishop, AZL Brewers 17
Glendon Rusch, Wilmington 17
Paul Wilson, Binghamton.................... 17
Keith Foulke, San Jose....................... 16

INDIVIDUAL FIELDING

MOST ERRORS
Hiram Bocachica, Albany..................... 58
Doug Bearden, Bristol.......................... 53
Bert Green, Savannah.......................... 51
Felix Martinez, Wichita......................... 50
Jason McDonald, Modesto 50

The road show began when the Colorado Rockies pushed the Denver Zephyrs out and the Southern League lost its Charlotte franchise when Charlotte won a Triple-A expansion team. Both clubs eyed New Orleans, but the Triple-A Zephyrs won territorial rights to the city, leaving the Double-A team without a home.

The former Charlotte franchise spent two years in Nashville, sharing a stadium with the Triple-A Sounds. While at its temporary home in Nashville, the franchise flirted with playing in Lexington, Ky., but that plan fell through. David Hersh offered to operate the franchise in Puerto Rico for two seasons while owner Dennis Bastien looked for another new home, but the parent Seattle Mariners vehemently rejected that plan.

The next permanent home was supposed to be Springfield, Mo., in 1997. But that effort was derailed because the city couldn't find money for a $9.5 million stadium.

Enter Ozark, a city a few miles south of Springfield. It proposed a half-cent sales tax that would pay for a stadium, though it first had to be approved by voters. City officials said the citizens craved a team and all but assured passage of the tax.

"We're just delighted that another option has potentially developed," league president Arnold Fielkow said. "They've been very open about how they're going to get funding for the stadium, about how they think the referendum will fare."

If voters approve the tax, the team plans to move for the 1997 season. Bastien also had to meet Southern League conditions regarding season-ticket sales and sponsorship. Whatever else happens, Fielkow said the team would play the 1996 season as the Port City Roosters.

Meanwhile, the situation in New Orleans is still uncertain as the Zephyrs' owners tried to jump start efforts to begin building a 10,000-seat stadium, overdue for construction in suburban Metairie.

Political haggling as well as delays in stadium design and getting out bids put the ballpark on hold. Meanwhile, the owners of the team were trying to get a lease agreement approved.

The Zephyrs were granted an extension to play at the University of New Orleans' Privateer Park for 1996. But with continued delays, American Association owners might be hesitant to renew that extension unless they see a signed lease and some serious work under way.

Rumors began flying late in the 1995 season that the franchise would move in 1996. There has been talk that the team would wind up in Austin; Long Island; or Greensboro, N.C., where Zephyrs minority owner Don Beaver is negotiating to buy the South Atlantic League franchise and there's talk of eventually moving up to the major leagues.

Attendance Holds Steady

The minors tried to stay above the furor caused by the major league strike, and for the most part they did. But it touched them a bit, because attendance stagnated after increases in every previous year in the 1990s.

Overall attendance in the National Association was 33,126,934, a drop of 0.7 percent from 1994's 33.4 million. That's still higher than any time since the postwar boom of the late 1940s, when there were more

ORGANIZATION OF THE YEAR
Resurgent Mets Stockpile Impressive Young Talent

The New York Mets were Baseball America's Organization of the Year in 1983 and 1984. By 1986 they were World Series champions.

With the quality of players throughout the organization now, it's not at all outlandish to think the  Mets could pull a repeat of that feat in the '90s.

The first half is complete: the Mets are Baseball America's 1995 Organization of the Year. Now all that remains is for those players to come through in the major leagues.

That's no small feat, of course, but the new Mets showed promise in the second half of the 1995 season. Jettisoning most of their expensive veterans, the Mets went from worst in the National League at the end of the first half (25-44) to tied for second in the NL East at the end of the season (69-75, or 44-31 in the second half).

Under the guidance of general manager Joe McIlvaine, the Mets finally gave up on trying to win again with free agents and rebuilt their organization from the ground up. The results are starting to show, as the minor league system's .536 winning percentage can attest.

At the top of the organization, the Triple-A Norfolk Tides were Baseball America's Minor League Team of the Year, and they had six of the International League's Top 10 Prospects as judged by IL managers. The Double-A Binghamton Mets had the Eastern League's top three prospects.

Righthanders Jason Isringhausen and Paul Wilson were 1-2 on both lists. Isringhausen also went 9-2 with the Mets when called up shortly after midseason and won 20 games overall in 1995. Wilson led the minor leagues in strikeouts.

The Mets have assembled the pieces. Now all that remains is to see how they're going to fit together.

PREVIOUS WINNERS

1982—Oakland Athletics	1989—Texas Rangers
1983—New York Mets	1990—Montreal Expos
1984—New York Mets	1991—Atlanta Braves
1985—Milwaukee Brewers	1992—Cleveland Indians
1986—Milwaukee Brewers	1993—Toronto Blue Jays
1987—Milwaukee Brewers	1994—Kansas City Royals
1988—Montreal Expos	

than 50 leagues and as many as 448 teams.

Attendance fell in every Double-A and Triple-A league except the Eastern, which experienced a significant gain, 19.7 percent. To be fair, the drops weren't huge. The biggest drop was in the Southern League, where without Michael Jordan attendance was off 12.9 percent.

"I think it was a combination of things," International League president Randy Mobley said. "I think many leagues experienced some tough weather early, which just happens every once in a while. And I think to an

MANAGER OF THE YEAR

Reds' Triple-A Skipper Honored

Indianapolis manager Marc Bombard is adding weight to the case for pitchers making the transition to managing.

Bombard's professional career as a pitcher didn't last very long—1971-76 in the Reds organization, the last two years as a player-coach—but it looks like he'll still have a long, fruitful run in dugouts. Baseball America's 1995 Minor League Manager of the Year led Cincinnati's Triple-A Indianapolis affiliate to the American Association playoffs with a league-best 88-56 record.

"I guess it was always a gut instinct that I wanted to be a manager," said Bombard, 45. "That was always first and foremost inside me, though when you're playing you never think of that."

Marc Bombard

BARBARA JEAN GERMANO

Bombard was a pitching coach in the organization until 1982, when he got his first managing job at Rookie-level Billings. He's been managing ever since, winning a Pioneer League championship in 1983 and a Midwest League championship in 1988.

He spent a year in the Brewers organization and three years in the Pirates organization, returning to the Reds in 1993 and taking over as the manager at Indianapolis.

Bombard led a veteran-laden club to an 86-57 record and the American Association championship last year. This season he had more prospects but the team faltered in the playoffs. He was named AA manager of the year on both occasions.

"Bomby is a great handler

of men, a great communicator," Reds farm director Chief Bender said. "He's great at putting young players in a position to better themselves, and he's always been a winner if he got decent material."

Bombard is a straightforward and self-deprecating man who's quick to give credit to his players and downplay his role. But the way winning seems to follow him around can't be coincidental.

"I'm not that smart," Bombard said. "The players are a lot smarter than I am. I just try to be honest and up-front with players. The bottom line is to try to get everybody to the majors, and since you can't really do that, to get the most out of everybody's ability."

Now after 25 seasons in the minor leagues, Bombard might be ready to move up to the majors. Ray Knight was groomed for the Reds' managing job, but other jobs will be open as well.

"Hopefully we can give him a major league opportunity," Bender said. "Maybe not managing, but coaching. He would be an ideal bench coach."

Bombard just wants to keep winning, wherever he is.

"You can't worry about what you can't control," Bombard said. "I hope the opportunity presents itself, but if not I just hope there's another opportunity available for me in baseball next year.

"If I didn't have baseball, I don't know what I'd do."

PREVIOUS WINNERS
1981—Ed Nottle, Tacoma (Athletics)
1982—Eddie Haas, Richmond (Braves)
1983—Bill Dancy, Reading (Phillies)
1984—Sam Perlozzo, Jackson (Mets)
1985—Jim Lefebvre, Phoenix (Giants)
1986—Brad Fischer, Huntsville (Athletics)
1987—Dave Trembley, Harrisburg (Pirates)
1988—Joe Sparks, Indianapolis (Expos)
1989—Buck Showalter, Albany (Yankees)
1990—Kevin Kennedy, Albuquerque (Dodgers)
1991—Butch Hobson, Pawtucket (Red Sox)
1992—Grady Little, Greenville (Braves)
1993—Terry Francona, Birmingham (White Sox)
1994—Tim Ireland, El Paso (Brewers)

---

extent there was some fallout from baseball's other problems."

Forty-four clubs and six leagues—the Eastern, Carolina, Midwest, South Atlantic, New York-Penn and Northwest—broke attendance records.

The West Michigan Whitecaps juggernaut continued as the franchise broke the Class A attendance record it set a year earlier, drawing 507,989—more than 30,000 over its record debut of 1994. The team has plans to expand its ballpark, so the record likely won't stand for long.

West Michigan actually beat all Double-A franchises in attendance as well. Bowie led Double-A teams with 463,976 fans. Buffalo was down from 1994 but still led Triple-A attendance with 900,782 fans. Portland led short-season teams with 249,696 fans in just 38 home dates.

The overall attendance ranks fifth all-time, with 1994's total in fourth place.

Seven cities took steps toward landing two Triple-A expansion franchises for 1998 when the Triple-A

expansion committee sent them applications.

But Double-A expansion continued to be delayed, with the possibility that those franchises might not play until 1999, the year after the Tampa Bay Devil Rays and Arizona Diamondbacks start play.

Randy Mobley, speaking for the Triple-A expansion committee, said applications had been sent to eight ownership groups in the seven cities.

The eight groups are from Birmingham; Bowie, Md.; Canton-Akron, Ohio; Durham, Greensboro and Winston-Salem, N.C.; and two ownership groups in San Juan, Puerto Rico.

There is a $15,000 application fee, and a $7.5 million expansion fee for the two winners.

Mobley said the committee hopes to meet with applicants and make on-site visits early in the 1996 season. The committee hopes to make its selections by mid-July.

Triple-A and Double-A must expand by two teams each because of the addition of Arizona and Tampa Bay to the major leagues. National Association spokesman Jim Ferguson said Double-A expansion is on hold because the Diamondbacks and Devil Rays haven't decided to field teams at that level in 1998.

Before the delay, 15 groups filled out questionnaires for Double-A franchises. They were in Albany and Long Island, N.Y.; Atlantic City, N.J.; Baton Rouge; Corpus Christi, Texas; Durham, Greensboro and Winston-Salem; three groups in Harrisburg, Pa; Lehigh Valley (Allentown), Pa.; Mobile and Montgomery, Ala.; and Springfield, Mass.

Fighting To The Top

The strike made 1995 a strange year in baseball from the beginning, and the minors were no exception. People were fighting left and right, and that was just the beginning of the strange behavior.

The most notable fight occurred when the Durham Bulls and Winston-Salem Warthogs (Carolina) had an ugly brawl on "Strike Out Domestic Violence Night" in Durham.

The fight erupted in the bottom of the third inning when Winston-Salem righthander Jason Kummerfeldt hit Bulls third baseman John Knott in the back after Durham hit consecutive home runs.

Knott charged the mound and both dugouts emptied. But this wasn't an average brawl. The players were out for blood.

Warthogs righthander Glen Cullop had his jaw broken and lost four teeth when Bulls reliever Earl Nelson kicked him in the face. Cullop missed the rest of the season, and Nelson was released by the Braves after serving a suspension.

Though they weren't as violent, many other fights tarnished the game in 1995. Charleston, W.Va. (South Atlantic) manager Razor Shines actually went into the Charleston, S.C., stands to defend his players

After a Texas League game in Wichita, Arkansas outfielder Dmitri Young approached fan Brian Holland in the box seats and punched him in the face, sending both men toppling to the ground. Young said Holland made racial slurs, which Holland denied.

Several fans converged, and fellow Travelers outfielder Keith Jones climbed into the stands waving a bat. "I wasn't going to do anything until I saw it was six on one," he said. He hit a fan in the back with the bat.

Both Young and Jones drew lengthy suspensions.

PBA Rules Prove Beneficial

After much hue and cry, the date for minor league clubs to comply with the facilities requirements of the Professional Baseball Agreement came and passed in 1995 with little fuss.

Most people agree that though the requirements have been a burden for some, the ultimate effect has been nothing but good for minor league baseball.

About 15 of the clubs that needed to make improvements missed the April 1 deadline, but they were not punished.

The facilities requirements that minor league teams have come under were part of the most recent PBA, passed in 1990. They range from clubhouse requirements to the required ratio of toilets to seats.

Clubs originally were to have the necessary improvements made by April 1994, but the deadline was extended a year.

TEAM OF THE YEAR
Talent-Laden Triple-A Club Emerges From The Pack

If you don't have a roster handy and want to know who played for the Norfolk Tides in 1995, just check a New York Mets box score. That should be a good representation of the players that Toby Harrah got to manage.

"It was a fun year for me," Harrah said. "We were winning, so many players made it to the big leagues and they had a lot of fun. It's a great indication of the good, young talent in this organization."

The Tides, named Baseball America's Team of the Year, did have it all in 1995. Not just solid players, but potential major league stars at many positions. Not just a winning season, but a record that was 10½ games better than the next-best team in the International League.

Shortstop Rey Ordonez, resurgent third baseman Butch Huskey and outfielders Carl Everett, Alex Ochoa and Jay Payton all spent time in Norfolk in 1995.

And the pitching. Oh my, the pitching.

"This was the best pitching I've ever seen on a minor league club," said veteran Norfolk general manager Dave Rosenfield, who has seen quite a few minor league clubs in his time.

Jason Isringhausen, Bill Pulsipher and Paul Wilson should form the foundation of the Mets rotation for years to come. And they were just the beginning.

The exodus of players to the majors finally took its toll in the playoffs, when the Tides lost to Ottawa in the championship series. But Harrah said the loss did little to take the shine off the season.

"I wish we had won, but it was still a great season," he said. "Getting these guys to the majors is what it's all about, and I got a big kick out of it. These kids are going to succeed."

PREVIOUS WINNERS
1993—Harrisburg (Expos)
1994—Wilmington, Del. (Royals)

THE TOP 10

Team (League)	W	L	PCT.
1. Norfolk (International)	86	56	.606
2. *Shreveport (Texas)	88	47	.652
3. Indianapolis (American Association)	88	56	.611
4. *Kinston (Carolina)	81	56	.591
5. Portland (Eastern)	86	56	.606
6. *Carolina (Southern)	89	55	.618
7. Tucson (Pacific Coast)	87	56	.608
8. *San Bernardino (California)	84	54	.609
9. Chattanooga (Southern)	83	60	.580
10. *Daytona (Florida State)	87	48	.644

*Won league championship.

The requirements made it easier for some clubs to move to new stadiums, either in their own cities or in new ones. The result was a building boom perhaps unprecedented in minor league history.

"I don't have any historical data, but I'd be shocked if there had ever been a bigger boom than this," said

TOP 100 PROSPECTS

Through consultation with baseball's scouting and player development fraternity, Baseball America annually selects a list of the game's top 100 major league prospects. The list emphasizes long-range major league potential and considers only players in professional baseball who have not exhausted their major league rookie status.

The list, complied prior to the 1995 season, identifies the highest level players attained in 1995.

1. Alex Rodriguez, ss, Mariners (Majors)
2. Ruben Rivera, of, Yankees (Majors)
3. Chipper Jones, 3b, Braves (Majors)
4. Derek Jeter, ss, Yankees (Majors)
5. Brian Hunter, of, Astros (Majors)
6. Shawn Green, of, Blue Jays (Majors)
7. Charles Johnson, c, Marlins (Majors)
8. Alex Gonzalez, ss, Blue Jays (Majors)
9. Johnny Damon, of, Royals (Majors)
10. Ben Grieve, of, Athletics (A)
11. Armando Benitez, rhp, Orioles (Majors)
12. Bill Pulsipher, lhp, Mets (Majors)
13. Todd Hollandsworth, of, Dodgers (Majors)
14. Alan Benes, rhp, Cardinals (Majors)
15. Antonio Osuna, rhp, Dodgers (Majors)
16. Paul Wilson, rhp, Mets (AAA)
17. Billy Wagner, lhp, Astros (Majors)
18. Dustin Hermanson, rhp, Padres (Majors)
19. Doug Million, lhp, Rockies (A)
20. Rey Ordonez, ss, Mets (AAA)
21. Andruw Jones, of, Braves (Majors)
22. Nomar Garciaparra, ss, Red Sox (AA)
23. Scott Ruffcorn, rhp, White Sox (Majors)
24. Josh Booty, 3b, Marlins (A)
25. James Baldwin, rhp, White Sox (Majors)
26. Roger Cedeno, of, Dodgers (Majors)
27. Ugueth Urbina, rhp, Expos (Majors)
28. Ray Durham, 2b, White Sox (Majors)
29. *Marc Newfield, of, Mariners (Majors)
30. LaTroy Hawkins, rhp, Twins (Majors)
31. Edgardo Alfonzo, 3b, Mets (Majors)
32. Michael Tucker, of, Royals (Majors)
33. Jose Silva, rhp, Blue Jays (AA)
34. Richard Hidalgo, of, Astros (AA)
35. *Alex Ochoa, of, Orioles (Majors)
36. *Frank Rodriguez, rhp, Red Sox (Majors)
37. Jason Isringhausen, rhp, Mets (Majors)
38. Paul Konerko, c, Dodgers (A)
39. Jim Pittsley, rhp, Royals (Majors)
40. Todd Walker, 2b, Twins (AA)
41. Chan Ho Park, rhp, Dodgers (Majors)

Yankees' Ruben Rivera

42. Jason Schmidt, rhp, Braves (Majors)
43. Trey Beamon, of, Pirates (AAA)
44. Julio Santana, rhp, Rangers (AAA)
45. Jimmy Haynes, rhp, Orioles (Majors)
46. Trot Nixon, of, Red Sox (AA)
47. Brian Barber, rhp, Cardinals (Majors)
48. Pokey Reese, ss, Reds (AAA)
49. Andy Pettitte, lhp, Yankees (Majors)
50. Jeff Suppan, rhp, Red Sox (Majors)
51. Orlando Miller, ss, Astros (Majors)
52. Bob Abreu, of, Astros (AAA)
53. John Wasdin, rhp, Athletics (Majors)
54. Terrell Wade, lhp, Braves (Majors)
55. *Juan Acevedo, rhp, Rockies (Majors)
56. Andy Larkin, rhp, Marlins (AA)
57. Benji Gil, ss, Rangers (Majors)
58. Everett Stull, rhp, Expos (AA)
59. *Phil Nevin, 3b, Astros (Majors)
60. Raul Casanova, c, Padres (AA)
61. Sergio Nunez, 2b, Royals (A)
62. *Ron Villone, lhp, Mariners (Majors)
63. Scott Elarton, rhp, Astros (A)
64. Antone Williamson, 3b, Brewers (AA)
65. Hiram Bocachica, ss, Expos (A)
66. Jaret Wright, rhp, Indians (A)
67. Paul Shuey, rhp, Indians (AAA)
68. Curtis Goodwin, of, Orioles (Majors)
69. Marc Kroon, rhp, Padres (Majors)
70. Marc Barcelo, rhp, Twins (AAA)
71. *Andrew Lorraine, lhp, Angels (Majors)
72. Shannon Stewart, of, Blue Jays (Majors)
73. J.R. Phillips, 1b, Giants (Majors)
74. Jeff Granger, lhp, Royals (AA)
75. Jimmy Hurst, of, White Sox (AA)
76. Glenn Williams, ss, Braves (A)
77. Sandy Martinez, c, Blue Jays (Majors)
78. Russ Davis, 3b, Yankees (Majors)
79. Matt Drews, rhp, Yankees (A)
80. Daron Kirkreit, rhp, Indians (AA)
81. Derrek Lee, 1b, Padres (AA)

Seattle's Alex Rodriguez

82. Brooks Kieschnick, 1b-of, Cubs (AAA)
83. Pat Watkins, of, Reds (AA)
84. Bret Wagner, lhp, Cardinals (AA)
85. Vladimir Guerrero, of, Expos (A)
86. Tony Clark, 1b, Tigers (Majors)
87. *C.J. Nitkowski, lhp, Reds (Majors)
88. Jermaine Dye, of, Braves (AA)
89. Marc Valdes, rhp, Marlins (Majors)
90. Dante Powell, of, Giants (A)
91. Scott Rolen, 3b, Phillies (AA)
92. Desi Relaford, ss, Mariners (AAA)
93. Garret Anderson, of, Angels (Majors)
94. Jose Malave, of, Red Sox (AAA)
95. Carl Everett, of, Mets (Majors)
96. Jay Payton, of, Mets (AAA)
97. Jose Herrera, of, Athletics (Majors)
98. Karim Garcia, of, Dodgers (Majors)
99. Damon Hollins, of, Braves (AA)
100. Chris Carpenter, rhp, Blue Jays (AA)

*Traded during 1995 season

Atlanta's Chipper Jones

Yankees' Derek Jeter

Tim Brunswick, the National Association's facilities coordinator.

An illustration of the boom comes from looking just at the last 10 years. From 1985-89, 20 new ballparks were built. Since 1990, and including parks scheduled to open in 1996, almost 50 new ballparks have gone up.

"It's night and day from before the requirements were passed," Brunswick said. "Clubhouses have improved, field conditions have improved for the play-

BOB FREITAS AWARDS

Albuquerque, Midland Saluted In AAA, AA

With the minor league baseball boom, popular new teams have sprung up alongside the traditionally successful operations. Baseball America, through the annual Bob Freitas Awards, recognizes those franchises that have stood the test of time.

Freitas was a longtime operator, promoter and minor league ambassador who died in 1989, and the award named for him annually honors teams at Triple-A, Double-A, Class A and short-season levels.

For the first time, one of the new breed of teams has been recognized—Class A Kane County (Midwest). But after five seasons, the franchise has proven that it has staying power, continuing to build on its initial success in suburban Chicago. Kane County drew 477,550 fans in 1995, second in Class A only to West Michigan, a fellow Midwest League member.

At Triple-A, Albuquerque (Pacific Coast) has been a model of stability, maintaining its affiliation with the Los Angeles Dodgers since the team debuted in the PCL in 1972.

Midland also opened in the Texas League in 1972 and is one of the reasons the league is one of the most stable in minor league baseball. That also explains why Texas League teams have won five of the seven Double-A awards.

A second Dodgers affiliate, Great Falls, won the short-season award for continuing to be one of the strongest draws year-in and year-out in the Pioneer League, even after being in the league since 1969.

ers. And it's overall much better for the fan."

Almost every team had to make at least minor changes to comply with the requirements. Those that had to do major renovations, projects that would have cost hundreds of thousands of dollars, often opted to take the next step.

"A lot of clubs figured why not spend another $3 million and get a whole new ballpark," Brunswick said.

Meanwhile, discussions of a new PBA stalled as the major league labor negotiations continued to push the major league-minor league relations on the back burner.

The current PBA does not expire until the end of the 1997 season, but negotiations for a new agreement could have been opened as soon as 1994. Both the National Association and Major League Baseball are interested in negotiating a new agreement as soon as possible, but the formal talks have been postponed since the strike began in 1994.

A Better Baseball Network

For the first time ever, the minor leagues had a national television contract, with ESPN2 broadcasting games from throughout the minors.

The two-year contract with the National Association required the network to broadcast at least one game from every league, and fans got a good assortment in the 25-game package.

The minors got a good deal of exposure in 1994 when the major leaguers went on strike, but those broadcasts often were the Michael Jordan game of the week.

With the "Baseball Across America" tour, ESPN2 did a better job of showing every level of the minor leagues and giving more of the flavor of the minor league experience.

Part of that was hiring two announcers who understand the minors well. Play-by-play man Matt Vasger-

sian's full-time job was with the Triple-A Syracuse Chiefs, and he had worked his way up through the minor league ranks.

Former major leaguer Steve Lyons proved to be a good match as the color man.

So Long, Clown Prince

Max Patkin, the clown prince of baseball whose career spanned five decades, officially retired in 1995.

Declining health forced Patkin, 75, to cancel his scheduled performances, but he returned at the end of the season for a farewell ceremony arranged by the Reading Phillies. Patkin usually finished his annual tour of the minors in Reading, only an hour from his home in suburban Philadelphia.

Patkin's health left him unable to perform, though he did one last routine for the crowd of 8,088, the classic bit in which he sips water and sprays a geyser into the air.

At the ceremony, Patkin donated one of his favorite jerseys, a baggy shirt with the Mets logo on the front and a question mark on the back, to the Hall of Fame.

"I wasn't a mascot, I played the game," he said.

Patkin pitched five years in the minors before joining the Navy in World War II. While stationed in Honolulu he played in pickup games and organized exhibitions between servicemen and major leaguers. That's when he began clowning around.

During the 1940s and '50s, Patkin performed at major league parks. He eventually moved on to the minors and performed at about 4,000 games overall.

Patkin's popularity increased with the minor leagues' resurgence during the 1980s and his appearance in the 1987 film "Bull Durham."

"If I get better I might come back and do some appearances," Patkin said. "One writer here told me, 'You've got to do something or you'll die.'"

MINOR LEAGUES
BEST TOOLS

	American Association (AAA)	International League (AAA)	Pacific Coast League (AAA)	Eastern League (AA)	Southern League (AA)	Texas League (AA)	California League (A)	Carolina League (A)	Florida State League (A)	Midwest League (A)	South Atlantic League (A)
Best Batting Prospect	Steve Gibralter, Indianapolis	Derek Jeter, Columbus	Karim Garcia, Albuquerque	Jay Payton, Binghamton	Jermaine Dye, Greenville	Johnny Damon, Wichita	Derrek Lee, Rancho Cucamonga	Richie Sexson, Kinston	Wendell Magee, Clearwater	Ryan Jackson, Kane County	Andruw Jones, Macon
Best Power Prospect	Brooks Kieschnick, Iowa	Glenn Murray, Pawtucket	Mike Busch, Albuquerque	Jay Payton, Binghamton	Jason Thompson, Memphis	Todd Greene, Midland	Steve Cox, Modesto	Richie Sexson, Kinston	Dan Held, Clearwater	Jake Patterson, Fort Wayne	Andruw Jones, Macon
Best Baserunner	Eric Owens, Indianapolis	Jim Buccheri, Ottawa	Trinidad Hubbard, Colorado Springs	Nomar Garciaparra, Trenton	Lonell Roberts, Knoxville	Jovino Carvajal, Midland	Jason McDonald, Modesto	Ricky Gutierrez, Kinston	Chris Latham, Vero Beach	Demond Smith, Cedar Rapids	Andruw Jones, Macon
Fastest Baserunner	Fernando Ramsey, Nashville	Curtis Goodwin, Rochester	Roger Cedeno, Colorado Springs	Terry Jones, New Haven	Lonell Roberts, Knoxville	Jovino Carvajal, Midland	Dante Powell, San Jose	Patricio Claudio, Kinston	Chris Latham, Vero Beach	Luis Castillo, Kane County	Derek Swafford, Augusta
Best Pitching Prospect	Alan Benes, Louisville	Jason Isringhausen, Norfolk	John Burke, Colorado Springs	Paul Wilson, Binghamton	Marc Kroon, Memphis	Billy Wagner, Jackson	William Percibal, High Desert	Bartolo Colon, Kinston	Matt Drews, Tampa	Marino Santana, Wisconsin	Jimmy Anderson, Augusta
Best Fastball	Alan Embree, Buffalo	Jason Isringhausen, Norfolk	Donne Wall, Tucson	Paul Wilson, Binghamton	Marc Kroon, Memphis	Billy Wagner, Jackson	Brad Rigby, Modesto	Bartolo Colon, Kinston	Dan Rios, Tampa	Jeff D'Amico, Beloit	Jaret Wright, Columbus
Best Breaking Pitch	James Baldwin, Nashville	Jason Isringhausen, Norfolk	John Burke, Colorado Springs	Jason Isringhausen, Binghamton	Todd Schmitt, Memphis	Carlos Valdez, Shreveport	Jon DeClue, Visalia	Rocky Coppinger, Frederick	Marty Janzen, Tampa	Carl Dale, Peoria	Wilmer Montoya, Columbus
Best Control	Rick Reed, Indianapolis	Dave Telgheder, Norfolk	Scott Watkins, Salt Lake	Bryan Rekar, New Haven	Elmer Dessens, Carolina	Carlos Valdez, Shreveport	Will Brunson, San Bernardino	Glendon Rusch, Wilmington	Jeff Davis, Charlotte	Tim Kester, Quad City	Larry Wimberly, Piedmont
Best Reliever	Cory Bailey, Louisville	Mike Christopher, Toledo	Ron Barnes, Tacoma	Jay Powell, Portland	Todd Schmitt, Memphis	Steve Montgomery, Arkansas	Doug Webb, Stockton	Danny Graves, Kinston	Joe Jacobsen, Vero Beach	Steve Rain, Rockford	Joe Maskivish, Augusta
Best Defensive C	Henry Mercedes, Omaha	Alberto Castillo, Norfolk	Ken Huckaby, Albuquerque	Mike Figga, Norwich	Jason Kendall, Carolina	Raul Chavez, Jackson	Willie Morales, Modesto	Robert Machado, Prince William	Eliezer Marrero, St. Petersburg	Jose Valentin, Fort Wayne	Julio Mosquera, Hagerstown
Best Defensive 1B	Mike Robertson, Nashville	Jon Zuber, Scranton/W-B	Chris Pritchett, Vancouver	Tim Clark, Portland	Jason Thompson, Memphis	Todd Landry, El Paso	Randy Jorgensen, Riverside	Richie Sexson, Kinston	Sean Freeman, Lakeland	Jesse Ibarra, Burlington	Craig Stone, Hagerstown
Best Defensive 2B	Eric Owens, Indianapolis	Steve Rodriguez, Pawtucket	Dave Hajek, Tucson	Ralph Milliard, Portland	Brian Koelling, Chattanooga	Miguel Cairo, San Antonio	Dickie Woodridge, Rancho Cuca.	Ricky Gutierrez, Kinston	Lionel Hastings, Brevard County	Luis Castillo, Kane County	Julio Zorilla, Columbia
Best Defensive 3B	Olmedo Saenz, Nashville	Howard Battle, Syracuse	Andy Sheets, Tacoma	Lou Lucca, Portland	Robert Smith, Greenville	Henry Blanco, San Antonio	Chad Tredaway, Rancho Cuca.	Raul Rodarte, Lynchburg	Willis Otanez, Vero Beach	Sean McNally, Springfield	Wes Helms, Macon
Best Defensive SS	Billy Ripken, Buffalo	Rey Ordonez, Norfolk	Denny Hocking, Salt Lake	Nomar Garciaparra, Trenton	Desi Relaford, Port City	Rich Aurilia, Shreveport	Keith Johnson, San Bernardino	Enrique Wilson, Kinston	Jason Maxwell, Daytona	Donnie Sadler, Michigan	Kyle Houser, Asheville
Best Infield Arm	Pokey Reese, Indianapolis	Rey Ordonez, Norfolk	Alex Rodriguez, Tacoma	Chad Roper, New Britain	Yuri Sanchez, Jacksonville	Felix Martinez, Wichita	Brett King, San Jose	Lou Collier, Lynchburg	Willis Otanez, Vero Beach	Wilson Delgado, Burlington	Guillermo Mota, Columbia
Best Defensive OF	Kevin Koslofski, New Orleans	Damon Buford, Rochester	Roger Cedeno, Albuquerque	Jay Payton, Binghamton	David Francisco, Huntsville	Calvin Murray, Shreveport	Earl Johnson, Rancho Cuca.	Edgard Velasquez, Salem	Kraig Hawkins, Tampa	Todd Dunwoody, Kane County	Andruw Jones, Macon
Best Outfield Arm	Duane Singleton, New Orleans	Alex Ochoa, Rochester	Karim Garcia, Albuquerque	Ruben Rivera, Norwich	Jermaine Dye, Greenville	Willie Romero, San Antonio	Armando Rios, San Jose	Edgard Velasquez, Salem	Ron Brown, Brevard County	Gary Matthews Jr., Clinton	Vladimir Guerrero, Albany
Most Exciting Player	Eric Owens, Indianapolis	Derek Jeter, Columbus	Alex Rodriguez, Tacoma	Jay Payton, Binghamton	Desi Relaford, Port City	Johnny Damon, Wichita	Dante Powell, San Jose	Enrique Wilson, Kinston	Chris Latham, Vero Beach	Ryan Jackson, Kane County	Andruw Jones, Macon
Best Umpire Prospect	Matt Malone, Nashville	Brian O'Nora, Norfolk	Don Long, Vancouver	Heath Jones	Jeff Schrupp	Kraig Sanders	Scott Gasaway	Jeff Head	Daryn Fredrickson	Brian McCraw	Sean McAnally
Best Manager Prospect	Rick Renick, Nashville	Toby Harrah, Norfolk		Carlos Tosca, Portland	Bruce Kimm, Orlando	Ron Johnson, Wichita	Ron Roenicke, San Bernardino	Dave Huppert, Prince William	Dave Trembley, Daytona	Steve Roadcap, Rockford	Jeff Banister, Augusta

Selected at midseason 1995 by minor league managers in consultation with Baseball America. Full-season leagues only

Confusion Rules '94 Rule V Draft, But 24 Players Picked

The confused and troubled state of baseball's unresolved labor dispute had a profound effect on the 1994 Rule V draft.

Traditionally one of the staples of baseball's Winter Meetings, the '94 draft was rescheduled twice by Major League Baseball before an awkward conference call was held Dec. 6. Farm and scouting directors and other player-development officials—but no general managers—called the shots for those clubs that had representatives in Dallas.

Despite the last-minute confusion and uncertainty, 24 players were selected in the major league phase, the highest number in years and more than double the 1993 total of 11.

"I don't think it's any coincidence," one scouting director said. "It's a factor of the money. A draft pick doesn't cost you as much."

Three kinds of players, if not protected on 40-man winter rosters, were eligible for selection: players with major league experience; players who have played parts of three seasons in National Association-affiliated minor leagues who were 19 or older on June 5 preceding their first contract; and players who have played parts of four seasons and were 18 or younger on June 5 preceding their first contract.

Major league draft picks cost $50,000 each, and players must be kept on the selecting team's 25-man major league roster all of the

Dodgers' Chad Fonville

next season or be offered back to their old team for $25,000.

By virtue of being the National League club with the worst record in 1994, the Padres had the draft's first pick. But San Diego's roster stood full at 40, so it wasn't entitled to make a selection. Only eight clubs made no selections, five of which were at their limit of 40.

With the second pick, the Angels selected shortstop Tomas Perez, 20, who hit .262 in 1994 for Montreal's Class A Burlington affiliate. The Angels then traded Perez to the Blue Jays.

Ten of the players selected remained in the big leagues throughout the 1995 season. Among the longshots was third baseman Freddy Garcia, selected by the Pirates from the Blue Jays. Though he spent the 1994 season at short-season St. Catharines, Garcia stuck with the Pirates, hitting .140 in 57 at-bats.

Other notable Rule V pickups included Chad Fonville, who was selected from the Giants by the Expos. Fonville began 1995 in Montreal and later moved to Los Angeles when the Expos tried to send him to the minors but couldn't sneak him through waivers. Fonville eventually took the starting shortstop job in Los Angeles from incumbent Jose Offerman.

Pirates' Freddy Garcia

1994 RULE V DRAFT

MAJOR LEAGUE DRAFT
Selection Price: $50,000

ROUND ONE

Selecting Club, Player, Pos., From

Angels. Tomas Perez, ss (Expos)
Cubs. Tanyon Sturtze, rhp (Athletics)
Marlins. Matt Mantei, rhp (Mariners)
Athletics. *Chris Eddy, lhp (Royals)
Rockies. Kevin Logsdon, lhp (Indians)
Rangers. Francisco Saneaux, rhp (Orioles)
Pirates. Freddy Garcia, 3b (Blue Jays)
Brewers. Alberto Reyes, rhp (Expos)
Cardinals. Rich DeLucia, lhp (Orioles)
Tigers. Todd Steverson, of (Blue Jays)
Phillies. *Craig Worthington, 3b (Reds)
Twins. *Brian Kowitz, of (Braves)
Red Sox. Vaughn Eshelman, lhp (Orioles)
Mets. *Kevin Lomon, rhp (Braves)
Dodgers. Ed Vosberg, lhp (Athletics)
Royals. Jon Nunnally, of (Indians)
Astros. *Nate Cromwell, lhp (Padres)
Orioles. *Russ Brock, rhp (Athletics)
Indians. Jim Lewis, rhp (Astros)
Expos. Chad Fonville, ss (Giants)

ROUND TWO

Selecting Club, Player, Pos., From

Marlins. *Matt Dunbar, lhp (Yankees)
Phillies. Mike Mimbs, lhp (Expos)
Red Sox. *Benji Simonton, of (Giants)
Mets. *Kevin Northrup, of (Expos)
*Returned to original organization

TRIPLE-A DRAFT
Selection Price: $12,000

ROUND ONE

Selecting Club, Player, Pos., From

Padres. Paul Russo, of (Twins)
Cubs. Steve Shiflett, rhp (Royals)
Mariners. Jeff Jackson, of (Phillies)
Marlins. Adrian Hollinger, rhp (Padres)
Rockies. Bobby Jones, lhp (Brewers)
Cardinals. Mark Mesewicz, lhp (Pirates)
Phillies. Chris Gambs, rhp (Giants)
Twins. Jay Maldonado, 3b (Blue Jays)
Giants. Randy Phillips, rhp (Blue Jays)
Red Sox. Antoine Henry, of (Cardinals)
Mets. Matt Anderson, lhp (Orioles)
Blue Jays. Todd Ingram, rhp (Athletics)
Dodgers. Dave Staton, 1b (Padres)
Royals. Bobby Bonds, of (Padres)
Orioles. Toby Lehman, rhp (White Sox)
Indians. Joe Biasucci, 2b (Cardinals)
White Sox. Joe Durso, c (Blue Jays)

ROUND TWO

Selecting Club, Player, Pos., From

Padres. Tim Killeen, c (Athletics)
Cubs. Shane Livsey, of-2b (Astros)
Giants. Shawn Purdy, rhp (Angels)
Red Sox. Hiram Ramirez, 1b (Giants)
Mets. Rich Turrentine, rhp (Yankees)
Dodgers. John Fritz, rhp (Rockies)
Orioles. Nerio Rodriguez, c (White Sox)
Indians. Mike Murphy, of (Blue Jays)

ROUND THREE

Selecting Club, Player, Pos., From

Padres. Michel LaPlante, rhp (Pirates)
Mets. Jason Hardtke, 2b (Padres)
Indians. Jim Chrisman, rhp (Royals)

DOUBLE-A DRAFT
Selection Price: $4,000

ROUND ONE

Selecting Club, Player, Pos., From

Padres. Dario Tena, of (Pirates)
Mariners. Kevin Booker, of (White Sox)
Athletics. Herbert Baxter, lhp (Dodgers)
Rockies. Frank Campos, rhp (White Sox)
Blue Jays. Kendall Rhine, rhp (Astros)
Dodgers. Chris Durkin, of (Astros)
Orioles. Ty Quillin, rhp-of (Mets)
White Sox. Chuck Smith, rhp (Astros)

ROUND TWO

Selecting Club, Player, Pos., From

Padres. Mitch Root, 3b (Tigers)

Louisville Rises Up When It Counts Most

By PETER BARROUQUERE

The Louisville Redbirds looked more like ugly ducklings when the 1995 American Association play-offs began.

They finished the regular season with a 74-70 record and had lost 15 of their last 20 games. They were about to get into the ring with the defending champion Indianapolis Indians, who finished the season with an 88-56 record—a .611 winning percentage, the best in Triple-A. The Indians also pretty much owned the Redbirds, having beaten them 16 times in 24 regular-season games.

But when it came time to be measured for championship rings, it was the Redbirds who held their hands out. They upset Indianapolis in the semifinals and finished off second-place Buffalo in the finals.

"I told the guys we had no chance against Indianapolis," said veteran third baseman Tracy Woodson before the Redbirds went out and swept three straight from the Indians.

"Then," said Woodson, knowing he had a good thing going motivationally, "I said we had no chance against Buffalo."

The Bisons also were 16-8 against the Redbirds during the season. But catcher Mike Difelice, a late-season callup from Double-A Arkansas, drove in four runs in the deciding game of the best-of-5 championship series to lead Louisville to an 8-2 victory and their first AA title since back-to-back triumphs in 1984-85. Buffalo has not won a league title of any kind since 1961.

Eric Owens

The Redbirds knocked out Buffalo's 17-game winner Joe Roa in the third inning to take a commanding 4-0 lead.

"We came out banging from the get-go," outfielder Ray Giannelli said. "A lot of guys didn't think we had a chance. And those teams did beat the heck out

Steve Gibralter. Indianapolis outfielder hit .316 and was voted the Association's top hitting prospect.

of us in the regular season. With each game we kept getting our confidence up."

Louisville scored only seven runs in splitting the first four games of the series, but a disturbance in Game Four seemed to fire up the Redbirds.

Defelice initiated the incident in the eighth inning by tagging out Buffalo's Luis Lopez on a third strike. Words were exchanged and Louisville pitcher John Frascatore hit the next batter.

Buffalo fans then got involved. One threw a baseball

STANDINGS

Page		W	L	PCT	GB	Manager	Attendance/Dates	Last Pennant
96	**Indianapolis Indians (Reds)**	88	56	.611	—	Marc Bombard	366,254 (69)	1994
102	**Buffalo Bisons (Indians)**	82	62	.569	6	Brian Graham	900,782 (68)	None
133	**Omaha Royals (Royals)**	76	68	.528	12	Mike Jirschele	404,156 (61)	1990
199	**Louisville Redbirds (Cardinals)**	74	70	.514	14	Joe Pettini	556,211 (69)	1995
90	**Iowa Cubs (Cubs)**	69	74	.483	18½	Ron Clark	466,320 (65)	1993
83	**Nashville Sounds (White Sox)**	68	76	.472	20	Rick Renick	355,133 (71)	None
147	**New Orleans Zephyrs (Brewers)**	63	79	.444	24	Chris Bando	143,728 (65)	None
225	**Oklahoma City 89ers (Rangers)**	54	89	.378	33½	Greg Biagini	259,518 (59)	1992

PLAYOFFS—Semifinals: Louisville defeated Indianapolis 3-0, and Buffalo defeated Omaha 3-1, in best-of-5 series. **Finals:** Louisville defeated Buffalo 3-2, in best-of-5 series.

NOTE: Team's individual batting and pitching statistics can be found on page indicated in lefthand column.

from the stands over the visitors' dugout. Redbirds third baseman Mike Gulan responded by throwing a roll of athletic tape into the stands.

League president Branch Rickey suspended Gulan, but the incident served as a wakeup call.

"We definitely used that," Woodson said. "We talked about it and used it."

The Bisons gave the Redbirds little trouble in the championship game. Lefthander Doug Creek got Brian Giles on a bases-loaded grounder to shortstop Aaron Holbert to work out of a jam in the seventh, protecting the victory for Mike Busby, who gave up two hits in the first six innings.

"It seemed like the whole playoffs, we'd do just enough to win," Louisville manager Joe Pettini said. "We really proved we're a team that wants to win this thing."

Nobody, it seemed, appreciated it more than catcher Marc Ronan, who raised his champagne bottle to his teammates in the clubhouse afterward.

"This is to everybody," said the usually reserved Ronan. "I've never won anything in my life. Thank you."

Owens Wins MVP

Indianapolis second baseman Eric Owens was selected the league's MVP, which probably took some of the hurt out of a season-ending injury. Owens, who was also selected Rookie of the Year, tore the anterior cruciate ligament in his left knee rounding first base on Aug. 14 against the Iowa Cubs.

He had been headed for an MVP season anyway,

Joe Roa. Buffalo ace led league with 17 victories.

LEE SCHMID

batting .314 with 12 home runs and 63 RBIs. Owens also led the league in stolen bases with 33.

"I had a lot of things going for me," said a disappointed Owens. "But for some reason, it wasn't meant for me to finish the season."

Roa (17-3) led the league in victories, becoming Buffalo's first 17-game winner since lefthander Walter Craddock went 18-8 in 1957. Nashville righthander Rod Bolton (14-3) easily led the league in ERA, winning his second AA title in three years with a 2.88 mark. Bolton would have led for a third straight year but missed winning the title by a single point in 1994.

And though Indianapolis made a quick departure from the playoffs, the Indians had their moments. They put together a 16-game road winning streak and hit nine of the league's 24 grand slam home runs.

Three were struck by outfielder Steve Gibralter, whose season ended after 79 games—just as he was about to be promoted to the parent Reds—when he tore ligaments in his left thumb. At the time, Gibralter was leading the league in homers and RBIs.

Louisville righthander Alan Benes and Gibralter were selected 1-2 as the league's top prospects in a poll of managers, even though Benes also was sidelined much of the season with a sore elbow.

Benes, who was 17-3 at four stops in the Cardinals system in 1994, made only 11 regular-season starts for Louisville. He made his presence known in the playoffs, however, spinning a 2-1 win over Buffalo in a pivotal third-game win. Benes also pitched a three-hit, 1-0 win over Indianapolis in the clinching game in the semifinals.

Attendance Drop

The league experienced its second straight attendance decline, drawing 3,452,102—a drop of 182,461 from 1994. Buffalo, which drew more than a million fans every year from 1988 to 1993, slipped to 900,782, its second straight year under a million. But it was still the minors' biggest draw.

Seven clubs suffered a dip in attendance, including New Orleans, whose meager total of 143,723 was the lowest in Triple-A. The Zephyrs, under local ownership for the first time since moving from Denver in 1993, were mired much of the season in political haggling over attempts to begin construction of a new 10,000 stadium in suburban Metairie.

The Zephyrs continued to use Privateer Park on the University of New Orleans campus, a facility considered grossly inadequate for Triple-A ball.

Front-office unrest led to the resignation of general manager Leanne Harvey, who was brought in to run the franchise shortly after local attorney Rob Couhig took over controlling interest of the Zephyrs.

LEAGUE CHAMPIONS

Last 25 Years

Year	Regular Season*	Pct.	Playoff
1971	Indianapolis (Reds)	.604	Denver (Senators)
1972	Wichita (Cubs)	.621	Evansville (Brewers)
1973	Iowa (White Sox)	.610	Tulsa (Cardinals)
1974	Indianapolis (Reds)	.578	Tulsa (Cardinals)
1975	Denver (White Sox)	.596	Evansville (Tigers)
1976	Denver (Expos)	.632	Denver (Expos)
1977	Omaha (Royals)	.563	Denver (Expos)
1978	Indianapolis (Reds)	.578	Omaha (Royals)
1979	Evansville (Tigers)	.574	Evansville (Tigers)
1980	Denver (Expos)	.676	Springfield (Cardinals)
1981	Omaha (Royals)	.581	Denver (Expos)
1982	Indianapolis (Reds)	.551	Indianapolis (Reds)
1983	Louisville (Cardinals)	.578	Denver (White Sox)
1984	Indianapolis (Expos)	.591	Louisville (Cardinals)
1985	Oklahoma City (Rangers)	.556	Louisville (Cardinals)
1986	Indianapolis (Expos)	.563	Indianapolis (Expos)
1987	Denver (Brewers)	.564	Indianapolis (Expos)
1988	Indianapolis (Expos)	.627	Indianapol (Expos)
1989	Indianapolis (Expos)	.596	Indianapolis (Expos)
1990	Omaha (Royals)	.589	Omaha (Royals)
1991	Buffalo (Pirates)	.566	Denver (Brewers)
1992	Buffalo (Pirates)	.604	Oklahoma City (Rangers)
1993	Iowa (Cubs)	.590	Iowa (Cubs)
1994	Indianapolis (Reds)	.601	Indianapolis (Reds)
1995	Indianapolis (Reds)	.611	Louisville (Cardinals)

*Best overall record

AMERICAN ASSOCIATION
1995 BATTING, PITCHING STATISTICS

CLUB BATTING

	AVG	G	AB	R	H	2B	3B	HR	BB	SO	SB
Buffalo	.276	144	4847	708	1338	261	41	129	461	660	63
Indianapolis	.275	144	4890	791	1344	286	29	193	492	1001	93
Omaha	.273	144	4772	698	1305	266	31	144	473	859	69
Iowa	.268	143	4790	552	1285	226	32	92	362	781	55
Nashville	.263	144	4906	621	1288	239	25	113	420	872	109
Louisville	.259	144	4697	617	1217	245	27	122	474	933	113
New Orleans	.253	142	4611	572	1166	206	30	85	442	862	107
Oklahoma City	.253	143	4696	572	1186	241	42	82	401	856	68

CLUB PITCHING

	ERA	G	CG	SHO	SV	IP	H	R	ER	BB	SO
Louisville	3.78	144	10	8	42	1241	1208	623	522	406	840
Buffalo	3.90	144	13	8	45	1251	1278	604	543	396	820
Indianapolis	3.91	144	12	8	41	1262	1178	642	548	434	883
New Orleans	3.98	142	11	8	32	1214	1274	606	537	445	806
Iowa	4.03	143	13	8	32	1240	1224	614	555	496	889
Nashville	4.04	144	8	11	39	1277	1338	673	573	405	931
Omaha	4.26	144	12	10	36	1238	1301	660	586	423	820
Oklahoma City	4.56	143	11	7	26	1221	1328	709	618	520	835

CLUB FIELDING

	PCT	PO	A	E	DP		PCT	PO	A	E	DP
New Orleans	.980	3641	1572	107	163	Louisville	.972	3723	1455	147	107
Buffalo	.979	3753	1592	115	137	Oklahoma City	.972	3662	1506	151	156
Iowa	.978	3721	1503	120	137	Nashville	.971	3830	1600	163	144
Omaha	.975	3715	1479	134	158	Indianapolis	.971	3786	1441	157	114

Brooks Kieschnick
23 home runs

Jeromy Burnitz
85 RBIs

INDIVIDUAL BATTING LEADERS
(Minimum 389 Plate Appearances)

	AVG	G	AB	R	H	2B	3B	HR	RBI	BB	SO	SB
Carter, Michael, Iowa	.325	107	421	57	137	16	3	8	40	14	46	12
Snopek, Chris, Nashville	.323	113	393	56	127	23	4	12	55	50	72	2
Owens, Eric, Indianapolis	.314	108	427	86	134	24	8	12	63	52	61	33
Ramsey, Fernando, Nashville	.310	98	406	61	126	19	3	5	45	13	47	26
Giles, Brian, Buffalo	.310	123	413	67	128	18	8	15	67	54	40	7
Marzano, John, Okla. City	.309	120	427	55	132	41	3	9	56	33	54	3
Saenz, Olmedo, Nashville	.304	111	415	60	126	26	1	13	74	45	60	0
Brady, Doug, Nashville	.298	125	450	71	134	15	6	5	27	31	76	32
Kieschnick, Brooks, Iowa	.295	138	505	61	149	30	1	23	73	58	91	2
Giannelli, Ray, Louisville	.295	119	390	56	115	19	1	16	70	44	85	3

INDIVIDUAL PITCHING LEADERS
(Minimum 115 Innings)

	W	L	ERA	G	GS	CG	SV	IP	H	R	ER	BB	SO
Bolton, Rod, Nashville	14	3	2.88	20	20	3	0	131	127	44	42	23	76
Reed, Rick, Indianapolis	11	4	3.33	22	21	3	0	135	127	60	50	26	92
Anderson, Mike, Iowa	7	9	3.46	27	27	3	0	172	156	71	66	69	123
Roa, Joe, Buffalo	17	3	3.50	25	24	3	0	165	168	71	64	28	93
Taylor, Scott, N.O.-Okla. City	8	8	3.55	24	21	1	0	129	132	62	51	41	74
Abbott, Paul, Iowa	7	7	3.67	46	11	0	0	115	104	50	47	64	127
Minchey, Nate, Louisville	8	7	3.73	26	24	1	0	147	153	77	61	42	67
Steenstra, Kennie, Iowa	9	12	3.89	29	26	6	0	171	174	85	74	48	96
Bell, Eric, Buffalo	13	9	3.90	28	24	3	0	161	177	76	70	47	86
De la Rosa, Francisco, Louis.	2	5	4.06	28	19	1	0	115	104	56	52	38	66

1996 ALMANAC • 255

DEPARTMENT LEADERS

BATTING

G	Mike Robertson, Nashville	139
AB	Kerry Valrie, Nashville	544
R	Eric Owens, Indianapolis	86
H	Brooks Kieschnick, Iowa	149
TB	Brooks Kieschnick, Iowa	250
2B	John Marzano, Okla. City	41
3B	Four tied at	8
HR	Brooks Kieschnick, Iowa	23
RBI	Jeromy Burnitz, Buffalo	85
SH	Shane Halter, Omaha	19
SF	Two tied at	8
BB	Jeff Grotewold, Omaha	82
IBB	Jeromy Burnitz, Buffalo	8
HBP	Drew Denson, Indianapolis	18
SO	Kerry Valrie, Nashville	107
SB	Eric Owens, Indianapolis	33
CS	Two tied at	15
GIDP	Two tied at	18
OB%	Jeff Grotewold, Omaha	.434
SL%	Jeromy Burnitz, Buffalo	.503

PITCHING

G	J.J. Munoz, Omaha	57
GS	John Farrell, Buffalo	28
CG	Kennie Steenstra, Iowa	6
ShO	Four tied at	2
GF	Rich Sauveur, Indianapolis	43
Sv	Cory Bailey, Louisville	25
W	Joe Roa, Buffalo	17
L	Two tied at	12
IP	John Farrell, Buffalo	184
H	John Farrell, Buffalo	198
R	John Farrell, Buffalo	97
ER	John Farrell, Buffalo	93
HR	James Baldwin, Nashville	27
BB	Mike Anderson, Iowa	69
HB	John Farrell, Buffalo	16
SO	Paul Abbott, Iowa	127
WP	Domingo Jean, Okla. City	14

FIELDING

C AVG	Marc Ronan, Louisville	.993
E	Brian Dorsett, Ind.	10
PB	Dean Borrelli, Okla. City	14
1B AVG	Mike Robertson, Nash.	.992
E	Jeff Grotewold, Omaha	15
2B AVG	Doug Brady, Nashville	.975
E	Eric Owens, Ind.	17
3B AVG	Olmedo Saenz, Nashville	.939
E	Olmedo Saenz, Nashville	24
SS AVG	Billy Ripken, Buffalo	.978
E	Aaron Holbert, Lou.	31
OF AVG	Kevin Koslofski, N.O.	.996
E	Two tied at	8

HONOR ROLL

OFFICIAL ALL-STAR TEAM

C—John Marzano, Oklahoma City. 1B—Jeff Grotewold, Omaha. 2B—Eric Owens, Indianapolis. 3B—Tracy Woodson, Louisville. SS—Mark Loretta, New Orleans. OF—Steve Gibralter, Indianapolis; Brian Giles, Buffalo; Brooks Kieschnick, Iowa. DH—Drew Denson, Indianapolis.

RHP—Joe Roa, Buffalo. LHP—Eric Bell, Buffalo. RP—Cory Bailey, Louisville. MVP—Eric Owens, Indianapolis. Manager of the Year—Marc Bombard, Indianapolis.

TOP 10 PROSPECTS
(Selected by league managers)

1. Alan Benes, rhp, Louisville
2. Steve Gibralter, of, Indianapolis
3. Eric Owens, 2b, Indianapolis
4. Pokey Reese, ss, Indianapolis
5. Brooks Kieschnick, of, Iowa
6. Alan Embree, lhp, Buffalo
7. Jim Pittsley, rhp, Omaha
8. Chris Snopek, 3b, Nashville
9. Mark Loretta, ss, New Orleans
10. Willie Greene, 3b, Indianapolis

INTERNATIONAL LEAGUE

Pitching-Rich Norfolk Shines In 1995

By TIM PEARRELL

The Tides kept coming in and going out during the 1995 International League season.

But despite supplying a boatload of prospects who should right the New York Mets, all the changing faces didn't keep Norfolk from establishing the league's high-water mark at 86-56 (.606), by far the best record in a circuit bloated with .500-level teams.

Norfolk was so impressive it commandeered six of the Top 10 prospect spots in a poll of managers and became the first team to sweep all the individual post-season awards in 19 years.

"This is only my third year as a manager, but it's the best talent I've been around," said Norfolk's Toby Harrah, who was named the IL's Manager of the Year.

About the only thing Norfolk failed to do was win the Governors' Cup championship. Ottawa, which joined the league in 1993 as an expansion team, became the first Canadian team to win the Cup since Toronto in 1966 by beating the Tides 3-1 in the final.

The championship put a nice ending on a rough season for Ottawa manager Pete Mackanin, whose wife, Nancy, was diagnosed with non-Hodgkin's lymphoma shortly before spring training. Mackanin used baseball as therapy while his wife underwent treatments.

"I've never seen a group of guys who want something so bad," said Mackanin. "It feels good to have your name on the trophy."

Norfolk, which had most of its team in place out of spring training while others relied on replacement players and Triple-A veterans, led the

Jason Isringhausen

Western Division virtually wire-to-wire. Anchored first by lefthander Bill Pulsipher, then by righthanders Jason Isringhausen and Paul Wilson, Norfolk featured a pitching staff that had few peers in the minors.

Rey Ordonez. Performed magic at shortstop for Norfolk.

They were backed by Rey Ordonez and his nightly magic show in the infield. Harrah called Ordonez the greatest fielding shortstop he had ever seen.

"Good players make a good manager, and great pitching makes better managers," Harrah said. "We had both."

East Up For Grabs

While Norfolk had little opposition in the West, the Eastern Division was sardine-packed. Four teams

STANDINGS

Page	EAST	W	L	PCT	GB	Manager(s)	Attendance/Dates	Last Pennant
62	Rochester Red Wings (Orioles)	73	69	.514	—	Marv Foley	394,035 (69)	1990
160	Ottawa Lynx (Expos)	72	70	.507	1	Pete Mackanin	482,144 (70)	1995
69	Pawtucket Red Sox (Red Sox)	70	71	.496	2½	Buddy Bailey	479,261 (69)	1984
186	Scranton/W-B Red Barons (Phillies)	70	72	.493	3	Mike Quade	479,030 (67)	None
231	Syracuse Chiefs (Blue Jays)	59	82	.418	13½	Bob Didier/Rich Hebner	303,208 (67)	1976

Page	WEST	W	L	PCT	GB	Manager(s)	Attendance/Dates	Last Pennant
173	Norfolk Tides (Mets)	86	56	.606	—	Toby Harrah	560,211 (69)	1985
55	Richmond Braves (Braves)	75	66	.532	10½	Grady Little	510,118 (68)	1994
166	Columbus Clippers (Yankees)	71	68	.511	13½	Bill Evers	541,451 (68)	1992
114	Toledo Mud Hens (Tigers)	71	71	.500	15	Tom Runnells	297,672 (65)	1967
121	Charlotte Knights (Marlins)	59	81	.421	26	Sal Rende	330,496 (67)	1993

PLAYOFFS—Semifinals: Norfolk defeated Richmond 3-2, and Ottawa defeated Rochester 3-2, in best-of-5 series. **Finals:** Ottawa defeated Norfolk 3-1 in best-of-5 series.

NOTE: Team's individual batting and pitching statistics can be found on page indicated in lefthand column.

scrambled into the final two weeks with a shot at first place. Mackanin called it "a pennant sack race."

"You keep falling, but you get up," Mackanin said. "Nobody takes the lead. You just trade places."

Rochester eventually landed on top, one game ahead of Ottawa. But the Lynx used a stingy bullpen and the hot bats of Curtis Pride, Chris Martin and Julian Yan to beat the Red Wings in five games in the semifinals.

Norfolk advanced by beating Richmond 3-2 in the other semifinal but had to use its remaining ace, Wilson, twice to do it. Wilson did not pitch in the championship series against Ottawa.

Isringhausen, who went 9-1 with a 1.55 ERA before being called to New York, was named the league's top prospect, its Most Valuable Pitcher and its Rookie of the Year. He was ineligible for the ERA crown because

Don Sparks

he didn't have enough innings. That was claimed by blossoming Richmond righthander Jason Schmidt, at 2.25.

Norfolk third baseman Butch Huskey enjoyed a resurgence after an abysmal, injury-plagued '94 season with the Tides and was named the league's MVP. Huskey, hitting .195 in late May, made some adjustments in his stance and finished at .284. He hit three homers in a game against Toledo and claimed the home run crown with 28.

Huskey finished second to Columbus' Don Sparks (90) in RBIs. Sparks, in his fifth season in Columbus, became the Clippers' all-time leader in hits, doubles, triples and at-bats.

Syracuse had its second straight batting champ, outfielder Robert Perez (.343). Chiefs outfielder Shawn

Butch Huskey. Norfolk slugging third baseman hit league high 28 homers.

Green earned the honor in '94.

Top Pitching Feats

Columbus righthander Mariano Rivera threw the league's only no-hitter, although it came in a rain-shortened, five-inning 3-0 win against Rochester.

Richmond righthander Chris Seelbach lost a no-hitter with two outs in the ninth against Norfolk, then lost the game 1-0. Seelbach was done in by Ricky Otero's opposite-field single and Jay Payton's run-scoring bloop double. Seelbach was traded to the Florida Marlins after the season.

Richmond's Grady Little topped 1,000 wins in his 16th season as a minor league manager. Little, 1,076-918 (.540) overall including the postseason, has guided his past four teams to a 336-232 (.592) mark. He has not managed a losing club since 1984.

After two seasons topping the 4.5-million mark in attendance, the turnstile count dropped slightly to just under 4.4 million. Norfolk led the way with 560,211, and two other clubs—Columbus and Richmond—each topped the 500,000 mark.

Money finally was allocated for stadiums in Rochester and Syracuse.

New York Gov. George Pataki had held up money that already had been approved for sports facilities projects throughout the state, including $16 million earmarked for a new $25.5 stadium to replace Syracuse's 50-year-old MacArthur Stadium and $15.25 million earmarked for a $33 million stadium to replace Rochester's 67-year-old Silver Stadium.

Rochester officials were hoping to begin play at Frontier Field in July 1996. Syracuse officials were shooting to be in their new digs by Opening Day, 1997.

LEAGUE CHAMPIONS

Last 25 Years

Year	Regular Season*	Pct.	Playoff
1971	Rochester (Orioles)	.614	Rochester (Orioles)
1972	Louisville (Red Sox)	.563	Tidewater (Mets)
1973	Charleston (Pirates)	.586	Pawtucket (Red Sox)
1974	Memphis (Expos)	.613	Rochester (Orioles)
1975	Tidewater (Mets)	.607	Tidewater (Mets)
1976	Rochester (Orioles)	.638	Syracuse (Yankees)
1977	Pawtucket (Red Sox)	.571	Charleston (Astros)
1978	Charleston (Astros)	.607	Richmond (Braves)
1979	Columbus (Yankees)	.612	Columbus (Yankees)
1980	Columbus (Yankees)	.593	Columbus (Yankees)
1981	Columbus (Yankees)	.633	Columbus (Yankees)
1982	Richmond (Braves)	.590	Tidewater (Mets)
1983	Columbus (Yankees)	.593	Tidewater (Mets)
1984	Columbus (Yankees)	.590	Pawtucket (Red Sox)
1985	Syracuse (Blue Jays)	.564	Tidewater (Mets)
1986	Richmond (Braves)	.571	Richmond (Braves)
1987	Tidewater (Mets)	.579	Columbus (Yankees)
1988	Tidewater (Mets)	.546	Rochester (Orioles)
	Rochester (Orioles)	.546	
1989	Syracuse (Blue Jays)	.572	Richmond (Braves)
1990	Rochester (Orioles)	.614	Rochester (Orioles)
1991	Columbus (Yankees)	.590	Columbus (Yankees)
1992	Columbus (Yankees)	.660	Columbus (Yankees)
1993	Charlotte (Indians)	.610	Charlotte (Indians)
1994	Richmond (Braves)	.567	Richmond (Braves)
1995	Norfolk (Mets)	.606	Ottawa (Expos)

*Best overall record

INTERNATIONAL LEAGUE
1995 BATTING, PITCHING STATISTICS

CLUB BATTING

	AVG	G	AB	R	H	2B	3B	HR	BB	SO	SB
Scranton/W-B	.272	142	4734	645	1286	248	48	73	459	777	95
Columbus	.271	140	4730	687	1281	222	61	105	456	911	104
Pawtucket	.264	142	4732	676	1249	240	19	156	456	951	94
Rochester	.262	142	4735	669	1242	256	36	122	446	820	125
Charlotte	.260	140	4695	620	1220	218	17	101	464	729	119
Norfolk	.260	142	4697	650	1219	229	40	90	434	823	132
Richmond	.259	141	4710	559	1222	194	33	78	441	794	70
Syracuse	.258	141	4764	615	1227	243	41	128	416	885	76
Ottawa	.257	142	4644	618	1195	225	35	87	454	824	161
Toledo	.257	142	4755	600	1222	224	35	108	442	962	93

CLUB PITCHING

	ERA	G	CG	SHO	SV	IP	H	R	ER	BB	SO
Norfolk	3.01	142	15	18	35	1259	1153	493	421	419	921
Richmond	3.46	141	4	14	41	1248	1196	545	480	466	898
Toledo	3.47	142	10	10	39	1253	1241	571	483	411	735
Rochester	3.80	142	9	5	36	1236	1263	616	522	398	899
Ottawa	3.92	142	9	11	28	1224	1190	611	533	410	761
Scranton/W-B	4.03	142	12	8	39	1236	1251	646	554	435	882
Columbus	4.07	140	5	8	33	1224	1220	643	553	478	822
Pawtucket	4.54	142	6	1	33	1230	1310	711	621	438	849
Syracuse	4.57	141	1	4	29	1230	1259	768	624	530	946
Charlotte	4.71	140	6	9	29	1225	1320	735	642	483	763

CLUB FIELDING

	PCT	PO	A	E	DP		PCT	PO	A	E	DP
Ottawa	.976	3673	1644	131	136	Charlotte	.973	3676	1630	145	154
Richmond	.975	3743	1558	134	122	Toledo	.972	3760	1735	157	168
Scranton/W-B	.975	3709	1467	133	134	Rochester	.971	3709	1477	154	127
Columbus	.975	3671	1606	137	149	Pawtucket	.971	3691	1425	152	104
Norfolk	.974	3776	1639	147	147	Syracuse	.964	3689	1490	195	116

Robert Perez
Top hitter

Jimmy Haynes
SO leader

Jason Schmidt
ERA leader

INDIVIDUAL BATTING LEADERS
(Minimum 383 Plate Appearances)

	AVG	G	AB	R	H	2B	3B	HR	RBI	BB	SO	SB
Perez, Robert, Syracuse	.343	122	502	70	172	38	6	9	67	13	60	7
Giovanola, Ed, Richmond	.321	99	321	45	103	18	2	4	36	55	37	8
Delgado, Carlos, Syracuse	.318	91	333	59	106	23	4	22	74	45	78	0
Jeter, Derek, Columbus	.317	123	486	96	154	27	9	2	45	61	56	20
Schall, Gene, Scranton	.313	92	320	52	100	25	4	12	63	49	54	3
Sparks, Don, Columbus	.312	137	545	67	170	26	10	7	90	29	75	2
Jordan, Kevin, Scranton	.310	106	410	61	127	29	4	5	60	28	36	3
Garcia, Omar, Norfolk	.309	115	430	55	133	21	7	3	64	21	58	3
Castleberry, Kevin, Ottawa	.294	118	428	65	126	18	4	7	56	52	59	9
Crespo, Felipe, Syracuse	.294	88	347	56	102	20	5	13	41	41	56	12

INDIVIDUAL PITCHING LEADERS
(Minimum 114 Innings)

	W	L	ERA	G	GS	CG	SV	IP	H	R	ER	BB	SO
Schmidt, Jason, Richmond	8	6	2.25	19	19	0	0	116	97	40	29	48	95
Murray, Matt, Richmond	10	4	2.78	19	19	0	0	123	108	41	38	34	78
Weston, Mickey, Toledo	11	7	2.90	28	27	2	0	180	170	68	58	41	69
Rueter, Kirk, Ottawa	9	7	3.06	20	20	3	0	121	120	50	41	25	67
Adamson, Joel, Charlotte	8	4	3.29	19	18	2	0	115	113	51	42	20	80
Haynes, Jimmy, Rochester	12	8	3.29	26	25	3	0	167	162	77	61	49	140
Deshaies, Jim, Scranton	7	8	3.45	19	19	2	0	117	105	51	45	26	79
Williams, Jimmy, Nor.-Rich.	12	6	3.48	32	16	0	2	119	110	55	46	65	100
Ilsley, Blaise, Scranton	8	10	3.88	29	29	2	0	185	210	96	80	34	103
Flener, Huck, Syracuse	6	11	3.94	30	23	1	0	135	131	70	59	41	83

Photo credits: BARBARA JEAN GERMANO, BARBARA JEAN GERMANO, MORRIS FOSTOFF

DEPARTMENT LEADERS

BATTING

G	Don Sparks, Columbus	137
AB	Don Sparks, Columbus	545
R	Derek Jeter, Columbus	96
H	Robert Perez, Syracuse	172
TB	Robert Perez, Syracuse	249
2B	Robert Perez, Syracuse	38
3B	Don Sparks, Columbus	10
HR	Butch Huskey, Norfolk	28
RBI	Don Sparks, Columbus	90
SH	Two tied at	11
SF	Don Sparks, Columbus	9
BB	Brad Tyler, Rochester	71
IBB	Carlos Delgado, Syracuse	7
HBP	Glenn Murray, Pawtucket	11
SO	Tony Clark, Toledo	129
SB	Jim Buccheri, Ottawa	43
CS	Three tied at	13
GIDP	Jose Munoz, Richmond	18
OB%	Ed Giovanola, Richmond	.417
SL%	Carlos Delgado, Syracuse	.610

PITCHING

G	Chuck Ricci, Scranton/W-B	68
GS	Blaise Ilsley, Scranton/W-B	29
CG	Three tied at	4
ShO	Jason Isringhausen, Norfolk	3
GF	Chuck Ricci, Scranton/W-B	48
Sv	Two tied at	25
W	Two tied at	12
L	Two tied at	13
IP	Blaise Ilsley, Scranton/W-B	185
H	Blaise Ilsley, Scranton/W-B	210
R	Dennis Springer, Scranton/W-B	101
ER	Two tied at	92
HR	Chris Roberts, Norfolk	24
BB	Jimmy Williams, Nor.-Rich.	65
HB	Tim Rumer, Columbus	16
SO	Jimmy Haynes, Rochester	140
WP	Steve Long, Charlotte	14

FIELDING

C AVG	Jorge Posada, Columbus	.993
E	Two tied at	8
PB	Jorge Posada, Columbus	14
1B AVG	Julian Yan, Ottawa	.997
E	Tony Clark, Toledo	13
2B AVG	Kevin Castleberry, Ottawa	.977
E	Felipe Crespo, Syracuse	25
3B AVG	Terry Jorgensen, Charlotte	.962
E	Craig Wilson, Toledo	28
SS AVG	Kevin Baez, Toledo	.975
E	Derek Jeter, Columbus	29
OF AVG	Bobby Moore, Richmond	1.000
E	Brent Bowers, Syracuse	9

HONOR ROLL

OFFICIAL ALL-STAR TEAM

C—Jorge Posada, Columbus. **1B**—Don Sparks, Columbus. **2B**—Kevin Jordan, Scranton/Wilkes-Barre. **3B**—Butch Huskey, Norfolk. **SS**—Derek Jeter, Columbus. **OF**—Alex Ochoa, Rochester-Norfolk; Robert Perez, Syracuse; Mark Smith, Rochester. **DH**—Carlos Delgado, Syracuse.

SP—Jason Isringhausen, Norfolk. **RP**—Rod Nichols, Richmond.

MVP—Butch Huskey, Norfolk. **Most Valuable Pitcher**—Jason Isringhausen, Norfolk. **Manager of the Year**—Toby Harrah, Norfolk.

TOP 10 PROSPECTS
(Selected by league managers)

1. Paul Wilson, rhp, Norfolk
2. Jason Isringhausen, rhp, Norfolk
3. Derek Jeter, ss, Columbus
4. Bill Pulsipher, lhp, Norfolk
5. Ruben Rivera, of, Columbus
6. Jason Schmidt, rhp, Richmond
7. Carlos Delgado, 1b, Syracuse
8. Rey Ordonez, ss, Norfolk
9. Alex Ochoa, of, Roch.-Norfolk
10. Butch Huskey, 3b, Norfolk

Colorado Sets Tone For Triple-A Affiliate

By JAVIER MORALES

News about an upstart team in Colorado in 1995 was not confined only to the Colorado Rockies.

Exemplifying their respectable scouting and player development operations, the Rockies assembled a Triple-A team at Colorado Springs that was good enough to win the Pacific Coast League championship. The Sky Sox became Colorado's affiliate just two years earlier, when the parent club played its inaugural season.

Much like the Rockies, the Sky Sox possessed a potent lineup, full of veteran power hitters. Colorado Springs tallied a club-record 157 home runs, including 97 at hitter-friendly Sky Sox Stadium.

Sky Sox left fielder Harvey Pulliam, a nine-year pro, was a triple crown candidate, but his .327 batting average was surpassed by three others, including .348 by winner Riccardo Ingram of Salt Lake. Pulliam led the league with 25 homers and 91 RBIs.

Harvey Pulliam. Sky Sox leftfielder hit .325 with 25 homers and 91 RBIs.

Trenidad Hubbard

Jay Gainer, in his third season with the Sky Sox, had a career year, batting .291 with 23 home runs and 86 RBIs. Trenidad Hubbard, who has played parts of six seasons in the PCL with Tucson and Colorado Springs, batted .340 and led the league in stolen bases (37), on-base percentage (.416) and runs (102). He led all of professional baseball with a 26-game hitting streak.

"Any pitcher facing our club had to be concerned about our lineup from top to bottom, especially when we played at home," Pulliam said.

Third baseman Jim Tatum, who was with the Rockies until August, became a more-than-adequate replacement in the lineup for Hubbard, a center fielder who was promoted to Colorado on Aug. 22. Tatum was the Sky Sox postseason hero, providing timely hits and a barrage of doubles.

After Hubbard was promoted, the Sky Sox went 4-7 and lost four of their last five games as the regular season came to a close. "Hubbard was our sparkplug," Colorado Springs manager Brad Mills said. "Without him, we lacked productivity."

That was until Tatum awoke the Sky Sox by going 10-for-18 with seven doubles in the semifinals against the Tucson Toros, who finished the season with a club record 87 victories. Colorado Springs won three straight after losing the first game of the series at home, and the clinching win told the story. The Sky Sox won 12-2 behind a club-record 10 doubles, four by Tatum.

Like Colorado Springs, Salt Lake reached the PCL championship with a talented lineup that offset a struggling pitching staff. Steve Dunn (.316-12-83), Ingram (.348-12-85) and Tom Quinlan (.279-17-88) made up the heart of the order.

The Buzz, in their second season in Salt Lake City after moving from Portland, faced a Vancouver team that due to promotions and trades didn't resemble the first-half champion in the Northern Division.

Salt Lake won the Northern Division playoffs in four games, advancing to play Colorado Springs, a team they beat nine of 16 times in the regular season. The Buzz overcame an 8-2 deficit to win the first game 9-8, setting the stage for a closely-played series that went the full five games.

STANDINGS: OVERALL

Page		W	L	PCT	GB	Manager(s)	Attendance/Dates	Last Pennant
127	**Tucson Toros (Astros)**	87	56	.608	—	Rick Sweet	301,963 (70)	1993
76	**Vancouver Canadians (Angels)**	81	60	.574	5	Don Long	305,739 (61)	1989
154	**Salt Lake Buzz (Twins)**	79	65	.549	8½	Phil Roof	637,332 (67)	1979
108	**Colorado Springs Sky Sox (Rockies)**	77	66	.538	10	Brad Mills	195,375 (60)	1995
140	**Albuquerque Dukes (Dodgers)**	75	69	.521	12½	Rick Dempsey	340,050 (70)	1994
180	**Edmonton Trappers (Athletics)**	68	76	.472	19½	Gary Jones	426,012 (63)	1984
219	**Tacoma Rainiers (Mariners)**	68	76	.472	19½	Steve Smith	316,103 (68)	1978
213	**Phoenix Firebirds (Giants)**	62	82	.431	25½	Keith Bodie/Jim Davenport	282,370 (70)	1977
206	**Las Vegas Stars (Padres)**	61	83	.424	26½	Tim Flannery	330,869 (71)	1988
192	**Calgary Cannons (Pirates)**	58	83	.411	28	Bobby Meacham	279,054 (63)	None

NOTE: Team's individual batting and pitching statistics can be found on page indicated in lefthand column.

A ninth-inning rally failed in Game Four as Salt Lake won 10-9, but the Sky Sox rallied late in Game Five. With two on and two out in the ninth, reliever Dan Naulty worked to a full count against Tatum.

Tatum hit a bloop single to left field, scoring two runs and giving the Sky Sox an 8-7 win and the championship, the first for any Rockies affiliate.

It was quite a day for Pulliam, whose wife Debbi gave birth to their third child. After the game he learned he had been called up to the Rockies.

"You couldn't ask for a better finish," he said. "Unbelievable!"

Attendance Decline

Although fans attended games at Edmonton's new 9,200-seat stadium in record numbers, attendance was down league-wide. The Trappers drew 426,012 fans to their park, which at the end of the season became TELUS Field, named after an Edmonton-based corporation. Edmonton drew 272,631 in 1994.

Donne Wall. Tucson righthander led the PCL with 17 wins and was named MVP.

The other nine teams declined in attendance. Salt Lake went from a PCL-record 713,224 in 1994 to 637,332. Colorado Springs attracted only 195,375 fans despite having a championship team.

Phoenix endured a 13-game losing streak which ultimately led to the reassignment of manager Keith Bodie. Third baseman Gary Scott and outfielder Brent Cookson, both of whom left the Giants organization in midseason trades, reportedly had personality clashes with Bodie as did many others.

Bodie became the Giants' coordinator of minor league instruction, a job he held in 1994. He was replaced by Jim Davenport, who managed Phoenix in 1971-73.

Two Prospects Stand Out

League managers were unanimous about the league lacking a good number of prospects, though two of the youngest players in Triple-A—Alex Rodriguez of

Tacoma and Karim Garcia of Albuquerque—were standouts. Both began the season at 19.

Garcia was among league leaders in batting average (.328), home runs (20) and RBIs (86). Rodriguez was shuffled between Seattle and Tacoma three times, but he managed to hit .362 with 15 homers in 213 at-bats.

One of the oldest players in the league, Rob Deer, 35, was one of two players to hit for the cycle. After his release from Vancouver he went to Las Vegas, where he hit for the cycle against Salt Lake. Deer finished the season batting .285 with 17 homers.

Mike Milchin of Albuquerque recorded the only no-hitter of the season, a seven-inning effort against Vancouver. It was the second game of a doubleheader. Milchin, a member of the U.S. team in the 1988 Olympics, had missed the 1994 season following reconstructive elbow surgery.

"I never consciously thought of the no-hitter," said Milchin, who finished the year at 8-4 with a 4.32 ERA. "They just kept hitting the ball at people. It just happened to come about."

STANDINGS: SPLIT SEASON

FIRST HALF					SECOND HALF				
NORTH	**W**	**L**	**PCT**	**GB**	**NORTH**	**W**	**L**	**PCT**	**GB**
Vancouver	45	27	.625	—	Salt Lake	41	31	.569	—
Salt Lake	38	34	.528	7	Vancouver	36	33	.522	3½
Tacoma	37	35	.514	8	Edmonton	33	39	.458	8
Edmonton	35	37	.486	10	Tacoma	31	41	.431	10
Calgary	30	41	.423	14½	Calgary	28	42	.400	12
SOUTH	**W**	**L**	**PCT**	**GB**	**SOUTH**	**W**	**L**	**PCT**	**GB**
Colo. Springs	39	33	.542	—	Tucson	50	22	.694	—
Albuquerque	38	34	.528	1	Colo. Springs	38	33	.535	11½
Tucson	37	34	.521	1½	Albuquerque	37	35	.514	13
Phoenix	34	38	.472	5	Las Vegas	35	37	.486	15
Las Vegas	26	46	.361	13	Phoenix	28	44	.389	22

PLAYOFFS—Semifinals: Salt Lake defeated Vancouver 3-2, and Colorado Springs defeated Tucson 3-1, in best-of-5 series. **Finals:** Colorado Springs defeated Salt Lake 3-2, in best-of-5 series.

LEAGUE CHAMPIONS

Last 25 Years

Year	Regular Season*	Pct.	Playoff
1971	Tacoma (Cubs)	.545	Salt Lake City (Angels)
1972	Albuquerque (Dodgers)	.622	Albuquerque (Dodgers)
1973	Tucson (Athletics)	.583	Spokane (Rangers)
1974	Spokane (Rangers)	.549	Spokane (Rangers)
1975	Hawaii (Padres)	.611	Hawaii (Padres)
1976	Salt Lake City (Angels)	.625	Hawaii (Padres)
1977	Phoenix (Giants)	.579	Phoenix (Giants)
1978	Tacoma (Yankees)	.584	Tacoma (Yankees)#
			Albuquerque (Dodgers)#
1979	Albuquerque (Dodgers)	.581	Salt Lake City (Angels)
1980	Albuquerque (Astros)	.595	Albuquerque (Dodgers)
1981	Albuquerque (Dodgers)	.712	Albuquerque (Dodgers)
1982	Albuquerque (Dodgers)	.594	Albuquerque (Dodgers)
1983	Albuquerque (Dodgers)	.594	Portland (Phillies)
1984	Hawaii (Pirates)	.621	Edmonton (Angels)
1985	Hawaii (Pirates)	.587	Vancouver (Brewers)
1986	Vancouver (Brewers)	.616	Las Vegas (Padres)
1987	Calgary (Mariners)	.596	Albuquerque (Dodgers)
1988	Albuquerque (Dodgers)	.605	Las Vegas (Padres)
1989	Albuquerque (Dodgers)	.563	Vancouver (White Sox)
1990	Albuquerque (Dodgers)	.641	Albuquerque (Dodgers)
1991	Albuquerque (Dodgers)	.580	Tucson (Astros)
1992	Colo. Springs (Indians)	.596	Colo. Springs (Indians)
1993	Portland (Twins)	.608	Tucson (Astros)
1994	Albuquerque (Dodgers)	.597	Albuquerque (Dodgers)
1995	Tucson (Astros)	.608	Colo. Springs (Rockies)

*Best overall record   #Co-champions

FRANK RAGSDALE

PACIFIC COAST LEAGUE
1995 BATTING, PITCHING STATISTICS

CLUB BATTING

	AVG	G	AB	R	H	2B	3B	HR	BB	SO	SB
Salt Lake	.304	144	4987	831	1516	332	45	107	455	712	132
Calgary	.302	141	4812	743	1451	306	35	106	398	704	98
Colorado Springs	.291	143	4819	821	1403	293	53	157	444	829	105
Tucson	.289	143	4816	786	1393	285	63	89	555	848	134
Albuquerque	.285	144	4901	754	1396	277	52	111	452	821	92
Vancouver	.281	141	4726	723	1328	237	43	76	504	755	114
Tacoma	.279	144	4874	682	1358	230	49	114	436	845	106
Edmonton	.278	144	4816	759	1340	295	43	86	541	811	80
Las Vegas	.271	144	4789	663	1300	254	32	83	437	840	77
Phoenix	.265	144	4871	658	1289	258	44	81	525	791	66

CLUB PITCHING

	ERA	G	CG	SHO	SV	IP	H	R	ER	BB	SO
Vancouver	4.08	141	14	11	26	1216	1242	620	551	421	782
Albuquerque	4.12	144	6	7	42	1249	1340	688	571	490	919
Tucson	4.50	143	1	8	41	1245	1425	698	623	427	859
Tacoma	4.54	144	10	8	40	1249	1354	734	631	471	771
Las Vegas	4.75	144	15	8	29	1230	1337	780	649	543	794
Phoenix	4.86	144	8	5	28	1276	1436	765	689	496	852
Colorado Springs	4.91	143	4	11	32	1212	1359	760	661	509	803
Salt Lake	5.03	144	10	5	40	1250	1446	773	698	448	754
Edmonton	5.13	144	6	5	32	1239	1384	790	706	541	703
Calgary	5.32	141	7	6	26	1195	1451	812	707	401	719

CLUB FIELDING

	PCT	PO	A	E	DP		PCT	PO	A	E	DP
Salt Lake	.981	3749	1647	103	131	Edmonton	.973	3718	1678	148	151
Vancouver	.978	3647	1459	117	131	Tucson	.973	3734	1592	148	146
Phoenix	.976	3827	1627	134	165	Tacoma	.971	3747	1576	159	130
Albuquerque	.974	3746	1663	144	152	Calgary	.968	3585	1667	174	150
Colo. Springs	.974	3636	1532	139	152	Las Vegas	.967	3691	1591	181	133

Bob Abreu
17 triples

Riccardo Ingram
.348 average

Karim Garcia
.319-20-91

INDIVIDUAL BATTING LEADERS
(Minimum 389 Plate Appearances)

	AVG	G	AB	R	H	2B	3B	HR	RBI	BB	SO	SB
Ingram, Riccardo, Salt Lake	.348	122	477	80	166	43	2	12	85	41	60	4
Hubbard, Trenidad, Colo. Spr.	.340	123	480	102	163	29	7	12	66	61	59	37
Beamon, Trey, Calgary	.334	118	452	74	151	29	5	5	62	39	55	18
Pulliam, Harvey, Colo. Spr.	.327	115	407	90	133	30	6	25	91	49	59	6
Hajek, Dave, Tucson	.327	131	502	99	164	37	4	4	79	39	27	12
Simons, Mitch, Salt Lake	.325	130	480	87	156	34	4	3	46	47	45	32
Garcia, Karim, Albuquerque	.319	124	474	88	151	26	10	20	91	38	102	12
Dunn, Steve, Salt Lake	.316	109	402	57	127	31	1	12	83	30	63	3
Ramos, Ken, Tucson	.315	112	327	57	103	24	8	3	47	51	27	14
Litton, Greg, Tacoma	.309	117	388	58	120	25	4	9	56	43	69	2

INDIVIDUAL PITCHING LEADERS
(Minimum 115 Innings)

	W	L	ERA	G	GS	CG	SV	IP	H	R	ER	BB	SO
Wall, Donne, Tucson	17	6	3.30	28	28	0	0	177	190	72	65	32	119
Williams, Shad, Vancouver	9	7	3.37	25	25	3	0	150	142	65	56	48	114
Johns, Doug, Edmonton	9	5	3.41	23	21	0	0	132	148	55	50	43	70
Sager, A.J., Colo. Springs	8	5	3.50	23	22	1	0	134	153	61	52	23	80
Hawkins, LaTroy, Salt Lake	9	7	3.55	22	22	4	0	144	150	63	57	40	74
Treadwell, Jody, Albuquerque	7	5	3.96	30	15	1	1	125	121	61	55	32	79
McFarlin, Terric, Las Vegas	7	6	3.96	58	2	0	7	123	120	67	54	59	85
Harriger, Denny, Las Vegas	7	9	4.07	29	28	7	0	177	187	94	80	60	97
Holt, Chris, Tucson	5	8	4.10	20	19	0	0	119	155	65	54	32	69
Taylor, Scott, Calgary	5	8	4.11	27	25	1	0	140	144	73	64	35	83

EASTERN
LEAGUE

Reading Wins Title, Ends 22-Year Drought

By ANDREW LINKER

So long the team to be beat, in the end the Reading Phillies were the team to beat. And no one did.

After a wait of 22 summers—most of them long and futile—the Phillies won the 1995 Eastern League playoffs.

They did so in a year that started in chaos in the aftermath of the major league strike. Nearly every team underwent extensive overhauls as many organizations were forced to supplement their initial Double-A rosters with replacement players or younger players not ready for the jump.

"It was strange at the start," Reading manager Bill Dancy said. "Everybody knew they weren't going to have the same club later. Some clubs that started off struggling came on strong at the end."

Reading stayed consistent, spending nearly the entire season either in first or second place in the Southern Division. The Phillies never fell more than four games off the pace before ending the season tied with the Trenton Thunder for the Southern title with a record of 79-63.

The tie, the first in the EL since Waterbury and Reading finished the 1970 regular season with identical records of 78-62, quickly was settled in the playoffs. The Phillies swept the Thunder in three games before using all five games to beat the New Haven Ravens in the finals.

Jay Payton. Eastern League MVP didn't slow down in 1995.

MORRIS FOSTOFF

The Phillies tagged New Haven for 13 of their 21 homers in the postseason. Second baseman David Doster and catcher-first baseman Tommy Eason combined in Reading's eight playoff games for 11 homers, 23 RBIs and 21 runs scored.

"We've had our good times and our bad times, but this is what it's all about," Doster said. "We just got hot in the playoffs."

Ironically, the 1995 Southern Division race was the closest in the EL since the 1973 Phillies—Reading's last playoff champion—finished one-half game ahead of the Sherbrooke Pirates in the league's National Division.

The Mighty Have Fallen

While Reading was climbing to its first title since Mike Schmidt's rookie season in Philadelphia, two of the league's perennial contenders were diving to the bottom.

The defending champion Binghamton Mets, despite having the league's top three prospects in righthanders Paul Wilson and Jason Isringhausen and outfielder Jay Payton, finished fourth in the Northern Division.

All three players were long gone from the EL by the time Reading won its title. Isringhausen (2-1, 2.85) found himself in New York's rotation by midseason while Wilson (6-3, 2.17) and Payton (.345-14-54) left for Triple-A Norfolk at the all-star break.

STANDINGS

Page	NORTH	W	L	PCT	GB	Manager	Attendance/Dates	Last Pennant
122	**Portland Sea Dogs (Marlins)**	86	56	.606	—	Carlos Tosca	429,763 (70)	None
108	**New Haven Ravens (Rockies)**	79	63	.556	7	Paul Zuvella	283,766 (70)	None
167	**Norwich Navigators (Yankees)**	70	71	.496	15½	Jimmy Johnson	281,473 (67)	None
174	**Binghamton Mets (Mets)**	67	75	.472	19	John Tamargo	200,077 (68)	1994
154	**Hardware City Rock Cats (Twins)**	65	77	.458	21	Sal Butera	124,560 (66)	1983

Page	SOUTH	W	L	PCT	GB	Manager	Attendance/Dates	Last Pennant
70	**Trenton Thunder (Red Sox)**	73	69	.514	—	Ken Macha	453,915 (71)	None
186	**Reading Phillies (Phillies)**	73	69	.514	—	Bill Dancy	383,984 (67)	1995
63	**Bowie Baysox (Orioles)**	68	74	.479	5	Bob Miscik	463,976 (67)	None
102	**Canton-Akron Indians (Indians)**	67	75	.472	6	Ted Kubiak	195,049 (62)	None
160	**Harrisburg Senators (Expos)**	61	80	.433	11½	Pat Kelly	240,488 (67)	1993

PLAYOFFS—Semifinals: New Haven defeated Portland 3-1, and Reading defeated Trenton 3-0, in best-of-5 series. **Finals:** Reading defeated New Haven 3-2 in best-of-5 series.

NOTE: Team's individual batting and pitching statistics can be found on page indicated in lefthand column.

Despite playing in only 85 games, Payton had enough plate appearances to win his second batting title in as many summers as a pro. He led the New York-Penn League in 1994.

Without their big three, the Mets finished at 67-75—19 games behind division-leading Portland and only two ahead of last-place Hardware City.

Meanwhile, the Harrisburg Senators, who had the EL's best record since moving from Nashua, N.H., in 1987, finished with the league's worst mark at 61-80.

On The Move

For the 12th time in the last 13 years, the EL had an affiliation switch or franchise relocation. The EL had both in 1995.

The Red Sox ended their 12-year stay in New Britain and replaced the Tigers in Trenton. The Twins moved their Double-A team from Nashville (Southern) to New Britain and became known as the Hardware City Rock Cats. The Yankees' affiliate began its first season as the Norwich Navigators after a 10-year run as the Albany-Colonie Yankees.

Led by Bowie's record of 463,976, the EL broke the 3 million mark in attendance for the first time in its 72-year history.

Top EL Performers. Portland outfielder Bill McMillon, left, led the Eastern League with 162 hits, while Binghamton righthander Paul Wilson led with a 2.17 ERA.

Reading, which set a franchise attendance record for the eighth straight season despite losing four openings to rainouts, came within 17,000 fans of joining Bowie, Trenton and Portland in drawing more than 400,000.

Each of the four surpassed the previous league single-season record of 375,197, set in 1994 by Portland.

Trenton enjoyed the benefits of playing an entire season at resodded Waterfront Park after a fragmented '94 season in which the Thunder played seven home games at neutral sites with a total of only 58 openings while Waterfront was under construction.

The only teams failing to draw at least 200,000 fans were Canton-Akron, which plans to move from Canton to Akron in 1997, and Hardware City, which plans to open a new stadium in 1996 in New Britain.

Soaring attendance throughout the league, however, was no guarantee of franchise stability.

Take the case of the Harrisburg Senators, who have drawn more than 200,000 fans for each of their nine summers since moving from Nashua. Despite their success at the gate, the Senators spent most of the season not knowing their future.

A quartet of investors from suburban Philadelphia, led by Nancy Stein, the wife of Reading Phillies owner Craig Stein, purchased the Senators in January from Jerome Mileur for $4.1 million and threatened to move the franchise to the Allentown-Easton area of Pennsylvania after the '96 season and later to Springfield, Mass.

Quick legislation by Pennsylvania Gov. Tom Ridge effectively blocked the first move. Harrisburg Mayor Stephen Reed prevented the second attempt by agreeing to have the city purchase the team for a record sum of $6.7 million.

LEAGUE CHAMPIONS

Last 25 Years

Year	Regular Season*	Pct.	Playoff
1971	Three Rivers (Reds)	.569	Elmira (Royals)
1972	West Haven (Yankees)	.600	West Haven (Yankees)
1973	Reading (Phillies)	.551	Reading (Phillies)
	Pittsfield (Rangers)	.551	
1974	Bristol (Red Sox)	.548	Thetford Mines (Pirates)
1975	Reading (Phillies)	.613	Bristol (Red Sox)
1976	Three Rivers (Reds)	.601	West Haven (Yankees)
1977	West Haven (Yankees)	.623	West Haven (Yankees)
1978	West Haven (Yankees)	.589	Bristol (Red Sox)
1979	West Haven (Yankees)	.597	None
1980	Bristol (Red Sox)	.568	Holyoke (Brewers)
1981	Glens Falls (White Sox)	.615	Bristol (Red Sox)
1982	West Haven (Athletics)	.614	West Haven (Athletics)
1983	Reading (Phillies)	.686	New Britain (Red Sox)
1984	Albany (Athletics)	.586	Vermont (Reds)
1985	Albany (Yankees)	.589	Vermont (Reds)
1986	Reading (Phillies)	.566	Vermont (Reds)
1987	Pittsfield (Cubs)	.630	Harrisburg (Pirates)
1988	Glens Falls (Tigers)	.583	Albany (Yankees)
1989	Albany (Yankees)	.657	Albany (Yankees)
1990	Albany (Yankees)	.568	London (Tigers)
1991	Harrisburg (Expos)	.621	Albany (Yankees)
1992	Canton-Akron (Indians)	.580	Binghamton (Mets)
1993	Harrisburg (Expos)	.681	Harrisburg (Expos)
1994	Harrisburg (Expos)	.633	Binghamton (Mets)
1995	Portland (Marlins)	.606	Reading (Phillies)

*Best overall record

EASTERN LEAGUE
1995 BATTING, PITCHING STATISTICS

CLUB BATTING

	AVG	G	AB	R	H	2B	3B	HR	BB	SO	SB
Portland	.269	142	4783	745	1286	223	45	93	577	846	140
New Haven	.261	142	4771	699	1243	226	27	87	471	951	145
Norwich	.258	141	4666	635	1206	237	46	89	559	1066	116
Binghamton	.256	142	4803	638	1231	247	35	74	488	864	103
Trenton	.256	142	4829	649	1234	239	33	103	529	935	135
Bowie	.255	142	4678	663	1193	229	16	92	542	838	126
Canton-Akron	.252	142	4599	557	1158	228	21	84	480	939	97
Reading	.252	142	4712	672	1186	236	29	118	494	853	100
Hardware City	.249	142	4717	627	1175	218	28	109	507	965	139
Harrisburg	.243	141	4591	587	1116	217	24	97	469	940	89

CLUB PITCHING

	ERA	G	CG	SHO	SV	IP	H	R	ER	BB	SO
New Haven	3.61	142	3	14	37	1240	1185	592	497	521	951
Trenton	3.78	142	15	8	35	1280	1197	624	538	452	905
Portland	3.78	142	6	9	40	1255	1183	592	528	497	979
Binghamton	3.91	142	15	10	28	1259	1162	625	547	487	897
Reading	3.99	142	7	8	31	1247	1211	634	553	513	991
Hardware City	4.01	142	7	12	26	1247	1236	653	555	500	935
Bowie	4.13	142	7	10	32	1231	1225	681	565	530	892
Canton-Akron	4.24	142	9	9	33	1215	1187	672	573	519	786
Harrisburg	4.31	141	7	6	26	1220	1176	682	584	543	981
Norwich	4.32	141	6	7	39	1232	1265	717	591	554	880

CLUB FIELDING

	PCT	PO	A	E	DP		PCT	PO	A	E	DP
Binghamton	.978	3778	1545	117	129	Canton-Akron	.968	3646	1512	173	136
Reading	.977	3741	1481	122	137	Hardware City	.967	3740	1549	180	120
Portland	.976	3765	1633	134	116	Harrisburg	.967	3659	1438	175	118
Trenton	.972	3839	1575	156	108	Norwich	.965	3695	1525	188	119
New Haven	.970	3719	1494	159	130	Bowie	.965	3693	1485	188	118

Dave Doster
254 total bases

Todd Walker
All-star 2B

Ryan McGuire
.333-7-59

INDIVIDUAL BATTING LEADERS
(Minimum 383 Plate Appearances)

	AVG	G	AB	R	H	2B	3B	HR	RBI	BB	SO	SB
Payton, Jay, Binghamton	.345	85	357	59	123	20	3	14	54	29	32	16
McGuire, Ryan, Trenton	.333	109	414	59	138	29	1	7	59	58	51	11
McMillon, Billy, Portland	.313	141	518	92	162	29	3	14	93	96	90	15
Jacobs, Frank, Bing.-Harr.	.312	101	337	56	105	22	0	13	60	58	56	1
Kennedy, David, New Haven	.306	128	484	75	148	22	2	22	96	48	131	4
Katzaroff, Rob, Portland	.304	116	441	87	134	16	4	10	49	43	33	18
Grable, Rob, Reading	.300	103	353	71	106	24	1	16	67	67	85	15
Echevarria, Angel, N.H.	.300	124	453	78	136	30	1	21	100	56	93	8
Horne, Tyrone, Harr.-Norwich	.291	133	460	82	134	33	5	16	69	84	101	18
Walker, Todd, Hard. City	.290	137	513	83	149	27	3	21	85	63	101	23

INDIVIDUAL PITCHING LEADERS
(Minimum 114 Innings)

	W	L	ERA	G	GS	CG	SV	IP	H	R	ER	BB	SO
Wilson, Paul, Binghamton	6	3	2.17	16	16	4	0	120	89	34	29	24	127
Falteisek, Steve, Harrisburg	9	6	2.95	25	25	5	0	168	152	74	55	64	112
Ludwick, Eric, Binghamton	12	5	2.95	23	22	3	0	143	108	52	47	68	131
Orellano, Rafael, Trenton	11	7	3.09	27	27	2	0	187	146	68	64	72	160
Moore, Joel, New Haven	14	9	3.20	27	26	1	0	157	156	69	56	67	102
Whitten, Casey, Canton	9	8	3.31	20	20	2	0	114	100	49	42	38	91
Serafini, Dan, Hard. City	12	9	3.38	27	27	1	0	163	155	74	61	72	123
Roberts, Brett, Hard. City	11	9	3.41	28	28	5	0	174	162	72	66	50	135
Mendoza, Reynol, Portland	9	10	3.43	27	27	1	0	168	163	73	64	69	120
Whisenant, Matt, Portland	10	6	3.50	23	22	2	0	129	106	57	50	65	107

DEPARTMENT LEADERS

BATTING
G	Billy McMillon, Portland	141
AB	David Doster, Reading	551
R	Ralph Milliard, Portland	104
H	Billy McMillon, Portland	162
TB	David Doster, Reading	254
2B	Jason Hardtke, Binghamton	42
3B	Jason Robertson, Norwich	10
HR	Fred McNair, Reading	23
RBI	Angel Echevarria, New Haven	100
SH	Ralph Milliard, Portland	13
SF	Two tied at	9
BB	Billy McMillon, Portland	96
IBB	Tim Clark, Portland	12
HBP	Nick Delvecchio, Norwich	23
SO	Nick Delvecchio, Norwich	133
SB	Terry Jones, New Haven	51
CS	Damian Jackson, Canton	22
GIDP	Lou Lucca, Portland	18
OB%	Billy McMillon, Portland	.423
SL%	Clyde Pough, Trenton	.543

PITCHING
G	Blake Doolan, Reading	60
GS	Garrett Stephenson, Bowie	29
CG	Three tied at	5
ShO	Mark Tranberg, Reading	3
GF	Jacob Viano, New Haven	49
Sv	Jay Powell, Portland	24
W	Joel Moore, New Haven	14
L	Four tied at	12
IP	Rafael Orellano, Trenton	187
H	Travis Miller, Hardware City	172
R	Mike Buddie, Norwich	102
ER	Neil Weber, Harrisburg	85
HR	Garrett Stephenson, Bowie	23
BB	Mike Buddie, Norwich	81
HB	Garrett Stephenson, Bowie	18
SO	Rafael Orellano, Trenton	160
WP	Reynol Mendoza, Portland	15

FIELDING
C AVG	Charlie Greene, Bing.	995
E	B.J. Waszgis, Bowie	16
PB	B.J. Waszgis, Bowie	23
1B AVG	Brian Daubach, Bing.	.992
E	David Kennedy, N.H.	16
2B AVG	Lamarr Rogers, N.H.	.984
E	Mike Neal, Canton	26
3B AVG	Lou Lucca, Portland	.952
E	Tom Schmidt, Hardware City	30
SS AVG	Neifi Perez, New Haven	.967
E	Damian Jackson, Canton	36
OF AVG	Matt Lawton, Hardware City	.991
E	Two tied at	10

SOUTHERN
LEAGUE

Mudcats Dominate SL From Start To Finish

By LARRY STARKS

The evidence of the Carolina Mudcats' strong—and sometimes spectacular—1995 season could be reduced to a tape for them to review on one of their long bus rides in 1996. They certainly will think it's worth a second look.

There were all those close wins in the first half. There was the great pitching. There was the strong hitting of catcher Jason Kendall and the surprising power numbers of veteran first baseman-DH George Canale.

Indeed, they could watch their thorough domination of the Southern League. The Mudcats led the Eastern Division for 128 of the season's 154 days and had the league's most dominant player and No. 1 prospect in Kendall.

The Mudcats, who won a league-best 89 games during the regular season, capped their year with two straight wins in the finals to capture the first league title in their five-year history, beating the Chattanooga Lookouts, 3-2, in the best-of-5 series.

An 11-7 win over Chattanooga gave the Mudcats their first SL title since moving from Columbus, Ga., to Zebulon, N.C., five years earlier. The final game looked good initially for the Lookouts, who took a 4-1 lead into the fifth inning. But the Mudcats scored six runs in the fifth, led by Omer Munoz and Rob Leary, who each hit two-run doubles to break the game open.

The Mudcats dominated the regular season despite staff ace Steve Parris being promoted to the Pittsburgh Pirates and pitchers Brian Shouse and Milt Hill, and shortstop Kevin Polcovich spending most of the second half at Triple-A Calgary.

Kendall, Canale and righthander Elmer Dessens, who spent the 1994 season in the Mexican League, picked up the slack. Kendall tied for second in the league with a .326 batting average, and Dessens led the league with 15 wins and a 2.49 ERA.

Canale, who played 44 games in the majors with the

Jason Kendall. Carolina catcher led Mudcats to first Southern League title and was named league MVP.

Milwaukee Brewers from 1989-91, had 21 home runs and a league-high 102 RBIs. He also had the league's only three-homer game, May 1 against Jacksonville, and was the only player with six hits in a contest, Aug. 12 against Port City.

Chattanooga Rallies

While the Mudcats played consistent baseball

STANDINGS: OVERALL

Page	Team	W	L	PCT	GB	Manager	Attendance/Dates	Last Pennant
193	Carolina Mudcats (Pirates)	89	55	.618	—	Trent Jewett	317,802 (70)	1995
97	Chattanooga Lookouts (Reds)	83	60	.580	5½	Dave Miley	290,002 (70)	1988
84	Birmingham Barons (White Sox)	80	64	.556	9	Terry Francona	303,066 (70)	1993
90	Orlando Cubs (Cubs)	76	67	.531	12½	Bruce Kimm	191,080 (66)	1991
115	Jacksonville Suns (Tigers)	75	69	.521	14	Bill Plummer	237,433 (69)	None
181	Huntsville Stars (Athletics)	70	74	.486	19	Dick Scott	243,179 (69)	1994
207	Memphis Chicks (Padres)	68	74	.479	20	Jerry Royster	221,302 (68)	1990
220	Port City Roosters (Mariners)	62	80	.437	26	Dave Myers	110,233 (66)	None
56	Greenville Braves (Braves)	59	83	.415	29	Bruce Benedict	223,225 (68)	1992
231	Knoxville Smokies (Blue Jays)	54	90	.375	35	Garth Iorg	123,428 (68)	1978

NOTE: Team's individual batting and pitching statistics can be found on page indicated in lefthand column.

throughout the season, Chattanooga started slowly, losing its first 10 games. A roster makeover enabled the Lookouts to finish with the league's second-best overall record.

The Lookouts shipped most of their young talent to Class A and raided the Triple-A Indianapolis roster. By the end of the season, their roster included 12 players who spent at least half of the 1994 season in Triple-A.

As a result, the Lookouts were 83-50 after the first 10 games, including 47-24 in the second half. Even with their sluggish start, they dominated the league offensively.

The Lookouts led the league with a .280 team batting average and averaged 9.5 hits and 5.1 runs a game. They also had four players among the top 10 hitters, led by journeyman outfielder Dan Rohrmeier, who hit .326.

They had the league's most consistent pitcher in Tommy Kramer, who went 12-1 after being added to the roster near the end of May.

There were plenty of other excellent performances throughout the league in 1995.

Birmingham pitcher Luis Andujar turned in the league's only no-hitter, beating the Memphis Chicks 1-0 on Aug. 8. It was merely the continuation of his strong turnaround. Andujar lost his first six games, then rebounded to go 14-8 and ended the season in the rotation of the parent Chicago White Sox.

The most unique pitching performance belonged to Chicks knuckleballer Rob Mattson, who started a game May 2 against Greenville and went four innings before the game was suspended by rain. He came back the following day to complete a 9-0 shutout.

STANDINGS: SPLIT SEASON

FIRST HALF

EAST	W	L	PCT	GB
Carolina	45	27	.625	—
Orlando	41	30	.577	3½
Greenville	35	37	.486	10
Port City	32	39	.451	12½
Jacksonville	32	40	.444	13

WEST	W	L	PCT	GB
Memphis	40	32	.556	—
Chattanooga	36	36	.500	4
Huntsville	35	37	.486	5
Birmingham	33	39	.458	7
Knoxville	30	42	.417	10

SECOND HALF

EAST	W	L	PCT	GB
Carolina	44	28	.611	—
Jacksonville	43	29	.597	1
Orlando	35	37	.486	9
Port City	30	41	.423	13½
Greenville	24	46	.343	19

WEST	W	L	PCT	GB
Chattanooga	47	24	.662	—
Birmingham	47	25	.653	½
Huntsville	35	37	.486	12½
Memphis	28	42	.400	18½
Knoxville	24	48	.333	23½

PLAYOFFS—Semifinals: Carolina defeated Orlando 3-2, and Chattanooga defeated Memphis 3-2, in best-of-5 series. **Finals:** Carolina defeated Chattanooga 3-2, in best-of-5 series.

George Canale. 103 RBIs led league.

Jacksonville first baseman Ivan Cruz led a power barrage by hitting 31 homers, 10 more than Canale. It was the most homers in the SL since Birmingham's Rondal Rollin hit 39 in 1987.

On the bases, Birmingham second baseman Essex Burton stole 60 bases, his fourth consecutive year with 60 or more.

Teams On The Move

Off the field, there was plenty of news as well.

The league waited until the last minute to find a home for the orphan Port City Roosters franchise, which spent the 1993-94 seasons sharing Nashville's Herschel Greer Stadium with the Triple-A Nashville Sounds.

The team has been without a permanent home since it was uprooted from Charlotte when that city was granted a Triple-A expansion franchise for the 1993 season. Efforts to locate the team in New Orleans, Lexington, Ky., and San Juan, P.R., fell through, forcing the league to settle for a makeshift stadium on the campus of the University of North Carolina-Wilmington little more than a month before the start of the '95 season.

The stadium fell far short of Double-A standards and the team drew only 110,233, the poorest attendance in Double-A.

The league thought it had a deal for the team to gain permanent residency in Springfield, Mo. However, a ballot initiative for a half-cent sales tax that would have been used to partly finance a new stadium failed.

League officials also had to deal with the prospect of losing the Memphis Chicks, who had been in the league since 1978. Chicks president David Hersh signed a letter of intent to swap franchises with the Triple-A Nashville Sounds, whose owner Larry Schmittou wanted to downgrade to Double-A. Hersh had wanted Memphis to become a Triple-A franchise for the 1996 season, but the White Sox, whose player development contract with Nashville runs through 1996, balked at the switch.

The league settled territorial concerns by the end of the season and the Chicks said their first year in Triple-A will be in 1997.

LEAGUE CHAMPIONS

Last 25 Years

Year	Regular Season*	Pct.	Playoff
1971	Charlotte (Twins)	.647	Charlotte (Twins)
1972	Asheville (Orioles)	.583	Montgomery (Tigers)
1973	Montgomery (Tigers)	.579	Montgomery (Tigers)
1974	Jacksonville (Royals)	.565	Knoxville (White Sox)
1975	Orlando (Twins)	.586	Montgomery (Tigers)
1976	Montgomery (Tigers)	.591	Montgomery (Tigers)
1977	Montgomery (Tigers)	.627	Montgomery (Tigers)
1978	Knoxville (White Sox)	.611	Knoxville (White Sox)
1979	Columbus (Astros)	.587	Nashville (Reds)
1980	Nashville (Yankees)	.678	Charlotte (Orioles)
1981	Nashville (Yankees)	.566	Orlando (Twins)
1982	Jacksonville (Royals)	.576	Nashville (Yankees)
1983	Birmingham (Tigers)	.627	Birmingham (Tigers)
1984	Greenville (Braves)	.567	Charlotte (Orioles)
1985	Knoxville (Blue Jays)	.552	Huntsville (Athletics)
1986	Huntsville (Athletics)	.553	Columbus (Astros)
1987	Jacksonville (Expos)	.590	Birmingham (White Sox)
1988	Greenville (Braves)	.604	Chattanooga (Reds)
1989	Birmingham (White Sox)	.615	Birmingham (White Sox)
1990	Orlando (Twins)	.590	Memphis (Royals)
1991	Greenville (Braves)	.611	Orlando (Twins)
1992	Greenville (Braves)	.699	Greenville (Braves)
1993	Birmingham (White Sox)	.549	Birmingham (White Sox)
1994	Huntsville (Athletics)	.587	Huntsville (Athletics)
1995	Carolina (Pirates)	.618	Carolina (Pirates)

*Best overall record

SOUTHERN LEAGUE
1995 BATTING, PITCHING STATISTICS

CLUB BATTING

	AVG	G	AB	R	H	2B	3B	HR	BB	SO	SB
Chattanooga	.280	143	4885	730	1366	259	36	127	480	808	91
Carolina	.270	144	5023	689	1358	257	31	86	445	826	129
Greenville	.268	142	4772	680	1278	263	29	132	431	1006	90
Birmingham	.264	144	4726	688	1249	225	23	83	554	868	155
Orlando	.261	143	4736	617	1235	233	28	82	454	786	83
Memphis	.258	142	4753	624	1225	205	39	116	389	1057	165
Port City	.253	142	4814	604	1216	229	24	93	500	948	107
Huntsville	.251	144	4779	643	1200	202	30	119	552	1027	113
Knoxville	.244	144	4619	577	1125	221	39	62	442	989	181
Jacksonville	.231	144	4720	620	1091	214	25	132	506	1055	103

CLUB PITCHING

	ERA	G	CG	SHO	SV	IP	H	R	ER	BB	SO
Orlando	3.41	143	6	14	43	1258	1174	563	477	413	892
Carolina	3.48	144	7	14	44	1322	1267	611	511	418	979
Port City	3.62	142	5	6	27	1264	1179	617	508	475	989
Birmingham	3.73	144	8	9	35	1248	1208	599	517	413	962
Jacksonville	3.73	144	13	8	36	1287	1303	621	533	476	854
Chattanooga	3.78	143	4	9	44	1258	1239	633	528	488	1033
Huntsville	4.03	144	1	7	39	1249	1230	637	559	433	865
Memphis	4.32	142	15	5	32	1236	1191	704	593	652	1058
Greenville	4.65	142	7	4	34	1235	1303	726	638	477	819
Knoxville	4.76	144	6	12	32	1222	1249	761	646	508	919

CLUB FIELDING

	PCT	PO	A	E	DP		PCT	PO	A	E	DP
Jacksonville	.976	3860	1779	139	167	Memphis	.971	3708	1411	155	122
Orlando	.973	3773	1531	146	121	Birmingham	.970	3745	1507	165	132
Huntsville	.971	3747	1663	161	151	Chattanooga	.969	3775	1358	163	122
Carolina	.971	3967	1639	168	139	Greenville	.969	3704	1466	165	111
Port City	.971	3792	1610	163	161	Knoxville	.966	3667	1479	183	129

Ivan Cruz
31 homers

Robin Jennings
.296-17-79

James Bonnici
246 total bases

INDIVIDUAL BATTING LEADERS
(Minimum 389 Plate Appearances)

	AVG	G	AB	R	H	2B	3B	HR	RBI	BB	SO	SB
Coughlin, Kevin, Birmingham	.385	96	327	56	126	29	2	3	49	34	43	5
Kendall, Jason, Carolina	.326	117	429	87	140	26	1	8	71	56	22	10
Rohrmeier, Dan, Chattanooga	.326	118	426	77	139	31	0	17	76	41	63	0
Swann, Pedro, Greenville	.324	102	339	57	110	24	2	11	64	45	63	14
Valdes, Pedro, Orlando	.300	114	426	57	128	28	3	7	68	37	77	3
Larregui, Ed, Orlando	.300	122	423	55	127	18	1	11	60	32	39	3
Koelling, Brian, Chattanooga	.296	107	432	71	128	21	7	3	44	40	63	30
Jennings, Robin, Orlando	.296	132	490	71	145	27	7	17	79	44	61	7
Santana, Ruben, Chattanooga	.293	142	556	89	163	23	10	11	79	50	77	2
Ladell, Cleveland, Chattanooga	.292	135	517	76	151	19	7	5	43	39	88	28

INDIVIDUAL PITCHING LEADERS
(Minimum 115 Innings)

	W	L	ERA	G	GS	CG	SV	IP	H	R	ER	BB	SO
Dessens, Elmer, Carolina	15	8	2.49	27	27	1	0	152	170	62	42	21	68
Sodowsky, Clint, Jacksonville	5	5	2.55	19	19	5	0	124	102	46	35	50	77
Miller, Trever, Jacksonville	8	2	2.72	31	16	3	0	122	122	46	37	34	77
Ruebel, Matt, Carolina	13	5	2.76	27	27	4	0	169	150	68	52	45	136
Wagner, Matt, Port City	5	8	2.82	23	23	0	0	137	121	.57	43	33	111
Andujar, Luis, Birmingham	14	8	2.85	27	27	2	0	167	147	64	53	44	146
Telemaco, Amaury, Orlando	8	8	3.29	22	22	3	0	148	112	60	54	42	151
Kramer, Tommy, Chattanooga	12	1	3.33	21	18	2	0	127	117	54	47	28	126
Ratliff, Jon, Orlando	10	5	3.47	26	25	1	0	140	143	67	54	42	94
Kroon, Marc, Memphis	7	5	3.51	22	19	0	2	115	90	49	45	61	123

BATTING

G	Three tied at	142
AB	Ruben Santana, Chatt.	556
R	Essex Burton, Birmingham	95
H	Ruben Santana, Chatt.	163
TB	James Bonnici, Port City	246
2B	James Bonnici, Port City	36
3B	Lorenzo De la Cruz, Knoxville	12
HR	Ivan Cruz, Jacksonville	31
RBI	George Canale, Carolina	102
SH	Two tied at	15
SF	Scott Spiezio, Huntsville	14
BB	Shannon Stewart, Knoxville	89
IBB	Two tied at	15
HBP	Lorenzo De la Cruz, Knoxville	15
SO	Glen Barker, Jacksonville	143
SB	Essex Burton, Birmingham	60
CS	Essex Burton, Birmingham	22
GIDP	Craig Wilson, Birmingham	21
OB%	Kevin Coughlin, Birmingham	.448
SL%	Ivan Cruz, Jacksonville	.564

PITCHING

G	John Kelly, Jacksonville	66
GS	Bobby Chouinard, Huntsville	29
CG	Rob Mattson, Memphis	11
ShO	Three tied at	3
Sv	Two tied at	29
W	Elmer Dessens, Carolina	15
L	Rob Mattson, Memphis	13
IP	Rob Mattson, Memphis	202
H	Rob Mattson, Memphis	199
R	Brad Kaufman, Memphis	112
ER	Two tied at	95
HR	Mike Hostetler, Greenville	24
BB	Brad Kaufman, Memphis	90
HB	Rob Mattson, Memphis	20
SO	Osvaldo Fernandez, Port City	160
WP	Robbie Beckett, Memphis	19

FIELDING

C AVG	Scott Vollmer, Birmingham	.992
E	Raul Casanova, Memphis	12
PB	Jason Varitek, Port City	21
1B AVG	James Bonnici, Port City	.995
E	D.J. Boston, Knoxville	17
2B AVG	Frank Catalanotto, Jack.	.974
E	Essex Burton, Birmingham	29
3B AVG	Greg Norton, Birmingham	.938
E	Scott Spiezio, Huntsville	29
SS AVG	Pablo Martinez, Green.	.966
E	Craig Wilson, Birmingham	34
OF AVG	Adam Hyzdu, Chatt.	.995
E	Ramon Espinosa, Carolina	11

HONOR ROLL

OFFICIAL ALL-STAR TEAM

C—Jason Kendall, Carolina. **1B**—James Bonnici, Port City. **2B**—Brian Koelling, Chattanooga. **3B**—Scott Spiezio, Huntsville. **SS**—Desi Relaford, Port City. **OF**—Jermaine Dye, Greenville; Robin Jennings, Orlando; Charles Poe, Birmingham; Pedro Valdes, Orlando. **DH**—Ivan Cruz, Jacksonville.

RHP—Luis Andujar, Birmingham; Elmer Dessens, Carolina. **LHP**—Matt Ruebel, Carolina.

MVP—Jason Kendall, Carolina.

Manager of the Year—Bruce Kimm, Orlando.

TOP 10 PROSPECTS
(Selected by league managers)
1. Jason Kendall, c, Carolina
2. Robert Smith, 3b, Greenville
3. Jermaine Dye, of, Greenville
4. Pedro Valdes, of, Orlando
5. Luis Andujar, rhp, Birmingham
6. Shannon Stewart, of, Knoxville
7. Robin Jennings, of, Orlando
8. Marc Kroon, rhp, Memphis
9. Desi Relaford, ss, Port City
10. Brian Lesher, of, Huntsville

TEXAS LEAGUE

Shreveport Overcomes Obstacles To Win

By GEORGE SCHROEDER

Despite uncertainty concerning the future of the franchise, the Shreveport Captains dominated the Texas League in 1995.

At one point, it appeared the Captains' 10th consecutive Texas League playoffs appearance might be a farewell to the city. After unsuccessful attempts to attract local buyers, Captains owner Taylor Moore had a tentative deal with investors from Austin, Texas, until it fizzled in midseason.

But the Captains were unfazed by the off-field rumors. Buoyed by pitching and defense, they won the Eastern Division title in both halves, then polished off Western Division champion Midland, 4-1, in the Texas League championship series.

"You never forget something like this," Captains manager Ron Wotus said. "It's a lot of hard work. We spent a long time when you look back to spring training."

The Captains were magnificent. They finished 88-47, the best record in club history. The Captains lost only two series all season, both to Arkansas, and never dropped more than three consecutive games.

In what has recently become tradition, the San Francisco Giants summoned three pitchers directly to the big leagues from Shreveport. Righthanders Jamie Brewington and Carlos Valdez made the jump at midseason; lefthander Shawn Estes was called up after the Texas League championship series.

Ron Wotus

Other key player moves included six promotions to Triple-A Phoenix. But the Captains never slowed down. They just plugged in new parts and kept winning, hitting .280 as a team even though no starter hit more than .300. Shreveport also led the league in ERA (3.28).

But Shreveport wasn't satisfied with a stellar regular season.

"Not to win a championship would be an unsuccessful season," outfielder Jacob Cruz said before the

George Arias. Midland third baseman had heavenly season with 30 homers, 104 RBIs.

series.

In the championship series, Shreveport showed its versatility, winning a pair of 1-0 games at Midland to return to Shreveport up two games to one. Cruz singled home the only run in both wins.

Back home, the Captains' offense revved up in a pair of victories, 7-2 and 5-1.

In the final game, four Shreveport pitchers allowed five hits. Desi Wilson's fifth-inning double pushed Shreveport ahead for good, and the Captains cruised home with the championship.

It was Shreveport's third TL championship in six years (1990, 1991), but manager Ron Wotus' first in three seasons despite reaching the playoffs each year.

The Captains even became the first Texas League club to host the Double-A all-star game, making the city's 100th season of professional baseball even better. Shreveport fans filled Fair Grounds Field to capacity (6,247) to watch the American League affiliates beat the National League affiliates, 3-1.

Midland's Mario Mendoza was the American League's skipper and Wotus was a coach for the

STANDINGS: OVERALL

Page		W	L	PCT	GB	Manager	Attendance/Dates	Last Pennant
213	**Shreveport Captains (Giants)**	88	47	.652	—	Ron Wotus	173,996 (67)	1995
134	**Wichita Wranglers (Royals)**	72	64	.603	16½	Ron Johnson	203,134 (66)	1992
200	**Arkansas Travelers (Cardinals)**	70	65	.519	18	Mike Ramsey	248,340 (56)	1989
148	**El Paso Diablos (Brewers)**	68	68	.500	20½	Tim Ireland	329,233 (68)	1994
77	**Midland Angels (Angels)**	66	70	.485	22½	Mario Mendoza	202,830 (66)	1975
141	**San Antonio Missions (Dodgers)**	64	72	.471	24½	John Shelby	387,090 (67)	None
128	**Jackson Generals (Astros)**	62	73	.459	26	Tim Tolman	171,508 (65)	1993
226	**Tulsa Drillers (Rangers)**	52	83	.385	36	Bobby Jones	321,662 (64)	1988

NOTE: Team's individual batting and pitching statistics can be found on page indicated in lefthand column.

National League.

Midland won the Western Division's first-half title behind the power hitting of George Arias and Todd Greene, who combined for 56 home runs and 194 RBIs. Greene was promoted to Triple-A Vancouver shortly after midseason.

In the second half, Wichita took the West, winning by eight games over El Paso, which was shut out of the playoffs for the first time in six years.

While Shreveport waited, Midland took the Western Division playoff, three games to two.

Attendance Holds Steady

Midland, El Paso and Jackson all set attendance records in 1995. Overall, attendance was down 3.4 percent from 1994's record, but Texas League commissioner Tom Kayser was more than satisfied with the third-highest total in league history: 2,037,793.

"We went over two million this year, only the fourth time we've ever done it," Kayser said. "You can't feel too badly about that."

Despite the best record of any full-season team in professional baseball, and despite winning the TL's Eastern Division in both halves of the split-season format, the Captains finished seventh in attendance, drawing an average of 2,597 and a total of 173,996 fans, down nearly 28,000 from 1994.

Moore said he expected some drop-off in 1995 and attributed much of the losses to the uncertainty sur-

Johnny Damon. Wichita all-star outfielder hit .343 with a career-best 16 homers, earning a promotion to Kansas City.

TOM DiPACE

rounding the Captains' future in Shreveport.

"Part of the reason was the sale (to the Austin group) was still alive and pending past April 30, past when most of our major promotions were booked," Moore said. "So we went the whole year with about as few promotions as a minor league club can go. We didn't have the Phillie Phanatic. We didn't have the Chicken. We had one buy-out the whole year.

"Given the marketing situation and all the potential negotiations, it didn't surprise me."

The Captains will remain in Shreveport for at least one more season. Moore continued negotiations with city officials in hopes of reaching an agreement on leasing Fair Grounds Field.

Damon Possession

Shreveport dominated team competition, but Wichita Wranglers outfielder Johnny Damon dominated league pitchers.

Damon ran, hit, caught and threw his way to no-contest awards as the league's top prospect and MVP.

"I could see he was special after four innings of the first game we played them, and that's no exaggeration," El Paso manager Tim Ireland said.

Damon hit .343 with a career-high 16 homers and finished among league leaders in five categories, despite missing most of the final month when he was called up by Kansas City. Damon was second in batting, third in hits (145), fourth in triples (9), third in runs scored (83) and first in on-base percentage (.434) and slugging (.534).

"He was just unbelievable," Tulsa manager Bobby Jones said. "He was fouling pitches off he didn't want. He was hitting home runs, getting walks and bunting for hits. He was so far ahead of the other guys it was unbelievable.

TEXAS LEAGUE
1995 BATTING, PITCHING STATISTICS

CLUB BATTING

	AVG	G	AB	R	H	2B	3B	HR	BB	SO	SB
El Paso	.286	136	4656	733	1331	274	67	84	527	889	83
Midland	.284	136	4681	726	1328	235	50	136	468	856	110
Wichita	.282	136	4701	685	1328	243	34	99	429	668	143
Shreveport	.280	135	4644	733	1302	267	35	85	546	742	108
Arkansas	.268	135	4387	617	1176	199	32	100	492	787	86
San Antonio	.265	136	4556	585	1209	228	34	86	446	833	119
Jackson	.262	135	4488	541	1174	203	24	86	427	689	78
Tulsa	.257	135	4513	540	1160	202	35	72	424	683	54

CLUB PITCHING

	ERA	G	CG	SHO	SV	IP	H	R	ER	BB	SO
Shreveport	3.28	135	6	14	44	1221	1181	530	445	432	748
San Antonio	3.76	136	6	5	38	1202	1214	586	503	482	783
Jackson	3.90	135	8	7	35	1186	1123	607	514	495	815
Arkansas	3.94	135	7	7	41	1154	1178	602	506	374	751
Wichita	4.30	136	3	5	45	1212	1243	668	579	478	821
Tulsa	4.55	135	9	6	24	1177	1318	692	596	485	651
El Paso	4.58	136	7	4	38	1199	1372	764	610	558	866
Midland	4.68	136	13	3	29	1196	1379	711	622	455	712

CLUB FIELDING

	PCT	PO	A	E	DP		PCT	PO	A	E	DP
Shreveport	.975	3663	1578	136	150	Midland	.971	3589	1624	158	169
Jackson	.973	3557	1538	144	144	Tulsa	.969	3532	1547	162	143
San Antonio	.972	3606	1568	148	137	Wichita	.968	3635	1512	169	125
Arkansas	.971	3462	1621	154	125	El Paso	.960	3598	1552	212	136

Wilton Guerrero
Batting champ

Todd Greene
All-star catcher

INDIVIDUAL BATTING LEADERS
(Minimum 367 Plate Appearances)

	AVG	G	AB	R	H	2B	3B	HR	RBI	BB	SO	SB
Guerrero, Wilton, San An.	.348	95	382	53	133	13	6	0	26	26	63	21
Damon, Johnny, Wichita	.343	111	423	83	145	15	9	16	54	67	35	26
Berblinger, Jeff, Arkansas	.319	87	332	66	106	15	4	5	29	48	40	16
Carvajal, Jovino, Midland	.313	79	348	58	109	13	5	2	23	18	42	39
Lopez, Roberto, El Paso	.312	114	417	80	130	22	8	1	44	77	63	9
Mueller, Bill, Shreveport	.309	88	330	56	102	16	2	1	39	53	36	6
Williamson, Antone, El Paso	.309	104	392	62	121	30	6	7	90	47	57	3
Banks, Brian, El Paso	.308	128	441	81	136	39	10	12	78	81	113	9
Myers, Rod, Wichita	.307	131	499	71	153	22	6	7	62	34	77	29
Monell, Johnny, Tulsa	.306	121	434	55	133	18	1	12	64	67	52	0

INDIVIDUAL PITCHING LEADERS
(Minimum 109 Innings)

	W	L	ERA	G	GS	CG	SV	IP	H	R	ER	BB	SO
Rath, Gary, San Antonio	13	3	2.77	18	18	3	0	117	96	42	36	48	81
Bourgeois, Steve, Shreveport	12	3	2.85	22	22	2	0	145	140	50	46	53	91
Narcisse, Tyrone, Jackson	5	14	3.24	27	27	2	0	164	140	76	59	60	93
Busby, Mike, Arkansas	7	6	3.29	20	20	1	0	134	125	63	49	35	95
Lidle, Cory, El Paso	5	4	3.36	45	9	0	2	110	126	52	41	36	78
Pyc, Dave, San Antonio	12	6	3.38	26	26	1	0	157	170	72	59	49	78
Soderstrom, Steve, Shreveport	9	5	3.41	22	22	0	0	116	106	53	44	51	91
Browne, Byron, El Paso	10	4	3.43	25	20	2	0	126	106	55	48	78	110
Simmons, Scott, Arkansas	11	9	3.43	22	22	1	0	139	145	66	53	28	73
Keling, Korey, Midland	8	5	3.46	29	12	1	1	122	113	53	47	52	101

DEPARTMENT LEADERS

BATTING
G	George Arias, Midland	134
AB	George Arias, Midland	520
R	George Arias, Midland	91
H	Rod Myers, Wichita	153
TB	George Arias, Midland	274
2B	Brian Banks, El Paso	39
3B	Leon Glenn, Midland	11
HR	George Arias, Midland	30
RBI	George Arias, Midland	104
SH	Ramon Martinez, Wichita	18
SF	Ramon Martinez, Wichita	9
BB	Brian Banks, El Paso	81
IBB	Johnny Damon, Wichita	13
HBP	Sal Fasano, Wichita	16
SO	Leon Glenn, Midland	126
SB	Felix Martinez, Wichita	44
CS	Wilton Guerrero, San Antonio	22
GIDP	Todd Landry, El Paso	21
OB%	Johnny Damon, Wichita	.434
SL%	Johnny Damon, Wichita	.534

PITCHING
G	Steve Montgomery, Arkansas	55
GS	Ryan Hancock, Midland	28
CG	Ryan Hancock, Midland	5
ShO	Two tied at	2
GF	Steve Montgomery, Arkansas	53
Sv	Steve Montgomery, Arkansas	36
W	Two tied at	13
L	Tyrone Narcisse, Jackson	14
IP	Ryan Hancock, Midland	176
H	Ryan Hancock, Midland	222
R	Ryan Hancock, Midland	107
ER	Ryan Hancock, Midland	89
HR	Chad Wiley, Tulsa	19
BB	Frankie Rodriguez, El Paso	80
SO	Frankie Rodriguez, El Paso	129
WP	Jeff Schmidt, Midland	17

FIELDING
C AVG	Paul Ellis, Arkansas	.998
E	Rogelio Nunez, Tulsa	17
1B AVG	Dan Melendez, San Antonio	.997
E	Frank Charles, Tulsa	19
2B AVG	Orlando Munoz, Midland	.994
E	Jay Canizaro, Shreveport	19
3B AVG	Bill Mueller, Shreveport	.977
E	George Arias, Midland	29
SS AVG	Russ Johnson, Jackson	.978
E	Felix Martinez, Wichita	50
OF AVG	Anthony Lewis, Arkansas	1.000
E	James Martin, San Antonio	12

HONOR ROLL

OFFICIAL ALL-STAR TEAM
C—Todd Greene, Midland. 1B—Todd Landry, El Paso. 2B—Jeff Berblinger, Arkansas. 3B—George Arias, Midland. SS—Wilton Guerrero, San Antonio. OF—Brian Banks, El Paso; Jacob Cruz, Shreveport; Johnny Damon, Wichita. DH—Oreste Marrero, San Ant.

P—Steve Bourgeois, Shreveport; Edwin Corps, Shreveport; Steve Montgomery, Arkansas; David Pyc, San Antonio; Gary Rath, San Antonio; Billy Wagner, Jackson.

Player of the Year—Johnny Damon, Wichita. **Pitcher of the Year**—Steve Bourgeois, Shreveport.

Manager—Ron Johnson, Wichita.

TOP 10 PROSPECTS
(Selected by league managers)
1. Johnny Damon, of, Wichita
2. Billy Wagner, lhp, Jackson
3. Jamie Brewington, rhp, Shreveport
4. Richard Hidalgo, of, Jackson
5. Todd Greene, c, Midland
6. George Arias, 3b, Midland
7. Gary Rath, lhp, San Antonio
8. Felix Martinez, ss, Wichita
9. Mike Gulan, 3b, Arkansas
10. Wilton Guerrero, ss, San Antonio

CALIFORNIA
LEAGUE

Dodgers Provide Magic Touch For Spirit

By MAUREEN DELANY

Once the most successful club in the California League, the San Bernardino Spirit had fallen on hard times the past few years. But all that changed in 1995.

The city of San Bernardino fueled a dramatic change in fortune for the Spirit by agreeing to build a new stadium, which lured the nearby Los Angeles Dodgers to switch their affiliation from Bakersfield to the Spirit, who finished 40 games under .500 in 1994.

The Spirit immediately turned things around on the field, winning their first-ever Cal League title. San Bernardino finished 30 games over .500, won the first half of the Southern Division and then swept Lake Elsinore and San Jose in the league's expanded playoffs to win the crown.

Within days of that triumph and after several delays in the financing, the city finally began construction of a $12 million, 5,000-seat stadium.

The Spirit, who set league attendance records in 1989 and 1990, lost their franchise following the 1992 season when it was relocated to Rancho Cucamonga. The city got another team when the Salinas Spurs moved to San Bernardino in December of that year, but the team was forced to operate as a co-op entry and continued to play in an old and inadequate stadium.

Paul Konerko

Spirit second baseman Adam Riggs was named the league's MVP, but it was catcher Paul Konerko who led the Spirit to the league title.

Konerko, the Dodgers' first-round draft pick in 1994, hit four home runs in three games against San Jose in the championship series. Konerko also set up the game-winning runs in decisive Game Three when he bunted over two runners in the top of the ninth, with the score tied 4-4. Shortstop Keith Johnson then drove in both runs with a single up the middle, for a 6-4 San Bernardino win.

MVP Season. Second baseman Adam Riggs led San Bernardino to the 1995 Cal League title, hitting .362 with 24 home runs.

"This is the kind of game you want to win a title on," Spirit manager Ron Roenicke said. "This is the way we've won all year."

The Spirit led the league in hitting (.284), home runs (154) and stolen bases (246).

Attendance Soared

Attendance in the Cal League continued to set records, again a result of beautiful new stadiums in Rancho Cucamonga and Lake Elsinore.

The Rancho Cucamonga Quakes broke their own

STANDINGS: OVERALL

Page		W	L	PCT	GB	Manager	Attendance/Dates	Last Pennant
142	San Bernardino Spirit (Dodgers)	84	54	.609	—	Ron Roenicke	119,434 (66)	1995
77	Lake Elsinore Storm (Angels)	81	57	.587	3	Mitch Seoane	383,297 (70)	None
181	Modesto A's (Athletics)	78	62	.557	7	Glenn Ezell	100,108 (69)	1984
214	San Jose Giants (Giants)	77	63	.550	8	Carlos Lezcano	140,976 (69)	1979
149	Stockton Ports (Brewers)	74	65	.532	10 ½	Bob Mariano	107,140 (67)	1992
220	Riverside Pilots (Mariners)	72	67	.518	12 ½	Dave Brundage	56,601 (69)	None
202	Rancho Cucamonga Quakes (Padres)	68	70	.493	16	Marty Barrett	446,146 (70)	1994
235	Bakersfield Blaze (Co-op)	58	82	.414	27	Greg Mahlberg	105,890 (70)	1989
235	Visalia Oaks (Co-op)	58	82	.414	27	Lyle Yates	71,513 (69)	1978
64	High Desert Mavericks (Orioles)	46	94	.329	39	Tim Blackwell	146,355 (70)	1993

NOTE: Team's individual batting and pitching statistics can be found on page indicated in lefthand column.

Top Pitcher. Lake Elsinore lefthander Matt Beaumont won 16 games and was selected the Cal League's top pitcher.

LEAGUE CHAMPIONS
Last 25 Years

Year	Regular Season*	Pct.	Playoff
1971	Modesto (Cardinals)	.597	Visalia (Mets)
1972	Bakersfield (Dodgers)	.629	Modesto (Cardinals)
1973	Lodi (Orioles)	.550	Lodi (Orioles)
	Salinas (Angels)	.550	
1974	Fresno (Giants)	.607	Fresno (Giants)
1975	Reno (Twins/Padres)	.614	None
1976	Salinas (Angels)	.650	Reno (Twins/Padres)
1977	Fresno (Giants)	.592	Lodi (Dodgers)
1978	Visalia (Twins)	.697	Visalia (Twins)
1979	San Jose (Mariners)	.636	San Jose (Mariners)
1980	Stockton (Brewers)	.638	Stockton (Brewers)
1981	Visalia (Twins)	.621	Lodi (Dodgers)
1982	Modesto (Athletics)	.671	Modesto (Athletics)
1983	Visalia (Twins)	.621	Redwood (Angels)
1984	Redwood (Angels)	.654	Modesto (Athletics)
1985	Salinas (Mariners)	.618	Fresno (Giants)
1986	Palm Springs (Angels)	.612	Stockton (Brewers)
1987	Stockton (Brewers)	.667	Fresno (Giants)
1988	Stockton (Brewers)	.657	Riverside (Padres)
1989	Stockton (Brewers)	.626	Bakersfield (Dodgers)
1990	Visalia (Twins)	.638	Stockton (Brewers)
1991	San Jose (Giants)	.676	High Desert (Padres)
1992	Stockton (Brewers)	.604	Stockton (Brewers)
1993	High Desert (Marlins)	.620	High Desert (Marlins)
1994	Modesto (Athletics)	.706	Rancho Cuca. (Padres)
1995	San Bern. (Dodgers)	.609	San Bern. (Dodgers)

*Best overall record

league record by almost 60,000 with 446,146 fans in 1995. Lake Elsinore, in its second season, wasn't far behind with 383,297.

Attendance in Riverside floundered for the third straight season, falling from 85,358 in 1994 to 56,601. That prompted the club to relocate to Lancaster after the 1995 season.

Michael Ellis had purchased the Pilots in November 1994 and hoped to revive the slumping franchise. But the Pilots continued to draw poorly, in part because they were one of only two clubs in the National Association that were not permitted to sell alcoholic beverages.

The city of Lancaster began construction of a new stadium in August, meaning that all five Southern Division teams would play in state-of-the-art facilities in 1996.

Attendance continued to falter in High Desert, despite a new working agreement with the Baltimore Orioles. The Mavericks won a league title in 1993 as a farm club of the Florida Marlins, but fell to the bottom of the standings as a co-op team in 1994 and continued to bring up the rear in 1995.

Bakersfield wasn't the only club without a major league affiliate in 1995. The Visalia Oaks also operated as a co-op after losing their affiliation with Colorado after the 1994 season. Both teams finished with identical 58-82 records, tied for eighth best in the league.

Visalia is partially owned by Japanese interests and had 11 Japanese players on its roster, including Masataka Endo, who led the league with 178 strikeouts and six complete games.

Offensive Cycle

Eight hitters finished above .320 for the season, as compared to one in 1994. The dominant offensive performer was Riggs, an obscure 22nd-round draft pick in 1994 who won the batting title (.362) and led the league in hits (196), doubles (39) and runs (111), and was third in homers (24) and RBIs (106).

Perhaps the most remarkable offensive feat of the season was that four players hit for the cycle—including two in one day. Rancho Cucamonga first baseman Derrek Lee and Lake Elsinore DH Earl Cunningham did it in May, and Modesto outfielder Gary Hust and Stockton infielder Brad Seitzer both hit for the cycle Sept. 1. Hitting for the cycle had been achieved only four times in the previous six years in the Cal League.

Riverside third baseman Rick Ladjevich had six hits in an April game. Lake Elsinore outfielder Greg Shockey twice had five hits in a game, and had three home runs in another.

Lee, San Diego's first-round pick in 1993, was named the league's top hitting prospect in a July survey of managers but finished the season in a prolonged slump. After hitting .352 in the first half, Lee batted just .233 in the second half.

The league uncharacteristically featured several first-round picks from the 1995 draft. Outfielder Darin Erstad, the first overall pick by the Angels, joined Lake Elsinore in early August and batted .363.

STANDINGS: SPLIT SEASON

FIRST HALF

NORTH	W	L	PCT	GB
Modesto	40	30	.571	—
San Jose	36	34	.514	4
Stockton	35	34	.507	4½
Visalia	35	35	.500	5
Bakersfield	31	39	.443	9

SOUTH	W	L	PCT	GB
San Bern.	44	25	.638	—
Lake Elsinore	37	32	.536	7
Riverside	35	34	.507	9
Rancho Cuca.	32	36	.471	11½
High Desert	22	48	.314	22½

SECOND HALF

NORTH	W	L	PCT	GB
San Jose	41	29	.586	—
Stockton	39	31	.557	2
Modesto	38	32	.543	3
Bakersfield	27	43	.386	14
Visalia	23	47	.329	18

SOUTH	W	L	PCT	GB
Lake Elsinore	44	25	.638	—
San Bern.	40	29	.580	4
Riverside	37	33	.529	7½
Rancho Cuca.	36	34	.514	8½
High Desert	24	46	.343	20½

PLAYOFFS—Quarterfinals: San Jose defeated Stockton 2-0, and Lake Elsinore defeated Riverside 2-1, in best-of-3 series. **Semifinals:** San Jose defeated Modesto 3-0, and San Bernardino defeated Lake Elsinore 3-0, in best-of-5 series. **Finals:** San Bernardino defeated San Jose 3-0, in best-of-5 series.

CALIFORNIA LEAGUE
1995 BATTING, PITCHING STATISTICS

CLUB BATTING

	AVG	G	AB	R	H	2B	3B	HR	BB	SO	SB
San Bernardino	.284	139	4803	823	1362	250	29	154	502	988	246
Stockton	.281	140	4778	730	1341	244	43	80	458	872	220
Lake Elsinore	.275	139	4773	800	1312	275	51	108	575	973	114
Riverside	.274	139	4813	799	1319	213	44	85	482	914	153
Rancho Cucamonga	.272	139	4733	742	1288	220	30	94	522	980	169
Modesto	.267	140	4678	773	1251	245	30	138	659	1064	137
Bakersfield	.267	140	4690	626	1250	229	21	76	475	952	149
San Jose	.260	140	4835	695	1256	227	54	70	528	1011	217
High Desert	.259	140	4710	669	1218	215	39	120	484	1033	181
Visalia	.255	140	4756	591	1211	210	38	66	459	1025	116

CLUB PITCHING

	ERA	G	CG	SHO	SV	IP	H	R	ER	BB	SO
San Jose	3.05	140	5	17	35	1270	1147	516	430	388	1013
Lake Elsinore	3.73	139	5	9	36	1227	1246	646	509	429	1022
Modesto	4.13	140	0	5	41	1234	1260	676	566	464	1077
San Bernardino	4.25	139	3	8	41	1248	1311	719	589	493	980
Stockton	4.30	140	5	7	40	1240	1311	694	592	555	880
Rancho Cucamonga	4.45	139	10	8	30	1216	1212	718	601	605	1074
Bakersfield	4.53	140	3	4	33	1222	1299	757	615	553	851
Riverside	4.53	139	2	6	34	1226	1290	767	618	577	981
Visalia	4.66	140	11	9	24	1243	1322	759	644	447	974
High Desert	5.78	140	3	2	30	1228	1410	996	789	633	960

CLUB FIELDING

	PCT	PO	A	E	DP		PCT	PO	A	E	DP
San Jose	.968	3810	1446	174	120	Rancho Cuca.	.963	3649	1463	199	128
San Bern.	.968	3744	1562	177	94	Riverside	.960	3679	1534	217	124
Stockton	.965	3719	1564	192	120	Bakersfield	.959	3666	1639	224	142
Visalia	.964	3730	1530	199	143	Modesto	.959	3703	1511	222	112
Lake Elsinore	.964	3682	1493	196	124	High Desert	.950	3683	1508	275	112

Raul Ibanez
All-star catcher

Steve Cox
30 HRs, 110 RBIs

Jason McDonald
70 steals

INDIVIDUAL BATTING LEADERS
(Minimum 378 Plate Appearances)

	AVG	G	AB	R	H	2B	3B	HR	RBI	BB	SO	SB
Riggs, Adam, San Bern.	.362	134	542	111	196	39	5	24	106	59	93	31
Hamlin, Jonas, Stockton	.332	99	388	65	129	32	5	16	69	17	86	5
Ibanez, Raul, Riverside	.332	95	361	59	120	23	9	20	108	41	49	4
McCall, Rod, Bakersfield	.330	96	345	61	114	19	1	20	70	40	90	2
Shockey, Greg, Lake Elsinore	.327	114	441	55	144	32	3	20	88	42	88	2
Ramirez, Alex, Bakersfield	.323	98	406	56	131	25	2	10	52	18	76	13
LaRocca, Greg, R.C.	.322	125	466	77	150	36	5	8	74	44	77	15
Nicholas, Darrell, Stockton	.320	87	350	54	112	16	3	5	39	23	75	26
Barger, Mike, Riverside	.317	82	344	77	109	10	1	2	41	38	45	33
Ladjevich, Rick, Riverside	.309	122	470	74	145	26	0	7	71	26	65	3

INDIVIDUAL PITCHING LEADERS
(Minimum 112 Innings)

	W	L	ERA	G	GS	CG	SV	IP	H	R	ER	BB	SO
Price, Tom, San Bernardino	10	5	2.20	42	13	2	3	152	145	49	37	14	82
Bonanno, Rob, Lake Elsinore	8	4	3.05	17	17	4	0	112	112	49	38	16	72
Janicki, Pete, Lake Elsinore	9	4	3.06	20	20	0	0	123	130	66	42	28	106
Moore, Trey, Riverside	14	6	3.09	24	24	0	0	148	122	65	51	58	134
Smith, Ryan, Riverside	10	7	3.11	23	23	2	0	142	142	68	49	50	108
Percibal, William, High Desert	7	6	3.23	21	20	2	0	128	123	63	46	55	105
Dixon, Bubba, R.C.	10	7	3.24	47	12	2	5	142	118	61	51	46	133
Beaumont, Matt, Lake Elsinore	16	9	3.29	27	26	0	0	175	162	80	64	57	149
Edwards, Wayne, Bakersfield	9	8	3.36	21	21	1	0	129	125	63	48	56	83
Foulke, Keith, San Jose	13	6	3.50	28	26	2	0	177	166	85	69	32	168

CAROLINA
LEAGUE

Kinston Dominates Awards, Wins Title

Indian Chiefs. Richie Sexson, left, and righthander Bartolo Colon led Kinston to the '95 Carolina League title. Sexson hit .306 and led the league in RBIs. Colon went 13-3 with a 1.96 ERA and league-leading 152 strikeouts.

By JAMES BAILEY

The Kinston Indians, who dominated everything in the Carolina League in 1995 from the all-star team to the postseason awards, swept through the playoffs to wrest the Mills Cup from the defending champion Wilmington Blue Rocks. The championship was Kinston's fourth in the Carolina League and its first since 1991.

Kinston, which earned a first-round bye after winning both halves in the Southern Division, won the third and final game 4-0 behind a brilliant performance by righthander Roland De la Maza. De la Maza carried a perfect game into the top of the eighth inning before

Blue Rocks outfielder Raul Gonzales lined a single into center field to lead off the inning. Righthander Johnny Martinez pitched a perfect ninth inning to combine with De la Maza on the one-hitter.

Despite the absence of the league's top prospect, righthander Bartolo Colon, the Indians had no shortage of pitching in the finals. Kinston allowed just two runs in the series.

The Blue Rocks played the postseason without catcher Mike Sweeney, who was the heart of their lineup. He received a promotion to Kansas City when major league rosters expanded in September. Sweeney hit a league-high .310 and was one of only two hitters to hit over .300.

The Blue Rocks, who finished with the best overall record in the league, swept by Prince William in two games in the semifinals. Wilmington won the second-half title in the Northern Division by 14 games, while the Cannons, who had edged the Blue Rocks by 1½ games in the first half, ran out of gas and faded to last place.

Kinston first baseman Richie Sexson, named the league's MVP, drove in five runs in the first two games of the final series to earn Mills Cup MVP honors as well. Sexson hit .306 with 22 homers and 85 RBIs in the regular season and was one of seven Kinston players to make the postseason all-star team. Kinston also secured the first three spots in a managers' survey of

STANDINGS: SPLIT SEASON

FIRST HALF					SECOND HALF			
NORTH	W	L	PCT	GB	**NORTH**	W	L	PCT	GB
Pr. William	37	33	.529	—	Wilmington	48	21	.696	—
Wilmington	35	34	.507	1½	Lynchburg	34	35	.493	14
Lynchburg	33	36	.478	3½	Frederick	31	38	.449	17
Frederick	27	41	.397	9	Pr. William	27	43	.386	21½
SOUTH	W	L	PCT	GB	**SOUTH**	W	L	PCT	GB
Kinston	45	24	.652	—	Kinston	36	32	.529	—
Win.-Salem	36	34	.514	9½	Win.-Salem	33	34	.493	2½
Salem	34	36	.486	11½	Salem	34	36	.486	3
Durham	30	39	.435	15	Durham	33	37	.471	4

PLAYOFFS—Semifinals: Wilmington defeated Prince William 2-0, in best-of-3 series. **Finals:** Kinston defeated Wilmington 3-0, in best-of-5 series.

the Top 10 prospects, with Colon, shortstop Enrique Wilson and Sexson.

"This is the best team I've ever managed," Kinston manager Gordy MacKenzie said. "There's going to be more guys off this club in the major leagues than any team I've ever been with."

Colon was named the league's Pitcher of the Year despite missing the final month of the season due to a bone bruise in his pitching elbow.

Kinston was the story of the league in the first half, winning the Southern Division by 9½ games. MacKenzie brought nearly half of his team to Lynchburg for the all-star game in July.

But it was hometown heroes Raul Rodarte and Reed Secrist who led the Northern Division to an 8-3 win. Rodarte hit the game's only home run and picked up MVP honors, while Secrist drove in two runs.

Mike Sweeney

No-Hitters Were Common

The league saw five no-hitters in 1995, four of which were combined efforts. Two Prince William hurlers got the flurry started April 8, combining for an 8-0 blanking of the Salem Avalanche. Righthander Brian Woods went the first seven innings before yielding to reliever Archie Vazquez, who finished off the first no-hitter in professional baseball in 1995.

One week later Wilmington lefthander Jose Rosado and righthander Pat Flury no-hit Winston-Salem 3-0. Durham Bulls righthanders Tommy Harrison and Earl Nelson turned in the league's third gem in April when they whitewashed Prince William 4-0 on April 30.

Cannons lefthander Rich Pratt threw the lone solo effort May 19 against Frederick, blanking the Keys 3-0 in a seven-inning game. Lynchburg righthanders John Dillinger and Jason Pfaff tossed the league's fifth and final no-hitter July 26, a 4-0 win over Kinston.

Wrestlemania

Unfortunately there were plenty of hits May 22 when Durham hosted Winston-Salem. And one vicious kick as well.

Durham's "Strike Out Domestic Violence" promotion was marred by an ugly brawl between the two clubs. Footage of the fight made highlight reels nationwide, including on ESPN and CNN.

The brouhaha erupted in the bottom of the third when Winston-Salem righthander Jason Kummerfeldt hit Bulls third baseman John Knott in the back with a pitch after surrendering consecutive home runs.

Knott charged the mound and both dugouts and bullpens emptied. But this was not your average baseball fracas. Virtually all the players on both teams were involved, and they seemed to be out for blood.

Warthogs righthander Glen Cullop had his jaw broken and lost four teeth when Bulls reliever Earl Nelson kicked him in the face. Cullop missed the rest of the season, and Nelson was released by the parent Atlanta Braves after serving a six-game suspension.

Two new stadiums made their debuts in 1995, although the opening of Salem's Memorial Baseball Stadium was delayed until Aug. 7, when a crowd of 6,421 saw the Avalanche beat Frederick 3-2 in 15 innings. The Avalance was forced to play the first four months of the season in its old park because of construction delays.

Durham Bulls Athletic Park was completed just in time for Opening Day. The Bulls drew a club-record crowd of 10,886 for the historic first game. Durham outfielder Wonderful Monds led off the bottom of the first inning with a blast over the 24-foot high Blue Monster in left field for the first home run in the new park.

Durham had a record-setting season attendance, narrowly missing the 400,000 mark. The Bulls drew 390,486 fans, a record for both the team and league.

STANDINGS: OVERALL

Page		W	L	PCT	GB	Manager	Attendance/Dates	Last Pennant
135	Wilmington Blue Rocks (Royals)	83	55	.601	—	John Mizerock	358,766 (65)	1994
103	Kinston Indians (Indians)	81	56	.591	1½	Gordy MacKenzie	140,116 (65)	1995
97	Winston-Salem Warthogs (Reds)	69	68	.504	13½	Mark Berry	158,842 (65)	1993
109	Salem Avalanche (Rockies)	68	72	.486	16	Bill Hayes	140,111 (65)	1987
194	Lynchburg Hillcats (Pirates)	67	71	.486	16	Marc Hill	111,654 (61)	1984
84	Prince William Cannons (White Sox)	64	76	.457	20	Dave Huppert	215,250 (64)	1989
56	Durham Bulls (Braves)	63	76	.453	20½	Matt West	390,486 (65)	1967
65	Frederick Keys (Orioles)	58	79	.449	24½	Mike O'Berry	300,968 (63)	1990

NOTE: Team's individual batting and pitching statistics can be found on page indicated in lefthand column.

CAROLINA LEAGUE
1995 BATTING, PITCHING STATISTICS

CLUB BATTING

	AVG	G	AB	R	H	2B	3B	HR	BB	SO	SB
Lynchburg	.264	138	4483	655	1185	214	27	107	501	880	156
Wilmington	.255	138	4591	550	1173	204	33	75	393	771	135
Kinston	.254	137	4509	605	1145	222	31	119	459	900	139
Salem	.252	140	4699	619	1186	231	29	109	516	991	69
Durham	.249	139	4447	566	1109	197	14	109	399	1007	150
Prince William	.247	140	4576	572	1130	210	28	90	477	878	96
Winston-Salem	.246	137	4508	601	1110	204	21	132	458	961	105
Frederick	.234	137	4430	497	1038	197	26	67	426	979	110

CLUB PITCHING

	ERA	G	CG	SHO	SV	IP	H	R	ER	BB	SO
Wilmington	2.84	138	2	17	46	1233	1017	459	389	405	1005
Kinston	3.24	137	8	10	37	1214	1056	500	437	408	943
Winston-Salem	3.33	137	12	11	30	1198	1065	538	443	427	850
Prince William	3.91	140	12	11	32	1206	1176	594	524	432	962
Frederick	3.92	137	10	11	32	1191	1123	617	518	487	1018
Salem	4.09	140	8	6	34	1237	1238	667	563	536	871
Lynchburg	4.16	138	5	9	27	1183	1213	640	547	393	893
Durham	4.25	139	6	3	39	1187	1188	650	560	541	825

CLUB FIELDING

	PCT	PO	A	E	DP		PCT	PO	A	E	DP
Kinston	.978	3642	1555	119	136	Win.-Salem	.969	3594	1543	165	127
Wilmington	.974	3698	1533	139	107	Durham	.968	3560	1353	160	134
Prince William	.970	3618	1525	157	99	Lynchburg	.967	3548	1569	175	130
Salem	.970	3711	1667	166	134	Frederick	.966	3572	1461	179	105

Glendon Rusch
14 victories, 1.74 ERA

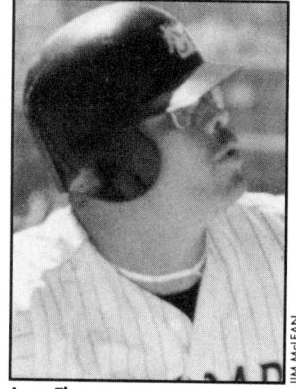

Juan Thomas
League-leading 26 homers

INDIVIDUAL BATTING LEADERS
(Minimum 378 Plate Appearances)

	AVG	G	AB	R	H	2B	3B	HR	RBI	BB	SO	SB
Sweeney, Mike, Wilmington	.310	99	332	61	103	23	1	18	53	60	39	6
Sexson, Richie, Kinston	.306	131	494	80	151	34	0	22	85	43	115	4
Velazquez, Edgard, Salem	.300	131	497	74	149	25	6	13	69	40	102	7
Zapata, Ramon, Lynchburg	.298	119	416	59	124	27	2	8	45	42	58	6
Rodarte, Raul, Lynchburg	.286	104	346	57	99	18	2	12	48	35	49	19
Medrano, Anthony, Wilmington	.285	123	460	69	131	20	6	3	43	34	42	11
Williams, Harold, Prince William	.282	129	472	56	133	30	1	14	72	48	98	4
Secrist, Reed, Lynchburg	.282	112	380	60	107	18	3	19	75	54	88	3
Culp, Brian, Salem	.279	128	459	69	128	33	1	8	63	71	80	8
Collier, Lou, Lynchburg	.276	114	399	68	110	19	3	4	38	51	60	31

INDIVIDUAL PITCHING LEADERS
(Minimum 112 Innings)

	W	L	ERA	G	GS	CG	SV	IP	H	R	ER	BB	SO
Rusch, Glendon, Wilmington	14	6	1.74	26	26	1	0	166	110	41	32	34	147
Colon, Bartolo, Kinston	13	3	1.96	21	21	0	0	129	91	31	28	39	152
Byrdak, Tim, Wilmington	11	5	2.16	27	26	0	0	166	118	46	40	45	127
Peters, Chris, Lynchburg	11	5	2.43	24	24	3	0	145	126	57	39	35	132
Wright, Jamey, Salem	10	4	2.47	26	26	2	0	171	160	74	47	72	95
Maduro, Calvin, Frederick	8	5	2.94	20	20	2	0	122	109	43	40	34	120
Lyons, Curt, W-S	9	9	2.98	26	26	0	0	160	139	66	53	67	122
Robbins, Jason, W-S	9	6	3.06	23	23	3	0	141	113	62	48	42	106
Rosado, Jose, Wilmington	10	7	3.13	25	25	0	0	138	128	53	48	30	117
Pratt, Rich, Prince William	5	11	3.14	25	25	2	0	152	139	66	53	42	120

FLORIDA STATE LEAGUE

Daytona Surges To '95 FSL Championship

By SEAN KERNAN

The Daytona Cubs weren't the best team from start to finish, but from May through Sept. 12—the night the Cubs captured the 1995 Florida State League championship—manager Dave Trembley's club was clearly the class of the Florida State League.

The Cubs gave their Eastern Division competitors a chance by starting the season with a 9-15 record in April. The rest of the way the Cubs were an incredible 81-34—a .704 winning percentage.

"The war is over and we won the war," said Trembley, who added the '95 FSL title to the '87 Eastern League championship won by his Harrisburg Senators. "More importantly, we did it the right way. The right way is to make sure when you come to the ballpark everyone is ready to play. There are a lot of guys who got us to this point."

A lot of guys but few top prospects, if any, if a league-wide evaluation of managers is considered. Yes, the Daytona Cubs had their own prospects in pitchers Jason Ryan, Brian Stephenson and Wade Walker, and a couple of everyday prospects in second baseman Bobby Morris and third baseman Kevin Orie.

But when measured against the league's other prospects, the Cubs didn't have a player or pitcher crack the Top 10. That made the end result that much more remarkable and a reason why Trembley was named Manager of the Year.

Matt Drews. Tampa righthander was voted the FSL's top pitching prospect.

The Cubs won both halves in the Eastern Division to earn a bye into the league championship series against the Western champion Fort Myers Miracle. Only the Shreveport Captains (Texas) had a better full-season record (88-47) than the Cubs' 87-48 mark. However, the Cubs matched the all-time best record by a Daytona Beach team in the 47 seasons an FSL club has played in the city, equaling a mark set in 1939.

When the Cubs' 1995 season came down to one game—the deciding contest of the best-of-5 championship series—Walker was in there for every out. The 23-year-old righthander took control early and went the distance in the 6-1 win that gave the Cubs organization only its third minor league championship of the 1990s.

"It's a great cap to a great season," Walker said. "I just had to go out there and throw strikes and let these guys play. This is a great team and it's great to be a part of a Cubs team that won a championship. Hopefully there will be more."

Walker coaxed the Miracle into 16 ground outs and third baseman Kevin Orie, who batted .611 in the series, made several sparkling plays in Game Five.

The Cubs took a 2-0 lead in the series by posting back-to-back shutouts at home. Walker and Geremis Gonzalez combined for a three-hitter in a 4-0 win in Game One. The next night Stephenson went eight innings. After facing one batter in the ninth, he gave way to Orlando Lopez,

STANDINGS: OVERALL

Page		W	L	PCT	GB	Manager	Attendance/Dates	Last Pennant
91	Daytona Cubs (Cubs)	87	48	.644	—	Dave Trembley	90,071 (63)	1995
155	Fort Myers Miracle (Twins)	75	55	.577	9½	Al Newman	78,431 (62)	1985
187	Clearwater Phillies (Phillies)	79	59	.572	9½	Don McCormack	71,761 (69)	1993
142	Vero Beach Dodgers (Dodgers)	74	59	.556	12	Jon Debus	42,702 (62)	1990
168	Tampa Yankees (Yankees)	72	64	.529	15½	Jake Gibbs	48,598 (61)	1994
226	Charlotte Rangers (Rangers)	65	67	.492	20½	Butch Wynegar	60,000 (64)	1989
71	Sarasota Red Sox (Red Sox)	65	68	.489	21	Tommy Barrett	65,223 (65)	1963
201	St. Petersburg Cardinals (Cards)	64	67	.489	21	Chris Maloney	100,035 (61)	1986
116	Lakeland Tigers (Tigers)	64	69	.481	22	Dave Anderson	21,633 (61)	1992
232	Dunedin Blue Jays (Blue Jays)	63	74	.460	25	Jim Nettles	65,764 (67)	None
175	St. Lucie Mets (Mets)	61	73	.455	25½	Rafael Landestoy	80,734 (64)	1988
122	Brevard Cty. Manatees (Marlins)	61	74	.452	26	Fredi Gonzalez	140,109 (68)	None
128	Kissimmee Cobras (Astros)	55	81	.404	32½	Dave Engle	41,091 (62)	None
161	West Palm Beach Expos (Expos)	54	81	.400	33	Gomer Hodge	71,446 (59)	1991

NOTE: Team's individual batting and pitching statistics can be found on page indicated in lefthand column.

who retired three straight batters to close out the six-hitter. Daytona won 6-0.

No Shortage Of No-Hitters

Three hurlers threw nine-inning no-hitters in the summer of '95.

When righthander Eric Moody of the Charlotte Rangers no-hit the Sarasota Red Sox in an 11-0 win on April 20, it marked the earliest no-hitter ever thrown in 76 FSL seasons. Steve Patterson had posted the earliest no-hitter in an April 22, 1972 outing for Miami in a game against West Palm Beach.

Brevard County's Clemente Nunez no-hit the Expos in a 2-0 win on May 28. The Manatees' righthander is best known as the first player ever signed by the Florida Marlins.

St. Lucie's Rafael Roque highlighted a strong second half by no-hitting the Dunedin Blue Jays in a 6-1 win on June 28. The southpaw also had a one-hitter.

Tampa outfielder Shane Spencer, in his fifth season in Class A, was named the league's MVP. He led the FSL in hits (150), total bases (235) and RBIs (88). Teammate Matt Drews was first in wins (15), second in strikeouts (140) and third in ERA (2.27).

Clearwater third baseman Scott Rolen was rated the league's top prospect in the poll of managers, despite playing in just 66 games. He missed the first part of the season with an injury and the last part when he was promoted to Double-A.

Rolen's teammates, outfielder Wendell Magee and first baseman Dan Held, also earned promotions to Double-A, but not before Magee won the batting title with a .353 average and Held led the league with 35 doubles and 21 homers.

Vero Beach Dodges Tragedy

A tragic situation created by Mother Nature was averted only because Father Time was on the side of the Vero Beach Dodgers. High winds kicked up during a thunderstorm split a light pole at Holman Stadium about 40 minutes before gates were scheduled to be opened on June 26.

"I don't even want to think what might have happened," Vero Beach general manager Tom Simmons said. "We're very fortunate it didn't happen after the gates were open. The lights ended up in the (third base) dugout."

No one was injured. The game between the West Palm Beach Expos and Dodgers was postponed. Other Dodgers home games were moved to one of the practice fields at the Dodgertown complex.

The weather was no match for Charlotte's County Stadium field, which was the true MVP of the league's 34th all-star game.

While the Port Charlotte area had been soaked by up to 15 inches of rain in a 48-hour period before the game, including a reported 11 inches in 15 hours, the only sign of rain on the spring training facility of the Texas Rangers was one small puddle.

STANDINGS: SPLIT SEASON

FIRST HALF

EAST	W	L	PCT	GB
Daytona	41	28	.594	—
Vero Beach	39	31	.557	2½
St. Lucie	33	35	.485	7½
Brevard	30	38	.441	10½
Kissimmee	28	41	.406	13
West Palm	25	44	.362	16

WEST	W	L	PCT	GB
Tampa	41	29	.586	—
Clearwater	38	32	.543	3
Lakeland	36	33	.522	4½
Dunedin	35	33	.515	5
Charlotte	35	33	.515	5
Fort Myers	34	34	.500	6
Sarasota	34	34	.500	6
St. Pete.	32	36	.471	8

SECOND HALF

EAST	W	L	PCT	GB
Daytona	46	20	.697	—
Vero Beach	35	28	.556	9½
Brevard	31	36	.463	15½
West Palm	29	37	.439	17
St. Lucie	28	38	.424	18
Kissimmee	27	40	.403	19½

WEST	W	L	PCT	GB
Fort Myers	41	21	.661	—
Clearwater	41	27	.603	3
St. Pete.	32	31	.508	9½
Sarasota	31	34	.477	11½
Tampa	31	35	.470	12
Charlotte	30	34	.469	12
Lakeland	28	36	.438	14
Dunedin	28	41	.406	16½

PLAYOFFS—Semifinals: Fort Myers defeated Tampa 2-1, in best-of-3 series. **Finals:** Daytona defeated Fort Myers 3-2, in best-of-5 series.

Shane Spencer (JOHN SPEAR)

LEAGUE CHAMPIONS

Last 25 Years

Year	Regular Season	Pct.	Playoff
1971	Miami (Orioles)	.667	Miami (Orioles)
1972	Daytona Beach (Dodgers)	.606	Miami (Orioles)
1973	West Palm Beach (Expos)	.580	St. Pete (Cardinals)
1974	Ft. Lauderdale (Yankees)	.626	W. Palm Beach (Expos)
1975	St. Petersburg (Cardinals)	.651	St. Pete (Cardinals)
1976	Tampa (Reds)	.559	Lakeland (Tigers)
1977	Lakeland (Tigers)	.616	Lakeland (Tigers)
1978	St. Petersburg (Cardinals)	.600	Miami (Orioles)
1979	Ft. Lauderdale (Yankees)	.643	Winter Haven (Red Sox)
1980	Daytona Beach (Astros)	.627	Ft. Lauderdale (Yankees)
1981	Ft. Lauderdale (Yankees)	.604	Daytona Beach (Astros)
1982	Ft. Lauderdale (Yankees)	.621	Ft. Lauderdale (Yankees)
1983	Daytona Beach (Astros)	.634	Vero Beach (Dodgers)
1984	Fort Myers (Royals)	.574	Ft. Lauderdale (Yankees)
1985	Fort Myers (Royals)	.589	Fort Myers (Royals)
1986	St. Petersburg (Cardinals)	.647	St. Pete (Cardinals)
1987	Ft. Lauderdale (Yankees)	.615	Ft. Lauderdale (Yankees)
1988	Osceola (Astros)	.605	St. Lucie (Mets)
1989	St. Lucie (Mets)	.589	Charlotte (Rangers)
1990	West Palm Beach (Expos)	.696	Vero Beach (Dodgers)
1991	Clearwater (Phillies)	.623	West Palm Beach (Expos)
1992	Sarasota (White Sox)	.639	Lakeland (Tigers)
1993	Charlotte (Rangers)	.632	Clearwater (Phillies)
1994	Tampa (Yankees)	.606	Tampa (Yankees)
1995	Daytona (Cubs)	.644	Daytona (Cubs)

*Best overall record

Mike Metcalfe. Speedster stole 60 bases for Vero Beach. (MORRIS FOSTOFF)

FLORIDA STATE LEAGUE
1995 BATTING, PITCHING STATISTICS

CLUB BATTING

	AVG	G	AB	R	H	2B	3B	HR	BB	SO	SB
Vero Beach	.261	133	4280	583	1119	182	22	65	451	755	184
Clearwater	.261	138	4565	653	1192	219	33	90	484	822	119
Lakeland	.261	135	4460	553	1162	190	38	65	388	935	133
Sarasota	.260	134	4400	551	1146	198	26	65	407	927	126
Daytona	.256	135	4355	638	1114	187	32	53	471	759	161
Charlotte	.253	133	4375	543	1106	210	32	56	449	839	96
Dunedin	.250	138	4616	621	1156	218	37	78	504	930	79
Brevard County	.248	135	4492	556	1113	197	23	58	502	891	83
Fort Myers	.248	131	4220	552	1045	196	22	54	440	784	84
Tampa	.247	136	4438	580	1098	191	31	73	557	911	98
West Palm Beach	.242	136	4324	510	1045	182	29	37	419	851	123
Kissimmee	.241	136	4452	508	1073	205	21	48	450	855	141
St. Lucie	.240	135	4313	484	1034	154	40	42	413	908	133
St. Petersburg	.234	131	4175	468	975	173	20	46	440	813	69

CLUB PITCHING

	ERA	G	CG	SHO	SV	IP	H	R	ER	BB	SO
Tampa	2.81	136	7	13	44	1188	1054	513	371	439	939
Daytona	2.82	135	3	13	49	1173	1020	484	368	382	980
Fort Myers	2.85	131	10	12	31	1136	978	450	360	409	823
St. Petersburg	3.03	131	7	12	34	1121	947	475	378	416	925
St. Lucie	3.25	135	18	16	27	1162	1085	504	419	412	793
Vero Beach	3.39	133	3	7	40	1137	990	521	429	563	939
Brevard County	3.44	135	5	14	29	1191	1123	582	456	462	828
West Palm Beach	3.49	136	8	7	29	1146	1110	550	445	478	745
Charlotte	3.50	133	7	8	35	1154	1120	538	449	394	758
Clearwater	3.55	138	8	10	36	1202	1202	583	474	416	891
Sarasota	3.81	134	6	10	34	1153	1142	606	488	466	819
Lakeland	3.87	135	5	7	44	1157	1181	617	498	450	887
Dunedin	4.02	138	4	5	30	1200	1205	668	536	541	840
Kissimmee	4.19	136	5	7	30	1184	1221	729	551	547	813

CLUB FIELDING

	PCT	PO	A	E	DP		PCT	PO	A	E	DP
Fort Myers	.974	3408	1382	129	135	Vero Beach	.967	3411	1415	165	102
St. Petersburg	.971	3364	1219	138	89	Brevard Cty.	.967	3574	1628	179	148
St. Lucie	.971	3485	1504	151	137	Lakeland	.966	3470	1522	177	117
Daytona	.969	3519	1384	158	120	West Palm	.963	3439	1446	186	110
Charlotte	.969	3463	1404	158	109	Dunedin	.963	3600	1482	194	122
Tampa	.967	3563	1497	170	106	Sarasota	.961	3459	1475	198	124
Clearwater	.967	3605	1425	169	102	Kissimmee	.955	3551	1520	240	119

INDIVIDUAL BATTING LEADERS
(Minimum 378 Plate Appearances)

	AVG	G	AB	R	H	2B	3B	HR	RBI	BB	SO	SB
Magee, Wendell, Clearwater	.353	96	388	67	137	24	5	6	46	33	40	7
Samuels, Scott, Daytona	.327	112	388	92	127	29	12	2	42	69	63	38
Nelson, Bryant, Kissimmee	.327	105	395	47	129	34	5	3	52	20	37	14
Saffer, Jon, West Palm Beach	.318	92	324	60	103	10	6	4	35	53	49	18
Morris, Bobby, Daytona	.308	95	344	44	106	18	2	5	55	38	46	22
Roberts, David, Lakeland	.303	92	357	67	108	10	5	3	30	39	43	30
Metcalfe, Mike, Vero Beach	.301	120	435	86	131	13	3	3	35	60	37	60
Spencer, Shane, Tampa	.300	134	500	87	150	31	3	16	88	61	60	14
Berg, David, Brevard	.298	114	382	71	114	18	1	3	39	68	61	9
Fick, Chris, St. Petersburg	.293	113	348	56	102	25	3	13	52	38	79	1

INDIVIDUAL PITCHING LEADERS
(Minimum 112 Innings)

	W	L	ERA	G	GS	CG	SV	IP	H	R	ER	BB	SO
Pincavitch, Kevin, Vero Beach	10	7	1.66	32	13	2	2	125	83	37	23	48	103
Bowers, Shane, Ft. Myers	13	5	2.16	23	23	1	0	146	119	43	35	32	103
Drews, Matt, Tampa	15	7	2.27	28	28	3	0	182	142	73	46	58	140
Nunez, Clemente, Brevard	7	7	2.48	19	19	4	0	123	99	48	34	22	79
Larson, Toby, St. Lucie	6	7	2.52	19	18	3	0	122	122	44	34	30	82
Walker, Wade, Daytona	8	6	2.53	25	24	2	0	135	113	50	38	36	117
King, Curtis, St. Petersburg	7	8	2.58	28	21	3	0	136	117	49	39	49	65
Janzen, Marty, Tampa	10	3	2.61	18	18	1	0	114	102	38	33	30	104
Guerra, Mark, St. Lucie	9	9	2.64	23	23	4	0	160	148	55	47	33	110
Winslett, Dax, V.B.-Daytona	12	6	2.78	26	25	0	0	152	148	59	47	39	111

MIDWEST LEAGUE

Pitching Propels Beloit To First Title

By CURT RALLO

There was no question who was king of the hill in the Midwest League in 1995.

Beloit used superior pitching to strong-arm the competition throughout the regular season and playoffs, capturing its first Midwest League title in the 14-year history of the franchise.

Beloit turned in a league-best 88-51 record in the regular season and then turned it up a notch in the playoffs, winning seven of eight games. The Snappers swept the Michigan Battle Cats, three games to none, in the championship series.

In addition to sweeping Michigan in the finals, manager Dub Kilgo's Beloit club beat Quad City, 2-1, in the second round and swept Rockford in two games in the first round.

Midwest League opponents would have had a better chance facing a firing squad than facing the pitcher's mound when the Snappers were on the field. Incredibly, Beloit pitchers gave up only three earned runs in 80 innings in the playoffs—a stunning 0.34 ERA.

Nobody scored an earned run in the playoffs against Beloit until Michigan outfielder Michael Coleman singled to score shortstop Donnie Sadler with two out in the eighth inning of the second game of the championship series—after 61 innings.

Beloit's 1-2 punch in the playoffs was Jeff D'Amico and Brian Tollberg, who led Beloit with 13 wins apiece in the regular season.

Tollberg pitched 15⅔ innings of scoreless ball in the playoffs, giving up just eight hits. He struck out 25 and walked one.

D'Amico, who made his professional debut in 1995, worked 18 innings in the playoffs and didn't allow a run. He only gave up eight hits, while striking out 17 and walking one. D'Amico was Milwaukee's first-round draft pick in 1993 but arm problems prevented him from pitching for almost two years.

"I think the reason we were successful was we were consistent," Kilgo said. "We were consistent with our pitching and our defense and we got timely hitting.

Jeff D'Amico. Beloit righthander won 13 games to lead Snappers to first Midwest League title.

FRANK RAGSDALE

Usually we were a club that didn't beat itself."

Skyrocketing Crowds

Off the field, the biggest news in the Midwest League in 1995 was the attendance.

West Michigan, which shattered the all-time Class A attendance record by drawing 475,212 fans in 1994, became the first Class A club to top the 500,000 mark. In all, the Midwest League ended up with 2,764,329

STANDINGS: OVERALL

Page		W	L	PCT	GB	Manager	Attendance/Dates	Last Pennant
150	Beloit Snappers (Brewers)	88	51	.633	—	Dub Kilgo	60,816 (59)	1995
129	Quad City River Bandits (Astros)	76	61	.555	11	Jim Pankovits	257,501 (63)	1990
78	Cedar Rapids Kernels (Angels)	76	62	.551	11 ½	Tom Lawless	135,840 (63)	1994
72	Michigan Battle Cats (Red Sox)	75	62	.547	12	DeMarlo Hale	171,794 (64)	None
156	Fort Wayne Wizards (Twins)	75	65	.536	13 ½	Dan Rohn	253,568 (70)	None
92	Rockford Cubbies (Cubs)	75	65	.536	13 ½	Steve Roadcap	110,052 (65)	None
123	Kane County Cougars (Marlins)	69	69	.500	18 ½	Lynn Jones	477,550 (65)	None
182	West Michigan Whitecaps (A's)	67	69	.493	19 ½	Jim Colborn	307,989 (67)	None
85	So. Bend Silver Hawks (White Sox)	66	69	.489	20	Fred Kendall	225,999 (60)	1993
136	Springfield Sultans (Royals)	65	74	.468	23	Brian Poldberg	39,467 (63)	None
201	Peoria Chiefs (Cardinals)	62	72	.463	23 ½	Roy Silver	195,056 (62)	None
221	Wisconsin Timber Rattlers (Mariners)	63	75	.457	24 ½	Mike Goff	209,159 (65)	1984
215	Burlington Bees (Giants)	54	81	.400	32	Mike Hart	69,412 (56)	1977
209	Clinton Lumber Kings (Padres)	51	86	.372	36	Ed Romero	50,126 (55)	1991

NOTE: Team's individual batting and pitching statistics can be found on page indicated in lefthand column.

fans, a league record. The previous attendance record was 2,469,999, set in 1994.

The 1995 season was one of change for the Midwest League as franchises moved, took on new major league affiliates and even new nicknames.

The league's new franchise was Michigan, which relocated to Battle Creek, Mich., from Madison, Wis., after the 1994 season. The team was originally going to be called the Golden Kazoos but legal problems forced it to change to Battle Cats.

The Boston Red Sox became Michigan's parent club after originally committing to Peoria. St. Louis agreed to swap affiliates, trading Michigan for Peoria.

Peoria had been a Chicago Cubs farm club through 1994, but the Cubs switched to Rockford for 1995, setting off a chain reaction. Kansas City, previously in Rockford, moved into Springfield, which previously was affiliated with San Diego.

The Padres then moved into Clinton, previously occupied by the San Francisco Giants, who shifted to Burlington to replace the Montreal Expos, who did not operate a team in the league in 1995.

The former Appleton Foxes franchise became known as the Wisconsin Timber Rattlers. Beloit dropped the Brewers name and became the Snappers.

And more changes are in the works for 1996. Springfield, which lost its team temporarily after the 1993 season—the team moved to Madison only to be replaced by Waterloo—is once again losing a franchise, this time to Lansing, Mich. Lansing will join the East Division with Peoria moving to the Central.

Individual Accomplishments

Outfielder Demond Smith, who had an insufficient number of plate appearances to qualify for the Midwest League batting title when he was promoted by the

STANDINGS: SPLIT SEASON

FIRST HALF

EAST	W	L	PCT	GB
Michigan	36	32	.529	—
West Mich.	35	33	.515	1
Fort Wayne	35	35	.500	2
South Bend	31	36	.463	4½

CENTRAL	W	L	PCT	GB
Beloit	45	25	.643	—
Kane County	39	31	.557	6
Rockford	34	36	.486	11
Wisconsin	30	38	.441	14

WEST	W	L	PCT	GB
Quad City	40	27	.597	—
Springfield	38	31	.551	3
Cedar Rapids	38	31	.551	3
Peoria	32	35	.478	8
Burlington	29	38	.433	11
Clinton	17	51	.250	23½

SECOND HALF

EAST	W	L	PCT	GB
Fort Wayne	40	30	.571	—
Michigan	39	31	.557	1
South Bend	35	33	.515	4
West Mich.	32	36	.471	7

CENTRAL	W	L	PCT	GB
Beloit	43	26	.623	—
Rockford	41	29	.586	2½
Wisconsin	33	37	.471	10½
Kane County	30	38	.441	12½

WEST	W	L	PCT	GB
Cedar Rapids	38	31	.551	—
Quad City	36	34	.514	2½
Clinton	34	35	.493	4
Peoria	30	37	.448	7
Springfield	27	43	.386	11½
Burlington	25	43	.368	12½

PLAYOFFS—Quarterfinals: Michigan defeated Fort Wayne 2-0, Beloit defeated Rockford 2-0, Quad City defeated Cedar Rapids 2-1, and West Michigan defeated Kane County 2-1, in best-of-3 series. **Semifinals:** Beloit defeated Quad City 2-1, and Michigan defeated West Michigan 2-1, in best-of-3 series. **Finals:** Beloit defeated Michigan 3-0, in best-of-5 series.

California Angels from Cedar Rapids to Lake Elsinore (California), got an unexpected reprieve when he was traded to the Oakland Athletics, who sent him back to the Midwest League to complete the season. He finished with a .338 average overall and gained the necessary at-bats with West Michigan to win the batting crown.

Burlington's Jesse Ibarra led the league with 34 home runs and finished second in the other two Triple Crown categories to earn selection as the league's MVP.

Quad City's Carlos Hernandez was the king of the basepaths with 58 stolen bases, beating Anton French by one theft. French, who started the season with Peoria, was traded by the Cardinals to the Braves organization with little more than a week remaining in the season.

Springfield righthander Javier Gamboa pitched a no-hitter—and lost. In the

JOHN SPEAR

Jesse Ibarra

first game of a doubleheader against Clinton, Gamboa held the Lumber Kings hitless until the eighth inning, when he gave up the game's only run. Because the game was scheduled to go seven innings, he was credited with a no-hitter.

Midwest League officials found themselves dealing with a rash of grooved bat incidents. Kane County third baseman Josh Booty, Fort Wayne outfielder Armann Brown, Rockford outfielder Marty Gazarek, Burlington outfielder Derek Reid and South Bend DH Melvin Rosario all were caught with grooved bats and faced fines and suspensions.

Burlington set a record with four consecutive home runs. Don Denbow, Kevin Watson, Jeff Poor and Raul Marval hit back-to-back-to-back-to-back homers in a victory over Michigan.

LEAGUE CHAMPIONS

Last 25 Years

Year	Regular Season*	Pct.	Playoff
1971	Appleton (White Sox)	.642	Quad City (Angels)
1972	Appleton (White Sox)	.598	Danville (Brewers)
1973	Clinton (Tigers)	.588	Wisconsin Rapids (Twins)
1974	Wisconsin Rapids (Twins)	.625	Danville (Brewers)
1975	Waterloo (Royals)	.726	Waterloo (Royals)
1976	Waterloo (Royals)	.600	Waterloo (Royals)
1977	Waterloo (Indians)	.579	Burlington (Brewers)
1978	Appleton (White Sox)	.708	Appleton (White Sox)
1979	Waterloo (Indians)	.600	Quad City (Cubs)
1980	Waterloo (Indians)	.609	Waterloo (Indians)
1981	Wausau (Mariners)	.636	Wausau (Mariners)
1982	Madison (Athletics)	.625	Appleton (White Sox)
1983	Appleton (White Sox)	.635	Appleton (White Sox)
1984	Appleton (White Sox)	.639	Appleton (White Sox)
1985	Appleton (White Sox)	.611	Kenosha (Twins)
1986	Springfield (Cardinals)	.621	Waterloo (Indians)
1987	Springfield (Cardinals)	.671	Kenosha (Twins)
1988	Cedar Rapids (Reds)	.621	Cedar Rapids (Reds)
1989	South Bend (White Sox)	.643	South Bend (White Sox)
1990	Cedar Rapids (Reds)	.656	Quad City (Angels)
1991	Clinton (Giants)	.583	Clinton (Giants)
1992	Quad City (Angels)	.664	Cedar Rapids (Reds)
1993	Clinton (Giants)	.597	South Bend (White Sox)
1994	Rockford (Royals)	.640	Cedar Rapids (Angels)
1995	Beloit (Brewers)	.633	Beloit (Brewers)

*Best overall record

MIDWEST LEAGUE
1995 BATTING, PITCHING STATISTICS

CLUB BATTING

	AVG	G	AB	R	H	2B	3B	HR	BB	SO	SB
Quad City	.269	137	4447	660	1195	226	33	78	438	767	206
Kane County	.264	138	4550	706	1201	235	38	82	535	935	171
Cedar Rapids	.263	138	4497	697	1184	234	28	101	525	880	195
Beloit	.263	139	4491	723	1181	234	35	92	560	860	194
Rockford	.263	140	4678	764	1229	275	30	83	524	894	184
Fort Wayne	.261	140	4786	691	1251	253	38	93	476	926	135
South Bend	.257	135	4507	630	1158	198	40	64	511	857	143
Michigan	.252	138	4601	684	1158	233	34	107	534	1058	175
Peoria	.249	134	4271	534	1065	175	37	53	356	738	131
Wisconsin	.245	138	4444	593	1089	230	31	55	452	926	166
Springfield	.245	139	4503	638	1101	217	41	90	425	980	187
Burlington	.240	135	4255	569	1022	166	18	113	429	960	103
Clinton	.234	137	4316	521	1011	188	18	36	510	910	160
West Michigan	.232	136	4304	650	1000	192	24	57	606	996	226

CLUB PITCHING

	ERA	G	CG	SHO	SV	IP	H	R	ER	BB	SO
Quad City	3.19	137	7	11	35	1166	1011	533	414	427	922
Wisconsin	3.75	138	14	8	35	1180	1055	599	492	501	917
South Bend	3.76	135	13	8	27	1184	1169	620	495	459	843
Peoria	3.80	134	6	9	36	1131	1039	605	478	466	937
Beloit	3.93	139	8	9	49	1196	1114	618	522	503	1064
West Michigan	3.95	136	1	9	36	1175	1146	664	515	550	893
Fort Wayne	4.03	140	4	8	41	1236	1187	660	554	515	1029
Michigan	4.05	138	9	5	31	1209	1130	665	544	502	975
Cedar Rapids	4.06	138	16	6	40	1185	1184	655	534	425	907
Rockford	4.12	140	4	5	29	1201	1136	663	550	508	829
Kane County	4.20	138	5	8	26	1182	1168	668	551	495	879
Springfield	4.32	139	4	5	22	1175	1248	680	564	429	729
Clinton	4.32	137	19	4	25	1129	1146	690	542	504	865
Burlington	4.44	135	6	4	35	1103	1112	710	545	597	898

CLUB FIELDING

	PCT	PO	A	E	DP		PCT	PO	A	E	DP
Beloit	.968	3587	1508	168	112	Kane County	.962	3545	1412	196	118
Michigan	.968	3626	1428	169	106	Quad City	.962	3499	1546	200	106
Cedar Rapids	.966	3554	1517	176	114	Fort Wayne	.962	3709	1542	210	115
Wisconsin	.965	3540	1555	184	114	Burlington	.961	3309	1451	194	111
South Bend	.964	3551	1488	186	107	Springfield	.960	3526	1579	215	105
Peoria	.964	3393	1403	178	103	West Michigan	.959	3524	1511	231	119
Rockford	.964	3603	1552	193	104	Clinton	.950	3387	1405	252	102

INDIVIDUAL BATTING LEADERS
(Minimum 378 Plate Appearances)

	AVG	G	AB	R	H	2B	3B	HR	RBI	BB	SO	SB
Smith, Demond, C.R.-W.M.	.338	87	349	70	118	26	8	9	44	34	69	40
Ibarra, Jesse, Burlington	.330	129	437	72	144	30	1	34	96	77	94	1
Mitchell, Donovan, Quad City	.329	111	383	72	126	23	1	4	42	29	38	21
Castillo, Luis, Kane County	.326	89	340	71	111	4	4	0	23	55	50	41
Hacopian, Derek, Beloit	.324	123	442	75	143	30	1	23	92	56	35	4
Valentin, Jose, Ft. Wayne	.321	112	383	59	123	26	5	19	65	47	75	0
Rodriguez, Noel, Quad City	.311	109	386	48	120	26	5	8	71	28	49	4
Koskie, Corey, Ft. Wayne	.310	123	462	64	143	37	5	16	78	38	79	2
Freire, Alejandro, Quad City	.305	125	417	71	127	23	1	15	65	50	83	9
Pico, Brandon, Rockford	.300	96	383	59	115	27	4	4	47	34	53	7

INDIVIDUAL PITCHING LEADERS
(Minimum 112 Innings)

	W	L	ERA	G	GS	CG	SV	IP	H	R	ER	BB	SO
Corrigan, Cory, Peoria	4	7	2.32	47	10	0	0	113	90	36	29	23	84
D'Amico, Jeff, Beloit	13	3	2.39	21	20	3	0	132	102	40	35	31	119
Mounce, Tony, Quad City	16	8	2.43	25	25	3	0	159	118	55	43	57	143
Smith, Charles, South Bend	10	10	2.69	26	25	4	0	167	128	70	50	61	145
Walters, Brett, Clinton	8	7	2.71	32	19	4	1	146	133	58	44	27	122
Dickson, Jason, Cedar Rapids	12	6	2.86	25	25	9	0	173	151	71	55	45	134
Dale, Carl, Peoria	9	9	2.94	24	24	2	0	144	124	66	47	62	104
Kester, Tim, Quad City	12	5	2.97	28	23	2	0	161	158	80	53	20	111
Bieniasz, Derek, Wisconsin	11	10	3.13	27	27	4	0	175	145	76	61	54	99
Cloude, Ken, Wisconsin	9	8	3.24	25	25	4	0	161	137	64	58	63	140

Jones, Guerrero Headline SAL Prospects

By GENE SAPAKOFF

Combined, Andruw Jones and Vladimir Guerrero make for a 10-tool prospect and an agent's dream. The pair of center fielders dominated the South Atlantic League in 1995, as their reputations preceded them into ballparks.

Jones, Baseball America's Minor League Player of the Year, hit 11 home runs for the Macon Braves in his first 36 games. For the season, the 18-year-old Netherlands Antilles native hit .277 with 25 home runs, 100 RBIs and a league-leading 56 stolen bases.

"Andruw can do everything and do everything well," Macon manager Nelson Norman said.

Jones homered in back-to-back at-bats against Columbus righthander Jaret Wright, the Cleveland Indians' first-round pick in 1994 and the No. 3 prospect in the league, according to a managers' survey. Jones and Guerrero ranked 1-2 in the same poll.

"What's not to like?" Albany manager Doug Sisson said. "He can go as far as desire will take him."

Like Jones, Guerrero was compared to Hall of Famer Roberto Clemente. Guerrero had the best throwing arm among SAL outfielders and threw out two runners at home plate in one game. Playing in Albany cut down on potential power numbers yet Guerrero won the league batting title, hitting .333. Only Hagerstown's Jeff Ladd had a better slugging percentage.

"He's going to be a star in the major leagues," Montreal Expos general manager Kevin Malone said.

SAL Stars. Albany's Vladimir Guerrero, left, and Macon's Andruw Jones.

Sisson, who got to put Guerrero's name in the lineup daily, said no Polecat worked harder.

"You have to see Vladimir everyday to appreciate him," Sisson said. "Even in early work, he tracks down fly balls in batting practice."

GreenJackets Take Title

The Augusta GreenJackets used something old, something new and something borrowed to make the rest of the league blue on their way to a 3-0 sweep of Piedmont in the SAL championship series.

The old: Championship game closer Rafael Chaves, 26, first pitched in the SAL in 1986 when one of his Charleston Rainbows teammates was Cleveland second baseman Carlos Baerga.

The new: First-year manager Jeff Banister led Augusta to a 76-62 record, including a first-half record of 43-25.

The borrowed: Pittsburgh Pirates management

STANDINGS: OVERALL

Page		W	L	PCT	GB	Manager	Attendance/Dates	Last Pennant
117	**Fayetteville Generals (Tigers)**	86	55	.610	—	Dwight Lowry	121,051 (65)	None
188	**Piedmont Phillies (Phillies)**	82	58	.586	3½	Roy Majtyka	115,649 (66)	None
104	**Columbus RedStixx (Indians)**	80	62	.563	6½	Jeff Datz	128,816 (70)	None
195	**Augusta GreenJackets (Pirates)**	76	62	.551	8½	Jeff Banister	171,166 (66)	1989
110	**Asheville Tourists (Rockies)**	76	63	.547	9	Bill McGuire	138,148 (63)	1984
98	**Charleston, W.Va., Alley Cats (Reds)**	77	65	.542	9½	Razor Shines	106,530 (63)	1990
233	**Hagerstown Suns (Blue Jays)**	73	68	.518	13	Omar Malave	113,438 (65)	None
175	**Columbia Bombers (Mets)**	72	68	.514	13½	Howie Freiling	152,207 (67)	1991
57	**Macon Braves (Braves)**	71	70	.504	15	Nelson Norman	113,825 (67)	None
169	**Greensboro Bats (Yankees)**	70	70	.500	15½	Trey Hillman	170,444 (68)	1982
162	**Albany Polecats (Expos)**	62	78	.443	23½	Doug Sisson	91,289 (65)	None
202	**Savannah Cardinals (Cardinals)**	56	83	.403	29	Scott Melvin	113,849 (68)	1994
227	**Charleston, S.C., RiverDogs (Rangers)**	50	89	.360	35	Mike Berger	101,280 (65)	None
85	**Hickory Crawdads (White Sox)**	49	89	.355	35½	Mike Rojas	265,017 (69)	None

NOTE: Team's individual batting and pitching statistics can be found on page indicated in lefthand column.

allowed pitcher Kevin Pickford, a first-half standout at Augusta, to come back from Lynchburg in the Carolina League for the SAL stretch drive and promoted outfielder Jose Guillen from Erie, where he led the New York-Penn League in home runs.

Chaves pitched a perfect final inning of the SAL season with tears in his eyes. His grandmother had died in Puerto Rico the night before.

"My body was here, but my heart was miles away," Chaves said.

Augusta led the league in batting (.256) and tied with Asheville for the league ERA lead (3.14). The GreenJackets swept by the Columbus RedStixx in two games in the semifinals while the Phillies knocked off Asheville two games to one.

No-Hitters A Team Effort

The league saw three no-hitters in 1995, though 11 pitchers joined in the no-hit fun.

Columbus' Wright started the first one against the Fayetteville Generals May 2 and went the first five innings. He was followed to the hill by teammates Wilmer Montoya, Noe Najera and Scot Donovan as the RedStixx won 4-1.

Charleston Alley Cats lefthander Cedric Allen tossed seven no-hit innings in a 4-0 win over Hagerstown June 22. Allen was relieved by Pete Magre and Emilio Giron who pitched one inning apiece to preserve the no-hitter.

On Aug. 18 it was Fayetteville's turn. Starter Brian Powell held the Columbia Bombers without a hit for six innings before being relieved by Jeff Siler, Adam Housley and Brandon Reed. The four combined on a 4-1 no-hitter.

Reed finished the season with a minor-league high 41 saves.

Meanwhile, Asheville outfielder Derrick Gibson was the only 30-30 player in the minor leagues in 1995. He hit .292 with 32 home runs and 31 stolen bases, while leading the league with 115 RBIs.

Doing The Charleston

A league-record 16 players plus Charleston, W.Va., Alley Cats manager Razor Shines were suspended and 51 players were fined a total of $7,150 for their roles in a brawl between the Alley Cats and the Charleston, S.C., RiverDogs at College Park in Charleston, S.C., on Aug. 15.

"In my 36 years as president (of the SAL), I've never seen anything like this," John H. Moss said.

The trouble started when Dom Gatti of the RiverDogs charged the mound after a close pitch from Alley Cats pitcher Clint Koppe. The benches and dugouts cleared. Shines and a group of Alley Cats ended up scuffling with fans in the stands near the visitors' dugout.

Shines, a former major leaguer said, "My sole inten-

STAN DENNY

Jaret Wright

tion was to protect my players. I didn't hit anybody. I didn't harm anybody. There was no charge led. It was blown out of proportion."

Holtzman Leaves Albany

Albany hosted the SAL all-star game even as rumors persisted that Polecats owner Rick Holtzman would buy his way out of a lease and move the team.

Sure enough, after the season ended Holtzman relocated his team to Salisbury, Md., and blasted Albany.

"Those who believe there is no such thing as a bad baseball town need only to examine Albany, Ga., closely," Holtzman said in a written statement.

Albany finished last in the SAL in attendance, drawing 91,289, but local officials blamed economic fallout from devastating floods that severely damaged the city during the summer of 1994.

"I don't know why you'd want to kick anybody when you leave," Albany mayor-elect Tommy Coleman said of Holtzman's attack.

SOUTH ATLANTIC LEAGUE
1995 BATTING, PITCHING STATISTICS

CLUB BATTING

	AVG	G	AB	R	H	2B	3B	HR	BB	SO	SB
Augusta	.256	138	4531	628	1158	203	37	48	411	940	215
Hagerstown	.255	141	4678	638	1191	244	34	95	461	1173	100
Columbus	.254	142	4748	630	1207	221	45	93	480	918	134
Albany	.254	140	4757	633	1206	251	44	66	510	1099	136
Fayetteville	.252	141	4633	660	1169	234	30	85	489	1025	158
Piedmont	.249	140	4595	683	1146	213	46	50	519	938	123
Greensboro	.249	140	4632	645	1154	223	26	86	525	1077	127
Charleston, W.Va.	.249	142	4551	633	1133	206	57	45	513	1002	230
Macon	.245	141	4876	739	1197	231	31	127	571	1225	172
Asheville	.243	139	4477	578	1086	210	24	81	438	928	130
Columbia	.241	140	4619	571	1111	183	34	73	387	1118	187
Charleston, S.C.	.234	139	4509	546	1054	220	20	46	514	939	218
Hickory	.227	138	4538	459	1030	198	29	57	397	1047	118
Savannah	.215	139	4534	448	977	138	28	50	544	1243	124

CLUB PITCHING

	ERA	G	CG	SHO	SV	IP	H	R	ER	BB	SO
Asheville	3.14	139	7	13	42	1212	1060	505	423	450	1011
Augusta	3.14	138	4	8	36	1199	1059	533	419	460	1000
Columbia	3.16	140	13	11	30	1236	1067	542	434	488	1045
Fayetteville	3.22	141	3	10	54	1232	1035	571	440	524	1183
Piedmont	3.26	140	7	12	38	1218	1087	574	442	460	1074
Columbus	3.41	142	3	17	48	1242	1085	598	471	569	1103
Hagerstown	3.52	141	11	8	41	1216	1178	599	476	391	906
Greensboro	3.58	140	5	11	38	1226	1137	595	488	450	1130
Charleston, W.Va.	3.59	142	10	11	42	1209	1166	559	483	443	930
Savannah	3.65	139	3	6	36	1229	1121	608	498	492	1118
Albany	3.90	140	6	5	31	1242	1282	713	538	460	1016
Macon	3.90	141	2	9	31	1270	1127	699	550	627	1136
Hickory	3.98	138	7	9	27	1222	1236	712	541	436	988
Charleston, S.C.	4.10	139	7	4	23	1201	1179	683	548	509	1032

CLUB FIELDING

	PCT	PO	A	E	DP		PCT	PO	A	E	DP
Asheville	.971	3636	1584	156	137	Piedmont	.961	3655	1467	208	113
Char., W.Va.	.968	3627	1525	169	112	Char., S.C.	.961	3604	1480	207	120
Columbus	.966	3727	1575	184	146	Macon	.960	3809	1586	226	122
Greensboro	.965	3678	1432	185	100	Fayetteville	.960	3695	1508	218	107
Columbia	.962	3707	1525	206	126	Hickory	.957	3666	1517	231	104
Savannah	.962	3686	1397	202	105	Augusta	.955	3598	1484	239	114
Hagerstown	.961	3648	1517	208	103	Albany	.945	3727	1519	303	118

INDIVIDUAL BATTING LEADERS
(Minimum 383 Plate Appearances)

	AVG	G	AB	R	H	2B	3B	HR	RBI	BB	SO	SB
Guerrero, Vladimir, Albany	.333	110	421	77	140	21	10	16	63	30	45	12
Fullmer, Brad, Albany	.323	123	468	69	151	38	4	8	67	36	33	10
Donato, Dan, Greensboro	.318	108	387	55	123	30	1	7	69	37	46	7
White, Eric, Columbus	.317	112	369	49	117	24	3	6	46	51	45	11
Ladd, Jeff, Hagerstown	.305	94	311	54	95	17	3	19	58	78	94	6
Tatis, Fernando, Char., S.C.	.303	131	499	74	151	43	4	15	84	45	94	22
Hall, Ronnie, Asheville	.299	130	448	64	134	20	4	4	46	44	78	26
Millan, Adam, Piedmont	.294	107	394	69	116	25	2	10	64	44	45	1
Rivers, Jonathon, Hag.	.294	123	429	54	126	16	6	6	48	40	104	18
Gibson, Derrick, Asheville	.292	135	506	91	148	16	10	32	115	29	136	31

INDIVIDUAL PITCHING LEADERS
(Minimum 114 Innings)

	W	L	ERA	G	GS	CG	SV	IP	H	R	ER	BB	SO
Kusiewicz, Mike, Asheville	8	4	2.06	21	21	0	0	122	92	40	28	34	103
Jordan, Jason, Fayetteville	10	4	2.28	24	24	0	0	138	128	48	35	43	103
Manning, Len, Piedmont	10	10	2.64	27	26	1	0	160	130	68	47	58	154
Wimberly, Larry, Piedmont	10	3	2.67	24	24	0	0	135	99	48	40	44	139
Herbert, Russell, Hickory	3	8	2.67	18	18	1	0	115	83	48	34	46	115
Moraga, David, Albany	8	8	2.68	25	24	1	0	148	136	63	44	46	109
Atwater, Joe, Columbia	9	6	2.69	27	18	3	1	147	106	52	44	28	127
Allen, Cedric, Char., W.Va.	13	7	2.85	27	27	5	0	170	143	64	54	46	108
Sievert, Mark, Hagerstown	12	6	2.91	27	27	3	0	161	126	59	52	46	140
Gooch, Arnold, Ashe.-C'bia	5	8	2.94	21	21	1	0	129	111	51	42	57	117

DEPARTMENT LEADERS

BATTING

G	Two tied at	139
AB	Wes Helms, Macon	539
R	Andruw Jones, Macon	104
H	Two tied at	151
TB	Derrick Gibson, Asheville	280
2B	Fernando Tatis, Char., S.C.	43
3B	Matt Guiliano, Piedmont	12
HR	Two tied at	32
RBI	Derrick Gibson, Asheville	115
SH	Jose Lobaton, Greensboro	11
SF	Andruw Jones, Macon	9
BB	Gus Kennedy, Macon	95
IBB	Daryle Ward, Fayetteville	11
HBP	Jamie Northeimer, Piedmont	20
SO	Chris Schwab, Albany	173
SB	Andruw Jones, Macon	56
CS	Ryan Rutz, Charleston, S.C.	26
GIDP	Aaron Royster, Piedmont	16
OB%	Jeff Ladd, Hagerstown	.454
SL%	Jeff Ladd, Hagerstown	.563

PITCHING

G	Matt Golden, Savannah	64
GS	Cam Smith, Fayetteville	29
CG	Cedric Allen, Char., W.Va.	5
ShO	Brent Crowther, Asheville	3
GF	Brandon Reed, Fayetteville	53
Sv	Brandon Reed, Fayetteville	41
W	Derrin Ebert, Macon	14
L	Rafael Ramirez, Savannah	15
IP	Derrin Ebert, Macon	182
H	Derrin Ebert, Macon	184
R	Luther Hackman, Asheville	95
ER	Luther Hackman, Asheville	85
HR	John Kelly, Columbia	16
BB	Two tied at	87
SO	Two tied at	177
WP	Cam Smith, Fayetteville	21

FIELDING

C AVG	Julio Mosquera, Hag.	.991
E	2 tied at	14
1B AVG	Craig Stone, Hagerstown	.991
E	Nate Brown, Albany	28
2B AVG	Epi Cardenas, Columbus	.978
E	Derek Swafford, Augusta	31
3B AVG	Pete Carranza, Asheville	.936
E	Andy Thompson, Hag.	43
SS AVG	Kyle Houser, Asheville	.973
E	Hiram Bocachica, Albany	58
OF AVG	Aaron Royster, Piedmont	.991
E	Ronnie Hall, Asheville	12

HONOR ROLL

OFFICIAL ALL-STAR TEAM

C—Julio Mosquera, Hagerstown. 1B—Daryle Ward, Fayetteville. 2B—Julio Zorrilla, Columbia. 3B—Wes Helms, Macon. SS—Hiram Bocachica, Asheville. OF—Derrick Gibson, Asheville; Vladimir Guerrero, Albany; Andruw Jones, Macon. DH—Jeff Ladd, Hagerstown.

RHP—Brent Crowther, Asheville. LHP—Larry Wimberly, Piedmont.

MVP—Andruw Jones, Macon. **Most Outstanding Pitcher**—Larry Wimberly, Piedmont.

Manager of the Year—Roy Majtyka, Piedmont.

TOP 10 PROSPECTS
(Selected by league managers)
1. Andruw Jones, of, Macon
2. Vladimir Guerrero, of, Albany
3. Jaret Wright, rhp, Columbus
4. Derrick Gibson, of, Asheville
5. Todd Helton, 1b, Asheville
6. Ron Wright, 1b, Macon
7. Larry Wimberly, lhp, Piedmont
8. Jimmy Anderson, lhp, Augusta
9. Brent Crowther, rhp, Asheville
10. Preston Wilson, of, Columbia

Watertown Survives Turmoil To Win Title

By BOB SUTTON

Off-field confusion never made it between the lines for the Watertown Indians in 1995.

While local owners were divided about selling the team and fans were distraught over a potential franchise relocation, the Indians remained united on the field. That resulted in the city's first New York-Penn League championship.

Coincidence or not, when the off-field controversy began to brew, the Indians made their move in the standings. By the time they were done, they had captured their third consecutive Pinckney Division championship and survived two close playoff series.

"What's real rewarding is the way the players came on the last six weeks," first-year Watertown manager Joel Skinner said. "You could see the whole thing kind of develop. They understood this was a marathon type of thing."

Far from stellar statistically, the Indians were opportunistic. At one point in August, they owned first place despite possessing the league's worst team batting average. Pitching carried the load, and then conveniently the hitting picked up during the final three weeks.

Joel Skinner

Watertown needed home victories in Games Two and Three to oust the Batavia Clippers in the semifinals. The championship round proved even more grueling against the Vermont Expos.

Three days into the series, only one game had been played—a Watertown home triumph. Rainouts hampered the series, so the final two games were played as a doubleheader. Vermont won Game Two to force a deciding game.

Game Three was scheduled to be seven innings, but it went nine, with Watertown winning 3-1. The Indians stymied several Vermont rallies and then scored two unearned runs in the ninth—in part, because of wet conditions caused by dew in Burlington, Vt. The final ended around 1 a.m.

Reliever Scott Winchester took part in all the postseason victories, with a couple of gutty performances typifying the Watertown season. He worked the final 3⅓ innings of the deciding game, retiring all 10 hitters and striking out five.

Skinner, a former catcher, became a championship manager 16 months after retiring as a player. For Vermont manager Jim Gabella, his former employer provided the final frustration. Gabella had spent the previous six years with the Cleveland organization, including two stints as manager in Watertown.

Vermont swept the four-game, regular-season series from Watertown en route to posting the league's best regular-season record at 49-27. Expos pitcher Chris Weidert led the league with an 11-1 record and 1.79 ERA.

It marked the fifth consecutive year in which the team with the best record in the regular season failed to win the league championship.

Strong At Third Base

Third baseman Tim Jorgensen played in every game for Watertown after coming off a record-setting NCAA Division III season for the University of Wisconsin-Oshkosh. Jorgensen led the league with 157 total bases, while finishing among the league leaders in

STANDINGS

Page	McNAMARA	W	L	PCT	GB	Manager	Attendance/Dates	Last Pennant
163	Vermont Expos (Expos)	49	27	.645	—	Jim Gabella	120,917 (37)	None
228	Hudson Valley Renegades (Rangers)	47	27	.635	1	Bump Wills	161,673 (37)	None
203	New Jersey Cardinals (Cardinals)	35	41	.461	14	Luis Melendez	176,788 (38)	1994
176	Pittsfield Mets (Mets)	34	42	.447	15	Ron Gideon	73,273 (38)	None

Page	PINCKNEY	W	L	PCT	GB	Manager	Attendance/Dates	Last Pennant
105	Watertown Indians (Indians)	46	27	.630	—	Joel Skinner	45,202 (35)	1995
130	Auburn Astros (Astros)	40	34	.541	6½	Manny Acta	58,972 (36)	1973
92	Williamsport Cubs (Cubs)	37	39	.487	10½	Oneri Fleita	63,192 (38)	None
169	Oneonta Yankees (Yankees)	34	41	.453	13	Rob Thomson	53,990 (37)	1990
72	Utica Blue Sox (Red Sox)	33	40	.452	13	Bob Geren	64,487 (37)	1983
123	Elmira Pioneers (Marlins)	25	51	.329	22½	Paul Kirsch	43,759 (37)	1976

Page	STEDLER	W	L	PCT	GB	Manager	Attendance/Dates	Last Pennant
188	Batavia Clippers (Phillies)	41	34	.547	—	Al LeBoeuf	38,313 (36)	1963
233	St. Catharines Stompers (Blue Jays)	38	37	.507	3	J.J. Cannon	50,528 (36)	1986
195	Erie SeaWolves (Pirates)	34	41	.453	7	Scott Little	181,815 (37)	1957
117	Jamestown Jammers (Tigers)	32	44	.421	9½	Bruce Fields	48,938 (37)	1991

PLAYOFFS—Semifinals: Watertown defeated Batavia 2-1, and Vermont defeated Hudson Valley 2-0, in best-of-3 series. **Finals:** Watertown defeated Vermont 2-1, in best-of-3 series.

NOTE: Team's individual batting and pitching statistics can be found on page indicated in lefthand column.

average (.325), home runs (9) and RBIs (52). He set several franchise marks.

He was upstaged by another third baseman, Cliff Brumbaugh of the Hudson Valley Renegades who won the batting title, hitting .358. Brumbaugh also was voted the league's MVP.

The two championship series teams advanced to post-season play without a couple of defections to college football.

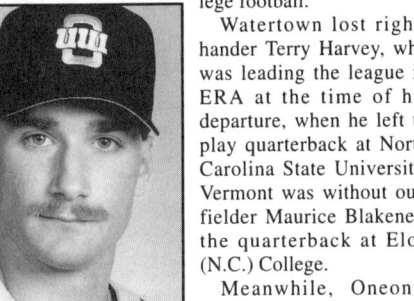

Tim Jorgensen

Watertown lost right-hander Terry Harvey, who was leading the league in ERA at the time of his departure, when he left to play quarterback at North Carolina State University. Vermont was without outfielder Maurice Blakeney, the quarterback at Elon (N.C.) College.

Meanwhile, Oneonta outfielder Shea Morenz gave up his college football career to sign as the first-round draft pick for the New York Yankees. Morenz was a quarterback for three years at the University of Texas.

Young Guns

The New York-Penn League is considered a good entry-level league for recently drafted college players, but teenagers made a surprising impact in 1995, particularly two first-round picks from the June draft.

Erie shortstop Chad Hermansen, 17, earned the immediate respect of the league's managers, who rated him the circuit's top major league prospect. Hermansen was Pittsburgh's first-round draft pick and displayed a steady bat and played solidly in the field.

Elmira outfielder Jaime Jones, Florida's first-round selection, was a threat at the plate, hitting .284, and a whiz in the field.

AL SOLOMON

Chris Weidert. Vermont righthander led the New York-Penn League in wins (11) and ERA (1.79).

Jose Guillen, a 19-year-old outfielder for Erie, belted a league-best 12 home runs while hitting .314.

Auburn Astros catcher Ramon Castro, who was drafted by Houston in the first round of the 1994 draft, became one of the most imposing players in the league. The 19-year-old's bat startled pitchers and his presence behind the plate caused heads to turn.

League Returns To Erie

After a season without an NY-P team, fans in Erie embraced a new Pirates affiliate, which played in a new ballpark after moving from Welland, Ontario. Erie, which drew a league-record 181,815 fans, might

Jose Guillen

have set itself up for a move to a higher classification. The city hosted a team in the independent Frontier League in 1994.

A new stadium welcomed fans and players in Auburn, where old Falcon Park was once considered the worst facility in the league.

Attendance remained strong for Vermont, New Jersey and Hudson Valley. All three of the second-year teams broke 100,000 in attendance. Altogether the league drew 1,181,847 fans.

LEAGUE CHAMPIONS

Last 25 Years

Year	Regular Season*	Pct.	Playoff
1971	Oneonta (Yankees)	.662	None
1972	Niagara Falls (Pirates)	.686	None
1973	Auburn (Phillies)	.667	None
1974	Oneonta (Yankees)	.768	None
1975	Newark (Brewers)	.701	None
1976	Elmira (Red Sox)	.714	None
1977	Oneonta (Yankees)	.671	Oneonta (Yankees)
1978	Oneonta (Yankees)	.729	Geneva (Cubs)
1979	Geneva (Cubs)	.725	Oneonta (Yankees)
1980	Oneonta (Yankees)	.662	Oneonta (Yankees)
1981	Oneonta (Yankees)	.658	Oneonta (Yankees)
1982	Oneonta (Yankees)	.566	Niagara Falls (White Sox)
1983	Utica (Independent)	.649	Utica (Independent)
	Newark (Orioles)	.649	
1984	Newark (Orioles)	.622	Little Falls (Mets)
1985	Oneonta (Yankees)	.705	Oneonta (Yankees)
1986	Oneonta (Yankees)	.766	St. Catharines (Blue Jays)
1987	Geneva (Cubs)	.632	Geneva (Cubs)
1988	Oneonta (Yankees)	.632	Oneonta (Yankees)
1989	Pittsfield (Mets)	.697	Jamestown (Expos)
1990	Oneonta (Yankees)	.667	Oneonta (Yankees)
1991	Pittsfield (Mets)	.662	Jamestown (Expos)
1992	Hamilton (Cardinals)	.737	Geneva (Cubs)
1993	St. Catharines (Jays)	.628	Niagara Falls (Tigers)
1994	Watertown (Indians)	.649	New Jersey (Cardinals)
1995	Vermont (Expos)	.645	Watertown (Indians)
	*Best overall record		

NEW YORK-PENN LEAGUE
1995 BATTING, PITCHING STATISTICS

CLUB BATTING

	AVG	G	AB	R	H	2B	3B	HR	BB	SO	SB
Auburn	.267	74	2444	383	653	112	18	32	258	410	71
Hudson Valley	.267	74	2512	376	670	105	25	24	252	465	107
Erie	.264	75	2503	368	661	92	25	46	232	502	81
Batavia	.262	75	2592	389	680	106	31	31	236	474	88
St. Catharines	.257	75	2557	344	658	119	25	28	248	570	96
Vermont	.257	76	2505	354	643	94	28	24	257	457	152
Watertown	.257	73	2456	360	630	127	26	29	299	529	49
Utica	.256	73	2425	358	622	98	23	33	191	479	125
Williamsport	.255	76	2561	379	654	122	34	21	275	523	85
Jamestown	.254	76	2544	368	646	117	29	35	338	526	104
New Jersey	.250	76	2603	370	651	105	27	13	280	477	93
Pittsfield	.249	76	2498	325	623	101	32	14	274	487	103
Elmira	.243	76	2534	316	616	106	30	34	253	552	111
Oneonta	.243	75	2489	312	604	125	30	18	259	553	87

CLUB PITCHING

	ERA	G	CG	SHO	SV	IP	H	R	ER	BB	SO
Vermont	2.86	76	1	9	30	668	558	282	212	251	479
Watertown	3.09	73	1	7	23	645	580	268	222	228	508
Williamsport	3.38	76	0	2	20	665	678	362	250	193	494
Oneonta	3.51	75	0	2	20	647	611	368	252	287	595
Erie	3.51	75	5	5	16	653	648	350	255	256	434
Hudson Valley	3.57	74	4	3	24	660	637	325	262	236	536
St. Catharines	3.71	75	1	3	19	670	652	341	276	292	461
Pittsfield	3.85	76	3	4	22	659	671	369	282	265	451
New Jersey	3.85	76	0	5	17	682	649	372	292	303	607
Batavia	3.93	75	4	8	14	666	716	369	291	194	507
Utica	4.00	73	7	2	19	636	643	379	283	300	500
Auburn	4.50	74	6	5	24	622	620	366	311	300	431
Elmira	4.55	76	0	2	16	658	675	424	333	293	507
Jamestown	4.59	76	1	1	15	667	673	427	340	254	494

CLUB FIELDING

	PCT	PO	A	E	DP		PCT	PO	A	E	DP
Watertown	.972	1936	894	83	72	Jamestown	.957	2000	896	131	63
Vermont	.962	2003	858	113	79	Elmira	.956	1974	894	133	64
Hudson Valley	.960	1980	864	120	64	Pittsfield	.955	1977	880	135	67
St. Catharines	.959	2009	917	126	72	Utica	.952	1909	827	138	62
Batavia	.959	1998	877	124	90	Erie	.950	1959	897	150	72
Auburn	.958	1865	832	119	71	Williamsport	.947	1996	828	158	57
New Jersey	.957	2046	739	124	55	Oneonta	.944	1940	827	165	50

INDIVIDUAL BATTING LEADERS
(Minimum 205 Plate Appearances)

	AVG	G	AB	R	H	2B	3B	HR	RBI	BB	SO	SB
Brumbaugh, Cliff, H.V.	.358	74	282	44	101	19	4	2	45	39	51	15
Bady, Ed, Vermont	.329	72	295	51	97	15	3	2	25	24	52	34
Casey, Sean, Watertown	.329	55	207	26	68	18	0	2	37	18	21	3
Wilcox, Luke, Oneonta	.327	59	223	25	73	16	7	1	28	20	28	9
Bates, Fletcher, Pittsfield	.326	75	276	52	90	14	9	6	37	41	72	17
Jorgensen, Tim, Watertown	.325	73	295	44	96	19	9	8	52	32	63	4
Vieira, Scott, Williamsport	.318	61	214	35	68	8	2	6	46	25	37	3
Rice, Andy, Erie	.316	70	269	44	85	15	2	8	33	19	59	7
Dawkins, Walter, Batavia	.315	58	203	46	64	11	4	1	31	27	36	15
Winn, Randy, Elmira	.315	51	213	38	67	7	4	0	22	15	31	19

INDIVIDUAL PITCHING LEADERS
(Minimum 61 Innings)

	W	L	ERA	G	GS	CG	SV	IP	H	R	ER	BB	SO
Weidert, Chris, Vermont	11	1	1.79	15	15	1	0	95	67	31	19	21	52
Dixon, Tim, Vermont	7	2	1.83	18	9	0	1	69	58	20	14	16	58
McNeese, John, Williamsport	5	3	1.86	13	12	0	0	73	73	24	15	10	47
Young, Joe, St. Catharines	6	5	2.04	15	15	0	0	84	72	29	19	35	73
Mudd, Scott, Hudson Valley	7	1	2.24	15	15	3	0	101	91	37	25	18	62
Bullock, Derek, Erie	4	4	2.35	11	11	1	0	65	65	21	17	15	27
Yeager, Gary, Batavia	9	4	2.56	19	8	1	0	81	74	33	23	16	57
Trumpour, Andy, Pittsfield	7	6	2.57	15	15	2	0	105	95	44	30	32	75
Stephens, Shannon, Elmira	8	5	2.58	17	12	0	0	91	72	38	26	17	74
Hamilton, Bo, Batavia	7	2	2.58	14	13	1	0	84	73	30	24	23	62

Hawks Tops On Field, Rockies At Gate

By SHANNON FEARS

In what proved to be a relatively quiet year on the field, the biggest noise made in the Northwest League in 1995 came from the turnstiles at Portland's Civic Stadium.

The Rockies drew a league-record 249,696 fans, an average of 6,571 per contest, allowing the league to eclipse the one-million mark in attendance for the first time.

The Colorado farm club, owned by the husband-and-wife team of Jack and Mary Cain, had spent the previous 14 years in Bend, a Central Oregon resort town with a population of about 30,000, and drew 69,225 there in 1994. Portland boasts a metropolitan area that contains nearly 2 million residents.

The move to Portland, the Cains' hometown, was made possible by the departure after the 1993 season of owner Joe Buzas' Pacific Coast League franchise, which ended up in Salt Lake City.

Buzas' last team in Portland, known as the Beavers and with a long, rich tradition of play in the PCL, drew 186,010 in 34 more dates. In fact, only two other Portland teams (1956 and 1983) ever drew more than the Cains were able to attract to Civic Stadium in 1995.

The reason may have been simple absence. Civic Stadium sat dark for a year (1994) while the PCL franchise in Calgary explored a move to Portland before deciding against it, and Rose City fans embraced the return of professional baseball by coming out 20,000 strong on Opening Night.

Portland fans reacted enthusiastically to the Cains' promotion-driven environment, even if short-season Class A baseball was a little hard to swallow for some in a community where the local National Basketball Association franchise is on a pedestal and the desire to be identified as major league is strong.

"I think we did a good enough job of entertaining the fans," Jack Cain said. "If they had a good time this season, chances are we can get them back next season, too."

Dynasty In Boise

The Rockies also gave their fans a team to cheer for, holding down the top spot in the league's South Divi-

Ryan Kane. Boise slugger swung a big bat for Northwest League champions, hitting 14 homers with 59 RBIs.

sion until August, thanks largely to a superb pitching staff that eventually would be decimated by call-ups.

When the Rockies faltered, the Boise Hawks passed them, winning the middle six games of a key eight-game series between the two teams in August. That signaled business as usual in the league as the Hawks went on to win the league championship for the fourth time in five years, all under manager Tom Kotchman.

Not that it was easy. Bellingham, which won 20 of 25 at one stretch midway through the season to nail down the North, won the first game of the best-of-3 championship series at home.

STANDINGS

Page	NORTH	W	L	PCT	GB	Manager	Attendance/Dates	Last Pennant
216	**Bellingham Giants (Giants)**	43	33	.566	—	Glenn Tufts	54,104 (35)	1992
221	**Everett AquaSox (Mariners)**	37	39	.487	6	Orlando Gomez	89,950 (38)	1985
136	**Spokane Indians (Royals)**	36	39	.480	6½	Al Pedrique	162,344 (38)	1990
143	**Yakima Bears (Dodgers)**	27	48	.360	15½	Joe Vavra	81,570 (38)	1964

Page	SOUTH	W	L	PCT	GB	Manager	Attendance/Dates	Last Pennant
79	**Boise Hawks (Angels)**	48	27	.640	—	Tom Kotchman	165,255 (36)	1995
111	**Portland Rockies (Rockies)**	41	34	.547	7	P.J. Carey	249,696 (38)	None
57	**Eugene Emeralds (Braves)**	37	39	.487	11½	Paul Runge	134,878 (38)	1980
182	**Southern Oregon Athletics (A's)**	33	43	.434	15½	Tony DeFrancesco	84,682 (37)	1983

PLAYOFFS—Boise defeated Bellingham 2-1, in best-of-3 series.

NOTE: Team's individual batting and pitching statistics can be found on page indicated in lefthand column.

Then the Giants took a 2-0 lead into the bottom of the ninth at Boise and were three outs away from the crown when the Hawks rallied with three in the ninth to force a third and deciding game.

The Hawks won that tilt 8-0, giving them their third straight league title. In six seasons under Kotchman, Boise has won five division crowns, being denied only in 1992 by Bend, and four NWL championships.

Young Talent

In contrast to the previous season, when a handful of high-profile draftees hit the league and made immediate waves, the '95 season offered a procession of younger players with perhaps more long-term potential.

Southern Oregon, which finished 10 games under .500, nonetheless had the league's top prospect in

Miguel Tejada

shortstop Miguel Tejada, a 19-year-old Dominican who impressed even the grizzled managers of the league with his range at shortstop and the pop in his bat.

Tejada (.245-8-44) was but one of a number of players under the legal drinking age who caught the eyes of opposing managers in the league. Eugene, in the first year of a new working agreement with Atlanta, had three such players in left fielder George Lombard, catcher Fernando Lunar and shortstop Glenn Williams.

Lombard, Lunar and Williams all began the season with Class A Macon but weren't quite ready for the

Kevin Gibbs. Yakima all-star outfielder swiped a Northwest League high 39 bases.

South Atlantic League. They proved they could hold their own in Eugene, though Lunar and Williams were just 18 and Lombard 19. Williams, who impressed managers with his power potential, muscled up for seven home runs and 36 RBIs.

The previous year, four first-rounders—Ben Grieve, Paul Konerko, Dante Powell and Doug Million—played significant parts of the season and left large impressions.

In '95, the only first-rounders to appear were Jose Cruz Jr., who was chosen by the Seattle Mariners with the No. 3 overall pick, and righthander Joe Fontenot, who was selected by the San Francisco Giants with the 16th overall choice. Cruz appeared in one three-game series with the Everett AquaSox before reporting to Class A Riverside (California). Fontenot worked just 19 innings for Bellingham after signing late and was 0-3 despite a 1.93 ERA.

Danny Buxbaum

The league MVP was Boise first sacker Danny Buxbaum, a 22-year-old Floridian who was an 11th-round pick by California out of the University of Miami. Buxbaum, who won the batting title with a .329 mark, hit eight home runs and had 51 RBIs.

Buxbaum's teammate Ryan Kane had a stellar debut season as well, leading the league with 14 home runs and 59 RBIs, while hitting .277.

LEAGUE CHAMPIONS

Last 25 Years

Year	Regular Season	Pct.	Playoff
1971	Tri-Cities (Padres)	.625	None
1972	Lewiston (Orioles)	.675	None
1973	Walla Walla (Padres)	.638	None
1974	Bellingham (Dodgers)	.619	Eugene (Independent)
1975	Eugene (Reds)	.684	Eugene (Reds)
1976	Walla Walla (Padres)	.639	Walla Walla (Padres)
1977	Portland (Independent)	.667	Bellingham (Mariners)
1978	Grays Harbor (Independent)	.671	Grays Harbor (Ind.)
1979	Bend (Phillies)	.606	Bend (Phillies)
1980	Bellingham (Mariners)	.643	Bellingham (Mariners)# Eugene (Reds)#
1981	Medford (Athletics)	.600	Medford (Athletics) •
1982	Medford (Athletics)	.757	Salem (Angels)
1983	Medford (Athletics)	.735	Medford (Athletics)
1984	Tri-Cities (Rangers)	.622	Tri-Cities (Rangers)
1985	Everett (Giants)	.541	Everett (Giants)
	Eugene (Royals)	.541	
1986	Bellingham (Mariners)	.608	Bellingham (Mariners)
	Eugene (Royals)	.608	
1987	Spokane (Padres)	.711	Spokane (Padres)
1988	Southern Oregon (Athletics)	.605	Spokane (Padres)
1989	Southern Oregon (Athletics)	.600	Spokane (Padres)
1990	Boise (Angels)	.697	Spokane (Padres)
1991	Boise (Angels)	.650	Boise (Angels)
1992	Bellingham (Mariners)	.566	Bellingham (Mariners)
	Bend (Rockies)	.566	
1993	Bellingham (Mariners)	.579	Boise (Angels)
1994	Yakima (Dodgers)	.645	Boise (Angels)
1995	Boise (Angels)	.640	Boise (Angels)

*Best overall record   #Co-champions

NORTHWEST LEAGUE
1995 BATTING, PITCHING STATISTICS

CLUB BATTING

	AVG	G	AB	R	H	2B	3B	HR	BB	SO	SB
Boise	.265	75	2523	411	669	117	16	49	350	506	68
Eugene	.249	76	2534	364	630	104	24	48	233	578	137
Yakima	.244	76	2560	288	624	116	25	21	260	565	122
Spokane	.242	76	2575	333	623	110	11	30	271	546	54
Everett	.241	76	2591	369	625	116	16	62	318	650	113
Bellingham	.239	76	2563	334	613	111	11	44	276	654	79
Southern Oregon	.237	76	2488	372	589	109	20	36	385	509	107
Portland	.223	75	2407	316	536	92	19	21	307	542	126

CLUB PITCHING

	ERA	G	CG	SHO	SV	IP	H	R	ER	BB	SO
Bellingham	3.05	76	0	8	21	685	618	297	232	285	591
Portland	3.06	75	4	4	23	662	531	284	225	277	561
Eugene	3.56	76	0	2	19	667	606	372	264	313	635
Everett	3.62	76	5	4	15	680	622	346	274	294	572
Spokane	3.65	76	1	4	20	681	653	345	276	269	522
Southern Oregon	3.72	76	0	3	13	669	667	374	277	237	542
Boise	3.90	75	4	5	20	654	575	343	283	329	590
Yakima	4.54	76	0	2	17	668	637	426	337	396	537

CLUB FIELDING

	PCT	PO	A	E	DP		PCT	PO	A	E	DP
Portland	.967	1987	909	100	68	Bellingham	.958	2056	860	129	55
Boise	.965	1961	808	99	66	So. Oregon	.954	2008	915	140	54
Everett	.963	2040	874	112	63	Yakima	.954	2003	878	139	63
Spokane	.962	2042	920	117	73	Eugene	.946	2001	844	161	54

Thad Chrismon
32 appearances

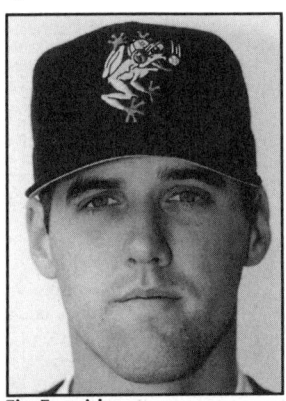

Tim Trawick
6-2, 3.14

INDIVIDUAL BATTING LEADERS
(Minimum 205 Plate Appearances)

	AVG	G	AB	R	H	2B	3B	HR	RBI	BB	SO	SB
Buxbaum, Danny, Boise	.329	68	231	46	76	15	0	8	51	49	31	1
Vida, James, Spokane	.323	74	291	38	94	13	1	4	39	19	32	0
Bilderback, Ty, Boise	.322	61	177	35	57	11	2	3	25	29	29	10
Ham, Kevin, Boise	.315	69	238	39	75	17	3	7	43	40	57	2
Gibbs, Kevin, Yakima	.313	52	182	36	57	6	4	1	18	36	46	38
Trippy, Joe, Eugene	.309	75	259	48	80	16	0	2	38	24	31	29
Hallmark, Patrick, Spokane	.304	56	227	36	69	11	0	4	25	13	37	5
Watson, Jon, Bellingham	.299	65	231	42	69	9	0	2	27	20	41	16
Cruz, Deivi, Bellingham	.296	62	223	32	66	17	0	3	28	19	21	6
Hodges, Randy, Eugene	.291	61	206	29	60	7	5	2	28	12	35	10

INDIVIDUAL PITCHING LEADERS
(Minimum 61 Innings)

	W	L	ERA	G	GS	CG	SV	IP	H	R	ER	BB	SO
Randall, Scott, Portland	7	3	1.99	15	15	1	0	95	76	35	21	28	78
Blood, Darin, Bellingham	6	3	2.54	14	13	0	0	74	63	26	21	32	78
Cruz, Charlie, Eugene	6	7	2.55	15	15	0	0	81	68	34	23	36	90
Niemeier, Todd, Everett	4	3	2.81	15	15	0	0	80	74	33	25	26	80
Villarreal, Modesto, Spokane	8	2	2.90	16	11	0	0	81	73	30	26	23	57
McKnight, Chris, Eugene	5	2	2.92	13	13	0	0	65	63	31	21	21	30
D'Alessandro, Marc, Portland	9	3	2.96	16	15	2	0	97	85	41	32	28	64
Thurmond, Travis, Boise	9	3	3.11	16	15	4	0	101	75	36	35	31	93
Kurtz, Danny, Everett	5	2	3.12	14	12	1	0	69	60	27	24	32	43
Trawick, Tim, Everett	6	2	3.14	16	13	3	0	86	66	34	30	30	63

APPALACHIAN
LEAGUE

Kingsport Wins Battle of Best Records

By JAMES BAILEY

When the two teams with the highest winning percentages in professional baseball in 1995 squared off in the Appalachian League playoffs, something had to give.

It did, in favor of the Kingsport Mets.

The Bluefield Orioles, who won 16 consecutive games and 23 of 24 during one stretch, finished the regular season with a .754 mark, winning the Northern Division by 17 games. They led the league in both pitching and hitting, finishing with a .293 team batting average, 30 points higher than the next best team.

Meanwhile, the Mets finished at .727 and captured the Southern Division crown by14 games.

The Mets emerged from the showdown as Appy League champions, taking the best-of-3 playoff series from Bluefield two games to one. It was their first title since 1988.

Kingsport center fielder Dan Ramirez launched a three-run homer in the eighth inning of Game Three to give the Mets an 11-6 win. Kingsport scored 33 runs in the series.

The two teams also combined to land four players on the managers list of Top 10 prospects, including three of the first four. Bluefield righthander Chris Fussell was chosen the No. 1 prospect after leading the league with nine wins and 98 strikeouts, in only 66 innings. Fussell, however, was rocked in the first game of the playoffs, losing 16-2 to Kingsport.

Martinsville outfielder Reggie Taylor was the lone 1995 first-round pick to play in the Appy League. He was taken 14th overall by Philadelphia.

JOANNE COLENZO

Jarrod Patterson

Three Appy League veterans finished atop the home run leaders. Princeton outfielder Darron Ingram hit 14, followed by Kingsport first baseman Jarrod Patterson,

the league's MVP, with 13 and Danville first baseman Ray McWhite with 12.

Danville righthander Winston Abreu threw one of two 1995 Appy no-hitters. On July 2, Abreu tossed a seven-inning 7-1 gem over Burlington in the second game of a doubleheader. For Abreu, who went 0-8 in the Gulf Coast League in 1994, it was his first professional victory.

River City Rumblers righthander Ty Young tossed the second no-hitter, blanking Elizabethton 4-0 in seven-innings on Aug. 3.

The Rumblers were forced to operate as a co-op in 1995 when they lost their affiliation with the Cubs organization. They had operated as the Huntington Cubs since 1990.

Bristol also saw a change in affiliation when the White Sox replaced the Tigers as parent club.

STANDINGS

Page	NORTH	W	L	PCT	GB	Manager	Attendance/Dates	Last Pennant
65	Bluefield Orioles (Orioles)	49	16	.754	—	Andy Etchebarren	45,127 (31)	1992
99	Princeton Reds (Reds)	31	32	.492	17	Brad Kelley	29,021 (29)	1994
189	Martinsville Phillies (Phillies)	30	37	.448	20	Ramon Henderson	46,155 (28)	None
105	Burlington Indians (Indians)	26	38	.406	22 ½	Harry Spilman	32,648 (30)	1993
58	Danville Braves (Braves)	27	40	.403	23	Max Venable	63,905 (30)	None

Page	SOUTH	W	L	PCT	GB	Manager	Attendance/Dates	Last Pennant
176	Kingsport Mets (Mets)	48	18	.727	—	John Gibbons	35,891 (30)	1995
156	Elizabethton Twins (Twins)	33	31	.516	14	John Russell	18,982 (29)	1990
203	Johnson City Cardinals (Cardinals)	35	33	.515	14	Steve Turco	41,449 (32)	1976
86	Bristol White Sox (White Sox)	28	39	.418	20 ½	Chris Cron	29,691 (32)	1985
238	River City Rumblers (Co-op)	22	45	.328	26 ½	Philip Wellman	20,631 (29)	None

PLAYOFFS—Kingsport defeated Bluefield 2-1, in best-of-3 series.

NOTE: Team's individual batting and pitching statistics can be found on page indicated in lefthand column.

APPALACHIAN LEAGUE
1995 BATTING, PITCHING STATISTICS

CLUB BATTING

	AVG	G	AB	R	H	2B	3B	HR	BB	SO	SB
Bluefield	.293	65	2174	437	637	120	22	42	241	416	128
Elizabethton	.263	64	2172	363	572	108	11	59	243	493	78
Kingsport	.263	66	2199	402	578	98	22	33	247	458	113
Danville	.258	67	2230	326	576	100	21	35	241	546	128
Bristol	.253	67	2209	296	559	91	18	29	210	546	95
Johnson City	.249	68	2261	357	562	119	23	28	304	583	70
Martinsville	.247	67	2131	325	526	98	17	27	257	531	91
Burlington	.238	64	2133	298	508	92	15	40	194	598	104
Princeton	.237	63	2098	330	497	100	13	53	210	546	71
River City	.237	67	2134	307	505	96	22	32	255	552	108

CLUB PITCHING

	ERA	G	CG	SHO	SV	IP	H	R	ER	BB	SO
Bluefield	3.22	65	2	3	28	561	511	269	201	227	531
Elizabethton	3.41	64	4	5	13	551	550	299	209	183	535
Kingsport	3.49	66	5	6	20	574	480	263	223	226	532
Princeton	4.19	63	1	4	15	543	538	339	253	267	506
Bristol	4.24	67	2	2	10	566	552	347	267	224	532
Danville	4.35	67	2	2	18	571	540	378	276	243	536
Martinsville	4.58	67	0	1	17	558	582	349	284	247	511
Johnson City	4.75	68	2	3	20	589	599	399	311	279	539
Burlington	4.87	64	4	4	12	550	538	373	298	272	582
River City	5.49	67	6	1	11	560	630	425	342	234	465

CLUB FIELDING

	PCT	PO	A	E	DP		PCT	PO	A	E	DP
Kingsport	.962	1723	687	94	45	Burlington	.947	1650	613	127	42
Bluefield	.956	1683	651	107	56	Johnson City	.946	1767	655	141	38
Martinsville	.953	1673	682	115	50	Princeton	.944	1630	657	136	47
Danville	.949	1712	650	126	49	Bristol	.941	1699	691	151	43
River City	.948	1681	704	131	40	Elizabethton	.934	1653	741	168	51

A.J. Pierzynski
All-star catcher

Carlos Lee
.346-7-45

Jamie Splittorff
5-4, 3.24

INDIVIDUAL BATTING LEADERS
(Minimum 205 Plate Appearances)

	AVG	G	AB	R	H	2B	3B	HR	RBI	BB	SO	SB
Munoz, Juan, Johnson City	.347	57	190	43	66	12	1	7	31	27	17	13
Lee, Carlos, Bristol	.346	67	269	43	93	17	1	7	45	8	34	17
Isom, Johnny, Bluefield	.344	59	212	47	73	14	4	6	56	25	27	9
Hooker, Kevin, Martinsville	.335	49	179	38	60	16	1	9	46	21	34	2
Pierzynski, A.J., Eliz.	.332	56	205	29	68	13	1	7	45	14	23	0
Mendoza, Carlos, Kingsport	.328	51	192	56	63	9	0	1	24	27	24	28
Simpson, Jeramie, Kingsport	.323	59	229	50	74	11	10	0	28	20	37	25
Rincones, Wuarnner, Bristrol	.317	61	189	25	60	10	4	1	25	32	29	2
Kingsale, Eugene, Bluefield	.316	47	171	45	54	11	2	0	16	27	31	20
Russin, Tom, Bluefield	.312	57	215	42	67	21	1	5	41	18	27	1

INDIVIDUAL PITCHING LEADERS
(Minimum 61 Innings)

	W	L	ERA	G	GS	CG	SV	IP	H	R	ER	BB	SO
Murphy, Chris, Princeton	7	1	1.55	10	10	1	0	64	51	23	11	19	52
Fussell, Chris, Bluefield	9	1	2.19	12	12	1	0	66	37	18	16	32	98
Abreu, Winston, Danville	6	3	2.31	13	13	1	0	74	54	29	19	13	90
Olson, Phil, Kingsport	6	2	2.42	12	10	2	1	67	47	24	18	23	45
Feliz, Bienvenido, Burlington	4	2	2.71	12	11	1	0	73	55	29	22	20	78
Sanders, Frankie, Burlington	3	5	2.96	12	12	3	0	70	48	31	23	32	80
Figueroa, Nelson, Kingsport	3	7	3.07	12	12	2	0	76	57	31	26	22	79
Roberts, Randy, Princeton	4	5	3.16	15	9	0	0	63	51	35	22	33	74
Wagner, Ken, Burlington	5	5	3.16	13	12	0	0	68	54	34	24	23	80
Splittorff, Jamie, Eliz.	5	4	3.24	13	12	1	0	72	64	40	26	29	72

Helena Takes Advantage Of Billings Slip

By JAMES BAILEY

The biggest story of the 1995 Pioneer League championship series was that the Billings Mustangs weren't in it.

Billings, which had won the previous three PL titles, finished with the league's best regular-season record for the third consecutive season. But the Mustangs (49-20) were upset in the first round of an expanded four-team playoff by Medicine Hat, two games to one.

Medicine Hat gained a playoff berth despite an overall 35-37 record. The Blue Jays finished well back of Billings in both halves of a new split-season schedule, but prevailed in the playoffs over Billings, winning the deciding game 11-6.

Meanwhile, the Helena Brewers won 13 games in a row in the second half then used the momentum to finish off the talent-laden Idaho Falls Braves in three games in the Southern Division to advance to the finals against Medicine Hat.

Helena, which had lost in the finals to Billings the two previous seasons, swept Medicine Hat in two games to win its first title since 1984.

With a team batting average of .304, the Brewers far outpaced the rest of the league in offense, scoring 558 runs in 71 games, an average of 7.9 runs per game.

Idaho Falls, which switched affiliations from the Braves to the Padres—yet kept Braves as its nickname to foster souvenir sales—dominated a managers survey of the league's best prospects. The Braves claimed five of the top six spots.

Catcher Ben Davis, the second pick overall in the

LEAGUE CHAMPIONS

Last 25 Years

Year	Regular Season*	Pct.	Playoff
1971	Great Falls (Giants)	.643	None
1972	Billings (Royals)	.694	None
1973	Billings (Royals)	.629	None
1974	Idaho Falls (Angels)	.569	None
1975	Great Falls (Giants)	.577	None
1976	Great Falls (Giants)	.577	None
1977	Lethbridge (Dodgers)	.629	None
1978	Billings (Reds)	.735	Billings (Reds)
1979	Helena (Phillies)	.623	Lethbridge (Dodgers)
1980	Lethbridge (Dodgers)	.740	Lethbridge (Dodgers)
1981	Calgary (Expos)	.657	Butte (Brewers)
1982	Medicine Hat (Blue Jays)	.629	Medicine Hat (Blue Jays)
1983	Billings (Reds)	.614	Billings (Reds)
1984	Billings (Reds)	.691	Helena (Independent)
1985	Great Falls (Dodgers)	.771	Salt Lake (Independent)
1986	Salt Lake (Independent)	.643	Salt Lake (Independent)
1987	Salt Lake (Independent)	.700	Salt Lake (Independent)
1988	Great Falls (Dodgers)	.754	Great Falls (Dodgers)
1989	Great Falls (Dodgers)	.791	Great Falls (Dodgers)
1990	Great Falls (Dodgers)	.706	Great Falls (Dodgers)
1991	Salt Lake (Independent)	.700	Salt Lake (Independent)
1992	Billings (Reds)	.697	Billings (Reds)
	Salt Lake (Independent)	.697	
1993	Billings (Reds)	.653	Billings (Reds)
1994	Billings (Reds)	.694	Billings (Reds)
1995	Billings (Reds)	.710	Helena (Brewers)

*Best overall record

1995 draft, was named the No. 1 prospect after hitting .279 with five homers. First baseman Sean Watkins was No. 2. He led in home runs (13) while finishing second in batting (.367) and RBIs (67).

Ogden outfielder Jamie Lopiccolo was the league's MVP. He led the league in hitting (.388), hits (101), total bases (154) and on-base percentage (.503).

For the second consecutive season, Ogden operated as an independent team, the only such designation in the National Association in 1995. Lethbridge and Butte also operated without major league affiliations, but players were provided to those clubs by Major League Baseball.

That arrangement will change in 1996 as MLB's two expansion teams, the Tampa Bay Devil Rays and Arizona Diamondbacks, have agreed to provide players for Lethbridge and Butte, respectively. The Milwaukee Brewers also moved their Rookie-level team from the Arizona League to Ogden.

STANDINGS: SPLIT SEASON

FIRST HALF

NORTH	W	L	PCT	GB
Billings	25	8	.758	—
Great Falls	18	15	.545	7
Medicine Hat	16	20	.444	10½
Lethbridge	15	21	.417	11½

SOUTH	W	L	PCT	GB
Idaho Falls	22	13	.629	—
Helena	20	15	.571	2
Ogden	14	20	.412	7½
Butte	8	26	.235	13½

SECOND HALF

NORTH	W	L	PCT	GB
Billings	24	12	.667	—
Medicine Hat	19	17	.528	5
Great Falls	13	23	.361	11
Lethbridge	10	26	.278	14

SOUTH	W	L	PCT	GB
Helena	29	7	.806	—
Idaho Falls	20	16	.556	9
Ogden	18	18	.500	11
Butte	11	25	.306	18

PLAYOFFS—Semifinals: Helena defeated Idaho Falls 2-1, and Medicine Hat defeated Billings 2-1, in best-of-3 series. **Finals:** Helena defeated Medicine Hat 2-0, in best-of-3 series

STANDINGS: OVERALL

Page		W	L	PCT	GB	Manager	Attendance/Dates	Last Pennant
99	Billings Mustangs (Reds)	49	20	.710	—	Donnie Scott	103,758 (34)	1994
150	Helena Brewers (Brewers)	49	22	.690	1	Alex Morales	36,224 (34)	1995
209	Idaho Falls Braves (Padres)	42	29	.592	8	Mike Basso	57,620 (36)	1974
234	Medicine Hat Blue Jays (Blue Jays)	35	37	.486	15½	Darren Balsley	19,603 (35)	1982
237	Ogden Raptors (Independent)	32	38	.457	17½	Willie Ambos	56,630 (36)	None
144	Great Falls Dodgers (Dodgers)	31	38	.449	18	John Shoemaker	62,312 (33)	1990
236	Lethbridge Mounties (Co-op)	25	47	.347	25½	Dan Simonds	47,607 (35)	1980
236	Butte Copper Kings (Co-op)	19	51	.271	30½	Billy Gardner	19,658 (32)	1981

NOTE: Team's individual batting and pitching statistics can be found on page indicated in lefthand column.

PIONEER LEAGUE
1995 BATTING, PITCHING STATISTICS

CLUB BATTING

	AVG	G	AB	R	H	2B	3B	HR	BB	SO	SB
Helena	.304	71	2428	558	739	160	14	55	387	424	119
Idaho Falls	.293	71	2525	519	741	133	26	55	361	485	83
Ogden	.291	70	2430	444	708	131	10	41	336	462	55
Billings	.289	69	2426	463	702	138	21	45	339	514	80
Great Falls	.272	69	2326	399	632	118	33	33	268	536	97
Butte	.266	70	2394	372	638	113	35	23	309	521	88
Medicine Hat	.261	72	2434	415	636	130	19	45	317	611	84
Lethbridge	.241	72	2404	340	580	92	28	20	290	531	98

CLUB PITCHING

	ERA	G	CG	SHO	SV	IP	H	R	ER	BB	SO
Billings	3.58	69	0	4	23	613	613	316	244	239	474
Medicine Hat	4.44	72	5	3	17	625	613	422	308	312	510
Great Falls	4.68	69	0	0	9	594	635	426	309	309	485
Helena	4.68	71	0	3	17	616	608	388	321	411	559
Lethbridge	4.89	72	5	2	14	632	710	446	344	297	595
Idaho Falls	5.25	71	1	3	17	635	669	455	370	344	564
Ogden	5.84	70	4	1	9	618	759	506	401	313	443
Butte	6.69	70	0	0	12	597	769	551	444	382	454

CLUB FIELDING

	PCT	PO	A	E	DP		PCT	PO	A	E	DP
Ogden	.959	1853	837	114	72	Lethbridge	.950	1896	786	142	49
Billings	.959	1839	780	112	75	Butte	.948	1792	775	142	60
Helena	.958	1848	798	117	78	Medicine Hat	.939	1874	732	170	60
Idaho Falls	.957	1904	861	123	91	Great Falls	.938	1783	744	168	55

Sean Watkins
.372-13-67

Rick Gama
All-star 2B

John Curl
26 doubles

INDIVIDUAL BATTING LEADERS
(Minimum 194 Plate Appearances)

	AVG	G	AB	R	H	2B	3B	HR	RBI	BB	SO	SB
Lopiccolo, Jamie, Ogden	.388	70	260	74	101	11	3	12	55	55	40	15
Watkins, Sean, Idaho Falls	.372	67	247	51	92	20	1	13	67	43	55	0
Gonzalez, Manuel, Great Falls	.360	59	197	35	71	9	3	4	30	9	27	16
Lopez, Louis, Ogden	.357	46	182	36	65	15	0	7	39	16	20	1
Parent, Gerald, Helena	.355	57	203	50	72	16	0	7	63	50	30	1
Kinkade, Mike, Helena	.353	69	266	76	94	19	1	4	39	43	38	26
Scott, Thomas, Billings	.353	67	252	68	89	24	4	7	43	46	65	17
Mealing, Al, Helena	.349	55	169	35	59	11	4	4	31	23	43	17
Goodhart, Steven, Billings	.340	65	250	48	85	12	4	0	45	28	34	9
Barkett, Andy, Butte	.333	45	162	33	54	11	5	5	51	33	39	1

INDIVIDUAL PITCHING LEADERS
(Minimum 58 Innings)

	W	L	ERA	G	GS	CG	SV	IP	H	R	ER	BB	SO
Veniard, Jay, Medicine Hat	4	1	2.71	11	10	0	0	63	67	34	19	21	43
Callahan, Damon, Billings	9	2	2.91	14	14	0	0	80	82	36	26	30	50
Bailey, Ben, Billings	6	4	2.96	13	13	0	0	79	74	32	26	29	68
Atchley, Justin, Billings	10	0	3.51	13	13	0	0	77	91	33	30	20	65
Neal, Billy, G.F.	3	3	3.72	16	9	1	0	65	74	42	27	24	55
Lapka, Rick, Billings	8	4	3.76	14	14	0	0	79	66	36	33	43	46
Rodriguez, Victor, M.H.	4	1	3.88	17	2	0	0	58	42	31	25	40	45
Novak, Troy, Ogden	5	1	3.88	15	15	2	0	97	101	50	42	41	71
Reed, Jason, Great Falls	2	5	4.09	15	12	0	1	73	79	42	33	28	45
Gooda, David, Helena	4	4	4.17	10	10	0	0	58	54	32	27	33	33

DEPARTMENT LEADERS

BATTING
G	Two tied at	72
AB	Shane Jones, Ogden	297
R	Mike Kinkade, Helena	76
H	Jamie Lopiccolo, Ogden	101
TB	Jamie Lopiccolo, Ogden	154
2B	John Curl, Medicine Hat	26
3B	Two tied at	7
HR	Sean Watkins, Idaho Falls	13
RBI	Shane Jones, Ogden	69
SH	Four tied at	6
SF	Rick Gama, Idaho Falls	10
BB	Andrew McCormick, Med. Hat	64
IBB	John Curl, Medicine Hat	8
HBP	Two tied at	12
SO	Collin Hinds, Lethbridge	87
SB	Mike Kinkade, Helena	33
CS	Mark Coca, Ogden	13
GIDP	Michael Peeples, Med. Hat	14
OB%	Jamie Lopiccolo, Ogden	.503
SL%	Sean Watkins, Idaho Falls	.619

PITCHING
G	Matt Schultea, Ogden	34
GS	Four tied at	15
CG	Three tied at	2
ShO	Five tied at	1
GF	Adam Bryant, Billings	26
Sv	Three tied at	11
W	Justin Atchley, Billings	10
L	Three tied at	8
IP	Troy Novak, Ogden	97
H	Two tied at	106
R	Two tied at	65
ER	Two tied at	50
HR	Miguel Gomez, Medicine Hat	10
BB	Ed Collins, Helena	63
SO	Casey Kirkman, Lethbridge	91
WP	Matt Clement, Idaho Falls	19

FIELDING
C AVG	Chris Keighley, Ogden	.986
E	Two tied at	12
PB	Rich Vallero, Ogden	15
1B AVG	Shane Jones, Ogden	.992
E	Sean Watkins, I.F.	12
2B AVG	Tom Hutchison, Leth.	.972
E	Michael Peeples, Med. Hat	26
3B AVG	Doyle Preston, Billings	.929
E	Andy Shatley, Med. Hat	32
SS AVG	Kelly Phair, Ogden	.948
E	Nelson Perez, Butte	31
OF AVG	Dave Elliott, Helena	1.000
E	Two tied at	9

HONOR ROLL

OFFICIAL ALL-STAR TEAM

C—Ben Davis, Idaho Falls. **1B**—Sean Watkins, Idaho Falls. **2B**—Rick Gama, Idaho Falls. **3B**—Mike Kinkade, Helena. **SS**—Mickey Lopez, Helena. **OF**—Manuel Gonzalez, Great Falls; Jamie Lopiccolo, Ogden; Shane Jones, Ogden; Gerald Parent, Helena. **RHP**—Damon Callahan, Billings. **LHP**—Justin Atchley, Billings. **RP**—John Mitchell, Medicine Hat.

MVP—Jamie Lopiccolo, Ogden.
Manager—Mike Basso, Idaho Falls.

TOP 10 PROSPECTS

(Selected by league managers)
1. Ben Davis, c, Idaho Falls
2. Sean Watkins, 1b, Idaho Falls
3. Rick Gama, 2b, Idaho Falls
4. Mickey Lopez, 2b-ss, Helena
5. Jake Remington, c, Idaho Falls
6. Domingo Guzman, rhp, Idaho Falls
7. Manuel Gonzalez, of, Great Falls
8. Kelvin Escobar, rhp, Medicine Hat
9. Justin Atchley, lhp, Billings
10. John Curl, 1b, Medicine Hat

Royals Take Care Of Unfinished Business

By JAMES BAILEY

One year after setting a Gulf Coast League record for best winning percentage, the Royals accomplished what they could not in 1994. They swept past the Tigers to capture the GCL title.

Despite winning at a .797 clip in the regular season in 1994, the Royals fell to the Astros in the championship series. Several of the players from that squad spent the 1995 season playing at Class A Wilmington, skipping two intermediate levels.

The 1995 Royals were not as dominant in the regular season, finishing with a mortal .649 percentage, third best in the league. But they won the newly revamped Southwest Division and swept through the playoffs with nary a call to the bullpen to win their second GCL title in four seasons.

Righthander Jeff Martin, who led the league with a 1.47 ERA, shut out the White Sox 3-0 in a one-game semifinal. In the other semifinal, the Tigers shut out the Marlins 2-0.

First baseman Gary Coffee, who hit .246 with one home run in the GCL in 1994, led the league with 11 home runs and 45 RBIs. Third baseman Jose Cepeda led the league with a .348 average, succeeding former Royals second baseman Sergio Nunez as the batting champion. Nunez hit .397 for the Royals in 1994.

Ten first-round picks from the 1995 draft played in the Gulf Coast League, though only four earned support from managers in a poll of the Top 10 prospects.

Pirates shortstop Chad Hermansen gained the most acclaim even though he left for the New York-Penn League after only 24 games. Red Sox righthander Andy Yount, Blue Jays righthander Roy Halladay and Expos shortstop Michael Barrett were the other first-rounders on the list.

Cubs righthander Kerry Wood and Marlins outfielder Jaime Jones both made very brief appearances in the league before moving up.

The Tigers fielded a GCL team for the first time since 1968, prompting a move to a four-division format, with each division composed of four clubs. Teams played only teams in their division during the regular season.

LEAGUE CHAMPIONS

Last 25 Years

Year	Regular Season*	Pct.	Playoff
1971	Royals	.755	None
1972	Cubs	.651	None
	Royals	.651	
1973	Rangers	.732	None
1974	Cubs	.702	None
1975	Rangers	.774	None
1976	Rangers	.704	None
1977	White Sox	.731	None
1978	Rangers	.600	None
1979	Astros	.635	None
1980	Royals Blue	.635	None
1981	Royals Gold	.688	None
1982	Yankees	.667	None
1983	Rangers	.645	Dodgers
1984	White Sox	.651	Rangers
1985	Yankees	.705	None
1986	Reds	.548	Dodgers
1987	Dodgers	.683	Dodgers
1988	Yankees	.714	Yankees
1989	Yankees	.651	Yankees
1990	Expos	.635	Dodgers
1991	Orioles	.593	Expos
1992	Royals	.695	Royals
1993	Rangers	.667	Rangers
1994	Royals	.797	Astros
1995	Marlins	.714	Royals

*Best overall record

STANDINGS

Page	EAST	Complex Site	W	L	PCT	GB	Manager	Last Pennant
124	Marlins	Melbourne	40	16	.714	—	Juan Bustabad	None
177	Mets	St. Lucie	38	19	.667	2 ½	John Stephenson	None
163	Expos	West Palm Beach	21	35	.375	19	Luis Dorante	1991
59	Braves	West Palm Beach	14	43	.246	26 ½	Jim Saul	1964

Page	NORTH	Complex Site	W	L	PCT	GB	Manager	Last Pennant
118	Tigers	Lakeland	33	24	.579	—	Kevin Bradshaw	None
170	Yankees	Tampa	32	26	.552	1 ½	Hector Lopez	1989
130	Astros	Osceola	32	26	.552	1 ½	Bobby Ramos	1994
234	Blue Jays	Dunedin	19	40	.322	15	Rocket Wheeler	None

Page	NORTHWEST	Complex Site	W	L	PCT	GB	Manager	Last Pennant
87	White Sox	Sarasota	36	22	.621	—	Mike Gellinger	1977
66	Orioles	Sarasota	34	25	.576	2 ½	Julio Garcia	None
228	Rangers	Port Charlotte	24	34	.414	12	Chino Cadahia	1993
196	Pirates	Bradenton	23	36	.390	13 ½	Woody Huyke	None

Page	SOUTHWEST	Complex Site	W	L	PCT	GB	Manager	Last Pennant
137	Royals	Fort Myers	37	20	.649	—	Bob Herold	1992
93	Cubs	Fort Myers	35	22	.614	2	Sandy Alomar	None
73	Red Sox	Fort Myers	21	36	.368	16	Felix Maldonado	None
157	Twins	Fort Myers	20	35	.364	16	Mike Boulanger	None

PLAYOFFS—Semifinals: Tigers beat Marlins and Royals beat White Sox in one-game series. **Finals:** Royals beat Tigers 2-0, in best-of-3 series.

NOTE: Team's individual batting and pitching statistics can be found on page indicated in lefthand column.

GULF COAST LEAGUE
1995 BATTING, PITCHING STATISTICS

CLUB BATTING

	AVG	G	AB	R	H	2B	3B	HR	BB	SO	SB
Marlins	.260	56	1835	289	478	72	23	11	213	306	95
Mets	.260	57	1875	306	487	92	26	25	205	360	63
Pirates	.256	59	1899	245	487	72	21	20	163	331	39
Royals	.256	57	1834	294	470	82	18	36	214	366	43
Cubs	.255	57	1793	276	457	73	28	23	199	397	128
Astros	.252	58	1784	268	449	68	19	15	173	381	114
Yankees	.246	58	1883	285	463	74	21	19	202	409	52
Orioles	.241	58	1856	260	448	85	13	14	212	375	59
White Sox	.241	58	1858	271	448	83	14	23	203	418	48
Tigers	.240	57	1715	237	411	50	24	19	189	467	122
Rangers	.232	58	1783	230	414	68	20	15	170	417	135
Twins	.222	55	1709	169	380	71	8	11	145	363	73
Red Sox	.221	57	1785	223	395	59	6	13	175	382	73
Blue Jays	.221	59	1819	259	402	82	21	17	258	467	47
Expos	.217	56	1727	195	375	75	15	8	175	425	62
Braves	.189	57	1721	141	326	53	2	14	161	401	36

CLUB PITCHING

	ERA	G	CG	SHO	SV	IP	H	R	ER	BB	SO
Cubs	2.07	57	0	5	11	483	369	184	111	189	344
Marlins	2.30	56	2	4	16	482	367	167	123	158	401
Mets	2.53	57	3	4	17	491	381	175	138	173	439
Orioles	2.66	59	6	7	17	490	407	223	145	190	377
Royals	2.75	57	1	5	15	483	406	223	148	142	423
Yankees	2.89	58	2	8	13	489	372	215	157	241	483
White Sox	2.91	58	3	5	13	483	438	217	156	155	400
Twins	3.11	55	5	6	9	453	406	244	157	232	357
Astros	3.21	58	2	4	12	476	429	228	170	199	492
Tigers	3.38	57	3	5	23	462	406	243	174	177	399
Rangers	3.67	58	3	5	13	477	456	274	195	196	385
Red Sox	3.93	57	7	3	9	477	494	287	208	181	400
Expos	3.99	56	1	6	12	466	470	275	207	179	310
Pirates	4.22	59	2	3	9	488	523	316	229	196	363
Braves	4.33	57	2	2	7	467	448	314	225	244	342
Blue Jays	4.87	59	3	5	7	480	518	363	260	205	350

CLUB FIELDING

	PCT	PO	A	E	DP		PCT	PO	A	E	DP
Mets	.966	1472	633	75	28	Tigers	.949	1386	574	105	42
Marlins	.961	1445	606	84	39	Red Sox	.948	1430	573	109	40
Rangers	.957	1432	589	91	47	Cubs	.947	1449	551	111	40
Yankees	.956	1468	641	96	51	Orioles	.947	1471	640	118	46
White Sox	.955	1448	606	97	49	Twins	.946	1360	621	113	45
Astros	.955	1429	600	96	35	Pirates	.946	1464	638	120	46
Royals	.954	1449	615	100	54	Braves	.942	1401	604	124	41
Expos	.952	1399	622	101	44	Blue Jays	.939	1440	664	137	47

INDIVIDUAL BATTING LEADERS
(Minimum 162 Plate Appearances)

	AVG	G	AB	R	H	2B	3B	HR	RBI	BB	SO	SB
Cepeda, Jose, Royals	.348	54	187	32	65	6	4	0	21	15	5	2
Gallagher, Shawn, Rangers	.338	58	210	34	71	13	3	7	40	19	44	17
Camilo, Jose, Marlins	.335	48	155	37	52	5	5	4	22	41	28	19
De la Cruz, Carlos, Tigers	.329	47	155	24	51	7	1	2	17	20	45	28
Coffee, Gary, Royals	.328	52	189	30	62	9	3	11	45	28	38	2
Samboy, Nelson, Astros	.313	55	192	39	60	12	2	1	22	26	19	21
Barrett, Michael, Eexpos	.311	50	183	22	57	13	4	0	19	15	19	7
Mifflin, Brian, Mets	.306	51	193	29	59	13	1	5	40	5	43	1
Bunkley, Antuan, Twins	.298	49	181	24	54	9	0	6	23	15	35	11
Gonzalez, Alex, Marlins	.294	53	187	30	55	7	4	2	30	19	27	11

INDIVIDUAL PITCHING LEADERS
(Minimum 48 Innings)

	W	L	ERA	G	GS	CG	SV	IP	H	R	ER	BB	SO
Martin, Jeffrey, Royals	3	1	1.47	11	10	1	0	55	35	12	9	11	53
Alicea, Patrick, Tigers	5	2	1.93	12	8	2	1	51	45	21	11	14	43
Dace, Derek, Astros	3	4	1.95	11	10	2	0	69	60	20	15	6	77
Pena, Juan, Red Sox	3	2	1.95	13	4	2	1	55	41	17	12	6	47
DeWitt, Scott, Marlins	5	3	1.98	11	10	1	0	64	48	15	14	9	70
White, Gary, Orioles	5	4	2.17	12	10	2	0	66	52	26	16	16	86
Dotel, Octavio, Mets	7	4	2.18	13	12	2	0	74	48	23	18	17	86
Kolb, Dan, Rangers	1	7	2.21	12	11	0	0	53	38	22	13	28	46
Perez, Odaliz, Braves	3	5	2.22	12	12	1	0	65	48	22	16	18	62
Robinson, Martin, Yankees	6	1	2.48	11	8	2	0	62	54	20	17	13	56

HONOR ROLL

OFFICIAL ALL-STAR TEAM

C—Brian Downs, White Sox. **1B**—Gary Coffee, Royals. **2B**—Elinton Jasco, Cubs. **3B**—Jose Cepeda. **SS**—Alex Gonzalez, Marlins. **OF**—Jose Camilo, Marlins; Carlos De la Cruz, Tigers; Thomas Peck, Blue Jays.

SP—Octavio Dotel, Mets. **RP**—Brent Stentz, Tigers.

TOP 10 PROSPECTS
(Selected by league managers)
1. Chad Hermansen, ss, Pirates
2. Andy Yount, rhp, Red Sox
3. Akex Gonzalez, ss, Marlins
4. Carlos Guillen, ss, Astros
5. Roy Halladay, rhp, Blue Jays
6. Michael Barrett, ss, Expos
7. Julio Ramirez, of, Marlins
8. D'Angelo Jiminez, ss, Yankees
9. Carlos Beltran, of, Royals
10. Gary Coffee, 1b, Royals

Hernandez-Led Athletics Regain Title

By JAMES BAILEY

In a league which places development ahead of victories, the Athletics have found a way to develop a winning attitude in their young players.

The A's won their fourth Arizona League title in the

Josh Bishop

past five years, sweeping a three-game, season-ending series from the Angels to finish two games ahead of the Angels in the regular season. There are no playoffs in the complex-based rookie league.

The key to the team's success in the Arizona League can be directly traced to Oakland's considerable presence in the Dominican Summer League. Fifteen players who were with the Athletics' DSL team in 1994 played in the Arizona League in '95, including league MVP and top prospect Ramon Hernandez.

Hernandez, a sound defensive catcher, nearly won the triple crown, finishing at .371 with four homers and 36 RBIs. After hitting .246 in the DSL in 1994, Hernandez blossomed in Arizona, leading the league in hitting.

He was joined on the league's postseason all-star team by five of his teammates, including shortstop Edward Lara, who was named the league's No. 5 prospect in a poll of managers. Lara led Oakland's DSL entry with a .363 average in 1994, but impressed Arizona League managers with his defense and speed, stealing 23 bases.

One player had a noteworthy season, though he didn't make the all-star team as picked by managers. Brewers righthander Josh Bishop set a league record with 134 strikeouts in 96 innings, shattering the previous mark of 105 set by Jason Myers for the Giants in 1993. Bishop was 8-2 with a 2.16 ERA for the season.

Many felt Bishop, who was drafted by Milwaukee out of the University of Missouri, should have spent the season at a higher level since he was three years older than most of his competitors in the Arizona League.

Brewers skipper Ralph Dickenson and Athletics manager Juan Navarette were honored as co-managers of the year. It was the third season in the league for Dickenson, Navarette's first.

While the Athletics recaptured their crown, they did so in a league with no defending champion. The Cardinals, who broke the A's string of three consecutive titles in 1994, chose not to field an Arizona League team in 1995. The Giants also pulled out of the league, cutting the number of teams from eight to six.

LEAGUE CHAMPIONS

Year	Regular Season*	Pct.	Playoff
1988	Brewers	.690	None
1989	Brewers	.727	None
1990	Brewers	.679	None
1991	Athletics	.650	None
1992	Athletics	.604	None
1993	Athletics	.636	None
1994	Cardinals	.607	None
1995	Athletics	.661	None

STANDINGS

Page		Complex Site	W	L	PCT	GB	Manager	Last Pennant
183	Athletics	Scottsdale	37	19	.661	—	Juan Navarrete	1995
79	Angels	Mesa	35	21	.625	2	Bruce Hines	None
151	Brewers	Chandler	34	22	.607	3	Ralph Dickenson	1990
210	Padres	Peoria	24	31	.436	12 ½	Dan Norman	None
222	Mariners	Peoria	24	32	.429	13	Tom LaVasseur	None
111	Rockies	Chandler	13	42	.236	23 ½	Jack Maloof	None

PLAYOFFS: None.

NOTE: Team's individual batting and pitching statistics can be found on page indicated in lefthand column.

ARIZONA LEAGUE
1995 BATTING, PITCHING STATISTICS

CLUB BATTING

	AVG	G	AB	R	H	2B	3B	HR	BB	SO	SB
Brewers	.265	56	1899	315	504	68	28	5	203	376	106
Angels	.263	56	1832	287	482	60	35	9	214	386	92
Mariners	.260	56	1959	304	510	93	28	13	224	477	71
Padres	.257	55	1822	254	469	78	27	18	177	482	69
Athletics	.256	56	1847	329	473	61	44	20	262	481	134
Rockies	.230	55	1819	237	418	60	17	8	194	503	63

CLUB PITCHING

	ERA	G	CG	SHO	SV	IP	H	R	ER	BB	SO
Angels	2.94	56	5	6	17	489	422	222	160	193	429
Brewers	3.28	56	5	2	16	494	444	238	180	199	536
Athletics	3.37	56	1	3	15	491	436	238	184	190	496
Padres	3.76	55	3	2	12	469	457	292	196	205	406
Mariners	4.30	56	1	1	10	494	528	326	236	244	448
Rockies	5.81	55	0	0	5	473	569	410	306	243	390

CLUB FIELDING

	PCT	PO	A	E	DP		PCT	PO	A	E	DP
Angels	.955	1467	654	100	53	Brewers	.944	1481	621	125	37
Athletics	.949	1474	602	111	54	Padres	.935	1408	571	137	43
Mariners	.945	1481	649	123	49	Rockies	.933	1420	628	146	43

INDIVIDUAL BATTING LEADERS
(Minimum 151 Plate Appearances)

	AVG	G	AB	R	H	2B	3B	HR	RBI	BB	SO	SB
Hernandez, Ramon, Athletics	.364	48	143	37	52	9	6	4	37	39	16	6
Johnson, Duan, Mariners	.351	43	174	33	61	9	3	0	28	8	14	3
Rutherford, Daryl, Padres	.333	47	186	29	62	12	4	5	27	11	28	13
Arias, David, Mariners	.332	48	184	30	61	18	4	4	37	23	52	2
Wilkerson, Adrian, Brewers	.331	54	160	22	53	1	1	0	28	16	28	18
Cesar, Dionys, Athletics	.322	48	171	41	55	11	4	2	29	23	29	17
Rodriguez, Miguel, Brewers	.313	49	163	24	51	12	1	1	18	11	34	9
Barnes, Larry, Angels	.310	56	197	42	61	8	3	3	37	27	40	12
Cruz, Cirilo, Mariners	.308	39	146	22	45	8	0	0	20	16	37	0
Stuart, Rich, Angels	.299	56	204	42	61	10	6	2	33	25	42	20

INDIVIDUAL PITCHING LEADERS
(Minimum 45 Innings)

	W	L	ERA	G	GS	CG	SV	IP	H	R	ER	BB	SO
Darrell, Thomas, Angels	4	3	1.71	18	5	0	2	63	51	18	12	14	49
Plant, David, Athletics	4	2	1.76	14	6	0	2	51	34	11	10	12	51
Clark, Chris, Padres	5	5	2.10	13	12	1	0	73	52	30	17	38	82
Bishop, Joshua, Brewers	8	2	2.16	14	13	3	0	96	64	34	23	29	134
Delossantos, Valerio, Brewers	4	6	2.20	14	12	0	0	82	81	34	20	12	57
Romero, John, Angels	7	3	2.41	18	6	2	1	71	57	29	19	18	64
Blevins, Jeremy, Angels	5	1	2.45	11	9	0	0	51	39	20	14	32	48
Volkman, Keith, Angels	5	2	2.53	13	10	0	0	68	61	30	19	25	49
Jacob, Russell, Mariners	6	2	2.88	12	11	0	0	56	47	29	18	31	54
Walker, Kevin, Padres	5	5	3.01	13	12	0	0	72	74	34	24	12	69

DEPARTMENT LEADERS

BATTING
G	Rich Stuart, Angels	56
AB	Juan Rodriguez, Angels	215
R	Two tied at	42
H	Juan Rodriguez, Angels	64
TB	David Arias, Mariners	99
2B	David Arias, Mariners	18
3B	Juan Rodriguez, Angels	8
HR	Two tied at	5
RBI	Three tied at	37
SH	Adam Wardrop, Angels	5
SF	Hipolito Martinez, Athletics	7
BB	Ramon Hernandez, Athletics	39
IBB	Roberto Jacobo, Padres	2
HBP	Ramon Hernandez, Athletics	8
SO	Pete Paciorek, Padres	58
SB	Rico Harris, Brewers	26
CS	Two tied at	10
GIDP	Carlos Vidal, Rockies	9
OB%	Ramon Hernandez, Athletics	.518
SL%	Ramon Hernandez, Athletics	.607

PITCHING
G	Robert Kazmirski, Athletics	28
GS	Three tied at	13
CG	Josh Bishop, Brewers	3
ShO	Four tied at	1
GF	Robert Kazmirski, Athletics	25
Sv	Two tied at	10
W	Two tied at	9
L	Cristy Rosa, Rockies	9
IP	Josh Bishop, Brewers	96
H	Gabe Ishee, Brewers	78
R	James Podjan, Rockies	58
ER	James Podjan, Rockies	45
HR	Jose Paulino, Athletics	5
BB	Gabe Ishee, Brewers	41
HB	Chris Druckrey, Rockies	8
SO	Josh Bishop, Brewers	134
WP	James Podjan, Rockies	14
Bk	Reggie Douglas, Rockies	11

FIELDING
C AVG	Ramon Hernandez, A's	.981
E	Miguel Rodriguez, Brewers	15
PB	Miguel Rodriguez, Brewers	17
1B AVG	David Arias, Mariners	.989
E	John Lindsey, Rockies	8
2B AVG	Adam Wardrop, Angels	.960
E	Rod Jackson, Padres	18
3B AVG	Steve Chavez, Padres	.871
E	Steve Chavez, Padres	23
SS AVG	Edward Lara, Athletics	.963
E	John Clark, Rockies	19
OF AVG	Rich Stuart, Angels	.976
E	Roberto Jacobo, Padres	14

HONOR ROLL

OFFICIAL ALL-STAR TEAM

C—Ramon Hernandez, Athletics. **1B**—David Arias, Mariners. **2B**—Dionys Cesar, Athletics. **3B**—Juan Polanco, Athletics. **SS**—Edward Lara, Athletics. **OF**—Salvador Duverge, Rockies; Juan Rodriguez, Angels; Rich Stuart, Angels. **DH**—Daryl Rutherford, Padres.

LHP—Keith Volkman, Angels. **RHP**—Jose Paulino, Athletics. **RP**—Bob Kazmirski, Athletics.

MVP—Ramon Hernandez, Athletics. **Manager of the Year**—Ralph Dickenson, Brewers; Juan Navarrete, Athletics.

TOP 5 PROSPECTS
(Selected by league managers)
1. Ramon Hernandez, c, Athletics
2. Rich Stuart, of, Angels
3. Chris Clark, rhp, Padres
4. Jeremy Blevins, rhp, Angels
5. Edward Lara, ss, Athletics

DOMINICAN SUMMER
LEAGUE

Third Time The Charm For Japanese Club

Japan's influence on baseball in the Dominican Republic produced its first tangible results in 1995 as a club sponsored by the Hiroshima Toyo Carp won its first Dominican Summer League title.

The Carp ran away with the San Pedro de Macoris Division, posting a league-best 58-13 record, then won four of five playoff games. They beat the Indians in two one-sided games in a best-of-3 final.

Japan began aggressively competing with major league clubs for Dominican Republic talent in the early '90s and intensified its efforts in 1993 when it entered a team in the 11-year-old Rookie league. It produced first-place clubs in both 1993 and 1994, both times the Carp was knocked off in the semifinals.

The Carp returned only six players from its '94 team, but five were pitchers who combined to go 42-9.

The group was led by righthander Francisco de la Cruz, who went 8-4 with a 1.71 ERA in 1994. He stepped up to lead the league with 11 wins in 1995 and added two more in the playoffs.

The Japanese-subsidized club also welcomed the return of outfielder Charlie Pena, the Dominican Summer League MVP and RBI leader in 1993. Pena did not play in 1994, but picked up where he left off. He hit .336 and led the league in RBIs (66).

The Carp's .817 winning percentage was the league's best since Toronto posted a professional baseball record 68-2, .971 mark in 1992.

The DSL fielded 22 clubs in 1995, including several with joint sponsorship by major league teams. All but three big league teams—the Reds, Red Sox and Twins—fielded teams.

STANDINGS

SANTO DOMINGO EAST	W	L	PCT	GB
Mariners	45	21	.682	—
Tigers	34	34	.500	12
Dodgers I	28	36	.438	16
Phillies/Cardinals	25	44	.362	21½
Expos	21	47	.309	25
SANTO DOMINGO CENTRAL	W	L	PCT	GB
Indians	48	20	.706	—
Athletics	44	21	.677	2½
Rangers	39	28	.582	8½
Marlins	26	42	.382	22
Cubs/Padres	22	45	.328	25½
SANTO DOMINGO WEST	W	L	PCT	GB
Blue Jays	44	24	.647	—
Mets	41	27	.603	3
Yankees	31	37	.456	13
Pirates	30	36	.455	13
Royals/Rockies	24	40	.375	18
SAN PEDRO de MACORIS	W	L	PCT	GB
Hiroshima Toyo Carp	58	13	.817	—
Dodgers II	44	25	.638	13
Angels	31	39	.443	26½
Orioles/White Sox	30	40	.429	27½
Astros/Brewers	28	39	.418	28
Giants	27	44	.380	31
Braves	26	44	.371	31½

PLAYOFF: Semifinals— Toyo Carp (Japan) defeated Blue Jays, 2-1 and Indians defeated Mariners 2-1, in best-of-3 series. **Finals—**Toyo Carp defeated Indians 2-0 in best-of-3 series.

ALL-STAR TEAM: C—Ignacio Suero, Blue Jays. **1B—**Pablo Sencion, Blue Jays. **2B—**Edwin Perez, Indians. **3B—**Marco Scuttaro, Indians. **SS—**Alfonso Guilleard, Toyo Carp. **OF—**Jesus Hernandez, Indians; Juan Moreno, Mets; Charlie Pena, Toyo Carp. **DH—**Ramon Pena, Blue Jays. **RHP—**Luis Vizcaino, Athletics. **LHP—**Ismel Zabala, Mariners.
Player of the Year: Jesus Hernandez, Indians. **Pitcher of the Year:** Luis Vizcaino, Athletics. **Manager of the Year:** Manny Castillo, Toyo Carp.

INDIVIDUAL BATTING LEADERS
(Minimum 170 Plate Appearances)

	AVG	AB	R	H	2B	3B	HR	RBI	SB
Hernandez, Jesus, Indians	.406	251	60	102	22	7	0	53	20
Scuttaro, Marco, Indians	.393	262	71	103	18	6	0	38	32
Fischer, Carlos, Angels	.378	155	25	51	3	0	0	13	10
Rodriguez, Miguel, Phils/Cards	.375	144	31	54	13	1	2	28	11
Guilleard, Alfonso, Carp	.366	227	52	83	12	3	4	55	8
Pena, Ramon, Blue Jays	.366	213	22	78	11	0	2	34	3
Guerrero, Wascar, Mariners	.364	173	37	63	14	1	10	43	1
Moreno, Juan, Mets	.360	228	59	82	14	1	13	36	15
Guzman, Martin, Toyo Carp	.349	229	58	80	16	1	7	54	0
Valera, Ramon, Mariners	.347	202	50	70	6	3	2	20	46
Encarnacion, Mario, A's	.345	229	56	79	11	5	8	44	17
Pena, Charlie, Toyo Carp	.336	241	80	81	27	0	8	66	17
Langagney, Shelwin, Blue Jays	.335	221	45	74	15	0	1	39	16
Mateo, Victor, Yankees	.335	248	34	83	17	4	2	37	5
Ozuna, Pedro, Yankees	.335	182	42	61	10	3	0	21	6
Castillo, Geramel, Rangers	.335	161	27	54	7	3	1	14	11
Espino, Fernando, Mariners	.335	203	41	68	15	1	6	33	3
Suero, Ignacio, Blue Jays	.333	243	37	81	13	0	15	61	2
Mejia, Renato, Marlins	.329	240	36	79	13	1	5	29	10
Fajardo, Alex, Phils/Cards	.328	183	31	60	11	3	1	21	17
Jimenez, Miguel, Mariners	.327	226	50	74	11	1	7	51	9
Olivares, Melvin, Mets	.326	236	39	77	12	1	10	54	3
Cruz, Luis, Toyo Carp	.325	271	75	88	14	3	5	51	18
Perez, Edwin, Indians	.322	239	58	77	9	7	3	37	14
Saturria, Arturo, Phils/Cards	.318	245	48	78	16	7	2	33	12
Martinez, Jose, Indians	.317	218	35	69	20	0	1	38	2
Cedeno, Ruddy, Astros/Brewers	.317	161	41	51	10	2	0	14	12
Hernandez, Rafael, Expos	.317	218	34	69	16	3	4	32	7
Taveras, Jose, Royals/Rockies	.315	178	35	56	8	4	5	24	12
Mejia, Oliver, Pirates	.313	179	30	56	9	3	0	25	4
Rosario, Carlos, Royals/Rockies	.313	217	31	68	8	3	1	32	6
#Peralta, Santiago, Carp	.279	225	46	62	4	9	2	46	11

INDIVIDUAL PITCHING LEADERS
(Minimum 50 Innings)

	W	L	ERA	G	SV	IP	H	BB	SO
Zabala, Ismel, Mariners	9	1	1.05	30	3	51	25	17	83
Patino, Leonardo, Angels	5	4	1.35	21	3	73	56	28	63
Guzman, Wilson, Pirates	5	0	1.47	16	4	55	52	17	48
De la Cruz, Francisco, Carp	11	1	1.56	16	1	104	73	31	80
Petigue, Marino, Toyo Carp	10	1	1.61	16	2	84	65	32	41
Henriquez, Roman, Dodgers I	4	1	1.81	37	8	60	56	31	40
Mota, Henry, Rangers	6	3	1.85	29	8	63	48	12	57
Baez, Miguel, Indians	7	2	1.99	15	0	95	64	24	74
Garcia, Jose, Indians	6	2	2.02	19	2	71	60	16	67
Aracena, Juan, Indians	6	2	2.06	24	5	57	39	18	31
#Guerrero, Jose, Mariners	4	1	2.09	29	15	39	23	17	57
Medina, Carlos, Marlins	2	3	2.18	12	0	62	59	30	47
Ortiz, Ramon, Angels	8	6	2.23	16	0	97	79	54	100
Vizcaino, Luis, Athletics	10	2	2.27	16	0	115	93	29	89
Zapata, Juan, Astros/Brewers	5	4	2.31	13	0	82	60	43	60
Diese, Jose, Toyo Carp	6	1	2.33	12	0	54	39	36	51
Delgado, Manuel, Blue Jays	4	4	2.36	25	9	53	34	15	60
Vargas, Jose, Toyo Carp	6	2	2.43	13	0	70	50	34	37
Peguero, Americo, Orioles/WhSox	8	3	2.48	15	1	102	64	47	120

INDEPENDENT LEAGUES

Independent Leagues Explode In '95, But Several Casualties

By WILL LINGO

The evolution of independent minor league baseball continued apace in 1995, with explosive growth and growing legitimacy in the upper ranks of the independent pecking order.

At the bottom of the order, though, problems continued, with several leagues either not getting started at all or folding up soon after their seasons were under way.

Several others that didn't fold made it through the season only on a shoestring, with some teams averaging about 100 fans per game.

The leagues at the top, the Northern League for example, continued to do well, drawing good players and good crowds. The Western League made a solid debut to join the upper echelon of independent leagues, and the Frontier League added some strong expansion teams that have given it new stability.

But for every good league or good team, there were a few that weren't so good. With so many new leagues, a few were bound to fail. The Atlantic Coast, Golden State and North Central leagues all suspended operations, the euphemism for shutting down.

Even in the relatively stable Texas-Louisiana League, the Laredo and Pueblo franchises drew poorly and the league shut them down before the season was half over.

And in the Western League, the Long Beach franchise filed for bankruptcy, though the team continued to operate and went on to win the league's first championship.

Limited Funds Doom Leagues

The Atlantic Coast League, with four franchises in North Carolina and South Carolina, and the Golden State League, with four teams in California and Arizona, were in their first seasons.

The Atlantic Coast League said a miscalculation of expenses, bad weather and poor attendance led to its shutdown.

The Golden State League's leaders, though they spent a great deal of time planning their league, said they just never had enough money.

"We were not able to raise sufficient investment capital, nor did we draw at the gate as well as we had projected," league president Bob Weinstein said. The league lost one of its chief investors shortly before the season began.

"Although we are continuing to talk with potential investors, it may be too little too late," Weinstein said when the league suspended play. "We need a major investor or we cannot resume the season."

They didn't get one, and the season didn't resume.

The North Central League was in its second season, but it was gutted by defections of its strongest franchises to the new Prairie League in the offseason. The league put together four franchises in Minnesota and Illinois but didn't draw well and also ran out of money.

League president George Vedder said the league was hurt by its late start, and by Vedder owning three of the franchises. At least one of the teams wanted to move into the Prairie League, which had a solid debut in the upper Midwest and Canada and plans to expand from eight to 10 teams for its second season.

The Texas-Louisiana League, which owns all of its teams, shut down the Laredo and Pueblo clubs due to poor attendance, giving the league eight teams.

"We made the decision to suspend play in two cities that weren't drawing well," league president Doug Theodore said. "There are no financial problems or insolvency or anything like that, but if you're drawing 600 people, what's the point?"

The league plans to get back to 10 teams for the 1996 season and might try to go to 12, he said.

The league had struggling franchises in San Antonio and Beaumont in 1994, but it kept them afloat through the season, moving them after the season ended.

"It's the same as the two losers we had last year," Theodore said. "Last year we said we were going to do the right thing and hope it gets better. It didn't, and no one really cared."

Independent leagues proved to be one of the biggest suppliers of replacement players as the strike of 1994-95 dragged through spring training.

The Northern League, for example, sold nearly 100 contracts to major league organizations. Other leagues supplied fewer players, but it seemed every one, even those that hadn't played yet, sold a player or two.

Most of the players returned to the leagues from whence they came, but a few made the most of their chances and stuck with the organizations they signed with.

NORTHERN LEAGUE

As the stormy independent seas swirled around it, the Northern League remained steady and stable, with the league's flagship franchise winning its second championship.

That would be the St. Paul Saints, the team under president Mike Veeck that increased its attendance for the third straight season, drawing 258,297. The Saints practically filled every seat they had available for every game.

The Saints were also the first team to win both halves of the season since the league was reborn in 1993. They faced the defending champion Winnipeg Goldeyes in the league championship, beating them three games to one.

Steve Morales shut down the Goldeyes 4-0 in the deciding game, pitching eight innings of one-hit ball. St. Paul outfielder Doug O'Neill, who batted .333 in the series, was the series MVP.

And Saints outfielder Darryl Motley, who hit the only home run in Game 7 of the 1985 World Series in Kansas City's rout of St. Louis, also hit the only home run of the deciding game of this championship, a solo shot in the ninth.

St. Paul won the league's first title in 1993, so became the first multiple-championship winner in the league. But Winnipeg manager Doug Simunic now has managed in each of the league's three championship series. Besides winning one and losing one with Winnipeg, he also led the Rochester Aces to the finals in 1993. Rochester relocated to Winnipeg after that season.

Terry Lee

"I'm not the greatest manager, I don't think," he said. "But I get a lot of people to come out on the field and give me a good effort."

The Goldeyes were led by league player of the year Terry Lee, a former Cincinnati Red who nearly won the triple crown. He hit .373 with 22 homers and 73 RBIs.

After three years of standing pat, the Northern League also announced its first expansion plans. Come 1996, Madison, Wis., and Fargo, N.D., will join the league.

"We are extremely proud to add two such strong markets to our league," league president Miles Wolff said. "It makes the league tremendously stable."

STANDINGS

FIRST HALF	W	L	PCT	GB
St. Paul Saints	26	16	.619	—
Winnipeg Goldeyes	25	17	.595	1
Sioux City Explorers	25	17	.595	1
Sioux Falls Canaries	20	22	.476	6
Duluth-Superior Dukes	16	26	.381	10
Thunder Bay Whiskey Jacks	14	28	.333	12

SECOND HALF	W	L	PCT	GB
St. Paul Saints	27	15	.643	—
Thunder Bay Whiskey Jacks	24	18	.571	3
Winnipeg Goldeyes	22	21	.512	5½
Sioux City Explorers	21	22	.488	6½
Sioux Falls Canaries	18	24	.429	9
Duluth-Superior Dukes	15	27	.357	12

CHAMPIONSHIP SERIES: St. Paul defeated Winnipeg 3-1, in best-of-5 series.

MANAGERS: Duluth-Superior—Tommy Thompson. St. Paul—Marty Scott. Sioux City—Ed Nottle. Sioux Falls—Frank Verdi. Thunder Bay—Doug Ault. Winnipeg—Doug Simunic.
ATTENDANCE: St. Paul, 258,297; Winnipeg, 196,460; Sioux City, 149,770; Sioux Falls, 102,328; Thunder Bay, 100,211; Duluth-Superior, 81,514.
ALL-STAR TEAM: C—Hank Manning, Winnipeg. **1B**—Dan Peltier, St. Paul. **2B**—Tommy Houk, Duluth-Superior. **3B**—Frank Valdez, Sioux Falls. **SS**—Greg D'Alexander, St. Paul. **OF**—Kevin Dattola, Winnipeg; Darryl Motley, St. Paul; Doug O'Neill, St. Paul. **DH**—Kevin Garner, Sioux Falls. **LHP**—Jeff Alkire, St. Paul. **RHP**—David Harris, Sioux City. **RP**—Bruce Walton, St. Paul.
Player of the Year: Terry Lee, Winnipeg. **Rookie of the Year:** Bobby Post, Sioux Falls. **Manager of the Year:** Ed Nottle, Sioux City.

INDIVIDUAL BATTING LEADERS
(Minimum 227 Plate Appearances)

	AVG	AB	R	H	2B	3B	HR	RBI	SB
Lee, Terry, Winnipeg	.373	314	62	117	15	2	22	73	0
Peltier, Dan, St. Paul	.366	325	63	119	29	1	9	56	6
Motley, Darryl, St. Paul	.358	268	69	96	21	1	13	50	11
Valdez, Frank, SF	.356	278	61	99	24	1	9	47	6
Powell, Corey, D-S	.344	253	36	87	18	1	7	40	1
Dattola, Kevin, Winn	.339	348	74	118	26	0	14	56	41
Proctor, Murph, SC	.322	342	50	110	26	1	8	62	1

Merchant, Mark, SC	.318	217	41	69	14	0	11	41	1
Castillo, Benny, SF	.316	297	51	94	29	1	10	60	6
Garner, Kevin, SF	.316	266	44	84	18	2	16	64	0

INDIVIDUAL PITCHING LEADERS
(Minimum 67 Innings)

	W	L	ERA	G	SV	IP	H	BB	SO
Harris, David, SC	11	4	3.01	19	0	123	104	48	102
Castro, Antonio, D-S	6	4	3.12	23	0	92	94	49	70
Tilmon, Pat, TB	4	4	3.27	13	0	85	87	18	85
Murdaugh, Reese, SC	8	5	3.27	17	0	99	114	28	39
Smith, Tim, Winnipeg	9	5	3.28	16	0	107	87	54	79
Jesperson, Bob, TB	5	3	3.30	25	2	95	86	32	63
McClellan, Darren, Winn	3	2	3.44	13	0	84	76	44	77
Wise, Andy, Sioux Falls	8	2	3.75	35	3	74	19	58
Doorneweerd, Dave, StP	10	4	3.79	18	0	114	95	36	104

BATTERS: 10 or more at-bats
PITCHERS: 5 or more innings

DULUTH-SUPERIOR

BATTING	AVG	AB	R	H	2B	3B	HR	RBI	SB
Allen, Matt, c-of	.277	278	49	77	11	4	9	49	1
Barsoom, Alan, ss-3b	.257	226	33	58	16	0	2	36	3
Bigler, Jeff, 1b	.262	263	37	69	19	0	4	34	0
Henderson, Lee, c	.259	116	9	30	7	0	0	17	1
Houk, Tom, 2b	.312	308	64	96	15	2	6	55	4
Hughes, Bobby, of	.256	121	13	31	5	2	1	5	3
Jensen, Jeff, of-1b	.279	183	19	51	7	2	2	28	0
Kemp, Tim, ss-of	.247	146	14	36	5	3	0	9	3
Kuld, Pete, dh-c	.297	148	23	44	7	2	11	39	0
2-team (42 TB)	.269	312	54	84	19	4	24	69	6
O'Halloran, Greg, c	.228	79	10	18	1	1	2	9	0
Powell, Corey, of	.344	253	36	87	18	1	7	40	1
Taylor, Jamie, 3b	.295	285	36	84	18	1	4	28	1
Vinyard, Derek, of	.229	315	47	72	5	2	0	14	35
Weary, Rodney, dh-of	.299	154	23	46	9	0	2	19	5
Zupcic, Bob, of	.314	35	4	11	3	0	1	5	1

PITCHING	W	L	ERA	G	SV	IP	H	BB	SO
Baldridge, James	0	0	11.81	6	0	5	7	10	1
Carroll, Sean	1	3	10.96	16	0	23	36	16	12
Castro, Antonio	6	4	3.27	20	0	88	86	48	65
2-team (3 SC)	6	4	3.12	23	0	92	94	49	70
Foreman, Toby	1	0	5.73	37	0	33	42	27	24
Gindorff, Matt	1	3	5.40	14	0	33	33	14	17
Hunt, Will	0	2	7.86	18	0	26	41	17	9
2-team (20 TB)	3	5	5.91	38	1	56	74	38	39
Linfante, Rob	3	6	6.22	42	1	51	50	40	50
Lyons, Steve	4	11	6.39	29	1	99	131	47	52
McGarity, Jeremy	6	8	3.87	21	0	123	135	38	78
McRoberts, Brian	4	1	1.88	40	11	43	37	14	24
Morrow, Eric	0	2	7.15	17	0	23	28	11	12
Simon, Mike	0	4	4.23	16	0	38	46	14	16
Tucker, Brett	1	3	5.77	11	0	48	61	26	22
Wiseman, Denny	4	6	5.74	18	0	102	149	15	39

ST. PAUL

BATTING	AVG	AB	R	H	2B	3B	HR	RBI	SB
Biernat, Joe, 2b-3b	.282	287	41	81	16	8	5	35	5
Castaldo, Vince, 3b	.304	171	22	52	15	1	6	36	4
D'Alexander, Greg, ss	.291	296	29	86	13	2	7	45	5
Dascenzo, Doug, of	.289	38	8	11	2	0	0	7	2
Frazier, Terance, of	.293	225	36	66	11	3	2	23	21
Gousha, Sean, c	.222	158	24	35	6	0	2	15	0
2-team (19 TB)	.223	206	29	46	9	0	2	21	0
Lopez, Luis, 3b	.111	27	4	3	0	0	0	0	0
Marillia, Greg, ss	.385	13	7	5	0	0	0	1	1
Miller, Joe, of	.286	140	24	40	8	0	2	18	3
Morris, Billy, ss	.265	34	4	9	1	0	0	7	2
Mota, Carlos, c	.207	111	18	23	5	0	0	8	3
Motley, Darryl, of-dh	.358	268	69	96	21	1	13	50	11
O'Neill, Doug, of	.312	356	75	111	20	2	17	58	24
Ortiz, Javier, of	.263	99	12	26	5	0	0	17	1
Peltier, Dan, 1b	.366	325	63	119	29	1	9	56	6
Shook, Wes, dh-c	.296	142	22	42	14	0	3	29	0
Stark, Matt, dh-1b	.311	45	5	14	6	0	3	11	0
Thomas, Tim, 2b	.266	169	23	45	19	0	0	26	0

PITCHING	W	L	ERA	G	SV	IP	H	BB	SO
Alkire, Jeff	8	3	4.25	19	0	114	123	40	81
Bullard, Jason	3	3	5.20	17	0	88	113	33	47
Caravelli, Mike	2	2	6.59	18	1	41	59	7	21
Centala, Scott	1	0	0.84	4	0	11	12	2	14
Curry, Steve	8	5	4.24	14	0	85	67	42	74
Doorneweerd, Dave	10	4	3.79	18	0	114	95	36	104

	W	L	ERA	G	SV	IP	H	BB	SO
Harris, Phil	0	0	2.08	5	0	9	7	6	5
Hebert, Jeff	2	0	3.20	8	0	20	15	12	7
Morales, Steve	6	4	4.03	26	0	80	68	39	52
Paskievitch, Tom	3	2	5.85	8	0	32	40	14	17
Ross, Craig	1	1	4.78	18	1	26	30	11	19
Stafford, Gerry	3	3	5.17	38	1	38	39	27	19
Turri, Shawn	3	1	3.90	27	1	30	22	18	17
Walton, Bruce	2	2	4.37	41	28	45	53	10	44

SIOUX CITY

BATTING	AVG	AB	R	H	2B	3B	HR	RBI	SB
DeStitger, Heath, c	.048	21	0	1	0	0	0	0	0
Farlow, Kevin, ss	.273	308	50	84	16	1	4	34	4
Konigsmark, Dave, 2b	.282	308	41	87	3	3	0	31	2
Lane, Nolan, of	.288	313	42	90	20	5	7	38	34
Merchant, Mark, dh-of	.318	217	41	69	14	0	11	41	1
Murphy, Sean, 2b	.341	44	6	15	0	0	1	8	4
Neff, Marty, of	.295	339	69	100	21	1	17	64	2
Nichols, Carl, c	.290	303	47	88	23	0	11	57	1
Proctor, Murph, 1b	.322	342	50	110	26	1	8	62	1
Robbins, Lance, 3b-of	.284	201	31	57	7	3	0	15	10
Wambach, James, dh	.210	119	11	25	6	0	3	14	1
Yamada, Jun, 3b	.178	146	16	26	3	0	1	10	0
Young, Gerald, of	.309	249	51	77	14	2	3	39	27

PITCHING	W	L	ERA	G	SV	IP	H	BB	SO
Blyleven, Todd	8	6	4.73	18	0	118	133	38	67
Boyd, Oil Can	6	6	5.03	17	0	107	129	28	62
Goldman, Barry	2	3	2.03	33	14	31	26	20	44
Harris, David	11	4	3.01	19	0	123	104	48	102
Lukas, Stephen	1	4	3.81	27	1	59	58	32	53
Murdaugh, Reese	8	5	3.27	17	0	99	114	28	39
Nishiguchi, Fumiya	3	1	1.83	6	0	39	27	14	41
Pricher, John	1	3	4.13	30	1	48	56	33	41
Shanahan, Chris	2	3	4.47	37	5	44	47	17	36
Tomioka, Hisaki	4	4	4.32	12	0	77	85	41	67

SIOUX FALLS

BATTING	AVG	AB	R	H	2B	3B	HR	RBI	SB
Ansley, Willie, of	.200	40	8	8	4	0	0	0	0
Burton, Mike, 1b	.294	306	37	90	22	1	7	39	2
Cannaday, Aaron, c	.245	245	37	60	12	0	8	41	0
Castillo, Benny, of	.316	297	51	94	29	1	10	60	6
Champoux, Beau, 2b-ss	.198	247	41	49	7	4	4	30	5
Davenport, Adell, of	.261	249	25	65	17	0	13	42	1
Davis, Matt, 2b-ss	.296	321	61	95	26	1	4	41	0
Frank, Nic, of	.160	25	5	4	2	0	0	1	0
Garner, Kevin, dh	.316	266	44	84	18	2	16	64	0
Gilmore, Kale, of	.167	30	3	5	3	0	0	2	0
Karle, Kurt, 3b-ss	.214	98	13	21	3	0	1	5	0
Lantigua, Eddie, of	.267	135	19	36	6	1	5	15	4
LaGreca, Paul, of	.190	42	5	8	3	0	0	0	0
Ollison, Scott, of	.333	33	6	11	1	0	0	7	0
Pence, Joe, ss-2b	.179	28	4	5	1	1	0	0	0
Perez, Raidel, of-2b	.339	109	24	37	9	2	3	20	2
Renteria, Edinson, ss-3b	.324	34	5	11	3	0	1	8	0
Tarter, Mike, c-of	.213	61	9	13	4	0	1	8	0
Valdez, Frank, 3b	.356	278	61	99	24	1	9	47	6

PITCHING	W	L	ERA	G	SV	IP	H	BB	SO
Andrakin, Rob	0	1	8.31	7	1	9	17	2	10
Brown, Dan	0	1	8.71	7	1	10	22	4	11
Coscia, Tony	5	8	4.57	18	0	87	99	38	56
Croxall, Rob	0	0	9.14	23	4	22	36	17	8
Franko, Kris	0	2	7.65	7	1	20	31	9	10
2-team (14 TB)	3	6	7.21	21	1	49	64	30	33
Gilmore, Joel	3	5	4.65	11	0	72	86	21	28
Harrington, Jody	0	1	4.15	5	0	9	11	11	4
Huffman, Rod	0	1	7.11	4	0	6	5	5	3
Jarolimek, Jon	2	3	8.40	11	0	30	37	14	11
Locklear, Jeff	2	1	4.97	5	0	25	33	7	21
Magnelli, Anthony	0	1	11.57	11	1	14	30	7	6
Meyers, Glenn	3	3	4.26	14	2	63	74	16	50
Mickel, Jason	1	5	5.85	25	6	52	54	35	25
Post, Bobby	8	2	4.00	15	0	97	108	23	49
Saylor, Jon	4	6	6.23	15	0	69	82	25	45
Valencia, Max	2	2	3.69	22	3	54	64	17	22
Wise, Andy	8	2	3.75	35	3	74	74	19	58

THUNDER BAY

BATTING	AVG	AB	R	H	2B	3B	HR	RBI	SB
Boston, Daryl, dh-of	.280	161	29	45	12	0	2	24	4
Cabrera, Francisco, dh-1b	.360	50	5	18	4	0	1	6	0
Cafferty, Jim, 2b	.203	69	9	14	0	0	4	4	0
Francois, Manny, ss	.313	134	23	42	8	2	4	20	2

BATTING	AVG	AB	R	H	2B	3B	HR	RBI	SB
Gousha, Sean, c	.229	48	5	11	3	0	0	6	0
Hearn, Sean, of	.303	323	55	98	12	2	19	58	20
Kraut, Jim, c-of	.262	42	8	11	5	0	1	7	0
Kuld, Pete, c-dh	.244	164	31	40	12	2	13	30	6
Marzano, David, of	.269	316	44	85	15	1	3	37	6
McLenaghan, Jason, ss-3b	.167	24	4	4	1	1	0	1	0
Montalvo, Rob, ss	.224	125	19	28	8	1	1	10	4
Robertson, Ryan, c	.191	141	9	27	8	0	0	17	0
Rosenthal, T.J., 1b	.240	150	12	36	5	0	0	16	2
Ross, Jackie, of	.279	355	57	99	11	5	2	39	15
Tisdale, Rodney, dh-of	.176	17	1	3	2	0	0	1	0
Tsoukalas, John, 3b	.293	290	34	85	13	0	3	38	4
Tunkin, Scott, 2b	.242	128	16	31	3	1	0	13	0
Vanek, Todd, 1b	.250	140	18	35	9	0	3	17	0
Waller, Casey, 2b	.298	171	27	51	11	0	6	26	0

PITCHING	W	L	ERA	G	SV	IP	H	BB	SO
Boynewicz, Jim	5	1	3.98	18	1	43	51	17	47
Browning, Mike	2	0	1.13	16	10	16	18	5	10
Butcher, Jason	1	1	5.19	4	0	17	20	11	15
Devereux, Charles	4	6	4.08	18	0	110	113	33	89
Franko, Kris	3	4	6.91	14	0	29	33	21	23
Hebert, Jeff	0	2	8.59	4	0	15	28	7	8
Hunt, Will	3	3	4.20	20	1	30	33	21	30
Jesperson, Bob	5	3	3.30	25	2	95	86	32	63
Martel, Ed	0	2	20.25	5	0	9	12	20	3
Martin, Doug	2	3	6.66	5	0	26	35	7	19
Miller, Marcus	0	1	6.12	16	0	32	36	37	21
Peterman, Ernie	2	1	1.25	4	0	22	15	10	18
Quinn, Aaron	3	7	4.26	33	4	74	81	31	38
Rohr, Mike	0	0	6.84	22	0	26	32	20	14
Tilmon, Pat	4	4	3.27	13	0	85	87	18	85
Ward, Anthony	3	5	5.92	10	0	59	73	19	42
Weber, Rob	0	0	6.94	12	0	23	24	17	8
Wilson, Mark	1	1	8.25	7	0	12	22	7	1

WINNIPEG

BATTING	AVG	AB	R	H	2B	3B	HR	RBI	SB
Arnold, Ken, ss	.230	322	43	74	12	1	1	31	6
Brinkley, Darryl, of	.336	131	22	44	2	1	4	19	6
Dattola, Kevin, of	.339	348	74	118	26	0	14	56	41
DeAngelis, Steve, dh	.281	317	40	89	21	1	11	65	2
De la Rosa, Juan, 3b-of	.328	134	27	44	7	1	4	13	4
Duva, Brian, 2b-of	.275	295	40	81	8	5	2	33	7
Halpenny, Andrew, c	.211	19	4	4	0	1	0	2	0
Hartung, Andy, 3b-1b	.270	137	22	37	7	1	3	21	1
Landstad, Rod, of	.071	14	4	1	1	0	0	0	0
Lee, Terry, 1b	.373	314	62	117	15	2	22	73	0
Lowery, Dave, 2b	.218	55	10	12	2	0	0	7	3
Manning, Henry, c	.284	334	55	95	24	0	19	57	0
Morris, Corey, of	.255	271	47	69	13	1	15	50	5
Springer, Steve, 3b	.161	31	4	5	0	0	0	0	0
Watts, Brent, of-3b	.298	245	50	73	18	3	7	44	21

PITCHING	W	L	ERA	G	SV	IP	H	BB	SO
Bailey, Mike	9	6	4.54	20	0	117	127	49	83
Bennett, Ricky	0	1	17.18	3	0	7	17	2	4
Bittiger, Jeff	8	5	3.99	20	0	124	131	46	106
Cather, Mike	4	2	1.45	27	8	31	18	12	35
Cochran, Jamie	2	1	5.82	9	0	17	22	12	14
Day, Steve	3	3	6.59	30	2	42	45	35	38
Donisthorpe, Randy	0	2	9.69	10	0	13	17	9	9
Futrell, Mark	1	0	15.43	4	0	7	16	7	6
Grieff, Todd	1	1	6.75	4	0	16	21	7	7
Harrington, Jody	0	0	18.00	3	0	1	1	2	0
2-team (5 SF)	0	1	5.59	8	0	10	12	13	4
Hayes, Chris	0	0	3.86	6	0	7	8	3	7
Hostetler, Tom	1	0	4.82	5	1	9	7	5	8
Magrini, Paul	2	3	7.55	9	0	31	39	13	21
Masterman, Tom	1	1	7.11	20	2	25	25	20	8
McClellan, Darren	3	2	3.44	13	0	84	76	44	77
Paskievitch, Tom	1	1	6.00	3	0	9	11	5	6
2-team (8 StP)	1	1	5.88	11	0	41	51	19	23
Sepeda, Jamie	0	3	10.13	4	0	19	31	10	6
Shenk, Larry	3	1	2.86	29	2	66	58	33	53
Smith, Tim	9	5	3.28	16	0	107	87	54	79
Smyth, Ken	0	1	6.10	5	0	10	14	5	6

TEXAS-LOUISIANA LEAGUE

It wasn't a sophomore slump, exactly, but the Texas-Louisiana League still is searching for the stability from top to bottom that will set it apart from the independent league pack.

The league replaced two franchises and added two more for the 1995 season, but only two of the four new teams survived the season (see above). The league planned to add at least two more teams for 1996.

Amarillo continued to be a big draw with 156,926 fans, though it was the only team to break 100,000. Overall attendance in the league increased from just over 600,000 to 680,725.

The most successful debut came from the Lubbock Crickets, who finished second in the league in attendance and first on the field.

The Crickets won the first-half title in the Northern Division, led by third baseman Frank Bolick, a former big leaguer, and his .355 average, and the acquisition of shortstop Rouglas Odor when the Laredo franchise folded.

Lubbock then squeezed by second-half champion Amarillo in the divisional playoffs and beat Alexandria in the final game of a best-of-5 series for the championship.

STANDINGS

FIRST HALF

NORTH	W	L	PCTGB
Lubbock	31	19	.620 —
Amarillo	30	20	.600 1
Tyler	28	22	.560 3
*Pueblo	21	29	.420 10
Abilene	17	33	.340 14

SOUTH	W	L	PCTGB
Alexandria	29	21	.580 —
Rio Grande	28	22	.560 1
Corp. Christi	27	22	.551 1½
Mobile	21	29	.420 8
*Laredo	17	32	.347 11½

SECOND HALF

NORTH	W	L	PCTGB
Amarillo	34	16	.680 —
Abilene	23	27	.460 11
Lubbock	22	28	.440 12
Tyler	20	30	.400 14

SOUTH	W	L	PCTGB
Alexandria	28	22	.560 —
Corp. Christi	28	22	.560 —
Rio Grande	25	24	.510 2½
Mobile	19	30	.388 8½

*Folded after first half

PLAYOFFS—Semifinals: Lubbock defeated Amarillo 2-1, in best-of-3 series. **Finals:** Lubbock defeated Alexandria 3-2, in best-of-5 series.

MANAGERS: Abilene—Charley Kerfeld. Alexandria—Stan Cliburn. Amarillo—Ross Grimsley. Corpus Christi—Mark Wasinger. Laredo—Jose Cruz. Lubbock—Greg Minton. Mobile—Butch Hobson. Pueblo—Jim Essian. Rio Grande Valley—Alan Ashby. Tyler—Wayne Krenchicki.

ATTENDANCE: Amarillo, 156,926; Lubbock, 94,367; Mobile, 81,378; Abilene, 73,954; Rio Grande Valley, 71,818; Corpus Christi, 61,793; Alexandria, 57,791; Tyler, 55,251; Laredo, 15,973; Pueblo, 11,474.

ALL-STAR TEAM: C—Kevin Tahan, Amarillo. 1B—Mike Cantu, Corpus Christi. 2B—Jorge Alvarez, Laredo-Amarillo. 3B—Fletcher Thompson, Alexandria. SS—Rouglas Odor, Laredo-Lubbock. OF—Dennis Hood, Amarillo; Lonnie Maclin, Amarillo; Kyle Shade, Alexandria. Util—Lino Connell, Corpus Christi. DH—Joe Ronca, Alexandria. SP—Daren Brown, Amarillo; Gary Eave, Corpus Christi; Kevin Henthorne, Corpus Christi. RP—Jerry Santos, Corpus Christi.

Most Valuable Player: Dennis Hood, Amarillo. **Most Valuable Pitcher:** Daren Brown, Amarillo.

INDIVIDUAL BATTING LEADERS
(Minimum 259 Plate Appearances)

	AVG	AB	R	H	2B	3B	HR	RBI	SB
Hood, Dennis, Amarillo	.372	376	100	140	37	5	11	83	56
Bolick, Frank, Lubbock	.355	214	42	76	17	1	7	56	1
Felder, Mike, CC	.352	307	68	108	15	6	4	37	11
Thompson, Fletcher, Alex	.343	353	106	121	28	2	15	66	47
Alvarez, Jorge, Amarillo	.343	359	60	123	33	1	10	59	8
Shade, Kyle, Alex	.338	382	60	129	28	1	10	85	1
Cedeno, Ramon, Mobile	.337	386	66	130	27	4	9	67	5
Tahan, Kevin, Amarillo	.333	393	82	131	26	3	13	95	8
Jones, Barry, Abilene	.332	383	58	127	13	5	10	80	7
DeLeon, Ray, CC	.328	357	46	117	17	1	9	70	11

INDIVIDUAL PITCHING LEADERS
(Minimum 77 Innings)

	W	L	ERA	G	SV	IP	H	BB	SO
Rambo, Dan, Tyler	10	5	1.90	17	0	128	127	18	68
Eave, Gary, CC	13	2	2.02	20	0	138	111	37	98
Henthorne, Kevin, CC	12	4	2.96	23	0	143	123	34	115

Moran, Eric, Alex	11	3	3.11	43	13	81	69	27	92
Brown, Daren, Amarillo	15	2	3.14	23	0	146	142	41	121
Satre, Jason, Rio Grande	4	4	3.27	16	1	94	92	34	58
Bicknell, Greg, Amarillo	10	6	3.74	19	0	125	135	41	80
Ahern, Brian, Rio Grande	10	10	3.78	24	0	150	152	51	101
Youngblood, Todd, Amar	11	5	3.90	19	0	111	116	23	68
Peery, Noah, Lubbock	3	2	3.91	51	1	78	77	54	87

BATTERS: 10 or more at-bats
PITCHERS: 5 or more innings

ABILENE

BATTING	AVG	AB	R	H	2B	3B	HR	RBI	SB
Bailey, Mark, dh	.287	265	41	76	22	0	9	53	2
Baker, Richard, ss	.130	46	2	6	1	0	0	3	0
Dando, Pat, 1b	.276	228	27	63	14	2	5	36	0
Evans, Chris, of	.246	57	11	14	3	0	2	6	0
3-team (51 CC, 3 Mob)	.285	246	46	70	14	0	11	27	1
Ferby, Ryan, ss-2b	.220	91	13	20	1	0	0	4	3
2-team (26 Mobile)	.265	185	29	49	5	0	1	9	9
Ferrante, Steve, c	.101	69	2	7	1	0	0	2	0
Harris, Vince, of	.312	263	61	82	8	2	1	21	45
Heller, Kyle, c	.214	14	1	3	2	0	0	2	0
Holland, Sidney, 2b-of	.266	237	39	63	15	4	3	24	4
Hunt, Chris, of	.267	251	29	67	11	1	1	26	1
Jackson, Karun, 2b	.189	37	0	7	0	0	1	0	0
Jones, Barry, of-1b	.332	383	58	127	13	5	10	80	7
Lindsey, Robin, c	.234	94	12	22	4	0	0	8	0
Madsen, Dan, of	.258	163	22	42	6	3	4	28	9
2-team (8 Pueblo)	.289	194	26	56	8	3	4	31	14
Nehls, Dale, ss-3b	.252	111	12	28	3	0	0	13	5
2-team (16 Mobile)	.253	178	19	45	7	1	0	21	6
Perez, Beban, of	.293	270	38	79	13	1	2	27	4
Ramon, Oscar, 3b	.204	49	1	10	1	0	0	1	0
Rich, Tony, 2b-ss	.265	166	23	44	4	0	0	9	2
Sigler, Brad, 3b-1b	.275	320	35	88	16	0	3	39	1
Yelding, Eric, ss-3b	.245	188	35	46	4	0	3	22	8

PITCHING	W	L	ERA	G	SV	IP	H	BB	SO
Arminio, Sam	6	3	3.96	11	0	77	82	22	38
2-team (9 Pueblo)	9	7	4.27	20	0	135	156	39	62
Bavousett, Brian	1	0	6.75	18	1	32	38	14	18
Bogart, Brady	1	3	5.86	8	0	35	44	20	20
2-team (9 Mobile)	2	4	4.98	17	0	56	68	36	26
Calero, Javier	0	1	9.82	5	0	15	28	6	7
Del Giacco, Chris	10	9	4.46	22	0	133	140	50	122
Gates, Leonard	0	0	13.50	4	0	5	6	11	4
Hartung, Mike	1	2	1.42	11	0	25	16	8	14
2-team (14 Mobile)	1	3	3.30	25	0	44	42	18	27
Jensen, Phil	1	2	5.92	17	0	24	28	4	18
Jones, Scott	2	3	4.04	13	2	49	46	17	32
Morgan, Mike	0	3	6.43	9	0	28	28	16	6
Piatt, Doug	4	6	3.66	37	15	52	52	18	45
Raney, Zachary	3	5	4.79	11	0	71	95	18	32
Smith, Mike	1	5	6.70	9	0	46	56	32	16
Steinmetz, Earl	5	13	4.40	23	0	139	155	62	77
Stone, Eric	1	0	5.03	12	1	20	25	10	15
2-team (8 CC)	1	1	5.27	20	1	27	41	13	19
Vaughn, Heath	2	3	5.67	13	0	46	45	21	26
Winkle, Ken	2	1	4.20	10	0	30	27	13	32
Yaughn, Kip	0	1	9.00	1	0	4	7	2	2
2-team (11 Pueblo)	5	3	3.21	12	0	53	51	18	41

ALEXANDRIA

BATTING	AVG	AB	R	H	2B	3B	HR	RBI	SB
Andrews, Jay, of	.314	392	78	123	30	4	11	58	26
Arntzen, Brian, c	.277	130	15	36	3	0	1	17	3
Bender, Rick, ss	.239	297	45	71	7	1	3	34	11
Colbert, Leighton, of	.252	163	26	41	2	0	0	14	4
Cole, Marvin, 2b	.299	394	72	118	22	2	2	52	22
Ford, Eric, 3b	.185	27	2	5	0	0	0	2	0
Glenn, Robby, 1b	.254	256	28	65	8	1	2	32	4
Matos, Malvin, of	.328	238	43	78	16	4	11	41	12
2-team (30 Mobile)	.315	352	62	111	21	8	13	54	16
Perozo, Jose, ss	.115	52	2	6	1	0	0	2	0
2-team (44 Pueblo)	.248	206	53	51	4	4	0	23	3
Riesgo, Nikco, of	.287	122	27	35	12	0	3	12	1
Ronca, Joe, dh	.325	412	67	134	24	1	14	82	3
Shade, Kyle, of	.338	382	60	129	28	1	10	85	1
Thompson, Fletcher, 3b	.343	353	106	121	28	2	15	66	47
White, Darrin, c	.236	233	35	55	18	1	2	33	3

PITCHING	W	L	ERA	G	SV	IP	H	BB	SO
Beauchamp, Jim	6	2	4.48	12	0	66	71	38	34
Doran, Sean	1	4	5.98	23	2	59	74	23	47
Douglas, Robert	0	1	6.75	3	0	8	7	4	2

	W	L	ERA	G	SV	IP	H	BB	SO
Fontenot, Lester	4	2	3.42	29	4	76	82	36	62
Hancock, Chris	3	5	5.36	10	0	45	55	28	32
2-team (6 Tyler)	4	6	5.79	16	0	79	95	50	62
Licursi, Rick	1	0	5.21	10	0	19	18	12	18
2-team (25 Lubb.)	4	0	4.00	35	8	54	46	33	50
Locey, Tony	0	0	3.71	10	0	27	18	19	25
Montgomery, Josh	3	2	3.00	11	0	42	31	21	36
2-team (11 Laredo)	3	3	2.91	22	2	56	41	37	51
Moran, Eric	11	3	3.11	43	13	81	69	27	92
Newman, Alan	10	8	5.19	23	0	137	141	74	129
Peters, Brannon	7	6	4.23	18	0	111	105	64	98
Rantz, Ronnie	0	1	6.75	4	0	4	4	8	5
2-team (13 Tyler)	0	4	6.39	17	0	25	27	31	20
Sodders, Mike	4	2	5.05	8	0	46	51	31	23
Thomas, Jeff	0	0	12.00	4	1	6	9	4	6
Varney, James	6	4	4.83	28	0	91	101	42	55
Viola, Dom	1	1	6.11	9	0	28	31	13	26
Wilson, Shon	0	2	9.00	8	0	13	14	11	2

AMARILLO

BATTING

	AVG	AB	R	H	2B	3B	HR	RBI	SB
Allen, Donald, of	.287	338	66	97	10	2	1	28	22
Alvarez, Jorge, 2b	.354	175	32	62	16	1	7	35	7
2-team (49 Laredo)	.343	359	60	123	33	1	10	59	8
Conreaux, Pat, of	.284	250	40	71	14	2	1	26	7
Elliott, Greg, of-dh	.292	250	51	73	15	3	2	28	5
Fernandez, Mike, 3b	.311	180	35	56	14	2	3	40	1
Gazeway, Jeff, 2b-dh	.220	50	3	11	0	1	0	6	0
Gunderson, Joe, c	.310	113	18	35	4	0	2	23	1
Hood, Dennis, of-2b	.372	376	100	140	37	5	11	83	56
Keith, Jason, ss	.288	372	64	107	22	1	3	51	8
Kiraly, John, 1b	.298	372	61	111	28	5	9	78	4
Maclin, Lonnie, of	.380	208	50	79	10	4	1	29	18
2-team (17 RGV)	.377	273	63	103	15	5	1	37	25
Meza, Larry, 3b-2b	.304	313	58	95	12	3	5	58	5
Pruitt, Jason, dh	.227	44	5	10	0	0	0	4	1
Ridner, Duston, dh-of	.220	59	7	13	0	0	0	6	11
Tahan, Kevin, c-1b	.333	393	82	131	26	3	13	95	8

PITCHING

	W	L	ERA	G	SV	IP	H	BB	SO
Bicknell, Greg	10	6	3.74	19	0	125	135	41	80
Bojan, Tim	0	3	6.27	27	2	52	61	29	33
Brown, Daren	15	2	3.14	23	0	146	142	41	121
Czarkowski, Mark	1	2	5.06	8	1	43	54	11	24
Duey, Kyle	6	4	3.24	21	3	67	66	24	65
Hanselman, Craig	0	2	6.65	18	4	23	36	10	16
Kermode, Al	14	4	4.11	22	0	151	171	26	92
Miller, Pat	1	1	3.12	4	0	9	5	3	2
Montoya, Al	2	1	4.18	31	4	52	58	14	28
Nelson, Bryan	0	0	3.95	10	0	14	14	10	9
2-team (22 Pueblo)	2	4	5.23	32	2	43	44	28	52
Perkins, Paul	3	1	5.10	21	4	42	50	12	30
Swan, Russ	1	2	6.75	7	1	7	10	6	4
Taylor, Tom	0	3	4.97	7	0	25	31	12	13
Youngblood, Todd	11	5	3.90	19	0	111	116	23	68

CORPUS CHRISTI

BATTING

	AVG	AB	R	H	2B	3B	HR	RBI	SB
Abercrombie, John, c	.236	72	10	17	3	2	0	5	0
Brakebill, Mark, 3b-of	.294	323	73	95	16	4	9	43	9
Cantu, Mike, 1b-dh	.317	338	51	107	15	0	24	79	0
Connell, Lino, 2b-ss	.301	196	35	59	9	2	2	25	18
2-team (50 Laredo)	.304	375	61	114	16	2	4	43	26
Cook, Steve, 2b-3b	.279	319	58	89	15	2	7	41	15
Cooper, Chris, c	.222	18	2	4	0	0	0	2	0
DeLeon, Ray, dh-1b	.328	357	46	117	17	1	9	70	11
Dotel, Mariano, ss	.184	206	26	38	5	2	3	21	4
Driskell, Jeff, c	.267	116	20	31	2	1	7	27	0
Evans, Chris, of	.302	182	35	55	11	0	9	20	1
Felder, Matt, of	.259	27	7	7	2	0	0	2	1
Felder, Mike, of	.352	307	68	108	15	6	4	37	11
Johnson, Herman, c	.211	38	8	8	1	0	0	4	1
Maldonado, Rafael, 2b	.171	35	7	6	1	1	0	5	1
Murphy, Sean, dh-of	.286	28	6	8	2	0	0	3	2
O'Neill, Tom, 3b-2b	.193	88	20	17	3	0	3	13	3
Olivas, Willie, of	.248	101	18	25	5	0	2	13	4
Reams, Ron, of	.297	387	59	115	16	4	11	63	19
Skeels, David, c	.294	119	18	35	4	0	2	20	1
2-team (1 Mobile)	.293	123	18	36	4	0	2	21	1
Tovar, Raul, of	.344	93	15	32	5	0	3	17	1

PITCHING

	W	L	ERA	G	SV	IP	H	BB	SO
Brown, Kevin	1	3	5.96	10	0	26	42	8	19
Caridad, Rolando	2	2	5.81	9	0	48	50	31	27
Curiel, Joe	0	1	12.38	6	0	8	14	9	6
DePriest, Jarrod	3	0	4.44	17	0	26	31	12	10
Dunlap, Travis	5	4	5.25	36	1	74	87	41	69
Eave, Gary	13	2	2.02	20	0	138	111	37	98
Gamble, James	0	0	8.31	5	0	9	14	5	6
Henthorne, Kevin	7	2	3.04	12	0	68	58	7	64
2-team (11 Laredo)	12	4	2.96	23	0	143	123	34	115
Kracl, Darin	0	0	7.07	14	0	14	23	5	13
LaRue, Shaun	0	0	11.81	5	1	5	9	3	2
Mack, Tony	6	4	4.09	15	0	88	84	16	68
Maldonado, Jay	0	3	7.85	6	0	18	20	16	14
Martineau, Yves	3	6	4.18	29	0	95	89	36	63
Niebla, Ruben	0	0	5.29	13	0	17	24	11	16
2-team (2 Laredo)	1	0	4.50	15	0	26	35	12	26
O'Neal, Randy	1	4	5.59	11	0	48	57	13	33
Santos, Jerry	5	5	2.15	51	24	59	50	15	68
Sepeda, Jamie	4	3	4.78	11	0	58	66	20	39
Stone, Carlos	0	1	5.87	8	0	8	16	3	4
Thomas, Carlos	3	0	2.63	21	2	27	16	16	36
Vogelgesang, Joe	1	2	9.31	9	0	10	18	3	7

LAREDO

BATTING

	AVG	AB	R	H	2B	3B	HR	RBI	SB
Alvarez, Jorge, 3b-2b	.332	184	28	61	17	0	3	24	1
Connell, Lino, 2b-ss	.307	179	26	55	7	0	2	18	8
Cruz, Jorge, 1b-dh	.260	131	15	34	7	1	3	16	3
DeFranco, Steve, 1b-p	.150	20	2	3	0	0	0	2	0
Mariucci, Rick, of	.190	21	4	4	0	1	1	1	3
2-team (10 Mobile)	.216	51	11	11	1	1	1	4	4
McDonald, James, dh-1b	.367	90	9	33	2	0	2	19	0
Morales, Jorge, c	.270	74	13	20	4	0	3	16	2
Odor, Rouglas, ss	.291	151	21	44	2	2	1	12	10
Owens, Clint, c	.276	29	2	8	0	0	0	3	1
Perozo, Ed, of-1b	.234	184	27	43	8	0	6	27	5
Reyes, Victor, c	.213	94	14	20	1	0	4	10	1
Riesgo, Nikco, 1b-of	.400	35	4	14	3	0	0	5	1
Rijo, Rafael, of	.289	190	26	55	8	4	4	18	11
Santana, Jose, of	.243	111	19	27	6	4	0	9	6
Seminoff, Rich, 1b-dh	.222	18	1	4	1	0	1	3	0
Shabosky, Brian, of-2b	.263	137	11	36	7	1	0	14	1

PITCHING

	W	L	ERA	G	SV	IP	H	BB	SO
Berzewski, O.	0	2	4.03	7	0	22	25	13	5
Calderon, Jose	1	6	4.78	15	2	32	45	14	19
Caridad, Rolando	0	1	15.00	2	1	3	6	2	2
2-team (9 CC)	2	3	6.35	11	1	51	56	33	29
DeFranco, Steve	2	2	3.94	7	0	16	13	12	5
Fargas, Hector	2	0	7.80	14	2	45	55	35	30
Gardenhire, Hal	1	0	4.15	9	0	13	15	9	12
Henthorne, Kevin	5	2	2.89	11	0	75	65	27	51
Maldonado, Jay	0	0	0.00	2	0	6	1	0	6
2-team (6 CC)	0	3	6.00	8	0	24	21	16	20
Montgomery, Josh	0	1	2.63	11	2	14	10	16	15
Mueller, Ryan	0	3	6.57	12	0	25	29	17	18
Niebla, Ruben	1	0	3.00	2	0	9	11	1	10
Ojeda, Jorge	2	6	5.57	10	0	53	66	28	26
Quiles, Henry	2	1	6.21	7	0	33	39	14	9
Rivera, Elvin	0	5	5.11	8	0	44	62	14	16
Zweig, Ivan	1	3	7.49	8	0	40	45	33	23

LUBBOCK

BATTING

	AVG	AB	R	H	2B	3B	HR	RBI	SB
Bogan, Tre, of	.263	138	18	35	5	2	0	19	10
Bolick, Frank, 3b	.355	214	42	76	17	1	7	56	1
Bonneau, Britt, 2b-of	.253	277	43	70	7	2	4	30	11
Cushman, Greg, dh-1b	.215	121	9	26	5	0	2	21	0
Dailey, Jason, of	.206	126	20	26	1	2	6	20	3
Demerson, Tim, of	.243	301	79	73	7	3	5	26	37
Hartung, Andy, 3b	.264	110	12	29	7	0	3	19	0
Hoyes, Scott, of	.182	159	29	29	4	4	3	15	7
Kilford, George, 2b-ss	.180	111	15	20	6	0	0	6	4
King, Mitch, of	.129	31	5	4	1	0	0	1	1
Lowery, Dave, 2b	.311	161	24	50	4	2	0	18	17
Norton, Chris, 1b	.291	327	61	95	16	3	21	61	6
Nunez, Dimerson, c	.245	53	3	13	4	0	0	5	0
Odor, Rouglas, ss	.287	181	27	52	12	6	2	31	9
2-team (39 Laredo)	.289	332	48	96	14	8	3	43	19
Ortiz, Ray, of-dh	.281	121	19	34	11	0	8	19	0
Reese, Mat, of	.299	97	10	29	1	1	2	19	2
Riesgo, Nikco, of-dh	.239	117	24	28	5	1	6	16	0
3-team (34 Alex, 9 Lar)	.281	274	55	77	20	1	9	33	2
Rowland, Lloyd, of	.225	138	17	31	5	0	0	11	4
Salvador, Felix, ss	.227	132	25	30	6	1	1	11	17
Stratton, John, c	.342	193	27	66	14	1	8	38	2
Sullivan, Glenn, of-1b	.255	165	22	42	6	2	3	20	2
2-team (34 Pueblo)	.297	293	41	87	10	3	6	37	10

PITCHING	W	L	ERA	G	SV	IP	H	BB	SO
Baine, David	0	1	5.64	11	0	22	21	19	22
Bryant, Phil	3	2	5.01	6	0	32	42	11	12
DiPino, Frank	9	5	3.39	36	12	64	58	17	49
Ferraro, Denny	0	0	5.63	33	1	62	71	30	41
Gienger, Craig	8	5	5.99	21	0	107	133	47	49
Huber, Jeff	1	2	3.79	12	1	19	21	7	10
Latter, David	9	7	4.58	20	0	118	155	39	70
Licursi, Rick	3	0	3.34	25	8	35	28	21	32
Macatee, John	0	0	8.68	6	0	9	10	7	12
Peery, Noah	3	2	3.91	51	1	78	77	54	87
Pelatowski, Keith	9	6	4.58	24	2	128	145	42	74
Pierce, Rob	4	5	5.02	11	0	66	70	27	49
Sadecki, Steve	4	12	5.76	22	0	105	130	56	40

MOBILE

BATTING	AVG	AB	R	H	2B	3B	HR	RBI	SB
Allen, Rick, 3b-of	.267	225	35	60	10	0	3	22	12
Becker, Tim, ss	.280	307	38	86	17	2	1	44	20
Black, Ryan, of	.300	20	5	6	1	0	0	3	0
Brown, Todd, of	.220	59	6	13	0	2	0	1	3
Burroughs, Eric, of	.275	131	20	36	4	2	1	15	8
Cedeno, Ramon, dh-of	.323	186	29	60	13	4	2	30	2
2-team (50 Pueblo)	.337	386	66	130	27	4	9	67	5
Dando, Pat, 1b	.308	117	12	36	8	0	5	22	0
2-team (59 Abil)	.287	345	39	99	22	2	10	58	0
Debrand, Juan, ss	.172	29	3	5	0	0	0	2	1
Fenton, Cary, 3b-c	.279	229	37	64	6	2	1	19	10
Ferby, Ryan, 2b-ss	.309	94	16	29	4	0	1	5	6
Fogg, Kevin, 2b	.258	31	4	8	2	0	0	1	0
Gonzalez, Rex, dh	.265	34	7	9	1	1	1	3	1
Halbruner, Rick, 1b	.171	41	8	7	0	0	3	3	0
Johnson, Derrick, 1b	.273	77	4	21	2	0	0	9	2
Mack, Anthony, 3b	.154	13	1	2	1	0	0	3	0
Mann, Kelly, c	.242	66	11	16	5	0	1	10	0
2-team (37 Pueblo)	.275	167	31	46	10	2	3	22	2
Mariucci, Rick, c	.233	30	7	7	1	0	0	3	1
Matos, Malvin, of	.289	114	19	33	5	4	2	13	4
Nehls, Dale, 2b	.254	67	7	17	4	1	0	8	1
Pledger, Kinnis, of	.268	299	57	80	17	3	21	61	14
Simpson, Jay, of	.183	104	10	19	3	0	2	12	4
Singer, Roberto, of	.182	132	20	24	3	1	7	13	0
Skeels, Andy, c	.214	220	34	47	7	1	6	20	0
Skeels, Mark, 3b-c	.311	132	20	41	11	0	5	21	2
Teal, Bart, dh-of	.260	77	11	20	2	1	1	8	1
Terilli, Joey, of	.241	108	19	26	4	0	1	7	0
Urban, Andy, 1b	.172	64	4	11	1	1	0	7	0
Venezia, Danny, 2b-ss	.182	11	1	2	0	0	1	1	1
Ward, Lance, 3b	.206	102	7	21	5	0	1	9	0
Webb, Kevin, 3b-1b	.222	162	12	36	4	0	1	12	2
Wilkerson, Willie, 2b	.344	32	4	11	0	0	0	0	0

PITCHING	W	L	ERA	G	SV	IP	H	BB	SO
Bogart, Brady	1	1	3.48	9	0	21	24	16	6
Carman, Don	5	5	3.18	12	0	76	70	19	69
Culberson, Calvain	4	5	4.30	21	0	88	81	38	62
Hartung, Mike	0	1	5.89	14	0	18	26	10	13
Hill, Chris	3	1	5.93	6	0	30	33	15	24
Johnson, Dom	2	2	5.24	9	0	45	56	22	29
Lee, Calvin	1	3	4.62	8	0	39	33	36	24
Locey, Tony	1	1	4.56	18	0	24	28	16	29
2-team (10 Alex)	1	1	4.11	28	0	50	46	35	54
Martel, Ed	2	4	5.50	7	0	34	40	29	11
Moore, Daryl	1	3	4.58	23	1	18	16	14	16
2-team (13 Pueblo)	1	3	3.94	36	5	30	25	20	25
Parks, Tommy	1	5	5.53	9	0	41	38	19	27
Porzio, Mike	0	3	5.40	16	0	28	32	13	15
Rodriguez, Mario	2	3	4.19	39	5	54	65	21	30
Sanders, Jeff	0	1	15.43	9	0	7	16	5	5
Seymour, Matt	3	2	2.34	48	7	73	59	34	40
Short, Ben	0	1	2.89	8	3	9	7	4	10
Simons, Doug	4	2	2.94	8	0	49	55	3	30
Smith, Jarod	3	4	5.66	24	1	35	36	23	27
Stanhope, Chuck	2	5	6.68	15	1	61	71	25	37
Stutz, Joe	4	4	5.19	15	0	69	82	33	28
Vaughn, Randy	1	2	9.45	3	0	13	25	4	5
Westbrook, Destry	0	1	6.92	8	0	13	13	13	11

PUEBLO

BATTING	AVG	AB	R	H	2B	3B	HR	RBI	SB
Cedeno, Ramon, of	.350	200	37	70	14	0	7	37	3
Cervantes, Ray, 2b-3b	.182	22	4	4	0	0	0	4	0
Collins, Sean, 3b-of	.379	169	27	64	8	2	0	24	17
Darnell, Rob, of-1b	.236	106	16	25	4	0	1	12	3
Dickerson, Robert, of	.228	79	12	18	2	2	2	10	3

	AVG	AB	R	H	2B	3B	HR	RBI	SB
Gomez, Fabio, 3b	.236	72	12	17	1	1	1	11	2
Gonzalez, Eddie, dh-1b	.281	135	19	38	11	0	5	22	0
Johnson, Andre, of	.269	134	28	36	7	2	2	15	10
Johnson, Jack, c-1b	.219	32	5	7	4	0	0	5	0
Kaber, Benji, c	.244	41	3	10	2	0	0	5	0
Lindsey, Robin, c	.167	6	2	1	1	0	0	1	0
2-team (26 Abil)	.230	100	14	23	5	0	0	9	0
Madsen, Dan, of	.452	31	4	14	2	0	0	3	5
Magallanes, Bobby, ss	.276	152	30	42	5	2	4	22	6
Mann, Kelly, c	.294	102	20	30	5	2	2	12	2
Mediavilla, Ricky, 2b-of	.313	48	8	15	1	0	1	5	2
Perez, Jorge, 3b-c	.100	10	1	1	0	0	0	0	1
Perozo, Jose, 2b-3b	.292	154	16	45	3	4	0	21	3
Sullivan, Glenn, 1b-of	.352	128	19	45	4	1	3	17	8
Wilkerson, Wayne, of	.262	42	7	11	0	0	0	3	2

PITCHING	W	L	ERA	G	SV	IP	H	BB	SO
Ahern, Brian	5	7	5.40	13	0	73	96	22	48
Alexander, Robby	3	5	3.96	13	0	64	76	30	36
Applegate, Bobby	0	1	8.42	16	0	26	40	11	14
Arminio, Sam	3	4	4.68	9	0	58	74	17	24
Boynewicz, Jim	3	3	4.26	19	1	51	59	19	22
Dawson, David	0	1	9.00	5	0	10	9	9	5
Martinez, Sean	0	2	6.94	3	0	12	12	10	8
Moore, Daryl	0	3	3.00	13	4	12	9	6	9
Nelson, Bryan	2	4	5.83	22	2	29	30	18	43
Rice, Eric	0	0	9.00	9	0	14	19	10	6
Tipton, Shawn	0	0	8.38	8	0	10	17	9	7
Vaughn, Kip	5	2	2.74	11	0	49	44	16	39

RIO GRANDE VALLEY

BATTING	AVG	AB	R	H	2B	3B	HR	RBI	SB
Cassels, Chris, dh-3b	.269	324	53	87	14	1	24	67	5
Connolly, John, ss-3b	.176	17	3	3	0	0	0	1	0
Cooley, James, c	.204	186	22	38	9	0	9	30	0
Fernandez, Mike, 3b	.203	128	9	26	5	0	0	8	0
2-team (46 Amar)	.266	308	44	82	19	2	3	48	1
Foss, Chris, of	.229	96	11	22	2	0	0	8	7
Garland, Tim, of	.301	376	85	113	20	0	9	44	37
Maclin, Lonnie, of	.369	65	13	24	5	1	0	8	7
Magallanes, Bobby, ss-3b	.273	121	17	33	5	0	7	21	1
2-team (40 Pueblo)	.275	273	47	75	10	2	11	43	7
Martinez, Joey, dh	.274	73	18	20	1	1	0	6	6
Moore, Tony, of	.236	140	21	33	4	0	7	25	6
Morgan, Randy, c	.160	25	3	4	1	0	0	1	0
O'Brien, John, 1b-3b	.276	355	60	98	29	1	21	81	0
Oster, Paul, of	.311	177	23	55	15	0	3	16	4
Pages, Javier, c	.172	29	2	5	1	0	1	5	0
Penn, Trevor, of-1b	.293	375	63	110	24	2	9	57	22
Skeels, Mark, c	.195	113	12	22	5	0	4	10	0
2-team (41 Mobile)	.257	245	32	63	16	0	9	31	2
Swindell, Mark, ss	.206	180	19	37	3	0	0	19	4
Tollison, David, 2b	.308	367	53	113	20	0	6	56	10
Viegas, Clark, 3b-ss	.275	138	21	38	6	1	2	17	0

PITCHING	W	L	ERA	G	SV	IP	H	BB	SO
Ahern, Brian	5	3	2.23	11	0	77	56	29	53
2-team (13 Pueblo)	10	10	3.78	24	0	150	152	51	101
Allen, Harold	2	1	4.76	11	0	28	31	8	20
Anderson, Clark	1	1	4.12	10	0	20	31	2	14
Clough, Ricky	6	3	3.92	41	1	57	53	29	54
Davis, Clint	3	2	2.70	38	21	40	29	9	59
DeJesus, Javy	1	2	3.46	17	1	26	17	14	21
2-team (1 Alex)	1	2	4.34	18	1	29	25	15	24
Duke, Kyle	7	9	4.43	21	0	106	112	60	57
Garcia, Luis	1	3	7.99	13	2	24	23	12	11
Lane, Kevin	8	9	4.34	23	0	156	154	65	128
Lundstrom, Carey	4	3	5.08	11	0	62	64	44	55
Osuna, Al	2	0	3.60	3	0	20	15	9	19
Richards, Dave	9	6	4.37	21	0	140	146	58	123
Satre, Jason	4	4	3.27	16	1	94	92	34	58

TYLER

BATTING	AVG	AB	R	H	2B	3B	HR	RBI	SB
Bertucci, Joe, of-2b	.152	33	3	5	0	0	0	2	1
Collins, Sean, of-2b	.267	146	19	39	4	1	1	13	19
2-team (44 Pueblo)	.327	315	46	103	12	3	1	37	36
Conkle, Troy, ss	.294	313	44	92	18	4	0	23	14
Dana, Derek, c	.237	215	22	51	12	2	2	29	3
Ford, Eric, 2b	.276	192	26	53	10	1	7	24	3
2-team (11 Alex)	.265	219	28	58	10	1	7	26	3
Gould, Clay, of	.280	300	47	84	25	2	4	39	11
Harris, James, 3b	.300	337	53	101	17	2	9	43	3
Norcross, Billy, 1b-dh	.270	163	24	44	7	0	2	13	2
Randle, Zach, 2b-ss	.272	268	34	73	16	3	2	23	4

	AVG	AB	R	H	2B	3B	HR	RBI	SB
Rhone, O.J., of	.216	97	14	21	3	1	1	10	3
Samples, Todd, of	.197	142	17	28	5	2	2	22	8
Shamburg, Ken, 1b	.292	360	68	105	32	2	20	80	4
Tewell, Terrance, c-dh	.255	239	30	61	13	2	7	31	1
Turner, John, 2b	.083	24	5	2	0	0	0	1	1
2-team (2 Lubb)	.125	32	7	4	0	0	0	1	1
Williams, Lanny, of	.279	136	22	38	5	1	9	24	4
Woodruff, Pat, of	.265	347	56	92	18	2	3	47	41

PITCHING	W	L	ERA	G	SV	IP	H	BB	SO
Batchler, Rob	7	5	4.24	21	0	127	161	28	44
Farr, Cody	2	1	6.08	8	0	13	24	4	19
Hancock, Chris	1	3	6.35	6	0	34	40	22	30
Haugh, Tim	2	6	3.92	33	1	60	76	38	51
Jones, Brett	1	2	10.03	9	0	12	24	8	10
Kelley, Rich	0	1	7.88	4	0	16	21	8	10
Knox, Kerry	4	2	2.44	11	0	48	49	4	32
Meador, Paul	10	7	4.28	21	0	139	155	53	62
Peck, Steve	3	4	5.00	12	0	63	85	19	36
Popple, Dan	0	0	5.13	23	0	53	67	18	22
Rambo, Dan	10	5	1.90	17	0	128	127	18	68
Rantz, Ron	0	3	6.33	13	0	21	23	23	15
Rivera, Elvin	0	1	5.40	3	0	10	14	3	1
Salmon, Fabian	4	3	2.22	34	11	45	38	19	47
Schneider, Tom	4	9	6.09	24	0	89	103	43	71

ATLANTIC COAST LEAGUE

STANDINGS

	W	L	PCT	GB
Gaston King Cougars	12	3	.800	—
Spartanburg Alley Cats	7	8	.467	5
Florence Flame	7	10	.412	6
Greenwood Grizzlies	6	11	.353	7

(League suspended play before completion of season)

INDIVIDUAL BATTING LEADERS
(Minimum 30 Plate Appearances)

	AVG	AB	R	H	2B	3B	HR	RBI	SB
Salcedo, Edwin, Spar	.360	25	2	9	2	0	0	4	0
Burroughs, Eric, Spar	.345	58	11	20	3	1	1	5	4
Singer, Roberto, Gastonia	.339	59	18	20	4	0	8	17	0
Mariucci, Rick, Gastonia	.328	64	13	21	4	0	0	4	11
Halbruner, Rick, Gastonia	.326	46	7	15	6	0	3	12	0
Hill, Howard, Green	.323	31	1	10	3	0	0	2	0
Clougherty, Pat, Flor	.318	66	15	21	4	1	2	14	1
Seminoff, Rich, Gastonia	.318	44	13	14	1	0	5	13	1
Jemson, Jackie, Gastonia	.315	54	10	17	3	1	4	12	3
Passaeu, Tippy, Flor	.314	70	6	22	2	0	1	9	2

INDIVIDUAL PITCHING LEADERS
(Minimum 10 Innings)

	W	L	ERA	G	SV	IP	H	BB	SO
Thomas, Jeff, Gastonia	1	0	0.00	8	2	13	5	3	14
Kown, John, Florence	1	0	0.00	3	0	10	6	3	5
Stutz, Joe, Gastonia	2	0	0.47	4	1	19	8	3	22
Cook, Alan, Greenwood	0	1	0.77	7	1	12	7	6	8
Morris, Chad, Flor	1	0	1.53	4	0	18	15	8	22
Hartung, Mike, Green	1	0	1.80	7	1	10	10	2	8
Keefe, Scotty, Flor	1	1	2.25	2	0	12	11	2	8

FRONTIER LEAGUE

The Frontier League, along with the Northern, started the whole independent league craze in 1993. But the league was beset by problems early and almost didn't survive its inaugural season.

But the league continued the growth and stability turnaround that began in 1994, moving weak franchises to better markets and establishing itself as one of the better independent leagues.

The addition of such teams as the Evansville Otters, Johnstown Steal and Richmond Roosters was a boon to the league, as those three teams led the way in attendance. Evansville drew 90,943 fans, far surpassing the 64,355 that led the league in 1994—by Erie, which returned to the New York-Penn League in 1995.

The Steal won back-to-back championships of sorts with their two-game sweep of Zanesville in the league championship series. The Steal played in Erie in 1994 and won the league crown before relocating.

Outfielder Mark Soto, who was on the University of Oklahoma's College World Series winner in 1994, led the Steal to the Frontier League championship with an MVP season. He finished the season hitting .313 with 12 homers and 62 RBIs.

The league had another claim to fame by welcoming Pete Rose back to his first appearance in a baseball park since he was banned from Organized Baseball for alleged gambling activities.

Rose appeared at a Richmond game, courtesy of Andy Furman, a Cincinnati newspaper columnist and sports radio personality who is a part owner of the Roosters and friend of Rose

STANDINGS

	W	L	PCT	GB
Johnstown Steal	46	23	.667	—
Newark Bison	39	29	.574	6½
Zanesville Greys	37	31	.544	8½
Richmond Roosters	38	32	.543	8½
Ohio Valley Redcoats	36	34	.514	10½
Evansville Otters	31	38	.449	15
Portsmouth Explorers	28	41	.406	18
Chillicothe Paints	21	48	.304	25

PLAYOFFS: Semifinals—Johnstown defeated Richmond 2-0, and Zanesville defeated Newark 2-0, in best-of-3 series. **Finals**—Johnstown defeated Zanesville 2-0 in best-of-3 series.

MANAGERS: Chillicothe—Rogers Hanners. Evansville—Boots Day. Johnstown—Mal Fichman. Newark—John Pacella. Ohio Valley—Greg Tagert. Portsmouth—Wayne Albury. Richmond—Larry Nolen. Zanesville—Eric Welch.

ATTENDANCE: Evansville, 90,943. Johnstown, 67,167. Richmond, 47,714. Chillicothe, 31,128. Zanesville, 25,515. Newark, 21,309. Ohio Valley, 21,093. Portsmouth, 11,931.

ALL-STAR TEAM: C—Stoney Burke, Richmond. **1B**—Morgan Burkhardt, Richmond. **2B**—Mark Johnson, Newark. **3B**—Steve Ruckman, Richmond. **SS**—Robert Camarillo, Portsmouth. **OF**—Thurston Rockmore, Johnstown; Jeff Snyder, Portsmouth; Mark Soto, Johnstown. **DH**—Johnny Booker, Richmond. **SP**—Sean Hogan, Johnstown. **RP**—Don Wolfe, Zanesville.

Most Valuable Player: Mark Soto, Johnstown. **Most Valuable Pitcher:** Don Wolfe, Zanesville. **Manager of the Year:** John Pacella, Newark.

INDIVIDUAL BATTING LEADERS
(Minimum 189 Plate Appearances)

	AVG	AB	R	H	2B	3B	HR	RBI	SB
Snyder, Jeff, Portsmouth	.398	221	39	88	13	2	1	34	20
James, Neill, Portsmouth	.349	241	45	84	16	2	4	39	2
Goble, Rodney, Johnstown	.345	197	37	68	8	3	1	25	22
Ruckman, Steve, Richmond	.342	237	38	81	10	1	2	32	6
Alkire, Ryan, Newark	.333	177	27	59	9	2	2	28	15
Yuen, Franz, Evansville	.332	244	27	81	19	5	6	33	3
Burkhardt, Morgan, Rich	.330	282	58	93	28	1	9	70	16
Rockmore, Thurston, John	.327	251	59	82	14	3	5	50	20
Coats, John, Johnstown	.320	206	36	66	20	3	6	38	4
Angulo, Gabby, Chillicothe	.320	222	27	71	12	0	1	26	1
Soto, Mark, Johnstown	.313	272	62	85	22	5	12	62	2
Range, J, Ohio Valley	.311	206	44	64	12	2	0	27	2
Hernandez, Carlos, Newark	.310	203	26	63	9	0	3	35	0
Zaragoza, Tony, Johnstown	.310	168	36	52	12	2	3	28	2
Johnson, Mark, Newark	.307	283	53	87	9	4	4	28	14
Venneman, Kurt, Evansville	.307	254	43	78	12	2	3	34	4
Gabbert, Chris, Ohio Valley	.306	219	49	67	12	3	10	60	8
Foss, Dirk, Ohio Valley	.305	249	54	76	12	2	4	40	30
Bolton, Doug, Richmond	.302	205	40	62	5	3	0	25	7
Alligood, Rusty, Zanesville	.302	245	39	74	6	1	0	25	37
Drabik, Josh, Richmond	.302	169	31	51	12	1	1	24	3
Prieto, Tony, Zanesville	.296	199	35	59	1	2	0	18	10
Koaster, Gerald, Johnstown	.295	190	36	56	6	3	0	18	16
Geffner, Steve, Portsmouth	.294	238	44	70	9	0	0	20	21
Booker, Johnny, Richmond	.289	256	49	74	18	0	11	46	8
Ponegalek, Chad, Zanes.	.272	158	46	43	6	0	2	15	39

INDIVIDUAL PITCHING LEADERS
(Minimum 56 Innings)

	W	L	ERA	G	SV	IP	H	BB	SO
Bonelli, Ralph, Newark	6	2	2.45	14	0	103	100	35	47
Hogan, Sean, Johnstown	7	1	2.48	15	0	94	85	43	86
Ainsworth, Chris, Newark	3	2	2.48	13	0	58	56	24	43
Arnold, Chad, Portsmouth	6	3	2.74	24	0	82	84	21	66
Mercado, Fernando, OV	8	4	2.82	15	0	105	97	32	91
Copp, Matt, Chillicothe	6	6	2.88	15	0	100	101	38	67
Boebert, Mike, Johnstown	7	5	2.94	15	0	95	87	55	84
Falcone, Dan, Richmond	2	1	3.07	15	0	59	61	29	36
McGill, Ron, Evansville	4	6	3.14	15	0	92	90	44	69
Pearson, Terry, Zanesville	6	2	3.23	14	0	84	80	37	55
Cancel, Rob, Zanesville	6	4	3.26	24	0	69	61	24	54
Bellows, Mike, Portsmouth	4	3	3.26	16	0	61	65	19	43
Smart, Kasey, Newark	5	4	3.28	14	0	91	96	16	69
Guehne, Dan, Evansville	6	3	3.32	11	0	76	87	7	51
Williams, Billy, Johnstown	9	4	3.32	15	0	100	107	36	64
Conlin, Sean, Zanesville	3	4	3.41	27	1	58	51	26	50
Carruth, Jason, Evansville	3	4	3.51	10	0	59	47	22	35
Moore, P.J., Evansville	1	4	3.58	14	0	88	104	27	40
Brantley, Jim, Portsmouth	4	2	3.63	9	0	57	61	19	26
McKinney, Burke, Ohio Valley	3	2	3.65	21	0	74	91	10	50

MID-AMERICA LEAGUE

STANDINGS

	W	L	PCT	GB
Lafayette Leopards	33	24	.579	—
Anderson Lawmen	33	26	.559	1
Merrillville Muddogs	27	31	.466	6½
East Chicago Conquistadors	23	35	.397	10½
PLAYOFFS: None.				

MANAGERS: Anderson—Jay Welker; East Chicago—Ron D'Auteuil; Merrillville—Ron Kittle; Lafayette—Jim Gonzalez.

ATTENDANCE: Merrillville, 18,351. Anderson, 12,579. Lafayette, 7,624. East Chicago, 5,444.

ALL-STAR TEAM: C—Donnie Diffenbaugh, Merrillville. **1B**—Larry Hisle Jr., East Chicago. **2B**—Ron D'Auteuil, East Chicago. **3B**—Craig Tucker, Merrillville. **SS**—Jeff Laschinski, Merrillville. **OF**—Darrio Green, East Chicago; Mike Shirley, Anderson; Kadir Villalona, Lafayette. **DH**—Brian Heigle, Anderson. **SP**—Javier Gomez, Merrillville; Ryan Lewis, Merrillville; Dustin Riggs, Anderson; Jason Taulman, Lafayette. **RP**—Aaron Magdeleno, Lafayette; Dylan Tedders, Anderson.

Most Valuable Player: Brian Heigle, Anderson. **Pitcher of the Year:** Javier Gomez, Merrillville. **Manager of the Year:** Jay Welker, Anderson.

INDIVIDUAL BATTING LEADERS
(Minimum 162 Plate Appearances)

	AVG	AB	R	H	2B	3B	HR	RBI	SB
Allen, Brandon, Lafayette	.391	151	31	59	6	4	4	24	4
Hisle, Larry, EC	.375	128	30	48	9	1	2	22	6
Villalona, Kadir, Laf	.369	233	40	86	10	6	3	47	28
Heigle, Brian, Anderson	.347	202	44	70	19	2	6	51	12
Padron, Jose, Lafayette	.335	185	37	62	10	1	2	27	11
Green, Darrio, EC	.330	206	47	68	12	1	4	21	24
Shirley, Mike, Anderson	.325	209	39	68	12	1	3	36	18
Martin, Lyle, Merr	.322	183	37	59	13	0	1	20	4
Diffenbaugh, Donnie, Merr	.322	199	30	64	6	1	4	31	4
Simmons, Brian, And	.301	206	33	62	6	0	0	22	23
Mayberry, Germaine, EC	.301	163	29	49	4	4	3	25	11
D'Auteuil, Ron, EC	.287	195	44	56	8	2	0	23	15
Alferman, Derek, And	.284	194	48	55	6	1	0	22	49
Newman, Bruce, EC	.282	181	30	51	16	2	5	43	9
Griffin, Vincent, Merr	.282	142	18	40	7	1	4	14	15
Tucker, Craig, Merr	.276	221	23	61	12	3	1	46	1
McKeeman, Rob, Laf	.276	156	34	43	13	0	2	27	5
Cruz, Brian, Anderson	.271	129	11	35	7	1	1	23	3
Rhinehart, Billy, And	.269	160	29	43	2	1	0	17	16

INDIVIDUAL PITCHING LEADERS
(Minimum 46 Innings)

	W	L	ERA	G	SV	IP	H	BB	SO
Gomez, Javier, Merr	5	4	2.43	10	0	67	59	27	68
Taulman, Jason, Lafayette	6	3	2.50	12	0	76	64	13	22
Towns, Brad, Lafayette	5	3	3.08	12	0	79	58	33	50
Lichtenstein, R.C., Merr	5	1	3.35	14	0	83	78	21	57
Riggs, Dustin, Anderson	8	4	3.36	14	0	104	103	42	83
Gamble, Rob, Anderson	3	3	3.66	8	0	47	48	13	19
Hall, Chris, Merrillville	2	5	3.75	12	0	58	64	14	41

Young, Mike, Anderson	4	3	3.88	9	0	53	55	16	42
Swank, Gary, Lafayette	2	4	3.90	19	3	60	73	15	33
Lewis, Ryan, Merrillville	3	2	4.08	11	0	46	50	27	22
Snure, Jeremy, East Chicago	3	2	4.18	9	1	47	46	21	26
Morehead, Dean, Anderson	3	3	4.30	13	1	46	50	15	31
Johnson, Chad, Lafayette	6	4	4.58	13	0	79	80	36	47
White, David, East Chicago	4	8	4.66	15	0	85	95	40	57
Ginder, Dave, Anderson	4	6	4.73	14	0	67	83	28	32

NORTH ATLANTIC LEAGUE

STANDINGS

	W	L	PCT	GB
Newark Barge Bandits	37	21	.638	—
Welland Aquaducks	32	27	.542	5½
Nashua Hawks	28	31	.475	9½
Niagara Falls Mallards	20	38	.345	17
PLAYOFFS: None.				

MANAGERS: Nashua—Allan Cupper. Newark—Dave Keylin. Niagara Falls—Ken Barna. Welland—Ellis Williams.

ATTENDANCE: Niagara Falls, 17,398; Newark, 15,005; Nashua, 14,339; Welland, 12,653.

ALL-STAR TEAM: C—Rob Zachman, Newark. **1B**—Doug Spofford, Nashua. **2B**—Erick Eckstein, Newark. **3B**—Rob Aziz, Nashua. **SS**—William Bellanger, Welland. **LF**—Keith Qualter, Nashua. **CF**—Doug Shumway, Welland. **RF**—Chris Neill, Welland. **LHP**—Jon Hinkle, Niagara. **RHP**—Jerry Hunter, Newark. **RP**—Tim McKenna, Newark.

Manager of the Year: Ellis Williams, Welland.

INDIVIDUAL BATTING LEADERS
(Minimum 162 Plate Appearances)

	AVG	AB	R	H	2B	3B	HR	RBI	SB
Qualter, Keith, Nashua	.354	178	37	63	15	2	2	37	7
Spofford, Doug, Nashua	.343	169	32	58	15	0	1	23	16
Eckstein, Erik, Newark	.342	146	18	50	8	0	0	20	8
Campaniello, Ed, Welland	.339	174	32	59	10	2	0	22	8
Neill, Chris, Welland	.337	175	32	59	6	3	0	14	34
Zachmann, Rob, Newark	.331	160	36	53	12	1	5	23	2
Telford, John, Niagara	.298	198	37	59	10	2	1	27	24
Bellanger, William, Well	.296	223	36	66	3	7	3	33	18
Shumway, Doug, Welland	.292	171	28	50	1	0	0	13	25
McClure, Jason, Newark	.292	130	24	38	8	2	2	19	7
Perez, Manny, Welland	.283	166	19	47	12	4	0	24	1
Sarno, Joseph, Nashua	.277	159	28	44	7	1	0	16	15
Hirst, Paul, Niagara	.273	150	18	41	7	0	0	18	2
Martenson, Blake, New	.273	150	13	41	11	1	1	23	10
Decker, Tim, Newark	.268	127	32	34	4	3	0	11	18
Strack, Steve, Niagara	.258	190	31	49	6	3	0	14	15
Bajzer, Gary, Niagara	.251	187	19	47	3	2	0	17	15
Zandt, Mike, Niagara	.250	200	17	50	11	0	3	27	5
Graham, Timothy, Nashua	.243	185	29	45	10	1	2	30	3
Key, Ken, Newark	.237	169	19	40	5	2	0	8	11

INDIVIDUAL PITCHING LEADERS
(Minimum 48 Innings)

	W	L	ERA	G	SV	IP	H	BB	SO
Hunter, Germaine, Newark	8	2	1.08	13	0	92	66	24	117
DeMartino, Joe, Niagara	3	4	1.70	11	0	74	75	27	49
Jones, Brett, Welland	7	2	1.76	13	0	97	72	35	46
McKeone, Chris, Niagara	3	3	1.79	12	0	65	57	27	54
Stewart, Stan, Newark	7	1	1.89	12	0	76	48	34	90
Schlee, Chad, Niagara	3	6	2.23	11	0	77	74	15	70
Marr, Jeff, Welland	5	3	2.44	8	0	63	57	11	46
Hinkle, Jon, Niagara	8	2	2.50	14	0	83	83	16	66
Rourke, Kevin, Nashua	6	4	2.68	11	0	77	75	15	59
Humphreys, Kevin, Newark	4	3	2.91	13	0	59	59	9	42
Golds, Aaron, Niagara	2	6	3.19	10	0	59	56	25	28
Dell'Oso, Vinny, Welland	4	3	3.23	15	0	70	67	36	40
Herrington, Todd, Nashua	4	3	3.50	10	0	74	72	44	47
Festa, Chris, Nashua	6	3	4.14	10	0	63	68	23	45

NORTH CENTRAL LEAGUE

STANDINGS

	W	L	PCT	GB
Chaska Valley Buccaneers	8	6	.571	—
Brainerd Bears	12	10	.545	—
Minnesota Skeeters	9	11	.450	2
Will County Claws	8	10	.444	2
(League suspended play before completion of season)				

INDIVIDUAL BATTING LEADERS
(Minimum 51 Plate Appearances)

	AVG	AB	R	H	2B	3B	HR	RBI	SB
Castro, Ernesto, CV	.444	54	12	24	7	1	3	20	0
Mueller, Jon, WC	.412	51	12	21	4	0	2	14	1
Durkac, Bo, Will County	.375	72	18	27	3	0	6	18	0
Tovar, Raul, Minn	.375	64	17	24	5	0	0	11	2
Smith, Luke, Brainerd	.373	67	17	25	7	0	2	9	2
Wickey, Menno, Brainerd	.366	82	22	30	6	2	2	13	10
Waller, Casey, Minn	.360	75	23	27	6	2	4	14	4
Underwood, Curtis, Brain	.351	74	13	26	5	1	1	12	0
Garife, Christopher, WC	.349	63	11	22	3	0	0	5	2
Sardinha, Eddie, Minn	.348	66	16	23	4	1	5	16	1

INDIVIDUAL PITCHING LEADERS
(Minimum 15 Innings)

	W	L	ERA	G	SV	IP	H	BB	SO
Martin, Doug, CV	3	0	0.75	3	0	24	21	2	10
Frace, Ryan, Brainerd	3	1	1.13	5	0	24	17	1	23
Brantley, Jim, WC	3	1	1.59	13	5	23	16	13	24
Hoffman, J.R., Brainerd	2	3	2.31	8	1	23	24	10	19
Stephens, Mark, Brainerd	3	1	3.10	5	0	29	25	11	24

NORTHEAST LEAGUE °

STANDINGS

	W	L	PCT	GB
Albany Diamond Dogs	52	18	.743	—
Mohawk Valley Landsharks	47	23	.671	5
Adirondack Lumberjacks	42	27	.609	9½
Newburgh Nighthawks	28	41	.406	23½
Sullivan Mountain Lions	23	43	.348	27
Yonkers Hoot Owls	12	52	.188	37

PLAYOFFS: Adirondack defeated Albany 2-1 in best-of-3 final.

MANAGERS: Adirondack—Dave LaPoint. Albany—Doc Edwards. Mohawk Valley—Ken Oberkfell. Newburgh—Ron LeFlore. Sullivan County—Howie Bedell. Yonkers—Paul Blair.
ATTENDANCE: Albany, 60,084; Adirondack, 51,543; Sullivan, 34,143; Newburgh, 21,978; Mohawk Valley, 12,507; Yonkers, 5,216.
ALL-STAR TEAM: None.
Most Valuable Player: Hugh Walker, Mohawk Valley. **Most Valuable Pitcher:** Jeff Letourneau, Albany. **Manager of the Year:** Doc Edwards, Albany.

INDIVIDUAL BATTING LEADERS
(Minimum 189 Plate Appearances)

	AVG	AB	R	H	2B	3B	HR	RBI	SB
Kokinda, Chris, Sullivan	.370	216	32	80	16	1	4	27	12
Walker, Hugh, Mohawk	.362	229	55	83	23	7	13	56	25
Haughney, Trevor, Sull	.351	248	52	87	12	4	0	16	35
Pineiro, Mike, Mohawk	.342	260	50	89	19	2	8	55	5
Coates, Tom, Adirondack	.342	234	53	80	14	2	8	50	26
Cooke, Jeff, Adirondack	.330	221	55	73	9	5	3	29	32
Gilliam, Sean, Albany	.327	284	55	93	15	6	13	64	1
Madden, Joey, Newburgh	.326	264	45	86	9	6	3	32	49
Wilson, Matt, Mohawk	.322	264	47	85	13	2	1	28	15
Mercado, Rafael, Albany	.316	215	30	68	18	3	2	39	1
DeLeon, Felix, Albany	.312	218	32	68	14	1	1	27	12
Jemison, Andrew, Yonkers	.311	219	41	68	20	2	8	47	7
Reinisch, Paul, Albany	.305	236	38	72	15	1	4	41	1
Furey, Mike, Mohawk	.304	207	34	63	10	4	2	28	6
Berlin, Randy, Albany	.304	184	24	56	11	0	4	24	3
Markiewicz, Brandon, MV	.298	265	49	79	18	3	11	59	3
Mitchell, Ed, Sullivan	.291	213	24	62	10	3	0	23	8
Durkac, Bo, Adirondack	.290	169	34	49	9	3	2	28	2
Zarate, Vince, Yonkers	.289	228	39	66	8	4	0	23	15
Wojtkowski, Steve, MV	.289	235	30	68	6	2	0	21	16
Bifone, Pete, Sullivan	.287	251	33	72	21	1	2	43	19
Burr, Chris, Albany	.286	241	43	69	14	1	4	50	1
Ojea, Alex, Newburgh	.286	280	33	80	7	2	3	33	21
Doucette, Darren, Adir	.282	216	30	61	8	3	8	44	0
Lockett, Ron, Albany	.282	220	46	62	14	6	3	27	21

INDIVIDUAL PITCHING LEADERS
(Minimum 54 Innings)

	W	L	ERA	G	SV	IP	H	BB	SO
Letourneau, Jeff, Albany	10	2	1.50	14	0	102	66	19	94
Rauth, Chris, Adirondack	9	6	2.47	15	0	106	102	18	54
Townsend, Rich, Mohawk	6	4	2.61	14	0	93	75	12	74
Meier, Pat, Mohawk	6	4	2.65	12	0	78	78	36	33

Bellcase, Bert, Newburgh	2	5	2.73	15	0	102	104	32	76
Sontag, Alan, Albany	9	3	2.92	15	0	117	109	13	102
Botkin, Alan, Albany	7	3	3.01	15	0	78	79	14	56
Grezlaczyk, Ken, Mohawk	8	4	3.16	13	0	91	96	26	63
Faile, William, Adirondack	6	3	3.27	13	0	72	57	39	35
Wood, Brian, Mohawk	7	2	3.65	14	0	81	75	23	69
Fleet, Kenyatta, Albany	11	1	3.68	13	0	86	80	34	66
Nelson, James, Yonkers	3	7	3.78	20	1	79	92	26	41
Bartnick, Mark, Sullivan	5	2	4.04	19	0	69	75	19	28
Knobloch, Mike, Newburgh	5	6	4.04	14	0	76	77	30	49
Farrar, Terry, Adirondack	8	5	4.05	14	0	87	87	30	79
Brosius, Paul, Sullivan	4	8	4.37	13	0	80	84	36	39
Clark, Doug, Adirondack	5	3	4.37	13	0	80	100	15	55
Nestor, Joe, Newburgh	7	4	4.80	25	3	69	72	29	40
Broome, John, Mohawk	4	3	5.30	15	0	71	88	16	42
Anastasi, Chris, Yonkers	4	9	5.53	20	1	68	100	27	22

PRAIRIE LEAGUE

STANDINGS

AMERICAN DIVISION	W	L	PCT	GB
Aberdeen Pheasants	56	13	.812	—
Minneapolis Loons	43	26	.623	13
Dakota Rattlers	30	42	.417	27½
Minot Mallards	24	47	.338	33

CANADIAN DIVISION	W	L	PCT	GB
Moose Jaw Diamond Dogs	44	28	.611	—
Regina Cyclones	40	30	.571	3
Saskatoon Riot	26	45	.366	17½
Brandon Grey Owls	19	51	.271	24

PLAYOFFS: Semifinals—Aberdeen defeated Minneapolis 2-0, and Regina defeated Moose Jaw 2-1, in best-of-3 series. **Finals**—Regina defeated Aberdeen 3-1 in best-of-5 final.

MANAGERS: Aberdeen—Bob Flori. Brandon—Darren Hursey. Dakota—John King. Minneapolis—Greg Olson. Minot—Mark Hebbeler. Moose Jaw—Mike Brocki. Regina—Jason Felice. Saskatoon—George Scott.
ATTENDANCE: Moose Jaw, 75,345; Regina, 49,223; Aberdeen, 40,036; Saskatoon, 38,711; Minneapolis, 32,351; Minot, 31,666; Dakota, 28,042; Brandon, 24,757.
ALL-STAR TEAM: C—Brad Gay, Aberdeen. **1B**—Ken Tirpack, Aberdeen. **2B**—Enrique Duncan, Aberdeen. **3B**—Shawn Wooten, Moose Jaw. **SS**—Bobby Holley, Aberdeen. **OF**—Brian Cornelius, Moose Jaw; Jason Felice, Regina; Ed Gerald, Aberdeen. **DH**—Boo Moore, Dakota. **LHP**—Chris Schmitt, Aberdeen. **RHP**—Darrin Reichle, Aberdeen. **RP**—Juan Berenguer, Minneapolis.
Most Valuable Player: Ken Tirpack, Aberdeen. **Most Valuable Pitcher:** Darrin Reichle, Aberdeen. **Manager of the Year:** Bob Flori, Aberdeen.

INDIVIDUAL BATTING LEADERS
(Minimum 130 Plate Appearances)

	AVG	AB	R	H	2B	3B	HR	RBI	SB
Cornelius, Brian, MJ	.403	308	82	124	19	1	20	73	23
Brocki, Mike, MJ	.402	259	81	104	13	1	5	35	33
Felice, Jason, Regina	.394	241	55	95	15	1	23	80	10
Tirpack, Ken, Aberdeen	.393	275	63	108	27	3	20	72	3
Kapano, Randy, Moose Jaw	.390	136	36	53	13	1	12	57	6
Holley, Bobby, Aberdeen	.382	288	67	110	26	1	13	64	8
Wooten, Shawn, MJ	.372	201	38	75	12	2	11	55	3
Gerald, Ed, Aberdeen	.352	273	75	96	20	2	23	77	18
Smith, Butch, Minot	.350	277	50	97	13	0	25	75	1
Moore, Boo, Dakota	.348	279	58	97	22	0	20	82	4
Smaler, Josh, Regina	.345	281	62	97	20	0	4	43	20
Vogel, Mike, Minn.	.343	137	27	47	9	0	6	25	2
Dong, Tommy, Dakota	.339	192	44	65	7	1	3	23	19
Paulsen, Matt, Moose Jaw	.337	169	25	57	12	0	1	18	5
Burrus, Daryl, Sask.-Reg.	.336	235	35	79	15	1	7	38	7
Duncan, Enrique, Aber.	.335	263	64	88	19	0	10	39	14
Srauss, Brad, Minot	.335	278	52	93	12	2	13	57	25
Griffith, Tommy, MJ-Reg.	.331	275	72	91	13	0	12	32	24
Shepard, Greg, Regina	.324	210	46	68	5	1	6	39	1
Wright, Pat, Minn.	.324	182	45	59	8	1	7	42	3
McKamie, Sean, Minn.	.322	264	66	85	12	1	9	39	18
Robinson, Darryl, Aber.	.321	290	47	93	13	1	6	40	0
Collum, Gary, Minot	.320	319	62	102	13	2	4	29	47
Jackson, Paul, Minn.	.317	252	59	80	10	0	10	55	11
Gravengoed, Jayson, Reg.	.316	253	52	80	17	0	17	56	1
Williams, Ted, MJ	.316	266	56	84	9	0	3	28	39

INDIVIDUAL PITCHING LEADERS
(Minimum 30 Innings)

	W	L	ERA	G	SV	IP	H	BB	SO
Berenguer, Juan, Minn.	2	3	0.82	26	9	33	23	2	32
Ehl, Kevin, Regina	3	1	2.02	32	13	36	34	11	40
Quillin, Kris, Aberdeen	3	1	2.16	23	7	42	38	12	32
Painter, Gary, Aberdeen	11	0	2.23	12	0	85	64	21	74
Salado, Tim, Regina	4	2	2.55	23	0	35	33	11	21
Schmitt, Chris, Aberdeen	11	3	2.65	17	0	126	109	37	74
Parkinson, Eric, Aber	10	2	2.71	15	0	110	103	35	69
Ligtenberg, Kerry, Minn........	11	2	2.73	17	0	109	101	26	100
Hayward, Steve, Aber...........	4	1	2.74	19	8	46	36	21	64
Reichle, Darrin, Aber............	14	0	2.77	16	0	107	100	30	86
Spurgeon, Steve, Minn...........	7	4	2.94	15	0	104	101	22	61
Wiesner, Chad, Minn.	2	3	3.02	33	1	48	38	20	33
Heil, Brian, Brandon	2	6	3.15	32	6	46	42	23	35
Nelson, Kevin, Minot	4	2	3.27	21	6	52	56	27	27
Pierce, Mike, Bran.-Sask.......	4	4	3.48	12	0	75	71	29	49
Matthews, Mark, Minot	7	7	3.57	16	0	106	110	20	79
Boggs, Brandon, Dakota	2	4	3.61	22	4	42	50	14	29
Prosser, David, Dakota	8	4	3.67	16	0	108	117	48	61
Angileri, Mike, Dakota	2	3	3.81	13	1	59	60	38	49
Fandel, Russ, Minn	8	5	3.94	16	0	103	97	30	81

WESTERN LEAGUE

The Western League made a big splash in its first season, attracting solid franchises, good players and fewer problems than usual for a first-year league.

The only real problem was in Long Beach, where the team's original owner-ship group had to file for bankruptcy protection. But the franchise emerged from that trouble with a new nickname (Riptide replaced Barracuda) and a deter-mined attitude, and won the league's first champi-onship.

To top it all off, the fran-chise's new ownership group includes Heather Locklear, Cheryl Miller and Susan Anton.

Ariel Prieto

The Riptide beat Tri-Cities three games to one in a championship series in which every game was decided by one run. Three of the games came down to the final at-bat.

Series MVP Eddie Christian went 4-for-4 in the decisive game and drove in the winning run with a single in the 10th inning. After he won the game, Christian ran into the outfield, away from his teammates.

"I saw those guys coming, and I thought they would crush me," he said.

No team in the league drew 100,000 fans, but attendance was solid throughout the league, and league officials planned expansion for 1996, with Reno, Nev., a good bet to join another new club in the league.

The league attracted interest early with former Dodgers GM Al Campanis leading the Palm Springs franchise and signing Cuban defector Ariel Prieto to his first professional contract. Prieto drew raves in the league and attracted legions of scouts before the Oakland Athletics used their first-round pick in the June draft to pluck him.

STANDINGS

FIRST HALF

NORTH	W	L	PCT	GB
Surrey	26	16	.619	—
Bend	22	23	.489	5½
Grays Harbor	18	26	.409	9
Tri-Cities	18	27	.400	9½

SOUTH	W	L	PCT	GB
Salinas	27	18	.600	—
Long Bch.	24	21	.533	3
Palm Spgs.	21	22	.488	5
Sonoma Cty.	21	24	.467	6

SECOND HALF

NORTH	W	L	PCT	GB
Tri-City	27	19	.587	—
Bend	26	20	.565	1
Grays Harbor	13	33	.283	14
Surrey	12	36	.250	16

SOUTH	W	L	PCT	GB
Salinas	33	12	.733	—
Long Bch.	28	17	.622	5
Sonoma Cty.	23	22	.511	10
Palm Spgs.	22	25	.468	12

PLAYOFFS: Semifinals—Long Beach defeated Salinas 2-0, and Tri-Cities defeated Surrey 2-0, in best-of-3 series. **Finals**—Long Beach defeated Tri-Cities 3-1 in best-of-5 series.

MANAGERS: Bend—Al Gallagher. Grays Harbor—Nate Colbert. Long Beach—Jeff Burroughs. Palm Springs—Bill Sudakis. Salinas—Dave Holt. Sonoma County—Paul Deese. Surrey—Dick Phillips. Tri-Cities—Tom Trebelhorn.

ATTENDANCE: Tri-Cities, 98,248; Grays Harbor, 82,450; Sonoma County, 84,173; Palm Springs, 61,595; Long Beach, 61,120; Salinas, 56,579; Surrey, 53,769; Bend, 53,465.

ALL-STAR TEAM: None.

Player of the Year: Kyle Washington, Sonoma County. **Pitcher of the Year:** John Weglarz, Tri-Cities. **Manager of the Year:** Dave Holt, Salinas.

INDIVIDUAL BATTING LEADERS
(Minimum 243 Plate Appearances)

	AVG	AB	R	H	2B	3B	HR	RBI	SB
Washington, Kyle, SC	.370	289	67	107	22	4	17	75	12
Tedder, Scott, Bend	.350	340	68	119	24	3	4	57	5
Christian, Eddie, LB..............	.339	333	66	113	27	2	1	50	27
Aldrete, Rich, Salinas	.337	332	54	112	26	1	6	54	0
Barbara, Don, LB...................	.335	221	31	74	16	1	5	48	7
Constantino, Kraig, PS	.334	299	48	100	16	2	9	41	5
Koehler, Jim, Bend................	.325	357	68	116	33	1	16	78	0
Peguero, Jose, PS	.322	320	50	103	20	3	13	55	28
Smedes, Mike, Bend	.321	290	51	93	18	2	6	57	0
Lewis, Dan, SC.....................	.317	268	45	85	21	1	11	56	1
Bobo, Elgin, Salinas	.316	234	31	74	22	3	10	51	2
Avery, Mark, PS	.316	244	37	77	12	2	7	44	3
Rosario, Victor, SC................	.310	342	49	106	27	2	5	55	10
Murphy, Jim, Surrey	.307	326	55	100	18	2	13	62	19
Dietz, Steve, GH....................	.306	268	46	82	13	2	1	32	15
Booker, Kevin, Tri-Cities........	.304	352	57	107	16	4	6	44	23
Nunez, Bernie, PS.................	.303	290	45	88	17	1	10	56	10
Turner, Shane, LB	.300	327	66	98	21	3	3	40	17
Pezzoni, Ron, T-C	.300	257	35	77	13	2	1	37	2
Gagliano, Manny, GH............	.298	332	61	99	27	0	16	50	3
Paul, Corey, GH	.297	256	54	76	10	0	9	36	2
Brice, Billy, Bend	.295	356	62	105	29	1	6	49	1
Bugg, Jason, Bend	.293	276	43	81	22	1	5	44	9
Burke, Alan, LB	.293	331	47	97	12	0	5	48	5
Chaffee, Jamie, SC	.292	322	54	94	14	3	6	48	10
Casey, Johnny, LB................	.292	288	39	84	15	0	5	50	1
Robinson, Don, LB	.289	332	68	96	26	3	7	61	20
Williams, Paul, GH	.289	332	58	96	14	0	22	79	2

INDIVIDUAL PITCHING LEADERS
(Minimum 72 Innings)

	W	L	ERA	G	SV	IP	H	BB	SO
Weglarz, John, Tri-Cities......	11	5	1.87	19	0	149	119	41	162
Patton, John, Salinas	11	6	2.01	22	0	134	108	53	112
Reardon, Kevin, Salinas........	14	2	2.29	21	0	138	109	27	93
Strong, Joe, Surrey	8	9	2.75	20	0	131	120	48	129
Singleton, Scott, LB..............	5	5	2.88	24	1	147	124	34	112
Warembourg, Scott, Salinas ...	9	3	2.98	28	0	124	123	37	69
Navarro, Rick, SC	4	6	3.24	15	0	94	87	13	74
Gogos, Keith, LB...................	6	2	3.44	12	0	84	93	14	36
McKinley, Leif, Bend	10	6	3.57	21	0	141	143	41	129
Gay, Steve, PS......................	5	8	3.69	19	0	132	137	44	83
Peltzer, Kurt, LB	13	5	3.75	22	0	163	158	35	118
Salcedo, Jose, T-C................	6	9	3.81	26	0	132	151	33	104
Johnson, Steve, T-C	7	9	3.81	21	0	141	150	20	86
Masi, Dave, Surrey................	3	8	3.86	19	0	98	99	40	61
O'Dea, Brett, PS....................	4	7	4.05	22	0	100	84	57	84
Pico, Jeff, Bend.....................	6	5	4.32	16	0	100	121	25	57
Loucks, Steve, T-C................	7	6	4.50	18	0	88	102	43	50

FOREIGN
LEAGUES

MEXICAN LEAGUE

Mexico's Economic Woes Plague League

By JAMES BAILEY

Major League Baseball was not alone in dealing with off-field problems in 1995. The Mexican League also took a major hit.

Severe financial problems, brought on by Mexico's economic troubles and fallout from the major league players' strike, forced league officials to scale back the regular-season schedule from 132 to 116 games. The first two weeks of the season were eliminated.

A grossly devalued peso, which resulted in rampant inflation and a 100 percent increase in interest rates, plagued the league. It made it especially difficult for teams to pay import players, who are paid in American dollars. The problem was compounded when big league clubs looked to the Mexican League for replacement players, many of whom were in major league spring training camps as the Mexican League season got underway.

"We're facing a crisis year," Nuevo Laredo vice president Samuel Lozano said. "Our economy is hurting. The buying power of the fan is limited."

On the field, the Mexico City Reds won at a .708 clip during the regular season but did not successfully defend their league title. The Monterrey Sultans stunned the Reds in the championship series by winning four straight games. It was Monterrey's seventh league title.

The Sultans, managed by American Derek Bryant, won the first two games in Monterrey, 7-3 and 8-3, and the next two in Mexico City, 3-0 and 9-7. The Reds had beaten Monterrey in seven games in 1994.

"We played a great team with great tradition," Bryant said. "We started playing great baseball the last month of the season, and took it into the playoffs."

The Sultans finished no higher than third in the North Zone in either half of the split-season schedule, but got hot in the playoffs and eliminated Saltillo and Reynosa.

The Reds, South Zone champions in both halves, beat Campeche and the Mexico City Tigers to reach the final round, but proved easy victims for the Sultans.

Monterrey won the deciding game by scoring six runs in the ninth inning to erase a 7-3 deficit and hand Reds righthander Francisco Cordoba his first loss in 26 decisions.

Cordoba, 23, hadn't lost since June 17, 1994. He was 13-0 during the regular season and 3-0 in the playoffs before the loss.

Triumphant Return For Gainey

Veteran Reds DH Ty Gainey, who returned to the Mexican League after playing two years in Japan, became the first triple crown winner in 39 years. He hit .411 with 27 home runs and 116 RBIs despite missing 25 early-season games with a hamstring injury. He also had a league-high .775 slugging percentage, but went hitless in the final three playoff games against Monterrey after homering twice in the opener.

Gainey became the sixth player to win a Mexican League triple crown. The last was also an American, Alonso Perry in 1956. Other winners include Cool Papa Bell (1940),

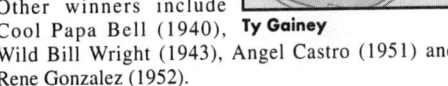
Ty Gainey

Wild Bill Wright (1943), Angel Castro (1951) and Rene Gonzalez (1952).

Gainey, who played with the Houston Astros from 1985-87, played for the Reds from 1990-92. He led the league with 47 home runs and 133 RBIs in 1992.

Because of the economic crisis that plagued Mexico, few Americans played in the Mexican League in 1995. Teams normally can have up to five imports on their rosters.

Legendary Mexican League slugger Andres Mora, who retired as a player in 1994, came back as a player-manager for Nuevo Laredo. He hit six home runs in 1995 to run his career total to 419, 34 shy of Hector Espino's record total of 453.

Mora wasn't the oldest fan favorite to make a comeback. Ramon Arano, 56, played briefly with Veracruz and became the first Mexican League player to appear in five decades. Though he appeared in only five games before accepting a role as the team's pitching coach, Arano proved he had something left by tossing a seven-inning, three-hit shutout in his first game back. Arano, who is enshrined in the Mexican League Hall of Fame, went 2-2 with a 6.86 ERA.

LEAGUE CHAMPIONS

Last 25 Years

Year	Regular Season*		Playoff
1971	Saltillo	.593	Jalisco
1972	Saltillo	.636	Cordoba
1973	Saltillo	.656	Mexico City Reds
1974	Jalisco	.627	Mexico City Reds
1975	Cordoba	.649	Tampico
1976	Cordoba	.595	Mexico City Reds
1977	Puebla	.640	Nuevo Laredo
1978	Cordoba	.655	Aguascalientes
1979	Saltillo	.704	Puebla
1980	Puebla	.716	None
1981	Mexico City Reds	.615	Reynosa
1982	Poza Rica	.623	Ciudad Juarez
1983	Mexico City Reds	.667	Campeche
1984	Mexico City Reds	.647	Yucatan
1985	Mexico City Reds	.606	Mexico City Reds
1986	Puebla	.682	Puebla
1987	Mexico City Reds	.604	Mexico City Reds
1988	Mexico City Reds	.646	Mexico City Reds
1989	Laredo	.621	Laredo
1990	Laredo	.618	Leon
1991	Monterrey Sultans	.683	Monterrey Sultans
1992	Mexico City Tigers	.594	Mexico City Tigers
1993	Mexico City Reds	.633	Tabasco
1994	Mexico City Reds	.646	Mexico City Reds
1995	Mexico City Reds	.708	Monterrey

*Best Overall Record

STANDINGS

NORTH ZONE

	W	L	PCT	GB
Reynosa Broncos (16)	73	40	.646	—
Monterrey Sultans (11)	65	49	.570	8½
Saltillo Sarape Makers (11.5)	63	53	.543	11½
Nuevo Laredo Owls (10.5)	62	54	.534	12½
Aguascalientes Railroadmen (9)	57	55	.509	15½
Union Laguna Cotton Pickers (10.5)	56	57	.496	17
Monclova Steelers (7.5)	46	69	.400	28
Jalisco Cowboys (6)	30	82	.268	42½

SOUTH ZONE

	W	L	PCT	GB
Mexico City Reds (16)	80	33	.708	—
Tabasco Olmecas (12)	61	50	.550	18
Mexico City Tigers (11.5)	62	54	.534	19½
Campeche Pirates (11)	60	54	.526	20½
Yucatan Lions (10)	59	55	.518	21½
Puebla Parrots (8.5)	52	63	.452	29
Veracruz Eagle (6.5)	45	71	.388	36½
Minatitlan Oilers (6.5)	41	73	.360	39½

NOTE: League played a split-season schedule. Points were awarded on basis of finish in each half (eight for first, seven for second, etc.) to determine playoff pairings.

PLAYOFFS—North Zone: Reynosa defeated Nuevo Laredo 4-3, and Monterrey defeated Saltillo 4-1, in best-of-7 semifinals. Monterrey defeated Reynosa 4-2 in best-of-7 final. **South Zone:** Mexico City Reds defeated Campeche 4-2, and Mexico City Tigers defeated Tabasco 4-1, in best-of-7 semifinals. Mexico City Reds defeated Mexico City Tigers 4-2 in best-of-7 final. **Finals:** Monterrey defeated Mexico City Reds 4-0 in best-of-7 series.

REGULAR-SEASON ATTENDANCE: Yucatan 261,179; Mexico City Tigers 229,732; Mexico City Reds 223,387; Reynosa 190,022; Monclova 164,962; Monterrey 156,145; Tabasco 152,567; Aguascalientes 137,124; Nuevo Laredo 135,330; Saltillo 127,933; Campeche 110,951; Union Laguna 110,568; Jalisco 109,455; Puebla 104,572; Minatitlan 102,982; Veracruz 100,287.

INDIVIDUAL BATTING LEADERS
(Minimum 313 Plate Appearances)

	AVG	AB	R	H	2B	3B	HR	RBI	SB
Gainey, Ty, Reds	.411	285	69	117	19	2	27	115	4
Canizalez, Juan, Mont.	.358	386	58	138	14	5	7	54	8
Mendez, Jesus, Tabasco	.356	399	54	142	21	3	4	54	2
Casillas, Adam, Reynosa	.356	382	82	136	22	3	2	53	0
Garcia, Cornelio, Mont.	.348	391	83	136	24	11	2	47	34
Romero, Oscar, Tabasco	.344	410	72	141	24	0	10	47	10
Tolentino, Jose, Mont.	.342	304	49	104	24	0	16	79	1
Gonzalez, Denio, Sal.	.341	384	74	131	23	1	24	95	4
Rivera, German, Puebla	.340	344	59	117	19	2	10	53	3
Arredondo, Luis, Reds	.340	421	90	143	19	3	8	58	15

INDIVIDUAL PITCHING LEADERS
(Minimum 93 Innings)

	W	L	ERA	G	SV	IP	H	BB	SO
Ruiz, Cecilio, Tabasco	13	5	1.71	24	0	163	132	33	92
Solarte, Jose, Minatitlan	8	4	1.72	45	4	115	93	42	64
Munoz, Ricardo, Tabasco	12	6	2.46	22	0	143	128	36	69
Ramirez, Roberto, Reds	13	3	2.56	20	0	137	125	35	70
Zappelli, Mark, Saltillo	6	8	2.63	33	6	106	109	47	45
Sierra, Abel, Campeche	11	9	2.64	24	0	153	132	48	80
Vazquez, Adrian, Cam.	11	6	2.64	21	0	136	118	72	39
Munoz, Miguel, Reynosa	11	3	2.67	20	0	138	140	22	62
Cuervo, Bernardo, Cam.	12	4	2.74	28	0	125	122	45	40
Martinez, Fili, Saltillo	8	5	2.76	19	0	108	98	57	57

AGUASCALIENTES

BATTING

	AVG	AB	R	H	2B	3B	HR	RBI	SB
Aguilar, Enrique, 3b	.325	428	59	139	21	1	15	74	2
Arevalo, Guadalupe, 3b-2b	.321	162	27	52	8	2	0	13	2
Arredondo, Jesus, ss	.322	388	79	125	16	8	0	49	7
Castillo, Juan, of	.335	376	73	126	16	8	7	58	6
Clements, Wes, 1b	.167	30	2	5	1	0	0	3	0
Enriquez, Graciano, of	.288	219	36	63	9	2	3	19	5
Guerrero, Jaime, 3b-of	.235	217	23	51	9	1	4	22	2
Guerrero, Javier, 1b	.251	203	30	51	9	2	7	27	3
Machiria, Pablo, of-1b	.333	406	61	135	21	1	12	72	3
Mendez, Ramon, c	.264	110	16	29	5	1	1	12	1
Quiroz, Jose, 1b-of	.239	155	21	37	9	1	3	28	1
Ramirez, Efren, c	.252	246	27	62	6	3	4	23	0

Valencia, Carlos, of	.269	160	19	43	9	0	2	27	2
Valenzuela, Jose, of	.311	106	15	33	4	3	0	7	1
Vizcarra, Roberto, 2b	.290	414	80	120	19	0	20	87	10

PITCHING

	W	L	ERA	G	SV	IP	H	BB	SO
Agosto, Juan	1	4	6.15	17	4	45	62	15	18
Brumley, Duff	1	3	3.86	7	0	28	25	20	22
Cano, Jose	9	7	5.02	21	0	118	137	53	73
Diaz, Octavio	0	0	18.00	4	0	5	9	7	5
Enriquez, Graciano	0	1	5.68	3	0	6	10	2	0
Enriquez, Martin	8	8	3.92	24	1	145	155	50	96
Franklin, Jay	9	6	3.52	22	0	123	127	57	60
Garibay, Salvador	0	0	3.00	23	0	54	60	24	31
Jimenez, German	6	4	3.25	18	0	102	121	32	43
Lopez, Jonas	3	3	4.06	20	0	44	55	9	19
Navarro, Adolfo	1	5	7.22	9	0	34	39	24	12
Quiroz, Jose	4	2	3.67	23	1	34	28	20	27
Ramirez, Martin	1	0	10.80	5	0	8	13	2	4
Rivera, Paul	2	1	5.82	14	0	39	45	34	27
Serna, Ramon	4	3	4.64	30	2	64	68	35	36
Vazquez, Aguedo	6	0	3.97	22	1	77	74	31	33
Villanueva, Luis	2	2	6.00	28	3	18	23	8	13
Villegas, Jose	9	7	3.70	52	7	82	86	46	35
Vizcarra, Rodrigo	0	0	3.60	3	0	5	8	3	0
Wagner, Hector	1	5	6.03	15	5	31	46	21	18

CAMPECHE

BATTING

	AVG	AB	R	H	2B	3B	HR	RBI	SB
Arvizu, Javier, 1b	.307	287	35	88	18	2	2	27	4
Brinkley, Darrell, of	.338	397	79	134	26	2	13	50	55
Canedo, Alberto, of	.179	39	7	7	2	0	1	4	0
Castaldo, Vince, 3b	.250	132	21	33	6	1	5	22	3
Espinoza, Javier, of	.247	198	24	49	7	1	1	19	2
Guizar, Hector, ss	.247	279	28	69	10	2	0	24	3
Hernandez, Martin, dh-1b	.287	101	9	29	2	0	4	15	2
Herrera, Isidro, of	.246	349	51	86	11	0	0	23	18
Jelks, Greg, dh-3b	.211	199	20	37	6	1	7	29	5
Laurencio, Rod, 2b	.182	22	2	4	0	0	0	0	0
Leal, Jose, of-dh	.269	308	37	83	12	2	4	51	1
Loredo, Jorge, 2b-ss	.257	269	27	69	10	2	4	31	0
Medina, Jose, of	.224	98	15	22	1	1	0	6	0
Michel, Domingo, 1b-of	.323	127	30	41	8	0	9	32	2
Payro, Edison, of-1b	.233	30	2	7	1	0	0	7	0
Renteria, Edinson, 2b-3b	.300	150	21	45	6	1	1	14	3
Reyes, Gilberto, c	.277	361	37	100	10	0	7	36	2
Sanchez, Roque, 3b-2b	.266	320	34	85	24	4	0	9	1

PITCHING

	W	L	ERA	G	SV	IP	H	BB	SO
Browning, Mike	1	3	6.14	9	3	7	10	5	4
Campos, Francisco	0	0	1.93	5	0	9	9	3	2
Cimorelli, Frank	1	3	3.26	19	4	30	38	13	13
Cuervo, Bernardo	12	4	2.74	28	0	125	122	45	40
Dominguez, Herminio	4	2	2.89	39	12	37	32	18	25
Lara, Hugo	8	5	4.14	24	1	126	126	53	54
Lizarraga, Hugo	3	4	2.78	24	3	68	70	32	36
Loaiza, Sabino	0	5	6.31	9	0	26	22	21	6
Mejia, Cesar	4	6	4.85	24	2	56	56	31	27
Sierra, Abel	11	9	2.64	24	0	153	132	48	80
Tejeda, Juan	3	4	3.24	27	2	67	75	17	18
Tinoco, Ruben	2	2	4.34	25	0	56	70	21	16
Toledo, Mario	2	4	4.15	26	0	43	45	28	16
Vazquez, Adrian	11	6	2.64	21	0	136	118	72	39

JALISCO

BATTING

	AVG	AB	R	H	2B	3B	HR	RBI	SB
Abrego, Jesus, of-c	.258	353	55	91	19	2	2	27	7
Agramon, Antonio, of	.244	131	16	32	7	0	5	21	1
Alvarez, Luis, 1b-of	.372	78	11	29	8	1	0	7	1
Arzate, Martin, of	.230	178	17	41	5	1	0	20	1
Cervera, Francisco, ss	.263	274	47	72	13	3	4	31	4
Fernandez, Carlos, of	.260	50	5	13	2	0	2	7	0
Gonzalez, Jesus, 2b-dh	.244	347	43	88	13	0	7	36	1
Jimenez, Ulises, 3b	.241	83	7	20	2	0	0	7	1
Lopez, Alfredo, of	.293	92	11	27	4	0	1	11	2
Lopez, Victor, c-of	.286	255	24	73	13	1	1	31	5
Naveda, Edgar, 1b-of	.290	352	45	102	25	1	2	37	8
Nunez Avina, Jose, ss-of	.191	47	7	9	1	0	0	7	1
Nunez Garcia, Jose, ss-2b	.125	40	1	5	0	0	0	1	0
Peralta, Amado, 3b-1b	.280	268	34	75	20	0	1	26	1
Pierce, Dom, dh	.160	25	0	4	1	0	0	0	0
Rivera, Alberto, 3b-ss	.263	133	18	35	2	1	0	9	4
Sabino, Miguel, of	.167	18	1	3	0	0	0	3	0
Santos, Julio, 2b-of	.285	130	15	37	6	0	1	11	2
Valenzuela, Horacio, 1b-dh	.196	235	19	46	17	0	3	24	0
Valverde, Raul, of-dh	.302	242	23	73	13	1	5	33	1
Villaescusa, Fernando, dh	.352	179	26	63	7	1	0	14	4

PITCHING	W	L	ERA	G	SV	IP	H	BB	SO
Alvarez, Ivan	0	4	7.27	6	1	17	20	8	8
Antunez, Martin	3	8	4.43	26	1	91	109	21	38
Arrington, Tom	5	9	5.26	16	0	92	129	32	47
Arzate, Martin	0	0	4.26	3	0	6	9	2	2
Bencomo, Omar	6	7	4.33	35	2	71	73	27	56
Benitez, Francisco	0	2	9.26	11	0	23	39	26	8
Burcham, Tim	1	2	3.18	6	0	28	25	9	17
Cano, Ezequiel	3	12	5.36	17	0	102	119	39	58
Castro, Leonel	3	10	6.04	19	0	107	141	45	49
Cruz, Juan	2	1	5.77	26	0	53	76	29	31
Espinoza, Rogelio	0	1	9.00	7	1	6	14	5	3
Gonzalez, Victor	1	6	7.21	32	2	87	133	49	34
Iniguez, Dario	2	7	10.47	11	0	39	76	22	34
Ledon, Juan	0	2	7.62	9	0	26	36	15	14
Moreno, Ricardo	0	2	1.85	9	1	24	26	10	11
Nunez Avina, Jose	0	1	7.62	17	0	28	41	15	11
Ramirez, Miguel	0	1	8.72	8	0	22	28	19	9
Sadecki, Steve	0	5	7.59	5	0	21	33	18	7
Sanchez, Jose	1	4	6.32	14	0	47	59	47	18

LAREDO

BATTING	AVG	AB	R	H	2B	3B	HR	RBI	SB
Arano, Wilfrido, of	.333	12	5	4	1	1	0	2	2
Carrasco, Ernesto, 2b-3b	.259	378	43	98	13	1	0	27	9
Castaneda, Rafael, 3b-1b	.278	406	52	113	16	3	5	43	5
Corrales, Virgilio, c	.111	18	2	2	2	0	0	3	0
Cruz, Marco, c	.240	333	32	80	12	1	4	36	0
Estrada, Ruben, 1b	.232	168	20	39	4	0	0	16	2
McCoy, Trey, dh	.321	28	7	9	0	0	2	3	0
Mora, Andres, dh-1b	.263	137	12	36	5	0	6	18	0
Morales, Florentino, dh-2b	.254	342	49	87	19	2	1	21	2
Noris, Rogelio, of	.205	122	15	25	4	1	1	13	2
Perez, Alejandro, 2b	.200	10	3	2	0	0	0	1	0
Pulido, Jesus, c	.118	17	0	2	0	0	0	0	0
Ramirez, Enrique, ss	.241	394	43	95	7	1	0	27	5
Rodriguez, Boi, of-1b	.307	293	54	90	18	2	22	77	2
Rodriguez, Genaro, 1b	.267	187	12	50	4	2	2	25	1
Saenz, Ricardo, of	.321	433	72	139	25	1	18	83	3
Sanchez, Gerardo, of	.323	400	72	129	24	1	11	59	5
Tejeda, Arturo, 2b-of	.116	43	6	5	1	0	0	1	0

PITCHING	W	L	ERA	G	SV	IP	H	BB	SO
Barfield, John	5	2	2.70	34	24	63	50	13	39
Cardenas, Benito	0	0	2.70	5	0	7	7	4	3
Diaz, Cesar	4	3	3.42	29	0	71	64	27	25
Garza, Roberto	2	3	6.71	19	0	51	54	31	20
Hernandez, Jose	7	4	3.19	47	6	99	94	38	52
Moreno, Alvarez	0	0	8.18	10	0	11	14	18	7
Moreno, Angel	16	3	3.20	22	0	160	136	44	108
Ochoa, Porfirio	0	1	8.22	7	0	8	15	2	1
Ortega, Pablo	0	1	5.93	5	0	14	11	5	7
Osuna, Roberto	6	13	4.45	25	0	127	148	55	74
Perry, Jeff	4	11	4.86	25	0	109	113	63	61
Quintanilla, Enrique	2	2	7.04	33	1	61	89	30	27
Quiroz, Aaron	11	7	3.11	23	0	139	136	56	108
Rodriguez, Rene	3	3	3.96	32	4	36	46	19	10
Valdez, Jose	2	1	3.80	15	0	21	28	5	11

MEXICO CITY REDS

BATTING	AVG	AB	R	H	2B	3B	HR	RBI	SB
Arredondo, Luis, of	.340	421	90	143	19	3	8	58	15
Barrera, Nelson, 1b-3b	.292	298	38	87	17	0	17	71	0
Duran, Felipe, 3b-ss	.279	136	29	38	6	0	1	11	2
Fernandez, Daniel, of	.316	386	89	122	14	7	6	45	23
Gainey, Ty, dh	.411	285	69	117	19	2	27	115	4
Horn, Sam, dh	.316	38	9	12	1	0	3	12	0
Lopez, Fabian, 2b	.214	14	2	3	0	0	0	1	1
Mendez, Roberto, of	.304	309	50	94	8	3	8	47	9
Ojeda, Miguel, c-of	.280	150	14	42	5	1	5	24	2
Paez, Raul, 1b	.341	232	32	79	19	3	3	28	1
Ramirez, Jesus, of	.175	40	13	7	1	0	0	4	2
Rojas, Homar, c	.332	319	51	106	13	0	5	53	3
Sandoval, Jose, ss	.311	354	52	110	22	1	8	59	3
Tatis, Bernardo, 3b	.303	304	69	92	13	2	4	45	17
Vazquez, Felipe, c	.333	27	3	9	2	0	0	1	0
Verdugo, Vicente, 2b	.285	358	48	102	14	0	4	35	2

PITCHING	W	L	ERA	G	SV	IP	H	BB	SO
Baller, Jay	0	1	2.37	16	6	19	10	17	13
Carrasco, Alejandro	2	2	4.91	30	1	48	54	18	13
Castillo, Felipe	3	1	1.75	17	5	26	19	18	15
Cordoba, Francisco	13	0	3.10	27	4	125	131	42	88
Flynt, Will	7	1	2.24	10	0	56	51	27	49
Hernandez, Manny	11	4	3.18	23	0	142	142	54	66
Moreno, Claudio	3	1	5.19	27	1	59	66	35	36
Moreno, Leobardo	6	1	5.02	21	0	52	61	23	41

Pina, Rafael	6	3	3.38	42	3	69	66	39	63
Ramirez, Roberto	13	3	2.56	20	0	137	125	35	70
Reyes, Dennis	5	5	6.60	17	0	59	76	41	44
Rincon, Ricardo	6	6	5.16	27	3	75	86	41	41
Walker, Mike	2	3	4.01	19	4	43	41	20	23

MEXICO CITY TIGERS

BATTING	AVG	AB	R	H	2B	3B	HR	RBI	SB
Bellazetin, Jose, dh	.192	26	8	5	0	0	0	2	0
Carrillo, Matias, of-1b	.331	338	81	112	14	4	20	78	20
Diaz, Luis, of-dh	.311	267	49	83	12	4	7	47	7
Heath, Lee, of	.321	305	40	98	12	5	2	30	10
Howell, Pat, of	.321	336	63	108	9	7	2	22	23
Mere, Pedro, 3b	.286	304	53	87	14	0	9	48	3
Montalvo, Ivan, of-dh	.285	144	18	41	8	3	2	22	1
Ochoa, Edgar, c	.228	92	10	21	6	0	3	12	0
Ortiz, Alejandro, 3b	.282	330	53	93	13	0	15	64	4
Roa, Hector, 3b	.250	128	18	32	9	0	3	22	0
Robles, Javier, ss	.311	409	93	127	24	8	17	53	7
Robles, Trinidad, of	.105	19	3	2	1	0	0	2	0
Romero, Marco, 1b	.297	381	61	113	18	2	21	96	5
Salgado, Eduardo, of	.231	13	2	3	0	1	0	2	0
Sparks, Greg, dh	.245	53	11	13	3	0	3	14	1
Trapaga, Miguel, 2b-ss	.202	109	17	22	4	0	2	9	0
Vega, Edgar, c	.208	192	16	40	3	2	0	9	2
Villanueva, Hector, c-dh	.374	182	41	68	11	0	12	47	1

PITCHING	W	L	ERA	G	SV	IP	H	BB	SO
Alvarez, Juan	12	8	3.70	23	0	153	158	59	65
Barraza, Ernesto	10	4	3.15	24	0	126	111	73	78
Castro, Gerardo	1	0	10.38	5	0	9	13	6	3
Couoh, Enrique	6	5	3.70	39	8	97	82	65	67
Delfin, Adolfo	1	6	5.19	37	3	69	81	30	30
Draper, Mike	4	4	3.62	22	5	32	26	16	11
Garcia Cruz, Jose	4	6	5.86	36	2	58	77	27	31
Garibay, Daniel	2	0	6.40	21	0	45	49	29	26
Leyva, Carlos	1	0	7.30	26	0	25	33	27	9
Lynch, Dave	2	2	2.75	8	0	36	32	15	31
Minutelli, Gino	2	3	8.26	12	1	28	43	15	15
Rios, Jesus	10	6	4.25	25	0	146	121	50	103
Salgado, Eduardo	0	0	3.86	11	0	14	16	7	6
Tunnell, Lee	4	5	5.91	14	0	35	34	14	25
Vega, Obed	5	5	5.75	18	0	77	78	58	41

MINATITLAN

BATTING	AVG	AB	R	H	2B	3B	HR	RBI	SB
Arce, Francisco, 3b-1b	.304	303	18	92	17	0	2	28	0
Balderas, Abelardo, 3b-ss	.183	104	12	19	1	0	0	10	0
Barrera, Jesus, 3b	.294	17	0	5	0	0	0	0	0
Beltran, Gerardo, of-dh	.253	265	22	67	11	1	5	22	1
Burguillos, Carlos, of	.252	337	41	85	14	2	4	35	10
Castro, Arnoldo, 2b	.253	380	39	96	9	1	4	32	2
Cecena, Manuel, of	.273	11	2	3	0	0	0	1	0
Cuevas, Angelo, of-dh	.270	371	44	100	14	1	7	33	2
Dominguez, David, of-dh	.297	263	36	78	11	1	9	37	1
Duarte, Rene, c	.264	197	23	52	7	0	2	16	2
Gastelum, Carlos, 2b	.239	163	11	39	3	0	0	1	1
Gavia, Jesus, 1b-c	.237	131	10	31	2	0	3	12	0
Hernandez, Gerardo, of	.216	218	21	47	14	1	0	12	2
Rubio, Marco, 3b-2b	.224	232	10	52	7	0	1	14	1
Sasser, Mackey, 1b	.286	56	4	16	1	0	2	11	0
Valle, Jose, ss	.221	339	36	75	10	1	4	35	1

PITCHING	W	L	ERA	G	SV	IP	H	BB	SO
Calderon, Manaces	0	0	1.59	3	0	6	2	4	3
Camacho, Adrian	2	2	5.40	22	0	38	43	22	14
Garcia, Miguel	4	3	3.39	38	0	74	72	32	26
Gomez, Martin	4	14	3.89	23	0	125	131	63	40
Lopez, Jose	4	7	2.57	36	16	56	46	23	37
Pinero, Hugh	0	0	5.40	3	0	7	4	3	3
Retes, Lorenzo	2	5	5.24	24	0	88	119	40	38
Rodriguez, Mario	9	4	4.53	26	0	109	131	46	31
Sandoval, Carlos	0	1	3.28	32	0	36	32	16	17
Solarte, Jose	8	4	1.72	45	4	115	93	42	64
Soto, Fernando	7	14	3.63	25	0	161	182	51	67
Velazquez, Israel	4	12	3.28	23	0	121	114	63	77

MONCLOVA

BATTING	AVG	AB	R	H	2B	3B	HR	RBI	SB
Aganza, Ruben, 1b-3b	.296	412	66	122	24	2	17	66	0
Arauz, Ignacio, c	.226	106	10	24	4	0	1	13	0
Carter, Steve, dh	.273	44	5	12	1	0	1	7	0
Chan, Armando, dh-1b	.274	201	31	55	8	2	1	19	0
Contreras, Cuitlahuac, ss-of	.202	94	10	19	1	1	3	12	2
Espinoza, Jose, of	.229	105	9	24	3	0	0	9	0
Gutierrez, Felipe, 2b-ss	.205	44	6	9	2	0	2	7	0

	AVG	AB	R	H	2B	3B	HR	RBI	SB
Harris, Donald, of	.271	188	26	51	7	4	8	31	5
Hecht, Steve, of	.333	18	2	6	0	0	0	2	1
Leyva, German, 3b	.285	358	49	102	13	2	3	39	3
Lopez, Gonzalo, of-ss	.323	362	35	117	18	5	5	66	1
Machorro, Roberto, c	.171	41	1	7	2	1	0	5	1
Martinez, Grimaldo, 2b	.272	393	55	107	10	6	2	45	7
Morones, Martin, of	.259	317	53	82	8	5	3	34	19
Olvera, Sergio, ss	.246	203	25	50	8	1	4	12	2
Rendina, Mike, 1b	.128	39	2	5	1	0	0	3	0
Rivera, Eleazar, c	.227	22	3	5	0	0	0	0	0
Rodriguez, Ruben, c	.258	62	8	16	4	0	0	4	1
Samaniego, Manuel, c	.327	171	19	56	9	3	1	30	1
Tovar, Jose, 2b-ss	.228	167	15	38	2	0	0	15	1
Wong, Julian, ss-2b	.228	114	11	26	3	1	1	10	0
Yuriar, Jesus, of	.278	313	40	87	9	4	0	35	2

PITCHING	W	L	ERA	G	SV	IP	H	BB	SO
Ayrault, Bob	0	2	8.60	7	0	30	43	17	15
Burlingame, Dennis	0	1	4.26	2	0	13	12	8	5
Castillo, Luis T.	1	1	10.13	4	0	13	20	6	8
Garcia, David	0	0	4.00	16	0	18	18	18	20
Gomez, Jesus	1	1	4.70	10	0	23	28	19	15
Hernandez, Dimas	0	0	4.81	13	0	24	21	19	12
Hernandez, Encarnacion	2	1	5.73	36	1	60	95	17	21
Herrera, Calixto	9	9	3.69	50	0	93	82	59	69
Jimenez, Cesar	3	6	3.87	14	0	74	84	28	26
Kelley, Rich	3	8	3.10	12	0	73	68	39	48
Leal, Gerardo	2	5	7.13	25	0	71	109	30	28
Lewis, Craig	0	2	6.28	3	0	14	19	11	10
Montano, Francisco	8	9	4.15	22	0	128	134	38	78
Murillo, Felipe	1	1	2.16	43	30	58	57	13	40
Pimental, Roberto	5	6	5.51	39	0	47	59	32	20
Pruneda, Armando	2	3	5.63	10	0	24	27	18	4
Raygoza, Martin	7	10	3.47	21	0	140	154	40	77
Rivera, Eleazar	1	0	0.00	1	0	8	6	4	6
Rivera, Lino	1	3	8.42	5	0	26	41	13	17
Veliz, Francisco	0	0	2.96	19	0	24	22	14	15
Wayne, Gary	4	5	3.41	22	2	58	60	14	51

MONTERREY

BATTING	AVG	AB	R	H	2B	3B	HR	RBI	SB
Canizalez, Juan, of	.358	386	58	138	14	5	7	54	8
Caraballo, Gary, dh-3b	.304	79	11	24	5	0	3	15	0
Diaz, Remigio, ss	.233	258	24	60	4	6	1	20	5
Fariss, Monty, of-1b	.259	112	20	29	7	0	3	14	1
Flores, Miguel, 2b	.292	120	20	35	8	1	1	18	8
Franco, Manuel, 3b	.280	225	29	63	14	4	3	41	7
Garcia, Cornelio, of	.348	391	83	136	24	11	2	47	34
Garcia, Jose, dh	.286	14	1	4	0	0	0	5	0
Gonzalez, Jose, of	.313	368	74	115	23	4	14	67	19
Hurtado, Hector,c	.245	163	13	40	5	0	1	18	0
Magallanes, Ever, ss-2b	.255	149	20	38	3	0	2	15	2
Martinez, Carmelo, dh	.296	142	23	42	12	0	10	30	1
Martinez, Enrique, of	.250	12	1	3	0	0	0	0	0
Meza, Alfredo, c	.172	58	5	10	0	0	1	2	0
Orantes, Ramon, 3b-of	.265	196	26	52	9	4	0	17	4
Quintero, Guillermo, 2b-ss	.377	69	24	26	2	1	0	6	7
Sanchez, Armando, 2b-3b	.293	290	35	85	13	1	0	29	2
Tolentino, Jose, 1b	.342	304	49	104	24	0	16	79	1
Trevino, Alex, c-of	.317	262	32	83	17	1	2	28	1
Velasquez, Guillermo, dh-1b	.252	119	16	30	9	0	4	18	0

PITCHING	W	L	ERA	G	SV	IP	H	BB	SO
Cazares, Juan	3	3	4.81	35	2	34	43	20	18
Diaz, Marcos	4	2	3.89	21	0	69	74	32	32
Elvira, Narciso	10	5	5.13	18	0	93	98	40	70
Esquer, Mercedes	7	3	2.64	13	0	72	72	21	33
Gonzalez, Arturo	7	8	4.55	18	0	97	108	37	39
Green, Otis	3	3	1.95	21	4	32	19	15	39
Heredia, Hector	9	9	3.30	22	0	142	148	40	66
Hernandez, Ramon	0	0	10.53	13	0	20	28	18	11
Hurst, Jonathan	4	1	2.16	28	9	50	40	13	49
Lewis, Scott	2	1	1.50	30	15	42	24	10	27
Olague, Jesus	0	0	4.58	7	0	20	20	14	9
Perez, Leonardo	8	4	2.48	34	4	83	69	47	56
Sanchez, Hector	2	3	5.44	24	1	45	60	11	16
Sandoval, Guillermo	2	4	5.03	33	1	59	62	31	36

PUEBLA

BATTING	AVG	AB	R	H	2B	3B	HR	RBI	SB
Alvarez, Hector, of	.295	413	77	122	27	1	3	58	5
Arias, Everardo, ss	.205	127	17	26	4	2	0	12	1
Arredondo, Hernando, 3b-2b	.291	158	16	46	4	1	0	12	1
Cabreja, Alexis, of	.297	212	42	63	10	4	1	19	9
Cantu, Gerardo, c-dh	.214	126	13	27	2	0	4	19	0
Estrada, Hector, c-dh	.313	418	51	131	23	0	11	78	1
Gutierrez, Andres, of	.196	97	16	19	4	1	0	6	1

	AVG	AB	R	H	2B	3B	HR	RBI	SB
Hernandez, Juan, 2b-ss	.167	66	15	11	4	0	0	3	2
Iturbe, Pedro, of	.323	440	77	142	21	8	2	61	4
Pardo, Victor, 2b	.260	288	36	75	12	2	6	27	2
Pena, Luis, 1b-dh	.310	326	36	101	18	0	11	61	1
Rivera, German, 3b-1b	.340	344	59	117	19	2	10	53	3
Rodriguez, Serafin, of	.286	14	2	4	0	0	0	0	0
Soto, Emison, of-dh	.286	304	54	87	21	2	13	52	2
Vargas, Trinidad, ss	.200	170	14	34	4	1	0	14	2
Zambrano, Roberto, of	.286	14	3	4	0	0	1	5	0

PITCHING	W	L	ERA	G	SV	IP	H	BB	SO
Cruz, Antonio	1	4	3.73	14	0	41	35	39	23
Garibay, Roberto	4	3	3.58	40	11	50	59	29	17
Guerra, Esmili	1	2	3.86	8	0	19	26	8	7
Henry, Jon	7	4	4.10	15	0	68	67	24	37
Huerta, Luis	9	7	3.28	22	0	145	134	48	55
Mansur, Jeff	0	0	4.50	13	1	12	16	10	4
Munoz, Pablo	0	0	6.35	10	0	6	8	3	1
Orozco, Jaime	8	10	4.24	23	0	140	154	48	67
Ramos, Jorge	1	4	3.97	23	1	48	53	19	19
Saenz, Alfredo	8	10	3.60	26	1	132	143	52	71
Valenzuela, Saul	10	8	3.94	22	0	146	156	54	52
Vargas, Ignacio	3	8	6.08	18	0	53	67	31	17
Villegas, Ramon	0	1	5.97	17	0	38	50	14	16

REYNOSA

BATTING	AVG	AB	R	H	2B	3B	HR	RBI	SB
Casillas, Adam, of-1b	.356	382	82	136	22	3	2	53	0
Castillo, Braulio, of	.312	356	77	111	30	7	15	81	3
Cruz, Luis, of-3b	.301	418	64	126	26	1	12	80	1
Esquer, Ramon, 2b	.289	287	52	83	11	7	1	40	3
Lopez, Salvador, of	.284	109	14	31	5	0	0	15	0
Merchant, Mark, 1b	.152	33	4	5	2	0	1	4	0
Monroy, Victor, c	.380	108	16	41	8	0	2	24	0
Munoz, Noe, c	.314	121	23	38	8	0	1	22	0
Perez, Francisco, 1b	.291	96	13	27	3	2	2	21	0
Rodriguez, Hector, 3b	.291	351	65	102	11	5	7	52	0
Stark, Matt, dh-1b	.332	322	66	107	26	0	12	83	0
Tellez, Alonso, of	.331	435	67	144	25	6	8	63	2
Valdez, Francisco, c	.267	217	36	58	12	1	1	30	0
Valenzuela, Armando, ss	.256	367	62	94	10	3	0	31	4
Vizcarra, Marco, 2b-ss	.294	177	32	52	1	0	1	16	1

PITCHING	W	L	ERA	G	SV	IP	H	BB	SO
Carranza, Javier	10	6	4.86	21	0	113	128	45	72
Cazares, Tomas	1	0	5.96	15	0	23	31	10	10
Chapin, Darrin	1	1	1.48	11	3	30	24	13	17
Cruz, Javier	5	4	4.32	35	2	90	99	37	51
Del Toro, Miguel	5	4	2.25	37	16	68	54	43	49
Guerrero, Omar	0	2	11.12	7	0	11	23	9	6
Lara, Jorge	7	2	2.33	39	4	73	53	38	45
Lind, Orlando	5	3	2.60	12	0	73	72	32	42
Mendez, Luis	6	6	4.57	21	0	106	129	41	68
Munoz, Miguel	11	3	2.67	20	0	138	140	22	62
Perez, Vladimir	1	1	2.82	14	6	22	17	13	6
Purata, Julio	13	5	3.60	22	0	133	126	50	74
Rodriguez, Mario	0	1	11.77	12	0	26	47	11	9
Rojo, Oscar	3	1	5.73	34	1	60	69	33	26

SALTILLO

BATTING	AVG	AB	R	H	2B	3B	HR	RBI	SB
Almeida, Shammar, 1b	.272	287	43	78	6	1	14	42	0
Castro, Eddie, 1b-dh	.246	191	16	47	7	0	3	24	0
Cornejo, Edgar, 3b-1b	.183	93	12	17	2	1	0	8	0
Escalante, Marcelo, of-dh	.245	220	19	54	10	2	3	29	1
Gonzalez, Denio, 3b-1b	.341	384	74	131	23	1	24	95	4
Gonzalez, Pedro, dh	.217	69	19	15	2	3	3	9	4
Jeter, Shawn, of-dh	.337	89	17	30	4	3	1	7	4
Jimenez, Houston, ss	.337	398	79	134	40	4	6	59	6
Luna, Jose, c	.224	254	21	57	12	1	0	26	0
Martinez, Luis, ss-2b	.227	66	10	15	4	0	0	4	0
Martinez, Raul, of	.357	14	0	5	0	0	0	1	0
Moreno, David, of	.133	15	0	2	1	0	0	0	0
Precichi, Jorge, 2b	.212	283	46	60	10	4	1	18	6
Torres, Eduardo, of-1b	.222	338	46	75	13	4	11	52	6
Valenzuela, Eduardo, c	.273	128	15	35	7	1	1	16	0
Villegas, Fernando, of	.323	375	65	120	12	11	5	40	9
Wearing, Mel, of-dh	.287	268	52	77	9	2	13	59	4
Wright, George, of	.333	409	70	137	23	2	12	76	12

PITCHING	W	L	ERA	G	SV	IP	H	BB	SO
Barron, Avelino	1	4	4.33	35	2	79	83	39	40
Cecena, Jose	4	4	4.40	38	14	45	34	40	47
Martinez, Fili	8	5	2.76	19	0	108	98	57	57
Martinez, Mauricio	0	1	4.87	11	0	21	20	16	12
Moreno, Jesus	10	4	4.95	22	0	131	147	50	60
Navarro, Luis	3	4	5.61	19	0	51	53	29	24

PITCHING	W	L	ERA	G	SV	IP	H	BB	SO
Rodriguez, Raul	14	4	3.30	23	0	145	126	55	106
Smith, Daryl	3	2	4.11	7	0	31	30	22	20
Sombra, Francisco	2	3	3.18	37	0	51	52	15	25
Valencia, Jorge	6	5	5.54	29	0	102	131	62	38
Velazquez, Ernesto	0	4	8.65	19	0	43	63	33	10
Zappelli, Mark	6	8	2.63	33	6	106	109	47	45

TABASCO

BATTING	AVG	AB	R	H	2B	3B	HR	RBI	SB
Almenda, Gregorio, of	.167	36	5	6	0	0	1	2	0
Cueta, Raul, c	.100	10	2	1	0	0	0	0	0
Delgado, Tomas, of	.284	67	13	19	1	1	2	6	0
DeLima, Rafael, of	.300	257	40	77	12	2	0	15	10
Fentanes, Oscar, of-dh	.311	341	33	106	11	4	7	51	1
Garzon, Eliseo, c	.223	292	31	65	11	0	7	37	0
Infante, Alexis, 2b	.299	354	52	106	10	3	0	26	3
Magallanes, Willie, of	.260	215	30	56	9	1	5	28	5
Marrujo, Hector, ss	.233	292	29	68	8	4	0	18	2
Mendez, Jesus, 1b	.356	399	54	142	21	3	4	54	2
Mitchell, Keith, of	.333	81	15	27	6	1	6	26	0
Ortega, Roberto, 1b-of	.218	193	15	42	11	0	3	16	0
Reyna, Marcos, of	.272	173	23	47	5	0	4	31	6
Ritchie, Gregg, of	.345	55	7	19	3	3	0	8	2
Rojas, Francisco, ss	.169	65	6	11	2	0	0	5	0
Romero, Oscar, 3b	.344	410	72	141	24	0	10	47	10
Ruiz, Demetrio, c	.214	84	4	18	1	1	0	7	0
Tiquet, Lazaro, of-dh	.281	352	35	99	29	3	4	52	4
Tillman, Rusty, of-1b	.248	202	30	50	7	0	11	34	6
Zazueta, Juan, 2b	.269	130	15	35	3	2	0	13	5
Zulueta, Felix, 1b	.140	43	4	6	0	0	0	0	0

PITCHING	W	L	ERA	G	SV	IP	H	BB	SO
Aguilar, Jose	4	10	6.91	24	0	72	94	37	36
Aguirre, Gaudencio	0	0	11.81	3	0	5	11	1	4
Cabrales, Gabriel	3	2	4.70	32	2	69	84	15	43
Cazares, Rosario	0	4	3.47	34	3	47	37	16	22
Cota, Armando	0	2	9.82	15	1	11	18	9	5
Dehesa, Noel	0	0	6.10	6	0	10	14	2	2
Garcia, Mike	2	1	1.94	26	14	46	36	6	30
Inzunza, Jorge	1	0	3.50	11	0	18	21	11	9
Lopez, Emigdio	14	6	3.09	25	0	163	169	38	82
Munoz, Ricardo	12	6	2.46	22	0	143	128	36	69
Osuna, Ricardo	2	4	4.26	8	0	38	45	20	16
Romero, Juan	3	5	3.49	29	1	70	71	29	23
Ruiz, Cecilio	13	5	1.71	24	0	163	132	33	92
Saldana, Edgardo	6	8	3.22	23	0	117	121	42	70
Strauss, Julio	2	2	2.13	12	2	13	9	10	9
Vargas, Joel	0	0	5.40	4	0	5	6	2	4

UNION LAGUNA

BATTING	AVG	AB	R	H	2B	3B	HR	RBI	SB
Avila, Ruben, 1b	.270	403	38	109	19	1	15	63	3
Dattola, Kevin, of	.265	117	15	31	2	1	2	13	3
Garcia, Hector, of	.294	405	60	119	11	7	0	42	11
Garza, Gerardo, c	.326	350	57	114	15	0	9	44	6
Guerrero, Francisco, ss	.267	270	44	72	12	3	0	33	4
Perez, Juan, c	.286	56	6	16	2	3	0	8	0
Pledger, Kinnis, of	.234	47	7	11	0	1	1	5	0
Rodriguez, Fernando, of-dh.	.320	347	49	111	17	2	12	49	3
Ruiz, Juan, 3b	.306	360	70	110	16	10	10	67	9
Salas, Heriberto, 2b-ss	.263	80	14	21	7	2	0	13	1
Snider, Van, of-dh	.325	302	61	98	22	0	24	67	0
Soriano, Ricardo, of	.143	28	6	4	0	0	0	2	1
Trafton, Todd, dh	.336	152	35	51	7	1	6	34	1
Valle, Jorge, of-3b	.292	325	46	95	13	3	3	36	2
Verdugo, Guadalupe, 2b-ss.	.222	45	7	10	2	0	0	5	1
Zazueta, Mauricio, 2b	.298	299	43	89	9	3	4	28	2

PITCHING	W	L	ERA	G	SV	IP	H	BB	SO
Acosta, Aaron	9	3	4.08	21	0	128	138	56	76
Alicea, Miguel	0	2	3.46	28	15	26	31	8	11
Figueroa, Fernando	11	5	4.72	17	0	114	124	46	54
Flores, Ignacio	0	2	6.44	21	0	29	42	19	12
Grajales, Norberto	4	1	3.41	41	1	69	71	35	31
Jones, Al	4	9	4.34	17	0	85	78	44	65
Juarez, Fernando	1	0	4.26	10	0	6	7	3	1
Klvac, David	0	0	10.80	3	1	5	5	6	4
Mack, Tony	0	2	7.20	4	0	10	19	6	2
Miranda, Julio	6	6	6.44	41	8	59	67	20	25
Molina, Joaquin	0	1	5.34	17	1	30	29	17	17
Neri, Braulio	1	1	12.56	21	0	14	26	20	5
Palafox, Juan	10	7	4.73	21	0	139	155	44	63
Puig, Benny	4	5	3.23	16	0	98	94	46	38
Quintero, Victor	1	0	6.75	5	0	8	10	3	5
Renteria, Hilario	5	10	6.00	22	0	111	146	31	58

PITCHING	W	L	ERA	G	SV	IP	H	BB	SO
Romo, Guillermo	1	3	5.96	15	0	45	59	38	15
Valdez, Armando	0	1	24.16	10	0	6	26	8	5

VERACRUZ

BATTING	AVG	AB	R	H	2B	3B	HR	RBI	SB
Ansley, Willie, of	.282	103	14	29	5	2	0	6	5
Campos, Oscar, c	.250	12	2	3	0	0	0	0	0
Cazarin, Manuel, c-3b	.244	386	28	94	22	1	4	38	2
Estrada, Ricardo, 1b	.206	107	10	22	5	0	1	8	0
Gamboa, Jose, of	.234	205	20	48	6	2	2	15	2
Garcia, Carlos, 2b-3b	.207	246	31	51	8	0	1	14	3
Garcia, Heriberto, ss	.284	433	55	123	7	5	1	25	14
Gutierrez, Jose, of	.247	227	18	56	6	0	1	21	0
Hernandez, Miguel, c	.257	152	10	39	3	0	0	9	1
Maclin, Lonnie, of	.236	140	27	33	4	3	0	10	13
Malpica, Enrique, 3b-of	.239	176	16	42	1	0	0	14	1
Mendiola, Juan, 2b	.098	51	3	5	2	0	0	3	0
Motley, Darryl, of	.276	116	16	32	8	0	2	22	1
Paredes, Johnny, 2b	.179	28	4	5	0	0	0	1	0
Reyes, Ramon, c	.077	13	0	1	0	0	0	0	0
Rodriguez, Jose, of	.241	237	13	57	12	0	0	12	3
Rodriguez, Juan, 2b	.178	174	18	31	2	0	0	12	0
Rodriguez, Noel, 3b	.316	19	3	6	0	0	0	1	1
Sommers, Jesus, dh-1b	.224	317	12	71	11	1	1	20	1
Velazquez, Armando, of	.222	45	2	10	0	0	0	5	0
Zamudio, Rafael, of-1b	.308	107	9	33	10	1	1	5	1

PITCHING	W	L	ERA	G	SV	IP	H	BB	SO
Arano, Ramon	2	2	6.86	5	0	21	28	6	7
Baez, Sixto	3	5	5.29	28	2	78	89	46	22
Cervantes, Lauro	3	5	7.25	14	0	58	88	24	25
Del Valle, Enrique	1	0	14.59	11	0	12	29	13	7
Diaz, Alejandro	2	4	4.01	24	2	52	52	20	22
Gutierrez, Arturo	0	1	4.19	8	0	19	19	13	6
Hernandez, Julio	5	11	4.33	21	0	100	98	53	53
Herrera, Enrique	2	4	2.64	34	1	72	83	23	35
Leyva, Filiberto	1	2	7.33	21	2	23	34	15	8
Lopez, Gilberto	0	0	7.43	8	0	13	16	9	6
Luevano, Juan	6	8	3.30	41	12	85	71	24	50
Macias, Abraham	0	1	9.58	6	1	10	15	11	4
Meza, Leobardo	2	1	0.69	7	0	26	15	5	13
Mora, Eleazar	6	10	4.53	23	0	117	133	43	58
Neri, Eduardo	4	5	3.59	51	4	103	86	71	61
Rivera, Hector	6	8	5.38	23	0	87	97	39	35
Soto, Ramon E.	0	0	1.80	3	0	5	3	3	4

YUCATAN

BATTING	AVG	AB	R	H	2B	3B	HR	RBI	SB
Cairo, Sergio, of	.313	195	26	61	2	0	6	35	3
Camacho, Adulfo, 2b	.245	372	69	91	14	2	3	34	4
Castaneda, Nick, dh	.395	43	7	17	4	1	1	9	0
Felix, Arturo, 3b	.246	333	42	82	14	3	0	32	7
Guzman, Marco, c	.269	316	28	85	15	0	3	43	1
Housie, Wayne, of	.239	184	27	44	5	6	1	21	6
Jimenez, Eduardo, of-dh	.316	373	67	118	26	3	24	90	4
Lopez, Miguel, 3b	.308	13	2	4	0	0	0	0	0
Magana, Gabriel, ss	.222	36	7	8	1	0	0	2	0
Mercedes, Luis, of	.316	196	35	62	5	2	1	10	7
Osuna, Hector, c	.185	54	7	10	0	0	0	11	0
Pacho, Juan, ss	.273	322	31	88	13	2	0	23	2
Pena, Carlos, c	.250	28	3	7	1	0	0	5	0
Quinones, Luis, of	.235	153	31	36	5	0	3	19	4
Quintana, Carlos, 1b-of	.325	268	47	87	9	2	4	37	2
Rubio, Sergio, of	.239	71	13	17	3	0	0	6	1
Sievers, Roberto, of	.158	19	1	3	0	0	1	2	0
Torres, Raymundo, dh-of	.233	309	45	72	11	1	15	62	2
Valdez, Jesus, 1b-of	.302	192	28	58	12	0	2	36	2

PITCHING	W	L	ERA	G	SV	IP	H	BB	SO
Cruz, Andres	4	11	4.73	23	0	126	146	48	61
Cruz, Juan	2	3	3.06	17	0	32	27	12	20
Hernandez, Martin	11	3	3.62	24	0	122	135	48	65
Jimenez, Issac	6	8	3.20	19	0	113	117	56	54
Leon, Danilo	1	3	9.00	5	1	8	12	5	4
Llanes, Emeterio	0	1	6.89	11	0	16	19	7	5
Quinones, Enrique	1	4	4.66	25	1	58	71	25	34
Rodriguez, Salvador	0	3	6.08	10	1	27	28	20	14
Segura, Jose	10	2	4.47	38	14	54	47	27	38
Solis, Ricardo	9	9	4.92	23	0	115	143	43	51
Uribe, Juan	6	3	1.93	43	6	70	52	30	43
Valdez, Rafael	8	1	5.51	22	0	96	124	49	67
Valenzuela, Aurelio	1	0	6.23	7	0	13	15	7	3
Villarreal, Antonio	5	2	2.95	34	1	76	78	35	43

Batters: 10 or more at-bats
Pitchers: 5 or more innings

JAPANESE LEAGUES

Yakult Wins Second Title In Three Years

By WAYNE GRACZYK

The Yakult Swallows of Tokyo defeated the Orix BlueWave of Kobe to win their second Japan Series title in three years in 1995. The Central League champions won the best-of-7 series, 4-1.

American first baseman Tom O'Malley was named Series MVP after hitting .529 with two homers. Teammate and countryman Terry Bross was selected the outstanding pitcher after winning Games One and Five.

Former Oakland A's players Doug Jennings and Troy Neel played in the Series for Orix. Jennings slammed two homers, including a game-winner in the fourth contest, the only game won by the BlueWave. Neel hit .308.

Tom O'Malley

For the Swallows, it was their third Japan Series championship. They beat the Hankyu Braves (currently the Blue Wave) in 1978 and the Seibu Lions in 1993.

The BlueWave, riding the "Spirit of the Kobe Comeback," were inspired by the city's recovery from the Great Hanshin Earthquake of Jan. 17, 1995, in which Kobe lost more than 5,500 citizens. Orix players wore a sleeve patch inscribed "Gambarou Kobe," meaning "Let's do our best, Kobe." Though the team did its best, the BlueWave fell to a stronger Yakult club.

An interesting development in the 1995 season was the hiring of former Texas Rangers manager Bobby Valentine to manage the Pacific League's Chiba Lotte Marines. Appearing in a computer commercial on Japanese TV at the beginning of the year, Valentine said, "We're gonna change this game. We're gonna change baseball."

He then changed the Marines from a perennial second division finisher in the six-team league, guiding them to a strong second place showing, 11 games over .500. Despite his effort, Valentine was fired after the season, reportedly because of a dispute with the team's front office, chiefly GM Tatsuro Hirooka, who had handpicked Valentine to manage the team in September 1994.

More than 14,000 fans signed a petition urging Lotte to retain the American as manager in 1996, but the club ignored those wishes.

Thirty-four North Americans played in Japan in 1995, with mixed performances. Chunichi Dragons outfielder Alonzo Powell, an ex-Mariners and Expos player, won his second consecutive Central League batting title, hitting .355. Nippon Ham Fighters righthander Kip Gross, a former Dodger, led the Pacific League in victories with 16.

Bross topped the Central with a 2.33 ERA while posting a 14-5 mark. He also became the first U.S. pitcher since 1964 to throw a no-hitter when he blanked the Yomiuri Giants 4-0 Sept. 9.

The best American in Japan in 1995 was O'Malley, who was named the Central League MVP after hitting .302 with 31 homers and 87 RBIs. He is a career .300 hitter in five Japan seasons.

In the Pacific League, Chiba's Julio Franco was third in the batting race at .306. Marines lefthander Eric Hillman was fourth with a 2.87 ERA while posting a 12-9 record.

The fabulous Ichiro led the Pacific League in hitting for the second year in a row with a .342 average. He also led with 179 hits, 104 runs, 285 total bases, 80 RBIs, 18 hit-by-pitches, 49 steals and a .432 on-base percentage. Ichiro, 21, hit 25 homers and won his second straight MVP.

The most disappointing development was the performance of Kevin Mitchell, who belted a grand slam in his first at-bat for the Fukuoka Daiei Hawks but soon went AWOL with a reported knee injury. Hawks officials doubted the severity of Mitchell's injury and the two sides squabbled through most of the season.

JAPAN SERIES

Last 25 Years

Year	Champion	Manager	Runner-Up	Result	MVP
1971	Yomiuri (CL)	Tetsuharu Kawakami	Hankyu (PL)	4-1	Toshimitsu Suetsugu, Yomiuri
1972	Yomiuri (CL)	Tetsuharu Kawakami	Hankyu (PL)	4-1	Tsuneo Horiuchi, Yomiuri
1973	Yomiuri (CL)	Tetsuharu Kawakami	Nankai (PL)	4-1	Tsuneo Horiuchi, Yomiuri
1974	Lotte (PL)	Masaichi Kaneda	Chunichi (CL)	4-2	Sumio Hirota, Lotte
1975	Hankyu (PL)	Toshiharu Ueda	Hiroshima (CL)	4-2	Takashi Yamaguchi, Hankyu
1976	Hankyu (PL)	Toshiharu Ueda	Yomiuri (CL)	4-3	Yutaka Fukumoto, Hankyu
1977	Hankyu (PL)	Toshiharu Ueda	Yomiuri (CL)	4-1	Hisashi Yamada, Hankyu
1978	Yakult (CL)	Tatsuro Hirooka	Hankyu (PL)	4-3	Katsuo Osugi, Yakult
1979	Hiroshima (CL)	Takeshi Koba	Kintetsu (PL)	4-3	Yoshihiko Takahashi, Hiroshima
1980	Hiroshima (CL)	Takeshi Koba	Kintetsu (PL)	4-3	Jim Lyttle, Hiroshima
1981	Yomiuri (CL)	Motoshi Fujita	Nippon (PL)	4-2	Takashi Nishimoto, Yomiuri
1982	Seibu (PL)	Tatsuro Hirooka	Chunichi (CL)	4-2	Osamu Higashio, Seibu
1983	Seibu (PL)	Tatsuro Hirooka	Yomiuri (CL)	4-3	Takuji Ota, Seibu
1984	Hiroshima (CL)	Takeshi Koba	Hankyu (PL)	4-3	Kiyoyuki Nagashima, Hiroshima
1985	Hanshin (CL)	Yoshio Yoshida	Seibu (PL)	4-2	Randy Bass, Hanshin
1986	Seibu (PL)	Masaaki Mori	Hiroshima (CL)	4-3-1	Kimiyasu Kudo, Seibu
1987	Seibu (PL)	Masaaki Mori	Yomiuri (CL)	4-2	Kimiyasu Kudo, Seibu
1988	Seibu (PL)	Masaaki Mori	Chunichi (CL)	4-1	Hiromichi Ishige, Seibu
1989	Yomiuri (CL)	Motoshi Fujita	Kintetsu (PL)	4-3	Norihiro Komada, Yomiuri
1990	Seibu (PL)	Masaaki Mori	Yomiuri (CL)	4-0	Orestes Destrade, Seibu
1991	Seibu (PL)	Masaaki Mori	Hiroshima (CL)	4-3	Koji Akiyama, Seibu
1992	Seibu (PL)	Masaaki Mori	Yakult (CL)	4-3	Takehiro Ishii, Seibu
1993	Yakult (CL)	Katsuya Nomura	Seibu (PL)	4-3	Kenjiro Kawasaki, Yakult
1994	Yomiuri (CL)	Shigeo Nagashima	Seibu (PL)	4-2	Hiromi Makihara, Yomiuri
1995	Yakult (CL)	Katsuya Nomura	Orix (PL)	4-1	Tom O'Malley, Yakult

CENTRAL LEAGUE

STANDINGS

	W	L	T	PCT	GB
Yakult Swallows	82	48	0	.631	—
Hiroshima Carp	74	56	1	.569	8
Yomiuri Giants	72	58	1	.554	10
Yokohama BayStars	66	64	0	.508	16
Chunichi Dragons	50	80	0	.385	32
Hanshin Tigers	46	84	0	.354	36

INDIVIDUAL BATTING LEADERS
(Minimum 403 Plate Appearances)

	AVG	AB	R	H	2B	3B	HR	RBI	SB
Powell, Alonzo, Dragons	.355	389	63	138	24	4	19	69	1
Rose, Bobby, BayStars	.315	492	76	155	32	4	22	97	3
Nomura, Kenjiro, Carp	.315	550	109	173	29	5	32	75	30
Ochiai, Hiromitsu, Giants	.311	399	64	124	15	1	17	65	1
Huru, Toshio, BayStars	.310	378	59	117	14	2	5	29	9
Ishii, Takuro, BayStars	.309	444	69	137	22	2	2	41	23
O'Malley, Tom, Swallows	.302	421	83	127	20	0	31	87	6
Tatsunami, Kazu, Dragons	.301	489	72	147	25	1	11	53	10
Sekikawa, Koichi, Tigers	.295	417	62	123	17	5	2	30	12
Furuta, Atsuya, Swallows	.294	487	88	143	18	1	21	76	6
Komada, Norihiro, BayStars	.289	499	45	144	29	4	6	66	0
Eto, Akira, Carp	.286	462	92	132	30	1	39	106	14
Matsui, Hideki, Giants	.283	501	76	142	31	1	22	80	9
Dobashi, Katsuyuki, Swallows	.281	459	66	129	32	1	9	54	7
Coolbaugh, Scott, Tigers	.278	468	56	130	25	1	22	77	1
Mack, Shane, Giants	.275	477	79	131	18	0	20	52	12
Shoda, Kozo, Carp	.274	449	62	123	17	2	3	38	7
Kanemoto, Tomoaki, Carp	.274	369	72	101	15	1	24	67	14
Braggs, Glenn, BayStars	.273	407	75	111	23	0	24	72	4
Oto, Shigeki, Carp	.267	404	49	108	15	2	9	49	4
Wada, Yutaka, Tigers	.267	509	49	136	22	4	1	35	4
Kuji, Teruyoshi, Tigers	.266	334	32	89	9	5	1	24	3
Ikeyama, Takahiro, Swallows	.263	456	64	120	24	2	19	70	8
Kawai, Masahiro, Giants	.261	371	51	97	13	0	2	19	3
Davis, Glenn, Tigers	.256	453	47	116	25	1	23	77	1
Ilda, Tetsuya, Swallows	.244	522	78	132	19	7	7	31	35

(Remaining U.S. Players)

	AVG	AB	R	H	2B	3B	HR	RBI	SB
Howell, Jack, Giants	.279	219	35	61	10	0	14	41	1
Meulens, Hensley, Swallows	.244	438	74	107	16	0	29	80	6
Hall, Mel, Dragons	.236	178	20	42	5	0	12	35	2
Medina, Luis, Carp	.223	103	9	23	3	0	4	11	0

INDIVIDUAL PITCHING LEADERS
(Minimum 130 Innings)

	W	L	ERA	G	SV	IP	H	BB	SO
Bross, Terry, Swallows	14	5	2.33	32	0	162	114	57	139
Saito, Masaki, Giants	18	10	2.70	28	0	213	166	50	187
Checo, Robinson, Carp	15	8	2.74	28	0	194	143	98	166
Ishii, Kazuhisa, Swallows	13	4	2.76	26	1	153	112	77	159
Makihara, Hiromi, Giants	11	8	2.88	26	0	191	167	44	145
Yabu, Keiichi, Tigers	7	13	2.98	27	0	196	185	50	118
Yamauchi, Yasuyuki, Carp	14	10	3.03	34	0	163	145	67	123
Kawajiri, Tetsuro, Tigers	8	11	3.10	29	0	148	130	36	105
Yoshii, Masato, Swallows	10	7	3.12	25	0	147	127	39	91
Imanaka, Shinji, Dragons	12	9	3.29	25	0	189	178	45	150

(Remaining U.S. Players)

	W	L	ERA	G	SV	IP	H	BB	SO
Birkbeck, Mike, BayStars	2	0	2.82	8	0	38	37	8	24
Jones, Jimmy, Giants	2	2	3.06	6	0	32	34	14	16
Schwarz, Jeff, BayStars	1	4	4.15	4	0	9	3	15	8
Monteleone, Rich, Dragons	2	4	6.55	11	0	44	55	17	19

Foreign stars. Alonzo Powell, left, led the Central League with a .355 average, while Terry Bross topped Central League pitchers with a 2.33 ERA.

INDIVIDUAL BATTING LEADERS
(Minimum 403 Plate Appearances)

	AVG	AB	R	H	2B	3B	HR	RBI	SB
Ichiro, Blue Wave	.342	524	104	179	23	4	25	80	49
Hori, Koichi, Marines	.309	457	71	141	18	4	11	67	16
Franco, Julio, Marines	.306	474	60	145	25	3	10	58	11
Hatsushiba, Kiyoshi, Marines	.301	458	60	138	27	5	25	80	1
Tanaka, Yukio, Fighters	.291	488	76	142	28	1	25	80	1
Morozumi, Kenji, Marines	.290	362	44	105	9	3	1	20	24
Jackson, Darrin, Lions	.289	506	66	146	28	3	20	68	9
Kokubo, Hiroki, Hawks	.286	465	72	133	20	9	28	76	14
Hamana, Chihiro, Hawks	.276	366	47	101	13	1	1	28	18
Ogawa, Hirofumi, Wave	.272	379	44	103	20	3	6	38	0
Sasaki, Makoto, Lions	.271	535	63	145	27	2	17	55	18
Mizuguchi, Eiji, Buffs	.268	107	31	98	5	1	2	26	6
Hirose, Tetsuro, Fighters	.267	442	50	118	11	1	2	35	4
Akiyama, Koji, Hawks	.267	476	61	127	25	1	21	66	13
Fujimoto, Hiroji, Hawks	.264	383	36	101	17	1	11	58	0
Baba, Toshifumu, Wave	.262	344	25	90	14	3	1	33	4
Hirai, Mitsuchica, Marines	.260	416	45	108	17	4	4	49	6
Suzuki, Takahisa, Buffs	.253	423	35	107	12	0	16	50	1
Suzuki, Ken, Lions	.252	416	39	105	10	0	12	42	0
Ducey, Rob, Fighters	.249	425	61	106	19	4	25	61	7
Taguchi, So, Blue Wave	.246	495	76	122	24	2	9	61	14
Ito, Tsutomu, Lions	.246	386	40	95	21	0	6	43	9
Stevens, Lee, Buffaloes	.246	476	54	117	29	1	23	70	0
Watanabe, Hiroshi, Fighters	.246	407	37	100	12	2	3	45	14
Kiyohara, Kazuhiro, Lions	.245	404	63	99	13	3	25	64	2

(Remaing U.S. Players)

	AVG	AB	R	H	2B	3B	HR	RBI	SB
Brito, Bernardo, Fighters	.313	214	31	67	6	0	21	50	0
Mitchell, Kevin, Hawks	.300	130	17	39	6	0	8	28	0
Jennings, Doug, Blue Wave	.266	335	44	89	22	1	16	60	2
Reimer, Kevin, Hawks	.254	351	31	89	11	3	10	52	0
Destrade, Orestes, Lions	.245	163	17	40	6	1	6	23	1
Neel, Troy, Blue Wave	.244	418	55	102	20	1	27	70	1
McIntosh, Tim, Fighters	.220	191	16	42	6	0	3	15	0
Bryant, Ralph, Buffaloes	.194	186	26	36	9	0	10	22	0
Incaviglia, Pete, Marines	.181	243	25	44	5	0	10	31	1

INDIVIDUAL PITCHING LEADERS
(Minimum 130 Innings)

	W	L	ERA	G	SV	IP	H	BB	SO
Irabu, Hideki, Marines	11	11	2.53	28	0	203	156	72	239
Kaku, Taigen, Lions	8	6	2.54	22	0	163	131	34	115
Komiyama, Satoru, Marines	11	4	2.60	25	0	187	150	53	169
Hillman, Eric, Marines	12	9	2.87	28	0	197	186	49	121
Hasegawa, Shietoshi, Wave	12	7	2.89	24	0	171	167	51	91
Shintani, Hiroshi, Lions	11	11	2.93	28	1	169	129	44	115
Gross, Kip, Fighters	16	13	3.04	31	0	231	219	59	114
Iwamoto, Tsutomu, Fighters	5	7	3.07	29	0	132	106	46	113
Noda, Koji, Blue Wave	10	7	3.08	26	0	184	145	69	208
Hoshino, Nobuyuki, Wave	11	8	3.39	24	0	157	133	51	112

(Remaining U.S. Players)

	W	L	ERA	G	SV	IP	H	BB	SO
Thigpen, Bobby, Hawks	1	1	1.96	20	8	23	22	10	10
Powell, Dennis, Buffaloes	2	7	3.67	23	3	83	84	33	54

Boldface type indicates league leader

PACIFIC LEAGUE

STANDINGS

	W	L	T	PCT	GB
Orix Blue Wave	82	47	1	.636	—
Chiba Lotte Marines	69	58	3	.543	12
Seibu Lions	67	57	6	.540	12½
Nippon Ham Fighters	59	68	3	.465	22
Fukuoka Daiei Hawks	52	72	4	.429	26½
Kintetsu Buffaloes	49	78	3	.386	32

CHINESE PROFESSIONAL
BASEBALL LEAGUE

President Lions Break Elephants' Grip

By JEFFREY WILSON

The President Lions broke the Brother Elephants' three-year domination of Taiwan's Chinese Professional Baseball League in 1995. The Lions won both half-season titles, marking the third time in four years that a team has claimed the league championship without the need for a postseason playoff.

The Lions were never seriously challenged the entire year, winning the first half by 6½ games over the China Times Eagles, and the second half by two games over the Mercury Tigers. The Brother Elephants were never a factor, finishing three games under .500 overall.

President relied on a strong pitching staff to carry it to the title, its second in the league's six-year

Luis de los Santos

history. The Lions compiled a 2.45 ERA and had the league's top two pitchers: righthanders Kuo Chin-hsing (20-7, 2.31), the only 20-game winner, and Jose Nunez (16-11, 1.88), the ERA leader for the second straight year.

Nunez, who formerly pitched for the Toronto Blue Jays and Chicago Cubs, has compiled a 56-25 record in three seasons in Taiwan. A native of the Dominican Republic, he is expected to play in Japan in 1996.

The Elephants never could reassert their dominance of 1995, in large part because ace pitcher Chen Yi-hsin fell to a disappointing 8-15 record after going 22-4 the year before.

The six-team league expanded its schedule to 100 games, an increase of 10. Nonetheless, few records were broken. Elephants third baseman Luis de los Santos broke the only significant record, for most hits in a season. He had 136, breaking his own record of 125 set in 1994.

De los Santos, who previously played for the Kansas City Royals, tied for the league lead in RBIs, with 72. He shared the lead with China Times outfielder George Hinshaw, the 1994 leader. Hinshaw also shared the lead in home runs with teammate Liao Min-hsiung, with 22.

Mercury second baseman Angel Gonzalez, a four-year veteran, edged out de los Santos for the batting title for the second straight year. He hit .354 and won by .002—the same margin that he beat de los Santos by in 1994.

STANDINGS

	W	L	T	PCT	GB
*President Lions	62	36	2	.633	—
Mercury Tigers	49	46	3	.505	12½
China Times Eagles	49	50	1	.495	13½
Brother Elephants	48	51	1	.485	14½
Weichuan Dragons	47	52	1	.475	15½
Jungo Bears	40	58	2	.408	22

*Won first- and second-half titles

INDIVIDUAL BATTING LEADERS
(Minimum 310 Plate Appearances)

	AVG	AB	R	H	2B	3B	HR	RBI	SB
Gonzalez, Angel, Tigers	.354	274	55	97	19	4	8	47	3
De los Santos, Luis, Elephants	.352	386	53	136	23	1	14	72	3
Chen Cheng-hsien, Lions	.333	342	47	114	33	1	11	46	1
Lu Ming-hsi, Dragons	.328	326	60	107	20	0	15	50	3
Iglesias, Luis, Tigers	.319	320	52	102	20	1	18	70	1
Wang Kuang-hui, Elephants	.316	297	45	94	16	0	8	48	1
Li Chu-ming, Elephants	.314	303	33	95	15	1	4	40	5
Tseng Kui-chang, Eagles	.306	415	70	127	26	4	5	38	9
Luo Shi-hsing, Dragons	.304	342	53	104	17	3	10	57	9
Garcia, Leo, Tigers	.303	366	67	111	27	5	11	49	14

(Remaining U.S. and Latin Players)

	AVG	AB	R	H	2B	3B	HR	RBI	SB
Figueroa, Bien, Lions	.436	39	6	17	2	0	0	4	2
Guerrero, Epy, Elephants	.320	278	39	89	13	2	4	25	7
Hernandez, Cesar, Lions	.301	372	47	112	24	2	10	57	17
Alvarez, Jorge, Elephants	.300	40	4	12	2	0	1	7	0
Jones, Ron, Bears	.299	304	41	91	15	0	12	54	2
Hinshaw, George, Eagles	.298	372	69	111	18	1	22	72	2
Laureano, Francisco, Lions	.292	349	51	102	18	1	9	41	4
Michel, Domingo, Lions	.274	62	6	17	3	0	1	7	1
Martinez, Julian, Eagles	.270	126	14	34	4	0	0	14	2
Espy, Cecil, Bears	.263	160	16	42	6	2	2	17	6
Giles, Brian, Eagles	.262	164	22	43	1	1	1	16	9
Campusano, Sil, Dragons	.259	359	66	93	17	1	17	56	13
Francois, Manny, Dragons	.242	66	15	16	2	0	1	12	4
Bishop, James, Bears	.238	206	16	49	10	0	4	14	0
Tiburcio, Freddie, Elephants	.222	126	12	28	6	0	2	9	8
Suero, William, Dragons	.200	140	26	28	4	0	3	13	11

INDIVIDUAL PITCHING LEADERS
(Minimum 100 Innings)

	W	L	ERA	G	SV	IP	H	BB	SO
Nunez, Jose, Lions	16	11	1.88	34	3	220	184	37	167
Liu Yi-chuan, Tigers	8	6	2.07	46	13	126	105	16	84
Kuo Chin-hsing, Lions	20	7	2.31	32	1	210	173	45	125
Garcia, Apolinar, Lions	10	5	2.44	19	0	132	105	49	94
Galvez, Balvino, Elephants	10	11	2.51	21	0	168	161	33	71
Hsieh Chang-heng, Lions	12	11	2.81	27	0	179	176	47	109
Chen Hsien-chang, Elephants	6	7	2.86	21	2	125	120	25	46
Clayton, Royal, Elephants	10	3	3.14	15	0	100	103	23	50
Chen Yi-hsin, Elephants	8	15	3.14	26	0	180	180	37	94
Lugo, Urbano, Dragons	9	10	3.22	29	4	142	130	26	106

(Remaining U.S. and Latin Players)

	W	L	ERA	G	SV	IP	H	BB	SO
Sanchez, Alex, Tigers	2	0	1.99	8	0	45	31	23	19
Moreno, Angel, Lions	1	0	2.25	2	0	12	10	1	3
Hernandez, Manny, Elephants	3	2	2.68	8	0	43	30	15	36
Vann, Brandy, Lions	2	1	2.79	41	14	80	65	37	72
Harris, Reggie, Dragons	3	5	3.00	9	0	63	53	47	32
Bennett, Chris, Elephants	4	5	3.02	15	1	86	89	24	54
Brito, Mario, Elephants	3	4	3.16	22	7	42	33	12	46
Perez, Dario, Dragons	13	9	3.22	27	0	196	186	64	120
Rivera, Carlos, Eagles	11	10	3.33	28	0	175	145	66	132
Toliver, Freddie, Dragons	9	11	3.42	24	1	173	163	90	93
August, Don, Bears	4	5	3.58	39	13	93	89	27	38
Franklin, Jay, Bears	2	6	3.76	16	1	69	69	36	19
Picota, Len, Tigers	8	8	3.99	26	2	144	153	39	79
Turgeon, Dave, Eagles	12	6	4.00	28	1	135	170	46	56
Barfield, John, Lions	1	0	4.15	11	0	26	34	8	17
Smith, Daryl, Bears	3	4	4.50	7	0	44	51	12	29
Solano, Julio, Dragons	5	2	4.50	25	6	42	43	14	29
Segura, Jose, Dragons	0	5	4.54	9	0	41	49	18	16
Lara, Jose, Tigers	1	1	4.67	4	0	17	19	7	9
Sangilbert, Mario, Eagles	2	6	4.76	16	0	58	67	33	19
Johnson, William, Dragons	5	2	4.89	9	0	46	51	38	21
Vasquez, Lioner, Tigers	0	2	4.93	9	0	49	64	22	32
Conde, Argenis, Tigers	0	0	5.09	11	3	23	32	12	14
Metoyer, Tony, Bears	5	11	5.14	19	0	110	132	38	57
Straker, Les, Bears	5	12	5.19	22	1	112	135	93	55
Diese, Juan, Eagles	0	1	5.84	4	0	12	11	5	7
Farmer, Gordon, Dragons	1	2	6.38	4	0	24	30	16	25

WINTER
LEAGUES

Puerto Rico's Dream Team Lineup Romps To Caribbean Series Crown

By ALLAN SIMPSON

With major leaguers embroiled in a players' strike that brought the game to its knees in the winter of 1994-95, Puerto Rico took advantage of a one-time opportunity to audition its version of a baseball Dream Team.

The powerful San Juan Senators not only monopolized the island nation's best native talent in winning their second straight league title, but then further reinforced a stacked roster to propel Puerto Rico, the host country, to its third Caribbean World Series title in four years.

A lineup that included the likes of all-stars Roberto Alomar, Carlos Baerga, Juan Gonzalez, Edgar Martinez and Ruben Sierra went undefeated in the 37th renewal of the four-nation event, beating the Dominican Republic 9-3 in the deciding game. The Senators outscored their opponents 49-15 in winning six straight games.

Never before had a winter league team—or possibly any team—assembled such a galaxy of stars.

"This is the strongest team I have ever played for, by far," said Milwaukee Brewers righthander Ricky Bones, who limited the Dominican Republic to two hits over the first six innings in the tournament's deciding game. A Puerto Rican loss would have forced a playoff game between the two teams.

Bones took a 5-0 lead to the sixth and got all the support he needed from outfielder Bernie Williams (Yankees), who doubled and homered twice, driving in three runs. Puerto Rico rocked starter Jose Rijo (Reds) and three Dominican relievers for 14 hits.

The deciding contest was seen by an overflow crowd in excess of 22,000 and electrified the entire island at a time when baseball was mired in a public relations backwash.

Puerto Rico also beat the Dominican Republic, 16-0, in a third-round matchup that proved to be the most one-sided game of the tournament. The two teams had entered the game unbeaten.

It was the 12th triumph in 37 tries for Puerto Rico, and its third on home soil. Caguas previously won in 1954 and Bayamon in 1975. The Series was last played in Puerto Rico in 1984.

The two losses to Puerto Rico were the only ones suffered by the defending champi-

Roberto Alomar

1995 CARIBBEAN WORLD SERIES

San Juan, Puerto Rico
Feb. 4-9, 1995

CHAMPIONSHIP STANDINGS	W	L	PCT.	GB
Puerto Rico (San Juan)	6	0	1.000	—
Dominican Republic (Azucareros)	4	2	.667	2
Venezuela (Caracas)	1	5	.167	5
Mexico (Hermosillo)	1	5	.167	5

INDIVIDUAL BATTING LEADERS
(Minimum 16 Plate Appearances)

	AVG	AB	R	H	2B	3B	HR	RBI	SB
Roberto Alomar, PR	.560	25	9	14	1	0	2	10	2
Jerry Brooks, DR	.435	23	7	10	5	0	1	8	0
Bernie Williams, PR	.417	24	8	10	2	0	3	4	0
Henry Rodriguez, DR	.400	20	6	8	1	0	2	5	0
Juan Gonzalez, PR	.375	24	3	9	1	0	2	6	0
Edgar Martinez, PR	.370	27	2	10	1	0	0	9	0
Ted Wood, Mexico	.364	22	4	8	3	0	1	5	0
Andujar Cedeno, DR	.333	24	3	8	2	0	1	5	0
Matt Franco, Mexico	.333	21	2	7	2	0	0	3	0
Rey Sanchez, PR	.333	21	6	7	1	1	0	3	0

INDIVIDUAL PITCHING LEADERS
(Minimum 5 Innings)

	W	L	ERA	G	SV	IP	H	BB	SO
Doug Brocail, PR	1	0	0.00	1	0	7	3	1	7
Urbano Lugo, Venezuela	1	0	0.00	1	0	7	3	3	4
Jose Alberro, PR	1	0	0.00	4	0	6	3	3	4
Pedro Astacio, DR	1	0	0.00	1	0	6	2	2	3
Juan Acevedo, Mexico	0	0	0.00	2	0	5	5	1	4
Eric Gunderson, PR	1	0	1.13	1	0	8	7	0	4
Antonio Alfonseca, DR	1	0	1.80	1	0	5	4	4	4
Jose Centeno, Venez.	0	0	1.80	3	0	5	2	2	4
Kevin Foster, Mexico	1	0	2.45	2	0	11	5	2	5
Chris Haney, PR	0	0	2.45	1	0	7	7	2	4

Most Valuable Player—Roberto Alomar, Puerto Rico.

---

on Dominican team, which featured a rotation that included Rijo, Pedro Martinez (Expos) and Pedro Astacio (Dodgers). Mexico and Venezuela tied for last place, winning only a game apiece.

Alomar was named the Series MVP after batting .560 (14-for-25). The 14 hits tied a Caribbean Series record.

Strike Paved The Way

Puerto Rico's Dream Team was largely a creation of the strike.

Most of the Caribbean country's best players normally perform sparingly in the winter season and rarely compete in the Caribbean Series because it infringes on spring training. But when the game ground to a halt, they were only too willing to continue playing.

A San Juan team that already included Alomar (Blue Jays), Baerga (Indians) and Martinez (Mariners) was bolstered by Gonzalez (Rangers), Sierra (Athletics) and relief ace Roberto Hernandez (White Sox), among other native players. Shortstop Rey Sanchez

(Cubs), who won the Puerto Rican League batting title with a .390 average, was dropped to No. 9 in the order to accommodate the pickups.

A team is entitled to make up to 10 changes to its roster for the Caribbean Series.

"We had everybody we needed, and just added a few more players," Sanchez said. "But I don't think that will happen again. I don't think the players that win the league championship are going to be happy to be replaced.

"I don't think I would want to do that either, take somebody else's job. They work so hard to win the title, and then all of a sudden somebody else takes their spot. I don't think we should do that again. This was the perfect year for it."

The strike impacted other countries as well, drawing a vastly greater number of established big leaguers to winter ball.

J.T. Snow

"The current winter league season will be difficult to repeat," said veteran Dominican catcher Tony Pena.

Among those who played winter ball who might otherwise have remained in California was Angels first baseman J.T. Snow, who hit .268 for Aragua of the Venezuelan League.

"When the strike began, I sat at home for two months and didn't do anything," Snow said. "I wanted to come here because I need to play and especially swing the bat more, and get experience.

"One of the reasons I went to Venezuela is to turn myself into a great hitter from the left side. The Angels want me to hit left only."

Snow used his winter performance as a springboard to a banner 1995 season, hitting .289 with 24 home

CARIBBEAN WORLD SERIES

Last 25 Years

Years	Site	Champion
1970-71	San Juan, P.R.	Licey (Dominican Republic)
1971-72	Santo Domingo, D.R.	Ponce (Puerto Rico)
1972-73	Caracas, Venez.	Licey (Dominican Republic)
1973-74	Hermosillo, Mexico	Caguas (Puerto Rico)
1974-75	San Juan, P.R.	Bayamon (Puerto Rico)
1975-76	Santo Domingo, D.R.	Hermosillo (Mexico)
1976-77	Caracas, Venez.	Licey (Dominican Republic)
1977-78	Mazatlan, Mexico	Mayaguez (Puerto Rico)
1978-79	San Juan, P.R.	Magallanes (Venezuela)
1979-80	Santo Domingo, D.R.	Licey (Dominican Republic)
1980-81	No Series	
1981-82	Hermosillo, Mexico	Caracas (Venezuela)
1982-83	Caracas, Venez.	Arecibo (Puerto Rico)
1983-84	San Juan, P.R.	Zulia (Venezuela)
1984-85	Mazatlan, Mexico	Licey (Dominican Republic)
1985-86	Maracaibo, Venez.	Mexicali (Mexico)
1986-87	Hermosillo, Mexico	Caguas (Puerto Rico)
1987-88	Santo Domingo, D.R.	Escogido (Dominican Republic)
1988-89	Mazatlan, Mexico	Zulia (Venezuela)
1989-90	Miami	Escogido (Dominican Republic)
1990-91	Miami	Licey (Dominican Republic)
1991-92	Hermosillo, Mexico	Mayaguez (Puerto Rico)
1992-93	Mazatlan, Mexico	Santurce (Puerto Rico)
1993-94	Puerto La Cruz, Venez.	Licey (Dominican Republic)
1994-95	San Juan, P.R.	San Juan (Puerto Rico)

runs and 102 RBIs, all career highs.

Delgado: Player of the Year

The best winter performance of all in 1994-95 was turned in by catcher Carlos Delgado, who hit .328 with 18 home runs and 70 RBIs for San Juan, including postseason play. He was selected Baseball America's Winter League Player of the Year.

Delgado led the Puerto Rican League with 12 homers and 47 RBIs during the regular season, and overshadowed many major league all-stars. In the Caribbean Series, Delgado hit cleanup on the Dream Team ahead of Gonzalez and Sierra.

Delgado, unfortunately, failed to capitalize on his strong winter showing. He spent most of the 1995 season in the minor leagues, playing for Toronto's Triple-A Syracuse affiliate, learning to play a new position.

1994-95 WINTER ALL-STAR TEAM

Selected by Baseball America

Player, Club (League)	Organiz.	PCT	AB	R	H	2B	3B	HR	RBI	SB
C Carlos Delgado, San Juan (PRico)	Blue Jays	.328	247	61	81	19	1	18	70	2
1B Domingo Martinez, Aguilas (Dom Rep)	White Sox	.326	215	32	70	15	0	13	53	2
2B Roberto Alomar, San Juan (PRico)	Blue Jays	.331	287	63	95	19	5	8	46	14
3B Carlos Baerga, San Juan (PRico)	Indians	.329	225	46	74	14	2	9	43	4
SS Rey Sanchez, San Juan (PRico)	Cubs	.353	289	51	102	17	4	3	45	6
OF Raul Mondesi, Azucareros (Dom Rep)	Dodgers	.301	216	37	65	8	1	13	31	4
OF Robert Perez, Lara (Venezuela)	Blue Jays	.299	251	27	75	13	1	6	43	3
OF Bernie Williams, Arecibo/San Juan (PR)	Yankees	.300	229	42	69	13	5	13	49	14
DH Dave Nilsson, Waverley (Australia)	Brewers	.388	160	41	62	12	1	16	56	7

		W	L	ERA	G	SV	IP	H	BB	SO
P Doug Brocail, Mayaguez/San Juan (PR)	Astros	10	4	2.18	19	0	99	71	33	54
P Rich Garces, Aragua (Venezuela)	Cubs	4	0	0.27	32	20	33	25	14	36
P Chris Haney, Mayaguez/San Juan (PR)	Royals	8	1	1.78	14	0	81	57	19	46
P Roberto Hernandez, May./San Juan (PR)	White Sox	4	2	1.47	41	21	49	26	6	58
P Antonio Osuna, Hermosillo (Mexico)	Dodgers	3	0	1.12	39	18	48	18	20	56

PLAYER OF THE YEAR: Carlos Delgado, San Juan (Puerto Rico).

Statistics include regular-season, playoff and Caribbean World Series games

Carlos Delgado
18 homers, 70 RBIs

Statistics in **boldface** indicate league leader.
#Indicates league leader in category other than batting/pitching.

Dream Team Rallies Down Stretch

San Juan may have fielded the equivalent of a Puerto Rican Dream Team as it marched to the Caribbean World Series crown, but it took a back seat to the Mayaguez Indians for most of the Puerto Rican winter season.

The Senators finished second to Mayaguez during regular-season play then placed second again to the Indians in the league's four-team, round-robin playoff. But the Senators went on to beat Mayaguez 5-3 in the best-of-9 championship series to advance to the Caribbean Series for the second year in a row.

San Juan wrapped up its eighth title overall when Mayaguez closer Roberto Hernandez (White Sox) served up a ninth-inning wild pitch with the bases loaded and Roberto Alomar (Blue Jays) at the plate, handing the Senators a 5-4 win.

San Juan catcher Carlos Delgado (Blue Jays) earned Baseball America Winter League Player of the Year honors. He led the league with 12 home runs, 47 RBIs, a .493 on-base percentage and a .658 slugging percentage, while hitting

Rey Sanchez

.323. Including the postseason, he hit .328 with 18 homers and 70 RBIs.

He was joined in the Senators everyday lineup by Alomar, third baseman Carlos Baerga (Indians), DH Edgar Martinez (Mariners) and shortstop Rey Sanchez (Cubs), who won the batting title with a .390 regular season mark. That was before the team unofficially became the Dream Team.

After the Puerto Rican playoffs ended, the Senators snapped up most of the remaining top talent from around the league for the CWS, which was conveniently played in San Juan. Many top major leaguers were playing winter ball in their native countries to stay in shape during the strike and players like Juan Gonzalez (Rangers), Ruben Sierra (Athletics) and Hernandez were added to San Juan's roster.

The Senators also picked up the league's two most successful pitchers: Mayaguez' Doug Brocail (Astros), who led the league with a 1.70 ERA, and Ponce's Eric Gunderson (Mets), who led with 62 strikeouts.

Caguas, which returned to the league after a three-year absence, had enough problems of its own. The Criollos went through three managers—including general manager Felix Millan.

Opening Day manager Mike Easler was fired four games into the season. Millan then disposed of Easler's replacement, Sixto Lezcano, 25 games later and finally took over the team himself when he couldn't find anyone else willing or able to do the job.

—JAMES BAILEY

STANDINGS

REGULAR SEASON	W	L	PCT	GB
Mayaguez Indians	33	21	.611	—
San Juan Senators	32	22	.593	1
Arecibo Wolves	28	26	.519	5
Ponce Lions	26	28	.481	7
Santurce Crabbers	22	32	.407	11
Caguas Criollos	21	33	.389	12

PLAYOFFS	W	L	PCT	GB
Mayaguez Indians	9	3	.750	—
San Juan Senators	6	6	.500	3
Arecibo Wolves	5	7	.417	4
Ponce Lions	4	8	.333	5

Championship Series: San Juan defeated Mayaguez, 5-3, in best-of-9 final.

INDIVIDUAL BATTING LEADERS
(Minimum 81 Plate Appearances)

	AVG	AB	R	H	2B	3B	HR	RBI	SB
Sanchez, Rey, San Juan	.390	177	33	69	10	3	0	26	4
Johnson, Brian, Mayaguez	.364	198	31	72	17	2	5	37	0
Martinez, Edgar, San Juan	.341	85	17	29	7	0	2	16	0
Cora, Joey, Ponce	.337	187	35	63	10	2	1	14	6
Baerga, Carlos, San Juan	.336	110	26	37	6	1	7	28	1
Rios, Armando, Mayaguez	.333	123	26	41	6	1	2	13	8
Gomez, Leo, Santurce	.329	140	23	46	6	0	3	20	1
Cangelosi, John, Mayaguez	.329	82	12	27	7	1	0	6	4
Battle, Allen, Arecibo	.329	76	16	25	2	2	0	11	6
Delgado, Carlos, San Juan	.323	155	39	50	14	1	12	47	1
Lowery, Terrell, Santurce	.316	79	14	25	4	0	1	10	4
Quinones, Luis, Ponce	.313	179	29	56	10	3	5	28	6
Garcia, Omar, Mayaguez	.310	200	21	62	7	3	0	26	13
Cordero, Wil, Mayaguez	.307	166	39	51	13	1	7	34	9
Echevarria, Angel, Arecibo	.303	76	10	23	2	0	2	10	0
Chimelis, Joel, Arecibo	.301	83	15	25	6	0	1	17	4
Alomar, Roberto, San Juan	.299	174	36	52	12	1	4	19	8
Crespo, Felipe, Caguas	.296	142	22	42	6	0	5	17	1
Valdes, Pedro, San Juan	.292	144	19	42	11	2	3	18	3
Vargas, Hector, Arecibo	.291	151	32	44	12	1	7	29	3
Ordonez, Rey, Santurce	.289	121	13	35	7	1	0	14	4
Durham, Ray, Arecibo	.288	163	29	47	6	5	4	21	18
Viera, Jose, Ponce	.286	77	8	22	4	1	1	8	2
Sierra, Ruben, Santurce	.285	144	25	41	11	0	3	24	1
Munoz, Pedro, Mayaguez	.283	152	23	43	9	0	8	35	2
Nieves, Melvin, Caguas	.283	92	11	26	5	1	4	14	3
Diaz, Mario, Caguas	.281	199	17	56	7	2	1	22	1
Maldonado, Candy, Arecibo	.278	158	30	44	12	1	4	21	3
Ortiz, Junior, Santurce	.277	166	16	46	11	1	5	22	1
Hubbard, Trenidad, San Juan	.276	192	42	53	13	1	6	32	8
Williams, Bernie, Arecibo	.269	160	26	48	9	3	7	37	13

INDIVIDUAL PITCHING LEADERS
(Minimum 27 Innings)

	W	L	ERA	G	SV	IP	H	BB	SO
Hernandez, Roberto, Mayaguez	.. 3	1	0.82	27	15	33	13	2	37
Valera, Julio, Mayaguez	2	2	1.13	8	0	40	22	16	24
Shifflett, Steve, Mayaguez	3	2	1.29	20	0	28	23	11	14
Brocail, Doug, Mayaguez	7	1	1.70	13	0	64	39	23	27
Alberro, Jose, Arecibo	5	1	1.75	26	8	36	20	16	29
Haney, Chris, Mayaguez	6	1	1.99	11	0	59	43	15	33
Nunez, Edwin, Ponce	2	1	2.25	8	0	32	22	5	22
Pierce, Jeff, Caguas	3	0	2.63	23	0	41	30	15	35
Corps, Edwin, San Juan	1	2	2.95	8	0	37	30	17	8
Reyes, Carlos, San Juan	6	3	3.00	11	0	72	69	13	46
Kiefer, Mark, San Juan	6	0	3.08	10	0	53	34	24	36
Scheid, Rich, Santurce	3	5	3.09	11	0	58	66	17	26
DeLeon, Luis, Mayaguez	1	0	3.19	19	0	31	30	6	26
Remlinger, Mike, Caguas	1	4	3.21	10	0	53	44	34	37
Gunderson, Eric, Ponce	7	1	3.21	12	0	70	70	23	62
Lind, Orlando, San Juan	3	1	3.24	8	1	33	22	15	18
Bones, Ricky, Ponce	4	3	3.65	12	0	62	60	24	34

DOMINICAN
LEAGUE

Upstart Azucareros Wins First Title

Azucareros was considered by many to be the weakest team at the start of the Dominican League season, but went on to capture the first title in its 12-year existence.

The La Romana-based team was coming off consecutive fourth-place finishes but won the regular-season pennant by a game over Aguilas. It then beat Aguilas again in the league's championship series, four games to two, to earn its first-ever appearance in the Caribbean World Series. Aguilas had previously won 11 championships.

Licey, the defending Caribbean World Series champion, finished last in the regular season and didn't even qualify for postseason play.

Azucareros was heavily stocked with young Los Angeles Dodgers prospects who played an influential role in the team's success in the regular season.

Outfielder Todd Hollandsworth finished fourth in the league in hitting at .320, while leading the circuit with 14 doubles and placing fourth in stolen bases with 12. He hit .350 with five more stolen bases in the championship series. Outfielder Jerry Brooks led the club with six home runs and 26 RBIs.

Righthander Jody Treadwell won six games on a staff where no one else won more than three, though closer Rudy Seanez went 3-1, with a 0.40 ERA while converting a league-high 10 save opportunities. Treadwell added three more wins in postseason play.

Domingo Martinez

Another Dodger, outfielder Raul Mondesi, played for rival Escogido and was impressive as well. Mondesi hit .317 with seven homers in the regular season and had a two-homer game in the playoffs. He became only the third professional player, joining Dick Stuart and Bernardo Brito (Twins), to clear Santo Domingo's Quisqueya Stadium's center-field fence, which is 411 feet away from home plate and 22 feet high.

Aguilas first baseman Domingo Martinez (Cardinals) earned league MVP honors. He narrowly missed winning a triple crown while becoming only the third player in league history to hit 10 or more home runs and have at least 40 RBIs, joining Alonzo Perry in 1953 and George Bell in 1984.

Martinez' 11 home runs were the highest total ever for a native player, topping Winston Llenas (1967) and Bell (1984), who both hit 10. Martinez also led the league with 94 total bases and a .610 slugging percentage, and hit two more homers and had 13 RBIs as Aguilas finished first in the round-robin playoff.

—JAMES BAILEY

STANDINGS

REGULAR SEASON	W	L	PCT	GB
Azucareros	29	19	.604	—
Aguilas	28	20	.583	1
Escogido	23	25	.479	6
Estrellas	22	26	.458	7
Licey	18	30	.375	11

PLAYOFFS	W	L	PCT	GB
Aguilas	11	7	.611	—
Azucareros	9	9	.500	2
Escogido	8	10	.444	3
Estrellas	8	10	.444	3

Championship Series: Azucareros defeated Aguilas, 4-2, in best-of-7 final.

INDIVIDUAL BATTING LEADERS
(Minimum 72 Plate Appearances)

	AVG	AB	R	H	2B	3B	HR	RBI	SB
Matos, Francisco, Licey	.361	119	12	43	7	0	0	10	2
Mercedes, Luis, Estrellas	**.352**	162	25	**57**	6	1	1	18	1
Jose, Felix, Licey	.348	89	19	31	3	2	2	12	0
Veras, Quilvio, Aguilas	.336	119	26	40	8	2	1	11	13
Martinez, Domingo, Aguilas	.331	154	23	51	10	0	**11**	**40**	1
Hollandsworth, Todd, Azu	.320	172	27	55	**14**	0	2	20	12
Offerman, Jose, Licey	.319	72	15	23	3	2	0	4	2
Mondesi, Raul, Escogido	.317	123	23	39	6	0	7	14	3
Hernandez, Cesar, Estrellas	.306	108	18	33	7	0	2	26	2
Rodriguez, Ruben, Estrellas	.299	77	8	23	2	0	1	10	0
Alexander, Manny, Estrellas	.297	145	19	43	5	2	0	14	**16**
Arias, Alex, Aguilas	.295	149	18	44	7	1	0	20	2
Carvajal, Jovino, Azucareros	.295	173	27	51	6	3	0	12	8
Herrera, Jose, Escogido	.290	107	13	31	9	1	0	15	1
Roa, Hector, Estrellas	.284	162	**28**	46	6	3	3	17	3
Ramirez, Omar, Aguilas	.272	81	9	22	1	2	0	4	3
Martinez, Manuel, Aguilas	.271	129	22	35	5	2	5	18	7
Bruno, Julio, Aguilas	.271	70	7	19	3	0	0	7	1
Bournigal, Rafael, Azucareros	.264	110	13	29	6	0	0	11	2
Fermin, Felix, Aguilas	.263	152	18	40	6	2	1	18	2
Gonzalez, Jose, Licey	.263	76	6	20	4	0	1	3	3
Ramirez, Manny, Aguilas	.261	134	19	35	6	3	1	14	0
Masteller, Dan, Licey	.260	123	11	32	7	0	0	13	1
Liriano, Nelson, Escogido	.260	100	13	26	5	2	0	7	3
Cedeno, Andujar, Azucareros	.259	166	15	43	5	0	5	22	4
Martin, Norberto, Aguilas	.256	121	16	31	2	0	1	13	2
Brooks, Jerry, Azucareros	.254	173	18	44	9	0	6	26	1
Devarez, Cesar, Estrellas	.253	79	6	20	1	0	0	5	2
Polonia, Luis, Aguilas	.253	79	13	20	5	4	1	12	5
#Cedeno, Domingo, Azu	.231	169	18	39	4	**5**	0	10	3

INDIVIDUAL PITCHING LEADERS
(Minimum 24 Innings)

	W	L	ERA	G	SV	IP	H	BB	SO
DeLeon, Ercilio, Azucareros	2	0	0.35	9	0	26	16	10	20
#Seanez, Rudy, Azucareros	3	1	0.40	17	**10**	23	13	4	20
De la Rosa, Francisco, Estrellas	0	1	1.15	14	0	31	23	7	16
Weber, Weston, Licey	2	2	**1.50**	9	0	48	30	13	17
Reyes, Alberto, Escogido	3	1	1.61	20	4	28	18	8	16
Mercedes, Jose, Estrellas	5	3	2.07	11	0	65	58	11	23
Pichardo, Hipolito, Aguilas	6	1	2.19	11	0	53	41	14	35
Kelly, John, Licey	0	3	2.20	22	4	29	23	10	9
Garcia, Apolinar, Aguilas	6	0	2.44	11	0	59	46	19	49
Perez, Yorkis, Licey	2	1	2.45	24	0	26	21	7	28
Bautista, Jose, Aguilas	3	3	2.50	11	0	36	33	8	19
Thomas, Royal, Estrellas	2	2	2.51	11	0	47	49	6	17
Heredia, Julian, Estrellas	6	2	2.53	23	1	53	40	15	48
Brosnan, Jason, Azucareros	3	4	2.72	11	0	56	60	20	35
Hernandez, Fernando, Aguilas	3	5	2.73	12	0	63	46	34	47
Heredia, Wilson, Azucareros	3	2	2.97	12	0	58	51	14	**58**
Treadwell, Jody, Azucareros	**6**	3	3.20	11	0	65	57	23	34
Perez, Carlos, Licey	4	3	3.23	14	0	53	52	12	44
Torres, Salomon, Licey	3	4	3.26	11	0	47	39	21	24
Veres, Dave, Escogido	3	3	3.33	10	0	49	55	16	29

Caracas Rallies To Win Elusive Title

The Caracas Lions turned the tables in the 1994-95 Venezuelan League championship series, spotting Zulia a two-game lead before roaring back to win four straight games and their first title since 1990.

A year earlier, Caracas took a 2-0 lead against Magallanes, only to lose the best-of-7 series, 4-3.

The championship clincher for Caracas, which went on to represent Venezuela in the Caribbean World Series, was a 5-3 win in 11 innings as shortstop Omar Vizquel (Indians) drove in the game-winning run. Vizquel, who missed the first two games, went 6-for-17 in the series with four RBIs.

Zulia took the first two games at home—with the aid of a garden hose.

Eagles manager Ruben Amaro (Tigers) decided to water down the basepath around first base to a swamp-like consistency, effectively slowing down speedy Caracas baserunners Curtis Goodwin (Orioles), Roger Cedeno (Dodgers) and Miguel Cairo (Dodgers), who had run at will on Eagles catcher Gregg Zaun (Orioles) during the round-robin semifinals. In one Zulia loss, the Lions made off with eight stolen bases.

The strategy worked until the series shifted to Caracas, where the Lions won all three games.

Caracas won the title despite having to change managers when Phil Regan

Eddie Perez

resigned early in the season to become skipper of the Baltimore Orioles. Regan, in his sixth season in Venezuela, turned the reins over to Venezuelan Pompeyo Davalillo, who successfully completed the task.

Zulia, Caracas and Magallanes each ended the four-team, round-robin with 7-5 records, forcing a three-way playoff. It was the first such tie since a round-robin playoff format was instituted in 1987-88.

To break the deadlock, the league decided on a two-game format with the two winners qualifying for the finals. Zulia beat Caracas 3-2 in the first game. The Lions then rebounded to beat Magallanes 5-4 in the second, scoring the winning run on a bases-loaded walk in the ninth inning.

Late in the season Lara appeared to have a lock on a playoff spot, but the Cardinals blew a seven-game lead and finished third in the Western Division.

Despite his team's collapse, Lara shortstop Luis Sojo (Mariners) held on to win his third consecutive league batting title and fourth overall, tying a record set by Vic Davalillo, Pompeyo's brother. Sojo hit .376.

MVP honors were earned by Aragua catcher Eddie Perez (Braves), who hit only .269 but had seven home runs and drove in 37 runs.

—JAMES BAILEY

STANDINGS

EAST	W	L	PCT	GB
Caracas Lions	33	27	.550	—
Magallanes Navigators	32	28	.533	1
Oriente Caribbeans	27	33	.450	6
La Guaira Tiburones	23	37	.383	10
WEST	**W**	**L**	**PCT**	**GB**
Zulia Eagles	36	24	.600	—
Aragua Tigers	34	26	.567	2
Lara Cardinals	33	27	.550	3
Cabimas Oilers	22	38	.367	14
PLAYOFFS	**W**	**L**	**PCT**	**GB**
*Caracas Lions	7	5	.583	—
Magallanes Navigators	7	5	.583	—
*Zulia Eagles	7	5	.583	—
Aragua Tigers	3	9	.250	4

* Won tiebreaker playoff
Championship Series: Caracas defeated Zulia, 4-2, in best-of-7 final.

INDIVIDUAL BATTING LEADERS
(Minimum 90 Plate Appearances)

	AVG	AB	R	H	2B	3B	HR	RBI	SB
Sojo, Luis, Lara	.376	197	35	74	9	0	1	24	7
Martinez, Carlos, La Guaira	.363	215	31	78	13	1	5	39	8
Hale, Chip, Aragua	.333	165	33	55	9	2	1	16	1
Soto, Emison, Zulia	.322	115	16	37	6	0	3	13	0
Alfonzo, Ed, Caracas	.321	190	18	61	9	0	3	21	3
Nava, Lipso, Zulia	.321	84	7	27	6	1	0	7	0
Cairo, Miguel, Caracas	.319	182	38	58	6	2	0	13	21
Bragg, Darren, Oriente	.315	203	40	64	15	1	0	21	6
Wachter, Derek, Cabimas	.314	185	19	58	6	0	5	22	0
Garcia, Carlos, Magallanes	.314	102	14	32	2	1	0	4	6
Infante, Alexis, Lara	.312	189	21	59	9	3	0	13	1
Amaro, Ruben, Zulia	.311	103	19	32	3	6	2	14	4
Vizquel, Omar, Caracas	.309	97	15	30	7	3	1	16	4
Butler, Rob, Lara	.308	78	11	24	5	3	0	8	1
Green, Shawn, Lara	.306	157	29	48	8	5	1	17	5
Quintana, Carlos, Zulia	.303	142	20	43	9	1	2	20	1
Marcano, Raul, Magallanes	.301	93	14	28	8	0	0	7	0
Ramos, Jairo, La Guaira	.301	166	16	50	7	1	0	16	2
Brown, Brant, Zulia	.300	120	13	36	6	0	4	19	6
Perez, Robert, Lara	.299	251	27	75	13	1	6	43	3
Espinoza, Alvaro, Magallanes	.298	168	15	50	10	2	0	15	2
Polidor, Wil, Oriente	.290	100	11	29	6	0	0	6	2
#Armas, Marcos, Lara	.276	181	21	50	7	2	11	39	0
#Cedeno, Roger, Caracas	.273	161	23	44	3	8	0	23	20
#Woods, Tyrone, Caracas	.267	322	31	86	6	1	11	33	0
#Diaz, Eddy, Magallanes	.255	204	30	52	6	2	0	15	23

INDIVIDUAL PITCHING LEADERS
(Minimum 30 Innings)

	W	L	ERA	G	SV	IP	H	BB	SO
Garces, Rich, Aragua	3	0	0.30	29	18	30	22	12	32
Machado, Julio, Zulia	2	0	0.88	26	10	31	15	12	20
Zimmerman, Mike, Caracas	1	0	1.39	6	0	32	24	17	13
Garcia, Miguel, Aragua	2	0	1.59	24	0	40	31	21	19
Solarte, Jose, Zulia	5	4	1.67	22	2	32	28	8	17
Hampton, Mike, Magallanes	4	2	1.79	8	0	45	34	11	47
Linares, Ifrain, Magallanes	2	0	1.88	17	0	43	30	25	14
Sanchez, Luis, Oriente	2	1	1.88	18	0	38	27	8	23
Gonzalez, Jeremy, Zulia	6	5	1.91	17	0	80	67	34	37
Daal, Omar, Caracas	6	2	2.00	15	1	95	82	34	67
Crabtree, Tim, Lara	1	2	2.02	26	8	36	23	13	32
Salazar, Luis, Cabimas	3	3	2.04	18	0	40	35	17	15
Torres, Dilson, Lara	5	2	2.14	11	0	59	54	17	34
Gonzales, Francisco, Zulia	5	1	2.27	14	0	71	63	30	43
Eshelman, Vaughn, Aragua	3	2	2.28	10	0	43	43	25	34
Lowe, Sean, Magallanes	2	1	2.30	6	0	31	28	11	16
Hurtado, Edwin, Lara	6	5	2.41	15	0	90	71	36	60
#Mejias, Fernando, Aragua	7	2	2.88	16	0	75	68	21	38
#Carrara, Giovanni, Lara	7	7	3.31	17	1	82	78	32	42

Orangegrowers Write Familiar Script

Hermosillo wrote a strikingly similar script in successfully defending its Mexican Pacific League title in 1994-95.

For the second year in a row, the Orangegrowers fired their manager at midseason, only to make a late-season surge to win all three playoff rounds and earn a familiar spot in the Caribbean World Series.

Again Hermosillo fared poorly at the CWS, going 1-5, following an 0-6 showing the previous year.

Hermosillo, winners of four Mexican Pacific League titles in six years and 12 overall, finished the first half of the league's reinstated split-season schedule in seventh place with an 11-17 record. It thereupon fired Marv Foley, who a year earlier had replaced Mario Mendoza after a poor early-season showing. Foley was replaced by Derek Bryant, best known as one of Mexico's premier hitters over the past decade.

The Orangegrowers responded to a change in leadership by finishing on top in the second half, qualifying for the six-team playoffs with a 28-28 overall record. They beat Culiacan 4-2 in a best-of-seven final, wrapping up the series with a 4-3 win in Game Six.

For the second year in a row, a team that lost in the first round of the playoffs came back to reach the final round. Culiacan was beaten by Mazatlan, 4-2, but earned a second chance in the second round by being the losing team in the first round with the best regular-season record. Culiacan then hit 11 home runs, including a postseason record five by shortstop Benji Gil (Rangers), to beat Mexicali 4-1 to reach the final.

Lefthanders Blaise Ilsley (Cubs) and Ed Vosberg (Dodgers) combined for a 4-0 shutout in the first game.

J.R. Phillips

FRANK RAGSDALE

Culiacan first baseman J.R. Phillips (Giants) led the league with 17 home runs and finished second to teammate Guillermo Velasquez (Indians) in RBIs with 50. Velasquez had 54.

Guasave outfielder Marquis Riley captured the batting crown by hitting .351. He was one of only six .300 hitters in the league.

Mazatlan righthander Aaron Acosta won the league's ERA title with a 1.69 mark, but Vosberg and Mexicali's Isidro Marquez (White Sox) were the more dominant pitchers. Vosberg and Marquez tied for the league lead with eight wins, while Marquez chipped in with a league best 13 saves. Vosberg was second in both ERA (1.95) and strikeouts (75), while Marquez had an ERA of 1.02 but did not have sufficient innings to qualify for the title.

—JAMES BAILEY

STANDINGS (Overall)

REGULAR SEASON	W	L	PCT	GB
Mexicali Eagles	34	22	.607	—
Culiacan Tomatogrowers	32	22	.593	1
Los Mochis Sugarcane Growers	31	25	.554	3
Mazatlan Deer	31	25	.554	3
Hermosillo Orangegrowers	28	28	.500	6
Obregon Yaquis	26	29	.473	7½
Guasave Cottoneers	20	35	.364	13½
Navojoa Mayos	19	35	.352	14

PLAYOFFS—Quarterfinals: Hermosillo defeated Los Mochis, 4-1; Mazatlan defeated Culiacan, 4-2; and Mexicali defeated Obregon, 4-2, in best-of-7 series. **Semifinals:** Culiacan defeated Mexicali, 4-1, and Hermosillo defeated Mazatlan, 4-2, in best-of-7 series. **Finals:** Hermosillo defeated Culiacan, 4-2, in best-of-7 series.

INDIVIDUAL BATTING LEADERS
(Minimum 84 Plate Appearances)

	AVG	AB	R	H	2B	3B	HR	RBI	SB
Herrera, Isidro, Mexicali	.366	93	19	34	6	1	0	16	4
Riley, Marquis, Guasave	.351	188	32	66	5	2	0	13	14
Sherman, Darrell, Culiacan	.339	180	45	61	5	2	0	10	16
Arredondo, Luis, Hermosillo	.317	82	12	26	5	0	1	17	5
Lott, Billy, Mexicali	.310	126	20	39	9	1	2	10	3
Jimenez, Eduardo, Mexicali	.309	165	40	51	11	1	14	46	0
Trafton, Todd, Mazatlan	.309	162	31	50	9	0	9	35	3
Barrera, Nelson, Culiacan	.308	172	19	53	7	0	9	26	4
Castilla, Vinny, Obregon	.306	209	35	64	9	0	14	36	3
Franco, Matt, Hermosillo	.305	82	6	25	5	0	0	12	1
Clark, Phil, Mazatlan	.298	191	33	57	6	0	7	36	6
Simmons, Nelson, LM	.298	161	34	48	8	1	14	40	1
Wood, Ted, Navojoa	.294	201	28	59	14	1	6	31	4
Casillas, Adam, Guasave	.293	184	22	54	5	1	1	19	1
Fernandez, Daniel, Mazatlan	.287	174	20	50	8	1	0	10	11
Garcia, Cornelio, Hermosillo	.286	199	21	57	3	0	1	22	13
Goodwin, Tom, Obregon	.286	206	32	59	2	4	2	16	26
Verdugo, Vicente, Mexicali	.282	117	13	33	3	0	3	15	1
Johnson, Mark, Obregon	.282	110	21	31	8	1	7	15	6
Magallanes, Ever, Mazatlan	.278	144	24	40	4	1	1	16	4
Martinez, Ray, Obregon	.278	144	21	40	2	1	5	20	4
Rhodes, Karl, Los Mochis	.277	130	28	36	9	3	8	19	12
Phillips, J.R., Culiacan	.274	190	34	52	8	0	17	50	1
Northrup, Kevin, Navojoa	.272	184	28	50	4	0	8	28	5
Carrillo, Matias, Mexicali	.271	192	29	52	8	2	6	25	20
Hosey, Steve, Mazatlan	.271	170	28	46	6	0	8	40	7
Gil, Benji, Culiacan	.270	185	47	50	7	3	9	29	15
#Flores, Miguel, Hermosillo	.267	210	39	56	14	1	4	17	12
#Velasquez, Guillermo, Cul	.225	187	26	42	8	0	10	54	0

INDIVIDUAL PITCHING LEADERS
(Minimum 28 Innings)

	W	L	ERA	G	SV	IP	H	BB	SO
Marquez, Isidro, Mexicali	8	1	1.02	25	13	35	20	18	25
Osuna, Antonio, Hermosillo	3	0	1.47	24	11	31	15	14	38
Garcia, Mike, Mazatlan	4	1	1.67	13	1	38	28	10	15
Acosta, Aaron, Mazatlan	7	1	1.69	22	3	59	35	21	46
Garibay, Daniel, Hermosillo	1	1	1.78	11	0	30	21	8	21
Vosberg, Ed, Los Mochis	8	2	1.95	11	0	78	60	28	75
Heredia, Hector, Navojoa	6	3	2.25	12	0	76	71	36	41
Palafox, Juan, Mazatlan	6	0	2.27	12	1	71	49	28	29
Bauer, Matt, Obregon	7	0	2.43	28	0	33	17	25	23
Vazquez, Adrian, Navojoa	0	1	2.43	14	0	30	19	17	12
Heredia, Gil, Hermosillo	5	1	2.49	12	0	69	54	15	55
Cruz, Javier, Guasave	1	2	2.54	22	0	28	25	9	19
Higuera, Ted, Guasave	4	3	2.61	8	0	52	37	21	37
Ruiz, Cecelio, Obregon	6	4	2.65	12	0	85	70	29	38
Osuna, Roberto, Mexicali	3	0	2.66	19	1	44	35	30	28
Valenzuela, Fernando, Navojoa	3	5	2.67	12	0	78	59	30	53
Hernandez, Jose, Culiacan	2	0	2.68	27	1	37	27	11	19
Sanchez, Hector, Guasave	1	1	2.74	21	0	43	38	22	27
#Palacios, Vicente, Mexicali	5	2	3.42	11	0	76	61	33	87

Nilsson Sparks Waverley To Second Title

The Waverley Reds became the first team in Australian Baseball League history to win two championships, beating the Perth Heat to capture the 1994-95 title.

The Reds, sixth-place finishers in 1993-94, won the regular-season title by winning 15 of their last 16 games, all on the road, to overtake Perth. Waverley then beat the Heat in the best-of-3 final series in two games, clinching the title with a 5-2 win behind the complete-game pitching of Phil Dale.

Dale, who formerly pitched and managed in the Cincinnati Reds system, restricted a powerful Heat lineup to four hits. He was named the championship series MVP.

The 32-year-old righthander also was selected the league's pitcher of the year. He went 12-2 with a 2.76 ERA in the regular season.

Waverley, which has a partial working agreement with the Atlanta Braves, was the ABL's first champion, in 1989-90.

Righthander Dirk Blair (Braves) pitched an outstanding game in the championship opener for Waverley, winning 5-1. Pitching at home, he went all nine innings and gave up six hits in winning his eighth straight decision.

"That was an absolute masterpiece," Reds manager Paul Runge (Braves)

Dave Nilsson

said. "You couldn't have asked for a better script to the story. It was as good an effort as he's given us all year."

Blair was matched against the Heat's Graeme Lloyd (Brewers), who also went the route. Lloyd allowed seven hits, including a two-run single to Milwaukee teammate David Nilsson that gave the Reds a 3-0 lead.

It was Nilsson's third championship with three different clubs. He was part of the Daikyo Dolphins team that won in 1992, then played third base and caught for the Brisbane Bandits in '94. He moved to the Reds prior to the 1994-95 season when he purchased a 25 percent interest in the team and was signed to a lifetime contract.

Nilsson had another strong season Down Under, winning the batting title while hitting .388. But winter ball was costly for Nilsson, who missed the first two months of the 1995 major league season after contracting Ross River Fever, a mosquito-borne virus unique to his native country.

If not for Nilsson, Perth outfielder Scott Metcalf would have captured the league's triple crown. Metcalf, a former Baltimore farmhand, set a new ABL record with 22 home runs, and also led the league with 67 RBIs while finishing second with a .365 average.

—JAMES BAILEY

STANDINGS

	W	L	PCT	GB
Waverley Reds	44	14	.759	—
Perth Heat	45	18	.714	1 ½
Sydney Blues	34	27	.557	11 ½
East Coast Cougars	33	28	.541	12 ½
Adelaide Giants	32	30	.516	14
Brisbane Bandits	26	34	.433	19
Melbourne Monarchs	27	36	.429	19 ½
Canberra Bushrangers	18	42	.300	27
Hunter Eagles	17	47	.266	30

PLAYOFFS—Semifinals: Perth defeated East Coast 2-0, and Waverley defeated Sydney 2-1, in best-of-3 series. **Finals:** Waverley defeated Perth, 2-0, in best-of-3 final.

INDIVIDUAL BATTING LEADERS
(Minimum 90 Plate Appearances)

	AVG	AB	R	H	2B	3B	HR	RBI	SB
Hinton, Steve, Brisbane	.403	144	46	58	9	4	12	41	10
Nilsson, Dave, Waverley	.388	160	41	62	12	1	16	56	7
Metcalf, Scott, Perth	.365	208	47	76	14	0	22	67	4
Tunkin, Scott, Sydney	.343	181	49	62	9	0	18	52	5
Bartee, Kimera, Perth	.328	198	57	65	5	1	15	38	26
Redington, Tom, East Coast	.324	176	31	57	8	0	3	39	1
Scott, Andrew, Adelaide	.322	171	34	55	8	1	10	34	2
Buckthorpe, David, Melbourne	.321	193	46	62	15	0	16	40	6
Sheldon-Collins, Simon, Wav	.319	185	30	59	7	2	4	37	8
Edmondson, Gavin, Perth	.316	171	46	54	11	2	8	30	5
Johnson, Ron, Brisbane	.315	184	37	58	14	0	15	55	2
Carothers, Ron, Melbourne	.315	181	33	57	11	0	7	29	6
Blum, Geoff, Hunter	.314	172	34	54	8	1	9	33	3
Jones, Sean, Perth	.312	186	38	58	14	0	17	39	2
LeGrand, Todd, Hunter	.310	168	32	52	10	0	9	24	2
Everingham, Matt, Canberra	.310	142	27	44	8	0	12	26	2
White, Gary, Sydney	.308	182	30	56	14	0	9	35	1
Adamson, Tony, Perth	.304	184	41	56	9	0	10	34	4
Wright, Nolan, Hunter	.303	155	21	47	7	0	14	40	1
Roberts, Lonell, Sydney	.302	212	50	64	11	7	8	23	33
Buckley, Matt, East Coast	.302	129	17	39	2	1	2	14	3
MacDonald, Ken, Brisbane	.302	169	18	51	8	0	9	36	5
Clarkson, David, Waverley	.302	179	34	54	12	0	10	45	5
Nichols, Todd, Hunter	.299	144	31	43	5	0	18	28	2
Vagg, Richard, Melbourne	.296	206	39	61	13	3	5	28	7
#Thompson, Stuart, East Coast	.293	198	28	58	17	0	5	39	2
#Holland, Tim, Perth	.291	199	57	58	8	6	15	43	9

INDIVIDUAL PITCHING LEADERS
(Minimum 30 Innings)

	W	L	ERA	G	SV	IP	H	BB	SO
Martinez, Jesus, Adelaide	6	8	2.17	15	0	87	69	45	88
Lloyd, Graeme, Perth	5	2	2.27	10	2	48	33	6	38
Radcliff, Brendan, Waverley	3	2	2.56	26	2	32	27	14	23
Dale, Phil, Waverley	12	2	2.76	17	2	101	104	19	75
Cederblad, Brett, East Coast	6	5	2.77	16	0	91	86	25	73
Lane, Aaron, Perth	3	3	2.93	19	3	40	42	32	28
Standish, Scott, Canberra	1	2	3.00	7	0	30	26	18	42
Walters, Brett, Perth	7	2	3.02	11	1	45	42	19	19
Eissens, Simon, Perth	8	1	3.24	14	1	67	59	18	44
Keling, Korey, East Coast	9	2	3.26	17	0	94	61	51	93
White, David, Canberra	6	8	3.50	18	1	108	106	17	75
Bennett, Shayne, East Coast	3	6	3.63	22	1	74	70	24	56
Jacobbson, Peter, Melbourne	7	7	3.82	16	0	99	85	41	71
Blair, Dirk, Waverley	12	3	3.93	15	0	92	87	16	57
Meagher, Adrian, East Coast	4	4	3.96	15	0	61	61	13	51
Nilsson, Bob, East Coast	6	4	3.98	24	8	32	26	17	20
Feledyk, Kris, Sydney	6	5	4.00	13	0	81	68	27	58
Boothby, John, Brisbane	6	5	4.04	18	0	85	87	26	53
Stull, Everett, Hunter	6	7	4.04	17	0	85	59	49	119
Conner, Scott, Perth	7	3	4.12	15	0	63	47	51	51
#Brandow, Derek, Sydney	8	7	4.38	15	0	88	64	42	119
#Jones, Ross, Melbourne	3	5	5.29	23	9	32	50	7	12

Jordan Stimulates Attendance Increase

The 1994 Arizona Fall League season was in jeopardy of being canceled when the players' strike hit and major league owners were looking for ways to cut back on expenses. But the show went on, and thanks to the presence of Michael Jordan, fans poured out in record numbers.

Jordan, who attracted large crowds while playing for the Double-A Birmingham Barons in 1994, hit .252 for the Scottsdale Scorpions and helped the league break its attendance record two weeks into its nine-week schedule. The league averaged 500 fans per game, up from 233 in 1993.

A specially arranged Scottsdale-Tempe game played in Tucson drew a record crowd of 7,836, though some fans were disappointed when Jordan was the DH and didn't play in the field.

Despite leading the league in attendance, the Scorpions finished six games behind the league-champion Peoria Javelinas in the Northern Division. The Mesa Saguaros ran away with the Southern Division, finishing 12 games ahead of the Chandler Diamondbacks.

Peoria made short work of the Saguaros in the playoffs, sweeping them in two games to capture the third AFL championship. Righthander Don Wengert pitched five shutout innings as the starter to win the second game.

The league's No. 1 prospect, as determined by a vote of managers, was Peoria outfielder Ruben Rivera (Yankees), who had never played higher than Class A. Most players in the league had at least Double-A experience.

Rivera hit only .236 but held his own, impressing managers with his speed and power.

"I've been in pro ball for 22 years and I've seen Hall of Famers, and he is the best talent I've seen," said Peoria skipper John Stearns. "But he's got to go out and do it."

—JAMES BAILEY

STANDINGS

NORTH	W	L	PCT	GB
Peoria Javelinas	32	19	.627	—
Scottsdale Scorpions	26	25	.510	6
Sun Cities Solar Sox	22	28	.440	9 ½

SOUTH	W	L	PCT	GB
Mesa Saguaros	32	18	.640	—
Chandler Diamondbacks	20	30	.400	12
Tempe Rafters	19	31	.380	13

Championship Series: Peoria defeated Mesa, 2-0, in best-of-3 final.

MANAGERS: Chandler—Lamar Johnson (Brewers). **Mesa**—Jerry Manuel (Expos). **Peoria**—John Stearns (Reds). **Scottsdale**—Terry Francona (White Sox). **Sun Cities**—Brian Graham (Indians). **Tempe**—Ken Macha (Angels).

TOP 10 PROSPECTS (Selected by league managers): **1.** Ruben Rivera, of, Peoria. **2.** Nomar Garciaparra, ss, Scottsdale. **3.** Derek Jeter, ss, Chandler. **4.** Desi Relaford, ss, Peoria. **5.** Brian Hunter, of, Mesa. **6.** Mark Grudzielanek, ss, Mesa. **7.** Stacy Hollins, rhp, Peoria. **8.** Dan Serafini, lhp, Chandler. **9.** Ron Villone, lhp, Peoria. **10.** Marty Cordova, of, Chandler.

INDIVIDUAL BATTING LEADERS
(Minimum 135 Plate Appearances)

	AVG	AB	R	H	2B	3B	HR	RBI	SB
Grudzielanek, Mark, Mesa	.365	148	26	54	8	3	1	32	5
Nevers, Tom, Mesa	.359	142	27	51	8	2	1	18	0
Jones, Dax, Chandler	.353	133	25	47	6	3	2	20	4
Garciaparra, Nomar, Scottsdale	.328	131	24	43	4	2	1	14	8
Kieschnick, Brooks, Mesa	.319	166	20	53	13	0	6	33	1
Randa, Joe, Scottsdale	.318	132	18	42	8	1	2	22	1
Carter, Michael, Mesa	.313	144	31	45	5	4	1	9	6
Relaford, Desi, Peoria	.309	178	37	55	4	1	2	18	21
Cordova, Marty, Chandler	.307	166	25	51	12	1	3	28	4
Snopek, Chris, Scottsdale	.303	145	26	44	10	1	5	26	0

INDIVIDUAL PITCHING LEADERS
(Minimum 40 Innings)

	W	L	ERA	G	SV	IP	H	BB	SO
Hancock, Lee, Chandler	2	1	2.20	9	0	41	40	8	24
Hollins, Stacy, Peoria	7	1	2.38	9	0	45	31	12	37
Person, Robert, Sun Cities	3	1	2.66	14	2	41	27	19	39
Bochtler, Doug, Sun Cities	4	2	2.70	10	0	50	33	37	44
Sackinsky, Brian, Scottsdale	3	1	2.74	10	0	43	35	7	27
Eischen, Joey, Mesa	1	1	3.29	10	0	41	40	21	30
Myers, Mike, Chandler	2	2	3.51	11	0	49	49	16	28
Baker, Scott, Peoria	2	1	3.59	10	0	43	53	16	20

CHANDLER

BATTING

	AVG	AB	R	H	2B	3B	HR	RBI	SB
5 Beamon, Trey, of	.269	104	11	28	5	0	0	5	1
5 Cordova, Marty, of	.307	166	25	51	12	1	3	28	4
7 Hinds, Robert, 2b	.176	51	5	9	1	0	0	4	0
2 Jensen, Marcus, c	.278	79	10	22	4	0	1	8	0
7 Jeter, Derek, ss	.278	54	11	15	3	1	0	9	2
3 Johnson, Charles, c-dh	.232	95	9	22	6	0	3	12	0
2 Jones, Dax, of	.353	133	25	47	6	3	2	20	4
5 Kendall, Jason, c	.307	88	8	27	6	1	1	16	1
7 Luke, Matt, of-1b	.228	127	11	29	4	4	2	17	7
3 Milliard, Ralph, 2b	.265	102	18	27	5	1	1	16	7
6 Raabe, Brian, ss-2b	.229	170	19	39	7	2	1	17	2
4 Saunders, Chris, 3b	.267	131	16	35	7	0	0	14	0
1 Singleton, Duane, of	.301	163	31	49	7	4	0	9	12
5 Stahoviak, Scott, 1b-3b	.301	93	18	28	6	3	0	13	0
1 Talanoa, Scott, 1b	.260	123	15	32	9	1	3	20	2

PITCHING

	W	L	ERA	G	SV	IP	H	BB	SO
1 Browne, Byron	1	4	6.11	10	0	35	35	28	21
5 Christiansen, Jason	0	0	3.86	13	0	21	22	4	14
3 Darensbourg, Victor	4	2	7.82	16	0	25	43	15	8
6 Gandarillas, Gus	1	1	2.63	16	5	27	27	8	14
5 Hancock, Lee	2	1	2.20	9	0	41	40	8	24
1 Karl, Scott	1	3	4.25	17	0	30	40	8	14
1 Kloek, Kevin	2	3	3.46	14	0	26	28	8	16
5 Konuszewski, Dennis	0	2	3.96	16	4	25	24	13	12
3 Long, Steve	2	4	5.51	15	0	33	30	21	27
3 Myers, Mike	2	2	3.51	11	0	49	49	16	28
3 Petersen, Matt	1	4	7.11	10	0	38	47	18	20
5 Pisciotta, Marc	0	2	6.86	14	0	21	19	26	7
6 Serafini, Dan	2	3	5.75	9	0	36	46	15	14
6 Watkins, Scott	1	0	4.28	16	1	27	29	6	21

Property of Brewers (1), Giants (2), Marlins (3), Mets (4), Pirates (5), Twins (6), Yankees (7).

MESA

BATTING

	AVG	AB	R	H	2B	3B	HR	RBI	SB
3 Ayrault, Joe, c	.242	95	11	23	5	0	1	8	0
1 Ball, Jeff, 2b-1b	.233	43	7	10	2	1	1	10	0
4 Carter, Michael, of	.313	144	31	45	5	4	1	9	6
4 Glanville, Doug, of	.299	164	31	49	8	1	3	19	13
3 Graffanino, Tony, 2b	.211	90	11	19	1	2	1	16	4
1 Groppuso, Mike, 3b-1b	.237	38	3	9	2	0	2	8	0
5 Grudzielanek, Mark, ss-2b	.365	148	26	54	8	3	1	32	5
1 Hunter, Brian, of	.257	171	30	44	6	1	2	21	11
4 Kieschnick, Brooks, 1b	.319	166	20	53	13	0	6	33	1
6 Luce, Roger, c	.244	86	5	21	5	0	0	12	0

	AVG	AB	R	H	2B	3B	HR	RBI	SB
1 Nevers, Tom, 3b-2b	.359	142	27	51	8	2	1	18	0
1 Nevin, Phil, 3b	.293	41	8	12	3	0	0	9	0
4 Petersen, Chris, ss-2b	.214	98	10	21	1	2	0	14	2
5 Pride, Curtis, dh-of	.299	164	41	49	8	2	5	33	11
6 Sagmoen, Marc, of	.337	95	14	32	9	2	0	10	0

PITCHING	W	L	ERA	G	SV	IP	H	BB	SO
4 Adams, Terry	6	0	3.90	20	1	28	26	25	18
3 Brock, Chris	3	2	2.33	11	0	39	30	10	25
3 Clontz, Brad	1	1	2.55	18	8	18	14	9	15
5 Eischen, Joey	1	1	3.29	10	0	41	40	21	30
1 Gardner, Chris	3	2	3.63	20	0	35	26	14	9
5 Gentile, Scott	3	3	2.88	20	1	25	19	9	9
2 Gray, Dennis	3	1	1.69	19	1	27	19	13	30
1 Henderson, Rod	1	1	3.89	9	0	37	39	11	19
1 Holt, Chris	1	1	4.50	6	0	26	29	6	8
3 Koller, Jerry	1	1	6.37	9	0	35	44	19	12
4 Smith, Ottis	1	1	2.59	21	0	24	26	9	9
5 Thobe, J.J	5	1	2.92	21	3	37	36	6	15
3 Wade, Terrell	1	2	4.54	10	0	42	40	22	43
2 Weber, Ben	2	1	8.03	13	0	25	31	12	13

Property of Astros (1), Blue Jays (2), Braves (3), Cubs (4), Expos (5), Rangers (6).

PEORIA

BATTING	AVG	AB	R	H	2B	3B	HR	RBI	SB
5 Dismuke, Jamie, 1b	.230	139	18	32	5	0	6	25	0
4 Eason, Tommy, c	.317	60	9	19	6	0	3	9	0
6 Fox, Andy, of-inf	.272	158	31	43	11	1	7	41	9
1 Geisler, Phil, dh-of	.285	123	20	35	7	1	1	22	2
1 Giambi, Jason, 3b	.283	113	17	32	9	1	2	21	0
4 Holifield, Rick, of	.297	148	34	44	2	4	2	22	24
2 Hughes, Bobby, c	.381	21	6	8	2	0	1	6	0
(2-team 18 Sun Cities)	.234	64	11	15	5	0	2	12	0
1 Lydy, Scott, dh-of	.241	79	19	19	1	0	4	8	2
4 Mouton, Lyle, of	.256	164	24	42	11	1	4	32	3
5 Owens, Eric, 3b-ss	.309	94	15	29	3	2	2	11	10
3 Relaford, Desi, ss-2b	.309	178	37	55	4	1	2	18	21
4 Rivera, Ruben, of	.236	161	31	38	3	4	7	24	14
4 Sefcik, Kevin, 2b	.303	142	24	43	6	2	0	12	9
2 Stefanski, Mike, c	.266	79	11	21	6	0	3	15	0
3 Widger, Chris, c	.254	63	8	16	0	1	3	13	0

PITCHING	W	L	ERA	G	SV	IP	H	BB	SO
1 Baker, Scott	2	1	3.59	10	0	43	53	16	20
5 Courtright, John	1	1	3.95	10	0	43	54	13	22
6 Dunbar, Matt	1	2	3.32	23	2	19	18	8	18
5 Ferry, Mike	4	0	4.32	10	0	42	50	10	13
5 Grott, Matt	1	2	2.48	16	1	36	25	11	26
4 Hill, Eric	1	0	4.91	10	0	18	15	12	19
1 Hollins, Stacy	7	1	2.38	9	0	45	31	12	37
3 Mecir, Jim	2	2	3.91	16	0	25	29	9	19
4 Mitchell, Larry	1	5	5.26	10	0	39	40	21	24
2 Phillips, Tony	3	1	1.89	23	1	33	27	3	15
5 Sullivan, Scott	1	1	5.09	16	3	18	24	7	13
1 Villone, Ron	3	1	2.57	17	6	21	18	11	26
1 Wengert, Don	2	1	2.38	18	2	34	36	4	20
3 Williams, Jeff	3	1	6.23	12	0	30	31	15	18

Property of Athletics (1), Brewers (2), Mariners (3), Phillies (4), Reds (5), Yankees (6).

SCOTTSDALE

BATTING	AVG	AB	R	H	2B	3B	HR	RBI	SB
5 Fryman, Troy, 1b-of	.208	96	10	20	4	0	0	11	2
3 Garciaparra, Nomar, ss	.328	131	24	43	4	2	1	14	8
2 Goodwin, Curtis, of	.250	160	18	40	6	3	1	12	9
4 Halter, Shane, 2b	.289	121	17	35	6	4	1	20	1
5 Jordan, Michael, of-dh	.252	123	24	31	4	1	0	8	6
1 McKeel, Walt, c	.291	55	5	16	5	0	0	3	0
2 Ochoa, Alex, of	.279	140	18	39	10	0	1	16	6
4 Randa, Joe, 3b-1b	.318	132	18	42	8	1	2	22	1
3 Rappoli, Paul, of	.263	95	18	25	8	2	1	15	1
5 Snopek, Chris, 3b-ss	.303	145	26	44	10	1	5	26	0
5 Sutton, Larry, 1b	.261	138	18	36	5	3	4	13	1
5 Tremie, Chris, c	.246	69	5	17	3	0	1	12	0
4 Tucker, Mike, of-dh	.244	131	19	32	9	3	1	16	5
1 Wilson, Craig, 2b-ss	.296	125	15	37	9	2	0	18	0
2 Zaun, Gregg, c	.232	56	9	13	3	0	0	6	1

PITCHING	W	L	ERA	G	SV	IP	H	BB	SO
3 Bennett, Joel	3	1	1.80	12	0	30	21	9	19
2 Bertotti, Mike	3	2	3.59	9	0	38	33	20	20
2 Borowski, Joe	1	0	6.54	18	1	32	41	14	15
1 Carlson, Dan	1	0	3.79	17	0	36	26	11	25
4 Evans, Bart	0	3	7.78	12	0	20	20	30	10
3 Gamez, Bob	3	0	1.99	21	0	23	20	10	12

	W	L	ERA	G	SV	IP	H	BB	SO
1 Hook, Chris	3	2	4.85	11	0	39	40	13	24
3 Hudson, Joe	1	0	2.53	21	10	21	19	8	11
2 Krivda, Rick	1	5	5.65	10	0	37	44	25	16
4 Myers, Rod	0	2	4.91	19	2	26	28	11	11
1 Pote, Lou	3	5	5.32	11	0	47	58	18	20
5 Ruffcorn, Scott	2	0	6.28	14	1	29	31	15	24
2 Sackinsky, Brian	3	1	2.74	10	0	43	35	7	27
2 Sullivan, Mike	2	4	7.29	21	2	21	28	9	16

Property of Giants (1), Orioles (2), Red Sox (3), Royals (4), White Sox (5).

SUN CITIES

BATTING	AVG	AB	R	H	2B	3B	HR	RBI	SB
5 Bates, Jason, 3b-ss	.247	150	23	37	6	2	3	11	3
4 Bush, Homer, 2b	.218	78	6	17	0	1	0	7	3
1 Butler, Rich, of	.269	130	18	35	3	3	2	16	2
4 Curtis, Randy, of-dh	.227	128	16	29	5	3	4	24	6
2 Giles, Brian, of	.282	142	24	40	8	2	5	17	3
4 Holbert, Ray, dh-ss	.136	22	2	3	0	1	0	2	0
3 Huskey, Butch, 3b-of	.286	161	29	46	14	3	4	23	5
2 Jackson, Damian, ss	.178	129	15	23	4	0	1	9	6
2 Mitchell, Tony, of-dh	.256	86	9	22	6	1	1	9	0
4 Mulligan, Sean, c	.270	111	13	30	8	0	0	15	0
1 Steverson, Todd, of	.255	98	16	25	2	2	2	13	1
2 Stynes, Chris, 2b	.245	155	17	38	9	2	3	20	2
5 Tatum, Jimmy, 1b-c	.265	136	25	36	3	1	7	19	1
1 Weinke, Chris, 1b	.193	119	15	23	4	0	3	16	0

PITCHING	W	L	ERA	G	SV	IP	H	BB	SO
4 Beckett, Robbie	1	2	5.16	21	2	30	23	31	30
4 Bochtler, Doug	4	2	2.70	10	0	50	33	37	44
5 Burke, John	0	0	9.39	3	0	8	11	8	6
2 Carter, John	0	1	3.75	5	0	24	21	10	16
2 Crawford, Carlos	0	3	5.16	6	0	23	26	7	8
2 Embree, Alan	0	0	2.00	15	0	18	16	15	16
2 Harris, Pep	2	3	6.16	8	0	19	16	13	11
3 Hiljus, Erik	2	2	6.65	10	0	46	42	38	33
4 Kroon, Marc	0	2	6.75	2	0	8	9	2	9
2 Logsdon, Kevin	1	0	6.07	8	0	13	17	6	9
4 Loiselle, Rich	1	0	7.07	5	0	14	23	5	3
5 Pedraza, Rodney	3	2	6.55	9	0	44	63	17	16
3 Person, Robert	3	1	2.66	14	2	41	27	19	39
3 Rogers, Bryan	1	0	3.18	3	1	6	4	2	7
3 Sellers, Jeff	0	2	11.25	4	0	8	9	8	8
2 Tam, Jeff	2	3	3.45	24	7	31	30	11	19
2 Viano, Jake	0	3	4.86	20	1	33	35	22	31
5 Voisard, Mark	0	0	1.08	11	0	17	14	7	3
3 Walker, Pete	2	2	5.56	10	0	11	13	7	14

Property of Blue Jays (1), Indians (2), Mets (3), Padres (4), Rockies (5).

TEMPE

BATTING	AVG	AB	R	H	2B	3B	HR	RBI	SB
3 Abbe, Chris, c	.194	62	7	12	3	0	1	10	0
4 Aurilia, Rich, ss	.211	123	15	26	6	0	1	15	1
4 Battle, Allen, of	.270	148	32	40	7	2	4	27	9
2 Bradshaw, Terry, of	.183	131	11	24	2	2	0	7	3
5 Clark, Tony, 1b	.239	159	21	38	6	0	4	28	0
3 Coomer, Ron, 3b	.293	123	18	36	9	3	3	15	0
1 Flora, Kevin, 2b	.333	63	12	21	3	1	0	5	1
1 Grebeck, Brian, 3b-ss	.205	44	3	9	3	0	0	4	2
1 Harkrider, Tim, inf	.269	104	12	28	8	1	0	17	1
2 Higginson, Bob, of-dh	.265	151	29	40	5	3	10	33	3
2 Mabry, John, of-1b	.283	145	21	41	9	2	2	15	3
5 Penn, Shannon, 2b	.247	146	24	36	4	3	2	13	16
4 Ronan, Marc, c	.233	60	5	14	1	0	1	4	1
4 Wilson, Desi, of	.267	101	14	27	7	2	1	10	1
5 Zinter, Alan, dh-c	.194	108	13	21	4	0	1	11	0

PITCHING	W	L	ERA	G	SV	IP	H	BB	SO
2 Barber, Brian	3	6	6.60	11	0	44	49	19	47
5 Blomdahl, Ben	0	0	4.58	20	3	35	42	7	28
2 Buckels, Gary	3	2	2.97	23	1	39	37	13	45
1 Edenfield, Ken	3	1	3.62	22	0	32	30	17	27
4 Geevé, Dave	1	3	4.22	9	0	32	39	9	16
1 Henderson, Ryan	0	1	5.46	20	0	31	38	25	28
1 Holzemer, Mark	3	1	5.40	20	2	20	25	9	18
4 Perez, David	0	6	5.72	12	0	39	51	12	28
3 Prado, Jose	2	2	9.74	10	0	20	36	17	10
3 Pyc, Dave	1	0	4.46	12	0	34	37	8	24
2 Ratekin, Mark	2	3	5.66	11	0	35	41	14	15
1 Schmidt, Jeff	2	0	2.57	10	1	14	10	13	6
5 Stidham, Phil	3	3	3.38	19	2	21	23	10	29
3 VanRyn, Ben	1	4	5.03	10	0	39	48	11	23

Property of Angels (1), Cardinals (2), Dodgers (3), Rangers (4), Tigers (5).

Kauai Slips In Through Back Door

For the second consecutive season, the team with the most wins in Hawaii Winter Baseball did not win the title, despite the league's no-playoff format.

The Kauai Emeralds (29-21) and the Maui Stingrays (30-22) ended in a virtual tie, but the Emeralds were crowned champions based on a better winning percentage. A year earlier, the Hilo Stars edged the Honolulu Sharks, despite winning one less game.

The difference in games played again was caused by rainouts that couldn't be made up during the days alloted for the winter season.

On the last night of the season, Maui defeated Hilo 3-1, giving the Stingrays a ½ game lead—for about an hour. In Honolulu, Emeralds second baseman Hiroki Kokubo ripped a 400-foot home run into a strong wind in the top of the sixth to break a scoreless tie. Kauai went on to win 2-0 and capture the league crown.

Kokubo, who was named league MVP on the strength of a .370 average and nine home runs, was happy to hit his pennant-winning blast in front of Sadaharu Oh, Japan's all-time home run king. Oh managed Kokubo with the Fukuoka Daiei Hawks during the 1995 Japanese season.

Kokubo, 23, wasn't the only Japanese player to excel in Hawaii. Kauai righthander Hidekazu Watanabe won the pitching equivalent of a triple crown, going 8-0 with a 0.98 ERA and 77 strikeouts in 64 innings. Watanabe was expected to be the leader of the Emeralds staff after going 8-4 with a 3.20 ERA for Daiei in 1994.

A year earlier, Ichiro Suzuki used his experience in Hawaii Winter Baseball to catapult himself into stardom in Japan. Ichiro hit .385 for the Orix Blue Wave in 1994 and set a Japanese record with 210 hits.

Like the inaugural season of 1993, players came from leagues all over the globe to play in Hawaii. Japan provided 22 players and they were spread throughout the league. They were joined by nine Koreans, all of whom played for the Honolulu Sharks.

Twelve players from the independent Northern League also made a splash in Hawaii, including home run and RBI champ David Kennedy, who hit .320 with 13 homers and 36 RBIs for Kauai. That performance earned Kennedy an opportunity with the Colorado Rockies and he went on to hit .306 with 22 home runs and 96 RBIs for their Double-A New Haven farm club in 1995.

In addition, the league broke new ground when two members of the all-female Colorado Silver Bullets barnstorming team suited up for the Stingrays.

Five-foot-4, 150-pound righthander Lee Anne Ketchum compiled a 6.75 ERA in nine relief appearances and 5-8, 130-pound first baseman Julie Croteau collected one hit in 12 at-bats while playing flawless defense.

Several major league organizations took advantage of the opportunity to place prospects who were not quite ready for more advanced winter leagues. The Pittsburgh Pirates contributed 10 players to the Emeralds alone, plus minor league manager Trent Jewett.

The second-year league saw attendance rise about 30 percent, to 69,533, but continued to be plagued by rainouts. Hilo had 14 postponements in 27 home dates.

—JAMES BAILEY

STANDINGS

REGULAR SEASON	W	L	PCT	GB
Kauai Emeralds	29	21	.580	—
Maui Stingrays	30	22	.577	—
Honolulu Sharks	21	28	.429	7½
Hilo Stars	17	26	.395	8½

PLAYOFFS: None.

INDIVIDUAL BATTING LEADERS
(Minimum 75 Plate Appearances)

	AVG	AB	R	H	2B	3B	HR	RBI	SB
Kokubo, Hiroki, Kauai	.370	200	32	74	21	2	9	27	5
Kennedy, David, Kauai	.320	147	31	47	11	1	13	36	0
Hanel, Marcus, Kauai	.319	94	10	30	7	2	1	14	1
Myrow, John, Maui	.305	190	26	58	10	0	2	25	5
Leary, Rob, Honolulu	.293	99	18	29	9	0	7	13	0
Luuloa, Keith, Maui	.288	163	26	47	11	2	1	24	1
Boone, Aaron, Honolulu	.288	170	21	49	14	2	2	16	1
Leach, Jalal, Hilo	.275	149	17	41	7	1	3	14	4
Robbins, Lance, Honolulu	.274	124	8	34	8	1	0	13	0
Allensworth, Jermaine, Kauai	.272	169	23	46	15	0	2	19	9
Lim, Soo Hyuk, Honolulu	.261	69	10	18	7	1	1	7	0
Franklin, Micah, Kauai	.258	124	23	32	7	1	5	23	4
Kelly, Pat, Maui	.253	194	24	49	14	2	3	20	3
Muramatsu, Arihito, Kauai	.252	111	12	28	3	0	0	13	6
Carpenter, Bubba, Hilo	.252	135	19	34	6	1	4	9	6
Wilson, Tom, Hilo	.252	139	16	35	12	0	2	15	0
McCracken, Quinton, Maui	.248	165	24	41	9	2	1	23	12
Cranford, Jay, Kauai	.248	161	26	40	8	0	3	23	5
Collier, Lou, Kauai	.246	171	33	42	12	0	5	23	4
Counsell, Craig, Maui	.244	176	22	43	9	3	1	15	6
Hurst, Jimmy, Honolulu	.241	87	10	21	5	1	1	3	2
#Gipson, Charles, Maui	.213	141	17	30	2	1	0	12	12
#DeBerry, Joe, Hilo	.203	128	13	26	4	3	3	13	1

INDIVIDUAL PITCHING LEADERS
(Minimum 25 Innings)

	W	L	ERA	G	SV	IP	H	BB	SO
Aminoff, Matt, Maui	2	1	0.91	16	4	30	19	10	24
Watanabe, Hidekazu, Kauai	8	0	0.98	10	0	64	46	18	77
Ishii, Takashi, Maui	4	2	1.60	11	1	62	42	14	75
Alston, Garvin, Maui	0	1	1.73	19	5	26	10	24	22
Cunnane, Will, Maui	3	2	1.94	8	0	42	32	17	32
Vierra, Joey, Maui	1	2	1.98	20	7	36	23	12	35
#Goldman, Barry, Honolulu	2	1	2.01	19	10	22	17	10	22
Iwasaki, Hisanori, Hilo	4	2	2.14	14	0	34	23	19	35
Hancock, Ryan, Honolulu	4	1	2.29	11	0	59	50	24	48
Imazeki, Masaru, Hilo	2	3	2.33	10	0	39	21	17	43
Bullinger, Kirk, Hilo	2	3	2.45	11	1	48	42	15	43
Bullard, Jason, Kauai	3	3	2.55	9	0	49	39	18	29
Monna, Tetsuhiro, Honolulu	3	3	2.58	11	0	66	52	16	61
Takagi, Kohgi, Kauai	3	0	2.61	13	0	41	45	19	23
Takeshita, Jun, Maui	3	2	2.68	10	0	47	37	11	46
Ward, Bryan, Maui	6	1	2.98	11	0	57	49	21	41
Brewer, Nevin, Kauai	1	3	3.04	21	7	27	24	11	15
Iwamoto, Tsutomu, Hilo	2	0	3.14	16	3	29	28	5	23
Atkinson, Neil, Kauai	3	2	3.25	22	2	28	23	8	27
Sullivan, Dan, Kauai	1	3	3.29	17	1	27	27	15	18
Maeda, Katsuhiro, Maui	4	1	3.34	17	1	35	23	21	42
Peters, Chris, Kauai	3	3	3.43	10	0	42	43	16	26
Kimura, Ryuji, Honolulu	4	6	3.71	13	0	70	71	20	59
Rekar, Bryan, Maui	5	3	3.76	11	0	55	59	12	46
Rawitzer, Kevin, Hilo	1	5	3.92	10	0	44	39	19	35

COLLEGE
BASEBALL

Titans Leave Mark On History By Overwhelming Competition

By JIM CALLIS

When Cal State Fullerton dispatched Southern California 11-5 in the College World Series championship game June 10, the Titans did more than win their third title. They stamped themselves as possibly the best college team of all time.

And Mark Kotsay established himself as almost certainly the best CWS performer ever.

Cal State Fullerton was rarely dazzling beyond its box scores. Its highest draft pick, righthander Jon Ward, went in the eighth round to the St. Louis Cardinals. But few teams have been as efficient.

Ranked No. 15 by Baseball America in the preseason, the Titans beat then top-rated Stanford in their first series of 1995, ascended to No. 1 by the end of February and stayed there for 13 of the season's final 15 weeks.

Prime-Time Performer. Cal State Fullerton's Mark Kotsay broke several CWS records in leading Titans to title.

Fullerton closed the year with 18 consecutive wins, sweeping the Big West Conference tournament, the South Regional and the CWS to finish 57-9.

"I have to admit I felt a little bit like David and Goliath out there," Tennessee coach Rod Delmonico said after Fullerton twice brushed off the Volunteers like lint on its shoulder. "They're an outstanding team, an unbelievable team. I kind of wonder why they lost nine games."

Ted Silva

The last team to exceed Fullerton's .864 winning percentage was Texas A&M, which went 58-9 (.866) in 1989 but failed to advance to Omaha. Only three CWS champions have better marks: Holy Cross (21-3, .875) in 1952, Arizona State (54-8, .871) in 1965 and Texas (56-6, .903) in 1975.

None of those teams played the schedule Fullerton did, certainly not on the road. The Titans played five nonconference games against CWS teams during the regular season, and another 12 against regional

participants (eight of those on the road). By contrast, Arizona State played two nonconference road games during the 1965 regular season. Texas, in 1975, played none.

Those teams also didn't have to contend with today's parity-inducing 11.7 scholarship limit.

Of Fullerton's nine losses, only one was to a team unranked at the time, San Jose State on March 26. Ace Ted Silva struck out 15 but was victimized by five Titans errors in a 6-3 loss.

Greatness was the farthest thing from Fullerton coach Augie Garrido's mind when the team gathered for offseason workouts during the fall of 1994. The mood was one of gloom after four of the five full-time position players and all four starting pitchers had departed from the Titans' 1994 third-place CWS team.

"I got on both recruiters when I saw the first three weeks," Garrido said. "I said, 'This isn't good enough.'"

Even the players didn't sense anything special. Senior first baseman D.C. Olsen, who had made trips to Omaha in 1992 and 1994, said they didn't even expect to go as far as the regionals.

Seven months later, Garrido admitted he was wrong.

"We rebuild fast," he said. "You sit around trying to build a house forever, and then you get it done in a hurry. Hell, I don't know how it happened."

The Mark Kotsay Show

Mark Kotsay happened. After platooning for much of 1994, the sophomore center fielder-lefthander couldn't have done much more in 1995.

Kotsay batted .422 with 18 home runs and 75 RBIs and went 2-1 with a 0.38 ERA and nine saves during the regular season, then drove in five runs and picked up a save as the Titans won the South Regional at Louisiana State. All that was nothing compared to the show he put on in Omaha.

Kotsay gave a preview in 1994, when he went 6-for-13 overall and tied a CWS record with seven RBIs against Florida State. Even those heroics paled in com-

COLLEGE WORLD SERIES

Omaha, Nebraska

June 2-10, 1995

STANDINGS

WEST BRACKET	W	L	RF	RA
Cal State Fullerton	4	0	39	11
Tennessee	2	2	10	25
Stanford	1	2	15	15
Clemson	0	2	4	11

West Bracket Final: Cal State Fullerton 11, Tennessee 0

EAST BRACKET	W	L	RF	RA
Southern California	4	2	54	49
Miami	2	2	27	26
Florida State	1	2	16	22
Oklahoma	0	2	6	12

East Bracket Final: Southern California 7, Miami 3

CHAMPIONSHIP GAME: Cal State Fullerton 11, Southern Cal 5

INDIVIDUAL BATTING LEADERS
(Minimum 15 At-Bats)

	AVG	AB	R	H	2B	3B	HR	RBI	SB
Mark Kotsay, CSF	.563	16	7	9	2	0	3	10	0
Scott Schroeffel, Tenn	.533	15	5	8	1	0	3	4	1
Geoff Jenkins, USC	.500	24	7	12	2	0	4	9	1
Bruce Thompson, Miami	.500	18	4	9	0	1	0	3	2
Rudy Gomez, Miami	.471	17	5	8	2	0	0	3	1
Wes Rachels, USC	.444	18	8	8	1	0	1	6	1
Brian Loyd, CSF	.412	17	3	7	1	0	2	6	0
Tony Miranda, CSF	.412	17	6	7	0	1	2	4	0
D.C. Olsen, CSF	.412	17	5	7	0	0	1	2	0
Greg Walbridge, USC	.391	23	5	9	3	0	2	7	0

INDIVIDUAL PITCHING LEADERS
(Minimum 9 Innings)

	W	L	ERA	G	SV	IP	H	BB	SO
Todd Helton, Tennessee	1	0	1.00	1	0	9	4	2	9
Jonathan Johnson, Fla. St.	1	0	2.00	1	0	9	6	1	5
Ryan Meyers, Tennessee	1	0	2.00	1	0	9	6	2	7
Randy Flores, USC	2	0	2.87	2	0	16	19	4	8
Kyle Peterson, Stanford	1	0	3.00	1	0	9	8	0	7

ALL-TOURNAMENT TEAM

C—Brian Loyd, Cal State Fullerton. **1B**—Doug Mientkiewicz, Florida State. **2B**—Wes Rachels, Southern California. **3B**—Tony Martinez, Cal State Fullerton. **SS**—Alex Cora, Miami. **OF**—J.D. Drew, Florida State; Geoff Jenkins, Southern California; Mark Kotsay, Cal State Fullerton. **DH**—Scott Schroeffel, Tennessee. **P**—Randy Flores, Southern California; Ted Silva, Cal State Fullerton.

Most Outstanding Player—Mark Kotsay, Cal State Fullerton.

CHAMPIONSHIP GAME

Titans 11, Trojans 5

USC	AB	R	H	BI	CSF	AB	R	H	BI
Dawkins cf	4	1	1	1	Miranda lf	4	2	2	2
Cruz dh	3	0	0	0	Ankrum dh	4	2	2	1
Ponchak ph	1	0	0	0	Chatham cf	0	0	0	0
Alvarez ss	4	0	0	0	Kotsay cf-p	4	2	2	5
Jenkins rf	4	2	2	1	Giambi rf	5	0	2	0
JqJones lf	3	1	1	0	Loyd c	5	0	1	0
Moeller c	4	0	1	0	Fraser 2b	4	1	1	0
Walbridge 1b	3	0	0	0	Olsen 1b	4	2	1	0
Carson ph	1	0	1	0	JkJones ss	3	1	0	0
Montoya pr	0	0	0	0	Martinez 3b	3	1	1	3
˙Diaz 3b	4	1	2	3					
Rachels 2b	3	0	0	0					
Totals	**34**	**5**	**8**	**5**	**Totals**	**36**	**11**	**12**	**11**

Southern California		032	000	000—	5
Cal State Fullerton		340	000	40x—	11

E—Alvarez (20), Etherton (1), Walbridge (10), Olsen (13). DP—Cal State Fullerton 1. LOB—Southern California 3, Cal State Fullerton 8. 2B—Diaz (8), Jenkins (15). HR—Dawkins (9), Diaz (9), Jenkins (23), Kotsay 2 (21), Martinez (7), Miranda (12). S—JqJones (7), Ankrum (6), Fraser (12), JkJones (19), Martinez (12).

USC	ip	h	r	er	bb	so	CSF	ip	h	r	er	bb	so
Cooper L	3⅓	7	7	3	1	0	Silva W	7⅓	6	5	2	0	5
Etherton	3⅓	4	0	2	3		Kotsay	1⅔	2	0	0	0	2
Krawczyk	1½	2	0	0	0	0							

WP—Etherton. T—3:01. A—22,027.

Happy Coach. Cal State Fullerton's Augie Garrido didn't like his team's chances, but it convincingly won the '95 national title.

parison to his 1995 performance:

■ In an opening-round 6-5 win over Stanford, Kotsay doubled and scored the tying run, sacrificed to set up the go-ahead run and got the last five outs for his 11th save.

■ In an 11-1 demolition of Tennessee in round two, he sacrificed to set up the first run, hit a grand slam in the second inning to put the game out of reach and added three more singles.

■ In an 11-0 drubbing of the Volunteers in a semifinal rematch, he walked during a seven-run first inning and added an RBI double in the fifth. Proving that he's mortal, Kotsay actually grounded into a double play in the seventh inning.

■ In the championship game, Kotsay essentially decided the outcome with his first two swings. He hit a three-run home run over the 26-foot-high center-field wall in the first inning, then added a two-run bomb to right to snap a 3-3 tie in the second. When Silva's back stiffened, Kotsay came on to record the last five outs.

Afterward, Southern California coach Mike Gillespie called Kotsay "The Messiah." Kotsay was named CWS most outstanding player in the biggest landslide since Reagan '84.

If there's a CWS record Kotsay doesn't own, he probably doesn't want it. He holds the marks for career batting average (.517), slugging percentage (1.103) and grand slams (two), and tied standards for career home runs (four) and championship-game homers (two) and RBIs (five).

About the only thing Kotsay can't do is explain what happens to him when he steps into the batter's box at Rosenblatt Stadium.

"I don't know," he said. "Coming in, I had a lot of confidence from last year. Maybe at the College World Series I'm more focused. Maybe it's a feeling I get."

While professional scouts haven't stamped Kotsay as a cinch first-round pick for the 1996 draft, there's no doubting his talent. He isn't dripping with athletic ability, but he isn't exactly dry either.

"He's not a tools guy," Horton said. "He doesn't have above-average major league power or above-average major league speed and he doesn't throw above average. But if they don't take Mark Kotsay in the first round next year, it's a mistake. He will play in the big leagues.

"What he does have is a way above-average heart, way above-average athletic ability, way above-average hand-eye coordination. He's put on an awesome display in practice and games. He's got things you can't teach. He hits for power, he hits the ball where it's pitched, lefthanders, righthanders, curveballs and changeups. What else can the guy do?

"If Pete Rose were playing college baseball, he wouldn't be a first-round pick either. But he'd still set the major league record for hits."

Coaching Milestones

Wichita State's Gene Stephenson made history May 13 by reaching the 1,000-victory mark faster than any coach in Division I history, which should have come as no surprise. He always has been in a hurry.

A 4-0 shutout of Creighton made Stephenson the 21st man to win 1,000 games, and the first Division I coach to do it in 18 seasons. Texas' Cliff Gustafson, who holds the Division I record for career wins, held the previous mark of 20 seasons.

When Stephenson arrived at Wichita State in March 1977, the Shockers had no team, no players, not much of a field and had to use the football film room as an office. Because he was so anxious to lead a program of his own, those handicaps didn't deter him. Nor did his $8,000 pay cut from his annual $20,000 salary as an Oklahoma assistant, or his mentor, Sooners coach Enos Semore, who thought Stephenson might be making a bad move.

COLLEGE WORLD SERIES
CHAMPIONS, 1947-95

Year	Champion	Coach	Record	Runner-Up	MVP
1947	California*	Clint Evans	31-10	Yale	None selected
1948	Southern Cal	Sam Barry	40-12	Yale	None selected
1949	Texas*	Bibb Falk	23-7	Wake Forest	Charles Teague, 2b, Wake Forest
1950	Texas	Bibb Falk	27-6	Washington St.	Ray VanCleef, of, Rutgers
1951	Oklahoma*	Jack Baer	19-9	Tennessee	Sid Hatfield, 1b-p, Tennessee
1952	Holy Cross	Jack Berry	21-3	Missouri	Jim O'Neill, p, Holy Cross
1953	Michigan	Ray Fisher	21-9	Texas	J.L. Smith, p, Texas
1954	Missouri	Hi Simmons	22-4	Rollins	Tom Yewcic, c, Michigan St.
1955	Wake Forest	Taylor Sanford	29-7	W. Michigan	Tom Borland, p, Oklahoma St.
1956	Minnesota	Dick Siebert	33-9	Arizona	Jerry Thomas, p, Minnesota
1957	California*	George Wolfman	35-10	Penn State	Cal Emery, 1b-p, Penn State
1958	Southern Cal	Rod Dedeaux	35-7	Missouri	Bill Thom, p, Southern Cal
1959	Oklahoma St.	Toby Greene	27-5	Arizona	Jim Dobson, 3b, Oklahoma St.
1960	Minnesota	Dick Siebert	34-7	Southern Cal	John Erickson, 2b, Minnesota
1961	Southern Cal*	Rod Dedeaux	43-9	Oklahoma St.	Littleton Fowler, p, Oklahoma St.
1962	Michigan	Don Lund	31-13	Santa Clara	Bob Garibaldi, p, Santa Clara
1963	Southern Cal	Rod Dedeaux	37-16	Arizona	Bud Hollowell, c, Southern Cal
1964	Minnesota	Dick Siebert	31-12	Missouri	Joe Ferris, p, Maine
1965	Arizona State	Bobby Winkles	54-8	Ohio State	Sal Bando, 3b, Arizona State
1966	Ohio State	Marty Karow	27-6	Oklahoma St.	Steve Arlin, p, Ohio State
1967	Arizona State	Bobby Winkles	53-12	Houston	Ron Davini, c, Arizona State
1968	Southern Cal*	Rod Dedeaux	45-14	S. Illinois	Bill Seinsoth, 1b, Southern Cal
1969	Arizona State	Bobby Winkles	56-11	Tulsa	John Dolinsek, of, Arizona State
1970	Southern Cal	Rod Dedeaux	51-13	Florida State	Gene Ammann, p, Florida St.
1971	Southern Cal	Rod Dedeaux	53-13	S. Illinois	Jerry Tabb, 1b, Tulsa
1972	Southern Cal	Rod Dedeaux	50-13	Arizona State	Russ McQueen, p, Southern Cal
1973	Southern Cal*	Rod Dedeaux	51-11	Arizona State	Dave Winfield, of-p, Minnesota
1974	Southern Cal	Rod Dedeaux	50-20	Miami (Fla.)	George Milke, p, Southern Cal
1975	Texas	Cliff Gustafson	56-6	South Carolina	Mickey Reichenbach, 1b, Texas
1976	Arizona	Jerry Kindall	56-17	E. Michigan	Steve Powers, dh-p, Arizona
1977	Arizona State	Jim Brock	57-12	South Carolina	Bob Horner, 3b, Arizona State
1978	Southern Cal*	Rod Dedeaux	54-9	Arizona State	Rod Boxberger, p, Southern Cal
1979	CS Fullerton	Augie Garrido	60-14	Arkansas	Tony Hudson, p, CS Fullerton
1980	Arizona	Jerry Kindall	45-21	Hawaii	Terry Francona, of, Arizona
1981	Arizona State	Jim Brock	55-13	Oklahoma St.	Stan Holmes, of, Arizona State
1982	Miami (Fla.)*	Ron Fraser	57-18	Wichita State	Dan Smith, p, Miami (Fla.)
1983	Texas*	Cliff Gustafson	66-14	Alabama	Calvin Schiraldi, p, Texas
1984	CS Fullerton	Augie Garrido	66-20	Texas	John Fishel, of, CS Fullerton
1985	Miami (Fla.)*	Ron Fraser	64-16	Texas	Greg Ellena, dh, Miami (Fla.)
1986	Arizona	Jerry Kindall	49-19	Florida State	Mike Senne, of, Arizona
1987	Stanford	Mark Marquess	53-17	Oklahoma St.	Paul Carey, of, Stanford
1988	Stanford	Mark Marquess	46-23	Arizona State	Lee Plemel, p, Stanford
1989	Wichita State	Gene Stephenson	68-16	Texas	Greg Brummett, p, Wichita St.
1990	Georgia	Steve Webber	52-19	Oklahoma St.	Mike Rebhan, p, Georgia
1991	Louisiana St.*	Skip Bertman	55-18	Wichita State	Gary Hymel, c, Louisiana St.
1992	Pepperdine*	Andy Lopez	48-11	CS Fullerton	Phil Nevin, 3b, CS Fullerton
1993	Louisiana St.	Skip Bertman	53-17	Wichita State	Todd Walker, 2b, Louisiana St.
1994	Oklahoma*	Larry Cochell	50-17	Georgia Tech	Chip Glass, of, Oklahoma
1995	CS Fullerton*	Augie Garrido	57-9	Southern Cal	Mark Kotsay, of-p, CS Fullerton

*Undefeated

Gene Stephenson

"I think, honestly, that everybody thought when I first came to Wichita it probably was a big mistake," said Stephenson, a two-time Baseball America Coach of the Year who won the College World Series in 1989. "I probably dug myself a grave when I

1995 COLLEGE ALL-AMERICA TEAM

Selected by Baseball America

Stanford catcher A.J. Hinch
.366-9-58

Nebraska outfielder Darin Erstad
.410-19-76

FSU righthander Jonathan Johnson
12-3, 2.89

FIRST TEAM

Pos	Player, School	YR	HT	WT	B-T	Hometown	AVG	AB	R	H	2B	3B	HR	RBI	SB
C	A.J. Hinch, Stanford	Jr.	6-1	200	R-R	Midwest City, Okla.	.366	238	61	87	21	6	9	58	13
1B	Todd Helton, Tennessee	Jr.	6-2	190	L-L	Knoxville, Tenn.	.407	258	86	105	27	4	20	92	11
2B	Marlon Anderson, South Alabama	Jr.	5-10	190	L-R	Prattville, Ala.	.362	246	60	89	18	3	7	46	31
3B	Clint Bryant, Texas Tech	Jr.	6-0	175	R-R	Lubbock, Texas	.422	258	91	109	24	4	16	93	25
SS	Mark Bellhorn, Auburn	Jr.	6-1	196	B-R	Oviedo, Fla.	.342	243	66	83	18	5	12	60	11
OF	Jose Cruz, Rice	Jr.	6-0	190	B-R	Houston	.377	223	77	84	17	2	16	76	19
OF	Darin Erstad, Nebraska	Jr.	6-2	195	L-L	Jamestown, N.D.	.410	251	84	103	20	7	19	76	11
OF	Geoff Jenkins, Southern Calif.	Jr.	6-1	200	L-R	Rancho Cordova, Calif.	.399	258	75	103	15	3	23	78	14
DH	Mark Kotsay, Cal State Fullerton	So.	6-0	180	L-R	Santa Fe Springs, Calif.	.422	263	85	111	20	5	21	90	15

Pos	Player, School	YR	HT	WT	B-T	Hometown	W	L	ERA	G	SV	IP	H	BB	SO
P	Jonathan Johnson, Florida State	Jr.	6-0	180	R-R	Ocala, Fla.	12	3	2.89	19	0	134	98	53	130
P	Matt Morris, Seton Hall	Jr.	6-5	210	R-R	Montgomery, N.Y.	10	3	2.68	14	0	94	64	54	104
P	Kyle Peterson, Stanford	Fr.	6-3	190	R-R	Omaha	14	1	2.96	20	1	143	129	35	112
P	Mark Redman, Oklahoma	Jr.	6-5	215	L-L	Del Mar, Calif.	15	3	2.22	20	0	142	109	35	158
P	Ted Silva, Cal State Fullerton	Jr.	6-1	170	R-R	Redondo Beach, Calif.	18	1	2.83	29	6	153	140	35	142

SECOND TEAM

Pos	Player, School	YR	HT	WT	B-T	Hometown	AVG	AB	R	H	2B	3B	HR	RBI	SB
C	Javier Flores, Oklahoma	So.	5-11	170	R-R	Broken Arrow, Calif.	.360	211	52	76	14	1	10	55	4
1B	Sean Casey, Richmond	Jr.	6-4	205	L-R	Pittsburgh	.461	193	63	89	26	1	14	70	2
2B	Jason Totman, Texas Tech	Sr.	6-0	175	R-R	McPherson, Kan.	.435	214	77	93	24	5	5	53	9
3B	Jeff Liefer, Long Beach State	Jr.	6-3	195	L-R	Upland, Calif.	.354	237	63	84	16	1	13	56	14
SS	Jason Adams, Wichita State	Sr.	5-11	185	R-R	Wichita, Kan.	.398	266	82	106	25	4	16	82	17
OF	David Dellucci, Mississippi	Sr.	5-10	180	L-L	Baton Rouge, La.	.410	229	67	94	15	6	17	63	31
OF	Shane Monahan, Clemson	Jr.	6-0	200	L-R	Marietta, Ga.	.388	273	82	106	22	5	12	52	21
OF	Mark Wulfert, New Mexico	Sr.	5-10	165	R-R	Farmington, N.M.	.438	201	63	88	24	4	15	80	39
DH	Steve Hacker, SW Missouri State	Jr.	6-5	233	R-R	St. Louis	.409	235	63	96	18	0	37	95	2

Pos	Player, School	YR	HT	WT	B-T	Hometown	W	L	ERA	G	SV	IP	H	BB	SO
P	Darin Blood, Gonzaga	Jr.	6-2	185	L-R	Post Falls, Idaho	13	3	2.57	16	0	119	92	46	145
P	Jamey Price, Mississippi	Sr.	6-7	205	R-R	Pine Bluff, Ark.	11	6	1.72	19	0	141	104	16	118
P	Evan Thomas, Florida Int'l	Jr.	5-10	170	R-R	Pembroke Pines, Fla.	15	2	1.70	20	0	127	76	45	146
P	Scott Winchester, Clemson	Jr.	6-1	190	R-R	Midland, Mich.	4	2	0.59	33	14	46	23	16	42
P	David Yocum, Florida State	So.	6-1	180	L-L	Miami	12	3	2.61	18	0	114	94	43	128

THIRD TEAM

C—Brian Loyd, So., Cal State Fullerton. **1B**—David Miller, Jr., Clemson. **2B**—Tom Sergio, So., North Carolina State. **3B**—Casey Blake, Jr., Wichita State. **SS**—Gabe Alvarez, Jr., Southern California. **OF**—Chad Alexander, Jr., Texas A&M; Ryan Christensen, Jr., Pepperdine; Tony Ellison, Jr., North Carolina State. **DH**—Tal Light, Jr., Oklahoma State.

P—R.A. Dickey, So., Tennessee; Mike Drumright, Jr., Wichita State; Ryan Halla, Jr., Auburn; Bryan Link, Sr., Winthrop; Scott Schultz, Sr., Louisiana State.

PLAYER OF THE YEAR

Reluctant Icon Carries Tennessee

Todd Helton, Baseball America's 1995 College Player of the Year and Tennessee's best player ever, did it all.

As the first baseman and No. 3 hitter in the Volunteers' lineup, Helton smacked home runs to all fields, rifled doubles into the gaps and drove in clutch runs. As a closer, he nailed down several of the most important wins in Tennessee history. The Volunteers needed him to start on the mound four times in 1995, and he responded with a complete-game victory each time.

Just don't ask him to admit that he has become an icon in Knoxville.

"People know who I am," said Helton, who was born and raised in Knoxville. "But I'm definitely not a celebrity or anything. It's

Todd Helton

just because I've been around so long in town."

Whether he's willing to admit it or not, the legacy Helton left behind extends beyond his 20 school records.

"Look at the programs around the country," Tennessee coach Rod Delmonico said. "Mississippi State had Rafael Palmeiro and Will Clark. Louisiana State had Albert Belle and Ben McDonald. Our two guys have been R.A. Dickey and Todd Helton. They've taken the program to where it is now."

Long a Southeastern Conference doormat, the Volunteers have had five consecutive winning seasons, culminating in 1995 with their first College World Series appearance in 44 years. Helton carried them to Omaha by batting .407 with 27 doubles, 20 homers and 92 RBIs—narrowly missing an SEC triple

crown—and going 8-2 with a 1.66 ERA and 12 saves on the mound. For the third straight year, Helton was named an All-American and was named MVP of the SEC Eastern Division postseason tournament.

"As a pure baseball player, he's right there at the top of players I've coached," said Delmonico, a former Florida State and Clemson assistant. "As far as athletes, there was Deion Sanders. This guy is just a baseball player. He can do so much to help you win.

"He's really old school. He's not caught up in wearing Oakleys and wristbands and necklaces. He loves to play the game."

That's all Helton wanted to do once he arrived on campus. He never saw himself as the cornerstone of a burgeoning baseball power, didn't care about becoming an icon.

"I really wasn't aware of it," said Helton, who was selected eighth overall in the 1995 draft by the Colorado Rockies. "I just wanted to come in and play as hard as I could. I wanted to set an example, play the game the way I thought it should be played."

Few have played it better in college, none at Tennessee. Helton might play his major league baseball on the other side of the country, but his legend won't be forgotten in Knoxville.

—JIM CALLIS

PREVIOUS WINNERS

1981—**Mike Sodders**, 3b, Arizona State
1982—**Jeff Ledbetter**, of-lhp, Florida State
1983—**Dave Magadan**, 1b, Alabama
1984—**Oddibe McDowell**, of, Arizona State
1985—**Pete Incaviglia**, of, Oklahoma State
1986—**Casey Close**, of, Michigan
1987—**Robin Ventura**, 3b, Oklahoma State
1988—**John Olerud**, 1b-lhp, Washington State
1989—**Ben McDonald**, rhp, Louisiana State
1990—**Mike Kelly**, of, Arizona State
1991—**David McCarty**, 1b, Stanford
1992—**Phil Nevin**, 3b, Cal State Fullerton
1993—**Brooks Kieschnick**, dh-rhp, Texas
1994—**Jason Varitek**, c, Georgia Tech

---

came here. There was no history of success in anything, and they hadn't even had baseball in eight years.

"There was no reason to think it could ever be successful, other than I was young enough and dumb enough. But Enos gave me enough experience at Oklahoma that I was confident I could do something."

Two other Division I coaches achieved their 1,000th victories in 1995.

Bill Freehan

Dave Bingham

Texas Tech's Larry Hays reached the plateau with a 6-4 win over Texas-Arlington on April 12, and Oklahoma's Larry Cochell did so with a 13-9 win over Texas on May 26 in the second round of the Midwest II Regional.

There were few significant coaching moves in 1995,

with the most noteworthy coming late in the summer.

Michigan's Bill Freehan resigned July 19 after going 166-167 record in six seasons, making him the only Wolverines baseball coach ever with a losing record. To be fair, Freehan's main task was to restore integrity.

Bud Middaugh, his predecessor, took the Wolverines to nine regionals and four College World Series before resigning in 1989, when it was learned that he had paid more than $45,000 to 24 players. The baseball team became the first Michigan athletic program to be placed on probation, and the Wolverines were banned from postseason play and had their scholarships reduced for three years.

Trojan Terror. Southern Cal outfielder Geoff Jenkins earned All-America honors, hitting .399 with 23 homers and 78 RBIs.

BILL SETLIFF

Freehan was surprised by the severity of the penalties, which were announced six months after he accepted the job and put a severe handicap on his recruiting ability. While Freehan erased the tarnish of Middaugh, he never could finish higher than a third-place tie in the Big Ten Conference and went 24-30 in 1995, his third straight losing season.

Freehan was replaced by another former major leaguer and Michigan alumnus, Pepperdine pitching coach Geoff Zahn, who was hired Sept. 6.

In contrast to Freehan, Dave Bingham was the most successful coach in Kansas history, leading the Jayhawks to the only two NCAA postseason appearances in the baseball program's 91 years. But after making a surprise trip to the College World Series in 1993 and returning to the regionals in 1994, Kansas went 24-33 in 1995, their worst record in Bingham's eight seasons.

Bingham said the frustrations of the 1995 season contributed to his resignation, which he announced Aug. 4. He described himself as physically exhausted and mentally wiped out, and said he had no definite plans for his future. He went 249-225 with the Jayhawks.

His successor is former Iowa State head coach Bobby Randall, who resigned Sept. 8 to accept the Kansas job. After his five-year big league career with the Minnesota Twins ended, Randall joined the Cyclones as an assistant in 1981. Taking over as head coach in 1985, he posted a 309-311 record in 11 seasons and led Iowa State to a second-place regular-sea-

COACH OF THE YEAR
Tennessee's Delmonico Recognized

Where others saw a moribund program, Rod Delmonico saw an opportunity.

When the Tennessee job came open in 1989, the Volunteers hadn't appeared in the College World Series since 1951, hadn't cracked a national poll since 1970. Lower Hudson Field rarely drew even 500 fans. Television, radio, promotions, baseball camps and a booster club were either primitive or nonexistent.

It was just what Delmonico was looking for. In November 1989, he was named the 20th baseball coach in Tennessee history.

"We didn't have tradition, we didn't have a good facility and we hadn't won," said Delmonico, who had all of those things as an assistant at Florida State. "We had to sell a dream. We thought it would be difficult, but it really wasn't."

It certainly isn't difficult any longer. Delmonico was named Baseball America's 1995 Coach of the Year after a season in which Tennessee finished third in its return to the CWS and set a school record with 54 victories.

Rod Delmonico

The program in no way resembles the one Delmonico inherited. The Volunteers now play in Lindsey Nelson Stadium, a $2.2 million facility with 4,000 seats that has hosted NCAA regional playoffs for three straight years. Tennessee averaged almost 2,000 fans per game for its 42 home dates in 1995.

About 50 games per year are broadcast on radio, and "The Rod Delmonico Show" appears on the SportSouth Cable Network eight times per year. The Famous Chicken made an appearance at Lindsey Nelson Stadium and Delmonico's baseball camps drew 1,300 players in 1995.

Progress came rapidly. After a 28-31 debut, Delmonico guided the Volunteers to a 41-19 record in 1991. Tennessee won its first-ever postseason title in 1993, capturing the Southeastern Conference Eastern Division tournament and advancing to the NCAA playoffs for the first time since 1952. The next year, the Volunteers won their first overall SEC championship since 1951.

In six seasons at Tennessee, Delmonico has gone 255-120 (.680). The consensus in college baseball is that this isn't a surprise given Delmonico's success as a recruiter at Florida State—among his signees were 10 eventual big leaguers—and more of the same should be expected in the future.

—JIM CALLIS

PREVIOUS WINNERS

1981—**Ron Fraser**, Miami
1982—**Gene Stephenson**, Wichita State
1983—**Barry Shollenberger**, Alabama
1984—**Augie Garrido**, Cal State Fullerton
1985—**Ron Polk**, Mississippi State
1986—**Skip Bertman**, Louisiana State
        Dave Snow, Loyola Marymount
1987—**Mark Marquess**, Stanford
1988—**Jim Brock**, Arizona State
1989—**Dave Snow**, Long Beach State
1990—**Steve Webber**, Georgia
1991—**Jim Hendry**, Creighton
1992—**Andy Lopez**, Pepperdine
1993—**Gene Stephenson**, Wichita State
1994—**Jim Morris**, Miami

son finish in 1990, the best in school history.

Cal State Northridge's Bill Kernen stepped down Aug. 31, probably the first time a college baseball coach resigned to become a playwright. Kernen, who went 240-154 in seven years and guided the Matadors to within a game of the College World Series in their first year in Division I in 1991, was accepted into a master's program at Columbia. Northridge promoted assistant coach Mike Batesole to replace him.

Two Programs Bid Farewell

Two Division I schools played their last baseball games in 1995. Stephen F. Austin State and Boston University cut baseball to better comply with Title IX, Congressional legislation enacted in 1972 that provides for equal opportunities throughout the educational system.

Stephen F. Austin State's board of regents decided in August 1994 to drop baseball and add women's soccer. The Lumberjacks went 2-40 in their final season.

Boston University athletic director Gary Strickler informed coach Bill Mahoney March 15 that the school was discontinuing its baseball program at the end of the season. The Terriers finished the year at 2-37.

On the positive side, Temple saved its program. Though Owls athletic director R.C. Johnson recommended that baseball be axed for gender-equity reasons, the program was spared at a December 1994 meeting of the school's board of trustees.

TV Deal Nixed

If not for the major league strike, college baseball might have had its first national television regular-season package since 1989.

John Askins, the Houston-based consultant who handles the television negotiations for a proposed Major College Baseball Alliance, said he had a verbal agreement from CBS to broadcast eight regular-season and two postseason games in 1995. But after the major league postseason was terminated the previous fall, advertisers lost interest and poured their money into the National Football League and other outlets.

"It wasn't the strike, but the cancellation of the playoffs and World Series that killed it," Askins said. "That pretty much poisoned the waters for the sport of baseball."

The last network to broadcast a college baseball game of the week was cable's ESPN in 1989. Over-the-air coverage has been limited to select College World Series by CBS, which began in 1988.

Askins also negotiated with PBS (over-the-air) and Prime Network (cable), but couldn't reach a deal in time for the 1995 season.

FRESHMAN OF THE YEAR

Stanford Pitcher Achieves Dream

Kyle Peterson had modest goals for 1995. He just hoped to pitch well enough to earn a regular spot in the Stanford bullpen.

The Cardinal was returning its top four starters from 1994 and was ranked No. 1 in the preseason. Peterson didn't figure a freshman had a chance to crack the rotation.

In the back of his mind was a fantasy shared by most kids who grow up in the Omaha area. Peterson has attended College World Series games as long as he can remember, sitting in section F behind the first-base dugout, and he dreamed of attending some in uniform before his college career ended.

His dreams became reality, and reality surpassed his dreams. Peterson became the ace of an injury-riddled Stanford staff, led the Cardinal to Omaha by force of will and pitched a complete-game CWS win.

His season numbers made him an easy choice for Baseball America's 1995 Freshman of the Year award: 14-1, 2.96 ERA, 10 complete games in 18 starts, 112 strikeouts in 143 innings. But years from now, the numbers won't be what Peterson remembers.

His thoughts will be of June 5, of the night he was the toast of Omaha. He defeated Clemson 8-3 to give Stanford its only victory of the CWS, allowing eight hits and no walks while striking out seven. The perfor-

Kyle Peterson

mance earned him a large chunk of the front page of the next day's Omaha World-Herald, complete with a huge photo showing him hugging his mother and a caption that read "Hometown Hero."

Using an outstanding change-up and an underrated fastball, Peterson broke Jack McDowell's Stanford record for victories by a freshman and tied Mike Mussina's mark for single-season wins. Peterson's best attribute might be his mound presence, which Cardinal coach Mark Marquess said is better than that of McDowell and Mussina when they were freshmen.

Baseball America's 1995 Freshman All-America first team:

C—Matt LeCroy, Clemson (.333-15-72).
1B—Ross Gload, South Florida (.347-15-78). **2B**—Kris Didion, Tulane (.337-6-45). **3B**—Ryan Hankins, Nevada-Las Vegas (.383-12-49). **SS**—Kip Harkrider, Texas (.300-0-55).
OF—Eric Byrnes, UCLA (.324-9-35, 18 SB); J.D. Drew, Florida State (.325-17-63); Jake Weber, North Carolina State (.326-10-54).
DH—Brad Winget, Brigham Young (.413-11-65).
P—Rocky Biddle, Long Beach State (6-1, 3.74, 108 IP, 122 SO); Eric DuBose, Mississippi State (8-4, 3.28, 113 IP, 109 SO); Jason Grilli, Seton Hall (8-2, 1.85, 78 IP, 63 SO); Kyle Peterson, Stanford (14-1, 2.96, 143 IP, 112 SO); Randy Wolf, Pepperdine (9-1, 2.15, 96 IP, 89 SO).

—JIM CALLIS

PREVIOUS WINNERS

1982—**Cory Snyder**, 3b, Brigham Young
1983—**Rafael Palmeiro**, of, Mississippi St.
1984—**Greg Swindell**, lhp, Texas
1985—**Jack McDowell**, rhp, Stanford
      Ron Wenrich, of, Georgia
1986—**Robin Ventura**, 3b, Oklahoma St.
1987—**Paul Carey**, of, Stanford
1988—**Kirk Dressendorfer**, rhp, Texas
1989—**Alex Fernandez**, rhp, Miami
1990—**Jeffrey Hammonds**, of, Stanford
1991—**Brooks Kieschnick**, rhp-dh, Texas
1992—**Todd Walker**, 2b, Louisiana State
1993—**Brett Laxton**, rhp, Louisiana State
1994—**R.A. Dickey**, rhp, Tennessee

RATINGS PERCENTAGE INDEX (RPI)

The Ratings Percentage Index is the criteria used by the NCAA Division I baseball committee to select and seed teams for the 48-team NCAA tournament. The RPI factors a team's record, strength of schedule and opponents' strength of schedule.

The top 100 teams for 1995:

1. **Cal State Fullerton**	52. Creighton
2. **Clemson***	53. **Lamar**
3. **Auburn***	54. Southern Mississippi
4. **Florida State**	55. George Mason
5. **Miami (Fla.)***	56. Kent State
6. **Tennessee**	57. UNC Greensboro
7. **Alabama***	58. Stetson
8. **Louisiana State***	59. Arkansas State
9. **Southern California**	60. Evansville
10. **Long Beach State***	61. Villanova
11. **Old Dominion**	62. Wake Forest
12. **Texas Tech**	63. Notre Dame
13. **North Carolina***	64. Rider
14. **Richmond***	65. **Pittsburgh**
15. **Oklahoma State**	66. UNC Wilmington
16. **Florida International***	67. **Central Michigan**
17. **Central Florida**	68. Radford
18. **Oklahoma***	69. Baylor
19. **Texas***	70. Santa Clara
20. **Stanford***	71. Northwestern
21. **Wichita State***	72. Akron
22. North Carolina State	73. Houston
23. **South Alabama***	74. Nevada-Las Vegas
24. **James Madison***	75. **Mid. Tennessee St.**
25. **Mississippi***	76. Western Michigan
26. **South Florida**	77. Virginia
27. **Arkansas***	78. **Troy State**
28. **Texas A&M***	79. Tulane
29. **Rice***	80. Virginia Tech
30. **Jacksonville***	81. Northeastern
31. Georgia	82. Penn State
32. Florida	83. Northwestern State
33. **California***	84. **Northeast Louisiana**
34. Arizona State	85. UC Santa Barbara
35. **Fresno State**	86. New Mexico State
36. Seton Hall	87. Kentucky
37. Delaware	88. McNeese State
38. South Carolina	89. **The Citadel**
39. Mississippi State	90. Northern Iowa
40. Nevada	91. Illinois State
41. **Winthrop**	92. Bowling Green
42. **Providence***	93. Siena
43. **Pepperdine**	94. Hawaii
44. **Ohio State**	95. San Diego State
45. **Indiana State**	96. Minnesota
46. **Massachusetts**	97. Cal State Northridge
47. **Georgia Tech***	98. George Washington
48. UNC Charlotte	99. Southeast Missouri St.
49. **SW Missouri State***	100. E. Carolina
50. UCLA	111. **Navy**
51. New Orleans	128. **Pennsylvania**

Boldface indicates selected to 1995 NCAA tournament.
*Selected as an at-large entry.

Based on 1995 RPI rankings for 1996 members, the following conferences have been granted automatic qualification for their 1996 champions (conference RPI rank in parentheses):

Atlantic Coast (2)	Mid-American (16)
Atlantic-10 (18)	Missouri Valley (6)
Big East (11)	North Atlantic (14)
Big Eight (7)	Pacific-10 (8)
Big South (12)	Southeastern (1)
Big Ten (13)	Southland (17)
Big West (4)	Southwest (3)
Colonial (5)	Sun Belt (9)
Conference USA (10)	Trans America (15)

NCAA REGIONALS

ATLANTIC I
Site: Tallahassee, Fla.
Participants: No. 1 Florida State (48-14, Atlantic Coast), No. 2 Mississippi (37-20, at large), No. 3 South Alabama (41-15, at-large), No. 4 Central Florida (48-11, Trans America), No. 5 Old Dominion (37-18, Colonial), No.6 Troy State (27-21, Mid-Continent).
Champion: Florida State (4-0).
Runner-Up: Mississippi (3-2).
Outstanding Player: Doug Mientkiewicz, 1b, Florida State.
Attendance: 17,317.

ATLANTIC II
Site: Coral Gables, Fla.
Participants: No. 1 Miami (42-14, at-large), No. 2 Texas A&M (40-20, at-large), No. 3 North Carolina (37-21, at-large), No.4 South Florida (38-23, Metro), No. 5 Florida International (49-9, at-large), No. 6 Massachusetts (38-12, Atlantic-10).
Champion: Miami (4-1).
Runner-Up: Texas A&M (4-2).
Outstanding Player: Jay Tessmer, rhp, Miami.
Attendance: 17,058.

EAST
Site: Clemson, S.C.
Participants: No. 1 Clemson (50-12, at-large), No. 2 Alabama (39-21, at-large), No. 3 Jacksonville (41-20, at-large), No. 4 Richmond (42-15, at-large), No. 5 Winthrop (39-15, Big South), No. 6 Navy (33-18, Patriot).
Champion: Clemson (4-0).
Runner-Up: Alabama (3-2).
Outstanding Player: Shane Monahan, of, Clemson.
Attendance: 21,352.

MIDWEST
Site: Knoxville, Tenn.
Participants: No. 1 Tennessee (48-14, Southeastern), No. 2 Oklahoma State (43-17, Big Eight), No. 3 California (31-23, at-large), No. 4 Georgia Tech (38-20, at-large), No. 5 Pittsburgh (37-14, Big East), No. 6 The Citadel (39-19, Southern).
Champion: Tennessee (4-0).
Runner-Up: Oklahoma State (3-2).
Outstanding Player: R.A. Dickey, rhp, Tennessee.
Attendance: 18,787.

MIDWEST I
Site: Wichita, Kan.
Participants: No. 1 Texas Tech (48-12, Southwest), No. 2 Wichita State (52-15, at-large), No. 3 Stanford (34-22, at-large), No. 4 Arkansas (38-21, at-large), No. 5 Lamar (36-22, Sun Belt), No. 6 Providence (44-13, at-large).
Champion: Stanford (5-1).
Runner-Up: Texas Tech (3-2).
Outstanding Player: Kyle Peterson, rhp, Stanford.
Attendance: 36,517.

MIDWEST II
Site: Oklahoma City.
Participants: No. 1 Auburn (47-11, at-large), No. 2 Oklahoma (38-14, at-large), No. 3 Texas (42-17, at-large), No. 4 Ohio State (40-21, Big Ten), No. 5 Indiana State (38-21, Missouri Valley), No. 6 Pennsylvania (25-19, Ivy).
Champion: Oklahoma (4-0).
Runner-Up: Auburn (3-2).
Outstanding Player: Ryan Minor, 1b-rhp, Oklahoma.
Attendance: 35,377.

SOUTH
Site: Baton Rouge, La.
Participants: No. 1 Cal State Fullerton (49-9, Big West), No. 2 Louisiana State (45-16, at-large), No. 3 Rice (40-17, at-large), No. 4 James Madison (42-15, at-large), No. 5 Central Michigan (40-17, Mid-American), No. 6 Northeast Louisiana (37-18, Southland).
Champion: Cal-State Fullerton (4-0).
Runner-Up: Rice (3-2).
Outstanding Player: Jack Jones, ss, Cal State Fullerton.
Attendance: 31,815.

WEST
Site: Fresno, Calif.
Participants: No. 1 Southern California (41-18, Pacific-10), No. 2 Long Beach State (35-23, at-large), No. 3 Fresno State (41-20, Western Athletic), No. 4 Pepperdine (34-17, West Coast), No. 5 Southwest Missouri State (37-19, at-large), No. 6 Middle Tennessee State (35-24, Ohio Valley).
Champion: Southern California (4-1).
Runner-Up: Long Beach State (4-2).
Outstanding Player: Brian Cooper, rhp, Southern Cal.
Attendance: 14,875.

COLLEGE BASEBALL

YEAR-BY-YEAR LEADERS

Since 1965

Joe Carter
120 RBIs in 1981

Bob Horner
47 homers in 1977-78

Greg Swindell
19 wins, 204 K's in 1985

Robin Ventura
110 RBIs in 1987

Year	Batting Average*	Home Runs	RBIs	Wins	ERA#	Strikeouts
1965	Rusty Adkins, Clemson .444	Terry Craven, CS Northridge 12	Luis Lagunas, Arizona State 68	Jim Merrick, Arizona State 13	Bruce Aitken, Fla. Southern 0.63	Steve Arlin, Ohio State 165
1966	Jimmy Yawn, Mississippi .408	Dale Ford, Washington St. 17	Eddie Leon, Arizona 75	John Stewart, USC 16	Bill Stoneman, Idaho 0.52	Bill Frost, California 169
1967	Tom Paciorek, Houston .435	Dennis Lamb, Brigham Young 17	Gary Gentry, Arizona State 51	Gary Gentry, Arizona State 17	Jim Johnson, W. Michigan 0.51	Gary Gentry, Arizona St. 229
1968	Ken Paciorek, Cal St. L.A. .440	Larry Romney, Brig. Young 13	John Schroeder, UCSB 60	John Schroeder, UCSB 12	Argo Meza, Loyola (La.) 0.39	Jeff Pryor, Fla. Southern 141
1969	Larry Pyle, Miami .431	Chris Chambliss, UCLA 15	Larry Ray Powell, Arizona St. 73	Larry Gura, Arizona St. 19	Stan Babieracki, St. John's 0.55	Larry Gura, Arizona St. 195
1970	Bob Prokopowicz, UTEP .471	Dan Stoligrosz, USC 14	Gene Ammann, Florida St. 58	Gene Ammann, Florida St. 15	Ron Hastings, East Carolina 0.56	Pat Osburn, Florida St. 154
1971	Glenn Borgmann, So. Alabama .471	Glenn Borgmann, So. Ala. 15	Roger Schmuck, Arizona St. 80	Jay Smith, Fla. Southern 15	Brian Herosian, Conn. 0.63	Burt Hooton, Texas 153
1972	Doug Ault, Texas Tech .473	Fred Lynn, USC 14	Alan Bannister, Arizona St. 90	Craig Swan, Arizona St. 16	Tom Farias, Amer. Int. 0.30	Eddie Bane, Arizona St. 213
1973	Mike Campbell, So. Florida .439	John Stearns, Colorado 15	Dick Harris, Arizona St. 72	Eddie Bane, Arizona St. 15	Roger Hatcher, Richmond 0.47	Eddie Bane, Arizona St. 192
1974	Ron Hassey, Arizona .421	Gene Delyon, Santa Clara 19	Rich Dauer, USC 92	Jim Gideon, Texas 19	Steve Ratzer, St. John's 0.84	Rich Wortham, Texas 135
1975	Randy Diaz-Gonzalez, N.M. St. .449	Jerry Maddox, Arizona St. 20	Jerry Maddox, Arizona St. 86	Jim Gideon, Texas 17	Al Holland, N.C. A&T 0.26	Floyd Bannister, Ariz. St. 217
1976	Ron McNeely, Memphis State .462	2 tied at 23	Ken Landreaux, Arizona St. 93	Floyd Bannister, Arizona St 19	Jack Taylor, Connecticut 0.44	Floyd Bannister, Ariz. St. 213
1977	Glenn Goya, Colorado St. .485	Bob Horner, Arizona State 22	Bob Horner, Arizona St. 87	Don Kainer, Texas 15	Mark Nipp, Oklahoma 0.72	Derek Tatsuno, Hawaii 146
1978	Mike Groh, SUNY Buffalo .464	Bob Horner, Arizona State 25	Chris Bando, Arizona State 102	Ron Meridith, Oral Roberts 14	Larry Brown, Harvard 0.95	Derek Tatsuno, Hawaii 161
1979	Jack Upton, Colorado St. .506	Jim Auten, UCLA 29	Tim Wallach, CS Fullerton 102	Derek Tatsuno, Hawaii 20	Dan Sijer, Washington 0.94	Derek Tatsuno, Hawaii 234
1980	Keith Hagman, New Mexico .551	Rick Siriano, Louisville 24	Mike Davis, Wichita State 98	Neal Heaton, Miami 18	Kevin Quirk, St. Joseph's 1.26	Ken Dayley, Portland 138
1981	Derrell Baker, Ga. Southern .462	Joe Carter, Wichita State 29	Joe Carter, Wichita State 120	Kendall Carter, Arizona St. 19	Jeff Keener, Kentucky 0.51	Neal Heaton, Miami 172
1982	Bill White, The Citadel .474	Jeff Ledbetter, Florida St. 42	Russ Morman, Wichita St. 130	Bryan Oelkers, Wichita St. 18	Kirk Killingsworth, Texas 0.80	Bryan Oelkers, Wichita St. 166
1983	Dave Magadan, Alabama .525	2 tied at 24	Russ Morman, Wichita St. 105	Jim Hickey, Texas-Pan Am 16	David Mills, The Citadel 1.13	Dennis Livingston, Okla. St. 180
1984	Steve Iannini, Georgetown .470	Mark McGwire, USC 32	Pete Incaviglia, Okla. St. 112	John Hoover, Fresno St. 18	Greg Brake, West. Michigan 0.95	John Hoover, Fresno St. 205
1985	Glen McElroy, Iona .472	Pete Incaviglia, Okla. St. 48	Pete Incaviglia, Okla. St. 143	Greg Swindell, Texas 19	Richard Lacko, Long Island 1.30	Greg Swindell, Texas 204
1986	Joe Kesselmark, Pace .487	George Canale, Va. Tech. 29	Robin Ventura, Okla. St. 96	Mike Loynd, Florida State 20	Mike Remlinger, Dartmouth 1.59	Richie Lewis, Florida St. 223
1987	Marteese Robinson, Seton Hall .529	Mike Willes, Brigham Young 31	Robin Ventura, Okla. St. 110	3 tied at 15	Gregg Olson, Auburn 1.26	Andy Benes, Evansville 196
1988	Scott Baerns, Tenn. Tech .476	Mike Willes, Brigham Young 35	Monty Fariss, Oklahoma St. 114	Linty Ingram, Arizona St. 17	Brian Evans, Jacksonville 1.19	Brian Barnes, Clemson 188
1989	Mike Pisacreta, Pace .476	Kevin Lofthus, UNLV 26	Scott Bryant, Texas 112	3 tied at 18	Jim Newlin, Wichita St. 1.08	Brian Barnes, Clemson 208
1990	Don Barbara, Long Beach St. .474	Paul Ellis, UCLA 29	Mike Daniel, Oklahoma St. 92	Joey Hamilton, Ga. South. 18	David Sinnes, Notre Dame 1.05	Steve Wolf, Fresno St. 171
1991	Gene Schall, Villanova .484	Mike Daniel, Oklahoma St. 27	Mike Daniel, Oklahoma St. 107	Kennie Steenstra, Wichita St. 17	Kirk Rueter, Murray St. 1.20	2 tied at 166
1992	Mike Smith, Indiana .490	Mike Smith, Indiana 27	Todd Walker, LSU 95	Mike Romano, Tulane 17	David Hawkins, Nicholls St. 1.38	Kenny Kendrena, CS North. 176
1993	Dickie Woodridge, LeMoyne .476	Ryan McGuire, UCLA 26	Daniel Choi, Long Beach St. 102	Daniel Choi, Long Beach St. 17	Brian Anderson, Wright St. 1.14	John Powell, Auburn 191
1994	Adrian Price, Coppin State .474	2 tied at 26	Jay Payton, Georgia Tech 102	R.A. Dickey, Tennessee 15	Danny Graves, Miami 0.89	Brad Rigby, Georgia Tech. 184
1995	Sean Casey, Richmond .461	Steve Hacker, SW Missouri 37	Tal Light, Oklahoma State 104	Ted Silva, CS Fullerton 18	Joseph Burns, Florida Int'l 1.20	Will Rushing, Ga. Southern 172

*Minimum 125 at-bats. #Minimum 60 Innings.

COLLEGE BASEBALL
NCAA DIVISION I LEADERS

Sean Casey
.461-14-70 for Richmond

TEAM BATTING

BATTING AVERAGE

	G	AVG
Texas Tech	65	.344
Indiana State	62	.340
Cal State Fullerton	66	.336
Central Michigan	60	.335
Air Force	54	.334
New Mexico	55	.333
Massachusetts	52	.333
Ohio State	63	.332
Grambling	39	.332
Wichita State	70	.331

RUNS SCORED

	G	R
Oklahoma State	65	686
Texas Tech	65	627
Wichita State	70	602
Cal State Fullerton	66	571
Clemson	68	570
Florida State	69	561
Nebraska	58	545
Georgia Tech	60	545
Tennessee	70	533
Rice	62	527

HOME RUNS

	G	HR
Southwest Missouri	58	103
Oklahoma State	65	101
Louisville	59	94
Texas A&M	67	88
Cal State Fullerton	66	88
Ohio State	63	84
Central Michigan	60	83
Texas Tech	65	83
Georgia Tech	60	82
Cal State Northridge	57	81
Louisiana State	65	81

STOLEN BASES

	G	SB	ATT
Wichita State	70	216	262
Florida State	69	162	207
California	57	159	209
Bethune-Cookman	48	157	176
Pittsburgh	55	150	194
Maryland-Eastern Shore	53	147	183
Texas Tech	65	146	202
Nicholls State	51	141	193
Evansville	57	139	199
Arkansas	61	138	161

TEAM PITCHING

WON-LOSS PERCENTAGE

	W	L	PCT
Cal State Fullerton	57	9	.864
Florida International	50	11	.820
Clemson	54	14	.794
Auburn	50	13	.794
Central Florida	49	13	.790
Texas Tech	51	14	.785
Tennessee	54	16	.771
Florida State	53	16	.768
Delaware	45	14	.763
Wichita State	53	17	.757
Providence	44	15	.746

EARNED RUN AVERAGE

	G	ERA
Florida International	61	2.40
Delaware	59	2.42
Florida State	69	2.72
McNeese State	57	3.08
Central Florida	62	3.14
Clemson	68	3.17
Seton Hall	54	3.21
The Citadel	60	3.26
Mississippi	62	3.36
Old Dominion	59	3.36

TEAM FIELDING

	G	AVG
Wake Forest	58	.974
Texas	63	.973
Stanford	65	.972
Cal State Fullerton	66	.971
Lamar	62	.971
Illinois	56	.971
Santa Clara	56	.970
Florida International	61	.970
Louisiana State	65	.970
Arkansas State	57	.969
Hawaii	54	.969

INDIVIDUAL BATTING

BATTING AVERAGE
(Minimum 125 At-Bats)

	AVG	G	AB	R	H	2B	3B	HR	RBI	BB	SO	SB
Sean Casey, Richmond	.461	55	193	63	89	26	1	14	70	37	13	2
Todd Tatlock, Indiana State	.460	58	213	49	98	19	0	6	70	10	20	0
Garrett Neubart, Columbia	.458	39	155	53	71	17	3	5	34	15	12	27
Cliff Brumbaugh, Delaware	.442	59	215	68	95	32	5	8	56	31	26	15
Mark Barron, Marist	.442	41	163	37	72	16	3	10	46	10	15	7
Mark Wulfert, New Mexico	.438	49	201	63	88	24	4	15	80	26	32	40
Lance Migita, Ga. Washington	.437	52	197	60	86	15	6	6	46	38	9	9
Jason Totman, Texas Tech	.435	61	214	77	93	24	5	5	53	53	15	9
Mike Wolger, California	.432	38	132	29	57	12	2	3	33	16	18	7
Jim Duffy, Seton Hall	.429	54	217	54	93	13	3	3	44	27	25	23
Lance Massey, Air Force	.429	51	191	73	82	12	6	18	51	41	20	8
Kevin Penwell, Boston College	.425	41	127	29	54	11	3	1	24	17	19	12
Dan Conroy, Fair. Dickinson	.424	40	144	42	61	13	3	0	42	20	5	14
Mike Crotty, Indiana	.423	56	194	48	82	18	2	12	64	25	42	4
Mark Kotsay, Cal State Fullerton	.422	66	263	85	111	20	5	21	90	39	15	15
Clint Bryant, Texas Tech	.422	65	258	91	109	24	4	16	93	50	35	25
Scott Weaver, Michigan	.418	50	170	44	71	13	2	10	42	30	10	13
Brian Church, Hofstra	.418	48	146	32	61	13	2	8	52	48	27	3
John Curl, Texas A&M	.415	43	212	61	88	21	2	18	58	35	51	1
Paul Wilders, Siena	.415	43	135	39	56	14	3	3	53	44	16	21
Brad Winget, Brigham Young	.413	58	208	57	86	17	0	11	65	23	29	7
Mike Miller, Hofstra	.411	48	158	59	65	11	4	20	57	38	27	7
Darin Erstad, Nebraska	.410	57	251	84	103	20	7	19	76	41	24	11
David Dellucci, Mississippi	.410	62	229	67	94	15	6	17	63	46	26	31
Travis Thornton, Coppin State	.410	48	178	45	73	11	1	3	22	25	11	18
Steve Hacker, SW Missouri	.409	58	235	63	96	18	0	37	95	27	23	2
Tom Whalen, Temple	.409	50	186	43	76	18	2	6	39	23	26	11
Toby Kominek, Cent. Michigan	.408	60	211	71	86	16	4	25	65	26	38	16
Todd Helton, Tennessee	.407	69	258	86	105	27	4	20	92	61	24	11
Mike Shannon, Penn	.407	46	172	37	70	15	5	4	47	8	26	6
Brian Zaun, Butler	.407	43	162	37	86	16	3	4	26	9	19	11
Scott Sollmann, Notre Dame	.406	61	229	73	93	9	11	1	32	34	18	23
Chris Moller, Alabama	.405	59	215	35	87	15	2	10	44	17	39	4
Terry Joseph, Northwestern St.	.404	51	193	70	78	13	5	14	54	27	24	33
Travis Janssen, New Mex. St.	.403	52	196	44	79	18	1	8	49	25	19	6
Mike Combs, Bowling Green	.403	47	159	30	64	9	1	5	31	23	30	3
Dan Thompson, Yale	.402	43	164	33	66	13	2	4	45	11	15	5
Jody Henson, W. Carolina	.401	52	202	46	81	21	3	1	36	24	27	25
Tim Howard, Ala.-Birmingham	.400	51	205	54	82	11	4	6	48	22	30	10
Marlon Stewart, Grambling	.400	38	135	39	54	7	2	8	40	15	17	3
Geoff Jenkins, Southern Cal	.399	70	258	75	103	15	3	23	78	51	32	14
Bill Mullee, Army	.399	45	158	39	63	15	1	1	31	24	4	17
Pat Pethel, Iowa State	.399	51	153	35	61	9	3	1	29	19	25	25
Jason Adams, Wichita State	.398	67	266	82	106	25	4	16	82	32	26	17
Tony Ellison, NC State	.398	60	246	72	98	14	1	24	79	24	45	7
Nelson Ubaldo, Massachusetts	.398	49	171	44	68	12	0	8	46	24	48	11
Ric Johnson, Indiana State	.397	62	252	82	100	14	5	7	49	25	35	27
Steve Smetana, Kent State	.397	58	194	46	77	27	1	5	50	21	21	6
Scott Ayotte, Michigan State	.397	51	179	65	71	16	7	13	60	25	31	5
Craig Caballero, Grand Canyon	.397	46	151	41	60	16	3	6	38	49	17	1
Jon Manuelian, Long Island	.397	45	151	52	60	12	2	8	40	44	28	2
Dan Seimetz, Ohio State	.396	57	197	50	78	20	3	10	58	23	22	0
John Shannon, Drexel	.396	58	192	49	76	12	7	8	56	39	22	1
Shawn McNally, Auburn	.396	46	187	39	74	10	1	6	44	23	23	10
Tom Owen, Northern Iowa	.394	55	193	56	76	23	1	10	53	37	21	2
Mike Stick, Creighton	.393	57	211	50	83	16	5	15	74	26	28	11
Joe Sarno, New Hampshire	.393	47	166	36	66	11	2	2	31	18	22	26
Randy DuRoss, Texas Tech	.392	61	240	79	94	17	4	9	55	30	39	10
Dave Murphy, Brown	.392	41	130	25	51	11	1	4	24	21	12	4
Ryan Rosplock, Sam Houston St.	.391	52	184	33	72	12	0	7	32	10	10	11

RUNS SCORED

	G	R
Clint Bryant, Texas Tech	65	91
Casey Blake, Wichita State	70	89
Todd Helton, Tennessee	69	86
Tripp MacKay, Okla. State	65	85
Mark Kotsay, CS Fullerton	66	85
Darin Erstad, Nebraska	57	84
Chris Richard, Okla. State	64	84
Peter Prodanov, Okla. State	65	84
Ric Johnson, Indiana State	62	82
Jason Adams, Wichita State	67	82
Shane Monahan, Clemson	67	82
Bob O'Toole, Providence	59	81
Randy DuRoss, Texas Tech	61	79
Tal Light, Oklahoma State	63	79
Chad Alexander, Texas A&M	66	79
David Miller, Clemson	68	79

HITS

	G	H
Mark Kotsay, CS Fullerton	66	111
Clint Bryant, Texas Tech	65	109
Chad Alexander, Texas A&M	66	106
Jason Adams, Wichita State	67	106
Shane Monahan, Clemson	67	106
Jacque Jones, Southern Cal	70	106
Todd Helton, Tennessee	69	105
Darin Erstad, Nebraska	57	103
David Miller, Clemson	68	103
Geoff Jenkins, Southern Cal	70	103

TOTAL BASES

	G	TB
Steve Hacker, SW Missouri	58	225
Mark Kotsay, CS Fullerton	66	204
Todd Helton, Tennessee	69	200
Darin Erstad, Nebraska	57	194
Geoff Jenkins, Southern Cal	70	193
Clint Bryant, Texas Tech	65	189
Jason Adams, Wichita State	67	187
Tony Ellison, NC State	60	186
Toby Kominek, Cent. Mich.	60	185
Chad Alexander, Texas A&M	66	184
Tal Light, Oklahoma State	63	180
Ryan Ritter, Georgia Tech	59	178
Mark Quinn, Rice	62	177
Doug Mientkiewicz, Fla. State	69	175
Shane Monahan, Clemson	67	174
David Dellucci, Mississippi	62	172

DOUBLES

	G	2B
Cliff Brumbaugh, Delaware	59	32
Steve Smetana, Kent State	58	27
Rob Morgan, Old Dominion	59	27
Gary Burnham, Clemson	66	27
Todd Helton, Tennessee	69	27
Sean Casey, Richmond	55	26
Lance Berkman, Rice	62	26
Scott Byers, Georgia Tech	56	25
Kevin Nehring, James Madison	58	25
Tyson Whitley, Ga. Southern	59	25
Jason Adams, Wichita State	67	25
Mark Wulfert, New Mexico	49	24

Clint Bryant
91 runs scored

Eric Pitt, San Jose St.	52	24
Brian August, Delaware	55	24
Jason Totman, Texas Tech	61	24
Kevin Chabot, Auburn	63	24
Clint Bryant, Texas Tech	65	24
Chad Cooley, Louisiana State	65	24

TRIPLES

	G	3B
Scott Sollmann, Notre Dame	61	11
Ron Green, Samford	51	10
David Miller, Clemson	68	10
Toph Lake, Navy	53	9
Andre Duffie, Delaware	58	9
Maika Symmonds, Old Dominion	59	9
Andrew McCormick, Gr. Canyon	62	9

HOME RUNS

	G	HR
Steve Hacker, SW Missouri	58	37
Tal Light, Oklahoma State	63	26
Toby Kominek, Cent. Mich.	60	25
Tony Ellison, NC State	60	24
Geoff Jenkins, Southern Cal	70	23
Matt Berger, Louisville	52	22
Mark Kotsay, CS Fullerton	66	21
Mike Miller, Hofstra	48	20
Alex Tolbert, West. Carolina	56	20
Ryan Ritter, Georgia Tech	59	20
Todd Helton, Tennessee	69	20
Bill Knight, Massachusetts	52	19
Steve Wilson, Ga. Southern	56	19
Darin Erstad, Nebraska	57	19
Bob O'Toole, Providence	59	19
Doug Mientkiewicz, Fla. State	69	19
Lou Deman, Long Island	46	18
Kevin Dotson, Detroit	46	18
Lawrence Scheffer, Detroit	46	18
Lance Massey, Air Force	54	18
Ryan Topham, Notre Dame	55	18
Mark Quinn, Rice	62	18
John Curl, Texas A&M	63	18

RUNS BATTED IN

	G	RBI
Tal Light, Oklahoma State	63	104
Steve Hacker, SW Missouri	58	95
Clint Bryant, Texas Tech	65	93
Todd Helton, Tennessee	69	92
Mark Kotsay, CS Fullerton	66	90

Mark Quinn, Rice	62	89
Chris Richard, Okla. State	64	85
Jason Adams, Wichita State	67	82
Mark Wulfert, New Mexico	49	80
Doug Mientkiewicz, Fla. State	69	80
Ryan Topham, Notre Dame	55	79
Tony Ellison, NC State	60	79
Ross Gload, South Florida	63	78
David Miller, Clemson	68	78
Geoff Jenkins, Southern Cal	70	78
Steve Carver, Stanford	65	77
Darin Erstad, Nebraska	57	76
Jose Cruz, Rice	62	76
Mike Stick, Creighton	57	74
Richie Taylor, Wichita State	68	74

BASES ON BALLS

	G	BB
Jose Cruz, Rice	62	76
Chris Richard, Okla. State	64	70
Tripp MacKay, Okla. State	65	67
Will Cook, Lamar	60	62
Mike Sak, Xavier	57	61
Hugh Lopes, South Alabama	58	61
Todd Helton, Tennessee	69	61

STRIKEOUTS

	G	SO
Kevin Chabot, Auburn	63	77
Craig Dour, South Carolina	56	76
Alex Tolbert, W. Carolina	56	73
Kevin Bentley, So. Mississippi	56	68
Will Bland, South Florida	59	68
Sean West, South Florida	62	68
Gio Cafaro, South Florida	63	68

TOUGHEST TO STRIKE OUT
(Minimum 125 At-Bats)

	AB	SO	Ratio
Kris Doiron, Drexel	221	3	73.7
Jason Stein, E. Kentucky	228	5	45.6
Kent Cox, Campbell	213	5	42.6
Kyle Morris, Bucknell	126	3	42.0
Bill Mullee, Army	158	4	39.5
Charles Pini, St. Peter's	149	4	37.3
Andy Johnson, Mich. State	162	5	32.4
Dan Conroy, Fair. Dick.	144	5	28.8
Tony Lawrence, La. Tech	170	6	28.3
Ryan Gorecki, Seton Hall	181	7	25.9

STOLEN BASES

	G	SB	ATT
Randy Young, Wichita State	68	64	71
Chad Green, Kentucky	60	54	70
Milton Anderson, Beth.-Cook.	43	52	56
Chad Meyers, Creighton	57	52	60
Kevin Gibbs, Old Dominion	52	48	52
Matt Kastelic, Texas Tech	61	46	60
Ivan Lewis, California	56	43	58
Carlos Akins, W. Kentucky	54	41	51
Mark Wulfert, New Mexico	49	40	43
Jermaine Clark, San Fran.	58	38	47
Aric Thomas, Oklahoma	58	38	48
Tim Decker, Kansas State	49	37	45
Dorian Speed, Fla. Int.	58	37	52

HIT BY PITCH

	G	HBP
Scott Vieira, Tennessee	69	25
Rusty McNamara, Okla. State	63	25
Ryan Reed, Ball State	48	24
Josh Mellor, Pittsburgh	51	23
David Crain, Nebraska	35	21

Steve Hacker
37 homers, 225 total bases

INDIVIDUAL PITCHING

EARNED RUN AVERAGE
(Minimum 60 Innings)

	W	L	ERA	G	GS	CG	SV	IP	H	R	ER	BB	SO
Joseph Burns, Fla. Int.	9	0	1.20	12	11	2	0	67	53	11	9	19	46
Curt Schnur, Delaware	11	3	1.21	16	13	10	1	104	76	23	14	24	83
Jay Tessmer, Miami	3	2	1.31	45	0	0	20	75	59	11	11	12	91
Brett Wheeler, Old Dominion	7	1	1.48	10	10	1	0	61	42	19	10	13	46
Greg Wooten, Portland St.	8	4	1.51	18	18	8	0	119	93	35	20	27	114
Michael Maroto, Southern	9	1	1.54	11	11	7	0	70	64	19	12	20	52
Don Morillo, The Citadel	6	2	1.60	32	0	0	13	67	48	17	12	25	75
Todd Helton, Tennessee	8	2	1.66	30	4	4	12	76	48	22	14	15	74

	W	L	ERA	G	GS	CG	SV	IP	H	R	ER	BB	SO
Evan Thomas, Fla. Int.	15	2	1.70	20	16	2	0	127	76	29	24	45	146
Jamie Wilson, Delaware	9	1	1.70	14	12	8	0	85	66	21	16	19	64
Willy Hilton, East. Illinois	4	3	1.71	27	0	0	10	63	48	15	12	28	39
Jamey Price, Mississippi	11	6	1.72	19	19	9	0	141	104	37	27	16	118
Bryan Link, Winthrop	12	3	1.74	21	17	10	4	134	94	37	26	41	135
Jason Grilli, Seton Hall	8	2	1.85	14	12	1	0	78	73	20	16	34	63
Jamie Puorto, NE Illinois	5	4	1.86	12	11	8	0	77	63	32	16	28	65
Frank Chibbaro, Pace	10	1	1.91	11	11	7	0	80	62	23	17	30	61
Britt Reames, The Citadel	10	3	1.93	14	14	3	0	98	65	28	21	37	123
Bob Pailthorpe, Santa Clara	10	4	1.96	18	17	6	0	124	102	36	27	49	126
Lou Vigliotti, Fairfield	6	4	1.97	13	13	9	0	81	75	24	18	17	45
Chad Clement, McNeese St.	6	3	1.97	31	5	1	7	73	57	19	16	33	61
Richard Palacios, Fla. Int.	9	1	1.99	24	7	1	2	86	62	22	19	37	58
Tommy Nuckols, Virginia Comm.	4	5	1.99	18	2	1	4	77	69	33	17	23	69
Jason Ramsey, UNC Wilmington	6	4	2.11	19	13	4	2	107	75	38	25	38	128
Randy Wolf, Pepperdine	9	1	2.16	31	0	0	6	96	69	26	23	36	69
Steve Stanson, New Orleans	8	3	2.20	20	10	4	1	82	58	28	20	26	72
Mike Maerten, St. John's	4	3	2.20	8	8	3	0	65	52	28	16	25	38
Mark Redman, Oklahoma	15	3	2.22	20	20	7	0	142	109	48	35	35	158
Kris Doiron, Drexel	9	3	2.24	14	12	9	0	84	69	32	21	41	64
Dan Galles, Penn	6	5	2.26	12	12	9	0	88	84	36	22	20	66
Keith Cooper, Vermont	7	3	2.28	15	10	5	2	75	64	29	19	29	57
Chip Pettit, Valparaiso	5	5	2.31	14	11	9	1	70	49	30	18	33	60
Adam Lancaster, Delaware	10	3	2.33	14	11	6	0	89	67	32	23	31	82
Jon Saylor, McNeese State	9	4	2.37	16	15	8	1	95	76	33	25	31	66
Stephen Prihoda, Sam Houston	8	4	2.41	15	12	7	0	105	76	39	28	40	88
Mark Chavez, CS Fullerton	4	2	2.45	37	0	0	6	62	56	18	17	24	35
Todd Incantalupo, Providence	10	1	2.47	17	10	6	0	87	81	25	24	20	51
Keiki Mattson, Hawaii-Hilo	4	3	2.48	12	11	4	1	76	58	29	21	32	44
Matt Anderson, Rice	11	2	2.51	28	4	0	1	72	46	27	20	52	63
Brian Field, Rider	6	2	2.51	13	10	0	0	72	68	29	20	32	51
Brian Sikorski, W. Michigan	10	2	2.52	14	12	7	2	79	63	30	22	31	69
Tim Bouch, Jas. Madison	4	1	2.52	16	7	1	0	64	64	29	18	22	64
Toby Moore, Navy	9	6	2.53	17	17	10	0	107	101	45	30	31	56
Darin Blood, Gonzaga	13	3	2.57	16	16	8	0	119	92	42	34	46	145
Travis Burgus, San Diego	10	6	2.58	17	16	8	1	122	115	50	35	42	73
Thomas Marks, New Orleans	5	4	2.59	14	12	1	0	80	80	33	23	15	61

WINS

	W	L
Ted Silva, CS Fullerton	18	1
Ryan Halla, Auburn	16	3
Evan Thomas, Fla. International	15	2
Mark Redman, Oklahoma	15	3
Tedde Campbell, Pittsburgh	15	4
Kyle Peterson, Stanford	14	1
R.A. Dickey, Tennessee	14	4
J.D. Smart, Texas	14	4
Tim Dixon, CS Fullerton	13	0
Darin Blood, Gonzaga	13	3
Randy Flores, Southern Cal	13	3
Kyle Wilson, Long Beach State	13	3
Kevin Gunther, Fresno State	12	2
Chris Morrison, Auburn	12	2
Allen Halley, South Alabama	12	3
Jonathan Johnson, Fla. State	12	3
Bryan Link, Winthrop	12	3
David Yocum, Florida State	12	3
Jason Bell, Oklahoma State	12	4
Scott Haws, Brigham Young	12	4
Jason Adge, Miami	12	6

LOSSES

	W	L
Glen Kimble, Stephen F. Austin	0	12
Matt Gies, Grand Canyon	3	11
Bruce Stanley, Ball State	4	11
Matt Barefield, Mercer	5	11

APPEARANCES

	G
Jay Tessmer, Miami	45
Gabe Gonzalez, Long Beach St.	39
Mark Chavez, CS Fullerton	37
Thad Chrismon, North Carolina	36
Alex Franklin, California	36

COMPLETE GAMES

	GS	CG
Brian Pisani, Coppin State	15	14
Chris Pollard, Davidson	14	11
Mike Nartker, Kent State	15	11
Curt Schnur, Delaware	13	10
Ryan VanDeWeg, W. Michigan	13	10
Willie Rivera, CS Sacramento	15	10
Dave Scranton, Bucknell	16	10
Ken Wagner, Fla. Atlantic	16	10
Bryan Link, Winthrop	17	10
Toby Moore, Navy	17	10
Kyle Peterson, Stanford	18	10

Will Rushing
172 strikeouts

SAVES

	G	SV
Gabe Gonzalez, Long Beach St.	39	20
Jay Tessmer, Miami	45	20
Finley Woodward, Auburn	33	19
Jamie Emiliano, Fla. Int.	27	16
Jason Garner, Southern Cal	31	15
Scott Winchester, Clemson	33	14
Braden Looper, Wichita State	27	13
Don Morillo, The Citadel	32	13
Tucker Barr, Georgia Tech	17	12
Kurt Belger, Iowa	24	12
Joe Witten, East. Kentucky	26	12
Todd Helton, Tennessee	30	12
Shannon Morgan, Cincinnati	31	12
Mike Nakamura, South Alabama	32	12
Thad Chrismon, North Carolina	36	12

INNINGS PITCHED

	G	IP
Will Rushing, Ga. Southern	20	160
R.A. Dickey, Tennessee	22	160
Ted Silva, CS Fullerton	29	153
Randy Flores, Southern Cal	20	150
Brian Powell, Georgia	19	147
Ryan Halla, Auburn	24	147
Jason Bell, Oklahoma State	21	145
Nate Yeskie, Nevada-Las Vegas	20	144
Kyle Peterson, Stanford	20	143
Mark Redman, Oklahoma	20	141
Jamey Price, Mississippi	19	141
Kevin Gunther, Fresno State	19	137
J.D. Smart, Texas	24	137

BASES ON BALLS

	IP	BB
Greg Dean, Oklahoma State	79	84
Mike Liloia, Monmouth	66	79
Joshua Farrow, Florida A&M	58	70
Sean Powell, Cleveland State	72	70
Don Martin, Temple	82	70
Sean Murphy, North Carolina	112	70
Scott Sladovnik, Creighton	89	68
Tedde Campbell, Pittsburgh	135	68

STRIKEOUTS

	IP	SO
Will Rushing, Ga. Southern	160	172
Mark Redman, Oklahoma	141	158
Scott Schultz, Louisiana St.	117	150
Ryan Halla, Auburn	147	148
Nate Yeskie, UNLV	144	147
Evan Thomas, Fla. Int.	127	146
Darin Blood, Gonzaga	119	145
Scott Rivette, Long Beach St.	130	144
Ted Silva, CS Fullerton	153	142
Brian Powell, Georgia	147	138
Bryan Link, Winthrop	134	135
Jason Dawsey, Clemson	129	133
Terry Harvey, NC State	121	131
Bob St. Pierre, Rchmond	129	130
Jonathan Johnson, Fla. State	134	130
Jason Ramsey, UNC Wilmington	107	128
David Yocum, Florida State	114	128
Mark Roberts, South Florida	102	127
Darren McClellan, Florida	122	126
Bob Pailthorpe, Santa Clara	124	126
Robby Crabtree, CS Northridge	126	126
Sean Murphy, North Carolina	112	125
Clark Maxwell, W. Carolina	123	124
Allen Halley, South Alabama	120	123
Rocky Biddle, Long Beach St.	108	122
R.A. Dickey, Tennessee	160	121
Jason Bell, Oklahoma State	145	120
Mike Eby, CS Sacramento	106	119
Charlie Cruz, Florida State	109	118
Ken Wagner, Fla. Atlantic	130	118
Jamey Price, Mississippi	141	118

STRIKEOUTS/9 INNINGS
(Minimum 50 Innings)

	IP	SO	AVG
J. O'Shaughnessy, N'eastern.	55	82	13.5
Matt Seely, Murray State	58	80	12.3
Scott Downs, Kentucky	76	102	12.0
Scott Schultz, LSU	117	150	11.5
Bill Koch, Clemson	87	111	11.5
Brian Hommel, Louisville	76	96	11.4
Britt Reames, The Citadel	98	123	11.3
Mark Roberts, South Florida	102	127	11.2
John Bale, Southern Miss.	70	86	11.1
Corey Lee, NC State	61	75	11.0
Gabe Gonzales, Long Beach St.	68	83	11.0
Darin Blood, Gonzaga	119	145	11.0
John Babson, UNCW	89	108	11.0
Jay Tessmer, Miami	75	91	10.9
Jason Ramsey, UNCW	107	128	10.8
Matt Carnes, Arkansas	93	111	10.8
Courtney Duncan, Grambling..	59	71	10.8

Baseball America's
COLLEGE TOP 25

BATTERS: 10 or more at-bats
PITCHERS: 5 or more innings

Boldface indicates selected in 1995 draft

Seminoles Slugger. First baseman Doug Mientkiewicz led Florida State to a No. 3 ranking, hitting .371 with 19 homers.

1 CAL STATE FULLERTON

Coach: Augie Garrido — Record: 57-9

BATTING	AVG	AB	R	H	2B	3B	HR	RBI	SB
Kotsay, Mark, of-p	.422	263	85	111	20	5	21	90	15
Loyd, Brian, c	.360	247	59	89	13	5	10	73	12
Miranda, Tony, dh-of	.352	247	66	87	21	3	12	53	19
Ankrum, C.J., of	.352	196	60	69	10	5	1	29	6
Giambi, Jeremy, of	.349	195	54	68	11	4	4	37	10
Fraser, Joe, 2b	.348	233	59	81	24	2	7	46	4
Matos, Robert, dh	.339	124	31	42	4	1	4	30	12
Olsen, D.C., 1b	.307	251	42	77	21	0	14	53	1
Chatham, Steve, of	.300	10	3	3	2	0	0	1	0
Martinez, Tony, 3b	.291	182	32	53	5	1	7	42	2
Jones, Jack, ss	.278	237	47	66	10	1	3	41	6
Hernandez, Ruben, dh-1b	.273	44	5	12	3	0	3	12	0
Lamb, Mike, 3b	.200	65	12	13	6	0	0	8	0

PITCHING	W	L	ERA	G	SV	IP	H	BB	SO
Kotsay, Mark	2	1	0.31	21	11	29	23	13	27
Chavez, Mark	4	2	2.45	37	6	62	56	24	55
Silva, Ted	18	1	2.83	29	6	153	140	35	142
Hild, Scott	2	0	3.23	13	0	31	32	9	20
Dixon, Tim	13	0	3.47	19	0	109	94	60	82
Ward, Jon	10	3	3.48	19	0	106	95	53	92
Hollibaugh, Kimson	2	1	4.68	13	0	25	32	8	19
Mitchell, John	3	0	5.92	21	2	59	59	33	48
Dillon, Tom	3	1	6.75	14	0	17	11	22	18

2 SOUTHERN CALIFORNIA

Coach: Mike Gillespie — Record: 49-21

BATTING	AVG	AB	R	H	2B	3B	HR	RBI	SB
Jenkins, Geoff, of	.399	258	75	103	15	3	23	78	14
Alvarez, Gabe, ss-2b	.361	269	73	97	14	2	13	59	7
Jones, Jacque, of	.353	300	59	106	16	4	7	53	14
Dawkins, Walter, of	.329	292	64	96	17	4	9	57	14
Moeller, Chad, c	.329	210	31	69	5	1	5	29	3
Walbridge, Greg, 1b	.302	222	34	67	11	0	9	47	4
Cruz, Paul, dh	.287	230	40	66	13	1	0	27	6
Montoya, Alfonso, pr	.286	7	10	2	1	0	0	1	12
Baker, Derek, 3b	.280	150	21	42	5	2	3	18	2
Rachels, Wes, 2b	.276	127	33	35	6	0	1	18	6
Diaz, Ernie, 3b-ss	.256	156	34	40	8	2	9	37	7
Ensberg, Morgan, 2b	.250	16	4	4	0	0	1	1	1
Carson, Glen, 1b	.245	53	5	13	2	0	0	8	0
Stromsborg, Ryan, 2b	.223	112	21	25	6	0	0	12	4
Brown, Jason, c	.222	36	3	8	0	0	0	4	0
Ponchak, Brian, dh-p	.182	22	1	4	2	0	0	4	0

PITCHING	W	L	ERA	G	SV	IP	H	BB	SO
Garner, Jason	6	1	3.12	31	15	49	50	19	36
Flores, Randy	13	3	3.24	20	1	150	142	34	86
Krawczyk, Jack	4	2	4.11	23	3	46	49	8	27
Tucker, Ben	7	2	4.19	21	0	105	111	45	81
Henderson, Scott	1	0	4.21	14	0	26	28	10	10
Parle, Justin	2	1	4.30	24	2	37	44	13	26
Mejia, Javier	6	2	4.30	27	0	46	51	15	39
Cooper, Brian	8	3	4.78	20	0	102	112	43	92
Etherton, Seth	2	4	5.66	13	0	41	44	28	28
Ponchak, Brian	0	3	6.59	14	0	29	36	16	15

3 FLORIDA STATE

Coach: Mike Martin — Record: 53-16

BATTING	AVG	AB	R	H	2B	3B	HR	RBI	SB
Mientkiewicz, Doug, 1b	.371	248	75	92	20	3	19	80	19
Zabala, Jose, 3b-ss	.339	56	6	19	3	0	0	11	0
Zech, Scott, 3b	.330	227	60	75	12	2	3	43	19
Drew, J.D., of	.325	209	54	68	7	3	17	63	11
Faurot, Adam, dh	.324	145	37	47	10	2	1	32	8
Hodges, Randy, of	.323	260	63	84	11	3	3	43	24
Lopez, Mickey, 2b	.290	272	65	79	19	3	7	50	32
Morris, Jeremy, of-dh	.271	207	37	56	9	3	5	46	9
Woodward, Matt, 1b	.261	23	4	6	1	0	0	2	0
Badeaux, Brooks, ss	.254	201	57	51	8	3	1	39	18
Salazar, Jeremy, c	.250	64	12	16	5	0	2	16	0
Martin, Mike, c	.221	217	41	48	14	1	9	47	13
Nedeau, Steve, of	.218	119	23	26	4	0	1	18	3
Senior, Bryan, of	.200	40	10	8	2	0	0	7	2
Adeeb, Josh, of	.200	35	10	7	1	0	0	6	4
Butler, Steve, p-ph	.083	12	4	1	1	0	0	0	0

PITCHING	W	L	ERA	G	SV	IP	H	BB	SO
Olson, Phil	3	2	1.19	29	7	38	23	13	38
Butler, Steve	0	0	1.23	8	0	7	7	6	7
Morgan, Scooby	4	3	1.46	25	1	56	33	24	50
Yocum, David	12	3	2.61	18	0	114	94	43	128
Johnson, Jonathan	12	3	2.89	19	0	134	98	53	130
Bell, Mike	7	3	2.90	13	0	62	61	22	53
Cruz, Charlie	8	1	2.98	18	0	109	101	51	118
Howell, Chuck	4	1	3.05	27	0	56	48	18	48
Niles, Randy	2	0	4.01	16	1	25	27	11	30
Choate, Randy	1	0	4.35	15	0	21	21	13	25

4 MIAMI

Coach: Jim Morris — Record: 48-17

BATTING	AVG	AB	R	H	2B	3B	HR	RBI	SB
Gomez, Rudy, 3b-of	.379	232	52	88	18	2	9	44	23
Rivero, Eddie, of	.324	176	31	57	6	1	8	44	4
Buxbaum, Danny, 1b	.324	210	38	68	15	0	14	60	6
Thompson, Bruce, of	.317	224	54	71	8	4	4	30	22
Lopez-Cao, Mike, dh	.316	38	9	12	3	0	1	5	1
Marcinczyk, T.R., dh-1b	.312	141	24	44	12	0	4	29	4
Gonzalez, Ricky, c	.305	210	29	64	3	1	3	34	12
Finnieston, Adam, of-dh	.301	186	38	56	11	4	4	34	8
Gama, Rick, 2b	.294	248	66	73	7	5	7	36	17
Torti, Mike, of-3b	.283	187	42	53	14	1	6	40	8
Cora, Alex, ss	.271	221	42	60	6	2	0	24	7
Moore, Tris, of	.258	31	7	8	0	0	0	7	1
Gargiulo, Jim, c	.242	33	5	8	0	0	1	6	0
Grimmett, Ryan, of	.237	97	23	23	4	0	3	10	13

PITCHING	W	L	ERA	G	SV	IP	H	BB	SO
Demorejon, Pete	0	0	0.82	6	0	11	10	6	11
Tessmer, Jay	3	2	1.31	45	20	75	59	12	91
Hoelker, Chad	0	0	3.12	8	0	9	8	1	5
Hoff, Eddie	0	0	3.14	11	0	14	10	7	9
Henderson, Kenny	11	3	3.15	18	0	106	91	45	102
Mestre, Marc	0	0	3.38	10	0	11	11	7	6
Westfall, Allan	7	0	3.45	39	0	60	53	30	65
Arteaga, J.D.	11	3	3.63	20	0	124	119	43	84
Adge, Jason	12	6	4.23	21	0	128	110	58	108
Brannan, Ryan	2	1	5.06	9	0	21	34	12	22
Gonzalez, Dorian	2	2	5.67	16	0	33	30	22	34

5 TENNESSEE

Coach: Rod Delmonico   **Record:** 54-16

BATTING	AVG	AB	R	H	2B	3B	HR	RBI	SB
Helton, Todd, 1b-p	.407	258	86	105	27	4	20	92	11
Lewis, Ed, 2b	.333	270	47	90	18	1	3	60	15
Vieira, Scott, c-3b	.333	228	56	76	15	1	11	56	12
Schroeffel, Scott, of-p	.331	266	63	88	13	5	9	52	15
Copley, Travis, dh-1b	.314	236	51	74	18	1	6	55	2
Whitley, Matt, ss	.300	293	71	88	10	0	2	24	30
Smith, Lance, of	.294	160	36	47	6	1	1	16	25
Christensen, Bryce, of	.289	225	45	65	4	1	0	25	14
McLuhan, Jonathan, dh-c	.289	45	11	13	1	0	3	15	0
Espinosa, Ray, c	.259	228	28	59	5	0	1	27	3
Franklin, Jason, 3b	.241	133	21	32	6	1	5	26	3
Figueroa, Eduardo, of	.167	72	12	12	3	0	2	13	6
Schlosser, Mark, ss	.133	30	5	4	1	0	0	1	1

PITCHING	W	L	ERA	G	SV	IP	H	BB	SO
Helton, Todd	8	2	1.66	30	12	76	48	15	74
Greene, Brad	0	1	2.57	22	1	28	23	7	16
Schroeffel, Scott	7	3	2.73	15	0	66	49	42	81
Meyers, Ryan	10	2	3.46	21	0	120	112	35	104
Alkire, John	7	2	3.97	20	1	79	70	44	51
Dickey, R.A.	14	4	4.28	25	1	160	169	60	121
Exum, Travis	6	0	4.56	25	1	49	55	24	44
Darlington, John	1	1	5.80	20	0	36	38	20	35
Nadeau, Joe	1	0	9.00	10	0	13	11	21	17
Miller, Tim	0	1	9.64	2	0	5	5	3	2

6 CLEMSON

Coach: Jack Leggett   **Record:** 54-14

BATTING	AVG	AB	R	H	2B	3B	HR	RBI	SB
Rhodes, Rusty, of	.390	59	18	23	1	1	0	12	2
Monahan, Shane, of	.388	273	82	106	22	5	12	52	21
Miller, David, 1b	.380	271	79	103	14	10	9	78	27
Burnham, Gary, of	.344	241	61	83	27	4	8	62	5
LeCroy, Matt, c-dh	.333	255	55	85	18	0	15	72	0
Galloway, Paul, 3b	.324	210	46	68	14	2	9	47	6
Duffie, Will, dh-c	.294	197	33	58	10	3	4	37	1
Schroeder, Bryan, dh	.294	51	15	15	1	3	2	7	0
DeMoura, Eric, 2b-3b	.281	64	17	18	3	0	0	8	1
Brizek, Seth, ss	.279	262	51	73	12	1	10	44	10
Robinson, Jerome, of	.268	179	30	48	4	0	2	15	2
Livingston, Doug, 2b	.262	260	67	68	15	1	3	38	12
Embler, Jason, 1b	.259	27	4	7	1	1	1	3	0
Dawsey, Jason, p-of	.216	37	7	8	1	0	0	3	1
Frantz, Tim, c	.182	22	4	4	0	0	0	2	0
Ward, Ryan, of	.000	11	1	0	0	0	0	1	0

PITCHING	W	L	ERA	G	SV	IP	H	BB	SO
Winchester, Scott	4	2	0.59	33	14	46	23	16	42
Eggleston, Jamie	6	1	2.42	24	0	45	49	13	26
Dawsey, Jason	11	4	2.78	19	0	129	101	45	133
Benson, Kris	8	3	3.20	14	0	79	75	23	79
Vining, Ken	4	0	3.39	22	2	69	53	25	78
Koch, Billy	7	2	3.72	16	0	87	70	37	111
Watson, Mark	7	1	3.75	12	0	50	33	35	42
Williams, Rodney	0	0	4.00	8	0	9	9	4	8
Sauve, Jeff	4	5	4.05	23	1	47	45	20	38
Matz, Brian	2	1	4.11	20	0	35	31	16	21
Hauser, Scott	0	0	6.17	11	0	12	11	8	9

7 OKLAHOMA

Coach: Larry Cochell   **Record:** 42-16

BATTING	AVG	AB	R	H	2B	3B	HR	RBI	SB
Galvin, David, c	.400	15	1	6	1	0	0	3	0
Brown, Bobby, of	.362	232	59	84	9	2	6	36	14
Flores, Javier, c	.360	211	52	76	14	1	10	55	4

ACC's Best. Clemson outfielder Shane Monahan hit .388 and was selected Atlantic Coast Conference Player of the Year.

Thomas, Aric, of	.357	244	63	87	8	2	2	29	38
Minor, Damon, 1b	.344	183	46	63	12	5	10	44	4
Paul, Tristan, dh-3b	.344	186	39	64	11	1	8	51	1
Shackelford, Brian, of-p	.317	167	25	53	8	2	7	41	2
Minor, Ryan, 1b-dh-p	.311	90	20	28	6	0	6	21	1
Hills, Rich, ss	.298	215	52	64	10	0	10	49	1
Bradshaw, Chris, of	.286	56	10	16	2	1	2	9	4
Hansen, Dustin, of	.243	70	19	17	2	0	2	13	8
Zepeda, Jesse, 2b	.234	197	33	46	9	3	5	38	11
Hill, Willy, ss	.231	26	5	6	0	0	0	2	4
Mariani, M.J., 3b	.207	140	21	29	7	0	0	15	1
Owens, Mike, of	.200	15	1	3	0	0	0	3	0
Linn, Eric, c	.182	11	3	2	1	0	0	2	0

PITCHING	W	L	ERA	G	SV	IP	H	BB	SO
Wilmot, Toby	4	1	1.82	24	4	35	35	17	27
Redman, Mark	15	3	2.22	20	0	142	109	35	158
Shackelford, Brian	1	2	2.60	11	4	17	15	6	15
Glascoe, Derek	2	0	2.96	13	0	24	19	16	22
Walton, Tim	3	1	2.97	12	1	39	33	27	26
Ortiz, Russell	3	2	4.53	18	1	52	47	35	56
Powell, Dax	2	1	4.81	18	0	39	35	19	34
Andra, Jeff	6	2	4.83	19	0	63	63	32	44
Pennington, Brett	1	0	5.85	14	1	20	17	14	21
Connelly, Steve	1	2	6.27	12	0	33	55	14	23
Snyder, Shawn	3	1	6.57	19	0	25	24	15	6
Williams, Jeff	0	0	7.20	3	0	5	5	3	3
Minor, Ryan	1	1	7.59	5	0	21	23	12	18
Reinecker, Jim	0	0	11.81	3	0	5	4	7	2

8 TEXAS TECH

Coach: Larry Hays   **Record:** 51-14

BATTING	AVG	AB	R	H	2B	3B	HR	RBI	SB
Totman, Jason, 2b	.435	214	77	93	24	5	5	53	9
Leonard, Neal, of	.429	14	3	6	2	0	0	5	0
Gonzales, Andy, dh	.427	124	45	53	14	2	4	40	0
Bryant, Clint, 3b	.422	258	91	109	24	4	16	93	25
DuRoss, Randy, 1b	.392	240	79	94	17	4	9	55	10
Kastelic, Matt, of	.352	253	68	89	15	3	2	37	46
Lindstrom, David, c	.335	188	38	63	18	0	12	56	2
McCain, Marcus, of	.333	129	31	43	8	1	2	28	17
Welch, Brandon, of	.313	198	56	62	10	2	11	65	7
Padron, Raul, 1b	.308	52	10	16	2	0	0	12	1
Miller, Logan, c	.296	54	10	16	1	0	1	18	2
Ruecker, Dion, ss	.276	257	47	71	13	2	17	68	6
Martinez, Sergio, of	.273	55	10	15	3	0	0	11	0
Holmstead, Dax, of	.238	126	30	30	5	2	2	20	9
Hernandez, Dominic, 2b	.234	94	23	22	5	1	2	8	7
Pfeifer, Scott, dh	.154	26	9	4	1	0	0	3	3

PITCHING	W	L	ERA	G	SV	IP	H	BB	SO
Frush, Jimmy	5	1	2.97	24	4	64	56	14	55
Davidson, Tim	2	0	3.33	8	0	24	18	7	13
Peck, Jeff	10	3	3.73	19	1	104	104	46	73
Smith, Travis	10	5	4.26	21	1	118	137	32	97
Kolb, Brandon	6	2	4.58	14	0	75	68	46	83
Miller, Matt	11	3	5.11	18	0	100	108	55	85
Brewer, Ryan	1	0	5.12	9	0	19	17	9	20
Free, Kelly	2	0	5.19	9	1	17	18	5	17
McCreary, Mike	1	0	5.30	7	1	19	23	11	16
Belovsky, Josh	1	0	5.56	3	0	11	11	5	10
Gonzales, Andy	2	0	5.93	5	0	14	14	8	8

9 AUBURN

Coach: Hal Baird   **Record:** 50-13

BATTING	AVG	AB	R	H	2B	3B	HR	RBI	SB
McNally, Shawn, of	.396	187	39	74	10	1	6	44	10
Bellhorn, Mark, ss	.342	243	66	83	18	5	12	60	11
Waggoner, Jay, 1b	.325	268	59	87	23	2	7	58	5
Chabot, Kevin, of	.317	218	52	69	24	0	12	66	3
Weeks, Mark, 3b	.317	227	37	72	20	1	2	39	2
Key, Ken, of	.306	245	65	75	19	3	2	31	11
Clark, Kirby, c	.301	206	36	62	11	2	4	38	0
Ruch, Dallan, dh-c	.297	175	31	52	16	1	3	47	0
Macrory, Rob, 2b	.268	213	45	57	3	1	0	21	4
Whittenburg, Russ, of	.237	76	24	18	5	0	0	7	2
Etheredge, Josh, 3b-1b	.214	84	19	18	3	1	2	19	0
Dews, David, ph	.214	14	5	3	0	0	0	1	0
Kanakis, Peter, c	.167	12	0	2	0	0	0	3	0

PITCHING	W	L	ERA	G	SV	IP	H	BB	SO
Morrison, Chris	12	2	2.70	19	0	117	108	15	75
Halla, Ryan	16	3	3.07	24	0	147	122	47	148
Humphreys, Kevin	9	2	3.75	18	0	94	106	24	54
Hebson, Bryan	7	1	5.69	13	0	62	66	16	39
Gober, Todd	0	0	2.22	10	1	24	18	16	28
Woodward, Finley	3	2	2.38	33	19	42	27	13	32
Dickinson, Rodney	0	0	2.57	7	0	14	8	6	10
LeBoeuf, Jason	0	0	3.86	13	0	23	33	4	21
Schardt, Mitch	3	2	5.05	19	3	36	40	17	34
Taylor, Matt	0	1	5.06	7	0	5	10	7	6

10 STANFORD

Coach: Mark Marquess   **Record:** 40-25

BATTING	AVG	AB	R	H	2B	3B	HR	RBI	SB
Hinch, A.J., c	.366	238	61	87	21	6	9	58	13
Carver, Steve, 3b	.341	258	49	88	21	3	14	77	3
VanWagenen, Brodie, dh	.333	18	3	6	0	0	1	2	0
Carter, Cale, of	.325	265	52	86	22	5	1	39	10
Dallimore, Brian, 2b	.323	257	42	83	16	2	3	35	8
Kilburg, Joe, of	.296	240	63	71	7	2	1	20	35
Schaeffer, Jon, dh	.294	180	27	53	4	0	2	34	5
Kent, Troy, 1b	.290	238	35	69	11	3	3	33	9
Pecci, Jay, ss	.275	51	9	14	2	0	0	7	4
Allen, Dusty, of-dh	.255	153	31	39	9	0	6	32	6
Sees, Eric, ss	.250	204	28	51	5	1	1	27	8
Crowe, Rich, of	.245	49	11	12	4	0	0	7	4
Draft, Chris, of	.214	28	5	6	0	2	1	5	0
Clark, Chris, of	.155	71	7	11	1	0	0	4	2

PITCHING	W	L	ERA	G	SV	IP	H	BB	SO
Peterson, Kyle	14	1	2.96	20	1	143	129	35	112
Brammer, J.D.	1	1	3.12	15	0	17	14	8	14
Robbins, Mike	6	4	3.66	21	2	111	121	41	78
Sullivan, Brendan	3	2	4.07	27	4	42	51	11	34
Iglesias, Mario	3	2	4.25	19	2	42	42	11	27
Middlebrook, Jason	1	5	4.78	9	0	43	45	18	42
Reed, Dan	4	4	4.96	14	0	74	75	33	60
Reimers, Tom	3	1	4.98	23	1	34	36	19	30
Bartels, Todd	4	5	5.09	17	0	58	71	14	37
Williams, Mark	1	0	8.00	7	0	9	9	9	11

11 OKLAHOMA STATE

Coach: Gary Ward   **Record:** 46-19

BATTING	AVG	AB	R	H	2B	3B	HR	RBI	SB
Prodanov, Peter, ss-3b	.388	250	84	97	22	1	9	73	17
Hardcastle, Mike, of	.362	177	51	64	17	1	10	46	3
Richard, Chris, 1b-of	.336	241	84	81	23	4	13	85	16
Light, Tal, 3b-1b	.335	254	79	85	13	2	26	104	1
MacKay, Tripp, 2b	.319	273	85	87	10	5	3	50	16
McNamara, Rusty, of-c	.315	213	60	67	9	3	2	26	7

Auburn All-American. Shortstop Mark Bellhorn led Auburn to a 50-13 record, hitting .342 with 12 home runs.

ROBERT GURGANUS

	AVG	AB	R	H	2B	3B	HR	RBI	SB
Steelmon, Wyley, dh	.314	185	45	58	15	0	13	61	0
Folmar, Ryan, c	.306	157	45	48	9	2	3	31	1
DiPace, Danny, of	.291	110	24	32	6	2	5	35	1
Champoux, Beau, ss	.276	105	32	29	5	1	5	27	4
Messick, J.T., 3b-c	.267	146	36	39	4	2	3	30	1
Cook, Jamie, 1b	.250	52	9	13	3	0	2	11	0
Tatum, Shane, ss	.250	36	7	9	0	0	0	10	1
Aylor, Brian, of	.246	134	34	33	5	3	5	26	16
Hernandez, Rob, c	.200	10	3	2	1	0	1	5	0

PITCHING	W	L	ERA	G	SV	IP	H	BB	SO
Harvey, Ian	1	0	2.89	1	0	9	10	4	6
Bell, Jason	12	4	3.10	21	0	145	138	48	120
Nelson, Chris	11	4	3.67	19	0	118	118	52	99
Dean, Greg	9	1	4.42	20	1	94	77	84	79
Maurer, David	0	1	5.79	14	0	14	19	7	8
Holding, Brook	2	1	6.00	24	0	33	41	36	22
Brown, Dan	1	0	6.06	15	2	16	13	8	10
Smith, Larry	2	4	6.45	14	1	67	81	39	36
Nichols, Brent	4	2	6.80	16	1	41	50	21	27
Gaiko, Rob	4	2	7.81	25	3	28	35	18	27
Fleetwood, Tony	0	0	15.32	15	1	12	24	13	16

12 RICE

Coach: Wayne Graham   **Record:** 43-19

BATTING	AVG	AB	R	H	2B	3B	HR	RBI	SB
Quinn, Mark, dh-p	.380	250	60	95	20	4	18	89	2
Cruz, Jose Jr., of	.377	223	77	84	17	2	16	76	19
Boni, Chris, 2b	.328	232	71	76	8	7	2	41	17
Brooks, David, ss	.325	209	42	68	14	1	6	49	16
Berkman, Lance, of-1b	.322	245	48	79	26	3	6	46	10
Landry, Jacques, 3b	.312	218	52	68	11	4	14	56	3
Doyle, Paul, 1b-p	.311	177	45	55	4	0	1	29	4
Herndon, Adam, p-of	.308	13	4	4	0	0	1	4	1
Venghaus, Jeff, of	.284	225	48	64	7	3	3	30	14
Hallmark, Patrick, c	.276	221	57	61	7	6	5	34	14
Joseph, Kevin, ss	.267	45	7	12	2	0	0	5	1
McLaughlin, Tim, c	.244	41	7	10	2	0	0	8	0
Cathey, Joseph, 2b	.222	18	4	4	2	0	0	3	0
Hicks, Jim, of	.111	27	4	3	1	0	0	1	0

PITCHING	W	L	ERA	G	SV	IP	H	BB	SO
Anderson, Matt	11	2	2.51	28	1	72	46	52	63
McClain, Brooks	2	1	2.73	14	1	26	19	20	18
Taylor, Mark	4	1	4.18	18	1	56	46	50	55
Shaddix, Jeff	2	0	4.74	10	0	25	20	18	15
Brown, Allen	4	2	5.01	20	1	65	71	24	41
Davis, Dana	8	3	5.33	20	0	76	64	58	58
Quinn, Mark	6	3	5.35	22	1	66	64	49	40
Herndon, Adam	2	2	5.46	18	0	57	60	43	30
Feris, Chad	2	2	5.64	9	0	22	21	20	28
Wilson, Mike	1	0	5.72	11	1	28	28	33	24
Doyle, Paul	0	3	7.54	19	3	23	19	19	30

13

WICHITA STATE

Coach: Gene Stephenson   **Record:** 53-17

BATTING	AVG	AB	R	H	2B	3B	HR	RBI	SB
Adams, Jason, ss	.398	266	82	106	25	4	16	82	17
Taylor, Richie, of	.385	244	65	94	19	2	9	74	12
Thomas, Ben, 1b-p	.368	182	45	67	11	1	7	44	10
Reese, Nathan, c	.367	177	38	65	13	0	3	45	3
Blake, Casey, 3b	.362	276	89	100	19	1	10	65	29
Davis, Casey, of-dh	.339	171	34	58	16	2	5	43	18
Stine, Jerry, of	.328	186	49	61	11	2	4	44	13
Young, Randy, of	.306	291	74	89	8	3	3	26	64
Bauer, Chris, 2b-p	.289	135	33	39	5	2	0	20	20
McCollough, Adam, c-dh	.285	144	26	41	5	0	8	22	4
Ficken, Jason, 2b	.270	126	22	34	7	1	0	23	11
Wyckoff, Travis, p-dh	.258	66	19	17	3	0	0	14	8
Bichelmeyer, Jason, 1b	.250	60	9	15	3	0	1	12	1
Adams, John, of	.220	41	7	9	2	0	0	6	3
Duplechain, Marty, 1b	.207	58	6	12	2	0	2	9	0
Cheatham, T.J., 2b	.111	18	4	2	0	0	0	2	3

PITCHING	W	L	ERA	G	SV	IP	H	BB	SO
Looper, Braden	3	3	1.77	27	13	56	44	18	45
Bauer, Chris	4	2	2.06	15	1	35	20	17	20
Foral, Steve	3	3	2.44	19	1	52	42	24	58
Evans, Mike	0	0	2.61	4	0	10	12	9	16
Wyckoff, Travis	6	0	3.50	25	4	64	45	32	55
Drumright, Mike	11	3	3.61	18	0	120	106	38	117
Baird, Brandon	11	3	3.72	18	0	102	107	27	74
Thomas, Ben	5	0	4.47	12	0	54	62	20	29
Dobson, Matt	2	0	4.60	10	0	16	17	10	12
Edwards, Tony	1	0	4.85	13	1	26	27	8	10
Krafft, Jason	3	1	6.52	9	1	29	35	9	29
Brandley, Mike	4	2	7.94	12	0	40	55	23	21

14

ALABAMA

Coach: Jim Wells   **Record:** 42-23

BATTING	AVG	AB	R	H	2B	3B	HR	RBI	SB
Moller, Chris, 1b	.405	215	35	87	15	2	10	44	4
Jordan, Jason, dh-1b	.332	241	42	80	16	2	6	36	0
Taft, Brett, ss	.306	235	50	72	18	1	7	30	5
Nodine, Todd, ph-pr	.300	10	7	3	0	0	1	1	1
Caruso, Joe, 2b	.298	198	38	59	13	2	5	26	5
Loflin, Rusty, of	.298	94	20	28	8	1	5	23	0
Mohr, Dustan, of	.293	246	38	72	7	4	12	44	3
Norris, Dax, c-dh	.283	254	45	72	18	2	3	34	1
Bounds, Drew, of	.282	85	22	24	3	3	1	14	7
Peterson, Tad, of-3b	.281	171	25	48	1	1	1	19	14
DuBose, Anthony, of	.276	221	35	61	3	1	2	25	6
Hill, Alan, c	.262	61	11	16	1	0	2	15	0
Campus, Joe, 2b	.250	44	5	11	3	0	1	7	2
Duncan, Nate, 3b	.165	139	18	23	2	0	0	14	4
Weil, Scott, dh	.133	15	6	2	0	0	1	4	0

PITCHING	W	L	ERA	G	SV	IP	H	BB	SO
Ainsworth, Craig	3	1	1.50	9	0	24	23	11	12
Young, Tim	6	3	1.67	26	7	54	37	23	51
Lamb, Neal	7	1	2.81	20	1	74	69	21	53
Eilers, Chris	6	3	3.48	17	1	101	90	30	86
Duman, Buster	3	0	3.62	15	2	37	40	11	32
Collins, John	5	5	3.62	15	0	92	87	35	66
Detoto, Rick	1	0	4.24	9	0	17	17	6	17
Colgrove, Joel	6	4	4.40	18	0	94	99	35	82
Schleuss, Will	4	6	5.18	14	0	73	80	47	75

15

LOUISIANA STATE

Coach: Skip Bertman   **Record:** 47-18

BATTING	AVG	AB	R	H	2B	3B	HR	RBI	SB
Morris, Warren, 2b	.369	252	70	95	17	3	8	50	18
Moore, Jeramie, 1b	.357	14	3	5	0	0	1	7	0
Klostermeyer, Mike, 1b-of	.349	235	65	82	20	6	10	62	17
Furniss, Eddy, dh-1b	.326	215	30	70	14	1	9	52	2
Williams, Jason, ss	.315	267	63	84	20	0	10	47	9
Berardi, Scott, c	.313	83	19	26	5	0	2	11	2
Cooley, Chad, of	.308	260	51	80	24	3	7	61	11
Dunn, Nathan, 3b	.303	208	58	63	12	2	15	50	12
Koerner, Mike, of	.294	160	40	47	4	2	6	33	8
Bowles, Justin, of	.278	198	42	55	12	2	6	37	4
Lanier, Tim, c	.250	164	28	41	11	2	4	26	3
Wilson, Brad, 3b	.214	42	9	9	2	0	0	3	2
Ainsworth, Kevin, of	.107	75	15	14	3	0	1	9	5
Reese, Stan, p-of	.174	23	2	4	0	0	1	0	0
Bernhardt, Tom, of	.137	51	11	7	2	0	2	9	2

LSU Mainstay. Righthander Scott Schultz led the Tigers with 11 wins and 150 strikeouts.

PITCHING	W	L	ERA	G	SV	IP	H	BB	SO
Reese, Stan	3	1	3.35	18	0	43	38	28	28
Zweig, Ivan	2	1	3.41	10	2	32	32	8	29
Yarnall, Eddie	5	0	3.45	16	0	60	46	36	87
Schultz, Scott	11	4	3.46	16	0	117	97	27	150
Coogan, Patrick	2	0	3.72	8	0	19	15	3	27
Berthelot, Eric	2	1	3.72	22	0	29	23	16	34
Fitterer, Scott	3	3	3.78	24	5	50	58	10	48
Daugherty, Brian	0	1	4.23	24	2	28	25	15	31
Laxton, Brett	4	4	4.37	13	0	68	65	42	65
McCabe, Bhrett	6	1	4.80	26	1	45	35	16	39
Winders, Brian	2	1	4.99	21	0	52	45	31	49
Tyson, Jeremy	3	1	5.81	9	0	26	27	7	24

TEXAS A&M

Coach: Mark Johnson   **Record:** 44-22

BATTING	AVG	AB	R	H	2B	3B	HR	RBI	SB
Curl, John, dh-1b	.415	212	61	88	21	2	18	58	1
Alexander, Chad, of	.387	274	79	106	17	5	17	70	16
Allen, Chad, of	.373	255	63	95	22	6	10	59	23
Bailey, Jeff, 1b-dh	.347	213	45	74	10	3	9	47	1
Barber, Paul, 3b	.313	147	23	46	8	2	1	26	4
Shiflett, William, c	.301	113	24	34	7	0	3	17	1
Huffman, Ryan, of	.296	125	33	37	5	4	5	26	8
Stephens, Jason, 2b	.291	158	33	46	9	2	7	41	3
Minor, David, of	.289	45	11	13	0	1	0	8	2
Petru, Rich, 2b	.276	105	17	29	4	0	1	14	3
Garrick, Matt, c	.276	98	21	27	3	1	3	18	5
Alvarez, Sean, of	.266	109	32	29	5	2	4	24	6
Harris, Robert, ss	.243	239	50	58	14	3	7	38	12
Claybrook, Stephen, of	.219	32	13	7	2	0	1	4	9
Stratta, Mark, inf	.208	48	7	10	1	0	0	6	3
Matzke, J.J., 3b	.200	50	4	10	1	0	2	8	1
Collard, Tommy, 2b	.200	25	4	5	0	0	0	2	0
Carroll, Billy, c	.200	10	2	2	1	0	0	1	0

PITCHING	W	L	ERA	G	SV	IP	H	BB	SO
Barrett, Scott	0	0	1.93	5	0	5	2	6	5
Codrington, John	1	0	2.25	5	0	8	8	2	6
Barber, Paul	4	0	2.76	18	3	33	18	22	29
Boring, Rich	0	0	3.68	4	0	7	7	11	2
Clarkson, Tim	4	1	3.86	15	0	42	36	13	24
Mitchell, Dean	8	1	4.33	19	0	73	76	23	46
Parker, Brian	2	5	4.78	22	4	49	54	21	49
Atchley, Justin	9	6	5.00	16	0	113	138	18	79
Rupe, Ryan	6	3	5.05	14	0	77	88	26	60
Sneed, John	6	3	5.08	17	0	78	76	46	52
Conrad, Chris	0	0	5.63	5	0	8	11	8	5
McIntyre, Spencer	2	1	6.35	15	1	23	20	15	14
King, Shane	1	1	7.46	12	0	41	50	19	26
Allen, Chad	1	0	10.13	9	0	11	14	4	5

Coach: Dave Snow   **Record:** 39-25

BATTING	AVG	AB	R	H	2B	3B	HR	RBI	SB
Liefer, Jeff, 3b	.354	237	63	84	16	1	13	56	14
Skett, Will, of	.340	141	26	48	13	2	4	38	5
Hodges, Jason, dh	.332	208	37	69	14	3	3	43	7
Pierce, Kirk, c	.326	176	34	58	8	1	7	34	1
Minici, Jason, of	.320	241	55	77	16	6	10	52	5
Frank, Nic, of	.319	207	43	66	11	0	0	28	19
Knupfer, Jason, ss	.300	180	27	54	6	1	0	19	11
Tagliaferri, Jeff, 1b	.297	148	21	44	8	0	7	32	4
Snow, Casey, of	.275	80	14	22	6	1	2	19	3
Martin, Casey, c-dh	.245	53	9	13	1	1	2	5	0
Falsken, Tim, 2b	.233	236	32	55	10	2	2	34	9
Rivera, Keith, of	.231	78	25	18	1	0	1	6	13
Montenegro, Jose, ss	.227	44	9	10	0	0	1	1	1
Watson, Al, 2b	.206	34	5	7	0	0	0	1	2
Stevenson, David, 1b	.192	52	6	10	1	1	2	16	0
Harrison, Dana, of	.154	13	9	2	0	0	0	1	1
Stembridge, Mike, 1b	.122	41	3	5	2	0	0	6	1

PITCHING	W	L	ERA	G	SV	IP	H	BB	SO
Steves, Ron	1	0	1.35	5	0	7	2	7	6
Rivette, Scott	9	5	2.91	18	0	130	121	49	144
Gonzalez, Gabe	3	7	3.31	39	20	68	66	25	83
Wilson, Kyle	13	3	3.74	22	0	101	116	25	60
Biddle, Rocky	6	1	3.74	18	0	108	94	49	122
Fitzpatrick, Luke	2	2	4.60	15	0	43	40	29	32
Hueston, Steve	2	2	5.23	20	1	65	56	44	52
Hecht, Geoff	1	0	5.25	12	0	12	11	6	6
Wyckoff, Ethan	0	0	5.40	9	0	10	11	5	6
Jones, Marcus	1	0	6.43	2	0	7	9	1	4
Sanchez, Alex	1	2	10.80	14	0	5	6	10	1
Siegel, Justin	0	3	12.00	20	0	21	28	17	12

Coach: Don Kessinger   **Record:** 40-22

BATTING	AVG	AB	R	H	2B	3B	HR	RBI	SB
Dellucci, David, of	.410	229	67	94	15	6	17	63	31
Mensik, Todd, 1b	.346	234	49	81	17	1	6	57	1
Morgan, Jim, of	.329	149	21	49	9	2	6	35	4
Harrelson, Richy, 3b	.327	202	35	66	12	0	2	31	3
Johnson, Jeff, ss	.300	237	46	71	18	3	5	37	10
Afenir, Tom, c	.299	174	29	52	14	2	2	28	4
Huisman, Jason, 2b-3b	.295	132	19	39	4	0	0	19	4
Abernathy, Matt, dh	.290	176	32	51	11	1	11	26	2
Swan, David, c	.273	33	4	9	3	0	0	7	0
Ignatius, Joe, of	.241	141	20	34	5	2	1	24	9
Knight, John, of	.241	133	35	32	3	2	0	8	13
Bryan, Doyle, dh	.232	69	10	16	1	1	1	13	0
Lewis, Keith, 2b	.226	146	25	33	6	0	1	14	4
MacMillan, Marc, of	.217	92	16	20	1	1	0	4	5

PITCHING	W	L	ERA	G	SV	IP	H	BB	SO
McKenzie, Jason	2	1	1.30	27	8	42	17	21	35
Price, Jamey	11	6	1.72	19	0	141	104	16	118
Callaway, Mickey	7	7	3.39	23	0	109	105	40	79
DeYoung, Dan	3	2	3.45	23	3	63	53	31	33
Young, Ryan	5	1	3.48	11	0	41	28	33	24
Easterling, Jason	0	0	4.70	8	0	15	10	15	11
Barbour, Charles	0	0	4.76	11	0	11	6	7	3
McNeese, John	10	4	5.29	18	0	99	113	32	71
Prine, Blaine	0	0	5.40	6	0	7	4	5	3
Vowell, Chris	2	1	5.67	12	0	27	33	11	12

Coach: Jay Bergman   **Record:** 49-13

BATTING	AVG	AB	R	H	2B	3B	HR	RBI	SB
Johnson, Adam, of	.365	203	44	74	21	0	8	66	9
Marrillia, Tony, of	.335	224	49	75	15	3	1	42	26
Morales, Alex, of	.329	225	60	74	12	8	6	28	19
King, Brad, dh-c	.310	168	33	52	12	0	3	31	1
Tocco, Todd, 1b	.303	201	36	61	10	0	4	39	11
Weaver, Jay, 2b	.300	10	1	3	0	0	0	1	0
Moser, Andy, 2b-3b	.278	97	18	27	6	1	0	12	4
Loubier, Scott, c	.260	204	26	53	18	1	5	48	2
Sheffer, Chad, ss	.243	206	39	50	10	2	3	21	26
Gage, Rookie, 2b	.227	141	29	32	3	0	0	17	7
Gladwin, Rob, dh-1b	.222	63	8	14	3	0	0	7	1
Bechtol, Billy, 3b	.211	95	16	20	4	0	0	6	3
Betancourt, George, of	.172	29	1	5	0	0	0	1	0
Bellhorn, Todd, of	.135	37	3	5	2	0	0	1	2

PITCHING	W	L	ERA	G	SV	IP	H	BB	SO
Lubozynski, Matt	1	0	1.23	8	0	15	9	2	12
Scutero, Brian	9	1	2.20	23	4	45	31	12	36
Golden, Steve	2	0	2.20	14	0	33	27	14	18
Gomes, Brian	8	1	2.95	15	0	82	75	14	51
Weeden, Carey	4	0	2.97	16	0	30	25	6	24
Riegert, Tim	2	1	3.10	11	1	29	29	14	25
Veniard, Jay	8	3	3.38	16	0	101	103	27	79
Cozart, Craig	10	2	3.59	17	0	90	97	22	60
Foran, John	1	3	3.81	22	7	26	18	17	29
Lawrence, Rich	4	2	3.81	12	0	59	56	18	58

Coach: Pat Harrison   **Record:** 36-19

BATTING	AVG	AB	R	H	2B	3B	HR	RBI	SB
Christenson, Ryan, of	.376	226	74	85	13	7	7	32	21
Newhan, David, of	.367	215	50	79	13	2	11	48	35
Hodgdon, Justin, 2b	.345	165	24	57	10	2	0	26	3
Gamboa, Ruben, 1b	.335	185	23	62	16	0	7	46	2
Gonzalez, Gerardo, dh-1b	.322	202	35	65	13	1	8	44	2
Luraschi, Clay, of	.320	50	9	16	2	0	1	5	0
Konrady, Dennis, ss	.292	209	43	61	8	1	1	36	3
Reid, Rob, 2b-ss	.274	113	15	31	4	1	0	9	1
Twombley, Dennis, c	.254	118	15	30	8	0	2	16	0
Lopez, Mark, of	.236	110	14	26	5	1	0	16	6
Cohen, Jason, 3b	.231	173	23	40	14	0	2	21	3
Ashley, Steve, c	.229	70	10	16	4	0	1	9	1
Oder, Josh, p-of	.217	23	6	5	0	0	0	3	0
Cosbey, Chris, of	.176	17	5	3	0	1	0	1	1
Tippin, Greg, of	.159	69	6	11	2	0	3	7	0

PITCHING	W	L	ERA	G	SV	IP	H	BB	SO
Brubaker, Eric	10	2	1.25	31	6	50	38	9	44
Wolf, Randy	9	1	2.16	15	0	96	69	36	89
Melcher, James	1	1	2.62	9	0	10	12	3	5
Oder, Josh	1	0	3.44	12	0	18	19	8	9
Workman, John	0	0	3.60	23	1	50	57	14	37
Vasquez, Tim	2	3	4.01	18	0	34	29	12	22
Wise, Matt	6	2	4.38	18	1	72	81	24	66
LeBlanc, Jason	3	3	5.01	18	1	79	90	29	49
Gregory, Greg	3	5	5.48	13	0	67	80	34	38
Gibbons, Jeff	1	1	6.86	13	0	22	35	4	13

Coach: Cliff Gustafson   **Record:** 44-19

BATTING	AVG	AB	R	H	2B	3B	HR	RBI	SB
Escamilla, Roman, c-dh	.392	51	4	20	2	0	1	2	1
Byers, MacGregor, 3b	.379	198	48	75	16	1	3	49	3
Edelstein, Chris, of	.372	199	36	74	8	1	4	44	10
Loeffler, Brett, of	.347	75	18	26	4	1	5	24	5
Peoples, Danny, 1b-dh	.343	175	47	60	15	0	11	62	5
Morenz, Shea, of	.336	226	61	76	22	4	9	52	4
Campbell, Wylie, 2b	.311	209	73	65	10	4	1	25	32
Kiemsteadt, Clint, dh	.309	81	25	25	3	1	1	23	4
Taylor, Jerry, of	.301	206	54	62	14	1	6	41	7
Harkrider, Kip, ss	.300	240	57	72	13	5	0	55	9
Randolph, Steve, of	.291	103	30	30	9	0	4	22	2
Blessing, Chad, 3b-of	.281	89	23	25	11	0	3	24	4
Salinas, Trey, c-dh	.255	55	11	14	3	0	0	10	0
Layne, Jason, 1b	.224	49	9	11	1	1	1	6	1
Webb, J.P., c	.187	107	20	20	4	1	0	18	2

PITCHING	W	L	ERA	G	SV	IP	H	BB	SO
Clements, Kelly	2	1	3.49	25	0	28	28	22	23
O'Dell, Jake	11	3	3.77	22	2	93	82	51	89
Senterfitt, Mark	8	4	4.56	17	0	99	110	60	52
Smart, J.D.	14	4	4.68	24	1	137	148	55	109
Hinojosa, JoJo	1	0	4.72	17	0	27	28	12	12
Cravey, Brian	4	3	4.81	22	7	39	37	16	30
Kjos, Ryan	0	0	4.96	11	0	16	12	26	18
French, Eric	2	0	5.40	17	0	40	38	20	38
McKinney, Brian	0	1	8.55	6	0	20	18	21	18
Weaver, Rad	1	2	9.00	14	1	19	21	20	15
Duke, Jason	1	1	11.93	10	0	14	25	14	8

22 FLORIDA INTERNATIONAL

Coach: Danny Price   **Record:** 50-11

BATTING	AVG	AB	R	H	2B	3B	HR	RBI	SB
Stewart, Paxton, of-1b	.358	148	36	53	13	3	3	33	9
Munoz, Juan, of	.344	192	44	66	10	3	1	28	10
Lowell, Mike, 2b	.338	216	40	73	15	1	3	34	12
Lebron, Francisco, 1b	.335	158	32	53	11	1	5	32	2
Speed, Dorian, of	.326	184	38	60	14	3	1	33	37
Warfield, Malcolm, 3b	.325	163	32	53	8	1	2	34	11
Ferrer, Eddie, dh-inf	.289	211	33	61	4	2	1	28	15
Vazquez, Manny, of	.272	173	32	47	8	5	3	25	13
Rodriguez, Ryan, ss	.253	150	21	38	8	0	1	26	5
McNally, Jason, c	.195	113	21	22	6	0	1	14	3
Hopler, Jimmy, 3b	.194	36	7	7	0	0	0	4	0
Suarez, Marc, c	.174	46	12	8	1	0	2	11	2
Mahoney, Sean, of	.154	13	3	2	1	0	0	5	0

PITCHING	W	L	ERA	G	SV	IP	H	BB	SO
Burns, Joseph	9	0	1.20	12	0	67	53	19	46
Rodriguez, Fernando	0	0	1.23	5	0	7	10	4	7
Thomas, Evan	15	2	1.70	20	0	127	76	45	146
Palacios, Richard	9	1	1.99	24	2	86	62	37	58
Poehnelt, Vito	1	1	2.84	10	0	13	6	5	11
Emiliano, Jamie	0	1	2.89	27	16	28	24	13	29
Burke, Jeff	3	1	3.22	7	0	22	18	11	13
Tidwell, Chris	5	3	3.70	12	0	66	57	27	52
Fernandez, Omar	8	2	3.79	16	0	74	70	29	45

23 FRESNO STATE

Coach: Bob Bennett   **Record:** 41-22

BATTING	AVG	AB	R	H	2B	3B	HR	RBI	SB
Rupcich, Larry, 2b	.357	14	3	5	1	0	0	2	0
Freitas, Joseph, of	.340	203	54	69	12	5	9	43	5
Curtis, Matt, c-3b	.337	243	55	82	22	2	5	40	0
Freitas, Jeremy, of	.333	24	3	8	0	0	0	4	0
Wood, Ryan, of	.323	251	52	81	11	4	0	27	33
Hennecke, Pete, 3b	.286	189	27	54	12	3	2	25	1
Borges, James, 1b	.285	172	33	49	7	0	1	33	1
Chiaramonte, Giuseppe, dh-c	.281	210	41	59	12	4	11	55	0
Reynoso, Ben, ss	.275	218	30	60	8	4	3	41	3
Feramisco, Derek, of	.271	70	11	19	2	4	1	11	1
Roberts, Noel, 2b	.263	80	11	21	2	0	0	5	1
Fisher, Jim, 2b	.262	183	31	48	13	1	4	34	3
Stone, Quentin, dh-1b	.253	91	14	23	3	0	1	13	1
Barnes, Larry, of-1b	.248	117	24	29	7	1	5	22	0
Kaitfors, Josh, of	.237	114	16	27	4	2	1	12	7
Brown, Chad, of	.200	20	4	4	0	0	0	2	0

PITCHING	W	L	ERA	G	SV	IP	H	BB	SO
Farfan, Shorty	1	4	2.86	28	10	57	55	31	40
Donnelly, Rob	7	5	2.98	23	3	91	70	56	91
Behn, Brendan	9	5	3.28	17	0	118	101	41	116
Gunther, Kevin	12	2	3.94	19	0	137	155	27	85
Naster, Jeff	3	0	3.94	15	1	30	30	8	26
Tucker, Brad	4	2	4.02	12	0	54	44	27	39
Enard, Tony	1	2	4.07	6	0	24	16	18	20
Navarro, Scott	3	1	4.32	17	2	33	32	16	33
Mercado, Victor	0	0	4.70	4	0	8	10	2	11
Powell, Michael	1	0	6.23	5	0	9	14	3	7

24 LAMAR

Coach: Jim Gilligan   **Record:** 38-24

BATTING	AVG	AB	R	H	2B	3B	HR	RBI	SB
Cook, Will, of	.383	188	56	72	15	0	8	43	7
Bunting, Chad, of	.354	223	59	79	16	2	1	32	24
Mapp, Eric, of	.332	232	55	77	14	6	13	68	9
Schroeder, Donny, 2b	.301	193	32	58	11	1	1	26	3
Lindsey, Robin, dh-c	.291	189	23	55	6	0	7	44	3
Rivera, Triny, 3b	.260	250	47	65	13	0	4	39	6

Lamar Leader. Lefthander Mike Pasqualicchio led Lamar to the NCAA regionals by winning 11 games.

	AVG	AB	R	H	2B	3B	HR	RBI	SB
Walker, Morgan, 1b	.236	225	40	53	8	0	10	48	4
Gafford, Cory, c	.235	149	25	35	8	1	2	16	2
Rauch, Bob, ss	.233	236	42	55	16	1	8	38	8
Van Wyk, Trevor, of-dh	.275	69	12	19	3	0	1	11	1
Duggen, David, p-of	.273	11	5	3	0	0	0	0	0
Cammack, Eric, p-of	.257	35	11	9	1	1	0	4	3
Jacobs, Ari, 2b	.086	35	13	3	1	0	0	0	0

PITCHING	W	L	ERA	G	SV	IP	H	BB	SO
Pasqualicchio, Mike	11	4	3.22	22	1	106	88	45	106
Smart, Kacey	9	2	3.40	16	0	103	104	27	51
Williams, Randy	4	0	3.46	15	1	52	50	21	51
Myhre, Owen	2	2	3.48	21	4	34	32	13	20
Cammack, Eric	4	1	3.91	11	0	51	40	21	38
Tyler, Jeffrey	1	1	3.93	11	0	18	21	9	15
King, Dustin	0	0	4.35	9	0	10	10	8	12
Dinkins, Jeff	2	2	4.40	16	1	47	53	15	21
Maas, Steve	0	1	5.16	10	1	23	20	8	14
Jensen, Phil	2	3	5.30	26	1	36	38	5	35
Lane, Kevin	3	6	6.42	21	1	41	55	20	34
Robinson, Jason	0	0	8.44	3	0	5	11	1	2

25 NORTH CAROLINA

Coach: Mike Roberts   **Record:** 39-23

BATTING	AVG	AB	R	H	2B	3B	HR	RBI	SB
Rowell, Josh, c	.381	155	32	59	10	1	2	27	1
Stoner, Mike, 1b-of	.320	253	47	81	15	1	12	41	8
Grimsley, Richie, of	.320	50	11	16	1	1	4	12	2
Smith, Antawan, of	.317	230	44	73	19	2	3	37	8
Kaplan, Brett, dh	.312	93	25	29	7	0	8	24	2
Boone, David, of	.305	220	42	67	11	2	10	51	7
Brown, Tyrone, of	.288	156	30	45	9	2	3	28	6
Torbett, Hanes, 3b-2b	.284	201	38	57	17	0	5	45	12
Raniszeski, Justin, 3b	.273	88	16	24	3	0	2	11	1
Husted, Larry, dh	.273	66	19	18	6	0	2	8	1
Whitlock, Brian, ss	.272	206	40	56	12	2	5	32	8
Coltrane, Crandel, dh-c	.262	61	9	16	4	0	3	8	1
McIver, Robby, 2b-3b	.259	58	11	15	4	1	3	9	1
Jones, Mitch, 2b-c	.228	158	26	36	4	2	1	15	11
Gonzalez, Gil, 1b-dh	.228	79	13	18	6	0	4	21	1

PITCHING	W	L	ERA	G	SV	IP	H	BB	SO
Chrismon, Thad	7	4	2.86	36	12	63	60	20	61
Murphy, Sean	11	4	3.21	20	0	112	91	70	125
Wallace, Jim	5	1	3.75	18	0	60	59	33	37
Stein, Ethan	6	4	4.20	19	1	75	86	17	52
Richardson, Corey	1	1	4.67	10	0	17	11	24	28
Potter, Josh	1	1	4.78	14	0	32	32	24	31
Willman, Brian	5	5	4.95	15	0	104	116	33	83
Yoder, A.Y.	1	1	7.63	15	0	46	57	23	38
McAllister, Scott	0	1	8.79	9	0	14	22	19	9
Severance, Eric	1	1	9.53	15	0	17	25	11	14

CONFERENCE STANDINGS, LEADERS

NCAA Division I Conferences

*Won conference tournament
Boldface: NCAA regional participant/conference leader
#Conference department leader who does not qualify for batting/pitching leaders

ATLANTIC COAST CONFERENCE

	Conference		Overall	
	W	L	W	L
Clemson	**20**	**4**	**54**	**14**
*Florida State	16	7	53	16
Georgia Tech	16	8	38	22
North Carolina	14	10	39	23
Wake Forest	13	11	34	24
North Carolina State	12	12	36	24
Virginia	8	15	26	29
Duke	4	20	30	27
Maryland	4	20	20	37

ALL-CONFERENCE TEAM: C—Tucker Barr, So., Georgia Tech. **1B**—David Miller, Jr., Clemson. **2B**—Tom Sergio, So., North Carolina State. **3B**—Brandon Hensley, Sr., Georgia Tech. **SS**—Mark Melito, Sr., Wake Forest. **OF**—Tony Ellison, Jr., North Carolina State; Shane Monahan, Jr., Clemson; Ryan Ritter, Jr., Georgia Tech. **DH**—Dave Lardieri, So., Wake Forest. **Util**—Matt Saier, Sr., Georgia Tech. **SP**—Jason Dawsey, Jr., Clemson; Jonathan Johnson, Jr., Florida State. **RP**—Scott Winchester, Jr., Clemson.
Player of the Year: Shane Monahan, Clemson.

INDIVIDUAL BATTING LEADERS
(Minimum 125 At-Bats)

	AVG	AB	R	H	2B	3B	HR	RBI	SB
Ellison, Tony, NC State	**.398**	246	72	98	14	1	**24**	79	7
Sergio, Tom, NC State	.391	233	70	91	8	6	3	33	17
Monahan, Shane, Clemson	.388	273	**82**	**106**	22	5	12	52	21
Ritter, Ryan, Georgia Tech	.383	256	76	98	12	4	20	69	6
Rowell, Josh, UNC	.381	155	32	59	10	1	2	27	1
Byers, Scott, Georgia Tech	.380	221	57	84	25	0	7	59	2
Miller, David, Clemson	.380	271	79	103	14	**10**	9	78	27
Lardieri, David, WF	.373	236	50	88	21	3	6	53	1
Mientkiewicz, Doug, Fla. St.	.371	248	75	92	20	3	19	**80**	19
Duarte, Luis, Duke	.367	218	46	80	18	2	4	38	10
King, Mike, Duke	.357	221	54	79	17	4	11	49	1
Melito, Mark, Wake Forest	.354	223	58	79	12	3	11	48	7
Thomas, J.J., Georgia Tech	.348	210	57	73	18	0	13	46	3
Sorrow, Michael, Ga. Tech	.347	236	63	82	13	5	4	41	4
Burnham, Gary, Clemson	.344	241	61	83	**27**	4	8	62	5
Fischer, Mark, Ga. Tech	.339	224	50	76	12	7	4	56	5
LeCroy, Matt, Clemson	.333	255	55	85	18	0	15	72	0
Lasater, Robby, NC State	.333	201	34	67	13	0	6	43	0
Zech, Scott, Florida State	.330	227	60	75	12	2	3	43	19
Counts, Justin, Virginia	.327	208	49	68	18	1	6	40	10
Weber, Jake, NC State	.326	258	71	84	11	4	10	54	10
Drew, J.D., Florida State	.325	209	54	68	7	3	17	63	11
Galloway, Paul, Virginia	.324	210	46	68	14	2	9	47	6
Faurot, Adam, Fla. State	.324	145	37	47	10	2	1	32	8
Hodges, Randy, Fla. State	.323	246	63	84	11	3	3	43	24
Hensley, Brandon, Ga. Tech	.322	208	56	67	13	1	7	48	1
Maluchnik, Gregg, Duke	.322	208	36	67	11	2	4	47	2
Drabik, Jeff, Wake Forest	.322	202	54	65	14	1	10	39	3
Guthrie, David, NC State	.321	190	37	61	7	1	0	17	4
Stoner, Mike, UNC	.320	253	47	81	15	1	12	41	8
Chiou, Frankie, Duke	.318	198	55	63	9	2	5	28	9
Smith, Antawan, UNC	.317	230	44	73	19	2	3	37	8
Galloway, John, Virginia	.317	161	44	51	9	3	3	22	9
Kramer, Jason, Wake Forest	.314	239	61	75	20	0	17	65	0
Itzoe, Josh, Wake Forest	.313	134	20	42	7	1	4	27	1
Bernard, Brian, WF	.312	202	35	63	14	2	6	29	1
Robinson, Adam, Virginia	.311	177	28	55	7	1	4	38	6
Seward, Donnie, Virginia	.310	145	42	45	15	2	0	10	8
Barkett, Andy, NC State	.306	219	49	67	17	1	9	59	5
Boone, David, UNC	.305	220	42	67	11	2	10	51	7
Hartman, Ron, Maryland	.302	199	30	60	13	1	4	35	3
Maddox, Garry, Maryland	.299	184	44	55	9	2	6	33	14
Gilleland, Ryan, Virginia	.297	192	25	57	9	0	2	28	10
Wagner, Jeff, Maryland	.296	213	45	63	9	2	9	39	22
Duffie, Will, Clemson	.294	197	33	58	10	3	4	34	1

Marciano, John, Maryland .... .292 202 36 59 12 1 7 34 2
Lopez, Mickey, Fla. State .... .290 272 65 79 19 3 7 50 **32**
Barr, Tucker, Ga. Tech .... .290 224 54 65 15 1 14 70 1
Brown, Tyrone, UNC .... .288 156 30 45 9 2 3 28 6

INDIVIDUAL PITCHING LEADERS
(Minimum 50 Innings)

	W	L	ERA	G	SV	IP	H	BB	SO
#Winchester, Scott, Clemson	4	2	0.59	33	**14**	46	23	16	42
Morgan, Scooby, Fla. State	4	3	1.46	25	1	56	33	24	50
Yocum, David, Florida State	**12**	3	**2.61**	18	0	114	94	43	128
Dawsey, Jason, Clemson	11	4	2.78	19	0	129	101	45	**133**
Chrismon, Thad, UNC	7	4	2.86	36	12	63	60	20	61
Johnson, Jonathan, Fla. St.	**12**	3	2.89	19	0	134	98	53	130
Bell, Mike, Florida State	7	3	2.90	13	0	62	61	22	53
Cruz, Charlie, Florida State	8	1	2.98	18	0	109	101	51	118
Howell, Chuck, Fla. State	4	1	3.05	27	0	56	48	18	48
Benson, Kris, Clemson	8	3	3.20	14	0	79	75	23	79
Murphy, Sean, UNC	11	4	3.21	20	0	112	91	70	125
Seaver, Mark, Wake Forest	6	4	3.26	15	0	99	80	32	97
Vining, Ken, Clemson	4	0	3.39	22	2	69	53	25	78
Wilson, Kris, Georgia Tech	8	2	3.46	18	0	112	109	35	101
Daneker, Pat, Virginia	4	4	3.57	13	0	88	88	26	66
Koch, Billy, Clemson	7	2	3.72	16	0	87	70	37	111
Watson, Mark, Clemson	7	1	3.75	12	0	50	33	35	42
Wallace, Jim, UNC	5	1	3.75	18	0	60	59	33	37
Starman, Craig, Duke	5	7	3.91	17	0	92	100	19	50
Cappelmann, John, Virginia	3	3	3.95	9	0	55	51	17	54
Lee, Corey, NC State	3	3	3.96	14	0	61	58	43	75
Stein, Ethan, UNC	4	4	4.20	19	0	75	86	17	52
Cronemeyer, Mike, NC State	6	3	4.34	30	8	56	51	24	58
Dishman, Richard, Duke	6	4	4.36	18	0	76	60	58	81
Darwin, David, Duke	6	4	4.55	19	0	93	111	35	59
Atkins, Ross, Wake Forest	10	7	4.67	17	0	104	108	44	91
Greisinger, Seth, Virginia	6	7	4.70	14	0	98	110	34	94
Harvey, Terry, NC State	9	4	4.77	19	0	121	129	41	131
Willman, Brian, UNC	5	4	4.85	15	0	104	116	33	83

ATLANTIC-10 CONFERENCE

	Conference		Overall	
	W	L	W	L
*Massachusetts	**19**	**5**	**38**	**14**
George Washington	17	7	27	25
St. Bonaventure	12	9	22	23
Rutgers	13	11	28	29
St. Joseph's	12	12	25	30
West Virginia	11	13	18	32
Temple	9	15	16	33
Duquesne	7	17	17	35
Rhode Island	5	16	12	31

ALL-CONFERENCE TEAM: C—Tom Tegeler, Sr., St. Bonaventure. **1B**—Eric Mullen, Jr., St. Joseph's. **2B**—Lance Migita, Sr., George Washington. **3B**—Tom Whalen, Jr., Temple. **SS**—Tony Myers, Jr., West Virginia. **OF**—Ryan Jette, Jr., Massachusetts; Bill Knight, Sr., Massachusetts; Danny Lauer, Jr., St. Joseph's. **DH**—Nelson Ubaldo, Jr., Massachusetts. **P**—Jamey Keysor, Jr., Duquesne; Jay Murphy, Sr., Massachusetts.
Player of the Year: Bill Knight, Massachusetts. **Pitcher of the Year:** Jay Murphy, Massachusetts.

INDIVIDUAL BATTING LEADERS
(Minimum 100 At-Bats)

	AVG	AB	R	H	2B	3B	HR	RBI	SB
Migita, Lance, Ga. Wash.	**.437**	197	60	**86**	15	**6**	6	46	9
Whalen, Tom, Temple	.409	186	43	76	18	2	6	39	11
Ubaldo, Nelson, UMass	.398	171	44	68	12	0	8	46	11
Jette, Ryan, UMass	.387	173	58	67	7	4	1	23	**32**
Knight, Bill, UMass	.374	195	**61**	73	15	1	**19**	**72**	6
Lauer, Danny, St. Joe	.373	217	51	81	10	2	3	49	17
Myers, Tony, West Virginia	.372	172	35	64	13	1	12	46	7
Swaney, Chris, West Va.	.361	183	30	66	12	1	2	29	11

	AVG	AB	R	H	2B	3B	HR	RBI	SB
Weingartner, Bill, St. Joe	.359	198	43	71	10	2	4	50	7
Dagliere, Muchie, UMass	.343	181	50	62	9	1	8	38	7
Mullen, Eric, St. Joseph's	.342	187	41	64	14	2	6	51	15
Bennett, Mike, St. Bona	.341	170	38	58	11	1	4	44	8
Giallella, Brian, Rutgers	.337	193	43	65	**20**	4	3	36	6
Pelis, Andy, UMass	.337	163	39	55	13	0	8	41	3
Tegeler, Tom, St. Bona	.335	155	40	52	8	3	5	36	4
Williamson, Josh, West Va.	.333	153	34	51	11	4	1	21	7
Pileski, Mark, UMass	.331	166	35	55	18	2	5	36	10

INDIVIDUAL PITCHING LEADERS
(Minimum 40 Innings)

	W	L	ERA	G	SV	IP	H	BB	SO
Bennett, Jason, UMass	8	0	2.63	13	1	51	45	14	26
Barnsley, Scott, UMass	5	2	3.02	11	0	48	49	27	27
Hoppel, Steve, Temple	5	3	**3.41**	14	2	69	58	43	27
Phillips, Tom, Rutgers	5	4	3.41	14	0	71	66	29	24
Keysor, Jamey, Duquesne	**8**	1	3.47	12	0	70	56	33	49
Williams, Matt, Ga. Wash.	4	0	3.86	15	0	54	56	28	25
Clark, Ryan, Ga. Washington	4	5	3.90	15	0	62	63	37	25
Ligi, Rick, Rhode Island	0	4	4.23	14	1	45	52	27	25
Prusiensky, Bob, Rutgers	2	1	4.25	8	0	42	46	21	26
Spencer, Chad, West Va.	2	7	4.46	15	0	71	73	40	45
Healy, Dennis, Ga. Wash.	5	7	4.47	16	0	90	89	22	**74**
Murphy, Jay, UMass	**8**	4	4.53	13	0	89	98	28	59
#Johnson, Jed, St. Joe	8	6	4.84	17	0	87	106	31	56
#Stegen, Brian, Rutgers	1	2	4.97	27	**9**	29	36	19	24

BIG EAST CONFERENCE

	Conference		Overall	
	W	L	W	L
Providence	16	5	44	15
Seton Hall	14	7	38	16
Villanova	14	7	40	16
*Pittsburgh	12	9	39	16
St. John's	12	9	18	16
Boston College	8	13	21	24
Georgetown	4	17	17	34
Connecticut	4	17	13	30

ALL-CONFERENCE TEAM: C—Bob O'Toole, Jr., Providence. **1B**—Brian Sankey, Jr., Boston College. **2B**—Scott Palmieri, So., Providence. **3B**—Jason Cassesa, Jr., Villanova. **SS**—Mike Moriarty, Jr., Seton Hall. **OF**—Tim Casey, Sr., Seton Hall; Brian Fili, So., Villanova; Ryan McGinty, Sr., Villanova. **DH**—John Garside, Sr., Providence. **Util**—Chris Lemonis, Sr., St. John's. **P**—Mike Macone, Jr., Providence; Matt Morris, Jr., Seton Hall; Curt Romboli, Sr., Boston College.

Player of the Year: Bob O'Toole, Providence. **Pitcher of the Year:** Mike Macone, Providence.

INDIVIDUAL BATTING LEADERS
(Minimum 125 At-Bats)

	AVG	AB	R	H	2B	3B	HR	RBI	SB
Duffy, Jim, Seton Hall	**.429**	217	54	**93**	13	3	4	44	23
Penwell, Kevin, Boston Coll.	.425	127	29	54	11	3	1	24	12
Womelsdorf, Kurt, Pitt	.377	151	35	57	6	3	0	28	31
McGinty, Ryan, Villanova	.376	197	66	74	13	4	1	35	3
Moriarty, Mike, Seton Hall	.371	186	48	69	15	3	7	42	9
Sankey, Brian, Boston Coll.	.365	137	41	50	14	0	6	41	4
O'Toole, Bob, Providence	.364	206	**81**	75	17	2	**19**	57	18
Young, Steve, Villanova	.360	186	43	67	5	0	2	44	3
Cassesa, Jason, Villanova	.347	196	58	68	14	3	8	56	1
Conti, Jason, Pittsburgh	.347	196	49	68	12	3	2	41	33
McDonald, John, Prov.	.347	245	59	85	**20**	1	3	44	26
Bisson, Chris, UConn	.341	167	35	57	11	0	9	31	4
Garside, John, Providence	.340	159	26	54	10	0	5	46	1
Clifford, John, Villanova	.337	208	60	70	13	2	10	**64**	19
Gorecki, Ryan, Seton Hall	.331	181	42	60	10	0	0	32	31
DeBernardis, Jon, Pitt	.327	199	39	65	16	2	4	52	5
Crowley, Sam, Pitt	.327	147	28	48	2	0	0	22	16
Casey, Tim, Seton Hall	.326	184	45	60	10	3	8	46	11
Fili, Brian, Villanova	.325	197	67	64	10	1	4	28	22
Dellaero, Jason, St. John's	.323	127	20	41	6	3	1	26	1
Delvecchio, T.J., Prov.	.320	219	51	70	**20**	1	5	41	4
Kleinz, Larry, Villanova	.320	203	41	65	19	2	2	40	1
#Harrington, Roger, G'town	.273	183	38	50	8	**6**	3	22	**34**

INDIVIDUAL PITCHING LEADERS
(Minimum 50 Innings)

	W	L	ERA	G	SV	IP	H	BB	SO
Grilli, Jason, Seton Hall	8	2	**1.85**	14	0	78	73	34	63
Maerten, Mike, St. John's	4	3	2.20	8	0	65	52	25	38
Klopp, John, Villanova	4	1	2.31	28	**9**	58	44	20	37

	W	L	ERA	G	SV	IP	H	BB	SO
Incantalupo, Todd, Prov.	10	1	2.47	17	0	87	81	20	51
O'Brien, Jim, Providence	8	1	2.65	10	0	68	46	29	58
Morris, Matt, Seton Hall	10	3	2.68	14	0	94	64	54	104
Gehring, Clint, Seton Hall	5	3	3.14	12	0	77	72	21	58
Flanagan, Paul, Georgetown	3	5	3.35	16	0	54	41	29	40
Romboli, Curt, Boston Coll.	5	5	3.39	10	0	74	72	27	77
Katz, Craig, Boston College	5	2	3.67	9	0	54	52	30	24
Campbell, Tedde, Pitt	**15**	4	3.73	26	2	135	123	68	**109**
Herr, David, Villanova	8	2	3.74	15	0	87	80	41	84
Macone, Mike, Providence	7	4	3.75	13	0	94	73	47	79
Adair, Derek, St. John's	3	4	3.94	8	0	48	42	10	31
Doody, Kevin, Geogetown	5	7	4.24	14	0	93	105	21	62
Dunlea, Steve, Boston Coll.	5	5	4.27	13	0	72	88	37	40

BIG EIGHT CONFERENCE

	Conference		Overall	
	W	L	W	L
Oklahoma	21	7	42	16
*Oklahoma State	18	10	46	19
Iowa State	13	12	28	24
Nebraska	13	14	35	23
Kansas State	13	14	29	24
Kansas	9	17	24	33
Missouri	7	20	19	34

ALL-CONFERENCE TEAM: C—Javier Flores, So., Oklahoma. **1B**—Chris Richard, Jr., Oklahoma State. **2B**—Scott Poepard, So., Kansas State. **3B**—Tal Light, Jr., Oklahoma State. **SS**—Rich Hills, Sr., Oklahoma. **OF**—Darin Erstad, Jr., Nebraska; Herb Hardcastle, Jr., Oklahoma State; Chris Hess, Jr., Kansas State; Aric Thomas, Sr., Oklahoma. **DH**—Alvie Shepard, Jr., Nebraska. **Util**—Peter Prodanov, Sr., Oklahoma State. **SP**—Jason Bell, Jr., Oklahoma State; Matt Koeman, Jr., Kansas State; Chris Nelson, Sr., Oklahoma State; Mark Redman, Jr., Oklahoma; Jamie Splittorff, Jr., Kansas. **RP**—Jonas Armenta, So., Nebraska; Dave Pollak, Sr., Iowa State.

Co-Players of the Year: Darin Erstad, Nebraska; Mark Redman, Oklahoma.

INDIVIDUAL BATTING LEADERS
(Minimum 125 At-Bats)

	AVG	AB	R	H	2B	3B	HR	RBI	SB
Erstad, Darin, Nebraska	.410	251	84	**103**	20	**7**	19	76	11
Pethel, Pat, Iowa State	.399	153	35	61	9	3	1	29	25
Prodanov, Peter, OSU	.388	250	84	97	22	1	9	73	17
Hess, Chris, Kansas State	.387	212	63	82	13	5	2	42	15
Hardcastle, Herb, OSU	.362	177	51	64	17	1	10	46	3
Brown, Bobby, Oklahoma	.362	222	59	84	9	2	6	36	14
Meyer, Matt, Nebraska	.362	185	48	67	12	6	9	52	1
Flores, Javier, Oklahoma	.360	211	52	76	14	1	10	55	4
Thomas, Aric, Oklahoma	.357	244	63	87	8	2	2	29	**38**
Motley, Mel, Nebraska	.357	227	68	81	16	4	7	58	13
Sears, Todd, Nebraska	.346	156	51	54	10	3	10	50	4
Minor, Damon, Oklahoma	.344	183	46	63	12	5	10	44	4
Paul, Tristan, Oklahoma	.344	186	39	64	11	1	8	51	1
Shepherd, Alvie, Nebraska	.343	230	60	79	22	1	12	70	3
Hendrix, David, Kansas State	.339	177	41	60	17	1	5	48	5
Dalton, Jed, Nebraska	.337	264	75	89	22	3	7	46	18
Richard, Chris, Okla. State	.336	241	84	81	**23**	4	13	85	16
Light, Tal, Oklahoma State	.335	254	79	85	13	2	**26**	**104**	1
Konigsmark, Dave, Iowa State	.332	184	38	61	10	2	2	37	1
Terrell, Jeff, Missouri	.327	147	30	48	9	3	2	30	7
Poepard, Scott, Kansas State	.326	221	51	72	**23**	0	10	55	8
Byrd, Isaac, Kansas	.321	165	48	53	14	2	3	28	16
MacKay, Tripp, Okla. State	.319	273	**85**	87	10	5	3	50	16
Buchman, Tom, Missouri	.318	173	29	55	14	1	4	28	0
Shackelford, Brian, Oklahoma	.317	167	25	53	8	2	7	41	2
McNamara, Rusty, OSU	.315	213	60	67	9	3	2	26	7
King, Alex, Kansas	.315	127	16	40	10	1	1	25	1
Steelmon, Wyley, Okla. State	.314	185	45	58	15	0	13	61	0
Logan, Troy, Iowa State	.309	149	33	46	6	2	3	39	0
Fereday, Todd, Kansas St.	.308	201	48	62	11	3	5	48	7

INDIVIDUAL PITCHING LEADERS
(Minimum 50 Innings)

	W	L	ERA	G	SV	IP	H	BB	SO
Redman, Mark, Oklahoma	**15**	1	**2.22**	20	0	142	109	35	**158**
Bell, Jason, Oklahoma State	4	4	3.10	21	0	145	138	48	120
Armenta, Jonas, Nebraska	9	3	3.49	25	0	67	57	32	64
Nelson, Chris, Okla. State	11	4	3.67	19	0	118	118	52	99
Splittorff, Jamie, Kansas	6	6	3.91	16	0	115	114	56	93
Pollak, Dave, Iowa State	6	1	4.40	17	5	51	43	28	35
Dean, Greg, Oklahoma State	9	1	4.42	20	1	94	77	84	79
Ortiz, Russell, Oklahoma	3	2	4.53	18	1	52	47	35	56

All-American Lefty. Oklahoma's Mark Redman led the Big Eight Conference with 15 wins, a 2.22 ERA and 158 strikeouts.

Callier, Jeremy, Missouri	5	6	4.55	16	0	89	85	36	60
Andra, Jeff, Oklahoma	6	2	4.83	19	0	63	63	32	44
Sebring, Jeff, Iowa State	4	3	4.85	12	0	65	57	35	38
Barnes, Brian, Missouri	3	3	4.89	14	0	57	72	18	24
Koeman, Matt, Kansas State	6	2	4.96	10	0	69	57	46	71
#Keens, Robert, Kansas	2	3	5.40	30	6	63	72	27	46

BIG SOUTH CONFERENCE

	Conference		Overall	
	W	L	W	L
Winthrop	18	6	41	17
Radford	17	7	30	24
UNC Greensboro	17	7	35	19
Liberty	15	9	33	20
Maryland-Baltimore County	13	11	25	23
Towson State	10	14	24	28
Charleston Southern	8	16	17	36
Coastal Carolina	6	17	17	37
UNC Asheville	3	20	12	37

ALL-CONFERENCE TEAM: C—John Canetto, Sr., Coastal Carolina. **1B**—Jason Pruitt, Sr., Maryland-Baltimore County. **2B**—Jeff Berman, So., Maryland-Baltimore County. **3B**—Mike Martin, Jr., Maryland-Baltimore County. **SS**—Chris Pond, Sr., Coastal Carolina. **OF**—Jason Baker, Jr., Liberty; Tony Costantino, Sr., Winthrop; Duane Filchner, Sr., Radford. **DH**—Eric Filipek, Sr., UNC Asheville. **P**—Jim Abbott, Sr., Radford; Bryan Link, Sr., Winthrop.

Player of the Year: Bryan Link, Winthrop.

INDIVIDUAL BATTING LEADERS
(Minimum 100 At-Bats)

	AVG	AB	R	H	2B	3B	HR	RBI	SB
Filchner, Duane, Radford	.389	208	60	81	19	0	15	51	12
Dean, Jeff, Radford	.386	132	23	51	14	0	6	34	1
Pond, Chris, Coastal Carolina	.377	199	37	75	20	1	7	38	14
Pruitt, Jason, UMBC	.375	168	39	63	9	1	11	40	2
Young, Scott, UNCG	.371	194	38	72	13	4	3	40	10
Costantino, Tony, Winthrop	.370	230	55	85	11	2	1	30	26
Keller, Jeremy, Winthrop	.359	209	52	75	19	2	10	54	8
Dampeer, Kelly, Radford	.358	212	47	76	22	1	16	58	9
Weisgerber, Chip, Coastal Car.	.349	196	30	68	14	1	5	32	2
Martin, Mike, UMBC	.349	189	43	66	8	0	10	51	1
Baker, Jason, Liberty	.342	184	42	63	16	1	14	52	4
Sturek, Ken, Towson St.	.340	144	34	49	6	2	1	18	1
Vallillo, James, Towson St.	.339	171	47	58	11	2	9	43	3
Landon, Tag, UMBC	.336	134	33	45	11	1	3	23	1
Reed, Mark, Liberty	.332	154	40	51	10	1	2	29	5
Phillips, Nicky, UNCG	.330	191	44	63	8	4	3	32	17
Hutchinson, Ryan, Liberty	.328	131	32	43	6	2	10	30	2
Giles, Tim, UNCG	.327	196	29	64	11	1	12	45	5
Hartshorn, Todd, Towson St.	.325	117	22	38	7	1	5	27	0
Cisar, Jeff, Winthrop	.325	228	49	74	21	2	3	46	6
Weaver, Terry, Liberty	.322	215	41	69	15	6	6	38	9
Hollingswith, Travis, Win.	.321	209	38	67	14	2	5	30	2
Brennan, Bill, Radford	.318	176	34	56	11	2	5	33	19
Turner, Stephen, CC	.317	221	45	70	13	1	6	26	35

INDIVIDUAL PITCHING LEADERS
(Minimum 40 Innings)

	W	L	ERA	G	SV	IP	H	BB	SO
Link, Bryan, Winthrop	12	3	1.74	21	4	134	94	41	135
Bickers, Tim, Liberty	4	1	1.91	28	2	43	46	16	29
Gunter, Brad, Liberty	6	3	3.12	14	1	78	65	29	36
Abbott, Jim, Radford	9	2	3.14	15	0	97	74	42	113
Brown, Mike, Liberty	6	4	3.15	16	2	74	74	25	72
Kuykendall, Jay, UNCG	7	3	3.22	27	3	67	74	15	38
Peek, David, Winthrop	7	2	3.48	15	0	52	50	22	41
Sylvester, Anthony, UNCG	7	5	3.57	23	1	88	77	40	72
Harrison, Donovan, Char. So.	3	10	3.67	18	1	108	102	44	110
Hasselhoff, Derek, Towson St.	3	7	3.76	10	0	67	77	18	58
Kowalski, Stan, Char. So.	9	4	3.77	17	0	86	85	43	60
Abbott, Jim, Winthrop	2	1	3.77	22	6	45	44	17	41
Harrell, Tim, Liberty	6	2	3.79	13	0	71	67	31	53
Condon, Mike, Winthrop	8	5	3.79	16	1	107	98	42	99
Parsons, Jason, UNCG	7	4	4.04	28	1	71	68	32	59
Tillmon, Darrell, UNCG	9	1	4.09	26	2	84	81	15	77

BIG TEN CONFERENCE

	Conference		Overall	
	W	L	W	L
*Ohio State	18	10	40	23
Minnesota	16	12	31	28
Northwestern	15	13	36	19
Purdue	15	13	27	30
Penn State	13	13	25	29
Illinois	14	14	25	31
Iowa	13	15	29	24
Indiana	12	16	33	23
Michigan State	12	16	24	27
Michigan	10	16	24	29

ALL-CONFERENCE TEAM: C—Shane Gunderson, Jr., Minnesota. **1B**—Brian Mannino, Sr., Ohio State. **2B**—Ron Rojas, Sr., Northwestern. **3B**—Tony Bender, Sr., Minnesota. **SS**—Josh Klimek, So., Illinois. **OF**—Scott Ayotte, Sr., Michigan State; Tom Sinak, Sr., Illinois; Scott Weaver, Jr., Michigan. **DH**—Dan Seimetz, Fr., Ohio State. **SP**—Kevan Cannon, Jr., Ohio State; Todd Jensen, Sr., Purdue; Brad Niedermaier, Jr., Northwestern; Chad Schroeder, Jr., Northwestern. **RP**—Kurt Belger, Jr., Iowa.

Co-Players of the Year: Shane Gunderson, Minnesota; Scott Weaver, Michigan. **Pitcher of the Year:** Chad Schroeder, Northwestern.

INDIVIDUAL BATTING LEADERS
(Minimum 125 At-Bats)

	AVG	AB	R	H	2B	3B	HR	RBI	SB
Crotty, Mike, Indiana	.423	194	48	82	18	2	12	64	4
Weaver, Scott, Michigan	.418	170	44	71	13	2	10	42	13
Ayotte, Scott, Michigan State	.397	179	65	71	16	7	13	60	5
Seimetz, Dan, Ohio State	.396	197	50	78	20	3	10	58	0
Johnson, Andy, Michigan St.	.389	162	24	63	7	0	3	34	2
Gunderson, Shane, Minn.	.389	193	55	75	12	6	13	65	19
Mannino, Brian, Ohio State	.389	193	50	75	13	0	8	50	0
Estep, Mike, Ohio State	.388	206	43	80	13	2	4	38	1
Riggins, Matt, Michigan State	.383	167	34	64	13	3	7	48	2
Klimek, Josh, Illinois	.361	158	36	57	18	0	5	24	8
Billotte, Kevin, Penn State	.355	169	33	60	8	6	2	18	12
Bender, Tony, Minnesota	.351	205	41	72	16	1	8	56	5
Reeder, Jim, Northwestern	.343	178	44	61	11	5	3	31	7
Bucci, Carmen, Northwestern	.338	195	48	66	4	3	1	19	15
Sinak, Tom, Illinois	.338	195	34	66	9	1	12	43	7
Kaczmar, Scott, Ohio State	.338	213	51	72	16	1	17	52	6
Fuller, Brian, Northwestern	.337	163	40	55	17	3	10	50	5
Piacenti, Neil, Northwestern	.333	183	46	61	10	3	2	26	6
Bochna, Derek, Penn State	.331	148	37	49	11	2	10	34	11
Carek, Mark, Ohio State	.330	203	57	67	8	3	6	48	2
Ostrom, Matt, Iowa	.328	189	43	62	13	4	8	37	4
Lewis, Jeremy, Iowa	.328	186	37	61	9	1	8	51	8
Rhodes, Dusty, Illinois	.327	159	28	52	6	1	0	15	8
Eckelman, Alex, Ohio State	.324	188	38	61	9	0	2	26	3
Fishman, Steve, Iowa	.324	176	28	57	11	0	4	36	2
Thieleke, C.J., Iowa	.324	176	43	57	11	0	5	38	6
Metzler, Rod, Purdue	.324	207	46	67	13	2	5	25	8
Goble, Rodney, Michigan	.322	205	46	66	15	5	2	28	18
Smith, Rob, Minnesota	.318	170	32	54	10	2	8	35	5
Rojas, Ron, Northwestern	.318	201	46	64	16	2	4	45	10
Simmons, Brian, Michigan	.317	183	48	58	10	5	13	45	5
Stritch, Mike, Northwestern	.316	158	30	50	8	4	10	43	4
Williams, Chris, Ohio State	.314	236	69	74	19	1	8	44	5
Schley, Jeff, Iowa	.314	137	30	43	9	1	3	19	5
Grigg, Tom, Michigan St.	.313	137	35	46	5	1	1	20	5
#Denning, Wes, Minnesota	.290	224	58	65	11	6	4	32	19

INDIVIDUAL PITCHING LEADERS
(Minimum 50 Innings)

	W	L	ERA	G	SV	IP	H	BB	SO
#Belger, Kurt, Iowa	3	3	2.28	24	12	43	35	7	31
Austin, Matt, Iowa	6	3	2.63	12	0	55	44	37	44
Schroeder, Chad, N'west	9	2	2.79	15	0	94	83	26	57
Niedermaier, Brad, N'west	10	5	2.93	17	0	104	89	58	109
Hedman, Mike, Purdue	6	5	3.03	13	0	92	88	30	50
Cummins, Brian, N'west	8	6	3.14	16	0	100	92	19	57
Romig, Chuck, Penn State	2	5	3.38	12	0	53	52	24	20
Billek, Tom, Penn State	3	5	3.71	16	0	63	63	35	28
Mudd, Scott, Indiana	7	3	3.86	18	0	96	110	35	89
Spears, Bob, Ohio State	7	4	3.96	33	4	86	93	21	60
Westfall, Joe, Minnesota	6	2	4.09	16	1	62	60	22	60
Jansen, Todd, Purdue	6	5	4.23	16	4	77	77	37	60
Ferrell, Dan, Indiana	5	6	4.26	16	0	87	86	31	65
Bloomer, Chris, Purdue	7	7	4.27	15	0	97	105	43	67
Oestreich, John, Illinois	6	5	4.29	25	3	78	71	41	70
Meccage, Jeremy, Iowa	5	4	4.34	14	0	66	59	33	55
Hammerschmidt, Andy, Minn.	5	8	4.40	19	0	90	99	22	61
Pederson, Justin, Minnesota	5	4	4.50	24	4	52	47	29	49
Cannon, Kevan, Ohio State	8	6	4.66	16	0	102	119	48	79

BIG WEST CONFERENCE

	Conference		Overall	
	W	L	W	L
*Cal State Fullerton	18	3	57	9
Long Beach State	16	5	39	25
Nevada	12	9	35	18
Nevada-Las Vegas	11	10	32	24
New Mexico State	9	12	32	22
UC Santa Barbara	8	13	24	26
Pacific	5	16	26	26
San Jose State	5	16	21	33

ALL-CONFERENCE TEAM: C—Brian Loyd, So., Cal State Fullerton. **1B**—Justin Drizos, Sr., Nevada. **2B**—Travis Janssen, Jr., New Mexico State. **3B**—Ryan Hankins, Fr., Nevada-Las Vegas; Jeff Liefer, Jr., Long Beach State. **SS**—Zach Elliott, Jr., UC Santa Barbara. **OF**—Mark Kotsay, So., Cal State Fullerton; Tony Miranda, Sr., Cal State Fullerton; Jorge Perez, Sr., New Mexico State. **DH**—Jason Hodges, Jr., Long Beach State. **Util**—Ron Lewis, Jr., Pacific. **SP**—Scott Rivette, Jr., Long Beach State; Ted Silva, Jr., Cal State Fullerton; Nate Yeskie, So., Nevada-Las Vegas. **RP**—Gabe Gonzalez, Jr., Long Beach State.

Player of the Year: Mark Kotsay, Cal State Fullerton. **Pitcher of the Year:** Ted Silva, Cal State Fullerton.

INDIVIDUAL BATTING LEADERS
(Minimum 125 At-Bats)

	AVG	AB	R	H	2B	3B	HR	RBI	SB
Kotsay, Mark, CS Fullerton	.422	263	85	111	20	5	21	90	11
Janssen, Travis, New Mexico St.	.403	196	44	79	18	1	8	49	6
Perez, Jorge, New Mexico St.	.388	188	50	73	13	2	11	49	17
Hankins, Ryan, UNLV	.383	240	51	92	18	2	12	49	7
Loyd, Brian, Cal State Fullerton	.360	247	66	89	13	5	10	73	12
Liefer, Jeff, Long Beach State	.354	237	63	84	16	1	12	56	14
Miranda, Tony, CS Fullerton	.352	247	66	87	21	3	12	53	19
Ankrum, C.J., CS Fullerton	.352	196	60	69	10	5	1	29	6
Jackson, Wade, Nevada	.351	211	56	74	17	5	5	40	10
Licon, Carlos, New Mexico St.	.350	143	28	50	6	2	8	31	5
Giambi, Jeremy, CS Fullerton	.349	195	64	68	11	4	4	37	10
Fraser, Joe, Cal State Fullerton	.348	233	59	81	24	2	7	46	4
Elliott, Zach, UCSB	.347	167	39	58	10	2	2	25	6
Briones, Chris, Nevada	.346	214	44	74	12	2	11	60	9
McClendon, Travis, UNLV	.343	216	47	74	16	6	9	44	20
Skett, Will, Long Beach State	.340	141	26	48	13	2	4	38	5
Wilson, Terrance, Nevada	.336	131	44	44	10	1	1	18	3
Erwin, Mat, Nevada	.333	204	41	68	12	2	5	33	2
Hodges, Jason, Long Beach St.	.332	208	37	69	14	3	3	43	7
Plughoff, Ryan, UNLV	.332	187	40	62	10	1	6	45	7
Slayton, Shane, Nevada	.332	184	41	61	10	0	7	46	2
Champagne, Andre, New Mex. St.	.331	181	41	60	5	4	0	24	19
Drizos, Justin, Nevada	.331	178	54	59	15	1	11	57	1
Willis, David, UCSB	.330	215	38	71	10	1	12	61	3
Hardy, Brett, UCSB	.330	188	46	62	12	3	2	28	10
Dominique, Jason, Nevada	.328	183	46	60	21	0	7	34	2
Pierce, Kirk, Long Beach State	.326	178	34	58	8	1	7	34	1
Tapia, Louis, UCSB	.324	185	20	60	12	0	0	27	2
Janke, Jared, UCSB	.323	158	36	51	8	0	13	49	1
Smaldino, Doug, UCSB	.321	159	52	51	13	1	6	30	15
Morgan, Darin, New Mexico St.	.321	156	41	50	13	0	7	28	10
Minici, Jason, Long Beach St.	.320	241	55	77	16	6	10	52	5
#Kershner, Jake, New Mexico St.	.268	149	37	40	3	0	13	24

INDIVIDUAL PITCHING LEADERS
(Minimum 50 Innings)

	W	L	ERA	G	SV	IP	H	BB	SO
Chavez, Mark, CS Fullerton	4	2	2.45	37	6	62	56	24	55
Lagattuta, Rico, Nevada	8	1	2.48	27	10	58	39	34	59
Silva, Ted, Cal State Fullerton	18	1	2.83	29	6	153	140	35	142
Mitchell, Scott, Pacific	4	6	2.87	16	2	85	81	42	80
Rivette, Scott, Long Beach St.	9	5	2.91	18	0	130	121	49	144
Lewis, Ron, Pacific	7	5	3.26	15	0	113	115	40	72
Gonzalez, Gabe, Long Beach St.	3	7	3.31	39	20	68	66	25	83
Dixon, Tim, Cal State Fullerton	13	0	3.47	19	0	109	94	60	82
Ward, Jon, Cal State Fullerton	10	3	3.48	19	0	106	95	53	92
Wilson, Kyle, Long Beach State	13	5	3.74	22	0	101	116	25	60
Biddle, Rocky, UNLV	6	1	3.74	17	0	108	94	4	122
Reichert, Dan, Pacific	8	5	3.91	16	1	99	100	35	81
Leslie, Sean, Nevada	5	5	4.34	14	0	77	89	41	58
Yeskie, Nate, UNLV	11	5	4.36	20	1	144	176	25	147
Ledeit, Rich, San Jose St.	6	4	4.66	25	4	83	92	26	42

COLONIAL ATHLETIC ASSOCIATION

	Conference		Overall	
	W	L	W	L
James Madison	14	4	42	17
UNC Wilmington	11	7	30	25
Richmond	11	7	43	17
George Mason	11	7	31	25
*Old Dominion	9	9	39	20
East Carolina	5	13	29	26
William & Mary	2	16	24	29

ALL-CONFERENCE TEAM: C—Matt Quatraro, Jr., Old Dominion. **1B**—Sean Casey, Jr., Richmond. **2B**—Kevin Nehring, Sr., James Madison. **3B**—Jay Johnson, Jr., James Madison. **SS**—Donny Burks, Sr., James Madison. **OF**—Mark Budzinski, Sr., Richmond; Kevin Gibbs, Jr., Old Dominion; Maika Symmonds, Sr., Old Dominion. **DH**—Ed Tober, Jr., Richmond. **LHP**—Brian McNichol, Jr., James Madison. **RHP**—John Babson, Sr., UNC Wilmington. **RP**—Mike Venafro, Sr., James Madison.

Player of the Year: Sean Casey, Richmond.

INDIVIDUAL BATTING LEADERS
(Minimum 125 At-Bats)

	AVG	AB	R	H	2B	3B	HR	RBI	SB
Casey, Sean, Richmond	.461	193	63	89	26	1	14	70	2
Quatraro, Matt, Old Dominion	.371	178	52	66	13	2	13	62	15
Morgan, Rob, Old Dominion	.366	243	54	89	27	0	9	46	6
Ginder, Chad, James Madison	.363	171	34	62	13	0	1	29	16
Budzinski, Mark, Richmond	.362	243	73	88	22	5	10	58	16
Nehring, Kevin, James Madison	.354	229	50	81	25	1	14	62	9
Symmonds, Maika, ODU	.353	224	65	79	16	9	10	61	13
Gibbs, Kevin, Old Dominion	.352	210	71	74	20	6	2	38	48
Laskofski, Mike, William & Mary	.342	196	36	67	16	2	4	36	6
Edwards, Lamont, East Carolina	.340	200	50	68	6	4	5	27	16
Johnson, Jay, James Madison	.333	213	32	71	13	3	3	54	9
Pennell, Ron, George Mason	.330	212	42	70	13	2	7	40	1
Goodwin, Joey, Ga. Mason	.314	207	39	65	17	0	3	46	3
Walker, Ron, Old Dominion	.314	210	51	66	8	2	5	47	2
Burkhart, Jay, Ga. Mason	.311	212	48	66	13	2	11	46	5
Tober, Ed, Richmond	.310	145	21	45	12	0	8	40	0
Riley, Jason, Old Dominion	.308	201	43	62	5	0	0	35	13
Finnerty, Keith, George Mason	.306	160	27	49	12	1	4	34	0
McGrory, P.J., Richmond	.306	160	21	49	11	1	3	36	1

INDIVIDUAL PITCHING LEADERS
(Minimum 50 Innings)

	W	L	ERA	G	SV	IP	H	BB	SO
Wheeler, Brett, Old Dominion	7	1	1.48	10	0	61	42	13	46
Butler, Adam, W&M	8	1	2.05	25	5	53	27	17	77
Ramsey, Jason, UNCW	6	4	2.11	19	2	106	75	38	128
#Venairo, Mike, James Madison	6	2	2.37	29	5	49	36	21	56
Bouch, Tim, James Madison	4	1	2.52	16	0	64	64	22	64
Hafer, Jeff, James Madison	6	2	2.75	13	0	85	93	29	61
McNichol, Brian, James Madison	8	2	3.08	17	0	99	92	22	91
Walker, Ron, Old Dominion	6	5	3.15	14	2	74	76	15	69
Pyrtle, Joey, UNCW	6	4	3.18	15	0	85	86	25	60
Dunham, Pat, East Carolina	7	5	3.28	20	2	71	45	41	60
Abraham, Adam, W&M	5	4	3.46	20	0	78	100	17	32
Babson, John, UNCW	6	5	3.55	20	2	88	90	28	108
Harper, Travis, James Madison	6	2	3.60	12	0	55	65	18	47
Eannacony, Anthony, ODU	6	4	3.63	20	0	87	75	53	83
Ogden, Henry, Richmond	8	2	3.76	19	3	81	70	35	39
Kreider, Justin, Old Dominion	6	3	3.78	19	2	95	106	20	55
Newton, Chad, East Carolina	2	3	3.88	17	1	67	67	21	36
#St. Pierre, Bob, Richmond	11	3	4.26	18	0	129	118	51	130

GREAT MIDWEST CONFERENCE

	Conference		Overall	
	W	L	W	L
Cincinnati	17	6	34	21
Alabama-Birmingham	13	9	34	22
*Memphis	12	11	32	28
Saint Louis	10	13	24	30
Dayton	5	18	11	44

ALL-CONFERENCE TEAM: C—Jay Jones, So., Alabama-Birmingham. **IF**—Brian Jersey, So., Alabama-Birmingham; Troy Muckerheide, Sr., Cincinnati; Jason Page, Sr., Alabama-Birmingham; Matt Primack, Jr., Cincinnati; Willie Viruet, Sr., Alabama-Birmingham. **OF**—Steve Barhorst, Jr., Cincinnati; Shayne Carnes, Fr., Alabama-Birmingham; Tim Howard, Jr., Alabama-Birmingham; Mike Huelsmann, So., Saint Louis. **DH**—Tony Hausladen, So., Saint Louis. **P**—Heath Henderson, Fr., Alabama-Birmingham; Chris Holt, Jr., Cincinnati; Shannon Morgan, So., Cincinnati.

Player of the Year: Chris Holt, Cincinnati.

INDIVIDUAL BATTING LEADERS
(Minimum 125 At-Bats)

	AVG	AB	R	H	2B	3B	HR	RBI	SB
Howard, Tim, UAB	.400	205	54	82	11	4	6	48	10
Carnes, Shayne, UAB	.386	189	44	73	14	2	9	43	2
Barhorst, Steve, Cincinnati	.386	220	61	85	20	2	5	42	25
Vaden, James, UAB	.368	171	35	63	7	1	0	20	10
Huelsmann, Mike, St.L.	.368	201	54	74	11	8	1	19	24
Hausladen, Tony, St.L.	.367	188	42	69	14	1	11	61	1
Merrill, Jerry, Cincinnati	.358	134	26	48	7	0	0	23	8
Muckerheide, Troy, Cinc.	.342	193	56	66	14	4	8	46	24
Howell, Rob, Dayton	.341	179	32	61	10	2	8	29	2
Barassi, Ronnie, Memphis	.333	150	28	50	13	1	8	42	6
Jersey, Brian, UAB	.332	205	60	68	14	4	7	51	1
Gabris, Adam, Saint Louis	.331	148	34	49	13	4	2	37	2

INDIVIDUAL PITCHING LEADERS
(Minimum 50 Innings)

	W	L	ERA	G	SV	IP	H	BB	SO
Morgan, Shannon, Cinc.	4	4	2.29	31	12	55	42	34	52
Henderson, Heath, UAB	9	4	2.69	16	1	84	87	35	51
Lyons, Jonathan, Memphis	5	3	3.29	15	1	66	69	23	68
Glass, Lonnie, Memphis	7	6	3.30	20	1	109	96	38	71
Tolbert, Lance, UAB	8	5	3.51	21	2	108	108	34	73
Moore, P.J., Memphis	3	3	3.72	16	0	58	61	17	42
Moriarty, John, Saint Louis	6	3	3.75	24	0	70	78	22	38
#Holt, Chris, Cincinnati	11	2	4.30	17	0	107	111	24	50

IVY LEAGUE

	Conference		Overall	
Gehrig	W	L	W	L
*Pennsylvania	13	5	25	21
Cornell	10	10	20	19
Columbia	9	9	15	24
Princeton	8	12	15	26
Rolfe				
Yale	13	7	23	20
Dartmouth	12	8	19	17
Brown	7	13	14	27
Harvard	6	14	10	25

ALL-CONFERENCE TEAM: C—Dave Murphy, Sr., Brown. **1B**—Eric Kirby, So., Cornell. **2B**—Armen Simonian, Fr., Pennsylvania. **3B**—Jake Isler, Jr., Dartmouth. **SS**—Bill Walkenbach, Fr., Cornell. **OF**—Dave Feuerstein, Sr., Yale; Garrett Neubart, Sr., Columbia; Bart Teal, Sr., Columbia; Dan Thompson, Jr., Yale. **DH**—Mike Shannon, Jr., Pennsylvania. **Util**—Derek Nemeth, Jr., Pennsylvania. **SP**—Ed Haughey, Sr., Pennsylvania; Dave Kahney, Sr., Princeton. **RP**—Frank Telesca, Jr., Columbia.

Player of the Year: Garrett Neubart, Columbia. **Pitcher of the Year:** Ed Haughey, Pennsylvania.

INDIVIDUAL BATTING LEADERS
(Minimum 100 At-Bats)

	AVG	AB	R	H	2B	3B	HR	RBI	SB
Teal, Bart, Columbia	.458	118	25	54	8	2	6	43	0
Neubart, Garrett, Columbia	.458	155	53	71	17	3	5	34	27
Shannon, Mike, Penn	.407	172	37	70	15	5	4	47	6
Thompson, Dan, Yale	.402	164	33	66	13	2	4	45	5
Murphy, Dave, Brown	.392	130	25	51	11	1	4	24	4
Simonian, Armen, Penn	.382	110	32	42	7	2	0	14	8
Feuerstein, Dave, Yale	.380	166	45	63	13	4	23	26	

Isler, Jake, Dartmouth	.378	135	28	51	9	4	0	27	0
Green, Michael, Penn	.368	114	16	42	6	4	1	28	5
Walkenbach, Bill, Cornell	.363	146	38	53	13	1	6	25	11
Weidenbach, Joe, Harvard	.356	104	15	37	2	1	0	9	1
Henwood, Tim, Penn	.354	161	41	57	11	2	2	28	3
Kirby, Eric, Cornell	.346	136	31	47	5	0	11	35	1
Spencer, Andrew, Dartmouth	.343	137	33	47	10	0	3	22	14
Horton, Travis, Dartmouth	.336	122	21	41	4	3	2	29	0

INDIVIDUAL PITCHING LEADERS
(Minimum 40 Innings)

	W	L	ERA	G	SV	IP	H	BB	SO
Galles, Dan, Penn	6	5	2.26	12	0	88	84	20	66
Walania, Eric, Dartmouth	4	1	2.34	12	1	47	49	14	9
Gutshall, Eric, Yale	4	3	3.03	14	0	62	54	21	35
Haughey, Ed, Penn	8	3	3.10	12	0	81	67	23	57
Kahney, Dave, Princeton	5	6	3.51	13	2	59	66	16	49
Shannon, Mike, Penn	4	2	3.67	8	0	49	44	13	34
Hogan, Frank, Harvard	2	3	3.75	8	0	50	49	6	38
Berger, Lance, Penn	5	2	3.78	12	0	50	59	28	26
#Stefanowicz, Dave, Dart.	2	3	5.26	17	5	29	30	12	16

METRO CONFERENCE

	Conference		Overall	
	W	L	W	L
UNC Charlotte	11	7	36	21
Southern Mississippi	11	7	36	24
*South Florida	11	7	38	25
Virginia Tech	11	7	34	24
Tulane	8	10	32	26
Virginia Commonwealth	7	11	23	35
Louisville	4	14	17	42

ALL-CONFERENCE TEAM: C—Derek Reams, Jr., Southern Mississippi. **1B**—Ross Gload, Fr., South Florida. **2B**—Mike Terhune, So., Virginia Tech. **3B**—Bo Durkac, Sr., Virginia Tech. **SS**—Chris, Heintz, Jr., South Florida. **OF**—Joey Anderson, Jr., UNC Charlotte; Kevin Barker, So., Virginia Tech; Brandon Snead, Jr., Virginia Commonwealth. **DH**—Dan McDonald, Jr., South Florida. **Util**—Keith English, Jr., UNC Charlotte. **P**—Tim Collie, Sr., UNC Charlotte; Matt McWilliams, Sr., UNC Charlotte.

Player of the Year: Tim Collie, UNC Charlotte.

INDIVIDUAL BATTING LEADERS
(Minimum 125 At-Bats)

	AVG	AB	R	H	2B	3B	HR	RBI	SB
McDonald, Dan, South Florida	.391	225	49	88	20	0	15	50	0
Martensen, Blake, Tulane	.359	217	30	78	10	1	3	22	8
English, Keith, UNCC	.348	178	32	62	13	1	8	36	6
Gload, Ross, South Florida	.347	236	50	82	15	0	15	78	2
Herman, Josh, Virginia Tech	.346	211	36	73	13	0	8	43	0
Durkac, Bo, Virginia Tech	.338	207	54	70	23	2	13	42	7
Didion, Kris, Tulane	.337	222	52	68	13	4	3	36	24
Heintz, Chris, South Florida	.335	257	58	86	21	2	6	56	0
Snead, Brandon, VCU	.330	209	35	69	10	2	5	42	12
Barker, Kevin, Virginia Tech	.325	228	41	74	13	6	8	44	4
Hughes, Brian, Tulane	.322	208	45	67	10	4	2	24	11
Allen, Clint, Tulane	.322	230	35	74	21	0	8	50	12
Nickel, Mark, Louisville	.319	147	38	47	13	4	7	31	5
Anderson, Jim, UNCC	.319	213	52	68	19	4	2	46	8
Terhune, Mike, Va. Tech	.319	238	50	76	11	2	3	35	10
Mason, Ryan, South Florida	.317	183	39	58	9	1	3	35	1
#Bland, Will, So. Florida	.303	211	62	64	14	2	8	44	12
#Anderson, Joey, UNCC	.294	214	57	63	10	6	4	32	22
#Berger, Matt, Louisville	.291	203	52	59	9	0	22	55	0
#Cafaro, Gio, So. Florida	.284	271	56	77	10	3	3	34	36

INDIVIDUAL PITCHING LEADERS
(Minimum 50 Innings)

	W	L	ERA	G	SV	IP	H	BB	SO
#Gillian, Charlie, Va. Tech	2	2	1.45	28	8	37	33	8	36
Nuckols, Tommy, VCU	4	5	1.99	28	4	77	59	23	69
Bale, John, USM	5	4	2.70	13	0	70	72	27	86
Colllie, Tim, UNC	9	3	2.94	17	0	125	102	21	102
Fitzgerald, Brian, Va. Tech	7	5	3.38	17	0	117	112	23	84
McGraw, Jeremy, Louisville	6	5	3.61	17	0	107	103	41	70
Player, Brannon, UNCC	4	1	3.69	12	0	63	58	30	38
Williamson, Jeremy, So. Miss.	6	3	3.77	16	0	103	95	41	91
Robinson, Jared, Tulane	4	3	3.77	18	0	60	63	15	49
Rath, Fred, South Florida	7	3	3.80	16	0	85	84	33	79
Lontayo, Alex, Tulane	4	3	3.82	18	0	75	64	40	77
Bell, Scott, Tulane	6	5	3.84	19	2	73	74	18	56
McWilliams, Matt, UNCC	10	5	3.86	19	1	121	119	39	90
#Roberts, Mark, South Fla.	8	7	5.19	18	0	102	95	52	127

METRO ATLANTIC CONFERENCE

North	Conference W	L	Overall W	L
*Siena	14	4	31	17
LeMoyne	12	6	19	21
Canisius	7	11	21	20
Niagara	3	15	14	26
South				
Fairfield	13	5	23	22
Iona	12	6	22	27
St. Peter's	10	8	18	24
Manhattan	1	17	5	42

MAAC North ALL-CONFERENCE TEAM: C—Carm Panaro, So., Niagara. **1B**—John Geis, Jr., LeMoyne. **2B**—Mark Drabik, Fr., Niagara; Dave Marek, Fr., Siena. **3B**—Paul Wilders, Jr., Siena. **SS**—Tim Fleischman, Jr., Siena. **OF**—James Burnett, Jr., LeMoyne; Brian Hennessey, So., Canisius; Rob McShinsky, Jr., Siena; Frank Tabsozynski, Fr., Niagara. **DH**—Todd Schell, Sr., Canisius. **P**—Dave Bunn, Jr., Niagara; Tim Christman, So., Siena; Dan Kurtz, Jr., LeMoyne.

Player of the Year: Paul Wilders, Siena.

MAAC South ALL-CONFERENCE TEAM: C—Marcelo Alcoba, Sr., Iona. **1B**—John Way, Jr., St. Peter's; Todd Wise, Sr., Fairfield. **2B**—John Johnson, Sr., Fairfield; Chris Nocera, Jr., St. Peter's. **3B**—Kevin Guinan, Sr., Fairfield. **SS**—Jeff Rowett, Fr., Manhattan. **OF**—John Penatello, Fr., Iona; Chris Pini, Sr., St. Peter's; Pat Polese, Jr., Iona; Rick Ranft, Sr., St. Peter's. **DH**—Mike Pike, Jr., Fairfield. **P**—Sean Breen, Jr., Iona; Victor Santos, Sr., St. Peter's; Matt Shinners, Sr., Manhattan; Lou Vigliotti, Sr., Fairfield.

Player of the Year: Marcelo Alcoba, Iona.

INDIVIDUAL BATTING LEADERS
(Minimum 100 At-Bats)

	AVG	AB	R	H	2B	3B	HR	RBI	SB
Wilders, Paul, Siena	.415	135	39	56	14	3	3	53	21
Riniolo, Brian, Canisius	.373	142	37	53	12	1	4	28	10
Penatello, John, Iona	.372	129	40	48	7	5	5	27	13
Phillips, Brian, LeMoyne	.370	127	23	47	6	0	2	14	2
Way, John, St. Peter's	.369	130	26	48	14	1	2	22	2
Pini, Chris, St. Peter's	.369	149	24	55	4	0	0	18	15
Drabik, Mark, Niagara	.360	135	28	49	15	1	1	18	3
Przybysz, Brian, Canisius	.353	102	28	36	8	1	0	17	4
Alcoba, Marcelo, Iona	.341	167	51	57	21	0	11	37	6
Fleischman, Tim, Siena	.337	178	36	60	9	1	6	32	8
Burnett, James, LeMoyne	.333	111	18	37	4	1	1	16	19
Connelly, Kyran, Iona	.331	139	35	46	9	0	7	39	2
Ranft, Rick, St. Peter's	.328	134	25	44	6	1	0	16	2
Wise, Todd, Fairfield	.327	162	19	53	9	0	2	28	0
Filippelli, Kevin, St. Peter's	.320	150	18	48	11	1	3	31	3
Johnson, John, Fairfield	.318	176	19	56	9	3	3	35	2
#Fiumfreddo, Tony, Siena	.243	140	49	34	6	1	0	13	30

INDIVIDUAL PITCHING LEADERS
(Minimum 40 Innings)

	W	L	ERA	G	SV	IP	H	BB	SO
Vigliotti, Lou, Fairfield	6	4	1.97	13	0	83	73	17	45
Breen, Sean, Iona	4	3	2.68	9	0	50	43	25	42
Santos, Victor, St. Peter's	4	4	3.00	11	0	66	47	27	58
Kurtz, Dan, LeMoyne	5	4	3.19	12	0	68	59	25	62
Wertman, Adam, Canisius	7	3	3.31	13	2	49	48	18	20
Plunkett, Jack, LeMoyne	1	2	3.46	10	0	42	36	15	32
Moore, Rob, Iona	7	3	3.50	11	0	64	78	14	36
Anderson, Mike, St. Peter's	5	5	3.55	11	0	46	50	26	35

MID-AMERICAN CONFERENCE

	Conference W	L	Overall W	L
Bowling Green State	22	8	34	20
Kent	19	10	40	18
*Central Michigan	19	12	41	19
Akron	18	12	36	22
Western Michigan	19	13	31	22
Eastern Michigan	18	13	22	31
Ohio	15	17	31	25
Toledo	9	21	21	32
Miami	8	23	21	35
Ball State	7	25	15	41

ALL-CONFERENCE TEAM: C—Shannon Swaino, So., Kent. **1B**—Steve Smetana, Sr., Kent. **2B**—Todd Staehle, Sr., Western Michigan. **3B**—Toby Kominek, Jr., Central Michigan. **SS**—Matt Engleka, Sr., Ohio. **OF**—Eric Camfield, Sr., Ohio; Jason LaJoice, Sr., Eastern Michigan; Luke Wilcox, Jr., Western Michigan. **DH**—Bill Bronikowski, So., Toledo. **Util**—Mike Combs, Jr., Bowling Green. **SP**—Chris Boggs, Sr., Bowling Green; Mike Nartker, Sr., Kent; Brian Sikorski, Jr., Western Michigan; Ryan VanDeWeg, Jr., Western Michigan. **RP**—Eric Stachler, Sr., Bowling Green.

Player of the Year: Toby Kominek, Central Michigan. **Co-Pitchers of the Year:** Mike Nartker, Kent; Brian Sikorski, Western Michigan.

INDIVIDUAL BATTING LEADERS
(Minimum 125 At-Bats)

	AVG	AB	R	H	2B	3B	HR	RBI	SB
Kominek, Toby, Cent. Mich.	.408	211	71	86	16	4	25	65	16
Combs, Mike, Bowl. Green	.403	159	30	64	9	1	5	31	3
Smetana, Steve, Kent	.397	194	46	77	27	1	5	50	6
Burke, Todd, Central Mich.	.391	203	53	79	15	2	3	34	13
LaJoice, Jason, East. Mich.	.383	154	42	59	13	5	2	25	5
Staehle, Todd, West. Mich.	.381	160	35	61	11	0	4	33	4
Haring, Brett, Cent. Mich.	.372	207	48	77	11	0	8	43	18
Swaino, Shannon, Kent	.364	132	24	48	9	0	7	28	0
Flynn, Sean, Miami	.363	160	42	58	10	1	8	34	5
Demetral, Scott, West. Mich.	.360	197	42	71	7	0	0	25	5
Camfield, Eric, Ohio	.360	189	40	68	12	3	9	30	22
Fails, Tim, Kent	.358	162	30	58	7	2	1	16	5
Burgei, Bill, Bowling Green	.357	171	37	61	9	0	0	20	8
Mighton, Art, Kent	.348	204	51	71	14	4	2	37	16
Putko, Jim, Akron	.348	161	28	56	15	1	2	40	0
Mahoney, Pat, Cent. Mich.	.347	170	38	59	11	1	11	46	6
Engleka, Matt, Ohio	.343	166	38	57	11	0	4	32	13
Smith, Rick, Cent. Mich.	.343	134	40	46	10	0	15	42	1
Marn, Kevin, Kent	.342	202	45	69	6	3	7	35	9
Baker, Curtis, East. Mich.	.341	185	29	63	10	2	5	42	6
Tessmer, Tim, East. Mich.	.341	179	26	61	8	2	2	37	3
Davis, Derrick, Miami	.340	162	28	55	15	1	5	32	12
Johnson, Anthony, Miami	.337	199	59	67	12	6	10	45	9
Petrucci, Brian, Akron	.326	184	35	60	14	3	6	38	7
Susey, Rob, Akron	.325	197	56	64	13	3	10	43	13
#Armetta, Jason, Miami	.263	205	38	54	9	0	2	30	33

INDIVIDUAL PITCHING LEADERS
(Minimum 50 Innings)

	W	L	ERA	G	SV	IP	H	BB	SO
Sikorski, Brian, West. Mich.	10	2	2.52	14	2	79	63	31	69
VanDeWeg, Ryan, West. Mich.	8	4	2.70	13	0	88	62	43	81
Houdeshell, Aaron, Ohio	8	3	2.76	12	0	75	83	24	36
Farrell, Jim, Kent	6	5	2.77	17	2	81	60	38	97
Header, Joe, Akron	8	3	2.81	14	1	74	67	46	39
Boggs, Chris, Bowling Green	8	3	2.86	16	0	79	74	24	42
Nartker, Mike, Kent	10	3	2.87	18	1	103	86	32	85
Tippie, Jason, Bowl. Green	6	4	2.92	17	0	74	70	44	48
Gardner, Lee, Cent. Mich.	4	3	2.96	17	1	76	70	23	51
Simon, Ben, East. Mich.	6	7	3.19	16	0	79	72	30	55
Rose, Ted, Kent	8	1	3.51	14	0	82	74	29	59
Hunt, John, Ohio	4	5	3.59	14	0	73	78	42	69
Singer, Ben, Akron	4	4	3.70	11	0	58	72	24	30
Roberts, Drew, Kent	7	1	3.75	12	1	50	45	35	52
Gluff, Chad, Toledo	5	3	3.82	15	0	61	66	31	39
Muck, Ken, Ohio	7	1	3.86	13	0	58	58	34	34
Braswell, Bryan, Toledo	5	3	3.92	14	0	64	53	35	75
Herbst, Steve, East. Mich.	5	4	3.98	20	4	64	71	31	54
#Rowland, Doug, Toledo	3	3	5.40	21	5	43	54	11	24
#Neal, Jack, Miami	0	0	7.71	17	5	23	34	10	17

MID-CONTINENT CONFERENCE

EAST	Conference W	L	Overall W	L
Youngstown State	16	4	37	17
*Troy State	13	6	27	23
Pace	10	10	21	26
New York Tech	7	13	23	22
Central Connecticut State	7	13	15	24
C.W. Post	6	13	18	29
WEST				
Eastern Illinois	15	5	28	19
Western Illinois	12	10	21	21
Northeastern Illinois	12	12	17	35
Valparaiso	10	14	23	29
Chicago State	7	15	15	28

EASTERN DIVISION ALL-CONFERENCE TEAM: C—Rob Zachman, Sr., Pace. **1B**—Steve Duncan, Jr., Troy State. **2B**—John Lipani, Sr., C.W. Post. **3B**—Peter Bezeredi, Jr., Troy State. **SS**—Mike Sidoti, Jr., Pace. **OF**—Bryan Kelly, Jr., Troy State; Clausel Milord, Sr., New York Tech; Jamie Palumbo, Jr., Youngstown State; Tom Raymond, Sr., Pace. **DH**—Cliff Brown, Jr., New York Tech. **P**—Frank Chibbaro, Sr., Pace; Jason Fawcett, So., Troy State; Matt Gervasio, Sr., C.W. Post.

WESTERN DIVISION ALL-CONFERENCE TEAM: C—Sam Antkiewicz, Sr., Valparaiso. **1B**—Shane Hesse, Jr., Eastern Illinois. **2B**—Melesio Salazar, Sr., Eastern Illinois. **3B**—Shawn Lemmons, Jr., Valparaiso. **SS**—Jim Morsovillo, Jr., Western Illinois. **OF**—Kerrick Leatherwood, Jr., Western Illinois; Jamie Sykes, Fr., Valparaiso; Ty Ziegler, So., Eastern Illinois. **DH**—Rob Nicholes, Sr., Eastern Illinois. **P**—Chuck Donley, Sr., Valparaiso; Willy Hilton, Sr., Eastern Illinois; Brian Quinn, So., Western Illinois.

Player of the Year: John Lipani, C.W. Post. **Pitcher of the Year:** Frank Chibbaro, Pace.

INDIVIDUAL BATTING LEADERS
(Minimum 100 At-Bats)

	AVG	AB	R	H	2B	3B	HR	RBI	SB
Sidoti, Mike, Pace	.390	164	36	64	13	4	4	33	6
Brown, Cliff, NY Tech	.384	151	33	58	14	1	9	36	1
Murphy, Andy, West. Ill.	.383	162	30	62	3	1	4	35	3
Lipani, John, C.W. Post	.368	174	38	64	8	4	9	40	28
Reimers, Mike, NY Tech	.357	140	30	50	8	1	1	27	17
Ziegler, Brad, Young	.345	119	25	41	5	1	5	24	2
Morseville, Jim, West. Ill.	.344	163	37	56	12	0	5	29	16
Sykes, Jamie, Valparaiso	.343	137	25	47	3	5	9	29	11
Brown, Tony, Troy State	.342	158	29	54	15	1	4	35	2
Lemmons, Shawn, Valp.	.341	144	37	56	7	5	11	41	4
Keller, Joseph, Chi. State	.341	126	19	43	6	1	4	28	0
Palumbo, Jamie, Young	.340	188	40	64	17	3	2	36	11
Nicholes, Rob, East. Illinois	.339	115	14	39	7	1	7	33	0
Furey, Mike, NY Tech	.338	136	29	46	10	1	5	22	6
Milord, Clausel, NY Tech	.333	156	46	52	10	2	2	16	35
Triveri, Jason, Young	.333	126	42	42	9	2	4	21	6
Albert, Jay, Cent. Conn.	.328	116	21	38	9	0	0	21	3
Raymond, Tom, Pace	.326	178	49	58	5	6	9	31	16
Kelly, Brian, Troy State	.326	190	37	62	12	0	6	32	5
Binder, Mark, Chi. State	.326	144	32	47	4	0	0	16	9
Duncan, Steve, Troy State	.324	173	45	56	12	2	8	41	5
Hadrick, Rob, Valparaiso	.323	167	34	54	8	4	3	26	16
Morgan, Marc, Young	.323	167	41	54	6	0	6	31	11
Gawitt, Nate, Cent. Conn.	.319	138	22	44	5	0	4	33	2
Herman, Frank, C.W. Post	.316	158	38	50	13	3	2	32	7
Antkiewicz, Sam, Valparaiso	.315	143	16	45	12	0	3	19	0
Daddona, Joe, Cent. Conn.	.314	137	31	43	9	0	5	31	1

INDIVIDUAL PITCHING LEADERS
(Minimum 40 Innings)

	W	L	ERA	G	SV	IP	H	BB	SO
#Morgan, Marc, Young	2	1	1.35	16	10	20	10	8	24
Hilton, Willy, Eastern Illinois	4	3	1.71	14	8	63	48	28	39
Puorto, Jamie, NE Illinois	5	4	1.86	12	0	77	63	28	65
Chibbaro, Frank, Pace	10	1	1.91	11	0	80	62	30	61
Pettit, Chip, Valparaiso	5	5	2.31	14	1	70	49	33	60
Schuberth, Jay, Cent. Conn.	4	3	2.79	11	1	52	52	6	37
Gervasio, Matt, C.W. Post	5	3	3.03	11	0	74	64	30	70
Quinn, Brian, West. Ill.	7	2	3.03	12	0	86	89	14	42
Hall, Chris, East. Illinois	6	3	3.38	12	0	56	51	22	40
Caldwell, John, Young	4	1	3.45	11	1	44	45	18	19
Seal, Beau, East. Illinois	5	4	3.67	11	0	54	46	37	52
Miller, Shawn, NE Illinois	6	6	3.69	12	0	78	69	53	51
Neal, Brian, East. Illinois	3	4	3.76	13	0	55	76	22	36
#Fawcett, Jason, Troy St.	6	9	4.71	19	0	109	114	37	112

MID-EASTERN CONFERENCE

	Conference		Overall	
NORTH	**W**	**L**	**W**	**L**
Maryland-Eastern Shore	14	4	25	28
*Coppin State	11	7	19	34
Delaware State	7	11	10	37
Howard	4	14	5	38
SOUTH				
Bethune-Cookman	8	4	27	19
Florida A&M	8	4	23	27
North Carolina A&T	2	10	10	45

ALL-CONFERENCE TEAM: C—Kippy Shockley, So., Maryland-Eastern Shore. **IF**—Marcus Hamilton, Sr., Coppin State; Freddie Little, Jr., Bethune-Cookman; Meryl Melendez, Jr., Bethune-

Cookman; Djuan Tinsley, So., Florida A&M. **OF**—Milton Anderson, Sr., Bethune-Cookman; Corey Battey, Jr., Florida A&M; Rufus Boykins, Sr., Florida A&M. **DH**—Dimas Padilla, Jr., Bethune-Cookman. **P**—Crawford Moser, Sr., North Carolina A&T.

Player of the Year: Rufus Boykins, Florida A&M.

INDIVIDUAL BATTING LEADERS
(Minimum 100 At-Bats)

	AVG	AB	R	H	2B	3B	HR	RBI	SB
Thornton, Travis, Coppin State	.410	178	45	73	11	1	3	22	18
Padilla, Dimas, Beth.-Cook.	.353	136	19	48	9	2	3	39	5
Clark, Bob, Delaware State	.348	161	36	56	10	4	7	38	6
Little, Freddie, Beth.-Cook.	.344	157	43	54	3	1	1	22	34
Boykin, Rufus, Florida A&M	.336	140	29	47	12	1	8	36	8
Tinsley, Djuan, Florida A&M	.333	150	34	50	8	6	4	34	11
Melendez, Meryl, Beth.-Cook.	.333	141	43	47	16	0	5	29	11
Cordrey, Keith, UMES	.325	169	43	55	7	5	1	31	15
Battey, Corey, Florida A&M	.324	142	39	46	7	3	0	17	9
Merced, Luis, Beth.-Cook.	.322	149	38	48	8	0	0	28	7
Shockley, Kippy, UMES	.318	176	44	56	10	2	7	30	24
McRae, Cullen, Florida A&M	.317	145	36	46	8	0	0	10	14
Aiken, Chris, Delaware State	.317	142	27	45	11	0	4	33	2
Watkins, Maurio, Florida A&M	.312	141	22	44	8	0	7	36	1
#Christwell, Cecil, Coppin St.	.288	184	31	53	8	0	9	42	1
#Anderson, Milton, Beth.-Cook.	.264	144	37	38	6	2	2	19	52

INDIVIDUAL PITCHING LEADERS
(Minimum 40 Innings)

	W	L	ERA	G	SV	IP	H	BB	SO
Robinson, Marcus, Beth.-Cook.	7	5	3.39	16	0	74	63	51	70
Davis, John, Beth.-Cook.	7	4	3.45	16	0	73	51	46	63
Kopajtic, John, UMES	7	3	3.63	13	0	62	53	52	37
Varnes, Brian, Florida A&M	4	4	3.67	12	1	69	64	29	52
Barnes, Fred, Beth.-Cook.	3	6	3.68	11	0	59	60	32	61
Scott, Joe, UMES	3	3	3.96	8	0	46	59	21	7
Thornton, Travis, Coppin State	6	5	4.55	14	0	93	106	42	42
Pisani, Brian, Coppin St.	8	7	5.57	19	0	118	130	66	83

MIDWESTERN CONFERENCE

	Conference		Overall	
EAST	**W**	**L**	**W**	**L**
Detroit	12	2	28	18
*Wright State	10	6	33	28
Xavier	7	9	28	30
La Salle	5	9	15	35
Cleveland State	4	12	13	41
WEST				
Notre Dame	11	4	40	21
Northern Illinois	9	7	29	27
Illinois-Chicago	7	9	21	28
Wisconsin-Milwaukee	6	9	21	24
Butler	6	10	22	27

ALL-CONFERENCE TEAM: C—Scooter Lange, Sr., Northern Illinois. **1B**—Craig DeSensi, Sr., Notre Dame. **2B**—Randall Brooks, So., Notre Dame. **3B**—Mike Amrhein, So., Notre Dame. **SS**—Brian Zaun, Jr., Butler. **OF**—Lawrence Scheffer, Sr., Detroit; Scott Sollmann, So., Notre Dame; Ryan Topham, Jr., Notre Dame. **DH**—Clint McKoon, Jr., Cleveland State. **P**—Jesse Richardson, Sr., Northern Illinois; Steve Ross, Sr., Detroit.

Player of the Year: Jesse Richardson, Northern Illinois.

INDIVIDUAL BATTING LEADERS
(Minimum 125 At-Bats)

	AVG	AB	R	H	2B	3B	HR	RBI	SB
Zaun, Brian, Butler	.407	162	37	66	16	3	4	26	11
Sollmann, Scott, Notre Dame	.406	229	73	93	9	11	1	32	23
Amrhein, Mike, Notre Dame	.386	220	58	85	16	3	7	59	2
Lopiccolo, Jamie, Detroit	.383	167	50	64	12	4	10	42	3
Piskor, Matt, Wright St.	.380	216	42	82	17	6	8	58	2
Scheffer, Lawrence, Detroit	.370	173	45	64	15	2	18	58	1
West, Sean, Xavier	.361	227	43	82	19	6	15	70	9
Carr, Bob, La Salle	.361	169	35	61	8	1	6	36	0
Morrison, Brock, North. Ill.	.360	172	43	62	9	2	4	35	15
Kraus, Jak, Wis.-Milwaukee	.357	143	46	51	9	2	9	32	2
Schaller, Brian, La Salle	.351	208	51	73	10	2	7	32	24
Jarosz, Kris, Wright St.	.346	182	52	63	20	4	4	51	11
DeSensi, Craig, Notre Dame	.345	232	76	80	20	2	8	48	5
Kravarik, John, Ill.-Chicago	.339	174	32	59	10	1	5	29	15
Beam, Tom, Wright St.	.338	216	46	73	13	5	10	50	6
Lange, Scooter, North. Ill.	.336	149	24	50	11	1	1	17	1
Gundry, Ed, Detroit	.335	173	31	58	17	3	3	29	1
Topham, Ryan, Notre Dame	.335	206	50	69	18	5	18	79	9

Brooks, Randall, Notre Dame ..	.333	171	42	57	5	3	2	25	5
Long, Phil, Wright St.	.333	171	43	57	9	4	1	37	21
Halpenny, Justin, Ill.-Chicago ..	.333	141	29	47	8	0	0	33	7
Sikora, Don, Detroit	.333	168	36	56	14	4	1	27	7
Roberts, Robin, Detroit	.331	148	32	49	10	3	3	23	4
Collinsworth, Brent, Butler	.331	151	23	50	8	2	5	40	2
Stoss, Jeff, Wis.-Milwaukee	.331	136	34	45	5	2	12	46	3
McKoon, Clint, Cleve. State	.328	177	27	58	12	2	3	41	7
#Stosik, Bill, Wright State	.266	214	49	57	8	2	3	24	**26**

INDIVIDUAL PITCHING LEADERS
(Minimum 50 Innings)

	W	L	ERA	G	SV	IP	H	BB	SO
Ross, Steve, Detroit	10	1	3.16	13	1	83	84	31	57
Richardson, Jesse, North. Ill.	9	3	3.43	14	1	94	81	44	88
Schmalz, Darin, Notre Dame	8	3	4.01	14	0	85	82	15	50
Schmack, Brian, North. Ill.	5	5	4.19	15	0	88	98	39	58
D'Antonio, Mark, Detroit	5	3	4.26	12	0	70	70	34	60
Guler, Jeremy, Butler	4	3	4.26	13	2	70	54	32	39
Schmitt, Jeff, North. Ill.	3	3	4.42	13	0	57	57	43	47
Henebry, Gregg, Notre Dame	4	2	4.47	12	0	52	69	14	32
Hayden, Terry, Detroit	4	2	4.56	10	0	51	57	28	16
Sullins, Sean, Wright St.	9	5	4.61	15	0	121	126	44	113
DeVault, Brandon, Xavier	3	3	4.65	28	6	62	65	27	44
Shields, Chris, Xavier	7	5	4.65	15	0	93	108	35	43
Callahan, Bob, Wis.-Milwaukee .	4	4	4.69	14	0	63	63	20	31
Powell, Sean, Cleve. State	1	9	4.79	22	1	72	76	70	59
Tardiff, Lance, Wis.-Milwaukee ..	1	3	5.46	18	9	30	36	13	16
#McAninch, Sam, Wright St.	3	2	7.46	30	**9**	45	59	36	32

MISSOURI VALLEY CONFERENCE

	Conference		Overall	
	W	L	W	L
Wichita State	**24**	**8**	**53**	**17**
Creighton	18	10	35	22
Evansville	18	13	32	25
Southwest Missouri State	**18**	**13**	**37**	**21**
*Indiana State	16	15	39	23
Bradley	13	19	30	27
Northern Iowa	12	20	28	27
Illinois State	12	20	25	28
Southern Illinois	8	21	21	30

ALL-CONFERENCE TEAM: C—Tim Kratochvil, Jr., Southern Illinois. **1B**—Steve Hacker, Jr., Southwest Missouri State. **2B**—Braden Gibbs, Sr., Southern Illinois. **3B**—Casey Blake, Jr., Wichita State. **SS**—Jason Adams, Sr., Wichita State. **OF**—Ric Johnson, Jr., Indiana State; Chad Meyers, So., Creighton; Mike Stick, Sr., Creighton. **DH**—Todd Tatlock, Jr., Indiana State. **Util**—Jeff Leaman, Sr., Indiana State. **SP**—Brandon Baird, Jr., Wichita State; Drue Councill, Fr., Creighton; Mike Drumright, Jr., Wichita State. **RP**—Braden Looper, So., Wichita State; Travis Wyckoff, Jr., Wichita State.

Player of the Year: Steve Hacker, Southwest Missouri State. **Pitcher of the Year:** Mike Drumright, Wichita State.

INDIVIDUAL BATTING LEADERS
(Minimum 125 At-Bats)

	AVG	AB	R	H	2B	3B	HR	RBI	SB
Tatlock, Todd, Indiana State	**.460**	213	49	98	19	0	6	70	0
Hacker, Steve, SMSU	.409	235	63	96	18	0	**37**	**95**	2
Adams, Jason, Wichita State	.398	266	82	**106**	**25**	4	16	82	17
Johnson, Ric, Indiana State	.397	252	82	100	14	5	7	49	27
Owen, Tom, Northern Iowa	.394	193	56	76	23	**6**	10	53	2
Stick, Mike, Creighton	.393	211	50	83	16	5	15	74	11
Taylor, Richie, Wichita State	.385	244	65	94	19	2	9	74	12
Slemmer, Dave, SMSU	.382	251	57	96	19	4	14	63	8
Musachio, John, Bradley	.381	139	32	53	10	1	5	33	5
Leaman, Jeff, Indiana State	.380	234	45	89	14	2	11	55	13
Ullery, David, Indiana State	.377	199	28	75	13	0	9	43	0
Olson, Dan, Indiana State	.368	220	51	81	15	5	10	62	18
Thomas, Ben, Wichita State	.368	182	45	67	11	1	7	44	10
Reese, Nathan, Wichita State	.367	177	38	65	13	0	3	45	3
Robertson, Doug, Bradley	.364	187	47	68	13	3	5	34	12
Blake, Casey, Wichita State	.362	276	**89**	100	19	1	10	65	29
Meyers, Chad, Creighton	.360	214	67	77	8	4	3	30	52
Markert, Josh, Bradley	.356	180	47	64	15	2	6	45	3
Hill, Jim, Indiana State	.356	216	65	77	14	1	9	36	1
Schaffer, Jacob, Bradley	.355	186	37	66	22	1	5	35	9
Kratochvil, Tim, SIU	.354	195	37	69	13	3	6	49	4
Carroll, Jamey, Evansville	.350	240	54	84	15	5	2	37	29
Rader, Matt, Bradley	.348	201	45	70	15	1	7	51	5
Gainer, Matt, Illinois State	.343	207	35	71	12	1	12	54	10
Davis, Casey, Wichita State	.339	171	34	58	16	2	5	43	18

Mote, Greg, Illinois State	.338	213	36	72	17	0	5	28	10
Howe, Dan, Creighton	.337	175	32	59	13	1	4	38	4
True, Bill, So. Illinois	.337	178	29	60	10	2	1	32	16
Kneeshaw, Dan, SMSU	.335	218	59	73	20	4	4	40	6
Manary, Alex, SMSU	.335	233	55	78	18	0	6	47	5
Stine, Jerry, Wichita State	.328	186	49	61	11	2	4	44	13
Schlosser, Pete, SIU	.328	180	39	59	20	2	7	41	3
Gadlage, Stephan, Ill. St.	.327	244	45	70	10	2	3	35	6
Barrett, Ryan, Evansville	.326	215	36	70	13	1	5	41	8
#Young, Randy, Wichita St.	.306	291	74	89	8	3	3	26	**64**

INDIVIDUAL PITCHING LEADERS
(Minimum 50 Innings)

	W	L	ERA	G	SV	IP	H	BB	SO
Looper, Braden, Wichita St.	3	3	1.77	27	**13**	56	44	18	45
Foral, Steve, Wichita State	3	3	2.44	19	1	52	42	24	58
Mays, Jarrod, SMSU	10	1	**2.90**	18	0	93	84	35	107
Okrasinski, Brian, Illinois St.	7	2	3.18	12	0	71	63	24	34
Fassbender, Brian, Creighton	6	4	3.24	14	0	75	70	26	60
Finken, Brad, Indiana State	8	2	3.47	22	1	70	69	30	51
Wyckoff, Travis, Wichita State	6	0	3.50	25	4	64	45	32	55
Drumright, Mike, Wichita State	**11**	3	3.61	18	0	120	106	38	**117**
Council, Drue, Creighton	10	3	3.61	15	0	107	116	43	77
Johannsen, Jeff, North. Iowa	6	3	3.63	13	0	84	70	47	72
Baird, Brandon, Wichita State	11	3	3.72	18	0	102	107	27	74
Lagerblade, Brett, North. Iowa	4	6	3.92	11	0	60	64	18	35
Blasingim, Joe, SMSU	8	5	4.00	17	0	90	91	46	87
Zidlicky, Tom, Creighton	6	0	4.13	25	2	52	52	17	51
Noblitt, Andy, Evansville	8	6	4.20	17	1	105	123	30	48
Leaman, Jeff, Indiana State	8	4	4.42	21	4	73	88	30	48

NORTH ATLANTIC CONFERENCE

	Conference		Overall	
	W	L	W	L
*Delaware	19	3	45	14
Northeastern	16	8	29	17
Vermont	15	9	27	18
New Hampshire	14	10	26	21
Drexel	11	12	32	27
Maine	11	13	20	37
Hartford	10	12	14	25
Hofstra	8	15	27	21
Boston University	1	23	2	37

ALL-CONFERENCE TEAM: C—John Shannon, Sr., Drexel. **1B**—Doug Spofford, Sr., New Hampshire. **2B**—Dennie Helkowski, Fr., Drexel. **3B**—Cliff Brumbaugh, Jr., Delaware. **SS**—Joe Sarno, Sr., New Hampshire. **OF**—Ethan Barlow, Jr., Vermont; T.J. Sheedy, Fr., Maine; Jeff Vallillo, Sr., Hofstra. **DH**—Kris Doiron, Jr., Delaware. **P**—Adam Lamanteer, Jr., Delaware; Jamie Wilson, Sr., Delaware.

Player of the Year: Cliff Brumbaugh, Delaware. **Pitcher of the Year:** Jamie Wilson, Delaware.

INDIVIDUAL BATTING LEADERS
(Minimum 100 At-Bats)

	AVG	AB	R	H	2B	3B	HR	RBI	SB
Spofford, Doug, New Hampshire	.451	113	29	51	9	3	0	20	4
Brumbaugh, Cliff, Delaware	.442	215	**68**	**95**	**32**	5	8	56	15
Church, Brian, Hofstra	.418	146	32	61	13	2	8	52	3
Miller, Mike, Hofstra	.411	158	59	65	11	4	**20**	57	7
Shannon, John, Drexel	.396	192	49	76	12	7	8	56	1
Sarno, Joe, New Hampshire	.393	168	36	66	11	2	2	31	**26**
Vallillo, Jeff, Hofstra	.386	158	45	61	11	3	10	49	20
Doiron, Kris, Delaware	.385	221	55	85	10	6	5	**59**	1
White, Adam, Drexel	.358	193	36	69	9	2	1	49	11
Puleo, Steve, Maine	.356	163	25	58	13	6	2	33	1
Barlow, Ethan, Vermont	.355	155	43	55	5	6	1	27	22
Kelkowski, Dennis, Drexel	.355	220	65	78	10	4	0	35	7
Russell, Kevin, Hartford	.346	133	30	46	11	1	3	17	13
Hammer, Dan, Delaware	.343	204	66	70	20	3	8	34	7
O'Donnell, Mike, Northeastern	.336	134	24	45	10	1	4	34	3
Brody, Mark, Hofstra	.336	143	43	48	7	1	4	21	1
Sheedy, T.J., Maine	.335	194	36	65	11	3	0	23	8
Hopkins, Mark, Northeastern	.329	155	33	51	5	3	0	12	11
Sperling, Matt, Drexel	.327	205	25	67	8	6	1	30	10
Watson, Alex, New Hampshire	.327	150	38	49	8	4	4	38	3
August, Brian, Delaware	.326	187	51	61	24	6	3	49	2
Gonzalez, Rich, Hofstra	.322	149	36	48	9	2	0	16	13
Ivens, Scott, New Hampshire	.320	178	33	57	13	5	0	38	2
Harris, Mike, Drexel	.319	138	30	44	12	4	1	28	3
Valentine, Anthony, New Hamp.	.318	179	43	57	12	7	0	22	4
Kelleher, Frank, Hofstra	.311	148	23	46	11	0	3	29	0
#Duffie, Andre, Delaware	.286	212	43	61	13	**9**	7	47	15

INDIVIDUAL PITCHING LEADERS
(Minimum 40 Innings)

	W	L	ERA	G	SV	IP	H	BB	SO
Schnur, Curt, Delaware	11	3	1.21	16	1	104	76	24	83
Wilson, Jamie, Delaware	9	1	1.70	14	0	85	66	19	64
Franzini, Steve, Delaware	3	2	2.01	12	0	45	33	15	43
Doiron, Kris, Drexel	9	3	2.24	14	0	84	69	41	64
Cooper, Keith, Vermont	7	3	2.28	15	2	75	64	29	57
Lamantea, Adam, Delaware	10	3	2.33	14	0	89	67	31	82
Ennico, Chris, Northeastern	5	2	2.39	9	1	53	39	24	45
O'Shaughnessy, Jay, N'eastern	5	3	2.63	9	0	55	22	43	82
McManus, Matt, Northeastern	4	2	2.91	7	0	53	59	15	26
Herrington, Todd, Vermont	7	0	2.44	10	0	52	44	26	31
#Rogers, Kevin, New Hamp.	2	4	3.12	21	7	26	20	10	17
O'Brien, Scott, Vermont	4	6	3.31	13	0	65	66	35	54
Dillon, Chris, Delaware	6	2	3.58	14	0	71	81	22	38
Zack, Chris, Northeastern	6	2	3.66	9	0	59	67	21	20
Messineo, Joe, Drexel	2	4	3.77	8	0	45	45	31	24
Houser, Paul, Northeastern	5	1	3.83	10	1	52	42	15	24
Decker, LeRoy, Maine	2	8	3.84	15	0	77	74	28	50
Putnam, Rob, Drexel	5	4	3.90	11	0	67	62	38	35
Jobin, Ken, New Hampshire	7	4	3.95	11	0	66	55	43	48
Forneiro, John, Northeastern	4	5	3.93	10	0	53	46	26	48

NORTHEAST CONFERENCE

	Conference W	L	Overall W	L
Rider	16	5	35	18
St. Francis	13	8	26	16
Long Island	10	11	18	28
Marist	10	11	14	26
Mount St. Mary's	9	12	13	25
Fairleigh Dickinson	9	12	20	24
Wagner	9	12	15	30
Monmouth	8	13	19	33

ALL-CONFERENCE TEAM: C—Lou Deman, Sr., Long Island. 1B—Jon Manuelian, Jr., Long Island. 2B—Jon Watson, Jr., Fairleigh Dickinson. 3B—Anthony Mauro, Sr., St. Francis. SS—Dan Conroy, Jr., Fairleigh Dickinson. OF—Mark Barron, Jr., Marist; Levi Miskolczi, So., Rider; Tom Porch, Sr., Mount St. Mary's. DH—Jason Koehler, So., Rider. P—Mark Barron, Jr., Marist; John Garrabrant, Sr., Monmouth; Chris O'Connor, Jr., Fairleigh Dickinson.
Player of the Year: Mark Barron, Marist. **Co-Pitchers of the Year:** Mark Barron, Marist; Chris O'Connor, Fairleigh Dickinson.

INDIVIDUAL BATTING LEADERS
(Minimum 100 At-Bats)

	AVG	AB	R	H	2B	3B	HR	RBI	SB
Barron, Mark, Marist	.442	163	37	72	16	3	10	48	7
Conroy, Dan, FDU	.424	144	42	61	13	3	0	42	14
Manuelian, Jon, Long Island	.397	151	52	60	12	2	8	40	2
Carlucci, Rob, St. Francis	.382	123	20	47	15	0	5	22	0
Larrick, Chris, Mt. St. Mary's	.370	135	28	50	12	0	4	33	4
Koehler, Jason, Rider	.366	186	50	63	17	1	17	52	2
Porch, Tom, Mt. St. Mary's	.358	137	28	49	6	0	2	26	5
Montelbano, Kevin, FDU	.350	160	38	56	12	2	6	52	7
Braun, Paul, Wagner	.350	137	24	48	9	1	1	18	1
Montelbano, Keith, FDU	.348	141	28	49	11	1	6	31	0
Falciglia, Anthony, FDU	.347	170	36	59	17	0	3	40	1
Deman, Lou, Long Island	.346	162	39	56	17	1	18	55	0
Cunningham, Dan, MSM	.342	111	21	38	11	0	2	23	0
Jenke, Dennis, MSM	.341	132	37	45	10	0	6	26	9
#Miskolczi, Levi, Rider	.328	193	48	63	8	8	6	50	12
#Gambale, John, St. Francis	.313	115	41	36	8	2	2	15	27

INDIVIDUAL PITCHING LEADERS
(Minimum 40 Innings)

	W	L	ERA	G	SV	IP	H	BB	SO
#Crane, John, Rider	3	1	1.49	19	4	36	25	16	26
Field, Brian, Rider	6	2	2.51	13	0	72	68	32	51
Garrabrant, John, Mon.	6	6	2.64	14	0	89	78	46	55
Vargas, Victor, FDU	3	4	2.87	16	0	69	50	42	54
Baggs, Mike, Monmouth	6	4	3.16	15	2	77	72	24	59
Gordon, Jim, Rider	6	2	3.28	9	0	47	50	22	34
Long, John, Rider	6	2	3.63	11	1	57	50	24	26
Rawa, Anthony, Rider	4	0	3.70	13	0	58	61	29	23
O'Connor, Chris, FDU	5	4	4.43	15	1	75	81	41	82
Doyle, Joe, Wagner	1	5	4.46	14	3	40	48	15	29
McConnell, Chris, StF	4	3	4.79	13	1	68	68	26	62
Calise, Frank, St. Francis	4	1	4.86	16	2	46	44	27	32
Stroub, James, Long Island	4	1	4.88	18	1	52	64	32	29
#Barron, Mark, Marist	6	4	6.01	13	0	76	85	37	65

OHIO VALLEY CONFERENCE

	Conference W	L	Overall W	L
*Middle Tennessee State	16	4	36	27
Southeast Missouri State	14	6	32	21
Eastern Kentucky	12	8	28	25
Morehead State	10	10	29	28
Murray State	10	10	21	28
Austin Peay State	9	12	24	32
Tennessee Tech	8	13	23	29
Tennessee-Martin	2	18	13	35

ALL-CONFERENCE TEAM: C—Rex Crosnoe, Sr., Southeast Missouri. 1B—Jamie Walker, Sr., Middle Tennessee. 2B—Kurt Muskopf, Sr., Murray State. 3B—Tom Breuer, Jr., Southeast Missouri. SS—Jason Stein, Sr., Eastern Kentucky. OF—Craig Reavis, Sr., Middle Tennessee; Kerry Robinson, Sr., Southeast Missouri; David Shoupe, Sr., Morehead State. DH—Josh Williams, So., Eastern Kentucky. Util—Jayson Gore, Sr., Morehead State. P—David Michel, Fr., Southeast Missouri; Troy Pehle, So., Southeast Missouri; Aaron Rider, Jr., Murray State.
Player of the Year: Rex Crosnoe, Southeast Missouri. **Pitcher of the Year:** David Michel, Southeast Missouri.

INDIVIDUAL BATTING LEADERS
(Minimum 100 At-Bats)

	AVG	AB	R	H	2B	3B	HR	RBI	SB
Shoupe, David, Morehead St.	.386	207	49	80	20	1	10	53	3
Robinson, Kerry, SE Mo.	.385	226	57	87	17	5	3	36	20
Bullington, Bryan, Tenn.-Martin	.377	167	36	63	14	1	11	44	1
Winn, Randy, E. Kentucky	.372	180	37	67	11	1	3	37	3
Reavis, Craig, Mid. Tenn.	.372	234	51	87	11	1	1	33	7
Crosnoe, Rex, SE Mo.	.369	195	53	72	18	3	8	42	1
Berger, Brandon, E. Kentucky	.365	189	44	69	15	1	7	47	22
Bennett, Ryan, Austin Peay	.366	188	40	67	17	3	5	43	5
Karem, Jason, Murray State	.353	133	27	47	5	2	3	23	6
Breuer, Tom, SE Mo.	.350	197	40	69	12	0	2	45	4
Pride, Billy, Tenn. Tech	.345	171	32	59	15	0	8	28	9
Walker, Jamie, Mid. Tenn.	.335	239	52	80	15	1	15	58	4
Stein, Jason, E. Kentucky	.333	228	48	76	11	0	0	31	14
Schaefer, Brian, SE Mo.	.333	198	46	66	16	4	12	67	8
Williams, Josh, E. Kentucky	.332	187	54	62	9	4	1	18	26
Barthol, Blake, E. Kentucky	.330	194	38	64	13	1	6	46	19
#Hopper, Scott, SE Mo.	.253	174	31	44	2	7	0	16	5

INDIVIDUAL PITCHING LEADERS
(Minimum 40 Innings)

	W	L	ERA	G	SV	IP	H	BB	SO
#Witten, Joe, E. Kentucky	1	0	3.10	26	12	29	28	9	19
Rider, Aaron, Murray State	6	4	3.16	14	0	77	78	37	51
Latta, Trent, Tenn.-Martin	2	1	3.35	16	1	48	52	26	29
Pehle, Troy, SE Mo.	9	2	3.38	22	4	56	66	10	40
Michel, David, SE Mo.	8	3	3.46	20	1	96	95	41	82
Walker, Jason, Murray State	6	3	3.63	13	0	69	73	31	48
Irwin, Jason, E. Kentucky	6	3	3.65	17	1	57	65	23	33
Hedrick, Keith, Tenn. Tech	3	3	3.65	12	0	67	57	43	42
Hamilton, Dan, Morehead St.	5	8	3.69	20	0	68	66	24	68
Seely, Matt, Murray State	4	4	3.70	25	7	58	65	14	80
Cornelison, Steve, Austin Peay	4	3	3.72	9	0	46	51	16	17
Logan, Steve, Morehead State	3	3	3.77	13	0	57	53	36	44

PACIFIC-10 CONFERENCE

	Conference W	L	Overall W	L
NORTH				
Washington State	18	12	28	30
Washington	16	14	24	30
Gonzaga	15	15	29	25
Oregon State	14	16	25	24
Portland	14	16	24	25
Portland State	13	17	19	36

ALL-CONFERENCE TEAM: C—Mike Kinkade, Sr., Washington State. 1B—Sean Spencer, So., Washington. 2B—Ron Naumu, Sr., Washington State. 3B—Pat Meiwes, Sr., Oregon State. SS—Les Dennis, Sr., Portland. OF—Ken Cameron, Jr., Washington State; Joe Trippy, Sr., Washington; Jon Vander Griend, Jr., Washington. DH—Shawn Mahle, Sr., Washington. Util—Kevin Hooker, Sr., Oregon State. SP—Darin Blood, Jr., Gonzaga; Kyle Kawabata, Sr., Washington State; Greg Wooten, So., Portand State. RP—Brett Merrick, Jr., Washington.
Player of the Year: Darin Blood, Gonzaga.

INDIVIDUAL BATTING LEADERS
(Minimum 125 At-Bats)

	AVG	AB	R	H	2B	3B	HR	RBI	SB
Cameron, Ken, WSU	.388	209	53	81	12	6	6	44	20
Vander Griend, Jon, UW	.385	192	45	74	17	3	11	49	8
Dennis, Les, Portland	.360	172	41	62	4	3	3	28	25
Trippy, Joe, Washington	.360	189	47	68	8	1	0	26	26
Kinkade, Mike, WSU	.343	216	44	74	17	3	9	60	15
Wicher, Ken, Portland	.335	155	33	52	4	3	5	35	10
Junkin, Ross, Washington	.330	215	39	71	16	1	2	37	12
Hare, Brendan, Gonzaga	.330	185	26	61	7	0	1	23	6
Ryan, Rob, WSU	.329	231	44	76	10	4	2	35	14
Schmidt, David, Oregon State	.320	128	27	41	5	0	8	25	2
Norton, Andy, Gonzaga	.320	175	33	56	10	1	0	27	4
Wakeland, Chris, Oregon St.	.311	164	31	51	8	3	5	33	3
Meiwes, Pat, Oregon State	.310	171	25	53	12	0	7	39	0
Jacobs, Casey, Gonzaga	.310	126	12	39	3	1	0	16	1
Hooker, Kevin, Oregon St.	.309	162	39	50	12	0	4	38	0
Morgan, Scott, Gonzaga	.308	133	30	41	6	1	7	25	7
Spencer, Sean, Wash.	.303	152	31	46	4	4	8	30	4
Naumu, Ron, Wash. St.	.303	195	34	59	15	2	4	34	7

INDIVIDUAL PITCHING LEADERS
(Minimum 50 Innings)

	W	L	ERA	G	SV	IP	H	BB	SO
Wooten, Greg, Portland State	8	4	1.51	18	0	119	93	27	114
Blood, Darin, Gonzaga	13	3	2.57	16	0	119	92	46	145
Kawabata, Kyle, WSU	11	3	2.76	17	1	111	121	28	58
Cleland, Troy, Gonzaga	7	4	3.20	17	0	84	76	26	40
Mickel, Jason, Portland	6	4	3.55	15	0	91	87	43	45
McMullen, Jerry, Portland St.	6	7	3.81	15	0	85	87	35	70
Poffenroth, Kyle, WSU	3	6	3.89	14	2	79	73	19	50
Lovinger, Eric, Oregon State	6	4	4.12	15	0	59	69	17	40
Wong, Jerrod, Gonzaga	6	8	4.45	13	0	87	96	27	59
Campbell, Tim, Washington	6	7	4.52	18	0	96	108	47	80
#Merrick, Brett, Wash.	3	4	4.61	31	10	41	33	35	44

SOUTH	W	L	W	L
*Southern California	21	9	49	21
Stanford	20	10	40	25
California	18	12	32	25
Arizona State	13	17	34	21
UCLA	12	18	29	28
Arizona	6	23	20	34

ALL-CONFERENCE TEAM: C—Tim DeCinces, So., UCLA; A.J. Hinch, Jr., Stanford. **1B**—Robbie Kent, Jr., Arizona State. **2B**—Scott Kidd, Jr., Arizona. **3B**—Steve Carver, Sr., Stanford. **SS**—Gabe Alvarez, Jr., Southern California. **OF**—Randy Betten, Sr., Arizona State; Eric Byrnes, Fr., UCLA; Cale Carter, Jr., Stanford; Walter Dawkins, Sr., Southern California; Geoff Jenkins, Jr., Southern California; Jacque Jones, So., Southern California. **Util**—Peter Zamora, Fr., UCLA. **P**—Randy Flores, So., Southern California; Jason Garner, Sr., Southern California; Kyle Peterson, Fr., Stanford; Kaipo Spenser, So., Arizona State.
Co-Players of the Year: A.J. Hinch, Stanford; Geoff Jenkins, Southern California. **Co-Pitchers of the Year:** Randy Flores, Southern California; Kyle Peterson, Stanford.

INDIVIDUAL BATTING LEADERS
(Minimum 125 At-Bats)

	AVG	AB	R	H	2B	3B	HR	RBI	SB
Wolger, Mike, California	.432	132	29	57	12	2	3	33	7
Jenkins, Geoff, USC	.399	258	75	103	15	3	23	78	14
Hinch, A.J., Stanford	.366	238	61	87	21	6	9	58	13
Alvarez, Gabe, USC	.361	269	73	97	14	2	13	59	7
Kidd, Scott, Arizona	.358	193	44	69	10	4	4	37	16
Jones, Jacque, USC	.353	300	59	106	16	4	7	53	14
Carver, Steve, Stanford	.341	258	49	88	21	3	14	77	3
Wickey, Menno, Arizona	.341	217	65	74	15	3	9	39	20
Kent, Robbie, Arizona St.	.341	223	53	76	21	1	7	47	10
Thrower, Jake, Arizona	.337	166	42	56	9	3	1	24	5
Dawkins, Walter, USC	.329	292	64	96	17	4	9	57	14
Moeller, Chad, USC	.329	210	31	69	5	1	5	29	3
Goodell, Steve, Ariz. St.	.328	183	43	60	8	2	6	40	6
McKinley, Dan, Ariz. St.	.325	126	29	41	10	2	1	7	9
Carter, Cale, Stanford	.325	265	52	86	22	5	1	39	10
Powers, John, Arizona	.324	204	26	66	13	2	3	37	8
Byrnes, Eric, UCLA	.324	238	45	77	11	2	9	35	18
Dallimore, Brian, Stanford	.323	257	42	83	16	2	3	35	8
Rico, Diego, Arizona	.322	214	34	69	6	5	1	28	13
Ammirato, Zak, UCLA	.322	199	23	64	10	1	3	28	4
Flowers, Travis, Ariz. St.	.321	168	29	54	7	2	4	34	4
Troilo, Darren, Ariz. St.	.321	196	42	63	19	1	4	54	10

Talented Trojan. USC outfielder Geoff Jenkins hit .399 and led the Pacific-10 South in homers (23) and RBIs (78).

BILL SETLIFF

	AVG	AB	R	H	2B	3B	HR	RBI	SB
Brown, Gavin, California	.321	196	39	63	13	0	11	45	12
Betten, Randy, Ariz. St.	.320	219	51	70	11	7	1	25	26
Lewis, Ivan, California	.318	214	47	68	8	1	1	30	43
McKay, Cody, Ariz. St.	.315	222	42	70	15	4	5	53	11
DeCinces, Tim, UCLA	.315	222	40	70	23	0	13	51	3
Gjerde, Jeff, Arizona	.312	221	44	69	8	4	4	50	4
Petke, Jonathan, California	.312	215	42	67	15	0	0	37	21
Heinrichs, Jon, UCLA	.303	195	32	59	15	1	1	29	11
Walbridge, Greg, USC	.302	222	34	67	11	0	9	47	4
Kilburg, Joe, Stanford	.296	240	63	71	7	2	1	20	35
Zamora, Pete, UCLA	.295	244	39	72	15	0	6	48	1
Schaeffer, Jon, Stanford	.294	180	27	53	4	0	2	34	5
Vallone, Gar, UCLA	.292	209	41	61	13	1	8	34	3
Matoian, Chad, UCLA	.291	134	24	39	5	0	0	15	1
Kent, Troy, Stanford	.290	238	35	69	11	3	3	33	9
Cey, Dan, California	.288	208	40	60	12	0	4	42	32
Cooper, Chris, Arizona	.288	191	40	55	7	1	5	42	5

INDIVIDUAL PITCHING LEADERS
(Minimum 50 Innings)

	W	L	ERA	G	SV	IP	H	BB	SO
Peterson, Kyle, Stanford	14	1	2.96	20	1	143	129	35	112
Spenser, Kaipo, Ariz. St.	8	5	3.05	22	3	106	100	55	112
#Garner, Jason, USC	6	1	3.12	31	15	49	50	19	36
Bradley, Ryan, Ariz. St.	6	3	3.18	30	6	57	56	23	38
Flores, Randy, USC	13	3	3.24	20	1	150	142	34	86
Robbins, Mike, Stanford	6	4	3.66	20	2	111	121	41	78
Parque, Jim, UCLA	3	6	3.94	14	0	89	90	35	84
Heineman, Rick, UCLA	7	4	4.00	16	0	90	101	40	62
Deakman, Josh, Ariz. St.	4	1	4.15	20	1	69	77	23	51
Tucker, Ben, USC	7	2	4.19	21	0	105	111	45	81
Evans, Keith, California	7	6	4.39	17	0	113	114	38	73
Vorhis, Jim, California	3	6	4.61	23	0	82	100	17	37
Neal, Billy, Ariz. St.	5	7	4.76	18	1	96	109	30	79
Cooper, Brian, USC	8	3	4.78	20	0	102	112	43	92
Reed, Dan, Stanford	4	4	4.96	14	0	74	75	33	60
Bartels, Todd, Stanford	4	5	5.09	17	0	58	71	14	37
Drese, Ryan, California	5	6	5.36	15	0	89	65	43	61
Lynch, Ryan, UCLA	3	4	5.50	20	0	70	85	40	47
Frace, Ryan, Arizona	4	6	5.70	16	0	85	101	22	63
Bond, Jason, Arizona St.	3	2	5.91	18	0	67	72	49	53

PATRIOT LEAGUE

	Conference		Overall	
	W	L	W	L
Navy	19	5	34	20
Fordham	16	8	30	20
Army	15	9	22	23
Lehigh	11	13	23	23
Bucknell	11	13	19	27
Lafayette	6	18	9	36
Holy Cross	6	18	10	33

ALL-CONFERENCE TEAM: C—Anthony Stringer, Sr., Fordham.
1B—Bill Mullee, Jr., Army. **2B**—Brian Yost, Jr., Lehigh. **3B**—Kevin Silverman, Jr., Bucknell. **SS**—Terrence Butt, Sr., Holy Cross. **OF**—Brian Bernth, Jr., Navy; Mark Houston, Sr., Army; Arthur O'Neal, Sr., Army. **DH**—Steve Mauro, Sr., Navy. **SP**—Jason Hance, Sr., Army; Toby Moore, Sr., Navy. **RP**—Charlie Cucchiara, Sr., Fordham.
Player of the Year: Brian Bernth, Navy. **Pitcher of the Year:** Toby Moore, Navy.

INDIVIDUAL BATTING LEADERS
(Minimum 100 At-Bats)

	AVG	AB	R	H	2B	3B	HR	RBI	SB
Mullee, Bill, Army	.399	158	39	63	15	1	1	31	17
Morris, Kyle, Bucknell	.389	126	17	49	10	1	3	35	2
Talbot, Ben, Lehigh	.389	144	28	56	13	3	3	45	10
Marchiano, Mike, Fordham	.378	148	48	56	7	2	8	22	10
O'Neal, Arthur, Army	.375	136	37	51	12	2	4	27	12
Geigle, Jerry, Fordham	.370	154	55	57	17	3	3	30	29
Silverman, Kevin, Bucknell	.369	160	31	59	12	0	5	39	5
Mauro, Steve, Navy	.353	136	23	48	10	2	4	32	1
Houston, Mark, Army	.350	143	34	50	7	1	5	34	5
Bernth, Brian, Navy	.344	192	39	66	15	6	0	36	6
DeHart, Chad, Bucknell	.337	104	36	35	6	4	2	15	9
Morris, Jon, Lafayette	.336	143	16	48	4	0	0	23	1
Butt, Terrence, Holy Cross	.333	138	16	46	8	2	2	28	1
Stringer, Anthony, Fordham	.331	163	34	54	14	2	3	36	8
Mendoza, Osvaldo, Fordham	.329	146	24	48	5	4	1	28	5
#Lake, Toph, Navy	.321	187	46	60	5	9	2	25	5

INDIVIDUAL PITCHING LEADERS
(Minimum 40 Innings)

	W	L	ERA	G	SV	IP	H	BB	SO
#Cucchiara, Charles, Ford.	1	1	2.38	26	9	34	28	9	25
Moore, Toby, Navy	9	6	2.53	17	0	107	101	31	56
McLemore, Tom, Navy	8	2	2.77	14	0	75	66	19	34
Couch, Bryan, Fordham	7	2	3.04	12	0	47	46	20	37
Murray, Kyle, Navy	8	5	3.21	17	0	90	86	30	56
Hance, Jason, Army	5	2	3.39	11	0	64	63	28	40
Querns, Chris, Lehigh	4	2	3.52	11	1	54	61	9	20
Carlson, Kevin, Navy	6	4	4.05	15	0	60	56	22	45
Angsteich, Dave, Lehigh	7	3	4.22	11	0	60	65	13	38
Scranton, Dave, Bucknell	7	8	4.58	16	0	92	108	25	34

SOUTHEASTERN CONFERENCE

	Conference		Overall	
EAST	**W**	**L**	**W**	**L**
*Tennessee	22	8	54	16
Florida	12	14	32	24
South Carolina	12	14	32	25
Georgia	9	17	29	29
Vanderbilt	10	19	29	32
Kentucky	8	19	26	30
WEST	**W**	**L**	**W**	**L**
Auburn	19	8	50	13
*Alabama	18	11	42	23
Louisiana State	17	12	47	18
Mississippi	14	12	40	22
Arkansas	13	15	38	23
Mississippi State	11	16	34	25

ALL-CONFERENCE TEAM: C—Todd Young, Jr., Kentucky.
1B—Todd Helton, Jr., Tennessee. **2B**—David Eckstein, So., Florida.
3B—Chris Wiggs, Sr., Florida. **SS**—Mark Bellhorn, Jr., Auburn. **OF**—Ty Bilderback, Sr., Arkansas; David Dellucci, Jr., Mississippi; Josh Paul, So., Vanderbilt. **DH**—Kit Pellow, Jr., Arkansas. **P**—Chris Morrison, Sr., Auburn; Jamey Price, Sr., Mississippi; Scott Schultz, Sr., Louisiana State.
Player of the Year: Todd Helton, Tennessee.

INDIVIDUAL BATTING LEADERS
(Minimum 125 At-Bats)

	AVG	AB	R	H	2B	3B	HR	RBI	SB
Dellucci, David, Mississippi	.410	229	67	94	15	6	17	63	31
Helton, Todd, Tennessee	.407	258	86	105	27	4	20	92	11
Moller, Chris, Alabama	.405	215	35	87	15	2	10	44	4
McNally, Shawn, Auburn	.396	187	39	74	10	1	6	44	10
Paul, Josh, Vanderbilt	.388	219	63	85	16	1	11	50	25
Wiggs, Chris, Florida	.374	219	48	82	16	2	4	42	4
Bilderback, Ty, Arkansas	.371	213	61	79	14	6	3	44	28
Morris, Warren, LSU	.369	252	70	93	17	3	8	50	13
Green, Chad, Kentucky	.350	263	58	92	17	4	5	43	54
Klostermeyer, Mike, LSU	.349	235	65	82	20	6	10	62	17
Eckstein, David, Florida	.348	224	58	78	14	2	6	41	24

SEC Leaders. Mississippi outfielder David Dellucci, left, led the conference with a .410 average while Auburn righthander Ryan Halla led with 16 wins.

	AVG	AB	R	H	2B	3B	HR	RBI	SB
Hazzard, Chuck, Florida	.347	144	34	50	6	1	7	35	3
Mensik, Todd, Mississippi	.346	234	49	81	17	1	6	57	1
Young, Todd, Kentucky	.344	209	33	72	14	0	0	29	7
Mapes, Mark, So. Carolina	.343	204	35	70	13	1	9	49	2
Bellhorn, Mark, Auburn	.342	243	66	83	18	5	12	60	11
Crane, Todd, Georgia	.340	244	60	83	18	3	3	37	22
Erickson, Matt, Arkansas	.335	206	33	69	11	2	1	28	7
Lewis, Ed, Tennessee	.333	270	47	90	18	1	3	60	15
Vieira, Scott, Tennessee	.333	228	56	76	15	1	11	56	12
Jordan, Jason, Alabama	.332	241	42	80	16	2	6	30	0
Pellow, Kit, Arkansas	.332	220	39	73	16	4	12	55	5
Schroeffel, Scott, Tenn.	.331	266	63	88	13	5	9	52	15
Whipple, Boomer, Vandy	.330	200	43	66	11	2	2	22	18
Morgan, Jim, Mississippi	.329	149	21	49	9	2	6	35	4
Harrelson, Richy, Mississippi	.327	202	35	66	12	0	2	31	3
Stegall, Randy, So. Carolina	.326	218	40	71	19	1	2	32	5
Furniss, Eddy, LSU	.326	215	30	70	14	1	9	52	2
Waggoner, Jay, Auburn	.325	268	59	87	23	2	7	58	5
Moore, Kendrick, Arkansas	.317	252	53	80	12	4	4	46	26
Weeks, Mark, Auburn	.317	227	37	72	20	1	2	39	2
Chabot, Kevin, Auburn	.317	218	52	69	24	0	12	66	3
Tamargo, John, Florida	.316	177	43	56	11	1	4	28	23
Williams, Jason, LSU	.315	267	63	84	20	0	10	47	9
Copley, Travis, Tenn.	.314	236	51	74	18	1	6	55	2
Clark, Brian, Miss. State	.314	175	42	55	13	1	5	38	4
Parsons, Jeff, Arkansas	.310	242	59	75	10	4	3	33	32
Stowers, Chris, Georgia	.309	204	39	63	8	1	3	48	20
Cooley, Chad, LSU	.308	260	51	80	24	3	7	61	11
Tedesco, Jay, Kentucky	.308	237	50	73	12	1	17	57	3
Clark, Chris, Arkansas	.307	192	32	59	7	5	5	30	16
Taft, Brett, Alabama	.306	235	50	72	18	1	7	30	5
Key, Ken, Auburn	.306	245	65	75	19	3	2	31	11
Hucks, Brian, So. Carolina	.306	157	29	48	15	0	3	33	0
Johnson, Brian, Georgia	.305	197	42	60	16	0	5	44	1
Lee, Richard, Miss. State	.304	194	20	59	17	0	2	35	4
Dunn, Nathan, LSU	.303	208	58	63	12	2	15	50	12
Clark, Kirby, Auburn	.301	206	36	62	11	2	4	38	0
Hauswald, Rob, Miss. State	.301	183	30	55	12	3	6	34	4
Pryor, Pete, Kentucky	.300	220	37	66	15	0	10	42	5
Johnson, Jeff, Mississippi	.300	237	46	71	18	3	5	37	10
#Montgomery, Ryan, Vandy	.293	205	43	60	13	6	5	49	10

INDIVIDUAL PITCHING LEADERS
(Minimum 50 Innings)

	W	L	ERA	G	SV	IP	H	BB	SO
Helton, Todd, Tennessee	8	2	1.66	30	12	76	48	15	74
Young, Tim, Alabama	6	3	1.67	26	7	54	37	23	51
Price, Jamey, Mississippi	11	6	1.72	19	0	141	104	16	118
Quarnstrom, Rob, Arkansas	4	2	2.20	16	0	57	48	32	56
#Woodward, Finley, Auburn	3	2	2.38	33	19	42	27	13	32
Lamb, Neal, Alabama	7	1	2.81	20	3	74	69	21	53
Morrison, Chris, Auburn	12	2	2.70	19	0	117	108	15	75
Schroeffel, Scott, Tenn.	7	3	2.73	15	0	66	49	42	81
Carnes, Matt, Arkansas	7	5	2.91	21	4	93	82	33	111
Tanksley, Scott, Miss. State	3	2	2.91	30	7	59	57	17	62
Halla, Ryan, Auburn	16	3	3.07	24	0	147	122	47	148
DuBose, Eric, Miss. State	8	4	3.28	18	0	113	107	43	109
Downs, Scott, Kentucky	5	5	3.30	13	0	76	74	23	102
Kennedy, Kyle, Miss. State	9	6	3.37	20	0	107	108	39	77
McClellan, Darren, Florida	11	4	3.38	18	0	122	110	36	126
Maynard, Wally, So. Carolina	6	3	3.39	16	0	80	68	22	84
Callaway, Mickey, Mississippi	7	7	3.39	23	0	109	105	40	79
DeYoung, Dan, Mississippi	3	2	3.45	23	3	63	53	31	33
Yarnall, Eddie, LSU	5	0	3.45	16	0	60	46	28	57

Meyers, Ryan, Tennessee 10 2 3.46 21 0 120 112 35 104
Schultz, Scott, LSU................. 11 4 3.46 16 0 117 97 27 **150**
Eilers, Chris, Alabama 6 3 3.48 17 1 101 90 30 86
Ortiz, Ray, Vanderbilt 2 3 3.60 19 0 55 48 14 31
Powell, Brian, Georgia............. 8 4 3.61 19 0 147 135 50 138
Collins, John, Alabama 5 5 3.62 15 0 92 87 35 66
Humphreys, Kevin, Auburn 9 2 3.75 18 0 94 106 24 54
McClellan, Sean, Florida 4 6 3.76 18 0 96 100 45 80
Fitterer, Scott, Louisiana State .. 5 3 3.78 24 5 50 58 10 48

SOUTHERN CONFERENCE

	Conference		Overall	
	W	L	W	L
*The Citadel	19	5	39	21
Georgia Southern	14	10	35	24
Western Carolina	13	11	32	24
Davidson	12	12	19	32
East Tennessee State	11	12	25	27
Appalachian State	10	13	17	30
Virginia Military Institute	10	14	19	28
Marshall	9	15	12	38
Furman	9	15	16	32

ALL-CONFERENCE TEAM: C—Steve Wilson, Jr., Georgia Southern. **1B**—Alex Tolbert, So., Western Carolina. **2B**—Adam Cross, Sr., East Tennessee. **3B**—Eric Whitson, Sr., Western Carolina. **SS**—David Groseclose, Sr., Virginia Military. **OF**—Ryan Glynn, Jr., Virginia Military; Garrick Haltiwanger, So., The Citadel; Jody Henson, Sr., Western Carolina. **DH**—Shane Owenby, Jr., Appalachian State. **P**—Britt Reames, Jr., The Citadel; William Rushing, Sr., Georgia Southern.

Player of the Year: Steve Wilson, Georgia Southern. **Pitcher of the Year:** Will Rushing, Georgia Southern.

INDIVIDUAL BATTING LEADERS
(Minimum 100 At-Bats)

	AVG	AB	R	H	2B	3B	HR	RBI	SB
Henson, Jody, West. Carolina ..	**.401**	202	46	81	21	3	1	36	25
Whitson, Eric, West. Carolina ..	.377	199	44	75	15	1	8	35	17
Wilson, Steve, Ga. Southern	.367	210	45	77	12	0	19	**61**	6
Whitley, Tyson, Ga. Southern	.351	245	**57**	**86**	**25**	1	5	40	6
Haltiwanger, Garrick, Citadel ..	.347	248	37	**86**	13	3	9	50	17
Edwards, Brad, Davidson	.342	193	29	66	14	0	12	45	0
Groseclose, David, VMI	.341	179	51	61	14	1	3	10	**33**
Martz, Dan, Furman	.340	144	25	49	9	3	4	25	5
Peterman, Tommy, Ga. South. ..	.333	249	53	83	13	1	13	59	4
Burwell, J.P., West. Carolina	.333	198	41	66	14	0	4	41	2
Moore, Chad, West. Carolina....	.329	170	31	55	14	2	0	23	9
McDaniel, Scott, ASU..............	.328	171	41	56	15	6	3	26	10
Hagy, Mike, Marshall	.324	176	24	57	19	1	1	25	2
Owenby, Shane, ASU	.323	164	43	53	21	1	5	34	2
Henzler, Kurt, Marshall	.320	175	36	56	8	1	5	23	5
Quattlebaum, Gus, Davidson....	.319	160	37	51	12	6	2	24	0
#Tolbert, Alex, West. Carolina ..	.296	216	47	64	9	1	**20**	55	3

INDIVIDUAL PITCHING LEADERS
(Minimum 40 Innings)

	W	L	ERA	G	SV	IP	H	BB	SO
Morillo, Don, The Citadel	6	2	**1.60**	32	**13**	67	48	25	75
Reames, Britt, The Citadel	10	3	1.93	14	0	98	65	37	123
Falco, Phil, ASU.....................	2	1	2.74	21	1	46	34	40	39
Hinkle, Jon, The Citadel	4	2	2.91	29	0	46	48	7	47
Rushing, Will, Ga. Southern	**11**	5	3.09	20	0	160	127	66	**172**
Maxwell, Clark, West. Carolina ..	8	6	3.43	18	0	123	107	56	124
Maxwell, Denny, ETSU	7	6	3.59	21	0	83	88	45	54
Pollard, Chris, Davidson.........	**11**	6	3.60	22	2	115	110	27	73
Callahan, Brian, Citadel	8	4	3.65	14	0	86	75	33	70
Hall, Daniel, ETSU..................	6	5	3.82	22	6	61	68	23	59

SOUTHLAND CONFERENCE

	Conference		Overall	
	W	L	W	L
Northwestern State	19	5	37	15
McNeese State	17	6	41	16
*Northeast Louisiana	16	7	37	20
Texas-Arlington	14	10	27	32
Texas-San Antonio	13	11	31	23
Southwest Texas State	10	14	23	31
Sam Houston State	10	14	22	32
Nicholls State	8	16	23	28
Stephen F. Austin State	0	24	2	40

ALL-CONFERENCE TEAM: C—Danny Ardoin, Jr., McNeese State. **1B**—Ryan Rosplock, Jr., Sam Houston State. **2B**—Mickey Perez, Sr., Texas-Arlington. **3B**—Matt Donner, Sr., Northwestern State. **SS**—Brett Elam, Sr., McNeese State. **OF**—Terry Joseph, Sr., Northwestern State; Jason LeCronier, Jr., McNeese State; Curt Lowry, Sr., McNeese State. **DH**—Ryan Robertson, Sr., McNeese State. **P**—Brian Dulin, Sr., Northwestern State; Stephen Prihoda, Sr., Sam Houston State; Jon Saylor, Sr., McNeese State.

Player of the Year: Terry Joseph, Northwestern State. **Pitcher of the Year:** Jon Saylor, McNeese State.

INDIVIDUAL BATTING LEADERS
(Minimum 125 At-Bats)

	AVG	AB	R	H	2B	3B	HR	RBI	SB
Joseph, Terry, Northwestern St..	**.404**	193	70	**78**	13	5	14	54	**33**
Rosplock, Ryan, Sam Houston ..	.391	184	33	72	12	0	7	32	11
Perez, Mickey, UTSA................	.371	194	54	72	13	**7**	5	40	34
Lowry, Curt, McNeese St.	.368	202	53	74	9	3	9	38	25
Elam, Brett, McNeese St...........	.362	163	38	59	10	5	5	22	7
Donner, Matt, Northwestern St.	.362	196	29	71	18	0	4	53	4
Wilson, B.G., UTA	.360	203	36	73	10	3	2	34	8
Lockwood, Brett, NSU	.347	190	32	66	9	3	4	41	11
Bonersbach, Joel, SW Texas ..	.342	161	31	55	16	5	3	25	8
Coffield, Cris, NE La.	.338	201	46	68	19	2	8	45	7
Wilcox, Stacey, NE La.	.332	199	45	66	**23**	2	6	**60**	22
Arevalos, Ryan, UTSA.............	.326	178	47	58	15	1	8	49	6
Russell, Andy, NE La.	.323	164	38	53	11	1	2	38	1
Garrett, Jason, UTA	.320	203	37	65	10	5	8	41	4
Rapp, Damon, McNeese St.	.313	166	29	52	6	1	3	29	12
Zepeda, Noel, SW Texas........	.312	154	34	48	7	1	3	22	8
Jensen, Clint, UTSA................	.312	128	32	40	4	2	2	19	7
Cooley, Shannon, NE La.	.311	235	49	73	13	2	1	34	15
Armenta, Ray, Nicholls St.	.311	151	38	47	9	1	2	30	7
LeCronier, Jason, McNeese St.	.309	188	42	58	12	1	**15**	51	12
Broussard, Brian, SW Texas	.308	198	20	61	12	3	0	38	7
Stelly, Duane, Northwestern St.	.305	131	25	40	12	4	4	23	2
Robertson, Ryan, McNeese St.	.303	155	28	47	8	0	2	23	4

INDIVIDUAL PITCHING LEADERS
(Minimum 50 Innings)

	W	L	ERA	G	SV	IP	H	BB	SO
Duffer, Chad, UTA	5	1	1.91	27	2	38	24	19	30
Clement, Chad, McNeese St.....	6	3	**1.97**	31	**7**	73	57	33	61
Saylor, Jon, McNeese State......	9	4	2.37	16	1	95	76	31	68
Prihoda, Stephen, SHS	8	4	2.41	15	0	105	76	40	88
Hebert, Jeff, McNeese State	9	0	2.62	11	0	65	51	30	45
Miller, Roy, UTA.....................	4	4	3.04	14	0	71	66	29	51
Glaze, Randy, UTA..................	5	4	3.12	12	0	75	59	27	35
Albright, Jeff, Sam Houston........	3	7	3.32	14	0	81	77	40	41
Reeder, Russel, McNeese St.....	7	3	3.39	16	0	77	64	34	73
Weaver, Andy, NE La.	9	6	3.41	18	0	106	120	24	79
Bond, Corey, Northwestern St....	4	1	3.57	19	1	53	46	36	47
Martin, Zach, Northwestern St...	7	6	3.64	17	1	94	91	40	77
#Dulin, Brian, Northwestern St..	**10**	2	4.15	17	1	87	92	36	71
#Cortez, Clint, Nicholls St........	6	5	6.29	21	1	93	97	64	**97**

SOUTHWEST CONFERENCE

	Conference		Overall	
	W	L	W	L
*Texas Tech	16	8	51	14
Rice	15	9	43	19
Texas A&M	15	9	44	22
Texas	14	10	44	19
Texas Christian	11	13	27	29
Baylor	7	17	25	28
Houston	6	18	26	29

ALL-CONFERENCE TEAM: C—David Lindstrom, Jr., Texas Tech. **1B**—Randy DuRoss, Sr., Texas Tech. **2B**—Jason Totman, Sr., Texas Tech. **3B**—Clint Bryant, Jr., Texas Tech. **SS**—David Brooks, Jr., Rice. **OF**—Chad Alexander, Jr., Texas A&M; Chad Allen, So., Texas A&M; Jose Cruz, Jr., Rice; Shea Morenz, Jr., Texas. **DH**—John Curl, Sr., Texas A&M. **Util**—Mark Quinn, Sr., Rice. **SP**—Jake O'Dell, Jr., Texas; Jeff Peck, So., Texas Tech; Tim Peters, Jr., Baylor. **RP**—Matt Anderson, Fr., Rice; Scott Atchison, Fr., Texas Christian; Jimmy Frush, So., Texas Tech.

Player of the Year: Clint Bryant, Texas Tech.

INDIVIDUAL BATTING LEADERS
(Minimum 125 At-Bats)

	AVG	AB	R	H	2B	3B	HR	RBI	SB
Totman, Jason, Texas Tech	**.435**	214	77	93	24	5	5	55	9
Bryant, Clint, Texas Tech........	.422	258	**91**	**109**	24	4	16	**93**	25
Curl, John, Texas A&M	.415	212	61	88	21	2	**18**	58	1
DuRoss, Randy, Texas Tech.....	.392	240	79	94	17	4	9	55	10

Alexander, Chad, Texas A&M ..	.387	274	79	106	17	5	17	70	16
Quinn, Mark, Rice	.380	250	60	95	20	4	18	89	2
Byers, MacGregor, Texas	.379	198	48	75	16	1	3	49	3
Cruz, Jose, Rice	.377	223	77	84	17	2	16	76	19
Allen, Chad, Texas A&M	.373	255	63	95	22	6	10	59	23
Edelstein, Chris, Texas	.372	199	36	74	8	6	1	44	10
Kastelic, Matt, Texas Tech.......	.353	253	68	89	15	3	2	37	46
Crawford, Marty, Baylor	.350	197	34	69	16	6	1	38	10
Bailey, Jeff, Texas A&M	.347	213	45	74	10	3	9	47	1
Peoples, Danny, Texas	.343	175	47	60	15	0	11	62	5
Morenz, Shea, Texas...............	.336	226	61	76	22	4	9	52	4
Lindstrom, David, Texas Tech ...	.335	188	38	63	18	0	12	56	2
McCain, Marcus, Texas Tech ..	.333	129	31	43	8	1	2	28	17
Farrow, Jason, Houston	.330	176	39	58	12	5	2	37	3
Boni, Chris, Rice.....................	.328	232	71	76	8	7	2	41	17
Maleski, Tom, Houston	.327	199	42	65	17	0	6	35	2
McClure, Jason, TCU...............	.327	196	41	64	17	3	11	45	5
Brooks, David, Rice	.325	209	42	68	14	1	6	49	16
Berkman, Lance, Rice	.322	245	48	79	26	3	6	46	10
Lunsford, Sam, TCU	.322	152	32	49	3	1	2	17	20
McCurdy, Jeff, TCU	.320	128	29	41	12	1	2	19	17
Barber, Paul, Texas A&M	.313	147	23	46	8	2	1	26	4
Welch, Brandon, Texas Tech ...	.313	198	56	62	10	2	11	65	7
Landry, Jacques, Rice	.312	218	52	68	11	4	14	56	3
Doyle, Paul, Rice	.311	177	45	55	4	0	1	29	4
Campbell, Wiley, Texas	.311	209	73	65	10	4	1	25	32
Millay, Gavin, TCU	.306	186	38	57	12	2	8	56	5
Perez, Carlos, Houston	.305	174	31	53	7	5	6	36	2
Smith, Casey, TCU	.304	138	28	42	9	0	2	16	5
Smith, Kerby, TCU	.303	201	44	61	16	4	7	39	12

INDIVIDUAL PITCHING LEADERS
(Minimum 50 Innings)

	W	L	ERA	G	SV	IP	H	BB	SO
Anderson, Matt, Rice	11	2	2.51	28	1	72	46	52	63
Frush, Jimmy, Texas Tech........	5	1	2.97	24	4	64	56	14	55
#Farrow, Jason, Houston	4	6	3.59	27	7	48	36	22	40
Peck, Jeff, Texas Tech.............	10	3	3.73	19	1	104	104	48	73
O'Dell, Jake, Texas	11	3	3.77	22	2	93	82	51	89
Peters, Tim, Baylor	8	5	3.87	19	0	105	102	41	68
Taylor, Mark, Rice	4	1	4.18	18	1	56	46	50	55
Box, John, Houston	4	3	4.26	17	0	57	70	17	36
Smith, Travis, Texas Tech........	10	5	4.26	21	1	118	137	32	97
Mitchell, Dean, A&M	8	1	4.33	19	0	73	76	23	46
Senterfitt, Mark, Texas	8	4	4.56	17	0	99	110	60	52
Kolb, Brandon, Texas Tech.......	6	2	4.58	14	1	75	68	46	83
Smart, J.D., Texas...................	14	4	4.68	24	1	137	148	55	109
#Cravey, Brian, Texas	4	3	4.81	22	7	39	37	16	30
Atchison, Scott, TCU	7	6	4.87	21	3	81	83	28	69
Wallace, Flint, TCU..................	5	4	4.93	17	0	91	96	27	69
Atchley, Justin, Texas A&M.......	9	6	5.00	16	0	113	138	18	79
Brown, Allen, Rice	4	2	5.01	20	1	65	71	24	41
Lambert, Kris, Baylor	3	5	5.02	17	0	81	87	41	65
Rupe, Ryan, Texas A&M...........	6	3	5.05	14	0	77	83	26	60
Sneed, John, Texas A&M..........	6	3	5.08	17	0	78	76	46	52
Miller, Matt, Texas Tech	11	5	5.11	18	0	100	108	55	85
McDonald, Jon, Houston	3	5	5.22	15	0	60	54	32	39
Davis, Dana, Rice	8	3	5.33	20	0	76	64	58	58
Quinn, Mark, Rice	6	3	5.35	22	1	66	64	49	40
Dollar, Toby, TCU....................	5	6	5.46	17	0	92	110	39	69

SOUTHWESTERN ATHLETIC CONFERENCE

	Conference		Overall	
EAST	**W**	**L**	**W**	**L**
*Jackson State	14	4	23	26
Alcorn State	13	7	19	18
Mississippi Valley State	7	11	10	23
Alabama State	4	16	10	27
WEST				
Southern	21	3	29	11
Grambling State	14	8	21	18
Prairie View A&M	7	15	7	27
Texas Southern	4	20	6	37

ALL-CONFERENCE TEAM: C—Bryan Graves, Jr., Southern. **1B**—Lincoln Williams, Fr., Southern. **2B**—Johnnie Pierce, So., Alcorn State. **3B**—Robert Fletcher, Jr., Grambling State. **SS**—Dejanerio Milhouse, Sr., Alabama State. **OF**—Andre Credit, So., Alcorn State; Michael Heard, Sr., Southern; Marlon Pequese, Jr., Grambling State. **DH**—Allen Dosty, Sr., Grambling State. **P**—Donnie Bradford, Sr., Alcorn State; Bradley Brommer, Jr., Alabama State; Courtney Duncan, So., Grambling State; Michael Maroto, Sr., Southern.

Player of the Year: Michael Maroto, Southern.

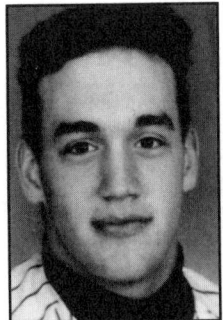

Texas A&M Twins. Outfielders Chad Alexander (.387-17-70), left, and Chad Allen (.373-10-59) were all-conference performers for the Aggies.

INDIVIDUAL BATTING LEADERS
(Minimum 100 At-Bats)

	AVG	AB	R	H	2B	3B	HR	RBI	SB
Pierce, Johnny, Alcorn State	.405	116	27	47	6	0	3	22	2
Stewart, Marlon, Grambling	.400	135	39	54	7	2	8	40	3
McAdory, Jamel, Jack. St.	.378	164	48	62	8	5	8	57	20
Heard, Michael, Southern.........	.371	132	35	49	11	3	3	27	6
Milhouse, Dejanerio, Ala. St.....	.367	128	32	47	4	2	0	19	30
Lewis, Marcus, Alcorn State	.363	113	24	41	7	3	3	23	2
Credit, Andre, Alcorn State	.359	103	21	37	8	0	0	13	7
Williams, Lincoln, Southern	.358	134	34	48	6	1	7	46	5
Dosty, Allen, Grambling	.350	120	27	42	4	3	1	28	1
Edmonds, James, Grambling	.333	117	33	39	9	0	3	27	4
Abner, Trennis, Texas Southern ..	.328	134	24	44	11	1	13	33	0
Daniel, Terrance, Alcorn St.......	.324	105	33	34	8	5	2	21	2
Chapman, Chris, Jack. St.........	.321	162	49	52	8	0	3	27	31

INDIVIDUAL PITCHING LEADERS
(Minimum 40 Innings)

	W	L	ERA	G	SV	IP	H	BB	SO
Maroto, Michael, Southern	9	1	1.54	11	0	70	64	20	52
Holmes, Shamar, Jack. St.........	4	1	2.85	10	0	47	34	48	29
Brommer, Bradley, Ala. St.	7	4	2.88	12	0	81	71	24	73
Walson, Hanif, Alabama St.	1	6	2.98	11	0	48	46	42	19
Smith, Donald, Jack. St.	3	2	3.14	13	0	52	45	31	33
Hill, Terrence, Southern............	6	1	3.35	12	0	54	44	17	53
Flowers, Ken, Alcorn St............	4	3	3.48	12	0	41	35	22	20
Washington, David, Grambling ..	3	4	3.54	12	1	53	47	19	49
Rey, Barrett, Southern..............	6	3	3.81	10	0	57	52	21	42
Taplin, Tyson, Alcorn State	4	5	3.86	11	0	68	61	29	56
Duncan, Courtney, Grambling....	7	3	4.25	15	0	59	46	51	71
Bradford, Donnie, Alcorn St.......	5	4	4.33	13	1	60	56	37	54
#Morrison, Marcus, Grambling...	1	1	6.15	13	4	34	40	22	23

SUN BELT CONFERENCE

	Conference		Overall	
	W	**L**	**W**	**L**
Jacksonville	21	6	41	22
South Alabama	20	7	41	17
Arkansas State	20	7	37	20
*Lamar	16	11	38	24
New Orleans	15	11	36	22
SW Louisiana	12	15	21	24
Arkansas-Little Rock	8	18	24	28
Texas-Pan American	8	19	17	37
Louisiana Tech	8	19	19	33
Western Kentucky	6	21	21	35

ALL-CONFERENCE TEAM: C—Chad Roney, Jr., Jacksonville. **1B**—Jason Washam, Jr., New Orleans. **2B**—Marlon Anderson, Jr., South Alabama. **3B**—Toby Anglen, Sr., Arkansas State. **SS**—Daniel Landry, Sr., New Orleans. **OF**—Shane Britt, Jr., South Alabama; Will Cook, Jr., Lamar; Eric Mapp, Sr., Lamar. **DH**—I.B. Stacy, So., South Alabama. **SP**—Keith Horn, Jr., Arkansas State; Mike Pasqualicchio, Jr., Lamar. **RP**—Greg Scheer, Sr., Jacksonville.

Player of the Year: Marlon Anderson, South Alabama.

INDIVIDUAL BATTING LEADERS
(Minimum 125 At-Bats)

	AVG	AB	R	H	2B	3B	HR	RBI	SB
Roney, Chad, Jacksonville........	.384	203	45	78	8	1	10	52	4
Cook, Will, Lamar.....................	.383	188	56	72	15	0	8	43	7

	AVG	AB	R	H	2B	3B	HR	RBI	SB
Lopes, Hugh, South Alabama	.366	202	**63**	74	17	1	2	29	22
Anderson, Marlon, So. Alabama	.362	246	60	**89**	**18**	3	7	46	31
Washam, Jason, New Orleans	.356	205	56	73	17	3	10	41	9
Bunting, Chad, Lamar	.354	223	59	79	16	2	1	32	24
Anglen, Toby, Arkansas State	.344	209	53	72	15	2	9	40	7
McKenzie, Shannon, West. Ky.	.342	193	33	66	10	2	2	28	3
Urban, Andy, South Alabama	.332	202	33	67	15	2	6	33	7
Mapp, Eric, Lamar	.332	232	55	77	14	**6**	**13**	**68**	9
Chabala, Chad, West. Ky.	.324	213	39	69	17	1	2	36	20
Allison, Cody, Arkansas St.	.323	164	29	53	7	1	2	36	1
Patton, Josh, West. Ky.	.321	212	24	68	17	3	4	57	0
Stacy, I.B., South Alabama	.321	187	39	60	17	2	11	47	6
Flody, Chris, Arkansas State	.320	219	48	70	13	0	1	32	0
Landry, Daniel, New Orleans	.319	207	49	66	13	3	11	53	11
Aguirre, Oswaldo, SW La.	.319	144	27	46	7	1	4	32	1
Akins, Carlos, West. Ky.	.319	204	64	65	22	4	2	30	**41**
Hayes, Chris, Jacksonville	.318	242	54	77	12	3	7	60	14
Britt, Shane, South Alabama	.317	227	48	72	10	3	11	52	18
Davis, James, West. Ky.	.317	205	56	65	16	4	11	45	7
Crow, Greg, Arkansas State	.316	174	30	55	10	3	1	29	1
Karolewicz, Steve, Ark.-LR	.316	155	31	49	9	0	0	12	11
Coca, Mark, Arkansas-LR	.315	168	39	53	11	0	1	34	10
Francia, David, So. Alabama	.315	178	38	56	5	2	4	28	12
Fogg, Kevin, New Orleans	.314	226	36	71	14	2	3	43	15
Wood, Eric, Jacksonville	.314	204	34	64	12	2	1	28	3
DiSalvo, Joe, New Orleans	.310	216	39	67	14	0	1	25	17

INDIVIDUAL PITCHING LEADERS
(Minimum 50 Innings)

	W	L	ERA	G	SV	IP	H	BB	SO
Stanson, Steve, New Orleans	8	3	**2.20**	20	1	82	58	26	72
Nakamura, Mike, So. Alabama	2	3	2.45	32	**12**	55	51	20	61
Marks, Thomas, New Orleans	5	4	2.59	14	0	80	80	15	61
Horn, Keith, Arkansas State	8	5	2.86	18	1	113	91	40	106
Ferguson, Chris, Jacksonville	7	1	2.99	30	2	81	80	27	39
Soden, Chad, Arkansas St.	4	8	3.18	15	1	82	81	28	67
Pasqualicchio, Mike, Lamar	11	4	3.22	22	1	106	88	45	106
Smart, Kacey, Lamar	9	2	3.40	16	0	103	104	27	51
Williams, Randy, Lamar	4	0	3.46	15	1	52	50	21	51
McKenna, Tim, Jacksonville	9	5	3.53	22	1	94	82	37	75
Sordo, Eddie, Jacksonville	10	4	3.70	20	0	109	111	40	67
Halley, Allen, So. Alabama	**12**	3	3.74	22	0	120	125	45	**123**
French, Jon David, Ark. St.	6	4	3.75	18	0	96	98	39	64
Harper, Terry, Arkansas-LR	6	4	3.90	22	0	85	91	44	65
Cammack, Eric, Lamar	4	1	3.91	11	0	51	40	21	38
Norton, Jason, So. Alabama	4	3	3.91	23	0	53	52	20	28
Key, Calvin, Arkansas State	7	3	3.92	20	2	78	70	39	64
Babineaux, Darrin, SW La.	7	5	3.95	13	0	80	62	38	67

TRANS AMERICA CONFERENCE

	Conference		Overall	
	W	L	W	L
Florida International	**27**	**3**	**50**	**11**
*Central Florida	23	7	49	13
Stetson	19	11	34	25
Florida Atlantic	17	13	27	31
Centenary	14	13	23	27
Campbell	12	18	26	29
Georgia State	11	17	20	33
SE Louisiana	10	18	17	31
Mercer	9	18	15	36
Samford	10	20	21	30
Charleston	8	22	17	29

ALL-CONFERENCE TEAM: C—Reggie Davis, So., Campbell. **1B**—Willy Kingsbury, Jr., Campbell. **2B**—Mike Lowell, Jr., Florida International. **3B**—Mitch Markham, Sr., Stetson. **SS**—Nick Presto, Jr., Florida Atlantic. **OF**—Adam Johnson, So., Central Florida; Dorian Speed, Jr., Florida International; David Turkoly, Sr., Centenary. **DH**—Frank McGarvey, Sr., Georgia State; Paxton Stewart, Jr., Florida International. **SP**—Evan Thomas, Jr., Florida International; Jay Veniard, Jr., Central Florida. **RP**—Jamie Emiliano, Jr., Florida International.

Player of the Year: Evan Thomas, Florida International.

INDIVIDUAL BATTING LEADERS
(Minimum 125 At-Bats)

	AVG	AB	R	H	2B	3B	HR	RBI	SB
McGarvey, Frank, Ga. State	**.374**	190	37	71	15	1	2	41	11
Johnson, Adam, Cent. Florida	.365	203	44	74	**21**	0	8	**66**	9
Gaea, Sonny, Centenary	.364	162	33	59	16	1	9	34	9
Cox, Kent, Campbell	.362	213	39	**77**	14	1	3	18	15
Stewart, Paxton, Fla. Int.	.358	148	36	53	13	3	3	33	9

	AVG	AB	R	H	2B	3B	HR	RBI	SB
Turkoly, David, Centenary	.352	179	35	63	12	0	12	58	5
Presto, Nick., Fla. Atlantic	.349	186	36	65	13	2	5	39	20
Sawyer, Chris, Stetson	.348	201	43	70	9	1	9	38	14
Munoz, Juan, Fla. Int.	.344	192	44	66	10	3	1	28	10
Lowell, Mike, Fla. Int.	.338	216	40	73	15	1	3	34	12
Lebron, Francisco, Fla. Int.	.335	158	32	53	11	1	5	32	2
Marrillia, Tony, Cent. Florida	.335	224	49	75	15	3	1	42	26
Brinson, Dennis, Campbell	.331	181	34	60	13	0	3	20	17
Davis, Reggie, Campbell	.331	172	42	57	10	2	**15**	48	7
Markham, Mitch, Stetson	.330	215	45	71	7	4	4	38	9
Morales, Alex, Cent. Florida	.329	225	**60**	74	12	8	6	28	19
Smith, Jeff, Stetson	.328	180	32	59	12	2	2	35	0
Speed, Dorian, Fla. Int.	.326	184	38	60	14	3	1	33	**37**
Mortimer, Mark, Georgia St.	.325	169	36	55	15	0	11	41	3
Warfield, Malcolm, FIU	.325	163	32	53	8	1	2	34	11
#Green, Ron, Samford	.270	174	54	47	12	**10**	6	22	16

INDIVIDUAL PITCHING LEADERS
(Minimum 50 Innings)

	W	L	ERA	G	SV	IP	H	BB	SO
Burns, Joe, Fla. Int.	9	0	**1.20**	12	0	67	53	19	46
Thomas, Evan, Fla. Int.	**15**	2	1.70	20	0	127	76	45	**146**
Palacios, Rich, Fla. Int.	9	1	1.99	24	2	86	62	37	58
Moore, Sam, Charleston	5	3	2.10	22	6	56	45	23	56
Monger, Mike, Campbell	7	4	2.75	12	0	69	72	23	44
#Emiliano, Jamie, Fla. Int.	0	1	2.89	27	**16**	28	24	13	29
Gomes, Brian, Cent. Florida	8	1	2.95	15	0	82	75	14	51
Beale, Chuck, Stetson	9	5	2.97	19	0	118	121	33	93
Wagner, Ken, Fla. Atl.	7	8	2.98	19	0	130	102	56	118
Hufstetler, James, Stetson	4	1	3.02	17	1	51	44	18	25
Collins, Ken, Campbell	2	5	3.23	13	0	70	63	40	40
Johnson, Chad, Charleston	3	9	3.34	15	0	89	76	29	66
Veniard, Jay, Cent. Florida	8	3	3.38	16	0	101	103	27	79
Ryan, B.J., Centenary	6	2	3.59	16	0	73	69	33	54
Cozart, Craig, Cent. Florida	10	2	3.59	17	0	90	97	22	60
Gomez, Javier, Stetson	6	4	3.59	20	1	100	88	36	85
Brown, Matt, Stetson	7	5	3.62	21	0	87	78	28	40
Tidwell, Chris, Fla. Int.	5	3	3.70	12	0	66	57	27	52
Groves, Brian, Charleston	3	4	3.75	14	0	84	83	46	70

WEST COAST CONFERENCE

	Conference		Overall	
	W	L	W	L
Pepperdine	23	3	36	19
Santa Clara	21	7	34	20
San Diego	14	14	25	27
Loyola Marymount	12	17	22	33
San Francisco	11	16	24	35
Saint Mary's	2	26	13	39

ALL-CONFERENCE TEAM: C—Karl Thompson, Jr., Santa Clara. **1B**—Andy Collett, Jr., Loyola Marymount; Ruben Gamboa, Jr., Pepperdine. **IF**—Jermaine Clark, Fr., San Francisco; Dennis Konrady, Jr., Pepperdine; Ross Parmenter, Jr., Santa Clara. **OF**—Ryan Christenson, Jr., Pepperdine; Brady Clark, Sr., San Diego; David Newhan, Sr., Pepperdine; Randy Winn, Jr., Santa Clara. **DH**—Gerardo Gonzalez, Jr., Pepperdine. **Util**—Mike Frank, So., Santa Clara. **SP**—Travis Burgus, Sr., San Diego; Bob Pailthorpe, Sr., Santa Clara; Randy Wolf, Fr., Pepperdine. **RP**—Eric Brubaker, So., Pepperdine.

Player of the Year: Ryan Christenson, Pepperdine. **Pitcher of the Year:** Bob Pailthorpe, Santa Clara.

INDIVIDUAL BATTING LEADERS
(Minimum 125 At-Bats)

	AVG	AB	R	H	2B	3B	HR	RBI	SB
Christenson, Ryan, Pepperdine	**.376**	226	**74**	**85**	13	**7**	7	32	21
Newhan, David, Pepperdine	.367	215	50	79	13	2	**11**	48	35
Weekley, Jason, St. Mary's	.347	193	27	67	15	6	4	32	6
Hodgdon, Justin, Pepperdine	.345	165	24	57	13	0	0	26	3
Gamboa, Ruben, Pepperdine	.335	185	23	62	**16**	0	7	46	2
Clark, Jermaine, San Francisco	.335	200	49	67	10	1	2	27	**38**
Mirizzi, Marc, Loyola Marymount	.332	232	42	77	13	1	3	36	8
Parmenter, Ross, Santa Clara	.330	194	34	64	10	2	4	33	8
Collett, Andy, Loyola Marymount	.329	207	32	68	11	2	**11**	**51**	1
Frank, Mike, Santa Clara	.327	217	55	71	15	4	3	23	19
Hoopii, Ikaika, Loyola Marymount	.326	221	57	72	12	2	7	29	16
Gonzalez, Gerardo, Pepperdine	.322	202	35	65	13	1	8	44	2
Peters, Mike, Loyola Marymount	.317	186	31	59	13	6	6	40	6
McDaniels, Paul, San Francisco	.316	174	45	55	15	3	2	32	14
Taclas, Jess, San Francisco	.314	229	45	72	7	2	1	29	28
Cole, Michael, Santa Clara	.314	172	32	54	9	4	3	19	7
Hernandez, Daryl, USF	.309	181	21	56	12	4	3	37	1
Clark, Brady, San Diego	.307	192	34	59	12	4	7	36	4

INDIVIDUAL PITCHING LEADERS
(Minimum 50 Innings)

	W	L	ERA	G	SV	IP	H	BB	SO
Brubaker, Eric, Pepperdine	10	2	1.25	31	6	50	38	9	44
Pailthorpe, Bob, Santa Clara	10	4	1.96	18	0	124	102	49	126
Wolf, Randy, Pepperdine	9	1	2.16	15	0	96	69	36	89
Burgus, Travis, San Diego	10	6	2.58	17	1	122	115	42	73
Hammett, Shawn, Loy. Mary.	5	8	3.25	24	4	105	109	32	84
Carmody, Brian, Santa Clara	7	0	3.48	13	0	65	51	23	53
Igou, Rich, San Francisco	6	4	3.52	13	0	87	94	45	70
Workman, John, Pepperdine	0	0	3.60	23	1	50	57	14	37
Harris, Jeff, San Francisco	4	6	3.62	12	1	80	84	21	70
Rizzo, John-Paul, Santa Clara	7	5	3.67	18	0	103	97	34	61
Halliburton, Chad, San Diego	5	4	4.08	13	1	71	71	35	66

WESTERN ATHLETIC CONFERENCE

	Conference		Overall	
EAST	W	L	W	L
Brigham Young	22	8	36	25
New Mexico	21	9	29	26
Grand Canyon	15	15	21	41
Wyoming	13	17	21	35
Air Force	10	18	29	25
Utah	7	21	15	39
WEST	W	L	W	L
*Fresno State	20	10	41	22
Sacramento State	16	13	28	26
Cal State Northridge	14	15	28	29
San Diego State	13	16	30	25
Cal Poly San Luis Obispo	13	17	21	29
Hawaii	12	17	30	24

All-Eastern Division Team: C—Jaime Garcia, Sr., New Mexico. **1B**—Aaron Fischer, Jr., Wyoming. **2B**—Travis Young, So., New Mexico. **3B**—Travis Parker, Sr., Utah. **SS**—Eric McDowell, Jr., Brigham Young. **OF**—Leroy Brown, Jr., Brigham Young; Lance Massey, Jr., Air Force; Mark Wulfert, Sr., New Mexico. **DH**—Glenn Harris, Sr., Air Force. **P**—Luis Gonzalez, Jr., New Mexico; Scott Haws, Jr., Brigham Young; Brian Knoll, Sr., Brigham Young; Dave Lyons, Jr., Air Force.
Player of the Year: Mark Wulfert, New Mexico.

All-Western Division Team: C—Matt Curtis, Jr., Fresno State. **1B**—Travis Lee, So., San Diego State. **2B**—Jody Napuunoa, Jr., Hawaii. **3B**—Jason Shanahan, Sr., Cal State Northridge. **SS**—Tony Zaragoza, Sr., San Diego State. **OF**—Joseph Freitas, Jr., Fresno State; Eric Gillespie, Sr., Cal State Northridge; Bret Mueller, Jr., Cal Poly San Luis Obispo; David Sanchez, Jr., San Diego State. **DH**—Andy Shaw, Jr., Cal State Northridge. **P**—Brendan Behn, So., Fresno State; Robby Crabtree, Jr., Cal State Northridge; Mike Eby, Jr., Sacramento State; Kevin Gunther, Sr., Fresno State.
Player of the Year: Mike Eby, Sacramento State.

INDIVIDUAL BATTING LEADERS
(Minimum 125 At-Bats)

	AVG	AB	R	H	2B	3B	HR	RBI	SB
Wulfert, Mark, New Mexico	.438	201	63	88	24	4	15	80	40
Massey, Lance, Air Force	.429	191	73	82	16	6	18	51	8
Winget, Brad, BYU	.413	208	57	86	17	0	11	65	7
Caballero, Craig, Gr. Can.	.397	151	41	60	16	3	6	38	1
Bracy, Kevin, Utah	.386	132	38	51	10	1	4	17	18
Hall, Andy, Cal Poly SLO	.380	187	34	71	5	3	1	27	10
Fischer, Aaron, Wyoming	.379	214	46	81	17	0	7	60	6
Balderramos, Armando, Sac St.	.376	202	43	76	17	0	1	29	7
Schied, Jeremy, Wyoming	.374	195	58	73	9	3	3	28	8
Zaragoza, Tony, SD State	.373	158	36	59	11	0	9	29	2
Hamilton, Ryan, Wyoming	.371	197	50	73	10	1	7	48	10
Shaw, Andy, CS Northridge	.371	159	45	59	14	1	13	53	1
Sharp, Mike, Air Force	.369	187	53	69	17	5	4	33	19
Young, Travis, New Mexico	.364	225	62	82	12	3	10	33	27
Sanchez, David, SD State	.362	174	39	63	12	4	4	33	9
Bayles, David, BYU	.362	130	41	47	10	0	3	26	0
Wright, Ryan, New Mexico	.361	169	42	61	10	5	2	32	2
Stratton, Kelly, Utah	.360	172	32	62	8	1	1	32	16
Kennedy, Adam, CS Northridge	.360	228	55	82	12	7	8	54	5
Garcia, Jaime, New Mexico	.358	173	44	62	13	2	13	54	3
Olson, Bob, Air Force	.357	143	34	51	10	2	9	37	3
Brown, Leroy, BYU	.356	177	44	63	10	1	11	49	9
Roberts, Ryan, BYU	.356	202	53	72	17	0	7	45	7
Gillespie, Eric, CS Northridge	.355	231	62	82	16	1	8	50	5
Johnson, Justin, Utah	.354	164	24	58	11	1	2	29	6
Mueller, Bret, Cal Poly SLO	.352	199	45	70	10	7	5	42	12
Sousa, Dan, New Mexico	.351	211	40	74	10	2	9	51	5
Lee, Travis, San Diego State	.350	200	48	70	13	4	7	41	19
Meng, Ronnie, New Mexico	.349	166	36	58	11	0	1	36	2
Harris, Glenn, Air Force	.347	176	47	61	16	3	16	58	9
Waller, Derric, San Diego State	.341	132	27	45	6	0	3	25	5
Shanahan, Jason, CS North.	.341	223	51	76	12	2	15	59	3
Freitas, Joseph, Fresno State	.340	203	54	69	12	5	9	43	5

INDIVIDUAL PITCHING LEADERS
(Minimum 50 Innings)

	W	L	ERA	G	SV	IP	H	BB	SO
Farfan, Shorty, Fresno State	1	4	2.86	28	10	57	55	31	40
Sheets, Ryan, Hawaii	6	2	2.96	22	0	79	74	29	82
Donnelly, Rob, Fresno State	7	5	2.98	23	3	91	70	56	91
Rivera, Willie, Sac. State	7	5	3.07	17	0	114	122	25	74
Behn, Brendan, Fresno State	9	5	3.28	17	0	118	101	41	116
Virchis, Adam, SD State	6	5	3.38	19	1	88	81	29	61
Eby, Mike, Sacramento State	9	4	3.41	16	0	106	104	55	119
Johnson, Mark, Hawaii	8	8	3.53	28	6	97	84	31	96
Gunther, Kevin, Fresno State	12	3	3.94	19	0	137	155	27	85
Umlauf, Keith, Air Force	2	6	3.96	33	11	52	64	24	53
Tucker, Brad, Fresno State	4	4	4.02	12	0	54	44	27	39
Nielsen, Mike, BYU	3	2	4.26	14	0	51	52	28	36
Robinson, Robby, Hawaii	5	4	4.32	16	0	83	93	29	66
Stephens, Shannon, CPSLO	6	6	4.37	14	0	95	100	29	78
Frank, Kris, Sacramento State	2	4	4.37	18	2	68	74	24	44
Crabtree, Robby, CSN	8	7	4.43	19	2	126	146	30	126
McNally, Andrew, Hawaii	5	4	4.69	13	0	79	88	19	73
Sagas, Mike, Utah	5	5	4.76	12	0	64	71	53	35
Haws, Scott, BYU	12	4	4.86	20	0	109	122	44	99
Ah Yat, Paul, Hawaii	4	2	4.92	16	0	60	71	22	45

INDEPENDENTS

	Overall	
	W	L
Miami	48	17
Hawaii-Hilo	21	26
Oral Roberts	21	34
West Chester	16	29
Colgate	6	16
Southern Utah	10	32

INDIVIDUAL BATTING LEADERS
(Minimum 100 At-Bats)

	AVG	AB	R	H	2B	3B	HR	RBI	SB
Gomez, Rudy, Miami	.379	232	52	88	18	2	9	44	23
Berish, Michael, West Chester	.368	155	29	57	13	1	0	27	2
Burke, Brolin, Hawaii-Hilo	.364	176	24	64	8	3	1	24	7
Morimoto, Ken, Hawaii-Hilo	.362	174	34	63	4	2	1	22	25
McGrath, Rob, So. Utah	.353	150	24	53	15	1	1	25	4
Pearson, Kit, Oral Roberts	.350	223	49	78	13	1	8	31	20
Rivero, Eddie, Miami	.324	176	31	57	6	1	8	44	4
Buxbaum, Danny, Miami	.324	210	38	68	15	0	14	60	6
Thompson, Bruce, Miami	.317	224	54	71	8	4	4	30	22
Schneider, Tom, West Ches.	.317	183	32	58	11	1	3	26	16
Marcinczyk, T.R., Miami	.312	141	24	44	12	0	4	29	4
Duncan, Derek, Oral Roberts.	.307	205	33	63	11	0	4	32	5
Gonzalez, Ricky, Miami	.305	210	29	64	3	1	3	34	12
Finnieston, Adam, Miami	.301	186	38	56	11	4	4	34	8
Schoonover, Danny, So. Utah	.301	163	25	49	5	0	0	18	2

INDIVIDUAL PITCHING LEADERS
(Minimum 40 Innings)

	W	L	ERA	G	SV	IP	H	BB	SO
Tessmer, Jay, Miami	3	2	1.31	45	20	75	59	12	91
Mattson, Keiki, Hawaii-Hilo.	4	3	2.48	12	1	76	58	32	44
Sedgwick, Chris, West Ches.	3	2	2.48	10	0	58	54	30	35
Coyaso, Ken, Hawaii-Hilo.	4	1	2.86	15	3	50	44	26	48
Henderson, Kenny, Miami	11	3	3.15	18	0	106	91	45	102
Dooley, Chris, Oral Roberts	6	6	3.35	17	0	118	113	41	90
Westfall, Allan, Miami	7	0	3.45	39	0	60	53	30	65
Arteaga, J.D., Miami	11	3	3.63	20	0	124	119	43	84
Kast, Nick, Oral Roberts	3	4	4.12	18	0	83	71	37	72
Adge, Jason, Miami	12	6	4.23	21	0	127	110	58	108
Miura, Blaine, Hawaii-Hilo	1	5	4.66	12	0	48	48	23	28

Florida Southern Wins Division II Title

By JIM CALLIS

Florida Southern junior righthander Brett Tomko, the Division II national player of the year, blanked Georgia College 15-0 June 3 in Montgomery, Ala., to lift the Moccasins to their eighth Division II College World Series title.

Tomko, the top pick (second round) of the Cincinnati Reds in the 1995 draft, allowed seven hits while striking out 11. He didn't allow a run in 19 Series innings, pitching two complete-game shutouts and picking up a save to earn tournament MVP honors. He finished the year 15-2 with a 1.35 ERA

Brett Tomko

and 154 strikeouts in 126 innings, winning the Division II pitching triple crown.

Senior shortstop Dave Burke sparked two key rallies for Florida Southern by going 4-for-5 with three runs, two stolen bases and one RBI. He led off a four-run second inning with a double and a two-run third with a single.

The Moccasins (51-10) solidified their reputation as a Division II powerhouse by winning four straight games. Florida Southern has won three titles in 13 years under coach Chuck Anderson and reached the postseason 26 times in the past 27 years.

FINAL POLL	
NCAA Division II	
1. Florida Southern	51-10
2. Georgia College	49-19
3. Central Missouri State	49-10
4. Valdosta State (Ga.)	41-22
5. North Alabama	43-15
6. Wingate (N.C.)	46-10
7. UC Riverside	43-16
8. Tampa	41-17
9. Bloomsburg (Pa.)	37-21
10. Kennesaw State (Ga.)	43-14

The Moccasins avenged a 14-9 loss to Central Missouri State in the 1994 championship game by eliminating the Mules in the fourth round with a 9-7 win. Georgia College (49-19) was unranked in the preseason, but reached the championship game in its fifth year in Division II.

■ Washburn (Kan.) threw back-to-back no-hitters March 11 and 12 against in-state rivals Bethany and Baker. Ichabods junior righthander Chad Jury blanked Bethany 3-0 and fanned nine in seven innings. Sophomore lefthander Jason Marsh and junior righthander Jason Valdivia combined to shut down Baker 8-1 with nine strikeouts in nine innings.

NCAA DIVISION III

LaVerne (Calif.) held off a late rally by Methodist (N.C.) to win its first Division III College World Series with a 5-3 triumph June 1 in Salem, Va.

The Leopards (39-9), making

just their second appearance ever in the Division III CWS, took a 5-0 lead into the ninth behind junior lefthander Jeff Doen. But Doen, who pitched a complete-game win over William Paterson (N.J.) in the tournament opener, ran out of gas and allowed the first four runners to reach base. Senior righthander J.D. Romero relieved Doen and struck out the first two hitters he faced, gave up two runs on a hit batter and a walk, then got the final out on a grounder.

LaVerne senior first baseman Jeff Polinsky was named tournament MVP. In five games, he went 10-for-20 with four home runs and nine RBIs.

Tim Jorgensen

The Monarchs (36-19) were playing their fourth game in two days because of rainouts. Earlier in the final day of the Series, Methodist disposed of defending-champion Wisconsin-Oshkosh, which handed LaVerne its only loss in the double-elimination tournament.

■ Wisconsin-Oshkosh senior shortstop Tim Jorgensen didn't earn another championship ring, but he did repeat as Division III player of the year. He also earned Baseball America's Small College Player of the Year award with one of the most spectacular college seasons ever.

In 44 games, Jorgensen batted .491 and shattered Division III records with 39 home runs, 121 RBIs, 218 total bases and a 1.275 slugging percentage. He also set the Division III career home run record with 70 and led all Division III players in runs (83) and hits (84).

The younger brother of former big leaguer Terry Jorgensen, Tim signed with the Cleveland Indians as an eighth-round pick in the 1995 draft.

■ Ohio Northern senior lefthander Brett Roehm set the Division III career strikeout record with his 336th on April 11. Fittingly, his opponent was Heidelberg (Ohio), whose Chris Reichert established the old record from 1976-79.

Roehm, who opened the 1995 season with a one-hitter and a no-hitter, also threatened the Division III consecutive scoreless innings mark before falling 3⅓ short at 26⅔. He went 14-1 with a 1.59

FINAL POLL	
NCAA Division III	
1. LaVerne (Calif.)	39- 9
2. Methodist (N.C.)	36-19
3. Wisconsin-Oshkosh	39- 5
4. Carthage (Wis.)	39- 8
5. Marietta (Ohio)	46- 9
6. Wm. Paterson (N.J.)	36- 9
7. Cortland State (N.Y.)	30-13
East. Connecticut St.	28-12
9. No. Car. Wesleyan	34-12
10. Montclair St. (N.J.)	29-13

NCAA DIVISION II

WORLD SERIES

Site: Montgomery, Ala.
Participants: Ashland, Ohio (36-18); Bloomsburg, Pa. (36-19); California-Davis (30-30); Central Missouri State (47-8); Florida Southern (47-10); Georgia College (46-18); New Haven, Conn. (31-5); Valdosta State, Ga. (39-20).
Champion: Florida Southern (4-0).
Runner-Up: Georgia College (3-1).
Outstanding Player: Brett Tomko, rhp, Florida Southern.

ALL-AMERICA TEAM

Pos.	Player, School	Yr.	AVG	HR	RBI
C	Ryan Coe, Kennesaw State (Ga.)	Sr.	.450	11	72
1B	James Vida, Florida Southern	Sr.	.383	13	92
2B	Greg Robertson, Mansfield (Pa.)	So.	.385	18	59
3B	Marc Rodriguez, Tampa	Jr.	.353	14	71
SS	Gene Stechschulte, Ashland (Ohio)	Jr.	.391	15	58
INF	Tom McCauley, Mansfield (Pa.)	Sr.	.429	15	63
OF	Darren Hayes, Wingate (N.C.)	Sr.	.434	24	90
	Andy Owen, UC Riverside	Sr.	.400	7	49
	Jerry Parent, Merrimack (Mass.)	Jr.	.445	5	43
	Juan Sanchez, Texas A&M-Kingsville	Jr.	.438	14	49
DH	Keith Daugherty, Columbus (Ga.)	Sr.	.407	15	59

		Yr.	W	L	ERA
P	Chad Arnold, Bloomsburg (Pa.)	Sr.	12	4	2.59
	Chris Macca, St. Leo (Fla.)	Jr.	2	0	2.16
	Bob Poisal, Central Missouri State	Sr.	13	3	4.20
	Scott Robinson, Ashland (Ohio)	Sr.	7	1	3.66
	Brett Tomko, Florida Southern	Jr.	15	2	1.35

Player of the Year—Andy Owen, UC Riverside. **Pitcher of the Year**—Brett Tomko, Florida Southern.

NATIONAL LEADERS

BATTING AVERAGE
(Minimum 125 At-Bats)

	AB	H	AVG
Schiltz, Chris, Morningside (Iowa)	116	56	.483
Sweeney, Kevin, Mercyhurst (Pa.)	120	56	.467
DeGraffenreid, Rico, Shaw (N.C.)	156	71	.455
Coe, Ryan, Kennesaw State (Ga.)	200	91	.455
Mamourish, Bill, Edinboro (Pa.)	155	70	.452
Tome, Jeff, Longwood (Va.)	151	68	.450
Darula, Bobby, Eckerd (Fla.)	165	74	.448
Buchner, Robert, Savannah State (Ga.)	96	43	.448
Foote, Jeff, North Alabama	177	79	.446
Parent, Jerry, Merrimack (Mass.)	164	73	.445

Department Leaders: Batting

Dept.	Player, School	G	Total
R	DeHaan, Dave, St. Francis (Ill.)	66	83
	Rydberg, David, St. Francis (Ill.)	65	83
H	Winters, Greg, Georgia College	69	102
TB	Hayes, Darren, Wingate (N.C.)	56	184
2B	Lynn, Jeremy, Coker (S.C.)	55	31
3B	Jones, Ivory, San Francisco State	52	11
	Snyder, Jeff, Carson-Newman (Tenn.)	48	11
	Wilson, Mike, Coker (S.C.)	54	11
HR	Hayes, Darren, Wingate (N.C.)	56	24
RBI	Vida, James, Florida Southern	61	92
SB	Shelton, David, North Alabama	57	59

EARNED RUN AVERAGE
(Minimum 60 Innings)

	IP	ER	ERA
Tomko, Brett, Florida Southern	126	19	1.35
Wallech, Ron, Shepherd (W.Va.)	74	12	1.47
Lail, Denny, Wingate (N.C.)	109	19	1.57
Bauer, Chuck, St. Rose (N.Y.)	120	21	1.58
Bost, Heath, Catawba (N.C.)	93	18	1.75
Brooks, Robb, Lynn (Fla.)	82	16	1.75
Diaz, Joey, San Francisco State	72	14	1.75

Department Leaders: Pitching

Dept.	Player, School	G	Total
W	Tomko, Brett, Florida Southern	24	15
SV	Macca, Chris, St. Leo (Fla.)	28	14
SO	Tomko, Brett, Florida Southern	24	154

NCAA DIVISION III

WORLD SERIES

Site: Salem, Va.
Participants: Carthage, Wis. (37-6); Cortland State, N.Y. (30-11); Eastern Connecticut State (28-10); LaVerne, Calif. (35-8); Marietta, Ohio (45-7); Methodist, N.C. (32-17); Wisconsin-Oshkosh (36-3); William Paterson, N.J. (35-7).
Champion: LaVerne (4-1).
Runner-Up: Methodist (4-2).
Outstanding Player: Jeff Polinsky, 1b, LaVerne.

ALL-AMERICA TEAM

Pos.	Player, School	Yr.	AVG	HR	RBI
C	John Zulegar, Carthage (Wis.)	Sr.	.374	15	49
1B	Craig Lieder, Wisconsin-Oshkosh	Sr.	.449	23	73
2B	Mark Johnson, Marietta, Ohio	Sr.	.394	6	39
3B	Chris Coste, Concordia-More., (Minn.)	Sr.	.484	9	41
SS	Chris Bryant, NC Wesleyan	Jr.	.469	15	59
	Joe Funaro, East. Connecticut St.	Sr.	.433	6	45
	Tim Jorgensen, Wisconsin-Oshkosh	Sr.	.491	39	121
OF	Jason Lariviere, Southern Maine	Sr.	.435	3	29
	Jim Mayer, Capital (Ohio)	Sr.	.444	8	47
	Toby Shamblin, Marietta (Ohio)	Sr.	.414	7	69
DH	Brian Caballero, Trenton (N.J.)	Sr.	.400	14	48

		Yr.	W	L	ERA
P	Chris Coste, Concordia (Minn.)	Sr.	7	2	1.27
	Brian Ford, Methodist (N.C.)	Sr.	15	1	1.41
	Keith Harvey, Ferrum (Va.)	Sr.	12	2	2.05
	Brett Roehm, Ohio Northern	Sr.	14	1	1.59
	Gary Yeager, Elizabethtown (Pa.)	Sr.	11	1	2.31

Player of the Year—Tim Jorgensen, Wisconsin-Oshkosh.

NATIONAL LEADERS

BATTING AVERAGE
(Minimum 100 At-Bats)

	AB	H	AVG
Reyes, Kiko, Lehman (N.Y.)	121	63	.521
Jorgensen, Tim, Wisconsin-Oshkosh	171	84	.491
Coste, Chris, Concordia-Morehead (Minn.)	126	61	.484
Bartucca, Scott, Oswego State (N.Y.)	108	52	.481
Taver, Corey, Wisconsin-Eau Claire	152	73	.480
Maraday, Jason, Mount St. Mary (N.Y.)	128	61	.477
Bryant, Chris, North Carolina Wesleyan	177	83	.469
Kula, Jarrod, Pomona-Pitzer (Calif.)	122	57	.467
Viggiano, Chris, Lehman (N.Y.)	123	57	.463
Roszell, John, Maryville (Tenn.)	139	64	.460

Department Leaders: Batting

Dept.	Player, School	G	Total
R	Jorgensen, Tim, Wisconsin-Oshkosh	44	83
H	Jorgensen, Tim, Wisconsin-Oshkosh	44	84
TB	Jorgensen, Tim, Wisconsin-Oshkosh	44	218
2B	Mu'min, Gary, Upper Iowa	44	21
3B	Fluck, Jesse, Franklin and Marshall (Pa.)	36	12
HR	Jorgensen, Tim, Wisconsin-Oshkosh	44	39
RBI	Jorgensen, Tim, Wisconsin-Oshkosh	44	121
SB	Yates, Chucky, Maryville (Tenn.)	38	46

EARNED RUN AVERAGE
(Minimum 50 Innings)

	IP	ER	ERA
Spedoske, Tim, Alma (Mich.)	60	8	1.21
Manthey, Jake, Lakeland (Wis.)	64	9	1.27
Coste, Chris, Concordia-Morehead (Minn.)	56	8	1.29
Wyllie, Graham, Allegheny (Pa.)	51	8	1.40
Ford, Brian, Methodist (N.C.)	127	20	1.41
Lynch, Tim, Stony Brook (N.Y.)	51	9	1.58

Department Leaders: Pitching

Dept.	Player, School	G	Total
W	Ford, Brian, Methodist (N.C.)	28	15
SV	Betley, Jody, Anderson (S.C.)	26	10
	Mohn, Stan, North Carolina Wesleyan	24	10
SO	Mayhew, Keith, Ferrum (Va.)	22	149

ERA and 134 strikeouts in 107 innings for the season, and 31-17 with a 2.76 ERA and 392 strikeouts in 320 innings for his career.

NAIA

Senior first baseman Chad Hopkins came alive just in time to help Bellevue (Neb.) win its first NAIA World Series championship.

After going 2-for-18 in his first five games of the tournament, Hopkins blasted a three-run homer in the bottom of the fifth inning of the June 2 title game at Sioux City, Iowa. The blow gave the Bruins (57-13) a 6-5 lead they wouldn't relinquish, and they cruised to an eventual 8-5 victory over Cumberland (Tenn.).

Bellevue senior shortstop Nic DeLuca won Series MVP honors after hitting .455 with four homers and nine RBIs in six games. DeLuca's homer started a four-run, eighth-inning rally which gave Bellevue a 7-5 semifinal win over Birmingham-Southern, avenging a first-round loss.

For Cumberland (49-19), junior righthander Kevin Hite set an NAIA World Series record with a 20⅓-inning scoreless streak. He allowed two runs in the bottom of the seventh of the final game.

After two consecutive years of missing the World Series, perennial NAIA power Lewis-Clark State (Idaho) returned and went 2-2 to finish fourth.

■ Southern Arkansas senior shortstop Tommy Stewart chased Robin Ventura's college hitting streak record before falling four games short. Stewart hit in an NAIA-record 54 consecutive games, including four in 1994, before being stopped May 16 against William Carey (Miss.) in the first round of the NAIA Southwest Regional.

The only streak longer in college history was the 58-game skein put together by Ventura at Oklahoma State in 1987. Stewart finished 1995 with a .474 batting average, which ranked fifth in the NAIA.

■ Gordie Gillespie, the all-time winningest coach in college baseball history, changed jobs at the end of the 1995 season. After leading St. Francis (Ill.) to a fifth-place finish at the NAIA World Series, he moved to Division III Ripon (Wis.) to replace his son Bob, who also is the school's athletic director and men's basketball coach.

Gillespie concluded his 43rd year of coaching with a 1,438-729 record. Close behind him is Cliff Gustafson, who has a 1,388-374 record in 28 years at Texas.

■ Brewton-Parker (Ga.) junior outfielder Mike Emerson was named NAIA player of the year. He batted .404 with 18 homers and 86 RBIs.

■ Southern California College sophomore lefthander Ila Borders continued her career with much less fanfare than in 1994, when she became the fourth woman to play college baseball, appeared on "The Tonight Show" and became a darling of the Japanese media.

After going 2-4 with a 2.92 ERA in nine games as a freshman, she struggled in 1995. Borders went 1-7 with a 7.20 ERA in 11 appearances.

JUNIOR COLLEGES

Middle Georgia became the first team to win the Junior College World Series after losing in the first round, beating Indian River (Fla.) 11-6 in the June 3 title game in Grand Junction, Colo.

Freshman left fielder Brian Davis, the tournament

NAIA

MVP, doubled, homered twice and drove in four runs in the final game for the Warriors (55-11). Sophomore righthander Derek Perkins, whose uncle Dwayne Cash won the 1979 title game for Middle Georgia, earned the victory.

The championship was the Warriors' fourth overall and first since 1982.

■ Volunteer State (Tenn.) shortstop Brian Conley was named Baseball America's Junior College Player of the Year. Conley led national juco players with 19 home runs and 83 RBIs, and ranked eighth in hitting at .467. After leading the Pioneers to a seventh-place finish at the Junior College World Series, he signed with the Chicago Cubs as a 16th-round draft pick.

■ Rancho Santiago won its second California community college championship in three years with a 12-2 win over host Fresno May 29. The Dons (42-9), who lost in the 1994 finals to Cypress, won 26 of 27 games to end 1995, including the last 15.

Freshman shortstop Tony Zuniga was named tournament MVP after going 8-for-13 with five RBIs. He doubled twice and homered in the final game.

Rancho Santiago dedicated its season to sophomore outfielder Ryan Lemmon, a projected starter who was killed in an automobile accident in September 1994. A banner that hung in the outfield at the Dons' baseball complex in Lemmon's memory was brought to Fresno and displayed after the game, and Lemmon's father was in the dugout at the game.

■ Potomac State became the first West Virginia school ever to win a national championship when it defeated Kirkwood (Iowa) in the final game of the Division II Junior College World Series May 25 in Millington, Tenn.

Sophomore Mike Duvall threw eight innings of three-hit ball for the Eagles (40-6), and tied a tournament record with 14 strikeouts. Potomac State freshman Chris Reyes was named Series MVP after winning two games, including an opening-round one-hitter against Delaware Tech.

■ Madison Area Tech (Wis.) beat defending champion Joliet (Ill.) for the second straight time May 26, capturing the Division III Junior College World Series with a 9-7 victory. The Trojans (41-12) lost to Joliet in the third round of the tournament before winning their final three games. Freshman catcher Bill Uelman was named Series MVP after hitting four homers and driving in 12 runs in six games.

Symonds Joins Elite Group

Bob Symonds became the fourth junior college coach to reach 1,000 victories when Triton (Ill.) defeated Morton (Ill.) 10-0 on April 13. Symonds finished 1995 with a 1,022-294 record in 25 seasons.

The only other juco coaches to reach that level are: Lloyd Simmons of Seminole (Okla.), 1,333-243; Bill Griffin of Howard (Texas), Panola (Texas) and Northeast Texas, 1,111-446; and Demie Mainieri of Miami-Dade North, 1,012-409. Griffin and Mainieri are retired.

■ Two Florida junior college righthanders tossed no-hitters against each other March 22. Seminole's Tony Von Dolteren defeated Valencia's David Rivera 1-0 as the Raiders scored the only run on a walk, an error and a wild pitch in the bottom of the ninth.

JUNIOR COLLEGE

NJCAA DIVISION I

WORLD SERIES

Site: Grand Junction, Colo.
Participants: Allegany, Md. (45-2); Dixie, Utah (39-19); Indian Hills, Iowa (38-11); Indian River, Fla. (41-12); Middle Georgia (50-10); Odessa, Texas (46-10); St. Louis-Meramec, Mo. (37-15); Seminole, Okla. (51-4); Triton, Ill. (42-11); Volunteer State, Tenn. (40-21).
Champion: Middle Georgia (5-1).
Runner-Up: Indian River (5-2).
Outstanding Player: Brian Davis, of, Middle Georgia.

ALL-AMERICA TEAM

C—Brent Whitlock, Jackson State (Tenn.). **INF**—Jim Chamblee, Odessa (Texas); Steve Chavez, Yavapai (Ariz.); Brian Conley, Volunteer State (Tenn.); Scott Seabol, Allegany (Md.). **OF**—Brandon Black, Pensacola (Fla.); Anthony Felston, Mississippi Delta; Frank Gappa, Fort Scott (Kan.). **DH**—Jackie Burnett, Northeastern Oklahoma A&M. **P**—Ricky Collins, Southern Union State (Ala.); Pete Fortune, Rockland (N.Y.); Cliff Politte, Jefferson (Mo.).

NATIONAL LEADERS

BATTING AVERAGE
(Minimum 100 At-Bats)

	AB	H	AVG
Zapata, Alexis, New Mexico	100	51	.510
Gappa, Frank, Fort Scott (Kan.)	151	75	.497
Rodriguez, John, Connors State (Okla.)	175	84	.480
Hunter, Johnny, Navarro (Texas)	127	61	.480
Martin, Gary, Barton County (Kan.)	110	52	.473

Department Leaders: Batting

Dept. Player, School	G	Total
HR Five tied at		19
RBI Conley, Brian, Volunteer State (Tenn.)	65	83

EARNED RUN AVERAGE
(Minimum 50 Innings)

	IP	ER	ERA
Whitekiller, Jerel, Connors State (Okla.)	64	8	1.13
Thompson, Doug, Mississippi Gulf Coast	96	13	1.22
Blank, Matt, Galveston (Texas)	102	14	1.24
Sanders, Frankie, Pasco-Hernando (Fla.)	97	14	1.29
Kingrey, Jarrod, Central Alabama	83	12	1.30

Department Leaders: Pitching

Dept. Player, School	Total
W Manwiller, Tim, Allegany (Md.)	14
Thompson, Doug, Mississippi Gulf Coast	14
SV Mastrolonardo, David, Central Florida	17
SO Spence, Cam, Lake City (Fla.)	160

NJCAA DIVISION II

WORLD SERIES

Site: Millington, Tenn.
Participants: Carl Albert (Okla.), Delaware Tech, Hinds (Miss.), Kirkwood (Iowa), Lincoln Land (Ill.), Macomb (Mich.), Massasoit (Mass.), Potomac State (W.Va.).
Champion: Potomac State (4-0).
Runner-Up: Kirkwood (4-2).
Outstanding Player: Chris Reyes, p, Potomac State.

NJCAA DIVISION III

WORLD SERIES

Site: Bavaria, N.Y.
Participants: Bronx (N.Y.), Gloucester (N.J.), Housatonic (Conn.), Joliet (Ill.), Madison (Wis.) Area, Mohawk Valley (N.Y.), Owens (Ohio), Richland (Texas).
Champion: Madison (5-1).
Runner-Up: Joliet (3-2).
Outstanding Player: Bill Uelmen, c, Madison Area.

CALIFORNIA JUCOS

STATE CHAMPIONSHIP

Site: Fresno.
Participants: Cerritos JC (37-12); Fresno CC (39-11); Rancho Santiago JC (39-9); Sacramento CC (42-8).
Champion: Rancho Santiago (3-0).
Runner-Up: Cerritos (2-2).
Outstanding Player: Tony Zuniga, ss, Rancho Santiago.

HIGH SCHOOL
BASEBALL

Tennessee School Piles Up 38 Wins In Row To Capture National Title

By CHRIS WRIGHT

Germantown (Tenn.) High School coach Phil Clark said his unbeaten national championship team was within one hit of losing. Not just a game. A whole bunch of them.

"We saw teams just as talented as we were," said Clark, whose Red Devils started a 38-0 year by winning the prestigious Upper Deck Classic in Orange, Calif., and ended it by claiming the Tennessee state 3-A title—and ultimately their first national title.

"This group never got rattled. We didn't pound people. All our games were close. We played tight games all year where one break and you get beat."

Unranked early in the 1995 season in the Baseball America/National High School Baseball Coaches Association poll, Germantown debuted at No. 2 after knocking off four California teams en route to the Upper Deck title. Included was a 10-6 victory over preseason No. 1 and tournament favorite Fountain Valley High.

Fountain Valley won the California Interscholastic Federation sectional title and ended the year at No. 6. It was one of eight teams to be ranked in the Top 25 for the second year in a row.

The others were No. 3 Mission Bay High of San Diego; No. 8 Green Valley High of Henderson, Nev.;

Rock At Shortstop. Jay Hood of national champion Germantown, Tenn.

No. 11 Calvert Hall (Md.) High; No. 13 Sarasota (Fla.) High; No. 18 New Hanover High of Wilmington, N.C.; No. 20 Farmington (N.M.) High; and No. 23 La Quinta High of Westminster, Calif.

Green Valley, Sarasota (the 1994 national champion) and New Hanover earned the honor for the third consecutive year.

Germantown sealed its season in typical fashion. At the Upper Deck Classic, it won a pair of two-run games and a one-run game. After rallying twice to win state playoff games, the Red Devils stared down defeat once more when finalist Montgomery Bell Academy of Nashville pushed the tying run to the plate before the Red Devils recorded the final out.

"The last out was the best part of the season," Clark said. "We were in a small ballpark. I told the guys, 'Let's get an out and we're the national champions.'

"We could play a little bit. We saw some great, great players. We were a scrappy little group which did the little things. And we had a rock at shortstop."

Jay Hood hit .460 with six homers as the Red Devils shortstop, but lasted until the fourth round of the draft in large part because he committed to Georgia Tech and teams considered him too high a risk to draft sooner.

Righthander Chad Hutchinson of Torrey Pines High in Encinitas, Calif., started the 1995 season as the nation's premier high school prospect and, aside from signing with Stanford, did little to hurt his draft status. The 6-foot-5, 220-pound two-sport star averaged 12 strikeouts per seven innings—recording single-game highs of 16 and 14—and finished 11-0 with a 1.10 ERA.

Atlanta, which once passed on another strong-armed pitching prospect, Todd Van Poppel, after he threatened to attend college, took a chance and drafted Hutchinson 26th overall. The $1.5 million gamble failed. While Hutchinson admitted being pumped at the prospect of playing for a pennant contender, he was even more excited about throwing strikes to receivers and catchers for Stanford's football and baseball teams and turned down the Braves' offer—the only first-round pick from the '95 draft not to sign.

One player Hutchinson didn't strike out was Rancho Bernardo High's All-American outfielder Jaime Jones, who was selected sixth overall in the draft by the Marlins. Scouts flocked to see Hutchinson and Jones square off during a regular-season game. Jones went 0-for-2 with a walk but flew out to the warning track and hit a

HIGH SCHOOL TOP 25

Baseball America's final 1995 Top 25, selected in conjunction with the National High School Baseball Coaches Association:

SCHOOL, CITY	W-L	Achievement
1. Germantown (Tenn.) HS	38-0	State 3-A champions
2. Elkins HS, Fort Bend, Texas	32-2	State 5-A champion
3. Mission Bay HS, San Diego	30-2	CIF sectional champion
4. Key West (Fla.) HS	35-2	State 4-A champion
5. Antioch (Calif.) HS	23-2	CIF sectional champion
6. Fountain Valley (Calif.) HS	26-3	CIF sectional champion
7. Petal (Miss.) HS	29-1	State 4-A champion
8. Green Valley HS, Henderson, Nev.	31-4	State 3-A champion
9. Grand Prairie (Texas) HS	33-4	
10. St. Thomas Aquinas HS, Ft. Lauderdale	27-4	State 5-A champion
11. Calvert Hall (Md.) HS	29-2	
12. Tottenville HS, Staten Island, N.Y.	37-2	Class A sectional champion
13. Sarasota (Fla.) HS	27-5	
14. Millikan HS, Long Beach, Calif.	23-3	
15. Norman (Okla.) HS	34-5	State 5-A champion
16. Kingwood (Texas) HS	24-4	
17. Pleasure Ridge Park HS, Louisville	39-3	State champion
18. New Hanover HS, Wilmington, N.C.	25-4	
19. Glen Oak HS, Canton, Ohio	28-2	State Division I champion
20. Farmington (N.M.) HS	22-2	State 5-A champion
21. Cherry Creek HS, Englewood, Colo.	25-1	State 5-A champion
22. Green Run HS, Virginia Beach, Va.	25-1	State 3-A champion
23. La Quinta HS, Westminster, Calif.	28-3	CIF sectional champion
24. Fontana (Calif.) HS	25-3	
25. Brainerd (Minn.) HS	23-3	State 2-A champion

1995 HIGH SCHOOL ALL-AMERICA TEAMS

Selected by Baseball America

FIRST TEAM

Pos., Player	School, Hometown	Drafted	AVG	AB	H	HR	RBI	SB
C Ben Davis	Malvern (Pa.) Prep	Padres (1)	.507	71	36	6	37	7
1B Nate Rolison	Petal (Miss.) HS	Marlins (2)	.548	84	46	8	55	14
IF Michael Barrett	Pace Academy, Atlanta	Expos (1)	.624	117	73	10	58	24
Chad Hermansen	Green Valley HS, Henderson, Nev.	Pirates (1)	.473	129	61	12	68	20
Jay Hood	Germantown (Tenn.) HS	Twins (4)	.460	100	46	6	40	15
OF Billy Brown	St. Thomas Aquinas HS, Fort Lauderdale	Athletics (3)	.444	90	40	11	26	15
*Eric Chavez	Mt. Carmel HS, San Diego	Not eligible	.537	117	63	9	35	51
Jaime Jones	Rancho Bernardo HS, San Diego	Marlins (1)	.475	80	38	10	30	26
DH Shawn Gallagher	New Hanover HS, Wilmington, N.C.	Rangers (5)	.591	110	65	19	61	10

Pos., Player	School, Hometown	Drafted	W	L	ERA	IP	H	BB	SO
P Joe Fontenot	Acadiana HS, Lafayette, La.	Giants (1)	10	2	0.62	66	22	26	126
Chad Hutchinson	Torrey Pines HS, Encinitas, Calif.	Braves (1)	10	0	1.32	64	33	28	102
Phill Lowery	Casa Grande HS, Petaluma, Calif.	Rangers (2)	13	0	0.58	85	30	15	182
Kerry Wood	Grand Prairie (Texas) HS	Cubs (1)	14	0	0.81	81	28	40	156
Andy Yount	Kingwood (Texas) HS	Red Sox (1)	10	0	2.41	76	46	27	124

SECOND TEAM

C—Ben Petrick, Glencoe HS, Hillsboro. Ore. (.513-11-46). **1B**—Jim Scharrer, Cathedral Prep, Erie, Pa. (.522-7-28). **IF**—*Joe Lawrence, Barbe HS, Lake Charles, La. (.412-5-21); Jeff Maloney, Ridge HS, Basking Ridge, N.J. (.474-6-37); Jason Woolf, American HS, Hialeah, Fla. (.526-2-21). **OF**—Richard Brown, Nova HS, Fort Lauderdale (.447-5-37, 37 SB); Reggie Taylor, Newberry, S.C., HS (.452-4-21); Chad Whitaker, St. Thomas Aquinas HS, Fort Lauderdale (.425-7-33). **DH**—Doug Blosser, Sarasota, Fla., HS (.447-12-39). **P**—Chuck Crowder, Crestwood HS, Mantua, Ohio (10-1, 0.09); Roy Halladay, West HS, Arvada, Colo. (10-1, 0.55); Ryan Mills, Horizon HS, Scottsdale, Ariz. (13-0, 0.86); Jimmy Osting, Trinity HS, Louisville (8-2, 0.09); *Bobby Seay, Sarasota, Fla., HS (10-1, 1.06).

*Junior

---

long drive foul with the bases loaded.

Gallagher Ties Records

No high school player gained more national attention in 1995 than New Hanover High's Shawn Gallagher, who tied two national records.

Gallagher hit four home runs in a game against Jordan High of Durham, N.C., and outdid himself less

Shawn Gallagher

than a month later when he tied a national mark by smashing five homers against Southern Wayne High of Dudley, N.C.

In pursuit all year of Stan Brown's 51-game hitting streak, Gallagher tied the record but was held hitless in Game 52 by crosstown rival Laney High. Gallagher went 0-for-2 and was intentionally walked his last time up as his team went down to a 3-2, extra-inning defeat. The Wildcats had won 35 games in a row at that point and were ranked No. 1 nationally ahead of Germantown.

The game also marked the first career loss in more than 30 decisions for junior righthander Eric Faulk.

Gallagher, drafted in the fifth round by the Texas Rangers, finished the 1995 season with a .591 average, 19 homers and 61 RBIs.

Other notable accomplishments in 1995:

■ Petal (Miss.) High All-American Nate Rolison (second round, Marlins) nearly hit for the cycle—in one inning. He singled, doubled and drilled a grand slam.

■ All-American lefthander Phill Lowery (second round, Rangers) of Casa Grande High in Petaluma, Calif., tossed his fourth career no-hitter and led the nation with 182 strikeouts.

■ Kingwood (Texas) High righthanders Jeff Austin (10th round, Expos) and Andy Yount (first round, Red Sox) struck out a combined 260 batters in 151 innings.

■ Grand Prairie (Texas) High All-American Kerry Wood (first round, Cubs), a transfer from nearby MacArthur High in Irving, no-hit his former team and made news when he started both ends of a Texas state playoff doubleheader and threw 175 pitches. Just to prove he wasn't one-dimensional, Wood added a grand slam that day, too.

Catcher Ben Davis, BA's High School Player of the Year, meanwhile, never really enjoyed a big day because he couldn't hit what he couldn't reach.

"I don't think he saw a fastball all season," Malvern Prep coach Mike Rooney said. Davis apparently can handle the curve because he hit .506 and drilled six

Ben Davis

homers playing on fields without a fence.

"They played me pretty deep," said Davis, who also had seven triples.

Players weren't the only ones earning accolades in 1995.

Bobby Moegle became just the second skipper ever to win 1,000 games when Monterey High of Lubbock, Texas, beat Permian High of Odessa 10-4. Moegle finished the season with a career mark of 1,002-235. He trails all-time leader Gene Schultz of Lansing Kee, Iowa, whose record is 1,083-227.

AMATEUR
BASEBALL

Team USA Raises Hopes For 1996 With Sweep Of Powerful Cuba

By JIM CALLIS

After six consecutive summers of disappointment, USA Baseball had one of its best seasons ever in 1995.

Gearing up for the 1996 Atlanta Olympics, the U.S. national team did nothing but fuel optimism that it could win a gold medal. Team USA finished 36-6 by winning its last 21 games, including an unprecedented four-game sweep of Cuba and a 7-0 run at the National Baseball Congress World Series.

"I don't think anybody could have anticipated this," Team USA general manager Mike Fiore said. "The worst thing about the summer was that it had to end."

The highlight of the summer was the four-game series with Cuba in Millington, Tenn., site of the national training base. Cuba, the defending Olympic champion and winner of 108 consecutive games in major international tournaments, never had lost more than three games in a row or been swept in a series.

Team USA put a dent in Cuba's invincibility by rallying three times in the ninth inning for victories, twice on RBI singles by UCLA third baseman Troy Glaus and once on a two-run homer by Cal State Fullerton catcher Brian Loyd.

"We probably will be married to history because nobody will beat Cuba four times again," U.S. head coach Skip Bertman (Louisiana State) said. "Nobody's done it before. It's an enormous feat."

Cuban head coach Jorge Fuentes noted that his team had a month off before working out in preparation for the July 29-Aug. 1 U.S. series and a subsequent Olympic qualifying tournament in Edmonton. But he did say that the 1995 version of Team USA was better than the 1992 U.S. Olympic team that finished fourth in Barcelona, but not quite as good as the 1988 U.S. team that won the gold medal in Seoul. Cuba beat the United States at the World Championships that year but boycotted the Olympics.

Skip Bertman

Bertman said the most important legacy of the sweep is dealing a blow to Cuba's considerable confidence.

"The No. 1 thing about Cuba is their hubris. They're certain they're going to win," Bertman said. "Now there's a chink that's going to be in place in the Cuban national team's thinking. Now we think we can win. That's the main value of the series."

Team USA was no less dominant at the National Baseball Congress World Series in Wichita. Making its first appearance ever at the tournament, the national team won all seven of its games and beat the Jayhawk League's Hays Larks 10-6 in the championship game.

Cal State Fullerton outfielder Mark Kotsay was voted top major league prospect after leading all hitters with a .600 batting average, while Hays first baseman Lance Berkman (Rice) was named MVP after hitting .571 with seven homers and a tournament-record 25 RBIs.

New Approach

After a disappointing fourth-place finish at the 1992 Barcelona Olympics, USA Baseball decided to rethink its approach. USA Baseball, which oversees the national teams, determined that continuity was important and viewed the building of the 1996 Olympic team as a two-year process.

Bertman returns in 1996 as head coach, as does his staff of assistants and a nucleus of players. He said he sees no reason why the 20-man Olympic roster can't match or exceed the total of nine veterans on the 1988 team, which won a gold medal at the Seoul Olympics, where baseball was a demonstration sport.

Only one player has been guar-

TEAM USA '95

OVERALL STATISTICS

BATTING	AVG	AB	R	H	2B	3B	HR	RBI	SB	College	Class
Travis Lee, 1b	.405	148	28	60	11	2	3	42	7	San Diego State	So.
*Javier Flores, c	.400	5	1	2	0	0	0	0	0	Oklahoma	So.
Jacque Jones, of	.376	157	40	59	12	2	8	44	8	Southern Cal	So.
Warren Morris, 2b	.361	144	46	52	11	2	5	21	7	Louisiana State	So.
Mark Kotsay, of-p	.358	134	32	46	11	1	3	31	5	Cal State Fullerton	So.
Troy Glaus, 3b	.306	111	19	34	3	0	2	15	0	UCLA	Fr.
Chad Allen, of	.295	105	13	31	3	1	4	18	5	Texas A&M	So.
Matt LeCroy, dh-c	.294	102	17	30	4	0	7	32	3	Clemson	Fr.
Augie Ojeda, ss	.287	80	20	23	3	0	1	10	6	Cypress (Calif.) JC	So.
Chad Meyers, of	.284	67	15	19	3	1	0	8	3	Creighton	So.
Brian Loyd, c	.271	59	12	16	1	0	2	5	1	Cal State Fullerton	So.
Brian Shackelford, of.	.269	67	13	18	6	1	3	12	0	Oklahoma	Fr.
A.J. Hinch, c	.265	83	12	22	4	0	1	11	2	Stanford	Jr.
Tom Sergio, 2b	.256	43	12	11	2	1	0	1	4	North Carolina St.	So.
*Chad Moeller, c	.200	5	1	1	1	0	0	0	0	Southern Cal	So.
Casey Blake, 3b	.174	69	10	12	3	0	1	8	3	Wichita State	Jr.
Derek Mitchell, ss	.171	41	7	7	1	0	0	6	0	Triton (Ill.) JC	So.
*Jason Williams, ss	.000	2	0	0	0	0	0	0	0	Louisiana State	So.

PITCHING	W	L	ERA	G	SV	IP	H	BB	SO	College	Class
Braden Looper	1	0	1.71	17	6	21	17	8	22	Wichita State	So.
Randy Wolf	4	0	1.90	12	1	24	26	8	30	Pepperdine	Fr.
Mark Kotsay	1	0	1.93	3	0	5	3	2	3	Cal State Fullerton	So.
R.A. Dickey	3	1	1.94	11	0	46	45	15	36	Tennessee	So.
Matt Anderson	2	0	1.96	14	5	16	16	10	14	Rice	Fr.
Ryan Drese	5	1	2.15	7	0	38	38	11	38	California	Fr.
Mark Johnson	5	0	2.34	13	2	42	32	5	36	Hawaii	So.
Jarrod Mays	2	0	2.38	10	0	34	26	11	29	SW Missouri State	So.
Mark Roberts	4	1	2.83	7	0	35	29	13	22	South Florida	So.
Rocky Biddle	1	0	2.93	4	0	15	9	6	11	Long Beach State	Fr.
Kaipo Spenser	3	1	3.27	11	0	44	37	20	43	Arizona State	So.
Eric DuBose	5	2	3.34	9	0	35	24	13	26	Mississippi State	Fr.

*Did not make traveling roster

ROBERT GURGAN JS

anteed a spot on the 1996 Olympic team. After turning down the Minnesota Twins, who drafted him in the third round in June, Stanford catcher A.J. Hinch committed to Team USA and Bertman reciprocated. Several others seem to have a stranglehold on starting jobs.

San Diego State first baseman Travis Lee, Baseball America's Summer Player of the Year, and Southern California left fielder Jacque Jones are near-locks to make the 1996 team. Ditto for Kotsay, the reigning College World Series MVP who offers much-needed versatility by doubling as a lefthanded reliever.

Pitching usually determines a team's success in international play, and Bertman couldn't be much more elated about his mound corps. Team USA finished the summer with a 2.47 ERA and never allowed more than six runs in a game.

Bertman was the pitching coach of the 1988 team, presiding over a staff that had Jim Abbott, Andy Benes and Ben McDonald in the rotation and Charles Nagy in the bullpen. He said it's a bit early to start comparing the 1995 staff to that group.

Travis Lee

"A year from now, you can ask me that question," Bertman said. "They're not as good as Abbott, McDonald, Nagy and Benes. But those guys were older and at the top of their game. Next year, these guys could be."

Bad Summer For Cuba

Bertman said he still considered Cuba the Olympic favorite, seconding the opinion of most international observers. But Cuba definitely isn't the virtual lock to win that it was in Barcelona.

After its stunning sweep at the hands of Team USA, Cuba extended its international winning streak to going 6-0 at the Aug. 5-13 Americas Baseball Challenge in Edmonton. But Cuba's play was especially ragged at times, even if it did secure an Olympic berth by beating Nicaragua 11-1 in the final.

Worse yet, the Cubans will come to Atlanta without two of its better pitchers. Righthander Osvaldo Fernandez defected in Millington July 29, the day Cuba began its series against Team USA. Fernandez, 28, had been a member of the Cuban national team since 1991 and had started twice against the United States at the 1992 Olympics.

Righthander Livan Hernandez, 20, left the team while it was training in Monterrey, Mexico, on Sept. 27. Hernandez eventually left Mexico for Venezuela, where he reportedly sought political asylum.

Fernandez is considered a decent prospect, but Hernandez is a cut above. He has excellent control and a fastball that consistently has been clocked in the mid-90s. He first came to the attention of international scouts when he dominated the United States in the title games of the 1992 and 1993 World Junior Championships.

Nine months before the start of the Olympic baseball tournament on July 20 in Atlanta, seven of the eight teams had been determined. In addition to

USA BASEBALL TRIALS ROSTER

Sixty-six of the nation's top baseball players were invited to the annual USA Baseball Trials Oct. 26-29 in Homestead, Fla. They underwent physical tests and performed in practice and games, part of the evaluation process for the 1996 U.S. Olympic team.

CATCHERS (9)	YR.	SCHOOL
*Tucker Barr	Jr.	Georgia Tech
Tim DeCinces	Jr.	UCLA
Jason Grabowski	So.	Connecticut
A.J. Hinch	Sr.	Stanford
Matt LeCroy	So.	Clemson
Brian Loyd	Jr.	Cal State Fullerton
Chad Moeller	Jr.	Southern California
Wyley Steelmon	Jr.	Oklahoma State
Dennis Twombley	Jr.	Pepperdine

INFIELDERS (18)	YR.	SCHOOL
Jerome Alviso (ss)	Jr.	Cal State Fullerton
Casey Blake (3b)	Sr.	Wichita State
Clint Bryant (3b)	Sr.	Texas Tech
Danny Cey (ss)	Jr.	California
Brian Dallimore (2b)	Sr.	Stanford
Troy Glaus (3b)	So.	UCLA
Kip Harkrider (ss)	So.	Texas
Jay Hood (ss)	Fr.	Georgia Tech
Travis Lee (1b)	Jr.	San Diego State
Warren Morris (2b)	Jr.	Louisiana State
Augie Ojeda (ss)	Jr.	Tennessee
Todd Sears (1b)	So.	Nebraska
Tom Sergio (2b)	Jr.	North Carolina State
John Tamargo (ss)	Jr.	Florida
Peter Tucci (1b)	Jr.	Providence
*Ron Walker (3b)	So.	Old Dominion
Jason Williams (ss)	Sr.	Louisiana State
Tony Zuniga (ss)	So.	Rancho Santiago (Calif.) JC

OUTFIELDERS (12)	YR.	SCHOOL
*Chad Allen	Jr.	Texas A&M
Lance Berkman	So.	Rice
J.D. Drew	So.	Florida State
*Chad Green	Jr.	Kentucky
Jacque Jones	Jr.	Southern California
*Mark Kotsay	Jr.	Cal State Fullerton
Jon Macalutas	Sr.	Cal Poly San Luis Obispo
Chad Meyers	Jr.	Creighton
Jason Michael	So.	Okaloosa-Walton (Fla.) CC
Jose Rio-Berger	Jr.	Lewis-Clark State (Idaho)
*Brian Shackelford	So.	Oklahoma
Eric Valent	Fr.	UCLA

PITCHERS (27)	YR.	SCHOOL
Matt Anderson (R)	So.	Rice
Jeff Austin (R)	Fr.	Stanford
John Bale (L)	Sr.	Southern Mississippi
Chris Bauer (R)	Sr.	Wichita State
Kris Benson (R)	Jr.	Clemson
Rocky Biddle (R)	So.	Long Beach State
Brad Blumenstock (R)	Jr.	Southern Illinois
Matt Carnes (R)	So.	Arkansas
R.A. Dickey (R)	Jr.	Tennessee
Ryan Drese (R)	So.	California
Eric DuBose (L)	So.	Mississippi State
Keith Evans (R)	Jr.	California
Mark Johnson (R)	Jr.	Hawaii
John Kaufman (L)	Jr.	Florida
Braden Looper (R)	Jr.	Wichita State
Matt Miller (L)	Jr.	Texas Tech
Eric Milton (L)	Jr.	Maryland
Jim Parque (L)	So.	UCLA
Kyle Peterson (R)	So.	Stanford
Dan Reichert (R)	So.	Pacific
Mark Seaver (R)	Jr.	Wake Forest
David Shepard (R)	Sr.	Mansfield State (Pa.)
Kaipo Spenser (R)	Jr.	Arizona State
*Brad Wilkerson (L)	Fr.	Florida
Kris Wilson (R)	Jr.	Georgia Tech
Randy Wolf (L)	So.	Pepperdine
Eddie Yarnall (L)	Jr.	Louisiana State

*Two-way player.
Boldface indicates played with Team USA in 1995.

SUMMER BASEBALL
CHAMPIONS

INTERNATIONAL

EVENT/Age Group	Location	Champion	Runner-Up
Pan American Games	Mar del Plata, Argentina	Cuba	Nicaragua
World Junior Championships	Cape Cod/Boston, Mass.	United States	Chinese Taipei
World University Games	Tokyo, Japan	Cuba	South Korea

NATIONAL

AAABA (21 & under)	Johnstown, Pa.	New Orleans	Johnstown, Pa.
American Legion Baseball (19 & under)	Fargo, N.D.	Aiea, Hawaii	Bellevue, Wash.
NBC World Series (open)	Wichita	Team USA	Hays, Kan.
U.S. Olympic Festival (18 & under)	Colorado Springs	USA West	USA South

AMERICAN AMATEUR BASEBALL CONGRESS

Pee Wee Reese (11-12)	Toa Baja, P.R.	Puerto Rico Gigantes	Levittown, P.R.
Sandy Koufax (13-14)	Jersey City, N.J.	Dallas	West Covina, Calif.
Mickey Mantle (15-16)	Kalamazoo, Mich.	Baltimore	Memphis
Connie Mack (17-18)	Farmington, N.M.	Dallas	Cincinnati
Stan Musial (open)	Battle Creek, Mich.	Sacramento	Bridgeview, Ill.

AMATEUR ATHLETIC UNION (AAU)

11 & under	Kenner, La.	Encinitas, Calif.	Chesapeake, Va.
12 & under	Burnsville, Minn.	Lake Mary, Fla.	Westlake Village, Calif.
13 & under	Norman, Okla.	San Diego	Monterey Park, Calif.
14 & under	Cocoa, Fla.	Hampton Roads, Va.	Kansas City, Kan.
15 & under	Millington, Tenn.	Middletown, N.J.	San Diego
16 & under	Des Moines	Fremont, Calif.	Lebanon, Tenn.
17 & under	Norman, Okla.	Greenfield, Wis.	Lawrence, Kan.
18 & under	Panama City, Fla.	Co-champions declared*	
20 & under	Daytona Beach, Fla.	Philadelphia	Mukwonago, Wis.

*Championship game postponed due to Hurricane Erin. Knoxville, and Hartsell, N.C., declared co-champions.

BABE RUTH BASEBALL

Bambino (11-12)	Abbeville, La.	Abbeville, La.	Kokomo, Ind.
13 Prep	Kinston, N.C.	Longwood, Fla.	Trumbull, Conn.
13-15	Millville, N.J.	Glendale, Ariz.	South Shore, N.Y.
16	Jamestown, N.Y.	Columbia Basin, Wash.	Iron Area, N.J.
16-18	Trail, B.C.	Vancouver, Wash.	San Luis Obispo, Calif.

CONTINENTAL AMATEUR BASEBALL ASSOCIATION

11 & under	Tarkio, Mo.	San Juan, P.R.	Omaha
12 & under	Omaha	Honolulu	Kansas City, Mo.
13 & under	Broken Arrow, Okla.	Encinitas, Calif.	Kansas City, Mo.
14 & under	Dublin, Ohio	Encinitas, Calif.	Seattle
15 & under	Crystal Lake, Ill.	Cucamonga, Calif.	Brunswick, Ohio
16 & under	Waukesha, Wis.	Springfield, Ill.	Cedar Rapids, Iowa
High School	Euclid, Ohio	Brooklyn	Miami
18 & under	Fort Wayne, Ind.	Baltimore	Wichita
College	Wheaton, Ill.	Wheaton, Ill.	Westerville, Ohio
Unlimited	Eau Claire, Wis.	Eau Claire, Wis.	Addison, Ill.

DIXIE BASEBALL

Youth (11-12)	Lexington, S.C.	Ville Platte, La.	Pensacola, Fla.
Boys (13-14)	Troy, Ala.	Valdosta, Ga.	Yazoo City, Miss.
Pre-Majors (15-16)	Mauldin, S.C.	Daphne, Ala.	Columbia County, Ga.
Majors (17-18)	Sebring, Fla.	Lake Charles, La.	Columbia County, Ga.

LITTLE LEAGUE BASEBALL

Little League (11-12)	Williamsport, Pa.	Chinese Taipei	Spring, Texas
Junior League (13)	Taylor, Mich.	So. Lake Charles, La.	Northridge, Calif.
Senior League (13-15)	Kissimmee, Fla.	Dunedin, Fla.	Clarksville, Ind.
Big League (16-18)	Fort Lauderdale	Chinese Taipei	Broward County, Fla.

NATIONAL AMATEUR BASEBALL FEDERATION

Freshman (11-12)	Sylvania, Ohio	Bartlett, Tenn.	Livonia, Mich.
Sophomore (13-14)	Miamisburg, Ohio	Renton, Wash.	Baltimore
Junior (15-16)	Northville, Mich.	Bayside, N.Y.	Lexington, Ky.
Senior (17-18)	Marietta, Ohio	Springfield, Ohio	Marietta, Ga.
High School	Fort Campbell, Ky.	Suffolk County, N.Y.	Apopka, Fla.
College (22 & under)	Cincinnati	Arlington, Va.	Fairfield, Ohio
Major (open)	Louisville	Pelham, N.Y.	Louisville

POLICE ATHLETIC LEAGUE

16 & under	Indianapolis	Metro Dade, Fla.	St. Petersburg, Fla.

PONY BASEBALL

Bronco (11-12)	Monterey, Calif.	Chinese Taipei	Bayamon, P.R.
Pony (13-14)	Washington, Pa.	Bayamon, P.R.	Hagerstown, Md.
Colt (15-16)	Lafayette, Ind.	Bayamon, P.R.,	Corona, Calif.
Palomino (17-18)	Greensboro, N.C.	Fort Worth, Texas	Little Creek, Va.

REVIVING BASEBALL IN INNER CITIES (RBI)

Junior (13-15)	Philadelphia	Atlanta	Newark, N.J.
Senior (16-17)	Philadelphia	Los Angeles	St. Louis

the United States, which received an automatic berth as the host nation, and Cuba the other qualifiers were: Holland and Italy, the 1-2 finishers at the European championships July 7-16 at Haarlem, the Netherlands; Japan and South Korea, the 1-2 finishers at the Asian Games Sept. 17-25 at Kurashiki City, Japan; and Nicaragua, the runner-up to Cuba at the Americas Baseball Challenge.

The remaining Olympic berth was to go to the winner of a playoff between Oceania champion Australia and Africa champion South Africa.

College Education

Team USA didn't play in any major international tournaments in 1995, chiefly because the timing wasn't right. The Pan American Games were played in the middle of the college season and the World University Games were held as colleges opened for the fall.

Unlike in past years, USA Baseball didn't put together national teams to send to those competitions, both of which were won by Cuba. St. John's and Florida State represented the United States instead and the results were disheartening.

St. John's went 0-6 and tied for ninth and last place at the March 11-22 Pan Am Games in Mar Del Plata, Argentina, in March. Along the way, the Red Storm became the second U.S. team in 12 Pan Am Games not to win a medal; the first to finish with a losing record; was a victim of the 10-run mercy rule against doormat Guatemala; and gave Guatemala and the Netherlands Antilles their only victories.

"Our worst fears came true," St. John's coach Joe Russo said. "We weren't going to be able to hit the more experienced pitchers of the other teams. They were ahead of us."

Florida State was much more respectable at the Aug. 26-Sept. 1 World University Games in Fukuoka, Japan. The Seminoles went 2-3 and finished fourth among eight teams, losing 7-3 to Japan in the bronze-medal game.

U.S. Juniors Win Fourth Title

The U.S. junior (16-18) team matched the success of the senior team. After coming within six outs of winning the World Junior Championships in 1994, Team USA finished the job in the Aug. 11-20 tournament in Cape Cod and Boston, Mass.

Tournament MVP Brad Wilkerson (Owensboro, Ky.) pitched a 10-0 three-hitter over Chinese Taipei in the finale to give the United States its fourth gold medal in the 15-year history of the tournament and first since 1989. Wilkerson also drove in the winning run in a 5-4 semifinal victory over Australia, and finished the tournament with three victories and three home runs.

Among the other U.S. stars were shortstop Jay Hood (Germantown, Tenn.), named the best defensive player in the tournament; outfielder Eric Valent (Anaheim Hills, Calif.), who led Team USA with a .394 batting average and nine RBIs; and righthander Matt White (Waynesboro, Pa.), who no-hit Italy during the round-robin.

Hood (Georgia Tech), Valent (UCLA) and Wilkerson (Florida) all headed to college and participated in the U.S. Olympic Trials in Homestead, Fla., in late October. White, a rising high school senior, is expected to be one

GOLDEN SPIKES AWARD
Kotsay Wins Amateur Honor

Mark Kotsay was so busy collecting awards in 1995 that it was hard to imagine he had the time to play baseball.

In June, the Cal State Fullerton two-way star picked up the MVP award at the College World Series. In August, he was named the top prospect at the National Baseball Congress World Series.

And in November he capped a banner year with the Golden Spikes Award, amateur baseball's highest honor.

A center fielder, Kotsay batted .422 with 21 home runs, 90 RBIs and 15 stolen bases as he led the Titans to the national championship. At the College World Series, he set or tied six records, including championship-game

Mark Kotsay

marks for home runs (two) and RBIs (five) in an 11-5 victory over Southern California.

Kotsay was equally outstanding as a pitcher, allowing a run in only one of his 21 appearances for Fullerton. Overall, he went 2-1 with a 0.31 ERA and 11 saves and closed out the title-game win over the Trojans.

Kotsay spent the summer with Team USA, primarily as a right fielder. He rebounded from a slow start to hit .358 with a team-high 11 doubles, three home runs and 31 RBIs in 37 games. He led all players with a .600 batting average at the National Baseball Congress World Series.

USA Baseball annually gives the award, college baseball's equivalent of the Heisman Trophy, to the nation's top amateur player. Other finalists were Texas Tech third baseman Clint Bryant, Rice outfielder Jose Cruz Jr., Nebraska outfielder Darin Erstad, Tennessee first baseman Todd Helton, Southern California outfielder Geoff Jenkins, Florida State righthander Jonathan Johnson, Clemson outfielder Shane Monahan and Oklahoma lefthander Mark Redman.

PREVIOUS WINNERS
1978—**Bob Horner**, 3b, Arizona State
1979—**Tim Wallach**, 3b, Cal State Fullerton
1980—**Terry Francona**, of, Arizona
1981—**Mike Fuentes**, of, Florida State
1982—**Augie Schmidt**, ss, New Orleans
1983—**Dave Magadan**, 1b, Alabama
1984—**Oddibe McDowell**, of, Arizona State
1985—**Will Clark**, 1b, Mississippi State
1986—**Mike Loynd**, rhp, Florida State
1987—**Jim Abbott**, lhp, Michigan
1988—**Robin Ventura**, 3b, Oklahoma State
1989—**Ben McDonald**, rhp, Louisiana State
1990—**Alex Fernandez**, rhp, Miami-Dade CC South
1991—**Mike Kelly**, of, Arizona State
1992—**Phil Nevin**, 3b, Cal State Fullerton
1993—**Darren Dreifort**, rhp-dh, Wichita State
1994—**Jason Varitek**, c, Georgia Tech

SUMMER PLAYER OF YEAR

Lee Excels Again

It was only a matter of time before Travis Lee won Baseball America's Summer Player of the Year award. He has made a habit of starring after school lets out.

In 1993, shortly after graduating from Capital High in Olympia, Wash., Lee more than held his own in the illustrious Alaska League, batting .365 with five home runs and 40 RBIs for the Alaska Goldpanners. He earned the reputation as the best high school player in the history of the Alaska leagues.

A year later, Lee returned to the Goldpanners and batted .299 with four homers, 41 RBIs and 33 stolen bases. Managers voted him the top professional prospect in Alaska baseball, ahead of future 1995 first-round draft picks Mike Drumright, Jeff Liefer and Alvie Shepherd.

Lee spent the summer of 1995 as Team USA's cleanup hitter and it was his best yet. Facing seasoned international pitching, the San Diego State first baseman led the U.S. team with a .405 batting average and ranked second with 11 doubles, 42 RBIs and seven stolen bases.

His performance helped Team USA win its final 21 games, including an unprecedented four-game sweep of Cuba and seven straight victories at the National Baseball Congress World Series. Though head coach Skip Bertman wouldn't tip his hand on the subject of the 1996 U.S. Olympic team, Lee has a firm hold on the first-base job.

The complete Summer All-America first team, with players' summer teams and leagues, colleges and summer statistics:

C—Reggie Davis, Wareham/Cape Cod (Campbell), .311-4-27.
1B—Travis Lee, Team USA (San Diego State), .405-3-42.
2B—Warren Morris, Team USA (Louisiana State), .361-5-21.
3B—Rob Hauswald, Danville/Central Illinois (Mississippi State), .405-5-41. **SS**—Augie Ojeda, Team USA (Cypress, Calif., JC/transferred to Tennessee), .287-1-10.
OF—Adam Kennedy, Goldpanners/Alaska (Cal State Northridge), .434-3-38, 25 SB; Jacque Jones, Team USA (Southern California), .376-8-44; Josh Paul, Cotuit/Cape Cod (Vanderbilt), .364-6-26.
DH—Lance Berkman, Hays/Jayhawk (Rice), .327-12-56.
P—R.A. Dickey, Team USA (Tennessee), 3-1, 1.94; Ryan Drese, Team USA (California), 5-1, 2.15; Braden Looper, Team USA (Wichita State), 1-0, 1.71, 6 SV; Jason Ramsey, Chatham/Cape Cod (UNC Wilmington), 5-1, 1.14, 63 IP, 74 SO; Eddie Yarnall, Harwich/Cape Cod (Louisiana State), 5-1, 1.85, 68 IP, 87 SO.

PREVIOUS WINNERS

1984—**Will Clark**, 1b, Team USA
　　—**Rafael Palmeiro**, of, Hutchinson (Jayhawk)
1985—**Jeff King**, 3b, Team USA
　　—**Bob Zupcic**, of, Liberal (Jayhawk)
1986—**Jack Armstrong**, rhp, Wareham (Cape Cod)
　　—**Mike Harkey**, rhp, Fairbanks (Alaska)
1987—**Cris Carpenter**, rhp, Team USA
1988—**Ty Griffin**, 2b, Team USA
　　—**Robin Ventura**, 3b, Team USA
1989—**John Olerud**, 1b-lhp, Palouse (Alaska)
1990—**Calvin Murray**, of, Anchorage Bucs (Alaska)
1991—**Chris Roberts**, of, Team USA
1992—**Jeffrey Hammonds**, of, Team USA
1993—**Geoff Jenkins**, of, Anchorage Bucs (Alaska)
1994—**Steve Carver**, 1b, Glacier Pilots (Alaska Central)

of the top picks in the 1996 draft.

Cuba, which won seven of the first 10 World Junior Championships it attended, went home without a medal for the second straight year. The Cubans lost four games during the round-robin by a total of five runs, and the buzz among scouts was that several top players were left in Cuba after pitchers Hansel Izquierdo and Michael Tejera defected on the way to the 1994 tournament in Brandon, Manitoba.

Team USA pitcher-shortstop Ryan Oase (Everett, Wash.) was the star of the final U.S. Olympic Festival, held July 22-26 in Colorado Springs. Oase led the West to the gold medal by driving in three runs in an 11-6 victory over the South, topped all hitters with an .818 batting average and even contributed five scoreless innings in his one pitching appearance.

Matt White

In October, the U.S. Olympic Committee decided to discontinue the Festival for financial reasons. USA Baseball likely will stage its own annual championships, which will become the new feeder program for the junior team.

Paul Dominates Cape

Vanderbilt outfielder-catcher Josh Paul accomplished just about everything possible in the Cape Cod League in 1995. He carried the Cotuit Kettleers to their first championship since 1985, winning the batting title, the regular-season and playoff MVP awards and top-prospect honors in separate surveys of managers and professional scouts.

"He can do all five things pro guys look for," Cotuit manager Mike Coutts (Maine) said. "Sometimes he looks a little awkward when he hits, but he can hit. The thing he does that other kids don't always do is keep his head on the ball."

Two lefthanders were named co-pitchers of the year. Chatham's Jason Ramsey (UNC Wilmington) went 5-1 with a Cape-best 1.14 ERA and 74 strikeouts in 63 innings. Harwich Mariners lefthander Eddie Yarnall (Louisiana State) threw a no-hitter, went 5-2 with a 1.85 ERA and led the Cape with 87 strikeouts in 68 innings.

Other Summer League Stars

Alaska Goldpanners outfielder-shortstop Adam Kennedy smashed Steve Kemp's 21-year-old team record with a .434 batting average, and led all players in Alaska in hitting, triples (11) and stolen bases (25). That earned him Alaska player-of-the-year honors and helped the Goldpanners share the Alaska Baseball Federation championship with the Anchorage Glacier Pilots.

Despite his success and quick bat, Kennedy didn't crack the annual managers' Top 10 Prospects list. No. 1 on that chart was Alvie Shepherd, a first-round pick of the Baltimore Orioles who joined the Anchorage Bucs when negotiations started to drag. A power-pitching righthander, Shepherd played sparingly, hit-

U.S. OLYMPIC FESTIVAL
Colorado Springs
July 22-26, 1995

ROUND-ROBIN STANDINGS

	W	L	RF	RA
West	3	0	36	16
South	2	1	32	24
North	1	2	23	38
East	0	3	16	29

BRONZE MEDAL: East 13, North 8. **GOLD MEDAL:** West 11, South 6.

INDIVIDUAL BATTING LEADERS
(Minimum 10 Plate Appearances)

	AVG	AB	R	H	2B	3B	HR	RBI	SB
Ryan Oase, West	.818	11	6	9	1	1	2	8	1
Brad Wilkerson, South	.500	14	5	7	1	1	2	9	1
Eric Valent, West	.444	18	8	8	4	0	2	7	1
Tony Schrager, North	.438	16	6	7	2	0	1	7	1
Nate Turner, East	.429	14	7	6	1	0	2	6	2
Brent Abernathy, South	.421	19	4	8	3	1	0	2	4
Robb Quinlan, North	.417	12	1	5	2	0	0	2	0
Kory Hartman, North	.412	17	3	7	0	0	1	6	1
Dustin Delucchi, West	.400	10	3	4	0	0	0	4	1
Jason Tyner, South	.389	18	3	7	0	0	0	3	3
Jody Gerut, North	.368	19	6	7	1	0	0	1	3
Jay Hood, South	.368	19	7	7	2	0	0	6	0

INDIVIDUAL PITCHING LEADERS
(Minimum 5 Innings)

	W	L	ERA	G	SV	IP	H	BB	SO
Ryan Oase, West	1	0	0.00	1	0	5	8	0	2
Doug Roper, South	2	0	0.00	2	0	6	5	3	5
Justin Lehr, West	0	0	1.50	2	1	6	2	0	3
Cliff Wren, South	0	0	1.69	1	0	5	6	3	2
Ben Evick, East	0	0	3.00	2	0	6	7	1	2
Brad Wilkerson, South	0	0	3.00	3	0	6	5	1	8

WORLD JUNIOR CHAMPIONSHIPS
Cape Cod, Mass./Boston
Aug. 11-20, 1995

ROUND-ROBIN STANDINGS

	W	L	RF	RA
South Korea	6	1	41	21
United States	6	1	42	11
Australia	4	3	44	29
Chinese Taipei	4	3	40	27
Canada	4	3	39	31
Cuba	3	4	32	20
*Netherlands	1	6	15	46
Italy	0	7	13	81

SEMIFINALS: United States 5, Australia 4; Chinese Taipei 4, South Korea 2.
BRONZE MEDAL: Australia 6, South Korea 5. **GOLD MEDAL:** United States 10, Chinese Taipei 0.

ALL-TOURNAMENT TEAM: C—Andrew Utting, Australia. **1B**—Park Bong Soo, South Korea. **2B**—Mark Paparella, Australia. **3B**—Peng Cheng-Min, Chinese Taipei. **SS**—Shih Chih-Wei, Chinese Taipei. **OF**—Brent Abernathy, United States; Yoandy Garlobo, Cuba; Eric Valent, United States. **P**—Kim Soo Sun, South Korea; Meng Hsien-Cheng, Chinese Taipei.
MVP—Brad Wilkerson, lhp-of, United States. **Best Defensive Player**—Jay Hood, ss, United States.

ROUND-ROBIN LEADERS
INDIVIDUAL BATTING
(Minimum 18 Plate Appearances)

	AVG	AB	R	H	2B	3B	HR	RBI	SB
Davide Dallospedale, Italy	.438	16	2	7	0	0	0	2	0
Peng Cheng-Min, CT	.419	31	6	13	0	0	3	9	2
Brent Abernathy, USA	.412	17	4	7	2	0	1	4	4
Shih Chih-Wei, CT	.400	30	5	12	0	0	1	4	5
Bobby Cripps, Canada	.385	26	3	10	0	0	0	3	2
Yoandy Garlobo, Cuba	.385	26	7	10	1	1	1	3	3
Jody Gerut, USA	.385	26	3	10	1	0	0	2	1
Park Bong Soo, Korea	.385	26	6	10	4	0	2	9	1
Shawn Pearson, Canada	.385	26	7	10	2	0	0	2	2
Daniele Frignani, Italy	.368	19	2	7	2	0	0	3	2
Matt Mason, Canada	.360	25	5	9	1	0	2	7	0
Eric Valent, USA	.360	25	7	9	2	0	1	7	1
Jay Hood, USA	.357	28	5	10	3	0	2	4	0
Jung Won Sok, Korea	.350	20	6	7	1	1	0	3	4
Jose Acevedo, Cuba	.344	32	6	11	1	0	0	3	1

INDIVIDUAL PITCHING
(Minimum 5 Innings)

	W	L	ERA	G	SV	IP	H	BB	SO
Chang Shih-Kai, CT	0	1	0.00	1	0	6	5	3	7
Doug Dent, USA	1	0	0.00	3	0	7	1	3	7
Perry Hoetjes, Neth	0	0	0.00	2	0	7	2	3	4
Kim Byoung Hyun, Korea	1	0	0.00	3	0	10	7	5	13
Aaron Myette, Canada	2	0	0.00	2	0	16	6	5	14
Matt White, USA	1	0	0.00	1	0	7	0	2	12
Maikel Quintero, Cuba	0	2	0.55	2	0	16	14	5	12
Rogier Rijnberk, Neth	0	0	0.87	2	0	10	4	7	3
Greg Bauer, USA	0	0	0.93	2	1	10	6	6	8
Jonder Martinez, Cuba	1	0	0.98	2	0	18	10	5	24

TEAM USA
OVERALL INDIVIDUAL BATTING

	AVG	AB	R	H	2B	3B	HR	RBI	SB
Eric Valent, rf	.394	33	9	13	4	1	1	9	1
Jay Hood, ss	.389	36	7	14	5	0	2	7	0
Tony Schrager, 3b	.375	8	2	3	1	0	0	0	0
Jody Gerut, cf	.361	36	3	13	1	1	0	3	1
Brad Wilkerson, lhp-lf	.360	25	7	9	3	0	3	8	0
Justin Lehr, c	.348	23	7	8	4	0	0	4	1
Brent Abernathy, lf	.346	26	7	9	1	0	1	5	4
Omar Moraga, 3b-rhp	.273	22	5	6	1	1	1	1	3
Ryan Oase, 1b-rhp	.238	21	2	5	1	0	0	2	0
David Matranga, 2b	.206	34	6	7	3	0	0	6	1
David Ross, c	.000	7	0	0	0	0	0	0	0

OVERALL INDIVIDUAL PITCHING

	W	L	ERA	G	SV	IP	H	BB	SO
Doug Dent, rhp	1	0	0.00	3	0	7	1	3	7
Joe Horgan, lhp	2	0	0.84	2	0	11	6	3	10
Brad Wilkerson, lhp-lf	3	0	0.90	3	0	20	11	3	26
Greg Bauer, rhp	0	0	0.93	2	1	10	6	6	8
Ryan Oase, 1b-rhp	1	0	1.35	3	2	7	5	1	3
Kory Hartman, rhp	0	0	1.50	1	0	6	4	3	7
Matt White, rhp	1	0	2.70	2	0	10	2	7	13
Omar Moraga, 3b-rhp	0	1	4.50	1	0	2	2	1	2
Gil Meche, rhp	0	0	6.23	1	0	4	3	3	6

ting .292 with four homers in 23 games as a DH and working three scoreless innings.

Righthander Jay O'Shaughnessy, who led NCAA Division I with 13.5 strikeouts per nine innings at Northeastern during the spring, continued to rack up the K's in the Northeastern Collegiate Baseball League. He fanned 15 in his first start for the Geneva Knights, a league-record 21 in his second (including 12 in a row) and broke his own mark with 24 in 10 innings in his final appearance. He went 2-0, 0.64 with 60 whiffs in 28 innings before signing with the Los Angeles Dodgers as an 18th-round pick.

Taiwan Back On Top

Chinese Taipei won its first Little League World Series since 1991 by demolishing Spring, Texas 17-3 in the second-most lopsided final ever.

Taiwan's Lin Chih-Hsiang pitched a four-hitter and hit two homers, giving him a record six for the tournament, staged Aug. 21-26 in Williamsport, Pa. Hsiang, who hit three homers in a 12-2 win over Canada during the round-robin, broke a record shared by former major leaguer Lloyd McClendon.

COLLEGE SUMMER LEAGUES

NCAA-AFFILIATED

ARIZONA SUMMER COLLEGIATE

	W	L	PCT	GB
Peoria Royals	22	13	.629	—
Glendale Angels	22	13	.629	—
Scottsdale Braves	17	18	.486	5
Phoenix Marlins	16	19	.457	6
Mesa Yankees	15	20	.429	7
Tempe Giants	13	22	.371	9

PLAYOFFS: Phoenix defeated Mesa 2-0 and Tempe defeated Scottsdale 2-1 in best-of-3 quarterfinals. Glendale defeated Phoenix 2-0 and Peoria defeated Tempe 2-0 in best-of-3 semifinals. Glendale defeated Peoria 2-1 in best-of-3 final.

INDIVIDUAL BATTING LEADERS
(Minimum 80 Plate Appearances)

	AVG	AB	R	H	2B	3B	HR	RBI	SB
Cronin, Shane, Mesa	.385	96	19	37	10	1	2	20	0
Hewes, Robert, Glendale	.378	98	28	37	5	3	0	16	8
Barnes, Nelson, Glendale	.372	78	23	29	4	1	1	18	8
Primack, Matt, Phoenix	.367	90	20	33	10	0	4	29	1
Bair, Rod, Scottsdale	.359	103	22	37	4	2	0	17	23
Roossien, Anthony, Peoria	.359	117	24	42	9	1	0	21	1
Johnson, Pat, Scottsdale	.356	87	19	31	1	0	2	17	11
Coppel, Rico, Peoria	.352	91	21	32	4	1	1	15	11
Altheide, Todd, Mesa	.351	77	16	27	6	3	1	7	0
Frick, Matt, Glendale	.347	101	21	35	9	1	2	24	5

INDIVIDUAL PITCHING LEADERS
(Minimum 20 Innings)

	W	L	ERA	G	SV	IP	H	BB	SO
Krawczyk, Jack, Peoria	4	2	1.85	7	0	39	34	7	26
Bubeck, Ben, Phoenix	3	2	2.18	9	2	21	21	15	15
Aledcoa, Ralph, Peoria	3	0	2.27	13	1	32	25	12	19
Oroz, Jason, Mesa	1	1	2.42	5	0	22	18	9	12
Bocock, Steve, Peoria	3	2	3.07	10	1	41	41	11	31

ATLANTIC COLLEGIATE LEAGUE

BELSON	W	L	PCT	GB
West Deptford Storm	23	13	.639	—
Quakertown Blazers	21	15	.584	2
Delaware Gulls	19	17	.528	4

KAISER	W	L	PCT	GB
New York Generals	24	12	.667	—
Nassau Collegians	9	27	.250	15
Brooklyn Clippers	8	28	.222	16

WOLFF	W	L	PCT	GB
Jersey Pilots	23	13	.639	—
Sussex Colonels	21	15	.584	2
Scranton/Wilkes-Barre Twins	15	21	.417	8

PLAYOFFS: Sussex defeated New York 2-1 and West Deptford defeated Jersey 2-1 in best-of-3 semifinals. West Deptford defeated Sussex in one-game final.

INDIVIDUAL BATTING LEADERS
(Minimum 90 Plate Appearances)

	AVG	AB	R	H	2B	3B	HR	RBI	SB
Manuelian, Jon, Brooklyn	.404	94	17	38	9	3	1	10	2
Harris, Mike, West Deptford	.376	109	15	41	7	0	1	23	6
Marchiano, Mike, Sussex	.359	197	23	42	5	2	1	25	11
Roof, Chris, Jersey	.358	95	18	34	1	2	1	18	4
Donahue, Greg, New York	.351	114	15	40	6	0	1	18	0
Vankoski, Brett, Delaware	.347	95	20	33	5	0	0	15	14
Rhodes, Dusty, Jersey	.331	118	25	39	5	1	0	10	5
Rooney, Mike, New York	.330	103	23	34	4	0	0	13	2
Stegen, Brian, Jersey	.327	113	20	37	7	2	2	23	0
Fitzsimmons, Brian, New York	.321	106	18	34	3	3	0	19	6

INDIVIDUAL PITCHING LEADERS
(Minimum 40 Innings)

	W	L	ERA	G	SV	IP	H	BB	SO
Rizzo, Nick, West Deptford	5	3	1.21	9	0	52	39	17	33
Connolly, Keith, New York	5	0	1.86	10	1	48	36	21	28
Rothfield, Eric, Jersey	4	2	1.94	11	1	60	53	26	20
Tull, Bill, West Deptford	2	3	2.03	8	0	44	34	21	36
Emerich, Ronald, Quakertown	5	2	2.09	12	2	43	38	16	35

CAPE COD LEAGUE

EAST	W	L	T	PCT	PTS
Chatham A's	25	17	1	.590	51
Orleans Cardinals	22	21	0	.512	44
Yarmouth-Dennis Red Sox	17	24	2	.419	36
Brewster Whitecaps	17	25	1	.407	35
Harwich Mariners	15	27	1	.360	31

WEST	W	L	T	PCT	PTS
Cotuit Kettleers	29	11	3	.709	61
Wareham Gatemen	28	15	1	.648	57
Hyannis Mets	22	20	1	.523	45
Bourne Braves	18	23	3	.443	39
Falmouth Commodores	16	26	1	.384	33

PLAYOFFS: Chatham defeated Orleans 2-1 and Cotuit defeated Wareham 2-1 in best-of-3 semfinals. Cotuit defeated Chatham 2-1 in best-of-3 final.

ALL-STAR TEAM: C—Reggie Davis, Wareham (Campbell). **1B**—Tim Giles, Orleans (UNC Greensboro). **2B**—Travis Young, Wareham (New Mexico). **3B**—Mark DeRosa, Bourne (Pennsylvania). **SS**—Jerome Alviso, Chatham (Canada, Calif., JC). **OF**—Josh Paul, Cotuit (Vanderbilt); Scott Sollman, Brewster (Notre Dame); Peter Tucci, Bourne (Providence). **Util**—Jason Koehler, Chatham (Rider). **P**—Chuck Beale, Orleans (Stetson); Jack Cressend, Cotuit (Tulane); Jason Ramsey, Chatham (UNC Wilmington); Eddie Yarnall, Harwich (Louisiana State). **RP**—Eric Parker, Yarmouth-Dennis (James Madison).

INDIVIDUAL BATTING LEADERS
(Minimum 114 Plate Appearances)

	AVG	AB	R	H	2B	3B	HR	RBI	SB
Paul, Josh, Cotuit	.364	132	37	48	8	6	6	26	16
Cey, Dan, Hyannis	.335	158	30	53	10	1	5	33	10
Amrhein, Mike, Bourne	.330	106	19	35	13	2	0	20	3
Tucci, Peter, Bourne	.325	169	37	55	8	1	11	43	18
Gillespie, Eric, Wareham	.325	151	24	49	11	1	5	25	3
Grimmett, Ryan, Hyannis	.322	115	34	37	4	2	0	19	17
Gload, Ross, Hyannis	.321	106	21	34	9	1	3	23	2
Young, Travis, Wareham	.318	170	30	54	2	0	0	21	24
Alviso, Jerome, Chatham	.311	183	29	57	8	1	0	10	2
Davis, Reggie, Wareham	.311	151	27	47	7	1	4	27	3
Johnson, Rick, Bourne	.309	139	23	43	6	2	0	21	9
Sollman, Scott, Brewster	.305	154	28	47	4	1	0	20	20
DeRosa, Mark, Bourne	.304	161	24	49	7	1	1	26	9
Koehler, Jason, Chatham	.297	145	43	13	0	8	37		1
Campbell, Wylie, Hyannis	.296	152	30	45	4	2	0	14	16
Matoian, Chad, Bourne	.294	102	20	30	2	0	1	10	8
Phoenix, Wynter, Brewster	.294	119	21	35	4	4	3	19	8
Barr, Tucker, Brewster	.289	128	16	37	7	0	6	25	2
Mirizzi, Marc, Wareham	.288	160	17	46	6	1	0	28	5
Byers, Scott, Falmouth	.287	136	15	39	7	0	2	26	2
Burnham, Gary, Orleans	.284	162	22	46	4	1	4	28	3
Peterman, Tom, Y-D	.283	166	17	47	9	1	4	25	2
McCuaig, Alex, Harwich	.283	138	21	39	2	1	0	8	11
Burke, Todd, Falmouth	.282	110	15	31	2	0	0	15	5
Giles, Tim, Orleans	.274	146	31	40	5	1	4	30	6
Olson, Dan, Hyannis	.274	146	23	40	4	2	4	29	6
Connacher, Kevin, Falmouth	.274	157	32	43	9	2	0	14	20
MacKay, Tripp, Orleans	.273	161	26	44	4	2	0	13	13
Fereday, Todd, Y-D	.270	159	28	43	12	0	1	16	18
Ferrer, Eddie, Wareham	.269	130	18	35	3	0	1	10	7

INDIVIDUAL PITCHING LEADERS
(Minimum 34 Innings)

	W	L	ERA	G	SV	IP	H	BB	SO
Ramsey, Jason, Chatham	5	1	1.14	8	0	63	35	17	74
Evans, Keith, Chatham	4	1	1.23	6	0	44	28	14	39
Wilson, Kris, Falmouth	3	0	1.28	7	0	42	33	22	40
Etherton, Seth, Chatham	4	2	1.29	8	0	49	28	17	65
Yarnall, Eddie, Harwich	5	1	1.85	9	0	68	35	31	87
Beale, Chuck, Orleans	5	0	1.88	11	2	72	52	22	62
Sebring, Jeff, Wareham	6	0	1.91	9	0	66	55	14	35
Cressend, Jack, Cotuit	7	1	2.44	9	0	70	52	26	63

Tisone, Jason, Falmouth 1 3 2.48 22 4 36 29 19 48
Ritter, Kyle, Wareham 3 5 2.48 10 0 58 55 7 30
Seaver, Mark, Chatham......... 3 1 2.52 9 0 54 39 18 55
Rose, Ted, Harwich 2 2 2.65 6 0 37 30 17 23
Flores, Randy, Chatham........ 0 2 2.68 7 0 47 41 11 29
Spencer, Sean, Brewster...... 3 3 2.76 8 0 49 41 23 39
Molina, Gabe, Orleans........... 1 0 3.02 14 2 42 29 31 56
Peck, Jeff, Wareham 2 1 3.03 11 0 39 38 16 22
Leese, Brandon, Harwich 1 7 3.04 10 0 68 54 34 73
Ramseyer, Mike, Cotuit 5 1 3.06 18 1 35 26 15 27
Lee, Corey, Falmouth 2 4 3.06 9 0 50 33 40 37
Gandy, Josh, Cotuit 4 0 3.16 8 0 51 44 24 34

CENTRAL ILLINOIS LEAGUE

FIRST	W	L	PCT	GB	SECOND	W	L	PCT	GB
Danville	15	6	.714	—	Twin City	17	2	.895	—
Springfield	12	8	.600	2½	Springfield	9	7	.563	6½
Twin City	11	9	.550	3½	Danville	10	9	.526	7
Decatur	8	13	.381	7	Champaign	5	14	.263	12
Champaign	5	15	.250	10½	Decatur	4	13	.235	12

PLAYOFFS: Twin City (2-0) won five-team tournament.

ALL-STAR TEAM: C—Jay Ahrendt, Twin City (Illinois Wesleyan); Tim Richardson, Springfield (Western Illinois). **1B**—Todd Mensik, Twin City (Mississippi). **2B**—Ryan Brownlee, Twin City (Evansville); Rob Hauswald, Danville (Mississippi State). **3B**—Dan Erickson, Danville (Arkansas). **SS**—Jim Morsovillo, Champaign County (Western Illinois). **OF**—Theo Fefee, Springfield (Lincoln Land, Ill., CC); Jason Hamrick, Springfield (Lincoln Land CC); Derrick Lankford, Decatur (Carson-Newman, Tenn.); Mark Power, Danville (Mississippi State). **DH**—Eddy Furniss, Champaign County (Louisiana State); Brian Mazurek, Twin City (St. Francis, Ill.). **P**—Neal Arnold, Springfield (Nebraska-Kearney); Randy Bromberek, Danville (Western Illinois); Billy Cusack, Twin City (St. Francis, Ill.); Chris Demouy, Danville (Louisiana State); Mick Fieldbinder, Springfield (Montevallo, Ala.); Derek Hart, Decatur (Lewis, Ill.); Tony Zettergren, Danville (St. Xavier, Ill.).

INDIVIDUAL BATTING LEADERS
(Minimum 90 Plate Appearances)

	AVG	AB	R	H	2B	3B	HR	RBI	SB
Hamrick, Jason, Springfield	.438	121	22	53	6	1	0	18	1
Hauswald, Rob, Danville	.405	148	24	60	5	3	5	41	3
Richardson, Tim, Spring	.392	125	18	49	8	0	3	27	0
Mensik, Todd, Twin City	.382	152	34	58	15	0	5	42	1
Brownlee, Ryan, TC	.380	158	37	60	3	1	0	27	12
Power, Mark, Danville.........	.370	146	18	54	6	2	0	20	7
Lankford, Derrick, Decatur...	.363	135	17	49	10	1	7	33	1
Mazurek, Brian, Twin City...	.356	104	20	37	11	1	5	25	0
Furniss, Eddy, Champaign .	.331	145	25	48	8	4	3	27	2
Erickson, Matt, Danville	.318	148	47	47	7	2	0	15	5

INDIVIDUAL PITCHING LEADERS
(Minimum 36 Innings)

	W	L	ERA	G	SV	IP	H	BB	SO
Zettergren, Tony, Danville	5	2	2.41	9	0	67	66	20	39
Arnold, Neal, Springfield.......	5	1	2.52	10	0	50	38	27	49
Bromberek, Randy, Danville....	4	3	2.91	11	0	74	77	22	44
Fieldbinder, Mick, Springfield .	6	1	2.94	9	0	49	52	15	31
Demouy, Chris, Danville	7	3	3.15	11	1	69	61	32	69

GREAT LAKES LEAGUE

NORTH	W	L	PCT	GB
Euclid Admirals	22	17	.564	—
Sandusky Bay Stars	21	18	.538	1
Lima Locos	19	20	.487	3
Sylvania Sox	13	27	.325	9½

SOUTH	W	L	PCT	GB
Columbus All-Americans	23	16	.590	—
Dayton Aviators	22	17	.564	1
Grand Lake Mariners	22	18	.550	1½
Central Ohio Cows	20	20	.500	3½
Springfield Electros	14	23	.378	8

PLAYOFFS: Grand Lake defeated Columbus 2-1 and Sandusky defeated Euclid 2-0 in best-of-3 semifinals. Sandusky defeated Grand Lake in one-game final.

ALL-STAR TEAM: C—Dave Lindstrom, Grand Lake (Texas Tech); Shannon Swaino, Lima (Kent). **1B**—Larry Husted, Dayton (North Carolina). **2B**—Adam Leggett, Sandusky (Georgia Tech).

3B—Peter Bezeredi, Lima (Troy State). **SS**—Greg Taylor, Grand Lake (Arkansas-Little Rock). **OF**—Bill Burgei, Lima (Bowling Green State); Kevin Marn, Euclid (Kent); Nicky Phillips, Columbus (UNC Greensboro). **Util**—John Burwell, Sandusky (Western Carolina); Brady Gick, Central Ohio (Ohio). **LHP**—Bryan Braswell, Dayton (Toledo); Brian Partenheimer, Dayton (Indiana). **RHP**—Scott Glazer, Springfield (South Florida); Clark Maxwell, Euclid (Western Carolina); Bob Spears, Central Ohio (Ohio State).

INDIVIDUAL BATTING LEADERS
(Minimum 100 Plate Appearances)

	AVG	AB	R	H	2B	3B	HR	RBI	SB
Husted, Larry, Dayton.........	.374	123	25	46	13	2	0	24	0
Marn, Kevin, Euclid.............	.352	125	30	44	4	0	1	7	10
Gick, Brady, Central Ohio...	.350	137	18	48	11	0	1	21	0
Bezeredi, Peter, Lima	.346	130	20	45	9	1	6	33	3
Burwell, John, Sandusky.....	.345	110	13	38	9	0	1	24	1
Swaino, Shannon, Lima.......	.344	90	13	31	3	0	3	16	2
Baker, Curtis, Columbus.....	.330	112	19	37	5	0	0	17	6
Lindstrom, David, Grand Lake	.324	111	18	36	10	0	5	27	2
Taylor, Greg, Grand Lake ...	.322	143	26	46	3	1	0	11	5
Farris, Ed, Sylvania	.318	129	13	41	8	1	5	23	0

INDIVIDUAL PITCHING LEADERS
(Minimum 36 Innings)

	W	L	ERA	G	SV	IP	H	BB	SO
Braswell, Bryan, Dayton	4	1	1.62	7	0	39	22	20	48
Oberschlake, Scott, Central Ohio	3	2	1.88	12	0	48	38	11	44
Marks, Thomas, Euclid	4	3	2.08	9	1	48	30	15	35
Borkowski, Mike, Sylvania	3	2	2.08	6	0	39	34	14	32
Spears, Bob, Central Ohio......	8	1	2.11	11	0	64	57	5	35

JAYHAWK LEAGUE

EAST	W	L	PCT	GB
Nevada Griffons	24	20	.545	—
Topeka Capitols	23	24	.489	2½
Red Oak Red Sox	14	34	.298	12
St. Joseph Cardinals	11	37	.229	15

SOUTH	W	L	PCT	GB
Wichita Broncos	36	8	.818	—
Elkhart Dusters	29	16	.644	7½
Liberal Bee Jays	26	15	.634	8½
Hays Larks	20	27	.426	17½

PLAYOFFS: Wichita defeated Nevada 2-0 in best-of-3 final.

INDIVIDUAL BATTING LEADERS
(Minimum 100 At-Bats)

	AVG	AB	R	H	2B	3B	HR	RBI	SB
Venghaus, Jeff, Liberal	.369	130	33	48	5	2	0	12	24
McCabe, Mike, Elkhart.......	.366	153	46	56	10	0	10	44	5
Barajas, Rodrigo, Elkhart....	.360	100	24	36	13	0	5	37	1
Byers, MacGregor, Liberal..	.357	126	32	45	9	2	3	22	13
Conti, Jason, Elkhart	.355	124	34	44	4	0	3	13	16
Jackson, Wade, Liberal	.351	114	25	40	6	2	4	29	12
Wilson, Andy, Hays	.351	114	26	40	4	1	1	14	17
Bennett, Marshall, Wichita...	.346	136	33	47	7	2	5	32	12
Young, Randy, Wichita	.343	105	23	36	4	0	0	11	27
West, Sean, Wichita	.343	143	22	49	13	1	4	36	6

INDIVIDUAL PITCHING LEADERS
(Minimum 36 Innings)

	W	L	ERA	G	SV	IP	H	BB	SO
Sneed, John, Wichita............	6	0	1.23	6	0	44	35	10	48
Weaver, Andy, Wichita	5	2	1.31	10	0	69	61	1	56
Schroeder, Chad, Liberal......	4	0	1.49	9	0	48	45	—	—
Smith, Andy, Red Oak	3	3	1.77	12	0	56	44	15	70
Keens, Robert, Hays	4	1	1.87	11	1	63	54	21	50

NORTHEASTERN LEAGUE

FIRST	W	L	PCT	GB	SECOND	W	L	PCT	GB
Cortland	13	8	.619	—	Cortland	12	9	.571	—
Geneva	11	10	.524	2	Mo. Valley	12	9	.571	—
Schenectady	11	10	.524	2	Hornell	11	10	.524	1
Cohocton	10	11	.476	3	Schenectady	11	10	.524	1
Hornell	10	11	.476	3	Cohocton	10	11	.476	2
Ithaca	10	11	.476	3	Ithaca	10	11	.476	2
Mo. Valley	8	13	.381	5	Geneva	8	13	.381	4

PLAYOFFS: Hornell (3-0) won four-team tournament.

INDIVIDUAL BATTING LEADERS
(Minimum 85 Plate Appearances)

	AVG	AB	R	H	2B	3B	HR	RBI	SB
Davis, Stacy, Hornell	.383	128	21	49	13	3	0	22	7
Greico, Tony, Mohawk Valley	.370	100	13	37	10	2	3	23	3
Johnson, Mike, Geneva	.343	99	10	34	8	0	2	17	0
Kim, David, Cortland	.328	128	18	42	4	3	3	19	4
Crawley, Dwayne, Schen.	.325	123	18	40	10	2	0	15	6
Falzarano, Heath, Cohocton	.322	115	21	37	6	4	4	14	5
McKitrick, Brian, Ithaca	.305	128	24	39	13	0	1	10	16
Granville, Earnie, Schen.	.304	79	8	24	6	1	0	7	5
Stoss, Jeff, Ithaca	.296	98	15	29	2	2	4	16	6
Doubleday, Mark, Hornell	.295	146	24	43	4	2	0	13	9

INDIVIDUAL PITCHING LEADERS
(Minimum 35 Innings)

	W	L	ERA	G	SV	IP	H	BB	SO
Salley, Anthony, Ithaca	5	1	1.23	9	0	51	34	30	37
Jordan, Todd, Hornell	4	2	1.82	14	1	39	29	15	27
Carlson, Garrett, Ithaca	2	4	2.05	7	0	48	31	17	45
Kelly, Doug, Mohawk Valley	6	1	2.11	15	5	55	42	30	42
Hreban, Mark, Cortland	6	0	2.12	8	0	47	38	12	34

NORTHWEST COLLEGIATE LEAGUE

FIRST	W	L	PCT	GB	SECOND	W	L	PCT	GB
Stars	10	5	.667	—	Dukes	10	5	.667	—
Ports	10	5	.667	—	Stars	9	6	.600	1
Dukes	9	6	.600	1	Ports	9	6	.600	1
Bucks	6	8	.429	3½	Toros	8	7	.533	2
Toros	5	10	.333	5	Lobos	7	8	.467	3
Lobos	4	10	.286	5½	Bucks	2	13	.133	8

PLAYOFFS: Dukes defeated Stars 2-1 in best-of-3 final.

INDIVIDUAL BATTING LEADERS
(Minimum 60 Plate Appearances)

	AVG	AB	R	H	2B	3B	HR	RBI	SB
Bailie, Matt, Stars	.406	69	22	28	4	0	6	21	2
Wakeland, Chris, Dukes	.402	82	25	33	9	1	1	15	16
Bertrand, Ben, Dukes	.384	73	13	28	4	2	1	21	3
Spitler, Jim, Stars	.362	58	9	21	4	0	2	15	2
Lubisch, Pete, Stars	.360	75	14	27	5	0	1	19	2
Beeler, Jeff, Dukes	.355	62	11	22	4	1	0	11	5
Uecker, Damian, Toros	.354	65	7	23	4	0	0	14	2
Smilowski, John, Lobos	.344	61	14	21	5	2	1	14	2
Hauskins, Randy, Ports	.344	96	13	33	4	1	0	18	7
Dorey, Matt, Ports	.338	65	6	22	1	0	0	8	1

INDIVIDUAL PITCHING LEADERS
(Minimum 25 Innings)

	W	L	ERA	G	SV	IP	H	BB	SO
Miadich, John, Dukes	7	2	0.91	11	0	61	38	17	45
Hajj, Scott, Ports	3	2	1.30	10	0	59	47	27	71
Hartman, Darren, Dukes	4	3	1.44	8	0	44	36	12	30
Oyler, Scott, Dukes	7	1	1.62	13	0	61	33	34	68
Messman, Joe, Ports	5	4	1.85	10	0	53	36	28	46

SAN DIEGO COLLEGIATE LEAGUE

FIRST HALF

AMERICAN	W	L	PCT	GB	NATIONAL	W	L	PCT	GB
South Bay	9	6	.600	—	El Cajon	10	5	.667	—
East County	6	8	.429	2½	Beach City	10	5	.667	—
San Diego	5	10	.333	4	North County	4	10	.286	6½

SECOND HALF

AMERICAN	W	L	PCT	GB	NATIONAL	W	L	PCT	GB
South Bay	10	4	.714	—	Beach City	10	5	.667	—
East County	6	8	.429	4	El Cajon	8	7	.533	2
San Diego	6	8	.429	4	North County	3	11	.214	6½

PLAYOFFS: Beach City defeated El Cajon in one-game semifinal. South Bay defeated Beach City 2-0 in best-of-3 final.

INDIVIDUAL BATTING LEADERS
(Minimum 72 Plate Appearances)

	AVG	AB	R	H	2B	3B	HR	RBI	SB
Barnes, John, El Cajon	.487	76	33	37	4	2	4	29	2
Bolton, Jason, East County	.397	68	13	27	3	0	0	10	7
Hudson, Brian, El Cajon	.379	66	21	25	3	1	1	5	6
Hammons, Ryan, El Cajon	.363	80	19	29	5	0	5	29	0
Acuna, Carlos, Beach City	.356	87	15	31	5	0	0	23	2
Palaez, Alex, South Bay	.356	90	13	32	5	3	0	18	6

Coddington, Rob, El Cajon	.351	77	12	27	4	1	0	11	0
Floyd, Chris, Beach City	.329	82	21	27	5	3	1	16	6
Betancourt, Oscar, Beach City	.321	81	8	26	4	1	0	9	3
Wright, Brad, North County	.319	69	11	22	0	0	0	10	2

INDIVIDUAL PITCHING LEADERS
(Minimum 30 Innings)

	W	L	ERA	G	SV	IP	H	BB	SO
Wise, George, Beach City	4	0	0.42	6	0	33	25	8	42
Silva, Ernie, El Cajon	1	1	0.92	8	1	30	24	16	20
Pamus, Javier, El Cajon	5	2	1.29	15	3	49	40	21	51
Plummer, Ray, Beach City	5	4	1.30	13	3	38	35	13	49
Neder, Rey, South Bay	4	0	1.33	13	3	42	29	11	31

SHENANDOAH VALLEY LEAGUE

	W	L	PCT	GB
Staunton Braves	29	11	.725	—
Waynesboro Generals	21	19	.525	8
New Market Rebels	19	21	.475	10
Winchester Royals	19	21	.475	10
Front Royal Cardinals	17	23	.425	12
Harrisonburg Turks	15	25	.375	14

PLAYOFFS: Staunton defeated New Market 3-1 and Waynesboro defeated Winchester 3-2 in best-of-5 semifinals. Staunton defeated Waynesboro 3-0 in best-of-5 final.

INDIVIDUAL BATTING LEADERS
(Minimum 100 Plate Appearances)

	AVG	AB	R	H	2B	3B	HR	RBI	SB
Robinson, Bo, Waynesboro	.398	93	18	37	9	0	1	16	3
Michaels, Jason, Staunton	.366	161	43	59	10	4	10	36	7
Weber, Jake, Winchester	.359	156	25	56	12	1	7	39	5
Thomas, Allen, Staunton	.331	151	33	50	10	2	4	27	9
Bush, Ronald, New Market	.330	103	20	34	4	3	1	15	2
Fernandez, Alex, Staunton	.327	113	30	37	6	4	0	15	11
Edwards, Lamont, Staunton	.324	136	34	44	4	2	3	28	9
Dampeer, Kelly, Front Royal	.320	153	22	49	7	0	3	24	6
Bird, Matthew, Waynesboro	.320	147	29	47	9	5	2	21	16
Sullivan, Adam, Waynesboro	.320	97	23	31	5	2	0	11	11

INDIVIDUAL PITCHING LEADERS
(Minimum 30 Innings)

	W	L	ERA	G	SV	IP	H	BB	SO
Chrysler, Clint, Waynesboro	2	2	1.85	16	7	39	23	12	52
Bohannon, Jason, Waynesboro	5	3	2.45	10	0	77	62	35	80
Harrison, Donovan, New Market	3	2	2.55	10	0	60	54	23	69
Cozart, Craig, Staunton	6	0	2.57	8	0	56	38	14	34
Brookens, Casey, Winchester	4	3	2.70	16	3	40	38	11	52

NON-AFFILIATED LEAGUES

ALASKA LEAGUES

		League				Overall	
ALASKA	W	L	PCT	GB		W	L
Alaska Goldpanners	11	5	.688	—		32	19
Anchorage Bucs	6	9	.400	4½		23	26
Hawaii Island Movers	6	9	.400	4½		19	21

		League				Overall	
ALASKA CENTRAL	W	L	PCT	GB		W	L
Anchorage Glacier Pilots	23	15	.605	—		31	20
Kenai Peninsula Oilers	16	19	.457	5½		26	26
Mat-Su Miners	16	19	.457	5½		20	24

PLAYOFFS: None.

ALASKA BASEBALL FEDERATION STANDINGS: Anchorage Glacier Pilots (14-10), Alaska Goldpanners (14-10), Anchorage Bucs (12-12), Kenai Peninsula Oilers (10-14), Mat-Su Miners (10-14).

ALL-ALASKA TEAM: C—David Schmidt, Anchorage Glacier Pilots (Oregon State). **1B**—Chris Shuffield, Mat-Su (Lubbock Christian, Texas). **2B**—Joe Dillon, Mat-Su (Santa Rosa, Calif., JC). **3B**—Jamie Ahu, Anchorage Bucs (Hawaii). **SS**—Brooks Badeaux, Kenai (Florida State). **OF**—J.D. Drew, Kenai (Florida State); Jon Macalutas, Glacier Pilots (Cal Poly San Luis Obispo); Adam Kennedy, Alaska (Cal State Northridge). **DH**—David Francia, Mat-Su (South Alabama). **Util**—Josh Kliner, Mat-Su (Kansas). **P**—Rob Crabtree, Kenai (Cal State Northridge); Toby Dollar, Kenai (Texas Christian); Brian Scott, Alaska (San Diego State); Flint Wallace, Bucs (Texas Christian).

INDIVIDUAL BATTING LEADERS
(Minimum 100 Plate Appearances)

	AVG	AB	R	H	2B	3B	HR	RBI	SB
Kennedy, Adam, Alaska	.434	222	63	96	15	11	3	38	25
Loeffler, Brett, Bucs	.378	98	23	37	6	2	4	26	3
Macalutas, Jon, Pilots	.370	184	40	68	8	0	5	48	2
Kliner, Josh, Mat-Su/Kenai	.356	132	32	47	10	3	9	32	8
Cermak, Jeff, Alaska	.352	159	40	56	9	6	1	27	9
Marquardt, A.J., Alaska	.351	145	29	51	8	5	3	38	7
Francia, David, Mat-Su	.342	149	34	51	8	2	8	26	15
Toro, Brandon, Hawaii	.338	136	26	46	7	3	4	22	11
Stanley, Todd, Mat-Su	.333	162	28	54	12	2	1	24	5
Reynoso, Ben, Alaska	.327	171	36	56	10	4	4	31	6
Hill, Willy, Bucs	.329	209	32	67	11	1	1	23	19
Fukuhara, Pete, Kenai	.322	118	23	38	6	0	2	21	14
Ammirato, Zak, Pilots	.320	153	34	49	16	0	3	34	2
DeMarco, Joe, Pilots	.314	188	51	59	9	1	2	36	26
Edelstein, Chris, Pilots	.312	125	11	39	6	0	1	23	2
Pickler, Jeff, Kenai	.309	178	33	55	6	0	0	17	13
Ahu, Jamie, Bucs	.308	163	26	50	3	0	1	26	1
Drew, J.D., Kenai	.307	140	31	43	6	3	11	33	9
Curtis, Matt, Alaska	.307	137	26	42	5	0	4	22	2
Badeaux, Brooks, Kenai	.305	141	28	43	5	1	1	18	11
Espada, Joe, Mat-Su	.295	95	22	28	3	0	4	11	10
Thieleke, C.J., Pilots	.290	131	33	38	2	0	3	21	1
Lewis, Ivan, Hawaii	.289	142	22	41	4	1	1	15	17
Ross, Jason, Hawaii	.289	121	19	35	6	0	1	15	14
Porter, Colin, Pilots	.288	156	31	45	5	1	1	16	8
Zech, Scott, Pilots	.288	132	25	38	7	0	0	17	13
Napuunoa, Jody, Hawaii	.286	147	27	42	7	1	2	25	9
Jones, Jack, Alaska	.285	130	22	37	0	2	4	25	4
Hagins, Steve, Alaska	.283	127	21	36	5	3	3	22	6
Konrady, Dennis, Kenai	.283	159	30	45	8	1	0	23	13

INDIVIDUAL PITCHING LEADERS
(Minimum 35 Innings)

	W	L	ERA	G	SV	IP	H	BB	SO
Scott, Brian, Alaska	4	1	2.11	9	1	60	38	16	56
Dollar, Toby, Kenai	7	2	2.33	11	0	70	63	20	61
Irvine, Kirk, Kenai	2	1	2.50	12	1	50	35	12	24
Bloomer, Chris, Alaska	4	2	2.90	9	0	59	50	19	39
Lee, Derek, Bucs	4	0	3.20	9	0	51	44	17	39
McDonald, Michael, Hawaii	5	2	3.20	13	0	45	43	17	23
Gardner, Mark, Alaska	5	2	3.22	17	0	53	45	21	29
Miller, Michael, Hawaii	3	5	3.32	10	0	62	74	11	32
Gilich, Denny, Pilots	6	2	3.36	11	1	62	69	23	38
O'Dell, Jake, Bucs	4	4	3.38	11	2	51	43	15	39
Crabtree, Rob, Kenai	4	4	3.39	13	2	61	70	15	47
Meyer, David, Bucs	1	6	3.61	13	0	47	50	11	34
Howell, Chuck, Kenai	1	3	3.83	6	0	42	43	19	21
Blank, Matt, Pilots	3	3	4.04	12	0	65	69	27	43
Callaway, Mickey, Kenai	2	4	4.07	6	0	49	42	26	23
Mullikin, Jamie, Mat-Su	1	2	4.11	16	3	35	30	24	23
Wallace, Flint, Bucs	5	4	4.23	11	0	72	68	24	54
Strickland, Scott, Mat-Su	5	1	4.24	10	0	68	75	32	43
Lee, Fletcher, Hawaii	2	2	4.26	12	1	38	45	12	29
Leslie, Sean, Pilots	6	1	4.33	14	0	52	58	23	32
Heineman, Rick, Pilots	4	1	4.47	10	0	44	46	17	33
Schmalz, Darin, Alaska	4	2	4.71	8	0	42	57	7	24
Parker, Christian, Alaska	3	4	4.78	11	0	70	68	24	43

CLARK GRIFFITH COLLEGIATE LEAGUE

	W	L	PCT	GB
Maryland Bombers	25	10	.714	—
Baltimore Oriolelanders	24	11	.686	1
Arlington Senators	17	18	.486	8
Reston Hawks	14	21	.400	11
Vienna Mavericks	13	22	.371	12
Prince William Gators	12	23	.343	13

PLAYOFFS: Arlington defeated Baltimore 2-0 and Maryland defeated Reston 2-0 in best-of-3 semifinals. Maryland defeated Arlington 3-1 in best-of-5 final.

INDIVIDUAL BATTING LEADERS
(Minimum 70 Plate Appearances)

	AVG	AB	R	H	2B	3B	HR	RBI	SB
Kansteiner, Lee, Baltimore	.363	113	26	41	9	1	3	26	2
Rikard, Will, Baltimore	.338	74	12	25	2	0	1	8	0
Smith, Larry, Maryland	.323	65	14	21	10	0	1	9	2
Berman, Jeff, Baltimore	.317	120	31	38	9	1	2	11	9
Marciano, John, Maryland	.315	89	15	28	5	2	0	20	6
Poss, John, Prince William	.311	122	17	38	8	0	1	18	4
Anderson, Jim, Maryland	.308	91	18	28	5	2	0	15	4

Walson, Steve, Reston .... .300 100 22 30 5 0 2 11 1

Walson, Steve, Reston	.300	100	22	30	5	0	2	11	1
Muller, Matt, Reston	.297	101	14	30	4	0	2	18	1
Turner, Natt, Vienna	.295	61	15	18	5	1	2	13	2

INDIVIDUAL PITCHING LEADERS
(Minimum 30 Innings)

	W	L	ERA	G	SV	IP	H	BB	SO
Cummings, Brian, Maryland	9	0	0.86	9	0	63	37	21	53
Daniels, Ben, Baltimore	5	1	1.37	8	0	53	36	9	27
Pollock, Jason, Baltimore	5	3	1.71	9	0	53	35	14	65
Jones, Brian, Maryland	5	1	1.76	7	0	46	35	10	33
O'Reilly, John, Maryland	5	2	1.81	8	1	50	30	17	62

NEW ENGLAND COLLEGIATE LEAGUE

	W	L	PCT	GB
Central Massachusetts Collegians	25	14	.641	—
Waterbury Barons	23	16	.590	2
Eastern Tides	19	21	.475	6½
Danbury Westerners	18	22	.450	7½
Bristol Nighthawks	18	22	.450	7½
Middletown Giants	16	24	.400	9½

PLAYOFFS: Central Massachusetts defeated Danbury 2-0 and Waterbury defeated Eastern 2-0 in best-of-3 semifinals. Central Massachusetts defeated Waterbury 2-0 in best-of-3 final.

INDIVIDUAL BATTING LEADERS
(Minimum 108 Plate Appearances)

	AVG	AB	R	H	2B	3B	HR	RBI	SB
Jette, Ryan, Cent. Mass.	.340	144	22	49	5	3	0	11	27
Carpenter, Jesse, Waterbury	.331	118	17	39	8	1	1	29	0
Valentine, Anthony, Danbury	.326	141	29	46	5	3	0	6	6
Dagliere, David, Middletown	.324	111	18	36	2	3	2	18	15
O'Brien, Mike, Cent. Mass.	.319	116	17	37	6	0	1	19	4
Kurasz, Jeremiah, Waterbury	.317	82	15	26	5	0	0	11	10
Dina, Allen, Waterbury	.309	110	15	34	3	3	1	15	12
Pericolosi, Frank, Middletown	.305	118	12	36	7	1	3	24	1
Reyes, Kiko, Danbury	.304	158	22	48	15	1	1	23	4
Samuelian, Adam, Middletown	.302	126	18	38	4	0	0	18	6

INDIVIDUAL PITCHING LEADERS
(Minimum 32 Innings)

	W	L	ERA	G	SV	IP	H	BB	SO
Taglienti, Jeffrey, Cent. Mass.	8	2	1.60	10	0	68	49	19	60
White, Dave, Eastern	3	1	1.74	7	0	41	29	16	24
Gieras, Kevin, Bristol	4	3	2.17	7	0	54	37	23	55
Alleman, Derek, Bristol	2	4	2.34	6	0	42	37	14	27
Stern, Daniel, Bristol	2	1	2.40	12	0	41	39	16	25

NORTHWOODS LEAGUE

FIRST	W	L	PCT	GB	SECOND	W	L	PCT	GB
Kenosha	19	8	.704	—	Manitowoc	20	9	.690	—
Waterloo	16	11	.593	3	Kenosha	21	10	.677	—
Manitowoc	13	13	.500	5½	Rochester	16	15	.516	5
Wausau	14	14	.500	5½	Waterloo	15	16	.484	6
Rochester	13	16	.448	7	Wausau	11	18	.379	9
Dubuque	6	19	.240	12	Dubuque	7	22	.241	13

PLAYOFFS: Kenosha defeated Manitowoc 2-0 in best-of-3 final.

INDIVIDUAL BATTING LEADERS
(Minimum 154 Plate Appearances)

	AVG	AB	R	H	2B	3B	HR	RBI	SB
Rivera, Luis, Waterloo	.437	245	47	107	21	3	3	60	23
Wold, Chris, Dubuque	.370	189	40	70	18	0	7	31	4
Frietas, Jeremy, Wausau	.370	200	48	74	25	0	7	44	1
Slayton, Shane, Kenosha	.365	126	27	46	10	0	6	32	4
Schaffer, Jake, Kenosha	.363	237	54	86	19	0	6	59	12
Johnson, David, Manitowoc	.361	133	25	48	7	0	2	23	4
Kneeshaw, Dan, Rochester	.353	221	51	78	13	3	10	54	16
Marshall, Brad, Kenosha	.345	232	53	80	15	5	4	37	30
Wycoff, Gabe, Waterloo	.342	193	41	66	3	2	1	30	17
Byas, Mike, Waterloo	.336	223	39	75	3	2	1	25	30

INDIVIDUAL PITCHING LEADERS
(Minimum 46 Innings)

	W	L	ERA	G	SV	IP	H	BB	SO
Erschen, Paul, Wausau	3	3	2.34	31	2	65	68	24	34
Guler, Jeremy, Kenosha	6	0	2.35	9	0	54	50	22	32
Hall, Brian, Waterloo	7	3	2.50	12	0	86	83	30	52
Marik, Tommy, Manitowoc	3	4	3.19	16	0	68	63	20	45
Ramirez, Erasmo, Kenosha	4	2	3.20	11	1	65	60	22	43

AMATEUR
DRAFT

Oakland Puts Unique Twist On Draft By Selecting Cuban Refugee

By ALAN SCHWARZ

For the first time in the amateur draft's 30-year history, the player talked about most before the affair wasn't a strong-armed Texan, power-hitting Californian or any player from the United States. It was, of all things, a Cuban refugee.

Ariel Prieto, a hard-throwing righthander who reportedly pitched on the Cuban national team, flew to the United States some six weeks before the draft in order to sign professionally with a major league organization. He didn't defect—he left with his government's permission by claiming he wanted to be with his wife's family in Florida—but immediately sent scouting departments buzzing.

Some organizations said they would have chosen Prieto with the draft's No. 1 overall selection. The California Angels, who owned that pick, weren't among them.

Prieto ultimately went No. 5 to Oakland, and he made his major league debut four weeks later—within days of signing a $1.2 million bonus contract. He became the 19th player in the draft era to enter the big leagues without any minor league experience.

"I did this because this is what I have dreamed of doing for years," said Prieto, who claimed to be 25 but was believed to be 28. He finished the 1995 season with a 2-6 record and 4.97 ERA for the A's.

Prieto, who became the oldest first-rounder ever by some six years, had signed with the the Palm Springs Suns of the independent Western League soon after arriving in the United States. He went 4-0 with a 0.97 ERA in six starts for the Suns, attracting in excess of 50 scouts to each of his pre-draft appearances.

Ariel Prieto

Prieto's agent, Gus Dominguez, said that before the draft several clubs offered him $2.3 million to sign Prieto on the open market. But Major League Baseball ruled that because he had achieved temporary residency in the United States, and because MLB subjects all independent league players to the draft if they had not yet gone through one before, Prieto entered the draft process.

Prieto's immediate financial windfall raised the possibility that more Cubans would choose to follow him. Cuban national-team pitchers Osvaldo Fernandez, 28, and Livan Hernandez, 20, defected

No. 1 Pick. The California Angels selected outfielder Darin Erstad with the top pick in the 1995 draft.

LARRY GOREN

within the next three months.

"(Prieto) saw the money. He pulled it off," said Sacramento Bee writer Pedro Gomez, a Cuban-American. "I don't know if baseball as we've known it under Castro will ever be the same."

Top Picks Excite Scouts

Other than the disruption of Prieto and his ability to pitch in the majors immediately, the first round unfolded with few surprises. Most encouraging to scouting staffs was the consensus that the 1995 draft pool was one of the deepest ever, comparable to the 1985 class that netted Barry Bonds, Barry Larkin, Rafael Palmeiro, Randy Johnson and a host of other major league standouts.

The Angels focused on University of Nebraska outfielder Darin Erstad all spring and didn't let Prieto's late presence dissuade them. Erstad, 21, was the consensus best player available, at least in terms of future potential.

Erstad hit .410 with 19 homers and 76 RBIs for the Cornhuskers in 1995 and was named a first-team All-American. More importantly, he displayed the best package of the five tools scouts crave: the

TOP 10 SIGNING BONUSES

Drafted Players Only

Player, Pos.	Club, Year (Rnd.)	Bonus
1. Josh Booty, ss	Marlins '94 (1)	$1,600,000
2. Darin Erstad, of	Angels '95 (1)	1,575,000
3. Brien Taylor, lhp	Yankees '91 (1)	1,550,000
Paul Wilson, rhp	Mets '94 (1)	1,550,000
5. Jaime Jones, of	Marlins '95 (1)	1,337,000
6. Ben Davis, c	Padres '95 (1)	1,300,000
Darren Dreifort, rhp	Dodgers '93 (1)	1,300,000
8. Jose Cruz Jr., of	Mariners '95 (1)	1,285,000
9. Kerry Wood, rhp	Cubs '95 (1)	1,265,000
10. Ben Grieve, of	Athletics '94 (1)	1,200,000
Ariel Prieto, rhp	Athletics '95 (1)	1,200,000

DRAFT '95
FIRST-ROUND PICKS

Team. Player, Pos.	School	Hometown	Bonus	B'date	B-T	Ht.	Wt.	AVG	AB	H	HR	RBI	SB	'95 Assignment*
1. Angels. Darin Erstad, of	U. of Nebraska	Jamestown, N.D.	$1,575,000	6-4-74	L-L	6-2	195	.410	251	103	19	76	11	Lake Elsinore (A)
2. Padres. Ben Davis, c	Malvern Prep	Malvern, Pa.	1,300,000	3-10-77	B-R	6-2	175	.507	71	36	6	37	7	Idaho Falls (R)
3. Mariners. Jose Cruz Jr., of	Rice U.	Houston	1,285,000	4-19-74	B-R	6-0	190	.377	223	84	16	76	19	Riverside (A)
6. Marlins. Jaime Jones, of	Rancho Bernardo HS.	San Diego	1,337,000	8-2-76	L-L	6-3	180	.475	80	38	10	30	26	Elmira (A)
8. Rockies. Todd Helton, 1b-lhp	U. of Tennessee	Knoxville	892,500	8-20-73	L-L	6-2	190	.407	258	105	20	92	11	Asheville (A)
9. Brewers. Geoff Jenkins, of	U. of Southern California	Rancho Cordova, Calif.	911,000	7-21-74	L-R	6-1	200	.399	258	103	23	78	14	El Paso (AA)
10. Pirates. Chad Hermansen, ss	Green Valley HS	Henderson, Nev.	1,150,000	9-10-77	R-R	6-2	175	.473	129	61	12	68	20	Erie (A)
14. Phillies. Reggie Taylor, of	Newberry HS	Newberry, S.C.	970,000	1-12-77	L-R	6-1	185	.452	73	33	4	21	24	Martinsville (R)
18. Mets. Ryan Jaroncyk, ss	Orange Glen HS	Escondido, Calif.	850,000	3-26-77	B-R	6-0	170	No high school team						Pittsfield (A)
19. Royals. Juan Lebron, of	Huyke HS	Arroyo, P.R.	650,000	6-7-77	R-R	6-4	185	.384	78	30	2	11	15	GCL Royals (R)
23. Indians. David Miller, 1b	Clemson U.	Philadelphia	620,000	12-9-73	L-L	6-4	200	.380	271	103	9	78	27	DNP—Signed late
24. Red Sox. Corey Jenkins, of	Dreher HS	Columbia, S.C.	575,000	8-25-76	R-R	6-2	195	.403	62	25	4	21	12	GCL Red Sox (R)
25. White Sox. Jeff Liefer, 3b	Long Beach State U.	Upland, Calif.	550,000	8-17-74	L-R	6-3	185	.354	237	84	13	56	14	DNP—Signed late
27. Yankees. Shea Morenz, of	U. of Texas	San Angelo, Texas	650,000	1-22-74	L-R	6-2	205	.336	226	76	9	52	4	Oneonta (A)
28. Expos. Michael Barrett, ss	Pace Academy	Atlanta	500,000	10-22-76	R-R	6-2	185	.624	117	73	10	58	24	Vermont (A)

SUPPLEMENTAL FIRST ROUND

Team. Player, Pos.	School	Hometown	Bonus	B'date	B-T	Ht.	Wt.	AVG	AB	H	HR	RBI	SB	'95 Assignment*
29. Cardinals. Chris Haas, 3b	St. Mary's HS	Paducah, Ky.	200,000	10-15-76	L-R	6-1	215	.554	65	38	7	29	26	Johnson City (R)

Team. Player, Pos.	School	Hometown	Bonus	B'date	B-T	Ht.	Wt.	W	L	ERA	IP	H	BB	SO	'95 Assignment
4. Cubs. Kerry Wood, p	Grand Prairie HS	Grand Prairie, Texas	$1,265,000	6-16-77	R-R	6-3	185	14	0	0.77	82	26	40	152	Williamsport (A)
5. Athletics. Ariel Prieto, p	Palm Springs#	Marianao, Cuba	1,200,000	10-22-69	R-R	6-3	220	4	0	0.97	37	23	7	48	Oakland
7. Rangers. Jonathan Johnson, p	Florida State U.	Ocala, Fla.	1,100,000	7-16-74	R-R	6-0	180	12	3	2.89	134	98	53	130	Charlotte (A)
11. Tigers. Mike Drumright, p	Wichita State U.	Valley Center, Kan.	970,000	4-19-74	R-R	6-3	210	11	3	3.61	120	106	38	117	Jacksonville (AA)
12. Cardinals. Matt Morris, p	Seton Hall U.	Montgomery, N.Y.	850,000	8-9-74	R-R	6-5	210	10	3	2.68	94	64	54	104	St. Petersburg (A)
13. Twins. Mark Redman, p	U. of Oklahoma	Del Mar, Calif.	830,000	1-5-74	L-L	6-5	210	15	3	2.22	142	109	35	158	Fort Myers (A)
15. Red Sox. Andy Yount, p	Kingwood HS	Kingwood, Texas	986,000	2-14-77	R-R	6-2	180	10	0	2.41	76	46	27	124	GCL Red Sox (R)
16. Giants. Joe Fontenot, p	Acadiana HS	Lafayette, La.	900,000	3-20-77	R-R	6-2	180	10	0	0.46	68	28	26	126	Bellingham (A)
17. Blue Jays. Roy Halladay, p	West HS	Arvada, Colo.	895,000	5-14-77	R-R	6-5	200	10	1	0.55	63	24	23	105	GCL Blue Jays (R)
20. Dodgers. David Yocum, p	Florida State U.	Miami	825,000	6-10-74	L-L	6-1	180	12	3	2.61	114	94	43	128	Vero Beach (A)
21. Orioles. Alvie Shepherd, p-1b	U. of Nebraska	Bellwood, Ill.	650,000	5-12-74	L-R	6-7	215	2	5	6.57	38	47	22	42	DNP—Signed late
22. Astros. Tony McKnight, p	Arkansas HS	Texarkana, Ark.	500,000	6-29-77	R-R	6-5	210	9	2	0.79	74	32	15	130	GCL Astros (R)
26. Braves. Chad Hutchinson, p	Torrey Pines HS	Encinitas, Calif.	DNS	2-21-77	R-R	6-6	230	10	0	1.32	64	33	28	102	Did not sign

SUPPLEMENTAL FIRST ROUND

Team. Player, Pos.	School	Hometown	Bonus	B'date	B-T	Ht.	Wt.	W	L	ERA	IP	H	BB	SO	'95 Assignment
30. Phillies. Dave Coggin, p	Upland HS	Upland, Calif.	415,000	10-30-76	R-R	6-3	190	9	2	1.83	76	50	30	83	Martinsville (R)

Signing bonuses do not include college scholarships, incentive bonus plans or salaries from a major league contract.
*Highest level attained   #Playing in independent Western League

Michael Barrett
Expos first-rounder

SIGNING BONUSES

SECOND-ROUND PICKS

31. Jarrod Washburn, lhp, Angels $355,000
32. Gabe Alvarez, ss, Padres 346,000
33. Shane Monahan, of, Mariners 315,000
34. Brian McNichol, lhp, Cubs 305,000
35. Mark Bellhorn, ss, Athletics 280,000
36. Nate Rolison, 1b, Marlins 610,000
37. Phil Lowery, lhp, Rangers DNS
38. Ben Petrick, c, Rockies 495,000
39. Mike Pasqualicchio, lhp, Brewers 250,000
40. Garrett Long, 1b, Pirates 400,000
41. Brian Powell, rhp, Tigers 270,000
42. Marlon Anderson, 2b, Phillies 225,000
43. Jason Bell, rhp, Twins 240,000
44. Jason Woolf, ss, Cardinals 191,500
45. Jose Olmeda, ss, Red Sox 225,000
46. Jason Brester, lhp, Giants 292,500
47. Craig Wilson, c, Blue Jays 292,500
48. Brett Herbison, rhp, Mets 285,000
49. Carlos Beltran, of, Royals 300,000
50. Damian Babineaux, rhp, Dodgers 240,000
51. Charles Alley, c, Orioles 325,000
52. Eric Ireland, rhp, Astros 240,600
53. Sean Casey, 1b, Indians 223,000
54. Brett Tomko, rhp, Reds 200,000
55. Brian Simmons, of, White Sox 210,000
56. Jim Scharrer, 1b, Braves 250,000
57. Richard Brown, of, Yankees 389,500
58. Henry Mateo, ss, Expos 200,000

SUPPLEMENTAL SECOND ROUND

59. Brian Buchanan, lhp, Yankees 300,000

ability to hit, hit with power, run, field and throw.

After two months of contract negotiations, the Angels signed Erstad to a $1.575 million bonus, second highest in draft history.

"It's just going to go into the bank, and I'll surprise my family one day," said Erstad, lauded equally for his talent as his professional and friendly demeanor. "I'm not going to change who I am or what kind of life I lead."

The newfound riches certainly didn't change Erstad's performance. In his first season as a professional, he hit .556 in an 18 at-bat cameo for the Angels' club in the complex-based Arizona League, then manhandled the California League by hitting .363 with five homers in 113 at-bats at Class A Lake Elsinore. He was named that loop's top prospect in a survey of managers.

The pick following Erstad was just as much of a lock. The San Diego Padres always had been infatuat-

Jaime Jones

ed with Ben Davis, widely considered the best high school catcher since Dale Murphy 21 years before, and snapped him up with the No. 2 selection. They signed him immediately for $1.3 million.

Davis hit .507 for Malvern (Pa.) Prep as a senior and won Baseball America's High School Player of the Year award. He batted .279 in his first pro summer, at Rookie-level Idaho Falls, and was named the top prospect in the Pioneer League in a managers survey.

The No. 3 pick was Rice University outfielder Jose Cruz Jr. The son of the former Astros all-star, Cruz was a two-time All-American who hit .377 with 16 homers and 76 RBIs in 1995 and was the hitter most scouts considered the closest to the major leagues.

"I started taking him to the ballpark when he was 3," the elder Cruz said. "He used to play with Phil Garner's son, Art Howe's son, Nolan Ryan's sons. He knows what the big leagues are about."

The Chicago Cubs followed with Grand Prairie (Texas) High righthander Kerry Wood, the consensus top pitcher in the draft. He went 14-0 with a 0.81 ERA as a high school senior. It marked the first time since 1978 that the first pitcher went as low as No. 4.

The No. 6 pick was Florida Marlins outfielder Jaime Jones, considered the best pure high school hitter available. He hit .475 with 10 home runs his senior season for San Diego's Rancho Bernardo High.

"I remember the first time I saw him," then-Marlins scouting director Gary Hughes said. "It was at the Area Code Games in San Diego when he was a sophomore. The first guy hit a ball to him in the outfield and he uncorked an unbelievable throw. I said, 'This Area Code stuff is pretty good.'

"He's got a great swing. He's a baseball player, period. He's got plus power. He's at least an average hitter. He's a plus baserunner with average speed. And he's

Mariners' Top Pick. With the No. 3 pick overall, Seattle went for Rice outfielder Jose Cruz Jr.

MEL BAILEY

got great instincts."

Florida State righthander Jonathan Johnson went No. 7 to the Texas Rangers. The Colorado Rockies followed by taking University of Tennessee first baseman Todd Helton, probably the most recognizeable name in the first round. He not only won BA's College Player of the Year award after batting .407 with 20 homers and 92 RBIs, and going 8-2 with a 1.66 ERA and 12 saves as a reliever, but also had been the Volunteers' starting quarterback the previous fall.

The thought of Helton someday hitting in the cozy confines of Coors Field made for great fantasy.

"Definitely not disappointed," Helton said of going No. 8. "People talk about where you want to go in the draft order, but really it's about the organization you're going to spend, hopefully, a big part of your life in."

Bonuses Keep Rising

Because the draft took place in the wake of the major league players strike, which sapped the industry of hundreds of millions of dollars in revenues, many executives predicted that signing bonuses for draft picks would decrease in 1995. They were wrong, but only in the sense that they increased at a lower rate than in previous years.

The average up-front payment for first-round picks climbed to $913,000, 15.6 percent higher than in 1994. The yearly surges in each of the past five years had been between 27 and 44 percent.

FIRST-ROUND BONUSES

Year	Average	% Increase
1995	$913,000	15.6
1994	790,000	29.3
1993	611,000	26.8
1992	482,000	35.7
1991	355,000	44.3
1990	246,000	39.7

Erstad led the way with his $1.575 million, while seven other players became instant millionaires. Possibly the most shocking of these was prep shortstop Chad Hermansen, who almost immediately after being taken 10th overall by the cash-strapped Pittsburgh Pirates was given $1.15 million.

"The draft doesn't appear to have been affected at all by the strike," Orioles scouting director Gary Nickels said. "It seems to be operating independent of the other problems the strike has created."

As usual, several players chosen beyond the first round received signing bonuses that made other major league teams shake their heads. Each was a top high school player who appeared headed to college before he came to terms.

The Marlins signed their second-round pick, power-hitting first baseman Nate Rolison, for $610,000. Garrett Long, another prep slugger, signed with the Pirates for $400,000 (plus almost $200,000 in education incentives) after being taken four picks after Rolison. He turned down a scholarship to Yale University but signed a contract that allows him to attend the Ivy League school during the offseason—at Pittsburgh's expense.

Hutchinson Rejects Braves

One player who surely would have raised the first-round bonus average was prep righthander Chad Hutchinson, the No. 26 pick by the Braves, but he became the only 1995 first-rounder not to sign.

The standout quarterback/pitcher from Torrey Pines High in San Diego declined the Braves' $1.5 million offer (his original demand) and enrolled at Stanford University to play football and baseball.

Chad Hutchinson

"It wasn't a money issue," Hutchinson said. "It was a lifestyle and education decision. Sure, it was hard to pass up all that money, but I know it'll be there eventually."

Hutchinson easily would have been one of the top 10 picks but his high price tag and a concern by some clubs that he had hurt his arm during the spring left him available only for a club willing to gamble on him. In two years on the Torrey Pines varsity, Hutchinson used his 97-mph fastball to go 23-2 with a 1.33 ERA and fan 182 batters in 152 innings. He went 11-0, 1.10 his senior year and averaged 12 strikeouts per seven innings.

Hutchinson said his decision not to sign with Atlanta was greatly influenced by his mother Martha. She watched as Chad's father Lloyd, once a top prospect himself, struggled in the Phillies minor league system without reaching the major leagues.

"After talking to my mom, it was a pretty easy decision," Hutchinson said. "She's seen minor league baseball first-hand, and knows how hard it is.

"At Stanford, I'm away from home, but I'm kind of sheltered. It's a good starting point for me. I'm sure three years here will help me mature and develop. And I'll be closer to the major leagues."

The Braves will receive a supplemental first-round pick in the 1996 draft as compensation for not signing Hutchinson.

Varitek Precedent Averted

The 1995 draft might have included an awfully familiar, and controversial, face had Jason Varitek not reached a compromise with the Mariners in April.

Varitek, a first-round pick by both Minnesota in 1993 and Seattle in 1994, reached an impasse with the Mariners soon after they picked him, and returned to Georgia Tech—with no eligibility remaining—that fall to complete his degree. He argued that Seattle held his rights only until a week before the 1995 draft, at which point he would become a free agent able to negotiate with any club.

Varitek made his eligibility for baseball's "amateur" draft even more murky in January by signing a professional contract with the St. Paul Saints of the independent Northern League. Major League Baseball, though, ruled that he would have to go through the draft again in 1995.

Jason Varitek

A pivotal arbitration hearing was avoided April 19 when Varitek and the Mariners agreed to a $650,000 bonus.

The Twins drafted Varitek No. 21 overall in 1993 but couldn't sign him. He played for the Yellow

Jackets as a senior and won Baseball America's College Player of the Year award. But after the Mariners picked him No. 14 overall in 1994 and he demanded an $800,000 signing bonus (the average first-round payment), while the Mariners offered just $400,000, all of baseball watched to see how well each side would hold the line.

A win for the Mariners would preserve baseball's bargaining power over college juniors—if they went back to school for their senior seasons, they would cost themselves bonus money—while a win for Varitek might have given future college juniors more leverege in negotiations.

Instead, the longest and most celebrated holdout in the 30-year history of the baseball draft ended when the Mariners and Varitek explored uncharted territory in 1990s baseball: compromise.

"They came up in their offer to the point where I thought it was fair," Varitek said. "It wasn't about money. It was about principle. This was justified. With the other college players I fit in, and I was the highest-paid college catcher."

Seattle scouting director Roger Jongewaard said he believed his hardline position also had been validated. "I think we held the line pretty well," he said. "When we have a high school player or a college junior, we always have to give them more because of their options. We in turn reversed the role. I don't think that's so bad. People don't seem to mind when they're not so nice to us."

Varitek, after playing no games for 10 months and working out all on his own, was assigned to Double-A Port City and hit .224 with 10 homers and 44 RBIs. He still was considered the Mariners' catcher of the future.

"We're not gloating. We're happy," Jongewaard said. "Isn't that the secret to the sale, that everyone thinks they came out OK?"

Owners Seek Bonus Plan

Trying to curb bonus inflation, baseball's owners have tried to implement new draft rules over the years, only to have them expunged by union grievances. In 1995 they devised a formula they planned to bargain over when the hibernating Basic Agreement discussions began again.

Major League Baseball wanted a cap on bonus payments allowed by each team for both draft and international signees during each calendar year. Under the proposal, the team with the first pick in the June draft would be allowed $1.302 million for all its amateur signees. The second team would have $1.290 million, with the caps decreasing down the line.

Teams would have specific spending limits on draft picks through the first five rounds. The first pick overall would receive up to $370,000, the second $365,000 and so on.

"This was a recommendation made by general managers, which was reviewed by the baseball operations committee and then recommended to the player relations committee to include in the bargaining process," said Bill Murray, MLB executive director of baseball operations. "It is only a proposal to be negotiated. It's on the table."

The plan would drastically curb the cost of procuring international talent. Teams no longer would have to bid anywhere near the $1 million top signees Glenn Williams (Braves) and Chan Ho Park (Dodgers) received because such a move would siphon most of their budget. The $2 million the Dodgers spent on Japanese free agent Hideo Nomo would be impossible under the cap.

MLB didn't implement the rules unilaterally because a similar effort in 1992 left an arbitration

NO. 1 DRAFT PICKS, 1965-95

Year	Club, Player, Pos.	School	Hometown	Highest Level (G*)	'95 Team	Bonus
1965	A's. Rick Monday, of	Arizona State U.	Santa Monica, Calif.	Majors (1,996)	Out of Baseball	$104,000
1966	Mets. Steve Chilcott, c	Antelope Valley HS	Lancaster, Calif.	Triple-A (2)	Out of Baseball	75,000
1967	Yankees. Ron Blomberg, 1b	Druid Hills HS	Atlanta	Majors (461)	Out of Baseball	75,000
1968	Mets. Tim Foli, ss	Notre Dame HS	Sherman Oaks, Calif.	Majors (1,696)	Out of Baseball	75,000
1969	Senators. Jeff Burroughs, of	Wilson HS	Long Beach, Calif.	Majors (1,689)	Out of Baseball	88,000
1970	Padres. Mike Ivie, c	Walker HS	Decatur, Ga.	Majors (857)	Out of Baseball	80,000
1971	White Sox. Danny Goodwin, c	Central HS	Peoria, Ill.	Majors (252)	Out of Baseball	DNS
1972	Padres. Dave Roberts, 3b	U. of Oregon	Corvallis, Ore.	Majors (709)	Out of Baseball	60,000
1973	Rangers. David Clyde, lhp	Westchester HS	Houston	Majors (84)	Out of Baseball	125,000
1974	Padres. Bill Almon, ss	Brown U.	Warwick, R.I.	Majors (1,236)	Out of Baseball	90,000
1975	Angels. Danny Goodwin, c	Southern U.	Peoria, Ill.	Majors (252)	Out of Baseball	125,000
1976	Astros. Floyd Bannister, lhp	Arizona State U.	Seattle	Majors (431)	Out of Baseball	100,000
1977	White Sox. Harold Baines, of	St. Michaels HS	St. Michaels, Md.	Majors (2,183)	Orioles	40,000
1978	Braves. Bob Horner, 3b	Arizona State U.	Glendale, Ariz.	Majors (1,020)	Out of Baseball	175,000
1979	Mariners. Al Chambers, of	Harris HS	Harrisburg, Pa.	Majors (57)	Out of Baseball	60,000
1980	Mets. Darryl Strawberry, of	Crenshaw HS	Los Angeles	Majors (1,384)	Yankees	210,000
1981	Mariners. Mike Moore, rhp	Oral Roberts U.	Eakly, Okla.	Majors (450)	Tigers	100,000
1982	Cubs. Shawon Dunston, ss	Jefferson HS	New York	Majors (1,138)	Cubs	100,000
1983	Twins. Tim Belcher, rhp	Mt. Vernon Naz. Coll.	Sparta, Ohio	Majors (260)	Mariners	DNS
1984	Mets. Shawn Abner, of	Mechanicsburg HS	Mechanicsburg, Pa.	Majors (392)	Mets (AAA)	150,000
1985	Brewers. B.J. Surhoff, c	U. of North Carolina	Rye, N.Y.	Majors (1,102)	Brewers	150,000
1986	Pirates. Jeff King, 3b	U. of Arkansas	Colorado Springs	Majors (739)	Pirates	160,000
1987	Mariners. Ken Griffey Jr., of	Moeller HS	Cincinnati	Majors (917)	Mariners	169,000
1988	Padres. Andy Benes, rhp	U. of Evansville	Evansville, Ind.	Majors (199)	Padres	235,000
1989	Orioles. Ben McDonald, rhp	Louisiana State U.	Denham Springs, La.	Majors (155)	Orioles	350,000
1990	Braves. Chipper Jones, ss	The Bolles School	Jacksonville	Majors (148)	Braves	275,000
1991	Yankees. Brien Taylor, lhp	East Carteret HS	Beaufort, N.C.	Double-A (27)	Yankees (R)	1,550,000
1992	Astros. Phil Nevin, 3b	Cal State Fullerton	Placentia, Calif.	Majors (47)	Tigers	700,000
1993	Mariners. Alex Rodriguez, ss	West. Christian HS	Miami	Majors (65)	Mariners	1,000,000
1994	Mets. Paul Wilson, rhp	Florida State U.	Orlando, Fla.	Triple-A (10)	Mets (AAA)	1,550,000
1995	Angels. Darin Erstad, of	U. of Nebraska	Jamestown, N.D.	Class A (25)	Angels (A)	1,575,000

*No. of games at that level   DNS—Did not sign

precedent that requires all changes to the draft to be negotiated through the Major League Baseball Players Association.

Brown Bros. Make History

Richard and Billy Brown in 1995 became the brother act to go highest in the same June draft in the 30-year history of the process. Richard went in the second round to the Yankees, and signed for $389,500, while Billy was taken by Oakland seven picks later, in the third round, but opted to attend Florida State University on a football scholarship.

The Abner brothers, Shawn (No. 1 overall pick, Mets, 1984) and Ben (fifth round, Expos) had been the highest-drafted brothers before the Browns. Todd Stottlemyre and his brother Mel Jr. were the Nos. 1 and 3 overall picks in the secondary phase of the old January draft, in 1985.

Both Brown brothers played outfield, but at different high schools. Billy starred at St. Thomas Aquinas High in Fort Lauderdale. Richard shined at rival Nova High.

Both Billy and Richard were enrolled at St. Thomas until their sophomore seasons, when Richard transferred to Nova to escape his brother's shadow. Billy is a year older than Richard but was held back for one year in elementary school.

"In my opinion, they are both going to play in the major leagues someday but Richard has the higher ceiling," said Demie Mainieri, a Brewers scout in south Florida. "Richard may hit 30 homers someday."

Cruz was the best known son of a former major leaguer drafted. Other such selections in the first five rounds were outfielder Chad Whitaker (son of Steve) in the third round by Cleveland and third baseman Cody McKay (son of Dave) in the fifth round by St. Louis.

Chris Haas, a supplemental first-round pick of St. Louis, is the nephew of ex-major leaguer Eddie Haas. Outfielder Shane Monahan, taken in the second round by Seattle, is the grandson of ex-hockey star Bernie "Boom Boom" Geoffrion.

The Requisite Draft Tidbits

There were 1,666 players selected in the 1995 draft, over 87 rounds. Oakland was the first team to drop out, in the 45th round, and the Marlins were the last.

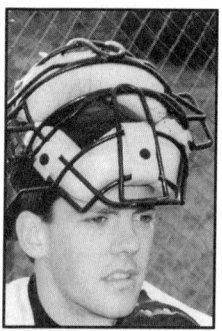

There were only two compensation picks between the first and second rounds, a reflection of the few number of major league free agents who were not offered arbitration by their former clubs the previous offseason. Normally, if a Type A free agent signs with another club, his former club receives that club's first- or second-round draft pick and a supplemental pick at the end of the first round—unless arbitration is not offered.

A.J. Hinch

With the strike in full bloom, few clubs were willing to offer arbitration.

A unique draft development took place when catch-

er A.J. Hinch, the Twins' third-round pick, decided to return to Stanford so he could captain the 1996 U.S. Olympic team. He turned down a $250,000 offer. "When I'm 45 and retired and look back, I think I'm going to be very happy that I stuck it out and played in the Olympics," Hinch said. "And if I'm not going to play in the big leagues, then I definitely want to play in the Olympics and live up all the life experiences I can. Add on that I'm going to graduate, and it seems like an easy decision to me."

The Mets took a flier on Ryan Minor, the slugging first baseman-righthander from the University of

Oklahoma more known for being the reigning Big Eight Conference basketball Player of the Year. He was selected in the seventh round but didn't sign with the Mets because of a snag that involved summer school.

Minor might have been a first-round selection if not for his basketball plans. A small forward, he appeared headed for top-20 selection in the National

Ryan Minor

Basketball Association draft in June 1996. Minor's twin brother Damon, a first baseman, was drafted by the Mets as well, in the 19th round, but didn't sign and followed Ryan back to the Sooners.

Detroit gambled its 16th-round pick on 6-foot-9 Washington State lefthander Mark Hendricksen, also a potential first-round pick in the 1996 NBA draft. It marked the fourth consecutive year that Hendricksen had been drafted, though he had pitched sparingly in three years at Washington State.

The Royals chose Puerto Ricans, Juan Lebron and Carlos Beltran, with their first- and second-round selections, the first team ever to do that. Each is a power-hitting outfielder.

The Marlins would have been tempted, if more as a public-relations measure, to select Prieto with the No. 6 overall selection in the first round had he not been selected by Oakland one pick before. But Florida pleased their local Cuban community by taking Cuban defectors Michael Tejara and Hansel Izquierdo, both pitchers for Miami's Southwest High, in the sixth and seventh rounds, respectively. The two had pitched for Cuba's national junior team before defecting to the U.S. in the summer of 1994.

When Jonathan Johnson and David Yocum went in the first round to the Rangers and Dodgers, respectively, it marked the fourth straight year that Florida State had a pitcher chosen in the first round. Chris Roberts (1992, Mets), John Wasdin (1993, Athletics) and Paul Wilson (1994, Mets) were the others.

The Yankees took a hit in April 1995 when Brian Buchanan, their first-round draft pick a year earlier, severely broke his ankle while playing at Class A Greensboro and was knocked out for the year. In a season of replacement players and umpires, the Yankees grabbed themselves a replacement Brian Buchanan with their supplemental second-round pick. This Brian Buchanan was a lefthander for Oviedo (Fla.) High.

DRAFT '95
CLUB-BY-CLUB SELECTIONS

ATLANTA BRAVES (26)

1. Chad Hutchinson, rhp, Torrey Pines HS, San Diego.
2. **Jim Scharrer, 1b, Cathedral Prep, Erie, Pa.**
3. **Robbie Bell, rhp, Marlboro Central HS, Marlboro, N.Y.**
4. **Jimmy Osting, lhp, Trinity HS, Louisville.**
5. Kevin McGlinchy, rhp, Malden (Mass.) HS.
6. Matt Middleton, ss, Graham HS, Conover, Ohio.
7. **Gerald Vecchioni, ss, Patapsco HS, Baltimore.**
8. Chad Mead, lhp-1b, Woodward (Okla.) HS
9. **Ben Wyatt, lhp, Fair HS, Little Rock, Ark.**
10. **Ryan Schurman, rhp, Tualatin (Ore.) HS.**
11. **Antone Brooks, lhp, Norfolk State U.**
12. **Joe Bauldree, rhp, Wake Forest-Rolesville HS, Wake Forest, N.C.**
13. **Charlie Cruz, lhp, Florida State U.**
14. **Steve Hacker, 1b, Southwest Missouri State U.**
15. **Matt McWilliams, rhp, UNC Charlotte.**
16. Casey Crawford, of, O'Connell HS, Falls Church, Va.
17. **Jason Shy, c, Butte (Calif.) JC.**
18. **Brian Rust, 3b, Lewis & Clark (Ore.) College.**
19. **Ben Fowler, rhp, Pace Academy, Alpharetta, Ga.**
20. Jason Hart, ss, Fair Grove (Mo.) HS.
21. David Noyce, lhp, Marietta (Ga.) HS.
22. **Oscar Otero, 3b, Cayey, P.R.**
23. **Keith Dougherty, 3b, Columbus (Ga.) College.**
24. **Skeeter Ellison, of, Dixie (Utah) JC.**
25. **James Wise, lhp, Abraham Baldwin (Ga.) CC.**
26. **Jerry McMullen, lhp, Portland State U.**
27. **Matthew Taylor, ss, Cal State Hayward.**
28. **Yan LaGrandeur, rhp, Granby, Quebec.**
29. Jacob Ruotsinoja, of, Seminole (Fla.) HS.
30. **Ariel Colon, 1b, Carolina, P.R.**
31. **Keith Mayhew, rhp, Ferrum (Va.) College.**
32. **Phillip Smith, of, Phillipsburg (N.J.) HS.**
33. **Corey Walker, of, Teikyo Westmar (Iowa) College.**
34. **Randy Hodges, of, Florida State U.**
35. **Curt Schnur, rhp, U. of Delaware.**
36. Mike Goldstein, of, Cherry Creek HS, Englewood, Colo.
37. Donnie Thomas, lhp, Andrew (Ga.) JC.
38. Troy Satterfield, lhp, Jonesboro (Ga.) HS.
39. **Mike Mahoney, c, Creighton U.**
40. Nathan Bennett, lhp, Coastal Christian HS, Arroyo Grande, Calif.
41. **Walker Reynolds, rhp, Berry (Ga.) College.**
42. Craig Cozart, rhp, U. of Central Florida.
43. Darren Blakely, of, Pensacola (Fla.) HS.
44. **Eric White, rhp, Enrico Fermi HS, Enfield, Conn.**
45. **Toby Anglen, 2b, Arkansas State U.**
46. Craig House, rhp, Christian Brothers HS, Memphis, Tenn.
47. **Pooh Hines, ss, DeKalb (Ga.) JC.**
48. **Jason Shiell, rhp, Windsor-Forest HS, Savannah, Ga.**
49. Luther Salinas, rhp-1b, LaVerne Lutheran HS, Whittier, Calif.
50. Robert Fishel, lhp, Pflugerville (Texas) HS.
51. **Andrew Cochrane, lhp, Pacific Lutheran (Wash.) U.**
52. **Kevin Loewe, lhp, U. of Maryland-Baltimore County.**
53. Jamel McAdory, 1b, Jackson State U.
54. Craig Owens, of, Chowan (N.C.) College.
55. Charlie Curry, ss-2b, Centennial HS, Portland, Ore.
56. **Brian Jolliffe, lhp, U. of Maine.**

BALTIMORE ORIOLES (21)

1. **Alvie Shepherd, rhp, U. of Nebraska.**
2. **Charles Alley, c, Palm Beach Lakes HS, West Palm Beach, Fla.**
3. **Darrell Dent, of, Montclair Prep, Panorama City, Calif.**
4. **Louis Fisher, rhp, Fremont HS, Oakland.**
5. Luke Hudson, rhp, Fountain Valley (Calif.) HS.
6. John Bale, lhp, U. of Southern Mississippi.
7. Kevin Miller, 3b, Ballard HS, Seattle.
8. **Scott Eibey, lhp, U. of Northern Iowa.**
9. **Joel Stephens, of, Notre Dame HS, Elmira, N.Y.**
10. **David Dellucci, of, U. of Mississippi.**
11. **Greg Dean, rhp, Oklahoma State U.**
12. **Carlos Akins, of, Western Kentucky U.**
13. **Bob O'Toole, c, Providence U.**
14. **Chris Bryant, 3b, North Carolina Wesleyan College.**
15. **Tim Olszewski, rhp, Triton (Ill.) JC.**
16. Zach Sorensen, ss, Highland HS, Salt Lake City.
17. **Jason Lecronier, of, McNeese State U.**
18. Lawrence Adams, 1b, Creekside HS, Fairburn, Ga.
19. **Brion King, of, Oviedo (Fla.) HS.**
20. Carlos Casillas, 1b, Santa Monica HS, Los Angeles.

Boston's Top Pick. Red Sox selected Texas schoolboy righthander Andy Yount with the first of two first-round picks.

21. **Dan Reed, lhp, Stanford U.**
22. Doug Thompson, rhp, Mississippi Gulf Coast JC.
23. Matthew Achilles, rhp, Black Hawk (Ill.) JC.
24. Jason Albert, 2b, Central Connecticut State U.
25. Gaylon Dixon, lhp, Seminole (Okla.) JC.
26. **Joaquin Serra, ss, Beverly Hills, Calif.**
27. **Robert Morseman, lhp, Salem-Teikyo (W.Va.) U.**
28. **Johnny Isom, of, Texas Wesleyan U.**
29. **Tom Russin, 1b, Eckerd (Fla.) College.**
30. **Chris Bray, rhp, Mount Olive (N.C.) College.**
31. A.J. Marquardt, of, Columbia Basin (Wash.) CC.
32. William Morstad, 3b, Windsor Academy, Macon, Ga.
33. Mike Cosgrove, rhp, Cypress (Calif.) JC.
34. Darin Moore, rhp, Lodi HS, Acampo, Calif.
35. **Calvin Pickering, of-1b, King HS, Temple Terrace, Fla.**
36. John Santos, rhp, Corcoran HS, Tulare, Calif.
37. **Avery Taylor, ss, Long Beach (Miss.) HS.**
38. Ken Sims, rhp, New Mexico JC.
39. Craig Jones, rhp, La Quinta HS, Westminster, Calif.
40. Cory Scott, rhp, Currituck County HS, Knotts Island, N.C.
41. Josh Taylor, ss, Shawnee (Okla.) HS.
42. Jerry Hairston, 2b, Naperville (Ill.) North HS.
43. Jason Glover, of, Georgia State U.
44. Mike Wooden, rhp, North County HS, Baltimore.
45. **Chris Paxton, c, Palmdale (Calif.) HS.**
46. Dan Keller, rhp, Fountain Valley (Calif.) HS.
47. Corey Coil, rhp, Francis Scott Key HS, Taneytown, Md.
48. **Wess Winn, ss, U. of Texas-Arlington.**
49. Robert Williams, c, Edgewater HS, Winter Park, Fla.

BOSTON RED SOX (15)

1. **Andy Yount, rhp, Kingwood (Texas) HS.**
1. **Corey Jenkins, of, Dreher HS, Columbia, S.C.** (Choice from Reds as compensation for Type B free agent Damon Berryhill).
2. **Jose Olmeda, ss, Fajardo, P.R.**
3. **Jay Yennaco, rhp, Pinkerton Academy, Windham, N.H.**
4. **Mike Spinelli, lhp, Revere (Mass.) HS.**
5. **Steve Lomasney, c, Peabody (Mass.) HS.**

6. Matt Kinney, rhp, Bangor (Maine) HS.
7. Cole Liniak, ss, San Dieguito HS, Encinitas, Calif.
8. Luis Cardona, c, San Sebastian, P.R.
9. Paxton Crawford, rhp, Carlsbad (N.M.) HS.
10. Lakevie Austin, rhp, Emmanuel (Ga.) College.
11. Jeff Sauve, rhp, Clemson U.
12. Jim Chamblee, ss, Odessa (Texas) JC.
13. Andy Noffke, rhp, Ohio State U.
14. Andrew Beinbrink, 3b, Scripps Ranch HS, San Diego.
15. Kevan Cannon, lhp, Ohio State U.
16. Rontrez Johnson, of, Marshall (Texas) HS.
17. Bobby Rodgers, rhp, Wake Forest U.
18. Felipe Roman, of, Rio Piedras, P.R.
19. Ben Stallings, rhp, Apollo HS, Owensboro, Ky.
20. Dwight Ferguson, of, Miami-Dade Christian HS, Carol City, Fla.
21. Curtis Romboli, lhp, Boston College.
22. Pete Prodanov, 3b-of, Oklahoma State U.
23. Chuck Lopez, of, Gahr HS, Cerritos, Calif.
24. Chris Toomey, of-rhp, Dana Hills HS, Dana Point, Calif.
25. Scott Jones, rhp, Miami (Ohio) U.
26. Moises Rojas, of, Brito Miami Private HS, Hialeah, Fla.
27. Juan Pena, rhp, Miami-Dade CC Wolfson.
28. Kaleb Harp, c, DeKalb (Texas) HS.
29. Bob Rauch, rhp-ss, Lamar U.
30. Mark Varriano, c, U. of North Dakota.
31. Cliff Brand, rhp, Central Gwinnett HS, Lawrenceville, Ga.
32. Cordele Mincey, rhp, Dodge County HS, Milan, Ga.
33. Matt Burch, rhp, Edison HS, Horseheads, N.Y.
34. Bart Vaughn, rhp, Mt. Dora Bible HS, Orlando, Fla.
35. Nick Gruber, c, Haddon Township HS, Westmont, N.J.
36. Derrick Lewis, rhp, Central Alabama CC.
37. Angel Diaz, c, Hillsborough (Fla.) JC.
38. Tim Boeth, ss, Leon HS, Tallahassee, Fla.
39. Jason Wilson, rhp, South Broward HS, Hollywood, Fla.
40. Jim Farrell, rhp, Kent U.
41. Brian Messer, rhp, Northwest HS, Shawnee, Kan.
42. Juan Chaidez, rhp, Miami-Dade Christian HS, Hialeah, Fla.
43. Pat Burrell, 3b, Bellarmine Prep, San Jose.
44. Bryan Wright, ss, Escambia HS, Pensacola, Fla.
45. Kris Brown, of, Central HS, Kalamazoo, Mich.

CALIFORNIA ANGELS (1)

1. Darin Erstad, of, U. of Nebraska.
2. Jarrod Washburn, lhp, U. of Wisconsin-Oshkosh.
3. Jeremy Blevins, rhp, Sullivan East HS, Bristol, Tenn.
4. Brian Cooper, rhp, U. of Southern California.
5. Justin Baughman, ss, Lewis & Clark (Ore.) College.
6. Ryan Kane, 3b, Presbyterian (S.C.) College.
7. Chris Pine, rhp, Tualatin (Ore.) HS.
8. Brian Scutero, rhp, U. of Central Florida.
9. Jason Stockstill, lhp, Katella HS, Anaheim, Calif.
10. Brandon McGuire, rhp-ss, Coahoma (Texas) HS.
11. Danny Buxbaum, 1b, U. of Miami (Fla.).
12. Kyle Wagner, c, Wake Forest U.
13. Jon Vander Griend, of, U. of Washington.
14. Josh Deakman, rhp, Arizona State U.
15. Darren Pomper, of, Aragon HS, San Mateo, Calif.
16. Mario Iglesias, rhp, Stanford U.
17. Michael Hughes, rhp, Fresno (Calif.) CC.
18. Greg Jones, c, Seminole (Fla.) HS.
19. Jed Dalton, 3b-of, U. of Nebraska.
20. Bryan Graves, c, Southern U.
21. Donnell Tate, ss-c, Oakland (Calif.) HS.
22. Jim O'Quinn, lhp, Florida CC.
23. Greg Millichap, c, Serra HS, Woodside, Calif.
24. Gar Vallone, ss, UCLA.
25. John Romero, rhp, Mission (Calif.) JC.
26. Randy Betten, 2b, Arizona State U.
27. Thomas Darrell, rhp, Garrett (Md.) CC.
28. Alex Llanos, 2b, Carolina, P.R.
29. Scott Prather, lhp, Lassiter HS, Marietta, Ga.
30. John McAninch, c, Lewis-Clark State (Idaho) College.
31. Ty Bilderback, of, U. of Arkansas.
32. E.J. Thoen, ss, Indian River (Fla.) CC.
33. Robb Quinlan, ss, Hill-Murray HS, Maplewood, Minn.
34. David Bittler, lhp, Florida CC.
35. Derrick Vargas, lhp, Memorial HS, Newark, Calif.
36. Douglas Hurst, rhp, Okaloosa Walton (Fla.) CC.
37. Mike Gauger, lhp, Wakulla HS, St. Marks, Fla.
38. Bobby Bystrowski, 3b-of, Jesuit HS, Fair Oaks, Calif.
39. Jake Jensen, ss-2b, Washington Union HS, Fresno, Calif.
40. Steve Mikesell, c, Glendale (Calif.) U.
41. Doug Blackman, c, Easton HS, New Orleans.
42. John Opina, ss, La Sierra HS, Riverside, Calif.
43. Michael Clarke, rhp, St. Petersburg (Fla.) JC.

First Pitcher. Drafting fourth, the Cubs selected Grand Prairie (Texas) High righthander Kerry Wood—the first pitcher picked.

44. Esteban Barrios, of, Miami-Dade CC New World Center.
45. Widd Workman, rhp-of, Brigham Young U.
46. Antonio Diaz, ss, Gulf Coast (Fla.) CC.
47. Sterling Bullock, 3b, Carson HS, Compton, Calif.
48. Matthew Koziara, rhp, Franklin (Pa.) HS.
49. Derek Ryder, c, Penn State U.
50. David Farfan, rhp, Fresno State U.
51. Stanisles James, of, Shanks HS, Quincy, Fla.
52. Joel Katte, 3b, North HS, Sheboygan, Wis.
53. Khalif Jefferson, ss, Serra HS, Compton, Calif.
54. Javier Baretti, c, Caguas, P.R.
55. Fernando Sordo, rhp, Spanish River HS, Boca Raton, Fla.
56. Eddie Marquez, 2b-ss, Gurabo, P.R.
57. Steve Maris, ss-2b, Oak Hall HS, Gainesville, Fla.
58. Moses Herrera, rhp, Colton (Calif.) HS.
59. Jason Townsell, rhp, Marianna (Fla.) HS.
60. Kurt Bultmann, ss-2b, Seminole HS, Largo, Fla.

CHICAGO CUBS (4)

1. Kerry Wood, rhp, Grand Prairie (Texas) HS.
2. Brian McNichol, lhp, James Madison U.
3. Jeff Yoder, rhp, Pottsville Area (Pa.) HS.
4. Adam Everett, ss, Harrison HS, Marietta, Ga.
5. Ismael Villegas, rhp, Guaynabo, P.R.
6. Tony Ellison, of, North Carolina State U.
7. Dorian Speed, of, Florida International U.
8. Denny Bair, rhp, Northeast Louisiana U.
9. Chad Ricketts, rhp, Polk (Fla.) CC.
10. Kasey Pressley, 1b, Dr. Phillips HS, Orlando.
11. Matt Hammons, rhp, Mission Bay HS, San Diego.
12. Barret Markey, rhp, St. Petersburg (Fla.) HS.
13. Terry Joseph, of, Northwestern State U.
14. Don Kinnie, of, Livingston (Ala.) U.
15. Kris Stading, lhp, Browne HS, Phoenix.
16. Brian Conley, rhp, Volunteer State (Tenn.) JC.
17. Chris Moller, 1b, U. of Alabama.
18. Jerry Connell, of, Colonia HS, Avenel, N.J.
19. Buck Gordon, c, Bridgewater (Va.) College.
20. Chris Booker, rhp, Monroe County HS, Monroeville, Ala.
21. Brandon Hammack, rhp, U. of Texas-San Antonio.
22. Andrew Mallory, rhp, Dixie Hollins HS, St. Petersburg, Fla.
23. Jim Putko, 1b, U. of Akron.
24. Kevin Bentley, of, U. of Southern Mississippi.
25. Dax Norris, c, U. of Alabama.
26. Brian Greene, rhp, Indiana U.
27. Tim Mosley, rhp, U. of Arkansas.
28. Scott Vieira, c, U. of Tennessee.

29. **Ashanti McDonald, ss-of, Olivet Nazarene (Ill.) U.**
30. **John McNeese, lhp, U. of Mississippi.**
31. **Ron Licciardi, lhp, U. of Connecticut-Avery Point.**
32. **Tom Maleski, 3b-c, U. of Houston.**
33. **Jason Martino, rhp, Vorhees HS, Pittstown, N.J.**
34. **Ryan Seidel, of, Southern California College.**
35. Chris Humpert, of, Arcadia (Calif.) HS.
36. Robert Kern, of, Central HS, Cape Girardeau, Mo.
37. Mark Taylor, lhp, Rice U.
38. Casey Burns, rhp, Hopewell Valley Central HS, Trenton, N.J.
39. Greg Strickland, of, Volunteer State (Tenn.) CC.
40. Brandon Ward, rhp, Cerro Coso (Calif.) JC.
41. Daniel Mooney, c, Monsignor Donovan HS, Forked River, N.J.
42. Michael Smosna, rhp, Burroughs HS, Ridgecrest, Calif.
43. Dave Phillips, 2b, Gloucester (N.J.) CC.
44. David Kelly, rhp, Leon HS, Tallahassee, Fla.
45. Tim Currens, of, Volunteer State (Tenn.) CC.
46. Lance Haver, c, Molalla Union HS, Molalla, Ore.
47. **Mickey Perez, 2b, U. of Texas-San Antonio.**
48. Brett Cornwell, rhp, Hobbs (N.M.) HS.
49. Jerry Zaffis, rhp, Eustis HS, Mt. Dora, Fla.
50. Aaron Armijo, 3b, Middle Georgia JC.
51. Chris Grubbs, c, West Orange HS, Ocoee, Fla.
52. Jack Koch, rhp, Miami-Dade CC North.
53. John Ogden, c, Palm Beach (Fla.) JC.
54. Arturo Mata, ss-2b, New Mexico JC.
55. **Justin Speier, c, Nicholls State U.**
56. Scott Stephens, lhp, Manatee (Fla.) JC.
57. Steven Bechard, rhp, Onieda (N.Y.) HS
58. Seth Spiker, c, Blinn (Texas) JC.
59. Bobby Sprague, c, Queen Of Peace HS, North Arlington, N.J.
60. Ryan Fuller, rhp, Monroe (N.Y.) CC.
61. Kris Williams, rhp, Westfield (N.J.) HS.

CHICAGO WHITE SOX (25)

1. **Jeff Liefer, 3b, Long Beach State U.**
2. **Brian Simmons, of, U. of Michigan.**
3. J.J. Putz, rhp, Trenton (Mich.) HS.
4. **Ryan Topham, of, U. of Notre Dame.**
5. **Tighe Brown, rhp, St. Xavier HS, Louisville.**
6. **John Hunt, lhp, Ohio U.**
7. **Jason Lakman, rhp, Woodinville (Wash.) HS.**
8. **Adam Virchis, rhp, San Diego State U.**
9. **Jason Secoda, rhp, Cal State Los Angeles.**
10. **Chuck Klee, ss, Cardinal Gibbons HS, Fort Lauderdale.**
11. **Kevin Beirne, rhp, Texas A&M U.**
12. **Daron Hollins, of, Sierra (Calif.) JC.**
13. **Brian Downs, c, Riverside (Calif.) CC.**
14. **Tom Buckman, rhp, Edison (Fla.) CC.**
15. Eric Stanton, 1b, Newberry (S.C.) HS.
16. **Erik Desrosiers, rhp, Grand Canyon U.**
17. **Derek Hasselhoff, rhp, Towson State U.**
18. **Mike Vota, rhp, Towson State U.**
19. **Jeff Johnson, ss, U. of Mississippi.**
20. Chris Beck, of, El Dorado HS, Placentia, Calif.
21. **Barry Shelton, 3b, West Virginia State College.**
22. **Jason Gray, rhp, Coconut Creek (Fla.) HS.**
23. **Frank Anderson, c, Southern Union State (Ala.) JC.**
24. **Tim Kraus, rhp, U. of Notre Dame.**
25. **John Strasser, ss, Mesa (Ariz.) CC.**
26. **Josh Fauske, c, Central Washington U.**
27. Aaron Gentry, ss, Labette (Kan.) CC.
28. **Brent Wilhelm, 3b, U. of Kansas.**
29. **Kelly Kruse, rhp, Southwest Missouri State U.**
30. **Allen Halley, rhp, U. of South Alabama.**
31. Brian Bullock, rhp, Itawamba (Miss.) JC.
32. **Joel Garber, lhp, U. of Nevada-Las Vegas.**
33. Chris Weekly, ss, Highland HS, Gilbert, Ariz.
34. Eric LeBlanc, rhp, College of St. Rose (N.Y.).
35. Nate Robertson, lhp, Maize (Kan.) HS.
36. Aaron Randle, 2b-ss, Northeast HS, Fort Lauderdale, Fla.
37. **Darren Hayes, of, Wingate (N.C.) College..**
38. Stephen Sparks, rhp, Faulkner State (Ala.) JC.
39. Andrew Tellez, of, Fullerton (Calif.) JC.
40. Matt Howe, ss, Mayde Creek HS, Houston.
41. Kereon Clarke, of-2b, South Plantation HS, Plantation, Fla.
42. **Pete Demorejon, rhp, U. of Miami.**
43. Justin Rayment, lhp, San Diego State U.
44. David Harden, lhp, Allen County (Kan.) CC.
45. **Jason Fennell, of, Baldwin HS, Pittsburgh.**
46. Nestor Gonzales, c, Rio Grande HS, Albuquerque.
47. David Hostetter, of, Fannett Metal HS, Fort Loudan, Pa.
48. Brian Thrash, of, Rising Sun HS, Elkton, Md.
49. Kris Conrad, rhp, Killian HS, Miami.
50. Wade Sterling, c, Allen County (Kan.) CC.

51. Brian Bowness, 1b-3b, Villanova U.
52. Peter Rodriguez, of, Broward (Fla.) JC.
53. **Manny Lutz, 3b, Southwestern (Calif.) JC.**
54. Mike Biasucci, 2b, South Broward HS, Hollywood, Fla.

CINCINNATI REDS (24)

1. (Choice to Red Sox as compensation for Type B free agent Damon Berryhill).
2. **Brett Tomko, rhp, Florida Southern College.**
3. **Andre Montgomery, ss, Pleasure Ridge Park HS, Louisville.**
4. **Mark Corey, rhp, Edinboro (Pa.) U.**
5. **Mike LaRue, c, Dallas Baptist U.**
6. **Andy Burress, c, Telfair County HS, McRae, Ga.**
7. **Herb Goodman, of, North Greenville (S.C.) JC.**
8. **Ray King, lhp, Lambuth (Tenn.) U.**
9. Bobby Walters, of, Salisaw (Okla.) HS.
10. **Ben Bailey, rhp, Glen Oaks (Mich.) CC.**
11. **Rich Lawrence, rhp, U. of Central Florida.**
12. **Justin Atchley, lhp, Texas A&M U.**
13. Michael Daniel, rhp, Calhoun (Ala.) CC.
14. Larfayette Stanley, rhp, Jordan HS, Columbus, Ga.
15. **Anthony Patellis, 3b, Kent U.**
16. **Lance Davis, lhp, Lake Gibson HS, Lakeland, Fla.**
17. **Todd Fehrenbach, c, Citrus HS, Inverness, Fla.**
18. **Justin Marine, rhp, Moorpark (Calif.) JC.**
19. **Eric Mapp, of, Lamar U.**
20. **James Davis, c, Western Kentucky U.**
21. Jason Johnson, of, Montclair (Calif.) HS.
22. **Gene Maddox, rhp, Florida CC.**
23. **Tony Cloud, rhp, Spartanburg Methodist (S.C.) JC.**
24. **Jeff Sparks, rhp, St. Mary's (Texas) U.**
25. **Stephen Claybrook, of, Texas A&M U.**
26. **David Guthrie, ss, North Carolina State U.**
27. **Steve Goodhart, 2b, Ohio Wesleyan U.**
28. Andrew Tracy, 1b, Bowling Green State U.
29. **Jason Parsons, 1b, Dallas Baptist U.**
30. Robert Mackoviak, ss-2b, South Suburban (Ill.) JC.
31. Brian Willman, rhp, U. of North Carolina.
32. **Scott MacRae, rhp, Valdosta State (Ga.) U.**
33. Zach Frachiseur, rhp, Rockdale County HS, Conyers, Ga.
34. **Lamont Mason, 2b-ss, Lubbock Christian U.**
35. Jeffery Juarez, cf, New Braunfels (Texas) HS.
36. **Will Schleuss, lhp, U. of Alabama.**
37. **Thomas Scott, of, Linfield (Ore.) College.**
38. Jason Hubbard, lhp, Angelina (Texas) JC.
39. Brian Loyd, c, Cal State Fullerton.
40. **Chris Murphy, lhp, U. of Cincinnati.**
41. **Scott Wright, rhp, Missouri Southern State U.**
42. **Joe Montgomery, rhp, Jacksonville State (Ala.) U.**
43. Chad Truby, 3b, Yavapai (Ariz.) JC.
44. **Dwayne Cushman, rhp, Valdosta State (Ga.) U.**

CLEVELAND INDIANS (23)

1. **David Miller, 1b, Clemson U.**
2. **Sean Casey, 1b, U. of Richmond.**
3. **Chad Whitaker, of, St. Thomas Aquinas HS, Fort Lauderdale.**
4. **Scott Harrison, rhp, Swett HS, Pinole, Calif.**
5. **Scott Schultz, rhp, Louisiana State U.**
6. **Jake Messner, of, Rio Americano HS, Sacramento.**
7. **Scott Morgan, of, Gonzaga U.**
8. **Tim Jorgensen, ss, U. of Wisconsin-Oshkosh.**
9. **Mike Edwards, ss, Mechanicsburg (Pa.) Area HS.**
10. **Jason Bennett, rhp, Shippensburg (Pa.) U.**
11. **Jewell Williams, of, Las Vegas (Nev.) HS.**
12. **Brett Merrick, lhp, U. of Washington.**
13. **Frankie Sanders, rhp, Pasco Hernando (Fla.) CC.**
14. **Scott Winchester, rhp, Clemson U.**
15. **Darren Loudermilk, rhp, Oklahoma City U.**
16. Luis Estrella, rhp, Rancho Santiago (Calif.) JC.
17. **Terry Harvey, rhp, North Carolina State U.**
18. **Keith Horn, rhp, Arkansas State U.**
19. **Jason Minici, of, Long Beach State U.**
20. **Marc Deschenes, ss, U. of Massachusetts-Lowell.**
21. **Mark Budzinski, of, U. of Richmond.**
22. **Mike Glavine, 1b, Northeastern U.**
23. **Jon Edwards, rhp, Whitman (Wash.) College.**
24. **Ken Wagner, rhp, Florida Atlantic U.**
25. **Jason Rakers, rhp, New Mexico State U.**
26. Frank Chapman, rhp, San Jacinto North (Texas) CC.
27. Gary Rodriguez, of, Seminole (Okla.) JC.
28. Michael Bishop, of-c, Willis (Texas) HS.
29. Corey Richardson, of, Daingerfield (Texas) HS.
30. **Jason Adge, rhp, U. of Miami.**
31. **Richy Gonzalez, c, U. of Miami.**

32. Michael Custer, rhp, Linn-Benton (Ore.) CC.
33. **Nathan Coats, c, San Francisco CC.**
34. Jamie Brown, rhp, West Lauderdale HS, Meridian, Miss.
35. **Bryan Hardy, 1b, Martin HS, Arlington, Texas.**
36. **Jerry Taylor, of, U. of Texas.**
37. **Chad Thornhill, ss, Cal State Northridge.**
38. **Ross Atkins, rhp, Wake Forest U.**
39. Thomas Blythe, c, North Little Rock (Ark.) HS.
40. Randy Keisler, lhp, Navarro (Texas) JC.
41. Mike Spiegel, lhp, Sacramento CC.
42. **Dennis Martinez Jr., rhp, Saint Thomas (Fla.) U.**
43. Bryan Ransom, ss, South Mountain (Ariz.) CC.
44. Albert Garza, rhp, Wapato (Wash.) HS.
45. Kirk Irvine, rhp, Rancho Santiago (Calif.) JC.
46. Rex Crosnoe, c, Southeast Missouri State U.
47. **Sam Mathis, rhp, Southern Arkansas U.**
48. Ryan Bailey, rhp, Rancho Bernardo HS, San Diego.
49. Brian Anderson, rhp, East Tennessee State U.
50. Peter Lopez, rhp, Central HS, Manchester, N.H.
51. **Tony Fleetwood, lhp, Oklahoma State U.**
52. Michael Ploharz, rhp, Clovis (Calif.) HS.
53. Kevin Eberwein, rhp, Green Valley HS, Henderson, Nev.
54. Damien Kolb, of, Capital HS, Olympia, Wash.
55. Brandon Driggers, rhp, Whitehouse (Texas) HS.

COLORADO ROCKIES (8)

1. **Todd Helton, 1b-lhp, U. of Tennessee.**
2. **Ben Petrick, c, Glencoe HS, Hillsboro, Ore.**
3. **Chris Macca, rhp, St. Leo (Fla.) College.**
4. **John Clark, ss, Clemens HS, Schertz, Texas.**
5. **Mike Vavrek, lhp, Lewis (Ill.) U.**
6. **Chandler Martin, rhp, U. of Portland.**
7. **Cristy Rosa, rhp, Guanica, P.R.**
8. **Tal Light, 3b, Oklahoma State U.**
9. **Jamie Emiliano, rhp, Florida International U.**
10. **Gary Gordon, of, Willingboro (N.J.) HS.**
11. **Scott Randall, rhp, Santa Barbara (Calif.) CC.**
12. **Brian Kirkpatrick, ss, King City (Calif.) HS.**
13. **John Lindsey, 1b, Hattiesburg (Miss.) HS.**
14. **Pat Williams, rhp, Mt. San Antonio (Calif.) JC.**
15. **John Mahlberg, rhp, Douglas HS, Dillard, Ga.**
16. **Chris Druckery, rhp, Kankakee (Ill.) JC.**
17. **Garrett Neubart, of, Columbia U.**
18. **Heath Bost, rhp, Catawba (N.C.) College.**
19. **John Clifford, c, Villanova U.**
20. **Bobby Bevel, lhp, Xavier U.**
21. **Blake Barthol, c, Eastern Kentucky U.**
22. **David Groseclose, ss, Virginia Military Institute.**
23. **David Lee, rhp, Mercyhurst (Pa.) College.**
24. **Carlos Vidal, c, Miami-Dade CC New World Center.**
25. **Reggie Douglas, rhp, Dorsey HS, Los Angeles.**
26. **Matt Whitley, ss, U. of Tennessee.**
27. J.J. Moore, rhp, Burnsville (Minn.) HS.
28. Rodney Nye, 3b, Cameron (Okla.) HS.
29. **Marc Brzozoski, of, Shorter (Ga.) College.**
30. **Brett Elam, ss, McNeese State U.**
31. **Sean Murphy, rhp, U. of North Carolina.**
32. **Brad Reitzenstein, rhp, U. of Portland.**
33. **David Feuerstein, of, Yale U.**
34. Ryan Kohlmeier, rhp, Chase County HS, Cottonwood Falls, Kan.
35. Brian Bowman, c, Garces Memorial HS, Bakersfield, Calif.
36. Jeremy Jones. c, Raymore Peculiar HS, Raymore, Mo.
37. Josh Kalinowski, lhp, Natrona County HS, Casper, Wyom.
38. Scott Brent, of, Linden (Calif.) HS.
39. Matt Montgomery, rhp, Rancho Santiago (Calif.) CC.
40. Brandon Lenox, ss, Red Mountain HS, Mesa, Ariz.
41. Jason Pozo, rhp, Ocean County (N.J.) CC.
42. Damione Merriman, of, Cheraw (S.C.) HS.
43. Anthony Taylor, rhp, Pueblo HS, Tucson.
44. Derek Corbett, rhp, Highland HS, Highley, Ariz.
45. Mike Medina, c, Moody HS, Corpus Christi, Texas.
46. Brad Schwartzbauer, c-3b, White Bear Lake (Minn.) Area HS.
47. Ali Samadani, rhp, CC of Marin (Calif.).
48. Kent Zweifel, 1b, Henley HS, Klamath Falls, Ore.
49. **Justin Drizos, 1b, U. of Nevada-Reno.**
50. Andres Mitchell, ss, Motlow State (Tenn.) CC.
51. Rodney Friar, c, Temecula Valley HS, Temecula, Calif.
52. Chris Rodriguez, c, Modesto (Calif.) JC.
53. Casey Kelley, 1b, Ellensburg (Wash.) HS.
54. Dan Ledesma, ss, Moody HS, Corpus Christi, Texas.
55. Derek Sawyer, ss, Paradise Valley HS, Phoenix.
56. James Slaughter, of, San Joaquin Delta (Calif.) JC.
57. John Garrison, rhp, San Joaquin Delta (Calif.) JC.
58. Gabriel Foster, rhp, Santa Rosa (Calif.) JC.

Detroit's Top Pick. The Tigers spent their first-round pick on Wichita State righthander Mike Drumright.

DETROIT TIGERS (11)

1. **Mike Drumright, rhp, Wichita State U.**
2. **Brian Powell, rhp, U. of Georgia.**
3. Chuck Crowder, lhp, Crestwood HS, Mantua, Ohio.
4. **Clay Bruner, rhp, Weatherford (Okla.) HS.**
5. **Rosario Ortiz, rhp, Arizona Western JC.**
6. **Jeremiah Lignitz, c, Davison (Mich.) HS.**
7. **Chris Manser, rhp-of, Hillsborough HS, Tampa.**
8. **Scott Weaver, of, U. of Michigan.**
9. Ron Marietta, lhp, Bishop Ford HS, Brooklyn.
10. **John Foran, rhp, U. of Central Florida.**
11. **Dave Borkowski, rhp, Sterling Heights (Mich.) HS.**
12. **Jason Lawrie, rhp, Independence HS, San Jose.**
13. Kevin Jordan, ss, Lee HS, Midland, Texas.
14. Steve Hartsburg, ss, Schaumburg (Ill.) HS.
15. Justin Lehr, rhp-c, West Covina (Calif.) HS.
16. Mark Hendricksen, lhp, Washington State U.
17. **Craig Caballero, c, Grand Canyon U.**
18. **Brian Fuller, c, Northwestern U.**
19. Lawyer Milloy, of, U. of Washington.
20. **Ron Rojas, 2b, Northwestern U.**
21. Clint Bryant 3b, Texas Tech.
22. J.P. Webb, c, U. of Texas.
23. **Jay Waggoner, 1b-of, Auburn U.**
24. **Peter Durkovic, lhp, Fordham U.**
25. **Robert Gray, of, Embry-Riddle Aeronautical (Fla.) U.**
26. Eric Valent, of, Canyon HS, Anaheim.
27. Matt Thornton, lhp, Centerville HS, Sturgis, Mich.
28. **Clausel Milord, of, New York Tech.**
29. **Mike Miller, 3b, Hofstra U.**
30. Jason Haynie, lhp, U. of South Carolina.
31. Darrell Hussman, rhp, Quartz Hill HS, Lancaster, Calif.
32. **Derek Mitchell, ss, Triton (Ill.) JC.**
33. **Derek Kopacz, 3b, Triton (Ill.) JC.**
34. Luke Bonner, rhp, Divine Child HS, Dearborn, Mich.
35. Chris Clark, of, U. of Arkansas.
36. **Tom Shipman, c, River Ridge HS, New Port Richey, Fla.**
37. Greg Sprehn, rhp, Bangor (Wis.) HS.
38. John Kremer, rhp, Chatard HS, Indianapolis.
39. Josh Davis, rhp, Pensacola (Fla.) Catholic HS.
40. Mike Davis, ss, Vocational HS, Chicago.
41. Phil Rosengren, rhp, Day HS, Rye, N.Y.
42. Mike Whiteman, lhp, Potomac State (W.Va.) JC.
43. Robert Fick, c, Cal State Northridge.
44. Jeremy Giambi, of, Cal State Fullerton.
45. Errick Lowe, of, Lake Worth (Fla.) HS.
46. **Doug Engleka, ss, Ohio U.**

47. Pedro Flores, lhp, Sierra Vista HS, Baldwin Park, Calif.
48. Brian Justine, lhp, Dwyer HS, Palm Beach Lakes, Fla.
49. Judd Van Winkle, lhp, Spartanburg Methodist (S.C.) JC.
50. Jose Nunez, 2b, Northeast Texas CC.
51. Greg Ryan, lhp, Divine Child HS, Dearborn, Mich.
52. Maurice Watkins, rhp, Osser HS, Chicago.
53. Bryan Houston, of, Escambia HS, Pensacola, Fla.
54. Chad Cook, rhp, Fallbrook (Calif.) HS.
55. Mark Mulder, 1b, Thornwood HS, South Holland, Ill.
56. Joe McFarlane, rhp, Anacortes (Wash.) HS.
57. Gabriel Kapler, 3b, Moorpark (Calif.) JC.
58. Brian Cummins, lhp, Northwestern U.
59. David Reinfelder, lhp, Michigan State U.

FLORIDA MARLINS (6)

1. Jaime Jones, of, Rancho Bernardo HS, San Diego.
2. Nate Rolison, 1b, Petal (Miss.) HS.
3. Randy Winn, of, U. of Santa Clara.
4. Mike Marriott, rhp, Spring (Texas) HS.
5. Rene Rascon, of, Sonoma State (Calif.) U.
6. Michael Tejera, lhp, Southwest HS, Miami.
7. Hansel Izquierdo, rhp, Southwest HS, Miami.
8. Mark Watson, lhp, Clemson U.
9. Tony Enard, rhp, Fresno State U,
10. Bob Pailthorpe, rhp, U. of Santa Clara.
11. Gary Knotts, rhp, Brewer HS, Somerville, Ala.
12. Jonathan Widerski, rhp, Academy of the Holy Angels, Richfield, Minn.
13. Jerrod Riggan, rhp, San Diego State U.
14. David Miller, rhp, UNC Wilmington.
15. Rick Garcia, rhp, Oklahoma City U.
16. Gabe Gonzalez, rhp, Long Beach State U.
17. Steve Goodell, ss, Arizona State U.
18. Travis Burgus, lhp, U. of San Diego.
19. Michael Duvall, lhp, Potomac State (W.Va.) JC.
20. Mat Erwin, c, U. of Nevada-Reno.
21. Joe Funaro, 2b, Eastern Connecticut State College.
22. Swan Austin, rhp, Douglasville, Ga.
23. Alex Morris, rhp, Westlake HS, Austin, Texas.
24. Jim Detwiler, lhp, Valley Forge Military Academy, Pottsville, Pa.
25. Kevin Fitzmaurice, rhp, Silver Creek HS, San Jose, Calif.
26. Ryan Tack, rhp, Durango HS, Las Vegas, Nev.
27. David Therneau, rhp, Navarro (Texas) JC.
28. Jorge Rodriguez, ss, Penuelas, P.R.
29. Gary Santoro, rhp, Flagler (Fla.) College.
30. Euclides Rojas, rhp, Palm Springs/Western League.
31. Mike Rose, rhp, Southwood HS, Shreveport, La.
32. George Oleksik, rhp, Middle Tennessee State U.
33. Todd Bramble, ss, Sprague HS, Salem, Ore.
34. Kevin Green, of, Mohawk Valley (N.Y.) CC.
35. Jason Shanahan, 3b, Cal State Northridge.
36. Tim McClaskey, rhp, Muscatine (Iowa) CC.
37. Brian Dallimore, 2b, Stanford U.
38. Ken Duebelbeis, lhp, De Anza (Calif.) JC.
39. Dion Battee, of, St. Bernard HS, Los Angeles.
40. Matt Blank, lhp, Galveston (Texas) JC.
41. Dwaine Neal, of, Norland HS, Miami.
42. Letarvius Copeland, of, Jackson HS, Miami.
43. Shannon Stephens, rhp, Cal Poly San Luis Obispo.
44. Jason Garrett, 1b, U. of Texas-Arlington.
45. Rob Hernandez, c, Oklahoma State U.
46. Jeff Cermak, of, Mesa (Ariz.) CC.
47. Rhett Ingerick, rhp, Davidson College.
48. Raymond Green, c, Sonoma State (Calif.) U.
49. Rafael Riguiero, rhp, North HS, Riverside, Calif.
50. William Reed, of, Westchester HS, Inglewood, Calif.
51. Aaron Cames, rhp, Sacramento CC.
52. Scott McKee, c, Riverdale Baptist HS, Bowie, Md.
53. Kerthatis Lovely, of, Glades Central HS, South Bay, Fla.
54. Howard Bell, rhp, Westchester HS, Los Angeles.
55. Darin Baker, of, Fallon (Nev.) HS.
56. Carl Jones, of, Andress HS, El Paso, Texas.
57. Joel Atwater, of, Southern Alamance HS, Graham, N.C.
58. Richard Circuit, ss, La Jolla (Calif.) HS.
59. Mark Greenlee, lhp, Triton (Ill.) JC.
60. William Fleck, rhp, Mercer County (N.J.) CC.
61. Scott Esker, 3b, JC of the Redwoods (Calif.).
62. Michael Laine, rhp, Connally HS, Waco, Texas.
63. Druen Mahony, ss, Hillcrest HS, Fountain Inn, S.C.
64. Quincy Foster, of, Spartanburg Methodist (S.C.) JC.
65. James Nederostek, lhp, St. Mary's HS, Lodi, Calif.
66. Robert Hammock, c, South Cobb HS, Marietta, Ga.
67. Matthew Pidgeon, ss, Eureka (Calif.) HS.
68. Andy Bair, lhp, Calvert Hall HS, Towson, Md.
69. Jason Berry, rhp, Mountain View HS, Orem, Utah.

70. William Tull, rhp, Gloucester County (N.J.) CC.
71. Derek Rowen, of, Mesa (Ariz.) CC.
72. William Boughey, rhp, Berkmar HS, Lawrenceville, Ga.
73. Jay Gospodarek, rhp, Pima (Ariz.) JC.
74. Stephen Blevins, 1b, Spotsylvania (Va.) HS.
75. Kevin Tolan, rhp, Citrus (Calif.) JC.
76. Dustin Keppen, rhp, Central Gwinnet HS, Lawrenceville, Ga.
77. Eric Kalie, ss, Martin County HS, Stuart, Fla.
78. Brett Schreyer, rhp, Paul VI HS, Waterford, N.J.
79. Joel Sajiun, of, Miami Springs HS, Hialeah, Fla.
80. Timothy Hicks, of, Gordon (Ga.) JC.
81. Shannon Carter, rhp, Gate City (Va.) HS.
82. Brian Bush, of, Howland HS, Warren, Ohio.
83. (voided selection)
84. Ryan Roberts, ss, Brigham Young U.
85. Andrew Lecrone, 3b, Downers Grove (Ill.) North HS.
86. John Schmitz, of, JC of San Mateo (Calif.).
87. Brian Haught, ss, Jesuit HS, Tampa.

HOUSTON ASTROS (22)

1. Tony McKnight, rhp, Arkansas HS, Texarkana, Ark.
2. Eric Ireland, rhp, Millikan HS, Long Beach, Calif.
3. Chad Alexander, of, Texas A&M U.
4. Brian Sikorski, rhp, Western Michigan U.
5. Mike Rose, c, Jesuit HS, Sacramento.
6. Scott Chapman, c, Alexander HS, Albany, Ohio.
7. Jason McCarter, rhp, Monterey Peninsula (Calif.) JC.
8. Eric Smith, rhp, Butler County (Kan.) CC.
9. Jason Adams, ss, Wichita State U.
10. Jeremy DeShazer, of, Lake Washington HS, Kirkland, Wash.
11. Ric Johnson, of, Indiana State U.
12. Eric Stachler, rhp, Bowling Green State U.
13. Marlon Mejia, ss, Westchester (N.Y.) CC.
14. Barry Wesson, of, Brandon HS, Pearl, Miss.
15. Mike Corominas, lhp, Arizona State U.
16. Aaron Vincent, rhp, Porterville (Calif.) JC.
17. Charles Wheeler, lhp, Connors State (Okla.) JC.
18. Derek Wallace, of, Neville HS, Monroe, La.
19. Aaron Miles, 2b, Antioch (Calif.)HS.
20. Eric Cole, 3b, Antelope Valley (Calif.) JC.
21. David Huggins, rhp, Galveston (Texas) CC.
22. Shawn Sonnier, rhp, Chipola (Fla.) JC.
23. Nelson Ubaldo, of, U. of Massachusetts.
24. Jerome Robertson, lhp, Exeter Union HS, Exeter, Calif.
25. Andy Bovender, 3b, UNC Charlotte.
26. James Alarcon, rhp, Jupiter (Fla.) Community HS.
27. Aaron McNeal, 1b, Castro Valley (Calif.) HS.
28. Adrian Taylor, ss, Tech HS, Oakland.
29. Troy Stoppa, lhp, Havre (Mont.) HS.
30. Robert Porter, lhp, McComb (Miss.) HS.
31. Caleb Brown, lhp, Howard (Texas) JC.
32. Tim Hamulack, of-lhp, Edgewood (Md.) HS.
33. Gregg Smyth, lhp, Rollins (Fla.) College.
34. Bryan King, rhp, Brawley Union HS, Brawley, Calif.
35. Eric Eckenstahler, lhp, Antioch HS, Lindenhurst, Ill.
36. Brian Moon, c, Newton County HS, Mansfield, Ga.
37. Javier Contreras, rhp, Rio Piedras, P.R.
38. Scott Sandusky, c, Seward County (Kan.) CC.
39. Corbett Leonard, c, Spring Grove (Pa.) HS.
40. Ryan Coe, c, Kennesaw State (Ga.) College.
41. Marty Godwin, of, Osceola HS, Kissimmee, Fla.
42. Jason Welch, of, Edison (Fla.) CC.
43. Brett Brown, lhp, Delaware Tech & CC.
44. Stephen Schwartz, rhp, Aurora (Ill.) U.
45. Brock Ashby, of, St. Francis Xavier HS, Edmonton, Alberta.
46. Troy Norrell, c, Brazoswood HS, Lake Jackson, Texas.
47. Mark Burnett, rhp, Bryant HS, Benton, Ark.
48. Luis Ramos, rhp, Rio Piedras, P.R.
49. Walter Harrington, rhp, Palomar (Calif.) JC.
50. Ryan Channel, lhp, Satellite Beach (Fla.) HS.
51. Jorge Mesa, rhp, Braddock HS, Miami.
52. Ryan Block, rhp, Walla Walla (Wash.) HS.
53. Corey Hart, 2b, Connors State (Okla.) JC.
54. Mark Chambers, of, Navarro (Texas) JC.
55. Stephen Dye, rhp, Middle Georgia CC.
56. Brian Berryman, rhp, Union HS, Redford, Mich.
57. Chris Hargett, 1b, Jeffersonville (Ind.) HS.
58. Juan Rivera, ss, Palm Beach (Fla.) JC.
59. Chris Meyer, rhp, Dakota Collegiate HS, Winnipeg, Manitoba.
60. Frank Bludau, rhp, Halletsville (Texas) HS.
61. Mark Tomse, lhp, Central Catholic HS, Aurora, Ill.
62. Josh Pascarella, rhp, Rancho Bernardo HS, San Diego.
63. Adam Bell, c, Helena (Mont.) HS.
64. James Crossley, 3b, Chabot (Calif.) JC.
65. Gabriel Garcia, c-rhp, Logan HS, Union City, Calif.

66. James Hawkins, rhp, Santa Margarita HS, Laguna Niguel, Calif.
67. Chris Oldham, c, Sullivan (Mo.) HS.
68. Brian Jordan, rhp, Gordon (Ga.) JC.
69. Blake Ricken, lhp, Fresno (Calif.) CC.
70. Josh Maloney, rhp, Central HS, Butte, Mont.
71. Chris Hill, rhp, Long Beach (Calif.) CC.
72. Michael Meyers, rhp, Annandale (Ontario) HS.
73. Chris Castleberry, c, Americus (Ga.) HS.
74. Peter Fukuhara, of, Canada (Calif.) JC.
75. Brian Fritz, 1b, Santa Ynez HS, Solvang, Calif.
76. Roger Foltynowicz, 3b, Lakeside HS, Evans, Ga.
77. Wayne Chinapen, rhp-of, York Mills Collegiate Institute, Willowdale, Ontario.
78. Scott Pasonage, rhp, Fullerton (Calif.) JC.
79. Jason Von Haefen, rhp, Blinn (Texas) JC.
80. Chris Sheldon, of, Glendale (Calif.) HS.
81. Darren Brown, rhp, Brophy Jesuit HS, Scottsdale, Ariz.
82. Shawn Jacob, c, Brandon (Miss.) HS.
83. Bill Eaton, ss-rhp, Indian River (Fla.) CC.
84. Brain Issett, of, Kimball HS, Royal Oak, Mich.
85. Charles Carter, 1b, McLennan (Texas) CC.
86. George Pickard, 1b, Hill (Texas) CC.

KANSAS CITY ROYALS (19)

1. **Juan Lebron of, Arroyo, P.R.**
2. **Carlos Beltran, of, Manati, P.R.**
3. **Doug Blosser, 1b, Sarasota (Fla.) HS.**
4. **Vic Radcliff, ss, North Augusta (S.C.) HS.**
5. **Steve Medrano, ss, Bishop Amat HS, La Puente, Calif.**
6. **Melvin Dasher, of, Palatka (Fla.) HS.**
7. **Allen Sanders, rhp, Lee (Texas) JC.**
8. **Jeff Martin, rhp, Bishop Gorman HS, Las Vegas, Nev.**
9. **Mike Robbins, lhp, Stanford U.**
10. **David Moore, rhp, Northeast HS, Oakland Park, Fla.**
11. **Mark Quinn, dh-rhp, Rice U.**
12. **Todd Meady, rhp, Milford (Conn.) Academy.**
13. Steve Donaghey, rhp, Woburn (Mass.) HS.
14. **Tony Penny, rhp, Newberry (S.C.) HS.**
15. **Matt Saier, rhp, Georgia Tech.**
16. **Jeremy Williamson, lhp, U. of Southern Mississippi.**
17. **Mark Melito, ss, Wake Forest U.**
18. **Patrick Hallmark, c, Rice U.**
19. Chad Schroeder, rhp, Northwestern U.
20. **Stephen Prihoda, lhp, Sam Houston State U.**
21. **Alonzo Aguilar, rhp, East Los Angeles JC.**
22. **James Vida, 1b, Florida Southern College.**
23. Randy Paulin, c, U. of the Pacific.
24. **Tony Miranda, of, Cal State Fullerton.**
25. **Jeff Wallace, lhp, Minerva (Ohio) HS.**
26. **Jon Albrecht, lhp, Kansas State U.**
27. **Steven Mullis, lhp, Brevard (N.C.) JC.**
28. **William Hodge, lhp, Jacksonville State (Ala.) U.**
29. **Emiliano Escandon, ss, Pomona-Pitzer (Calif.) College.**
30. **Taylor Bales, c, Lee (Texas) JC.**
31. **Scott Kortmeyer, of, Grand Canyon U.**
32. **Bret Schafer, of, UCLA.**
33. **Francis Key, rhp, Pensacola (Fla.) JC.**
34. **Jesus Liz, lhp, Miami-Dade CC North.**
35. **Craig Sanders, rhp, U. of Nebraska.**
36. **Adam Finnieston, of, U. of Miami.**
37. **Bobby Shannon, lhp, Shippensburg Area (Pa.) HS.**
38. Jeremy Albritton, c, Parklane Academy, Bogue Chitto, Miss.
39. Brian Wiese, rhp, Central HS, Baton Rouge, La.
40. Cliff Wilson, 3b, Byrnes HS, Lyman, S.C.
41. Seth Tate, ss, Wenatchee (Wash.) HS.
42. Jamison Powers, rhp, Sullivan East HS, Bluff City, Tenn.
43. Alan Bundy, rhp, Smith HS, Mansfield, Conn.
44. Adam Bolthouse, lhp, Spring Lake (Mich.) HS.
45. Brandon Buckley, c, San Ramon HS, Danville, Calif.
46. James Scarborough, of, Elkins HS, Fort Bend, Texas.
47. Dustin Wilson, rhp, Columbia Basin (Wash.) CC.
48. Denton McDaniel, lhp, Lake Travis HS, Austin, Texas.
49. Greg Arnold, lhp, Smithtown HS, Nesconset, N.Y.
50. Glen School, of, Brookdale (N.J.) CC.
51. Rudy Bulgar, of, New Bedford (Mass.) HS.
52. Brian Starcich, rhp, Blinn (Texas) JC.
53. Paul Stryhas, 3b, Sarasota (Fla.) HS.
54. Michael Cabales, rhp, East Islip (N.Y.) HS.
55. MerrellLigons, 2b, Palisades HS, Culver City, Calif.
56. Stephen Watson, rhp, Galveston (Texas) JC.
57. Andy Lynch, lhp, Bridgton Academy, North Bridgton, Me.
58. Lance Awbrey, c, Sinagua HS, Flagstaff, Ariz.
59. Paul Phillips, c, West Lauderdale HS, Bailey, Miss.
60. Tommy Worthy, ss, Etowah HS, Attalla, Ala.
61. Jaime Bonilla, lhp, Villalba, P.R.

62. Michael Rodriguez, ss, Chaffey HS, Ontario, Calif.
63. Courtney Thornton, rhp, Tallassee (Ala.) HS.
64. Scott Ham, c, Palestine (Ill.) HS.
65. Adam Reikowski, rhp, Providence HS, Charlotte, N.C.
66. **Brian Winders, rhp, Louisiana State U.**
67. Michael Degruy, rhp, Harrison Central HS, Gulfport, Miss.
68. Robert Shabansky, lhp, Bishop Gorman HS, Las Vegas, Nev.
69. Ralph Cadima, of, Mt. San Antonio (Calif.) JC.
70. Jason Van Curen, rhp, Monte Vista HS, San Ramon, Calif.

LOS ANGELES DODGERS (20)

1. **David Yocum, lhp, Florida State U.**
2. **Darrin Babineaux, rhp, U. of Southwestern Louisiana.**
3. **Onan Masaoka, lhp, Waiakea HS, Hilo, Hawaii.**
4. **Judd Granzow, of, Faith Baptist HS, Granada Hills, Calif.**
5. **Sef Soto, rhp, Palomar (Calif.) JC.**
6. **Kevin Gibbs, of, Old Dominion U.**
7. **Trent Cuevas, ss, El Dorado HS, Placentia, Calif.**
8. **Jon Tucker, 1b, Chatsworth (Calif.) HS.**
9. **Eric Brown, ss, East St. John HS, LaPlace, La.**
10. **Mike Carpentier, ss, Cal State Sacramento.**
11. **Craig Taczy, lhp, Shepard HS, Crestwood, Ill.**
12. Kenny Miller, ss, Providence Catholic HS, New Lenox, Ill.
13. Brad Wilkerson, lhp, Apollo HS, Owensboro, Ky.
14. Spencer Micunek, rhp, Henry Ford (Mich.) CC.
15. **J.J. Pearsall, lhp, U. of South Carolina.**
16. **Eric Flores, ss, Rio Mesa HS, Oxnard, Calif.**
17. **Antonio Mota, of, Miami Springs HS, Miami.**
18. **Jay O'Shaughnessy, rhp, Northeastern U.**
19. David Ross, c, Florida HS, Tallahassee, Fla.
20. Jeffrey Rodriguez, c, Coral Gables HS, Miami.
21. **Dennis Mauch, c, Cosumnes River (Calif.) JC.**
22. **A..J. Walkanoff, c, Creighton U.**
23. **Brett Illig, 3b, Phoenixville (Pa.) HS.**
24. **Travis Meyer, c, East Carolina U.**
25. **Peter Cervantes, rhp, East Los Angeles JC.**
26. Peyton Warren, rhp, West Florence HS, Florence, S.C.
27. **Mike Sanchez, rhp, Chaffey (Calif.) JC.**
28. **Ken Morimoto, of, U. of Hawaii.**
29. Greg Clark, c, Paradise Valley HS, Phoenix.
30. **Mitch McNeely, lhp, Centenary (La.) College.**
31. **Pedro Feliciano, lhp, Dorado, P.R.**
32. **Andy Owen, of, UC Riverside.**
33. Lazaro Gutierrez, lhp, Brito Miami Private HS, Hialeah, Fla.
34. **Scott Chambers, lhp, Logan (Ill.) JC.**
35. **Jeff Keppen, rhp, Georgia Southern U.**
36. Trevor Bishop, rhp, Assiniboia (Sask.) Composite HS.
37. David Schmidt, c, Oregon State U.
38. **Terrence McClain, ss, Cumberland (Tenn.) U.**
39. Chad Roney, c, Jacksonville U.
40. Bobby Cripps, c, Cameron HS, Powell River, B.C.
41. **John Davis, rhp, Bethune-Cookman (Fla.) College.**
42. Jason Smith, rhp, Demopolis HS, Coatopa, Ala.
43. Rabell Rivera, ss, Las Lomas, P.R.
44. Jeffrey Deno, lhp, Franklin HS, Los Angeles.
45. Brad Block, rhp, Lake Michigan (Mich.) JC.
46. **Michael Bourbakis, rhp, Roosevelt HS, Brooklyn, N.Y.**
47. Steve Green, rhp, Longueuil, Quebec.
48. Xavier Curley, 3b, Marshall County HS, Lewisburg, Tenn.
49. Andrew Dougherty, c, Glassboro (N.J.) HS.
50. Kevin Hodge, ss, Bryan (Texas) HS.
51. Mark Paschal, of, Fontana HS, Bloomington, Calif.
52. Maurice Hightower, lhp, Arlington (Texas) HS.
53. Christian Keating, rhp, Brother Rice HS, Country Club Heights, Ill.
54. Cesar Acosta, of, Yuma (Ariz.) HS.
55. Justin Rumfield, ss-3b, McLennan (Texas) CC.
56. Vance Cozier, rhp, Pickering HS, Ajax, Ontario.
57. Joel Ainsworth, lhp, Sarnia (Ontario) Collegiate Institute.
58. Cesar Castenada, 3b, Lincoln HS, Los Angeles.
59. Jose Rijo-Berger, of, Walla Walla (Wash.) CC.
60. Charles Koone, of, Spartanburg Methodist (S.C.) JC.
61. **Cash Riley, of, Trinity Christian Academy, Irving, Texas.**
62. Brian Oliver, ss, Antioch (Calif.) HS.
63. Chris Vollaro, rhp, Alvin (Texas) HS.
64. Mark Vallecorsa, lhp, Damien HS, San Dimas, Calif.
65. Stephen Dupont, rhp, Nicholls State U.
66. Gregory Conley, c, Sequim (Wash.) HS.
67. Paul Auton, c, Ainlay HS, Edmonton, Alberta.
68. Brian Dawson, rhp, San Bernardino Valley (Calif.) JC.
69. Tim Hackman, rhp, Vernon (B.C.) HS.
70. Brian Wagner, c, Sacramento CC.
71. Joseph Thomas, rhp, West Covina HS, La Puente, Calif.
72. Tony James, 2b, Chaffey (Calif.) JC.
73. Ryan Cail, rhp, Kwantlen (B.C.) College.
74. Craig Allen, rhp, U. of Notre Dame.

75. Todd Sutton, of, Angola HS, Pleasant Lake, Ind.
76. Neal Atchison, rhp, Central Huron HS, Clinton, Ontario.
77. Scott Oliver, rhp, Richland Northeast HS, Columbia, S.C.
78. Harold Featherstone, rhp, Hendersonville (N.C.) HS.
79. **Larry Bethea, 1b, Red Springs (N.C.) HS.**
80. Brandon Bowe, rhp, San Joaquin Delta (Calif.) CC.
81. Michael Tablit, rhp, Yuba (Calif.) CC.
82. Cary Stover, rhp, American River (Calif.) JC.
83. Brad Brewer, ss, Sacramento CC.
84. Mathew Randel, rhp, Ridgefield (Wash.) HS.
85. Ryan Moskau, 1b-lhp, Sabino HS, Tucson.

MILWAUKEE BREWERS (9)

1. **Geoff Jenkins, of, U. of Southern California.**
2. **Mike Pasqualicchio, lhp, Lamar U.**
3. **Greg Schaub, rhp, Solanco HS, Oxford, Pa.**
4. **Jeff Alfano, c, Mt. Whitney HS, Visalia, Calif.**
5. **Jared Camp, rhp, Indian River (Fla.) JC.**
6. **Toby Kominek, of, Central Michigan U.**
7. **Sam Singleton, ss, DuPont HS, Rand, W.Va..**
8. **Ryan Ritter, 2b-of, Georgia Tech.**
9. **Mike Kinkade, c-of, Washington State U.**
10. **Jason Dawsey, lhp, Clemson U.**
11. **Darren Berninger, rhp, Nicholls State U.**
12. **Chris Walther, of, Gaither HS, Tampa.**
13. **Mickey Lopez, 2b, Florida State U.**
14. **Shawn Miller, rhp, Northeastern Illinois U.**
15. **Jonathan Guzman, lhp, Levittown, P.R.**
16. **Donald Moore, of, Dallastown HS, York, Pa.**
17. **Alex Andreopoulos, c, Seton Hall U.**
18. **Ledowick Johnson, of, North Carolina State U.**
19. **Travis Smith, rhp, Texas Tech.**
20. **Sergio Guerrero, 2b, Laredo (Texas) JC.**
21. **Brian Hommel, lhp, U. of Louisville.**
22. Brad Pautz, rhp, Reedsville (Wis.) HS.
23. **Dave Elliott, of, Western Michigan U.**
24. **Jesse Richardson, lhp, Northern Illinois U.**
25. **Michael Roche, 2b, Brevard (Fla.) JC.**
26. **Derek Torres, rhp, Miami-Dade CC North.**
27. Beau Johnson, 1b-of, Mendocino (Calif.) CC.
28. **Rick Smith, 1b, Central Michigan U.**
29. **Ryan Arevalos, ss, U. of Texas-San Antonio.**
30. Scott Kirby, 3b, Lake Gibson HS, Lakeland, Fla.
31. **Gerald Parent, of, Merrimack (Mass.) College.**
32. Travis Bailey, ss, Wellington Community HS, West Palm Beach, Fla.
33. Anthony Rodriguez, rhp, Cooper City HS, Pembroke Pines, Fla.
34. Eric Leiser, of, Antioch (Calif.) HS.
35. Jonathan Rose, lhp, Brevard (N.C.) JC.
36. Migues Rodriguez, ss, Sonora HS, Brea, Calif.
37. Doug Wakefield, lhp, Victor Valley (Calif.) CC.
38. **Josh Bishop, rhp, U. of Missouri (dropout).**
39. Zane Curry, c, Ball HS, Galveston, Texas.
40. Austin Lawes, of, North Miami HS, Miramar, Fla.
41. George Phillips, ss, Demopolis (Ala.) HS.
42. Carlos Barbosa, c, Dinuba (Calif.) HS.
43. Mark Cridland, of, Galveston (Texas) JC.
44. Walter Ward, of, Northern HS, Chesapeake Beach, Md.
45. Blair Murphy, rhp, De Anza (Calif.) JC.
46. Byron Tribe, rhp, Galveston (Texas) JC.
47. Richard Cercy, rhp, Seabreeze HS, Ormond Beach, Fla.
48. Edward French, of, Seabreeze HS, Ormond Beach, Fla.
49. Michael Leach, rhp, Palm Beach (Fla.) CC.
50. James Landingham, of, South Miami HS, Miami.
51. Stanford Woods, of, Boone HS, Orlando.
52. Alain Cruz, c, Miami-Dade CC North.
53. Eric Armour, of, Palm Beach (Fla.) CC.
54. Kenny Avera, rhp, Pace (Fla.) HS.
55. Robert Cornett, c, North Hall HS, Gainesville, Ga.
56. Monty Ward, rhp, Monterey HS, Lubbock, Texas.
57. Paul Turco, ss, Sarasota (Fla.) HS.
58. Kip Wells, rhp, Elkins HS, Fort Bend, Texas.
59. Charlie Hunter, rhp, Notre Dame HS, Ooltewah, Tenn.
60. Steven Lawson, rhp, Damien HS, La Verne, Calif.
61. Lance Jordan, rhp, Whittier Christian HS, La Habra, Calif.
62. James Leary, rhp, South Grand Prairie HS, Grand Prairie, Texas.
63. Dirk Lewallen, 1b, Victor Valley (Calif.) JC.
64. Ara Petrosian, rhp, Cypress (Calif.) JC.
65. Jason Ross, of, U. of Hawaii.
66. Richard Jennings, ss, Overland HS, Aurora, Colo.
67. Kevin McDougal, of, West HS, Arvada, Colo.
68. Eric McMaster, 2b, West HS, Arvada, Colo.

MINNESOTA TWINS (13)

1. **Mark Redman, lhp, U. of Oklahoma.**
2. **Jason Bell, rhp, Oklahoma State U.**

3. A.J. Hinch, c, Stanford U.
4. Jay Hood, ss, Germantown (Tenn.) HS.
5. **Doug Mientkiewicz, 1b, Florida State U.**
6. **Shane Gunderson, c-1b, U. of Minnesota.**
7. **Mike Moriarty, ss, Seton Hall U.**
8. **Will Rushing, lhp, Georgia Southern U.**
9. **Joe McHenry, of, Oakland HS, Murfreesboro, Tenn.**
10. Kyle Kane, of, Linfield HS, Temecula Valley, Calif.
11. **Jamaal Harrison, 1b, Palo Alto (Calif.) HS.**
12. **Jason McKenzie, of, U. of Mississippi.**
13. **Jamie Splittorff, rhp, U. of Kansas.**
14. Josh Holliday, c, Stillwater (Okla.) HS.
15. **Brad Neidermaier, rhp, Northwestern U.**
16. **Alan Mahaffey, lhp, U. of Arkansas.**
17. Rob Ramsay, lhp, Washington State U.
18. **Freddy Reyes, 1b-3b, Levittown, P.R.**
19. **Carlisle Johnson, ss-of, Taylor HS, Pierson, Fla.**
20. **Jeff Smith, c, Stetson U.**
21. **David Orndorff, c, Shippensburg Area (Pa.) HS.**
22. **Scott Tanksley, rhp, Mississippi State U.**
23. Jamie Vallis, lhp, Allen HS, Bedford, N.S.
24. **John Blank, lhp, William Carey (Miss.) College.**
25. **Kevin Nelson, 1b, Bryant (Ark.) HS.**
26. **Tim Peters, lhp, Baylor U.**
27. **Joe Fraser, 2b, Cal State Fullerton.**
28. **Jeff Harris, rhp, U. of San Francisco.**
29. **Sean Reilly, lhp, Aldershot HS, Burlington, Ontario.**
30. **Travis Johnson, of, U. of North Dakota.**
31. **Todd Bartels, rhp, Stanford U.**
32. **Lee Marshall, rhp, Enterprise (Ala.) HS.**
33. Javier Mejia, rhp, U. of Southern California.
34. Matthew Noe, lhp, Riverside (Calif.) CC.
35. **Ivory Jones, of, San Francisco State U.**
36. **Harold Boggs, rhp, West Virginia State College.**
37. Adam Danner, rhp, U. of South Florida.
38. John Chapman, lhp, St. Joseph's (Ind.) College.
39. Scott Dobson, rhp, West Potomac HS, Alexandria, Va.
40. **Matt Vanderbush, lhp, William Paterson (N.J.) College.**
41. Leo Torres, lhp, Cibola HS, Somerton, Ariz.
42. Edmond Daniels, rhp, Polk (Fla.) CC.
43. Gary Forster, rhp, Montesano (Wash.) HS.
44. **Jeff Garff, rhp, Dixie (Utah) JC.**
45. Toby Wilmot, lhp, U. of Oklahoma.
46. **Andres Cruz, c, Salinas, P.R.**
47. Brian Mitchell, 3b, Iowa City (Iowa) HS.
48. Edgar Oropeza, rhp, CC of San Francisco.
49. Brian Bodwell, rhp, Ocosta HS, Westport, Wash.
50. Nelson Correa, 1b, Florida Air Academy HS, Melbourne, Fla.
51. (selection voided)
52. Michael Brunet, rhp, Land O'Lakes (Fla.) HS.
53. **Bryan Malko, rhp, Piscataway (N.J.) HS.**
54. Craig Black, 2b, Palm Beach Lakes HS, West Palm Beach, Fla.
55. Paul Boykin, of, Columbine HS, Littleton, Colo.

MONTREAL EXPOS (28)

1. **Michael Barrett, ss, Pace Academy, Atlanta.**
2. **Henry Mateo, ss, Santurce, P.R.**
3. **Kenny James, of, Sebring (Fla.) HS.**
4. **J.D. Smart, rhp, U. of Texas.**
5. **Brian Schneider, c, Northampton HS, Cherryville, Pa.**
6. **Ronney Daniels, of-lhp, Lake Wales (Fla.) HS.**
7. **Peter Fortune, lhp, Rockland (N.Y.) JC.**
8. **Trey Martin, rhp, Arcadia HS, Phoenix.**
9. **Bienvenido Sanchez, rhp, Arecibo, P.R.**
10. Jeff Austin, rhp, Kingwood (Texas) HS.
11. Jimmy Turman, rhp, Shelton State (Ala.) CC.
12. **Robert Marquez, rhp, McNeese State U.**
13. **David Herr, rhp, Villanova U.**
14. **Tim Dixon, lhp, Cal State Fullerton.**
15. **D.C. Olsen, lhp, Cal State Fullerton.**
16. **Pierre Laforest, ss-3b, Gatineau, Quebec.**
17. **Wes Denning, of, U. of Minnesota.**
18. Tom Brady, c, Serra HS, San Mateo, Calif.
19. **Jake Steinkemper, c, Arizona State U.**
20. **Mike Bell, lhp, Florida State U.**
21. Stan Baston, of-3b, North Florida Christian HS, Tallahassee, Fla.
22. **Scott Mitchell, rhp, U. of the Pacific.**
23. **Mo Blakeney, of, Elon (N.C.) College.**
24. **Mike Wolger, of-lhp, U. of California.**
25. **Jaime Garcia, c, U. of New Mexico.**
26. **Ryan Van Oeveren, ss, U. of Michigan.**
27. Noah Hall, of, Aptos (Calif.) HS.
28. **Jarrett Shearin, of, Wake Forest-Rolesville HS, Wake Forest, N.C.**
29. **Jeremiah Colson, of, St. Paul's (N.C.) HS.**
30. **James Lacey, rhp, Coconut Creek (Fla.) HS.**

Turns To Baseball. The Yankees spent their first-round pick on ex-Univerity of Texas quarterback Shea Morenz.

31. Toby McDermott, lhp, Tacoma (Wash.) CC.
32. Joe Kerrigan Jr., ss, Radnor HS, Rosemont, Pa.
33. Shawn Peterson, c-of, Orem (Utah HS.
34. Scott Porter, rhp, Middleburg (Fla.) HS.
35. Mitch Wylie, rhp, North Scott HS, Princeton, Iowa.
36. Aaron Underwood, rhp, Lehigh HS, Lehigh Acres, Fla.
37. Matt Dehner, 3b, El Dorado HS, Las Vegas, Nev.
38. Brandon Gadke, of, Orange (Ohio) HS.
39. Bruno Vaillancourt, lhp, Le Gardeur, Quebec.
40. Shane Wright, rhp, Hayden HS, Topeka, Kan.
41. Robert Everett, rhp, Lake City (Fla.) CC.
42. Torrance Davis, of, Liberty Eylau HS, Texarkana, Texas.
43. Jesse Crespo, c, Camuy, P.R.
44. Phil Derryman, rhp, Moorpark (Calif.) JC.
45. Adam Huxhold, lhp, Lindbergh HS, Maple Valley, Wash.
46. Daniel Prata, lhp, Repentigny, Quebec.

NEW YORK METS (18)

1. Ryan Jaroncyk, ss, Orange Glen HS, Escondido, Calif.
2. Brett Herbison, rhp-ss, Central HS, Burlington, Ill.
3. Ryan Bowers, c, Pineview HS, St. George, Utah.
4. Corey Erickson, ss, Lanphier HS, Springfield, Ill.
5. Jeff Parsons, ss, U. of Arkansas.
6. Todd Cutchins, lhp, Tallahassee (Fla.) CC.
7. Ryan Minor, 1b-rhp, U. of Oklahoma.
8. Allan Burnett, rhp, Central Arkansas Christian HS, North Little Rock, Ark.
9. Tydus Meadows, of, Evans (Ga.) HS.
10. Dan Murray, rhp, San Diego State U.
11. Grant Roberts, rhp, Grossmont HS, El Cajon, Calif.
12. Mark Pileski, ss, U. of Massachusetts.
13. Erick Torres, rhp, Mayaguez, P.R.
14. Eric McQueen, c, North Cobb HS, Alworth, Ga.
15. Anthony Johnson, c-of, Oakland (Calif.) HS.
16. Lindsay Gulin, lhp, Issaquah (Wash.) HS.
17. Scott Proctor, rhp, Martin County HS, Stuart, Fla.
18. Chris Adolph, of, Clovis West HS, Fresno, Calif.
19. Damon Minor, 1b, U. of Oklahoma.
20. Phil Olson, rhp, Florida State U.
21. Joey Pyrtle, rhp, UNC Wilmington.

22. Andrew Zwirchitz, rhp, Okaloosa Walton (Fla.) CC.
23. Brooks Stephens, 1b, Florida HS, Tallahassee, Fla.
24. Jeff Howatt, rhp, UCLA.
25. Ben Hickman, rhp, Bryant (Ark.) HS.
26. Paul Yoder, of, Alvernia (Pa.) College.
27. Preston Ballew, lhp, Carlsbad (N.M.) HS.
28. Chadwick Cooper, rhp, Potomac State (W.Va.) JC.
29. Mark Enloe, lhp, Tarkington HS, Cleveland, Texas.
30. Nelson Figueroa, rhp, Brandeis (Mass.) U.
31. Matt Ferullo, rhp, U. of Michigan.
32. Brandon Copeland, of, Washburn HS, Topeka, Kan.
33. Mike Blang, rhp, Southern Illinois U.
34. Brandon Black, of, Pensacola (Fla.) JC.
35. John Mattson, rhp, South Kitsap HS, Port Orchard, Wash.
36. Jacob Handy, rhp, Arvin HS, Bakersfield, Calif.
37. Ryan Morrison, of, Onondaga (N.Y.) CC.
38. Clifton Wren, c, Petal (Miss.) HS.
39. Richard Martinez, c, St. Mary's (Texas) U.
40. Aaron Rowand, ss, Glendora (Calif.) HS.
41. Tim Tessmar , lhp, Eastern Michigan U.
42. Donald Loland, rhp, Ascension Catholic HS, Donaldsonville, La.
43. Casey Patterson, rhp, Fresno (Calif.) CC.
44. Randy Young, of, Wichita State U.
45. Sean Gill, of, Wright State U.
46. Tylor More, of, East HS, Cheyenne, Wyom.
47. Stephen Minus, rhp-c, Judson HS, San Antonio, Texas.
48. Cory Patton, of, Olney Central (Ill.) JC.
49. Jacob Bailey, rhp, Hutchinson (Kan.) CC.
50. Clinton Johnston, 1b, Carroll HS, Vero Beach, Fla.
51. Jaime Rodgers, rhp, Friendship Christian HS, Mt. Juliet, Tenn.
52. Chris Dewitt, rhp, St. Andrews Presbyterian (N.C.) College.
53. Shawn Hannah, rhp, Clovis (Calif.) HS.
54. Luis Castillo, c, American HS, Miami Lakes, Fla.
55. Chris Reinike, rhp, Long Beach (Miss.) HS.
56. Corey Brittan, rhp, Hutchinson (Kan.) CC.
57. Derek Daugherty, of, Kingfisher (Okla.) HS.
58. Quinn Cravens, of, Valley Center (Kan.) HS.
59. Jerrell Carver, 1b, Northeastern HS, Elizabeth City, N.C.
60. Tony Moreno, c, Riverside HS, El Paso, Texas.
61. Robert Piercy, c, Crest HS, Shelby, N.C.
62. Hector Esparza, 3b, San Jose (Calif.) CC.
63. Darren Dyt, of, Porterville (Calif.) JC.

NEW YORK YANKEES (27)

1. Shea Morenz, of, U. of Texas.
2. Richard Brown, of, Nova HS, Fort Lauderdale, Fla.
2. Brian Buchanan, lhp, Oviedo (Fla.) HS (Supplemental choice—59th—for loss of Type C free agent Matt Nokes).
3. Luke Wilcox, of, Western Michigan U.
4. Eric Boardman, rhp, Cerritos (Calif.) JC.
5. Jason Wright, rhp, Martinsville (Ind.) HS.
6. Brad Williams, lhp, Sabino HS, Tucson.
7. Bob St. Pierre, rhp, U. of Richmond.
8. Scott Brand, rhp, McLennan (Texas) JC.
9. Mike Judd, rhp, Grossmont (Calif.) JC.
10. Jeff Saffer, of, Pima (Ariz.) CC.
11. Darrell Einertson, rhp, Iowa Wesleyan College.
12. Cam Spence, rhp, Lake City (Fla.) CC.
13. Ryan Mills, lhp, Horizon HS, Scottsdale, Ariz.
14. Cesar Verdin, lhp, Crawford HS, San Diego.
15. Josh Hochgesang, ss, Sunny Hills HS, Fullerton, Calif.
16. Dana Davis, rhp, Rice U.
17. Jerry Lail, rhp, Wingate (N.C.) College.
18. Steve Randolph, lhp, U. of Texas.
19. Jay Tessmer, rhp, U. of Miami.
20. Mike Lowell, 2b, Florida International U.
21. Scott Emmons, c, U. of California.
22. Donzell McDonald, of, Yavapai (Ariz.) JC.
23. Cody McCormick, c, U. of California.
24. Ryan Snellings, lhp, Seminole HS, Largo, Fla.
25. Dan Kanell, rhp, Florida State U.
26. Daunte Culpepper, of, Vanguard HS, Ocala, Fla.
27. Patrick Antrim, ss, Saddleback (Calif.) CC.
28. Les Dennis, ss, U. of Portland.
29. Jason Ryan, lhp, Indian River (Fla.) CC.
30. Michael Schnautz, lhp, San Jacinto North (Texas) JC.
31. Chris Crawford, rhp, Wheeler HS, Marietta, Ga.
32. Tim Spindler, rhp-ss, Orange County (N.Y.) CC.
33. Brian Aylor, of, Oklahoma State U.
34. Richard Cremer, lhp, West Frankfort (Ill.) HS.
35. Orlando Carey, of, Motlow State (Tenn.) CC.
36. Ben Phillips, rhp, Howard (Texas) JC.
37. Travis Brummitt, rhp, Cleveland State (Tenn.) CC.
38. Barry Brown, of, Grossmont (Calif.) JC.
39. Lisnardo DeCastro, 1b-of, Florida Bible Christian HS, Sunrise, Fla.

40. Lateef Vaughn, ss, Southwestern (Calif.) JC.
41. Ben Chestnut, of, Sacramento CC.
42. Joseph Horgan, lhp, Cordova HS, Rancho Cordova, Calif.
43. Jason Imrisek, c, U. of Evansville.
44. Jared Hoerman, rhp, Plainview HS, Armore, Okla.
45. Casey Blake, 3b, Wichita State U.
46. Deris Pujals, rhp, U. of Miami.
47. Jason Ellison, rhp, Navarro (Texas) JC.
48. Scott Kingston, 1b, Columbus (Ga.) HS.
49. Philip Haigler, rhp, Vanderbilt U.
50. Lance Hawkins, of, Lake Charles-Boston HS, Lake Charles, La.
51. Brandon James, of, Sacramento CC.
52. Brian Hervey, rhp, Tallahassee (Fla.) CC.
53. Chad Clements, ss, Centreville HS, Fairfax, Va.
54. Jason Becker, 2b, Bremen HS, Midlothian, Ill.
55. Michael Hamm, c, Shoals (Ala.) CC.
56. Darryl Craig, lhp-1b, Douglas (B.C.) College.
57. Dorian Cameron, ss, Northern HS, Durham, N.C.
58. Jude Campbell, of, Chabot (Calif.) JC.
59. Daniel Thomas, rhp, Poway (Calif.) HS.
60. Nathan Koepke, of, Long Beach (Calif.) CC.
61. Brandon Hemmings, of, Columbus (Ga.) HS.
62. Charles Shipp, of, Vocational HS, Chicago.
63. Jeremiah Johnson, rhp, Homer (Mich.) HS.
64. Doug Dixon, rhp, Northside HS, Belhaven, N.C.
65. Scott Hardesty, rhp, U. of Illinois-Chicago.
66. Jake Zajc, rhp, Bradley-Bourbonnais HS, Bourbornais, Ill.
67. Justin Carpenter, rhp, Prague (Okla.) HS.
68. Charles Thomas, of, Harlan (Ky.) HS.
69. Peter Fisher, rhp, Stoneham (Mass.) HS.
70. Daniel Washburn, rhp, Nova HS, Pembroke Pines, Fla.
71. William Duncan, c, Burlington-Edison HS, Burlington, Wash.

OAKLAND A's (5)

1. Ariel Prieto, rhp, Palm Springs/Western League.
2. Mark Bellhorn, ss, Auburn U.
3. Billy Brown, of, St. Thomas Aquinas HS, Fort Lauderdale.
4. Wayne Nix, rhp, Monroe HS, North Hills, Calif.
5. Danny Ardoin, c, McNeese State U.
6. Jamey Price, rhp, U. of Mississippi.
7. Tim Jones, of, Buena Park (Calif.) HS.
8. Tom Bennett, rhp, Ohlone (Calif.) HS.
9. Tom Knickerbocker, of, Kirkwood (Ia.) JC.
10. Ryan Christensen, of, Pepperdine U.
11. Scott Rivette, rhp, Long Beach State U.
12. Troy Rauer, of, Arizona State U.
13. Willie Hilton, rhp, Eastern Illinois U.
14. Kevin Mlodik, rhp, U. of Wisconsin-Oshkosh.
15. David Shepard, rhp, Mansfield (Pa.) U.
16. Robert Harris, ss, Texas A&M U.
17. David Newhan, of, Pepperdine U.
18. Mike Klostermeyer, 1b, Louisiana State U.
19. Jason Hill, c, Monte Vista HS, Danville, Calif.
20. David Slemmer, ss-2b, Southwest Missouri State U.
21. Bill Knight, of, U. of Massachusetts.
22. T.J. Costello, lhp, Montclair State (N.J.) College.
23. Duane Filchner, of, Radford U.
24. Steve Connelly, rhp, U. of Oklahoma.
25. Brian Callahan, rhp, The Citadel.
26. Jeff Davanon, of-2b, San Diego State U.
27. Ryan Kjos, rhp, U. of Texas.
28. Victor Hernandez, of, Ciales, P.R.
29. Stephen Bess, rhp, Montgomery Bell Academy, Nashville, Tenn.
30. Bill Batchelder, rhp, U. of New Hampshire.
31. Kevin Gunther, rhp, Fresno State U.
32. Jace Johnson, of, Scottsdale (Ariz.) CC.
33. Byron Embry, rhp, Madison Central HS, Richmond, Ky.
34. Chris Morrison, rhp, Auburn U.
35. Jon French, rhp, Arkansas State U.
36. Ryan Gill, rhp, Woodlawn HS, Baton Rouge, La.
37. Rodney Clifton, rhp, Elgin (Ill.) HS.
38. Greg Halvorson, c, Canyon Del Oro HS, Tucson, Ariz.
39. Matthew Dornfeld, of, Arizona Western JC.
40. Robert Norman, rhp, Columbia Academy, Mt. Pleasant, Tenn.
41. Chris Nelson, rhp, Oklahoma State U.
42. Brandon Welch, of, Texas Tech.
43. Victor Chambers, 2b-of, CC o f San Francisco.
44. Todd Abbott, rhp, U. of Arkansas.

PHILADELPHIA PHILLIES (14)

1. Reggie Taylor, of, Newberry (S.C.) HS.
1. Dave Coggin, rhp, Upland (Calif.) HS (Supplemental choice—30th—for loss of Type A free agent Danny Jackson).
2. Marlon Anderson, 2b, U. of South Alabama (Choice from Cardinals as compensation for Type A free agent Danny Jackson).

Phillies Phenom. Philadelphia had the 14th overall choice in the draft and went for South Carolina high school outfielder Reggie Taylor.

2. (Choice to Cardinals as compensation for Type A free agent Gregg Jefferies).
3. Randy Knoll, rhp-3b, Corona (Calif.) HS.
4. Steve Carver, 3b, Stanford U.
5. Pee Wee Lopez, c, Westminster Christian HS, Miami.
6. Caleb Martinez, lhp, Florida Bible Christian HS, Miami.
7. Chris Bauer, rhp-ss, Wichita State U.
8. Erick Williams, ss, Patrick Henry HS, San Diego.
9. Kirk Pierce, c, Long Beach State U.
10. Brian Mensink, rhp, U. of Minnesota.
11. Jason Wallace, of, Callaway HS, Jackson, Miss.
12. Jason Kershner, lhp, Saguaro HS, Scottsdale, Ariz.
13. Mark Raynor, ss, Barton (N.C.) College.
14. Marty Barnett, rhp, U. of South Alabama.
15. Walter Dawkins, of, U. of Southern California.
16. Melvin Pizarro, lhp, Carolina, P.R.
17. Ryan Lentz, 3b, Woodinville (Wash.) HS.
18. Matt Buckles, c, Palatka (Fla.) HS.
19. Christopher Snusz, c, Mercyhurst (Pa.) College.
20. Brian Miller, rhp, Marian College of Fond Du Lac (Wisc.).
21. Tyson Kimm, ss, Creighton U.
22. Brian Ford, lhp, Methodist (N.C.) College.
23. Anthony Shumaker, lhp, Cardinal Stritch (Wisc.) College.
24. Jared Janke, 1b, UC Santa Barbara.
25. Tim Walton, rhp, U. of Oklahoma.
26. Todd Crane, of, U. of Georgia.
27. Gary Yeager, rhp, Elizabethton (Pa.) College.
28. Casey Brookens, rhp, James Madison U.
29. Zachary Elliot, 2b-ss, UC Santa Barbara.
30. Kyle Kawabata, rhp, Washington State U.
31. Kevin Hooker, 2b, Oregon State U.
32. Kory Kosek, rhp, Mankato State (Minn.) U.
33. Brian Dunne, lhp, Kansas Newman College.
34. Richard O'Connor, ss, Valparaiso U.
35. Charles Cox, c, U. of Texas -Pan American.

36. Scott Tebbetts, rhp, UC Riverside.
37. Bill Noone, rhp, Wilkes (Pa.) U.
38. Justin Kennedy, of, Bastrop (La.) HS.
39. David Robinson, of, U. of Rio Grande (Ohio).
40. Courtney Moore, of, Shoals (Ala.) CC.
41. Rob Gaiko, rhp, Oklahoma State U.
42. Jonathon Cornelius, of, Cal State Los Angeles.
43. Jeff Leaman, 3b, Indiana State U.
44. Clyde Livingston, c, Newberry (S.C.) College.
45. Bryan Williamson, rhp, Kamiakin HS, Kennewick, Wash.
46. Jaime Mendes, rhp, New Mexico State U.
47. Josh Glenn, rhp, Riley HS, South Bend, Ind.
48. Marques Meshack, rhp, Lincoln HS, San Diego.
49. Jason Bell, of, Atwater (Calif.) HS.
50. Charles Marino, of, Kennedy HS, La Palma, Calif.
51. Jose Sandoval, ss, Poly HS, Sun Valley, Calif.
52. Benito Lemos, c, Royal HS, Simi Valley, Calif.
53. Mike Heidemann, 1b, Yavapai (Ariz.) JC.

PITTSBURGH PIRATES (10)

1. Chad Hermansen, ss, Green Valley HS, Henderson, Nev.
2. Garrett Long, 1b, Bellaire HS, Houston.
3. Bronson Arroyo, rhp, Brooksville-Hernando HS, Brooksville, Fla.
4. Alex Hernandez, of, Levittown, P.R.
5. Dawan Elliott, of, Long Branch (N.J.) HS.
6. O.J. Cook, rhp, Liberty HS, Bethlehem, Pa.
7. Josh Loggins, c, Harrison HS, West Lafayette, Ind.
8. Brad Weber, of, DeKalb HS, Auburn, Ind.
9. Fred May, of, Kennedy HS, Seattle.
10. Daniel Delgado, ss, Killian HS, Miami.
11. Brian O'Connor, lhp, Redding (Ohio) HS.
12. Al Benjamin, of, Milby HS, Houston.
13. Brian Settle, rhp, Wilson HS, Portsmouth, Va.
14. Travis Gaerte, rhp, Fremont (Ind.) HS.
15. Elton Pollock, of, Presbyterian (S.C.) College.
16. Ian Rauls, of, Ewing HS, Trenton, N.J.
17. Jason Saenz, lhp, Mater Dei HS, Santa Ana, Calif.
18. Ryan Gillispie, rhp, Rancho Bernardo HS, San Diego.
19. Maika Symmonds, lhp, Old Dominion U.
20. Derek Bullock, rhp, Briar Cliff (Iowa) College.
21. Steven Flanigan, c, California (Pa.) U.
22. Chris Miyake, ss, UC San Diego.
23. Cory Bigler, rhp, U. of Wisconsin-Milwaukee.
24. Tim Collie, rhp, UNC Charlotte.
25. John Canetto, 3b, Coastal Carolina College.
26. Chris Heck, lhp, Northeast Catholic HS, Philadelphia.
27. Jason Farrow, rhp, U. of Houston.
28. George Hlodan, rhp, Forward HS, Elizabeth, Pa.
29. Neal McDade, rhp, Florida CC.
30. Brock Hundt, 3b, Logan (Ill.) JC.
31. Chris Miller, rhp-3b, Winter Haven (Fla.) HS.
32. Ronald Brooks, rhp, Leon HS, Tallahassee, Fla.
33. Travis Siegel, of, Choctaw HS, Midwest City, Okla.
34. Jacob Whitfield, lhp, Tallahassee (Fla.) CC.
35. Matt Hoffman, rhp, Claremore (Okla.) HS.
36. Ronald Ricks, rhp, Tallahassee (Fla.) CC.
37. Michael Carney, lhp, Merritt Island (Fla.) HS.
38. Brandon Larson, ss, Blinn (Texas) JC.
39. Joseph Wroble, lhp, South Suburban (Ill.) College.
40. Arthur Young, of, New Rochelle (N.Y.) HS.
41. Jason Wright, rhp, Palomar (Calif.) JC.
42. Scott Beach, rhp, Pittsburg State (Kan.) College.
43. Rob Thomas, lhp, Texas A&M U.
44. Jason Shelley, ss, Plainfield (Ill.) HS.

ST. LOUIS CARDINALS (12)

1. Matt Morris, rhp, Seton Hall U.
1. Chris Haas, 3b, St. Mary's HS, Paducah, Ky. (Supplemental choice—29th— for loss of Type A free agent Gregg Jefferies).
2. (Choice to Phillies as compensation for Type A free agent Danny Jackson).
2. Jason Woolf, ss, American HS, Hialeah, Fla. (Choice from Phillies as compensation for Jefferies).
3. Billy Deck, 1b, Potomac HS, Dumphries, Va.
4. Rodney Barfield, rhp, DeKalb (Ga.) JC.
5. Cody McKay, 3b, Arizona State U.
6. Joe Freitas, of, Fresno State U.
7. Matt King, rhp, Galveston (Texas) JC.
8. Jon Ward, rhp, Cal State Fullerton.
9. Ryan McHugh, of, Florida Southern College.
10. Matt DeWitt, rhp-3b, Valley HS, Las Vegas, Nev.
11. Robert Cooke, rhp, Mount Oliver (N.C.) College.
12. Kevin Miedreich, rhp, St. Thomas Aquinas (N.Y.) College.
13. Shawn McNally, of-ss, Auburn U.

Cardinal Catch. St. Louis had the 12th overall pick in the draft, and used it on Seton Hall righthander Matt Morris.

14. Ken Cameron, of, Washington State U.
15. Jason Lee, of, Burlington (Iowa) HS.
16. Andy Hall, 2b, Cal Poly San Luis Obispo.
17. Britt Reames, rhp, The Citadel.
18. Lou Deman, c, Long Island U.
19. Chris Richard, of-1b, Oklahoma State U.
20. Adam Benes, rhp, U. of Evansville.
21. Tom Truselo, rhp, Delcastle HS, New Castle, Del.
22. Travis McClendon, c, U. of Nevada-Las Vegas.
23. Jorge Roque, rhp, Santurce, P.R.
24. Andy Schofield, of, Illinois State U.
25. Mike Kimbrell, lhp, Southeastern Louisiana U.
26. Darrell Betts, ss, Ball State U.
27. Matt Wagner, rhp, Lewis-Clark State (Idaho) College.
28. Ernest Spivey, 2b, Cowley County (Kan.) CC.
29. Chris Mazur, lhp, East Bladen HS, Elizabethtown, N.C.
30. Rusty Sarnes, lhp, Lincoln Land (Ill.) CC.
31. Miguel Insunza, ss, Lewis-Clark State (Idaho) College.
32. Gavin Brown, of, U. of California.
33. Juan Munoz, of, Florida International U.
34. Kerry Robinson, of, Southeast Missouri State U.
35. Dean Brueggemann, lhp, Belleville Area (Ill.) JC.
36. Jeff Ryan, ss, Grand Prairie (Texas) HS.
37. Tony Falciglia, c, Farleigh Dickinson U.
38. Jose Villafana, rhp, Mission (Calif.) JC.
39. Mike Swenson, lhp, U. of South Florida.
40. Bryce Darnell, c, Missouri Southern State U.
41. Scott Spaulding, rhp, Eastern Connecticut State U.
42. Kyle West, ss, Pineview HS, St. George, Utah.
43. Wade Jackson, 2b, U. of Nevada-Reno.
44. Jason Lariviere, of-2b, U. of Southern Maine.
45. Brian Clark, lhp, Mississippi State U.
46. Bret Mueller, of, Cal Poly San Luis Obispo.
47. Michael Gray, rhp, North Florida JC.
48. Nick Deluca, ss, Bellevue (Neb.) College.
49. Ruben Cardona, 2b, Bellhaven (Miss.) College.
50. Brandon Folkers, 1b, Pasco-Hernando (Fla.) JC.
51. Michael Hogan, of, Middle Georgia JC.
52. George Burgos, of, American HS, Miami.
53. Brian Jorgensen, 3b, U. of Missouri.
54. Clifford Politte, rhp, Jefferson (Mo.) JC.
55. Cheron Farley, 2b, Lincolnton (N.C.) HS.
56. Nick Roberts, rhp, South Sevibic HS, Annabella, Utah.
57. Michael Delano, lhp, North Hollywood (Calif.) HS.
58. Nolan Vincent, 3b-of, Hollister (Mo.) HS.
59. Ryan Gladwin, of, Martin County HS, Stuart, Fla.
60. Nick Kast, lhp, Oral Roberts U.
61. Rob Donnelly, rhp, Fresno State U.
62. James Birr, ss, U. of North Florida.
63. Ryan Pene, lhp, Grand County HS, Moab, Utah.
64. Michael Glendenning, 3b-of, Pierce (Fla.) JC.
65. Craig Moore, 3b, Bergail HS, Freemont, Neb.

SAN DIEGO PADRES (2)

1. Ben Davis, c, Malvern (Pa.) Prep.
2. Gabe Alvarez, ss, U. of Southern California.
3. Ryan Van de Weg, rhp, Western Michigan U.
4. Brandon Kolb, rhp, Texas Tech.
5. Kenny Henderson, rhp, U. of Miami.
6. Kevin Walker, lhp, Grand Prairie (Texas) HS.
7. Jason Totman, 2b, Texas Tech.
8. Sean Watkins, 1b, Bradley U.
9. Mike Martin, c, Florida State U.
10. James Sak, rhp, Illinois Benedictine College.
11. Mark Wulfert, of, U. of New Mexico.
12. Curt Lowry, of, McNeese State U.
13. Rick Gama, 2b, U. of Miami.
14. Andy Hammerschmidt, lhp, U. of Minnesota.
15. Steven Hoff, lhp, Mills HS, San Bruno, Calif.
16. John Rodriguez, ss, Miller HS, Corpus Christi, Texas.
17. Michael Irvine, rhp, U. of Northern Iowa.
18. Don Kirkendoll, lhp, Bacone (Okla.) JC.
19. Brandon Pernell, of, St. Bernard HS, Torrance, Calif.
20. Rich Hills, ss, U. of Oklahoma.
21. Aaron Looper, rhp, Byng HS, Ada, Okla.
22. Anthony Marnell, c, U. of Arizona.
23. Matt Abernathy, of, U. of Mississippi.
24. James Moore, of, Ranger (Texas) JC.
25. Anthony Felston, of, Mississippi Delta JC.
26. Damon Minor, of, Green River (Wash.) CC.
27. Enrique Lazu, rhp, Trujillo Alto, P.R.
28. Carmen Bucci, ss, Northwestern U.
29. Clint Weibl, rhp, Odessa (Texas) JC.
30. Dusty Allen, of-1b, Stanford U.
31. Joe Victory, rhp, Eastern Oklahoma State U.
32. Damond Nash, rhp, Texarkana (Texas) JC.
33. Ken Jones, c, Western Michigan U.
34. Ryan Brown, rhp, Grapevine HS, Colleyville, Texas.
35. Andrew Hunter, of, Arlington (Texas) HS.
36. Jesse Cornejo, lhp, Wellington (Kan.) HS.
37. Brandon Brown, lhp, Ranger (Texas) JC.
38. Robert Gorr, ss, Rancho Buena Vista HS, Vista, Calif.
39. Chuck Crumpton, rhp, Poteet HS, Mesquite, Texas.
40. Brian Jacobus, of , Rogers HS, Puyallup, Wash.
41. Scott Pratt, ss, Tooele (Utah) HS.
42. William Alexander, rhp, Northwest Shoals (Ala.) CC.
43. Rico Lagattuta, lhp, U. of Nevada-Reno.
44. John Robertson, rhp, Rockdale (Texas) HS.
45. Brett Kondro, lhp, Fort Saskatchewan (Alberta) HS.
46. Davis Kile, rhp, Friday Harbor (Wash.) HS.
47. Wilbert Nieves, c, Condado, P.R.
48. Allen Goudy, of, Lake Michigan JC.
49. Joel Vega, lhp, Cidra, P.R.
50. Chad Reynolds, rhp, Friendship HS, Lubbock, Texas.
51. Justin Sellers, rhp, Evergreen HS, Vancouver, Wash.
52. Adrian Stewart, 1b, Claremont (Calif.) HS.

SAN FRANCISCO GIANTS (16)

1. Joe Fontenot, rhp, Acadiana HS, Lafayette, La.
2. Jason Brester, lhp, Burlington-Edison HS, Burlington, Wash.
3. Darin Blood, rhp, Gonzaga U.
4. Russ Ortiz, rhp, U. of Oklahoma.
5. Jim Woodrow, rhp, Flagler (Fla.) College.
6. Joe Nathan, rhp, SUNY Stonybrook.
7. Alex Morales, of, U. of Central Florida.
8. Ben Tucker, rhp, U. of Southern California.
9. Manny Bermudez, rhp, Antioch (Calif.) HS.
10. Jeff Hutzler, rhp, U. of Texas-San Antonio.
11. Ian Rand, of, Helix HS, La Mesa, Calif.
12. Bruce Thompson, of, U. of Miami.
13. Philip Bailey, lhp, Central Arkansas U.
14. Jon Watson, 2b, Fairleigh Dickinson U.
15. Nathan Forbush, c-1b, Central Arizona JC.
16. Brian Knoll, rhp, Brigham Young U.
17. Duane Eason, rhp, Brookdale (N.J.) CC.
18. Rogelio Colon, rhp, Caguas, P.R.
19. Kurt Takahashi, rhp, Fresno (Calif.) CC.
20. Andy Norton, c, Gonzaga U.
21. Terry Weaver, ss, Liberty (Va.) U.
22. Danny Harmon, rhp, Midland HS, Floral, Ark.
23. Mark Peer, of, St. Louis CC-Meramec.
24. Toby Hall, c, American River (Calif.) JC.
25. Marc Mosman, rhp, Cal State Dominguez Hills.
26. Jeffrey Pohl, rhp, Three Rivers (Mo.) CC.
27. Billy Coleman, rhp, Davidson (Okla.) HS.
28. Jeremy Jackson, of, Indian Hills (Iowa) CC.
29. Kelly Ireland, of, Mt. Hood (Ore.) CC.

30. John McMurray, 3b, Monticello (Ark.) HS.
31. Shawn Lindsey, of, Franklin HS, Portland, Ore.
32. Brian Phelan, c, East Denver HS, Denver.
33. Brian Little, 3b, Tulare Union HS, Tulare, Calif.
34. Justin Miller, rhp, Torrance (Calif.) HS.
35. Matt Schuldt, c, Howard (Texas) JC.
36. Brandon Hayes, rhp, McLane HS, Fresno, Calif.
37. Jason Dewey, c, Brandon HS, Valrico, Fla.
38. LaJuan Rice, of, McNair HS, Atlanta.
39. Tom Topaum, c, Centennial HS, Gresham, Ore.
40. Michael Lincoln, rhp, American River (Calif.) JC.
41. Mike Littlefield, rhp, Central Arizona JC.
42. Brad Lidge, rhp, Cherry Creek HS, Englewood, Colo.
43. Jason Huth, ss, Cherry Creek HS, Englewood, Colo.
44. Mike Davis, rhp, Tallahassee (Fla.) CC.
45. Eric Thompson. rhp, Greenon HS, Fairborn, Ohio.
46. Casey Bookout, 1b, Stroud (Okla.) HS.
47. Joe Blasingim, rhp, Southwest Missouri State U.
48. Kirk Bolling, rhp, West Torrance HS, Torrance, Calif.
49. David Townsend, rhp, Delta State (Miss.) U.
50. Eduard Guzman, 3b, Naranjito, P.R.

SEATTLE MARINERS (3)

1. Jose Cruz Jr., of, Rice U.
2. Shane Monahan, of, Clemson U.
3. Greg Wooten, rhp, Portland State U.
4. Duan Johnson, ss, St. Paul's (N.C.) HS.
5. Gary Kinnie, rhp, Chippewa Valley HS, Clifton Township, Mich.
6. Karl Thompson, c, U. of Santa Clara.
7. Branden Nogowski, lhp, Hood River (Ore.) Valley HS.
8. Seth Brizek, ss, Clemson U.
9. Marty Weymouth, rhp, Brother Rice HS, Bloomfield Hills, Mich.
10. Ernest Tolbert, of, Lincoln HS, San Diego.
11. Russ Koehler, rhp, Chemeketa (Ore.) CC.
12. Dan Kurtz, rhp, LeMoyne College.
13. Andy Collett, rhp-1b, Loyola Marymount U.
14. Chad Sheffer, ss, U. of Central Florida.
15. Lawrence Severence, p, Bryan HS, Archbold, Ohio.
16. Kevin Gryboski, rhp, Wilkes (Pa.) U.
17. Aaron Myette, rhp, Johnston Heights HS, Surrey, B.C.
18. Wynter Phoenix, of, UC Santa Barbara.
19. Justin Kaye, rhp, Bishop Gorman HS, Las Vegas, Nev.
20. Greg Scheer, lhp, Jacksonville U.
21. Chad Soden, lhp, Arkansas State U.
22. Scott Maynard, c, Dana Hills HS, Laguna Niguel, Calif.
23. Rob Morrison, rhp, Wellington Community HS, Loxahatchee, Fla.
24. Brett Laxton, rhp, Louisiana State U.
25. Brian Fuentes, lhp, Merced (Calif.) JC.
26. Keith Law, ss, East Paulding HS, Hiram, Ga.
27. Ramon Vazquez, ss, Indian Hills (Iowa) CC.
28. Greg Donahue, c, Rockland (N.Y.) JC.
29. Charles Christianson, rhp, Chaffey (Calif.) JC.
30. Juan Pierre, of, Alexandria (La.) HS.
31. Adam Walker, lhp, Yavapi (Ariz.) JC.
32. Harold Frazier, rhp, Oral Roberts U.
33. Yusef Hamilton, of, St. Martin Deporres HS, Detroit.
34. Richard Sundstrom, rhp, Kennedy HS, La Palma, Calif.
35. Nathan Burnett, rhp, Rutherford HS, Panama City, Fla.
36. Todd Niemeier, lhp, U. of Southern Indiana.
37. Anthony Rice, 3b, CC of San Francisco.
38. Joseph Hunt, of, Sante Fe (Fla.) CC.
39. Brian Nelson, c, Edison (Fla.) CC.
40. Michael Campbell, of, Coronado HS, Mesa, Ariz.
41. Shaylar Hatch, rhp, Gilbert (Ariz.) HS.
42. Brian Grubbs, rhp, Cooper HS, Abilene, Texas.
43. Travis Ray, rhp, Cairo (Ga.) HS.
44. Leron Cook, of, Fresno (Calif.) CC.
45. Joe DeVisser, ss, Mattawan HS, Schoolcraft, Mich.
46. Tim Burton, rhp, St. Thomas Aquinas HS, Fort Lauderdale.
47. Jeremy Palki, rhp, Clackamas (Ore.) CC.
48. James Pietraszko, c, Forest Heights HS, Kitchener, Ontario.
49. Brian Smith, of, Granite Hills HS, El Cajon, Calif.
50. Zachary Tharp, 1b, Boone HS, Orlando, Fla.
51. Jacob Hermann, lhp, Eagle Point (Ore.) HS.
52. Joel Greene, lhp, Linn-Benton (Ore.) CC.
53. Brandon McNab, 1b, Boerne HS, Fair Oaks Ranch, Texas.
54. Jeffrey Hammond, of, Flomaton (Ala.) HS.
55. Jason Balcom, of, Mt. Desales HS, Macon, Ga.
56. Brian Cawaring. of, Alhambra HS, Martinez, Calif.
57. Roy Roundy, c, Coronado HS, Scottsdale, Ariz.
58. Todd Ozias, rhp, Miami-Dade CC Kendall.
59. Jason Marr, rhp, Cerritos (Calif.) JC.
60. Rafael Rivera, rhp, Miami-Dade CC New World Center.
61. Ray Farmer, rhp, Duke U.
62. Eric Moten, of, Grant HS, Portland, Ore.

63. Joseph Seymour, c, Southside HS, Elmira, N.Y.
64. Damon Warren, rhp, Lower Columbia (Wash.) CC.
65. Sean Hansen, 1b, Norco (Calif.) HS.
66. Isaac Burton, rhp, Arizona State U.
67. Sean Kelley, rhp, Miramar HS, Miami.
68. Steve Kokinda, 3b, Palm Beach (Fla.) JC.
69. Gerald Eady, of, Seminole (Fla.) CC.
70. Sean Hamilton, rhp, Dunedin (Fla.) HS.
71. Eric Lloyd, rhp, Charlton County HS, Folkston, Ga.
72. Brian Shultz, of, Blinn (Texas) JC.
73. Travis Knight, 2b, Kent Meridian HS, Kent, Wash.
74. Tim Henley, rhp, Eastside HS, Gainesville, Fla.
75. Wendell Simmons, rhp, Southwest HS, Macon, Ga.
76. Michael Anderson, of, Jones County HS, Gray, Ga.
77. Shane Roland, of, Cook County HS, Adel, Ga.

TEXAS RANGERS (7)

1. Jonathan Johnson, rhp, Florida State U.
2. Phill Lowery, lhp, Casa Grande HS, Petaluma, Calif.
3. Ryan Dempster, rhp, Elphinstone HS, Gibson's, B.C.
4. Ryan Glynn, rhp, Virginia Military Institute.
5. Shawn Gallagher, 1b, New Hanover HS, Wilmington, N.C.
6. Dan Kolb, rhp, Sauk Valley (Ill.) CC (dropout).
7. George Carrion, rhp-ss, DeWitt Clinton HS, Bronx, N.Y.
8. Craig Monroe, ss, Texarkana (Texas) HS.
9. Juan Rivera, c, Rio Grande, P.R.
10. Julio Mercado, of, Brook Pointe HS, Stafford, Va.
11. Brian Martineau, rhp, Rancho Santiago (Calif.) JC.
12. Bryan Link, lhp, Winthrop U.
13. Cliff Brumbaugh, 3b, U. of Delaware.
14. Brandon Knight, rhp, Ventura (Calif.) JC.
15. Ryan Gorecki, 2b, Seton Hall U.
16. Nathan Vopata, 3b-2b, Lewis-Clark State (Idaho) College.
17. Brian Llibre, c, West Covina (Calif.) HS.
18. Damian Rose, of, Overfelt HS, San Jose, Calif.
19. Charles Bauer, rhp, College of St. Rose (N.Y.).
20. Joe Goodwin, c, George Mason U.
21. Ted Silva, rhp, Cal State Fullerton.
22. Bobby Styles, rhp, East Henderson HS, Hendersonville, N.C.
23. Robert Moore, rhp, U. of Hawaii.
24. Manny Torres, rhp, St Joseph's HS, Trumbull, Conn.
25. Mike McHugh, lhp, Penn State U.
26. Chris Briones, c, U. of Nevada-Reno.
27. David Brazeal, c, Mustang (Okla.) HS.
28. Gary Johnson, of, East Los Angeles JC.
29. Mike Venafro, lhp, James Madison U.
30. Scott Mudd, rhp, Indiana U.
31. Kelly Stratton, of, U. of Utah.
32. Scooter Bryant, lhp, Sulphur (La.) HS.
33. Joe Garibaldi, lhp, Terra Nova HS, Pacifica, Calif.
34. John McAulay, c, William Carey (Miss.) College.
35. Bobby Kahlon, rhp, U. of California.
36. Joseph Williams, 3b, Chaffey HS, Ontario, Calif.
37. Emar Fleming, rhp, Allegany (Md.) CC.
38. Russell Bratton, rhp, Central HS, Columbia, Tenn.
39. Danny Carrasco, rhp, Hayward (Calif.) HS.
40. Billy Reed, ss, Auburn U.
41. Mandell Echols, of, William Carey (Miss.) College.
42. Brent Sagedal, rhp, Carthage (Wis.) College.
43. Amury Leon, ss, Tucson (Ariz.) HS.
44. Tom Smith, rhp, Petaluma (Calif.) HS.
45. Mark Draeger, rhp, Slippery Rock (Pa.) U.
46. Tim Codd, rhp, Edinboro (Pa.) U.
47. Ryan Haley, rhp, Loxahachee, Fla.

TORONTO BLUE JAYS (17)

1. Roy Halladay, rhp, West HS, Arvada, Colo.
2. Craig Wilson, c, Marina HS, Huntington Beach, Calif.
3. Jeff Maloney, ss, Ridge HS, Basking Ridge, N.J.
4. Mike Whitlock, 1b, San Lorenzo (Calif.) HS.
5. Jay Veniard, lhp, U. of Central Florida.
6. Blaine Fortin, c, Lundar (Manitoba) HS.
7. Jeremi Rudolph, of, Apopka (Fla.) HS.
8. Dave Marciniak, ss, Woodbridge (N.J.) HS.
9. Kyle Burchart, rhp, Bixby (Okla.) HS.
10. Ryan Freel, 2b, Tallahassee (Fla.) CC.
11. Allen Levrault, lhp, Westport (Mass.) HS.
12. John Curl, 1b, Texas A&M U.
13. Ted Lilly, lhp, Fresno (Calif.) CC.
14. Jason Pomar, rhp, Vero Beach (Fla.) HS.
15. Robert Corraro, rhp, Xavier (Conn.) HS.
16. Bill Brabec, rhp, Illinois State U.
17. Johnny Byrd, rhp, University Christian HS, Jacksonville.
18. Doug Dent, rhp, San Juan HS, Citrus Heights, Calif.
19. Jaron Seabury, rhp, Bellevue (Wash.) CC.

Rangers Get Their Man. Texas selected Florida State All-American righthander Jonathan Johnson with its first-round pick.

20. James Whitehead, 1b-c, Meridian (Miss.) CC.
21. Logan Miller, c, Texas Tech.
22. Scott Fitterer, rhp, Louisiana State U.
23. Brian Bejarano, 3b, Central Arizona JC.
24. Mark Curtis, lhp, Bellerose HS, St. Albert, Alberta.
25. John Mitchell, rhp, Cal State Fullerton.
26. John Kehoe, 2b, Cumberland (Tenn.) U.
27. Robert Medina, c, Caguas, P.R.
28. Chris Hayes, 3b, Jacksonville U.
29. Brian Williams, c, Southwest Texas State U.
30. Brandon Duckworth, rhp, JC of Southern Idaho.
31. John Douglas, ss, Catholic U., Washington D.C.
32. Stanley Gay, lhp, Covington (Tenn.) HS.
33. Todd Moser, lhp, Manatee (Fla.) JC.
34. Andrew McCormick, of, Grand Canyon U.
**35. Jonathan Herring, lhp, Alabama Christian Academy,
Montgomery, Ala.**
36. Randy Albaral, of, Jesuit HS, River Ridge, La.
37. Thomas Taylor, ss, Tate HS, Gonzales, Fla.
38. Tyrone Gracia, 3b, Yarmouth Regional HS, Dennis, Mass.
39. Eduardo Marquez, of, Mater Dei HS, Orange, Calif.
40. Brian Leach, rhp, Osceola HS, Seminole, Fla.
41. Jesse Bechard, ss, Washington HS, Massillon, Ohio.
42. Thomas Peck, of, Rollins (Fla.) College.
43. Justin Johnson, of, Diamond Bar (Calif.) HS.
· 44. Brian Fitts, rhp, Gallatin (Tenn.) HS.
45. Joe Pierson, ss, Huntington (W.Va.) HS.
46. Ryan Cisar, ss, Magnolia HS, New Martinsville, W.Va.
47. Antonio Jackson, of, Parker HS, Birmingham, Ala.
48. Paxton Stewart, 1b, Florida International U.
49. Derek Hines, of, West HS, Arvada, Colo.
50. Jeremy Satterfield, rhp, JC of Southern Idaho.
51. Kyle Adams, lhp, Creighton Prep, Omaha.
52. Albert Colon, of, Apopka (Fla.) HS.
53. Ryan Bundy, c, Lake Stevens HS, Everett, Wash.
54. Claude Greene, 1b, O'Dea HS, Seattle.
55. Travis Grant, rhp, Skyline HS, Salt Lake City, Utah.
56. Sidney Harden, rhp, Middle Georgia HS.
57. Pat Schultz, c, CC of Rhode Island.
58. Doug Franklin, 2b, Pensacola (Fla.) JC.
59. Andy Tarpley, rhp, U. of California.

OBITUARIES/
INDEX

OBITUARIES
November 1994-October 1995

Bob Allison, the 1959 American League rookie of the year, died April 9 in Rio Verde, Ariz. He was 60. An outfielder, Allison batted .255 with 256 home runs and 796 RBIs in 1,541 big league games from 1958-70. He hit .261 with 30 homers as a rookie with the Washington Senators, and was a three-time all-star. He hit the game-winning home run for the Twins in Game Six of the 1965 World Series, won in seven games by the Dodgers.

Dick "Rowdy Richard" Bartell, the National League's starting shortstop in the first All-Star Game in 1933, died of Alzheimer's disease Aug. 4 in Alameda, Calif. He was 87. Bartell, whose feisty play earned him his nickname, batted .284 with 79 home runs in 2,016 major league games.

Gus Bell, a four-time National League all-star outfielder and part of the major leagues' second three-generation family, died May 7 in Cincinnati. He was 66. Bell batted .281 with 206 home runs and 942 RBIs in 1,741 big league games from 1950-64. He hit the first home run in Mets history in 1962. Bell's son Buddy was a five-time all-star third baseman during an 18-year big league career from 1972-89, and Buddy's son David, an infielder with the Cardinals, made his major league debut in 1995. The Boones (Ray, Bob and Bret) are the only other three-generation major league family.

Glenn Burke, the only major leaguer known to have revealed his homosexuality, died from AIDS complications May 30 in San Leandro, Calif. He was 42. An outfielder, Burke hit .237 with two homers and 38 RBIs in 225 major league games from 1976-79. He admitted to being gay in 1982, and said that prejudice drove him out of the game. He also is credited with inventing the high-five gesture.

Jim Campbell, the Tigers general manager and president who presided over Detroit's World Series titles of 1968 and 1984, died Oct. 31 in Lakeland, Fla. He was 71. Campbell was named Tigers GM in 1962 and was promoted to president in 1983. It was his suggestion to pair Alan Trammell and Lou Whitaker, the longest-running double-play combination in big league history.

Harry Chozen, who hit safely in 49 consecutive games in the minor leagues, died Sept. 16 in Houston. He was 78.

Harry Craft, the first manager of the Houston Colt .45s, died Aug. 3 in Conroe, Texas. He was 80. An outfielder, Craft batted .253 with 44 homers and 267 RBIs in 566 big league games from 1937-42. He managed three big league teams, the Kansas City Athletics (1957-59), the Cubs (1961, as part of their infamous College of Coaches) and the Colt .45s (1962-64, the first three years of existence for the franchise now known as the Astros). His managerial record was 360-485.

Tony Cuccinello, who nearly won the American League batting title in his final big league season, died of congestive heart failure Sept. 21 in Tampa. He was 87. A second and third baseman, Cuccinello hit .280 with 94 homers and 888 RBIs in 1,704 big league games from 1930-40 and 1942-45. A member of the first National League all-star team in 1933, he led the AL batting race going into the final day of the 1945 season. But a controversial scoring change gave the Yankees' Snuffy Stirnweiss an extra hit, and he edged Cuccinello .309-.308. Cuccinello was released by the White Sox after the season and never played in the majors again.

Leon Day, the last Negro Leaguer elected to the Hall of Fame, died March 13 in Baltimore. He was 78. Day was named to the Hall by the Veterans Committee six days before his death.

David Eggert, an Expos minor league righthander, died after apparently falling asleep at the wheel of his car and crashing into a tree Dec. 4 near his Ventura, Calif., home. He was 24. Eggert went 3-1, 3.82 with three saves at Class A West Palm Beach in 1994.

Don Elston, who helped inspire the official save statistic, died Jan. 2 in Evanston, Ill. He was 65. A righthander, Elston went 49-54, 3.63 with 63 unofficial saves in 450 big league games in 1953 and from 1957-64. He led the National League in appearances twice and relief wins once for the Cubs. His work inspired longtime Chicago writer Jerome Holtzman to push for a save statistic, which became official in 1973.

George Fanning, general manager of Bluefield's Appalachian League franchise since 1954, died Sept. 7 in Bluefield, W.Va. He was 86. A mainstay of Bluefield baseball since 1948, Fanning died hours after Cal Ripken broke Lou Gehrig's consecutive-game streak. Ripken began his pro career in Bluefield in 1978.

Rick Ferrell, a Hall of Fame catcher, died of arrhythmia July 27 in Bloomfield Hills, Mich. He was 89. Ferrell batted .281 with 28 homers and 734 RBIs in 1,884 big league games from 1929-45 and 1947. A six-time American League all-star, he started the first All-Star Game in 1933. He established an AL record with 1,806 games caught, since broken by Bob Boone and Carlton Fisk. After his playing career ended, Ferrell served in several capacities with the Tigers from 1950-92, including general manager. He was elected to the Hall of Fame by the Veterans Committee in 1984.

Dan Galbreath, president of the Pirates from 1970-85 and a prominent horse owner, died of cancer Sept. 3 in Galloway, Ohio. He was 67. Galbreath is credited with saving the Pirates for Pittsburgh by taking half of market value in return for assurances the team wouldn't move.

Alex Gamez, a star outfielder in the independent Frontier League, died in an auto accident July 13 in Zanesville, Ohio. He was 23.

Ed Gill, the second-oldest living major league player, died Oct. 10 in Brockton, Mass. He was 100. A righthander, Gill went 1-1 with a 4.82 ERA in 16 games with the 1919 Washington Senators. The only older living major league player at the time of Gill's death was former Yankees and St. Louis Browns lefthander Chet Hoff, 104.

Walter Haas, who owned the Athletics for 15 years before selling them in 1995, died of cancer Sept. 20 in San Francisco. He was 79. Haas saved the team for Oakland when he bought the franchise from Charlie Finley during the 1980 season. Under his ownership, the Athletics won five American League West titles, three pennants and one World Series. His sale of the A's to Bay Area businessmen Ken Hofmann and Steven Schott was approved shortly before Haas' death.

Walter Haas

Bill Haber, one of the 16 founding members of the Society for American Baseball Research, died after an asthma attack June 4 in Brooklyn. He was 53. Haber helped organize SABR in 1971 at a meeting in Cooperstown. He worked with the Topps baseball-card company, and had a reputation for being able to find biographical information on the most obscure players. He was the leading authority on baseball obituaries, which he compiled for Baseball America.

Thelma Griffith Haynes, a former co-owner of the Twins, died Oct. 15 in Orlando. She was 82. Haynes and her brother Calvin Griffith were adopted by their uncle Clark Griffith, a Hall of Fame pitcher and owner of the Washington Senators, in 1922. She worked as a secretary for her uncle until his death in 1955, after which she and Calvin each inherited 26 percent of the team. The family sold the team to Carl Pohlad in 1985. Haynes' late husband Joe pitched 14 seasons in the major leagues with the Senators and White Sox from 1939-52.

Ed Holtz, general manager of the South Atlantic League's Macon Braves, died Oct. 7 in Macon, Ga. He was 65.

Willie James, a Jackson State University second baseman, died in an auto accident June 3 in Jackson, Miss. James batted .253 in 1995. Teammate Henry Wallace also was killed in the accident.

Vernal "Nippy" Jones, the key figure in one of the most famous World Series incidents of all time, died of a heart attack Oct. 3 in Sacramento. He was 70. Jones batted .267 with 25 homers and 209 RBIs in 412 big league games from 1946-52 and 1957. Though he went 0-for-2 as a pinch-hitter in the 1957 Series, Jones made a large contribution to the Milwaukee Braves' title. After the Yankees won two of the first three games, they scored four runs in the ninth inning to tie Game Four and took the lead on a Hank Bauer triple in the top of the 10th. Jones pinch-hit for Warren Spahn to lead off the bottom half, and Bob Grim threw a pitch in the dirt. Jones insisted the ball hit him, but plate umpire Augie Donatelli didn't agree initially. Then Jones, known for meticulously shining his spikes, showed Donatelli that there was shoe polish on the ball. He was awarded first base, keying a three-run rally and helping the Braves win in seven games.

Jack Kramer, a two-time American League all-star pitcher, died of a brain hemorrhage May 18 in Metairie, La. He was 77. A righthander, Kramer went 95-103 with a 4.24 ERA in 322 big league games from 1939-41 and 1943-51.

Roland LeBlanc, the scout who signed two-time American League MVP Robin Yount for the Brewers in 1973, died May 13 in La Habra, Calif. He was 74.

Bobby Lewis, the University of Pittsburgh's baseball coach for 36 years, died Feb. 22 in Pittsburgh. He was 65.

Ron Luciano, a former American League umpire known for his flamboyance, died in what was ruled suicide by carbon monoxide poisoning Jan. 18 in Endicott, N.Y. He was 57. A star offensive lineman at Syracuse University, where he blocked for the great Jim Brown, Luciano began umpiring in 1964 in the Class A Florida State League. He reached the AL in 1969 and worked one World Series and three Championship Series before retiring in 1980.

Mickey Mantle, Hall of Fame outfielder for the Yankees and possibly the nation's most beloved baseball player ever, died of cancer Aug. 13 in Dallas. He was 63. (For more on Mantle, please see Page 15.)

Terry Moore, the center fielder on the Cardinals' World Series championship teams of 1942 and 1946, died March 29 in Collinsville, Ill. He was 82. Moore batted .280 with 80 homers and 513 RBIs in 1,298 big league games form 1935-42 and 1946-48. He went 35-42 as Phillies manager in 1954.

Lindsey Nelson, a legendary broadcaster, died of complications from Parkinson's disease and pneumonia June 10 in Atlanta. He was 76. Nelson was one of three announcers hired by the expansion Mets in 1962, and stayed with the team for 17 years. He was honored with the 1988 Ford C. Frick Award, the highest honor a baseball broadcaster can receive.

Chet Nichols, who led the National League in ERA as a rookie, died March 27 in Lincoln, R.I. He was 64. Nichols went 34-36 with a 3.64 ERA in 189 major league games in 1951 and from 1954-56 and 1960-64. Nichols went 11-8, 2.88 for the Boston Braves in 1951, finishing second to Willie Mays in NL rookie-of-the-year balloting.

Vada Pinson, a two-time all star outfielder, died Oct. 21 in Oakland. He was 59. Pinson batted .286 with 256 homers and 1,170 RBIs with 305 steals in 2,469 big league games from 1958-75. He was one of only six players in major league history to hit at least 250 homers with 300 steals. Pinson made the National League all-star team in each of his first two full seasons in 1959 and 1960, and won a Gold Glove in 1961. He led the NL in hits, doubles, triples and outfield fielding percentage

Vada Pinson

twice each, and runs once.

Gus Polidor, a former big league infielder who tried to make the Expos' replacement team in spring training, was shot and killed April 28 in Caracas, Venezuela. He was 34. Polidor was shot twice in the head when two men attempted to steal his car and take his 1-year-old son. His son wasn't injured and was safe. Polidor batted .207 in 229 major league games from 1985-90 and 1993. His brother Wil is a shortstop in the White Sox organization.

Bob Prentice, a Blue Jays scout and member of the Canadian Baseball Hall of Fame, died of a respiratory illness Feb. 9 in Scarborough, Ontario. He was 66.

Dale Ramsburg, head coach at West Virginia University, died after a year-long battle with leukemia Nov. 3 in Morgantown, W.Va. He was 53.

Allie "Superchief" Reynolds, one of the best World Series pitchers ever, died of cancer Dec. 27 in Oklahoma City. He was 77. Reynolds won games in six World Series for the Yankees from 1947-53, winning or saving the final game in three as New York won all six. Reynolds went 182-107 with a 3.30 ERA in 13 big league seasons from 1942-54. In 1951, he became the first American League pitcher to throw two no-hitters in one season. A four-time all-star, he led the AL in shutouts and strikeouts twice each, and winning percentage and ERA once each.

Tony Rubello, the scout who signed Hall of Fame catcher Johnny Bench for the Reds in 1965, died Dec. 25 in Fort Worth. He was 91.

Frank Secory, a former big league outfielder and umpire, died April 7 in Port Huron, Mich. He was 82. Secory batted .228 in 93 big league games in 1940, 1942 and from 1944-46. He became an umpire after his playing career ended in 1947. He joined the NL in 1952 and worked six All-Star Games and four World Series before retiring in 1970.

David Shotkoski, a Braves replacement player, was shot and killed during a robbery March 24 in West Palm Beach. He was 30. Shotkoski was drafted by the Braves in the fourth round of the January 1985 draft and played in three organizations before topping out in Triple-A and playing the 1990 season in Italy. Though he appeared in just one spring-training game, he would have made Atlanta's replacement team, which was scuttled when the players ended their strike. Replacement teammate Terry Blocker was instrumental in tracking down the suspect charged with Shotkoski's murder.

John "Hi" Simmons, who coached the University of Missouri to the 1954 College World Series championship, died Jan. 12 in Columbia, Mo. He was 89. Simmons coached from 1937-73, going 481-294 and winning 11 conference championships.

Zoilo Versailles, the 1965 American League MVP, died June 9 in Bloomington, Minn. He was 55. A shortstop, Versailles hit .242 with 95 homers and 810 RBIs in 1,400 big league games from 1959-69 and 1971. In 1965, he led the Twins to the World Series by hitting .273 with 19 homers and 77 RBIs and leading the AL in at-bats, runs, doubles and triples. He also led the AL in triples in 1963 and 1964.

Jason Walker, a Point Loma Nazarene (Calif.) College pitcher, died in an automobile accident Sept. 12 in Temecula, Calif. He was 23.

Bob Wellman, who won four consecutive minor league home run crowns, died Dec. 20 in Covington, Ky. He was 69. Wellman played 15 big league games with the Philadelphia Athletics in 1948 and 1950, but had a much more extensive career in the minors. He batted .315 with 219 homers and 1,141 RBIs in 1,536 games in 1942 and from 1946-59, winning homer titles in the lower minors from 1954-57. He also managed 25 years in the minors, going 1,663-1,440, and worked as a scout. Among his signees was Roger McDowell.

Woody Williams, who tied a still-standing National League record with 10 consecutive hits in 1943, died Feb. 24 in Appomattox, Va. He was 82. A second baseman, Williams batted .250 in 338 big league games in 1938 and 1943-45.

GENERAL INFORMATION

MAJOR, MINOR LEAGUE CLUBS